BALDWIN'S
OHIO PRACTICE

SOWALD & MORGANSTERN
DOMESTIC RELATIONS LAW

Volume 1

Chs. 1-21

REVISED FOURTH EDITION

By
Beatrice K. Sowald
and
Stanley Morganstern
General Editors

A Thomson Reuters business

For Customer Assistance Call 1-800-328-4880

Mat #40893248

Authors' Acknowledgments

This book is the product of the efforts of many people, individuals who have contributed their time and expertise collectively to provide guidance to practitioners throughout Ohio. I gratefully acknowledge these contributors, those from prior editions of this work, those who are new to the project, and those who have returned to update and revise this text to reflect the changing needs of family law attorneys. Our profession and our clients benefit from their sharing of their experience, time, and effort.

Beatrice K. Sowald

Columbus, Ohio
December 2009

I gratefully acknowledge the contributions of my partner, Pamela J. MacAdams, firm associates and members of our office staff who have assisted in research writing, and clerical preparation. It would not have been possible for me to devote the time and effort to this project without their support and assistance.

Stanley Morganstern

Cleveland, Ohio
December 2009

About the General Editors

Beatrice K. Sowald [co-General Editor, and author, Chapter 9, "Separation Agreements," Chapter 10, "Dissolution of Marriage," Chapter 27, "Jurisdiction and Venue," Chapter 34, "Role of Attorney: Ethics"] is a partner in the Columbus law firm of Sowald, Sowald & Clouse, practicing mainly in the area of family law. She received both undergraduate and law degrees from The Ohio State University. In 1967, she joined the Columbus Legal Aid Society, and from 1972 to 1980 was Supervising Attorney of the Family Law Unit. She has chaired the Family Law (1979-81) and Professional Ethics (1985-87) Committees of the Columbus Bar Association, and the Family Law (1982-84) and the Legal Ethics and Professional Conduct (2000-02) Committees of the Ohio State Bar Association. Mrs. Sowald has lectured on domestic relations law and practice for the Ohio Legal Center Institute's Continuing Legal Education Program and has been an Adjunct Professor at the Ohio State University College of Law. She served as a Judge of the Franklin County Court of Common Pleas, Domestic Relations Division, in 1984, and as a Judge of the Franklin County Municipal Court in 1985. She is a member of Women Lawyers of Franklin County, of the Family Law, Alternative Dispute Resolution, and Bankruptcy Committees of the Columbus Bar Association, of the Council of Delegates and the Family Law and Legal Ethics and Professional Conduct Committees of the Ohio State Bar Association, and has served as a member of the Ohio Board of Bar Examiners.

Stanley Morganstern [co-General Editor, and author, Chapter 8, "Legal Separation", Chapter 24, "Relief from Judgment"] is a partner in the Cleveland law firm of Morganstern, MacAdams & DeVito Co., L.P.A., and a certified specialist in family law. He received his undergraduate degree from the Ohio State University and law degree (magna cum laude) from the Cleveland-Marshall College of Law. He is the Editor-In-Chief of West's *Domestic Relations Journal of Ohio* (DRJO) and writes regular articles for *DRJO*. He is also the editor of *Baldwin's Ohio Practice, Elements of an Action*. He has published several articles in other publications on corporate and consumer law. Mr. Morganstern is a fellow in the American Academy of Matrimonial

Lawyers and has completed matrimonial arbitration training. He is a former adjunct professor at the University of Phoenix and currently President of the Orange City School District Board of Education. He is a frequent speaker for the Ohio CLE Institute and is a member of the Cleveland Metropolitan Bar Association and a member of the Family Law Committee of the Ohio State Bar Association. He has served as Chair of the OSBA Specialization Committee.

About the Contributors

Deborah R. Akers [co-author, Chapter 12, "Marital and Separate Property"] is a partner in the Cleveland law firm of Wolf & Akers, practicing in the area of domestic relations law. She received her undergraduate degree from Washington University and her law degree from Cleveland-Marshall College of Law. She was a Trial Referee in the Court of Common Pleas of Medina County, Division of Domestic Relations, from 1983 to 1984. Mrs. Akers has chaired the Family Law Committee of the Ohio State Bar Association, as well as several of its subcommittees, and was the Primary Draftsperson of 1990 House Bill 514, which revised the laws regarding spousal support and property division. She has lectured extensively on domestic relations law, particularly on the subject of Marital Property and Property Division. She is a member of the Editorial Advisory Board of West's Domestic Relations Journal of Ohio and has contributed to DRJO and many other publications in the area of domestic relations. A Fellow of the American Academy of Matrimonial Lawyers, she also served as chair of the Family Law Section of the Cleveland Bar Association and as Trustee of the Family Law Section of the Cuyahoga County Bar Association.

Joyce E. Barrett [author, Chapter 25, "Pleading and Practice"] is engaged in the private practice of law in Cleveland, practicing mainly in the area of family law. She received both her undergraduate and law degrees from Cleveland State University. She has been a member of the Supreme Court Advisory Committee on Child Support Enforcement. Ms. Barrett is an adjunct professor of Law at Cleveland-Marshall College of Law and has lectured extensively on domestic relations law and practice for: the Cleveland-Marshall Law Alumni Association, the Ohio Family Law Institute, Inc., the Cleveland Women Lawyers' Association, the Ohio Association of Common Pleas Court Judges, the Ohio Academy of Trial Lawyers, Ohio Legal Center Institute's Continuing Legal Education Program, and various bar associations. A Fellow of the American Academy of Matrimonial Lawyers, she has chaired the Family Law Section of the Cuyahoga County Bar Association and served as co-chair of the Certification and Specialization Committee of the Family Law Section of the American Bar Association.

Randal S. Bloch [co-author, Chapter 17, "Uniform Child Custody Jurisdiction Act; Parental Kidnapping Prevention Act; International Child Abduction Remedies Act"] is a partner in the Cincinnati law firm of Wagner & Bloch. She received her undergraduate degree from the University of Wisconsin and her law degree from Brooklyn Law School. She has served on the Hamilton County Community Action

Agency Board of Trustees and for the Women Advocates for Divorce Education. Ms. Bloch has served as Secretary of and has chaired the Juvenile Court Section and the Civil Rights Committee of the Cincinnati Bar Association, and she has taught paralegal courses at the College of Mount St. Joseph. She is a member of the Cincinnati, Ohio State, and American Bar Associations.

V. Michael Brigner [author, Chapter 2, "Marriage"] is a Judge of the Court of Common Pleas of Montgomery County, Division of Domestic Relations. He received his undergraduate degree from Wright State University and his law degree from the Salmon P. Chase College of Law. Judge Brigner was in private practice in the area of general family law from 1977 to 1990. He has taught various programs for the Ohio Judicial College, Ohio CLE Institute, Ohio Domestic Relations Judges Association, Ohio Magistrates Association, and Sinclair Community College. Judge Brigner is a member of the Editorial Advisory Board of West's Domestic Relations Journal of Ohio, to which he contributes regularly, and has written numerous articles for the Dayton Bar Association's Bar Briefs and the ABA Family Law Section's Family Advocate. He is a member of the Dayton and Ohio State Bar Associations as well as the Family Law Section of the American Bar Association.

Douglas M. Brill [author, Chapter 15, "Parental Rights and Shared Parenting"] is a partner in the law firm of Spike, Meckler, Brill, Illner, & Couch. He received his undergraduate degree from The Ohio State University and his law degree from the University of Toledo Law School. Mr. Brill is a Certified Mediator and a Certified Specialist in Family Relations Law. He was the Ohio State Bar Association appointee to the Family Parenting Task Force and the Ohio Supreme Court Task Force on Family Law and Children. Mr. Brill lectures for such groups as the Ohio CLE Institute, the Ohio Judicial College, the Ohio Academy of Trial Lawyers, the Lorain County Bar Association, the National Business Institute, the Family Law Institute, and also serves as a guest lecturer at The Ohio State University Law School. Mr. Brill is a Fellow of the American Academy of Matrimonial Lawyers, and a member of the Lorain County and Ohio Bar Associations. He serves as Secretary of the Family Law Committee of the Ohio State Bar Association, and is a member of the Legislative Drafting and Legislative Review Committees.

Timothy M. Flanagan [author, Chapter 11, "Divorce"] is Administrative Judge, Cuyahoga County Court of Common Pleas, Domestic Relations Division-a position he has held since 1982. In 1983, he received the Ohio Supreme Court Award for Superior Judicial Service. A graduate of The Ohio University and the Cleveland-Marshall College of Law, where he was a member of law review, he was engaged in private practice before his election to the bench. Judge Flanagan has been a frequent lecturer at seminars sponsored by Cleveland-Marshall and by the Ohio State Bar Association's Continuing Legal Education Association. During 1985 to 1986, he served on the Ohio Supreme Court Advisory Committee on Child Support Enforcement.

Robert J. Frankart [co-author, Chapter 22, "Child Support Enforcement Agencies"] is Deputy Legal Counsel of the Office of Legal Services of the Ohio Department of Human Services, a position he assumed in 1987. He received his undergraduate degree from Denison University and his law degree from Vanderbilt University. Mr. Frankart has previously served as Managing Attorney of the Domestic Relations Unit of the Legal Aid Society of Columbus. He has also contributed to several publications including West's Domestic Relations Journal of Ohio.

June Rose Galvin [author, Chapter 21, "Enforcement of Parenting Time Rights and Allocation of Parental Rights"] is a retired Judge of the Court of Common Pleas of Lucas County, Division of Domestic Relations. She received her undergraduate and law degrees from the University of Toledo. From 1964 until her election to the bench in 1976, she was engaged in the private practice of law in Toledo. Judge Galvin has served as President of the Toledo Legal Aid Society and the Ohio Bureaus of Support Association. She has chaired the Family Law Committee of the Toledo Bar Association and is a founding member of Toledo United Against Rape. A member of the Toledo, Lucas County, Ohio State, and American Bar Associations, and serving on the Alternative Dispute Resolution Committee, the Family Law Committee, and the Guardian Ad Litem Subcommittee of the Ohio State Bar Association, she is also a member of the Association of Family and Conciliation Courts, the Ohio Association of Juvenile and Family Court Judges, the National Association of Women Judges, the Ohio Association of Domestic Relations Judges, the Child Support Shareholders' Reform Group, and the National Child Support Association, and has served on the Joint Gender Fairness Task Force of the Ohio State Bar Association and the Ohio Supreme Court.

Gary J. Gottfried [co-author, Chapter 17, "Uniform Child Custody Jurisdiction Act; Parental Kidnapping Prevention Act; International Child Abduction Remedies Act"] is engaged in the private practice of law in Columbus. He received his undergraduate degree from Marietta College and his law degree from Capital University Law School. Mr. Gottfried has lectured on Domestic Relations law for Professional Education Systems, Inc., the Columbus Bar Association, Chalfee and Associates, and the Rossen Bar Review Course. He is a member of the American, Ohio State, and Columbus Bar Associations, and of the American Trial Lawyers Association.

Melissa A. Graham-Hurd [author, Chapter 29, "Government Retirement Benefits"] is engaged in the private practice of law in Akron, primarily in the area of family law. She received both her undergraduate and law degrees from the University of Akron. She has presented seminars for the Akron Bar Association, the Ohio State Bar Association, the Ohio Academy of Trial Lawyers, and the National Business Institute on several occasions. Ms. Graham-Hurd has chaired the Akron Bar Association's Family Law Committee and the Ohio State Bar Association Family Law Committee. She is a member of the family law committees of the Akron, Ohio State, and American Bar Associations.

Michael A. Hochwalt [author, Chapter 37, "Mental Health Experts"] is a Magistrate in the Montgomery County Common Pleas Court, Domestic Relations Division, where he has served since 1987. He received his undergraduate, Master of Education, and Doctorate of Education degrees from the University of Cincinnati, and his law degree from the University of Dayton. Mr. Hochwalt has served as an assistant prosecutor for Montgomery County, and since 1992 he has been licensed by the state of Ohio as a Licensed Professional Clinical Counselor. He has written and taught frequently in the area of counseling and mental health in the context of the legal system, and he is a member of the Ohio State and Dayton Bar Associations, the International Association of Marriage and Family Counselors, the American Counseling Association, and the American Mental Health Counseling Association.

Richard L. Innis [author, Chapter 18, "Parenting Time and Visitation"] is a partner in the Columbus law firm of Innis & Barker. He received his undergraduate degree from The Ohio State University and his law degree from Capital University. Mr. Innis is on the Editorial Advisory Board of West Group's Domestic Relations Journal of Ohio and is a regular contributor to DRJO. He also lectures frequently on Domestic Relations law for the Columbus Bar Association and Ohio Legal Center Institute. Mr. Innis is vice chair of the Ohio State Bar Association Family Law Committee, and he is also a member of the Family Law Committees of the American, Ohio State, and Columbus Bar Associations.

Douglas R. Jennings [author, Chapter 32, "Appeals"] is associated with the Columbus law firm of Carlile Patchen & Murphy LLP. He received both his undergraduate and law degrees from The Ohio State University. Mr. Jennings served as a Law Clerk for the Tenth District Court of Appeals, and an adjunct Legal Writing Instructor with The Ohio State University College of Law. He is a member of the Columbus, Ohio State, and American Bar Associations, and chaired a subcommittee of the Columbus Bar Association's Professionalism Committee.

Michael J. Johrendt [author, Chapter 28, "Tax Considerations"] is a partner in the Columbus law firm of Johrendt, Cook & Eberhart, practicing mainly in the areas of business and tax law. He received his undergraduate and law degrees from The Ohio State University. Mr. Johrendt has taught several courses on business and tax topics, including "Tax Aspects of Divorce" for the Columbus Bar Association. He is a member of the Ohio State and Columbus Bar Associations.

David I. Kelley [co-author, Chapter 30, "Dividing Private Retirement Benefits in Divorce"] is a Certified Financial Planner with QDRO

Consultants and Kelley, Shulman & Co. in Medina, Ohio. He received his undergraduate degree from Manhattan College and his Master degree from the University of Connecticut. Mr. Kelley specializes in the drafting of QDROs and Qualified Medical Child Support Orders, and he has prepared over 20,000 reports on the present value of pensions and presented expert testimony over 700 times. He frequently lectures and writes on present values, and he is a co-author of Dividing Pensions in Divorce.

James R. Kirkland [author, Chapter 4, "Marital Obligations and Property Rights"] is engaged in the private practice of law in Dayton. He received his undergraduate degree from Ohio Wesleyan University and his law degree from The Ohio State University College of Law. Mr. Kirkland is on the Editorial Advisory Board of West's Domestic Relations Journal of Ohio and has been a regular contributor to that and many other publications in Domestic Relations law. He is a frequent lecturer for numerous Bar Associations and Continuing Education organizations, and he has also been honored by the Ohio State Bar Association for his lectures on domestic relations law and practice. He lectures nationally, having given the Divorce Law Updates at seminars sponsored by the Law Education Institute on several occasions. He is a Fellow of the American Academy of Matrimonial Lawyers and past president of the Academy's Ohio Chapter. He is a member of the American, Ohio State, and Dayton Bar Associations.

James Leonard [co-author, Chapter 23, "Interstate and Foreign Support Practice"] is Professor of Law and Associate Dean for Legal Information Services at The University of Alabama School of Law and formerly Professor of Law at Ohio Northern University. He received his undergraduate, Master of Library Science, and law degrees from the University of North Carolina at Chapel Hill, where he was elected to Phi Beta Kappa and served as a member of the law review. Professor Leonard has taught courses in legal research and writing, domestic relations, remedies, property, disability law, federal jurisdiction and employment discrimination. He is a member of the Ohio State Bar Association and its Family Law and Disability Law Committees.

Mary C. LoPresti [co-author, Chapter 31, "Magistrates"] is a Trial Magistrate in the Court of Common Pleas of Cuyahoga County, Division of Domestic Relations. She received her undergraduate degree from Ursuline College and her law degree from Cleveland-Marshall College of Law. Ms. LoPresti served as the Director of the Legal Department of the Court of Common Pleas of Cuyahoga County, Division of Domestic Relations, after having served there as a Law Clerk from 1985 to 1988. She has lectured on Domestic Relations Law for the Cuyahoga County Bar Association Guardian ad Litem Seminars, the Cleveland Bar Association Family Law Section, and the Ohio Judicial College.

Pamela J. MacAdams [author, Chapter 3, "Parentage"] is a partner in the Cleveland law firm of Morganstern, MacAdams &

DeVito, with whom she has been affiliated since 1984. She received her undergraduate degree from Baldwin-Wallace College and her law degree from Cleveland-Marshall College of Law. She is a member of the Editorial Advisory board of West's Domestic Relations Journal of Ohio and writes a Practice Pointer column for each issue of DRJO. She is a member of the Ohio State Bar Association Family Law Committee, and a Fellow in the American Academy of Matrimonial Lawyers. She is also a Certified Specialist in Family Law by the Ohio State Bar Association.

Don W. Martin [author, Chapter 15, "Parental Rights and Shared Parenting"] is Deputy Court Director of the Common Pleas Court of Franklin County, Division of Domestic Relations and Juvenile Court, where he has served since 1991. He received his undergraduate degree from The Ohio State University and his law degree from Capital University. Mr. Martin previously served on the Common Pleas Court of Franklin County, Division of Domestic Relations and Juvenile Court, as Administrative Referee from 1989 to 1991 and Referee from 1982 to 1989. He has also been a Staff Attorney for the Franklin County Public Defender. He has lectured on Domestic Relations law for the Ohio Judicial College, the Columbus Bar Association, and the Ohio CLE Institute.

Denise Herman McColley [author, Chapter 6, "Alternative Forms of Dispute Resolution"] has been the judge of the Henry County Common Pleas Court, Domestic Relations and Juvenile Divisions since 2005. From 1996 until becoming judge, she acted as magistrate in both the Fulton and Henry County Common Pleas Courts. She received her Bachelor of Science in Education and Master of Education degrees from Bowling Green State University and her law degree from The Ohio State University College of Law. From 1981 until becoming magistrate, she was engaged in the private practice of law and from 1989 she was also engaged in a mediation practice. Judge McColley is a past president of the Association of Family and Conciliation Courts (AFCC), a past member of the Herny County Court Appointed Special Advocate (CASA)/Guardian ad Litem (GAL) Board, and a past president of the Board of Trustees for the Center for Child and Family Advocacy, Inc. Judge McColley has frequently lectured on family law and on dispute resolution topics for various entities, including AFCC, the Ohio CLE Institute, the Ohio State Bar Association, the Toledo Bar Association, and the Ohio Judicial College. She is a member of the Henry County, Ohio (member of the Dispute Resolution and Family Law Committees) and American Bar Associations (where she was member of the Child Custody Pro Bono Project Task Force), the Boards of Directors of both the Ohio Association of Juvenile Court Judges and the Ohio Association of Domestic Relations Court Judges, the Ohio Judicial Conference (Juvenile Law and Procedure and Domestic Law and Procedure Commitees), the Ohio Judicial College Board of Trustees, and the National Council of Juvenile and Family Court Judges. She also served on the Ohio Task Force for Family Law and Children.

Tom H. Nagel [author, Chapter 20, "Enforcement of Spousal and Child Support"] is a partner in the Columbus law firm of Britt, Campbell, Nagel & Sproat, with which he has been affiliated since 1976. He received his undergraduate and law degrees from The Ohio State University. Mr. Nagel has lectured on Domestic Relations law for the Columbus Bar Association. He is a member of the Ohio State Bar Association and the Family Law Committee of the Columbus Bar Association.

Diane M. Palos [author; Chapter 19, "Child Support"] is a Judge in the Domestic Relations Division of the Court of Common Pleas in Cuyahoga County. She received her law degree from Case Western Reserve University. Judge Palos is an adjunct professor for Cleveland-Marshall College of Law, and frequently lectures for the Ohio CLE Institute, the Ohio Judicial College, the Cleveland-Marshall College of Law Alumni Association, the Ohio CSEA Directors Association, the Center for Principled Family Advocacy, and the Cleveland Metropolitan Bar Association. She is a former member of the Board of Trustees for the Ohio Judicial College, an Executive Committee member for the Center for Principled Family Advocacy, a member of the Advisory Board of West's Domestic Relations Journal of Ohio, a former member of the Supreme Court of Ohio Advisory Committee on Children, Families and Courts, and a former member of the Ohio Child Support Council. Judge. Palos is a member of the Ohio Association of Domestic Relations Judges, the Ohio Association of Magistrates, the Association of Family and Conciliation Courts, the International Academy of Collaborative Professionals, the Center for Principled Family Advocacy, and the American Bar Association, Family Law and Dispute Resolution Sections.

Michael Partlow [author, Chapter 5, "Domestic Violence"] is of counsel with the Cleveland law firm of Morganstern, MacAdams & DeVito, practicing mainly in the area of family law. He received his undergraduate and law degrees from the University of Akron, where he was a member of the Jessup International Moot Court team. Mr. Partlow served as a Law Clerk to Judge Edward Mahoney of the Ninth District Court of Appeals from 1986 to 1988 and has been previously published in the Akron Law Review. He is a member of the American Bar Association.

David W. Robertson [co-author, Chapter 22, "Child Support Enforcement Agencies"] graduated from Cleveland-Marshall College of Law in 1983. Mr. Robertson was engaged in private practice before joining the Wood County Child Support Enforcement Agency. He became a Staff Attorney at the Ohio Department of Job and Family Services Office of Legal Services in 1999 and a Senior Staff Attorney in 2001, specializing in Child Support Policy and Litigation.

Nancy Hardin Rogers [author, Chapter 6, "Mediation and Conciliation"] is Platt Professor of Law at The Ohio State University College of Law. She received her undergraduate degree from the

University of Kansas and her law degree from Yale Law School. Before joining the OSU faculty, she served as a law clerk to U.S. District Judge Thomas D. Lambros (1972 to 1975) and as a Staff Attorney with the Cleveland Legal Aid Society (1974 to 1975). Professor Rogers has co-authored three books and numerous articles on the subject of Mediation and was twice awarded the Book Prize by the Center for Public Resources. She served as chair of the American Bar Association Standing Committee on Dispute Resolution and is currently co-chair of the Editorial Board of the American Bar Association's Dispute Resolution Magazine. She is also a member of the Board of Directors of the Legal Services Corporation.

Joel F. Sacco [co-author, Chapter 13, "Spousal Support"] is a Trial Magistrate in the Court of Common Pleas of Cuyahoga County, Division of Domestic Relations, a position he assumed in 1987. He received his undergraduate degree from Cornell University and his law degree from xiii the Cleveland-Marshall College of Law. Prior to his appointment with the court, he was a partner in the Cleveland law firm of Sacco and Serrat. Before entering private practice in 1983, he served as Bailiff to Judge James D. Sweeney of the Cuyahoga County Court of Common Pleas, Domestic Relations Division and General Division. Mr. Sacco has lectured at numerous continuing education seminars and is a member of the Cleveland and American Bar Associations.

Lynn B. Schwartz [author, Chapter 1, "Antenuptial Agreements," Chapter 7, "Annulment"] is associated with the Cleveland law firm of Morganstern, MacAdams & DeVito. She received her undergraduate degree from the State University of New York at Potsdam, her Master degree from Northwestern University, and her law degree from Cleveland-Marshall College of Law. Ms. Schwartz has contributed several articles to West's Domestic Relations Journal of Ohio and is a member of the Family Law Committee of the Ohio State Bar Association.

Michael R. Shanabruch [co-author, Chapter 13, "Spousal Support"] is a staff attorney with the Court of Common Pleas of Cuyahoga County, Domestic Relations Division. He received his undergraduate degree from Ohio University and his law degree from Case Western Reserve University School of Law.

Gary Shulman [co-author, Chapter 30, "Dividing Private Retirement Benefits in Divorce"] is an ERISA attorney with QDRO Consultants and Kelley, Shulman & Co. in Medina, Ohio. He received his undergraduate degree from The Ohio State University and his law degree from the Cleveland-Marshall College of Law. Mr. Shulman specializes in the drafting of QDROs and Qualified Medical Child Support Orders, and serves as a consultant to attorneys and plan administrators in preparing and reviewing QDROs. With twenty years of experience in the benefits and actuarial field, he has written and co-authored numerous publications, including the Qualified Domestic Relations Order Handbook and the Qualified Medical Child Support Order Handbook.

Sharon A. Skirbunt [author, Chapter 16, "Modification of Parental Rights and Responsibilities"] is a partner in the Cleveland law firm of Skirbunt & Skirbunt, practicing mainly in the area of Domestic Relations law. She received her undergraduate degree from Kent State University and her law degree from Case Western Reserve University School of Law. Prior to her present position, she was an associate with McDonald, Hopkins, Burke & Haber in Cleveland. She has lectured on Family Law for the Ohio CLE Institute and the National Business Institute and is a contributing author of the NBI publication Family Law Litigation in Ohio. Mrs. Skirbunt is a member of the Family Law Sections of the Cleveland, Cuyahoga County, Ohio State, and American Bar Associations.

Heather G. Sowald [contributing author, Chapter 34, "Role of Attorney: Ethics"] is a partner in the Columbus law firm of Sowald, Sowald, Anderson & Hawley, practicing in the area of family law. She received her undergraduate degree from Case Western Reserve University and her law degree from Capital University Law School. She has chaired the Family Law Committee, the Juvenile Law Committee, and the Ethics Committee of the Columbus Bar Association. She has chaired two task forces for the Columbus Bar Association, in 1995 and again in 2008, reviewing and making recommendations for improvement to the Franklin County Court of Common Pleas, Domestic Relations and Juvenile Court Divisions. She has served as the president of the Columbus Bar Association, the Franklin County Trial Lawyers Association, the Ohio Metropolitan Bar Association, and the Ohio State Bar Association. She has served on the Supreme Court of Ohio's Task Force on the Rules of Professional Conduct and on the Supreme Court of Ohio's Advisory Committee on Children, Families and the Courts. She has written and lectured extensively on family law, professionalism, and ethics topics.

Sheldon Stein [author, Chapter 33, "Bankruptcy"] is engaged in the private practice of law in Cleveland, primarily in the area of bankruptcy law. He received his undergraduate degree from Case Western Reserve University and his law degree from the Cleveland-Marshall College of Law. He is a member of the Ohio State Bar Association's Bankruptcy Committee, the Association of Trial Lawyers of America, and the Cuyahoga County, Cleveland, and Ohio State Bar Associations.

Mark Edward Stone [author, Chapter 14, "Modification of Spousal Support"] is a sole practitioner in Beavercreek. He concentrates his practice in family law matters. He received his B.S. degree from Bowling Green State University and his J.D. from the University of Dayton School of Law. He is a member of the Dayton Bar Association and its Family Law and Certified Grievance Committees (past chair of one of the two DBA Certified Grievance Committees), the Greene County Bar Association and the Ohio State Bar Association (and its Family Law Committee). He was certified in 1999 as a family law specialist by the Ohio State Bar Association Family Relations

Law Specialty Board. He is a Fellow of the American Academy of Matrimonial Lawyers and is a member of its Ohio Chapter. Mr. Stone is also a contributing writer to and member of the Ohio Domestic Relations Journal Editorial Advisory Board.

Edward J. Sukol [author, Chapter 36, "Jewish Divorce"] is the rabbi of Congregation Bethaynu in Pepper Pike, Ohio. He received his undergraduate degree from Temple University and his Rabbinic Ordination from the Hebrew Union College-Jewish Institute of Religion. Rabbi Sukol is a Certified Chaplain of the National Association of Jewish Chaplains, and he has completed specialized training in Clinical Pastoral Care. He has been the Hillel director at Ohio University, and was a board member of the Southeastern Ohio Foodbank and the Athens (Ohio) AIDS Task Force. He currently serves on the Pediatric Ethics Committee at Rainbow Babies and Children's Hospital.

Adam J. Thurman [author, Chapter 26, "Discovery"] is a sole practitioner engaged in the practice of law in Cleveland, primarily in the area of domestic relations law. Previously, he was an associate with the Law Offices of Herbert Palkovitz, a former author of this chapter. Mr. Thurman received his undergraduate degree from John Carroll University and his law degree from the Cleveland-Marshall College of Law, where he was an executive editor of the Cleveland State Law Review. He is a frequent lecturer on domestic relations law topics and a former chair of the Family Law Section of the Cleveland Bar Association.

Craig P. Treneff [co-author, Chapter 12, "Marital and Separate Property"] is engaged in the private practice of law in Columbus, Ohio. He is a graduate of The Ohio State University and Capital University Law School, where he was elected to Law Review. Prior to entering private practice in 1983, he was judicial law clerk to Justice William B. Brown of the Ohio Supreme Court and served as chief legislative assistant to the Chairman of the Finance-Appropriations Committee of the Ohio House of Representatives. He is certified by the Ohio State Bar Association as a family relations specialist. In addition, he is a Fellow of the American Academy of Matrimonial Lawyers, a Director of the Collaborative Family Law Council of Central Ohio, and a member of the family law committees of the Columbus, Ohio State and American Bar Associations. He is also a member of the Editorial Advisory Board of the Domestic Relations Journal of Ohio.

Gary D. Yanus [author, Chapter 35, "Catholic Declaration of Nullity"] is Adjutant Judicial Vicar of The Tribunal of the Diocese of Cleveland. He received his undergraduate degree from Baldwin-Wallace College, his M.Div. from St. Mary's Seminary, and his J.C.D. in Canon Law from the University of St. Thomas in Urbe (Rome) in 1990. Prior to his present position, he was Defender of the Bond for the Diocese of Cleveland, and has been Associate Pastor of St. Joseph's Church in Collinwood.

Ann Weatherhead [author, Chapter 13, "Spousal Support"] received her B.A. from Yale and her J.D. from Case Western Reserve Law School. She has been a Magistrate in the Domestic Relations Division of the Cuyahoga County Court of Common Pleas since 1988.

Foreword

This Revised Fourth Edition to Baldwin's Ohio Practice, Domestic Relations Law, together with its companion volume, Baldwin's Ohio Practice, Ohio Domestic Relations Laws and Rules Annotated, provides a thorough and contemporary guide to the complex laws that impact changing family relationships.

As in prior editions, the primary focus is on domestic relations practice in Ohio's Courts of Common Pleas, particularly within Divisions of Domestic Relations. Over the past decade, however, the forums in which family law issues are resolved have expanded to include more frequent contact with Juvenile Courts and an evolving administrative process that touches many more aspects of family relationships than ever before. The discussion in this edition is expanded accordingly in the context of parent and child issues. Other types of family law matters heard in other courts such as the adjudication of cases involving neglected or dependent children (Juvenile Court) or adoption (Probate Court)—are not within its scope. (For coverage of these matters, see Giannelli & Yeomans Salvador, Ohio Juvenile Law, and Carlin, Baldwin's Ohio Practice, Merrick-Rippner Probate Law.)

Baldwin's Ohio Practice, Domestic Relations Law, is the product of many talented individuals. Under the General Editorship of Beatrice K. Sowald of the Columbus Bar and Stanley Morganstern of the Cleveland Bar, it contains contributions from over forty authors, each an expert in a particular area of domestic practice or related field. Rapidly changing areas, such as enforcement of child support, parenting issues, treatment of retirement benefits in divorce, alternative forms of dispute resolution and tax considerations, have been extensively revised.

Each chapter of the text continues to provide many practice-oriented features, such as checklists, practice tips, and new forms, as well as forms from prior editions, incorporated into the textual discussion of the relevant issue. All of the author-drafted forms are also provided on CDROM, to allow practitioners to select forms and adapt them for use on their word-processing systems. The forms included on the CD-ROM are designated by a disc icon at the end of the section heading. Instructions on the use of the disc are included in its envelope.

A detailed Index provides ready access to each topic covered, including popular names, legal terminology, and common phrases, to create multiple entry points for research. A Table of Cases, Table of Laws and Rules, and numerous cross references point to related documents, both within the work and in other publications. The Appendix provides a useful Correlation Table of recently amended, enacted and repealed sections of the Revised Code related to child support.

About the Contributors contains a biographical sketch of each author. We are grateful to all of them for their work and extremely proud of the result of their collective efforts. Because of their expertise, Baldwin's Ohio Practice, Domestic Relations Law, is the definitive work on the ever-changing subject of family law in Ohio.

The Publisher

Cleveland, Ohio
December 2009

Table of Abbreviations

Bd.	Board
Bhd.	Brotherhood
Bldg.	Building
B.R.	Bankruptcy Reporter
Broad.	Broadcast; Broadcasting
Bros.	Brothers
Bull.	Ohio Weekly Law Bulletin
Bus.	Business
Cal.	California; California Reports
Cal.2d	California Reports, Second Series
Cal.3d	California Reports, Third Series
Cal. App.	California Appellate Reports
Cal. App.2d	California Appellate Reports, Second Series
Cal. App.3d	California Appellate Reports, Third Series
Cal. App.4th	California Appellate Reports, Fourth Series
Cal. Fam. Code	West's Annotated California Code, Family
Cal. Rptr.	West's California Reporter
Cal. Rptr.2d	West's California Reporter, Second Series
Capital L. Rev.	Capital University Law Review
Cas.	Casualty
CASA	Court Appointed Special Advocate
Case W. Res. L. Rev.	Case Western Reserve Law Review
C.C.	Ohio Circuit Court Reports
C.C.(n.s.)	Ohio Circuit Court Reports, New Series
C.C.H.	Commerce Clearing House
CCPA	Consumer Credit Protection Act
C.D.	Ohio Circuit Decisions
Cent.	Central
cert. denied	certiorari denied
C.F.R.	Code of Federal Regulations
Ch.	Chapter
Chem.	Chemical
Cin. L. Rev.	Cincinnati Law Review
Cir.	Circuit Court
Civ. R.	Ohio Rules of Civil Procedure
Clev. Bar J.	Cleveland Bar Journal
Clev.-Marshall L. Rev.	Cleveland-Marshall Law Review
Clev. St. L. Rev.	Cleveland State Law Review
Co.	Company
Colo.	Colorado
Colo. App.	Colorado Court of Appeals Reports
Comm.	Committee
Comm'n	Commission
Comm'r	Commissioner
Comm'rs	Commissioners
Cong.	Congress
Conn.	Connecticut
Conn. Supp.	Connecticut Supplement
Consol.	Consolidated

Const.	Constitution
Constr.	Construction
Coop.	Cooperative
Corp.	Corporation
C.P.	Common Pleas Court
CPO	Civil Protection Order
C.P. Sup. R.	Rules of Superintendence for Court of Common Pleas
Crim. R.	Ohio Rules of Criminal Procedure
CSEA	Child Support Enforcement Agency
CSPC	Child Support Payment Central
CSRS	Civil Service Retirement System
Ct.	Court
Ctr.	Center; Centre
Cuy. R.	Cuyahoga County Common Pleas Court Rule
Dayton L. Rev.	University of Dayton Law Review
D.C.	District Court; District of Columbia
D.C. Intrafamily R.	District of Columbia Superior Court Rules of the Family Division, Intrafamily Proceedings
Del.	Delaware
Dep't	Department
Dev.	Development
DHS	Department of Human Services
Dir.	Director
Dist.	District
Dist. Ct. App.	District Court of Appeals
Distrib.	Distributing; Distributor
Div.	Division
Dom. Rel.	Domestic Relations Court
D.R.	Disciplinary Rules, Code of Professional Responsibility
D.R. R.	Domestic Relations Court Rule
Duq. L. Rev.	Duquesne Law Review
DUUCCJA	Declaration Under Uniform Child Custody Jurisdiction Act
DV-TRO	Domestic Violence-Temporary Restraining Order
E.	East; Eastern
Econ.	Economic; Economical; Economy
E.D.	Eastern District
ed.	edition; editor
Educ.	Education; Educational
eff.	effective
e.g.	exempli gratia (for example)
Elec.	Electric; Electrical; Electricity; Electronic
Eng'g	Engineering
Eng'r	Engineer
Enter.	Enterprise
Env't	Environment
Envtl.	Environmental

Equal.	Equality
Equip.	Equipment
ERISA	Employee Retirement Income Security Act of 1974
et seq.	et sequeates (and the following)
Evid. R.	Ohio Rules of Evidence
Exam'r	Examiner
Exch.	Exchange
Ex'r	Executor
Ex'x	Executrix
F.	Federal Reporter
F.2d	Federal Reporter, Second Series
F.3d	Federal Reporter, Third Series
Fam.	Family
Fam. Advoc.	Family Advocate
Fam. L. Q.	Family Law Quarterly
Fam. L. Rep.	Family Law Reporter
Fed.	Federal Reporter
Fed. Civ. R.	Federal Civil Rule
Fed'n	Federation
FERS	Federal Employees' Retirement System
FFCCSOA	Full Faith and Credit for Child Support Orders Act
FIDM	Financial Institution Data Match
Fin.	Finance; Financial; Financing
Fla.	Florida
F.L.R.	Federal Law Reporter
Found.	Foundation
FPLS	Federal Parent Locator Service
Frank. R.	Franklin County Common Pleas Court Rule
F.R.D.	Federal Rules Decisions
F.Supp.	Federal Supplement
F.Supp.2d	Federal Supplement, Second Series
Ga.	Georgia; Georgia Reports
GAL	Guardian Ad Litem
GATT	General Agreement on Tariffs and Trade
GC	General Code of Ohio
Gen.	General
Geo. L. J.	Georgetown Law Journal
Gov't	Government
Guar.	Guaranty
Ham.	Hamilton County
Harv. L. Rev.	Harvard Law Review
H.B.	House Bill
H. Con. Res.	U.S. House of Representatives Congressional Resolution
Hen. 8	English statute enacted under Henry VIII
HLA	Human Leukocyte Antigens
Hosp.	Hospital
Hous.	Housing
HPRS	Highway Patrol Retirement System

Mass.	Massachusetts Reports
M.C. Sup. R.	Rules of Superintendence for Municipal Courts and County Courts
Md.	Maryland Reports
Md. App.	Maryland Appellate Reports
Me.	Maine
Med.	Medical; Medicine
Mem'l	Memorial
Mem. St. L. Rev.	Memphis State Law Reivew
Metro.	Metropolitan
Mfg.	Manufacturing
Mfr.	Manufacturer
Mgt.	Management
Mich.	Michigan
Mich. App.	Michigan Appeals Reports
Mich. L. Rev.	Michigan Law Review
Minn.	Minnesota
Misc.	New York Miscellaneous Reports
Misc.2d	New York Miscellaneous Reports, Second Series
Mkt.	Market
Mktg.	Marketing
Mo.	Missouri; Missouri Reports
Mont.	Montana; Montana Reports
Mont. R.	Montgomery County Common Pleas Court Rule
Mt.	Mount
Mun.	Municipal
Muni.	Municipal Court
Mut.	Mutual
N.	North; Northern
NASW	National Association of Social Workers
Nat'l	National
N.C.	North Carolina; North Carolina Reports
N.D.	North Dakota; North Dakota Reports; Northern District
N.E.	North Eastern Reporter
N.E.2d	North Eastern Reporter, Second Series
New Eng. L. Rev.	New England Law Review
N.J.	New Jersey; New Jersey Reports
N.J. Eq.	New Jersey Equity Reports
N.J. Misc.	New Jersey Miscellaneous Reports
N.J. Super.	New Jersey Superior Court Reports
No.	Number
N.P.	Ohio Nisi Prius Reports
N.W.	Northwestern Reporter
N.W.2d	North Western Reporter, Second Series
N.W. L. Rev.	Northwestern University Law Review
N.Y.	New York; New York Reports
N.Y.2d	New York Reports, Second Series
N.Y. Misc.2d	New York Miscellaneous Reports, Second Series

N.Y.S.	West's New York Supplement
N.Y.S.2d	West's New York Supplement, Second Series
OAC	Ohio Administrative Code
O.A.G.	Ohio Opinions of the Attorney General
O. Const.	Ohio Constitution
ODHS	Ohio Department of Human Services
Ohio	Ohio Reports
Ohio App.	Ohio Appellate Reports
Ohio App.2d	Ohio Appellate Reports, Second Series
Ohio App.3d	Ohio Appellate Reports, Third Series
Ohio B.	Ohio Bar Reports
Ohio C.C.	Ohio Circuit Court Reports
Ohio C.C. Dec.	Ohio Circuit Court Decisions
Ohio C.C.(n.s.)	Ohio Circuit Court Reports, New Series
Ohio Cir. Dec.	Ohio Circuit Decisions
Ohio Dec.	Ohio Decisions
Ohio Dec. Reprint	Ohio Decisions, Reprint
Ohio Jur.2d	Ohio Jurisprudence, Second Series
Ohio Jur.3d	Ohio Jurisprudence, Third Series
Ohio Law Abs.	Ohio Law Abstract
Ohio L. Rep.	Ohio Law Reporter
Ohio Misc.	Ohio Miscellaneous Reports
Ohio Misc.2d	Ohio Miscellaneous Reports, Second Series
Ohio N.P.	Ohio Nisi Prius Reports
Ohio N.P.(n.s.)	Ohio Nisi Prius Reports, New Series
Ohio N. U. L. Rev.	Ohio Northern University Law Review
Ohio Op.	Ohio Opinions
Ohio Op.2d	Ohio Opinions, Second Series
Ohio Op.3d	Ohio Opinions, Third Series
Ohio St.	Ohio State Reports
Ohio St.2d	Ohio State Reports, Second Series
Ohio St.3d	Ohio State Reports, Third Series
Ohio St. L. J.	Ohio State Law Journal
Ohio Supp.	Ohio Supplement
OJI	Ohio Jury Instructions
Okla.	Oklahoma
Op.	Opinion
OPA	Ohio Parentage Act
OPLS	Ohio Parent Locator Service
Or.	Oregon; Oregon Reports
Or. App.	Oregon Reports, Court of Appeals
Org.	Organization; Organizing
OWF	Ohio Works First
p.	page
P.	Pacific Reporter
P.2d	Pacific Reporter, Second Series
Pa.	Pennsylvania State Reports
Pac.	Pacific
Pa. Super.	Pennsylvania Superior Court Reports

PERS	Public Employees Retirement System
PFDPF	Police and Fireman's Disability and Pension Fund
Pharm.	Pharmaceutical; Pharmaceutics
PKPA	Parental Kidnapping Prevention Act
Prob.	Probate
Prod.	Product; Production
Prof'l	Professional
PSERS	Public School Employees Retirement System
Pub.	Public
Publ'g	Publishing
QDRO	Qualified Domestic Relations Order
QJSA	Qualified (post-retirement) Joint and Survivor Annuity
QPSA	Qualified Pre-retirement Survivor Annuity
RC	Ohio Revised Code
Rd.	Road
REA	Retirement Equity Act
Ref.	Refining
Reg'l	Regional
Rep. R.	Supreme Court Rules for the Reporting of Opinions
Reprod.	Reproduction; Reproductive
Rev.	Review; Revised
Rev. Rul.	Revenue Ruling
Rptr.	Reporter
R.R.	Railroad
RS	Revised Statutes of Ohio
RSDHI	Retirement, Survivors, Disability Health Insurance Program
Rts.	Rights
RURESA	Revised Uniform Reciprocal Enforcement of Support Act
Ry.	Railway
S.	South; Southern
Sav.	Savings
S.B.	Senate Bill
S.C.	South Carolina; South Carolina Reports
Sch.	School; Schools
S.Ct.	United States Supreme Court Reporter
S.D.	South Dakota Reports
S.E.	South Eastern Reporter
S.E.2d	South Eastern Reporter, Second Series
Sec.	Securities; Security
SEP	Simplified Employee Pension Plan
Serv.	Service
Servs.	Services
SETS	Support Enforcement Tracking System
SMM	Summary of Material Modification
So.	Southern Reporter
So.2d	Southern Reporter, Second Series

Soc.	Social
Soc. Work	Social Work
Soc'y	Society
S.S.	Steamship; Steamships
SSI	Supplemental Security Income
St.	Street
Stark R.	Stark County Common Pleas Court Rule
Stat.	Statutes
STRS	State Teachers Retirement System
Subcomm.	Subcommittee
Super.	Superior Court
Sup. R.	Rules of Superintendence for the Courts of Ohio
Sur.	Surety
S.W.	South Western Reporter
S.W.2d	South Western Reporter, Second Series
Sys.	System; Systems
T.C.	Tax Court
T.C.M.	Tax Court Memorandum Decisions
Tech.'	Technology
Tel.	Telegraph; Telephone
Telecomm.	Telecommunication
Temp.	Temporary
Tenn. App.	Tennessee Appeals
Tex.	Texas; Texas Reports
Tex. Civ. App.	Texas Civil Appeals Reports
Tex. Crim.	Texas Criminal Reports
Tol. L. Rev.	Toledo Law Review
TPO	Temporary protection order
Traf. R.	Ohio Traffic Rules
Transcon.	Transcontinental
Transp.	Transport; Transportation
TRO	Temporary Restraining Order
TSA	Tax Sheltered Annuity
Twp.	Township
U.	University
UCCJA	Uniform Child Custody Jurisdiction Act
UCCJEA	Uniform Child Custody Jurisdiction and Enforcement Act
UEFJA	Uniform Enforcement of Foreign Judgments Act
UIFSA	Uniform Interstate Family Support Act
Unif.	Uniform
URESA	Uniform Reciprocal Enforcement of Support Act
U.S.	United States Supreme Court Reports
U.S.C.A.	United States Code, Annotated
U.S. Const.	United States Constitution
Util.	Utility
v.	versus
VA	Veterans Administration
Va. L. Rev.	Virginia Law Review

vol. .... volume
W. .... West; Western
Wash. .... Washington Reports
Wash.2d .... Washington Reports, Second Series
W.D. .... Western District
Wis. .... Wisconsin; Wisconsin Reports
Wis.2d .... Wisconsin Reports, Second Series
Wis. L. Rev. .... Wisconsin Law Review
WL .... Westlaw
Women & Pol. .... Women and Politics
Women's Rts. L. Rep. .. Women's Rights Law Reporter
Wyo. .... Wyoming
Yale L.J. .... Yale Law Journal

Westlaw® Electronic Research Guide

Westlaw—Expanding the Reach of Your Library

Baldwin's Ohio Practice Series, Domestic Relations Law is an essential aid to legal research. Westlaw is West's online legal research service. With Westlaw, you experience the same quality and integrity that you have come to expect from West books, plus quick, easy access to West's vast collection of statutes, case law materials, public records, and other legal resources, in addition to current news articles and business information. For the most current and comprehensive legal research, combine the strengths of West books and Westlaw.

When you research with westlaw.com you get the convenience of the Internet combined with comprehensive and accurate Westlaw content, including exclusive editorial enhancements, plus features found only in westlaw.com such as ResultsPlus™ or StatutesPlus.™

This guide will focus on a few aspects of Westlaw use to supplement research begun in this publication, and will direct you to additional sources of assistance.

Accessing Databases Using the Westlaw Directory

A database is a collection of documents with some features in common. It may contain statutes, court decisions, administrative materials, commentaries, news or other information. Each database has a unique identifier, used in many Westlaw commands to select a database of interest.

The Westlaw Directory lists all databases on Westlaw and contains links to detailed information relating to the content of each database. Click **Directory** on the westlaw.com toolbar. There are several ways to access a database even when you don't know the database identifier. Browse a directory view. Scan the directory. Type all or part of a database name in the *Search these databases* text box. Or click **Find a Database Wizard** to help you select relevant databases for your search. You can access up to ten databases at one time for user-defined multibase searching.

The Ohio case law database identifier is OH-CS.

Annotated and unannotated versions of the Ohio statutes are searchable on Westlaw (identifiers OH-ST-ANN and OH-ST), as are Ohio court rules (OH-RULES) and the Ohio Administrative Code, Approved Edition (OH-ADC). Documents used to update Ohio statutes are also searchable in Ohio Legislative Service (OH-LEGIS). Those used to update rules are searchable in Ohio Court Orders (OH-ORDERS).

The United States Code and United States Code Annotated are searchable databases on Westlaw (identifiers USC and USCA, respectively), as are federal court rules (US-RULES) and regulations (CFR). Documents used to update federal statutes, rules, and regulations are searchable in the United States Public Laws (US-PL), Federal Orders (US-ORDERS) and Federal Register (FR) databases, respectively.

Other databases of potential interest in connection with your research include:

OH-AG	Ohio Attorney General Opinions
WLD-OH	West Legal Directory—Ohio
ATR-TP	Antitrust & Trade Regulation—Law Reviews, Texts & Bar Journals
OHCML-CS	Commercial Law & Contracts—Ohio Cases
WLD-ATR	West Legal Directory—Antitrust & Trade Regulation
FATR-BRL	Federal Antitrust & Trade Regulation—Department of Justice Business Review Letters
FATR-CODREG	Federal Antitrust & Trade Regulation—Code and Regulations
FATR-CPSC	Consumer Product Safety Commission Materials
FATR-FTC	Federal Antitrust & Trade Regulation—Federal Trade COmmission Decisions
FATR-NR	Federal Antitrust & Trade Regulation—News Releases
FATR-CS	Federal Antitrust & Trade Regulation—Federal Cases
AGELINE	American Association of Retired Persons (AARP) Database (DIALOG)
ANMALR	Andrews Mergers & Acquisitions Litigation Reporter (Andrews Publications)
BNA-ATD	BNA Antitrust & Trade Regulation Daily (Bureau of National Affairs, Inc.)
BNA-ATR	BNA Antitrust & Trade Regulation Database
CONFLQR	Consumer Finance Law Quarterly Report (The Conference on Consumer Finance Law)
LYCLREV	Loyola Consumer Law Review (Loyola University of Chicago School of Law)
DPLBCLJ	DePaul Business and Commercial Law Journal
HAWKLAND	Uniform Commercial Code Series (Hawkland)
PLI-COMM	Commercial Law and Practice Course Handbook Series (Practicing Law Institute)
REST-CONTR	Restatement of the Law—Contracts (American Law Institute)
UCC-CS+	Uniform Commercial Code Cases Plus (Clark Boardman Callaghan)
UCC-OH	Ohio Uniform Commercial Code Records

For information as to content, currentness and search tips regarding any Westlaw database, use the Scope feature.

Westlaw Highlights

Use of this publication may be supplemented through the Westlaw Bulletin (WLB), the Westlaw Ohio State Bulletin (WSB-OH) and various Topical Highlights. Highlights databases contain summaries of significant judicial, legislative and administrative developments and are updated daily; they are searchable both from an automatic list of recent documents and using general Westlaw search methods for documents accumulated over time. Consult the Westlaw Directory for a complete, current listing of highlights databases.

Retrieving a Specific Document

To retrieve a specific document by citation or title on westlaw.com, click **Find** on the toolbar to display the Find a Document page. If you are unsure of the correct citation format, type the publication abbreviation, e.g., **xx st** (where xx is a state's two-letter postal abbreviation), in the *Find this document by citation* text box and click **Go** to display a fill-in-the-blank template. To retrieve a specific case when you know one or more parties' names, click **Find a Case by Party Name**.

Updating Research Using KeyCite®

KeyCite, West's citation research service on Westlaw, makes it easy to trace the history of your case, statute, administrative decision or regulation to determine if there are recent updates, and to find other documents that cite your document. KeyCite will also find pending legislation relating to federal or state statutes. Access the powerful features of KeyCite from the westlaw.com toolbar, the **Links for** tab or KeyCite flags in a document display. KeyCite's red and yellow warning flags tell you at a glance whether your document has negative history. Depth-of-treatment stars help you focus on the most important citing references. KeyCite Alert allows you to monitor the status of your case, statute or rule, and automatically sends you updates at the frequency you specify.

Using Westlaw as a Citator

For research beyond the coverage of any citator service, go directly to the databases (OH-CS, for example) containing citing documents and use standard Westlaw search techniques to retrieve documents citing specific constitutional provisions, statutes, standard jury instructions or other authorities.

Fortunately, the specific portion of a citation is often reasonably distinctive, such as 22:636.1, 301.65, 401(k), 12-21-5, 12052. When it is, a search on that specific portion alone may retrieve applicable documents without any substantial number of inapplicable ones (unless the number happens to be coincidentally popular in another context). Ohio statutes fall into this category.

Similarly, if the citation involves more than one number, such as 42 U.S.C.A. § 1201, a search containing both numbers (e.g., 42 /5 1201) is likely to produce mostly desired information, even though the component numbers are common.

If necessary, the search may be limited in several ways:

A. Switch from a general database to one containing mostly documents within the subject area of the cite being researched;

B. Use a connector (&, /s, /p, etc.) to narrow the search to documents including terms which are highly likely to accompany the correct citation in the context of the issue being researched;

C. Include other citation information in the query. Because of the variety of citation formats used in documents, this option should be used primarily where other options prove insufficient. Below are illustrative queries for any database containing Ohio cases:

Civ.Rule Civ Civil O.R.C.P. R.C.P. /7 56

will retrieve cases citing Civil Procedure Rule 56; and

(appellate /2 procedure rule) App.Proc! App.Rule R.A.P. /7 9

will retrieve cases citing Appellate Procedure Rule 9.

Alternative Retrieval Methods

A Natural Language search allows you to frame your issue in plain English to retrieve documents:

[May a creditor retain collateral and sue for deficiency?]

Alternatively, retrieval may be focused by use of the Terms and Connectors method:

[HE(RETAIN! KEEP SURRENDER REPOSSESSES! /P COLLATERAL /P DEFICIENCY]

In databases with Key Numbers, either of the above examples will identify [Secured Transactions ☞ 240] as a Key Number collecting headnotes relevant to this issue if there are pertinent cases. Since the Key Numbers are affixed to points of law by trained specialists based on conceptual understanding of the case, relevant cases that were not retrieved by either of the language-dependent methods will often be found at a Key Number.

Similarly, citations in retrieved documents (to cases, statutes, rules, etc.) may suggest additional, fruitful research using other Westlaw databases (e.g., annotated statutes, rules) or services (e.g., KeyCite).

Key Number Search and KeySearch

Frequently, case law research rapidly converges on a few topics, headings and Key Numbers within West's Key Number System that are likely to contain relevant cases. These may be discovered from known, relevant cases from any jurisdiction; Library References in West publications; browsing in a digest; or browsing the KeySearch feature on westlaw.com.

Once discovered, topics, subheadings or Key Numbers are useful as search terms (in databases containing cases) alone or with other search terms, to focus the search within a narrow range of potentially relevant material.

For example, to retrieve cases with at least one headnote classified to [Secured Transactions ☞ 240], sign on to a case law database and enter

[[349Ak240] [use with other search terms, if desired]

The topic name [(Secured Transactions)] is replaced by its numerical equivalent [(349A)] and the ☞ by the letter k. A list of topics and their numerical equivalents can be found on westlaw.com by clicking the drop down arrow in the upper right hand corner of the toolbar and selecting "Key Numbers & Digest." Other topics of special interest include: [Assignment (38), Bankruptcy (56), Banks and Banking (52), Bills and Notes (56), Carriers (70), Chattel Mortgages (76), Consumer Credit (92B), Consumer Protection (92H), Contracts (95), Debtor and Creditor (117T), Fraudulent Conveyances (186), Interest (219), Novation (278), Reformation of Instruments (328), Sales (343), Trade Regulation (382), and Warehousemen (403).]

KeySearch, powered by the West Key Number System, identifies relevant key numbers and their underlying concepts and runs a query for you. KeySearch can retrieve reported cases as well as documents that don't contain key numbers, such as law reviews and unpublished cases.

To use KeySearch, complete these steps:

1. Click **KeySearch** on the toolbar.
2. Browse the topics and subtopics in the right frame by clicking the closed folder icons. Search option: You can also search the KeySearch topics and subtopics for specific terms. Type the terms in the text box in the left frame of the KeySearch page and click **GO**. A list of topics and subtopics containing the terms in their hierarchy is displayed. (**Note:** You can use the traditional Westlaw connectors between terms when using the search feature, except for the **/p** connector, which KeySearch does not recognize.)
3. Select a topic or subtopic to search by clicking the open folder icon next to the topic or subtopic.
4. Choose the source you want to retrieve documents from and type additional search terms (optional) in the *Add search terms* text box. KeySearch provides a query for you based on the topic or subtopic you selected and on any search terms you entered in the *Add search terms* text box.
5. Click **Search** to run the KeySearch query. **Note:** If you add search terms to the KeySearch query, Westlaw will automatically look for typographical, spelling, and usage errors in your query. If errors are found, an updated *Did You Mean* search will be displayed at the top of the Result page. You may also see a list of alternative search terms and databases at the top of the page; adding these terms to your query or running your query in these databases may help you retrieve more documents that are relevant to your issue.

Using Westlaw's Extensive Linking Features

Westlaw allows you to move from one document to another or from one part of a document to another, then easily return to your original place, without losing your original result. Opportunities to move in this manner are indicated by blue, underlined text ("link"). Whenever you see these links, you may move to the document designated by the text of the link (e.g. another case, statute, etc.) by clicking on the link with your mouse. You can return to your original place by either closing the box that opened after clicking the link or, if you maximized the new document, by clicking **Back** on your internet service browser.

Within the text of a court opinion, there are numerous links to case and statute cites, and to bracketed number links marking discussions corresponding to headnotes. On a screen containing the text of a headnote, the bracketed number links allow movement to the corresponding discussion in the text of the opinion,

[2]

and allow browsing West's Key Number System beginning at various heading levels:

☞ [349A Secured Transactions]
☞ [349AVII Default and Enforcement]
☞ [349Ak240 k. Deficiency and personal liability]

ResultsPlus™

ResultsPlus is a Westlaw technology that automatically suggests additional information related to your search. The suggested materials are accessible by a set of links that appear to the right of your westlaw.com search results:

- Go directly to relevant ALR® articles and Am Jur® annotations.

- Find on-point resources by key number.

- See information form related treatises and law reviews.

StatutesPlus™

When you access a statutes database in westlaw.com you are brought to a powerful Search Center which collects, on one toolbar, the tools that are most useful for fast, efficient retrieval of statutes documents:

- Have a few key terms? Click **Index**.

- Know the common name? Click **Popular Name Table**.

- Familiar with the subject matter? Click **Table of Contents**.

- Have a citation or section number? Click **Find by Citation**.

- Or, simply search with **Natural Language** or **Terms and Connectors**.

When you access a statutes section, click on the **Links for** tab for all relevant links for the current document that will also include a

KeyCite section with a description of the KeyCite status flag. Depending on your document, links may also include administrative, bill text, and other sources that were previously only available by accessing and searching other databases.

Additional Information

Westlaw is available on the Web at http://www.westlaw.com.

The information provided above illustrates some of the ways Westlaw can complement research using this publication. However, this brief overview illustrates only some of the power of Westlaw. The full range of Westlaw search techniques is available to support your research.

For search assistance, call the West Reference Attorneys at 1-800-REF-ATTY (1-800-733-2889).

For technical assistance, call West Customer Technical Support at 1-800-WESTLAW (1-800-937-8529).

RELATED PRODUCTS FROM WEST

STATUTES, CONSTITUTIONS, AND COURT RULES

Baldwin's Ohio Revised Code Annotated

Baldwin's Ohio Legislative Service Annotated

Ohio Constitution Handbook

Ohio Rules of Court, State and Federal

United States Code Annotated

CASE LAW, REPORTERS, DIGESTS, ATTORNEY GENERAL OPINIONS

Ohio Official Reports

West's Ohio Digest

Ohio Attorney General Opinions

SERB Official Reporter

Federal Reporter

Federal Supplement

West's Supreme Court Reporter

ADMINISTRATIVE LAW

Baldwin's Ohio Administrative Code

Ohio Administrative Law Handbook
and Agency Directory
Fenton and McNeil

Baldwin's Ohio Monthly Record

Administrative Law and Practice 2d

Administrative Law: Practice and Procedure

GENERAL LEGAL REFERENCES

Ohio Jurisprudence 3d

American Jurisprudence 2d

American Law Reports

Corpus Juris Secundum

OHIO DATABASES ON WESTLAW

Cases, General & Topical
Statutes & Court Rules
Legislative Service, Bills & Bill Tracking
Administrative & Executive Materials
Public Information, Records & Filings
Baldwin's Ohio Practice Series
Ohio Jurisprudence 3d
Ohio Forms, Legal & Business
Law Reviews, Bar Journals & Legal Periodicals
Newspapers & Periodicals
Miscellany

CD-ROM

Baldwin's Ohio Revised Code Annotated with
Ohio Administrative Code, and
SERB Official Reporter

Ohio Reports
Ohio Unreported Appellate Decisions
Baldwin's Ohio Practice Library
West's Ohio Digest
Ohio Jurisprudence 3d
United States Code Annotated
West's Sixth Circuit Reporter
West's Federal District Court Reporter—Sixth Circuit
West's Supreme Court Reporter
Federal Reporter, 1st, 2d, and 3d Series
Federal Supplement
Federal Rules Decisions
Wright & Miller, Federal Practice and Procedure
Topical CD-ROM Libraries
Ohio Jurisprudence Pleading and Practice Forms
Ohio Criminal Defense Motions
Hennenberg and Reinhart

CIVIL PRACTICE AND PROCEDURE

Baldwin's Ohio Practice, Civil Practice 2d
Klein, Darling, and Terez

Baldwin's Ohio Practice, Civil Practice Laws & Rules Annotated

Ohio Personal Injury Practice
O'Reilly

Baldwin's Ohio Practice, Tort Law
Ernst

Trial Handbook for Ohio Lawyers
Markus

CRIMINAL LAW AND PRACTICE

Baldwin's Ohio Practice, Criminal Law 3d
Katz, Giannelli, Lipton and Crocker

Baldwin's Ohio Practice, Statutory Charges
Terez

Ohio Arrest, Search and Seizure
Katz

Baldwin's Ohio Practice, Ohio Criminal Laws and Rules
Katz and Giannelli (Eds.)

Ohio Domestic Violence Law
Adrine and Ruden

Ohio Driving Under the Influence Law
Weiler and Weiler

Ohio Felony Sentencing Law
Griffin and Katz

Trial Handbook for Ohio Lawyers
Markus

TRIAL AND APPELLATE PRACTICE

Baldwin's Ohio Practice, Evidence 2d
Giannelli and Snyder

Baldwin's Ohio Practice, Rules of Evidence Handbook
Giannelli and Snyder

Ohio Appellate Practice
Painter and Dennis

Ohio Trial Objections
Giannelli and Snyder

Trial Handbook for Ohio Lawyers
Markus

DOMESTIC RELATIONS AND FAMILY LAW

Baldwin's Ohio Practice, Domestic Relations Law 4th
Sowald and Morganstern

Baldwin's Ohio Practice, Domestic Relations Laws and Rules Annotated

Ohio Domestic Violence Law
Adrine and Ruden

Ohio Elder Law
Kreiner

Domestic Relations Journal of Ohio
Morganstern

PROBATE AND JUVENILE LAW

Baldwin's Ohio Practice, Merrick-Rippner Probate Law 7th
Carlin

Ohio Probate Code Annotated

Probate Law Journal of Ohio
Brucken

Ohio Juvenile Law
Giannelli and Yeomans Salvador

REAL ESTATE

Ohio Landlord Tenant Law
White

Baldwin's Ohio Practice, Ohio Real Estate Law 3d
Kuehnle and Levey

Ohio Condominium Law
Kuehnle and Williams

BUSINESS AND LEGAL

Baldwin's Ohio Practice, Business Organizations 2d
Blackford

Baldwin's Ohio Practice, Business Organizations Laws & Rules
Ekonomon and Heinle (Eds.)

Ohio Consumer Law
Legal Aid Society of Cleveland, Williams (Ed.)

LEGAL FORMS

Ohio Forms Legal and Business

Ohio Forms and Transactions

Ohio Jurisprudence Pleading and Practice Forms

West's Legal Forms, 2d

TAX LAW

Baldwin's Ohio Tax Law and Rules
Engel

LABOR LAW

**Ohio Civil Service & Collective Bargaining Laws & Rules
Annotated**

Ohio Employment Practices Law
Siegel and Stephen

Ohio Workers' Compensation Law
Wasil and Mastrangelo

Workers' Compensation Journal of Ohio
Harris

GOVERNMENT

Baldwin's Ohio Practice, Local Government Law—Township
Princehorn

Baldwin's Ohio Practice, Local Government Law—Municipal
Gotherman, Babbit and Lang

Baldwin's Ohio Practice, Local Government Law—County
Conard II

Finley's Ohio Municipal Service
Finley

Ohio Election Laws Annotated

Ohio Planning and Zoning Law
Meck and Pearlman

SCHOOL LAW

Baldwin's Ohio School Law
Hastings, Manoloff, Sharb, Sheeran and Jaffe

Ohio School Law Handbook
Hastings, Manoloff, Sharb, Sheeran and Jaffe

Baldwin's Ohio School Law Journal
Lentz

Lentz School Security
Lentz

United States School Laws and Rules

BUILDING CONSTRUCTION AND CODE ENFORCEMENT

Ohio Building Code and Related Codes

Know Your Code: A Guide to the OBC

Ohio Construction and Code Journal
Harris

Ohio Construction Law Manual

Code News

If you would like to inquire about these West publications or place an order, please call 1–800–344–5009.

WEST®
A Thomson Reuters business

West
610 Opperman Drive
Eagan, MN 55123

Visit West on the Internet:
http://west.thomson.com

Summary of Contents

Table of Contents

CHAPTER 1. ANTENUPTIAL AGREEMENTS

CHAPTER 2. MARRIAGE

CHAPTER 3. PARENTAGE

CHAPTER 4. MARITAL OBLIGATIONS AND PROPERTY RIGHTS

CHAPTER 5. DOMESTIC VIOLENCE

CHAPTER 6. ALTERNATIVE FORMS OF DISPUTE RESOLUTION

CHAPTER 7. ANNULMENT

CHAPTER 8. LEGAL SEPARATION

CHAPTER 9. SEPARATION AGREEMENTS

I.   SEPARATION AGREEMENTS—FORMS

II.   PRELIMINARY CLAUSES—FORMS

VII. PARENTAL RIGHTS AND RESPONSIBILITY CLAUSES—FORMS

VIII. PARENTING TIME CLAUSES—FORMS

CHAPTER 12. MARITAL AND SEPARATE PROPERTY

CHAPTER 13. SPOUSAL SUPPORT

CHAPTER 14. MODIFICATION OF SPOUSAL SUPPORT

CHAPTER 15. PARENTAL RIGHTS AND SHARED PARENTING

CHAPTER 16. MODIFICATION OF PARENTAL RIGHTS AND RESPONSIBILITIES

CHAPTER 17. UNIFORM CHILD CUSTODY JURISDICTION ACT; PARENTAL KIDNAPPING PREVENTION ACT; UNIFORM CHILD CUSTODY JURISDICTION AND ENFORCEMENT ACT; INTERNATIONAL CHILD ABDUCTION REMEDIES ACT

CHAPTER 18. PARENTING TIME AND VISITATION

CHAPTER 19. CHILD SUPPORT

CHAPTER 20. ENFORCEMENT OF SPOUSAL AND CHILD SUPPORT

I. THE BASIC TOOL

II. THE ANCIENT TOOL

III. THE RUSTY TOOL

IV. THE AWKWARD TOOL

V. THE TRENDY TOOL

CHAPTER 21. ENFORCEMENT OF PARENTING TIME RIGHTS AND ALLOCATION OF PARENTAL RIGHTS

Chapter 1

Antenuptial Agreements

By Lynn B. Schwartz, Esq.[*]

KeyCite®: Cases and other legal materials listed in KeyCite Scope can be researched through the KeyCite service on Westlaw®. Use KeyCite to check citations for form, parallel references, prior and later history, and comprehensive citator information, including citations to other decisions and secondary materials.

---

§ 1:1 Function and nature

An antenuptial agreement is a contract entered into by persons about to be married, who wish to resolve issues of support, distribution of wealth, and identification, separation, and/or division of prop-

---

[*]Updated for the Fourth Edition by Stanley Morganstern, Esq.

erty, in the event of the death of either spouse or the failure of the proposed marriage.[1] Antenuptial agreements are recognized in every common law jurisdiction, and Ohio is no exception.[2] Generally, antenuptial agreements are enforced as to the rights and obligations of the parties when the marriage ends in death.[3] Where the marriage is terminated by divorce and provision for such an event is made in the antenuptial agreement, the court will examine the issue of fairness at the time of execution for purposes of property division and fairness at the time of divorce for purposes of spousal support.[4] Such contracts are enforceable, even by the party found at fault.[5]

Antenuptial agreements can be used to divest the parties of statutory rights in each other's property which would normally arise by virtue of marriage.[6] Consequently, they are commonly employed by persons possessed of substantial wealth who wish to (1) preserve all or part of the wealth from a spouse, or (2) keep the wealth in the same family that generated it. In addition, antenuptial agreements are commonly used by (1) those who have been previously married

---

[Section 1:1]

[1]Hook v. Hook, 69 Ohio St. 2d 234, 23 Ohio Op. 3d 239, 431 N.E.2d 667 (1982); Southern Ohio Sav. Bank & Trust Co. v. Burkhart, 148 Ohio St. 149, 35 Ohio Op. 166, 74 N.E.2d 67 (1947); Dearbaugh v. Dearbaugh, 110 Ohio App. 540, 13 Ohio Op. 2d 351, 170 N.E.2d 262 (2d Dist. Shelby County 1959); Kennedy v. Kennedy, 11 Ohio App. 399, 1919 WL 906 (8th Dist. Cuyahoga County 1919); Kosik v. George, 253 Or. 15, 452 P.2d 560 (1969).

[2]RC 2106.22, RC 3103.05; Hook v. Hook, 69 Ohio St. 2d 234, 23 Ohio Op. 3d 239, 431 N.E.2d 667 (1982).

[3]Hook v. Hook, 69 Ohio St. 2d 234, 23 Ohio Op. 3d 239, 431 N.E.2d 667 (1982); Gross v. Gross, 11 Ohio St. 3d 99, 464 N.E.2d 500, 53 A.L.R.4th 139 (1984); Southern Ohio Sav. Bank & Trust Co. v. Burkhart, 148 Ohio St. 149, 151, 35 Ohio Op. 166, 74 N.E.2d 67 (1947) ("It would be monstrous to hold that a woman could collect an annuity settled upon her by contract in contemplation of marriage, when after the marriage, without cause, she utterly refused to live with her husband longer than seven weeks and three days. This is the precise case before us." (quoting Jacobs v. Jacobs, 42 Iowa 600, 1876 WL 442 (1876)); Conley v. Conley, 45 Ohio App. 2d 1, 74 Ohio Op. 2d 6, 340 N.E.2d 430 (1st Dist. Hamilton County 1975) (where agreement contains no recital of or any provision for consideration to support obligations, is expressly conditioned on continued legal existence of marriage, and termination of marriage by divorce removes condition, both parties are relieved of agreement); Dearbaugh v. Dearbaugh, 110 Ohio App. 540, 542, 13 Ohio Op. 2d 351, 170 N.E.2d 262 (2d Dist. Shelby County 1959) ("If one party fails to perform a promise made in an antenuptial agreement, such failure may justify granting relief [alimony] to the other party."); Kennedy v. Kennedy, 11 Ohio App. 399, 1919 WL 906 (8th Dist. Cuyahoga County 1919) (husband guilty of breach of contract (or has not substantially performed), wife not barred by such antenuptial contract of right to alimony given to her by statutes of state). But see Benza v. Benza, 1978 WL 216102 (Ohio Ct. App. 1st Dist. Warren County 1978) (terms of antenuptial agreement followed at time of divorce). See also Kosik v. George, 253 Or. 15, 452 P.2d 560 (1969); Text § 1:8, Considerations for possible divorce, dissolution.

[4]See Text § 1:8, Considerations for possible divorce, dissolution.

[5]Gross v. Gross, 11 Ohio St. 3d 99, 464 N.E.2d 500, 53 A.L.R.4th 139 (1984).

[6]Troha v. Sneller, 169 Ohio St. 397, 8 Ohio Op. 2d 435, 159 N.E.2d 899 (1959).

and wish to see that their property goes to the issue of the prior marriage upon the termination of the proposed marriage, and (2) those who have had a bad experience in a prior divorce, in regard to property and/or spousal support, and have no wish to repeat the experience. As a modern trend, more persons are choosing to marry later in life, which means they have acquired more individual property prior to the marriage, and they would most likely prefer to retain control of such property, until they are certain of the marriage.[7]

Antenuptial agreements are contractual in nature.[8] However, the Ohio courts have traditionally treated antenuptial agreements differently from other contracts because of their confidential nature and the possibility of overreaching.[9] Historically, Ohio courts have, and most American jurisdictions perceive the woman to be the weaker party in these agreements. The following language from *Stilley v. Folger*[10] was typical:

> What person so exposed to imposition as a woman, contracting personally with her intended husband, just on the eve of marriage—at a time when all prudential considerations are likely to be merged in a confiding attachment, or suppressed from an honorable instinct and sentiment of delicacy.

> It would be a reproach to the law, if the very virtues and graces of a woman were thus allowed to become the successful means of overreaching and defrauding them in bargains.[11]

RC 3103.05 specifically states that contracts between married persons are "subject 'to the general rules which control the actions of persons occupying confidential relations with each other.' " The same rules apply to separation agreements.[12] Although the statute and

---

[7]See Text Ch 12, Marital and Separate Property. For the effect on the survivor benefit of a pension plan, see Michael D. Rose, *Caveat: Antenuptial Agreements Cannot Affect Pension Plan Survivor Benefits*, 4 Dom. Rel. J. Ohio 101 (Nov./Dec. 1992).

[8]Hook v. Hook, 69 Ohio St. 2d 234, 23 Ohio Op. 3d 239, 431 N.E.2d 667 (1982); Southern Ohio Sav. Bank & Trust Co. v. Burkhart, 148 Ohio St. 149, 35 Ohio Op. 166, 74 N.E.2d 67 (1947); Juhasz v. Juhasz, 134 Ohio St. 257, 12 Ohio Op. 57, 16 N.E.2d 328, 117 A.L.R. 993 (1938); Dearbaugh v. Dearbaugh, 110 Ohio App. 540, 13 Ohio Op. 2d 351, 170 N.E.2d 262 (2d Dist. Shelby County 1959); Osborn v. Osborn, 10 Ohio Misc. 171, 39 Ohio Op. 2d 275, 226 N.E.2d 814 (C.P. 1966), judgment aff'd, 18 Ohio St. 2d 144, 47 Ohio Op. 2d 310, 248 N.E.2d 191 (1969) (antenuptial agreements are prima facie valid and binding); Vadakin v. Vadakin, 1997 WL 325319 (Ohio Ct. App. 4th Dist. Washington County 1997). See also Stilley v. Folger, 14 Ohio 610, 1846 WL 153 (1846), for a discussion of the origins and nature of antenuptial agreements.

[9]Rudrick v. Thull, 39 Ohio App. 69, 10 Ohio L. Abs. 542, 177 N.E. 513 (5th Dist. Richland County 1931).

[10]Stilley v. Folger, 14 Ohio 610, 613, 1846 WL 153 (1846).

[11]See also Hook v. Hook, 69 Ohio St. 2d 234, 23 Ohio Op. 3d 239, 431 N.E.2d 667 (1982).

[12]Lowman v. Lowman, 166 Ohio St. 1, 1 Ohio Op. 2d 152, 139 N.E.2d 1 (1956); Nellis v. Nellis, 98 Ohio App. 247, 57 Ohio Op. 281, 129 N.E.2d 217 (6th Dist. Lucas County 1955); Brewer v. Brewer, 84 Ohio App. 35, 39 Ohio Op. 89, 52 Ohio L. Abs. 116, 78 N.E.2d 919 (2d Dist. Montgomery County 1948).

cases apply to separation agreements rather than antenuptial agreements, this basic principle of confidential relationship is the same.[13]

Since antenuptial agreements are contracts, the law of contracts will generally apply as to their application and interpretation. The terms of an agreement to share household expenses were satisfied with each contributing during their joint occupancy of the marital home and payment of their respective expenses after separation.[14]

When terms are not defined in an agreement, they are to be given their common sense meaning. The term "financial contribution" was held to include the pledge of stock to acquire other stock. The court should consider whether or not there has been a substantial circumstance from the time the agreement was entered into so as to render the spousal support provisions unconscionable.[15]

In dealing with antenuptial agreements, the courts are more likely to give more weight to the adequacy of the supporting consideration and the circumstances surrounding their execution than they would in the case of a conventional contract.[16] Consequently, counsel should not handle these agreements as they would a conventional contract.

§ 1:2   Requirement of writing

Like other contracts, antenuptial agreements cannot seek to accomplish ends contrary to public policy or alter statutory duties of ei-

---

[13]Zimmie v. Zimmie, 11 Ohio St. 3d 94, 464 N.E.2d 142, 53 A.L.R.4th 75 (1984); Gross v. Gross, 11 Ohio St. 3d 99, 464 N.E.2d 500, 53 A.L.R.4th 139 (1984); Kennedy v. Kennedy, 11 Ohio App. 399, 400, 1919 WL 906 (8th Dist. Cuyahoga County 1919) ("We are quite aware of the rule that ante-nuptial contracts will be scrutinized closely by the courts in order to ascertain whether the parties thereto fully understood the nature and terms of the same, and the property possessed by each, and whether any improper advantage was taken of either to induce the making of the contract."); Osborn v. Osborn, 10 Ohio Misc. 171, 39 Ohio Op. 2d 275, 226 N.E.2d 814 (C.P. 1966), judgment aff'd, 18 Ohio St. 2d 144, 47 Ohio Op. 2d 310, 248 N.E.2d 191 (1969).

[14]Badger v. Badger, 2002-Ohio-448, 2002 WL 185306 (Ohio Ct. App. 9th Dist. Medina County 2002).

[15]Fox v. Fox, 2002-Ohio-2010, 2002 WL 722804(Ohio Ct. App. 10th Dist. Franklin County 2002).

[16]Hook v. Hook, 69 Ohio St. 2d 234, 23 Ohio Op. 3d 239, 431 N.E.2d 667 (1982) ("The agreement, however, must meet certain minimum levels of good faith, and will be set aside as invalid as a matter of law if the agreement is not fair and reasonable under the circumstances.'); Southern Ohio Sav. Bank & Trust Co. v. Burkhart, 148 Ohio St. 149, 35 Ohio Op. 166, 74 N.E.2d 67 (1947) ("[The wife] cannot in sound reason and good conscience require performance of a contract which she herself has failed and refused to perform."); Kennedy v. Kennedy, 11 Ohio App. 399, 1919 WL 906 (8th Dist. Cuyahoga County 1919) ("We are quite aware of the rule that ante-nuptial contracts will be scrutinized closely by the courts in order to ascertain whether the parties thereto fully understood the nature and terms of the same, and the property possessed by each, and whether any improper advantage was taken of either to induce the making of the contract."). See also Text § 1:4, Discloure requirements.

ther party during the marriage.[1] In addition, because they are made at least partially in consideration of marriage, antenuptial agreements are within the statute of frauds and hence must be in writing.[2] However, as is true of contracts generally, the writing fulfills an evidentiary requirement and is not essential to the formation of the antenuptial contract. Consequently, it is possible for the parties to adopt a writing after the marriage, encompassing the terms of the prenuptial contract.[3] However, a writing after the marriage is valid only if shown to be a memorandum of the agreement reached prior to the marriage,[4] or as an agreement pursuant to a separation. In *Logan v. Logan*,[5] a postnuptial agreement did not contain a statement that it was a memorandum of an oral antenuptial agreement and was given no effect. If the requirements of *Gross v. Gross*[6] are met, an oral antenuptial agreement reduced to a writing after marriage may be valid.[7]

§ 1:3 Consideration, disproportionate provisions

Because of the confidential nature of antenuptial agreements, the courts of all jurisdictions, including Ohio, tend to carefully scrutinize the adequacy, sufficiency, and nature of the consideration supporting these agreements.[1]

Traditionally, Ohio courts viewed the marriage or promise to marry

---

[Section 1:2]

[1]Dearbaugh v. Dearbaugh, 110 Ohio App. 540, 13 Ohio Op. 2d 351, 170 N.E.2d 262 (2d Dist. Shelby County 1959). See Randolph Carl Oppenheimer, *The Antenuptial Contract in Ohio*, 28 Case W. Res. L. Rev. 1040 (1978); Sabin, *Some Practical Aspects of the Antenuptial Agreement Under the Laws of Ohio*, 18 Cin. L. Rev. 53 (1949); Clark, The Law of Domestic Relations in the United States § 1.9. See also Text § 1:5, Terms.

[2]RC 1335.05.

[3]In re Weber's Estate, 170 Ohio St. 567, 11 Ohio Op. 2d 415, 167 N.E.2d 98 (1960); In re Jones' Estate, 44 Ohio L. Abs. 339, 64 N.E.2d 609 (Ct. App. 3d Dist. Van Wert County 1943). For application of the partial performance exception to the statute of frauds to antenuptial agreements, see Henry v. Henry, 27 Ohio St. 121, 1875 WL 155 (1875).

[4]In re Weber's Estate, 170 Ohio St. 567, 11 Ohio Op. 2d 415, 167 N.E.2d 98 (1960); Brewsaugh v. Brewsaugh, 23 Ohio Misc. 2d 19, 491 N.E.2d 748 (C.P. 1985) (agreement held invalid from inception where parties entered into postnuptial agreement in New Mexico (where valid) but Ohio was their domicile).

[5]Logan v. Logan, 1985 WL 7999 (Ohio Ct. App. 8th Dist. Cuyahoga County 1985).

[6]Gross v. Gross, 11 Ohio St. 3d 99, 464 N.E.2d 500, 53 A.L.R.4th 139 (1984).

[7]Dobbins v. Dobbins, 1992 WL 341001 (Ohio Ct. App. 12th Dist. Clermont County 1992).

[Section 1:3]

[1]Alexander Lindey, *Separation Agreements and Ante-nuptial Contracts,* § 90-51-54 (2d rev. ed. 1967); Clark, The Law of Domestic Relations in the United States § 1.9. See also Zimmie v. Zimmie, 11 Ohio St. 3d 94, 464 N.E.2d 142, 53 A.L.R.4th 75 (1984); Hook v. Hook, 69 Ohio St. 2d 234, 23 Ohio Op. 3d 239, 431 N.E.2d 667 (1982) (importance of confidential relations factor); Southern Ohio Sav. Bank & Trust Co. v.

as the highest form of consideration known to law and hence presumed it to be the primary consideration supporting an antenuptial contract. This is the primary reason that Ohio courts have refused to strictly enforce antenuptial agreements when the marriage ends in divorce.[2] However, the more modern and realistic view is to consider the marriage as a condition precedent to the antenuptial agreement, with other considerations being the basis for the contractual obligations imposed by the agreement.[3] There are no reported Ohio cases in which the marriage, by itself, was the only consideration for the other spouse's renunciation of all claims arising by virtue of marriage.[4] Consequently, the agreement should be based on other considerations besides the marriage or promise to marry. The courts have held that mutual promises to forbear from making claims to the other's property,[5] inter vivos or testamentary transfer to real property,[6] inter vivos

Burkhart, 148 Ohio St. 149, 35 Ohio Op. 166, 74 N.E.2d 67 (1947); Juhasz v. Juhasz, 134 Ohio St. 257, 12 Ohio Op. 57, 16 N.E.2d 328, 117 A.L.R. 993 (1938); Dearbaugh v. Dearbaugh, 110 Ohio App. 540, 13 Ohio Op. 2d 351, 170 N.E.2d 262 (2d Dist. Shelby County 1959); Osborn v. Osborn, 10 Ohio Misc. 171, 39 Ohio Op. 2d 275, 226 N.E.2d 814 (C.P. 1966), judgment aff'd, 18 Ohio St. 2d 144, 47 Ohio Op. 2d 310, 248 N.E.2d 191 (1969) (antenuptial agreements are prima facie valid and binding); Stilley v. Folger, 14 Ohio 610, 1846 WL 153 (1846) (discussion of the origins and nature of antenuptial agreements).

[2]See Gross v. Gross, 11 Ohio St. 3d 99, 464 N.E.2d 500, 53 A.L.R.4th 139 (1984) (upheld antenuptial agreement as to property allocation); Southern Ohio Sav. Bank & Trust Co. v. Burkhart, 148 Ohio St. 149, 35 Ohio Op. 166, 74 N.E.2d 67 (1947); Rudrick v. Thull, 39 Ohio App. 69, 10 Ohio L. Abs. 542, 177 N.E. 513 (5th Dist. Richland County 1931). See also Text § 1:8, Considerations for possible divorce, dissolution.

[3]Hook v. Hook, 69 Ohio St. 2d 234, 23 Ohio Op. 3d 239, 431 N.E.2d 667 (1982) and Troha v. Sneller, 169 Ohio St. 397, 8 Ohio Op. 2d 435, 159 N.E.2d 899 (1959) (Ohio Supreme Court did not discuss marriage as being primary consideration supporting agreement, but operated on assumption that mutual covenants to waive all rights in other's property formed consideration for contracts). See also Clark, The Law of Domestic Relations in the United States § 1.9; Dearbaugh v. Dearbaugh, 110 Ohio App. 540, 13 Ohio Op. 2d 351, 170 N.E.2d 262 (2d Dist. Shelby County 1959) ("The consideration of an antenuptial agreement is the marriage contract."); Cantor v. Cantor, 15 Ohio Op. 2d 148, 86 Ohio L. Abs. 452, 174 N.E.2d 304 (Prob. Ct. 1959).

[4]But see Conley v. Conley, 45 Ohio App. 2d 1, 74 Ohio Op. 2d 6, 340 N.E.2d 430 (1st Dist. Hamilton County 1975) (agreement contains no recital of or any provision for consideration to support obligations, and is expressly conditioned on continued legal existence of marriage, and termination of marriage by divorce removes condition, both parties are relieved of agreement); Dearbaugh v. Dearbaugh, 110 Ohio App. 540, 13 Ohio Op. 2d 351, 170 N.E.2d 262 (2d Dist. Shelby County 1959) ("The consideration of an antenuptial agreement is the marriage contract.").

[5]Hook v. Hook, 69 Ohio St. 2d 234, 23 Ohio Op. 3d 239, 431 N.E.2d 667 (1982); Troha v. Sneller, 169 Ohio St. 397, 8 Ohio Op. 2d 435, 159 N.E.2d 899 (1959); Cohen v. Cohen, 82 Ohio App. 260, 37 Ohio Op. 565, 51 Ohio L. Abs. 189, 80 N.E.2d 813 (1st Dist. Hamilton County 1947); Herman v. Soal, 71 Ohio App. 310, 26 Ohio Op. 188, 37 Ohio L. Abs. 527, 49 N.E.2d 109 (1st Dist. Hamilton County 1942); Osborn v. Osborn, 10 Ohio Misc. 171, 39 Ohio Op. 2d 275, 226 N.E.2d 814 (C.P. 1966), judgment aff'd, 18 Ohio St. 2d 144, 47 Ohio Op. 2d 310, 248 N.E.2d 191 (1969); Hawkins v. Hawkins, 89

or testamentary payments of cash or other securities,[7] or some combination of these constitute sufficient consideration to make the agreement enforceable.

While there may be sufficient consideration to support an antenuptial agreement in a technical sense, the courts may refuse to enforce such an agreement if they feel that the consideration is grossly inadequate, absent a showing of complete disclosure of the parties' relative wealth and the effect of the agreement.[8] The courts tend to discuss this concept in terms of disproportionateness and to place such emphasis on the overall fairness of the contract and the circumstances surrounding its execution.[9]

The courts have held that whether a particular agreement makes an unreasonable or disproportionate provision for the surviving spouse is a question of fact and must be decided on the circumstances of the particular case.[10] However, the Ohio Supreme Court in *Hook v. Hook*[11] held that whenever an antenuptial agreement bars a surviving spouse from any claim to the decedent's estate and where the amount the surviving spouse would receive under the antenuptial agreement is wholly disproportionate to the amount the survivor would take under the law, then the agreement would only be upheld if it was entered into voluntarily, with full knowledge of the nature, extent, and value of the other spouse's property.[12]

The courts have considered such factors as the relative wealth of

---

Ohio L. Abs. 161, 185 N.E.2d 89 (Prob. Ct. 1962), judgment aff'd, 176 Ohio St. 469, 27 Ohio Op. 2d 435, 200 N.E.2d 300 (1964).

[6]Juhasz v. Juhasz, 134 Ohio St. 257, 12 Ohio Op. 57, 16 N.E.2d 328, 117 A.L.R. 993 (1938); Pniewski v. Przybysz, 89 Ohio L. Abs. 385, 183 N.E.2d 437 (Ct. App. 8th Dist. Cuyahoga County 1962).

[7]Rudrick v. Thull, 39 Ohio App. 69, 10 Ohio L. Abs. 542, 177 N.E. 513 (5th Dist. Richland County 1931); Rocker v. Rocker, 13 Ohio Misc. 199, 42 Ohio Op. 2d 184, 42 Ohio Op. 2d 241, 232 N.E.2d 445 (Prob. Ct. 1967); Cantor v. Cantor, 15 Ohio Op. 2d 148, 86 Ohio L. Abs. 452, 174 N.E.2d 304 (Prob. Ct. 1959).

[8]Zimmie v. Zimmie, 11 Ohio St. 3d 94, 464 N.E.2d 142, 53 A.L.R.4th 75 (1984); Hook v. Hook, 69 Ohio St. 2d 234, 23 Ohio Op. 3d 239, 431 N.E.2d 667 (1982); Juhasz v. Juhasz, 134 Ohio St. 257, 12 Ohio Op. 57, 16 N.E.2d 328, 117 A.L.R. 993 (1938); Kennedy v. Kennedy, 11 Ohio App. 399, 1919 WL 906 (8th Dist. Cuyahoga County 1919). See Text § 1:4, Disclosure requirements.

[9]See Zimmie v. Zimmie, 11 Ohio St. 3d 94, 464 N.E.2d 142, 53 A.L.R.4th 75 (1984); Stilley v. Folger, 14 Ohio 610, 1846 WL 153 (1846) (thorough discussion of the origins and early history of antenuptial agreements). See also Randolph Carl Oppenheimer, *The Antenuptial Contract in Ohio*, 28 Case W. Res. L. Rev. 1040 (1978); Clark, The Law of Domestic Relations in the United States § 1.9; Kennedy v. Kennedy, 11 Ohio App. 399, 1919 WL 906 (8th Dist. Cuyahoga County 1919).

[10]Juhasz v. Juhasz, 134 Ohio St. 257, 12 Ohio Op. 57, 16 N.E.2d 328, 117 A.L.R. 993 (1938); Grogan v. Garrison, 27 Ohio St. 50, 1875 WL 148 (1875); Garver v. Miller, 16 Ohio St. 527, 1866 WL 15 (1866).

[11]Hook v. Hook, 69 Ohio St. 2d 234, 23 Ohio Op. 3d 239, 431 N.E.2d 667 (1982).

[12]See also Rocker v. Rocker, 13 Ohio Misc. 199, 42 Ohio Op. 2d 184, 42 Ohio Op. 2d 241, 232 N.E.2d 445 (Prob. Ct. 1967).

each party,[13] the relative provisions for the surviving spouse with and without the agreement,[14] and the proportionate relationship of the provision made in the agreement to the decedent's total worth.[15] In determining whether a particular provision is disproportionate, the courts have historically seemed to favor the female party to the agreement.[16] However, even if the court finds that the particular agreement makes a disproportionate or unreasonable provision for the surviving spouse, if the court is convinced that he or she knowingly and freely agreed to such provision, after a full and fair disclosure of the nature and extent of the other party's assets and property, and the effect of the contract, the court will still enforce the agreement.[17] An antenuptial agreement containing a clause that the surviving spouse shall have no right in the deceased spouse's estate is valid and enforceable where full and fair disclosure of assets was made prior to the signing of the agreement.[18] An antenuptial agreement that did not disclose the value of ninety-eight acres of land owned by appellant husband nor the existence of a mortgage on another parcel of property was found to be void and unenforceable by the Fourth District Court of Appeals.[19] The party claiming unconscionability has the burden of proof.[20]

---

[13]Juhasz v. Juhasz, 134 Ohio St. 257, 12 Ohio Op. 57, 16 N.E.2d 328, 117 A.L.R. 993 (1938); Mettler v. Warner, 11 Ohio N.P. (n.s.) 363, 21 Ohio Dec. 184, 1910 WL 809 (C.P. 1910); Johnson v. Johnson, 1 Ohio C.D. 291, 1886 WL 2562 (Ohio Cir. Ct. 1886), dismissed by 18 W.L.B. 18.

[14]Hook v. Hook, 69 Ohio St. 2d 234, 23 Ohio Op. 3d 239, 431 N.E.2d 667 (1982); Juhasz v. Juhasz, 134 Ohio St. 257, 12 Ohio Op. 57, 16 N.E.2d 328, 117 A.L.R. 993 (1938).

[15]Juhasz v. Juhasz, 134 Ohio St. 257, 12 Ohio Op. 57, 16 N.E.2d 328, 117 A.L.R. 993 (1938); Grogan v. Garrison, 27 Ohio St. 50, 1875 WL 148 (1875); Rocker v. Rocker, 13 Ohio Misc. 199, 42 Ohio Op. 2d 184, 42 Ohio Op. 2d 241, 232 N.E.2d 445 (Prob. Ct. 1967); Mettler v. Warner, 11 Ohio N.P. (n.s.) 363, 21 Ohio Dec. 184, 1910 WL 809 (C.P. 1910). But see Herman v. Soal, 71 Ohio App. 310, 26 Ohio Op. 188, 37 Ohio L. Abs. 527, 49 N.E.2d 109 (1st Dist. Hamilton County 1942); Ross v. Ross, 2 Ohio Dec. Rep. 181, 2 West. L. Monthly 17, 1859 WL 4448 (Ohio C.P. 1859).

[16]Rudrick v. Thull, 39 Ohio App. 69, 10 Ohio L. Abs. 542, 177 N.E. 513 (5th Dist. Richland County 1931) (contract between man and woman ambiguous, construction most favorable to woman should be adopted). But see Southern Ohio Sav. Bank & Trust Co. v. Burkhart, 148 Ohio St. 149, 35 Ohio Op. 166, 74 N.E.2d 67 (1947) (citing holding in Jacobs v. Jacobs).

[17]Hook v. Hook, 69 Ohio St. 2d 234, 23 Ohio Op. 3d 239, 431 N.E.2d 667 (1982); Juhasz v. Juhasz, 134 Ohio St. 257, 12 Ohio Op. 57, 16 N.E.2d 328, 117 A.L.R. 993 (1938). See also Text § 1:4, Disclosure requirements.

[18]Sasarak v. Sasarak, 66 Ohio App. 3d 744, 586 N.E.2d 172 (8th Dist. Cuyahoga County 1990).

[19]McDole v. McDole, 1990 WL 105436 (Ohio Ct. App. 4th Dist. Washington County 1990).

[20]Zimmie v. Zimmie, 11 Ohio St. 3d 94, 464 N.E.2d 142, 53 A.L.R.4th 75 (1984); Cohen v. Estate of Cohen, 23 Ohio St. 3d 90, 491 N.E.2d 698 (1986).

§ 1:4 Disclosure requirements

All American courts that have dealt with antenuptial agreements have traditionally required that both parties enter into such agreements with full knowledge of each other's assets, rights, and property.[1] The courts have reasoned that since an engagement to marry creates a confidential relationship, particular precautions should be taken to avoid any overreaching.[2] The Ohio courts have always followed this approach, being especially careful to protect surviving widows.[3] The anachronistic treatment of women may no longer be constitutionally valid.[4] However, no Ohio case has ever held that a husband has been overreached.[5]

Because of the confidential nature of antenuptial agreements, the Ohio courts have consistently required that both parties be fully aware of the nature of their involvement. They have always required that each party be aware of the other's assets and the extent of their rights in those assets without the agreement.[6] This scrutiny has been especially strict when the agreement makes a disproportionate or unrea-

---

[Section 1:4]

[1]Zimmie v. Zimmie, 11 Ohio St. 3d 94, 464 N.E.2d 142, 53 A.L.R.4th 75 (1984); Alexander Lindey, *Separation Agreements and Ante-nuptial Contracts* § 90-47(A) (2d rev. ed. 1967); Clark, The Law of Domestic Relations in the United States § 1.9; Hook v. Hook, 69 Ohio St. 2d 234, 23 Ohio Op. 3d 239, 431 N.E.2d 667 (1982) ("The agreement, however, must meet certain minimum levels of good faith, and will be set aside as invalid as a matter of law if the agreement is not fair and reasonable under the circumstances."); Gottfried v. Gottfried, 1981 WL 5592 (Ohio Ct. App. 6th Dist. Lucas County 1981) (antenuptial agreement upheld as proper and valid as to property settlement in divorce, since no evidence of fraud, gross misrepresentation, or coercion on part of either party).

[2]Hook v. Hook, 69 Ohio St. 2d 234, 23 Ohio Op. 3d 239, 431 N.E.2d 667 (1982); Juhasz v. Juhasz, 134 Ohio St. 257, 12 Ohio Op. 57, 16 N.E.2d 328, 117 A.L.R. 993 (1938); Stilley v. Folger, 14 Ohio 610, 1846 WL 153 (1846); In re Mosier's Estate, 58 Ohio Op. 369, 72 Ohio L. Abs. 268, 133 N.E.2d 202 (Prob. Ct. 1954); Stotler v. Stotler, 19 Ohio N.P. (n.s.) 369, 27 Ohio Dec. 303, 1916 WL 986 (C.P. 1916); Duttenhofer v. Duttenhofer, 12 Ohio Dec. 736, 1902 WL 984 (Super. Ct. 1902). See also Annot., 27 A.L.R. 2d 883.

[3]Stilley v. Folger, 14 Ohio 610, 1846 WL 153 (1846). See also Osborn v. Osborn, 10 Ohio Misc. 171, 39 Ohio Op. 2d 275, 226 N.E.2d 814 (C.P. 1966), judgment aff'd, 18 Ohio St. 2d 144, 47 Ohio Op. 2d 310, 248 N.E.2d 191 (1969).

[4]See Orr v. Orr, 440 U.S. 268, 99 S. Ct. 1102, 59 L. Ed. 2d 306 (1979); Craig v. Boren, 429 U.S. 190, 97 S. Ct. 451, 50 L. Ed. 2d 397 (1976); Reed v. Reed, 404 U.S. 71, 92 S. Ct. 251, 30 L. Ed. 2d 225 (1971).

[5]Pniewski v. Przybysz, 89 Ohio L. Abs. 385, 183 N.E.2d 437 (Ct. App. 8th Dist. Cuyahoga County 1962).

[6]Zimmie v. Zimmie, 11 Ohio St. 3d 94, 464 N.E.2d 142, 53 A.L.R.4th 75 (1984); Stotler v. Stotler, 19 Ohio N.P. (n.s.) 369, 27 Ohio Dec. 303, 1916 WL 986 (C.P. 1916); Duttenhofer v. Duttenhofer, 12 Ohio Dec. 736, 1902 WL 984 (Super. Ct. 1902); Speckman v. Speckman, 15 Ohio App. 283, 1921 WL 1138 (5th Dist. Coshocton County 1921); Postiy v. Postiy, 2003-Ohio-2146, 2003 WL 1962410 (Ohio Ct. App. 5th Dist. Stark County 2003) (appellate court upheld trial court's decision to invalidate antenuptial agreement where husband omitted an airplane worth $130,000, gold assets worth between $10,000-$20,000, undervalued his business by $300,000, and failed to

sonable provision for the surviving spouse.[7] Consequently, counsel should make sure that (1) both parties fully disclose their assets and holdings to each other; (2) each party understands the extent of the other's holdings; and (3) the parties understand the effect the agreement would have on their rights in regard to such property.

There are several methods that counsel can employ to ensure that each party is aware of the other's assets/property and the contract's effect on their rights in the assets/property. One would be to question orally each party as to his general knowledge of the other's financial status and the effect of the contract. While this practice may be efficient and economical, and may truly satisfy the interrogating attorney, one may be certain that on death of the financially dominant party, the survivor's memory of the events will differ from the memory of the interrogating attorney. In *Sheets v. Sheets*,[8] the widow challenged the antenuptial agreement alleging nondisclosure of assets. The parties had discussed their assets in deceased husband's attorney's office. The court found the attorney's testimony more credible and enforced the agreement. Thus, while this practice is initially friendly, efficient, and economical, there is a built-in guarantee of inevitable dispute and possible litigation. There should be independent corroboration, preferably a writing, videotape, or reporter transcript, where the agreement ventures into serious fiscal divestments, rather than mere clarifications.

A more practical and useful option would be to include, by physical attachment and incorporation into the agreement, a complete inventory of each party's principal assets, accounts, properties, etc. This approach has been held to refute any accusations of nondisclosure.[9] Although the presence of independent counsel is not required for the

---

include a value for his oil wells on a financial statement showing a net worth of $1,500,000). See also Annot., 27 A.L.R. 2d 883.

[7]Hook v. Hook, 69 Ohio St. 2d 234, 23 Ohio Op. 3d 239, 431 N.E.2d 667 (1982); Juhasz v. Juhasz, 134 Ohio St. 257, 12 Ohio Op. 57, 16 N.E.2d 328, 117 A.L.R. 993 (1938); Troha v. Sneller, 169 Ohio St. 397, 8 Ohio Op. 2d 435, 159 N.E.2d 899 (1959); Southern Ohio Sav. Bank & Trust Co. v. Burkhart, 148 Ohio St. 149, 35 Ohio Op. 166, 74 N.E.2d 67 (1947); Grogan v. Garrison, 27 Ohio St. 50, 1875 WL 148 (1875); Garver v. Miller, 16 Ohio St. 527, 1866 WL 15 (1866); Stilley v. Folger, 14 Ohio 610, 1846 WL 153 (1846); Conley v. Conley, 45 Ohio App. 2d 1, 74 Ohio Op. 2d 6, 340 N.E.2d 430 (1st Dist. Hamilton County 1975); Dearbaugh v. Dearbaugh, 110 Ohio App. 540, 13 Ohio Op. 2d 351, 170 N.E.2d 262 (2d Dist. Shelby County 1959); Cohen v. Cohen, 82 Ohio App. 260, 37 Ohio Op. 565, 51 Ohio L. Abs. 189, 80 N.E.2d 813 (1st Dist. Hamilton County 1947); Herman v. Soal, 71 Ohio App. 310, 26 Ohio Op. 188, 37 Ohio L. Abs. 527, 49 N.E.2d 109 (1st Dist. Hamilton County 1942); Rudrick v. Thull, 39 Ohio App. 69, 10 Ohio L. Abs. 542, 177 N.E. 513 (5th Dist. Richland County 1931); Kennedy v. Kennedy, 11 Ohio App. 399, 1919 WL 906 (8th Dist. Cuyahoga County 1919).

[8]Sheets v. Sheets, 1995 WL 404997 (Ohio Ct. App. 4th Dist. Pickaway County 1995).

[9]In re Mosier's Estate, 58 Ohio Op. 369, 72 Ohio L. Abs. 268, 133 N.E.2d 202 (Prob. Ct. 1954); Osborn v. Osborn, 10 Ohio Misc. 171, 39 Ohio Op. 2d 275, 226 N.E.2d 814 (C.P. 1966), judgment aff'd, 18 Ohio St. 2d 144, 47 Ohio Op. 2d 310, 248 N.E.2d 191 (1969); Rocker v. Rocker, 13 Ohio Misc. 199, 42 Ohio Op. 2d 184, 42 Ohio

enforcement of an antenuptial agreement,[10] the use of the independent counsel would also be strong evidence to dispel any charges of overreaching.

In *Hook v. Hook*,[11] the Ohio Supreme Court has seemed to relax significantly the disclosure requirements in regard to antenuptial agreements. The court held that an explanation of the agreement's effect consisting of " 'Never mind, just sign it. It means what is mine is mine and what is yours is yours,' " coupled with a cursory description of the husband's assets, was sufficient disclosure to make enforceable an antenuptial agreement which totally severed the widow's claims to the decedent's estate. The court reasoned that since she signed the contract she was presumed to know its content and was therefore bound by it, in spite of her protests that she had not read it and consequently did not know what its effect would be. This holding indicates the court applied a commercial contract standard to this situation. While such an approach may be helpful to counsel attempting to prove the validity of a previously executed agreement, sound practice would seem to be to follow the guidelines laid down by the older cases.

§ 1:5 Terms

The primary purpose of an antenuptial agreement is to control the property rights of the parties and their successors in interest[1] upon the termination of the marriage.[2] Consequently, the terms of such agreements typically focus upon the rights of each spouse in both their own and the other's property. The Ohio courts have recognized that an antenuptial agreement can be used to cut off all of the surviving spouse's rights in the property/estate of the deceased spouse[3] and have also allowed parties to cut off certain specific rights, while allow-

Op. 2d 241, 232 N.E.2d 445 (Prob. Ct. 1967); Hook v. Hook, 69 Ohio St. 2d 234, 23 Ohio Op. 3d 239, 431 N.E.2d 667 (1982); Vlad v. Vlad, 2005-Ohio-2080, 2005 WL 1007252 (Ohio Ct. App. 11th Dist. Trumbull County 2005) (antenuptial agreement was held to be unenforceable because it lacked a comprehensive list of the parties' assets and their values at the time of the marriage—as a result, the party seeking to enforce the antenuptial agreement failed to show that there was a full disclosure of the nature, value, and extent of the property at the time the agreement was signed); Gearheart v. Cooper, 2007-Ohio-25, 2007 WL 29552 (Ohio Ct. App. 1st Dist. Hamilton County 2007) (court invalidated antenuptial agreement after the death of the parties where agreement contained no description or listing of the parties' properties or assets.).

[10]Hook v. Hook, 69 Ohio St. 2d 234, 23 Ohio Op. 3d 239, 431 N.E.2d 667 (1982).

[11]Hook v. Hook, 69 Ohio St. 2d 234, 23 Ohio Op. 3d 239, 431 N.E.2d 667 (1982).

[Section 1:5]

[1]See Text § 1:7, Enforcing or attacking the antenuptial contract.

[2]See Text § 1:1, Function and nature. See also RC 3103.05, RC 3103.06.

[3]Troha v. Sneller, 169 Ohio St. 397, 8 Ohio Op. 2d 435, 159 N.E.2d 899 (1959). See Wilson v. Rudolph Wurlitzer Co., 48 Ohio App. 450, 2 Ohio Op. 48, 18 Ohio L. Abs. 449, 194 N.E. 441 (1st Dist. Hamilton County 1934) (postnuptial agreements will not cut off all of surviving spouse's rights in property/estate of deceased spouse).

ing others to remain. Among the specific rights which the courts have allowed the surviving spouse to waive by prenuptial contract are dower,[4] a statutory share in the deceased spouse's testate or intestate estate,[5] exemption of certain property from administration,[6] rights to rent from or residence in the mansion house,[7] rights to purchase the mansion house or the decedent's personal property,[8] priority in administration of the decedent's estate,[9] and year's allowance.[10]

While the Ohio courts have allowed parties to bar these rights by contract, the Ohio Supreme Court has held that such agreements must contain "strong and unmistakable language" to obtain such results.[11] Consequently, counsel should make specific reference to the rights which the parties wish to bar by contract.[12]

When terms are not defined in an agreement, they are to be given their common sense meaning. The term "financial contribution" was

---

[4]Osborn v. Osborn, 10 Ohio Misc. 171, 39 Ohio Op. 2d 275, 226 N.E.2d 814 (C.P. 1966), judgment aff'd, 18 Ohio St. 2d 144, 47 Ohio Op. 2d 310, 248 N.E.2d 191 (1969); Troha v. Sneller, 169 Ohio St. 397, 8 Ohio Op. 2d 435, 159 N.E.2d 899 (1959); Mintier v. Mintier, 28 Ohio St. 307, 1876 WL 10 (1876); RC 2103.02.

[5]Hook v. Hook, 69 Ohio St. 2d 234, 23 Ohio Op. 3d 239, 431 N.E.2d 667 (1982); Osborn v. Osborn, 10 Ohio Misc. 171, 39 Ohio Op. 2d 275, 226 N.E.2d 814 (C.P. 1966), judgment aff'd, 18 Ohio St. 2d 144, 47 Ohio Op. 2d 310, 248 N.E.2d 191 (1969); Juhasz v. Juhasz, 134 Ohio St. 257, 12 Ohio Op. 57, 16 N.E.2d 328, 117 A.L.R. 993 (1938); RC 2105.06, RC 2107.03.

[6]Cohen v. Cohen, 82 Ohio App. 260, 37 Ohio Op. 565, 51 Ohio L. Abs. 189, 80 N.E.2d 813 (1st Dist. Hamilton County 1947); RC 2113.03.

[7]See RC 2106.15. Troha v. Sneller, 169 Ohio St. 397, 8 Ohio Op. 2d 435, 159 N.E.2d 899 (1959); Juhasz v. Juhasz, 134 Ohio St. 257, 12 Ohio Op. 57, 16 N.E.2d 328, 117 A.L.R. 993 (1938).

[8]See RC 2106.16. Hook v. Hook, 69 Ohio St. 2d 234, 23 Ohio Op. 3d 239, 431 N.E.2d 667 (1982); Troha v. Sneller, 169 Ohio St. 397, 8 Ohio Op. 2d 435, 159 N.E.2d 899 (1959); Juhasz v. Juhasz, 134 Ohio St. 257, 12 Ohio Op. 57, 16 N.E.2d 328, 117 A.L.R. 993 (1938).

[9]Gionfriddo v. Palatrone, 26 Ohio Op. 2d 158, 93 Ohio L. Abs. 257, 196 N.E.2d 162 (Prob. Ct. 1964); RC 2113.06.

[10]See RC 2106.13. Hook v. Hook, 69 Ohio St. 2d 234, 23 Ohio Op. 3d 239, 431 N.E.2d 667 (1982); Troha v. Sneller, 169 Ohio St. 397, 8 Ohio Op. 2d 435, 159 N.E.2d 899 (1959); Juhasz v. Juhasz, 134 Ohio St. 257, 12 Ohio Op. 57, 16 N.E.2d 328, 117 A.L.R. 993 (1938); Jacobsen v. Cleveland Trust Co., 6 Ohio Misc. 173, 35 Ohio Op. 2d 366, 217 N.E.2d 262 (C.P. 1965).

[11]Troha v. Sneller, 169 Ohio St. 397, 402, 8 Ohio Op. 2d 435, 159 N.E.2d 899 (1959) (adult man and woman, each owning substantial amount of property, and each having grown children by prior marriages, may lawfully enter into prenuptial agreement whereby each relinquishes every and all rights in property of other; if husband dies, widow is barred from any part of his estate, where agreement by its clear wording shows that such result intended); In re Estate of Armstrong, 1997 WL 139441 (Ohio Ct. App. 4th Dist. Hocking County 1997); In re Estate of Taris, 2005-Ohio-1516, 2005 WL 736627 (Ohio Ct. App. 10th Dist. Franklin County 2005).

[12]Beverly v. Parilla, 165 Ohio App. 3d 802, 2006-Ohio-1286, 848 N.E.2d 881 (7th Dist. Columbiana County 2006) (Antenuptial agreement that did not reference spousal support did not constitute a waiver of a party's right to seek support, therefore spousal support could be awarded if justified by the statute.).

held to include the pledge of stock to acquire other stock. The court should consider whether or not there has been a substantial circumstance from the time the agreement was entered into so as to render the spousal support provisions unconscionable.[13]

While the Ohio courts have been tolerant in allowing parties to waive rights arising after marriage, they have not shown the same liberality when parties wish to change their rights and obligations during the marriage. This seems to be the pattern in most jurisdictions and is based on both statutory and public policy grounds.[14] Furthermore, Ohio courts have been reluctant to enforce terms in antenuptial contracts which do not deal with property rights. They have refused to enforce covenants to educate children in a particular religion,[15] and which seek to preserve tort claims of one spouse against another.[16] In view of the Ohio Supreme Court's decision in *Shearer v. Shearer*[17] and the judicial elimination of the interspousal tort immunity doctrine, parties may be able to preserve tort claims. Obviously, this would depend on the availability of insurance to cover such a claim. Finally, the courts have refused to allow parties to alter the statutory scheme of descent and distribution, although they have allowed parties to incorporate this scheme by reference.[18]

The Tenth District Court of Appeals has upheld a clause in an antenuptial agreement requiring the parties, in the event of a divorce or separation, to resolve disputed issues through binding arbitration, even though that would deprive the court of such decision making.[19]

The effect of an invalid provision on the entire agreement is unclear. The Ohio cases dealing with invalid provisions in antenuptial agreements present no clear pattern. The cases in which the entire agreement was struck down because a particular provision of the contract was invalid concerned provisions relating to the substance of the

---

[13]Fox v. Fox, 2002-Ohio-2010, 2002 WL 722804 (Ohio Ct. App. 10th Dist. Franklin County 2002).

[14]Du Bois v. Coen, 100 Ohio St. 17, 125 N.E. 121 (1919); Pashko v. Pashko, 45 Ohio Op. 498, 63 Ohio L. Abs. 82, 101 N.E.2d 804 (C.P. 1951); In re Slight's Estate, 467 Pa. 619, 359 A.2d 773 (1976); Isaacs v. Isaacs, 71 Neb. 537, 99 N.W. 268 (1904). See RC 3103.05 and RC 3103.06.

[15]Hackett v. Hackett, 78 Ohio L. Abs. 485, 150 N.E.2d 431 (Ct. App. 6th Dist. Lucas County 1958).

[16]Tanno v. Eby, 78 Ohio App. 21, 33 Ohio Op. 384, 46 Ohio L. Abs. 600, 68 N.E.2d 813 (8th Dist. Cuyahoga County 1946) (antenuptial agreement that attempts to preserve to wife a tort claim against husband, for tort committed prior to marriage, is unenforceable as against public policy with respect to interspousal immunity).

[17]Shearer v. Shearer, 18 Ohio St. 3d 94, 480 N.E.2d 388 (1985).

[18]Cantor v. Cantor, 15 Ohio Op. 2d 148, 86 Ohio L. Abs. 452, 174 N.E.2d 304 (Prob. Ct. 1959).

[19]Kelm v. Kelm, 73 Ohio App. 3d 395, 597 N.E.2d 535 (10th Dist. Franklin County 1992).

contract.[20] The one Ohio case which has dealt with an unenforceable provision in an antenuptial/separation agreement that did not relate to the substance of the agreement did not state whether the entire contract would fail.[21] However, there is authority in other jurisdictions that holds that antenuptial agreements should be construed so as to render them valid if possible.[22] Furthermore, the Ohio courts have repeatedly held that the intent of the parties is controlling in the enforcement of antenuptial contracts.[23] Therefore, it would seem that, if such contracts were drafted to include a provision stating the intention of the parties that the rest of the contract should be enforced regardless of the invalidity of some nonessential provisions, the courts would probably enforce the rest of the contract in spite of its minor infirmities.

Once an antenuptial agreement has been found to be valid, the court should closely adhere to the terms of the agreement with respect to property division. In *Vail v. Vail*, the parties each attached a copy of the antenuptial agreement to their pleadings and prayed for its enforcement.[24] The antenuptial agreement provided that a parcel of real estate owned by the parties should be sold in the event the parties' marriage terminated and they could not agree on the value of the property. When the parties were unable to agree on the value, the court ordered an appraisal, allocated the real property to husband, and ordered husband to pay one half of the appraised value to wife. The Eighth District Court of Appeals found that the trial court should have ordered to property to be sold and the proceeds to be divided between the parties in accordance with the terms of their antenuptial agreement.

---

[20]Tanno v. Eby, 78 Ohio App. 21, 33 Ohio Op. 384, 46 Ohio L. Abs. 600, 68 N.E.2d 813 (8th Dist. Cuyahoga County 1946); Dearbaugh v. Dearbaugh, 110 Ohio App. 540, 542, 13 Ohio Op. 2d 351, 170 N.E.2d 262 (2d Dist. Shelby County 1959) ("If one party fails to perform a promise made in an antenuptial agreement, such failure may justify granting relief [alimony] to the other party."); Southern Ohio Sav. Bank & Trust Co. v. Burkhart, 148 Ohio St. 149, 153, 35 Ohio Op. 166, 74 N.E.2d 67 (1947) ("[The wife] cannot in sound reason and good conscience require performance of a contract which she herself has failed and refused to perform.").

[21]Hackett v. Hackett, 78 Ohio L. Abs. 485, 150 N.E.2d 431 (Ct. App. 6th Dist. Lucas County 1958) (involving separation agreement which incorporated questionable provision from antenuptial agreement that parties had entered into prior to their marriage).

[22]Barham v. Barham, 33 Cal. 2d 416, 202 P.2d 289 (1949); McClain's Estate v. McClain, 133 Ind. App. 645, 183 N.E.2d 842 (1962); Sanders v. Sanders, 40 Tenn. App. 20, 288 S.W.2d 473, 57 A.L.R.2d 932 (1955).

[23]Southern Ohio Sav. Bank & Trust Co. v. Burkhart, 148 Ohio St. 149, 35 Ohio Op. 166, 74 N.E.2d 67 (1947); Dearbaugh v. Dearbaugh, 110 Ohio App. 540, 13 Ohio Op. 2d 351, 170 N.E.2d 262 (2d Dist. Shelby County 1959); Troha v. Sneller, 169 Ohio St. 397, 8 Ohio Op. 2d 435, 159 N.E.2d 899 (1959). See also Randolph Carl Oppenheimer, *The Antenuptial Contract in Ohio*, 28 Case W. Res. L. Rev. 1040 (1978).

[24]Vail v. Vail, 2004–Ohio–2158, 2004 WL 906132 (Ohio Ct. App. 8th Dist. Cuyahoga County 2004).

In *Reams v. Reams*[25] the antenuptial agreement contained two inconsistent paragraphs. Paragraph four of the agreement provided that "after the proposed marriage and during said marriage," all property and increments in value thereon owned by the parties "before said proposed marriage or which each may thereafter separately acquire, shall be divided equally between them."[26] Paragraph 7 stated that in the event the marriage was terminated, "it is mutually agreed between said parties that they both hereby release and surrender any and all rights to receive any property settlement from the other."[27]

The Sixth District Court of Appeals did not invalidate the entire antenuptial agreement due to the conflicting provisions. The Court of Appeals, following the mandate that it should attempt to harmonize all provisions of the agreement and give reasonable, lawful and effective meaning to all of its terms, concluded that paragraph four governed initially, taking precedence over paragraph seven during the course of the marriage. However, upon the initiation of divorce proceedings, paragraph seven became applicable, superceding and nullifying paragraph four.

§ 1:6   Voluntary and involuntary rescission, modification

There is no definitive authority in Ohio on the ability of the parties to an antenuptial agreement to voluntarily rescind the agreement. An early Ohio case held that it was not possible to rescind the agreement, but this is probably not true today.[1] This result was based on the common law inability of a husband and wife to contract with each other. At common law, the husband and wife were considered one entity. Since one could not contract with one's self, it was held impossible for the spouses to contract with each other. The court reasoned that, as an agreement to rescind a contract is a contract in and of itself (in this case, the rescission agreement was written on the back of the antenuptial agreement), and as this was impossible between a husband and wife, any rescission was impossible. However, the enactment of RC 3103.05 impliedly invalidated this rationale.

One appellate court has held that parties may rescind an antenuptial agreement that expressly provides for such a rescission but has held that the party asserting the rescission did not offer adequate

---

[25]Reams v. Reams, 2005-Ohio-5264, 2005 WL 2415936 (Ohio Ct. App. 6th Dist. Lucas County 2005).

[26]Reams v. Reams, 2005-Ohio-5264, 2005 WL 2415936, at *3 (Ohio Ct. App. 6th Dist. Lucas County 2005).

[27]Reams v. Reams, 2005-Ohio-5264, 2005 WL 2415936, at *3 (Ohio Ct. App. 6th Dist. Lucas County 2005).

[Section 1:6]

[1]Ross v. Ross, 2 Ohio Dec. Rep. 181, 2 West. L. Monthly 17, 1859 WL 4448 (Ohio C.P. 1859).

proof that such a rescission had taken place.[2] However, RC 3103.05 allows husbands and wives to contract with each other so it would seem that they could effect a rescission of a contract with each other, as rescission is a form of contract.[3] RC 3103.05 states that contracts between a husband and wife shall be treated as would any contract between persons in a confidential relationship. Therefore, it would follow that the same special considerations which are present in the formation of an antenuptial contract would be present in its rescission.[4]

Execution of a will that provides a party a greater interest in property of the other spouse than a previously executed antenuptial agreement does not automatically invalidate the agreement.[5] The Third District Court of Appeals, following *Cantor v. Cantor*, held that appellant failed to prove a rescission of the agreement by a preponderance of the evidence.[6] In addition to the property provided for in the agreement, appellant was awarded $20,000 in recognition for her contribution of time, effort, and direct financial contributions to the marriage. The agreement had not defined the rights of the parties in the event of a divorce.

While there is no clear case law pattern in regard to voluntary rescission of an antenuptial contract, the opposite is true in regard to involuntary rescissions. The Ohio courts have held that divorce may effect an involuntary rescission of an antenuptial agreement on the basis of failure of consideration.[7] Similarly, failure of one party to perform his obligations under the agreement will be grounds for involuntary rescission if such nonperformance is in relation to the

---

[2]Dalgarn v. Leonard, 41 Ohio Op. 506, 55 Ohio L. Abs. 149, 87 N.E.2d 728 (Prob. Ct. 1948), judgment aff'd, 55 Ohio L. Abs. 405, 90 N.E.2d 159 (Ct. App. 2d Dist. Franklin County 1949).

[3]Corbin on Contracts § 1236.

[4]See Text § 1:1, Function and nature; Text § 1:3, Consideration, disproportionate provisions; Text § 1:4, Disclosure requirements.

[5]Cantor v. Cantor, 15 Ohio Op. 2d 148, 86 Ohio L. Abs. 452, 174 N.E.2d 304 (Prob. Ct. 1959).

[6]Nighswander v. Nighswander, 1990 WL 4242 (Ohio Ct. App. 3d Dist. Seneca County 1990).

[7]Southern Ohio Sav. Bank & Trust Co. v. Burkhart, 148 Ohio St. 149, 35 Ohio Op. 166, 74 N.E.2d 67 (1947) (former wife may not enforce performance of antenuptial contract, which provided for annuity on death of husband, where she had failed and refused to perform); Dearbaugh v. Dearbaugh, 110 Ohio App. 540, 542, 13 Ohio Op. 2d 351, 170 N.E.2d 262 (2d Dist. Shelby County 1959) ("If one party fails to perform a promise made in an antenuptial agreement, such failure may justify granting relief [alimony] to the other party."); Kennedy v. Kennedy, 11 Ohio App. 399, 1919 WL 906 (8th Dist. Cuyahoga County 1919) (husband found guilty of breach of contract (or has not substantially performed), antenuptial contract will not bar wife from right to alimony given to her by statutes of state). See Text § 1:3, Consideration, disproportionate provisions; Text § 1:8, Considerations for possible divorce, dissolution. But see Benza v. Benza, 1978 WL 216102 (Ohio Ct. App. 1st Dist. Warren County 1978) (terms of antenuptial agreement followed at time of divorce).

substance of the contract.[8] Fraud in the inducement of the agreement is also grounds for rescission,[9] as is fraud in the factum.[10] According to strict contract theory, fraud in the factum is not grounds for rescission, as such fraud prevents the formation of a contract; hence, there is nothing to rescind. However, since the practical result is almost indistinguishable, it is treated as a rescission.

An antenuptial agreement was found to have been rescinded when the parties could not produce it during divorce proceedings, and there was testimony that husband had instructed his attorney to destroy it.[11]

As is true of the subject of voluntary rescission, there is no definitive case law on the ability of spouses to modify the terms of an antenuptial contract. However, it would appear that, for the reasons discussed in regard to voluntary rescission, an antenuptial contract could be voluntarily modified. The law is clear that antenuptial and separation agreements are permitted, and RC 3103.05 permits contracts between married persons. However, the contracts between married persons may not vary the legal obligations within the marriage. Thus, for example, while antenuptial and separation agreements can provide for spousal support, such an agreement cannot be made during a continuing marriage. If a wife needs spousal support during a marriage, an action for legal separation is the proper vehicle. If the parties make an spousal support agreement and live by it, the question of enforcement does not arise. Not until one side defaults and the other seeks to enforce the agreement will the problem arise. The agreement cannot be enforced under current law.

The parties may mutually agree to rescind the contract. If the parties can rescind the entire contract, then it logically follows that they can partially rescind. Partial rescission may be labeled as a modification, but a rescission is a restoration of legal rights, not a compromise or waiver of existing legal rights.

For example, assume an agreement whereby each party waives interest in any property in the estate of the other. Assume further that the husband subsequently elects to make a bequest to the wife in his will. In effect, this is a partial rescission. It is unilateral and ex

---

[8]Cantor v. Cantor, 15 Ohio Op. 2d 148, 86 Ohio L. Abs. 452, 174 N.E.2d 304 (Prob. Ct. 1959); Kennedy v. Kennedy, 11 Ohio App. 399, 1919 WL 906 (8th Dist. Cuyahoga County 1919); Southern Ohio Sav. Bank & Trust Co. v. Burkhart, 148 Ohio St. 149, 35 Ohio Op. 166, 74 N.E.2d 67 (1947); Dearbaugh v. Dearbaugh, 110 Ohio App. 540, 13 Ohio Op. 2d 351, 170 N.E.2d 262 (2d Dist. Shelby County 1959).

[9]Juhasz v. Juhasz, 134 Ohio St. 257, 12 Ohio Op. 57, 16 N.E.2d 328, 117 A.L.R. 993 (1938).

[10]Petrich v. Petrich, 44 Ohio Op. 457, 58 Ohio L. Abs. 566, 97 N.E.2d 56 (Ct. App. 8th Dist. Cuyahoga County 1950).

[11]Simoni v. Simoni, 102 Ohio App. 3d 628, 657 N.E.2d 800 (8th Dist. Cuyahoga County 1995).

parte, but nevertheless valid.[12] In effect, this is an example of a modification of an agreement in the form of a rescission or waiver by the party who would be charged with the liability, and is a gain to the party who would otherwise be the injured party. It would thus appear that a modification by a rescission or waiver which would restore a party to rights that would have existed absent the agreement would not be objectionable to either of the parties or the court. However, a modification during marriage which alters such legal rights, by giving one party less rights than already exist, is the precise reason for the prohibition of such agreements during marriage. RC 3103.05, which permits married persons to contract with each other, has not been construed to mean a contractual modification of already existing marital rights.

Thus, if an antenuptial agreement limited a wife to $100 per week spousal support pursuant to a divorce, a subsequent modification that would cancel this provision and leave the matter to a separation agreement or a court would cause no legal problem. A modification raising the amount to $200 would most likely be enforced, unless it is shown that it was an inducement to a divorce by the husband or that the wife precipitated the divorce in order to get the spousal support.[13] As previously stated, since contracts between husband and wife involve a confidential relationship, the same considerations would be pertinent to the modification of the contract as in the formation of the original contract.

Property that is designated to be separate under a valid antenuptial agreement may become marital property by the execution of an instrument such as a joint and survivorship deed. An antenuptial agreement may provide for the gift of separate property during marriage.[14] Further, although an antenuptial agreement may provide that separate property brought into the marriage by either party would remain that party's separate asset, separate property may still be deemed to be marital property if it can be shown that it has been commingled and transmutation occurred.[15]

§ 1:7 Enforcing or attacking the antenuptial contract

RC 2106.22 requires that any action to contest the validity of an antenuptial agreement be brought within four months of the appointment of an executor or administrator of the deceased spouse's estate. The statute states, and the courts have ruled, that unless an action

---

[12]See Gionfriddo v. Palatrone, 26 Ohio Op. 2d 158, 93 Ohio L. Abs. 257, 196 N.E.2d 162 (Prob. Ct. 1964).

[13]See Jacobs v. Jacobs, 42 Iowa 600, 1876 WL 442 (1876), as cited in Southern Ohio Sav. Bank & Trust Co. v. Burkhart, 148 Ohio St. 149, 151, 35 Ohio Op. 166, 74 N.E.2d 67 (1947).

[14]Hippely v. Hippely, 2002-Ohio-3015, 2002 WL 1370795(Ohio Ct. App. 7th Dist. Columbiana County 2002).

[15]Dudich v. Dudich, 2005-Ohio-889, 2005 WL 488910 (Ohio Ct. App. 8th Dist. Cuyahoga County 2005).

directly attacking such an agreement is brought within this time period, the antenuptial agreement will conclusively be presumed to be valid,[1] in spite of inadequate provision for the surviving spouse,[2] inadequate disclosure,[3] minority of a party,[4] or fraud in the inducement.[5] However, a showing of fraud in the factum has been held to justify the waiver of this statute of limitations. In *Petrich v. Petrich*,[6] two arguments were presented to allow a party to attack an antenuptial agreement in spite of the six-month statute of limitations which was then in effect. The attacking party convinced the court that the executor had lulled the surviving spouse into "sleeping on her rights" and hence was either estopped from raising the statute as a defense or had waived such a defense. The other argument is based on contract theory. The court reasoned that since fraud in the factum rendered the contract void rather than merely voidable, no agreement existed and hence the six-month statute of limitations did not apply.

The party attacking the agreement must attack it directly. The Ohio Supreme Court has held that a mere repudiation of a widow's right of election is not sufficient.[7] However, a lower court has held that a widow's objection to exceptions of other heirs or will beneficiaries that are based on the validity of the agreement is sufficient to meet the requirements of RC 2106.22.[8] The best device to attack the agreement would appear to be a declaratory judgment.[9]

[Section 1:7]

[1]Juhasz v. Juhasz, 134 Ohio St. 257, 12 Ohio Op. 57, 16 N.E.2d 328, 117 A.L.R. 993 (1938); Osborn v. Osborn, 10 Ohio Misc. 171, 39 Ohio Op. 2d 275, 226 N.E.2d 814 (C.P. 1966), judgment aff'd, 18 Ohio St. 2d 144, 47 Ohio Op. 2d 310, 248 N.E.2d 191 (1969) (antenuptial contracts are prima facie valid and binding); Cantor v. Cantor, 15 Ohio Op. 2d 148, 86 Ohio L. Abs. 452, 174 N.E.2d 304 (Prob. Ct. 1959).

[2]Juhasz v. Juhasz, 134 Ohio St. 257, 12 Ohio Op. 57, 16 N.E.2d 328, 117 A.L.R. 993 (1938).

[3]Juhasz v. Juhasz, 134 Ohio St. 257, 12 Ohio Op. 57, 16 N.E.2d 328, 117 A.L.R. 993 (1938).

[4]Burlovic v. Farmer, 96 Ohio App. 403, 54 Ohio Op. 399, 115 N.E.2d 411 (8th Dist. Cuyahoga County 1953), judgment aff'd, 162 Ohio St. 46, 54 Ohio Op. 5, 120 N.E.2d 705 (1954) (using same standards to attack separation agreement).

[5]Cantor v. Cantor, 15 Ohio Op. 2d 148, 86 Ohio L. Abs. 452, 174 N.E.2d 304 (Prob. Ct. 1959).

[6]Petrich v. Petrich, 44 Ohio Op. 457, 58 Ohio L. Abs. 566, 97 N.E.2d 56 (Ct. App. 8th Dist. Cuyahoga County 1950).

[7]Juhasz v. Juhasz, 134 Ohio St. 257, 12 Ohio Op. 57, 16 N.E.2d 328, 117 A.L.R. 993 (1938).

[8]In re Estate of Shafer, 77 Ohio App. 105, 32 Ohio Op. 380, 65 N.E.2d 902 (3d Dist. Hancock County 1944).

[9]Osborn v. Osborn, 10 Ohio Misc. 171, 39 Ohio Op. 2d 275, 226 N.E.2d 814 (C.P. 1966), judgment aff'd, 18 Ohio St. 2d 144, 47 Ohio Op. 2d 310, 248 N.E.2d 191 (1969) (antenuptial agreements are prima facie valid and binding).

The action attacking the antenuptial agreement must be brought in a court of competent jurisdiction.[10] While the majority of actions concerning antenuptial agreements are brought in probate court, if the action is framed in terms of a declaratory judgment, it may be brought in either common pleas or probate court.[11] An action to enforce the provisions of an antenuptial agreement is properly brought in probate court when a party to a divorce dies during the pendency of the divorce.[12]

The introduction of an antenuptial agreement into domestic relations court is common, usually to prevent spousal support and property distributions.[13] When parties do not attack the validity of an antenuptial agreement, they frequently require the court to interpret provisions of the agreement.[14] When enforcing an antenuptial agreement in a domestic relations court that provides each party waives any rights to the other party's property acquired prior to or after the marriage, and the parties assets were always separately maintained, no tracing is required. In *Avent v. Avent*,[15] the parties entered into an antenuptial agreement stating that they each desired to keep their financial estates separate and that property owned by each party prior to and acquired after the marriage would remain separate. The trial court determined that all of the wife's assets held in her own name were marital because she failed to adequately trace her "separate property" owned prior to the marriage to her present assets. However, the record established that the parties always maintained their separate accounts in their own names and never commingled their separate funds in joint bank accounts. As a result, the Sixth District Court of Appeals reversed the trial court's decision, holding

---

[10]RC 2106.22.

[11]See RC 2721.02, RC 2721.04; Hook v. Hook, 69 Ohio St. 2d 234, 23 Ohio Op. 3d 239, 431 N.E.2d 667 (1982); Natl. City Bank v. de Laville, 170 Ohio App. 3d 317, 2006-Ohio-5909, 867 N.E.2d 416 (6th Dist. Lucas County 2006) (a probate court has jurisdiction in an action for declaratory judgment to determine a widow's right to share in her husband's estate—not just under the terms of a trust instrument, but also under the terms of an antenuptial agreement).

[12]Kascak v. Diemer, 112 Ohio App. 3d 635, 679 N.E.2d 1140 (8th Dist. Cuyahoga County 1996) (husband's spousal support obligations set forth in antenuptial agreement were triggered by divorce, not the parties' separation, and thus could not be enforced upon wife's death prior to decree of divorce).

[13]Zimmie v. Zimmie, 11 Ohio St. 3d 94, 464 N.E.2d 142, 53 A.L.R.4th 75 (1984); Gross v. Gross, 11 Ohio St. 3d 99, 464 N.E.2d 500, 53 A.L.R.4th 139 (1984); Osborn v. Osborn, 10 Ohio Misc. 171, 39 Ohio Op. 2d 275, 226 N.E.2d 814 (C.P. 1966), judgment aff'd, 18 Ohio St. 2d 144, 47 Ohio Op. 2d 310, 248 N.E.2d 191 (1969). See Text § 1:8, Considerations for possible divorce, dissolution.

[14]Pol v. Miller, 2007-Ohio-2954, 2007 WL 1713216 (Ohio Ct. App. 1st Dist. Hamilton County 2007), appeal not allowed, 116 Ohio St. 3d 1411, 2007-Ohio-6140, 876 N.E.2d 969 (2007) (antenuptial agreement's terms were unambiguous, as such, trial court erred in its determination of payments in lieu of spousal support and property division).

[15]Avent v. Avent, 166 Ohio App. 3d 104, 2006-Ohio-1861, 849 N.E.2d 98 (6th Dist. Lucas County 2006).

that a tracing was not required and that wife's assets were separate as there was no evidence of commingling.

If the antenuptial agreement is not carefully worded, appreciation on separate property can be determined to be marital.[16]

One seeking to set aside an antenuptial agreement on the basis of fraud, duress, coercion or overreaching must plead those affirmative defenses. Failure to plead them or amend an answer to include them constitutes a waiver of those defenses.[17]

The trier of fact, as the sole judge of the credibility of the witnesses, may determine whether or not an agreement is enforceable.[18] In *Bisker v. Bisker*,[19] the Supreme Court concluded that the validity of the agreement was an issue of fact to be determined by the trier of fact, and that the trial court's decision to invalidate the agreement due to lack of full disclosure was not an abuse of discretion.

Anyone having a pecuniary interest in the validity or invalidity of an antenuptial agreement has standing in an action concerning its validity. The Ohio courts have allowed executors,[20] administrators,[21] and administrators de bonis non[22] standing, presumably because the outcome of the action necessarily affects the manner in which they would distribute the estate. The courts have also allowed heirs[23] and will[24] and trust[25] beneficiaries to be parties to such suits, presumably

---

[16]Graham v. Graham, 2007-Ohio-1091, 2007 WL 730063 (Ohio Ct. App. 3d Dist. Allen County 2007) (although husband's 401(k) and railroad retirement was listed as husband's separate property in the antenuptial agreement, the trial court determined that contributions made during the marriage and the growth were to be divided as marital property). See also Steinke v. Steinke, 2006-Ohio-4185, 2006 WL 2337647 (Ohio Ct. App. 3d Dist. Auglaize County 2006), appeal not allowed, 112 Ohio St. 3d 1443, 2007-Ohio-152, 860 N.E.2d 767 (2007) (where antenuptial agreement provides that husband's pension is his separate property as well as increases in value, regardless of the reason for the increases, the trial court erred in awarding wife a portion of the growth of the pension).

[17]Todd v. Todd, 2000 WL 552311 (Ohio Ct. App. 10th Dist. Franklin County 2000).

[18]Bisker v. Bisker, 1992 WL 335202 (Ohio Ct. App. 7th Dist. Mahoning County 1992), judgment rev'd, 69 Ohio St. 3d 608, 1994-Ohio-307, 635 N.E.2d 308 (1994).

[19]Bisker v. Bisker, 69 Ohio St. 3d 608, 1994-Ohio-307, 635 N.E.2d 308 (1994).

[20]Hook v. Hook, 69 Ohio St. 2d 234, 23 Ohio Op. 3d 239, 431 N.E.2d 667 (1982).

[21]Troha v. Sneller, 169 Ohio St. 397, 8 Ohio Op. 2d 435, 159 N.E.2d 899 (1959).

[22]Cantor v. Cantor, 15 Ohio Op. 2d 148, 86 Ohio L. Abs. 452, 174 N.E.2d 304 (Prob. Ct. 1959).

[23]Verbsky v. Burger, 146 Ohio St. 235, 32 Ohio Op. 255, 65 N.E.2d 695 (1946).

[24]Gross v. Gross, 11 Ohio St. 3d 99, 464 N.E.2d 500, 53 A.L.R.4th 139 (1984). See also Beverly v. Parilla, 2007-Ohio-2756, 2007 WL 1630186 (Ohio Ct. App. 7th Dist. Columbiana County 2007) (even though antenuptial agreement did not reference spousal support, trial court on remand was required to consider the factors of RC 3105.18 in its determination that wife was not entitled to spousal support).

[25]Osborn v. Osborn, 10 Ohio Misc. 171, 39 Ohio Op. 2d 275, 226 N.E.2d 814 (C.P. 1966), judgment aff'd, 18 Ohio St. 2d 144, 47 Ohio Op. 2d 310, 248 N.E.2d 191 (1969).

because they, as third party donee beneficiaries of the contract,[26] have a pecuniary interest in the outcome of the suit. In addition, the courts have permitted surviving spouses[27] and the representatives of the estate of a spouse who died simultaneously with the deceased, defending spouse[28] to be parties to such suits. The courts have also allowed divorced spouses standing.[29] In Ohio, the law of the state in which the couple was domiciled during the marriage will be applied in any action concerning the validity of an antenuptial agreement.[30]

The elements of the first condition may be read with their generally accepted meaning being applicable. Accordingly, the term "overreaching" is used in the sense of one party by artifice or cunning, or by significant disparity to understand the nature of the transaction, to outwit or cheat the other. The first condition of the Gross test invalidated an antenuptial agreement where wife was a "mail order bride," not fluent in English and who was presented with the agreement a few days before the wedding and two weeks before her visa expired.[31]

The legal fiction of retroactive nullification was applied in *Lang v. Reetz-Lang*[32] to declare an antenuptial agreement rescinded for failure of consideration. The marriage in *Lang* was never consummated and was subsequently annulled. In the annulment proceedings, the court found that consummation was an implied condition of the agreement. The court did not apply the reasoning of *Gross v. Gross*,[33] that "[i]f the parties had intended that the subsequent marital misconduct would extinguish the mutual promises . . . [they] could very well have made this clear within the terms of the agreement."

§ 1:8 Considerations for possible divorce, dissolution

Antenuptial agreements have traditionally been used to control the

---

[26]Cantor v. Cantor, 15 Ohio Op. 2d 148, 86 Ohio L. Abs. 452, 174 N.E.2d 304 (Prob. Ct. 1959).

[27]Hook v. Hook, 69 Ohio St. 2d 234, 23 Ohio Op. 3d 239, 431 N.E.2d 667 (1982); In re Weber's Estate, 170 Ohio St. 567, 11 Ohio Op. 2d 415, 167 N.E.2d 98 (1960); Troha v. Sneller, 169 Ohio St. 397, 8 Ohio Op. 2d 435, 159 N.E.2d 899 (1959); Juhasz v. Juhasz, 134 Ohio St. 257, 12 Ohio Op. 57, 16 N.E.2d 328, 117 A.L.R. 993 (1938).

[28]Rudrick v. Thull, 39 Ohio App. 69, 10 Ohio L. Abs. 542, 177 N.E. 513 (5th Dist. Richland County 1931).

[29]Southern Ohio Sav. Bank & Trust Co. v. Burkhart, 148 Ohio St. 149, 35 Ohio Op. 166, 74 N.E.2d 67 (1947); Dearbaugh v. Dearbaugh, 110 Ohio App. 540, 13 Ohio Op. 2d 351, 170 N.E.2d 262 (2d Dist. Shelby County 1959); Kennedy v. Kennedy, 11 Ohio App. 399, 1919 WL 906 (8th Dist. Cuyahoga County 1919); Benza v. Benza, 1978 WL 216102 (Ohio Ct. App. 1st Dist. Warren County 1978).

[30]Osborn v. Osborn, 10 Ohio Misc. 171, 39 Ohio Op. 2d 275, 226 N.E.2d 814 (C.P. 1966), judgment aff'd, 18 Ohio St. 2d 144, 47 Ohio Op. 2d 310, 248 N.E.2d 191 (1969) (prima facie valid).

[31]Azarova v. Schmitt, 2007-Ohio-653, 2007 WL 490908 (Ohio Ct. App. 1st Dist. Hamilton County 2007).

[32]Lang v. Reetz-Lang, 22 Ohio App. 3d 77, 488 N.E.2d 929 (10th Dist. Franklin County 1985).

[33]Gross v. Gross, 11 Ohio St. 3d 99, 464 N.E.2d 500, 53 A.L.R.4th 139 (1984).

rights of the parties when the marriage ends because of the death of one of the spouses. They have not always been strictly enforced when the marriage ends in divorce, annulment, or dissolution.[1] The courts have based this on three different rationales: (1) to allow parties to plan for divorce would undermine the strong public interest in the preservation of marriage as an institution;[2] (2) the courts should not allow the parties to change their statutory duties by contract;[3] and (3) the termination of the marriage destroys the primary consideration for the agreement, thus causing the agreement to lapse for failure of consideration.[4] With the exception of one unreported court of appeals decision,[5] the Ohio courts have uniformly refused to give effect to antenuptial agreements after the divorce of the parties, where the party asserting the agreement is the one that (initially) breached the

---

[Section 1:8]

[1]Hook v. Hook, 69 Ohio St. 2d 234, 23 Ohio Op. 3d 239, 431 N.E.2d 667 (1982); Southern Ohio Sav. Bank & Trust Co. v. Burkhart, 148 Ohio St. 149, 151, 35 Ohio Op. 166, 74 N.E.2d 67 (1947); Conley v. Conley, 45 Ohio App. 2d 1, 74 Ohio Op. 2d 6, 340 N.E.2d 430 (1st Dist. Hamilton County 1975) (agreement lacks consideration to support obligations and is expressly conditioned on continued legal existence of marriage, and where termination of marriage by divorce removes condition, both parties are relieved of agreement); Dearbaugh v. Dearbaugh, 110 Ohio App. 540, 542, 13 Ohio Op. 2d 351, 170 N.E.2d 262 (2d Dist. Shelby County 1959) ("If one party fails to perform a promise made in an antenuptial agreement, such failure may justify granting relief [alimony] to the other party."); Kennedy v. Kennedy, 11 Ohio App. 399, 1919 WL 906 (8th Dist. Cuyahoga County 1919) (husband found guilty of breach of contract (or has not substantially performed), antenuptial contract will not bar wife from right to alimony given to her by statutes of state). But see Benza v. Benza, 1978 WL 216102 (Ohio Ct. App. 1st Dist. Warren County 1978) (terms of antenuptial agreement followed at time of divorce); Alexander Lindey, *Separation Agreements and Ante-nuptial Contracts* § 90.33 (2d rev. ed. 1967); Clark, The Law of Domestic Relations in the United States § 1.9; Kosik v. George, 253 Or. 15, 452 P.2d 560 (1969).

[2]Fricke v. Fricke, 257 Wis. 124, 42 N.W.2d 500 (1950); In re Gudenkauf's Marriage, 204 N.W.2d 586 (Iowa 1973). But see Tomlinson v. Tomlinson, 170 Ind. App. 331, 352 N.E.2d 785 (1976) (disapproved of by, In re Marriage of Boren, 475 N.E.2d 690 (Ind. 1985)) and Unander v. Unander, 265 Or. 102, 506 P.2d 719 (1973) (antenuptial agreements encourage elimination of risk involved with marriage by delineating rights of parties upon divorce).

[3]In re Gudenkauf's Marriage, 204 N.W.2d 586 (Iowa 1973); Garlock v. Garlock, 279 N.Y. 337, 18 N.E.2d 521, 120 A.L.R. 1331 (1939).

[4]Southern Ohio Sav. Bank & Trust Co. v. Burkhart, 148 Ohio St. 149, 35 Ohio Op. 166, 74 N.E.2d 67 (1947) (former wife may not enforce performance of antenuptial contract, which provided for annuity on death of husband, where she failed and refused to perform); Dearbaugh v. Dearbaugh, 110 Ohio App. 540, 13 Ohio Op. 2d 351, 170 N.E.2d 262 (2d Dist. Shelby County 1959) ("The consideration of an antenuptial agreement is the marriage contract."); Kennedy v. Kennedy, 11 Ohio App. 399, 1919 WL 906 (8th Dist. Cuyahoga County 1919) (husband found guilty of breach of contract (or has not substantially performed), antenuptial contract will not bar wife from right to alimony given to her by statutes of state).

[5]Benza v. Benza, 1978 WL 216102 (Ohio Ct. App. 1st Dist. Warren County 1978).

agreement.[6] The Ohio opinions have rested upon failure of consideration and, to a lesser extent, lack of clear intention of the parties that the agreement should survive divorce.[7]

As Ohio courts apparently do not feel that there is any public policy prohibiting the enforcement of antenuptial agreements upon divorce (focusing instead on failure of consideration and lack of intent), it would seem that with proper drafting one could frame an antenuptial agreement that would survive divorce.[8] The starting point in drafting such an agreement would be to express in clear and unambiguous language that it is the intention of the parties that the agreement should continue to control and govern their respective rights in spite of the fact that the marriage ends in divorce, annulment, or dissolution, rather than death. The agreement would also have to be designed to provide sufficient consideration, aside from the marriage itself, to support the agreement after the termination of the marriage. Perhaps the use of insurance policies, annuities, inter vivos cash payments, conveyances of real estate, or the creation of inter vivos trusts would suffice. Again, the draftsman should make clear that the parties do not view the marriage itself as either the fundamental consideration or a condition precedent to the agreement.[9] Finally, counsel would be well advised to provide sufficient support for the estranged spouse and children, in order to avoid any conflict with the statutory duty of support.[10]

If the courts do not hold the parties' rights upon divorce to be totally

---

[6]Dearbaugh v. Dearbaugh, 110 Ohio App. 540, 542, 13 Ohio Op. 2d 351, 170 N.E.2d 262 (2d Dist. Shelby County 1959); Kennedy v. Kennedy, 11 Ohio App. 399, 1919 WL 906 (8th Dist. Cuyahoga County 1919).

[7]See Southern Ohio Sav. Bank & Trust Co. v. Burkhart, 148 Ohio St. 149, 35 Ohio Op. 166, 74 N.E.2d 67 (1947); Dearbaugh v. Dearbaugh, 110 Ohio App. 540, 13 Ohio Op. 2d 351, 170 N.E.2d 262 (2d Dist. Shelby County 1959). See also Will Kuhlmann & Larry D. Rhodebeck, *The Drafting and Enforcement in Ohio of Antenuptial Agreements in Anticipation of Divorce*, 53 Ohio B. 463 (3-24-80); Randolph Carl Oppenheimer, *The Antenuptial Contract in Ohio*, 28 Case W. Res. L. Rev. 1040 (1978).

[8]Benza v. Benza, 1978 WL 216102 (Ohio Ct. App. 1st Dist. Warren County 1978); In re Needles' Estate, 39 Ohio Op. 381, 54 Ohio L. Abs. 433, 437, 87 N.E.2d 489 (Prob. Ct. 1949).

[9]Southern Ohio Sav. Bank & Trust Co. v. Burkhart, 148 Ohio St. 149, 35 Ohio Op. 166, 74 N.E.2d 67 (1947) (former wife may not enforce performance of antenuptial contract, which provided for an annuity on death of husband, where she failed and refused to perform); Dearbaugh v. Dearbaugh, 110 Ohio App. 540, 13 Ohio Op. 2d 351, 170 N.E.2d 262 (2d Dist. Shelby County 1959) ("The consideration of an antenuptial agreement is the marriage contract."); Kennedy v. Kennedy, 11 Ohio App. 399, 1919 WL 906 (8th Dist. Cuyahoga County 1919) (husband found guilty of breach of contract (or has not substantially performed), antenuptial contract will not bar wife from right to alimony given to her by statutes of state). See also Will Kuhlmann & Larry D. Rhodebeck, *The Drafting and Enforcement in Ohio of Antenuptial Agreements in Anticipation of Divorce*, 53 Ohio B. 463 (3-24-80); Randolph Carl Oppenheimer, *The Antenuptial Contract in Ohio*, 28 Case W. Res. L. Rev. 1040 (1978).

[10]RC 3103.03; Juhasz v. Juhasz, 134 Ohio St. 257, 12 Ohio Op. 57, 16 N.E.2d 328, 117 A.L.R. 993 (1938); Mettler v. Warner, 11 Ohio N.P. (n.s.) 363, 21 Ohio Dec. 184, 1910 WL 809 (C.P. 1910); Johnson v. Johnson, 1 Ohio C.D. 291, 1886 WL 2562

controlled by the agreement, the courts would be more likely to hold that the distribution of their property would be controlled by the agreement, as this is the traditional function of an antenuptial agreement.[11] As an alternative, counsel could urge the court to take the agreement into consideration when determining the terms of the spousal support and property division pursuant to a divorce under RC 3105.18 and RC 3105.171.[12]

On June 13, 1984, the Ohio Supreme Court announced a landmark decision in *Gross v. Gross*.[13] The Court held that "provisions contained within antenuptial agreements providing for the disposition of property and awarding sustenance alimony upon a subsequent divorce of the parties are not void *per se* as being against public policy."[14]

The *Gross* decision most likely will stand as the benchmark for future interpretations of antenuptial agreements. In *Sciance v. Sciance*,[15] the Fourth District Court of Appeals, relying on *Gross*, determined that a trial court erred in disregarding an antenuptial agreement as it pertained to a property division of premarital assets. Since the agreement was silent as to jointly owned property acquired during the marriage, the trial court did not err in overriding a division of those marital assets which included pension rights. The Sixth District Court of Appeals affirmed a trial court decision which had invalidated an antenuptial agreement on the basis of fraud.[16] Where an antenuptial agreement was signed three weeks before the wedding and the wife was given an opportunity to ask questions, even though she was not represented by counsel, voluntariness and disclosure tests of *Gross* and *Hook* were met.[17]

The court added that antenuptial agreements containing such event-

---

(Ohio Cir. Ct. 1886), dismissed by 18 W.L.B. 18; Unander v. Unander, 265 Or. 102, 506 P.2d 719 (1973).

[11]Will Kuhlmann & Larry D. Rhodebeck, *The Drafting and Enforcement in Ohio of Antenuptial Agreements in Anticipation of Divorce*, 53 Ohio B. 463 (3-24-80).

[12]Will Kuhlmann & Larry D. Rhodebeck, *The Drafting and Enforcement in Ohio of Antenuptial Agreements in Anticipation of Divorce*, 53 Ohio B. 463 (3-24-80); Unander v. Unander, 265 Or. 102, 506 P.2d 719 (1973).

[13]Gross v. Gross, 11 Ohio St. 3d 99, 464 N.E.2d 500, 53 A.L.R.4th 139 (1984).

[14]Gross v. Gross, 11 Ohio St. 3d 99, 464 N.E.2d 500, 53 A.L.R.4th 139 (1984) (emphasis added).

[15]Sciance v. Sciance, 1987 WL 26249 (Ohio Ct. App. 4th Dist. Washington County 1987).

[16]Matter of Estate of Fels, 1989 WL 1611 (Ohio Ct. App. 6th Dist. Lucas County 1989).

[17]Baksa v. Baksa, 1988 WL 68699, at *1 (Ohio Ct. App. 3d Dist. Paulding County 1988). See In re Estate of Gates v. Gates, 2007-Ohio-5040, 2007 WL 2782626 (Ohio Ct. App. 7th Dist. Columbiana County 2007), appeal not allowed, 116 Ohio St. 3d 1509, 2008-Ohio-381, 880 N.E.2d 484 (2008) where the court held no overreaching even though wife was presented with antenuptial agreement on the day of the marriage with no opportunity to consult with counsel. Wife could have postponed the wedding and there is no strict rule that she must be instructed to consult an attorney. But see Zawahiri v. Alwattar, 2008-Ohio-3473, 2008 WL 2698679 (Ohio Ct. App. 10th Dist. Franklin County 2008), appeal not allowed, 120 Ohio St. 3d 1487, 2009-Ohio-

of-divorce clauses will be valid and enforceable if (1) they have been entered into freely without fraud, duress, coercion, or overreaching; (2) there was a full disclosure, or full knowledge and understanding, of the nature, value, and extent of the prospective spouse's property; and (3) the terms do not promote or encourage divorce or profiteering by divorce.

The elements of the first condition may be read with their generally accepted meaning being applicable. Accordingly, the term "overreaching" is used in the sense of one party by artifice or cunning, or by significant disparity to understand the nature of the transaction, to outwit or cheat the other.

The elements of the second condition would be satisfied either by the exhibiting of the attachment to the antenuptial agreement of a listing of the assets of the parties to the agreement, or alternatively a showing that there had been a full disclosure by other means. The Eighth District Court of Appeals in *Parr v. Parr* went further to hold that a mere listing of assets would not meet the *Gross* test, and that the agreement must disclose the value of the assets.[18] The Ohio Supreme Court in *Gross* did not distinguish within its hypothetical which party leaves the marriage or who would benefit under the agreement. As such, the validity of the agreement does not depend upon who abandons the marriage.[19]

A hypothetical example of the type of situation which condition three seeks to avoid is where the parties enter into an antenuptial agreement which provides a significant sum either by way of property settlement or spousal support at the time of a divorce, and after the lapse of an undue short period of time one of the parties abandons the marriage or otherwise disregards the marriage vows.

Gross appears to have indirectly abolished the theory that there is a failure of consideration when a marriage ends in divorce or dissolution, such that any antenuptial agreement the parties may have entered into is null and void.

Finally, the court said that if an agreement meets the three conditions set out in its opinion and is otherwise valid, it will not be "abrogated as to either party for marital misconduct arising after

---

278, 900 N.E.2d 198 (2009) where court did not enforce religious contract as a valid prenuptial agreement where husband agreed to pay a $25,000.00 mahr (dowry) on the day of the wedding without an opportunity to consult with counsel.

[18]Parr v. Parr, 1997 WL 97231 (Ohio Ct. App. 8th Dist. Cuyahoga County 1997). See Millstein v. Millstein, 2002-Ohio-4783, 2002 WL 31031676 (Ohio Ct. App. 8th Dist. Cuyahoga County 2002) which held that the full disclosure requirement of Gross is satisfied if the spouse challenging the prenuptial agreement has a general knowledge of the nature and extent of the other's wealth and assets.

[19]Gartrell v. Gartrell, 181 Ohio App. 3d 311, 2009-Ohio-1042, 908 N.E.2d 1019 (5th Dist. Tuscarawas County 2009), appeal not allowed, 122 Ohio St. 3d 1479, 2009-Ohio-3625, 910 N.E.2d 478 (2009).

[the] marriage."[20] Fault which might precipitate a divorce or dissolution will not also serve the ironic purpose of invalidating the very provisions of the agreement designed to deal with those eventualities.

The standard of judicial review of event-of-divorce clauses in antenuptial agreements was also dealt with in *Gross*. The Court held that provisions concerning the division of property are to be subjected to a different standard of review from provisions concerning spousal support. In reviewing provisions relating to the division or allocation of property at the time of a divorce, the applicable standards must relate back to the time of the execution of the contract and not to the time of the divorce. As to these provisions, if it is found that the parties have freely entered into an antenuptial agreement, fixing the property rights of each, a court should not substitute its judgment and amend the contract. A perfect or equal division of the marital property is not required to withstand scrutiny under this standard. This is in keeping with this Court's standard of review of provisions contained in antenuptial agreements providing for the devolution of property at the time of the death of one of the parties. The Court distinguished the property rights provisions from the sustenance alimony (now known as spousal support) provisions:

> [However, in reviewing] provisions in antenuptial agreements regarding maintenance or sustenance alimony, a further standard of review must be applied—one of conscionability of the provisions at the time of the divorce or separation. Although we have held herein that such provisions in an antenuptial agreement generally may be considered valid, and even though it is found in a given case upon review that the agreement had met all of the good faith tests, the provisions relating to maintenance or sustenance may lose their validity by reason of changed circumstances which render the provisions unconscionable as to one or the other at the time of the divorce of the parties. Accordingly, such provisions may, upon a review of all of the circumstances, be found to have become voidable at the time of the divorce or dissolution.[21]

The Court found that the maintenance provisions of the Gross's antenuptial agreement were unconscionable and therefore voidable and remanded the case to the trial court which was directed to review the antenuptial agreement's sustenance alimony clause for conscionability and reasonableness, using "the same factors that govern the allowance of alimony."[22] Unconscionability in this case was based on an increase in Mr. Gross's net assets from $550,000 at the time of the marriage to $6,000,000 at the time of the divorce when he was earn-

---

[20]Baksa v. Baksa, 1988 WL 68699 (Ohio Ct. App. 3d Dist. Paulding County 1988). See also *Special Issue on Prenuptial Agreements,* 6 Fam. Advoc. 3 (Winter 1984).

[21]Gross v. Gross, 11 Ohio St. 3d 99, 464 N.E.2d 500, 53 A.L.R.4th 139 (1984).

[22]Gross v. Gross, 11 Ohio St. 3d 99, 464 N.E.2d 500, 53 A.L.R.4th 139 (1984). See In re Estate of Gates v. Gates, 2007-Ohio-5040, 2007 WL 2782626 (Ohio Ct. App. 7th Dist. Columbiana County 2007), appeal not allowed, 116 Ohio St. 3d 1509, 2008-Ohio-381, 880 N.E.2d 484 (2008) (the unconscionable standard does not apply to the review of allocation of property, only to spousal support); Hampton v. Hampton, 2008-Ohio-868, 2008 WL 564724 (Ohio Ct. App. 12th Dist. Clermont County 2008) (the issue of

ing $250,000 annually. The Gross's antenuptial agreement had specified that in the event of divorce, Mrs. Gross was to receive no more than $200 per month for a period of ten years, as sustenance alimony, and that she was not entitled to any division of property. The antenuptial agreement was found to be valid when entered into; the husband could enforce all provisions except those pertaining to sustenance and maintenance, which the court found to be unconscionable. The case was remanded to the trial court for alternative sustenance orders.

On the same day, June 13, 1984, the Ohio Supreme Court set aside another antenuptial agreement in *Zimmie v. Zimmie*,[23] holding that "[a]lthough antenuptial agreements are not *per se* invalid, they must meet certain minimum standards of good faith and fair dealing . . . .. The prospective spouse must be fully and accurately apprised of the nature, value, and extent of the property affected by the agreement, and must enter into it voluntarily."[24] The evidence in *Zimmie* indicated that (1) the wife saw the antenuptial agreement for the first time just one day prior to the wedding; (2) there had been no previous discussion of the agreement's contents; (3) soon after receiving the agreement in the mail, she was taken to the office of her husband's attorney and signed the agreement without reading its entire contents; (4) no one explained to her the value of her husband's assets or that her signing of the agreement waived her rights in his property; and (5) she thought that she had no choice but to sign the agreement. The Court found sufficient evidence to support the conclusion that the wife did not voluntarily enter into the agreement after full disclosure of her husband's financial worth.[25]

The Tenth District Court of Appeals has upheld an arbitration provision contained in an antenuptial agreement. The agreement required any dispute as to spousal support, child support, and the nature, extent, and division of real or personal property acquired during the marriage be submitted to binding arbitration. The trial court granted a stay of proceedings in the divorce action to accomplish the arbitration.[26]

An antenuptial agreement may be unenforceable if a party was a victim of "overreaching." "Overreaching" was defined in *Gross v. Gross*.[27] " '[O]verreaching' is used in the sense of one party by artifice or cunning, or by significant disparity [in the] understand[ing of] the nature of the transaction, [outwitting or cheating] the other." The

---

an antenuptial agreement's fairness at the time of the divorce is only relevant to matters involving spousal support).

[23]Zimmie v. Zimmie, 11 Ohio St. 3d 94, 464 N.E.2d 142, 53 A.L.R.4th 75 (1984).

[24]Zimmie v. Zimmie, 11 Ohio St. 3d 94, 464 N.E.2d 142, 53 A.L.R.4th 75 (1984) (footnotes omitted).

[25]See Text § 9:47, In-court agreements—Confidential relationship.

[26]Kelm v. Kelm, 73 Ohio App. 3d 395, 597 N.E.2d 535 (10th Dist. Franklin County 1992).

[27]Gross v. Gross, 11 Ohio St. 3d 99, 464 N.E.2d 500, 53 A.L.R.4th 139 (1984).

requirement of full disclosure can be met by attaching an exhibit to the agreement or by showing there was full disclosure by other means. The Ohio Supreme Court held that although the antenuptial agreement was valid and enforceable, the trial court erred in not granting spousal support. Changed circumstances during the marriage, which began in 1983, should have led the trial court to hold the provision waiving spousal support unconscionable.[28]

The Supreme Court in *Fletcher v. Fletcher*[29] held that one who seeks to set aside an antenuptial agreement on the basis of fraud, duress, coercion, or overreaching has the burden of proof in establishing the claim. If, however, the party challenging the agreement is to receive disproportionately less under the agreement than he or she would have under an equitable distribution, then the party seeking to enforce the agreement has the burden of proving that there has been full disclosure and a meaningful opportunity for independent counsel.[30]

An antenuptial agreement may provide for a waiver of rights to share in appreciation of separate property that a party may have been otherwise entitled to under RC 3105.171.[31]

An antenuptial agreement waiving and releasing all rights and interests a spouse may have in the property or estate of the other, by virtue of their marriage, will control and take precedence over a provision in an earlier IRA contract that states that benefits will be paid to the surviving spouse of the contract-holder.[32]

The trial court improperly awarded sole ownership of the marital home to husband based upon an antenuptial agreement entered between the parties. The antenuptial agreement discussed only division of assets upon death of a spouse and made no reference to divorce. The appellate court held that such an agreement is inapplicable to a divorce proceeding.[33] The Third District Court of Appeals held in 1995 that the trial court properly held the parties' antenuptial agreement unenforceable in its allocation of their property division. The agree-

---

[28]Fletcher v. Fletcher, 1992 WL 206646 (Ohio Ct. App. 2d Dist. Montgomery County 1992), judgment rev'd, 68 Ohio St. 3d 464, 1994-Ohio-434, 628 N.E.2d 1343 (1994).

[29]Fletcher v. Fletcher, 68 Ohio St. 3d 464, 1994-Ohio-434, 628 N.E.2d 1343 (1994).

[30]Fletcher v. Fletcher, 68 Ohio St. 3d 464, 1994-Ohio-434, 628 N.E.2d 1343 (1994).

[31]Matter of Estate of Radcliff-Umstead, 1994 WL 587972 (Ohio Ct. App. 11th Dist. Portage County 1994).

[32]Kinkle v. Kinkle, 83 Ohio St. 3d 150, 1998-Ohio-119, 699 N.E.2d 41 (1998). But see Bowman v. Bowman, 2001 WL 28663 (Ohio Ct. App. 2d Dist. Montgomery County 2001) (antenuptial agreement which lists 401(k) as premarital asset fails to satisfy ERISA which requires a waiver to be executed by a spouse, not spouse-to-be).

[33]Stokes v. Stokes, 98 Ohio App. 3d 238, 648 N.E.2d 83 (8th Dist. Cuyahoga County 1994); Barnes v. Barnes, 1995 WL 453136 (Ohio Ct. App. 11th Dist. Geauga County 1995); see Devault v. Devault, 80 Ohio App. 3d 341, 609 N.E.2d 214 (10th Dist. Franklin County 1992) and Fletcher v. Fletcher, 68 Ohio St. 3d 464, 1994-Ohio-434, 628 N.E.2d 1343 (1994).

ment listed certain property as separate, but failed to provide how this separate property was to be disposed of in the event of a divorce or dissolution, nor did it define marital property for purposes of the antenuptial agreement and how it was to be divided.[34]

A trial court does not err in reducing the amount payable to wife pursuant to the terms of the antenuptial agreement by the amount of wife's portion of marital debt when the agreement does not contain a provision regarding marital debt.[35] The court may also award temporary support for the pendency of the divorce proceeding when the antenuptial agreement does not provide for it.[36]

An antenuptial agreement provided for a lump-sum property settlement of $20,000 per year for each full year of marriage. Husband was convicted of domestic violence and removed from the marital home nine months after marriage. The trial court erred in entering summary judgment in husband's divorce action, holding that husband owed wife nothing under the antenuptial agreement as the marriage terminated de facto when husband vacated marital residence prior to the end of the first full year. Wife was entitled to her rights under the contract until their marriage was terminated de jure. Equity did not allow husband to limit or extinguish his contract obligations by his own actions.[37]

In an action to enforce an antenuptial agreement after the death of one of the parties to a pending divorce, the trial court properly determined that jurisdiction was with the probate division rather than the domestic relations division.[38] The domestic relations division has jurisdiction only during proceedings for divorce or legal separation and in the absence of such proceedings, including where the death of a party abates a pending divorce action, the domestic relations court lacks jurisdiction to enforce an antenuptial agreement.[39]

---

[34]Osborne v. Osborne, 1995 WL 407402 (Ohio Ct. App. 3d Dist. Allen County 1995).

[35]Mulvey v. Mulvey, 1996 WL 724759 (Ohio Ct. App. 9th Dist. Summit County 1996).

[36]Mulvey v. Mulvey, 1996 WL 724759 (Ohio Ct. App. 9th Dist. Summit County 1996).

[37]Langer v. Langer, 123 Ohio App. 3d 348, 704 N.E.2d 275 (2d Dist. Montgomery County 1997), cause dismissed, 80 Ohio St. 3d 1473, 687 N.E.2d 470 (1997).

[38]Diemer v. Diemer, 99 Ohio App. 3d 54, 649 N.E.2d 1285 (8th Dist. Cuyahoga County 1994).

[39]See RC 3105.171.

§1:9 Arbitration of antenuptial agreements

Agreements to arbitrate disputes under an antenuptial agreement are enforceable.[1] If the parties agree to arbitrate, the procedure used must resemble arbitration pursuant to RC Chapter 2711 or other court rules.[2] The parties should have a written agreement to arbitrate and have an opportunity to move the trial court to vacate, modify or correct the award.

There are certain issues that cannot be arbitrated. The Tenth District Court of Appeals interpreted the Supreme Court's ruling in *Kelm v. Kelm*[3] as holding that matters of child custody and visitation are not subject to arbitration. The Supreme Court affirmed the Tenth District and specifically held that matters of child custody and parental visitation are not subject to arbitration in a domestic relations case.[4] The ruling followed *Pulfer v. Pulfer*.[5] Property, child support and spousal support issues may be submitted to the arbitration process.

An order compelling arbitration under RC 2711.02 is a final appealable order. The law favors and encourages arbitration. It is meant to be a final and binding process, only modified or corrected on grounds set forth in RC 2711.01 and RC 2711.11.

§1:10 Antenuptial agreements and temporary spousal support

It is axiomatic that antenuptial agreements are contracts to which the law applies.[1] If an antenuptial agreement provides that there is to be no temporary support or that the total spousal support is to be in a stated amount, may the court ignore that provision and award temporary support pursuant to RC 3105.18? That issue was considered by the Eighth and Ninth District Courts of Appeal in *Cangemi v.*

[Section 1:9]

[1]Kelm v. Kelm, 68 Ohio St. 3d 26, 1993-Ohio-56, 623 N.E.2d 39, 38 A.L.R.5th 845 (1993).

[2]Cangemi v. Cangemi, 2005-Ohio-772, 2005 WL 433529 (Ohio Ct. App. 8th Dist. Cuyahoga County 2005) (the Court of Appeals vacated the arbitrator's decision and remanded the case to the trial court for further proceedings because the parties' agreement to arbitrate issues arising under the antenuptial agreement was found to be inadequate).

[3]Kelm v. Kelm, 2000 WL 664720 (Ohio Ct. App. 10th Dist. Franklin County 2000), aff'd, 92 Ohio St. 3d 223, 2001-Ohio-168, 749 N.E.2d 299 (2001).

[4]Kelm v. Kelm, 92 Ohio St. 3d 223, 2001-Ohio-168, 749 N.E.2d 299 (2001).

[5]Pulfer v. Pulfer, 110 Ohio App. 3d 90, 673 N.E.2d 656 (3d Dist. Allen County 1996).

[Section 1:10]

[1]Fletcher v. Fletcher, 68 Ohio St. 3d 464, 1994-Ohio-434, 628 N.E.2d 1343 (1994).

Cangemi[2] and *Fields v. Fields*,[3] respectively. In *Fields*, the parties' antenuptial agreement provided that the wife would not receive any distribution from the husband until after the granting of a divorce. It effectively, therefore, provided that there would be no temporary support during the pendency of the action which, in that case, was two years. Both the trial court and the Ninth District Court of Appeals concluded that under RC 3105.18, relating to temporary support issues, the trial court had authority to grant temporary support and was not bound by the terms of the antenuptial agreement. The test, however, is the conscionability of the award at the time of the divorce or separation.[4] The Ninth District Court of Appeals noted that "[U]nconscionability can be found in a number of circumstances including a changed standard of living occasioned by the marriage, where a return to the prior living standard would work a hardship on the spouse."[5]

In *Cangemi*,[6] the parties' antenuptial agreement provided that husband would pay to wife a sum of Sixty Thousand Dollars payable in twelve monthly installments as spousal support. The agreement further stated that "the parties fully understand that there will not be any other alimony paid in the event of termination of marriage except for that which has been specifically agreed to" within the antenuptial agreement. The trial court ordered husband to pay temporary support *pendente lite.* Husband paid temporary support to wife for a period in excess of six years while the litigation was pending, an amount substantially exceeding Sixty Thousand Dollars. In the final divorce decree, the trial court held that husband should pay to wife an additional Sixty Thousand Dollars, in addition to the temporary spousal support already paid, pursuant to the terms of the antenuptial agreement.

Husband argued that he should not have to pay spousal support to wife in excess of Sixty Thousand Dollars, including temporary support. Husband further argued that he should have received a credit for the amount he paid in excess of Sixty Thousand Dollars toward the amount he must pay to wife as her share of the property division. The Eighth District Court of Appeals rejected Husband's arguments, finding that the spousal support award was appropriate, holding: "There is no set formula under R.C. 3105.18 to guide courts to arrive at an appropriate temporary support. The only explicit limitation in R.C. 3105.18(B) is that the award must be 'reasonable'." Courts are giving

---

[2]Cangemi v. Cangemi, 2006-Ohio-2879, 2006 WL 1555461 (Ohio Ct. App. 8th Dist. Cuyahoga County 2006).

[3]Fields v. Fields, 1992 WL 74207, at *5 (Ohio Ct. App. 9th Dist. Summit County 1992).

[4]Gross v. Gross, 11 Ohio St. 3d 99, 464 N.E.2d 500, 53 A.L.R.4th 139 (1984).

[5]Fields v. Fields, 1992 WL 74207 (Ohio Ct. App. 9th Dist. Summit County 1992).

[6]Cangemi v. Cangemi, 2006-Ohio-2879, 2006 WL 1555461 (Ohio Ct. App. 8th Dist. Cuyahoga County 2006).

discretion in deciding what is reasonable support because that determination is dependent on the unique facts and circumstances of each case."[7]

Other jurisdictions have considered the issue. In *Rubin v. Rubin*,[8] the New York Court of Appeals held that the trial court erred in granting wife temporary support when provisions of an antenuptial agreement specifically waived such payments. On the other hand, the Supreme Court of Nevada held that a provision in an antenuptial agreement setting forth the amount of spousal support in the event of dissolution was a separate issue from that of temporary spousal support.[9]

Following *Fields v. Fields*, the Ninth District Court of Appeals in *Mulvey v. Mulvey*[10] held that the trial court had not erred in granting spousal support despite the parties' prenuptial agreement which provided for payment upon the granting of a divorce. The court noted that the disparity in the parties' incomes justified the temporary support order. The trial court also refused to credit the temporary support payments against the lump sum payment provided for by the prenuptial agreement. At the time the temporary support order was issued, wife was earning $40,000 per year and husband over $400,000. The disparity in the income was apparently the decisive factor in awarding temporary support contrary to the provisions of the agreement.

While there is no Ohio Supreme Court case on the issue, and few court of appeals' cases, it may reasonably be assumed that a trial court faced with the issue could ignore the specific provisions of the antenuptial agreement. Justification for the decision can be found under the court's broad statutory discretion on the matter, the goal of preserving the status quo, and the conscionability of the temporary support provision or a lack thereof at the time of hearing. A trial court may, however, enforce the parties' waiver of spousal support if the issue of the validity of the agreement is not raised.[11] Presumably the waiver could be applied to all spousal support including temporary support. In *Dever v. Dever*,[12] an antenuptial agreement provided for 100 months of permanent support. The trial court offset a portion of those payments by the temporary support paid after the "termination date" of the marriage.

[7]Cangemi v. Cangemi, 2006-Ohio-2879, 2006 WL 1555461 (Ohio Ct. App. 8th Dist. Cuyahoga County 2006). (Citation omitted).

[8]Rubin v. Rubin, 262 A.D.2d 390, 690 N.Y.S.2d 742 (2d Dep't 1999).

[9]Dimick v. Dimick, 112 Nev. 402, 915 P.2d 254 (1996).

[10]Mulvey v. Mulvey, 1996 WL 724759 (Ohio Ct. App. 9th Dist. Summit County 1996).

[11]Mauser v. Mauser, 2001 WL 822678 (Ohio Ct. App. 11th Dist. Portage County 2001).

[12]Dever v. Dever, 2000 WL 1902195 (Ohio Ct. App. 12th Dist. Clermont County 2000).

§ 1:11   Antenuptial agreement—Basic—Form⊚

This is an Agreement entered into on *[date]*, at *[city and state]*, by and between *[name of spouse]*, *[number of years old]* years of age, and *[name of spouse]*, *[number of years old]* years of age, who represent that:

(A) *[Name of spouse]* has *[no / number of children]* children of a former marriage, all adults, namely, *[name(s) and date(s) of birth of children]*.

(B) *[Name of spouse]* has *[no / number of children]* children of a former marriage, all adults, namely, *[name(s) and date(s) of birth of children]*.

(C) The parties contemplate marrying each other.

(D) Each party possesses real and personal property in his/her own right and each has fully disclosed in the financial statements attached hereto as Exhibits A and B, which are hereby made a part hereof, the nature, extent and probable value of all property presently owned by each party, together with the nature and extent of his/her liabilities. Furthermore, each party hereby warrants to the other the accuracy of his/her financial statement, and acknowledges that the other is relying upon such statement in entering into this Agreement.

(E) The parties desire and intend to, and do, waive, renounce, and relinquish any and all rights each may be or become entitled to, under the law, as a spouse and as a surviving spouse in the property and in the estate of the other by virtue of entering into the aforesaid proposed marriage.

(F) Each party is represented by his/her own legal counsel and each fully understands all provisions of this Agreement.

Therefore, in consideration of the proposed marriage and foregoing premises, and mutual promises, the parties agree as follows:

(1) In the event of the death of either party:

(a) The surviving party shall not present, make, or assert any claim or right to share or participate in any manner in the other party's estate.

(b) The surviving party hereby waives, renounces, and relinquishes his/her right to statutory exemptions and his/her statutory right to an interest in the mansion house, and further waives, renounces, and relinquishes any and all other rights, benefits, and privileges of whatever kind or nature conferred upon him/her by law to share or participate in the other party's estate, as a surviving spouse.

(2) All property, real or personal, tangible or intangible, which each of the parties owned before the parties' proposed marriage, or which each may thereafter acquire (including, without limitation, dividends, interest, rents, profits, or increments in value thereof) shall be and remain the personal estate of such party, free from any claim whatsoever on the part of the other by the way of dower, statutes of descent and distribution, or other applicable laws as though no marriage had been entered into between them.

(3) Each party may make such disposition of his/her property acquired before or during the parties' marriage by sale, gift, will, or otherwise during his/her lifetime as he/she may desire.

(4) If either party desires to sell, encumber, transfer, or otherwise dispose of his/her own property, real or personal, tangible or intangible, in whole or in part, then the other, upon request, shall join in, and execute, any and all papers, documents, and legal instruments necessary to effectuate such transaction.

(5) This Agreement constitutes the entire understanding between the parties. It may not be changed, modified, altered, or revoked except in writing signed by both parties.

(6) This Agreement and all of its provisions shall be construed and enforced in accordance with the laws of Ohio.

(7) In the event of a termination of the parties' marriage by annulment, divorce, or dissolution proceedings in a court of competent jurisdiction, this Agreement shall thereupon *[be deemed null and void and of no effect/be conclusive as to the ownership of property brought into the marriage and shall determine the distribution of such assets]*.

(8) This Agreement becomes effective when the parties' proposed marriage is duly *[consummated/solemnized]*, and thereupon this Agreement shall bind the parties hereto, and their respective administrators, executors, heirs, assigns, and legal representatives.

(9) If any provision or clause of this Agreement or application thereof to any person or circumstances is held to be invalid, such invalidity shall not affect any other provisions or applications of the Agreement, each of which shall be given effect, and to this end the provisions of this Agreement are declared to be severable.

IN WITNESS WHEREOF, the parties have affixed their signatures to four counterparts of this Agreement, each of which shall constitute an original.

_____
Husband

_____
Wife

Signed and acknowledged
in the presence of:

_____

Witness

_____

Witness

State of Ohio   :
                       : SS.   AFFIDAVIT
County of [_____]   :

[Name], having been duly sworn, acknowledges that [he/she] did sign this Antenuptial Agreement as [his/her] free act and deed, and does hereby specifically aver and represent that [his/her] financial statement referred to in paragraph (D) hereof is accurate and correctly portrays [his/her] financial condition.

[Jurat]

NOTES TO FORM

Drafter's Notes

Exhibits A and B, listing each party's declared assets, preferably with approximate value stated, should be attached to this Agreement.

§ 1:12 Antenuptial agreement—Detailed—Form⊚

This is an Antenuptial Agreement entered into between [name of spouse] (hereinafter referred to as "_____") and [name of spouse] (hereinafter referred to as "_____"). It becomes effective upon the marriage of the parties, and in the event that there is no such marriage then it shall be null and void and have no effect whatever.

(1) Background

[Name of spouse] is [number of years old] years old, [single/divorced/widowed], and the [father/mother] of [no / number of children] children, namely, [name(s) and date(s) of birth of children]. [Name of child] resides with [name of spouse], and [name of child] and [name of child] reside with their [father/mother], to whom [name of spouse] is paying $[dollar amount] per year in [spousal support/child support]. [Name of spouse] is [number of years old] years old, [single/divorced/widowed], and the [father/mother] of [no/number] children, namely, [name(s) and date(s) of birth of children] who [lives/live] with [name of spouse]. [Name of spouse] owns and lives in a single-family residence located at [street address, city, state]. [Name of spouse] owns and lives in a single-family residence located at [street address, city, state]. [Name of spouse] and [name of spouse] intend to marry sometime during [year]. Each owns individually various assets and property, real and personal, tangible and intangible, and the parties intend that each shall retain any such property free and clear of any claim by the other, as though each were remaining single, subject only to the provisions set forth herein.

(2) Present assets

Attached hereto, and made a part hereof, are financial statements provided by each party to the other reflecting, in each party's instance, a description of such party's assets and the approximate value thereof, together with such party's indebtedness and the nature thereof. Each party warrants to the other that such financial statements set forth, in general, the nature and extent of his/her assets and liabilities and contain a full disclosure of such assets and liabilities. Also attached hereto is a summary description of the pension plan established for benefit of [name of spouse] by [name of company]. Each party understands that the other is entering into this Agreement with the understanding that such statements do in fact constitute such full disclosure.

(3) Recitals

In consideration of the foregoing, and in consideration of the marriage of the parties and of the disclosure by each to the other of the character and extent of his or her property and worth, the parties agree as follows: _____.

(4) Division of estate of [name of spouse]

(A) In the event of death of [name of spouse] while the parties are still married, and providing that no dissolution, divorce, or annulment proceedings are then pending between the parties in any jurisdiction and further providing that the parties are not legally separated at the time of death of [name of spouse], [name of spouse] shall receive from the estate of [name of spouse][percentage amount]% of such estate. In this context "estate" means gross estate of [name of spouse] for federal estate tax purposes and shall include any and all death benefits and other benefits payable according to the terms of any pension or profit sharing plan in which [name of spouse] is, at the time of [his/her] death, a participant, including specifically, without limitation, any pension or profit sharing plans established by any professional corporation of which [he/she] is now, or in the past has been, or in the future may become, a shareholder, whether or not any such pension or profit sharing plan benefits are includible in the estate of [name of spouse] for federal estate tax purposes. The share of [name of spouse] in the estate of [name of spouse] shall, if [he/she] elects, include any interest that [name of spouse] owns in any residential real estate occupied by the parties as their principal residence at the time of [his/her] death together with all improvements thereon, and shall also include, if [name of spouse] so elects, all household furnishings, utensils, appliances, and other items of personal property located in and about such residential property. In the event that [name of spouse] elects to take, as a portion of *[his/her]* share of the estate of *[name of spouse]*, interest in such residential real estate and the household furnishings and other items of personal property referred to, then the value thereof, as appraised in the estate of *[name of spouse]*, shall be credited against the *[percentage amount]*% interest of *[name of spouse]* in the estate of *[name of spouse]*, provided, however, that if such value exceeds *[percentage amount]*% of the estate of *[name of spouse]*, *[name of spouse]* shall nevertheless be entitled to such residential real estate and the household furnishings and other items of personal property referred to without accounting to, or having to reimburse, the estate of *[name of spouse]* for the amount by which such value exceeds *[percentage amount]*%. In the event that the value of such residential real estate, household furnishings and other items of personal property referred to is less than *[percentage amount]*% of estate of *[name of spouse]*, then the estate of *[name of spouse]* shall pay over and deliver to *[name of spouse]*, within *[number of months]* months after the death of *[name of spouse]*, an amount in money equal to the difference between such value and *[percentage amount]*% of the estate of *[name of spouse]*.

(B) In the event of the death of *[name of spouse]* survived by *[name of spouse]* at a time when dissolution, divorce, or annulment proceedings are pending between the parties in any jurisdiction or at a time when the parties are legally separated, then *[name of spouse]* shall receive, on account of the death of *[name of spouse]*, *[percentage amount]*% of the estate of *[name of spouse]* and in all other respects the provisions of subparagraph (A) of this paragraph (4) shall apply.

(C) *[Name of spouse]* shall, within *[number of days]* days after the execution of this Agreement by both parties, cause a will and other appropriate estate planning instruments to be drawn and executed reflecting the provisions set forth in this paragraph (4), and for such purposes, this Agreement shall be deemed an enforceable agreement to make a will under the law of Ohio. Furthermore, regardless of whether *[name of spouse]* does in fact execute such instruments, *[name of spouse]* shall, in the event of the death of *[name of spouse]*, have a claim against the estate of *[name of spouse]* (as defined in paragraph (4)(A) to the extent set forth in this paragraph (4)).

(5) Division of estate of *[name of other spouse]*

(A) In the event of the death of *[name of spouse]* while the parties are still married, providing that no dissolution, divorce, or annulment proceedings are then pending between the parties in any jurisdiction and further providing that the parties are not legally separated at the time of *[his/her]* death, *[name of spouse]* shall be entitled to receive from the estate of *[name of spouse]* any interest that *[he/she]* has in and to any residential real estate occupied by the parties as their principal residence at the time of *[his/her]* death, together with all improvements thereon and also all household furnishings, furniture, utensils, appliances, and other items of personal property located in and about such residential property, except such items of furnishings, furniture, and silverware that *[he/she]* specifically designates in writing, shall go to members of *[his/her]* family other than *[name of spouse]*. Under no circumstances, unless *[name of spouse]* otherwise provides by will or other instrument, shall *[name of spouse]* be entitled to any assets acquired by *[name of spouse]*, either before or after *[his/her]* marriage to *[name of spouse]*, by way of inheritance, or by way of gift from any person. For this purpose, "assets" mean not only the assets acquired by *[name of spouse]* in their original form, but also accretions thereto or other assets to which such original assets have been converted.

(B) In the event of the death of *[name of spouse]* survived by *[name of spouse]* at a time when dissolution, divorce, or annulment proceedings are pending between the parties in any jurisdiction or at a time when the parties are legally separated, then *[name of spouse]* shall not be entitled to any share of the estate of *[name of spouse]*.

(C) *[Name of spouse]* shall, within *[number of days]* days after the execution of this Agreement by both parties, cause a will and other appropriate estate planning instruments to be drawn and executed reflecting the provisions set forth in this paragraph (5), and for such purposes, this Agreement shall be deemed an enforceable agreement to make a will under the law of Ohio. Furthermore, regardless of whether *[name of spouse]* does in fact execute such instruments, *[name of spouse]* shall, in the event of the death of *[name of spouse]*, have a claim against the estate of *[name of spouse]* to the extent set forth in subparagraph (A) of this paragraph (5), provided that the provisions of subparagraph (B) do not apply.

(6) Maintenance of pension and profit sharing plans

As to any pension or profit sharing plans in which *[name of participant spouse]* is a participant including specifically without limitation the pension plan established by the *[name of company]*, *[name of participant spouse]* shall cause *[his/her]* professional corporation, or any successor thereto, to continue to make contributions to such plan or plans upon the same basis and according to the same formulas upon which the amounts of such contributions were determined for the year *[year]* or, if the total contributions for *[year]* have already been made, for the year *[year]*. As to any and all such plans in which *[name of participant spouse]* is a participant, *[name of participant spouse]* shall not in any way deplete or reduce the assets held by such plan, or cause any such reduction to be made, without the express prior written consent of *[name of nonparticipant spouse]*. Furthermore, *[name of participant spouse]* shall, immediately upon the parties' marriage, take any and all steps necessary to assure the payment to *[name of nonparticipant spouse]* of all benefits payable to *[him/her]* from, or on account of, any and all such pension and profit sharing plans pursuant to the provisions of this paragraph (6), including specifically, without limitation, provisions for the payment of death benefits to *[him/her]* in the event of *[his/her]* death and the payment to *[him/her]*, on a joint annuity basis or otherwise, of installment payments (by way of annuity or otherwise) after *[his/her]* death. It is the parties' intention that *[name of nonparticipant spouse]* be assured that *[name of participant spouse]* will continue to participate in, and make contributions to, *[his/her]* existing pension and profit sharing plans upon the same basis as that which has prevailed in the past; that, in the event of the death of *[name of participant spouse]* before *[he/she]* begins to draw retirement payments from any such plan, *[he/she]* receive at least *[percentage amount]*% of the death benefits pursuant to the terms of any and all such plans; and that, in the event of the death of *[name of participant spouse]* at a time when *[name of nonparticipant spouse]* is drawing retirement benefits from any and all such plans, such payments (by way of annuity or otherwise) shall, in effect, be on a joint annuity basis so as to assure to *[name of nonparticipant spouse]* the continued payment of all such payments to *[him/her]* after the death of *[name of participant spouse]*.

(7) Divorce, dissolution, separation

(A) Within *[number of years]* years

In the event that the parties' marriage is dissolved by means of a decree or judgment entry entered by a court of competent jurisdiction within *[number of years]* years after the date upon which the parties are married, or in the event that the parties enter into a formal separation agreement, the effective date of which is within *[number of years]* years of such date, then the following provisions shall apply: (1) each party shall retain, free and clear of any claim by the other, any and all assets owned by him/her on the date of the parties' marriage; (2) each party shall retain, free and clear of any claim by the other, any assets acquired by him/her by means of inheritance or gift from others; (3) neither party shall be required to pay to the other any spousal support or periodic support payments of any kind; (4) except as hereinafter provided, the parties will divide equally the assets which they have accumulated during the course of their marriage; (5) in the event that *[name of spouse]* has made a contribution toward the purchase of a new home for the parties (whether before or after their marriage), then *[name of spouse]* shall pay to *[him/her]* an amount equal to such contribution plus interest thereon, compounded at the rate of *[percentage amount]*% per month for each month *(or part of a month)* from the date on which such contribution was made to the date on which *[name of spouse]* makes such repayment to *[him/her]*; and (6) *[name of spouse]* and *[his/her]* children may remain in the parties' residence for a period not to exceed *[number of days]* days after repayment of *[name of spouse]* to *[him/her]* of the sum owed to *[him/her]* pursuant to the terms of clause (5) of this paragraph (7)(A).

(B) After *[number of years]* years

In the event that the parties' marriage is dissolved by means of a decree or judgment entry entered by a court of competent jurisdiction *[number of years]* years or more after the date upon which the parties are married, or in the event that the parties enter into a formal separation agreement, the effective date of which is *[number of years]* years or more after such date of marriage, then the provisions set forth in subparagraph (A) of this paragraph (7) shall apply, and, in addition, *[name of spouse]* shall pay to *[name of spouse]*, in a lump sum and within *[number of months]* months after such entry date or effective date, a sum equal to *[percentage amount]*% of the total amount contributed to any pension or profit sharing plan in which *[name of spouse]* is, or has been, a participant from the date of the parties' marriage to such entry date or effective date for each year *(or portion of a year)* during which the parties have been married, provided, however, that under no circumstances shall such payment be less than *[percentage amount]*%, nor more than *[percentage amount]*%, of such contributions.

(8) Gifts and bequests

This Agreement shall not be construed to prevent *[name of spouse]* and *[name of spouse]* from voluntarily giving property to the other during *[his/her]* lifetime or from voluntarily leaving assets to the other upon *[his/her]* death to an extent beyond that which is required by the strict terms hereof. Either may name the other as beneficiary under any trust agreement or insurance contract, or as legatee or devisee under *[his/her]* will. The parties may hold property in the names of both of them under any estate or contractual arrangement whereby the entire ownership of, or right to, the property in question shall vest in the survivor of them. Either party may serve as executor of the other's estate if *[he/she]* is so designated in such other's will, and either may serve as trustee of any trust established by the other.

(9) Additional instruments

[Name of spouse] and *[name of spouse]* shall, from time to time, upon the other's request, execute, acknowledge and deliver any and all instruments of release or conveyance which may be necessary or desirable to enable the other to dispose of any and all property belonging to such other, whether now owned or subsequently acquired, free and clear of any right of dower or other spousal rights, and such further instruments as may reasonably be requested by the other. Upon the death of either party, the survivor shall furnish to decedent's personal representative, and to his/her heirs or assigns, such instruments as may be requested in order to evidence and carry into effect the releases and waivers provided for herein.

(10) Taxes

Unless they otherwise agree, *[name of spouse]* and *[name of spouse]*, and their respective personal representatives, shall file joint federal, state, and local income tax returns for any period for which such joint returns may be filed, the applicable regulations permitting. As to each such period each party shall bear and pay, as his/her portion of the tax due under any such joint return, that amount which is in the same proportion to the total joint income tax due as is that party's portion of the aggregate which would be due if the parties had filed separate tax returns. Each party shall freely and fully cooperate with the other in instituting and prosecuting any contest of any joint tax liability and in seeking refund of any tax upon joint returns. The requesting party shall save the other harmless as to any expenses incurred in prosecuting such contest or seeking any such refund.

(11) Definitions

As used herein, the words "property" and "assets" mean and include money and every other form of property and interest in property, tangible and intangible, real and personal.

(12) Partial invalidity; survival

This Agreement is effective during the lifetime of each of the parties and shall survive the death of each. In the event that any portion hereof is found to be contrary to law by a court of competent jurisdiction, then the other provisions hereof shall nevertheless remain in full force and effect and, as to the portions deemed contrary to law, such language and provisions shall be substituted therefor as shall effectuate the parties' intentions as expressed herein.

(13) Living expenses; income of [name of spouse]

Except as herein otherwise expressly provided, the parties agree that as long as they are residing together as husband and wife, [name of spouse] shall provide the reasonable living expenses for both parties, provided, however, that [name of spouse] shall pay [his/her] children's educational and clothing expenses.

(14) Entire understanding; amendment

This Agreement sets forth the parties' entire understanding with reference to its subject matter. There is no other or further or different understanding, undertaking, agreement, representation or warranty, express or implied, in any way limiting, extending, defining or relating to any provision of this Agreement. However, the parties reserve the right to amend and alter this Agreement, and to revoke it, both before and after their marriage. No agreement altering, modifying or waiving or releasing the terms of this Agreement shall be valid or binding unless it extends and increases the rights of a party, is in writing and duly executed by the parties in the same manner and with the same formalities as the execution of this Agreement.

(15) Legal counsel

The parties acknowledge that [name of spouse] was represented by [name of attorney], attorney, [city and state], and [name of spouse] was represented by [name of attorney], attorney, [city and state], as their respective legal counsel, in the execution of this Agreement and that each such counsel was freely and voluntarily chosen by each of the respective parties.

(16) Binding effect

This Agreement shall inure to the benefit of, and shall be binding upon, the heirs, executors, administrators and successors of the parties.

(17) Confidentiality

The parties agree that the information set forth in the financial statements and other attachments hereto is confidential and that they will not disclose such information to any person other than their respective legal counsel unless such disclosure is essential in connection with later negotiations or litigation relating to this Agreement.

IN WITNESS WHEREOF, said parties have affixed their signatures at *[city and state]* this *[date]* to *[number]* copies of this Agreement, each of which shall constitute an original.

In the presence of:

Witness	Date	Husband
Witness	Date	Date

[Jurat]

In the presence of:

Witness	Date	Wife
Witness	Date	Date

[Jurat]

Each of us acknowledges that we have advised our respective clients concerning the foregoing Antenuptial Agreement.

Attorney for Wife	Attorney for Husband

NOTES TO FORM

Drafter's Notes

Paragraphs (4) and (5), or subparagraphs thereof, may be used in the alternative.

§ 1:13 Alternate clauses—Children—Form⊛

(1) The parties agree that the responsibility for raising the parties' children rests upon both parents, and believe that any restrictions on this responsibility would deprive them of experiences and opportuni-

ties both as individuals and parents, and would be detrimental to the growth and development of their children. Therefore, the parties agree that child care and rearing should be a mutual privilege and responsibility. In allocating time and duties, the parties shall take into account the demands of their respective careers, their needs as individuals to establish, maintain, and cultivate social and business contacts outside of the marriage, their individual skills and desires, and the best interests of their children.

(2)   Should the marriage terminate after the birth or adoption of a child or children, the parties agree that *[name of spouse]* will remain in the family home with the children and that *[name of spouse]* will pay the costs of maintaining the family home until the children become emancipated. The parties agree to share the privileges of the care of the children and shall provide for the support of the children *[in the same proportion as their earnings shall bear to each other/ equally]*. Reasonable expenses incident to amenities such as summer camps, special lessons, travel, etc., shall be borne by *[the party desiring that the child have the advantage of said musical, athletic, or educational experiences/other named individual]*. Health insurance for the benefit of the children will be carried by *[name of spouse]* unless the health insurance coverage available to *[name of spouse]* offers more comprehensive coverage (e.g., dental care, etc.). Upon the emancipation of the youngest of the parties' children, property acquired during the marriage will be divided equally. In the case of a child over twelve, the parties agree to let the child choose the party with whom *[he/she]* desires to live and shall respect the decision of the child. Should any dispute as to allocation of parental rights and responsibilities of the child arise, the parties agree to submit such dispute to *[arbitration pursuant to the rules and procedures of the American Arbitration Association/mediation prior to court action]*.

(3)   The parties recognize that, under the laws of the state of Ohio, the court has jurisdiction during the minority of the children to require both parties to provide support for children in sufficient amounts. The parties by this Agreement do not intend any limitation of such power, but an extension and augmentation of court-imposed responsibilities.

§ 1:14   Alternate clauses—Debts and expenses—Form⊚

(1)   The parties agree to share *[equally/proportionally to their income]* their normal living expenses (including such items as food, utilities, taxes, housing, medical expenses, transportation, clothing, and insurance). The parties shall maintain a joint/survivorship checking account out of which such expenses shall be paid, and each party shall contribute *[his/her proportionate share/fifty percent]* of all amounts deposited therein necessary to pay such expenses on a timely basis. *[Name of spouse]* shall bear the responsibility for writing checks on such account and balancing all statements pertaining thereto.

(2)   In the event either party is involuntarily unemployed or voluntarily unemployed by agreement of the parties, or is unable to work during a period of injury, infirmity, maternity, or illness, then the

earnings, salaries and income of the working party during said periods shall be deemed to be jointly held property subject to control by both parties.

(3)   Neither party shall expect reimbursement from jointly held funds for any amount expended from their individually held funds for the maintenance and expansion of their household.

(4)   Debts and liabilities incurred by the parties acting as individuals will be the liability of the party incurring the debt. One party may refuse to guarantee or co-sign for the debts of the other party.

(5)   The parties agree that debts, both joint and individual, may cause a strain upon their marriage and therefore agree that incurrence of debts will be mutually made only after serious consideration of its effects on the welfare of the marriage. Furthermore, expenditures over $*[dollar amount]* will be made by mutual consent, except in cases of emergency.

§ 1:15   Alternate clauses—Property and assets—Form⊚

(1)   All assets and property held by the parties at the time of the marriage shall continue to be separately held. All gifts, bequests, or devises to either party individually during the course of the marriage shall also be separately held by such party, subject to the control and management of such party as if no marriage had been entered into.

[(2)   During their marriage, the parties may contract and agree from time to time to change certain items of property from individually held property to jointly held property by a written contract duly acknowledged by the parties or by oral contract if the contract is fully confirmed, and ratified by both parties.]

or

[(2) All assets owned by the parties at the time of the marriage shall be merged and jointly held and managed.]

(3)   The parties have made full disclosure to each other of all properties and assets (including expectancies) presently owned by each of them and of the income derived therefrom and from all other sources and agree that each party shall have sole management, control, and disposition of the property so owned as described in Exhibits A and B which are thereby made a part of this contract. The parties agree to make good faith efforts to update schedules of assets annually. Likewise, the parties shall prepare, review, and amend during January of each year, beginning in *[year]*, an Exhibit C that shall accurately reflect the extent of their marital assets and liabilities as to which they share equally. The parties may by mutual agreement determine their respective interests in an item of property on a basis other than by financial contribution, but such agreement shall not be effective until reduced to writing in Exhibit A, B, or C.

(4)   All tangible assets acquired after the marriage is performed, including wedding presents, real estate, interest, stock dividends, and other income and assets, will be deemed marital property in which each party shall have a fifty percent interest.

(5) All property acquired during the marriage shall be marital property in which each party shall have a fifty percent interest, regardless of the source of funds used to acquire such assets, but shall be managed by [name of spouse].

(6) The parties shall have joint control and ownership of all assets acquired by either or both during the marriage and neither shall dispose of any such assets, or any interest therein, without the voluntary written consent of the other party.

§ 1:16 Alternate clauses—Wills/estates—Form⊚

(1) If [name of spouse] survives [name of spouse], then [he/she] shall not as [his/her] surviving spouse assert or make any claim whatever to the parcel of real estate now owned by [name of spouse], which consists of a brick single residence bearing address [street address] and is further described as follows:

[legal description]

(2) Also, if [name of spouse] should survive [name of spouse], then [he/she] shall not, as [his/her] surviving spouse, assert or make any claim to any part of the furnishings, furniture, fixtures, or to any other items of personal property owned by [him/her] as listed in Exhibit A and now in [his/her] home situated on aforesaid parcel of real estate.

(3) Except as otherwise provided in preceding paragraphs (1) and (2), each party shall have all the rights, benefits, and privileges and the right to share in the estate of the other, as provided by law, or as each may provide by Last Will and Testament, the same as though the marriage had taken place without the execution of this Agreement.

(4) Each party shall forthwith take all steps necessary to assure that, at [his/her] death, there is in existence a valid will by the terms of which the other party is the sole primary devisee and legatee of [his/her] probate estate, or in such other proportions as the parties may have agreed upon. This Agreement shall be deemed an enforceable agreement to make a will under the law of the State of Ohio.

(5) Each party shall have the free and uncontrolled use, enjoyment, and right to dispose of any and all property held by [him/her] individually by means of conveyance, devise, or bequest as if single, irrespective of any laws or statutes which otherwise provide.

(6) This Agreement shall be binding upon the parties hereto and their respective administrators, executors, heirs, assigns, and legal representatives.

§ 1:17 Alternate clauses—Termination of marriage—Form⊚

(1) When the parties' proposed marriage has been duly solemnized, this Agreement shall constitute the entire understanding between the parties and shall not be changed, modified, altered, or revoked unless done in writing signed by both parties.

(2) Termination of the parties' marriage shall be sought only after good faith attempts at marriage counseling and reconciliation. Should

such good faith efforts fail, the parties agree to terminate the marriage as specified above.

(3) In the case of unresolved disputes between the parties over this contract or any portion thereof, they will seek mediation, professional or otherwise, by a neutral third party and be bound by the decisions of such third party.

[(4) If the marriage terminates prior to the birth of any children, the jointly held property of the parties will be divided equally and each shall retain *[his/her]* individually held property.]

or

> [(4) If the dissolution occurs prior to the birth of any children, all property shall be divided equally. Any differences as to such division will be solved by arbitration. *[Name of spouse]* shall pay spousal support to *[name of spouse]* while *[name of spouse]* undergoes job training and is self-supporting; however, the period of the said spousal support payments shall not exceed the duration of the marriage.]

(5) Each of the parties waives and releases the other from any claim for spousal support or maintenance, after the termination of marriage, whether such rights arise by statute or common law and irrespective of fault by the other party.

(6) In the event of termination of the marriage, each party shall retain sole ownership of his/her own property inherited during the marriage, whether said property is in the same form or is in another form due to conversion, trade, sale and reinvestment, or has increased in value, irrespective of the cause of the increase, such as from improvements, infusion of funds, or inflation.

NOTES TO FORM

Drafter's Notes

Clause (5) can be used to show the intent of the parties, even though the court will follow RC 3105.18 and Gross v. Gross, 11 Ohio St. 3d 99, 464 N.E.2d 500, 53 A.L.R.4th 139 (1984), in determining the equity of providing or denying spousal support.

§ 1:18 Alternate clauses—Retirement benefits—Form⊚

(1) *[Future spouse]* acknowledges that *[spouse-participant]* has listed in Schedule *[name of schedule]* that *[he/she]* is a participant in *[name of (pension/profit sharing) plan]*, and also that, pursuant to the *[divorce/dissolution]* decree rendered in *[court, case number]*, *[participant spouse's former spouse]* is entitled to receive certain benefits from said plan. *[Future spouse]* agrees to execute all consents and waivers necessary to effectuate the terms of the qualified domestic relations order.

[(2) *[Future spouse]* agrees to consent to permit *[participant spouse]* complete discretion in naming the beneficiaries of the interest of *[participant spouse]* in *[name of (pension/retirement benefit) plan]*.]

or

[(2) *[Name of future spouse]* agrees to consent to permit *[name of participant spouse]* discretion to name *[name of beneficiary]* or *[name of beneficiary]* as beneficiaries of *[his / her]* interest in *[name of (pension / retirement benefit) plan].]*

(3)   Each party waives all spousal rights in the other party's retirement plans, as listed in the schedules attached hereto and any successor plans, including the right to be an alternate payee should the marriage terminate. This waiver includes any additions to or increases in value of said plan. Each spouse further agrees to sign all necessary waivers of spousal benefits subsequent to the marriage, in a timely fashion, as and when requested by the participant spouse. Nothing in this paragraph shall prevent one spouse from naming the other spouse as a designated beneficiary, and such designation shall prevail over this paragraph.

NOTES TO FORM

Drafter's Notes

The consents and waivers called for above cannot be signed until after the marriage and must be witnessed by the plan administrator or signed in front of a notary.

§ 1:19   Alternate clauses—Taxes—Form⊚

(1)   During the marriage, each party agrees to cooperate in maximizing the tax advantage that may result from the marital status, including joint tax returns where such would result in lower total tax due, and each consents that any gift made by either will be considered as made one-half by each, to maximize benefits from tax-free gift-splitting provisions of the Internal Revenue Code. Nothing in this paragraph shall be construed to require either party to make any specific provision or disposition by gift or will to maximize estate tax advantages.

§ 1:20   Alternate clauses—Arbitration—Form⊚

In the event of a termination of marriage, by divorce or dissolution, the parties agree to refer any dispute regarding the nature, extent and division of real or personal property acquired during their marriage, allocation of parental rights and responsibilities, spousal support, debt obligations, or related matters to binding arbitration under the procedures of the Ohio Arbitration Act (RC Ch. 2711) and the rules of the American Arbitration Association. The parties shall not, however, be required to use members of that association as arbitrators.

§ 1:21   Alternate clauses—Miscellaneous—Form⊚

(1)   The consideration of this Agreement is the mutual promises herein contained and the marriage about to be solemnized. If the marriage does not take place, this Agreement shall in all respects be null and void.

(2)   The parties agree to retain and use the given family names of each party to wit: *[name of husband]* and *[name of wife]*. They will

employ the titles of address, Mr. *[name of husband]* and Ms. *[name of wife]* and will henceforth be known as PARTNERS IN THIS RELATIONSHIP.

(3) The parties agree that each shall have the right to maintain his/her own legal residence or domicile notwithstanding the legal residence or domicile of the other. The parties hereby waive whatever right each may have solely to determine the legal domicile of the parties.

[(4) The parties recognize and respect each other's individual religious beliefs and practices and therefore agree to permit each other freedom of and from the exercise of religion. The parties agree to make no demands on each other to change their religious preferences or practices. Contributions to any church or denomination shall be made from individual funds only.]

or

[(4) The parties agree to attend and become members of the *[name of church]* church. Contributions and dues to said church will be paid from jointly held funds.]

(5) In any event, this contract is intended to effect a complete settlement of any and all claims that either party may have against the other arising from this marriage.

(6) The parties accept the conditions heretofore set forth and solemnly promise to love, cherish and honor each other and agree to preserve and promote their marriage to the best of their ability.

(7) If any portion of this contract be unenforceable under the laws of the State of Ohio, it is the intention of the parties that the remaining portions thereof shall remain in full force and effect.

(8) *[Name of spouse]* is represented by legal counsel and *[name of spouse]* chooses to be unrepresented by legal counsel. Each party fully understands the provisions of this Agreement.

(9) Each party shall, upon request of the other party, execute, acknowledge, and deliver any additional instruments required in order to accomplish the provisions or intent of this Agreement.

§ 1:22 Amendment to antenuptial agreement—Form⊙

This Agreement is made between *[name of spouse]* and *[name of spouse]*, both residing at *[street address, city, state]*.

On *[date]*, the parties entered into an Antenuptial Agreement, the "Agreement." The parties were married on *[date of marriage]*. They desire to modify the Agreement as hereinafter set forth.

Now, therefore, in consideration of the premises, and for other good and valuable consideration, the parties agree as follows:

1. Item () of the Agreement is hereby amended to read as follows:
   [Provision constituting amendment]

2. Item () of the Agreement is hereby amended to read as follows:
   [Provision constituting amendment]

3. Item () of the Agreement is hereby stricken therefrom in its entirety.

4. Except as herein expressly modified, the Agreement shall continue in full force and effect.

The parties have hereto affixed their signatures this *[date]*.

Witness   Husband

Witness   Wife

NOTES TO FORM

Drafter's Notes

There is some question as to the enforceability of an amendment, particularly where the modification is more restrictive than the original agreement, by virtue of the fact that the modification takes place after the marriage which was the consideration for the original agreement.

§ 1:23   Complaint to set aside antenuptial agreement—Form⊚

[Title of Court]

[Caption]

Case No. [_____]
COMPLAINT TO SET ASIDE
ANTENUPTIAL AGREEMENT

(1)   Plaintiff and *[name of spouse]* (hereinafter sometimes referred to as Decedent) entered into a written Antenuptial Agreement on *[date]*, by means of which they settled and adjusted their respective rights relating to each other as well as matters which might arise as a result of their later marriage. A copy of such Agreement, marked Exhibit A, is attached hereto and is hereby made a part hereof.

(2)   Plaintiff, having confidence and trust in Decedent, was persuaded and induced by *[him/her]* to enter into such Agreement, and on *[date]*, Plaintiff and Decedent were married. They lived together as husband and wife until Decedent's death on *[date]*. Plaintiff did not have the benefit of counsel due to lack of time and insistence of the Decedent.

(3)   Defendant, *[name of defendant]*, *[administrator/executor]*, is the duly appointed and acting *[administrator/executor]* of Decedent's estate, having been so appointed in the course of proceedings in Case No. *[case number]*, Probate Court, *[name of county]* County, Ohio.

(4)   Defendants *[name of defendant]* and *[name of defendant]* (individually) are the heirs at law and next of kin of Decedent and are also devisees and legatees named in Decedent's will.

(5)   Decedent concealed material facts from Plaintiff at the time of the execution of the aforementioned Antenuptial Agreement, and Plaintiff was not aware of certain facts relating to the extent of Decedent's income and the extent and value of the assets owned by *[him/her]* at the time of *[his/her]* execution of the said Agreement. Plaintiff did not become aware of such facts until Defendant, *[name of*

defendant], as executor of Decedent's estate, filed the inventory as to such estate with the Probate Court of *[name of county]* County, Ohio.

(6) Plaintiff relied on the disclosures made by Decedent to *[him/her]* as to the value and extent of *[his/her]* property and income and was induced to execute the said Antenuptial Agreement by reason of such reliance.

(7) The terms of the said Antenuptial Agreement are unjust and unfair to Plaintiff considering the nature and extent of Decedent's estate now revealed to *[him/her]* and considering the further fact that *[he/she]* was induced to enter into the said Antenuptial Agreement by reason of Decedent's false representations to *[him/her]*.

WHEREFORE, Plaintiff demands that: (a) the aforesaid Antenuptial Agreement be set aside; (b) *[he/she]* be restored to all legal, equitable, and statutory rights relative to Decedent's estate; (c) Defendants be ordered to pay all costs herein and all costs and expenses, including attorney's fees, incurred by Plaintiff in connection with *[his/her]* prosecution of this action; and (d) *[he/she]* be granted such further relief to which *[he/she]* may be entitled.

———————————————

Attorney for Plaintiff

[EXHIBIT A]

NOTES TO FORM

Drafter's Notes

A long form caption should be used on the complaint.

If service other than pursuant to Civ. R. 4 is desired, a written request for service (usually a court form) should accompany the complaint when it is filed.

The complaint must be filed within four months of the appointment of an executor or administrator. There is no tolling for minority (RC 2106.22).

§ 1:24 Will clause referring to antenuptial agreement—Form⊚

AGREEMENT

On *[date]*, and prior to my marriage to *[name of spouse]*, we entered into an Antenuptial Agreement. In accordance with the terms of the Agreement, *[name of spouse]* waived and relinquished all rights in and to my property, waived and relinquished the right of election to take against any last will and testament of mine, as well as any other statutory right to my estate; in consideration thereof I agreed that upon my death *[name of spouse]* would receive $*[dollar amount]* from my estate if *[name of spouse]* survived me. I hereby direct my executors to carry out all the provisions of the Antenuptial Agreement.

In addition, and apart from my obligations under the Antenuptial Agreement, I give and bequeath to *[name of spouse]* the sum of $*[dollar amount]* if *[name of spouse]* survives me.

Chapter 2

Marriage

*By Hon. V. Michael Brigner**

---

*With research assistance of Rebecca Barton, Esq.

§ 2:1 The nature of marriage

Marriage contemplates a twofold definition. First and historically,[1] marriage is a civil contract between two competent persons of opposite gender, based upon mutual promises to live together for life discharging to each other and the community those duties imposed by law upon the relationship of husband and wife, with a view toward mutual support and procreation of children.[2] It is no mere sacrament; unless founded on a civil contract, there is no marriage.[3] While general contract law is applicable, the marriage contract is regarded as more important and sacred than ordinary contracts.[4] A special body of contract law has developed to govern the creation[5] and termination[6] of matrimonial contracts, the capacity of parties,[7] and most other elements of the relationship. Also, the state is considered an interested party in the marriage contract and makes itself part of the agreement by imposing certain requirements, obligations, and prohibitions on the parties, as if expressly included in the contract.[8]

Although parties contemplating marriage may enter into a binding

---

[Section 2:1]

[1]For a discussion of the historical development of marriage in western culture, see Samuel Green & John V. Long, *Marriage and Family Law Agreements* 1.01 et seq. (1997). See also 52 Am. Jur. 2d, Marriage § 1; Hugh A. Ross, *The Ohio Law of Marriage*, 14 Case W. Res. L. Rev. 724 (1963). For an excellent historical review of how marriage has progressed from a legal status with state-imposed terms to a partnership of autonomous persons largely free from external regulations, see M. Dickerson, *Family Values and the Bankruptcy Code: A Proposal to Eliminate Bankruptcy Benefits Awarded on the Basis of Marital Status*, 67 Fordham Law Review 69, at 73–83 (1998).

[2]Umbenhower v. Labus, 85 Ohio St. 238, 97 N.E. 832 (1912); Waymire v. Jetmore, 22 Ohio St. 271, 1872 WL 1 (1872); Cox v. Cox, 19 Ohio St. 502, 1869 WL 84 (1869).

[3]Roberts v. Roberts, 8 West. L.J. 372, 1 Ohio Dec. Rep. 368, 1850 WL 2921 (Ohio C.P. 1850); Conley v. Conley, 28 Ohio Op. 289, 14 Ohio Supp. 22, 1943 WL 6289 (C.P. 1943).

[4]Charrier v. State, 30 Ohio C.D. 578, 1918 WL 902 (Ohio Ct. App. 8th Dist. Summit County 1918); Meyer v. Meyer, 4 Ohio Dec. Rep. 345, 7 Ohio Dec. Rep. 561, 1 Cleve. Law Rep. 347, 3 W.L.B. 985, 1878 WL 7379 (Ohio C.P. 1878), aff'd, 7 Ohio Dec. Rep. 627, 4 W.L.B. 368, 1879 WL 6394 (Ohio Dist. Ct. 1879); Pashko v. Pashko, 45 Ohio Op. 498, 63 Ohio L. Abs. 82, 101 N.E.2d 804 (C.P. 1951).

[5]See Text §§ 2:6 et seq., Ceremonial marriage; Text §§ 2:35 et seq., Common law marriage.

[6]See Text § 2:65, Termination of marriage.

[7]See Text §§ 2:16 et seq., Capacity to marry.

[8]Basickas v. Basickas, 93 Ohio App. 531, 51 Ohio Op. 229, 114 N.E.2d 270 (9th Dist. Summit County 1953); Hardin v. Davis, 30 Ohio Op. 524, 16 Ohio Supp. 19,

prenuptial contract[9] or separation agreement,[10] the law limits the extent to which individuals may change the civil contract of marriage as defined by law.

Despite common talk of the "marriage contract," family and contract law doctrines historically have served primarily to prevent the use of contract rules and exchange norms in the family. [Footnote: See generally Restatement (Second) of Contracts §§ 189–91 (1981) (mandating that promises in restraint of marriage, changing the essential nature of the marital relationship, or affecting the right to custody of a minor are unenforceable on the grounds of public policy); Restatement of Contracts §§ 581–87 (1932) (establishing the illegality of certain bargains concerning domestic relations); E. Allan Farnsworth, Contracts §§ 3.7, 5.4 (2d ed. 1990) (discussing policies against enforcement of family or social promises or agreements that might impair family relations)].[11]

Religious vows that conflict with civil law will not be enforced. Responding to a wife's contention that the parties were married in the Catholic Church, and both agreed to be bound by Catholic canon law regarding their marriage and any issues regarding their children, an Ohio appellate court rules that even if this "somehow created an oral antenuptial agreement to arbitrate disputes regarding their marriage, any such oral agreement is barred by the Statute of Frauds, as set forth in RC 1335.05, which states that agreements 'made upon consideration of marriage' must be in writing to be enforceable."[12]

Second, marriage is a civil status, created by the marriage contract of husband and wife, which fixes upon the union all of the rights and duties the law provides.[13]

1945 WL 5519 (C.P. 1945); Hickle v. Hickle, 3 Ohio C.D. 552, 1892 WL 300 (Ohio Cir. Ct. 1892); Allen, *An Inquiry into the State's Role in Marriage*, 13 J. Econ. Behav. & Organ 171 (1990).

[9]See Text Ch 1, Antenuptial Agreements.

[10]See Text Ch 9, Separation Agreements.

[11]Ann Laquer Estin, *Love and Obligation: Family Law and the Romance of Economics*, 36 Wm. & Mary L. Rev. 989, 1039 (March 1995).

[12]MacFarlane v. MacFarlane, 2006-Ohio-3155, 2006 WL 1704531 (Ohio Ct. App. 8th Dist. Cuyahoga County 2006), appeal not allowed, 111 Ohio St. 3d 1472, 2006-Ohio-5625, 855 N.E.2d 1260 (2006).

[13]Hardin v. Davis, 30 Ohio Op. 524, 16 Ohio Supp. 19, 1945 WL 5519 (C.P. 1945); Siebert v. Siebert, 32 Ohio App. 487, 7 Ohio L. Abs. 435, 168 N.E. 223 (6th Dist. Lucas County 1929); Belk v. Belk, 13 Ohio App. 2d 212, 42 Ohio Op. 2d 376, 235 N.E.2d 530 (1st Dist. Hamilton County 1968); In re Soeder's Estate, 7 Ohio App. 2d 271, 36 Ohio Op. 2d 404, 220 N.E.2d 547 (8th Dist. Cuyahoga County 1966). For a detailed discussion of marriage as a contract versus marriage as a status, see Samuel Green & John V. Long, *Marriage and Family Law Agreements* 1.35 (1997).

Stated another way, marriage is a legal Janus, being both a fundamental relationship that precedes the state[14] and a state conferred legal status that does not exist apart from the state.[15]

The right to marry is a fundamental one, protected by the Due Process Clause. "[t]he freedom to marry has long been recognized as one of the vital personal rights essential to the orderly pursuit of happiness by free men."[16] Marriage is a "natural right" not created by state law, merely governed by it.[17] Regulations which substantially interfere with the decision to marry are unconstitutional unless closely tailored to meet sufficiently important state interests,[18] but regulations which do not significantly interfere with the decision to marry may be legitimately imposed.[19]

"Married persons enjoy a wide range of benefits, including pension benefits, immigration preferences, tax preferences, health insurance benefits, tort rights in each other, intestate succession preferences, and conjugal visits, to name a few."[20]

In governing marriage, Ohio has created a detailed statute regulating the creation of marriages.[21] But the Ohio General Assembly has not adopted the Uniform Marriage and Divorce Act, originally drafted in 1970.[22]

---

[14]Griswold v. Connecticut, 381 U.S. 479, 486, 85 S. Ct. 1678, 14 L. Ed. 2d 510 (1965) (marriage is "a right of privacy older than the Bill of Rights").

[15]Baehr v. Lewin, 74 Haw. 530, 74 Haw. 645, 852 P.2d 44 (1993), reconsideration granted in part, 74 Haw. 650, 875 P.2d 225 (1993) and as clarified on reconsideration, (May 27, 1993) (on remand now styled *Baehr v. Miike*).

[16]Loving v. Virginia, 388 U.S. 1, 12, 87 S. Ct. 1817, 18 L. Ed. 2d 1010 (1967).

[17]Courtright v. Scringem, 53 Ohio St. 685, Ohio Sup. Ct. Dec. Unrep. 388, 44 N.E. 1134 (1895); Carmichael v. State, 12 Ohio St. 553, 1861 WL 66 (1861); Bank of Toledo v. City of Toledo, 1 Ohio St. 622, 1853 WL 59 (1853); Zablocki v. Redhail, 434 U.S. 374, 98 S. Ct. 673, 54 L. Ed. 2d 618, 24 Fed. R. Serv. 2d 1313 (1978).

[18]Zablocki v. Redhail, 434 U.S. 374, 98 S. Ct. 673, 54 L. Ed. 2d 618, 24 Fed. R. Serv. 2d 1313 (1978); In re Pieper Children, 85 Ohio App. 3d 318, 619 N.E.2d 1059 (12th Dist. Preble County 1993) (derogation of right of marriage found in juvenile court order which prohibited mother any contact with father whose parental rights had been terminated for abuse).

[19]Califano v. Jobst, 434 U.S. 47, 98 S. Ct. 95, 54 L. Ed. 2d 228 (1977) (termination of dependent child's social security benefits upon marriage); Pena v. Northeast Ohio Emergency Affiliates, Inc., 108 Ohio App. 3d 96, 670 N.E.2d 268 (9th Dist. Lorain County 1995), dismissed, appeal not allowed, 75 Ohio St. 3d 1494, 664 N.E.2d 1291 (1996) (permitting evidence of remarriage by surviving spouse in wrongful death action); Mishlen v. Mishlen, 305 N.J. Super. 643, 702 A.2d 1384 (App. Div. 1997) (divorce decree forbidding custodial parent from exposing children to her abusive paramour does not infringe on her fundamental right to marry him).

[20]Steven K. Homer, *Against Marriage*, 29 Harv. C.R.-C.L. L. Rev. 505, 515 (1994) (citation omitted).

[21]RC Ch. 3101.

[22]Am. Jur. 2d Desk Book, Item 124; 52 Am. Jur. 2d, Marriage §§ 1 et seq.

In 2005, Ohio found itself dealing with the unintended consequences that are a result of adopting what is commonly called the Marriage Amendment to the Ohio Constitution.[23] The new provision states:

> Definition of marriage. Only a union between one man and one woman may be a marriage valid in or recognized by this state and its political subdivisions. This state and its political subdivisions shall not create or recognize a legal status for relationships of unmarried individuals that intends to approximate the design, qualities, significance or effect of marriage.[24]

Criminal proceedings based upon Ohio's domestic violence law[25] have subsequently been challenged, based upon an alleged conflict between the statute and the Marriage Amendment. The criminal statute protects a more limited class of victims than general assault laws. The statute prohibits causing or attempting to cause "physical harm to a family or household member."[26] The statute's definition of "family or household member" includes one who is "residing or has resided with" the alleged offender, and who is either a "spouse, [or] a person living as a spouse."[27] And the definition of "a person living as a spouse" is "a person who is living or has lived with the offender in a common law marital relationship, who otherwise is cohabiting with the offender, or who. . . has cohabited with the offender within five years prior to the date of the alleged commission of the act in question."[28]

The Supreme Court of Ohio was called upon to resolve conflicts among appellate districts concerning this issue. Some defendants convicted of violating civil protection orders issued to protect unmarried cohabitants claimed that the criminal statute, RC 2919.25, enforcing Ohio's civil protection order statute, RC 3113.31, conflicts with the Ohio Marriage Amendment by creating a legal status approximating marriage. The court rejected this argument. "While the intent of the domestic-violence statute is to protect persons from violence by close family members or residents of the same household, the intent of the marriage amendment was to prevent the creation or recognition of a legal status that approximates marriage through judicial, legislative, or executive action. The statute and the constitution are not in conflict."[29] Thus, the Ohio Marriage Amendment does not prevent the state from enforcing domestic violence orders against non-married cohabitants.

Ohio recognizes a foreign marriage as valid if it was valid under the

---

[23] Adopted by popular vote on Nov. 2, 2004.

[24] O. Const. Art. XV, § 11.

[25] RC 2919.25.

[26] RC 2919.25(A), (B), (C).

[27] RC 2919.25(F).

[28] RC 2919.25(F)(2).

[29] State v. Carswell, 114 Ohio St. 3d 210, at § 36, 2007-Ohio-3723, 871 N.E.2d 547 (2007).

laws of the place where entered or solemnized.[30] Where the parties
failed to comply with statutory procedures in the foreign jurisdiction
(South Korea), and the moving party could not establish a de facto
marriage under South Korean case law, Ohio could not recognize a
valid marriage for purposes of a divorce action.[31]

A trial court may not refuse to take judicial notice of foreign law,
specifically the Hindu Marriage Act of 1955 of the Republic of India,
during divorce proceedings. The parties, natives of India, were married in a 2005 civil ceremony in that country. The wife's evidence of a
1994 marriage was rejected by the trial court, in part because the
husband had entered an intervening marriage and fathered a child in
that relationship. But the appellate court reversed for new property
and support orders based upon the wife's sufficient evidence of the
earlier marriage, one that was valid under foreign law.[32]

A new brand of state-sanctioned relationship, the "covenant marriage" has gained foothold in three states. Louisiana was the first to
adopt it in 1997, followed by Arizona and Arkansas. Ohio's only
venture into this area died in the General Assembly.[33] Covenant marriage laws require special premarital counseling, and severely restrict
a party's right to terminate a covenant marriage with a divorce. At
the time of application for a marriage license, parties may elect this
new form of marriage, or choose to exercise existing marriage laws.
Grounds for terminating a covenant marriage are limited. For
example, the Louisiana statute as originally drafted did not even allow divorce for physical or sexual abuse. As passed, the statute allows
a "non-breaching" spouse to obtain a divorce on the grounds of
adultery, commission of a felony, abandonment for one year, physical
or sexual abuse of the spouse or child, or continuous physical separation for two years.[34] The basic idea behind the covenant marriage
concept is to save the family by making it harder to get divorced. One
commentator calls it "a sort of 'marriage deluxe' that would be slightly
harder to enter and much harder to exit than a 'regular marriage.' "[35]
The insignificant number applications it has generated (26 of the first
3,000 applications in Louisiana), led noted Professor Ellman to

---

[30]Hardin v. Davis, 30 Ohio Op. 524, 16 Ohio Supp. 19, 1945 WL 5519 (C.P.
1945); In re Zemmicks Estate, 49 Ohio L. Abs. 353, 76 N.E.2d 902 (Ct. App. 7th Dist.
Belmont County 1946); Weintraub, *Is This Marriage Legal?*, 3 Fam. Advoc. 20 (Spring
1981).

[31]Lee v. Melanson, 2007-Ohio-1784, 2007 WL 1114012 (Ohio Ct. App. 11th Dist.
Trumbull County 2007).

[32]Verma v. Verma, 179 Ohio App. 3d 637, 2008-Ohio-6244, 903 N.E.2d 343 (2d
Dist. Greene County 2008).

[33]H.B. 567, 122d Gen. Assembly, 1997-98 Reg. Sess. (Ohio 1997).

[34]La. Rev. Stat. Ann. §§ 9:272–73 (West Supp. 1998).

[35]Amy L. Stewart, *NOTE: Covenant Marriage: Legislating Family Values*, 32
Ind. L. Rev. 509, at 509 (1999).

observe, "[t]he two states adopting covenant marriage have found that their constituents have little interest in it."[36]

§ 2:2 Federal laws affecting marriage

It has been frequently stated that the states exclusively may govern family law[1] as there is no federal domestic relations law.[2] However, federal tax law allows the Internal Revenue Service to determine dependency exemptions, support versus property settlement, alimony versus child support, and similar issues without regard to state law and to prior state court determinations as to the same matters and the same parties.[3] Federal bankruptcy law permits bankruptcy courts the same latitude to ignore state law and case rulings.[4] Federal child support legislation obliges the states to comply.[5] Thus, it can no longer be said that the subject of family law belongs exclusively to the states.[6]

In 2003, Congress considered the reauthorization of the Welfare Reform Act of 1996.[7] Part of that legislation included the addition of nearly $2 billion to promote the institution of marriage. States would be required to invest even more money into "marriage initiatives" to obtain the funds. The proposal to spend significant public funds on promoting marriage has drawn criticism, mostly along the lines that the potential benefits are overstated, that other social services may suffer, and that it constitutes conservative social engineering.[8] Daniel T. Lichter, an Ohio State University professor who has written

---

[36]Ira Mark Ellman, *Divorce Rates, Marriage Rates, and The Problematic Persistence of Traditional Marital Roles*, 34 Fam. L.Q. 1, 15 (2000).

[Section 2:2]

[1]Butner v. U.S., 440 U.S. 48, 99 S. Ct. 914, 59 L. Ed. 2d 136 (1979); State of Ohio ex rel. Popovici v. Agler, 280 U.S. 379, 50 S. Ct. 154, 74 L. Ed. 489 (1930).

[2]Crouch v. Crouch, 566 F.2d 486 (5th Cir. 1978); Simms v. Simms, 175 U.S. 162, 20 S. Ct. 58, 44 L. Ed. 115 (1899); Clark, The Law of Domestic Relations in the United States; Restatement (Second) of Conflicts § 283 (1971).

[3]Bardwell v. C.I.R., 318 F.2d 786 (10th Cir. 1963); *Divorce Taxation*10,003, 10,004 (P-H 1985); Kittrell, *Property Transfer*, 7 Fam. Advoc. 22 (Fall 1984).

[4]11 U.S.C.A. § 523(C); In re Calhoun, 715 F.2d 1103 (6th Cir. 1983); *Collier on Bankruptcy* 523.15(6) (15th ed. 1985).

[5]Child Support Enforcement Amendments of 1984, 45 C.F.R. pt. 301 to 307.

[6]McCarty v. McCarty, 453 U.S. 210, 101 S. Ct. 2728, 69 L. Ed. 2d 589 (1981) (overruling recognized by, Dunham v. Dunham, 602 So. 2d 1139 (La. Ct. App. 1st Cir. 1992)) and (overruling recognized by, Porter v. Porter, 1996 SD 6, 542 N.W.2d 448 (S.D. 1996)), superseded by statute as explained in Cameron v. Cameron, 641 S.W.2d 210 (Tex. 1982); Samuel Green & John V. Long, *Marriage and Family Law Agreements* 1.10 (1997).

[7]2003 CONG US HR 4.

[8]Michael Tanner, *Wedded to Poverty, The New York Times*, 2003 WL 60382577 (7-29-03); *Can Marriage Cure Poverty? Conservatives Now Welcome Government Social Engineering*, Pittsburgh Post-Gazette, 2003 WL 3891872 (2-26-03); *A bad pitch for getting hitched*, The Denver Post, 2003 WL 5518565 (8-3-03); *Back to Marriage, or to Servitude?* Newsday (New York), 2003 WL 17814615 (4-13-03); Pamela J. Smock

extensively on the subject of public policies toward marriage, was quoted in one news report as questioning whether marriage should be regarded as an economic panacea. Dr. Lichter recently published a report finding that although marriage benefited most low-income mothers, subsequent divorce left them worse off than never-married women.[9]

§ 2:3 Engagement

An engagement to marry is a bilateral executory contract; it is the executory nature of the contract that distinguishes it from a common law marriage contract, which contemplates an immediate existing marriage.[1]

A confidential relationship is assumed by the parties on engagement,[2] but rights of consortium do not apply to engaged couples.[3] A marriage brokerage contract has been held to be unenforceable in Ohio as contrary to public policy.[4] A suit by a disappointed husband against a marriage broker alleging breach of a negotiated marriage contract did not constitute an obsolete amatory action barred by RC 2305.29, yet still could be dismissed as an attempt to enforce a contract which treats women as chattel, against public policy.[5]

§ 2:4 Amatory actions abolished

The law's interest in engagement contracts in Ohio used to include such issues as consideration, the capacity of the parties, the necessity of a writing under the Statute of Frauds, and tender of performance. These concerns are now of primarily historical interest, since the Ohio Criminal Code was revised effective January 1, 1974, to repeal ancient

---

and Stephanie Coontz, *U.S. Congress Marriage Promotion Programs Offer No Quick Fix to Welfare Families' Dilemmas: A Balanced Anti-Poverty Program Requires More Than Marriage Education*, AScribe Newswire, 2003 WL 5499360 (2-25-03).

[9]Cheryl Wetzstein, *Federal official urges promoting marriage; Bush to seek funds to enhance wedlock*, The Washington Times, 2003 WL 7714601 (6-2-03).

[Section 2:3]

[1]See Text §§ 2:35 et seq., Common law marriage. See also Text Ch 1, Antenuptial Agreements.

[2]Juhasz v. Juhasz, 134 Ohio St. 257, 12 Ohio Op. 57, 16 N.E.2d 328, 117 A.L.R. 993 (1938); In re Mosier's Estate, 58 Ohio Op. 369, 72 Ohio L. Abs. 268, 133 N.E.2d 202 (Prob. Ct. 1954); Bearns-Lane v. Lane, 1992 WL 386005 (Ohio Ct. App. 10th Dist. Franklin County 1992).

[3]Haas v. Lewis, 8 Ohio App. 3d 136, 456 N.E.2d 512 (10th Dist. Franklin County 1982); Kris Treu, *Loss of Consortium and Engaged Couples: The Frustrating Fate of Faithful Fiancees*, 44 Ohio St. L.J. 219 (1983).

[4]Anonymous, 11 Ohio Dec. Rep. 745, 29 W.L.B. 49, 1892 WL 1054 (Ohio C.P. 1892).

[5]Singh v. Singh, 81 Ohio App. 3d 376, 611 N.E.2d 347 (8th Dist. Cuyahoga County 1992).

crimes related to breach of promise to marry,[1] and since the common law cause of action for breach of promise was abolished on June 26, 1978, because of the fear that some actions were used for blackmail purposes.[2]

Although half of the states have adopted such "heart balm" statutes, those laws have been criticized as providing too much protection to parties who dishonor promises to marry, thereby insulating them from responsibility for the consequences of their actions. One author suggests an alternate remedy to the common law breach of promise to marry action. "Instead, a more appropriate approach lies on middle ground presently unoccupied by any state court or legislature: parties who breach promises to marry should bear responsibility for their conduct, but only to the extent they have induced reliance by those to whom they were formerly engaged. Promissory estoppel provides the framework for reaching this compromise."[3] The proponent admits that no state has yet adopted this approach, and that legislation might be needed to clear the way in states like Ohio that have already adopted heart balm statutes.

Part of Ohio's "heart balm" act abolishing amatory actions banned tort suits on the common law causes of alienation of affections, criminal conversation, and seduction. Attempts to circumvent this bar by bringing such actions under the guise of the independent tort of intentional infliction of emotional distress were rejected by a majority of the Ohio Supreme Court, over strong dissent, in *Strock v. Pressnell*.[4] One Ohio trial judge waxed poetic in following this precedent:

> The Court determines upon proper review
> That Doris' complaint is an amatory action;
> That the same is barred by RC 2305.29,
> And thus denies Doris satisfaction.
>
> . . .
>
> The within cause is hereby ordered dismissed
> With the Plaintiff bearing the cost,
> And with this advice in the parting,
> Love never won can't be lost.[5]

One avenue for recovery from a broken marriage promise may still

---

[Section 2:4]

[1]See former RC 2905.09, RC 2905.15, RC 2911.19, repealed by 1972 H.B. 511, eff. 1-1-74.

[2]RC 2305.29. The Ohio Supreme Court upheld the constitutionality of Ohio's "heart balm" act in Strock v. Pressnell, 38 Ohio St. 3d 207, 527 N.E.2d 1235, 75 A.L.R.4th 729 (1988).

[3]Neil G. Williams, *What To Do When There's No "I Do": A Model For Awarding Damages Under Promissory Estoppel*, 70 Wash. L. Rev. 1019, 1021–22 (1995) (footnote omitted).

[4]Strock v. Pressnell, 38 Ohio St. 3d 207, 527 N.E.2d 1235, 75 A.L.R.4th 729 (1988) (footnotes omitted).

[5]Irvin v. Smith, 71 Ohio Misc. 2d 18, 21–22, 654 N.E.2d 189 (C.P. 1993).

be available. One Ohio court found, even considering the precedent of the Strock decision, that RC 2305.29 does not bar a claim for fraud merely because the fraudulent misrepresentation involves an intention to marry.[6]

A good analysis of the legal relationship of parties when their engagement is broken is found in the Third Appellate District case of *Dixon v. Smith*.[7] After the parties agreed to be married, the plaintiff moved in with the defendant and they began commingling bank accounts. The plaintiff borrowed $18,750 on her own rental property to improve defendant's real estate, resulting in a $57,000 increase in value. When plaintiff learned of defendant's affair, she moved out and sued him for the borrowed funds and her "sweat equity," on claims of unjust enrichment and constructive trust. The defense asserted unclean hands, gift, and that the claims were barred as constituting palimony. Defendant admitted he had no intention of marrying plaintiff. The trial court awarded $18,750 for unjust enrichment, but denied any constructive trust. Plaintiff received no interest and no share of the increased property value which defendant retained. The court of appeals ruled that Ohio law barring civil damages for breach of a promise to marry does not preclude recovery of property transferred in contemplation of marriage. Even if a gift, it is a conditional gift; if the condition fails, the property must be returned. Plaintiff's claim is not barred as palimony, since it seeks recovery of previously owned property. Constructive trust is also available as a remedy in such circumstances, but the court ruled that plaintiff's other lost money was not traceable, so her recovery was limited to the $18,750 unjust enrichment award. Prejudgment interest was denied.

The recovery of property transferred in reliance on a promise to marry is permitted based on the theory of preventing unjust enrichment, and this was held not to violate Ohio's "heart balm" statute barring the recovery of civil damages based upon a broken promise of marriage.[8]

Creative pleading to state the tort of intentional infliction of emotional distress against a former wife and her paramour relating to the severe emotional distress a husband sustained in learning the child born during his marriage was not his biological child, allowed a case to survive the prohibition of amatory claims.[9] The court must examine whether the claim is a "disguised substitute" for one of the actions barred by RC 2305.29 and whether the harm to the claimant is serious.

---

[6]Turner v. Shavers, 96 Ohio App. 3d 769, 645 N.E.2d 1324 (10th Dist. Franklin County 1994).

[7]Dixon v. Smith, 119 Ohio App. 3d 308, 695 N.E.2d 284 (3d Dist. Logan County 1997).

[8]Jury v. Ridenour, 1999 WL 436843 (Ohio Ct. App. 5th Dist. Richland County 1999), dismissed, appeal not allowed, 87 Ohio St. 3d 1416, 717 N.E.2d 1104 (1999).

[9]Bailey v. Searles-Bailey, 140 Ohio App. 3d 174, 746 N.E.2d 1159 (7th Dist. Mahoning County 2000).

§ 2:5 Engagement and wedding gifts

Broken engagements still come before the courts when there are disputes over the disposition of gifts. Most courtship gifts are considered absolute, but an engagement gift in specific contemplation of marriage, such as a ring, may be considered conditional and ordered returned upon nonfulfillment of the (marriage) condition.[1] With the exception of an engagement ring, gifts given to a fiancè and her mother, including home improvements, were deemed irrevocable by the Fourth Appellate District Court.[2] A wedding gift is owned by one party solely or both parties jointly, depending on how the gift was addressed and delivered.[3]

§ 2:6 Ceremonial marriage—Statutory basis

A legal marriage in Ohio may be created either by complying with the ceremonial requirements of RC Chapter 3101 or by meeting the case law definition of a nonceremonial or "common law marriage."[1] For the practitioner, the difference lies in proof. A ceremonial marriage creates an official record of the matrimonial contract, while a

---

[Section 2:5]

[1]Patterson v. Blanton, 109 Ohio App. 3d 349, 672 N.E.2d 208 (10th Dist. Franklin County 1996) (unjust enrichment doctrine required return of gifts even though donor was married to another at time of gift and theoretically had unclean hands); Zsigmond v. Vandemberg, 1995 WL 815349 (Ohio Ct. App. 11th Dist. Portage County 1995) (gifts in contemplation of marriage must be returned even if parties married, where marriage was subsequently annulled); Sigrist v. Lyons, 100 Ohio App. 3d 252, 653 N.E.2d 744 (10th Dist. Franklin County 1995); Lyle v. Durham, 16 Ohio App. 3d 1, 473 N.E.2d 1216 (1st Dist. Hamilton County 1984); Wilson v. Dabo, 10 Ohio App. 3d 169, 461 N.E.2d 8 (10th Dist. Franklin County 1983); Somple v. Livesay, No. 78 CA 16 (Ohio Ct. App. 7th Dist. Mahoning County 1979) (if gift was not made in contemplation of marriage, but was made as part of courtship, it is considered absolute and need not be returned when engagement is terminated); Unger v. Atkinson, 6 Ohio L. Abs. 463, 1928 WL 3181 (Ct. App. 8th Dist. Cuyahoga County 1928); Annot., 24 A.L.R. 2d 579; Annot., 46 A.L.R. 3d 578. But see also Coconis v. Christakis, 70 Ohio Misc. 29, 24 Ohio Op. 3d 178, 435 N.E.2d 100 (County Ct. 1981) (return of ring depends on who broke engagement); Wion v. Henderson, 24 Ohio App. 3d 207, 494 N.E.2d 133 (2d Dist. Miami County 1985); Dillon v. Dillon, 1991 WL 271344 (Ohio Ct. App. 4th Dist. Pickaway County 1991) (wife's placing her engagement ring and wedding band on husband's table before walking out on him merely symbolic of her desire to end marriage and not her intent to make them a gift to husband); Coddington v. Leesman, 1999 WL 63990 (Ohio Ct. App. 2d Dist. Montgomery County 1999) (signed general release prevails over man's demand for return of engagement ring); also see RC 3105.171(A)(6)(a)(ii) and (vii).

[2]Cooper v. Smith, 155 Ohio App. 3d 218, 2003-Ohio-6083, 800 N.E.2d 372 (4th Dist. Lawrence County 2003).

[3]Ward v. Ward, 63 Ohio St. 125, 57 N.E. 1095 (1900) (disapproved of by, MacLean v. J. S. MacLean Co., 57 Ohio Op. 454, 70 Ohio L. Abs. 102, 123 N.E.2d 761 (Prob. Ct. 1955)) and (overruled in part by, Perlberg v. Perlberg, 18 Ohio St. 2d 55, 47 Ohio Op. 2d 167, 247 N.E.2d 306 (1969)); Oskamp v. Oskamp Jewelry Co., 1925 WL 2532, 23 Ohio Law Rep. 77 (Ohio Com.Pl., Feb 18, 1925).

[Section 2:6]

[1]See Text §§ 2:35 et seq., Common law marriage.

common law marriage does not and requires proof of the requisite elements.[2] Ohio will not recognize common law marriages entered into in Ohio after October 10, 1991.[3]

§ 2:7   Ceremonial marriage—License to marry

RC 3101.05 sets forth marriage license requirements. A license may be obtained by application to the probate court in the county where either applicant resides, or in the case of non-Ohio residents, in the county where the marriage is to be solemnized.[1] Since there is no length of residency defined in the statute, a day or even an hour is sufficient.[2] The parties must appear personally to make the application upon their oaths.[3] Personal appearance may be waived by a probate judge upon a physician's affidavit of illness or physical disability of an applicant.[4]

The court's authority to waive personal appearance for the application does not include the authority to waive the appearance for an incarcerated aspiring applicant. Nor is the warden required to transport an inmate for that purpose. Nor is the clerk required to travel to the jail to accommodate a marriage-minded inmate.[5]

The marriage license application must include the party's name, age, residence, place of birth, occupation, father's name, and mother's maiden name, if known, and the name of the person who is expected to solemnize the marriage. If either party has been previously married, the application must include the names of the parties to any previous marriage and of any minor children, and if divorced, the jurisdiction, date, and case number of the decree.[6]

The statute requires that if either applicant is under the age of eighteen years, the judge shall require the applicants to state that they received marriage counseling satisfactory to the court.[7]

Ohio's marriage license statute now states that the license application shall include each party's social security number, but allows the probate court to retain that information in a separate record while us-

---

[2]See Text §§ 2:52 et seq., Proof of marriage.

[3]RC 3105.12, eff. 10-10-91. See Text §§ 2:35 et seq., Common law marriage.

[Section 2:7]

[1]RC 3101.05(A).

[2]Stern v. Stern, 33 Ohio App. 281, 168 N.E. 478 (1st Dist. Hamilton County 1929).

[3]RC 3101.05(A). See RC 3101.99(A) for penalties.

[4]RC 3101.05(A). See RC 3101.99(A) for penalties.

[5]State ex rel. Leach v. Schotten, 73 Ohio St. 3d 538, 653 N.E.2d 356 (1995).

[6]RC 3101.05(A). Mayo v. Mayo, 172 N.C. App. 844, 617 S.E.2d 672 (2005), review denied, 360 N.C. 65, 623 S.E.2d 586 (2005) (trial court did not err in annulling marriage based on wife's false statement on marriage license that she had two prior marriages, when in fact she had seven prior marriages).

[7]RC 3101.05(A).

ing another number for reference purposes.[8] If the court uses a separate record for retaining social security numbers, that separate record is deemed not to be a public record under RC 149.43, except for limited law enforcement purposes.[9]

From July 1, 1996 to February 12, 2001, RC 3101.05(A) included the requirement: "Each marriage license issued shall include the social security number of each party to the marriage, as stated on the marriage license application." A statutory amendment and addition[10] in 2001 barred probate courts from publishing the applicants' social security numbers in the marriage license, but retained the requirement that those numbers be disclosed on the marriage license application. Interpretation of the statute was quickly sought, and the Franklin County Court of Appeals decided that in regard to the inclusion of social security numbers on marriage license applications, the statute is directory, not mandatory; it ordered the probate court to issue marriage licenses to ten applicants who did not or could not provide a social security number.[11] Less than a year later the Ohio Supreme Court ruled that, as a matter of statutory interpretation, RC 3101.05(A) does not require social security numbers from marriage license applicants who do not have a social security number.[12] This decision did not specifically address whether an individual who has a social security number may refuse to disclose that information on the marriage license application.

Finding that marriage is a fundamental right protected by the Due Process Clause, the Court of Appeals for Stark County issued a writ of mandamus to prevent the probate court from requiring a state-issued photo identification as a condition for approval of an applicant's marriage license. The probate judge refused to accept the applicant's Yugoslavian passport, but the appeals court ruled, at headnote 5, that, "There is no discretion provided in RC 3101.05(A). The language is mandatory and absent a legal impediment, the probate court must issue the license." The statute provides only three valid legal impediments, and the probate court is not free to invent its own. The three statutory requirements are: (1) the applicants must be of the opposite sex; (2) the applicants must meet the age requirements or have consent if they are minors; and, (3) the applicants cannot be nearer in

---

[8]RC 3101.05(A).

[9]RC 3101.05(A).

[10]RC 3101.051.

[11]State ex rel. Ten Residents of Franklin Cty. Who Are Fearful of Disclosing Their Names v. Belskis, 142 Ohio App. 3d 296, 755 N.E.2d 443 (10th Dist. Franklin County 2001).

[12]Vasquez v. Kutscher, 95 Ohio St. 3d 280, 2002-Ohio-2125, 767 N.E.2d 267 (2002).

kin than second cousins. Absent these legal impediments, the probate court is required to issue a marriage license.[13]

Immediately upon receipt of an application for a marriage license, the court shall place the parties' record in a book kept for that purpose. If the probate judge is satisfied that there is no legal impediment and if one or both of the parties are present, the probate judge shall grant the marriage license.[14] Effective in 2001, the General Assembly eliminated the statute's five-day waiting period between the application and the issuance of the license,[15] and the court may now issue the license on the same day the application is submitted.

A license may not be granted where either applicant is "under the influence of an intoxicating liquor or controlled substance or is infected with syphilis."[16] A probate court may not require an IQ test or refuse to grant a license on the grounds of present inability to support a family or arrearages due in child support of a prior marriage.[17]

The United States Supreme Court struck down a Wisconsin statute that prevented state residents from marrying if they were behind in child support obligations. Despite the state's contention that the statute assisted the state to counsel residents on their financial obligations and protected the children to whom support was owed, the Court ruled that the statute violated equal protection by substantially interfering with the fundamental right to marry and found that the effect of the statute was that more illegitimate children would be born.[18]

Where one party, Jacob B. Nash, had undergone surgery to reassign her gender from female to male, and another state had issued an amended birth certificate to designate Nash as male, an Ohio probate court refused to issue a marriage license for Nash to marry a female. The appellate court upheld the decision, stating, "Since the Ohio Legislature clearly has neither changed the public policy regarding marriages and transsexuals. . . nor expanded the definition of male or female beyond their common and traditional interpretations, a marriage between a post-operative female-to-male transsexual and a biological female is void as against public policy."[19]

---

[13]State ex rel. Valero v. Park, 2007 WL 4105589, 2007-Ohio-6179 (Ohio App. 5 Dist. Nov 19, 2007).

[14]RC 3101.05(A).

[15]See RC 3101.05(A) prior to 2-12-01.

[16]RC 3101.06.

[17]OAG 69-051.

[18]Zablocki v. Redhail, 434 U.S. 374, 98 S. Ct. 673, 54 L. Ed. 2d 618, 24 Fed. R. Serv. 2d 1313 (1978).

[19]In re Marriage License for Nash, 2003-Ohio-7221, 2003 WL 23097095 (Ohio Ct. App. 11th Dist. Trumbull County 2003).

The license permits the parties to marry; the person who solemnizes a marriage can rely on a license proper in form.[20]

A marriage license expires sixty days after issuance, and no marriage ceremony may be performed based upon that license thereafter.[21]

A purported marriage performed without a marriage license was decreed "absolutely void" by a New Jersey court, even though it was solemnized by an authorized cleric.[22]

§ 2:8   Ceremonial marriage—Blood test

The requirement that both parties submit to a standard laboratory blood test for syphilis was eliminated effective November 15, 1981, by amendment of RC 3101.05. However, the General Assembly left in place the prohibition against granting a license to one infected with syphilis,[1] leaving verification dependent solely upon the oaths of the parties.[2] Ohio has not addressed the issue of testing marriage applicants for HIV/AIDS infection.[3]

§ 2:9   Ceremonial marriage—Solemnization

Solemnization of a marriage must occur within sixty days of the issuance of the license, or the license expires.[1] RC 3101.08 provides who may solemnize a marriage, which includes ordained or licensed ministers, county court judges,[2] municipal court judges,[3] probate court judges,[4] and mayors of municipal corporations. Many county court and municipal courts specified in the statute will upon request appoint an attorney as an "acting judge for a day" for purposes of

---

[20]Annot., 61 A.L.R. 2d 847.

[21]RC 3101.07.

[22]Yaghoubinejad v. Haghighi, 384 N.J. Super. 339, 894 A.2d 1173 (App. Div. 2006).

[Section 2:8]

[1]RC 3101.06.

[2]RC 3101.05.

[3]For further discussion of this issue, see Michael Closen, et al., *Mandatory Premarital HIV Testing: Political Exploitation of the AIDS Epidemic*, 69 Tul. L. Rev. 71 (1994).

[Section 2:9]

[1]RC 3101.07.

[2]See RC 1907.18(C), which authorizes county court judges to perform marriage ceremonies anywhere in the state.

[3]See RC 1901.14(A)(1), which authorizes municipal court judges to perform marriage ceremonies anywhere in the state.

[4]See RC 2101.27, which authorizes probate court judges to perform marriage ceremonies anywhere in the county.

performing a wedding.[5] The procedure for a minister to obtain a license to solemnize marriages is set forth in RC 3101.10. An Ohio wedding was deemed valid by an Indiana appellate court, even though it was performed without an Ohio license by a minister not authorized to perform Ohio marriages. The court found that the couple had complied with the requisite statutes in obtaining and filing their Indiana marriage license and certificate, and the reverend could have solemnized the marriage under Indiana law had the ceremony taken place there. So the marriage was not void under Indiana law, despite the failure to comply with Ohio statutes.[6] These statutes do not provide how a marriage is to be solemnized. While a minister may be licensed by the state to solemnize marriages generally, that license bestows no specific right to do so within a county courthouse.[7]

After an Ohio man died, it was discovered that the marriage to his surviving spouse six years earlier was solemnized by a minister who had failed to obtain the necessary license to solemnize marriages. The Fourth District Court of Appeals found three states have ruled that a marriage performed by one without a valid license is void; three others have decided that such a marriage is merely voidable. In the Ohio case, the appellate court found that the decedent's marriage was not void, but voidable, as the marriage was not against public policy.[8]

The parties may decide how to solemnize or celebrate the marriage; a personal appearance of the parties before a person authorized by law to perform marriages, and the performance of the marriage rites by the parties in the presence of each other and one or more witnesses, are said to fulfill the ceremonial function.[9] Sample forms for solemnizing a marriage in a civil ceremony are provided in the following sections.

§ 2:10 Ceremonial marriage—Solemnization—Appointment of acting judge to perform marriage ceremony—Form⊛

[Title of Court]

In re Appointment of Acting Judge

Under the authority and power vested in me as *[Administrative/*

---

[5]See Text § 2:10, Ceremonial marriage—Solemnization—Appointment of acting judge to perform a marriage ceremony—Form.

[6]McPeek v. McCardle, 866 N.E.2d 387 (Ind. Ct. App. 2007), transfer granted, opinion vacated, IN RAP 58(A), (Aug. 7, 2007).

[7]Wright v. Courthouse Facilities Committee, 1999 WL 1022873 (Ohio Ct. App. 6th Dist. Lucas County 1999).

[8]Dodrill v. Dodrill, 2004-Ohio-2225, 2004 WL 938476 (Ohio Ct. App. 4th Dist. Vinton County 2004), appeal not allowed, 103 Ohio St. 3d 1463, 2004-Ohio-5056, 815 N.E.2d 678 (2004).

[9]Respole v. Respole, 34 Ohio Op. 1, 70 N.E.2d 465, 170 A.L.R. 942 (C.P. 1946). A Louisiana appellate court determined that the fact that the witnesses to a wedding ceremony were minors did not warrant declaring the marriage a nullity. (Tennison v. Nevels, 2006-2124 La. App. 1 Cir. 6/8/07, 2007 WL 1651241 (La. Ct. App. 1st Cir. 2007)).

Presiding] Judge of the *[Title of Court]*, and pursuant to the provisions of the Ohio Revised Code governing appointment of acting judges in this court, I hereby appoint *[name of attorney]* as Acting Judge of the *[Title of Court]* without compensation, to serve on *[date of marriage]*, for the sole purpose of performing a marriage ceremony in the State of Ohio in accordance with the provisions of RC 3101.08.

_____
Judge

State of Ohio, *[County]*

Before me the undersigned, personally appeared *[Name of Attorney]* who being duly sworn, upon *[his/her]* oath says that *[he/she]* will support the Constitution of the United States and the Constitution of the State of Ohio, and that *[he/she]* will faithfully, honestly, and impartially discharge the duties of the office of Acting Judge of the *[Title of Court]* to which said office *[he/she]* has been appointed, according to the law and to the best of *[his/her]* skill and ability.

_____
[Name of Attorney]

In testimony whereof I have hereunto set my hand and affixed my seal this *[date]*.

_____
Clerk of Court

§ 2:11 Ceremonial marriage—Solemnization—Traditional wedding ceremony—Form⊚

WEDDING CEREMONY *[HUSBAND]* AND *[WIFE]* *[DATE]*

We are gathered here in the presence of these witnesses to join together this man and this woman in matrimony. Into this state of marriage these two people come now to be united. *[Optional: Who gives this bride away?]*

Today you make solemn promises to each other. By truly observing these promises, your life together will be full of happiness and peace. Let no promises be as sacred as these you are about to make. Are you ready to proceed with the vows? Please join hands:

I, *[Husband]*, take you, *[Wife]*, to be my wedded wife, to have and to hold, from this day forward, for better or for worse, for richer or poorer, in sickness and in health, to love and to cherish, for as long as we both shall live.

I, *[Wife]*, take you, *[Husband]*, to be my wedded husband, to have and

an annulment of the marriage.[1] At least two Ohio appellate courts have ruled that nonconsummation makes a ceremonial marriage voidable, but not void ab initio.[2] An Ohio trial court found that consummation by coition is not necessary to the validity of a marriage, nor is cohabitation.[3] Another Ohio trial court found such a position potentially unfair in *Hardin v. Davis*:[4]

> To hold that cohabitation is necessary to create a marriage status following a proven marriage ceremony would be deciding that a marriage relationship is non-existent in a case in which a husband, immediately following a ceremony, was called into military service and died before he could cohabit with his wife, or in any case in which death or other circumstances prevented cohabitation on the part of the parties. Such a conclusion would be unfair and illogical.[5]

§ 2:15   Choice of surname

Although by tradition the wife upon marriage adopts the husband's surname, there is no legal requirement that she do so. Unless an intent to defraud is shown, married individuals are free to continue to use their individual premarital surnames, or to adopt a common surname.[1]

§ 2:16   Capacity to marry—Legal age

RC 3101.01 specifies that males eighteen years old and females sixteen years old may enter into marriage, and that minors must first obtain consent to marry.[1] Since the age of majority in Ohio is eigh-

---

[Section 2:14]

[1]RC 3105.31(F).

[2]Lang v. Reetz-Lang, 22 Ohio App. 3d 77, 488 N.E.2d 929 (10th Dist. Franklin County 1985); Darling v. Darling, 44 Ohio App. 2d 5, 73 Ohio Op. 2d 5, 335 N.E.2d 708 (8th Dist. Cuyahoga County 1975).

[3]Anderson v. Anderson, 8 Ohio Misc. 97, 37 Ohio Op. 2d 108, 219 N.E.2d 317 (C.P. 1966).

[4]Hardin v. Davis, 30 Ohio Op. 524, 16 Ohio Supp. 19, 1945 WL 5519 (C.P. 1945).

[5]Hardin v. Davis, 30 Ohio Op. 524, 16 Ohio Supp. 19, 26, 1945 WL 5519 (C.P. 1945); See also Kugel v. Kugel, 1991 WL 270412 (Ohio Ct. App. 6th Dist. Huron County 1991) (nonconsummation due to known prostate cancer does not render marriage void).

[Section 2:15]

[1]State ex rel. Krupa v. Green, 114 Ohio App. 497, 19 Ohio Op. 2d 341, 177 N.E.2d 616 (8th Dist. Cuyahoga County 1961); State ex rel. Bucher v. Brower, 21 Ohio Op. 208, 7 Ohio Supp. 51, 1941 WL 3383 (C.P. 1941); Annot., 67 A.L.R. 3d 1266.

[Section 2:16]

[1]See Hugh A. Ross, *The Ohio Law of Marriage*, 14 Case W. Res. L. Rev. 724 (1963). See also Robert F. Drinan, *The Loving Decision and the Freedom to Marry*, 29 Ohio St. L.J. 358 (1968); Samuel Green & John V. Long, *Marriage and Family Law Agreements* 1.14 (1997).

teen,[2] females aged sixteen and seventeen comprise the only category of persons needing consent.

Marriage of persons under the statutory age is void in Ohio.[3] The only exceptions involve out-of-state marriages and pregnant teenagers. An out-of-state marriage that was valid where made is valid in Ohio unless expressly prohibited by law.[4] The pregnant teenager exception is found in RC 3101.04, which allows a juvenile court to give consent in a probate court for the marriage of a minor female who is pregnant or delivered of an illegitimate child. The probate court may then issue a marriage license notwithstanding that either or both contracting parties are minors. RC 3101.05(A) requires that, upon application by a minor for a marriage license, the probate judge "shall require the applicants to state that they received marriage counseling satisfactory to the court."

A minor seeking to marry must first obtain the consent of her parents, surviving parent, guardian of her person, legal custodian, or in some circumstances a juvenile court.[5] However, the marriage of a minor solemnized without consent is valid if ratified.[6] Parents who assisted their 11-year old daughter to misrepresent her age and consented to the issuance of a marriage license to her could be found guilty of acting in a way tending to cause delinquency in a child, though the child marriage thus created was a valid marriage.[7] The marriage of a minor does not excuse compulsory school attendance for minors from age 6 to age 18 as required by RC 3321.03.[8] The Department of Youth Services does not stand in the legal status as a parent of a minor incarcerated under its custody, and has no authority to consent or withhold consent to the marriage of such a minor.[9]

Statutes similar to Ohio's, creating disparate age eligibilities for marriage, have been struck down as unconstitutional elsewhere.[10]

Marriage is generally considered to be an emancipating event for a minor, especially if accompanied by establishment of a separate resi-

---

[2]RC 3109.01.

[3]Carlton v. Carlton, 76 Ohio App. 338, 32 Ohio Op. 82, 64 N.E.2d 428 (6th Dist. Wood County 1945); State v. Wilcox, 26 Ohio N.P. (n.s.) 343, 1926 WL 2503 (Juv. Ct. 1926). For a discussion of underage marriages attaining voidability status see Text § 2:60, Void and voidable marriages—Specific impediments—Nonage.

[4]Peefer v. State, 42 Ohio App. 276, 12 Ohio L. Abs. 583, 182 N.E. 117 (2d Dist. Greene County 1931) (marriage of Ohio residents in Kentucky, followed by cohabitation in Ohio, held voidable only by minor female).

[5]RC 3101.01 & RC 3101.04. See also Juv. R. 42.

[6]See Text § 2:60, Void and voidable marriages—Specific impediments—Nonage.

[7]State v. Gans, 168 Ohio St. 174, 5 Ohio Op. 2d 472, 151 N.E.2d 709, 68 A.L.R.2d 736 (1958).

[8]1977 Ohio Att'y Gen. Op. No. 77-001.

[9]1989 Ohio Att'y Gen. Op. No. 89-046.

[10]Stanton v. Stanton, 421 U.S. 7, 95 S. Ct. 1373, 43 L. Ed. 2d 688 (1975); Phelps v. Bing, 58 Ill. 2d 32, 316 N.E.2d 775 (1974).

dence from the parents and achieving a self-supporting status.[11] One of the effects of emancipation is to relieve parents of their duty to support the minor pursuant to RC 3109.10. It is possible for that parental responsibility to be reestablished. An Arizona court has ruled that the annulment of a child's marriage during her minority and before she would have otherwise become emancipated serves to revive child's unemancipated status, thereby reviving her father's child support obligation.[12]

§ 2:17 Capacity to marry—Legal age—Application for consent of parent/guardian—Form⊚

[Title of Court]

[Caption]   Case No. [_____]
                                             CONSENT

The undersigned, being the [parents/father, the other parent being dead/mother, the other parent being dead/parent named residential parent and legal custodian by a court of competent jurisdiction/ guardian of the person/person or organization awarded permanent custody in a court exercising juvenile jurisdiction] of [name], a minor of the age of [age in years] years, do hereby give [our/my] consent to the marriage of [our/my] said [son/daughter/ward] with [name of prospective spouse].

In Testimony Whereof, [we/I] have hereunto subscribed [our/my] name this [date].

Witnessed by

_____   _____
Witness   Parent

_____   _____
Witness   Parent

The State of Ohio, [Name of county].

[Name of witness], one of the attesting witnesses to the foregoing marriage consent, being duly sworn, says that [he/she][saw/heard] the [parents/father, the other parent being dead/mother, the other parent being dead/parent named residential parent and legal custodian by a court of competent jurisdiction/guardian of the person/ person or organization awarded permanent custody by a court exercising juvenile jurisdiction] of said [name of applicant] and whose name is annexed to such certificate [subscribes to/acknowledges] the same.

---

[11]Albert v. Ellis, 59 Ohio App. 2d 152, 13 Ohio Op. 3d 188, 392 N.E.2d 1309 (8th Dist. Cuyahoga County 1978).

[12]State ex rel. Dept. of Economic Sec. v. Demetz, 212 Ariz. 287, 130 P.3d 986 (Ct. App. Div. 1 2006).

_____

Witness

Sworn to before me and signed in my presence, this *[date]*.

_____

Probate Judge

NOTES TO FORM

Drafter's Notes

The forms in this section can usually be obtained from the juvenile court. The application should be captioned "In the matter of . . ." or "In re . . .".

§ 2:18 Capacity to marry—Legal age—Application for consent of non-resident parent/guardian (with judge's certificate)—Form⊚

[Title of Court]

[Caption]   Case No. *[_____]*
                                    CONSENT

The undersigned, being *[name]* and *[name]*, the *[parents/father, the other parent being dead/mother, the other parent being dead/parent named residential parent and legal custodian by a court of competent jurisdiction/guardian of the person/person or organization awarded permanent custody in a court exercising juvenile jurisdiction]* of *[name]*, a minor of the age of *[number]* years, do hereby give *[our/my]* consent to the marriage of *[our/my]* said *[son/daughter/ward]* to *[name of prospective spouse]*.

In Testimony Whereof, *[we/I]* have hereunto subscribed *[our/my]* name this *[date]*.

Witnessed by

_____   _____
Witness   Parent

_____   _____
Witness   Parent

I, the undersigned Judge of the *[name of court]* Court, a Court of Record of *[name of county]* County, do hereby certify that on *[date]*, *[names]*, the *[parents/father, the other parent being dead/etc.]* of said *[name of minor]* personally appeared before me and gave consent in writing to the marriage of *[name of minor]*, said *[son/daughter/ward]*, to *[name of prospective spouse]*; which consent duly attested by two witnesses is hereto attached.

In Testimony Whereof, I have hereunto subscribed my name and caused the seal of said Court to be affixed, this *[date]*.

_____
Judge

§ 2:19 Capacity to marry—Legal age—Application for consent of juvenile court (with consent of parents)—Form⊛

[Title of Court]

[Caption]   Case No. *[_____]*
                              <u>APPLICATION</u>

The undersigned respectfully make application to the Juvenile Court for consent to their marriage.

They state that the undersigned *[name]* is *[if the male is of age, insert full age and efface the remainder of the sentence; otherwise insert under age and give other required information]* being of the age of *[age in years]* years on *[date]*, and has no parents, custodian or legal guardian. *[If parent is alive give address and reason consent is not possible]*.

They state that the undersigned *[name]* resides in this County and is *[if the female is of age, insert full age and efface the remainder of the sentence; otherwise insert under age and give other required information]* being of the age of *[age in years]* years on *[date]* and has no parents, custodian or legal guardian. *[If parent is alive give address and reason consent is not possible]*.

They further state that they have had marital counseling as required by law and on terms satisfactory to the juvenile court.

_____
Husband

_____
Wife

Sworn to before me and subscribed in my presence this *[date]*.

_____
Notary Public—Deputy Clerk

The undersigned parents consent to the granting of this application.

_____

Parent

_____

Parent

§ 2:20   Capacity to marry—Legal age—Application for consent of juvenile court, alternate, maternity—Form⊚

[Title of Court]

[Caption]   Case No. [_____]
                                      <u>APPLICATION</u>

The undersigned respectfully make application to the Juvenile Court for consent to their marriage.

They state that the undersigned [name] [if the male is of age, state full age, if not, insert under age], is of the age of [age in years] years on [date].

They state that the undersigned [name] resides in this County, [if the female is of age, state full age, if not, insert under age], is of the age of [age in years] years [date], and that her condition is such as imperatively to impel the marriage estate by reason of [a child having been born on [date]/approaching maternity].

[State whether either applicant is already a ward of the Court.]

They further state that they have had marital counseling as required by law and on terms satisfactory to the juvenile court.

_____

Husband

_____

Wife

Sworn to before me and subscribed in my presence this [date].

_____

Notary Public—Deputy Clerk

The undersigned [parents/ward/guardian] consent to the granting of this application.

_____

[Parent / Ward / Guardian]

_____

[Parent / Ward / Guardian]

NOTES TO FORM

Drafter's Notes

Certificate from physician verifying pregnancy, or birth certificate, should be attached.

§ 2:21 Capacity to marry—Legal age—Consent order of juvenile court—Form⊚

[Title of Court]

[Caption]   Case No. *[_____]*
                              <u>CONSENT</u>

This day said applicants appeared in open court and made application to the court for consent for their marriage; and

It appearing that the statements in the application are true; that the parties have received marriage counseling satisfactory to the Court; and that the Application ought to be granted;

It is ORDERED that consent for said marriage be and hereby is granted.

_____

Judge

§ 2:22 Capacity to marry—Physical capacity

Impotence or any other physical incapacity of either party that prevents consummation of the marriage renders the marriage voidable and subject to annulment.[1] Impotence has been defined in other jurisdictions to include partial, imperfect, unnatural, or painful intercourse; however, the definition of impotence does not include sterility.[2]

_____

[Section 2:22]

[1]McDowell v. Sapp, 39 Ohio St. 558, 1883 WL 213 (1883); Kugel v. Kugel, 1991 WL 270412 (Ohio Ct. App. 6th Dist. Huron County 1991) (voidable only by person aggrieved). See also Text Ch 7, Annulment; Text Ch 11, Divorce.

[2]See Samuel Green & John V. Long, *Marriage and Family Law Agreements* 1.17 (1997).

Ratification of a marriage to one physically incapable of consummation may occur by cohabitation after removal of the disability.[3]

No marriage license may be granted where either applicant is
infected with syphilis that is communicable or likely to become
communicable.[4]

§ 2:23   Capacity to marry—Same gender

Only persons of opposite gender may obtain a marriage license in
Ohio.[1] Homosexual marriage is not recognized in Ohio;[2] thus, a
homosexual couple may not obtain a divorce in Ohio.[3] Though commentators have raised equal protection issues, no state to date has
recognized homosexual marriages,[4] and the United States Supreme
Court has refused to hear a case on point.[5]

Marriage of a surgically changed transsexual raises different issues
(as to consummation, illegality, public policy, etc.), and the capacity of
a postoperative female to marry a male has been approved in at least
one state.[6] Ohio law does not allow a postoperative male to female
transsexual to marry a male.[7]

In a case that may presage the anticipated legal conflict over
whether states are bound by comity to recognize same-sex marriages
performed in other states, an Ohio appellate court ruled that a Massachusetts birth certificate which amended a woman's designation
from female to male after gender reassignment surgery created only a
rebuttable presumption concerning the individual's gender. The court
then refused to give full faith and credit to the foreign birth certificate, found that Ohio was free to disregard it, and made its own determination of the transsexual individual's gender, based upon "Ohio
common definition." The Ohio appeals court upheld a probate court

---

[3]McDowell v. Sapp, 39 Ohio St. 558, 1883 WL 213 (1883).

[4]RC 3101.06.

[Section 2:23]

[1]RC 3101.01. See also Text § 2:76, Same sex marriage.

[2]Charrier v. State, 30 Ohio C.D. 578, 1918 WL 902 (Ohio Ct. App. 8th Dist.
Summit County 1918); see Michael Brigner, *Same Gender Couples: Legal Disabilities
and Strategies*, 10 DRJO 1 (Jan./Feb. 1998).

[3]Irwin v. Lupardis, No. 41379 (Ohio Ct. App. 8th Dist. Cuyahoga County 1980).

[4]See Samuel Green & John V. Long, *Marriage and Family Law Agreements* 1.17
(1997); Joel E. Smith, Annot., Property Rights Arising from Relationship of Couple
Cohabitating Without Marriage, 63 A.L.R. 3d 1199.

[5]Baker v. Nelson, 291 Minn. 310, 191 N.W.2d 185 (1971). See also Text § 2:76,
Same sex marriage.

[6]M. T. v. J. T., 140 N.J. Super. 77, 355 A.2d 204 (App. Div. 1976).

[7]In re Ladrach, 32 Ohio Misc. 2d 6, 513 N.E.2d 828 (Prob. Ct. 1987); Gajovski v.
Gajovski, 81 Ohio App. 3d 11, 610 N.E.2d 431 (9th Dist. Summit County 1991) (hold-
ing transsexual may not marry as member of new gender, nor create a legal status of
concubinage which would terminate other partner's alimony rights); Dial v. Dial, 92
Ohio App. 3d 513, 636 N.E.2d 361 (9th Dist. Summit County 1993); see Samuel
Green & John V. Long, *Marriage and Family Law Agreements* 1.17 (1997).

refusal to grant a marriage license to the transgendered applicant and a female applicant.[8]

There appears to be no legal bar to a divorce or dissolution of marriage action between two married persons, one of whom has surgically changed genders during the marriage. The postoperative result, in the more common circumstance where the husband undergoes the surgical procedure, is that two women are legally married, then legally divorced.

§ 2:24 Capacity to marry—Mental capacity

Until 1981, imbecility and insanity were grounds for denying a marriage license.[1] Since those grounds were repealed, questions are unanswered regarding how one who has been adjudged insane or incompetent to handle his own affairs may be said to be competent to garner the intent or grant the consent necessary to enter into a marriage contract, or even to take the oath to apply for a license to marry. Perhaps the answers lie in the law's attempt to squeeze the complex marriage relationship into the standard law of contracts.[2] Prior to the statutory change, it was held that guardianship alone did not render a marriage contract void, as long as the mentally ill person comprehended the nature and consequences of marriage.[3]

Even if a marriage contract is challenged for reasons related to mental incapacity, RC 3105.31(C) and Ohio case law indicate the marriage can be ratified by cohabitation after removal of the disability, provided that sanity is in fact restored and the party acts with full knowledge of all material facts relevant to the ratification.[4]

While RC 3105.32(C) permits a relative of an incompetent to sue for annulment of a marriage, such proceedings must take place during

---

[8]In the Matter of the Application for a Marriage License for Jacob B. Nash and Erin A. Barr, 2003 WL 23097095, 2003-Ohio-7221 (Ohio Ct. App. 11th Dist. Trumbull County 2003). A Florida court took a contrary view in Kantaras v. Kantaras, #98-5375C (Cir. Ct. Paseo Co., Fla. 2003).

[Section 2:24]

[1]RC 3101.06. See also Text Ch 11, Divorce.

[2]For review and criticism of restrictions on marriage based on mental capacity, see Samuel Green & John V. Long, *Marriage and Family Law Agreements* 1.19 (1997); Brian J. Linn & Lesly A. Bowers, *The Historical Fallacies Behind Legal Prohibitions of Marriages Involving Mentally Retarded Persons—The Eternal Child Grows Up*, 13 Gonz. L. Rev. 625 (1978); Herbert I. Lazerow, *Mental Incompetency as Grounds for Annulment*, 7 J. Fam. L. 442 (1967); Lois Guller Jacobs, *The Right of the Mentally Disabled to Marry: A Statutory Evaluation*, 15 J. Fam. L. 463 (1977).

[3]Seabold v. Seabold, 84 Ohio App. 83, 39 Ohio Op. 112, 84 N.E.2d 521 (9th Dist. Lorain County 1948); Dozer v. Dozer, 8 Ohio L. Abs. 507, 1930 WL 2189 (Ct. App. 4th Dist. Gallia County 1930); Boyd v. Edwards, 4 Ohio App. 3d 142, 446 N.E.2d 1151 (8th Dist. Cuyahoga County 1982).

[4]McDowell v. Sapp, 39 Ohio St. 558, 1883 WL 213 (1883); Goodheart v. Ransley, 11 Ohio Dec. Rep. 655, 28 W.L.B. 227, 1892 WL 356 (Ohio C.P. 1892), aff'd, 7 Ohio C.D. 47, 1893 WL 324 (Ohio Cir. Ct. 1893); Heath v. Heath, 25 Ohio N.P. (n.s.) 123, 1924 WL 2200 (C.P. 1924).

the lifetime of the alleged incompetent. The trial court did not err in dismissing the complaint for annulment filed by the decedent's son to annul his father's marriage after the death of the father.[5]

§ 2:25 Capacity to marry—Prior undissolved marriage

RC 3101.01 provides that a person having a husband or wife living may not marry another person. Additionally, RC 2919.01 provides criminal penalties for bigamy. A prior marriage, whether ceremonial or common law, renders the subsequent marriage void ab initio,[1] at least until the prior marriage is discovered and terminated, when the newer marriage becomes ratifiable.[2] Neither deceit on the part of the previously married spouse nor good faith on the part of the innocent spouse will save the second marriage from the legal status as void, adulterous, and bigamous.[3] Bigamy is also a crime under RC 2919.01. Of course, the second marriage is not legally jeopardized if the prior relationship was a void marriage,[4] was dissolved,[5] or was merely meretricious.[6]

Three options are available to an innocent spouse who discovers that his or her mate has a husband or wife still living. First, the innocent spouse may separate without legal action; the innocent spouse needs no divorce or annulment action as to the void marriage and

---

[5]Hall v. Nelson, 41 Ohio App. 3d 138, 534 N.E.2d 929 (9th Dist. Summit County 1987).

[Section 2:25]

[1]Carmichael v. State, 12 Ohio St. 553, 1861 WL 66 (1861); Wright v. Lore, 12 Ohio St. 619, 1861 WL 76 (1861); Industrial Commission of Ohio v. Dell, 104 Ohio St. 389, 135 N.E. 669, 34 A.L.R. 422 (1922); Johnson v. Wolford, 117 Ohio St. 136, 5 Ohio L. Abs. 402, 157 N.E. 385 (1927); Pappalardo v. Pappalardo, 6 Ohio App. 291, 30 Ohio C.D. 285, 1917 WL 1410 (1st Dist. Hamilton County 1917); Blaustein v. Blaustein, 77 Ohio App. 281, 33 Ohio Op. 46, 45 Ohio L. Abs. 4, 66 N.E.2d 156 (1st Dist. Hamilton County 1946); Williams v. Williams, 90 Ohio App. 369, 48 Ohio Op. 21, 106 N.E.2d 655 (8th Dist. Cuyahoga County 1951); Darling v. Darling, 44 Ohio App. 2d 5, 73 Ohio Op. 2d 5, 335 N.E.2d 708 (8th Dist. Cuyahoga County 1975); In re Zemmicks Estate, 49 Ohio L. Abs. 353, 76 N.E.2d 902 (Ct. App. 7th Dist. Belmont County 1946).

[2]See Text § 2:61, Void and voidable marriages—Specific impediments—Bigamy.

[3]Kennelly v. Cowle, 4 Ohio N.P. 105, 6 Ohio Dec. 170, 1897 WL 778 (C.P. 1897); Williams v. Williams, 90 Ohio App. 369, 48 Ohio Op. 21, 106 N.E.2d 655 (8th Dist. Cuyahoga County 1951); Starr v. Knights of Maccabees of the World, 6 Ohio C.C.(n.s.) 473, 17 Ohio Cir. Dec. 475 (Cir., Lucas 1905), affirmed sub nom Styre v. Starr, 74 Ohio St. 501, 78 N.E. 1139 (1906); In re Roth's Estate, 6 Ohio N.P. 498, 9 Ohio Dec. 429, 1899 WL 779 (Prob. Ct. 1899). For discussion of how such marriages may become voidable and thus ratifiable see Text § 2:61, Void and voidable marriages—Specific impediments—Bigamy.

[4]Evans v. Reynolds, 32 Ohio St. 163, 1877 WL 100 (1877); State v. Moore, 3 West. L.J. 134, 1 Ohio Dec. Rep. 171, 1845 WL 2693 (Ohio C.P. 1845).

[5]Ives v. McNicoll, 59 Ohio St. 402, 53 N.E. 60 (1899); Sharp v. Sharp, 9 Ohio N.P.(n.s.) 461, 29 Ohio Dec. 255 (C.P., Montgomery 1910).

[6]Charrier v. State, 30 Ohio C.D. 578, 1918 WL 902 (Ohio Ct. App. 8th Dist. Summit County 1918).

may legally remarry.[7] However, a judicial determination of legal status is preferred.[8] Second, an annulment may be sought.[9] Third, a divorce can be filed.[10]

Where a court discovers, in a pending divorce case, that one party was still married at the time of the parties' wedding, the court may dismiss the divorce case, or even grant an annulment. Either option places the parties in the same legal position as if their marriage had not taken place.[11]

An annulment is properly granted where one party's former spouse was living at the time of the second marriage, and where such party's "Mexican Divorce" was invalid and void because it was procured without either party leaving the United States.[12]

In some states, estoppel theories have been invoked to deny annulments to spouses who assert a prior defective divorce only to escape marital responsibilities at the time of a divorce action.[13]

At times, it is not until the death of one of the parties that the prior undisclosed marriage becomes disclosed. The Lorain County Court of Appeals recently overturned a probate judge who decided that both marriages were valid, and remanded the case for a determination of which wife is the surviving spouse.[14] The appeals court relied on an Ohio Supreme Court which held that:

> Where it is stipulated that both marriages have been lawfully solemnized, and the record is silent as to whether there has been a divorce of the parties to the first marriage, there is a presumption that the status of the parties to the first marriage continues, and the burden is upon the parties claiming the validity of the second marriage to overcome such presumption.[15]

A divorce litigant sued to terminate spousal support to his ex-wife,

---

[7]Williams v. Williams, 90 Ohio App. 369, 48 Ohio Op. 21, 106 N.E.2d 655 (8th Dist. Cuyahoga County 1951); White v. Industrial Commission, 102 Ohio App. 236, 2 Ohio Op. 2d 264, 142 N.E.2d 549 (10th Dist. Franklin County 1956).

[8]Abelt v. Zeman, 16 Ohio Op. 2d 87, 86 Ohio L. Abs. 109, 173 N.E.2d 907 (C.P. 1961).

[9]RC 3105.31(B). See also Text Ch 7, Annulment.

[10]RC 3105.01(A). See also Text Ch 11, Divorce. Bubsey v. Oleyar, 2000 WL 680447 (Ohio Ct. App. 8th Dist. Cuyahoga County 2000) (A divorce could have been granted even though defendant lacked capacity to marry because she had a spouse living at the time of the marriage; although the second marriage may have been void, plaintiff could obtain a divorce to declare judicially that the marital relation did not exist).

[11]Tabler v. Tabler, 2007 WL 969421, 2007-Ohio-1579 (Ohio App. 5 Dist. Mar 26, 2007).

[12]Haska v. Haska, 1989 WL 11272 (Ohio Ct. App. 11th Dist. Portage County 1989).

[13]See Heuer v. Heuer, 152 N.J. 226, 704 A.2d 913 (1998).

[14]Bajurczak v. Estate of Bajurczak, 139 Ohio App. 3d 78, 742 N.E.2d 1191 (9th Dist. Lorain County 2000).

[15]Industrial Commission of Ohio v. Dell, 104 Ohio St. 389, 135 N.E. 669, 34 A.L.R. 422 (1922).

based upon her remarriage. He was rebuffed by the Second District Court of Appeals. It found that even though the wife and a "paramour" were married in a Muslim religious ceremony, no marriage license was secured through the state, and the "marriage" occurred while the wife was still legally married to the husband. Thus, the wife's second marriage was held to be void, and could not be the basis of termination of her support.[16]

§ 2:26 Capacity to marry—Relationships of the parties

Persons nearer of kin than second cousins are forbidden to marry by RC 3101.01,[1] following social policy that is centuries old prohibiting incestuous marriages, marriages within certain degrees of consanguinity (blood relationship), and marriages within certain degrees of affinity (relationship through marriage).[2] Ohio courts have ruled that a marriage in violation of RC 3101.01 is void,[3] cannot be ratified by cohabitation,[4] and may be annulled even if the party seeking annulment entered the marriage knowingly and willfully.[5] However, the voidness of these prohibited marriages has been brought into question.[6] Marriage within a prohibited degree of relationship is not specified by statute as a ground for annulment.[7]

In *State ex rel. Soley v. Dorrell,*[8] the Supreme Court stated, "While R.C. 3101.01 limits the right of marriage to those 'not nearer of kin than second cousins,' no statute or decision of this court states that a marriage between first cousins is void *ab initio.*" The court denied a writ of prohibition designed to declare first-cousin marriages invalid.

§ 2:27 Capacity to marry—Consent of parties

Although the issue of agreement or consent usually arises in common law marriage disputes, voluntary consent remains an essential

---

[16]Rihan v. Rihan, 2006-Ohio-2671, 2006 WL 1461097 (Ohio Ct. App. 2d Dist. Greene County 2006).

[Section 2:26]

[1]For a review of the development and modern criticism of such laws, see Samuel Green & John V. Long, *Marriage and Family Law Agreements* 1.15 (1997).

[2]52 Am. Jur. 2d, Marriage §§ 62–65.

[3]In re Stiles Estate, 59 Ohio St. 2d 73, 13 Ohio Op. 3d 62, 391 N.E.2d 1026 (1979).

[4]Basickas v. Basickas, 93 Ohio App. 531, 51 Ohio Op. 229, 114 N.E.2d 270 (9th Dist. Summit County 1953); Heyse v. Michalske, 18 Ohio Op. 254, 31 Ohio L. Abs. 484, 6 Ohio Supp. 33 (Prob. Ct. 1940).

[5]52 Am. Jur. 2d, Annulment of Marriage § 10.

[6]See Text § 2:63, Void and voidable marriages—Specific impediments—Consanguinity.

[7]RC 3105.31.

[8]State ex rel. Soley v. Dorrell, 1994-Ohio-103, 69 Ohio St. 3d 514, 515-16, 634 N.E.2d 215 (1994).

element of all marriages, including ceremonial ones.[1] Marriages have been voided where it was proved that the parties went through the ceremony for purposes other than to create a permanent husband and wife relationship.[2] A marriage for hire for purposes of allowing the husband to obtain a U.S. Visa was intended to circumvent the immigration and naturalization laws of the U.S. government, according to a probate court judge, who voided the marriage license and the marriage itself. This action was reversed by the court of appeals, which found that RC 2101.24 does not indicate that the probate court has authority to determine issues regarding immigration and naturalization.[3]

§ 2:28 Marriage brokerage contract

A marriage brokerage contract between fathers of the bride and groom was held invalid due to the illegality of the subject matter, and a suit for return of a dowry and monetary gifts between parents was dismissed.[1]

An Ohio court considered an arrangement where the Lebanese friend of a Lebanese-born American suitor acted as the suitor's agent in a divorce in Lebanon, stood in for the absent suitor in a marriage to a new bride in Lebanon, then acted as the suitor's agent in a divorce from the new bride in Lebanon. The Sixth District Court of Appeals found these extraordinary services to be nothing more than the equivalent of hiring a minister to perform a wedding ceremony or a caterer for the reception. Absent clear evidence that a marriage brokerage agreement had been created, the court said these services did not constitute an "agreement made upon consideration of marriage" barred under the statute of frauds, RC 1335.05. The jury verdict for the services of the suitor's Lebanese friend was upheld.[2]

The issue of "mail order brides," women brought to the United States for marriage purposes, often through the unregulated, Internet-based marriage brokerage industry, is gaining national attention. Congress began considering regulations after a mail order bride was

---

[Section 2:27]

[1]Solomon v. Solomon, 1 Ohio N.P. (n.s.) 113, 13 Ohio Dec. 517, 1903 WL 1093 (C.P. 1903), rev'd, 16 Ohio C.D. 307, 1904 WL 1146 (Ohio Cir. Ct. 1904).

[2]Conley v. Conley, 28 Ohio Op. 289, 14 Ohio Supp. 22, 1943 WL 6289 (C.P. 1943); see Text § 2:33, Sham marriage.

[3]Matter of Ababseh, 1996 WL 116148 (Ohio Ct. App. 7th Dist. Mahoning County 1996).

[Section 2:28]

[1]Muflahi v. Musaad, 205 Mich. App. 352, 522 N.W.2d 136 (1994).

[2]Akl v. El Chafehi, 120 Ohio App. 3d 110, 696 N.E.2d 1103 (6th Dist. Lucas County 1997), appeal allowed, 80 Ohio St. 3d 1413, 684 N.E.2d 705 (1997) and appeal dismissed as improvidently allowed, 1998-Ohio-241, 82 Ohio St. 3d 1219, 695 N.E.2d 262 (1998).

killed in Washington state.[3] This effort produced several new federal laws, most significantly the International Marriage Broker Regulation Act of 2005[4]. This law attempts to regulate international marriage brokers ("IMBs"), informally known as "mail-order bride" companies. As analyzed by one author, "IMBRA limits individuals' and criminal organizations' opportunities to abuse the fiancée visa process, whether for purposes of human smuggling, sex trafficking, or individual exploitation in servile marriages."[5]

§ 2:29 Defenses to marriage contract

As in any other contract, marriage is subject to the defenses of duress[1] and fraud.[2] However, the fraud must relate directly to such essential elements of the marriage as the identity of the spouse,[3] and not to such ancillary matters as the deceitful party's social status or wealth,[4] or his physical infirmities, such as false teeth and glass eyes.[5] Misrepresentation as to chastity is insufficient to invalidate a marriage;[6] however, undisclosed pregnancy creates a voidable marriage,[7] except where the husband knows of the pregnancy or has engaged in

---

[3]David Crary; *The Associated Press, Mail-order-brides bill pending; Washington murder prompting legislation to regulate industry*, The Seattle Times, 2003 WL 3640792 (7-6-03); see also Suzanne H. Jackson, *To Honor and Obey: Trafficking in "Mail-Order Brides"*, 70 Geo. Wash. L. Rev. 475, June 2002.

[4]8 U.S.C.A. § 1375a(d)(2) and (e)(4).

[5]Suzanne H. Jackson, Marriages of Convenience: International Marriage Brokers, "Mail-order Brides," and Domestic Servitude, 38 U. Tol. L. Rev. 895, 907-908 (Spring, 2007).

[Section 2:29]

[1]Shafher v. State, 20 Ohio 1, 1851 WL 1 (1851); Abelt v. Zeman, 16 Ohio Op. 2d 87, 86 Ohio L. Abs. 109, 173 N.E.2d 907 (C.P. 1961). See also Robert Kingsley, *Duress as a Ground for Annulment of Marriage*, 33 S. Cal. L. Rev. 1 (1959); Samuel Green & John V. Long, *Marriage and Family Law Agreements* 1.25 (1997).

[2]Harry W. Vanneman, *Annulment of Marriage for Fraud*, 9 Minn. L. Rev. 497 (1925); Robert Kingsley, *Fraud as a Ground for Annulment of a Marriage*, 18 S. Cal. L. Rev. 213 (1945); Samuel Green & John V. Long, *Marriage and Family Law Agreements* 1.24 (1997).

[3]Meyer v. Meyer, 4 Ohio Dec. Rep. 345, 7 Ohio Dec. Rep. 561, 1 Cleve. Law Rep. 347, 3 W.L.B. 985, 1878 WL 7379 (Ohio C.P. 1878), aff'd, 7 Ohio Dec. Rep. 627, 4 W.L.B. 368, 1879 WL 6394 (Ohio Dist. Ct. 1879). See also 4 Am. Jur. 2d, Annulment of Marriage § 14.

[4]Meyer v. Meyer, 4 Ohio Dec. Rep. 345, 7 Ohio Dec. Rep. 561, 1 Cleve. Law Rep. 347, 3 W.L.B. 985, 1878 WL 7379 (Ohio C.P. 1878), aff'd, 7 Ohio Dec. Rep. 627, 4 W.L.B. 368, 1879 WL 6394 (Ohio Dist. Ct. 1879); Kraus v. Kraus, 6 Ohio N.P. 248, 9 Ohio Dec. 515, 1899 WL 785 (C.P. 1899).

[5]Kraus v. Kraus, 6 Ohio N.P. 248, 9 Ohio Dec. 515, 1899 WL 785 (C.P. 1899).

[6]Meyer v. Meyer, 4 Ohio Dec. Rep. 345, 7 Ohio Dec. Rep. 561, 1 Cleve. Law Rep. 347, 3 W.L.B. 985, 1878 WL 7379 (Ohio C.P. 1878), aff'd, 7 Ohio Dec. Rep. 627, 4 W.L.B. 368, 1879 WL 6394 (Ohio Dist. Ct. 1879); Joy v. Joy, 12 Ohio Dec. 574, 1900 WL 1285 (C.P. 1900).

[7]Anderson v. Anderson, 8 Ohio Misc. 97, 37 Ohio Op. 2d 108, 219 N.E.2d 317 (C.P. 1966); Meyer v. Meyer, 4 Ohio Dec. Rep. 345, 7 Ohio Dec. Rep. 561, 1 Cleve.

premarital sexual relations with the wife.[8] Fraud is established by statute as a ground for both annulment[9] and divorce.[10]

§ 2:30   Proxy marriages

There is no statutory authorization in Ohio for creation of a marriage by proxy, in which one or both parties are represented at the ceremony by an authorized agent or proxy.[1] RC 3101.05 does require personal appearance and oath by both parties to obtain the license to marry, but the details of the ceremony are left to the discretion of the prospective bride and groom. By definition, a common law marriage cannot be created by proxy.

While Ohio law does not authorize proxy marriages, it does not prohibit such marriages; the state will recognize a foreign proxy marriage if it was valid in the state where performed.[2] However, if the law of the state of performance fails to authorize proxy marriages, an Ohio court will find such a marriage voidable.[3]

Proxy marriages often involve persons detained overseas. With no statutory prohibition in Ohio, it is surprising that in this modern age a "video marriage," where one or both parties "appear" at the ceremony by electronic means, has not been brought to the attention of the state's courts.

Proxy marriages are authorized by section 206 of the Uniform Marriage and Divorce Act.[4]

§ 2:31   Incarceration and marriage

Incarceration may make marriage somewhat inconvenient, but not unlawful. Prison regulations restricting the right of adult prisoners to marry must be reasonably related to legitimate penological interests. As the U.S. Supreme Court has noted: "The right to marry, like many other rights, is subject to substantial restrictions as a result of incarceration. Many important attributes of marriage remain, however, after taking into account the limitations imposed by prison

---

Law Rep. 347, 3 W.L.B. 985, 1878 WL 7379 (Ohio C.P. 1878), aff'd, 7 Ohio Dec. Rep. 627, 4 W.L.B. 368, 1879 WL 6394 (Ohio Dist. Ct. 1879).

[8]Meyer v. Meyer, 4 Ohio Dec. Rep. 345, 7 Ohio Dec. Rep. 561, 1 Cleve. Law Rep. 347, 3 W.L.B. 985, 1878 WL 7379 (Ohio C.P. 1878), aff'd, 7 Ohio Dec. Rep. 627, 4 W.L.B. 368, 1879 WL 6394 (Ohio Dist. Ct. 1879); See also Tyminski v. Tyminski, 8 Ohio Misc. 202, 37 Ohio Op. 2d 263, 221 N.E.2d 486 (C.P. 1966).

[9]RC 3105.31(D).

[10]RC 3105.01(E).

[Section 2:30]

[1]See Ernest G. Lorenzen, *Marriage by Proxy and the Conflict of Laws*, 32 Harv. L. Rev. 473 (1919).

[2]Hardin v. Davis, 30 Ohio Op. 524, 16 Ohio Supp. 19, 1945 WL 5519 (C.P. 1945).

[3]Respole v. Respole, 34 Ohio Op. 1, 70 N.E.2d 465, 170 A.L.R. 942 (C.P. 1946).

[4]Unif. Marriage and Divorce Act § 206, 9A Uniform Laws Annotated p 107.

life."[1] Among attributes other than living together, the court listed emotional support, public commitment, spiritual significance with respect to many religions, expectation of full consummation upon release, and the effect of marriage with respect to children born out of wedlock, government benefits, and property rights.[2]

The refusal of the Department of Rehabilitation and Correction to allow a woman to marry a male prison inmate after questioning her gender resulted in an unsuccessful intentional infliction of emotional distress claim, where the woman had no documentary proof of gender and refused to submit to a medical examination.[3]

In a case that was unreported except in the popular press, a Massachusetts judge ruled that a sheriff did not have authority to deny a jail inmate the right to marry, despite the fact that the man was serving a four year sentence for assaulting a previous girlfriend by dragging her from a car and threatening to beat her with a baseball bat.[4]

§ 2:32 Military regulation of marriage

Current U.S. military policy states that all active duty personnel have basically the same rights to enter into a marriage as any other Unites States citizen, but requires that overseas military personnel obtain written approval from their senior area commander prior to marrying.[1] This type of regulation has not gone uncriticized.[2]

§ 2:33 Sham marriage

The issue of marriage ceremonies entered into by the parties with no intent to be "really married" arises where the parties intend for the marriage to serve only limited purposes, such as furthering a career, or legitimizing children[1] Most often however, the limited purpose involves manipulation of immigration laws, and court cases

---

[Section 2:31]

[1]Turner v. Safley, 482 U.S. 78, 95, 107 S. Ct. 2254, 96 L. Ed. 2d 64 (1987).

[2]See Samuel Green & John V. Long, *Marriage and Family Law Agreements* 1.21 (1997).

[3]Saffell v. Department of Rehabilitation and Correction, 91 Ohio Misc. 2d 30, 696 N.E.2d 1126 (Ct. Cl. 1997).

[4]Casey Ross, *Wedding planning tough for bride; Fiance in jail for abusing ex-girlfriend*, The Patriot Ledger (Quincy, MA), 2003 WL 9746455 (5-20-03).

[Section 2:32]

[1]Army Regulation 600-240, "Marriage in Overseas Commands;" see Samuel Green & John V. Long, *Marriage and Family Law Agreements* 1.22 (1997).

[2]Johns, *The Right to Marry: Infringement by the Armed Forces*, 10 Fam. L.Q. 357 (1977); Murphy, *The Soldier's Right to a Private Life*, 24 Mil. L. Rev. 97 (1964).

[Section 2:33]

[1]Conley v. Conley, 28 Ohio Op. 289, 14 Ohio Supp. 22, 1943 WL 6289 (C.P. 1943); see Samuel Green & John V. Long, *Marriage and Family Law Agreements* 1.27 to 1.29 (1997).

have resulted in inconsistent opinions.[2] The Sixth Circuit Court of Appeals recently decided that, where the federal Board of Immigration Appeals (BIA) validly determines that an alien obtained permanent resident status in the United States on the basis of a fraudulent marriage, entered into solely for the purpose of procuring the alien's admission as an immigrant, the BIA may find that the alien is removable from the U.S.[3]

Limited purpose marriages should be distinguished from marriages in jest, where the parties go through a ceremony as a joke or upon a dare, but never actually intend to consent to marriage.[4]

§ 2:34 Contract in restraint of marriage

A divorce decree provision prohibiting the ex-husband from allowing one particular woman to reside in the former marital residence (which was awarded to him by the decree) was held in *Beechler v. Beechler*[1] not to constitute an unlawful restraint of marriage, as the ex-husband could still marry the woman in question and reside elsewhere. In deciding the matter, the court discussed the lawful limits on contractual restrictions on marriage:

> Generally, contracts in absolute restraint of marriage are void because they violate public policy. King v. King, 63 Ohio St. 363, 59 N.E. 111 (1900). However, where the restraint is not absolute, but limited as to person, group or time, it is generally considered valid unless the remaining sphere of permissible marriage is so small that a permitted marriage is not likely to occur. 52 Am. Jur. 2d, Marriage § 181. A limited restraint on marriage may or may not be void depending on whether or not it is reasonable; a court should determine reasonableness not on the terms of the condition alone, but on the relation of the parties, and the purpose behind the restraint. Saslow v. Saslow, 104 Ohio App. 157, 162, 4 Ohio Op. 2d 230, 232–233, 147 N.E.2d 262 (2d Dist. Montgomery County 1957).[2]

---

[2]See Samuel Green & John V. Long, *Marriage and Family Law Agreements* 1.27 to 1.29 (1997).

[3]Fang Huang v. Mukasey, 523 F.3d 640 (6th Cir. 2008).

[4]See Samuel Green & John V. Long, *Marriage and Family Law Agreements* 1.26 (1997).

[Section 2:34]

[1]Beechler v. Beechler, 95 Ohio App. 3d 121, 641 N.E.2d 1189 (12th Dist. Fayette County 1994).

[2]Beechler v. Beechler, 95 Ohio App. 3d 121, 127–128, 641 N.E.2d 1189 (12th Dist. Fayette County 1994). Interestingly, colonial America adopted the 18th century European practice for men to disinherit their widows if they remarried. Patriot Patrick Henry's will cut off a generous bequest to his widow Dorothea if she were to remarry after his death in 1799. She said, in effect, "Give me liberty," and married Henry's cousin Judge Winston. German poet Heinrich Heine took the opposite approach, leaving his entire estate to his wife, but only if she remarried after his death in 1856. His will explained the reason: "Because then there will be at least one man to regret my death."

§ 2:35 Common law marriage and its demise

A common law marriage entered into in Ohio prior to October 10, 1991, constitutes a valid legal marriage in Ohio.[1] After this date, new common law marriages are prohibited in Ohio.[2] Protection is provided in RC 3105.12(B)(3) for such marriages that came into existence prior to October 10, 1991, or were entered into in another state or country that recognizes common law marriage. A few states continue to recognize such nonceremonial marital arrangements. Most authorities, including the American Bar Association and the Commission on Uniform State Laws, favor abolition of common law marriage.[3]

The elimination of common law marriages by the Ohio General Assembly may in the future reduce claims in probate court, the arena where the issues arise when claimed surviving spouses assert their spousal rights.[4] However, the elimination of common law marriage without providing any legislative remedies to assist non-married cohabitants settle their affairs when their relationships break up leaves those citizens to the mercies of "frontier justice"; all assets will go to the biggest or swiftest partner (or to the one who holds a weapon). Non-married cohabitants will find help from Ohio courts almost as scarce as help from the General Assembly.[5]

More than a decade after the abolition of new common law marriages in Ohio, the existence of old common law marriages—those formed prior to October 10, 1991—continues to create litigation for Ohio courts. For example, the Clermont County Court of Appeals found that the plaintiff proved by competent, credible evidence that she was the common law wife of an intestate decedent, and thus qualified as his heir.[6] The Summit County Court of Appeals found no agreement of marriage in praesenti, despite a 21-year cohabitation, and dismissed the divorce complaint of the alleged common law wife.[7] The Franklin County Court of Appeals decided that a wife proved all elements of a common law marriage and upheld the decree of legal separation awarded to her; it also upheld the award of the nonresi-

---

[Section 2:35]

[1]RC 3105.12(B)(3), as amended by 1991 H.B. 32, eff. 10-10-91.

[2]RC 3105.12(B)(1).

[3]See Samuel Green & John V. Long, *Marriage and Family Law Agreements* 1.33 (1997).

[4]See, e.g., Henderson v. Harshman, 1990 WL 121891 (Ohio Ct. App. 2d Dist. Montgomery County 1990); Bank One, Mansfield v. Conner, 1992 WL 91667 (Ohio Ct. App. 5th Dist. Holmes County 1992).

[5]See Text § 2:69, Cohabitants' legal remedies—Few available in Ohio.

[6]Polly v. Coffey, 2003-Ohio-509, 2003 WL 231293 (Ohio Ct. App. 12th Dist. Clermont County 2003).

[7]Glover v. Glover, 2003-Ohio-1292, 2003 WL 1240107 (Ohio Ct. App. 9th Dist. Summit County 2003); Sulfridge v. Kindle, 2005-Ohio-3929, 2005 WL 1806482 (Ohio Ct. App. 4th Dist. Adams County 2005).

dent husband's Ohio real estate to the wife as spousal support.[8] The Cuyahoga County Court of Appeals reversed a trial court judgment that failed to find a common law marriage. The parties had cohabited since 1989, and when the husband divorced a prior wife in 1990, all legal impediments to common law marriage status at that time were removed.[9] The Cuyahoga County Court of Appeals also rejected a common law marriage claim of a purported wife despite over a quarter century of cohabitation and the fact that the parties had a son together. Cohabitation was deemed proven, but agreement and holding out as husband and wife were not; the son was deemed irrelevant.[10] In 2005 the Court of Appeals for Lucas County ruled on a common law marriage that allegedly occurred in 1977, when a couple had a son and began living together. They remained together, held a ceremonial marriage in 1998, and entered divorce court in 2003. Despite the birth of the child and the fact that the husband had referred to his wife as "his wife" 10 or 15 times prior to the ceremonial marriage, the court found no evidence of the necessary element of an agreement to marry in praesenti. The appeals court affirmed the trial court's rejection of the wife's claim to property and support rights for the period prior to 1998.[11] A similar decision the same year in Cuyahoga County additionally found that the putative wife's claim was barred by laches because she had delayed more than eight years after the parties separated before bringing suit.[12]

Ohio courts will also entertain common law marriage disputes pursuant to RC 3105.12(B)(3), where a common-law marriage came into existence in another state that does recognize common-law marriage, and it is in accordance with the laws of that state.[13]

§ 2:36 Common law marriage concept defended

Strong arguments exist for recognizing the institution of common law marriage. For example, Ohio appellate Judge Lawrence Grey, in a concurring opinion, explained his objections to abolishing common law marriage:

I cannot agree with the suggestion that common-law marriages no lon-

---

[8]Kvinta v. Kvinta, 2003-Ohio-2884, 2003 WL 21291049 (Ohio Ct. App. 10th Dist. Franklin County 2003). See Bevan v. Bevan, 2006-Ohio-2775, 2006 WL 1519654 (Ohio Ct. App. 11th Dist. Lake County 2006) (common law marriage proven, spousal support warranted).

[9]Spencer v. Harmon, 2002-Ohio-4909, 2002 WL 31087419 (Ohio Ct. App. 8th Dist. Cuyahoga County 2002).

[10]Winthrop v. Harden, 2002-Ohio-6217, 2002 WL 31528720 (Ohio Ct. App. 8th Dist. Cuyahoga County 2002).

[11]Reyes v. Vasquez, 2005-Ohio-2948, 2005 WL 1389076 (Ohio Ct. App. 6th Dist. Lucas County 2005).

[12]Faison v. Faison, 2005-Ohio-2733, 2005 WL 1303344 (Ohio Ct. App. 8th Dist. Cuyahoga County 2005).

[13]Fuentes v. Fuentes, 2007-Ohio-820, 2007 WL 613751 (Ohio Ct. App. 8th Dist. Cuyahoga County 2007).

ger be recognized. The ultimate philosophical question, as I see it, is should we have laws which reflect the way we want people to behave, or should we have laws which reflect the way they actually behave? Some common-law marriages are of long duration, and have brought stability and happiness into the lives of the parties. Whatever the reason parties do not chose a ceremonial marriage, the unmistakable fact of life is that there are many long-term common-law marriages, which are real marriages in every sense of the word.

. . .

If we refuse to recognize these kinds of marriages, we will often work a terrible injustice. A woman may have lived with a man for forty years, held herself out as his wife, borne his children, helped him through the bad times, celebrated the good times, and done everything a good and faithful wife might have done. But when he dies, we will ignore the fact of their life together, deny her survivor benefits, her right to share in his estate, even her right to bury him, for in the eyes of the law, this helpmate of a lifetime is only a legal stranger. We will do all this and call it just, solely so a court can avoid having to decide, every now and then, a close case such as we have here.

The issue is not whether common-law marriages are antiquated, because we still get them regularly. The question is whether we will continue to have the common decency to recognize them.[1]

One year after Judge Grey's opinion was published, the General Assembly voted to abolish common law marriages in Ohio.

Contrary to recent trends, the Utah legislature amended its marriage statute in 1987 to specifically validate common law marriage.[2]

§ 2:37 Common law marriage defined

As recently as 1984, the Ohio Supreme Court had confirmed the legality and requisites of common law marriage as follows:

A common law marriage is the marital joinder of a man and a woman without the benefit of formal papers or procedures. Such marriages are not favored in Ohio, but have long been recognized as lawful if certain elements or circumstances are found to be present.

The necessary elements in order to establish a common law marriage were set forth by this court in *Umbenhower*, . . . as follows: "An agreement of marriage *in praesenti* when made by parties competent to contract, accompanied and followed by cohabitation as husband and wife, they being so treated and reputed in the community and circle in which they move, establishes a valid marriage at common law. "

[Section 2:36]

[1]In re Estate of Hall, 67 Ohio App. 3d 715, 721–22, 588 N.E.2d 203 (4th Dist. Washington County 1990).

[2]Utah Code Ann. § 30-1-4.5 (Supp. 1987); see Samuel Green & John V. Long, *Marriage and Family Law Agreements* 1.33 (1997).

The fundamental requirement to establish the existence of a common law marriage is a meeting of the minds between the parties who enter into a mutual contract to presently take each other as man and wife.[1]

The concept of common law marriage was recognized by the Ohio General Assembly in 1953, at least for purposes of divorce proceedings, through the adoption of RC 3105.12: "Proof of cohabitation and reputation of the marriage of the parties is competent evidence to prove such marriage, and within the discretion of the court, may be sufficient therefor."

The five essential elements of a common law marriage, as itemized in Ohio case law, will be discussed below, as follows: (1) a mutual agreement of marriage in praesenti; (2) made by persons competent to marry; (3) followed by cohabitation; (4) a holding out as husband and wife; and (5) a reputation as being husband and wife.

A common law marriage should be distinguished from a putative marriage, wherein one or both parties believe a valid legal marriage exists, but in fact an impediment exists which renders the "marriage" unlawful.[2]

Both common law marriage and putative marriage are clearly distinguishable from a relationship that involves cohabitation with intercourse but with no intention by the parties to have marital status.[3]

§ 2:38 Common law marriage elements—Agreement

A mutual contract between the parties to presently take each other as man and wife (marriage in praesenti) is the first and most important element of a common law marriage. As the Ohio Supreme Court stated in *Nestor v. Nestor*:[1]

> The agreement to marry in praesenti is the essential element of a common law marriage. Its absence precludes the establishment of such a relationship even though the parties live together and openly engage in cohabitation. Although cohabitation and reputation are necessary elements of a common law marriage, . . . standing alone they do not constitute a common law marriage.

The *Nestor* court went on to note, "Where there is no direct proof in reference to the formation of the contract of marriage in *praesenti*,

---

[Section 2:37]

[1]Nestor v. Nestor, 15 Ohio St. 3d 143, 145-46, 472 N.E.2d 1091 (1984) (citations omitted). See Samuel Green & John V. Long, *Marriage and Family Law Agreements* 1.31–1.35 (1997).

[2]See Text § 2:50, Putative marriage.

[3]See Text § 2:66, Cohabitation.

[Section 2:38]

[1]Nestor v. Nestor, 15 Ohio St. 3d 143, 472 N.E.2d 1091 (1984).

testimony regarding cohabitation and community reputation tends to raise an inference of the marriage."[2]

While no particular words or ceremony is necessary to contract a common law marriage,[3] and while there need not be a writing,[4] the agreement must be in praesenti (in the present tense, expressing a current agreement by the parties that they are married)[5] and must be for life.[6] A contract to marry in the future does not create a common law marriage.[7] Proof of intercourse or children is not conclusive proof of a common law marriage, since these factors may be present in nonmarital relationships as well.[8]

The timing of the agreement may be critical. If one of the parties is already married at the time of the agreement, the prior marriage is an impediment to the creation of a common law marriage. If that party then divorces, should the common law arrangement then be deemed to blossom into a marriage? The Ohio Supreme Court in *Johnson v. Wolford*[9] held that there must be a new agreement in praesenti. However, *Jenkins v. Jenkins*,[10] a later and better-reasoned decision of the Sixth District Court of Appeals, held that if the other necessary elements are present, the law imputes an agreement upon removal of the impediment.

In *Hatfield v. Hatfield*,[11] the issue was whether the *in praesenti* requirement of a common law marriage could be defeated by a belief, mistaken or not, that one is already married to the same spouse. The question arose after summary judgment was awarded to the party

---

[2]Nestor v. Nestor, 15 Ohio St. 3d 143, 472 N.E.2d 1091 (1984).

[3]In re Barrett, 49 Bull. 222 (Prob., Hamilton 1904).

[4]Eagleson v. McKee, 19 Ohio Op. 362, 33 Ohio L. Abs. 33, 1 Ohio Supp. 321 (Prob. Ct. 1939), aff'd, 33 Ohio L. Abs. 38, 33 N.E.2d 417 (Ct. App. 2d Dist. Franklin County 1940).

[5]Knight v. Shields, 19 Ohio L. Abs. 37, 1935 WL 3195 (Ct. App. 2d Dist. Montgomery County 1935); Holmes v. Pere Marquette R. Co., 28 Ohio App. 297, 6 Ohio L. Abs. 628, 162 N.E. 675 (6th Dist. Lucas County 1927).

[6]Holmes v. Pere Marquette R. Co., 28 Ohio App. 297, 6 Ohio L. Abs. 628, 162 N.E. 675 (6th Dist. Lucas County 1927). See also In re Zemmicks Estate, 49 Ohio L. Abs. 353, 76 N.E.2d 902 (Ct. App. 7th Dist. Belmont County 1946); Bates v. State, 9 Ohio C.C.(n.s.) 273, 19 Ohio Cir. Dec. 189 (Cir., Allen 1906), affirmed by 77 Ohio St. 622, 84 N.E. 1132 (1907); In re Hammonds' Estate, 39 Ohio Misc. 96, 67 Ohio Op. 2d 27, 68 Ohio Op. 2d 267, 315 N.E.2d 843 (C.P. 1973).

[7]Duncan v. Duncan, 10 Ohio St. 181, 1859 WL 67 (1859); Carmichael v. State, 12 Ohio St. 553, 1861 WL 66 (1861); Umbenhower v. Labus, 85 Ohio St. 238, 97 N.E. 832 (1912); Johnson v. Wolford, 117 Ohio St. 136, 5 Ohio L. Abs. 402, 157 N.E. 385 (1927).

[8]Ryan v. Ryan, 84 Ohio App. 139, 39 Ohio Op. 166, 86 N.E.2d 44 (5th Dist. Stark County 1948).

[9]Johnson v. Wolford, 117 Ohio St. 136, 5 Ohio L. Abs. 402, 157 N.E. 385 (1927).

[10]Jenkins v. Jenkins, 30 Ohio App. 336, 6 Ohio L. Abs. 596, 164 N.E. 790 (6th Dist. Sandusky County 1928).

[11]Hatfield v. Hatfield, 1995 WL 23984 (Ohio Ct. App. 4th Dist. Gallia County 1995).

challenging the common law marriage claim based upon a prior divorce which the parties believed was not decreed. In reversing, the court quoted extensively and favorably from Clark,[12] and concluded that the *in praesenti* requirement "pertains solely to an intent of the parties to conduct their affairs as if they are presently married."[13]

Likewise, the formation of the agreement to be married in another jurisdiction that does not recognize common law marriages, followed by continuous cohabitation and functioning as a marital unit in Ohio, can sustain a finding that the parties did have a meeting of the minds in Ohio concerning their desire to presently take each other as husband and wife.[14]

§ 2:39   Common law marriage elements—Competence to marry

Competency of the parties is essential for creation of a common law marriage.[1] The rules governing capacity to marry are the same for common law marriages as for ceremonial ones.[2]

While recognizing that one component of a valid common law marriage requires parties competent to contract marriage and that a person married to another would not be able to establish a valid common law marriage, the Fourth District Court of Appeals held that "although the parties' common law marriage was void in that appellee lacked the capacity to marry due to her continuing marriage to [her husband], appellant could still maintain his divorce action and, if granted a divorce, the court would have jurisdiction to grant to him alimony and other relief."[3] Therefore, since there were issues of fact in dispute, the sustaining of a summary judgment motion was reversed.

A common law marriage cannot arise, even with all the other incidents such as present intent, reputation and cohabitation, so long as one party is under a legal disability due to at the same time being married to another.[4]

---

[12]Clark, Law of Domestic Relations in the United States (2d ed.).

[13]Hatfield v. Hatfield, 1995 WL 23984, at *5 (Ohio Ct. App. 4th Dist. Gallia County 1995).

[14]Bowman v. Senne, 1995 WL 312713 (Ohio Ct. App. 9th Dist. Summit County 1995).

[Section 2:39]

[1]Johnson v. Wolford, 117 Ohio St. 136, 5 Ohio L. Abs. 402, 157 N.E. 385 (1927); Duncan v. Duncan, 10 Ohio St. 181, 1859 WL 67 (1859).

[2]Johnson v. Wolford, 117 Ohio St. 136, 5 Ohio L. Abs. 402, 157 N.E. 385 (1927). See also Text §§ 2:6 et seq., Ceremonial marriage.

[3]Bolin v. Bolin, 1987 WL 17301, at *3 (Ohio Ct. App. 4th Dist. Jackson County 1987).

[4]Hill v. Hill, 2008 WL 2572681, 2008-Ohio-2774 (Ohio App. 5 Dist. Jun 09, 2008).

§ 2:40 Common law marriage elements—Cohabitation

In *Nestor v. Nestor*,[1] the Ohio Supreme Court settled a long-standing dispute over whether proof of cohabitation and reputation is necessary where the agreement of the parties is already proven; the court said "yes":

> There is a noted difference among authorities as to whether evidence of the remaining elements which constitute a common law marriage, cohabitation and a reputation in the community as being husband and wife, is necessary when there exists direct proof of a contract of marriage *in praesenti*.
>
> . . .
>
> [T]his court has consistently required proof of both cohabitation and reputation following the contract in order to establish the existence of a common law marriage. Today, we again choose to follow this time-tested rationale.

In modern usage, "cohabitation" usually refers to the nonmarital arrangement of a man and woman sharing the same residence with no intention of creating a present marriage; in fact, the arrangement is often intended as a trial of the relationship preliminary to a decision about marriage.[2] In the context of proof of common law marriage, however, the definition of cohabitation is more specific and closely tied to the parties' intent ("holding out") and public acceptance ("reputation") as man and wife. Cohabitation must follow the agreement of marriage,[3] must be constant and exclusive,[4] and must include sexual relations[5] to qualify as proof of a common law marriage. No specific amount of time is required to create a common law marriage. Arguably, it could be as little as a day and in fact has been held to be as little as twelve days.[6]

§ 2:41 Common law marriage elements—"Holding out"

Although the "holding out" element of a common law marriage usually finds itself mingled with case law language about reputation (often combined under the general label of "notoriety"), the two elements deserve separate attention. "Holding out" focuses on the actions of the parties to make known publicly their marriage contract and cohabitation, while "reputation" is the public conception of the relationship.

[Section 2:40]

[1]Nestor v. Nestor, 15 Ohio St. 3d 143, 472 N.E.2d 1091 (1984) (footnotes omitted).

[2]For further discussion of nonmarital cohabitation, see Text §§ 2:66 et seq., Cohabitation.

[3]Nestor v. Nestor, 15 Ohio St. 3d 143, 472 N.E.2d 1091 (1984).

[4]Williams v. Williams, 90 Ohio App. 369, 48 Ohio Op. 21, 106 N.E.2d 655 (8th Dist. Cuyahoga County 1951).

[5]Nestor v. Nestor, 15 Ohio St. 3d 143, 472 N.E.2d 1091 (1984).

[6]Gatterdam v. Gatterdam, 86 Ohio App. 29, 40 Ohio Op. 459, 54 Ohio L. Abs. 271, 85 N.E.2d 526 (2d Dist. Franklin County 1949).

The jumbling of these elements is well illustrated by the Ohio Supreme Court's decision in *Nestor v. Nestor*:[1]

> As to the element of cohabitation, there must be proof that the parties had sexual activity in the open manner of husband and wife in a marital state. Secret cohabitation with its attendant indicium of concealment concerning the sexual activity of the parties will not suffice as evidence of a valid common law marriage.
>
> As to the element surrounding the reputation of the parties in the community as being man and wife, in order to establish a common law marriage it is not necessary that they disseminate information to all society generally, or to all of the community in which they reside. Rather, there must be a holding out to those with whom they normally come in contact. A common law marriage will not necessarily be defeated by the fact that all persons in the community within which the parties reside are not aware of the marital arrangement, nor by the fact that all persons with whom they normally come in contact are also unaware of the arrangement.

It may be concluded from *Nestor* and prior cases[2] that secrecy defeats a claim of common law marriage. Thus, the failure of a wife to adopt her husband's surname reflects negatively on proof of the agreement and the holding out elements of a common law marriage.[3] As *Nestor* indicates, however, it is not necessary for the parties to publish their marriage to all the world, as long as they hold out as man and wife to the persons with whom they normally come in contact.[4]

Proof of holding out as husband and wife for a long time can even rescue a defective ceremonial marriage or one where the license and certificate cannot be located.[5]

§ 2:42 Common law marriage elements—Reputation

The result of holding out as married at common law is the reputation of marriage created in the community. Of course, proof of reputation also helps to establish the existence and intent of the parties' agreement and confirms their success in holding themselves out as married.

Reputation is one of the two elements of proof (along with cohabita-

---

[Section 2:41]

[1]Nestor v. Nestor, 15 Ohio St. 3d 143, 472 N.E.2d 1091 (1984).

[2]Roberts v. Roberts, 8 West. L.J. 372, 1 Ohio Dec. Rep. 368, 1850 WL 2921 (Ohio C.P. 1850); Borton v. Burns, 11 Ohio Misc. 200, 40 Ohio Op. 2d 480, 230 N.E.2d 156 (Prob. Ct. 1967).

[3]State v. Durham, 49 Ohio App. 2d 231, 3 Ohio Op. 3d 280, 360 N.E.2d 743 (1st Dist. Hamilton County 1976).

[4]Gatterdam v. Gatterdam, 86 Ohio App. 29, 40 Ohio Op. 459, 54 Ohio L. Abs. 271, 85 N.E.2d 526 (2d Dist. Franklin County 1949); In re McLaughlin's Estate, 29 Ohio Op. 2d 218, 93 Ohio L. Abs. 228, 197 N.E.2d 578 (Prob. Ct. 1963); In re Madia's Estate, 6 Ohio Misc. 109, 35 Ohio Op. 2d 234, 215 N.E.2d 72 (Prob. Ct. 1966).

[5]Kontner v. Kontner, 103 Ohio App. 360, 3 Ohio Op. 2d 384, 74 Ohio L. Abs. 97, 139 N.E.2d 366 (10th Dist. Franklin County 1956).

tion) which RC 3105.12 specifies as competent evidence in a divorce case to establish a marriage. Ohio courts are unanimous in holding that reputation in the community as husband and wife is an essential element of a common law marriage.[1]

§ 2:43 Common law marriage—Degree of proof

A common law marriage must be proven by clear and convincing evidence.[1] Since common law marriage cases often arise in the context of contested divorce and estate matters, proof of the elements, especially the agreement and cohabitation, is often subject to dispute. Courts generally allow the marriage to be proved by circumstantial evidence.[2] The burden of proof is on the party attempting to prove the common law marriage.[3]

Summary judgment declaring a common law marriage nonexistent is inappropriate where there are conflicting affidavits and there is a factual issue of its existence.[4] A wife is competent to give testimony concerning her marital reputation in the community. A subsequent marriage application, upon which a person states that he has no living spouse, does not contradict an existing common law marriage where the question can be interpreted to ask if the applicant had any "other" husband or wife.

The claim of a woman that she was the surviving spouse of a decedent, based upon a common law marriage ostensibly established in September 1959 and continuing to his death thirty-three years later was rejected by the Probate Court of Columbiana County. After the parties' separation in 1963, the claimant remarried twice. The court held that under Ohio law a party may be estopped by his or her remarriage to take a legal position inconsistent with the validity of that marriage.[5]

§ 2:44 Common law marriage—Termination

Once established, a common law marriage may only be terminated

---

[Section 2:42]

[1]See Nestor v. Nestor, 15 Ohio St. 3d 143, 472 N.E.2d 1091 (1984).

[Section 2:43]

[1]Nestor v. Nestor, 15 Ohio St. 3d 143, 472 N.E.2d 1091 (1984); see also In re Maynard's Estate, 117 Ohio App. 315, 24 Ohio Op. 2d 95, 192 N.E.2d 281 (4th Dist. Lawrence County 1962); Jolley v. Jolley, 46 Ohio Misc. 40, 75 Ohio Op. 2d 350, 347 N.E.2d 557 (C.P. 1975); Makeever v. Makeever, 20 Ohio Misc. 2d 13, 485 N.E.2d 1071 (C.P. 1984).

[2]In re Madia's Estate, 6 Ohio Misc. 109, 35 Ohio Op. 2d 234, 215 N.E.2d 72 (Prob. Ct. 1966); Dibble v. Dibble, 88 Ohio App. 490, 45 Ohio Op. 251, 100 N.E.2d 451 (5th Dist. Richland County 1950).

[3]Molitor v. Gaddis, 1998 WL 347067 (Ohio Ct. App. 5th Dist. Morrow County 1998).

[4]Ruscilli v. Ruscilli, 90 Ohio App. 3d 753, 630 N.E.2d 745 (10th Dist. Franklin County 1993).

[5]In re Estate of Dalton, 68 Ohio Misc. 2d 78, 647 N.E.2d 581 (C.P. 1995).

as ceremonial marriages are, by death, divorce, or annulment.[1] It cannot be terminated at the will of the parties, by separation, by adulterous conduct, or even by a deathbed repudiation.[2]

§2:45 Common law marriage—Effects of cohabitation subsequent to ceremonial marriage

Where the two parties to an alleged common law marriage were previously married ceremonially, then divorced, courts have been cautious about holding subsequent cohabitation to create a new marriage at common law between the ex-spouses.[1] However, a quantum meruit claim was sustained in one case where a woman lived with and cared for her sick ex-husband for six years.[2]

A decision based on a record replete with evidence in support of the formation of a common law marriage in 1987, following a 1985 divorce, was upheld in *Baker v. Baker*.[3] The appellants in that case were the husband's parents, as third party title owners to property transferred to them by their son without the wife's signature or knowledge.

§2:46 Common law marriage—Effects of cohabitation prior to ceremonial marriage—In general

The same legal effects as a common law marriage are sometimes created when the parties cohabited and operated as an economic or

---

[Section 2:44]

[1]Dibble v. Dibble, 88 Ohio App. 490, 45 Ohio Op. 251, 100 N.E.2d 451 (5th Dist. Richland County 1950). See RC 3105.12(B)(2).

[2]Umbenhower v. Umbenhower, 12 Ohio C.C.(n.s.) 289, 21 Ohio Cir. Dec. 317 (Cir., Stark 1909), affirmed sub nom Umbenhower v. Labus, 85 Ohio St. 238, 97 N.E. 832 (1912); In re Zemmick's Estate, 32 Ohio Op. 504, 44 Ohio L. Abs. 390, 17 Ohio Supp. 15 (Prob. Ct. 1945), aff'd, 49 Ohio L. Abs. 353, 76 N.E.2d 902 (Ct. App. 7th Dist. Belmont County 1946); Ryan v. Ryan, 84 Ohio App. 139, 39 Ohio Op. 166, 86 N.E.2d 44 (5th Dist. Stark County 1948); Howard v. Central Nat. Bank of Marietta, 21 Ohio App. 74, 4 Ohio L. Abs. 700, 152 N.E. 784 (4th Dist. Washington County 1926); In re Barrett, 49 Bull. 222 (Prob., Hamilton 1904).

[Section 2:45]

[1]Holmes v. Pere Marquette R. Co., 28 Ohio App. 297, 6 Ohio L. Abs. 628, 162 N.E. 675 (6th Dist. Lucas County 1927); Minnix v. Brantner, 48 Ohio Op. 450, 64 Ohio L. Abs. 327, 107 N.E.2d 562 (Prob. Ct. 1952); Kuhls v. Kuhls, 162 Ohio St. 146, 54 Ohio Op. 68, 120 N.E.2d 718 (1954); In re Hammonds' Estate, 39 Ohio Misc. 96, 67 Ohio Op. 2d 27, 68 Ohio Op. 2d 267, 315 N.E.2d 843 (C.P. 1973); Dean v. Cowan, 1985 WL 8640 (Ohio Ct. App. 12th Dist. Clermont County 1985). See also Annot., 82 A.L.R. 2d 688 1962; Annot., 79 A.L.R. 213; Fields v. Fields, 39 Ohio App. 3d 187, 530 N.E.2d 933 (2d Dist. Montgomery County 1987); Levy v. Levy, No. 77AP-918 (Ohio Ct. App. 10th Dist. Franklin County 1978). However, where the parties entered an actual partnership agreement, a partition action was allowed, in Purdy v. Purdy, 1993 WL 185580 (Ohio Ct. App. 12th Dist. Butler County 1993).

[2]Hartley v. Hartley, No. 96-CA-132 (Ohio Ct. App. 5th Dist. Licking County 1997).

[3]Baker v. Baker, 2000 WL 1336700 (Ohio Ct. App. 12th Dist. Clinton County 2000).

marital partnership prior to the date of a ceremonial marriage. This type of result can occur in two circumstances: (1) where the court, in determining the "duration of the marriage," uses a commencement date prior to the ceremonial date of the marriage; and (2) where the court "tacks" a prior marriage to one currently being dissolved in a divorce action for purposes of determining property and/or support rights.[1]

§ 2:47 Common law marriage—Effects of cohabitation prior to ceremonial marriage—Duration of marriage determination

One of the factors a domestic relations court must consider upon termination of a marriage is "the duration of the marriage." This determination is necessary for analysis of spousal support[1] and property division issues.[2] Duration of the marriage is defined at RC 3105.171(A) as follows:

(2) "During the marriage" means whichever of the following is applicable:

(a) Except as provided in division (A)(2)(a) of this section, the period of time from the date of the marriage through the date of the final hearing in an action for divorce or in an action for legal separation;

(b) If the court determines that the use of either or both of the dates specified in division (A)(2)(a) of this section would be inequitable, the court may select dates that it considers equitable in determining marital property. If the court selects dates that it considers equitable in determining the marital property, "during the marriage" means the period of time between those dates selected and specified by the court.

The duration of marriage may include a period of cohabitation by the parties prior to the ceremonial marriage. Such inclusion was affirmed where the record showed that the parties lived together, supported one another emotionally and financially, and filed joint federal tax returns during that period.[3]

The selection of a de facto date of marriage some two years prior to the ceremonial marriage was upheld by the Cuyahoga County Court of Appeals. "It was at this time, as recognized by the court, that the parties started functioning as husband and wife, both socially and economically. At that time, their finances were, substantially, as one. . . . They had effectively pooled their resources and worked toward a common purpose, to the extent of purchasing property in

---

[Section 2:46]

[1]Jones v. Jones, 2000 WL 1513980 (Ohio Ct. App. 2d Dist. Montgomery County 2000) (finding that a common law marriage existed prior to their ceremonial marriage supported by evidence).

[Section 2:47]

[1]RC 3105.18(C)(1)(e).

[2]RC 3105.171(F)(1).

[3]Lott v. Lott, 1993 WL 389453 (Ohio Ct. App. 8th Dist. Cuyahoga County 1993).

anticipation of wedding. The parties were truly interdependent emotionally from that point, with appellee starting to work in the appellant's medical office and effect changes and efficiencies therein which, as the income records indicate, demonstrably aided the growth of the medical practice, appellant's income, and, in turn, the parties' lifestyle. These attachments, emotionally and financially, buttress the court's use of the de facto date of marriage commencement."[4]

Other states have found the period of premarital cohabitation to be a valid factor for consideration in dividing marital property,[5] thus creating in effect, if not legal fact, a common law marriage prior to a ceremonial marriage.

§ 2:48 Common law marriage—Effects of cohabitation prior to ceremonial marriage—Tacking of marriage periods

Where parties have engaged in serial matrimony, Ohio courts have sometimes held that factual circumstances might allow the tacking of the period of the first marriage onto the period of the second marriage for purposes of spousal support determination[1] and property division.[2]

§ 2:49 "Common law divorce"

"While Ohio law accepts the concept of a common-law marriage, it has no counterpart in a common-law divorce," according to one appellate court. A decedent's first wife was not estopped from challenging the validity of a Mexican divorce, even though the wife acquiesced in

---

[4]D'Hue v. D'Hue, 2002-Ohio-5857, ¶ 90, 2002 WL 31401993, at *12 (Ohio Ct. App. 8th Dist. Cuyahoga County 2002), appeal not allowed, 98 Ohio St. 3d 1490, 2003-Ohio-1189, 785 N.E.2d 472 (2003).

[5]Nielsen v. Nielsen, 179 Mich. App. 698, 446 N.W.2d 356 (1989); Matter of Marriage of Lindsey, 101 Wash. 2d 299, 678 P.2d 328 (1984); Warden v. Warden, 36 Wash. App. 693, 676 P.2d 1037 (Div. 1 1984); In re Marriage of Goldstein, 97 Ill. App. 3d 1023, 53 Ill. Dec. 397, 423 N.E.2d 1201 (1st Dist. 1981). Contra: Crouch v. Crouch, 88 Ill. App. 3d 426, 43 Ill. Dec. 580, 410 N.E.2d 580 (3d Dist. 1980). See also Barbara Freedman Wand, *The Relevance of Premarital Cohabitation to Property Division Awards in Divorce Proceedings: An Evaluation of Present Trends and a Proposal for Legislative Reform*, 63 B.U.L. Rev. 105 (1983); Aaron R. Haimowitz, *Classifying Property Subject to Equitable Distribution: Evaluating the Alternative Marriage Termination Dates*, 10 Am. J. Fam. L. 221 (1996).

[Section 2:48]

[1]Moore v. Moore, 83 Ohio App. 3d 75, 79, 613 N.E.2d 1097 (9th Dist. Summit County 1992) (with caveat that facts of the case strongly favored tacking, and "we do not mean to indicate that any premarital relationship is relevant to a decision to award spousal support").

[2]Swartz v. Swartz, 1997 WL 86308 (Ohio Ct. App. 12th Dist. Warren County 1997).

the divorce for 25 years by living separate and apart and countenanced the husband's subsequent remarriage.[1]

§ 2:50   Putative marriage

A putative (or reputed) marriage is the standard equitable device used in those states that do not recognize common law marriages and have no other way to satisfactorily determine property division, probate claims of the (reputed) surviving spouse, etc.[1] Though the finding of a common law marriage would usually resolve such matters in Ohio, the concept of putative marriage may still be useful where a legal impediment prevents the creation of common law marital status, or where the relationship began after October 10, 1991, when common law marriages were legislatively abolished in Ohio.[2]

The putative marriage concept does not create or validate a marriage but creates the fiction of a marriage as an equitable remedy, based upon a good faith belief in the existence of a valid marriage.[3]

If a marriage is voidable rather than void ab initio, a court may find putative marriage to remedy apparent or attempted injustice. For instance, one court found that a marriage between first cousins by blood was merely voidable as such marriages, while disapproved, are not forbidden by Ohio law. The finding prevented a husband from avoiding the obligations of a twenty-year marriage.[4] Mistake or fraud pertaining to the validity of a marriage may be the basis for restitution or other remedies for a putative spouse.[5] The party asserting a putative marriage must have entered into the putative marriage in good faith, specifically with an honest and reasonable belief that the

---

[Section 2:49]

[1]In re Estate of Newton, 65 Ohio App. 3d 286, 288, 583 N.E.2d 1026 (5th Dist. Muskingum County 1989).

[Section 2:50]

[1]See Christopher L. Blakesley, *The Putative Marriage Doctrine*, 60 Tul. L. Rev. 1 (1985); Joel E. Smith, Annot., Property Rights Arising from Relationship of Couple Cohabiting Without Marriage, 3 A.L.R. 4th 13; Francis M. Dougherty, Annot., Waiver of Statutory Demand-for-Rent Due or of Notice-to-Quit Prerequisite of Summary Eviction of Lessee for Nonpayment of Rent—Modern Cases, 31 A.L.R. 2d 1255; Samuel Green & John V. Long, *Marriage and Family Law Agreements* 1.34, 3.02 (1997).

[2]RC 3105.12(B)(3).

[3]See Christopher L. Blakesley, *The Putative Marriage Doctrine*, 60 Tul. L. Rev. 1 (1985); Annot., 3 A.L.R. 4th 13; Francis M. Dougherty, Annot., Waiver of Statutory Demand-for-Rent Due or of Notice-to-Quit Prerequisite of Summary Eviction of Lessee for Nonpayment of Rent—Modern Cases, 31 A.L.R. 2d 1255; Samuel Green & John V. Long, *Marriage and Family Law Agreements* 1.34, 3.02 (1997). See also Uniform Marriage & Divorce Act § 209, 94 Uniform Laws Annotated p 115.

[4]Soley v. Soley, 101 Ohio App. 3d 540, 655 N.E.2d 1381 (6th Dist. Lucas County 1995), dismissed, appeal not allowed, 73 Ohio St. 3d 1410, 651 N.E.2d 1308 (1995).

[5]Santos v. Santos, 32 Cal. App. 2d 62, 89 P.2d 164 (4th Dist. 1939); Roberts v. Roberts, 64 Wyo. 433, 196 P.2d 361 (1948).

marriage was valid at its inception and that no legal impediment existed.[6]

The putative spouse doctrine is found in the social security regulations for purposes of determining eligibility for insurance benefits. Those regulations define a "deemed valid marriage" as follows: "You will be deemed to be the wife, husband, widow, or widower of the insured if, in good faith, you went through a marriage ceremony with the insured that would have resulted in a valid marriage except for a legal impediment. A legal impediment includes only an impediment which results because a previous marriage had not ended at the time of the ceremony or because there was a defect in the procedure followed in connection with the intended marriage."[7] This provision was applied by the Sixth Circuit Court of Appeals in *Lawson v. Heckler*[8] to award benefits to a surviving spouse despite the invalidity of her marriage due to her husband's prior undissolved marriage.

§ 2:51 Quasi-estoppel as preventing denial of putative marriage

Even where the marriage is void, or where the party asserting a putative marriage had knowledge of a defect in the marriage when it was entered and cannot thus claim "good faith," the court might rely on the concept of quasi-estoppel to provide relief to the aggrieved party. "There is a difference between declaring a marriage void and preventing a party from asserting its invalidity," stated a dissenting Alaska Supreme Court justice in advocating relief upon the basis of quasi-estoppel where he thought it would be "unconscionable" to allow one party to reap the benefits of holding himself out as married for more than twenty years, then allow him to assert the marriage was void.[1] The dissenting justice described the concept of quasi-estoppel:

Quasi-estoppel "precludes a party from taking a position inconsistent with one he [or she] has previously taken where circumstances render assertion of the second position unconscionable." Jamison v. Consolidated Utilities, Inc., 576 P.2d 97, 102 (Alaska 1978). Quasi-estoppel does not require the injured party to have relied on the estopped party's conduct or statements, nor does it require the injured party to be ignorant of the truth. Id. at 102. In determining if quasi-estoppel applies, the court considers "whether the party asserting the inconsistent position has gained an advantage or produced some disadvantage through the first

---

[6]Rakestraw v. City of Cincinnati, 69 Ohio App. 504, 24 Ohio Op. 214, 37 Ohio L. Abs. 159, 44 N.E.2d 278 (1st Dist. Hamilton County 1942); Batey v. Batey, 933 P.2d 551 (Alaska 1997); Covington v. Covington, 421 Pa. Super. 328, 617 A.2d 1318 (1992); Watts v. Watts, 250 Neb. 38, 547 N.W.2d 466 (1996); Cardwell v. Cardwell, 195 S.W.3d 856 (Tex. App. Dallas 2006).

[7]20 C.F.R. § 404.346(a).

[8]Lawson v. Heckler, 771 F.2d 169 (6th Cir. 1985). See also Fontana v. Callahan, 999 F. Supp. 304 (E.D. N.Y. 1998).

[Section 2:51]

[1]Batey v. Batey, 933 P.2d 551, 555 (Alaska 1997).

position; whether the inconsistency was of such significance as to make the present assertion unconscionable; and whether the first assertion was based on full knowledge of the facts." Id.[2]

Quasi-estoppel, or estoppel by election of remedies, is rarely cited but is a long established feature of the Ohio legal landscape,[3] although it does not appear to have been applied in family law cases in this state.

§ 2:52 Proof of marriage—Burden of proof

The burden of establishing the existence of a marriage rests upon the party asserting the marriage or claiming some rights or benefits by virtue of it.[1] This is equally true for proof of a common law marriage.[2]

Similarly, the party asserting the invalidity of a marriage is charged with the burden of proving such invalidity, whether a ceremonial or a common law marriage is being challenged.[3]

Since Ohio follows the presumption that a prior marriage continues, the burden falls upon a second spouse to rebut that presumption with proof of termination of the first marriage, in order to eliminate the first marriage as a legal bar to the second.[4]

---

[2]Batey v. Batey, 933 P.2d 551, 554–55 (Alaska 1997). The dissent also relied upon the authority of In re Marriage of Recknor, 138 Cal. App. 3d 539, 187 Cal. Rptr. 887, 34 A.L.R.4th 805 (2d Dist. 1982); Annot., 34 A.L.R. 4th 805. A Tennessee trial court decreed a marriage by estoppel, upon proof that when the parties married twenty years and four children ago, the wife's first divorce in Mexico was not final. The state supreme court reversed, finding the husband had rebutted the presumption that the parties' marriage was valid and had established that the marriage was bigamous. (Guzman v. Alvares, 205 S.W.3d 375 (Tenn. 2006).).

[3]Hampshire County Trust Co. of North Hampton, Mass. v. Stevenson, 114 Ohio St. 1, 4 Ohio L. Abs. 74, 150 N.E. 726 (1926); McCahan v. Whirlpool Corp., 1986 WL 9661 (Ohio Ct. App. 3d Dist. Hancock County 1986); Dayton Securities Assoc. v. Avutu, 105 Ohio App. 3d 559, 664 N.E.2d 954 (2d Dist. Montgomery County 1995).

[Section 2:52]

[1]Rea v. Fornan, 26 Ohio Op. 485, 37 Ohio L. Abs. 135, 46 N.E.2d 649 (Ct. App. 2d Dist. Franklin County 1942).

[2]In re Soeder's Estate, 7 Ohio App. 2d 271, 36 Ohio Op. 2d 404, 220 N.E.2d 547 (8th Dist. Cuyahoga County 1966); Jolley v. Jolley, 46 Ohio Misc. 40, 75 Ohio Op. 2d 350, 347 N.E.2d 557 (C.P. 1975); Dirion v. Brewer, 20 Ohio App. 298, 4 Ohio L. Abs. 534, 151 N.E. 818 (8th Dist. Cuyahoga County 1925).

[3]Evans v. Reynolds, 32 Ohio St. 163, 1877 WL 100 (1877); Rea v. Fornan, 26 Ohio Op. 485, 37 Ohio L. Abs. 135, 46 N.E.2d 649 (Ct. App. 2d Dist. Franklin County 1942).

[4]Evans v. Reynolds, 32 Ohio St. 163, 1877 WL 100 (1877); Industrial Commission of Ohio v. Dell, 104 Ohio St. 389, 135 N.E. 669, 34 A.L.R. 422 (1922); In re Soeder's Estate, 7 Ohio App. 2d 271, 36 Ohio Op. 2d 404, 220 N.E.2d 547 (8th Dist. Cuyahoga County 1966).

In *Wilson v. Brown*,[5] the referee had reported at an initial hearing that there was a valid common law marriage between the parties. That report was approved by the court and was not appealed. During the divorce trial, the trial court set aside its prior order and reviewed evidence on the issue of common law marriage. After trial, it dismissed the complaint for divorce for failure to prove a common law marriage. The procedure was found to be in error, although the appellate court did recognize that Civil Rule 75 orders were interlocutory and that so long as the parties and the subject matter remain before the court, it has the inherent power to reopen issues previously determined.

Where parties cohabited and used "Mr. and Mrs." when traveling, but each party had a separate phone and the "wife" took out loans and had bank accounts in both her maiden name and in the man's name, the burden of proving common law marriage was not met.[6] In *Summers v. Summers*,[7] common law remarriage of the same parties was not established by clear and convincing evidence. Had common law marriage been found to exist, it would have acted as a revocation of the prior separation agreement. In *Barger v. Barger*,[8] the appeals court ruled that the trial court erred in finding a common law marriage where the only evidence of the parties' reputation in the community as husband and wife was (1) several greeting cards addressed to the couple, and (2) a few bills referring to plaintiff as "Karen Barger" (defendant's surname), and where even plaintiff's daughter testified she only considered the parties to be married because of the length of time they lived together and not because of their actions.

§ 2:53 Proof of marriage—Presumptions

Ohio courts have developed a number of presumptions that apply, through Evidence Rule 301, to proof of issues related to marriage. Once established, a marriage relationship is presumed valid and presumed to continue until the contrary is shown, whether a ceremonial[1] or common law marriage is involved.[2]

This presumption as to validity and continuation of marriage sets

---

[5]Wilson v. Brown, 41 Ohio App. 3d 77, 534 N.E.2d 883 (10th Dist. Franklin County 1987).

[6]Ogletree v. Ogletree, 1988 WL 67532 (Ohio Ct. App. 7th Dist. Columbiana County 1988). See also Stebbins v. Stebbins, 1989 WL 148057 (Ohio Ct. App. 5th Dist. Stark County 1989) (application by defendant for health insurance coverage for "wife" and joint checking account insufficient to overcome failure to provide reputation evidence or "in praesenti" agreement).

[7]Summers v. Summers, 1988 WL 72373 (Ohio Ct. App. 2d Dist. Clark County 1988).

[8]Barger v. Barger, 1988 WL 125696 (Ohio Ct. App. 12th Dist. Clermont County 1988).

[Section 2:53]

[1]Industrial Commission of Ohio v. Dell, 104 Ohio St. 389, 135 N.E. 669, 34 A.L.R. 422 (1922); McHenry v. McHenry, 19 Ohio App. 187, 1 Ohio L. Abs. 406, 1923 WL 2711 (1st Dist. Hamilton County 1923); Olijan v. Lublin (Gudlin), 38 Ohio L. Abs.

the stage for a battle of presumptions when the continuation of a prior marriage is pitted against the validity of a subsequent one. Ohio follows the minority view in holding that the prior marriage continues, so the second marriage is deemed invalid unless the party challenging the prior marriage can overcome the presumption of its continuation.[3]

Additionally, no presumption of divorce exists in Ohio to support the legality of a subsequent marriage.[4]

A strong legal bias toward legitimacy creates a presumption of marriage wherever possible to serve this end.[5]

§ 2:54   Proof of marriage—Judicial notice

Ohio courts may take judicial notice of the validity of common law marriages established prior to October 10, 1991 in Ohio, by virtue of the common law and the directive of Evidence Rule 201 that courts take judicial notice of adjudicative facts. Evidence Rule 201, read with the terms of RC 3105.12, allows judicial notice of the validity of common law marriages established in other states or nations, "in accordance with all relevant aspects of the law of that state or nation."[1] Judicial notice of the validity of marriages in other states is mandated by Civil Rule 44.1. " 'In Ohio, in accordance with the rule prevailing in all jurisdictions, the validity of a marriage is determined by the law of the place where the contract is entered into. If valid where it is solemnized, it is valid everywhere; if invalid there, it is invalid elsewhere. * * * The better rule, however, is that capacity or incapacity to marry depends on the law of the place where the marriage is

---

393, 50 N.E.2d 264 (Ct. App. 8th Dist. Cuyahoga County 1943), judgment aff'd, 143 Ohio St. 417, 28 Ohio Op. 354, 55 N.E.2d 658 (1944). See also 52 Am. Jur. 2d, Marriage §§ 133 et seq.

[2]Dibble v. Dibble, 88 Ohio App. 490, 45 Ohio Op. 251, 100 N.E.2d 451 (5th Dist. Richland County 1950); In re Clark's Estate, 69 Ohio L. Abs. 435, 128 N.E.2d 437 (Ct. App. 2d Dist. Darke County 1954).

[3]Domany v. Otis Elevator Co., 369 F.2d 604, 13 Ohio Misc. 161, 41 Ohio Op. 2d 355, 42 Ohio Op. 2d 183 (6th Cir. 1966). See also Industrial Commission of Ohio v. Dell, 104 Ohio St. 389, 135 N.E. 669, 34 A.L.R. 422 (1922); McHenry v. McHenry, 19 Ohio App. 187, 1 Ohio L. Abs. 406, 1923 WL 2711 (1st Dist. Hamilton County 1923); Olijan v. Lublin (Gudlin), 38 Ohio L. Abs. 393, 50 N.E.2d 264 (Ct. App. 8th Dist. Cuyahoga County 1943), judgment aff'd, 143 Ohio St. 417, 28 Ohio Op. 354, 55 N.E.2d 658 (1944); Annot., 14 A.L.R. 2d 24; Bajurczak v. Estate of Bajurczak, 139 Ohio App. 3d 78, 742 N.E.2d 1191 (9th Dist. Lorain County 2000).

[4]Olijan v. Lublin (Gudlin), 38 Ohio L. Abs. 393, 50 N.E.2d 264 (Ct. App. 8th Dist. Cuyahoga County 1943), judgment aff'd, 143 Ohio St. 417, 28 Ohio Op. 354, 55 N.E.2d 658 (1944). See also Smith v. Smith, 5 Ohio St. 32, 1855 WL 40 (1855); Bajurczak v. Estate of Bajurczak, 139 Ohio App. 3d 78, 742 N.E.2d 1191 (9th Dist. Lorain County 2000).

[5]Dirion v. Brewer, 20 Ohio App. 298, 4 Ohio L. Abs. 534, 151 N.E. 818 (8th Dist. Cuyahoga County 1925); Johnson v. Dudley, 3 Ohio N.P. 196, 4 Ohio Dec. 243, 1896 WL 663 (C.P. 1896); Joseph v. Alexander, 12 Ohio St. 3d 88, 465 N.E.2d 448 (1984). See also Annot., 57 A.L.R. 2d 729.

[Section 2:54]

[1]RC 3105.12(B)(3)(a).

celebrated, and not on that of the domicil of the parties.' "[2] In the absence of evidence to the contrary, Ohio courts will presume that the common law of marriage is the same in a foreign state as in Ohio.[3]

§ 2:55 Proof of marriage—Records and documentary evidence

If properly identified and authenticated under the Ohio Rules of Evidence,[1] a marriage may be proven by the marriage register or similar records of the county or probate court.[2] A marriage certificate is admissible for the same purpose, but since such a document is not self-authenticating, the signature of the official who performed the marriage must be proven.[3]

Other documentary evidence may be admitted, such as a marriage contract, antenuptial agreement, deed records, letters, license and insurance applications, driver's license, wills, and income tax returns, either to establish or to disprove the existence of a marriage.

§ 2:56 Proof of marriage—Obtaining marriage records

In Ohio, marriage records may be obtained from the probate court of the county which issued the marriage license, where such records are required to be kept by RC 3101.13. Information on obtaining marriage records in other states is available from the United States Department of Health and Human Services.[1]

§ 2:57 Proof of marriage—Parol and other evidence

Marriage may be proven without production of the marriage certificate or other documentary evidence by reliance upon competent parol

---

[2]Abbott v. Industrial Commission, 80 Ohio App. 7, 13, 35 Ohio Op. 406, 74 N.E.2d 625 (5th Dist. Muskingum County 1946) (citation omitted).

[3]Respole v. Respole, 34 Ohio Op. 1, 70 N.E.2d 465, 170 A.L.R. 942 (C.P. 1946).

[Section 2:55]

[1]Evid. R. 901 to Evid. R. 903.

[2]Lipen v. Lipen, 7 Ohio Dec. Rep. 141, 1 W.L.B. 164, 1876 WL 7273 (Ohio C.P. 1876); In re Clark's Estate, 69 Ohio L. Abs. 435, 128 N.E.2d 437 (Ct. App. 2d Dist. Darke County 1954); 52 Am. Jur. 2d, Marriage §§ 154 et seq.

[3]Hanley v. State, 5 Ohio C.D. 488, 1896 WL 558 (Ohio Cir. Ct. 1896); Evid. R. 901, Evid. R. 902.

[Section 2:56]

[1]*Where to Write for Vital Records: Births, Deaths, Marriages & Divorces*, DHHS Publication No. (PHS) 84-1142 (1992), United States Dep't of Health & Human Services, Public Health Service, National Center for Health Statistics, Hyattsville, Maryland, (301) 436-8500.

evidence,[1] including testimony by the official who performed the marriage ceremony.[2] Testimony by the parties in question is also admissible,[3] at least until the marriage is consummated and cohabitation begins. Additionally, the parties' own admissions and declarations may be admitted either to help prove[4] or disprove the establishment of a marriage.[5]

Testimony as to the parties' cohabitation and reputation as husband and wife is specifically allowed by RC 3105.12 as competent evidence in a divorce case to establish the marriage,[6] and such testimony is admissible in other types of cases to prove not only a common law marriage[7] but also to prove a ceremonial marriage where no written record is available.[8]

§ 2:58 Void and voidable marriages—Definitions

Certain incapacities and impediments cause a marriage to be void or voidable.[1] Usually these terms are raised in the context of ceremonial marriages, since many of the disabilities to marriage are

---

[Section 2:57]

[1]Umbenhower v. Labus, 85 Ohio St. 238, 97 N.E. 832 (1912); Markley v. Hudson, 143 Ohio St. 163, 28 Ohio Op. 81, 54 N.E.2d 304 (1944); Eagleson v. McKee, 19 Ohio Op. 362, 33, 33 Ohio L. Abs. 33, 1 Ohio Supp. 321 (Prob. Ct. 1939), aff'd, 33 Ohio L. Abs. 38, 33 N.E.2d 417 (Ct. App. 2d Dist. Franklin County 1940).

[2]Pappalardo v. Pappalardo, 6 Ohio App. 291, 30 Ohio C.D. 285, 1917 WL 1410 (1st Dist. Hamilton County 1917).

[3]Pappalardo v. Pappalardo, 6 Ohio App. 291, 30 Ohio C.D. 285, 1917 WL 1410 (1st Dist. Hamilton County 1917); see also Eagleson v. McKee, 19 Ohio Op. 362, 33, 33 Ohio L. Abs. 33, 1 Ohio Supp. 321 (Prob. Ct. 1939), aff'd, 33 Ohio L. Abs. 38, 33 N.E.2d 417 (Ct. App. 2d Dist. Franklin County 1940).

[4]Umbenhower v. Labus, 85 Ohio St. 238, 97 N.E. 832 (1912); Dirion v. Brewer, 20 Ohio App. 298, 4 Ohio L. Abs. 534, 151 N.E. 818 (8th Dist. Cuyahoga County 1925); Rea v. Fornan, 26 Ohio Op. 485, 37 Ohio L. Abs. 135, 46 N.E.2d 649 (Ct. App. 2d Dist. Franklin County 1942).

[5]In re Redman's Estate, 135 Ohio St. 554, 14 Ohio Op. 426, 21 N.E.2d 659 (1939); In re Maynard's Estate, 117 Ohio App. 315, 24 Ohio Op. 2d 95, 192 N.E.2d 281 (4th Dist. Lawrence County 1962); In re Speeler's Estate, 6 Ohio Op. 529, 22 Ohio L. Abs. 223, 1 Ohio Supp. 227 (Prob. Ct. 1936).

[6]RC 3105.12.

[7]Bruner v. Briggs, 39 Ohio St. 478, 1883 WL 202 (1883); Howard v. Central Nat. Bank of Marietta, 21 Ohio App. 74, 4 Ohio L. Abs. 700, 152 N.E. 784 (4th Dist. Washington County 1926); Lynch v. Romas, 74 Ohio L. Abs. 1, 139 N.E.2d 352 (Ct. App. 10th Dist. Franklin County 1956); Stewart v. Welch, 41 Ohio St. 483, 1885 WL 5 (1885).

[8]Kontner v. Kontner, 103 Ohio App. 360, 3 Ohio Op. 2d 384, 74 Ohio L. Abs. 97, 139 N.E.2d 366 (10th Dist. Franklin County 1956); Umbenhower v. Labus, 85 Ohio St. 238, 97 N.E. 832 (1912); Rea v. Fornan, 26 Ohio Op. 485, 37 Ohio L. Abs. 135, 46 N.E.2d 649 (Ct. App. 2d Dist. Franklin County 1942).

[Section 2:58]

[1]See Goda, *The Historical Evolution of the Concepts of Void and Voidable Marriages*, 7 J. Fam. L. 297 (1967).

statutory ones. However, certain impediments that cause a void or voidable marital status, such as a prior existing marriage, fraud,[2] and prohibited family relationship, may also be raised in a common law marriage dispute. It is the nature of the impediment that distinguishes void and voidable marriages. Specific impediments are discussed below.

A "void" marriage is regarded at common law or by statute as an absolute nullity, creating no legal rights and incapable of ratification; it is as if no marriage ever existed.[3] Though divorce or annulment of a void marriage is possible and advisable,[4] it is not required by law, and either party to a void marriage is free without legal action to terminate the relationship and even remarry.[5] A void marriage may be attacked either by the parties to it or by third parties, directly or collaterally, during the parties' lifetimes. A finding that a remarriage is void may be used to reinstate alimony rights which were terminated by that remarriage.[6] A void marriage, such as an incestuous one between uncle and niece, may even be challenged after the death of the parties.[7]

Ohio statutes relating to marriage, divorce, and annulment do not mention "void" or "voidable" marriages. It has been suggested by foreign courts that statutes legitimizing children born of void and voidable marriages (such as Ohio's former RC 3105.33)[8] are irreconcilable with the view that a marriage is void.[9]

---

[2]The Ninth Appellate District Court found a wife's alleged false representation as to wealth and external conditions when the parties met in an internet chat room did not constitute such fraud as would justify an annulment or the award of attorney fees to the husband. Stepp v. Stepp, 2004-Ohio-1617, 2004 WL 626116 (Ohio Ct. App. 9th Dist. Medina County 2004).

[3]Mazzolini v. Mazzolini, 168 Ohio St. 357, 7 Ohio Op. 2d 123, 155 N.E.2d 206 (1958); Nyhuis v. Pierce, 65 Ohio L. Abs. 73, 114 N.E.2d 75 (Ct. App. 8th Dist. Cuyahoga County 1952); Short v. Short, 61 Ohio L. Abs. 49, 102 N.E.2d 719 (Ct. App. 8th Dist. Cuyahoga County 1951). But see Eggleston v. Eggleston, 156 Ohio St. 422, 46 Ohio Op. 351, 103 N.E.2d 395 (1952) (second, bigamous marriage held not legal marriage).

[4]See Text Ch 7, Annulment; Text Ch 11, Divorce.

[5]Williams v. Williams, 90 Ohio App. 369, 48 Ohio Op. 21, 106 N.E.2d 655 (8th Dist. Cuyahoga County 1951).

[6]Watts v. Watts, 250 Neb. 38, 547 N.W.2d 466 (1996); generally, concerning rights and liabilities arising from void marriages, see Annot., 2 A.L.R. 2d 637; Annot., 14 A.L.R. 2d 918; Annot., 72 A.L.R. 2d 956; Annot., 81 A.L.R. 3d 281.

[7]Heyse v. Michalske, 18 Ohio Op. 254, 31, 31 Ohio L. Abs. 484, 6 Ohio Supp. 33 (Prob. Ct. 1940).

[8]See RC 3111.03 (presumptions as to father and child relationships).

[9]Perlstein v. Perlstein, 152 Conn. 152, 204 A.2d 909 (1964).

A voidable marriage differs from a void marriage in that it may be
either annulled or ratified upon removal of the impediment.[10] A voidable marriage is valid until set aside by court decree.[11] A voidable
marriage may only be terminated by annulment during the life of the
parties and may not be attacked collaterally or after either party's
death.[12]

§ 2:59 Void and voidable marriages—Specific impediments— In general

Most impediments to marriage have been held to create a voidable
legal status, terminable always by annulment[1] and sometimes by
divorce,[2] depending on the specific grounds raised by the impediment.
The following defects create a voidable marriage: fraud, jest, or lack of
consent;[3] duress or force;[4] nonconsummation;[5] and physical incapacity.[6]
A defect in the marriage license procedure was ruled to make a marriage voidable, but not void, by an Ohio appeals court. The issue arose
when the adult children of a decedent attempted to have his marriage
a decade earlier declared invalid because the minister who solemnized
the marriage did not obtain a license for the purpose of solemnizing
marriages. The minister was a licensed minister, but had failed to
comply with RC 3101.08 to obtain a second license for purpose of
solemnizing marriages. Because this defect made the marriage voidable rather than void, the court determined that the wife was the

---

[10]Mazzolini v. Mazzolini, 168 Ohio St. 357, 7 Ohio Op. 2d 123, 155 N.E.2d 206
(1958); Heyse v. Michalske, 18 Ohio Op. 254, 31, 31 Ohio L. Abs. 484, 6 Ohio Supp. 33
(Prob. Ct. 1940).

[11]Johnson v. Wolford, 117 Ohio St. 136, 5 Ohio L. Abs. 402, 157 N.E. 385 (1927).

[12]Heyse v. Michalske, 18 Ohio Op. 254, 31 Ohio L. Abs. 484, 6 Ohio Supp. 33
(Prob. Ct. 1940). See also Hitchens v. Hitchens, 47 F. Supp. 73 (D. D.C. 1942); In re
Guthery's Estate, 205 Mo. App. 664, 226 S.W. 626 (1920).

[Section 2:59]

[1]See RC 3105.31 (grounds for annulment).

[2]See RC 3105.01 (grounds for divorce).

[3]RC 3105.01(F), RC 3105.31(D). See also Meyer v. Meyer, 4 Ohio Dec. Rep. 345,
7 Ohio Dec. Rep. 561, 1 Cleve. Law Rep. 347, 3 W.L.B. 985, 1878 WL 7379 (Ohio C.P.
1878), aff'd, 7 Ohio Dec. Rep. 627, 4 W.L.B. 368, 1879 WL 6394 (Ohio Dist. Ct. 1879);
Conley v. Conley, 28 Ohio Op. 289, 14 Ohio Supp. 22, 1943 WL 6289 (C.P. 1943);
Annot., 14 A.L.R. 2d 624.

[4]RC 3105.31(E). See also Annot., 16 A.L.R. 2d 1430.

[5]RC 3105.31(F). See also Meyer v. Meyer, 4 Ohio Dec. Rep. 345, 7 Ohio Dec.
Rep. 561, 1 Cleve. Law Rep. 347, 3 W.L.B. 985, 1878 WL 7379 (Ohio C.P. 1878), aff'd,
7 Ohio Dec. Rep. 627, 4 W.L.B. 368, 1879 WL 6394 (Ohio Dist. Ct. 1879); Text § 2:14,
Ceremonial marriage—Consummation.

[6]McDowell v. Sapp, 39 Ohio St. 558, 1883 WL 213 (1883). See also Text § 2:22,
Capacity to marry—Physical capacity; Annot., 52 A.L.R. 3d 589.

surviving spouse of the decedent and entitled to inherit accordingly under decedent's estate.[7]

The impediments that create void marital status, which may at the option of either party be annulled or simply abandoned without court action, are limited to the most serious violations of statute or public policy. Based upon strong presumptions in favor of marriage, courts have gradually come to recognize that even these serious impediments may be removed in most cases, and the marriage thus becomes subject to ratification. This appears inconsistent with the void/voidable distinctions; it is a voidable marriage which is characterized as subject to later ratification, while marriage void ab initio cannot, in theory, be salvaged by any act of the parties. The simplest example is the absolutely void union of underage partners, which can be declared a nullity by either of them during nonage, but which Ohio courts say can also be ratified by them upon their attainment of the age of consent. As explained below, the best resolution for this decisional inconsistency is to recognize that most void marriages at some stage lose their void status and become instead voidable. This carries legal implications with respect to such matters as collateral attack,[8] but more importantly with respect to the necessity of divorce or annulment before remarriage.

§ 2:60   Void and voidable marriages—Specific impediments— Nonage

Marriage by a male under eighteen or a female under sixteen is said to be void in Ohio,[1] but the state's courts also say that such marriages become ratifiable upon expiration of the disability; at that time the "void" marriage ripens into a "voidable" one and continued cohabitation as husband and wife or other affirmative act will serve to ratify it.[2] No new marriage or agreement is necessary to make the marriage valid.[3] In light of these rulings finding voidability rather than voidness in such unions, simple abandonment of the marriage is

---

[7]Dodrill v. Dodrill, 2004-Ohio-2225, 2004 WL 938476 (Ohio Ct. App. 4th Dist. Vinton County 2004), appeal not allowed by 103 Ohio St.3d 1463, 2004-Ohio-5056, 815 N.E.2d 678 (2004).

[8]See Text § 2:58, Void and voidable marriages—Definitions.

[Section 2:60]

[1]See Text § 2:16, Capacity to marry—Legal age. This view is contrary to that of a majority of states.

[2]RC 3105.31(A). Shafher v. State, 20 Ohio 1, 1851 WL 1 (1851); Holtz v. Dick, 42 Ohio St. 23, 1884 WL 197 (1884); McDowell v. Sapp, 39 Ohio St. 558, 1883 WL 213 (1883); Peefer v. State, 42 Ohio App. 276, 12 Ohio L. Abs. 583, 182 N.E. 117 (2d Dist. Greene County 1931); In re Zemmick's Estate, 32 Ohio Op. 504, 44, 44 Ohio L. Abs. 390, 17 Ohio Supp. 15 (Prob. Ct. 1945), aff'd, 49 Ohio L. Abs. 353, 76 N.E.2d 902 (Ct. App. 7th Dist. Belmont County 1946); Matter of Ababseh, 1996 WL 116148 (Ohio Ct. App. 7th Dist. Mahoning County 1996).

[3]State v. Wilcox, 26 Ohio N.P. (n.s.) 343, 1926 WL 2503 (Juv. Ct. 1926); In re Zemmick's Estate, 32 Ohio Op. 504, 44, 44 Ohio L. Abs. 390, 17 Ohio Supp. 15 (Prob.

inadvisable; annulment is called for, at least where the parties have attained statutory age before one decides to end the relationship.[4]

§ 2:61   Void and voidable marriages—Specific impediments— Bigamy

A bigamous marriage, wherein either party has a spouse from a prior undissolved marriage living, is also deemed absolutely void in Ohio.[1] A prior wife has even been deemed to have standing to bring an action for annulment of a subsequent ceremonial marriage by her alleged common law husband to another woman, provided she could prove the existence of the common law marriage at the time of the remarriage.[2]

But once again, in an effort to enforce public policies favoring marriage, courts view the void bigamous marriage as becoming a voidable (and thus ratifiable) marriage upon removal of the disability[3] by the divorce,[4] death,[5] or presumed death[6] of the former spouse.

Some divorced parties have found themselves suddenly classified as bigamists through no intent of their own, when one or both remarried after their dissolution was entered, but their dissolution decree was subsequently vacated upon a Civil Rule 60(B) motion. After a thorough discussion of the Ohio precedents on this matter, one court held that "when one or both of the parties have remarried, 60(B) is not the proper recourse [because it interferes with one's fundamental right to marry]. Instead, the aggrieved party may seek relief in a damages action or in any other appropriate action at common law. In the present case, this would mean that [the aggrieved party] could possibly bring, for example, an action for an accounting, declaratory judgment,

---

Ct. 1945), aff'd, 49 Ohio L. Abs. 353, 76 N.E.2d 902 (Ct. App. 7th Dist. Belmont County 1946).

[4]RC 3105.31(A).

[Section 2:61]

[1]See Text § 2:16, Capacity to marry—Legal age. See also Moore v. Moore, 2000 WL 1782328 (Ohio Ct. App. 12th Dist. Brown County 2000) (alleged bigamous marriage of wife prior to divorce cannot render the issue of spousal support moot, because a second, bigamous marriage is void ab initio).

[2]Thomas-Schafer v. Schafer, 111 Ohio App. 3d 779, 677 N.E.2d 374 (1st Dist. Hamilton County 1996).

[3]Ryan v. Ryan, 84 Ohio App. 139, 39 Ohio Op. 166, 86 N.E.2d 44 (5th Dist. Stark County 1948); Hale v. Graham, 85 Ohio App. 447, 40 Ohio Op. 305, 86 N.E.2d 330 (9th Dist. Summit County 1948); In re Partlow's Estate, 105 Ohio App. 189, 6 Ohio Op. 2d 29, 77 Ohio L. Abs. 59, 146 N.E.2d 147 (8th Dist. Cuyahoga County 1957).

[4]But such divorce must be proven; it will not be presumed. See Text § 2:53, Proof of marriage—Presumptions.

[5]Johnson v. Wolford, 117 Ohio St. 136, 5 Ohio L. Abs. 402, 157 N.E. 385 (1927); Jenkins v. Jenkins, 30 Ohio App. 336, 6 Ohio L. Abs. 596, 164 N.E. 790 (6th Dist. Sandusky County 1928).

[6]See Text § 2:65, Termination of marriage.

conversion, damages, or unjust enrichment."[7] Taking a different approach to this dilemma, the Colorado Supreme Court has ruled that when a divorce court enters a divorce decree it is a final order with respect to the marital status of the parties—provided that grounds were not contested—even though it is not final for purposes of appellate review. The court analyzed the case in terms of the Uniform Marriage and Divorce Act, and found that parties need finality as to their marital status, even though financial matters may remain contested on appeal.[8]

Bigamy, the offense of willfully and knowingly contracting a second marriage while the first marriage, to the knowledge of the offender, is still subsisting and undissolved,[9] should be distinguished from polygamy, the offense of having several husbands or wives at the same time, or the practice of simultaneous marriage of one man with two or more women.[10]

§ 2:62 Void and voidable marriages—Specific impediments— Mental incompetence

Mental incompetence appears to be another disability that can render a marriage void,[1] yet it is capable of ratification if cohabitation follows recovery of mental stability.[2] In a Nebraska case, *Homan v. Homan*,[3] a marriage was deemed ratified where cohabitation occurred during a "recovery" that was in fact only a period of lucidity. In light of the muddled state of the law in this area, compounded by changing societal, medical, and legal views of mental disabilities, it is safer to seek annulment of such a marriage under RC 3105.31(C) where applicable, or divorce under RC Chapter 3105, rather than allow one

---

[7]Whitman v. Whitman, 1996 WL 276379, at *5 (Ohio Ct. App. 3d Dist. Hancock County 1996), appeal allowed, 77 Ohio St. 3d 1478, 673 N.E.2d 141 (1996) and judgment rev'd, 1998-Ohio-466, 81 Ohio St. 3d 239, 690 N.E.2d 535 (1998).

[8]Estate of Burford v. Burford, 935 P.2d 943 (Colo. 1997).

[9]Black's Law Dictionary (5th ed.) p 148; see Samuel Green & John V. Long, *Marriage and Family Law Agreements* 1.18 (1997).

[10]Black's Law Dictionary (5th ed.) p 1044; see Samuel Green & John V. Long, *Marriage and Family Law Agreements* 1.18 (1997). Recent efforts to eliminate polygamy in the United States, and to redefine and defend it, are examined in *Maura I. Strassberg, The Challenge of Post-Modern Polygamy: Considering Polyamory*, 31 Cap. U.L. Rev. 439 (2003).

[Section 2:62]

[1]See Text § 2:24, Capacity to marry—Mental capacity. See also Waymire v. Jetmore, 22 Ohio St. 271, 1872 WL 1 (1872); Short v. Short, 61 Ohio L. Abs. 49, 102 N.E.2d 719 (Ct. App. 8th Dist. Cuyahoga County 1951).

[2]McDowell v. Sapp, 39 Ohio St. 558, 1883 WL 213 (1883); Goodheart v. Ransley, 11 Ohio Dec. Rep. 655, 28 W.L.B. 227, 1892 WL 356 (Ohio C.P. 1892), aff'd, 7 Ohio C.D. 47, 1893 WL 324 (Ohio Cir. Ct. 1893); Heath v. Heath, 25 Ohio N.P. (n.s.) 123, 1924 WL 2200 (C.P. 1924). But see Goodheart v. Ransley, 11 Ohio Dec. Rep. 655, 28 W.L.B. 227, 1892 WL 356 (Ohio C.P. 1892), aff'd, 7 Ohio C.D. 47, 1893 WL 324 (Ohio Cir. Ct. 1893) (attempted ratification nullity where insanity recurred afterwards).

[3]Homan v. Homan, 181 Neb. 259, 147 N.W.2d 630 (1967).

party to simply abandon the marriage as void and risk a subsequent contrary court opinion.

The issue of what constitutes sufficient mental competence to contract a valid marriage often arises in the case of challenges by heirs to marriages entered into by the elderly.[4] One court held that the test is whether there is capacity to understand the nature of the contract and the duties and responsibilities which it creates.[5] An Ohio court refused to let relatives annul a marriage which occurred two days prior to the husband's death, as the decedent was never during his lifetime judged mentally incompetent. "We decline to enlarge the category of 'party aggrieved' [per RC 3105.22] under fraud and failure to consummate to include relatives who believe they have been cheated of their inheritance."[6]

§ 2:63 Void and voidable marriages—Specific impediments— Consanguinity

Equally muddled is the status of marriage within prohibited degrees of relationship.[1] RC 3101.01 denies a marriage license to certain types of relatives, but a marriage in violation of this statute is not declared to be void. Further, such a marriage is not cited as a ground for either annulment[2] or divorce.[3] Perhaps the legislature saw no reason to annul what courts have called a void incestuous relationship.[4] But the legislature in 1974 repealed criminal sanctions for fornication and adultery between kin closer than cousins.[5] Earlier cases relied on this felony statute as well as public policy to declare such marriages void ab initio.[6] In *Mazzolini v. Mazzolini*,[7] the Ohio Supreme Court held that a first-cousin marriage was not void in the absence of a statute so declaring. Once again, it appears prudent not to rely on an assumption of voidness and to instead seek an annulment or divorce in such cases.

---

[4]See Samuel Green & John V. Long, *Marriage and Family Law Agreements* 1.19 (1997).

[5]In re Estate of Hendrickson, 248 Kan. 72, 805 P.2d 20 (1991).

[6]Hilt v. Diedrich, 1990 WL 121487 (Ohio Ct. App. 3d Dist. Mercer County 1990).

[Section 2:63]

[1]See Text § 2:26, Capacity to marry—Relationships of the parties.

[2]RC 3105.31.

[3]RC 3105.01.

[4]In re Stiles Estate, 59 Ohio St. 2d 73, 13 Ohio Op. 3d 62, 391 N.E.2d 1026 (1979); Basickas v. Basickas, 93 Ohio App. 531, 51 Ohio Op. 229, 114 N.E.2d 270 (9th Dist. Summit County 1953); Heyse v. Michalske, 18 Ohio Op. 254, 31, 31 Ohio L. Abs. 484, 6 Ohio Supp. 33 (Prob. Ct. 1940); 52 Am. Jur. 2d, Annulment of Marriage § 10.

[5]RC 2905.07, repealed by 1972 H.B. 511, eff. 1-1-74.

[6]Basickas v. Basickas, 93 Ohio App. 531, 51 Ohio Op. 229, 114 N.E.2d 270 (9th Dist. Summit County 1953); Heyse v. Michalske, 18 Ohio Op. 254, 31, 31 Ohio L. Abs. 484, 6 Ohio Supp. 33 (Prob. Ct. 1940).

[7]Mazzolini v. Mazzolini, 168 Ohio St. 357, 7 Ohio Op. 2d 123, 155 N.E.2d 206 (1958).

After the Ohio Supreme Court in *State ex rel. Soley v. Dorrell*[8] approved the authority of a trial court to determine the law of marriage between first cousins, the trial court did so, finding a valid marriage. In affirming, the court of appeals in *Soley v. Soley*[9] distinguished a marriage between uncle and niece and blood first cousins, the latter being voidable rather than void.

In *Soley v. Soley*,[10] the Wood County trial court permitted intervention by a first wife following a dissolution between the husband and purported second wife. The husband had married the second wife in Hungary while his first marriage was being litigated in Lucas County, and after he had ostensibly obtained a Dominican Republic divorce. The intervenor was successful in having the dissolution decree vacated based upon a bigamous marriage which was void and ineffective. The court of appeals affirmed the intervention and the vacating of the decree.

§ 2:64 Void marriage as criminal defense

Several criminal defendants charged with sex crimes have unsuccessfully claimed error on appeal by the failure of the state to prove that they were not married to the victim of the crime, where the criminal statute excludes "the spouse of the offender." Where the rape victim of the male defendant was a 12-year old boy, and the defendant was already married, the court found it not appropriate to give a jury instruction as to the spousal status between defendant and victim, as it was legally impossible for them to be married.[1] Where the six-year old gross sexual imposition victim was the defendant's stepson, it was a legal impossibility for the two to be legally married, so there was no need for the state to present evidence as to their spousal relationship.[2]

§ 2:65 Termination of marriage

Termination of marriage occurs only through court actions of divorce,[1] dissolution,[2] or annulment,[3] or due to death, or presumption of

---

[8]State ex rel. Soley v. Dorrell, 1994-Ohio-103, 69 Ohio St. 3d 514, 634 N.E.2d 215 (1994).

[9]Soley v. Soley, 101 Ohio App. 3d 540, 655 N.E.2d 1381 (6th Dist. Lucas County 1995), dismissed, appeal not allowed, 73 Ohio St. 3d 1410, 651 N.E.2d 1308 (1995).

[10]In Matter of Soley, 1995 WL 84691 (Ohio Ct. App. 6th Dist. Wood County 1995), dismissed, appeal not allowed, 73 Ohio St. 3d 1410, 651 N.E.2d 1308 (1995).

[Section 2:64]

[1]State v. Bock, 28 Ohio St. 3d 108, 502 N.E.2d 1016 (1986).

[2]State v. Bodine, 1990 WL 106456 (Ohio Ct. App. 6th Dist. Sandusky County 1990).

[Section 2:65]

[1]See Text Ch 11, Divorce.

[2]See Text Ch 10, Dissolution of Marriage.

death. Marriage is not terminable at the will of either party or by their mutual agreement.[4]

For estate purposes, the Presumed Decedents' Law[5] sets a period of five years' absence to create a presumption of death, but this law has been held inapplicable to other legal circumstances,[6] which are governed by the common law presumption of death arising seven years after disappearance.[7] This common law presumption, which may be rebutted by contrary evidence,[8] requires an unexplained continuous absence from the home without any contrary intelligence from or about the person in question for a full seven years.[9] The time of death is not established by the presumption; it is simply presumed that the absentee is, at the end of the seven years, dead.[10]

In some instances, a sudden disappearance under circumstances that strongly suggest death has been held to create the presumption of death after a period shorter than seven years.[11]

§ 2:66 Cohabitation

The U.S. Census Bureau estimated in 2007 that unmarried cohabitants comprised 4.7% of the country's 111 million households, or about 10 million individuals, and unmarried cohabitants comprised 4.8 percent of Ohio's 4.5 million households, or about 432,000 individuals. These figures do not include the children of those unmar-

---

[3]See Text Ch 7, Annulment.

[4]Burke v. Burke, 36 Ohio App. 551, 8 Ohio L. Abs. 682, 173 N.E. 637 (6th Dist. Lucas County 1930); Hardin v. Davis, 30 Ohio Op. 524, 16 Ohio Supp. 19, 1945 WL 5519 (C.P. 1945).

[5]RC 2121.01.

[6]White v. Industrial Commission, 102 Ohio App. 236, 2 Ohio Op. 2d 264, 142 N.E.2d 549 (10th Dist. Franklin County 1956).

[7]In re McWilson's Estate, 155 Ohio St. 261, 44 Ohio Op. 262, 98 N.E.2d 289 (1951).

[8]Brunny v. Prudential Ins. Co. of America, 151 Ohio St. 86, 38 Ohio Op. 533, 84 N.E.2d 504 (1949); Jones v. Industrial Commission, 30 Ohio L. Abs. 7, 1939 WL 3247 (Ct. App. 2d Dist. Franklin County 1939).

[9]Jones v. Industrial Commission, 30 Ohio L. Abs. 7, 1939 WL 3247 (Ct. App. 2d Dist. Franklin County 1939); see also In re McWilson's Estate, 155 Ohio St. 261, 44 Ohio Op. 262, 98 N.E.2d 289 (1951); Stover's Heirs v. Bounds' Heirs, 1 Ohio St. 107, 1853 WL 1 (1853); Supreme Commandery of Order of Knights of Golden Rule v. Everding, 11 Ohio C.D. 419, 1893 WL 333 (Ohio Cir. Ct. 1893), dismissed by 29 W.L.B. 415.

[10]Thompson v. Parrett, 82 Ohio App. 366, 38 Ohio Op. 42, 52 Ohio L. Abs. 16, 78 N.E.2d 419 (2d Dist. Franklin County 1948); Young v. Young, 10 Ohio App. 351, 1918 WL 1133 (2d Dist. Franklin County 1918).

[11]Jones v. Industrial Commission, 30 Ohio L. Abs. 7, 1939 WL 3247 (Ct. App. 2d Dist. Franklin County 1939); Travelers' Ins. Co. v. Rosch, 13 Ohio Cir. Dec. 491, 3 Ohio C.C.(n.s.) 156 (Cir., Lorain 1902), affirmed by 69 Ohio St. 561, 70 N.E. 1133 (1903); see RC 2121.01(A)(2); Skele v. Mutual Ben. Life Ins. Co., 20 Ohio App. 3d 213, 485 N.E.2d 770 (2d Dist. Miami County 1984).

ried cohabitants, or same-gender-couple households.[1] The number of unmarried cohabitant households ballooned a thousand percent, from about a half million in 1970, to over 5 million in 2000.[2]

Perhaps no other area of family relationships has received less attention from courts and legislatures than nonmarital cohabitation, compared to the pervasiveness of this lifestyle in modern American society[3] and the extensive attention the subject receives from legal authorities.[4] The only Ohio statutory reference to the rights and duties of nonmarital partners appears in the domestic violence statutes, which extend coverage to "persons living as spouses" in a cohabiting relationship.[5] Case law on nonmarital cohabitation is limited to such matters as the effect of such arrangements on post-decree alimony rights.[6] Ohio courts have not yet reported a decision defining the rights and duties of cohabitants, though in *Haas v. Lewis*,[7] one appel-

---

[Section 2:66]

[1]U.S. Census Bureau (www.census.gov), American Community Survey, S1101. Households and Families, Data Set: 2005-2007 American Community Survey 3-Year Estimates.

[2]Jason Fields & Lynne M. Casper, U.S. Census Bureau, P20-537, America's Families and Living Arrangements: Population Characteristics (2001).

[3]See Samuel Green & John V. Long, *Marriage and Family Law Agreements* 3.01 (1997). News sources say the number of households of unmarried couples has increased 600% since 1970, now totalling 4% to 6% of all U.S. households.

[4]See J. Thomas Oldham & David S. Caudill, *A Reconnaissance of Public Policy Restrictions upon Enforcement of Contracts Between Cohabitants*, 18 Fam. L.Q. 93 (Spring 1984); Charles F. Crutchfield, *Nonmarital Relationships and Their Impact on the Institution of Marriage and the Traditional Family Structure*, 19 J. Fam. L. 247 (1981); Phyllis W. Beck, *Nontraditional Lifestyles and the Law*, 17 J. Fam. L. 685 (1978–79); Ward, *Settlement of Property Rights upon Termination of Cohabitation Arrangement*, 46 Cin. L. Rev. 924 (1977); H. Jay Folberg & William P. Buren, *A Proposal for Dividing the Property of Unmarried Families*, 12 Willamette L.J. 453 (1976); Mary DeNevi, Note, *Reasonable Expectations in Nonmarital Cohabitation: A Proposal for Recovery*, 21 B.C.L. Rev. 889 (1980); Craig A. Bowman & Blake M. Cornish, *A More Perfect Union: A Legal and Social Analysis of Domestic Partnership Ordinances*, 92 Colum. L. Rev. 1164 (1992); William A. Reppy, Jr., *Property and Support Rights of Unmarried Cohabitants: A Proposal for Creating A New Legal Status*, 44 La. L. Rev. 1677 (1984); Annot., 3 A.L.R. 4th 13; Jane Massey Draper, Annot., Recovery for Services Rendered by Persons Living in Apparent Relation of Husband and Wife Without Express Agreement for Compensation, 94 A.L.R. 3d 552.

[5]RC 2919.25(D)(2), RC 3113.31(A)(4), RC 3113.33(D).

[6]Taylor v. Taylor, 11 Ohio App. 3d 279, 465 N.E.2d 476 (1st Dist. Hamilton County 1983); Fuller v. Fuller, 10 Ohio App. 3d 253, 461 N.E.2d 1348 (10th Dist. Franklin County 1983); Fahrer v. Fahrer, 36 Ohio App. 2d 208, 65 Ohio Op. 2d 330, 304 N.E.2d 411 (1st Dist. Hamilton County 1973). See also Samuel Green & John V. Long, *Marriage and Family Law Agreements* 3.24 (1997).

[7]Haas v. Lewis, 8 Ohio App. 3d 136, 456 N.E.2d 512 (10th Dist. Franklin County 1982).

late court ruled that consortium rights cannot be claimed without marriage.[8]

Despite the number of citizens choosing to live together unwed, nonmarital cohabitation still finds itself as an "illicit" (prohibited) or "meretricious" (pertaining to an unlawful sexual connection, from the Latin for prostitute) relationship, though cohabitation is illegal in only thirteen states.[9] Courts in at least one state, Washington, use the term "meretricious relationship" to recognize serious cohabiting relationships in the way Ohio courts used to recognize "common law marriage." Washington courts define a meretricious relationship as a stable, marital-like relationship where both parties cohabit with knowledge that they are not lawfully married.[10] Use of the disparaging term "meretricious" in discussing unmarried persons living together has come under judicial fire:

> Much of the case law speaks of such a relationship as "meretricious". Defined as "Of or pertaining to a prostitute; having a harlot's traits" (Webster's Third New International Dictionary Unabridged, p. 1413), that word's pejorative sense makes it no longer, if it ever was, descriptive of the relationship under consideration, and we, therefore, decline to use it.[11]

Cohabitation is not illegal in Ohio, except in cases of bigamy,[12] and Ohio has abolished adultery and fornication as crimes.[13] The Model Penal Code drafters opposed criminal sanctions for adultery, fornication, and cohabitation.[14] Virginia's criminal fornication and cohabitation statutes have even been struck down as an unconstitutional inva-

---

[8]Annot., 40 A.L.R. 4th 553. Contra Ledger v. Tippitt, 164 Cal. App. 3d 625, 210 Cal. Rptr. 814 (2d Dist. 1985) (disapproved of by, Elden v. Sheldon, 46 Cal. 3d 267, 250 Cal. Rptr. 254, 758 P.2d 582 (1988)) (cause of action for loss of consortium exists in favor of common law marriage partner); Lauper v. Harold, 23 Ohio App. 3d 168, 492 N.E.2d 472 (12th Dist. Butler County 1985) (court has no authority to divide assets of parties based on cohabitation without marriage).

[9]As of 1996, cohabitation was illegal in Alabama, Arizona, Florida, Idaho, Illinois, Kansas, Massachusetts, Michigan, New Mexico, North Carolina, South Carolina, West Virginia, and Wisconsin. The constitutionality of such laws is drawn into question by the federal court ruling striking down Virginia's fornication and cohabitation statutes on privacy grounds. Doe v. Duling, 603 F. Supp. 960 (E.D. Va. 1985), decision vacated, 782 F.2d 1202 (4th Cir. 1986); see Samuel Green & John V. Long, *Marriage and Family Law Agreements* 3.14 (1997).

[10]Connell v. Francisco, 127 Wash. 2d 339, 898 P.2d 831, 69 A.L.R.5th 705 (1995).

[11]Morone v. Morone, 50 N.Y.2d 481, 486 n.2, 429 N.Y.S.2d 592, 413 N.E.2d 1154, 1156 (1980).

[12]RC 2919.01.

[13]Former RC 2905.08, repealed by 1972 H.B. 511, eff. 1-1-74 ("No person shall cohabit in a state of adultery or fornication."). State v. Brown, 47 Ohio St. 102, 23 N.E. 747 (1890) (single sexual act held not to constitute violation). See also Latham v. Latham, 274 Or. 421, 547 P.2d 144 (1976); Robert A. Brazener, Annot., Validity of Statute Making Adultery and Fornication Criminal Offenses, 41 A.L.R. 3d 1338.

[14]Model Penal Code § 213.6 note on adultery and fornication (ALI 1980).

sion of privacy rights.[15] Thus, to obey the precedent of cases denying relief to cohabitants upon termination, often with cruelly unfair results,[16] based on the legal theory that the agreements of the partners rest upon the void consideration of sexual services,[17] appears unjustifiable under modern statutes and social conditions.

§ 2:67 Cohabitants' legal remedies—In other states

Those courts that have aided cohabitants in sorting out their property rights upon breaking up, and occasionally by awarding support for so-called "palimony," have relied on a variety of legal and equitable theories,[1] including express contract,[2] implied contract,[3] joint venture/implied partnership,[4] equitable distribution based on "quasi-marital" relationship,[5] "just and equitable distribution,"[6] equitable

---

[15]Doe v. Duling, 603 F. Supp. 960 (E.D. Va. 1985), decision vacated, 782 F.2d 1202 (4th Cir. 1986).

[16]Rehak v. Mathis, 239 Ga. 541, 238 S.E.2d 81 (1977); Wellmaker v. Roberts, 213 Ga. 740, 101 S.E.2d 712 (1958); Hewitt v. Hewitt, 77 Ill. 2d 49, 61, 31 Ill. Dec. 827, 394 N.E.2d 1204, 3 A.L.R.4th 1 (1979) (fifteen-year relationship; woman helped put man through dental school and bore him three children; alleged contract held unenforceable to "preserve the integrity of marriage").

[17]See Samuel Green & John V. Long, *Marriage and Family Law Agreements* 3.14 (1997).

[Section 2:67]

[1]See Samuel Green & John V. Long, *Marriage and Family Law Agreements* 3.16 et seq. (1997); Joel E. Smith, Annot., Property Rights Arising from Relationship of Couple Cohabiting Without Marriage, 3 A.L.R. 4th 13; Francis M. Dougherty, Annot., Waiver of Statutory Demand-for-Rent Due or of Notice-to-Quit Prerequisite of Summary Eviction of Lessee for Nonpayment of Rent—Modern Cases, 31 A.L.R. 2d 1255; Charles W. Bohmfalk, *Property Rights of Nonmarital Partners in Meretricious Cohabitation,* 13 New Eng. L. Rev. 453 (1978); Bruce K. Childers & Marianne M. Jennings, *Legal Theories Available for a Marvin Case,* 3 Fam. Advoc. 30 (Summer 1980).

[2]Marvin v. Marvin, 18 Cal. 3d 660, 134 Cal. Rptr. 815, 557 P.2d 106 (1976); Whorton v. Dillingham, 202 Cal. App. 3d 447, 248 Cal. Rptr. 405 (4th Dist. 1988); Morone v. Morone, 50 N.Y.2d 481, 429 N.Y.S.2d 592, 413 N.E.2d 1154 (1980); Hay v. Hay, 100 Nev. 196, 678 P.2d 672 (1984); Kozlowski v. Kozlowski, 80 N.J. 378, 403 A.2d 902 (1979); Fernandez v. Garza, 88 Ariz. 214, 354 P.2d 260 (1960); Wilcox v. Trautz, 427 Mass. 326, 693 N.E.2d 141 (1998).

[3]Marvin v. Marvin, 18 Cal. 3d 660, 134 Cal. Rptr. 815, 557 P.2d 106 (1976); Carlson v. Olson, 256 N.W.2d 249 (Minn. 1977); Boland v. Catalano, 202 Conn. 333, 521 A.2d 142 (1987); see Jane Massey Draper, Annot., Recovery for Services Rendered by Persons Living in Apparent Relation of Husband and Wife Without Express Agreement for Compensation, 94 A.L.R. 3d 552.

[4]Marvin v. Marvin, 18 Cal. 3d 660, 134 Cal. Rptr. 815, 557 P.2d 106 (1976); In re Thornton's Estate, 81 Wash. 2d 72, 499 P.2d 864 (1972); Leek v. Powell, 884 S.W.2d 118 (Tenn. Ct. App. 1994).

[5]Zion Const., Inc. v. Gilmore, 78 Wash. App. 87, 895 P.2d 864 (Div. 1 1995), review granted, cause remanded, 127 Wash. 2d 1022, 904 P.2d 1157 (1995).

[6]Connell v. Francisco, 127 Wash. 2d 339, 898 P.2d 831, 69 A.L.R.5th 705 (1995); In re Sutton and Widner, 85 Wash. App. 487, 933 P.2d 1069 (Div. 3 1997).

distribution of property but no spousal maintenance,[7] partition,[8] constructive trust,[9] resulting trust,[10] unjust enrichment based upon confidential fiduciary relationship,[11] quasi-contractual theory of quantum meruit,[12] equitable lien,[13] and community property-like presumption.[14]

Foreign courts have applied other legal tools to protect the legal rights of cohabiting citizens. A U.S. federal district court ruled that cohabitation is a protected activity for which an employer may not discriminate absent a showing that it creates a material conflict of interest with the employer's business.[15] In doing so, the court struck down a New York state appellate division ruling that upheld the firing of two former Wal-Mart employees on the basis that dating was not a protected legal recreational activity. In a decision that put children's interests ahead of some social agendas, the District of Columbia Court of Appeals granted unmarried cohabitants, whether heterosexual or homosexual, the right to jointly adopt a child.[16] The court held that the D.C. Code should be liberally construed to allow adoptions that are in the children's best interests.

Other courts have declined to use legal or equitable tools to help cohabitants dismantle the legal structure of their relationships.[17] Georgia courts have twice struck down attempts by the city of Atlanta to enact a domestic partnership ordinance to provide benefits to the unmarried partners of city employees.[18] A New Jersey court made a similar ruling as to dependents of homosexual state employees.[19] Although the Restatement of the Law of Restitution says it is unjust for

---

[7]Rance v. Rance, 587 N.E.2d 150 (Ind. Ct. App. 3d Dist. 1992).

[8]Carroll v. Lee, 148 Ariz. 10, 712 P.2d 923 (1986).

[9]Evans v. Wall, 542 So. 2d 1055 (Fla. Dist. Ct. App. 3d Dist. 1989); Williams v. Lynch, 245 A.D.2d 715, 666 N.Y.S.2d 749 (3d Dep't 1997).

[10]Collins v. Davis, 68 N.C. App. 588, 315 S.E.2d 759 (1984), decision aff'd, 312 N.C. 324, 321 S.E.2d 892 (1984).

[11]Nini v. Sullivan, No. 95 DR 52 (Colo. 12-31-96), 23 Fam. L. Rep. (BNA) 1127.

[12]Suggs v. Norris, 88 N.C. App. 539, 364 S.E.2d 159 (1988); Middlecoff v. Middlecoff, 160 Cal. App. 2d 22, 324 P.2d 669 (1st Dist. 1958).

[13]Marvin v. Marvin, 18 Cal. 3d 660, 134 Cal. Rptr. 815, 557 P.2d 106 (1976).

[14]Koher v. Morgan, 93 Wash. App. 398, 968 P.2d 920 (Div. 1 1998).

[15]Pasch v. Katz Media Corp., 10 I.E.R. Cas. (BNA) 1574, 1995 WL 469710 (S.D. N.Y. 1995).

[16]In re M.M.D., 662 A.2d 837 (D.C. 1995).

[17]Miller v. Ratner, 114 Md. App. 18, 688 A.2d 976 (1997); Hewitt v. Hewitt, 77 Ill. 2d 49, 31 Ill. Dec. 827, 394 N.E.2d 1204, 3 A.L.R.4th 1 (1979); Rehak v. Mathis, 239 Ga. 541, 238 S.E.2d 81 (1977); Succession of Llula, 44 La. Ann. 61, 10 So. 406 (1892); Davis v. Davis, 643 So. 2d 931 (Miss. 1994).

[18]Morgan v. Atlanta, Ga. Super. Ct. Fulton County, No. E-52854 (12-31-96), 23 Fam. L. Rep. (BNA) 1131; City of Atlanta v. McKinney, 265 Ga. 161, 454 S.E.2d 517 (1995).

[19]Rutgers Council of AAUP Chapters v. Rutgers, The State University, 298 N.J. Super. 442, 689 A.2d 828, 116 Ed. Law Rep. 731 (App. Div. 1997); but see contra

a party to go without compensation where he has conferred a benefit in order to protect the life, health, or property of another,[20] restitution is founded in commercial norms. Claims in the family law setting generally have proven unsuccessful, because acts seen rooted in love or obligation are deemed already compensated by the relationship itself.[21]

For most of the millions of American citizens whose cohabiting relationships dissolve, the law of the jungle prevails. Without access to court remedies, except in those rare circumstances where cohabitants contracted against the contingency of a break up, or where other arcane legal remedies are available, any disputed interests accumulated during while the couple lived together will often go to the biggest, or the swiftest, or the one with a gun. The American Law Institute takes the position that upon the termination of "Domestic Partner" relationships, justice should entitle cohabitants to the same property and support rules applicable to divorcing spouses, unless they have contractually opted out of such remedies in advance.[22]

Among commentators there appears to be growing support for recognition of termination rights for unmarried cohabitants. "Marvin is not a California oddity. Other jurisdictions, with and without the encouragement of Marvin, have recognized the futility and injustice of ignoring the legal problems associated with nonmarital relationships."[23] Opposition to the trend toward providing equitable remedies to unmarried cohabitants can also be found,[24] as well as disinterested discussion of the legal issues which cohabitation creates.[25]

The Supreme Court of New Mexico unanimously ruled that a claim for the loss of companionship of a partner is not limited to married couples.[26] In a tort case involving a loss of consortium claim, the court gave a presumption of a close familial relationship to couples who meet the common law marriage elements in those states that allow such marriages, and said this same presumption would be afforded couples engaged to be married and living together. For all other

---

holding in University of Alaska v. Tumeo, 933 P.2d 1147, 117 Ed. Law Rep. 314 (Alaska 1997).

[20]Restatement of Restitution §§ 112–17 (1937).

[21]Ann Laquer Estin, *Love and Obligation: Family Law and the Romance of Economics,* 36 Wm. & Mary L. Rev. 989, 1044–47 (1995).

[22]Am. Law Inst., Principles of the Law of Family Dissolution: Analysis and Recommendations, Ch. 6 (2003).

[23]P. Beth Enos, *The Fearful and Wonderful Ramifications of* Marvin v Marvin, 10 Mem. St. Univ. L. Rev. 61, 74 (1979); see also Carol S. Bruch, *Property Rights of De Facto Spouses Including Thoughts on the Value of Homemakers' Services,* 10 Fam. L.Q. 101 (1976).

[24]See Ruth L. Deech, *The Case Against Legal Recognition of Cohabitation,* 29 Int'l & Comp. L.Q. 480 (1980); Marsha Garrison, *Nonmarital Cohabitation: Social Revolution and Legal Regulation,* 42 Fam. L.Q. 309 (Fall 2008).

[25]See Samuel Green & John V. Long, *Marriage and Family Law Agreements* 3.01 et seq. 1997).

[26]Lozoya v. Sanchez, 2003-NMSC-009, 133 N.M. 579, 66 P.3d 948 (2003).

couples, by a preponderance of the evidence, claimants would be required to prove an intimate familial relationship. The standard for such proof would include the duration of the relationship; the degree of mutual dependence; the extent of common contributions to a life together; and the extent and quality of shared experience. The relationship would also have to be exclusive.

§ 2:68   Cohabitants' legal remedies—Where action brought

Where should claims arising from a cohabitation arrangement or cohabitation agreement be brought: in a general division court which has jurisdiction over contract actions, or in a domestic relations division court which has jurisdiction over termination of marriage statutes? Absent a comprehensive statutory remedy for resolving the disputes of unmarried cohabitants upon termination of their relationships, litigants can easily find themselves in a variety of forums: juvenile court for parenting issues, common pleas court for real estate partition, municipal court for replevin of a vehicle, and small claims court for recovery of personal property. One court to discuss the issue of jurisdiction in such cases found that as a court of equity, the domestic relations court has the power to determine questions of custody, support, and partition of real and personal property between unmarried cohabitants.[1]

In Ohio "[t]he court of common pleas including divisions of courts of domestic relations, has full equitable powers and jurisdiction appropriate to the determination of all domestic relations matters."[2] The purpose of domestic relations laws in Ohio has been held to serve society through protecting and maintaining the family,[3] and a family has been held not to be exclusively defined by biological relationships,[4] so domestic relations courts can be argued to be the proper forum for such disputes. As a practical matter as well, the expertise of domestic relations courts in dealing with the laws of equity and the wreckage of personal relationships would make them preferable for cohabitation cases, where allowed.

§ 2:69   Cohabitants' legal remedies—Few available in Ohio

To date, the Ohio General Assembly has ignored the legal needs of the vast and growing segment of the state population who live

---

[Section 2:68]

[1]Metten v. Benge, 366 N.W.2d 577 (Iowa 1985).

[2]RC 3105.011.

[3]Pashko v. Pashko, 45 Ohio Op. 498, 63 Ohio L. Abs. 82, 101 N.E.2d 804 (C.P. 1951).

[4]Smith v. Organization of Foster Families For Equality and Reform, 431 U.S. 816, 97 S. Ct. 2094, 53 L. Ed. 2d 14 (1977).

together without getting married,[1] apparently on the assumption that legislative disdain will encourage cohabitants to marry.

Ohio courts are equally unaccommodating to those citizens. The Ohio judicial system has generally refused to adopt any of the available legal mechanisms that court of other states have used in order to provide assistance to unmarried cohabitants who turn to the law seeking assistance in dissolving their legal entanglements. Denying relief to a woman cohabitant based upon a claim of unjust enrichment, the court in *Tarry v. Stewart*[2] additionally refused to impose a constructive trust upon assets in the man's name, even though acquired and improved during the parties' cohabitation. The court rejected the argument that Ohio public policy supports the enforcement of contracts between cohabiting individuals, denied that there is any fiduciary relationship between cohabiting individuals, and found no precedent for dividing assets or property based on mere cohabitation without marriage. It has also been held in Ohio that cohabitation will not give rise to a claim for relief on the following grounds: breach of implied contract, a claim of partnership/joint venture, or palimony.[3]

The only chink in Ohio's armor-clad refusal to assist cohabitants in resolving disputes upon termination of their relationships might be found in the theory of unjust enrichment. In *Seward v. Mentrup*, the court acknowledged that a claim of unjust enrichment is possible "in any type of relationship." However, the court brushed off Ms. Seward's claim to nine years' worth of improvements to Mr. Mentrup's real estate, stating she had already enjoyed the benefits by living in the home, and upon termination of the relationship she "received all that she expected."[4] So the court in *Seward* recognized a legal remedy for cohabitants, but denied relief to the plaintiff. Actual damages were awarded in a Logan County case to a woman who lived with her fiance for four years and contributed significant sums to improving his home. The court rejected a constructive trust claim but granted relief based upon unjust enrichment.[5] A "quantum meruit" claim was

---

[Section 2:69]

[1]Best estimates put the proportion of cohabitant households at 4% to 6%. With 15.6 million total households, the number of Ohio citizens living together unwed can be estimated at 1.2 to 1.9 million.

[2]Tarry v. Stewart, 98 Ohio App. 3d 533, 649 N.E.2d 1 (9th Dist. Lorain County 1994).

[3]Lauper v. Harold, 23 Ohio App. 3d 168, 492 N.E.2d 472 (12th Dist. Butler County 1985); Seward v. Mentrup, 87 Ohio App. 3d 601, 622 N.E.2d 756 (12th Dist. Clermont County 1993).

[4]Seward v. Mentrup, 87 Ohio App. 3d 601, 603-04, 622 N.E.2d 756 (12th Dist. Clermont County 1993).

[5]Dixon v. Smith, 119 Ohio App. 3d 308, 695 N.E.2d 284 (3d Dist. Logan County 1997).

sustained by another Ohio appeals court where a woman lived with and cared for her sick ex-husband for six years.[6]

Ohio's judicial disdain for unmarried cohabitants extends into the realm of torts. A loss of consortium claim by an unmarried cohabitant was thrown out in *Haas v. Lewis*.[7] This rule denying a loss of consortium claim has been extended to the affianced. Finding it a "well-settled rule" in Ohio that only a married individual has standing to sue for loss of consortium, another court denied relief to a woman whose fiance was injured in an automobile accident just ten days before their marriage.[8] In so holding, the Ohio courts ignored rulings from other states that an unmarried cohabitant may state a cause of action for loss of consortium by evidence of a deep and significant relationship, or longstanding relational interests, or by demonstrating that "the nonmarital relationship is both stable and significant"[9] and has those characteristics of "significance which one may expect to find in what is essentially a de facto marriage."[10]

In a case where there was no dispute between the cohabitants themselves, an Ohio court upheld the beneficiary designation by a male to his female cohabitant for retirement system death benefits, even though the man died legally married to another woman.[11]

Ohio domestic violence laws extend protection to a "person living as a spouse," including a cohabitant.[12]

§ 2:70 Cohabitation agreements—And related documents[1]

In the controversy that surrounded the "palimony" award in the landmark *Marvin* divorce case, it was widely overlooked that the California Supreme Court specifically upheld the right of unmarried

---

[6]Hartley v. Hartley, No. 96-CA-132 (Ohio Ct. App. 5th Dist. Licking County 1997).

[7]Haas v. Lewis, 8 Ohio App. 3d 136, 456 N.E.2d 512 (10th Dist. Franklin County 1982).

[8]Reygaert v. Palmer, 1986 WL 1340 (Ohio Ct. App. 2d Dist. Montgomery County 1986).

[9]Butcher v. Superior Court, 139 Cal. App. 3d 58, 188 Cal. Rptr. 503, 40 A.L.R. 4th 539 (4th Dist. 1983) (disapproved of by, Elden v. Sheldon, 46 Cal. 3d 267, 250 Cal. Rptr. 254, 758 P.2d 582 (1988)).

[10]Butcher v. Superior Court, 139 Cal. App. 3d 58, 188 Cal. Rptr. 503, 40 A.L.R. 4th 539 (4th Dist. 1983) (disapproved of by, Elden v. Sheldon, 46 Cal. 3d 267, 250 Cal. Rptr. 254, 758 P.2d 582 (1988)); Bulloch v. U. S., 487 F. Supp. 1078 (D.N.J. 1980); Sutherland v. Auch Inter-Borough Transit Co., 366 F. Supp. 127 (E.D. Pa. 1973).

[11]Rakestraw v. City of Cincinnati, 69 Ohio App. 504, 24 Ohio Op. 214, 37 Ohio L. Abs. 159, 44 N.E.2d 278 (1st Dist. Hamilton County 1942).

[12]RC 2919.25, RC 3113.31.

[Section 2:70]

[1]Credit belongs to L. Anthony Lush, Esq. for editorial contributions to this section, including the cohabitation agreement form included below.

couples to enter written or oral contracts.[2] The Ohio Revised Code contains no specific recognition of cohabitation agreements. Several states have considered legislation concerning the rights of unmarried cohabitants, but those proposals have more often been punitive in nature rather than remedial, aimed at denying relief to cohabitants who did not enter a contract, rather than providing a cause of action to assist those individuals.[3] Oregon and Washington appear to be the only states that are considering legislation to define the rights of non-married cohabitants and to provide remedies to protect those rights.[4]

Cohabitants are at great legal risk if they fail to prepare proper legal documents, since they cannot rely on the default civil contract provided by state laws governing marriage. However, cohabitants might actually find it easier simply to get married when they realize how extensive such contracts must be if they are to address the myriad rights and duties which marriage automatically confers, and when they consider the various benefits of marriage which cannot be acquired by contract alone. Nonetheless, in the absence of a valid marriage, written contracts are the best available means for cohabitants to determine their own legal future.[5]

Among the legal documents that will help cohabiting couples structure their legal relationship are a will,[6] trusts, powers of attorney,[7] a durable power of attorney for health care,[8] a living will declaration,[9] contracts to jointly purchase property, real property titles, insurance beneficiary designations, legal adoption decrees for minor children,[10] and a written cohabitation agreement.

A cohabitation agreement should cover all of the essential elements of a domestic partnership: property and debts brought into the cohab-

---

[2]Marvin v. Marvin, 18 Cal. 3d 660, 134 Cal. Rptr. 815, 557 P.2d 106 (1976).

[3]Minnesota's statutes, at M.S.A. §§ 513.075–513.076, now prohibit any property or support claims absent a written contract, while providing no guidance for drafting such contracts, and providing no other protection for cohabitants.

[4]See Samuel Green & John V. Long, *Marriage and Family Law Agreements* 3.25 (1997); Cohabitation Agreements—State Survey, 37 Brandeis Law J. 245 (1988-99).

[5]See Samuel Green & John V. Long, *Marriage and Family Law Agreements* 3.25 (1997); Edward L. Winer & Lewis Becker, *Premarital and Marital Contracts: A Lawyer's Guide to Drafting and Negotiating Enforceable Marital and Cohabitation Agreements* (1993). See also Bradley A. Friedman, *Cohabitation Agreements: Practical and Ethical Considerations,* 13 Am. J. of Fam. Law 246 (1999).

[6]See Joseph W. deFuria, Jr., *Testamentary Gifts Resulting from Meretricious Relationships: Undue Influence or Natural Beneficence?,* 64 Notre Dame L. Rev. 200 (1989).

[7]See Samuel Green & John V. Long, *Marriage and Family Law Agreements* 3.26 (1997).

[8]RC Ch. 1337.

[9]RC Ch. 2133.

[10]A non-biological "parent"—whether of the same or opposite gender—may have no standing to continue a relationship with a child absent a legal adoption. See Nancy S. v. Michele G., 228 Cal. App. 3d 831, 279 Cal. Rptr. 212 (1st Dist. 1991) (disapproved of by, Watkins v. Nelson, 163 N.J. 235, 748 A.2d 558 (2000)); D.G. v.

itation, property ownership and management, income and support, monetary arrangements including payment of debts, tax issues, residence, division of household duties and expenses, insurance, health and medical care, dispute resolution, issues arising upon possible termination of the relationship including support rights, issues arising upon death, issues relating to children,[11] birth control,[12] and pension rights.[13]

§ 2:71   Cohabitation agreements—Form⊚

COHABITATION AGREEMENT

THIS AGREEMENT is made at *[location]*, Ohio, this *[date]*, by and between *[Male]*, (hereinafter referred to as "*[_____]*"), and *[Female]*, (hereinafter referred to as "*[_____]*"), and both being sometime referred to in this Agreement as the "parties," or the "cohabitants."

RECITALS:

1. *[Male]* and *[Female]* contemplate cohabiting with each other.

2. *[Male]* and *[Female]* each own separate items of property, and each of them wishes to enter into an agreement regarding the future disposition of such property.

3. If *[Male]* and *[Female]* do cohabit with each other as they presently intend, each will want such cohabitation to continue, and each is of the opinion that this agreement will constitute a solid foundation for their intended cohabitation and will contribute toward that cohabitation being permanent, on the basis that this agreement makes it clear that any cohabitation will occur because of the love each has for the other and not from any desire to obtain a share of the property of the other.

4. *[Male]* and *[Female]* are both aware that, in the absence of a cohabitation agreement, their cohabitation will give neither of them any

---

D.M.K., 1996 SD 144, 557 N.W.2d 235 (S.D. 1996); Titchenal v. Dexter, 166 Vt. 373, 693 A.2d 682 (1997).

[11]Stanley v. Illinois, 405 U.S. 645, 92 S. Ct. 1208, 31 L. Ed. 2d 551 (1972) (denial of due process to presume all unmarried fathers unfit custodians); Heyer v. Peterson, 307 N.W.2d 1 (Iowa 1981).

[12]See Diane M. Carlton, *Fraud Between Sexual Partners Regarding the Use of Contraceptives*, 71 Ky. L.J. 593 (1982–83); Eisenstadt v. Baird, 405 U.S. 438, 92 S. Ct. 1029, 31 L. Ed. 2d 349 (1972) (dissimilar statutory treatment of unmarried person as to right to obtain contraceptives violates equal protection clause).

[13]See Samuel Green & John V. Long, *Marriage and Family Law Agreements* 3.25 (1997). For sample language that may be used or modified for use in cohabitation agreements, see Text § 2:71, Cohabitation agreements—Form, and the antenuptial agreement forms in Text Ch 1, Antenuptial Agreements. Also, for a useful discussion of cohabitant contracts for both heterosexual and homosexual couples, including a checklist and draft forms, see Brooke Oliver, *Contracting for Cohabitation: Adapting the California Statutory Marital Contract to Life Partnership Agreements Between Lesbian, Gay or Unmarried Heterosexual Couples*, 23 Golden Gate U.L. Rev. 899 (1993). See also Oliphant, *Drafting Live-In Contracts*, 38 Bench and Bar No. 6, p. 49 (April 1982); Harry G. Prince, *Public Policy Limitations on Cohabitation Agreements*, 70 Minn. L. Rev. 163 (1985).

specific rights in the estate of the other (i.e. in the property owned by the other person at the time of his or her death), and may not give either of them any rights in the property of the other in the event the cohabitation is terminated.

5. Both *[Male]* and *[Female]* intend that this Agreement will release and surrender all rights that either of them may have or acquire in the present and future property of the other, except such rights as are specifically given one another by this Agreement.

6. The parties have used the services of an attorney or attorneys merely to place into writing the understanding which *[Male]* and *[Female]* have arrived at between themselves, so as to cause their understanding to constitute a valid cohabitation agreement between them.

7. *[Male]* and *[Female]* have been informed that the validity of agreements such as this depends in part upon each person understanding the nature and extent of the rights which are released or surrendered, and that each party must make a full disclosure to the other of the property which he or she owns and of the value of such property, a disclosure of his or her income level, and a disclosure of his or her debts and current liabilities; this disclosure has been made in Exhibit "A" for *[Male]* and in Exhibit "B" for *[Female]*.

8. To complete the understanding communicated to *[Male]* and *[Female]* of the nature and extent of the rights which are being released or surrendered, there is set forth an explanation of the rights each party would have (in the absence of a cohabitation agreement) upon the death of the other without a cohabitation agreement, and if they were married to one another instead of cohabiting, or if the parties separated without a written cohabitation agreement.

9. The parties have been advised that the various states in the United States may have differing rules as to procedures regarding the validity of, and the effect given to, cohabitation agreements, and further have been advised that the law governing cohabitation agreements in Ohio and other states is subject to change in the future which might affect the validity and enforceability of this Agreement.

10. The parties have also been advised that the various states customarily (although not always) will give effect to an agreement which complies with the law(s) of some other state, as long as the agreement identifies that other state and specifies the agreement is to be interpreted and applied in accordance with the law of that particular state.

11. To provide certainty with regard to the interpretation, construction, and application of this Agreement, *[Male]* and *[Female]* desire and intend (and it is hereby so stipulated) that all aspects of this Agreement shall be interpreted, construed, and applied in accordance with the law(s) of the State of Ohio.

12. In the absence of a cohabitation agreement, and upon the death of the other, the parties in Ohio would have no rights or claims to the property of the deceased party unless specifically provided in that party's will, trust, or other similar document.

13. If *[Male]* and *[Female]* would marry one another, and upon the death of the other while still married, a husband or wife in Ohio would at this point in time have the following rights and claims to the property of the deceased spouse. (These are the major rights of a surviving spouse; there may be additional, although possibly less important, rights):

(A) Each would be entitled to receive a share of the assets in the estate of the other, even if the decedent-spouse's will states that no property whatsoever was to be left to the surviving spouse; and

(B) To receive a family allowance of Twenty-five Thousand Dollars ($25,000).

The items listed in (A) and (B) above are the major rights of a surviving spouse in the State of Ohio; any other state in which the parties may eventually be domiciled may provide different, lesser, and/or greater rights to a surviving spouse. However, because the parties are not getting married but are instead electing to cohabit, they both acknowledge that neither will be entitled to the benefits/rights listed in items (A) and (B) above.

14. If the parties would marry one another, *[Male]* and *[Female]* would have the following claims on or rights in the assets and income of the other in the event of a "marital dispute" between them, those words being defined in this Agreement to mean a divorce, dissolution, or other legal termination of their marriage, or a legal separation accompanied by a written separation agreement ("legal separation"). (These are the major claims or rights; there may be additional, although possibly less important, claims). Further, each party has been made aware of the following matters regarding such claims:

(A) Each would be entitled to claim a share in all interests in property owned by the other, and also to make a claim for spousal support.

(B) An Ohio court making a decision upon such claims would be entitled to consider a number of facts including, but not limited to, the duration of the marriage, the relative amounts of property, income, and liabilities of the parties, the assets each owned prior to the marriage and any appreciation thereon, the respective standards of living, ages, and conditions of physical and mental health of the parties at the time, and the amounts of property acquired after the marriage;

(C) The tendency of Ohio courts would be to grant a claim or right in property acquired after the marriage, but not to grant a claim in property owned prior to the marriage, except to consider granting a share of any appreciation in previously owned property;

(D) The division of property made by Ohio courts frequently results in each party receiving fifty percent (50%) of the property accumulated during the marriage, but seldom grants either husband or wife a share in property owned by the other prior to the marriage or acquired by gift or inheritance during the marriage (except to consider granting a share of any appreciation in such property);

(E) Spousal support is not often granted by Ohio courts if the marriage is of relatively short duration, and/or if the property and income of the party requesting spousal support are such that he or she will be able to maintain approximately the same standard of living that person enjoyed during the marriage. Ability to pay is one factor considered by courts making spousal support awards, and for this purpose, all the income will be considered, even though it comes from property owned prior to the marriage.

The items listed in (A) through (E) immediately above are the major rights of a spouse in Ohio in the event of a marital dispute, and any other state in which a marital dispute occurs might provide different, lesser, and/or greater rights and liabilities. However, because the parties are not getting married but are instead electing to cohabit, they both acknowledge that neither will be entitled to the benefits/rights listed in items (A) through (E) immediately above.

15. Both *[Male]* and *[Female]*, understanding that they would have the rights set out above should they marry, state that it is not their intent to become married at this time. The parties understand that common law marriages have been specifically abolished in the State of Ohio, and state that it is not their intent that their cohabitation be viewed as a basis in any state or country to constitute a common law marriage. The parties agree that this Agreement will become null and void upon their subsequent formal and ceremonial marriage.

THEREFORE, in consideration of (1) the matters set forth in the above recitals (all of which shall be deemed to be part of the substantive provisions of this agreement, (2) their contemplated cohabitation, and (3) the mutual promises set forth below (each of these three considerations being independent and adequate in and of itself, even if the other did not exist), *[Male]* and *[Female]* agree as follows:

1. SUPPORT

[Male] and *[Female]* waive any claim for support against the other and the issue of support shall not be subject to the further jurisdiction of any court. However, during their cohabitation, they agree to equally contribute to the household and living expenses, in proportion to their incomes.

2. PROPERTY OWNED PRIOR TO COHABITATION

[Male] and *[Female]* shall each retain his or her separate and independent ownership of all property that he or she may now own. That property is described in Exhibit "A" for *[Male]* and in Exhibit "B" for *[Female]*, both exhibits being attached to and made a part of this Agreement. This retention of separate and independent ownership shall include all income from such property and all appreciation in value of that property, and shall include any change of form through items of property being traded or being sold and the proceeds invested in new forms of property.

To make this provision effective, each party hereby waives, renounces, and relinquishes all legal and equitable claims and rights, actual and implied and contingent, that he or she may now have in the separate property of the other or that he or she may acquire in that property if the parties do cohabit with one another, except those rights granted by this Agreement.

3. PROPERTY ACQUIRED AFTER COHABITATION

All property acquired by either *[Male]* or *[Female]* in their separate names after this Agreement is signed shall be and remain the sole property of that person, including any income from that property, all appreciation in value of that property, and any change of form through such property being traded or sold. All property acquired after this Agreement is signed that is in the joint names of *[Male]* and *[Female]* (e.g., a house they may own as tenants in common, with both of their names on the deed) shall be divided between them on a 50-50 basis in the event of a dispute, unless otherwise stated in the deed for said property. Notwithstanding the provisions of this paragraph to the contrary, any and all property acquired by gift or inheritance by either *[Male]* or *[Female]* after this Agreement is signed shall be and remain the sole property of the party receiving the gift or inheritance, including any income from that property, all appreciation in value of that property, and any change of form of that property by being traded or sold. Such property acquired by gift or inheritance shall be excluded from any division between the parties in the event of a dispute.

To make this provision effective, each party hereby waives, renounces and relinquishes all legal and equitable claims and rights, actual and implied and contingent, that he or she might otherwise have in property subsequently acquired by the other, except those rights granted by this paragraph as to a dispute and except as may be granted elsewhere in this Agreement.

Any property, such as furniture, furnishings, equipment, and appliances which are acquired by the parties during their relationship shall be divided by mutual agreement upon a termination of the parties cohabitation by means other than marriage, as set out above. Should the parties be unable to mutually agree to a division of said property, then they shall employ one of the following options below in order to effectuate a division of said property:

(A) Coin Toss: The parties shall toss a coin with the winner selecting the first item of disputed property, regardless of price, and the parties shall alternate thereafter until all disputed items are divided. Should there be a debt associated with the particular item of property, then the party choosing that item shall be solely responsible for the timely payment of said debt and shall hold the other party harmless and blameless thereon.

(B) Valuation and Buy-Out: The parties shall hire an appraiser, splitting the cost of said appraiser equally, and the appraiser shall appraise all disputed items of property. Either party shall have the right to buy all of the property from the other at one-half of the appraisal value, within seven (7) days of the appraisal. If both parties should be willing and able to purchase the interest of the other, and both should choose to do so, then the parties will flip a coin with the winner being entitled to purchase said property.

(C) Sale of Property: The parties may mutually sell all disputed property and then split equally the equity proceeds therefrom.

Each party's items of personal property such as clothing and jewelry shall remain the property of that person regardless of any other provisions herein.

4. RETIREMENT BENEFITS WAIVER

Any retirement benefit, account, or right, including any distributions or other payments to a party, and any increase in such benefit or account during the term of the marriage, either by contributions, earnings, or appreciation, whether the Participant or others make investment decisions ("Retirement Benefit"), will be the separate property of the person who is the participant or owner of the benefit or account (the "Participant"), except as otherwise specifically provided in this Agreement. The Participant shall receive 100% of the Retirement Benefit and the non-Participant cohabitant will receive none of the Retirement Benefit, regardless of when it is paid.

The Participant and non-Participant cohabitant agree that neither will seek the imposition of any qualified domestic relations order or other order which would attempt to assign any rights in the Retirement Benefits to the non-Participant cohabitant. The non-Participant cohabitant hereby specifically agrees to consent in writing with his or her signature, duly witnessed by a notary public, to any election by the Participant to waive any and all forms of survivor benefits, specifically including, but not limited to, any pre-retirement survivor annuity and joint and survivor retirement annuity waivers and beneficiary designations. The non-Participant cohabitant shall complete such consents to any waivers of these benefits completed by the Participant at any such time as requested by the Participant, whether currently or any time in the future.

5. DEATH OF EITHER PARTY AFTER COHABITATION

[Male] and *[Female]* each waives, relinquishes, and renounces all rights and claims he or she might otherwise have upon the death of the other and against the estate or property of the other. This waiver and renunciation shall include every right, claim, and debt the other may be entitled to enforce against the estate and/or against the property of the other upon the death of the other, including all rights and claims, procedural and substantive.

6. RIGHT TO SELL OR TRANSFER PROPERTY

Each party shall have the right at all times to sell or transfer any interest in his or her own property by deed, will, mortgage, or any other manner whatsoever, on his or her sole signature and to any person or entity. Each is hereby barred from and releases all claims of dower in the property of the other, and each agrees to sign and deliver at any time(s) and without additional consideration any deeds, releases, or other documents necessary (or merely appropriate or helpful) to evidence that he or she has no claim in the property of the other.

7. GIFT OR DEVISE OF PROPERTY

This Agreement is not intended to block or prohibit *[Male]* or *[Female]* from giving property to the other by will, by gift, by designating the other as beneficiary of insurance, by designating the other party as a recipient of retirement benefits, or by any other lawful method whatsoever.

8. CONDITION TO GIVE AGREEMENT EFFECT

This Agreement shall not become effective unless *[Male]* and *[Female]* begin to cohabit with each other. Said cohabitation shall be recognized and acknowledged by the parties by living together in one common residence wherein one address is acknowledged as the home of both parties. Evidence of said cohabitation shall include the common residence, listing the same address for mailing purposes, having a driver's license listed at the same address, and other similar factors common to traditionally married couples. Invalidation of any one or more of the provisions of this agreement by any court shall in no way affect the remaining provisions, each and every one of which shall remain in full force and effect.

9. TERMINATION OF AGREEMENT

This Agreement shall terminate upon the following events and/or conditions:

(A) Marriage of the parties in this or any jurisdiction;

(B) Written notification of either party, his or her agent, representative, or other party acting in a similar legal status for either party; or,

(C) Living separate and apart, other than vacations, work, or other obligations of a similar nature, for more than thirty (30) days.

10. GENERAL PROVISIONS

[Male] and *[Female]* each make the following statements and declarations with regard to himself or herself:

(A) He or she has read this Agreement, and understands its effect on his or her rights. Further, the items of property and income and liabilities listed in Exhibit "A" and "B" have been discussed by and between the parties and are fully understood.

(B) He or she signs this Agreement of his or her own free will and accord, there having been no oral or written representations, inducements, pressure, or influence made to or exerted upon either to persuade him or her to enter into this Agreement.

(C) This Agreement constitutes the entire understanding between them on the subject, there being no prior to contemporaneous oral or written promises, obligations, or conditions between them on these matters. Any amendment or alteration of this Agreement, to be effective against either party, must be in writing and signed by the party against whom (or against whose property or income) it is sought to be enforced, with said signature being duly notarized.

(D) Under all circumstances, this Agreement is fair and reasonable for each party.

(E) This Agreement has been prepared by *[name of attorney]* as attorney for *[Male/Female]*, and it represents the agreement of both *[Male]* and *[Female]* and is not to be construed or applied against *[Male/Female]* by reason of the fact that it was drafted by *[Male/Female]*'s attorney.

(F) *[Male]* and *[Female]* were each given a separate copy of this Agreement before it was signed, and each had an opportunity to review and analyze the same. *[Male/Female]* has consulted with *[name of attorney]*, attorney at law, for the purpose of obtaining independent legal counsel as to his/her rights and to the terms and effects of this Agreement.

(G) Each party hereby waives any and all equitable and or legal claims one against the other by virtue of entering into this Agreement. The parties specifically intend to limit their recoveries and rights one to the other to the express terms and conditions set out herein.

11. SEVERABILITY

In the event any provision of this Agreement is found to be contrary to law by a court of competent jurisdiction, the remaining provisions shall remain in full force and effect and be severable from those portions deemed contrary to law, and shall continue to be valid and enforceable to effectuate the parties' intentions as expressed in the recitals.

12. MISCELLANEOUS

This Agreement shall be binding upon and shall inure to the benefit of *[Male]* and *[Female]* and their respective heirs, executors, administrators, and assigns. The titles in this Agreement are for convenience only and shall not be deemed to have substantive effect.

13. ENFORCEMENT

Should it become necessary to enforce the terms and conditions of this Agreement in a court of competent jurisdiction, the party found to be at fault for breach of the terms and conditions set forth herein shall be responsible for the costs of enforcement for the prevailing party, to include attorney fees, court costs, and any related expenses.

IN WITNESS WHEREOF, this Agreement has been signed by the parties in duplicate on the day and year first mentioned above, with each signed copy to be deemed to be an original.

In the presence of:

_____   _____
Witness   *[Male]*

_____   _____

Witness   *[Female]*

State of Ohio, *[County]*
Sworn to before me and signed in my presence, this *[date]*.

_____
                                           Notary Public

§ 2:72   Cohabitation agreements—Consideration

In drafting such agreements it is important to observe that other states have held such agreements to be unenforceable if they are founded on the illegal consideration of "illicit sexual intercourse."[1] Thus the contract should exclude any mention of sex or sexuality. However, the issue of consideration should not be ignored; a carefully drafted statement of valid consideration is essential to any contract. Mutual promises, such as for one partner to provide financial support and for the other to provide homemaking activities, is required. A promise to perform homemaking services has been deemed a lawful and adequate consideration for a contract.[2] Another court held that the consideration for the partners' agreement was their intention to become married, notwithstanding the fact that they did not do so.[3] An itemization of the investments of time, money, and personal services by each partner into the joint enterprise should be included in any cohabitation agreement. However, clients should be advised that courts are much more likely to enforce financial provisions of contracts, and that provisions relating to personal behavior are unenforceable.

A severability clause specifically agreeing that any part of the agreement found legally unenforceable is severable has been used by at least one court to uphold the remainder of a nonmarital cohabitation agreement,[4] Even in implied contract cases,[5] and express unwritten

_____

[Section 2:72]

[1]See Suggs v. Norris, 88 N.C. App. 539, 541, 364 S.E.2d 159 (1988); Jones v. Daly, 122 Cal. App. 3d 500, 176 Cal. Rptr. 130 (2d Dist. 1981); Morone v. Morone, 50 N.Y.2d 481, 429 N.Y.S.2d 592, 413 N.E.2d 1154 (1980).

[2]Marvin v. Marvin, 18 Cal. 3d 660, 134 Cal. Rptr. 815, 557 P.2d 106 (1976); contra Featherston v. Steinhoff, 226 Mich. App. 584, 575 N.W.2d 6 (1997) (household services in meretricious relationship are presumed gratuitous and do not constitute consideration for breach of contract after eight-year cohabitation and one child), appeal dismissed by 459 Mich. 920, 589 N.W.2d 774 (1998).

[3]Cook v. Cook, 142 Ariz. 573, 691 P.2d 664 (1984).

[4]Whorton v. Dillingham, 202 Cal. App. 3d 447, 248 Cal. Rptr. 405 (4th Dist. 1988). See Samuel Green & John V. Long, *Marriage and Family Law Agreements* 3.15 (1997).

[5]Cook v. Cook, 142 Ariz. 573, 691 P.2d 664 (1984).

contract cases,[6] the severance doctrine has been applied by courts to disregard any implication that sexual services comprise part of the consideration for the contract, and to enforce the remaining terms of the parties' "agreement." Including a severability clause in a written cohabitation agreement is highly advisable.

§ 2:73 Cohabitation agreements—Limitations

The limitations of cohabitation agreements should be clearly explained to the parties to such agreements. Many of the rights and privileges associated with marriage are difficult or impossible for cohabiting partners to establish by contract or other document. For instance, the tax treatment of married couples cannot be created under the law of contracts. When one partner supports a nonworking partner, the working partner cannot claim head-of-household status,[1] cannot claim the other partner as a dependent,[2] and cannot count the support as a gift.[3] Other rights and benefits which cannot be created by contract include workers' compensation benefits, social security benefits, step-parent adoption rights,[4] credit rights,[5] consortium claims,[6] pension benefits, testamentary benefits, spousal testimonial privileges,[7] name changes, inheritance rights,[8] insurability of spouses, next-of-kin status for making medical, guardianship, or burial arrangements, and the right to demand a final resolution of all issues between the parties by a court of domestic relations.[9]

There are 1,049 federal laws in which marital status is a factor, according to the federal General Accounting Office in Washington, D.C. This does not count state benefits and private sector benefits. The GAO counts these benefits in thirteen categories:

Social Security, housing and food stamps

---

[6]Hierholzer v. Sardy, 128 Mich. App. 259, 340 N.W.2d 91 (1983).

[Section 2:73]

[1]Newsom v. C. I. R., T.C. Memo. 1974-265, 1974 WL 2359 (1974).

[2]Angstadt v. C.I.R., T.C. Memo. 1968-140, 1968 WL 1243 (T.C. 1968).

[3]Jones v. C.I.R., T.C. Memo. 1977-329, 1977 WL 3055 (1977). See also Randall, *Living Together Can Be Very Taxing,* 2 Fam. Advoc. 2 (Winter 1979).

[4]RC 3107.03.

[5]See Markham v. Colonial Mortg. Service Co., Associates, Inc., 605 F.2d 566, 55 A.L.R. Fed. 448 (D.C. Cir. 1979) (extended certain Equal Credit Opportunity Act rights to unmarried couples).

[6]For example, the District of Hawaii federal trial court held that Hawaii law denied an unmarried partner standing to bring a common law loss of consortium claim based upon a severe injury to the other partner, ruling that a person who witnesses a severe injury to their unmarried partner has no right of action for negligent infliction of emotional distress. Milberger v. KBHL, LLC, 486 F. Supp. 2d 1156 (D. Haw. 2007).

[7]RC 2921.22(E), RC 2945.42; Annot., 4 A.L.R. 4th 422.

[8]RC 2105.06, RC 2107.39.

[9]RC 2105.06, RC 2107.39.

Veteran's benefits

Taxation

Federal civilian and military service benefits

Employment benefits and related laws

Immigration, naturalization and alien affairs

Indian affairs

Trade, commerce and intellectual property

Financial disclosure and conflict of interest

Domestic crimes and family violence

Loans, guarantees and payments in agriculture

Federal natural resources and related laws

Miscellaneous[10]

One author advocating contractual agreements between cohabitants points out:

> Individuals may contract to regulate matters only between themselves; they may not contract for a legislatively granted privilege, such as the privilege not to testify against a spouse. Parties cannot create for themselves a legal privilege the legislature has not seen fit to extend to them. The courts have expressly denied other marital rights and privileges to same gender or unmarried heterosexual partners, including the marital communications privilege, the right to bring a wrongful death action if a third party kills the other partner, and the right to sue for loss of consortium and negligent infliction of emotional distress. Other rights, such as the right to divide community property and to seek spousal support on the termination of marriage, have been denied to same gender or unmarried heterosexual partners, but may be created by contract.[11]

§ 2:74 Cohabitation by same-sex couples

Since homosexual couples in Ohio are denied the legal ability to marry,[1] they might succeed in gaining some rights by raising the equitable issues listed above.[2] However, it is imperative that they prepare cohabitation agreements and related legal documents if they want any legal protection of their property rights and other legal interests.[3] It is unlikely that the states will take any action to protect such interests since they are unanimous in refusing to recognize

---

[10]Mariella Savidge, *The 1,049 beneficial reasons, financial and otherwise, to marry, Morning Call* (Allentown, PA) Mar. 9, 2004, A.M. Magazine Section, Pg. E1.

[11]Brooke Oliver, *Contracting for Cohabitation: Adapting the California Statutory Marital Contract to Life Partnership Agreements Between Lesbian, Gay or Unmarried Heterosexual Couples,* 23 Golden Gate U.L. Rev. 899, 901–902 (1993) (footnotes omitted).

[Section 2:74]

[1]See Text § 2:23, Capacity to marry—Same gender.

[2]See Text § 2:67 Cohabitants' legal remedies—In other states; see also Samuel Green & John V. Long, *Marriage and Family Law Agreements* 3.04 (1997).

[3]See Text § 2:75 Cohabitation agreements for same-sex couples.

homosexual "marriage,"[4] and considering that at least 16 states have already adopted statutes similar to the federal 1996 Defense of Marriage Act,[5] and further considering United States Supreme Court opinions allowing the states to regulate private consensual homosexual activity.[6]

Courts must sometimes determine who to include in the definition of family when resolving visitation rights,[7] eligibility for public entitlement, and housing and zoning cases. Some states have adopted a functional definition of a family for such purposes. For instance, a New York court established a four-factor test emphasizing the functions of a family unit in a case involving an eviction: (1) the exclusivity and longevity of the relationship, (2) the level of emotional and financial commitment, (3) the manner in which the parties conducted their everyday lives and held themselves out to society, and (4) the reliance placed upon one another for daily family services.[8] Such an approach to determining family matters could be expected to assist same gender as well as heterosexual cohabitants, especially those who have documented the family nature of their relationship with cohabitation agreements and related legal documents.[9]

In one respect Ohio has acted to protect the interests of same-sex cohabitants. Same-sex couples have been held to be living in a "spousal relationship" for purposes of the state's domestic violence statute.[10]

In 2005, Defendants charged with violation of the domestic violence criminal and protection order laws alleged the law has been made unconstitutional by the Marriage Amendment,[11] because it recognizes a legal status for relationships of unmarried individuals that ap-

---

[4]See Samuel Green & John V. Long, *Marriage and Family Law Agreements* 1.17, 1.17A (1997).

[5]Feingold, "Gay Marriage Battle Rocks Union's Foundations," Nat'l L.J. (1-27-97, at A24).

[6]Bowers v. Hardwick, 478 U.S. 186, 106 S. Ct. 2841, 92 L. Ed. 2d 140 (1986); Doe v. Commonwealth's Attorney for City of Richmond, 403 F. Supp. 1199 (E.D. Va. 1975), judgment aff'd, 425 U.S. 901, 96 S. Ct. 1489, 47 L. Ed. 2d 751 (1976).

[7]Annot., 8 A.L.R. 5th 1 2000.

[8]Braschi v. Stahl Associates Co., 74 N.Y.2d 201, 544 N.Y.S.2d 784, 543 N.E.2d 49, 55 (1989).

[9]For further discussion of the functional definition of family, as well as the contrary view of other courts that emphasize the evidentiary desirability of the "bright line" of legal marriage to objectively verify the family relationship of individuals, see Brooke Oliver, *Contracting for Cohabitation: Adapting the California Statutory Marital Contract to Life Partnership Agreements Between Lesbian, Gay or Unmarried Heterosexual Couples,* 23 Golden Gate U.L. Rev. 899, 905–908 (1993).

[10]State v. Linner, 77 Ohio Misc. 2d 22, 665 N.E.2d 1180 (Mun. Ct. 1996); State v. Hadinger, 61 Ohio App. 3d 820, 573 N.E.2d 1191 (10th Dist. Franklin County 1991); State v. Yaden, 118 Ohio App. 3d 410, 692 N.E.2d 1097, 71 A.L.R.5th 749 (1st Dist. Hamilton County 1997).

[11]The marriage amendment reads: "Definition of marriage. Only a union between one man and one woman may be a marriage valid in or recognized by this state and

proximate the status of marriage. The only appellate decisions to date rejected this contention, finding that Ohio's domestic violence law refers to, but does do not create, a legal status that approximates marriage.[12] The court relied in part upon the reasoning of the first reported Ohio decision on the subject, *State v. Rodgers*.[13] The issue of whether Ohio's domestic violence protection order law is rendered unconstitutional by virtue of the Marriage Amendment created a split in authority among appellate districts, requiring resolution by the Supreme Court of Ohio. On December 12, 2006, the justices heard oral argument in an appeal in one of those cases from the Warren County Court of Appeals. The appellate court upheld the domestic violence protection order law, overturning a trial judge, who had ruled the law was unconstitutional as applied to an unmarried individual.[14]

None of the Ohio cases decided to date have discussed whether the Marriage Amendment itself is unconstitutional, as violating equal protection rights. Similar arguments have been raised in other states, with inconsistent results. An unpublished California trial court decision found that the state's Family Code Section 300, which provides that marriage is between a man and a woman, and Section 308.5, which provides that California will recognize as a marriage only a union between a man and a woman, violate the equal protection clause of the California Constitution.[15] To the contrary, a New York trial court found that New York's Domestic Relations Law exclusion of same sex couples from the definition of who may marry is rationally related to a legitimate state interest, procreation and child rearing, and is thus constitutional.[16]

§ 2:75 Cohabitation agreements for same-sex couples

If cohabitation agreements and related legal documents are legally advisable for opposite-gender couples, they are indispensable for same-gender couples, at least for those who want a degree of predictability

---

its political subdivisions. This state and its political subdivisions shall not create or recognize a legal status for relationships of unmarried individuals that intends to approximate the design, qualities, significance or effect of marriage." O. Const. Art. XV, § 11.

[12]State v. Newell, 2005-Ohio-2848, 2005 WL 1364937 (Ohio Ct. App. 5th Dist. Stark County 2005).

[13]State v. Rodgers, 131 Ohio Misc. 2d 1, 2005-Ohio-1730, 827 N.E.2d 872 (C.P. 2005).

[14]State v. Carswell, 2005-Ohio-6547, 2005 WL 3358882 (Ohio Ct. App. 12th Dist. Warren County 2005), appeal allowed, 109 Ohio St. 3d 1423, 2006-Ohio-1967, 846 N.E.2d 533 (2006).

[15]Coordination Proceeding, Special Title [Rule 1550 (c)], Marriage Act, Judicial Council Coordination Proceeding No. 4365 (California Superior Court, County of San Francisco, March 14, 2005), unpublished, available at http://www.sftc.org/Docs/marriage.pdf.

[16]Seymour v. Holcomb, 7 Misc. 3d 530, 790 N.Y.S.2d 858 (Sup 2005).

and control over their legal affairs.[1] A striking example of what can happen when available legal mechanisms are ignored can be seen in a case where one of two "life partners" was seriously injured in a car wreck, placed under a legal guardianship by her parents, and kept apart from her partner for three years.[2] And a California court ruled that state law does not permit granting visitation rights with a former lesbian partner's child born during the couple's relationship.[3]

The legal documents that will help same-sex couples structure their legal relationships, and the provisions which should be included in cohabitation agreements for same-sex couples, are very similar to those described under "Cohabitation Agreements," above.[4] Cohabitation agreements between same-sex partners specifically have been upheld in in other states.[5]

Given the strong public policy favoring heterosexual marriage, same gender couples face a more difficult legal challenge than married couples in securing the court's recognition of the legitimacy of their relationships and their rights as a family. Establishing and documenting the nature of their relationship through all legal means available provides evidence for a court to use in determining their true intent vis a vis each other, their children and their property. Legal means of documenting the "marriage-like" nature of their relationship currently available to same gender life partners include life partnership contracts, durable powers of attorney for financial matters and health care, co-parenting agreements, wills, trusts, beneficiary designations on life insurance or pension plans, second parent adoption of children, and domestic partner registration where possible.[6]

Structuring of the legalities and other aspects of the cohabiting relationship of same-gender couples may be pursued through mediation.[7]

§ 2:76 Same sex marriage

American social and legal concepts of marriage are restructuring

---

[Section 2:75]

[1]David L. Chamber, *What If? The Legal Consequences of Marriage and the Legal Needs of Lesbian and Gay Male Couples,* 95 Mich. L. Rev. 447 (Nov. 1996); Mary Patricia Treuthart, *Adopting a More Realistic Definition of "Family,"* 26 Gonz. L. Rev. 91 (1990/1991).

[2]In re Guardianship of Kowalski, 382 N.W.2d 861 (Minn. Ct. App. 1986).

[3]West v. Superior Court, 59 Cal. App. 4th 302, 69 Cal. Rptr. 2d 160 (3d Dist. 1997).

[4]See Text § 2:70 Cohabitation agreements—And related documents.

[5]Crooke v. Gilden, 262 Ga. 122, 414 S.E.2d 645 (1992); Whorton v. Dillingham, 202 Cal. App. 3d 447, 248 Cal. Rptr. 405 (4th Dist. 1988); Posik v. Layton, 695 So. 2d 759 (Fla. Dist. Ct. App. 5th Dist. 1997); Silver v. Starrett, 176 Misc. 2d 511, 674 N.Y.S.2d 915, 176 (Sup 1998); but see Jones v. Daly, 122 Cal. App. 3d 500, 176 Cal. Rptr. 130 (2d Dist. 1981).

[6]Brooke Oliver, *Contracting for Cohabitation: Adapting the California Statutory Marital Contract to Life Partnership Agreements Between Lesbian, Gay or Unmarried Heterosexual Couples,* 23 Golden Gate U.L. Rev. 899, 905 (1993) (footnotes omitted).

[7]Clark Freshman, *Privatizing Same-Sex 'Marriage' Through Alternative Dispute Resolution,* 44 UCLA L. Rev. 1687 (August 1997).

themselves at the start of the 21st century as the issue of same-sex marriage pinballs among federal and state legislative, judicial, and electoral venues. Massachusetts became the first state to allow same-sex marriage when its highest court ruled in 2003 that the state's marriage statute violated the state constitution[1] Five years later, the Supreme Court of California similarly struck down the state law restricting marriage to a man and a woman that violated the Equal Protection Clause of that state's constitution.[2] Subsequently, California voters passed Proposition 8, amending the state constitution to ban same-sex marriage. Later in 2008, the Connecticut Supreme Court relied on its state constitution to declare that failure to grant same-sex couples the full rights, responsibilities and name of marriage violated the guarantee of equal protection of the law.[3] And in spring of 2009, the Iowa Supreme Court legalized same-sex marriage in that state when it held that a one-man-one-woman marriage statute violated the equal protection clause of the Iowa state constitution[4]

The supreme courts of three states have ruled to the contrary. Claims that state marriage laws violated their state constitutions were rejected in New York[5] Washington[6] and Maryland[7]

With variations on definitional themes, three New England states became the first in the U.S. to legalize same-sex marriage by legislative act rather than judicial decree. The State of Vermont became the first of those when it replaced its civil union law with a civil marriage law in 2009.[8] The second state to recognize same-sex marriage by legislation is Maine. Barring a public referendum, the amendment to Maine's domestic relation law was scheduled to take effect in September of 2009.[9] The third New England state in 2009 to legalize same-sex marriage through the legislative process was New

---

[Section 2:76]

[1]Goodridge v. Department of Public Health, 440 Mass. 309, 798 N.E.2d 941 (2003).

[2]In re Marriage Cases, 43 Cal. 4th 757, 76 Cal. Rptr. 3d 683, 183 P.3d 384 (2008).

[3]Kerrigan v. Commissioner of Public Health, 289 Conn. 135, 957 A.2d 407 (2008).

[4]Varnum v. Brien, 763 N.W.2d 862 (Iowa 2009).

[5]Hernandez v. Robles, 7 N.Y.3d 338, 821 N.Y.S.2d 770, 855 N.E.2d 1 (2006).

[6]Andersen v. King County, 158 Wash. 2d 1, 138 P.3d 963 (2006).

[7]Conaway v. Deane, 401 Md. 219, 932 A.2d 571 (2007), opinion extended after remand, 2008 WL 3999843 (Md. Cir. Ct. 2008).

[8]2009 Vt. S. 115, eff. 9-1-09, amending Vt. Stat. Ann. Tit. 15 § 8 to read: "MARRIAGE DEFINITION. Marriage is the legally recognized union of two people. When used in this chapter or in any other statute, the word 'marriage' shall mean a civil marriage. Terms relating to the marital relationship shall be construed consistently with this section for all purposes throughout the law, whether in the context of statute, administrative or court rule, policy, common law, or any other source of civil law."

[9]2009 Me. S.B. 384, amending Title 19A Me. Rev. Stat. Ann. § 650-A to read: "Codification of Marriage. Marriage is the legally recognized union of 2 people.

Hampshire. The state already had a civil union statute in effect and the state legislature provided that any existing civil union will automatically be deemed a marriage on January 1, 2011.[10]

In addition to those states that have judicially or legislatively recognized same-sex marriage, several states have enacted civil union or domestic partnership laws that establish legal recognition of same-sex couple relationships. Those states include, as of July, 2009, New Jersey, Oregon, Washington, Nevada and the District of Columbia.[11]

A more limited legal status for same-sex partners was adopted in Hawaii, where they may register with the state as "reciprocal beneficiaries" and obtain limited rights and benefits of marriage. This arrangement was created by state law.[12] combined with an amendment to the Hawaii Constitution.[13]

The impetus for these changes in Hawaii law is the State Supreme Court decision in *Baehr v. Lewin*[14] but the impact of this case extends far beyond the Hawaiian Islands. In what must certainly be regarded as a landmark decision due to its continuing shock waves across the field of family law, the Hawaii Supreme Court found the state law that denied the civil right of marriage to same-sex couples was presumptively invalid under the equal protection clause of the Hawaii Constitution. This decision ignited across the nation a firestorm of political debate, prompted a host of state electoral referendums, resulted in legislative changes in Congress and a majority of states, and fueled litigation that shows no sign of abating.

Congress responded to *Baehr* with the Defense of Marriage Act (DOMA) in 1996. This law redefined marriage for purposes of federal law, as follows: "In determining the meaning of any Act of Congress, or of any ruling, regulation, or interpretation of the various administrative bureaus and agencies of the United States, the word 'marriage' means only a legal union between one man and one woman as husband and wife, and the word 'spouse' refers only to a person of the

---

Gender-specific terms relating to the marital relationship or familial relationships, including, but not limited to, 'spouse,' 'family,' 'marriage,' 'immediate family,' 'dependent,' 'next of kin,' 'bride,' 'groom,' 'husband,' 'wife,' 'widow' and 'widower,' must be construed to be gender-neutral for all purposes throughout the law, whether in the context of statute, administrative or court rule, policy, common law or any other source of civil law."

[10]N.H. H.B. 436, eff. 1-1-10, enacting N.H. Rev. Stat. Ann. § 457:1-a, to read: "Equal Access to Marriage. Marriage is the legally recognized union of 2 people. Any person who otherwise meets the eligibility requirements of this chapter may marry any other eligible person regardless of gender. Each party to a marriage shall be designated 'bride,' 'groom,' or 'spouse.'"

[11]Ann Laquer Estin, Golden Anniversary Reflections: Changes in Marriage After Fifty Years, 42 Fam. L.Q. 333, 348 (Fall 2008); and Steve Friess, Nevada Partnership Bill Now Law, N.Y. Times (June 1, 2009).

[12]Haw. Rev. Stat. § 572-1 (2007).

[13]Haw. Const. art. 1 § 23.

[14]Baehr v. Lewin, 74 Haw. 530, 74 Haw. 645, 852 P.2d 44 (1993).

opposite sex who is a husband or a wife."[15] DOMA also undercut the Full Faith and Credit Clause of the United States Constitution, which addresses the duties that states within the United States have to respect the "public acts, records, and judicial proceedings" of other states,[16] by providing that no state would be required to give legal effect to a "relationship between persons of the same sex that is treated as a marriage under the laws of such other state."[17]

The first state to challenge DOMA in court was the first state to legalize gay marriage. Massachusetts. In July, 2009, the state filed suit in the U.S. District Court, District of Massachusetts, alleging that the federal Act is an unconstitutional assault on the right of the state to regulate marriage, forces the state to discriminate against 16,000 same-sex married couples, and exceeds Congress' legislative authority.[18]

In addition to the federal passage of DOMA, some thirty states have enacted laws or amended their constitutions to limit recognition of same-sex-couple relationships, actions commonly called "mini-DOMA" provisions.[19] Ohio joined ranks with the states that deny marriage rights to same-sex couples, twice. First, the General Assembly took legislative action in 2004. Later the same year, Ohio voters passed a sweeping ballot initiative amending the state constitution.

An Ohio legislative initiative to declare same sex marriages as being against the strong public policy of the state, failed to pass both houses of the General Assembly.[20] Upon reconsideration in 2004, Ohio H.B. 272 amended RC 3101.01 and 3105.12 "to specifically declare that same sex marriages are against the strong public policy of the state, [and] to declare that the recognition or extension by the state of the specific statutory benefits of legal marriage to nonmarital relationships is against the public policy of the state." The governor signed this legislation within 24 hours of its passage. The new law also declared that Ohio would not give full faith and credit to a marriage entered into by persons of the same sex in any other jurisdiction.[21] The new law did, however, exempt from its prohibitions any statutory benefits extended to persons of the same sex or different sexes who are in non-marital relationships.[22] The new law also allowed the exten-

---

[15]1 U.S.C.A. § 7.

[16]Article IV, Section 1.

[17]28 U.S.C.A. § 1738C (2006).

[18]*Nandini Jayakrishna*, Mass. is 1st to fight US marriage law, Boston Globe (July 9, 2009).

[19]Ann Laquer Estin, Golden Anniversary Reflections: Changes in Marriage After Fifty Years, 42 Fam. L.Q. 333, 347 (Fall 2008).

[20]2001 Ohio H.B. 234.

[21]RC 3101.01(C)(2).

[22]RC 3101.01(C)(3).

sion of partnership benefits to unmarried couples by private employers.[23]

Following the Ohio General Assembly's anti-same-sex-marriage legislation in 2004 voters approved a constitutional amendment in the November, 2004 election, Ohio State Issue 1. In sweeping language, this ballot initiative banned same-sex marriage and civil unions in the state. The newly enacted Ohio Const. art. XV, § 11 reads: "Only a union between one man and one woman may be a marriage valid in or recognized by this state and its political subdivisions. This state and its political subdivisions shall not create or recognize a legal status for relationships of unmarried individuals that intends to approximate the design, qualities, significance or effect of marriage." The broad wording of State Issue 1 immediately created litigation seeking to restrict two types of government benefits to unmarried couples. First, the Court of Appeals for Butler County dismissed, on grounds of lack of standing, a taxpayer suit to block Miami University from offering domestic-partner benefits to members of its faculty and staff[24] Secondly, the Supreme Court of Ohio decided that the all-encompassing language of the new amendment does not prevent the state from enforcing domestic violence orders against non-married cohabitants[25]

As states continue to sort out the legal ramifications within their own borders of the new laws embracing or condemning same-sex couple relationships, the stage is set for a wave of litigation to resolve the legal rights of those couples when they cross state borders.

This picture is far more complex than indicated by a simple counting of states with DOMA laws, on the one hand, and states in which courts have mandated recognition for same-sex relationships on the other. Taken collectively, there are now 10 to 12 U.S. jurisdictions in which same-sex couples have access to many or all of the legal rights and obligations of marriage. These jurisdictions have a combined population of more than eighty-two million people, or more than one fourth of the nation's residents. In view of this diversity, conflict-of-laws questions will return to a prominent position in family law in the years ahead.[26]

Examples of the conflict-of-laws issues and other complications arising from the same-sex marriage legal landscape are already emerging from court opinions. A same-sex Rhode Island couple married in Mas-

---

[23]RC 3101.01(C)(4).

[24]Brinkman v. Miami Univ., 139 Ohio Misc. 2d 114, 2005-Ohio-7161, 861 N.E.2d 925, 216 Ed. Law Rep. 612 (C.P. 2005).

[25]State v. Carswell, 114 Ohio St. 3d 210, 2007-Ohio-3723, 871 N.E.2d 547 (2007).

[26]Ann Laquer Estin, Golden Anniversary Reflections: Changes in Marriage After Fifty Years, 42 Fam. L.Q. 333, 348 (Fall 2008), citing generally Andrew Koppelman, Interstate Recognition of Same-Sex Marriages and Civil Unions: A Handbook for Judges, 153 U. Pa. L. Rev. 2143 (2005).

sachusetts found they were barred from divorcing in Rhode Island[27] The Connecticut appellate court found that full faith and credit clause of the United States Constitution impinges on the independent sovereignty of the state, determined it is a discretionary concept that states can obey as they choose, and denied a resident the right to file a divorce to dissolve a civil union entered into in Vermont[28] New Yorkers of the same gender married in Canada are entitled to spousal health care benefits from a community college according to a court decision that noted New York never enacted a "mini-DOMA" law.[29] Michigan found that its "mini-DOMA" law prohibits public employers from providing health insurance benefits to their employee's same-sex domestic partners.[30] New York's answer to the conflict-of-laws issue came not through court order, but gubernatorial decree, when Governor David Paterson directed state agencies to recognize same-sex marriages performed in other jurisdictions.[31]

Challenges to DOMA are now being brought in federal courts. For example, a lesbian couple who were legally married in Massachusetts sought a declaration that the Defense of Marriage Act is unconstitutional. A federal trial court disagreed that DOMA violates the Full Faith and Credit Clause, due process, equal protection, the Privileges and Immunities Clause, or the Commerce Clause. The court ruled the ability to marry someone of the same sex is not a fundamental right, homosexuality a not suspect class, and the statute was rationally related to the legitimate governmental interest of encouraging the raising of children in homes consisting of a married mother and father.[32]

If a same-sex couple is legally married in another jurisdiction, the question arises as to whether they can be divorced in the state of Ohio. Ohio courts have not yet addressed that issue, but a few states have been called upon to decide similar matters arising out of Vermont's civil union law for homosexual couples.[33] Several courts have sidestepped full faith and credit questions by ruling that a civil union is not a marriage, and thus state divorce laws do not apply. One Texas circuit court judge decided to recognize a Vermont civil union in a dissolution of marriage action, but later reversed himself. And in an unreported West Virginia case, a divorce was granted to a lesbian couple who had been united in Vermont. Parties who have entered a Vermont civil union may be divorced there, but Vermont

---

[27]Chambers v. Ormiston, 935 A.2d 956 (R.I. 2007).

[28]Rosengarten v. Downes, 71 Conn. App. 372, 802 A.2d 170 (2002).

[29]Martinez v. County of Monroe, 50 A.D.3d 189, 850 N.Y.S.2d 740 (4th Dep't 2008).

[30]National Pride At Work, Inc. v. Governor of Michigan, 481 Mich. 56, 748 N.W.2d 524 (2008).

[31]Jeremy W. Peters, New York to Back Same-Sex Unions from Elsewhere, N.Y. Times (May 29, 2008).

[32]Wilson v. Ake, 354 F. Supp. 2d 1298, 1 A.L.R. Fed. 2d 611 (M.D. Fla. 2005).

[33]Vt. Stat. Ann. tit. 15, § 1201 et. seq.

divorce law requires a six month residency in that state by at least one of the parties before a divorce or dissolution action may be filed, plus continued residency until the case is finalized.[34]

An unmarried couple who had been denied relief by lower courts were permitted by the Ohio Supreme Court to adopt a common last name. The Supreme Court said two women in a committed relationship could change their surnames to the same last name. The court held that the name change was proper since there was no criminal or fraudulent purpose shown, and found that the appellants did not intend to create the appearance of a state-sanctioned marriage.[35] This result was similar to the decision reached in a New Jersey court,[36] and overturned the Ohio appellate court opinion that said barring the name change would serve a legitimate governmental interest in "promoting solemnized marriage."[37] The appeals court had upheld the trial court's ruling that was based in part upon Ohio's abolition of common law marriage. The trial court had ruled that it was not "reasonable and proper"[38] to change the names of unmarried cohabitants because to do so would give an "aura of propriety and official sanction" to their cohabitation.

An Ohio trial court's denial of requests by long-term cohabiting females to change their last names to a common last name was upheld as constitutionally advancing a legitimate governmental interest in "promoting solemnized marriage."[39] Relying in part upon Ohio's abolition of common law marriage, the trial court found that it was not "reasonable and proper" (a statutory standard for name changes under RC 2717.01(A)) to change the names of unmarried cohabitants because to do so would give an "aura of propriety and official sanction" to their cohabitation. A contrary result was reached in New Jersey.[40]

For same gender cohabitants, the questions raised by lawsuits over civil marriage rights go far beyond turn of the century debates regarding government control over private relationships. No degree of contracting and estate planning can accomplish the level of favorable treatment married couples enjoy under federal and state laws.

---

[34]Janice G. Inman, *Dissolving a Same-Sex Marriage*, NO. 10 N.Y. Fam. L. Monthly 1 (July 11, 2003); Molly McDonough, *Court Oks Divorce Without Recognizing 'Marriage': Gay Couple's Civil Union, Created in Vermont, Is Dissolved in Texas*, 2 NO. 11 A.B.A. J. E-Report 2 (March 21, 2003).

[35]In re Bicknell, 96 Ohio St.3d 76, 2002-Ohio-3615, 771 N.E.2d 848 (2002).

[36]In re Application for Change of Name by Bacharach, 344 N.J. Super. 126, 780 A.2d 579 (App. Div. 2001).

[37]In re Bicknell, 2001-Ohio-4200, 2001 WL 121147 (Ohio Ct. App. 12th Dist. Butler County 2001), rev'd, 96 Ohio St. 3d 76, 2002-Ohio-3615, 771 N.E.2d 846 (2002).

[38]"Reasonable and proper" is a statutory standard for name changes under RC 2717.01(A).

[39]In re Bicknell, 2001-Ohio-4200, 2001 WL 121147 (Ohio Ct. App. 12th Dist. Butler County 2001), appeal allowed, 93 Ohio St. 3d 1432, 755 N.E.2d 355 (2001).

[40]In re Application for Change of Name by Bacharach, 344 N.J. Super. 126, 780 A.2d 579 (App. Div. 2001).

For example, under federal tax laws, spouses have the right to file a joint tax return and the ability to reduce certain gift and estate taxes. They also have the right to receive certain federal entitlements that are granted based on marital status (including social security benefits), and they receive favorable privileges in immigration decisions. Spouses have the right under state laws to sue for loss of consortium and for wrongful death, and the right not to be forced to testify against each other in criminal proceedings. State laws also give spouses the right to receive property from each other when one dies intestate and in many states, souses can rely on state laws to shield their assets from individual creditors by owning property as tenants by the entirety. In addition to receiving quantifiable state and federal benefits, married couples receive certain status-based entitlements, including the right to visit each other in hospitals and in jails. Finally, although many unmarried workers have successfully convinced both public and private employers to extend employee benefit coverage to their non-spouse partners, in most instances only married employees receive workplace employee benefits for their dependents.

* * *

Although bankruptcy laws are designed to regulate debtors' economic affairs with their creditors, and not their sexual affairs with their significant others, the [Bankruptcy] Code grants several benefits to debtors based solely on their decision or ability to marry. . . .[41]

An Ohio commentator describes a "laundry list of state benefits and protections that accompany marriage" that cannot be attained by private contracting, civil unions, or domestic partnership laws.[42]

Some of the economic benefits withheld or specifically denied to same gender couples by statutory law have been offset in limited situations by actions of employers to grant employee benefits to heterosexual and homosexual couples alike. Most courts have denied

---

[41]Mechele Dickerson, *Family Values and the Bankruptcy Code: A Proposal to Eliminate Bankruptcy Benefits Awarded on the Basis of Marital Status*, 67 Fordham L. Rev. 69, 88-89 (1998) (internal footnotes omitted).

[42]See, e.g., Goodridge v. Department of Public Health, 440 Mass. 309, 798 N.E.2d 941 955–56 (2003) (citing a lengthy list of benefits and protections accorded to married couples; some of the more important ones include joint state income tax filing, automatic inheritance rights under intestacy statutes, entitlement of wages owed to deceased employees, right to share the medical policy of one's spouse, access to veterans' spousal benefits and preferences, equitable division of marital property on divorce, right to bring claims for wrongful death, presumption of legitimacy of children, evidentiary rights such as not being required to testify against one's spouse, automatic "family member" preference to make medical decisions for an incompetent spouse, and predictable rules of child custody and visitation). See also Hernandez v. Robles, 7 N.Y.3d 338, 821 N.Y.S.2d 770, 855 N.E.2d 1, 6–7 (2006) (listing marriage benefits under New York law); Craig A. Bowman & Blake M. Cornish, Note, A More Perfect Union: A Legal and Social Analysis of Domestic Partnership Ordinances, 92 Colum. L. Rev. 1164, 1167 (1992) (noting that marriage status imposes support obligations on the parties and also legally affects, among other things, workers' compensation, unemployment compensation, the right to bring tort actions for wrongful death or loss of consortium, legal presumptions in inheritance, and communications privileges); Brodie M. Butland, Note: The Categorical Imperative: Romer as the Groundwork for Challenging State "Defense of Marriage" Amendments, 68 Ohio St. L.J. 1419, n. 54 (2007).

discrimination claims and declined to find any obligation on the part of employers to offer domestic-partner benefits.[43] The Supreme Court of Alaska held to the contrary, finding that state law forbade marital-status discrimination by employers.[44] While this case was still pending, the Alaska legislature amended the state's Human Rights Act to allow employers to grant different benefits to married and nonmarried employees.[45]

Where employers voluntarily provide domestic partner benefits, nonmarried employees still do not gain the same advantage as married employees. The tax advantages granted for spouses and legal dependents are absent, so domestic partner benefits are generally taxable to the employee.[46]

The *Baehr* case has also inspired a wave of thoughtful law review articles on conflicts of laws issues, equal rights issues, privacy issues, and same-sex marriage issues.[47] These articles are digested in the "Marriage" section of the *Annual Survey of Periodical Literature* published in the Winter edition of the American Bar Association's *Family Law Quarterly*.[48]

---

[43]Rutgers Council of AAUP Chapters v. Rutgers, The State University, 298 N.J. Super. 442, 689 A.2d 828, 116 Ed. Law Rep. 731 (App. Div. 1997); Ross v. Denver Dept. of Health and Hospitals, 883 P.2d 516 (Colo. Ct. App. 1994); Phillips v. Wisconsin Personnel Com'n, 167 Wis. 2d 205, 482 N.W.2d 121 (Ct. App. 1992).

[44]University of Alaska v. Tumeo, 933 P.2d 1147, 117 Ed. Law Rep. 314 (Alaska 1997).

[45]Alaska Stat. § 18.80.220(c)(1). See also Annot., 74 A.L.R. 5th 439.

[46]See Bruce J. Kasten, Linda M. Doyle and Edward J. Pisarcik, *Domestic-Partner Benefits Plans Raise Legal Issues*, National Law Journal, June 8, 1998, at p. B7.

[47]Samuel Marcosson, *The Lesson of the Same-Sex Marriage Trial*, 35 U. Louisville J. Fam. L. 721 (Fall 1996–97); Farabee, *Marriage, Equal Protection, and New Judicial Federalism: A View from the States*, 14 Yale L. & Pol'y Rev. 237 (1996); Ettelbrick, *Wedlock Alert: A Comment on Lesbian and Gay Family Recognition*, 5 J.L. & Pol'y 107 (Fall 1996); Curt Pham, *Let's Get Married in Hawaii: A Story of Conflicting Laws, Same-Sex Couples, and Marriage*, 30 Fam. L.Q. 727 (Fall 1996); Lynn D. Wardle, *A Critical Analysis of Constitutional Claims for Same-Sex Marriage*, 1996 BYU L. Rev. 1; Allen, *Same-Sex Marriage: A Conflict-of-Laws Analysis for Oregon*, 32 Willamette L. Rev. 619 (Summer 1996); Note, *In Sickness and In Health, In Hawaii and Where Else?: Conflict of Laws and Recognition of Same-Sex Marriages*, 109 Harv L. Rev. 2038 (June 1996); Barbara J. Cox, *Same-Sex Marriage and Choice-of-Law: If We Marry in Hawaii, Are We Still Married When We Return Home*, 1994 Wis. L. Rev. 1033; Thomas M. Keane, *Aloha, Marriage? Constitutional and Choice of Law Arguments for Recognition of Same-Sex Marriages*, 47 Stan. L. Rev. 499 (1995); Mohr, *The Case for Gay Marriage*, 9 Notre Dame J.L. Ethics & Pub. Pol'y 215 (1995); Candace L. Sage, *Sister-State Recognition of Valid Same-Sex Marriages: Baehr v. Lewin—How Will it Play in Peoria*, 28 Ind. L. Rev. 115 (1994); Steven K. Homer, *Against Marriage*, 29 Harv. C.R.-C.L. L. Rev. 505 (1994).

[48]For example, one of the most comprehensive articles digested in the Winter, 2006 edition is Phyllis G. Bossin, *Same-Sex Unions: The New Civil Rights Struggle or an Assault on Traditional Marriage?*, 40 Tulsa L. Rev. 381 (2005).

Chapter 3

Parentage

By Pamela J. MacAdams, Esq.

§ 3:1   Ohio Parentage Act—History and origin

The Ohio Parentage Act (OPA), originally enacted in 1982 as RC Chapter 3111, is a modified version of the Uniform Parentage Act,[1] which completely replaced the former paternity statutes. Prior Ohio law distinguished between legitimate and illegitimate children and conditioned many of a child's rights on the marital status of his or her

---

[Section 3:1]

[1]Approved by the National Conference of Commissioners on Uniform State Laws in 1973 and adopted as of March 1987, with various modifications, in Alabama, California, Colorado, Delaware, Hawaii, Illinois, Kansas, Minnesota, Montana, Nevada, New Jersey, North Dakota, Rhode Island, Washington, and Wyoming.

parents.[2] The OPA abolished the statutory and common law classifications of legitimate and illegitimate and provided that the parent-child relationship extends equally to all children for whom parentage has been established, regardless of the marital status of their parents.[3]

In abolishing distinctions between legitimate and illegitimate children, the OPA is consistent with US Supreme Court decisions. The United States Constitution ensures that illegitimate children whose parentage has been legally determined have rights similar to those afforded to legitimate children, including the rights to support and inheritance.[4] Acknowledged fathers also have rights and obligations comparable to those of fathers of legitimate children.[5]

§ 3:2 Administrative determination of parentage—Purpose

In 1992 statutory enactments changed the method by which a parent-child relationship is established. Counsel may no longer file a complaint to establish a parent-child relationship pursuant to RC 3111.01 to RC 3111.18 in the juvenile court until the administrative procedure enacted by RC 3111.38 is followed, unless one of the following exceptions apply.

RC 3111.381 initially allowed three exceptions to the required use of the administrative procedure before suit. They are where (1) the probate court retains jurisdiction over the parent-child relationship when the alleged father is deceased and the probate of his estate is or can be commenced, and may determine the parent-child relationship without the administrative determination through CSEA; (2) the issue of paternity arises in a domestic relations action for divorce, dissolution of marriage, or legal separation, that court may determine the parent-child relationship without an administrative determination through CSEA; and (3) an acknowledgment of paternity in probate court pursuant to RC 2105.18 prior to January 1, 1998, or an acknowledgment filed with the department of human services under

---

[2]See Robert J. Frankart, *The Determination of Parentage Under the New Ohio Parentage Act,* 55 Ohio B. 1248 (7-26-82).

[3]RC 3111.01(B).

[4]Lalli v. Lalli, 439 U.S. 259, 99 S. Ct. 518, 58 L. Ed. 2d 503 (1978) (paternal inheritance rights); Gomez v. Perez, 409 U.S. 535, 93 S. Ct. 872, 35 L. Ed. 2d 56 (1973) (right to paternal support); Levy v. Louisiana, 391 U.S. 68, 88 S. Ct. 1509, 20 L. Ed. 2d 436 (1968) (wrongful death recovery). Classifications based on illegitimacy have not been held to be suspect classifications subject to "strict scrutiny," but they command an intermediate level of protection and are invalid under U.S. Const. amend. XIV if they are not substantially related to permissible state interests: Weber v. Aetna Cas. & Sur. Co., 406 U.S. 164, 92 S. Ct. 1400, 31 L. Ed. 2d 768 (1972); Mathews v. Lucas, 427 U.S. 495, 96 S. Ct. 2755, 49 L. Ed. 2d 651 (1976); Mills v. Habluetzel, 456 U.S. 91, 102 S. Ct. 1549, 71 L. Ed. 2d 770 (1982).

[5]RC 3111.13; Stanley v. Illinois, 405 U.S. 645, 92 S. Ct. 1208, 31 L. Ed. 2d 551 (1972); Caban v. Mohammed, 441 U.S. 380, 99 S. Ct. 1760, 60 L. Ed. 2d 297 (1979).

RC 5101.314 after January 1, 1988, and before March 22, 2001,[1] results in a juvenile court support order pursuant to RC 2151.231, any parentage issue arising during the course of those support proceedings may be adjudicated by the juvenile court issuing the support order without a CSEA administrative determination being made first.

Ohio House Bill 136, effective on May 17, 2006, added two more exceptions to the rule that the administrative parentage determination must precede a parentage action in juvenile court.

The first of these new exceptions is codified in RC 3111.381(B). It permits a child's mother to bring a parentage action in the juvenile court, without first requesting an administrative determination, if the child's mother is bringing the action "in order to request an order to determine the allocation of parental rights and responsibilities, the payment of all or any part of the reasonable expenses of the mother's pregnancy and confinement, or support of the child." When such an action is commenced, the clerk of court shall forward a copy of the complaint to the child support enforcement agency of the county in which the complaint is filed.

The second new exception is in RC 3111.381(C) and provides that a putative father may bring a parentage action in court without first exhausting his administrative remedy if he brings the action "in order to request an order to determine the allocation of parental rights and responsibilities." Again, the clerk of courts must forward a copy of the complaint to CSEA.

In both instances of the new exceptions, the action must still be brought in the county in which the child resides.

Absent one of the above exceptions, counsel must follow the procedures set forth in RC Chapter 3111 to commence a parentage action.[2] The objective behind the administrative procedure is to establish more swiftly the legal relationship between the parent and child in order to then establish a support order for the child as soon as possible. Since the success of the administrative procedure is largely dependent upon cooperation and admissions of the parties, the ultimate goal of child support will be reached at variable times. There is a possibility the process will be slow, and ultimately lead to litigation to establish the parent-child relationship if the parties are uncooperative.

§ 3:3 Administrative determination of parentage—Initial procedure

RC 3111.38 is the current procedural reference for the administra-

---

[Section 3:2]

[1]After March 22, 2001, the acknowledgment statute is RC 3111.23.

[2]But see State ex rel. Jackson County Child Support Enforcement Agency v. Long, 2004-Ohio-2184, 2004 WL 914640 (Ohio Ct. App. 4th Dist. Jackson County 2004).

tive process to establish parentage. All notice requirements of the Rules of Civil Procedure also apply.[1] To initiate the establishment of paternity through CSEA:

(1) A parent or alleged parent must request an administrative determination of parentage through the child support enforcement agency (CSEA). This request must contain certain identifying information regarding each parent and/or alleged parent, and the child. The applicant must supply the name, birthdate, current address, or last known address of the alleged father. The application must include the mother's name, social security number, and current address.[2]

(2) The CSEA shall assign an officer who may schedule a conference with the mother and the alleged father to provide information and an opportunity to sign an acknowledgment under RC 5101.324.[3]

The CSEA is to schedule testing, then call the parties in, and cancel the tests if they sign the acknowledgment. If service of notice (now required pursuant to the Civil Rules) is not accomplished by the genetic testing date, then the CSEA has to proceed to test those persons present.[4] Notice of the administrative support hearing must now be attached to the Administrative Finding of Parentage.

The CSEA must give notice of the genetic testing in accordance with the Ohio Rules of Civil Procedure. The notice must contain all of the following information:

(1) That the CSEA has been requested to determine the parent-child relationship;

(2) The child's name and birthdate;

(3) The mother and alleged father's names;

(4) Parental rights and responsibilities;

(5) That the child, mother and alleged father must submit to genetic testing at a stated time, date, and place;

(6) The administrative procedure for determining the existence of a parent and child relationship;

(7) That if the alleged father or natural mother willfully fails to submit to genetic testing, or the alleged father, natural mother or the custodian of the child willfully fails to submit the child to genetic testing, the agency will issue an order that it is inconclusive whether the alleged father is the child's natural father;

(8) That if the alleged father or natural mother willfully fails to submit to genetic testing, or the alleged father, natural mother

---

[Section 3:3]

[1]RC 3111.421.

[2]RC 3111.40.

[3]RC 3111.22(C)(1).

[4]RC 3111.44.

or custodian of the child willfully fails to submit the child to genetic testing, they may be found in contempt of court.[5]

Presumably, the failure of a party to appear at this information conference will result in a genetic testing order. RC 3111.44 does not directly address a failure to appear at the conference, but does authorize the genetic testing order and RC 3111.47 states that failure to submit to genetic testing shall result in an inconclusive parentage order.[6] Some agencies are simply dismissing the administrative action where a party fails to appear.[7]

RC 3111.38 requires that the CSEA be used in the county in which the child or the child's guardian or legal custodian resides.[8]

When genetic test results generate a probability of paternity of 99% or greater, CSEA issues an order that the man is the father. If test results generate less than 99% probability of paternity, then CSEA shall issue an order that the man is not the father.[9] The right of a party to raise the parentage issue in a later court or administrative proceeding to establish support is eliminated if not raised when the action arises. This occurs in those instances when CSEA is asked to establish a support order based upon a presumption of parentage. Under former RC 3111.20 (now repealed), the issuance of a support order on this basis did not preclude a parent from raising the issue later.

§ 3:4   Administrative determination of parentage—
Acknowledgment, support order, and birth record

If both parties attend the information conference, the CSEA must explain the allegation, the administrative procedure for establishing paternity, the parental rights and responsibilities, and the right to acknowledge parentage and assume the duty of support.[1]

If at this conference both parents sign an acknowledgment of paternity, an administrative finding of paternity is made in a written order that advises both parties of their right to object to such finding within thirty days by filing a complaint under RC 3111.01 to RC 3111.18,[2] in the juvenile court or other court with jurisdiction under RC 2101.022 or RC 2301.03, in the county in which the child support enforcement agency that employs the administrative officer who issued the order is located. If the action is not brought within the thirty-day period, the administrative order is final and enforceable by a court and may not be challenged in an action under RC 3111.

---

[5]RC 3111.42.

[6]RC 3111.44 to RC 3111.47.

[7]See Text § 3:7, Administrative determination of parentage—Dismissal.

[8]RC 3111.44.

[9]RC 3111.46, eff. 3-22-01.

[Section 3:4]

[1]RC 3111.44.

[2]RC 3111.49.

However, RC 3111.28 permits challenge to an acknowledgment of parentage within one year of it becoming final on the basis of fraud, duress, or material mistake of fact. The action shall be treated as an initial parentage determination by the court as if brought under RC 3111.01 et seq. and may be brought where the child, guardian or custodian of the child or either party who signed the acknowledgement resides. If an acknowledgment is not proven to have been filed with the office of child support, then it does not become a final or enforceable establishment of parentage.[3]

A distinction between post-decree and post-acknowledgment rules as to vacation of paternity is made in Galan v. Holbert, 2008-Ohio-1586, 2008 WL 853302 (Ohio Ct. App. 2d Dist. Greene County 2008). An action to rescind an acknowledgment must be brought within one year after it becomes final and a post-decree paternity action cannot be brought on a child's behalf absent an express determination by the court that such action is in the best interests of the child.[4]

RC 3111.381 is the administrative establishment of parentage process. It remains in effect such that to establish parentage, the administrative process must be exhausted prior to jurisdiction vesting at the court level unless an exception applies.[5] Note that two statutes are inconsistent with one another. RC 3111.47 instructs the CSEA hearing officer to issue an "inclusive" finding where a party fails to present for genetic testing. However, RC 3111.54 requires CSEA to file a contempt action against the party failing to present for testing. Due to this discrepancy, a party who prefers to use the court as opposed to the administrative process could register at CSEA, fail to appear, and demand an "inclusive" finding for use as basis to file in court. Without an order, there should be no contempt process available to CSEA.

If after the administrative determination of parentage, a support order is requested by a party, then the CSEA must issue notice of an administrative support hearing to be held not later than sixty days from the request for same, and not earlier than thirty days from issuance of notice of such a hearing.[6]

An administrative support order must comply with current statutory support schedules or with statutes permitting annuities in lieu thereof. The order must also include notice of procedure to be followed to object to the administrative support order by bringing an action under RC 2151.231 within thirty days of the administrative support order. If no such action is brought within this thirty-day period, then

---

[3]Jennifer C. v. Tony M.D., 2005-Ohio-5050, 2005 WL 2335332 (Ohio Ct. App. 12th Dist. Clermont County 2005).

[4]Broxterman v. Broxterman, 101 Ohio App. 3d 661, 656 N.E.2d 394 (1st Dist. Hamilton County 1995).

[5]See Text § 3:2, Administrative determination of parentage—Purpose.

[6]RC 3111.80.

the administrative support order is final and modifiable and may not be challenged in an RC 3111 proceeding.[7]

CSEA may also change the surname and birth record of a child at issue if it finds that the father is a man other than that named on the birth record.[8]

§ 3:5 Administrative determination of parentage—No acknowledgment and support order

After March 22, 2001, after issuing an order for genetic testing, the administrative hearing officer may schedule a conference with both mother and alleged father to provide information and an opportunity to sign an acknowledgment of parentage pursuant to RC 3111.31. If they sign the acknowledgment, the genetic testing is canceled. No acknowledgment can be signed, however, if there is a presumption of parentage with another man under RC 31l1.03. If no acknowledgment is signed, then the parties shall submit to genetic testing under the prior order.[1]

The results of the genetic tests shall prompt the administrative hearing officer to issue one of two orders. If the test results indicate a probability of parentage of 99% or greater, then the hearing officer shall issue an administrative finding of parentage between the alleged father and the child. However, if the test results are less than 99% probability of parentage, then the administrative hearing officer shall issue an administrative order that the alleged father is not the father of the child.[2]

Any order issued in accordance with RC 3111.46 shall be served in accordance with the Civil Rules governing service of pleadings subsequent to the initial complaint.[3]

Each party has thirty days from the issuance of one of the above orders to appeal, by filing suit under RC 3111.01 to RC 3111.18 in the court of proper jurisdiction.[4]

After the establishment of paternity, an administrative support hearing shall be scheduled with proper notice and within the time limits as described after an administrative acknowledgment of paternity, that is, within sixty days of request but not prior to thirty days after notice.[5] Appeal from an administrative support order at this stage is taken by filing a support suit under RC 2151.231 within thirty days or else the order is final and modifiable only under RC 3113.21 to RC 3113.219 or RC 3111.27.

---

[7]RC 3111.49.

[8]RC 3111.58 and RC 3111.52.

[Section 3:5]

[1]RC 3111.44.

[2]RC 3111.46.

[3]RC 3111.46.

[4]RC 3111.49. See also Text §§ 3:9 et seq., Judicial parentage action.

[5]RC 3111.80.

§ 3:6 Administrative determination of parentage—Finality

RC 3111.49 specifies that an administrative order is final if neither party brings an action in court within thirty days of the determination. Thus, where the alleged father did not object to the determination within that period, he could not later bring a complaint to determine whether he was the father.[1] The administrative order was res judicata. The court properly denied a putative father's motion for an HLA test where he did not challenge an administrative determination of paternity thirty days after the determination. "Finality is particularly compelling in a case involving determinations of parentage, visitation and support of a minor child."[2]

§ 3:7 Administrative determination of parentage—Dismissal

Under RC 3111.47, the CSEA hearing officer shall issue "inclusive" findings of parentage where a party fails to present for genetic testing. However, RC 3111.56 requires CSEA to file contempt action against the party failing to present for genetic testing. If a party prefers to use the court instead of the administrative process to establish parentage, they could fail to appear and demand an "inclusive" finding for use as a basis to file in court. Without an order, there should be no contempt process available to CSEA.

§ 3:8 Jurisdiction and venue

The OPA grants the juvenile court original jurisdiction in parentage actions.[1] Venue is proper in the juvenile court of the county in which the child, the child's mother, or the alleged father resides or is found, or in the county in which the child is being provided support by the department of human services. If the alleged father is deceased, venue is found in the county in which his estate has been or can be probated.[2] The action may be brought by the child or the child's personal representative, the mother or her personal representative, the man alleged or alleging himself to be the child's father, or the CSEA may bring the action if the mother is a recipient of public assistance.[3]

While juvenile court jurisdiction is not exclusive, and the court of common pleas may properly assume jurisdiction over parentage mat-

---

[Section 3:6]

[1]Richards v. Kazleman, 1994 WL 249826 (Ohio Ct. App. 5th Dist. Stark County 1994). RC 3111.49.

[2]See Strack v. Pelton, 70 Ohio St. 3d 172, 175, 1994-Ohio-107, 637 N.E.2d 914 (1994). See also State ex rel. Fulton Cty. Dept. of Human Serv. v. Kenneth J., 99 Ohio App. 3d 475, 651 N.E.2d 27 (6th Dist. Fulton County 1994). But see Text § 3:30, Res judicata and vacation of parentage orders.

[Section 3:8]

[1]RC 3111.06(A).

[2]RC 3111.06(A).

[3]RC 3111.04.

ters,[4] actions which encompass only parentage claims usually should be filed in juvenile court. RC Chapter 3111 is not the exclusive procedure for determining the paternity of an illegitimate child. Before January 1, 1998, an action seeking custody and support could be based on an acknowledgment of paternity under RC 2105.18.[5] An acknowledgment of paternity was filed in the probate court, stating that the natural mother or other custodian or guardian of a child and the natural father acknowledge that the father is the child's natural father and that he assumes the duty of support for the child. This was filed by either parent, a guardian, custodian, the CSEA or a hospital staff member, pursuant to RC 3727.17. 1997 House Bill 352 amended and recodified this acknowledgment procedure in RC 5101.314, moving it from probate court to the department of human services.[6] Parental rights and responsibility are conferred upon all concerned as if the child were born in wedlock, including the right of any party with standing under RC 3109.12 to apply for companionship or visitation rights with the child. It has been held that a court did not err in accepting an RC 2105.18 probate court legitimation as a basis for a custody and support award where the acknowledged father fails to avail himself of an opportunity to challenge paternity in a juvenile court proceeding.[7]

Parties who assent by filing pleadings, attending hearings, and stipulating to an agreed entry are properly within the court's jurisdiction.[8]

If a divorce, dissolution, or legal separation action is pending in which parentage of a child is at issue, the domestic relations court has original jurisdiction.[9] A party to a UFISA action may raise the issue of parentage in response to litigation to establish a child support order. Such a defense entitles the defendant to paternity testing at his

---

[4]Standifer v. Arwood, 17 Ohio App. 3d 241, 479 N.E.2d 304 (12th Dist. Warren County 1984) ("The Common Pleas Court being a court of general jurisdiction . . . has jurisdiction of all actions unless its jurisdiction is taken away by statute," quoting State ex rel. Mastracci v. Rose, 79 Ohio App. 556, 558, 72 N.E.2d 582 (2d Dist. Franklin County 1947)). See also Niarhos v. Niarhos, 1986 WL 3490 (Ohio Ct. App. 2d Dist. Montgomery County 1986); Reed v. Reynolds, 1985 WL 8168 (Ohio Ct. App. 12th Dist. Clermont County 1985).

[5]In re Custody of Davis, 41 Ohio App. 3d 81, 534 N.E.2d 945 (5th Dist. Guernsey County 1987).

[6]Effective March 22, 2001, acknowledgments of paternity are now codified under RC 3111.23, and filed with the Office of Child Support.

[7]See Pamela J. MacAdams, *Determination of Paternity*, 1 Dom. Rel. J. Ohio 8 (May/June 1989).

[8]Smith v. Quigg, 2000 WL 873543 (Ohio Ct. App. 5th Dist. Fairfield County 2000).

[9]RC 3111.06(A), RC 3111.22(A)(2). Corrigan v. Corrigan, 1999 WL 304523 (Ohio Ct. App. 8th Dist. Cuyahoga County 1999).

request.[10] Jurisdiction of that court depends on the facts existing at the time the suit was brought. Thus, the Eighth District Court of Appeals held in *Slavin v. Slavin*[11] that the domestic relations court does not lose jurisdiction over parentage claims and other matters concerning children if the complaint for divorce is dismissed on the day of trial.[12]

In addition to parties physically within the state, anyone who has had sexual intercourse in Ohio is within the court's jurisdiction in an action involving the parentage of a child who may have been conceived by that act of intercourse.[13] Consent or lack of consent to sexual intercourse is irrelevant to jurisdiction.[14] Limited long-arm jurisdiction has also been applied to a putative father who was not present in Ohio and who did not engage in sexual intercourse in Ohio, but who had previously visited the child, sent support money to the child's mother, and sent a birthday gift to the child in Ohio.[15] However, *State ex rel. Stone v. Court of Common Pleas of Cuyahoga County, Juvenile Division*[16] held that simple allegations of tortious failure to support are insufficient to uphold long-arm jurisdiction when the putative father and Ohio had no other contacts.

Under the UCCJEA, Ohio does not have jurisdiction to establish paternity or custody of a child, though such child has lived in Ohio since birth, when the child is conceived during the marriage of spouses whose divorce and custody issues are pending in another state, and the other state has not relinquished jurisdiction. In *In re Craig* the biological mother who was divorcing her husband in North Carolina, gave birth to her daughter in Michigan. From birth, the child was delivered to the mother's sister in Ohio, where the child was raised for a number of years. The biological father (husband) did not know of the whereabouts of the child until the child's aunt and uncle sought custody in Ohio. The aunt and uncle refused to comply with the North

---

[10]Beam v. Beam, 2002-Ohio-2910, 2002 WL 1331989 (Ohio Ct. App. 2d Dist. Darke County 2002).

[11]Slavin v. Slavin, 1985 WL 6893 (Ohio Ct. App. 8th Dist. Cuyahoga County 1985).

[12]See also Minneapolis & St. L. R. Co. v. Peoria & P. U. Ry. Co., 270 U.S. 580, 46 S. Ct. 402, 70, 70 L. Ed. 743 (1926); St. Paul Mercury Indem. Co. v. Red Cab Co., 303 U.S. 283, 58 S. Ct. 586, 82, 82 L. Ed. 845 (1938).

[13]RC 3111.06(B). Verber v. Wilson, 1997 WL 304403 (Ohio Ct. App. 10th Dist. Franklin County 1997).

[14]Van Pham v. Redle, 29 Ohio App. 3d 213, 504 N.E.2d 1147 (9th Dist. Summit County 1985).

[15]Yarnick v. Stegkamper, 1985 WL 6574 (Ohio Ct. App. 4th Dist. Lawrence County 1985).

[16]State ex rel. Stone v. Court of Common Pleas of Cuyahoga County, Juvenile Div., 14 Ohio St. 3d 32, 470 N.E.2d 899 (1984) (mother and child moved to Ohio after conception and birth; putative father had never been a resident of Ohio and did not engage in relevant sexual intercourse in Ohio; court rejected tortious failure to support as authority for jurisdiction because the injury, the failure to support, is ancillary to a determination of an obligation to support by reason of paternity).

Carolina order for genetic testing. The Ohio and North Carolina courts conferred pursuant to the terms of the UCCJEA. North Carolina refused to relinquish jurisdiction, though the child never lived there, until the mother and/or aunt and uncle submitted the child to genetic testing.[17]

Also, where a child was born in Texas, the alleged father was served with a complaint in his state of residence of Oklahoma, and the conception of the child took place in Texas, the mother and child's residence in Ohio is insufficient to confer in personam jurisdiction over the defendant on an Ohio court.[18]

The juvenile court has subject matter jurisdiction to change a child's name after a parent-child relationship has been established under the Ohio Parentage Act.[19] The standard for decision as to whether to order such a change when a parent objects to such change of name is best interest of the child.[20]

A second voluntary dismissal of a parentage action must be with prejudice.[21]

Under 2000 S.B. 180, new RC 2151.23(B)(6) grants the juvenile court jurisdiction to hear and determine actions filed under new RC 3119.961 (relief from paternity judgments). RC 2151.231 specifies that no child support action may be brought against a person presumed to be a parent based upon an acknowledgment of paternity, until that acknowledgment becomes final.[22]

§ 3:9   Judicial parentage action—Initial procedure

After compliance with the procedures mandated by RC 3111.38, parentage actions can be brought pursuant to RC 3111 to establish the parentage of a nonmarital child or a child born to a mother who, at the time of the child's birth, was married to a man other than the biological father. RC 3111 actions are usually the preferable method of establishing parentage, because they can be brought by any party without the consent of the other parties, and because child support, visitation, and other related issues can be adjudicated in conjunction with or following the parentage determination.

Parent-child relationships can also be established by legitimation or acknowledgment pursuant to RC 3111.23 which places this authority in the department of human services. Acknowledgment must be filed by the natural father with the consent of the mother. However, a

---

[17]In re Craig, 2007-Ohio-3843, 2007 WL 2164532 (Ohio Ct. App. 11th Dist. Trumbull County 2007).

[18]Gaisford v. Swanson, 83 Ohio App. 3d 457, 615 N.E.2d 266 (3d Dist. Paulding County 1992).

[19]Bobo v. Jewell, 1987 WL 12245 (Ohio Ct. App. 4th Dist. Athens County 1987).

[20]See Text § 3:51, Related issues—Name.

[21]Liptay v. Feruski, 1994 WL 11323 (Ohio Ct. App. 8th Dist. Cuyahoga County 1994).

[22]Finality is determined by the factors in RC 3111.25 et seq.

mother may not arbitrarily withhold her consent to the legitimation of her child, where she has previously indicated agreement with the court's order for support and visitation by the natural father.[1] If the department of human services is satisfied that the applicant is the natural father and that the establishment of the relationship is in the best interest of the child, the court or agency can make such a finding in its records and, thereafter, the child is legally the child of the natural father. Parent-child relationships can also be established by adoption[2] or by a domestic relations court when the issue arises in an action for divorce, dissolution, legal separation, or annulment.[3] An agreed judgment entry which finds a defendant to be the "reputed father" and orders support is not a valid legal determination of parentage.[4]

One Ohio common pleas court has held RC 3111.04(A) to be an unconstitutional infringement on marital privacy when an alleged father attempted to rebut the presumption of paternity which arises by virtue of marriage.[5] This, however, is not the prevailing viewpoint.[6]

§ 3:10 Judicial parentage action—Parties

Parent-child relationships include the mother and child relationship and the father and child relationship.[1] The mother's relationship may be established by proof that she gave birth to the child, or pursuant to RC 3111.01 to RC 3111.19, or RC 3111.20 to RC 3111.29;[2] the parent-child relationship between a child and its natural father may have been established pursuant to RC 2105.18 (RC 5101.314 after 1-1-98 and before 3-22-01, and RC 3111.23 after 3-22-01), or RC 3111.01 to RC 3111.19, or RC 3111.20 to RC 3111.29.[3] court may properly dismiss an action to be declared the legal mother of a child where she is not the biological mother and no surrogate agreement existed, even

---

[Section 3:9]

[1]In re Legitimation of Conn, 7 Ohio App. 3d 241, 455 N.E.2d 16 (10th Dist. Franklin County 1982).

[2]RC 3111.02. See also RC 3107.01 et seq.

[3]RC 3111.22(A)(2), repealed eff. 3-22-01; Slavin v. Slavin, 1985 WL 6893 (Ohio Ct. App. 8th Dist. Cuyahoga County 1985).

[4]Glass By Glass v. Campbell, 1993 WL 195104 (Ohio Ct. App. 3d Dist. Van Wert County 1993).

[5]Merkel v. Doe, 63 Ohio Misc. 2d 490, 635 N.E.2d 70 (C.P. 1993).

[6]Joseph v. Alexander, 12 Ohio St. 3d 88, 465 N.E.2d 448 (1984).

[Section 3:10]

[1]RC 3111.01(A).

[2]RC 3111.02. See also RC 3111.17.

[3]RC 3111.02.

though she had an oral agreement that she would be the child's legal parent.[4]

After January 1, 1998, RC 3109.042, added by 1997 House Bill 352, states that an unmarried female who gives birth to a child is the child's sole residential parent, until a court of competent jurisdiction issues an order otherwise.

The child, the child's mother, each man alleged to be the father, each man alleging himself to be the father, or the personal representative of any of these individuals may bring an action to determine the existence or nonexistence of a father-child relationship.[5] The natural mother of the child, each man presumed by RC 3111.03 to be the father of the child, and each man alleged to be the father of the child shall all be parties to the parentage action.[6] The CSEA may bring the action if the mother is a recipient of public assistance.[7] However, this statutory provision has been interpreted to allow the CSEA to bring an action on behalf of a non-public assistance recipient, and on behalf of a putative father. The court reasoned that to retain federal funds, each court must compose its own comprehensive system to establish paternity. It would be unconstitutional for the CSEA to reject representation of a putative father seeking to establish paternity.[8] Since the ruling in *Belsito*,[9] acknowledgments of paternity are now filed with CSEA, not with probate court. Consequently, after *Belsito* (which allowed a declaratory judgment action to define parentage of an unborn child being carried by a surrogate mother), it has been held that there is no statutory or constitutional authority for a probate court declaratory judgment of parentage.[10]

Previous to Ohio H.B. 136, the CSEA of the county in which the child resides must be made a party. Effective May 17, 2006, this provision is deleted from RC 3111.07(A), which has been amended to remove the child support enforcement agency as a necessary party when the party who initiates the action is a recipient of public assistance or if the responsibility for the collection of support has been assumed by the agency under Title IV D of the Social Security Act. Under the amended RC 3111.07(A), CSEA shall be given notice of the action pursuant to the Civil Rules and an opportunity to be heard.

A defendant may not be ordered to reimburse the department of human services for birth costs if the department is not made a party to

---

[4]Seymour v. Stotski, 82 Ohio App. 3d 87, 611 N.E.2d 454 (10th Dist. Franklin County 1992).

[5]RC 3111.04.

[6]RC 3111.07(A).

[7]RC 3111.04.

[8]Shockley v. Hedges, 2005-Ohio-6948, 2005 WL 3537682 (Ohio Ct. App. 5th Dist. Fairfield County 2005).

[9]Belsito v. Clark, 67 Ohio Misc. 2d 54, 644 N.E.2d 760 (C.P. 1994).

[10]Nemcek v. Paskey, 137 Ohio Misc. 2d 1, 2006-Ohio-2059, 849 N.E.2d 108 (C.P. 2006).

the action.[11] Thus, the department of human services must also be a party if money is due it for Medicaid-paid bills.

A former husband has no standing to intervene in the paternity case of his former wife once the spouses' decree of divorce, or other parentage proceedings, adjudicate that former husband is not the biological father of the child at issue. Thus, the trial court did not err in finding it had no jurisdiction to entertain former husband's motions for custody or visitation in mother's paternity action.[12]

Grandparents supporting a child of their own minor child have standing to establish parentage in order to enforce support rights and responsibilities under RC 3109.19.[13]

Other non-parent custodians of a minor child have standing to bring a post-decree paternity action, subject to an express determination that such action is in the best interest of the child.[14]

The child shall also be a party unless one of the other parties shows the court good cause for not joining the child.[15] A child may bring a parentage action separately from his mother.[16] Additionally, a county welfare department which has provided financial assistance to the child may be joined for the purpose of collecting or recovering support.[17] The court may align the parties to the parentage action and may add and drop parties sua sponte.[18] A proper party may intervene in a paternity action brought under RC 3111.04, per Civil Rule 24. No notice of other pending or prior litigation is required in an RC 3111.04 action.[19]

A parentage action may be brought before the birth of the child; however, if the action is contested, all proceedings (except the service of process and the taking of depositions to preserve testimony) may be stayed until after the birth. The stay allows the parties to perform ge-

---

[11]Fenton v. McElhatten, 1990 WL 200301 (Ohio Ct. App. 5th Dist. Richland County 1990).

[12]Strope v. Wells, 171 Ohio App. 3d 658, 2007-Ohio-1962, 872 N.E.2d 363 (5th Dist. Licking County 2007).

[13]See Text § 3:47, Effect of judgment—Grandparent duty of support; Text § 3:54, Complaint to establish father-child relationship—By grandparent, with request for support—Form.

[14]Broxterman v. Broxterman, 101 Ohio App. 3d 661, 656 N.E.2d 394 (1st Dist. Hamilton County 1995).

[15]McMullen v. Muir, 34 Ohio App. 3d 241, 517 N.E.2d 1381 (8th Dist. Cuyahoga County 1986).

[16]RC 3111.04; Rees v. Heimberger, 60 Ohio App. 3d 45, 573 N.E.2d 189 (8th Dist. Cuyahoga County 1989).

[17]RC 3111.07(B); Toth v. Leasure, 1986 WL 4767 (Ohio Ct. App. 5th Dist. Guernsey County 1986) (a judgment for support cannot be made in favor of the welfare department unless it is joined as a party).

[18]Carpenter v. Valez, 1986 WL 2390 (Ohio Ct. App. 4th Dist. Hocking County 1986).

[19]Hardman v. Chiaramonte, 39 Ohio App. 3d 9, 528 N.E.2d 1270 (9th Dist. Summit County 1987).

netic tests and to present the birth date, the medical records, and other information which would not have been available before the birth.[20]

No mention is made in RC 3111.38 of using the CSEA administrative procedure before birth. However, as the legislature left in the statute the right to bring suit before birth,[21] and a suit cannot be brought before using the RC 3111.38 procedure, it follows that the CSEA must accept applications for determination of parentage prior to birth. As a practical matter, a CSEA dismissal entry is required to file a complaint with the court. Thus, the mother of an unborn child should go to CSEA to begin the administrative process, but instead will receive a dismissal notice.

§ 3:11   Judicial parentage action—Pleading

Under RC 3111.13(C), a party must request the relief sought in the prayer of the complaint. The complaint, other initial pleading, or a subsequent pleading, must state a short and plain statement of each claim showing that the pleader is entitled to relief and a demand for judgment for the relief claimed, pursuant to Civil Rule 8(A). Failure to state a claim precludes the court from granting relief. If an order for a likely claim such as past care, health coverage or name change is desired, it must be requested in pleading form. court errs in granting past care support if a claim for such relief is not made in pleading.[1]

§ 3:12   Judicial parentage action—Procedure before hearing

A parentage suit is a civil action to which the Ohio Rules of Civil Procedure apply unless specified otherwise.[1] If the defendant admits the parentage allegations in the complaint, the court may enter judgment accordingly.[2] If the defendant denies the parentage allegations, the court holds a pretrial hearing at which each party is informed of the right to request genetic testing.[3] The action is not set for trial until all pretrial matters have been completed.[4] If the defendant does not file an answer after proper service, he is not entitled to notice of a

---

[20]RC 3111.04(C).

[21]RC 3111.04(C).

[Section 3:11]

[1]Woods v. Mt. Castle, 2002-Ohio-1878, 2002 WL 628888 (Ohio Ct. App. 2d Dist. Clark County 2002).

[Section 3:12]

[1]RC 3111.08(A).

[2]RC 3111.08(B).

[3]RC 3111.11.

[4]RC 3111.11.

default hearing.[5] If a party fails to appear at trial, the court does not err in dismissing the matter without prejudice.[6] A trial court also does not err in establishing parentage where the putative father failed to appear for genetic testing ordered on two separate occasions and failed to appear for trial when his motion for continuance was denied.[7]

After January 1, 1998, the jury demand provisions of RC 3111.12 were deleted by 1997 House Bill 352. Because parentage actions are governed by the Civil Rules, it is uncertain whether this change is intended to eliminate the right to jury trial, or to conform the demand procedures generally to the Civil Rules.

At least one Ohio appellate court has determined that the right to a jury trial in parentage actions existed prior to the addition, and thus exists after the deletion of the jury trial language formerly found in RC 3113.12, which is now silent as to juries. In *Kennedy v. Sherwood*[8], the court held that the former statutory language allowing a jury to be demanded by filing the demand within three days after the action is set for trial, merely established a procedure for requesting a jury. The statute did not create the right to a jury, as parentage proceedings are governed by the Civil Rules, and Civil Rule 38 outlines the procedure for exercising the right to a jury in a parentage case.

The juvenile court must make an order determining parentage within 120 days of the filing of the complaint.[9] The statute fails to address service, and probably should have given courts four months from service rather than filing, since service problems are common in parentage cases.

§ 3:13 Judicial parentage action—Presumptions of parentage—Creating

"[T]he strongest presumption of the law, [is] the presumption of legitimacy."[1] RC 3111.03, which sets forth the situations in which paternity is presumed, reflects this premise. Legislation has eliminated many of the previous presumptions of parentage. Only three presumptions remain:

---

[5]Long v. Bartlett, 73 Ohio App. 3d 764, 598 N.E.2d 197 (10th Dist. Franklin County 1992). See Text § 3:29, Resolution without trial. Fleming v. Plummer, 2002-Ohio-624, 2002 WL 233538 (Ohio Ct. App. 10th Dist. Franklin County 2002).

[6]State ex rel. Cody v. Bradley, 123 Ohio App. 3d 397, 704 N.E.2d 307 (2d Dist. Montgomery County 1997).

[7]Spradlin v. Montgomery, 2007-Ohio-2704, 2007 WL 1584578 (Ohio Ct. App. 12th Dist. Fayette County 2007).

[8]Kennedy v. Sherwood, 2001-Ohio-3355, 2001 WL 1122071 (Ohio Ct. App. 7th Dist. Columbiana County 2001).

[9]RC 3111.12(F).

[Section 3:13]

[1]Thompson v. Nichols, 286 A.D. 810, 141 N.Y.S.2d 590 (1st Dep't 1955) (where mother and husband were living together at the times of conception and birth of a child, evidence of paternity in another man was not sufficient to overcome the strongest presumption of the law, the presumption of legitimacy).

(1) The man and the child's mother are or have been married to one another, and the child is born during or within 300 days of the termination of the marriage;

(2) The man and the child's mother attempted to marry, but the marriage could be, or is, invalid and (a) the marriage can only be declared invalid by a court and the child is born during or within 300 days after the termination of the marriage; or (b) the attempted marriage is invalid without a court order and the child is born within 300 days after termination of cohabitation; and

(3) An acknowledgment of paternity has been filed under RC 3111.23 or former RC 5101.314 and has not become final under former section 3111.211 or 5101.314 or section 2151.232, 3111.25, or 3111.821 of the Revised Code.

Former presumptions of parentage that arose before this change are still valid unless rebutted pursuant to the provisions of the new law. The fact that a child bears a man's surname, is not a presumption of paternity, nor an establishment of paternity. Consequently, the trial court properly proceeded to order genetic testing and enter default judgment of paternity when father failed to appear at hearings after genetic test results did not exclude him as father.[2]

RC 3111.03 is the statutory listing of presumptions of parentage. The presumption formerly created by an acknowledgment is no longer a presumption, but is a final and enforceable determination of parentage unless the acknowledgment is rescinded.[3]

Acknowledgments are more commonplace than ever. It used to be that they only arose when parents voluntarily went to probate court and signed affidavits saying they are the parents of an illegitimate child. Now, however, because the statutes require hospital personnel to try to establish a father of an illegitimate child, this form of establishment is seen more frequently. In fact, hospitals are rewarded with a fee for each acknowledgment they get signed, though there is not any licensed legal advice involved in the process.[4]

The repeated changes in law related to the establishment of parentage; presumptions and the effect of each on finality of parentage rulings requires awareness of the history of such changes in order to apply the correct rules of law even today. Because the changes have taken place in a span of time less than the minority of some of the children at issue, it is imperative that the sequence of events which comprise the facts of a paternity case be compared to the law at the time of each event. For example, while today there are only three presumptions of paternity, historically there were many more.

---

[2]State ex rel. K.S. v. T.M., 2007-Ohio-984, 2007 WL 701038 (Ohio Ct. App. 8th Dist. Cuyahoga County 2007).

[3]RC 3111.28.

[4]RC 3111.03(A)(1).

Likewise, there were statutory methods of establishment of paternity
in the past which have been eliminated.

The legislature has sought to protect these former establishments
and presumptions by identifying in RC 3111.03 that those presumptions and findings of parentage which arose under prior law remain
recognized as final orders, despite the fact that the laws have changed.[5]

A presumption of paternity was created by the probate court entering an acknowledgment upon its journal as provided in RC 2105.18
until January 1, 1998, and by the department of human services under
RC 5101.314 from January 1998 until 3-21-01, and pursuant to RC
3111.23 from 3-22-01 to date. There was statutory conflict regarding
the effect of the probate court acknowledgment because former RC
2105.18 treated the acknowledgment of paternity as an establishment
of paternity, yet RC 3111.03(A)(5) listed the acknowledgment as only
a presumption.

The presumption that an acknowledgment is a presumption is now
as follows: It is a presumption for just a short window of time, then it
becomes a final enforceable finding of parentage. Under prior law,
these acknowledgments could not be attacked under the new Motion
for Relief from Parentage Actions created by RC 3119.961. Now,
however, after the window of time when they become final, they are
like any other finding of parentage. Thus, they can be subject to such
a motion for relief.

The presumption established by RC 3111.03 is not overcome by evidence of a husband's vasectomy where he failed to return for a sterility test prior to the date of conception.[6] A sworn affidavit raises no
presumption of paternity where the putative father and the child's
mother were not married.[7]

1997 House Bill 352 addressed this conflict by adding to RC
3111.03(B)(1) that where presumptions and determinations conflict,
the determination of parentage is controlling. Also effective January
1, 1998, new language was added to RC 3111.20 which eliminated the
ability of a party to raise parentage as an issue in a support action if
there has been a final acknowledgment of paternity under RC 2151.23,
RC 3111.211, or RC 5101.314, and RC 3111.25 after 3-22-01.[8] If the
acknowledgment was not final, however, the acknowledgment could
be rescinded by raising the issue of parentage before finalization.[9]
However, the Tenth District Court of Appeals distinguished the finality of an acknowledgment, holding that *res judicata* did not apply to

[5]RC 3111.03(A)(3); RC 3111.03(B); RC 3111.03(C)(1) and RC 3111.03(C)(2).

[6]Walkup v. Walkup, 31 Ohio App. 3d 248, 511 N.E.2d 119 (12th Dist. Brown
County 1986).

[7]McMullen v. Muir, 34 Ohio App. 3d 241, 517 N.E.2d 1381 (8th Dist. Cuyahoga
County 1986).

[8]RC 3111.20(C), repealed eff. 3-22-01.

[9]RC 3111.211(A), repealed eff. 3-22-01. See also RC 5101.314(A)(3) and RC
5101.314(A)(4)(b). See now RC 3111.82.

bar a challenge to an acknowledgment of paternity, where RC 3113.03(C)(1) created only a presumption of parentage. Here, the child was born in 1990, the parents married thereafter, and in 1992 the putative father signed an acknowledgment of paternity. Pursuant to RC 2105.18, the Franklin County Probate Court entered the acknowledgment of paternity upon its journal. The parties divorced in 1997 by dissolution of marriage which made no mention whatsoever of the child, and did not order child support. In 2004, mother sought child support and father contested paternity. The trial court ruled denied his motion for genetic testing, asserting that the issue of parentage was *res judicata,* as he had acknowledged paternity years prior. The Court of Appeals reversed, ruling that the doctrine of *res judicata* neither barred his paternity action nor precluded genetic testing. Their reasoning was that RC 3111.03 provided that a journalized acknowledgment of paternity "does not result in an unassailable, conclusive determination of paternity but, instead, renders only a rebuttable presumption of paternity.[10]

Ascertainment of the truth as a policy objective overrides general policy of law in favor of legitimacy. The use of a Civil Rule 75(D) investigation to challenge a prior finding of parentage where the man married the pregnant mother was upheld in a motion brought five years after the dissolution decree ordering support.[11]

These presumptions arise regardless of the validity or invalidity of the marriage, provided it was solemnized in apparent compliance with the law of the state in which it took place.[12] A man who never marries the child's mother, but who knowingly signs the child's birth certificate as informant, was also the child's presumed father[13] until January 1, 1998, when House Bill 352 removed this presumption prospectively.[14] The presumptions of paternity arising out of RC 3111.03 may be overcome by clear and convincing evidence.[15] Such evidence may be adduced through any of the methods contained in RC 3111.10,[16] but must include the results of genetic testing.[17] A presumption arising out of RC 3111.03(A)(1) or (2) is conclusive and cannot be rebutted as provided in RC 3111.37(A) where it is stated that the

---

[10]M.L. v. M.R., 2007-Ohio-4665, 2007 WL 2633616 (Ohio Ct. App. 10th Dist. Franklin County 2007)

[11]Carson v. Carson, 62 Ohio App. 3d 670, 577 N.E.2d 391 (12th Dist. Brown County 1989).

[12]RC 3111.03(A)(2), (A)(3), (B).

[13]RC 3111.03(A)(4); Hernandez v. Rivera, 1985 WL 10844 (Ohio Ct. App. 9th Dist. Lorain County 1985) (knowing consent is crucial; evidence that a man who signed the birth certificate could not read English and was not aware of the nature of the document he signed must be considered).

[14]RC 3111.03(A)(5), RC 3111.03(B)(3), eff. 1-1-98.

[15]RC 3111.03(B).

[16]Hulett v. Hulett, 45 Ohio St. 3d 288, 544 N.E.2d 257 (1989).

[17]RC 3111.03(B). Crawford County Child Support Enforcement Agency v. Sprague, 1997 WL 746770 (Ohio Ct. App. 3d Dist. Crawford County 1997).

spouse, not the donor for nonspousal artificial insemination, is the biological father.

After January 1, 1998, but before March 22, 2001, a presumption that the man is the natural father arises where the results of genetic tests indicate a probability of ninety-nine percent or greater that the man is the biological father of the child.[18]

It has been held that the rebuttable presumption of parentage need not include the results of genetic tests of the presumed father.[19]

RC 3111.27 eliminated the requirement that more than 60 days must elapse after the last signature, before an acknowledgment becomes final. Now under RC 3111.27, the acknowledgment can be rescinded within 60 days of the last signature by either parent by either requesting an administrative determinate of the existence or non-existence of parent-child relationship, or by either parent giving the Office of Child Support notice of the request for an administrative determination and CSEA making that determination.

Rescission is accomplished by requesting an administrative determination of whether there is a parent-child relationship between the man who signed the acknowledgment and the child subject of it.

An administrative determination that no parent child relationship exists must be issued before there is a rescission. The Office of Child Support must verify that an administrative determination request has been made, which causes the acknowledgment to be subject to rescission, instead of being actually rescinded as formerly was the procedure.[20]

The action for rescission may be brought within one year on the basis of fraud, duress, material mistake of fact, or by motion for relief from judgment under RC 3119.961.

Other eliminated presumptions include: the presumption created by father's agreement to pay child support by court order or written promise; the presumption created by 99% genetic test results ordered by the court, CSEA, or agreed to between the parties.

The law remains that a presumption can only be rebutted by clear and convincing evidence that includes the results of genetic testing.

§ 3:14 Judicial parentage action—Presumptions of parentage—Rebutting

Under the former parentage provisions, the presumption of legitimacy of a child born to a married mother was so strong that a man who alleged that he was the natural father of a child born during the mother's marriage to another had no standing to assert his claim unless the mother's husband disavowed paternity and a court found that

---

[18]RC 3111.03(A)(5), repealed.

[19]Matter of Feister v. Lee, 1993 WL 472868 (Ohio Ct. App. 5th Dist. Tuscarawas County 1993).

[20]RC 3111.27.

the husband was not the father of the child. Former RC 3111.01 to RC 3111.03 provided that only an unmarried woman, her legal representative, or the executor of her estate, if she was deceased, had standing to bring a paternity action. Courts desired to preserve intact families and to avoid rendering illegitimate a child who was previously legitimate.[1]

In contrast, RC 3111.04 allows a man alleging himself to be the child's father to bring an action to determine the existence of the relationship.[2] In *Joseph v. Alexander*,[3] the Ohio Supreme Court upheld the constitutionality of RC 3111.04(A) and stated:

> While every child conceived in lawful wedlock is presumed legitimate, such presumption is not conclusive and may be rebutted by clear and convincing evidence that there were no sexual relations between husband and wife during the time in which the child must have been conceived.

By this holding, the Court appeared to be reaffirming the traditional requirement; that is, when the mother's husband asserts paternity, the only evidence sufficient to overcome the presumption of legitimacy is that the husband and wife had no sexual relations during the probable period of conception.[4] On remand, the Fifth District Court of Appeals in *Joseph v. Alexander*[5] reversed a jury verdict that found that Joseph was the father of Alexander's child on the ground that Alexander and her husband had engaged in sexual relations during the time period in which the child was conceived. In *Jewett v. Jewett*,[6] the husband's assertion that he had not engaged in conjugal relations with his wife for more than 300 days prior to the birth of a child was insufficient to rebut the presumption of paternity.

Similarly, in *Nelson v. Nelson*,[7] the court held that a stipulation and affidavit are not clear and convincing evidence sufficient to overcome the presumption of legitimacy when other factors support the presumption that the husband is the legal father, including the husband's rearing of the child from birth. The court explained:

[Section 3:14]

[1]See State ex rel. Hoerres v. Wilkoff, 157 Ohio St. 286, 47 Ohio Op. 174, 105 N.E.2d 39 (1952); Franklin v. Julian, 30 Ohio St. 2d 228, 59 Ohio Op. 2d 264, 283 N.E.2d 813 (1972).

[2]RC 3111.04(A). Other states have also granted standing to an alleged biological father to dispute the presumption of paternity in a mother's husband. See, e.g., R. McG. v. J. W., 200 Colo. 345, 615 P.2d 666 (1980).

[3]Joseph v. Alexander, 12 Ohio St. 3d 88, 465 N.E.2d 448 (1984).

[4]See State ex rel. Walker v. Clark, 144 Ohio St. 305, 29 Ohio Op. 450, 58 N.E.2d 773 (1944). Compare Joseph v. Alexander, 12 Ohio St. 3d 88, 465 N.E.2d 448 (1984) (alleged biological father granted standing to dispute presumption of paternity in a mother's husband).

[5]Joseph v. Alexander, 1986 WL 5263 (Ohio Ct. App. 5th Dist. Stark County 1986).

[6]Jewett v. Jewett, 1991 WL 116988 (Ohio Ct. App. 11th Dist. Ashtabula County 1991).

[7]Nelson v. Nelson, 10 Ohio App. 3d 36, 38, 460 N.E.2d 653 (10th Dist. Franklin County 1983).

The possible harm is not merely the illegitimation of a heretofore legitimate child, but the disruption of the normal psychological and sociological relationship between father and child which is nurtured by support
and association.

. . .

Due to the length of time that defendant considered the oldest child to
be his son and the natural mother's concomitant assent thereto, both
parties are effectively estopped from denying parentage by stipulation.

In reaching this conclusion, the court noted that since the parties
were married before the child was conceived, the husband was
presumed to be the father and thus adoption was not necessary.

In *Slavin v. Slavin*,[8] the Eighth District Court of Appeals held that
the husband had standing to assert another man's paternity of a child
born to his wife during their marriage because the husband was the
presumed father. However, the Ohio Supreme Court in *Weinman v.
Larsh*[9] refused to find a cause of action under either common law or
RC Chapter 3111 to allow a husband to maintain an action against
the alleged father of the child for past necessaries furnished. In *In re
Feister v. Lee*,[10] the presumption that the husband was the father was
overcome without testing the father when the defendant's genetic
tests resulted in a 99.93% probability of paternity.

These cases, while still good law, must be read in conjunction with
the revised statutes effective July 15, 1992 requiring results of genetic
testing to successfully overcome a presumption under RC 3111.03.[11]

Before the OPA, the presumption that a man who knowingly married a pregnant woman was the father of her child was irrebuttable
even though the presumption as to a child conceived and born during
a marriage was not.[12] The rationale for this irrebuttable presumption,
as set forth in *Hall v. Rosen*,[13] was that the husband had voluntarily
assumed the role of father and the duty of supporting the child under
circumstances that were tantamount to adoption, and that to allow
the presumption to be rebutted would encourage "father shopping."
However, following the enactment of the OPA (which made the
presumption rebuttable), the Court in *Johnson v. Adams*[14] overruled
Hall for all children, including those born prior to the enactment of
the OPA. The Court noted that the risk of "father shopping" is
diminished by the "medical and legal acceptance of [HLA] tests" and
held that the child's welfare should be placed ahead of any "moral

---

[8]Slavin v. Slavin, 1985 WL 6893 (Ohio Ct. App. 8th Dist. Cuyahoga County
1985).

[9]Weinman v. Larsh, 5 Ohio St. 3d 85, 448 N.E.2d 1384 (1983).

[10]Matter of Feister v. Lee, 1993 WL 472868 (Ohio Ct. App. 5th Dist. Tuscarawas
County 1993).

[11]RC 3111.03(B).

[12]Miller v. Anderson, 43 Ohio St. 473, 3 N.E. 605 (1885); Hall v. Rosen, 50 Ohio
St. 2d 135, 4 Ohio Op. 3d 336, 363 N.E.2d 725 (1977).

[13]Hall v. Rosen, 50 Ohio St. 2d 135, 4 Ohio Op. 3d 336, 363 N.E.2d 725 (1977).

[14]Johnson v. Adams, 18 Ohio St. 3d 48, 51-52, 479 N.E.2d 866 (1985).

disparagement . . . [or] suddenly increased financial responsibilities" a man might incur as the result of being ordered to support a child.

Under this change in the law, a man who marries a woman pregnant by someone else can disavow the presumption of his paternity at any time until the child's twenty-third birthday, unless he legally adopts the child. If the marriage occurred before the OPA was enacted, however, the husband could not have adopted the child or established paternity, since he was conclusively presumed to be the child's father. Some children may, as a result, be caught in a parentage limbo, between presumptions.[15]

Under similar circumstances, the Eighth District Court of Appeals held that the trial court did not err in establishing a parent-child relationship after genetic testing demonstrated that a child born during a marriage was not the child of the husband. Mother, husband and biological father agreed to treat the child as husband's child, placed husband's name on the birth certificate and biological father executed a consent to adoption. Years later when husband attempted to adopt the child, his petition was denied, as he was already named on the birth certificate as father. Mother proceeded to establish the parent-child relationship between biological father and child in the juvenile court. Father objected, but was overruled and relationship was established, and support ordered.[16]

Even where a husband and wife object to the establishment of parentage by an alleged third party father, the trial court errs in refusing to order genetic testing which would enable the alleged father to establish the burden of proof which would overcome the presumption that a child born during a marriage is the husband's child.[17]

§ 3:15 Evidence—In general

Where the HLA test excludes the man as the father, he has no right to pursue parentage or visitation.[1] Proof by a preponderance of the evidence is the standard for establishing paternity.[2] RC 3111.10 provides that in a parentage action evidence relating to a putative father's paternity may include evidence of sexual intercourse between the alleged father and the mother at a time when conception was possible; expert evidence on the statistical probability of the alleged father's

---

[15]See Viera v. Viera, 1986 WL 8672 (Ohio Ct. App. 10th Dist. Franklin County 1986).

[16]H.N.H. v. H.M.F., 2005-Ohio-1869, 2005 WL 927004 (Ohio Ct. App. 8th Dist. Cuyahoga County 2005).

[17]David P. v. Kim D., 2007-Ohio-1865, 2007 WL 1165711 (Ohio Ct. App. 6th Dist. Lucas County 2007).

[Section 3:15]

[1]Sherburn v. Reichert, 97 Ohio App. 3d 120, 646 N.E.2d 255 (3d Dist. Van Wert County 1994).

[2]McMullen v. Muir, 34 Ohio App. 3d 241, 517 N.E.2d 1381 (8th Dist. Cuyahoga County 1986).

paternity based on the length of the mother's pregnancy; genetic test results; and medical evidence or other evidence which is relevant to the issue of the child's paternity. However, pursuant to RC 3111.12(C), testimony relating to the mother's sexual activities at any time other than the probable time of conception is inadmissible unless it is offered by the mother. Any evidence intended to rebut a presumption rising from RC 3111.03 must be clear and convincing and include the results of genetic testing,[3] except in donor cases where the presumption is conclusive.[4]

§ 3:16 Evidence—Witnesses

RC 3111.12(A) provides that the mother of the child and the alleged father are competent to testify in a parentage action, and they may be compelled to testify by subpoena. A witness may be compelled to give self-incriminatory testimony upon a grant from the court of "immunity from having [this] testimony . . . used against [him or her] in subsequent criminal proceedings."[1] Physicians also may testify concerning the medical circumstances of the mother's pregnancy and the characteristics of the child upon birth, and, pursuant to RC 3111.12(B), such testimony may not be excluded on the grounds of physician-patient privilege.

A court may determine paternity in a hearing under former RC 3115.24 without the defendant's presence where the defendant willfully disregards a subpoena and the issue of paternity was raised in the support proceeding.[2]

Testimony of the child may not be excluded without cause. In *Philpot v. Williams*,[3] the First District Court of Appeals held that it was error to refuse to permit a ten-year-old child to testify on the issue of his own parentage without first examining the child to determine his competency under Evidence Rule 601.

§ 3:17 Evidence—Genetic tests—Background

RC 3111.09(E) states that genetic tests are serological tests which include, but are not limited to, tests for the presence or absence of the common blood group antigens, the red blood cell antigens, human lymphocyte antigens, serum enzymes, serum proteins and genetic markers, and for the comparison of the deoxyribonucleic acid (DNA). Genetic testing is a relatively recent breakthrough, making possible,

---

[3]RC 3111.03(B).

[4]RC 3111.03(B); RC 3111.37.

[Section 3:16]

[1]RC 3111.12(A).

[2]RC 3115.24(A); McMullen v. Muir, 34 Ohio App. 3d 241, 517 N.E.2d 1381 (8th Dist. Cuyahoga County 1986).

[3]Philpot v. Williams, 8 Ohio App. 3d 241, 456 N.E.2d 1315 (1st Dist. Hamilton County 1983).

in many cases, virtually certain identification of the biological father. Antigens are genetic markers found in each person's chromosomes, and each antigen must be inherited from a parent. No one can have an antigen which is not present in either his or her biological mother or father.[1] The human leukocyte antigen (HLA) test is an extremely accurate test which examines and identifies HLA antigens of the mother, child, and alleged father.[2]

Therefore, once the antigen markers of a child and its mother are identified, the child's antigen genetic markers which could be inherited only from the father can generally be determined. If the child has antigens which are not present in the mother or the alleged father, then that alleged father can be excluded. On the other hand, if the alleged father and the child share antigens that are not present in the mother, the probability of the alleged father's paternity can be statistically determined, usually to a very accurate degree.[3]

A joint report of the American Medical Association and the American Bar Association recommends that six red blood cell antigen systems (ABO, Rh, MNS, Kell, Duffy, and Kidd) and the HLA be used in combination for paternity testing.[4] These seven tests can completely exclude a man erroneously alleged to be the father of a child in ninety-one to ninety-seven percent of the cases, and can predict the likelihood of paternity in cases in which the man is not excluded.[5] The HLA test is not meaningful in distinguishing between two biologically related, nonexcluded fathers, but it often predicts the likelihood of paternity in ninety percent of other cases.[6] To maximize accuracy, these tests can be done in a double blind format, which involves two completely independent tests of the blood samples. DNA testing, however, will distinguish between two biologically related persons (except identical twins) because no two people have the same DNA protein. DNA is found in every cell in the body.

Simple blood grouping tests (ABO tests), used prior to HLA and DNA tests, could only exclude a man as a possible father for a specific

---

[Section 3:17]

[1] Lester B. Herzog, *The HLA Test: New Method for Resolving Disputed Paternity Cases*, 55 N.Y. St. Bar J. 34 (May 1983).

[2] Richard E. Armitage & Donald E. Cross, *Paternity Testing in a Judicial Setting*, 39 J. Mo. Bar 477 (1983).

[3] Richard E. Armitage & Donald E. Cross, *Paternity Testing in a Judicial Setting*, 39 J. Mo. Bar 477 (1983).

[4] ABA and AMA, *Joint AMA-ABA Guidelines: Present Status of Serologic Testing in Problems of Disputed Parentage*, 10 Fam. L.Q. 247 (1976).

[5] Richard E. Armitage and Donald E. Cross, *Paternity Testing in a Judicial Setting*, 39 J. Mo. Bar 477 (1983); RC 3111.09.

[6] Lester B. Herzog, *The HLA Test: New Method for Resolving Disputed Paternity Cases*, 55 N.Y. St. Bar J. 34 (May 1983).

child.[7] Therefore, under the former paternity statute, the results of blood tests were admissible only to exclude a defendant and could not be used as affirmative evidence of a defendant's paternity.[8] RC 3111.10(C) specifically provides that genetic tests may be used as affirmative evidence of paternity. RC 3111.03(B) requires genetic test results as evidence to overcome presumptions of parentage. In *Owens v. Bell*,[9] the Ohio Supreme Court held that genetic tests are significantly different from blood grouping tests and that these tests would have been admissible even under the former statutory provisions. Therefore, genetic test results could be used in cases brought prior to the adoption of the OPA as well as those brought pursuant to the OPA.

§ 3:18 Evidence—Genetic tests—Testing procedure

RC 3111.09(A) also provides that a court may order the child's mother, the child, the alleged father, and any other person who is a defendant in the action to submit to genetic tests within thirty days of its order for testing.[1] A court need not be presented with a prima facie showing of paternity before ordering genetic testing.[2] "[A]ll that is required before court may order such testing is that a complaint be filed and that 'the person against whom the action is brought does not admit the existence . . . of the father and child relationship.' " As the Tenth District Court of Appeals explained in *Henry v. Miller*,[3] the good cause requirement of Civil Rule 35(A) has been legislatively determined, and "good cause for requiring the genetic tests exists in every paternity case in which the alleged father has denied paternity of the child."

After January 1, 1998, the court may also use any DNA records from a database maintained by the state bureau of criminal identification and investigation under RC 109.573 to determine the child's parentage,[4] and the results of genetic tests conducted in a proceeding under former RC 3111.21 or RC 3111.22.

Responding to a challenge of the constitutionality of the require-

---

[7]Lester B. Herzog, *The HLA Test: New Method for Resolving Disputed Paternity Cases,* 55 N.Y. St. Bar J. 34 (May 1983).

[8]Former RC 3111.16.

[9]Owens v. Bell, 6 Ohio St. 3d 46, 451 N.E.2d 241 (1983).

[Section 3:18]

[1]RC 3111.09(A); Dukes v. Cole, 23 Ohio App. 3d 65, 491 N.E.2d 374 (9th Dist. Lorain County 1985) (dismissal of a complaint with prejudice for the failure of plaintiff to appear for genetic testing ordered by the court on defendant's motion is an abuse of discretion where there is no showing that plaintiff's absence was intentional).

[2]Smith v. Sturt, 1985 WL 7603, at *6 (Ohio Ct. App. 6th Dist. Lucas County 1985).

[3]Henry v. Miller, 1984 WL 5952, at *2 (Ohio Ct. App. 10th Dist. Franklin County 1984).

[4]RC 3111.09(A)(1), eff. 1-1-98.

ment of complying with an order to submit to genetic testing, the appellate court in *McCarty v. Kimmel*[5] held that " 'the requirement to submit to the withdrawal of blood is not susceptible to a right of privacy challenge,' " even where it was the mother who refused the test on behalf of herself and the child.

The violation of a putative father's constitutional rights were further addressed as relates to his religious beliefs, and his assertion that the testing was performed under force, threat of force or coercion in *State ex rel. Maxwell v. Trikilis*, where the putative father claimed that his religious beliefs forbade the extraction of any substance from his body if not for medical purposes, and that he was compelled to undergo buccal swab testing by force. The facts of the case indicate that Appellant-putative father in fact held religious beliefs as he described, but that there was no real force of threat thereof involved in the testing process. The Court of Appeals held that the state proved a compelling interest in establishing paternity, and that the method of extraction of the putative father's dna was the least restrictive means available to further the state's interest, thus Appellant's right to free exercise of his religion was not violated.[6] Likewise, a trial court properly orders the CSEA to use genetic testing results from a prior action to ascertain parentage in a pending action, where alleged father asserts a religious opposition to genetic testing.[7]

The probate court may permit disinterment of an alleged parent in an effort to determine paternity by genetic testing, under a discovery motion filed in an action to determine heirship.[8] The Franklin County Probate Court reasoned, "The accuracy and infallibility of the DNA test are nothing short of remarkable." In an effort to have the law keep pace with modern developments, the court extended to the illegitimate child this procedure so that he could prove his right to share in his father's estate.[9]

RC 3111.09 allows a court to order genetic testing on its own motion and requires a court to order such testing on the motion of a party.[10] If a party or the court requests genetic testing, the court order for testing must include an order that the mother, child, alleged

---

[5]McCarty v. Kimmel, 62 Ohio App. 3d 775, 781, 577 N.E.2d 665 (2d Dist. Montgomery County 1989), quoting State v. Meacham, 93 Wash. 2d 735, 612 P.2d 795 (1980).

[6]State ex rel. Maxwell v. Trikilis, 2007-Ohio-1355, 2007 WL 879670 (Ohio Ct. App. 9th Dist. Medina County 2007).

[7]In re My'Kavellie E., 2008-Ohio-5035, 2008 WL 4409430 (Ohio Ct. App. 6th Dist. Lucas County 2008).

[8]Alexander v. Alexander, 42 Ohio Misc. 2d 30, 34, 537 N.E.2d 1310 (Prob. Ct. 1988).

[9]See also Alexander v. Alexander, 54 Ohio App. 3d 77, 560 N.E.2d 1337 (10th Dist. Franklin County 1989) for a concurring opinion and a relevant comment on trial court's procedure.

[10]State ex rel. Jason V. v. Cubbon, 180 Ohio App. 3d 595, 2009-Ohio-267, 906 N.E.2d 502 (6th Dist. Lucas County 2009).

father, and any other defendant submit to testing on the date in accordance with RC 3111.09.[11] Willful failure to submit is contempt of court.[12] RC 3111.09(A) provides that if a party shows "good cause" for failure to submit to genetic testing, the refusal is not "willful" and, thus, the trial court shall not enter a default judgment on that basis.[13]

If the CSEA is not a party to an action, then the clerk of courts must schedule tests within thirty days of a court order for testing.[14] If the CSEA is a party, tests should comply with rules under RC 3125.

If the mother willfully fails to submit herself or the child to genetic tests, then the court must issue an order determining the parent-child relationship without tests, where the father is the plaintiff. If the mother is the plaintiff, and the alleged father willfully fails to submit to tests, or if he is custodian and fails to submit the child for testing, the court must issue an order finding him to be the father without tests.[15]

RC 3111.09 allows a party to demand a second set of genetic tests. A court need not grant repeated continuances for this purpose.[16]

§ 3:19 Evidence—Genetic tests—Results of test

If all the experts conclude that the alleged father is not the father of the child, the court must enter a judgment of nonpaternity pursuant to RC 3111.09(D). However, the results of genetic tests supporting a finding of paternity are not conclusive, and a court could weigh these test results with the other evidence.

After January 1, 1998, the right to jury trial in parentage actions will be governed by the Civil Rules, because RC 3111.12(E), which defined jury trial demands in parentage actions was repealed.[1] When a court orders genetic tests which are not performed or introduced at trial, the court may proceed with the case and reach a judgment on the basis of whatever evidence is presented.[2]

The admissibility of the HLA and DNA tests does not obviate the need for laying a proper evidentiary foundation for the introduction of the results of the test at trial. The Seventh District Court of Appeals

---

[11]RC 3111.09(A).

[12]RC 3111.09(A).

[13]Marsh v. Clay, 125 Ohio App. 3d 518, 708 N.E.2d 1073 (8th Dist. Cuyahoga County 1998).

[14]RC 3111.09(A)(2).

[15]RC 3111.09(A).

[16]Merle v. Stantz, 1998 WL 667021 (Ohio Ct. App. 5th Dist. Richland County 1998).

[Section 3:19]

[1]Former RC 3111.12(E) was repealed by 1997 H.B. 352, eff. 1-1-98.

[2]Pless v. McGowan, 1986 WL 1724 (Ohio Ct. App. 8th Dist. Cuyahoga County 1986); Ewing v. Lenegar, 1985 WL 9459 (Ohio Ct. App. 4th Dist. Jackson County 1985); Richard v. Bell, No. C-840794 (Ohio Ct. App. 1st Dist. Hamilton County 1986).

has held that court errs when it allows a report of HLA tests results to be entered into evidence without a foundation being laid and without hearing testimony by the examiner performing the tests.[3] The genetic test examiners may be called, pursuant to RC 3111.09(B), to testify as to their findings and procedures. The extent of the necessary foundation seems to be within the discretion of the court, at least under the rationale of the Clark County Court of Appeals.[4] HLA test results were held to be admissible with minimal foundation as to (1) identification of blood as that of the parties, (2) reliability of samples, and (3) unbroken chain of custody of the samples. At trial, any party may also produce other expert evidence, including evidence of independent genetic tests.[5]

§ 3:20   Evidence—Genetic tests—Costs of testing

The costs of genetic tests usually are paid in advance by the party requesting them and later taxed as costs of the action.[1] If the parties stipulate to other arrangements for payment, the court may uphold the agreement.[2] Sometimes privately represented parties agree to split the costs of testing and that neither party will be reimbursed regardless of results. In these cases the court will abide by such agreement and not tax the costs if the agreement is journalized. Genetic testing shall not be delayed due to a dispute about who should pay. Instead, the CSEA should advance the costs and determine reimbursements due later,[3] when the court may tax them as costs. However, after January 1, 1998, CSEA need not advance the costs of genetic testing to parties previously tested pursuant to a former RC 3111.21 or RC 3111.22 proceeding.[4]

Indigent paternity defendants cannot prepay the cost of genetic tests; nevertheless, they face the state as an adversary when the complainant mother and her child are recipients of public assistance. According to *Anderson v. Jacobs*,[5] due process requires that such defendants be entitled to genetic or blood grouping tests at state

---

[3]Stewart v. Six, 1987 WL 14028 (Ohio Ct. App. 7th Dist. Columbiana County 1987).

[4]Camden v. Miller, 34 Ohio App. 3d 86, 517 N.E.2d 253 (2d Dist. Clark County 1986).

[5]RC 3111.09(B), (C). See also David H. Kaye & Ronald Kanwischer, *Admissibility of Genetic Testing in Paternity Litigation: A Survey of State Statutes*, 22 Fam. L.Q. 109 (Summer 1988).

[Section 3:20]

[1]See RC 3111.14; Reed v. Pace, 1985 WL 7978 (Ohio Ct. App. 8th Dist. Cuyahoga County 1985).

[2]Frase v. Albright, 1985 WL 6498 (Ohio Ct. App. 5th Dist. Licking County 1985).

[3]RC 3111.09(A).

[4]RC 3111.12(D) eff. 1-1-98.

[5]Anderson v. Jacobs, 68 Ohio St. 2d 67, 22 Ohio Op. 3d 268, 428 N.E.2d 419 (1981).

expense.[6] According to *Keeney v. Lawson*,[7] the entitlement to state-paid blood or genetic tests is "clearly designed to aid the court in the 'truth-finding' function," and, therefore, it must be applied retroactively. The costs of a second expert seriologist, however, must be borne by the party requesting other expert evidence.[8]

The absence of genetic tests may be asserted in a Civil Rule 60(B) proceeding.[9] These holdings are supported and strengthened by RC 3111.09(A) which now forbids delay in testing due to disputes over payment for testing. The CSEA or a party advancing the fees may seek reimbursement as court costs.

It is a denial of due process for a court to fail to provide an alleged father with sufficient time to accumulate funds necessary to pay for blood tests and time to have them performed.[10] All CSEA departments must have an on-site genetic testing program to facilitate the obtaining of blood samples for genetic testing.[11]

§ 3:21 Evidence—Other types of evidence

While scientific data are prominent in OPA practice, more traditional evidence also must be considered. For example, in *Domigan v. Gillette*,[1] the Second District Court of Appeals held that under RC 3111.10(E) a jury may be permitted to view the child to compare physical characteristics with those of the putative father.

§ 3:22 Burden of proof and weight of the evidence

A parentage action is a civil action in which the plaintiff need only prove the case by a preponderance of the evidence.[1] However, in cases in which a presumption arises, that presumption can be rebutted only by clear and convincing evidence that includes the results of genetic

---

[6]See also Little v. Streater, 452 U.S. 1, 101 S. Ct. 2202, 68 L. Ed. 2d 627 (1981).

[7]Keeney v. Lawson, 19 Ohio App. 3d 318, 321, 484 N.E.2d 745 (1st Dist. Hamilton County 1984).

[8]Langston v. Miller, 1997 WL 72103 (Ohio Ct. App. 9th Dist. Summit County 1997); E.B. v. T.J., 2006-Ohio-441, 2006 WL 242507 (Ohio Ct. App. 8th Dist. Cuyahoga County 2006).

[9]Keeney v. Lawson, 19 Ohio App. 3d 318, 321, 484 N.E.2d 745 (1st Dist. Hamilton County 1984).

[10]Hamilton County Dept. of Human Services v. Ball, 36 Ohio App. 3d 89, 521 N.E.2d 462 (1st Dist. Hamilton County 1986).

[11]RC 2301.35(D)(2).

[Section 3:21]

[1]Domigan v. Gillette, 17 Ohio App. 3d 228, 479 N.E.2d 291 (2d Dist. Clark County 1984).

[Section 3:22]

[1]Domigan v. Gillette, 17 Ohio App. 3d 228, 479 N.E.2d 291 (2d Dist. Clark County 1984). See also RC 3111.08(A).

testing.[2] Once a presumption is rebutted by clear and convincing evidence, the plaintiff can proceed to establish his or her case by a preponderance of the evidence. For example, in *Howard v. Jofferion*,[3] a case involving the parentage of a child born during the mother's marriage to another, the appellate court held that the trial court erred in using the preponderance standard to find that the husband was not the father.[4] The court stated that only after clear and convincing evidence had established that the husband was not the father could the court find that a preponderance of evidence proved that the alleged father was the biological father.

Since the burden of proof is by a preponderance of evidence, the jury verdict in *Lillie v. Dawson*,[5] adjudging a defendant to be the father of the child, was upheld in the absence of blood tests, even though the mother admitted to having had sexual intercourse with other men during the possible period of conception. A judgment notwithstanding the verdict was held to be proper to establish parentage where genetic test results were 95% or greater.[6] Once genetic testing has excluded an individual as father, the trial court lacks discretion to consider any other evidence of paternity. It is required to enter judgment that he is not the father.[7]

§ 3:23 Criminal interference with establishment of paternity

RC 3111.19 establishes that a criminal offense has been committed if one attempts to prevent the establishment of a parent-child relationship. RC 3111.99 defines the violation of RC 3111.19 as a first degree misdemeanor. Likewise, the interference with establishing or modifying a support order is a first degree misdemeanor under RC 2919.231, or if the defendant was previously convicted of violating RC 2919.231 or RC 3111.19, the new offense is a fifth degree felony.[1]

---

[2]RC 3111.03(B).

[3]Howard v. Jofferion, 1985 WL 4591 (Ohio Ct. App. 8th Dist. Cuyahoga County 1985).

[4]See also Domigan v. Gillette, 17 Ohio App. 3d 228, 479 N.E.2d 291 (2d Dist. Clark County 1984).

[5]Lillie v. Dawson, 1984 WL 7751 (Ohio Ct. App. 7th Dist. Columbiana County 1984).

[6]Filkins v. Cales, 86 Ohio App. 3d 61, 619 N.E.2d 1156 (3d Dist. Logan County 1993).

[7]See RC 3111.09(D).

[Section 3:23]

[1]RC 3111.19 and RC 3111.99.

§ 3:24   Defenses—Statute of limitations

A parentage action may be brought any time prior to a child's twenty-third birthday.[1] This long statute of limitations avoids the equal protection infirmities of the shorter statutes which the United States Supreme Court declared unconstitutional in *Mills v. Habluetzel*[2] and *Pickett v. Brown*.[3] Ohio's provision was held to be constitutional by the Ohio Supreme Court in *Wright v. Oliver*.[4] Since nonmarital children often depend on the state for all or part of their support, the long statute of limitations serves the public interest as well.[5]

In *Garrison v. Smith*,[6] the plaintiff attempted to establish paternity by an application to determine heirship filed more than five years after the child's age of majority. Her application was barred by the statute of limitations in RC 3111.05 and RC Chapter 2123.

§ 3:25   Defenses—Laches

Traditionally, laches is invoked to avoid problems with stale evidence caused by the absence of witnesses or by failure of their memories.[1] In most parentage cases, genetic tests, the most accurate evidence of paternity, can be performed at any time, and delay is usually not harmful to an alleged father's ability to present a defense.[2] Most courts have not invoked laches to limit parentage actions within the statutory period, reasoning that a child needs parental support for his or her entire minority and, therefore, has a continuing interest in establishing parentage.[3]

[Section 3:24]

[1]RC 3111.05.

[2]Mills v. Habluetzel, 456 U.S. 91, 102 S. Ct. 1549, 71 L. Ed. 2d 770 (1982) (court held that Texas' one-year statute of limitations in paternity actions violated an illegitimate child's equal protection rights).

[3]Pickett v. Brown, 462 U.S. 1, 103 S. Ct. 2199, 76 L. Ed. 2d 372 (1983) (court held that a two-year statute of limitations was unconstitutional).

[4]Wright v. Oliver, 35 Ohio St. 3d 10, 517 N.E.2d 883 (1988); See also Furman v. Waggoner, 1997 WL 45059 (Ohio Ct. App. 9th Dist. Summit County 1997); Pound, v. Fracker, 1984 WL 7511 (Ohio Ct. App. 5th Dist. Licking County 1984).

[5]Washington v. Dickey, 1985 WL 11152 (Ohio Ct. App. 4th Dist. Scioto County 1985).

[6]Garrison v. Smith, 55 Ohio App. 3d 14, 561 N.E.2d 1041 (6th Dist. Lucas County 1988).

[Section 3:25]

[1]Russell v. Fourth Nat. Bank, 102 Ohio St. 248, 131 N.E. 726 (1921).

[2]Washington v. Dickey, 1985 WL 11152 (Ohio Ct. App. 4th Dist. Scioto County 1985).

[3]Washington v. Dickey, 1985 WL 11152 (Ohio Ct. App. 4th Dist. Scioto County 1985); Manley v. Howard, 25 Ohio App. 3d 1, 495 N.E.2d 436 (3d Dist. Marion County 1985); Still v. Hayman, 153 Ohio App. 3d 487, 2003-Ohio-4113, 794 N.E.2d 751 (7th Dist. Jefferson County 2003).

In *Wright v. Oliver*,[4] the First District Court of Appeals' ruling that laches could be applied in a paternity case prior to the expiration of the statute of limitations was reversed by the Ohio Supreme Court. In 1996, the Fourth District found that court abused its discretion in failing to find that a plaintiff's claim was barred by laches when a complaint to establish a parent-child relationship was inactive for 14 years before activity resumed.[5] The Supreme Court held that the defense is available only where material prejudice can be shown.[6] Incurrence of financial obligations and unavailability of witnesses are not sufficient material prejudice.[7] The Second District Court of Appeals has held that the assumption of debt by a father is insufficient basis to allow a defense of laches.[8]

In *Shumaker v. Smith*,[9] the Third District Court of Appeals held that laches did not bar an action for child support arrearages where the child's mother did not seek to have paternity established until the child was sixteen, the parties lived in a small town, and the defendant father never denied paternity. In *Cooper v. Russell*,[10] the court held that the laches defense was properly rejected, though the mother did not bring the action until the child was fourteen years old. She had attempted to inform the father of his parentage, and the father failed to demonstrate any material prejudice. In determining whether a laches defense is equitable, a court may consider the reason for the delayed action by the plaintiff. If the plaintiff's delay is for valid reasons, such as being unable to locate or serve the father during the period of delay, a laches defense often fails.[11]

An opposite result was reached in *Stephenson v. Potts*[12] where the mother and sixteen-year-old plaintiff son sought past care retroactive to the child's birth. The court of appeals held that laches was a valid

---

[4]Wright v. Oliver, 1986 WL 14887 (Ohio Ct. App. 1st Dist. Hamilton County 1986). See also Fisher v. Call, 1994 WL 313650 (Ohio Ct. App. 5th Dist. Morrow County 1994).

[5]Adams County Adams County Child Support Enforcement Agency v. Osborne, 1996 WL 230038 (Ohio Ct. App. 4th Dist. Adams County 1996).

[6]Kinney v. Mathias, 10 Ohio St. 3d 72, 461 N.E.2d 901 (1984); Newbauer v. Bertrand, 2003-Ohio-5109, 2003 WL 22227372 (Ohio Ct. App. 12th Dist. Clermont County 2003).

[7]In re O'Herron, 2000 WL 896376 (Ohio Ct. App. 2d Dist. Montgomery County 2000).

[8]In re O'Herron, 2000 WL 896376 (Ohio Ct. App. 2d Dist. Montgomery County 2000).

[9]Shumaker v. Smith, 1990 WL 68028 (Ohio Ct. App. 3d Dist. Wyandot County 1990).

[10]Cooper v. Russell, 1995 WL 520773 (Ohio Ct. App. 12th Dist. Warren County 1995).

[11]See Seegert v. Zietlow, 95 Ohio App. 3d 451, 642 N.E.2d 697 (8th Dist. Cuyahoga County 1994); Johnson v. Johnson, 71 Ohio App. 3d 713, 595 N.E.2d 388 (11th Dist. Portage County 1991).

[12]Stephenson v. Potts, 1993 WL 150496 (Ohio Ct. App. 10th Dist. Franklin County 1993).

defense against appellants' claims for sixteen years of support. The Eleventh Appellate District in *Ryan v. Osman*[13] reversed the trial court's denial of a laches defense where the father of a twelve-year-old child had earned substantially more in the child's early years than at the time of the past care judgment. At the time of judgment, the father had lost his business to bankruptcy and suffered an illness which left him with social security as his only source of income. The mother's delay in bringing the action barred her request for retroactive child support. In *Park v. Ambrose*,[14] however, while the mother's claim for retroactive support was barred by laches, the child's claim was held to be timely. It has been held that absent a showing of material prejudice, a laches defense will not prevail.[15]

§ 3:26 Defenses—Waiver

Waiver has also been held inapplicable to the establishment of paternity and future support.[1] However, in *State ex rel. Engel v. Church*,[2] the trial court denied the mother past care during the period of her marriage to another man on the basis of estoppel and waiver.

§ 3:27 Defenses—Lack of choice regarding birth

A father's argument that he should not have to support a child he did not want was rejected by the court.[1] The father argued that although he urged abortion or adoption, he had no choice or control over the mother's decision to raise the child so should have no support obligation. In rejecting his argument, the appellate court reasoned that even the husband of a married woman cannot make the choice for abortion,[2] so neither can an unmarried partner choose abortion for the mother. Furthermore, under RC 3103.03(A) and RC 3103.031, and *Johnson v. Adams*,[3] a father's obligation extends to both the child and the state. As to his adoption argument, the appellate court noted that

---

[13]Ryan v. Osman, 1996 WL 702472 (Ohio Ct. App. 11th Dist. Lake County 1996).

[14]Park v. Ambrose, 85 Ohio App. 3d 179, 619 N.E.2d 469 (4th Dist. Ross County 1993).

[15]Owens v. Burgess, 1994 WL 424075 (Ohio Ct. App. 7th Dist. Columbiana County 1994).

[Section 3:26]

[1]Washington v. Dickey, 1985 WL 11152 (Ohio Ct. App. 4th Dist. Scioto County 1985).

[2]State ex rel. Engel v. Church, 2000 WL 727540 (Ohio Ct. App. 9th Dist. Medina County 2000).

[Section 3:27]

[1]Bryant v. Hacker, 116 Ohio App. 3d 860, 689 N.E.2d 609 (1st Dist. Hamilton County 1996).

[2]Planned Parenthood of Central Missouri v. Danforth, 428 U.S. 52, 96 S. Ct. 2831, 49 L. Ed. 2d 788 (1976); People in Interest of S. P. B., 651 P.2d 1213 (Colo. 1982).

[3]Johnson v. Adams, 18 Ohio St. 3d 48, 479 N.E.2d 866 (1985).

an adoption can be granted only if written consent is provided by both mother and father; thus, there is no unequal treatment between parents.

§ 3:28   Defenses—Surrogate father

The claim of a father, that he had agreed to be a "surrogate" father for a woman who wanted to become pregnant, did not care who the father might be, said she would try to raise the child herself, and never told appellant she would seek support, did not insulate him from liability for support.[1] The Fifth District Court of Appeals rejected the designation of "surrogate" and stated that he could be identified as an "accommodation maker," hence "primarily liable" on the obligation.[2]

§ 3:29   Resolution without trial

Since parentage actions are civil actions, the Civil Rules pertaining to summary judgment apply.[1] Default judgments are also explicitly permitted by RC 3111.08(B), which provides that if the defendant fails to plead or otherwise defend against the action, the opposing party may make an oral or written motion requesting a default judgment. The motion for default is governed by the Civil Rules.[2] After hearing satisfactory evidence of the truth of the statements in the complaint, the court will render a default judgment against the defendant.[3]

The trial court may properly deny a Civil Rule 60(B) motion filed later than one year after a default judgment.[4] The trial court may properly refuse to order genetic tests, and may grant default judgment where the alleged father failed to answer the complaint, failed to appear at the pretrial, and at the default hearing, although he had

---

[Section 3:28]

[1]Gorley v. Pack, 1987 WL 7167, at 1*(Ohio Ct. App. 5th Dist. Licking County 1987).

[2]Gorley v. Pack, 1987 WL 7167 (Ohio Ct. App. 5th Dist. Licking County 1987).

[Section 3:29]

[1]Milum (Nancy A.) v. Saldusky (Dennis W.), 1986 WL 8680 (Ohio Ct. App. 3d Dist. Wyandot County 1986). But see DeSalvo v. Sukalski, 8 Ohio App. 3d 337, 457 N.E.2d 349 (11th Dist. Geauga County 1983); State of W. Va. ex rel. Lewis v. Klein, 1993 WL 148807 (Ohio Ct. App. 4th Dist. Meigs County 1993).

[2]RC 3111.08.

[3]RC 3111.08(B). See Potts v. Wilson, 1985 WL 11144 (Ohio Ct. App. 4th Dist. Adams County 1985).

[4]See Long v. Bartlett, 73 Ohio App. 3d 764, 598 N.E.2d 197 (10th Dist. Franklin County 1992).

been served. The alleged father's only appearance in the matter was a letter to the court requesting blood testing.[5]

§ 3:30 Res judicata and vacation of parentage orders

◆ **Note:** Content of Text § 3:30, Res judicata and vacation of parentage orders, must be read in conjunction with the provisions of 2000 H.B. 242 (as outlined in Text § 3:31, Relief from paternity or support judgment, under RC 3119.961), which legislated a remedy for relief from judgment under RC 3119.961.

Judgments in paternity actions are final judgments and are, therefore, res judicata as to future proceedings between the original parties on the issue of the parentage of the child. Similarly, affirmative adjudications of parentage in divorce and dissolution proceedings are res judicata between the parties as to future attempts to litigate the parentage of a child.[1] As in all matters in which a party seeks to assert the doctrine of res judicata, there must be privity of parties and identity of issues.[2] Thus, a finding in a divorce or dissolution order that a child was born as issue of a marriage is not res judicata as to anyone not a party to that action.[3] Consequently, in *Gatt v. Gedeon*,[4] a man who alleged himself to be the father of a child was not precluded from bringing a parentage action even though the child's parentage was determined in a prior dissolution between the mother of the child and her husband, because the man asserting parentage was not a party to those proceedings, nor was he in privity with a party. Similarly, it appears that a child who was not a party to a pre-OPA

---

[5]Harvey v. Mynatt, 94 Ohio App. 3d 619, 641 N.E.2d 291 (9th Dist. Summit County 1994).

[Section 3:30]

[1]McDonald v. McDonald, 1996 WL 741403 (Ohio Ct. App. 4th Dist. Ross County 1996); Gatt v. Gedeon, 20 Ohio App. 3d 285, 485 N.E.2d 1059 (8th Dist. Cuyahoga County 1984); In re Mancini, 2 Ohio App. 3d 124, 440 N.E.2d 1232 (9th Dist. Lorain County 1981); Kashnier v. Donnelly, 81 Ohio App. 3d 154, 610 N.E.2d 519 (9th Dist. Medina County 1991); Williams v. Dye, 1985 WL 11109 (Ohio Ct. App. 4th Dist. Jackson County 1985); Kinder v. Sams, 1985 WL 8642 (Ohio Ct. App. 12th Dist. Butler County 1985).

[2]Gatt v. Gedeon, 20 Ohio App. 3d 285, 485 N.E.2d 1059 (8th Dist. Cuyahoga County 1984); In re Mancini, 2 Ohio App. 3d 124, 440 N.E.2d 1232 (9th Dist. Lorain County 1981); Kashnier v. Donnelly, 81 Ohio App. 3d 154, 610 N.E.2d 519 (9th Dist. Medina County 1991); Williams v. Dye, 1985 WL 11109 (Ohio Ct. App. 4th Dist. Jackson County 1985); Kinder v. Sams, 1985 WL 8642 (Ohio Ct. App. 12th Dist. Butler County 1985).

[3]Gatt v. Gedeon, 20 Ohio App. 3d 285, 485 N.E.2d 1059 (8th Dist. Cuyahoga County 1984); In re Mancini, 2 Ohio App. 3d 124, 440 N.E.2d 1232 (9th Dist. Lorain County 1981); Kashnier v. Donnelly, 81 Ohio App. 3d 154, 610 N.E.2d 519 (9th Dist. Medina County 1991); Williams v. Dye, 1985 WL 11109 (Ohio Ct. App. 4th Dist. Jackson County 1985); Kinder v. Sams, 1985 WL 8642 (Ohio Ct. App. 12th Dist. Butler County 1985); Amy F. v. George J., 1997 WL 614985 (Ohio Ct. App. 6th Dist. Lucas County 1997).

[4]Gatt v. Gedeon, 20 Ohio App. 3d 285, 485 N.E.2d 1059 (8th Dist. Cuyahoga County 1984).

parentage action could file suit under the OPA even if the child's mother brought a prior action and dismissed it with prejudice.[5]

A party may not raise a res judicata defense by way of a Civ. R. 12(B)(6) motion to dismiss.[6] In *Melissa M. v. Jeffrey J.*, the Sixth District reversed and remanded the trial court's decision granting a defendant's motion to dismiss based on res judicata, where the plaintiff's complaint to establish parentage was brought twenty years after her dissolution decree named the child as issue of her marriage to another man. The appellate court ruled that Civ. R. 12(B) enumerates the defenses that can be raised by motion, and res judicata is not one of them.[7] The defendant should have raised his res judicata defense in a summary judgment motion.

A party may also not assert res judicata as a defense when the establishment of paternity was previously barred by a "good cause" assertion under Ohio Admin. Code § 5101:1-32-02 and Ohio Admin. Code § 5101:1-29-962. The "good cause" remedy does not preclude either party, nor the child, from later resuming attempt at establishing paternity. It simply delays the process.[8]

However, a divorce decree that fails to specifically find that a child was "issue of the marriage" may be subject to attack under Civil Rule 60(B). In *LaBonte v. LaBonte*,[9] the decree stated that a child was born during the marriage but did not specifically say as issue from the marriage. This language permitted a Civil Rule 60(B) motion to stand on the issue of the child's parentage. Ascertainment of the truth as a policy objective overrides general policy of law in favor of legitimacy. In *Bottke v. Bottke*,[10] the Ninth Appellate District vacated a finding of parentage on a Civil Rule 60(B) motion. Subsequent genetic tests indicated that the adjudicated father in fact was not the father of the children at issue. Civil Rule 60(B) allows a judgment to be vacated upon motion of a party when it is "no longer equitable that the judgment should have prospective application."

Where a 1993 juvenile court order held that the husband is the father of the wife's child, but a 1996 dissolution decree held that the

---

[5]Johnson v. Norman, 66 Ohio St. 2d 186, 20 Ohio Op. 3d 196, 421 N.E.2d 124 (1981); Stephens v. Paris, 1993 WL 265414 (Ohio Ct. App. 2d Dist. Clark County 1993).

[6]Melissa M. v. Jeffrey J., 1997 WL 28343 (Ohio Ct. App. 6th Dist. Wood County 1997).

[7]Melissa M. v. Jeffrey J., 1997 WL 28343 (Ohio Ct. App. 6th Dist. Wood County 1997).

[8]Mossing v. Dye, 2002-Ohio-4689, 2002 WL 31006140 (Ohio Ct. App. 3d Dist. Seneca County 2002).

[9]LaBonte v. LaBonte, 61 Ohio App. 3d 209, 572 N.E.2d 704 (4th Dist. Meigs County 1988).

[10]Bottke v. Bottke, 1993 WL 28578 (Ohio Ct. App. 9th Dist. Summit County 1993).

husband is not the father, the latter of the two inconsistent orders prevails.[11]

Where a divorce decree fails to name a child born or conceived during the marriage as issue of the marriage, the juvenile court and the CSEA have jurisdiction to establish parentage, and are not barred by res judicata, even though the parents are the same parents, because CSEA and the child were not parties to the divorce.[12]

Also, where a prior dissolution decree, which did determine parentage, is vacated, the trial court in a parentage action may properly order genetic testing of an alleged father not a party to the divorce action.[13]

Postjudgment challenges to parentage orders have become the subject of conflicting appellate rulings. It has been consistently held that the only proper procedural vehicle to challenge paternity after judgment is a 60(B) motion to vacate.[14] The motion must be timely filed under Civil Rule 60(B), and the evidence of nonpaternity must be clear and convincing. In *Taylor v. Haven*,[15] the court allowed a 60(B) motion to proceed 10 years after judgment. In contrast, the court in *Bates v. Bates*[16] refused to set aside a parentage order where both mother and father agreed it was erroneous. In *Davis v. Nikitin*,[17] the appellate court held that a six-year delay in filing a 60(B) motion presents reasonable basis for overruling the motion.

A compromise position between denial and granting of a Civ. R. 60(B) motion appears in *Douglas v. Boykin*,[18] where the trial court's order to vacate the paternity finding, but still hold the alleged father responsible for child support to the date of the order vacating, was upheld. He no longer had any rights or responsibilities for the child

---

[11]State ex rel. Musselman v. Musselman, 1998 WL 855426 (Ohio Ct. App. 2d Dist. Montgomery County 1998).

[12]State ex rel. Smith v. Smith, 110 Ohio App. 3d 336, 674 N.E.2d 398 (8th Dist. Cuyahoga County 1996); State ex rel Willacy v. Smith, 1996 WL 355286 (Ohio Ct. App. 8th Dist. Cuyahoga County 1996). See Pamela J. MacAdams, *When Does Divorce Decree Bar Parentage Action?* 8 Dom. Rel. J. Ohio 95 (Nov./Dec. 1996).

[13]Amy F. v. George J., 1997 WL 614985 (Ohio Ct. App. 6th Dist. Lucas County 1997).

[14]Matter of Springer, 1992 WL 389943 (Ohio Ct. App. 2d Dist. Clark County 1992); Tatom v. Tatom, 19 Ohio App. 3d 198, 482 N.E.2d 1339 (2d Dist. Montgomery County 1984); Stevens v. Stevens, 1990 WL 116157 (Ohio Ct. App. 2d Dist. Montgomery County 1990).

[15]Taylor v. Haven, 91 Ohio App. 3d 846, 633 N.E.2d 1197 (12th Dist. Butler County 1993).

[16]Bates v. Bates, 1993 WL 385304 (Ohio Ct. App. 5th Dist. Guernsey County 1993). See also Philabaum v. Singleton, 1993 WL 535494 (Ohio Ct. App. 5th Dist. Stark County 1993).

[17]Davis v. Nikitin, 1994 WL 11023 (Ohio Ct. App. 9th Dist. Summit County 1994).

[18]Douglas v. Boykin, 121 Ohio App. 3d 140, 699 N.E.2d 123 (12th Dist. Butler County 1997).

after the 60(B) ruling, but was still obligated for accrued arrears up to that date.

Similarly, in *Wood v. Wood*[19] the trial court's ruling was upheld which granted reversal of a judgment of paternity, but left the door open for the teenaged child's "psychological father" to be awarded parenting time, despite his non-paternity. In this same case, mother asserted that the trial court erred in granting relief from paternity judgment, because the man "knew" he was not the father long before he sought relief pursuant to RC 3119.962(B)(3). The appellate court was unconvinced that he knew he was not the father, which knowledge would have precluded his relief, given prior acknowledgments of parentage. (See Text § 3:31, Relief from paternity or support judgment, under RC 3119.961, for further law on this topic).

Conversely, in *Leguillon v. Leguillon*[20] the court refused to allow the reversal of a parentage determination two years after divorce where the father alleged the results of a post-vasectomy sperm analysis proved he could not have fathered the child at issue. The ruling was upheld as in the best interests of the child.

The Fifth District Court of Appeals upheld a trial court ruling permitting a rescission of an acknowledgment holding that the judgment allowing rescission was res judicata. The mother had been ordered three separate times to submit herself and the twin children to genetic testing. She failed to do so; alleged father was granted summary judgment, with a finding that the paternity acknowledgments were rescinded, and that no parent-child relationship existed. Mother had moved to California, where she filed actions for paternity on behalf of the twins. The California Court refused to accord full faith and credit to the Ohio ruling and established paternity. Genetic testing done under the California case evidenced 99.99% probability of paternity. Still, the Ohio court held that the Ohio ruling was final and enforceable, and res judicata as to later actions. Additionally, the California court had no authority to overturn the Ohio ruling.

In *Poskarbiewicz v. Poskarbiewicz*,[21] the Sixth District Court of Appeals reversed and remanded court's grant of a 60(B) motion filed nearly 20 years after the original establishment of parentage. Father had his twenty-year old daughter submit to genetic testing which resulted in a zero percent probability of parentage. As a result of the genetic tests, the trial court granted his motion to vacate the parentage finding, which he filed upon the CSEA's stepping up arrearage collection efforts. The Court of Appeals, while reversing the order granting his motion to vacate, remanded for the trial court's consideration of the issue under newly enacted RC 3119.961, which is a statutory relief from judgment vehicle specific to parentage.

---

[19]Wood v. Wood, 2007-Ohio-5052, 2007 WL 2781891 (Ohio Ct. App. 5th Dist. Tuscarawas County 2007).

[20]Leguillon v. Leguillon, 124 Ohio App. 3d 757, 707 N.E.2d 571 (12th Dist. Clermont County 1998).

[21]Poskarbiewicz v. Poskarbiewicz, 2002-Ohio-3666, 2002 WL 445058 (Ohio Ct. App. 6th Dist. Lucas County 2002).

The trial court was upheld in its denial of Civil Rule 60(B) relief where the motion was filed 10 years after admission of paternity and seven years after father-appellant and mother-appellee apparently knew father may not be the biological father. The appellate ruling, however, was based not on res judicata, but on laches.[22]

The appellate court reversed the trial court's grant of father's 60(B) motion in *State ex rel. Minnis v. Lewis*.[23] The basis of the grant was that father had not been served with notice of the default judgment. The appellate court held, however, that his failure to appear at pre-trial divested him of the right to such notice.

The use of a Civil Rule 75(D) investigation to challenge a prior finding of parentage where the man married the pregnant mother was upheld in a motion brought five years after the dissolution decree ordering support.[24]

The Ohio Supreme Court has specifically held that a paternity action is barred by res judicata where determination of parentage has been made in a previous litigation, including a dissolution proceeding.[25] In the absence of fraud, a Civil Rule 60(B) motion for relief from judgment should not be granted. A declaration of paternity filed for the purpose of obtaining a new birth certificate is not, however, res judicata in a legitimation proceeding.[26]

Paternity adjudications made in connection with a parentage action or a divorce or dissolution order can also be set aside pursuant to Civil Rule 60(B). In *Niarhos v. Niarhos*,[27] the Second District Court of Appeals overruled the trial court's refusal to hear a Civil Rule 60(B) motion, alleging that parentage was not adjudicated in a dissolution proceeding because the trial court mistakenly believed it did not have jurisdiction to hear parentage claims in a dissolution. Some courts have been lenient about reopening divorce and dissolution decrees to make parentage determinations or to provide for child custody, support, and visitation, especially when the party seeking to reopen the divorce or dissolution shows fraud (such as concealment of a pregnancy). In *In re Dissolution of Watson*,[28] the court justified this le-

---

[22]Cooper v. Data, 1999 WL 1072169 (Ohio Ct. App. 5th Dist. Stark County 1999).

[23]State ex rel. Minnis v. Lewis, 1993 WL 546584 (Ohio Ct. App. 10th Dist. Franklin County 1993).

[24]Carson v. Carson, 62 Ohio App. 3d 670, 577 N.E.2d 391 (12th Dist. Brown County 1989).

[25]In re Gilbraith, 32 Ohio St. 3d 127, 512 N.E.2d 956 (1987).

[26]Collett v. Cogar, 35 Ohio St. 3d 114, 518 N.E.2d 1202 (1988).

[27]Niarhos v. Niarhos, 1986 WL 3490 (Ohio Ct. App. 2d Dist. Montgomery County 1986).

[28]In re Marriage of Watson, 13 Ohio App. 3d 344, 469 N.E.2d 876 (9th Dist. Lorain County 1983).

niency by citing the best interests of the child. Other courts, however, refuse to reopen the issue.[29]

A father fails to allege a basis for relief under a Civil Rule 60(B) motion by his failure to allege fraud after blood tests showed that he could not be the child's biological father.[30] Still, a motion for relief from judgment must be brought within one year of adjudication if based on newly discovered evidence produced by genetic tests.[31] The Ohio Supreme Court has held that a Civ. R. 60(B) motion based on the results of genetic tests falls under 60(B)(2), newly discovered evidence, and thus, must be brought within one year.[32] This restriction is further defined as one year from judgment, as opposed to one year from discovery of new evidence.[33]

Where the record fails to support appellant's ability to provide a meritorious defense, and a significant length of time elapsed between original ruling and a 60(B) motion, court does not abuse its discretion in overruling the motion for relief from judgment.[34]

In *Smith v. Ohio Department of Human Services*,[35] the judgment was affirmed where appellant successfully set aside a parentage order ten years after its inception then sought to recover child support collected by ODHS. The Court of Claims denied his claim. The court of appeals affirmed the reasoning that the unjust impoverishment which appellant suffered did not correspond to any unjust enrichment by the State. Additionally, restitution was inappropriate because appellant contributed to his alleged wrong by voluntarily acknowledging paternity instead of demanding genetic testing ten years earlier.

A distinction between post-decree and post-acknowledgment rules as to vacation of paternity is made in Galan v. Holbert, 2008-Ohio-1586, 2008 WL 853302 (Ohio Ct. App. 2d Dist. Greene County 2008). An action to rescind an acknowledgment must be brought within one year after it becomes final and a post-decree paternity action cannot

---

[29]Clippinger v. Clippinger, 1998 WL 8682 (Ohio Ct. App. 12th Dist. Preble County 1998).

[30]Matter of Belden, 1993 WL 179254 (Ohio Ct. App. 2d Dist. Miami County 1993); Caron v. Manfresca, 1998 WL 832163 (Ohio Ct. App. 10th Dist. Franklin County 1998).

[31]Gosink v. Hamm, 111 Ohio App. 3d 495, 676 N.E.2d 604 (1st Dist. Hamilton County 1996).

[32]Strack v. Pelton, 70 Ohio St. 3d 172, 1994-Ohio-107, 637 N.E.2d 914 (1994); Kay B. v. Timothy C., 117 Ohio App. 3d 598, 690 N.E.2d 1366 (6th Dist. Wood County 1997).

[33]In re Hawkins, 1998 WL 31518 (Ohio Ct. App. 2d Dist. Montgomery County 1998).

[34]Woodward v. Woodward, 1993 WL 512368 (Ohio Ct. App. 12th Dist. Butler County 1993).

[35]Smith v. Ohio Dept. of Human Serv., 103 Ohio App. 3d 149, 658 N.E.2d 1100 (10th Dist. Franklin County 1995).

be brought on a child's behalf absent an express determination by the court that such action is in the best interests of the child.[36]

Parties to a parentage action could arrive at a compromise settlement under a former version of RC 3111.19, no longer in effect, which allowed the alleged father to undertake financial obligations in favor of a child without a determination of parentage. This type of agreement, if journalized in a court of proper jurisdiction, is also res judicata as to the issue of parentage between the parties of the action at issue, even though parentage was left undetermined.[37] Parties may not, however, compromise a settlement without court approval.[38]

In *Cuyahoga Support Enforcement Agency v. Guthrie*,[39] a case certified to the Ohio Supreme Court to resolve conflicting appellate rulings, the Ohio Supreme Court held that genetic test results obtained after a final parentage adjudication do not constitute newly discovered evidence under Civil Rule 60(B)(2) or (4) and, thus, do not justify vacating a parentage finding. However, the Court held that under RC 3111.16, court does have authority to vacate a paternity finding upon proper evidence, and to grant relief from a prospective support obligation. A court may not, however, retroactively relieve an obligor of a support duty or eliminate an arrearage that accrued while the support order was in effect. In overturning a post-decree denial of a motion for genetic testing, the Third District Court of Appeals has held that the *Guthrie* ruling, plus the language of RC 3111.09(A)(1), leaves court no discretion to deny a motion for genetic testing at any stage of the proceedings and certainly not without a hearing.[40]

Effective 1–25–02 RC 3119.961(A) authorizes 60(B) relief from judgment of parentage, including relief from the support order. Relief shall be granted by the court if there are 0.00% DNA test results issued within six months of the application for 60(B) relief; and no adoption has taken place, and the child was not conceived by artificial insemination.

Relief shall be denied if the court finds that the person knew he was not the father before any of the following occurred:

(1) The person or male minor was required to support the child by a child support order

(2) The person or male minor validly signed the child's birth certificate as an informant as provided in RC 3705.09 (as that section existed prior to 1-1-98);

---

[36]Broxterman v. Broxterman, 101 Ohio App. 3d 661, 656 N.E.2d 394 (1st Dist. Hamilton County 1995).

[37]Nelson v. Pleasant, 73 Ohio App. 3d 479, 597 N.E.2d 1137 (4th Dist. Lawrence County 1991).

[38]Phelps v. Fowler, 107 Ohio App. 3d 263, 668 N.E.2d 558 (8th Dist. Cuyahoga County 1995).

[39]Cuyahoga Support Enforcement Agency v. Guthrie, 84 Ohio St. 3d 437, 1999-Ohio-362, 705 N.E.2d 318 (1999); Benford v. Smith, 2005-Ohio-2561, 2005 WL 1220737 (Ohio Ct. App. 10th Dist. Franklin County 2005).

[40]Lightner v. Perkins, 2000-Ohio-1898, 2000 WL 924806 (Ohio Ct. App. 3d Dist. Hardin County 2000).

(3) The person or male minor was named in an acknowledgment of paternity of the child that a court entered upon its journal pursuant to former RC 2105.18;

(4) The person or male minor was named in an acknowledgment of paternity that has become final under RC 2151.232; RC 3111.25; RC 3111.821 or former RC 3111.211 or 5101.314;

(5) The person or male minor was presumed to be the natural father of the child under any of the circumstances listed in:

  (i)   RC 3111.03(A)(3) as that division existed prior to January 1, 1998;

  (ii) RC 3111.03(A)(3) as that division existed on and after January 1, 1998, and prior to the effective date of RC 3119.962 (March 22, 2001);

  (iii) RC 3111.03(A)(5) as that division existed prior to the effective date of RC 3119.962 (March 22, 2001)

(6) The person or male minor was presumed to be the natural father of the child under any of the circumstances listed in divisions RC 3111.03(A)(1) to (3); or

(7) The person or male minor otherwise admitted or acknowledged himself to be the child's father.

RC 3119.963 authorizes the court to grant 60(B) relief where mother is the child's custodian and fails to submit herself or the child to genetic testing, or where father is the custodian and fails to submit himself or the child to genetic testing.

RC 3119.964(A) addresses parenting time and child support post 60(B) relief. If relief from parentage judgment is granted, but the person had parenting time before relief, then the court shall determine whether to continue, modify, or terminate those rights. If the person had a support order before relief from judgment, then the court may cancel the order and rescind any support arrears. The payor may seek recovery of support paid under the order.

RC 3119.964(A) allows a person relieved from a parentage judgment to seek recovery of support paid, and allows the court to cancel arrears owed. However, in *Hoose v. Brown*,[41] the appellate court upheld the trial court's denial of recovery of support paid. The court held that absent any showing that the mother had no legal or equitable right to retain the support monies, former father's claim will fail. Since there was a previously valid parentage and support order, the court held that there was no question that mother had the right to the monies when received.

§ 3:31   Relief from paternity or support judgment, under RC 3119.961

Relief from judgment estabilishing parentage or child support is now available under RC 3119.961 by virtue of 2000 S.B. 180, effective

---

[41]Hoose v. Brown, 2004-Ohio-4701, 2004 WL 1961661 (Ohio Ct. App. 3d Dist. Hardin County 2004).

March 22, 2001. It grants an adjudged father relief from judgment when genetic tests result in an exclusion.

The statutory language allowing the court to vacate a finding of parentage if the court receives genetic test results excluding the moving party as a parent, has caused something of a procedural dilemma. It is common that a party wishing to move to vacate a parentage order cannot obtain cooperation for genetic testing. In *Rojas v. Guilfu*,[1] the court ruled that the moving party may alleviate such a dilemma by showing that attempt to gain genetic tests was denied, and then under RC 3119.963(B), may seek remedies against a party who willfully fails to submit to testing. It follows, then, that a party moving to vacate a parentage order, may first wish to seek testing outside the court system before expecting to gain an order for testing in conjunction with the motion to vacate.

Effective October 27, 2000, 2000 H.B. 242 amended RC 3111.13 and RC 3111.17 and enacted RC 3113.2111: The effective date is irrelevant as the act provides relief both retroactively and prospectively. Less than one year later, however, 2000 S.B. 180 repealed RC 3113.2111. Analogous statutory authority for vacating a parentage finding now is codified at RC 3119.961 through RC 3119.967.

Recently enacted RC 3119.961(A) states, in pertinent part:

> Notwithstanding the provisions to the contrary in Civil Rule 60(B) and in accordance with this section, a person may file a motion for relief from a final judgment, court order, or administrative determination or order that determines that a person . . . is the father of a child or from a child support order under which the person or male minor is the obligor. The person shall file the motion in the juvenile court or other court with jurisdiction under section 2101.022 or 2301.03 of the Revised Code of the county in which the original judgment, court order, or administrative determination or child support order was made.

Some critics have argued that the legislature supplanted the exclusive powers of the Supreme Court to make rules and procedures as provided by the Ohio constitution by abrogating Civil Rule 60(B). In fact, the statutory provision has been challenged constitutionally and upheld by the Ohio Supreme Court.

Constitutional conflict resolved. The Ohio Supreme Court upheld the constitutionality of the controversial 60(B) statute, RC 3119.961 in *State ex rel. Loyd v. Lovelady*,[2] decided February 1, 2006.

Revised Code 3119.961 was enacted effective 3-22-01 permitting relief from judgments establishing paternity by filing a 60(B) motion, notwithstanding provisions to the contrary in Ohio Civil Rule 60(B).

RC 3119.962 provides:

[Section 3:31]

[1]State ex rel. Ohio Child Support Enforcement Agency, 2004-Ohio-6707, 2004 WL 2891907 (Ohio Ct. App. 8th Dist. Cuyahoga County 2004).

[2]State ex rel. Loyd v. Lovelady, 108 Ohio St. 3d 86, 2006-Ohio-161, 840 N.E.2d 1062 (2006).

Upon the filing of a motion for relief under section 3119.961 of the Revised Code, a court shall grant relief from . . . a child support order under which a person or male minor is the obligor if all of the following apply:

    a. the court receives genetic test results from a genetic test administered no more than six months prior to the filing of the motion for relief that finds there is a zero percent probability that the person or male minor is the father of the child.

    b. the person or male minor has not adopted the child.

    c. the child was not conceived as a result of artificial insemination in compliance with sections 3111.88 or 3111.961(A) of the Revised Code.

Since the enactment of this statute, the various Ohio Appellate Courts have differed on whether RC 3119.961, a legislated statute, unconstitutionally violates the separation of powers of the constitution and the Supreme Court's exclusive authority to prescribe rules governing practice and procedure in courts.

Willa Loyd gave birth in 1985 to DL. In 1995, the Cuyahoga County Child Support Enforcement Agency initiated a paternity case, to which the alleged father, Lovelady, failed to respond. The court entered default judgment establishing parentage and issued a child support award to the mother.

Seven years later, Lovelady filed for relief from judgment under RC 3119.961, asserting that a recent genetic test result excludes him as father of this child.

The trial court denied his motion, relying upon *Van Dusen v. Van Dusen*,[3] which had held that RC 3119.961 is an unconstitutional violation of separation of powers.

Lovelady appealed. The Eighth District Court of Appeals reversed and remanded on the basis that because the statute established a substantive right, not a procedural right, it does not violate the constitution.

Section 5(B), Article IV of the Ohio Constitution states that the Supreme Court is vested with "exclusive authority to prescribe rules governing practice and procedure in all courts of the state, which rules shall not abridge, enlarge or modify any substantive right . . ."

The Ohio Supreme Court accepted CSEA's discretionary appeal. CSEA argued that RC 3119.961(A) conflicts with Ohio Civ R 60(B) by expressly overriding Civ. R. 60(B)'s provisions and thus is an intrusion on the Supreme Court's authority granted under Art. IV, Sec. 5(B). For example, a motion for relief from judgment under RC 3119.961 can be filed well after the frame of time allotted for filing a 60(B) motion under the Ohio Civil Rules.

---

[3]Van Dusen v. Van Dusen, 151 Ohio App. 3d 494, 2003-Ohio-350, 784 N.E.2d 750 (10th Dist. Franklin County 2003).

The Ohio Supreme Court in *State ex rel. Loyd v. Lovelady*,[4] reasoned that although RC 3119.961 and RC 3119.962 are necessarily couched in procedural terms, clearly, the General Assembly intended to create a substantive right. Consequently, no intrusion on the Supreme Court's exclusive authority over procedural matters exists, and thus there is no violation of the separation of powers.

The Ohio Supreme Court affirmed the Eighth District's ruling that RC 3119.961 et seq. is not unconstitutional.

Conversely, a trial court properly grants a 60(B) motion relieving one from a parentage judgment obtained in default divorce proceedings where subsequent genetic testing identifies a zero percent probability of parentage.[5]

A trial court errs in denying a motion for relief from judgment where the moving party submits genetic test results obtained within six months of the filing, and which preclude the possibility of his parentage of the child.[6]

Prior to *Lloyd v. Lovelady*,[7] in *Prendergast v. Prendergast*,[8] the trial court denied a post-decree challenge to parentage under this new law. The trial court's basis for denial included the fact that the movant did not have exclusionary genetic test results prior to the filing of his motion, and that thus, the prior decree finding parentage controls.[9]

The Sixth District Court of Appeals held that RC 3119.961, RC 3119.962 and RC 3119.967 are unconstitutional violations of Article IV Section 5(B) of the Ohio Constitution, as they permit a party to bypass Civil Rule 60(B) and the policy of res judicata. The appellate court held the trial court erred in granting elimination of child support arrearages and the return of IRS intercepted funds on the basis of exclusionary genetic test results. Paternity had been unsuccessfully contested on two prior occasions.[10]

Conversely, the Eighth District Court of Appeals has held that the statute providing that a person may file a motion for relief from a parentage judgment provides a substantive right and not a procedural

---

[4]State ex rel. Loyd v. Lovelady, 108 Ohio St. 3d 86, 2006-Ohio-161, 840 N.E.2d 1062 (2006).

[5]Barber v. Gross, 2005-Ohio-7056, 2005 WL 3610477 (Ohio Ct. App. 11th Dist. Lake County 2005).

[6]Sloat v. Sloat, 2006-Ohio-5552, 2006 WL 3020334 (Ohio Ct. App. 5th Dist. Stark County 2006).

[7]State ex rel. Loyd v. Lovelady, 108 Ohio St. 3d 86, 2006-Ohio-161, 840 N.E.2d 1062 (2006).

[8]Prendergast v. Prendergast, No. 81-CV 865 (Ohio Ct. App. 7th Dist. Columbiana County 2001).

[9]See *Constitutionality Challenge to RC 3113.2111*, Domestic Relations J. of Ohio, Vol. 13, Issue 4.

[10]Poskarbiewicz v. Poskarbiewicz, 152 Ohio App. 3d 307, 2003-Ohio-1626, 787 N.E.2d 688 (6th Dist. Lucas County 2003).

right, and thus, the statue is constitutional and does not violate the separation of powers provision of the State Constitution.[11]

While under RC 3119.961(A) a person may have his establishment of parentage vacated and support order terminated, some courts will not eliminate the arrears of support which have accrued between the establishment and the vacated orders.[12] If visitation or companionship rights were granted in an order later vacated, the court "shall determine whether the order granting those rights shall be terminated, modified, or continued."[13]

Likewise, an action filed against CSEA for reimbursement of support monies paid between the adjudication of parentage and the vacating of that finding, is properly dismissed for lack of jurisdiction. The agency does not retain funds paid for child support, nor have control over them. Instead, the agency serves as trustee to remit the monies to the person entitled to receive payments.[14]

Additional basis for criticism of RC 3119.961 has been that although the Ohio Supreme Court has held that juvenile courts may vacate their own orders of paternity based on their continuing jurisdiction, the Court has specifically held that domestic relations courts do not have continuing jurisdiction as to paternity after a divorce is final.

RC 3119.961 was held unconstitutional by the Franklin County Court of Appeals in *Van Dusen v. Van Dusen*[15] where father was awarded residential parent status, but the children fled his home, asserting that he was not their father. Genetic testing was then performed which excluded him as the father of one of the children. The trial court overruled father's motion under RC 3119.96. The Ohio Attorney General intervened due to the questionable constitutionality of RC 3119.96. On appeal, the Tenth District upheld the trial court's ruling and specifically held RC 3119.96 et seq. unconstitutional. The Tenth District considered the provisions of RC 3119.96 a disregard of the traditional powers of the other branches of government and furthermore stated that parentage established at the time of divorce is res judicata.

Since the 10th District has held RC 3119.961 unconstitutional, it extends its logic to attorney fees in defense of a 60(B) motion brought under this statute. RC 3119.966 allows attorney fees where relief is denied under RC 3119.962. The Franklin County Court of Appeals

---

[11]C.S.E.A. ex rel. Lloyd v. Lovelady, 2004-Ohio-3617, 2004 WL 1532275 (Ohio Ct. App. 8th Dist. Cuyahoga County 2004).

[12]Newton v. Dunn, 2003-Ohio-5523, 2003 WL 22369276 (Ohio Ct. App. 4th Dist. Ross County 2003); Benford v. Smith, 2005-Ohio-2561, 2005 WL 1220737 (Ohio Ct. App. 10th Dist. Franklin County 2005).

[13]RC 3119.964(A).

[14]Lynette T. v. Terrance C., 2006-Ohio-6292, 2006 WL 3458088 (Ohio Ct. App. 6th Dist. Lucas County 2006).

[15]Van Dusen v. Van Dusen, 151 Ohio App. 3d 494, 2003-Ohio-350, 784 N.E.2d 750 (10th Dist. Franklin County 2003); Blystone v. Blystone, 2003-Ohio-5667, 2003 WL 22415636 (Ohio Ct. App. 10th Dist. Franklin County 2003).

has held that court errs in awarding attorney fees to former husband in a post-decree divorce proceeding wherein former wife's 60(B) motion challenging his parentage was dismissed. If the portion of the statute allowing a 60(B) challenge to parentage is unconstitutional, so must be any related statute allowing an award of fees for defending it.[16]

Added to the list of appellate courts holding RC 3119.961 unconstitutional is the 2nd District. The Greene County Court of Appeals, in *Hittle v. Palbas* [17] adopted the reasoning of the 10th District in *Van Dusen*.[18] Additionally, the court was persuaded that it would not be in the child's best interest to allow an award of genetic testing under RC 3119.961 because the child was well-bonded and had been in the father's custody for some time, and it would not be in the child's best interest to place him in the mother's custody, even if former husband were not father.

The 3119.961(A) remedy has been held unavailable to a mother when she attempted to assert it as a challenge to a child support modification. The Lake County Court held it applies only to putative fathers.[19]

The procedural provisions of RC 3119.962 provide time lines to bring actions, burdens of proof between mother and adjudged father, retroactivity, costs of paternity tests, the action and attorney fees, as follows:

The court is prohibited from denying relief if the father *did not know* he was not the father when:

(1) The person or male minor was required to support the child by a child support order.

(2) The person or male minor validly signed the child's birth certificate as an informant as provided in RC 3705.09 as that section existed prior to January 1, 1998.

(3) The person or male minor was named in an acknowledgment of paternity of the child that a court entered upon its journal pursuant to former RC 2105.18.

(4) The person or male minor was named in an acknowledgment of paternity that has become final under RC 2151.232; RC 3111.25; RC 3111.821 or former RC 3111.211 or RC 5101.314.

(5) The person or male minor was presumed to be the natural father of the child under any of the circumstances listed in RC 3111.03.

---

[16]Blystone v. Blystone, 2003-Ohio-5667, 2003 WL 22415636 (Ohio Ct. App. 10th Dist. Franklin County 2003).

[17]Hittle v. Palbas, 2003-Ohio-5843, 2003 WL 22462141 (Ohio Ct. App. 2d Dist. Greene County 2003).

[18]Van Dusen v. Van Dusen, 151 Ohio App. 3d 494, 2003-Ohio-350, 784 N.E.2d 750 (10th Dist. Franklin County 2003).

[19]Demore v. Demore, 2008-Ohio-1328, 2008 WL 754891 (Ohio Ct. App. 11th Dist. Lake County 2008).

(6) The person or male minor was presumed to be the natural father of the child under any of the circumstances listed in:

    (i)   Division (A)(3) of RC 3111.03 as that division existed prior to January 1, 1998;

    (ii)   Division (A)(3) of RC 3111.03 as that division existed on and after January 1, 1998, and prior to March 22, 2001 (the effective date of RC 3119.962);

    (iii) Division (A)(5) of RC 3111.03 as that division existed prior to March 22, 2001 (the effective date of RC 3119.962.

(7) The person or male minor was determined to be the father of the child in a parentage action under RC Chapter 3111.

(8) The person or male minor otherwise admitted or acknowledged himself to be the child's natural father.

A trial court errs in vacating a paternity judgment where the basis of their finding of non-paternity is genetic testing acquired greater than six months before the filing of the motion for relief from judgment.[20] Additionally the court is prohibited from granting relief if the father did know he was not the father and he did all the above. In *Caldwell v. Eyler*,[21] a man entered into a consent judgment acknowledging paternity and reducing his child support, though he knew based on exclusionary genetic testing that he was not the father. The trial court's denial of relief from judgment under RC 3119.962 was upheld. Two separate statutory sections of RC 3119.962 preclude relief under such circumstances. RC 3119.962(B) provides that a court shall not grant relief if it finds that, knowing he was not the natural father of the child, the person or male minor otherwise admitted or acknowledged himself to be the child's father. Additionally, RC 3119.962(B)(1) provides that relief from judgment shall not be granted if the adjudicated father agreed to pay child support.

The granting of a 60(B) motion does not preclude the mother from bringing other actions under RC Ch. 3111 to establish paternity (one per two-year period)[22] but if she loses, "the court shall require the person who filed the motion for relief to pay all costs of the action and the reasonable attorney's fees of the opposing party."[23] If movant loses on his 60(B) action, he is liable for court costs and attorney fees. If a 60(B) is granted, arrearages are vacated and father may bring action to recoup child support payments made.

Likewise, where a mother seeks to set aside the portion of an agreed divorce decree finding "issue" of the marriage, though she knew at the time of the divorce that her husband was not the child's father, she is

---

[20]Hardy v. Wilson, 2006-Ohio-4532, 2006 WL 2528510 (Ohio Ct. App. 9th Dist. Lorain County 2006).

[21]Caldwell v. Eyler, 2002-Ohio-5124, 2002 WL 31151604 (Ohio Ct. App. 2d Dist. Miami County 2002); Rozhon v. Rozhon, 2006-Ohio-3118, 2006 WL 1686747 (Ohio Ct. App. 9th Dist. Medina County 2006); Vah v. Mahan, 2006-Ohio-3476, 2006 WL 1851732 (Ohio Ct. App. 7th Dist. Belmont County 2006).

[22]RC 3119.965

[23]RC 3119.966(A).

prohibited from relief. In *Myers v. Myers*,[24] during custody modification proceedings, mother filed a 60(B) motion under RC 3119.961, because she was concerned that she would lose custody. Both she and her former husband had entered into an agreed judgment of divorce naming her child as issue of the marriage, but knowing that husband was not the father. The Court of Appeals affirmed the trial court's denial of her 60(B) motion.

Actions have been brought in common pleas divisions of Ohio courts by husbands who have learned that a child they are raising is not a child of the marriage, but instead the product of the wife's extramarital affair. While RC Ch. 3111 authorizes a mother to bring such an action against the biological father, it does not authorize the husband to do so. Thus, a trial court properly dismisses such an action for failure to state a claim.[25]

Other provisions of RC 3119.963 provide for genetic tests to be done by court-authorized testing labs, ordered by the clerk of courts, with payment made by the requesting party, unless represented by CSEA and CSEA orders the test. However, any party, including CSEA, may request reimbursement from the party assessed with the costs of the action.

Further amendments to RC 3111.13 include the addition of subsections (F)(3)(a) to (c), which provide that a new finding of paternity and orders of support shall not include support from the date of the child's birth if the child is over three years of age at the time of the initial filing *and* the father had no knowledge of, and no reason to have knowledge of, the possibility of parentage. RC 3111.13(F)(3)(b) shifts the burden to mother to prove by a preponderance of the evidence that she "performed a reasonable and documented effort to contact and notify the alleged father of his paternity." RC 3111.13(F)(3)(c) provides for modification of any existing child support order.

§ 3:32 Right to counsel

The Ohio Supreme Court held in *State ex rel. Cody v. Toner*[1] that an indigent paternity defendant who faces the state as an adversary is entitled to a court-appointed attorney when the complainant-mother and the child are recipients of public assistance and are represented by the prosecuting attorney. Upon finding that the child's interests conflict with those of the mother, the court may appoint separate counsel for the child pursuant to RC 3111.07(A). The defendant-

---

[24]Myers v. Myers, 153 Ohio App. 3d 243, 2003-Ohio-3552, 792 N.E.2d 770 (7th Dist. Columbiana County 2003).

[25]Weinman v. Larsh, 5 Ohio St. 3d 85, 448 N.E.2d 1384 (1983); Phillips v. Cochrum, 2007-Ohio-247, 2007 WL 162850 (Ohio Ct. App. 9th Dist. Summit County 2007).

[Section 3:32]

[1]State ex rel. Cody v. Toner, 8 Ohio St. 3d 22, 456 N.E.2d 813 (1983).

alleged father, however, does not have standing to assert that conflict.[2] Some courts interpret this provision liberally and routinely require the appointment of a guardian ad litem for children in contested parentage proceedings.

In *State ex rel. Armstrong v. Hall*,[3] the Third District Court of Appeals held that a complainant mother who was not represented by the prosecuting attorney was not entitled to court-appointed counsel or a transcript of proceedings at public expense. Her interests, the child's interests, and the state's interests must meet the due process standards outlined in *Mathews v. Eldridge*.[4] However, the court found that the child's need for financial support and for the establishment of a family relationship mandated that the *child* should have counsel appointed.

Though there is a constitutional right to counsel in the establishment of parentage,[5] that right does not extend necessarily to establishment of child support.[6]

The *Toner*[7] ruling was expanded in *Post v. Caycedo*,[8] which held that the right to counsel is not limited to indigent parties, nor to parties involved with public assistance. When a party's counsel withdraws, the trial court errs in compelling a party to proceed without counsel in a parentage and child support litigation.

§ 3:33 Attorney fees and costs

Formerly, attorney fees were not generally granted in parentage actions at least at the stage of establishing the legal relationship.[1] Absent some provision in a statute, a rule of court, or some contractual provision or stipulation, a litigant was held to have no inherent right

---

[2]Phelps v. Fowler, 107 Ohio App. 3d 263, 668 N.E.2d 558 (8th Dist. Cuyahoga County 1995).

[3]State ex rel. Armstrong v. Hall, 33 Ohio App. 3d 1, 514 N.E.2d 424 (3d Dist. Marion County 1986).

[4]Mathews v. Eldridge, 424 U.S. 319, 335, 96 S. Ct. 893, 47 L. Ed. 2d 18 (1976).

[5]State ex rel. Cody v. Toner, 8 Ohio St. 3d 22, 456 N.E.2d 813 (1983).

[6]Geauga Cty. Dept. of Human Serv. v. Hall, 68 Ohio Misc. 2d 75, 647 N.E.2d 579 (C.P. 1995).

[7]State ex rel. Cody v. Toner, 8 Ohio St. 3d 22, 456 N.E.2d 813 (1983).

[8]Post v. Caycedo, 2005-Ohio-161, 2005 WL 100785 (Ohio Ct. App. 9th Dist. Summit County 2005).

[Section 3:33]

[1]Jelen v. Price, 9 Ohio App. 3d 174, 458 N.E.2d 1267 (8th Dist. Cuyahoga County 1983); Williams v. Dye, 1985 WL 11109 (Ohio Ct. App. 4th Dist. Jackson County 1985); Stevenson v. Woods, 1985 WL 8364, at 3*, (Ohio Ct. App. 6th Dist. Lucas County 1985) ("Ohio courts have repeatedly and specifically held that attorney fees are not to be considered either as part of the costs of prosecution or as necessary expenses caused by pregnancy and childbirth under R.C. 3111.17"); Baugh v. Carver, 3 Ohio App. 3d 139, 444 N.E.2d 58 (1st Dist. Hamilton County 1981).

to have attorney fees paid by his opponent.[2] The Uniform Parentage
Act, after which the Ohio Parentage Act is modeled, provides for payment of attorney fees in establishing parent-child relationships. The
Ohio version conspicuously omits the provision. The expenses for
which a party may be taxed are set forth in RC 3111.14, but a
complaining party's right to recover attorney fees is not mentioned,[3]
except in conjunction with obtaining or enforcing support orders.[4]
However, it can be argued in some instances, that all stages of a parentage action are toward the goal of securing the child's support. A
parent cannot apply for support without first establishing the parent-
child relationship that creates a duty of support. In *Zartman v. Swad*,[5]
the Court of Appeals held that the trial court did not err in awarding
attorney fees in a parentage action because the statute provides
authority to award fees in any proceeding in which support is
established, and support was ordered in this case.

Where parentage is contested for the apparent purpose of delaying
a support order, the trial court may properly award fees under RC
2323.51 due to frivolous conduct.[6]

Where relief from judgment is not granted under RC 3119.961, the
court shall require the party who filed for relief to pay all court costs
of the action and the reasonable attorney fees of the opposing party.[7]
Where a motion for relief from a parentage judgment is filed under
RC 3119.961 and granted, a subsequent action under RC Ch. 3111
may be filed against the person granted relief from judgment. If such
an action is filed, but the court determines that there is no parent-
child relationship, the court shall require the person who filed the action to pay all court costs and attorney fees.[8]

Former RC 3111.14(B), as enacted by 1990 House Bill 591, and in
effect from April 12, 1990, to July 15, 1992, provided remedies for
wrongfully accused males to recover their monetary losses resulting
from the paternity suit, including but not limited to lost wages, attorney fees, expert fees, genetic or other medical test costs, and court
costs. These remedies would still be available to any defendant wrongfully accused in a parent-child relationship complaint filed between
April 12, 1990, and July 15, 1992, if the evidence indicates that the

---

[2]See Sorin v. Board of Ed. of Warrensville Heights School Dist., 46 Ohio St. 2d
177, 75 Ohio Op. 2d 224, 347 N.E.2d 527 (1976); Sutherland v. Sutherland, 61 Ohio
App. 3d 154, 572 N.E.2d 215 (10th Dist. Franklin County 1989).

[3]Stevenson v. Woods, 1985 WL 8364 (Ohio Ct. App. 6th Dist. Lucas County
1985).

[4]RC 3123.17(B).

[5]Zartman v. Swad, 2003-Ohio-4140, 2003 WL 21804426 (Ohio Ct. App. 5th Dist.
Fairfield County 2003).

[6]Surface v. Grottlla-Kennedy, 2003-Ohio-3978, 2003 WL 21716183 (Ohio Ct.
App. 2d Dist. Clark County 2003).

[7]RC 3119.966.

[8]RC 3119.966(B).

plaintiff knew or should have known that the defendant could not be the child's father.[9]

Custodial parents seeking child support are entitled to federally funded services, which include legal assistance in establishing parentage and enforcing support.[10] Where a putative father argued that the prosecutor's office should not be permitted to represent both the plaintiff-mother and the Department of Human Services because they could have conflicting interests, the court held that defendant had no standing to complain of such a conflict, if any.[11]

Attorney fees and costs are clearly authorized by statute where a payor is found in contempt of a support order.[12] At least one Ohio appellate court recognized the prior gap in availability of attorney fees to parents seeking support for children born out of wedlock. In *McQueen v. Hawkins*,[13] the Sixth District Court of Appeals held that the legislature's failure to include a provision for payment of attorney fees in the Parentage Act denied the mother equal protection of the law, and remanded the case to the trial court to determine whether an award of fees was equitable.[14] Attorney fees have also been awarded as costs in contempt proceedings resulting from failure to comply with genetic testing orders.[15]

A trial court errs in assessing attorney fees to the child support enforcement agency without a motion and without a hearing when CESA failed to terminate a support order for an emancipated child.[16]

§ 3:34 Soldiers' and Sailors' Relief Act

The Soldiers' and Sailors' Civil Relief Act of 1940[1] provides:

At any stage thereof any action or proceeding in any court in which a

---

[9]See former RC 3111.14(B), deleted by 1992 S.B.10.

[10]42 U.S.C.A. § 651.

[11]Phelps v. Fowler, 107 Ohio App. 3d 263, 668 N.E.2d 558 (8th Dist. Cuyahoga County 1995); Morgan v. North Coast Cable Co., 63 Ohio St. 3d 156, 586 N.E.2d 88 (1992).

[12]RC 3105.21(C), RC 3109.05(C); In re Adler, 1994 WL 284988, at *3, (Ohio Ct. App. 8th Dist. Cuyahoga County 1994) (judgment for attorney fees in contempt proceeding is finding of contempt even though judge did not use the words "found in contempt").

[13]McQueen v. Hawkins, 63 Ohio App. 3d 243, 578 N.E.2d 539 (6th Dist. Lucas County 1989).

[14]See Pamela J. MacAdams, *Counsel Fees in Paternity Actions*, 4 Dom. Rel. J. Ohio 3 (Jan./Feb. 1992); Pamela J. MacAdams, *Attorney Fees Available in Parentage Cases*, 7 Dom. Rel. J. Ohio 3 (May/June 1995).

[15]Persinger v. Miller, 1993 WL 65750 (Ohio Ct. App. 2d Dist. Darke County 1993).

[16]Huffman v. Medina County Child Support Enforcement Agency, 2004-Ohio-729, 2004 WL 298696 (Ohio Ct. App. 9th Dist. Medina County 2004).

[Section 3:34]

[1]50 App. U.S.C.A. § 521.

person in military service is involved, either as plaintiff or defendant, during the period of such service or within sixty days thereafter may, in the discretion of the court in which it is pending, on its own motion, and shall, on application to it by such person or some person on his behalf, be stayed as provided in this Act [sections 501 to 591 of this Appendix], unless, in the opinion of the court, the ability of plaintiff to prosecute the action or the defendant to conduct his defense is not materially affected by reason of his military service.

The stay provided by the Soldiers' and Sailors' Civil Relief Act is not automatic. It is within the trial court's discretion to grant or deny a stay of proceedings.[2]

The United States Supreme Court has held "[t]he Act cannot be construed to require continuance on mere showing that the defendant was . . . in the military service."[3] The serviceman must show that he is unavailable for trial and that his rights would be materially affected if the stay is denied and the trial goes forward.

In *Phelps v. Fowler*,[4] the defendant failed to show that he was unavailable and, in fact, failed to present any evidence that he attempted to request leave to be present for his trial. Therefore, the appellate court overruled his assignment of error and affirmed the lower court's denial of the stay of proceedings.

§ 3:35 Effect of judgment—Allocation of parental rights and responsibilities, visitation, and companionship rights— As between parents

RC 3111.13(C) specifies that the court may issue certain orders "upon the request of a party and if not prohibited under federal law," which it used to be authorized to issue, period. Thus, the prayer of the parentage complaint should now specify relief requested, such as reimbursement of maternity expenses. The court used to automatically address these issues, but may now only award them if prayed for in the complaint.

This revision also allows the court to assess birth costs to the appropriate party. The former version only permitted the court to assess all or a portion to the father.

Also, this section clarifies that the father's or relative's actions for parenting time are separate complaints, not to be considered in the parentage action. Pursuant to the provisions of Ohio H.B. 136, the court is permitted under RC 3109.043 to consider making a temporary order regarding the allocation of parental rights and responsibilities for a child, companionship rights or temporary custody to the putative father while the parentage action is pending in the event that a par-

---

[2]Nurse v. Portis, 36 Ohio App. 3d 60, 520 N.E.2d 1372 (9th Dist. Summit County 1987); Olsen v. Olsen, 87 Ohio App. 3d 12, 621 N.E.2d 830 (8th Dist. Cuyahoga County 1993).

[3]Boone v. Lightner, 319 U.S. 561, 565, 63 S. Ct. 1223, 87 L. Ed. 1587 (1943).

[4]Phelps v. Fowler, 107 Ohio App. 3d 263, 668 N.E.2d 558 (8th Dist. Cuyahoga County 1995).

ent and child relationship has not yet been established, where father is named on the birth record, child has father's last name, or a "clear pattern of a parent child relationship between the child and the putative father exists."

A parent-child action is intended to establish the parent-child relationship and to provide support. It is not a custody proceeding, and therefore an affidavit pursuant to RC 3127.23 (UCCJEA) is not required.[1]

A judgment or order of the court determining the existence of a parent-child relationship may contain any other provision in the best interest of the child.[2] After entry of the parentage order, a father may petition to be named the child's residential parent, or for visitation of the child in a proceeding separate from the original parentage action.[3] However, the natural father of a nonmarital child who has participated in the nurturing process of the child has equal standing with the mother regarding custody of the child, even if paternity has not been adjudicated, where the mother admits that the custody applicant is the child's father.[4] A court errs in dismissing the application for custody of an acknowledged father. A court has jurisdiction to hear the complaint for custody of a father who has acknowledged parentage. An acknowledged father has the same rights, responsibilities and due process rights as a father of a child born in wedlock.[5] A natural parent has standing as a parent, and nonmarital children have the same right as marital children to live with the parent who can better care for them. The best interest of the child is the applicable standard in a custody determination between the parents of a nonmarital child.[6]

Note that under S.B. 180, RC 3109.051(D)(15) adds a new best-interest standard. When determining companionship or visitation rights requested by a non-parent, the wishes and concerns of the child's parents shall be considered.

[Section 3:35]

[1]Hardman v. Chiaramonte, 39 Ohio App. 3d 9, 528 N.E.2d 1270 (9th Dist. Summit County 1987).

[2]RC 3111.13(C). As amended by 2000 S.B. 180, a party must request relief before court may grant it.

[3]RC 3111.13(C). See Mercer v. Channell, 1986 WL 6051, at 3*, (Ohio Ct. App. 4th Dist. Jackson County 1986) (court found that while same trial court number was used in custody order, "the bastardy proceeding was already completed," and thus the custody was a proceeding separate from the paternity action).

[4]In re Byrd, 66 Ohio St. 2d 334, 20 Ohio Op. 3d 309, 421 N.E.2d 1284 (1981); Pruitt v. Jones, 62 Ohio St. 2d 237, 16 Ohio Op. 3d 276, 405 N.E.2d 276 (1980); Matter of Crawford, 1986 WL 13689 (Ohio Ct. App. 8th Dist. Cuyahoga County 1986); Madison v. Jameson, 1997 WL 416319 (Ohio Ct. App. 9th Dist. Summit County 1997).

[5]Walters v. Johnson, 2002-Ohio-2680, 2002 WL 1162340 (Ohio Ct. App. 5th Dist. Licking County 2002).

[6]In re Byrd, 66 Ohio St. 2d 334, 20 Ohio Op. 3d 309, 421 N.E.2d 1284 (1981); Pruitt v. Jones, 62 Ohio St. 2d 237, 16 Ohio Op. 3d 276, 405 N.E.2d 276 (1980); Matter of Crawford, 1986 WL 13689 (Ohio Ct. App. 8th Dist. Cuyahoga County 1986).

This seems to be our legislature's response to *Troxel v. Granville*,[7] wherein the U.S. Supreme Court held the Washington visitation statute unconstitutional, because, among other reasons, they failed to consider the parents' wishes in granting visitation to a non-parent.

However, if paternity has been adjudicated, and the parents have not lived together during the life of the child, a father petitioning the court for custody formerly needed to meet the standards of RC 3109.04(F)(1) for custody modification, because a support order in a paternity action "impliedly and necessarily" recognized a mother's legal custody of a child who lives with her.[8] This provision is codified in RC 3109.042, effective January 1, 1998. Similarly, the conduct of the parents in allowing a child to live with the mother for a substantial period of time will be viewed by a court as vesting sole legal custody in the mother.[9] The effect of RC 3109.042 (eff. 1-1-98) is to negate the rulings in *In the Matter Ragland*,[10] *In re Yates*,[11] and similar rulings, as the new statute places parents on equal footing in any initial custody litigation. Additionally, the *In the Matter Ragland* and *In re Yates* rulings were essentially reversed by the ruling of the Tenth District in *Ellen v. Deal*,[12] which held that the trial court erred in applying the standards for modification of custody to an initial custody litigation, even though the child had been in the care of the mother, and even though a prior visitation order was in effect for the father but such visitation order did not designate custody. A similar rationale supported the Eighth District Court of Appeals in *In re Crawford*,[13] in which custody was awarded to a putative father who admitted parentage during a habeas corpus proceeding in which a mother sought return of her child. The court recognized that the child had lived with her father and his family for most of her life and, therefore, awarded him legal custody even though parentage had not been established in a formal proceeding.

---

[7]Troxel v. Granville, 530 U.S. 57, 120 S. Ct. 2054, 147 L. Ed. 2d 49 (2000).

[8]In the Matter Ragland, 1983 WL 3653 at 3*, (Ohio Ct. App. 10th Dist. Franklin County 1983). See also Lucas v. Estes, 1989 WL 13529 (Ohio Ct. App. 2d Dist. Montgomery County 1989) (subsequent modification of custody pursuant to RC 3113.13(C) is the functional equivalent of an RC 3109.04(B)(1) proceeding, which requires proof of change of circumstances).

[9]In re Yates, 18 Ohio App. 3d 95, 481 N.E.2d 646 (10th Dist. Franklin County 1984).

[10]In the Matter Ragland, 1983 WL 3653 at 3*, (Ohio Ct. App. 10th Dist. Franklin County 1983).

[11]In re Yates, 18 Ohio App. 3d 95, 481 N.E.2d 646 (10th Dist. Franklin County 1984).

[12]State ex rel. Ellen v. Deal, 1994 WL 723377 (Ohio Ct. App. 10th Dist. Franklin County 1994).

[13]Matter of Crawford, 1986 WL 13689 (Ohio Ct. App. 8th Dist. Cuyahoga County 1986).

§ 3:36 Effect of judgment—Allocation of parental rights and responsibilities, visitation, and companionship rights— Relatives and nonparents

Visitation may be granted to nonparents under RC 3109.051(B).[1] RC 3109.12 now permits an award of visitation with a minor child of an unmarried woman to the father, his parent and/or relative, and the parent or relative of the mother when they file a complaint pursuant to RC 3109.12.[2] A request for custody initiated by grandparents during the pendency of the parentage proceedings is not authorized by statute. A separate complaint is necessary under RC 3109.12.[3] However, a court may not issue a shared parenting plan between nonparents.[4]

Where grandparents are named as day care providers in a parenting plan, court may enforce their right of visitation even absent a day care provision, pursuant to RC 3109.12.[5]

When the natural parents of a child have remained married throughout the child's lifetime, the doctrine of parental autonomy applies to remove the rights other interested parties may have under RC 3109.12.[6] However, parents of a nonmarital child who marry after the child's birth are not protected by the parental autonomy doctrine, and, therefore, are subject to companionship requests by parties qualified under RC 3109.12.[7]

Under RC 3109.12, unless and until parentage is established, only the parent or relative of the unmarried woman may file for visitation, not the putative father's family. The court is governed in its actions by the criteria set out in RC 3109.051(F). Hence, if visitation is denied, the court shall make findings of fact and conclusions of law pursuant to Civil Rule 52.

The effects of a decree of adoption upon the rights of interested parties were expanded by S.B. 180 under RC 3107.15(C), where a grandparent's right to companionship or visitation pursuant to RC 3109.11 is not restricted or curtailed by an adoption, if a parent-child

---

[Section 3:36]

[1]Riddlebarger v. Workman, 1988 WL 50508 (Ohio Ct. App. 4th Dist. Scioto County 1988).

[2]RC 3111.13(C).

[3]Mary B. v. Zollie M., 1997 WL 90612 (Ohio Ct. App. 6th Dist. Lucas County 1997).

[4]Lorence v. Goeller, 2000 WL 988760 (Ohio Ct. App. 9th Dist. Lorain County 2000).

[5]Borkosky v. Mihailoff, 132 Ohio App. 3d 508, 725 N.E.2d 694 (3d Dist. Wyandot County 1999).

[6]In re Gibson, 61 Ohio St. 3d 168, 573 N.E.2d 1074 (1991).

[7]Stout v. Kline, 1997 WL 219099 (Ohio Ct. App. 5th Dist. Richland County 1997).

relationship has not been terminated between the parent and that parent's child, when the spouse of the other parent adopts the child.[8]

RC 3109.11 has been amended to include additional language that offers grandparents or other relatives the right to move for companionship time if the parent-child relationship between the child and deceased parent has not been terminated prior to the parent's death, even if the surviving parent's new spouse adopts the child.[9]

Legal custody of a child may not be awarded to a non-parent without first a finding of parental unsuitability.[10] The constitutional custodial right of a parent must be protected by conducting custody litigation pursuant to the procedures that are fundamentally fair under the due process clause of the 14th Amendment to the United States Constitution and Section 16, Article I of the Ohio Constitution which protect the natural parents' fundamental liberty to have the care, custody and management of their children. After a finding of unsuitability of the natural parent, then the "best interests of the child" standard applies.

Likewise, visitation rights shall not be awarded a non-parent where biological parents do not agree, and where biological parents are not first found unfit. When genetic testing revealed during a divorce action that the husband was not the father of a minor child, the domestic relations court referred to matter to the juvenile division to address parentage. In that action husband requested visitation rights after there was an establishment of parentage between the child and his biological father (not husband, who was excluded). The court of appeals upheld the trial court's ruling that husband is precluded from visitation rights with the child if the child's parents did not agree that he should have visitation. The juvenile court must consider the parents' wishes under RC 3109.051(D).[11]

A trial court errs in applying the standard for custody between a parent and a non-parent as set forth in *In Re Perales*,[12] when after the death of a biological mother, her relatives sought custody of a child legitimized pursuant to former RC 2105.18. During the custody trial, the father admitted that he did not meet mother until after the child's birth, thus admitting that he obtained the legitimization by fraud.

---

[8]A parent's rights may be terminated before his/her death if by adoption prior to death or by legal custody being removed prior to death.

[9]Note: This statute applies only to unmarried, not divorced, parents.

[10]In re Hockstok, 98 Ohio St. 3d 238, 2002-Ohio-7208, 781 N.E.2d 971 (2002); Lorence v. Goeller, 2005-Ohio-2678, 2005 WL 1283713 (Ohio Ct. App. 9th Dist. Lorain County 2005); In re C.R., 2004-Ohio-4465, 2004 WL 1899219 (Ohio Ct. App. 8th Dist. Cuyahoga County 2004).

[11]Collins v. Collins, 2004-Ohio-5653, 2004 WL 2380992 (Ohio Ct. App. 12th Dist. Fayette County 2004).

[12]In re Perales, 52 Ohio St. 2d 89, 6 Ohio Op. 3d 293, 369 N.E.2d 1047 (1977).

Therefore, the trial court erred in applying the *Perales*, supra. standard to this custody case.[13]

§ 3:37   Effect of judgment—Child support—In general

A father's duty to support extends to his marital and nonmarital children alike,[1] and judgment in a parentage case usually includes child support.[2] When there are two children, and there is a finding of likelihood of paternity only as to one, the duty of support attaches only that child.[3] Child support may be ordered from the date of birth,[4] even where paternity is denied and there has been a delay in the filing of the paternity proceeding.[5] The Ninth District Court of Appeals held in *Edwards v. Sadusky*[6] that a court abuses its discretion when it fails to award child support from the date of birth, absent some compelling circumstances which ought reasonably to relieve the father of obligation and the child of this entitlement.

In parentage actions, RC 3111.13(E) governs the determination of support orders, which are now based on RC Ch. 3119. These are the same child support statutes used in domestic relations courts, and specifically require the juvenile court to provide the children in parentage cases the same socioeconomic status that would have been available to them if the parents had married.[7] The Ohio Supreme Court has held that whether establishing an initial support order, or modifying an existing order based upon the parties' agreement that

---

[13]Biggs v. Balosky, 2002-Ohio-3859, 2002 WL 1766603 (Ohio Ct. App. 9th Dist. Medina County 2002).

[Section 3:37]

[1]See RC 3103.031. See Gomez v. Perez, 409 U.S. 535, 93 S. Ct. 872, 35 L. Ed. 2d 56 (1973); Franklin v. Julian, 30 Ohio St. 2d 228, 59 Ohio Op. 2d 264, 283 N.E.2d 813 (1972); Johnson v. Norman, 66 Ohio St. 2d 186, 20 Ohio Op. 3d 196, 421 N.E.2d 124 (1981).

[2]See RC 3111.13.

[3]Stacey v. Lacey, 1988 WL 81341 (Ohio Ct. App. 11th Dist. Lake County 1988).

[4]RC 3111.13, RC 3111.15. Beach v. Poole, 111 Ohio App. 3d 710, 676 N.E.2d 1254 (5th Dist. Muskingum County 1996).

[5]Gilbert v. Ucker, 1988 WL 38792 (Ohio Ct. App. 5th Dist. Licking County 1988); Edwards v. Sadusky, 4 Ohio App. 3d 297, 448 N.E.2d 506 (9th Dist. Summit County 1982) (obligation to support a nonmarital child begins at child's birth, not at the date paternity is established); Baugh v. Carver, 3 Ohio App. 3d 139, 444 N.E.2d 58 (1st Dist. Hamilton County 1981); Parker v. Slivinski, 1986 WL 6766 (Ohio Ct. App. 12th Dist. Madison County 1986); Brown v. Snyder, 51 Ohio St. 3d 704, 555 N.E.2d 321 (1990).

[6]Edwards v. Sadusky, 4 Ohio App. 3d 297, 448 N.E.2d 506 (9th Dist. Summit County 1982).

[7]RC 3113.215(B)(3). For a comprehensive overview, see Pamela J. MacAdams, *Support Issues in Paternity Cases*, 7 Dom. Rel. J. Ohio 6 (Nov./Dec. 1995).

the residential parent shall provide all support, the statutory child support guidelines must be followed as laid out in *Marker v. Grimm*.[8]

RC 3111.13(E) formerly set forth standards in determining the amount of support to be paid by the obligor, including the standard of living the child would have enjoyed had the parents been married[9] and the educational opportunities that would have been available to the child. Now, all paternity support orders issued must comply with RC Ch 3119, RC Ch 3121, RC Ch 3123 and RC Ch 3125[10] and are subject to the courts' continuing jurisdiction to modify.[11]

A court may not take judicial notice of CSEA support proceedings. Thus, a certified copy of the order must be admitted into evidence or a records custodian of CSEA must testify to the order.[12]

A claim of nonpaternity is not a defense and cannot be an issue in a nonsupport action.[13] The Ohio legislature has removed paternity as an element of the crime of nonsupport by the enactment of RC 2919.21(B), which provides that the basis for establishing an accused's duty to support is the introduction of a prior court order or a decree requiring support. However, nonpaternity is a defense to a Uniform Reciprocal Enforcement of Support Act (URESA) action or a Uniform Interstate Family Support Act (UIFSA) action, and the court may adjudicate parentage in the URESA or UIFSA proceeding if both parties are present or the evidence indicates that their presence is not necessary; otherwise, the court may adjourn the hearing until parentage has been established.[14]

RC 3103.031 governs the duration of the obligation, extending the duty of support even beyond the age of majority if a child continually attends an accredited high school.

§ 3:38 Effect of judgment—Child support—Past care

In assessing support from date of birth, courts shall consider any payments, in-kind benefits and other contributions of an obligor made before issuance of a support order.[1] Interest shall accrue at the statutory interest rate on past care judgments not paid pursuant to court

---

[8]Marker v. Grimm, 65 Ohio St. 3d 139, 601 N.E.2d 496 (1992); DePalmo v. DePalmo, 78 Ohio St. 3d 535, 1997-Ohio-184, 679 N.E.2d 266 (1997).

[9]RC 3119.23(L).

[10]RC 3111.13(E).

[11]Ward v. Goodman, 1990 WL 152096 (Ohio Ct. App. 7th Dist. Columbiana County 1990).

[12]Chapman v. Muetzel, 2002-Ohio-563, 2002 WL 207105 (Ohio Ct. App. 10th Dist. Franklin County 2002).

[13]State v. Brown, 5 Ohio App. 3d 220, 451 N.E.2d 1232 (5th Dist. Stark County 1982).

[14]RC 3115.24, as in effect until 1-1-98, and RC 3115.52 thereafter.

[Section 3:38]

[1]RC 3111.13(F)(2).

order.[2] The Eighth District has held that court errs in failing to award interest on a substantial past care award.[3] However, where a parent fails to request child support back to the child's birth in his or her pleadings, the court does not abuse its discretion in failing to award past care support.[4]

The retroactivity of child support back to the date of birth has been held to be barred by laches under circumstances where the mother declined offers of support, changed the child's surname, and discouraged visitation requests.[5] An adult child's claim for paternal support brought in a parentage action under RC Ch 3111 is separate from the mother's claim. The barring of the mother's claim by laches does not necessarily bar the child's recovery of support.[6]

The proper method of calculation of past care (child support back to birth date) is to apply the appropriate statutory support formula for each year of the child's life. The installment re-payment plan must not be unreasonably short or long.[7] It has been held that court errs in failing to complete child support computation worksheets for each year of a child's life in calculating past care.[8] Conversely, where a court makes findings of fact sufficient to support a finding that the obligor met the child's needs prior to the court's support order it is not error to fail to order support retroactive to birth.[9]

RC 3119.05(J) clarifies that manner in which courts should handle past care issues in parentage cases. The fact finder is to apply the worksheets, schedule, and law which are in effect at each respective time period. For example, past care issues in parentage actions often go back many years, some of which may not resemble the current year's income. The fact finder now must review the income and other guideline factors like day care and health care costs, and apply those numbers for each respective year at issue to the guideline worksheets then in effect. A trial court abuses it's discretion in assessing past care based upon current earnings, even where the relevant factors to

---

[2]Neilsen v. Meeker, 1997 WL 337628 (Ohio Ct. App. 8th Dist. Cuyahoga County 1997).

[3]Cicchini v. Crew, 2000 WL 1876397 (Ohio Ct. App. 8th Dist. Cuyahoga County 2000).

[4]Michael v. Chesnut, 1997 WL 254142 (Ohio Ct. App. 2d Dist. Greene County 1997).

[5]Stephenson v. Potts, 1993 WL 150496 (Ohio Ct. App. 10th Dist. Franklin County 1993).

[6]Park v. Ambrose, 85 Ohio App. 3d 179, 619 N.E.2d 469 (4th Dist. Ross County 1993).

[7]State ex rel. Donovan v. Zajac, 2000 WL 816249 (Ohio Ct. App. 11th Dist. Geauga County 2000).

[8]Yeager v. Kane, 1998 WL 429620 (Ohio Ct. App. 5th Dist. Guernsey County 1998); Rebecca A. v. Joseph A, 2000 WL 770137 (Ohio Ct. App. 6th Dist. Ottawa County 2000); Hills v. Patton, 2008-Ohio-1343, 2008 WL 755305 (Ohio Ct. App. 3d Dist. Allen County 2008).

[9]Shockey v. Blackburn, 1999 WL 326174 (Ohio Ct. App. 12th Dist. Warren County 1999).

calculate support pursuant to each years' then existing guidelines is not presented as evidence. The child support statutes must be followed literally and technically. Thus, failure to apply the guidelines in effect for each year of past care is reversible error.[10]

In *Lewis v. Chapin*,[11] the court held that the trial court erred in dismissing a mother's motion for child support arrears after a probate court acknowledgment. The trial court based its ruling on the doctrine of res judicata. The appellate court reasoned that res judicata did not apply as the issue was not parentage, but was past care. Likewise, a trial court errs in dismissing a mother's claim for past care due to her failure to object to an administrative support order, where the administrative agency had no authority to award past care.[12]

Absent a finding that one parent made voluntary contributions to the support of a child prior to a support order, court abuses its discretion in not awarding past care back to the date of birth. Where court does not award past care back to birth, findings of fact must be made in support of its decision.[13]

A trial court errs in failing to award child support retroactive to the date of filing a complaint except as authorized under RC 3111.13(F)(3)(a). An appellate court found that the duty of support under RC 3103.03(A) commences at birth and support orders generally are made retroactive to the date of birth.[14]

Exceptions to child support awards retroactive to birth are now found in RC 3111.13(F)(3)(a). This statutory authority disallows inclusion of a past care order to the date of the child's birth if the child is over three years of age at the time of the initial filing *and* the father had no knowledge or reason to know of the possibility of parentage.[15]

Some courts treat this provision as a statute of limitations. As such assertion of it is a defense, which must be pled as an affirmative defense in the initial responsive pleading, or it may be treated as waived. Thus, where a father fails to state in his answer the affirmative defense that he did not know, or should not have known, of his parentage, or that the past care claim is barred by the statute of limitations, he may have waived the provisions of RC 3111.13(F)(3) which

[10]Kreitzer v. Anderson, 157 Ohio App. 3d 434, 2004-Ohio-3024, 811 N.E.2d 607 (3d Dist. Auglaize County 2004).

[11]Lewis v. Chapin, 93 Ohio App. 3d 695, 639 N.E.2d 848 (8th Dist. Cuyahoga County 1994).

[12]Nicely v. Kline, 2006-Ohio-951, 2006 WL 496004 (Ohio Ct. App. 10th Dist. Franklin County 2006).

[13]Baugh v. Carver, 3 Ohio App. 3d 139, 444 N.E.2d 58 (1st Dist. Hamilton County 1981); Magee v. Robinson, 1998 WL 646677 (Ohio Ct. App. 9th Dist. Summit County 1998).

[14]Brightwell v. White, 1999 WL 1127392 (Ohio Ct. App. 2d Dist. Montgomery County 1999).

[15]Dixon v. Walcutt, 152 Ohio App. 3d 372, 2003-Ohio-1667, 787 N.E.2d 1237 (5th Dist. Muskingum County 2003)

forbid the court to issue a past care order when the action is brought after the child's third birthday.[16]

Under RC 3111.13(F)(3)(b), the mother has the burden of proving by a preponderance of the evidence that she "performed a reasonable and documented effort to contact and notify the alleged father of his paternity."

It has been held that mother met her burden un RC 3111.13(F)(3)(b) based upon her testimony that she and father discussed the pregnancy at the time she became pregnant, and that mother made occasional attempts to contact father thereafter, including leaving messages with his roommate and searching for his contact data about twice per year. Mother's testimony without written documentation was held sufficient.[17]

A constitutional challenge was made to RC 3111.13(F)(3)(a) in *Smith v. Smith*.[18] Mother moved the trial court to declare RC 3111.13(F)(3)(a) unconstitutional. Her motion was overruled. She appealed and the 3rd District Court of Appeals reversed the trial court reasoning that the statute is "substantive" and thus unconstitutionally retroactive.[19]

§ 3:39   Effect of judgment—Child support—Past care—Claim brought after child is emancipated

Various Ohio jurisdictions had differing precedent on the issue of whether an adult child had the right to bring a past care claim prior to age 23. In *Carnes v. Kemp*,[1] with a five to three decision, the Ohio Supreme Court ruled that an adult emancipated child, unlike his or her mother, may be awarded past care after the establishment of parentage when that establishment is not made until after the child's 18th birthday.

The question was certified to the Ohio Supreme Court when the Auglaize County Court of Appeals reversed the trial court's ruling that an 18 year old could be awarded retroactive child support when parentage was established after she was an adult. In *Carnes v. Kemp*, Jessica Schaefer was born to Deborah Carnes on June 12, 1982. Mother never established parentage during the child's minority. When Jessica was 18, she sought and found her father, established parent-

---

[16]Kreitzer v. Anderson, 157 Ohio App. 3d 434, 2004-Ohio-3024, 811 N.E.2d 607 (3d Dist. Auglaize County 2004); Pfeifer v. Shannon, 2004-Ohio-7241, 2004 WL 3090215 (Ohio Ct. App. 11th Dist. Portage County 2004); Hills v. Patton, 2008-Ohio-1343, 2008 WL 755305 (Ohio Ct. App. 3d Dist. Allen County 2008).

[17]Osgood v. Dzikowski, 2008-Ohio-5065, 2008 WL 4416653 (Ohio Ct. App. 10th Dist. Franklin County 2008).

[18]Smith v. Smith, 157 Ohio App. 3d 778, 2004-Ohio-3552, 813 N.E.2d 740 (3d Dist. Hancock County 2004).

[19]See also Dixon v. Walcutt, 152 Ohio App. 3d 372, 2003-Ohio-1667, 787 N.E.2d 1237 (5th Dist. Muskingum County 2003).

[Section 3:39]

[1]Carnes v. Kemp, 104 Ohio St. 3d 629, 2004-Ohio-7107, 821 N.E.2d 180 (2004).

age, sought and was awarded past care of more than $52,000. Jessica's father, Barrett Kemp, II, argued at the trial level that Carnes was not entitled to past care, as she had failed to bring the action before Jessica was 18. The trial court held that it had no jurisdiction to award Carnes past support because Jessica was an adult before the action commenced. However, the trial court ruled that it did have jurisdiction to make the award to Jessica.

The Court of Appeals reversed, holding that the trial court had no jurisdiction to award retroactive child support to an adult emancipated child. Recognizing that it's decision was in conflict with other jurisdictions, the Court of Appeals certified the conflict.

The precise issue certified was: "Does a court have subject-matter jurisdiction to award retroactive child support payments in a paternity action initiated after the child has reached the age of majority?"

RC 3111.06 authorizes juvenile courts to hear parentage actions. RC 3111.05 outlines the statute of limitations stating in relevant part: "An action to determine the existence or nonexistence of the father and child relationship may not be brought later than five years after the child reaches the age of eighteen." RC 3113.13(C) provides authority for the trial court, once it establishes parentage, to make orders against the appropriate party concerning the duty of support, including past care awards for minor children.

The conflict among jurisdictions was that when RC 3111.05 is read in conjunction with RC 3111.13, it is interpreted that the juvenile court retains jurisdiction to award past child support when a parentage action is brought by the child before his or her 23rd birthday. Cases in support of this interpretation include: *In re Buechter,*[2] *Sexton v. Conley,*[3] *Elzey v. Springer,*[4] *Hudgins v. Mitchell,*[5] *Spires v. Moore,*[6] and *Seegert v. Zietlow.*[7]

These courts reason that since the legislature extended the time to file a parentage action beyond age 18, and since the remedies outlined in the parentage statute include retroactive support, the legislature must have intended that an adult child establishing parentage between the ages of 18 and 23 is entitled to recoup back child support.

Courts who held the opposing view reasoned that once a child

---

[2]In re Buechter, 2002-Ohio-5598, 2002 WL 31341567 (Ohio Ct. App. 2d Dist. Miami County 2002).

[3]Sexton v. Conley, 2002-Ohio-6346, 2002 WL 31630766 (Ohio Ct. App. 4th Dist. Scioto County 2002).

[4]Elzey v. Springer, 2004-Ohio-1373, 2004 WL 549805 (Ohio Ct. App. 12th Dist. Fayette County 2004).

[5]Hudgins v. Mitchell, 128 Ohio App. 3d 403, 715 N.E.2d 213 (9th Dist. Summit County 1998).

[6]Spires v. Moore, 2000 WL 1545 (Ohio Ct. App. 5th Dist. Muskingum County 1999).

[7]Seegert v. Zietlow, 95 Ohio App. 3d 451, 642 N.E.2d 697 (8th Dist. Cuyahoga County 1994).

reaches age 18, he or she is no longer a child and the juvenile court has no jurisdiction to order a parent to pay support obligations. The courts who adopted this interpretation reason that there is no provision in RC Ch. 3111 allowing retroactive support to an adult child. Additionally, the purpose of child support is to meet the current needs of a minor, and the duty of support exists only during a child's minority. Neither mother nor child may attempt to first establish support after age of majority. Cases making this interpretation include: *Snider v. Lillie*,[8] *Park v. Ambrose*,[9] and *In re Livingston*.[10]

To weigh the soundness of the two viewpoints, the Supreme Court looked to the doctrine of *in pari materia*, a rule of statutory construction which seeks to interpret legislative intent by construing statutes together and giving full application to both statutes unless they are irreconcilable.

RC 3111.05 expressly provides that a paternity action may be commenced by an adult child up to age 23. RC 3111.13(C) authorizes among the remedies after parentage judgment, the award of child support.

Thus, the Supreme Court reasoned that the combined effect of these two statutes is to authorize retroactive support payments when an adult child files to establish parentage before age 23. Thus, the judgment of the Court of Appeals was reversed and remanded as the juvenile court has jurisdiction to award retroactive child support payments to an adult emancipated child if a parentage action is filed prior to the child's 23rd birthday.

The dissent asserted that the doctrine of *in pari materia* is simply inapplicable, because the statutes which the majority attempt to reconcile are actually in conflict. A juvenile court's jurisdiction is limited by statute. RC 2151.23 defines the juvenile court's jurisdiction and refers only to support orders for a "child," which is defined as a person under 18. While RC 3111.05 extends the statute to allow juvenile courts to determine parentage for persons up to age 23, no where does it extend the right to child support. The dissent points out that the legislature specifically extends child support obligations in certain circumstances, such as when a child is over 18 and still in high school,[11] and if they intended to extend it under these circumstances they certainly would have known how, but chose not to.

RC 2105.06 demonstrates legislative intent *not* to provide jurisdiction to award child support after adulthood. It states at Division (C): "After issuance of an order under this section, the adult child shall be

---

[8]Snider v. Lillie, 131 Ohio App. 3d 444, 722 N.E.2d 1036 (1st Dist. Hamilton County 1997).

[9]Park v. Ambrose, 85 Ohio App. 3d 179, 619 N.E.2d 469 (4th Dist. Ross County 1993).

[10]In re Livingston, 115 Ohio App. 3d 613, 685 N.E.2d 1285 (8th Dist. Cuyahoga County 1996).

[11]RC 3103.03.

considered the child of the man declared to be the father as if born to him in lawful wedlock, except that the adult child and the adult child's mother shall not be awarded child support from the man from the time the adult child was a minor." RC 3103.031 manifests no duty for parents to support adult children.

There are reasons, other than to obtain support, that the legislature may have extended the right to establish parentage beyond 18. Those may include inheritance rights, exploration of medical history or to reach governmental benefits. The dissent criticizes the majority for creating a category of "adult emancipated children" to find jurisdiction, and for failing to recognize that RC 3111.05 is only a statute of limitations, not authority for extension of support clearly prohibited.

As admonished by the dissent, there may be practical problems resulting from this ruling. Potential questions likely to arise include: To whom is the support due if a court orders retroactive support? The adult child or the child's care giver during minority? Will governmental agencies who supplied assistance during the child's minority be entitled to recoup those monies until the child is 23, thus seeking out young adults to sue their fathers for parentage? What about RC 3111.13(F)(3)(a), the controversial statute which forbids a juvenile court from awarding past care where a mother knew or should have known father's identity, but failed to establish parentage before the child was age three?[12] Will this statute apply to adult children seeking to establish parentage? If so, will adult children have a cause of action against mothers for failure to protect their interests? If not, will adult children be encouraged to bring claims because mother is barred? If counsel fails on the mother's past care claim, may we bring it again on behalf of the child? Are we negligent if we fail to add the adult child as a party to ensure the claim when the child is under age 23?

§ 3:40 Effect of judgment—Child support—Other remedies

Lost wages as a result of pregnancy and confinement after childbirth are awardable under RC 3111.13.[1] Birthing expenses are also recoverable in a parentage action.[2]

The trial court erred in refusing to grant child support retroactive to the date of birth of the child, but did not err in refusing to grant plaintiff's request for reimbursement of reasonable expenses of pregnancy and confinement of the relator. The action was commenced under RC 2151.23(B)(4) and captioned "Motion for Order of Child Support: With Prior Legitimization; RC 2151.23(B)(4)." Apparently, because of the statutory authority under which the pleadings were

---

[12]RC 3111.13(F)(3)(a).

[Section 3:40]

[1]Horner v. Dible, 1994 WL 319071 (Ohio Ct. App. 6th Dist. Sandusky County 1994).

[2]Walk v. Bryant, 2004-Ohio-1295, 2004 WL 540919 (Ohio Ct. App. 4th Dist. Lawrence County 2004).

filed, the court had no jurisdiction to access RC 3111.13(C) which would have specifically directly the court to address payment of reasonable expenses of the mother's pregnancy and confinement.[3] After January 1, 1998, any request for reimbursement of maternity expenses must be in writing and include copies of invoices or documents as evidence to support the claim.[4]

RC 3111.13(D) specifies that any annuity purchased in lieu of periodic payments of support will be authorized only if the remaining principal will be transferred to the ownership of the child on the child's attainment of the age of majority. This revision seems to defeat those opportunities formerly available to have annuity pay out through college. For example, occasionally a negotiated settlement bargained for an annuity using as leverage the payout through college, though the court cannot otherwise address college expenses. This new provision seems to take away those opportunities by compelling the payout at age 18 to the child. The other remedies available, instead of periodic payments of support under the typical support statutes, must be carefully examined for compliance with this new law.

RC 3111.19 has been repealed. This former law permitted parents to compromise a settlement without a finding of parentage. RC 3111.19 now is former RC 3111.29, Interference with Establishment of Paternity, which prohibits persons from harassing others in order to discourage pursuing a parentage action.

RC 3111.13(D) allows the purchase of an annuity to be ordered in lieu of periodic payments of support when the same is found to be in the child's best interest. RC 3111.16 specifically allows the court to render support nonmodifiable and irrevocable if ordered pursuant to RC 3111.13(D).[5] It is error, however, for a court to combine a periodic child support obligation together with a lump-sum payment. In *Frazier v. Daniels*,[6] the trial court ordered periodic support payments, plus the finding of a trust account for future needs. The payor was a professional ball-player, and the court was anticipating large fluctuations in his income. Still, the court's order was not authorized by law. The court must choose either modifiable periodic payments of support, or a non-modifiable annuity in law thereof.

The father is also required to pay the mother for her support and maintenance during pregnancy and the necessary expenses caused by

---

[3]State ex rel. County of Summit, Dept. of Human Services and Child Support Enforcement Agency v. Paynther, 1994 WL 665512 (Ohio Ct. App. 9th Dist. Summit County 1994).

[4]RC 3111.12(E), eff. 1-1-98.

[5]Wallace v. Milgrim, 1990 WL 82146 (Ohio Ct. App. 8th Dist. Cuyahoga County 1990).

[6]Frazier v. Daniels, 118 Ohio App. 3d 425, 693 N.E.2d 289 (1st Dist. Hamilton County 1997).

pregnancy and childbirth.[7] In determining the sums necessary for the mother to pay medical expenses and to support herself during pregnancy, delivery, and postnatal convalescence, court may consider insurance payments and disability benefits received by a mother.[8]

§ 3:41 Effect of judgment—Child support—Administrative support order

RC 3111.80 creates a statutory vehicle for administrative support orders based on voluntary acknowledgment of paternity. This section allows the CSEA to progress to support orders after an administrative determination of parentage.

Administrative support orders must also address payment of medical expenses and provide for health insurance coverage where available. Obligors must provide obligees all necessary forms and cards to use health insurance coverage. If the obligor fails to comply with an order for coverage when it is available through his/her employer, the CSEA can order the employer to enroll the employee's dependent children and deduct the costs from the obligor's pay. Welfare recipients must notify medical providers of any insurance coverage and providers must use it before using welfare coverage. If an obligor fails to comply with a health insurance order, he or she must be liable for medical expenses resulting.[1]

The department of human services must have established procedures to review administrative support orders.[2] Orders shall be governed by the support schedules in the Revised Code, and administrative support officers shall not deviate therefrom.[3]

RC 3121.02 requires the CSEA to issue appropriate security for administrative support orders just as in court ordered support orders. Income sources who fail to withhold pursuant to an order are liable for the sums not withheld, except where pay cycles make compliance impossible.[4]

§ 3:42 Effect of judgment—Child support—Temporary support order

Effective January 1, 1998, RC 3111.111 provides for the issuance of a temporary child support order during the period of objections to a CSEA administrative order under former RC 3111.21 or RC 3111.22

---

[7]RC 3111.13(C). See also Jelen v. Price, 9 Ohio App. 3d 174, 458 N.E.2d 1267 (8th Dist. Cuyahoga County 1983).

[8]Jelen v. Price, 9 Ohio App. 3d 174, 458 N.E.2d 1267 (8th Dist. Cuyahoga County 1983).

[Section 3:41]

[1]RC 3119.56.

[2]RC 3119.024 and RC 3119.76.

[3]RC 3119.61.

[4]RC 3121.38.

or RC 3111.38 to RC 3111.54. If a payor is later found not to be the child's father, the court shall order reimbursement of any sums paid under such a temporary order.

Likewise, if an acknowledgment under RC 5101.314 or RC 3111.23 has been entered but is not yet final, either signatory to the acknowledgment may request a temporary administrative support order.[1]

When the issue of parentage is raised by a party at this stage of the proceedings, the acknowledgment is considered rescinded and the request for establishment of parentage shall proceed according to RC 3111.38. If no issue is raised as to parentage of this stage, then the acknowledgment shall be considered final as of the date the order is issued.

§ 3:43 Effect of judgment—Compromise settlements

Pursuant to former RC 3111.19, the alleged father and the mother were previously allowed—subject to the approval of the court—to compromise a paternity action by an agreement in which the parent and child relationship is not determined, but in which the alleged father undertakes a specific economic obligation in favor of the child.[1] The trial court could refuse to accept such a settlement, however, if the court did not deem the compromise settlement to be in the child's best interest. In *Phelps v. Fowler*,[2] the trial court properly rejected the parties' compromise settlement which would have paid mother a lump sum as child support, dismiss the parentage action without prejudice, and make no finding of paternity. Conclusive genetic test results of 99.99% weighed in favor of adjudicating parentage for the child's future benefit, such as inheritance rights. The accuracy of HLA and DNA testing today offers little reason not to adjudicate parentage.

A compromise agreement was dispositive of issues between the mother and alleged father only, and does not bar a subsequent action brought on behalf of the child.[3] Thus, under this former statute a putative father could agree to support a child without admitting to or being bound by a paternity determination. The Second District Court

---

[Section 3:42]

[1]RC 3111.211, repealed eff. 3-22-01.

[Section 3:43]

[1]Former RC 3111.19, repealed eff. 3-22-01. Compromise settlements are no longer permitted.

[2]Phelps v. Fowler, 107 Ohio App. 3d 263, 668 N.E.2d 558 (8th Dist. Cuyahoga County 1995).

[3]Carpenter v. Digman, 1991 WL 148107 (Ohio Ct. App. 5th Dist. Knox County 1991); Payne v. Cartee, 111 Ohio App. 3d 580, 676 N.E.2d 946 (4th Dist. Ross County 1996); Cornell v. Brumfield, 115 Ohio App. 3d 259, 685 N.E.2d 270 (4th Dist. Lawrence County 1996).

of Appeals held in *In re Smith*[4] that such a support agreement can later be vacated on the grounds that it is unjust, when all the parties agree that the putative father is not the biological father. A compromise agreement need not determine the paternity of a child to be res judicata as to a subsequent parentage action where a support obligation was imposed.[5]

A governmental agency such as the CSEA which is providing support to a child may intervene in a parentage action for the purposes of collecting or recovering that support.[6]

§ 3:44 Effect of judgment—Dependency exemption

A supporting parent may be awarded the income tax dependency exemption at the time of the original order[1] and in any modification proceeding.[2] The test for awarding a dependency exemption to a non custodial parent is to determine whether such an award will produce a net tax savings for the parents, thereby furthering the child's best interest.[3] court errs in allocating the tax exemption to the non-residential parent without a finding that it would produce a net tax savings for the parents.[4]

§ 3:45 Effect of judgment—Retrospective effect

The Ohio legislature expressly provided that the provisions of the OPA were to be applied retrospectively. 1982 House Bill 245, effective June 29, 1982, provides for the commencement of an action under RC 3111.01 to RC 3111.19 regardless of whether the child is born prior to, or on or after, the effective date of the act. In *Standifer v. Arwood*,[1] the Twelfth District Court of Appeals held that the retrospective nature of RC 3111.09 and RC 3111.10 did not violate Article II, section 28 of the Ohio Constitution since the new provisions affected

---

[4]In re Smith, 16 Ohio App. 3d 75, 474 N.E.2d 632 (2d Dist. Miami County 1984).

[5]Nelson v. Pleasant, 73 Ohio App. 3d 479, 597 N.E.2d 1137 (4th Dist. Lawrence County 1991).

[6]RC 3111.07(B).

[Section 3:44]

[1]Bobo v. Jewell, 1987 WL 12245 (Ohio Ct. App. 4th Dist. Athens County 1987).

[2]RC 3113.21(B)(10), repealed eff. 3-22-01. Thereafter see RC 3119.82.

[3]Singer v. Dickinson, 63 Ohio St. 3d 408, 588 N.E.2d 806 (1992); State ex rel. Jackson County Dept. of Human Services v. Strickland, 1997 WL 360745 (Ohio Ct. App. 4th Dist. Jackson County 1997).

[4]Yeager v. Kane, 1998 WL 429620 (Ohio Ct. App. 5th Dist. Guernsey County 1998).

[Section 3:45]

[1]Standifer v. Arwood, 17 Ohio App. 3d 241, 479 N.E.2d 304 (12th Dist. Warren County 1984).

procedural and not substantive rights.[2] However, in *Johnson v. Adams*,[3] the Ohio Supreme Court stated that this retrospective effect does not allow the reversal, on appeal, of a *judgment* rendered prior to the effective date of the statute. Thus, the OPA cannot be used to set aside paternity judgments entered prior to its effective date. Fathers whose paternity was adjudicated under the old law may file for custody, visitation, or other rights made available under the subsequent amendments.[4] Today, the administrative procedures under RC 3111.38 must be followed first, but the litigation rights remain where issues are not resolved at the administrative level.

§ 3:46   Effect of judgment—Inheritance

A parent can provide for a nonmarital child in a will regardless of whether the child's parentage has been established. However, when the parent dies intestate, the descent and distribution statutes apply.[1] RC 2105.17 provides that a nonmarital child can inherit from and transmit inheritance to his or her mother to the same extent as a marital child. A nonmarital child whose parentage has been established pursuant to the OPA or a probate court legitimation or acknowledgment under RC 3111.38 can inherit from, and transmit inheritance to, his or her father to the same extent as a marital child.[2] For the purposes of bringing a will contest, "child," as used in RC 2105.06, includes nonmarital children for whom the parent-child relationship has been established. Thus, a nonmarital child will not usually inherit from a putative father who dies intestate unless the father's paternity was established prior to his death or the father leaves a will in which he specifically provides for the child.

There are conflicting decisions regarding the applicability of the presumptions set forth in RC 3111.03 to inheritance cases, prior to the amendments effective January 1, 1998. In *In re Estate of Roberts*,[3] an illegitimate son whom the decedent had supported was not allowed to be listed as an heir to the estate, since his right to inherit had not been established under RC Ch. 3111 or the Ohio statute of descent

---

[2]See also Russell v. Rayburn, 1985 WL 9475 (Ohio Ct. App. 4th Dist. Jackson County 1985).

[3]Johnson v. Adams, 18 Ohio St. 3d 48, 479 N.E.2d 866 (1985).

[4]Mercer v. Channell, 1986 WL 6051, at 3*, (Ohio Ct. App. 4th Dist. Jackson County 1986). See also RC 3111.13(C).

[Section 3:46]

[1]RC 2105.06. Byrd v. Trennor, 157 Ohio App. 3d 358, 2004-Ohio-2736, 811 N.E.2d 549 (2d Dist. Clark County 2004).

[2]Former RC 2105.18.

[3]Re Estate of Roberts (Cyril Dunlop), 1986 WL 8689 (Ohio Ct. App. 7th Dist. Mahoning County 1986).

and distribution.[4] Since the appellant had been born in 1927, he was barred by the statute of limitations from now filing an action under the OPA, and that result was held not to be unconstitutionally discriminatory. However, in *Fry v. Doran*,[5] which involved a determination of parentage for life insurance proceeds of a deceased child, the court stated that although "the court below was not entertaining paternity proceedings under R.C. Chapter 3111 et seq., we agree with the parties that R.C. 3111.03 is an instructive guide to resolving the present case," and the probate court, in effect, made a paternity determination. In *Beck v. Jolliff*,[6] no question of retroactive application was raised in finding standing where a jury had, many years earlier, found the decedent the "reputed father." The statutes conflict somewhat, in that RC 3111.02 specifically creates a parent-child relationship by virtue of filing an acknowledgment with the department of human services under RC 5101.314, a process formerly done in the probate court. However, RC 3111.03 lists such an acknowledgment merely as a presumption of parentage, although effective January 1, 1998, this presumption may only be rebutted under RC 5101.314(B)(2).

Ohio law on intestate inheritance for nonmarital children, then, appears to be in accord with United States Supreme Court cases deciding nonmarital children's equal protection challenges to state descent and distribution laws. In *Trimble v. Gordon*,[7] the Supreme Court invalidated an Illinois intestate succession statute which prevented nonmarital children from inheriting from their father unless he had married the child's mother, holding that the statute was not substantially related to a permissible state interest. In turn, the Court has upheld statutes which premise a child's right to intestate inheritance on the establishment of the child's parentage in a judicial proceeding prior to the putative father's death, citing the underlying state interests in both the orderly adjudication of intestate estates and the avoidance of problems of proof and spurious claims.[8]

§ 3:47 Effect of judgment—Grandparent duty of support

Beginning November 15, 1995, when a minor bears or fathers a child, the parents of the minor parent have a statutory duty to support that baby, their grandchild, under RC 3109.19. The CSEA or the

---

[4]See also In re Estate of Vaughan, 90 Ohio St. 3d 544, 2001-Ohio-222, 740 N.E.2d 259 (2001).

[5]Fry v. Doran, 1985 WL 8822 at 4*, (Ohio Ct. App. 1st Dist. Hamilton County 1985).

[6]Beck v. Jolliff, 22 Ohio App. 3d 84, 489 N.E.2d 825 (5th Dist. Knox County 1984).

[7]Trimble v. Gordon, 430 U.S. 762, 97 S. Ct. 1459, 52 L. Ed. 2d 31 (1977).

[8]Lalli v. Lalli, 439 U.S. 259, 99 S. Ct. 518, 58 L. Ed. 2d 503 (1978). See also Labine v. Vincent, 401 U.S. 532, 91 S. Ct. 1017, 28 L. Ed. 2d 288 (1971). See also Garrison v. Smith, 55 Ohio App. 3d 14, 561 N.E.2d 1041 (6th Dist. Lucas County 1988).

court shall calculate the support order based upon the income of the grandparents, not the parents.[1]

§ 3:48   Effect of judgment—Appealability

A finding of parentage is not a final appealable order where the court's entry establishing paternity continues the matter for an evidentiary hearing on the issues of current support and medical coverage. The appeal was, therefore, properly dismissed under Civil Rule 54(B) when there was no expression in the entry that there is no just reason for delay and when all claims presented were not disposed of.[1]

A court's order requiring genetic testing is not a final appealable order.[2]

§ 3:49   Related issues—Adoption

A father established pursuant to the OPA is a child's legal parent and has the same right to grant or refuse consent to the adoption of his child as does the mother.[1] Thus, unless one of the statutory exceptions that make parental consent unnecessary applies, a child cannot be adopted absent the consent of a father whose paternity has been established.[2] However, a putative father whose parentage has not been established under the OPA is not a "parent" as defined in the adoption statute, and the circumstances requiring a putative father's consent are different from those in which a parent must consent.[3] Generally, a putative father's consent is necessary when he has developed some relationship with his child, in addition to the biological one. Specifically, a putative father's consent to the adoption is required if he has signed the child's birth certificate as informant, or if, prior to the child's placement for adoption, he acknowledged the child in a notarized statement, filed an objection to the adoption, or was alleged to be the child's father in a proceeding brought pursuant

---

[Section 3:47]

[1]For a complete summary, see Pamela J. MacAdams, *Grandparents' Duty to Support Grandchild*, 8 Dom. Rel. J. Ohio 3 (May/June 1996).

[Section 3:48]

[1]Marsh v. Clay, 1995 WL 428569 (Ohio Ct. App. 8th Dist. Cuyahoga County 1995).

[2]Smith v. Tackett, 1996 WL 666731 (Ohio Ct. App. 12th Dist. Butler County 1996).

[Section 3:49]

[1]RC 3107.06.

[2]RC 3107.06.

[3]See RC 3107.07. See also In Re: Schwartz, 1985 WL 7416 (Ohio Ct. App. 8th Dist. Cuyahoga County 1985).

to the OPA.[4] The consent of a putative father is not required if, prior to the child's adoptive surrender or placement, he failed to file an objection with the court or the agency who had custody of the child; if he abandoned the mother of the child during her pregnancy; or if he abandoned and failed to care for and support the child from the time of the child's birth until the child's adoptive placement or surrender;[5] or if he has failed to register as the minor's father with Ohio's purative father's registry within 30 days of the child's birth.[6] A putative father has no obligation to support and therefore cannot fail to support under RC Chapter 3111 until an adjudication of paternity is made. A court errs when it finds a failure to support by a putative father is a basis for not requiring his consent to adoption.[7]

Under RC 3103.031, however, the parental duty of support is no longer created by acknowledgment of parentage on the child's birth certificate as provided in RC 3705.09, but does arise from an acknowledgment filed with the department of human services under RC 5101.314 and RC 3111.23.

Thus, in adoption matters, consent requirements are premised on the nature of the relationship between the father and child, not merely on their biological connection. This focus differs from that of the OPA, which primarily considers the biological relationship. The emphasis of the adoption statutes on the nature of the relationship is consistent with the approach of the United States Supreme Court, which has extended constitutional protections to established relationships between unwed fathers and their children.[8] The Court held in *Lehr v. Robertson*[9] that a substantial relationship between parent and child, not a mere biological link, is the relevant criterion in evaluating both the rights of the parent and the best interests of the child.[10] An unwed father who lived with and supported his children has a cognizable and substantial interest in retaining parental rights to his children which is protected under the due process clause even if his paternity was

---

[4]RC 3107.06(F).

[5]RC 3107.07(B). See also West v. Nelson, 1986 WL 12849 (Ohio Ct. App. 6th Dist. Lucas County 1986).

[6]In re Adoption of A.N.L., 2005-Ohio-4239, 2005 WL 1949678 (Ohio Ct. App. 12th Dist. Warren County 2005).

[7]In re Adoption of Toth, 33 Ohio App. 3d 265, 515 N.E.2d 950 (9th Dist. Summit County 1986).

[8]Quilloin v. Walcott, 434 U.S. 246, 98 S. Ct. 549, 54 L. Ed. 2d 511 (1978); Caban v. Mohammed, 441 U.S. 380, 99 S. Ct. 1760, 60 L. Ed. 2d 297 (1979); Lehr v. Robertson, 463 U.S. 248, 103 S. Ct. 2985, 77 L. Ed. 2d 614 (1983).

[9]Lehr v. Robertson, 463 U.S. 248, 103 S. Ct. 2985, 77 L. Ed. 2d 614 (1983).

[10]See also Stanley v. Illinois, 405 U.S. 645, 92 S. Ct. 1208, 31 L. Ed. 2d 551 (1972); Quilloin v. Walcott, 434 U.S. 246, 98 S. Ct. 549, 54 L. Ed. 2d 511 (1978); Caban v. Mohammed, 441 U.S. 380, 99 S. Ct. 1760, 60 L. Ed. 2d 297 (1979).

never established legally.[11] In *Caban v. Mohammed*,[12] the Supreme Court held that a man acquires this interest when he acts as a father to his children and comes forward to participate in their rearing.

The significance of the biological connection is that it offers the natural father an opportunity that no other male possesses to develop a relationship with his offspring.[13] Where the biological father neither establishes his paternity nor develops a relationship with the child, the court looks to the availability of procedures by which he could have indicated his desire to acknowledge paternity or establish a relationship with the child. When such a system exists and is easy to use, the putative father must avail himself of it in order to merit constitutional protection.[14] Thus, due process requires the consent of a biological father who has exercised significant responsibility for the child, but it does not require such consent when the father has not developed a relationship with the child.[15] The father's exercise of some parental contact or effort to acknowledge the child appears to be the keystone of this distinction between fathers who must consent to an adoption and those who do not need to do so.[16]

In *Smith v. Smith*,[17] the judge was prohibited from establishing a parent-child relationship between the putative father and his alleged minor child for the reason that the mother placed her child for adoption in South Africa in accordance with the laws in South Africa. The judge believed he was permitted to go forward because the establishment of parentage was a separate issue than the adoption. The court of appeals stated that because our court must recognize the validity of another court's order under RC 3107.18, and because the establishment of parentage would be completely inconsistent with the public policy determinations made in conjunction with an adoption, the judge was prohibited from proceeding with the parentage action. On appeal to the Ohio Supreme Court, the Eighth District ruling was reversed, denying appellee the writ of prohibition because appellee failed to establish the inadequacy of the post-judgment appeal process.

---

[11]Stanley v. Illinois, 405 U.S. 645, 92 S. Ct. 1208, 31 L. Ed. 2d 551 (1972); Caban v. Mohammed, 441 U.S. 380, 99 S. Ct. 1760, 60 L. Ed. 2d 297 (1979). See also Elizabeth Buchanan, *The Constitutional Rights of Unwed Fathers Before and After Lehr v. Robertson*, 45 Ohio St. L.J. 313 (1984).

[12]Caban v. Mohammed, 441 U.S. 380, 99 S. Ct. 1760, 60 L. Ed. 2d 297 (1979).

[13]Caban v. Mohammed, 441 U.S. 380, 99 S. Ct. 1760, 60 L. Ed. 2d 297 (1979). See also Wisconsin v. Yoder, 406 U.S. 205, 231–33, 92 S. Ct. 1526, 32 L. Ed. 2d 15 (1972); Smith v. Organization of Foster Families For Equality and Reform, 431 U.S. 816, 844, 97 S. Ct. 2094, 53 L. Ed. 2d 14 (1977) ("[T]he importance of the familial relationship to the individuals involved and to the society . . . stems from the emotional attachments that derive from the intimacy of daily association.").

[14]Lehr v. Robertson, 463 U.S. 248, 103 S. Ct. 2985, 77 L. Ed. 2d 614 (1983).

[15]Lehr v. Robertson, 463 U.S. 248, 103 S. Ct. 2985, 77 L. Ed. 2d 614 (1983); Quilloin v. Walcott, 434 U.S. 246, 98 S. Ct. 549, 54 L. Ed. 2d 511 (1978).

[16]Caban v. Mohammed, 441 U.S. 380, 99 S. Ct. 1760, 60 L. Ed. 2d 297 (1979).

[17]Smith v. Smith, 1995 WL 264613 (Ohio Ct. App. 8th Dist. Cuyahoga County 1995).

Writs of prohibition have been sought in cases where a putative father seeks to establish his legal relationship during the pendency of an adoption proceeding. Such a writ was properly denied in *State ex rel Jason V. v. Cubbon*,[18] where the adoptive parents sought to preclude the juvenile court judge from ordering and proceeding with genetic testing while the adoption was pending. The paternity action was properly and timely initiated by the putative father, hence the writ was denied.

In *State ex rel Furnas v. Monnin*[19] the putative father sought to establish paternity after a final decree of adoption. The adoptive parents sought a writ of prohibition. The Ohio Supreme Court denied the writ and held that the adoption does not divest the juvenile court of jurisdiction to determine paternity for the limited purpose of allowing the biological father to exercise statutory rights to provide information regarding his social and medical history for placement in the adoption records.

§ 3:50   Related issues—Artificial insemination and surrogate mothers

The husband of a woman who is artificially inseminated with the semen of another is, if the husband consented to the artificial insemination, pursuant to RC 3111.95(A), "treated in law and regarded as the natural father of a child conceived as a result of the artificial insemination."[1] This presumption is conclusive, and no action under RC Chapter 3111 can affect this father-child relationship. A child conceived as a result of artificial insemination of an unmarried woman "shall not be treated in law or regarded as the natural child of the donor," and the donor shall not be treated or regarded as the natural father of the child.[2]

In *Brooks v. Fair*,[3] the husband was given leave to amend his answer so as to avoid a default judgment. He was not the biological father; his wife was artificially inseminated during the marriage with his consent, and he was listed on the birth certificate as the father. The trial court properly refused to find nonexistence of father-child relationship, basing its decision on (1) the finding that the legislature did not intend for RC 3111.04 to be applied retroactively to determine

---

[18]State ex rel. Jason V. v. Cubbon, 180 Ohio App. 3d 595, 2009-Ohio-267, 906 N.E.2d 502 (6th Dist. Lucas County 2009).

[19]State ex rel. Furnas v. Monnin, 120 Ohio St. 3d 279, 2008-Ohio-5569, 898 N.E.2d 573 (2008).

[Section 3:50]

[1]Gillem v. Gillem, 1997 WL 106318 (Ohio Ct. App. 12th Dist. Clermont County 1997). See also Susan Garner Eisenman, *Fathers, Biological and Anonymous, and Other Legal Strangers: Determination of Parentage and Artificial Insemination by Donor Under Ohio Law*, 45 Ohio St. L.J. 383 (1984).

[2]RC 3111.95, RC 3111.03(B).

[3]Brooks v. Fair, 40 Ohio App. 3d 202, 532 N.E.2d 208 (3d Dist. Van Wert County 1988).

the *nonexistence* of a father and child relationship; (2) the public
policy in favor of legitimacy of children; (3) the public policy against
making a child a ward of the state; and (4) the mother's intent that
the father-child relationship be more than temporary, as evidenced by
her awareness of the husband's name listed on the child's birth certificate, her claim in dissolution proceedings that the child was an issue
of the marriage, the length of the father-child relationship, and the
mother's acceptance of child support and compliance with visitation.

Ohio's RC 3111.89 states specifically that the sections regulating
artificial insemination do not apply to surrogate motherhood. A 1983
Attorney General's Opinion found that the business of arranging surrogate contracts was prohibited by RC 5103.17.[4] The opinion, which
had been requested by the department of health and human services
pursuant to its mandate under RC 5103.03 to regulate child-placing
agencies, stated that activities such as arranging pregnancies,
negotiating surrogate contracts, and paying for surrogate services and
subsequent adoptions, when carried out by agencies unlicensed by the
department, violated provisions prohibiting separation of children
from parents except by duly licensed adoption agencies in the same
manner as "baby-brokering" or adoption for fee.

In the much discussed New Jersey case involving "Baby M," the
trial court upheld a surrogate contract using both contract theory and
a best interests test.[5] The Supreme Court of New Jersey reversed the
lower court, holding that a surrogate parenting contract is unenforceable and illegal, and provides no basis for requiring a mother to turn
over custody to a natural father. The Supreme Court, however, after
settling the invalidity of the surrogate contract, upheld the trial
court's award of custody to the father based on the best interest test.[6]
In the wake of the "Baby M" case, many legislative bodies are looking
into the issues surrounding surrogate contracts. Limits on fees,
regulation by courts, and safeguards for both surrogates who change
their minds and children who are refused by the prospective parents
are some of the recommendations of the staff of the New York State
Senate Judiciary Committee, which conducted a study of the practice.[7]

Where a mother solicits the participation of a co-worker as sperm
donor each agreeing that his involvement in the child's life be
considered as a "friend" or "uncle" to the child, the court did not err in
finding that mother could not invoke the protections of the nonspousal
artificial insemination statutes to preclude father's rights in visitation
litigation. Mother had failed to object to the establishment of

---

[4]OAG 83-001. But see Surrogate Parenting Associates, Inc. v. Com. ex rel.
Armstrong, 704 S.W.2d 209 (Ky. 1986) (surrogate arrangement and adoption were
upheld as serving best interests of child, and adopting parents were awarded $3,500
in attorney fees).

[5]Matter of Baby M., 217 N.J. Super. 313, 525 A.2d 1128 (Ch. Div. 1987).

[6]Matter of Baby M, 109 N.J. 396, 537 A.2d 1227, 77 A.L.R.4th 1 (1988).

[7]Debra Cassens Moss, *Surrogate Parent Debate: "Baby M" Case Lawyers Outline
Views to Family Law Section*, 73 A.B.A. J. 25 (4-1-87).

paternity, and only attempted to invoke the artificial insemination statutes when father sought parenting time.[8]

A trial court held that the artificial insemination statutes did not apply to prevent a paternity adjudication when the mother solicited the participation of the donor, who was known to her, and where the mother and donor agreed that there would be a relationship between donor and child. The artificial insemination statutes are designed to provide anonymity and protection to both the donor and the mother. However, the statute does not contemplate a complete circumvention by the donor and the mother of the element of anonymity.[9]

When husband and wife were advised by the hospital that the child resulting from wife's egg and husband's sperm, but being carried by a gestational surrogate through the in vitro fertilization process, would be considered illegitimate and the gestational surrogate would be listed on the birth certificate as the child's mother, they filed a declaratory judgment action.[10] They requested they be declared genetic and natural parents of the child and that the birth certificate reflect the legitimate status of the child. The court held that when a child is delivered by a gestational surrogate who has been impregnated through the in vitro fertilization process, the natural parents shall be identified by a determination as to which individuals have provided the genetic imprint for that child. If those individuals have not relinquished or waived their rights to assume legal status of natural parents, they shall be considered natural and legal parents of that child. As such, the plaintiffs were declared the natural and legal parents. The birth certificate should list them as father and mother.

§ 3:51 Related issues—Name

An unmarried mother's child, whose birth certificate was signed by his or her natural father, may be given the surname of either parent, according to the wishes of the parents. If the natural father is not named on the birth certificate, the child is given the mother's surname. Any future change of the child's surname can be accomplished only in a probate court procedure pursuant to RC 2717.01,[1] or during the

---

[8]In the In re R.A.S., 2007-Ohio-6238, 2007 WL 4146828 (Ohio Ct. App. 12th Dist. Warren County 2007).

[9]C.O. v. W.S., 64 Ohio Misc. 2d 9, 639 N.E.2d 523 (C.P. 1994).

[10]Belsito v. Clark, 67 Ohio Misc. 2d 54, 644 N.E.2d 760 (C.P. 1994); Rice v. Flynn, 2005-Ohio-4667, 2005 WL 2140576 (Ohio Ct. App. 9th Dist. Summit County 2005).

[Section 3:51]

[1]In re Paternity, 4 Ohio Misc. 193, 33 Ohio Op. 2d 299, 211 N.E.2d 894 (C.P. 1965). See also Monteux v. Monteux, 5 Ohio App. 2d 34, 34 Ohio Op. 2d 92, 213 N.E.2d 495 (10th Dist. Franklin County 1966); In re Russek, 38 Ohio App. 2d 45, 67 Ohio Op. 2d 260, 312 N.E.2d 536 (8th Dist. Cuyahoga County 1974); Dolgin v. Dolgin, 1 Ohio App. 2d 430, 30 Ohio Op. 2d 435, 205 N.E.2d 106 (6th Dist. Lucas County 1965).

pendency of the parentage action.[2] In a post-parentage custody, support, and visitation hearing, the court has no jurisdiction to deal with that issue,[3] although the statute provides that the court may order the issuance of a new birth certificate.[4] The Scioto County Court of Appeals refused to set aside an agreement of the parties to change the child's birth certificate. The agreement arose out of a paternity action brought by the putative father who had signed the birth certificate.[5]

In addition, a probate court name change requires the consent of both living, legal parents. In the absence of consent, a hearing is required to determine whether the name change is in the best interest of the child.[6] The parent who does not consent must be given notice of this hearing.[7]

The Supreme Court held in *Bobo v. Jewell*[8] that a court of common pleas, including the juvenile court, has jurisdiction to order a change in the child's name. The Court found that the court is authorized, pursuant to RC 3111.13(B), to order a new birth certificate issued, stating such "denotes legislative recognition that a court has the power to order a change in the child's name."[9] The Court emphasized that the determination must be made after considering certain factors to ascertain the best interest of the child.[10] Factors to be considered in a name change include the following:

(1) Length of time child has used a surname;
(2) Effect of change of name on child's relationship with each parent;
(3) Identification of child as part of the family unit;
(4) Child's association with the residential parent;
(5) Child's preference;
(6) Parental failure to maintain contact with and support of the child;[11]
(7) The embarrassment, discomfort, or inconvenience that may

---

[2]Bobo v. Jewell, 1987 WL 12245 (Ohio Ct. App. 4th Dist. Athens County 1987). RC 3111.52, eff. 3-22-01, now permits the agency to alter a surname as part of the administrative process.

[3]West v. Nelson, 1986 WL 12849 (Ohio Ct. App. 6th Dist. Lucas County 1986).

[4]RC 3111.13(B), RC 3111.18.

[5]Riddlebarger v. Workman, 1988 WL 50508 (Ohio Ct. App. 4th Dist. Scioto County 1988).

[6]In re Newcomb, 15 Ohio App. 3d 107, 472 N.E.2d 1142 (10th Dist. Franklin County 1984); In re Russek, 38 Ohio App. 2d 45, 67 Ohio Op. 2d 260, 312 N.E.2d 536 (8th Dist. Cuyahoga County 1974).

[7]RC 2717.01.

[8]Bobo v. Jewell, 38 Ohio St. 3d 330, 528 N.E.2d 180 (1988).

[9]Bobo v. Jewell, 38 Ohio St. 3d 330, 528 N.E.2d 180 (1988).

[10]Bobo v. Jewell, 38 Ohio St. 3d 330, 528 N.E.2d 180 (1988); Geer v. Toth, 1993 WL 544308 (Ohio Ct. App. 5th Dist. Licking County 1993) (trial court properly refused to change child's surname after establishing parentage).

[11]In re Willhite, 85 Ohio St. 3d 28, 1999-Ohio-201, 706 N.E.2d 778 (1999).

result when a child's surname is different from the residential parent's;[12]

(8) Any other factors relevant to child's best interest.[13]

Under RC 2717.01(A) the court must determine whether there is "reasonable and proper cause" for changing the name. In *In re Willhite*[14] the Supreme Court interpreted this statutory provision to mean that a court must consider the best interests of a child when it determines whether reasonable and proper cause exists to change a surname. That determination is based on the *Bobo v. Jewell* factors.[15] Where a non-residential parent has lost contact with a child, the court properly changed child's surname to match the residential parent and half-siblings.[16] court errs in failing to consider the specific factors set forth in *Willhite* when ruling upon a name change.[17] Evidence demonstrating that a name change will not be harmful to a child does not rise to the level of demonstrating that the child's best interests are served by a name change. Thus, where the father (non-residential parent) demonstrates that the mother's relationship with the child would not be harmed by a name change and that the child was too young to express a preference or have friends who know him by a given surname, the court did not err in finding the evidence inadequate to meet the standard of proof that it was in the child's best interest to change his surname to father's.[18]

Furthermore, the ruling must be supported with findings as to the *Bobo v. Jewell* factors which support the change of name being in the child's best interest. A general finding that the best interest test is met is inadequate without findings under the *Bobo* test.[19]

In fact, it has been held reversible error to change a child's surname where father's testimony was that mother had been uncooperative in his relationship with the child thus far; he had other children bearing his name, but they lived out of state, and had no nearby relatives who bore his surname; his relationship with the child would not be adversely affected by his son bearing the mother's surname, but that

[12]In re Willhite, 85 Ohio St. 3d 28, 1999-Ohio-201, 706 N.E.2d 778 (1999).

[13]Bobo v. Jewell, 38 Ohio St. 3d 330, 528 N.E.2d 180 (1988). See also Sharp v. Sayre, 1990 WL 178111 (Ohio Ct. App. 4th Dist. Scioto County 1990) (court erred in changing child's surname where father failed to express interest in child before birth).

[14]In re Willhite, 85 Ohio St.3d 28, 1999-Ohio-201, 706 N.E.2d 778 (1999).

[15]In re Willhite, 85 Ohio St.3d 28, 1999-Ohio-201, 706 N.E.2d 778 (1999); In re Budenz, 133 Ohio App. 3d 359, 728 N.E.2d 24 (2d Dist. Clark County 1999).

[16]In re Name Change of Savers, 2000 WL 1124068 (Ohio Ct. App. 9th Dist. Summit County 2000).

[17]Provchy v. Casteel, 2000 WL 1124069 (Ohio Ct. App. 9th Dist. Summit County 2000).

[18]In re Dayton, 155 Ohio App. 3d 407, 2003-Ohio-6397, 801 N.E.2d 531 (7th Dist. Jefferson County 2003). See also In re Application for Change of Name of McGowan, 2005-Ohio-2938, 2005 WL 1385734 (Ohio Ct. App. 7th Dist. Harrison County 2005).

[19]Erin C. v. Christopher R., 2000 WL 125792 (Ohio Ct. App. 6th Dist. Sandusky County 2000).

he had no other sons to carry on his family name. Mother testified that her son carried her surname, as did her son's half-sibling who went to the same school; that the child's maternal family members lived in the same town and bore the same name; that the child had medical records under her name, and would be embarrassed by not sharing a surname with his custodial parent.[20]

A trial court errs in ruling that the court may only change a child's surname in a paternity action if the parties are in agreement to such. In fact, while the administrative agency can only change a name by agreement, the court is not under the same restriction.[21]

§ 3:52   Complaint to establish father-child relationship—By mother—Form⊚

[Title of Court]

[Caption]   Case No. [_____]
                                                 COMPLAINT

1. Plaintiff, [name of plaintiff], is the [mother/guardian] of the minor child, [name of minor child], born on [date], in [name of city], Ohio.

2. [Name of minor child] is a minor child aged [age of minor child] and brings this action by and through [his/her] [mother/guardian] and next friend, [name of next friend].

3. Plaintiff(s) state that Defendant, [name of defendant], is the natural father of said minor child and [is a resident of [name of county] County/said child was born as the result of sexual intercourse in the state of Ohio between Plaintiff [name of plaintiff] and Defendant [name of defendant] and thus jurisdiction may be obtained upon said Defendant by virtue of RC 3111.06(B).]

4. The plaintiff has attempted to resolve this matter through the child support enforcement agency pursuant to RC 3111.821 and [has been unsuccessful in resolving the matter/the parties have reached an agreement regarding the matter].The [dismissal entry/parentage adjudication order of the child support enforcement agency] in attached hereto as Exhibit [designation of exhibit].

WHEREFORE, Plaintiff(s) demand a judgment against Defendant establishing the existence of a father/child relationship between them; an order requiring Defendant to pay all reasonable expenses of Plaintiff [name of plaintiff]'s pregnancy; an order requiring Defendant to pay reasonable child support as of the date of birth of said child; an order requiring Defendant to obtain and maintain an appropriate policy of hospitalization and major medical insurance for the benefit

---

[20]Charles B. v. Jennifer S., 2008-Ohio-4276, 2008 WL 3878493 (Ohio Ct. App. 6th Dist. Erie County 2008).

[21]Eagleson v. Hall, 2008-Ohio-3647, 2008 WL 2840602 (Ohio Ct. App. 5th Dist. Guernsey County 2008).

of said minor child; an order allocating uncovered medical expenses for the minor child; an order requiring the issuance of a new birth certificate herein reflecting the father/child relationship and substituting it for the existing birth certificate, as provided by law; an order requiring Defendant to pay all costs herein expended; an award of attorney fees; and for such other and further relief to which the Plaintiff(s) may be entitled.

_____
Attorney for Plaintiff

NOTES TO FORM

Drafter's Notes

A long form caption should be used on the complaint. Include in caption, as parties, all necessary parties, including the child, as plaintiff or defendant, and all alleged and presumed fathers.

If service other than pursuant to Civ. R. 4 is desired, a written request for service (usually a court form) must accompany the complaint when it is filed.

A parentage action is not a custody (parenting) proceeding, and an RC 3127.23 affidavit is not required. Hardman v. Chiaramonte, 39 Ohio App. 3d 9, 528 N.E.2d 1270 (9th Dist. Summit County 1987).

RC 3123.17 permits the court to make an order of attorney fees in any support proceeding, including RC 3111.13 parentage orders.

§ 3:53   Complaint to establish father-child relationship—By father—Form⊚

[Title of Court]

[Caption]   Case No. *[_____]*

<u>COMPLAINT</u>

1.   Plaintiff *[name of plaintiff]* states that Defendant *[name of defendant]* gave birth to a child *[name of minor child]* on *[date]* in *[name of city, state]*.

2.   Plaintiff further states that he is the natural father of said child.

3.   The plaintiff has attempted to resolve this matter through the child support enforcement agency pursuant to RC 3111.381 and *[has been unsuccessful in resolving the matter/the parties have reached an agreement regarding the matter]*. The *[dismissal entry/parentage adjudication order of the child support enforcement agency]* is attached hereto as Exhibit *[designation of exhibit]*.

WHEREFORE, Plaintiff demands a judgment establishing the existence of the parent/child relationship between *[child's name]* and Plaintiff, the issuance of a new birth certificate reflecting such relationship and such other relief to which Plaintiff may be entitled.

_____

Attorney for Plaintiff

NOTES TO FORM

Drafter's Notes

A long form caption should be used on the complaint. Include in caption, as parties, all necessary parties, including the child, as plaintiff or defendant, and all alleged and presumed fathers.

If service other than pursuant to Civ. R. 4 is desired, a written request for service (usually a court form) must accompany the complaint when it is filed.

§ 3:54 Complaint to establish father-child relationship—By grandparent, with request for support—Form⊚

[Title of Court]

[Name of Grandparent]
            and
[Name of Minor Child], a minor,
by and through his/her next
friend
and grandparent,
[Name of Grandparent]
            Plaintiffs,   Case No. [_____]
vs.   COMPLAINT TO ESTABLISH
                                       FATHER/CHILD RELATION-
                                       SHIP
                                       AND FOR SUPPORT

[Name of Minor Father / Mother]
            and
[Parent of Minor Father / Mother]
            Defendants.

1. Plaintiff, *[name of grandparent]*, is the *[mother / father]* of *[name of minor child / parent]*, a minor born *[date]*, who is the *[mother / father]* of *[name of minor child]*, born *[date]*.

2. Plaintiff states that *[he / she]* is providing support for *[name of minor child]*.

3. Plaintiff states that *[he / she]* believes *[name of minor father]* is the father of the minor child, *[name of minor child]*.

4. Plaintiff states that *[he / she]* is bringing this action pursuant to RC 3109.19(B) for the determination of the parent-child relationship between *[name of minor father]*, and *[name of minor child]*.

5. Plaintiff has complied with the requirements of RC 3111.381 to attempt to establish parentage through the Child Support Enforcement Agency, but no resolution was reached. The dismissal entry of the child support enforcement agency is attached hereto as Exhibit *[designation of exhibit]*.

6. Plaintiffs state that defendant(s), *[name(s) of parent(s) of minor father or mother][is/are]* the parent(s) of *[minor father/minor mother]*, and the *[maternal/paternal]* grandparent(s) of *[name of minor child]*.

Wherefore, Plaintiffs demand a judgment establishing the existence of the parent-child relationship between *[name of minor father]* and *[name of minor child]* and for an order requiring *[minor father's/ mother's parents]* to pay support for the child, and for such other relief to which Plaintiffs may be entitled.

_____
Attorney for Plaintiff

NOTES TO FORM

Drafter's Notes

1995 H.B. 167 enacted RC 3109.19 to permit a grandparent to file a parentage action if that grandparent is providing support for a minor child of a minor parent. That act did *not*, however, add such grandparents as necessary parties under RC 3111.07.

A long form caption should be used on the complaint. Include the grandparent's and grandchild's names as plaintiffs, minor mother, minor father, (if not named as plaintiff), and grandparents from whom support is sought as defendants, and provide addresses for all.

Note the requirements of Civil Rule 17(B) for service on minor defendants, and the requirement for appointment of guardian ad litem for the protection of a minor defendant.

§ 3:55 Answer—Admission—Form⊚

[Title of Court]

[Caption]   Case No. *[_____]*
ANSWER

1. Defendant, *[name]*, states that he is in receipt of the Complaint to establish the father/child relationship.

2. Defendant says that he has read each and every allegation contained in said Complaint and further that he understands all of said allegations.

3. Defendant further states that he knowingly and voluntarily elects to waive his rights to any genetic and/or blood tests of all of the parties hereto as provided by law.

4. Defendant admits the allegations contained in said Complaint and states that he is the natural father of the minor child, *[name of child]*, born to Plaintiff *[name of plaintiff]* on *[date]*.

_____

Attorney for Defendant

[Certificate of Service]

§ 3:56   Answer—Denial by father—Form⊚

[Title of Court]

[Caption]   Case No. *[_____]*
                                         ANSWER

1.   Defendant, *[name of defendant]*, *[admits/neither admits nor denies for want of personal knowledge]* that Plaintiff is the mother of the minor child *[name of minor child]*.

2.   Further answering, Defendant denies that he is the father of said minor child.

3.   Defendant demands that the court order genetic testing to be conducted and paid for by Plaintiff.

Wherefore, Defendant prays that the court determine the nonexistence of the parent/child relationship between this Defendant and the minor child; that he be awarded his costs, attorney fees, and fees for genetic tests, pursuant to RC 3123.17; and that the action be dismissed as to him; and that he be granted such relief as is equitable.

_____

Attorney for Defendant

[Certificate of Service]

§ 3:57   Answer—Denial by mother—Form⊚

[Title of Court]

[Caption]   Case No. *[_____]*
                                         ANSWER

1.   Defendant *[name of defendant]*, in answer to Plaintiff's complaint herein, admits that she is the mother of the minor child, *[name of minor child]*, born *[date]* in *[name of city, state]*.

2.   Further answering, Defendant denies that Plaintiff is the father of said child.

[Optional] [3. Further answering, Defendant states that *[name of father]* is the father and that Plaintiff has failed to join an indispensable party.]

Wherefore, Defendant demands that the court find and declare the nonexistence of the parent/child relationship between Plaintiff and the minor child.

_____

Attorney for Defendant

[Certificate of Service]

§ 3:58   Journal entry—Establishing father-child relationship—Form⊚

[Title of Court]

[Caption]   Case No. *[_____]*
                                               <u>JUDGMENT ENTRY</u>

This matter came before the Court upon Plaintiff's Complaint to establish the father/child relationship between *[Plaintiff/Defendant]* *[name of plaintiff/defendant]* and the minor child, *[name of minor child]*, born on *[date]*. All parties herein have appeared before the Court, and Defendant herein has filed an Answer *[admitting/denying]* that *[Plaintiff/Defendant]* is the natural father of said minor child.

[The Court, being fully aware of the premises herein and based upon the pleadings and evidence adduced in open Court, finds that Plaintiff, [name of plaintiff], is the mother of the minor child, [name of minor child], born to her on [date] in [name of city, county], Ohio. The Court further finds that Defendant has [been properly served/waived service of summons] as provided by law and that he is at least eighteen years of age and not under any legal disability. The Court further finds that Defendant was duly advised of all of his rights herein and that he has knowingly and voluntarily waived said rights. The Court also finds [from the testimony and evidence presented, upon a preponderance thereof/ that Defendant has admitted the allegations contained in the Complaint herein and] that Defendant is the natural father of said minor child.]

[or]

[Alternate][The Court, being fully aware of the premises herein and based upon the pleadings and evidence adduced in open Court, finds that Defendant, [name of defendant], is the mother of the minor child, [name of minor child], born on [date] in [name of city, county], Ohio. The Court further finds that Defendant has [been properly served/ waived service of summons] as provided by law and that she is at least eighteen years of age and not under any legal disability. The Court further finds that Defendant was duly advised of all of her rights herein and that she has knowingly and voluntarily waived said rights. The Court also finds that Defendant has admitted the allegations contained in the Complaint herein and that Plaintiff is the natural father of said minor child.]

It is therefore ordered that:

1. *[Plaintiff/Defendant]* pay the reasonable expenses of *[Plaintiff's/ Defendant's]* pregnancy in the sum of $*[dollar amount]*.

2. *[Plaintiff/Defendant]* obtain and maintain, for so long as he is obligated to support said minor child, a policy of hospitalization and major medical insurance for the benefit of said minor child, and *[Plaintiff/Defendant]* shall pay *[percentage amount]*% of any future uncovered medical, dental, hospital, optical, or prescription expenses of the minor child.

[Optional][3. The Department of Health prepare a new birth certificate consistent with the findings herein and that said birth certificate shall be substituted for the original certificate of birth issued herein.]

4. *[Plaintiff/Defendant]* pay as and for child support, the sum of $*[dollar amount]* per month until such time as said child shall reach the age of eighteen years and shall continue so long as the child continuously attends on a full-time basis any recognized and accredited high school, as provided by Ohio law. *[Insert all statutorily mandated CSEA language for support orders.]*

5. The arrearages from the date of birth of the child to the date of this order are in the sum of $*[dollar amount]*, which shall be paid by the *[Plaintiff/Defendant]* by payroll withholding along with the child support ordered herein, at the rate of $*[dollar amount]* per month until paid in full.

6. The above child support payments, together with the processing charge, shall be paid by withholding to *[Plaintiff/Defendant]*, *[name]*, through the Child Support Enforcement Agency, *[address of agency]*, then to be forwarded to *[Plaintiff/Defendant]* at an address provided by *[her/him]*.

7. *[Plaintiff/Defendant]* shall pay the sum of $*[dollar amount]*, as and for attorney fees, to the *[Defendant/Plaintiff]*. Payment shall be made as follows: _____.

8. *[Plaintiff/Defendant]* shall *[pay/reimburse]* the Child Support Enforcement Agency for the cost of genetic testing.

9. *[Plaintiff/Defendant]* shall be entitled to the IRS dependency exemption for the minor child. *[Plaintiff/Defendant]* shall sign all forms necessary to effectuate this order.

10. *[Plaintiff/Defendant]* is hereby ordered to pay the court costs of this case.

11. All child support and spousal support under this order shall be withheld or deducted from the wages or assets of the obligor pursuant to a withholding or deduction notice or appropriate court order issued in accordance with section 3121.27 of the Revised Code, and shall be forwarded to the obligee in accordance with sections 3121.035 to 3121.27 of the Revised Code.

This order shall be effective from *[date]*.

_____
Judge

Approved:

_____

Attorney for Plaintiff

_____

Attorney for Defendant

NOTES TO FORM

Drafter's Notes

The duty to support beyond the age of eighteen until the completion of high school is found under RC 3103.03, pertaining to husband and wife, and in RC 3103.031, pertaining to a biological parent of a child, a man determined to be the natural father in a parentage case, and an adoptive parent.

RC 3123.17 permits the court to order either party to pay the costs of the action including attorney fees and genetic testing fees.

§ 3:59 Journal entry—Establishing father-child relationship and ordering grandparent support—Form⊚

[Title of Court]

[Caption]   Case No. *[_____]*
                                                  <u>JUDGMENT ENTRY</u>

This matter came before the Court upon Plaintiff's *[Grandparent's name]* Complaint to establish the father/child relationship between *[Plaintiff/Defendant][Minor Father/Mother]* *[name of minor father/mother]* and the minor child, *[name of minor child]*, born on *[date]*. All parties herein have appeared before the Court, and Defendant *[name of defendant]* herein has filed an Answer *[admitting/denying]* that *[Plaintiff/Defendant][name of plaintiff/defendant]* is the natural father of said minor child. The *[Defendant(s)-Other grandparent's name(s)][have/have not]* filed an answer.

*[The Court, being fully aware of the premises herein and based upon the pleadings and evidence adduced in open Court, finds that *[Plaintiff/Defendant]*, *[name of plaintiff/defendant]*, is the mother of the minor child, *[name of minor child]*, born to her on *[date]* in *[name of city, county]*, Ohio. The Court further finds that Defendant-Minor Father *[name of minor father]* has *[been properly served/waived service of summons]* as provided by law. The Court further finds that Defendant-Minor Father was duly advised of all of his rights herein and that he has knowingly and voluntarily waived said rights. The Court also finds [from the testimony and evidence presented, upon a preponderance thereof/that Defendant-Minor Father *[name of minor father]* has admitted the allegations contained in the Complaint herein and] that Defendant-Minor Father *[name of minor father]* is the natural father of said minor child.]*

[or]

[Alternate][The Court, being fully aware of the premises herein and based upon the pleadings and evidence adduced in open Court, finds that Defendant, [name of minor mother], is the mother of the minor child, [name of minor child], born on [date] in [name of city, county], Ohio. The Court further finds that Defendant-Mother has [been properly served/waived service of summons] as provided by law. The Court further finds that Defendant-Mother was duly advised of all of her rights herein and that she has knowingly and voluntarily waived said rights. The Court also finds that Defendant-Mother has admitted the allegations contained in the Complaint herein and that [Plaintiff/ Defendant] is the natural father of said minor child.]

It is therefore ordered that:

1. *[Plaintiff/Defendant] [name of plaintiff/defendant]* pay the reasonable expenses of *[Plaintiff's/Defendant's] [name of plaintiff/ defendant]* pregnancy in the sum of *$[dollar amount]*.

2. *[Plaintiff/Defendant] [name of plaintiff/defendant]* obtain and maintain, for so long as he is obligated to support said minor child, a policy of hospitalization and major medical insurance for the benefit of said minor child.

[Optional][3. The Department of Health prepare a new birth certificate consistent with the findings herein and that said birth certificate shall be substituted for the original certificate of birth issued herein.]

4. *[Defendant-Minor father's/mother's parent(s)] [names of parents]*, shall pay the sum of *$[dollar amount]* per month as and for support for the minor child.

5. Said support order for grandparents to pay shall terminate upon the occurrence of any of the following:

a. *[Name of minor parent who resides with Defendant-grandparents]* reaches the age of eighteen years, dies, marries, enlists in the armed services, is deported, gains legal or physical custody of the child, or is otherwise emancipated.

b. *[Name of minor child]* dies, is adopted, is deported, or is transferred to the legal or physical custody of *[name of minor parent who resides with defendant grandparents]*.

c. Plaintiff-Grandparent is no longer providing any support for *[name of minor child]*.

[Include statutory notices from Text § 15:77, Statutory notices for parents—Form.]

6. The arrearages from the date of birth of the child to the date of this order are in the sum of *$[dollar amount]*, which shall be paid by the *[Defendant][name of defendant]* by payroll withholding along with the child support ordered herein, at the rate of *$[dollar amount]* per month until paid in full.

7. The above child support payments, together with the processing charge, shall be paid by withholding to *[Plaintiff]*, *[name]*, through the Child Support Enforcement Agency, *[address of agency]*, then to be forwarded to *[Plaintiff][name of plaintiff]* at an address provided by *[her/him]*.

8. *[Plaintiff / Defendant] [name of plaintiff / defendant]* shall pay the sum of $*[dollar amount]*, as and for attorney fees, to the *[Defendant / Plaintiff][name of defendant / plaintiff]*. Payment shall be made as follows: _____.

9. *[Plaintiff / Defendant] [name of plaintiff / defendant]* shall *[pay / reimburse]* the Child Support Enforcement Agency for the cost of genetic testing.

10. *[Plaintiff / Defendant] [name of plaintiff / defendant]* shall be entitled to the IRS dependency exemption for the minor child. *[Plaintiff / Defendant] [name of plaintiff / defendant]* shall sign all forms necessary to effectuate this order.

11. *[Plaintiff / Defendant] [name of plaintiff / defendant]* is hereby ordered to pay the court costs of this case.

This order shall be effective from *[date]*.

_____
                                      Judge

Approved:

_____
Attorney for Plaintiff
[Name of Plaintiff]

_____
Attorney for Defendant
[Name of Defendant]

NOTES TO FORM

Drafter's Notes

RC 3123.17 permits the court to order either party to pay the costs of the action including attorney's fees and genetic testing fees.

In calculating support, the income of the minor's parents is used. Any support ordered to be paid by a minor parent is deducted from that parent's parents' obligation.

Due to the potentially large number of parties, specifying each party's name at each instance where intended will reduce confusion.

§ 3:60   Complaint for custody, support, and visitation— Form⊚

[Title of Court]

[Caption]   Case No. *[_____]*
                                   COMPLAINT FOR CUSTODY,

SUPPORT, AND VISITATION
OR
SHARED PARENTING

Now comes *[name]*, Plaintiff, and states that:

1. He is the father as determined in [Case No. *[case number]*, *[title of court]* on *[date]*/an administrative proceeding through the *[name of county]* County Child Support Enforcement Agency in administrative order number *[administrative order number]*, and that *[name of defendant]*, Defendant, is the mother of the minor child *[name of child]*, born *[date]* in *[name of city, county, state]*. A copy of the adjudication of parentage is attached hereto as Exhibit *[designation of exhibit]*.

2. Plaintiff's address is *[address of plaintiff]* and respondent's address is *[address of respondent]*.

3. Said child is not a ward of another court of the state.

4. This complaint is being brought pursuant to RC 3111.13(C) and RC 2151.23(A)(2).

5. It is in the best interest of the minor child that the custody, visitation, and support rights of the parties and the child be determined.

WHEREFORE, Plaintiff requests an order *[naming the defendant mother the residential parent and legal custodian of the minor child/ adopting the plaintiff's shared parenting plan filed herein/awarding the plaintiff specific visitation rights with the minor child]* and setting a reasonable amount of support for said child, including allocating medical expenses and the IRS dependency exemption.

_____

                                                       Plaintiff

NOTES TO FORM

Drafter's Notes

If the caption is entitled "In the matter of *[name of child]*," the body of the complaint should set forth the names and addresses of the parties. If the caption is entitled "*[Name]*, Plaintiff v. *[Name]*, Defendant," the addresses will appear in the caption.

As with all proceedings involving the custody of minor children, an affidavit under RC 3127.23 (UCCJEA) must accompany the complaint.

A request for shared parenting should be accompanied with a proposed shared parenting plan, pursuant to RC 3109.04(G).

§ 3:61 Answer and counterclaim to complaint for custody, support, and visitation—Form⊚

[Title of Court]

[Caption]   Case No. *[_____]*

ANSWER AND COUNTERCLAIM TO COMPLAINT FOR CUSTODY, SUPPORT, AND VISITATION

1. Now comes the Defendant and in answer to the complaint herein admits the allegations in paragraphs *[designation of paragraphs]* of the complaint.

2. Further answering, the Defendant neither admits nor denies the allegations contained in paragraphs *[designation of paragraphs]*.

WHEREFORE, Defendant prays Plaintiff's complaint be dismissed; that Defendant be named residential parent and legal custodian of, and awarded support for, the minor child; and that Defendant be granted such other relief as may be equitable.

_____
Attorney for Defendant

COUNTERCLAIM

1. The Defendant states that on or about *[date]*, and pursuant to RC 3111.38, the father-child relationship was established between the Plaintiff, *[name of plaintiff]*, and the minor child, *[name of child]*. A copy of said Order is attached as Exhibit *[designation of exhibit]*.

2. Further, Defendant states that pursuant to subsequent hearing held on *[date]*, child support was set, effective as of that day, for the minor child.

3. Further, Defendant states that it is necessary for this court to set the amount of support due and owing to the Defendant from the date of birth and for medical expenses of the pregnancy, pursuant to RC 3111.13.

4. Further, pursuant to RC 3123.17, the Defendant states she is entitled to an award of attorney fees necessary to obtain appropriate support and retroactive support.

WHEREFORE, Defendant prays for an order determining the correct amount of child support for the minor child; for an order setting child support retroactive to the child's birth; for an order requiring Plaintiff to pay for all of Defendant's unreimbursed medical and hospital costs; for an order requiring the Plaintiff, *[name of plaintiff]*, to pay the Defendant's attorney fees in this matter; and for an order specifying the Plaintiff's right of visitation with the regard for the needs of the child.

_____

Attorney for Defendant

[Certificate of Service]

Chapter 4

Marital Obligations and Property Rights

By James R. Kirkland, Esq.[*]

KeyCite®: Cases and other legal materials listed in KeyCite Scope can be researched through the KeyCite service on Westlaw®. Use KeyCite to check citations for form, parallel references, prior and later history, and comprehensive citator information, including citations to other decisions and secondary materials.

---

[*]The author acknowledges the assistance of Kathryn Shields and Courtney Mohn, law clerks, in the preparation of this chapter.

§ 4:1   History of marital property rights and obligations

At common law, husband and wife were said to be one, and that one was the husband.[1] Each spouse had obligations to the other, but the wife had no property rights.[2] The common law stripped the wife of her personal property, transferred to the husband the income from her real estate, vested in the husband the right to the wife's earnings, denied to her the right to contract and merged her legal identity with his. To compensate her for these disabilities, the common law absolved her from nearly every legal obligation and duty, including that of maintaining her children. She had no legal control over them or right to their services, and even her widowhood did not restore this control or right.[3]

Early legislation gave the wife a separate estate in her personal property but still did not disturb the doctrine of the legal unity of husband and wife.[4] It was not until passage of the Married Women's Act in 1861 that the common law doctrine of the unity of husband and wife was effectively nullified. This legislation recognized the wife as a distinct person competent to have separate property, contracts, debts and credits, and other personal, legally protected rights which were under her sole control.[5]

Women's role in present-day society has changed the entire structure of the American family and, thereby, the nature of the marital relationship. A wife no longer has a symbiotic relationship to her husband, wholly dependent upon him for all of her needs. Today a husband and wife are equals. Both may enter the work force and provide financially for their family, and both are expected to share the responsibilities of keeping a home and raising children.

The Ohio Revised Code acknowledges the equality of the wife. RC 3103.03 provides that each spouse is equally responsible for mutual and self-support, and for the support of any minor children. If one spouse is unable to do so, the other must assist as far as he or she is able.[6] RC 3103.04 and RC 3103.07 separate a wife's property interest from her husband's. RC 3103.04 states that spouses hold no interest in each other's property except the rights of support and dower and the right to remain in the mansion house following the death of the other. RC 3103.07 entitles each spouse to take, hold, and dispose of property, real or personal, the same as if unmarried. This is an alteration of the common law rule.

[Section 4:1]

[1]State v. Phillips, 85 Ohio St. 317, 97 N.E. 976 (1912).

[2]Prosser and Keeton on the Law of Torts (5th ed.) § 122.

[3]Fulton v. Fulton, 52 Ohio St. 229, 39 N.E. 729 (1895).

[4]State v. Parker, 3 Ohio Dec. Rep. 551, 1882 WL 7468 (Ohio C.P. 1882).

[5]Westlake v. Westlake, 34 Ohio St. 621, 1878 WL 69 (1878); Dillingham v. Dillingham, 9 Ohio App. 284 (Hamilton 1917) (analysis of married woman's common law property rights and subsequent statutory changes).

[6]See also RC 3103.01.

§ 4:2 Support obligations during marriage—Equality of spouses—In general

The "necessity" theory of support is dying out in a society where both spouses work and provide the necessities which were once supplied only by the husband. There is now a partnership relationship, other than a master-servant relationship, upon entering marriage. Under this theory, each spouse voluntarily and impliedly accepts rights, duties, and contributions of equal value.

The marital relationship is no longer viewed as creating an implied agency. Courts, however, have not eliminated the possibility that a spouse may act on the authority of the other spouse. If the spouses agree to act for each other by an express agreement, there is no proscription against this. However, there is no longer a presumption that the husband has the authority to act on behalf of the wife. A husband and wife are separate individuals. RC 3103.08 states that "[n]either . . . is answerable for the acts of the other."[1] Neither is bound by the other's acts in relation to his or her property unless the other spouse is acting as agent. A husband has no inherent power to act as his wife's agent, and in order to bind his wife by his acts he must be expressly authorized by her appointment, his acts must subsequently be ratified by her, or his authority must be implied. There is no presumption of his authority to act for her, and his agency must be proved by evidence, as does any other fact. The mere relationship of husband and wife does not give rise to any presumption of agency.[2]

This current view of the marital relationship has changed the interaction of and support obligations between husband and wife as well as the relation of each to third party creditors. In a case not involving necessaries, the Hancock County Municipal Court found a former wife liable on her husband's credit card based on the theory of her use of the credit card and prior payments on the card having been made from a joint checking account. The Third District Court of Appeals reversed, finding the wife was an authorized user, which imposed liability only on the cardholder who was liable under the agreement with the issuing bank.[3] The appellate court held that paying debts from a joint account, a common practice, does not create or impose liability on the party not responsible.

In recognition of the decisions and comments that either found RC

[Section 4:2]

[1]See Y. & O. Coal Co. v. Paszka, 20 Ohio App. 248, 251, 4 Ohio L. Abs. 82, 152 N.E. 31 (7th Dist. Jefferson County 1925); Sowers v. Birkhead, 108 Ohio App. 507, 9 Ohio Op. 2d 491, 80 Ohio L. Abs. 84, 157 N.E.2d 459 (10th Dist. Franklin County 1958).

[2]Sowers v. Birkhead, 108 Ohio App. 507, 9 Ohio Op. 2d 491, 80 Ohio L. Abs. 84, 157 N.E.2d 459 (10th Dist. Franklin County 1958); McSweeney v. Jackson, 117 Ohio App. 3d 623, 691 N.E.2d 303 (4th Dist. Lawrence County 1996).

[3]First Nat. Bank of Findlay v. Fulk, 57 Ohio App. 3d 44, 566 N.E.2d 1270, 13 U.C.C. Rep. Serv. 2d 1134 (3d Dist. Hancock County 1989).

3103.03 as it stood unconstitutional or reformed it to be gender neutral,[4] the legislature amended this statute, effective April 11, 1991, to make each married person responsible for his or her own support and for the support of the spouse.[5]

§ 4:3 Support obligations during marriage—Equality of spouses—Spousal support

RC 3103.01 states that the spousal obligation of support is mutual. This was strengthened by the 1991 replacement of RC 3103.03, which placed the primary duty of support on the husband, with RC 3103.03(A).[1] RC 3103.03(A) imposes equal duties of mutual support, self-support, and child support on both marital partners. Where a husband is unable to support himself, his wife must aid in his support to the extent she is able.[2] Neither spouse is unconditionally liable for necessaries furnished to the other.

A credit card issuer may not hold a husband liable for his wife's charges when evidence fails to show that the wife acted as the husband's agent or that the husband ratified her conduct.[3] 15 U.S.C.A. § 1601 controls the extent of liability for the unauthorized use of a credit card. The creditor who allows purchases by one spouse on the credit of the other spouse, absent some evidence of authorization, does so at his own risk.[4] However, a third party creditor may recover against both husband and wife if he establishes a joint undertaking, contribution, or benefit.[5]

A spouse's duty of support does not preclude him or her from transferring assets to a third party.[6] Such transfers will be set aside only when the other spouse can demonstrate that his or her present right to support has been hindered.[7] A showing by the other spouse

---

[4]Cleveland Metropolitan General Hosp. v. Oleksik, 38 Ohio App. 3d 21, 525 N.E.2d 831 (8th Dist. Cuyahoga County 1987) (disapproved of by, Ohio State University Hosp. v. Kinkaid, 48 Ohio St. 3d 78, 549 N.E.2d 517 (1990)).

[5]RC 3103.03(A), as amended by 1990 S.B. 3, eff. 4-11-91.

[Section 4:3]

[1]See Text Ch 13, Spousal Support.

[2]State v. Butler, 48 Ohio St. 3d 78, 549 N.E.2d 516 (1990).

[3]Society Natl. Bank v. Kienzle, 11 Ohio App. 3d 178, 463 N.E.2d 1261 (8th Dist. Cuyahoga County 1983).

[4]McFarland v. Purper, 31 Ohio C.D. 694, 1908 WL 606 (Ohio Cir. Ct. 1908).

[5]Clarke v. Cannon, 33 Ohio C.D. 161, 1911 WL 1662 (Ohio Cir. Ct. 1911); Farm Bureau Agr. Credit Corp. v. Dicke, 29 Ohio App. 2d 1, 58 Ohio Op. 2d 3, 277 N.E.2d 562 (3d Dist. Auglaize County 1972) (when husband and wife sign promissory note, both estates will be liable to third party creditor).

[6]RC 3103.04, RC 3103.07.

[7]Mark v. Mark, 145 Ohio St. 301, 30 Ohio Op. 534, 61 N.E.2d 595, 160 A.L.R. 608 (1945).

that there might be a failure of support in the future is not sufficient to establish a breach of duty under the statute.[8]

Necessaries under today's law are generally the same as they were at common law. Included in the definition are such articles and services as will maintain the spouse according to the position and condition of the spouse and the means of the other spouse. Not included in this definition are extravagances, luxuries, or expeditions for pleasure and personal enjoyment.[9] The word "support," as used in RC 3103.03, includes medical and hospital services.[10] Liability may arise under the following circumstances:

(1) Where there is an express or implied contract between the husband and the medical provider;

(2) Where, by a course of conduct or express authority, the wife is authorized as the agent of the husband and pledges his credit; or

(3) Where the husband fails to perform his legal duty in furnishing necessary medical expenses.[11]

While a spouse may be liable for legal services rendered to the other spouse for purposes of spousal or child support under the claim that the services constitute "necessaries" supplied to the spouse, a husband may not be liable for legal services rendered to his wife for divorce. Holding that a determination of the reasonableness of legal expenses is a prerequisite to imposing liability upon a spouse for necessaries, and that such a determination of necessity and reasonableness is best suited to domestic relations proceedings, the court in *Rust v. Takacs*[12] ruled against an attorney who sought to recover his fees for services rendered to his former client, the wife, from her husband.

The probate court has subject matter jurisdiction over an action by a spouse against his or her spouse's legal guardian to enforce the ward's statutory duty under RC 3103.03 to pay his or her medical expenses.[13]

The Eighth District Court of Appeals led the way to the amendment

---

[8]Mark v. Mark, 145 Ohio St. 301, 30 Ohio Op. 534, 61 N.E.2d 595, 160 A.L.R. 608 (1945).

[9]Smith v. Sutter, 90 Ohio App. 320, 47 Ohio Op. 427, 106 N.E.2d 658 (6th Dist. Huron County 1951); Blum v. Blum, 9 Ohio St. 2d 92, 38 Ohio Op. 2d 224, 223 N.E.2d 819 (1967) (necessaries include reasonable attorney fees incurred in enforcing father's obligation to support his minor children); Wolf v. Friedman, 20 Ohio St. 2d 49, 49 Ohio Op. 2d 306, 253 N.E.2d 761 (1969) (legal fees for criminal defense held to be necessaries).

[10]Surgical and Medical Neurology Associates, Inc. v. Levan, 7 Ohio Misc. 2d 11, 454 N.E.2d 604 (Mun. Ct. 1982).

[11]Surgical and Medical Neurology Associates, Inc. v. Levan, 7 Ohio Misc. 2d 11, 454 N.E.2d 604 (Mun. Ct. 1982).

[12]Rust v. Takacs, 70 Ohio Misc. 2d 1, 650 N.E.2d 193 (Mun. Ct. 1994).

[13]Passoni v. Breehl, 29 Ohio Op. 220, 41 Ohio L. Abs. 315, 14 Ohio Supp. 100 (Prob. Ct. 1944).

of RC 3103.03 by finding the statute unconstitutional as being gender-based discrimination and remanded a case to make a gender-neutral determination as to the ability of the parties to pay.[14]

The wife of a decedent was held responsible for the necessaries of her husband's last illness where his estate was unable to pay, irrespective of RC 3103.03 and RC 3103.05.[15] The court found that "a surviving spouse, whether male or female, even though no written contractual obligation exists, should be required to pay for the deceased spouse's expenses for the last illness and necessities provided by third parties."[16]

Finding a strong public policy argument that the responsibility of support between a husband and wife should be of mutual and equal obligation, the Supreme Court in *Ohio State University Hospital v. Kinkaid*[17] found a wife liable for her deceased husband's medical bills when his estate was insufficient.

Necessaries for support include burial expenses. Where an adult son signed to be personally responsible for payment of a funeral bill, he was entitled to recover from the surviving spouse, his stepmother, where the estate was insolvent.[18]

According to RC 3103.03(E), if a decedent purchased an irrevocable preneed funeral contract pursuant to RC 4717.34, then the duty of support owed to a spouse does not include an obligation to pay the funeral expenses of the deceased spouse. RC 3103.03(E) does not preclude a surviving spouse from assuming by contract the obligation to pay for the funeral expenses of the deceased spouse.

§ 4:4 Property rights during marriage—Individual ownership—In general

The common law disabilities which once restricted a wife's property rights have been removed. However, the statutes do not eliminate the possibility that the husband may control the wife's property (or vice-versa), but only eliminate the possibility that such domination and control will be the result of the legal structure of the marital relationship alone. If the spouses agree to transfer of control, by an express or implied agreement, where property is titled to a wife but is controlled

---

[14]In re Rauscher, 40 Ohio App. 3d 106, 531 N.E.2d 745 (8th Dist. Cuyahoga County 1987) (disapproved of by, Ohio State University Hosp. v. Kinkaid, 48 Ohio St. 3d 78, 549 N.E.2d 517 (1990)).

[15]Cleveland Metropolitan General Hosp. v. Oleksik, 38 Ohio App. 3d 21, 525 N.E.2d 831 (8th Dist. Cuyahoga County 1987) (disapproved of by, Ohio State University Hosp. v. Kinkaid, 48 Ohio St. 3d 78, 549 N.E.2d 517 (1990)).

[16]Cleveland Metropolitan General Hosp. v. Oleksik, 38 Ohio App. 3d 21, 23, 525 N.E.2d 831 (8th Dist. Cuyahoga County 1987) (disapproved of by, Ohio State University Hosp. v. Kinkaid, 48 Ohio St. 3d 78, 549 N.E.2d 517 (1990)).

[17]Ohio State University Hosp. v. Kinkaid, 48 Ohio St. 3d 78, 549 N.E.2d 517 (1990).

[18]Davis-Turner Funeral Home, Inc. v. Chaney, 61 Ohio Misc. 2d 82, 573 N.E.2d 1242 (Mun. Ct. 1991).

by her husband, there is an agency relationship, with the result that between spouses and third parties, agency law controls.

The property rights of a husband and wife during their marriage depend upon the characterization of their property as separate or marital. Property owned solely by one spouse upon entering the marriage or acquired during the marriage may remain his or her separate property. Property owned by both spouses, whether before or during the marriage, establishes a confidential relation between them, requiring their best efforts to protect the property. The nature of this relation and the rights of each spouse in their jointly owned property will depend upon the type of joint ownership that exists in the property.

Title held by one spouse upon entering marriage will continue as such unless title is transferred to the other or both spouses. A husband or wife who owns real or personal property in his or her name alone may freely dispose of that property as if unmarried. The husband or wife need not obtain the consent of the other spouse. However, under Ohio's dower statute, RC Chapter 2103, anyone taking real property without the spouse's waiver of dower does so at the risk of a claim by such spouse.

A spouse has an interest in the property of the other spouse which includes a right to dower,[1] an interest under the descent and distribution statutes,[2] the present right of support,[3] and the right to remain in the mansion house free of charge for up to one year after the death of the other spouse.[4]

§ 4:5 Property rights during marriage—Individual ownership—Dower

RC 2103.02 has abolished all vested dower except in real property (1) conveyed during coverture, without the spouse joining in the deed, and (2) to the extent that such property during coverture was encumbered by a mortgage without the spouse joining in the mortgage or by a judgment lien, or otherwise without the surviving spouse having relinquished or having been barred from dower.[1]

A husband cannot convey his real property, held under such cir-

---

[Section 4:4]

[1]RC Ch. 2103.

[2]RC 2105.06.

[3]RC 3103.03.

[4]RC 2106.15.

[Section 4:5]

[1]See Perlberg v. Perlberg, 18 Ohio St. 2d 55, 47 Ohio Op. 2d 167, 247 N.E.2d 306 (1969) (spouse who has not relinquished or been barred from dower is endowed with estate for life in one-third of real property of which consort is seized at any time during marriage; conveyance of realty to children of former marriage, without consideration other than love and affection, by man engaged to be married, without disclosure of conveyance to intended wife, whom he later marries, does not defraud her right to dower under RC 2103.02).

cumstances that dower attaches, so as to defeat his wife's right to dower, without her joining in the deed.[2] Even where the real property is relieved of the wife's legal claim for dower, Ohio courts refuse to recognize a husband's attempt to defeat the wife's rights if they can accomplish this without interfering with the rights of bona fide purchasers.[3] Where a buyer has notice of a husband's fraud, property which a husband attempts to dispose of in order to defeat his wife's rights passes to a trust in favor of his wife.[4] In *Chittenden v. Chittenden*,[5] a mortgage which a wife was induced to sign upon false representations was held to be a fraud upon her marital rights and invalid as against her claim for alimony. RC 2103.06 codifies this rule stating, "If a husband or wife gives up real property by collusion or fraud, or loses it by default, the widow or widower may recover dower therein."

A spouse's dower interest terminates upon the granting of an absolute divorce in favor or against him or her by a court of competent jurisdiction within or without the state of Ohio.[6] Under RC 2103.05, a husband or wife who leaves the other and dwells in adultery will be barred from dower in the real property of the other, unless the offense is condoned by the injured consort.[7]

§ 4:6 Property rights during marriage—Individual ownership—Descent and distribution

A surviving spouse is entitled to a distributive share provided by RC 2105.06 in lieu of the dower interest, which terminates upon the death of the consort.[1] These statutory rights are overridden by the right to control one's own property before and during marriage.[2] During a marriage, either spouse may bring an action in partition against the other with regard to jointly owned property.[3] A spouse may transfer property during his or her lifetime, free of the other spouse's

---

[2]See RC Ch. 2103.

[3]Iddings v. Whitacre, 1 Ohio App. 223, 24 Ohio C.D. 427, 1913 WL 877 (7th Dist. Carroll County 1913).

[4]Tate v. Tate, 19 Ohio C.C. 531, 10 Ohio Cir. Dec. 321 (6th Cir. Lucas 1898).

[5]Chittenden v. Chittenden, 12 Ohio C.D. 526, 1901 WL 769 (Ohio Cir. Ct. 1901).

[6]RC 2103.02.

[7]Taylor v. Taylor, 11 Ohio App. 3d 279, 465 N.E.2d 476 (1st Dist. Hamilton County 1983).

[Section 4:6]

[1]RC 2103.02.

[2]In re Kusar's Estate, 5 Ohio Misc. 23, 34 Ohio Op. 2d 32, 211 N.E.2d 535 (Prob. Ct. 1965) (court held transfer of real estate prior to marriage not an attempt to defraud wife of dower rights).

[3]Shafer v. Shafer, 30 Ohio App. 298, 6 Ohio L. Abs. 481, 163 N.E. 507 (1st Dist. Hamilton County 1928) (wife may seek partition of real estate jointly owned with husband); Shively v. Shively, 54 Ohio L. Abs. 527, 88 N.E.2d 615 (Ct. App. 2d Dist. Montgomery County 1948) (husband may seek partition of real estate jointly owned by wife).

right to a distributive share and one year's allowance, since these claims of the surviving spouse do not come into existence until after the death of the spouse. However, a spouse who did not consent to the transfer of the property has a one-third interest in the property, in the form of an estate for life. In practicality, this creates a lien on the property. Therefore, dower makes transfer of such property impractical and nearly impossible.

In regard to the husband's personal property, the interest of the wife as a statutory heir or distributee of her husband is the same as that of the children; that is, she has no vested or quasi-vested right in the husband's property during his lifetime, apart from a creditor relationship.[4] The same is true of the husband's right in the personal property of his wife. Either spouse may dispose of his or her separate personal property voluntarily,[5] even though the effect is to deprive the surviving spouse of his or her distributive share, so long as the disposition is not colorable or indicative of fraud arising from an absolute transfer of property to avoid having any interest therein after the death of the other.[6] Where the husband retains control during his lifetime, and the transfer is a device to deprive his wife of her distributive share in his personal property, it is ineffective against the wife and may be set aside.[7] The surviving spouse's distributive share in personal property cannot be defeated by the absence of a provision for the surviving spouse in the will of the decedent, since in regard to the right of distribution in personal property, the decedent is considered to have died intestate.[8]

The surviving spouse has the right to purchase the mansion house, including the parcel of land on which the same is situated, at the appraised value.[9] Under RC 2106.16, the probate court must approve the action of a surviving spouse to purchase the mansion house of a decedent at the value determined by the court-appointed appraisers, unless it is affirmatively shown that the price to be paid is so inadequate as to prejudice the rights of heirs or creditors.[10]

The right to receive from or convey title to a third person by will independently of the other spouse is limited by fraud. A husband may not receive conveyance of title to property, by will or otherwise, when

---

[4]Ostrander v. Preece, 129 Ohio St. 625, 3 Ohio Op. 24, 196 N.E. 670, 103 A.L.R. 218 (1935).

[5]Mark v. Mark, 145 Ohio St. 301, 30 Ohio Op. 534, 61 N.E.2d 595, 160 A.L.R. 608 (1945).

[6]Brodt v. Rannells, 7 Ohio N.P. 79, 9 Ohio Dec. 503, 1890 WL 3581 (C.P. 1890); In re Lackman's Estate, 26 Ohio N.P. (n.s.) 387, 1927 WL 2761 (C.P. 1927).

[7]Hayes v. Lindquist, 22 Ohio App. 58, 5 Ohio L. Abs. 276, 153 N.E. 269 (6th Dist. Lucas County 1926).

[8]RC 2105.06.

[9]In re Reed's Estate, 65 Ohio L. Abs. 129, 114 N.E.2d 314 (Prob. Ct. 1952).

[10]Passoni v. Breehl, 29 Ohio Op. 220, 41 Ohio L. Abs. 315, 14 Ohio Supp. 100 (Prob. Ct. 1944).

it would work fraud upon his wife.[11] In such a case, the husband is deemed to hold property as trustee for the wife. In modern practice, it is easier and more appropriate for a spouse in these circumstances to allege a purchase money resulting trust which, when shown, converts the spouse wrongfully holding title into a trustee of the asset for the benefit of the injured spouse and the marriage; that is, the asset becomes marital property irrespective of the locus of the title for purposes of valuation and division of marital property. The principal advantage of this approach is the ease of proof and lack of necessity to affirmatively prove fraud.

Where a husband purchases land with money borrowed by the wife, with the understanding that the land will be in her name, and takes the deed in his own name, it is fraud, and he becomes her trustee.[12] Also, where the land set apart by a decedent for his daughter is conveyed by fraud or mistake to his daughter and her husband jointly, as between the co-grantees, the husband holds the legal title to an undivided interest in trust for his wife.[13] It is not fraudulent, however, for a husband to take a deed to property purchased with the proceeds of a sale of the wife's realty in his own name, when the deed is executed in her presence and explained to her, without any objection on her part.[14]

Where a husband and wife have separated, or their relationship is such as to make separation inevitable or highly probable, the wife may be regarded as a quasi-creditor. Therefore, a conveyance made by a husband for the purpose of depriving his wife of spousal support and avoiding his marital obligations in reference thereto is not governed by the general rule. Under such circumstances, the conveyance is fraudulent and may be set aside by the wife.[15]

§ 4:7 Property rights during marriage—Individual ownership—Support for self

There exists a strong public policy in Ohio that the responsibility of support between a wife and a husband should be one of mutual and

---

[11]Newton v. Taylor, 32 Ohio St. 399, 1877 WL 132 (1877); Farmers' & Merchants' Nat. Bank v. Wallace, 45 Ohio St. 152, 12 N.E. 439 (1887).

[12]Newton v. Taylor, 32 Ohio St. 399, 1877 WL 132 (1877).

[13]Farmers' & Merchants' Nat. Bank v. Wallace, 45 Ohio St. 152, 12 N.E. 439 (1887).

[14]Ramsdall v. Craighill, 9 Ohio 197, 1839 WL 53 (1839) (defrauded spouse pleaded fraud and lost; had she pleaded purchase money resulting trust, she might have prevailed).

[15]Rose v. Rose, 34 Ohio App. 89, 7 Ohio L. Abs. 666, 8 Ohio L. Abs. 105, 170 N.E. 181 (9th Dist. Summit County 1929); Daniels v. Daniels, 17 Ohio N.P. (n.s.) 605, 26 Ohio Dec. 575, 1915 WL 1364 (C.P. 1915).

equal obligation.[1] Under RC 3103.03, the Ohio legislature as well as the Ohio Supreme Court has recognized that it is a desirable goal to have autonomy and equality regardless of gender.[2] Where a husband is unable to provide for his own support, pursuant to RC 3103.03 a wife must aid in the support of her husband to the extent she is able. The determination as to a wife's ability to aid in the support of her husband is a matter to be decided within the sound discretion of the trial court.[3]

Each married person must support himself or herself and his or her spouse out of his or her property or by his or her labor. If a married person is unable to do so, the spouse of that married person must assist in the support so far as the spouse is able.[4] If a married person neglects to support his or her spouse, any other person, in good faith, may supply the spouse with necessaries for the support of the spouse and recover the reasonable value of the necessaries supplied from the married person who neglected to support his or her spouse unless the spouse requiring the necessaries abandons the supporting person without cause.[5]

§ 4:8 Property rights during marriage—Individual ownership—Mansion house—In general

RC 3103.04 states in relevant part that neither a husband nor wife "can be excluded from the other's dwelling, except upon a decree or order of injunction made by a court of competent jurisdiction." The term "dwelling" used in the statute refers to any place of abode that has been used as the matrimonial home, and even a three-year absence from the home by a wife in whose name title is vested does not destroy its character as her "dwelling."[1] Since "dwelling" denotes ownership of residence, rather than title to property, it would seem that the state of title, i.e., in one or the other or joint, is irrelevant. Thus, the

[Section 4:7]

[1]Ohio State University Hosp. v. Kinkaid, 48 Ohio St. 3d 78, 549 N.E.2d 517 (1990) (wife held liable for payment of medical expenses incurred by husband prior to his death when, at husband's death, assets were insufficient to pay such expenses). See also Riverside Methodist Hosp. v. Payne, 48 Ohio App. 3d 123, 548 N.E.2d 987 (10th Dist. Franklin County 1988).

[2]Ohio State University Hosp. v. Kinkaid, 48 Ohio St. 3d 78, 549 N.E.2d 517 (1990).

[3]Ohio State University Hosp. v. Kinkaid, 48 Ohio St. 3d 78, 549 N.E.2d 517 (1990).

[4]RC 3103.03(A).

[5]RC 3103.03(C).

[Section 4:8]

[1]Slansky v. Slansky, 33 Ohio App. 2d 127, syl.1, 62 Ohio Op. 2d 235, 293 N.E.2d 302 (8th Dist. Cuyahoga County 1973).

husband can be evicted from his own house, so long as the wife is "dwelling" in it.[2]

It had been held that since one spouse cannot be excluded from the other spouse's dwelling without a court order barring the spouse, a court can make neither a finding of criminal trespass against a spouse,[3] nor a finding of guilty of violating the burglary statute, since burglary requires a trespass.[4] However, the Supreme Court, in *State v. Lilly*,[5] held that a spouse may be criminally liable for trespass and/or burglary committed in the residence of the other spouse who is exercising custody or control over that dwelling. The court concluded that RC 3103.04 is inapplicable in criminal cases.

The phrase "of competent jurisdiction" refers to the courts having jurisdiction in domestic relations cases, and not to any court having authority to decide questions touching property rights, per se.

§ 4:9 Property rights during marriage—Individual ownership—Mansion house—Procecdural devices for eviction

There are three procedural devices to effect eviction: (1) motion to vacate the premises; (2) domestic violence relief; and (3) motion for a temporary restraining order.

A motion for an ex parte order to vacate can be filed where there is physical violence or a threat of physical violence.[1] An ex parte hearing on the motion to vacate the premises will be set to determine whether an order should be given. Immediate and present danger of domestic violence constitutes good cause for an order to vacate. Immediate and present danger includes, but is not limited to, situations where the respondent has threatened the family, or a particular household member, with bodily harm.[2] If the respondent previously has engaged in domestic violence against the family or household member, such history will weigh in favor of a finding of good cause. Counsel representing a potentially abused spouse should use a domestic violence complaint, civil or criminal, with a request that possession of

---

[2]Slansky v. Slansky, 33 Ohio App. 2d 127, syl.1, 62 Ohio Op. 2d 235, 293 N.E.2d 302 (8th Dist. Cuyahoga County 1973).

[3]State v. Herder, 65 Ohio App. 2d 70, 19 Ohio Op. 3d 47, 415 N.E.2d 1000 (10th Dist. Franklin County 1979).

[4]State v. Middleton, 85 Ohio App. 3d 403, 619 N.E.2d 1113 (4th Dist. Vinton County 1993).

[5]State v. Lilly, 87 Ohio St. 3d 97, 1999-Ohio-251, 717 N.E.2d 322 (1999); State v. O'Neal, 87 Ohio St. 3d 402, 2000-Ohio-449, 721 N.E.2d 73 (2000). See also State v. Shinn, 2000 WL 781106 (Ohio Ct. App. 4th Dist. Washington County 2000).

[Section 4:9]
[1]RC 3113.31.
[2]RC 3113.31(D).

the premises be given exclusively to the petitioning spouse. A full hearing on the matter is then held within seven days.[3]

When a domestic violence petition has been filed in domestic relations court, and there has been domestic violence, one of the available remedies is the eviction of the wrongdoer and the granting of exclusive possession to the injured party. One must assume that the eviction will not be granted ex parte without proper affidavit of true facts. A domestic violence petition should not be used for purposes of tactical advantage. Courts faced with counsel that have taken advantage of this process invoke the sanctions of Civil Rule 11.

Civil Rule 75(I)(2) permits the issue of a restraining order against a party. Where the affiant party is "about to suffer physical abuse, annoyance, or bodily injury by the other party, the court may allow a temporary restraining order, with or without bond, to prevent that action."

This clause has been used by counsel and judges to justify eviction of a spouse from the premises, in spite of the fact that Civil Rule 75(H) was not specifically designed for that use. The rule does not require de facto harm, injury, etc., but only the possibility of it. The order is not punitive for acts committed, but is a preventive measure. In addition, Civil Rule 75(H) permits a restraining order against presumed harm, if a party to the action or a child of any party is about to suffer physical abuse, annoyance, or bodily injury by the other party, which could mean a restraining order against future wrongful conduct. Until the passage of the Domestic Violence Act,[4] the temporary restraining order was the only fast, efficient way to protect wives and children from abusive husbands.

§ 4:10   Property rights during marriage—Individual ownership—Mortgages, deeds, and insurance

The mortgage of any interest of a married person in real property must be signed, attested, acknowledged, and certified as provided in RC 5301.01. A wife has the same power as her husband to execute a deed or mortgage to her separate property. Therefore, she may execute such deeds and mortgages without joining her husband and may bind whatever interests she has in lands, including release of her dower.[1]

A creditor is required by law to extend credit to a husband and wife equally. RC 4112.021 has been amended to conform with the Ohio an-

---

[3]See Text Ch 5, Domestic Violence.

[4]1978 H.B. 835, eff. 3-27-79, enacting RC 3113.31 and RC 3113.32; 1979 S.B. 46, eff. 1-18-80, enacting RC 3113.33 to RC 3113.39.

[Section 4:10]

[1]Straman v. Rechtine, 58 Ohio St. 443, 51 N.E. 44 (1898).

tidiscrimination laws with the federal Equal Credit Opportunity Act.[2] RC 4112.021(B)(1)(g) provides that it shall be an unlawful discriminatory practice for any creditor to

> [f]ail or refuse . . . to print on or firmly attach to each application for credit, in a type size no smaller than that used throughout most of the application form, the following notice: "The Ohio laws against discrimination require that all creditors make credit equally available to all credit worthy customers, and that credit reporting agencies maintain separate credit histories on each individual upon request. The Ohio civil rights commission administers compliance with this law."

The statute also prohibits any creditor from failing or refusing on the basis of race, color, religion, age, sex, marital status, national origin, handicap, or ancestry to maintain, upon the request of the individual, a separate account for each individual to whom credit is extended.

Under RC 1319.06, a husband and/or wife cannot create any lien, by chattel mortgage or otherwise, on personal household property owned by a husband or wife or both unless both join in the execution of such transaction. This provision does not apply, however, to any mortgage or lien for the purchase price of such property. Since no mortgage on personal household property is valid unless executed by both spouses, the signature of a wife, even if living apart from her husband, is needed to obtain a chattle mortgage on a filed financial statement on furniture given by the husband, so long as the relationship of husband and wife exists. A mortgage not so signed is invalid.[3]

A married woman who is the beneficiary of an insurance policy taken out by the husband on his life may legally transfer, before the death of her husband, her interest in the certificate in good faith and for valuable consideration or may pledge it for the payment of a valid debt.[4]

§ 4:11 Property rights during marriage—Individual ownership—Gifts and inheritances

Under the provisions of RC 3103.05 and RC 3103.07, a husband and wife may enter into any engagement or transaction with each other as if unmarried and may take, hold, and dispose of real or personal property without regard to the marital relationship. Therefore, either may properly convey his or her separate property to the other. Such transfers are effective in law and pass legal title to the property. A

---

[2]15 U.S.C.A. § 1691.

[3]See also Pietro v. Leonetti, 26 Ohio App. 2d 221, 55 Ohio Op. 2d 383, 270 N.E.2d 660 (8th Dist. Cuyahoga County 1971), judgment aff'd, 30 Ohio St. 2d 178, 59 Ohio Op. 2d 186, 283 N.E.2d 172 (1972) (surviving spouse entitled to contribution from estate of deceased husband for his share of joint obligation, evidenced by joint and several mortgage note and secured by mortgage on property held as joint tenants with right of survivorship, which property passed to surviving spouse on death of husband).

[4]Klinckhamer Brewing Co. v. Cassman, 12 Ohio C.D. 141, 1900 WL 1177 (Ohio Cir. Ct. 1900).

spouse making a gift of real property must secure the release of his or her spouse's right to dower in order to insure the validity of such a gift. Apart from the question of the rights of the creditors of the donor, one spouse may make a valid gift of real or personal property to the other spouse, just as though the parties were unmarried.[1] The validity of such gratuitous transfers will be measured by the usual criteria pertaining to gifts inter vivos and causa mortis.[2]

When a husband transfers property or funds to his wife, it is presumed to be a gift unless shown to the contrary,[3] and the burden is on the party attacking the transfer.[4] If a wife fails to show donative intent on the husband's part when wife's name was placed on deeds during the marriage, the transfer will not be considered a gift. To prove the elements of donative intent the party must show that (1) there was an intention on the part of the donor to transfer title, and right of possession to the wife, (2) there was a delivery to the donee of the gift to the extent practical with the relinquishment of ownership, dominion and control over it. The burden of proof is on the donee to show by clear and convincing evidence that the donor intended to make an inter vivos gift of an interest in property.[5] Evidence during divorce proceeding supported finding that vacant lot was marital property, despite husband's claim that the lot was a gift to him from his mother; though husband's mother testified that the gift of the land was intended solely for husband, wife's name was on the deed, and all real estate taxes on the lot were paid from marital funds.[6] Undue influence is not presumed by the mere relation of the parties but must be shown either by direct proof or by circumstances from which it may be fairly inferred.[7]

The presumption is that when a spouse makes advancements to the other spouse, in view of the mutual benefits which are likely to accrue from such advancements, the spouse who made the advancement has

---

[Section 4:11]

[1]In re Shangle's Estate, 8 Ohio L. Abs. 621, 1930 WL 2217 (Ct. App. 5th Dist. Perry County 1930).

[2]Bender v. Cleveland Trust Co., 123 Ohio St. 588, 10 Ohio L. Abs. 190, 176 N.E. 452 (1931); Barrett v. Barrett, 91 F. Supp. 680, 42 Ohio Op. 465, 58 Ohio L. Abs. 244 (N.D. Ohio 1950); Meyer v. Bigler, 27 Ohio N.P. (n.s.) 375, 1929 WL 2386 (Prob. Ct. 1929).

[3]Cosgrove v. Pendleton, 24 Ohio L. Abs. 417, 1937 WL 2284 (Ct. App. 2d Dist. Franklin County 1937); Van Hoose v. French, 75 Ohio App. 342, 31 Ohio Op. 110, 62 N.E.2d 259 (5th Dist. Fairfield County 1944); Sweeny v. Palus, 16 Ohio Op. 2d 373, 86 Ohio L. Abs. 29, 172 N.E.2d 925 (Prob. Ct. 1961).

[4]Van Hoose v. French, 75 Ohio App. 342, 31 Ohio Op. 110, 62 N.E.2d 259 (5th Dist. Fairfield County 1944).

[5]Smith v. Smith, 2004-Ohio-408, 2004 WL 193041 (Ohio Ct. App. 5th Dist. Muskingum County 2004).

[6]Stacy v. Stacy, 2005-Ohio-5289, 2005 WL 2416666 (Ohio Ct. App. 11th Dist. Ashtabula County 2005).

[7]RC 3105.171.

no claim against his or her spouse or his or her estate unless there was an express promise to repay him or her. Therefore, an otherwise valid gift from a husband to a wife will not be set aside without proof of undue influence, no presumption of which arises from the marital relation alone.[8]

A gift from one spouse to another cannot be made in disregard of creditors of the donor, and a creditor prejudiced by the transfer may, in a proper case, have it set aside.[9] Ordinarily, a spouse who is insolvent cannot make a valid gift or conveyance without consideration to the other spouse. Such a transfer is fraudulent as to the creditors and may be set aside.[10] Clearly, the transfer of a husband's property to his wife for nominal consideration for the purpose of defeating his creditors is subject to nullification. However, a voluntary conveyance from husband to wife is not void as to subsequent creditors, although the husband subsequently becomes insolvent, unless actual fraud is shown.[11]

A wife may transfer to her father property inherited from her mother's estate, where her father transferred the property to the mother, and such transfer will not be fraudulent as to the husband's marital property rights.[12] Courts will require that any gift by a wife of her personal property, which would deprive her husband of his marital property rights, meet the requirements of a valid gift.[13] When a wife holds property purchased by her husband in her name, with the understanding that he will receive it upon her death, she does not possess the power to devise to him only an estate for life. In such circumstances, a court will decree that the wife's entire interest pass to the husband.[14]

§ 4:12   Property rights during marriage—Joint ownership— Joint tenancy and survivorship—Tenancy by entirety

RC 5302.17, as amended effective April 4, 1985,[1] sets forth the

---

[8]Dozer v. Dozer, 8 Ohio L. Abs. 507, 1930 WL 2189 (Ct. App. 4th Dist. Gallia County 1930).

[9]Oliver v. Moore, 23 Ohio St. 473, 1872 WL 87 (1872).

[10]Allen v. Toth, 22 Ohio L. Abs. 457, 1935 WL 2006 (Ct. App. 2d Dist. Montgomery County 1935); Vilas v. Christopher, 8 Ohio L. Abs. 521, 1930 WL 2711 (Ct. App. 8th Dist. Cuyahoga County 1930).

[11]Flora v. Glander, 10 Ohio L. Abs. 572, 1931 WL 2639 (Ct. App. 2d Dist. Preble County 1931); Commonwealth Oil Co. v. Turk, 118 Ohio St. 273, 6 Ohio L. Abs. 191, 160 N.E. 856 (1928).

[12]Ambler v. Boone, 3 Ohio App. 87, 24 Ohio C.D. 512, 1914 WL 1155 (7th Dist. Columbiana County 1914).

[13]Ambler v. Boone, 3 Ohio App. 87, 24 Ohio C.D. 512, 1914 WL 1155 (7th Dist. Columbiana County 1914).

[14]Stopplekamp v. Stopplekamp, 8 Ohio Dec. 699, 1898 WL 751 (C.P. 1898).

[Section 4:12]

[1]1984 S.B. 201.

requirements for creating a survivorship interest in property. Any person who is the sole owner of real property, or persons who are tenants with a right to survivorship under the common or statutory law of this state, or as tenants in common, may create in themselves and in any other person or persons a survivorship tenancy in the real property, by executing a deed as provided for in RC 5302.17 conveying their entire, separate interests in the real property to themselves and to such other person or persons. The deed form set forth in RC 5302.17 creates a form of co-ownership which transfers by operation of law to the survivor(s) upon the death of any co-owner. The RC 5302.17 survivorship deed has replaced all other forms of survivorship ownership in Ohio.

Survivorship deeds are frequently used by husbands and wives, and replace tenancies by the entireties as the means for spouses to jointly own property with survivorship rights. Existing tenancies by the entireties will be recognized but after April 4, 1985, RC 5302.17 is the only means by which to create new survivorship interests.

Title to either real or personal property by technical joint tenancy has been abolished in Ohio. Where an instrument includes the term "joint tenancy" without any effort to expressly provide for survivorship, ownership will be construed as a tenancy in common.[2] However, if a donor or grantor, by the operative words of gift or grant, clearly expresses an intention to give the right of survivorship, the expression "joint tenancy" will not be disregarded.[3] Therefore, where a husband and wife take title to real estate by a joint and survivorship deed, such deed will be a valid and effective means of transferring the entire fee simple title to the surviving grantee.[4] Express mention of survivorship rights in sufficiently clear language is necessary for joint tenancy to exist.

Prior to April 4, 1985, if a husband and wife wished to create in themselves a tenancy by the entirety, they could do so by complying with RC Chapter 5301 and RC 5302.17. Former RC 5302.17 applied to and could be used to create a tenancy by the entirety in property previously owned by only one of the spouses.

The difference between the tenancy in common and tenancy by the entirety is that upon the death of one spouse, the tenancy by the entirety operates like a joint tenancy; that is, full title automatically passes to the surviving spouse and not the heirs and devisees. In the-

---

[2]In re Hutchison's Estate, 120 Ohio St. 542, 7 Ohio L. Abs. 333, 166 N.E. 687 (1929).

[3]In re Hutchison's Estate, 120 Ohio St. 542, 7 Ohio L. Abs. 333, 166 N.E. 687 (1929).

[4]Ross v. Bowman, 32 Ohio Op. 27, 17 Ohio Supp. 59, 1945 WL 5793 (C.P. 1945); Lewis v. Baldwin, 11 Ohio 352, 1842 WL 26 (1842) (joint tenancy, when created by act of grantor in deed and clearly expressed to show intention to create right of survivorship, is not contrary to Ohio law); In re Dennis' Estate, 30 Ohio N.P. (n.s.) 118, 1928 WL 2753 (C.P. 1928). See also Ewing O. Cossaboom, *Survivorship Deeds in Ohio*, 17 Cin. L. Rev. 191 (1948).

ory, the parties to a tenancy in common are individual owners of the joint property while they are alive. In the tenancy by the entirety, however, the marriage is the owner. Thus, an inter vivos conveyance or bequest by will by only one of the parties is a nullity unless the other spouse joins, or unless the other spouse has predeceased the transferor.

In an estate by the entirety both spouses have an equal undivided interest in the whole property, not just in half of the property. In essence, each owns the entire estate. The distinguishing characteristics of the tenancy by the entirety are as follows:

(1) The owners must be husband and wife;

(2) The owners have rights of survivorship;

(3) During the owners' lives, title can be conveyed only by deed signed by both parties (one party cannot convey a one-half interest); and

(4) There is generally no right to partition.

A tenancy by the entirety prevents the creditor of only one spouse from attaching that spouse's interest in the estate or from levying on the tenancy property. However, even if otherwise validly created, the estate held by husband and wife as tenants by the entirety could be set aside as a fraudulent conveyance if its creation rendered the debtor spouse insolvent, or if it was created with the intent to hinder, delay, or defraud present or future creditors.[5] Tenancies by the entireties created before April 4, 1985 are recognized as valid in Ohio. However, no new tenancies by the entireties can be created after that date.

§ 4:13 Property rights during marriage—Joint ownership— Joint bank accounts and other funds

A husband and wife may be joint owners of a bank deposit in their joint names subject to withdrawal by either survivor.[1] *Gillota v. Gillota*[2] has muddied these waters. The general proposition of this case is that the proceeds of a joint and survivorship bank account, during the lifetime of the parties, belong to the parties in proportion to the net contributions of each, unless there is clear and convincing evidence of a different intent. A bank account in the names of husband and wife with a specific provision that the funds may be paid to either or the

---

[5]Wagner v. Galipo, 50 Ohio St. 3d 194, 553 N.E.2d 610 (1990).

[Section 4:13]

[1]Tax Commission of Ohio v. Hutchison, 120 Ohio St. 361, 166 N.E. 352 (1929); Osterland v. Schroeder, 22 Ohio App. 213, 4 Ohio L. Abs. 581, 153 N.E. 758 (8th Dist. Cuyahoga County 1926); In re Shangle's Estate, 8 Ohio L. Abs. 621, 1930 WL 2217 (Ct. App. 5th Dist. Perry County 1930); Ryan v. Henney, 20 Ohio L. Abs. 518, 1935 WL 1928 (Ct. App. 2d Dist. Franklin County 1935) (husband and wife may contract as joint owners of bank deposit in their joint names, subject to withdrawal by either or survivor, to which both have contributed, and balance passes to survivor and his or her heirs).

[2]Gillota v. Gillota, 4 Ohio St. 3d 222, 448 N.E.2d 802 (1983).

survivor is a clear instance of joint ownership with right of survivorship.[3] Such an account is a joint and survivorship account, even where provision is made that both must sign, and the husband retains the passbook.[4] However, if a deposit account is carried in the names of both husband and wife, and no mention is made of survivorship rights, both spouses have an equal interest in the property as tenants in common, and neither has survivorship rights.[5]

A surviving wife is not entitled to any portion of a bank account established by her husband in his own name during the marriage, where the only evidence of joint ownership is that she gave him small sums of money from her earnings, without any proof of the specific amount, instructions, or arrangements about making deposits in his name, or other disposition of the money.[6]

Spouses may also become joint owners with right of survivorship of bonds,[7] building and loan certificates,[8] and stock accounts[9] by placing both spouses' names on the title and including the words "rights of survivorship."

Where a husband and wife have created a valid joint and survivorship account, the husband cannot alter his wife's interest by will,[10] nor can he assign his interest in the account to a third party.[11] Similarly, a wife cannot change the joint ownership of an investment simply by converting it into cash.[12] Where an account consists entirely of the husband's money, this fact may be shown to prevent a creditor

---

[3]Ryan v. Henney, 20 Ohio L. Abs. 518, 1935 WL 1928 (Ct. App. 2d Dist. Franklin County 1935) (form of account is not conclusive as to joint ownership); Union Properties, Inc. v. Cleveland Trust Co., 152 Ohio St. 430, 40 Ohio Op. 425, 89 N.E.2d 638 (1949) (wife entitled to deposit certificate in name of husband or wife without mention of survivorship rights, where husband told bank before his death that he intended his wife to be able to draw either before or after his death); In re Burns' Estate, 21 Ohio L. Abs. 148, 1935 WL 1976 (Ct. App. 2d Dist. Darke County 1935).

[4]In re Vollmer's Estate, 30 Ohio N.P. (n.s.) 289, 1933 WL 1654 (C.P. 1933).

[5]Bender v. Cleveland Trust Co., 123 Ohio St. 588, 10 Ohio L. Abs. 190, 176 N.E. 452 (1931); Foraker v. Kocks, 41 Ohio App. 210, 11 Ohio L. Abs. 545, 180 N.E. 743 (5th Dist. Perry County 1931); In re Chittock's Estate, 47 Ohio Op. 226, 65 Ohio L. Abs. 432, 106 N.E.2d 320 (Prob. Ct. 1952).

[6]Clark v. Clark, 23 Ohio App. 68, 5 Ohio L. Abs. 279, 155 N.E. 409 (1st Dist. Hamilton County 1926).

[7]Gladieux v. Parney, 93 Ohio App. 117, 50 Ohio Op. 246, 63 Ohio L. Abs. 289, 106 N.E.2d 317 (6th Dist. Lucas County 1951).

[8]Riley v. Keel, 84 Ohio App. 313, 39 Ohio Op. 468, 53 Ohio L. Abs. 257, 85 N.E.2d 123 (1st Dist. Hamilton County 1946).

[9]Schwartz v. Sandusky County Savings & Loan Co., 65 Ohio App. 437, 19 Ohio Op. 43, 30 N.E.2d 556 (6th Dist. Sandusky County 1939).

[10]In re Shangle's Estate, 8 Ohio L. Abs. 621, 1930 WL 2217 (Ct. App. 5th Dist. Perry County 1930); Bennett v. Bennett, 70 Ohio App. 187, 24 Ohio Op. 510, 45 N.E.2d 614 (9th Dist. Summit County 1942).

[11]Schwartz v. Sandusky County Savings & Loan Co., 65 Ohio App. 437, 19 Ohio Op. 43, 30 N.E.2d 556 (6th Dist. Sandusky County 1939).

[12]Barrett v. Barrett, 91 F. Supp. 680, 42 Ohio Op. 465, 58 Ohio L. Abs. 244 (N.D. Ohio 1950) (when evidence establishes government bonds issued in name of husband

of the wife from levying on the account.[13] A court will not divide equally the money in a joint and survivorship account without giving the parties an opportunity to show the source of the money in the account.[14]

§ 4:14   Support obligations while separated

RC 3103.03 controls spousal support obligations while a couple is married, despite the fact that the couple may be separated. Upon separation, a husband and wife may provide for their own support and that of their children during the separation.[1] If an agreement does not contain a provision reciting the intention of the parties to separate or live apart, it will be viewed as an unenforceable attempt to alter their legal relationship.[2] The parents' agreement may relieve them of their support obligations for each other, but they cannot relieve themselves of the obligation to support their children.[3] The husband and wife may release each other from claims for future care, support, and maintenance.[4] The agreement may include provisions which terminate the right to dower and distributive shares as well as obligations of support or maintenance.[5] Agreements providing for division of property and containing provisions for spousal support, if

---

or wife are joint property of both and not property of wife by gift, mere conversion of bonds into cash does not change joint ownership in investment or proceeds).

[13]Fayen v. Cleveland Trust, 23 Ohio Op. 563, 9 Ohio Supp. 148, 1942 WL 3125 (C.P. 1942).

[14]Ulmer v. Society for Savings, 35 Ohio L. Abs. 525, 41 N.E.2d 578 (Ct. App. 8th Dist. Cuyahoga County 1942).

[Section 4:14]

[1]RC 3103.03, RC 3103.06.

[2]Smith v. Smith, 50 Ohio Op. 175, 67 Ohio L. Abs. 489, 493, 112 N.E.2d 346 (C.P. 1953) (agreement not containing required provision "subject to the approval of the court in the event of an award of alimony").

[3]RC 3103.06. See also Smith v. Smith, 50 Ohio Op. 175, 67 Ohio L. Abs. 489, 112 N.E.2d 346 (C.P. 1953) (agreement between parents does not terminate liability of either); Rutter v. Rutter, 24 Ohio Misc. 7, 53 Ohio Op. 2d 32, 261 N.E.2d 202 (C.P. 1970); Rand v. Rand, 18 Ohio St. 3d 356, 481 N.E.2d 609, 26 Ed. Law Rep. 1198 (1985) (judicial enforcement of separation agreement incorporated into divorce decree, which requires non-residential parent to pay tuition for child's religious education, does not offend O. Const. Art. I § 7).

[4]Phillips v. Pelton, 10 Ohio St. 3d 52, 461 N.E.2d 305 (1984) (separation agreement, incorporated into decree of dissolution, which includes release of life insurance beneficiary rights, will exclude such benefits even though no specific change of beneficiary was made under policy); Bednar v. Bednar, 20 Ohio App. 3d 176, 485 N.E.2d 834 (9th Dist. Summit County 1984) (separation agreement incorporated into dissolution decree which requires party to divide and pay over his (expectancy) inheritance to other party is valid and enforceable).

[5]Hoagland v. Hoagland, 113 Ohio St. 228, 3 Ohio L. Abs. 388, 148 N.E. 585 (1925) (upholding separation agreement in which husband and wife released all claims to dower, support, and distributive share); Gilford v. Wurster, 24 Ohio App. 3d 77, 493 N.E.2d 258 (9th Dist. Lorain County 1983) (where parties' separation agreement extends child support beyond obligor's death, said support becomes charge

otherwise found to be valid, are not abrogated as to either party for marital misconduct arising after the marriage, unless the agreement provides that marital misconduct will invalidate the agreement.[6]

A separation agreement will be unenforceable if the provisions are not fair and reasonable.[7] As with contracts entered into between a husband and wife during their marriage, the parties are subject "to the general rules which control the actions of persons occupying confidential relations with each other."[8] The husband is often thought to be in a position to dominate his wife, and, therefore, transactions between them will be scrutinized for fairness.[9] Questions of fairness can often be resolved by insertion of a clause in the agreement stating that the parties entered into it voluntarily, with full knowledge of each other's assets, and with an explanation of the terms of the agreement by counsel. Despite the inclusion of such a provision, a separation agreement will likely be voided if there is a complex financial settlement and one of the parties was not represented by counsel.[10] Each party can insure fairness by creating a written list of assets and all other financial data, and exchanging these lists prior to entering into an agreement.

The marital relationship can be altered by a separation agreement without creating a presumption of unfairness and fraud.[11] It is

---

against decedent's estate, subject to credit for social security benefits paid to child); In re Estate of Hogrefe, 30 Ohio App. 3d 238, 507 N.E.2d 414 (3d Dist. Henry County 1986) (separation agreement may, by its terms, survive dismissal of dissolution action and bind party's estate as to any matters covered by agreement).

[6]Gross v. Gross, 11 Ohio St. 3d 99, 464 N.E.2d 500, 53 A.L.R.4th 139 (1984).

[7]DiPietro v. DiPietro, 10 Ohio App. 3d 44, 460 N.E.2d 657 (10th Dist. Franklin County 1983) (separation agreement, pursuant to RC 3103.05, is required to be fair and equitable to wife deemed to be party in need when parties dealt at arm's length; test is whether agreement is product of fraud, duress, or undue influence upon party in weaker bargaining position; fact that separation agreement does not equally divide property of parties does not require finding that agreement is unenforceable).

[8]RC 3103.05. See also Brewer v. Brewer, 84 Ohio App. 35, 39 Ohio Op. 89, 52 Ohio L. Abs. 116, 78 N.E.2d 919 (2d Dist. Montgomery County 1948) (separation agreement drafted after two days of intense negotiations between parties and without legal advice to wife was unreasonable and unfair).

[9]Hasselschwert v. Hasselschwert, 90 Ohio App. 331, 47 Ohio Op. 494, 106 N.E.2d 786 (3d Dist. Defiance County 1951).

[10]In re Marriage of Kesler, 59 Ohio Misc. 33, syl. 4, 13 Ohio Op. 3d 105, 392 N.E.2d 905 (C.P. 1978) (court invalidated separation agreement and stated that "[t]he equitable principle requiring a husband to procure independent advice for his wife in transactions between them does not require a showing of a design founded in evil purpose on the part of the husband").

[11]Meyer v. Meyer, 153 Ohio St. 408, 41 Ohio Op. 415, 91 N.E.2d 892 (1950) (provision in separation agreement barring spouse from seeking alimony not void but enforceable until court determines it to be unfair); In Re: Estate of Robinson, 1985 WL 6929 (Ohio Ct. App. 2d Dist. Greene County 1985) (trial court erred in denying spouse's right to elect against will where separation agreement incorporated into decree of alimony only but no explicit release of right of each to take against other's will).

important to draft with specificity and clarity in order to avoid any settlement which appears to cause hardship to one of the parties.

Except as to the allocation of parental rights and responsibilities, the parties and the court will be bound by the terms of a separation agreement where it has been incorporated into a divorce decree.[12] Parents have no statutory authority to determine the allocation of parental rights and responsibilities for their minor children. While a court may uphold their decision, the best interest of the children is the court's first concern; it is not bound by the parental rights provisions of the separation agreement.[13]

Executory portions of a separation agreement may become unenforceable upon the reconciliation of the parties and the resumption of a normal married life, by agreement or by operation of law.[14] However, a separation agreement will not be invalidated because of the minority of the executing parties[15] or because the decree makes no reference to it.[16] A separation agreement will not be rendered ineffective by the withdrawal of a petition for dissolution and the filing of a divorce complaint by one of the parties.[17]

§ 4:15 Support obligations upon divorce—Spousal support— Initial award

RC 3103.03(A) provides that each spouse must provide mutual and self-support equally during the marriage. Upon divorce, RC 3105.18 provides the considerations the court must make when determining which spouse, if either, will be awarded spousal support.

As a general rule, the duty of a spouse to support the other spouse survives a separation by mutual consent.[1] RC 3103.03(A) refers to a husband and wife and their mutual support obligations to each other

---

[12]Bastian v. Bastian, 13 Ohio Op. 2d 267, 81 Ohio L. Abs. 408, 160 N.E.2d 133, 73 A.L.R.2d 1440 (Ct. App. 8th Dist. Cuyahoga County 1959).

[13]Stadalsky v. Stadalsky, 1987 WL 7885 (Ohio Ct. App. 8th Dist. Cuyahoga County 1987).

[14]In re Price's Estate, 1 Ohio Op. 459, 22 Ohio L. Abs. 639, 1 Ohio Supp. 173 (Prob. Ct. 1935); Rutter v. Rutter, 24 Ohio Misc. 7, 53 Ohio Op. 2d 32, 261 N.E.2d 202 (C.P. 1970) (provision for custody, support, and maintenance of minor child found to be executory).

[15]Burlovic v. Farmer, 96 Ohio App. 403, 54 Ohio Op. 399, 115 N.E.2d 411 (8th Dist. Cuyahoga County 1953), judgment aff'd, 162 Ohio St. 46, 54 Ohio Op. 5, 120 N.E.2d 705 (1954).

[16]Mendelson v. Mendelson, 123 Ohio St. 11, 8 Ohio L. Abs. 754, 173 N.E. 615 (1930); Greiner v. Greiner, 61 Ohio App. 2d 88, 15 Ohio Op. 3d 95, 399 N.E.2d 571 (8th Dist. Cuyahoga County 1979) (separation agreement not incorporated into divorce decree valid, binding, enforceable contract).

[17]Carey v. Carey, 9 Ohio App. 3d 243, 459 N.E.2d 626 (3d Dist. Shelby County 1983).

[Section 4:15]

[1]41 Am. Jur. 2d, Husband and Wife § 175; 331; Block v. Block, 165 Ohio St. 365, 60 Ohio Op. 1, 135 N.E.2d 857 (1956) (Supreme Court stated that wife separated

and to their minor children, in contrast to RC 3109.05, which refers to "parents" who are separated or divorced.

In *Wolfe v. Wolfe*,[2] the Court had stated that

> we end our quest for an ascertainable and legitimate basis for post-marital alimony, properly so-called, because we are confident that modern legal principles cannot harbor such an anachronistic notion. Rather, it is our considered opinion that most awards of property incident to a final divorce are readjustments of the party's property rights, and . . . "[w]hether in the judgment such adjustment is called 'alimony or' 'division of property' . . . [has not been considered] important . . . [T]he General Assembly, although continually authorizing the award of 'alimony,' has never defined that term, but in referring to it imbues it with somewhat more force than mere sustenance."

RC 3105.18 defines the duties of one spouse where the other spouse is entitled to spousal support.[3] RC 3105.18 was amended effective January 1, 1991, at the same time the Ohio legislature created RC 3105.171. The effect of this amendment and creation of the new section was to clear up the area of the law dealing with spousal support by separating it distinctly from the area of law dealing with property division. After the 1991 changes, support obligations are no longer termed "alimony" but are now referred to as spousal support. Old RC 3105.18 was titled "alimony" and listed eleven factors for the court to consider when deciding whether to grant alimony. Amended RC 3105.18 provides fourteen factors for the court to consider when deciding whether to award spousal support.[4]

§ 4:16 Support obligations upon divorce—Spousal support—Modification

It is the duty of the trial court to determine if spousal support is appropriate and reasonable under the factors set forth in RC 3105.18(C), after the division or disbursement of property under RC 3105.171. A subsequent substantial increase in the obligor's income may be sufficient to merit an increase in spousal support if the court's decree reserves jurisdiction over spousal support. A party must show a change in circumstances to justify a modification of spousal support. The definition of change in circumstances includes an increase or involuntary decrease in either party's wages, salary, bonuses, living ex-

---

from her husband is in position of creditor, in regard to support, and may set aside voluntary conveyance made by husband without consideration).

[2]Wolfe v. Wolfe, 46 Ohio St. 2d 399, 410-11, 75 Ohio Op. 2d 474, 350 N.E.2d 413 (1976) (footnote omitted), superseded by statute as stated in Heslep v. Heslep, 2000 WL 818909 (Ohio Ct. App. 7th Dist. Monroe County 2000)).

[3]Klump v. Klump, 96 Ohio App. 93, 54 Ohio Op. 202, 121 N.E.2d 273 (6th Dist. Lucas County 1954).

[4]See Text §§ 4:15, 4:16, Support obligations upon divorce—Spousal support; Text Ch 13, Spousal Support.

penses, or medical expenses.[1] However, the court must modify the amount of spousal support if the obligor's circumstances make it impossible to meet the amount awarded.[2] Denial of such a modification would be an abuse of the court's discretion.[3]

In 1951, all reference to aggression was eliminated from the domestic relations statutes. The deletion of specific reference to aggression in the statutes does not preclude a court from considering it in an award of spousal support. The General Assembly intended to eliminate the element of aggression as controlling the discretion of the court, but not as one element affecting the discretion of the court.[4]

In divorce and legal separation proceedings, upon the request of either party and after the court determines the division or disbursement of property under RC 3105.171, the court of common pleas may award reasonable spousal support to either party. During the pendency of any divorce, or legal separation proceeding, the court may award reasonable temporary spousal support to either party.[5] In determining whether spousal support is appropriate and reasonable, and in determining the nature, amount and terms of payment, and duration of spousal support, which is payable either in gross or in installments, the court shall consider the fourteen factors listed under RC 3105.18(C)(1).

Although at common law and by statute a husband's support obligation may continue upon divorce, on proper evidence spousal support may be awarded to the husband.[6] The court should use the same criteria for determining a husband's need for spousal support as it uses in determining a wife's.

§ 4:17 Property rights upon divorce—In general

When a husband and wife are divorced, they stand as equals before the court, which must then determine their property rights. The court's responsibility, similar to that in deciding support obligations, is to divide equitably the assets of the parties based upon what prop-

---

[Section 4:16]

[1]RC 3105.18(F). But see Gross v. Gross, 64 Ohio App. 3d 815, 582 N.E.2d 1144 (10th Dist. Franklin County 1990) (court-ordered support is just and proper despite obligor's ability to afford larger award; substantial increase in obligor's income insufficient to merit increased support).

[2]Haase v. Haase, 64 Ohio App. 3d 758, 582 N.E.2d 1107 (8th Dist. Cuyahoga County 1990) (obligor's early retirement, severe medical condition sufficient cause for modification of spousal support).

[3]Haase v. Haase, 64 Ohio App. 3d 758, 582 N.E.2d 1107 (8th Dist. Cuyahoga County 1990) (obligor's early retirement, severe medical condition sufficient cause for modification of spousal support).

[4]Esteb v. Esteb, 173 Ohio St. 259, 19 Ohio Op. 2d 80, 181 N.E.2d 462 (1962).

[5]See RC 3105.18(B).

[6]Sharkey v. Sharkey, 73 Ohio L. Abs. 321, 137 N.E.2d 575 (Ct. App. 2d Dist. Montgomery County 1955); Orr v. Orr, 440 U.S. 268, 99 S. Ct. 1102, 59 L. Ed. 2d 306 (1979) (unconstitutionality of alimony statute for women only).

erty was acquired during the marriage through either the division of labor of the parties or their joint labors.

Prior to 1991, RC 3105.18 combined property division and spousal support in a single statute and the cases interpreting RC 3105.18 had evolved into an inconsistent and unpredictable body of law. For this reason the Ohio legislature sought to refine and renovate the Code.

Effective January 1, 1991, the legislature amended RC 3105.18 and enacted RC 3105.171. The effect was to divide former RC 3105.18 into two distinct sections, separating property division and spousal support. In doing so, the legislature recognized that the nature of family law proceedings does not lend itself to rigid application of rules; however, it was also recognized that discretion should remain in the trial court so that each case would be treated fairly on its facts. The goal of RC 3105.18 and RC 3105.171 was to promote a reasonable degree of uniformity among the courts in Ohio, while preserving the sanctity of the court's judgment on a case-by-case basis.

The 1991 statutes made technical changes in the law, such as changing the words "alimony" to "spousal support" and "alimony only" to "legal separation" throughout the Code. In addition, the amendments made substantive changes to Title 31 of the Ohio Revised Code, including:

(1) RC 3105.10(B) sets forth the jurisdiction of the common pleas court to enforce a separation agreement upon motion of either party.

(2) RC 3105.17 changed the grounds for alimony only, now known as legal separation, to conform with the grounds for divorce in RC 3105.01, and states that the filing of a complaint for legal separation does not bar a subsequent complaint for divorce or annulment.

(3) RC 3105.63 directs the court to use the factors under RC 3105.18 when modifying spousal support awards under a dissolution decree where the jurisdiction for modification has been reserved.

When the trial court divides property other than equally (equitably) the trial court must make a written finding of fact to support such a distribution.[1] RC 3105.171 is comprised of sections (A) through (J). RC 3105.171(C) is the heart of the statute, requiring that the division of property be equal, unless an equal division would be inequitable, in which case the court must determine an equitable division. The court has also found that private agreements are not binding upon the court and a trial court is not relieved of the duty to divide a marital

---

[Section 4:17]

[1]Raff v. Raff, 2005-Ohio-3348, 2005 WL 1532354 (Ohio Ct. App. 5th Dist. Stark County 2005).

estate equitably simply because the parties have an agreement regarding the division of debt or property.[2]

The statute also requires that courts issue findings of fact in certain situations. RC 3105.171(D) requires findings of fact to be issued where the court disburses separate property of one spouse to the other. RC 3105.171(G) requires findings of fact to support the determination that marital property has been equitably divided. It further requires the court to specify the dates the court uses in determining the beginning and end of the marriage. This provision is for the purposes of determining the dates of valuation of property and the nature of the property as separate or marital.

House Bill 535, effective January 1, 2002, added an amendment to RC 3105.171, dealing with the following five state retirement systems; the State Teachers, Public Employees, State Employees, Police and Firemen, and Ohio Highway Patrol Retirement Systems. The systems may now, pursuant to a court order to divide marital property, make payments to members' former spouses in order to divide a retirement benefit or lump sum payment. This amendment does not, however, appear to allow cost of living adjustments, survivorship, guaranteed payments, or early commencement.

§ 4:18 Property rights upon divorce—Characterizing property as separate or marital

RC 3105.171(B) states that the court shall determine what constitutes marital property and what constitutes separate property in a divorce proceeding. The court may, upon request of either spouse, determine marital and separate property in a legal separation proceeding.

The commingling of property between a husband and wife does not automatically cause separate property to lose its status as "separate". Separate property, as defined by RC 3105.171(A)(6)(a), whether commingled or not, as long as traceable, remains the separate property of that individual.

The Supreme Court held in *Middendorf v. Middendorf*,[1] that where property can be traced to one spouse's separate property and neither spouse has made efforts that caused any appreciation in value or income, then the appreciation or income will be deemed as separate property. The ruling in *Middendorf* aligns with RC 3105.171(A)(3)(a)(iii), which states that premarital property becomes marital if "labor, monetary, or in-kind contribution of either or both of the spouses" occurred during the marriage. Routine or regular main-

---

[2]Kershner v. Kershner, 2004-Ohio-1523, 2004 WL 605169 (Ohio Ct. App. 11th Dist. Portage County 2004), see also Szerlip v. Szerlip, 2000 WL 1682548 (Ohio Ct. App. 5th Dist. Knox County 2000).

[Section 4:18]

[1]Middendorf v. Middendorf, 82 Ohio St. 3d 397, 1998-Ohio-403, 696 N.E.2d 575 (1998).

tenance even when combined with the payment of property taxes and utilities is generally insufficient proof that marital residence's increase in value was due to the spouse's "labor, monetary, or in kind contribution" for the purposes of creating a marital interest pursuant to RC 3105.171(A)(3)(a).[2]

Income and appreciation from a separate asset, which produced income or appreciated in value without any monetary, in-kind, or labor contribution by either party during the marriage, are defined in the statute as "passive income" under RC 3105.171(A)(4). Passive income has been defined by the courts as income acquired through means other than the labor, monetary, or in-kind contribution of either spouse. Similarly, passive appreciation has been defined by the courts as an increase in market value which results from inflation or market changes rather than from marital efforts or the expenditure of marital funds.[3]

Spouses can change one type of property, such as separate property, to a different type, such as marital property, "based on actions during the marriage."[4] This is primarily done through inter vivos gift from one spouse to the other. An inter vivos gift is an "immediate, voluntary, gratuitous and irrevocable transfer of property by a competent donor to another."[5] If the elements of an inter vivos gift have been met, marital property may then be considered transmuted into a spouse's separate property.[6]

§ 4:19 Property rights upon divorce—RC 3105.171— Definitions—Distributive award

The distributive award is an award from separate property made (1) to "facilitate, effectuate, or supplement"[1] the division of marital property, (2) to achieve equity where there is hardship in reaching an

---

[2]Pressler v. Pressler, 2005-Ohio-1408, 2005 WL 694480 (Ohio Ct. App. 12th Dist. Butler County 2005).

[3]Hansen v. Hansen, 1992 WL 366885 (Ohio Ct. App. 11th Dist. Lake County 1992); Barkley v. Barkley, 119 Ohio App. 3d 155, 694 N.E.2d 989 (4th Dist. Pickaway County 1997); Weithman v. Weithman, 2001-Ohio-2181, 2001 WL 730736 (Ohio Ct. App. 3d Dist. Crawford County 2001) (stating that because there was no evidence the husband was a "decision maker" or that his role contributed directly to the increased value of stock, the appreciation in stock value was classified as passive income and therefore separate property).

[4]Helton v. Helton, 114 Ohio App. 3d 683, 685, N.E.2d 1157 (2d Dist. Montgomery County 1996).

[5]Helton v. Helton, 114 Ohio App. 3d 683, 685, 683 N.E.2d 1157 (2d Dist. Montgomery County 1996); Fricke v. Martin-Fricke, 2001 WL 523946 (Ohio Ct. App. 2d Dist. Greene County 2001).

[6]See Sweeney v. Sweeney, 2000 WL 799095 (Ohio Ct. App. 9th Dist. Summit County 2000); Snyder v. Snyder, 2000 WL 1876614 (Ohio Ct. App. 11th Dist. Geauga County 2000); West v. West, 2002-Ohio-1118, 2002 WL 388845 (Ohio Ct. App. 9th Dist. Wayne County 2002).

[Section 4:19]

[1]RC 3105.171(E)(1).

equitable division comprised of marital property alone, or (3) to compensate the offended spouse where the other spouse engaged in financial misconduct.

The distributive award involves *only* separate property and income, including future income. The provisions pertaining to the distributive award are set out in RC 3105.171(A) and (E). Although these subsections are physically separated in the statute, when read together they provide a clear definition.

Under RC 3105.171(A)(1), a distributive award must be made in a fixed amount, and may not be contingent upon any future event. However, this does not prohibit a fixed percentage in an equitable distribution award.

RC 3105.171(E) defines financial misconduct as, among other things, dissipation, destruction, concealment, or fraudulent disposition of assets. The subsection states that a spouse may be compensated with a distributive award, or with a greater award of marital property, where financial misconduct is proved. Although evidence in a divorce action supported trial court's determination that husband engaged in financial misconduct by setting fire to the parties' rental property, there was no evidence that he "personally gained or profited from his misconduct, or that wife was harmed financially from the misconduct," and thus, trial court's award to wife of the entirety of the insurance proceeds from the fire was not warranted; although the arson resulted in a diminished value of the property, the insurance proceeds compensated for that loss.[2] The purpose of RC 3105.171(E)(3) is the neutralize the losses caused by the offending spouse and not to reward one spouse for the other spouse's wrongdoing.[3]

This section additionally prescribes the use of the distributive award to achieve equity where a strict division of marital property would be impractical or burdensome. For example, funds received by wife in settlement related to a workplace injury suffered by her prior to marriage and used to pay husband's premarital debts remained wife's separate property and were subject to repayment upon divorce, where wife paid off husband's debts only in expectation that marriage would continue and did not intend that such funds be treated as gift to husband.[4] It would be impractical to make a strict division of marital property when a spouse relieves the other spouse's debt with her separate property believing at the time of the debt relief the husband would continue to support her.

---

[2]Eggeman v. Eggeman, 2004-Ohio-6050, 2004 WL 2588343 (Ohio Ct. App. 3d Dist. Auglaize County 2004).

[3]Eggeman v. Eggeman, 2004-Ohio-6050, 2004 WL 2588343 (Ohio Ct. App. 3d Dist. Auglaize County 2004).

[4]Stonehill v. Stonehill, 2004-Ohio-3022, 2004 WL 1302458 (Ohio Ct. App. 3d Dist. Allen County 2004).

A lien on any property, marital or separate, may be used to secure a distributive award.[5]

§4:20 Property rights upon divorce—RC 3105.171—Definitions—During the marriage

The term "during the marriage," as defined in RC 3105.171(A)(2), requires that the parties and the court specify the dates when the marriage began and ended. These dates are essential to determining the appropriate dates of valuation. The statute presumes that the date of valuation or for determining marital property will be through the date of the final hearing (or a date practicably close), unless the court selects another date it considers equitable.[1] While findings of fact must be provided when marital property has been equitably divided, there is no specific statutory requirement that the court issue written findings of fact to explain its reasoning for not using the date of final hearing to consider the "duration of the marriage."[2]

§4:21 Property rights upon divorce—RC 3105.171—Definitions—Marital property

Marital property is defined in RC 3105.171(A)(3). Marital property is distinct from all separate property. There are four subdivisions within the definition of marital property:

(3)(a) "Marital property" means, subject to division (A)(3)(b) of this section, all of the following:

(i) All real and personal property that currently is owned by either or both of the spouses, including, but not limited to, the retirement benefits of the spouses, and that was acquired by either or both of the spouses during the marriage;

(ii) All interest that either or both of the spouses currently has in any real or personal property, including, but not limited to, the retirement benefits of the spouses, and that was acquired by either or both of the spouses during the marriage;

(iii) Except as otherwise provided in this section, all income and appreciation on separate property, due to the labor, monetary, or in-kind contribution of either or both of the spouses that occurred during the marriage;

(iv) A participant account, as defined in section 148.01 of the Revised Code, of either of the spouses, to the extent of the following: the moneys

---

[5]See Shehata v. Shehata, 2005-Ohio-3659, 2005 WL 1685099 (Ohio Ct. App. 2d Dist. Montgomery County 2005).

[Section 4:20]

[1]See also RC 3105.171(G).

[2]Kohler v. Kohler, 1996 WL 132369, at *2 (Ohio Ct. App. 5th Dist. Coshocton County 1996) (while statute does not require that trial court set forth its reasoning for not using date of final hearing, appellate court stated such a statement would be of assistance to the court for review purposes); Dunlap v. Dunlap, 1996 WL 134543 (Ohio Ct. App. 1st Dist. Hamilton County 1996) (trial court erred in finding de facto termination of marriage based on unilateral conduct).

that have been deferred by a continuing member or participating employee, as defined in that section, and that have been transmitted to the Ohio public employees deferred compensation board during the marriage and any income that is derived from the investment of those moneys during the marriage; the moneys that have been deferred by an officer or employee of a municipal corporation and that have been transmitt4ed to the governing board, administrator, depository, or trustee of the deferred compensation program of the municipal corporation during the marriage and any income that is derived from the investment of those moneys during the marriage; or the moneys that have been deferred by an officer or employee of a government unit, as defined in section 148.06 of the Revised Code, and that have been transmitted to the governing board, as defined in that section, during the marriage and any income that is derived from the investment of those moneys during the marriage.

(3)(b) "Marital property" does not include any separate property.

§ 4:22   Property rights upon divorce—RC 3105.171— Definitions—Separate property

Personal property, as defined in RC 3105.171(A)(5), includes both tangible and intangible personal property. The definition of separate property in RC 3105.171(A)(6) lists seven specific types of separate property.[1] Other provisions pertaining to separate property include:

(1) Separate property which is commingled does not lose its identity as separate property unless it is not traceable.[2]

(2) Unless the court makes a distributive award from separate property, it must be disbursed to its owner. If the court awards separate property other than to its title owner, the court must make specific findings of fact to explain its determination.[3]

(3) The manner in which the title to property is held, either by one spouse individually or by both spouses in a form of co-ownership, does not determine whether it is marital or separate.[4] Whether property has been commingled, therefore, does not determine its status as marital or separate property.

In most cases, this resolves a disagreement among courts regarding the transmutation of property.

Inheritances, premarital property, and passive income are all

---

[Section 4:22]

[1]See RC 3105.171(A)(6)(a).

[2]RC 3105.171(A)(6)(b); Matic v. Matic, 2001 WL 848530 (Ohio Ct. App. 11th Dist. Geauga County 2001); Best v. Best, 1999 WL 1140067 (Ohio Ct. App. 10th Dist. Franklin County 1999) (the act of tracing need not be supported by physical documentation such as bank statements).

[3]RC 3105.171(D).

[4]RC 3105.171(H); Jakab v. Jakab, No. 90-CA-02 (Ohio Ct. App. 2d Dist. Miami County 1991) (where separate property is later retitled jointly, courts will use a "source of funds" or tracing method rather than simply assume a gift was made from one spouse to another; public policy favors a rule allowing courts to make equitable considerations regarding jointly titled property rather than one encouraging couples to keep their separate property isolated during the marriage in case of divorce).

presumed to be separate property, as long as they are traceable, whether or not they have been commingled.[5] Appreciation is separate property as long as the property is separate property and the increase is not due to the labor, monetary, or in kind contribution of either or both spouses that occurred during the marriage.[6] The burden of proof is on the party seeking to show that the appreciation was passive and therefore non-marital.[7] Compensation for personal injury is separate property unless attributable to expenses paid from marital funds, whether or not it has been commingled, if it is traceable.[8] Additionally, compensation for a non-compete provision in an employment contract settlement has been held to be separate property.[9] Severance payments paid during the marriage are marital property, however, a severance payment intended to compensate the spouse for future wages after the marriage has ended is separate property.[10] Any gift to a spouse, whether from the other spouse or from a third party, is presumed to be marital property, unless it can be proved otherwise by clear and convincing evidence.[11] If the elements of an inter vivos gift from one spouse to the other are met (an intent to donate the property to another, and delivery and relinquishment of control over the property by the donor to the donee), marital property may then be transmuted into a spouse's separate property.[12]

[5]RC 3105.171(A)(6)(a)(i) to (iii).

[6]See RC 3105.171(A)(3)(a)(iii); Middendorf v. Middendorf, 82 Ohio St. 3d 397, 1998-Ohio-403, 696 N.E.2d 575 (1998); Rothwell v. Rothwell, 2001 WL 502982 (Ohio Ct. App. 12th Dist. Warren County 2001) (when either spouse makes contributions causing an increased value in the fair market value of separate property, there must be evidence to show the labors caused the increase in value before it is deemed marital property; here, simply renting apartments was not sufficient to classify the increased value as marital property).

[7]Volk v. Volk, 2004-Ohio-1433, 2004 WL 573952 (Ohio Ct. App. 9th Dist. Summit County 2004).

[8]RC 3105.171(A)(6)(a)(vi).

[9]Gergacz v. Gergacz, 2000 WL 429613 (Ohio Ct. App. 1st Dist. Hamilton County 2000).

[10]McKenzie v. McKenzie, 2006-Ohio-6841, 2006 WL 3759837 (Ohio Ct. App. 2d Dist. Greene County 2006).

[11]RC 3105.171(A)(6)(a)(vii). This provision originated among proponents of the statute who feared that a parent who gave an asset to both parties during a marriage would testify otherwise when faced with the divorce of his or her offspring. The provision is a compromise between those who support the tenet that all gifts are separate property and those who believe that all gifts given during marriage should be marital property. Wilkinson v. Wilkinson, 2001-Ohio-3426, 2001 WL 1199046 (Ohio Ct. App. 7th Dist. Columbiana County 2001) (ten percent of husband's personal injury settlement represented compensation for the wife's loss of consortium and was therefore her separate property).

[12]See Helton v. Helton, 114 Ohio App. 3d 683, 685, N.E.2d 1157 (2d Dist. Montgomery County 1996); Fricke v. Martin-Fricke, 2001 WL 523946 (Ohio Ct. App. 2d Dist. Greene County 2001); Sweeney v. Sweeney, 2000 WL 799095 (Ohio Ct. App. 9th Dist. Summit County 2000); Snyder v. Snyder, 2000 WL 1876614 (Ohio Ct. App.

§ 4:23 Property rights upon divorce—RC 3105.171—Jurisdiction to divide

RC 3105.171(B) contains an express grant of jurisdiction to the domestic relations court to allocate both marital and separate property. However, once allocated, property settlements are final and the court does not have continuing jurisdiction to modify an award in the nature of a property settlement Thus, modification of a property division is expressly prohibited.[1]

RC 3105.171(C)(2) provides that each party must be considered to have contributed equally to the production and acquisition of marital assets.[2] The phrase "shall be considered to have contributed" may prove problematic, and this concept may be interpreted differently from court to court. The logical interpretation is, however, that the language creates a rebuttable presumption.

RC 3105.171(F) sets out ten factors which the court must consider in dividing property. The court must consider all ten factors, and these factors do not apply to an award of support, but apply only to a division of property.[3] Those ten factors are the following:

(1) The duration of the marriage;
(2) The assets and liabilities of the spouses;
(3) The desirability of awarding the family home, or the right to reside in the family home for reasonable periods of time, to the spouse with custody of the children of the marriage;
(4) The liquidity of the property to be distributed;
(5) The economic desirability of retaining intact an asset or an interest in an asset;
(6) The tax consequences of the property division upon the respective awards to be made to each spouse;
(7) The costs of sale, if it is necessary that an asset be sold to effectuate an equitable distribution of property;
(8) Any division or disbursement of property made in a separation agreement that was voluntarily entered into by the spouses;
(9) Any retirement benefits of the spouses, excluding the social security benefits of a spouse except as may be relevant for purposes of dividing a public pension;

11th Dist. Geauga County 2000); West v. West, 2002-Ohio-1118, 2002 WL 388845 (Ohio Ct. App. 9th Dist. Wayne County 2002).

[Section 4:23]

[1]Mettler v. Mettler, 61 Ohio App. 3d 14, 572 N.E.2d 127 (4th Dist. Ross County 1988); RC 3105.171(I).

[2]RC 3105.171(C)(3) specifies that a division of property shall be made prior to and without regard to any award of spousal support.

[3]Under RC 3105.18 prior to 1991, the court was required to consider all relevant factors, including the eleven factors set out therein. It was within the discretion of the trial court to apply any one of those factors as a criterion for support or for property division, as the court saw fit.

(10) Any other factor that the court expressly finds to be relevant and equitable.

Ten of the factors from the previous alimony statute were intentionally deleted, and six new factors were added. Both the current and previous statutes direct the court to consider all other relevant factors.

Although consideration of retirement benefits has been deleted from 3105.171(F), RC 3105.171(A)(3)(a) specifically refers to retirement benefits as part of the marital estate.[4] Also, inheritances as well as property brought into the marriage are now covered in the separate property section of RC 3105.171(A)(6)(a)(i) and (ii), respectively. There will be no monetary relief from a final judgment for which mutual mistake is asserted as a basis for the relief.[5] A QDRO must meet the terms of an agreement in a divorce decree[6] Additionally, the Ohio Supreme Court has ruled that a divorce decree that requires the filing of a QDRO, is a final appealable order before the QDRO is filed. The filing of the QDRO does not affect the orders set forth in the decree, rather it implements those orders.[7]

§ 4:24   Property rights upon divorce—RC 3105.18 spousal support—In general

RC 3105.18 defines "spousal support" as any payment(s) made to a spouse or former spouse, or to a third party for the benefit of a spouse or former spouse, that is both for the sustenance and support of the spouse or former spouse. The statute expressly provides that "spousal support" does not include any payment that is made as a division or distribution of property under RC 3105.171. Future business earnings used in a property division calculation cannot then be used to calculate spousal support.[1]

RC 3105.18(B) expressly grants the court of common pleas jurisdiction to award spousal support, but only after the court has first determined the division of property under RC 3105.171.

Unlike a division of property, a divorce decree may provide that the court of common pleas will retain jurisdiction to modify an award of spousal support upon the showing of a change in the circumstances of

---

[4]Neville v. Neville, 99 Ohio St. 3d 275, 2003-Ohio-3624, 791 N.E.2d 434 (2003).

[5]Senoyuit v. Senoyuit, 2008-Ohio-2003, 2008 WL 1849613 (Ohio Ct. App. 11th Dist. Trumbull County 2008), appeal not allowed, 119 Ohio St. 3d 1475, 2008-Ohio-4911, 894 N.E.2d 333 (2008).

[6]Kelley v. Kelley, 2005-Ohio-2355, 2005 WL 1131587 (Ohio Ct. App. 3d Dist. Defiance County 2005).

[7]Wilson v. Wilson, 116 Ohio St. 3d 268, 2007-Ohio-6056, 878 N.E.2d 16 (2007).

[Section 4:24]

[1]Heller v. Heller, 2008-Ohio-3296, 2008 WL 2588064 (Ohio Ct. App. 10th Dist. Franklin County 2008), appeal not allowed, 120 Ohio St. 3d 1421, 2008-Ohio-6166, 897 N.E.2d 654 (2008).

either party.[2] A change of circumstances of a party includes, but is not limited to, any increase or involuntary decrease in the party's wages, salary, bonuses, living expenses, or medical expenses.[3]

§ 4:25 Property rights upon divorce—RC 3105.18 spousal support—Factors for awarding

An award of spousal support must be both appropriate and reasonable. In determining whether spousal support is reasonable and the amount and terms of payment of spousal support, each party shall be considered to have contributed equally to the production of marital income.[1] Furthermore, the statute requires that the court shall consider all of the following fourteen factors:

(1)   The income of the parties, from all sources, including, but not limited to, income derived from property divided, disbursed, or distributed under RC 3105.171;

(2)   The relative earning abilities of the parties;

(3)   The ages and the physical, mental, and emotional conditions of the parties;

(4)   The retirement benefits of the parties;

(5)   The duration of the marriage;

(6)   The extent to which it would be inappropriate for a party, because he will be custodian of a minor child of the marriage, to seek employment outside the home;

(7)   The standard of living of the parties during the marriage:

(8)   The relative extent of education of the parties;

(9)   The relative assets and liabilities of the parties, including, but not limited to, any court-ordered payments by the parties;

(10) The contribution of each party to the education, training, or earning ability of the other party, including, but not limited to, any party's contribution to the acquisition of a professional degree of the other party;

(11) The time and expense necessary for the spouse who is seeking spousal support to acquire education, training, or job experience so that the spouse will be qualified to obtain appropriate employment, provided the education, training, or job experience, and employment is, in fact, sought;

(12) The tax consequences for each party of an award of spousal support;

(13) The lost income production capacity of either party that resulted from that party's marital responsibilities; and

---

[2]RC 3105.18(E).

[3]RC 3105.18(F).

[Section 4:25]

[1]RC 3105.18(C)(2).

(14) Any other factor that the court expressly finds relevant and equitable.[2]

When a trial court makes an award of spousal support, it must set forth in the judgment, with sufficient detail, the basis for the award so that the reviewing court can properly review the judgment.[3] Courts have held cohabitation as a factor in determining the spousal support award even though not specifically listed in RC 3105.18.[4]

§ 4:26 Property rights upon annulment

Marital property rights and the concomitant right to have the court make an equal or an equitable division do not arise where the marriage is annulled.[1]

§ 4:27 Common law intrafamily immunity abolished

Intrafamily immunity from suit existed at common law in certain cases. Neither spouse could be prosecuted for the larceny of the goods of the other.[1] Neither spouse could sue the other for injury sustained by the other's negligent acts. If, for example, a person had two passengers in an automobile, one of whom was the driver's spouse, and both were injured in an accident, Ohio permitted the third party to recover damages from the negligent driver, but the spouse could not recover damages. This rule existed in the case of negligent but not intentional acts.[2]

The interspousal immunity doctrine was based on the theory that permitting suits between family members would tend to disrupt family harmony or that there might be collusion to defraud an insurance company. The injured spouse had to look to the marital assets for compensation.[3] This immunity from suit also extended to the children who were barred from bringing suit against a parent.

Today, a husband and wife are treated as separate individuals. RC

---

[2]RC 3105.18(C)(1). See also Roach v. Roach, 61 Ohio App. 3d 315, 572 N.E.2d 772 (8th Dist. Cuyahoga County 1989).

[3]Schneider v. Schneider, 61 Ohio App. 3d 164, 572 N.E.2d 221 (6th Dist. Lucas County 1989).

[4]Yarnell v. Yarnell, 2006-Ohio-3929, 2006 WL 2141564 (Ohio Ct. App. 5th Dist. Delaware County 2006).

[Section 4:26]

[1]Liming v. Liming, 117 Ohio App. 3d 617, 691 N.E.2d 299 (4th Dist. Adams County 1996); see also Text Ch 7, Annulment.

[Section 4:27]

[1]State v. Phillips, 85 Ohio St. 317, 97 N.E. 976 (1912).

[2]Kobe v. Kobe, 61 Ohio App. 2d 67, 15 Ohio Op. 3d 86, 399 N.E.2d 124 (8th Dist. Cuyahoga County 1978); Green v. Green, 4 Ohio App. 3d 133, 446 N.E.2d 837 (6th Dist. Lucas County 1982).

[3]Lyons v. Lyons, 2 Ohio St. 2d 243, 31 Ohio Op. 2d 504, 208 N.E.2d 533 (1965) (overruling recognized by Shearer v. Shearer, 18 Ohio St. 3d 94, 480 N.E.2d 388 (1985)).

3103.08 states that "neither . . . is answerable for the acts of the other." Therefore, the husband is no longer answerable for his wife's negligent act,[4] unless an actual agency relationship was established between them with regard to the specific activity that resulted in an accident. Unless direct or circumstantial evidence can prove that a husband acted as the agent of his wife, she will not be liable for his negligent acts on her property, and vice versa.[5]

The Ohio Supreme Court, in a series of decisions beginning in 1984, has abrogated the common law concepts of interspousal tort immunity, parental tort immunity, and intrafamily tort immunity.[6] Each spouse is now free to sue the other for injuries resulting from their negligent and/or intentional conduct. They no longer need look to the marital assets for compensation. A child also has a right of action against his parent for injuries resulting from parental negligence or intentional misconduct. Parents may also sue their unemancipated minor children for negligence.[7]

A spouse's cause of action against his spouse for intentional infliction of emotional distress resulting from disclosure of their child's paternity should be considered independently from their divorce action.[8] It is inconsistent to combine the two, since a party to a divorce

---

[4]Damm v. Elyria Lodge No. 465, Benev. Protective Order of Elks, 158 Ohio St. 107, 48 Ohio Op. 54, 107 N.E.2d 337 (1952).

[5]Sowers v. Birkhead, 108 Ohio App. 507, 9 Ohio Op. 2d 491, 80 Ohio L. Abs. 84, 157 N.E.2d 459 (10th Dist. Franklin County 1958); Marks v. Robins, 23 Ohio L. Abs. 538, 1936 WL 2181 (Ct. App. 7th Dist. Mahoning County 1936); Bretzfelder v. Demaree, 102 Ohio St. 105, 130 N.E. 505 (1921) (although wife had permission to drive husband's car, he was not liable as principal for her negligence, absent showing that she acted at his direction or to benefit his business).

[6]Kirchner v. Crystal, 15 Ohio St. 3d 326, 474 N.E.2d 275 (1984) (parental tort immunity abolished; rationales underlying doctrine of parental immunity are outdated, highly questionable, and unpersuasive; doctrine of parental immunity abolished in toto: abolition of parental immunity as a public policy will provide the innocent victims of tortious conduct the forum they deserve in attempting to redress their claims; widespread availability of liability insurance from a variety of sources operates to eradicate any perceived problems which the absence of immunity may have presented); Shearer v. Shearer, 18 Ohio St. 3d 94, 480 N.E.2d 388 (1985) (interspousal tort immunity abolished; child also has a right of action against a parent for injuries resulting from negligence. "Interspousal immunity is a doctrine of the common law, a creation of the courts, not the legislature. . . . When feudal concepts of [the] marital entity evolve to the modern concept of the marital partnership, it is the court's duty to see that the law reflects the changing face of society."); Price v. Price, 19 Ohio App. 3d 245, 483 N.E.2d 1222 (9th Dist. Lorain County 1985) (when Court abolished doctrine of parental immunity without reservation in *Kirchner*, it also abolished corollary rule prohibiting a parent from prosecuting a tort action against his unemancipated minor child; in addition, holdings in *Kirchner* were given retroactive application).

[7]Price v. Price, 19 Ohio App. 3d 245, 483 N.E.2d 1222 (9th Dist. Lorain County 1985) (*Kirchner* applied retroactively to permit parents to sue emancipated children for negligence).

[8]Koepke v. Koepke, 52 Ohio App. 3d 47, 556 N.E.2d 1198 (6th Dist. Wood County 1989).

action cannot recover damages, which is the main objective of tort litigation.

Citing *Shearer v. Shearer*[9] and its holding that public policy does not bar interspousal torts, the Ninth District Court of Appeals upheld a husband's conviction for arson for burning his wife's automobile, even though the parties were married and living together at the time.[10]

An action for assault and battery must be brought within the one-year statute of limitations applicable to such torts,[11] but if the cause of action is alleged to be the intentional infliction of emotional distress, it is governed by a four-year statute of limitations.[12]

---

[9]Shearer v. Shearer, 18 Ohio St. 3d 94, 480 N.E.2d 388 (1985).

[10]State v. Regan, 51 Ohio App. 3d 214, 555 N.E.2d 987 (9th Dist. Wayne County 1988).

[11]RC 2305.111; Green v. Green, 4 Ohio App. 3d 133, 446 N.E.2d 837 (6th Dist. Lucas County 1982) (statute is not tolled during continuation of marriage).

[12]RC 2305.09(D); Steiner v. Steiner, 85 Ohio App. 3d 513, 620 N.E.2d 152 (4th Dist. Scioto County 1993).

Chapter 5

Domestic Violence

By Michael A. Partlow, Esq.[*]

KeyCite®: Cases and other legal materials listed in KeyCite Scope can be researched through the KeyCite service on Westlaw®. Use KeyCite to check citations for form, parallel references, prior and later history, and comprehensive citator information, including citations to other decisions and secondary materials.

---

§ 5:1   Nature and history

Domestic violence, especially in the form of spousal abuse, has existed for hundreds of years. At least until the late 1800s, male violent responses to familial problems were both "legally protected and

---

[*]Yan Liang and Darla Krapinski, research assistants for 2009 update.

socially condoned."[1] Until fairly recent times, only spouses could seek any sort of injunctive relief in conjunction with a divorce or legal separation proceeding in most jurisdictions.[2] As of 1990, approximately four million acts of domestic violence were estimated to occur against women on an annual basis.[3]

1978 H.B. 835, effective March 27, 1979, established the criminal offense of domestic violence[4] and a civil remedy for domestic violence as well.[5] Both of these statutes were broad departures from former statutory and common law, in that remedies were provided for those to whom any remedy had either been extremely elusive or totally unavailable in the past. Further, both statutes create provisions for support and maintenance which enable and encourage dependent victims to come forward. Since first established, both the civil and criminal provisions have been amended on numerous occasions to address specific problems which have arisen in prosecution of domestic violence actions and to expand the coverage of the statutes.

After the recent passage of the Marriage Amendment in the Ohio Constitution, there have been a few cases in which defendants have based arguments against being charged with domestic violence by claiming that the domestic violence statute is unconstitutional as being violative of the Amendment. Presumably, the same arguments would apply to the civil domestic violence statutes. In the Marriage Amendment, it is stated that "This state and its political subdivisions shall not create or recognize a legal status for relationships of unmarried individuals that intends to approximate the design, qualities, significance or effect of marriage."[6] In three of the cases on this topic, the argument has been rejected based upon the rational that the language in the Marriage Amendment was not intended to exclude unmarried co-habitants from being protected under the Domestic Violence statute.[7] However, in *State v. Burk*, the court held that the language in the Marriage Amendment and the Domestic Violence statute were not compatible without the clear meaning of either being distorted. This court reasoned that "the clear purpose of adding the second

---

[Section 5:1]

[1]*Legal Responses to Domestic Violence* 106 Harv. L. Rev. 1498, 1528 (1993).

[2]*Legal Responses to Domestic Violence* 106 Harv. L. Rev. 1498, 1528 (1993).

[3]*Legal Responses to Domestic Violence* 106 Harv. L. Rev. 1498, 1501 (1993), citing Women and Violence: *Hearings Before the Senate Comm. on the Judiciary*, 101st Cong., 2d Sess. 119 (1990) (testimony of Angela Browne, Ph.D.).

[4]RC 2919.25.

[5]RC 3113.31.

[6]O. Const. Art. XV § 11.

[7]State v. Rodgers, 131 Ohio Misc. 2d 1, 2005-Ohio-1730, 827 N.E.2d 872 (C.P. 2005); State v. Newell, 2005-Ohio-2848, 2005 WL 1364937 (Ohio Ct. App. 5th Dist. Stark County 2005); City of Cleveland v. Knipp, 2005 WL 1017620 (Ohio Mun. Ct. 2005).

sentence [in the amendment] is to restrict the legal recognition of other relationships between unmarried individuals."[8]

However, the Supreme Court of Ohio hearing this issue stated that RC 2919.25 merely identifies a particular class of persons for purposes of the domestic violence statute and, therefore, is not unconstitutional and does not create a quasi-marital relationship in violation of Section 11, Article XV of the Ohio Constitution. The Court reasoned that satisfying the "living as a spouse" category employed in the domestic violence statute provides no rights, duties, or benefits of marriage. It is simply a classification with relevance only to the domestic violence statute.

Yet, a dissent to the decision emphasizes that Section 11, Article XV prohibits a legal status that intends to approximate the design, qualities, significance, or effect of marriage. The dissent argues that under the domestic violence statute persons living as spouses do attain a legal status, in that each person may sue the other for domestic violence and this is a special status that, for example, unmarried roommates do not enjoy.[9]

The legislation is attempting to deal with this discrepancy by enacting amendments to RC 2919.25, 3113.31, and 3113.33 that are still pending. The new language, if eventually enacted, will modify the definition of a "family or household member" to include unmarried cohabitants that are not living as a spouse.[10] This would appear to be the legislature's response to allegations that being charged with domestic violence is unconstitutional according to the language in the Marriage Amendment if the defendant and victim are not legally married.

§ 5:2   Criminal domestic violence—Elements of the offense

RC 2919.25, the statute defining the criminal offense of domestic violence, provides, in part:

(A) No person shall knowingly cause or attempt to cause physical harm to a family or household member.

(B) No person shall recklessly cause serious physical harm to a family or household member.

(C) No person, by threat of force, shall knowingly cause a family or household member to believe that the offender will cause imminent physical harm to the family or household member.

RC 2919.25(E), defining "family or household member" and "person living as a spouse," provides:

(E) As used in this section and sections 2919.251 and 2919.26 of the Revised Code:

---

[8]State v. Burk, 2005 WL 786212 (Ohio C.P. 2005), judgment rev'd, 164 Ohio App. 3d 740, 2005-Ohio-6727, 843 N.E.2d 1254 (8th Dist. Cuyahoga County 2005), judgment aff'd, 114 Ohio St. 3d 430, 2007-Ohio-4552, 872 N.E.2d 1212 (2007).

[9]State v. Carswell, 114 Ohio St. 3d 210, 2007-Ohio-3723, 871 N.E.2d 547 (2007).

[10]See 2005 H.B. 161.

(1) "Family or household member" means any of the following:

(a) Any of the following who is residing or has resided with the offender:

(i) A spouse, a person living as a spouse, or a former spouse of the offender;

(ii) A parent or a child of the offender, or another person related by consanguinity or affinity to the offender.

(iii) A parent or a child of a spouse, person living as a spouse, or former spouse of the offender, or another person related by consanguinity or affinity to a spouse, person living as a spouse, or former spouse of the offender;

(b) The natural parent of any child of whom the offender is the other natural parent or is the putative other natural parent.

(2) "Person living as a spouse" means a person who is living or has lived with the offender in a common law marital relationship, who otherwise is cohabiting with the offender, or who otherwise has cohabited with the offender within five years prior to the date of the alleged commission of the act in question.[1]

In order to sustain a conviction pursuant to RC 2919.25(A), proof beyond a reasonable doubt must indicate that the accused either caused or attempted to cause "physical harm" to the victim. Pursuant to RC 2901.01(A)(3), "physical harm" has been defined as "any injury, illness, or other physiological impairment, regardless of its gravity or duration" and this definition has been employed for purposes of the criminal domestic violence statute.[2] The term "injury" has been defined as an "invasion of any legally protected interest of another."[3]

Conviction for a violation of RC 2919.25(A) also requires proof that the accused acted "knowingly." RC 2901.22(B) defines the culpable mental state of "knowingly" and provides:

A person acts knowingly, regardless of his purpose, when he is aware that his conduct will probably cause a certain result or will probably be of a certain nature. A person has knowledge of circumstances when he is aware that such circumstances probably exist.

In addition RC 2901.22(B) requires, the evidence must not only show that the defendant acted "knowingly", but also that defendant was subjectively aware that a specified result was probable.[4] Unlike the provisions contained in RC 2919.25(C), the requirement that the

---

[Section 5:2]

[1]RC 2919.25(E), as amended by 1994 H.B. 335, eff. 12-9-94, 1995 S.B. 2, eff. 7-1-96, and 1997 S.B. 1, eff. 10-21-97.

[2]State v. Mills, 1997 WL 133430 (Ohio Ct. App. 1st Dist. Hamilton County 1997).

[3]State v. Mills, 1997 WL 133430 (Ohio Ct. App. 1st Dist. Hamilton County 1997) (citing State v. Suchomski, 58 Ohio St. 3d 74, 567 N.E.2d 1304 (1991)).

[4]State v. Berry, 2007-Ohio-7082, 2007 WL 4554948 (Ohio Ct. App. 12th Dist. Warren County 2007).

perpetrator act "knowingly" contained in section (A) focuses upon the mind-set of the perpetrator as opposed to the perception of the victim.[5]

Unlike RC 2919.25(A), section (B) requires that the offender actually succeed in causing "*serious* physical harm to a family or household member." Emphasis added. This section contains no prohibition against a mere "attempt" to cause harm. Further, evidence beyond a reasonable doubt must be presented to establish that the offender acted "recklessly." This culpable mental state is defined in RC 2901.22(C), which provides:

> A person acts recklessly when, with heedless indifference to the consequences, he perversely disregards a known risk that his conduct is likely to cause a certain result or is likely to be of a certain nature. A person is reckless with respect to circumstances when, with heedless indifference to the consequences, he perversely disregards a known risk that such circumstances are likely to exist.

Perhaps the most perplexing provision contained in RC 2919.25 is the prohibition against causing a family or household member "to believe" that physical harm is imminent by virtue of a "threat of force."[6] This is due to the fact that the evidence necessary to prove a violation of this section beyond a reasonable doubt requires a journey into the mind of the victim to establish "a reasonable belief by the victim that the accused will cause imminent physical harm."[7] In determining the reasonableness of the victim's belief of imminent physical harm, evidence of a defendant's prior acts of violence may be admissible.[8] At least one Ohio appellate court has defined "imminent" for purposes of the criminal domestic violence statute as "threatening to occur immediately."[9]

Pursuant to the test established in *State v. Deem*,[10] none of the sections contained in RC 2919.25 appear to be lesser included offenses of one another. At least one reviewing court has specifically recognized that RC 2919.25(C) is not a lesser included offense of RC 2919.25(A).[11] Since RC 2919.25(A) and RC 2919.25(B) are both first degree misdemeanors,[12] it also appears that neither of these sections is a lesser

---

[5]State v. Robinette, 1997 WL 88926 (4th Dist. Ct. App., Jackson, 2-26-97).

[6]RC 2919.25(C).

[7]State v. Taylor, 79 Ohio Misc. 2d 82, 85, 671 N.E.2d 343 (Mun. Ct. 1996). See also State v. Collie, 108 Ohio App. 3d 580, 671 N.E.2d 338 (1st Dist. Hamilton County 1996).

[8]State v. Collie, 108 Ohio App. 3d 580, 671 N.E.2d 338 (1st Dist. Hamilton County 1996).

[9]State v. Collie, 108 Ohio App. 3d 580, 583, 671 N.E.2d 338 (1st Dist. Hamilton County 1996).

[10]State v. Deem, 40 Ohio St. 3d 205, 533 N.E.2d 294 (1988) (holding modified by, State v. Smith, 117 Ohio St. 3d 447, 2008-Ohio-1260, 884 N.E.2d 595 (2008)).

[11]State v. Corrill, 133 Ohio App. 3d 550, 729 N.E.2d 403 (12th Dist. Butler County 1999).

[12]See Text § 5:4, Criminal domestic violence—Sentencing.

included offense of the other as they both carry the same potential penalty.[13]

Although the language of the statute provides a definition of "family or household member" which includes a rather wide range of potential victims, a great deal of litigation has occurred concerning this issue. At least one Ohio court has concluded that the offender need not have actually resided with the "family or household member" at any time after the enactment of the statute.[14] In the past, Ohio authority supported the preposition that RC 2919.25 is applicable to same sex couples.[15] However, since the Defense of Marriage Amendment was passed, the application of RC 2919.25 to cohabiting homosexual couples becomes more difficult to anticipate. The actual intent of the Amendment was to recognize a marriage only between one man and one woman. As a result of this, some courts out of the Third District have refused to apply RC 2919.25 to unmarried, heterosexual couples.[16] However, other courts outside of this district will allow a relationship of cohabiting individuals to be recognized for purposes of the domestic violence statute.[17] Due to the inconsistencies that exist, it is difficult to say whether or not a court will recognize a relationship for purposes of the domestic violence statute for same sex cohabitants.

Another Ohio reviewing court has determined that a foster parent does not qualify as a "parent" for purposes of prosecution under RC 2919.25.[18] This opinion appears to be consistent with other authority which indicates that the mere fact that a victim may be or have been in a "loco parentis" relationship with the perpetrator is insufficient to

---

[13]See State v. Deem, 40 Ohio St. 3d 205, 533 N.E.2d 294 (1988) (holding modified by, State v. Smith, 117 Ohio St. 3d 447, 2008-Ohio-1260, 884 N.E.2d 595 (2008)).

[14]State v. Mrus, 71 Ohio App. 3d 828, 595 N.E.2d 460 (11th Dist. Trumbull County 1991) (overruled by, State v. James, 1997 WL 269139 (Ohio Ct. App. 11th Dist. Portage County 1997)) and (overruled by, State v. Fleming, 1997 WL 269141 (Ohio Ct. App. 11th Dist. Portage County 1997)) and (abrogated by, State v. Uher, 1997 WL 269407 (Ohio Ct. App. 11th Dist. Portage County 1997)) and (abrogated by, State v. Wyand, 1997 WL 269143 (Ohio Ct. App. 11th Dist. Portage County 1997)) and (overruled by, State v. Musick, 119 Ohio App. 3d 361, 695 N.E.2d 317 (11th Dist. Portage County 1997)).

[15]State v. Linner, 77 Ohio Misc. 2d 22, 665 N.E.2d 1180 (Mun. Ct. 1996); State v. Yaden, 1997 WL 106343 (1st Dist. Ct. App., Hamilton, 3-5-97); State v. Hadinger, 61 Ohio App. 3d 820, 573 N.E.2d 1191 (10th Dist. Franklin County 1991).

[16]State v. McKinley, 2006-Ohio-2507, 2006 WL 1381635 (Ohio Ct. App. 3d Dist. Logan County 2006), judgment rev'd, 114 Ohio St. 3d 430, 2007-Ohio-4552, 872 N.E.2d 1212 (2007); State v. Shaffer, 2006-Ohio-2662, 2006 WL 1459769 (Ohio Ct. App. 3d Dist. Union County 2006), judgment rev'd, 114 Ohio St. 3d 430, 2007-Ohio-4552, 872 N.E.2d 1212 (2007).

[17]State v. Rodriguez, 2006-Ohio-3378, 2006 WL 1793688 (Ohio Ct. App. 6th Dist. Huron County 2006), judgment aff'd, 114 Ohio St. 3d 430, 2007-Ohio-4552, 872 N.E.2d 1212 (2007).

[18]In Matter of Whitley, 1996 WL 488806 (Ohio Ct. App. 5th Dist. Stark County 1996).

satisfy the statutory definition of family or household member.[19] Ohio law does permit an affirmative defense to a criminal domestic violence charge if the evidence indicates that the perpetrator was merely employing "reasonable parental discipline," even if the child suffers some form of injury.[20]

In September 1997, the Ohio Supreme Court clarified the definition of "cohabiting" as the term is used in RC 2919.25(E)(2).[21] The Court concluded that a person is a "cohabitant" and, therefore, a "family or household member" if the following essential elements are shown: (1) "sharing of familial or financial responsibilities," and (2) "consortium."[22] The question of whether an offender is a "cohabitant" is to be made "on a case-by-case basis."[23] While it is difficult to determine how far this definition of cohabitation will be extended, it is noteworthy that the Ohio Supreme Court relied upon a variety of common law cases from both Ohio and elsewhere in establishing this definition of cohabitation. As a result of the Defense of Marriage Amendment, courts are split on whether they can recognize a relationship between heterosexual cohabiting couples under RC 2919.25. Courts from the Fourth, Fifth, Sixth, Seventh, Eighth, Ninth, Tenth and Twelfth Districts have said that a relationship under the criminal statute can still be recognized regardless of the Amendment.[24] One court in the Fifth District went so far as to say that the Defense of Marriage Amendment has no application to criminal statutes in gen-

---

[19]State v. Harris, 109 Ohio App. 3d 873, 673 N.E.2d 237 (1st Dist. Hamilton County 1996). See also State v. Rhodes, 2005-Ohio-2293, 2005 WL 1109693 (Ohio Ct. App. 10th Dist. Franklin County 2005).

[20]State v. Hicks, 88 Ohio App. 3d 515, 624 N.E.2d 332 (10th Dist. Franklin County 1993); State v. Hart, 110 Ohio App. 3d 250, 673 N.E.2d 992 (3d Dist. Defiance County 1996); accord State v. Suchomski, 58 Ohio St. 3d 74, 567 N.E.2d 1304 (1991).

[21]State v. Williams, 79 Ohio St. 3d 459, 1997-Ohio-79, 683 N.E.2d 1126 (1997).

[22]State v. Williams, 79 Ohio St. 3d 459, 465, 1997-Ohio-79, 683 N.E.2d 1126 (1997). Cf. State v. Toles, 1999 WL 1232092 (Ohio Ct. App. 4th Dist. Gallia County 1999).

[23]State v. Williams, 79 Ohio St. 3d 459, 465, 1997-Ohio-79, 683 N.E.2d 1126 (1997).

[24]State v. Goshorn, 2006-Ohio-2755, 2006 WL 1495256 (Ohio Ct. App. 4th Dist. Ross County 2006); State v. Adams, 2005-Ohio-6333, 2005 WL 3196850 (Ohio Ct. App. 5th Dist. Stark County 2005); State v. Rodriguez, 2006-Ohio-3378, 2006 WL 1793688 (Ohio Ct. App. 6th Dist. Huron County 2006), judgment aff'd, 114 Ohio St. 3d 430, 2007-Ohio-4552, 872 N.E.2d 1212 (2007); State v. McClaslin, 2006 WL 459621 (Ohio Ct. App. 7th Dist. Columbiana County 2006); State v. Douglas, 2006-Ohio-2343, 2006 WL 1304860 (Ohio Ct. App. 8th Dist. Cuyahoga County 2006), judgment aff'd, 114 Ohio St. 3d 430, 2007-Ohio-4552, 872 N.E.2d 1212 (2007); State v. Nixon, 165 Ohio App. 3d 178, 2006-Ohio-72, 845 N.E.2d 544 (9th Dist. Summit County 2006); State v. Rodgers, 166 Ohio App. 3d 218, 2006-Ohio-1528, 850 N.E.2d 90 (10th Dist. Franklin County 2006); State v. Carswell, 2005-Ohio-6547, 2005 WL 3358882 (Ohio Ct. App. 12th Dist. Warren County 2005), judgment aff'd, 114 Ohio St. 3d 210, 2007-Ohio-3723, 871 N.E.2d 547 (2007).

eral, RC 2919.25 included.[25] Although so many districts have held
that RC 2919.25 is Constitutional even under the Defense of Marriage
Amendment, the Second and Third Districts have consistently held
that application of RC 2919.25 to unmarried cohabiting couples would
be unconstitutional.[26] So, where the lawsuit is brought will weigh
heavily on the outcome of the case. Conceivably, this could impact
upon totally unrelated areas, such as post-decree termination of
spousal support based upon cohabitation. However, courts appear to
disagree in that regard.[27]

§ 5:3 Criminal domestic violence—Practice and procedure

As a practical matter, many domestic violence prosecutions are initiated either by the victim or by another family or household member
executing a complaint alleging that the accused committed the crime
of domestic violence.[1] Additionally, police officers have been granted
expanded authority to arrest in response to domestic violence calls.
The peace officer need only have "reasonable ground to believe" that
the offense of domestic violence has been committed.[2] Such reasonable
grounds exist where a written statement is executed either by the
victim of the alleged domestic violence or by a parent of the alleged
victim indicating that the accused has committed domestic violence
against the victim.[3] Reasonable grounds for arrest also exist where
the arresting officer's "own knowledge and observation of the facts
and circumstances" indicate that the offense has been committed.[4]
Obviously, a police officer may arrest anyone whom the officer actually
witnesses committing domestic violence.[5] In fact, arrest of the
perpetrator is "the preferred course of action in this state" if any of

---

[25]State v. Edwards, 2005-Ohio-7064, 2005 WL 3642716 (Ohio Ct. App. 5th Dist.
Stark County 2005).

[26]State v. Hill, 2006-Ohio-1811, 2006 WL 925176 (Ohio Ct. App. 2d Dist.
Montgomery County 2006); State v. Logsdon, 2006-Ohio-2938, 2006 WL 1585447
(Ohio Ct. App. 3d Dist. Seneca County 2006), judgment rev'd, 114 Ohio St. 3d 430,
2007-Ohio-4552, 872 N.E.2d 1212 (2007); State v. McIntosh, 2006-Ohio-1815, 2006
WL 925179 (Ohio Ct. App. 2d Dist. Montgomery County 2006), judgment rev'd, 114
Ohio St. 3d 430, 2007-Ohio-4552, 872 N.E.2d 1212 (2007); State v. Steineman,
2006-Ohio-1818, 2006 WL 925166 (Ohio Ct. App. 2d Dist. Greene County 2006); State
v. Ward, 166 Ohio App. 3d 188, 2006-Ohio-1407, 849 N.E.2d 1076 (2d Dist. Greene
County 2006), judgment rev'd, 114 Ohio St. 3d 430, 2007-Ohio-4552, 872 N.E.2d 1212
(2007).

[27]Compare Thurston v. Thurston, 2000 WL 423987 (Ohio Ct. App. 10th Dist.
Franklin County 2000) with Schmidt v. Schmidt, 2000 WL 1867396 (Ohio Ct. App.
8th Dist. Cuyahoga County 2000).

[Section 5:3]

[1]See Crim. R. 3.

[2]RC 2935.03(B)(1).

[3]RC 2935.03(B)(3)(a)(i).

[4]RC 2935.03(B)(3)(a)(ii).

[5]RC 2935.03(B)(3)(a)(iii).

the bases for reasonable grounds for belief exist, and a peace officer must file a report if an arrest is not made under these circumstances.[6]

After a criminal complaint alleging domestic violence has been filed, the Revised Code provides that a "temporary protection order" (TPO) may be sought.[7] A motion for a TPO may be filed either by the complainant or by "a person who made an arrest for the alleged violation," if the complainant is unable to file in an emergency situation.[8] The clerk of court in the jurisdiction in which the complaint was filed must accept the motion and, further, provide a sample form for the motion that substantially complies with the form set forth in the statute.[9] The Code also provides that the court issue a TPO, sua sponte, in the event that the court finds that it is necessary for the "safety and protection" of the victim.[10]

A trial court must address a motion for a TPO within 24 hours after it is filed, and conduct a hearing to determine whether to issue the protection order.[11] The person seeking the TPO must appear or, if that person is unable to do so due to physical impairment resulting from the alleged domestic violence, another may appear on the complainant's behalf, so long as the alternate person is able to provide the trial court with sufficient information upon which to base its decision.[12]

The Code is clear that a TPO may be issued as a pretrial condition of release which is in addition to, and not as part of, bail under Criminal Rule 46.[13] Further, the statute specifically provides that once a TPO is issued, the defendant and victim cannot waive or nullify its terms by agreement.[14]

Ohio trial courts are given discretion as to the precise terms of a TPO. A non-exhaustive list of potential terms includes a prohibition against the accused from "entering the residence, school, business, or place of employment" of the victim or complainant.[15] A TPO will only remain effective as long as the criminal proceeding is pending and any disposition of such automatically renders the TPO ineffective.[16] The fact that a trial court issues a TPO does not constitute a finding that the accused committed domestic violence, and may not be

---

[6]See RC 2935.03(B)(3)(b) et seq.

[7]RC 2919.26.

[8]RC 2919.26(A)(1).

[9]RC 2919.26(B).

[10]RC 2919.26(D)(1).

[11]RC 2919.26(C).

[12]RC 2919.26(C).

[13]See RC 2919.26(D)(1), RC 2919.26(E)(1).

[14]RC 2919.26(C)(2)(a).

[15]RC 2919.26(C). See Sup. R. 10, 10.01, 10.02.

[16]See RC 2919.26(E)(2).

introduced as evidence against the accused at trial.[17] Further, in order to issue a temporary protection order, the State must "demonstrate the due process requirements of statute RC 2919.26 were complied with the issuance of the temporary protection order."[18] This is a pre-requisite to a defendant being convicted of violating such an order.

A trial court is permitted to issue a TPO on an ex parte basis. However, if it does so, it must then conduct a hearing in the presence of the accused "as soon as possible after the issuance of the order."[19] At the hearing, the trial court will determine whether the TPO should remain in effect, or be modified or revoked.[20]

A trial court is also permitted, under certain circumstances, to issue a TPO directed at the "complainant or another family or household member of the defendant."[21] However, a trial court may only issue such an order if two conditions are met. First, the accused in the underlying criminal domestic violence proceeding must file a separate complaint against the complainant or the other family or household member.[22] Second, the trial court must determine that *both* the accused and the perpetrator alleged in the complaint filed by the accused "acted primarily as aggressors" and neither "acted primarily in self-defense."[23]

Another preliminary issue which must be addressed in any criminal proceeding is the subject of pre-trial bail. While most Domestic Violence cases involve misdemeanor charges, a personal appearance will be required before bail can be established if one of the following apply:

(1) At the time of the offense, the accused was already subject to a TPO or a CPO;

(2) The accused has already been convicted of a Domestic Violence charge or related crime;

(3) The accused has already been convicted for violating a TPO or a CPO;

(4) The accused has already been convicted of one of several other offenses established by statute and the victim of the offense was a family or household member; or

(5) The arresting officer indicates in the police report that he either

    (a) Observed the objective manifestations of physical harm to the victim that the arresting officer reasonably believed to be a result of the offense

---

[17]RC 2919.26(E)(3).

[18]State v. Mohabir, 2005-Ohio-78, 2005 WL 66484 (Ohio Ct. App. 5th Dist. Fairfield County 2005).

[19]RC 2919.26(D)(2).

[20]RC 2919.26(D)(2).

[21]RC 2919.26(I)(2).

[22]RC 2919.26(I)(2)(a).

[23]RC 2919.26(I)(2)(b).

   (b) Reasonably relieved that the offender possessed a deadly
      weapon or dangerous ordinance on his or her person at the
      time of the offense, or
   (c) Reasonably believed that the offender presents a credible
      threat of serious physical harm to the victim or any other
      person.[24]

A common problem after a TPO has been issued involves situations
where the victim, or other person protected by the TPO, has a change
of heart and does not wish for the TPO to be enforced. Such circumstances can result in the victim actually inviting the respondent to
violate the terms of the TPO. While this may prove frustrating for
courts and law enforcement officials, in *State v. Lucas*,[25] the Supreme
Court of Ohio specifically held that a person "who is the protected
subject of a temporary protection order may not be prosecuted for aid-
ing and abetting the restrainee under the protection order in violating
said order." The same analysis would apply in the context of a CPO.[26]

Presumably, the affirmative defense of "self-defense" would apply to
a criminal domestic violence charge.[27] At least one reviewing court has
held that the affirmative defense of "defense of others" could apply if
supported by the evidence.[28] Additionally, the law recognizes the right
of a parent to administer reasonable corporal punishment.[29] However,
corporal punishment in a domestic violence proceeding is only an affirmative defense if the child/victim is under eighteen years of age and
not suffering from a mental or physical handicap.[30]

Practitioners should be aware that these statutes have been
amended on several occasions, and carefully evaluate holdings in any
older cases prior to citing the cases in a pending proceeding. In 1992,
RC 2919.26 et seq. were amended to include "stalking"[31] and "aggravated trespass"[32] violations as both a basis for the issuance of a
TPO and a basis for finding a violation of a TPO previously issued.[33]
The statute was also extensively amended in 1994, including both
substantive changes and renumbering certain existing provisions.[34]
Substantive changes to RC 2919.26 include:

---

[24]RC 2919.251.

[25]State v. Lucas, 100 Ohio St. 3d 1, syl., 2003-Ohio-4778, 795 N.E.2d 642 (2003).

[26]State v. Youngpeter, 2005-Ohio-329, 2005 WL 196754 (Ohio Ct. App. 3d Dist.
Van Wert County 2005)

[27]See State v. Maine, 2005-Ohio-3742, 2005 WL 1713371 (Ohio Ct. App. 4th Dist.
Washington County 2005).

[28]State v. Sochor, 1999 WL 547927 (Ohio Ct. App. 5th Dist. Stark County 1999).

[29]State v. Suchomski, 58 Ohio St. 3d 74, 567 N.E.2d 1304 (1991).

[30]See State v. Miller, 134 Ohio App. 3d 649, 731 N.E.2d 1192 (1st Dist. Hamilton
County 1999).

[31]RC 2903.211.

[32]RC 2911.211.

[33]1992 H.B. 536, eff. 11-5-92.

[34]1994 H.B. 335, eff. 12-9-94.

(1) Addition of language to former RC 2919.26(A), now known as RC 2919.26(A)(1), and to RC 2919.26(D)(1) to include "a violation of a municipal ordinance substantially similar to" the other Revised Code sections cited in the statute as a basis for both the issuance of a TPO and a finding of a violation of a TPO previously issued;

(2) Addition of a new section, RC 2919.26(A)(2), which clarifies that all stages of a proceeding brought pursuant to section RC 2919.26(A)(1) are "critical stages" and provides that a "complainant" may be "accompanied by a victim advocate" at any hearings arising from the complaint;

(3) Substitution of a new form for a motion for a TPO, RC 2919.26(B), which is designed to accommodate the substantive changes made to the statute;

(4) Addition of new language to former RC 2919.26(C) which permits "another person who is able to provide the court with the information it requests" to appear on behalf of the complainant at the initial hearing on the motion for a TPO if the court finds that the complainant's failure to appear is due to the complainant's "hospitalization or medical condition resulting from the offense alleged in the complaint";

(5) Changes to RC 2919.26(D)(2) to require that a hearing be conducted "not later than the next day on which the court is scheduled to conduct business after the day on which the alleged offender was arrested or at the time of the appearance of the alleged offender pursuant to summons" if a TPO has been issued on an ex parte basis. Formerly, the statute required a hearing within 24 hours of the issuance of an ex parte TPO;

(6) Complete revision of RC 2919.26(G)(3) which now: (1) provides for registering a TPO in a county other than the county in which the order is issued; and (2) permits law enforcement agencies in counties other than that in which a TPO has been issued to enforce the TPO, regardless of whether the TPO has actually been registered in the other county;

(7) Complete revision of RC 2919.26(I) which now defines the term "defendant" and contains provisions which strictly control when a TPO may be issued against the complainant in addition to the defendant; and

(8) Addition of RC 2919.26(K) which defines "victim advocate" as "a person who provides support and assistance for a victim of an offense during court proceedings."

In 1997, various sections were amended in order to clarify that a TPO issued by a municipal court has continuing effect even if an accused is subsequently bound over to a common pleas court for felony prosecution.[35]

Prior to the Ohio Supreme Court's ruling in *State v. Busch*,[36] appellate courts had held that a trial court did not have the authority to dismiss a domestic violence charge against a defendant upon the request of the prosecuting witness when the prosecuting attorney objected to the dismissal and indicated that the state was prepared to proceed.[37] The prosecuting witness is not a party, just a witness. A contrary ruling existed from the Eighth Appellate District.[38]

Crim. R. 48(B) requires a court to state its reasons for a dismissal over objection by the state. Thus, the Supreme Court in *Busch* reasoned that a trial court necessarily has the inherent power to dismiss a prosecution if it serves the interests of justice. In exercising its discretion in dismissing the case, the trial court must consider "[t]he seriousness of the injuries, the presence of independent witnesses, the status of counseling efforts, whether the complainants's refusal to testify is coerced, and whether the defendant is a first-time offender."[39]

Effective October 21, 1997, Ohio courts are authorized to enforce a protection order that has been issued by a court in another state.[40] However, it is an affirmative defense to a charge for violation of such an order that the order fails to comply with 18 U.S.C.A. § 2265(b).[41] Protection orders from other states may also be registered with Ohio authorities.[42]

§ 5:4 Criminal domestic violence—Sentencing

The potential sentence a defendant in a criminal domestic violence action faces depends upon precisely which section the defendant was charged with violating. RC 2919.25(D), as amended effective April 7, 2009, provides:

> (D)(1) Whoever violates this section is guilty of domestic violence, and the court shall sentence the offender as provided in divisions (D)(2) to (6) of this section.
> (2) Except as otherwise provided in division (D)(3) to (5) of this section, a violation of division (C) of this section is a misdemeanor of the fourth degree, and a violation of division (A) or (B) of this section is a misdemeanor of the first degree.

---

[35]See RC 2919.26(D)(4), RC 2919.26(E)(2), RC 2919.26(G)(1).

[36]State v. Busch, 76 Ohio St. 3d 613, 1996-Ohio-82, 669 N.E.2d 1125 (1996).

[37]See State v. Wise, 99 Ohio App. 3d 239, 650 N.E.2d 191 (10th Dist. Franklin County 1994).

[38]City of Cleveland v. Hall, 1983 WL 5829 (Ohio Ct. App. 8th Dist. Cuyahoga County 1983).

[39]State v. Busch, 76 Ohio St. 3d 613, 616, 1996-Ohio-82, 669 N.E.2d 1125 (1996).

[40]RC 2919.27(A)(3).

[41]RC 2919.27(C).

[42]RC 2919.272, RC 3113.31(N)(1).

(3) Except as otherwise provided in division (D)(4) of this section, if the offender previously has pleaded guilty to or been convicted of domestic violence, a violation of an existing or former municipal ordinance or law of this or any other state or the United States that is substantially similar to domestic violence, a violation of section 2903.14, 2909.06, 2909.07, 2911.12, 2911.211, or 2919.22 of the Revised Code if the victim of the violation was a family or household member at the time of the violation, a violation of an existing or former municipal ordinance or law of this or any other state or the United States that is substantially similar to any of those sections if the victim of the violation was a family or household member at the time of the commission of the violation, or any offense of violence if the victim of the offense was a family or household member at the time of the commission of the offense, a violation of division (A) or (B) of this section is a felony of the fourth degree, and, if the offender knew that the victim of the violation was pregnant at the time of the violation, the court shall impose a mandatory prison term on the offender pursuant to division (A)(6) of this section, and a violation of division (C) of this section is a misdemeanor of the second degree.

(4) If the offender previously has pleaded guilty to or been convicted of two or more offenses of domestic violence or two or more violations or offenses of the type described in division (D)(3) of this section involving a person who was a family or household member at the time of the violations or offenses, a violation of division (A) or (B) of this section is a felony of the third degree, and, if the offender knew that the victim of the violation was pregnant at the time of the violation, the court shall impose a mandatory prison term on the offender pursuant to division (A)(6) of this section, and a violation of division (C) of this section is a misdemeanor of the first degree.

(5) Except as otherwise provided in division (D)(3) or (4) of this section, if the offender knew that the victim of the violation was pregnant at the time of the violation, a violation of division (A) or (B) of this section is a felony of the fifth degree, and the court shall impose a mandatory prison term on the offender pursuant to division (A)(6) of this section, and a violation of division (C) of this section is a misdemeanor of the third degree.

(6) If division (A)(3), (4), or (5) of this section requires the court that sentences an offender for a violation of division (A) or (B) of this section to impose a mandatory prison term on the offender pursuant to this division, the court shall impose the mandatory prison term as follows:

(a) If the violation of division (A) or (B) of this section is a felony of the fourth or fifth degree, except as otherwise provided in division (A)(6)(b) or (c) of this section, the court shall impose a mandatory prison on the offender of at least six months.

(b) If the violation of division (A) or (B) of this section is a felony of the fifth degree and the offender, in committing the violation, caused serious physical harm to the pregnant woman's unborn or caused the termination of the pregnant woman's pregnancy, the court shall impose a mandatory prison term on the offender of twelve months.

(c) If the violation of division (A) or (B) of this section is a felony of the fourth degree and the offender, in committing the violation, caused serious physical harm to the pregnant woman's unborn or caused the termination of the pregnant woman's pregnancy, the court shall impose a mandatory prison term on the offender of at least twelve months.

(d) If the violation of division (A) or (B) of this section is a felony of the third degree, except as otherwise provided in division (A)(6)(e) of this section and notwithstanding the range of prison terms prescribed in section 2929.14 of the Revised Code for a felony of the third degree, the court shall impose a mandatory prison term on the offender of either a definite term of six months or one of the prison terms prescribed in section 2929.14 of the Revised Code for felonies of the third degree.

(e) If the violation of division (A) or (B) of this section is a felony of the third degree and the offender, in committing the violation, caused serious physical harm to the pregnant woman's unborn or caused the termination of the pregnant woman's pregnancy, notwithstanding the range of prison terms prescribed in section 2929.14 of the Revised Code for a felony of the third degree, the court shall impose a mandatory prison term on the offender of either a definite term of one year or one of the prison terms prescribed in section 2929.14 of the Revised Code for felonies of the third degree.

Violation of RC 2919.25(C), being a misdemeanor of the fourth degree, results in the least serious potential penalty. An accused who is convicted of violating this section may be incarcerated for a definite term of no more than thirty days and may be fined no more than $250, plus court costs.[1] Violations of either division (A) or (B) of RC 2919.25, being first degree misdemeanors, may result in much more serious sanctions being imposed. The defendant may be incarcerated for a definite term of up to six months and fined a maximum of $1,000, along with court costs.[2] If the defendant has previously been convicted of either domestic violence, felonious assault, aggravated assault, negligent assault, aggravated menacing, menacing by stalking, menacing, aggravated trespass, or endangering children, or any substantially similar municipal ordinance, then a subsequent conviction is enhanced by one degree. Thus, violations of sections (A) or (B) of RC 2919.25 become felonies of the fourth degree. The defendant may then be sentenced to a definite term of incarceration of either 6, 7, 8, 9, 10, 11, 12, 13, 14, 15, 16, 17, or 18 months and fined up to $5,000, along with court costs.[3] A prior conviction elevates a violation of RC 2919.25(C) to a second degree misdemeanor. The defendant may be sentenced to a definite term of incarceration of no more than ninety days and fined no more than $750, plus court costs.[4]

A new Section (4) has been added to RC 2919.25(D) which provides for further elevation if the offender has previously been convicted of two or more offenses of either domestic violence or the other statutorily defined related offenses. Under these new provisions, a violation of division (A) or (B) becomes a felony of the third degree and a violation of division (C) becomes a misdemeanor of the first degree. A felony of the third degree is punishable by a definite term of incarceration of 1,

---

[Section 5:4]

[1]RC 2929.21(B)(4); RC 2929.21(C)(4).

[2]RC 2929.21(B)(1); RC 2929.21(C)(1).

[3]RC 2929.14(A)(5); RC 2929.18(A)(3)(e).

[4]RC 2929.21(B)(3); RC 2929.21(C)(3).

2, 3, 4, or 5 years and a maximum fine of $15,000. A misdemeanor of the first degree is punishable by a definite term of incarceration of not more than six months and a maximum fine of $1,000. While the enhancement provisions of the statute are desirable as a deterrent for future acts, there is no actual requirement that they be employed in a given case.[5]

Effective April 7, 2009, penalties have been enhanced based upon knowledge by the offender that the victim was pregnant at the time of the offense.

While a trial court has discretion in establishing terms of probation after an offender has been convicted, this discretion is not unbridled. Generally, probation terms must: 1) reasonably relate to rehabilitating the offender; 2) have some relationship to the offense in question; and 3) relate to conduct which is either criminal or reasonably related to future criminal conduct and serves the ends of probation established by statute.[6] Hence, while a trial court may order that the offender have no contact with the victim involved, a trial court has been held to have abused its discretion by ordering that an offender have no contact with his children where the children were not victims of domestic violence.[7] Further, a trial court may not order a change of title to property as a condition of probation.[8] Effective April 7, 2009, electronic monitoring of the offender for a period not to exceed five (5) years may be ordered pursuant to RC 2919.27(B)(5).

Practitioners should recognize that the penalty provisions for criminal domestic violence may place the victim in a quagmire. If the defendant is convicted and sentenced to a term of incarceration, the victim may then lose a valuable source of support for a significant period of time. Additionally, the enhancement provisions contained in the statute can often be quite confusing. For example, a criminal defendant who is initially charged with domestic violence and subsequently pleads to a lesser offense, such as disorderly conduct, does not face an enhanced sentence in any subsequent criminal domestic violence proceedings.[9] Even more troubling, from a practical standpoint, is that a prior conviction for one of the enumerated offenses may not be sufficient to enhance a subsequent charge if the prior

---

[5]City of Maple Heights v. Spearman, 1998 WL 355850 (Ohio Ct. App. 8th Dist. Cuyahoga County 1998).

[6]State v. Donnelly, 109 Ohio App. 3d 604, 672 N.E.2d 1034 (9th Dist. Lorain County 1996).

[7]State v. Brillhart, 129 Ohio App. 3d 180, 717 N.E.2d 413 (9th Dist. Wayne County 1998).

[8]State v. Mueller, 122 Ohio App. 3d 483, 702 N.E.2d 139 (1st Dist. Hamilton County 1997).

[9]See, e.g., City of Parma v. Peyatt, 1996 WL 199843 (Ohio Ct. App. 8th Dist. Cuyahoga County 1996).

conviction resulted from an uncounseled plea of guilty or no contest plea by the defendant.[10]

§ 5:5   Civil proceeding—Jurisdiction, venue

The civil code sections, RC 3113.31 et seq., provide a plethora of possible solutions and define domestic violence more broadly than RC 2919.25.[1] As defined by RC 3113.31(A)(1):

(1) "Domestic violence" means the occurrence of one or more of the following acts against a family or household member:

(a) Attempting to cause or recklessly causing bodily injury;

(b) Placing another person by the threat of force in fear of imminent serious physical harm or committing a violation of section 2903.211 or 2911.211 of the Revised Code;

(c) Committing any act with respect to a child that would result in the child being an abused child, as defined in section 2151.031 of the Revised Code.

The domestic relations division of the court of common pleas, in counties that have such a division, or the court of common pleas, in those counties that do not have a domestic relations division, has jurisdiction over all proceedings under RC 3113.31(B).[2] The jurisdiction of the common pleas court remains intact even where the petitioner in a domestic violence action changes residences in order to avoid future acts of violence.[3] Obviously, the same should be true if the respondent moves in order to avoid future allegations of domestic violence.

RC 3113.31 contains no residency requirements for either party. However, service must be obtainable upon the respondent under the Ohio Rules of Civil Procedure.[4] The proper venue can be any county where Civil Rule 3 authorizes filing.[5] The most commonly used venue provision is the county where the respondent resides.[6] However, Civil Rule 3 now specifically provides that venue is proper in a county in which the petitioner either "currently" or "temporarily" resides.[7]

§ 5:6   Civil proceeding—Parties

The civil domestic violence statute provides expansive coverage for

---

[10]See State v. Snider, 1996 WL 368216 (Ohio Ct. App. 4th Dist. Meigs County 1996).

[Section 5:5]

[1]Stanzak v. Stanzak, 1990 WL 129456 (Ohio Ct. App. 12th Dist. Butler County 1990) (verbal threats of violence, without any attempt to cause physical harm, do not constitute domestic violence within the meaning of RC 3113.31(A)(1)).

[2]RC 3113.31(A)(2).

[3]RC 3113.31(B).

[4]RC 3113.31(G). See also Civ. R. 4.

[5]RC 3113.31(G).

[6]Civ. R. 3(B)(1).

[7]Civ. R. 3(B)(10).

a wide variety of potential petitioners. The victim need only be a "family or household member."[1] A relationship such as that between a mother-in-law and a son-in-law has been held sufficient for the issuance of a CPO.[2] The actual petitioner may be either the victim or "any parent or adult household member" on behalf of the victim.[3] Further, a "victim advocate" may assist the petitioner in bringing and prosecuting the action.[4] "Family or household member" and "person living as a spouse" are defined as follows:

(3) "Family or household member" means any of the following:

(a) Any of the following who is residing with or has resided with the respondent:

(i) A spouse, a person living as a spouse, or a former spouse of the respondent;

(ii) A parent or a child of the respondent, or another person related by consanguinity or affinity to the respondent;

(iii) A parent or a child of a spouse, person living as a spouse, or former spouse of the respondent, or another person related by consanguinity or affinity to a spouse, person living as a spouse, or former spouse of the respondent.

(b) The natural parent of any child of whom the respondent is the other natural parent or is the putative other natural parent.

(4) "Person living as a spouse" means a person who is living or has lived with the respondent in a common law marital relationship, who otherwise is cohabiting with the respondent, or who otherwise has cohabited with the respondent within five years prior to the date of the alleged occurrence of the act in question.[5]

It is important to note that the in at least one Ohio district, the Defense of Marriage Amendment has not prevented the court from issuing a CPO when unmarried, cohabiting, heterosexual adults were involved.[6]

However, the expansive coverage provided for in the statute does have limits. For example, the Third District Court of Appeals has held that a paternal uncle does not have standing to bring a civil domestic violence proceeding on behalf of his fourteen year old niece, with

---

[Section 5:6]

[1]RC 3113.31(A)(1).

[2]Williams v. Workman, 2005-Ohio-5388, 2005 WL 2514239 (Ohio Ct. App. 9th Dist. Summit County 2005).

[3]RC 3113.31(C).

[4]RC 3113.31(A)(5).

[5]RC 3113.31(A)(3) to (A)(4).

[6]Noggle v. Smith, 2005-Ohio-5636, 2005 WL 2727128 (Ohio Ct. App. 5th Dist. Ashland County 2005). See, also State v. McCaslin, 2006-Ohio-891, 2006 WL 459261 (Ohio Ct. App. 7th Dist. Columbiana County 2006).

whom he had never resided.[7] However, testimony by a child's mother as to the paternity of the Respondent has been held to be sufficient to establish the Respondent as a "family or household member", despite the fact that no paternity test had ever been conducted.[8]

§ 5:7 Civil proceeding—The petition

The petition must contain or state allegations that the respondent engaged in domestic violence against a family or household member including the nature and extent of the domestic violence, the relationship between the respondent and the petitioner (and to the victim if other than the petitioner), and a request for relief.[1] The petition may request an ex parte order,[2] in which case the description of the domestic violence incident should be clearly explained. It is good practice to accompany the petition with an affidavit, and the petitioner should be prepared to present oral testimony immediately. If temporary custody of a minor child is involved, it may be necessary to file a UCCJEA Parenting Proceeding Affidavit.[3] Multiple copies of the petition should be prepared so that service can be effected as soon as possible, preferably immediately after the hearing.

Most jurisdictions have local rules which usually prove to be of great assistance to those practitioners careful enough to check them first.[4] These local rules are extremely important in civil domestic violence proceedings. Most provide quite specific instructions for everything from the contents of a petition for domestic violence relief to presentation of evidence. However, the unwary may suffer if local procedures are not consulted.[5]

RC 3113.31 does not appear to prohibit the preparation and filing of a two-count petition seeking a divorce and alleging domestic violence. However, no filing fee may be charged for a petition which merely addresses civil domestic violence.[6]

Provisions concerning the expiration of the provisions contained in a civil protection order (CPO) were amended in 1994.[7] RC 3113.31(E)(3)(a) provides that a CPO will expire either on a date

---

[7]Seibert v. Seibert, 2003-Ohio-3758, 2003 WL 21658309 (Ohio Ct. App. 3d Dist. Crawford County 2003).

[8]See State v. Mills, 2005-Ohio-2128, 2006 WL 1132543 (Ohio Ct. App. 2d Dist. Montgomery County 2006).

[Section 5:7]

[1]RC 3113.31(C)(1) to (3).

[2]RC 3113.31(D).

[3]RC 3127.23.

[4]See, e.g., Cuy. Loc. R. 26; Ham. Loc. R. 18.2, 19.1; Lucas Loc. R. 7.10, 7.13; Mahoning Loc. R. 18; Mont. Loc. R. 4.22, 4.56; Summit Loc. R. 8.

[5]See, e.g., Summit Loc. R. 8.04 (petition seeking ex parte CPO which is filed after 3:00 p.m. will not be heard until following business day).

[6]RC 3113.31(J).

[7]1994 H.B. 335, eff. 12-9-94.

certain set forth in the order itself or five years from the date of issuance of the order. A trial court may only extend the expiration of a CPO after conducting a new hearing.[8] With regard to provisions in CPOs which allocate parental rights and responsibilities and establish child support, RC 3113.31(E)(3)(b) provides that such orders will terminate either on a date certain set forth in the order itself, on the date that a court of competent jurisdiction makes a new award concerning these subjects (i.e., a domestic relations or juvenile court), or five years from the date that the order is initially filed. If a court of competent jurisdiction does subsequently issue an order allocating parental rights, the provisions in the original CPO not specifically addressed in the new order remain in effect.[9]

The language contained in RC 3113.31 does not specify how long after the act of domestic violence is committed a petitioner has to file a complaint. At least one court has stated that there is no time bar for filing a motion for a Civil Protection Order. However, the court was also quick to point out that it is the petitioner's burden to show a fear of imminent harm before a Civil Protection Order may be granted. Obviously a time gap between the date of an incident and the filing will impact upon this finding.[10] Most courts addressing the question have concluded that "staleness" of a claim is merely an evidentiary matter that a trial court may consider in determining whether to issue a civil protection order.[11]

RC 3113.31 does not specify any requirement for an answer to be filed. The court does not disallow the filing of an answer, but this is generally not done as a practical matter given the time constraints of the legislation.[12]

Pursuant to 1994 House Bill 335 § 4 (uncodified), the Supreme Court of Ohio has been directed to create a form which may be employed by pro se petitioners seeking a CPO. In response, the Court amended the Rules of Superintendence for the Courts of Ohio effective January 1, 1998. New rules 10.01 and 10.02 set forth standard forms for both civil and criminal protection orders, and directs that courts provide packets of forms with instructions to those who request them.

§ 5:8   Civil proceeding—Hearing procedure

The domestic violence statute specifically addresses time frames for

---

[8]Saari v. Saari, 2000 WL 1729455 (Ohio Ct. App. 9th Dist. Lorain County 2000).

[9]Hershberger v. Hershberger, 2000-Ohio-1716, 2000 WL 1675568 (Ohio Ct. App. 3d Dist. Seneca County 2000).

[10]Oliver v. Johnson, 2007-Ohio-5880, 2007 WL 3227668 (Ohio Ct. App. 4th Dist. Jackson County 2007).

[11]See Maccabee v. Maccabee, 1999 WL 430943 (Ohio Ct. App. 10th Dist. Franklin County 1999); Trent v. Trent, 1999 WL 298073 (Ohio Ct. App. 12th Dist. Preble County 1999).

[12]See Text § 5:8, Civil proceeding—Hearing procedure.

ex parte and full hearings.[1] If a person who files a petition pursuant to RC 3113.31 requests an ex parte order, the court shall hold an ex parte hearing on the same day that the petition is filed. While it is apparent that the general assembly intended to provide immediate civil relief to the petitioner, it remained silent as to how the petitioner would proceed in a court that traditionally necessitates the use of attorneys to draft and file proceedings and represent parties. Because of this, courts have established their own local procedures in order to comply with the law.[2]

The court may, for good cause shown, at the ex parte hearing, enter any temporary orders, with or without bond, that the court finds necessary to protect the family or household member from domestic violence. RC 3113.31(D) states:

> Immediate and present danger of domestic violence to the family or household member constitutes good cause for purposes of this section. Immediate and present danger includes, but is not limited to, situations in which the respondent has threatened the family or household member with bodily harm or in which the respondent previously has been convicted of or pleaded guilty to an offense that constitutes domestic violence against the family or household member.

Pursuant to RC 3113.31(D), if the court, after an ex parte hearing, issues an order requiring the respondent to leave the premises, the court shall schedule a full hearing that shall be held within seven court days after the ex parte hearing. If any other type of protection order is issued by the court after an ex parte hearing, the full hearing shall be held within ten days after the ex parte hearing. The statute provides for continuances of the full hearing based on failure of service, by agreement of the parties, the need of a party to obtain counsel, or other "good cause."[3]

Domestic violence situations frequently involve allegations of violence, abuse, or threats of violence levied by both parties against each other. A question arises as to whether the petitioner must "come into court with clean hands" in order to be considered a proper party. While there is no case law on point, the sole legal issue before the court should be whether the respondent committed an act of domestic violence as alleged, and not who was more at fault. Furthermore, mere aggressive or offensive conduct may not sustain a request for a civil protection order (CPO). The conduct complained of must "meet the minimal requirements of the statute defining domestic violence."[4] Extreme offensive language coupled with threats of physical abuse

---

[Section 5:8]

[1]RC 3113.31(D).

[2]See, e.g., Cuya. Loc. R. 26; Ham. Loc. R. 18.2, 19.1; Lucas Loc. R. 7.10, 7.13; Mahoning Loc. R. 18; Mont. Loc. R. 4.22, 4.56; Summit Loc. R. 8.

[3]RC 3113.31(D)(2)(a).

[4]Beach v. Beach, 1992 WL 328642, at *1 (Ohio Ct. App. 10th Dist. Franklin County 1992).

may be sufficient.[5] In short, there must have been a threat of force that has one party in fear of imminent, serious bodily harm.[6] There appears to be a conflict among appellate districts as to whether a subjective or an objective test should be employed to assess a petitioner's fear of imminent serious physical harm.[7] The respondent will have an opportunity to present evidence at full hearing regarding any acts of the petitioner which would also constitute domestic violence, and the court may direct orders toward both parties.[8] A "full hearing" requires that the respondent be provided with a "reasonable opportunity to know the claims"[9] made by the petitioner and to present evidence in response to those claims.[10] Parents are able to call children as witnesses in a hearing if they so choose. But, if that child is under 10, the court can decide if the child testifies or not but can not just dismiss the child. Some sort of inquiry must occur because "[i]t is the duty of the trial judge to conduct a voir dire examination of a child less than ten years of age to determine the child's competency to testify."[11]

In *Spigos v. Spigos*,[12] a trial court did not permit the petitioner/wife to complete the presentation of her evidence prior to denying her petition for a civil protection order. On appeal, the Franklin County Court of Appeals reversed and held that where the issuance of such an order is contested, a full presentation of evidence and argument must be allowed prior to ruling.

Initially, some courts held that civil domestic violence must be established by "clear and convincing" evidence.[13] However, the Ohio Supreme Court has now held that the petitioner must show that either the petitioner or other household members are in danger of do-

---

[5]Eichenberger v. Eichenberger, 82 Ohio App. 3d 809, 613 N.E.2d 678 (10th Dist. Franklin County 1992).

[6]Young v. Young, 2006-Ohio-978, 2006 WL 515522 (Ohio Ct. App. 2d Dist. Greene County 2006).

[7]See Tyler v. Tyler, 2004-Ohio-5784, 2004 WL 2436594 (Ohio Ct. App. 2d Dist. Montgomery County 2004).

[8]See Text §§ 5:9 et seq., Civil proceeding—Remedies.

[9]Deacon v. Landers, 68 Ohio App. 3d 26, 29, 587 N.E.2d 395 (4th Dist. Ross County 1990).

[10]Deacon v. Landers, 68 Ohio App. 3d 26, 587 N.E.2d 395 (4th Dist. Ross County 1990).

[11]Brandt v. Brandt, 2006-Ohio-883, 2006 WL 456716 (Ohio Ct. App. 3d Dist. Auglaize County 2006) (citing State v. Frazier, 61 Ohio St. 3d 247, 574 N.E.2d 483 (1991)).

[12]Spigos v. Spigos, 2004-Ohio-757, 2004 WL 308098 (Ohio Ct. App. 10th Dist. Franklin County 2004).

[13]O'Hara v. Dials, 1996 WL 38810, at *2 (Ohio Ct. App. 6th Dist. Erie County 1996) (abrogated by, Felton v. Felton, 79 Ohio St. 3d 34, 1997-Ohio-302, 679 N.E.2d 672 (1997)), abrogated by Felton v. Felton, 79 Ohio St. 3d 34, 1997-Ohio-302, 679 N.E.2d 672 (1997).

mestic violence by a preponderance of the evidence.[14] Ohio authority also supports the use of substantial, credible evidence to support the grant of a CPO.[15] Also, when there is good cause, evidence, and a specific petition with description of acts of domestic violence, a CPO can properly be issued.[16] An order either granting or denying a CPO after a full hearing is a final appealable order.[17] Even if the CPO is appealed, the discretion and findings of the trial court will be presumed to be correct.[18]

§ 5:9 Civil proceeding—Remedies—In general

The civil relief available under RC 3113.31 is similar to, but far more comprehensive than, the criminal remedies of RC 2919.26 in almost every instance. The court at an ex parte or full hearing may grant the following relief:

(1) Direct the respondent to refrain from abusing the family or household members;[1]

(2) Grant possession of the residence to the petitioner or other household member by evicting the respondent, when the petitioner or other household member solely owns or leases the residence;[2]

(3) Grant possession of the residence to the petitioner by ordering the respondent to vacate the residence when both the respondent and the petitioner (or other household member) jointly own or lease the residence;[3]

(4) Grant possession of the residence to the petitioner by ordering the respondent to vacate the residence where the respondent has a duty to support the petitioner (or other household member), and the respondent is the sole owner or lessee of the

---

[14]Felton v. Felton, 79 Ohio St. 3d 34, 1997-Ohio-302, 679 N.E.2d 672 (1997), paragraph two of the syllabus; Williams v. Workman, 2005-Ohio-5388, 2005 WL 2514239 (Ohio Ct. App. 9th Dist. Summit County 2005); Wilburn v. Wilburn, 2006-Ohio-2553, 2006 WL 1409784 (Ohio Ct. App. 9th Dist. Lorain County 2006); U.S. v. Mendoza-Escobedo, 2005 WL 2840674 (S.D. Tex. 2005).

[15]Brubaker v. Farr, 2006-Ohio-2001, 2006 WL 1062102 (Ohio Ct. App. 3d Dist. Shelby County 2006).

[16]Ferris v. Ferris, 2006-Ohio-878, 2006 WL 456811 (Ohio Ct. App. 12th Dist. Clermont County 2006).

[17]RC 3113.31(G).

[18]Gibson v. Gibson, 2006-Ohio-2880, 2006 WL 1555935 (Ohio Ct. App. 4th Dist. Washington County 2006).

[Section 5:9]

[1]RC 3113.31(E)(1)(a). See Text § 5:10, Civil proceeding—Remedies—Restraining orders.

[2]RC 3113.31(E)(1)(b). See Text § 5:11, Civil proceeding—Remedies—Orders to vacate, eviction.

[3]RC 3113.31(E)(1)(b). See Text § 5:11, Civil proceeding—Remedies—Orders to vacate, eviction.

residence[4] or, alternatively, allow the respondent to arrange for suitable housing for the petitioner or other family or household member.

(5) Award temporary custody of minor children, provided no other court has assumed jurisdiction, and award visitation and companionship rights;[5]

(6) Award support if the respondent has a duty to support the petitioner, or if the respondent customarily provides for, or contributes to, the support of the family or household member;[6]

(7) Require the respondent, petitioner, or victim to seek counseling;[7]

(8) Require the respondent to refrain from entering the residence, school, business, or place of employment of the petitioner, or other household member;[8] and

(9) Grant any other relief that the court considers equitable and proper, including division of household and family personal property, and ordering respondent to permit the use of a motor vehicle to petitioner.[9] A division of property made pursuant to RC 3113.31, however, does not necessarily operate as a total property settlement in a related divorce proceeding.[10]

On occasion, jurisdictional issues do arise in civil domestic violence proceedings. In such circumstances, Ohio's long-arm statute, RC 2307.382 governs. For example, in *Dobos v. Dobos*,[11] the Twelfth District Court of Appeals held that an evidentiary hearing would be required in order to determine whether threatening phone calls were made to the Petitioner in Ohio from Hungary. If so, the jurisdictional requirements of the statute could be fulfilled.

§ 5:10   Civil proceeding—Remedies—Restraining orders

A request that the respondent refrain from abusing a family member is the remedy ordered in most cases. It is also the most common order by agreement at the full hearing when the parties allow the respondent to return to the residence. Where the parties have

---

[4]RC 3113.31(E)(1)(c). See Text § 5:11, Civil proceeding—Remedies—Orders to vacate, eviction.

[5]RC 3113.31(E)(1)(d). See Text § 5:12, Civil proceeding—Remedies—Temporary custody, support, visitation (a parenting affidavit must be filed pursuant to RC 3127. 23).

[6]RC 3113.31(E)(1)(e). See Text § 5:12, Civil proceeding—Remedies—Temporary custody, support, visitation.

[7]RC 3113.31(E)(1)(f). See Text § 5:13, Civil proceeding—Remedies—Counseling.

[8]RC 3113.31(E)(1)(g).

[9]RC 3113.31(E)(1)(h).

[10]Cooley v. Cooley, 90 Ohio App. 3d 706, 630 N.E.2d 417 (2d Dist. Montgomery County 1993).

[11]Dobos v. Dobos, 2008-Ohio-5665, 2008 WL 476081 (Ct. App. 12 Dist. Clermont Cty. 2008)

been mutually combative, the appropriate remedy may be to enjoin both parties from abuse upon the court's own initiative.[1] However, a court does not have unbridled discretion regarding what are sometimes known as mutual restraining orders. RC 3113.31(E)(4) provides that all of the following must apply:

(a) The respondent files a separate petition for a protection order in accordance with this section.

(b) The petitioner is served notice of the respondent's petition at least forty-eight hours before the court holds a hearing with respect to the respondent's petition, or the petitioner waives the right to receive this notice.

(c) If the petitioner has requested an ex parte order pursuant to division (D) of this section, the court does not delay any hearing required by that division beyond the time specified in that division in order to consolidate the hearing with a hearing on the petition filed by the respondent.

(d) After a full hearing at which the respondent presents evidence in support of the request for a protection order and the petitioner is afforded an opportunity to defend against that evidence, the court determines that the petitioner has committed an act of domestic violence or has violated a temporary protection order issued pursuant to section 2919.26 of the Revised Code, that both the petitioner and the respondent acted primarily as aggressors, and that neither the petitioner nor the respondent acted primarily in self-defense.

The mere filing of an action for divorce is not a basis on which to deny a civil protection order pursuant to RC 3113.31.[2] The Tenth District Court of Appeals, in *Thomas v. Thomas*, reversed the trial court and held that the purpose of a civil protection order issued under RC 3113.31 is in addition to and not in lieu of any other civil order made pursuant to Civ. R. 75, when the parties are involved in a pending divorce. The purpose of such order is to provide protection from domestic violence and, incidental to that relief, to provide for support and shelter, custody, and visitation, to require counseling, and to provide a broad range of relief the court considers necessary.

Violation of a restraining order issued under RC 3113.31(D) or (E) subjects the offender to criminal prosecution under RC 3113.31(L)(1)(a) and to punishment for contempt under RC 3113.31(L)(1)(b). The statute further provides that punishment for contempt does not bar criminal prosecution for the same offense, but the violator is entitled to credit for the punishment imposed upon conviction.[3] In *State v. Vanselow*,[4] the Hamilton County Municipal Court found this section to be unconstitutional and stated:

[Section 5:10]

[1]Clum v. Searcy, 1993 WL 535383 (Ohio Ct. App. 5th Dist. Tuscarawas County 1993).

[2]Thomas v. Thomas, 44 Ohio App. 3d 6, 540 N.E.2d 745 (10th Dist. Franklin County 1988). See also Judith A. Nicely, *Temporary Restraining Order or Protective Order—Which Is More Effective?*, 2 Dom. Rel. J. of Ohio 3, at 37 (May/June 1990).

[3]RC 3113.31(L)(2).

[4]State v. Vanselow, 61 Ohio Misc. 2d 1, 9, 572 N.E.2d 269 (Mun. Ct. 1991).

The legislature obviously attempted to remedy the double jeopardy problem with R.C. 3113.31(L)(2), which allows credit for any time served on one case to be applied against the other. While this credit provision might avoid the prohibited double punishment for the same offense, it does not avoid the constitutional prohibition against multiple prosecutions.

The statute now provides that a person that has been criminally convicted may not subsequently be found in contempt for conduct "arising out of the same activity."[5]

Even though protection orders can be extremely beneficial, the enforcement can be difficult at times. The Supreme Court has ruled that if a law enforcement official fails to enforce an order, that officer can not be held liable under § 1983 of the Civil Rights Act for negative results that stem from the lack of enforcement.[6] In the *Town of Castle Rock v. Jessica Gonzalez* case, Gonzalez tried to bring suit under § 1983 against the police officers that refused to enforce her valid protective order that covered her and her three children. As a result of the police officers refusal to enforce the order, her three children were murdered. However, the Supreme Court held that (1) the officer's were not liable under § 1983 because they had discretionary power in regard to when to enforce an order and (2) that the enforcement of the protective order was not something that Gonzalez was "entitled" to. More specifically, in his opinion, Scalia stated, "[t]he creation of a personal entitlement on something so vague and novel as enforcing a restraining order cannot go without saying. . ." While Gonzalez was unable to recover in federal court under § 1983, it is possible that she could seek damages in state court but that would depend on the state's interpretation of relevant statutes.

§ 5:11 Civil proceeding—Remedies—Orders to vacate, eviction

The petitioner's request for either an order to vacate or eviction of the respondent should receive close scrutiny at the ex parte hearing because of the extraordinary nature of the relief. The respondent may be evicted or required to vacate when the petitioner owns or leases the property solely or jointly with respondent. However, no order to vacate may issue against a respondent solely owning or leasing property unless there is also a duty to support.[1] This provision poses some questions, such as whether a male respondent may be ordered to vacate a residence owned solely by him on the female petitioner's motion to vacate where they are cohabiting, and have produced a minor child, but there is no judicial determination of paternity of the child.

---

[5]RC 3113.31(L)(2).

[6]Town of Castle Rock, Colo. v. Gonzales, 545 U.S. 748, 125 S. Ct. 2796, 162 L. Ed. 2d 658 (2005).

[Section 5:11]

[1]RC 3113.31(E)(1)(c).

Valid arguments can be made in this case that there is a duty to support established by statute.

In determining whether to grant an ex parte order to vacate or evict, courts should be concerned with such factors as (1) the date the violence occurred in relation to the date of the petition; (2) the behavioral history between the two parties and the respondent's history, e.g., any assaults upon others or prior criminal record; (3) the nature and extent of injury, and any injury to minor children in addition to the petitioner; and (4) whether the petitioner is reasonably afraid of the respondent, especially where threats of harm are alleged. The court should also inquire into the competency and minority of the respondent.

§ 5:12 Civil proceeding—Remedies—Temporary custody, support, visitation

An award of temporary custody is requested nearly as often as a protection order against abuse. The court should grant temporary custody at the ex parte hearing, when requested, in order to resolve another issue likely to cause further disagreement between the parties. Like eviction, the award of temporary custody is not always granted by the court until the full hearing. Along with temporary custody, the court may also order temporary visitation at the ex parte hearing.[1] Visitation issues, however, are better left to the full hearing, in order to avoid immediate contact between the parties. At the full hearing, visitation issues should be thoroughly discussed. However, a court hearing a domestic violence petition may not allocate parental rights or address visitation if another court has already determined such or is in the process of doing so.[2] However, it is important to note that a domestic violence conviction is not an automatic reason to deny parental rights.[3]

A petitioner who requests temporary custody usually requests an award of support as well. All payments of child or spousal support must be paid through the child support enforcement agency and paid out of wages when the obligor is employed, or out of other resources, as provided in RC 3113.31(K). However, a court must calculate child support pursuant to RC 3119.021 et seq. A copy of the child support worksheet must be attached to the journal entry granting child sup-

---

[Section 5:12]

[1]RC 3113.31(E)(1)(d).

[2]RC 3113.31(E)(1)(b); Kiedrowicz v. Kiedrowicz, 1999 WL 197793 (Ohio Ct. App. 6th Dist. Huron County 1999).

[3]Hussein v. Hussein, 2005-Ohio-6399, 2005 WL 3249490 (Ohio Ct. App. 5th Dist. Morrow County 2005).

port, even if the award is made pursuant to a petition for a CPO, rather than a divorce filing.[4]

Special treatment is afforded petitioners who are not entitled to support pursuant to Ohio law. Under this section, the petitioner may be awarded support where the respondent customarily provides for or contributes support without a legal duty to do so.[5]

Interestingly, a temporary allocation of parental rights or visitation order made in a civil domestic violence proceeding may not be dispositive in a subsequent divorce proceeding. In *Schmidt v. Schmidt*,[6] the court of appeals upheld the trial court's order of shared parenting, despite the fact that the appellee-father had previously been convicted of domestic violence against the appellant-mother. The reviewing court concluded that since the father had not committed any acts of domestic violence against the children and since the evidence indicated that shared parenting was in the best interests of the children, the trial court had not abused its discretion by ordering shared parenting. Another peculiarity arises when a divorce decree conflicts with a Civil Protection Order. The Supreme Court of Ohio has stated that a subsequently filed divorce decree can modify a pre-existing Civil Protection Order. The Court found that a divorce decree that allowed for visitation and was executed after the Civil Protection Order properly allowed such visitation without repercussion under the Civil Protection Order.[7]

§ 5:13 Civil proceeding—Remedies—Counseling

Another remedy available under this provision which may be included as part of the temporary protection order is to require the respondent, petitioner, victim of domestic violence, or any combination of those persons to seek counseling.[1] Although this may be requested at the ex parte hearing, it is more properly an issue left for complete discussion at the full hearing. The parties are often in need of this remedy, especially where the parties wish to remain together.

Every order to seek counseling should contain the name of the agency, mental health facility, or therapist. The court should provide for a review to insure compliance. Unfortunately, many communities do not have these resources available or there are few counselors who are able or willing to treat violent families. Another problem is the resistance of the parties, usually the respondent, to agree to seek counseling. While contempt charges are available to enforce the order

---

[4]Halley v. Ashley, 1997 WL 760662 (Ohio Ct. App. 9th Dist. Summit County 1997).

[5]RC 3113.31(E)(1)(e).

[6]Schmidt v. Schmidt, 1999 WL 225157 (Ohio Ct. App. 12th Dist. Clermont County 1999).

[7]State v. Price, 118 Ohio St. 3d 144, 2008-Ohio-1974, 886 N.E.2d 852 (2008).

[Section 5:13]

[1]RC 3113.31(E)(1)(f).

to counseling, they do not provide a very willing candidate for therapy. Practically speaking, the success of such an order is dependent upon the parties' voluntary cooperation with the therapist. The most effective use of court-ordered counseling in these cases may be through the use of the criminal procedure, either as an alternative to prosecution or as a condition of probation.

§ 5:14 Civil proceeding—Remedies—Property division

RC 3113.31(E)(1)(h) enables the court to "[g]rant other relief that the court considers equitable and fair, including, but not limited to, ordering the respondent to permit the use of a motor vehicle by the petitioner or other family or household member and the apportionment of household and family personal property." Necessary property, e.g., children's clothes, is usually requested or ordered at the ex parte hearing. The respondent should always be awarded clothing (and tools of his trade, if applicable) at the ex parte hearing. A division of (limited) personal property, using guidelines from divorce proceedings, may be ordered at full hearing.

Regarding this provision of the domestic violence statute, it does not seem proper or logical to construe this "division of property" to mean the same as a general division of RC 3105.171 marital property. RC 3105.171 does not permit such a general division. There is no termination of the marriage and the parties are not necessarily even involved in a marital relationship. Thus, the division of marital property is unwarranted. The intent is to provide the dependent person or persons with such support as is reasonable and necessary during the proceedings.

§ 5:15 Enforcement

Prior versions of RC 3113.31 were somewhat unclear as to whether law enforcement agencies could immediately enforce a CPO without resort to further judicial proceedings. However, RC 3113.31(F) now provides:

(F)(1) A copy of any protection order, or consent agreement, that is issued or approved under this section shall be issued by the court to the petitioner, to the respondent, and to all law enforcement agencies that have jurisdiction to enforce the order or agreement. The court shall direct that a copy of an order be delivered to the respondent on the same day that the order is entered.

(2) All law enforcement agencies shall establish and maintain an index for the protection orders and the approved consent agreements delivered to the agencies pursuant to division (F)(1) of this section. With respect to each order and consent agreement delivered, each agency shall note on the index, the date and time that it received the order or consent agreement.

(3) Regardless of whether the petitioner has registered the order or agreement in the county in which the officer's agency has jurisdiction pursuant to division (N) of this section, any officer of a law enforcement agency shall enforce a protection order issued or consent agreement ap-

proved by any court in this state in accordance with the provisions of the order or agreement, including removing the respondent from the premises, if appropriate.

Pursuant to the provisions contained in RC 3113.31(N), a petitioner who successfully obtains a civil protection order may register the order in any county and have such enforced by any law enforcement agency. Common pleas court clerks and municipal court clerks are required to maintain a registry of all orders submitted to them pursuant to RC 3113.31(N)(3).

Violation of a civil protection order is punishable by either a contempt proceeding in the court which issued the order or through a criminal charge made pursuant to RC 2919.27, or both.[1] If the offender has not previously been convicted of or pleaded guilty to two or more violations of RC 2903.211 or RC 2911.211 involving the same victim, and has not previously been convicted of or pleaded guilty to any violation of RC 2919.27, a conviction for violation of RC 2919.27(A) is a misdemeanor of the first degree.[2] However, if either of these contingencies do apply, violation of RC 2919.27(A) is a fifth degree felony.[3]

Generally, enforcement through the contempt remedy is not as speedy a process as should be available given the extraordinary nature of relief granted. If the victim wishes to stay within the civil case, a motion for contempt can be filed and served,[4] and upon the hearing with the respondent present, a finding of contempt can result in the same penalty as other contempt actions. Upon a first violation, RC 2705.05(A)(1) provides that the court may impose a sentence of up to thirty days' incarceration and a fine of up to $250. Increased penalties of fines and incarceration are provided for subsequent offenses of contempt. RC 2705.05(A)(2) mandates a fine of not more than $500, up to sixty days in jail, or both for a second offense, and RC 2705.05(A)(3) provides for a fine of not more than $1,000, up to ninety days in jail, or both for subsequent offenses.

Another informal method of enforcement available at the court's discretion is to schedule a review hearing within sixty to ninety days of the order to determine if the terms are being complied with, or need to be modified or amended. Unfortunately, this is not practical for most jurisdictions which already have overcrowded dockets.

In addition to the statutory civil and criminal procedures provided to the victim of domestic violence, there is also available a civil tort

---

[Section 5:15]

[1] RC 3113.31(L)(1).

[2] RC 2919.27(B).

[3] RC 2919.27(B).

[4] RC 3113.31(L)(1)(b).

suit for assault, personal injury, etc., in light of the abrogation of the doctrine of interspousal immunity.[5]

§ 5:16 Civil versus criminal

Criminal and civil sanctions are clearly complementary to each other, providing the victim with alternatives not previously available. Both actions may be commenced by a victim simultaneously. Some commentators clearly feel that the civil remedy is superior to the criminal proceeding.[1]

Finally, jurisdiction in domestic relations court over domestic violence, as defined, does not replace the notice requirements required by RC 2151.421 where the petition alleges violence against minor children.[2] If a petition alleges violence against minor children, the court must report it pursuant to RC 2151.421.[3]

There is concurrent jurisdiction[4] for both municipal and common pleas courts over the parties to domestic violence in order to provide an option to the victim/claimant/petitioner as to which remedy would be more appropriate for that person. Filing in both forums is permitted. However, the criminal temporary protection order ceases to be effective once a civil protection order is issued or a consent agreement arising out of the same activities as those that were the basis of the complaint is approved.[5] At least one Ohio appellate court has agreed that a convicted offender may be subjected to a "no contact" order as a term of probation.[6] If a domestic relations court rejects a petition for a CPO after a full hearing on the merits, this decision does not necessarily bar criminal prosecution under RC 2919.25.[7]

In determining whether the more appropriate action is civil, criminal, or possibly both, attorneys should consider the following:

Criminal:
 (1) Was the offender arrested on a warrantless arrest shortly following the violent episode?

---

[5]See Text § 4:1, History of marital property rights and obligations.

[Section 5:16]

[1]See, e.g., Michael Brigner, *Civil Protection Orders In Ohio Domestic Relations Cases*, 9 Dom. Rel. J. of Ohio 3, at 37 (May/June 1997). However, practitioners should be mindful that only the criminal remedy may be employed to obtain *immediate* relief after the courthouse doors have closed for the day or weekend and should advise their clients accordingly.

[2]RC 3113.31(H).

[3]RC 3113.31(H).

[4]RC 2919.25, RC 3113.31(A)(2).

[5]RC 2919.26(E)(2).

[6]State v. Conkle, 129 Ohio App. 3d 177, 717 N.E.2d 411 (9th Dist. Wayne County 1998).

[7]Cleveland v. Hogan, 92 Ohio Misc. 2d 34, 699 N.E.2d 1020 (Mun. Ct. 1998).

(2) Is the claimant seriously interested in criminal prosecution?

(3) What impact or effect will criminal sanctions have on the offender's behavior, e.g., has he been through the system before?

(4) Generally, this remedy is free, requires no private attorney, and is speedy.

Civil:

(1) The victim/petitioner is extremely reluctant to pursue criminal remedy, but the violence problem needs intervention.

(2) The civil remedies available are broader and more creative.

(3) The protection order may be effective for five years, subject to renewal, in contrast to the criminal order, which is effective until the case is disposed of.[8]

(4) The victim/petitioner has been seriously considering separation or divorce.

RC 2919.26(I) prohibits any court from charging a fee for filing a motion for a temporary protection order in the criminal context, and RC 3113.31(J) prohibits any such charge for filing a petition for relief in the civil context.

In conclusion, too much emphasis in the past has been placed on the victim's dismissal of criminal charges. In Lucas County, tentative results of civil protection orders indicate that the mere obtaining of such an order has caused a cessation of violence in some cases. Victims also report that the granting of an assortment of remedies (including the court's telling the respondent that domestic violence is against the law) has resulted in a cessation of violence in more difficult cases. The value of this statute should be measured by the violence stopped and not by the rate of dismissal in criminal cases.

§ 5:17 Warning concerning domestic violence—Protection orders—Form⊚

WARNING CONCERNING THE ATTACHED DOMESTIC VIOLENCE PROTECTION ORDER

NOTE: Rules of Superintendence 10.01 and 10.02 require this Warning to be attached to the FRONT of all civil and criminal domestic violence protection orders issued by the courts of the State of Ohio.

WARNING TO RESPONDENT/DEFENDANT
Violating the attached Protection Order is a crime, punishable by imprisonment or fine or both, and can cause your bond to be revoked or result in a contempt of court citation against you.

---

[8]See RC 3113.31(E)(3). However, a criminal trial court may impose conditions of probation which last for several years and may offer protection to the victim which is similar to that provided in a temporary protection order. See State v. Sutley, 1990 WL 208811 (Ohio Ct. App. 11th Dist. Ashtabula County 1990).

WARNING TO RESPONDENT/DEFENDANT

This Protection Order is enforceable in all 50 states, the District of Columbia, tribal lands, and U.S. Territories pursuant to the Violence Against Women Act of 1994, 18 U.S.C. Section 2265. Violating this Protection Order may subject you to federal charges and punishment. You may also be subject to federal penalty for possessing, transporting, or accepting a firearm under the Gun Control Act, 18 U.S.C. Section 922(g)(8).

Only the Court can change this order. The Petitioner cannot give you legal permission to change this order. If you go near the Petitioner, even with the Petitioner's consent, you may be arrested. If you and the Petitioner/Complainant/Victim want to resume your relationship you must ask the Court to modify or dismiss this Protection Order. Unless the Court modifies this order, you can be arrested for violating this Protection Order. <u>You act at your own risk if you disregard this WARNING</u>.

WARNING TO PETITIONER/COMPLAINANT/VICTIM

You cannot change the terms of this order by your words or actions. Only the Court can allow the Respondent/Defendant to contact you or return to your residence. If you and the Respondent want to resume your relationship, you must ask the Court to modify or dismiss this Protection Order.

<u>NOTICE TO ALL LAW ENFORCEMENT AGENCIES AND OFFICERS</u>

The attached Protection Order is enforceable in all jurisdictions. Violation of this Protection Order, regardless of whether it is a criminal or civil Protection Order, is a crime under R.C. 2919.27. Law enforcement officers with powers to arrest under R.C. 2935.03 for violations of the Ohio Revised Code must enforce the terms of this Protection Order as required by R.C. 2919.26, 2919.27 and R.C. 3113.31. If you have reasonable grounds to believe that Respondent/Defendant has violated this Protection Order, it is the preferred course of action in Ohio under R.C. 2935.03 to arrest and detain Respondent/Defendant until a warrant can be obtained.

---

§ 5:18 Petition and affidavit for civil protection order—Basic—Form⊚

[Title of Court]

[Caption]

Case No. *[_____]*
<u>PETITION AND AFFIDAVIT</u>
<u>FOR</u>
<u>CIVIL PROTECTION ORDER</u>

Now comes Petitioner, being first duly sworn, and states that the following facts are true:

[1. Petitioner and Respondent were married on *[date]* and that *[no/number]* children have been born issue of said marriage.]

or

[1. Petitioner is a family or household member of Respondent, as defined in RC 3113.31(A)(3).]

2. Petitioner and Respondent *[own/lease as co-tenants/etc.]* the premises at *[address]*, Ohio.

3. Respondent attempted to cause serious bodily injury to Petitioner on *[date]*, by *[description of attempt]*.

4. Respondent has placed Petitioner in fear of imminent serious physical harm by *[description of reason for fear]*.

5. Petitioner is in immediate and present danger of domestic violence from Respondent and the relief requested is necessary to protect Petitioner from domestic violence.

WHEREFORE, Petitioner respectfully requests the Court for the following protective relief:

[1. Enjoin Respondent from abusing Petitioner.]

and/or

[2. Grant exclusive possession of said residence by evicting Respondent from said property.]

and/or

[3. Award Petitioner temporary custody of the children of the parties.]

and/or

[4. Require Respondent to maintain support of both Petitioner and *[his/her]* children.]

and/or

[5. Enjoin Respondent from entering the residence, school or business of Petitioner or the children.]

Petitioner prays that this Court will grant an ex parte hearing in the above matter.

_____
Petitioner

[Jurat]

NOTES TO FORM

Drafter's Notes

The parties should be designated as "Petitioner" and "Respondent."

A long form caption should be used on the petition.

A RC 3127.23 affidavit (court form) should accompany the initial filing where there are minor children of the marriage.

If service other than pursuant to Civ. R. 4 is desired, a written request for service (usually a court form) should accompany the petition when it is filed.

The petition can also request an order for visitation, child support, spousal support, counseling, and use of an automobile/household goods.

§ 5:19 Petition for domestic violence civil protection order—Form⊛

IN THE _____ COURT

_____ COUNTY, OHIO

_____		
Petitioner	:	Case No. _____
_____		
Address	:	Judge _____
_____		
City, State, Zip Code	:	
Date of Birth:		PETITION FOR
_____		DOMESTIC
	:	VIOLENCE CIVIL
		PROTECTION
v.	:	ORDER (R.C.
		3113.31)
_____		
Respondent	:	**Notice to**
		Petitioner:
		Throughout
_____		**this form, mark**
		every ☐ that
		applies.
Address	:	
		Do NOT write your
_____		**address at left**
City, State, Zip Code	:	**or below if you are**
Date of Birth:		**requesting**
_____		**confidentiality.**

☐ 1. Petitioner is a family or household member of Respondent and a victim of domestic violence and seeks relief on Petitioner's own behalf. The relationship of Petitioner to Respondent is that of:

☐ Spouse of Respondent

☐ Former spouse of Respondent

☐ The natural parent of Respondent's child

☐ Other relative (by blood or marriage) of Respondent

☐ Child of Respondent

☐ Parent of Respondent

☐ Person "living as a spouse of Respondent" defined as:

● now cohabiting; or
● cohabited within five years prior to the alleged act of domestic violence.

☐ 2. Petitioner seeks relief on behalf of the following family or household members who are victims of domestic violence:

NAME	AGE/DOB	HOW RELATED TO PETITIONER	RESPONDENT	RESIDES WITH

3. Respondent has engaged in the following act(s) of domestic violence (describe the acts as fully as possible):

_____

_____

_____

_____

4. Petitioner requests that the Court grant relief under Ohio Revised Code 3113.31 to stop domestic violence against Petitioner and the family or household members named in this Petition by granting a civil protection order that:

☐ (a) Directs Respondent not to abuse Petitioner and the family or household members named in this Petition by harming, attempting to harm, threatening, molesting, following, stalking, bothering, harassing, annoying, contacting, or forcing sexual relations upon them.

☐ (b) Requires Respondent to leave and not return to the following residence and grants Petitioner exclusive possession of the residence: _____

☐ (c) Divides household and family personal property and directs Respondent not to remove, damage, hide, or dispose of any property or funds that Petitioner owns or possesses.

☐ (d) Temporarily allocates parental rights and responsibilities for the care of the following minor children and suspends Respondent's visitation rights until a full hearing is held (include names and birth dates of the minor children):

_____

_____

☐ (e) Establishes temporary visitation rights with the following minor children and requires visitation to be supervised or occur under such conditions that the Court determines will insure the safety of Petitioner and the minor children (include names and birth dates of the minor children):

_____

_____

☐ (f) Requires Respondent to provide financial support for Petitioner and the other family or household members named in this Petition.

☐ (g) Requires Respondent to complete batterer counseling, substance abuse counseling, or other counseling as determined necessary by the Court.

☐ (h) Requires Respondent to refrain from entering, approaching, or contacting (including contact by telephone, fax, e-mail, and voice mail) the residence, school, business, and place of employment of Petitioner and the family or household members named in this Petition.

☐ (i) Requires Respondent to permit Petitioner or other family or household member to have exclusive use of the following motor vehicle: _____

☐ (j) Requires Respondent to pay all costs of this action.

☐ (k) Includes the following additional provisions: _____

☐ 5. Petitioner further requests that the Court issue an *ex parte* (emergency) protection order under Ohio Revised Code 3113.31(D) and (E) and this Petition.

6. Petitioner further requests that the Court issue no mutual protection orders or other orders against Petitioner unless all of the conditions of Ohio Revised Code 3113.31(E)(4) are met.

7. Petitioner further requests that if Petitioner has a victim advocate, the court permit the victim advocate to accompany Petitioner at all stages of these proceedings as required by Ohio Revised Code 3113.31(M).

8. Petitioner further requests that the Court grant such other relief as the Court considers equitable and fair.

9. Petitioner lists here all present court cases and pertinent past court cases (including civil, criminal, divorce, juvenile, custody, visitation, and bankruptcy cases) that relate to you, your children, your family, or household members:

CASE NAME				
CASE NUMBER				
COURT/COUNTY				
TYPE OF CASE				
RESULT OF CASE				

I hereby swear or affirm that the answers above are true, complete and accurate to the best of my knowledge. I understand that falsification of this document may result in a contempt of court finding against me which could result in a jail sentence and fine, and that falsification of this document may also subject me to criminal penalties for perjury under Ohio Revised Code 2921.11.

Sworn to and subscribed before me on this

_____ _____ day of _____,
                                    _____.

SIGNATURE OF PETITIONER

                                    _____

                                    NOTARY PUBLIC

                        _____

Signature of Attorney for Petitioner (if applicable)

_____

Name

_____

Address

_____

Attorney Registration Number

INSTRUCTIONS FOR COMPLETING THE INFORMATION FOR PARENTING PROCEEDING AFFIDAVIT

These instructions will help you prepare the information For Parenting Proceeding Affidavit. The Affidavit must be filed if you are requesting a parenting (custody) order in a Petition for a Domestic Violence Civil Protection Order. IF YOU ALREADY HAVE A DIVORCE OR DISSOLUTION CASE FILED, CUSTODY ISSUES WILL BE HANDLED IN THAT CASE, NOT THE DOMESTIC VIOLENCE CASE, SO YOU DO NOT NEED TO FILE THIS AFFIDAVIT FORM IN THE DOMESTIC VIOLENCE CASE.

> **FILLING OUT THE FORM: Mark each instruction below after you read and complete it.**

☐ Print or type only. Attach an additional page to the Affidavit for your answers if you need more room.

☐ At the top of the front page, fill in the names. YOU are the "Petitioner." The person you want protection from is the "Respondent." Leave the Case No. and Judge lines blank for the clerk of court to complete. Fill in your name again as the "Affiant."

☐ Paragraph 1: Fill in the names and other information requested about the children involved in this action.

☐ Paragraph 2: Write the address where the children are living now. If you do not want to have this address know, write "address confidential."

☐ Paragraph 3: Write the names of all adults that the children are now living with, including you, if applicable.

☐ Pagaraph 4: List every address where the children have lived in the past 5 years. Also list the names of all adults who lived with the children at each address. Attach an additional page if you need more room.

☐ Paragraph 5: List the current address of every adult whose name appears in your answers to Questions 3 and 4.

☐ Paragraph 6: Answer "YES" or "NO". If you answer "YES", then write the details in Question 7.

☐ Paragraph 7: If now or in the past, there has been a court case concerning the custody, visitation, or care of the children, write as many details as you know. If you do not know of any case, write "NONE".

☐ Paragraph 8: List the name and address of anyone who is not a party to this case who might have some claim to child custody or visitation. If none, write "NONE".

☐ Paragraph 9: State if you or any other party to this case has been involved in any other case where child abuse, child neglect, or domestic violence was an issue. Fill in as many details as you know. If you do not know of ay cases, write "NONE".

☐ Paragraph 10: State if you have any domestic violence protection orders or any other court restraining orders in effect now, either against you or on your behalf. Fill in as many details as you know. If you are not aware of any cases, write "NONE".

SIGNING THE FORM: Fill out this form before you go to the courthouse. AFTER YOU HAVE FILLED OUT THE FORM, TAKE THE FORM TO THE CLERK OF COURT'S OFFICE OR TO A NOTARY PUBLIC TO HAVE YOUR SIGNATURE NOTARIZED. *DO NOT SIGN THE FORM UNLESS YOU ARE IN FRONT OF A NOTARY PUBLIC*.

---

§ 5:20 Parenting Proceeding Affidavit—Form ⊚

IN THE _____ COURT

_____ COUNTY, OHIO

_____ :

Petitioner   Case No. _____

                                        :

                                        Judge _____

v.

                                        : INFORMATION FOR
                                        PARENTING
_____   PROCEEDING AFFIDAVIT
                                        (R.C. 3127.23)

Respondent   :
                                        (Filed with Petition for
                                        Domestic
                                    :   Violence Civil Protection Order)

NOTE: By law, this affidavit **must** be filed and served
with the first pleading filed by each party in every
parenting (custody/visitation) proceeding in this Court,
including a Petition for a Domestic Violence Civil Protection Order. Each party has a continuing duty while this
case is pending to inform the Court of any parenting
proceeding concerning the child(ren) in any other court in
this or any other sate. **If more space is needed, attach
an additional page.**

Affiant, _____, states as follows:
1. The name, birth date, and Social Security Number [if any] of
each child whose custody/visitation is at issue in this case is:

_____

_____

2. The present home address of the child(ren) is:

_____

_____

3. The child(ren) currently reside(s) with what adult(s)?

_____

_____

4. All other places and dates where the child(ren) have lived during
the last 5 years, and the names of all adult(s) with whom they lived at
each address are as follows:

_____

_____

_____

_____

5. The name(s) and current address of all adults listed above are:

_____

_____

_____

6. Do you know of any litigation anywhere, past or present, which
concerns the custody, visitation, or care of the child(ren)?

7. If the answer to]6 is "yes", state any other information you have
about any parenting proceeding concerning the child(ren) now pending in a court of this or any other state. Include the case number, the
name of the court and the address of the court.

_____

8. State the name and address of any person who is **not** a party to this proceeding: (A) who has physical possession of the child(ren); or (B) who claims to be a parent of the child(ren) and is either the residential parent and legal custodian, or has visitation rights with the child; or (C) who is a person other than a parent of the child(ren) who has custody or visitation rights.

_____

_____

_____

9. Are you now, or have you ever been, a party to any civil or criminal case or any investigation concerning child abuse, child neglect, or domestic violence? If so, state each court, case name, case number, date, type of case and result of the case.

_____

_____

_____

10. Do you have any domestic violence protection orders or any other restraining orders issued against you, or on your behalf against any other person? If so, state each court, case name, case number, date, type of case and result of the case.

_____

_____

_____

OATH OF AFFIANT

I hereby swear or affirm that the answers above are true, complete and accurate. I understand that falsification of this document may result in a contempt of court finding against me which could result in a jail sentence and fine, and that falsification of this document may also subject me to criminal penalties for perjury (R.C. 2921.11).

_____

AFFIANT

Sworn to and subscribed before me on this _____ day of _____,

_____

_____

NOTARY PUBLIC

§ 5:21 **Ex parte civil protection order—Form**⊙

IN THE _____COURT

_____ COUNTY, OHIO

_____	:	Case No. _____
Petitioner		
Date Of Birth:	:	Judge _____
_____		
v.		
	:	**DOMESTIC VIOLENCE *EX PARTE* CIVIL PROTECTION ORDER R.C. 3113.31**
_____	:	
Respondent		
Date Of Birth:		
_____		

> **NOTICE TO RESPONDENT: SEE THE ATTACHED WARNING AND NOTICE OF FULL HEARING BELOW.**

> **PERSON(S) PROTECTED BY THIS ORDER:**
> **PETITIONER:** _____ **DOB** _____
> **FAMILY OR HOUSEHOLD MEMBER(S):**
> _____ **DOB** _____
> _____ **DOB** _____
> _____ **DOB** _____
> **RESIDENCE:**_____

This proceeding came on for an *ex parte* hearing on _____, _____. The Court finds: 1) the facts contained in the Petition are true in that Respondent engaged in domestic violence against the family household member(s) named in the Petition as defined in R.C. 3113.31; and 2) the following orders are equitable and fair, necessary to protect the family or household member(s) named in the Petition from domestic violence, and supported by good cause as shown in the *ex parte* hearing. Violence Against Women Act, 42 U.S.C. 13981, Full Faith and Credit Declaration: The Court further finds that it has jurisdiction over the parties and matter under Ohio law and that notice and an opportunity to be heard will be provided to Respondent within the time required by Ohio law.

The Court hereby issues the following orders to Respondent (the applicable orders are marked in the boxes below):

☐ 1. **RESPONDENT SHALL NOT ABUSE** the family or household member(s) named in this Order by harming, attempting to harm, threatening, molesting, following, stalking, bothering, harassing, annoying, contacting, or forcing sexual relations on them. [NCIC 01 and 02]

☐ 2. **RESPONDENT SHALL IMMEDIATELY VACATE** the following residence: _____

☐ 3. **EXCLUSIVE POSSESSION OF THE RESIDENCE** located at: _____ is granted to: _____. Respondent shall not interfere with this individual's right to occupy the residence by canceling utilities or insurance, interrupting phone service, mail delivery, or the delivery of any other documents or items [NCIC 03]

☐ 4. **RESPONDENT SHALL SURRENDER** all keys and garage door openers to the above residence at the earliest possible opportunity to the law enforcement officer who serves Respondent with this Order or as follows: _____

_____

☐ 5. **RESPONDENT SHALL STAY AWAY FROM THE FAMILY OR HOUSEHOLD MEMBER(S) NAMED IN THIS ORDER.** Respondent shall not be present within _____ (distance) of them, and shall refrain from entering any place where they may be found. This order to stay away includes, but is not limited to, the buildings, grounds, and parking lots of their residences, schools, businesses, places of employment, day care centers, and babysitters. If Respondent accidentally comes in contact with the family or household member(s) named in this Order in any public or private place, Respondent must depart immediately. [NCIC 04]

☐ 6. **RESPONDENT SHALL NOT CONTACT**, the family or household member(s) named in this Order or their residences, businesses, places of employment, schools, day care centers, and babysitters. Contact includes, but is not limited to, telephone, fax, e-mail, and voice mail. [NCIC 05]

☐ 7. **RESPONDENT SHALL IMMEDIATELY SURRENDER POSSESSION OF AND ALL KEYS TO THE FOLLOWING MOTOR VEHICLE:** _____ to: _____, who is granted exclusive use of this motor vehicle.

☐ 8. **RESPONDENT SHALL NOT REMOVE, DAMAGE, HIDE, OR DISPOSE OF ANY PROPERTY OR PETS** owned or possessed by the family or household member(s) named in this Order. Household and family personal property shall be apportioned as follows: _____

_____

_____

☐ 9. **RESPONDENT SHALL NOT CAUSE OR ENCOURAGE ANY PERSON** to do any act prohibited by this order.

☐ 10. **RESPONDENT SHALL NOT POSSESS, USE, CARRY, OR OBTAIN ANY DEADLY WEAPON**. Respondent shall turn over all deadly weapons in Respondent's possession at the earliest possible opportunity to the law enforcement officer who serves Respondent with this Order or as follows: _____ _____.

Any law enforcement agency receiving such deadly weapon(s) shall hold them in protective custody until further Court order. [NCIC 07]

☐ 11. **PARENTAL RIGHTS AND RESPONSIBILITIES ARE TEMPORARILY ALLOCATED AS FOLLOWS:**

_____

_____

This order applies to the following child(ren): _____

12. **VISITATION ORDERS DO NOT PERMIT RESPONDENT TO VIOLATE THE TERMS OF THIS ORDER.** If there is a visitation order, Respondent should bring it to the full hearing for the Court to review. Until the full hearing is held.

☐ (A) Respondent's visitation rights are suspended; or

☐ (B) as a limited exception to paragraph 5, temporary visitation rights are established as follows:

_____

_____ .

This order applies to the following child(ren): _____

_____ .

Law enforcement officers shall assist Petitioner in gaining custody of the child(ren) if necessary.

☐ 13. **RESPONDENT SHALL SUPPORT** the family or household member(s) named in this Order by following the attached Support Order, which is incorporated herein by reference.

☐ 14. **RESPONDENT MAY PICK UP CLOTHING** and personal items from the above residence only upon reasonable notice to Petitioner and in the company of a uniformed law enforcement officer within 7 days of the filing of this Order.

Arrangements may be made by contacting: _____

☐ 15. **IT IS FURTHER ORDERED** that: _____

_____

☐ 16. **THIS MATTER IS REFERRED TO A MAGISTRATE FOR A FULL HEARING PURSUANT TO CIVIL RULE 53.**

☐ 17. **THIS MATTER SHALL PROCEED TO A FULL HEARING PURSUANT TO OHIO REVISED CODE 3113.31(D)(3).**

☐ 18. **NOTICE TO RESPONDENT: ONLY THE COURT CAN CHANGE THIS ORDER. THE PETITIONER CANNOT GIVE YOU LEGAL PERMISSION TO CHANGE THIS ORDER. IF YOU GO NEAR THE PETITIONER, EVEN WITH THE PETITIONER'S CONSENT, YOU MAY BE ARRESTED. IF YOU AND THE PETITIONER/COMPLAINANT/VICTIM WANT TO RESUME YOUR RELATIONSHIP YOU MUST ASK THE COURT TO MODIFY OR DISMISS THIS PROTECTION ORDER. UNLESS THE COURT MODIFIES THIS ORDER, YOU CAN BE ARRESTED FOR VIOLATING THIS PROTECTION ORDER. YOU ACT AT YOUR OWN RISK IF YOU DISREGARD THIS WARNING.**

☐ 19. **IT IS FURTHER ORDERED** that the Clerk of Court shall cause a copy of the Petition and this Order to be delivered to the Respondent as required by law. "Delivered" for this purpose means service in accordance with Rules 4 through 4.6 of the Rules of Civil Procedure. The Clerk of Court shall also provide certified copies of the Petition and this Order to Petitioner upon request. This Order is granted without bond, and is **effective through the following date:** _____.

IT IS SO ORDERED.

_____   _____
MAGISTRATE   **JUDGE**

A FULL HEARING on this Order, and on all other issues raised by the Petition, shall be held before Judge/Magistrate _____, on _____, _____ at _____ a.m./p.m. at the following location: _____

SERVICE OF ALL DOCUMENTS TO:
☐ Respondent (by personal service)

---

§ 5:22 Domestic violence full hearing civil protection order—Form⊚

IN THE _____ COURT

_____ COUNTY, OHIO

_____	:	Case No. _____
Petitioner		
Date of Birth:	:	CSEA No. _____
_____		
	:	Judge _____
v.	:	Magistrate _____
	:	**DOMESTIC VIOLENCE FULL HEARING CIVIL PROTECTION ORDER (R.C. 3113.31)**
_____	:	
Respondent	:	☐ **WITH SUPPORT ORDER**
Date of Birth: _____	:	

NOTICE TO RESPONDENT:
SEE THE ATTACHED WARNING.

PERSON(S) PROTECTED BY THIS ORDER:
PETITIONER: ———— **DOB** ————
FAMILY OR HOUSEHOLD MEMBER(S):
———————— **DOB** ————
———————— **DOB** ————
———————— **DOB** ————
RESIDENCE:————————

This proceeding came on for a hearing on ————, ———— before the Court or the undersigned Magistrate pursuant to Civil Rule 53 and the *Ex parte* Order filed on ————, ————. The following individuals were present: ————————.

The Court/Magistrate hereby makes the following findings of fact: —
————————————————————————————————
————————————————————————————————
————————————————————————————————
————————————————————————————————

The Court finds by a preponderance of the evidence: 1) that the Petitioner or Petitioner's family or household member(s) are in danger of or have been a victim of domestic violence, as defined in Ohio Revised Code 3113.31(A), committed by Respondent; and 2) the following orders are equitable, fair, and necessary to bring about a cessation or prevention of domestic violence against the family or household member(s) named in the Petition. Violence Against Woemn Act, 42 U.S.C. 13981, Full Faith and Credit Declaration: The Court finds that it has jurisdiction over the parties and matter under Ohio law and that notice and an opportunity to be heard were provided to Respondent.

Upon the evidence submitted, the Court hereby ORDERS as follows (the applicable orders are marked below):

☐ 1. **RESPONDENT SHALL NOT ABUSE** the family or household member(s) named in this Order by harming, attempting to harm, threatening, molesting, following, stalking, bothering, harassing, annoying, contacting, or forcing sexual relations upon them. [NCIC 01 and 02]

☐ 2. **RESPONDENT SHALL IMMEDIATELY VACATE** the following residence: ————.

☐ 3. **EXCLUSIVE POSSESSION OF THE RESIDENCE** located at ———— is given to: ————. Respondent shall not interfere with this individual's right to occupy the residence by canceling utilities or insurance and interrupting phone service, mail delivery, or the delivery of any other documents or items. [NCIC 03]

☐ 4. **RESPONDENT SHALL SURRENDER** all keys and garage door openers to the above residence at the earliest possible opportunity to the law enforcement officer who serves Respondent with this Order or as follows:

————————————————.

☐ 5. **RESPONDENT SHALL STAY AWAY FROM THE FAMILY OR HOUSEHOLD MEMBER(S) NAMED IN THIS ORDER.** Respondent shall not be present within _____ (distance) of them, and shall refrain from entering any place where they may be found. This order to stay away includes, but is not limited to, the buildings, grounds, and parking lots of their residences, schools, businesses, places of employment, day care centers, and babysitters. If Respondent accidentally comes in contact with these family or household member(s) in any public or private place, Respondent must depart immediately. [NCIC 04]

☐ 6. **RESPONDENT SHALL NOT CONTACT**, the family or household member(s) named in this Order or their residences, businesses, places of employment, schools, day care centers, and babysitters. Contact includes, but is not limited to, telephone, fax, e-mail, and voice mail. [NCIC 05]

☐ 7. **RESPONDENT SHALL IMMEDIATELY SURRENDER POSSESSION OF AND ALL KEYS TO THE FOLLOWING MOTOR VEHICLE:** _____ to: _____, who is granted exclusive use of this motor vehicle.

☐ 8. **RESPONDENT SHALL NOT REMOVE, DAMAGE, HIDE, OR DISPOSE OF ANY PROPERTY OR PETS** owned or possessed by the family or household member(s) named in this Order. Household and family personal property shall be apportioned as follows: _____

_____

_____.

☐ 9. **RESPONDENT SHALL NOT CAUSE OR ENCOURAGE ANY PERSON** to do an act prohibited by this order.

☐ 10. **RESPONDENT SHALL NOT POSSESS, USE, CARRY, OR OBTAIN ANY DEADLY WEAPON**. Respondent shall turn over all deadly weapons in Respondent's possession at the earliest possible opportunity to the law enforcement officer who serves Respondent with this Order or as follows: _____

_____.

Any law enforcement agencies receiving deadly weapons shall hold them in protective custody until further Court order. [NCIC 07]

☐ 11. **PARENTAL RIGHTS AND RESPONSIBILITIES ARE TEMPORARILY ALLOCATED AS FOLLOWS:**

_____

_____.

This order applies to this/these child(ren): _____.

☐ 12. **VISITATION ORDERS DO NOT PERMIT RESPONDENT TO VIOLATE THE TERMS OF THIS ORDER.**

   ☐ (A) Respondent's visitation rights are suspended; or

   ☐ (B) as a limited exception to paragraph 5, temporary visitation rights are established as follows:

_____

_____.

This order applies to the following child(ren): _____
_____

Law enforcement officers shall assist Petitioner in gaining custody of the child(ren) if necessary.

☐ 13. **RESPONDENT SHALL SUPPORT** the family or household member(s) named in this Order by following the attached Support Order, which is incorporated into this Order by reference.

☐ 14. **RESPONDENT MAY PICK UP CLOTHING** and personal items from the above residence only upon reasonable notice to Petitioner and in the company of a uniformed law enforcement officer within 7 days after this Order is filed. Arrangements may be made by contacting _____.

☐ 15. **RESPONDENT SHALL NOT CONSUME, USE, OR POSSESS** illegal drugs or beverages containing alcohol.

☐ 16. **RESPONDENT SHALL COMPLETE THE FOLLOWING COUNSELING PROGRAM:** _____
_____

Respondent shall contact this program within _____ **days after receiving this Order and immediately arrange for an initial appoiintment.** The counseling program is requested to provide the Court a written notice if Respondent fails to attend the initial appointment and a written report when Respondent completes the program. Any program reports shall be accepted into evidence by the Court at the next scheduled hearing as the direct examination of the author of each report, subject to cross-examination by the parties. The party wishing to conduct such cross-examination must subpoena the appropriate individuals for the hearing.

☐ **Respondent is ordered to appear before Judge/Magistrate** _____**, on** _____**,** _____ **at** _____**m., to review Respondent's compliance with this counseling order. Respondent is warned: If you fail to attend the counseling program you may be held in contempt of court. If you fail to appear at this hearing, the court may issue a warrant for your arrest.**

☐ 17. **IT IS FURTHER ORDERED THAT:** _____
_____
_____
_____

18. **NOTICE TO RESPONDENT: ONLY THE COURT CAN CHANGE THIS ORDER. THE PETITIONER CANNOT GIVE YOU LEGAL PERMISSION TO CHANGE THIS ORDER. IF YOU GO NEAR THE PETITIONER, EVEN WITH THE PETITIONER'S CONSENT, YOU MAY BE ARRESTED. IF YOU AND THE PETITIONER/COMPLAINANT/VICTIM WANT TO RESUME YOUR RELATIONSHIP YOU MUST ASK THE COURT TO MODIFY OR DISMISS THIS PROTECTION ORDER. UNLESS THE COURT MODIFIES THIS ORDER, YOU CAN BE ARRESTED FOR VIOLATING THIS PROTECTION ORDER. YOU**

ACT AT YOUR OWN RISK IF YOU DISREGARD THIS WARNING.

19. **IT IS FURTHER ORDERED** that Respondent shall pay the remaining court costs in this action.

20. **IT IS FURTHER ORDERED** that the Clerk of Court shall cause a copy of the Petition and this Order to be delivered to the Respondent as required by law. "Delivered" for this purpose means service in accordance with Rule 5 of the Rules of Civil Procedure. The Clerk of Court shall also provide certified copies of the Petition and this Order to Petitioner upon request. This Order is granted without bond.

21. **ALL OF THE TERMS OF THIS ORDER REMAIN IN FULL FORCE AND EFFECT UNTIL** _____ unless earlier modified, vacated, or extended by order of this Court. Except for paragraphs 11, 12, and 13 above, this order survives a divorce, dissolution of marriage, or legal separation. Until this order is delivered to Respondent, the terms of the *Ex parte* CPO remain in effect.

IT IS SO ORDERED.

_____   _____
MAGISTRATE   **JUDGE**

NOTICE OF FINAL APPEALABLE ORDER
Copies of the foregoing Order, which is a final
appealable order, were mailed by ordinary U.S.
mail or hand delivered to the parties indicated
on the following date:_____, _____
By:_____
         CLERK OF COURT

A time-stamped copy of this Order
shall be mailed or handed to:

_____   _____
Signature of Attorney for   Signature of Attorney for
Petitioner (if applicable)   Respondent (if applicable)

_____   _____
Name   Name

_____   _____
Address   Address

_____   _____
Attorney Registration Number   Attorney Registration Number

§ 5:23 Final judgment entry granting civil protection order—Form⊚

IN THE _____ COURT

_____ COUNTY, OHIO

_____	:
Petitioner	: Case No. _____
Date Of Birth:	: CSEA No. _____
_____	
	: Judge _____
	: Magistrate _____
v.	: **CONSENT AGREEMENT**
	AND
	DOMESTIC VIOLENCE
	CIVIL
	PROTECTION ORDER
_____	: **(R.C. 3113.31)**
Respondent	☐ **WITH SUPPORT ORDER**
Date Of Birth:	:
_____	

NOTICE TO RESPONDENT: SEE THE
ATTACHED WARNING.

PERSON(S) PROTECTED BY THIS ORDER:
PETITIONER: _____ **DOB** _____
FAMILY OR HOUSEHOLD MEMBER(S):
_____ DOB _____
_____ DOB _____
_____ DOB _____
RESIDENCE:_____

This proceeding came on for a hearing on _____, _____ before the Court or the undersigned Magistrate pursuant to Civil Rule 53 and the *Ex Parte* Order filed on _____, _____. The following individuals were present: _____. The parties agree to waive their notice and hearing rights under Civil Rule 53, including the right to request findings of fact and conclusions of law and to file objections to the Magistrate's Decision in this matter. Violence Against Women Act, 42 U.S.C. 13981, Full Faith and Credit Declaration: The Court has jurisdiction over the parties and matter under Ohio law and that notice and an opportunity to be heard were provided to Respondent.

Pursuant to R.C. 3113.31(E)(1), the parties hereby agree as follows:

☐ 1. **RESPONDENT SHALL NOT ABUSE** the family or household member(s) named in this Order by harming, attempting to harm, threatening, molesting, following, stalking, bothering, harassing, annoying, contacting, or forcing sexual relations upon them. [NCIC 01 and 02]

☐ 2. **RESPONDENT SHALL IMMEDIATELY VACATE** the following residence: _____.

☐ 3. **EXCLUSIVE POSSESSION OF THE RESIDENCE** locaed at _____ is granted to: _____. Respondent shall not interfere with this individual's right to occupy the residence by canceling utilities or insurance and interrupting phone service, mail delivery, or the delivery of any other documents or items. [NCIC 03]

☐ 4. **RESPONDENT SHALL SURRENDER** all keys and garage door openers to the above residence at the earliest possible opportunity to the law enforcement officer who serves Respondent with this Order or as follows: _____
_____.

☐ 5. **RESPONDENT SHALL STAY AWAY FROM THE FAMILY OR HOUSEHOLD MEMBER(S) NAMED IN THIS ORDER.** Respondent shall not be present within _____ (distance) of them, and shall refrain from entering any place where they may be found. This order to stay away includes, but is not limited to, the buildings, grounds, and parking lots of their residences, schools, businesses, places of employment, day care centers, and babysitters. If Respondent accidentally comes in contact with these family or household member(s) in any public or private place, Respondent must depart immediately. [NCIC 04]

☐ 6. **RESPONDENT SHALL NOT CONTACT,** the family or household member(s) named in this Order or their residences, businesses, places of employment, schools, day care centers, and babysitters. Contact includes, but is not limited to, telephone, fax, e-mail, and voice mail contact. [NCIC 05]

☐ 7. **RESPONDENT SHALL IMMEDIATELY SURRENDER POSSESSION OF AND ALL KEYS TO THE FOLLOWING MOTOR VEHICLE:** _____ to: _____, who is granted exclusive use of this motor vehicle.

☐ 8. **RESPONDENT SHALL NOT REMOVE, DAMAGE, HIDE, OR DISPOSE OF ANY PROPERTY OR PETS** owned or possessed by the family or household member(s) named in this Order. Household and family personal property shall be apportioned as follows: _____
_____
_____.

☐ 9. **RESPONDENT SHALL NOT CAUSE OR ENCOURAGE ANY PERSON TO DO AN ACT PROHIBITED ABOVE.**

☐ 10. **RESPONDENT SHALL NOT POSSESS, USE, CARRY, OR OBTAIN ANY DEADLY WEAPON.** Respondent shall turn over all deadly weapons in Respondent's possession at the earliest possible opportunity to the law enforcement officer who serves Respondent with this Order or as follows: _____
_____.

Any law enforcement agencies receiving deadly weapons shall hold them in protective custody until further Court order. [NCIC 07]

☐ 11. **PARENTAL RIGHTS AND RESPONSIBILITIES ARE TEMPORARILY ALLOCATED AS FOLLOWS:**

_____

_____.

This order applies to the following child(ren): _____.

12. **VISITATION ORDERS DO NOT PERMIT RESPONDENT TO VIOLATE THE TERMS OF THIS ORDER.**

☐ (A) Respondent's visitation rights are suspended; or

☐ (B) as a limited exception to paragraph 5, temporary visitation rights are established as follows:

_____

_____.

This order applies to the following child(ren):

_____ _____.

Law enforcement officers shall assist Petitioner in gaining custody of the child(ren) if necessary.

☐ 13. **RESPONDENT SHALL SUPPORT** the family or household member(s) named in this Order by following the attached Support Order, which is incorporated into this Order by reference.

☐ 14. **RESPONDENT MAY PICK UP CLOTHING** and personal items from the above residence only upon reasonable notice to Petitioner and in the company of a uniformed law enforcement officer within 7 days after this Order is filed. Arrangements may be made by contacting: _____.

☐ 15. **RESPONDENT SHALL NOT CONSUME, USE, OR POSSESS** illegal drugs or beverages containing alcohol.

☐ 16. **RESPONDENT SHALL COMPLETE THE FOLLOWING COUNSELING PROGRAM:** _____

_____.

Respondent shall contact this program within _____ days after receiving this Order and immediately arrange for an initial appointment. The counseling program is requested to provide the Court a written notice if Respondent fails to attend the initial appointment and a written report when Respondent completes the program. Any program reports shall be accepted into evidence by the Court at the next scheduled hearing as the direct examination of the author of each report, subject to cross-examination by the parties. The party wishing to conduct such cross-examination must subpoena the appropriate individuals for the hearing.

☐ **Respondent is ordered to appear before Judge/Magistrate _____, on _____, _____ at _____ m., to review Respondent's compliance with this counseling order. Respondent is warned: If you fail to attend the counseling program you may be held in contempt of court. If you fail to appear at this hearing, the Court may issue a warrant for your arrest.**

☐ 17. **IT IS FURTHER ORDERED THAT:** _____

_____

_____

_____

☐ 18. **<u>NOTICE TO RESPONDENT</u>: ONLY THE COURT CAN CHANGE THIS ORDER. THE PETITIONER CANNOT GIVE YOU LEGAL PERMISSION TO CHANGE THIS ORDER. IF YOU GO NEAR THE PETITIONER, EVEN WITH THE PETITION-ER'S CONSENT, YOU MAY BE ARRESTED. IF YOU AND THE PETITIONER/COMPLAINANT/VICTIM WANT TO RESUME YOUR RELATIONSHIP YOU MUST ASK THE COURT TO MODIFY OR DISMISS THIS PROTECTION ORDER. UNLESS THE COURT MODIFIES THIS ORDER, YOU CAN BE AR-RESTED FOR VIOLATING THIS PROTECTION ORDER. <u>YOU ACT AT YOUR OWN RISK IF YOU DISREGARD THIS WARNING</u>.**

19. **IT IS FURTHER ORDERED** that Respondent shall pay the remaining court costs in this action.

20. **IT IS FURTHER ORDERED** that the Clerk of Court shall cause a copy of the Petition and this Order to be delivered to the Respondent as required by law. "Delivered" for this purpose means service in accordance with Rule 5 of the Rules of Civil Procedure. The Clerk of Court shall also provide certified copies of the Petition and this Order to Petitioner upon request. This Order is granted without bond.

21. **ALL OF THE TERMS OF THIS ORDER SHALL REMAIN IN FULL FORCE AND EFFECT UNTIL** _____ unless earlier modified, vacated, or extended by order of this Court. Except for paragraphs 11, 12, and 13 above, this order survives a divorce, dissolution of marriage, or legal separation. Until this order is delivered to Respondent, the terms of the *Ex Parte* CPO remain in effect.

IT IS SO ORDERED.

MAGISTRATE	JUDGE
I have read this Consent Agreement and Civil Protection Order and agree to its terms.	**I have read this Consent Agreement and Civil Protection Order and agree to its terms.**
Signature of Petitioner	Signature of Respondent
Address of Petitioner	Address of Respondent
Signature of Attorney for Petitioner	Signature of Attorney for Respondent

_____   _____

Address of Attorney for Petitioner   Address of Attorney for
                                      Respondent

NOTICE OF FINAL APPEALABLE ORDER
Copies of the foregoing Order, which is a final
appealable order, were mailed by ordinary U.S.
mail or hand delivered to the parties indicated
on the following date:_____, _____
By:_____
         CLERK OF COURT

A time-stamped copy of this Order
shall be mailed or handed to:

---

§ 5:24   Criminal temporary protection order—Form⊚

IN THE _____ COURT

_____ COUNTY, OHIO

State of Ohio	:	Case No. _____
	:	
v.	:	Judge _____
	:	
	:	
Defendant	:	**CRIMINAL**
		TEMPORARY
		PROTECTION
		ORDER
		R.C. 2919.26

NOTICE TO DEFENDANT:
SEE THE ATTACHED WARNING.

PERSON(S) PROTECTED BY THIS ORDER:
COMPLAINANT/VICTIM: _____ **DOB** _____
FAMILY OR HOUSEHOLD MEMBER(S):
_____ **DOB** _____
_____ **DOB** _____
_____ **DOB** _____
RESIDENCE:_____

Upon a hearing held on _____, _____, the Court finds that the motion of Complainant/Victim for a Temporary Protection Order is well taken. The Court finds that the safety and protection of Complainant/Victim and the other family or household members named above may be impaired by the continued presence of Defendant. Therefore, the following orders, which are designed to ensure the safety and protection of Complainant/Victim and the family or household members, are issued to Defendant as pretrial conditions of release in addition to any bail set under Criminal Rule 46. **All of the orders that are marked in the boxes below apply to Defendant:**

☐ 1. **DEFENDANT SHALL NOT ABUSE COMPLAINANT/ VICTIM AND THE OTHER FAMILY OR HOUSEHOLD MEMBERS NAMED IN THIS ORDER** by harming, attempting to harm, threatening, molesting, following, stalking, bothering, harassing, annoying, contacting, or forcing sexual relations upon them.

☐ 2. **DEFENDANT SHALL NOT ENTER** the buildings, grounds, and parking lots of the residences, schools, businesses, and places of employment of Complainant/Victim and the other family or household members named in this Order.

☐ 3. **DEFENDANT SHALL STAY AWAY FROM THE COMPLAINANT/VICTIM AND THE OTHER FAMILY OR HOUSEHOLD MEMBERS NAMED IN THIS ORDER.** Defendant shall not be present within _____ (distance) of them. If Defendant accidentally comes in contact with Complainant/Victim or the other family or household members named in this Order in any public or private place, Defendant must depart immediately.

☐ 4. **DEFENDANT SHALL NOT INTERFERE** with Complainant's/Victim's right to occupy the residence indicated above by canceling utilities or insurance and interrupting phone service, mail delivery, or the delivery of any other documents or items. Defendant shall surrender all keys and garage door openers to the residence indicated above at the earliest possible opportunity to the law enforcement officer who serves Defendant with this order or as follows:

_____.

☐ 5. **DEFENDANT SHALL NOT INITIATE ANY CONTACT WITH COMPLAINANT/VICTIM OR THE OTHER FAMILY OR HOUSEHOLD MEMBERS NAMED IN THIS ORDER.** This contact includes, but is not limited to, telephone, fax, e-mail, and voice mail contact with their residences, schools, businesses, and places of employment except as provided:

_____.

☐ 6. **DEFENDANT SHALL NOT CAUSE OR ENCOURAGE ANY OTHER PERSON** to do any act prohibited in this order.

☐ 7. **DEFENDANT MAY PICK UP CLOTHING** and personal items from the above residence only upon reasonable notice to Complainant/Victim and in the company of a uniformed law enforcement officer within 7 days of the filing of this Order or the date of Defendant's release on bond in connection with this charge, whichever is later. Arrangements may be made by contacting: _____.

☐ 8. **DEFENDANT SHALL NOT POSSESS, USE, CARRY, OR OBTAIN ANY DEADLY WEAPON.** Defendant shall turn over any deadly weapon in Defendant's possession at the earliest possible opportunity to the law enforcement officer who serves Defendant with this Order or as follows: _____.

Any law enforcement agencies receiving deadly weapons shall hold them in protective custody until further Court order. [NCIC 07]

☐ 9. **DEFENDANT SHALL NOT CONSUME, USE, OR POSSESS** illegal drugs or beverages containing alcohol.

☐ 10. **IT IS FURTHER ORDERED THAT:** _____

☐ 11. **DEFENDANT IS ADVISED THAT VISITATION ORDERS DO NOT PERMIT DEFENDANT TO VIOLATE ANY OF THE TERMS OF THIS ORDER.**

12. **IT IS FURTHER ORDERED** that defendant shall pay the remaining court costs in this action.

13. **NOTICE TO DEFENDANT: IF THIS ORDER REQUIRES YOU TO VACATE A RESIDENCE OR REFRAIN FROM ENTERING THE RESIDENCE, SCHOOL, BUSINESS, OR PLACE OF EMPLOYMENT OF THE FAMILY OR HOUSEHOLD MEMBER(S) NAMED IN THIS ORDER, THIS ORDER CANNOT BE WAIVED OR NULLIFIED BY AN INVITATION TO YOU TO ENTER THEIR RESIDENCE, SCHOOL, BUSINESS, OR PLACE OF EMPLOYMENT OR YOUR ENTRY INTO ONE OF THOSE PLACES OTHERWISE UPON THEIR CONSENT.**

14. **NOTICE TO DEFENDANT: ONLY THE COURT CAN CHANGE THIS ORDER. THE COMPLAINANT/VICTIM CANNOT GIVE YOU LEGAL PERMISSION TO CHANGE THIS ORDER. IF YOU GO NEAR THE COMPLAINANT/VICTIM, EVEN WITH THE COMPLAINANT/VICTIM'S CONSENT, YOU MAY BE ARRESTED. IF YOU AND THE COMPLAINANT/VICTIM WANT TO RESUME YOUR RELATIONSHIP YOU MUST ASK THE COURT TO MODIFY OR DISMISS THIS PROTECTION ORDER. UNLESS THE COURT MODIFIES THIS ORDER, YOU CAN BE ARRESTED FOR VIOLATING THIS PROTECTION ORDER. YOU ACT AT YOUR OWN RISK IF YOU DISREGARD THIS WARNING.**

15. **IT IS FURTHER ORDERED THAT** a copy of this Order shall be delivered to Defendant on the same day that the Order is entered. "Delivered" for this purpose means service in accordance with Rule 4 of the Rules of Criminal Procedure.

IT IS SO ORDERED.

MAGISTRATE **JUDGE**

COPIES SHALL BE ISSUED TO:

DEFENDANT: DATE: _____

_____

Chapter 6

Alternative Forms of Dispute Resolution

*By Hon. Denise Herman McColley**

---

§ 6:1 Introduction

In recent years, Ohio, like many other states, has seen a dramatic increase in the use of what are called "alternative dispute resolution" processes to resolve disputes in family cases, as well as other matters. Many of these disputes would have previously been resolved through

---

*Based on the original work of Prof. Nancy Hardin Rogers.

litigation or attorneys' negotiation and settlement prior to litigation. Processes most typically used to resolve family cases include mediation, arbitration, mediation-arbitration ("med-arb"), the use of parenting coordinators (sometimes called parent coordinators or special masters), collaborative law, and early neutral evaluation ("ENE").[1] In addition, the process of conciliation, which has been allowed in Ohio since 1969, is sometimes used to resolve marital disputes, with an emphasis on preserving the marriage.[2]

Some now argue that as part of legal representation an attorney should have a duty to discuss the various dispute resolution processes with a client.[3] There is no doubt that the practice of law has changed in the face of the various methods of dispute resolution.[4]

§ 6:2 Definitions

Arbitration is a process in which a third person is designated to make a finding or provide a decision or award for the disputing parties. The process is adjudicatory in nature, but normally less formal than traditional litigation.

Collaborative law is a process in which parties engage attorneys to assist in the negotiation and settlement of their dispute. In most collaborative law models, attorneys are retained with the understanding that, in the event the dispute is not resolved and it appears the matter will proceed to litigation, the collaborative attorney will withdraw and the parties must retain other counsel to represent them in litigation or proceed on a pro se basis.

Conciliation is a process whereby the court may order parties to participate in counseling for a prescribed period of time, generally in an effort to preserve their marriage.

Early neutral evaluation ("ENE") is a non-binding form of dispute resolution in which parties meet before a neutral third party who has experience in the subject matter being litigated. The neutral offers the parties a confidential opinion regarding the likely outcome of the case and an analysis of strengths and weaknesses of each side's arguments

---

[Section 6:1]

[1] For a discussion of different dispute resolution alternatives, suitable for clients' reading, see *Q & A—The Road to Settlement: ADR Offers Cost-Effective Alternatives to Trial*, 28 Family Advocate 10 (Summer 2005).

[2] For a discussion of dispute resolution in Ohio and Colorado, *see* Eileen Pruett and Cynthia Savage, *Statewide Initiatives to Encourage Alternative Dispute Resolution and Enhance Collaborative Approaches to Resolving Family Issues*, 42 Family Court Review 232 (April 2004).

[3] Thomas D. Vu, Going to Court as a Last Resort: Establishing a Duty for Attorneys to Discuss Alternative Dispute Resolution With Their Clients, 47 Family Court Review 586 (July 2009).

[4] Julie Macfarlane, The New Lawyer: How Settlement is Transforming the Practice of Law, Vancouver Canada: UBC Press, 2008.

in an effort to give parties a realistic view of the case, identify issues, speed up discovery and encourage settlement.[1]

Med-Arb (or mediation-arbitration) is a hybrid process, in which the parties agree in advance that they will first attempt to mediate their dispute and, if the mediation is unsuccessful, will then arbitrate. In med-arb, upon reaching the decision that there is an impasse and the mediation cannot proceed, either the mediator "changes hats" and acts as an arbitrator or a second individual enters the process and arbitrates the dispute.

Mediation is a "process in which a mediator facilitates communication and negotiation between parties to assist them in reaching a voluntary agreement regarding their dispute."[2] The mediator is not authorized to make a decision for the parties.

Parenting coordination is a process that is sometimes used to resolve ongoing and continuing high conflict parenting disputes. In this process, an individual is appointed as "parenting coordinator" (sometimes referred to as "parent coordinator" or "special master") by court order or through the written agreement of the parties. Terms outlining the parenting coordinator's scope of authority, the judicial review process, how he or she is to be paid, and the length of the appointment are set out in the order or agreement. Typically, parenting coordinators use a med-arb model in which, once a dispute is identified, the coordinator first uses mediative techniques with the parents in an effort to reach resolution of a dispute. If that effort is not successful, the coordinator issues a decision or an award.

§ 6:3   Mediation

RC 3109.052 provides the framework for the court to use in ordering mediation in certain cases. In outlining which cases are subject to such an order, subsection (A) of the statute provides the following direction:

> If a proceeding for divorce, dissolution, legal separation, annulment, or the allocation of parental rights and responsibilities for the care of a child involves one or more children, if the parents of the children do not agree upon an appropriate allocation of parental rights and responsibilities for the care of their children or do not agree upon a specific schedule of parenting time for their children, the court may order the parents to mediate their differences on those matters in accordance with mediation procedures adopted by the court by local rule . . . .

Subsection (D) of the statute makes it plain that the court may not order mediation to resolve issues other than those set out above. In other words, the parties may agree to subject other issues of

---

[Section 6:2]

[1]Jordan Leigh Santeramo, *Early Neutral Evaluation in Divorce Cases*, 42 Family Court Review 321, 325 (April 2004).

[2]RC 2710.01(A).

controversy to mediation (e.g., determination of duration of the marriage, division of property, division of debts, spousal support, payment of attorney fees, court costs, etc.); however, the court may not require them to do so.

In addition, subsection (A) of the statute indicates that if one of the parties has been convicted of or pleaded guilty to domestic violence or been determined to be a perpetrator of an abusive act that is the basis of an adjudication that a child is an abused child, the court may order mediation only if the court determines that it is in the best interests of the parties to order mediation and makes specific written findings of fact to support its determination.

Subsection (B) of the statute provides that if a mediation order is issued and the order requires the parties to file a mediation report, the mediator and the parties must file a report of the results of the mediation with the court. A mediation report is required to indicate only whether agreement has been reached on any of the issues subject to the mediation, and, if agreement has been reached, the content and details of the agreement. Mediation reports are not to contain any background information or any information discussed or presented in the process. In practice, in cases in which parties are represented by counsel and agreements have been reached, mediators will generally not ask the parties to sign a mediation report or file a report with the content and details of the mediation agreement unless and until counsel have reviewed the agreement with the parties and, following the review, both parties have signed the agreement and/or report of mediation. In the event agreement has not been reached, a mediation report indicating the failure to reach agreement and referring the case back to the court for further action is appropriate.

RC 2710.06 provides that a mediator is prohibited from making a report, assessment, evaluation, recommendation or finding to a court, department, agency or officer of the state that may make a ruling on the dispute that is the subject of the mediation. The statute enumerates certain exceptions to this prohibition, one of which is that the mediator may report whether the mediation has occurred or was terminated, whether a settlement was reached and who attended the mediation session(s).

The court is not bound by any agreements which have been reached by the parties in mediation; however, the mediation report must be considered by the court when it allocates parental rights and responsibilities for the children and/or when it establishes a parenting time schedule. Ultimately, the court is required to consider the best interest of the children when making that allocation or establishing the parenting time schedule.

§ 6:4 Communications made in mediation

RC 3109.052(C) describes the limited mediation privilege available for mediators acting under a court order in a proceeding for divorce, dissolution, legal separation, or annulment in which the allocation of parental rights and responsibilities, or the award of parenting time is being determined, as follows:

(T)he mediator shall not be made a party to, and shall not be called as a witness or testify in, any action or proceeding, other than a criminal, delinquency, child abuse, child neglect, or dependent child action or proceeding, that is brought by or against either parent and that pertains to the mediation process, to any information discussed or presented in the mediation process, to the allocation of parental rights and responsibilities for the care of the parent's children, or to the awarding of parenting time rights in relation to their children. The mediator shall not be made a party to, or be called as a witness or testify in, such an action or proceeding even if both parents give their prior consent to the mediator being made a party to or being called as a witness or to testify in the action or proceeding.

In addition, RC 2317.02(H) provides that a mediator acting under a mediation order issued under RC 3109.052(A) or an order otherwise issued in any proceeding for divorce, dissolution, legal separation, annulment (presumably orders regarding mediation for determination of division of property and debts, support issues, duration of marriage, etc.), or the allocation of parental rights and responsibilities for the care of children, shall not testify "in any action or proceeding, other than a criminal, delinquency, child abuse, child neglect, or dependent child action or proceeding, that is brought by or against either parent who takes part in mediation in accordance with the order and that pertains to the mediation process, to any information discussed or presented in the mediation process, to the allocation of parental rights and responsibilities for the care of the parents' children, or to the awarding of parenting time rights in relation to their children."

Ohio's version of the Uniform Mediation Act (UMA)[1] became effective October 29, 2005. The act repealed RC 2317.023 which previously governed disclosure of mediation communications and provided a qualified privilege.

RC 2710.01(B) defines "mediation communication" as "a statement, whether oral, in a record, verbal or nonverbal, that occurs during a mediation or is made for purposes of considering, conducting, participating in, initiating, continuing, or reconvening a mediation or retaining a mediator."

RC 2710.06 of the UMA prohibits mediators from sharing substantive information with a court, department or agency subject to certain exceptions, two of which are that the mediator may report any communications that the parties agreed are not confidential[2] and that the mediator may disclose "communications that evidence abuse, neglect, abandonment or exploitation of an individual to a public agency

---

[Section 6:4]

[1]RC 2710.01 et seq.

[2]RC 2710.06(A)(2) and RC 2710.07.

responsible for protecting individuals against abuse, neglect, abandonment or exploitation."[3]

According to RC 2710.03, three types of persons may hold a privilege against disclosure of mediation communications: a mediation party, a mediator or a nonparty participant. A mediation party may refuse to disclose, and may prevent any other person from disclosing, a mediation communication. A mediator may refuse to disclose a mediation communication and may prevent any other person from disclosing a mediation communication of the mediator. A non-party participant may refuse to disclose, and may prevent any other person from disclosing a mediation communication of the nonparty participant.

Finally, it is important to be aware of the provisions of RC 2151.421(A), commonly referred to as the "mandatory reporting law," as they may effect a mediator's duty to report certain disclosures which are made during mediation sessions. That Code section applies to certain professionals, including attorneys, licensed psychologists and persons engaged in social work or the practice of counseling, many of whom also have mediation practices. The section requires that any of the named professionals who is "acting in an official or professional capacity and knows or suspects that a child under eighteen years of age or a mentally retarded, developmentally disabled, or physically impaired child under twenty-one years of age has suffered or faces a threat of suffering any physical or mental wound, injury, disability, or condition of a nature that reasonably indicates abuse or neglect of the child" must "immediately report that knowledge or suspicion to the public children services agency or a municipal or county peace officer in the county in which the child resides or in which the abuse or neglect is occurring or has occurred." Even though the mediator may not be acting as an attorney, psychologist or social worker when he or she mediates, the mediator is acting in "an official or professional capacity" which would appear to make the provisions of RC 2151.421(A) applicable.

§ 6:5   Motion for mediation—Form

(RC 3109.052)

[Title of Court]

[Caption]   Case No. [_____]
                                                                MOTION FOR
                                                                MEDIATION

Plaintiff/Defendant, [name], by and through his undersigned attorney, says the following:

    1. That this case involves the allocation of parental rights and re-

---

[3]RC 2710.06(A)(3).

sponsibilities for the care of the parties' children, [names and dates of birth].

2. That the Plaintiff and Defendant have not agreed upon [an appropriate allocation of parental rights and responsibilities for the care of their children] and/or [a specific schedule of parenting time for their children].

3. *Option one:*

That neither party has been previously convicted of or pleaded guilty to a violation of section 2919.25 of the Revised Code involving a victim who at the time of the commission of the offense was a member of the family or household that is the subject of the proceeding; that neither party previously has been convicted of or pleaded guilty to an offense involving a victim who at the time of the commission of the offense was a member of the family or household that is the subject of the proceeding and caused physical harm to the victim in the commission of the offense; and that neither party has been determined to be the perpetrator of the abusive act that is the basis of an adjudication that a child is an abused child.

Option two (select those of the following phrases which are applicable):

_____That the [Plaintiff] [Defendant] has previously been convicted of or pleaded guilty to a violation of section 2919.25 of the Revised Code involving a victim who at the time of the commission of the offense was a member of the family or household that is the subject of the proceeding;

_____That the [Plaintiff] [Defendant] previously has been convicted of or pleaded guilty to an offense involving a victim who at the time of the commission of the offense was a member of the family or household that is the subject of the proceeding and caused physical harm to the victim in the commission of the offense;

_____That the [Plaintiff] [Defendant] has been determined to be the perpetrator of the abusive act that is the basis of an adjudication that a child is an abused child.

And that, despite the [guilty plea(s)] [conviction(s)] [determination] referred to above, it is in the best interests of the parties for the court to order mediation in this case.

4. Mediation is appropriate in this proceeding.

Now, therefore, the Plaintiff, moves the Court for an order referring the matter to mediation in accordance with the Court's mediation procedures.

_____
Plaintiff/Defendant/Attorney

§ 6:6 Court order for mediation—Form⊚

(RC 3109.052)

[Title of Court]

[Caption]

Case No. *[_____]*
<u>JUDGMENT
ENTRY /
MAGISTRATE'S
ORDER
REQUIRING
MEDIATION</u>

This matter came on for consideration upon a motion to have this matter submitted to mediation. Pursuant to section 3109.052 of the Revised Code, the following findings are made:

1. That this case involves the allocation of parental rights and responsibilities for the care of the parties' children, [names and dates of birth].

2. That the Plaintiff and Defendant have not agreed upon [an appropriate allocation of parental rights and responsibilities for the care of their children] and/or [a specific schedule of parenting time for their children].

3. *Option one:*

That neither party has been previously convicted of or pleaded guilty to a violation of section 2919.25 of the Revised Code involving a victim who at the time of the commission of the offense was a member of the family or household that is the subject of the proceeding; that neither party previously has been convicted of or pleaded guilty to an offense involving a victim who at the time of the commission of the offense was a member of the family or household that is the subject of the proceeding and caused physical harm to the victim in the commission of the offense; and that neither party has been determined to be the perpetrator of the abusive act that is the basis of an adjudication that a child is an abused child.

Option two (select those of the following phrases which are applicable):

_____That the [Plaintiff] [Defendant] has previously been convicted of or pleaded guilty to a violation of section 2919.25 of the Revised Code involving a victim who at the time of the commission of the offense was a member of the family or household that is the subject of the proceeding;

_____That the [Plaintiff] [Defendant] previously has been convicted of or pleaded guilty to an offense involving a victim who at the time of the commission of the offense was a member of the family or household that is the subject of the proceeding and caused physical harm to the victim in the commission of the offense;

_____That the [Plaintiff] [Defendant] has been determined to be the perpetrator of the abusive act that is the basis of an adjudication that a child is an abused child.

4. *Select those of the following phrases which are applicable if there has been plea(s), conviction(s), or determination as referred to above (if there has not been such a plea, conviction or determination, proceed to paragraph 5, below)* :

_____That the [Plaintiff] [Defendant] has completed a domestic violence or other appropriate counseling program as a term and condition of his/her probation and/or pursuant to court order issued in case number *[number of case]*, in the *[title of court]* Court of *[name of county]*, Ohio.

_____That both the Plaintiff and the Defendant have consented to this matter being referred to mediation and have consented to attend any required mediation screening sessions.

_____That both parties believe it would be in their best interest and the best interest of their child(ren) if the matter were referred to mediation.

_____That both parties' attorneys have indicated they believe it is in the parties' best interest to mediate this matter.

_____That

_____.

Therefore, despite the [guilty plea(s)] [conviction(s)] [determination] referred to above, it is in the best interests of the parties that mediation be ordered in this case.

5. Mediation is appropriate in this proceeding.

It is, therefore, ORDERED that this matter is hereby referred to *[name of mediator]* for mediation of the disputes relative to the allocation of parental rights and responsibilities for the care of the parties' children and/or regarding parenting time for the children. Upon the conclusion of such mediation, the parties and mediator shall provide an appropriate report to the court.

It is further ORDERED that the parties shall attend all mediation screening sessions established by the mediator and shall attend all mediation sessions scheduled until such time as mediation is concluded or terminated.

If appropriate, the following order may be added:

It is further ORDERED that counsel shall attend all mediation sessions.

_____

Judge / Magistrate

§ 6:7 Mediation report—Agreement—Form⊛

[Title of Court]

[Caption]

Case No.

[_____]

<u>MEDIATION</u>
<u>REPORT</u>

Now come the mediator, [name], the Plaintiff and the Defendant [by and through their undersigned attorneys], and say that the parties have reached an agreement settling [all matters at issue in this case] [settling some of the matters at issue in this case]. The agreement is attached hereto as "Exhibit A" and the parties hereby request that the court adopt their agreement as its order.

If agreement on all issues has not been reached, add the following sentence:

[The parties hereby request that the court set those matters which have not been resolved for hearing at the earliest date available.]

_____   _____
Mediator   Plaintiff/Attorney

                                           _____
                                           Defendant/Attorney

§ 6:8 Mediation report—No agreement—Form⊛

[Title of Court]

[Caption]

Case No.

[_____]

<u>MEDIATION</u>
<u>REPORT</u>

Now come the mediator, [name], the Plaintiff and the Defendant [by and through their undersigned attorneys], and say that the parties have attempted to resolve their differences through mediation, but that they have been unable to do so.

The parties hereby request that the court set this case for hearing at the earliest date available.

_____   _____
Mediator   Plaintiff/Attorney

                                           _____
                                           Defendant/Attorney

NOTES TO FORM

Drafter's Notes

Always check your local rules, since some counties have a mediation program and their own forms for referral, assessment and reporting.

§ 6:9 Mediator qualifications

In Ohio, there are no legally prescribed qualifications or certification standards which entitle an individual to be deemed a mediator.[1] However, Revised Code 3109.52(A) provides that "[a]ny mediation procedures adopted by local court rule for the use under this division shall include, but are not limited to, provisions establishing qualifications for mediators who may be employed or used and provisions establishing standards for the conduct of the mediation."

Rule 16(A) of the Rules of Superintendence for the Courts of Ohio further expands on that code section by requiring every court in Ohio to consider a local rule for mediation, which then may be adopted by the court.

Rule 16(C) of the Rules of Superintendence sets out the required qualifications to be included in any local rule for mediation of disputes concerning the allocation of parental rights and responsibilities or of delinquency or status offenses, which are applicable to any mediator employed by the court or to whom the court makes referrals. Those requirements are, as follows:

(1) A bachelor's degree, or equivalent educational experience, as is satisfactory to the court, and at least two years of professional experience with families. "Professional experience with families" includes counseling, casework, legal representation in family law matters, or equivalent experience as is satisfactory to the court;

(2) Completion of at least twelve hours of basic mediation training or equivalent experience as a mediator, as is satisfactory to the court;

(3) After completing the twelve hours of basic mediation training, completion of at least forty hours of specialized family or divorce mediation training conducted in a program approved by the Dispute Resolution Section of the Supreme Court;

(4) All mediators who mediate any cases for domestic relations or juvenile courts must have fourteen hours of additional special-

---

[Section 6:9]

[1]For a general discussion of issues related to regulation, certification of, and voluntary standards for mediators, see Forrest S. Mosten, Institutionalization of Mediation, 42 Family Court Review 292 (April 2004). See also Dorothy J. Della Noce, *The Beaten Path to Mediator Quality Assurance: The Emerging Narrative of Consensus and Its Institutional Functions*, Vol. 19, No. 3, Ohio State J. on Disp. Resol. 937 (2004); Robert A. Baruch Bush, *One Size Does Not Fit All: A Pluralistic Approach to Mediator Performance Testing and Quality Assurance*, Vol. 19, No. 3, Ohio State J. on Disp. Resol. 965 (2004).

ized training in domestic abuse issues and mediation through an approved training program unless the mediator is co-mediating with another mediator who has completed the training;[2]

(5) Mediators who mediate abuse, dependency and neglect cases must also have significant mediation experience and 32 hours of specialized training;[3]

(6) Domestic relations and juvenile courts with mediation programs shall encourage mediators to comply with the Model Standards of Practice for Family and Divorce Mediation.[4]

In assisting a client to choose a mediator, in addition to those items set out in Rule 16 and those which might be established by local court rule, an attorney may want to consider other criteria as follows:

(1) Training in domestic abuse issues. As set out above, in order to receive court referrals or to be employed by a court as a mediator, the mediator must have completed training in domestic abuse issues. Those mediating issues in family cases should be trained to recognize signs of domestic abuse and, if domestic abuse is or has been a factor in a relationship, to institute appropriate precautions in the mediation or, if necessary, to terminate the mediation. The training entitled "Domestic Abuse Issues: Training for Mediators and other Professionals," developed by the Ohio Supreme Court through its Judicial and Court Services Division, Office of Dispute Resolution Section[5] has been and is being offered in various areas of the state. In court-connected programs, mediation participants should be screened for domestic abuse issues prior to the mediation's commencement.[6]

(2) Continuing education and mediation experience. In choosing a mediator, a legitimate question is how long and in how many cases has the mediator provided mediation services. A second

[2]Rule 16(C)(2).

[3]Rule 16(C)(3).

[4]See http://afccnet.org/resources/resources_model_mediation.asp and Rule 16(D).

[5]For more information, contact The Supreme Court of Ohio, Judicial and Court Services Division, Office of Dispute Resolution Programs Services, (800) 826-9010, (614) 752-4700, http://www.sconet.state.oh.us. Elizabeth Clemants and Alan Gross, *Why Aren't We Screening? A Survey Examining Domestic Violence Screening Procedures and Training Protocols in Community Mediation Centers*, vol. 24, no. 4 Conflict Resolution Quarterly (Summer 2007). Desmond Ellis and Noreen Stuckless, *Domestic Violence, DOVE, and Divorce Mediation*, vol. 44, no. 4 Family Court Review 658 (October 2006). Desmond Ellis and Noreen Stuckless, *Separation, Domestic Violence and Divorce Mediation*, vol. 23, no. 4 Conflict Resolution Quarterly 461 (Summer 2006); Connie J.A. Beck, Michele E. Walsh and Rose Weston, Analysis of Mediation Agreements of Families Reporting Specific Types of Intimate Partner Abuse, 47 Family Court Review 401 (July 2009).

[6]See http://afccnet.org/resources/resources_model_mediation.asp and Rule 16(D).

question is whether or not the mediator has continued his mediation education beyond that required to receive referrals by the court (see above).

(3) Liability insurance. Prior to the adoption of Rule 16, Rule 81 of the Rules of Superintendence provided that those mediators employed by or receiving referrals from the court were required to maintain "appropriate liability insurance specifically covering the activities of the individual as a mediator." This provision was eliminated with the enactment of Rule 16. Comments to the rule indicate that "[w]hile the Committee recognizes the possible threat of liability, the actual occurrence of malpractice suits against mediators has been extremely rare . . . . The Committee does not feel it necessary to mandate liability insurance in a minimum qualifications rule. Instead, the Committee encourages flexibility for local courts which may wish to consider the issue and retain the insurance requirement for their individual programs."

(4) Adherence to ethical standards or standards of conduct. It is certainly reasonable to ask if a prospective mediator adheres to certain ethical standards or standards of conduct.

The Model Standards of Conduct for Mediators were prepared from 1992 through 1994 and revised in 2005 by a committee composed of delegates from the American Arbitration Association, the American Bar Association ("ABA") and the Society of Professionals in Dispute Resolution (now merged into the Association for Conflict Resolution). These standards have been approved by the American Arbitration Association, the Society of Professionals in Dispute Resolution and the ABA and can be found at http://www.abanet.org. The standards apply to mediators in general and are not specific to family mediators. They have not been adopted in Ohio, but may be considered persuasive as to acceptable practice for mediators.

RC 2710.08 (part of Ohio's version of the Uniform Mediation Act) also sets out ethical concerns and required disclosures in mediation.

The Model Standards of Practice for Family and Divorce Mediation came about through a collaborative effort by family mediation professionals and organizations to create standards of practice to increase public confidence in the profession and to provide guidance for mediators. In the past, various groups developed their own standards of practice [For example, the ABA's 1984 *Standards of Practice for Lawyer Mediators in Family Law Disputes*, and the 1984 *Model Standards of Practice for Family and Divorce Mediation* which was developed as the result of national symposia convened by the Association of Family and Conciliation Courts ("AFCC"), and various other standards of practice developed by national and statewide organizations].

From 1998 to 2000, AFCC acted as the convener of the Model

Standards Symposium with the ABA's Family Law Section and the National Council of Dispute Resolution Organizations [an umbrella organization including the Academy of Family Mediators, the Society of Professionals in Dispute Resolution, and Conflict Resolution Education Network (now merged to form the Association for Conflict Resolution or "ACR"), the ABA Section of Dispute Resolution, AFCC, the National Association for Community Mediation, and the National Conference on Peacemaking and Conflict Resolution] all acting as co-conveners. Representatives from over twenty family mediation organizations were a part of the Symposium which resulted in the Model Standards of Practice for Family and Divorce Mediation.[7] The Standards have been adopted by ACR, by the ABA Family Section and by AFCC. Rule 16(D) of the Rules of Superintendence for the State of Ohio states that "[e]ach division that adopts a local rule providing for mediation of family cases shall encourage mediators to comply with the Model Standards of Practice for Family and Divorce Mediation. . .and the Special Policy Considerations for State Regulation of Family Mediators and Court Affiliated Programs. . .."[8]

Questions sometimes arise as to whether mediation constitutes the practice of law. The American Bar Association Section on Dispute Resolution issued its Resolution on Mediation and the Unauthorized Practice of Law in February 2002. The Resolution encourages the interpretation of statutes and regulations on the unauthorized practice of law "in such a manner as to permit all individuals, regardless of whether they are lawyers, to serve as mediators," and sets out various principles which should be used in the interpretation and application of such statutes and regulations.[9] The Resolution contains commentary comparing the Resolution with state guidelines and with ethical considerations for mediators and lawyers. The principles set out in the Resolution are worth consideration by any individual acting as a mediator.

(5) Involvement of children in mediation.[10] If one of the issues to be resolved in mediation is the allocation of parental rights and re-

---

[7]For more information, contact The Supreme Court of Ohio, Judicial and Court Services Division, Office of Dispute Resolution Programs Services, (800) 826-9010, (614) 752-4700, http://www.sconet.state.oh.us.

[8]For more information, see Ann Milne and Andrew Schepard, *Does Your Mediator Measure Up? Standards of Practice for Family and Divorce Mediation*, vol. 24, no. 4 Family Advocate 22 (Spring 2002). Also see Appendix F and Appendix G of The Rules of Superintendence.

[9]See ABA Section of Dispute Resolution: Resolution on Mediation and the Unauthorized Practice of Law Adopted by the Section on February 2, 2002, at http://www.abanet.org/dispute/resolution2002.pdf.

[10]For a discussion on the involvement of children in mediation, see Dona Lansky, Leslie H. Swift, E. Elizabeth Manley, Amy Elmore & Christine Gerety, *The Role of Children in Mediation*, 14 Mediation Quarterly 147 (Winter 1996); Jennifer McIntosh,

sponsibilities for the care of or parenting time for children, some mediators will involve the children in the mediation in some fashion, either directly, through a mediator interview, or via the child's guardian ad litem or attorney. Other mediators will not involve the children, instead relying upon the parents to make agreements they determine to be in the best interests of their children. If a client has a strong feeling about the involvement of the children in the mediation, the mediator should be asked in advance as to his or her policy on that matter.

(6) Mediator's style and policies. Mediators may approach mediation in different ways.[11] Two primary styles which have been identified are "evaluative" and "facilitative." One or the other may be more conducive to a settlement or be more comfortable for mediation participants in a given case. In general, a mediator who is more evaluative in style will, through the use of his or her training, background and objectivity, identify the issues, evaluate the case and provide some guidance to the participants as to reasonable parameters of settlement. A mediator who has a more facilitative style will try not to impose his or her own ideas of a fair settlement upon the participants and will, instead, encourage the participants to identify the issues, clarify their options and develop their own settlement agreement.[12] A third type of mediation style which is sometimes identified is "transformative" mediation. A transformative mediator's role is to empower parties to identify issues and determine settlement

---

Child-Inclusive Mediation: Report on a Qualitative Research Study, 18 Mediation Quarterly 55 (Fall 2000); Bruce Menin, *The Party of the Last Part: Ethical and Process Implications for Children in Divorce Mediation*, 17 Mediation Quarterly 281 (Spring 2000); Peggy Beck, Nancee Biank, *Broadening the Scope of Divorce Mediation to Meet the Needs of Children*, 14 Mediation Quarterly 179 (Spring 1997); Donald T. Saposnek, *The Value of Children in Mediation: A Cross-Cultural Perspective*, 8 Mediation Quarterly 325 (Summer 1991); Ernest A. Sanchez and Sherrie Kibler-Sanchez, *Empowering Children in Mediation*, 42 Family Court Review 554 (July 2004); Melissa J. Schoffer, *Bringing Children to the Mediation Table: Defining a Child's Best Interest in Divorce Mediation*, 43 Family Court Review 323 (April 2005); Alicia M. Hehr, *A Child Shall Lead Them: Developing and Utilizing Child Protection Mediation to Better Serve the Interests of the Child*, Vol. 22, No. 2 Ohio St. J. on Disp. Resol. 443 (2007).

[11]See vol. 6, issue 2 ACResolution (Winter 2007) in which the entire publication, entitled *Paradigms of Practice: A Mosaic of Approaches* reviews various mediation styles. Kenneth Kressel, *The Strategic Style in Mediation*, vol. 24, no. 3 Conflict Resolution Quarterly 251 (Spring 2007); Lorig Charkoudian, Cristian DeRitis, Romona Buck, Carrie L. Wilson, Mediation by Any Other Name Would Smell as Sweet—or Would It? The Struggle to Define Mediation and Its Various Approaches, 26 Conflict Resolution Quarterly 293 (Spring 2009).

[12]Leonard L. Loeb, *New Forms of Resolving Disputes*, 33 Family Law Quarterly 581, 583-584 (Fall 1999).

terms while assisting each of them to a better understanding of
the other's positions.[13]

An attorney referring a client to mediation should also ask the
mediator what policies he or she has regarding communication
with attorneys. Some mediators may have made it a policy to
have little or no communication with attorneys during the
mediation process. Others may make it a policy to communicate
regularly with attorneys representing mediation participants.
In addition, an attorney should ask how communications are
made. Are they made via a writing to all attorneys representing
parties or are they made through telephone calls or other means
of communication?

Generally, mediators in private practice will ask mediation
participants to sign an agreement engaging their services,
agreeing to make payment and spelling out the obligations of
the mediator and the participants. An attorney should ask
whether a client will be required to sign such an agreement
and, if so, for a copy to review before the client signs it.

(7) Referral source. Many courts maintain their own court-
sponsored mediation programs. Others provide lists of approved
mediators. When choosing a mediator, one should review the
items set out above and ask for referrals from other
practitioners. In addition, lists of mediators are maintained on
the websites of the Association for Conflict Resolution[14] and the
Ohio Mediation Association[15] Another source is the Ohio Directory of Court and Not-for-Profit Programs[16] and Consumer Guide
for Selecting a Mediator.[17] Practitioners may also want to check
an on-line directory of dispute resolution professionals maintained by the Ohio State Bar Association at http//www.ohiobar.
org/pub/adr/.

(8) Mediator's racial and cultural sensitivity. "Mediation involving
issues of race and/or culture requires a mediator who is aware
of and sensitive to these issues. To increase the possibility of a
successful mediation, i.e., one that produces a successful

---

[13]Leonard L. Loeb, *New Forms of Resolving Disputes*, 33 Family Law Quarterly
581, 584 (Fall 1999); Lisa P. Gaynier, *Transformative Mediation: In Search of a The-
ory of Practice*, 22 Conflict Resolution Quarterly 397 (Spring 2005). For a different
concept of mediator styles, see John Wood, *Mediation Styles: Subjective Description of
Mediators*, 21 Conflict Resolution Quarterly 437 (Summer 2004). Dorothy J. Della
Noce, *From Practice to Theory to Practice: A Brief Retrospective on the Transformative
Mediation Model*, Vol. 19, No. 3 Ohio State J. on Disp. Resol. 925 (2004); Dorothy J.
Della Noce, James R. Antes and Judith A. Saul, *Identifying Practice Competence in
Transformative Mediators: An Interactive Rating Scale Assessment Model*, Vol. 19,
No. 3, Ohio State J. on Disp. Resol. 1005 (2004). Ann Milne, *A Facilitative Mediation
Process*, vol. 6, issue 2 ACResolution 10 (Winter 2007).

[14]See http://www.acresolution.org.

[15]See http://www.mediateohio.org.

[16]http://disputeresolution.ohio.gov/nfpmap.htm.

[17]http://disputeresolution.ohio.gov/Brochures/cgmediator.htm.

outcome as defined by the parties, the mediator must have technical expertise as well as training and experience with regard to race and cultural awareness in the context of mediation."[18]

§ 6:10 Advantages of mediation

Mediation has come into the forefront of dispute resolution processes during the last thirty years. Research indicates there are many advantages to the use of mediation to settle disputes.[1] These include, the following:

(1) Parties are likely to be more satisfied with a resolution they have reached as opposed to one which is imposed upon them by a court or other decision-maker.[2] In mediation, the responsibility for settlement of family conflict is placed upon the parties who are most closely involved, those who are in the best position to know what is best for their family and who have the best knowledge of those terms upon which they might settle. Through mediation, participants are able to fashion settlement agreements with a greater level of specificity than those settlements resulting from attorney-negotiations or litigation. Because of their satisfaction with mediation and the agreements reached through the process, mediation participants are more likely to remain satisfied with the agreement and less likely to return to court.[3]

(2) It appears that mediation may reduce the conflict between the

---

[18]Marjorie H. O'Reilly, *Race, Culture and Mediation*, 27 Family Advocate, 37, 38 (Fall 2004).

[Section 6:10]

[1]Robert E. Emery, David Sbarra, Tara Grover, *Divorce Mediation: Research and Reflections*, 43 Family Court Review 22 (January 2005); Joan B. Kelly, *Family Mediation Research: Is There Empirical Support for the Field?*, 22 Conflict Resolution Quarterly 3 (Fall-Winter 2004); Kent B. Scott, Cody W. Wilson, *Questions Clients Have About Whether (and How) to Mediate and How Counsel Should Answer Them*, 63 JUL Disp. Resol. J. 26 (May-July 2008).

[2]Chris Guthrie and James Levin, *A "Party Satisfaction" Perspective on a Comprehensive Mediation Statute*, 13 Ohio St. J. On Disp. Resol. 885 (1998); Joan B. Kelly, *Mediated and Adversarial Divorce: Respondents' Perceptions of Their Processes and Outcomes*, No. 24 Mediation Quarterly 71 (Summer 1989). Also see Jo Daugherty Bailey and Susan P. Robbins, *Couple Empowerment in Divorce: A Comparison of Mediated and Nonmediated Outcomes*, 22 Conflict Resolution Quarterly 453 (Summer 2005).

[3]Nina R. Meierding, *Does Mediation Work? A Survey of Long-Term Satisfaction and Durability Rates for Privately Mediated Agreements*, 11 Mediation Quarterly 157 (Winter 1993), indicating, at page 169, a "high level of satisfaction of participants in the private, voluntary, and confidential mediation process. Despite the high levels of stress, anxiety, and fear associated with the breakup of a marriage, the vast majority of the parties in mediation believed that their needs and interests had been considered by the mediator and that the agreements reached in mediation were substantively fair to both parties . . . . Long-term satisfaction with the agreements was demonstrated by the continued compliance with the original agreements and changes by

parties and assist them in resuming a workable relationship with one another.[4] Because of this, mediation is ideally suited to the resolution of conflicts between or among individuals who must maintain a relationship following the resolution of the immediate dispute.

(3) The use of mediation may reduce costs for the participants.[5]

(4) In many cases the use of mediation allows the resolution of a dispute in a more timely[6] and more private fashion than which would take place were the conflict to be resolved through court processes.

Of course, there are those who would indicate that the reported advantages are not what they would seem to be, particularly in those cases in which there is domestic abuse present or in which there is a "power imbalance" due to one parties' fear of the other, his or her lack of knowledge or experience or developmental, mental or emotional disability. Some of those issues may be addressed by having attorneys attend mediation with their clients or by allowing a mediation participant to have an advocate of some sort present during the mediation.[7]

---

mutual consent, modifications that were reached through constructive private discussion or by a return to mediation." Joan B. Kelley, *A Decade of Divorce Mediation Research: Some Answers and Questions*, 34 Family and Conciliation Courts Review 373, 377 (July 1996); Michael Benjamin & Howard H. Irving, *Research in Family Mediation: Review and Implications*, 13 Mediation Quarterly 53, 58, 63 (Fall 1995).

[4]Joan B. Kelley, *A Decade of Divorce Mediation Research: Some Answers and Questions*, 34 Family and Conciliation Courts Review 373, 379 - 380 (July 1996); Michael Benjamin & Howard H. Irving, *Research in Family Mediation: Review and Implications*, 13 Mediation Quarterly 53, 62 (Fall 1995).

[5]Joan B. Kelly, *Is Mediation Less Expensive?: Comparison of Mediated and Adversarial Divorce Costs*, 8 Mediation Quarterly 15 (Fall 1990), indicating that in study conducted in Marin County, California, couples obtaining divorces using the two-attorney adversarial process spent 134 percent more in total fees than couples using a comprehensive divorce mediation process to resolve all issues; Joan B. Kelly, *A Decade of Divorce Mediation Research: Some Answers and Questions*, 34 Family and Conciliation Courts Review, 373, 376 (July 1996); Michael Benjamin & Howard H. Irving, *Research in Family Mediation: Review and Implications*, 13 Mediation Quarterly 53, 62 (Fall 1995).

[6]Joan B. Kelly, *A Decade of Divorce Mediation Research: Some Answers and Questions*, 34 Family and Conciliation Courts Review, 373, 376 (July 1996).

[7]For a discussion of issues related to power imbalances and other issues creating problems in mediation, see: Ann L. Milne, Peter Salem & Kristin Koeffler, *When Domestic Abuse is an Issue*, vol. 14, no. 4, Family Advocate 34 (Spring 1992); Peter Salem & Ann L. Milne, *Making Mediation Work in a Domestic Violence Case*, vol. 17, no. 3, Family Advocate 34 (Winter 1995); Madeleine B. Simborg and Joan B. Kelly, *Beware of Stereotypes in Mediation*, vol. 17, no. 1, Family Advocate 69 (Summer 1994); Sheila F. G. Schwartz, *To Mediate or Not to Mediate: When Should You Begin the Process and When Should You End It?*, vol. 24, no. 4, Family Advocate 14 (Spring 2002); Becky Hoover Herrnstein, *Women and Mediation: A Chance to Speak and to Be Heard*, 13 Mediation Quarterly 229 (Spring 1996); Joan B. Kelly, *Power Imbalance in Divorce and Interpersonal Mediation Assessment and Intervention*, 13 Mediation Quarterly 85 (Winter 1995); Nancy Thoennes, Peter Salem, and Jessica Pearson, *Mediation and Domestic Violence: Current Policies and Practices*, 33 Family and

§ 6:11 Representing clients in mediation

The role of an attorney is very important in mediation. It is imperative that the attorney representing a client who is going through mediation not abdicate the responsibility to be an advocate for the client.[1]

An attorney should review the pros and cons of mediation with a client[2] and, if it is determined to proceed with mediation, assist the client in conjunction with opposing counsel or the opposing party in choosing a mediator.[3]

In many areas, particularly in court-connected programs, it is customary that the parties attend the mediation without their attorneys. However, an attorney should always evaluate whether his or her attendance would be appropriate in a given case. Before making a decision about whether or not to attend mediation with a client, the attorney and the client should determine whether opposing counsel intends to attend, whether there are difficult issues which might require the advice of counsel as the mediation progresses, whether the mediator prefers the attendance of counsel, or whether there is a power imbalance between the client and the opposing party due to domestic abuse, developmental, mental or emotional disability, or lack of knowledge or information about property or debts which would make attendance of counsel helpful or necessary. Before making a final determination, counsel should discuss the added fees necessary

---

Conciliation Courts Review 6 (January 1995); Diane Neumann, *How Mediation Can Effectively Address the Male-Female Power Imbalance in Divorce*, 9 Mediation Quarterly 227 (Spring 1992); Jessica Pearson, *Mediating When Domestic Violence is a Factor: Policies and Practices in Court-Based Mediation Programs*, 14 Mediation Quarterly 319 (Summer 1997).

[Section 6:11]

[1]See Andrew Schepard, *Supporting Parent-Clients in Mediation of Child Custody Disputes*, ALI–ABA's Practice Checklist Manual on Alternative Dispute Resolution, American Law Institute—American Bar Association Committee on Continuing Professional Education 135 (2002) and also see http://www.ali-aba.org; Barbara Kahn Stark, *Your Lawyer as Mediation Coach*, vol. 24, no. 4, Family Advocate 18 (Spring 2002); *Mediation: The Lawyer's Role* and *Mediation: What the Client Needs to Know*, vol. 16, no. 4, Family Advocate 31 (Spring 1994); Althea Lee Jordan, *Maybe You Should Mediate: A Cost-Effective Alternative to Trial*, vol. 22, no. 1, Family Advocate 19 (Summer 1999); Mori Irvine, *Some "Do's" and "Don'ts" of Mediation Advocacy*, Vol. 58, No. 6, Dispute Resolution Journal 45 (Feb.-Apr. 2003); Maurice Jay Kutner and Kathryn Devane Hamilton, *Successful Mediation Techniques*, Vol. 28, No. 3, Family Advocate 6 (Winter 2006); Carol Gertsten, *Mediate the Move*, Vol. 28, No. 4, Family Advocate 30 (Spring 2006); Kent B. Scott, Cody W. Wilson, *Questions Clients Have About Whether (and How) to Mediate and How Counsel Should Answer Them*, 63 JUL Disp. Resol. J. 26 (May-July 2008).

[2]Carol S. Bruch, *When to Use and When to Avoid Mediation: A Lawyer's Guide*, 31 Family and Conciliation Courts Review 101 (January, 1993); John Wade, *Don't Waste My Time on Negotiation and Mediation: This Dispute Needs a Judge*, 18 Mediation Quarterly 259 (Spring 2001); Michael W. Hawkins, *Putting the Pieces Together: How to Effectively Mediate Disputes*, Vol. 17, No. 2, Ohio Lawyer (March/April 2003).

[3]See Consumer Guide: What You Need to Know When Selecting a Mediator, http://disputeresolution.ohio.gov/Brochures/cgmediator.htm.

for him or her to attend the mediation session(s). If it is determined that counsel should attend the mediation, he or she should inform opposing counsel and the mediator. It is important that be done, as it is possible the mediator may not allow the mediation to proceed if one party attends with counsel and the other does not, due to a potential power imbalance or the mediator's policy.

Whether counsel does or does not attend, it is important that the client be adequately prepared for mediation in advance of the first session. Mediation is normally structured in different stages. Typically, several stages such as the following are identified:[4]

Stage 1: Introduction

In this stage the participants are introduced to the mediation process and to the mediator, information is gathered, mediation guidelines are reviewed and, if appropriate, an employment or mediation retainer agreement is reviewed and may be executed.

Stage 2: Fact Finding and Isolation of Issues

In this stage the mediator and participants identify the nature of the participants' conflict. Together, they determine a set of goals, objectives and strategies for the conduct of the mediation, and create an "agenda" for review and determination of issues.

Stage 3: Creation of Options and Alternatives

The mediator assists the participants in defining the options available for resolution of the dispute and the participants, with the mediator's help, develop new settlement alternatives for consideration.

Stage 4: Negotiation and Decision Making

The participants, with the mediator's assistance, review options, discuss the pros and cons of the alternatives and define the effect of each upon others who may be affected (e.g., children, other family members), with the goal of arriving at a resolution of the dispute.

Stage 5: Clarification and Writing a Plan

The participants and mediator review the agreed-upon terms and then, with the mediator's assistance, may determine the wording of their proposed agreement or plan. Another option is for the mediator to memorialize the understandings reached by the parties in the form of a letter or proposed agreement or memorandum of understanding to be forwarded to the parties' attorneys for review with the participants. If the parties have not reached agreement on all matters at issue, a partial settlement plan, agreement, or memorandum of understanding may be drafted.

Stage 6: Legal Review / Processing

---

[4]Jay Foldberg and Alison Taylor, *Mediation: A Comprehensive Guide to Resolving Conflicts Without Litigation*, pages 38–72 (Jossey-Bass, 1984); Jay Foldberg and Ann Milne, *Divorce Mediation: Theory and Practice*, pages 8–9 (The Guilford Presss, 1988). *See also* Jay Foldberg, Ann Milne and Peter Salem (eds.), *Divorce and Family Mediation: Models, Techniques and Applications* (The Guilford Press, 2004).

The participants review the proposed agreements with their legal counsel. If all is satisfactory, the proposed agreements should be incorporated into the appropriate pleading to be filed with the court or in appropriate form to be presented at hearing. If there are matters which are not satisfactory after review with counsel, the parties may return to mediation for further negotiation or, with counsel's help, may resolve the remaining dispute(s), prior to filing with the court or appearing for hearing.

Stage 7: Implementation, Review, and Revision

At this stage, the participants implement the plan they have adopted. If the agreement deals with the allocation of parental rights and responsibilities or parenting time, it may be necessary to make changes as circumstances change and as the parties work under its terms. The mediated agreement should allow for review and revision, as may be appropriate.

An attorney should be aware of the mediation stages, counsel his or her clients about them in advance and prepare the client with appropriate information prior to mediation sessions. Most importantly, an attorney should assist a client in identifying possible alternatives for settlement, the cost of the various options (in time, financially and emotionally) and ensure that the client has a clear understanding of various positions. If a client (or an attorney and his or her client) attends a mediation session without information necessary for an adequate discussion of a topic or without an appropriate understanding of possible alternatives, in many instances the mediation is not effective and if "agreements" are reached, they are later negated after review by counsel.

§ 6:12 Planning for post-decree mediation

Attorneys representing clients in a parenting proceeding should consider negotiating a mediation clause to be included in the parties' shared parenting plan, separation agreement or consent entry that would require the use of mediation to resolve future disputes between the parties prior to resorting to litigation.

The Supreme Court has not ruled directly on the use and enforceability of mediation clauses but a 1996 case indicated that trial court rulings regarding mediation clauses in separation agreements may be reviewed on appeal of the judgment. The Court declined to issue an extraordinary writ as a way of reviewing the trial judge's ruling.[1] Although not controlling, in his concurring opinion in the *Kelm II* case (see discussion below in Text § 6:13, Uniform Mediation Act), Chief Justice Moyer indicated his concurrence in the majority decision

---

[Section 6:12]

[1]State ex rel. Hunter v. Patterson, 75 Ohio St. 3d 512, 1996-Ohio-203, 664 N.E.2d 524 (1996). See also State ex rel. Gibson v. Ray, 1995 WL 428475 (Ohio Ct. App. 6th Dist. Lucas County 1995) (order to mediate reviewable on appeal).

indicating that the parties' agreement to arbitrate custody and visitation disputes would not be enforced but that the ruling "is confined to arbitration and does not apply to agreements reached regarding visitation and custody through the process of mediation."[2]

If a mediation clause is to be used, the following terms should be considered for inclusion: (1) the identity of the mediator or the entity designated to provide mediation services or how the mediator will be selected; (2) how any mediation fees will be paid or divided or how that will be determined; (3) what constitutes compliance with the mediation clause (attendance by each party at a certain number of sessions, providing certain records, making full disclosure, etc.); (4) what consequences result from noncompliance (inability to proceed with court filings, dismissal of any pending motions, payment of all expenses for mediator and/or attorney fees, etc.); (5) whether and what things said in mediation may be disclosed; (6) when mediation must be instituted (e.g., prior to the filing of a motion) and what notice to the other party is required (e.g., 30 days in advance of any mediation to be scheduled); (7) whether attorneys will attend the sessions or how a determination will be reached as to whether attorneys will attend; (8) whether children will be included in the mediation or, if not, if someone else will represent their wishes and concerns within the mediation (e.g., guardian ad litem); (9) whether and under what circumstances mediation may be waived and what exceptions there will be to the requirement of participation in mediation (motions arising from domestic violence or child abuse situations, matters in which the parties are entitled to court-sponsored mediation if a motion is first filed, etc.).

A party who has previously agreed to a mediation clause should be aware that if he or she files a motion with the court or participates in a proceeding initiated by the other party without requesting mediation, the court may rule that he or she has waived the protection of the clause.[3]

The appellate court in *Spickler v. Spickler*[4] affirmed the trial court's refusal to find a parent in contempt of a provision in the parties' separation agreement that required mediation before bringing a post decree motion. The court reasoned that the provision could not divest the trial court of jurisdiction over the request to increase child support. Inserting a provision requiring mediation by a date certain following

---

[2]Kelm v. Kelm, 92 Ohio St. 3d 223, 228, 2001-Ohio-168, 749 N.E.2d 299 (2001). Also see Rex v. Conner, 2003-Ohio-4561, 2003 WL 22019537 (Ohio Ct. App. 8th Dist. Cuyahoga County 2003), in which the court approved the trial court's adoption of an arbitration award regarding the allocation of parental rights and responsibilities, finding that the "adoption" was appropriate because the trial court completed an independent analysis of the statutory factors set out in RC 3109.04.

[3]Dugach v. Dugach, 1995 WL 237040 (Ohio Ct. App. 11th Dist. Lake County 1995).

[4]Spickler v. Spickler, 2003-Ohio-3553, 2003 WL 21518732 (Ohio Ct. App. 7th Dist. Columbiana County 2003).

the court's adoption of a plan for the allocation of parental rights and responsibilities, may make an order temporary rather than final. In *Smith v. Smith*,[5] the trial court adopted a shared parenting plan in October 2004 containing a provision that the plan was to be maintained "through August 2005" and that "the parents agree to mediate a subsequent parenting schedule . . . not later than June 15, 2005." In March 2005, the appellant filed her motion requesting either continuation of the shared parenting plan or modification of it in her favor. After hearing, the trial court modified the plan in appellee's favor and appellant appealed claiming there had been no change of circumstances and, therefore, the plan should not have been modified. In affirming the trial court, the appellate court indicated that because "the shared parenting order of October 15, 2004, pursuant to the parties' agreement, called for further mediation of the issue no later than June 15, 2005, Appellant had previously agreed to further review of shared parenting issues, and . . . is judicially estopped from now asserting a lack of change of circumstances. . . .. The October 15, 2004 shared parenting order, which foresaw further negotiation or litigation by the parties by a date certain, is in the nature of a temporary order, despite the trial court's labeling of it as a final shared parenting decree."

§ 6:13 Uniform Mediation Act

In August, 2001, the National Conference of Commissioners on Uniform State Laws ("NCCUSL") approved the Uniform Mediation Act and recommended its enactment in all fifty states. The Act was drafted by NCCUSL and the ABA Section of Dispute Resolution, and with Ohio-specific modifications became effective in this state on October 29, 2005.[1]

Essentially the UMA defines how and under what circumstances mediation communications are confidential;[2] what mediations are subject to the act;[3] how and under what circumstances mediation communications are privileged;[4] how and under what circumstances privilege may be waived;[5] and under what circumstance there is no privilege.[6] Portions of the UMA have been discussed above in Text § 6:3, Mediation; § 6:4, Communications made in mediation and § 6:9, Mediator qualifications.

---

[5]Smith v. Smith, 2006-Ohio-3251, 2006 WL 1728050 (Ohio Ct. App. 5th Dist. Muskingum County 2006).

[Section 6:13]

[1]For a copy of the Uniform Mediation Act as enacted in Ohio, RC 2710.01 to 2710.10, see http://www.legislature.state.oh.us/bills.cfm?ID=125_HB_303.

[2]RC 2710.07.

[3]RC 2710.02.

[4]RC 2710.03.

[5]RC 2710.04.

[6]RC 2710.05.

In a change from what has previously been the practice in many areas of the state, the UMA emphasizes the rights of the parties to determine certain aspects of the mediation. For example, the UMA allows a mediation party to designate an attorney or another individual to accompany him or her and to participate in the mediation.[7] In addition, the Ohio law provides that, with certain exceptions, "mediation communications are confidential to the extent agreed by the parties. . .."[8] Finally, with certain exceptions, the UMA sets out the right of the parties to determine what is privileged, in other words, if mediation communications may be disclosed in court, department or agency proceedings.[9]

The UMA emphasizes the difference between confidentiality and privilege. Pursuant to RC 2710.07, the extent of confidentiality is something the parties must agree upon. (The writer suggests that any confidentiality agreement be set forth in writing). For instance, the parties may agree that all mediation communications are confidential with the exception that they may divulge the information to their attorneys (but not their families).

On the other hand, with limited exceptions, pursuant to RC 2710.03, mediation parties, mediators and nonparty mediation participants hold certain privileges and, based upon those privileges, mediation communications are not subject to discovery or admissible in evidence in a proceeding unless waived or precluded pursuant to RC 2710.04. Specifically, with limited exceptions, a mediation party may refuse to disclose, and may prevent any other person from disclosing, any mediation communications made by any party. A mediator may refuse to disclose any communications made by any party and may prevent any other person from disclosing the mediator's mediation communications. In addition, a non-party participant may refuse to disclose, and may prevent any other person from disclosing, a mediation communication of the nonparty participant. However, once a "mediation communication is contained in a written agreement evidenced by a record signed by all parties to the agreement," there is no longer any privilege with regard to the contents of that agreement.[10] It is important to note, however that RC 2710.01(H) states that " '[r]ecord' means information that is inscribed on a tangible medium or that is stored in an electronic or other medium and is retrievable in perceivable form." Subsection (I) of that same section provides that " '[s]ign' means either of the following: (1) [t]o execute or adopt a tangible symbol with the present intent to authenticate a record; (2) [t]o attach or logically associate an electronic symbol, sound or process to or with a record with the present intent to authenticate a record." Therefore,

---

[7]RC 2710.09.
[8]RC 2710.07.
[9]RC 2710.03.
[10]RC 2710.05(A)(1).

it appears that a "signed" agreement does not need to be on paper. Instead, it may be an acknowledged recording of some sort.[11]

With regard to exceptions to privilege and/or to confidentiality, please review the UMA to determine what may apply in a given circumstance.

§ 6:14 Arbitration

Pursuant to Rule 15(B) of the Rules of Superintendence for the Courts of Ohio, a judge of a division of a common pleas court may, at the request of all parties, refer a pending case or a designated issue to arbitration in a juvenile or domestic relations matter. The rule sets out the procedure for arbitration in these cases and specifies that any party may appeal the arbitration report and award. In other words, in these matters, arbitration is not binding, and, pursuant to Rule 15, a party may appeal an award and seek a de novo hearing or challenge the award due to "misconduct or corruption."[1]

In addition, RC Chapter 2711 sets out procedure and requirements for enforcement of agreements to arbitrate and it is important that the procedure be followed in order to make the resulting arbitration award enforceable through a court order.[2] Individuals have inserted arbitration clauses in antenuptial agreements, separation agreements or separate writings executed after a divorce. As described below, in this section, questions have arisen as to which items in family cases may properly be subject to arbitration and which, as a matter, of law are not.

In *Kelm v. Kelm*[3] ("*Kelm I*"), the Supreme Court ruled that arbitration clauses in antenuptial contracts are enforceable in family cases, even for those issues typically falling within the court's jurisdiction such as issues of temporary spousal and child support. The Court recognized that, in those cases, courts and "arbitrators for that matter" have a duty to protect a child's best interest and ensure that a spouse's needs are met.[4] The Court determined that it could exercise its oversight responsibilities by ensuring that arbitration in spousal and child support matters "is accomplished in an expeditious, efficient

---

[11]Hon. Richard T. Payne (ret.), *All Things Considered*, 51 MAR Res Gestae 32 (March 2008); Thomas J. Campbell, *Reversal in Uniform Mediation Act Case*, Vol. 14 No. 2 Disp. Resol. Mag. 33 (Winter 2008)

[Section 6:14]

[1]For a discussion of the use of arbitration in domestic relations cases, see Andre R. Imbrogno, *Arbitration as an Alternative to Divorce Litigation: Redefining the Judicial Role*, 31 Capital University Law Review 413 (2003).

[2]See Cangemi v. Cangemi, 2005-Ohio-772, 2005 WL 433529 (Ohio Ct. App. 8th Dist. Cuyahoga County 2005) for discussion of a case in which proper arbitration procedure was not followed, making the award unenforceable.

[3]Kelm v. Kelm, 68 Ohio St. 3d 26, 1993-Ohio-56, 623 N.E.2d 39, 38 A.L.R.5th 845 (1993).

[4]Kelm v. Kelm, 68 Ohio St. 3d 26, 30, 1993-Ohio-56, 623 N.E.2d 39, 38 A.L.R. 5th 845 (1993).

and reasonable manner" and concluded by indicating that the trial court could use its contempt powers to ensure the timely and reasonable conclusion of the case if arbitration failed to protect the child or the spouse.[5]

In *Kelm v. Kelm*,[6] a case in which the trial court had confirmed an arbitrator's award increasing child support upon motion of the child support obligee, the Franklin County Appeals Court ruled that, pursuant to RC 2711.09 and RC 2711.13, "upon application of a party to confirm an arbitrator's award the court must confirm the award unless another party files a motion to vacate, modify or correct the award."

In *Ellsworth v. Ellsworth*,[7] the trial court issued an order requiring the parties to arbitrate the issue of where the children would attend school in accordance with a mediation and arbitration clause included in the parties' shared parenting plan which was incorporated in the court's decree. The trial court's inherent power to enforce those provisions was affirmed by the appellate court.

However, in *Pulfer v. Pulfer*,[8] the Allen County Court of Appeals refused to extend *Kelm I* in a post-decree request to modify the allocation of parental rights and responsibilities for a child due to a parent's relocation, indicating that "certain issues are not arbitrable as a matter of law."[9] The court distinguished this sort of case from the support disputes which were the focus of the *Kelm I* case, by citing a New York case in indicating that this case involved "the delicate balancing of the factors composing the best interests of a child,' a determination that could only be made by a trial court."[10] The court went on to cite

---

[5]Kelm v. Kelm, 68 Ohio St. 3d 26, 30, 1993-Ohio-56, 623 N.E.2d 39, 38 A.L.R. 5th 845 (1993).

[6]Kelm v. Kelm, 2004-Ohio-1004, 2004 WL 396325 (Ohio Ct. App. 10th Dist. Franklin County 2004).

[7]Ellsworth v. Ellsworth, 1998 WL 892139 (Ohio Ct. App. 1st Dist. Hamilton County 1998).

[8]Pulfer v. Pulfer, 110 Ohio App. 3d 90, 673 N.E.2d 656 (3d Dist. Allen County 1996).

[9]Pulfer v. Pulfer, 110 Ohio App. 3d 90, 93, 673 N.E.2d 656 (3d Dist. Allen County 1996).

[10]Nestel v. Nestel, 38 A.D.2d 942, 943, 331 N.Y.S.2d 241, 243 (2d Dep't 1972); Pulfer v. Pulfer, 110 Ohio App. 3d 90, 94, 673 N.E.2d 656 (3d Dist. Allen County 1996). See also Hirsch v. Hirsch, 4 A.D.3d 451, 774 N.Y.S.2d 48 (2d Dep't 2004), (the New York appellate court affirmed the trial court in finding that disputes regarding child custody are not subject to arbitration, even though husband and wife had originally agreed to arbitration through a Bais Din, pursuant to Jewish law). Also see MacFarlane v. MacFarlane, 2006-Ohio-3155, 2006 WL 1704531 (Ohio Ct. App. 8th Dist. Cuyahoga County 2006), in which the appellate court cited *Kelm II* in finding the trial court was correct in not ceding its jurisdiction to a Catholic canonical court for arbitration despite wife's arguments that, because she and husband were married in the Catholic church and agreed to be bound by Catholic canon law regarding their marriage and children, the canonical court should be allowed to assume jurisdiction. The appellate court confirmed that disputes relative to the allocation of parental

the case of *Nester v. Nester*,[11] in which a domestic arbitration regarding economic issues was enforced. The court indicated that review of arbitration awards is governed by RC 2711.11 and that under that statute, review is limited to "material mistake or extensive impropriety."[12]

In *Malkoski v. Leonhardt*,[13] the parties entered into a shared parenting plan adopted by the court that called for them to submit any dispute under the plan to arbitration. The appellant filed a motion to terminate the shared parenting plan and the dispute was referred to arbitration. The trial court adopted the arbitrator's decision which declined to terminate the plan. On appeal the court cited the *Pulfer* decision in finding that, despite the parties' agreement, the arbitrator did not have the authority to determine issues relating to the custody of the parties' children.

The Supreme Court addressed the issue of arbitration of the allocation of parental rights and responsibilities for a child in *Kelm v. Kelm (Kelm II)*.[14] In that case, the Court indicated that "[i]n a domestic relations case, matters of child custody and parental visitation are not subject to arbitration." The court acknowledged that there is a variance of opinions among the states as to whether arbitration in these matters should be permitted. However, it rejected the argument that, because the arbitrator's decisions are subject to de novo review by the courts, the process allows for the court's ultimate authority. The Court believed that a two-stage process composed of an arbitrator's decision followed by de novo judicial review was wasteful of time and expense and would result in a duplication of effort.

Further, the Court indicated that even though a party may have agreed to arbitration in a parenting plan, he or she may challenge the arbitration agreement as it relates to child custody or visitation disputes. The Court did not focus on the parents' rights but on the duty of the courts under the parens patriae doctrine to protect the children's best interests.

Finally, the Court stated that a "trial court has a continuing responsibility under R.C. 3109.04(B)(1) and (E)(1)(a) to protect the best interests of the children . . . . [T]he parties' agreement to

---

rights and responsibilities are not subject to arbitration, that even thought the parties may have made agreements with one another through their marital vows, an antenuptial agreement to arbitrate must be in writing, and that wife had waived any right she may have had to demand arbitration when she invoked the court's jurisdiction by filing a complaint and then participating in the divorce litigation.

[11]Nester v. Nester, 1995 WL 318737 (Ohio Ct. App. 10th Dist. Franklin County 1995).

[12]Pulfer v. Pulfer, 110 Ohio App. 3d 90, 95, 673 N.E.2d 656 (3d Dist. Allen County 1996).

[13]Malkoski v. Leonhardt, 1997 WL 799816 (Ohio Ct. App. 6th Dist. Lucas County 1997).

[14]Kelm v. Kelm, 92 Ohio St. 3d 223, 2001-Ohio-168, 749 N.E.2d 299 (2001).

arbitrate custody and visitation disputes impermissibly interferes with the court's ability to carry out this responsibility."[15]

Therefore, at this point, the law in Ohio appears to be that issues related to the custody or placement of children and parenting time with them are not subject to arbitration and must be referred to the Court. However, under the reasoning of the Court in both *Kelm I* and *Kelm II*, it would seem that those matters such as division of property and debts, valuation of property (including businesses and professional practices), the duration of the marriage, the determination of what is separate or marital property, and issues related to spousal and child support may all be properly subject to determination via arbitration.[16]

§ 6:15   High conflict families and parenting coordination

Courts have been increasingly troubled by the continued conflict exhibited in what are termed "high conflict families," and the resulting distress suffered by children within those families.[1] "Interparental conflict has been consistently identified as a significant predictor of adjustment difficulties in children following divorce."[2] "Research indicates in divorce, or in intact but high-conflict families, the greatest damage to children occurs when the children are subjected to conflict, particularly when they are used as a medium through which the conflict takes place."[3]

Courts see this conflict when parents continue to file motions with the court over various disputes and demonstrate apparent inability to resolve what appear to be even the simplest disagreements.[4] In addition to the continued stress upon the family and particularly the children, these families repeatedly draw upon limited court resources, in many instances with no long-term resolution in sight.

The recognition of this problem throughout the United States and,

---

[15]Kelm v. Kelm, 92 Ohio St. 3d 223, 228, 2001-Ohio-168, 749 N.E.2d 299 (2001).

[16]For further discussion of the use of arbitration in family cases, see Robin M. Kennedy & Ron L. Rimelspach, *Arbitration in Domestic Relations: The Neglected Alternative*, vol. 13, no. 5, Ohio Lawyer 18 (1999).

[Section 6:15]

[1]John H. Grych, *Interparental Conflict as a Risk Factor for Child Maladjustment: Implications for the Development of Prevention Program*, 43 Family Court Review 97 (January 2005); William A. Eddy, *Handling High Conflict Personalities in Family Mediation*, 4 ACResolution 14 (Summer 2005).

[2]Catherine C. Ayoub, Robin M. Deutsch, & Andronicki Maraganore, *Emotional Distress in Children of High-Conflict Divorce: The Impact of Marital Conflict and Violence*, 37 Family and Conciliation Courts Review 297, 299 (July 1999).

[3]M.A. Baris, C.A. Coates, B.B. Duvall, C.B. Garrity, E.T. Johnson, E.R. LaCrosse, *Working with High-Conflict Families of Divorce*, page 13 (Jason Aronson, Inc., 2001).

[4]Ralph A. Peeples, Suzanne Reynolds, Catherine T. Harris, *It's the Conflict Stupid: An Empirical Study of Factors that Inhibit Successful Mediation in High-Conflict Custody Cases*, 43 Wake Forest L. Rev. 505 (Summer 2008).

in fact, throughout the world, was demonstrated in September 2000, when the American Bar Association and the Johnson Foundation sponsored what has become known as the "Wingspread Conference," an interdisciplinary, international conference convened "to develop recommendations for changes in the legal and mental health systems to reduce the impact of high conflict custody cases on children."[5] The report from that conference sets out many recommendations for professionals dealing with these families, including recommendations for lawyers and the court system.

In response to the concerns generated by high conflict families, courts in other jurisdictions and in some counties in Ohio, are using what are sometimes called "parenting coordinators," "parent coordinators," or "special masters" (hereinafter referred to as "parenting coordinators").[6] Although there are variations on how parenting coordination is implemented, in general for a parenting coordinator to be used, the parties must agree to the appointment of the parenting coordinator for a specific term and execute an agreement and/or submit a consent judgment entry setting out the terms of his or her appointment (e.g., how much the parenting coordinator will charge, who will pay the parenting coordinator's fees, what is the scope of the parenting coordinator's authority, what are the responsibilities of the parties and of the parenting coordinator, what matters are subject to judicial review and under what circumstances, etc.).[7]

In many instances, a parenting coordinator will use what might be called a "med-arb" (mediation-arbitration) method of assisting the parents in resolving conflicts as they arise in their case. Under this protocol, if a dispute arises, one or both parties contact the parenting coordinator. The coordinator attempts to assist the parties in resolving the dispute through the use of mediation or by using mediative techniques. If the parties are unable to reach agreement, the parenting coordinator then acts as an arbitrator and issues a decision or

---

[5]*High-Conflict Custody Cases: Reforming the System for Children—Conference Report and Action Plan*, 39 Family Court Review 146 (April 2001).

[6]For a general discussion of parenting coordination, see E. Robert LaCrosse, *Parenting Coordination: Developing a Definition*, 48 The Ohio Psychologist 29 (2000-2001); Matthew J. Sullivan, *Have a Problem? Hire a Special Master as Decision-Maker*, vol.21, no. 1, Family Advocate 41 (Summer, 1998); Christine A. Coates, Robin Deutsch, Hugh Starnes, Matthew J. Sullivan and Bea Lisa Sydlik, *Parenting Coordination for High Conflict Familes*, 42 Family Court Review 246 (April 2004); Matthew J. Sullivan, *Ethical, Legal and Professional Practice Issues Involved in Acting as a Psychologist Parent Coordinator in Child Custody Cases*, 42 Family Court Review 576 (July 2004). Christine A. Coates, *Parenting Coordination: What Mediators Need to Know*, vol. 6, issue 1 ACResolution (Fall 2006). Debra Carter, Linda Fieldstone and Hugh Starnes, *Parenting Coordinators Promote Accord for High Conflict Families*, vol. 6, issue 1 ACResolution 32 (Fall 2006). Eve Orlow, *Working with Parenting Coordinators*, vol. 30, no. 1 Family Advocate (Summer 2007). Dale R. Koch and Amy Pincolini-Ford, *Parenting Coordination in Domestic Violence Cases*, vol. 15, no. 2 Juvenile and Family Justice Today 16 (Summer 2006).

[7]Karl Kirkland and Matthew Sullivan, Parenting Coordination (PC) Practice: A Survey of Experienced Professionals, 46 Family Court Review 622 (October 2008).

award. Whether and under what circumstances such a decision or award is subject to judicial review should be set out in the parenting coordination agreement or order. Based on the Supreme Court's decision in *Kelm II* (see discussion in Text § 6:13, Uniform Mediation Act), it appears that the parenting coordinator would not be able to issue a decision or award on the issue of change in the custody or placement of a child or in parenting time.

Nevertheless, the use of a parenting coordinator is worth considering in cases in which a coordinator might be able to assist parents in determining day-to-day issues that arise regarding their child and which, in many instances, need immediate decisions (e.g., whether the child will participate in Little League or swim lessons, whether the child will go for Thanksgiving dinner with his mother when the father is claiming the distance he is to travel is too great, whether the child is to go to camp when one party does not want him to go, which physician should treat a child, etc.).

The Ohio Supreme Court has not yet addressed the issue of parenting coordination and those courts or parties using parenting coordination appear to take their authority from a combination of RC 3109.052 (allowing the court to order parents to participate in mediation in matters involving the allocation of parental rights and responsibilities and parenting time—see Text § 6:2, Definitions) together with the parties' ability to submit issues to mediation by agreement; from Rule 15(B) of the Rules of Superintendence for the Courts of Ohio (allowing pending matters to be submitted to arbitration—see Text § 6:13, Uniform Mediation Act); and from the Ohio Arbitration Act (allowing for agreements to arbitrate certain disputes—see Text § 6:13, Uniform Mediation Act).[8]

The Delaware County Court of Appeals dealt with the appointment of a parenting coordinator to resolve visitation (parenting time) conflicts after entry of the final decree in the case of *Beatley v. Block*.[9] In that case, "[t]he parties had a history of extensive conflict, including physical confrontation, surveillance, searching of appellee's trash, and appellee receiving cockroaches in the mail."[10] The court's decision does not specifically describe the terms and conditions of the parenting coordination order; however the court overruled the appellant father's claim that the court abused its discretion in appointing a

---

[8]For more information on parenting coordination, please see AFCC Task Force on Parenting Coordinators and Special Masters Resource List at http://www.afccnet.o rg/pdfs/parenting_coordinator_resources.pdf, and the report of that task force entitled, *"Parenting Coordination: Implementation Issues,"* 41 Family Court Review 533 (October 2003). For parenting coordination guidelines, see *Guidelines for Parenting Coordination Developed by The AFCC Task Force on Parenting Coordination*, Vol. 44, No. 1, Family Court Review 164 (January 2006) or see http://www.afccnet.org/pdf s/AFCCGuidelinesforParentingCoordinationnew.pdf.

[9]Beatley v. Block, 2000 WL 699653 (Ohio Ct. App. 5th Dist. Delaware County 2000).

[10]Beatley v. Block, 2000 WL 699653 (Ohio Ct. App. 5th Dist. Delaware County 2000).

parenting coordinator "to work with the parties on stabilizing their relationship as it relates to the children." The appellate court stated, as follows:

> It is apparent from the order that the court did not abdicate any judicial responsibility to the parenting coordinator. In Section 4.6 (*referring to the entry appointing the parent coordinator*) the court states that the parenting coordinator does not have authority to evaluate custody. In Section 4.5, the order states that the parenting coordinator's fundamental role is to minimize the conflict to which the children are exposed by the parties. Given the history of discord between the parties, appellant has not demonstrated error in the appointment of a neutral person to assist the parties in minimizing conflict.

The court also noted that there was no demonstration of prejudice from the appointment of the parenting coordinator, in that the coordinator had not usurped the role of the trial court as demonstrated by the fact that the appellant had filed several motions upon which the court ruled after the appointment of the parent coordinator.

In 2001, a group of family lawyers and mental health professionals organized in Franklin County for the purpose of creating a parenting coordinator project. The Franklin County Parenting Coordinator Pilot Project has developed standards and training for participants in the project and a Model Parenting Coordinator Agreement. The project is designed so that parenting coordinators will act in post-decree disputes using a "med-arb" model to assist high conflict parents in resolving disputes over the enforcement or minor modifications of their parenting plan or decree.

§ 6:16   Parenting coordinator agreement—Form[1]⊚

PARENTING COORDINATOR AGREEMENT

We, *[name of parent]* and *[name of parent]* (PARENTS), hereby appoint *[name of Parenting Coordinator]* to function as Parenting Coordinator (PC) for us pursuant to the terms of this agreement.

1. **Parenting Coordination:** We understand that the function of the PC is to help parents resolve their differences regarding their child(ren) and their care in a manner that serves the best interests of the child(ren), minimizes conflict between the parents that could harm the child(ren) and fosters cooperation between parents. The PC may assess the situation and educate us as necessary regarding child development and communication, and facilitate communication between us and with others involved with our child(ren). The PC also may coach us on strategies of dealing with each other and/or with our child(ren), and may refer either or both of us, and/or our child(ren), to other professionals, such as therapists or counselors.

[Section 6:16]

[1]This form has been provided by the Franklin County Parenting Coordinator Pilot Project.

2. **Professional Advice:** We understand that the PC does not offer legal advice or offer legal counsel, and that we have been advised to consult separate attorneys in order to be properly counseled about our legal interests, rights and responsibilities. In addition, we understand that the PC does not provide mental health services or counseling of any kind, and that we have been advised to consult separate mental health professionals regarding any mental health issue that might arise during the parenting coordination process.

3. **Releases for Information:** We agree that we shall provide appropriate written releases to the PC and any attorneys, Guardian Ad Litem, school employee, health care provider and/or mental health professionals involved with us or our child(ren), so that they may communicate with each other about any relevant subject involving us and/or our child(ren).

4. **Confidentiality Waiver:** Because the PC may need to use information acquired from either or both of us, and from other sources, in order to perform the PC functions and responsibilities, pursuant to this agreement, we understand and agree that there will not be any confidentiality or privilege regarding any of our oral or written communications with the PC or with each other during mediation and arbitration sessions or otherwise. Also, it is understood that the statutory law of Ohio requires the PC to report to the appropriate authorities any information that would give the PC reason to believe that a child is in need of protection; that either parent or another person is in danger of bodily harm; or, that there is intent to commit a felony.

5. **Joint Parenting Decisions:** Notwithstanding the appointment of the PC, we understand that we may make joint parenting decisions in our child(ren)'s best interests at any time, without the PC's assistance.

6. **Dispute Resolution—Mediation:** We understand that the PC is a trained and experienced mediator who may mediate any disputes between us involving our parental responsibilities, as necessary to help us make our own decisions; provided however, this mediation service is not the regular type of mediation which would be subject to the statutory privilege of confidentiality, as provided above in paragraph 4. In the event that mediation is unsuccessful after not less than 60 minutes of mediation time and effort, we appoint the PC to become an Arbitrator, as provided below in paragraph 7; provided however, the PC has discretionary authority to extend the mediation time, before the PC becomes the Arbitrator.

7. **Dispute Resolution—Arbitration:** Although it is our intent to resolve disputes through mediation as much as possible, in the event that we are unable to reach a mutually satisfactory resolution of a dispute, we agree to seek arbitration with the PC also acting as the ARBITRATOR, pursuant to Sections 2711.01 through 2711.16, inclusive, of the Revised Code, copies of which are attached hereto as Appendix A. If the PC is at any time unable to serve as Arbitrator, the parents may appoint another qualified professional to act

temporarily as the Arbitrator; provided however, if the parents cannot agree on the choice of another Arbitrator, each parent will name a Court Approved Mediator practicing in *[name of county]* County, Ohio, and those two mediators will appoint the temporary Arbitrator, taking into consideration the particular training and qualifications necessary to serve the needs of the parents and their child(ren) in this case.

In the event mediation fails, as provided above in paragraph 6, we specifically grant to the PC the authority to arbitrate and decide any dispute between us related to the interpretation, enforcement and/or modification of the terms of any prior parenting plan, decree or order involving our child(ren), with the exception of the following excluded subjects:

1. Termination of a shared parenting plan.
2. Modification of a prior parenting plan, decree or order in a manner that would reduce the total parenting time of either parent during a calendar year, or that would change the designation of the residential parent for school purposes.
3. Supervised parenting time for either parent.
4. Relocation of the residence of a child.
5. The formal or informal religious education of a child.
6. Other: _____.

The PC will have discretion to determine the level of formal procedures to use for each issue addressed in arbitration, bearing in mind that more serious or significant issues require a higher level of procedural protection. We specifically waive the right to have a separate, formal arbitration hearing and agree that the communications and information shared with the PC by us, our child(ren) and/or other persons shall serve as an arbitration hearing; provided however, upon written notice to the parents at least seven days in advance, the PC may exercise the discretionary authority to hold a formal arbitration hearing pursuant to Section 2711.06 of the Revised Code. In addition, the PC and/or either parent may request submission of written statements of position and facts to the PC. Then, either parent may respond in writing to the other parent's statement. Thereafter, the PC shall review the information, statements and responses, and shall issue a written arbitration award regarding any disputed issue, as provided in Section 2711.08 of the Revised Code, with 14 days following the date the arbitration process finally is completed and submitted to the PC.

The award/decision of the PC shall be effective immediately upon issuance of the arbitration award, and shall continue in effect until and unless the award is vacated, modified or corrected, as prescribed in Sections 2711.10 and 2711.11 of the Revised Code. In addition to any such statutory remedy for vacation, modification or correction of the arbitration award, within 30 days following the date of issuance of the arbitration award, either parent may file in the court that issued the prior parenting decree or order a motion seeking a hearing de novo on the subject of the arbitration award, subject to the continuing jurisdiction of the court; provided however, the non-prevailing party shall pay the reasonable and necessary attorney fees and other litigation expenses of the prevailing party, unless the court finds such an order would be manifestly unjust.

8. **Influencing Children**: The PC is authorized to interview our child(ren) privately, in order to ascertain the child(ren)'s needs as to the issues being arbitrated. In conducting such an interview, the PC shall avoid forcing the child(ren) to choose between us.

During any period in which we are engaged in a mediation or arbitration process, the parent with residential parenting time of a child shall take no substantial action in the area of disagreement that would prejudice or take unfair advantage of the other parent.

9. **Conferences and Communications:** Copies of all correspondence from either parent to the PC must be mailed, e-mailed, faxed or hand-delivered to the other parent, with "cc:" noted on the correspondence, unless otherwise directed by the PC.

Office and/or telephone conferences between the PC and either or both parents shall be scheduled or conducted only during weekdays and the regular business office hours of the PC. We agree to make a good faith effort to be available for telephone and/or office conferences, as scheduled by the PC.

The PC is authorized to tell either or both of us that an unnecessary amount of time is being taken by either or both of us in this process. We agree that the amount of time spent on resolving a dispute be in proportion to the nature of the dispute, as determined by the PC.

10. **Payment for PC Services:** We agree to pay the PC for services and expenses by the PC in working with us in accordance with the terms of this agreement, including, but not limited to, the time spent by the PC reviewing/drafting documents and correspondence; meetings and phone conferences with us, our child(ren), our attorneys and any other people involved with us or our child(ren), and deliberation and issuance of arbitration awards, at the rate of $[dollar amount] per hour. We also agree to pay the expenses incurred by the PC, including, but not limited to, long-distance phone calls, photocopies, fax charges, etc. This hourly rate will remain in effect for at least one year; provided however, after 12 months from the date of execution of this agreement (date of PC's signature), the PC may change the hourly rate regularly charged for such services by the PC at such time, upon written notice to the parents.

We shall pay the PC's fees and expenses in the following manner: Each of us shall be responsible separately for payment for our individual time spent with the PC in office and/or telephone conferences. For any services by the PC for us jointly, e.g. mediation, arbitration, drafting, joint phone/office conferences, conferences with our child(ren) and other involved third parties, etc., Father shall pay [percentage amount]% and Mother shall pay [percentage amount]%; provided however, the PC shall have discretionary authority to reallocate the fees and expenses for any arbitrated matter, considering the relative merits of each parent's position.

We understand that in the event we must reschedule or cancel an office appointment with the PC, we shall be charged for one hour of the PC's time, unless we notify the PC at least 24 hours prior to the scheduled appointment. In the event that one of us does not appear for a scheduled appointment, or does not give 24 hours advance notice, and the other parent does appear or is prepared to appear, the parent who does not appear or give adequate notice shall be responsible for paying the full fee for the hour charged by the PC.

We each shall deposit with the PC an advance deposit for fees and expenses of $*[dollar amount]*, upon the signing of this agreement, and we shall replenish such deposit balance to the same level per parent upon its depletion. **Accounts past due 30 days will be charged finance charges at the rate of at 1.5% compounded monthly (19.6% Annual Percentage Rate).** Non-payment of fees shall be grounds for the resignation of the PC.

We agree that all fees and expenses of the PC are in the nature of additional child support, as a necessary part of our parental responsibilities, and they are not dischargeable in bankruptcy.

11. **Term and Reports:** The term of the PC's service shall be a period of *[number of months]* months from the date of execution of this agreement by the PC. At the end of the term, if either parent and/or the PC desires to terminate the professional relationship with the PC, this agreement shall be terminated. The services of the PC may be terminated prior to the end of such term if both parents agree that they wish to terminate the PC's services, or if the PC requests to withdraw prior to the termination date. At least 30 days prior to the end of a term, the PC shall prepare and serve upon the parents, and GAL, if any, a summary report of the history of services rendered to the family, including all decisions and any recommendations for the future involvement of a PC with the family. At his/her own expense, a parent may make a record of any information submitted to the PC during the term covered by such report. The PC also may provide parents, their attorneys and the GAL with written interim reports of developments, at the PC's discretion. Any written communication with a parent must be copied to the other parent, the GAL and any attorneys for the parents.

12. **Other Terms**

_____

_____

_____

Agreed and Accepted:

Father:*[name of father]* Date*[date]*. Mother:*[name of mother]* Date-*[date]*

Parenting Coordinator:*[name of parenting coordinator]* Date:*[date]*

§ 6:17   Collaborative law

The use of collaborative law in family law cases in Ohio is a relatively new but growing alternative to traditional family litigation. Collaborative family law is a process which focuses on resolving family disputes through negotiation by specially trained family lawyers who contract with their clients not to litigate, but rather to settle the disputes involved in marital dissolution or divorce.

> Going to court is "off the table" as an option for resolving differences. This principle is so fundamental to the process that the parties, as well as their counsel, sign a Collaborative Law Participation Agreement, promising not to go to court while they are negotiating a resolution to their conflict. If the collaborative-law process breaks down because one party or his or her attorney feels compelled to litigate, the collaborative counsel who represents that party must withdraw. The Collaborative Law Participation Agreement states explicitly that collaborative counsel is hired for the sole purpose of negotiating a settlement and not for representing the client in court.
>
> Once the threat of litigation is gone, a profound change takes place in participants and their lawyers. Suspicion, fear, mistrust, and other barriers to settlement are replaced by cooperation, information sharing, and creative problem-solving.[1]

In collaborative law, "[t]he parties' lawyers work together to provide agendas for four-way settlement meetings, to set realistic deadlines for document exchanges, and to create a safe, open, and fair environment for resolving conflicts."[2]

In Ohio, the model most frequently used for collaborative law is, as described above, a model which focuses entirely on settlement and

---

[Section 6:17]

[1]Rita S. Pollak, *Collaborative Law: Take the Cat-and-Dog Fight Out of Your Divorce*, vol. 24, no. 4, Family Advocate 28 (Spring 2002).

[2]Rita S. Pollak, *Collaborative Law: Take the Cat-and-Dog Fight Out of Your Divorce*, vol. 24, no. 4, Family Advocate 28 (Spring 2002); for a critique of collaborative law, see Rhonda Murphy, *Is the Turn Toward Collaborative Law a Turn Away from Justice?*, 42 Family Court Review 460 (July 2004). See also James K.L. Lawrence, *Collaborative Lawyering: A New Development in Conflict Resolution*, 17 Ohio State J. on Disp. Resol. 431 (2002); Sandra S. Beckwith and Sherri Goren Slovin, *The Collaborative Lawyer as an Advocate: A Response*, 18 Ohio State J. on Disp. Resol. 497 (2003); Christopher M. Fairman, *Ethics and Collaborative Lawyering: Why Put Old Hats on New Heads?*, 18 Ohio State J. on Disp. Resol. 505 (2002); Christopher M. Fairman, *A Proposed Model Rule for Collaborative Law*, 21 Ohio State J. on Disp. Resol. 73 (2005); Jill Schachner Chanen, *Collaborative Counselors: Newest ADR Option Wins Converts While Suffering Some Growing Pains*, 92 ABA Journal 52 (June 2006). John Lande, *Principles for Policymaking About Collaborative Law and Other ADR Processes*, vol. 22, no. 3 Ohio State Journal on Dispute Resolution 619. Christopher M. Fairman, *Why We Still Need a Model Rule for Collaborative Law: A Reply to Professor Lande*, vol. 22, no. 3 Ohio State Journal on Dispute Resolution 709. Stuart G. Webb and Ronald D. Ousky, *The Collaborative Way to Divorce: The Revolutionary Method that Results in Less Stress, Lower Costs, and Happier Kids—Without Going to Court* (Hudson Street Press, the Penguin Group, 2006); Susan Zaidel, How Collaborative is Collaborative Divorce?, Family Mediation Newsletter (Summer 2008).

requires the lawyer to withdraw from representation of the client if an agreement is not reached and the matter must proceed to litigation. However, there are some locations in which a model of collaborative law is being used which does not require the withdrawal of counsel if the parties determine to litigate the matter.[3]

Collaborative law groups exist in the northwest Ohio counties and in Clinton, Clermont, Cuyahoga, Franklin, Hamilton and Warren Counties.

§ 6:18 Collaborative law—Participation agreement—Form⊚

COLLABORATIVE LAW PARTICIPATION AGREEMENT

PURPOSE

[WIFE] and [HUSBAND] (hereinafter sometimes referred to as "the parties") have chosen to use the principles of Collaborative Law to settle the issues arising from the dissolution of their marriage. The primary goal of Collaborative Law is to settle in a nonadversarial manner the issues of the parties' separation and dissolution of their marriage. The parties have retained lawyers who agree to use the principles of Collaborative Law to assist them in reaching this goal.

COMMUNICATION

The parties and their lawyers intend to effectively communicate with each other to efficiently and economically settle the dissolution of their marriage. Written and verbal communications will be respectful and constructive and will not make accusations or claims not based in fact.

It is agreed that communications during settlement meetings will be focused on the economic and parenting issues (if applicable) in the dissolution and the constructive resolution of those issues. The parties and their lawyers understand that the costs for settlement meetings are substantial and require everyone's cooperation to make the best possible use of available resources. To achieve this goal, the parties agree not to engage in unnecessary discussions of past events.

To maintain an objective and constructive settlement process, the parties agree to discuss settlement of their dissolution issues only in the settlement conference setting. Discussions outside of the conference setting must be agreed to by the parties and their lawyers. Settlement issues will not be discussed in the presence of the parties' children, nor at unannounced times by telephone calls or appearances at the other party's residence.

---

[3]For an excellent discussion regarding ethical considerations and issues inherent in collaborative law and for suggestions as to the formulation of collaborative law participation agreements see: ABA Formal Opinion 07-417, August 9, 2007, *Ethical Considerations in Collaborative Law Practice*, and Scott R. Peppel, *The New Ethics of Collaborative Law*, Vol. 14, No. 2 Disp. Resol. Mag. 23 (Winter 2008).

The parties acknowledge that inappropriate communications regarding their dissolution can be harmful to their children. Communication with the children regarding these issues will occur only if it is appropriate and done by mutual agreement. By mutual agreement, the parties may together seek the advice of a neutral child specialist. (See section on "Experts" below.) The parties specifically agree that their children will not be included in any discussion regarding the dissolution except as described in this Agreement.

The parties agree that all statements made during any settlement meeting are intended to be taken as being in furtherance of settlement, and therefore, not admissible as evidence in court. Further, neither party shall call either attorney as a witness should either or both parties resort to litigation.

EXPERTS

When appropriate and needed, the parties will use neutral experts for purposes of valuation, cash flow analysis, parenting issues and any other issue which requires expert advice and/or recommendations. The parties will agree in advance as to how the costs of the third-party expert will be paid. If the parties resort to litigation, either party may call any neutral expert who has participated in the Collaborative Law process as a witness in court, and the expert's report may be submitted to the court.

INFORMATION

The parties and their lawyers agree to deal with each other in good faith to promptly provide all necessary and reasonable information requested. No formal discovery procedures (e.g., depositions, interrogatories, document requests, requests for admissions) will be used during the Collaborative Law process.

The parties acknowledge that by using informal discovery, they are giving up certain investigative procedures and methods that would be available to them in the litigation process. They give up these measures with the specific understanding that both parties make full and fair disclosure of all assets, income, debts and other information necessary for a fair settlement. Participation in the Collaborative Law process, and the settlement reached, is based upon the assumption that both parties have acted in good faith and have provided complete and accurate information to the best of their ability. The parties agree to sign a sworn statement making full and fair disclosure of their income, assets and debts.

ENFORCEABILITY OF AGREEMENTS

In the event that either party requires a temporary agreement for any purpose, the agreement will be put in writing and signed by the parties and their lawyers. If either party withdraws from the Collaborative Law process, the written agreement shall not be submitted to the court.

ATTORNEY FEES

The parties acknowledge and agree that each party must have funds available for payment of attorney fees. The parties agree to make funds available for this purpose.

LEGAL PROCESS

Court Proceedings: Unless otherwise agreed, or in the case of an emergency, prior to reaching final agreement on all issues, no Summons and Complaint will be served or filed, nor will any other motion or document be prepared or filed which would initiate court intervention unless otherwise agreed. When the parties have reached a final agreement, the parties will file jointly for a dissolution of marriage. Alternatively, by agreement of the parties, one party may file for an uncontested divorce. Neither party nor their lawyer will use the court during the Collaborative Law process unless it is mutually agreed, or in the case of an emergency.

Withdrawal from Collaborative Law Process: If a party decides to withdraw from the Collaborative Law process, prompt written notice will be given to the other party through his or her lawyer. Upon withdrawal from the Collaborative Law process, there will be a thirty (30) day waiting period (unless there is an emergency) before any court hearing, to permit the other party to retain another lawyer and make an orderly transition. All temporary agreements will remain in full force and effect during this period. The intent of this provision is to avoid surprise and prejudice to the rights of the other party. It is therefore mutually agreed that either party may bring this provision to the attention of the court in requesting a postponement of a hearing.

The parties understand and agree that, if either party withdraws from the Collaborative Law process and the case proceeds to litigation, neither attorney who has represented the parties in the Collaborative Law process shall represent the party in the litigation process.

OTHER RIGHTS AND OBLIGATIONS PENDING SETTLEMENT

The parties understand that, without filing a court action, neither party is restrained by court order from any act. However, the parties agree to the following, until further written agreement by the parties:

(1) Neither party will harass, annoy, interfere with, harass by telephone, assault, or cause bodily harm to the other party.

(2) Neither party will sell, damage, destroy, remove, encumber, dispose of, lessen the value of, or in some manner hide any asset belonging to either or both of the parties.

(3) Neither party will change beneficiaries on any life insurance policies, fail to pay the premiums thereon, cancel or cash in said policies, or permit said policies to lapse, or otherwise change the status of said policies.

(4) Neither party will withdraw, spend, encumber, or dispose of funds deposited in financial institutions, including but not limited to bank accounts (except checking accounts), savings ac-

counts, money markets, credit unions, pension plans, or certificates of deposit.

(5) Neither party will change beneficiaries on any insurance policies, fail to pay the premiums thereon, cancel or cash in said policies, or permit said policies to lapse, or otherwise change the status of said policies.

(6) Neither party will contract upon the other's credit in some manner, or incur any debt to which the other may be obligated.

(7) Neither party will relocate any of the parties' minor children from the county in which they now reside or to a location that would interfere with school attendance in their present school district.

(8) Neither party will conceal the whereabouts of any of their minor children during the pendency of the Collaborative Law process.

ACKNOWLEDGMENT OF RIGHTS

The parties have chosen the Collaborative Law process to reduce emotional and financial costs, and to generate a final agreement that addresses their concerns. They agree to work in good faith to achieve these goals. The parties acknowledge that, by dissolving their marriage by agreement, they will be waiving the following rights that would otherwise be available to them through the litigation process:

(1) The right to formal discovery, including but not limited to discovery of assets and liabilities.

(2) The right to have each and every item of marital property valued and to have the court resolve any disputes between them with respect to valuation.

(3) The right to have a court divide the marital property in a manner that the court determines to be equitable under Ohio law.

By signing below, both parties and their lawyers acknowledge that they have read this Agreement and agree to abide by its terms.

Dated:_____   Dated:_____

_____   _____
Wife's Name   Husband's Name
Address   Address

_____   _____
Attorney for Wife   Attorney for Husband
Attorney Registration No.   Attorney Registration No.
Street Address   Street Address
City, State, Zip   City, State, Zip
Office Phone   Office Phone
Fax Number   Fax Number

Collaborative Family Law Council of Central Ohio

Revised 1/6/98

§ 6:19 Conciliation

Since 1969, Ohio statutes have authorized a conciliation process that promotes reconciliation of parties experiencing marital discord. RC 3117.01 empowers common pleas courts to determine "that social conditions and the number of domestic relations cases in the county render the conciliation procedures provided necessary to proper consideration of such cases or to effectuate conciliation of marital controversies." If a court makes such a determination, its judge(s) are to hear conciliation cases filed in the court[1] and, in counties with populations over one hundred thousand, the court is entitled to appoint one or more conciliation counselors to assist the court in carrying out its functions in conciliation.[2] RC 3117.05 indicates that a petition for conciliation may be filed as a separate claim for relief prior to or during the pendency of a divorce, annulment or legal separation action by one or both spouses in an effort "to preserve the marriage by effecting a reconciliation, or to amicably settle the controversy between the spouses, so as to avoid further litigation over the issues involved."[3] RC Chapter 3117 also establishes the rules and procedure for conciliation actions and when and under what circumstances such actions are terminated.[4] During the period commencing with the filing of the petition for conciliation and continuing until the expiration of any court order for reconciliation, pending divorce, annulment and legal separation actions are stayed and neither spouse may file such an action during that period.[5]

RC 3105.091 sets out the procedure that is to be used in pending actions for divorce, annulment, legal separation or dissolution of marriage if one or both of the parties request or if the court, on its own motion, orders conciliation and/or, if children are involved, family counseling. Unlike an action under RC Chapter 3117, which is brought as a separate action by petition either before or during an action for divorce, legal separation or annulment, a proceeding under RC3105.091, is brought by motion during the pendency of a divorce, dissolution, legal separation or annulment action. Under RC 3105.091, the court may refer a conciliation matter to its conciliation office established under RC 3117.03 (if it has such an office) or may refer the parties to "public or private marriage counselors, family service agencies, community health services, physicians, licensed psycholo-

---

[Section 6:19]

  [1]RC 3117.02.
  [2]RC 3117.03.
  [3]RC 3117.05(A).
  [4]RC 3117.05 and RC 3117.06.
  [5]RC 3117.07.

gists, or clergymen."[6] Orders requiring the parties to undergo conciliation may be for a period of time not exceeding ninety days; however,
the court "may" establish the length of time for family counseling
which may be "during the course of the proceeding or for any reasonable period of time as directed by the court."[7]

§ 6:20 Petition for conciliation—Form⊚

(RC Ch. 3117)

[Title of Court]

[Caption]   Case No. [_____]
                                               PETITION FOR
                                               CONCILIATION

   Now comes the Petitioner, *[name]*, and for this Petition for Conciliation says as follows:
   1. That the parties were married on *[date]* at *[city and state]*, and
that *[no/number]* children were born as issue of said marriage,
namely *[name(s) and date(s) of birth of children]*.
   2. That controversy between the parties has arisen which, unless
a reconciliation or settlement is achieved, may result in dissolution
of the marriage or disruption of the household and that the following are facts showing the same:
   [a._____.]
      [b._____.]
   Wherefore, the Petitioner requests the aid of the court to effect
a reconciliation or an amicable settlement of the controversy between the parties by ordering the parties to obtain counseling
from _____.

                                               _____
                                               Petitioner

NOTES TO FORM
Drafter's Notes
   The caption must state the names and addresses of the parties. A petition for
conciliation is available only in counties in which the common pleas court has
determined, pursuant to RC 3117.01, to apply the statutes. RC 3117.05(D)
provides that the clerk of court of common pleas provide (without charge) blank
forms for filing petitions and RC 3227.05(E) provides that no fee may be charged
for filing.

§ 6:21 Motion for conciliation—Form⊚

(RC 3105.091)

----

   [6]RC 3105.091(A).
   [7]RC 3105.091(A)

[Title of Court]

[Caption]

Case No. *[_____]*
MOTION FOR
CONCILIATION
[AND FAMILY
COUNSELING]

Now comes the *[Plaintiff] [Defendant]* and moves the Court for an order requiring the parties to undergo conciliation with *[name of conciliator]* and family counseling with *[name of counselor]* for the reasons set out in the affidavit of *[Plaintiff] [Defendant]* attached hereto.

_____

Plaintiff/Defendant/Attorney

State of Ohio   :

       :   SS.   AF-
                                       FIDAVIT

County of *[_____]*   :

[Affiant], being first duly sworn, deposes and says as follows:

1. *[He] [She]* is the *[Plaintiff] [Defendant]* in this action and that *[his] [her]* spouse, *[name]*, is the *[Plaintiff] [Defendant]*;

2. The parties have been married for *[number of years]* years, and *[number of children]* children have been born as issue of their marriage, namely *[names and dates of birth of children]*;

3. *(Use only if there are children)* Because children are involved, family counseling would benefit all family members;

4. The parties have acquired many assets and liabilities during the term of their marriage for which they are jointly responsible; and

5. Many common bonds exist between the parties and among their family. Affiant believes that it is not necessary to terminate their marriage at this time and that professional conciliation services could result in saving the relationship between the parties *[and family counseling could assist the children in adjusting and responding to the marital conflict between the parties]*;.

Further affiant says naught.

_____

Affiant

§ 6:22 Order for conciliation, stay—Form⊚

(RC 3105.091 and Ch. 3117)

[Title of Court]

[Caption]   Case No. [_____]
                                             ORDER FOR CONCILI-
                                             ATION
                                             [AND FAMILY
                                             COUNSELING]

Pursuant to *[RC Chapter 3117] [RC 3105.091]*, and pursuant to conciliation proceedings, the Court finds that conciliation is appropriate in this case.

Therefore, it is hereby ORDERED, as follows:

1. The *[divorce] [legal separation] [annulment][dissolution]* proceedings are stayed pending the following conciliation actions in which the parties are directed to participate:

[State procedure, name of conciliator, length of time and type of conciliation counseling]

[In addition, the parties and their children are directed to participate in the following family counseling:

State procedure, name of counselor, length of time and type of counseling];

2. The costs of the conciliation *[and/or family counseling]* procedures shall be paid *[describe who will pay the costs or how they will be divided between the parties].*

                                      _____
                                      Judge

§ 6:23 Early neutral evaluation

Early neutral evaluation ("ENE") is being used in some contested divorce proceedings in order to provide parties and attorneys with a realistic view of the case in an effort to identify issues, speed up discovery and encourage settlement of the case.

If a determination is made that the use of ENE would be helpful in the resolution of a case, the parties agree to meet before a neutral third party (the "evaluator") who has experience in domestic relations matters. Each party's case is presented to the evaluator and, at the conclusion of the presentation, he or she offers the parties a confidential opinion regarding the likely outcome of the case and an analysis of its strengths and weaknesses. The evaluator's opinion is strictly that—an opinion—and is not binding in any way upon the parties.

However, in many instances, upon hearing the evaluator's opinion, the parties will settle some or all of the contested issues, thereby eliminating a portion of the costs associated with the action, shortening the time of the proceeding and reducing the personal and familial conflict and stress related to protracted litigation.[1]

[Section 6:23]

[1]See Jordan Leigh Santeramo, *Early Neutral Evaluation in Divorce Cases*, 42 Family Court Review 321 (April 2004). Yvonne Pearson, with contributions from Gunnar Bankovics, Maryellen Bauman, Nancy Darcy, Susan DeVries, James Goetz and Greg Kowalsky, *Early Neutral Evaluation: Applications to Custody and Parenting Time Cases Program Development and Implementation in Hennepin County, Minnesota*, vol. 44, no. 4 Family Court Review 672 (October 2006).

Chapter 7

Annulment

By Lynn B. Schwartz, Esq.[*]

---

[*]Updated for the Fourth Edition by Laurel G. Stein, Esq.

KeyCite®: Cases and other legal materials listed in KeyCite Scope can be researched through the KeyCite service on Westlaw®. Use KeyCite to check citations for form, parallel references, prior and later history, and comprehensive citator information, including citations to other decisions and secondary materials.

---

§ 7:1 Nature of marriage and annulment

An annulment decree is an order of a court declaring that a marriage is legally invalid or defective because of some impediment or defect which existed at the time the marriage was formed. Annulment is a legal action. As used in this chapter, annulment refers to a civil action in the civil court system. The term is used elsewhere to describe a similar action within the judicial system of a church.[1] Thus, any consideration of the nature of annulment requires a brief summary of the nature of marriage.[2]

Entry into the marital status consists of a contract, evidenced by formalities[3] in its execution, consisting of a mutual agreement between parties who are legally eligible to marry. Where any of these three factors is absent, the absence is referred to as a defect or impediment, and the marriage is void or voidable.

Certain factors which impair the validity of a marriage relate to the agreement itself. Like other contracts, the marriage contract must be made by persons who have legal and mental capacity to contract. The rules relating to insanity and intoxication are essentially the same for both types of contracts (contract voidable for lack of capacity to contract). Similarly, nonmarital and marital contracts by minors are voidable. However, for policy reasons, the rules are different. The term "nonage" is used when referring to marriage because the alternatives, "infancy" or "minority," have a technical meaning in contract law; those terms refer to someone who is not yet an adult. While the age of majority was twenty-one at common law, by statute it is now eighteen.[4] Finally, marriages, like other contracts, may be avoided if the agreement is the result of fraud, duress, or mistake. In contrast to

---

[Section 7:1]

[1]For a discussion of Catholic annulment, see Text § 35:7, Formal process for declaration of nullity.

[2]See Text §§ 2:6 to 2:14, Ceremonial marriage; Text §§ 2:35 to 2:48, Common law marriage.

[3]The problem of formalities is discussed in the sections on common law and statutory marriage. See Text §§ 2:6 to 2:14, Ceremonial marriage; Text §§ 2:35 to 2:48, Common law marriage.

[4]RC 3109.01.

other contracts, marriage is more difficult to avoid on these grounds because of a strong public policy in favor of preserving an existing marital status.

Although the parties have complied with the formalities and have made a valid agreement, certain defects relating to eligibility will render a marriage void. The first defect relates to the physical health of the parties. A second defect includes factors which make it unlawful for a person to marry anyone who comes from a specified group or class. The final defect is a disability imposed by law, which makes it impossible for a person who is already married to contract a valid marriage with another.

§ 7:2   History of annulment

On September 24, 1963 Ohio adopted an annulment code.[1] Prior to this date, Ohio courts relied upon the common law to annul marriages. The statute itself lists six specific grounds for annulment. Other bases for annulment which the common law courts have utilized and which are still used today are referred to as nonstatutory grounds.[2]

§ 7:3   Effect of void or voidable disability

Generally, the older decisions classified each defect as void or voidable, the choice resting largely on historical precedent. Under early common law, canon law disabilities apparently rendered a marriage voidable, and the marriage was valid for all purposes until avoided by court decree. Where the court was faced with a civil defect, the usual solution was to adopt the comparable rule from contract law. The normal contract rule is that insanity voids a contract, while fraud, duress, and minority render a contract voidable. These rules, to some extent, have been assimilated into marriage law.

Where a court concludes that a defect renders a marriage voidable, the usual consequences attached by the law are as follows:

(1) The marriage can be ratified by acts or conduct of the parties after the defect is removed.

(2) The marriage is valid until avoided by a court decree. Self-help is not permitted. The parties cannot disaffirm the marriage by walking away from it.

(3) The marriage can be disaffirmed only in a direct suit between the parties to the marriage. Collateral attack on the marriage is not permitted.

Where a court concludes that a marriage is void, the usual incidents are the converse of the above. That is, ratification is ineffective, the marriage is invalid without the necessity of a court decree, and collateral attack on the marriage is permitted.

[Section 7:2]

[1]RC 3105.31, RC 3105.32, RC 3105.34.

[2]See Text §§ 7:12 to 7:15, Common law grounds.

It should be apparent that the terms void and voidable are simply verbal labels used to describe the three factors listed above. The three factors listed are not the only incidents of the labels void and voidable, although they are the most common. Generally, equitable defenses, such as unclean hands, laches, and estoppel, are available as defenses in an annulment action based on a voidable marriage, but not in an action based on a void marriage. Further, the annulment decree declaring a void marriage is sometimes related back to the time of the marriage, whereas it becomes effective only when rendered in the case of a voidable marriage.[1] It is also clear that there is no logical necessity for classifying marriage in only two ways, void or voidable, in terms of the above rules. Thus, it would be possible to hold that a marriage is void, in that no court decree is necessary and collateral attack is permitted, and still hold that ratification is possible. This is exactly what the Ohio Supreme Court has done regarding nonage marriages.[2]

A court should not blindly attach the label void or voidable to a defect without understanding the effect of the label. Fortunately, most modern courts look to the effects of the label and decide that the marriage is void or voidable on the basis of policy considerations. Thus, if there is very strong sentiment against a particular marriage (for example, bigamy), the court will usually declare the marriage void. If the marriage is between first cousins, the court will usually hold such a marriage voidable as there is no strong public bias against a marriage between first cousins.[3]

Another factor which often influences the court is the relative ease of proof. Where a defect is difficult to prove and is of the type which could be invented years after the marriage to evade obligations of support, the court may hold such marriage voidable and bar the plaintiff on the basis of unclean hands or ratification. The defects of fraud and insanity are examples of this situation.

In most judicial opinions, the statement that a marriage is void or voidable is dictum. In the typical annulment case, the suit is between the parties, collateral attack or ratification is not involved, and the de-

---

[Section 7:3]

[1]For a discussion of the extent to which an annulment decree relates back to the date of the marriage, see Note, *The Void and Voidable Marriage: A Study in Judicial Method*, 7 Stan. L. Rev. 529 (1955). See also Text §§ 7:22 to 7:25, Effect of annulment decree.

[2]Shafher v. State, 20 Ohio 1, 1851 WL 1 (1851) (although *Shafher* has been criticized, it has not been expressly overruled). (Acts of marriage contracted under the age of consent, after arriving at that age, must be shown, in order to bind the party contracting such marriage). See also Text § 7:6, Statutory grounds—Underage marriage.

[3]See Mazzolini v. Mazzolini, 168 Ohio St. 357, 7 Ohio Op. 2d 123, 155 N.E.2d 206 (1958). (The policy of the law is to sustain marriages, where they are not incestuous, polygamous, shocking to good morals, unalterably opposed to a well-defined public policy, or prohibited). See also Text §§ 7:6 to 7:11, Statutory grounds.

cision would be the same whether the marriage was treated as void or voidable.

§ 7:4 Annulment versus divorce

Conceptually, a decree of divorce terminates the marital status because of some cause or event which arose after the status was created. On the other hand, an annulment decree is one which either terminates the status (in the case of a voidable marriage) or which declares that there never was a marital status (in the case of a void marriage). However, in both cases the basis of the action is some event or condition which existed at the time the alleged marriage was contracted. Accordingly, most states hold that the two actions are mutually exclusive. That is, there can be no annulment of a legally valid marriage. Conversely, there can be no divorce where the marriage is defective, or as it is more commonly phrased, a valid marriage is a jurisdictional prerequisite to a divorce action.

The difficulty in Ohio arises from the fact that since 1853 the divorce statute has included three grounds for divorce which are traditionally grounds for annulment. These were impotency, fraud, and bigamy.[1] In 1989, impotency was deleted as a ground for divorce.[2] Bigamy and fraud remain as grounds for divorce under RC 3105.01 as well as grounds for annulment under RC 3105.31. RC 3105.01 does not explain whether these grounds refer to events which happened at the time of the marriage or subsequently. However, bigamy and fraud, by their very nature, refer to entry into the marital status. Prior to 1989 House Bill 129, impotency was an additional ground for divorce, which could be construed as impotency occurring after entry into the status. However, the Ohio courts have never followed this line of reasoning. In addition, the three grounds were not defined in the statute, but the Ohio courts have always incorporated the substantive law of annulment in arriving at definitions of the statutory terms.[3]

Prior to 1952, there was no speculation in the Ohio opinions as to the dual nature of these three grounds and little discussion as to the reason why the legislature designated three of the many grounds for annulment as grounds for divorce. There is a passing reference in one Ohio Supreme Court case[4] suggesting that this was done so that the good faith victim of a bigamous marriage could terminate the marriage and also obtain spousal support. This suggestion, based on the fault of the defendant, could logically explain the special treatment of

---

[Section 7:4]

[1]See former RC 3105.01(A), (D), (F).

[2]1989 H.B. 129, eff. 8-25-89.

[3]See Text §§ 7:6 to 7:11, Statutory grounds; Text §§ 7:12 to 7:15, Common law grounds. See also Meyer v. Meyer, 4 Ohio Dec. Rep. 345, 7 Ohio Dec. Rep. 561, 1 Cleve. Law Rep. 347, 3 W.L.B. 985, 1878 WL 7379 (Ohio C.P. 1878), aff'd, 7 Ohio Dec. Rep. 627, 4 W.L.B. 368, 1879 WL 6394 (Ohio Dist. Ct. 1879).

[4]Smith v. Smith, 5 Ohio St. 32, 1855 WL 40 (1855).

bigamy and fraud. However, the applicability of this rationale is questionable in cases involving impotency, which does not involve fault and, for this reason, is no longer available as grounds for divorce. The suggested rationale of the statute was strengthened by an 1869 Ohio Supreme Court opinion,[5] holding that the victim of a bigamous marriage, without knowledge of the defect, was entitled to alimony when she sued for divorce on the grounds of bigamy. The holding in that opinion suggests that the bigamous spouse is able to obtain an annulment of the second marriage (because the marriage is void, not voidable), and the other spouse has an option: to sue for annulment without spousal support or, if she married in good faith, unaware of the impediment, to sue for divorce and spousal support.

Apparently, the implications of this suggestion were never pursued. The lower courts seemed to follow the practice of granting either a divorce or an annulment, depending on the request of the plaintiff, without any distinctions based on good faith, knowledge of the impediment, or comparative fault.

This situation changed in 1952 with the decision in *Eggleston v Eggleston*.[6] In that case, the husband married the wife at a time when he had a prior wife living. The second wife had no knowledge of the bigamy. The parties lived together for ten years and had two children. The second wife discovered that her marriage was bigamous and sued for divorce on the grounds of bigamy, cruelty, and neglect. As an alternative to divorce she asked for an annulment. The trial court held that she was entitled to an annulment but denied her a divorce, alimony, or child support on the theory that no divorce can be granted for a void marriage. The wife appealed and the Ohio Supreme Court reversed, indicating that this is the exact situation for which the statute was intended, i.e., a divorce in addition to alimony for the good faith victim of bigamy.

Apparently, the decision in the *Eggleston* case was correct in light of the facts. However, subsequent difficulty was caused by the Court's additional ground for the decision. The additional provision stated that where the legislature has set forth a marital defect as a ground for divorce, the divorce statute provides the exclusive remedy. The statement was unnecessary to the decision of the case and, if read literally, would indicate that the courts no longer have jurisdiction to grant annulments for bigamy or fraud.

Between 1952 and 1963, the lower court decisions in regard to the "*Eggleston* problem" were conflicting. *Basickas v. Basickas*[7] and *Abelt*

---

[5]Vanvalley v. Vanvalley, 19 Ohio St. 588, 1869 WL 105 (1869).

[6]Eggleston v. Eggleston, 156 Ohio St. 422, 46 Ohio Op. 351, 103 N.E.2d 395 (1952).

[7]Basickas v. Basickas, 93 Ohio App. 531, 51 Ohio Op. 229, 114 N.E.2d 270 (9th Dist. Summit County 1953).

v. Zeman[8] followed the dictum in the *Eggleston* case and indicated that divorce is the only remedy for all three grounds then in effect, regardless of other factors such as good faith of the parties. *Nyhuis v. Pierce*[9] and *Schwartz v. Schwartz*[10] granted annulments for bigamy in spite of the *Eggleston* rule. Partly to settle this problem, the 105th General Assembly enacted Ohio's first annulment act, a fairly detailed annulment code which became effective in September 1963.[11] The Annulment Act amended many sections of the divorce chapter, RC Chapter 3105, to specify that the divorce rules on venue, jurisdiction, and procedure apply to annulment. In addition, four new sections were created: RC 3105.31, setting forth grounds for annulment; RC 3105.32, setting forth rules on time limitations and standing for annulment actions; former RC 3105.33, later moved to RC 3111.03, providing a presumption of legitimacy for the children of the annulled marriage; and RC 3105.34, providing for the restoration of the wife's maiden name.[12] Unfortunately, the act was poorly drafted and hastily enacted, and, while it solved many problems, it created a number of new ones which remain unresolved.

The logical way to have solved the problem created by the *Eggleston* case would have been to delete the three annulment grounds from the divorce statute, as they existed when the Annulment Act was enacted. However, the new statute left the divorce section unchanged and listed bigamy, fraud, and impotency among the grounds for annulment. Thus, the "*Eggleston* problem" has been resolved because the legislature no longer lists an exclusive remedy for the three defects. The legislature now lists two separate and conceptually inconsistent remedies for each of the three defects. Neither the statute nor the legislative history gives any hint as to the policy factors which should govern the choice of remedy in a specific case.

A more recent decision emphasizes another aspect of the problem. In *Liming v. Liming*,[13] the trial court's decree of annulment and division of property was reversed because the property division statute does not apply to annulment proceedings. The Court stated that property division in annulment is not based on legal status such as marriage, but is more like adjustment of property interests between parties, similar in nature to dissolution of a business partnership.

_____

[8]Abelt v. Zeman, 16 Ohio Op. 2d 87, 86 Ohio L. Abs. 109, 173 N.E.2d 907 (C.P. 1961).

[9]Nyhuis v. Pierce, 65 Ohio L. Abs. 73, 114 N.E.2d 75 (Ct. App. 8th Dist. Cuyahoga County 1952) (Where an annulment is justified, the divorce statutes should not be construed as being involved).

[10]Schwartz v. Schwartz, 113 Ohio App. 275, 17 Ohio Op. 2d 267, 173 N.E.2d 393 (1st Dist. Hamilton County 1960).

[11]130 Laws of Ohio H.B. 467, eff. 9-24-63.

[12]The Annulment Act and the legislative history are discussed in Andrew M. Fishman, *The Ohio Annulment Law: A Beginning But Not an End*, 16 Case W. Res. L. Rev. 915 (1965).

[13]Liming v. Liming, 117 Ohio App. 3d 617, 691 N.E.2d 299 (4th Dist. Adams County 1996).

No cases subsequent to the enactment of the statute discuss this issue. Even so, the problem of a choice of remedies can and should be resolved by reviewing the original reason for including annulment grounds in the divorce statute, i.e., the provision for a divorce with spousal support for the unwitting victim of a defective marriage. Where the party who knew of the bigamy, or was the party guilty of fraud or bigamy, sues for divorce, the action should be barred by estoppel. In this case, annulment is the only appropriate remedy. Where the purpose of the action is to set the record straight as to the invalidity of a bigamous marriage, or where the parties, for personal or religious reasons, prefer annulment to divorce and are willing to forego spousal support, there should be no objection to an annulment. Where the party is the innocent victim of a defective marriage, that party should be able to choose annulment or divorce, notwithstanding the objection of the defendant spouse.

§ 7:5   Exclusivity of remedy

On its face, the Ohio Annulment Act, RC 3105.31 to RC 3105.34, appears to be a comprehensive annulment code. If comprehensive, by implication the act displaces the courts' equity jurisdiction in annulment existing for over a century and a half prior to enactment of the act.

To date, no reported decisions have resolved this issue. It is probable that when the issue comes before an Ohio court, the court should and will hold that the act is not exclusive. Specifically, the statute should be interpreted as follows:

(1) The statute is exclusive of the common law in that the procedural rules in RC 3105.32 apply where a ground for annulment is listed in RC 3105.31; and

(2) The statute is nonexclusive in that it does not list all grounds for annulment which were available under the common law. Therefore, a party should be able to obtain an annulment on grounds not listed in RC 3105.31.

There are two reasons for the latter interpretation. First, too many established grounds for annulment are omitted from RC 3105.31 which, in the interests of justice, ought to be grounds for annulment. For example, the statute provides for annulment where one spouse was adjudicated to be mentally incompetent at the time of the marriage. A provision for an unadjudicated incompetent is omitted. Where one party was in fact mentally incompetent at the time of entry into marriage and is still incompetent, either the party or his or her guardian ought to be able to annul the marriage. Other examples of grounds which are not covered by the statute, include incestuous marriages, marriages entered into in a state of alcohol or narcotic intoxication, and mistake or lack of mutual consent.

The second reason to support the contention that a party should be able to obtain an annulment on grounds not listed in RC 3105.31 is that the scant legislative history indicates that the statute is not exclusive. The chairman of the House Judiciary Committee at the time of enactment has stated in writing, "It was not intended that this statute provide exclusive remedies and I am going to suggest to the 106th General Assembly that the grounds such as incest, mistake and lack of mutual consent be added and that the courts be permitted to retain equitable jurisdiction."[1] Whether this suggestion was made to the legislature is unknown. If made, no formal action was taken, but lack of action should not invalidate the chairman's conclusion that at least the committee assumed that the statute was nonexclusive.

The question should be settled either by amendment of RC 3105.31 or by judicial decision. Lacking such a decision, one may assume that annulment is available as part of equity jurisprudence, for grounds not mentioned in the statute.

§ 7:6 Statutory grounds—Underage marriage

The age of consent is the age at which a person can enter into a valid marriage, and is not necessarily the same as the age of majority. A marriage in which one or both of the parties are below the age of consent is referred to as a "nonage" marriage. Unlike other contracts, a marriage entered into by a minor who is over the age of consent cannot be avoided when the minor reaches majority because marriage is not only a contract but also a status involving social interests and interests of third persons, such as children. However, a minor's promise to marry can be avoided like any other contract, as none of the incidents of the status have attached.

The age of consent under the common law was fourteen for males and twelve for females. A marriage below the age of seven was void, and a marriage over age seven and below the age of consent was voidable. The present statute, RC 3101.01, provides that males age eighteen and females age sixteen may marry. Ohio is one of the few states which continues to set different ages of consent for men and women. The statute may be unconstitutional under the rationale of *Stanton v. Stanton*,[1] which held a state statute unconstitutional which provided that the age of majority for males was twenty-one and for females eighteen for purposes of requiring parental support. Federal courts in the Sixth Circuit and some Ohio courts have adopted the ra-

---

[Section 7:5]

[1]Letter from Judson Hoy, Esq. to Andrew Fishman, Esq. (February 8, 1965), available from files of the Case Western Reserve Law Review. See also Andrew M. Fishman, *The Ohio Annulment Law*, 16 Case W. Res. L. Rev. 915, 932 (1965).

[Section 7:6]

[1]Stanton v. Stanton, 421 U.S. 7, 95 S. Ct. 1373, 43 L. Ed. 2d 688 (1975).

tionale of *Stanton,* but RC 3101.01 has not been directly challenged as unconstitutional.[2]

Other statutes relating to marriage in RC Chapter 3101 have been held to be directory rather than mandatory. Thus, the lack of a license did not invalidate an otherwise valid common law marriage entered into prior to October 10, 1991, until common law marriages were abolished by RC 3105.12.[3] One might assume that the age statute would be construed the same way. However, the Ohio courts have held, without exception, that the statute does more than fix the age at which a license may issue; it fixes the age of consent.[4] Thus, it is clear that a marriage below the statutory age is invalid whether it is a ceremonial or a common law marriage. RC 3101.01 also provides, in equally mandatory terms, that the consent of the parents must be obtained if the party is a minor. RC 3109.01 declares persons eighteen or more of "full age for all purposes." Yet, Ohio holds that lack of parental consent has no effect on the validity of the marriage.[5]

Although a nonage marriage is invalid, it may be ratified, that is, approved and sanctioned, when the underage party reaches the age of consent.[6] Most of the ratification cases involve continued cohabitation, but any unambiguous act is sufficient. Thus, in one case the court held that the wife, although presently living apart from her husband, could ratify her nonage marriage by a letter addressed "Dear Husband."[7] RC 3105.31 lists underage marriage as a ground for annulment "unless after attaining such age such party cohabited with the other." As only one form of ratification is listed in the statute, a court might conclude that cohabitation is the only type of ratification effective. The question is the extent to which the statute displaces the common law.[8]

Absent ratification, it is clear that the underage spouse can have the marriage annulled either before or after reaching the age of consent. Courts and commentators have disapproved of the right of a person under the age of consent to avoid a marriage which has been

---

[2]In re Netherton, 2 B.R. 50 (Bankr. M.D. Tenn. 1979); In re Rauscher, 40 Ohio App. 3d 106, 531 N.E.2d 745 (8th Dist. Cuyahoga County 1987) (disapproved of by, Ohio State University Hosp. v. Kinkaid, 48 Ohio St. 3d 78, 549 N.E.2d 517 (1990)).

[3]1991 H.B. 32, eff. 10-10-91.

[4]Holtz v. Dick, 42 Ohio St. 23, 1884 WL 197 (1884); Shafher v. State, 20 Ohio 1, 1851 WL 1 (1851).

[5]Holtz v. Dick, 42 Ohio St. 23, 1884 WL 197 (1884).

[6]Holtz v. Dick, 42 Ohio St. 23, 1884 WL 197 (1884); State v. Wilcox, 26 Ohio N.P. (n.s.) 343, 1926 WL 2503 (Juv. Ct. 1926) (a marriage contracted in Ohio by a female under the age of sixteen years is void and remains void, unless confirmed by her cohabitation, or some other ratification, at the time she becomes sixteen years of age or afterward). In re Zemmick's Estate, 32 Ohio Op. 504, 44 Ohio L. Abs. 390, 17 Ohio Supp. 15 (Prob. Ct. 1945), aff'd, 49 Ohio L. Abs. 353, 76 N.E.2d 902 (Ct. App. 7th Dist. Belmont County 1946).

[7]Holtz v. Dick, 42 Ohio St. 23, 26, 1884 WL 197 (1884).

[8]See Text § 7:5, Exclusivity of remedy.

consummated. However, the general rule is to grant the annulment as a matter of right, regardless of the equitable rule of clean hands. There are several cases in which an underage male lies about his age, perjures himself in a marriage license application, marries, fathers a child, and deserts the mother just before reaching the statutory age, and nevertheless is granted a decree of annulment from an equity court.[9]

There is little case law in Ohio regarding the right of anyone other than the underage party to avoid the marriage. The general rule is that such a marriage is voidable, not void, so that only the underage party can annul. The other spouse cannot avoid the marriage simply because his spouse has such a privilege.[10] Although there are no cases on the subject, it is possible that the spouse who is over the age of consent could annul for fraud if the underage party had misrepresented his or her age.

In addition, most states have held that the parents of the underage party cannot annul the marriage. This was the Ohio law prior to 1963.[11] The Annulment Act includes underage marriage as a ground for annulment and provides that the underage party or the parent or guardian of the underage party has standing to annul.[12]

At common law the underage party could annul if still underage or could annul after reaching the age of consent if he or she acted prior to ratification and within a reasonable time period. The present statute allows the parent to annul before the minor reaches the age of consent. The minor can annul prior to reaching the age of consent or within two years after arriving at the age of consent. Whether the underage party is over the age of consent or not, if he or she is a minor, suit must be brought by the "next friend" or other representative pursuant to Civil Rule 17(B).

It is not clear whether a nonage marriage in Ohio is void or voidable. The question has not been resolved by the Annulment Act. The confusion stems from the earliest case to reach the Ohio Supreme Court, *Shafher v. State*,[13] which is still the leading Supreme Court opinion on this subject. The Court held that an underage marriage could be disaffirmed or avoided by the underage party by means other than a judicial decree. The normal rule is that a voidable marriage is treated as valid until it is declared invalid by a court decree.[14] In the *Shafher* case, the boy married while underage, deserted his wife, and remar-

---

[9]Carlton v. Carlton, 76 Ohio App. 338, 32 Ohio Op. 82, 64 N.E.2d 428 (6th Dist. Wood County 1945); Swenson v. Swenson, 179 Wis. 536, 192 N.W. 70 (1923).

[10]Clark, The Law of Domestic Relations in the United States § 2.10.

[11]Peefer v. State, 42 Ohio App. 276, 12 Ohio L. Abs. 583, 182 N.E. 117 (2d Dist. Greene County 1931); Klinebell v. Hilton, 2 Ohio L. Abs. 637, 1924 WL 2613, 2 (Ct. App. 2d Dist. Franklin County 1924).

[12]RC 3105.32(A).

[13]Shafher v. State, 20 Ohio 1, 1851 WL 1 (1851).

[14]See Text § 7:1, Nature of marriage and annulment.

ried without having his first marriage annulled. A conviction of criminal bigamy was set aside, and the Court said that an underage marriage was void but could be ratified. The decision did not indicate whether the operative act of avoidance was the desertion of the first wife or the later marriage. In either case, the theory is irreconcilable with the orthodox view that a nonage marriage is only voidable. For this reason, the Ohio view has been sharply criticized by commentators and courts of other states as contrary to both reason and the weight of authority.[15]

If the *Shafher* case is still the law in Ohio, a nonage marriage is void because no annulment is necessary and is also voidable as it is not subject to collateral attack.[16] Since the *Shafher* decision, lower courts which have dealt with the problem have reached conflicting decisions. Some courts have said that the marriage is void,[17] while others have held it voidable.[18] In many of the cases, the language used was dictum, and the same result would have been reached under either theory. The problem of the *Shafher* case, i.e., the right to avoid without judicial action, was not considered in any of the cases. Cases which squarely hold the marriage voidable are cases denying collateral attack. For example, *Peefer v. State*[19] held that the state cannot attack the marriage by convicting one spouse of contributing to the delinquency of his child bride.[20] Also, *Courtright v. Courtright*,[21] which was affirmed without opinion by the Supreme Court, held that where the underage wife dies before reaching the age of consent, her brothers cannot attack the marriage in an heirship proceeding.

---

[15]Owen v. Coffey, 201 Ala. 531, 78 So. 885 (1918); Walls v. State, 32 Ark. 565, 1877 WL 1674 (1877); State v. Cone, 86 Wis. 498, 57 N.W. 50 (1893).

[16]Holtz v. Dick, 42 Ohio St. 23, 1884 WL 197 (1884) (parents cannot collaterally attack an underage marriage).

[17]Carlton v. Carlton, 76 Ohio App. 338, 32 Ohio Op. 82, 64 N.E.2d 428 (6th Dist. Wood County 1945); Gill v. Gill, 2 Ohio L. Abs. 14, 1923 WL 2378, 2 (Ct. App. 9th Dist. Summit County 1923); State v. Wilcox, 26 Ohio N.P. (n.s.) 343, 1926 WL 2503 (Juv. Ct. 1926); Ott v. Ott, 3 Ohio N.P. 161, 3 Ohio Dec. 684, 1893 WL 391 (C.P. 1893); Vernon v. Vernon, 9 Ohio Dec. Rep. 365, 12 W.L.B. 237, 1883 WL 6769 (Ohio C.P. 1883).

[18]In re Zemmick's Estate, 32 Ohio Op. 504, 44 Ohio L. Abs. 390, 17 Ohio Supp. 15 (Prob. Ct. 1945), aff'd, 49 Ohio L. Abs. 353, 76 N.E.2d 902 (Ct. App. 7th Dist. Belmont County 1946); Peefer v. State, 42 Ohio App. 276, 12 Ohio L. Abs. 583, 182 N.E. 117 (2d Dist. Greene County 1931); Klinebell v. Hilton, 2 Ohio L. Abs. 637, 1924 WL 2613 (Ct. App. 2d Dist. Franklin County 1924); Allen v. Allen, 1923 WL 2060, 21 Ohio Law Rep. 313 (Ohio Com.Pl., 1923); Pearlman v. Pearlman, 27 Ohio N.P. (n.s.) 46, 1928 WL 3312 (C.P. 1928).

[19]Peefer v. State, 42 Ohio App. 276, 12 Ohio L. Abs. 583, 182 N.E. 117 (2d Dist. Greene County 1931).

[20]But see State v. Gans, 168 Ohio St. 174, 184, 5 Ohio Op. 2d 472, 151 N.E.2d 709, 68 A.L.R.2d 736 (1958) (parents of the nonage bride were convicted of " 'acting in a way tending to cause delinquency' " when they encouraged her to enter into an out-of-state marriage which was apparently valid where made; every argument the Court used to convict the parents applied with equal force to the husband).

[21]Courtright v. Scringem, 53 Ohio St. 685, Ohio Sup. Ct. Dec. Unrep. 388, 44 N.E. 1134 (1895).

Those criticizing the *Shafher* decision have assumed that the doctrine is too deeply entrenched in Ohio law to be overturned. Surprisingly, no one focused on the flaw in the reasoning of the Supreme Court in *Shafher*. The Court stated that the parties could avoid the marriage without a decree because equity courts did not have annulment jurisdiction and no statute authorized annulment for this cause. "For our law furnishes no method of obtaining a judicial sentence for annulling such a marriage; unless the parties have the means of escape in their own hands, none exist."[22] This rule was clearly repudiated by the same Court in the later case of *Waymire v. Jetmore.*[23] Thus, it appears that the rule in *Shafher* rests on an incorrect assumption of law.

§ 7:7 Statutory grounds—Bigamy

In Ohio, bigamy is both a ground for annulment and a ground for divorce.[1] The Ohio marriage statute expressly states that persons "not having a husband or wife living, may be joined in marriage."[2] Case law illustrates that Ohio has adopted the general rule that a prior undissolved marriage is a complete bar to a valid marriage and renders the second marriage void. The rule applies with equal force where the first marriage was a common law union.[3]

The second bigamous marriage is treated as a nullity, and neither the marital status nor the usual incidents of the status can arise from it. Thus, the second wife is not entitled to dower or support,[4] and the innocence or good faith of one or both of the spouses is immaterial.[5] Further, the lack of good faith on the part of one of the spouses will not bar his or her annulment action on the ground of estoppel or unclean hands.[6] As the second marriage is void rather than voidable, the spouses technically need not seek a divorce or annulment but can terminate the relationship by separation. Thus, the innocent spouse could enter into a valid marriage with another without waiting for the

---

[22]Shafher v. State, 20 Ohio 1, 6, 1851 WL 1 (1851).

[23]Waymire v. Jetmore, 22 Ohio St. 271, 1872 WL 1 (1872).

[Section 7:7]

[1]The problems which result from this dual position are treated in Text § 7:4, Annulment versus divorce; Text § 7:5, Exclusivity of remedy.

[2]RC 3101.01.

[3]In re Zemmick's Estate, 32 Ohio Op. 504, 44 Ohio L. Abs. 390, 17 Ohio Supp. 15 (Prob. Ct. 1945), aff'd, 49 Ohio L. Abs. 353, 76 N.E.2d 902 (Ct. App. 7th Dist. Belmont County 1946).

[4]Smith v. Smith, 5 Ohio St. 32, 1855 WL 40 (1855).

[5]Williams v. Williams, 90 Ohio App. 369, 48 Ohio Op. 21, 106 N.E.2d 655 (8th Dist. Cuyahoga County 1951).

[6]Smith v. Smith, 72 Ohio App. 203, 27 Ohio Op. 79, 38 Ohio L. Abs. 531, 50 N.E.2d 889 (1st Dist. Hamilton County 1943).

dissolution of the bigamous marriage.[7] As a practical matter, this should not be the recommendation of an attorney, who should be diligent in clearing up the record. Somewhere there is a record of the marriage of the innocent spouse to the bigamous party which should be resolved.

As a bigamous marriage is void rather than voidable, there can be no ratification by continued cohabitation after the dissolution of the first marriage. Under certain circumstances, however, the practical effect of continued cohabitation after dissolution of the first marriage may be similar to ratification, if the requirements of a common law marriage are satisfied.[8]

In Ohio, if the first marriage was dissolved and the new agreement was made prior to October 10, 1991, a valid common law marriage may be recognized.[9] After October 10, 1991, no common law marriage can be created by cohabitation or otherwise in Ohio. Ohio courts will, however, recognize a common law marriage entered into in another state or country, as long as the marriage is valid under the law of that jurisdiction.[10] If the jurisdiction in which the parties lived when the first marriage was dissolved and the new agreement made recognized the new marriage under common law, it will be recognized in Ohio.

Where there is evidence that the parties have entered into a bigamous common law or ceremonial marriage at a time when one or both are ineligible to marry because of another existing marriage, and the parties continue to live together after the impediment is removed (i.e., by death or divorce of the other spouse), the cases can be divided into three general categories:

(1) Where both parties were aware of the impediment, the courts apply the presumption that a relationship meretricious in its origin is presumed to continue as such, so that no new agreement of common law marriage will be presumed.

(2) Where neither party was aware of the impediment, the courts presume that a new agreement for a common law marriage, if applicable, was entered into when the impediment was removed (or more accurately, that the original agreement was a continuing one).

(3) Where one party, but not both, was aware of the impediment, the courts are split. However, the Ohio Supreme Court has held that under these circumstances, continued cohabitation is equiv-

---

[7]Williams v. Williams, 90 Ohio App. 369, 48 Ohio Op. 21, 106 N.E.2d 655 (8th Dist. Cuyahoga County 1951).

[8]See Text §§ 2:35 et seq., Common law marriage.

[9]RC 3105.12, eff. 10-10-91.

[10]RC 3105.12(B)(3).

alent to a new agreement for purposes of the applicable law regarding common law marriage.[11]

No rules of standing or time limitation are set forth in RC 3105.01 which authorizes a divorce for bigamy. As to standing, the divorce action can be filed only by a spouse. The court may hold that the bigamous spouse (or the nonbigamous spouse who knew the marriage was bigamous when entered into) may be barred by estoppel from filing the action or more likely may have standing to obtain a divorce but be barred by estoppel from obtaining spousal support incident to such a divorce.[12]

The statute authorizing annulment for bigamy[13] contains specific rules on standing and limitation. The action can be filed by either party to the bigamous marriage during the life of the other party to the bigamous marriage.[14] In addition, the action can be filed, presumably against both spouses to the bigamous marriage, by the other spouse who was a party to the prior valid marriage. RC 3105.32(B) refers to the "former husband or wife." This is an error in terminology. The first spouse is still a spouse, not a former spouse. One of the requirements of the bigamy statute, RC 3105.31(B), is that "the marriage with such former husband or wife was then and still is in force." If it is still in force, the parties are still spouses. Accordingly, the first (former) spouse has standing to bring an action to annul the marriage.[15]

An annulment is properly granted where one party's former spouse was living at the time of the second marriage, and where such party's "Mexican Divorce" was invalid and void because it was procured without either party leaving the United States.[16]

§ 7:8 Statutory grounds—Mental incompetency

The Ohio Annulment Act lists among the grounds for annulment that "either party has been adjudicated to be mentally incompetent, unless such party after being restored to competency cohabited with

---

[11]Johnson v. Wolford, 117 Ohio St. 136, 5 Ohio L. Abs. 402, 157 N.E. 385 (1927). See also Hale v. Graham, 85 Ohio App. 447, 40 Ohio Op. 305, 86 N.E.2d 330 (9th Dist. Summit County 1948); Ryan v. Ryan, 84 Ohio App. 139, 39 Ohio Op. 166, 86 N.E.2d 44 (5th Dist. Stark County 1948); Mieritz v. Metropolitan Life Ins. Co., 8 Ohio N.P. 422, 11 Ohio Dec. 759, 1901 WL 872 (C.P. 1901). See generally Text §§ 2:35 et seq., Common law marriage.

[12]See Text § 7:4, Annulment versus divorce.

[13]RC 3105.31(B).

[14]RC 3105.32(B). See Tabler v. Tabler, 2007-Ohio-1579, 2007 WL 969421 (Ohio Ct. App. 5th Dist. Stark County 2007) (where husband of wife's second and bigamous marriage was granted an annulment on the grounds of bigamy thirty years after the wife's first marriage ended).

[15]Thomas-Schafer v. Schafer, 111 Ohio App. 3d 779, 677 N.E.2d 374 (1st Dist. Hamilton County 1996).

[16]Haska v. Haska, 1989 WL 11272 (Ohio Ct. App. 11th Dist. Portage County 1989).

the other as husband or wife."[1] It is not clear what constitutes an adjudication of incompetency. Almost certainly, a probate court determination that a person is mentally incompetent,[2] followed by appointment of a general guardian of both person and estate, is such an adjudication. "Mental incompetent" is not defined in the statute, but "incompetent" is defined in RC 2111.01(D)[3] to include persons who are so mentally impaired by a mental or physical illness or disability, or mental retardation, or chronic substance abuse that they cannot take proper care of themselves, their property, or those they are required by law to support. This definition also includes any person confined to a correctional institution. Clearly some of these groups might or might not be included within the phrase "adjudicated to be mentally incompetent."[4] Arguably, a probate court determination that a person is mentally ill and needs hospitalization[5] is also an adjudication of mental incompetence. However, it seems that a judicial hospitalization order is not an adjudication of incompetence in view of the clear policy expressed in the "Patient's Bill of Rights" sections[6] of the Ohio Hospitalization Act that even judicially committed patients retain their civil rights, including the right to legal competency.[7]

RC 3105.32(C), governing standing and time limitations, provides that the action may be filed "by the party aggrieved or a relative or guardian of the party adjudicated mentally incompetent at any time before the death of either party." The statute seems ambiguous. The "party aggrieved" may be the mentally ill spouse after termination of the guardianship, or it may refer to the other spouse. The latter interpretation seems to be consistent with the grammatical construction of the statute but inconsistent with the general view that mental incompetency renders a marriage voidable, not void. Further, the statute allows a "relative" to sue. It is not clear why a relative who is not a guardian should have standing to annul a marriage.

While RC 3105.32(C) permits a relative of an incompetent to sue for annulment of a marriage, such proceedings must take place during the lifetime of the alleged incompetent. The trial court did not err in dismissing the complaint for annulment filed by the decedent's son to annul his father's marriage after the death of the father.[8] The Third District Court of Appeals held that a brother and sister did not have

---

[Section 7:8]

[1] RC 3105.31(C).

[2] RC Ch. 2111.

[3] As amended by 1994 H.B. 571, eff. 10-6-94.

[4] RC 3105.31(C).

[5] RC Ch. 5122. See definition in RC 5122.01(B) and judicial procedures in RC 5122.11 to RC 5122.16.

[6] RC 5122.27 to RC 5122.31.

[7] RC 5122.301.

[8] Hall v. Nelson, 41 Ohio App. 3d 138, 534 N.E.2d 929 (9th Dist. Summit County 1987).

standing to seek an annulment on behalf of a deceased brother under RC 3105.31. They had claimed that the marriage had not been consummated, that the consent of the decedent was obtained by fraud, and that he did not have the mental capacity to enter into the marriage. Possible loss of their inheritance did not make them aggrieved parties under RC 3105.32.[9]

The statute applies only to persons adjudicated mentally incompetent, apparently disregarding whether they were incompetent in fact at the time of the entry into marriage. The converse situation of the marriage of someone who was at the time of the marriage mentally incompetent in fact, but not then under an adjudication of incompetency, raises questions. In principle, such a marriage should be subject to annulment. Under general law, it is clear that such marriage is voidable and can be annulled by the incompetent spouse. In Ohio, the availability of annulment in this case depends on whether the Annulment Act sets forth the exclusive list of grounds.[10]

A person who is mentally incompetent by reason of mental illness, mental retardation, or intoxication at the time of the marriage agreement cannot contract a valid marriage. The mental incapacity must exist at the time of the ceremony. Therefore, if the ceremony takes place during a lucid interval, the marriage will be valid. The test of capacity to marry is essentially the same as the test used in cases of capacity to make a contract, deed, or will. The language used to describe the test is essentially the same as that used by the Ohio Supreme Court to describe testamentary capacity. In one case, the court said that each party to the marriage must understand the nature of the marital contract and the duties and responsibilities of the marital status.[11]

The Ohio cases are in accord with the weight of authority in other states that neither guardianship nor commitment by the probate court is conclusive on the issue of mental capacity.[12] The current statutes on guardianship say nothing about the legal capacity of persons under guardianship. The current statute on patients in mental hospitals, RC 5122.301, states that unless specifically denied in an order of adjudication a patient retains all civil rights, including the right to marry. This statute reverses the prior statute, former RC 5122.36,[13] which stated that indeterminate hospitalization under court order was equiv-

---

[9]Hilt v. Diedrich, 1990 WL 121487 (Ohio Ct. App. 3d Dist. Mercer County 1990).

[10]See Text § 7:4, Annulment versus divorce; Text § 7:5, Exclusivity of remedy.

[11]Dozer v. Dozer, 8 Ohio L. Abs. 507, 1930 WL 2189 (Ct. App. 4th Dist. Gallia County 1930). See also Niemes v. Niemes, 97 Ohio St. 145, 119 N.E. 503 (1917).

[12]Dozer v. Dozer, 8 Ohio L. Abs. 507, 1930 WL 2189 (Ct. App. 4th Dist. Gallia County 1930); Heath v. Heath, 85 N.H. 419, 159 A. 418 (1932); Goodheart v. Ransley, 11 Ohio Dec. Rep. 655, 28 W.L.B. 227, 1892 WL 356 (Ohio C.P. 1892), aff'd, 7 Ohio C.D. 47, 1893 WL 324 (Ohio Cir. Ct. 1893); McCleary v. Barcalow, 3 Ohio C.D. 547, 1891 WL 304 (Ohio Cir. Ct. 1891).

[13]Repealed by 1976 H.B. 244, eff. 8-26-76.

alent to an adjudication of incompetency. In *Seabold v. Seabold*,[14] the earlier statute was construed to mean that a mentally ill patient, on a "trial visit" from an Ohio hospital, could annul a marriage contracted in Ohio. The court denied the annulment in that case because the marriage took place outside of Ohio, and the court applied the law of the place of the contract as to the effect of a hospitalization decree.

Generally, the cases hold that the burden of proving incompetency is on the person attacking the marriage, as competency is presumed and a strong presumption favors the validity of a marriage complying with legal formalities. Where marriage occurs during a period when the person is under guardianship for mental incompetency or is subject to a judicial commitment order, the courts hold that the decree is prima facie evidence of incompetency, and competency must be proved by clear and convincing evidence.[15]

There are no Ohio cases directly on point on whether the marriage of a mental incompetent is void or voidable, although the cases contain dicta both ways.[16] The lower courts in Ohio have held that the incompetent party to the marriage can ratify the marriage after he becomes competent, thus indicating that the marriage is merely voidable.[17] There are no Ohio cases in which the issue involved a collateral attack on such a marriage, nor are there any cases involving the right of the parties to disaffirm the marriage by actions other than court decree.

Suit to annul the marriage may be brought by the guardian or by the party who was incompetent, provided he is competent at the time he brings the action.[18] If the competent spouse sues the spouse under guardianship for divorce, the guardian may cross-petition for an an-

---

[14]Seabold v. Seabold, 84 Ohio App. 83, 84, 39 Ohio Op. 112, 84 N.E.2d 521 (9th Dist. Lorain County 1948).

[15]Heath v. Heath, 85 N.H. 419, 159 A. 418 (1932).

[16]McDowell v. Sapp, 39 Ohio St. 558, 1883 WL 213 (1883) (marriage voidable and may be ratified); Waymire v. Jetmore, 22 Ohio St. 271, 1872 WL 1 (1872) (marriage void); Heath v. Heath, 85 N.H. 419, 159 A. 418 (1932) (marriage void, but could be ratified); Goodheart v. Ransley, 11 Ohio Dec. Rep. 655, 28 W.L.B. 227, 1892 WL 356 (Ohio C.P. 1892), aff'd, 7 Ohio C.D. 47, 1893 WL 324 (Ohio Cir. Ct. 1893) (marriage void, but could be ratified); Benton v. Benton, 26 Ohio C.D. 613, 1909 WL 663 (Ohio Cir. Ct. 1909) (marriage void).

[17]McDowell v. Sapp, 39 Ohio St. 558, 1883 WL 213 (1883) (marriage voidable and may be ratified); Waymire v. Jetmore, 22 Ohio St. 271, 1872 WL 1 (1872) (marriage void); Heath v. Heath, 85 N.H. 419, 159 A. 418 (1932) (marriage void, but could be ratified); Goodheart v. Ransley, 11 Ohio Dec. Rep. 655, 28 W.L.B. 227, 1892 WL 356 (Ohio C.P. 1892), aff'd, 7 Ohio C.D. 47, 1893 WL 324 (Ohio Cir. Ct. 1893) (marriage void, but could be ratified); Benton v. Benton, 26 Ohio C.D. 613, 1909 WL 663 (Ohio Cir. Ct. 1909) (marriage void).

[18]Murphy v. Murphy, 85 Ohio App. 392, 40 Ohio Op. 254, 54 Ohio L. Abs. 116, 87 N.E.2d 102 (1st Dist. Hamilton County 1948) (incompetent ward cannot maintain action in his own name, but must be represented by his guardian); Pace v. Pace, 32 Ohio App. 3d 47, 513 N.E.2d 1357 (10th Dist. Franklin County 1986) (incompetent cannot maintain action in his own name as long as adjudication of incompetency continues); Boyd v. Edwards, 4 Ohio App. 3d 142, 446 N.E.2d 1151 (8th Dist.

nulment without the consent of his ward.[19] In one case, the guardian filed the action prior to the death of the ward. The court held that the action did not abate on the death of the ward but could be continued by the administrator of the decedent's estate.[20]

There are no cases in Ohio involving the right of the competent spouse to sue for annulment. Generally, the right of the competent party to annul depends on whether the defect renders the marriage void or voidable. Those states which by statute or case law hold the marriage void permit the competent partner to sue unless he had knowledge of the facts at the time of the marriage.[21]

§ 7:9 Statutory grounds—Fraud

Outside of Ohio, fraud is probably the most common ground for annulment. There are very few Ohio cases on fraud, probably because the Ohio courts were historically liberal in granting divorces for cruelty and gross neglect. In Ohio, fraud is a ground for both annulment and divorce.[1]

The general rules on fraud are easy to state but difficult to apply. When men and women are courting each other, they may exaggerate or evade answers in respect to matters regarding past history, character, or future prospects. If every misrepresentation were a ground for annulment, few marriages would be safe from attack. A certain amount of "puffing" is allowable and inevitable in the courtship, just as it is in commercial transactions. The real question is how much fraud is necessary to justify an annulment, and the answer will depend largely on the facts of a particular case.

Generally, a marriage which is induced by fraud is voidable rather than void. Cohabitation after knowledge of the fraud is treated as an act of ratification or as a waiver of the defect and will defeat any claim for annulment.[2] An action for annulment is not the exclusive remedy of the fraud victim; he may also bring an action for damages.[3]

Although the rule is seldom stated, the cases clearly indicate that if

---

Cuyahoga County 1982) (guardian may not demand divorce where ward, if able to express his desire, might not want divorce). See also Civ. R. 17(B) on how an incompetent sues.

[19]Duncan v. Duncan, 88 Ohio App. 243, 44 Ohio Op. 453, 99 N.E.2d 510 (9th Dist. Lorain County 1950).

[20]Heath v. Heath, 85 N.H. 419, 159 A. 418 (1932).

[21]See Hoadley v. Hoadley, 244 N.Y. 424, 155 N.E. 728, 51 A.L.R. 844 (1927). See also Friedman v. Friedman, 187 Misc. 689, 64 N.Y.S.2d 660 (Sup 1946).

[Section 7:9]

[1]For a discussion of the problems which result from this dual position, see Text § 7:4, Annulment versus divorce; Text § 7:5, Exclusivity of remedy.

[2]Fenicchia v. Fenicchia, 110 N.Y.S.2d 110 (Sup 1952).

[3]Heath v. Heath, 85 N.H. 419, 159 A. 418 (1932); Cohen v. Kahn, 177 Misc. 18, 28 N.Y.S.2d 847 (Sup 1941), order aff'd, 263 A.D. 728, 30 N.Y.S.2d 875 (2d Dep't 1941).

the marriage has not been consummated, it may be annulled for such fraud as would render an ordinary contract voidable, at least in cases where the marriage is promptly disaffirmed before any change of status has occurred.[4] Thus, the minimum essentials for such an annulment would be the following:

(1) A deception, which may be either an affirmative false representation or concealment of a fact where the law holds that there is a duty to speak, must have been made.

(2) The deception must have been intentionally or negligently made. Innocent misrepresentation is not a ground for annulment.

(3) The deception must have been a material element in inducing the deceived party to enter the marriage and must have been relied on.

In analyzing fraud cases from other states, it is important to distinguish the New York cases. Since the turn of the century, the New York courts have treated the marriage contract as any other contract. Whether the marriage is consummated or not, the only requirements for annulment are the three listed above. The test applied is that the deception must have been so material that if it had not taken place, the victim would not have consented to the marriage. Also, the fraud must have been of such a nature as to deceive a person of reasonable prudence. This test of fraud is still referred to as the "New York rule" or "materiality test."

The majority of states, including Ohio, have adopted the stricter "essentials test" or "essentialia doctrine." Under this concept, the fraud not only must be material but must also relate to the very essence of the marital relation, at least in cases where the marriage has been consummated. The justification for the essentials test is that the state has a special interest in the preservation of the marital status.

The advantage of the New York rule is that it is relatively easy to administer. There is a substantial body of general contract law regarding what is material. The principal disadvantage of the New York rule is that the relative ease of obtaining an annulment for fraud is an invitation to perjury or collusion. In some New York cases, the fraud appears to have been invented long after the marriage, and the action is used as a substitute for divorce, without the provisions for continued financial support which apply to the usual divorce case.

The essentials rule is difficult to apply because there is a wide area of disagreement as to what constitutes the essentials of the marital relation. However, some of the factors which clearly relate to the essentials of marriage and which are generally held to justify annulment of a consummated marriage are as follows:

(1) A concealed intent not to engage in sexual intercourse;[5]

---

[4]Akrep v. Akrep, 1 N.J. 268, 63 A.2d 253 (1949).

[5]Miller v. Miller, 1 Ohio Dec. 354, 1893 WL 370 (C.P. 1893).

(2) Concealment of sterility, or the inability to procreate;[6]

(3) Concealment of the fact that one spouse is afflicted with a disease which is both serious and communicable, such as tuberculosis,[7] or a disease which would seriously interfere with the attainment of certain physical objects of marriage, namely intercourse and the birth of healthy children. On this last basis, it is generally held that concealment of a venereal disease is justification for annulment;[8] and

(4) Concealment of the fact that the wife is pregnant by another man at the time of the marriage.[9] Where the husband engaged in sexual intercourse with the wife prior to marriage, the general rule is to deny the husband an annulment. This is true both where the woman induced the marriage by falsely claiming pregnancy when in fact she was not pregnant,[10] and where she claimed to be pregnant by the husband when in fact she was pregnant by another.[11]

However, in *Slavin v. Slavin*,[12] the Eighth District Court of Appeals affirmed the granting of an annulment to a husband where he relied on the wife's denial of sexual relations with another man during the relevant time period. The wife had failed to disclose her uncertainty concerning whether she had such relations; both she and the possible father had been highly intoxicated and had no clear memory on the morning after.

It is generally held that the following types of fraud do not relate to the essentials and do not justify annulment, except possibly in New York:

(1) Concealment or misrepresentation as to premarital lack of chastity. Thus, where the wife had been the mistress of another man, had been previously divorced for her own adultery, or had given birth to an illegitimate child, concealment of this activity did not justify annulment.[13]

(2) Concealment or misrepresentation of a previous marriage or

---

[6]Aufort v. Aufort, 9 Cal. App. 2d 310, 49 P.2d 620 (1st Dist. 1935).

[7]Davis v. Davis, 90 N.J. Eq. 158, 106 A. 644 (Ch. 1919).

[8]Stone v. Stone, 136 F.2d 761 (App. D.C. 1943).

[9]Anderson v. Anderson, 4 Ohio App. 2d 90, 33 Ohio Op. 2d 145, 212 N.E.2d 643 (8th Dist. Cuyahoga County 1965); Vorvilas v. Vorvilas, 252 Wis. 333, 31 N.W.2d 586 (1948). See Annot., Westfall v. Westfall, 100 Or. 224, 197 P. 271, 13 A.L.R. 1428 (1921).

[10]Tyminski v. Tyminski, 8 Ohio Misc. 202, 37 Ohio Op. 2d 263, 221 N.E.2d 486 (C.P. 1966); Mason v. Mason, 164 Ark. 59, 261 S.W. 40 (1924).

[11]Kawecki v. Kawecki, 67 Ohio App. 34, 21 Ohio Op. 76, 35 N.E.2d 865 (6th Dist. Lucas County 1941); Foss v. Foss, 94 Mass. 26, 12 Allen 26, 1866 WL 4794 (1866). See Annot., Westfall v. Westfall, 100 Or. 224, 197 P. 271, 13 A.L.R. 1428 (1921).

[12]Slavin v. Slavin, 1985 WL 6893 (Ohio Ct. App. 8th Dist. Cuyahoga County 1985).

[13]Joy v. Joy, 12 Ohio Dec. 574, 1900 WL 1285 (C.P. 1900); Foy v. Foy, 57 Cal. App. 2d 334, 134 P.2d 29 (2d Dist. 1943); Anonymous v. Anonymous, 45 Del. 458, 85

divorce. Thus, no annulment was permitted where the wife represented herself to be a widow, although in fact she was a divorcee with a living ex-husband, and her second husband was a Roman Catholic.[14] The few cases which relax this harsh rule are generally those involving an unconsummated marriage, an express misrepresentation as opposed to a concealment, or a youthful or weak-willed victim of the fraud.[15]

(3) Concealment or misrepresentation of past insanity or commitment to a mental hospital.[16] If the marriage is entered into at a time when the spouse is mentally incompetent, the lack of mental capacity will excuse the fraud, but the marriage may be annulled for insanity.

(4) Concealment or misrepresentation as to age, health, or physical characteristics. An Ohio court denied an annulment where the bride wore glasses to conceal a glass eye.[17]

(5) Concealment or misrepresentation as to past or present financial condition, social position, occupation, education, etc.[18] Thus, an annulment was denied where the husband represented himself as wealthy, when in fact his business was bankrupt.[19] The strict rule denying annulment is sometimes relaxed where the fraud is gross and the victim is young and immature or aged and feeble.[20]

(6) Concealment or misrepresentation as to nationality or citizenship. Generally, fraud as to national origin, race, or citizenship does not go to the essence of the marriage,[21] but New York courts have held that a false representation of American citizenship

---

A.2d 706 (1951), affirmed sub nom DuPont v. DuPont, 47 Del. 231, 90 A.2d 468 (1952), cert. denied 344 U.S. 836, 73 S.Ct. 46, 97 L.Ed.2d 651 (1952); contra McAndrew v. McAndrew, 194 Ky. 755, 240 S.W. 745 (1921).

[14]Cassin v. Cassin, 264 Mass. 28, 161 N.E. 603, 58 A.L.R. 319 (1928); Oswald v. Oswald, 146 Md. 313, 126 A. 81 (1924). See also Annot., 58 A.L.R. 319.

[15]Christlieb v. Christlieb, 71 Ind. App. 682, 125 N.E. 486 (1919).

[16]Robertson v. Roth, 163 Minn. 501, 204 N.W. 329, 39 A.L.R. 1342 (1925). See Annot., Concealment of insanity or diseased mental condition as ground of annulment of marriage, 39 A.L.R. 1345 (1925).

[17]Kraus v. Kraus, 6 Ohio N.P. 248, 9 Ohio Dec. 515, 1899 WL 785 (C.P. 1899).

[18]Meyer v. Meyer, 4 Ohio Dec. Rep. 345, 7 Ohio Dec. Rep. 561, 1 Cleve. Law Rep. 347, 3 W.L.B. 985, 1878 WL 7379 (Ohio C.P. 1878), aff'd, 7 Ohio Dec. Rep. 627, 4 W.L.B. 368, 1879 WL 6394 (Ohio Dist. Ct. 1879); Stepp v. Stepp, 2004-Ohio-1617, 2004 WL 626116 (Ohio Ct. App. 9th Dist. Medina County 2004) (general rule that false representation as to character, health, wealth and external conditions do not constitute such fraud as will annul a marriage contract; fraud must affect the marital relation in its essential parts).

[19]Marshall v. Marshall, 212 Cal. 736, 300 P. 816, 75 A.L.R. 661 (1931). See Annot., Misrepresentation or mistake as to identity or condition in life of one of the parties as affecting validity of marriage, 75 A.L.R. 663 (1931).

[20]Entsminger v. Entsminger, 99 Kan. 362, 161 P. 607 (1916); Brown v. Scott, 140 Md. 258, 117 A. 114, 22 A.L.R. 810 (1922); Dooley v. Dooley, 93 N.J. Eq. 22, 115 A. 268 (Ch. 1921). See Annot., 58 A.L.R. 319.

[21]Wetstine v. Wetstine, 114 Conn. 7, 157 A. 418 (1931).

warrants annulment, especially where the guilty husband was subject to deportation for illegal entry.[22]

(7) Concealment or misrepresentation of an ulterior or unworthy motive, such as a marriage for money alone, a marriage to gain a new citizenship or to avoid deportation, or a marriage entered into for the sole purpose of legitimatizing a child born of the parties.[23] A number of courts have allowed annulment where the fraud was extreme and the victim was immature or was not in a position to investigate the truth of the representations.[24]

There are four areas of fraud where the rules have not yet crystallized. The few cases involved are divided on whether the fraud relates to the essence of the marriage. These are as follows:

(1) Concealment of a past history of serious criminal activity. The Ohio courts have not discussed this problem, and the decisions from other jurisdictions are in conflict. A California court stated as dictum that concealment of a prior conviction would justify annulment.[25] New York and Utah courts held that concealment of a prior criminal record related to the essence of the marriage,[26] although Florida and Washington, D.C. have held to the contrary.[27]

(2) Concealment of an illness which results in permanent disability. It already has been noted that concealment of a serious illness which is communicable or which could be inherited by children is a ground for annulment. There are numerous illnesses which do not fall into these categories but which prevent a husband from supporting his wife. There are no cases which have determined whether the successful concealment of an illness which results in permanent disability is a ground for annulment. The issue was raised but not decided in a Connecticut case.[28]

(3) False promises relating to religious faith. As to false promises relative to present or future religious faith, the cases are in conflict. The problem is complicated by the constitutional provisions relative to freedom of worship and separation of church and state. Gener-

---

[22]Damaskinos v. Damaskinos, 325 Mass. 217, 89 N.E.2d 766 (1950) (application of New York law); Protopapas v. Protopapas, 47 N.Y.S.2d 460 (Sup 1943), judgment aff'd, 267 A.D. 804, 47 N.Y.S.2d 287 (4th Dep't 1943); Laage v. Laage, 176 Misc. 190, 26 N.Y.S.2d 874 (Sup 1941); Truiano v. Truiano, 121 Misc. 635, 201 N.Y.S. 573 (Sup 1923).

[23]Salzberg v. Salzberg, 107 N.J. Eq. 524, 153 A. 605 (Ct. Err. & App. 1931); Campbell v. Moore, 189 S.C. 497, 1 S.E.2d 784 (1939); Harding v. Harding, 11 Wash. 2d 138, 118 P.2d 789 (1941).

[24]Security-First Nat. Bank of Los Angeles v. Schaub, 71 Cal. App. 2d 467, 162 P.2d 966 (2d Dist. 1945); Titcomb v. Titcomb, 160 Fla. 320, 34 So. 2d 742 (1948); Sampson v. Sampson, 332 Mich. 214, 50 N.W.2d 764 (1952).

[25]Douglass v. Douglass, 148 Cal. App. 2d 867, 307 P.2d 674 (2d Dist. 1957).

[26]Lockwood v. Lockwood, 29 Misc. 2d 114, 220 N.Y.S.2d 718 (Sup 1961); Haacke v. Glenn, 814 P.2d 1157 (Utah Ct. App. 1991).

[27]Savini v. Savini, 58 So. 2d 193 (Fla. 1952); Craun v. Craun, 168 A.2d 898 (Mun. Ct. App. D.C. 1961), judgment rev'd, 300 F.2d 737 (D.C. Cir. 1962).

[28]Nerini v. Nerini, 11 Conn. Supp. 361, 1943 WL 771 (Super. Ct. 1943).

ally, breach of a premarital agreement to renounce a religious faith, to accept a new faith, or to raise children in a specified faith is not a ground for annulment.[29] In Ohio, a common pleas court held that breach of a prenuptial agreement by the wife to renounce her religious faith could not be considered gross neglect of duty. The court said that to allow such a ground for divorce would violate the wife's constitutional right to freedom of religion.[30] A number of courts have allowed annulments for fraud where both parties were already of the same faith and one spouse violated an agreement to follow a civil ceremony with a religious ceremony. Two New Jersey cases granted annulment where, after a civil ceremony, the husband refused to be married in the Roman Catholic church.[31] In one case, both parties were Catholics, and in the other the wife was Catholic and the husband falsely represented that he was of the same religion.

(4) Concealed intent not to engage in sexual intercourse. As stated above, a concealed intent not to consummate a marriage by refraining from intercourse or concealment of the fact of sterility are both recognized grounds for annulment. In recent years, a number of courts have been faced with the problem of a concealed intent held by one spouse at the time of the marriage not to engage in sexual intercourse unless contraceptives are used. Most of the courts passing on this problem have held that such fraud relates to the essence of the marriage.[32] The problem of proof is a difficult one in a case of this type,[33] and the plaintiff is sometimes denied relief because of acquiescence in the use of contraceptives.[34] In some states, an unjustified insistence on the use of contraceptive devices has also

---

[29]Hickman v. Hickman, 10 S.W.2d 738 (Tex. Civ. App. Waco 1928); contra Williams v. Williams, 194 Misc. 201, 86 N.Y.S.2d 490 (Sup 1947).

[30]Apple v. Apple, 28 Ohio N.P. (n.s.) 620, 1931 WL 2788 (C.P. 1931). See Hackett v. Hackett, 78 Ohio L. Abs. 485, 150 N.E.2d 431 (Ct. App. 6th Dist. Lucas County 1958) (problem of the relation between the constitutional doctrine of freedom of religion and domestic relations law); Note, *Hackett v. Hackett*, 72 Harv. L. Rev. 372 (1958); Note, *Survey of Ohio Law*, 9 Case W. Res. L. Rev. 397 (1958).

[31]Akrep v. Akrep, 1 N.J. 268, 63 A.2d 253 (1949); Nocenti v. Ruberti, 17 N.J. Misc. 21, 3 A.2d 128 (Ch. 1933). See also Bilowit v. Dolitsky, 124 N.J. Super. 101, 304 A.2d 774 (Ch. Div. 1973); Samuelson v. Samuelson, 155 Md. 639, 142 A. 97 (1928); Labbate v. Labbate, 189 Misc. 447, 69 N.Y.S.2d 867 (Sup 1947); Brillis v. Brillis, 4 N.Y.2d 125, 173 N.Y.S.2d 3, 149 N.E.2d 510 (1958).

[32]Maslow v. Maslow, 117 Cal. App. 2d 237, 255 P.2d 65 (2d Dist. 1953) (abrogated by, Liodas v. Sahadi, 19 Cal. 3d 278, 137 Cal. Rptr. 635, 562 P.2d 316 (1977)), abrogated by Liodas v. Sahadi, 19 Cal. 3d 278, 137 Cal. Rptr. 635, 562 P.2d 316 (1977).

[33]See Richardson v. Richardson, 200 Misc. 778, 103 N.Y.S.2d 219 (Sup 1951); Witten v. Witten, 109 N.Y.S.2d 254 (Sup 1951).

[34]Maslow v. Maslow, 117 Cal. App. 2d 237, 255 P.2d 65 (2d Dist. 1953) (abrogated by, Liodas v. Sahadi, 19 Cal. 3d 278, 137 Cal. Rptr. 635, 562 P.2d 316 (1977)), abrogated by Liodas v. Sahadi, 19 Cal. 3d 278, 137 Cal. Rptr. 635, 562 P.2d 316 (1977) (acquiescence for six months barred the action); Baxter v. Baxter, 117 L.J.H.L.(n.s.) 479 (1948) (ten years' acquiescence was not a bar).

been treated as a ground for divorce under the heading of desertion, cruelty, or gross neglect.

Fraud is included as a ground for annulment in the Ohio Annulment Act.[35] RC 3105.32(D) provides that the "party aggrieved" may annul within two years after discovery of the fraud. Presumably, this means the party who is the victim of the fraud may annul and has up to two years to sue, although the plaintiff may be barred before the two-year period expires if such party, "with full knowledge of the facts constituting the fraud, cohabited with the other as husband or wife."[36]

§ 7:10 Statutory grounds—Duress

In general, where the consent of a party has been obtained by violence or threats of physical harm, the victim of the coercion may have the resulting marriage annulled. The threat need not be directed at the victim. Thus, threats of harm directed toward another in whose welfare a party has a vital interest may be duress.[1] Generally, a threat of harm to reputation or to financial condition is insufficient. In an Arkansas case, annulment was denied where the woman threatened that if the man did not marry her she would commit suicide and would publicly involve his name in her death.[2] The majority of courts rely on a subjective standard, and the annulment will be granted if the will of the particular plaintiff was overcome, even though a person of ordinary firmness would not have relented.[3]

To warrant annulment, the coercion must have been present throughout the entire transaction. If the plaintiff had a reasonable opportunity to escape, relief will be denied.[4] The threats need not come from the defendant in the annulment action. Annulment will be granted where the coercion is exercised by friends or relations of the defendant. A New York court has held that annulment will not be granted unless the defendant was a party to the duress or was aware of it.[5] This seems wrong in principle, as annulment is granted to allow the plaintiff to escape from a marriage to which he did not consent,

---

[35]130 Laws of Ohio H.B. 467, eff. 9-24-63. See RC 3105.31(D).

[36]RC 3105.31(D).

[Section 7:10]

[1]Warren v. Warren, 199 N.Y.S. 856 (Sup 1900); Fratello v. Fratello, 118 Misc. 584, 193 N.Y.S. 865 (Sup 1922); contra Capasso v. Colonna, 95 N.J. Eq. 35, 122 A. 378 (Ch. 1923), aff'd, 96 N.J. Eq. 385, 124 A. 760 (Ct. Err. & App. 1924).

[2]Feigenbaum v. Feigenbaum, 210 Ark. 186, 194 S.W.2d 1012 (1946); accord Fluharty v. Fluharty, 38 Del. 487, 193 A. 838 (Super. Ct. 1937); contra Scott v. Sebright, 57 L.T.R.(n.s.) 421 (1886).

[3]Smith v. Smith, 47 Bull. 137 (C.P., Franklin 1902); Cannon v. Cannon, 7 Tenn. App. 19, 1928 WL 1990 (1928).

[4]See Annot., Phipps v. Phipps, 216 S.C. 248, 57 S.E.2d 417, 16 A.L.R.2d 1426 (1950).

[5]Sherman v. Sherman, 20 N.Y.S. 414 (C.P. 1892).

rather than as a punishment for misconduct of the defendant. One case so holds.[6]

There are some cases where it is clear that the consent of the party was obtained by duress. Yet, the demands of public policy will override the interests of the plaintiff and the court will find that there was no duress. Therefore, where a man has had intercourse with a girl and consents to marriage to avoid prosecution for bastardy, seduction, or statutory rape, annulment will not be granted unless the charge of duress was made without probable cause.[7] In this situation, an annulment will usually be denied the man. However, in one Ohio case the court granted the wife an annulment on the ground that the man, the victim of the duress, never intended to consummate the marriage and was therefore guilty of fraud.[8] The strict rule denying annulment where the threatened prosecution is based on probable cause, even though the man is in fact innocent, is sometimes relaxed where the man is immature and is given no chance to consult with friends or counsel.[9] The rule may also be overlooked where the man is ill and believes that, if convicted of nonsupport of the illegitimate child, his term in the workhouse will kill him.[10]

Although there is dictum on both sides in Ohio cases, it is generally held that a coerced marriage is voidable rather than void, and annulment will not be granted if the parties ratify the marriage.[11] Consummation is strong evidence of intent to ratify, but consummation under duress will not ratify the marriage.[12]

The Ohio Annulment Act does not include duress, which is the threat of force, as one of the grounds but does include "[t]hat the consent to the marriage of either party was obtained by force."[13] Presumably, the draftsmen meant "threat of force," and the courts will apply the common law rules of duress in construing the statute. RC 3105.32(E) requires the action be brought by the "party aggrieved," presumably the party subject to duress, within two years of the marriage.

§ 7:11 Statutory grounds—Nonconsummation

In Ohio, impotency, without any definition or qualification, was,

---

[6]Lee v. Lee, 176 Ark. 636, 3 S.W.2d 672 (1928).

[7]Smith v. Saum, 324 Ill. App. 299, 58 N.E.2d 248 (1st Dist. 1944). See Annot., Phipps v. Phipps, 216 S.C. 248, 57 S.E.2d 417, 16 A.L.R.2d 1426 (1950).

[8]Miller v. Miller, 1 Ohio Dec. 354, 1893 WL 370 (C.P. 1893).

[9]Smith v. Smith, 51 Mich. 607, 17 N.W. 76 (1883).

[10]Smith v. Smith, 47 Bull. 137 (C.P., Franklin 1902).

[11]Norvell v. State, 149 Tex. Crim. 213, 193 S.W.2d 200 (1946). See also Annot., Marriage to which consent of one of parties was obtained by duress as void or only voidable, 91 A.L.R. 414 (1934).

[12]Fowler v. Fowler, 131 La. 1088, 60 So. 694 (1913).

[13]RC 3105.31(E).

until August 25, 1989, listed among the grounds for divorce.[1] Impotency as such is not listed among the grounds in the Annulment Act. However, RC 3105.31(F) includes the following language: "That the marriage between the parties was never consummated although otherwise valid."

There is no legislative history indicating why this language was chosen. It certainly includes impotency, but it may include other grounds. There are at least three possible constructions of the statute:

(1) It means impotency only. The difficulty with this argument is that the draftsmen would have specified impotency if that was all that was intended. Following the logic that the statute does not use the word "impotency," the Tenth District Court of Appeals has held that "the pre-existence of a condition preventing consummation is not a requisite for annulment for nonconsummation."[2]

(2) England and a few American jurisdictions have by statute established a new ground for annulment, "willful refusal to consummate the marriage." This is in addition to impotency. Conceptually, such conduct is grounds for divorce rather than annulment, because it involves conduct which occurred after entry into the marriage.[3] Such willful refusal should qualify as marital misconduct and justify divorce for mental cruelty or gross misconduct. Under the statutory ground for annulment, however, where one spouse refuses to consummate the marriage without good cause, the other spouse can have the marriage annulled.[4] This may have been the intention of the draftsmen. This construction is aided by the fact that the section on standing and time limits[5] provides that the action may be brought within two years of the marriage "by the party aggrieved." In other areas, "party aggrieved" is used to describe the victim of fraud or duress; therefore, its use may imply fault on the part of the defendant. In *Kugel v. Kugel*,[6] the trial court grant of a decree of annulment to a plaintiff husband who was physically incapable of consummating the marriage because of prostate cancer was reversed. Relying on RC 3105.32(F), the appellate court held that where only the party aggrieved may bring on an action based on

---

[Section 7:11]

[1]RC 3105.01(D).

[2]Lang v. Reetz-Lang, 22 Ohio App. 3d 77, 79, 488 N.E.2d 929 (10th Dist. Franklin County 1985).

[3]See discussion of the difference between divorce and annulment in Text § 7:4, Annulment versus divorce.

[4]Lang v. Reetz-Lang, 22 Ohio App. 3d 77, 488 N.E.2d 929 (10th Dist. Franklin County 1985) (willful or knowing refusal or avoidance of consummation is a proper ground for annulment).

[5]RC 3105.32(F).

[6]Kugel v. Kugel, 1991 WL 270412 (Ohio Ct. App. 6th Dist. Huron County 1991). Anderson v. Anderson, 8 Ohio Misc. 97, 37 Ohio Op. 2d 108, 219 N.E.2d 317 (C.P. 1966) (marriage will not be annulled based upon lack of consummation if defendant wife was ready and willing to live with plaintiff husband, who refused).

nonconsummation, it was error to grant an annulment where the defendant-wife was not at fault.

(3) The statute may be construed literally. Thus, the fact that a marriage has not been consummated is sufficient, and the reasons for this nonconsummation are irrelevant.[7] For example, if, after a valid ceremonial marriage, the parties leave for their honeymoon and prior to consummation there is an automobile accident and the husband is permanently physically disabled, then, under this construction of the statute, the wife can live with her husband. However, at any time within two years she can change her mind and have the marriage annulled. This result seems both unfair to the husband and inconsistent with the conceptual basis of annulment.

§ 7:12   Common law grounds—Mistake and lack of mutual consent

Mistake and lack of mutual consent are not included in the Ohio Annulment Act.[1]

A mistake as to the name, character, or past history of a party to a marriage will not ordinarily affect the validity of a marriage, either under the doctrine of mistake or fraud. Thus, the mere assumption of a false name by one party will not justify annulment. A true mistake as to identity, however, as where a person is substituted for the one who intended to marry, will render the marriage voidable.[2]

A mistaken belief by one or both parties that the ceremony performed is not a marriage but is a religious or engagement ceremony is a sufficient ground for annulment by the mistaken party.[3] In such case, there is no real consent, even though the formal prerequisites of marriage are complied with.

When the marriage is contracted as a joke or jest, a few courts have denied annulment,[4] but the weight of authority today is that such marriage is voidable when there is clear evidence that both parties

---

[7]Lang v. Reetz-Lang, 22 Ohio App. 3d 77, 488 N.E.2d 929 (10th Dist. Franklin County 1985) (the fact that the marriage was not consummated is sufficient to support a decree of annulment).

[Section 7:12]

[1]130 Laws of Ohio H.B. 467, eff. 9-24-63. See also Text § 7:4, Annulment versus divorce; Text § 7:5, Exclusivity of remedy.

[2]Meyer v. Meyer, 4 Ohio Dec. Rep. 345, 7 Ohio Dec. Rep. 561, 1 Cleve. Law Rep. 347, 3 W.L.B. 985, 1878 WL 7379 (Ohio C.P. 1878), aff'd, 7 Ohio Dec. Rep. 627, 4 W.L.B. 368, 1879 WL 6394 (Ohio Dist. Ct. 1879). See Annot., Misrepresentation or mistake as to identity or condition in life of one of the parties as affecting validity of marriage, 75 A.L.R. 663 (1931).

[3]Mehta v. Mehta, 2 All E.R. 690 (1945).

[4]See Hand v. Berry, 170 Ga. 743, 154 S.E. 239 (1930). See also Annot., Validity of marriage as affected by intention of the parties that it should be only a matter of form or jest, 14 A.L.R.2d 624.

lacked real intent to enter a permanent marriage.[5] The majority view has been cited with approval in an Ohio case.[6]

The most difficult problem in this area is the requirement of mutual consent. The majority of courts hold that when both parties intend to enter the legal status of matrimony, the marriage is valid, and a mutual understanding that the marriage was not to be consummated and would be annulled will be disregarded. Thus, a Connecticut decision held that recognition of such an agreement would be contrary to public policy.[7] In a few states, including Ohio, the opposite view is taken. In *Stone v. Stone*,[8] a young girl became pregnant. The father of the child was unavailable for marriage, so it was agreed that a family friend would marry her to give a name to the child. Both parties intended that they would never assume any relationship as husband and wife and separated immediately after the ceremony. The court held that the marriage, rather than the reservations, was contrary to public policy and granted the annulment. In a similar Ohio case, the court granted an annulment, stating, "A child needs help in a social order that styles him, instead of his guilty parents, as being 'illegitimate.' . . . The court prefers not to punish either party for their honorable conduct in formulating a plan that permitted the child to be born in wedlock."[9]

§ 7:13 Common law grounds—Incest

For religious and eugenic reasons, marriages are prohibited where the parties are within a specified degree of kinship. The term "incestuous" is applied to such marriage, but the rules governing incest are not the same in domestic relations law as in the criminal law. The prohibited relationship may exist by reason of consanguinity (blood relationship) or by affinity (relation by marriage). A man's relations by affinity are the blood relations of his wife. The rules of consanguin-

---

[5]Davis v. Davis, 119 Conn. 194, 175 A. 574 (1934); McClurg v. Terry, 21 N.J. Eq. 225, 1870 WL 5173 (Ch. 1870); Meredith v. Shakespeare, 96 W. Va. 229, 122 S.E. 520 (1924).

[6]Conley v. Conley, 28 Ohio Op. 289, 14 Ohio Supp. 22, 1943 WL 6289 (C.P. 1943) (mere words without any intention corresponding thereto will not make a marriage, but the words are evidence of such intention, and where marriage vows have been exchanged, it must be clearly shown that both parties intended and understood that they were not to have effect).

[7]Schibi v. Schibi, 136 Conn. 196, 69 A.2d 831, 14 A.L.R.2d 620 (1949). See Annot., Validity of marriage as affected by intention of the parties that it should be only a matter of form or jest, 14 A.L.R.2d 624. See also Comment, *Sham Marriages*, 20 U. Chi. L. Rev. 710 (1953).

[8]Stone v. Stone, 159 Fla. 624, 32 So. 2d 278 (1947).

[9]Conley v. Conley, 28 Ohio Op. 289, 14 Ohio Supp. 22, 1943 WL 6289 (C.P. 1943).

ity apply to relatives of the half blood[1] and to illegitimate relations,[2] although apparently not to relatives by adoption.[3]

In England, a series of statutes enacted during the reign of Henry VIII established first-cousin marriage as valid and marriage between those closer than cousins by consanguinity or affinity as voidable.[4] Some courts have held that the English statutes are a part of our common law and therefore follow them. The majority of courts hold, however, that the disability is a canon law impediment and that a marriage between relatives is valid in the absence of statute, unless the relation is so close as to shock the conscience, such as a marriage between brother and sister or within lineage.[5]

Generally, all American states prohibit marriage by persons closer than first cousins, except that a few states permit marriage between uncle and niece. About half the states prohibit first-cousin marriage.

In Ohio, two statutes deal with incest, but they are both unclear as to whether such a marriage is void or voidable, or whether affinity is a defect. The marriage statute, RC 3101.01, provides that persons "not nearer of kin than second cousins" may join in marriage. The negative implication of the statute is that persons who are nearer of kin than second cousins, i.e., first cousins or closer, may not marry. There is no longer any general criminal statute relating to incest, but the criminal statute on sexual battery, RC 2907.03(A)(5), provides that no person shall engage in sexual conduct with another who is not the spouse of the offender when the offender is the other person's natural or adoptive parent, stepparent, guardian, custodian, or person in loco parentis.

In 1958, when a criminal statute prohibited sex relations (and thus by inference marriage) between persons closer than first cousins,[6] the Ohio Supreme Court in *Mazzolini v. Mazzolini*[7] construed the two statutes and indicated that a marriage prohibited only by the marriage statute would be voidable, but that a marriage within the degree prohibited by the criminal statute was void. The annulment of a first-cousin marriage was denied because it took place in another state whose law provided it was valid unless void under the law of the domicile (Ohio). Thus, the holding of the *Mazzolini* case is as follows: (1) Ohio looks to the law of the place of the marriage, including that

---

[Section 7:13]

[1]Audley v. Audley, 196 A.D. 103, 187 N.Y.S. 652 (1st Dep't 1921).

[2]State v. Lee, 196 Miss. 311, 17 So. 2d 277, 151 A.L.R. 1143 (1944).

[3]Morgan v. State, 11 Ala. 289, 1847 WL 182 (1847).

[4]Statutes of 25 Hen. 8, ch. 22; 28 Hen. 8, ch. 7; and 32 Hen. 8, ch. 38.

[5]Wightman v. Wightman, 4 Johns. Ch. 343, 1 N.Y. Ch. Ann. 861, 1820 WL 1618 (N.Y. Ch. 1820).

[6]RC 2905.07 enacted by 1953 H.B. 1, eff. 10-1-53, repealed by 1972 H.B. 511, eff. 1-1-74.

[7]Mazzolini v. Mazzolini, 168 Ohio St. 357, 7 Ohio Op. 2d 123, 155 N.E.2d 206 (1958).

state's conflict of law rules, even though one of the parties is a domiciliary of Ohio and Ohio is the intended matrimonial domicile; and (2) the internal substantive law of Ohio is that a first-cousin marriage is not void.

In 1979, the question of whether a marriage prohibited by the marriage statute because of kinship was void, voidable, or valid was again before the Ohio Supreme Court in *In re Stiles Estate*.[8] The Court held that, notwithstanding the repeal of the incest statute, RC 2905.07, by 1972 House Bill 511, effective January 1, 1974, and the inapplicability of the criminal statute, RC 2907.03, sexual battery, to the uncle-niece relationship, on general public policy grounds such a marriage was void. Based on this case and on other earlier Ohio Supreme Court cases cited therein, it seems that the present law is as follows:

(1) A marriage contracted in Ohio between first cousins is voidable, not void, and subject to annulment during the life of both spouses.[9]

(2) A marriage contracted outside Ohio by first cousins is valid in Ohio[10] unless it was invalid in the state where contracted, in which case it is voidable in Ohio.[11]

(3) A marriage contracted in Ohio by parties closer than first cousins is void, not voidable,[12] and is subject to annulment.[13]

(4) A marriage contracted outside of Ohio by parties closer than first cousins is void in Ohio, whether or not it is valid in the state where contracted.[14]

(5) Ohio does not follow the strict English rule under which affinity was a permanent bar. The relation by affinity ceases when the marriage which created the relation ceases. Thus, a man could

---

[8]In re Stiles Estate, 59 Ohio St. 2d 73, 13 Ohio Op. 3d 62, 391 N.E.2d 1026 (1979).

[9]Mazzolini v. Mazzolini, 168 Ohio St. 357, 7 Ohio Op. 2d 123, 155 N.E.2d 206 (1958). See also Soley v. Soley, 101 Ohio App. 3d 540, 655 N.E.2d 1381 (6th Dist. Lucas County 1995).

[10]Mazzolini v. Mazzolini, 168 Ohio St. 357, 7 Ohio Op. 2d 123, 155 N.E.2d 206 (1958).

[11]Mazzolini v. Mazzolini, 168 Ohio St. 357, 7 Ohio Op. 2d 123, 155 N.E.2d 206 (1958).

[12]In re Stiles Estate, 59 Ohio St. 2d 73, 13 Ohio Op. 3d 62, 391 N.E.2d 1026 (1979).

[13]In re Stiles Estate, 59 Ohio St. 2d 73, 13 Ohio Op. 3d 62, 391 N.E.2d 1026 (1979) (arose after the act, but was an attack on the marriage in a probate court proceeding, not an annulment); Mazzolini v. Mazzolini, 168 Ohio St. 357, 7 Ohio Op. 2d 123, 155 N.E.2d 206 (1958) (annulment action arising prior to the enactment of the act). See also discussion in Text § 7:5, Exclusivity of remedy, on the availability of annulment for grounds not listed in the Annulment Act.

[14]State v. Brown, 47 Ohio St. 102, 23 N.E. 747 (1890).

marry his stepdaughter or sister-in-law after termination of the first marriage by death or divorce.[15]

While under general law it is clear that a marriage either void or voidable because of kinship is subject to annulment, in Ohio, incest is not one of the grounds included in the Annulment Act.[16] Therefore, the availability of annulment depends on the question of whether the statutory list of grounds is exclusive.[17]

§ 7:14 Common law grounds—Physical health

There are two physical conditions which may give rise to a defective marriage: impotency[1] and syphilis. The annulment of a marriage for either of these defects should not be confused with annulment for fraudulent concealment of a serious illness or physical disability.[2] The distinction is clearly illustrated by the rule that sterility or the inability to procreate is not a defect, but concealment of sterility is fraud relating to the essentials of the marriage and may be a ground for annulment.[3] The justification for the different treatment of the two situations lies in the presence of fault in the fraud case. On occasion, the courts confuse the two doctrines. In *Tompkins v. Tompkins*,[4] the court referred to impotency as a type of fraud, in spite of the fact that the impotent husband was apparently unaware of his condition at the time of the marriage.

As to syphilis, RC 3101.06 prohibits issuance of a marriage license to a person infected with syphilis in a form that is communicable or likely to become communicable. The statute is silent as to the validity of a marriage contracted in violation of its provisions, and no Ohio cases indicate whether such a marriage would be valid. The few cases from other jurisdictions hold that where the legislature has clearly indicated that a syphilitic should not marry, such a marriage is voidable.[5]

Impotency was a canon law disability recognized by the English ecclesiastical courts. The theory was that an annulment would be granted to the nonimpotent spouse to discourage the possible temptation to commit adultery if the annulment were denied. A canon law

---

[15]State v. Brown, 47 Ohio St. 102, 23 N.E. 747 (1890); Noble v. State, 22 Ohio St. 541, 1872 WL 39 (1872). Ohio cases are discussed in Back v. Back, 148 Iowa 223, 125 N.W. 1009 (1910).

[16]130 Laws of Ohio H.B. 467, eff. 9-24-63.

[17]See Text § 7:4, Annulment versus divorce; Text § 7:5, Exclusivity of remedy.

[Section 7:14]

[1]See Text § 7:11, Statutory grounds—Nonconsummation.

[2]See Text §§ 7:12 to 7:15, Common law grounds.

[3]See Text §§ 7:12 to 7:15, Common law grounds.

[4]Tompkins v. Tompkins, 92 N.J. Eq. 113, 111 A. 599 (Ch. 1920).

[5]Doe v. Doe, 35 Del. 301, 165 A. 156 (Super. Ct. 1933); Christensen v. Christensen, 144 Neb. 763, 14 N.W.2d 613 (1944). See also Clark, The Law of Domestic Relations in the United States § 2.11.

disability requires some expression of legislative policy disapproving of such marriage before an equity court can grant an annulment.[6]

Although there are no cases on point, it can be assumed that impotency as a ground for divorce incorporates the substantive rules of impotency as developed in annulment actions. In a similar situation, an Ohio court held that when the legislature included "fraudulent contract" as a ground for divorce without defining the term, the statute incorporated the substantive annulment law of fraud.[7]

As a general proposition, the legal definition of impotence refers to the inability of the parties to participate in ordinary or natural and complete sexual intercourse.[8] It is also referred to as sexual incapacity. The origin of impotency is immaterial, and an annulment may be granted where the inability is caused by venereal disease,[9] physical deformity,[10] or psychiatric factors.[11] Some persons are impotent as to their spouse but are able to have intercourse with others. This condition, known as "impotency quod hanc," justifies a decree of annulment.[12]

Impotency as a ground for annulment must have existed at the time of the marriage, continued to the time of the trial, and be incurable. If the defect can be cured, but only by a dangerous or painful operation, the impotency is considered incurable and an annulment will be granted.[13] Where the defect can be remedied by a simple surgical operation and the defendant refuses to submit to treatment, there is a split of authority. The New York cases hold that failure to submit to treatment for impotency is not a ground for annulment,[14] while other courts have held that impotency is nonetheless grounds for annulment, as incurable, if the impotent party willfully and without justification refuses treatment.[15]

Proof of impotency is difficult, especially if the defendant is a woman, and usually expert medical or psychiatric testimony is required. Thus, in one case a psychiatrist was allowed to testify as to his conclusions relative to impotency, although the basis of his

---

[6]See Text § 7:1, Nature of marriage and annulment.

[7]Meyer v. Meyer, 4 Ohio Dec. Rep. 345, 7 Ohio Dec. Rep. 561, 1 Cleve. Law Rep. 347, 3 W.L.B. 985, 1878 WL 7379 (Ohio C.P. 1878), aff'd, 7 Ohio Dec. Rep. 627, 4 W.L.B. 368, 1879 WL 6394 (Ohio Dist. Ct. 1879).

[8]Donati v. Church, 13 N.J. Super. 454, 80 A.2d 633 (App. Div. 1951).

[9]Ryder v. Ryder, 66 Vt. 158, 28 A. 1029 (1894).

[10]Anonymous, 89 Ala. 291, 7 So. 100 (1890).

[11]Kaufman v. Kaufman, 164 F.2d 519 (App. D.C. 1947).

[12]Kaufman v. Kaufman, 164 F.2d 519 (App. D.C. 1947); S_____ v. S_____, 192 Mass. 194, 77 N.E. 1025 (1906); Tompkins v. Tompkins, 92 N.J. Eq. 113, 111 A. 599 (Ch. 1920).

[13]Anonymous, 158 N.Y.S. 51 (Sup 1916).

[14]Anonymous, 158 N.Y.S. 51 (Sup 1916) (discussion of New York cases).

[15]Griffith v. Griffith, 162 Ill. 368, 44 N.E. 820 (1896); Mutter v. Mutter, 123 Ky. 754, 30 Ky. L. Rptr. 76, 97 S.W. 393 (1906).

testimony depended on what the spouses had told him.[16] In a few cases, American courts have applied a presumption developed in the English courts known as "the rule of 'triennial cohabitation.' "[17] Under this doctrine, proof that the wife is potent and is still a virgin three years after marriage raises a presumption that the husband is impotent. The presumption was conclusive in England, but a New Jersey court used it to shift the burden of going forward with evidence.[18] In impotency cases, the courts have often asserted the power to order both parties to submit to a medical examination,[19] and apparently this practice applies in Ohio.[20] In a Delaware case, the court held that the refusal of the defendant to submit to a physical examination was evidence of his impotency.[21]

As a general proposition, impotency renders a marriage voidable rather than void. Therefore, the impotent party cannot annul the marriage,[22] and cohabitation after knowledge of the defect amounts to ratification.[23] If the lack of capacity is known before the marriage, or if it might reasonably have been expected because of the age or known physical condition of the parties, no annulment will be granted.[24]

§ 7:15 Common law grounds—Intoxication

Intoxication caused by alcohol or narcotics at the time of marriage invalidates the marriage for the same reason that mental illness avoids it: the lack of intelligent consent. RC 3101.06 prohibits issuance of a marriage license when either of the applicants is under the influence of an intoxicating liquor or controlled substance. Although no Ohio cases have been decided on the subject, the rules of mental incompetency would most probably apply. Cases from other states indicate that intoxication alone will seldom serve to invalidate a marriage. As stated by a Texas court, "To avoid a contract on [the ground that the obligor was drunk when he entered into it], the obligor must have been so drunk as to have dethroned reason, memory, and

---

[16]Griffith v. Griffith, 162 Ill. 368, 44 N.E. 820 (1896).

[17]Griffith v. Griffith, 162 Ill. 368, 372, 44 N.E. 820 (1896).

[18]Tompkins v. Tompkins, 92 N.J. Eq. 113, 111 A. 599 (Ch. 1920). See also Heller v. Heller, 116 N.J. Eq. 543, 174 A. 573 (Ct. Err. & App. 1934).

[19]D. v. D., 41 Del. 263, 20 A.2d 139 (Super. Ct. 1941).

[20]S.S. Kresge Co. v. Trester, 123 Ohio St. 383, 9 Ohio L. Abs. 349, 175 N.E. 611 (1931). Regarding psychiatric examinations, see Kelley v. Smith & Oby Co., 70 Ohio L. Abs. 202, 129 N.E.2d 106 (C.P. 1954).

[21]S. v. S., 42 Del. 192, 29 A.2d 325 (Super. Ct. 1942).

[22]Anonymous v. Anonymous, 69 Misc. 489, 126 N.Y.S. 149 (Sup 1910).

[23]Kirschbaum v. Kirschbaum, 92 N.J. Eq. 7, 111 A. 697 (Ch. 1920).

[24]Steerman v. Snow, 94 N.J. Eq. 9, 118 A. 696 (Ch. 1922); Hatch v. Hatch, 58 Misc. 54, 110 N.Y.S. 18 (Sup 1908).

judgment."[1] As a practical matter, suits to avoid a marriage for intoxication are almost never successful. In these cases, judges and jurors view with extreme skepticism the plaintiff who testifies that he was so drunk that he did not know what he was doing and yet admits that he was able to stand up before the minister without falling.[2]

§7:16 Relief incident to annulment—Temporary spousal support and Temporary Restraining Orders (TROs)

When no rule or statute governed the matter, the general approach regarding relief was to grant the defendant spousal support pendente lite (pending trial), but to deny it to the plaintiff as the plaintiff was asserting there was no marriage. This is assuming that other factors such as need and ability to pay indicate that spousal support would be granted if divorce, rather than annulment, were the issue. Spousal support is now available to either spouse, both by rule[1] and by constitutional right.[2]

Generally, when the wife is the defendant, she is entitled to support during marriage and, therefore, to temporary spousal support until her marriage is declared invalid. This is true, at least where she can make a prima facie case of a marriage by denying her husband's charge of invalidity. This is inconsistent with the retroactive nature of annulment, but the policy in favor of support for de facto wives outweighs the need for logical consistency. However, if she concedes his claim or fails to deny it, there is no marriage, no duty of support, and no temporary spousal support.[3]

Where the wife is the plaintiff, the traditional rule was that she could not maintain inconsistent positions, alleging she was not mar-

---

[Section 7:15]

[1]Wells v. Houston, 23 Tex. Civ. App. 629, 647, 57 S.W. 584 (1900). See Annot., Validity, construction, and effect of provision in antenuptial contract forfeiting property rights of innocent spouse on separation or filing of divorce or other matrimonial action, 57 A.L.R.2d 942 (superseded by Modern status of views as to validity of premarital agreements contemplating divorce or separation, 53 A.L.R.4th 22, and Enforceability of premarital agreements governing support or property rights upon divorce or separation as affected by circumstances surrounding execution--modern status, 53 A.L.R.4th 85, and Enforceability of premarital agreements governing support or property rights upon divorce or separation as affected by fairness or adequacy of those terms--modern status, 53 A.L.R.4th 161).

[2]Feigenbaum v. Feigenbaum, 210 Ark. 186, 194 S.W.2d 1012 (1946) (annulment denied where plaintiff allegedly under influence of codeine appeared normal to license clerk and justice of peace); Christoph v. Sims, 234 S.W.2d 901 (Tex. Civ. App. Dallas 1950), writ refused n.r.e. (plaintiff intoxicated but could drive his car); Price v. Price, 38 Del. 172, 190 A. 104 (Super. Ct. 1937). But see Mahan v. Mahan, 88 So. 2d 545, 57 A.L.R.2d 1246 (Fla. 1956). See also Annot., Mahan v. Mahan, 88 So. 2d 545, 57 A.L.R.2d 1246 (Fla. 1956).

[Section 7:16]

[1]Civ. R. 75(N).

[2]Orr v. Orr, 440 U.S. 268, 99 S. Ct. 1102, 59 L. Ed. 2d 306 (1979).

[3]Clark, The Law of Domestic Relations in the United States § 3.5.

ried and never had been, yet asking for support which is a duty owed only to a spouse.[4] The general rules evolved at a time when inconsistent pleadings were prohibited and prior to the recent emphasis on rational and humane rules of intrafamily support.

In Ohio, Civil Rule 75(N) provides that during the pendency of an action for divorce, annulment, or legal separation, the court may grant spousal support pendente lite for good cause shown. It is possible to construe "good cause" to mean that the court has discretion to continue to apply the old rules referred to above. It is more likely that "good cause" refers to need and ability to pay, and that the rule will be construed to allow the wife temporary spousal support where there is a strong showing of need, whether she is plaintiff or defendant. Certainly, the trend is to provide economic protection to the de facto family where real need exists. The argument that Civil Rule 75(N) applies to all annulment actions is strengthened by Civil Rule 75(A), which says that with certain exceptions all civil rules apply to both divorce and annulment, presumably with equal effect.

Civil Rule 75(I) provides that in both annulment and divorce actions, Civil Rule 65(A), relating to temporary restraining orders, does not apply. The rule further provides that when a party is about to dispose of property to defeat spousal or child support, or where a party or child may suffer abuse, the court may grant a motion for a TRO to enjoin such action, with or without bond. The argument in favor of construing Civil Rule 75(I) to give the court authority to protect the de facto family seems even stronger than the argument for granting temporary spousal support. An argument by analogy is that the Ohio Domestic Violence Act, RC 3113.31 to RC 3113.39, provides protection for de facto families.[5] To date, no Ohio decisions have treated either temporary spousal support or other temporary orders incident to annulment. A judgment can be rendered on temporary spousal support arrearages along with the granting of an annulment.[6]

§ 7:17   Relief incident to annulment—Spousal support

The general rule is that there can be no spousal support incident to annulment. Here "spousal support" means a judicially created obligation to furnish future support to an ex-spouse. RC 3105.18 was amended to provide for spousal support instead of "alimony."[1] Spousal support, as post-termination support or maintenance for an ex-spouse, is a substitute for the obligation of support imposed by the law as

---

[4]Clark, The Law of Domestic Relations in the United States § 3.5.

[5]See RC 3113.31(A)(3), RC 3113.31(A)(4).

[6]Haska v. Haska, 1989 WL 11272 (Ohio Ct. App. 11th Dist. Portage County 1989).

[Section 7:17]

[1]1990 H.B. 514, eff. 1-1-91. See also Text §§ 7:22 to 7:25, Effect of annulment decree.

incident to a legal marriage. As was held in *Short v Short*,[2] if the marriage is not valid, there was never an obligation of support, and thus no spousal support is allowed.[3]

Since that case was decided, the statutes on spousal support were amended and Civil Rule 75 was adopted by the Ohio Supreme Court. The relevant provisions are as follows:

(1) RC 3105.18 regarding spousal support refers to actions for divorce or legal separation and does not mention actions for annulment, thus indicating adherence to the traditional doctrine.

(2) Civil Rule 75(O) provides, "When a party who is entitled to a decree of divorce or annulment is ordered to pay spousal support or child support . . . the court may delay entering a decree for divorce or annulment until the party . . . secures the payment of the spousal support or child support of the child."

This language could be construed to mean that spousal support refers to divorce and child support to divorce and annulment. More likely, the language means that spousal support is available as an incident to annulment.

The argument in favor of granting spousal support in an appropriate case is strengthened by RC 3105.011, stating that in all domestic relations matters the court has full equitable powers. While now statutory, annulment has traditionally been an equitable action. Therefore, the grant of post-annulment support is almost always based on strong equitable considerations, such as a change of position by a wife who leaves her job in reliance on the validity of a marriage which later turns out to be invalid.

A growing number of states recognize the harshness of the traditional rule and its drastic effect on wives who have become dependent in fact as a result of a defective marriage. In most such states, express statutes exist relating to spousal support for the good faith victim of an invalid marriage. In addition, in some states general spousal support statutes have recently been construed to include such spousal support.[4]

As a practical matter, counsel for the deserving victim of a defective marriage should be able to get spousal support by converting the annulment action to a divorce action based on one of the two annulment grounds in the divorce statute: fraud and bigamy.[5] This conversion could be effected by amendment under Civil Rule 15 if the wife is the

---

[2]Short v. Short, 61 Ohio L. Abs. 49, 102 N.E.2d 719 (Ct. App. 8th Dist. Cuyahoga County 1951).

[3]See also Annot., Right to allowance of permanent alimony in connection with decree of annulment, 54 A.L.R.2d 1410; Revlon, Inc. v. Buchanan, 271 F.2d 795, 2 Fed. R. Serv. 2d 733, 81 A.L.R.2d 222 (5th Cir. 1959).

[4]See Annot., Right to allowance of permanent alimony in connection with decree of annulment, 81 A.L.R.3d 281. See also Roth v. Roth, 49 Md. App. 433, 433 A.2d 1162 (1981).

[5]See Text § 7:4, Annulment versus divorce. See also Vanvalley v. Vanvalley, 19 Ohio St. 588, 1869 WL 105 (1869).

plaintiff in annulment or by a counterclaim for divorce under Civil Rule 13, where the wife is the defendant.

§ 7:18   Relief incident to annulment—Property division

RC 3105.171 provides for division of property acquired during marriage. This section refers only to divorce and legal separation so its application to annulment is questionable.

In principle, it is clear that a court granting an equitable annulment should be able to exercise its equitable powers to divide marital property. A property division is not based on a legal status such as marriage. It is an adjustment of property interests, returning to each party what is his or hers regardless of title. The analogy is the division of assets relating to a dissolution of a business partnership.[1]

There is one Ohio case, *Walker v. Walker*,[2] in which the court stated that, in an annulment action, the court has jurisdiction to make an equitable division of the property acquired by the parties during cohabitation. As a practical matter, it is suggested that where a division of property acquired during the invalid marriage is sought, the suit should be brought as a divorce action. If this action cannot be taken, counsel should plead an equitable property division, based on restitution, unjust enrichment, and general principles of equity, as suggested by RC 3105.011 and *Walker*.[3]

In *Zsigmond v. Vandemberg*,[4] the court looked at the one item of property at issue between the parties in an annulment action, a television set, and compared it to an engagement ring. The court relied on Ohio law requiring the return of an engagement ring because it is a conditional gift, made in contemplation of marriage, and the television set was ordered to be returned to the purchaser.

In the 1996 case of *Liming v. Liming*,[5] the trial court's division of property pursuant to RC 3105.171 in its annulment decree was reversed. RC 3105.171 is expressly applicable to divorce and legal separation, and not to annulment. The trial court was advised to place the parties in the same position that they would have been had the annulled marriage not taken place and return property interests to each party if possible.

[Section 7:18]

[1]Liming v. Liming, 117 Ohio App. 3d 617, 691 N.E.2d 299 (4th Dist. Adams County 1996).

[2]Walker v. Walker, 54 Ohio L. Abs. 153, 84 N.E.2d 258 (C.P. 1948).

[3]Walker v. Walker, 54 Ohio L. Abs. 153, 84 N.E.2d 258 (C.P. 1948).

[4]Zsigmond v. Vandemberg, 1995 WL 815349 (Ohio Ct. App. 11th Dist. Portage County 1995). See also Kelly v. Kelly, 163 Ohio App. 3d 260, 2005-Ohio-4740, 837 N.E.2d 811 (2d Dist. Clark County 2005) (wedding ring was a conditional gift which became former husband's after annulment).

[5]Liming v. Liming, 117 Ohio App. 3d 617, 691 N.E.2d 299 (4th Dist. Adams County 1996).

§ 7:19   Relief incident to annulment—Children of an annulled marriage—Child support and custody

Prior to the adoption of the Civil Rules and the 1963 Annulment Act,[1] it was not clear whether the annulment court had authority to enter a child support and custody decree or whether the parties had to file a separate action in juvenile court under RC 2151.23(A)(2).

There are no doubts today. RC 3105.21(A) provides that if the annulment is granted, the court must make an order for the disposition, care, and maintenance of the children of the alleged marriage. If the court denies the annulment it may, but need not, make such an order.[2] If the court does make an order, it must apply the basic rules applied in divorce cases.[3]

Where minor children are involved, the Civil Rules provide that the procedures applying to the allocation of parental rights and responsibilities, including child support incident to divorce also apply to the allocation of parental rights and responsibilities, including child support incident to annulment.[4] Specifically, the case worker investigation,[5] subpoena,[6] and temporary child support, maintenance, and allocation of parental rights and responsibilities[7] rules apply. In addition, if minor children are involved, the Uniform Child Custody Jurisdiction and Enforcement Act[8] applies, and counsel must file the affidavit required by RC 3127.23 and inform the court of any out-of-state parenting proceedings.

§ 7:20   Relief incident to annulment—Children of an annulled marriage—Legitimacy of the child

At early common law, the annulment was given retroactive effect for all purposes, so that the effect of an annulment decree was to make the children illegitimate. In Ohio, this rule was rejected in 1805.[1] The statute was modeled on a Virginia act of 1785. The history is discussed in *Santill v Rossetti*.[2]

Prior to the adoption of the Uniform Parentage Act, RC 2105.18

[Section 7:19]

[1]Ohio Rules of Civil Procedure, adopted eff. 7-1-70; Annulment Act, 130 Laws of Ohio H.B. 467, eff. 9-24-63.

[2]RC 3105.21(B).

[3]RC 3105.21, RC 3109.03 to RC 3109.05, RC 3113.21 to RC 3113.219.

[4]Civ. R. 75(A).

[5]Civ. R. 75(D).

[6]Civ. R. 75(E).

[7]Civ. R. 75(H), (N).

[8]RC 3127.01 to RC 3127.53.

[Section 7:20]

[1]3 Laws of Ohio 281 (1805).

[2]Santill v. Rossetti, 18 Ohio Op. 2d 109, 87 Ohio L. Abs. 400, 178 N.E.2d 633 (C.P. 1961).

stated, "The issue of parents whose marriage is null in law are nevertheless legitimate." RC 3111.01(B) provides, "The parent and child relationship extends equally to all children and all parents, regardless of the marital status of the parents." Both statutes apply to any de facto marriage, whether void or voidable,[3] and whether annulled or not. There are two interesting cases on the scope of the statute in nonannulment cases. The question is what is a "marriage null in law,"[4] which is a contradiction in terms if marriage is considered as a legal status. *Santill* held that children were legitimate where the parties agreed to a bigamous common law marriage, where one party knew of the defect and the other did not. The statute was extended by *Wolf v. Gardner*,[5] a social security case which turned on Ohio law. The court held the children legitimate as children of a "null marriage," where both parents knew of the defect of bigamy but held themselves out as married. Thus, the children of a simple *"Marvin* type"[6] cohabitation might be legitimate because many cohabitation arrangements involve some appearance of marriage.[7] The 1963 Annulment Act expressly provided, "A judgment of nullity of marriage does not affect the legitimacy of offspring conceived before the judgment, and the issue of such marriage are legitimate."[8]

§ 7:21 Relief incident to annulment—Restoration of name

RC 3105.34 provides that on annulment, the court may restore to either party any name the party had prior to marriage. It is not necessary to request this in the complaint, although it is good practice to do so.

§ 7:22 Effect of annulment decree—In general

The annulment decree is a kind of declaratory judgment finding a particular marriage not legally valid as a marriage because of some defect which existed at the time of entry into the attempted status.[1] Thus, according to strict logic, every annulment decree is totally retroactive and declares that there never was a marriage. Therefore, no legal rights can arise from such a "nonmarriage."

Fortunately, the law has never been completely logical. The fact is

---

[3]Wright v. Lore, 12 Ohio St. 619, 1861 WL 76 (1861).

[4]Wolf v. Gardner, 386 F.2d 295, 296, 15 Ohio Misc. 161, 43 Ohio Op. 2d 179 (6th Cir. 1967).

[5]Wolf v. Gardner, 386 F.2d 295, 15 Ohio Misc. 161, 43 Ohio Op. 2d 179 (6th Cir. 1967).

[6]Marvin v. Marvin, 18 Cal. 3d 660, 134 Cal. Rptr. 815, 557 P.2d 106 (1976).

[7]See also Text § 2:40, Common law marriage elements—Cohabitation; Text § 3:1, Ohio Parentage Act—History and origin.

[8]Former RC 3105.33, repealed by 1982 H.B. 245, eff. 6-29-82. See RC 3111.03 for provisions analogous to former RC 3105.33.

[Section 7:22]

[1]See Text § 7:1, Nature of marriage and annulment.

that the parties did enter into what they thought was a valid status, and the putative spouses and others have usually changed their circumstances, often to their detriment, in reliance on the supposed marriage. The issue is essentially one of policy, i.e., whether the law should insist on consistency of doctrine or should recognize the legitimate expectations of parties. Over the past two centuries, the trend has been clearly in favor of the latter approach. Thus, the distinction between void and voidable marriages, in which the voidable marriage is not subject to attack by nonspouses, is a repudiation of the logical concept of total retroactivity.[2] That Ohio had, since 1857, included three grounds for annulment (fraud, impotency, and bigamy) and has retained two of them (fraud and bigamy) among the grounds for divorce[3] and authorizes spousal support for the good faith victim of a bigamous marriage[4] is even less consistent with the retroactive theory.

Since 1805, Ohio law has provided that an annulment does not have the effect which it did in England, i.e., to make the children of the parties retroactively illegitimate.[5]

The annulment decree may have a retroactive effect in that the parties are considered never married, but it also has a prospective effect in terminating the marriage, if any. Thus, as is the case with an absolute divorce, following annulment neither spouse has any obligation to support the other, except as such obligation is incorporated into the decree which terminates the marriage. The possibility that spousal support is available as an incident to an annulment[6] is also an indication that Ohio law does not insist on a retroactive effect in all cases.

The Tenth District Court of Appeals in *Lang v. Reetz-Lang*[7] agreed with the Eighth District's decision in *Darling v. Darling*[8] and held that "an annulment decree operates to hold the marriage as a nullity as though it had never existed with the limitation that the legal fiction of retroactive nullification should not be applied to work an injustice."[9]

In *Darling*, retroactive nullification

would have been an injustice because the first husband would have been required to pay alimony to his former wife after nullification of her

---

[2]See Text § 7:1, Nature of marriage and annulment.

[3]See Text § 7:4, Annulment versus divorce.

[4]Vanvalley v. Vanvalley, 19 Ohio St. 588, 1869 WL 105 (1869).

[5]See Text §§ 7:19 to 7:20, Relief incident to annulment—Children of an annulled marriage.

[6]See Text § 7:17, Relief incident to annulment—Spousal support.

[7]Lang v. Reetz-Lang, 22 Ohio App. 3d 77, 488 N.E.2d 929 (10th Dist. Franklin County 1985).

[8]Darling v. Darling, 44 Ohio App. 2d 5, 73 Ohio Op. 2d 5, 335 N.E.2d 708 (8th Dist. Cuyahoga County 1975).

[9]Lang v. Reetz-Lang, 22 Ohio App. 3d 77, 80, 488 N.E.2d 929 (10th Dist. Franklin County 1985).

second marriage. . . . In this case, retroactive nullification is the only way to achieve justice.

. . .

Consummation of the marriage was an inherent part of the marriage contract and was an implied condition of the [antenuptial] agreement.[10]

A dissent in *Lang* argued that the parties did not provide that the promise to convey was conditioned on a consummated marriage, but provided only that it was conditioned on a marriage. Citing *Gross v. Gross*,[11] the dissent noted that the promises contained in an antenuptial agreement are enforceable even by one at fault "when the agreement [contemplates] future misconduct or fault, [and does not] expressly provide that such misconduct or fault would extinguish the promises in the agreement."[12]

§ 7:23 Effect of annulment decree—Resumption of a prior support obligation

The problem raised by a prior support obligation can be outlined by a simple and fairly common hypothetical case. A husband and wife are divorced, or their marriage is subject to dissolution. The wife is dependent in fact and needs spousal support for her future support. Accordingly, the decree, whether based on a separation agreement or not, provides for continuing spousal support of $500 per month until the wife's remarriage. The word "remarriage" is not defined in the decree or contract, if any. The wife remarries on January 1, 1992, notifies her ex-husband of the fact, and he ceases monthly payments. One year later, January 1, 1993, the second marriage is annulled. The wife then demands (1) $500 per month for the twelve months of 1992, i.e., $6,000 arrears; and (2) a decree ordering her ex-husband to resume paying $500 per month, starting with January 1993.

The wife's argument is simple and logical: there never was a marriage, so there never was a remarriage. The annulment is retroactive to the date of the second marriage, January 1, 1992. Therefore, from that date she was a single woman and, by the terms of the decree, the ex-husband must pay her spousal support.

The ex-husband will argue as follows:

(1) During the term of the defective marriage, 1992, she was in fact supported by her supposed husband. Therefore, enforcing his spousal support obligation for this period results in double support

---

[10]Lang v. Reetz-Lang, 22 Ohio App. 3d 77, 80, 488 N.E.2d 929 (10th Dist. Franklin County 1985) (wife did not invest any money in the property transferred on marriage and would have received a windfall).

[11]Gross v. Gross, 11 Ohio St. 3d 99, 464 N.E.2d 500, 53 A.L.R.4th 139 (1984).

[12]Lang v. Reetz-Lang, 22 Ohio App. 3d 77, 81, 488 N.E.2d 929 (10th Dist. Franklin County 1985). See Text § 1:8, Considerations for possible divorce, dissolution.

for her, a windfall which is inequitable, unfair, and contrary to public policy.[1]

(2) As to future support, it is unfair to require resumption of spousal support. The wife was the one who elected to remarry, and her election to marry constitutes an assumption of the risk that her second marriage may turn out invalid. As between husband and wife, that burden should be placed on her because she is in a better position to evaluate the validity of her second marriage before entering into it. Further, in good faith reliance on the notice of her remarriage, the ex-husband had committed his available funds elsewhere, as by buying a business on terms or entry into his own remarriage. The courts are not agreed on the answers to the two questions indicated above, but it is possible to suggest some tentative answers.

The most obvious although often overlooked point is that the issue is essentially one of construction of language, i.e., if the word "remarriage" in the decree or contract meant marriage in its technical legal sense or marriage in the nontechnical sense which might include a de facto relationship. If a husband can persuade the court that the latter was meant, either by a dictionary definition or by use of extrinsic evidence of the intent of the parties, there was a remarriage. This argument is easier to use where a separation decree is involved than where the obligation to pay is in a judicial decree.

Where the wife's own conduct contributed to the defective nature of the second marriage, or where she knew of the defect, or in the exercise of reasonable care ought to have known of it, she should be estopped by her own misconduct or negligence.[2] In Ohio, estoppel can validate for some purposes a relationship which is not a legal marriage.[3]

Despite the equitable arguments outlined above, a substantial number of courts have followed the strictly logical view that an annulment is completely retroactive. Probably the best-known case is *Sutton v Leib*,[4] where, following annulment, the wife was entitled to a judgment against her first husband both for the period she lived with

---

[Section 7:23]

[1]Sleicher v. Sleicher, 251 N.Y. 366, 167 N.E. 501 (1929). See also Hunt v. Hunt, 169 Ohio St. 276, 8 Ohio Op. 2d 286, 159 N.E.2d 430 (1959) (overruled by, In re Adams, 45 Ohio St. 3d 219, 543 N.E.2d 797 (1989)) (court held that it was contrary to public policy to require an ex-husband to pay alimony where the ex-wife is in fact supported by another); Wolfe v. Wolfe, 46 Ohio St. 2d 399, 75 Ohio Op. 2d 474, 350 N.E.2d 413 (1976).

[2]Gevis v. Gevis, 147 N.Y.S.2d 489 (Sup 1955) (second marriage was annulled because of the wife's fraud; she was estopped from claiming a resumption of prior alimony).

[3]See Edgar v. Richardson, 33 Ohio St. 581, 1878 WL 29 (1878).

[4]Sutton v. Leib, 199 F.2d 163, 33 A.L.R.2d 1451 (7th Cir. 1952) (application of Illinois law). See also cases cited in Annot., Annulment of later marriage as reviving prior husband's obligation under alimony decree or separation agreement, 45 A.L.R.3d 1033.

her second husband following a defective marriage and for the period after that marriage was annulled up to the time of a valid third marriage. The equities of the husband were protected by not charging him interest on the arrears. An old Ohio case seems to take the same approach.[5]

A substantial number of courts take the position that an annulment of a void marriage is retroactive, but the annulment of a voidable marriage[6] is like a divorce and does not have the effect of reviving a prior spousal support decree.[7] Such decisions are consistent with the retroactive nature of annulment if the marriage is void but is inconsistent with the retroactive effect of annulment if the marriage is voidable. An Ohio case, *Darling v. Darling*,[8] takes this approach. In that case, the second marriage was annulled for lack of consummation under RC 3105.31(F).[9] The trial court applied the doctrine of *Sutton* and granted judgment for both the period of the second marriage and the period following the annulment. The court of appeals reversed, holding that such a defect rendered the second marriage voidable, and that prior alimony is not revived on annulment of a voidable marriage. It seems that the result was correct, but the rationale was not. The case indicates, as dicta, that if the second marriage were void, the annulment would be retroactive. It would seem that the equitable factors, such as the wife's assumption of the risk of an invalid marriage and the husband's change of position, are essentially the same whether the second marriage is characterized as void or voidable.

Another position is illustrated in a case from Massachusetts. In *Glazer v. Silverman*,[10] the second marriage was annulled as bigamous and void, but the court refused to adopt the void-voidable distinction, and the first husband did not prove any specific change of position. Instead, the court took the position that if the wife can get support from her second husband as an incident to the annulment action, she should try to do so, and if she fails to make the attempt, she should not be allowed to revive a prior support obligation. The wife was barred because she annulled her second marriage in New York, which by statute allows spousal support in annulment actions.

---

[5]Brenholts v. Brenholts, 19 Ohio L. Abs. 309, 1935 WL 1824 (Ct. App. 2d Dist. Franklin County 1935) (following annulment, the court revived the prior alimony decree, which incorporated a separation agreement; it is not clear from the opinion whether the wife claimed back alimony for the period of her defective marriage or only from the date of annulment).

[6]See discussion of the void-voidable distinction in Text § 7:1, Nature of marriage and annulment.

[7]See Annot., Annulment of later marriage as reviving prior husband's obligation under alimony decree or separation agreement, 45 A.L.R.3d 1033; Flaxman v. Flaxman, 57 N.J. 458, 273 A.2d 567, 45 A.L.R.3d 1026 (1971).

[8]Darling v. Darling, 44 Ohio App. 2d 5, 73 Ohio Op. 2d 5, 335 N.E.2d 708 (8th Dist. Cuyahoga County 1975).

[9]See discussion of this statutory ground in Text § 7:11, Statutory grounds—Nonconsummation.

[10]Glazer v. Silverman, 354 Mass. 177, 236 N.E.2d 199 (1968). See also McConkey v. McConkey, 216 Va. 106, 215 S.E.2d 640 (1975), and cases cited therein.

The applicability of this doctrine to the Ohio annulment situation should be noted. The law on spousal support in annulment is unsettled, but, at least until there is a clear decision from the Supreme Court denying spousal support in annulment, it is possible to apply for it.[11] Further, at least where the second marriage is annulled for fraud, bigamy, or impotency, it is possible for the wife to obtain support from her second husband by converting her annulment action to a divorce based on annulment grounds.[12]

A small minority of jurisdictions hold that whether or not the wife could have received spousal support in the annulment action, the probability that the husband changed his position in reliance on the second marriage is sufficient justification to refuse to reinstate a prior decree.[13]

In conclusion, it would seem logical and reasonable that the courts should both reject the void-voidable distinction and the total retroactivity position and adopt a combination of these approaches. Thus, the court should consider the construction of the language of the initial decree, the fault or negligence of the wife in remarrying, her ability to get support from her second husband, and the first husband's actual or probable change of position. Such a "balancing of the equities" approach is indicated in several cases[14] and seems to be the most appropriate approach in light of RC 3105.011, preserving the full equitable power of the domestic relations court in all domestic relations matters. Further, as a practical matter, counsel should try to avoid the problem by drafting the separation agreement or legal separation decree so that spousal support terminates not just on remarriage, but on any attempted entry into marital status regardless of the validity of the new marriage and also on establishing a settled or long-term cohabitation arrangement.

§ 7:24 Effect of annulment decree—Resumption of prior benefits

There are a number of programs, both public and private, providing monthly payments to individuals, usually widows, until their remarriage. The private programs include pension and life insurance plans. The public programs include public employees retirement and social security retirement. When the question of resumption of such benefits following annulment of a defective "remarriage" comes before the courts, the approach taken is similar to the approach taken in the spousal support cases, with two important exceptions. In contrast to

---

[11]See Text §§ 7:16 to 7:21, Relief incident to annulment.

[12]See Text § 7:4, Annulment versus divorce.

[13]Keeney v. Keeney, 211 La. 585, 30 So. 2d 549 (1947); Chavez v. Chavez, 82 N.M. 624, 485 P.2d 735 (1971).

[14]Ferguson v. Ferguson, 564 P.2d 1380 (Utah 1977); Flaxman v. Flaxman, 57 N.J. 458, 273 A.2d 567, 45 A.L.R.3d 1026 (1971), cited with approval in Darling v. Darling, 44 Ohio App. 2d 5, 73 Ohio Op. 2d 5, 335 N.E.2d 708 (8th Dist. Cuyahoga County 1975).

the spousal support cases, the intent of the party who creates the benefit program is often recognized as critical. Thus, in a private pension case, the court should look to the purpose of the pension program. In a public program case, this involves determining the purpose of the statute. In both cases, the purpose is usually the same: to provide long-term support for a defined class, usually widows of retired employees. Recognition of this policy usually results in giving retroactive effect to the annulment and a resumption of benefits, but only for the period following the annulment. The leading case is on resumption of social security benefits. In *Nott v. Fleming*,[1] the court emphasized that the legislative purpose was to provide support for the widow, and that her remarriage provided that support even though the marriage was defective, because the annulment took place in a state where spousal support can be granted incident to annulment. As she no longer needed social security, the annulment was not given retroactive effect.[2]

The principal reason for the avoidance of retroactivity in spousal support cases is the possibility that on learning of the "remarriage" the first husband will act in reliance on the knowledge by committing his limited funds to other purposes. Therefore, a resumption of spousal support following annulment would work a major hardship on him. This factor does not apply to the large pension or social security fund, where the claims of this particular widow are only one of thousands (or in the case of social security, millions) of similar claims. Thus, resumption of the benefits following annulment works no hardship on the fund and retroactivity is the rule. The leading case is *Folsom v. Pearsall*,[3] where social security benefits were revived following annulment, notwithstanding the fact that the annulment occurred in California, whose courts had decided that annulment would not revive a prior spousal support decree.[4]

The Ohio Supreme Court recently addressed the issue of restoration of a spouse's worker's compensation death benefits following the annulment of a remarriage.[5] In *White v. Conrad*, wife was awarded workers' compensation death benefits pursuant to RC 4123.59(B), which would continue until her death or remarriage. She remarried several years later, but the marriage was annulled for fraud. Wife filed for reinstatement of her death benefits with the Bureau of Workers' Compensation, but was denied restoration of her benefits. The

---

[Section 7:24]

[1]Nott v. Flemming, 272 F.2d 380 (2d Cir. 1959).

[2]See also Cottam v. City of Los Angeles, 184 Cal. App. 2d 523, 7 Cal. Rptr. 734, 85 A.L.R.2d 238 (2d Dist. 1960) (resumption of benefits for widow and minor children of police officer killed in line of duty).

[3]Folsom v. Pearsall, 245 F.2d 562 (9th Cir. 1957).

[4]See also cases cited in Clark, The Law of Domestic Relations in the United States § 3.6; Annot., Effect of divorce, remarriage, or annulment, on widow's pension or bonus rights or social security benefits, 85 A.L.R.2d 242.

[5]White v. Conrad, 102 Ohio St. 3d 125, 2004-Ohio-2148, 807 N.E.2d 327 (2004).

trial court reversed the administrative order and found that wife was entitled to the benefits and they should be retroactive to the date they had been terminated. The basis of the trial court's decision was that because wife obtained an annulment, she must be treated as if she never remarried. The appellate court reversed the trial court's decision finding that the trial court lacked subject matter jurisdiction to determine whether wife was entitled to benefits. The Supreme Court reversed and remanded for a determination of the substantive question of whether an annulment of a remarriage puts a deceased employee's surviving spouse back in the position where she is entitled to receive death benefits.

On remand, the Ninth District Court of Appeals upheld the trial court's decision that the widow was entitled to the restoration of her benefits due to the annulment of her second marriage. The appellate court stated, "The annulled marriage is treated as though it never existed. If, in the eyes of the law, Appellee's [wife's] second marriage never existed, it follows that her death benefits cannot be terminated on the basis of this marriage, and that she is entitled to a restoration of those benefits retroactive to the date of termination."[6]

§ 7:25 Effect of annulment decree—Tax considerations

Marital status is a factor in determining tax liability under state and federal income tax, gift, estate, inheritance, and, more rarely, excise tax laws. While the taxing authority could define marital status for tax purposes, normally it does not. Thus, the usual rule is to look to the state law of the domicile of the taxpayer. Thus, under Revenue Ruling 79-330, 1979-2 Cum. Bul. 391, the effect of an interlocutory divorce decree on the right to file a joint return depends on whether under state law the decree is final when granted, even though the parties cannot remarry for a period, or whether it is final at the end of the period.

No cases have settled the issue of the retroactive tax impact of an annulment. However, a 1976 revenue ruling[1] involved taxpayers who filed joint returns while married and in the following year "a state court of competent jurisdiction annulled the marriage and decreed that no valid marriage ever existed." The ruling follows the retroactive theory and states that, as the taxpayers were both single persons for the tax year prior to the annulment, they must file amended returns as single persons for that year. The ruling does not indicate what the defect was, whether it rendered the marriage void or voidable, or the state law involved. With an Ohio annulment, it may be possible to avoid the ruling by arguing that Ohio law does not treat an annulled marriage as void for all purposes, so it should not be for

---

[6]White ex rel. White v. Conrad, 2005-Ohio-17, 2005 WL 17889 (Ohio Ct. App. 9th Dist. Medina County 2005).

[Section 7:25]

[1]Rev. Rul. 76-255, 1976-2 Cum. Bul. 40.

this purpose. Further, the ruling was an attempt by the Internal Revenue Service to force amendment of joint returns at a time when filing a joint return resulted in a lower tax than filing separate returns. The reverse is true where both spouses have income because the rates for persons who are married filing separately are substantially higher than the combined rate for two single persons. Thus, the retroactivity issue is now more likely to come up at the behest of the taxpayers. A couple who have filed joint returns and who annul the marriage can attempt to use the revenue ruling to avoid the "marriage penalty" by filing amended returns as single persons.

There are no cases or rulings on the retroactive effect of an annulment on the marital deduction under the federal estate tax. The issue is not likely to come up because marital status as of the date of death controls, and normally a marriage cannot be annulled after the death of a spouse, although there are exceptions.[2]

§ 7:26 Jurisdiction

By statute, jurisdiction in annulment is vested in the court of common pleas.[1] If a common pleas court has both a general division and a domestic relations division,[2] the domestic relations division has jurisdiction in annulment actions based on grounds listed in the annulment statute, RC 3105.31. Presumably, the same division has jurisdiction where the grounds are not listed in the statute.[3] However, the statute is not clear on this, and possibly the general division may have concurrent jurisdiction on the theory that nonstatutory annulment is equitable in nature.

A six-month residency is required of the plaintiff before filing the complaint, with venue according to the Ohio Civil Rules.[4]

In other states, there have been conflicting decisions on whether jurisdiction in annulment is in personam (i.e., annulment is transitory, and the plaintiff must sue where the defendant is) or whether it is quasi in rem (i.e., plaintiff may or must sue in the state where the marriage occurred and personal jurisdiction over the defendant is not required). There are no decisions on this in Ohio, and the issue is now settled by statute. Specifically, the Annulment Act[5] applies the divorce rules relating to jurisdiction over annulment actions. Jurisdiction in annulment is based on the residence of the plaintiff for at least six

---

[2]See Text §§ 7:27 to 7:39, Practice and procedure.

[Section 7:26]

[1]RC 3105.10(A). See also RC 3105.011, RC 3105.03.

[2]RC 2301.03.

[3]See Text § 7:5, Exclusivity of remedy; Text §§ 7:12 to 7:15, Common law grounds, for a discussion of annulment grounds not set forth in the statute.

[4]RC 3105.03.

[5]130 Laws of Ohio H.B. 467, eff. 9-24-63.

months;[6] the court of the domicile of the plaintiff has jurisdiction over the case even though the marriage or cause of action occurred outside Ohio.[7] RC 3105.03 uses the term "residence," but "residence" has been construed to mean "domicile" in divorce cases. Presumably, the same rule applies to annulment. Based on the divorce analogy, domicile in Ohio is jurisdictional. In addition, the Ohio court has jurisdiction even though the defendant spouse is a non-resident of the state.[8]

§ 7:27 Practice and procedure—In general

The traditional annulment action is an action in equity to declare that a marriage is invalid.[1] The function of the action is to provide the parties with a judicial decree to the effect that an alleged marriage, a legal and public status, is not legally a marriage. Functionally, annulment is equivalent to a declaratory judgment action. Because the action antedates the modern declaratory judgment action, the procedures set forth in the Ohio Declaratory Judgment Act[2] do not apply. The action is equitable in origin, so the rules of practice and procedure which apply to equity actions apply to annulment. In 1963, the legislature enacted a statute which applies most of the procedural rules in the divorce act to annulment actions. Thus, procedure in annulment actions is governed by (1) the few specific rules, mainly jurisdiction and venue, found in RC Chapter 3105; (2) the rules which apply to equitable actions generally; and (3) the Ohio Rules of Civil Procedure, which apply to equity actions generally[3] and to annulment actions specifically.[4]

§ 7:28 Practice and procedure—Venue

Under the Annulment Act,[1] actions for annulment must be brought in the proper county pursuant to the Civil Rules.[2] Civil Rule 3(B) provides several venue alternatives. These include (1) the county in which the defendant resides (Civil Rule 3(B)(1)) or has his principal place of business (Civil Rule 3(B)(2)); (2) the county in which the plaintiff resides and has resided for at least ninety days (Civil Rule 3(B)(9)); (3) the county where the marriage occurred or where other facts giving rise to the cause of action occurred, such as where the

---

[6]RC 3105.03.
[7]RC 3105.03.
[8]RC 3105.06.

[Section 7:27]
[1]See Text § 7:1, Nature of marriage and annulment.
[2]RC Ch. 2721.
[3]Civ. R. 1(A).
[4]Civ. R. 75(A).

[Section 7:28]
[1]130 Laws of Ohio H.B. 467, eff. 9-24-63.
[2]RC 3105.03.

fraud or deceit occurred (Civil Rule 3(B)(6)); and (4) if division of property is sought as incidental to the annulment and there is no other venue available, in the county where the defendant's property is located (Civil Rule 3(B)(11)).

§ 7:29 Practice and procedure—Parties

With a few exceptions, the two spouses are the only parties in an annulment action. As to parties plaintiff, the spouse is the only proper plaintiff, subject to four exceptions:

(1) If the plaintiff spouse is under a disability, such as minority or mental incompetency, the action is prosecuted by a representative who may be a general guardian, next friend, or guardian ad litem.[1] In addition to the representatives referred to in Civil Rule 17(B), RC 3105.32(C) allows a relative to commence an action to annul a marriage of an adjudicated incompetent. Presumably, the relative acts as a representative and not in his own right, although this is not clear from the language of the statute.

(2) The Annulment Act allows the parent, guardian, or other person having charge of an underage spouse to bring the action.[2] It is unclear whether the parent can annul in his own right, or whether the parent acts on behalf of the child. If the action is brought by the parent as next friend, the statute seems superfluous. Whether the parent sues in his own name or on behalf of the minor child, and the child objects to the annulment, it is suggested that the court appoint a guardian ad litem for the child, either on motion of a party or on its own motion.[3]

(3) An action to annul a bigamous marriage may be filed by the other party to the first and still valid marriage.[4]

(4) As to grounds for annulment which are not covered by statute, if the defect renders the marriage void, any person with an interest sufficient to justify standing may collaterally attack the marriage.[5]

As to parties defendant, the spouse is always a defendant, except (1) where the defendant spouse is under disability, the action lies against a general guardian, or, if none exists, a guardian ad litem;[6] and (2) where the plaintiff's spouse is dead.

Civil Rule 75(B) provides that Civil Rules 14, 19, 19.1, and 24 do not apply to annulment actions. However, Civil Rule 20 applies, since it is not specifically excluded. Where the annulment involves a child of the marriage, the child may be made a party defendant and a guard-

---

[Section 7:29]

[1]Civ. R. 17(B).

[2]RC 3105.32(A).

[3]Civ. R. 17(B) (last sentence).

[4]RC 3105.32(B). See also Text § 7:7, Statutory grounds—Bigamy.

[5]See Text § 7:1, Nature of marriage and annulment.

[6]Civ. R. 17(B).

ian ad litem appointed.[7] Any person having property in his possession which may be subject to a child support or spousal support order may be made an additional defendant. An employer of a party may be joined after notice to the party ordered to pay support and to his employer.[8]

§ 7:30 Practice and procedure—Service of process

By statute, service of process in annulment is identical to service of process in divorce. The only serious issue in the process area is whether an Ohio plaintiff can annul a marriage where the other spouse is outside the state. The plaintiff can always go to the state of residence of the defendant and sue there. If the Ohio resident sues in Ohio, RC 3105.06 appears to allow quasi in rem jurisdiction based on service by publication where the defendant's residence is unknown. Civil Rule 4.4 was amended effective July 1, 1991, to provide that where the plaintiff is proceeding in forma pauperis, service by publication in an annulment action may be accomplished by posting in the courthouse and two other public places and by mail to the last known address, rather than by publication in a newspaper of general circulation.[1] In addition, the "long arm rule" probably justifies in personam jurisdiction based on "[l]iving in the marital relationship within this state."[2]

§ 7:31 Practice and procedure—Pleadings

The normal rules of pleading, set forth in Civil Rules 7 to 13, and 15, apply to annulment actions.[1] A party may plead alternative and inconsistent claims, such as a request for an annulment if the marriage is invalid and for divorce if it is valid. If the case involves allocation of parental rights and responsibilities for a minor child, the Uniform Child Custody Jurisdiction and Enforcement Act, RC 3127.01 to RC 3127.53, applies and the pleadings must include the information required by RC 3127.23(A).

---

[7]Civ. R. 75(B)(1) to (3).

[8]Civ. R. 75(B)(1) to (3).

[Section 7:30]

[1]Civ. R. 4.4(A)(2).

[2]Civ. R. 4.3(A)(8).

[Section 7:31]

[1]Civ. R. 75(B).

§ 7:32   Practice and procedure—Pleading defenses

It is an open question whether the adoption of statutory grounds for annulment preempts the equitable grounds.[1] If such equitable actions exist, specific equitable defenses to them, such as unclean hands by the plaintiff, estoppel, and laches, also exist. Presumably, these are all affirmative defenses and must be pleaded under Civil Rule 8(C).

As to statutory actions, RC 3105.32 lists for each ground the persons who have standing to sue and the statute of limitations for that ground. The separate causes, and in some instances the possible initiators, have different time periods within which an annulment action must be commenced.

(1) Where the action is based on nonage:
- (a) If brought by the party who was under the age set forth in RC 3101.01 for eligibility to marry, it must be brought within two years of arriving at the statutory age.
- (b) Cause is extinguished if the underage spouse cohabits with the other spouse after reaching the age of majority.
- (c) If brought by parent, guardian, or person having charge of the underage spouse, it must be commenced before that spouse reaches the age of majority.

(2) Where the action is based on the existence of a living spouse at the time of the marriage, there is no time limitation, except that the action must be brought during the life of the other spouse.

(3) Where the action is based on mental incompetency:
- (a) During the incompetency, any designated person may commence the action so long as *both* spouses are alive.
- (b) After the restoration of competency, if there has been no subsequent cohabitation, the action may be brought any time, so long as *both* spouses are alive.
- (c) After the restoration of competency, if there is subsequent cohabitation, the cause is extinguished.

(4) Where the action is based on consent by fraud:
- (a) It must be brought within two years of the discovery of the facts constituting the fraud.
- (b) Cohabitation after the aggrieved party learns the facts extinguishes the cause.

(5) Where the action is based on consent obtained under duress:
- (a) It must be brought within two years of the date of the marriage.
- (b) Cohabitation after the forced consent extinguishes the cause. Ostensibly, consent to cohabit may also be obtained by force and it can be presumed that forced nonconsensual cohabitation would not serve to bar the action.

(6) Where the action is based on nonconsummation, it must be

[Section 7:32]

[1]See Text § 7:4, Annulment versus divorce; Text § 7:5, Exclusivity of remedy.

brought by the aggrieved party within two years of the date of the marriage. In fact, both parties may be aggrieved by this circumstance.

In addition to the affirmative defense of statutory time limitation specified in Civil Rule 8(C), under the rule's catchall wording of "and any other matter constituting an avoidance or affirmative defense," both cohabitation after the specific event and lack of standing are likely to be deemed affirmative defenses which must be pleaded.

§ 7:33   Practice and procedure—Pretrial practice

The normal rules of pretrial discovery set forth in Civil Rules 26 to 37 apply to annulment actions.[1] Prior to trial of an annulment, the court may order conciliation efforts and refer the parties to a public or private conciliation service for up to ninety days. The case may not be heard until conciliation has been concluded.[2] Conciliation would be applicable to a voidable marriage and a moot point as to a void marriage.

Where the allocation of parental rights and responsibilities or child support for a minor child is involved, the court may order a pretrial social investigation of the family, as in a divorce action.[3] In a case where children are involved, the Uniform Child Custody Jurisdiction Act applies, and counsel must file the affidavit required by RC 3127.23 and inform the court of any out-of-state parenting proceedings.

The Civil Rules do not require a pretrial conference,[4] but where local rules require them, counsel should check their applicability to annulment cases. For example, in Cuyahoga County both General Division Rule 21 and Domestic Relations Rules on "Pretrial and Case Management Procedures" apply to annulment actions and require both pretrial statement and pretrial conferences.

A default judgment may not be entered in an annulment action.[5] If the defendant does not answer or is not subject to personal jurisdiction, the plaintiff can obtain the same result by a motion for summary judgment under Civil Rule 56.

[Section 7:33]

[1]Civ. R. 75(B).

[2]RC 3105.091. See Text Ch 6, Alternative Forms of Dispute Resolution.

[3]Civ. R. 75(D).

[4]Civ. R. 16.

[5]Civ. R. 75(F).

§ 7:34   Practice and procedure—Trial

As in divorce, trial of an annulment action is before a judge or a magistrate without a jury.[1] If trial is before a magistrate, the magistrate prepares a decision and counsel have fourteen days to object to the report.[2] The six-week waiting period after service is the same for trial of annulment as for divorce.[3] At the trial, the court may not grant an annulment on the testimony of a party unless it is supported by other credible evidence.[4] The spouses are competent to testify, notwithstanding the marital relation.[5]

§ 7:35   Practice and procedure—Judgment

Civil Rules 54 and 58 apply to annulment actions. The judgment should state that because of a specific defect, "the marriage is annulled." This is the language suggested in the opening phrase of RC 3105.31. However, RC 3105.32 refers to a "decree of nullity," and RC 3105.33 and RC 3105.34 refer to a "judgment of nullity." The judgment could also use the language of RC 3105.10(A) that the marriage is dissolved and the parties released from their obligations. If there are minor children of the parties and the court grants the annulment, the court must include an appropriate order allocating parental rights and responsibilities and ordering child support in the judgment.[1] If the court denies the annulment, it may make an order allocating parental rights and responsibilities and ordering child support[2] and normally should do so.

If the judgment affects real property outside the county of trial, as in the case of a property division incident to an annulment, the judgment should describe the property, and a certified copy of the judgment should be filed in the county where the property is located, as provided in the lis pendens statutes.[3]

If the judgment allocates parental rights and responsibilities and orders child support, the court may delay entry of the judgment for annulment until the spouse who must pay child support secures pay-

---

[Section 7:34]

   [1]Civ. R. 75(C).

   [2]Civ. R. 53.

   [3]Civ. R. 75(K).

   [4]Civ. R. 75(M).

   [5]Civ. R. 75(M).

[Section 7:35]

   [1]RC 3105.21(A).

   [2]RC 3105.21(B).

   [3]RC 2703.26, RC 2703.27.

ment or until the party who had possession of the child prior to the decree surrenders the child to the residential parent.[4]

If the annulment is granted, the judgment may include, and normally should include, a provision restoring the maiden name of the wife or the name she used prior to the annulled marriage.[5]

A judgment can be rendered on temporary spousal support arrearages along with the granting of an annulment.[6]

§ 7:36   Practice and procedure—Effect of death of a spouse

The effect of the death of a spouse on an annulment action is, at best, undecided in Ohio. As to both divorce and annulment, the statutes are confusing and the few cases point different ways. Conceptually, there are two aspects of the problem:

(1) Where one spouse dies before the annulment action is filed, can an action for annulment be filed either by or against the estate of the deceased spouse? The problem of survival is governed by RC 2305.21, an ancient and poorly drafted statute.

(2) Where a spouse dies after the annulment action is commenced,[1] can the action be continued by or against the estate of the deceased? The problem of abatement is governed by RC 2311.21.

Neither survival nor abatement is mentioned in the Annulment Act or in RC Chapter 3105. The Civil Rules do not settle either issue. They merely provide that if an action does not abate on the death of a party, certain procedures are set forth to substitute the estate of the deceased as a new party.[2]

As to the first question, the survival statute provides that certain causes of action survive the death of the party entitled to bring the action or the death of the person liable thereto. Those actions listed are actions for profits, injuries to person or property, actions for deceit or fraud, and those actions which survive at common law. Neither annulment nor divorce fits any of these categories, with the possible exception that annulment for fraud might be held an action for fraud or deceit. It seems inconsistent to allow one type of annulment action to survive and hold that all others do not.

Other states tend to disregard the survival statutes and to apply ad hoc rules to the annulment situation. The leading case is *Patey v.*

---

[4]Civ. R. 75(N).

[5]RC 3105.34.

[6]Haska v. Haska, 1989 WL 11272 (Ohio Ct. App. 11th Dist. Portage County 1989).

[Section 7:36]

[1]See Civ. R. 3(A) (Action is "commenced" when the complaint is filed with the court if service is obtained within a year.).

[2]Civ. R. 25(A), (E).

Peaslee,[3] which held that the answer to the survival question depends on the classification of the marriage as void or voidable. If merely voidable, the annulment action may not be brought after death of either spouse. If void, it may be brought after the death of a spouse, not because the action survived at common law, and not because a statute covers the issue, but because being void the marriage can be collaterally attacked by anyone who has standing, including the estate of the deceased spouse or the heirs. The case was filed by the heirs of a deceased wife who allegedly married while mentally incompetent. The court held that a marriage of a mental incompetent was voidable only, so the annulment action did not survive death. The only Ohio case on the issue is a lower court opinion which follows the rationale of the *Patey* case. *Heyse v. Michalske*[4] involved an uncle-niece marriage. The court held that such a marriage is void and could be annulled by the heirs, even though both spouses were dead. However, in *Hilt v. Diedrich*,[5] the Third District Court of Appeals held that the brother and sister of a decedent did not have standing to bring an annulment action on the grounds of fraud or nonconsummation because they were not "the party aggrieved" as required by RC 3105.32(D) or (F).

Professor Homer Clark further addressed the subject:

> Since, as has been demonstrated in other sections, the void-voidable distinction is both confusing and unworkable, it is regrettable that it has been made the crucial factor here. . . . The kinds of cases in which posthumous attack on a marriage is to be permitted should be severely limited if not forbidden entirely. Such attack usually occurs in the course of a struggle between the surviving "spouse" and the deceased's relatives over the inheritance of the deceased's estate, in which the "spouse's" moral claims are generally superior. . . . [A] spouse's claims do have the virtue that they are based on a de facto marriage. . . . Legal recognition of the status quo is the better policy.[6]

As to the effect of death of a spouse during pendency of the action, the general tendency is to disregard the abatement statutes and treat annulment as a special case. In general, if the marriage was void so it could have been commenced by the heirs, it can be continued by the heirs under the collateral attack rationale. If the marriage is voidable and death occurs prior to judgment, the suit abates and is dismissed. If the marriage is voidable and death occurs after judgment and prior to the time for filing an appeal runs, it does not abate, and the heirs or estate may perfect a pending appeal or file a new appeal.[7]

The Ohio abatement statute simply provides, "Unless otherwise

---

[3]Patey v. Peaslee, 99 N.H. 335, 111 A.2d 194, 47 A.L.R.2d 1388 (1955).

[4]Heyse v. Michalske, 18 Ohio Op. 254, 31 Ohio L. Abs. 484, 6 Ohio Supp. 33 (Prob. Ct. 1940).

[5]Hilt v. Diedrich, 1990 WL 121487 (Ohio Ct. App. 3d Dist. Mercer County 1990).

[6]Clark, The Law of Domestic Relations in the United States § 3.3.

[7]Clark, The Law of Domestic Relations in the United States § 3.3. See also Annot., Right to attack validity of marriage after death of party thereto, 47 A.L.R.2d 1393.

provided, no action . . . shall abate by the death of either or both parties."[8] Nowhere is it "otherwise provided" by any express statute. Therefore, annulment, once started, should not abate. There are no Ohio cases relating to this subject, but one case in the analogous area of divorce suggests an additional policy factor which ought to be weighed in the balance in abatement issues and possibly in the survival area.

Porter v. Lerch[9] involved an action for divorce and for a property division. After a trial and an appeal which resulted in a remand, the husband died before final judgment was entered. The court referred to the abatement statute and indicated that, the statute notwithstanding, if the action is for a divorce alone (i.e., a declaration that the marriage is terminated prospectively), it must abate by death, because circumstances have accomplished the result sought by the parties. However, if the action also involves the adjustment of property rights between the parties, the entire action did not abate and the estate is substituted as a party, presumably for all purposes, including additional appeals.

A later case, *Delaney v. Delaney*,[10] applied the analogy in *Porter v. Porter*[11] to an action for legal separation under RC 3105.17. No property adjustment or prior rights were involved. Only future support was asked. Since a dead husband has no obligation to support his wife, the action abated on the husband's death.

An annulment decree may include an equitable division of property acquired during the defective marriage.[12] It seems that in principle, the rationale of *Porter* should also apply to an annulment action. Therefore, if counsel wants to avoid the possibility of abatement if death occurs while the action is pending, the complaint should include a request for division of marital property, even though very little property is involved and the parties are agreed on its division.

§ 7:37 Practice and procedure—Complaint for annulment— Form⊚

[Title of Court]

[Caption]   Case No. [_____]
                                            COMPLAINT

1. Plaintiff has been a resident of Ohio for at least six months immediately preceding the filing of this complaint.

---

[8]RC 2311.21.

[9]Porter v. Lerch, 129 Ohio St. 47, 1 Ohio Op. 356, 193 N.E. 766 (1934); accord Coffman v. Finney, 65 Ohio St. 61, 61 N.E. 155 (1901).

[10]Delaney v. Delaney, 102 Ohio App. 249, 2 Ohio Op. 2d 271, 73 Ohio L. Abs. 545, 133 N.E.2d 915 (8th Dist. Cuyahoga County 1956).

[11]Porter v. Porter, 25 Ohio St. 2d 123, 54 Ohio Op. 2d 260, 267 N.E.2d 299 (1971).

[12]See Text §§ 7:16 to 7:21, Relief incident to annulment.

2.   Plaintiff and Defendant were married at *[city]*, Ohio, on *[date]*, and there are *[no/number of children]* children as issue of such marriage, namely, *[name(s) and date(s) of birth of children]*.

3.   Plaintiff says that [grounds pursuant to RC 3105.31].

Wherefore, Plaintiff demands that *[she/he]* be granted an annulment from Defendant and be named residential parent and legal custodian of their minor *[child/children]*; that *[she/he]* be granted reasonable spousal support and support for their minor *[child/children]*; [that she be restored to her former name of *[former name]*;] and for costs herein, including a reasonable sum for expenses and attorney fees in this action, and for such other relief as shall be proper and necessary.

_____

Attorney for Plaintiff

NOTES TO FORM

Drafter's Notes

A long form caption should be used on the complaint.

Under his/her signature on the complaint, counsel should list his/her business address, Supreme Court registration number, and phone number.

If service other than pursuant to Civ. R. 4 is desired, a written request for service (usually a court form) should accompany the complaint when it is filed.

A RC 3127.23 affidavit (court form) should accompany the initial filing where there are minor children of the marriage.

As in other civil cases, the complaint in a domestic relations matter may plead in the alternative, i.e., for annulment or legal separation, or for annulment or divorce.

§ 7:38   Practice and procedure—Complaint for annulment by minor plaintiff—Form⊚

[Title of Court]

[Caption]   Case No. *[_____]*

COMPLAINT

1.   Plaintiff, a minor, brings this action by *[name]*, *[his/her]* parent and next friend.

2.   Plaintiff has been a resident of Ohio for at least six months immediately preceding the filing of this complaint.

3.   On *[date]*, at the time of *[his/her]* marriage, Plaintiff was [grounds for annulment pursuant to RC 3105.31].

4.   There is no issue of such marriage.

WHEREFORE, Plaintiff demands a judgment of the Court annulling the marriage between Plaintiff and Defendant, costs and such other relief as the Court may deem proper.

_____
Attorney for Plaintiff

NOTES TO FORM

Drafter's Notes

Caption should have name of minor, with designation as minor, and name of parent and/or next friend as plaintiff.

§ 7:39 Practice and procedure—Judgment entry granting decree of annulment—Form⊚

[Title of Court]

[Caption]

Case No. *[_____]*
<u>JUDGMENT ENTRY</u>

This cause came on for hearing this *[date]*, upon the complaint of Plaintiff and the evidence, Defendant being in default of answer or other pleading although duly served with process according to law.

Upon due consideration thereof, the Court finds that the parties were purportedly married as alleged, and that *[no/number]* *[child was/children were]* legally born of the marriage.

The Court further finds that *[statutory ground upon which annulment was rendered]* and that by reason thereof Plaintiff is entitled to an annulment of said marriage;

IT IS THEREFORE ORDERED, ADJUDGED AND DECREED THAT:

1. The said marriage contract be and the same is hereby canceled and declared null and void as of the date of said marriage.

2. The Plaintiff be named the residential parent and legal custodian of the minor *[child/children]* until further order of Court, with visitation to Defendant as follows: *[state visitation provisions]*.

3. Defendant pay to Plaintiff the sum of $*[dollar amount]* per month towards the support and maintenance of the minor *[child/children]*, plus all reasonable medical, dental and hospital expenses, until further order of Court. Payment of support shall be made, plus processing charge, by payroll withholding through the Child Support Enforcement Agency, *[address]*.

4. Except as expressly provided to the contrary herein, Plaintiff and Defendant are fully released and discharged from said marriage contract.

5. Defendant pay the costs of this proceeding for which sum judgment is rendered and execution may issue.

_____

Judge

Approved:

_____

Attorney for Plaintiff

_____

Attorney for Defendant

Chapter 8

Legal Separation

By Stanley Morganstern, Esq.*

KeyCite®: Cases and other legal materials listed in KeyCite Scope can be researched through the KeyCite service on Westlaw®. Use KeyCite to check citations for form, parallel references, prior and later history, and comprehensive citator information, including citations to other decisions and secondary materials.

---

§ 8:1 "Alimony only" now "legal separation"

Effective January 1, 1991, RC 3105.17 was amended. All references to "alimony only" as a proceeding were replaced by the term "legal separation," a term found to be more familiar than "alimony only." RC 3105.17(A) allows a court to grant a legal separation for the following causes:

(1) Either party had a husband or wife living at the time of the marriage from which legal separation is sought;

(2) Willful absence of the adverse party for one year;

(3) Adultery;

(4) Extreme cruelty;

(5) Fraudulent contract;

(6) Any gross neglect of duty;

(7) Habitual drunkenness;

(8) Imprisonment of the adverse party in a state or federal correctional institution at the time of filing the complaint;

(9) On the application of either party, when husband and wife have, without interruption for one year, lived separate and apart without cohabitation;

---

*Based on the 1984 Edition by Hon. Patrick F. Gallagher.

(10) Incompatibility, unless denied by either party.

RC 3105.17(B) provides:

The filing of a complaint or counterclaim for legal separation or the granting of a decree of legal separation under this section does not bar either party from filing a complaint or counterclaim for a divorce or annulment or obtaining a divorce or annulment.

Civil Rule 75 was amended, effective July 1, 1991, to reflect the change in terminology from "alimony only" to "legal separation," as were numerous local court rules.

§ 8:2   Nature of action, jurisdiction

While RC 3105.03 states that plaintiffs in divorce and annulment actions must have been residents of the state for at least six months prior to filing an action, there is no such limitation for actions for legal separation. The statute only requires that an action for legal separation be brought in the proper county pursuant to Civil Rule 3(B)(1) to (13).

In *Taylor v. Taylor*,[1] the wife's complaint for legal separation was dismissed by the trial court for failing to satisfy the residency rule of Civil Rule 3(B)(9). The court of appeals reversed, holding that where there was no other county under Civil Rules 3(B)(1) to 3(B)(9) where venue would be proper, the plaintiff could avail herself of Civil Rule 3(B)(11), even though her residency prior to filing in Montgomery County was only eighteen days.

Jurisdiction for spousal support in a legal separation action is found in RC 3105.18, which specifically authorizes a court to award spousal support. Spousal support pursuant to a divorce is also subject to this section, and is discussed elsewhere.[2]

RC 3105.17 provides that legal separation is available regardless of whether the parties are living separately at the time the complaint is filed. At the time of the final hearing the parties must be living separate and apart in order for the separation and spousal support to be awarded. If they are not living separately, legal separation would be an incorrect remedy.

Eight of the ten grounds for a legal separation award include an element of intentional/willful fault on the part of the defendant.[3] Abandonment is no longer a ground for legal separation. Willful absence for one year or the parties living separate and apart for one year will constitute sufficient grounds as in the divorce statute.[4] In-

---

[Section 8:2]

[1]Taylor v. Taylor, 84 Ohio App. 3d 445, 616 N.E.2d 1199 (2d Dist. Montgomery County 1992).

[2]See Text Ch 13, Spousal Support.

[3]RC 3105.17.

[4]RC 3105.01.

compatibility, unless denied by the other party, is also available.[5] Ill treatment by the adverse party has also been eliminated as a ground for legal separation by the amendment to RC 3105.17.[6]

A legal separation decree does not have the effect of terminating the marriage and, in that respect, the public interest in requiring a "cooling-off" period between the filing of a complaint and the final decree may be less than for a divorce. Nonetheless, Civil Rule 75(K) requires a forty-two-day period and such period is nonwaivable,[7] even though other statutory requirements are less stringent. The defenses of recrimination and condonation, although not specifically eliminated by RC 3105.10(C), are not available in a legal separation action.[8]

In *Zhao v. Zeng*,[9] the court held that Husband's complaint for legal separation should not have been dismissed by reason of the "jurisdictional priority rule," as wife had filed for a divorce in China. The rule only pertains to state courts with concurrent jurisdiction. On remand, the trial court was instructed to consider whether to apply the doctrine of forum convenience.

Foreign divorce decrees may be recognized under the principle of comity, therefore divesting a court of jurisdiction to hear a complaint for legal separation. In *Yu v. Zhang*,[10] a trial court lacked jurisdiction to hear a claim for legal separation because the parties had previously been divorced in China. The parties were married in China and husband moved to the United States in 1992. Wife subsequently moved to the United States in 2000. A divorce was granted in China on October 17, 2000, although Wife testified that she was unaware of the proceedings. Wife argued that the Ohio court should not recognize the Chinese divorce decree because husband lacked jurisdiction to file in China, as neither party resided there at the time the divorce was granted. Wife was unable to refute evidence that the Chinese divorce was commenced prior to her move to the United States. The trial court recognized the Chinese divorce under the principle of comity, found that the Chinese court had subject matter jurisdiction to hear the complaint, and dismissed wife's complaint for legal separation.

---

[5]RC 3105.17(A)(10).

[6]1990 H.B. 514. See Maughan v. Maughan, 21 Ohio Op. 2d 121, 89 Ohio L. Abs. 282, 184 N.E.2d 628 (C.P. 1961); Picker v. Picker, 46 Ohio App. 82, 16 Ohio L. Abs. 64, 187 N.E. 749 (6th Dist. Sandusky County 1933).

[7]Robinette v. Robinette, 41 Ohio App. 3d 25, 534 N.E.2d 386 (5th Dist. Licking County 1988) (original complaint for alimony alone was filed with waiver of service and on same day trial court granted decree of alimony, with judgment approved by both parties; decree had ordered conveyance of real property, provisions for distributions of proceeds of sale, other orders respecting property, and periodic support).

[8]Allen v. Allen, 1989 WL 30738 (Ohio Ct. App. 12th Dist. Butler County 1989).

[9]Zhao v. Zeng, 2003-Ohio-3060, 2003 WL 21360804 (Ohio Ct. App. 1st Dist. Hamilton County 2003).

[10]Yu v. Zhang, 175 Ohio App. 3d 83, 2008-Ohio-400, 885 N.E.2d 278 (2d Dist. Greene County 2008)

In *Kvinta v. Kvinta*,[11] the court found that the trial court correctly held it had in rem jurisdiction to grant wife's complaint for legal separation and award her spousal support from marital property in Ohio although not having personal jurisdiction over husband. There was sufficient evidence to establish a common law marriage and the trial court did not err in using the presumptive statutory trial date rather than an earlier de facto termination date.

If a later files a complaint for divorce after obtaining a legal separation, any jurisdictional issues arising during the legal separation cannot be re-litigated. In *Kvinta v. Kvinta*,[12] wife subsequently filed a complaint for divorce in a different county from where she acquired a decree of legal separation, attempting to re-litigate issues of personal jurisdiction pursuant to the long-arm statute. The Fifth District Court of Appeals held that wife could not re-litigate jurisdictional issues prior to the legal separation as they are *res judicata*, but the trial court could determine if it acquired jurisdiction over husband during the time between the journalization of the legal separation decree and the divorce filing.

Further, parties may be added to the divorce proceedings who were not part of the original legal separation proceedings. It is alleged that husband had remarried during the course of the proceedings. In the *Kvinta* divorce action, wife named husband's purported new wife as a defendant, although she did not reside in the State of Ohio, in order to divide a Charles Schwab brokerage account that had been transferred to purported wife by husband. Purported new wife admitted that she paid nothing for the transfer of the Charles Schwab brokerage account into her name and that the purpose of the transfer was to defeat or eliminate any claims wife may have had to the account. The Court of Appeals held that the trial court had personal jurisdiction over purported wife under Ohio Civil Rule 4.3(A)(9), as she caused tortious injury by an act outside of the State of Ohio that she would reasonably expect may injure a resident of the State. The trial court's determination that the account was marital property and award of half of the account to wife was upheld.

§ 8:3   Legal separation versus divorce

Both legal separation and divorce actions can provide temporary and continuing support. The major difference is that after a legal separation action the parties remain married. This presents the applicant with the practical problem of choice of remedy. Since there is no jurisdictional residency time requirement prior to filing a legal separation action, it is occasionally used for immediate relief, such as a restraining order or temporary order, until the complaint can be

---

[11]Kvinta v. Kvinta, 2003-Ohio-2884, 2003 WL 2129049 (Ohio Ct. App. 10th Dist. Franklin County 2003).

[12]Kvinta v. Kvinta, 2009-Ohio-828, 2009 WL 449145 (Ohio Ct. App. 5th Dist. Richland County 2009), appeal not allowed, 122 Ohio St. 3d 1456, 2009-Ohio-3131, 908 N.E.2d 946 (2009)

amended to a divorce. However, if a party violates a restraining order in a legal separation action that is subsequently dismissed, the other party does not have any remedy to have the property returned in a subsequently filed divorce action even though the other party violated the court order. In *Michelson v. Michelson*,[1] Husband filed an action for legal separation and the trial court issued temporary restraining orders preventing either party from disposing of assets during the pendency of the litigation. The complaint for legal separation was dismissed for lack of prosecution. Wife subsequently filed for divorce. Before temporary restraining orders were imposed, Husband died. Wife learned that she was no longer the named beneficiary on Husband's life insurance policies, and that the beneficiary designation had been changed while the temporary restraining orders in the legal separation action had been in effect. Wife argued that she was entitled to the proceeds of the life insurance policies because the judicial prohibition against the change in beneficiary was in force at the time it was changed. The Sixth District Court of Appeals held that the dismissal of the legal separation complaint removed all claims that arose from the court's jurisdiction and placed the parties in a position as if no suit had ever been brought.

The first factor to be considered in deciding what remedies to request is whether the applicant wants to continue or terminate the marriage. The cooperation of the defendant is a major consideration. While the applicant may wish to preserve the marriage, there is nothing to prevent the defendant/respondent from cross-complaining for divorce. If the defendant proves the grounds alleged in the cross-complaint for divorce, a divorce will be granted.[2] The Eleventh District Court of Appeals held that when granting a legal separation the trial court should consider the parties estates, particularly where there are children from a previous marriage. The best interests of the parties' overall are to be considered. A trial court has discretion to deny a divorce and grant a legal separation even though grounds for divorce have been proven.[3]

The court may also grant a divorce where one party seeks a legal separation and the other a divorce. Where wife sought a legal separation on the grounds of gross neglect of duty and husband sought a

---

[Section 8:3]

[1]Michelson v. McMillan, 2006-Ohio-3063, 2006 WL 1667744 (Ohio Ct. App. 6th Dist. Williams County 2006).

[2]Brennan v. Brennan, 1995 WL 803613 (Ohio Ct. App. 11th Dist. Portage County 1995). But see Duffy v. Duffy, 1994 WL 476456 (Ohio Ct. App. 5th Dist. Licking County 1994) (husband did not present evidence in support of grounds for divorce so court awarded wife a legal separation).

[3]Mahon v. Mahon, 1999 WL 1483438 (Ohio Ct. App. 11th Dist. Trumbull County 1999).

divorce on the same grounds, the trial court did not err in granting the divorce. The marriage had been deteriorating for a long time.[4]

The various advantages of the marriage relationship may have some impact on the choice of remedy. For example, a wife may be covered by her husband's medical insurance policy, which may be far less expensive to maintain than two separate policies. Congress attempted to alleviate the impact of loss of coverage of employee's beneficiaries by enacting the Consolidated Omnibus Budget Reconciliation Act (COBRA), effective July 1, 1986.[5] Under COBRA, the former spouse may elect to continue to be covered with the same group policy and benefits as the employed spouse. The problem is that the maximum period of coverage is thirty-six months. Beyond the thirty-six months, the nonemployed spouse may be able to convert group policy coverage to individual coverage (without any gap in coverage, thus assuring coverage for preexisting conditions) but at an increased rate with fewer benefits.

The parties may want to continue the marriage in order to assure that life insurance, annuity, retirement, or payable-on-death account benefits will be payable as intended. Prior to May 31, 1990, a divorce alone did not automatically defeat the rights of a named beneficiary. Subsequent to that date, however, there is a revocation of spousal beneficiary by operation of law. Unless the decree provides otherwise or there is a renaming after the marriage termination, the designated beneficiary spouse is deemed to have predeceased the designating spouse.[6]

A very important consideration is the loss or retention of spousal benefits for disability, medicare, and/or retirement under the social security laws.[7] The law permits the divorced spouse to be eligible for such benefits based on the credits of the other spouse. In effect, this is to protect the standard working husband and homemaker/wife, where the husband, as the worker, has such credits to his name, but the homemaker/wife, who is technically unemployed in the labor force, obtains no credits of her own. Thus, in the event of the termination of the marriage, the husband retains his credits, but the wife, after the divorce, as a legal stranger, is left with no social security credit. The current law permits such a wife to be eligible for benefits as a spouse in the event of a sustained ten-year marriage.[8] For a wife who is approaching retirement, in ill health, or otherwise unemployable, and who has been married nine years, it may be more advantageous to

---

[4]Pelanda v. Pelanda, 2002-Ohio-1123, 2002 WL 398667 (Ohio Ct. App. 5th Dist. Delaware County 2002).

[5]Pub. L. No. 99-272, 100 Stat. 82 (1986) (amended various sections of 26 U.S.C.A.).

[6]Former RC 1339.63, now RC 5815.33.

[7]See Text Ch 29, Government Retirement Benefits.

[8]42 U.S.C.A. § 402, 42 U.S.C.A. § 416. See also 20 C.F.R. § 404.331, 20 C.F.R. § 404.336.

elect the legal separation action, at least until such time as the social security benefits vest in the wife.

In *Tedrow v. Tedrow*,[9] the Court of Appeals held that the trial court erred in refusing to grant husband a divorce when the evidence was clear that the parties had lived separate and apart for more than one year. Wife was granted a legal separation primarily because of her ill health and the trial court's conclusions that medical coverage for her could not be obtained at a reasonable cost and that drug costs would be prohibitive if husband's provided health care coverage terminated.

The Court of Appeals held that the record did not sufficiently support the trial court's findings. While the granting of a legal separation instead of a divorce may be justified in "some rare instances", the ruling must be supported by clear and unequivocal evidence as such a ruling deprives the party seeking a divorce the right to marry in the future.

Religious beliefs may be a significant consideration in the election. It may be that the applicant subscribes to a religion that does not permit divorce, or only permits it under certain conditions, such as for adultery. Where this situation exists, the choice for the applicant is narrowed.

Often, a party will choose to file a complaint for legal separation, rather than request a divorce, because health care coverage is either unavailable or cost prohibitive for that individual. When issues of health care are involved, a court of appeals may defer to a trial court's decision to grant a legal separation rather than grant the other party's request for a divorce. However, such a ruling must be clearly and unequivocally supported by evidence in the record that health care coverage was clearly not available or affordable post decree, since the party seeking the divorce is deprived of the right to marry in the future.[10]

Possible reconciliation or reform of an errant spouse may be another consideration. If the only requirement or preference of the applicant is for support, reconciliation may be the better remedy.

Another consideration may be the retention of the marital status while the homemaker/wife engages in vocational rehabilitation. When and if the marriage terminates, she will better be able to become and remain independent.

There are other considerations; those listed are only the major ones. If and when a spouse, especially a homemaker/wife, is seeking advice on a divorce or other remedy with respect to her present marital problems, the choice of legal separation should be considered as a viable alternative to absolute termination.

---

[9]Tedrow v. Tedrow, 2003-Ohio-3693, 2003 WL 21638280 (Ohio Ct. App. 11th Dist. Trumbull County 2003).

[10]Tedrow v. Tedrow, 2003-Ohio-3693, 2003 WL 21638280 (Ohio Ct. App. 11th Dist. Trumbull County 2003); Sabo v. Sabo, 2003-Ohio-6586, 2003 WL 22900633 (Ohio Ct. App. 9th Dist. Lorain County 2003).

§ 8:4 Spousal support and division of property

Prior to the amendment of RC 3105.18, effective January 1, 1991, Ohio courts regarded the term "alimony" as synonymous with a division of property belonging to the parties at the time of the separation.[1] The Ohio alimony statute concerning property distribution authorized the court to liquidate the marriage and to distribute marital assets and liabilities.[2] Such a judgment was neither void nor subject to collateral attack.[3]

However, a 1980 court of appeals decision, *Turek v. Turek*,[4] held that a domestic relations court was without authority to make a division of property in an alimony only action. This holding appeared to be erroneous, but there was merit in the public policy arguments put forth in *Turek*. RC 3105.10(E) empowered the court to award real estate to one party in an alimony proceeding and to bar the other party from exercising the rights of dower. The fact that the legislature enacted a section specifically for real estate implied that the court could allocate other property.[5]

The view of the Ohio Supreme Court was that an alimony only action permitted division of property as well as support alimony.[6] The better view should have been to recognize the court's jurisdiction and to permit the division of marital property. Because of the generally unusual circumstances of each situation (especially one that would cause a party to elect legal separation rather than divorce), the division of marital property should have been a matter of judicial discretion, but with such discretion to be exercised in light of the public policy view of *Turek*.

While the court could make a property division, it was permissive and not necessarily a condition precedent to an award of spousal sup-

---

[Section 8:4]

[1]Desjardins v. Desjardins, 193 F. Supp. 210, 16 Ohio Op. 2d 226, 4 Fed. R. Serv. 2d 80 (E.D. Ky. 1961), judgment modified, 308 F.2d 111, 22 Ohio Op. 2d 98, 91 Ohio L. Abs. 111 (6th Cir. 1962).

[2]See William Louis Tabac, *Alimony and Child Support in Ohio: New Directions After Dissolution,* 26 Clev. St. L. Rev. 395 (1977).

[3]Wade v. Wade, 1982 WL 2920 (Ohio Ct. App. 5th Dist. Stark County 1982).

[4]Turek v. Turek., 1980 WL 355488 (Ohio Ct. App. 8th Dist. Cuyahoga County 1980).

[5]RC 3105.10(E), as enacted by 1974 H.B. 233, eff. 9-23-74.

[6]See Griste v. Griste, 171 Ohio St. 160, 12 Ohio Op. 2d 176, 167 N.E.2d 924 (1960); Goetzel v. Goetzel, 169 Ohio St. 350, 8 Ohio Op. 2d 355, 159 N.E.2d 751 (1959); Brewer v. Brewer, 117 Ohio App. 263, 24 Ohio Op. 2d 60, 183 N.E.2d 250 (1st Dist. Warren County 1962); Turek v. Turek., 1980 WL 355488 (Ohio Ct. App. 8th Dist. Cuyahoga County 1980). See also Crum v. Howard, 1 Ohio Op. 2d 399, 73 Ohio L. Abs. 111, 137 N.E.2d 654 (C.P. 1956); Cable v. Cable, 57 Ohio Op. 495, 70 Ohio L. Abs. 187, 127 N.E.2d 433 (C.P. 1955) (implied in judgment even though denied on the facts). But see Hetrick v. Hetrick, 101 Ohio App. 334, 1 Ohio Op. 2d 282, 139 N.E.2d 674 (6th Dist. Ottawa County 1954); Martin v. Martin, 1979 WL 210624 (Ohio Ct. App. 8th Dist. Cuyahoga County 1979).

port under RC 3105.17 before its amendment in 1991.[7] RC 3105.18(B) now requires that there be a division of property before the court considers the issue of spousal support.

While Ohio case law was divided as to whether a trial court could make distribution of property in a legal separation proceeding under the statute prior to January 1, 1991, the court may now make a determination as to what constitutes marital or separate property on the request of either party.[8] A party to a legal separation claiming that property to be divided should be characterized as separate bears the burden of proof to establish the validity of his or her claim, however, oral testimony without documentary evidence may suffice to identify specific property as the separate property of one spouse.[9] If the court does make such determination, the distribution is to be equitable.[10] The duration of the marriage is to be determined in accordance with RC 3105.171(A)(2).[11]

§ 8:5 Determination of need, amount

After the determination of the division of property, the court may award spousal support under RC 3105.18.[1] Jurisdiction to award spousal support is found in RC 3105.18. The factors to be analyzed in determining need and amount of spousal support are set forth in RC 3105.18. The factors are the same whether or not the marriage is being terminated and are fully discussed in the spousal support chapter.[2] Likewise, an award of attorney fees in a legal separation action is governed by RC 3105.18(H).[3]

A trial court does not abuse its discretion by declining to set a specific termination date for a spousal support award in a legal separation and retains jurisdiction over the issue of spousal support. In *Gordon v. Gordon*,[4] the trial court granted the parties a legal separation, after the parties had resolved all issues except for spousal

---

[7]Poulias v. Poulias, 1986 WL 723 (Ohio Ct. App. 12th Dist. Butler County 1986).

[8]RC 3105.171(B).

[9]Gosser v. Gosser, 2007-Ohio-3201, 2007 WL 1810521 (Ohio Ct. App. 11th Dist. Trumbull County 2007), appeal not allowed, 116 Ohio St. 3d 1438, 2007-Ohio-6518, 877 N.E.2d 990 (2007).

[10]Leathem v. Leathem, 94 Ohio App. 3d 470, 640 N.E.2d 1210 (3d Dist. Hancock County 1994).

[11]King v. King, 1997 WL 106898 (Ohio Ct. App. 4th Dist. Washington County 1997); Parr v. Parr, 1997 WL 97231 (Ohio Ct. App. 8th Dist. Cuyahoga County 1997).

[Section 8:5]

[1]For a full discussion of RC 3105.171 and RC 3105.18 as they relate to divorce and legal separation actions see Text Ch 13, Spousal Support.

[2]For a full discussion of RC 3105.171 and RC 3105.18 as they relate to divorce and legal separation actions see Text Ch 13, Spousal Support.

[3]DeLevie v. DeLevie, 1997 WL 35537 (Ohio Ct. App. 10th Dist. Franklin County 1997); Bauer v. Bauer, 1997 WL 72113 (Ohio Ct. App. 6th Dist. Wood County 1997).

[4]Gordon v. Gordon, 2006-Ohio-51, 2006 WL 39069 (Ohio Ct. App. 11th Dist. Trumbull County 2006).

support. The evidence established that although the parties' son had reached the age of majority, he had a mental disability and functioned at the intelligence level of a five year old. Wife had to provide continuous care for the son and his special needs prevented her from acquiring employment. Husband was ordered to pay spousal support to Wife due to these circumstances. Husband appealed the trial court's decision, arguing that the court abused its discretion by failing to specify a termination date for the spousal support award. The Eleventh District Court of Appeals held that absent the resources, ability and potential to be self supporting, a termination date is not required.[5]

§ 8:6 Parental rights and child support

A trial court in a legal separation case has the same power and duty it has in a divorce case to make an order with regard to the disposition of the children of the marriage. This duty is imposed on the trial court by RC 3105.21 and RC 3109.04.

The court can make an order upon a request for determination of parental rights and responsibilities for the minor children which is included with the complaint for legal separation.[1] In a case where there is no request for determination of parental rights and responsibilities, the court still has a duty to make a disposition with regard to the care and custody of the minor children of the marriage. In addition, when the court does not grant the complaint for divorce or legal separation because of failure to prove grounds, the court still may make an order for the disposition and care of the children. Before the enactment of present RC 3105.21,[2] the court was without jurisdiction to make an order regarding the care and custody of children when complaints for divorce or legal separation were denied.[3] Now, the duty is clearly mandatory when a divorce is granted and discretionary when the divorce grounds fail.[4]

In most cases, the parties to a legal separation action are living separate and apart, and it only makes sense that a determination regarding the disposition of the children be made in order to provide for their best interests. The duty of the court as set out in RC 3105.21

---

[5]Gordon v. Gordon, 2006-Ohio-51, 2006 WL 39069 (Ohio Ct. App. 11th Dist. Trumbull County 2006).

[Section 8:6]

[1]Gasior v. Gasior, 67 Ohio App. 84, 21 Ohio Op. 105, 35 N.E.2d 1021 (6th Dist. Lucas County 1940); Hiler v. Hiler, 14 Ohio App. 174, 1921 WL 1093 (1st Dist. Butler County 1921); Bignell v. Bignell, 1997 WL 254150 (Ohio Ct. App. 2d Dist. Greene County 1997).

[2]1974 H.B. 233, eff. 9-23-74.

[3]Lewis v. Lewis, 103 Ohio App. 129, 3 Ohio Op. 2d 199, 144 N.E.2d 887 (2d Dist. Fayette County 1956); Whitecotton v. Whitecotton, 103 Ohio App. 149, 3 Ohio Op. 2d 210, 144 N.E.2d 678 (6th Dist. Lucas County 1955).

[4]RC 3105.21; Matthews v. Matthews, 37 Ohio L. Abs. 283, 46 N.E.2d 833 (Ct. App. 9th Dist. Summit County 1940); Lewis v. Lewis, 103 Ohio App. 129, 3 Ohio Op. 2d 199, 144 N.E.2d 887 (2d Dist. Fayette County 1956).

and RC 3109.04 is clear. Civil Rule 75(M) addresses temporary custody and support during the pendency of an action. Temporary orders may be granted when properly requested in a legal separation action.[5]

The difficulty arises when the parties to a legal separation action are still living together and the judge grants temporary residential parent status to one parent over the other, even though they are both in the home. There is no statutory requirement that the parties be living separate and apart before the court has a duty to make a disposition with regard to the care and custody of the children. Following the best interests of the child standard set out in RC 3105.21, the court should make a decision as to the care and custody of the children.[6] The "best interests of the child" provision of RC 3105.21 refers to the criteria of RC 3109.04. The court can grant shared parenting to both parents, award custody to one or the other, or award custody to a relative.[7] As in a divorce case the court has continuing jurisdiction over the custody of these children in subsequent proceedings.[8]

A court can allocate parental rights and responsibilities to a nonparent if there is evidence that the natural parents are unsuitable pursuant to In re Perales, 52 Ohio St. 2d 89, 6 Ohio Op. 3d 293, 369 N.E.2d 1047 (1977). In Riley v. Riley,[9] mother and father obtained a legal separation. Mother passed away and maternal grandmother sought custody of the parties' child. The parties entered into an agreement providing that grandmother would have temporary custody of the child in May 2006. In August 2006, father filed a motion seeking to allocate parental rights and responsibilities solely to him. The trial court did not find father to be unsuitable and granted father's motion for custody. Grandmother appealed, arguing that *Perales* does not apply in an action which originated from a complaint for legal separation, therefore the best interest test contained in RC 3109.04(D)(2) should have been applied. The *Riley* court noted that a trial court must first make a finding of parental unsuitability in a child custody case between a natural parent and a nonparent. The Court of Appeals disagreed with grandmother's assertion that only the best interest standard should be utilized. The Court of Appeals found that the trial court apparently believed that returning the child to father would serve her best interest and it would not be in the child's best interest

---

[5]Office v. Office, 1997 WL 18043 (Ohio Ct. App. 2d Dist. Montgomery County 1997).

[6]See, e.g., Ham. R. 15.0, which states that custody and support orders are not to be granted when parties are in the same household.

[7]See Text Ch 15, Parental Rights and Shared Parenting; Text Ch 19, Child Support.

[8]See Text Ch 15, Parental Rights and Shared Parenting; Text Ch 16, Modification of Parental Rights and Responsibilities.

[9]Riley v. Riley, 2008-Ohio-859, 2008 WL 556818 (Ohio Ct. App. 4th Dist. Washington County 2008), appeal not allowed, 119 Ohio St. 3d 1444, 2008-Ohio-4487, 893 N.E.2d 516 (2008).

to return the child to an unsuitable parent. As a result, the trial court's decision was affirmed.

§ 8:7 Effect of decree

A decree of legal separation essentially reaffirms the marital status, indicates that the defendant has been committing wrongful acts against the plaintiff, and orders the defendant to treat the plaintiff differently in the future. It would be very difficult to conceptualize a post-decree situation where the parties continue to live together. Therefore, the decree has one essential element: that the plaintiff, although still married, has the right to live separate and apart from the defendant, with legal permission to deny/refuse marital rights, without the denial/refusal being later considered as grounds for a divorce. On the other hand, the defendant has been severed from his or her marital rights but not from his or her marital obligations, and it is questionable whether the fact of the severance can later be used as grounds for divorce.[1] The majority of the court of appeals approved the granting of a divorce to husband on the ground of having lived separate and apart for more than one year under RC 3105.01(J). A decree of legal separation had been rendered in favor of wife several months before husband filed for divorce. He had been denied a divorce in the first case. Judge Harsha, dissenting, would have denied the divorce as the separation was legally sanctioned by a court of another county. The fact of the separation, legal or not, as long as it is de facto, is sufficient grounds for a divorce pursuant to RC 3105.01(J).

Parental rights and child support awarded in a legal separation action are modifiable and enforceable in that action, the court having assumed jurisdiction. Similarly, any division of property is res judicata and not subject to subsequent modification.[2] Since spousal support provisions in a legal separation are subject to modification under RC 3105.18(D), a subsequent action for divorce could ostensibly have jurisdiction limited to marital status.

Where there is a complaint for legal separation and a counterclaim for divorce, it was held in *Hobbs v. Hobbs*[3] that the dismissal of the divorce complaint does not prevent an award of legal separation. It should be noted, however, that the case was decided prior to the enactment of RC 3105.01(J). Thus, if the counterclaim is for reasons other than living separate and apart, there is always the risk of dismissal.

[Section 8:7]

[1]Payton v. Payton, 1997 WL 354797 (Ohio Ct. App. 4th Dist. Scioto County 1997).

[2]Hirt v. Hirt, 2006-Ohio-2851, 2006 WL 1544322 (Ohio Ct. App. 9th Dist. Medina County 2006) (Wife was granted a legal separation in which the duration of the marriage was determined and the family business' stock was assigned a value. Wife was precluded from relitigating these issues when Husband filed for divorce due to the doctrines of res judicata and issue preclusion.).

[3]Hobbs v. Hobbs, 115 Ohio App. 536, 21 Ohio Op. 2d 200, 186 N.E.2d 134 (2d Dist. Greene County 1961).

Considering that the nature of the decree is to sustain the marriage, it is no surprise to find a decision that terminated the spousal support when the recipient spouse engaged in marital misconduct.[4] It may be assumed that any conduct by the recipient spouse that is contrary to the marital contract, other than mere legal separation, would be evidence that the plaintiff was no longer concerned about the marriage per se, but only about the support. Although the statute does not expressly so provide, this could easily be a changed circumstance with respect to spousal support modification.[5]

Counsel should consider the possibility that one of the spouses may die during the period of legal separation. There is a split among the jurisdictions regarding whether a legal separation terminates the rights of a surviving spouse. The Second District Court of Appeals has held that a separation agreement incorporated into a decree of legal separation which does not specifically provide a release of the right of each party to take against the other's will does not prohibit such an election.[6] However, in the case In Re: Estate of Ramminger, the surviving spouse applied for a family allowance pursuant to RC 2106.13 after his deceased wife's will was admitted to probate.[7] The Twelfth District Court of Appeals held that, although a judgment entry granting a legal separation fails to include a clause waiving the rights of a surviving spouse to participate in the deceased spouse's estate, the grant of a legal separation implicitly terminates such rights. Also, in Hering v. Hering, the trial court granted a legal separation without including a provision waiving the rights of the surviving spouse in the decree.[8] The Ninth District Court of Appeals found that, except where there is contrary language in a will, termination of the rights of a surviving spouse is implicit in the grant of a legal separation pursuant to RC 2107.33(D). As a result, the trial court did not need to include an express provision waiving said rights in the final legal separation decree.

Further, a court may retroactively grant a legal separation if one of the parties dies prior to journalization of the final legal separation decree. In Ramminger v. Ramminger, the Twelfth District Court of Appeals held that a trial court may enter a nunc pro tunc entry granting a legal separation back to a date prior to the death of one of the

---

[4]Bishop v. Bishop, 18 Ohio Misc. 177, 47 Ohio Op. 2d 417, 248 N.E.2d 641 (C.P. 1969).

[5]Neal v. Neal, 53 Ohio L. Abs. 329, 85 N.E.2d 147 (C.P. 1949).

[6]In Re: Estate of Robinson, 1985 WL 6929 (Ohio Ct. App. 2d Dist. Greene County 1985).

[7]In re Estate of Ramminger, 2003-Ohio-3697, 2003 WL 21637943 (Ohio Ct. App. 12th Dist. Butler County 2003).

[8]Hering v. Hering, 2005-Ohio-262, 2005 WL 161171 (Ohio Ct. App. 9th Dist. Lorain County 2005).

parties.[9] In *Ramminger,* the matter had been adjudicated but not journalized prior to the death.

A final decree of legal separation is a final judgment, subject to appeal. If it is not appealed within thirty days, it is res judicata as to the issues decided which could have been appealed and which are not modifiable.

§ 8:8 Enforcement and modification

Once a spousal support award has been made in a legal separation decree, it is enforced as any other spousal support award. As to periodic payments of support, it is subject to the provisions of 1986 House Bill 509, effective December 1, 1986, requiring payments to be made, plus processing change, through the child support enforcement agency.[1] Property division provisions are enforced in the same manner as in a decree of divorce.[2]

RC 3105.18(D) specifically grants continuing jurisdiction in cases brought under RC 3105.17 for legal separation as to periodic payments, for review or modification on changed circumstances of either party. That power, however, is limited to the court that originally made the order and retained jurisdiction to modify the spousal support award.[3]

In *Mikluscak v. Mikluscak,*[4] a decree of legal separation was entered and a subsequent divorce decree recognized and referred to the prior decree. It ordered that the legal separation orders of spousal support and maintenance of a hospitalization plan should remain in force, but did not incorporate the prior decree. The appellate court affirmed the trial court's later modification of the hospitalization provision. The court found that the provision was modifiable under either the earlier decree of legal separation or the subsequent divorce decree. The Second District Court of Appeals in *Eversole v. Eversole*[5] held that a trial court must consider matters of spousal support, child support, custody, and debt allocation in a divorce action filed subsequent to the conclusion of a legal separation action. The finalization of the divorce

---

[9]Ramminger v. Ramminger, 2001 WL 649757 (Ohio Ct. App. 12th Dist. Butler County 2001).

[Section 8:8]

[1]See Text Ch 20, Enforcement of Spousal and Child Support; Jacobs v. Jacobs, 1988 WL 140559 (Ohio Ct. App. 8th Dist. Cuyahoga County 1988).

[2]See Text Ch 20, Enforcement of Spousal and Child Support; Jacobs v. Jacobs, 1988 WL 140559 (Ohio Ct. App. 8th Dist. Cuyahoga County 1988).

[3]Payton v. Payton, 1997 WL 354797 (Ohio Ct. App. 4th Dist. Scioto County 1997).

[4]Mikluscak v. Mikluscak, 1988 WL 30524 (Ohio Ct. App. 8th Dist. Cuyahoga County 1988).

[5]Eversole v. Eversole, 1989 WL 94556 (Ohio Ct. App. 2d Dist. Montgomery County 1989).

action rendered the prior legal separation decree void.[6] However, the Fourth District Court of Appeals, noting that divorce and legal separation are distinct actions, concluded that an award of spousal support made by one court cannot be modified by another. If the original court retained jurisdiction, it has exclusive jurisdiction to modify the award upon changed circumstances. If there was no reservation of jurisdiction, the issue would be barred by res judicata.[7]

In *Robinson v. Robinson*,[8] the parties' legal separation judgment entry was vacated after a hearing on husband's Civil Rule 60(B) motion. He claimed that he had not understood the agreement; could not hear a portion of what was read into the record by counsel; and that wife had not made disclosure of her pension and deferred compensation plans. The trial court did not, however, grant the motion as it related to the parties' shared parenting plan.

Although failure to file a financial affidavit as required by local court rule would, in and of itself, not be a basis for vacating a judgment, failure to make disclosure of assets supported husband's claim that he did not understand the agreement.

It was not error to grant the motion with respect to property division and deny it with respect to the shared parenting plan.

In *Welch v. Welch*,[9] the court entered a decree of legal separation in which husband was required to pay wife a sum of money in installment payments as her portion of the property division, for which husband executed a promissory note secured by a mortgage. Husband ceased payment on the obligation and wife filed both a motion to show cause in the domestic relations court and a foreclosure action in the general division. The trial court found husband in contempt and sentenced husband to a fifteen day jail sentence, suspended in the event that husband purged his contempt by making full payment of the remainder of his obligation. Husband failed to pay the purge and wife moved the court to impose the suspended sentence while the foreclosure action was still pending. The Eleventh District Court of Appeals found that wife's procedure of using simultaneous legal proceedings to enforce the same debt did not violate the doctrine of election of remedies as the remedies were neither inconsistent nor repugnant. Nonetheless, the Court of Appeals found that "[e]quity precludes [wife's] filing of a motion to impose [sanctions] until the appeal of the foreclosure action is determined with finality." As a result, the Court of Appeals concluded that the trial court acted within its discretion when delaying imposition of sanctions while the foreclosure

---

[6]Aukland v. Aukland, 17 Ohio Op. 387, 30 Ohio L. Abs. 461, 31 Ohio L. Abs. 101, 31 N.E.2d 731 (Ct. App. 2d Dist. Franklin County 1939).

[7]Payton v. Payton, 1997 WL 354797 (Ohio Ct. App. 4th Dist. Scioto County 1997).

[8]Robinson v. Robinson, 2002-Ohio-5760, 2002 WL 31386243 (Ohio Ct. App. 5th Dist. Stark County 2002).

[9]Welch v. Welch, 2006 WL 3833849 (Ohio Ct. App. 11th Dist. Lake County 2006).

proceedings, or any other potentially determinative actions, were pending.

§ 8:9   Complaint for legal separation—Form⊚

[Title of Court]

[Caption]   Case No. *[_____]*
                                              COMPLAINT

1.   Plaintiff and Defendant were married at *[city and state]* on *[date]*, and there are *[no/number]* children, the issue of such marriage, namely, *[name(s) and date(s) of birth of children]*.

2.   Defendant has been guilty of [grounds for legal separation pursuant to RC 3105.17].

3.   The parties are the owners of, and each has an interest in, the following property: *[list property]*.

Wherefore, Plaintiff demands that *[he/she]* be granted a decree of legal separation and be named residential parent and legal custodian of and be awarded support for their minor *[child/children]*; that *[he/she]* be granted reasonable spousal support; that *[he/she]* be awarded Defendant's right, title and interest in the *[personal/real]* property; and costs herein, including a reasonable sum for expenses and attorney fees in this action, and for such other and further relief as shall be proper and necessary.

                                         _____
                                         Attorney for Plaintiff

NOTES TO FORM

Drafter's Notes

A long form caption should be used on the complaint.

A RC 3127.23 affidavit (court form) should accompany the initial filing where there are minor children of the marriage.

As in other civil cases, the complaint in a domestic relations matter may plead in the alternative, i.e., for legal separation or annulment, or for legal separation or divorce.

§ 8:10   Judgment entry, decree of legal separation—Form⊚

[Title of Court]

[Caption]   Case No. *[_____]*
                                              JUDGMENT ENTRY

This cause came on for hearing this *[date]*, upon the complaint of Plaintiff and the evidence, *[Defendant being in default of answer or other pleading although duly served with process according to law/*

Defendant having filed an answer and cross-complaint and having failed to present testimony or evidence].

Upon due consideration thereof, the Court finds that the parties were married as alleged, and that *[no/number]* children were born as issue of the marriage.

The Court further finds that Defendant has been guilty of [ground for legal separation pursuant to RC 3105.17] and that by reason thereof Plaintiff is entitled to a decree of legal separation.

The Court further finds:

(1) The duration of the marriage was from *[date]* to *[date]*;

(2) The parties have the following marital property: _____;

(3) Each party has the following separate property: _____; and

(4) The order below divides the marital property equitably.

The Court further finds that Plaintiff and Defendant voluntarily entered into and executed a certain written Agreement dated *[date]*, which Agreement was admitted into evidence, and this Court after proper examination and full consideration thereof finds it fair, just, and equitable, and by reason thereof, said Agreement should be approved and made an order of this Court in its entirety.

IT IS THEREFORE ORDERED, ADJUDGED AND DECREED that:

1. Plaintiff be and is hereby granted a decree of legal separation from Defendant;

2. *[Plaintiff/Defendant]* is designated as the residential parent and legal custodian of the minor *[child/children]* until further order of the Court. *[Plaintiff/Defendant]* shall have the following visitation rights: _____.

[3. The Court makes no determination of marital or separate property.]

or

[3. The Court grants to *[Plaintiff/Defendant]* the following property: _____.]

or

[3. The aforesaid Agreement between Plaintiff and Defendant marked Exhibit A attached hereto and made a part hereof as if fully rewritten herein is hereby approved and adopted by this Court in its entirety, and said Agreement and all of its terms and provisions are made the order of this Court, and each party to said Agreement is hereby ordered and directed to comply with all the terms and provisions thereof.]

4. *[Plaintiff/Defendant]* shall pay and save *[Plaintiff/Defendant]* harmless on the following debts: _____.

5. Defendant shall pay the costs of this proceeding for which judgment is rendered and execution may issue.

_____
Judge

Approved:

_____
Attorney for Plaintiff

_____
Attorney for Defendant

NOTES TO FORM

Drafter's Notes

It is discretionary with the trial court in a legal separation to determine what constitutes marital property and what is separate property. If it makes such a determination, then the court shall divide the property. RC 3105.17(B). In such circumstances, the court must also make various written findings of fact. RC 3105.171(G).

Where parental rights and responsibilities are allocated and child support is ordered, various statutory notices are required in the decree. Local rules may also specify the form of such notices.

Chapter 9

Separation Agreements

*By Beatrice K. Sowald, Esq.**

---

*Based on the 1984 Edition by William S. Friedman, Esq.

I. SEPARATION AGREEMENTS—FORMS

II. PRELIMINARY CLAUSES—FORMS

III. PERSONAL PROPERTY CLAUSES—FORMS

IV. REAL ESTATE CLAUSES—FORMS

VII. PARENTAL RIGHTS AND RESPONSIBILITY CLAUSES—FORMS

VIII. PARENTING TIME CLAUSES—FORMS

IX. CHILD SUPPORT CLAUSES—FORMS

X. INCOME TAX CLAUSES—FORMS

XI. MARITAL DEBT CLAUSES—FORMS

XII. MUTUAL RELEASE CLAUSES—FORMS

XIII. MISCELLANEOUS CLAUSES—FORMS

XIV. COURT DOCUMENTS—FORMS

> **KeyCite®:** Cases and other legal materials listed in KeyCite Scope can be researched through the KeyCite service on Westlaw®. Use KeyCite to check citations for form, parallel references, prior and later history, and comprehensive citator information, including citations to other decisions and secondary materials.

§ 9:1   Agreements pursuant to separation only

There are a number of statutes forming the general legal background against which Ohio separation agreements are viewed. Pursuant to RC 3103.01, marriage partners mutually contract obligations of respect, fidelity, and support. A separation agreement is an interparty contract which changes these mutual statutory obligations.

RC 3103.05 permits husband and wife to contract with each other. Their contracts are governed by the general rules which govern persons who share confidential relationships.[1] RC 3103.05 is further modified by RC 3103.06, which prevents a married couple from altering their statutory duties stated in RC 3103.01 and RC 3103.03, except that a married couple may enter an agreement providing for immediate separation which may include provisions for support of either party and their minor children.[2]

A spouse contemplating a de facto separation from his or her mate should be informed of the various legal consequences which will occur on their separation, as well as the marital obligations that will not terminate on separation. For example, even though a spouse is living separate and apart from the other spouse and/or children, each spouse has a duty of support for himself or herself and for his or her spouse;[3] if one spouse is unable to support himself or herself, the other spouse will be required to provide support.[4] Neither party can relinquish this duty of support of the children and spouse by a separation agreement if factual circumstances show such support is necessary.[5] RC 3103.03 formerly provided that the husband had the primary duty of support for the family. Under the former law, where the husband/father was under a physical disability at the time of separation and had no property, he was found to be required to provide support when he recovered

---

[Section 9:1]

[1]See Text Ch 4, Marital Obligations and Property Rights.

[2]See Lowman v. Lowman, 166 Ohio St. 1, 1 Ohio Op. 2d 152, 139 N.E.2d 1 (1956); Hawgood v. Hawgood, 33 Ohio Misc. 227, 62 Ohio Op. 2d 427, 294 N.E.2d 681 (C.P. 1973).

[3]Hickle v. Hickle, 3 Ohio C.D. 552, 1892 WL 300 (Ohio Cir. Ct. 1892).

[4]RC 3103.03(A); Hickle v. Hickle, 3 Ohio C.D. 552, 1892 WL 300 (Ohio Cir. Ct. 1892); RC 3103.03, as amended by 1990 S.B. 3, eff. 4-11-91.

[5]Bowen v. State, 56 Ohio St. 235, 46 N.E. 708 (1897). See also Text Ch 19, Child Support.

and was capable of providing support.[6] If a third party provides the necessaries for a spouse's or child's support, the neglectful spouse may be liable to pay for such necessaries.[7] A spouse's duty to provide support for the other spouse continues after legal separation,[8] except if the neglected spouse abandoned the other spouse without cause.[9]

To resolve these issues and other matters which may arise, a formal separation agreement is necessary when a husband and wife decide to live separate and apart. The main purpose of the agreement is to determine the parties' future obligations and rights in relation to each other and their children. It should be noted that a separation agreement must be fair and entered into voluntarily, with full disclosure and understanding by each side.[10] If a court decides that a separation agreement is not fair to both parties under all circumstances, it may withhold approval of the agreement. Alternatively, if the parties have proceeded to judgment, the court may set aside the agreement.[11] When a party proposes a separation agreement, he or she should advise the other spouse to seek legal counsel for assistance. With both parties well represented, the possibility of a separation agreement being rejected by the court may be avoided.[12] Both parties must fully recognize the importance of the separation agreement.

An additional reason to have the agreement in writing is to establish, for income tax purposes, that certain payments made pursuant to the agreement are considered spousal support and thereby deductible by the payor and taxable to the payee.[13]

A separation agreement continues to be enforceable, including be-

[6]State ex rel. Person v. Industrial Commission of Ohio, 126 Ohio St. 85, 183 N.E. 920 (1932).

[7]RC 3103.03(C), RC 3103.03(D); Wolf v. Friedman, 20 Ohio St. 2d 49, 49 Ohio Op. 2d 306, 253 N.E.2d 761 (1969). For a discussion of "necessaries," see Text §§ 4:2 to 4:3, Support obligations during marriage—Equality of spouses.

[8]Klump v. Klump, 96 Ohio App. 93, 54 Ohio Op. 202, 121 N.E.2d 273 (6th Dist. Lucas County 1954). For a discussion of the interparty marital and parental obligations, see Text Ch 4, Marital Obligations and Property Rights.

[9]RC 3103.03(C).

[10]Brewer v. Brewer, 117 Ohio App. 263, 24 Ohio Op. 2d 60, 183 N.E.2d 250 (1st Dist. Warren County 1962). For a discussion of the concept of "fair and equitable," see Text § 9:39, Effect of signed agreement—Modification; Text § 9:40, Effect of signed agreement—Enforcement; Text Ch 10, Dissolution of Marriage.

[11]Brewer v. Brewer, 117 Ohio App. 263, 24 Ohio Op. 2d 60, 183 N.E.2d 250 (1st Dist. Warren County 1962). For a discussion of the concept of "fair and equitable," see Text § 9:39, Effect of signed agreement—Modification; Text § 9:40, Effect of signed agreement—Enforcement; Text Ch 10, Dissolution of Marriage. See also Nellis v. Nellis, 98 Ohio App. 247, 57 Ohio Op. 281, 129 N.E.2d 217 (6th Dist. Lucas County 1955); Text Ch 24, Relief from Judgment.

[12]See also In re Marriage of Kesler, 59 Ohio Misc. 33, 13 Ohio Op. 3d 105, 392 N.E.2d 905 (C.P. 1978) (agreement set aside in spite of three attorney waiver clauses because judge subsequently believed that "complex" economic structure required independent legal advice to wife).

[13]I.R.C. § 71(b)(1)(A) and I.R.C. § 71(b)(2)(B); see also Text §§ 28:2 to 28:12, Alimony—Payments as deductible.

ing subject to incorporation into a decree by a trial court, for an indefinite period of time. The fact that a party, subsequent to the execution of an agreement, acquires assets which are not included in the separation agreement does not invalidate the prior agreement.[14]

An agreement from which the words "intend to separate" were deleted is invalid because it lacks an agreement between the parties to separate immediately. A party's subsequent unilateral separation does not meet statutory requirements so as to validate the writing as an enforceable separation agreement.[15]

A separation agreement is valid and enforceable until and unless a court declares the agreement invalid because of fraud in the procurement or breach of a confidential relationship.[16] However, a separation agreement, unless such agreement provides otherwise, terminates on the spouses' reconciliation and resumption of cohabitation.[17] A husband and wife living together, with the intent to remain together, cannot enter into a binding agreement disposing of all rights and obligations of the marital relationship.[18]

Separation agreements providing only for separation and maintenance are contingent on the condition that the parties live separate and apart; when cohabitation and marital relations resume, the separation agreement is automatically revoked by RC 3103.06, which only provides for the disposition of marital rights and obligations when the parties live separate and apart.[19] However, a separation agreement which includes a division of property or a property settlement is an executed agreement, and the property division is not revoked because the spouses reconcile and resume the marital

---

[14]Ralstin v. Ralstin, 1988 WL 94378 (Ohio Ct. App. 11th Dist. Portage County 1988).

[15]Kauffman v. Kauffman, 1992 WL 208930 (Ohio Ct. App. 10th Dist. Franklin County 1992).

[16]Lowman v. Lowman, 166 Ohio St. 1, 1 Ohio Op. 2d 152, 139 N.E.2d 1 (1956); Nellis v. Nellis, 98 Ohio App. 247, 57 Ohio Op. 281, 129 N.E.2d 217 (6th Dist. Lucas County 1955); Brewer v. Brewer, 117 Ohio App. 263, 24 Ohio Op. 2d 60, 183 N.E.2d 250 (1st Dist. Warren County 1962). For further discussion on confidential relationships, see Text §§ 9:42 to 9:50, In-court agreements.

[17]In re Carnathan's Estate, 27 Ohio N.P. (n.s.) 65, 1928 WL 2736 (Prob. Ct. 1928). See Text § 9:37, Effect of signed agreement—Revocation by reconciliation.

[18]In re Carnathan's Estate, 27 Ohio N.P. (n.s.) 65, 1928 WL 2736 (Prob. Ct. 1928). See Text § 9:37, Effect of signed agreement—Revocation by reconciliation; Smith v. Smith, 50 Ohio Op. 175, 67 Ohio L. Abs. 489, 112 N.E.2d 346 (C.P. 1953); Hornberger v. Hornberger, 1986 WL 14404 (Ohio Ct. App. 7th Dist. Carroll County 1986) (continued cohabitation after execution of separation agreement voids agreement).

[19]Rutter v. Rutter, 24 Ohio Misc. 7, 53 Ohio Op. 2d 32, 261 N.E.2d 202 (C.P. 1970); In re Price's Estate, 1 Ohio Op. 459, 22 Ohio L. Abs. 639, 1 Ohio Supp. 173 (Prob. Ct. 1935). But see contra Leedy v. Malcolm, 8 Ohio L. Abs. 640, 1930 WL 2220 (Ct. App. 8th Dist. Cuyahoga County 1930).

relationship.[20] The spouses should execute a separate writing to revoke such separation agreement.

§ 9:2 Agreements pursuant to dissolution

A separation agreement pursuant to a dissolution of marriage is only slightly different from one for a separation only. The principal difference is that the dissolution agreement must provide for the termination of all marital relationships, including a division of all property, spousal support, allocation of parental rights, child support, and visitation rights and privileges,[1] while the separation only agreement is limited to those matters agreed to by the parties. One may view the agreement pursuant to immediate separation as fully executed and enforceable on execution, while the agreement pursuant to a dissolution, if so worded, may be viewed as executory only until subsequently ratified by the parties in open court and approved by the court. After execution of the dissolution agreement, it may be subsequently amended by the parties, and the amendment may be filed any time prior to the hearing.[2]

Agreements written expressly for a dissolution are contingent on the dissolution. Therefore, in the event the dissolution is terminated or dismissed, the agreement becomes a nullity. However, if the agreement has expressly provided that it is to survive any dismissal and is to have independent significance, or if the parties by their conduct and performance have demonstrated an intent that it is not dependent on the obtaining of a dissolution, it may continue as a valid separation agreement between two persons pursuant to RC 3103.06.[3] If the language of a separation agreement expresses an intent that the agreement survive the dismissal of a dissolution petition, a trial court in a subsequent divorce action must consider the agreement, but need not be bound by it.[4]

The Fifth District Court of Appeals has held that the trial court did

---

[20]Rutter v. Rutter, 24 Ohio Misc. 7, 53 Ohio Op. 2d 32, 261 N.E.2d 202 (C.P. 1970); In re Price's Estate, 1 Ohio Op. 459, 22 Ohio L. Abs. 639, 1 Ohio Supp. 173 (Prob. Ct. 1935). But see contra Leedy v. Malcolm, 8 Ohio L. Abs. 640, 1930 WL 2220 (Ct. App. 8th Dist. Cuyahoga County 1930). See also Greiner v. Greiner, 61 Ohio App. 2d 88, 15 Ohio Op. 3d 95, 399 N.E.2d 571 (8th Dist. Cuyahoga County 1979).

[Section 9:2]

[1]RC 3105.63. See Text Ch 10, Dissolution of Marriage.

[2]RC 3105.63. See Text Ch 10, Dissolution of Marriage.

[3]Greiner v. Greiner, 61 Ohio App. 2d 88, 15 Ohio Op. 3d 95, 399 N.E.2d 571 (8th Dist. Cuyahoga County 1979); Flint v. Flint, 1990 WL 8465 (Ohio Ct. App. 12th Dist. Clinton County 1990) (partial performance of terms of agreement evidences intent of parties that agreement should survive dismissal of dissolution petition). See also the discussion of the "independent significance" factor in Text §§ 9:35 to 9:41, Effect of signed agreement. See also Text § 9:58, Separation agreement—Basic—Form; Text § 9:59, Separation agreement—Detailed—Form.

[4]Covault v. Covault, 1987 WL 17521 (Ohio Ct. App. 10th Dist. Franklin County 1987).

not err in adopting a separation agreement even though the agreement had been executed in contemplation of a dismissed dissolution. There was no provision in the agreement that it would survive the dissolution, but it had been amended after the dissolution was dismissed.[5]

Dissolution agreements can be drafted by a single attorney. However, an attorney cannot represent both parties. Even if it is a friendly dissolution, there is the potential for subsequent changes of memory, creating a conflict of interest for the attorney. The attorney must always identify one party as the client and require that the other party sign an attorney waiver.[6] There is the possibility of future discord as in any marital termination, and the agreement may be challenged on grounds of lack of representation and may be set aside.[7] A judge is not required to approve the terms of the agreement.[8]

The agreement, even though drafted by an attorney, is between the parties and therefore subject to the "confidential relationship" mandate of RC 3103.05. In addition, it is subject to future reconsideration if a judge later determines that one party received an advantage which does not appear fair on later judicial scrutiny.[9]

A decision by the First District Court of Appeals, *In re Murphy*,[10] held that when a separation agreement is drawn up, it must divide *all* property belonging to the spouses. It is mandatory that husband and wife concur in the separation agreement and that such agreement cover all points of potential controversy between them.

---

[5]Henry v. Henry, 1988 WL 38639 (Ohio Ct. App. 5th Dist. Stark County 1988).

[6]See discussion of the attorney waiver in Text § 9:33, Elements of agreement—Attorney waiver. See In re Marriage of Kesler, 59 Ohio Misc. 33, 13 Ohio Op. 3d 105, 392 N.E.2d 905 (C.P. 1978) (agreement set aside in spite of three attorney waiver clauses, because judge subsequently believed that "complex" economic structure required independent legal advice to wife).

[7]See RC 3103.05; In the Matter Of: Fugazzi, 1983 WL 3535 (Ohio Ct. App. 10th Dist. Franklin County 1983) (where husband unrepresented by counsel, and wife was represented, and agreement drafted by wife's attorney and agreement had ambiguities, such ambiguities should be construed in favor of husband). See also Text Ch 4, Marital Obligations and Property Rights; In re Marriage of Kesler, 59 Ohio Misc. 33, 13 Ohio Op. 3d 105, 392 N.E.2d 905 (C.P. 1978).

[8]Shalkhauser v. Shalkhauser, 1981 WL 10388 (Ohio Ct. App. 8th Dist. Cuyahoga County 1981) (court not required to adopt any settlement agreement between parties if court finds it is not fair, just, and reasonable); Mollencamp v. Mollencamp, 18 Ohio L. Abs. 90, 1934 WL 2587 (Ct. App. 2d Dist. Franklin County 1934); Stark v. Stark, 28 Ohio N.P. (n.s.) 36, 8 Ohio L. Abs. 287, 1929 WL 2380 (C.P. 1929).

[9]Lowman v. Lowman, 166 Ohio St. 1, 1 Ohio Op. 2d 152, 139 N.E.2d 1 (1956); In re Marriage of Kesler, 59 Ohio Misc. 33, 13 Ohio Op. 3d 105, 392 N.E.2d 905 (C.P. 1978). See also McClain v. McClain, 15 Ohio St. 3d 289, 473 N.E.2d 811 (1984) (separation agreements pursuant to dissolution not modifiable as to support alimony); Wolfe v. Wolfe, 46 Ohio St. 2d 399, 75 Ohio Op. 2d 474, 350 N.E.2d 413 (1976) (property alimony not modifiable in any event).

[10]In re Murphy, 10 Ohio App. 3d 134, 461 N.E.2d 910 (1st Dist. Hamilton County 1983).

In *Carey v. Carey*,[11] the Third District Court of Appeals agreed with the Eighth District's decision in *Greiner v. Greiner*[12] that a separation agreement may survive the withdrawal of a petition for dissolution but held that a dispute over the validity of a separation agreement is not resolved by a summary judgment.[13] A separation agreement which is intended to bind the parties independently of a dissolution proceeding is enforceable even if one party dies prior to the dissolution being granted. Specifically, a release of rights in a decedent's estate will be binding if the agreement was meant to survive a dismissal of the dissolution proceeding.[14]

The parties in *Evanoff v. Evanoff*[15] entered into a separation agreement which was incorporated into a dissolution decree. Nine months after the dissolution, the parties resumed living together for almost three years. The Eighth District Court of Appeals held that since the parties did not intend to reconcile and resume a normal life together, the separation agreement was not abrogated and should not be held for naught.

§ 9:3 Agreements pursuant to divorce—In general

There is no provision for an agreement pursuant to a divorce in the statutes. The agreements between married persons pursuant to RC 3103.05 pertain to contracts in regard to matters that the parties could contract, as well as with third parties, and do not contemplate a modification agreement of marital obligations.[1] The agreements permitted by RC 3103.06, allowing modifications of marital obligations, are contingent on a de facto separation. The agreements of RC 3105.63 permit separation agreements pursuant to a dissolution of the marriage.

Separation agreements in preparation for a divorce are common and are submitted regularly where there is a default divorce or an uncontested divorce. As used here, a "default" is where one party fails to answer a complaint. The matter proceeds as if uncontested. "Uncontested" means that one party is not contesting the divorce by

---

[11]Carey v. Carey, 9 Ohio App. 3d 243, 459 N.E.2d 626 (3d Dist. Shelby County 1983) (over seventy percent of assets omitted).

[12]Greiner v. Greiner, 61 Ohio App. 2d 88, 15 Ohio Op. 3d 95, 399 N.E.2d 571 (8th Dist. Cuyahoga County 1979).

[13]See also Text § 10:8, Incorporation of agreement.

[14]In re Estate of Hogrefe, 30 Ohio App. 3d 238, 507 N.E.2d 414 (3d Dist. Henry County 1986).

[15]Evanoff v. Evanoff, 1985 WL 8962 (Ohio Ct. App. 8th Dist. Cuyahoga County 1985).

[Section 9:3]

[1]Lowman v. Lowman, 166 Ohio St. 1, 1 Ohio Op. 2d 152, 139 N.E.2d 1 (1956); Mendelson v. Mendelson, 123 Ohio St. 11, 8 Ohio L. Abs. 754, 173 N.E. 615 (1930); Hoagland v. Hoagland, 113 Ohio St. 228, 3 Ohio L. Abs. 388, 148 N.E. 585 (1925); Brewer v. Brewer, 84 Ohio App. 35, 39 Ohio Op. 89, 52 Ohio L. Abs. 116, 78 N.E.2d 919 (2d Dist. Montgomery County 1948).

failing to appear at the scheduled hearing where the other party proceeds. The party failing to appear may have done so because of lack of concern, subsequent interparty agreement, or by a withdrawal of the complaint or answer/counterclaim as was agreed to by the parties. An agreement can be valid even though the divorce filings may have already taken place.

§ 9:4 Agreements pursuant to divorce—Requirement of fairness

A court may refuse to approve a separation agreement at the time of divorce if it determines that the agreement is unfair or unreasonable.[1] One party's misconception of the terms of the agreement is not cause to find it unfair or to set it aside.[2] Further, the agreement may have become unfair by reason of changed circumstances since the time it was executed.

> [T]he court must independently assess the fairness of [a separation] agreement with respect to periodic support or maintenance provisions at time of divorce in light of the circumstances then existing, and if unfair, refuse to approve it and enter such orders [as] are appropriate.[3]

§ 9:5 Agreements pursuant to divorce—Choice of remedies

When an agreement is reached in a contested divorce proceeding, it is important to elect the choice of remedy: (1) to continue with the divorce with one party at fault or under the grounds of incompatibility or (2) to convert to a dissolution.[1] This decision is frequently part of the negotiations of the agreement. In the event one party is unable or unwilling to appear, then a divorce is the only alternative, since a dissolution requires the appearance of both parties. The advantage of both parties appearing is to handle a situation where a problem arises due to unexpected events such as the nonaccepting by the court of the proposed agreed decree and agreement. In most situations, there is no problem. However, it may be worthwhile to be at the hearing to be sure nothing interferes with completion of the case.

From a procedural point of view, there are several ways for the rec-

---

[Section 9:4]

[1]RC 3105.10(B)(2); Sinclair v. Sinclair, 98 Ohio App. 308, 57 Ohio Op. 347, 129 N.E.2d 311 (2d Dist. Preble County 1954); Brewer v. Brewer, 84 Ohio App. 35, 39 Ohio Op. 89, 52 Ohio L. Abs. 116, 78 N.E.2d 919 (2d Dist. Montgomery County 1948); Sentelik-Roberts v. Roberts, 1993 WL 547178 (Ohio Ct. App. 1st Dist. Hamilton County 1993).

[2]Kostrevski v. Kostrevski, 1993 WL 268434 (Ohio Ct. App. 10th Dist. Franklin County 1993).

[3]Medas v. Medas, 1985 WL 11143 (Ohio Ct. App. 4th Dist. Gallia County 1985) (fifteen-month lapse between signing of separation agreement and filing of complaint for divorce).

[Section 9:5]

[1]RC 3105.08.

ord to be cleared. Where one party is not going forward with a pleading, either the complaint or counterclaim, the decree should recite that it is withdrawn, or that a party failed to proceed on such pleading and that the divorce was heard on the remaining pleading. One party may file a motion to withdraw, accompanied by the appropriate judgment entry. This is a matter of local procedure. In the alternative, some jurisdictions will permit the record to be the motion to withdraw, accompanied by a stipulated judgment entry, signed by both attorneys. As a protective device the stipulated judgment entry should be signed by the parties.

The agreement is presented to the court for its findings, approval, and adoption into the divorce decree. As with the agreement pursuant to a dissolution, there is no requirement that the court must approve it.[2]

If both parties elect to convert the divorce to a dissolution, the parties file a motion in the divorce case, which contains a petition for dissolution.[3] There is no filing fee nor assessment of filing costs.

As to whether divorce or dissolution is a better remedy, note that spousal support in a dissolution formerly was nonmodifiable.[4] The Ohio legislature has addressed this issue and RC 3105.18(E) now provides as follows:

> the court that enters the decree of . . . dissolution . . . does not have jurisdiction to modify the amount or terms of the alimony or spousal support unless . . .
>
> (2) . . . the separation agreement that is approved by the court and incorporated into the decree contains a provision specifically authorizing the court to modify the amount or terms of alimony or spousal support.

Similarly, RC 3105.18 now specifies that spousal support awarded in a divorce action will only be modifiable where the decree or separation agreement incorporated into the decree expressly authorizes the court to modify the amount or terms of spousal support.[5] These provisions are prospective only, from May 2, 1986, and apply to decrees entered on and after that date. Removal of the distinction removes that factor in making the decision between the two remedies.

---

[2]Sinclair v. Sinclair, 98 Ohio App. 308, 57 Ohio Op. 347, 129 N.E.2d 311 (2d Dist. Preble County 1954); Brewer v. Brewer, 117 Ohio App. 263, 24 Ohio Op. 2d 60, 183 N.E.2d 250 (1st Dist. Warren County 1962); Shalkhauser v. Shalkhauser, 1981 WL 10388 (Ohio Ct. App. 8th Dist. Cuyahoga County 1981) (court not required to adopt any settlement agreement between parties if court finds it is not fair, just, and reasonable).

[3]RC 3105.08. See Text § 10:4, Motion for conversion and complaint for divorce—Form.

[4]McClain v. McClain, 15 Ohio St. 3d 289, 473 N.E.2d 811 (1984); Alban v. Alban, 1 Ohio App. 3d 146, 439 N.E.2d 963 (10th Dist. Franklin County 1981); Ashley v. Ashley, 1 Ohio App. 3d 80, 439 N.E.2d 911 (8th Dist. Cuyahoga County 1981) (no jurisdiction to modify dissolution alimony). See also In the Matter of Black, 1981 WL 5481 (Ohio Ct. App. 6th Dist. Fulton County 1981) (court extended concept of no jurisdiction to modify, to modification of support).

[5]See Text Ch 13, Spousal support.

§ 9:6 Elements of agreement—In general

A separation agreement is a contract between two parties which provides for an alteration of the parties' marriage contract.[1] As with any other contract, the agreement must be supported by consideration.[2] A separation agreement may be binding even if the parties are under the age of eighteen, as RC 3103.06 makes no age distinction.[3] In order to be valid, the separation agreement must be made in contemplation of an immediate separation[4] and must be followed by an actual separation.[5]

RC 3103.06 does not differentiate between oral and written contracts. In *Pawlowski v. Pawlowski*,[6] the 10th District Court of Appeals found that the parties were bound by an oral separation agreement, stating that RC 3103.06 "does not on its face bar an oral contract or separation agreement."

To prepare a well-drafted separation agreement, the attorney must perform an in-depth interview and investigation. It is an excellent idea for each practitioner to design and develop a checklist that will follow the criteria of RC 3105.171 and RC 3105.18. Items to be determined include assets, liabilities, general health of each family member, earning capacity of each party, the education of the parties, length of marriage, children (including names, ages, physical condition, schooling, and related special requirements), prior marriages, children by prior marriages, the physical and mental condition of each party, employment (including history and sources of income), property brought to the marriage by each spouse, property acquired during the marriage by gift, inheritance, or otherwise, the financial needs of the parties, safe deposit boxes or other places of safekeeping, and tax returns. After the draftsman has examined and analyzed the information received, a tentative separation agreement may be prepared for negotiation with the other party's attorney.

It is extremely important that the parties reach an agreement if at all possible. Divorce litigation may be protracted and very costly to

---

[Section 9:6]

[1]See Text § 9:1, Agreements pursuant to separation only; Text § 9:2, Agreements pursuant to dissolution; Text §§ 9:3 to 9:5, Agreements pursuant to divorce.

[2]Garver v. Miller, 16 Ohio St. 527, 1866 WL 15 (1866).

[3]Burlovic v. Farmer, 96 Ohio App. 403, 54 Ohio Op. 399, 115 N.E.2d 411 (8th Dist. Cuyahoga County 1953), judgment aff'd, 162 Ohio St. 46, 54 Ohio Op. 5, 120 N.E.2d 705 (1954).

[4]Du Bois v. Coen, 100 Ohio St. 17, 125 N.E. 121 (1919); Wilson v. Rudolph Wurlitzer Co., 48 Ohio App. 450, 2 Ohio Op. 48, 18 Ohio L. Abs. 449, 194 N.E. 441 (1st Dist. Hamilton County 1934); Tefft v. Tefft, 73 Ohio App. 399, 29 Ohio Op. 99, 54 N.E.2d 423 (9th Dist. Summit County 1943). See also Text § 9:1, Agreements pursuant to separation only.

[5]Meyer v. Meyer, 153 Ohio St. 408, 41 Ohio Op. 415, 91 N.E.2d 892 (1950); Hoagland v. Hoagland, 113 Ohio St. 228, 3 Ohio L. Abs. 388, 148 N.E. 585 (1925).

[6]Pawlowski v. Pawlowski, 83 Ohio App. 3d 794, 615 N.E.2d 1071 (10th Dist. Franklin County 1992).

both parties. Further, the adversarial nature of the proceedings will create negative feelings between the parties. This is an undesirable result, particularly where there must necessarily be an ongoing relationship between the parties, subsequent to the separation, because of children or a joint business venture. As an agreement between the parties is more likely to be responsive to the needs and abilities of the parties than a court-imposed settlement, the possibility of voluntary compliance by both parties is enhanced.

While the attorney must strive for terms most favorable to his or her client, it is essential to be certain that the agreement is fair and reasonable with respect to both parties. If it is not fair and reasonable, the court may reject (or refuse to approve) the agreement. The written agreement should be carefully drafted, stating clearly and concisely the intentions of the parties. Identification of all the parties involved and a statement that the relationship is being terminated are essential.

Provisions should be made for the allocation of parental rights and responsibilities concerning the minor children, the division of property between the parties, and the payment of spousal support.[7] The agreement may provide for shared parenting between the parties.[8] The agreement should also provide for payment of the marital debts, tax matters, release of inheritance rights, responsibility for attorney fees, and the execution of the agreement.

To avoid future problems, all contingencies, such as the death or remarriage of one of the parties, reconciliation between the parties, failure or refusal by the court to incorporate the agreement into the divorce decree, and the failure of either party to abide by the agreement, should be considered and provided for in the separation agreement.

A carefully negotiated settlement can be impaired by a poorly drafted agreement. A well-drafted document will minimize the possibility of future arguments and litigation because of ambiguity in terminology. No matter how well drafted, the agreement per se cannot prevent future arguments or some finding of a flaw or technicality to justify an attempt to have the matter judicially reviewed and modified.

§ 9:7 Elements of agreement—Declaration and consideration

A contract has been defined by Ohio courts as an agreement on sufficient consideration between two or more persons to do or refrain from doing a particular thing.[1] A separation agreement is a special

---

[7]RC 3105.63.

[8]See Text Ch 15, Parental Rights and Shared Parenting.

[Section 9:7]

[1]Greiner v. Greiner, 61 Ohio App. 2d 88, 15 Ohio Op. 3d 95, 399 N.E.2d 571 (8th Dist. Cuyahoga County 1979).

type of contract. Therefore, the rules governing contracts in general, as well as the provisions of RC 3103.06, are also applicable to the creation of separation agreements.[2]

The opening statement of a separation agreement should contain the contract elements of (1) sufficient consideration, (2) lawful subject matter, (3) two persons with the capacity to contract, and (4) a declaration by these parties that they intend to contract.[3] The opening statement should also clearly identify the parties to the agreement and the parties affected by the agreement.

The opening statement should indicate that an agreement has been reached and that the writing signed by the parties represents the total and final agreement of the parties. Both parties should be informed that the written agreement will control in regard to property, parental rights, visitation, spousal support, and other matters. The parties should also be informed that prior oral agreements concerning these matters are no longer viable after a written agreement has been finalized. It is most important that a party be convinced that he or she can live with the agreement as written.

The lawful subject matter of the contract must also be identified in the agreement. The agreement should therefore include the date of the marriage or the date on which the parties established a common law marriage. The children of the marriage should also be identified by name, age, and date of birth. The listing of children should include both natural-born children and children adopted during the course of the marriage.

An essential element of any contract is consideration. A recital of consideration is generally placed in the agreement before parental rights allocations and property divisions are included. Consideration for the separation agreement is not necessarily the same as for an ordinary contract.[4] A domestic relations court has the ability to set the contract aside for fraud, overreaching, or unfairness to one of the contractual parties.[5] Therefore, the consideration must be found from the express provisions of the contract.[6] The consideration exchanged in a separation agreement is the mutual written promises of the parties which release the parties from the obligations and rights imposed

---

[2]Greiner v. Greiner, 61 Ohio App. 2d 88, 15 Ohio Op. 3d 95, 399 N.E.2d 571 (8th Dist. Cuyahoga County 1979).

[3]For examples of declaration and consideration terminology, see Text § 9:60, Recitals—Parties—Form; Text § 9:61, Recitals—Marriage, children, and separation—Form; Text § 9:62, Recitals—Consideration—Form.

[4]Brewer v. Brewer, 84 Ohio App. 35, 39 Ohio Op. 89, 52 Ohio L. Abs. 116, 78 N.E.2d 919 (2d Dist. Montgomery County 1948).

[5]In re Marriage of Kesler, 59 Ohio Misc. 33, 13 Ohio Op. 3d 105, 392 N.E.2d 905 (C.P. 1978) (agreement set aside in spite of three attorney waiver clauses because judge subsequently believed that "complex" economic structure required independent legal advice to wife).

[6]Brewer v. Brewer, 84 Ohio App. 35, 39 Ohio Op. 89, 52 Ohio L. Abs. 116, 78 N.E.2d 919 (2d Dist. Montgomery County 1948).

by marriage in exchange for the new obligations and rights imposed by the separation agreement, subject to the actual separation.

§ 9:8   Elements of agreement—Separation and nonmolestation

RC 3103.06 provides that a husband and wife cannot contract to alter their legal marriage relationship, except that they may agree to an immediate separation and may provide for the support of the dependent spouse and the minor children. An agreement which attempts to alter the marriage relationship is not valid except in the case where the parties agree to immediately separate. The word used in the statute is "immediate." Anything short of immediate separation renders the agreement void. In practice this may create a problem, especially in dissolutions. Occasionally, marital parties still living together inquire whether they can execute the agreement and continue to reside together until the final hearing. It would appear that this procedure produces a legally void agreement. Better practice is to advise parties to separate soon after signing. Some courts require the parties to a divorce or dissolution to have resided separate and apart for a specified period of time prior to the final hearing.[1] RC 3105.65 impliedly makes the agreement pursuant to dissolution an executory instrument until subsequently ratified by the parties, approved and adopted by the court, and journalized. In legal theory, there is no agreement until that time.

The separation agreement should include a statement that the parties intend to live separate and apart, or that they have done so. Failure to separate immediately, or at least soon after executing the agreement, can cause the whole agreement to be unenforceable as a valid separation agreement.[2]

This portion of the agreement may also include a nonmolestation clause which states that neither party shall harass or otherwise bother the other.[3] A nonmolestation clause may not prevent subsequent molestation, but including the clause in the agreement subsequently merged into the decree allows one to seek a contempt citation if molestation occurs, with the sanction being the same as a direct contempt of a court order.

[Section 9:8]

[1]See, e.g., Franklin County C.P. Dom. Rel. R. 5.

[2]Carlisle v. T & R Excavating, Inc., 123 Ohio App. 3d 277, 704 N.E.2d 39 (9th Dist. Medina County 1997).

[3]For examples of separation and nonmolestation terminology, see Text § 9:60, Recitals—Parties—Form; Text § 9:61, Recitals—Marriage, children, and separation—Form; Text § 9:62, Recitals—Consideration—Form; Text § 9:63, Recitals—Nonmolestation—Form.

The ability to enforce a non-molestation clause in a separation agreement incorporated into a decree of dissolution does not preclude bringing a domestic violence claim.[4]

§ 9:9 Elements of agreement—Allocation of parental rights and responsibilities

Whether termed custodial rights, parental rights, residential rights, or allocation of such rights, the separation agreement must identify the intention of the parties regarding care of their minor children. Parties may also provide for shared parenting for the minor children within the separation agreement.[1]

The agreement should provide for the allocation of "parenting time,"[2] child support, medical provisions, and education.[3] Ideally, an agreement may be reached where both parents are identified as fit custodians, in which it is noted that both parents desire to be the residential parent, but, because of existing circumstances, the parties have agreed that one parent would be the better custodian at the time of separation.[4] A positive approach in the parental rights clause may prevent further unnecessary grief, as children may read their parents' separation agreement.

Mutual cooperation between the residential parent and the non-residential parent cannot be created in a separation agreement. Even so, the drafter of the agreement should include several mutual promises relating to the welfare of the children. Mutual promises to cooperate for the children's benefit, notifying the other party of a substantial change in any child's location, and a promise to always exchange phone numbers of the child should be included in the agreement. The residential parent may also promise to advise the other of school functions, reports, activities, and consequential doctors' appointments; not to change the children's present last name; or not to permanently remove the children from the city or state without the other's permission or court order.

As required by RC 3103.06, the separation agreement must also state that the support of minor children and of the dependent spouse has been resolved in the agreement. Further, RC 3109.05(A)(2) states, "The court . . . shall include in each support order . . . the requirement that one or both of the parents provide for the health care needs of the child to the satisfaction of the court." RC 3103.03 provides that each married person must support himself or herself and his or her

---

[4]Felton v. Felton, 79 Ohio St. 3d 34, 1997-Ohio-302, 679 N.E.2d 672 (1997).

[Section 9:9]

[1]RC 3105.63, RC 3105.65(B) (for dissolutions).

[2]RC 3109.057 as effective 3-22-01.

[3]See Text Ch 15, Parental Rights and Shared Parenting; Text Ch 16, Modification of Parental Rights and Responsibilities; Text Ch 18, Parenting Time; Text Ch 19, Child Support.

[4]See Text Ch 15, Parental Rights and Shared Parenting.

spouse and their minor children out of his or her property or by his or her labor. The obligations imposed by this section are not altered by a de facto separation of the parties. Therefore, it must be provided for in the agreement.

RC 3109.051(G), (H), (I), and (J) grant rights of notice of relocation to the non-residential parent and at the same time prohibit schools, day care centers and keepers of records from withholding from the non-residential parent privileges that the residential parent has.[5]

The draftsman must know that parental rights is one of the most highly charged areas of pre-decree and post-decree conflict.[6] A carefully drafted agreement can prevent future combat. RC 3119.08[7] requires a court that issues a child support order to include in the order specific provisions for parenting time and special visitation.

Parental rights arrangements can vary.[8] Theoretically, visitation is a portion of the custody concept, since as one parent takes the child for a visit, de facto custody has been modified for the duration of the visit. The greater the visitation rights, the lesser the de facto custody. It is not possible to consider custody separate from visitation.

Parental rights agreement terminology may be written with the express or implied suggestion to either party that it is modifiable. Even so, this is misleading. Property divisions can never be changed, child support can always be modified, and spousal support can sometimes be changed. Changes in parental rights allocations are somewhere between the "never" of property and the "sometimes" of spousal support.[9] The parties can always subsequently agree to change the agreement, but the court may not be bound by it.[10] Parental rights terms should be designed by examining each and every contingency.

§ 9:10 Elements of agreement—Parenting Time

Allocating parenting time is an area where every detail of the agreement must be spelled out for the parties.[1] A well-drafted agreement will provide for both "reasonable" and "specific" time. Pursuant to RC 3119.08,[2] when a court issues a child support order, specific provisions for parenting time must be included. Thus, for a trial court to approve

---

[5]See Text § 15:77, Statutory notices for parents—Form.

[6]See Text Ch 15, Parental Rights and Shared Parenting.

[7]Formerly RC 3113.215(C).

[8]See Text Ch 15, Parental Rights and Shared Parenting.

[9]See Text Ch 15, Parental Rights and Shared Parenting; Text Ch 16, Modification of Parental Rights and Responsibilities.

[10]See Text Ch 15, Parental Rights and Shared Parenting; Text Ch 16, Modification of Parental Rights and Responsibilities.

[Section 9:10]

[1]For a discussion of the applicable law, see Text Ch 18, Parenting Time and Visitation. For examples of visitation clauses, see Text §§ 9:129 to 9:137, Parenting time.

[2]Formerly RC 3113.215(C).

a separation agreement for a divorce or a dissolution, which makes a support order, the agreement must also set forth parenting time and specific visitation. Where a non-residential parent is out of state, travels, a child is disabled, or such factors exist as to make "reasonable and liberal" parenting time the best description, the agreement should spell out such circumstances. The parties may also be referred to local rules or guidelines for parenting time allocation.

A specific parenting time schedule should provide for overnight parenting time for the non-residential parent and alternating weekends. In some cases, one or more evenings during the week could be designated for parenting time by the non-residential parent. Additionally, the specific schedule should provide for parenting time on holidays. Traditionally, the holidays considered are New Year's, Easter, Memorial Day, Fourth of July, Labor Day, Thanksgiving, Christmas, plus religious holidays relevant to the parties. The agreement should provide that the non-residential parent will receive holiday parenting time in addition to specified parenting time if the holiday does not fall on the non-residential parent's alternating weekend.

The drafter of the agreement should consider a number of other special occasions (for example, Mother's Day, Father's Day, the mother's birthday, the father's birthday, the children's birthday, ethnic holidays, and other regularly celebrated family events). The drafter should also provide for each parent's desire to go on vacation with the children. The cost of the vacation should be assumed by the parent taking the children on vacation, and this should be specified in the agreement.

The agreement should include a provision for other reasonable parenting time by the non-residential parent. During the initial periods of separation, agreement on additional nonspecified parenting time is generally not achieved. However, if the parties overcome the bitterness of the separation, an "other times by agreement" clause may become a very viable alternative to the specified parenting time. Where counsel for the intended parenting time parent has any suspicion that there may be post-decree acrimony which would affect normal parenting time, the terminology of "reasonable and liberal" should never be used, as there is a possibility that such terms will be construed as meaning what is "reasonable" to the custodian, rather than what is "reasonable" for the children and "other parent." The drafter should include provision for advance notice of a request for additional parenting time and for notice when specified parenting time will not be exercised.

Trial courts are vested with authority under RC 3109.051(B) to grant visitation or companionship rights to persons other than the natural parents, if it is in the best interests of the children.[3] Where it is appropriate, such rights can be granted to the spouse who is the

---

[3]Hollingsworth v. Hollingsworth, 34 Ohio App. 3d 13, 516 N.E.2d 1250 (10th Dist. Franklin County 1986).

stepparent to the other spouse's children and has become, in some cases, a substitute for a natural parent and wishes to continue to have contact.

Finally, where the non-residential parent has other than customary employment, such as a traveling salesman, rotating shifts, essentially weekend work, or where distance is a problem, provisions should be made to provide for these contingencies.

§ 9:11 Elements of agreement—Child support—In general

The separation agreement must provide for support of the minor children until their emancipation.[1] All orders of child support made or modified after December 1, 1986, were governed by RC 3113.21 through RC 3113.219, until March 22, 2001, when the statutes were rewritten.[2] While it is possible that the separation agreement ultimately may not become part of a decree of dissolution, divorce, or legal separation, in most instances this is intended. Provision must therefore be made to comply with all the requirements of RC 3121.01 et seq. for withholding and with RC 3119.01 et seq. for calculation of amounts.

The agreement should set out the amount to be paid, as a monthly amount due[3] per unemancipated child. While withholding or payments may be made in a different cycle, the statute presently requires the amount of the support order to be specified as a monthly amount. If it is not set forth as a per child amount, it will be an "in gross" order and continue in the full amount until modified. For example, the phrase "$100 per month for the support of the children" could result in a judicial ruling that the amount remain constant, even after the emancipation of one or more of the children. Alternatively, it could be construed to mean $100 for each of the children or construed as $100 to be divided among all of the children.

In addition to detailing the precise amounts, consideration should be given to periodic or contingency adjustments, sometimes labeled escalator clauses. The concept considers automatic increases and discounts decreases. There is nothing to prevent negotiation for de-escalation clauses as a trade for escalation clauses. It is fair to both parties. The only problem would be the contingencies and adjustment rates. Even if a problem, it is better to provide escalator clauses in the agreement than to provide for escalation in subsequent and periodic motions for support modification.

[Section 9:11]

[1]For a discussion of the applicable law, see Text Ch 8, Legal Separation; Text Ch 19, Child Support; Text Ch 20, Enforcement of Spousal and Child Support; Text Ch 22, Child Support Enforcement Agencies; Text Ch 23, Interstate and Foreign Support Practice; Text Ch 28, Tax Considerations. For examples of support clauses, see Text §§ 9:138 to 9:149, Child support.

[2]RC 3109.05(A)(1); 2000 S.B. 180, eff. 3-22-01 enacted Chapters 3119, 3121, 3123, and 3125 to deal with child support.

[3]RC 3119.02.

All orders of spousal support and child support must be made payable to the child support enforcement agency, and after implementation of 1997 House Bill 352, to what is now called the Department of Job and Family Services.[4] The agreement should specify who is to pay the processing charge, formerly called "poundage." As a general rule, if unexpressed, the payor is liable for the processing charge, but there is nothing to prevent an agreement of a set figure, where the processing charge is to be taken from that figure so long as the amount complies with the child support guidelines.

Other contingencies concerning the payment of child support should be delineated in the agreement. For example, a clause could be included in the agreement which states whether child support must be paid during extended periods of parenting time with an obligor.

§ 9:12   Elements of agreement—Child support—Education expenses

RC 3103.03 provides that a parent must support his or her minor children until the age of majority, or so long as the children continuously attend, on a full-time basis, a recognized and accredited high school. If the parties are satisfied with the minimum statutory requirements, the attorney need go no further. However, many parents consider a college education as part of basic support. The expense of college should at least be considered at the time of separation. Once agreed to, the obligation for college education of an adult child becomes enforceable.[1]

Another issue which should be considered at the time of separation is the cost of private versus public education. Many people will assume that the cost of private education will continue to be paid by the non-residential parent. However, unless specified in the agreement, problems may arise.

Each client should be thoroughly questioned about the lifestyle of the children and the manner in which the separation will affect the child's lifestyle. The subject of private education, colleges, trade schools, music, other private lessons, sports costs, camp, vacations, religious affiliation, training costs, and other matters should be examined for applicability and provided for, either by express exclusion or inclusion, with the payor's responsibility defined whenever possible, including direct and related costs.

---

[4]See Text Ch 22, Child Support Enforcement Agencies. See also RC 2301.35.

[Section 9:12]

[1]Kaltenbach v. Kaltenbach, 1987 WL 15494 (Ohio Ct. App. 4th Dist. Ross County 1987); Hyder v. Pizer, 2002-Ohio-1744, 2002 WL 570256 (Ohio Ct. App. 9th Dist. Summit County 2002) (where separation agreement is clear and unambiguous requiring ex-husband to pay one-half of all college expenses, error for court to consider the equities).

§ 9:13 Elements of agreement—Child support—Medical expenses

Major medical, hospitalization, and dental insurance, or its equivalent, should also be provided in the agreement. While the court is prohibited from ordering an amount of child support for reasonable and ordinary uninsured medical and dental expenses when it is entering a support order based on the child support guidelines, it is required to issue a separate order for extraordinary medical and dental expenses, as well as appropriate private education.[1] RC 3119.01(C)(4) defines extraordinary medical expenses as uninsured expenses incurred for a child during a calendar year that exceed $100 for that child during that year. However, parties to a separation agreement may allocate both ordinary and extraordinary uncovered expenses, and define the terms for purposes of their agreement.[2] Are pierced ears a medical expense, or a "necessary" medical expense? Is an abortion authorized by the custodial parent without the knowledge or consent of the obligor parent a medical or necessary expense?[3] If possible, the drafter should avoid use of any limiting words.

Generally, the party receiving insurance coverage through an employer will continue to provide the coverage after the separation. However, these policies usually list deductible amounts to be paid prior to coverage, and there are coverage ceilings providing maximum limits on insurance coverage. In addition, certain medical procedures are not covered by insurance in some cases.

The drafter of the support clause should allocate medical and related expenses not covered by insurance to one or both of the parties. This includes deductible amounts and amounts in excess of the ceilings to the party carrying the insurance coverage. A well-drafted agreement will also provide for items not covered by the terms "medical and dental." For example, post-separation counseling for the children or the spouse, conducted by a psychologist or a social worker, could be viewed by the court as nonmedical treatment. In addition, the drafter should also consider the expense of other specialists such as optometrists, psychologists, and therapists. Orthodontists are generally covered by dental, unless specifically excluded or separately addressed.

◆ **Practice Tips:** If you are representing the parent who is to be reimbursed for uncovered extraordinary expenses, provide your client with a form and instructions on how to keep a record of expenses for each child, when the $100.00 per child per year floor is met,

---

[Section 9:13]

[1]RC 3113.215(B)(5)(f).

[2]See McFadden v. McFadden, 1981 WL 3369 (Ohio Ct. App. 10th Dist. Franklin County 1981).

[3]See Akron City Hospital v. Anderson, 68 Ohio Misc. 14, 22 Ohio Op. 3d 238, 428 N.E.2d 472 (Mun. Ct. 1981).

and accompanying receipts. The most frequent complaint and or defense of the other parent is "I never got any bills, receipts, or he/she waited too long."

§ 9:14 Elements of agreement—Child support—Medical expense—Form⊚

Child _____

DOCU-MENT NO.	DATE OF SERVICE	PROVIDER	AMOUNT BILLED	INSURER PAYMENT	AMOUNT PAID BY ME	OTHER PARTY OWES

§ 9:15 Elements of agreement—Child support—Medical expenses—Collection agencies

The legislature has provided protection to the non-liable parent for unpaid medical expenses where a decree terminating the marriage requires a party, who is a resident of the state, to be responsible for obtaining health insurance coverage for the former spouse or children. Where the responsible party fails to obtain such coverage, no provider or collection agency shall collect or attempt to collect from the former spouse or children any reimbursement of such expenses as would have been covered.[1] The former spouse or children must provide a copy of the court order, and assistance in locating the responsible party. In addition, if the party follows the statutory procedure, the collection agency may not report the nonpayment by the former spouse to a credit-reporting agency.

§ 9:16 Elements of agreement—Child support—Insurance to protect[1]

Another problem which arises in this area is the effect of the death of the supporting parent, which will generally cause his duty of support to end, and his estate will not be chargeable with the duty of

---

[Section 9:15]

[1]RC 1349.01(B).

[Section 9:16]

[1]See, also, Text § 9:134, Spousal support security—Life insurance as guarantee—Form; Text § 9:175, Life insurance to be maintained—Form, and Text § 9:176, Life insurance—Additional Policy—Form.

support.[2] This situation is subject to change by written agreement and must therefore be addressed by the drafter. One of the most common ways to address this question is to provide that the supporting parent maintain, through emancipation (or college for a child, if provided), a life insurance policy naming the children as primary beneficiaries. In the agreement, if this provision is intended only as "additional security" to guarantee the support of the child, it may be interpreted to limit the amount of proceeds payable to the amount of support. In the alternative, the attorney may provide that the supporting parent's estate continue to pay the support, or that the will name the children as beneficiaries of the estate in a specified amount.

In either case, enforcement of the provisions is difficult. A party may agree to maintain a policy, to name the children in the will, or to provide a charge on his estate. He or she may also terminate the policy, die intestate, leave all to his or her new spouse, or arrange to die insolvent.[3] The problems are enforcement and sanctions that can be agreed on, recognizing that in the event of contest, the court cannot provide the requested guarantees.

When an agreement provided that child support was to increase in an amount proportionate to the husband's "net income," which was not defined in the agreement, the Tenth District Court of Appeals in *Chaney v. Chaney*[4] held that "net income means gross income less expenses and taxes" and not adjusted gross income for tax purposes.

§ 9:17 Elements of agreement—Child support—Life Insurance to protect—Form⊚

The *wife/husband (party insured)* is the insured and owner of the following life insurance policies *list policy names and numbers*. The *wife/husband (party maintaining life insurance)* shall maintain, in full force and effect, said life insurance *policy/policies* currently issued on *his/her (party w/life insurance)* life and shall designate the *wife/husband/child/children/a trust for the benefit of the minor child/children (designated beneficiary)* as the sole *beneficiary/beneficiaries* of said policy, until the *child/children reach/reaches* the age of *cut-off age*

OPTION

and thereafter until *each/such/the* child completes or terminates *his/her* higher education or training.

---

[2]Billow v. Billow, 97 Ohio App. 277, 56 Ohio Op. 80, 125 N.E.2d 558 (9th Dist. Summit County 1953).

[3]Studley v. Studley, 32 Ohio App. 3d 1, 513 N.E.2d 811 (8th Dist. Cuyahoga County 1986) (court imposed constructive trust on proceeds); Kelly v. Medical Life Ins. Co., 31 Ohio St. 3d 130, 509 N.E.2d 411 (1987) (constructive trust appropriate remedy where insured fails to name beneficiaries as required by decree; where no limitation on amount of obligation, "so long as support obligation exists" only limits duration of obligation, thus all proceeds subject to trust).

[4]Chaney v. Chaney, 24 Ohio App. 3d 169, 493 N.E.2d 997 (10th Dist. Franklin County 1985).

OPTION

so long as *he/she (obligor)* has any obligations to the *wife/husband (obligee)* hereunder.

§ 9:18 Elements of agreement—Division of marital property—Disclosure

Any property division is dependent on the spousal support portion of the agreement and vice versa.[1] The focus of the division of marital property should therefore be on the final, combined result of the property and support provisions.[2]

In determining a property settlement, each side must make a full disclosure of his or her assets and debts.[3] A separation agreement should therefore include a complete recitation of the assets and liabilities of either or both parties, including when they were acquired, how they are presently titled, and where they are located. It should contain a statement as to the most recent gross income of both parties, stated in a yearly, monthly, or weekly figure. If necessary, verification may be required. Each side must fully explain to the other the details and significance of each item of property and its transfer, including tax implications. The agreement should list each item of property and the method of ownership, or the same should be incorporated by reference to earlier provisions. For persons with moderate or extensive wealth, there may be a preference not to include a precise listing in the agreement per se, as, in the event of a divorce or dissolution, the total agreement will become a matter of public record. In many cases, this is not a viable consideration, and other methods for full disclosure of assets may be appropriate.

For instance, assume full disclosure has taken place between the parties and they are satisfied. Also assume that the parties have agreed to a disposition of the tangibles. It is possible that each could take possession of the tangibles prior to the hearing. Intangibles (stocks, bonds, bank accounts, etc.) and realty can also be accounted in the final hearing. For instance, each brings the documents and appropriate assignments to the court for the hearing, and the court puts them in escrow. After the dissolution (or uncontested hearing), the court assures that each party takes the appropriate documents. The risk is that after distribution of the tangibles, one of the parties might renege on the dissolution. In this event, assuming the document has

---

[Section 9:18]

[1]For a discussion of the applicable law, see Text Ch 12, Marital and Separate Property; Text Ch 28, Tax Considerations. For examples of division of property clauses see Text §§ 9:65 to 9:72, Personal property; Text §§ 9:73 to 9:79, Real estate; Text §§ 9:80 to 9:86, Retirement benefits.

[2]See Text Ch 12, Marital and Separate Property; Text Ch 13, Spousal Support. See also RC 3105.18(C)(1)(i).

[3]RC 3105.171(C)(2). See In re Murphy, 10 Ohio App. 3d 134, 461 N.E.2d 910 (1st Dist. Hamilton County 1983) (court may set aside decree where separation agreement fails to identify and allocate all assets).

been drafted with an independent significance clause, it could be used in a divorce proceeding.

Real property should be listed according to mailing address and legal description. Boats, motor vehicles, and trailers should be listed by model, year, and serial number. Other items of value should be specifically identified to avoid the possibility of confusion as to which items are meant.

The parties should warrant that they have specifically disclosed all assets in their possession. The agreement should further provide that, if a court of competent jurisdiction later determines that either party failed to disclose an item of property within the agreement, of which either had possession when disclosure was requested, the nondisclosing party shall pay an agreed percentage of value (generally one-half) to the other party. Value of the item should be determined either at the time of discovery or at the time of agreement, whichever is more equitable.[4] A warranty clause should prevent nondisclosure by placing the risk of market fluctuation and inapplicability of related debts or liens on the nondisclosing party.[5]

§ 9:19 Elements of agreement—Division of marital property— Personal property

A division of property will usually give to each party his or her personal possessions and divides the other assets, both real and personal, which represent the wealth of the marriage. Personal possessions generally include clothing, sports equipment, tools, jewelry, and other personal effects.

The actual division of the assets should begin tentatively with the household goods, furnishings, and other items of personal property located in the family home. The entire contents may be allocated to one party, or the items should be specifically identified and allocated to the appropriate party. Provision should be made for the parties to take possession of their respective property, with notice to the other party residing in the home.

Whenever practical, the parties should physically divide the property. The party not living in the residence should remove the property as soon as possible, at least before the final hearing. Failure to do so frequently creates actions where the resident spouse objects to the non-resident spouse entering the home and otherwise refuses to deliver. Additionally, the non-resident spouse may enter and forcibly take property not rightfully his or hers or otherwise allocated to the resident. Finally, as the agreement will most likely include an "abandonment" clause (property not removed by a certain date will be

---

[4]For a discussion of the problems associated with valuation dates, see Text § 12:29, Valuation date. See also Berish v. Berish, 69 Ohio St. 2d 318, 23 Ohio Op. 3d 296, 432 N.E.2d 183 (1982).

[5]For further discussion on valuations and risks, see Text § 12:28, Methods of valuation.

considered as having been abandoned and will become the property of the resident), it is always better to have the property removed before the hearing, or immediately after the hearing but before the decree is recorded. A clause may be added permitting or requiring removal within a specified time (e.g., within ten days of the hearing).

If the draftsperson feels that waste or theft of his or her client's possessions may occur, the agreement should provide that the property will be delivered in undamaged condition by the spouse in possession to the spouse receiving possession. Generally, household goods, furnishings, etc., are the areas where couples going through the process of altering their marital relationship can first agree.

The next item of division may be intangibles (for example, cash, bank deposits, and corporate stocks and bonds). The drafter should identify the stocks, allocate the appropriate stocks and bonds to the appropriate parties, and require the transferring party to perform all necessary actions to transfer or release title. Further, the drafter should allocate all accrued dividends and interest to one of the parties. Cash and bank accounts should be divided in a similar manner.

Automobiles, boats, or other vehicles covered by applicable motor vehicle registration statutes should be identified by year, model, and serial number. The agreement should require that the transferring party deliver good title, free and clear of all liens, if that is the intent. In some cases, the parties may agree to retain the automobiles already in their name, or one of the parties may agree to accept a vehicle subject to a lien. This condition should be clearly expressed.

§ 9:20　Elements of agreement—Division of marital property— Real property

Real property should be transferred by deed (generally a quitclaim deed, although in some situations a limited warranty deed should be considered), in which the transferor conveys all right, title, and interest in the real estate. The agreement should identify the property both by mailing address and legal description.

The drafter should anticipate and provide for lack of post-decree cooperation on the part of the transferor. Where, for example, the counsel or party may have reason to believe that the transferor may fail to execute and provide for delivery of the deed to the real property, the agreement should provide that the agreement may be filed as a conveyance, in which case the agreement should be witnessed by two witnesses and a notary.[1] The court has this authority to enforce compliance by contempt or by entry of judgment which has the effect

---

[Section 9:20]

[1]For deeds or documents of conveyance of real estate entered into subsequent to February 1, 2002, RC 5301.01 requires only a notary. The prior requirement of two witnesses was removed.

of a conveyance, without this type of clause,[2] but the clause serves a twofold purpose. First, the mere existence of the clause in the agreement may deter the transferring party from attempting to stall. Second, in the event the transfer is stalled, the existence of an agreed alternative procedure for the transfer of the real property will provide the court with a ready-made remedy. Where a parcel of property is to be physically divided in some manner between the parties in the future, the agreement should state the method of division, the allocation of costs for any necessary surveying and responsibility for preparation of deeds.

In line with the concept that there should be nothing left for post-decree, interparty performance, there is a procedure for transfer of titled property. The property has been allocated, and rights have been granted by the agreement. The title papers (e.g., quitclaim deed) must be drafted. Practically speaking, there is no reason why the drafting cannot be completed by the hearing date. If the parties to an agreed termination have not reneged, they will most likely not do so at that date. If counsel know the hearing is to go forward, nothing will prevent all such documents from being drafted, executed (in court if necessary), and brought to the hearing. The documents will be placed on the judge's bench as exhibits so that the judge may examine them. If the termination is granted, the judge will transfer the papers to the intended party. If the termination is not granted, the papers will be returned. It is better to transfer title at the hearing than to leave the transfer to post-decree performance.

A former spouse of a decedent, who had never transferred residence real property pursuant to the agreement of the parties incorporated under the 1977 decree of divorce, recorded the divorce judgment 26 years later in 2003. The probate court magistrate concluded that the wife had become the sole owner of the property at the time of divorce, as the filing of divorce judgment with clerk's office gave notice and the filing with the recorder's office was ministerial, not substantive. Due to the circumstances, laches didn't apply.[3] A deed does not have to be recorded to pass title, but an unrecorded deed is unenforceable against a subsequent bona fide purchaser for value without actual knowledge.

Any liabilities on the real property are generally allocated to the party taking possession of the property. The agreement should specifically allocate all liabilities on the property. It must be made clear to the parties that they can make any agreement they wish as to liabilities on mortgages, liens, and notes, but the assumption of liability by one party does not mean that the creditor will release the other on the obligation. The joint liability to the creditor continues despite any interdebtor agreements. Taxes, as well as tax escrow balance, should be specifically provided for in the agreement. The agreement should provide for continuing house insurance coverage during

---

[2]Civ. R. 70.

[3]In re Estate of Dinsio, 159 Ohio App. 3d 98, 2004-Ohio-6036, 823 N.E.2d 43 (7th Dist. Mahoning County 2004).

the period of transfer. Generally, the transferor would provide insurance until the time the transfer takes place, at which time the party in possession assumes responsibility. If the property is to be sold at a loss (pay to close), the liability for a negative equity must be allocated.

The tax law change in 1997 effectively removed any tax on the capital gain on personal residences, when it created an exemption of $250,000.00 of gain per person.[4] However, that only applies to personal residences. If the real property is unimproved land or other real property, the liability for paying taxes on and reporting gain or adjustment of basis should be addressed.

Other alternatives for the disposition of real property can include (1) use by a party for a period of time and then sale, with provision for distribution of gross and resulting net sale proceeds; (2) use by a party for a period of time with an option to purchase at a certain defined rate; or (3) sale on a failure to exercise such option.

In any arrangement regarding the division of real property, the agreement should always specify the time at which required actions are to take place and an alternative remedy if required actions are not completed. Further, the agreement regarding any property should always provide for the allocation of liabilities, taxes, and insurance. In addition, the agreement should provide whether new liabilities can be incurred to encumber the property.

The agreement should also provide for the orderly physical transfer of the property from one party to the other. Specific dates for vacating the premises, surrendering all keys, etc., should be provided for in the agreement. The agreement should further specify that neither party will commit waste or in any way hinder the orderly process of transfer. If the property is to be transferred prior to or contemporaneously with a final hearing, the deed of transfer should be prepared, ready for review and signing along with the agreement.

To prevent future problems, where the realty is subject to a future transfer, and the interest of the other party in the cash value of that realty is to be vested in possession (paid) at that future time, it is essential that counsel consider that the reserved cash interest be represented by a mortgage note, with or without interest on the "loan," as the parties may agree. As additional security, the mortgage note should be secured by a mortgage deed from the resident new owner in favor of the mortgagee. This gives a date certain and a security to prevent subsequent alienation or compromise of that asset by the owner. If the owner party or counsel refuses to agree to such note and security, counsel for the mortgagee should be immediately put on notice and insist on it. The realty interest should not be transferred without this point being seriously considered.

---

[4]I.R.C. § 121(b).

§ 9:21 Elements of agreement—Division of marital property— Retirement benefits

Retirement plans are marital property, subject to division.[1] In the past, it was generally unrealistic to physically divide these plans. A division of a retirement plan usually resulted in a substantial penalty for early withdrawal. Additionally, tax consequences further depleted the available assets. As a result, most separation agreements attempted to resolve these problems by having the original party maintain his or her retirement accounts and to compensate by making other adjustments or provisions for the other party.

While the above-noted procedure is still an acceptable practice, the way in which retirement plans are dealt with in a separation agreement has been substantially altered by a number of statutes. The statute having the most dramatic effect on the issue of retirement plans in separation agreements is the Retirement Equity Act of 1984 (REA).[2] Prior to the enactment of REA,[3] the general rule was that private pension plans were not subject to assignment. This general rule in a number of cases worked an undue hardship on those attempting to enforce family support obligations, including child support, spousal support, and division of marital property. REA created a specific exception to the general rule against assignability in order to address the unique needs of this area of domestic relations law. REA applies to private pension plans and attempts to provide for the spouses and dependents of private pension plan participants by creating a vehicle by which spouses and dependents can receive the benefit of the private pension plan, which in many cases is the largest family asset.

The vehicle created by REA is the "qualified domestic relations order" (QDRO). A QDRO is a domestic relations order which creates or recognizes the right or rights of a spouse, former spouse, child, or other dependent to receive all or a portion of the benefits payable from a private pension plan for the provision of or payment of child support, spousal support, or marital property rights due from the private pension plan participant. A QDRO must clearly specify the name and last known mailing address of the private pension plan participant and the name and mailing address of each alternate payee (spouse, former spouse, child, or other dependent) covered by the QDRO. Further, the QDRO must identify the amount or percentage of the participant's benefits to be paid by the private pension plan to each alternate payee or the manner in which such amount or percentage is to be determined and the number of payments or, in the alternative,

---

[Section 9:21]

[1]See Text Ch 30, Dividing Private Retirement Benefits in Divorce.

[2]Pub. L. No. 98-397, codified at 29 U.S.C.A. § 1001.

[3]Benson v. Benson, 1998 WL 28002 (Ohio Ct. App. 2d Dist. Clark County 1998) (trial court has inherent power to issue QDRO to effectuate division of retirement asset in pre-REA separation agreement).

the time period to which the order is to apply. Also, each private pension plan affected by the order must be identified in the order.

A QDRO cannot require that a pension plan provide benefits not normally offered. Further, a QDRO cannot increase benefits, and existing QDROs take precedent over any subsequent attempts to assign private pension plan benefits.

A QDRO may provide that benefits be paid to an alternate payee at the earliest retirement date of the participant without violating the requirement that a QDRO cannot require a pension plan to provide benefits not normally offered. Finally, it should be noted that a separation agreement in and of itself does not constitute a QDRO. The separation agreement may contain all of the necessary provisions to be a valid QDRO on incorporation into a decree, or the agreement may provide that each party will execute a separate judgment entry with all pension plan provisions. This eliminates the need for the plan administrator to go through all other provisions of the separation agreement. A failure to include retirement benefits in a separation agreement may result in the granting of a subsequent Civil Rule 59 or 60(B) motion since the court must consider pension plans.[4]

In addition to the REA, there are a number of federal retirement plan statutes which provide for alternate payee options pursuant to a domestic court order.[5]The civil service retirement system of the federal government is governed by 5 U.S.C.A. § 8345(j)(1), which provides as follows:

> Payments under this subchapter which would otherwise be made to an employee, member, or annuitant based upon his service shall be paid (in whole or in part) by the Office to another person if and to the extent expressly provided for in the terms of any court decree of divorce, annulment, or legal separation, or the terms of any court order or court-approved property settlement agreement incident to any court decree of divorce, annulment, or legal separation. Any payment under this paragraph to a person bars recovery by any other person.

The issue of payment of spousal support, child support, or property settlement for a military family is addressed in 10 U.S.C.A. § 1408(c)(1), which provides as follows:

> Subject to the limitations of this section, a court may treat disposable retired or retainer pay payable to a member for pay periods beginning after June 25, 1981, either as property solely of the member or as property of the member and his spouse in accordance with the law of the jurisdiction of such court.

This section specifically requires that the court have personal jurisdiction over the plan member.

The foreign service retirement system of the federal government also provides for and recognizes that a retirement plan is marital property subject to division at 22 U.S.C.A. § 4044.

---

[4]Malone v. Malone, 126 Ohio App. 3d 685, 711 N.E.2d 262 (4th Dist. Scioto County 1998).

[5]See Text Ch 29, Government Retirement Benefits.

Provisions for the division of a federal railroad retirement plan are contained at 45 U.S.C.A. § 231(A).

42 U.S.C.A. § 416 recognizes the right of a divorced spouse to participate in social security benefits earned by a prior spouse, if said divorced spouse had been married to the individual for a period of ten years immediately before the date the divorce or dissolution became effective.

In light of REA and the various federal statutory enactments, virtually all pension funds are subject to assignment for the purposes of spousal support, child support, and division of marital property. Ohio state government funds are subject to assignment, after commencement of benefits, for all of these purposes.[6] State plans in Ohio have some problematic features, such as no survivorship benefits, and must be evaluated in respect to the best way to address in a separation agreement.

In 1986, the Ohio legislature provided for the first time for withholding for child and spousal support from state retirement benefit plans which were in pay status.[7] Effective January 1, 2002,[8] a participant's state retirement benefits became subject to court orders dividing property rights.[9] Effective October, 2006, a participant can name up to four survivor beneficiaries for up to 50% survivor benefits when retiring and can include a former spouse.[10]

The Ohio Public Employees Deferred Compensation fund, which involves voluntary employee contributions, can be subject to property division under certain circumstances.[11]

§ 9:22 Elements of agreement—Division of marital property—Business interests

Another problem is the closely held corporation, small partnership, or sole proprietorship.[1] In many marriages, this business may provide the parties' livelihoods and constitute the largest asset they possess. If that asset is transferred to the party who is not familiar with the business, the business may quickly lose value. However, the nonman-

---

[6]See Text Ch 29, Government Retirement Benefits.

[7]RC 3113.21(D)(3) as enacted in 1986 H.B. 509.

[8]2000 H.B. 535, eff. 1-1-02.

[9]For a comprehensive discussion, see Text §§ 29:48 et seq.

[10]To review these plans see RC 145.46 for PERS, RC 3309.46 for SERS, and RC 3307.60 for STRS.

[11]See Text § 29:73, Ohio Public Employees Deferred Compensation Fund.

[Section 9:22]

[1]See Text §§ 12:18 to 12:26, Specific types of property; Text Ch 28, Tax Considerations.

aging party is entitled to a part of the value of the business if the business was operating during the marriage.[2]

There are several possible approaches to this problem. The first possibility is for the managing party to buy out the nonmanaging party. In this case, the agreement should contain a formula to which the parties agree for the valuation of the shares of the corporation. The drafter should consider whether this sale should occur before or after the divorce and whether the sale should be accompanied by a consent from the Internal Revenue Service that all proceeds be recognized as long-term gains. As in the transfer of real property, the agreement should provide for the delivery of all necessary documents, a specific time for performance, and a remedy in the event of nonperformance.

In the case of a sole proprietorship, the drafter is again faced with the question of valuation. The agreement should contain a formula for determining value. The agreement should also require all necessary performance (payment, etc.) within a specified period. In the event of nonperformance, the agreement should provide a remedy.

In considering closely held corporations, sole proprietorships, and general or limited partnerships, there may be an agreement in which no transfer for value is made. It may be preferable for (1) one spouse to hold a portion of the entity in trust for the other; (2) only the income of the entity to be shared on a pro rata, before or after tax, basis; (3) one spouse to receive all the business interests and the other spouse to receive a compensating offsetting interest in nonbusiness assets; or (4) one spouse to receive a note and security interest against the business assets retained or received by the other. Further, it is not unusual for a husband and wife to be equal partners in a business where both parties play key roles in the management of the business. In this case, it may not be possible to alter their business relationship in the separation agreement.

§ 9:23   Elements of agreement—Spousal support

Prior to January 1, 1991, Ohio had one statute under which property was divided and alimony was awarded.[1] Subsequently, the term spousal support[2] supplanted the concept of the support portion of the

---

[2]Wolfe v. Wolfe, 46 Ohio St. 2d 399, 75 Ohio Op. 2d 474, 350 N.E.2d 413 (1976). See also Text § 12:30, Methods of distribution.

[Section 9:23]

[1]Former RC 3105.18.

[2]For a discussion of the applicable law, see Text Ch 8, Legal Separation; Text Ch 13, Spousal Support; Text Ch 14, Modification of Spousal Support; Text Ch 20, Enforcement of Spousal and Child Support; Text Ch 22, Child Support Enforcement Agencies; Text Ch 23, Interstate and Foreign Support Practice; Text Ch 28, Tax Considerations; Text Ch 33, Bankruptcy. For examples of spousal support clauses, see Text §§ 9:87 to 9:120, Spousal Support.

prior alimony statute, and a new statute reflected all considerations for division of property.[3]

There are several possible approaches to the spousal support issue. In a short-term marriage, depending on the property settlement, spousal support may not be appropriate. In this case, the agreement would simply state that neither party shall pay spousal support to the other party.

Another approach to the spousal support issue is the lump-sum or in-gross settlement. The IRS may or may not view the lump-sum approach as spousal support.[4] This approach would most properly work in a situation where the needs of both parties can be accommodated by a division of marital property. In general, this would be a couple who had acquired a measurable degree of wealth during the course of the marriage.

The most common approach to the spousal support question is the periodic payment of spousal support on a specified cyclic term (monthly, weekly, bi-monthly) over a period of years, generally contingent on its termination when the party receiving payment dies or remarries. The payor will also generally want any periodic spousal support to cease upon the payee's cohabitation with an unrelated adult of the opposite sex. As counsel for the payee, it is wise to resist this provision, unless cohabitation is defined to require, for instance, that it be with "same person, in payee's residence, continuously for six months," to avoid termination upon short-term trial relationships, and to avoid litigation to determine if the relationship constituted "cohabitation."

However, there are several pitfalls to be considered in drafting this portion of the separation agreement. First, the attorney must consider whether spousal support will result in an equitable division of marital property. If the client intends to remarry or cohabit in the near future, a large monthly spousal support payment terminating on remarriage or cohabitation is of little support value, although it may be an excellent deterrent. In this case, the drafter should consider (1) whether the spousal support should continue wholly or partly after remarriage; (2) whether the agreement should have a built-in escalation and/or de-escalation provision based on an objective contingency, such as a cost of living index, a set sum or percentage, or a combination thereof; and (3) whether a clause should permit the spousal support recipient to earn up to a set figure per year without reducing the spousal support. As previously noted, if the client intends to remarry or cohabit in the near future, the appropriate place to look for equitable division (at least for that person) is in the property division.[5]

If the parties intend the spousal support to be modifiable in the future, the agreement must state that the court shall have continuing

---

[3]RC 3105.171.

[4]See Text Ch 28, Tax Considerations; Text Ch 33, Bankruptcy.

[5]See Text Ch 13, Spousal Support; Text Ch 14, Modification of Spousal Support.

jurisdiction to modify.[6] The parties should also specify whether the spousal support is to be taxable to the recipient and deductible by the payor.[7]

Ohio Revised Code Chapter 3121[8] replaced former RC 3105.18(G) which required all spousal support orders made after December 1, 1986 to have withholding from payroll or other identifiable sources. Provisions for withholding should be included in the agreement if applicable.

In cases where there are no minor children, RC 3121.441, as effective January 25, 2002, permits the parties to agree to direct payment of spousal support.[9]

The statute authorizing the direct payment provides protection by providing that, in the event of the default in making any payment, the court may rescind the provision. The benefit of not having to pay a processing fee is of real value when the amount of the support order is high. Payments must be made by check, money order, or in a form that establishes a clear record of payment.

§ 9:24 Elements of agreement—Spousal support—Insurance to protect

Parties may agree to a provision that protects the obligee from the financial loss of spousal support in the event of the death of the obligor. Where a spousal support award specifies it terminates upon obligee's death but omits obligor's death and expresses the intent for spousal support to continue after death of obligor, the trial court may secure the spousal support order with life insurance.[1]

§ 9:25 Elements of agreement—Marital debts

Substantial financial obligations are likely to have been incurred by the parties over the course of their marriage.[1] To prevent future problems between the parties and from third parties (creditors), the satisfaction of these debts must be addressed. The separation agreement, therefore, should contain a list of every such obligation and

---

[6]RC 3105.18(E).

[7]I.R.C. § 71(b)(1)(B).

[8]RC Ch. 3121, placing all withholding provisions in a separate chapter, was enacted by 2000 S.B. 180, eff. 3-22-01.

[9]2001 H.B. 208. See Text § 9:95, Spousal support—Method of payment—Direct—Form.

[Section 9:24]

[1]Forbis v. Forbis, 2005-Ohio-5881, 2005 WL 2931851 (Ohio Ct. App. 6th Dist. Wood County 2005). See Text § 9:120, Spousal support security—Life insurance as guarantee—Form.

[Section 9:25]

[1]For sample marital debt clauses, see Text §§ 9:166 to 9:171, Marital debts; See also Text Ch 28, Tax Considerations.

identify, in each instance, which spouse will assume responsibility for payment. Additionally, it is recommended that the parties provide for responsibility or the division of responsibility for undetermined liabilities, such as for previously filed joint income tax returns. A post-decree notice of deficiency may come as a surprise. Without prior allocation, one party may be the person pursued, without recourse against the other party. One or more of these debts may remain a joint obligation of the parties if they so desire. The agreement may also specify a source for satisfying the debt (for example, withdrawals from a bank account or the sale of property and application of the proceeds).

Additionally, a clause should be inserted in which both parties warrant that there are no other outstanding obligations for which the other party may be held responsible. The agreement should nevertheless anticipate that undisclosed debts may arise. The agreement, therefore, should provide for payment by the party who fails to disclose. The logical approach is to place the responsibility for repayment on the party who incurred the obligation, if possible. As a further incentive toward full disclosure, a clause should be added requiring the party incurring the obligation to indemnify and hold the other party harmless against any action brought by the undisclosed creditor and also to bear the cost of defending such an action.

As with a specific listing of marital properties, there may be the situation where the parties, or at least one of them, may not want all the debts and creditors listed in the agreement, which will shortly become a public document. Some courts require, by local rule, full disclosure to the court.[2] The general conceptual requirement is de facto disclosure of the debts to the other party. There is no requirement that such debts become a matter of public record. If such is the case, the listing could be a separate instrument, incorporated by reference into the agreement, rather than physically attached: in other words, a collateral agreement. In that event, the agreement could list the fact and amount of the debts, or merely disclosure of the fact of the agreed full disclosure. If both parties are represented by counsel, the disclosure listing could be held by the attorneys in a form of escrow. As the party not wanting the disclosure is most likely the one that is liable, the possibility of subsequent disclosure in a show cause proceeding is an adequate deterrent. There is no suggestion that any of the alternative procedures be used or preferred, but only that they are for use as each situation demands.

---

[2]See, e.g., Stark County R. 31.02, Montgomery County C.P. Dom. Rel. R. 4.08, Franklin County C.P. Dom. Rel. R. 17.

§ 9:26   Elements of agreement—Use of other's credit

Ohio law does not impose pecuniary liability on a spouse strictly by virtue of the marriage relationship.[1] RC 3103.08 incorporates the abolition of the common law legal identity of husband and wife.[2] However, joint credit accounts and various other circumstances may have created an agency relationship whereby one or both spouses are capable of legally obligating the other. This agency relationship, if allowed to exist subsequent to the separation, can only be a source of trouble. Hence, the separation agreement should provide for the closing out of all such credit accounts. Credit cards issued in the names of both spouses should be returned or destroyed and the accounts closed. Businesses that had previously been authorized to grant one spouse credit on the other's account must be notified that an agency relationship no longer exists. Further, the separation agreement should contain mutual promises not to create debts subsequent to the separation, or after a specified date, for which the other party may be held liable. If this promise is breached, a clause in the agreement should require the party incurring the obligation to indemnify and hold harmless the other party and to bear the costs of defending any action brought against the party.

§ 9:27   Elements of agreement—Resumption of former name

One or both spouses may wish to resume their former prenuptial names subsequent to the divorce or dissolution. Usually, this involves restoration of the wife's maiden name. Any complications that may arise from a name change should be considered and explained to the client. If it is still desired, a provision may be made for it in the separation agreement. Thereafter, if the divorce or dissolution is granted, the court must accommodate the party and restore his or her former name in the decree. RC 3105.16 does not require a resumption of the maiden name but permits any name used prior to the marriage. Thus, if the person has used other names, such as in a prior marriage, the party can use any of those prior names. A change of name to one other than any previously used is a probate procedure. If a change of name is requested, the order granting the restoration to a prior name should be in the decree itself.

§ 9:28   Elements of agreement—Mutual releases

Parties should be advised regarding the legal consequences of mutual releases and relinquishment of marital rights pending

---

[Section 9:26]

[1]For applicable law, see Text §§ 4:2 to 4:3, Support obligations during marriage.

[2]Damm v. Elyria Lodge No. 465, Benev. Protective Order of Elks, 158 Ohio St. 107, 48 Ohio Op. 54, 107 N.E.2d 337 (1952). See also Text Ch 4, Marital Obligations and Property Rights; RC 3103.05 (permits "transactions" with others as if unmarried, which implies ability to incur individual nonmarital financial obligations).

termination of marriage. There may be situations where it is not desired.[1]

The separation agreement may and usually should contain a clause which mutually releases the parties from their former marital obligations.[2] This clause, in effect, states that the parties' relationship is now governed by the separation agreement and that all other marital rights and duties have been discharged. The mutual release clause should specifically note that all rights or claims of dower, inheritance, descent and distribution, allowance for a year's support, rights to remain in the mansion house, other claims as widow, widower, heir, distributee, survivor, or next of kin, and any other estate rights connected with the marital relationship are now barred. Whether this result is desired before an actual termination of the marriage should be thoroughly discussed and evaluated. Finally, the parties should release any rights to administer the estate of the other.

In the event of a contrary intention, the parties may agree that either or both execute a will which provides for specific items or amounts to be devised to each other, to their children, or to others. Since the agreement itself is adequate consideration, the provision would be enforceable.[3]

A mutual release "from any present and future claims and demands" contained in a separation agreement incorporated into a decree can extinguish an obligee's rights to child support which arose out of a prior proceeding between the parties.[4] While the domestic relations court would not otherwise have authority to erase an arrearage, the court does have the power to give effect to and enforce such an agreement.[5]

The abrogation of the doctrine of interspousal immunity for negligent or intentional torts makes it appropriate to provide mutual releases from tort claims.[6]

§ 9:29   Elements of agreement—Expenses and fees

A well-drafted separation agreement should include a clause establishing responsibility for all expenses incurred in the negotiation, drafting, and execution of the agreement and/or obtaining of the

---

[Section 9:28]

[1]See, e.g., In re Estate of Hogrefe, 30 Ohio App. 3d 238, 507 N.E.2d 414 (3d Dist. Henry County 1986) (inferred waiver from general language).

[2]For sample mutual release clauses, see Text §§ 9:172 to 9:174, Mutual release.

[3]Longo v. Longo, 1996 WL 664883 (Ohio Ct. App. 7th Dist. Mahoning County 1996) (enforcement of a will clause is a contract issue).

[4]Fout v. Fout, 1993 WL 485119 (Ohio Ct. App. 10th Dist. Franklin County 1993).

[5]Fout v. Fout, 1993 WL 485119 (Ohio Ct. App. 10th Dist. Franklin County 1993).

[6]See Text § 4:1, History of marital property rights and obligations.

divorce or dissolution.[1] Attorney fees, accounting fees, appraiser fees, court costs, and all other expenses should be enumerated and assigned to one or both parties. This will minimize, if not eliminate, argument over such matters in the future.

As a general rule, the court has a wide range of discretion in allowing for expenses in the final decree. However, where a separation agreement is found to be fair and equitable and is incorporated into the decree by reference, the court has no authority to alter a provision made by the parties regarding the payment of fees and expenses. Such an agreement may be upheld even though it totally bars the wife from receiving further expense money. Thus, a provision dividing the expenses incurred in the separation and subsequent proceedings is likely to be binding on the court and may prevent a court settlement less desirable to both parties. The court has the obligation to approve the agreement before adoption.[2]

§ 9:30 Elements of agreement—Applicable law

It is important that a clause be inserted into the separation agreement that states what law will be controlling on the agreement.[1] The effect of such a provision is to avoid future controversies and choice of law entanglements. Even if one or both parties take up residence in a different state, their respective rights under the agreement and decree will be governed by the same law and will remain unchanged. On the other hand, the failure to include a clause in the agreement may result in prolonged litigation just to determine which state's law applies. Thus, to avoid future problems, the agreement should declare a state under whose law the agreement will be construed and governed.

However, no matter how expertly drafted, a clause will not prevent the operation of the provisions of URESA, UIFSA, UCCJA, and UCCJEA, which give another state the jurisdiction to apply its laws and discretion as to modifications of spousal and child support, and custody. The parties should be advised of this contingency.

§ 9:31 Elements of agreement—Modification provisions

The possibility of reconciliation should be considered in the

---

[Section 9:29]

[1]For a discussion of the applicable law, see Text Ch 13, Spousal support.

[2]See Sinclair v. Sinclair, 98 Ohio App. 308, 57 Ohio Op. 347, 129 N.E.2d 311 (2d Dist. Preble County 1954); Brewer v. Brewer, 84 Ohio App. 35, 39 Ohio Op. 89, 52 Ohio L. Abs. 116, 78 N.E.2d 919 (2d Dist. Montgomery County 1948); Shalkhauser v. Shalkhauser, 1981 WL 10388 (Ohio Ct. App. 8th Dist. Cuyahoga County 1981) (court not required to adopt any settlement agreement between parties if court finds it is not fair, just, and reasonable).

[Section 9:30]

[1]For sample clauses, see Text § 9:58, Separation agreement—Basic—Form; Text § 9:59, Separation agreement—Detailed—Form; Text § 9:180, Governing law—Form.

agreement.[1] The drafter of the agreement should include a provision which allows for modification or waiver of the separation agreement, or of any part of the agreement, but is effective only if made in writing and executed with the same formality as the original agreement. It should specifically note that the failure by either party to insist on strict performance of any of the provisions in the agreement does not constitute a waiver or modification of said agreement.

RC 3105.18 was amended by 1986 House Bill 358, effective May 2, 1986, to deny a court jurisdiction to modify periodic payments of money as spousal support unless the divorce decree or a separation agreement of the parties incorporated into the decree of divorce or dissolution *specifically* authorizes the court to modify the amount or term of spousal support.[2]

The parties should be advised that nothing in the agreement can prevent the inherent and statutory continuing jurisdiction to modify matters of child support and parental rights on application for that continuing jurisdiction by either party.

While RC 3105.63 and RC 3105.65 do not create continuing jurisdiction for a trial court to modify property divisions in dissolutions, nothing in the statutes precludes the parties from voluntarily including a provision for continuing jurisdiction in their separation agreement.[3] Where the court has approved the agreement and incorporated it into a decree of dissolution, the court has the power to enforce the clause.

§ 9:32 Elements of agreement—Full understanding

A clause should be inserted into the agreement which memorializes the advice and negotiation which resulted in drafting of the agreement. This clause should clearly indicate that the separation agreement contains the entire understanding of the parties and that there are no representations, warranties, covenants, or understandings except those expressly contained in the agreement. This is an expression of basic contract law and the parol evidence rule.

§ 9:33 Elements of agreement—Attorney waiver

The agreement should contain a provision in which both parties acknowledge that they were advised to seek legal counsel of their own choice in order to understand the effect and consequences of the terms and conditions of the agreement. Additionally, the agreement should provide that both parties have read and understand the agreement. If

---

[Section 9:31]

[1]For a discussion of the applicable law, see Text Ch 8, Legal Separation; Text Ch 14, Modification of Spousal Support; Text Ch 16, Modification of Parental Rights and Responsibilities; Text Ch 18, Parenting Time; Text Ch 24, Relief from Judgment; See Text § 9:64, Effect of reconciliation—Form.

[2]1986 H.B. 358 also amended RC 3105.63 and RC 3105.65.

[3]In re Whitman, 81 Ohio St. 3d 239, 1998-Ohio-466, 690 N.E.2d 535 (1998).

one party does not obtain counsel, this provision should note that the drafter only represents one party, both parties were advised to seek counsel, and the party in question voluntarily entered into the agreement without the advice of counsel.[1]

The fact that a separation agreement was prepared by the other party's attorney does not require the court to construe the provisions against the party who prepared it, where there is no ambiguity in the terms.[2]

§ 9:34 Elements of agreement—Execution

The agreement should further provide that the provisions of the agreement and their legal effect have been fully explained and that the parties are voluntarily entering into the agreement. Finally, the agreement could have signature lines on every page of the agreement to further substantiate that the parties have read, understand, and are entering into the agreement voluntarily. Its legal effect is the same as in general contract law. If the agreement disposes of realty, it must be executed with the formality of a deed to be able to file the agreement in the event it is not contingent and is never incorporated in a decree, which would render it a court order.

§ 9:35 Effect of signed agreement—Incorporation, integration, and merger

A matter can be incorporated into any written instrument by any of the three standard methods of incorporation:

(1) Actual incorporation is where a matter, such as a real estate deed description, is repeated verbatim in the instrument, giving the fact of the transfer and full legal description in the agreement. This is the best method but is sometimes unnecessary or impractical. This procedure is common in separation agreements, where counsel will include the legal description of the realty to be transferred in the agreement as a precaution against the failure of one party on post-decree performance as to execution of the agreed deed. In most instances, this is unnecessary if counsel has the deeds ready for transfer at the hearing, contingent on the granting of the decree.

(2) Physical attachment is where the fact of the transfer, etc., is on a separate instrument, such as the existing deed, which is physically attached to the agreement. Physical attachment is incorporation and is legal, but where the agreement does not state the fact (the fact of, and reason for, the physical attachment) of incorpora-

---

[Section 9:33]

[1]In re Carnathan's Estate, 27 Ohio N.P. (n.s.) 65, 1928 WL 2736 (Prob. Ct. 1928). But see In re Marriage of Kesler, 59 Ohio Misc. 33, 13 Ohio Op. 3d 105, 392 N.E.2d 905 (C.P. 1978) (agreement set aside in spite of three attorney waiver clauses, because judge subsequently believed that "complex" economic structure required independent legal advice to wife).

[2]Jobe v. Jobe, 1989 WL 13570 (Ohio Ct. App. 12th Dist. Clinton County 1989).

tion by reference, there can always be the litigation issue of whether the mere physical attachment was intended to be a legal incorporation. It is good practice to physically attach and incorporate by reference.

This practice is also common to antenuptial agreements, where the agreement incorporates the listing of party assets by reference to each as a specific exhibit, which is physically attached to the agreement and specifically incorporates them into the agreement by reference.

(3) Incorporation by reference is where an existing memorandum, deed, text, or other writing or document is incorporated into the agreement by a specific reference to it and where a statement of the incorporation is in the main body of the agreement.[1] The standard terms of incorporation by reference are the same as any practitioner uses when a standard motion incorporates a brief and affidavit into the motion by reference,[2] or when a matter is incorporated by reference into a will.[3] In law, it may not be necessary to attach the writing to the agreement physically, but it is good practice to do so.

Any agreement that has more than one page or more than one written instrument, such as an agreement with a deed and list of certain assets, with the other documents incorporated by reference and physically attached, is considered to be a single integrated instrument. Accumulations of instruments executed at different times or under different circumstances are viewed in law as matters of relatively independent significance, leaving the finder of fact with the problem of determining which document prevails, or whether one is designed or intended to supplement or replace the other. When properly physically attached and specifically incorporated by reference, the cumulation of pages and/or documents is viewed as one ("integer") and is to be construed as one ("integrated") under standard rules of construction.

The legal theory of merger applies in domestic relations when any prior instruments are considered as merged into a judgment. It generally applies in two domestic relations law situations. In time sequence, a judgment (order) for temporary spousal support is considered to have merged into the judgment for divorce and permanent spousal support whether there was an award or not, as long as the matter was resolved.[4] The practitioner should be aware of this if there are any accrued temporary spousal support arrearages. If the arrearages

---

[Section 9:35]

[1]See RC 2107.05 (although this is a probate code section, it does an excellent job of summarizing the matter for domestic relations purposes).

[2]See generally Text Ch 25, Pleading and Practice.

[3]See RC 2107.05.

[4]Colom v. Colom, 58 Ohio St. 2d 245, 12 Ohio Op. 3d 242, 389 N.E.2d 856 (1979); Wolfe v. Wolfe, 46 Ohio St. 2d 399, 75 Ohio Op. 2d 474, 350 N.E.2d 413 (1976). See also Text § 13:7, Temporary support (pendente lite)—Modification and termination.

are not specifically reserved in the subsequent spousal support judgment, they will be considered as having been merged into the final decree and no longer actionable.

A second merger application is where a separation agreement has been incorporated by reference into the final judgment and physically attached. The separation agreement is no longer viewed in law as a private agreement but one that has been merged into the judgment and is to be enforced as a judgment.[5]

In practice, it may be viewed as error to draft a separation agreement without incorporation by reference and physical attachment to the judgment entry so it can be merged into the judgment and enforced as such.

§ 9:36 Effect of signed agreement—Independent review by court

In a divorce, a trial court may choose to ignore a separation agreement and may make its own orders. A trial court must determine whether the separation agreement is fair, just, and equitable at the time the parties present it to the court.[1] The court should base its determination on evidence of the parties' current circumstances, rather than when they entered into the agreement.[2] The trial court may reject some terms "as unfair, unjust, unreasonable or inequitable, make an independent ruling on the issues embraced by those terms, and incorporate the independent rulings and the remaining terms of the separation agreement into the divorce decree."[3] An unequal division of marital assets, where made upon an informed choice, voluntarily entered into, can be approved by the court.[4]

In dissolution proceedings the trial court has no duty to review the separation agreement and determine its fairness. The parties just need to be "satisfied" with the agreement. If either party is not "satisfied" with the agreement, the court must dismiss and refuse to validate the agreement.[5]

The standard of review of a trial court's decision to enforce or to set aside a separation agreement as contrary to interest of justice and

----

[5]Wolfe v. Wolfe, 46 Ohio St. 2d 399, 75 Ohio Op. 2d 474, 350 N.E.2d 413 (1976).

[Section 9:36]

[1]RC 3105.10(B)(2).

[2]Ellman v. Ellman, 1996 WL 562815 (Ohio Ct. App. 2d Dist. Greene County 1996).

[3]Ellman v. Ellman, 1996 WL 562815 (Ohio Ct. App. 2d Dist. Greene County 1996); Hune v. Hune, 2000 WL 1859831 (Ohio Ct. App. 9th Dist. Lorain County 2000) (trial court may reject proposed agreement even if both parties request its approval).

[4]Overholser v. Overholser, 1998 WL 22040 (Ohio Ct. App. 2d Dist. Miami County 1998).

[5]RC 3105.65(A).

equity is abuse of discretion.[6] In *Busse v. Busse*,[7] failure of an agreement to disclose fully and specifically the assets of the parties, the parties' failure to abide by the provisions of the agreement, and the parties' lack of intent to separate permanently combined to indicate fraud and duress in the formation of the agreement and justified the trial court's imposition of a property settlement different from that of the parties' agreement.

§ 9:37 Effect of signed agreement—Revocation by reconciliation

Separation agreements which do not provide for a division of property and do not have clauses changing the statutory requirements[1] terminate on the parties' return to marital cohabitation.[2] However, the courts reserve the right to determine whether it is a bona fide reconciliation.[3] Such separation agreements are considered as contingent only, which means the separation agreements are effective only while the parties are actually living separate and apart.[4]

A separation agreement designed to terminate on reconciliation would differ from other separation agreements by the lack of clauses providing for property division and would generally only provide for child support, parental rights and responsibilities, spousal support, and include (1) identification provisions, (2) separation clauses, (3) child custody and visitation, (4) child support, (5) spousal support, and (6) effectuation provisions.[5] The spousal support clause should be designed so that property is not divided in such a way as to make reconciliation practically impossible.[6]

Remarriage of the parties acts as a revocation of a separation agree-

---

[6]Schneider v. Schneider, 110 Ohio App. 3d 487, 674 N.E.2d 769 (11th Dist. Geauga County 1996).

[7]Busse v. Busse, 1985 WL 7112 (Ohio Ct. App. 6th Dist. Lucas County 1985).

[Section 9:37]

[1]RC 3103.06. See also Text § 9:1, Agreements pursuant to separation only.

[2]In re Carnathan's Estate, 27 Ohio N.P. (n.s.) 65, 1928 WL 2736 (Prob. Ct. 1928). See also Greiner v. Greiner, 61 Ohio App. 2d 88, 15 Ohio Op. 3d 95, 399 N.E.2d 571 (8th Dist. Cuyahoga County 1979); Rutter v. Rutter, 24 Ohio Misc. 7, 53 Ohio Op. 2d 32, 261 N.E.2d 202 (C.P. 1970); In re Price's Estate, 1 Ohio Op. 459, 22 Ohio L. Abs. 639, 1 Ohio Supp. 173 (Prob. Ct. 1935). But see contra Leedy v. Malcolm, 8 Ohio L. Abs. 640, 1930 WL 2220 (Ct. App. 8th Dist. Cuyahoga County 1930).

[3]Mendelson v. Mendelson, 123 Ohio St. 11, 8 Ohio L. Abs. 754, 173 N.E. 615 (1930) (must be finding by court that marital cohabitation has resumed; not per se); Leedy v. Malcolm, 8 Ohio L. Abs. 640, 1930 WL 2220 (Ct. App. 8th Dist. Cuyahoga County 1930) (subsequent reconciliation may be of "little significance").

[4]In re Price's Estate, 1 Ohio Op. 459, 22 Ohio L. Abs. 639, 1 Ohio Supp. 173 (Prob. Ct. 1935).

[5]For examples of these items, see Text §§ 9:6 to 9:34, Elements of agreement.

[6]For a discussion of judicial attitudes on the reconciliation matters in a parallel issue, see Text Ch 8, Legal Separation.

ment incorporated into a decree of dissolution.[7] Reconciliation after execution of a separation agreement but while the parties are still married abrogates the agreement. Even though the reconciliation may be conditioned upon specified behavior or conduct, violation of that condition does not resuscitate the invalidated agreement.[8] However, in *Johnson v. Johnson*[9] the court affirmed the trial court's analysis that an executed separation agreement containing property division provisions is not subject to rescission, revocation or abrogation, solely by reconciliation of the parties and resumption of the marital relationship. There must be direct evidence of a clear agreement between the parties that the agreement be revoked.[10]

§ 9:38   Effect of signed agreement—Revocation by abandonment

Separation agreements, like other contracts, can be abandoned. Abandonment requires an intentional relinquishment of rights. Neither breach of some conditions nor failure to sue for enforcement necessarily constitutes abandonment.[1]

§ 9:39   Effect of signed agreement—Modification

When modification of a separation agreement is being considered, the attorney should first determine whether the separation agreement has been incorporated into a court decree. If the parties are separated, or the separation agreement was not incorporated into a decree, the modification of the separation agreement will be governed by contract principles.

The modification of a separation agreement, as with any other contract, is an alteration of the agreement, which leaves the basic

---

[7]Summers v. Summers, 1988 WL 72373 (Ohio Ct. App. 2d Dist. Clark County 1988) (although appellate court reversed finding of remarriage of common law, court concluded that remarriage would revoke separation agreement and property determinations), citing Lowman v. Lowman, 166 Ohio St. 1, 1 Ohio Op. 2d 152, 139 N.E.2d 1 (1956). Fout v. Fout, 1993 WL 485119 (Ohio Ct. App. 10th Dist. Franklin County 1993) (remarriage is sufficient to extinguish the collectibility of a debt for arrearages from first decree; general release provision in separation agreement in second divorce barred prosecution for arrearages from prior decree); Annarino v. Annarino, 1991 WL 6208 (Ohio Ct. App. 5th Dist. Licking County 1991), cause dismissed, 63 Ohio St. 3d 1201, 584 N.E.2d 1218 (1992). But see Benner v. Benner, 1990 WL 25697 (Ohio Ct. App. 12th Dist. Butler County 1990) (subsequent remarriage had no effect on prior separation agreement in decree of dissolution).

[8]Garver v. Garver, 1995 WL 231414 (Ohio Ct. App. 9th Dist. Wayne County 1995).

[9]Johnson v. Johnson, 1999 WL 976170 (Ohio Ct. App. 5th Dist. Ashland County 1999).

[10]See Text § 9:67, Effect of reconciliation—Form.

[Section 9:38]

[1]Medas v. Medas, 1985 WL 11143 (Ohio Ct. App. 4th Dist. Gallia County 1985).

goals of the agreement unchanged.[1] Those portions of the separation agreement which remain to be fulfilled are the subject of modification.[2] Modification may be accomplished through provisions of the separation agreement itself, which set up a modification procedure. Generally, however, modification is a new agreement which must be supported by new consideration.[3] The consideration may be the mutual promises of the parties.[4] A written separation agreement should be modified by a new writing.[5]

A trial court may, in a divorce action, modify a separation agreement prior to incorporating it into a decree, without first finding the agreed division to be unfair or inequitable. Citing *Greiner v. Greiner,*[6] the Sixth District Court of Appeals underscored that a trial court could "reject some of the terms of the separation agreement, make an independent ruling on those issues, and incorporate the independent rulings and partial separation agreement into the decree."[7]

There are different considerations when a separation agreement is incorporated into a decree and merged with the judgment of the domestic relations court. These considerations include modification of parental rights and responsibilities, child support, visitation, and spousal support. Child support, parental rights and responsibilities, and visitation are subject to modification by statute.[8] An action for legal separation, formerly alimony only, is subject to modification by statute as well.[9] Spousal support awards may or may not be within the court's continuing jurisdiction depending on the nature of the particular decree involved.

RC 3105.18 was amended by 1986 House Bill 358, effective May 2, 1986, to deny a court jurisdiction to modify periodic payments of money as spousal support unless the divorce decree or a separation agreement of the parties incorporated into the decree of divorce or dis-

---

[Section 9:39]

[1]Thurston v. Ludwig, 6 Ohio St. 1, 1856 WL 14 (1856).

[2]Wolfe v. Wolfe, 46 Ohio St. 2d 399, 75 Ohio Op. 2d 474, 350 N.E.2d 413 (1976); Phelps v. Logan Natural Gas & Fuel Co., 101 Ohio St. 144, 128 N.E. 58 (1920).

[3]Heriott v. Marine, 96 Ohio App. 174, 54 Ohio Op. 238, 121 N.E.2d 305 (3d Dist. Union County 1953) (expresses novation concept of contract law); Rainier v. Rainier, 1981 WL 3575 (Ohio Ct. App. 10th Dist. Franklin County 1981) (subsequent agreement to terminate separation agreement set aside on grounds plaintiff received no consideration).

[4]White v. Snodgrass, 1 Ohio L. Abs. 76, 1922 WL 2058 (Ct. App. 9th Dist. Summit County 1922).

[5]Hotchner v. Neon Products, 163 F.2d 672 (C.C.A. 6th Cir. 1947) (restates basic contract law with respect to oral revisions and/or revocation of written contract).

[6]Greiner v. Greiner, 61 Ohio App. 2d 88, 15 Ohio Op. 3d 95, 399 N.E.2d 571 (8th Dist. Cuyahoga County 1979).

[7]Welly v. Welly, 55 Ohio App. 3d 111, 562 N.E.2d 914 (6th Dist. Williams County 1988).

[8]RC 3105.65(B), RC 3109.04(E), RC 3109.051, RC 3113.215(B)(4); Civ. R. 75(I).
[9]RC 3105.18(D).

solution *specifically* authorizes the court to modify the amount or term of spousal support.

However, continuing jurisdiction is construed under statute, and the method of its exercise is dictated by the Rules of Civil Procedure. Absent a provision in the agreement permitting modification of the property division upon written agreement of the parties or proper application to the court,[10] the court has no jurisdiction to modify a property division.[11] The method of exercising the continuing jurisdiction is dictated by the Rules of Civil Procedure.[12]

A possible method of modifying a decree, in which a separation agreement is incorporated, if timely filed, may be by the application of Civil Rule 60(B). The grounds provided by this rule include (1) mistake, inadvertence, surprise, excusable neglect; (2) newly discovered evidence which could not have been discovered with reasonable diligence prior to trial; and (3) fraud or any other reason which would justify relief.

When considering subsequent spousal support modification, counsel should consider a specification in a spousal support award in regard to portions which constitute and are intended as a division of property not subject to modification.[13] If a separation agreement incorporated into a decree provides for support of the other party during that party's lifetime, the agreement will constitute a charge against the obligor's estate if the agreement is binding on heirs and the estate.[14] A permanent spousal support award based on the agreement of the parties and intended for a property division is not subject to modification.[15]

Two cases decided before *Wolfe v. Wolfe*[16] asserted the following propositions: (1) an agreed indefinite award of permanent spousal support in which the court does not reserve continuing jurisdiction was not subject to modification; and (2) if there was no agreement, and the court made a spousal support award after an evidentiary determination, the court has continuing jurisdiction to modify its

---

[10]In re Whitman, 81 Ohio St. 3d 239, 1998-Ohio-466, 690 N.E.2d 535 (1998).

[11]RC 3105.171(I).

[12]Civ. R. 75(J).

[13]Wolfe v. Wolfe, 46 Ohio St. 2d 399, 75 Ohio Op. 2d 474, 350 N.E.2d 413 (1976); Channel v. Channel, 1982 WL 3024 (Ohio Ct. App. 5th Dist. Stark County 1982) (court has no jurisdiction to alter, modify, or reconsider provision of separation agreement concerning division of property).

[14]White v. White, 48 Ohio App. 2d 72, 2 Ohio Op. 3d 48, 355 N.E.2d 816 (6th Dist. Erie County 1975); Platt v. Davies, 82 Ohio App. 182, 37 Ohio Op. 533, 50 Ohio L. Abs. 225, 77 N.E.2d 486 (2d Dist. Franklin County 1947) (agreement will constitute charge against obligor's estate unless alimony is found or intended to be personal to payor only).

[15]Wolfe v. Wolfe, 46 Ohio St. 2d 399, 75 Ohio Op. 2d 474, 350 N.E.2d 413 (1976); Drossman v. Drossman, 48 Ohio App. 2d 81, 2 Ohio Op. 3d 63, 355 N.E.2d 891 (6th Dist. Erie County 1975).

[16]Wolfe v. Wolfe, 46 Ohio St. 2d 399, 75 Ohio Op. 2d 474, 350 N.E.2d 413 (1976).

decree.[17] The Tenth District Court of Appeals decided that the correct interpretation of dissolution law is that domestic relations courts do not have jurisdiction to modify spousal support which was established in a dissolution.[18]

Therefore, to determine whether a court has jurisdiction to modify spousal support contained in a separation agreement incorporated into a decree, the attorney must determine the date of the decree, whether the decree was for divorce or dissolution, and the manner in which the decree provided for a division of assets and liabilities and must then consider the date of *Wolfe*[19] and the effective date of amended RC 3105.18.[20]

If the court has continuing modification jurisdiction, a motion to modify must be filed with the court and served in the same manner as service is obtained on a defendant in a non-domestic relations case.[21] Evidence must thereafter be submitted to sustain the modification request. A separation agreement granting to the trial court continuing jurisdiction to modify spousal support is enforceable, irrespective of when it was entered.[22]

§ 9:40 Effect of signed agreement—Enforcement

In an action for dissolution of marriage, when the court grants a judgment which incorporates a settlement agreement between parties

---

[17]Hunt v. Hunt, 169 Ohio St. 276, 8 Ohio Op. 2d 286, 159 N.E.2d 430 (1959) (overruled by, In re Adams, 45 Ohio St. 3d 219, 543 N.E.2d 797 (1989)); McClain v. McClain, 26 Ohio App. 2d 10, 55 Ohio Op. 2d 28, 268 N.E.2d 294 (8th Dist. Cuyahoga County 1971).

[18]See Alban v. Alban, 1 Ohio App. 3d 146, 439 N.E.2d 963 (10th Dist. Franklin County 1981); Ashley v. Ashley, 1 Ohio App. 3d 80, 439 N.E.2d 911 (8th Dist. Cuyahoga County 1981) (dissolution alimony not modifiable by court except by agreement of both parties, and any modification by court without that joint consent is void). See also Text § 10:16 to 10:18, Modification of dissolution decree; Text Ch 14, Modification of Spousal Support; Text Ch 24, Relief from Judgment.

[19]June 23, 1976.

[20]1986 H.B. 358, eff. 5-2-86. See also McClain v. McClain, 15 Ohio St. 3d 289, 473 N.E.2d 811 (1984) (trial court lacks authority to modify amount of alimony payments in dissolution); In the Matter Of: Fugazzi, 1983 WL 3535 (Ohio Ct. App. 10th Dist. Franklin County 1983); Price v. Price, 4 Ohio App. 3d 217, 447 N.E.2d 769 (8th Dist. Cuyahoga County 1982) (foreign divorce and alimony decree is enforceable under the concept of full faith and credit, and a separation agreement, being a contract, is subject to the same general rules governing other contracts, and particular questions must be resolved by reference to the particular language of the agreement; but where the language of the agreement indicates that the maintenance and support payments are modifiable only on the approval of the parties, then the Ohio courts cannot modify the agreement because the agreement is unmodifiable in the jurisdiction where it was reduced to judgment because of the express limitation). See Text Ch. 14, Modification of Spousal Support, for full discussion.

[21]Civ. R. 75(J). See Text §§ 25:54 to 25:56, Post-decree motions.

[22]Colley v. Colley, 43 Ohio St. 3d 87, 538 N.E.2d 410 (1989).

into the decree of dissolution,[1] the separation agreement becomes a part of the dissolution decree. If the separation agreement is presented to the court and approved by the court, in an action for divorce, the separation agreement will merge with the decree if it is set forth within the decree or incorporated into the decree with a copy of the separation agreement attached thereto. After merger, the provisions of the separation agreement are enforced in the same manner as a decree or order of the court.[2]

A separation agreement is considered valid and binding, if properly executed, until a court passes on the validity of the decree.[3] Therefore, a separation agreement need not be presented to a court in a divorce proceeding and be approved first by the court in order to be enforceable.[4] An appropriate court can enforce the separation agreement without prior approval by a court.[5] Courts have both statutory and common law jurisdiction to enforce separation agreements.[6]

RC 3105.10(B) gives statutory authority for the enforcement of separation agreement provisions on the filing of a motion with the court of common pleas. Where a court of common pleas has a domestic relations division, all cases brought for enforcement of a separation agreement are to be assigned to that division.[7]

A post-dissolution decree agreement, which modified the separation agreement, is a valid and enforceable contract. The domestic relations court is the court with jurisdiction to determine whether the agreement, which had not been submitted to or approved by the court, was enforceable.[8]

The manner of enforcement of the provisions of a separation agree-

---

[Section 9:40]

[1]RC 3105.65.

[2]Wolfe v. Wolfe, 46 Ohio St. 2d 399, 75 Ohio Op. 2d 474, 350 N.E.2d 413 (1976); Wierwille v. Wierwille, 34 Ohio St. 2d 17, 63 Ohio Op. 2d 41, 295 N.E.2d 200 (1973); Hassaurek v. Hassaurek's Adm'r, 68 Ohio St. 554, 67 N.E. 1066 (1903); Rahm v. Rahm, 39 Ohio App. 2d 74, 68 Ohio Op. 2d 225, 315 N.E.2d 495 (8th Dist. Cuyahoga County 1974); Istnick v. Istnick, 37 Ohio Misc. 91, 66 Ohio Op. 2d 244, 307 N.E.2d 922 (C.P. 1973); Noble v. Noble, 80 Ohio L. Abs. 581, 160 N.E.2d 426 (C.P. 1959). See also Text § 9:2, Agreements pursuant to dissolution; Text §§ 9:3 to 9:5, Agreements pursuant to divorce.

[3]Danner v. Danner, 43 Ohio Op. 181, 57 Ohio L. Abs. 30, 93 N.E.2d 54 (Ct. App. 8th Dist. Cuyahoga County 1950). See Text § 9:1, Agreements pursuant to separation only.

[4]Mendelson v. Mendelson, 123 Ohio St. 11, 8 Ohio L. Abs. 754, 173 N.E. 615 (1930).

[5]Tefft v. Tefft, 73 Ohio App. 399, 29 Ohio Op. 99, 54 N.E.2d 423 (9th Dist. Summit County 1943). RC 3105.10(B).

[6]Hawgood v. Hawgood, 33 Ohio Misc. 227, 62 Ohio Op. 2d 427, 294 N.E.2d 681 (C.P. 1973).

[7]RC 3105.10(B)(3).

[8]In re Dunn, 101 Ohio App. 3d 1, 654 N.E.2d 1303 (12th Dist. Clinton County 1995).

ment varies according to whether the agreement is incorporated into the decree. If the separation agreement has been incorporated into the decree, a party's failure to obey the provisions of the agreement is disobedience of an order of the court. The method of enforcement is a contempt proceeding in the court that issued the order.[9] If the disobedient party fully disobeys an order of court yet has the ability to comply with the order, the court may punish him.[10]

The failure to pay a lump-sum or periodic payment will result in a lump-sum judgment of the entire unpaid amount accrued to the date of the action, which can be enforced by execution on the defendant.[11] The power of contempt can be used to compel the transfer of property according to the provisions of the separation agreement incorporated into the decree.[12] In addition, use of Civil Rule 70 to cause conveyance of land, transfer of title or possession, delivery of deeds, and performance of other acts is proper as an alternative to or in conjunction with a contempt proceeding.

If the separation agreement has not been presented to a court and approved by a court, the method of enforcement is by an action based on the agreement, as it is a contractual remedy based on the breach of an agreement.[13] Such action is brought in a court of common pleas.[14] In addition, minor children of the parties who are third party beneficiaries of the agreement can bring a claim for relief to enforce the agreement provisions relating to them.[15] These remedies are in addition to administrative support enforcement procedures.

Specific performance can be required when one party has tendered

---

[9]RC 2705.02; Harris v. Harris, 58 Ohio St. 2d 303, 12 Ohio Op. 3d 291, 390 N.E.2d 789 (1979). See also Text §§ 25:43 to 25:53, Motions by obligee regarding enforcement of judgments; Text Ch 20, Enforcement of Spousal and Child Support.

[10]State ex rel. Cook v. Cook, 66 Ohio St. 566, 64 N.E. 567 (1902).

[11]Roach v. Roach, 164 Ohio St. 587, 59 Ohio Op. 1, 132 N.E.2d 742, 59 A.L.R.2d 685 (1956); Sexton v. Sexton, 32 Ohio App. 2d 344, 61 Ohio Op. 2d 514, 291 N.E.2d 542 (1st Dist. Clermont County 1971); De Milo v. Watson, 166 Ohio St. 433, 2 Ohio Op. 2d 433, 143 N.E.2d 707 (1957) (separation agreement incorporated into court decree provides for support alimony and obligor dies, judgment operates to bind estate of obligor according to terms of agreement). See also Harris v. Harris, 58 Ohio St. 2d 303, 12 Ohio Op. 3d 291, 390 N.E.2d 789 (1979); State ex rel. Cook v. Cook, 66 Ohio St. 566, 64 N.E. 567 (1902).

[12]Harris v. Harris, 58 Ohio St. 2d 303, 12 Ohio Op. 3d 291, 390 N.E.2d 789 (1979); Dahunsi, Formerly Craig v. Aetna Life Insurance Co, 1981 WL 4875 (Ohio Ct. App. 7th Dist. Columbiana County 1981) (where a separation agreement required the husband to keep the plaintiff as a beneficiary of his life insurance policy and the husband secretly and without approval of the court changed the beneficiary and subsequently died, the common pleas court correctly ordered distribution of the insurance proceeds to the plaintiff).

[13]Harvith v. Harvith, 17 Ohio App. 2d 216, 46 Ohio Op. 2d 308, 245 N.E.2d 736 (7th Dist. Columbiana County 1969); Calkins v. Calkins, 11 Ohio Op. 141, 26 Ohio L. Abs. 327, 5 Ohio Supp. 161, 1938 WL 3184 (C.P. 1938).

[14]RC 3105.10(B).

[15]Smith v. Smith, 7 Ohio App. 2d 4, 36 Ohio Op. 2d 27, 218 N.E.2d 473 (3d Dist. Seneca County 1964).

performance under the separation agreement, the other party has failed to perform, and the required performance is unique. For example, where there is a transfer of the family residence to the wife and children, specific performance may lie.[16] If the separation agreement is breached, the party against whom the breach was committed may sue in quantum meruit to recover the value of his performance, a rescissionary remedy.[17] A party may attempt to recover on the contract or consider the contract terminated and sue for the benefit of the bargain.[18]

§ 9:41   Effect of signed agreement—Presumption of validity

A separation agreement, being a contract, is enforceable until or unless a court declares it invalid. The party challenging the enforceability of an agreement has the burden of proving the invalidity, due, for instance to fraud, duress, breach of a confidential relationship, overreaching, undue influence, or incapacity. Assertion of duress must have been the result of the other party's conduct, not the result of the complaining party's necessities.[1]

§ 9:42   In-court agreements—In general

A common procedure in a contested divorce is for the parties to reach an agreement while waiting for a hearing or during the hearing. An important impetus for reaching an agreement is not only the certainty of result, but also the avoidance of an appeal. It is presumed that the consent agreement operates as a waiver of the right to appeal.[1] In the event of an agreement, it may be reduced to a writing on the spot. Alternatively, if a court reporter is available, the agreement will be recited to the reporter, and the writing will follow. Finally, the parties may testify in court as to the agreement, and the writings will follow.

Any of these procedures produces an in-court agreement. The questions that sometimes follow are in two categories: (1) issues of fact, and (2) issues of law. The issue of fact will arise when one party complains that the agreement as written by the other counsel is not an accurate representation of the agreement, is the result of duress or

---

[16]Board of Education of Bath Tp. v. Townsend, 63 Ohio St. 514, 59 N.E. 223 (1900).

[17]Buschmeyer v. Advance Machinery Co., 7 Ohio App. 202, 29 Ohio C.D. 207, 1916 WL 1312 (6th Dist. Lucas County 1916).

[18]Albright v. Meredith, 58 Ohio St. 194, 50 N.E. 719 (1898).

[Section 9:41]

[1]Brooks-Lee v. Lee, 2005-Ohio-2288, 2005 WL 1109755 (Ohio Ct. App. 10th Dist. Franklin County 2005).

[Section 9:42]

[1]Kerwin v. Kerwin, 2004-Ohio-4676, 2004 WL 1949431 (Ohio Ct. App. 6th Dist. Lucas County 2004).

coercion,[2] is unfair, unjust, inequitable,[3] or is incomplete.[4] Further negotiations may follow, or the judge or magistrate will decide the issue and order the agreement to be written as understood by the court.[5]

Where the parties reach a settlement agreement as to all issues and the agreement is read into the record and agreed to by both parties under oath, the court may enter judgment incorporating that agreement even without the written consent of one of the parties.[6] The court should not reduce an agreement to judgment where there is a dispute over its existence, where the proceedings lack clarity, and nei-

---

[2]Buza v. Buza, 1981 WL 3870 (Ohio Ct. App. 9th Dist. Summit County 1981) (a challenge to a separation agreement entered into at a pre-trial conference, challenged on the basis that the wife signed the agreement under duress and coercion from her husband and former attorney, was found to be unwarranted based on the facts and the subsequent failures to object to the referee's report and failure to contest the divorce by not appearing).

[3]Thomas v. Thomas, 5 Ohio App. 3d 94, 449 N.E.2d 478 (5th Dist. Licking County 1982) (in-court agreements are enforceable; court will not vacate in-court agreements made by a party who wishes to now contend that the agreement was unfair when it was voluntary on his part with full knowledge of the terms of the agreement, and they were read into the record and adopted by the court; statute of frauds does not apply to an in-court settlement or to the order of the court, as they do not constitute a contract of sale or an interest in real estate; RC 3105.18 controls alimony proceedings in a contested divorce but does not control in-court settlements); Head v. Head, 1989 WL 35527 (Ohio Ct. App. 6th Dist. Lucas County 1989), dismissed, 45 Ohio St. 3d 702, 543 N.E.2d 807 (1989) (no authority requires a court incorporating the terms of an "in-court" settlement to consider the factors set out in RC 3105.18(B)); Bauer v. Bauer, No. 42805 (Ohio Ct. App. 8th Dist. Cuyahoga County 1981) (where the parties entered into an in-court settlement agreement and defendant was expressly given an opportunity to object to the settlement agreement by the court, the defendant may not later challenge the settlement as being unjust, unfair, or inequitable, where those allegations were not raised previously).

[4]Holland v. Holland, 25 Ohio App. 2d 98, 54 Ohio Op. 2d 175, 266 N.E.2d 580 (10th Dist. Franklin County 1970) (in-court agreement of the parties concerning division of property and alimony adopted by the court as its judgment thereon is enforceable by the court and may be incorporated into the judgment entry even in the absence of an agreement in writing or an approval of the judgment entry signed by a party or his attorney; such an in-court settlement agreement is enforceable by the court even where one of the parties to such settlement intended to include additional provisions or limitations which were neither included in the settlement agreement nor expressed by such party at the time of making such agreement). See also Melvald v. Melvald., 1979 WL 209895 (Ohio Ct. App. 8th Dist. Cuyahoga County 1979) (in-court agreement not void merely because agreement dictated in court, and no formal paper signing).

[5]Holland v. Holland, 25 Ohio App. 2d 98, 54 Ohio Op. 2d 175, 266 N.E.2d 580 (10th Dist. Franklin County 1970); see also Melvald v. Melvald., 1979 WL 209895 (Ohio Ct. App. 8th Dist. Cuyahoga County 1979) (in-court agreement not void merely because agreement dictated in court, and no formal paper signing).

[6]Gulling v. Gulling, 70 Ohio App. 3d 410, 591 N.E.2d 349 (9th Dist. Lorain County 1990), cause dismissed, 60 Ohio St. 3d 706, 573 N.E.2d 674 (1991); Head v. Head, 1989 WL 35527 (Ohio Ct. App. 6th Dist. Lucas County 1989), dismissed, 45 Ohio St. 3d 702, 543 N.E.2d 807 (1989).

ther party's proposed entry conformed to the terms.[7] The trial court does not have to review the statutory factors of RC 3105.18 to justify approving an "in-court" settlement agreement.[8]

In *Kelley v. Kelley*,[9] the appellate court found an in-court settlement agreement which was specifically conditioned on certain performance prior to journalization, was, nevertheless, properly incorporated into a final decree, where partial performance had provided sufficient evidence of an enforceable agreement.

A trial court commits reversible error where it enters a judgment clearly inconsistent with the separation agreement orally entered into at the final hearing and confirmed by the parties at that time.[10]

§ 9:43   In-court agreements—Validity

The issue of law that will frequently appear post-decree is the enforceability of in-court agreements. The courts that have faced this issue have consistently held that such in-court agreements are valid and binding, although subject to a proper motion to vacate, the same as any judgment.[1] Unless vacated or modified, it is enforceable and not subject to challenge solely because it was an in-court agreement and not a formal separation agreement.[2]

It is also possible that the memorandum of the agreement was signed or initialed in the office of one of the party's counsel. There is no question of its validity as a memorandum of an agreement, but it may happen that between the initialing (signing) of the memorandum and the time for the signing of the formal agreement, one party may have second thoughts and may refuse to sign the formal agreement. The question arises as to whether the court would accept the initialed

---

[7]Zigmont v. Toto, 47 Ohio App. 3d 181, 547 N.E.2d 1208 (8th Dist. Cuyahoga County 1988), cause dismissed, 38 Ohio St. 3d 715, 533 N.E.2d 783 (1988).

[8]Thomas v. Thomas, 5 Ohio App. 3d 94, 449 N.E.2d 478 (5th Dist. Licking County 1982); Barker v. Barker, 2000-Ohio-1873, 2000 WL 1373963 (Ohio Ct. App. 3d Dist. Union County 2000).

[9]Kelley v. Kelley, 76 Ohio App. 3d 505, 602 N.E.2d 400 (8th Dist. Cuyahoga County 1991).

[10]Koontz v. Koontz, 1985 WL 7611 (Ohio Ct. App. 6th Dist. Wood County 1985).

[Section 9:43]

[1]Spercel v. Sterling Industries, Inc., 31 Ohio St. 2d 36, 60 Ohio Op. 2d 20, 285 N.E.2d 324 (1972) (where the parties in an action for an accounting and royalties voluntarily enter into an oral settlement agreement in the presence of the court, such agreement constitutes a binding contract; in order to effect a rescission of a binding settlement entered into in the presence of the court, a party must file a motion to set the agreement aside; and, in the absence of such motion, a trial court may properly sign a journal entry reflecting the settlement agreement).

[2]Spercel v. Sterling Industries, Inc., 31 Ohio St. 2d 36, 60 Ohio Op. 2d 20, 285 N.E.2d 324 (1972); Holland v. Holland, 25 Ohio App. 2d 98, 54 Ohio Op. 2d 175, 266 N.E.2d 580 (10th Dist. Franklin County 1970); Thomas v. Thomas, 5 Ohio App. 3d 94, 449 N.E.2d 478 (5th Dist. Licking County 1982); Bauer v. Bauer, No. 42805 (Ohio Ct. App. 8th Dist. Cuyahoga County 1981); Buza v. Buza, 1981 WL 3870 (Ohio Ct. App. 9th Dist. Summit County 1981).

memorandum as the agreement between the parties and give it the same status as one signed in an open courtroom. One case held it was the same as one signed in an open court, before a judge or magistrate, and would be enforced in the same manner.[3]

In *Bolen v. Young*,[4] the court stated as follows:

> Where the settlement agreement is arrived at by the parties in open court and preserved by being read into the record or being reduced to writing and filed, then the trial judge may, *sua sponte,* approve a journal entry which accurately reflects the terms of the agreement, adopting the agreement as his judgment. . . . Where an agreement is purportedly arrived at in the presence of the trial judge and approved by the parties, but its terms are not memorialized on the record and one of the parties later disputes the terms of the agreement by refusing to approve an entry journalizing the agreement, the trial judge may not adopt the terms of the agreement as he recalls and understands them in the form of a judgment entry. Instead, the party disputing the agreement is entitled to an evidentiary hearing before another judge . . . —in which the trial judge may be called as a witness to testify as to his recollection and understanding of the terms of the agreement—and, if the court concludes that the parties entered into a binding contract, the settlement may be enforced.

§ 9:44   In-court agreements—Effect of stipulations

When the parties enter into stipulations at court, the court must use the stipulations. They could be as to duration of marriage, valuation dates and amounts, grounds such as incompatibility or one year living separate and apart.[1]

§ 9:45   In-court agreements—Enforcement and avoidance

A review of the reported cases indicates little question that in-court agreements are as enforceable as separation agreements reached out of court.[1]

---

[3]Hawgood v. Hawgood, 33 Ohio Misc. 227, 62 Ohio Op. 2d 427, 294 N.E.2d 681 (C.P. 1973) (court held that two yellow, legal, lined sheets, in addition to testimony that these sheets were prepared during a meeting of the parties' counsel and were approved by the parties, are admissible as evidence of a separation agreement between the husband and wife; as dicta, the court indicated that such an agreement would be enforceable whether oral or in writing).

[4]Bolen v. Young, 8 Ohio App. 3d 36, 37-38, 455 N.E.2d 1316 (10th Dist. Franklin County 1982).

[Section 9:44]

[1]Snyder v. Snyder, 2007-Ohio-2676, 2007 WL 1584010 (Ohio Ct. App. 3d Dist. Union County 2007).

[Section 9:45]

[1]See Text § 9:40, Effect of signed agreement—Enforcement.

A general proposition of Ohio law is that incorporated separation agreements are enforced as judgments.[2] This general rule makes no distinction between in-court and out-of-court agreements. Once incorporated, it is the judgment that is in issue. Civil Rule 60(B) applies to judgments.

A separation agreement incorporated into a judgment is still an agreement between the parties. Basic contract law permits contracts between parties to be rescinded or vacated for cause.[3] The legal issue is whether, as a matter of Ohio law, a party asserting fraud, misrepresentation, or one of the many reasons permitted for rescission has a right to a hearing to determine whether the allegations are true.[4] There is no legal or rational basis for excluding separation agreements from this basic contract remedy. While RC 3103.06 permits such agreements (contracts) between a husband and wife, there is no exclusion of such agreements from the application of RC 3103.05 (contracts between husband and wife subject to rule of confidential relationship).[5] Rather, there is every reason to believe that RC 3103.05 and RC 3103.06 are to be read together when considering separation agreements.[6]

The court in *Szmania v. Szmania*[7] held that the trial court's decision whether to enforce an in-court settlement agreement was discretionary and the court did not have to determine pursuant to RC 3105.10(B)(2) if it was fair and equitable prior to incorporating it in a divorce decree. The court need only be satisfied that it was not procured by fraud, duress, overreaching or undue influence.

Unilateral repudiation of an in-court agreement before it is journalized, evidencing a change of mind, is insufficient cause to render the

---

[2]Wolfe v. Wolfe, 46 Ohio St. 2d 399, 75 Ohio Op. 2d 474, 350 N.E.2d 413 (1976). See also Text §§ 9:3 to 9:5, Agreements pursuant to divorce; Text § 9:35, Effect of signed agreement—Incorporation, integration, and merger; Text § 9:40, Effect of signed agreement—Enforcement.

[3]See Restatement (Second) of Contracts (1981); Franchini v. Franchini, 2003-Ohio-6233, 2003 WL 22763520 (Ohio Ct. App. 11th Dist. Geauga County 2003) (where there is a mutual mistake of a material fact, trial court erred in overruling a motion to rescind).

[4]See Buza v. Buza, 1981 WL 3870 (Ohio Ct. App. 9th Dist. Summit County 1981); Thomas v. Thomas, 5 Ohio App. 3d 94, 449 N.E.2d 478 (5th Dist. Licking County 1982); Bauer v. Bauer, No. 42805 (Ohio Ct. App. 8th Dist. Cuyahoga County 1981); Holland v. Holland, 25 Ohio App. 2d 98, 54 Ohio Op. 2d 175, 266 N.E.2d 580 (10th Dist. Franklin County 1970); Melvald v. Melvald., 1979 WL 209895 (Ohio Ct. App. 8th Dist. Cuyahoga County 1979); Spercel v. Sterling Industries, Inc., 31 Ohio St. 2d 36, 60 Ohio Op. 2d 20, 285 N.E.2d 324 (1972); Hawgood v. Hawgood, 33 Ohio Misc. 227, 62 Ohio Op. 2d 427, 294 N.E.2d 681 (C.P. 1973). See also Ohio Jur. 3d, Cancellation and Reformation of Instruments §§ 7, 10 to 14, 27.

[5]For a discussion of the confidential relationship factor, see Text § 9:47, In-court agreements—Confidential relationship.

[6]See Text § 4:14, Support obligations while separated; Text § 4:23.

[7]Szmania v. Szmania, 2008-Ohio-4091, 2008 WL 3522345 (Ohio Ct. App. 8th Dist. Cuyahoga County 2008).

agreement a nullity.[8] *Spercel v. Sterling Industries, Inc.*[9] certainly indicates such a right, at least in situations where the motion is made prior to judgment. A motion to rescind or refusal to proceed after an in-court settlement agreement would require a hearing to determine if the agreement was procured by fraud, duress, overreaching, or undue influence, but not require a finding that it be fair and equitable.[10] Neither a change of heart nor poor legal advice would be a ground to set aside the agreement, since a party may not unilaterally repudiate a binding settlement agreement. The rescission in domestic relations cases usually occurs after the in-court agreement but prior to the filing of the judgment entry.

It is error for the trial court, in ruling on objections to a magistrate's order, to set aside the settlement agreement of the parties. Where the parties have entered into a fully enforceable settlement agreement before the magistrate, the agreement should have been deemed to preclude objections. Minor discrepancies between the agreement and the magistrate's decisions do not nullify an agreement clearly stated in the record.[11]

In *Brown v. Brown*,[12] the court held that the death of a party following the filing of a dissolution action does not affect the binding nature of a separation agreement, even where there is reference to a specific date for performance and such performance was not completed.

In-court agreements, when reduced to judgment, are subject to motions under Civil Rule 60(B). Note that this is in addition to the *Spercel* remedy of a motion to rescind prior to the judgment.

In *Gregory v. Gregory*,[13] the husband attended the final hearing while handcuffed and shackled. In his appeal, he claimed duress,

---

[8]Ellyson v. Ellyson, 1993 WL 205022 (Ohio Ct. App. 7th Dist. Columbiana County 1993).

[9]Spercel v. Sterling Industries, Inc., 31 Ohio St. 2d 36, 60 Ohio Op. 2d 20, 285 N.E.2d 324 (1972).

[10]Walther v. Walther, 102 Ohio App. 3d 378, 657 N.E.2d 332 (1st Dist. Hamilton County 1995); Dubinsky v. Dubinsky, 1995 WL 106119 (Ohio Ct. App. 8th Dist. Cuyahoga County 1995) (emotional and economic duress not caused by other party is insufficient cause; attorney's threat to withdraw if no agreement is insufficient cause to rescind agreement); Grubic v. Grubic, 1999 WL 703053 (Ohio Ct. App. 8th Dist. Cuyahoga County 1999) (trial court errs in not holding evidentiary hearing on fraud, duress and actual terms of agreement as opposed to final judgment entry); Haas v. Bauer, 156 Ohio App. 3d 26, 2004-Ohio-437, 804 N.E.2d 80 (9th Dist. Lorain County 2004).

[11]Brilla v. Mulhearn, 168 Ohio App. 3d 223, 2006-Ohio-3816, 859 N.E.2d 578 (9th Dist. Summit County 2006).

[12]Brown v. Brown, 90 Ohio App. 3d 781, 630 N.E.2d 763 (11th Dist. Geauga County 1993), cause dismissed, 68 Ohio St. 3d 1441, 626 N.E.2d 124 (1994); In Matter of Driggers v. Osdyke, 1996 WL 704339 (Ohio Ct. App. 11th Dist. Portage County 1996) (error of probate court in setting aside separation agreement leads to error in appointing surviving spouse as administrator in spite of waiver of right in agreement).

[13]Gregory v. Gregory, 2007-Ohio-1033, 2007 WL 706757 (Ohio Ct. App. 2d Dist. Miami County 2007), referencing Blodgett v. Blodgett, 49 Ohio St. 3d 243, 551 N.E.2d 1249 (1990) and its citations.

which should make the negotiated court agreement unconscionable and unenforceable. The appellate court disagreed, although a dissenting judge questioned the equity of the decree.

To establish duress, a party must prove three elements, which are common to duress situations:

1) That one side involuntarily accepted the terms of another;
2) That circumstances permitted no other alternative; and
3) That such circumstances were the result of coercive acts of the other party.

§ 9:46   In-court agreements—Court-imposed agreements

There is, of course, no such concept in the law as a "court-imposed agreement." It is strictly an invention to describe a situation that exists in courts generally, including domestic relations courts.

When the parties appear for a trial on the merits, or possibly a pretrial, it is not uncommon practice for the trier of fact, the judge or magistrate, to determine if the matter can be resolved without a contest. There is no question that such a practice is in the best interests of the court and the parties.[1] It not only saves court time, but resolution of the ancillary divorce issues by the parties will always be better than court-imposed orders.

It does happen on occasion that the judge or magistrate may become too enthusiastic in seeking a solution as an alternative to trial and actually may force a solution on the parties which is then written into the judgment as an in-court agreement. That "force" or "determined persuasion" could be a result of an in-chambers conference with counsel only, or on occasion a result of an in-chambers conference with the parties absent counsel. The former is less excessive than the latter, but in either case the result could be from duress, coercion, or undue influence. Therein lies the problem.

One case that deals with the problem is *In re Marriage of Hitchcock*,[2] indicating the following problem and result:

> Under the record, a finding would be justified that during the noon recess Judge Missildine announced his views as to what would constitute a fair and just distribution of the assets of the parties. The alternative for Mrs. Hitchcock was to follow the judge's suggestion and settle the matter in accordance therewith or proceed to try her case on its merits before a tribunal which had apparently prejudged the issue to be determined by the court as mandated by section 598.21, The Code. In our opinion, this is a far cry from a reasonable alternative as contemplated by the Restatement. We agree with Mrs. Hitchcock she did not have a reasonable alternative to succumbing.

[Section 9:46]

[1]Dale A. Oesterle, *Dangers of Judge-Imposed Settlements*, 9 Litig. 29 (Spring 1983); Propriety and prejudicial effect of suggestion or comments by judge as to compromise or settlement of civil case, 6 A.L.R.3d 1457; In re Marriage of Hitchcock, 265 N.W.2d 599 (Iowa 1978).

[2]In re Marriage of Hitchcock, 265 N.W.2d 599, 606 (Iowa 1978).

Insofar as we are able to determine from the record the remarks attributed to Judge Missildine were made by the judge in the presence of both parties and their counsel.

From our de novo review we conclude the purported settlement relative to the distribution of the assets of the parties as set forth in the decree is voidable by Mrs. Hitchcock. It cannot be logically maintained that she ratified the settlement agreement in any manner or to any extent, particularly in view of her promptness in filing the motion to vacate.

The *Hitchcock* case does bring out other essential legal and factual elements where such court-imposed agreements are determined: (1) confidential relationship, (2) burden of proof, (3) no reasonable alternative, and (4) remedy.

§ 9:47 In-court agreements—Confidential relationship

When an agreement is challenged by a disadvantaged party, Ohio law will look closely at the agreement once a confidential relationship has been shown.[1] Such reported relationships include brother/sister, patient/physician, uncle/nephew, attorney/client, principal/agent, administrator/beneficiary, and close personal friends.[2] To date, there have been no cases indicating that the relationship between a judge or magistrate and a party, exclusive of counsel, is a confidential relationship.

Where the confidential relationship does exist, certain general rules follow:

(1) The party has a right to assume that the confidant will not act against the party's best interests;[3]

(2) The party has a right to rely on any representations of fact or law;[4]

(3) The burden of proof of the fairness of the agreement shifts to the dominant party of the relationship and agreement;[5]

[Section 9:47]

[1]RC 3103.05 (contracts between husband and wife are subject to confidential relationship rule); Ohio Jur. 3d, Cancellation and Reformation of Instruments § 27.

[2]Ohio Jur. 3d, Cancellation and Reformation of Instruments § 27.

[3]See Ohio Jur. 3d, Cancellation and Reformation of Instruments §§ 13, 14. See also Restatement (Second) of Contracts §§ 175, 177 (1981).

[4]See Ohio Jur. 3d, Cancellation and Reformation of Instruments §§ 13, 14. See also Restatement (Second) of Contracts §§ 175, 177 (1981).

[5]See McCluskey v. Burroughs, 4 Ohio App. 3d 182, 446 N.E.2d 1143 (7th Dist. Belmont County 1982) (where there is a confidential relationship between the parties to an agreement such as a deed, the party who has the superior position has the burden of proof to establish the fairness of the transaction while the asserted victim retains the risk of nonpersuasion). See also Gavin v. Gavin, 71 Ohio L. Abs. 361, 123 N.E.2d 666 (Ct. App. 8th Dist. Cuyahoga County 1955).

(4) It is irrelevant who benefits by any undue influence exerted by the judge or magistrate;[6] and

(5) The courts must be liberal in construing against the dominant party if that party received the benefit of an unfair agreement.[7]

§ 9:48   In-court agreements—Burden of proof

Where a confidential relationship exists, such as between the judge or magistrate and a party, and a party seeks a rescission based on an unfair agreement, the burden shifts to the party gaining the advantage to show lack of undue influence, duress, or coercion.[1]

The principal problem here is that the party who received the benefit of the bad bargain is the other party, not the judge or magistrate who exerted the undue influence. The general rule requires the other party to show the lack of undue influence, and in this case it would not be hard to show; in fact, the allegation is against someone other than the spouse. To suggest that the judge or magistrate prove the lack of undue influence would require the testimony of that judge or magistrate. This presents some practical problems for the attorney presenting the case. If the confidant was a magistrate, the judge may be willing to listen. If the confidant was the judge, then there is a real problem, and most likely it could be resolved only at the appellate level.

In *Veronesi v. Veronesi*,[2] the court decided, "Transactions between parties in a confidential relationship will be examined with great care by the courts and will be rescinded unless the party benefitting can clearly show the fairness and justice of the transaction."[3] The test is whether an agreement was reached due to fraud, duress, or undue influence.[4] Where a husband threatens his wife with bodily harm, or threatens to humiliate, embarrass, or disgrace her, the husband's ac-

---

[6]Ohio Jur. 3d, Cancellation and Reformation of Instruments § 7. Propriety and prejudicial effect of suggestion or comments by judge as to compromise or settlement of civil case, 6 A.L.R.3d 1457; In re Marriage of Hitchcock, 265 N.W.2d 599 (Iowa 1978).

[7]Ohio Jur. 3d, Cancellation and Reformation of Instruments §§ 7, 27.

[Section 9:48]

[1]Ohio Jur. 3d, Cancellation and Reformation of Instruments §§ 7, 27; Annot., 6 A.L.R. 2d 1457; In re Marriage of Hitchcock, 265 N.W.2d 599 (Iowa 1978).

[2]Veronesi v. Veronesi, 1983 WL 3001 (Ohio Ct. App. 8th Dist. Cuyahoga County 1983).

[3]Veronesi v. Veronesi, 1983 WL 3001 (Ohio Ct. App. 8th Dist. Cuyahoga County 1983) (addenda to a separation agreement given no effect because they were not equitable, just, or fair).

[4]DiPietro v. DiPietro, 10 Ohio App. 3d 44, 460 N.E.2d 657 (10th Dist. Franklin County 1983) (evidence on these issues must be confined to a reasonable time before and after the execution of the agreement).

tions constitute duress if the wife is thereby induced to act in a manner contrary to her best interests.[5]

The standard for proving duress or mental incompetence sufficient to avoid an agreement is clear and convincing evidence. Where the allegation was that the complaining party's attorney, not the opposing counsel, allegedly created the duress, such duress is not grounds for relief.[6] The coercive acts must be those of the opposite party.[7]

§ 9:49 In-court agreements—No reasonable alternative

This concept, as it applies to an in-court court agreement, is best explained in *In re Marriage of Hitchcock*,[1] where once the judge announced his decision as to division of property, prior to a hearing on the merits, appellant had only two choices: accept the prejudged settlement announced by the judge, or reject the settlement and go to trial before the same judge who had already prejudged the case. Either way, the result would be the same.

It is one thing to assert "no reasonable alternative" from negotiations between counsel,[2] and quite another to assert it where there has been such a predetermined result announced by the judge.[3]

§ 9:50 In-court agreements—Remedy

There is only one remedy in a situation where there has been abuse of a confidential relationship, a prejudgment settlement, and "no reasonable alternative." The law must permit the victim the right to rescind the agreement. The major problem is the promptness of the victim in pursuit of the remedy. In the usual undue influence/duress/coercion situation, the victim does not really know what has happened until sometime after the effect has worn off. If the victim did realize it, he or she could have been stopped in time. More often than not, the realization comes sometime after the event. It may be in the brief

---

[5]Young v. Young, 8 Ohio App. 3d 52, 455 N.E.2d 1360 (10th Dist. Franklin County 1982) (fact wife employs counsel does not necessarily negate possibility of undue influence, where husband has exerted influence over period of years). See also Text § 10:8, Incorporation of agreement.

[6]Davis v. Davis, 1996 WL 191785 (Ohio Ct. App. 8th Dist. Cuyahoga County 1996).

[7]Blodgett v. Blodgett, 49 Ohio St. 3d 243, 551 N.E.2d 1249 (1990) (satisfaction of judgment, signed while an appeal is pending to allow release of escrowed funds, terminates the appeal; economic duress is irrelevant since satisfaction of judgment puts an end to the controversy).

[Section 9:49]

[1]In re Marriage of Hitchcock, 265 N.W.2d 599 (Iowa 1978).

[2]The most likely remedy is a malpractice suit.

[3]See also Restatement (Second) of Contracts § 175(b) (1981).

time span between hearing and judgment, in which case *Spercel*[1] provides the Ohio remedy, but more than likely it happens after judgment.

Where an in-court agreement failed to include pension benefits, a timely-filed Civil Rule 59 motion for a new trial was the proper method for the court to consider the omitted asset.[2] The Supreme Court, in *Bisker v. Bisker*,[3] remanded a divorce action for the trial court to consider pension plans, saying that they must be considered.

A claim of ineffective assistance of counsel by failing to negotiate the terms of an agreement effectively, is insufficient grounds to reverse a judgment in a civil case where the litigant employed the attorney.[4]

If it happens after judgment, then Civil Rule 60(B) appears to apply. However, it is not expressly covered. The rule expressly applies to fraud, etc., from an adverse party. It makes no provision for relief when the fraud, etc., is from a third party, or if the fraud, etc., is from the judge or magistrate. In this event, the one-year rule appears to apply. Even so, there is a question of whether the time limit for equitable relief from fraud, duress, coercion, or undue influence should run from the time of the event or the time of the discovery of the fraud, duress, etc. Reason suggests that it run from the time of discovery and thus fall under Civil Rule 60(B)(5), which has no express time limit. Unfortunately, there is no case law or statute on point.

§ 9:51 Out-of-court agreements—Negotiated but unsigned

Because settlement agreements are favored in the law, the appellate court in *Shetler v. Shetler*[1] affirmed the trial court's enforcement of a settlement agreement arrived at following a deposition and read into the deposition record. The parties did not sign the agreement, but the appellant had agreed under oath to the terms. Citing numerous cases regarding agreements made out of the presence of the court, including oral agreements,[2] the court looked only to whether the terms were established by clear and convincing evidence.

Where, however, the terms of an agreement are disputed or where

---

[Section 9:50]

[1]Spercel v. Sterling Industries, Inc., 31 Ohio St. 2d 36, 60 Ohio Op. 2d 20, 285 N.E.2d 324 (1972).

[2]Malone v. Malone, 126 Ohio App. 3d 685, 711 N.E.2d 262 (4th Dist. Scioto County 1998).

[3]Bisker v. Bisker, 69 Ohio St. 3d 608, 1994-Ohio-307, 635 N.E.2d 308 (1994).

[4]Castro v. Castro, 2000-Ohio-2602, 2000 WL 1714448 (Ohio Ct. App. 7th Dist. Mahoning County 2000).

[Section 9:51]

[1]Shetler v. Shetler, 2001 WL 542318 (Ohio Ct. App. 9th Dist. Wayne County 2001).

[2]Pawlowski v. Pawlowski, 83 Ohio App. 3d 794, 615 N.E.2d 1071 (10th Dist. Franklin County 1992).

the existence of a settlement agreement is contested, the trial court must conduct an evidentiary hearing.[3]

§ 9:52 Interpretation of separation agreements

It is not uncommon for a party to question the interpretation of clauses in a separation agreement. When parties dispute the meaning, the court must first examine the contract to determine whether an ambiguity exists. When a separation agreement is deemed ambiguous, the trial court has the power and responsibility to clarify and interpret such clauses by considering the intent of the parties as well as the equities.[1]

A separation agreement is subject to the same rules of construction as other contracts.[2] When interpreting the agreement and the intent of the parties, the court may look to the placement of clauses.[3] The construction and interpretation of a separation agreement that is incorporated into a decree is a question of law. As such, an appellate court will apply a *de novo* standard when reviewing a lower court's ruling. Thus, the appellate court affords no deference to the trial court and conducts its own review to ascertain the meaning of the agreement.[4]

Where there is ambiguity in or a conflict over the provisions of a

---

[3]Depman v. Kuhn, 2001 WL 376380 (Ohio Ct. App. 6th Dist. Wood County 2001) (citing Rulli v. Fan Co., 79 Ohio St. 3d 374, 1997-Ohio-380, 683 N.E.2d 337 (1997)).

[Section 9:52]

[1]In re Marriage of Seders, 42 Ohio App. 3d 155, 536 N.E.2d 1190 (9th Dist. Summit County 1987). See, e.g., Guerrieri v. Guerrieri, 1991 WL 43127 (Ohio Ct. App. 7th Dist. Mahoning County 1991) (meaning of "net cash flow"); O'Hara v. O'Hara, 1990 WL 100418 (Ohio Ct. App. 8th Dist. Cuyahoga County 1990) (court interpreted agreement to pay mortgage not to include insurance and taxes even though included in mortgage payment); Trout v. Trout, 1991 WL 33111 (Ohio Ct. App. 7th Dist. Belmont County 1991) (interpretation of job promotion or transfer not to include bonus); Leibowitz v. Leibowitz, 1991 WL 43313 (Ohio Ct. App. 9th Dist. Summit County 1991) (reasonable expenses at a local private school include room and board); Matter of Klingenberg, 1993 WL 48746 (Ohio Ct. App. 3d Dist. Marion County 1993) (court gave word "profit" its ordinary meaning and refused to award portion of proceeds of house sale to husband, where there was no gain on sale); Wesselman v. Wesselman, 88 Ohio App. 3d 338, 623 N.E.2d 1300 (12th Dist. Butler County 1993) (absent restrictive language in agreement, court could not place conditions on parent's obligation to pay expenses for education); Urban v. Spriestersbach, 1995 WL 81975 (Ohio Ct. App. 3d Dist. Seneca County 1995).

[2]Forstner v. Forstner, 68 Ohio App. 3d 367, 588 N.E.2d 285, 73 Ed. Law Rep. 226 (11th Dist. Lake County 1990); Klug v. Klug, 2003-Ohio-3042, 2003 WL 21360893 (Ohio Ct. App. 2d Dist. Montgomery County 2003).

[3]Rubins v. Rubins, 1993 WL 76886 (Ohio Ct. App. 8th Dist. Cuyahoga County 1993); Foith v. Foith, 2005-Ohio-490, 2005 WL 299846 (Ohio Ct. App. 5th Dist. Stark County 2005) (words "at retirement" interpreted to refer to wife's retirement, not husband's, due to placement).

[4]Drake v. Drake, 1998 WL 321296 (Ohio Ct. App. 4th Dist. Highland County 1998).

separation agreement, the court may take testimony regarding the parties' intention to assist in construing the language of a separation agreement.[5] The court may consider parol evidence.[6]

In *Saeks v. Saeks*,[7] a separation agreement provided that the wife would receive permanent spousal support calculated on the basis of the husband's business income. A year after the parties were divorced, the husband incorporated his solely owned and operated business. Thereafter, his "income" was greatly reduced, while the corporation received substantial commissions. After incorporating, the husband paid spousal support based on his "income," rather than the actual earnings of the business. The Second District Court of Appeals upheld the trial court's action in piercing the corporate veil to calculate support on the basis of all of the husband's business income on the grounds that the corporation had no identity separate from its shareholder. The husband knew that by incorporating he would reduce the support owed to his wife. This was not the intent of the separation agreement, and to hold otherwise would have been unjust to the wife.

The court may not construe, clarify, nor interpret language which is not ambiguous.[8] A party's intent is not relevant to a court's resolution of a contract dispute when the terms are unambiguous.[9] In addition, the court may not extend a party's obligation by implication from one paragraph continuing child support beyond age 18 to another paragraph regarding medical expenses, which does not specify beyond such age simply because the paragraphs are in the same section.[10]

Further, where there is no uncertainty, but only an absence in the agreement of a provision about a particular matter, the court must not construe as included something intended to be excluded nor make the contract speak where it was silent.[11] Thus, where an agreement did not provide for division of all the property, the ensuing decree is fatally flawed, the court is barred from indulging its equitable powers, and the decree may only be attacked through a motion to vacate.[12]

---

[5]Brewer v. Brewer, 1993 WL 323547 (Ohio Ct. App. 2d Dist. Greene County 1993).

[6]Williams v. Williams, 2001 WL 823650 (Ohio Ct. App. 8th Dist. Cuyahoga County 2001).

[7]Saeks v. Saeks, 24 Ohio App. 3d 67, 493 N.E.2d 280 (2d Dist. Montgomery County 1985).

[8]In Matter of Leonhart v. Nees, 1993 WL 313604 (Ohio Ct. App. 6th Dist. Erie County 1993).

[9]Urban v. Spriestersbach, 1995 WL 81975 (Ohio Ct. App. 3d Dist. Seneca County 1995) (disagreement over interpretation does not equate to ambiguity).

[10]Matter of Howard, 1993 WL 437690 (Ohio Ct. App. 12th Dist. Clermont County 1993).

[11]Morgan v. Morgan, 1994 WL 265899 (Ohio Ct. App. 7th Dist. Columbiana County 1994).

[12]Morgan v. Morgan, 1994 WL 265899 (Ohio Ct. App. 7th Dist. Columbiana County 1994).

§ 9:53 Interpretation of separation agreements—Oral hearing

Where there is ambiguity in the terms of a separation agreement, the trial court has the inherent authority to interpret the terms. The court should hold an evidentiary hearing to resolve any dispute regarding the existence of an agreement and its terms.[1]

§ 9:54 Interpretation of separation agreements—Q.D.R.O

A substantial number of cases requiring interpretation arise out of the failure of counsel to obtain an approved QDRO at the time of the marriage termination.[1] Sketchy or incomplete provisions, regarding the rights of the party entitled to a portion of the other party's retirement pension benefits, without a concomitant signing of a QDRO which include all provisions, have created situations where the trial court or appellate court have ordered the creation of a QDRO.

In *Bush v. Bush*,[2] the dissolution was in 1998. Not until 2002 was a proposed QDRO presented. The agreement had "minimalist language" providing that alternate payee, wife, was to receive one-half of the participant's pension. The wife's attorney tried to "fill in the gaps" by providing additional benefits in the submitted QDRO. The appellate court found error in the trial court's adoption of the QDRO which went beyond clarification.

Typical of the disputes that later arise when the separation agreement is sketchy in its description of the rights of the parties and there is no agreed QDRO filed or accompanying the decree is *Pohl v. Pohl*.[3] The dispute as to meaning of words "benefits . . . accrued through 6/30/88" resulted in the wife not receiving a coverture fraction amount.

[Section 9:53]

[1]Zigmont v. Toto, 47 Ohio App. 3d 181, 547 N.E.2d 1208 (8th Dist. Cuyahoga County 1988), cause dismissed, 38 Ohio St. 3d 715, 533 N.E.2d 783 (1988); Michelle S. v. Eduardo T., 2006-Ohio-2119, 2006 WL 1120684 (Ohio Ct. App. 6th Dist. Erie County 2006).

[Section 9:54]

[1]Cunningham v. Cunningham, 2003-Ohio-5711, 2003 WL 22429038 (Ohio Ct. App. 11th Dist. Trumbull County 2003) (first QDRO rejected by plan administrator; court approved QDRO, filed 6 years later with modification, reversed by appellate court); Kistler v. Kistler, 2004-Ohio-2309, 2004 WL 1047444 (Ohio Ct. App. 11th Dist. Trumbull County 2004).

[2]Bush v. Bush, 2003-Ohio-2781, 2003 WL 21257970 (Ohio Ct. App. 12th Dist. Butler County 2003). See also McKinney v. McKinney, 142 Ohio App. 3d 604, 756 N.E.2d 694 (2d Dist. Montgomery County 2001); Tabor v. Tabor, 2003-Ohio-1432, 2003 WL 1466277 (Ohio Ct. App. 7th Dist. Mahoning County 2003) (oral separation agreement in 1986; QDRO can be issued anytime so long as it does not modify decree); Maiorana v. Maiorana, 2004-Ohio-3925, 2004 WL 1662217 (Ohio Ct. App. 11th Dist. Lake County 2004) (Appellate court found no error in trial court approving a QDRO, which fleshed out the agreement in more detail). See also, Text §§ 30:24 et seq, Separation Agreements.

[3]Pohl v. Pohl, 2004-Ohio-3790, 2004 WL 1588110 (Ohio Ct. App. 2d Dist. Montgomery County 2004).

This problem would have been avoided if the separation agreement had spelled out or specified a coverture formula. The additional problem in *Pohl* is that the participant elected to withdraw his benefits in a lump sum.

In *Yarder v. Scherer*,[4] a 1996 decree awarded the wife a portion of the husband's State Teacher's Retirement System. Five years later, after the former wife learned that the husband had begun receiving his retirement benefits, she filed a motion in contempt and hired an evaluator.

The evaluator calculated the wife's benefits based on the husband receiving a single life annuity even though the participant had selected a joint and survivorship payment. The appellate court affirmed the trial court's interpretation of the separation agreement. The court agreed that "one-half the value . . . as accrued through the date of this agreement" was somewhat ambiguous.

Another important reason for spelling out the intended terms in the separation agreement and the avoidance of disputes as to the meaning is the problem of filing a decree of divorce without an accompanying QDRO. Appropriate wording without ambiguity, can ostensibly avoid the procedural quagmire of *Mishler v. Mishler*,[5] where the divorce was in 1992, the first QDRO was filed in 1995 and subsequently was amended three times, the last in 2004.

Where a QDRO differs from the separation agreement which provided property division, the QDRO is void ab initio and can be vacated by the court in accordance with its inherent authority. Thus a motion to vacate the QDRO does not have to comply with general requirements of Civ. R. 60(B) motions. It is void where in conflict with terms of the separation agreement.[6]

The issue in *Stare v. Stare*[7] was whether parties intended the QDRO (really a COAP for federal pension purposes) on the federal pension to state that the former spouse's death would cause her benefits to go to her estate or revert to participant. The appeal did not resolve the issue because the appellate court held there was no final appealable order due to the lack of a QDRO.[8]

Agreement for QDRO to be based on equalizing values in both par-

---

[4]Yarder v. Scherer, 2003-Ohio-6744, 2003 WL 22946151 (Ohio Ct. App. 6th Dist. Lucas County 2003).

[5]Mishler v. Mishler, 2005-Ohio-634, 2005 WL 375459 (Ohio Ct. App. 5th Dist. Stark County 2005) (was a separation agreement in decree).

[6]Himes v. Himes, 2004-Ohio-4666, 2004 WL 1948704 (Ohio Ct. App. 5th Dist. Tuscarawas County 2004); Bagley v. Bagley, 181 Ohio App. 3d 141, 2009-Ohio-688, 908 N.E.2d 469 (2d Dist. Greene County 2009), appeal not allowed, 122 Ohio St. 3d 1455, 2009-Ohio-3131, 908 N.E.2d 946 (2009).

[7]Stare v. Stare, 2004-Ohio-4770, 2004 WL 2004152 (Ohio Ct. App. 5th Dist. Licking County 2004).

[8]See Wilson v. Wilson, 116 Ohio St. 3d 268, 2007-Ohio-6056, 878 N.E.2d 16 (2007) (Appellate decisions which held not final appealable order without QDRO were in error).

ties' retirement assets as of a specific date should not be set aside just because husband claims an improper calculation based on husband's belief that pre-divorce withdrawals would be factored into computation.[9]

In addition to the task of determining the intent of the parties,[10] the process itself can present a procedural quagmire. This is especially so when the plan rejects the proposed orders and amended orders are necessary.[11]

> ◆ **Practice Tips:** Many pension plans will provide the attorney with approved formats. Some will reject any substantive alterations of their forms. To the extent possible have the QDRO pre-approved by all parties and attorneys for filing with the final decree of divorce or dissolution.[12]

§ 9:55   Action to set aside separation agreement

RC 2106.22 provides that a separation agreement to which a decedent was a party will be deemed valid unless an action to set aside the separation agreement is begun within four months after the appointment of the executor or administrator of the estate of the party-decedent or unless the validity of the separation agreement is attacked on another basis within the four-month time period. A court will generally bar all evidence regarding the formation of the agreement after the four months has tolled. This bar will even prevent an attorney from introducing evidence of fraud regarding the assets of any party or other fraud in the formation of the agreement. Any attorney would be well advised to be aware of RC 2106.22 when representing the spouse or the estate of a party who has entered into a separation agreement.[1]

§ 9:56   Rescission

A separation agreement may be impliedly rescinded when parties file for divorce and assert rights that are contrary to the prior agreement. However, when the agreement itself expressly states that it will survive into a divorce action, merely filing a divorce complaint

---

[9]Mamula v. Mamula, 2006-Ohio-4176, 2006 WL 2337467 (Ohio Ct. App. 11th Dist. Trumbull County 2006).

[10]Stare v. Stare, 2004-Ohio-4770, 2004 WL 2004152 (Ohio Ct. App. 5th Dist. Licking County 2004) (question whether alternate payee's share would revert to alternate payee's estate or participant's estate upon death of alternate payee).

[11]Mishler v. Mishler, 2005-Ohio-634, 2005 WL 375459 (Ohio Ct. App. 5th Dist. Stark County 2005).

[12]See Cleveland Bar Assn. v. Clavner, 99 Ohio St. 3d 53, 2003-Ohio-2464, 788 N.E.2d 1065 (2003), for consequences of failing to obtain an approved QDRO.

[Section 9:55]

[1]Burlovic v. Farmer, 162 Ohio St. 46, 54 Ohio Op. 5, 120 N.E.2d 705 (1954).

does not rescind the agreement. An express written declaration of rescission, signed by both parties, would be necessary.[1]

§ 9:57 Expiration of agreement

A separation agreement that by its own terms states that it will be of no effect if the parties have not been granted a decree of divorce or dissolution within a stated period of time, will expire and become null and void.[1]

I. SEPARATION AGREEMENTS—FORMS

§ 9:58 Separation agreement—Basic—Form⊚

This Agreement is made between *[name of spouse]* and *[name of spouse]*, who represent that:

The parties were married on or about *[date]*, at *[city and state]*.

There has been no issue of the marriage and none is expected.

In consequence of disputes and irreconcilable differences, the parties have separated and are now living apart. In view of their intention to live separate and apart the parties are desirous of settling their respective rights.

Now, Therefore, the parties agree as follows:

(1) The parties shall live apart for the rest of their lives. Each shall be free from interference, direct or indirect, by the other, as fully as though unmarried. Each may, for his or her separate benefit, engage in any employment, business, or profession he or she may choose. The parties shall not molest or malign each other.

(2) The parties have divided their personal property to their mutual satisfaction. Henceforth each of them shall own and enjoy, independently of any claim or right of the other, all items of real and personal property of every kind, whether now or hereafter owned by him or her, with full power to dispose of the same as fully and effectually as if he or she were unmarried.

(3) Neither party shall be responsible in any manner whatsoever for the support and maintenance of the other. This provision is intended and shall operate as a waiver of the right to periodic support or spousal support that either spouse may have against the other.

(4) The parties mutually release each other from any and all claims and demands, except as otherwise herein provided.

[Section 9:56]

[1]Estate of Driggers, 1998 WL 258169 (Ohio Ct. App. 11th Dist. Portage County 1998).

[Section 9:57]

[1]Phillips v. Phillips, 2005-Ohio-231, 2005 WL 121657 (Ohio Ct. App. 5th Dist. Stark County 2005); Greiner v. Greiner, 61 Ohio App. 2d 88, 15 Ohio Op. 3d 95, 399 N.E.2d 571 (8th Dist. Cuyahoga County 1979). See Text § 9:182, Expiration clause—Form.

(5) Each party hereby waives and relinquishes any and all rights that each may now or hereafter have to share as spouse in the other party's estate, or to act as the legal representative thereof. It is the intention of the parties that this provision shall serve as a mutual waiver of the right of election to take against each other's last will and testament under the present or future laws of the State of Ohio or any other jurisdiction.

(6) If either party or both parties should institute an action for divorce, legal separation or for dissolution of marriage in this state or elsewhere, this entire Agreement shall be disclosed and presented to the Court in such proceeding, with the request that it be adjudicated to be fair, just and proper, and this Agreement and all its terms and provisions shall then be adopted by said Court, and embodied in, and made a part of, the Order of said Court in the final Decree entered in such proceeding.

(7) The parties acknowledge that they have had the advice of counsel and that each is entering into this Agreement voluntarily and with full knowledge of the other party's income and property.

IN WITNESS WHEREOF, the parties have signed on the dates noted.

Witnessed by

Witness	Date	Husband	Date
Witness	Date		
Witness	Date	Wife	Date
Witness	Date		

§ 9:59 Separation agreement—Detailed—Form⊚

This is a Separation Agreement made by and between *[name of spouse]*, presently residing at *[street address, city, [name of county] County, state]* (sometimes hereinafter referred to as "*[_____]*") and *[name of spouse]*, presently residing at *[street address, city, [name of county] County, state]* (sometimes hereinafter referred to as "*[_____]*"). It is effective *[date]*, although either or both parties may have signed it before or after that date.

The parties were married on *[date]*, at *[city and state]*. *[Number]* children have been born of the said marriage: *[name of child A]*, born on *[date]*; *[name of child B]*, born on *[date]*; *[name of child C]*, born on *[date]*; and *[name of child D]*, born on *[date]*. *[Name of child A]* is an adult college student and, except to the extent that *[name of spouse]* is voluntarily making a contribution toward *[his/her]* educational expenses, is no longer dependent upon either of the parties. *[Name of child B]* is an adult high school senior and, after *[date]*, will no longer be dependent upon either of the parties, except to the extent that

531

[name of spouse] hereafter voluntarily contributes toward the expenses associated with *[his/her]* post-high school education. *[Name of child C]* and *[name of child D]* are both minors, living with *[name of spouse]*, and are dependent upon the parties. They are sometimes hereinafter referred to as "[_____]" and "[_____]" or as "the minor children."

As the result of disputes and irreconcilable differences, the parties have separated and are now living apart. They intend to continue to live apart and they are desirous of settling their property rights and agreeing upon terms for the support of *[name of spouse]*, the payment of support for the minor children, and the division of their property. In view of the foregoing and in consideration of the premises and of the mutual promises and undertakings hereinafter set forth, and for other good and valuable considerations, the parties agree as follows:

ARTICLE I. Freedom of action; noninterference

The parties may and shall continue to live apart. Each shall be free from interference, direct or indirect, by the other as fully as though unmarried. Neither party shall molest or interfere with the other. Each may, for his or her separate benefit, engage in any employment, business, or profession that he or she may choose.

ARTICLE II. Allocation of parental rights and responsibilities

(A) The *[wife/husband]* is designated as the residential parent and legal custodian of the minor children.

[or]

(A) The parties agree to share in the parental rights and responsibilities associated with the care of the minor *[child/children]*, and attach hereto a Shared Parenting plan which is incorporated herein, providing for all matters regarding the *[child/children]*.

(B) *[Name of spouse]* shall have the right to parenting time with said children at reasonable times and places, upon *[name of spouse]* giving reasonable advance notice to *[name of spouse]* of *[his/her]* intentions as to, and plans for, such parenting time. More specifically, as to parenting time which *[name of spouse]* anticipates will extend over a period exceeding three consecutive days, *[he/she]* shall give *[name of spouse]* at least *[fifteen]* days' advance notice as to any such proposed parenting time; and as to parenting time which *[he/she]* anticipates will extend over a period exceeding *[one]* week(s), *[he/she]* shall give *[name of spouse]* at least *[thirty]* days' advance notice.

[or]

(B) The parenting time rights of *[name of spouse]* shall be in accordance with the parenting time / visitation schedule of the *[name of court]* Court, with the following exceptions: [_____].

(C) Both parties expect that both of the said children and *[name of spouse]* shall at all times have reasonable access to one another, and each party will act in such a way as to encourage liberal and frequent parenting time between *[name of spouse]* and the said children.

(D) *[Name of spouse]* shall consult with *[name of spouse]*, and shall keep *[name of spouse]* advised, as to the general health and welfare of *[name of child]* and *[name of child]*, and shall inform *[name of spouse]* as quickly as possible in the event of either such child's major illness or accident. Further, *[name of spouse]* shall keep *[name of spouse]* informed as to each such child's educational progress and shall take any and all steps necessary to assure access of *[name of spouse]* to each such child's school record, report cards, and the like.

(E) Child support

(1) *[Name of spouse]* shall pay to *[name of spouse]*, as and for the support of *[name of child]* and *[name of child]*, the sum of $*[dollar amount]* per child per month ($*[dollar amount]* per month total at the outset), the first such payment to be made on or before *[date]*, and each subsequent payment to be made on or before the *[day of month]* day of each month as to which it is due. Until this agreement becomes a court order, the *[name of payor spouse]* shall pay directly to the *[name of payee spouse]* said *[monthly/weekly]* sums. After this agreement is incorporated into a court decree, all child support payments shall be made, plus the processing charge, by payroll withholding due and owing the *[name of obligor]* spouse, through the Ohio Child Support Payment Central (C.S.P.C.), P.O. Box 182394, Columbus, OH, 43218-2394, and shall continue as to each child to age eighteen years and through the month of the year during which such child graduates from high school. *[Said sum was computed under the child support guidelines and is in conformity therewith.][or] [Said sum deviates from the child support guidelines. The parties agree that application of the guideline amount would be unjust or inappropriate to the [child/children] or either parent and would not be in the best interest of the [child/children] based upon the following factors: [list or specify factors].]*

(Statutory support notices may be included here)

(2) Medical and dental expenses

[Name of spouse] shall pay, either directly or by reimbursement to *[name of spouse]*, and shall hold *[name of spouse]* harmless as to, all reasonable medical, dental (including orthodontic), hospitalization and optical expenses as to each minor child, *[his/her]* obligation in this regard to continue, as to each child, until *[he/she]* is no longer obligated to pay support for such child under the terms of this Agreement. Further, *[name of spouse]* shall maintain, and keep in full force and effect, a policy or policies of health and hospitalization insurance at least equivalent to that under which the parties' minor children are now insured, *[his/her]* obligation in this regard to continue, as to each child, until *[he/she]* no longer has any obligation to pay any medical, dental, hospitalization, or optical expenses as to such child pursuant to

the terms of this paragraph.

[or]

(2) Medical and dental expenses

[Name of spouse] shall maintain health and hospitalization
insurance coverage for the minor *[child/children]* as available through *[his/her]* place of employment. In the event
medical insurance is not available through employment, *[he/
she]* shall obtain coverage for the *[child/children]* that is
comparable to the present coverage. All uncovered medical,
dental, psychological, optical, and prescription drug expenses
which are extraordinary, as defined herein as being over $100
per year per child, shall be paid *[all/one-half/proportionately]*
by the *[husband/wife/parties]*.

(3) Education

Both parties recognize the value and desirability of making
available to their children a post-high school education. To the
extent that any of the children desires to obtain such an education, the parties agree to consult with each other and with such
child with respect to such education and to make such education
available to the extent that the parties are reasonably able to do
so under the circumstances then prevailing as to parties and the
child in question. It is understood, however, that neither party is,
nor shall be deemed to be, undertaking any legally enforceable
obligation to provide or pay for all or any part of any expenses associated with any such child's post-high school education.

ARTICLE III. Property and property division

(A) Real estate

[Name of spouse] is the record owner of the premises known as
[street address, city, [name of county] County, state], and more fully
described as *[legal description]*. *[Name of spouse]* shall remain the
owner thereof, free and clear of any claim by *[name of spouse]*, and
shall be free to deal with, and to dispose of, such property in any
way and at any time that *[he/she]* sees fit. *[Name of spouse]* shall
be solely responsible for, and shall hold *[name of spouse]* harmless
as to, all expenses and debts associated with such property and
[his/her] occupancy thereof, including, without limitation, the
mortgage presently encumbering such property, taxes, insurance,
maintenance, and repairs.

(B) Automobiles

[Name of spouse] now has in *[his/her]* possession an automobile
used by *[him/her]* pursuant to the terms of a lease in which *[he/
she]* is named as the lessee. *[Name of spouse]* shall continue in possession of such automobile and *[name of spouse]* shall pay all lease
payments relative thereto and, upon expiration of the present lease
term (in *[date]*) shall purchase such automobile and cause title
thereto to be transferred to *[name of spouse]*, free and clear of any
encumbrances. Until such transfer of title takes place, *[name of*

spouse] shall maintain insurance on such automobile in accordance with the terms of the policy under which such automobile is now insured. Except as otherwise herein provided, on and after [date], [name of spouse] shall be solely responsible for, and shall hold [name of spouse] harmless as to all expenses associated with [his/her] ownership of such automobile, including, without limitation, the cost of maintenance and repairs.

(C) Household goods and personal property

The parties have heretofore physically divided their personal property and possessions, and each acknowledges that he or she has in his or her possession all of such items to which he or she is entitled, and neither claims any interest in such items now held by the other. More specifically, [name of spouse] shall retain, free and clear of any claim by [name of spouse], all of the furniture, furnishings, utensils, appliances, and other items of personal property located in and about the premises located at [address], [city], [name of county] County, [state], and likewise, [name of spouse] shall retain, free and clear of any claim by [name of spouse], all items located in and about the premises at [address], [city], [name of county] County, [state].

(D) Checking and savings accounts

Each party shall retain, free and clear of any claim by the other, any checking account, savings account, certificates of deposit, or any other account of any kind now registered in his or her name.

(E) Investments and other assets

[Name of spouse] shall retain, free and clear of any claim by [name of spouse], any and all interests that [he/she] has in any partnerships (limited or general), retirement plans, real estate and other investment vehicles or devices, and [name of spouse] specifically relinquishes any claims or rights that [he/she] might otherwise have or claim therein.

(F) Life insurance

(1) [Name of spouse] has the following life insurance policies of which [he/she] is the owner and insured: [list here].

(2) So long as [name of payor] has any obligation for the payment of support as to either [name of child] or [name of child], [name of payor] shall maintain, and keep in full force and effect, a policy or policies of life insurance which will, upon death of [name of payor], pay (either directly or in trust) to each such child a net amount of at least $[dollar amount]. The obligation of [name of payor] to maintain such insurance shall cease, as to each child, when [name of payor] no longer has any obligation to pay support as to that child. Upon request of [name of payee], [name of payor] shall provide to [name of payee], from time to time, whatever documentation or other proof that [name of payee] may reasonably request to assure [name of payee] that [name of payor] is carrying out the terms of this paragraph. In the event that [name of payor] fails to provide such information to [name of payee] within

[number of days] days after request of *[name of payee]* therefor, then *[name of payor]* does hereby irrevocably empower *[name of payee]* to make inquiry of any insurance company issuing any insurance policy or policies under which *[name of payor]* is insured and as to which either such child is the beneficiary. In the event that *[name of payor]* fails to keep a policy or policies in full force and effect so as to provide payment to, or for the benefit of, such children as provided herein, then the estate of *[name of payor]* shall be liable to each child entitled to such benefits for the difference between the net amount so payable and the amount or amounts actually paid to such child or for such child's benefit, by any insurer or insurers on account of death of *[name of payor]*.

(3) *[Name of spouse]* shall maintain, and keep in full force and effect, a policy or policies of life insurance which will, upon his death, pay directly to *[name of spouse]*:

(a) A net amount of at least $*[dollar amount]*, provided, however, that as obligation of *[name of payor]* to pay lump-sum spousal support pursuant to the provisions of Article *[designation of Article]* hereof is reduced, *[name of payor]* may reduce the net amount payable to *[name of payee]* to the reduced amount so payable; plus

(b) A net amount of at least $*[dollar amount]*, such insurance to be maintained at that level until *[name of payor]* no longer has any obligation to pay periodic spousal support to *[name of payee]* pursuant to the provisions of Article *[designation of Article]* hereof. When *[name of payor]* no longer has an obligation to pay spousal support of any kind under Article *[designation of Article]* or Article *[designation of Article]* hereof, then the obligation of *[name of payor]* for the maintenance of life insurance pursuant to the terms of this Article *[designation of Article]* shall cease entirely. However, under no circumstances shall the net amount payable to *[name of payee]* under any policy or policies of which *[name of payee]* is a beneficiary pursuant to the terms of this paragraph be reduced to less than $*[dollar amount]* so long as *[name of payor]* is obligated to continue to make periodic spousal support payments to *[name of payee]* pursuant to the provisions of Article *[designation of Article]* hereof. In the event that *[name of payor]* fails to keep a policy or policies in full force and effect so as to provide payment to *[name of payee]* of the benefits provided for herein, the estate of *[name of payor]* shall be liable to *[name of payee]* for the difference between the net amount so payable and the amount or amounts actually paid to *[name of payee]* by any insurer or insurers on account of death of *[name of payor]*. Upon request of *[name of payee]*, *[name of payor]* shall, from time to time, provide to *[name of payee]* whatever documentation or other proof that *[name of payee]* may reasonably request to assure *[name of payee]* that *[name of payor]* is carrying out the terms of this paragraph. In the event that *[name of payor]* fails to provide such information to *[name of payee]* within *[number of days]* days after request of *[name of payee]* therefor, then *[name of payor]* does hereby irrevocably empower *[name of payee]* to make inquiry of any insurance company issuing life insurance policies on the life of *[name of payor]* as to the status of any such policy under which *[name of payee]* is the beneficiary pursuant to the provisions hereof, the payment of premiums due thereon, and the like. The provision herein placing potential liability upon the estate of *[name of payor]* shall not prevent, preclude, nor be a defense to any action brought by *[name of payee]* to enforce this requirement of insurance by contempt or otherwise.

(G) Property division

[Name of spouse] shall pay to *[name of spouse]* as lump sum division of property the sum of $*[dollar amount]*, such sum to be paid in *[number of installments]* equal yearly installments of $*[dollar amount]*, the first such payment to be made on or before *[date]* and each subsequent payment to be made on or before *[day of month]* day of *[month]* of the year as to which it is due. All such payments shall be made directly to *[name of payee]*. The lump sum property division provided for herein shall be due and payable to *[name of payee]* in all events, whether or not *[name of payee]* or *[name of payor]* dies before payment of the full amount and whether or not *[name of payee]* remarries prior to the payment in full thereof and regardless of any change in the financial circumstances of either party. The balance due on the obligation imposed upon *[name of payor]* by the terms of this paragraph shall constitute a charge against estate of *[name of payor]* in the event of death of *[name of payor]* before the payment thereof in full and shall be an asset of estate of *[name of payee]* in the event of death of *[name of payee]* prior to such payment in full. However, any such balance shall be reduced by the net amount paid to *[name of payee]* in life insurance proceeds pursuant to the provisions of Article *[designation of Article]* hereof. The parties recognize this sum is not taxable to the *[name of payee]* nor deductible by the *[name of payor]*.

(H) Retirement benefits

The *[name of participant-spouse]* has accumulated retirement benefits, through *[his/her]* employment, and such benefits shall be *[his/hers]*, free and clear of any claims of the *[name of nonparticipant-spouse]*.

ARTICLE IV. Spousal support

[Name of spouse] shall pay to *[name of spouse]* as spousal support the sum of $*[dollar amount]* per month, the first such payment to be made on or before *[date]*, and each subsequent payment to be made on or before the *[day of month]* day of each month thereafter. Such spousal support payments shall continue until the first to happen of the following: (a) death of *[name of payee]*; (b) remarriage of *[name of payee]*; or (c) death of *[name of payor]*. Until this agreement is

incorporated in an order of court, the *[name of payor]* shall pay said sum directly to the *[name of payee]*. Thereafter, all payments by *[name of payor]* to *[name of payee]*, plus the processing charge, shall be made by *[payroll withholding from the wages due payor/withholding from ([name of bank, account no. [account number], other income source, etc.)] through the [name and address of agency]*. Said spousal support shall be *[modifiable/nonmodifiable]* by the court.

[or]

[Name of spouse] shall pay to *[name of spouse]*, as spousal support, the sum of $*[dollar amount]*, payable in installments of $*[dollar amount]* each and every month beginning on *[date]*, and continuing for a total of *[number of months]* months, each payment to be made on or before the *[day of month]* day of the month as to which it is due. The obligation of *[name of payor]* to pay *[name of payee]* pursuant to the terms of this paragraph will end, and *[name of payor]* will be released from the obligation of payment, after the earliest of the death of either party or the remarriage of *[name of payee]*. All payments by *[name of payor]* to *[name of payee]* pursuant to the terms of this paragraph shall be made, plus the processing charge, by *[payroll withholding from the wages due payor/withholding from ([name of bank, account no. [account number], other income source, etc.)] through the [name and address of county agency]*. Said spousal support shall be nonmodifiable by the court.

[or]

[Name of spouse] shall pay to *[name of spouse]*, as spousal support, a sum equal to *[percentage amount]*% of his total gross income for the immediately preceding month, the first such payment to be made on or before *[date]*, and each subsequent payment to be made on or before the *[day of month]* day of each month thereafter. All such payments shall be made, plus the processing charge, by *[payroll withholding from the wages due payor/withholding from ([name of bank, account no. [account number], other income source, etc.)] through the [name and address of agency]*. Said spousal support shall be *[modifiable/nonmodifiable]* by the court. The obligation of *[name of payor]* to pay *[name of payee]* pursuant to the terms of this paragraph shall end, and *[name of payor]* will be released from the obligation of payment, after death of *[name of payee]*. The parties expressly agree that such payments *[shall/shall not]* be deductible by *[name of payor]* for income tax purposes and *[shall/shall not]* be included by *[name of payee]* for such purposes.

[or]

Neither party shall pay spousal support to the other party. This provision has been arrived at after consideration of all statutory factors, and shall not be modifiable by the court.

ARTICLE V. Income tax

(A) The parties agree, in the event they are still married on December 31st of any year, to cooperate in the filing of income returns, either jointly or as married filing separately and to file in the manner which will result in the greater overall tax savings. In so doing, neither party shall be required to pay more than he or she would have had to pay had he or she filed separately, and shall be reimbursed by the other party for such refund he or she could have received. If the savings exceeds the benefit to each, such excess refund (and only to the extent there is a refund) shall be divided *[equally/proportionately]*.

(B) *[Name of spouse]* shall pay, and shall indemnify and hold *[name of spouse]* harmless as to, any cost or expense associated with any asserted claim with respect to any joint federal, state, or local income tax or state personal property tax returns heretofore and hereafter filed by the parties.

(C) As to *[year]* and all years thereafter, *[name of payor]* shall be entitled to claim each of the parties' children as a dependent for federal and state income tax purposes, the applicable regulations permitting. *[Name of payee]* shall sign any declaration required by the Internal Revenue Service to implement the terms of this paragraph and agrees to provide such declaration to *[name of payor]*.

ARTICLE VI. Payment of debts

(A) The husband shall pay and save the wife harmless on the following debts: *[_____]*.

(B) The wife shall pay and save the husband harmless on the following debts: *[_____]*.

(C) Except as herein otherwise specified, each party shall pay any and all debts incurred by him or her prior to *[date]*. On and after *[date]*, neither party shall incur any debt or obligation upon the credit of the other and each shall indemnify and save the other harmless as to any such debt or obligation so charged or otherwise incurred.

ARTICLE VII. Attorney fees

[Name of spouse] shall forthwith pay to *[name of spouse]*, or directly to attorney of *[name of spouse]*, the reasonable attorney fees (not to exceed $*[dollar amount]*) incurred by *[name of spouse]* for the negotiation and drafting of this Agreement and representation in connection with the divorce action presently pending between the parties.

ARTICLE VIII. Disposition of estates

Other than as herein set forth, each party shall at all times be at full liberty to dispose of his or her property, real, personal, or mixed, tangible or intangible, by last will and testament or otherwise, free from any claim, interest, or right in favor of the other.

ARTICLE IX. Mutual release

Except as otherwise herein expressly provided, the parties shall and do mutually release and forever discharge each other from any and all actions, suits, debts, claims, demands, and obligations whatsoever, both in law and in equity, which either of them ever had, now has, or may hereafter have or assert against the other upon or by reason of any matter, cause, or thing up to the date of the execution of this Agreement.

Each party waives all rights of inheritance and in the estate of the other, and all rights which would otherwise be available as a surviving spouse, except payments or rights expressly accruing in this agreement.

ARTICLE X. Waiver and modification

No modification or waiver of any of the terms hereof shall be valid unless in writing and signed by both the parties. No waiver of any breach hereof or default hereunder shall be deemed a waiver of any subsequent breach or default of the same or similar nature.

ARTICLE XI. Execution of additional instruments

Each party shall, at any time and from time to time hereafter, take any and all steps and execute, acknowledge, and deliver to the other party any and all further instruments and assurances, that the other party may reasonably request for the purpose of giving full force and effect to the provisions of this Agreement.

ARTICLE XII. Notices

Except as herein otherwise expressly provided, any and all notices given hereunder or pursuant to the terms hereof, or on account hereof, shall be in writing and shall be sent by first-class mail to either party at his or her residence address, and each party agrees to keep the other informed of any change in his or her residence address.

The following Notices are hereby incorporated into this separation agreement by agreement of the parties, and made an ORDER of the Court:

I. RELOCATION NOTICE: Pursuant to RC 3109.051(G), the parties hereto are hereby notified as follows:

If the "residential parent," namely *[name of residential parent]*, intends to move to a residence other than the residence specified in the parties' separation agreement, said "residential parent" shall file a notice of intent to relocate with this court. Except as provided in RC 3109.051(G)(2), (3), and (4), a copy of such notice shall be mailed by the court to *[name of non-residential parent]*. On receipt of the notice, the court, on its own motion or the motion of *[name of non-residential parent]*, may schedule a hearing with notice to both parties to determine whether it is in the best interest of the child or children to revise the visitation or parenting schedule for the child or children.

II. RECORDS ACCESS NOTICE: Pursuant to RC 3109.051(H) and RC 3319.321(B)(5)(a), the parties hereto are hereby notified as follows:

Excepting as specifically modified or otherwise limited by the parties' separation agreement, and subject to RC 2301.35(F)(2) and RC 3319.321(F), the "non-residential" parent, namely *[name of non-residential parent]*, is entitled to access, under the same terms and conditions as the "residential parent," namely *[name of residential parent]*, to any record that is related to the child or children and to which said residential parent of the child or children legally is provided access, including school records. Any keeper of a record, public or private, who knowingly fails to comply with this order, is in contempt of court.

III. DAY CARE CENTER ACCESS NOTICE: Pursuant to RC 3109.051(I), the parties hereto are hereby notified as follows:

Excepting as specifically modified or otherwise limited by court order, and in accordance with RC 5104.011, *[name of non-residential parent]*, the parent who is not the residential parent, is entitled to access to any day care center that is or will be attended by the child or children with whom visitation is granted, to the same extent that *[name of residential parent]*, the residential parent, is granted access to the center.

IV. SCHOOL ACTIVITIES NOTICE: Pursuant to RC 3109.051(J), the parties hereto are hereby notified as follows:

Excepting as specifically modified or otherwise limited by the parties' separation agreement, and subject to RC 3319.321, the "non-residential" parent, namely *[name of non-residential parent]*, is entitled to access, under the same terms and conditions as the "residential parent," namely *[name of residential parent]*, to any student activity that is related to the child or children and to which the "residential parent" of the child or children legally is provided access.

ARTICLE XIII. Partial invalidity

If any provision of this Agreement is held to be invalid or unenforceable, all other provisions shall nevertheless continue in full force and effect.

ARTICLE XIV. Incorporation into decree

There is presently pending in the *[name of county]* County Court of Common Pleas, Division of Domestic Relations, an action in which both parties seek a divorce. In the event that the parties are hereafter divorced pursuant to such action or pursuant to any action instituted in any court of competent jurisdiction, this

Agreement shall be incorporated into, and shall become a part of, the decree of the court rendering such action, and neither party will demand a settlement in connection with such action for divorce other than as provided herein.

[or]

If either the Husband or the Wife should institute an action for divorce or legal separation, or if they jointly institute proceedings for a dissolution, in this state or elsewhere, this Agreement shall be disclosed and presented to the court in such proceeding with the request that it be adjudicated to be fair, just, and proper, and that this Agreement and all its terms and provisions be incorporated into the Decree of said court.

ARTICLE XV. Compliance with existing orders

The parties shall comply with any court orders relative to temporary allocation of parental rights and responsibilities, child support, spousal support, and the like now in effect, and any payment due pursuant to any such order shall be made by *[name of spouse]* to *[name of spouse]* through *[date]*.

ARTICLE XVI. Warranty as to financial statements

[Name of spouse] has furnished to *[name of spouse]* and to the attorney of *[name of spouse]* various financial statements reflecting the parties' financial condition as of *[date]*, and the parties agree and understand that they have arrived at the settlement set forth in this Agreement on the basis of, and in light of, the information set forth in such financial statements. *[Name of spouse]* represents and warrants to *[name of spouse]* that there have been no substantial changes in *[his/her]* financial circumstances since *[date]*, and that such financial statements correctly, accurately, and fully reflect *[his/her]* financial condition as of the date upon which *[he/she]* signed this Agreement.

In the event it is hereafter discovered that either party has failed to disclose, whether knowingly or inadvertently, an asset the value of which is substantial (herein defined as having a value in excess of $*[dollar amount]*) the other party shall be entitled to one-half if it is a divisible asset or 50% of the value, as independently ascertained, of said asset.

ARTICLE XVII. Entire agreement

The parties have incorporated herein their entire understanding. There are no representations, warranties, covenants, or undertakings other than those expressly set forth herein. No oral statements or prior written matter extrinsic to this Agreement shall have any force or effect. Each party acknowledges that he or she fully understands the terms hereof, and each acknowledges that he or she is signing this Agreement freely and voluntarily.

ARTICLE XVIII. Binding of heirs

Each party hereby makes this agreement binding upon the heirs, estate, executor and administrator of his or her respective estate and all obligations created hereunder shall be a charge upon his or her estate.

ARTICLE XIX. Effective date

This Agreement shall be effective upon the date last signed by a party.

IN WITNESS WHEREOF, the parties have hereunto set their hands to four counterparts of this Agreement, each of which shall constitute an original.

In the presence of:

Witness	Date	Husband
Witness	Date	Date
[Jurat]		

In the presence of:

Witness	Date	Wife
Witness	Date	Date
[Jurat]		

NOTES TO FORM

Drafter's Notes

Article II, paragraph (E)(3) is not enforceable and merely states the parties' concern for the well-being of their offspring.

A jurat is technically unnecessary, as are witnesses. However, if real estate is to be transferred pursuant to the agreement, compliance with the formalities of conveyances (requiring a notary) will permit the filing of the separation agreement to effectuate a transfer upon failure of the transferor to sign the deed.

II. PRELIMINARY CLAUSES—FORMS

§ 9:60   Recitals—Parties—Form⊚

This Agreement is made between *[name]*, residing at *[street address, city, state]*, hereinafter called the Husband, and *[name]*, residing at *[street address, city, state]*, hereinafter called the Wife.

§ 9:61   Recitals—Marriage, children, and separation—Form⊚

The parties were married on *[date]*, in *[city and state]*. There *[is/are]* *[number]* *[child/children]* of the marriage, namely, *[name]*, born *[birthdate]*; *[name]*, born *[birthdate]*; and *[name]*, born *[birthdate]*.

In consequence of disputes and irreconcilable differences between them, the parties *[have separated and are living apart and]* intend to live separate and apart for the remainder of their lives. They desire, by this Agreement, to settle their respective property rights, agree on terms for spousal support and maintenance, and provide for the allocation of parental rights and responsibilities of their *[child/children]*.

§ 9:62 Recitals—Consideration—Form⊚

In consideration of the above premises and of the mutual promises and undertakings set forth herein, *[and of the payments to be made from time to time pursuant to certain provisions of this Agreement,]* the parties agree:

§ 9:63 Recitals—Nonmolestation—Form⊚

The parties shall hereafter *[continue to]* live separate and apart from each other and each shall go his or her own way without direction, molestation, or interference from the other, the same as though unmarried, and neither shall annoy or harass the other in any manner whatsoever.

NOTES TO FORM

Drafter's Notes

An essential requirement for validity of a separation agreement is that the parties intend to and actually do separate. Where the parties sign a separation agreement but continue to share the marital home, the IRS has considered it a sham transaction. The agreement would fail also for lack of the primary requirement of separation.

§ 9:64 Effect of reconciliation—Form⊚

If the parties reconcile after the date of the execution of this Agreement, this Agreement shall nevertheless continue in full force until it is modified or abrogated by another written instrument to that effect signed by each of the parties.

III. PERSONAL PROPERTY CLAUSES—FORMS

§ 9:65 Personal property—Nondisclosed and nondivided—Form⊚

If it is later ascertained or discovered that either party owned or had an interest in property, of any kind, not disclosed by such party and not divided or allocated herein, whether such nondisclosure was by virtue of purposeful, negligent, or innocent omission, and such property is substantial (defined herein as worth more than $*[dollar amount]*), the other party shall be entitled to one-half of said property, if it is divisible, or one-half of the value of such property, if not divisible. The nonowner party shall be entitled to enforce this provision in court if there is not compliance and to recover his or her attorney fees in obtaining compliance.

§ 9:66 Personal property—Furniture, household furnishings, and effects—Form⊚

(a) Except as otherwise provided herein all the furniture, furnishings, household goods and appliances, fixtures and appurtenances, books and works of art, and other items of personal property located in the marital dwelling at *[street address, city, state]*, shall be the sole and exclusive property of *[name of spouse]* free and clear of any claim on behalf of *[name of spouse]*.

(b) The following items presently located at the aforesaid dwelling shall be the sole and exclusive property of *[name of spouse]*: *[specify]*.

[Name of spouse] shall, within *[number]* days after the execution of this Agreement, remove these items from the aforesaid dwelling at *[his/her]* own expense. If *[he/she]* fails to do so within this period of time, all such items not so removed shall thereafter be the sole property of *[name of spouse]*, free and clear of any claim by *[name of spouse]*.

(c) Each party shall hereafter own, have, and enjoy, independently of any claim on behalf of the other party, all items of real and personal property (tangible and intangible) now owned or hereafter acquired by him or her and not otherwise disposed of herein, with power to use or dispose of the same as fully and effectually as though he or she were unmarried.

§9:67 Personal property—To be divided per list—Form⊚

The parties agree that the furniture, furnishings, household goods and appliances, fixtures and appurtenances, books and works of art, and other items of personal property located in the marital dwelling at *[street address, city, state]*, as listed in Exhibit "A," attached hereto, shall be the property of *[name of spouse]* and the items in Exhibit "B" shall be the property of *[name of spouse]* and *[he/she]* shall be entitled to remove *[his/her]* items by *[date]*.

§9:68 Personal property—Already divided—Form⊚

All the furniture, furnishings, household goods and appliances, fixtures and appurtenances, books and works of art, and other items of personal property located, or once located, in the marital dwelling at *[street address, city, state]*, have previously been divided by and between the parties and each party shall hereafter own, have and enjoy, free of any claim on behalf of the other, all items of personal property now in his or her possession, respectively, and each party hereby relinquishes any claim that *[he/she]* might otherwise have as to the personal property now in the other's possession.

§9:69 Personal property—Insurance for contents of marital home—Form⊚

[Name of spouse] hereby represents that the contents of the marital home of the parties located at *[street address, city, state]*, are insured against various risks under a policy with *[name of insurance company]* issued to *[name of spouse]*, under Policy No. *[policy number]* issued by the *[name of insurance company]* on *[date]*, that it will not expire

until *[date]*, that it is in full force and effect, and that all premiums on it to *[date]* have been paid. *[Name of spouse]* hereby assigns and transfers to *[name of spouse]* all *[his/her]* right, title, and interest in and to the aforesaid insurance, and simultaneously herewith has delivered the policy to *[name of transferee]*, together with a letter addressed to the insurance company apprising it of the assignment. On and after *[date]*, *[name of transferee]* shall be responsible for any such premium costs regarding the contents of the marital home.

§ 9:70   Personal property—Transfer of auto and auto insurance—Form⊚

[Name of spouse] hereby assigns and transfers to *[name of spouse]* all *[his/her]* right, title, and interest in the *[make, model, year]* automobile registered in *[his/her]* name. *[Name of transferor]* shall simultaneously herewith execute and deliver a document of transfer to *[name of transferee]*. Certain bodily injury liability and property damage liability insurance is currently in full force and effect in *[name of transferor]*'s name with respect to the aforesaid automobile; such insurance is represented by Policy No. *[policy number]*, issued to *[name of transferor]* on *[date]* by the *[name of insurance company]*. All premiums thereon have been paid to *[date]*. *[Name of transferor]* assigns and transfers to *[name of transferee]* all *[his/her]* right, title, and interest in and to the aforesaid insurance, and simultaneously herewith has delivered the aforesaid policy to *[name of transferee]*, together with a letter addressed to the insurance company apprising it of the assignment.

§ 9:71   Personal property—Copyrights and royalties—Form⊚

A. *[Name of spouse]* is a *[poet/author/inventor/composer]*.

B. *[Name of spouse]* agrees that all *[works/books/inventions]*, completed subsequent to the signing of this Agreement shall be the sole property of *[name of spouse]*.

C. Each party agrees that payments received by *[name of spouse]* which are in the nature of *[royalties/copyrights]* from works completed during marriage shall be *[sole property of the creator/divided evenly between the parties/deposited to the account of [name of party]/ irrevocably assigned to the minor children/paid to [name of party] as a division of property settlement]*.

§ 9:72   Personal property—Professional licenses—Form⊚

In recognition of the contribution of *[nonprofessional spouse]* to the obtaining by *[professional spouse]* of *[his/her][medical/legal/ optometric]* degree and further recognizing that such license to practice is not subject to division and that such license requires the personal efforts and attention of *[professional spouse]*, *[professional spouse]* agrees to pay to *[nonprofessional spouse]* and *[nonprofessional spouse]* agrees to accept the sum of $*[dollar amount]* payable as follows: *[terms]*.

IV.   REAL ESTATE CLAUSES—FORMS

§ 9:73   Real estate—Disclaimer of interest in property titled to one spouse—Form⊚

[Name of spouse] hereby acknowledges that *[he/she]* has no right, title, or interest whatsoever in certain real property titled in the name of *[name of spouse]*, which property is located at *[street address]* and is further described as follows:

[legal description]

Said real estate shall be the sole and exclusive property of *[title holder]*, free and clear of any claim whatsoever on behalf of *[nontitle holder]*, and *[nontitle holder]* covenants and agrees to execute and deliver any and all documents required in order to release any rights *[he/she]* may have in the aforesaid real estate.

NOTES TO FORM

Drafter's Notes

No statute requires that separation agreements be either witnessed or notarized. In the event that a real property transfer is incorporated into the separation agreement, however, it is recommended that the agreement be signed in the presence of two witnesses and notarized so that the county recorder is able to convey the real estate. See Text § 9:59, Separation agreement—Detailed—Form, for an example of signatures, witnesses, and jurat.

§ 9:74   Real estate—Immediate sale with proceeds divided—Form⊚

The parties are presently joint owners of the marital home located at *[street address]* and further described as follows:

[legal description]

The parties shall immediately list said real estate for sale with a real estate broker of their mutual choice. In the event the parties are unable to agree upon an acceptable real estate broker, then in that event said real estate shall be listed for sale with *[name of broker]* at a sales price of $*[dollar amount]*. In the event that said real estate is not sold within *[time]*, then the sales price shall be reduced to $*[dollar amount]* until sold.

Until said property is sold, *[name of spouse]* shall pay all amounts due for *[mortgage/taxes/insurance/repairs]*. Upon sale, *[name of spouse]* shall be reimbursed from the proceeds, for that amount by which payments made by *[name of spouse]* reduced the mortgage principal from the date of this Agreement to the date of sale.

Upon closing, and after payment of the first mortgage due and owing upon said real estate, any real estate commissions payable and the normal and customary costs of closing, the net proceeds realized therefrom shall be divided *[equally/[[percentage amount]% to Husband and [[percentage amount]% to the Wife]*. The parties hereby authorize and direct the escrow agent to distribute funds directly to the parties and others as provided for in this Agreement.

§ 9:75   Real estate—Sale upon specified event or after term of years with proceeds divided—Form⊚

(a) The parties are joint owners of certain real estate constituting the marital home located at *[street address]*, and further described as follows:

[legal description]

(b) *[Name of spouse]* [and minor *[child/children]* shall enjoy the exclusive use and occupancy of said home until:

(1) *[Number of years]* years from the date of this Agreement,

(2) Death of *[name of occupant]*,

(3) No minor child making his or her residence in said home,

(4) Remarriage of *[name of occupant]*,

(5) Cohabitation by occupant with an adult unrelated person of the opposite sex (For the purposes of this agreement, cohabitation is defined to mean residence by such person in occupant's home in excess of *[number of months]* months; said months need not be consecutive.),

(6) *[Name of occupant]* desires to sell,

(7) Both parties desire to sell,

(8) The last of the children reaches the age of eighteen years and has completed high school, or

(9) *[Name of occupant]* abandons said home as *[his/her]* principal residence.

Until said premises are sold, *[name of occupant]* shall maintain said property. All maintenance and repair expenses in excess of $*[dollar amount]* shall be paid one-half by each party.

Upon the first occurrence of the events enumerated, the marital home shall be listed for sale at a price then to be agreed upon by and between the parties, and the net proceeds realized after payment of the first mortgage, any real estate commissions due and owing and other normal and customary costs of closing, *[shall be divided equally/ shall be divided, [percentage amount]% to the Husband, [percentage amount]% to the Wife][or] [name of spouse]* shall be paid the sum of $*[dollar amount]* and all remaining proceeds shall be paid to *[name of spouse]*. The escrow agent is hereby authorized and directed to distribute funds upon sale of the marital home as provided for in this Agreement.

(c) *[Name of occupant]* assumes and agrees to pay the remaining unpaid balance on a certain promissory note jointly executed by the parties, the payment of which was secured by a first mortgage on the aforesaid real estate. Said note and mortgage are held by *[name of mortgagee]* and are in the original sum of $*[dollar amount]* with a present unpaid balance of not more than $*[dollar amount]*; and further, *[name of occupant]* shall indemnify and hold absolutely harmless *[name of non-occupant-spouse]* from any expense, loss, claim or liability whatever arising from, or in any way connected with, said note and mortgage; and

Until the occurrence of the earliest of these contingencies, *[name of occupant]* will pay the taxes, assessments, insurance, and the balance due on the note and mortgage securing said premises, though each month, *[name of non-occupant-spouse]* will pay *[name of occupant]*, in addition to child support payments, a payment equal to that month's principal payment owed to *[name of mortgagee]* on the parties' present mortgage, the parties understanding that at present this principal payment is approximately $*[dollar amount]*.

[Name of occupant] shall be entitled to the federal income tax deduction for the mortgage interest and real estate tax payments on the above-described premises, together with any similar deduction as to state or local income tax.

[Name of occupant] agrees that *[he/she]* will not allow the mortgage payments to become more than *[number of days]* days in arrears and further agrees that if they become more than *[number of days]* days in arrears the premises may be sold and the proceeds divided equally between the parties in the fashion set forth above.

(d) The parties warrant that said real estate is free and clear of all encumbrances except as aforesaid, and the parties covenant and agree that until the sale of said real estate neither of them shall cause any further encumbrances to be placed upon said real estate unless there is a mutual agreement of the parties to do so.

NOTES TO FORM

Drafter's Notes

Where property is left in the parties' joint names, the post-decree problems are numerous, such as remarriage of the nonoccupying spouse (if the nonoccupying spouse dies and the new spouse is the co-estate holder), inability to obtain a new spouse's signature on a deed for sale, bankruptcy of the nonoccupying spouse, creditors of the nonoccupying spouse putting judgment liens on the nonoccupying spouse's interest, etc.

§ 9:76 Real estate—Transfer of interest by deed in exchange for note and mortgage back—Form⊚

(a) *[Name of spouse]* shall convey forthwith, by sufficient deed, all *[his/her]* right, title, and interest in and to the parcel of real estate located at *[address]*, and further described as:

[legal description]

(b) *[Name of transferee]* assumes and agrees to pay the remaining unpaid balance on a certain promissory note jointly executed by *[names of parties]* as Husband and Wife, the payment of which was secured by a first mortgage on aforesaid real estate. Said note and mortgage are held by *[name of mortgagee]* and are in the original sum of $*[dollar amount]*, with a present unpaid balance of not more than $*[dollar amount]*; and further, *[name of transferee]* shall indemnify and hold absolutely harmless *[name of transferor]* from any expense, loss, claim or liability whatever arising from, or in any way connected with, said note and mortgage.

(c) The parties warrant said real estate is free and clear of all encumbrances except as aforesaid.

(d) Concurrently with the execution of this Agreement and receipt of such sufficient deed from *[name of transferor]*, *[name of transferee]* shall execute and deliver to *[name of transferor]* a mortgage deed and note in favor of *[name of transferor]* in the principal amount of $*[dollar amount]*, *[bearing interest at the rate of [percentage amount]% / with no interest]* which shall become due and payable to *[name of transferor]* on *[date]*.

[or]

(d) Concurrently with the execution of this Agreement and transfer of sufficient deed from *[name of transferor]*, *[name of transferee]* shall execute and deliver to the *[name of transferor]* a mortgage deed and non-interest-bearing note in favor of *[name of transferor]*. Said note shall provide that its value and payment price shall be determined at the time of sale pursuant to the following computations:

After payment of

1. Balance due on the mortgage(s);

2. Commissions;

3. Cost of sale including attorney fees, inspections, points, transfer taxes;

4. Repayment to *[name of payor of mortgage]* of the amount by which *[his / her]* mortgage payments from this date to the date of sale reduced the principal balance of the mortgage;

5. Repayment to *[name of payor of expenses]* of the cost of all repairs and replacements on the residence;

6. Balance to be divided *[equally / [percentage amount]% to the husband, [percentage amount]% to the wife]*.

NOTES TO FORM

Drafter's Notes

See Text § 9:78, Real estate—Automatic conveyance—Form; § 9:79, Real estate—Survival of obligation as charge on payor's estate—Form.

Preparation of the deed and note in advance permits all documents to be signed at same time as the separation agreement.

§ 9:77 Real estate—Transfer of interest by sufficient deed after hearing—Form⊚

In the event that a Court of competent jurisdiction should grant a divorce to the parties, or in the event the marriage of the parties is otherwise dissolved, then after journalization of any such judgment or decree, *[name of spouse]* shall convey to *[name of spouse]* by sufficient deed, all *[his / her]* right, title, and interest in and to real estate located at *[street address, city, state]*, and further described in the legal description attached hereto as Exhibit B and incorporated herein.

[Name of transferee] shall be responsible from and after *[date]* and shall hold *[name of transferor]* harmless on any and all liens, mortgages, and encumbrances placed upon the aforesaid real estate, in ad-

dition to any and all real estate taxes on and after *[date]*. *[Name of transferee]* shall also be responsible and shall hold *[name of transferor]* harmless on a certain obligation to *[name]* for the acquisition of the land lease from the owners, developers, lessors, and their assigns of the land upon which the aforesaid real estate is located. Said obligation is in the total amount of $*[dollar amount]*].

Said real estate shall be the sole property of *[name of transferee]* in fee simple absolute and shall be construed to be a division of property and not spousal support.

§ 9:78   Real estate—Automatic conveyance—Form⊚

Upon *[name of transferor]*'s failure to convey all *[his/her]* right, title, and interest in and to said real estate to *[name of transferee]* within *[amount of time]* after the execution hereof, thereupon this Agreement when incorporated into a Decree of a Court of competent jurisdiction shall be, constitute, and operate as such conveyance, and the County *[title of county official]* is hereby authorized and directed to record same for a public record of such conveyance.

NOTES TO FORM

Drafter's Notes

This type of provision should be considered and included whenever a quitclaim deed is called for.

If the Agreement is intended to convey an interest in real estate, it should include a complete legal property description and must be executed with the formality of a deed.

§ 9:79   Real estate—Survival of obligation as charge on payor's estate—Form⊚

The obligation of *[name of obligor-spouse]* hereunder to *[make mortgage payments/pay spousal support in the amount of $[dollar amount]/make property settlement/convey certain properties]* shall not terminate upon the death of *[name of obligor-spouse]* and shall be a charge against *[his/her]* estate, shall be binding upon *[his/her]* heirs or executor/administrator, and shall be paid or conveyed to *[name of party]* as required herein.

[Optional] To insure the payment of this obligation, *[name of obligor-spouse]* shall purchase and maintain *[adequate insurance/decreasing term insurance/insurance in the amount of $[dollar amount]/mortgage cancellation insurance]* and name *[name of payee]* as beneficiary in a sum sufficient to complete payments of any amounts remaining unpaid upon *[name of obligor]*'s death. *[Name of obligor-spouse]* shall *[annually furnish/upon demand furnish][name of obligee-spouse]* proof of coverage, maintenance of premium payments, and designation of beneficiary of said insurance.

NOTES TO FORM

Drafter's Notes

This type of provision should be considered and included whenever there is the expectation that a sum certain is to be paid over a period of time and in all events.

V.   RETIREMENT BENEFITS—CLAUSES—FORMS

§ 9:80   Retirement benefits—Each party to keep own—Form⊚

1. *[Name of party]* has accumulated benefits in the *[retirement system]*, and such benefits shall be *[his/hers]*, free and clear of all claims of *[name of party]*.

2. *[Name of party]* has accumulated benefits in the *[name of retirement system]*, and such benefits shall be *[his/hers]*.

3. The parties agree that each contemplates that such retirement funds shall be necessary for retirement.

§ 9:81   Retirement benefits—Pension reduced to present value and divided—Form⊚

[Name of spouse] is a participant in the *[name of pension plan]*. *[Name of participant]* asserts that the present value of such account is approximately $*[dollar amount]*. The parties agree that *[name of non-participating spouse]*'s interest in such account is the sum of $*[dollar amount]*. The parties agree that the sum of $*[dollar amount]*, representing *[name of nonparticipating spouse]*'s interest shall be payable to *[him/her]* as follows: *[specify]*.

It is understood that in the event *[name of nonparticipating spouse]* is still receiving payments in the nature of child support or spousal support at the time *[name of participant]* commences receiving income from *[name of pension plan]*, any funds received by *[name of participant]* *[shall / shall not]* be discounted in evaluating the appropriateness of payments of child support and/or spousal support by *[name of payor]* to *[name of payee]*.

[Name of participant] agrees to name and maintain the children of the parties as primary beneficiaries under the *[name of pension plan]* in the event of *[his/her]* death prior to retirement or receipt of funds.

§ 9:82   Retirement benefits—Qualified domestic relations order—Form⊚

(1) *[Husband/Wife]* as participant in the *[name of pension or retirement plan(s)]* agrees to assign to the *[wife/husband]* as an alternate payee certain benefits, as delineated below, from *[his/her]* interest in the plan. *[Husband/Wife]* agrees to sign an order, for the court's approval, which order shall comply with the requirements of the Retirement Equity Act of 1984 to establish a qualified domestic relations order, and both parties agree they will make any modifications necessary to qualify the order.

(2) The participant's name, address, social security number, and date of birth are:

(3) The alternate payee's name, address, social security number, and date of birth are:

(4) *[Name of nonparticipant-spouse]* shall be entitled, from the interest of *[name of participant-spouse]* in the plan:

    (a) Commencing on the retirement of *[name of participant-spouse]*;

(b) Commencing no later than sixty days from the date of retirement of *[name of participant-spouse]*; or

(c) Commencing on the date *[name of participant-spouse]* attains the earliest retirement age under the plan or under I.R.C. § 414, whichever is sooner, whether *[name of participant-spouse]* actually retires or separates from service, as follows:

[Here provide benefits, as available under specific plan, making sure amount and form of payments conform to permissible options, e.g.,

(i) Lump-sum distribution of $*[dollar amount]* which represents *[percentage amount]*% of present accrued benefits, or

(ii) Lump-sum distribution of amount calculated by using following formula: *[describe]*, or

(iii) Lump-sum distribution of *[percentage amount]*% of participant's accrued benefits as of *[date]*, or

(iv) Annuity in amount of $*[dollar amount]* /*[percentage amount]*%, or

(v) Joint and survivor annuity in amount of $*[dollar amount]*/*[percentage amount]*%, or

(vi) *[Monthly / quarterly / annual]* payments calculated by reference to following formula: *[describe]*, or

(vii) Monthly payments of *[percentage amount]*% of monthly payments which would be payable to *[name of participant-spouse]* if *[he/she]* retired on that date.]

(5) *[Name of nonparticipant-spouse]* agrees to name *[name of child / name of children]* as *[his/her]* beneficiaries to receive the benefits payable as above in the event that *[he/she]* dies before receipt of said benefits.

(6) *[Name of participant-spouse]* further agrees that *[name of nonparticipant-spouse]* shall qualify as "surviving spouse" under I.R.C. § 410(a)(11) and 417 and that *[name of nonparticipant-spouse]* shall be entitled to benefits in the event of death of *[name of participant-spouse]* before retirement.

(7) *[Name of participant-spouse]* agrees to protect rights of *[name of nonparticipant-spouse]* to receive benefits as beneficiary.

NOTES TO FORM

Drafter's Notes

This provision spells out the rights of the participant and alternate payee to the benefits in the plan. A separate qualified domestic relations order must be prepared for submission to the court along with a separate Decree of Divorce or Dissolution. The plan administrator must review the order pertaining to the plan and not the whole decree and agreement, which would have matters not relevant to their determination of qualification and instructions. See Text Ch 30, Dividing Private Retirement Benefits in Divorce.

§ 9:83 Retirement benefits—State government retirement plans⊚

The *[Husband/Wife]* has accumulated retirement benefits, through the *[Name of Plan]* Fund. The *[Husband/Wife]* agrees that there be a Division of Property Order (DPO), to be submitted for the Court's approval. Said DPO shall provide that the *[Wife/Husband]* shall be entitled to *[percentage amount]%* of the *[Husband/Wife]*'s accumulated value as of *[date]*, as defined below, and, if allowed in the DPO, the *[Wife/Husband]* shall be designated as "surviving spouse". The *[Husband/Wife]* will have the remaining *[percentage amount]%*. The *[Husband/Wife]* agrees that the *[Wife/Husband]* shall be entitled to said amount of *[Husband/Wife]*'s benefits in said plan as and when they are available to be distributed, and that the Plan Administrator shall be directed, by virtue of the DPO, to make distribution to the *[Wife/Husband]* in the same manner and at the same time as to the *[Husband/Wife]*, or if the plan so permits when the *[Wife/Husband]* so elects. The parties further agree that while the provisions of this Agreement otherwise may or may not be modifiable, that any DPO or order of the court may be modifiable, in order to make the DPO acceptable to the Plan Administrator and effectuate the intent of the parties.

The parties understand that the state government plan automatically provides COLA benefits (based on participant's first year of receipt of benefits) both to the participant and to the alternate payee in the same percentage as in the DOPO.

The participant agrees to name the *[wife/husband]* as survivor for no less than the same percentage as the alternate payee is entitled to under the DOPO.

The parties understand that the DPOs require that income taxes on these amounts, if any are due, are the responsibility of the recipient.

§ 9:84   Retirement benefits—Public Employees Deferred Compensation Fund—Form⊚

QUALIFIED DOMESTIC RELATIONS ORDER

IT IS HEREBY ORDERED AS FOLLOWS:

1. **Effect of This Order as a Qualified Domestic Relations Order:** This Order creates and recognizes the existence of an Alternate Payee's right to receive a portion of the Participant's benefits payable under a government-sponsored retirement plan that is qualified under Section 457 of the Internal Revenue Code (the "Code"). It is intended to constitute a Qualified Domestic Relations Order ("QDRO") under Section 414(p) of the Code and Section 206(d)(3) of ERISA.

2. **Participant Information:** The name, last known address, birth date and social security number of the plan "Participant" are:

Name:
Address:
Social Security Number:
Birth Date:

3. **Alternate Payee Information:** The name, last known address, social security number and date of birth of the "Alternate Payee" are:

Name:
Address:
Social Security Number:
Birth Date:

The Former Spouse shall have the duty to notify in writing the Ohio Public Employees Deferred Compensation Program (located at 250 Civic Center Drive, Suite 350, Columbus, Ohio 43215-5450) of any changes in her mailing address subsequent to the entry of this Order and within thirty (30) days of any such change of address.

4. **Plan Name:** The name of the Plan to which this Order applies is the **Ohio Public Employees Deferred Compensation Program** (hereinafter referred to as "Plan"). Further, any successor plan to the Plan or any other plan(s) to which liability for provision of the Participant's benefits described above is incurred, shall also be subject to the terms of this Order.

5. **Pursuant to State Domestic Relations Law:** This Order is entered pursuant to the authority granted in the applicable domestic relations laws of the State of Ohio.

6. **For Provision of Marital Property Rights:** This Order relates to the provision of marital property rights and/or spousal support to the Alternate Payee as a result of the Order of Divorce between Participant and Alternate Payee.

7. **Amount of Alternate Payee's Benefit:** This Order assigns to Alternate Payee ***(1) ($*[dollar amount]*) **or*****(2) (an amount equal to **Fifty Percent (50%)**) of the Participant's Total Account Balance accumulated under the Plan as of *** date *** (or the closest valuation date thereto), plus any interest and investment earnings or losses attributable thereon subsequent to the date of acknowledged receipt of this order by OPEDCP, until the date of total distribution. Such Total Account Balance shall include all amounts maintained under all of the various accounts and/or investment funds established on behalf of the Participant. The Alternate Payee's share of the benefits shall be allocated on a "pro-rata" basis among all of the Participant's accounts maintained on his behalf under the Plan.

8. **Commencement Date and Form of Payment to Alternate Payee:** If the Alternate Payee so elects, she shall be paid her benefits as soon as administratively feasible following the date this Order is approved as a QDRO by the Plan Administrator, or at the earliest date permitted under the Plan or Section 414(p) of the Internal Revenue Code, if later. Benefits will be payable to the Alternate Payee in any form or permissible option otherwise available to participants and alternate payees under the terms of the Plan, including, but not limited to, a single lump-sum cash payment.

9. **Alternate Payee's Rights and Privileges:** On or after the date that this Order is deemed to be a Qualified Domestic Relations Order, but before the Alternate Payee receives her total distribution under the Plan, the Alternate Payee shall be entitled to all of the rights and election privileges that are afforded to Plan beneficiaries, including, but not limited to, the rules regarding the right to designate a beneficiary for death benefit purposes.

10. **Death of Alternate Payee:** In the event of Alternate Payee's death prior to Alternate Payee receiving the full amount of benefits called for under this Order, such Alternate Payee's beneficiary(ies), as designated on the appropriate form provided by the Plan Administrator (or in the absence of a beneficiary designation, her estate), shall receive the remainder of any unpaid benefits under the terms of this Order.

11. **Death of Participant:** In the event that the Participant dies **before>** the Alternate Payee receives her distribution in accordance with the terms of this QDRO, or before the establishment of separate account(s) in the name of the Alternate Payee, such Alternate Payee shall be treated as the surviving spouse of the Participant for any death benefits payable under the Plan to the extent of the full amount of her benefits as called for under Paragraph 7 of this Order. Should the Participant predecease the Alternate Payee **after** the new account(s) have been established in her behalf, such Participant's death shall not affect Alternate Payee's right to the portion of her benefits as stipulated herein.

12. **Savings Clause:** This Order is not intended, and shall not be construed in such a manner as to require the Plan:

(a) to provide any type or form of benefit option not otherwise provided under the terms of the Plan:

(b) to require the Plan to provide increased benefits determined on the basis of actuarial value; or

(c) to require the payment of any benefit to the Alternate Payee which are required to be paid to another alternate payee under another death order which was previously deemed to be a QDRO.

13. **Tax Treatment of Distributions Made Under This Order:** For purposes of Sections 402(a)(1) and 72 of the Internal Revenue Code, any Alternate Payee who is the spouse or former spouse of the Participant shall be treated as the distributee of any distribution or payments made to the Alternate Payee under the terms of this Order, and as such, will be required to pay the appropriate federal income taxes on such distribution.

14. **Constructive Receipt:** In the event that the Plan Trustee inadvertently pays to the Participant any benefits which are assigned to the Alternate Payee pursuant to the terms of this Order, the Participant shall immediately reimburse the Alternate Payee to the extent that he has received such benefit payments, and shall forthwith pay such amounts so received directly to the Alternate Payee within ten (10) days of receipt.

15. **Continued Jurisdiction:** The Court shall retain jurisdiction with respect to this Order to the extent required to maintain its qualified status and the original intent of the parties as stipulated herein. The Court shall also retain jurisdiction to enter such further orders as are necessary to enforce the assignment of benefits to Alternate Payee as set forth herein.

16. **Plan Termination:** In the event of a Plan termination, the Alternate Payee shall be entitled to receive her portion of Participant's benefits as stipulated herein in accordance with the Plan's termination provisions for participants and beneficiaries.

17. **Actions By Participant:** The Participant shall not take any actions, affirmative or otherwise, that can circumvent the terms and provisions of this Qualified Domestic Relations Order, or that could diminish or extinguish the rights and entitlements of the Alternate Payee as set forth herein. Should the Participant take any action or inaction to the detriment of the Alternate Payee, he shall be required to make sufficient payments **directly** to the Alternate Payee to the extent necessary to neutralize the effects of his actions or inactions and to the extent of her full entitlements hereunder.

IT IS SO ORDERED.

_____

JUDGE

APPROVED:

_____

Attorney for Participant

_____

Attorney for Alternate Payee

NOTES TO FORM

Drafter's Notes

Pursuant to RC 3105.171(A)(3)(a)(iv) and (C)(4), the amount specified in this paragraph may not exceed the total amount of money that has been deferred by the Program Participant and transmitted to the Ohio Public Employees Deferred Compensation Program during the marriage and any income that is derived from the investment of those moneys during the marriage. See, also, Text § 29:40, Military benefits—Benefits as spousal support.

By this agreement, _[name of participant-spouse]_ authorizes the Program to disclose to _[name of nonparticipant-spouse or designee]_ that information contained in the Participant's Account necessary for the proper execution of this agreement.

[Name of nonparticipant-spouse] agrees to notify in writing the Ohio Public Employees Deferred Compensation Program, 172 East State Street, Columbus, Ohio 43215, of any change of address within thirty days of any such change of address.

Drafter's Notes

*= this amount is the total amount currently deferred, including any increases due to earnings on the deferrals.

**= this amount is calculated by identifying the deferrals and earnings thereon from date of the marriage to the time of separation or dissolution.

***= this amount is a fixed dollar amount, established by the court or by the parties, which shall be distributed to the ex-spouse at the time the participant begins distribution from the account.

In order to provide the parties with information needed to divide this account, the Program will need to be advised of the date of the participant's marriage, and the date the parties agree shall be considered as the date of dissolution or separation. Pursuant to OAC 145:1-1-01(C)(6), the Program also will need to be provided written authorization from the participant to permit it to disclose the account history to the ex-spouse.

See also Text § 29:74, Ohio Public Employees Deferred Compensation Fund—Qualified Domestic Relations Order—Form, for alternate order on deferred compensation fund.

§ 9:85   Retirement benefits—Division of military benefits—Form⊙

[Name of spouse] is a member of the *[branch of armed services]* and has been a member for *[number of years]* during the marriage. *[Name of spouse-member]* agrees that *[name of other spouse]* shall be entitled to benefits from *[his/her]* retirement as follows: *[specify]*. This award to *[name of other spouse]* shall apply to any severance pay, continuance pay, or Voluntary Separation Incentive pay to which *[name of member-spouse]* may be entitled. A survivor benefit plan *[shall/shall not]* not provide for benefits to *[name of other spouse]*. *[Name of spouse]* shall be responsible for payment of *[all/one-half]* of cost of survivor benefit plan.

§ 9:86   Retirement benefits—Division of federal employee benefits—Form⊙

[Name of employee-spouse] is a participant in the Civil Service Retirement System (CSRS). *[Name of employee-spouse]* agrees that there be a Court Order Dividing Employee Annuity (CODEA), to be submitted for the court's approval. Said order shall provide that *[name of former spouse]* shall be entitled to benefits calculated under the Office of Personnel Management (OPM) terminology of pro rata share, including COLAs, and *[name of former spouse]* shall be designated as "surviving spouse." *[Name of employee-spouse]* agrees that *[name of former spouse]* shall be entitled to a pro rata share of *[his/her]* benefits in said annuity, as and when they are available to be distributed, and that the OPM shall be directed, by virtue of the order, to make distribution to *[name of former spouse]* in the same manner and at the same time as to *[name of employee-spouse]*. The parties further agree that while the provisions of this agreement may or may not otherwise be modifiable, that any order of the court may be modifiable to make that order acceptable to the OPM and to effectuate the intent of the parties.

[Name of employee-spouse] when *[he/she]* retires, expressly agrees that *[he/she]* will select a joint and survivor annuity with *[name of former spouse]* named as survivor for the maximum possible former

spouse survivor annuity. The parties acknowledge that said designation of joint and survivor benefits will, during the lifetime of *[name of employee-spouse]*, result in lower monthly payments to *[name of employee-spouse]* and to *[name of former spouse]*, but that such designation is appropriate and equitable under the circumstances.

[Name of former spouse] shall have the same rights to benefits in the event of *[name of employee-spouse]*'s receipt of disability retirement benefits.

OPTIONAL

The benefits payable to the *[name of former spouse]* from the CSRS shall be calculated by the following formula: one-half times a fraction, the numerator of which equals the number of months of federal civilian and military service that *[name of employee-spouse]* performed during the marriage, and the denominator being the total number of months of federal civilian and military service performed by *[name of employee-spouse]* pursuant to the federal regulations and pursuant to the OPM.

[Name of employee-spouse] shall not take any action which would defeat, reduce, or limit the *[name of former spouse]*'s right to receive *[her/his]* share of *[name employee-spouse]*'s civil service retirement, aside from electing a joint and survivor (50%) annuity with *[name of former spouse]*, including merging retirement pay with other pensions or waiving any portion of *[his/her]* retirement. In the event *[name of employee-spouse]* breaches this provision, *[he/she]* shall indemnify and pay directly to *[name of former spouse]* any sums reduced by such action.

NOTES TO FORM

Drafter's Notes

The U.S. Office of Personal Management has published a handbook providing all acceptable paragraphs and defining the terms to be used in preparing the court order, *A Handbook For Attorneys On Court-ordered Retirement and Health Benefits Under the Civil Service Retirement System, Federal Employers Retirement System, and Federal Employees Health Benefits Program*(October, 1992). For a copy, mail to: New Orders Superintendent of Documents, P.O. Box 371954, Pittsburgh, PA 15250-7954 and enclose $19.00; Phone 1-202-512-1800; Stock # 006-000-01408-9. See also Text Ch 29, Government Retirement Benefits.

VI. SPOUSAL SUPPORT CLAUSES—FORMS

§ 9:87 Spousal support—Definite amount for unspecified period—Form⊚

[Name of payor] shall pay to *[name of payee]* as and for *[spousal support/(his/her) support and maintenance]* the sum of $*[dollar amount]* per *[period]*, such payments to commence *[date]*. All payments shall terminate upon the death of *[name of payee]*, and no payments or substitutions therefor shall be made after death of *[name of payee]*.

Said payments *[shall/shall not]* be modifiable by the court.

§ 9:88 Spousal support—Lump sum with receipt acknowledged—Form⊚

In full and final settlement and satisfaction of any and all claims and rights of *[name of spouse]* for support and maintenance, and otherwise, *[name of spouse]* has simultaneously herewith paid *[him/ her]* the sum of $*[dollar amount]*, receipt whereof is hereby duly acknowledged by *[him/her]*.

§ 9:89 Spousal support—Lump sum in specified installments—Form⊚

In full and final settlement and satisfaction of any and all claims and rights of *[name of spouse]* for support and maintenance, and otherwise, *[name of spouse]* shall pay to *[him/her]* the sum of $*[dollar amount]* as follows:

(a) The sum of $*[dollar amount]* herewith, receipt whereof if hereby acknowledged by *[him/her]*;

(b) The sum of $*[dollar amount]* on or before *[date]*; and

(c) The sum of $*[dollar amount]* on or before *[date]*.

Concurrently herewith *[name of payor]* has delivered to *[name of payee][his/her]* negotiable promissory notes payable to *[his/her]* order, evidencing the deferred payments mentioned above.

§ 9:90 Spousal support—Lump sum in installments, ending at payee's death or remarriage—Form⊚

[Name of payor] shall pay to *[name of payee]*, as spousal support, the sum of *[e.g., $160,000]*. Such shall be paid in monthly installments of *[e.g., $2,222]* each, and each such payment shall be made on or before the *[day of month]* day of the month as to which it is due, beginning *[date]*, and continuing for *[number]* months through *[date]*. However, the obligation of *[name of payor]* to pay such installments to *[name of payee]* shall cease upon *[death/remarriage or death]* of *[name of payee]*, and under no circumstances shall *[name of payor]* be obliged to pay, or pay, any such installments, or any part thereof or any substitutes therefor, after death of *[name of payee]*. The estate, successors, and heirs of *[name of payee]* shall have no right to any such payments which otherwise would have been due to *[name of payee]* in the event that *[he/she]* had lived.

§ 9:91 Spousal support—Amount as percentage of annual gross income—Form⊚

[Name of spouse] shall pay to *[name of spouse]* for *[his/her]* separate maintenance and support a sum in each calendar year commencing with *[year]* and continuing to and including *[year]* equal to *[percentage amount]%* of the gross income of *[name of payor]* (as hereinafter defined) for that year to a maximum of $*[dollar amount]*, payable in twelve equal monthly installments and adjusted annually after filing of the federal income tax return of *[name of payor]*. In no

event shall any payments or substitutions therefor be made after death of *[name of payee]*.

The term "gross income" as herein used shall mean "adjusted gross income" for federal income tax purposes.

[or]

The term "gross income" as herein used shall include all income, earned and unearned, unreduced by taxes, deductions, credits, losses, etc.

[Name of payee] shall be entitled to verify the sufficiency of any and all payments hereunder by referring to the annual federal income tax returns of *[name of payor]*, either personally or through an accountant.

NOTES TO FORM

Drafter's Notes

See Text Ch 28, Tax Considerations. I.R.C. § 71(f), enacted as part of the Tax Reform Act of 1984, and further amended in 1986, is designed to prevent "front-end loading" of spousal support payments exceeding $15,000 per year during the first three post-separation years. If the agreement provides for declining payments during that year, be sure that it is not framed in such a way as to run afoul of the recapture rules imposed by I.R.C. § 71(f). To avoid the recapture rules, keep the spousal support payments level, or have them escalate over the first three years, or make certain that the highest early year's payment is not more than $15,000 higher than the lowest later year's payment.

There are important qualifications and exceptions that may be applicable. One is set forth in I.R.C. § 71(f)(5)(C)—the so-called "fluctuating payment" exception. If the agreement is correctly drawn, the three-year recapture trap set by I.R.C. § 71(f)(2) can be avoided by tying spousal support payments to some extrinsic condition, e.g., a percentage of the income from a business or partnership.

§ 9:92   Spousal support—Amount as percentage of monthly gross income—Form⊚

[Name of payor-spouse] shall pay to *[name of payee-spouse]*, as spousal support, a monthly amount equal to *[percentage amount]*% of *[his/her]* total income (from whatever source) for the immediately preceding month. Each such payment shall be made on or before the *[day of month]* day of the month as to which it is due, beginning on *[date]*. The obligation of *[name of payor]* to pay *[name of payee]* pursuant to the terms of this paragraph will cease upon death of *[name of payee]*, and under no circumstances shall *[he/she]* be obliged to make any such payments after death of *[name of payee]*. Payments, plus processing charge, shall be made *[by payable withholding/by withholding from bank account]* through *[agency]*.

§ 9:93   Spousal support—Medical benefits for spouse under COBRA—Form⊚

[Name of employed spouse] presently has health insurance coverage through employment which covers *[name of unemployed spouse]*. Said health plan is subject to the provisions of Pub. L. No. 99-272 (COBRA) and as amended. The *[name of unemployed spouse]* is eligible for

continuing coverage, after the termination of the marriage, for a period of time not in excess of thirty-six months, subject to earlier termination in the event *[he/she]* becomes employed and covered under a health plan or remarries and becomes covered under the new spouse's health plan.

[Name of employed spouse] agrees to maintain *[name of unemployed spouse]* as a covered beneficiary on *[his/her]* policy so long as the parties remain married. Thereafter, in the event *[name of unemployed spouse]* notifies *[name of employed spouse]* that *[he/she]* wishes to continue coverage, *[name of employed spouse]* shall be responsible to obtain and provide to *[name of unemployed spouse]* all of the necessary documents in a prompt manner and within the time requirement for election of coverage and premium payment. *[Name of employed spouse]* agrees to make all premium payments required to maintain coverage for *[name of unemployed spouse][for a minimum of [[number of months]] months/until [name of unemployed spouse] remarries/until coverage terminates by operation of law/whichever occurs first]*. Thereafter *[name of unemployed spouse]* shall maintain all premium payments if *[he/she]* desires to continue the coverage.

[Optional][Notwithstanding that the "continuation" features of COBRA coverage will terminate, at the latest, thirty-six months from a decree of divorce or dissolution, [name of employed spouse] agrees to maintain the premium payments thereafter for "conversion" coverage for [name of unemployed spouse].]

Such payments by *[name of employed spouse][shall/shall not]* be as and for spousal support *[and deductible as spousal support]*. This spousal support payment *[shall/shall not]* be subject to modification by the court.

NOTES TO FORM

Drafter's Notes

   If conversion coverage is available to employees, and the employee meets the requirements of COBRA (20 employees or more), then the conversion option must be available to qualified beneficiaries.

§ 9:94   Spousal support—Method of payment—Form⊚

After the incorporation of this agreement into an order of court, all spousal support shall be made pursuant to the provisions of RC 3105.18(E) requiring payments to be through the *[agency designated for collection]*. The parties shall comply with the notice requirements. Payments, plus the processing charge, shall be deducted from *[wages/bank accounts/workers' compensation, etc.]* for forwarding to the *[agency]*.

All child support and spousal support under this order shall be withheld or deducted from the wages or assets of the obligor pursuant to a withholding or deduction notice or appropriate court order issued in accordance with RC 3113.21, and shall be forwarded to the obligee in accordance with RC 3113.21 to 3113.213.

§ 9:95   Spousal support—Method of payment—Direct—Form⊚

The parties agree that the *[name of obligor-spouse]* shall pay the spousal support order as set forth herein directly to the *[name of obligee-spouse]*. The *[name of obligor]* shall make such payment as a check, money order or in any other form that establishes a clear record of payment.

If the *[name of obligor]* should be in default of making any spousal support payments to the *[name of obligee]*, the Court, upon motion of the *[name of obligee]* or on its own motion, may rescind the permission granted under this order pursuant to R.C. 3121.441.

§ 9:96   Spousal support—Acknowledgment by payee of adequacy of support—Form⊚

[Name of payee] hereby knowingly and voluntarily accepts the provisions herein made for *[him/her]* in place of, and in full, final, fair and adequate settlement of, any and all claims against *[name of payor]* for *[his/her]* support.

§ 9:97   Spousal support—Waiver of spousal support—Form⊚

Except as expressly provided to the contrary herein, neither the Husband nor the Wife shall be responsible in any manner whatsoever for the support and maintenance of the other spouse. This provision is intended and shall operate as a waiver of the right to spousal support and support which either spouse may have as against the other.

[or]

Neither party shall pay spousal support to the other party. This provision has been arrived at after considering all the factors listed in RC 3105.18.

§ 9:98   Spousal support—Annual adjustment—Tied to index—Form⊚

The parties recognize and agree that by reason of monetary inflation or deflation the purchasing power of the dollar may be impaired or increased at any time hereafter. In consideration thereof, *[name of spouse]* agrees to pay to *[name of spouse]* for the calendar year *[year]* the sum of $*[dollar amount]* in twelve equal monthly installments of $*[dollar amount]* payable on the first day of each month. At the expiration of calendar year *[year]* and for each and every succeeding year thereafter for a period of *[number of years]* total years, *[name of payor]* shall pay to *[name of payee]* in each such calendar year a total sum equal to $*[dollar amount]* in *[year]* as adjusted in the Consumer Price Index of the U.S. Bureau of Labor Statistics.

§ 9:99   Spousal support—Annual adjustment—Percentage formula—Form⊚

[Name of spouse] shall pay to *[name of spouse]* during *[his/her]* lifetime:

(a) So long as *[name of payee]* does not remarry, or cohabit with a person of the opposite sex for more than *[period]* and until December 31, [_____],

>   *[percentage amount]%* of *[his/her]* annual income up to *[e.g., $25,000]*; plus

>   *[percentage amount]%* of *[his/her]* annual income above *[e.g., $25,000]*, but in no event less than *[e.g., $8,000]* per annum.

(b) So long as *[name of payee]* does not remarry or cohabit with a person of the opposite sex for more than *[period]*, continuously, *[name of payor]* shall pay to *[him/her]* commencing January 1, [_____],

>   *[percentage amount]%* of *[his/her]* annual income up to *[e.g., $25,000]*; plus

>   *[percentage amount]%* of *[his/her]* annual income above *[e.g., $25,000]*, but in no event less than *[e.g., $6,000]* per annum.

(c) If *[name of payee]* remarries or cohabits with a person of the opposite sex for more than *[period]* continuously, all payments hereunder by *[name of payor]* to *[him/her]* shall cease, except that *[he/she]* shall be liable for arrears.

(d) In the event of *[name of payee]'s* remarriage or cohabitation as described herein, appropriate pro rata adjustment shall be made in the amounts payable to *[him/her]* under subdivisions (a) and (b) for the year in which *[he/she]* remarries or cohabits as described herein.

(e) Notwithstanding anything herein contained to the contrary, the aggregate payment to be made by *[name of payor]* hereunder in any calendar year, when added to any income which *[name of payee]* may derive from any other source during such calendar year, shall not exceed one-half of the combined income of the parties for such calendar year. *[Name of payee]'s* income shall be defined in the same manner as *[name of payor]'s* income in subdivision (f) next following.

(f) For the purpose of this Agreement, *[name of payor]'s* annual income shall be *[his/her]* annual "adjusted gross income" for federal income tax purposes, except that all capital gains and losses shall be disregarded.

§ 9:100 Spousal support—Annual adjustment—Incremental formula—Form⊚

(a) *[Name of spouse]* shall pay to *[name of spouse]* for *[his/her]* separate maintenance and support the sum of $*[dollar amount]* per month, commencing on the day this Agreement is executed, and a like amount on the first day of each month thereafter *[for a period of [number of years] years/until [he/she] dies/until [he/she] remarries if the parties become divorced/until [name of payor] dies]*, then whichever of these events occurs first, *[name of payor]'s* obligation to pay or furnish such support shall thereupon absolutely cease and terminate, and

(b) Said monthly payments for the separate maintenance and support of *[name of payee]* shall be increased or decreased on the following basis:

[Name of payor]'s current total annual earnings (before taxes) from all sources are approximately $*[dollar amount]*, and using said sum as a base, then for every increase of $*[dollar amount]* over said base sum in any calendar year, *[name of payor]* shall pay to *[name of payee]* an additional sum of $*[dollar amount]* per month, and for every decrease of $*[dollar amount]* in *[name of payor]*'s total annual earnings (before taxes) from whatever source derived in any calendar year, monthly payments to *[name of payee]* shall be reduced by $*[dollar amount]* per month, and

Said adjustments are to be made as here illustrated:

Earnings in calendar year	Monthly payments
[e.g., $10,000] but less than *[e.g., $12,500]*	*[e.g., $225]*
[e.g., $12,500] but less than *[e.g., $15,000]*	*[e.g., $275]*
[e.g., $15,000] but less than *[e.g., $17,500]*	*[e.g., $325]*
[e.g., $17,500] but less than *[e.g., $20,000]*	*[e.g., $375]*
[e.g., $20,000] but less than *[e.g., $22,500]*	*[e.g., $425]*

Said adjustments shall take place on the first day of each *[e.g., February]*, based upon *[name of payor]*'s earnings for the prior calendar year.

After adjusted as aforesaid, the monthly payments for *[name of payee]*'s separate maintenance and support shall continue to be made by *[name of payor]* in the total sum as adjusted until a further adjustment is in order as herein provided, but

In no event shall *[name of payor]* pay to *[name of payee]* less than $*[dollar amount]* per month or more than $*[dollar amount]* per month for *[his/her]* separate maintenance and support, and

[Name of payor] shall, upon request by *[name of payee]* therefor, furnish *[him/her]* true and correct information as to *[his/her]* total annual earnings from whatever source derived.

§ 9:101   Spousal support—Termination contingencies— Payments for payee's life—Form⊚

[Name of spouse] will pay to *[name of spouse]* the sum of $*[dollar amount]* every month, each such payment to be made on or before the *[name of spouse]*] day of the month as to which it is due, beginning on *[date]*. The obligation of *[name of payor]* to pay such payments to *[name of payee]* pursuant to the terms of this paragraph will end upon *[death/remarriage or death]* of *[name of payee]*.

§ 9:102   Spousal support—Termination contingencies— Payments ending at payee's death—Form⊚

[Name of spouse] shall pay to *[name of spouse]*, as spousal support, *[e.g., $1,500]* per month, each such payment to be made on or before the *[day of month]* day of the month as to which it is due, beginning

on *[date]*. The obligation of *[name of payor]* to make such payments shall cease upon the death of either party.

§ 9:103 Spousal support—Termination contingencies—Death of either party or payee's remarriage—Form⊚

During the life of *[name of payee]* and so long as *[he / she]* does not *[remarry / cohabit with a person of the opposite sex for more than [_____] months continuously]*, *[name of payor]* shall pay to *[name of payee]* for *[his / her]* maintenance and support the sum of $*[dollar amount]* per month in advance on the first day of each and every month commencing *[date]*. Such payments shall cease upon death of *[name of payee]* and in no event shall any such payments, or any substitutions therefor, in any form, be made after such death of *[name of payee]*.

NOTES TO FORM

Drafter's Notes

Periodic payments in the nature of spousal support made by one spouse to the other spouse under a written Separation Agreement are deductible by the payor and taxable to the payee, so long as the parties do not file a tax return jointly and the agreement does not provide to the contrary. The tax consequences commence with the effective date of the written Agreement. Clients should be advised regarding the filing of estimated quarterly taxes when the amount of spousal support will have a tax impact.

See Text Ch 28, Tax Considerations, as to the requirements of the Tax Reform Act of 1984 in order to qualify payments for spousal support (still known as alimony for IRS purposes) treatment under I.R.C. § 71 and 215. It is very important to review the current Code provisions and regulations in order to make certain that the payments qualify.

§ 9:104 Spousal support—Termination contingencies— Payee's employment—Form⊚

[Name of payor] shall pay to *[name of payee]* the sum of $*[dollar amount]* per *[period]*, as and for spousal support. At such time as the *[name of payee]* becomes gainfully employed the spousal support shall be modified as follows:

(a) When the gross earnings of *[name of payee]* are $*[dollar amount]* or more per *[period]*, the spousal support shall be reduced to $*[dollar amount]* per *[period]*.

(b) When the gross earnings of *[name of payee]* are $*[dollar amount]* or more per *[period]*, the spousal support shall be further reduced to $*[dollar amount]* per *[period]*.

(c) When the gross earnings of *[name of payee]* exceed $*[dollar amount]* per *[period]* the spousal support shall be terminated forever.

[or]

(c) When the gross earnings of *[name of payee]* exceed $*[dollar amount]* per *[period]* the payment of spousal support shall be suspended and not subject to reinstatement until or unless the gross earnings of *[name of payee]* are thereafter less than $*[dollar amount]* per *[period]*.

All payments of spousal support shall, however, terminate upon the remarriage or death of *[name of payee]*.

Said payments *[shall / shall not]* be modifiable by the court.

§9:105 Spousal support—Termination contingencies—Payee's cohabitation—Form☉

[Name of payor] shall pay to *[name of payee]* the sum of $*[dollar amount]* per month as and for spousal support until the death of either party, the remarriage of *[name of payee]*, or the cohabitation by *[name of payee]* with an unrelated adult *[male / female]*, whichever comes first. For the purposes of this Agreement, cohabitation shall require the cohabitation with the same unrelated adult *[male / female]* for a period in excess of six months, whether consecutive or nonconsecutive.

§9:106 Spousal support—Reduction contingencies—Payor's unemployment—Form☉

In the event, however, that *[name of payor]* shall become unemployed by reason of ill health or inability to sustain or secure gainful employment, the obligation of *[name of payor]* to *[name of payee]* during such period of hardship shall be *[reduced by [percentage amount]% / subject to appropriate modification]*.

NOTES TO FORM

Drafter's Notes

See Text Ch 28, Tax Considerations, re "front-end loading rules" of I.R.C. 71(f). Downward modification of spousal support during the first three post-decree years, for whatever reason, may result in income recapture taxable to the payor.

Where a separation agreement is to be incorporated into a decree of dissolution, any power of court modification must be specific. For any decree entered after May 2, 1986, the parties may agree on the court's modification powers (RC 3105.18(E)).

§9:107 Spousal support—Reduction contingencies—Payor's income decrease—Form☉

If at any time after calendar year *[year]* (but not before) the gross income of *[name of payor]*, as hereinafter defined, shall fall below $*[dollar amount]*, *[he / she]* shall pay to *[name of payee]*, instead of $*[dollar amount]* per month as provided above, the following amounts:

[here specify]

The term "gross income" as herein used shall mean "adjusted gross income" for federal income tax purposes.

NOTES TO FORM

Drafter's Notes

See Text Ch 28, Tax Considerations, re "front-end loading rules" of I.R.C. §71(f). Downward modification of spousal support during the first three postdecree years, for whatever reason, may result in income recapture taxable to the payor.

§ 9:108 Spousal support—Reduction contingencies—Payee's remarriage—Form⊚

[Name of spouse] shall pay in cash to *[name of spouse]*, as spousal support, *[e.g., $1,500]* per month, each such payment to be made on or before the [_____] day of the month as to which it is due, beginning on *[date]*. In the event of remarriage of *[name of payee]*, *[name of payor]* shall pay to *[name of payee][e.g., $750]* per month. However, the obligation of *[name of payor]* to make such spousal support payments to *[name of payee]* shall cease upon the death of *[name of payee]*.

§ 9:109 Spousal support—Modification—Jurisdiction reserved—Form⊚

The parties agree that paragraphs *[designation of paragraph]* and *[designation of paragraph]* relating to the payment of spousal support by *[name of payor]* to *[name of payee]* *[shall/shall not]* be subject to modification by the court.

§ 9:110 Spousal support—Modification—Limited jurisdiction reserved—Form⊚

The parties agree that paragraphs *[designation of paragraph]* and *[designation of paragraph]*, relating to the payment of spousal support by *[name of payor]* to *[name of payee]* shall be subject to modification by the court. However, such modification must be based upon substantial change of circumstances and

(1) No modification may be sought or granted within *[number of years]* years of *[date of agreement/date of decree]* and no more frequently than within *[number of years]* years by same party.

(2) No modification may be sought or granted which would lower the monthly amount of spousal support below $*[dollar amount]*, nor raise the monthly amount of spousal support above $*[dollar amount]*.

§ 9:111 Spousal support—Modification—Pre-1985 agreement to be taxable—Form⊚

The parties, by this document and pursuant to paragraph *[designation of paragraph]* of the Agreement dated *[date]*, which paragraph permits modification by agreement of both parties, hereby modify said Agreement as follows:

Payments under paragraph *[designation of paragraph]* of the aforesaid Separation Agreement shall be treated as spousal support under I.R.C. § 71, as amended by the Deficit Reduction Act of 1984. This modification is effective as of *[date]*.

§ 9:112 Spousal support—Modification—Pre-1985 agreement not to be taxable—Form⊚

In modification of the Separation Agreement dated *[date]*, the parties hereby agree that payments made by *[name of payor]* to *[name of payee]* pursuant to the terms of paragraph *[designation of paragraph]* shall be designated as nonincludable in gross income of *[name of payee]* under I.R.C. § 71(b)(1)(B), and not allowable as a deduction to *[name of payor]* under I.R.C. § 215, effective as of *[date]*.

§ 9:113 Spousal support trust—Trust created to pay support—Form⊚

[Name of spouse] hereby makes the following provision for *[name of spouse]*'s support and maintenance:

(a) *[Name of payor]* has paid to *[name of payee]* the sum of $*[dollar amount]* simultaneously herewith.

(b) In addition, *[he/she]* has, by a separate trust deed (herein called the Trust Deed) created an irrevocable trust for *[his/her]* benefit and has delivered to *[name]* and *[name]*, as trustees, securities having a market value of $*[dollar amount]* as of this date. The Trust Deed is hereby incorporated in this Agreement by reference, with the same force and effect as if it were fully set forth herein.

NOTES TO FORM

Drafter's Notes

Payments to the payee will be taxable income when received, but not deductible by the payor-grantor.

§ 9:114 Spousal support trust—Annuity trust to pay support—Form⊚

In full and final settlement and satisfaction of obligation of *[name of spouse]* to support and maintain *[name of spouse]*, and in consideration of *[his/her]* relinquishing all *[his/her]* rights against *[him/her]* for support and maintenance, *[policy owner]* has simultaneously herewith delivered to *[him/her]* an annuity policy bearing No. *[policy number]*, dated *[date]*, issued by *[insurance company]*, wherein and whereby *[name of payee]* is to receive the sum of $*[dollar amount]* per annum for life. *[Policy owner]* represents and warrants that the policy is fully paid and nonassessable. *[He/she]* guarantees that *[name of payee]* shall receive the specified annuity thereunder for life. *[Name of payee]* acknowledges receipt of the policy.

NOTES TO FORM

Drafter's Notes

Payments to the payee will be taxable income when received, but not deductible by the payor. The amount received by the payee will be taxable under the annuity rules.

§ 9:115 Spousal support trust—Trust agreement under I.R.C.§ 682 (alimony trust)—Form⊚

This is a Trust Agreement entered into at *[name of city]*, Ohio on *[date]*, by and between *[name of spouse]* (hereinafter referred to as "Grantor") and *[name of trustee]* (hereinafter referred to as "Trustee").

Background

Grantor and *[his/her]* former spouse, *[name of spouse]* (hereinafter referred to as "Beneficiary") entered into a Separation Agreement on *[date]*, pursuant to the terms of which Grantor is required to establish a trust for the purpose of providing support to Beneficiary during *[his/her]* lifetime, subject to certain terms and conditions relative to termination and otherwise. After entering into the said Separation Agreement, Grantor and Beneficiary filed a Petition for Dissolution in the Court of Common Pleas of *[name of county]* County, Ohio, Division of Domestic Relations (Case No. *[number of case]*), and pursuant to proceedings in that case the said Court entered a Judgment dissolving the marriage of Grantor and Beneficiary and adopting the said Separation Agreement as a part of the said Judgment Entry. This Trust Agreement is entered into for the purpose of meeting the requirements of such Separation Agreement and Judgment Entry.

The trust established by means of this Trust Agreement is intended to qualify for treatment in accordance with the terms of I.R.C. § 682, as amended, or any substitute therefor hereinafter enacted.

Grantor has delivered to Trustee certain assets, identified and listed on Exhibit A attached hereto and hereby made a part hereof, and, in consideration of the mutual covenants and agreements contained herein, it is agreed between Grantor and Trustee that Trustee shall hold and administer all such assets, together with any other assets which may hereafter come into the trust created hereby, in accordance with the terms, provisions and conditions set forth herein.

ARTICLE I. Disposition of trust estate during Beneficiary's lifetime

1.01. All income to Beneficiary

Trustee shall pay to, or for the benefit of, Beneficiary, in monthly installments, all of the income of this trust until such time as the happening of one of the events referred to in paragraph 2.01 hereof.

1.02. Minimum annual payment to Beneficiary

Beneficiary shall be entitled to receive from the trust not less than $*[dollar amount]* as to each month (or a prorated amount as to any part of a month) during which this trust remains in existence but in no event beyond the happening of any of the events referred to in paragraph 2.01. Within sixty-five days after the end of each trust fiscal year, Trustee shall determine whether or not, as to the preceding year, Beneficiary has in fact received the total amount due to *[him/her]* in accordance with such formula. In the event that the amount paid to Beneficiary during such preceding year is less than the amount to which *[he/she]* is entitled, Trustee shall, on or before February 15 of each year, pay to Beneficiary a sum equal to the difference between the amount *[he/she]* actually received during the preceding year and the amount to which *[he/she]* is entitled. For this purpose Trustee may make such payment out of principal.

ARTICLE II. Termination of trust

2.01. Remarriage, cohabitation, death of Beneficiary

Subject to the provisions of paragraph 2.03, this trust shall terminate upon the first to happen of any of the following events:

(a) Beneficiary's remarriage; (b) Beneficiary's cohabitation with an unrelated adult; or (c) Beneficiary's death.

2.02. Disposition of income accrued

All income of the trust accrued to and including the date of termination pursuant to the provisions of paragraph 2.01 shall be paid to or for the benefit of Beneficiary or, in the event of *[his/her]* death prior to *[his/her]* having received all such income, to Beneficiary's estate. All income accrued thereafter shall be disposed of in accordance with the terms of paragraph 2.03.

2.03. Disposition of trust assets upon termination

As soon as practicable after the happening of any of the events referred to in paragraph 2.01, Trustee shall pay over and distribute to Grantor all assets remaining in such trust (including income accrued after such termination). However, in the event that, at the time of the happening of any such event, Grantor is deceased, then this trust shall continue in accordance with the terms hereinafter set forth.

[Hereafter, set forth dispositive and trust administration provisions according to Grantor's estate plan, or simply provide, in section 2.03 above, for some other direct disposition upon the happening of one of the events set forth in section 2.01.]

IN WITNESS WHEREOF, Grantor has signed this Trust Agreement and Trustee has caused its corporate signature to be affixed hereto by its proper officers thereunto duly authorized, at *[name of city]*, Ohio, on the date first above written.

_____

Grantor

_____

Trustee, By Trust Officer

[Exhibit A]

NOTES TO FORM

Drafter's Notes

The Tax Reform Act of 1984 simplifies the tax rules applicable to what had theretofore been referred to as "alimony trusts." In essence, it eliminates the I.R.C. § 71 requirements as to trusts and makes I.R.C. § 682 the sole section relevant to trusts in divorce or separation. In cases involving substantial assets and proposed "alimony" payments, serious consideration should be given to the use of a " Section 682 trust," under which the payee-beneficiary may receive income from the trust in the same form as it was received by the trust (e.g., tax-free income from municipal bonds). Under I.R.C. § 1041, the "payor" spouse can: (a) transfer assets to such a trust without incurring a capital gains tax; (b) provide income for the payee-spouse from the trust in lieu of what would traditionally be called alimony; and (c) provide for the passage of the trust assets to his/her children, or back to himself/herself, upon the payee-spouse's death.

Additional articles may treat such matters as powers of trustee, duties of trustee, irrevocability of trust, trustee bond or waiver, payment of fee or waiver, successor trustee, exoneration, etc.

§ 9:116 Spousal support tax treatment—No payments as taxable spousal support—Form⊚

Payments by *[name of spouse]* to *[name of spouse]* pursuant to the terms of this paragraph are specifically designated as not includable in gross income of *[name of payee]* under I.R.C. § 71(b)(1)(B), and not allowable as a deduction to *[name of payor]* under I.R.C. § 215. *[Name of payor]* and *[name of payee]* shall treat all such payments consistently with this designation for their respective federal income tax purposes.

§ 9:117 Spousal support tax treatment—Some payments not taxable spousal support—Form⊚

Any payment in excess of [e.g., $15,000] in any calendar year made by *[name of payor]* to *[name of payee]* pursuant to the terms of this paragraph is hereby designated as not includable in gross income of *[name of payee]* under I.R.C. § 71(b)(1)(B), and not allowable as a deduction to *[name of payor]* under I.R.C. § 215. The parties shall treat all such excess payments consistently with this designation for federal income tax purposes.

§ 9:118 Spousal support tax treatment—Percentage of payments not taxable spousal support—Form⊚

[Fifty, e.g.] percent of the payments made by *[name of payor]* to *[name of payee]* pursuant to the terms of this paragraph are hereby designated as not includable in gross income of *[name of payee]* under I.R.C. § 71(b)(1)(B), and not allowable as a deduction to *[name of payor]* under I.R.C. § 215. The parties shall treat such payments consistently with this designation for their respective federal income tax purposes.

§ 9:119 Spousal support security—Support as charge against payor's estate—Form⊚

[Name of spouse] shall pay to *[name of spouse]* for *[his/her]* separate maintenance and support during *[his/her]* life or until *[his/her]* remarriage or cohabitation with a person of the opposite sex for more than *[period]* continuously, the sum of $*[dollar amount]* per *[period]* commencing *[date]*, notwithstanding the earlier death of *[name of payor]*. In the event *[name of payor]* dies before *[name of payee]* remarries, cohabits as herein described, or dies, the remaining unpaid balance of the monthly installments payable to *[name of payee]* hereunder shall be paid from *[name of payor]*'s estate in the following manner:

[specify]

§ 9:120   Spousal support security—Life insurance as guarantee—Form⊚

If *[name of payor]* dies before *[name of payee]* remarries or cohabits as herein described or dies, then, the remaining unpaid balance of the monthly installments, for *[name of payee]*'s spousal support during the period of time specified above, shall be paid to *[name of payee]* from the proceeds of an insurance policy issued on *[name of payor]*'s life.

[Name of payor] shall forthwith duly procure from an insurance company duly licensed to do business in the State of Ohio a "reducing term" insurance policy on *[his/her]* life, effective for the period of time set forth above. Said policy shall be issued in the sum of $*[dollar amount]* with a reducing or declining monthly balance which shall co-incide with, and never be less than, the amount needed to pay the monthly installments of spousal support to *[name of payee]* as specified above. The *[name of payor]* shall provide to *[name of payee]* the name of the insurance company and the policy number.

Further, said policy shall provide that from and after *[name of payor]*'s death, the insurance company shall pay directly to *[name of payee]* each month the sum of $*[dollar amount]* during the effective period of time set forth above, including all accrued and unpaid installments at time of *[name of payor]*'s death. *[Name of payor]* shall designate and thereafter maintain *[name of payee]* as the primary beneficiary in said policy until *[he/she]* dies or remarries or cohabits as herein described or until the total sum of $*[dollar amount]* has been fully paid to *[him/her]*, whichever occurs first. Thereafter, *[name of payor]* shall be restored as full owner of the policy free from any claim on part of *[name of payee]*. Said policy shall contain a "Waiver of Premium Disability Benefit" clause. *[Name of payor]*, at *[his/her]* sole expense, shall maintain said policy in full force and effect and keep same free and clear of any encumbrances whatsoever. All dividends hereafter paid on said policy, if any, shall be applied by the insurance company toward the payment of premiums chargeable on said policy.

Said policy shall further obligate the insurance company to give *[name of payee]* due notice when each premium becomes due, and when such premium has been paid. The insurance company should be notified of this provision.

The insurance provision herein made for *[name of payee]* is solely to secure and guarantee payment of the spousal support for *[name of payee]* as specified above.

NOTES TO FORM

Drafter's Notes

Where a spouse has been named as beneficiary of a life insurance policy prior to a divorce or dissolution, such designation will not, by statute, survive the termination of marriage unless the decree or the agreement incorporated into the decree specifically provides that such former spouse will continue to be or will be named the beneficiary. RC 5815.33.

VII. PARENTAL RIGHTS AND RESPONSIBILITY CLAUSES—FORMS

§ 9:121 Parental rights—Basic clause including parenting time—Form⊚

[Name of spouse] shall be designated as the residential parent and legal custodian of the minor *[child / children]*. *[Name of spouse]* shall have the right to parenting time of the *[child / children]* at all reasonable times upon notice to the *[residential parent]*, including, but not limited to the following: *[_____]*

NOTES TO FORM

Drafter's Notes

RC 3119.08 requires a court that issues a child support order to include specific provisions for regular, holiday, vacation, parenting time, and special visitation consistent with Ohio statutes.

§ 9:122 Parental rights—Basic clause with one parent support—Form⊚

[Name of spouse] shall be the residential parent and legal custodian of the minor *[child / children]*. *[Name of spouse]* shall have the right to parenting time of the *[child / children]* at all reasonable times as may be agreed to by and between the parties, including the following:

_____.

[name of non-residential parent] shall pay to *[name of residential parent]*, as and for the support of the parties' children, the sum of $*[dollar amount]* per child per month, each such payment to be made on or before the *[day of month]* day of each month as to which it is due. Payments, plus the processing charge, shall be made through the *[name and address of designated agency]* by payroll deduction. Such support payments shall continue as to each child until such child dies, marries, becomes self-supporting, or reaches eighteen, whichever event first occurs, provided that, if at the time such child reaches eighteen *[he / she]* is enrolled as a full-time student in high school, such payments shall continue [until *[he / she]* graduates from, or ceases to be enrolled as a full-time student in, high school/through *[month]* of the year during which such child graduates from high school.]

[non-residential parent] shall maintain *[medical / hospital / health]* insurance for the minor *[child / children]* and shall be responsible for payment of all uncovered *[medical / counseling / dental / optometric / orthodontic / prescription drug]* expenses.

[or]

Each party shall pay one-half of the uncovered medical expenses of the minor *[child / children]*.

[or]

Each party shall pay one-half of the uncovered extraordinary medical and dental expenses of the minor *[child / children]*.

NOTES TO FORM

Drafter's Notes

RC 3119.08 requires a court that issues a child support order to include specific provisions for regular, holiday, vacation, and special visitation consistent with Ohio statutes.

The parties may define "extraordinary" in their agreement. RC 3119.01(C)(4) identifies extraordinary medical expenses as uninsured medical expenses incurred for a child during a calendar year that exceed $100 for that child.

§ 9:123 Parental rights—Basic clause with joint support—Form⊙

[Name of spouse] shall be the residential parent and legal custodian of the minor *[child/children]*. *[Name of spouse]* shall have the right to visit the *[child/children]* at all reasonable times as may be agreed to by and between the parties, including the following: _____

Both parents shall be responsible for the care, support, maintenance and education of the said minor *[child/children]*, the same as if married, except as specifically otherwise detailed herein. *[Residential parent]* shall have primary liability for support, and shall provide for room, board, maintenance, clothing, and incidentals. *[non-residential parent]* shall contribute to the support in the amount of $*[dollar amount]* per month per child until *[each]* such child is eighteen and out of high school, such amounts to be paid to *[residential parent]* beginning the first day of the month following approval of this Separation Agreement by a competent court. Payments, plus the processing charge, shall be made by *[income withholding/bank accounts/etc.]* pursuant to RC 3121.03. *[Said sum was computed under the child support guidelines and is in conformity therewith.] [or]* [Said sum deviates from the child support guidelines. The parties agree that application of the schedule would be unjust or inappropriate to the *[child/children]* or either parent and would not be in the best interest of the child based upon the following factors: *[list or specify factors]*.]

Notwithstanding the provision above, *[non-residential parent]* agrees to continue said support with respect to *[each]* such child so long as the child continues to live with *[residential parent]* or, being in college, maintains his or her principal residence with *[residential parent]*, or until he or she reaches *[number of years]* years.

In addition to the payments above, *[non-residential parent]* shall provide insurance to cover medical, dental, optical, and prescription appliances and drugs, and to the extent such items are not covered by insurance, shall reimburse *[residential parent]* for any such expenses incurred for *[each]* such child until he or she is eighteen years of age, except that such insurance coverage shall continue if he or she is in a college or other institution of higher education, until age twenty-three. *[Residential parent]* shall send any requests for reimbursement for medical expenses not covered by a medical insurance plan to *[non-residential parent]*, who shall reimburse *[him/her]*.

NOTES TO FORM

Drafter's Notes

RC 3119.08 requires a court that issues a child support order to include specific provisions for regular, holiday, vacation, parenting time, and special visitation consistent with Ohio statutes.

§ 9:124 Parental rights—Child not to be removed from locale—Form⊚

The parties agree that frequent and ongoing contact by both parents is in the best interest of the minor *[child/children]* and therefore *[residential parent]* agrees not to move the residence of the minor *[child/children]* from *[name of county]* County/adjacent counties/further than fifty miles from *[name of county]* County without the consent of *[non-residential parent]* or further order of the Court.

NOTES TO FORM

Drafter's Notes

RC 3109.051(G)(1) requires the residential parent to notify the court of an intention to relocate.

§ 9:125 Parental rights—Non-residential parent's right to records—Form⊚

[non-residential parent] shall have the right to request, inspect, and receive copies of all school and medical records of minor *[child/children]* as would be available to *[residential parent]*. In addition, *[residential parent]* agrees to encourage the minor *[child/children]* to advise *[non-residential parent]* regarding school and sports activities and said *[non-residential parent]* shall be encouraged and permitted to attend and participate in said events. *[non-residential parent]* agrees, when school is in session during visitation, to assist and encourage the *[child/children]*, when visiting, to complete homework assigned over such period encompassed by visitation, even as *[he/she]* would if the parents were still living together.

NOTES TO FORM

Drafter's Notes

RC 3109.051(H)(1) requires record keepers to allow the non-residential parent access to child's records equal to residential parent's rights.

RC 3109.051(J)(1) entitles the non-residential parent access to any school activity to which the residential parent has access.

§ 9:126 Parental rights—Fostering affection and respect for both parents—Form⊚

The parties shall exert every reasonable effort to maintain free access between themselves and the *[child/children]* and to foster a feeling of affection between themselves and the *[child/children]*. Neither party shall do anything to interfere with the natural development of the *[child/children]*'s love and respect for the other.

NOTES TO FORM

Drafter's Notes

This provision may be inserted in any paragraph which allocates parental rights and responsibilities.

§ 9:127 Parental rights—Provision against adoption—Form⊚

The allocation of the parental rights and responsibilities of the residential parent and legal custodian of the *[child / children]* to *[name of spouse]* shall not be construed to operate as *[non-residential parent]*'s consent to the adoption of the said *[child / children]* by any other person, nor shall such relinquishment confer upon *[residential parent]* any authority, in case of *[his / her]* death, to appoint a guardian for the *[child / children]* to the exclusion of *[non-residential parent]*, nor to change the *[child / children]*'s surname(s) without *[his / her]* consent.

§ 9:128 Parental rights—Sample findings of fact and conclusions of law—Form⊚

[Caption]

Findings of Fact and Conclusions of Law

This cause came on to be heard upon the Complaint of the Plaintiff and the Cross-Complaint of the Defendant for Divorce in the above-captioned action.

The Court hereby makes the following Findings of Fact and Conclusions of Law:

1. That the child support guidelines would result in child support being paid from the Plaintiff to the Defendant in the amount of $*[dollar amount]* per month;

2. That the amount is unjust and inappropriate and it would not be in the best interest of the minor child for the Plaintiff to pay this amount; and

3. That the Court in considering the factors in R.C. § 3119.23 finds that:

(here list reasons)

The Court finds that it is in the best interest of the minor child/children of the parties to have no child support of $*[dollar amount]*, per month as proposed in the Shared Parenting Plan; and it would therefore be inappropriate to pay guideline support.

IT IS SO ORDERED.

_____

Judge

Approved:

_____

_____

VIII. PARENTING TIME CLAUSES—FORMS

§ 9:129   Parenting time—Adopting court's guidelines—Form⊚

The parties hereby agree to adopt the *[visitation guidelines/model visitation/parenting time schedule]* as provided under Local Rule *[designation of Local Rule]*, with the following exceptions and changes: *[_____]*.

NOTES TO FORM

Drafter's Notes

Pursuant to RC 3109.051(F)(2), each court must have standard parenting time guidelines. Consult local court rules.

§ 9:130   Parenting time—Alternating weekends and holidays—Form⊚

(A) *[non-residential parent]* shall have parenting time with the *[child/children]* on alternating weekends from Friday 6:00 p.m. to Sunday 6:00 p.m. commencing with *[date]*;

(B) *[non-residential parent]* shall have parenting time with the *[child/children]* on the following alternating legal holidays: Christmas Day, *[_____]*, New Year's Day, Easter Sunday, Memorial Day, 4th of July, Labor Day, and Thanksgiving;

(C) *[non-residential parent]* shall have every reasonable opportunity to spend some time with the *[child/children]* and to have the *[child/children]* visit *[him/her]*.

§ 9:131   Parenting time—Detailed schedule—Form⊚

[Name of spouse] shall be named residential parent and legal custodian of the *[child/children]* and shall supervise their care, subject to the following rights on *[name of spouse]*'s part:

(A) Up to each child's *[ordinal number of birthday]* birthday, the following provisions shall apply to such child:

(1) *[non-residential parent]* shall have the right to parenting time with the child upon twenty-four hours' notice to *[residential parent]*.

(2) *[He/she]* shall also have the child spend either Saturday or Sunday with *[him/her]* each week, from *[time, day]* to *[time, day]*.

(B) Between each child's *[ordinal number of birthday]* and *[ordinal number of birthday]* birthdays, the following provisions shall apply to such child:

(1) *[non-residential parent]* shall have the right to visit the child upon twenty-four hours' notice to *[residential parent]*.

(2) *[He/She]* shall also have the right to have the child spend up to *[number of weekends]* weekends each calendar year with *[him/her]*. For the purposes hereof, weekends shall be deemed to run from Friday evening to Sunday evening. *[non-residential parent]* shall give *[residential parent][number of days]* days' notice in advance of each such weekend.

(3) *[non-residential parent]* shall also have the right to have the child spend with *[him/her]* each year a vacation not exceeding *[number of days]* consecutive days. Such vacations shall take place during the summer vacation period. *[non-residential parent]* shall give *[number of weeks]* weeks' notice in advance of each such vacation.

(C) After each child's *[ordinal number of birthday]* birthday, the parties shall confer with each other to arrive at mutually satisfactory arrangements concerning *[non-residential parent's]* rights of parenting time with respect to weekends and vacations. In default of agreement, *[his/her]* rights shall be fixed by arbitration hereunder.

§9:132 Parenting time—Parents living far apart—Form⊚

When the *[child is/children are]* to be with *[non-residential parent]* pursuant to the terms of this Agreement, all the traveling and incidental expenses of said *[child/children]* (and of the adult required to accompany *[him/her/them]*) *[shall be paid by [non-residential parent]/shall be shared equally by the parties]*. *[non-residential parent]* is responsible for making all arrangements for the transportation, safety, and convenience of the *[child/children]*.

NOTES TO FORM

Drafter's Notes

Pursuant to RC 3109.051(F)(2), each court must have standard parenting time guidelines. Consult local court rules.

§9:133 Parenting time—In the event of non-residential parent's illness—Form⊚

If *[non-residential parent]* is unable to visit the *[child/children]*, because of noncontagious illness, then *[child/children]* shall be sent to *[non-residential parent]*, attended, if necessary, at *[non-residential parent]*'s expense, at such reasonable times and to such reasonable place or places as may be consistent with *[child/children]*'s welfare.

§9:134 Parenting time—In the event of child's illness—Form⊚

In the event of the illness of the *[child/children]* at any time, the party then having possession of the *[child/children]* shall immediately communicate with the other party by telephone, if possible; and during such illness each party shall have the right to parenting time with the said *[child/children]* as often as the "visiting" parent desires without unduly inconveniencing the residential parent. The word "illness" as herein used shall mean any illness which confines the *[child/children]* to bed for more than one day.

§ 9:135   Parenting time—Modification due to employment schedule change—Form⊛

The parties recognize that *[non-residential parent]* has an employment schedule subject to fluctuation, and in an effort to provide *[him/her]* and the *[child/children]* with the advantage and opportunity for maintaining an ongoing relationship, *[non-residential parent]* agrees to give *[residential parent]*, as and when available, and in advance, a copy of *[his/her]* projected schedule. *[Residential parent]* agrees, to the extent it does not burdensomely interfere with the plans and arrangements of *[residential parent]* and the school and activity schedules of the minor *[child/children]*, to permit, provide and encourage parenting time during *[non-residential parent]*'s available times.

§ 9:136   Parenting time—Procedure when residential parent relocates—Form⊛

[Residential parent] shall reside within a radius of fifty miles of *[place]*. Except for brief visits, camp or vacations, *[he/she]* shall not take the *[child/children]* out of the State of *[name]* without *[non-residential parent]*'s consent; and in default of such consent, the question *[arbitrated/mediated]*. If *[residential parent]*, for reasons of remarriage, health or business, desires to establish a residence beyond the radius specified herein, the parties will confer with each other with a view to working out, in advance of *[residential parent]*'s removal, mutually satisfactory arrangements governing *[non-residential parent]*'s rights as to parenting time, weekends and vacations. In default of agreement, *[non-residential parent]*'s rights with respect thereto shall be fixed by *[arbitration/mediation]* hereunder. The costs of *[arbitration/mediation]* shall be paid by each party in proportion to their incomes. Both parties recognize that the court continues to have jurisdiction to order modification of parenting time, and both agree to resolve matters without court intervention if possible.

NOTES TO FORM

Drafter's Notes

RC 3109.051(G)(1) requires the residential parent of a child to notify the court of his or her intention to relocate.

Provisions requiring arbitration or mediation of child-related matters may be more precatory than enforceable, but are not inappropriate.

§ 9:137   Parenting time—Provision against waiver of rights—Form⊛

The failure of *[non-residential parent]* to exercise *[his/her]* rights to parenting time hereunder shall in no event be deemed a waiver of such rights.

NOTES TO FORM

Drafter's Notes

This provision may be inserted in any parenting time paragraph.

IX. CHILD SUPPORT CLAUSES—FORMS

§ 9:138   Child support—Basic agreement—Form⊚

1. The *husband/wife* shall pay the sum of $*[dollar amount]* per month per child as and for child support until the *child/children reach/reaches* the age of eighteen, or is otherwise emancipated, and such support is to continue beyond the age of 18 years if said child continuously attends, on a full-time basis, any recognized and accredited high school, including seasonal vacation periods,

OPTION 1 for over age 19:

and shall continue beyond the date the child has reached the age of 19 years so long as he/she is still attending high school. Payments, plus processing charge, shall be made by payroll withholding from the wages due and owing the *husband/wife,* to be paid through the Ohio Child Support Payment Central (C.S.P.C.), P.O. Box 182394, Columbus, OH, 43218-2394, to be forwarded to the *wife/husband.*[1]

OPTION 2 for over age 19:

and such support is to continue beyond the age of 18 years if said child continuously attends on a full-time basis any recognized and accredited high school, including seasonal vacation periods, but not beyond the date the child has reached the age of 19 years. Payments, plus processing charge, shall be made by *payroll withholding from the wages due and owing the husband/wife, /bank account* to be paid through the Ohio Child Support Payment Central (C.S.P.C.), P.O. Box 182394, Columbus, OH, 43218-2394, to be forwarded to the *wife/ husband.*

2. Until such time as the Separation Agreement of the parties becomes an order of the Court, the *husband/wife* agrees that *he/she* shall make child support payments directly to the *wife/husband.* At such time as the court orders the *husband/wife* to make payments directly through the Ohio Child Support Payment Center (C.S.P.C.), P.O. Box 182394, Columbus, OH, 43218-2394, *he/she* shall do so until the first payment is made from wages.

3. Further, at such time as the first deduction is made from the *husband/wife's funds*, the parties will determine if any shortage or overpayment in child support exists, and any additional money owed by the *husband/wife* or owed to the *wife/husband* shall be paid immediately. If neither party makes written demand upon the other, concerning any shortage or overpayment, within sixty (60) days of the

---

[Section 9:138]

[1]2000 S.B. 180 removed the "over 19" language from RC 3103.03. However, RC 3119.86 contains the default limitation on support orders at age 19 unless a court order or agreement provides otherwise.

first support deduction from the *husband/wife's* funds, then it shall be conclusively presumed that all payments made prior to the first deduction from the *husband/wife's* funds were correct.

4. To facilitate recomputation of child support, each party agrees to exchange income tax information annually, upon request from the other party, and to provide the other party with copies of his or her IRS 1040 and all accompanying schedules, along with W-2s or 1099s, within fourteen (14) days of said request of the filing of his or her 1040 return.

[Said sum was computed under the child support guidelines and is in conformity therewith.][or] [Said sum deviates from the child support guidelines. The parties agree that application of the schedule would be unjust or inappropriate to the *[child/children]* or either parent and would not be in the best interest of the child based on the following factors: *[list or specify factors]*.]

NOTES TO FORM

Drafter's Notes

Consult the Child Support Schedule set forth in RC 3119.021 to compute child support. If the amount in the agreement deviates from the guidelines amount, the reasons may be included in the agreement. In addition, the court must enter in its journal the amount computed under the guidelines and its determination that such amount is unjust or inappropriate and not in the best interest of the (1) child (RC 3119.22); (2) child, obligor, or obligee when gross income over $150,000 (RC 5119.04(B)); or (3) child or either parent when shared parenting (RC 3119.24), and enter findings of fact in all cases of deviation.

See Text § 19:3, Support obligations—In general; Wiest v. Wiest, 2000 WL 262665 (Ohio Ct. App. 2d Dist. Darke County 2000) (statute in effect at time of order controls).

§ 9:139 Child support—Automatic increases—Form⊚

[non-residential parent] shall pay the sum of $*[dollar amount]* per *[period]* as *[his/her]* contribution to child support for *[number of years]* years from the date of signing hereof; thereafter, *[non-residential parent]* shall pay the sum of $*[dollar amount]* per *[period]* for *[number of years]* years; thereafter, *[non-residential parent]* shall pay the sum of $*[dollar amount]* per *[period]* for *[number of years]* years.

[or]

[non-residential parent] shall pay the sum of $*[dollar amount]* per *[period]* as and for child support for *[number of years]* years. Thereafter the amount of support shall be automatically adjusted annually in the same percentage as *[non-residential parent]*'s income (defined elsewhere) increases. In the event *[non-residential parent]*'s income decreases, the support shall, however, not be less than $*[dollar amount]* per *[period]*.

NOTES TO FORM

Drafter's Notes

This requires that the non-residential parent provide the residential parent annually with relevant information.

Consult the Child Support Guidelines set forth in RC 3119.021 to compute child support. If the amount in the agreement deviates from the guidelines amount, the reasons may be included in the agreement. In addition, the court must enter in its journal the amount computed under the guidelines and its determination that such amount is unjust or inappropriate and not in the best interest of the (1) child (RC 3119.22); (2) child, obligor, or obligee when gross income over $150,000 (RC 3119.04(B)); or (3) child or either parent when shared parenting (RC 3119.24), and enter findings of fact in all cases of deviation.

§ 9:140   Child support—Modification when child support guidelines revised—Form⊚

The payments herein provided have been based upon the present Child Support Guidelines. If there is a change in the Guidelines in the future, upward or downward, of *[percentage amount]%*, a corresponding adjustment of *[percentage amount]%*, by way of increase or reduction, shall be made in the payments that *[non-residential parent]* is obligated to make hereunder at that time.

NOTES TO FORM

Drafter's Notes

Consult the Child Support Guidelines set forth in RC 3119.024 to compute child support. If the amount in the agreement deviates from the guidelines amount, the reasons may be included in the agreement. In addition, the court must enter in its journal the amount computed under the guidelines and its determination that such amount is unjust or inappropriate and not in the best interest of the (1) child (RC 3119.22); (2) child, obligor, or obligee when gross income over $150,000 (RC 3119.04(B)); or (3) child or either parent when shared parenting (RC 3119.24), and enter findings of fact in all cases of deviation.

§ 9:141   Child support—Medical, dental, and optical—Both parents have medical plans—Form⊚

Both parties presently have medical insurance plans which provide coverage for the minor *[child/children]* and each agrees to continue carrying such insurance. In the event such coverage is no longer available to either party by reason of circumstances not related to a voluntary act of such party, such party shall promptly notify the other party. Uncovered medical expenses, including deductibles and percentage disallowances, shall be paid *[one-half/proportionately]* by each party.

NOTES TO FORM

Drafter's Notes

RC 3119.30 sets forth health insurance requirements.

§ 9:142   Child support—Medical, dental, and optical—No medical plan available—Form⊚

In the event *[name of obligor]* is unable to obtain medical insurance coverage for the minor *[child/children]* *[or elects not to do so]*, *[name of obligor]* shall be responsible for prompt payment of all medical, dental, optical, prescription drugs, and appliance expenses of the minor *[child/children]*.

§ 9:143   Child support—Education expenses—No limitations— Form⊚

In addition to the foregoing, *[non-residential parent]* shall pay *[all / one-half]* of the costs and expenses for the education of *[each child / said child]* in a college, university, and/or school of higher learning and training until *[he / she]* *[attains the age of [age in years] / marries / without limitation]*. Said expenses and costs shall include clothing, transportation, tuition, board, lodging, books, and other necessary expenses directly related thereto. *[Each child / Said child]* may attend the college, university, and/or school of higher learning or training of *[his / her]* own choice after prior consultation with both the Husband and Wife.

§ 9:144   Child support—Education expenses—Specific limitation on costs—Form⊚

In addition to the foregoing, *[non-residential parent]* shall pay all costs and expenses for the education of *[each child / said child]* in a college, university, and/or school of higher learning and training during the time *[each such child / he / she]* is in attendance at any such college, university and/or school of higher learning and training until *[each such child / he / she]* *[attains the age of [[age in years] / marries]*, but such costs shall be limited in amount to costs comparable to those of a state-supported college or university in Ohio. Said expenses and costs shall include clothing, transportation, tuition, board, lodging, books, and other necessary expenses directly related thereto. *[Each child / Said child]* may attend the college, university, and/or school of higher learning or training of *[his / her]* own choice after prior consultation with both the Husband and Wife. It is further provided, that in the event a child is not eighteen during the time *[each child / said child]* is in attendance at a college, university or school of higher learning or training, and *[non-residential parent]* is not in default of *[his / her]* obligation to pay the costs and expenses therefor, as herein set forth, then the support payments provided above for *[that child / him / her]* shall be reduced *[to $[dollar amount] / by [percentage amount]%]* if the child is living away from *[residential parent]*'s home. Payments to be made under this paragraph are, except as specified, independent of the obligations set forth above.

§ 9:145   Child support—Education expenses—Limitation if unable to pay—Form⊚

Subject to *[non-residential parent]*'s financial ability to do so, and in addition to the foregoing, *[non-residential parent]* shall pay all costs and expenses for the education of *[name]* beyond high school, limited, however to the following:

(1) Not to exceed four years;

(2) Tuition, books, lab fees;

(3) Tuition comparable to *[highest / lowest]* state-supported college or university in Ohio;

(4) Transportation not exceeding *[number of miles]* miles;

(5) Dormitory residence, room, and board.

§ 9:146   Child support—Abatement during extended visitation—Form⊚

Notwithstanding any provision to the contrary contained herein, during those periods of time that the minor *[child is/children are]* visiting with the *[non-residential parent]* for longer than *[number of days or weeks]* days/weeks*[non-residential parent's]* obligation to *[residential parent]* for the total of any such periods shall be abated by *[percentage amount]*% of the then applicable child support obligation of *[non-residential parent]* to the *[residential parent]*.

NOTES TO FORM

Drafter's Notes

With payments mandatorily paid through payroll withholding or automatic withholding from a bank account, it may now be too cumbersome to structure an abatement, much less to provide notices to the employer or withholder each time an abatement should occur.

§ 9:147   Child support—Life insurance as guarantee—Form⊚

[non-residential parent] owns and has in *[his/her]* possession and in force and effect an insurance policy issued on *[his/her]* life issued by *[name of insurance carrier]* Policy No. *[number of policy]* in the sum of $*[dollar amount]*, and *[he/she]* warrants that same is unencumbered, and that all premiums thereon have been paid to date. *[non-residential parent]* shall designate and forthwith and thereafter maintain *[residential parent]* as the sole beneficiary of said policy until the *[child reaches/children reach]* the age of eighteen years and thereafter until *[each such child/he/she]* completes or terminates *[his/her]* college or university education or completes the program of study at a school of higher education or training. Said policy shall contain a "Waiver of Premium Disability Benefit" clause. Upon execution of this agreement *[insured]* shall deliver said policy to *[beneficiary]*, and at *[his/her]* sole expense *[he/she]* shall keep same in force and effect, free and clear of any encumbrance, and *[he/she]* shall not transfer or assign the policy or any interest therein during the time aforesaid; and said insurance company shall furnish to *[beneficiary]* due notice when each premium becomes due and when each premium has been paid on said policy and proof of designation of beneficiary. When the above time period has expired, *[beneficiary]* shall refund said policy to *[insured]* and *[he/she]* shall be full owner from that time, with all rights, from any claim on behalf of *[residential parent]*.

The aforesaid insurance provision is provided to secure the care, maintenance, support, and education of the minor *[child/children]* of the parties in the event of *[non-residential parent]*'s death.

NOTES TO FORM

Drafter's Notes

Where a spouse has been named as beneficiary of a life insurance policy prior to a divorce or dissolution, such designation will not, by statute, survive the termination of marriage unless the decree or the agreement incorporated into the decree specifically provides that such former spouse will continue to be or will be named the beneficiary. RC 5815.33. The payee should be advised to notify the insurance company of this provision.

§ 9:148   Child support—Waiver of contribution—Form⊚

In consideration of all promises and adjustment of rights herein, *[residential parent]* hereby waives any contribution to child support from *[non-residential parent]* and expressly agrees to be solely responsible for the maintenance and support of the *[child/children]*. *[Residential parent]* further agrees that such noncontribution shall not be usable against *[non-residential parent]* for any purpose, including visitation rights and adoption.

Said sum deviates from the child support guidelines. The parties agree that application of the schedule would be unjust or inappropriate to the *[child/children]* or either parent and would not be in the best interest of the child based upon the following factors: *[list or specify factors]*.

NOTES TO FORM

Drafter's Notes

Where a child is not made a party, nor represented in the action by a guardian ad litem, a subsequent provider of support of such child would not be precluded from later asserting a right to support. A court might not approve such a provision in a separation agreement submitted for incorporation into a decree, especially if there is a question about the residential parent's ability to support. Also, where incorporated into a decree, the court retains jurisdiction to modify child support provisions.

§ 9:149   Child support—Automobile expenses

In the event the parents agree that a child be allowed to drive, both parents shall assist in getting the child's driver's permit, provide parent supervised driving for required hours, pay one half of lesson and license fees, and equally pay any premium cost for insuring premium coverage until said child is 18 and has graduated from high school.

X.   INCOME TAX CLAUSES—FORMS

§ 9:150   Income tax exemption—Residential parent to use— Form⊚

[Residential parent] shall be entitled to claim the minor *[child/children]* as dependent(s) for purposes of all applicable federal, state and local tax purposes notwithstanding any financial contribution made by *[non-residential parent]* for the support and maintenance of the minor *[child/children]*.

§ 9:151   Income tax exemption—Non-residential parent to use—Form⊚

[Residential parent] agrees that at all times that *[non-residential*

parent] is in full compliance with this Agreement or any amendment to this Agreement or subsequent modification to this Agreement, *[non-residential parent]* shall be entitled to declare the *[child/children]* in *[his/her]* federal, state, or other tax returns as dependent(s). *[Residential parent]* shall sign any declaration required by the Internal Revenue Service to implement the terms of this paragraph and shall provide such declaration to *[non-residential parent]*.

§ 9:152 Income tax exemption—Phase-out of dependency exemption—Form⊚

However, in the event the *[husband/wife]* in effect loses the benefit of the dependency exemption due to the phase-out of said dependency over specified incomes, pursuant to I.R.C. § 151(d)(3), then the *[other parent]* shall be entitled to claim the *[child/children]* as *[his/her]* dependents in such year.

§ 9:153 Income tax exemption—Parents to divide exemptions—Form⊚

(1) The parties agree that, for calendar year *[year]* and each year thereafter, so long as *[name of eligible party]* is complying with the support order herein and the *[child/children]* continue to reside with *[name of residential parent]*, *[name of eligible party]* shall be entitled to claim *[name(s) of child(ren)]* as *[his/her]* dependent(s) for all tax purposes and *[name of other spouse]* shall be entitled to claim *[name(s) of other child(ren)]* as *[his/her]* dependent(s). Each party shall sign any declaration required by the Internal Revenue Service to implement the terms of this paragraph and shall provide such declaration to the other.

[or]

[(1) The parties agree that, commencing with the tax return filed for calendar year *[year]*, and so long as the parties continue to abide by the terms of the *[agreement/shared parenting plan]* herein, the parties will alternate the dependency deduction of the minor *[child/children]* with *[name of spouse]* being entitled to claim the deduction for the even numbered years and *[name of spouse]* being entitled to claim the deduction for the odd numbered years. Each party shall sign any declaration required by the Internal Revenue Service to implement the terms of this paragraph and shall provide such declaration to the other.]

§ 9:154 Income tax exemption—Post emancipation—Form⊚

The parties recognize that a dependency exemption may be claimed by a parent for a child up to the child's age of 24 years so long as the child is full time student for at least 5 months of the year and so long as said child does not claim himself/herself as a dependent. In view of said entitlement and the provisions herein for a parent's contribution/payment of post high school education costs, and to avoid later disagreements or confusion, the parties agree that the Wife/Husband shall be entitled to claim name of child/children as his/her dependent so long as he/she is in compliance with all the terms of this agreement and the I.R.C.[1]

§ 9:155 Income tax—Status—Head of household—Form⊛

The parties agree that so long as they are operating under the shared parenting plan incorporated in this agreement, the [mother/father] shall be entitled to claim head of household status for the minor child, irrespective of [his/her] waiver of the dependency exemption, and so long as such parent has not remarried and such status is in conformity with IRC provisions.

§ 9:156 Income tax credits—Earned income credit—Form⊛

Irrespective of [residential parent]'s waiver of [his/her] right to claim the minor [child/children] as [his/her] dependent[s], said residential parent shall be permitted to claim earned income credit for the [child/children] residing with [him/her].

§ 9:157 Income tax credits—Child tax credit—Form⊛

The parties agree that the [name of spouse] shall be entitled to claim the child tax credit which accompanies the dependency exemption for [all children/specified child] beginning in [year]. The parties agree that the dependency exemption and child tax credit shall continue to be claimed by [name of spouse] so long as it does not phase out. If, however, [name of spouse] becomes subject to the phase-out provision, the parties agree that [name of other spouse] shall be entitled to receive the dependency exemption and child tax credit.

§ 9:158 Income tax credits—Education tax credit—Form⊛

The parties having agreed in Article [designation of Article] above to provide for the costs of tuition and fees for post-high-school education expenses for their [child/children], the parties further agree that [name of spouse] shall be entitled to claim the [hope scholarship/lifetime learning] credit for allowable education expenses paid for the [child/children].

§ 9:159 Income tax returns—Filing joint return—Form⊛

[Name of spouse] agrees, upon being requested by [name of spouse], to join in the filing of joint federal, state, and local income tax returns for any year in which the law permits the filing of said joint returns.

[Name of spouse] agrees to indemnify and hold [name of spouse] harmless from any [liability/additional liability] which may be assessed with regard to taxes, penalties, or interest arising from the fil-

---

[Section 9:154]

[1]I.R.C. § 152(c)(3)(A)(ii) and (f)(2)(A) and (B).

ing of joint income tax returns for any year in which joint returns may be or have been filed in the past.

The parties agree that they will divide equally any refund from the tax authorities to the extent such refunds exceed the total liabilities from other taxing authorities.

NOTES TO FORM

Drafter's Notes

Marital status for IRS filing purposes is determined as of December 31 of the tax year. To the extent counsel can control the hearing date, this timing factor can save or cost additional taxes.

§ 9:160   Income tax returns—Select manner of filing to maximize tax savings—Form⊛

The parties agree to compute their income tax liability, both as married filing separately as well as filing jointly, and thereafter to file in a manner which results in the greater overall tax saving. In the event they file jointly, neither party shall pay more than such party would have paid in his or her respective total tax liability had that party filed separately. The tax savings by filing jointly shall be shared *[equally/proportionately to the total savings]*.

NOTES TO FORM

Drafter's Notes

Marital status for IRS filing purposes is determined as of December 31 of the tax year. To the extent counsel can control the hearing date, this timing factor can save or cost additional taxes.

§ 9:161   Income tax liability—One spouse to hold the other harmless—Form⊛

At the option of *[name of spouse]*, Husband and Wife shall file joint federal, state, and local income tax returns for any year for which the law permits the filing of said joint returns, and *[name of spouse]* alone shall be liable for the payment of any tax due.

[Name of spouse] shall notify *[name of spouse]* no later than *[e.g., February 15]* of *[his/her]* exercise of *[his/her]* option to require the joint filing. *[Name of spouse]* shall be reimbursed by *[name of spouse]* for any refund *[he/she]* would have been entitled to had *[he/she]* filed in a different manner. *[Name of spouse]* shall indemnify and shall hold *[name of spouse]* harmless as to any costs or expenses associated with any asserted claim with respect to any joint federal, state, or local income tax or personal property tax returns heretofore or hereafter filed by the parties.

§ 9:162   Income tax liability—Acknowledgment of tax consequences—Form⊛

The parties recognize that the transfer by *[name of transferor-spouse]* to *[name of transferee-spouse]* of the real estate hereunder (and the later receipt by *[name of transferor-spouse]* of *[his/her]* equity) is a property transfer incident to a termination of marriage and thus, pursuant to I.R.C. § 1041, has no tax consequences for *[name of transferor-spouse]*. *[Name of transferee-spouse]* acknowledges that when and if *[he/she]* sells the property, *[he/she]* will report the sale and, to the extent any gain is not avoided by exclusion under 1997 Tax Reform Act, *[he/she]* will be liable for the tax consequences of any gain on the sale.

NOTES TO FORM

Drafter's Notes

If the principal residence is sold after May 6, 1997, a universal exclusion of $250,000 ($500,000 if joint filing) of gain is available so long as the home was used as a principal residence for a total of two years of the five years before sale.

§ 9:163 Income tax liability—Mortgage interest and real estate tax deduction—Form⊚

In the event the parties are not married as of December 31 in the year of this agreement, or being still married, file their tax returns as married filing separately, each party shall be entitled to claim, as an itemized deduction, one-half of the mortgage interest payments and real estate taxes (paid from mortgage escrow) for the property located at *[address of property]* for said year. Thereafter, the *[husband/wife]* shall be entitled to the entire deduction.

§ 9:164 Income tax liability—Reporting of gain—Form⊚

The parties sold their prior residence, located at *[address]*, in calendar year *[year]*. Both parties agree to share all documentation relating to the original purchase price and costs, all records of improvements, and the closing documents for the purpose of reporting the sale on his or her return. In the event the parties are not married as of December 31, or, if still married, they do not file jointly, then each party shall be responsible for the reporting and payment of the taxes on one-half of the capital gain incident to the ownership and sale of the prior marital residence.

NOTES TO FORM

Drafter's Notes

If the principal residence is sold after May 6, 1997, a universal exclusion of $250,000 ($500,000 if joint filing) of gain is available so long as the home was used as a principal residence for a total of two years of the five years before sale.

§ 9:165 Income tax liability—Deductibility of spousal support payments—Form⊚

The parties acknowledge that the effective date of this agreement will be the date last signed by a party and all payments of periodic spousal support hereunder shall immediately be reportable by the parties and appropriately deducted and claimed, pursuant to I.R.C.

§ 71(b)(1)(A) and I.R.C. § 71(b)(2)(B), notwithstanding the fact that they are made prior to an order of court.

XI. MARITAL DEBT CLAUSES—FORMS

§ 9:166 Marital debts—Each party assumes debts in individual's own name—Form⊚

Except as expressly provided to the contrary in this Agreement, each party agrees to hold the other party harmless from all debts, obligations and/or claims incurred in that party's name prior to the date of this Agreement provided, however, that this clause shall not become effective until each party has made a full disclosure of all known liabilities that may come within this provision. Except as may be otherwise provided in writing, each party shall be responsible for all such debts, obligations and/or claims as are in that party's name.

Except for those debts and obligations created under this Agreement, each party agrees to pay and hold the other party harmless from all debts, liabilities and obligations incurred by him or her from the effective date of this Agreement.

§ 9:167 Marital debts—Each party to pay specified debts— Form⊚

With respect to the financial obligations incurred by the parties during the marriage, the following shall apply:

(a) *[Name of spouse]* shall pay the following obligations: *[list debts]*.

(b) *[Name of spouse]* shall pay the following obligations: *[list debts]*.

(c) If the other party is called upon to pay and does pay any bills, debts, or obligations other than those listed herein, *[such party shall have the right to deduct the same, together with all incidental expenses, from any payments that he or she is to make to the other party under the provisions of this Agreement / such party shall have the right to indemnification from the other party]*.

§ 9:168 Marital debts—One party to pay specified debts— Form⊚

[Name of spouse] hereby assumes the obligation to pay the balance due, $*[dollar amount]*, on a certain note here made and delivered by the parties to *[name of bank]*; and *[name of spouse]* hereby assumes the obligation to pay the indebtedness of the parties to *[name of creditor]*, in the sum of $*[dollar amount]*. The obligor hereunder shall hold *[name of other party]* harmless from any and all liability of every kind on the aforesaid obligations, and shall indemnify *[him / her]* for any expense *[he / she]* may necessarily incur in connection therewith.

NOTES TO FORM

Drafter's Notes

See Text Ch 33 Bankruptcy, for domestic settlement orders for dischargeability or non-dischargeability in bankruptcy of decretal obligations to make payments to creditors.

§ 9:169   Marital debts—One party assumes all liabilities and holds the other harmless—Form⊚

[Name of spouse] shall pay and discharge all debts, claims and obligations of the marriage incurred prior to the date of this Agreement, and shall hold *[name of spouse]* harmless thereon and otherwise indemnify *[him/her]* with respect to such debts, claims and obligations.

§ 9:170   Marital debts—Acknowledgment of no outstanding debts—Form⊚

Each party represents and warrants that he or she has not incurred any debt or made any commitment for which the other or the other's estate may be liable, and neither party shall at any time hereafter incur any such debt or make any such commitment.

§ 9:171   Marital debts—Survival of liability for debts after bankruptcy—Form⊚

Any payments required herein to be made by one party to third parties for payment of debts shall be in the nature of support and/or maintenance for the other party, but shall not be included as gross income of the payor party, unless otherwise provided for herein. The payments are intended to be an integral part of the financial support settlement of the parties and not a specific division of property, but are not modifiable by the court absent agreement of the parties. With respect to each part's responsibility to pay and/or hold the other party harmless for the payment thereof, the parties intend these specific debts and liabilities to be nondischargeable under sections 523(a)(5) and 523(a)(15) of the Bankruptcy Code of the United States.

XII.   MUTUAL RELEASE CLAUSES—FORMS

§ 9:172   Mutual release—Estates—Form⊚

Except as otherwise herein provided, each party hereby waives, releases and relinquishes any and all rights that he or she may now have or may hereafter acquire as the other party's spouse under the present or future laws of any jurisdiction (a) to elect to take against any will or codicil of the other party now or hereafter in force; (b) to share in the other party's estate in case of intestacy; and (c) to act as executor or administrator of the other party's estate.

[or]

Each of the parties waives any and all rights to inherit any part of the estate of the other at his or her death; any right to elect to take against the will of the other, and the right to act as executor or administrator of the other's estate, unless so nominated by a will or codicil dated subsequently to the effective date of this agreement; and any right to receive property from the estate of the other by bequest or devise, except under a will or a codicil dated subsequently to the effective date of this agreement; and each party releases any and all rights or claims to dower, descent, a distributive share, statutory allowance for support, statutory exemptions, right to reside in the residence, and all rights as widow, widower, or next of kin to the estate of the other. Each party also completely and forever releases the other from all rights as to any other property, privileges, or benefits accruing to either by benefit of their marriage, whether the foregoing are conferred by statutory or common law of any state.

§ 9:173   Mutual release—Detailed—Form⊚

Except as herein otherwise provided, each party hereto additionally, completely and forever releases the other party from any and all rights each has, or may have:

(a) To past, present and future support from the other;

(b) To division of property in the estate of the other;

(c) To dower in the estate of the other, past, present, or future including but not limited to real estate acquired subsequent to this Agreement;

(d) To act as administrator or executor in the estate of the other;

(e) As legatee or devisee in the last will and testament of the other;

(f) To any statutory distributive share in the estate of the other;

(g) As a beneficiary of any life insurance, or other type of insurance policy of the other, except as may be provided otherwise in this Agreement;

(h) To statutory exemptions, statutory mansion house rights, and statutory year's allowance in the estate of the other; and to any other property, privileges, or benefits accruing to the other by virtue of the marriage, or accruing to either from any other source, act, matter, or agreement whatsoever, whether the foregoing are conferred by the Statutory or Common Law of any State, or of the United States of America, or of any other country, except as may be otherwise provided in this Agreement;

(i) To rights, claims, demands, or causes of action that each may now have arising out of their marriage, or from any other act, agreement, or cause whatsoever occurring prior to the date of this Agreement.

§ 9:174   Mutual release—No release during separation— Form⊚

The parties hereto do not by this Agreement intend to waive, release, or relinquish statutory rights of a spouse that might accrue by virtue of the death of a party while the marriage continues. Each party intends to retain such rights of a spouse until the marriage is terminated by a court decree.

XIII.   MISCELLANEOUS CLAUSES—FORMS

§ 9:175   Life insurance to be maintained—Form⊚

During the lifetime of *[name of beneficiary spouse]* and as long as *[he/she]* does not remarry or cohabit with a person of the opposite sex, *[name of insured spouse]* shall keep in full force and effect insurance covering *[his/her]* life, in a principal sum not less than $*[dollar amount]*, and name *[name of beneficiary spouse]* as beneficiary thereof. This sum shall be payable to *[name of beneficiary]* outright upon *[name of insured]*'s death. If *[name of party insured]* fails to do so, *[his/her]* estate shall be liable to *[name of beneficiary]* in the sum of $*[dollar amount]*, provided *[he/she]* survives *[name of insured]*, and has not remarried, or cohabited with a person of the opposite sex prior to *[insured]*'s death. If for any reason *[name of beneficiary]* receives less than $*[dollar amount]* from the insurance, *[name of insured]*'s estate shall be liable to *[him/her]* for the deficiency.

NOTES TO FORM

Drafter's Notes

Where a spouse has been named as beneficiary of a life insurance policy prior to a divorce or dissolution, such designation will not, by statute, survive the termination of marriage unless the decree or the agreement incorporated into the decree specifically provides that such former spouse will be or will continue to be the beneficiary. RC 5815.33.

§ 9:176   Life insurance—Additional policy—Form⊚

The parties recognize that the *[Wife/Husband]* has an insurable interest in the *[Husband/Wife]*. The *[Wife/Husband]* may, at *[her/his]* option, obtain an additional life insurance policy on the *[Husband/Wife]*, at *[her/his]* cost. The *[Husband/Wife]* shall cooperate in any manner to facilitate such coverage, including signing all documents and participating in requested medical exams.

§ 9:177   Effect of breach, nonwaiver—Form⊚

The failure of either party to insist in any one or more instances upon the strict performance of any of the terms of this Agreement by the other party shall not be construed as a waiver or relinquishment of such term or terms for the future, and the same shall nevertheless continue in full force and effect.

§ 9:178   Arbitration provision—Form⊚

Any controversy or claim arising between the parties out of or relating to this Agreement shall be settled by arbitration in accordance with the Rules of the American Arbitration Association, and the decision rendered by the arbitrators may be entered in any court having jurisdiction thereof. The cost of arbitration shall be paid as the decision may direct.

§ 9:179   Agreement to make will—Form⊚

[Name of spouse] hereby agrees to make a will which will provide that *[insert specific provisions]*. This provision is supported by all the consideration of this agreement and is binding upon *[name of spouse]*'s

estate. *[Name of spouse shall take no action to defeat or reduce the benefits provided herein]*.

§ 9:180   Governing law—Form⊚

This agreement shall be interpreted and governed by the laws of the state of Ohio. It is intended that the court in which a decree terminating the marriage is granted shall continue to have jurisdiction to enforce all matters related to this agreement.

§ 9:181   Effective date—Form⊚

This agreement shall be effective upon the date last signed by a party.

§ 9:182   Expiration clause—Form⊚

The purpose of this Agreement is to resolve all issues between the parties for inclusion in a dissolution of marriage. If no dissolution of marriage is granted within ninety days after signing of this Agreement, then this Agreement and all of the provisions herein shall be null and void and of no further effect, irrespective of any part or full performance by either party.

§ 9:183   Amendment of agreement—Form⊚

Whereas, *[name of spouse]* and *[name of spouse]* have previously entered into a Separation Agreement dated *[date]*; and

Whereas, the parties desire to amend and modify said Separation Agreement in certain respects; in consideration of the above premises and of the mutual promises and undertakings set forth herein, the parties do agree as follows:

[set forth modifications desired]

§ 9:184   Modification of agreement—Form⊚

This agreement may be amended or modified only by a written instrument signed by both parties. [OPTION: except with respect to Article *[designation of Article]* (parental rights), Article *[designation of Article]* (spousal support), over which the court shall continue to have jurisdiction.] The court *[shall / shall not]* have the jurisdiction to alter any property division.

§ 9:185   Obligation to obtain a Get (form)—Form[1]

The Husband agrees that he will cooperate in obtaining a Get, timely making all arrangements, appearing and participating as directed and paying all costs associated therewith. The Wife agrees to

---

[Section 9:185]

[1]See Text § 36:2, The Get document and its meaning, for discussion.

appear in person or, if permitted, by a personal representative to receive the Get.

XIV. COURT DOCUMENTS—FORMS

§ 9:186 Judgment entry of divorce incorporating agreement—Form⊚

[Title of Court]

[Caption]   Case No. [_____]
                                             JUDGMENT ENTRY

This cause, regularly assigned, came before the Court on [date], on the Complaint of the Plaintiff, and the testimony of the Plaintiff and [his/her] witness.

THE COURT FINDS THAT:

1. Defendant was duly served pursuant to law and has [failed to answer/filed an answer in which he or she has withdrawn/filed an answer but failed to offer testimony].

2. Plaintiff on the date of filing [his/her] Complaint had been a resident of the State of Ohio for more than six months and of [name of county] County for more than ninety days preceding such filing.

3. The parties were married on [date] at [city and state], and [no / number of children] children were born as issue of said marriage, namely, [name(s) and date(s) of birth of children]. The duration of the marriage was from [date] to [date].

4. The parties have entered into a Separation Agreement, allocating their parental rights and responsibilities as to their minor children and all other matters arising out of the marriage relationship, which agreement the Court finds to be fair and equitable. The parties waived appraisal of the marital property. The property division is equitable.

5. Defendant has been guilty of [grounds for divorce], and by reason thereof, Plaintiff is entitled to a Decree of Divorce as prayed for in [his/her] Complaint.

[or]

5. The parties are incompatible, which incompatibility is not denied by either party, and by reason thereof the parties are entitled to a decree of divorce.

IT IS THEREFORE ORDERED, ADJUDGED AND DECREED THAT:

1. [Plaintiff is hereby awarded a divorce from Defendant / Both parties are awarded a divorce from each other.] The marriage contract heretofore existing between the parties is terminated and both parties are discharged from the obligations of the same.

2. The Separation Agreement executed by the parties, attached hereto, is hereby approved and validated and incorporated as if fully

rewritten herein, and the parties are ORDERED to fulfill each and every obligation imposed by the Separation Agreement upon them.

_____
Judge

Approved:

_____
Attorney for Plaintiff

_____
Attorney for Defendant
        Presiding

§ 9:187   Complaint to enforce separation agreement—Form⊚

[Title of Court]

[Caption]   Case No. [_____]
                                       COMPLAINT TO ENFORCE
                                       SEPARATION AGREEMENT

Plaintiff states that [she/he] and Defendant entered into a separation agreement, dated [date], a copy of which is attached hereto and incorporated herein for reference.

Plaintiff [moves/prays/demands] that the court enforce the provisions of said agreement as follows: _____.

_____
Attorney for Plaintiff

NOTES TO FORM

Drafter's Notes

RC 3105.10(B)(2) states that a separation agreement may be enforceable on the motion of either party. However, to "bring a case," the initial pleading would be called a "complaint." Civ. R. 7.

§ 9:188   Complaint to set aside separation agreement—Form⊚

[Title of Court]

[Caption]   Case No. [_____]

COMPLAINT TO SET ASIDE
SEPARATION AGREEMENT

(1) Plaintiff and *[name of spouse]* (hereinafter sometimes referred to as Decedent) entered into a written Separation Agreement on *[date]*, by means of which they settled and adjusted their respective rights relating to each other as well as matters which arose as a result of their marriage. A copy of such Agreement, marked Exhibit A, is attached hereto and is hereby made a part hereof.

(2) Plaintiff, having confidence and trust in Decedent, was persuaded and induced by *[him/her]* to enter into such Agreement, Plaintiff did not have the benefit of counsel due to confidence in decedent.

(3) Defendant, *[name of defendant]*, *[administrator/executor]*, is the duly appointed and acting *[administrator/executor]* of Decedent's estate, having been so appointed in the course of proceedings in Case No. *[case number]*, Probate Court, *[name of county]* County, Ohio.

(4) Defendants *[name of defendant]* and *[name of defendant]* (individually) are the heirs at law and next of kin of Decedent and are also devisees and legatees named in Decedent's will.

(5) Decedent concealed material facts from Plaintiff at the time of the execution of the aforementioned Agreement, and Plaintiff was not aware of certain facts relating to Decedent's and the parties' assets at the time of *[his/her]* execution of the said Agreement. Plaintiff did not become aware of such facts until Defendant, *[name of defendant]*, as executor of Decedent's estate, filed the inventory as to such estate with the Probate Court of *[name of county]* County, Ohio.

[or]

(5) Decedent made threats to Plaintiff regarding consequences to the children if Plaintiff did not acquiesce in the agreement.

(6) Plaintiff relied on the referendums made by Decedent to *[him/her]* as to the value and extent of *[his/her]* property and income and was induced to execute the said Agreement by reason of such reliance.

(7) The terms of the said Agreement are unjust and unfair to Plaintiff considering the nature and extent of Decedent's estate now revealed to *[him/her]* and considering the further fact that *[he/she]* was induced to enter into the said Agreement by reason of Decedent's false representations to *[him/her]*.

WHEREFORE, Plaintiff demands that: (a) the aforesaid Agreement be set aside; (b) *[he/she]* be restored to all legal, equitable, and statutory rights relative to Decedent's estate; (c) Defendants be ordered to pay all costs herein and all costs and expenses, including attorney's fees, incurred by Plaintiff in connection with *[his/her]* prosecution of this action; and (d) *[he/she]* be granted such further relief to which *[he/she]* may be entitled.

_____

Attorney for Plaintiff

[EXHIBIT A]

NOTES TO FORM

Drafter's Notes

A long form caption should be used on the complaint.

If service other than pursuant to Civ. R. 4 is desired, a written request for service (usually a court form) should accompany the complaint when it is filed.

The complaint must be filed within four months of the appointment of an executor or administrator. There is no tolling for minority (RC 2106.22).

Chapter 10

Dissolution of Marriage

By Beatrice K. Sowald, Esq.[*]

> **KeyCite®:** Cases and other legal materials listed in KeyCite Scope can be researched through the KeyCite service on Westlaw®. Use KeyCite to check citations for form, parallel references, prior and later history, and comprehensive citator information, including citations to other decisions and secondary materials.

§ 10:1   History of dissolution

In the late 1960s, after California had enacted a no fault divorce law, there was a major move to pass similar legislation in Ohio. There was also resistance to such a liberal concept of termination of marriage. Out of this conflict arose a compromise. Included as part of the compromise was a new concept of termination of marriage, upon agreement of the parties, called a dissolution. Ohio was the first state

---

[*]Based on the 1984 Edition by Judge Clayton W. Rose.

to enact such a statute[1] and to use such an action. Thus far, no other states have enacted similar legislation. While California may be the first state to have a dissolution procedure, it is not the first state to have a no fault divorce procedure. A dissolution is a form of no fault divorce. It has the advantages of not being a "divorce," not having a "plaintiff and defendant," and not having the court determine spousal support, property matters, and allocate parental rights and responsibilities.

The dissolution of marriage replaces the traditional adversary lawsuit to terminate a marriage with a joint petition where both parties are requesting the court for the same relief, i.e., that their agreement be reviewed and approved and that their marriage be terminated by judicial order. As a purely statutory remedy, dissolution is an alternative to divorce.[2]

§ 10:2   Jurisdiction

An action for dissolution is filed in the common pleas court.[1] In counties providing a domestic relations division, the petition should be filed in that division. Where no division of domestic relations exists, the petition should be filed in the general division.

Effective June 13, 1990, spouses may convert a divorce action to a dissolution proceeding prior to final judgment.[2] RC 3105.08 requires the filing of a motion which contains a petition for dissolution. The action then proceeds with the parties redesignated as petitioners.

To file a petition for dissolution of a marriage, one of the parties must have been a resident of Ohio for at least six months immediately preceding the filing of the petition.[3] A similar requisite exists for divorce and annulment in Ohio.[4] While there have been no cases decided on what constitutes a six-month continuous residence necessary for a dissolution filing, the law should be the same as that for divorce and annulment.

[Section 10:1]

[1]RC 3105.61, enacted by 1974 H.B. 233, eff. 9-23-74.

[2]See Ashley v. Ashley, 1 Ohio App. 3d 80, 439 N.E.2d 911 (8th Dist. Cuyahoga County 1981) and Alban v. Alban, 1 Ohio App. 3d 146, 439 N.E.2d 963 (10th Dist. Franklin County 1981) (Courts of Appeals of Eighth and Tenth Districts held alimony pursuant to dissolution agreement not modifiable because dissolution statute does not expressly grant such authority). 1986 H. 358 enacted 3105.18(E) to give a court power to modify under specific circumstances, whether divorce or dissolution.

[Section 10:2]

[1]RC 3105.61.

[2]RC 3105.08, as enacted by 1990 S.B. 25, § 1, eff. 6-13-90.

[3]RC 3105.62.

[4]RC 3105.03.

The term "residence" means bona fide domiciliary residence. That is, there must be an actual physical presence in Ohio and an intent to have Ohio as a domiciliary residence.[5]

Temporary absence from the state, so long as there is no intent to change domiciliary residence, does not interrupt the continuous period of residency.[6] Thus, absence while serving in the military outside of Ohio does not interrupt the residency period.[7]

Although venue is no longer jurisdictional in Ohio, some mention should be made of the venue requirements in regard to dissolution. RC 3105.62 requires that the action be brought in the proper county for commencement of actions pursuant to the civil rules. The only problem is that the dissolution procedure was enacted after the civil rules, and no civil rule exactly applies to the proceeding. Civil Rule 3(B) gives some guidelines for determination of proper venue in dissolution actions. Civil Rules 3(B)(1) and (2), make available the county in which the defendant resides or has a principal place of business. Technically, neither party in a dissolution is a defendant; both are petitioners. Civil Rule 3(B)(6) specifies the county in which all or part of the claims arise. This would probably include the county in which the parties were married or at any time thereafter resided. Civil Rule 3(B)(9), which is probably the section the legislature intended should govern, states, "In actions for divorce, annulment or for legal separation, in the county in which the plaintiff is and has been a resident for at least ninety days immediately preceding the filing of the complaint."

Civil Rule 3(B)(10) provides, "If there is no available forum in divisions (B)(1) to (B)(9) of this rule, [proper venue lies] in the county in which plaintiff resides, has his principal place of business, or regularly and systematically conducts business activity."

Some courts, particularly where there is a large spill over from one county to another, have restrictively interpreted the law in regard to venue requirements. Most jurisdictions will hear the dissolution if there is some color of venue. Counsel should inquire into local custom prior to filing.

RC 3105.62 further requires that personal jurisdiction be obtained over the petitioners. This requirement seems redundant in that the parties are joint petitioners. RC 3105.62 states in part, "For purposes

---

[5]Saalfeld v. Saalfeld, 86 Ohio App. 225, 41 Ohio Op. 94, 55 Ohio L. Abs. 156, 89 N.E.2d 165 (1st Dist. Clermont County 1949) (relevant evidence of domiciliary residence might include voting registration, driver's license, auto license, ownership of property, employment, etc.). See also Text §§ 27:26 to 27:36, Jurisdiction over marital status, for discussion of domicile and residence.

[6]Saalfeld v. Saalfeld, 86 Ohio App. 225, 41 Ohio Op. 94, 55 Ohio L. Abs. 156, 89 N.E.2d 165 (1st Dist. Clermont County 1949); Draper v. Draper, 107 Ohio App. 32, 7 Ohio Op. 2d 354, 78 Ohio L. Abs. 5, 151 N.E.2d 379 (10th Dist. Franklin County 1958); Redrow v. Redrow, 94 Ohio App. 38, 51 Ohio Op. 266, 114 N.E.2d 293 (1st Dist. Clermont County 1952).

[7]Draper v. Draper, 107 Ohio App. 32, 7 Ohio Op. 2d 354, 78 Ohio L. Abs. 5, 151 N.E.2d 379 (10th Dist. Franklin County 1958).

of service of process, both parties in an action for dissolution of marriage shall be considered as defendants and subject to service of process as defendants pursuant to the Rules of Civil Procedure." The parties are defendants only for purposes of service of process. This does not mean that either or both must be denominated as "defendant" on the petition for dissolution. The personal jurisdiction requirement is usually met by having adult petitioners waive service and acknowledge receipt of a copy of the petition by including a waiver paragraph within the petition.[8]

§ 10:3   Dissolution versus divorce

A dissolution proceeding contemplates a complete settlement of all property disputes and support and parental rights and responsibilities. It cannot be used if any of these issues are unresolved by the parties.[1] In a divorce, legal separation, or annulment action, the court may be called on to resolve one or any number of these issues.[2] In a contested divorce, it is rare that the debate is whether there are grounds and a divorce should be granted.[3] Rather, the debate relates to spousal support, property, or parenting matters. In a dissolution, all matters must be resolved in advance in a separation agreement before the judicial proceedings are initiated.

The legal effect of a divorce and a dissolution is the same. In both, the marital status is terminated, as are the attendant property rights of the parties, including rights of dower and inheritance.[4]

In the divorce action, it is often necessary that one party allege that the other party was at fault. This has a negative effect and often causes problems in negotiations. In a dissolution, this acrimony is minimized, although it is not eliminated. In a dissolution action a separation agreement is prepared in advance of filing a petition. Preparation of the separation agreement results in a more positive attitude and a better spirit of cooperation between the parties. This spirit of cooperation may continue after the decree of dissolution, and the ongoing relationship between the parties often helps in avoiding post-decree problems of parental rights, support, and visitation.

The dissolution action avoids court conflict and the expense of lengthy litigation, as both parties at the outset are relatively sure of the outcome. The dissolution process is also more expedient than the divorce process. In actions for divorce, Civil Rule 75(K) requires that at least forty-two days elapse from service of process until the hearing on the divorce complaint. A dissolution may be heard after thirty days

---

[8]See Text § 10:9, Petition for dissolution—Form.

[Section 10:3]

[1]RC 3105.65(A).

[2]RC 3105.171, RC 3105.18, RC 3109.04.

[3]RC 3105.21.

[4]RC 3105.65(B).

have elapsed from the filing of the action.[5] In a divorce, if any issue is contested, proceedings may take several months, or even years, depending on the court dockets and availability of trial counsel. The maximum time for a dissolution is ninety days and the average in-court time is about ten minutes.[6]

The dissolution requires that both husband and wife appear before the court at the dissolution hearing. In the event that a party has moved out of state and does not wish to return, there can be no dissolution. This does not prevent a separation agreement, but it means that the procedure would be an uncontested divorce with the agreement submitted to the court for approval and adoption. Divorce may be the only option if one of the parties is unable to appear in court.

At any time after the filing of a petition for dissolution prior to a decree, either party may convert the action to a divorce action by filing a motion that includes a complaint for divorce. The divorce action then must comply with the Rules of Civil Procedure including the issuance and service of summons.[7]

A motion to convert a dissolution to a divorce, filed more than 90 days after the petition for dissolution was filed, is timely filed so long as the case has not been dismissed and a decree has not been entered.[8] While a trial court must dismiss the petition if at the time of hearing either party does not want a dissolution, the statute does not require immediate dismissal.

§ 10:4 Motion for conversion and complaint for divorce—Form⊚

[Title of Court]

[Caption]

Case No. [_____]
MOTION FOR CONVERSION
AND COMPLAINT FOR
DIVORCE

or

[Title of Court]

[Caption of Dissolution]
[Names and addresses]

---

[5]RC 3105.64.

[6]If your county allows private judges to preside over dissolutions or divorces, court time can be eliminated by having the final hearing conducted by the private judge in your office. RC 2701.10. See State ex rel. Huffman v. Cox, 2003-Ohio-3642, 2003 WL 21545128 (Ohio Ct. App. 10th Dist. Franklin County 2003).

[7]RC 3105.65(C).

[8]Smith v. Smith, 101 Ohio App. 3d 62, 654 N.E.2d 1342 (4th Dist. Highland County 1995).

MOTION FOR CONVERSION AND COMPLAINT FOR DIVORCE

Petitioner *[husband/wife]* hereby moves the Court to convert the within dissolution action to a divorce proceeding.

[Here insert a complete complaint for divorce.]

NOTES TO FORM

Drafter's Notes

The statute requires that Civil Rules 4 to 4.6 be used to issue and serve summons, not Civil Rule 5. Thus, mailing a copy to the other party's attorney would be courteous, but it is not a substitute for proper service. The complaint must state grounds.

§ 10:5   Entry for conversion and complaint for divorce—Form⊚

[Title of Court]

[Caption]   Case No. *[_____]*
                                          ENTRY

Upon motion of the *[petitioner-wife/petitioner-husband]*, the within dissolution action is hereby converted to a divorce proceeding and said *[petitioner-wife/petitioner-husband]* shall be redesignated as Plaintiff, and the *[petitioner-husband/petitioner-wife]* shall be redesignated as Defendant. The Clerk of Courts shall correct its records to reflect the redesignation.

_____

Judge

§ 10:6   Procedure

A prerequisite to the commencement of a dissolution proceeding is the execution of a valid separation agreement which must provide for a division of all real and personal property.[1] It must also provide for spousal support.[2] If the parties have no property or no spousal support is to be paid to either party, the agreement should so state. The agreement should make provisions for allocation of parental rights and responsibilities, child support, and visitation rights,[3] if the parties

_____

[Section 10:6]

[1]RC 3105.63; In re Murphy, 10 Ohio App. 3d 134, 461 N.E.2d 910 (1st Dist. Hamilton County 1983) (failure to include division of all property renders decree voidable).

[2]RC 3105.63.

[3]RC 3105.63.

have minor children, and any other adjustments between the parties normally provided for in a separation agreement.[4]

RC 3105.63(A)(2) further provides that if either spouse owns a participant account as defined by RC 145.71, i.e., the Public Employees Retirement System or Public Employees Deferred Compensation Programs, then the separation agreement shall include the account and the income derived from the investment to the extent that eligible individuals have deferred income during the marriage.

If there is a possibility the marriage may continue, consideration should be given to whether the separation agreement should have a section providing for its invalidation in the event either party elects not to proceed with the ultimate dissolution of the marriage.[5]

As in all separation agreements, the parties should make full financial disclosure to one another, and the agreement must be entered into voluntarily.[6] The agreement may be amended at any time prior to or during the hearing on the petition for dissolution.[7] Because the original agreement will not necessarily be the same as the final agreement, some courts require a newly executed agreement for inclusion in the judgment entry and sometimes a re-execution before the court. Local rules should be checked in advance.[8]

In contrast to other pleadings, the petition for dissolution need not be signed by the attorney for one of the parties or by the attorneys for both parties; the petition must be signed by both the husband and wife.[9] If only one party is represented by counsel, a waiver of counsel should be filed with the documents.

The agreement with all amendments or addenda must be attached to the petition for dissolution.[10] The petition for dissolution, with the agreement attached, is filed in the general division of the common pleas court or the division of domestic relations if one has been established in the county in which it is to be filed.[11] Some counties may require that an extra copy or copies of the petition and separation agreement be filed to facilitate an investigation by court personnel or to permit study of the contents of the agreement. Some counties

---

[4]See Text §§ 9:6 to 9:342, Elements of agreement.

[5]Carey v. Carey, 9 Ohio App. 3d 243, 459 N.E.2d 626 (3d Dist. Shelby County 1983); In re Estate of Hogrefe, 30 Ohio App. 3d 238, 507 N.E.2d 414 (3d Dist. Henry County 1986) (separation agreement may, by its terms, survive dismissal of dissolution action and bind party's estate as to any matters covered by agreement).

[6]RC 3105.64.

[7]RC 3105.63.

[8]See Text §§ 9:42 to 9:50, In-court agreements.

[9]RC 3105.63 (petition must be signed by parties, whether or not attorney elects to sign). See Civ. R. 11 which requires attorney signature on "pleading" and Civ. R. 7(A) which does not include a "petition" as a pleading. Interestingly, Civ. R. 7(A) does not list a "counterclaim" or "cross claim" as a pleading, but does list a "reply" or "answer" to such as allowed pleadings.

[10]RC 3105.63.

[11]RC 3105.61.

may also require the parties to file a financial disclosure statement along with the pleadings.

RC 3105.62 provides that service of process be made on both parties pursuant to the Rules of Civil Procedure. This is usually done by including a waiver of service with or within the petition. Many attorneys follow the practice of a notarized signature on the waiver. Although the Civil Rules do not require the waiver to be notarized, local court rules may require a notarized signature.

A hearing date will be obtained or assigned according to local custom. The hearing must be not less than thirty days or more than ninety days after the filing of the petition.[12]

Both parties must be present at the hearing on the petition.[13] In some counties the judge makes inquiry of the parties without aid of counsel. In others, counsel is expected to interrogate the parties. Inquiry must be made under oath as to whether each of the parties voluntarily entered into the separation agreement, is still satisfied with its terms, and still wants the dissolution of the marriage.[14]

In *In re Murphy*,[15] the court stated:

> Each party must appear at the court hearing on dissolution and acknowledge under oath that he or she voluntarily entered into the separation agreement, which is amendable up to the hearing date, and that he or she is satisfied with its terms and seeks dissolution of the marriage. If either one fails to do so, the court must dismiss the petition and refuse to validate the agreement. If both are agreed, the court may grant the decree. . . .

> The statutory provisions requiring agreement on both the separation agreement and the dissolution of the marriage are obviously mandatory.[16]

Where a separation agreement that was the basis of a dissolution is later modified, the decree of dissolution will be modified accordingly. The decree and the agreement cannot be treated separately; an attack on one is an attack on the other. As the First District Court of Appeals noted in *Murphy*:

> Among the factors to be considered by the trial court in determining

---

[12]RC 3105.64; Starr v. Starr, 26 Ohio App. 3d 134, 498 N.E.2d 1092 (12th Dist. Madison County 1985) (thirty-day waiting period mandatory, but court held decree voidable, not void, and not subject to collateral attack); Smith v. Smith, 101 Ohio App. 3d 62, 654 N.E.2d 1342 (4th Dist. Highland County 1995) (party may convert dissolution to divorce beyond 90 days so long as trial court has not dismissed case).

[13]RC 3105.64; Starr v. Starr, 26 Ohio App. 3d 134, 498 N.E.2d 1092 (12th Dist. Madison County 1985) (thirty-day waiting period mandatory, but court held decree voidable, not void, and not subject to collateral attack).

[14]RC 3105.64; Starr v. Starr, 26 Ohio App. 3d 134, 498 N.E.2d 1092 (12th Dist. Madison County 1985) (thirty-day waiting period mandatory, but court held decree voidable, not void, and not subject to collateral attack).

[15]In re Murphy, 10 Ohio App. 3d 134, 461 N.E.2d 910 (1st Dist. Hamilton County 1983).

[16]In re Murphy, 10 Ohio App. 3d 134, 137, 461 N.E.2d 910 (1st Dist. Hamilton County 1983) (citation omitted).

whether relief from a decree of dissolution based on an incomplete separation agreement should be granted under Civ.R. 60(B) in the first instance (factors that will also be used by a reviewing court in determining whether the trial court abused its discretion) are the following: what caused the delay in making the motion; whether the delay was reasonable; what personal knowledge the movant had about the nature, extent and value of all the marital assets (whether included or omitted); what the movant should have known about them in the exercise of ordinary care; whether the movant expressly or implicitly concurred in the property provisions of the separation agreement; what deceptions, if any, were used by the other spouse; and what has intervened between the decree and the motion (such as, remarriage of either spouse or both spouses).[17]

In the event the dissolution is the result of a divorce action that has been converted by the parties to a dissolution, the motion to convert will contain the petition for dissolution. Where there are children, the original parenting affidavit should not have to be refiled.[18] A new deposit for court costs is not to be charged. The thirty days required prior to hearing after filing may be counted from the date of the original divorce filing, but the ninety-day maximum does not commence until the filing of the conversion.[19]

§ 10:7 Representation by counsel

One attorney cannot represent both parties in a dissolution even if both parties want to agree. While parties are free to proceed without counsel, when only one party has an attorney, the retained attorney should make it clear to the unrepresented spouse that the attorney represents only his or her client and should provide an appropriate waiver signed and filed with the pleadings.[1]

§ 10:8 Incorporation of agreement

After the testimony of the parties has been presented, the court must decide if the requirements have been met, and whether the separation agreement should be approved.[1] A separation agreement pursuant to a dissolution, pursuant to a divorce, or an in-court settle-

---

[17]In re Murphy, 10 Ohio App. 3d 134, 138, 461 N.E.2d 910 (1st Dist. Hamilton County 1983). See also Text § 9:2, Agreements pursuant to dissolution.

[18]RC 3105.08.

[19]RC 3105.64(B).

[Section 10:7]

[1]See Text § 10:10, Waiver of Attorney—Form, pursuant to Ohio State Bar Association Formal Opinion No. 30.

[Section 10:8]

[1]RC 3105.65(B) (does not require that court make finding of "fair and equitable," but only that court "approve"); Charlton v. Charlton, 1990 WL 222992 (Ohio Ct. App. 11th Dist. Lake County 1990).

ment is a contract.[2] A contract does not have to be fair or equitable to be enforceable; it can be unfair or favor one side over the other, so long as it is not procured by fraud, duress, overreaching, or undue influence.[3] If the court is satisfied, a decree of dissolution incorporating the separation agreement and any amendments is entered.[4] The decree of dissolution, together with the agreement, terminates the marriage and fixes the property and other rights of the parties. Pursuant to RC 3105.65(B), rights to dower and inheritance are terminated.

A separation agreement incorporated into a dissolution decree will supersede the terms of a prior insurance agreement.[5]

§ 10:9   Petition for dissolution—Form⊚

[Title of Court]

[Caption]   Case No. [_____]
                                        PETITION FOR DISSOLUTION

1. [Parties/Petitioner/Husband/Wife] [has/have] been resident(s) of Ohio for at least six months preceding the filing of this petition.

2. The parties were married at [city and state] on [date], and [no/number] children have been born as issue of said marriage, namely, [name(s) and date(s) of birth of children].

3. The parties have agreed to and signed the attached Separation Agreement, and the same together with all amendments hereafter made, is hereby incorporated into this Petition as if fully set forth herein.

4. The parties, each being over eighteen years of age and not under any disability, and each entitled to receive summons as a party in the above action for Dissolution of Marriage, do each hereby waive service of summons in accordance with Rule 4(D) of the Ohio Civil Rules and state that they each have received a copy of this Petition and voluntarily enter their appearance herein.

WHEREFORE, the parties petition the court for a Decree of Dissolution of their marriage incorporating their Separation Agreement.

_____   _____
Petitioner-Wife   Attorney for [name of Petitioner]

_____   _____
Petitioner-Husband   Attorney for [name of Petitioner]

---

[2]See Text Ch 9, Separation Agreements.

[3]Walther v. Walther, 102 Ohio App. 3d 378, 657 N.E.2d 332 (1st Dist. Hamilton County 1995).

[4]RC 3105.65(B).

[5]See Phillips v. Pelton, 10 Ohio St. 3d 52, 461 N.E.2d 305 (1984) (separation agreement specifically addressed issue of life insurance).

NOTES TO FORM

Drafter's Notes

A long form caption should be used on the petition, with the names and addresses of both parties, the parties being designated as "petitioners." The petition should be captioned "In the matter of [_____]" or "In re the Dissolution of Marriage of [_____]."

An RC 3127.23 affidavit (court form) should accompany the initial filing where there are minor children of the marriage.

Under his/her signature on the petition, counsel should list his/her Supreme Court registration number, business address, and phone number.

§ 10:10 Waiver of attorney—Form⊚

[Title of Court]

[Caption]   Case No. [_____]
ACKNOWLEDGMENT, WAIVER
AND CONSENT

I, *[name of petitioner]*, am fully aware that Attorney *[name]* does not represent me, that *[he/she]* is attorney for *[name of petitioner]*.

I understand that I have the right to have my own attorney to advise me and represent my interest, and, after consideration, have decided that I do not need an attorney, that this is my own decision and that I have not been advised by my spouse's attorney.

I hereby consent to Attorney *[name]* representing *[name of other petitioner]*.

_____
Petitioner

_____
Petitioner (Optional)

NOTES TO FORM

Drafter's Notes

This waiver should be filed with the petition when only one petitioner is represented by counsel. Only the waiving petitioner needs to acknowledge that he or she is not represented.

§ 10:11 Judgment entry—Simple decree of dissolution— Form⊚

[Title of Court]

[Caption]   Case No. [_____]
JUDGMENT ENTRY

This matter came on for hearing upon the Petition of the parties for dissolution of marriage and the Separation Agreement of the parties and any amendments attached thereto, and upon consideration thereof, the Court finds that both parties have waived service of summons, as provided in the Civil Rules, that the matter was set for hearing not less than thirty days nor more than ninety days after the filing of the Petition, that both parties appeared before the Court at said hearing and acknowledged under oath that they voluntarily entered into a Separation Agreement appended to the Petition and any amendments and sought dissolution of their marriage, and that the facts set forth in the Petition are true.

IT IS THEREFORE ORDERED, ADJUDGED AND DECREED that the marriage heretofore existing between *[names of parties]* be, and the same is hereby dissolved and the Separation Agreement and any amendments are approved and incorporated as a part of this decree. Costs paid or costs to be paid by parties equally.

_____
Judge

APPROVED:

_____
Petitioner-Wife

_____
Attorney for *[name of Petitioner]*

_____
Petitioner-Husband

_____
Attorney for *[name of Petitioner]*

PRAECIPE: TO THE CLERK OF COURTS

Pursuant to Civil Rule 58(B), you are hereby instructed to serve upon all parties not in default for failure to appear, notice of the judgment and its date of entry upon the journal.

§ 10:12 Judgment entry—Detailed decree of dissolution—Form ⊚

[Title of Court]

[Caption]

Case No. *[_____]*
<u>JUDGMENT ENTRY</u>

This cause came on for hearing in this Court on *[date of hearing]*, upon the petition of the parties.

The Court finds that Petitioner(s) *[name if only one]* *[was a/were]* resident(s) of the State of Ohio for a period of more than six months preceding the filing of the Petition herein, and that service thereof was waived by both parties as provided in the Civil Rules.

The Court finds that the parties were married in *[city and state]* on *[date]*, and that there are *[no/number]* children born as issue of the marriage, namely *[name(s) and date(s) of birth of children]*.

The Court finds that the parties have entered into a Separation Agreement that provides for the division of marital property and the support and maintenance of each of them (and for an allocation of parental rights and responsibilities for their minor children), and that the Agreement was attached to and filed with the Petition herein.

The Court FINDS that Petitioner *[name]* has petitioned this Court for leave to resume her former/maiden name.

The Court FINDS that the parties appeared in open Court on this date and acknowledged that they had entered into the Separation Agreement that was filed with the Petition herein, that it was their free and voluntary act, that they have reaffirmed the Agreement and Petition, that there had been full disclosure of all marital assets, and that such Agreement is full, fair, and equitable.

It is therefore ORDERED, ADJUDGED, AND DECREED that:

1. The marriage contract between the parties is dissolved.

2. The said Separation Agreement, attached hereto, is approved and incorporated into this Decree the same as if fully rewritten herein.

[3. *[Name of spouse]* will be the residential parent and legal custodian of the minor children.]

or

[3. The parties will share the parenting of the minor children pursuant to their shared parenting plan and decree.]

4. *[Insert standard notices required by statute (see local court rules).]*

5. *[Optional]* [Petitioner-wife be granted restoration of her former/maiden name of *[insert here]*.]

6. Costs paid.

_____
Judge

Approved:

_____   _____
Petitioner-Wife   Attorney for *[name of Petitioner]*

_____   _____
Petitioner-Husband   Attorney for *[name of Petitioner]*

PRAECIPE: TO THE CLERK OF COURTS

Pursuant to Civil Rule 58(B), you are hereby instructed to serve upon all parties not in default for failure to appear, notice of the judgment and its date of entry upon the journal.

§ 10:13 Judgment entry—Alternate recitation clauses— Form⊚

[(1) The Court further finds that the Petition for Dissolution of Marriage was filed on *[date]*, that service was waived thereon pursuant to law, and that attached thereto was a Separation Agreement signed by the parties, which is fair, just, and equitable.]

[(2) The Court further finds that in open Court this *[date]* the parties acknowledge that they are still in agreement as to the terms thereof, and that there has been a full disclosure by each of the parties of all of his/her assets.]

[(3) The Court further finds that the copy of said Agreement attached to the Petition is incorporated herein as if fully rewritten.]

§ 10:14   Judgment entry—Alternate provisions for decree— Form⊚

[(1)   The marriage contract heretofore existing between the parties be and the same is hereby dissolved and the terms of the attached Separation Agreement ordered into execution.]

[(2)   The *[wife/husband]* shall be the residential parent and legal custodian of the minor children of the parties.]

[(3)   Until further order of the Court, the *[husband/wife]* shall pay to the *[wife/husband]* as and for support of the said minor children the sum of $*[dollar amount]* per *[period of time]* for each child. Payments, plus processing charge, shall be made through the *[name and address of the county agency]* to be forwarded to the petitioner *[husband/wife]*.]

[(4)   The *[husband/wife]* shall pay to the *[wife/husband]* the sum of $*[dollar amount]* per month for the support of the minor children. Payments, plus processing charge, shall be made through the Child Support Enforcement Agency, *[address]*, to be forwarded to the *[wife/husband]*.]

[(5)   All child support and spousal support ordered by this decree shall be withheld or deducted from the wages or assets of the obligor under the order in accordance with RC 3113.21 and shall be forwarded to the obligee under the decree in accordance with RC 3113.21 to RC 3113.219.]

[(6)   IT IS FURTHER ORDERED, ADJUDGED AND DECREED that *[name of spouse]* pay the costs of this proceeding, for which judgment is rendered and execution may issue.]

§ 10:15   Enforcement of dissolution decree

On entering the decree of dissolution incorporating a separation agreement, the terms of the separation agreement become court orders and can be enforced as such. RC 3105.65(B) states that "[t]he court has full power to enforce its decree." Decrees of dissolution can be enforced by all the methods used to enforce judgment entries of divorce and spousal support.[1] Included in these enforcement provisions is the right to have arrearages reduced to judgment.[2] On the court's rendering a judgment for arrearages, execution can be issued, garnishment proceedings instituted, and judgment liens placed on property, etc.

[Section 10:15]

[1]See Text §§ 20:1 to 20:6, Statutory history; Text §§ 20:20 to 20:42, Contempt; Text §§ 20:43 to 20:54, Reduction to judgment and execution; Text § 20:71, Criminal nonsupport; Text §§ 22:8 to 22:12, Support order enforcement; Text Ch 23, Interstate and Foreign Support Practice.

[2]See RC 2301.38. See also Text §§ 20:43 to 20:54, Reduction to judgment and execution.

The show cause or contempt proceedings[3] can be used for failure to transfer property pursuant to the terms of the agreement or failure to comply with spousal support, child support, or visitation provisions. The show cause is a civil contempt and is governed by RC 2705.02 et seq.

A separation agreement used in a dissolution can also provide for a judicial transfer of property if the property is located within Ohio. Then, once the separation agreement is approved and incorporated into the decree, the real estate may be transferred.[4] As a court order, the separation agreement may be used in the event one of the parties fails to execute a deed required in the separation agreement. The agreement should contain a property description, last recording data, and provisions authorizing such documents as conveyances subject to their being filed in the recorder's office. Because of potential post-decree problems, it is good practice to have all documents transferred at the hearing where they may be passed to the parties before termination of the hearing. Civil Rule 70 is also available as an aid in enforcing separation agreements incorporated into a decree of dissolution.

§ 10:16 Modification of dissolution decree—Parental rights

The court retains jurisdiction to modify all matters of parental rights and responsibilities, child support, and visitation.[1] This is done by motion with notice given to the opposing party pursuant to Civil Rule 4 to 4.6. Civil Rule 75(J) describes the procedures for invoking the trial court's continuing jurisdiction. A trial court is not required to transfer the case to a consenting transferee court, even when both parties no longer reside in the original county.[2]

§ 10:17 Modification of dissolution decree—Spousal support

In addition, the court now retains jurisdiction to modify spousal support if such authority is specifically reserved by the parties in the separation agreement.

Previously, there was no specific statutory authority to modify spousal support provisions. In fact, the legislative history of RC 3105.65 indicated an intent that the court not have authority to modify spousal support in dissolution agreements.

In the original enactment of the law by 1974 House Bill 233, effec-

---

[3]See Text §§ 20:20 to 20:42, Contempt; Text § 25:45, Motions by obligee regarding enforcement of judgments—Motion for order to show cause.

[4]RC 3105.63; Kungle v. Equitable General Ins. Co., 27 Ohio App. 3d 203, 500 N.E.2d 343 (9th Dist. Summit County 1985) (insurance proceeds held in trust for transferee of property under decree of dissolution).

[Section 10:16]

[1]RC 3105.65(B).

[2]Bieniek v. Bieniek, 27 Ohio App. 3d 28, 499 N.E.2d 356 (9th Dist. Medina County 1985).

tive September 23, 1974, it was stated, "The court has full power to enforce its decree, and retains jurisdiction to modify all matters of custody, child support, visitation, and periodic alimony payments."

In 1975, House Bill 370, effective August 1, 1975, amended RC 3105.65 to read, "The court has full power to enforce its decree, and retains jurisdiction to modify all matters [of custody, child support, and visitation]." This change left out the authority to modify spousal support provisions, which indicated the legislative intent to take away the court's authority to modify spousal support provisions. Several courts of appeals found this legislative intent and held that, in fact, the court was without authority to modify spousal support provisions in dissolution proceedings.[1]

This intent was considered by the Ohio Supreme Court in *McClain v. McClain*,[2] and the Court reached the conclusion that spousal support in a dissolution was not modifiable.

However, since the *McClain* decision, significant amendments have been made to RC 3105.18, RC 3105.63, and RC 3105.65. It is now possible to modify spousal support in dissolution cases so long as certain key words appear in the separation agreement.

RC 3105.18(E) reads as follows:

If a continuing order for periodic payments of money as alimony is entered in a divorce or dissolution of marriage action that is determined on or after May 2, 1986, and before January 1, 1991, or if a continuing order for periodic payments of money as spousal support is entered in a divorce or dissolution of marriage action that is determined on or after January 1, 1991, the court that enters the decree of divorce or dissolution of marriage does not have jurisdiction to modify the amount or terms of the alimony or spousal support unless the court determines that the circumstances of either party have changed and unless one of the following applies:

(1) In the case of a divorce, the decree or a separation agreement of the parties to the divorce that is incorporated into the decree contains a provision specifically authorizing the court to modify the amount or terms of alimony or spousal support.

(2) In the case of a dissolution of marriage, the separation agreement that is approved by the court and incorporated into the decree contains a provision specifically authorizing the court to modify the amount or terms of alimony or spousal support.

It is important to note that the amendment's effective date is May 2, 1986, and that it is applicable only to decrees entered after that date. Case law will control prior decrees.

[Section 10:17]

[1]See Ashley v. Ashley, 1 Ohio App. 3d 80, 439 N.E.2d 911 (8th Dist. Cuyahoga County 1981); Alban v. Alban, 1 Ohio App. 3d 146, 439 N.E.2d 963 (10th Dist. Franklin County 1981). See also In the Matter Of: Fugazzi, 1983 WL 3535 (Ohio Ct. App. 10th Dist. Franklin County 1983) (court has no jurisdiction to modify alimony provisions pursuant to dissolution, even where separation agreement provides for continuing jurisdiction).

[2]McClain v. McClain, 15 Ohio St. 3d 289, 473 N.E.2d 811 (1984).

The issue may be further complicated by the enactment of RC 3105.63(C) which provides:

> If a petition for dissolution of marriage contains an authorization for the court to modify the amount or terms of spousal support provided in the separation agreement, the modification shall be in accordance with section 3105.18 of the Revised Code.

This raises the question whether the authorization to modify spousal support must appear in the original petition as well as in the separation agreement itself. Good practice would require the inclusion of such language in both the petition and the separation agreement.

§ 10:18 Modification of dissolution decree—Property division

Courts have held that they could not grant Civil Rule 60(B) relief to correct a property division awarded under a dissolution decree without setting aside the entire dissolution.[1] The Supreme Court, however, held in *In re Whitman*,[2] that where the parties had given the court the power in the separation agreement attached to the decree to make "further orders," the court has continuing jurisdiction to enforce that clause.

§ 10:19 Vacation of dissolution decree

A dissolution decree, incorporating the separation agreement of the parties, wherein the parties agree to the court's continuing jurisdiction over sustenance alimony or spousal support payments, is subject to the court's jurisdiction to modify the spousal support terms pursuant to the express authority provided in the agreement, regardless of when the decree was entered.[1]

A decree of dissolution can be vacated by authority of Civil Rule 60.[2] Civil Rule 60(B) states in part:

> On motion and upon such terms as are just, the court may relieve a party or his legal representative from a final judgment, order or proceeding for the following reasons: (1) mistake, inadvertence, surprise or excusable neglect; (2) newly discovered evidence which by due diligence could not have been discovered in time to move for a new trial under Rule 59(B); (3) fraud (whether heretofore denominated intrinsic or extrinsic), misrepresentation or other misconduct of an adverse party; (4) the judgment has been satisfied, released or discharged, or a prior judgment upon which it is based has been reversed or otherwise vacated, or it is no longer equitable that the judgment should have prospective application; or (5) any other reason justifying relief from the judgment. The

---

[Section 10:18]

[1]Ashley v. Ashley, 1 Ohio App. 3d 80, 439 N.E.2d 911 (8th Dist. Cuyahoga County 1981).

[2]In re Whitman, 81 Ohio St. 3d 239, 1998-Ohio-466, 690 N.E.2d 535 (1998).

[Section 10:19]

[1]Colley v. Colley, 43 Ohio St. 3d 87, 538 N.E.2d 410 (1989).

[2]See Text Ch 24, Relief From Judgment.

motion shall be made within a reasonable time, and for reasons (1), (2) and (3) not more than one year after the judgment, order or proceeding was entered or taken.

In *Knapp v. Knapp*,[3] the Ohio Supreme Court refused to allow a party to avoid the nonmodifiability of spousal support as declared in *McClain*, by bringing his claim under Civil Rule 60(B)(4). The court said that Ohio's public policy is to deprive the courts of jurisdiction to modify dissolution spousal support agreements and held, "The '. . . it is no longer equitable . . .' clause of Civ.R. 60(B)(4) will not relieve a litigant from the consequences of his voluntary, deliberate choice to enter into a separation agreement in a dissolution of marriage proceeding."[4]

To obtain relief under Civil Rule 60, grounds for relief must be established within the time limitations specified by that section.[5] It has been held that where a Civil Rule 60(B) motion is granted, the court must dismiss the petition and decree; the court cannot realign the parties and grant other relief.[6] Thus, the parties are still married, a result that can cause problems when one or both of the parties have remarried. Several courts of appeals have determined that when one or both of the parties have remarried, a Civ. R. 60(B) motion requesting that the dissolution decree be vacated is not the proper recourse.[7]

If the claim asserted is that the incorporated separation agreement omitted substantial and material pieces of property, the aggrieved party may seek relief in an action for accounting, declaratory judgment, conversion, damages, or unjust enrichment.[8]

However, the Supreme Court, in *In re Whitman*[9] rejected the court of appeals decision that found remarriage of a party to be a complete

---

[3]Knapp v. Knapp, 24 Ohio St. 3d 141, 493 N.E.2d 1353 (1986).

[4]Knapp v. Knapp, 24 Ohio St. 3d 141, 493 N.E.2d 1353 (1986); Matter of Dissolution of Marriage of Jewell v. Jewell, 1994 WL 718351 (Ohio Ct. App. 4th Dist. Jackson County 1994).

[5]Civ. R. 60(B). See Text Ch 24, Relief From Judgment.

[6]Ashley v. Ashley, 1 Ohio App. 3d 80, 439 N.E.2d 911 (8th Dist. Cuyahoga County 1981) (court must vacate entire decree or not, but it cannot change agreement of parties without their consent); Gustin v. Gustin, 1985 WL 3967 (Ohio Ct. App. 12th Dist. Clermont County 1985) (court must dismiss petition where no agreement); Alban v. Alban, 1 Ohio App. 3d 146, 439 N.E.2d 963 (10th Dist. Franklin County 1981); Barros v. Barros, 1981 WL 6483 (Ohio Ct. App. 5th Dist. Stark County 1981) (not error to vacate dissolution where court finds fraud or misrepresentation); Gregory v. Gregory, No. 9743 (Ohio Ct. App. 9th Dist. Summit County 1980).

[7]LaBeau v. LaBeau, 1993 WL 323541 (Ohio Ct. App. 2d Dist. Montgomery County 1993); Henry v. Edwards, 1996 WL 220885 (Ohio Ct. App. 2d Dist. Montgomery County 1996).

[8]Whitman v. Whitman, 1996 WL 276379 (Ohio Ct. App. 3d Dist. Hancock County 1996), judgment rev'd, 81 Ohio St. 3d 239, 1998-Ohio-466, 690 N.E.2d 535 (1998).

[9]In re Whitman, 81 Ohio St. 3d 239, 1998-Ohio-466, 690 N.E.2d 535 (1998).

bar to awarding any relief under Civ. R. 60(B). The court held it would only be a factor that might weigh against relief.[10]

The decree may be vacated under Civil Rule 60(B)(5), where the one-year limitation does not apply, if there was not a division of *all* property, that is, all property owned by the husband or wife, not just property jointly owned.[11] Noncompliance with the enabling statute is a fatal defect which renders the dissolution decree voidable.

The decree is also subject to being vacated where it was obtained under duress, under the broad coverage of Civil Rule 60(B)(5). A finding that a party did not enter into the agreement freely would invalidate the agreement and thus the dissolution. Citing *Blodgett v. Blodgett*,[12] the Ninth District Court of Appeals in *Quebodeaux v. Quebodeaux*[13] found three elements necessary to establish duress: first, that one side involuntarily accepted the terms of another; second, that circumstances permitted no other alternative; and third, that the opposite party's coercive acts caused those circumstances.

---

[10]See also Thompson v. Thompson, 1998 WL 274847 (Ohio Ct. App. 4th Dist. Pickaway County 1998) (remarriage of both parties is not an automatic bar to granting relief).

[11]In re Murphy, 10 Ohio App. 3d 134, 461 N.E.2d 910 (1st Dist. Hamilton County 1983); Byrd v. Byrd, 1985 WL 8807 (Ohio Ct. App. 1st Dist. Hamilton County 1985); Gustin v. Gustin, 1985 WL 3967 (Ohio Ct. App. 12th Dist. Clermont County 1985). Morgan v. Morgan, 1994 WL 265899 (Ohio Ct. App. 7th Dist. Columbiana County 1994).

[12]Blodgett v. Blodgett, 49 Ohio St. 3d 243, 551 N.E.2d 1249 (1990).

[13]Quebodeaux v. Quebodeaux, 102 Ohio App. 3d 502, 657 N.E.2d 539 (9th Dist. Lorain County 1995).

Chapter 11

Divorce

*By Hon. Timothy M. Flanagan**

---

*The author gratefully acknowledges the assistance of Sherry A. Naegele, Esq. in preparing this chapter.

Research References

Additional References

FinPlan's Divorce Planner CD-ROM

KeyCite®: Cases and other legal materials listed in KeyCite Scope can be researched through the KeyCite service on Westlaw®. Use KeyCite to check citations for form, parallel references, prior and later history, and comprehensive citator information, including citations to other decisions and secondary materials.

---

§ 11:1   Historical background

At early common law, divorce was the exclusive jurisdiction of the ecclesiastical courts. At the outset, a divorce was granted only for adultery. This was known as a divorce a mensa et thoro, which literally meant a divorce from bed and board; the parties could live separately, but they were still married to each other and thus could not remarry. A divorce a mensa et thoro is similar to Ohio's legal separation action.

The divorce a mensa et thoro was inadequate to meet the needs of parties who wished to sever their marital ties completely. In response to this problem, the English Parliament initiated the divorce a vinculo matrimonii, the basis for which was that the marriage was invalid at its inception. It was a forerunner of the annulment.

Since neither of these divorce actions was a common law action, courts in the United States believed that they did not have the inherent jurisdiction to grant divorces. As a result, divorce in the United States is a creation of statutory law blended with equitable principles and ecclesiastical law.[1]

§ 11:2   Preliminary considerations—In general

In Ohio, the equitable power and exclusive jurisdiction to grant di-

---

[Section 11:1]

[1]Clark, The Law of Domestic Relations in the United States § 13.11.

vorces rests in the courts of common pleas.[1] To grant a divorce, the court of common pleas must find the following:

(1) That the plaintiff has been a resident of the state of Ohio for at least six months prior to the filing of the complaint;[2]

[Section 11:2]

[1]RC 3105.011; Wagner v. Wagner, 1983 WL 6884 (Ohio Ct. App. 6th Dist. Lucas County 1983) (domestic relations exclusive jurisdiction may terminate upon granting of divorce decree and concurrent jurisdiction may exist with general division of common pleas court); In re Rutan, 2004-Ohio-4022, 2004 WL 1718160 (Ohio Ct. App. 3d Dist. Union County 2004) (division of domestic relations has exclusive jurisdiction over a matter unless it is certified to juvenile court); Recker v. Hohenbrink, 1998 WL 682256 (Ohio Ct. App. 3d Dist. Putnam County 1998); Pyle v. Pyle, 2007-Ohio-110, 2007 WL 92377 (Ohio Ct. App. 3d Dist. Allen County 2007); Frantz v. Martin, 2009-Ohio-2378, 2009 WL 1424024 (Ohio Ct. App.8th Dist. Cuyahoga County 2009); Howard v. Lawton, 2009-Ohio-639, 2009 WL 353327 (Ohio Ct. App.10th Dist. Franklin County 2009); Townsend v. Townsend, 2008-Ohio-6701, 2008 WL 5265677 (Ohio Ct. App.4th Dist. Lawrence County 2008); Daufel v. Daufel, 2008-Ohio-3868, 2008 WL 2942220 (Ohio Ct. App. 2d Dist. Montgomery County 2008); Mitchell v. Mitchell, 2008-Ohio-833, 2008 WL 553246 (Ohio Ct. App. 11th Dist. Portage County 2008); Nedel v. Nedel, 2008-Ohio-1025, 2008 WL 625102 (Ohio Ct. App. 11th Dist. Portage County 2008); Robbins v. Robbins, 2008-Ohio-495, 2008 WL 344143 (Ohio Ct. App. 2d Dist. Clark County 2008); Whitten v. Whitten, 2008-Ohio-3446, 2008 WL 2681139 (Ohio Ct. App. 8th Dist. Cuyahoga County 2008), and Dvorak v. Dvorak, 2006-Ohio-6875, 2006 WL 3772295 (Ohio Ct. App. 11th Dist. Portage County 2006) (common pleas court has original and continuing exclusive jurisdiction over divorce matters); Lisboa v. Karner, 167 Ohio App. 3d 359, 2006-Ohio-3024, 855 N.E.2d 136 (8th Dist. Cuyahoga County 2006) (in a divorce proceeding, any collateral claim, involving the rights of a third party, must be brought in a separate action in the appropriate court/division); Seitz v. Kozma, 2006-Ohio-3591, 2006 WL 1934547 (Ohio Ct. App. 8th Dist. Cuyahoga County 2006) (the equitable doctrine of unclean hands can be employed as a defense in a domestic relations action since the court has full equitable powers under RC 3105.011); In re Staats, 2007-Ohio-111, 2007 WL 92376 (Ohio Ct. App. 3d Dist. Allen County 2007) (juvenile court's jurisdiction terminates upon marriage of the parents, and if parents file to terminate their marriage, any issues regarding the children born of the relationship shall be within the jurisdiction of domestic relations).

[2]RC 3105.03; McMaken v. McMaken, 96 Ohio App. 3d 402, 645 N.E.2d 113 (2d Dist. Montgomery County 1994); Weightman v. Weightman, 1999 WL 354405 (Ohio Ct. App. 10th Dist. Franklin County 1999) and Collins v. Collins, 2005-Ohio-89, 2005 WL 66590 (Ohio Ct. App. 5th Dist. Tuscarawas County 2005) (decree is void for lack of subject matter jurisdiction where plaintiff fails to satisfy six-month residency requirement); Franklin v. Franklin, 5 Ohio App. 3d 74, 449 N.E.2d 457 (7th Dist. Mahoning County 1981) (plaintiff must be actual resident of state, that is, one who has his place of abode within state); Husein ex rel. Estate of Husein v. Husein, 2001 WL 842023 (Ohio Ct. App. 5th Dist. Stark County 2001) (Ohio does not give comity to a divorce decree of foreign jurisdiction when residency was never acquired there); Heiney v. Heiney, 157 Ohio App. 3d 775, 2004-Ohio-3453, 813 N.E.2d 738 (6th Dist. Williams County 2004) (husband in military established Ohio residency where he maintained Ohio as his "home of record", Ohio driver's license and wife averred that she would be returning to Ohio in another year); Holtz v. Holtz, 2006-Ohio-1812, 2006 WL 925164 (Ohio Ct. App. 2d Dist. Greene County 2006), Rahawangi v. Alsamman, 2004-Ohio-4083, 2004 WL 1752957 (Ohio Ct. App. 8th Dist. Cuyahoga County 2004), appeal not allowed, 104 Ohio St. 3d 1460, 2005-Ohio-204, 821 N.E.2d 577 (2005) and Heath v. Heath, 1997 WL 103832 (Ohio Ct. App. 6th Dist. Lucas County 1997) (plaintiff has the burden of proving domiciliary residence by a preponderance of the

(2) That the county is the proper county for commencement of the action in accordance with Civil Rule 3(B);[3] and

(3) That grounds exist pursuant to RC 3105.01.

Once the jurisdiction of the court is invoked, it continues as to all the issues raised in the pleadings until adjudicated or reserved. By statute, the trial court retains continuing jurisdiction over various domestic relations matters. For example, RC 3105.65(B) and RC 3105.18(E) provides for the trial court's continuing jurisdiction to modify certain provisions relating to parental rights and responsibilities, parenting time, child support and spousal support, if jurisdiction is specifically retained.[4] Continuing jurisdiction is invoked by motion filed in the

---

evidence); Barth v. Barth, 2006-Ohio-1094, 2006 WL 562188 (Ohio Ct. App. 8th Dist. Cuyahoga County 2006), motion to certify allowed, 110 Ohio St. 3d 1462, 2006-Ohio-4288, 852 N.E.2d 1211 (2006) and rev'd, 113 Ohio St.3d 27, 2007-Ohio-973, 862 N.E.2d 496 (2007) (strict residency test in regards to filing a complaint for divorce; plaintiff must have been an Ohio resident for six months *immediately* before filing a complaint); Rickenbrode v. Rickenbrode, 1986 WL 13594 (Ohio Ct. App. 8th Dist. Cuyahoga County 1986) (the filing of an amended complaint does not cure an initial jurisdictional defect); Ortiz v. Ortiz, 2006-Ohio-3488, 2006 WL 1851730 (Ohio Ct. App. 7th Dist. Jefferson County 2006); Hall v. Hall, 2007-Ohio-2449, 2007 WL 1463358 (Ohio Ct. App. 5th Dist. Licking County 2007); and Pandya v. Pandya, 1986 WL 13177 (Ohio Ct. App. 6th Dist. Williams County 1986) (plaintiff has the requisite intent to make Ohio his permanent home); Thomas v. Thomas, 2004-Ohio-2136, 2004 WL 886892 (Ohio Ct. App. 10th Dist. Franklin County 2004) (six-month residency period is defined with certainty and specificity); Mir v. Birjandi, 2007-Ohio-3444, 2007 WL 1934219 (Ohio Ct. App. 2d Dist. Greene County 2007) (if plaintiff delivered complaint for divorce upon the court prior to relocating to Maryland, but complaint was not filed until after plaintiff relocated, residency requirement would be satisfied).

[3]Venue is waivable if not raised. Civ. R. 12(H). Herrmann v. Herrmann, 1983 WL 5494 (Ohio Ct. App. 8th Dist. Cuyahoga County 1983) and Pickel v. Ghouati, 2009 Ohio 1644, 2009 WL 903299 (Ohio Ct. App.2d Dist. Montgomery County 2009).

[4]Page v. Page, 2008-Ohio 3011, 2008 WL 2469176 (Ohio Ct. App. 2d Dist. Clark County 2008) and Rogers v. Rogers, 2008-Ohio-1790, 2008 WL 1700440 (Ohio Ct. App. 6th Dist. Huron County 2008) (trial court has continuing jurisdiction to modify allocation of parental rights and responsibility orders during the minority of the child); Hanna v. Hanna, 177 Ohio App. 3d 233, 2008-Ohio-3523, 894 N.E.2d 355 (10th Dist. Franklin County 2008) (a child may not invoke continuing jurisdiction over a custody matter); Sunday v. Sunday, 2008-Ohio-2307, 2008 WL 2026420 (Ohio Ct. App. 10th Dist. Franklin County 2008) (invoking trial court's continuing jurisdiction to review child support does not preclude a party from obtaining relief during an administrative review process, which also invokes the court's continuing jurisdiction); Jones v. Jones, 179 Ohio App.3d 618, 2008-Ohio-6069, 903 N.E.2d 329 (2008); Swinehart v. Swinehart, 2007-Ohio-6174, 2007 WL 4105634 (Ohio Ct. App. 5th Dist. Ashland County 2007) (trial court lacks continuing jurisdiction over issues of property division); Nemeth v. Nemeth, 2008-Ohio-4678, 2008 WL 4216408 (Ohio Ct. App. 11th Dist. Geauga County 2008), Noble v. Noble, 2008-Ohio-4685, 2008 WL 4233915 (Ohio Ct. App. 10th Dist. Franklin County 2008), Hiscox v. Hiscox, 2008-Ohio-5209, 2008 WL 4456964 (Ohio Ct. App. 7th Dist. Columbiana County 2008), McLaughlin v. McLaughlin, 178 Ohio App.3d 419, 2008-Ohio-5284, 898 N.E.2d 79 (2008), Shreyer v. Shreyer, 2008-Ohio-7013, 2008 WL 5451376 (Ohio Ct. App. 5th Dist. Fairfield County 2008), Ebbinghaus v. Ebbinghaus, 2009-Ohio-1000, 2009 WL 580793 (Ohio Ct. App. 11th Dist. Geauga County 2009) and Mandelbaum v. Mandelbaum, 121 Ohio St.3d 433, 2009-Ohio-1222, 905 N.E.2d 172 (2009) (trial court only retains continuing juris-

original action with limited exceptions.[5] The motion must be served in
accordance with the rules for service of process in an original action.[6]

diction over spousal support if specifically stated within the decree), and Davis v.
Mendez, 2008-Ohio-5768, 2008 WL 4823367 (Ohio Ct. App. 2d Dist. Greene County
2008).

[5]Redman v. Francis, 2006-Ohio-3640, 2006 WL 1976215 (Ohio Ct. App. 5th Dist.
Licking County 2006) (trial court granted wife relief she requested, based upon
husband's motion to show cause, even though she failed to file a motion to invoke the
court's continuing jurisdiction).

[6]Civ. R. 75(J) (providing service of process in accordance with Civ. R. 4 to 4.6);
Blake v. Heistan, 99 Ohio App. 3d 84, 649 N.E.2d 1304 (3d Dist. Mercer County
1994); State ex rel. Soukup v. Celebrezze, 83 Ohio St. 3d 549, 1998-Ohio-8, 700
N.E.2d 1278 (1998); Farley v. Farley, 2000 WL 1231091 (Ohio Ct. App. 10th Dist.
Franklin County 2000); Whaley v. Whaley, 2006-Ohio-770, 2006 WL 400139 (Ohio Ct.
App. 2d Dist. Montgomery County 2006); Eden v. Eden, 2003-Ohio-356, 2003 WL
187527 (Ohio Ct. App. 9th Dist. Lorain County 2003); Wellman v. Kisel, 2003-Ohio-
1919, 2003 WL 1877823 (Ohio Ct. App. 9th Dist. Lorain County 2003); Fuller v.
Fuller, 2000 WL 807224 (Ohio Ct. App. 4th Dist. Lawrence County 2000); Giffen v.
Giffen, 2002-Ohio-5477, 2002 WL 31259936 (Ohio Ct. App. 5th Dist. Stark County
2002); Grubic v. Grubic, 2003-Ohio-3680, 2003 WL 21570497 (Ohio Ct. App. 8th Dist.
Cuyahoga County 2003); Corrao v. Corrao, 2006-Ohio-1686, 2006 WL 847119 (Ohio
Ct. App. 11th Dist. Lake County 2006); State ex rel. Seaton v. Holmes, 100 Ohio St.
3d 265, 2003-Ohio-5897, 798 N.E.2d 375 (2003); Morell v. Morell, 2004-Ohio-3478,
2004 WL 1472071 (Ohio Ct. App. 8th Dist. Cuyahoga County 2004); Szymczak v.
Szymczak, 136 Ohio App. 3d 706, 737 N.E.2d 980 (8th Dist. Cuyahoga County 2000);
Cowgill v. Cowgill, 2003-Ohio-610, 2003 WL 264327 (Ohio Ct. App. 2d Dist. Darke
County 2003); Nicholson v. Nicholson, 2001 WL 1167151 (Ohio Ct. App. 8th Dist.
Cuyahoga County 2001); Hansen v. Hansen, 21 Ohio App. 3d 216, 486 N.E.2d 1252
(3d Dist. Seneca County 1985); Pulice v. Collins, 2006-Ohio-3950, 2006 WL 2170601
(Ohio Ct. App. 8th Dist. Cuyahoga County 2006); Hamad v. Hamad, 2008-Ohio-4111,
2008 WL 3522450 (Ohio Ct. App. 10th Dist. Franklin County 2008); Regueiro v.
Regueiro, 2008-Ohio-4046, 2008 WL 3271022 (Ohio Ct. App. 9th Dist. Medina County
2008); Stuber v. Stuber, 2007-Ohio-3981, 2007 WL 2231445 (Ohio Ct. App. 3d Dist.
Allen County 2007), appeal not allowed, 116 Ohio St. 3d 1476, 2008-Ohio-153, 879
N.E.2d 784 (2008); Bierce v. Howell, 2007-Ohio-3050, 2007 WL 1748517 (Ohio Ct.
App. 5th Dist. Delaware County 2007) and Evans v. Evans, 2008-Ohio-2640, 2008 WL
2572025 (Ohio Ct. App. 5th Dist. Fairfield County 2008) (after initial service of motion, pursuant to Civ. R. 4 through 4.6, service of hearing notices for contempt actions
shall be upon a party's attorney, if represented); Redman v. Francis, 2006-Ohio-3640,
2006 WL 1976215 (Ohio Ct. App. 5th Dist. Licking County 2006) and Bellamy v.
Bellamy, 110 Ohio App. 3d 576, 674 N.E.2d 1227 (6th Dist. Erie County 1996) (by one
party filing a contempt motion for nonpayment of support and properly invoking the
court's continuing jurisdiction, the court held that the filing of the motion extended
its jurisdiction to consider other aspects related to the motion, including modification
of support, as long as proper notice); Mastandrea v. Spiros, 1995 WL 428545 (Ohio
Ct. App. 8th Dist. Cuyahoga County 1995) and Safranek v. Safranek, 2002-Ohio-
5066, 2002 WL 31123864 (Ohio Ct. App. 8th Dist. Cuyahoga County 2002) (court
holds that a motion to show cause is not sufficient to modify a support order); Hansen
v. Hansen, 132 Ohio App. 3d 795, 726 N.E.2d 557 (1st Dist. Hamilton County 1999)
and Ewing v. Ewing, 2007-Ohio-7108, 2007 WL 4563458 (Ohio Ct. App. 5th Dist.
Licking County 2007) (contempt proceedings during the pendency of a divorce action
is a separate independent proceeding wherein service shall be upon the party pursuant to Civ. R. 4 through Civ. R. 4.6); Hiscox v. Hiscox, 2007-Ohio-1124, 2007 WL
755384 (Ohio Ct. App. 7th Dist. Columbiana County 2007) (contempt proceedings
during the pendency of a divorce action shall be served upon the party, pursuant to

Therefore, only the issues raised in the properly served motion(s) will be addressed at time of hearing. The court keeps jurisdiction to enforce post-decree matters, even if both parties have subsequently established residency elsewhere,[7] until another court properly assumes jurisdiction.

§ 11:3 Preliminary considerations—Jurisdiction—Subject matter jurisdiction

The legitimate extent of the trial court's jurisdiction in divorce cases depends on four factors: (1) the court's subject matter jurisdiction over the marital relationship; (2) the court's ability to obtain personal jurisdiction over the defendant; (3) the location of the parties' property; and (4) the determination of which court has proper jurisdiction to establish a custody and parenting time order when the parties have minor children.

In order for a trial court to grant a divorce, the court must have subject matter jurisdiction over the marital relationship.[1] The trial court may exercise subject matter jurisdiction in a divorce action if the plaintiff has satisfied the six-month residency requirement set forth in RC 3105.03.[2] Once the residency requirement is satisfied, the trial court may enter a decree terminating the plaintiff's marriage

---

Civ. R. 4 through Civ. R. 4.6, unless contemptor is proven to have actual notice of the contempt proceedings); Laver v. Laver, 2008-Ohio-6068, 2008 WL 4965168 (Ohio Ct. App. 3rd Dist. Henry County 2008) and Tuckosh v. Cummings, 2008-Ohio-5819, 2008 WL 4838127 (Ohio Ct. App. 7th Dist. Belmont County 2008) (trial court's continuing jurisdiction is invoked by filing a post decree motion to modify child support with service pursuant to Civ. R. 4 through 4.6), and Heary v. Heary, 2009-Ohio-2272, 2009 WL 1346618 (Ohio Ct. App. 8th Dist. Cuyahoga County 2009).

[7]RC 3127.16 and RC 3127.17 (a court of this state has exclusive, continuing jurisdiction over child custody matters until a court of another state properly assumes jurisdiction by determining that the child, child's parents, and any person acting as a parent do not presently reside in the initiating state); Weinberger v. Weinberger, 43 Ohio App. 2d 129, 72 Ohio Op. 2d 325, 334 N.E.2d 514 (9th Dist. Summit County 1974); Crockett v. Crockett, 9th Dist. No. 9487 (May 28, 1980) (holding that requirement of Civ. R. 4.3 that one party in an action be an Ohio resident before process provision regarding non-resident service may be used does not apply in action for modification or enforcement of divorce decree); Ashburn v. Roth, 2007-Ohio-2995, 2007 WL 1731426 (Ohio Ct. App. 12th Dist. Butler County 2007); North v. North, 2008-Ohio-6438, 2008 WL 5159844 (Ohio Ct. App. 9th Dist. Summit County 2008), and Lafi v. Lafi, 2008-Ohio-1871, 2008 WL 1759083 (Ohio Ct. App. 2d Dist. Miami County 2008), appeal not allowed, 119 Ohio St. 3d 1413, 2008-Ohio-3880, 891 N.E.2d 771 (2008).

[Section 11:3]

[1]Williams v. State of N. C., 325 U.S. 226, 65 S. Ct. 1092, 89 L. Ed. 1577, 157 A.L.R. 1366 (1945); Donovan v. Templeton, 1997 WL 337657 (Ohio Ct. App. 2d Dist. Montgomery County 1997); Ramsey v. Ramsey, 1992 WL 127679 (Ohio Ct. App. 2d Dist. Montgomery County 1992).

[2]McMaken v. McMaken, 96 Ohio App. 3d 402, 645 N.E.2d 113 (2d Dist. Montgomery County 1994); Rijo v. Rijo, 1995 WL 35730 (Ohio Ct. App. 1st Dist. Hamilton County 1995); Bandell v. Bandell, 1996 WL 199563 (Ohio Ct. App. 9th Dist. Lorain County 1996); Reese v. Reese, 1997 WL 272368 (Ohio Ct. App. 8th Dist.

even if the court is unable to obtain personal jurisdiction over the defendant.[3]

§ 11:4 Preliminary considerations—Jurisdiction—Personal jurisdiction

Where the defendant resides out of the state of Ohio, the court must have a basis for asserting personal jurisdiction over him or her. The Court may obtain personal jurisdiction if the defendant is amenable to service under the rules governing long-arm jurisdiction[1] and if so, the court must determine whether granting jurisdiction under the statute and rule would deprive the non-resident defendant of due process under the Fourteenth Amendment of the United States Constitution.[2] The Court held in *Fraiberg v. Cuyahoga Cty. Ct. of*

Cuyahoga County 1997); Wetzel v. Spears, 2001-Ohio-2536, 2001 WL 1913874 (Ohio Ct. App. 4th Dist. Scioto County 2001); Polakova v. Polak, 107 Ohio App. 3d 745, 669 N.E.2d 498 (1st Dist. Hamilton County 1995); Dobson v. Dobson, 1998 WL 519255 (Ohio Ct. App. 5th Dist. Stark County 1998); Ahmad v. Ahmad, 2001 WL 1518116 (Ohio Ct. App. 6th Dist. Lucas County 2001); Barth v. Barth, 113 Ohio St. 3d 27, 2007-Ohio-973, 862 N.E.2d 496 (2007); Ortiz v. Ortiz, 2006-Ohio-3488, 2006 WL 1851730 (Ohio Ct. App. 7th Dist. Jefferson County 2006); Mir v. Birjandi, 2007-Ohio-3444, 2007 WL 1934219 (Ohio Ct. App. 2d Dist. Greene County 2007); Hall v. Hall, 2007-Ohio-2449, 2007 WL 1463358 (Ohio Ct. App. 5th Dist. Licking County 2007); Rosen v. Celebrezze, 172 Ohio App. 3d 478, 2008-Ohio-3771, 875 N.E.2d 659 (8th Dist. Cuyahoga County 2007), cause dismissed, 115 Ohio St. 3d 1470, 2007-Ohio-5735, 875 N.E.2d 625 (2007), order vacated, 115 Ohio St. 3d 1476, 2007-Ohio-5820, 875 N.E.2d 629 (2007) and judgment rev'd, 117 Ohio St. 3d 241, 2008-Ohio-853, 883 N.E.2d 420 (2008); Pickel v. Ghouati, 2009-Ohio-1644, 2009 WL 903299 (Ohio Ct. App. 2d Dist. Montgomery County 2009).

[3]Estin v. Estin, 334 U.S. 541, 68 S. Ct. 1213, 92 L. Ed. 1561, 1 A.L.R.2d 1412 (1948); McGill v. Deming, 44 Ohio St. 645, 11 N.E. 118 (1887); Collins v. Collins, 165 Ohio App. 3d 71, 2006-Ohio-181, 844 N.E.2d 910 (1st Dist. Hamilton County 2006); Depaulitte v. Depaulitte, 138 Ohio App. 3d 780, 742 N.E.2d 659 (2d Dist. Montgomery County 2000); Cornelius v. Cornelius, 1999 WL 999798 (Ohio Ct. App. 2d Dist. Darke County 1999); Stanek v. Stanek, 1994 WL 519826 (Ohio Ct. App. 12th Dist. Butler County 1994); Nain v. Nain, 1994 WL 411690 (Ohio Ct. App. 9th Dist. Lorain County 1994); Hager v. Hager, 79 Ohio App. 3d 239, 607 N.E.2d 63 (2d Dist. Greene County 1992); Kvinta v. Kvinta, 2009-Ohio-828, 2009 WL 449145 (Ohio Ct. App. 5th Dist. Richland County 2009).

[Section 11:4]

[1]Civ. R. 4.3(A) and RC 2307.382.

[2]Hudgins v. Hudgins, 80 Ohio App. 3d 707, 610 N.E.2d 582 (3d Dist. Henry County 1992) citing, Ohio State Tie & Timber, Inc. v. Paris Lumber Co., 8 Ohio App. 3d 236, 456 N.E.2d 1309 (10th Dist. Franklin County 1982); Depaulitte v. Depaulitte, 138 Ohio App. 3d 780, 742 N.E.2d 659 (2d Dist. Montgomery County 2000); Kvinta v. Kvinta, 2003-Ohio-2884, 2003 WL 21291049 (Ohio Ct. App. 10th Dist. Franklin County 2003); Keller v. Keller, 2005-Ohio-5258, 2005 WL 2416022 (Ohio Ct. App. 6th Dist. Erie County 2005); Stanek v. Stanek, 1994 WL 519826 (Ohio Ct. App. 12th Dist. Butler County 1994); State ex rel. Toma v. Corrigan, 92 Ohio St. 3d 589, 2001-Ohio-1289, 752 N.E.2d 281 (2001); Toma v. Toma, 2003-Ohio-4344, 2003 WL 21957022 (Ohio Ct. App. 8th Dist. Cuyahoga County 2003); State ex rel. Atty. Gen. v. Grand Tobacco, 171 Ohio App. 3d 551, 2007-Ohio-418, 871 N.E.2d 1255 (10th Dist. Franklin County 2007), appeal not allowed, 114 Ohio St. 3d 1426, 2007-Ohio-2904, 868 N.E.2d

Common Pleas, Domestic Relations Div.,[3] that it possessed personal jurisdiction over the defendant because he owned property in Ohio (Civ. R. 4.3(A)(6)) and because he had previously resided in the marital relationship in Ohio (Civ. R. 4.3(A)(8)). Merely visiting Ohio for one week with the intention to relocate here was held to be insufficient to confer personal jurisdiction over the defendant even though the defendant attempted to purchase real estate during that trip.[4] However, a husband's repeated visits to the State of Ohio and his threatening telephone calls were sufficient to obtain personal jurisdiction over husband, pursuant to Civ. R. 4.3(A)(9) and RC 2307.382, for a civil protection order.[5]

Although the trial court may terminate the marriage without first obtaining personal jurisdiction over the defendant, the court must have in personam jurisdiction over the defendant before it can impose a personal obligation or duty, or terminate the defendant's rights.[6] Thus, the trial court cannot order child and/or spousal support,[7] award

---

680 (2007); Signom v. Schenck Fuels, Inc., 2007 WL 1726492 (S.D. Ohio 2007); West v. Trace Am., Inc., 2007-Ohio-3311, 2007 WL 1859262 (Ohio Ct. App. 1st Dist. Hamilton County 2007); Buflod v. Von Wilhendorf, LLC, 2007-Ohio-347, 2007 WL 210790 (Ohio Ct. App. 12th Dist. Warren County 2007); Beegle v. Beegle, 2007-Ohio-4314, 2007 WL 2398480 (Ohio Ct. App. 10th Dist. Franklin County 2007); Prouse, Dash & Crouch, L.L.P. v. DiMarco, 175 Ohio App. 3d 467, 2008-Ohio-919, 887 N.E.2d 1211 (8th Dist. Cuyahoga County 2008), appeal not allowed, 119 Ohio St. 3d 1415, 2008-Ohio-3880, 891 N.E.2d 772 (2008); Dobos v. Dobos, 179 Ohio App.3d 173, 2008-Ohio-5665, 901 N.E.2d 248 (2008).

[3]Fraiberg v. Cuyahoga Cty. Court of Common Pleas, Domestic Relations Div., 76 Ohio St. 3d 374, 1996-Ohio-384, 667 N.E.2d 1189 (1996).

[4]Depaulitte v. Depaulitte, 138 Ohio App. 3d 780, 742 N.E.2d 659 (2d Dist. Montgomery County 2000), appeal dismissed as improvidently allowed, 91 Ohio St. 3d 1201, 2001-Ohio-229, 740 N.E.2d 1103 (2001).

[5]Haas v. Semrad, 2007-Ohio-2828, 2007 WL 1653032 (Ohio Ct. App. 6th Dist. Lucas County 2007) and Dobos v. Dobos, 179 Ohio App.3d 173, 2008-Ohio-5665, 901 N.E.2d 248 (2008).

[6]International Shoe Co. v. State of Wash., Office of Unemployment Compensation and Placement, 326 U.S. 310, 66 S. Ct. 154, 90 L. Ed. 95, 161 A.L.R. 1057 (1945); Stanek v. Stanek, 1994 WL 519826 (Ohio Ct. App. 12th Dist. Butler County 1994); Woods v. Woods, 1982 WL 3609 (Ohio Ct. App. 4th Dist. Lawrence County 1982); Knotts v. Anderson, 2001-Ohio-7083, 2001 WL 1658121 (Ohio Ct. App. 2d Dist. Clark County 2001); Tagg v. Tagg, 7th Dist. No. 80-J-9 (July 16, 1980); Kvinta v. Kvinta, 2009-Ohio-828, 2009 WL 449145 (Ohio Ct. App. 5th Dist. Richland County 2009).

[7]Estin v. Estin, 334 U.S. 541, 68 S. Ct. 1213, 92, 92 L. Ed. 1561, 1 A.L.R.2d 1412 (1948); Crozier v. Hafer, 1999 WL 194205 (Ohio Ct. App. 9th Dist. Wayne County 1999); Cornelius v. Cornelius, 1999 WL 999798 (Ohio Ct. App. 2d Dist. Darke County 1999); Meadows v. Meadows, 73 Ohio App. 3d 316, 596 N.E.2d 1146 (3d Dist. Hancock County 1992); Wayne Cty. Bur. of Support v. Wolfe, 71 Ohio App. 3d 765, 595 N.E.2d 421 (9th Dist. Wayne County 1991); Bigley v. Bigley, 90 Ohio App. 3d 310, 629 N.E.2d 45 (9th Dist. Wayne County 1993); Hudgins v. Hudgins, 80 Ohio App. 3d 707, 610 N.E.2d 582 (3d Dist. Henry County 1992); Ades v. Ades, 70 Ohio App. 487, 25 Ohio Op. 214, 37 Ohio L. Abs. 58, 45 N.E.2d 416 (1st Dist. Hamilton County 1942); Watson v. Watson, 2007-Ohio-468, 2007 WL 314380 (Ohio Ct. App. 11th Dist. Portage County 2007); Beegle v. Beegle, 2007-Ohio-4314, 2007 WL 2398480

custody and/or parenting time,[8] or divide property[9] unless the defendant is under the trial court's jurisdiction.

The court may obtain personal jurisdiction over a defendant, who resides in Ohio, either by (1) service of process pursuant to Civ. R. 4 to 4.2, (2) the voluntary appearance and submission of the defendant or his legal representative, or (3) certain acts of the defendant or his legal representative, which constitute an involuntary submission to the jurisdiction of the court. If defendant fails to assert lack of personal jurisdiction, it is waived.[10] Any judgment rendered by a court

---

(Ohio Ct. App. 10th Dist. Franklin County 2007) (however, in personam jurisdiction over obligee is not necessary for Ohio courts to accept registration of another state's child support order for enforcement purposes, but will not allow modification of a foreign decree unless the Ohio Court has in personam jurisdiction over obligee).

[8]Kulko v. Superior Court of California In and For City and County of San Francisco, 436 U.S. 84, 98 S. Ct. 1690, 56 L. Ed. 2d 132 (1978); May v. Anderson, 345 U.S. 528, 73 S. Ct. 840, 97 L. Ed. 1221, 67 Ohio L. Abs. 468 (1953); Harvey v. Bentley, 74 Ohio App. 3d 375, 599 N.E.2d 284 (2d Dist. Montgomery County 1991); Van Kan v. Mattheus, 1999 WL 476139 (Ohio Ct. App. 11th Dist. Geauga County 1999); Smith v. Smith, 1993 WL 370824 (Ohio Ct. App. 5th Dist. Guernsey County 1993); Lonigro v. Lonigro, 1988 WL 79315 (Ohio Ct. App. 2d Dist. Montgomery County 1988); James v. James, 1978 WL 217531 (Ohio Ct. App. 5th Dist. Stark County 1978); A.S. v. D.G., 2007-Ohio-1556, 2007 WL 959902 (Ohio Ct. App. 12th Dist. Clinton County 2007); In re B.P.H., 2007-Ohio-1366, 2007 WL 881546 (Ohio Ct. App. 12th Dist. Butler County 2007).

[9]Stanek v. Stanek, 1994 WL 519826 (Ohio Ct. App. 12th Dist. Butler County 1994); Nain v. Nain, 1994 WL 411690 (Ohio Ct. App. 9th Dist. Lorain County 1994); Collins v. Collins, 165 Ohio App. 3d 71, 2006-Ohio-181, 844 N.E.2d 910 (1st Dist. Hamilton County 2006); Seevers v. Seevers, 1990 WL 210852 (Ohio Ct. App. 12th Dist. Clinton County 1990); Maffucci v. Maffucci, 1986 WL 14568 (Ohio Ct. App. 11th Dist. Ashtabula County 1986); Watson v. Watson, 2007-Ohio-468, 2007 WL 314380 (Ohio Ct. App. 11th Dist. Portage County 2007).

[10]Maryhew v. Yova, 11 Ohio St. 3d 154, 464 N.E.2d 538 (1984); Beachler v. Beachler, 2007-Ohio-1220, 2007 WL 805526 (Ohio Ct. App. 12th Dist. Preble County 2007); Jones v. Jordan, 2007-Ohio-2519, 2007 WL 1508255 (Ohio Ct. App. 8th Dist. Cuyahoga County 2007); Citibank (South Dakota) N.A. v. Fischer, 2007-Ohio-1322, 2007 WL 866996 (Ohio Ct. App. 6th Dist. Sandusky County 2007); Kostoglou v. D & A Trucking and Excavating Inc., 2007-Ohio-3399, 2007 WL 1898510 (Ohio Ct. App. 7th Dist. Mahoning County 2007); In re Guardianship of Tracey, 2007-Ohio-2310, 2007 WL 1395479 (Ohio Ct. App. 11th Dist. Trumbull County 2007); In re B.P.H., 2007-Ohio-1366, 2007 WL 881546 (Ohio Ct. App. 12th Dist. Butler County 2007); Schilling v. Ball, 2007-Ohio-889, 2007 WL 634418 (Ohio Ct. App. 11th Dist. Lake County 2007); Rahawangi v. Alsamman, 2006-Ohio-3163, 2006 WL 1705125 (Ohio Ct. App. 8th Dist. Cuyahoga County 2006); Gliozzo v. Univ. Urologists of Cleveland, Inc., 114 Ohio St. 3d 141, 2007-Ohio-3762, 870 N.E.2d 714 (2007); Beegle v. Beegle, 2007-Ohio-4314, 2007 WL 2398480 (Ohio Ct. App. 10th Dist. Franklin County 2007); Abuhilwa v. O'Brien, 2007-Ohio-4328, 2007 WL 2405723 (Ohio Ct. App. 2d Dist. Montgomery County 2007), appeal not allowed, 116 Ohio St. 3d 1459, 2007-Ohio-6803, 878 N.E.2d 35 (2007); Smoske v. Sicher, 2007-Ohio-5617, 2007 WL 3052208 (Ohio Ct. App. 11th Dist. Geauga County 2007); State ex rel. Athens Cty. Dept. of Job & Family Servs. v. Martin, 2008-Ohio-1849, 2008 WL 1758896 (Ohio Ct. App. 4th Dist. Athens County 2008), appeal not allowed, 119 Ohio St. 3d 1448, 2008-Ohio-4487, 893 N.E.2d 518 (2008); In re Guardianship of Thomas, 2008-Ohio-2409, 2008 WL 2081274 (Ohio Ct. App. 7th Dist. Monroe County 2008); Regueiro v. Regueiro, 2008-Ohio-4046, 2008 WL 3271022 (Ohio Ct. App. 9th Dist. Medina County 2008);

that has not acquired personal jurisdiction, and defendant has not waived, is void ab initio, not merely voidable. Service by publication, pursuant to Civil Rule 4.4, is not sufficient to establish personal jurisdiction over the defendant.[11]

Where the defendant resides in a foreign country, compliance with any applicable Hague Service Convention sections is mandatory.[12] In *Ward v. Ludwig*,[13] the court held that because West Germany had rejected Article 10 of the Hague Service Convention and chose to follow Article 5 instead, it was mandatory that divorce papers be served to a central authority who would serve the papers only if they had been translated into German. However, the trial court, in *In re D.C.*,[14] held that service of a motion for permanent custody by registered mail, directly upon the defendant, satisfied Civ. R. 4.3 and 4.5's requirements since Italy recognized Article 10 of the Hague Service Convention.

§ 11:5 Preliminary considerations—Jurisdiction—Property division

The trial court in a divorce action is required to equitably divide all of the parties' property.[1] The court has broad discretion to divide and

---

Evans v. Evans, 2008-Ohio-5695, 2008 WL 4787582 (Ohio Ct. App. 10th Dist. Franklin County 2008).

[11]Sutovich v. Sutovich, 120 Ohio App. 473, 29 Ohio Op. 2d 371, 200 N.E.2d 716 (1st Dist. Hamilton County 1964); Kurtz v. Kurtz, 71 Ohio App. 3d 176, 593 N.E.2d 322 (6th Dist. Erie County 1991); Salyer v. Salyer, 1990 WL 16510 (Ohio Ct. App. 3d Dist. Marion County 1990); Fancher v. Fancher, 8 Ohio App. 3d 79, 455 N.E.2d 1344 (1st Dist. Hamilton County 1982); Shonk v. Shonk, 16 Ohio Misc. 123, 45 Ohio Op. 2d 86, 241 N.E.2d 178 (C.P. 1968); Wellman v. Wellman, 1978 WL 215292 (Ohio Ct. App. 9th Dist. Lorain County 1978); Meadows v. Meadows, 73 Ohio App. 3d 316, 596 N.E.2d 1146 (3d Dist. Hancock County 1992).

[12]Collins v. Collins, 165 Ohio App. 3d 71, 2006-Ohio-181, 844 N.E.2d 910 (1st Dist. Hamilton County 2006); Okubo v. Shimizu, 2002-Ohio-2624, 2002 WL 1042086 (Ohio Ct. App. 2d Dist. Greene County 2002); Meek v. Nova Steel Processing, Inc., 124 Ohio App. 3d 367, 706 N.E.2d 374 (2d Dist. Miami County 1997); Linquist v. Drossel, 2006-Ohio-5712, 2006 WL 3087705 (Ohio Ct. App. 5th Dist. Stark County 2006).

[13]Ward v. Ludwig, 149 Ohio App. 3d 687, 2002-Ohio-5948, 778 N.E.2d 650 (4th Dist. Pike County 2002).

[14]In re D.C., 2007-Ohio-2344, 2007 WL 1427471 (Ohio Ct. App. 9th Dist. Summit County 2007).

[Section 11:5]

[1]RC 3105.171. Berish v. Berish, 69 Ohio St. 2d 318, 23 Ohio Op. 3d 296, 432 N.E.2d 183 (1982); Patterson v. Patterson, 2006-Ohio-1786, 2006 WL 902414 (Ohio Ct. App. 12th Dist. Preble County 2006); Hanna v. Hanna, 2005-Ohio-4868, 2005 WL 2249584 (Ohio Ct. App. 6th Dist. Lucas County 2005); Didisse v. Didisse, 2004-Ohio-6811, 2004 WL 2914102 (Ohio Ct. App. 7th Dist. Belmont County 2004); O'Brien v. O'Brien, 2004-Ohio-5780, 2004 WL 2438831 (Ohio Ct. App. 2d Dist. Greene County 2004); Merriman v. Merriman, 2004-Ohio-3511, 2004 WL 1486837 (Ohio Ct. App. 11th Dist. Portage County 2004); Didick v. Didick, 2002-Ohio-5182, 2002 WL 31163775 (Ohio Ct. App. 7th Dist. Carroll County 2002); Newsom v. Newsom,

distribute property.[2] The division of property located within the state

2002-Ohio-1317, 2002 WL 433578 (Ohio Ct. App. 10th Dist. Franklin County 2002); Weaver v. Weaver, 2006-Ohio-4698, 2006 WL 2598393 (Ohio Ct. App. 5th Dist. Licking County 2006); Weisbecker v. Weisbecker, 2006-Ohio-5840, 2006 WL 3187157 (Ohio Ct. App. 12th Dist. Butler County 2006); Lawson v. Lawson, 2006-Ohio-6890, 2006 WL 3775827 (Ohio Ct. App. 5th Dist. Coshocton County 2006); Hepfner v. Hepfner, 2007-Ohio-595, 2007 WL 446050 (Ohio Ct. App. 7th Dist. Columbiana County 2007); Metz v. Metz, 2007-Ohio-549, 2007 WL 431014 (Ohio Ct. App. 1st Dist. Hamilton County 2007), appeal not allowed, 114 Ohio St. 3d 1480, 2007-Ohio-3699, 870 N.E.2d 732 (2007); Wayland v. Wayland, 2007-Ohio-1149, 2007 WL 764814 (Ohio Ct. App. 5th Dist. Delaware County 2007), appeal not allowed, 114 Ohio St. 3d 1482, 2007-Ohio-3699, 870 N.E.2d 733 (2007); Thomas v. Thomas, 171 Ohio App. 3d 272, 2007-Ohio-2016, 870 N.E.2d 263 (1st Dist. Hamilton County 2007); Grosnickle v. Grosnickle, 2007-Ohio-3613, 2007 WL 2028919 (Ohio Ct. App. 12th Dist. Warren County 2007); Beagle v. Beagle, 2008-Ohio-764, 2008 WL 501092 (Ohio Ct. App. 10th Dist. Franklin County 2008); Brady v. Brady, 2008-Ohio-1657, 2008 WL 919685 (Ohio Ct. App. 11th Dist. Portage County 2008); Dewsnap v. Dewsnap, 2008-Ohio-4433, 2008 WL 4058100 (Ohio Ct. App. 12th Dist. Clermont County 2008); Downey v. Downey, 2007-Ohio-6294, 2008 WL 4179863 (Ohio Ct. App. 9th Dist. Summit County 2007); Downs v. Downs, 2008-Ohio-3702, 2008 WL 2853675 (Ohio Ct. App. 4th Dist. Ross County 2008); Grove v. Grove, 2008-Ohio-1552, 2008 WL 852476 (Ohio Ct. App. 7th Dist. Jefferson County 2008); Harkey v. Harkey, 2008-Ohio-1027, 2008 WL 625218 (Ohio Ct. App. 11th Dist. Lake County 2008); Kestner v. Kestner, 173 Ohio App. 3d 632, 2007-Ohio-6222, 879 N.E.2d 849 (7th Dist. Columbiana County 2007); Lewis v. Lewis, 2008-Ohio-3342, 2008 WL 2609462 (Ohio Ct. App. 7th Dist. Jefferson County 2008); Moore v. Moore, 2007-Ohio-4355, 2007 WL 2410543 (Ohio Ct. App. 12th Dist. Clermont County 2007); Stump v. Stump, 2007-Ohio-6553, 2007 WL 4293302 (Ohio Ct. App. 3d Dist. Logan County 2007); Wenger v. Wenger, 2007-Ohio-6003, 2007 WL 3342443 (Ohio Ct. App. 9th Dist. Wayne County 2007); Westhoven v. Westhoven, 2008-Ohio-2875, 2008 WL 2390817 (Ohio Ct. App. 6th Dist. Ottawa County 2008); Worrell v. Worrell, No. 06 AP 1147 (10th Dist. March 4, 2008); Clemens v. Clemens, 2008-Ohio-4730, 2008 WL 4278216 (Ohio Ct. App. 2d Dist. Greene County 2008); Comella v. Comella, 2008-Ohio-6673, 2008 WL 5259731 (Ohio Ct. App. 8th Dist. Cuyahoga County 2008); Faller v. Faller, 2008-Ohio-6638, 2008 WL 5245571 (Ohio Ct. App. 7th Dist. Mahoning County 2008); Hackman v. Hackman, 2009-Ohio-820, 2009 WL 444336 (Ohio Ct. App. 10th Dist. Franklin County 2009); Harrington v. Harrington, 2008-Ohio-6888, 2008 WL 5393138 (Ohio Ct. App. 4th Dist. Gallia County 2008); Haynes v. Owens-Haynes, 2008-Ohio-4963, 2008 WL 4379589 (Ohio Ct. App. 12th Dist. Clermont County 2008); Hittle v. Hittle, 2009-Ohio-1286, 2009 WL 726028 (Ohio Ct. App. 2d Dist. Darke County 2009); Najmi v. Najmi, 2008-Ohio-4405, 2008 WL 4023719 (Ohio Ct. App. 9th Dist. Lorain County 2008); Ulliman v. Ulliman, 2008-Ohio-3876, 2008 WL 2942213 (Ohio Ct. App. 2d Dist. Montgomery County 2008).

[2]Martin v. Martin, 18 Ohio St. 3d 292, 480 N.E.2d 1112, 18 O.B.R. 342 (1985); Middendorf v. Middendorf, 82 Ohio St. 3d 397, 1998-Ohio-403, 696 N.E.2d 575 (1998); Koblitz v. Koblitz, 2005-Ohio-6723, 2005 WL 3475771 (Ohio Ct. App. 8th Dist. Cuyahoga County 2005); Drake v. Drake, 2002-Ohio-6106, 2002 WL 31502073 (Ohio Ct. App. 12th Dist. Butler County 2002); Siefker v. Siefker, 2006-Ohio-5154, 2006 WL 2795596 (Ohio Ct. App. 3d Dist. Putnam County 2006); Biro v. Biro, 2007-Ohio-3191, 2007 WL 1810478 (Ohio Ct. App. 11th Dist. Lake County 2007); Doyle v. Doyle, 2007-Ohio-2554, 2007 WL 1531419 (Ohio Ct. App. 12th Dist. Warren County 2007); Phillips v. Phillips, 2007-Ohio-3368, 2007 WL 1881318 (Ohio Ct. App. 11th Dist. Ashtabula County 2007); Galloway v. Khan, 2006-Ohio-6637, 2006 WL 3703360 (Ohio Ct. App. 10th Dist. Franklin County 2006), appeal not allowed, 113 Ohio St. 3d 1490, 2007-Ohio-1986, 865 N.E.2d 914 (2007); Cardiff v. Cardiff, 2006-Ohio-6624, 2006 WL 3691658 (Ohio Ct. App. 4th Dist. Jackson County 2006); Woofter v. Woofter,

may be accomplished either directly or indirectly. The court may indirectly affect the distribution of property by declaring the extent of the parties' rights with respect to the property in question, and ordering the parties to perform whatever acts are necessary to complete the distribution of property, such as conveying title to the other party. The court may also directly affect the division of the parties' property by including in the decree language, i.e. legal description of real property or VIN number of a motor vehicle, which serves as a conveyance of particular items of property.[3] When this method is utilized, the judgment entry of divorce acts as a substitute for a quit claim deed to transfer title of real property and/or acts as a substitute for a title to transfer ownership of a motor vehicle.

The trial court's power to divide and distribute property located outside of the state is more limited. The general rule is that the trial court is without jurisdiction to directly affect the title of property lo-

---

2006-Ohio-5177, 2006 WL 2796779 (Ohio Ct. App. 11th Dist. Trumbull County 2006); Brown v. Bordenkircher, 2006-Ohio-3904, 2006 WL 2110746 (Ohio Ct. App. 7th Dist. Jefferson County 2006); Baker v. Baker, 2007-Ohio-7172, 2007 WL 4615953 (Ohio Ct. App. 4th Dist. Washington County 2007); Bils v. Bils, 2008-Ohio-4125, 2008 WL 3582803 (Ohio Ct. App. 6th Dist. Wood County 2008); Boggs v. Boggs, 2008-Ohio-1411, 2008 WL 795305 (Ohio Ct. App. 5th Dist. Delaware County 2008); David v. David, 2007-Ohio-6942, 2007 WL 4485572 (Ohio Ct. App. 11th Dist. Ashtabula County 2007); El-Badewi v. El-Badewi, 2007-Ohio-3800, 2007 WL 2163970 (Ohio Ct. App. 5th Dist. Stark County 2007); Hart v. Hart, 2007-Ohio-4905, 2007 WL 2745208 (Ohio Ct. App. 6th Dist. Huron County 2007); Kenning v. Gundrum, 2007-Ohio-4706, 2007 WL 2683515 (Ohio Ct. App. 1st Dist. Hamilton County 2007); Musleve v. Musleve, 2008-Ohio-3961, 2008 WL 3009863 (Ohio Ct. App. 5th Dist. Stark County 2008); Oberly v. Oberly, 2007-Ohio-4571, 2007 WL 2483518 (Ohio Ct. App. 2d Dist. Greene County 2007), appeal not allowed, 116 Ohio St. 3d 1478, 2008-Ohio-153, 879 N.E.2d 785 (2008); Scott v. Scott, 2008-Ohio-530, 2008 WL 351665 (Ohio Ct. App. 11th Dist. Trumbull County 2008); Smith v. Smith, 2008-Ohio-799, 2008 WL 525420 (Ohio Ct. App. 10th Dist. Franklin County 2008); Soulsby v. Soulsby, 2008-Ohio-1019, 2008 WL 623952 (Ohio Ct. App. 4th Dist. Meigs County 2008); Bostick v. Bostick, 2008-Ohio-5119, 2008 WL 4434986 (Ohio Ct. App. 8th Dist. Cuyahoga County 2008); Brickner v. Brickner, 2009-Ohio-1164, 2009 WL 683706 (Ohio Ct. App. 12th Dist. Butler County 2009); Clark v. Clark, 2009-Ohio-2803, 2009 WL 1655430 (Ohio Ct. App. 12th Dist. Butler County 2009); Cooper v. Cooper, 2008-Ohio-4731, 2008 WL 4278215 (Ohio Ct. App. 2d Dist. Greene County 2008); Day v. Day, 2009-Ohio-638, 2009 WL 353307 (Ohio Ct. App. 10th Dist. Franklin County 2009); Faller v. Faller, 2008-Ohio-6638, 2008 WL 5245571 (Ohio Ct. App. 7th Dist. Mahoning County 2008); Gordon v. Gordon, 2009-Ohio-177, 2009 WL 106653 (Ohio Ct. App. 5th Dist. Muskingum County 2009); Roberts v. Roberts, 2008-Ohio-6121, 2008 WL 5049808 (Ohio Ct. App. 10th Dist. Franklin County 2008); Nichols-Ross v. Ross, 2009-Ohio-1723, 2009 WL 975756 (Ohio Ct. App. 12th Dist. Butler County 2009); Shilling v. Shilling, 2009-Ohio-1476, 2009 WL 806856 (Ohio Ct. App. 6th Dist. Ottawa County 2009); Smith v. Smith, 2009-Ohio-2326, 2009 WL 1393351 (Ohio Ct. App. 2d Dist. Greene County 2009); Zollar v. Zollar, 2009-Ohio-1008, 2009 WL 580798 (Ohio Ct. App. 12th Dist. Butler County 2009).

[3]See Civ. R. 70; Roth v. Roth, 2008-Ohio-927, 2008 WL 599324 (Ohio Ct. App. 8th Dist. Cuyahoga County 2008).

cated in another state.[4] The court, however, may indirectly affect the title of property located outside of Ohio.[5] Thus, while an Ohio court lacks the authority to convey property located in another state, the court may order one of the parties to convey the out-of-state property. An order directing a party to convey property located in another state is entitled to full faith and credit, provided the Ohio court obtained personal jurisdiction over the party.[6]

§ 11:6 Preliminary considerations—Jurisdiction—Parental rights and responsibilities

The trial court in a divorce action is also required to make an award of custody.[1] Although the Ohio Revised Code confers jurisdiction to allocate custody upon the trial court, the court will not necessarily exercise this jurisdiction. The Uniform Child Custody Jurisdiction and Enforcement Act (UCCJEA),[2] approved by the Ohio General Assembly on January 10, 2005 and effectively replacing the UCCJA on April 11, 2005, acknowledges that several states might exercise jurisdiction over the issue of child custody.[3] The purpose of the UCCJEA is to promote cooperation between state courts and to avoid jurisdictional conflict by establishing criteria for determining which jurisdiction, among several jurisdictions, is the appropriate forum to determine the best interest of a child in a custody matter.[4] Under the UCCJEA and Parental Kidnapping Prevention Act (PKPA), Ohio courts must give

---

[4]Fall v. Eastin, 215 U.S. 1, 30 S. Ct. 3, 54 L. Ed. 65 (1909); also see 34 A.L.R. 3d 962.

[5]Groza-Vance v. Vance, 162 Ohio App. 3d 510, 2005-Ohio-3815, 834 N.E.2d 15 (10th Dist. Franklin County 2005).

[6]34 A.L.R. 3d 962.

[Section 11:6]

[1]RC 3109.04(A).

[2]RC 3127.01 to RC 3127.53.

[3]See Text Ch 17, Uniform Child Custody Jurisdiction and Enforcement Act; Parental Kidnapping Prevention Act; International Child Abduction Remedies Act.

[4]State ex rel. Morenz v. Kerr, 104 Ohio St. 3d 148, 2004-Ohio-6208, 818 N.E.2d 1162 (2004); Harper v. Harper, 2005-Ohio-3989, 2005 WL 1840019 (Ohio Ct. App. 10th Dist. Franklin County 2005), appeal not allowed, 107 Ohio St. 3d 1699, 2005-Ohio-6763, 840 N.E.2d 204 (2005); Rodriguez v. Frietze, 2004-Ohio-7121, 2004 WL 3001067 (Ohio Ct. App. 4th Dist. Athens County 2004), appeal not allowed, 105 Ohio St. 3d 1519, 2005-Ohio-1880, 826 N.E.2d 316 (2005); State ex rel. Seaton v. Holmes, 100 Ohio St. 3d 265, 2003-Ohio-5897, 798 N.E.2d 375 (2003); Graves v. Graves, 2002-Ohio-3740, 2002 WL 1626144 (Ohio Ct. App. 9th Dist. Medina County 2002); Durgans v. Durgans, 2001 WL 114983 (Ohio Ct. App. 11th Dist. Portage County 2001); Hochmuth v. Hochmuth, 1995 WL 12070 (Ohio Ct. App. 6th Dist. Huron County 1995); In re Craig, 2007-Ohio-3843, 2007 WL 2164532 (Ohio Ct. App. 11th Dist. Trumbull County 2007); Rosen v. Celebrezze, 117 Ohio St. 3d 241, 2008-Ohio-853, 883 N.E.2d 420 (2008); Trevino v. Trevino, 2007-Ohio-1874, 2007 WL 1160889 (Ohio Ct. App. 6th Dist. Lucas County 2007); Beck v. Sprik, 2008-Ohio-3197, 2008 WL 2581385 (Ohio Ct. App. 9th Dist. Medina County 2008); Lafi v. Lafi, 2008-Ohio-1871, 2008 WL 1759083 (Ohio Ct. App. 2d Dist. Miami County 2008), appeal not allowed, 119 Ohio St. 3d 1413, 2008-Ohio-3880, 891 N.E.2d 771 (2008); In

full faith and credit to valid child custody determinations of sister states.[5]

It should be noted, however, that the UCCJEA merely serves to resolve jurisdictional disputes between several states, each of which could otherwise properly exercise jurisdiction. It neither confers jurisdiction upon Ohio courts nor divests Ohio courts of the jurisdiction conferred upon them by RC 3109.04(A). Moreover, the UCCJEA does not supersede the rule that the trial court must have personal jurisdiction over the party before it may issue an order which affects a substantive right of the party.[6] However, RC 3127.07(A) allows that service of notice may be accomplished by publication on out-of-state parties if there is no other way to serve them.

§ 11:7   Preliminary considerations—Venue

Litigants must bring their action in the proper county for commencement of a divorce case. Venue connotes the locality, within the state, where an action should be heard and is governed by Civil Rule 3(B). Civil Rule 3(B)(9) specifically addresses divorce actions. However, it is not exclusive; subsections 3(B)(1) through (13) are on equal status, and any county specified therein may be an appropriate venue.[1] If venue is proper in several counties, pursuant to Rule 3(B), the plaintiff may choose the venue he or she prefers from among the several counties.[2] As a practical matter, however, venue is ordinarily based on Rule 3(B)(1) or (9) in divorce actions. The defense of improper venue,

---

re S.K., 2008-Ohio-1256, 2008 WL 740573 (Ohio Ct. App. 8th Dist. Cuyahoga County 2008); In re M.T., 178 Ohio App.3d 546, 2008-Ohio-5174, 899 N.E.2d 162 (2d Dist. Montgomery County 2008); Thebeau v. Thebeau, 2008-Ohio-4751, 2008 WL 4278127 (Ohio Ct. App. 4th Dist. Lawrence County 2008).

[5]Ashburn v. Roth, 2007-Ohio-2995, 2007 WL 1731426 (Ohio Ct. App. 12th Dist. Butler County 2007); In re Collins, 2007-Ohio-4582, 2007 WL 2492731 (Ohio Ct. App. 5th Dist. Guernsey County 2007); In re M.T., 178 Ohio App.3d 546, 2008-Ohio-5174, 899 N.E.2d 162 (2d Dist. Montgomery County 2008).

[6]See Text § 11:4, Preliminary considerations—Jurisdiction—Personal jurisdiction.

[Section 11:7]

[1]Morrison v. Steiner, 32 Ohio St. 2d 86, 61 Ohio Op. 2d 335, 290 N.E.2d 841 (1972); Reese v. Reese, 1997 WL 272368 (Ohio Ct. App. 8th Dist. Cuyahoga County 1997); Motorists Mut. v. Grimes, 2004-Ohio-1287, 2004 WL 540314 (Ohio Ct. App. 5th Dist. Stark County 2004); Rusk Industries v. Alexander, 2002-Ohio-2171, 2002 WL 850232 (Ohio Ct. App. 6th Dist. Lucas County 2002); State ex rel. Davis v. Ohio Adult Parole Authority, 2000 WL 1227298 (Ohio Ct. App. 11th Dist. Portage County 2000); Reder v. Public Employees Retirement System of Ohio, 1999 WL 315407 (Ohio Ct. App. 11th Dist. Portage County 1999); Matthews v. D'Amore, 2006-Ohio-5745, 2006 WL 3095817 (Ohio Ct. App. 10th Dist. Franklin County 2006), appeal not allowed, 113 Ohio St. 3d 1442, 2007-Ohio-1266, 863 N.E.2d 658 (2007); DeRosa v. Elliott Leveling, Inc., 2008-Ohio-3502, 2008 WL 2700006 (Ohio Ct. App. 6th Dist. Lucas County 2008); Wood v. Estate of Thomas Batta, 2008-Ohio-1400, 2008 WL 795127 (Ohio Ct. App. 8th Dist. Cuyahoga County 2008).

[2]General Motors Acceptance Corp. v. Jacks, 27 Ohio Misc. 115, 56 Ohio Op. 2d 93, 56 Ohio Op. 2d 343, 268 N.E.2d 833 (Mun. Ct. 1971); Rusk Industries v. Alexan-

pursuant to Civ. R. 12(B)(3), must be made at the inception of a case or it is waived.[3]

Civil Rule 3(B)(9) provides that proper venue in a divorce lies in the county where the plaintiff is and has been a resident for at least ninety days immediately preceding the filing of the complaint.[4] Civil Rule 3(B)(1) provides that proper venue lies in the county in which the defendant resides. Thus, if the plaintiff has been a resident of Ohio for six months and a certain county for ninety days, but the defendant is a resident of a different county, the plaintiff can file for divorce where he or she resides, where the defendant resides, or in another county if one of the other venue provisions applies. Since jurisdiction is statewide, an out-of-county defendant poses none of the problems that the out-of-state defendant poses.

The appropriate venue for an incarcerated person is the county where the party lived prior to incarceration and not the county in which the prison is located.[5]

§ 11:8 Grounds—In general

Statutory grounds, as set forth in RC 3105.01, must exist to terminate a marriage by divorce. A majority of Ohio cases state that

---

der, 2002-Ohio-2171, 2002 WL 850232 (Ohio Ct. App. 6th Dist. Lucas County 2002); Clermont County Adamh Boards v. Hogan, 1995 WL 631641 (Ohio Ct. App. 12th Dist. Clermont County 1995); Thompson v. G & D Transport, Inc., 1989 WL 98506 (Ohio Ct. App. 4th Dist. Gallia County 1989); Piqua Pizza Supply Co., Inc. v. Rutherford, 1986 WL 9088 (Ohio Ct. App. 2d Dist. Darke County 1986); American Bank of Central Ohio v. Carson, 1980 WL 353731 (Ohio Ct. App. 10th Dist. Franklin County 1980); Mentor Lagoons, Inc. v. Geldart, 1979 WL 208017 (Ohio Ct. App. 11th Dist. Lake County 1979); Nagy v. Swann, 56 Ohio Misc. 33, 10 Ohio Op. 3d 69, 385 N.E.2d 331 (C.P. 1978).

[3]Lappert v. Lappert, 1981 WL 4159 (Ohio Ct. App. 9th Dist. Summit County 1981); Smith v. Smith, 1979 WL 207363 (Ohio Ct. App. 7th Dist. Carroll County 1979); Kelly v. Kelly, 1977 WL 199733 (Ohio Ct. App. 1st Dist. Hamilton County 1977); Citibank (South Dakota) N.A. v. Fischer, 2007-Ohio-1322, 2007 WL 866996 (Ohio Ct. App. 6th Dist. Sandusky County 2007); Portman v. Mabe, 2008-Ohio-3508, 2008 WL 2718506 (Ohio Ct. App. 3d Dist. Van Wert County 2008); Morgan v. Ramby, 2008-Ohio-6194, 2008 WL 5052777 (Ohio Ct. App. 12th Dist. Warren County 2008); Pickel v. Ghouati, 2009-Ohio-1644, 2009 WL 903299 (Ohio Ct. App. 2d Dist. Montgomery County 2009).

[4]Swearingen v. Swearingen, 2007-Ohio-1241, 2007 WL 828691 (Ohio Ct. App. 10th Dist. Franklin County 2007).

[5]Wernert v. Wernert, 61 Ohio Misc. 2d 436, 579 N.E.2d 800 (C.P. 1991); State ex rel. Saunders v. Court of Common Pleas of Allen County, 34 Ohio St. 3d 15, 516 N.E.2d 232 (1987); In re Guardianship of Goins, 2003-Ohio-931, 2003 WL 685878 (Ohio Ct. App. 7th Dist. Mahoning County 2003); Gonzalez, Jr. v. Gonzalez, 1983 WL 3964 (Ohio Ct. App. 9th Dist. Lorain County 1983); Bowers v. Baughman, 29 Ohio App. 2d 277, 58 Ohio Op. 2d 492, 281 N.E.2d 201 (3d Dist. Allen County 1972).

there must be testimony from the party seeking the divorce.[1] In lieu of oral testimony at the time of hearing, the deposition of the party seeking the divorce may be presented.[2] In addition, the party seeking the divorce must support this testimony with other evidence.[3] Supporting evidence may be in the form of testimony of a corroborating witness,[4] admissions of the other party[5] or documentary evidence.[6] A minority of courts have held that a divorce may be granted, without the

---

[Section 11:8]

[1]Daniels v. Daniels, No. 2989 (Ohio Ct. App. 9th Dist. Summit County 1980) (plaintiff did not testify at trial; there were no grounds upon which to grant divorce); Brown v. Brown, 2003-Ohio-4878, 2003 WL 22120269 (Ohio Ct. App. 7th Dist. Mahoning County 2003); Ware v. Ware, 1994 WL 675685 (Ohio Ct. App. 4th Dist. Ross County 1994); Boyd v. Edwards, 1982 WL 2372 (Ohio Ct. App. 8th Dist. Cuyahoga County 1982); Reynolds v. Court of Common Pleas, Probate-Domestic Division, 1981 WL 6680 (Ohio Ct. App. 3d Dist. Marion County 1981); Hubbard v. Hubbard, 1980 WL 352002 (Ohio Ct. App. 3d Dist. Defiance County 1980), opinion vacated on reconsideration, 1980 WL 352003 (Ohio Ct. App. 3d Dist. Defiance County 1980).

[2]Wernert v. Wernert, 61 Ohio Misc. 2d 436, 579 N.E.2d 800 (C.P. 1991); Elkins v. Elkins, 1999 WL 939 (Ohio Ct. App. 12th Dist. Clermont County 1999); Reynolds v. Court of Common Pleas, Probate-Domestic Division, 1981 WL 6680 (Ohio Ct. App. 3d Dist. Marion County 1981); Ware v. Ware, 1994 WL 675685 (Ohio Ct. App. 4th Dist. Ross County 1994); Brown v. Brown, 2003-Ohio-4878, 2003 WL 22120269 (Ohio Ct. App. 7th Dist. Mahoning County 2003). Civ. R. 30(A) and 32.

[3]Civ. R. 75(M). Lesh v. Lesh, 138 Ohio St. 492, 21 Ohio Op. 362, 37 N.E.2d 383 (1941); Brooks-Lee v. Lee, 2005-Ohio-2288, 2005 WL 1109755 (Ohio Ct. App. 10th Dist. Franklin County 2005), appeal not allowed, 106 Ohio St. 3d 1545, 2005-Ohio-5343, 835 N.E.2d 727 (2005); Damschroder v. Damschroder, 1998 WL 46376 (Ohio Ct. App. 6th Dist. Lucas County 1998); Zamos v. Zamos, 1991 WL 45622 (Ohio Ct. App. 11th Dist. Portage County 1991); Brooks v. Brooks, 1989 WL 33107 (Ohio Ct. App. 2d Dist. Miami County 1989); Frick v. Frick, 1981 WL 2699 (Ohio Ct. App. 7th Dist. Columbiana County 1981).

[4]Hobbs v. Hobbs, 115 Ohio App. 536, 21 Ohio Op. 2d 200, 186 N.E.2d 134 (2d Dist. Greene County 1961); Selby v. Hershey, 1994 WL 200805 (Ohio Ct. App. 9th Dist. Summit County 1994); Mathews v. Laci, 1992 WL 93077 (Ohio Ct. App. 12th Dist. Clermont County 1992); Moser v. Moser, 72 Ohio App. 3d 575, 595 N.E.2d 518 (3d Dist. Allen County 1991); Smith v. Smith, 1985 WL 7665 (Ohio Ct. App. 2d Dist. Montgomery County 1985); Welge v. Welge, 87 Ohio App. 93, 42 Ohio Op. 315, 58 Ohio L. Abs. 314, 94 N.E.2d 208 (1st Dist. Hamilton County 1950).

[5]Thomas v. Thomas, 5 Ohio App. 3d 94, 449 N.E.2d 478 (5th Dist. Licking County 1982) (divorce may be granted upon testimony of plaintiff supported by admissions of defendant which are not the product of collusion); Toth v. Toth, 1982 WL 5805 (Ohio Ct. App. 11th Dist. Lake County 1982); Zimmie v. Zimmie, 1983 WL 5747 (Ohio Ct. App. 8th Dist. Cuyahoga County 1983), judgment aff'd in part, rev'd in part, 11 Ohio St. 3d 94, 464 N.E.2d 142, 53 A.L.R.4th 75 (1984); DeMeo v. DeMeo, 1985 WL 7438 (Ohio Ct. App. 8th Dist. Cuyahoga County 1985); Minnick v. Minnick, 1990 WL 102363 (Ohio Ct. App. 12th Dist. Madison County 1990); Marvin v. Marvin, 1997 WL 123914 (Ohio Ct. App. 11th Dist. Portage County 1997); Ahwajee v. Ahwajee, 2008-Ohio-6844, 2008 WL 5381689 (Ohio Ct. App. 5th Dist. Stark County 2008).

[6]Briers v. Briers, 1983 WL 3993 (Ohio Ct. App. 9th Dist. Summit County 1983); Taylor v. Taylor, 1989 WL 65309 (Ohio Ct. App. 2d Dist. Montgomery County 1989).

testimony of the party seeking the divorce, if other sufficient evidence is presented to establish grounds for the divorce.[7]

It is not necessary for the supporting evidence to substantiate every detail of the testimony of the party seeking the divorce.[8] The evidence, however, must substantiate the existence of the material elements essential to prove the ground for divorce alleged in the pleading.[9]

The first nine grounds for divorce are basically "fault" grounds. The tenth, living separate and apart without cohabitation for one year, is often considered "no fault ground"[10] Incompatibility, under RC 3105.01(K), is technically not a "ground" of divorce that has to be proven so much as a status that must be agreed on by both parties.[11] A no fault ground for divorce is part of the trend toward facilitating

---

[7]Wohlers v. Wohlers, 111 Ohio App. 405, 14 Ohio Op. 2d 415, 168 N.E.2d 608 (1st Dist. Hamilton County 1960) and Gordon v. Gordon, 1984 WL 6396 (Ohio Ct. App. 8th Dist. Cuyahoga County 1984).

[8]Wiley v. Wiley, 78 Ohio L. Abs. 597, 153 N.E.2d 784 (Ct. App. 7th Dist. Columbiana County 1957); Sindel v. Sindel, 1975 WL 181946 (Ohio Ct. App. 10th Dist. Franklin County 1975); Yurick v. Yurick, 1978 WL 217965 (Ohio Ct. App. 8th Dist. Cuyahoga County 1978); Butler v. Butler, 1980 WL 354106 (Ohio Ct. App. 5th Dist. Licking County 1980); Telep v. Telep, 1982 WL 2813 (Ohio Ct. App. 9th Dist. Medina County 1982); Price v. Price, 3rd Dist. No. 5-86-19 (March 13, 1987); Camera v. Camera, 1987 WL 19526 (Ohio Ct. App. 9th Dist. Lorain County 1987); Kaminski v. Kaminski, 1997 WL 89156 (Ohio Ct. App. 12th Dist. Clermont County 1997).

[9]Brown v. Brown, 50 Ohio L. Abs. 90, 76 N.E.2d 730 (Ct. App. 2d Dist. Franklin County 1947); Toth v. Toth, 1982 WL 5805 (Ohio Ct. App. 11th Dist. Lake County 1982); Weber v. Weber, 7th Dist. No. 462 (April 3, 1973); Widdowson v. Widdowson, 1985 WL 6950 (Ohio Ct. App. 2d Dist. Montgomery County 1985); Brinker v. Brinker, 1987 WL 19457 (Ohio Ct. App. 9th Dist. Summit County 1987); Hurchanik v. Hurchanik, 1987 WL 10360 (Ohio Ct. App. 12th Dist. Warren County 1987); Taylor v. Taylor, 1989 WL 65309 (Ohio Ct. App. 2d Dist. Montgomery County 1989); Zamos v. Zamos, 1991 WL 45622 (Ohio Ct. App. 11th Dist. Portage County 1991); Young v. Young, 1995 WL 912747 (Ohio Ct. App. 10th Dist. Franklin County 1995); Damschroder v. Damschroder, 1998 WL 46376 (Ohio Ct. App. 6th Dist. Lucas County 1998).

[10]Sproull v. Sproull, 1978 WL 216393 (Ohio Ct. App. 1st Dist. Hamilton County 1978); Murray v. Murray, 1989 WL 106338 (Ohio Ct. App. 7th Dist. Belmont County 1989); Ross v. Ross, No. 97AP030022 (5th Dist. Oct. 22, 1997) (The court held that RC 3105.01(H) [Imprisonment of the adverse party in a state or federal correctional institution at the time of filing the complaint] is a no-fault ground, and appears to be a minority.); Harding v. Harding, 2005-Ohio-3010, 2005 WL 1406293 (Ohio Ct. App. 8th Dist. Cuyahoga County 2005); Nolan v. Nolan, 2006-Ohio-3409, 2006 WL 1817075 (Ohio Ct. App. 11th Dist. Geauga County 2006); Broach v. Broach, 177 Ohio App. 3d 664, 2008-Ohio-4132, 895 N.E.2d 640 (2d Dist. Montgomery County 2008).

[11]Hirt v. Hirt, 2003-Ohio-2425, 2003 WL 21078093 (Ohio Ct. App. 9th Dist. Medina County 2003); Rodgers v. Henninger Rodgers, 2003-Ohio-2642, 2003 WL 21185784 (Ohio Ct. App. 5th Dist. Licking County 2003); Mahon v. Mahon, 1999 WL 1483438 (Ohio Ct. App. 11th Dist. Trumbull County 1999); Lehman v. Lehman, 72 Ohio App. 3d 68, 593 N.E.2d 447 (4th Dist. Hocking County 1991); Galloway v. Khan, 2006-Ohio-6637, 2006 WL 3703360 (Ohio Ct. App. 10th Dist. Franklin County 2006), appeal not allowed, 113 Ohio St. 3d 1490, 2007-Ohio-1986, 865 N.E.2d 914 (2007); Mathewson v. Mathewson, 2007-Ohio-574, 2007 WL 431480 (Ohio Ct. App. 2d Dist. Greene County 2007), appeal not allowed, 114 Ohio St. 3d 1427, 2007-Ohio-2904, 868 N.E.2d 680 (2007); Stump v. Stump, 2007-Ohio-6553, 2007 WL 4293302 (Ohio Ct. App. 3d Dist. Logan County 2007); Broach v. Broach, 177 Ohio App. 3d 664,

an individual's ability to obtain a divorce. In *Pasqualone v. Pasqualone*,[12] the Ohio Supreme Court stated in dicta, "In a divorce action, the desire of one party to break the marital bonds constitutes a sufficient basis for divorce regardless of the other spouse's desires. It is fair and reasonable to allow a divorce on the basis of one spouse's unilateral acts."

With the advent of no fault, fault as a basis for awarding and dividing property has been minimized.[13] In addition, the defenses of condonation and recrimination have been abolished by the Ohio legislature.[14] In the past, under the "clean hands" doctrine, if both parties were guilty of a marital fault, then the courts would not grant a divorce. Now, not only is this no longer the case, but recently courts have granted divorces to *both* parties.[15]

§ 11:9   Grounds—Spouse living at time of marriage

In Ohio, a plural or bigamous marriage is grounds for divorce.[1] If either party had a spouse living at the time of the marriage ceremony,

---

2008-Ohio-4132, 895 N.E.2d 640 (2d Dist. Montgomery County 2008), *in dissent*, [court held incompatibility a ground that requires a finding of fault based upon objective proof]; Ahwajee v. Ahwajee, 2008-Ohio-6844, 2008 WL 5381689 (Ohio Ct. App. 5th Dist. Stark County 2008).

[12]Pasqualone v. Pasqualone, 63 Ohio St. 2d 96, 17 Ohio Op. 3d 58, 406 N.E.2d 1121 (1980) (primarily custody case under UCCJA, now known as UCCJEA).

[13]Herbert R. Whiting, et al., *Principles and Guidelines for the Division of Property in Actions for Divorce in Ohio,* 54 Ohio B. 491 (3-16-81). Limited to RC 3105.171(E) (3), 3105.171(F)(9), 3105.18(C)(1)(n). Hysell v. Hysell, 1980 WL 350952 (Ohio Ct. App. 4th Dist. Meigs County 1980); Fisher v. Fisher, 1984 WL 6412 (Ohio Ct. App. 11th Dist. Lake County 1984); Krutz v. Krutz, 1985 WL 7828 (Ohio Ct. App. 11th Dist. Portage County 1985).

[14]RC 3105.10(C). Mahle v. Mahle, 27 Ohio App. 3d 326, 500 N.E.2d 907 (10th Dist. Franklin County 1985); Murray v. Murray, 1988 WL 38879 (Ohio Ct. App. 7th Dist. Belmont County 1988); Allen v. Allen, 1989 WL 30738 (Ohio Ct. App. 12th Dist. Butler County 1989).

[15]See Blankenship v. Blankenship, 2003-Ohio-4551, 2003 WL 22017252 (Ohio Ct. App. 4th Dist. Hocking County 2003); Bruggeman v. Bruggeman, 2000 WL 1726845 (Ohio Ct. App. 2d Dist. Montgomery County 2000); Snyder-Forsyth v. Forsyth, 1996 WL 535299 (Ohio Ct. App. 2d Dist. Clark County 1996), dismissed, appeal not allowed, 77 Ohio St. 3d 1517, 674 N.E.2d 371 (1997); Eitel v. Eitel, 1996 WL 482703 (Ohio Ct. App. 4th Dist. Pickaway County 1996); Carlin v. Carlin, 1996 WL 139486 (Ohio Ct. App. 6th Dist. Williams County 1996); Decker v. Decker, 1995 WL 236005 (Ohio Ct. App. 3d Dist. Defiance County 1995); Ortega v. Ortega, 1987 WL 10602 (Ohio Ct. App. 8th Dist. Cuyahoga County 1987); Juranko v. Juranko, 1978 WL 215918 (Ohio Ct. App. 11th Dist. Lake County 1978); Westhoven v. Westhoven, 2008-Ohio-2875, 2008 WL 2390817 (Ohio Ct. App. 6th Dist. Ottawa County 2008); Slobody v. Friedland-Slobody, 2008-Ohio-3395, 2008 WL 2635496 (Ohio Ct. App. 11th Dist. Geauga County 2008); Burns v. Burns, 2008-Ohio-2483, 2008 WL 2152625 (Ohio Ct. App. 6th Dist. Sandusky County 2008); Teaberry v. Teaberry, 2008-Ohio-3334, 2008 WL 2609618 (Ohio Ct. App. 7th Dist. Mahoning County 2008).

[Section 11:9]

[1]RC 3105.01(A).

that spouse was under a disability to contract the subsequent marriage. Such a marriage is void ab initio.[2] Although the marriage is void, children born of the marriage are legitimate.[3]

Either party may be granted a divorce based on the bigamous nature of the marriage even if both parties knew of the possibility of an impediment prior to their marriage.[4] This is true even if the marriage was a common law marriage, rather than a ceremonial marriage,[5] provided that the marital relationship was established prior to October 10, 1991.[6] A common law marriage was found void where the wife had another husband living at the time of the second marriage.[7] However, RC 3105.01(A) specifies that as a ground for divorce, a trial court should not dismiss a complaint for divorce under those circumstances.[8]

If a marriage is void, based on either party having a husband or a wife living at the time of the marriage, ratification, by continuous cohabitation of the parties, is not permitted after the impediment, the former marriage, is removed/dissolved.[9] However, before common law marriage was abolished on October 10, 1991, the continued cohabitation of the parties after the dissolution of the prior marriage was

---

[2]Abelt v. Zeman, 16 Ohio Op. 2d 87, 86 Ohio L. Abs. 109, 173 N.E.2d 907 (C.P. 1961); Brenholts v. Brenholts, 19 Ohio L. Abs. 309, 1935 WL 1824 (Ct. App. 2d Dist. Franklin County 1935); Basile v. Basile, 86 Ohio App. 535, 42 Ohio Op. 205, 93 N.E.2d 564 (9th Dist. Summit County 1948); Williams v. Williams, 90 Ohio App. 369, 48 Ohio Op. 21, 106 N.E.2d 655 (8th Dist. Cuyahoga County 1951); Darling v. Darling, 44 Ohio App. 2d 5, 73 Ohio Op. 2d 5, 335 N.E.2d 708 (8th Dist. Cuyahoga County 1975); Bubsey v. Oleyar, 2000 WL 680447 (Ohio Ct. App. 8th Dist. Cuyahoga County 2000).

[3]RC 3111.03. Garner v. B. F. Goodrich Co., 136 Ohio St. 397, 16 Ohio Op. 568, 26 N.E.2d 203 (1940); Abelt v. Zeman, 16 Ohio Op. 2d 87, 86 Ohio L. Abs. 109, 173 N.E.2d 907 (C.P. 1961); Wolf v. Gardner, 386 F.2d 295, 15 Ohio Misc. 161, 43 Ohio Op. 2d 179 (6th Cir. 1967).

[4]Smith v. Smith, 72 Ohio App. 203, 27 Ohio Op. 79, 38 Ohio L. Abs. 531, 50 N.E.2d 889 (1st Dist. Hamilton County 1943); Nyhuis v. Pierce, 65 Ohio L. Abs. 73, 114 N.E.2d 75 (Ct. App. 8th Dist. Cuyahoga County 1952).

[5]Bolin v. Bolin, 1987 WL 17301 (Ohio Ct. App. 4th Dist. Jackson County 1987); Bubsey v. Oleyar, 2000 WL 680447 (Ohio Ct. App. 8th Dist. Cuyahoga County 2000); Nyhuis v. Pierce, 65 Ohio L. Abs. 73, 114 N.E.2d 75 (Ct. App. 8th Dist. Cuyahoga County 1952); In re Zemmick's Estate, 32 Ohio Op. 504, 44 Ohio L. Abs. 390, 17 Ohio Supp. 15 (Prob. Ct. 1945), aff'd, 49 Ohio L. Abs. 353, 76 N.E.2d 902 (Ct. App. 7th Dist. Belmont County 1946); Smith v. Smith, 5 Ohio St. 32, 1855 WL 40 (1855).

[6]RC 3105.12(B). Fuentes v. Fuentes, 2007-Ohio-820, 2007 WL 613751 (Ohio Ct. App. 8th Dist. Cuyahoga County 2007); Bevan v. Bevan, 2006-Ohio-2775, 2006 WL 1519654 (Ohio Ct. App. 11th Dist. Lake County 2006).

[7]Tabler v. Tabler, 2007-Ohio-1579, 2007 WL 969421 (Ohio Ct. App. 5th Dist. Stark County 2007); Hill v. Hill, 2008-Ohio-2774, 2008 WL 2572681 (Ohio Ct. App. 5th Dist. Perry County 2008).

[8]Bubsey v. Oleyar, 2000 WL 680447 (Ohio Ct. App. 8th Dist. Cuyahoga County 2000); Eggleston v. Eggleston, 156 Ohio St. 422, 46 Ohio Op. 351, 103 N.E.2d 395 (1952).

[9]Heyse v. Michalske, 18 Ohio Op. 254, 31 Ohio L. Abs. 484, 6 Ohio Supp. 33 (Prob. Ct. 1940).

considered similar to ratification, if and only if, the requirements of a common law marriage were satisfied.[10] Today, if the impediment is removed after the date common law was abolished, ratification of a common law marriage established in the state of Ohio is not possible. However, if a common law marriage is established in another state or country that currently recognizes common law marriage, the parties continue to reside together after the impediment is removed, and the parties subsequently relocate to Ohio, Ohio court's may find that the parties have "ratified" their marriage.[11]

A bigamous marriage is also grounds for annulment.[12] The two causes of action may be joined, with a prayer for relief in the alternative, or a party may initially elect either a divorce or an annulment.[13] If a party is granted a divorce, the court can award spousal support and divide the marital property.[14] Thus, a propertied party might seek an annulment to avoid financial obligation, while a financially insecure party might opt for a divorce to obtain spousal support and/or a division of marital property.[15]

§ 11:10   Grounds—Willful absence

A second ground for divorce is the willful absence of a party from the marital home for one year.[1] Willful absence is an intentional and voluntary act performed with the intent to cease cohabitation, which

---

[10]Johnson v. Wolford, 117 Ohio St. 136, 5 Ohio L. Abs. 402, 157 N.E. 385 (1927); Williams v. Williams, 90 Ohio App. 369, 48 Ohio Op. 21, 106 N.E.2d 655 (8th Dist. Cuyahoga County 1951); Egan v. Egan, 1978 WL 217719 (Ohio Ct. App. 8th Dist. Cuyahoga County 1978); Crozier v. Hafer, 1999 WL 194205 (Ohio Ct. App. 9th Dist. Wayne County 1999).

[11]In re Zemmick's Estate, 32 Ohio Op. 504, 44 Ohio L. Abs. 390, 17 Ohio Supp. 15 (Prob. Ct. 1945), aff'd, 49 Ohio L. Abs. 353, 76 N.E.2d 902 (Ct. App. 7th Dist. Belmont County 1946).

[12]RC 3105.31(B). Tabler v. Tabler, 2007-Ohio-1579, 2007 WL 969421 (Ohio Ct. App. 5th Dist. Stark County 2007).

[13]Civ. R. 8(A). Eggleston v. Eggleston, 156 Ohio St. 422, 46 Ohio Op. 351, 103 N.E.2d 395 (1952); Tyminski v. Tyminski, 8 Ohio Misc. 202, 37 Ohio Op. 2d 263, 221 N.E.2d 486 (C.P. 1966); Cosic v. Cosic, 2002-Ohio-2030, 2002 WL 745397 (Ohio Ct. App. 8th Dist. Cuyahoga County 2002).

[14]See Eggleston v. Eggleston, 156 Ohio St. 422, 46 Ohio Op. 351, 103 N.E.2d 395 (1952); Minor v. Minor, 1994 WL 590341 (Ohio Ct. App. 5th Dist. Tuscarawas County 1994), dismissed, appeal not allowed, 71 Ohio St. 3d 1491, 646 N.E.2d 467 (1995); Vanvalley v. Vanvalley, 19 Ohio St. 588, 1869 WL 105 (1869); Treadway v. Treadway, 97 Ohio App. 248, 56 Ohio Op. 35, 125 N.E.2d 552 (1st Dist. Hamilton County 1954); Kizer v. Kizer, 1975 WL 182353 (Ohio Ct. App. 6th Dist. Williams County 1975); Bolin v. Bolin, 1987 WL 17301 (Ohio Ct. App. 4th Dist. Jackson County 1987); Liming v. Liming, 117 Ohio App. 3d 617, 691 N.E.2d 299 (4th Dist. Adams County 1996).

[15]Liming v. Liming, 117 Ohio App. 3d 617, 691 N.E.2d 299 (4th Dist. Adams County 1996).

[Section 11:10]

[1]RC 3105.01(B).

is against the will of the other spouse.[2] This ground is available only to the nonabsent party.[3]

The key elements are willfulness and absence for the statutory period of one year. Any reconciliation between the parties stops the running of the one-year period; if the parties separate again, the time period begins to run all over again.[4] The one-year statutory time period must be continuous and not an accumulation of various separations. However, a shorter period of time may constitute gross neglect of duty if aggravating circumstances are present.[5] It has been held that an absence is willful if it is intentional and voluntary by a spouse who purposely and designedly carries out such an absence.[6]

The absence from the home must be by choice, but it need not be hostile or malicious on the part of the absent party. For example, the refusal of a wife to live with her husband has been held to be willful absence,[7] including a situation where the wife remained in the previous marital home after refusing to move with her husband into a newer home.[8] Where the court finds that one of the parties deserted the other, this holding may be used as proof of willful absence.[9] Willful absence may also be proved by an offer to resume marital rela-

---

[2]Hanover v. Hanover, 34 Ohio App. 483, 171 N.E. 350 (6th Dist. Lucas County 1929); Ferree v. Ferree, 8 Ohio Dec. Rep. 405, 7 W.L.B. 302, 1882 WL 7631 (Ohio C.P. 1882); Murphy v. Murphy, 8 Ohio Dec. Rep. 406, 7 W.L.B. 303, 1882 WL 7502 (Ohio C.P. 1882); Mason v. Mason, 30 Ohio Op. 27, 42 Ohio L. Abs. 286, 15 Ohio Supp. 48 (C.P. 1945); Shuster v. Shuster, 1988 WL 140565 (Ohio Ct. App. 8th Dist. Cuyahoga County 1988).

[3]RC 3105.01(B). Mason v. Mason, 30 Ohio Op. 27, 42 Ohio L. Abs. 286, 15 Ohio Supp. 48 (C.P. 1945); Nolan v. Nolan, 2006-Ohio-3409, 2006 WL 1817075 (Ohio Ct. App. 11th Dist. Geauga County 2006).

[4]Shuster v. Shuster, 1988 WL 140565 (Ohio Ct. App. 8th Dist. Cuyahoga County 1988) (sexual relations between the parties during the one-year period of "willful absence" is irrelevant and does not stop the running of said time period).

[5]Porter v. Lerch, 129 Ohio St. 47, 1 Ohio Op. 356, 193 N.E. 766 (1934); Jones v. Jones, 77 Ohio App. 551, 33 Ohio Op. 364, 47 Ohio L. Abs. 53, 68 N.E.2d 680 (1st Dist. Hamilton County 1945); Casbarro v. Casbarro, 66 Ohio L. Abs. 505, 118 N.E.2d 209 (Ct. App. 2d Dist. Franklin County 1953); Sullivan v. Sullivan, 105 Ohio App. 457, 6 Ohio Op. 2d 200, 152 N.E.2d 761 (2d Dist. Greene County 1957); Fischer v. Fischer, 8th Dist. No. 42589 (Feb. 5, 1981); Simpson v. Simpson, 2002-Ohio-6266, 2002 WL 31546221 (Ohio Ct. App. 5th Dist. Ashland County 2002).

[6]Hanover v. Hanover, 34 Ohio App. 483, 171 N.E. 350 (6th Dist. Lucas County 1929); Mason v. Mason, 30 Ohio Op. 27, 42 Ohio L. Abs. 286, 15 Ohio Supp. 48 (C.P. 1945); Wiley v. Wiley, 78 Ohio L. Abs. 597, 153 N.E.2d 784 (Ct. App. 7th Dist. Columbiana County 1957).

[7]Sullivan v. Sullivan, 105 Ohio App. 457, 6 Ohio Op. 2d 200, 152 N.E.2d 761 (2d Dist. Greene County 1957) (RC 3103.02, which required wife to conform to husband's place of residence, was in effect at this time; repealed by 1974 H.B. 233, eff. 9-23-74).

[8]Casbarro v. Casbarro, 66 Ohio L. Abs. 505, 118 N.E.2d 209 (Ct. App. 2d Dist. Franklin County 1953).

[9]Nelson v. Nelson, 3 Ohio App. 2d 293, 32 Ohio Op. 2d 391, 210 N.E.2d 137 (1st Dist. Hamilton County 1964); Mason v. Mason, 30 Ohio Op. 27, 42 Ohio L. Abs. 286, 15 Ohio Supp. 48 (C.P. 1945); Newell v. Newell, 23 Ohio App. 2d 149, 52 Ohio Op. 2d 178, 261 N.E.2d 278 (5th Dist. Stark County 1970).

tions, which remains unaccepted or rejected by the adverse party.[10] No other aggravating circumstances need be shown to assert this ground.[11]

When the absence is not intentional or by choice, then the absence is not willful as required by statute. Thus, if a party to a marriage is hospitalized for one year, serves in the military, or is absent for a similar reason, the required intent is missing and a divorce asserting this ground must fail. If the parties separate under a decree for legal separation or an agreement between the parties for separate support or maintenance, such separation cannot be a basis for this ground.[12]

§ 11:11 Grounds—Adultery

Adultery[1] is defined as the "[v]oluntary sexual intercourse of a married person with a person other than the offender's [spouse]."[2] If the adultery is with the spouse's consent, then that consenting spouse is not legally aggrieved, and the permission serves as a defense against the adultery.[3]

The difficulty of asserting adultery as a ground for divorce is the burden of proof. Adultery can be established by a preponderance of evidence upon proof of circumstances from which guilt can be inferred, but the proof must be clear, positive, and sufficiently definite to show the circumstances under which it was committed.[4] The charge cannot be sustained by suspicion or innuendo; the evidence must be of a

---

[10]Mason v. Mason, 30 Ohio Op. 27, 42 Ohio L. Abs. 286, 15 Ohio Supp. 48 (C.P. 1945).

[11]Sullivan v. Sullivan, 105 Ohio App. 457, 6 Ohio Op. 2d 200, 152 N.E.2d 761 (2d Dist. Greene County 1957); Fischer v. Fischer, 8th Dist. No. 42589 (Feb. 5, 1981); Casbarro v. Casbarro, 66 Ohio L. Abs. 505, 118 N.E.2d 209 (Ct. App. 2d Dist. Franklin County 1953); Slusser v. Slusser, 68 Ohio L. Abs. 7, 121 N.E.2d 317 (Ct. App. 9th Dist. Summit County 1952).

[12]Condon v. Condon, 8 Ohio App. 189, 1917 WL 1438 (1st Dist. Hamilton County 1917); Murphy v. Murphy, 8 Ohio Dec. Rep. 406, 7 W.L.B. 303, 1882 WL 7502 (Ohio C.P. 1882); Tiberghein v. Tiberghein, 8 Ohio Dec. Rep. 464, 8 W.L.B. 89, 1882 WL 7518 (Ohio C.P. 1882); Lichtwadt v. Lichtwadt, 2 Ohio L. Abs. 597, 1924 WL 1998 (Ct. App. 1st Dist. Hamilton County 1924); Moody v. Moody, 76 Ohio L. Abs. 477, 142 N.E.2d 276 (Ct. App. 8th Dist. Cuyahoga County 1957).

[Section 11:11]

[1]RC 3105.01(C).

[2]Black's Law Dictionary (6th ed.) p 51.

[3]Backenstoe v. Backenstoe, 14 Ohio Dec. 353, 1904 WL 728 (C.P. 1904).

[4]Ashley v. Ashley, 118 Ohio App. 155, 25 Ohio Op. 2d 13, 193 N.E.2d 535 (6th Dist. Lucas County 1962); Geiger v. Geiger, 80 Ohio App. 161, 35 Ohio Op. 490, 48 Ohio L. Abs. 587, 72 N.E.2d 766 (2d Dist. Montgomery County 1947); Taylor v. Taylor, 2000 WL 329669 (Ohio Ct. App. 5th Dist. Guernsey County 2000); Kampfer v. Kampfer, 1990 WL 237481 (Ohio Ct. App. 5th Dist. Stark County 1990); Brock v. Brock, 1977 WL 199377 (Ohio Ct. App. 3d Dist. Auglaize County 1977).

substantial nature and worthy of belief.[5] Weight of the evidence is not the proper standard of review in determining whether a spouse committed adultery.[6] The ground of adultery failed in *Hoag v. Hoag*,[7] where a plaintiff husband alleged adultery, defendant wife denied it, and no corroborating witnesses were called; the court weighed the credibility of the witnesses and other evidence and failed to grant the divorce for adultery.

An admission by the errant partner may be adequate evidence of adultery.[8] However, the court will carefully scrutinize any evidence tending to prove adultery, particularly alleged admissions.[9] Additionally, the simple fact that a married person is living with a person of the opposite sex is not proof of adultery; other evidence must be introduced.[10] Like several of the other grounds identified in RC 3105.01, adultery is predicated on the misconduct of the other spouse in relation to the obligations a marital relationship imposes.[11] The issue of misconduct is a factual issue to be determined by the trial court.[12]

When a person is divorced and that divorce decree is later set aside, sexual intercourse during the time the person believed the divorce to

---

[5]Ashley v. Ashley, 118 Ohio App. 155, 25 Ohio Op. 2d 13, 193 N.E.2d 535 (6th Dist. Lucas County 1962); Geiger v. Geiger, 80 Ohio App. 161, 35 Ohio Op. 490, 48 Ohio L. Abs. 587, 72 N.E.2d 766 (2d Dist. Montgomery County 1947); Taylor v. Taylor, 2000 WL 329669 (Ohio Ct. App. 5th Dist. Guernsey County 2000); Farnsworth v. Farnsworth, 8 Ohio Dec. 171, 1895 WL 657 (C.P. 1895).

[6]Moser v. Moser, 2006-Ohio-5381, 2006 WL 2939929 (Ohio Ct. App. 12th Dist. Warren County 2006), appeal not allowed, 113 Ohio St. 3d 1415, 2007-Ohio-1036, 862 N.E.2d 844 (2007).

[7]Hoag v. Hoag, 1984 WL 4705 (Ohio Ct. App. 10th Dist. Franklin County 1984).

[8]Moser v. Moser, 5 Ohio App. 3d 193, 450 N.E.2d 741 (9th Dist. Lorain County 1982); Casbarro v. Casbarro, 66 Ohio L. Abs. 505, 118 N.E.2d 209 (Ct. App. 2d Dist. Franklin County 1953); Milyard v. Milyard, 1980 WL 352527 (Ohio Ct. App. 2d Dist. Montgomery County 1980); Sgro v. Sgro, 1988 WL 131438 (Ohio Ct. App. 6th Dist. Fulton County 1988); Minnick v. Minnick, 1990 WL 102363 (Ohio Ct. App. 12th Dist. Madison County 1990); Young v. Young, 1995 WL 912747 (Ohio Ct. App. 10th Dist. Franklin County 1995).

[9]Moser v. Moser, 5 Ohio App. 3d 193, 450 N.E.2d 741 (9th Dist. Lorain County 1982); Geiger v. Geiger, 80 Ohio App. 161, 35 Ohio Op. 490, 48 Ohio L. Abs. 587, 72 N.E.2d 766 (2d Dist. Montgomery County 1947); Ashley v. Ashley, 118 Ohio App. 155, 25 Ohio Op. 2d 13, 193 N.E.2d 535 (6th Dist. Lucas County 1962).

[10]Helms v. Helms, 1982 WL 6886 (Ohio Ct. App. 3d Dist. Hancock County 1982).

[11]Robbins v. Robbins, 2008-Ohio-495, 2008 WL 344143 (Ohio Ct. App. 2d Dist. Clark County 2008) (however, the husband's adultery was not *financial* misconduct allowing an increase in the wife's share of the marital estate); Shreyer v. Shreyer, 2008 Ohio 7013, 2008 WL 5451376 (Ohio Ct. App. 5th Dist. Fairfield County 2008) (a trial court did not error in considering a husband's infidelity in awarding spousal support since marital conduct could be a relevant factor in determining support).

[12]Cobb v. Cobb, 78 Ohio L. Abs. 229, 152 N.E.2d 123 (Ct. App. 10th Dist. Franklin County 1958) (overnight guest sleeping in separate bedroom not sufficient evidence of adultery).

be valid is not adultery.[13] Older cases have held that sodomy and bes-
tiality do not constitute adulterous sexual intercourse within the
meaning of the statute.[14] In addition, a victim of rape is not committing adultery, as the requisite voluntariness is absent.

§ 11:12 Grounds—Extreme cruelty

Extreme cruelty[1] has been defined as acts and conduct calculated to
destroy the peace of mind and happiness of one of the parties to the
marriage.[2] The conduct must be such that it so seriously affects the
household as to render the marital relationship intolerable.[3] Moreover, the conduct must be voluntary or intentional.[4] Thus, extreme
cruelty cannot be committed by a spouse who is insane and incapable
of understanding the nature of his or her conduct.[5] However, a divorce
may be granted on the ground of extreme cruelty where the insane
person engaged in the offensive conduct while sane.[6]

---

[13]Holmes v. Holmes, 82 Ohio App. 33, 37 Ohio Op. 360, 51 Ohio L. Abs. 316, 80
N.E.2d 507 (1st Dist. Hamilton County 1948).

[14]Anonymous, 2 Ohio N.P. 342, 3 Ohio Dec. 450, 1895 WL 1426 (C.P. 1895).

[Section 11:12]

[1]RC 3105.01(D).

[2]Buess v. Buess, 89 Ohio App. 37, 45 Ohio Op. 331, 100 N.E.2d 646 (3d Dist.
Hardin County 1950); Verplatse v. Verplatse, 17 Ohio App. 3d 99, 477 N.E.2d 648 (3d
Dist. Hancock County 1984); Miller v. Miller, 1995 WL 14794 (Ohio Ct. App. 12th
Dist. Madison County 1995); Parks v. Parks, 1989 WL 35134 (Ohio Ct. App. 9th Dist.
Lorain County 1989); Warrick v. Warrick, 1990 WL 26093 (Ohio Ct. App. 2d Dist.
Darke County 1990); Clark v. Clark, 2004-Ohio-1577, 2004 WL 615708 (Ohio Ct. App.
7th Dist. Noble County 2004); Rendina v. Rendina, 2005-Ohio-4772, 2005 WL 2211113
(Ohio Ct. App. 11th Dist. Lake County 2005), cause dismissed, 107 Ohio St. 3d 1689,
2005-Ohio-6637, 839 N.E.2d 408 (2005); Doody v. Doody, 2007-Ohio-2567, 2007 WL
1532083 (Ohio Ct. App. 11th Dist. Lake County 2007).

[3]Ginn v. Ginn, 112 Ohio App. 259, 16 Ohio Op. 2d 164, 175 N.E.2d 848 (4th
Dist. Lawrence County 1960); Kaminski v. Kaminski, 1997 WL 89156 (Ohio Ct. App.
12th Dist. Clermont County 1997); Rice v. Rice, 2001 WL 1400012 (Ohio Ct. App. 8th
Dist. Cuyahoga County 2001); Bernard v. Bernard, 2002-Ohio-552, 2002 WL 206411
(Ohio Ct. App. 7th Dist. Columbiana County 2002); Wuebker v. Wuebker, 2003-Ohio-
2954, 2003 WL 21341412 (Ohio Ct. App. 3d Dist. Auglaize County 2003); McConnell
v. McConnell, 2004-Ohio-1955, 2004 WL 830961 (Ohio Ct. App. 3d Dist. Union County
2004).

[4]Heim v. Heim, 35 Ohio App. 408, 8 Ohio L. Abs. 166, 172 N.E. 451 (6th Dist.
Lucas County 1930); Hossler v. Hossler, 1979 WL 207865 (Ohio Ct. App. 3d Dist.
Seneca County 1979); Denning v. Denning, 72 Ohio L. Abs. 14, 132 N.E.2d 774 (Ct.
App. 2d Dist. Montgomery County 1955).

[5]Heim v. Heim, 35 Ohio App. 408, 8 Ohio L. Abs. 166, 172 N.E. 451 (6th Dist.
Lucas County 1930); Wolcott v. Wolcott, 22 Ohio C.D. 587, 1911 WL 675 (Ohio Cir.
Ct. 1911); Douglas v. Douglas, 46 Ohio L. Abs. 9, 68 N.E.2d 237 (Ct. App. 2d Dist.
Franklin County 1944).

[6]Heim v. Heim, 35 Ohio App. 408, 8 Ohio L. Abs. 166, 172 N.E. 451 (6th Dist.
Lucas County 1930); Wolcott v. Wolcott, 22 Ohio C.D. 587, 1911 WL 675 (Ohio Cir.
Ct. 1911); Douglas v. Douglas, 46 Ohio L. Abs. 9, 68 N.E.2d 237 (Ct. App. 2d Dist.
Franklin County 1944).

Extreme cruelty is not limited to acts of physical violence.[7] Rather, extreme cruelty encompasses a broad range of hostile, aggressive, or disruptive acts which may affect the physical, emotional, or psychological well-being of the victim-spouse, including:

(1) physical abuse;[8]
(2) excessive or abnormal sexual demands, provided such acts are against complaining party's will;[9]
(3) refusal to engage in sexual relations;[10]
(4) homosexuality;[11]
(5) excessive marijuana smoking;[12]
(6) insistence on attending adult movies, in addition to gambling with household funds;[13]

---

[7]Hoppert v. Hoppert, 1977 WL 199354 (Ohio Ct. App. 11th Dist. Lake County 1977); Porter v. Porter, 1979 WL 207823 (Ohio Ct. App. 3d Dist. Allen County 1979); Hilton v. Hilton, 1979 WL 209253 (Ohio Ct. App. 10th Dist. Franklin County 1979); Vaughn v. Vaughn, 7th Dist. No. 503 (Nov. 19, 1985); Frye v. Frye, 1986 WL 14822 (Ohio Ct. App. 6th Dist. Fulton County 1986); Thomas v. Thomas, 1987 WL 33002 (Ohio Ct. App. 5th Dist. Guernsey County 1987); Parks v. Parks, 1989 WL 35134 (Ohio Ct. App. 9th Dist. Lorain County 1989); Baker v. Baker, 1990 WL 19390 (Ohio Ct. App. 2d Dist. Darke County 1990); Beaver v. Beaver, 1990 WL 131529 (Ohio Ct. App. 7th Dist. Monroe County 1990); Kerstetter v. Kerstetter, 1993 WL 98040 (Ohio Ct. App. 4th Dist. Lawrence County 1993); Brennan v. Brennan, 1995 WL 803613 (Ohio Ct. App. 11th Dist. Portage County 1995).

[8]Baishnab v. Baishnab, 1981 WL 4596 (Ohio Ct. App. 8th Dist. Cuyahoga County 1981); Amole v. Amole, 71 Ohio L. Abs. 111, 129 N.E.2d 860 (Ct. App. 2d Dist. Greene County 1955); Weaver v. Weaver, 1978 WL 215762 (Ohio Ct. App. 3d Dist. Union County 1978); Sherman v. Sherman, 1978 WL 218357 (Ohio Ct. App. 8th Dist. Cuyahoga County 1978); Walls v. Walls, 1983 WL 7249 (Ohio Ct. App. 3d Dist. Putnam County 1983); Reese v. Reese, 1997 WL 272368 (Ohio Ct. App. 8th Dist. Cuyahoga County 1997).

[9]Johnston v. Johnston, 76 Ohio L. Abs. 29, 143 N.E.2d 498 (C.P. 1957); Merta v. Merta, 45 Ohio L. Abs. 186, 63 N.E.2d 847 (Ct. App. 2d Dist. Montgomery County 1945); Ullom v. Ullom, 72 Ohio L. Abs. 97, 133 N.E.2d 427 (Ct. App. 7th Dist. Mahoning County 1954); Osborn v. Osborn, 1976 WL 188995 (Ohio Ct. App. 9th Dist. Summit County 1976); Gallo v. Gallo, 1981 WL 4780 (Ohio Ct. App. 7th Dist. Columbiana County 1981).

[10]DeMeo v. DeMeo, 1985 WL 7438 (Ohio Ct. App. 8th Dist. Cuyahoga County 1985); Jones v. Jones, 1981 WL 3890 (Ohio Ct. App. 9th Dist. Summit County 1981); Rambaud v. Rambaud, 1987 WL 19078 (Ohio Ct. App. 5th Dist. Stark County 1987); Brinker v. Brinker, 1987 WL 19457 (Ohio Ct. App. 9th Dist. Summit County 1987); Moser v. Moser, 72 Ohio App. 3d 575, 595 N.E.2d 518 (3d Dist. Allen County 1991); Brennan v. Brennan, 1995 WL 803613 (Ohio Ct. App. 11th Dist. Portage County 1995).

[11]Bales v. Hack, 31 Ohio App. 3d 111, 509 N.E.2d 95 (2d Dist. Clark County 1986).

[12]Parks v. Parks, 1989 WL 35134 (Ohio Ct. App. 9th Dist. Lorain County 1989).

[13]Pearson v. Pearson, 1985 WL 7656 (Ohio Ct. App. 2d Dist. Montgomery County 1985); Marvin v. Marvin, 1997 WL 123914 (Ohio Ct. App. 11th Dist. Portage County 1997); Woodworth v. Woodworth., 1977 WL 201176 (Ohio Ct. App. 8th Dist. Cuyahoga County 1977).

(7)   threats of divorce combined with alcoholism,[14] nagging,[15] and involvement with another person;[16]

(8)   attacks on spouse's character and self-respect;[17]

(9)   bad faith attempt to have spouse placed in mental institution;[18]

(10)   religious faith which disrupts and destroys marriage;[19]

(11)   verbal abuse;[20]

(12)   general failure to provide companionship and emotional support;[21]

(13)   continuous quarreling and nagging, combined with making false, malicious, and derogatory statements to friends and business associates;[22]

(14)   attempting to have spouse arrested for leaving home with parties' minor child as well as refusing to allow spouse and spouse's father to visit with minor child;[23] and

(15)   repeated attempts at suicide.[24]

Although cruelty is usually predicated upon a series of cruel acts, it is possible to establish it from one incident if the act was outrageous

---

[14]Corrigan v. Corrigan., 1979 WL 210487 (Ohio Ct. App. 8th Dist. Cuyahoga County 1979) (Court determined that alcoholism alone is not sufficient to establish extreme cruelty).

[15]Stark v. Stark, 28 Ohio N.P. (n.s.) 36, 8 Ohio L. Abs. 287, 1929 WL 2380 (C.P. 1929); Mallett v. Mallett, 1978 WL 214770 (Ohio Ct. App. 6th Dist. Lucas County 1978); Schiff v. Schiff, 36 Ohio L. Abs. 626, 45 N.E.2d 132 (Ct. App. 2d Dist. Franklin County 1942); Gugle v. Gugle, 40 Ohio L. Abs. 230, 57 N.E.2d 156 (Ct. App. 2d Dist. Franklin County 1943); Purmort v. Purmort, 32 Ohio N.P. (n.s.) 313, 17 Ohio L. Abs. 63, 1933 WL 1648 (C.P. 1933).

[16]O'Leary v. O'Leary, 1983 WL 2735 (Ohio Ct. App. 8th Dist. Cuyahoga County 1983).

[17]Eddy v. Eddy, 14 Ohio L. Abs. 277, 1932 WL 2488 (Ct. App. 7th Dist. Monroe County 1932).

[18]Ginn v. Ginn, 112 Ohio App. 259, 16 Ohio Op. 2d 164, 175 N.E.2d 848 (4th Dist. Lawrence County 1960).

[19]Pater v. Pater, 1990 WL 162021 (Ohio Ct. App. 1st Dist. Hamilton County 1990), judgment rev'd, 63 Ohio St. 3d 393, 588 N.E.2d 794 (1992); Hoppes v. Hoppes, 5 Ohio Misc. 159, 34 Ohio Op. 2d 329, 214 N.E.2d 860 (C.P. 1964).

[20]Ogletree v. Ogletree, 1990 WL 40656 (Ohio Ct. App. 2d Dist. Miami County 1990); Bonner v. Bonner, 1988 WL 30498 (Ohio Ct. App. 6th Dist. Wood County 1988); Jones v. Jones, 1996 WL 715441 (Ohio Ct. App. 2d Dist. Champaign County 1996); Vaughn v. Vaughn, 7th Dist. No. 503 (Nov. 19, 1985); Chance v. Chance, 2002-Ohio-5767, 2002 WL 31386736 (Ohio Ct. App. 9th Dist. Wayne County 2002).

[21]Warrick v. Warrick, 1990 WL 26093 (Ohio Ct. App. 2d Dist. Darke County 1990) (cruelty extreme in degree albeit subtle in its manifestation); Winnard v. Winnard, 62 Ohio App. 351, 16 Ohio Op. 51, 23 N.E.2d 977 (2d Dist. Franklin County 1939).

[22]Groff v. Groff, 33 Ohio App. 309, 169 N.E. 39 (1st Dist. Hamilton County 1929).

[23]Yankovich v. Yankovich, 1988 WL 104408 (Ohio Ct. App. 9th Dist. Medina County 1988).

[24]Liedorff v. Liedorff, 67 Ohio L. Abs. 36, 113 N.E.2d 127 (C.P. 1953); McConnell v. McConnell, 2004-Ohio-1955, 2004 WL 830961 (Ohio Ct. App. 3d Dist. Union County

in itself, was dangerous and might be repeated, or produced an irreconcilable alienation between the parties.[25]

Whether the conduct of a spouse constitutes extreme cruelty is a question which is left to the sound discretion of the trial court.[26]

A husband's admissions may sufficiently corroborate a wife's allegation of extreme cruelty without the need for other corroborative testimony.[27] A civil or criminal domestic violence protective order may also be used to corroborate an allegation of extreme cruelty.[28]

§ 11:13   Grounds—Fraudulent contract

Fraudulent contract[1] relates to the validity of the marriage.[2] The fraud can relate to the personal disclosures as to essential elements between the individuals making the marriage contract,[3] or it can

---

2004); Glimcher v. Glimcher, 29 Ohio App. 2d 55, 58 Ohio Op. 2d 37, 278 N.E.2d 37 (10th Dist. Franklin County 1971).

[25]Annot., 7 A.L.R. 3d 761. Mcgrew v. Mcgrew, 1981 WL 6725 (Ohio Ct. App. 3d Dist. Wyandot County 1981); Hummel v. Hummel, 7 Ohio Dec. Rep. 138, 1 W.L.B. 153, 1876 WL 7462 (Ohio C.P. 1876).

[26]Verplatse v. Verplatse, 17 Ohio App. 3d 99, 477 N.E.2d 648 (3d Dist. Hancock County 1984); Harshbarger v. Harshbarger, 1993 WL 221269 (Ohio Ct. App. 5th Dist. Licking County 1993); Camera v. Camera, 1987 WL 19526 (Ohio Ct. App. 9th Dist. Lorain County 1987); Miller v. Miller, 1995 WL 14794 (Ohio Ct. App. 12th Dist. Madison County 1995); Schuster v. Schuster, 1989 WL 36274 (Ohio Ct. App. 11th Dist. Portage County 1989); Frye v. Frye, 1986 WL 14822 (Ohio Ct. App. 6th Dist. Fulton County 1986); Clark v. Clark, 2004-Ohio-1577, 2004 WL 615708 (Ohio Ct. App. 7th Dist. Noble County 2004); Kerstetter v. Kerstetter, 1993 WL 98040 (Ohio Ct. App. 4th Dist. Lawrence County 1993); Huelsman v. Huelsman, 1988 WL 122899 (Ohio Ct. App. 8th Dist. Cuyahoga County 1988).

[27]Ogletree v. Ogletree, 1990 WL 40656 (Ohio Ct. App. 2d Dist. Miami County 1990); Slyh v. Slyh, 72 Ohio L. Abs. 537, 135 N.E.2d 675 (Ct. App. 2d Dist. Madison County 1955); Weaver v. Weaver, 1978 WL 215762 (Ohio Ct. App. 3d Dist. Union County 1978); Brooks v. Brooks, 1988 WL 118814 (Ohio Ct. App. 10th Dist. Franklin County 1988); Doody v. Doody, 2007-Ohio-2567, 2007 WL 1532083 (Ohio Ct. App. 11th Dist. Lake County 2007).

[28]Baishnab v. Baishnab, 1981 WL 4596 (Ohio Ct. App. 8th Dist. Cuyahoga County 1981).

[Section 11:13]

[1]RC 3105.01(E).

[2]Eggleston v. Eggleston, 156 Ohio St. 422, 46 Ohio Op. 351, 103 N.E.2d 395 (1952) (court observed fraudulent contract goes to validity of marriage); Dagostino v. Dagostino, 165 Ohio App. 3d 365, 2006-Ohio-723, 846 N.E.2d 582 (4th Dist. Athens County 2006); Nyhuis v. Pierce, 65 Ohio L. Abs. 73, 114 N.E.2d 75 (Ct. App. 8th Dist. Cuyahoga County 1952).

[3]See Miller v. Miller, 1 Ohio Dec. 354, 1893 WL 370 (C.P. 1893); Dagostino v. Dagostino, 165 Ohio App. 3d 365, 2006-Ohio-723, 846 N.E.2d 582 (4th Dist. Athens County 2006).

relate to one or both of the parties entering the marital relationship when there is an impediment resulting in a fraud upon the court.[4]

A party will be granted a divorce if he or she was induced into marriage as a result of a fraudulent representation that affects the essential elements of the marriage.[5] The most common example would be the misrepresentation of pregnancy by a party. If the husband married the wife knowing she was pregnant and believing that the child was his based on her statements, but the child was not his, then a divorce on the ground of fraudulent contract would be possible.[6] The concealment of pregnancy by another man is fraud that would entitle a husband to a divorce. Fraudulent contract is also grounds for annulment.[7]

A marriage, which is prohibited by law, is a fraudulent contract. In *Basickas v. Basickas*,[8] an uncle and niece married after stating under oath that they were no nearer than second cousins. A marriage between parties so closely related is prohibited; therefore, the marriage was void ab initio. The court held that even though both parties knew they were perpetrating a fraud, the divorce would be granted for fraudulent contract.

§ 11:14   Grounds—Gross neglect of duty

The next ground for divorce in Ohio is "[a]ny gross neglect of duty."[1] There is no all-inclusive definition of gross neglect;[2] however, the Ohio Supreme Court has held that gross neglect is limited to acts which

---

[4]See Basickas v. Basickas, 93 Ohio App. 531, 51 Ohio Op. 229, 114 N.E.2d 270 (9th Dist. Summit County 1953); Dagostino v. Dagostino, 165 Ohio App. 3d 365, 2006-Ohio-723, 846 N.E.2d 582 (4th Dist. Athens County 2006).

[5]Joy v. Joy, 12 Ohio Dec. 574, 1900 WL 1285 (C.P. 1900); Kraus v. Kraus, 6 Ohio N.P. 248, 9 Ohio Dec. 515, 1899 WL 785 (C.P. 1899).

[6]Meyer v. Meyer, 7 Ohio Dec. Rep. 627, 4 W.L.B. 368, 1879 WL 6394 (Ohio Dist. Ct. 1879).

[7]RC 3105.31(D). Anderson v. Anderson, 8 Ohio Misc. 97, 37 Ohio Op. 2d 108, 219 N.E.2d 317 (C.P. 1966); Slavin v. Slavin, 1985 WL 6893 (Ohio Ct. App. 8th Dist. Cuyahoga County 1985); Stepp v. Stepp, 2004-Ohio-1617, 2004 WL 626116 (Ohio Ct. App. 9th Dist. Medina County 2004); Benton v. Benton, 26 Ohio C.D. 613, 1909 WL 663 (Ohio Cir. Ct. 1909); Tyminski v. Tyminski, 8 Ohio Misc. 202, 37 Ohio Op. 2d 263, 221 N.E.2d 486 (C.P. 1966).

[8]Basickas v. Basickas, 93 Ohio App. 531, 51 Ohio Op. 229, 114 N.E.2d 270 (9th Dist. Summit County 1953).

[Section 11:14]

[1]RC 3105.01(F).

[2]Simpson v. Simpson, 2002-Ohio-6266, 2002 WL 31546221 (Ohio Ct. App. 5th Dist. Ashland County 2002); Edwards v. Edwards, 1978 WL 217970 (Ohio Ct. App. 8th Dist. Cuyahoga County 1978); Porter v. Lerch, 129 Ohio St. 47, 1 Ohio Op. 356, 193 N.E. 766 (1934); Buess v. Buess, 89 Ohio App. 37, 45 Ohio Op. 331, 100 N.E.2d 646 (3d Dist. Hardin County 1950); Harshbarger v. Harshbarger, 1993 WL 221269 (Ohio Ct. App. 5th Dist. Licking County 1993); Demarco v. Demarco, 1983 WL 6201 (Ohio Ct. App. 11th Dist. Geauga County 1983); Rice v. Rice, 2001 WL 1400012 (Ohio Ct. App. 8th Dist. Cuyahoga County 2001); Glick v. Glick, 1985 WL 4426 (Ohio Ct.

constitute an omission to perform a legal duty.[3] Therefore, an appropriate analysis for whether gross neglect is present would be (1) was there an affirmative duty to act which the spouse omitted; and (2) did the omission rise above ordinary neglect so as to be gross neglect.[4] The trial court has broad discretion to interpret what is gross neglect based on the peculiar facts and circumstances of each case.[5] In *Smith v. Smith*,[6] the Second District Court of Appeals characterized gross neglect as a "nebulous" concept but found the aggravating circumstances of the case were sufficient for a finding of gross neglect. In *Vanatta v. Aten*, the Fifth District Court of Appeals acknowledged that gross neglect is open to subjective interpretation, and where one trial court might find gross neglect, another may reject it.[7]

The Ohio Revised Code sets forth several legal duties and obligations for spouses. RC 3103.01 sets forth respect, fidelity, and support as the legal duties of one spouse to another.[8] Additionally, a spouse must support himself or herself, his or her spouse and minor children out of his or her property or by his or her labor, but if either spouse is unable to do so, then the other must assist as far as he or she is able.[9] A spouse also has the duty not to exclude the other spouse from the

---

App. 12th Dist. Clermont County1985); Mallett v. Mallett, 1978 WL 214770 (Ohio Ct. App. 6th Dist. Lucas County 1978); Clark v. Clark, 2004-Ohio-1577, 2004 WL 615708 (Ohio Ct. App. 7th Dist. Noble County 2004); Deuri v. Deuri, 1987 WL 14429 (Ohio Ct. App. 9th Dist. Summit County 1987).

[3]Mark v. Mark, 145 Ohio St. 301, 30 Ohio Op. 534, 61 N.E.2d 595, 160 A.L.R. 608 (1945).

[4]Warrick v. Warrick, 1990 WL 26093 (Ohio Ct. App. 2d Dist. Darke County 1990).

[5]Porter v. Lerch, 129 Ohio St. 47, 1 Ohio Op. 356, 193 N.E. 766 (1934); Harshbarger v. Harshbarger, 1993 WL 221269 (Ohio Ct. App. 5th Dist. Licking County 1993); Watkins v. Watkins, 1989 WL 47237 (Ohio Ct. App. 6th Dist. Huron County 1989); Simpson v. Simpson, 2002-Ohio-6266, 2002 WL 31546221 (Ohio Ct. App. 5th Dist. Ashland County 2002); Coleman v. Coleman, 68 Ohio App. 410, 23 Ohio Op. 126, 41 N.E.2d 734 (5th Dist. Guernsey County 1941); Eldridge v. Eldridge, 1986 WL 12363 (Ohio Ct. App. 3d Dist. Hardin County 1986); Demarco v. Demarco, 1983 WL 6201 (Ohio Ct. App. 11th Dist. Geauga County 1983); Ison v. Ronald, 1981 WL 5989 (Ohio Ct. App. 4th Dist. Pike County 1981); Taylor v. Taylor, 1982 WL 5357 (Ohio Ct. App. 8th Dist. Cuyahoga County 1982).

[6]Smith v. Smith, 1988 WL 37891, at *1 (Ohio Ct. App. 2d Dist. Clark County 1988).

[7]Vanatta v. Aten, 1995 WL 347903 (Ohio Ct. App. 5th Dist. Licking County 1995), dismissed, appeal not allowed, 73 Ohio St. 3d 1425, 652 N.E.2d 798 (1995).

[8]Vogt v. Vogt, 67 Ohio App. 3d 197, 586 N.E.2d 242 (6th Dist. Lucas County 1990); Corrigan v. Corrigan., 1979 WL 210487 (Ohio Ct. App. 8th Dist. Cuyahoga County 1979); Glick v. Glick, 1985 WL 4426 (Ohio Ct. App. 12th Dist. Clermont County 1985); Milyard v. Milyard, 1980 WL 352527 (Ohio Ct. App. 2d Dist. Montgomery County 1980); Slater v. Slater, 1988 WL 136936 (Ohio Ct. App. 7th Dist. Noble County 1988); Pemberton v. Pemberton, 1988 WL 48035 (Ohio Ct. App. 4th Dist. Lawrence County 1988).

[9]RC 3103.03. Edwards v. Edwards, 1978 WL 217970 (Ohio Ct. App. 8th Dist. Cuyahoga County 1978); Glimcher v. Glimcher, 29 Ohio App. 2d 55, 58 Ohio Op. 2d 37, 278 N.E.2d 37 (10th Dist. Franklin County 1971); Schwenk v. Schwenk, 1979 WL

marital home;[10] however, the wife no longer has a duty to conform to her husband's place of living.[11] RC 3103.03 also provides that either or both of the spouses must support their children.[12] Any party alleging gross neglect of duty must prove that the other spouse failed to perform at least one of his or her duties.[13]

While the Ohio Supreme Court has said that the term gross neglect of duty is elusive of any concrete definition, it would seem that any elusiveness can only be found in the word gross.[14] A simple or ordinary neglect of a marital duty is not sufficient to constitute grounds for

---

210473 (Ohio Ct. App. 8th Dist. Cuyahoga County 1979); Fulton Cty. Health Center v. Jones, 2007-Ohio-6523, 2007 WL 4277583 (Ohio Ct. App. 6th Dist. Fulton County 2007); Kracker v. Kracker, 2008-Ohio-3751, 2008 WL 2878325 (Ohio Ct. App. 5th Dist. Stark County 2008); Hutta v. Hutta, 177 Ohio App. 3d 414, 2008-Ohio-3756, 894 N.E.2d 1282 (5th Dist. Delaware County 2008); Hutchings v. Childress, 119 Ohio St.3d 486, 2008-Ohio-4568, 895 N.E.2d 520 (2008).

[10]RC 3103.04.

[11]RC 3103.02 was repealed by 1974 H.B. 233, eff. 9-23-74. Dabney v. Dabney, 1976 WL 189489 (Ohio Ct. App. 1st Dist. Hamilton County 1976); Rouault v. Rouault, 1976 WL 190961 (Ohio Ct. App. 8th Dist. Cuyahoga County 1976).

[12]Klump v. Klump, 96 Ohio App. 93, 54 Ohio Op. 202, 121 N.E.2d 273 (6th Dist. Lucas County 1954); Corrigan v. Corrigan., 1979 WL 210487 (Ohio Ct. App. 8th Dist. Cuyahoga County 1979); Edwards v. Edwards, 1978 WL 217970 (Ohio Ct. App. 8th Dist. Cuyahoga County 1978); Glimcher v. Glimcher, 29 Ohio App. 2d 55, 58 Ohio Op. 2d 37, 278 N.E.2d 37 (10th Dist. Franklin County 1971); In re Staats, 2007-Ohio-111, 2007 WL 92376 (Ohio Ct. App. 3d Dist. Allen County 2007); Howell v. Howell, 167 Ohio App. 3d 431, 2006-Ohio-3038, 855 N.E.2d 533 (2d Dist. Clark County 2006); Davis v. Davis, 115 Ohio St. 3d 180, 2007-Ohio-5049, 873 N.E.2d 1305 (2007); Berthelot v. Berthelot, 2007-Ohio-3884, 2007 WL 2192963 (Ohio Ct. App. 9th Dist. Summit County 2007); Hose v. Gatliff, 176 Ohio App. 3d 356, 2008-Ohio-2430, 891 N.E.2d 1263 (9th Dist. Summit County 2008); Swinehart v. Rutter, 2008-Ohio-3121, 2008 WL 2571694 (Ohio Ct. App. 5th Dist. Muskingum County 2008); In re Adoption of J.M.N., 2008-Ohio-4394, 2008 WL 3990828 (Ohio Ct. App. 2d Dist. Clark County 2008); Garner v. Greenwalt, 2008-Ohio-5963, 2008 WL 4918231 (Ohio Ct. App. 5th Dist. Stark County 2008).

[13]Glimcher v. Glimcher, 29 Ohio App. 2d 55, 58 Ohio Op. 2d 37, 278 N.E.2d 37 (10th Dist. Franklin County 1971); Kennedy v. Kennedy, 111 Ohio App. 432, 12 Ohio Op. 2d 201, 165 N.E.2d 454 (1st Dist. Clermont County 1959); Sladoje v. Sladoje, 1988 WL 38118 (Ohio Ct. App. 10th Dist. Franklin County 1988).

[14]Berry v. Berry, 18 Ohio N.P. (n.s.) 521, 27 Ohio Dec. 242, 18, 1915 WL 1369 (C.P. 1915); Addison v. Addison, 15 Ohio L. Abs. 51, 1933 WL 1471 (Ct. App. 2d Dist. Montgomery County 1933); Coleman v. Coleman, 68 Ohio App. 410, 23 Ohio Op. 126, 41 N.E.2d 734 (5th Dist. Guernsey County 1941).

termination of a marriage.[15] The neglect must be gross in that it must contain some element of willfullness, design, or aggression.[16]

RC 3105.01(F) does not prescribe time or duration limits for the occurrence of gross neglect.[17] The fact that the statute states that "*any* gross neglect" (emphasis added) is sufficient seems to ascribe a liberal amount of latitude to the court for determining what constitutes gross neglect.[18] Again, the facts and circumstances of each case must be interpreted by the court.

Generally, a court may grant a decree of divorce for gross neglect where there is proof of failure to support: where the husband voluntarily quits his job and fails to maintain steady employment;[19] or where the husband gambles[20] and fails to secure employment;[21] but not where the wife works from time to time to supplement the husband's income;[22] nor where the husband transfers property to his children of a former marriage, thus potentially undermining the wife's future eco-

---

[15]Glimcher v. Glimcher, 29 Ohio App. 2d 55, 58 Ohio Op. 2d 37, 278 N.E.2d 37 (10th Dist. Franklin County 1971); Sullivan v. Sullivan, 105 Ohio App. 457, 6 Ohio Op. 2d 200, 152 N.E.2d 761 (2d Dist. Greene County 1957); Fowler v. Fowler, 1983 WL 4847 (Ohio Ct. App. 2d Dist. Miami County 1983); Devereaux v. Devereaux, 1983 WL 4037 (Ohio Ct. App. 9th Dist. Lorain County 1983); Wise v. Wise, 1984 WL 14354 (Ohio Ct. App. 6th Dist. Lucas County 1984); Kniffen v. Kniffen, 1985 WL 7443 (Ohio Ct. App. 8th Dist. Cuyahoga County 1985).

[16]Glimcher v. Glimcher, 29 Ohio App. 2d 55, 58 Ohio Op. 2d 37, 278 N.E.2d 37 (10th Dist. Franklin County 1971).

[17]Coleman v. Coleman, 68 Ohio App. 410, 23 Ohio Op. 126, 41 N.E.2d 734 (5th Dist. Guernsey County 1941).

[18]Conner v. Conner, 1981 WL 6290 (Ohio Ct. App. 5th Dist. Richland County 1981); Glick v. Glick, 1985 WL 4426 (Ohio Ct. App. 12th Dist. Clermont County 1985).

[19]Kent v. Kent, 20 Ohio L. Abs. 61, 1935 WL 3271 (Ct. App. 7th Dist. Mahoning County 1935).

[20]Vinas v. Vinas, 1977 WL 200988 (Ohio Ct. App. 5th Dist. Stark County 1977) (Husband's gambling habits and misuse of family funds constitutes gross neglect of duty.); Pearson v. Pearson, 1985 WL 7656 (Ohio Ct. App. 2d Dist. Montgomery County 1985) (Husband forced wife to attend adult movies, and he gambled excessively.); Klump v. Klump, 96 Ohio App. 93, 54 Ohio Op. 202, 121 N.E.2d 273 (6th Dist. Lucas County 1954) (Husband habitually sought the society of person other than the members of his family, including woman; that he spent much of his time playing golf, gambling and being away from home at night.); Holland v. Holland, 8 Ohio Dec. Rep. 460, 8 W.L.B. 86, 1882 WL 7516 (Ohio C.P. 1882) (Husband, for several years, willfully withheld support from his wife and gambled away his wages.); Whitecotton v. Whitecotton, 103 Ohio App. 149, 3 Ohio Op. 2d 210, 144 N.E.2d 678 (6th Dist. Lucas County 1955) (defendant is guilty of gross neglect of duty when his drinking, gambling and affairs with woman kept him away from home and prevented him from performing his marital duties).

[21]Krider v. Krider, 1986 WL 1367 (Ohio Ct. App. 5th Dist. Stark County 1986).

[22]Hamilton v. Hamilton, 65 Ohio L. Abs. 261, 114 N.E.2d 487 (Ct. App. 2d Dist. Montgomery County 1952).

nomic security.[23] The refusal to live together as husband and wife has been held to be gross neglect. Examples of this refusal include the wife's moving out within two weeks of the marriage and never thereafter performing marital duties[24] and the wife's moving out despite a request to stay and an offer to pay her tuition.[25] Refusing a request to resume cohabitation where the requesting spouse had previously voluntarily left the marital residence, however, is not gross neglect.[26] Poor housekeeping is not gross neglect unless it is flagrant, atrocious, heinous, or shameful.[27] Gross neglect of duty is demonstrated, however, when there is evidence that a spouse consistently neglected her housekeeping and child-care duties so as to require the husband to perform those chores after work and that the poor household conditions were detrimental to the children.[28] Further, a wife who failed to cook and keep a clean house; spent too much money and abused credit cards; failed to communicate or listen to husband, and was depressed and refused help is guilty of gross neglect of duty.[29] *Glick v. Glick*[30] held that name-calling in front of the children, discussion of marital problems with others, and spying on each other constitute gross neglect of duty. Likewise, failure to communicate and failure to engage in sexual relations for over two years was deemed to be grounds of gross neglect of duty where the parties also had no social or professional life together.[31] The Seventh District Court of Appeals in *Murray v. Murray*[32] held that the trial court erred in not granting either party a divorce. The court held that Ohio should pursue a modified doctrine of comparative rectitude and grant a divorce to the party least at fault. A finding that neither party is entitled to divorce limits the trial court's power regarding spousal support and property divisions.

Sometimes gross neglect of duty is the sum of a variety of acts. For

---

[23]Mark v. Mark, 145 Ohio St. 301, 30 Ohio Op. 534, 61 N.E.2d 595, 160 A.L.R. 608 (1945).

[24]Tyminski v. Tyminski, 8 Ohio Misc. 202, 37 Ohio Op. 2d 263, 221 N.E.2d 486 (C.P. 1966).

[25]Thompson v. Thompson, 1985 WL 9420 (Ohio Ct. App. 4th Dist. Lawrence County 1985).

[26]Walters v. Walters, 4 Ohio App. 3d 162, 446 N.E.2d 1173 (10th Dist. Franklin County 1982).

[27]Willis v. Willis, 19 Ohio App. 3d 45, 482 N.E.2d 1274 (11th Dist. Geauga County 1984); Glimcher v. Glimcher, 29 Ohio App. 2d 55, 58 Ohio Op. 2d 37, 278 N.E.2d 37 (10th Dist. Franklin County 1971); Combs v. Combs, 1979 WL 208447 (Ohio Ct. App. 2d Dist. Montgomery County 1979).

[28]Penate v. Penate, 1989 WL 62052 (Ohio Ct. App. 8th Dist. Cuyahoga County 1989).

[29]Clark v. Clark, 2004-Ohio-1577, 2004 WL 615708 (Ohio Ct. App. 7th Dist. Noble County 2004).

[30]Glick v. Glick, 1985 WL 4426 (Ohio Ct. App. 12th Dist. Clermont County 1985).

[31]See Pelanda v. Pelanda, 2002-Ohio-1123, 2002 WL 398667 (Ohio Ct. App. 5th Dist. Delaware County 2002).

[32]Murray v. Murray, 1988 WL 38879 (Ohio Ct. App. 7th Dist. Belmont County 1988).

instance, the Eighth District Court of Appeals affirmed the trial court's decision to grant a divorce on the ground of gross neglect of duty where the husband physically and verbally abused his wife, had his wedding ring melted down by a jeweler, and refused to speak to wife for period of time.[33] The Third District Court of Appeals has held that a divorce may be granted on the ground of gross neglect of duty where the wife assaulted her husband and refused to involve him in important events during the course of her pregnancy such as doctor visits and LaMaze classes.[34] Evidence that a husband is frequently absent from the marital home, that he verbally abuses his wife and that he physically assaulted his wife on one occasion is sufficient to establish gross neglect.[35] Gross neglect of duty has also been found where a husband failed to look for work in over one year, refused to have marital relations with wife, inflicted physical violence upon wife in private and in public, and generally degraded wife for no apparent reason.[36]

Ohio courts have been reluctant to find gross neglect of duty in cases of in-laws' interference with the marital relationship,[37] failure to adopt a particular religious faith or adoption of a religious faith which causes a strain on the marriage,[38] or sexual incompatibility.[39] Additionally, where a husband is merely neglectful of his wife, so that she loses all love for him and no longer wants to be married to him, but where the husband continues to live in and maintain the family home and his wife and child, gross neglect is not established.[40] The entire transcript must establish that the grievances complained of are not trivial or are not sufficiently disputed.[41]

---

[33]Moro v. Moro, 68 Ohio App. 3d 630, 589 N.E.2d 416 (8th Dist. Cuyahoga County 1990).

[34]Frizzell v. Frizzell, 1991 WL 271705 (Ohio Ct. App. 3d Dist. Logan County 1991).

[35]Elder v. Elder, 1993 WL 481433 (Ohio Ct. App. 3d Dist. Seneca County 1993).

[36]Ison v. Ronald, 1981 WL 5989 (Ohio Ct. App. 4th Dist. Pike County 1981).

[37]Miller v. Miller, 56 Ohio L. Abs. 280, 91 N.E.2d 804 (Ct. App. 2d Dist. Franklin County 1949); DeMeo v. DeMeo, 1985 WL 7438 (Ohio Ct. App. 8th Dist. Cuyahoga County 1985) (Eighth District granted husband a divorce based on in-law interference when coupled with wife's termination of sexual relations, refusal to cook when she did not work and a one time act of physical violence).

[38]Glimcher v. Glimcher, 29 Ohio App. 2d 55, 58 Ohio Op. 2d 37, 278 N.E.2d 37 (10th Dist. Franklin County 1971); Patterson v. Patterson, 12 Ohio N.P. (n.s.) 601, 1912 WL 842 (Insolv. 1912); Apple v. Apple, 28 Ohio N.P. (n.s.) 620, 1931 WL 2788 (C.P. 1931).

[39]Stephens v. Stephens, 78 Ohio L. Abs. 300, 156 N.E.2d 159 (Ct. App. 10th Dist. Franklin County 1957).

[40]Wise v. Wise, 1984 WL 14354 (Ohio Ct. App. 6th Dist. Lucas County 1984).

[41]Hunt v. Hunt, 63 Ohio App. 3d 178, 578 N.E.2d 498 (2d Dist. Montgomery County 1989).

§ 11:15 Grounds—Habitual drunkenness

The term "[h]abitual drunkenness"[1] has been defined as "[t]he custom or habit of getting drunk; the constant indulgence in stimulants, whereby intoxication is produced; . . . [t]hat degree of intemperance from the use of intoxicating drinks which disqualifies the person a great portion of the time from properly attending to business, or which would reasonably inflict a course of great mental anguish upon the innocent party."[2]

The few reported cases on habitual drunkenness have held that there must be a showing of frequent and regular recurrence of intoxication or drunkenness.[3] Occasional or sporadic indulgence is insufficient to establish habitual drunkenness.[4] Habitual drunkenness cases are sparse because often evidence of alcoholism or drunkenness is introduced with other aggravating circumstances to establish gross neglect of duty or extreme cruelty.[5]

§ 11:16 Grounds—Imprisonment of adverse party

RC 3105.01(H) defines this ground as "[i]mprisonment of the adverse party in a state or federal correctional institution at the time of filing the complaint." As the statute is specific to "adverse party" the incarceration of the plaintiff will not constitute grounds for divorce.[1] This ground includes a time limitation; the complaint must be filed while the defendant is imprisoned. However, there are no other requirements concerning the length of the prison term or the possibility of release of the defendant. The defendant's proclamation of innocence and expectations of prevailing on a petition for post-conviction relief have no impact on the ground for divorce.[2]

If a divorce is granted on this ground, but the couple subsequently

---

[Section 11:15]

[1]RC 3105.01(G).

[2]Black's Law Dictionary (6th ed.) p 711; Murphy v. Murphy, 85 Ohio App. 392, 40 Ohio Op. 254, 54 Ohio L. Abs. 116, 87 N.E.2d 102 (1st Dist. Hamilton County 1948).

[3]E.g., Eddy v. Eddy, 14 Ohio L. Abs. 277, 1932 WL 2488 (Ct. App. 7th Dist. Monroe County 1932); Burner v. Burner, 7 Ohio Dec. Rep. 140, 1 W.L.B. 164, 1876 WL 7271 (Ohio C.P. 1876).

[4]Collins v. Collins, 13 Ohio N.P. (n.s.) 114, 22 Ohio Dec. 342, 1912 WL 1580 (C.P. 1912); Cadwell v. Cadwell, 32 Ohio C.D. 266, 1911 WL 764 (Ohio Cir. Ct. 1911).

[5]Duff v. Duff, 69 Ohio L. Abs. 496, 126 N.E.2d 466 (Ct. App. 2d Dist. Montgomery County 1954); Sharkey v. Sharkey, 73 Ohio L. Abs. 321, 137 N.E.2d 575 (Ct. App. 2d Dist. Montgomery County 1955); Diemer v. Diemer., 1978 WL 218109 (Ohio Ct. App. 8th Dist. Cuyahoga County 1978); Zabolotny v. Zabolotny, 1979 WL 210665 (Ohio Ct. App. 8th Dist. Cuyahoga County 1979); Taylor v. Taylor, 1989 WL 65309 (Ohio Ct. App. 2d Dist. Montgomery County 1989).

[Section 11:16]

[1]Ware v. Ware, 1994 WL 675685 (Ohio Ct. App. 4th Dist. Ross County 1994).

[2]Vild v. Vild, 2000 WL 301005 (Ohio Ct. App. 8th Dist. Cuyahoga County 2000).

remarries while the defendant is on parole, the plaintiff is not entitled to a divorce on this ground if the paroled spouse returns to prison under the same sentence.[3]

The term "correctional institution" is not defined by the statute. The term has been defined elsewhere as "[a] generic term describing prisons, jails, reformatories and other places of correction and detention."[4] For the purposes of RC 3105.01(H), the term "correctional institution" means, at a minimum, penitentiaries and reformatories.[5]

An incarcerated defendant may seek transportation to attend civil proceedings by filing a petition for a writ of habeas corpus ad testificandum.[6] An incarcerated defendant has no absolute due process right to attend a civil/divorce proceeding to which he is a party.[7] However, the issuance of a writ of habeas corpus ad testificandum is a matter within the trial court's discretion.

When considering a writ of habeas corpus ad testificandum, the trial court shall weigh the nine *Mancino* factors in determining whether to permit an incarcerated party to attend the civil/divorce

---

[3]Miller v. Miller, 19 Ohio App. 518, 4 Ohio L. Abs. 108, 1926 WL 2923 (5th Dist. Muskingum County 1926).

[4]Black's Law Dictionary (6th ed.) p 344.

[5]Bowers v. Bowers, 114 Ohio St. 568, 4 Ohio L. Abs. 275, 151 N.E. 750 (1926).

[6]In re Colburn, 30 Ohio St. 3d 141, 507 N.E.2d 1138 (1987); Wall v. Wall, 1999 WL 978666 (Ohio Ct. App. 6th Dist. Williams County 1999); Brown v. Brown, 2003-Ohio-4878, 2003 WL 22120269 (Ohio Ct. App. 7th Dist. Mahoning County 2003); Harden v. City of Dayton, 2008-Ohio-1599, 2008 WL 867734 (Ohio Ct. App. 2d Dist. Montgomery County 2008).

[7]Dragojevic-Wiczen v. Wiczen, 101 Ohio App. 3d 152, 655 N.E.2d 222 (11th Dist. Trumbull County 1995), dismissed, appeal not allowed, 72 Ohio St. 3d 1539, 650 N.E.2d 479 (1995); Kampfer v. Donnalley, 125 Ohio App. 3d 359, 708 N.E.2d 750 (7th Dist. Columbiana County 1998); Quimby v. Quimby, 1988 WL 96630 (Ohio Ct. App. 7th Dist. Columbiana County 1988); Bissell v. Bissell, 1990 WL 56795 (Ohio Ct. App. 6th Dist. Huron County 1990); Meadows v. Meadows, 1990 WL 65374 (Ohio Ct. App. 7th Dist. Belmont County 1990); Waites v. Waites, 1994 WL 102396 (Ohio Ct. App. 11th Dist. Lake County 1994); Fraley v. Fraley, 1999 WL 960963 (Ohio Ct. App. 2d Dist. Montgomery County 1999); Sweet v. Sweet, 2001 WL 1775387 (Ohio Ct. App. 5th Dist. Richland County 2001); Dale v. Dale, 2003-Ohio-1113, 2003 WL 959891 (Ohio Ct. App. 10th Dist. Franklin County 2003); Brown v. Weidner, 2006-Ohio-6852, 2006 WL 3771981 (Ohio Ct. App. 3d Dist. Seneca County 2006), appeal not allowed, 113 Ohio St. 3d 1512, 2007-Ohio-2208, 866 N.E.2d 511 (2007), petition for cert. filed (U.S. Aug. 9, 2007); Lonergan v. State Med. Bd. of Ohio, 2006-Ohio-6790, 2006 WL 3743097 (Ohio Ct. App. 10th Dist. Franklin County 2006); Waters v. Lattany, 2007-Ohio-1047, 2007 WL 707519 (Ohio Ct. App. 6th Dist. Lucas County 2007); Alexander v. Alexander, 2007-Ohio-3933, 2007 WL 2206856 (Ohio Ct. App. 5th Dist. Muskingum County 2007); Faith v. Scuba, 2007-Ohio-6563, 2007 WL 4292740 (Ohio Ct. App. 11th Dist. Geauga County 2007), appeal not allowed, 117 Ohio St. 3d 1478, 2008-Ohio-1841, 884 N.E.2d 1109 (2008); Gaietto v. Noveck, 2008-Ohio-519, 2008 WL 351460 (Ohio Ct. App. 3d Dist. Seneca County 2008); Hageman v. Brown, 2008-Ohio-3218, 2008 WL 2596298 (Ohio Ct. App. 3d Dist. Hancock County 2008); Lopshire v. Lopshire, 2008-Ohio-5946, 2008 WL 4901772 (Ohio Ct. App. 11th Dist. Portage County 2008); Anderson v. Holskey, 2009-Ohio-3053, 2009 WL 1813800 (Ohio Ct. App. 7th Dist. Belmont County 2009); In re P.J., 2009-Ohio-182, 2009 WL 119811 (Ohio Ct. App. 11th Dist. Ashtabula County 2009).

proceeding. The nine factors are: (1) whether the inmate's request to be present at trial reflects something more than a desire to be temporarily freed from prison; (2) whether the inmate is capable of conducting an intelligent and responsive argument; (3) the cost and convenience of transporting the inmate to court; (4) any security risk posed by the inmate's presence; (5) the substantiality of the litigated issues; (6) the need for resolution of those issues; (7) the possibility of delaying the trial until the prisoner is released; (8) the probability of success on the merits, and (9) the inmate's interest in presenting evidence in person, rather than via deposition.[8]

Deposition testimony may be used as an alternative to the in-court testimony of an incarcerated party.[9] The existence of this alternative has been cited as justification for the denial of a writ of habeas corpus ad testificandum.[10]

§ 11:17 Grounds—Out-of-state divorce

The procurement of a divorce outside Ohio, where the party who procured it is released from the obligations of the marriage while those same obligations remain binding upon the other party, is grounds for divorce in Ohio.[1]

Any state in which either party is domiciled has jurisdiction to terminate the marital relationship; however, without the minimum contacts necessary to establish personal jurisdiction over the defendant, determinations of allocation of parental rights and responsibilities, child support, spousal support, and property settlement may not

---

[8]In re Colburn, 30 Ohio St. 3d 141, 507 N.E.2d 1138 (1987); Nye v. Nye, 1997 WL 346110 (Ohio Ct. App. 1st Dist. Hamilton County 1997); Brown v. Brown, 2003-Ohio-4878, 2003 WL 22120269 (Ohio Ct. App. 7th Dist. Mahoning County 2003); Savage v. Savage, 2004-Ohio-6341, 2004 WL 2697281 (Ohio Ct. App. 11th Dist. Lake County 2004); Mancino v. City of Lakewood, 36 Ohio App. 3d 219, 523 N.E.2d 332 (8th Dist. Cuyahoga County 1987); Alexander v. Alexander, 2007-Ohio-3933, 2007 WL 2206856 (Ohio Ct. App. 5th Dist. Muskingum County 2007); Rowe v. Stillpass, 2006-Ohio-3789, 2006 WL 2045904 (Ohio Ct. App. 4th Dist. Lawrence County 2006); State ex rel. Maxwell v. Trikilis, 2007-Ohio-1355, 2007 WL 879670 (Ohio Ct. App. 9th Dist. Medina County 2007); Carrion v. Carrion, 2007-Ohio-6142, 2007 WL 4083308 (Ohio Ct. App. 9th Dist. Lorain County 2007); Abuhilwa v. Board, 2008-Ohio-5326, 2008 WL 4561209 (Ohio Ct. App. 4th Dist. Pickaway County 2008).

[9]Wernert v. Wernert, 61 Ohio Misc. 2d 436, 579 N.E.2d 800 (C.P. 1991); Perdue v. Perdue, 1979 WL 209131 (Ohio Ct. App. 10th Dist. Franklin County 1979); Dragojevic-Wiczen v. Wiczen, 101 Ohio App. 3d 152, 655 N.E.2d 222 (11th Dist. Trumbull County 1995); Vild v. Vild, 2000 WL 301005 (Ohio Ct. App. 8th Dist. Cuyahoga County 2000); Stookey v. Stookey, 2002-Ohio-3352, 2002 WL 1396888 (Ohio Ct. App. 12th Dist. Warren County 2002); In re C.M., 2007-Ohio-3999, 2007 WL 2255232 (Ohio Ct. App. 9th Dist. Summit County 2007); In re P.J., 2009-Ohio-182, 2009 WL 119811 (Ohio Ct. App. 11th Dist. Ashtabula County 2009); In re M.M., 2009-Ohio-3400, 2009 WL 2004387 (Ohio Ct. App. 6th Dist. Wood County 2009); In re Destiny H.K., 2009-Ohio-771, 2009 WL 426432 (Ohio Ct. App. 6th Dist. Williams County 2009).

[10]Ware v. Ware, 1994 WL 675685 (Ohio Ct. App. 4th Dist. Ross County 1994).

[Section 11:17]

[1]RC 3105.01(I).

be ordered.[2] If such orders are made without personal jurisdiction over the defendant, then they are not entitled to full faith and credit.[3] The result is that the party who was divorced in the other jurisdiction can seek relief on matters such as allocation of parental rights and responsibilities, child support, spousal support, and property settlement in Ohio if Ohio has jurisdiction.[4] The result is the same where the spouse obtained a divorce in a foreign country.[5]

§ 11:18 Grounds—Living separate and apart

RC 3105.01(J) provides that a divorce will be granted on the application of either party when husband and wife have, without interruption, for one year, lived separate and apart without cohabitation. This provision is based on the theory living apart for a long period of time is the best evidence that a marriage has failed.[1] RC 3105.01(J) is considered Ohio's no-fault grounds for divorce.[2] This ground recog-

---

[2]See Text §§ 11:2 to 11:7, Preliminary considerations; Text Ch 27, Jurisdiction and Venue.

[3]Williams v. State of North Carolina, 317 U.S. 287, 63 S. Ct. 207, 87 L. Ed. 279, 143 A.L.R. 1273 (1942) (overruling recognized by, Beck v. Board of Ed. of City of New York, 182 Misc. 886, 50 N.Y.S.2d 19 (Sup 1944)); Ahmad v. Ahmad, 2001 WL 1518116 (Ohio Ct. App. 6th Dist. Lucas County 2001); Watson v. Watson, 2007-Ohio-468, 2007 WL 314380 (Ohio Ct. App. 11th Dist. Portage County 2007); Muter v. Muter, 2008-Ohio-6794, 2008 WL 5340876 (Ohio Ct. App. 9th Dist. Summit County 2008) (trial court did not give the North Carolina judgment for absolute divorce full faith and credit since the North Carolina decree reserved jurisdiction for all remaining issues and therefore was not a final order).

[4]Peterson v. Peterson, 1981 WL 2974 (Ohio Ct. App. 10th Dist. Franklin County 1981), reconsideration overruled, 1981 WL 3207 (Ohio Ct. App. 10th Dist. Franklin County 1981); Linck v. Linck, 31 Ohio Misc. 224, 60 Ohio Op. 2d 388, 288 N.E.2d 347 (C.P. 1972); Edwards v. Edwards, 1983 WL 2414 (Ohio Ct. App. 2d Dist. Montgomery County 1983); Trevino v. Trevino, 2007-Ohio-1874, 2007 WL 1160889 (Ohio Ct. App. 6th Dist. Lucas County 2007).

[5]Rousculp v. Rousculp, 17 Ohio App. 2d 101, 46 Ohio Op. 2d 125, 244 N.E.2d 512 (10th Dist. Franklin County 1968).

[Section 11:18]

[1]Dailey v. Dailey, 11 Ohio App. 3d 121, 463 N.E.2d 427 (2d Dist. Montgomery County 1983); Nolan v. Nolan, 2006-Ohio-3409, 2006 WL 1817075 (Ohio Ct. App. 11th Dist. Geauga County 2006); Harding v. Harding, 2005-Ohio-3010, 2005 WL 1406293 (Ohio Ct. App. 8th Dist. Cuyahoga County 2005), appeal not allowed, 107 Ohio St. 3d 1683, 2005-Ohio-6480, 839 N.E.2d 403 (2005); Tedrow v. Tedrow, 2003-Ohio-3693, 2003 WL 21638280 (Ohio Ct. App. 11th Dist. Trumbull County 2003); Sabo v. Sabo, 2003-Ohio-6586, 2003 WL 22900633 (Ohio Ct. App. 9th Dist. Lorain County 2003); Cline v. Cline, 1991 WL 38904 (Ohio Ct. App. 2d Dist. Greene County 1991); Tapfer v. Tapfer, 1990 WL 106148 (Ohio Ct. App. 9th Dist. Medina County 1990); Murray v. Murray, 1989 WL 106338 (Ohio Ct. App. 7th Dist. Belmont County 1989); Launsbach v. Launsbach, 1988 WL 128237 (Ohio Ct. App. 8th Dist. Cuyahoga County 1988); Mahle v. Mahle, 27 Ohio App. 3d 326, 500 N.E.2d 907 (10th Dist. Franklin County 1985).

[2]Mahle v. Mahle, 27 Ohio App. 3d 326, 500 N.E.2d 907 (10th Dist. Franklin County 1985); Mahon v. Mahon, 1999 WL 1483438 (Ohio Ct. App. 11th Dist. Trumbull County 1999); Payton v. Payton, 1997 WL 354797 (Ohio Ct. App. 4th Dist. Scioto

nizes the societal interest in terminating dead marriages regardless of blame.[3] A trial court does not abuse its discretion by refusing to hear evidence of other grounds when the parties have lived separate and apart for more than one year.[4]

One or both of the parties must leave the marital residence with the intent to abandon the marital relationship. Thus, where a husband and wife resided on the same property, but in different structures, and the husband continued to visit the marital home to assist and support the wife and to carry out household chores, the requisite intent to separate was absent.[5] Additionally, where one spouse was temporarily in a foreign city because of immigration problems, RC 3105.01(J) was inapplicable as grounds for divorce;[6] the one-year period does not begin to run until at least one party voluntarily desires the separation.[7] Furthermore, if the physical separation of the parties is because of reasons beyond their control, or if the absent party is incapable of forming an intent to leave, there is no abandonment of the marriage and a divorce cannot be granted. Thus, where one party suffers a stroke and is placed in a nursing home,[8] or where one party

---

County 1997); Jenkins v. Jenkins, 1988 WL 86763 (Ohio Ct. App. 8th Dist. Cuyahoga County 1988); Stoll v. Stoll, 1980 WL 354536 (Ohio Ct. App. 8th Dist. Cuyahoga County 1980); Ross v. Ross, 5th Dist. No. CA-5227 (June 11, 1980); Sproull v. Sproull, 1978 WL 216393 (Ohio Ct. App. 1st Dist. Hamilton County 1978); Broach v. Broach, 177 Ohio App. 3d 664, 2008-Ohio-4132, 895 N.E.2d 640 (2d Dist. Montgomery County 2008).

[3]Cassaro v. Cassaro, 50 Ohio App. 2d 368, 4 Ohio Op. 3d 320, 363 N.E.2d 753 (8th Dist. Cuyahoga County 1976); Harding v. Harding, 2005-Ohio-3010, 2005 WL 1406293 (Ohio Ct. App. 8th Dist. Cuyahoga County 2005), appeal not allowed, 107 Ohio St. 3d 1683, 2005-Ohio-6480, 839 N.E.2d 403 (2005); Boyd v. Edwards, 4 Ohio App. 3d 142, 446 N.E.2d 1151 (8th Dist. Cuyahoga County 1982); Maslach v. Maslach, 1979 WL 209930 (Ohio Ct. App. 8th Dist. Cuyahoga County 1979); Sproull v. Sproull, 1978 WL 216393 (Ohio Ct. App. 1st Dist. Hamilton County 1978).

[4]Murray v. Murray, 1989 WL 106338 (Ohio Ct. App. 7th Dist. Belmont County 1989); Sattler v. Sattler, 1983 WL 5869 (Ohio Ct. App. 8th Dist. Cuyahoga County 1983).

[5]Bennington v. Bennington, 56 Ohio App. 2d 201, 10 Ohio Op. 3d 201, 381 N.E.2d 1355 (10th Dist. Franklin County 1978).

[6]Coreano v. Coreano, 1984 WL 5497 (Ohio Ct. App. 8th Dist. Cuyahoga County 1984).

[7]Coreano v. Coreano, 1984 WL 5497 (Ohio Ct. App. 8th Dist. Cuyahoga County 1984); Heskett v. Heskett, 1991 WL 256136 (Ohio Ct. App. 2d Dist. Champaign County 1991); Launsbach v. Launsbach, 1988 WL 128237 (Ohio Ct. App. 8th Dist. Cuyahoga County 1988); Zalewski v. Zalewski, 1987 WL 5660 (Ohio Ct. App. 8th Dist. Cuyahoga County 1987); King v. King, 1984 WL 3692 (Ohio Ct. App. 6th Dist. Wood County 1984).

[8]Dailey v. Dailey, 11 Ohio App. 3d 121, 463 N.E.2d 427 (2d Dist. Montgomery County 1983).

is incompetent and placed in a nursing home,[9] the voluntary intent to live apart is absent.[10]

The effect of this statutory ground, when one of the parties is confined to a mental institution, is unclear. The statute no longer requires that the parties live separate and apart four years when one of the parties is continuously confined to a mental institution.[11] While in existence, that extended time requirement appeared to eliminate the need to show an intent to abandon the marital relationship when one of the parties was continuously confined to a mental institution.[12] Unresolved at this time are questions as to whether such an intent must exist and be proven,[13] whether a person confined to a mental institution can form such an intent, and whether the voluntariness or involuntariness of the commitment is important.

The presence or absence of sexual intercourse within the one-year period is not necessarily determinative of grounds under RC 3105.01(J).[14] Sexual intercourse one time during the one-year period does not destroy the grounds for divorce; "cohabitation" requires some regularity of functioning as husband and wife, sexually or otherwise.[15] Even several isolated acts of sexual intercourse, without other aspects of living together, have been held not to negate an assertion of living separate and apart without cohabitation.[16] In *Smith v. Smith*,[17] the trial court erred in denying a divorce on grounds of living separate and apart for more than one year. The relationship, which included "intermittent sex," did not constitute cohabitation.

The statutory time period that the parties are to live separate and apart must be continuous and without interruption. Acts of friendship, especially where parties share a mutual interest in a child, do

---

[9]Laube v. Laube, No. 5-80-3 (Ohio Ct. App. 3d Dist. Hancock County 1980).

[10]See Heskett v. Heskett, 1991 WL 256136 (Ohio Ct. App. 2d Dist. Champaign County 1991).

[11]1982 H.B. 477, eff. 7-12-82.

[12]O'Dell v. O'Dell, 55 Ohio App. 2d 149, 9 Ohio Op. 3d 296, 380 N.E.2d 723 (4th Dist. Scioto County 1977).

[13]Laube v. Laube, No. 5-80-3 (Ohio Ct. App. 3d Dist. Hancock County 1980).

[14]Pandya v. Pandya, 1986 WL 13177 (Ohio Ct. App. 6th Dist. Williams County 1986).

[15]Prather v. Prather, 1 Ohio Op. 188, 33 Ohio L. Abs. 336, 4 Ohio Supp. 243 (C.P. 1934); Brown v. Bordenkircher, 2006-Ohio-3904, 2006 WL 2110746 (Ohio Ct. App. 7th Dist. Jefferson County 2006); Fuller v. Fuller, 10 Ohio App. 3d 253, 461 N.E.2d 1348 (10th Dist. Franklin County 1983).

[16]Sindel v. Sindel, 1975 WL 181946 (Ohio Ct. App. 10th Dist. Franklin County 1975); Shapiro v. Shapiro, 1980 WL 353808 (Ohio Ct. App. 10th Dist. Franklin County 1980); Johnson v. Johnson, 1976 WL 188752 (Ohio Ct. App. 9th Dist. Summit County 1976).

[17]Smith v. Smith, 1997 WL 586707 (Ohio Ct. App. 6th Dist. Lucas County 1997).

not constitute interruption unless they constitute cohabitation.[18] The fact that a party, who abandons the marital home, has a change of heart and attempts to reenter the residence will not interrupt the time period if the attempt is unsuccessful, this is true even where it is unsuccessful because the other spouse has changed the locks.[19] In *Jenkins v. Jenkins*,[20] RC 3105.01(J) requirements were met where a party admitted in his answer that the parties had lived apart more than a year. The trial court, which had incorrectly relied on Civil Rule 75(M), was reversed.

RC 3105.01 provides that a court *may* grant a divorce on any of the enumerated grounds. Therefore, a trial court does not err when it grants a wife's complaint for legal separation instead of husband's counterclaim for divorce, although the evidence establishes that the parties have lived separate and apart for more than one year.[21] The use of the word *may* instead of the word *shall* gives the trial court discretion to determine whether a legal separation or a divorce is more appropriate.[22]

A party may file an amended complaint to include this ground during divorce proceedings on other grounds, if the statutory one-year time period expires while the divorce action is pending.[23] However, trial courts have held that if, during the pendency of a divorce proceeding, parties have lived separate and apart over one year and both parties openly admit to said fact, the trial court may grant the parties a

---

[18]Sindel v. Sindel, 1975 WL 181946 (Ohio Ct. App. 10th Dist. Franklin County 1975).

[19]Cassaro v. Cassaro, 50 Ohio App. 2d 368, 4 Ohio Op. 3d 320, 363 N.E.2d 753 (8th Dist. Cuyahoga County 1976).

[20]Jenkins v. Jenkins, 1988 WL 86763 (Ohio Ct. App. 8th Dist. Cuyahoga County 1988).

[21]Mahon v. Mahon, 1999 WL 1483438 (Ohio Ct. App. 11th Dist. Trumbull County 1999).

[22]Nolan v. Nolan, 2006-Ohio-3409, 2006 WL 1817075 (Ohio Ct. App. 11th Dist. Geauga County 2006); Harding v. Harding, 2005-Ohio-3010, 2005 WL 1406293 (Ohio Ct. App. 8th Dist. Cuyahoga County 2005), appeal not allowed, 107 Ohio St. 3d 1683, 2005-Ohio-6480, 839 N.E.2d 403 (2005); Harcourt v. Harcourt, 1998 WL 683811 (Ohio Ct. App. 11th Dist. Ashtabula County 1998).

[23]Shapiro v. Shapiro, 1980 WL 353808 (Ohio Ct. App. 10th Dist. Franklin County 1980); Cline v. Cline, 1991 WL 38904 (Ohio Ct. App. 2d Dist. Greene County 1991); Gordon v. Gordon, 1984 WL 6396 (Ohio Ct. App. 8th Dist. Cuyahoga County 1984); Nozik v. Nozik, 1977 WL 201385 (Ohio Ct. App. 8th Dist. Cuyahoga County 1977). Mathewson v. Mathewson, 2007-Ohio-574, 2007 WL 431480 (Ohio Ct. App. 2d Dist. Greene County 2007), appeal not allowed, 114 Ohio St. 3d 1427, 2007-Ohio-2904, 868 N.E.2d 680 (2007); Galloway v. Khan, 2006-Ohio-6637, 2006 WL 3703360 (Ohio Ct. App. 10th Dist. Franklin County 2006), appeal not allowed, 113 Ohio St. 3d 1490, 2007-Ohio-1986, 865 N.E.2d 914 (2007); Nolan v. Nolan, 2008-Ohio-1505, 2008 WL 835817 (Ohio Ct. App. 11th Dist. Geauga County 2008).

divorce based upon RC 3105.01(J) without the parties amending their complaint or counterclaim.[24]

§ 11:19   Grounds—Amendment of complaint

Rule 15 of the Ohio Rules of Civil Procedure states the proper procedure to follow when amending a pleading. Amendment of a complaint, as to grounds for divorce, cannot be permitted by oral motion unless the adverse party is given proper notice and an opportunity to prepare a defense.[1]

However, trial courts have held that if, during the pendency of a divorce proceeding, parties, by express or implied consent, allege and sufficiently prove grounds not raised by either parties' pleadings, the grounds shall be treated as if they had been raised in said pleadings. Failure of the party to amend the complaint and/or counterclaim for divorce, does not prevent the trial court from granting a divorce based upon the established grounds.[2] However, once a party objects to the evidence being presented at trial, since said issue and/or grounds were not plead in either party's complaint and/or counterclaim, the party raising the new issue must properly request the trial court to amend his/her pleading.[3] If not properly amended, said issue(s) cannot be addressed and/or the divorce cannot be granted on grounds not alleged in the complaint and/or counterclaim.

---

[24]Civ. R. 15(B). Mathewson v. Mathewson, 2007-Ohio-574, 2007 WL 431480 (Ohio Ct. App. 2d Dist. Greene County 2007), appeal not allowed, 114 Ohio St. 3d 1427, 2007-Ohio-2904, 868 N.E.2d 680 (2007); Galloway v. Khan, 2006-Ohio-6637, 2006 WL 3703360 (Ohio Ct. App. 10th Dist. Franklin County 2006), appeal not allowed, 113 Ohio St. 3d 1490, 2007-Ohio-1986, 865 N.E.2d 914 (2007).

[Section 11:19]

[1]Smith v. Smith, 1975 WL 182991 (Ohio Ct. App. 8th Dist. Cuyahoga County 1975); Pandya v. Pandya, 1986 WL 13177 (Ohio Ct. App. 6th Dist. Williams County 1986); McCree v. McCree, 1997 WL 16194 (Ohio Ct. App. 7th Dist. Mahoning County 1997); Nolan v. Nolan, 2008-Ohio-1505, 2008 WL 835817 (Ohio Ct. App. 11th Dist. Geauga County 2008) (husband had no objection to wife orally amending her Complaint for Divorce during the pendency of the trial).

[2]Civ. R. 15(B). Mathewson v. Mathewson, 2007-Ohio-574, 2007 WL 431480 (Ohio Ct. App. 2d Dist. Greene County 2007), appeal not allowed, 114 Ohio St. 3d 1427, 2007-Ohio-2904, 868 N.E.2d 680 (2007); Galloway v. Khan, 2006-Ohio-6637, 2006 WL 3703360 (Ohio Ct. App. 10th Dist. Franklin County 2006), appeal not allowed, 113 Ohio St. 3d 1490, 2007-Ohio-1986, 865 N.E.2d 914 (2007); Krepfl v. Krepfl, 1992 WL 190166 (Ohio Ct. App. 11th Dist. Lake County 1992); Moser v. Moser, 5 Ohio App. 3d 193, 450 N.E.2d 741 (9th Dist. Lorain County 1982); Sgro v. Sgro, 1988 WL 131438 (Ohio Ct. App. 6th Dist. Fulton County 1988); Shoemaker v. Shoemaker, 1992 WL 226349 (Ohio Ct. App. 4th Dist. Pike County 1992) (an implied amendment of the pleadings will not be permitted where it results in substantial prejudice to a party); Dickson v. Dickson, 1982 WL 5380 (Ohio Ct. App. 8th Dist. Cuyahoga County 1982).

[3]Pemberton v. Pemberton, 1988 WL 48035 (Ohio Ct. App. 4th Dist. Lawrence County 1988).

§ 11:20   Grounds—Incompatibility, unless denied by either party

Incompatibility, under RC 3105.01(K), is really not a "ground" that has to be proven so much as a status that must be agreed on by both parties.[1] It is a consensual ground and not intended to be litigated.[2]

Incompatibility is typically alleged where (1) all matters are agreed upon, but the parties cannot proceed with a dissolution of marriage because one of the parties is unable to attend the dissolution hearing; (2) the alternative no fault ground of living separate and apart for one year has not occurred; or (3) the parties come to an agreement on terms for divorce at a final hearing and there is an aversion to imposing or declaring other fault grounds.

The requirement that the allegation of incompatibility not be denied by either party was included to prevent the unilateral declaration of incompatibility by one party, which would otherwise give the court the jurisdiction to terminate the marriage and make all concomitant orders.[3] However, a party's failure to appear at trial will not be deemed a denial of incompatibility, and a court may grant a divorce on grounds of incompatibility with the testimony of the appearing

---

[Section 11:20]

[1]Rodgers v. Henninger Rodgers, 2003-Ohio-2642, 2003 WL 21185784 (Ohio Ct. App. 5th Dist. Licking County 2003); Byers v. Byers, 2001 WL 111776 (Ohio Ct. App. 5th Dist. Stark County 2001); Lehman v. Lehman, 72 Ohio App. 3d 68, 593 N.E.2d 447 (4th Dist. Hocking County 1991); Galloway v. Khan, 2006-Ohio-6637, 2006 WL 3703360 (Ohio Ct. App. 10th Dist. Franklin County 2006), appeal not allowed, 113 Ohio St. 3d 1490, 2007-Ohio-1986, 865 N.E.2d 914 (2007); Stump v. Stump, 2007-Ohio-6553, 2007 WL 4293302 (Ohio Ct. App. 3d Dist. Logan County 2007); Ahwajee v. Ahwajee, 2008-Ohio-6844, 2008 WL 5381689 (Ohio Ct. App. 5th Dist. Stark County 2008).

[2]Vanatta v. Aten, 1995 WL 347903 (Ohio Ct. App. 5th Dist. Licking County 1995), dismissed, appeal not allowed, 73 Ohio St. 3d 1425, 652 N.E.2d 798 (1995); Hirt v. Hirt, 2003-Ohio-2425, 2003 WL 21078093 (Ohio Ct. App. 9th Dist. Medina County 2003); Bernard v. Bernard, 2002-Ohio-552, 2002 WL 206411 (Ohio Ct. App. 7th Dist. Columbiana County 2002); Sancho v. Sancho, 1994 WL 369488 (Ohio Ct. App. 3d Dist. Union County 1994); Galloway v. Khan, 2006-Ohio-6637, 2006 WL 3703360 (Ohio Ct. App. 10th Dist. Franklin County 2006), appeal not allowed, 113 Ohio St. 3d 1490, 2007-Ohio-1986, 865 N.E.2d 914 (2007); Stump v. Stump, 2007-Ohio-6553, 2007 WL 4293302 (Ohio Ct. App. 3d Dist. Logan County 2007); Ahwajee v. Ahwajee, 2008-Ohio-6844, 2008 WL 5381689 (Ohio Ct. App. 5th Dist. Stark County 2008).

[3]Hirt v. Hirt, 2003-Ohio-2425, 2003 WL 21078093 (Ohio Ct. App. 9th Dist. Medina County 2003); Rodgers v. Henninger Rodgers, 2003-Ohio-2642, 2003 WL 21185784 (Ohio Ct. App. 5th Dist. Licking County 2003); Bernard v. Bernard, 2002-Ohio-552, 2002 WL 206411 (Ohio Ct. App. 7th Dist. Columbiana County 2002); Byers v. Byers, 2001 WL 111776 (Ohio Ct. App. 5th Dist. Stark County 2001); Lehman v. Lehman, 72 Ohio App. 3d 68, 593 N.E.2d 447 (4th Dist. Hocking County 1991); Galloway v. Khan, 2006-Ohio-6637, 2006 WL 3703360 (Ohio Ct. App. 10th Dist. Franklin County 2006), appeal not allowed, 113 Ohio St. 3d 1490, 2007-Ohio-1986, 865 N.E.2d 914 (2007).

party and a corroborating witness.[4] Both the majority and dissenting opinions in *Lehman v. Lehman*[5] suggested that RC 3105.01 should address the issue of a unilateral desire of one spouse to terminate the marriage, especially under unique circumstances such as in *Lehman* where one of the parties denied the couple's obvious incompatibility.[6]

In *Consorte v. Consorte*,[7] although wife had denied incompatibility was a ground for divorce in her answer, she was deemed to have waived the denial when she left the courthouse on the day of trial without permission. The trial proceeded and her request for a continuance through counsel was properly denied. Conversely, in *Hamrick v. Hamrick* and *Mathewson v. Mathewson*,[8] the appellate courts held it to be error to grant the wife a divorce pursuant to RC 3105.01(K) where the husband had denied the same in his written answer to the complaint for divorce. Likewise, the appellate court in *Hirt v. Hirt*[9] held that a divorce could not be granted on the grounds of incompatibility where the wife stated that they would not be incompatible "[I]f he would get rid of his girlfriend." The opinion in *Rodgers v. Henninger Rodgers*,[10] held that it was proper for the trial court to grant a divorce on the grounds of incompatibility where both parties had testified that they were incompatible, even though the wife subsequently objected to the magistrate's recommendation to grant the divorce on the grounds of incompatibility. However, it was clarified in

---

[4]Lindsey v. Lindsey, 1994 WL 123523 (Ohio Ct. App. 4th Dist. Lawrence County 1994); Byers v. Byers, 2001 WL 111776 (Ohio Ct. App. 5th Dist. Stark County 2001).

[5]Lehman v. Lehman, 72 Ohio App. 3d 68, 593 N.E.2d 447 (4th Dist. Hocking County 1991).

[6]See also Dudon v. Dudon, 1993 WL 224494 (Ohio Ct. App. 2d Dist. Montgomery County 1993) (when complaint for divorce is filed alleging incompatibility and later amended to include gross neglect of duty and extreme cruelty, trial court's inadvertently stating the original rather than amended grounds in its final judgment and decree will not be abuse of discretion, even if parties do not agree they are incompatible, providing other grounds are proven); Swihart v. Swihart, 1994 WL 704475 (Ohio Ct. App. 3d Dist. Union County 1994) (it is not error for the trial court to preclude evidence on any other grounds when the complaint for divorce alleges incompatibility and the responsive pleading does not deny it). But see Sancho v. Sancho, 1994 WL 369488 (Ohio Ct. App. 3d Dist. Union County 1994) (harmless error to grant divorce on grounds of incompatibility when husband denied incompatibility where evidence supported other grounds asserted in complaint).

[7]Consorte v. Consorte, 1998 WL 196184 (Ohio Ct. App. 8th Dist. Cuyahoga County 1998).

[8]Hamrick v. Hamrick, 2001 WL 1782883 (Ohio Ct. App. 5th Dist. Stark County 2001); Mathewson v. Mathewson, 2007-Ohio-574, 2007 WL 431480 (Ohio Ct. App. 2d Dist. Greene County 2007), appeal not allowed, 114 Ohio St. 3d 1427, 2007-Ohio-2904, 868 N.E.2d 680 (2007).

[9]Hirt v. Hirt, 2003-Ohio-2425, 2003 WL 21078093 (Ohio Ct. App. 9th Dist. Medina County 2003).

[10]Rodgers v. Henninger Rodgers, 2003-Ohio-2642, 2003 WL 21185784 (Ohio Ct. App. 5th Dist. Licking County 2003).

Bernard v. Bernard[11] that where both parties pled incompatibility that the court is not bound to grant the divorce based on that ground. Based on the evidence presented, the court may grant the divorce on other grounds, if other grounds are proven. Since marital misconduct is no longer a factor in spousal support assessment, the court's granting the divorce on grounds of gross neglect of duty and extreme cruelty was not prejudicial to the wife.

§ 11:21 Defenses—In general

Generally, defenses either in the form of denials or affirmative defenses must be pleaded in the answer or other responsive pleadings as required by Civil Rule 8 except the listed defenses in Civ. R. 12(B), which may be made by motion.[1] Failure to timely assert a defense constitutes a waiver of that defense.[2] Similarly, a failure to respond to a particular allegation contained in the pleading of an opposing party

---

[11]Bernard v. Bernard, 2002-Ohio-552, 2002 WL 206411 (Ohio Ct. App. 7th Dist. Columbiana County 2002).

[Section 11:21]

[1]Poe v. Poe, 99 Ohio App. 542, 59 Ohio Op. 441, 135 N.E.2d 484 (3d Dist. Auglaize County 1954); Lehman v. Hubbard, 2006-Ohio-6906, 2006 WL 3783461 (Ohio Ct. App. 9th Dist. Summit County 2006); Hills v. Patton, 2008-Ohio-1343, 2008 WL 755305 (Ohio Ct. App. 3d Dist. Allen County 2008); Ramsey v. Rutherford, 2008-Ohio-124, 2008 WL 142507 (Ohio Ct. App. 4th Dist. Ross County 2008); Gliozzo v. Univ. Urologists of Cleveland, Inc., 114 Ohio St. 3d 141, 2007-Ohio-3762, 870 N.E.2d 714 (2007); Hedrick v. Spitzer Motor City, Inc., 2007-Ohio-6820, 2007 WL 4442689 (Ohio Ct. App. 8th Dist. Cuyahoga County 2007); Guillory v. Ohio Dept. of Rehab. & Corr., 2008-Ohio-2299, 2008 WL 2026101 (Ohio Ct. App. 10th Dist. Franklin County 2008); UAP-Columbus JV326132 v. O. Valeria Stores, Inc., 2008-Ohio-588, 2008 WL 384236 (Ohio Ct. App. 10th Dist. Franklin County 2008); JP Morgan Chase Bank, N.A. v. Brown, 2008-Ohio-200, 2008 WL 186680 (Ohio Ct. App. 2d Dist. Montgomery County 2008); Property Asset Management, Inc. v. Shaffer, 2008-Ohio-4645, 2008 WL 4193251 (Ohio Ct. App. 3d Dist. Union County 2008); Boylen v. Ohio Dept. of Rehab. & Corr., 2009-Ohio-1953, 2009 WL 1114215 (Ohio Ct. App. 5th Dist. Richland County 2009); Thayer v. Diver, 2009-Ohio-2053, 2009 WL 1167888 (Ohio Ct. App. 6th Dist. Lucas County 2009).

[2]Civ. R. 12(H). State ex rel. The Plain Dealer Publishing Co. v. Cleveland, 75 Ohio St. 3d 31, 1996-Ohio-379, 661 N.E.2d 187 (1996) (holding modified by, Jim's Steak House, Inc. v. City of Cleveland, 81 Ohio St. 3d 18, 1998-Ohio-440, 688 N.E.2d 506 (1998)); Lehman v. Hubbard, 2006-Ohio-6906, 2006 WL 3783461 (Ohio Ct. App. 9th Dist. Summit County 2006); Timms v. Timms, 1991 WL 57167 (Ohio Ct. App. 5th Dist. Fairfield County 1991); Kindred v. Kindred, 1999 WL 462370 (Ohio Ct. App. 8th Dist. Cuyahoga County 1999); Asad v. Asad, 2001 WL 1612099 (Ohio Ct. App. 8th Dist. Cuyahoga County 2001); Pinotti v. Pinotti, 2003-Ohio-3104, 2003 WL 21386277 (Ohio Ct. App. 6th Dist. Lucas County 2003); Davis v. Davis, 2003-Ohio-4657, 2003 WL 22052785 (Ohio Ct. App. 8th Dist. Cuyahoga County 2003); State ex rel. Athens Cty. Dept. of Job & Family Servs. v. Martin, 2008-Ohio-1849, 2008 WL 1758896 (Ohio Ct. App. 4th Dist. Athens County 2008), appeal not allowed, 119 Ohio St. 3d 1448, 2008-Ohio-4487, 893 N.E.2d 518 (2008); Stafford v. Columbus Bonding Ctr., 177 Ohio App.3d 799, 2008-Ohio-3948, 896 N.E.2d 191 (10th Dist. Franklin County 2008); Mitchell v. Thompson, 2007-Ohio-5362, 2007 WL 2897752 (Ohio Ct. App. 4th Dist. Gallia County 2007); Portman v. Mabe, 2008-Ohio-3508, 2008 WL 2718506 (Ohio Ct. App. 3d Dist. Van Wert County 2008); Business Data Sys., Inc. v. Gourmet Cafe Corp., 2008-Ohio-409, 2008 WL 315600 (Ohio Ct. App. 9th Dist. Summit County

is deemed an admission of that allegation; however, the initiating party must still prove the truth of the pleading's averments to the court's satisfaction before judgment can be granted, and the trial court should not deny the opposing party, who appears at a hearing but fails to file a responsive pleading, the right to present evidence on his behalf.[3] Civil Rule 9 should also be consulted when pleading special matters such as capacity, fraud, judgment, and time and place.[4] The burden of proving affirmative defenses falls upon the party asserting

---

2008); Snyder Computer Sys., Inc. v. Stives, 175 Ohio App. 3d 653, 2008-Ohio-1192, 888 N.E.2d 1117 (7th Dist. Jefferson County 2008); Abuhilwa v. O'Brien, 2007-Ohio-4328, 2007 WL 2405723 (Ohio Ct. App. 2d Dist. Montgomery County 2007), appeal not allowed, 116 Ohio St. 3d 1459, 2007-Ohio-6803, 878 N.E.2d 35 (2007); Walton v. Higginbottom, 2007-Ohio-7056, 2007 WL 4554458 (Ohio Ct. App. 9th Dist. Summit County 2007); Marok v. The Ohio State Univ., 2008-Ohio-3170, 2008 WL 2553055 (Ohio Ct. App. 10th Dist. Franklin County 2008); O'Brien v. City of Olmsted Falls, 2008-Ohio-2658, 2008 WL 2252527 (Ohio Ct. App. 8th Dist. Cuyahoga County 2008); Lewis v. Buxton, 2007-Ohio-5986, 2007 WL 3317481 (Ohio Ct. App. 2d Dist. Greene County 2007); Broach v. Broach, 177 Ohio App.3d 664, 2008-Ohio-4132, 895 N.E. 2d 640 (2d Dist. Montgomery County 2008); Hicks v. Estate of Mulvaney, 2008-Ohio-4391, 2008 WL 3990811 (Ohio Ct. App. 2d Dist. Montgomery County 2008); Neighbor v. Nalepka, 2008-Ohio-4708, 2008 WL 4263562 (Ohio Ct. App. 8th Dist. Cuyahoga County 2008); State ex rel. Deiter v. McGuire, 119 Ohio St.3d 384, 2008-Ohio-4536, 894 N.E.2d 680 (2008); Nat'l City Commercial Capital Corp. v. Page, 2009-Ohio-1161, 2009 WL 683773 (Ohio Ct. App. 12th Dist. Butler County 2009); U.S. Bank Nat'l Assoc. v. Golf Course Mgt., Inc., 2009-Ohio-2807, 2009 WL 1655395 (Ohio Ct. App. 12th Dist. Clermont County 2009).

[3]Civ. R. 8(D). Heffernan v. Heffernan, 1981 WL 4115 (Ohio Ct. App. 9th Dist. Summit County 1981); Skaggs v. Skaggs, 1995 WL 368838 (Ohio Ct. App. 3d Dist. Marion County 1995); Rochow v. Rochow, 1996 WL 227763 (Ohio Ct. App. 7th Dist. Mahoning County 1996); Weightman v. Weightman, 1999 WL 354405 (Ohio Ct. App. 10th Dist. Franklin County 1999); Riley v. Riley, 2000 WL 554478 (Ohio Ct. App. 12th Dist. Butler County 2000); Rue v. Rue, 169 Ohio App. 3d 160, 2006-Ohio-5131, 862 N.E.2d 166 (2d Dist. Greene County 2006); Discover Bank v. Hicks, 2007-Ohio-4448, 2007 WL 2453293 (Ohio Ct. App. 4th Dist. Washington County 2007); Roark v. Rydell, 174 Ohio App. 3d 186, 2007-Ohio-6873, 881 N.E.2d 333 (1st Dist. Hamilton County 2007); Harper v. New England Handpiece Repair, Inc., 2007-Ohio-6307, 2007 WL 4200602 (Ohio Ct. App. 8th Dist. Cuyahoga County 2007); Capital One Bank v. Zavatchen, 2008-Ohio-4224, 2008 WL 3870619 (Ohio Ct. App. 8th Dist. Cuyahoga County 2008); Doepker v. Willo Security, Inc., 2008-Ohio-2008, 2008 WL 1850970 (Ohio Ct. App. 5th Dist. Stark County 2008), appeal not allowed, 119 Ohio St. 3d 1448, 2008-Ohio-4487, 893 N.E.2d 518 (2008); Sharp v. Thompson, 2008-Ohio-4990, 2008 WL 4382678 (Ohio Ct. App. 5th Dist. Knox County 2008); Fitworks Holding, LLC v. Sciranko, 2008-Ohio-4861, 2008 WL 4356098 (Ohio Ct. App. 8th Dist. Cuyahoga County 2008); Turner v. Progressive Ins. Co., 2008-Ohio-4988, 2008 WL 4382698 (Ohio Ct. App. 5th Dist. Holmes County 2008); In re Guardianship of Schnierle v. Schnierle, 2009-Ohio-1580, 2009 WL 840393 (Ohio Ct. App. 5th Dist. Stark County 2009); Whited v. Whited, 2006-Ohio-5551, 2006 WL 3020335 (Ohio Ct. App. 5th Dist. Stark County 2006) and Gordon v. Gordon, 2009-Ohio-177, 2009 WL 106653 (Ohio Ct. App. 5th Dist. Muskingum County 2009) (trial court may limit the non responsive party's presentation of evidence if he/she failed to file an answer or responsive pleading).

[4]Cayten v. Cayten, 103 Ohio App. 3d 354, 659 N.E.2d 805 (11th Dist. Trumbull County 1995); Becker v. Becker, 1997 WL 451381 (Ohio Ct. App. 12th Dist. Clermont County 1997); Broach v. Broach, 177 Ohio App. 3d 664, 2008-Ohio-4132, 895 N.E.2d 640 (2d Dist. Montgomery County 2008).

the defense.[5] An affirmative defense must be proven by a preponderance of the evidence.[6]

Civil Rule 8(C) allows a defendant to affirmatively plead "any other matter constituting an avoidance or affirmative defense."[7] The effect of this language is to allow a defendant to plead matters defensively, which are more factual in nature if the case so requires. Also, the liberal amendment mechanism provided in Civil Rule 15 may be used in a proper situation.[8] This permits either party to adjust the pleadings as new facts are discovered and is very commonly used in divorce litigation. A trial court, however, cannot unilaterally raise affirmative defenses, specifically statute of limitations, on behalf of a party that fails to do so.[9]

---

[5]Lehman v. Hubbard, 2006-Ohio-6906, 2006 WL 3783461 (Ohio Ct. App. 9th Dist. Summit County 2006); Eyre v. Eyre, 2006-Ohio-6492, 2006 WL 3544820 (Ohio Ct. App. 11th Dist. Portage County 2006); Faubel v. Faubel, 2006-Ohio-4679, 2006 WL 2590604 (Ohio Ct. App. 7th Dist. Mahoning County 2006); Nolan v. Nolan, 2008-Ohio-1505, 2008 WL 835817 (Ohio Ct. App. 11th Dist. Geauga County 2008); Hills v. Patton, 2008-Ohio-1343, 2008 WL 755305 (Ohio Ct. App. 3d Dist. Allen County 2008); Van Beusecum v. Continental Builders, Inc., 2008-Ohio-2141, 2008 WL 1932310 (Ohio Ct. App. 5th Dist. Delaware County 2008), cause dismissed, 119 Ohio St. 3d 1403, 2008-Ohio-3825, 891 N.E.2d 765 (2008).

[6]Hanlon v. J. E. Miller Transfer & Storage Co., 149 Ohio St. 387, 37 Ohio Op. 87, 79 N.E.2d 220 (1948); Piciacchia v. Piciacchia, 2007-Ohio-2328, 2007 WL 1413216 (Ohio Ct. App. 5th Dist. Stark County 2007); Walters v. Murphy, 2007-Ohio-3426, 2007 WL 1934730 (Ohio Ct. App. 5th Dist. Ashland County 2007); Jay v. Massachusetts Cas. Ins. Co., 2008-Ohio-846, 2008 WL 555440 (Ohio Ct. App. 5th Dist. Stark County 2008), appeal not allowed, 119 Ohio St. 3d 1409, 2008-Ohio-3880, 891 N.E.2d 769 (2008); Adams v. Disbennett, 2008-Ohio-5398, 2008 WL 4615623 (Ohio Ct. App. 3d Dist. Marion County 2008) (trial court held that defendant must prove affirmative defenses by clear and convincing evidence).

[7]A husband was unsuccessful in halting a divorce where he claimed that the court would be violating his "right to free exercise of his religion" if they granted the divorce when his religion does not recognize divorce. Hogan v. Hogan, 140 Ohio App. 3d 301, 747 N.E.2d 299 (12th Dist. Butler County 2000).

[8]Callihan v. Callihan, 1979 WL 210731 (Ohio Ct. App. 8th Dist. Cuyahoga County 1979); Waterfield v. Waterfield, 1979 WL 206879 (Ohio Ct. App. 4th Dist. Brown County 1979); Kassoy v. Kassoy, 1985 WL 9882 (Ohio Ct. App. 10th Dist. Franklin County 1985); Pandya v. Pandya, 1986 WL 13177 (Ohio Ct. App. 6th Dist. Williams County 1986); Dean v. Dean, 2008-Ohio-754, 2008 WL 498476 (Ohio Ct. App. 2d Dist. Clark County 2008); Gannon v. Gannon, 2008-Ohio-4484, 2008 WL 4093687 (Ohio Ct. App. 6th Dist. Wood County 2008).

[9]Lehman v. Hubbard, 2006-Ohio-6906, 2006 WL 3783461 (Ohio Ct. App. 9th Dist. Summit County 2006); Thrower v. Olowo, 2003-Ohio-2049, 2003 WL 1924652 (Ohio Ct. App. 8th Dist. Cuyahoga County 2003); O'Brien v. City of Olmsted Falls, 2008-Ohio-2658, 2008 WL 2252527 (Ohio Ct. App. 8th Dist. Cuyahoga County 2008); Walton v. Higginbottom, 2007-Ohio-7056, 2007 WL 4554458 (Ohio Ct. App. 9th Dist. Summit County 2007); Welch v. Staggs, 2009-Ohio-379, 2009 WL 223414 (Ohio Ct. App. 4th Dist. Scioto County 2009).

Generally, the evidence, which may be introduced at trial, is limited to facts, which were in existence prior to the filing of the pleading.[10] However, upon the filing of a motion pursuant to Civil Rule 15(E), the trial court may permit a party to file and serve a supplemental pleading.[11] If the supplemental pleading alleges facts, which came into existence after the filing of the initial pleading, the trial court's inquiry will extend to evidence, which tends to prove or disprove these new allegations.[12] The trial court must provide sufficient notice and opportunity to prepare to defend the new allegations stated in a supplemental pleading.[13]

§ 11:22 Defenses—Condonation and recrimination

Condonation and recrimination have been abolished as defenses in a divorce proceeding.[1] Condonation is the voluntary forgiveness, either express or implied, of a marital wrong with the expectation that the wrong will not be repeated.[2] The legal consequence of condonation was to prevent the wrong or injury, which was forgiven, from later being used as a ground or cause for divorce.[3] Thus, the effect of condonation was to encourage reconciliation.

Recrimination is an equitable doctrine based on "clean hands," which prevents a plaintiff, who is also guilty of marital fault, from

---

[10]Zatko v. Zatko, 100 Ohio App. 223, 60 Ohio Op. 200, 136 N.E.2d 358 (6th Dist. Lucas County 1953); Nissen v. Nissen, 1983 WL 6898 (Ohio Ct. App. 6th Dist. Lucas County 1983).

[11]Stoll v. Stoll, 1980 WL 354536 (Ohio Ct. App. 8th Dist. Cuyahoga County 1980); Pemberton v. Pemberton, 1988 WL 48035 (Ohio Ct. App. 4th Dist. Lawrence County 1988).

[12]See Text § 25:9, Pleadings—Amended and supplemental pleadings. Tompkins v. Tompkins, 107 Ohio App. 229, 8 Ohio Op. 2d 129, 157 N.E.2d 755 (2d Dist. Montgomery County 1958); Brock v. Brock, 1977 WL 199377 (Ohio Ct. App. 3d Dist. Auglaize County 1977).

[13]McCree v. McCree, 1997 WL 16194 (Ohio Ct. App. 7th Dist. Mahoning County 1997); Pemberton v. Pemberton, 1988 WL 48035 (Ohio Ct. App. 4th Dist. Lawrence County 1988).

[Section 11:22]

[1]RC 3105.10(C). Dabney v. Dabney, 1976 WL 189489 (Ohio Ct. App. 1st Dist. Hamilton County 1976); Juranko v. Juranko, 1978 WL 215918 (Ohio Ct. App. 11th Dist. Lake County 1978); Gerlach v. Gerlach, 1979 WL 209399 (Ohio Ct. App. 10th Dist. Franklin County 1979); Floyd v. Floyd, 1980 WL 352632 (Ohio Ct. App. 2d Dist. Montgomery County 1980); Epperly v. Epperly, 1982 WL 5070 (Ohio Ct. App. 9th Dist. Summit County 1982); Helms v. Helms, 1982 WL 6886 (Ohio Ct. App. 3d Dist. Hancock County 1982); Wernert v. Wernert, 61 Ohio Misc. 2d 436, 579 N.E.2d 800 (C.P. 1991).

[2]Maughan v. Maughan, 21 Ohio Op. 2d 121, 89 Ohio L. Abs. 282, 184 N.E.2d 628 (C.P. 1961); Mears v. Mears, 30 Ohio Op. 177, 42 Ohio L. Abs. 346, 15 Ohio Supp. 61 (C.P. 1945); Rouault v. Rouault, 1976 WL 190961 (Ohio Ct. App. 8th Dist. Cuyahoga County 1976); Ross v. Ross, 5th Dist. No. CA-5227 (June 11, 1980).

[3]Duff v. Duff, 69 Ohio L. Abs. 496, 126 N.E.2d 466 (Ct. App. 2d Dist. Montgomery County 1954); Dase v. Dase, 78 Ohio L. Abs. 144, 152 N.E.2d 20 (C.P. 1958).

obtaining a divorce.[4] The legal consequence of recrimination was that neither party could obtain a divorce because both were guilty. In 1985, *Mahle v. Mahle*[5] held that evidence of condonation and recrimination is inadmissible.

§ 11:23 Defenses—Collusion and connivance

Collusion is still a valid defense in Ohio.[1] An example of collusion is an agreement between the parties to obtain a divorce by suppressing facts or manufacturing evidence.[2] With the advent of no-fault divorce and dissolution of marriage, the reason for collusive behavior between parties has disappeared. Under Civil Rule 75(M), an admission by a party will now be held to be corroboration rather than collusion, unless the court determines the admission is obtained by fraud, connivance, coercion or other improper means.[3] In *Jenkins v. Jenkins*,[4] RC 3105.01(J) requirements were met where a party admitted in answer that the parties had lived apart more than a year. The trial court, which had incorrectly relied on Civil Rule 75(L), was reversed.

Connivance may be described as one party agreeing to certain conduct of the other party, which conduct later becomes the basis of the complaint for divorce.[5] The essential element is the plaintiff's consent to the conduct. Equity precludes such acts from being the basis for a divorce since one cannot complain of that to which one consents.[6] It might also be argued that the plaintiff has become an accomplice in the defendant's conduct. Thus, equity dictates that a party cannot be relieved from a situation tainted by his or her own wrong.

Connivance may be proven directly or may be inferred from the facts. It may also include acquiescence to a known wrongful act.

---

[4]Shepard v. Shepard, 7th Dist. No. 966 (Feb. 27, 1973); Hilton v. Hilton, 1979 WL 209253 (Ohio Ct. App. 10th Dist. Franklin County 1979); Allen v. Allen, 1989 WL 30738 (Ohio Ct. App. 12th Dist. Butler County 1989).

[5]Mahle v. Mahle, 1985 WL 3877 (Ohio Ct. App. 10th Dist. Franklin County 1985).

[Section 11:23]

[1]Thomas v. Thomas, 5 Ohio App. 3d 94, 449 N.E.2d 478 (5th Dist. Licking County 1982); Dutton v. Dutton, 127 Ohio App. 3d 348, 713 N.E.2d 14 (7th Dist. Mahoning County 1998).

[2]Campbell v. Campbell, 36 Ohio Op. 232, 50 Ohio L. Abs. 9, 75 N.E.2d 698 (C.P. 1947); Maimone v. Maimone, 55 Ohio L. Abs. 566, 90 N.E.2d 383 (Ct. App. 8th Dist. Cuyahoga County 1949).

[3]Thomas v. Thomas, 5 Ohio App. 3d 94, 449 N.E.2d 478 (5th Dist. Licking County 1982); Born v. Born, 1977 WL 200404 (Ohio Ct. App. 10th Dist. Franklin County 1977); Weaver v. Weaver, 1978 WL 215762 (Ohio Ct. App. 3d Dist. Union County 1978); Haska v. Haska, 1989 WL 11272 (Ohio Ct. App. 11th Dist. Portage County 1989); Minnick v. Minnick, 1990 WL 102363 (Ohio Ct. App. 12th Dist. Madison County 1990).

[4]Jenkins v. Jenkins, 1988 WL 86763 (Ohio Ct. App. 8th Dist. Cuyahoga County 1988).

[5]Backenstoe v. Backenstoe, 14 Ohio Dec. 353, 1904 WL 728 (C.P. 1904).

[6]Backenstoe v. Backenstoe, 14 Ohio Dec. 353, 1904 WL 728 (C.P. 1904).

§ 11:24 Defenses—Insanity

When pleaded as an affirmative defense, the party asserting the defense of insanity has the burden of proof.[1] If proven, an insanity defense will operate as a bar to a divorce decree, since any acts by the defendant, which may, under ordinary circumstances, constitute a ground for divorce, were done without the requisite mental capacity.[2] For example, extreme cruelty requires voluntary or intentional conduct, and cannot be committed by an insane person who does not understand the nature of his acts.[3] However, a divorce may be granted against an insane person on the basis of acts, which were committed by him while he was sane.[4]

Mental capacity is a question of fact. An adjudication of insanity prior to the divorce proceeding is not a necessary prerequisite to the use of insanity as a defense.[5]

§ 11:25 Defenses—Res judicata

The doctrine of res judicata prohibits parties or those in privity with them from relitigating issues, which have already been litigated and reduced to judgment.[1] Thus, where the parties have been granted a decree of divorce by a court of competent jurisdiction, the doctrine

---

[Section 11:24]

[1]Nelson v. Nelson, 108 Ohio App. 365, 9 Ohio Op. 2d 318, 79 Ohio L. Abs. 602, 154 N.E.2d 653 (8th Dist. Cuyahoga County 1958); State v. Leisure, 2008-Ohio-6386, 2008 WL 5124019 (Ohio Ct. App. 12th Dist. Preble County 2008).

[2]Nelson v. Nelson, 108 Ohio App. 365, 9 Ohio Op. 2d 318, 79 Ohio L. Abs. 602, 154 N.E.2d 653 (8th Dist. Cuyahoga County 1958); Laube v. Laube, No. 5-80-3 (Ohio Ct. App. 3d Dist. Hancock County 1980).

[3]Heim v. Heim, 35 Ohio App. 408, 8 Ohio L. Abs. 166, 172 N.E. 451 (6th Dist. Lucas County 1930).

[4]Heim v. Heim, 35 Ohio App. 408, 8 Ohio L. Abs. 166, 172 N.E. 451 (6th Dist. Lucas County 1930); Butler v. Butler, 19 Ohio Misc. 2d 1, 482 N.E.2d 998 (C.P. 1984); Lewis v. Lewis, 6 Ohio N.P. (n.s.) 242, 18 Ohio Dec. 408, 1908 WL 643 (C.P. 1908); Benton v. Benton, 26 Ohio C.D. 613, 1909 WL 663 (Ohio Cir. Ct. 1909); Williams v. Williams, 19 Ohio L. Abs. 527, 1935 WL 3241 (Ct. App. 2d Dist. Franklin County 1935); Douglas v. Douglas, 46 Ohio L. Abs. 9, 68 N.E.2d 237 (Ct. App. 2d Dist. Franklin County 1944).

[5]Nelson v. Nelson, 108 Ohio App. 365, 9 Ohio Op. 2d 318, 79 Ohio L. Abs. 602, 154 N.E.2d 653 (8th Dist. Cuyahoga County 1958); Manning v. Manning, 1985 WL 11137 (Ohio Ct. App. 4th Dist. Pike County 1985).

[Section 11:25]

[1]Filip v. Filip, 1989 WL 21404 (Ohio Ct. App. 8th Dist. Cuyahoga County 1989), dismissed, 44 Ohio St. 3d 709, 542 N.E.2d 347 (1989); Gross v. Gross, 64 Ohio App. 3d 815, 582 N.E.2d 1144 (10th Dist. Franklin County 1990); Broxterman v. Broxterman, 101 Ohio App. 3d 661, 656 N.E.2d 394 (1st Dist. Hamilton County 1995); Fitzpatrick v. Fitzpatrick, 126 Ohio App. 3d 476, 710 N.E.2d 778 (12th Dist. Clermont County 1998); Bailey v. Bailey, 2000 WL 1785942 (Ohio Ct. App. 9th Dist. Lorain County 2000); Pisani v. Pisani, 2001 WL 280076 (Ohio Ct. App. 8th Dist. Cuyahoga County 2001); Teiberis v. Teiberis, 2005-Ohio-999, 2005 WL 544827 (Ohio Ct. App. 9th Dist. Lorain County 2005); King v. King, 2006-Ohio-183, 2006 WL 146063 (Ohio

prevents either party from maintaining a subsequent action regarding issues adjudicated in the final divorce decree.[2] The defense of res judicata also applies when a party voluntarily dismisses an appeal. All issues raised in the appeal are deemed waived and barred from subsequent litigation.[3] The doctrine is inapplicable, however, where there has been no final determination on the merits by a court of competent jurisdiction.[4] This is true even if the action has been tried

---

Ct. App. 4th Dist. Adams County 2006); Hirt v. Hirt, 2006-Ohio-2851, 2006 WL 1544322 (Ohio Ct. App. 9th Dist. Medina County 2006); Smith v. Smith, 2007-Ohio-512, 2007 WL 397283 (Ohio Ct. App. 9th Dist. Summit County 2007); Danforth v. Danforth, 2006-Ohio-2890, 2006 WL 1554821 (Ohio Ct. App. 8th Dist. Cuyahoga County 2006), appeal not allowed, 111 Ohio St. 3d 1469, 2006-Ohio-5625, 855 N.E.2d 1258 (2006); Kean v. Kean, 2006-Ohio-3222, 2006 WL 1725933 (Ohio Ct. App. 11th Dist. Trumbull County 2006); O'Connor v. O'Connor, 2008-Ohio-2276, 2008 WL 2025267 (Ohio Ct. App. 10th Dist. Franklin County 2008); Bartlett v. Sobetsky, 2008-Ohio-4432, 2008 WL 4058103 (Ohio Ct. App. 12th Dist. Clermont County 2008); Clagg v. Clagg, 2009-Ohio-328, 2009 WL 190049 (Ohio Ct. App. 10th Dist. Franklin County 2009); Carlisle v. Carlisle, 180 Ohio App.3d 569, 2009-Ohio-215, 906 N.E.2d 483 (4th Dist. Lawrence County 2009).

[2]Ashley v. Ashley, 118 Ohio App. 155, 25 Ohio Op. 2d 13, 193 N.E.2d 535 (6th Dist. Lucas County 1962); Arndt v. Arndt, 1988 WL 64745 (Ohio Ct. App. 5th Dist. Stark County 1988); Bartram v. Bartram, 1992 WL 349835 (Ohio Ct. App. 9th Dist. Medina County 1992); Walls v. Walls, 1995 WL 293831 (Ohio Ct. App. 4th Dist. Highland County 1995); Scott v. Scott, 1995 WL 495311 (Ohio Ct. App. 5th Dist. Morgan County 1995); Hatfield v. Hatfield, 1991 WL 110004 (Ohio Ct. App. 4th Dist. Gallia County 1991); Eyre v. Eyre, 2006-Ohio-6492, 2006 WL 3544820 (Ohio Ct. App. 11th Dist. Portage County 2006); Campbell v. Campbell, 2007-Ohio-2175, 2007 WL 1309553 (Ohio Ct. App. 5th Dist. Licking County 2007); Galvin v. Adkins, 2008-Ohio-3202, 2008 WL 2581682 (Ohio Ct. App. 9th Dist. Lorain County 2008); Flanagan v. Flanagan, 174 Ohio App. 3d 77, 2007-Ohio-6209, 880 N.E.2d 962 (9th Dist. Lorain County 2007); Murphy-Kesling v. Kesling, 2009-Ohio-2560, 2009 WL 1539039 (Ohio Ct. App. 9th Dist. Summit County 2009); Kvinta v. Kvinta, 2009-Ohio-828, 2009 WL 449145 (Ohio Ct. App. 5th Dist. Richland County 2009) (in a subsequent action, a party cannot once again argue in personam jurisdiction; it would be considered res judicata).

[3]Weisberg v. Sampson, 2006-Ohio-3646, 2006 WL 1976735 (Ohio Ct. App. 11th Dist. Portage County 2006); Chasko v. Chasko, 2007-Ohio-5451, 2007 WL 2955585 (Ohio Ct. App. 8th Dist. Cuyahoga County 2007) (since Wife failed to timely file an appeal on a motion for new trial and division of property [QDRO], the Wife was barred from raising the issue years later in an unrelated appeal); State ex rel. Mowen v. Mowen, 119 Ohio St.3d 462, 2008-Ohio-4759, 895 N.E.2d 163 (2208); Carlisle v. Carlisle, 180 Ohio App.3d 569, 2009-Ohio-215, 906 N.E.2d 483 (4th Dist. Lawrence County 2009).

[4]Walls v. Walls, 1995 WL 34788 (Ohio Ct. App. 4th Dist. Highland County 1995), on reconsideration, 1995 WL 293831 (Ohio Ct. App. 4th Dist. Highland County 1995); Foster v. Foster, 1986 WL 10318 (Ohio Ct. App. 2d Dist. Montgomery County 1986); Perala v. Perala, 1987 WL 19753 (Ohio Ct. App. 11th Dist. Lake County 1987); Davis v. Davis, 1992 WL 47299 (Ohio Ct. App. 8th Dist. Cuyahoga County 1992); Kuba v. Compola, 1995 WL 491129 (Ohio Ct. App. 8th Dist. Cuyahoga County 1995); Dever v. Dever, 2000 WL 1902195 (Ohio Ct. App. 12th Dist. Clermont County 2000); Witmer-Lewis v. Lewis, 2007-Ohio-240, 2007 WL 162834 (Ohio Ct. App. 9th Dist. Summit County 2007) and Kiehborth v. Kiehborth, 169 Ohio App. 3d 308, 2006-Ohio-5529, 862 N.E.2d 863 (5th Dist. Delaware County 2006) (res judicata does not apply to matters pertaining to custody and support since the trial court retains continuing

and the decision has been announced. For example, the doctrine does not apply to the decision of a magistrate issued pursuant to Civil Rule 53, if the plaintiff subsequently dismisses the action before the court journalizes a decree based on the magistrate's decision.[5]

There are two exceptions to the general application of res judicata to final decrees of divorce. The first exception is where the decree has been vacated.[6] The second exception is where a divorce is procured outside of Ohio, which releases the party who procured the divorce from the obligations of the marriage while the same obligations remain binding upon the other party.[7] Further, a dismissal of a divorce action, pursuant to Civ. R. 12(B)(1), is not a valid judgment on the merits of a case, and therefore, a subsequent action for divorce is not barred by res judicata.[8]

§ 11:26 Defenses—Limitations and laches

With the exception of an action based on the defendant's imprisonment in a state or federal institution, no statutory limitation exists regarding the time when a divorce action must be filed. The right to assert a particular ground is not lost or defeated because of the pas-

---

jurisdiction over these matters); Kean v. Kean, 2006-Ohio-3222, 2006 WL 1725933 (Ohio Ct. App. 11th Dist. Trumbull County 2006), Danforth v. Danforth, 2006-Ohio-2890, 2006 WL 1554821 (Ohio Ct. App. 8th Dist. Cuyahoga County 2006), appeal not allowed, 111 Ohio St. 3d 1469, 2006-Ohio-5625, 855 N.E.2d 1258 (2006) and Cramblett v. Cramblett, 2006-Ohio-4615, 2006 WL 2574561 (Ohio Ct. App. 7th Dist. Harrison County 2006) (a motion to modify child support will be barred by res judicata where a party previously moved to modify the support obligation on the same basis and presents no new evidence); Weisberg v. Sampson, 2006-Ohio-3646, 2006 WL 1976735 (Ohio Ct. App. 11th Dist. Portage County 2006), Eggleston v. Eggleston, 2007-Ohio-2692, 2007 WL 1584221 (Ohio Ct. App. 11th Dist. Trumbull County 2007) and Salisbury v. Salisbury, 2006-Ohio-3543, 2006 WL 1882298 (Ohio Ct. App. 11th Dist. Portage County 2006) (a change in circumstance determination in an allocating parental rights and responsibilities is a barrier meant to operate as the 'domestic relations version of the doctrine of res judicata'); Zamos v. Zamos, 2009-Ohio-1321, 2009 WL 738023 (Ohio Ct. App. 11th Dist. Portage County 2009).

[5]Walls v. Walls, 1995 WL 34788 (Ohio Ct. App. 4th Dist. Highland County 1995), on reconsideration, 1995 WL 293831 (Ohio Ct. App. 4th Dist. Highland County 1995); Dennis v. Dennis, 1989 WL 101651 (Ohio Ct. App. 12th Dist. Butler County 1989) (the trial court failed to rule on the magistrate's decision, therefore when the wife refiled the motion to show cause, res judicata was inapplicable).

[6]Coulson v. Coulson, 5 Ohio St. 3d 12, 448 N.E.2d 809 (1983); Millhon v. Millhon, 1991 WL 42472 (Ohio Ct. App. 10th Dist. Franklin County 1991); Poskarbiewicz v. Poskarbiewicz, 2002-Ohio-3666, 2002 WL 445058 (Ohio Ct. App. 6th Dist. Lucas County 2002); Civ. R. 60(B) (relief from judgment); vacation of void judgment at common law.

[7]RC 3105.01(I); see Text § 11:4, Preliminary considerations—Jurisdiction—Personal jurisdiction; see also Text § 11:17, Grounds—Out-of-state divorce.

[8]McKenzie v. Vickers-McKenzie, 2006-Ohio-7005, 2006 WL 3825216 (Ohio Ct. App. 6th Dist. Lucas County 2006).

sage of time. In fact, if the parties are separated, such passage of time may constitute an additional ground for divorce.[1]

Even though the equitable defense of laches cannot prevent a person from initiating a divorce proceeding, laches, on rare occasions, may be presented as an affirmative defense to a finding of contempt / the enforcement of a previously established court order (for example, child support), if the delay in asserting the claim materially prejudices the nonmovant.[2] Laches must be pled as an affirmative defense. If not properly raised, the defense is barred.[3] However, laches cannot be raised against the State or against a county child support enforcement agency attempting to recover payment of child support arrearages.[4]

[Section 11:26]

[1]RC 3105.01(J).

[2]Walker v. Walker, 2006-Ohio-1179, 2006 WL 625969 (Ohio Ct. App. 9th Dist. Summit County 2006); Riley v. Riley, 2006-Ohio-3572, 2006 WL 1901011 (Ohio Ct. App. 5th Dist. Knox County 2006); Marcum v. Marcum, 2003-Ohio-7012, 2003 WL 22998229 (Ohio Ct. App. 7th Dist. Columbiana County 2003); Atwater v. King, 2003-Ohio-53, 2003 WL 77181 (Ohio Ct. App. 2d Dist. Greene County 2003); Rhyne v. Rhyne, 1998 WL 180568 (Ohio Ct. App. 10th Dist. Franklin County 1998); Brooks v. Brooks, 1992 WL 188344 (Ohio Ct. App. 11th Dist. Portage County 1992); Troxell v. Troxell, 1986 WL 5963 (Ohio Ct. App. 1st Dist. Hamilton County 1986); Mermer v. Clark, 1984 WL 7858 (Ohio Ct. App. 6th Dist. Lucas County 1984); Kinney v. Mathias, 10 Ohio St. 3d 72, 461 N.E.2d 901 (1984); Wiley v. Wiley, 2007-Ohio-6423, 2007 WL 4225506 (Ohio Ct. App. 3d Dist. Marion County 2007); Post v. Caycedo, 2008-Ohio-111, 2008 WL 142449 (Ohio Ct. App. 9th Dist. Summit County 2008); Barker v. Jarrell, 2007-Ohio-7024, 2007 WL 4554177 (Ohio Ct. App. 9th Dist. Lorain County 2007); Fisk v. Paris, 2008-Ohio-884, 2008 WL 569034 (Ohio Ct. App. 5th Dist. Stark County 2008); Howell v. Howell, 2008-Ohio-6639, 2008 WL 5245570 (Ohio Ct. App. 7th Dist. Columbiana County 2008).

[3]Lehman v. Hubbard, 2006-Ohio-6906, 2006 WL 3783461 (Ohio Ct. App. 9th Dist. Summit County 2006); Coder v. Coder, 1996 WL 257215 (Ohio Ct. App. 2d Dist. Montgomery County 1996); Sassen v. Sassen, 1995 WL 100590 (Ohio Ct. App. 2d Dist. Clark County 1995); Ucker v. Ucker, 1999 WL 253439 (Ohio Ct. App. 5th Dist. Fairfield County 1999); Mary D. v. Frank H., 2000 WL 1752761 (Ohio Ct. App. 6th Dist. Lucas County 2000); Spain v. Hubbard, 2003-Ohio-2555, 2003 WL 21134700 (Ohio Ct. App. 7th Dist. Belmont County 2003); State v. Roman, 1982 WL 5378 (Ohio Ct. App. 8th Dist. Cuyahoga County 1982); Hills v. Patton, 2008-Ohio-1343, 2008 WL 755305 (Ohio Ct. App. 3d Dist. Allen County 2008); Welch v. Staggs, 2009-Ohio-379, 2009 WL 223414 (Ohio Ct. App. 4th Dist. Scioto County 2009).

[4]Campbell v. Campbell, 87 Ohio App. 3d 48, 621 N.E.2d 853 (9th Dist. Wayne County 1993); Furman v. Waggoner, 1997 WL 45059 (Ohio Ct. App. 9th Dist. Summit County 1997); Yeater v. Yeater, 1998 WL 574429 (Ohio Ct. App. 7th Dist. Belmont County 1998); Bellamy v. Bellamy, 2000 WL 638949 (Ohio Ct. App. 6th Dist. Erie County 2000); Weber v. Weber, 2001-Ohio-2648, 2001 WL 1682945 (Ohio Ct. App. 4th Dist. Jackson County 2001); Mizell v. Mizell, 2001-Ohio-3409, 2001 WL 1667865 (Ohio Ct. App. 7th Dist. Jefferson County 2001); Still v. Hayman, 153 Ohio App. 3d 487, 2003-Ohio-4113, 794 N.E.2d 751 (7th Dist. Jefferson County 2003) (trial court held that there is not an absolute bar against applying the doctrine of laches as a defense against the state; it is merely disfavored); Monroe Cty. Child Support Enforcement Agency on Behalf of Ullman v. Ullman, 2005-Ohio-4692, 2005 WL 2174005 (Ohio Ct. App. 7th Dist. Monroe County 2005); Rice v. Rice, 177 Ohio App. 3d 476,

§ 11:27 Death of party

The death of a party to a divorce during the pendency raises several issues. Generally, a divorce action abates where one or both parties to the divorce action die before a final decree has been entered.[1] Conversely, a final decree is unaffected by the subsequent death of a party to the divorce action.[2] The Ohio Supreme Court and various courts of appeals, however, have recognized an exception to the general rule[3] where the trial court renders judgment but the death occurs before the judgment is journalized.[4] Under this exception, the decree may be journalized by an entry nunc pro tunc.[5] Thus, it is within the trial court's discretion to enter a decree of divorce after the death of a

---

2008-Ohio-3518, 895 N.E.2d 198 (5th Dist. Stark County 2008); Cosby v. Franklin Cty. Dept. of Job and Family Servs., 2007-Ohio-6641, 2007 WL 4340280 (Ohio Ct. App. 10th Dist. Franklin County 2007), appeal not allowed, 117 Ohio St. 3d 1498, 2008-Ohio-2028, 885 N.E.2d 955 (2008); Cerreta v. Ohio Dept. of Commerce, 2009-Ohio-1760, 2009 WL 990545 (Ohio Ct. App. 5th Dist. Stark County 2009).

[Section 11:27]

[1]Porter v. Lerch, 129 Ohio St. 47, 1 Ohio Op. 356, 193 N.E. 766 (1934); Gregg v. Gregg, 145 Ohio App. 3d 218, 762 N.E.2d 434 (12th Dist. Clermont County 2001); Taylor v. Taylor, 1992 WL 166076 (Ohio Ct. App. 1st Dist. Hamilton County 1992); Ondak v. Ondak, 1999 WL 179477 (Ohio Ct. App. 8th Dist. Cuyahoga County 1999); Hook v. Hook, 35 Ohio App. 3d 51, 519 N.E.2d 687 (8th Dist. Cuyahoga County 1987); Guardianship of Schnierle v. Schnierle, 2009-Ohio-1580, 2009 WL 840393 (Ohio Ct. App. 5th Dist. Stark County 2009).

[2]Porter v. Lerch, 129 Ohio St. 47, 1 Ohio Op. 356, 193 N.E. 766 (1934); King v. King, 2002-Ohio-1060, 2002 WL 398716 (Ohio Ct. App. 4th Dist. Adams County 2002); Endejann v. Endejann, 1983 WL 8807 (Ohio Ct. App. 1st Dist. Hamilton County 1983).

[3]Concepcion v. Concepcion, 131 Ohio App. 3d 271, 722 N.E.2d 176 (3d Dist. Seneca County 1999) (the court held that since Husband violated a temporary restraining order, the issue of who was the proper beneficiary of a life insurance policy did not abate upon the death of the Husband even though no evidence was heard and no facts were adjudicated prior to Husband's death).

[4]Caprita v. Caprita, 145 Ohio St. 5, 30 Ohio Op. 238, 60 N.E.2d 483, 158 A.L.R. 1201 (1945); Ingram v. Ingram, 1975 WL 181650 (Ohio Ct. App. 2d Dist. Montgomery County 1975).

[5]Caprita v. Caprita, 145 Ohio St. 5, 30 Ohio Op. 238, 60 N.E.2d 483, 158 A.L.R. 1201 (1945); Brooks v. Brooks, 2003-Ohio-5177, 2003 WL 22232962 (Ohio Ct. App. 6th Dist. Lucas County 2003); King v. King, 2002-Ohio-1060, 2002 WL 398716 (Ohio Ct. App. 4th Dist. Adams County 2002); Grashel v. Grashel, 2002-Ohio-4612, 2002 WL 2030907 (Ohio Ct. App. 4th Dist. Scioto County 2002); Miller v. Trapp, 20 Ohio App. 3d 191, 485 N.E.2d 738 (2d Dist. Miami County 1984); Ramminger v. Ramminger, 2001 WL 649757 (Ohio Ct. App. 12th Dist. Butler County 2001); Current v. Current, 1991 WL 128226 (Ohio Ct. App. 3d Dist. Shelby County 1991); Koch v. Koch, 1994 WL 69358 (Ohio Ct. App. 6th Dist. Sandusky County 1994) (the Court held that since the trial court had made no previous rulings on the issues of support, custody and property division, the trial court lacked authority to journalize a nunc pro tunc entry on those issues after the death of a party).

party where the trial court rendered its decision before the party died.[6]

The exception to the general rule recognized in *Caprita* does not apply where the action was pending at the time of the death but where no evidence was heard and no facts were adjudicated.[7] Nor does the exception apply where objections to the magistrate's decision are pending at the time of the death of a party.[8] This is because the decision of the magistrate is merely a recommendation, and does not represent the final decision of the trial court.[9]

Where a party dies after a judgment has been rendered but before the judgment has been journalized, the surviving party may move for a dismissal of the action. The surviving party, however, is not entitled to a dismissal as a matter of right. Rather, the granting or overruling of such a motion rests with the sound discretion of the trial court.[10]

§ 11:28 Incompetent party

Another interesting issue is whether an incompetent person can maintain an action for divorce.[1] Pursuant to Civ. R. 17(B), a guardian

---

[6]Miller v. Trapp, 20 Ohio App. 3d 191, 485 N.E.2d 738 (2d Dist. Miami County 1984); Current v. Current, 1991 WL 128226 (Ohio Ct. App. 3d Dist. Shelby County 1991); Ramminger v. Ramminger, 2001 WL 649757 (Ohio Ct. App. 12th Dist. Butler County 2001).

[7]State ex rel. Litty v. Leskovyansky, 77 Ohio St. 3d 97, 1996-Ohio-340, 671 N.E.2d 236 (1996); Diemer v. Diemer, 99 Ohio App. 3d 54, 649 N.E.2d 1285 (8th Dist. Cuyahoga County 1994); Hook v. Hook, 35 Ohio App. 3d 51, 519 N.E.2d 687 (8th Dist. Cuyahoga County 1987); Driggers v. Driggers, 115 Ohio App. 3d 229, 685 N.E.2d 252 (11th Dist. Portage County 1996); Gregg v. Gregg, 145 Ohio App. 3d 218, 762 N.E.2d 434 (12th Dist. Clermont County 2001); Ondak v. Ondak, 1999 WL 179477 (Ohio Ct. App. 8th Dist. Cuyahoga County 1999); Williams v. Williams, 1998 WL 201738 (Ohio Ct. App. 2d Dist. Greene County 1998) (trial court held the divorce abated since at least one issue of the pending divorce was outstanding).

[8]Endejann v. Endejann, 1983 WL 8807 (Ohio Ct. App. 1st Dist. Hamilton County 1983).

[9]See Endejann v. Endejann, 1983 WL 8807 (Ohio Ct. App. 1st Dist. Hamilton County 1983); Johnson v. Johnson, 1992 WL 209320 (Ohio Ct. App. 3d Dist. Crawford County 1992). (However, this court followed the logic of Caprita and held that when the parties have fully presented their case to the court/ magistrate, a party's untimely death will not prevent the trial court from exercising its discretion and enter a nunc pro tunc entry). See also Text Ch 31, Magistrates.

[10]Caprita v. Caprita, 145 Ohio St. 5, 30 Ohio Op. 238, 60 N.E.2d 483, 158 A.L.R. 1201 (1945); Brooks v. Brooks, 2003-Ohio-5177, 2003 WL 22232962 (Ohio Ct. App. 6th Dist. Lucas County 2003); Taylor v. Taylor, 1992 WL 166076 (Ohio Ct. App. 1st Dist. Hamilton County 1992); Grashel v. Grashel, 2002-Ohio-4612, 2002 WL 2030907 (Ohio Ct. App. 4th Dist. Scioto County 2002); Miller v. Trapp, 20 Ohio App. 3d 191, 485 N.E.2d 738 (2d Dist. Miami County 1984); Kress v. Kress, 1987 WL 14066 (Ohio Ct. App. 5th Dist. Stark County 1987).

[Section 11:28]

[1]State ex rel. Downs v. Panioto, 107 Ohio St. 3d 347, 2006-Ohio-8, 839 N.E.2d 911 (2006); Banez v. Banez, 2007-Ohio-4584, 2007 WL 2493441 (Ohio Ct. App. 5th

may bring and/or defend a suit on behalf of an incompetent ward.[2] If an action is brought against or filed by a person adjudged to be incompetent, a guardian must be appointed to be a substitute for the incompetent party in the pending matter.[3] In *Boyd v. Edwards*,[4] a guardian sued for divorce on behalf of her incompetent ward alleging that the parties had lived separate and apart for one year. The court held that the trial court must first ascertain whether the incompetent party can communicate and express his feelings.[5] If the incompetent party is lucid, the court must take his testimony as to his desire for a divorce. Where the party has no lucid moments, a divorce under former RC 3105.01(K) could not be granted because the requisite voluntary intent to live separate was absent.[6]

Although an incompetent person cannot be sued for divorce for acts committed while incompetent, he may be sued for divorce for acts committed prior to his infirmity.[7] An action, against an incompetent, must be defended by his or her duly appointed guardian, not a next friend or trustee; and any cross-complaint must be maintained by said guardian.[8] Moreover, where there is substantial evidence that the marriage had failed prior to a defendant becoming incompetent, and

---

Dist. Stark County 2007), appeal not allowed, 116 Ohio St. 3d 1507, 2008-Ohio-381, 880 N.E.2d 483 (2008).

[2]Boyd v. Edwards, 4 Ohio App. 3d 142, 446 N.E.2d 1151 (8th Dist. Cuyahoga County 1982); Broach v. Broach, 177 Ohio App. 3d 664, 2008-Ohio-4132, 895 N.E.2d 640 (2d Dist. Montgomery County 2008); Shenk v. Shenk, 100 Ohio App. 32, 59 Ohio Op. 471, 135 N.E.2d 436 (3d Dist. Allen County 1954) and Prather v. Prather, 1 Ohio Op. 188, 33 Ohio L. Abs. 336, 4 Ohio Supp. 243 (C.P. 1934) (*Shenk* and *Prather* both stated that a guardian could not maintain an action for divorce, but these matters were decided prior to institution of Civ. R. 17(B)).

[3]Civ. R. 25(B). Boyd v. Edwards, 4 Ohio App. 3d 142, 446 N.E.2d 1151 (8th Dist. Cuyahoga County 1982); Banez v. Banez, 2007-Ohio-4584, 2007 WL 2493441 (Ohio Ct. App. 5th Dist. Stark County 2007), appeal not allowed, 116 Ohio St. 3d 1507, 2008-Ohio-381, 880 N.E.2d 483 (2008).

[4]Boyd v. Edwards, 4 Ohio App. 3d 142, 446 N.E.2d 1151 (8th Dist. Cuyahoga County 1982).

[5]Civ. R. 9(A) (capacity is a concern only if the opposing party raises the issue of whether the other party is incompetent by way of a specific negative averment); Banez v. Banez, 2007-Ohio-4584, 2007 WL 2493441 (Ohio Ct. App. 5th Dist. Stark County 2007), appeal not allowed, 116 Ohio St. 3d 1507, 2008-Ohio-381, 880 N.E.2d 483 (2008); Heskett v. Heskett, 1991 WL 256136 (Ohio Ct. App. 2d Dist. Champaign County 1991); Boyd v. Edwards, 4 Ohio App. 3d 142, 446 N.E.2d 1151 (8th Dist. Cuyahoga County 1982). Ohio R. Evid. 601.

[6]Prather v. Prather, 1 Ohio Op. 188, 33 Ohio L. Abs. 336, 4 Ohio Supp. 243 (C.P. 1934); Jack v. Jack, 49 Ohio L. Abs. 207, 75 N.E.2d 484 (Ct. App. 8th Dist. Cuyahoga County 1947); Shenk v. Shenk, 100 Ohio App. 32, 59 Ohio Op. 471, 135 N.E.2d 436 (3d Dist. Allen County 1954); Kerecman v. Kerecman, 5th Dist. No. CA-3041 (1984).

[7]Butler v. Butler, 19 Ohio Misc. 2d 1, 482 N.E.2d 998 (C.P. 1984); State ex rel. Broer v. Alexander, 175 Ohio St. 24, 23 Ohio Op. 2d 298, 190 N.E.2d 923 (1963). See also Text § 11:24, Defenses—Insanity.

[8]Murphy v. Murphy, 85 Ohio App. 392, 40 Ohio Op. 254, 54 Ohio L. Abs. 116, 87 N.E.2d 102 (1st Dist. Hamilton County 1948); Duncan v. Duncan, 88 Ohio App. 243,

that he had left home, it is within the discretion of the trial court to allow the guardian of the defendant to amend defendant's counterclaim to allege that the parties lived separate and apart for more than a year. The parties' separation was deemed to be voluntary.[9]

An Ohio trial court cannot grant a divorce on any ground to a person adjudged incompetent in a sister state without the appointment of a guardian. The judgment of incompetency is entitled to full faith and credit. Nor could the Ohio court readjudicate competency to determine whether the party could file a divorce action in his own name without his guardian.[10] A divorce action is not abated by the appointment of a guardian.[11]

§ 11:29   Amendment of claim

1990 Senate Bill 25, effective June 13, 1990, enacted RC 3105.08 and amended RC 3105.62, RC 3105.64, and RC 3105.65 to allow conversion of a divorce action to one for dissolution and vice versa.[1]

Pursuant to 1990 House Bill 514, effective January 1, 1991, RC 3105.17(B) now provides that the filing of a claim for legal separation does not bar either party from filing a complaint or counterclaim for divorce.

§ 11:30   Complaint for divorce—Basic—Form⊚

[Title of Court]

[Caption]   Case No. *[_____]*
                                      Judge *[_____]*
                                      <u>COMPLAINT</u>

1. Plaintiff has been a resident of the State of Ohio for at least six (6) months and a bona fide resident of *[name of county]* County for

---

44 Ohio Op. 453, 99 N.E.2d 510 (9th Dist. Lorain County 1950); Wozniak v. Wozniak, 6th Dist. No. L-85-147 (Jan. 31, 1986).

[9]Heskett v. Heskett, 1991 WL 256136 (Ohio Ct. App. 2d Dist. Champaign County 1991).

[10]Pace v. Pace, 32 Ohio App. 3d 47, 513 N.E.2d 1357 (10th Dist. Franklin County 1986).

[11]State ex rel. Broer v. Alexander, 175 Ohio St. 24, 23 Ohio Op. 2d 298, 190 N.E.2d 923 (1963); Heskett v. Heskett, 1991 WL 256136 (Ohio Ct. App. 2d Dist. Champaign County 1991); State ex rel. Downs v. Panioto, 107 Ohio St. 3d 347, 2006-Ohio-8, 839 N.E.2d 911 (2006); Friedman v. Friedman, 1990 WL 51998 (Ohio Ct. App. 9th Dist. Summit County 1990); Banez v. Banez, 2007-Ohio-4584, 2007 WL 2493441 (Ohio Ct. App. 5th Dist. Stark County 2007), appeal not allowed, 116 Ohio St. 3d 1507, 2008-Ohio-381, 880 N.E.2d 483 (2008); Broach v. Broach, 177 Ohio App. 3d 664, 2008-Ohio-4132, 895 N.E.2d 640 (2d Dist. Montgomery County 2008).

[Section 11:29]

[1]Smith v. Smith, 101 Ohio App. 3d 62, 654 N.E.2d 1342 (4th Dist. Highland County 1995); Galley v. Galley, 1994 WL 191431 (Ohio Ct. App. 2d Dist. Miami County 1994).

more than ninety (90) days immediately preceding the filing of this Complaint.

2. Plaintiff and Defendant were married at *[city and state]* on *[date]*, and there were *[no/number]* child(ren) born as issue of this marriage, namely *[name(s) and date(s) of birth of children]*, and *[Plaintiff/ Defendant] [is/is not]* presently pregnant.

3. The parties are the joint owners of various parcels of real estate, as described in Exhibit A attached, and other marital assets from which Plaintiff seeks a division of property and/or spousal support.

4. Plaintiff states that *[set forth statutory grounds for divorce]*:

[(a) *[Plaintiff/Defendant]* had a *[wife/husband]* living at the time of the marriage herein;] or

[(b) *[_____]* is guilty of willful absence for over one year;] or

[(c) *[_____]* is guilty of adultery;] or

[(d) *[_____]* is guilty of extreme cruelty;] or

[(e) *[_____]* is guilty of fraudulent contract;] or

[(f) *[_____]* is guilty of gross neglect of duty;] or

[(g) *[_____]* is guilty of habitual drunkenness;] or

[(h) *[_____]* is presently imprisoned in a *[state/federal]* correctional institution;] or

[(i) *[_____]* has procured a divorce outside this state, by virtue of which the Defendant is released from the obligations of the marriage, while such obligations remain binding upon the Plaintiff;] or

[(j) *[He/She]* and the Defendant have, without interruption for one year, lived separate and apart without cohabitation;] or

[(k) The parties are incompatible, which incompatibility is not denied by either party.]

WHEREFORE, the Plaintiff demands that *[he/she]* be granted an absolute divorce from the Defendant; that *[he/she]* be awarded temporary and permanent spousal support; that *[he/she]* be named residential parent and legal custodian of and awarded support for the minor *[child/children]* of the parties; that *[he/she]* be awarded *[his/ her]* equitable share of the marital real and personal property; that *[he/she]* be awarded the household furnishings and effects; that *[he/ she]* be awarded a reasonable amount for attorney fees and further expenses in the prosecution of this action; that the costs of this action be assessed against the Defendant; and for such other and further relief as the court may deem proper.

_____
[Attorney for] Plaintiff

NOTES TO FORM

Drafter's Notes

A long form caption should be used on the complaint, which includes the parties' names, addresses, dates of birth and number of marriages.

Under his/her signature on the complaint, counsel shall list his/her Supreme Court registration number, business address, phone number, and facsimile number. When a party represents him/herself, he/she should list their telephone number underneath their signature.

A written request for service (usually a court form) shall accompany the complaint when it is filed, pursuant to Civ. R. 4.

A RC 3109.27 Parenting Proceeding Affidavit (court form) should accompany the initial filing where there are minor children of the marriage.

As in other civil cases, the complaint in a domestic relations matter may plead in the alternative, i.e., for divorce and annulment, or for divorce and legal separation.

§ 11:31   Complaint for divorce—Common law marriage—Form⊚

[Title of Court]

[Caption]   Case No. [_____]
                                         Judge [_____]
                                         <u>COMPLAINT</u>

1.   Plaintiff has been a resident of The State of Ohio for at least six (6) months and a bona fide resident of [name of county] County for more than ninety (90) days immediately preceding the filing of the Complaint.

2.   Plaintiff and Defendant on or about [date] entered into a common law marriage in [city], [state].

3.   Plaintiff and Defendant on said date commenced to live together and held themselves out to the community as husband and wife.

4.   There are [no/number] children born as the issue of such marriage, namely, [name(s) and date(s) of birth of children], and [Plaintiff/ Defendant] [is/is not] presently pregnant.

5.   The parties are the joint owners of various personal and real property [list address(es) of property] and other marital assets from which Plaintiff seeks a division of property and/or spousal support.

6.   Plaintiff states that [set forth one or more of the statutory grounds for divorce as provided by law].

WHEREFORE, Plaintiff demands that [he/she] be granted a divorce from Defendant; that [he/she] be named residential parent and legal custodian of their minor children; that [he/she] be granted reasonable spousal support and support for their minor children; that [he/she] be awarded an equitable division of the marital property (including household furnishings); and for [his/her] costs herein, including a reasonable sum for [his/her] expenses and attorney fees in this action, to be assessed against the Defendant, and for such other relief as shall be proper and necessary.

_____

[Attorney for] Plaintiff

NOTES TO FORM

Drafter's Notes

Common law marriages, entered into validly in Ohio prior to October 10, 1991, should continue to be recognized as valid, pursuant to RC 3105.12(B)(1), effective October 10, 1991.

Please see Drafter's Notes from Text § 11:30 Complaint for divorce—Basic—Form.

§ 11:32   Complaint for divorce—With temporary restraining order as to personal property—Form⊚

[Title of Court]

[Caption]   Case No. [_____]
                                   Judge [_____]
                                   COMPLAINT AND TEMPORARY
                                   RESTRAINING ORDERS

1.   Plaintiff has been a resident of the State of Ohio for at least six (6) months and a bona fide resident of *[name of county]* County for more than ninety (90) days immediately preceding the filing of this Complaint.

2.   Plaintiff and Defendant were married at *[city and state]* on *[date]*, and there were *[no/number]* child(ren) born as issue of this marriage, namely, *[name(s) and date(s) of birth of children]*, and *[Plaintiff/Defendant] [is/is not]* presently pregnant.

3.   Plaintiff states that *[set forth statutory grounds for divorce]*.

4.   The parties hereto own the household furnishings and effects now located in the marital premises at *[street address, city, state]*.

5.   The *[Plaintiff/Defendant] [is/are]* the title owner(s) of a *[year, make, model]* automobile(s) and a *[year, make, model]* automobile(s).

6.   The Plaintiff says that unless the Defendant is restrained from doing so, *[he/she]* may attempt to remove, destroy, or otherwise encumber the household contents and effects and automobiles in the aforesaid marital premises as more fully appears in the affidavit of Plaintiff attached hereto and marked Exhibit A.

WHEREFORE, the Plaintiff demands that *[he/she]* be granted an absolute divorce from the Defendant; that *[he/she]* be awarded temporary and permanent spousal support; that *[he/she]* be named residential parent and legal custodian of the minor child(ren) of the parties and awarded temporary and permanent child support; that *[he/she]* be awarded the household furnishings and effects; that *[he/she]* be awarded a reasonable amount for attorney fees and further expenses in the prosecution of this action; that the Defendant be restrained from removing for sale, destroying, or otherwise encumbering the household furnishings and effects; that *[he/she]* be awarded one of the automobiles, and for costs in this action be assessed against the Defendant; and such other and further relief as the court may deem proper.

_____

[Attorney for] Plaintiff

State of Ohio   :
                                     : SS.   <u>AFFIDAVIT</u>
County of *[_____]*   :

[Name of Plaintiff], being first duly sworn, deposes and says that *[he/she]* is the Plaintiff in the within divorce action filed in the Court of Common Pleas, Domestic Relations Division, *[name of county]* County, Ohio.

Affiant further states that during *[his/her]* marriage to the Defendant, the parties owned personal property consisting of household furnishings and effects which are located in the premises at *[street address, city, state]*.

Affiant further states that the *[Affiant and/or Defendant]* *[is/are]* the title owner(s) of a *[year, make, model]* automobile(s) and a *[year, make, model]* automobile(s).

Affiant further states that *[he/she]* has reason to believe that unless the Defendant is restricted from doing so, *[he/she]* will sell, dispose of, or otherwise encumber such household furnishings and effects and such automobiles all to the irreparable damage of the Affiant.

Affiant further requests that the Court restrain the Defendant from doing so.

Further Affiant sayeth naught.

_____

Affiant

[Jurat]

NOTES TO FORM

Drafter's Notes

A proposed order should accompany this filing.

Please see Drafter's Notes from Text § 11:30 Complaint for divorce—Basic—Form.

§ 11:33   Complaint for divorce—With temporary restraining order as to person—Form⊚

[Title of Court]

[Caption]

Case No. [_____]
Judge [_____]
COMPLAINT AND TEMPORARY
RESTRAINING ORDERS

1.   Plaintiff has been a resident of the State of Ohio for at least six (6) months and a bona fide resident of *[name of county]* County for more than ninety (90) days immediately preceding the filing of this Complaint.

2.   Plaintiff and Defendant were married at *[city and state]* on *[date]* and there were *[no/number]* child(ren) born as issue of this marriage, namely, *[name(s) and date(s) of birth of children]*, and *[Plaintiff/ Defendant] [is/is not]* presently pregnant.

3.   Plaintiff states that Defendant has been guilty of *[set forth statutory grounds for divorce]*.

4.   Plaintiff states that the parties are the joint owners of miscellaneous household goods and furnishings.

5.   Plaintiff further states that the parties are the joint owners of certain real estate located at *[street address, city, state]* and more fully described as follows: *[here describe]*. Said real estate is encumbered by a mortgage to *[mortgagee]*.

6.   The Plaintiff states that unless the Defendant is restrained from doing so, *[he/she]* may molest, threaten, harass or bother the Plaintiff, or interfere with the Plaintiff during pendency of the action.

WHEREFORE, the Plaintiff demands that *[he/she]* be granted an absolute divorce from the Defendant; that *[he/she]* be awarded temporary and permanent *[spousal/child]* support; that *[he/she]* be named residential parent and legal custodian of the minor child(ren) of the parties; that *[he/she]* be awarded the household goods and furnishings and effects; that *[he/she]* be awarded an one-half undivided interest in the above described real estate; that *[he/she]* be awarded a reasonable amount for attorney fees and further expenses in the prosecution of this action; that the Defendant be restrained from molesting, threatening, harassing, bothering or interfering with the Plaintiff; and that the costs of this action be assessed against the Defendant and such other and further relief as may be just and equitable in the cause.

_____
[Attorney for] Plaintiff

NOTES TO FORM

Drafter's Notes

An affidavit of plaintiff in support of the motion for a restraining order, together with a proposed order, should be filed with the complaint.

Please see Drafter's Notes from Text § 11:30 Complaint for divorce—Basic—Form.

§ 11:34 Temporary restraining order—Basic motion—Form⊚

[Title of Court]

[Caption]   Case No. *[_____]*
                                     Judge *[_____]*
                                     <u>MOTION FOR TEMPORARY
                                     RESTRAINING ORDER</u>

Plaintiff moves that Defendant forthwith be restrained and enjoined from (1) striking, threatening, assaulting, or molesting Plaintiff; (2) disposing of, attempting to dispose of, moving, damaging, or encumbering any of either party's or both parties' property, real or personal, tangible or intangible; (3) changing the ownership of, or beneficiaries named in, any and all life insurance policies under which Defendant is the insured; (4) changing the coverage of or insureds under any policy of insurance, including health and automobile, all until further order herein.

Plaintiff requests that no bond be required of *[him/her]*.

_____

[Attorney for] Plaintiff

State of Ohio   :
                          : SS. <u>AFFIDAVIT</u>
County of *[_____]*   :

[Name of Plaintiff], having been first duly sworn, says that *[he/she]* is the Plaintiff herein; that on several occasions during the past six months, Defendant has struck *[him/her]*, threatened *[him/her]* with physical violence and otherwise molested *[him/her]* both physically and emotionally; that, unless *[he/she]* is restrained from doing so, Defendant may attempt to dispose of some of the parties' assets and to change the ownership of, or the beneficiaries on, life insurance policies under which *[he/she]* is presently the insured and Affiant is the beneficiary, thus jeopardizing Affiant's ability to receive spousal support and a division of the parties' assets, and may terminate Affiant's coverage under present medical and automobile policies.

_____
Affiant

[Jurat]

§ 11:35 Temporary restraining order—Basic judgment entry—Form⊚

[Title of Court]

[Caption]   Case No. [_____]
                                             Judge [_____]
                                             JUDGMENT ENTRY

Upon motion of Plaintiff, supported by affidavit, and for good cause shown, it is ORDERED that Defendant forthwith be, and [he/she] hereby is, restrained and enjoined from (1) striking, threatening, assaulting, or molesting Plaintiff in any way; (2) disposing of, or attempting to dispose of, any of either party's or both parties' property, real or personal, tangible or intangible, until further order herein, and (3) changing the ownership of, or the beneficiaries presently named in, any and all insurance policies under which Plaintiff or Defendant is the insured, until further order herein.

Notice of hearing and bond are hereby dispensed with.

IT IS SO ORDERED.

_____
Judge

§ 11:36 Temporary restraining order—Detailed motion—Form⊚

[Title of Court]

[Caption]   Case No. [_____]
                                             Judge [_____]
                                             MOTION FOR TEMPORARY
                                             RESTRAINING ORDER

Now comes the [Plaintiff/Defendant] and respectfully moves this Court for an order restraining the [Defendant/Plaintiff] during the pendency of this action from directly or indirectly harassing, annoying, interfering with, harassing by telephone, assaulting, or doing bodily harm to [Plaintiff/Defendant] at the residence or elsewhere.

Further, the [Plaintiff/Defendant] moves this Court for an order restraining the [Defendant/Plaintiff] from selling, damaging, destroying, encumbering, disposing of, lessening the value of, or in some manner secreting the assets of the marriage of the parties, including but not limited to, real estate, household furniture and furnishings, or appliances.

Further, the *[Plaintiff/Defendant]* moves this Court for an order restraining the *[Defendant/Plaintiff]* from selling, damaging, destroying, encumbering, disposing of, or lessening the value of the automobiles or other vehicles of the parties.

Further, the *[Plaintiff/Defendant]* moves this Court for an order restraining the *[Defendant/Plaintiff]* from directly or indirectly changing beneficiaries, making loans on, terminating or otherwise closing out, or reducing life insurance policies, including benefits and values, on the life of the Plaintiff or Defendant or the *[child/children]* thereof.

Further, the *[Plaintiff/Defendant]* moves this Court for an order restraining the *[Defendant/Plaintiff]* from withdrawing, spending, encumbering, or disposing of funds deposited in any financial institution, including but not limited to bank accounts, savings accounts, money markets, credit unions, pension plans, or certificates of deposit (except checking/business accounts and except mandated security transactions).

Further, the *[Plaintiff/Defendant]* moves this Court for an order restraining the *[Defendant/Plaintiff]* from directly or indirectly causing the hospitalization and/or medical, dental or any other insurance, including automobile insurance, previously in effect for the benefit of the Plaintiff or Defendant or the *[child/children]* thereof to be terminated or lessened as to benefits or value.

Further, the *[Plaintiff/Defendant]* moves this Court for an order restraining the *[Defendant/Plaintiff]* from contracting upon *[Plaintiff's/Defendant's]* credit in any manner.

Further, the *[Plaintiff/Defendant]* moves this Court for an order restraining the *[Defendant/Plaintiff]* from permanently removing the minor *[child/children]* of the parties from the jurisdiction of this Court or concealing the whereabouts of the minor *[child/children]* of the parties during the pendency of this action.

Plaintiff further moves this Court that no bond be required of *[him/ her]*.

This Motion is supported by the Affidavit below.

_____
[Plaintiff/Defendant] or *[Attorney for Plaintiff/Defendant]*

State of Ohio   :
                       : SS.   <u>AFFIDAVIT</u>
County of *[_____]* :

[Name of Plaintiff/Defendant], being first duly sworn, deposes and says that *[he/she]* is the *[Plaintiff/Defendant]* herein and that:

(1) *[He/She]* fears that, unless restrained, the *[Defendant/Plaintiff]* will directly or indirectly harass, annoy, interfere with, harass by telephone, assault, or do bodily harm to *[Plaintiff/Defendant]* at the residence or elsewhere as *[he/she]* has on occasion done.

(2) *[Plaintiff/Defendant]* fears that, unless restrained, the *[Defendant/Plaintiff]* will sell, damage, destroy, encumber, dispose of, lessen the value of, or in some manner secrete the assets of the marriage of the parties, including but not limited to real estate, household furniture and furnishings, or appliances.

(3) *[He/She]* fears that, unless restrained, the *[Defendant/Plaintiff]* will sell, damage, destroy, encumber, dispose of or lessen the value of the automobiles or other vehicles of the parties.

(4) *[He/She]* fears that, unless restrained, the *[Defendant/Plaintiff]* will directly or indirectly change beneficiaries, make loans on, terminate or otherwise close out or reduce life insurance policies, including benefits and values, on the life of the Plaintiff or Defendant or the *[child/children]* thereof.

(5) *[He/She]* fears that, unless restrained, the *[Defendant/Plaintiff]* will withdraw, spend, encumber, or dispose of funds deposited in any financial institution, including but not limited to, bank accounts, savings accounts, money markets, credit unions, pension plans, or certificates of deposit *(except checking/business accounts and except mandated security transactions).*

(6) *[He/She]* fears that, unless restrained, the *[Defendant/Plaintiff]* will directly or indirectly cause the hospitalization and/or medical, dental or any other insurance, including automobile insurance, previously in effect for the benefit of the Plaintiff or Defendant or the *[child/children]* thereof to be terminated or lessened as to benefits or value.

(7) *[He/She]* fears that, unless restrained, the *[Defendant/Plaintiff]* will contract upon *[Plaintiff's/Defendant's]* credit in any manner.

(8) *[He/She]* fears that, unless restrained, the *[Defendant/Plaintiff]* will permanently remove the minor *[child/children]* of the parties from the jurisdiction of this Court, except removing the parties' minor *[child/children]* from the jurisdiction of this Court for a period no longer than fourteen (14) days for the purpose of travel, vacation or recreation, or conceal the whereabouts of the minor *[child/children]* of the parties, during the pendency of this action.

Further, Affiant sayeth naught.

_____
Name of *[Plaintiff/Defendant]*

Sworn to before me and subscribed in my presence this *[date]*.

_____

Notary Public

§ 11:37 Temporary restraining order—Detailed judgment entry—Form⊚

[Title of Court]

[Caption]   Case No. *[_____]*
                                               Judge *[_____]*
                                               <u>JUDGMENT ENTRY</u>

Upon Application and Affidavit of the *[Plaintiff/Defendant]* and for good cause shown, the *[Defendant/Plaintiff]* is restrained from directly or indirectly harassing, annoying, interfering with, harassing by telephone, assaulting, or doing bodily harm to *[Plaintiff/Defendant]* at the residence or elsewhere.

It is further ordered that *[Defendant/Plaintiff]* is restrained from selling, damaging, destroying, encumbering, disposing of, lessening the value of, or in some manner secreting the assets of the marriage of the parties, including but not limited to real estate, household furniture and furnishings, or appliances.

It is further ordered that *[Defendant/Plaintiff]* is restrained from selling, damaging, destroying, encumbering, disposing of, or lessening the value of the automobiles or other vehicles of the parties.

It is further ordered that *[Defendant/Plaintiff]* is restrained from directly or indirectly changing beneficiaries, making loans on, or terminating or otherwise closing out or reducing life insurance policies, including benefits and values, on the life of the Plaintiff or Defendant or the *[child/children]* thereof.

It is further ordered that *[Defendant/Plaintiff]* is restrained from withdrawing, spending, encumbering, or disposing of funds deposited in any financial institution, including but not limited to, bank accounts, savings accounts, money markets, credit unions, pension plans, or certificates of deposit (except checking/business accounts and except mandated security transactions).

It is further ordered that *[Defendant/Plaintiff]* is restrained from directly or indirectly causing the hospitalization and/or medical, dental or any other insurance, including automobile insurance, previously in effect for the benefit of the Plaintiff or Defendant or the *[child/children]* thereof to be terminated or lessened as to benefits or value.

It is further ordered that *[Defendant/Plaintiff]* is restrained from contracting upon *[Plaintiff's/Defendant's]* credit in some manner.

It is further ordered that *[Defendant/Plaintiff]* is restrained from permanently removing the minor *[child/children]* of the parties from the jurisdiction of this Court, except removing the parties' minor *[child /children]* from the jurisdiction of this Court for a period no longer than fourteen (14) days for the purpose of travel, vacation or recreation, or concealing the whereabouts of the minor *[child/children]* of the parties during the pendency of this action.

No bond shall be required of *[Plaintiff/Defendant]*.

IT IS SO ORDERED.

_____
Judge

Approved:

_____
[Plaintiff/Defendant] or [Attorney for Plaintiff/Defendant]

§ 11:38 Conversion to dissolution—Motion—Form⊚

[Title of Court]

[Caption of Divorce Proceeding]	Case No. *[case number]* Judge *[name of judge]* <u>MOTION FOR CONVERSION</u> <u>AND PETITION FOR DISSOLU-</u> <u>TION INSTANTER</u>

The parties hereto, *[name of spouse]* and *[name of spouse]*, respectfully move the Court to convert the within action from a divorce proceeding to a dissolution proceeding and for an order requiring the Clerk of Courts to correct its records to reflect that the parties are redesignated as petitioners.

_____ _____
[Plaintiff/Attorney for Plaintiff]   *[Defendant/Attorney for Defendant]*

NOTES TO FORM

Drafter's Notes

A Petition for Dissolution, Separation Agreement and, if applicable, Shared Parenting Plan should accompany this motion.

§ 11:39 Conversion to dissolution—Judgment entry—Form⊚

[Title of Court]

[Caption] Case No. *[case number]*

Judge *[name of judge]*
JUDGMENT ENTRY

Upon motion of both parties, the within action is hereby converted from a divorce proceeding to a dissolution, and the parties shall be redesignated as petitioners.

IT IS SO ORDERED.

_____

Judge

§ 11:40   Answer—Basic—Form⊚

[Title of Court]

[Caption]	Case No. *[case number]*
	Judge *[name of judge]*
	ANSWER

1.   The Defendant admits the allegations contained in paragraph(s) *[designation of paragraph]* and *[designation of paragraph]* of the Plaintiff's complaint.

2.   The Defendant denies for want of knowledge the allegations contained in paragraph(s) *[designation of paragraph]* and *[designation of paragraph]* of the Plaintiff's complaint.

3.   The Defendant denies the allegations contained in paragraph(s) *[designation of paragraph]* and *[designation of paragraph]* of the Plaintiff's complaint and all other allegations contained in the Plaintiff's complaint not specifically admitted to be true.

WHEREFORE, the Defendant demands that the Plaintiff's complaint be dismissed at Plaintiff's cost and such other relief as the Court may deem proper.

_____

[Attorney for] Defendant

NOTES TO FORM

Drafter's Notes

Under his/her signature on the answer, counsel should list his/her Supreme Court registration number, business address, phone number, and facsimile number. When a party represents him/herself, he/she should list their telephone number underneath their signature.

A proof/certificate of service shall be attached to the answer.

§ 11:41 Answer—Detailed—Form©

[Title of Court]

[Caption]   Case No. *[case number]*
                                     Judge *[name of judge]*
                                     ANSWER

1. Defendant *[admits / denies]* that Plaintiff has been a resident of the state of Ohio for more than six (6) months and a bona fide resident of *[name of county]* County for more than ninety (90) days immediately preceding this action.

2. Defendant *[admits / denies]* that Plaintiff and Defendant were married on *[date]* at *[city and state]*.

3. Defendant *[admits / denies]* there *[is/are]* *[no/number]* of child(ren) living, as a result of the said marriage, namely, *[name(s) and date(s) of birth of child(ren)]*.

4. Defendant *[admits / denies]* the mutual ownership of various items of household furniture, cash, savings, and other items of personal property.

5. Defendant denies all other allegations of Plaintiff's Complaint not herein admitted.

WHEREFORE, Defendant prays that Plaintiff's request for divorce should be denied; *[his/her]* request to be named residential parent and legal custodian of the minor child(ren) should be denied; *[his/her]* request for support for *[herself/himself]* and the minor child(ren) should be denied; that Defendant be named residential parent and legal custodian of and awarded support for the minor child(ren); and that the court grant such other relief to *[him/her]* as may be just and equitable and that the Defendant go hence with *[his/her]* costs.

_____
[Attorney for] Defendant

NOTES TO FORM

Drafter's Notes

Under his/her signature on the answer, counsel should list his/her Supreme Court registration number, business address, phone number, and facsimile number. When a party represents him/herself, he/she should list their telephone number underneath their signature.

§ 11:42 Answer—With motions and counterclaim for divorce—Form©

[Title of Court]

[Caption]   Case No. *[case number]*
                                     Judge *[name of judge]*

ANSWER, COUNTERCLAIM (or CROSS-COMPLAINT), AND REQUEST FOR TEMPORARY RESTRAINING ORDER AND ATTORNEY FEES

(1) Now comes the Defendant *[name]* and for *[his/her]* Answer denies each and every allegation of the Plaintiff except as otherwise admitted herein.

(2) Defendant admits the allegation(s) of the Complaint paragraph(s) *[designation of paragraph]* and *[designation of paragraph]*.

(3) Defendant substantially admits the allegations of Complaint paragraph *[designation of paragraph]*. Although three of the dates are, and one of the names is, in error, the allegation is substantially correct.

(4) Defendant denies the allegation of Complaint paragraph *[designation of paragraph]*.

(5) Defendant denies the allegation of Complaint paragraph *[designation of paragraph]*.

[COUNTERCLAIM] or *[CROSS-COMPLAINT]*

(6) Defendant states that *[he/she]* is and has been a resident of the state of Ohio for more than six (6) months and a bona fide resident of *[name of county]* County for more than ninety (90) days immediately preceding this action.

(7) Defendant states that *[he/she]* and the Plaintiff were married on *[date]* at *[city and state]* and *[no/number]* child(ren) were born as issue of said marriage, namely, *[name(s) and date(s) of birth of child(ren)]*.

(8) Plaintiff and Defendant are joint owners of the real property of the marriage [described in Complaint paragraph(s) *[designation of paragraph]* / more fully described as: [_____].

(9) Plaintiff states that Defendant *[set forth one or more of the statutory grounds for divorce as provided by law]*.

WHEREFORE, Defendant prays that:

(1) Plaintiff's claim be dismissed;

(2) Defendant be granted a divorce from the Plaintiff on the grounds stated;

(3) Defendant be awarded the marital home as spousal support;

(4) Defendant be named residential parent and legal custodian of the minor child(ren);

(5) Defendant be awarded an amount that will adequately provide for the support of the minor child(ren);

(6) Defendant be awarded an amount for spousal support in such amount and for such time as the facts of this case and the Court deem reasonable;

(7) Defendant be awarded attorney fees, as additional spousal support, in this case;

(8) Costs be taxed to the Plaintiff;

(9) An order restraining the Plaintiff from *[state activities sought to be restrained]*, for the reasons set forth in the attached affidavit "Exhibit A"; and

(10) Such other relief which may be just and equitable in consideration of the facts and circumstances of this case.

_____

[Attorney for] Defendant

EXHIBIT A.

State of Ohio   :
                    :   SS.   <u>AFFIDAVIT</u>
County of *[name of*   :
county]

[Name of Defendant] being first duly sworn, deposes and says that *[he/she]* is the Defendant in the within divorce action filed in the Court of Common Pleas, Domestic Relations Division, *[name of county]* County, Ohio.

Affiant further states that during *[his/her]* marriage to the Plaintiff the parties owned personal property consisting of household furnishings and effects which are located in the premises at *[street address, city, state]*.

Affiant further states that *[he/she]* has reason to believe that unless the Plaintiff is restrained from doing so, *[he/she]* will sell, dispose of, or otherwise encumber such household furnishings and effects all to the irreparable damage of the Defendant.

Affiant further requests that the Court restrain the Defendant from doing so.

Further Affiant sayeth naught.

_____

Affiant

NOTES TO FORM

Drafter's Notes

A long form caption should be used on the counterclaim.

Under his/her signature on the counterclaim, counsel shall list his/her Supreme Court registration number, business address, phone number, and facsimile number. When a party represents him/herself, he/she should list their telephone number underneath their signature. A written request for service (usually a court form) shall accompany the counterclaim when it is filed, pursuant to Civ. R. 4. A RC 3127.23 Parenting Proceeding Affidavit (court form) shall accompany the counterclaim where there are minor children of the marriage.

A proposed order should be prepared and presented with Answer/Counterclaim and Motion for Temporary Restraining Order.

§ 11:43   Reply to counterclaim—Form⊚

[Title of Court]

[Caption]   Case No. [case number]
                                        Judge [name of judge]
                                        REPLY

1.   The Plaintiff admits the allegations contained in paragraphs [designation of paragraph] and [designation of paragraph] of the Defendant's counterclaim.

2.   The Plaintiff denies the allegation contained in paragraph [designation of paragraph] of the Defendant's counterclaim.

3.   The Plaintiff denies for want of knowledge the allegations contained in paragraphs [designation of paragraph] and [designation of paragraph] of the Defendant's counterclaim.

WHEREFORE, the Plaintiff demands that the Defendant's counterclaim be dismissed and that judgment be rendered in accordance with the complaint filed herein.

_____

                                        [Attorney for] Plaintiff

[Proof/certificate of service]

§ 11:44   Judgment entry—Divorce before a judge with no children—Form⊚

[Title of Court]

[Caption]   Case No. [case number]
                                        Judge [name of judge]
                                        JUDGMENT ENTRY OF
                                        DIVORCE WITHOUT CHIL-
                                        DREN

This cause came on for hearing on [date of hearing] and was duly heard before the Honorable [name of Judge], Judge of the Domestic Relations Division of the Court of Common Pleas upon the [1) Complaint of Plaintiff and the evidence, Defendant being in default of Answer or other pleading although duly served with process, according to law; 2) Complaint of Plaintiff and the evidence, Defendant having withdrawn his Answer and Counterclaim; 3) Complaint of Plaintiff, and Counterclaim of Defendant, and the evidence, OR 4) Counterclaim of Defendant, and the evidence].

Upon due consideration thereof, the Court finds that [Plaintiff/Defendant/both parties] [was/were] (a) resident(s) of the State of Ohio for more than six (6) months and a bona fide resident of [name of County] County for more than ninety (90) days, both immediately preceding the filing of the Complaint; the parties were married on *[date of marriage]* at *[city and state]*; no minor children were born as issue of the marriage, and *[Plaintiff/Defendant]* is not currently pregnant.

The Court further finds that *[Plaintiff/Defendant/both parties]* *[has/have]* established the cause of *[set forth statutory grounds for divorce]*, and by reason thereof *[Plaintiff/Defendant/both parties]* *[is/are]* entitled to a divorce.

[CHOOSE ONE OF THE FOLLOWING THREE ALTERNATIVES]

[ALTERNATIVE ONE]

The Court further finds that the parties have, prior to this hearing, entered into a Separation/In Court Agreement which is fair, just and equitable, and orders said agreement, a copy of which is attached hereto and for identification purposes marked as Exhibit A, be included herein as if fully rewritten and its terms ordered into execution.

IT IS THEREFORE ORDERED, ADJUDGED AND DECREED that *[Plaintiff/Defendant/both parties]* *[is/are]* hereby granted a divorce from *[Plaintiff/Defendant/each other]*, and that the marriage contract heretofore existing between the parties be and is hereby dissolved and set aside and that the terms of the attached Separation Agreement/In Court Agreement be and are ordered into execution.

[ALTERNATIVE TWO]

The Court further finds that the "duration of the marriage is from *[date of marriage]* until *[date of hearing]*.

The Court further finds that based on the evidence presented, the following: that each party has received any separate property that he/she may have and that the parties have divided their marital property to their mutual satisfaction. Each party shall pay the debts that he or she has incurred and hold the other harmless for those debts. Neither party owns any real property.

IT IS THEREFORE ORDERED, ADJUDGED AND DECREED that *[Plaintiff/Defendant/both parties]* *[is/are]* hereby granted a divorce from *[Plaintiff/Defendant/each other]*, and that the marriage contract heretofore existing between the parties be and is hereby dissolved and set aside.

IT IS FURTHER ORDERED, ADJUDGED AND DECREED that each party shall retain any marital property in his or her possession and shall pay any debts in his or her name and hold the other party harmless.

[OR ALTERNATIVE THREE]
Based upon the evidence presented, the Court further finds

that the parties are joint owners of a parcel of real estate, located at *[address of joint property]* and being more fully described as *[legal description of joint property]*, known as a one-family dwelling, valued at approximately $*[dollar amount of value of property]* and is mortgaged in the approximate sum of $*[dollar amount of remaining mortgage]*.

The Court further finds that the Plaintiff has a *[savings/checking]* account(s) with *[name of Plaintiff's bank]* Bank in the amount of $*[dollar value of Plaintiff's bank account]*, and that the Defendant has a *[savings/checking]* account(s) with *[name of Defendant's bank]* Bank in the amount of $*[dollar value of Defendant's bank account]*. There is a joint *[savings/checking]* account(s) in the *[name of bank]* Bank in the amount of $*[dollar value of joint bank account]*.

The Court further finds that Plaintiff has retirement or pension assets in the amount of approximately $*[dollar value of Plaintiff's retirement/pension assets]*. Defendant has retirement or pension assets in the amount of approximately $ *dollar value of Defendant's retirement/pension assets]*.

IT IS THEREFORE ORDERED, ADJUDGED AND DECREED that *[Plaintiff/ Defendant/both parties]* *[is/are]* hereby granted a divorce from *[Plaintiff/Defendant/each other]*, and that the marriage contract heretofore existing between the parties be and is hereby dissolved and set aside.

IT IS FURTHER ORDERED, ADJUDGED AND DECREED that *[Plaintiff/Defendant]* is hereby awarded *[Plaintiff's/Defendant's]* interest in the marital residence, located at *[address of marital residence]* and being more fully described as *[legal description of marital residence]*, and *[Plaintiff/Defendant]* is hereby ordered to execute a quit claim deed in favor of *[Plaintiff/Defendant]* to said property; on *[his/her]* failure to do so within *[number of days]* days of the journalization of this order, the decree shall operate as a conveyance thereof and the Clerk is directed to certify so much as is necessary of this decree to effectuate such conveyance to the County Auditor and County Recorder. Further, *[Plaintiff/Defendant]* shall refinance any and all mortgages associated with said property, within *[state a specific time period]* to hold *[Plaintiff/Defendant]* harmless. If *[Plaintiff/Defendant]* is unable to refinance, the marital property shall be sold to satisfy the obligation. If the property must be sold, the proceeds from the sale of the real property shall be divided as follows: *[set forth terms for dividing the proceeds of the sale]*.

IT IS FURTHER ORDERED, ADJUDGED AND DECREED that *[Plaintiff/Defendant]* is awarded all of the household furniture and appliances located in the marital home located at *[street address, city and state]*.

IT IS FURTHER ORDERED, ADJUDGED AND DECREED that the joint *[savings/checking]* account(s) deposited with *[name of financial institution]* is awarded to *[Plaintiff/Defendant]* and the *[savings/checking]* account(s) deposited with *[name of financial insti-*

tution] shall be awarded to *[Plaintiff/Defendant]* and the *[savings/ checking]* account(s) deposited with *[name of financial institution]* shall be awarded to *[Plaintiff/Defendant]*.

IT IS FURTHER ORDERED, ADJUDGED AND DECREED that the *[Plaintiff/ Defendant]* is awarded *[$[dollar amount] / [percentage amount]% of benefits accrued]* of *[Defendant's/Plaintiff's]* interest in the *[name of retirement plan]*, under the following terms: *[specification of terms]*.

IT IS FURTHER ORDERED, ADJUDGED AND DECREED that any Qualified Domestic Relations Order (QDRO) or Division of Property Order that is necessary to implement the orders herein, and was not submitted at the time of this final hearing pursuant to Local Rule 28(E)(1) of the Court of Common Pleas, Division of Domestic Relations, Cuyahoga County, Ohio, shall be prepared by the party noted in that Rule or *[Plaintiff/Defendant]*, no later than *[number of days]* days from this date.

IT IS FURTHER ORDERED, ADJUDGED AND DECREED that the Court retains jurisdiction with respect to the Qualified Domestic Relations Order or Division of Property Order to the extent required to maintain its qualified status and the original intent of the parties. The Court also retains jurisdiction to enter further orders as are necessary to enforce the assignment of benefits to the non-participant as set forth herein, including the recharacterization thereof as a division of benefits under another plan, as applicable, or to make an award of spousal support, if applicable, in the event that the participant fails to comply with the provisions of this order.

IT IS FURTHER ORDERED, ADJUDGED AND DECREED that the participant shall not take actions, affirmative or otherwise, that can circumvent the terms and provisions of the Qualified Domestic Relations Order or Division of Property Order, or that may diminish or extinguish the rights and entitlements of the non-participant.

IT IS FURTHER ORDERED, ADJUDGED AND DECREED that *[Plaintiff/Defendant]* is ordered to pay and hold *[Defendant/ Plaintiff]* harmless on the following debts: *[list debts]*; and the *[Defendant/Plaintiff]* shall pay and hold *[Plaintiff/Defendant]* harmless on the following debts: *[list debts]*.

[FOR ALL ORDERS]

[CHOOSE ONE OF THE FOLLOWING TWO ALTERNATIVES]

[ALTERNATIVE ONE]

The Court determines that the foregoing constitutes an equal division of the property.

[OR ALTERNATIVE TWO]

The Court determines that the foregoing division of property, though not equal, is equitable and makes the following findings of fact in support of that determination: *[specifically state facts that support an equitable division of property]*.

[FOR ALL ORDERS]

SPOUSAL SUPPORT

[CHOOSE ONE OF THE FOLLOWING TWO ALTERNATIVES]

[ALTERNATIVE ONE]

The Court further finds, upon considering the factors set forth in Ohio Revised Code § 3105.18 and in particular, those specified below, that it is appropriate for *[Plaintiff/Defendant]* to pay spousal support to *[Plaintiff/Defendant]*. The Court further finds that the following factors support this award: *[list the specific factors considered]*.

IT IS FURTHER ORDERED, ADJUDGED AND DECREED that *[Plaintiff/Defendant]* shall pay spousal support to *[Plaintiff/Defendant]* in the sum of $*[dollar amount for spousal support]* per month, plus 2% processing charge, for a term of *[number or year(s) or month(s)]* commencing *[date of commencement]*. Pursuant to Ohio Revised Code § 3105.18(B), all payments shall terminate upon the death of either party *[and the remarriage of the spouse receiving support]* *[and list any other reason spousal support shall terminate]*. The Court shall *[retain/not retain]* jurisdiction to modify this order.

[OR ALTERNATIVE TWO]

IT IS FURTHER ORDERED, ADJUDGED AND DECREED that neither party shall receive spousal support. The Court does not retain jurisdiction over this matter.

[FOR ALL ORDERS]

IT IS FURTHER ORDERED, ADJUDGED AND DECREED that all restraining orders previously issued by this Court are hereby dissolved and set aside.

IT IS FURTHER ORDERED, ADJUDGED AND DECREED that the *[Plaintiff/ Defendant]*, *[date of birth of party]*, be and she is hereby restored to her former name of *[full maiden name of wife]*.

IT IS FURTHER ORDERED, ADJUDGED AND DECREED that the costs of this proceeding shall be paid by *[Plaintiff/Defendant/ the parties equally]*, for which judgment is rendered and execution may issue.

IT IS SO ORDERED.

JUDGE

Approved by:

[Attorney for Plaintiff / Plaintiff]

[Attorney for Defendant / Defendant

§ 11:45 Judgment entry—Divorce before a magistrate with children—Form⊚

◆ **Author's Note:** The following is the form used in Cuyahoga County after the enactment of the applicable sections of House Bill 119 effective July 21, 2008.

[Title of Court]

[Caption]   Case No. *[case number]*
                               Judge *[name of judge]*
                               <u>JUDGMENT ENTRY OF</u>
                               <u>DIVORCE WITH CHILDREN</u>

This cause came on for hearing on *[date of hearing]* and was duly heard before Magistrate *[name of Magistrate]* to whom this cause was referred under provisions of Civil Rule 75 and 53 by the Honorable *[name of Judge]*, Judge of the Domestic Relations Division of the Court of Common Pleas upon the *[1) Complaint of Plaintiff and the evidence, Defendant being in default of Answer or other pleading although duly served with process, according to law; 2) Complaint of Plaintiff and the evidence, Defendant having withdrawn his Answer and Counterclaim; 3) Complaint of Plaintiff, and Counterclaim of Defendant, and the evidence, OR 4) Counterclaim of Defendant, and the evidence]*.

Upon due consideration thereof, the Court finds that *[Plaintiff / Defendant / both parties]* *[was / were]* (a) resident(s) of the State of Ohio for more than six (6) months and a bona fide resident of *[name of County]* County for more than ninety (90) days, both immediately preceding the filing of the Complaint; the parties were married on *[date of marriage]*; there *[is / are]* *[number of child(ren)]* child(ren) born as issue of the marriage, to wit: *[full name(s) and date(s) of birth of child(ren)]*, and *[Plaintiff / Defendant]* *[is / is not]* currently pregnant.

The Court further finds that *[Plaintiff / Defendant / both parties]* *[has / have]* established the cause of *[set forth statutory grounds for divorce]*, and by reason thereof *[Plaintiff / Defendant / both parties]* *[is / are]* entitled to a divorce.

[CHOOSE ONE OF THE FOLLOWING THREE ALTERNATIVES]

[ALTERNATIVE ONE]

The Court further finds that the parties have, prior to this hearing, entered into a Separation/In Court Agreement which is fair, just and equitable, and orders said agreement, a copy of which is attached hereto and for identification purposes marked as Exhibit A, be included herein as if fully rewritten and its terms ordered into execution.

IT IS THEREFORE ORDERED, ADJUDGED AND DECREED that *[Plaintiff/Defendant/both parties] [is/are]* hereby granted a divorce from *[Plaintiff/Defendant/each other]*, and that the marriage contract heretofore existing between the parties be and is hereby dissolved and set aside and that the terms of the attached Separation Agreement/In Court Agreement be and are ordered into execution.

[ALTERNATIVE TWO]

The Court further finds that based on the evidence presented, the following: that each party has received any separate property that he/she may have and that the parties have divided their marital property to their mutual satisfaction. Each party shall pay the debts that he or she has incurred and hold the other harmless for those debts. Neither party owns any real property.

IT IS THEREFORE ORDERED, ADJUDGED AND DECREED that *[Plaintiff/Defendant/both parties] [is/are]* hereby granted a divorce from *[Plaintiff/Defendant/each other]*, and that the marriage contract heretofore existing between the parties be and is hereby dissolved and set aside.

[OR ALTERNATIVE THREE]

The Court further finds that the parties are joint owners of a parcel of real estate, located at *[address of joint property]* and being more fully described as *[legal description of joint property]*, known as a one-family dwelling, valued at approximately $*[dollar amount of value of property]* and is mortgaged in the approximate sum of $*[dollar amount of remaining mortgage]*.

The Court further finds that the Plaintiff has a *[savings/checking]* account(s) with *[name of Plaintiff's bank]* Bank in the amount of $*[dollar value of Plaintiff's bank account]*, and that the Defendant has a *[savings/checking]* account(s) with *[name of Defendant's bank]* Bank in the amount of $*[dollar value of Defendant's bank account]*. There is a joint *[savings/checking]* account(s) in the *[name of bank]* Bank in the amount of $*[dollar value of joint bank account]*.

The Court further finds that Plaintiff has retirement or pension assets in the amount of approximately $*[dollar value of Plaintiff's retirement/pension assets]*. Defendant has retirement or pension assets in the amount of approximately $*[dollar value of Defendant's retirement/pension assets]*.

IT IS THEREFORE ORDERED, ADJUDGED AND DECREED that *[Plaintiff/ Defendant/both parties] [is/are]* hereby granted a divorce from *[Plaintiff/Defendant/each other]*, and that the marriage contract heretofore existing between the parties be and is hereby dissolved and set aside.

[FOR ALL ORDERS]

SPOUSAL SUPPORT

[CHOOSE ONE OF THE FOLLOWING TWO ALTERNATIVES]

[ALTERNATIVE ONE]

The Court further finds, upon considering the factors set forth in Ohio Revised Code § 3105.18 and in particular, those specified below, that it is appropriate for *[Plaintiff/Defendant]* to pay spousal support to *[Plaintiff/Defendant]*. The Court further finds that the following factors support this award: *[list the specific factors considered]*.

IT IS FURTHER ORDERED, ADJUDGED AND DECREED that *[Plaintiff/Defendant]* shall pay spousal support to *[Plaintiff/ Defendant]* in the sum of $*[dollar amount for spousal support]* per month, plus 2% processing charge, for a term of *[number or year(s) or month(s)]* commencing *[date of commencement]*. Pursuant to Ohio Revised Code § 3105.18(B), all payments shall terminate upon the death of either party *[and the remarriage of the spouse receiving support] [and list any other reason spousal support shall terminate]*. The Court shall *[retain/not retain]* jurisdiction to modify this order.

[OR ALTERNATIVE TWO]

IT IS FURTHER ORDERED, ADJUDGED AND DECREED that neither party shall receive spousal support. The Court does not retain jurisdiction over this matter.

[FOR ALL ORDERS]

ALLOCATION OF PARENTAL RIGHTS AND RESPONSIBILITIES FOR THE CARE OF THE CHILD(REN)

[CHOOSE ONE OF THE FOLLOWING THREE ALTERNATIVES]

[ALTERNATIVE ONE]

The Court finds that a pleading or motion requesting shared parenting was filed by *[at least one parent/both parents jointly]* and a plan for shared parenting was filed at least 30 days prior to hearing, which plan the Court determines to be in the best interest of the child(ren).

[OR ALTERNATIVE TWO]

The Court finds that the parents have waived the requirement of a written request for shared parenting and plan for shared parenting filed at least 30 days before hearing. The Court finds that the parents have agreed to shared parenting and have jointly submitted a plan on the date of hearing, which plan the Court finds is in the best interest of the child(ren).

[APPLICABLE TO ALTERNATIVES ONE AND TWO]

IT IS FURTHER ORDERED, ADJUDGED AND DECREED that this Judgment Entry shall constitute an ORDER FOR SHARED PARENTING pursuant to Ohio Revised Code § 3109.04(A), (D) and (G) and the parties shall share the rights and responsibilities for the care of the child(ren) in accordance with the attached approved shared parenting plan, which is adopted and incorporated herein by reference.

[OR ALTERNATIVE THREE]

IT IS FURTHER ORDERED, ADJUDGED AND DECREED that parental rights and responsibilities are allocated primarily to *[Plaintiff/Defendant]* who is hereby designated the residential parent and legal custodian of the minor child(ren). The parent who is not the residential parent, *[Plaintiff/Defendant]*, shall have parenting time *[in accordance with the schedule attached hereto/in accordance with the Standard Parenting Time Guidelines attached hereto]* as Exhibit *[exhibit designator]* and incorporated herein by reference.

[FOR ALL ORDERS]

IT IS FURTHER ORDERED, ADJUDGED AND DECREED that each parent shall file a notice of intent to relocate if he/she intends to move to a residence other than the one specified in this order. Pursuant to the determination made under Ohio Revised Code § 3109.051(G)(2) and subject to further order of the Court, the other parent *[shall/shall not]* be sent a copy of any notice of relocation filed with the Court.

CHILD SUPPORT

For purposes of this order *[Plaintiff/Defendant]* is the Child Support Obligor and *[Plaintiff/Defendant]* is the Child Support Obligee.

This order for child support and cash medical support is effective *[date child support and/or cash medical is to commence]*.

The worksheet used to compute child support and cash medical support under Ohio Revise Code § 3119.022 or § 3119.023 is attached as Exhibit *[exhibit designator]*.

IT IS FURTHER ORDERED, ADJUDGED AND DECREED that when private health insurance **IS** being provided by a party in accordance with this order for the child(ren) named above, the Child

Support Obligor shall pay **child support** for the minor child(ren) in the sum of $*[dollar amount of child support]* per month ($*[dollar amount]* per month, per child) to the Child Support Obligee, and/or *[his/her]* assignee(s), **plus 2% processing charge**. (Line 29, Child Support Computation Worksheet-Sole Residential Parent or Shared Parenting Order **or** Line 27, Child Support Computation Worksheet-Split Parental Rights and Responsibilities)

IT IS FURTHER ORDERED, ADJUDGED AND DECREED that when private health insurance **IS NOT** being provided by a party in accordance with this order for the child(ren) named above, the Child Support Obligor shall pay **child support** for the minor child(ren) in the sum of $*[dollar amount of child support]* per month ($*[dollar amount]* per month per child) to the Child Support Obligee, and/or *[his/her]* assignee(s), **plus 2% processing charge**. (Line 29, Child Support Computation Worksheet-Sole Residential Parent or Shared Parenting Order **or** Line 27, Child Support Computation Worksheet-Split Parental Rights and Responsibilities)

[INCLUDE FOLLOWING PARAGRAPH IF APPICABLE]

The above child support deviates from the amount of child support that would otherwise result from the use of the Basic Child Support Schedule and the applicable worksheet, through the line establishing the actual annual obligation because, pursuant to Ohio Revised Code § 3119.22, the amount would be unjust and inappropriate and would not be in the best interest of the minor child(ren) for the following reason(s): *[state reason(s) for deviation from child support worksheet]*.

CASH MEDICAL SUPPORT

[CHOOSE ONE OF THE FOLLOWING TWO ALTERNAcTIVES]

[ALTERNATIVE ONE]

The Court finds that the Child Support Obligor's total annual gross income (Line 7a, Child Support Computation Worksheet) is less than 150% of the federal poverty guideline for an individual. Pursuant to Ohio Revised Code § 3119.30(C) the cash medical support obligation is $0.00.

[OR ALTERNATIVE TWO]

The Court finds that the Child Support Obligor's total annual gross income (Line 7a, Child Support Computation Worksheet) is 150% or more of the federal poverty guideline for an individual. Pursuant to Ohio Revised Code § 3119.30(C) the cash medical support obligation is 5% of the Child Support Obligor's adjusted gross income (line 14a) or the amount of cash medical support to be paid according to the Ohio Department of Job and Family Services USDA Cash Medical Support

Schedule created pursuant to Ohio Revised Code § 3119.302(B), which-ever is the lower amount.

[FOR ALL ORDERS]

IT IS FURTHER ORDERED ADJUDGED AND DECREED that when private health insurance **IS NOT** being provided by a party in accordance with this order for the child(ren) named above, the Child Support Obligor shall pay **cash medical support** in the sum of $*[dollar amount of cash medical]* per month (*[dollar amount]* per month, per child), **plus 2% processing charge.** (Line 31, Child Support Computation Worksheet-Sole Residential Parent or Shared Parenting Order **or** Line 29, Child Support Computation Worksheet-Split Parental Rights and Responsibilities)

If private health insurance coverage is being provided and becomes unavailable or is terminated, the Child Support Obligor SHALL BEGIN paying cash medical support commencing the first day of the month immediately following the month in which private health insurance coverage became unavailable or is terminated, and SHALL CEASE paying cash medical support on the last day of the month immediately preceding the month in which private health insurance coverage begins or resumes. Cash medical support shall be paid in addition to child support.

[COMPLETE THE FOLLOWING TWO PARAGRAPHS ONLY IF PARTIES OBTAINED AN ADMINISTRATIVE ORDER FROM CHILD SUPPORT ENFORCEMENT AGENCY]

The Court finds that the parties have an administrative support order, case number *[P-_____]*, *[SETS #_____]* issued by the *[name of County]* County Child Support Enforcement Agency (COPY ATTACHED HERETO AS EXHIBIT *[EXHIBIT DESIGNATOR]*) that requires *[Plaintiff/Defendant]* to pay child support in the amount of $*[dollar amount of child support]* per month when health insurance IS being provided by a party, and $*[dollar amount of child support]* per month plus cash medical support in the amount of $*[dollar amount of cash medical]* when health insurance IS NOT being provided by a party, plus 2% processing charge, for the support of the above—named child(ren). The Court finds it appropriate to adopt this order for the purpose of preserving and determining arrearage accrued under the administrative order.

IT IS FURTHER ORDERED, ADJUDGED AND DECREED that the administrative order is hereby adopted and any arrears and overpayments accrued under the administrative order are hereby preserved. The *[name of county]* County CSEA shall terminate any support withholding or deduction notice issued in case number *[P-_____]*. All support paid hereafter shall be under *[name of county]* County Domestic Relations case number *[divorce case number]*.

The Child Support Obligor shall be given credit for any payments received under the administrative order.

[IF THERE IS AN ARREARAGE INCLUDE FOLLOWING PARAGRAPH AND EITHER ALTERNTIVE ONE OR TWO]

The Court further finds that as of *[date]* the arrearage is $*[dollar amount of arrearage]*. This sum <u>includes</u> all accrued child support, cash medical support, spousal support, processing charges and arrearage accrued under the above-referenced administrative order, if any. This sum supercedes all prior determinations of arrearage. The Support Obligor has been credited with all support payments made through the CSEA, payments made directly to and acknowledged by the Child Support Obligee, credit acknowledged by the Child Support Obligee for support provided directly to the child(ren), and credit for support waived by the Child Support Obligee, as of the computation date, *[and the arrearage also includes the Child Support Obligor's share of health care expenses not covered by private health insurance or cash medical support]*.

[ALTERNATIVE ONE]

IT IS FURTHER ORDERED, ADJUDGED AND DECREED that the Child Support Obligor shall pay an additional $*[dollar amount]* per month toward the existing arrearage.

[OR ALTERNATIVE TWO]

IT IS FURTHER ORDERED, ADJUDGED AND DECREED that judgment in the amount of $*[dollar amount of arrearages]* as and for support arrears is hereby entered in favor of *[Plaintiff/Defendant]* and against *[Plaintiff/Defendant]*, and upon which execution may issue.

[FOR ALL ORDERS]

The duty of support shall continue until further order of Court or until the above-named child(ren) reach(es) age 18 or so long as the child(ren) continuously attend(s), on a full-time basis, any recognized and accredited high school, however, no later than age 19, or as otherwise provided in Ohio Revised Code § 3119.86.

Total monthly order is $*[total dollar amount of support owed by Obligor]* when health insurance <u>is</u> provided, including 2% processing charge.

This includes: $*[dollar amount]* current child support (including 2% processing charge)

$*[dollar amount]* current spousal support (including 2% processing charge)

$*[dollar amount]* arrearage payment (including 2% processing charge).

Total monthly order is $*[total dollar amount of support owed by Obligor]* when health insurance <u>is not</u> provided, including 2% processing charge.

This includes: $*[dollar amount]* current child support (including 2% processing charge)

$*[dollar amount]* current spousal support (including 2% processing charge)

$*[dollar amount]* current cash medical support (including 2% processing charge).

$*[dollar amount]* arrearage payment (including 2% processing charge).

All support shall be paid through Ohio Child Support Payment Central (OCSPC), P.O. Box 182372, Columbus, Ohio 43218-2372. Any payments not made through OCSPC shall not be considered as payment of support. Checks or money orders shall be made payable to "OCSPC". Cash payments to OCSPC may be made at the *[name of county]* County Treasurer's Office, *[address of County Treasurer's Office]*. All payments shall include the following: Obligor's name, Social Security Number, SETS case number, and Domestic Relations Court case number.

All support under this order shall be withheld or deducted from the income or assets of the obligor pursuant to a withholding or deduction notice or appropriate order issued in accordance with Chapters 3119., 3121., 3123., and 3125. of the Revised Code or a withdrawal directive issued pursuant to sections 3123.24 to 3123.38 of the Revised Code and shall be forwarded to the obligee in accordance with Chapters 3119., 3121., 3123., and 3125. of the Revised Code.

To secure the support obligations, the Court finds that:

[CHOOSE ONE OF THE FOLLOWING FOUR ALTERNATIVES]

[ALTERNATIVE ONE]

The Child Support Obligor receives income from an income source. A withholding notice shall issue in the amount of $*[total dollar amount to be withheld from Obligor's income source]* per month.

INCOME SOURCE	*[name of income source/ Obligor's employer]*
ADDRESS	*[address of income source/Obligor's employer]*

The income source shall be notified not to withhold a total amount, including all fees, in excess of the amount allowed under Section 303(b) of the "Consumer Credit Protection Act," 15 U.S.C. 1673(B).

Until the income source begins withholding in the appropriate amount, the Child Support Obligor shall make payments directly to OCSPC.

[OR ALTERNATIVE TWO]

The Child Support Obligor has nonexempt funds on deposit in an account at a financial institution. A deduction notice shall issue upon the account in the amount of $*[total dollar amount to be deducted from financial account]* per month.

FINANCIAL INSTITUTION	*[name of Obligor's financial institution where support is to be withheld]*
ADDRESS	*[address of Obligor's financial institution where Support is to be withheld]*

The Obligor shall immediately notify the CSEA of the number of the account from which support shall be deducted, and the name, branch, location and routing number of the financial institution if not set forth above.

[OR ALTERNATIVE THREE]

The Child Support Obligor has no attachable income source and has the ability to post a cash bond. An order to post bond in the amount of $*[dollar amount of cash bond]* shall issue.

[OR ALTERNATIVE FOUR]

The Child Support Obligor has no attachable income and has no assets to post a bond. An order to seek work and report income shall issue.

[FOR ALL ORDERS]

IT IS FURTHER ORDERED, ADJUDGED AND DECREED that the Obligor immediately notify the CSEA, in writing, of any change in employment (including self-employment), receipt of additional income/monies or termination of benefits. The Obligor shall include a description of the nature of the employment and the name, business address and telephone number of any employer. The Obligor shall immediately notify the CSEA of any change in the status of an account from which support is being deducted or the opening of a new account with any financial institution.

IT IS FURTHER ORDERED, ADJUDGED AND DECREED that pursuant to Revised Code § 3119.82 the *[Mother/Father/both Mother and Father pursuant to agreement specifically stated herein]* shall claim the child(ren) who *[is/are]* the subject of this order as (a) dependent(s) for federal income tax purposes. *[State specific agreement if both parties are to claim child(ren)]*.

IT IS FURTHER ORDERED, ADJUDGED AND DECREED

that the parties shall take whatever action is necessary pursuant to section 152 of the "Internal Revenue Code of 1986," 100 Stat. 2085, 26 U.S.C. 1, as amended, to enable the parent who has been awarded the right to claim the exemption(s) to claim the child(ren) as (a) dependent(s) for federal income tax purposes in accordance with this order. Failure of a party to comply with the order may be considered contempt of Court.

MEDICAL SUPPORT OF CHILDREN

Pursuant to Ohio Revised Code § 3119.30(A) both parents are liable for the health care of the child(en) who *[is / are]* not covered by private health insurance or cash medical support as calculated in accordance with § 3119.022 or § 3119.023, as applicable.

IT IS FURTHER ORDERED, ADJUDGED AND DECREED that the child support **OBLIGOR** shall pay *[% of money Obligor shall pay for medical]* and the child support **OBLIGEE** shall pay *[% of money Obligee shall pay for medical]* of the costs of the health care needs of the child(ren) that exceed the amount of cash medical support ordered to be paid, if any, when private health insurance coverage is not available or is not being provided in accordance with this order, OR of the uninsured health care costs or co-payment or deductible cost required under the health insurance policy, contract, or plan that covers the child(ren), when private health insurance coverage is being provided in accordance with this order.

Private Health Insurance Findings

A list of any private health insurance policies, contracts or plans available to the parties including a description of any private health insurance in which the Child Support Obligor, the Child Support Obligee, and the child(ren) are enrolled (Private Health Insurance Questionnaire) is attached hereto.

[CHOOSE ONE OF THE FOLLOWING TWO ALTERNATIVES]

[ALTERNATIVE ONE]

The Court finds that neither parent has private health insurance available to cover the child(ren) at a reasonable cost.

[OR ALTERNATIVE TWO]

The Court finds that the Mother and/or Father have the following private health insurance available for the child(ren) through a group policy, contract, or plan: *[Insurance company's name(s) available to Mother / Father / both Mother and Father].*

(Accessibility)

The Court further finds that the private health insurance available to the Mother and/or the Father:

Mother Father **(Check all applicable boxes)**

☐ ☐ **provides primary care services within thirty miles from the residence of the child(ren) subject to the child support order.**

[OR]

☐ ☐ **is accessible because residents in part or all of the child(ren)'s immediate geographic area customarily travel farther distances than thirty miles for primary care services.**

☐ ☐ **is accessible because primary care services are only available to the child(ren) by public transportation.**

(Reasonableness of Cost)

The Court further finds that the contributing cost (cost of adding the child(ren) to existing coverage or difference between self-only and family coverage) of the private health insurance available to the Mother and/or the Father:

Mother Father (At least one box MUST be checked if private health insurance is available)

☐ ☐ does not exceed **that party's Health Insurance Maximum (line 7b of Child Support Computation Worksheet).**

[OR]

☐ ☐ exceeds **that party's Health Insurance Maximum (line 7b of Child Support Computation Worksheet).**

*[CHOOSE ONE OF THE FOLLOWING FOUR CHOICES **ONLY** IF APPLICABLE]*

[CHOICE ONE]

The Court further finds that **both parents agree** that *[Mother/ Father/both parents]* shall obtain or maintain private health insurance that **exceeds** the Health Insurance Maximum for that parent.

[CHOICE TWO]

The Court further finds that *[Mother/Father]* has requested to obtain or maintain private health insurance that **exceeds** the Health Insurance Maximum for that parent.

[CHOICE THREE]

The Court further finds that <u>it is in the best interest</u> of the child(ren) for *[Mother/Father]* to obtain or maintain private health insurance the contributing cost of which **exceeds** that party's health insurance maximum because: *[State reason why it is in the best interest of child(ren)]*.

[CHOICE FOUR]

The Court further finds that <u>it is not in the best interest</u> of the child(ren) for the parties to obtain or maintain the private health insurance coverage that **does not exceed** the parties' respective health insurance maximums because: *[State reason why it is not in best interest of child(ren)]*.

[APPLICABLE TO ALL ORDERS—CHOOSE EITHER ALTERNATIVE ONE OR TWO]

[ALTERNATIVE I]

IT IS FURTHER ORDERED, ADJUDGED AND DECREED that the **Child Support Obligor and the Child Support Obligee** shall immediately inform the CSEA if private health insurance coverage for the child(ren) becomes available to either the Obligor or the Obligee. The CSEA shall determine if the private health insurance is available at a reasonable cost and if coverage is reasonable, order the Obligor or the Obligee to obtain private health insurance.

[OR ALTERNATIVE II]

IT IS FURTHER ORDERED, ADJUDGED AND DECREED that the *[Mother/Father/both Mother and Father]* *[is/are]* hereby designated as the **Health Insurance Obligor(s)**, until further order of Court.

The Health Insurance Obligor(s) shall provide private health insurance through:

Mother

Name of employer/group/individual	*[name of employer/group/individual]*
Address of employer/group/individual	*[address of employer/group/individual]*
Name of health plan	*[name of health plan]*
Name of insurance company	*[Name of insurance company]*

Claims address of insurance company	[address of insurance company]
Customer service telephone number	[telephone number of ins. company]
Group number	[group number]
Identification/Subscriber number	[identification number]

[and/or]

Father

Name of employer/group/individual	[name of employer/group/individual]
Address of employer/group/individual	[address of employer/group/individual]
Name of health plan	[name of health plan]
Name of insurance company	[Name of insurance company]
Claims address of insurance company	[address of insurance company]
Customer service telephone number	[telephone number of ins. company]
Group number	[group number]
Identification/Subscriber number	[identification number]

and shall designate the following child(ren) as covered dependents under the private health insurance policy, contract or plan: [name(s) and date(s) of birth of each child subject to the Medical Support Order].

IT IS FURTHER ORDERED, ADJUDGED AND DECREED that pursuant to Ohio Revised Code § 3119.30 the parent(s) ordered to provide private health insurance for the child(ren) shall, not later than thirty (30) days after the issuance of the order, supply the other parent with information regarding the benefits, limitations and exclusions of the health insurance coverage, copies of any insurance forms necessary to receive reimbursement, payment, or other benefits under the health insurance coverage and a copy of any necessary insurance cards.

The following individual shall be reimbursed for covered out-of-pocket medical, optical, hospital, dental or prescription expenses paid for the above-named child(ren): [name, address and telephone number of the party to be reimbursed for out-of-pocket medical].

The health plan administrator(s) of the health insurer(s) that provide(s) the private health insurance coverage for the child(ren) may continue making payment for medical, optical,

hospital, dental, or prescription services directly to any health care provider in accordance with the applicable private health insurance policy, contract, or plan.

The employer(s) of the person(s) required to obtain private health insurance coverage is/are required to release to the other parent, any person subject to an order issued under § 3109.19 of the Revised Code, or the CSEA, on written request, any necessary information on the private health insurance coverage, including the name and address of the health plan administrator and any policy, contract or plan number, and to otherwise comply with Ohio Revised Code § 3119.32 and any order or notice issued under this section.

If the person(s) required to obtain private health insurance coverage for the child(ren) subject to this child support order obtain(s) new employment, the agency shall comply with the requirements of section 3119.34 of the Revised Code, which may result in the issuance of a notice requiring the new employer to take whatever action is necessary to enroll the child(ren) in private health insurance coverage provided by the new employer.

Any employer who receives a copy of an order issued under Ohio Revised Code § 3119.30, § 3119.33 or § 3119.34 shall notify the CSEA of any change in or the termination of the Child Support Obligor's or the Child Support Obligee's private health insurance coverage that is maintained pursuant to the order.

Upon receipt of notice by the CSEA that private health insurance coverage is not available at a reasonable cost, cash medical support shall be paid in the amount as determined by the child support computation worksheets in § 3119.022 or § 3119.023 of the Revised Code, as applicable. **The CSEA may change the financial obligations of the parties to pay child support in accordance with the terms of the court order and cash medical support without a hearing or additional notice to the parties.**

[APPLICABLE TO ALL ORDERS]

IT IS FURTHER ORDERED, ADJUDGED AND DECREED that the **Child Support Obligor and the Child Support Obligee** shall comply with the request of the CSEA in advance of an administrative review of a support order to provide the following: copy of federal income tax return from the previous year, copy of all pay stubs within the preceding six (6) months, copy of all other records evidencing the receipt of any other salary, wages or compensation within the preceding six (6) months, and, if the Obligor is a member of the uniformed services and on active military duty, a copy of the Obligor's Internal Revenue Service Form W-2, "Wage and Tax Statement," and a copy of a statement detailing the Obligor's earnings and leave with the uniformed services. The **Child Support Obligor and the Child Support Obligee** shall also provide a list of available group health insurance and health care policies, contracts and plans, and their costs, the current health insurance or health care policy, contract, or plan under which the Obligee and/or Obligor is/are enrolled, and their costs, including any Tricare program offered by the United States Department of Defense available to the Obligee, and any other information necessary to properly review the child support order.

IT IS FURTHER ORDERED, ADJUDGED AND DECREED that the **residential parent and legal custodian of the child(ren)** immediately shall notify, and the obligor under a child support order may notify, the CSEA of any reason for which the child support order should terminate, including but not limited to the child(ren)'s death, marriage, emancipation (age 18 or high school completion/ termination), enlistment in the Armed Services, deportation, or change of legal custody. A willful failure to notify the CSEA is contempt of court.

The following information is provided for the use of the CSEA in accordance with § 3121.24 and § 3121.30 of the Ohio Revised Code:

CHILD SUPPORT OBLIGEE:

NAME:	*[name of Obligee]*
MAILING ADDRESS:	*[mailing address of Obligee]*
RESIDENCE ADDRESS:	*[residence address of Obligee]*
RESIDENCE PHONE NO.:	*[telephone number of Obligee]*
SOCIAL SECURITY NO.:	*[last 4 digits of Obligee's social security number]*
DATE OF BIRTH:	*[date of birth of Obligee]*
DRIVER'S LICENSE NO.:	*[driver's license number of Obligee]*

CHILD SUPPORT OBLI- GOR:

NAME:	*[name of Obligor]*
MAILING ADDRESS:	*[mailing address of Obligor]*
RESIDENCE ADDRESS:	*[residence address of Obligor]*
RESIDENCE PHONE NO.:	*[telephone number of Obligor]*
SOCIAL SECURITY NO.:	*[last 4 digits of Obligor's social security number]*
DATE OF BIRTH:	*[date of birth of Obligor]*
DRIVER'S LICENSE NO.:	*[driver's license number of Obligor]*

The parties affected by the support order shall inform the CSEA of any change of name or other change of conditions that may affect the administration of the order. Willful failure to inform the CSEA of the above information and any changes is contempt of court.

EACH PARTY TO THIS SUPPORT ORDER MUST NOTIFY THE CHILD SUPPORT ENFORCEMENT AGENCY IN WRITING OF HIS OR HER CURRENT MAILING ADDRESS, CURRENT RESIDENCE ADDRESS, CURRENT RESIDENCE TELEPHONE NUMBER, CUR-

RENT DRIVER'S LICENSE NUMBER, AND OF ANY CHANGES IN THAT INFORMATION. EACH PARTY MUST NOTIFY THE AGENCY OF ALL CHANGES UNTIL FURTHER NOTICE FROM THE COURT OR AGENCY, WHICHEVER ISSUED THE SUPPORT ORDER. IF YOU ARE THE OBLIGOR UNDER A CHILD SUPPORT ORDER AND YOU FAIL TO MAKE THE REQUIRED NOTIFICATIONS, YOU MAY BE FINED UP TO $50 FOR A FIRST OFFENSE, $100 FOR A SECOND OFFENSE, AND $500 FOR EACH SUBSEQUENT OFFENSE. IF YOU ARE AN OBLIGOR OR OBLIGEE UNDER ANY SUPPORT ORDER ISSUED BY A COURT AND YOU WILLFULLY FAIL TO GIVE THE REQUIRED NOTICES, YOU MAY BE FOUND IN CONTEMPT OF COURT AND BE SUBJECTED TO FINES UP TO $1,000 AND IMPRISONMENT FOR NOT MORE THAN 90 DAYS.

IF YOU ARE AN OBLIGOR AND YOU FAIL TO GIVE THE REQUIRED NOTICES, YOU MAY NOT RECEIVE NOTICE OF THE FOLLOWING ENFORCEMENT ACTIONS AGAINST YOU: IMPOSITION OF LIENS AGAINST YOUR PROPERTY; LOSS OF YOUR PROFESSIONAL OR OCCUPATIONAL LICENSE, DRIVER'S LICENSE, OR RECREATIONAL LICENSE; WITHHOLDING FROM YOUR INCOME; ACCESS RESTRICTION AND DEDUCTION FROM YOUR ACCOUNTS IN FINANCIAL INSTITUTIONS; AND ANY OTHER ACTION PERMITTED BY LAW TO OBTAIN MONEY FROM YOU TO SATISFY YOUR SUPPORT OBLIGATION.

Failure to comply with this support order can result in a contempt action; and, as provided in Ohio Revised Code § 2705.05, the penalty for which may be imprisonment for not more than thirty (30) days in jail and/or fine of not more than $250.00 for a first offense, not more than sixty (60) days in jail and/or fine of not more than $500.00 for a second offense, and not more than ninety (90) days in jail and/or not more than $1,000.00 fine for a third or subsequent offense.

<u>DIVISION OF PROPERTY</u>

IT IS FURTHER ORDERED, ADJUDGED AND DECREED that the marital property acquired during the marriage, which period is from *[date of marriage until date of final hearing]*, shall be divided in accordance with this order.

[CHOOSE ONE OF THE FOLLOWING THREE ALTERNATIVES]

[ALTERNATIVE ONE]

IT IS FURTHER ORDERED, ADJUDGED AND DECREED that the terms of the attached separation agreement be ordered into execution.

[OR ALTERNATIVE TWO]

IT IS FURTHER ORDERED, ADJUDGED AND DECREED

that each party shall receive any separate property that he/she may have and that each party shall pay the debts that he or she has incurred and hold the other harmless for those debts.

[OR ALTERNATIVE THREE]

IT IS FURTHER ORDERED, ADJUDGED AND DECREED that *[Plaintiff/Defendant]* is hereby awarded *[Plaintiff's/Defendant's]* interest in the marital residence, located at *[address of marital residence]* and being more fully described as *[legal description of marital residence]*, and *[Plaintiff/Defendant]* is hereby ordered to execute a quit claim deed in favor of *[Plaintiff/Defendant]* to said property; on *[his/her]* failure to do so within *[number of days]* days of the journalization of this order, the decree shall operate as a conveyance thereof and the Clerk is directed to certify so much as is necessary of this decree to effectuate such conveyance to the County Auditor and County Recorder. Further, *[Plaintiff/Defendant]* shall refinance any and all mortgages associated with said property, within *[state a specific time period]* to hold *[Plaintiff/Defendant]* harmless. If *[Plaintiff/Defendant]* is unable to refinance, the marital property shall be sold to satisfy the obligation. If the property must be sold, the proceeds from the sale of the real property shall be divided as follows: *[set forth terms for dividing the proceeds of the sale]*.

IT IS FURTHER ORDERED, ADJUDGED AND DECREED that *[Plaintiff/Defendant]* is awarded all of the household furniture and appliances located in the marital home located at *[street address, city and state]*.

IT IS FURTHER ORDERED, ADJUDGED AND DECREED that the joint *[savings/checking]* account(s) deposited with *[name of financial institution]* is awarded to *[Plaintiff/Defendant]* and the *[savings/checking]* account(s) deposited with *[name of financial institution]* shall be awarded to *[Plaintiff/Defendant]* and the *[savings/checking]* account(s) deposited with *[name of financial institution]* shall be awarded to *[Plaintiff/Defendant]*.

IT IS FURTHER ORDERED, ADJUDGED AND DECREED that the *[Plaintiff/Defendant]* is awarded *[$[dollar amount] / [percentage amount]% of benefits accrued]* of *[Defendant's/Plaintiff's]* interest in the *[name of retirement plan]*, under the following terms: *[specification of terms]*.

IT IS FURTHER ORDERED, ADJUDGED AND DECREED that any Qualified Domestic Relations Order (QDRO) or Division of Property Order that is necessary to implement the orders herein, and was not submitted at the time of this final hearing pursuant to Local Rule 28(E)(1) of the Court of Common Pleas, Division of Domestic Relations, Cuyahoga County, Ohio, shall be prepared by the party noted in that Rule or *[Plaintiff/Defendant]*, no later than *[number of days]* days from this date.

IT IS FURTHER ORDERED, ADJUDGED AND DECREED **that**

the Court retains jurisdiction with respect to the Qualified Do-mestic Relations Order or Division of Property Order to the extent required to maintain its qualified status and the origi-nal intent of the parties. The Court also retains jurisdiction to enter further orders as are necessary to enforce the assign-ment of benefits to the non-participant as set forth herein, including the recharacterization thereof as a division of benefits under another plan, as applicable, or to make an award of spousal support, if applicable, in the event that the participant fails to comply with the provisions of this order.

IT IS FURTHER ORDERED, ADJUDGED AND DECREED that the participant shall not take actions, affirmative or otherwise, that can circumvent the terms and provisions of the Qualified Domestic Relations Order or Division of Property Order, or that may diminish or extinguish the rights and entitlements of the non-participant.

IT IS FURTHER ORDERED, ADJUDGED AND DECREED that *[Plaintiff/Defendant]* is ordered to pay and hold *[Defendant/ Plaintiff]* harmless on the following debts: *[list debts]*; and the *[Defendant/Plaintiff]* shall pay and hold *[Plaintiff/Defendant]* harm-less on the following debts: *[list debts]*.

IT IS FURTHER ORDERED, ADJUDGED AND DECREED that *[Plaintiff/Defendant]* shall pay to *[Defendant/Plaintiff]*, as ad-ditional spousal support, the sum of $*[dollar amount of spousal sup-port]* as and for *[Defendant's/Plaintiff's]* attorney fees for which judg-ment is rendered and execution may issue.

[FOR ALL ORDERS]
[CHOOSE ONE OF THE FOLLOWING TWO ALTERNATIVES]
[ALTERNATIVE ONE]

The Court determines that the foregoing constitutes an equal divi-sion of the property.

[OR ALTERNATIVE TWO]

The Court determines that the foregoing division of property, though not equal, is equitable and makes the following findings of fact in sup-port of that determination: *[specifically state facts that support an eq-uitable division of property]*.

[INCLUDE THE FOLLOWING PARAGRAPH IF APPLICABLE]

IT IS FURTHER ORDERED, ADJUDGED AND DECREED that *[Plaintiff/Defendant]* shall pay to *[Plaintiff/Defendant]* as ad-ditional spousal support the expenses for *[his/her]* counsel fees in the sum of $*[dollar amount for fees]*, for which judgment is rendered and execution may issue.

IT IS FURTHER ORDERED, ADJUDGED AND DECREED that all restraining orders previously issued by this Court are hereby dissolved and set aside.

IT IS FURTHER ORDERED, ADJUDGED AND DECREED that the *[Plaintiff/ Defendant]*, *[date of birth of party]*, be and she is hereby restored to her former name of *[full maiden name of wife]*.

IT IS FURTHER ORDERED, ADJUDGED AND DECREED that the costs of this proceeding shall be paid by *[Plaintiff/Defendant/ the parties equally]*, for which judgment is rendered and execution may issue.

IT IS SO ORDERED.

_____

MAGISTRATE

                            _____

                                    JUDGE

Approved by:

_____

[Attorney for Plaintiff/Plaintiff]

_____

[Attorney for Defendant/Defendant]

Chapter 12

Marital and Separate Property

By Deborah R. Akers, Esq.[*]

Research References

Additional References
FinPlan's Divorce Planner CD-ROM

---

[*]Updates for the 2004, 2005, 2006, 2007, 2008 and 2009 pocket parts are attributed to Craig P. Treneff, Esq.

§ 12:1   Jurisdiction—Appellate review

The courts of common pleas in Ohio have full power and jurisdiction to equitably divide the property of married parties[1] upon their divorce, dissolution, or legal separation, but in the latter case only if requested.[2] The trial court is charged with the duty of valuing and distributing all property of the parties, marital and separate.[3]

In carrying out its duty under RC 3105.171(B), a court must address and distribute *all* of the property owned by the parties. Even though an order on foreign property might not be enforceable overseas, the court must still determine the value of such property and allocate the rights of the parties.[4]

If any property is not distributed, the entry is not a final order and wil be remanded for the trial court to complete the property division. Where an entry divided most of the parties' property but did not make a final determination as to five bank accounts, but instead ordered their attorneys 1) to determine whether the accounts were duplicative or genuine, then 2) to determine whether any funds remained, and then 3) to divide the funds between the parties, the order was too "vague and speculative" to be a final and appealable order.[5]

The discretion allowed the trial courts is broad but not unlimited.[6] This breadth of discretion is validated by the test upon the appeal of a division of property: whether the trial court abused its discretion in

---

[Section 12:1]

[1]RC 2301.03 (organization of courts), RC 2305.01 (general jurisdiction in civil cases), RC 3105.01 (divorce jurisdiction), RC 3105.011 (divorce jurisdiction), RC 3105.17 (jurisdiction to grant legal separation), RC 3105.171(B) (jurisdiction to distribute property); RC 3105.63 (dissolution jurisdiction); O. Const. Art. II § 32, (legislature forbidden from granting divorces).

[2]RC 3105.171(B). See Text § 12:30, Methods of distribution.

[3]RC 3105.171(B); Rowe v. Rowe, 69 Ohio App. 3d 607, 591 N.E.2d 716 (6th Dist. Lucas County 1990).

[4]Dabis v. Dabis, 1998 WL 391938 (Ohio Ct. App. 3d Dist. Mercer County 1998).

[5]Briskey v. Briskey, 120 Ohio App. 3d 302, 697 N.E.2d 1061 (8th Dist. Cuyahoga County 1997); see also Burton v. Burton, 1998 WL 800939 (Ohio Ct. App. 6th Dist. Wood County 1998) (court erred by failing to dispose of the parties' stock in a country club).

[6]Bisker v. Bisker, 69 Ohio St. 3d 608, 1994-Ohio-307, 635 N.E.2d 308 (1994); Worthington v. Worthington, 21 Ohio St. 3d 73, 488 N.E.2d 150 (1986), superseded by statute as stated in Bryant v. Bryant, 1999 WL 98110 (Ohio Ct. App. 5th Dist. Coshocton County 1999); Holcomb v. Holcomb, 44 Ohio St. 3d 128, 541 N.E.2d 597 (1989).

applying the law to the factual findings;[7] the appellate issue is not whether the trial court's decision was equitable. Abuse of discretion is defined as an arbitrary, unreasonable, or unconscionable attitude of the court, not simply an error of law or of judgment.[8] It is beyond the scope of the authority of a reviewing court to substitute its judgment for that of the trial court, absent such an abuse of discretion.[9] However, a trial court abuses its discretion if it does not address at least those factors set forth in the applicable statute.[10]

Whether a finding of fact is against the manifest weight of the evidence is a separate test applied to an appeal on the factual findings rather than on the application of law. For example, the standard of review of the trial court's decision characterizing specific property as marital or separate is whether that decision is against the manifest weight of the evidence.[11] The Court in *C.E. Morris v. Foley Constr. Co.*[12] held that if there is a scintilla of evidence supporting the finding of the trial court, distinguished from a conclusion of law, the judgment will be affirmed.

§ 12:2   Evolution of RC 3105.171

Ohio is an equitable distribution jurisdiction as opposed to a community property state. No precedent or statute requires that property of the marriage be distributed equally between husband and wife.[1] Over decades of societal change, the courts and legislature have come to treat spouses as equal partners, working together for their common benefit, while retaining their individual rights and assuming individual duties toward each other.[2] However, the marital partnership is

---

[7]Booth v. Booth, 44 Ohio St. 3d 142, 541 N.E.2d 1028 (1989); Martin v. Martin, 18 Ohio St. 3d 292, 480 N.E.2d 1112 (1985); Briganti v. Briganti, 9 Ohio St. 3d 220, 459 N.E.2d 896 (1984); Jelen v. Jelen, 86 Ohio App. 3d 199, 620 N.E.2d 224 (1st Dist. Hamilton County 1993).

[8]Blakemore v. Blakemore, 5 Ohio St. 3d 217, 450 N.E.2d 1140 (1983).

[9]Martin v. Martin, 18 Ohio St. 3d 292, 480 N.E.2d 1112 (1985).

[10]Bisker v. Bisker, 69 Ohio St. 3d 608, 1994-Ohio-307, 635 N.E.2d 308 (1994) (the Supreme Court applied RC 3105.18 because the case was filed before 1-1-91, the effective date of RC 3105.171, the successor of RC 3105.18 as it relates to property division).

[11]Wilson v. Wilson, 1995 WL 695063 (Ohio Ct. App. 4th Dist. Washington County 1995); Murphy v. Murphy, 1996 WL 629522 (Ohio Ct. App. 2d Dist. Montgomery County 1996); James v. James, 101 Ohio App. 3d 668, 656 N.E.2d 399 (2d Dist. Greene County 1995); Foster v. Foster, 1993 WL 63382 (Ohio Ct. App. 4th Dist. Pike County 1993).

[12]C. E. Morris Co. v. Foley Const. Co., 54 Ohio St. 2d 279, 8 Ohio Op. 3d 261, 376 N.E.2d 578 (1978).

[Section 12:2]

[1]But see the language of RC 3105.171(C). See also Text § 12:3, Equitable distribution.

[2]Wolfe v. Wolfe, 46 Ohio St. 2d 399, 75 Ohio Op. 2d 474, 350 N.E.2d 413 (1976).

not the equivalent of the business partnership under Ohio law.[3] The parties enter a fiduciary relationship upon their marriage that is unique to the marital institution.[4] It is this delicate relationship that the legislature and courts strive to protect.

On January 1, 1991, 1990 House Bill 514 took effect in Ohio and significantly changed the statutory scheme of property division in family law cases.[5]

Previously, RC 3105.18 governed what was then called alimony, in the nature of both support and property division. The legislature then, as now, deemed the broad discretion of the courts to be of the utmost importance in balancing the equities of the parties in the sensitive area of divorce and family relations.[6] The effect of former RC 3105.18, as interpreted in this discretionary scheme, was to handicap a party on appeal. For example, it was not always possible to discern which portion of a judgment was granted as support and which as property division.[7] Thus, on appeal the law regarding one could not effectively be argued in preference to the other. The trial courts did not always adequately set forth their rationale in findings of fact and conclusions of law,[8] which impeded the ability of a party to assign error. Different courts of appeals allowed the application of different factors listed in RC 3105.18 to property division on the one hand and to support determinations on the other.[9] The range of property distributions upheld on appeal was great. Many Ohio court holdings were irreconcilable.[10] Prior to the mid-1980s,[11] the distribution of un-

---

[3]Cherry v. Cherry, 66 Ohio St. 2d 348, 20 Ohio Op. 3d 318, 421 N.E.2d 1293 (1981).

[4]Du Bois v. Coen, 100 Ohio St. 17, 125 N.E. 121 (1919).

[5]The enactment of the Bill rendered Cuyahoga County's *Principles and Guidelines for the Division of Property in Actions for Divorce in Ohio*, 54 Ohio B. 491 (1981), archaic in many regards.

[6]Cherry v. Cherry, 66 Ohio St. 2d 348, 20 Ohio Op. 3d 318, 421 N.E.2d 1293 (1981).

[7]Kaechele v. Kaechele, 1986 WL 13922 (Ohio Ct. App. 10th Dist. Franklin County 1986), judgment aff'd and remanded, 35 Ohio St. 3d 93, 518 N.E.2d 1197 (1988); Buckles v. Buckles, 46 Ohio App. 3d 102, 546 N.E.2d 950 (10th Dist. Franklin County 1988); Slorgie v. Slorgie, 5 Ohio App. 3d 202, 450 N.E.2d 721 (9th Dist. Wayne County 1982) (court under no duty to differentiate between property and support awards). But see Scherer v. Scherer., 1980 WL 355307 (Ohio Ct. App. 8th Dist. Cuyahoga County 1980) (every award clearly designated as property division or support).

[8]Russell v. Russell, 14 Ohio App. 3d 408, 471 N.E.2d 810 (12th Dist. Warren County 1984).

[9]Cherry v. Cherry, 66 Ohio St. 2d 348, 20 Ohio Op. 3d 318, 421 N.E.2d 1293 (1981).

[10]Verplatse v. Verplatse, 17 Ohio App. 3d 99, 477 N.E.2d 648 (3d Dist. Hancock County 1984); Martin v. Martin, 18 Ohio St. 3d 292, 480 N.E.2d 1112 (1985); Campitelli v. Campitelli, 65 Ohio App. 3d 307, 583 N.E.2d 1322 (5th Dist. Stark County 1989); Householder v. Householder, 1988 WL 59819 (Ohio Ct. App. 7th Dist. Jefferson County 1988); Garrett v. Garrett, 1988 WL 141706 (Ohio Ct. App. 12th Dist. Clermont

valued property was affirmed on appeal,[12] rendering a judgment virtually unassailable.

The result of these applications of RC 3105.18 was to preclude the development of clear precedent in Ohio family law property division decisions. This, in turn, inhibited settlement, because the outcome of a family law case could not logically be predicted. It clouded a practitioner's ability to judge what evidence would likely establish the legal position of the client. Further, it rendered the right of appeal virtually meaningless in many instances.

As American society has evolved, the issues considered by domestic courts have become more and more complex. Taxation, valuation, transmutation, appreciation, and many other issues are now raised more frequently than in the past. This, compounded by the mounting difficulties cited above, motivated the movement to overhaul the law of property division in Ohio, which resulted in the enactment of RC 3105.171.[13] The amended RC 3105.18 separately and distinctly addresses spousal support, in sharp contrast to its predecessor.

Although RC 3105.171 simply codifies a great deal of Ohio case law, it also settles conflicting decisions; it changes certain areas of law, and clarifies others. The statute goes a great distance toward a cure for the problems discussed above. However, the spirit of family law in Ohio remains unaltered by RC 3105.171. The drafters recognized and employed the prevailing philosophy[14] that the delicate, fiduciary nature of the marital relationship does not lend itself to hard and fast rules. Each case is distinct, and discretion must remain with the judiciary to treat each family law case according to its unique facts, most certainly in parental rights and responsibilities determinations, but even in division of property.

§ 12:3 Equitable distribution

The format of RC 3105.171(A) to (J) is a bit complicated; however, overall it is a very concise, straightforward, and practical tool.

The essence of the statute is contained in RC 3105.171(C), requiring

---

County 1988); Metro v. Metro, 1981 WL 4968 (Ohio Ct. App. 8th Dist. Cuyahoga County 1981); Mochko v. Mochko, 63 Ohio App. 3d 671, 579 N.E.2d 773 (8th Dist. Cuyahoga County 1990); Diefenthaler v. Diefenthaler, 63 Ohio App. 3d 845, 580 N.E.2d 477 (6th Dist. Ottawa County 1989); Malanowski v. Malanowski, 1990 WL 3164 (Ohio Ct. App. 8th Dist. Cuyahoga County 1990); Moody v. Moody, 1981 WL 6210 (Ohio Ct. App. 5th Dist. Tuscarawas County 1981); Mowery v. Mowery, 1981 WL 3557 (Ohio Ct. App. 10th Dist. Franklin County 1981); Williamson v. Williamson, 1981 WL 6566 (Ohio Ct. App. 5th Dist. Fairfield County 1981).

[11]Briganti v. Briganti, 9 Ohio St. 3d 220, 459 N.E.2d 896 (1984); Willis v. Willis, 19 Ohio App. 3d 45, 48, 482 N.E.2d 1274 (11th Dist. Geauga County 1984); Eisler v. Eisler, 24 Ohio App. 3d 151, 493 N.E.2d 975 (11th Dist. Geauga County 1985).

[12]Crouser v. Crouser, 1985 WL 4485 (Ohio Ct. App. 5th Dist. Muskingum County 1985); Briganti v. Briganti, 9 Ohio St. 3d 220, 459 N.E.2d 896 (1984).

[13]1990 H.B. 514, eff. 1-1-91.

[14]Cherry v. Cherry, 66 Ohio St. 2d 348, 20 Ohio Op. 3d 318, 421 N.E.2d 1293 (1981).

that division of property must be equal, unless such a division is inequitable. In the latter case, the court must divide the property equitably rather than equally.[1] This is a codification of the landmark holding in *Cherry v. Cherry*,[2] with a slightly stronger limit on the discretion of the court. The *Cherry* Court held that it did not intend to create a "presumption, rebuttable or irrebuttable, that property be divided equally upon divorce; rather a potentially equal division should be the starting point of analysis for the trial court."[3] Under RC 3105.171, an equal division is not just a starting point for analysis; an equal division of marital property is required unless it would be inequitable.[4] Courts have held that certain unequal divisions are not inequitable[5] and that an equal division may constitute an abuse of discretion.[6]

An equal but inequitable award was reversed in *Weithman v. Weithman*.[7] Husband was awarded only illiquid assets, including a pension and the marital home. Husband was then ordered to pay wife over $46,000 to "equalize" the division on a dollar-for-dollar basis. The court of appeals reversed because husband had no assets from which to pay the $46,000 to wife without liquidating his pension or selling the house. Each of these sources would carry with it a tax or other

---

[Section 12:3]

[1]Shaffer v. Shaffer, 109 Ohio App. 3d 205, 671 N.E.2d 1317 (3d Dist. Crawford County 1996); Wyum v. Wyum, 1997 WL 97235 (Ohio Ct. App. 8th Dist. Cuyahoga County 1997); Sellman v. Sellman, 1996 WL 557553 (Ohio Ct. App. 4th Dist. Highland County 1996); Thompson v. Thompson, 1993 WL 218394 (Ohio Ct. App. 5th Dist. Delaware County 1993); Fields v. Fields, 1992 WL 329451 (Ohio Ct. App. 12th Dist. Butler County 1992); Wollum v. Wollum, 1993 WL 268879 (Ohio Ct. App. 12th Dist. Clermont County 1993).

[2]Cherry v. Cherry, 66 Ohio St. 2d 348, 20 Ohio Op. 3d 318, 421 N.E.2d 1293 (1981).

[3]Cherry v. Cherry, 66 Ohio St. 2d 348, 20 Ohio Op. 3d 318, 421 N.E.2d 1293 (1981).

[4]Shannon v. Shannon, 1993 WL 19572 (Ohio Ct. App. 8th Dist. Cuyahoga County 1993) (trial court abused its discretion by awarding 75% of all assets to wife); Gullia v. Gullia, 93 Ohio App. 3d 653, 639 N.E.2d 822 (8th Dist. Cuyahoga County 1994), cause dismissed, 70 Ohio St. 3d 1409, 637 N.E.2d 6 (1994) (trial court's award to wife of two-thirds of the marital property while ordering the husband to pay real estate taxes, temporary support arrearages and attorney fees is inequitable and constitutes an abuse of discretion), appeal dismissed by 70 Ohio St.3d 1409, 637 N.E.2d 7 (1994).

[5]Mullen v. Mullen, 1998 WL 391385 (Ohio Ct. App. 12th Dist. Warren County 1998) (unequal division of pension found equitable); Roberts v. Roberts, 1993 WL 49461 (Ohio Ct. App. 4th Dist. Highland County 1993); Stafford v. Stafford, 1995 WL 118172 (Ohio Ct. App. 2d Dist. Greene County 1995); Modon v. Modon, 115 Ohio App. 3d 810, 686 N.E.2d 355 (9th Dist. Summit County 1996); Randall v. Randall, 1997 WL 133342 (Ohio Ct. App. 6th Dist. Williams County 1997).

[6]Barrett v. Barrett, 1996 WL 307236 (Ohio Ct. App. 12th Dist. Butler County 1996); Cooper v. Cooper, 1996 WL 575981 (Ohio Ct. App. 5th Dist. Stark County 1996).

[7]Weithman v. Weithman, 1995 WL 363760, at *1 (Ohio Ct. App. 3d Dist. Crawford County 1995).

cost which the trial court had not addressed in finding the division to be equitable. Therefore, the trial court had failed to "indicate the basis for its award in sufficient detail to enable a reviewing court to determine that the award is fair, equitable and in accordance with the law."[8]

In contrast, where wife was awarded no amount representing her half interest in husband's business, the court found that the distribution was not equal, but was equitable, because husband had been ordered to pay a substantial income tax liability which offset wife's interest in the business.[9]

To support a decision that property has been equitably divided, a court must make specific findings of fact. Findings of fact are required to support an award of any portion of a party's separate property to the other spouse[10] and to support the determination that marital property has been equitably divided in consideration of the factors listed in RC 3105.171(F).[11] Where a court finds financial misconduct by one spouse, an unequal division of property may be equitable.[12]

The court is also required to specify the dates it uses in determining the beginning and end of the marriage.[13]

The court need not, however, make findings of fact where parties have submitted an agreement as to the terms of their division of property. It was not the intent of the legislature that the courts make findings of fact on all issues when the parties have reached an agree-

---

[8]Weithman v. Weithman, 1995 WL 363760 (Ohio Ct. App. 3d Dist. Crawford County 1995); See Kaechele v. Kaechele, 35 Ohio St. 3d 93, 518 N.E.2d 1197 (1988), superseded by statute as stated in Heslep v. Heslep, 2000 WL 818909 (Ohio Ct. App. 7th Dist. Monroe County 2000).

[9]Cooper v. Cooper, 1996 WL 575981 (Ohio Ct. App. 5th Dist. Stark County 1996).

[10]RC 3105.171(D).

[11]RC 3105.171(G); Allen v. Allen, 109 Ohio App. 3d 640, 672 N.E.2d 1056 (12th Dist. Butler County 1996); Gibson v. Gibson, 87 Ohio App. 3d 426, 622 N.E.2d 425 (4th Dist. Scioto County 1993); Wilson v. Wilson, 1996 WL 411631 (Ohio Ct. App. 9th Dist. Wayne County 1996); Weilbacher v. Weilbacher, 1996 WL 145495 (Ohio Ct. App. 10th Dist. Franklin County 1996); Williams v. Williams, 1993 WL 243058 (Ohio Ct. App. 8th Dist. Cuyahoga County 1993), cause dismissed, 67 Ohio St. 3d 1509, 622 N.E.2d 657 (1993).

[12]RC 3105.171(E)(3). Loeffler v. Loeffler, 1998 WL 800951 (Ohio Ct. App. 6th Dist. Lucas County 1998); Leadingham v. Leadingham, 120 Ohio App. 3d 496, 698 N.E.2d 465 (12th Dist. Warren County 1997); Sears v. Sears, 1992 WL 71550 (Ohio Ct. App. 5th Dist. Guernsey County 1992); Spicer v. Spicer, 1996 WL 204115 (Ohio Ct. App. 12th Dist. Butler County 1996); Crues v. Crues, 2004-Ohio-6757, 2004 WL 2895986 (Ohio Ct. App. 5th Dist. Stark County 2004); Osborn v. Osborn, 2004-Ohio-6476, 2004 WL 2785554 (Ohio Ct. App. 11th Dist. Trumbull County 2004).

[13]RC 3105.171(G). This provision is ostensibly for purposes of determining the dates of valuation of property and the nature of property as separate or marital. See Text § 12:6, Statutory terms of art—During the marriage.

ment on those issues.[14] A contract such as an agreed judgment entry or separation agreement does not have to be equitable to be enforceable, so long as it has not been procured by fraud, duress, or undue influence.[15]

§ 12:4 Statutory terms of art—In general

RC 3105.171(A) contains definitions of six terms of art: distributive award, during the marriage, marital property, passive income, personal property, and separate property. All, with the exception of distributive award[1] and, for the most part, separate property[2] embody principles previously set forth in statutory or case law. The greatest changes to prior case law took place in the definition of separate property, which is more clearly defined than it was prior to 1991; and separate property is afforded more protection from transmutation than before.[3] Except in certain appellate districts, transmutation of separate property to marital property has been virtually abolished as a rule of law in Ohio.[4]

§ 12:5 Statutory terms of art—Distributive award

Although RC 3105.171(A)(1), (E)(1) to (3), (F), (G), and (I), addressing the distributive award, are distantly positioned, if read together

---

[14]Pawlowski v. Pawlowski, 83 Ohio App. 3d 794, 615 N.E.2d 1071 (10th Dist. Franklin County 1992); Stegawski v. Stegawski, 1994 WL 197232 (Ohio Ct. App. 8th Dist. Cuyahoga County 1994); Melendrez v. Melendrez, 1993 WL 134893 (Ohio Ct. App. 5th Dist. Delaware County 1993). Many judges, however, do not recognize this principle and require findings as to duration of marriage and equal division of property in all agreed judgment entries.

[15]Walther v. Walther, 102 Ohio App. 3d 378, 657 N.E.2d 332 (1st Dist. Hamilton County 1995).

[Section 12:4]

[1]See Text § 12:5, Statutory terms of art—Distributive award.

[2]See Text § 12:10, Statutory terms of art—Separate property.

[3]See Text § 12:10, Statutory terms of art—Separate property.

[4]Transmutation was considered and defined prior to the passage of RC 3105.171 in cases such as Kahn v. Kahn, 42 Ohio App. 3d 61, 536 N.E.2d 678 (2d Dist. Montgomery County 1987) and Kuehn v. Kuehn, 55 Ohio App. 3d 245, 564 N.E.2d 97 (12th Dist. Clinton County 1988); Morgan v. Morgan, 1993 WL 418495 (Ohio Ct. App. 11th Dist. Portage County 1993); Cataline v. Cataline, 1993 WL 452093 (Ohio Ct. App. 6th Dist. Sandusky County 1993) (unless the financial history of an asset cannot be traced, there is no longer transmutation in Ohio); Pruitt v. Pruitt, 1996 WL 221893 (Ohio Ct. App. 9th Dist. Medina County 1996); Stern v. Stern, 1996 WL 451056 (Ohio Ct. App. 12th Dist. Clinton County 1996); Moore v. Moore, 2000 WL 1782328 (Ohio Ct. App. 12th Dist. Brown County 2000) (The enactment of RC 3105.171 "virtually abolished" the concept of transmutation as a rule of law. Separate property may be commingled with marital property and will retain its character as separate property so long as it is traceable.); Arden Lynn Achenberg, Ohio Revised Code Section 3105. 171; *An Equitable Distribution Statute Maintaining Judicial Discretion and Transmutation*, 17 U. Dayton L. Rev. 697, 717 (Winter 1992).

they clearly define the term.[1] Distributive award defines a preexisting concept that has not been uniformly applied among courts.[2] It is an award from separate property made in order to achieve equity, (1) to compensate a party for the financial misconduct of the other party;[3] (2) to provide relief where it is impractical or burdensome to reach an equitable division comprised of marital property alone;[4] or (3) to ef-

---

[Section 12:5]

[1]During the course of the public hearings on the Bill, the legislature was asked to change this new term to a term that would be less confusing. Rather than do so, the legislature deemed the terms "disburse property" and "divide property" to apply to awards of marital property. The term "distribute property" applies *only* to distributive awards. This distinction will no doubt increase rather than diminish confusion.

[2]Ranz v. Ranz, 51 Ohio App. 3d 66, 554 N.E.2d 142 (1st Dist. Hamilton County 1988); Carpenter v. Carpenter, 61 Ohio App. 3d 584, 573 N.E.2d 698 (9th Dist. Lorain County 1988).

[3]RC 3105.171(E)(3); Holmes v. Holmes, 1994 WL 68490 (Ohio Ct. App. 6th Dist. Erie County 1994) (disproportionate award may be made to compensate for financial misconduct); Shelar v. Shelar, 910 F. Supp. 1307 (N.D. Ohio 1995); Soley v. Soley, 101 Ohio App. 3d 540, 655 N.E.2d 1381 (6th Dist. Lucas County 1995); Bouillon v. Bouillon, 1996 WL 65600 (Ohio Ct. App. 3d Dist. Seneca County 1996); Lewis v. Lewis, 1994 WL 581545 (Ohio Ct. App. 3d Dist. Auglaize County 1994); Grime v. Grime, 1996 WL 673516 (Ohio Ct. App. 6th Dist. Fulton County 1996); Eggeman v. Eggeman, 2004-Ohio-6050, 2004 WL 2588343 (Ohio Ct. App. 3d Dist. Auglaize County 2004); Bucalo v. Bucalo, 2005-Ohio-6319, 2005 WL 3193851 (Ohio Ct. App. 9th Dist. Medina County 2005) (irresponsible investing by husband of wife's inheritance, while irresponsible and bordering on dishonesty, did not rise to the level of financial misconduct); Brent v. Brent, 2006-Ohio-1960, 2006 WL 1044458 (Ohio Ct. App. 5th Dist. Licking County 2006) (financial misconduct may result from serious gambling habit); Carpenter v. Carpenter, 2007-Ohio-1238, 2007 WL 827720 (Ohio Ct. App. 7th Dist. Noble County 2007); Parker v. Parker, 2006-Ohio-4110, 2006 WL 2300797 (Ohio Ct. App. 10th Dist. Franklin County 2006); Robbins v. Robbins, 2008-Ohio-495, 2008 WL 344143 (Ohio Ct. App. 2d Dist. Clark County 2008); Hiscox v. Hiscox, 2008-Ohio-5209, 2008 WL 4456964 (Ohio Ct. App. 7th Dist. Columbiana County 2008); Najmi v. Najmi, 2008-Ohio-4405, 2008 WL 4023719 (Ohio Ct. App. 9th Dist. Lorain County 2008); Putman v. Putman, 2009-Ohio-97, 2009 WL 57621 (Ohio Ct. App. 12th Dist. Clermont County 2009); Day v. Day, 2009-Ohio-638, 2009 WL 353307 (Ohio Ct. App. 10th Dist. Franklin County 2009); Taub v. Taub, 2009-Ohio-2762, 2009 WL 1653823 (Ohio Ct. App. 10th Dist. Franklin County 2009); Fillis v. Fillis, 2009-Ohio-2808, 2009 WL 1663978 (Ohio Ct. App. 12th Dist. Clermont County 2009).

[4]RC 3105.171(E)(2). For example, the sole asset of the marriage is the business run by husband. The marital dwelling is mortgaged to the full extent of its value, and the parties have depleted all bank accounts and other assets. The court does not want to destroy the sole source of income, the business, by ordering that it be sold; nor is the husband's income from the business sufficient to pay both support and property payments. The husband has inherited separate property. In order to surmount this hardship and preserve the business intact, the court can invade the inheritance and award the wife the equivalent of her half interest in the business. This is known as a distributive award. See also Babka v. Babka, 83 Ohio App. 3d 428, 615 N.E.2d 247 (9th Dist. Summit County 1992) (distributive award to wife from husband's separate portion of proceeds of sale of marital dwelling is appropriate to offset wife's interest in husband's pension and protect the pension from penalties for early withdrawal); Obermyer v. Obermyer, 1996 WL 28001 (Ohio Ct. App. 6th Dist. Wood County 1996).

fectuate, facilitate, or supplement the disbursement of marital property.[5]

Findings of fact are mandatory if the court makes a distributive award.[6] The trial court erred by failing to delineate what portion of the parties' marital residence retained its character as separate property and what portion was to be considered marital property. The trial court's judgment did not indicate that the trial court considered the factors of RC 3105.171(F). The appellate court was unable to determine if the trial court's division of marital property was equal or equitable.[7] In *Clark v. Lintner-Clark*,[8] the trial court, while awarding wife an "equitable share" of the parties' farm property, erred by not classifying the asset as separate or marital property. RC 3105.171(B) requires a court to determine what constitutes marital property and what constitutes separate property. If a trial court fails to set forth sufficient findings to justify a distributive award, the decision is in error and will be reversed for further proceedings.[9] While a court must make written findings of fact supporting an equitable division of property, it need not address every factor of RC 3105.171 in the findings so long as the record reflects they have been considered. The trial court must, however, assign a value to all of the assets.[10] The same factors which determine an award of marital property determine a distributive award.[11]

However, it is imperative to understand that the distributive award is issued from separate property and income only, including future income.

A distributive award must be made in a fixed amount. For example, it must not be contingent upon any future event.[12] It is not subject to future modification.[13]

A lien on any property, marital or separate, is authorized in order

---

[5]Swartz v. Swartz, 110 Ohio App. 3d 218, 673 N.E.2d 972 (12th Dist. Warren County 1996) (grossly disproportionate distributive award constitutes an abuse of discretion); Guziak v. Guziak, 80 Ohio App. 3d 805, 610 N.E.2d 1135 (9th Dist. Summit County 1992). See also RC 3105.171(F)(3) and (J); RC 3105.171(E)(1); Smallwood v. Smallwood, 1993 WL 191982 (Ohio Ct. App. 12th Dist. Butler County 1993); Chance v. Chance, 2002-Ohio-5767, 2002 WL 31386736 (Ohio Ct. App. 9th Dist. Wayne County 2002).

[6]RC 3105.171(G).

[7]Heslep v. Heslep, 2000 WL 818909 (Ohio Ct. App. 7th Dist. Monroe County 2000).

[8]Clark v. Lintner-Clark, 2000 WL 875364 (Ohio Ct. App. 7th Dist. Carroll County 2000).

[9]Stewart v. Stewart, 1998 WL 177558 (Ohio Ct. App. 2d Dist. Montgomery County 1998).

[10]Carl v. Carl, 1999 WL 552673 (Ohio Ct. App. 4th Dist. Ross County 1999).

[11]RC 3105.171(F).

[12]RC 3105.171(A)(1).

[13]RC 3105.171(I). Krisher v. Krisher, 82 Ohio App. 3d 159, 611 N.E.2d 499 (3d Dist. Logan County 1992) (trial court erred in awarding set-off against spousal support to compensate husband for cash award he was entitled to receive; proper ap-

to secure a distributive award.[14] The amount of security for delayed payments of a distributive award is within the trial court's sound discretion.[15]

§12:6 Statutory terms of art—During the marriage

The definition of the term during the marriage[1] requires the court specifically to address the dates when the marriage began and ended. These dates are instrumental in determining the appropriate dates of property valuation and distinguishing marital, premarital, and post-separation assets and liabilities.[2] The statute creates a presumption that the date of valuation will be the date of hearing,[3] and the period of acquisition of marital property will fall between the date of formal marriage and the date of hearing, or a date practicably close, unless the court states why different dates are equitable. The court is required to specify the dates that the marriage began and ended, if relevant and if different from the dates prescribed by statute.[4] Case law decided both before and after the passage of the statute has held that it is within the discretion of the trial court to determine the period of the marriage for purposes of valuing and classifying property as marital or separate, and recent cases have ruled that it is error for the court to omit specific findings.[5]

A court's discretion is not unlimited in determining the duration of

---

proach is distributive award). See also Swartz v. Swartz, 110 Ohio App. 3d 218, 673 N.E.2d 972 (12th Dist. Warren County 1996).

[14]RC 3105.171(E)(1).

[15]Clark v. Clark, 1995 WL 48408 (Ohio Ct. App. 9th Dist. Summit County 1995); Greene v. Greene, 2004-Ohio-3529, 2004 WL 1486346 (Ohio Ct. App. 5th Dist. Licking County 2004).

[Section 12:6]

[1]RC 3105.171(A)(2).

[2]See Text §12:29, Valuation date.

[3]RC 3105.171(A)(2)(a).

[4]RC 3105.171(G); Budd v. Budd, 2009-Ohio-2674, 2009 WL 1607820 (Ohio Ct. App. 9th Dist. Summit County 2009); Hittle v. Hittle, 181 Ohio App. 3d 703, 2009-Ohio-1286, 910 N.E.2d 1042 (2d Dist. Darke County 2009).

[5]Gullia v. Gullia, 93 Ohio App. 3d 653, 639 N.E.2d 822 (8th Dist. Cuyahoga County 1994), cause dismissed, 70 Ohio St. 3d 1409, 637 N.E.2d 6 (1994); Day v. Day, 40 Ohio App. 3d 155, 532 N.E.2d 201 (10th Dist. Franklin County 1988); Wilson v. Wilson, 1996 WL 411631 (Ohio Ct. App. 9th Dist. Wayne County 1996); Kohler v. Kohler, 1996 WL 455850 (Ohio Ct. App. 9th Dist. Lorain County 1996); Landry v. Landry, 105 Ohio App. 3d 289, 663 N.E.2d 1026 (3d Dist. Auglaize County 1995); Murphy v. Murphy, 1996 WL 629522 (Ohio Ct. App. 2d Dist. Montgomery County 1996); Wyum v. Wyum, 1997 WL 97235 (Ohio Ct. App. 8th Dist. Cuyahoga County 1997); Carpenter v. Carpenter, 61 Ohio App. 3d 584, 573 N.E.2d 698 (9th Dist. Lorain County 1988); Connolly v. Connolly, 70 Ohio App. 3d 738, 591 N.E.2d 1362 (8th Dist. Cuyahoga County 1990); Peters v. Peters, 14 Ohio St. 2d 268, 43 Ohio Op. 2d 441, 237 N.E.2d 902 (1968); Berish v. Berish, 69 Ohio St. 2d 318, 23 Ohio Op. 3d 296, 432 N.E.2d 183 (1982); Day v. Day, 1985 WL 10789 (Ohio Ct. App. 9th Dist. Lorain County 1985); Josselson v. Josselson, 52 Ohio App. 3d 60, 557 N.E.2d 835 (8th Dist. Cuyahoga County 1988); Guidubaldi v. Guidubaldi, 64 Ohio App. 3d 361, 581 N.E.2d

a marriage. Where a court determined that the duration of the parties' marriage included two years the parties lived together before their ceremonial marriage, the decision was reversed and remanded for the court to explain why it held that period to be equitable.[6]

Even where a court makes findings to support its decision that a de facto termination occurred, a reviewing court may find that those findings are inequitable and may reverse that decision. In *Langer v. Langer*,[7] the parties' antenuptial agreement provided for a lump-sum property settlement of $20,000 per year for each full year of marriage. The husband was convicted of domestic violence and removed from the marital home nine months after marriage. The trial court granted summary judgment in the husband's divorce action, holding that husband owed nothing to wife under their antenuptial agreement, finding that the marriage terminated de facto when the husband vacated the marital residence prior to the end of the first full year. The court of appeals reversed, holding that the wife was entitled to her rights under the contract until their marriage was terminated de jure. Equity did not allow the husband to limit or extinguish his contract obligations by his own actions.

Recent cases discussing termination date of the marriage include:

Where the court held it was not an abuse of discretion for the trial court to use the date of divorce filing to value real estate and the separation date, five years earlier, for valuing the remainder of the marital assets. The court provided adequate explanation for its inconsistent valuation dates.[8]

In *McMaken v. McMaken*,[9] the court found that although the parties separated in 1990, the trial court did not err in adopting the date of filing a divorce complaint in 1993 as the date of termination of the marriage. The parties had continued to visit and there was insufficient evidence to establish a clear and bilateral decision to terminate their marriage until filing.[10]

---

621 (11th Dist. Portage County 1990); Schoonover v. Schoonover, 1992 WL 217986 (Ohio Ct. App. 10th Dist. Franklin County 1992).

[6]Hoover v. Hoover, 1998 WL 879496 (Ohio Ct. App. 6th Dist. Williams County 1998).

[7]Langer v. Langer, 123 Ohio App. 3d 348, 704 N.E.2d 275 (2d Dist. Montgomery County 1997), cause dismissed, 80 Ohio St. 3d 1473, 687 N.E.2d 470 (1997).

[8]Kramer v. Kramer, 1999 WL 561527 (Ohio Ct. App. 8th Dist. Cuyahoga County 1999).

[9]McMaken v. McMaken, 1999 WL 126065 (Ohio Ct. App. 12th Dist. Butler County 1999).

[10]*But see*, Boggs v. Boggs, 2008-Ohio-1411, 2008 WL 795305 (Ohio Ct. App. 5th Dist. Delaware County 2008), in which the Court of Appeals affirmed a trial court decision to follow the statutory presumption of RC § 3105.171(A)(2) that the date of final hearing constitutes the end point for the duration of the marriage despite the fact that both parties were responsible for their own debts and liabilities at an earlier date.

In *O'Brien v. O'Brien*,[11] the trial court did not err in using the date of the divorce filing as the date of termination of the marriage. Factors to be considered in choosing such a date include the parties having separate residences, utilizing separate bank accounts, not being financially intertwined, and not attempting reconciliation.

In *Jackson v. Jackson*, evidence was presented at trial which supported the trial court's finding that a marriage lasted thirty months, and not one year, with respect to property division, even though the wife moved out of marital residence ten months after marriage began and made no further financial contributions to it. The final hearing was held forty-one months after parties' marriage and the wife moved out of marital residence only to re-establish her residence in the preferred school district for her daughter's educational and medical needs, and parties continued to engage in sexual relations and attend functions as a family until termination date determined by court.[12]

The court in *Zoldan v. Zoldan*,[13] held that parties may stipulate a valuation date other than the trial date. It is not an abuse of discretion for the trial court to accept that date.

A trial court erred by ordering an equal division of the equity in the parties' marital home as of the time of trial. The court had defined the duration of the marriage as ending as of the *de facto* termination in 1991. The equity in the home should have been decided as of that date.[14] It was not error for a court to conclude the *de facto* date of the end of the marriage was the filing of a counterclaim for divorce as that was the point at which it appears that both parties evidenced the irreconcilability of the marriage.[15]

A trial court held that the de facto termination of the marriage occurred on the date that the Husband murdered his girlfriend and their young child even though the Husband maintained involved in a family business following his incarceration.[16]

In *Fillis v. Fillis*, the trial court did not err in determining the *de facto* termination date based upon evidence that the husband and wife stayed significantly financially involved despite the wife's claim

---

[11]O'Brien v. O'Brien, 1999 WL 355836 (Ohio Ct. App. 10th Dist. Franklin County 1999). Rogers v. Rogers, 1997 WL 559479 (Ohio Ct. App. 10th Dist. Franklin County 1997).

[12]Jackson v. Jackson, 2003-Ohio-7095, 2003 WL 23011368 (Ohio Ct. App. 2d Dist. Greene County 2003).

[13]Zoldan v. Zoldan, 1999 WL 397918 (Ohio Ct. App. 7th Dist. Mahoning County 1999).

[14]Crowder v. Crowder, 1999 WL 569277 (Ohio Ct. App. 10th Dist. Franklin County 1999).

[15]Loeffler v. Loeffler, 167 Ohio App. 3d 737, 2006-Ohio-3060, 857 N.E.2d 150 (6th Dist. Wood County 2006).

[16]Doyle v. Doyle, 2007-Ohio-2554, 2007 WL 1531419 (Ohio Ct. App. 12th Dist. Warren County 2007), appeal not allowed, 115 Ohio St. 3d 1473, 2007, 2007-Ohio-5735, 875 N.E.2d 627 (2007).

that she was subjected to abuse and her financial involvement with husband was neither voluntary nor bilateral.[17]

§ 12:7   Statutory terms of art—Marital property

Marital property[1] is distinct from all separate property. It is error for the trial court to fail to expressly classify each asset of the parties as marital or separate.[2] There are three subdivisions within the section of the statute that defines marital property:

(1) Property owned by either or both parties on the date of hearing, which was acquired during the marriage;[3]

(2) An interest in same (contemplating a mortgage interest or something different from absolute ownership);[4]

(3) The income and appreciation accruing during the marriage on separate property, if, and only if, that income or appreciation is attributable to a monetary, in-kind, or labor contribution of both or either party;[5] and

---

[17]Fillis v. Fillis, 2009 WL 1663978 (Ohio App. 12th Dist.).

[Section 12:7]

[1]RC 3105.171(A)(3).

[2]Vajdich v. Vajdich, 1993 WL 62157 (Ohio Ct. App. 9th Dist. Medina County 1993); Schoonover v. Schoonover, 1992 WL 217986 (Ohio Ct. App. 10th Dist. Franklin County 1992).

[3]RC 3105.171(A)(3)(a)(i). Under this subsection property owned at date of hearing, but acquired outside the period found to be "during the marriage" is not marital property. Baker v. Baker, 83 Ohio App. 3d 700, 615 N.E.2d 699 (9th Dist. Summit County 1992) (where husband purchased real property with funds from unnamed source, placed property in his and son's name and son resided therein rent-free, property was marital); Leathem v. Leathem, 94 Ohio App. 3d 470, 640 N.E.2d 1210 (3d Dist. Hancock County 1994) (where husband transferred marital property into son's name as trustee five months before wife filed for legal separation, the transfer was void *ab initio* as an attempt to defeat wife's interest); Bils v. Bils, 2008-Ohio-4125, 2008 WL 3582803 (Ohio Ct. App. 6th Dist. Wood County 2008), appeal not allowed, 120 Ohio St. 3d 1490, 2009-Ohio-278, 900 N.E.2d 200 (2009).

[4]RC 3105.171(A)(3)(a)(ii).

[5]RC 3105.171(A)(3)(a)(iii); Jakab v. Jakab, No. 90-CA-02 (Ohio Ct. App. 2d Dist. Miami County 1991); Edgell v. Edgell, 1993 WL 55978 (Ohio Ct. App. 2d Dist. Clark County 1993) (trial court properly divided accumulated appreciation of premarital real estate where efforts of both spouses during marriage caused its increase in value); Slutzker v. Slutzker, 1996 WL 132256 (Ohio Ct. App. 5th Dist. Stark County 1996) (appreciation of a nonmarital business and home deemed marital due to spouse's contribution to each during the marriage, award of appreciated value to contributing spouse alone was abuse of discretion); Baker v. Baker, 83 Ohio App. 3d 700, 615 N.E.2d 699 (9th Dist. Summit County 1992) (wife insulated, cleaned, and maintained husband's premarital real estate, stained cabinets, installed a drop ceiling; this contribution of labor during the marriage rendered the appreciation on the property marital in nature); Miller v. Miller, 1997 WL 10143 (Ohio Ct. App. 9th Dist. Summit County 1997); Henley v. Henley, 2006-Ohio-3336, 2006 WL 1790915 (Ohio Ct. App. 9th Dist. Wayne County 2006); Smith v. Smith, 2006-Ohio-2136, 2006 WL 1132850 (Ohio Ct. App. 12th Dist. Butler County 2006); Teaberry v. Teaberry, 2008-Ohio-3334, 2008 WL 2609618 (Ohio Ct. App. 7th Dist. Mahoning County 2008),

(4) Participant accounts in state and municipal deferred compensation plans, to the extent set forth.[6]

Even though the owner of premarital or other separate property is the only contributor to the appreciation on that separate property, if the contribution is made during the marriage and that contribution is not from separate property, the appreciation is marital.[7]

Any remaining doubts on this issue were resolved by the Ohio Supreme Court in *Middendorf v. Middendorf*.[8] In this case, the husband argued that the increase in the value of his pre-marital stockyard business was separate property based on the "joint-efforts" analysis in *Worthington v. Worthington*.[9] Because only he participated in the business, not his wife, he maintained that any increase in its value was his separate property. The Supreme Court flatly rejected his argument, finding that the definition of separate property in RC 3105.171(A)(3)(a)(iii) supersedes *Worthington*. The contribution of either spouse, whether of labor, money, or in kind, results in marital property. The husband's claim that the appreciation was passive, attributable to "market changes," and therefore separate property, was also rejected because he actively managed the business while his wife's contributions at home made that possible.[10]

Where a husband presented no documentation or other evidence to the trial court to sufficiently trace his separate property, the trial court properly concluded that property was marital.[11] Although proceeds from the sale of a premarital home are arguably premarital assets, if the premarital aspect cannot be traced, the separate prop-

---

appeal not allowed, 120 Ohio St. 3d 1419, 2008-Ohio-6166, 897 N.E.2d 654 (2008); Miller v. Miller, 2009-Ohio-3330, 2009 WL 1915169 (Ohio Ct. App. 7th Dist. Jefferson County 2009).

[6]RC 3105.171(A)(3)(a)(iv), as amended by 1992 S.B. 300, eff. 11-5-92. See Text § 12:18, Specific type of property—Retirement funds and other deferred compensation.

[7]RC 3105.171(A)(3)(a)(iii); Schoonover v. Schoonover, 1992 WL 217986 (Ohio Ct. App. 10th Dist. Franklin County 1992). But see Ames v. Ames, 1993 WL 95607 (Ohio Ct. App. 5th Dist. Holmes County 1993). See also Text § 12:10, Statutory terms of art—Separate property.

[8]Middendorf v. Middendorf, 82 Ohio St. 3d 397, 1998-Ohio-403, 696 N.E.2d 575 (1998).

[9]Worthington v. Worthington, 21 Ohio St. 3d 73, 488 N.E.2d 150 (1986), superseded by statute as stated in Bryant v. Bryant, 1999 WL 98110 (Ohio Ct. App. 5th Dist. Coshocton County 1999).

[10]Husband claimed that appreciation in a premarital business interest was attributable to his brother and a third party. The trial court and appeals court disagreed and found that the business appreciated due to Husband's active participation. Schalk v. Schalk, 2008-Ohio-829, 2008 WL 553283 (Ohio Ct. App. 3d Dist. Seneca County 2008); Entingh v. Entingh, 2008-Ohio-756, 2008 WL 498978 (Ohio Ct. App. 2d Dist. Montgomery County 2008).

[11]Knight v. Knight, 2000 WL 426167 (Ohio Ct. App. 4th Dist. Washington County 2000).

erty has lost its separate character after being commingled with marital property.[12]

Where a fund is in the name of a child of the marriage on the date that the court finds is the end of the marriage and where the court finds that both parties intended the fund to be in the name of the child, the fund is not a marital asset.[13]

But, in Moser v. Moser, the assets of a Family Limited Partnership that had been employed for estate planning purposes were determined to be marital property due to a finding that the Husband had not relinquished control of the assets consistent with the intent to make a gift.[14]

RC 3105.171(A)(3), which defines marital property, expressly states that retirement benefits are marital assets. It may have been more logical to add retirement benefits to the list of nine factors to be considered for property division under RC 3105.171(F); however, the effect is the same.

RC 3105.171(A)(3)(a)(iv)[15] defines the extent to which a participant account in a state or municipal deferred compensation plan can be classified as marital property.

The burden to show that property is separate property is upon the proponent.[16]

The interests of third parties must also be considered in determining whether property is marital. Where a wife and her mother were co-owners of a certain asset, the trial court erred in finding that asset to be entirely marital property and dividing it between the husband and the wife. The court should have joined the wife's mother as a party and allowed her to present evidence of her interest in the property, to provide her due process to protect her property rights.[17]

§ 12:8 Statutory terms of art—Passive income and appreciation

Where a separate asset produces income or appreciates in value,

---

[12]Peck v. Peck, 96 Ohio App. 3d 731, 645 N.E.2d 1300 (12th Dist. Butler County 1994).

[13]Henderson v. Henderson, 1995 WL 653827 (Ohio Ct. App. 1st Dist. Hamilton County 1995); Marini v. Marini, 2006-Ohio-3775, 2006 WL 2042984 (Ohio Ct. App. 11th Dist. Trumbull County 2006). See Text § 12:10, Statutory terms of art—Separate property; Miller v. Miller, 2008-Ohio-4297, 2008 WL 3892154 (Ohio Ct. App. 9th Dist. Wayne County 2008).

[14]Moser v. Moser, 2007-Ohio-4109, 2007 WL 2296413 (Ohio Ct. App. 11th Dist. Portage County 2007), appeal not allowed, 116 Ohio St. 3d 1459, 2007, 2007-Ohio-6803, 878 N.E.2d 35 (2007).

[15]As amended by 1992 S.B. 300, eff. 11-5-92. See Text § 12:18, Specific types of property—Retirement funds and other deferred compensation.

[16]See Text § 12:10, Statutory terms of art—Separate property; Fisher v. Fisher, 1997 WL 407853 (Ohio Ct. App. 3d Dist. Putnam County 1997).

[17]Koval v. Koval, 129 Ohio App. 3d 68, 716 N.E.2d 1217 (11th Dist. Portage County 1998).

but there is no monetary, in-kind, or labor contribution by either party during the marriage, the income or appreciation is separate property.[1] Income and appreciation of this nature are defined as passive.[2] The origin of this property classification is found in case law which preceded the enactment of the statute,[3] as well as subsequent decisions.[4] The formula for determining the amount of separate property of appreciated real estate is first to ascertain the percentage of separate investment to total investment and apply that percentage to the amount the property has appreciated, not to the total equity in the premises. The amount of separate property is then the amount of original investment and the separate amount of appreciation.[5] In *Knight v. Knight*,[6] the trial court erred by crediting husband with a non-marital contribution of $24,000 towards the construction of a new home. Husband did not meet his burden to establish that the $24,000 was his separate property. He failed to adequately trace the source of the money to pre-marital funds. Mortgage payments made by one party during the marriage represent a marital investment and are to be considered part of the marital equity of a marital home.[7]

Depreciation of separate property creates a separate, nonmarital loss, where there is no marital contribution to or marital diminution

---

[Section 12:8]

[1]Waltzer v. Waltzer, 1992 WL 329426 (Ohio Ct. App. 6th Dist. Lucas County 1992). See also Ames v. Ames, 1993 WL 95607 (Ohio Ct. App. 5th Dist. Holmes County 1993); Lancione v. Lancione, 1994 WL 521242 (Ohio Ct. App. 10th Dist. Franklin County 1994). See Text § 12:10, Statutory terms of art—Separate property.

[2]RC 3105.171(A)(4). See also Roberts v. Roberts, 1993 WL 49461 (Ohio Ct. App. 4th Dist. Highland County 1993).

[3]Worthington v. Worthington, 21 Ohio St. 3d 73, 488 N.E.2d 150 (1986), superseded by statute as stated in Bryant v. Bryant, 1999 WL 98110 (Ohio Ct. App. 5th Dist. Coshocton County 1999); Palmer v. Palmer, 7 Ohio App. 3d 346, 455 N.E.2d 1049 (12th Dist. Warren County 1982); Sanzenbacher v. Sanzenbacher, 3 Ohio App. 3d 180, 444 N.E.2d 454 (6th Dist. Lucas County 1981); Kassouf v. Kassouf, 1988 WL 37120 (Ohio Ct. App. 8th Dist. Cuyahoga County 1988); McCalmont v. McCalmont, 1985 WL 6761 (Ohio Ct. App. 1st Dist. Hamilton County 1985).

[4]Schoonover v. Schoonover, 1992 WL 217986 (Ohio Ct. App. 10th Dist. Franklin County 1992). See Text § 12:10, Statutory terms of art—Separate property.

[5]Munroe v. Munroe, 1999 WL 401366 (Ohio Ct. App. 8th Dist. Cuyahoga County 1999).

[6]Knight v. Knight, 2000 WL 426167 (Ohio Ct. App. 4th Dist. Washington County 2000).

[7]Goebel v. Werling, 1999 WL 548969 (Ohio Ct. App. 9th Dist. Summit County 1999); Mansell v. Mansell, 2003-Ohio-4643, 2003 WL 22049136 (Ohio Ct. App. 5th Dist. Fairfield County 2003) (appreciation on rental property owned by husband prior to marriage was not due to labor, monetary, or in-kind contribution of wife, and thus appreciation remained husband's separate property upon divorce, where wife's contributions were cleaning and painting the property and showing it to prospective tenants; increase in value of property was passive appreciation).

in value of the separate asset.[8] RC 3105.171(A)(3)(a)(iii) does not suggest that depreciation in separate property during marriage is a marital loss.[9]

Many courts require additional direct evidence of what appreciation to separate property occurred due to market forces alone (passive) and what appreciation occurred due to improvements, labor, or the efforts of the parties during the marriage (active).[10]

§ 12:9   Statutory terms of art—Personal property

Both tangible and intangible personal property are included in this definition, which did not change with the enactment of RC 3105.171.

§ 12:10   Statutory terms of art—Separate property

Contained within the definition of separate property is a list of seven specific types.[1] In addition, scattered throughout RC 3105.171 are the following rules pertaining to separate property:

(1) The commingling of separate property does not destroy its identity as separate property, except when its identity is not traceable;[2]

(2) Separate property must be disbursed to its owner, unless a distributive award is made therefrom. If the court does not award separate property to its titled owner, the court must make specific findings of fact;[3] and

---

[8]Parks v. Parks, 1993 WL 346183 (Ohio Ct. App. 12th Dist. Butler County 1993).

[9]Tanagho v. Tanagho, 1993 WL 540277 (Ohio Ct. App. 10th Dist. Franklin County 1993) (rejected by, Bryant v. Bryant, 1999 WL 98110 (Ohio Ct. App. 5th Dist. Coshocton County 1999)).

[10]Ray v. Ray, 2003-Ohio-6323, 2003 WL 22798100 (Ohio Ct. App. 9th Dist. Medina County 2003); Smith v. Smith, 2008-Ohio-799, 2008 WL 525420 (Ohio Ct. App. 10th Dist. Franklin County 2008); Cooper v. Cooper, 2008-Ohio-4731, 2008 WL 4278215 (Ohio Ct. App. 2d Dist. Greene County 2008); Miller v. Miller, 2009-Ohio-3330, 2009 WL 1915169 (Ohio Ct. App. 7th Dist. Jefferson County 2009).

[Section 12:10]

[1]RC 3105.171(A)(6)(a)(i) to (vii).

[2]RC 3105.171(A)(6)(b). Neel v. Neel, 113 Ohio App. 3d 24, 680 N.E.2d 207 (8th Dist. Cuyahoga County 1996) (where husband's mother loaned husband $16,000 to purchase marital home, and wife repaid the $16,000 from her separate property, the sum is traceable, and it is an abuse of discretion to fail to award that separate property to wife); Shaffer v. Shaffer, 1993 WL 390161 (Ohio Ct. App. 7th Dist. Jefferson County 1993) (separate property loses its identity as separate property if both commingled and nontraceable).

[3]RC 3105.171(D). See Knowles v. Knowles, 1992 WL 371915 (Ohio Ct. App. 6th Dist. Lucas County 1992); Dewalt v. Dewalt, 1993 WL 95618 (Ohio Ct. App. 5th Dist. Tuscarawas County 1993). See Text § 12:5, Statutory terms of art—Distributive award.

(3) Title to property, in and of itself, does not determine whether property is marital or separate.[4]

Thus, the act of commingling will not be determinative. This is a concept which puts to rest, in most cases, a major controversy among the courts regarding the transmutation of property. It is perhaps the most remarkable change in the law as a result of the enactment of RC 3105.171.[5]

The burden of proof that specific property is separate property is upon the proponent of the claim.[6] Oral testimony as evidence of the

[4]RC 3105.171(H). Leathem v. Leathem, 94 Ohio App. 3d 470, 640 N.E.2d 1210 (3d Dist. Hancock County 1994) (conveyance of marital home to a trust by husband was fraud upon wife); Landphair v. Landphair, 1996 WL 420876 (Ohio Ct. App. 6th Dist. Huron County 1996); Baker v. Baker, 83 Ohio App. 3d 700, 615 N.E.2d 699 (9th Dist. Summit County 1992) (where husband purchased real property with funds from an unnamed source, placed the property in his and his son's name and his son resided therein rent-free, the property was marital); Kohus v. Kohus, 2003-Ohio-2551, 2003 WL 231135479 (12th Dist. Clermont County, 2003) (husband's acts of placing wife's name on title of home that he owned prior to marriage and refinancing the property twice during the marriage did not convert his separate property interest in the home into marital property, where the mortgage was not used to finance the purchase of the home, but was used to build an addition onto home and pay off credit card debt); Schiesswohl v. Schiesswohl, 2004-Ohio-1615, 2004 WL 626110 (Ohio Ct. App. 9th Dist. Summit County 2004); Wygant v. Wygant, 2006-Ohio-1660, 2006 WL 846270 (Ohio Ct. App. 3d Dist. Wyandot County 2006). Business begun before the marriage but incorporated after the marriage was found to be marital property. Schalk v. Schalk, 2008-Ohio-829, 2008 WL 553283 (Ohio Ct. App. 3d Dist. Seneca County 2008). Jones v. Jones, 2008-Ohio-2476, 2008 WL 2152054 (Ohio Ct. App. 4th Dist. Athens County 2008).

[5]The logical analysis is that, if property can be traced, it is always separate property. If it cannot, there is no issue of intent to be determined; the property is commingled beyond identification, whether this was or was not intended. However, the court retains the discretion to balance the equities with an unequal division of property, a distributive award, or other means if the strict application of the statute results in an inequitable division of property. Findings of fact are required. See Fergus v. Fergus, 117 Ohio App. 3d 432, 690 N.E.2d 949 (7th Dist. Mahoning County 1997); Cox v. Cox, 1995 WL 399419 (Ohio Ct. App. 12th Dist. Clermont County 1995); Deaton v. Deaton, 1995 WL 746230 (Ohio Ct. App. 12th Dist. Butler County 1995).

[6]Peck v. Peck, 96 Ohio App. 3d 731, 645 N.E.2d 1300 (12th Dist. Butler County 1994); Gibson v. Gibson, 87 Ohio App. 3d 426, 622 N.E.2d 425 (4th Dist. Scioto County 1993); Ramirez v. Ramirez, 1996 WL 748167 (Ohio Ct. App. 6th Dist. Lucas County 1996); Balogh v. Balogh, 1995 WL 815504 (Ohio Ct. App. 11th Dist. Portage County 1995); Cokonougher v. Loring, 1996 WL 560523 (Ohio Ct. App. 4th Dist. Hocking County 1996); Croftcheck v. Croftcheck, 1996 WL 492261 (Ohio Ct. App. 8th Dist. Cuyahoga County 1996); Franklin v. Franklin, 1994 WL 246156 (Ohio Ct. App. 9th Dist. Summit County 1994); Kane v. Kane, 1995 WL 869955 (Ohio Ct. App. 11th Dist. Lake County 1995); Landphair v. Landphair, 1996 WL 420876 (Ohio Ct. App. 6th Dist. Huron County 1996); Modon v. Modon, 115 Ohio App. 3d 810, 686 N.E.2d 355 (9th Dist. Summit County 1996); Nance v. Nance, 1996 WL 104741 (Ohio Ct. App. 4th Dist. Pike County 1996); Obermyer v. Obermyer, 1996 WL 28001 (Ohio Ct. App. 6th Dist. Wood County 1996); Rinehart v. Rinehart, 1995 WL 762925 (Ohio Ct. App. 4th Dist. Gallia County 1995); Tupler v. Tupler, 1994 WL 6003 (Ohio Ct. App. 1st Dist. Hamilton County 1994); Duffey v. Duffey, 2002-Ohio-785, 2002 WL 264595 (Ohio Ct. App. 10th Dist. Franklin County 2002); Ray v. Ray, 2003-Ohio-6323, 2003

separate nature of property, without documentary proof, may[7] or may not be sufficient to carry the burden.[8] The burden must be sustained by a preponderance of the evidence.[9] The proponent of the claim that property is premarital must meet a two-prong test: first, that the property existed prior to marriage; and second, that the property can be traced.[10]

The protection afforded separate property in divorce is enunciated not only in the provisions above, but also in RC 3105.171(A)(6)(a)(i) to (vii):

(1) Traceable inheritances are presumed to be separate property, whether or not they have been commingled;[11]

(2) Traceable premarital property is presumed to be separate property, whether or not it has been commingled;[12]

WL 22798100 (Ohio Ct. App. 9th Dist. Medina County 2003); Maloney v. Maloney, 160 Ohio App. 3d 209, 2005-Ohio-1368, 826 N.E.2d 864 (2d Dist. Montgomery County 2005); Spier v. Spier, 2006-Ohio-1289, 2006 WL 696093 (Ohio Ct. App. 7th Dist. Mahoning County 2006); Dennis v. Dennis, 2007-Ohio-6758, 2007 WL 4395150, 2007 (Ohio Ct. App. 5th Dist. Guernsey County 2007); Cooper v. Cooper, 2008-Ohio-4731, 2008 WL 4278215 (Ohio Ct. App. 2d Dist. Greene County 2008).

[7]Perrine v. Perrine, 1996 WL 490253 (Ohio Ct. App. 9th Dist. Summit County 1996); Ramirez v. Ramirez, 1996 WL 748167 (Ohio Ct. App. 6th Dist. Lucas County 1996); Slutzker v. Slutzker, 1994 WL 822539 (Ohio Ct. App. 5th Dist. Stark County 1994) (where appellee conceded that appellant's property was separate, it was error to find that separate property could not be traced, even if there was no documentary evidence offered).

[8]Wylie v. Wylie, 1996 WL 292044 (Ohio Ct. App. 4th Dist. Lawrence County 1996); Wolfangel v. Wolfangel, 1995 WL 312697 (Ohio Ct. App. 9th Dist. Summit County 1995); Bechara v. Essad, 2004-Ohio-3042, 2004 WL 1325636 (Ohio Ct. App. 7th Dist. Mahoning County 2004).

[9]Tupler v. Tupler, 1994 WL 6003 (Ohio Ct. App. 1st Dist. Hamilton County 1994); Johnson v. Johnson, 2006-Ohio-5901, 2006 WL 3231256 (Ohio Ct. App. 5th Dist. Guernsey County 2006), appeal not allowed, 113 Ohio St. 3d 1443, 2007, 2007-Ohio-1266, 863 N.E.2d 659 (2007).

[10]Guenther v. Guenther, 1994 WL 577751 (Ohio Ct. App. 9th Dist. Wayne County 1994).

[11]RC 3105.171(A)(6)(a)(i). Southworth v. Southworth, 1998 WL 896293 (Ohio Ct. App. 8th Dist. Cuyahoga County 1998) (court erred in finding traceable inheritance to be marital); Holman v. Holman, 1997 WL 458046 (Ohio Ct. App. 6th Dist. Ottawa County 1997); Earick v. Earick, 1994 WL 66890 (Ohio Ct. App. 5th Dist. Ashland County 1994) (nontraceable commingled inheritances are marital).

[12]RC 3105.171(A)(6)(a)(ii). This section is widely applied in Hoyt v. Hoyt, 53 Ohio St. 3d 177, 559 N.E.2d 1292 (1990) (pensions); Kassouf v. Kassouf, 1988 WL 37120 (Ohio Ct. App. 8th Dist. Cuyahoga County 1988) (investments); McCalmont v. McCalmont, 1985 WL 6761 (Ohio Ct. App. 1st Dist. Hamilton County 1985) (premarital dwellings occupied during remarriage). See also Stepich v. Stepich, 1993 WL 266954 (Ohio Ct. App. 8th Dist. Cuyahoga County 1993) (premarital downpayment on real property); Dionne v. Dionne, 1994 WL 115927 (Ohio Ct. App. 5th Dist. Stark County 1994) (real estate purchased partly with nonmarital funds); Schneider v. Schneider, 1999 WL 173000 (Ohio Ct. App. 12th Dist. Brown County 1999) (husband traced his separate interest in equity in marital home, court's failure to award it as his separate property was error); Avent v. Avent, 166 Ohio App. 3d 104, 2006-Ohio-1861, 849 N.E.2d 98 (6th Dist. Lucas County 2006).

(3) Traceable passive income and appreciation are presumed to be separate property, whether or not they have been commingled;[13]

(4) Property acquired after date of filing of a decree of legal separation and property excluded from marital property by antenuptial agreement are separate, whether or not the property has been commingled, if it can be traced;[14]

(5) Compensation for personal injury not attributable to expenses paid from marital funds is separate property, whether or not it has been commingled, if it can be traced;[15] A claim for loss of consortium is the claimant's separate property. The amount of the claim, if not clearly delineated, should be calculated after deduction of lost wages, attorney fees and expenses for prosecuting the claim.[16]

(6) A gift received by a spouse during the marriage is presumed to be marital property, unless it can be proved otherwise by clear and convincing evidence.[17]

The trial court did not err in concluding that the parties' marital

---

[13]RC 3105.171(A)(4), RC 3105.171(A)(6)(a)(iii). Ames v. Ames, 1993 WL 95607 (Ohio Ct. App. 5th Dist. Holmes County 1993) (trial court errs in failing to award as separate property to wife the appreciated value of real property purchased by wife with her separate inheritance); Lancione v. Lancione, 1994 WL 521242 (Ohio Ct. App. 10th Dist. Franklin County 1994). See Text § 12:8, Statutory terms of art—Passive income and appreciation; May v. May, 2008-Ohio-634, 2008 WL 434998 (Ohio Ct. App. 5th Dist. Richland County 2008); Smith v. Smith, 2008-Ohio-799, 2008 WL 525420 (Ohio Ct. App. 10th Dist. Franklin County 2008).

[14]RC 3105.171(A)(6)(a)(iv), (v). Steinke v. Steinke, 2006-Ohio-4185, 2006 WL 2337647 (Ohio Ct. App. 3d Dist. Auglaize County 2006), appeal not allowed, 112 Ohio St. 3d 1443, 2007, 2007-Ohio-152, 860 N.E.2d 767 (2007).

[15]RC 3105.171(A)(6)(a)(vi). Cox v. Cox, 1999 WL 74573 (Ohio Ct. App. 12th Dist. Fayette County 1999); Modon v. Modon, 115 Ohio App. 3d 810, 686 N.E.2d 355 (9th Dist. Summit County 1996); Hartzell v. Hartzell, 90 Ohio App. 3d 385, 629 N.E.2d 491 (2d Dist. Darke County 1993); Bartram v. Bartram, 1991 WL 199907 (Ohio Ct. App. 9th Dist. Medina County 1991); Wroblewski v. Wroblewski, 1993 WL 256326 (Ohio Ct. App. 4th Dist. Gallia County 1993); Marcum v. Marcum, 116 Ohio App. 3d 606, 688 N.E.2d 1085 (2d Dist. Montgomery County 1996); Nafziger v. Nafziger, 1996 WL 608537 (Ohio Ct. App. 6th Dist. Fulton County 1996); Wright v. Wright, 1994 WL 649271 (Ohio Ct. App. 4th Dist. Hocking County 1994) (overruled by, Liming v. Liming, 2005-Ohio-2228, 2005 WL 1056263 (Ohio Ct. App. 4th Dist. Athens County 2005)).

[16]Lee v. Lee, 1999 WL 317338 (Ohio Ct. App. 2d Dist. Montgomery County 1999); Kondik v. Kondik, 2009-Ohio-2300, 2009 WL 1365259 (Ohio Ct. App. 11th Dist. Portage County 2009).

[17]RC 3105.171(A)(6)(a)(vii). This provision originated among proponents of the bill who feared that a parent who gave an asset to both parties during marriage would testify otherwise when faced with his offspring's divorce and those who feared that, if the marital home is the sole asset of the parties, one spouse, whose parent had provided a down payment, could succeed to the entire marital estate. The provision is a compromise between proponents of the tenet that all gifts are separate property in accord with the original draft of this statute, and those who advocate that all gifts given during the marriage should be marital property. Congrove v. Congrove, 2000 WL 1349809 (Ohio Ct. App. 9th Dist. Summit County 2000) (it was error for the trial court to conclude that funds received by husband during the marriage from his mother were an advance against inheritance rather than a loan which constituted a marital debt); Helton v. Helton, 114 Ohio App. 3d 683, 683 N.E.2d 1157 (2d Dist.

residence was husband's separate property although he had executed a survivorship deed to wife. There was no donative intent by husband to convert the separate property to marital property. Husband's intent in executing the deed was to give wife a possessory interest and to provide for his child upon death. Wife did not prove by clear and convincing evidence husband's donative intent.[18] In *Lowry v. Lowry*,[19] the trial court erred in finding that a transfer of real estate for no consideration to the parties was not a gift. The evidence did not support a finding that there was an obligation to repay the transferor for the property. The evidence supported a determination that the transfer was a valid gift.

The court must award a spouse's separate property to him or to her. If the court does not do so, it must supply findings of fact to support the award.[20]

The term duration of the marriage[21] is relevant to defining what specific assets are marital and what are separate. Assets acquired before or after the period which the court defines as the duration of

---

Montgomery County 1996) (husband deeded an interest in his premarital real estate to wife during marriage; court found the transfer to be a gift, not an aspect of his estate planning). Note that it could be argued that only the interest transferred, not the interest retained, is subject to division as marital property. But see Dooley v. Dooley, 1998 WL 454112 (Ohio Ct. App. 1st Dist. Hamilton County 1998) (husband provided sufficient evidence through written loan documents and testimony to establish that funds received from his parents were loans and advancements of inheritance and not gifts to both parties); Mayer v. Mayer, 110 Ohio App. 3d 233, 673 N.E.2d 981 (3d Dist. Allen County 1996) (because title does not determine whether property is marital or separate, husband's premarital real estate held in the name of both parties was traceable and was therefore separate property), appeal dismissed by 77 Ohio St.3d 1413, 670 N.E.2d 1002 (1996). Accord, Schultheis v. Schultheis, 1996 WL 666726 (Ohio Ct. App. 3d Dist. Allen County 1996). See also Neel v. Neel, 113 Ohio App. 3d 24, 680 N.E.2d 207 (8th Dist. Cuyahoga County 1996) (court defines a gift); Michael v. Michael, 1997 WL 72108 (Ohio Ct. App. 6th Dist. Sandusky County 1997); Obermyer v. Obermyer, 1996 WL 28001 (Ohio Ct. App. 6th Dist. Wood County 1996); Reed v. Reed, 1996 WL 76150 (Ohio Ct. App. 8th Dist. Cuyahoga County 1996); Rinehart v. Rinehart, 1995 WL 762925, at *3 (Ohio Ct. App. 4th Dist. Gallia County 1995); Roberts v. Roberts, 1993 WL 49461 (Ohio Ct. App. 4th Dist. Highland County 1993); Barker v. Barker v. Kaiser, 1996 WL 529534 (Ohio Ct. App. 7th Dist. Belmont County 1996); Wolfangel v. Wolfangel, 1995 WL 312697 (Ohio Ct. App. 9th Dist. Summit County 1995); Humphrey v. Humphrey, 2002-Ohio-3121, 2002 WL 1357108 (Ohio Ct. App. 11th Dist. Ashtabula County 2002); Stonehill v. Stonehill, 2004-Ohio-3022, 2004 WL 1302458 (Ohio Ct. App. 3d Dist. Allen County 2004); Ockunzzi v. Ockunzzi, 2006-Ohio-5741, 2006 WL 3095754 (Ohio Ct. App. 8th Dist. Cuyahoga County 2006), appeal not allowed, 113 Ohio St. 3d 1443, 2007, 2007-Ohio-1266, 863 N.E.2d 658 (2007); Dudley v. Dudley, 2008-Ohio-3760, 2008 WL 2896657 (Ohio Ct. App. 5th Dist. Guernsey County 2008).

[18]Sweeney v. Sweeney, 2000 WL 799095 (Ohio Ct. App. 9th Dist. Summit County 2000); Neighbarger v. Neighbarger, 2006-Ohio-796, 2006 WL 416371 (Ohio Ct. App. 10th Dist. Franklin County 2006).

[19]Lowry v. Lowry, 1999 WL 435175 (Ohio Ct. App. 6th Dist. Wood County 1999).

[20]RC 3105.171(D). See Text § 12:5, Statutory terms of art—Distributive award.

[21]RC 3105.171(A)(2). See Text § 12:6, Statutory terms of art—During the marriage.

the marriage are separate. The courts exercised their discretion to determine the *de facto* period of marriage prior to the enactment of RC 3105.171.[22] Even under the statute, where the parties divorced and remarried each other, property acquired during the period of time between the marriages may or may not be considered as separate property.[23]

By definition, the distributive award can be made from only separate property.[24] Separate property may also be the subject of an order[25] to allow the use by the nonowner spouse of the separate property for a reasonable time.[26] The court has the discretion to order that separate property be sold or used as security for a loan to bring about equity in the property division.[27]

The application of the separate property sections of RC 3105.171 has resulted in a substantial body of case law. The recent precedent supports the conclusion that transmutation occurs under only limited circumstances.

Transmutation is defined and discussed in *Kuehn v. Kuehn*[28] and *Kahn v. Kahn*,[29] both predecessors of RC 3105.171. Transmutation is the process by which nonmarital property is converted to marital property. Whether property which would otherwise be separate had suffered transmutation was based, prior to 1991,[30] upon six factors: (1) intent of the parties; (2) source of funds used to acquire the property; (3) circumstances of the acquisition; (4) dates of acquisition, marriage, alleged transmutation, and breakup of the marriage; (5) inducement for and purpose of the transactions giving rise to the alleged transmutation; and (6) value of the property and significance to the parties.

Such criteria as intent, inducement, purpose, and significance are extremely subjective. The law of separate property begged for more precise elements and for requisite findings of fact.

The purpose for the change in the law of transmutation implemented in RC 3105.171 is not to limit the discretion of the courts, but to bet-

---

[22]Day v. Day, 1985 WL 10789 (Ohio Ct. App. 9th Dist. Lorain County 1985).

[23]Mitchell v. Mitchell, 1998 WL 225043 (Ohio Ct. App. 9th Dist. Summit County 1998).

[24]RC 3105.171(A)(1). See Text § 12:5, Statutory terms of art—Distributive award.

[25]RC 3105.171(J).

[26]An example might be a shed used for equipment storage by the husband in his business. Although the property is the wife's premarital separate real estate, the husband might be granted limited use if the court deems it fair to do so. The classic example, however, is the use of the marital dwelling granted to the residential parent. See Text § 12:15, Other equitable orders. See also RC 3105.171(F)(3) regarding use of the marital home by the spouse who is granted custody.

[27]RC 3105.171(J).

[28]Kuehn v. Kuehn, 55 Ohio App. 3d 245, 564 N.E.2d 97 (12th Dist. Clinton County 1988).

[29]Kahn v. Kahn, 42 Ohio App. 3d 61, 536 N.E.2d 678 (2d Dist. Montgomery County 1987).

[30]January 1, 1991, the effective date of RC 3105.171.

ter define the criteria for disposition of separate property. Decisions among Ohio counties regarding separate property were disparate. Grounds for appeal were so clouded that effective argument was precluded. The lawyer's ability to clearly advise clients was impeded by the absence of the predictability of results.

The source of funds rule of RC 3105.171 has supplanted the multi-factor rule of *Kuehn v. Kuehn*[31] and *Kahn v. Kahn*.[32] The policy adopted by the Ohio legislature is two-fold. First, the multi-factor rule is contrary to public policy because it encourages a spouse to isolate his or her separate property in contemplation of divorce, which the legislature deemed detrimental to the marital relationship. Second, the legislature ratified a policy which was set forth in cases decided prior to the enactment of RC 3105.171: If the right to hold separate property is to be "meaningful," the characterization of property as marital or nonmarital must be determined by the source of contributions.[33]

Courts, after 1991, should rarely enter appellate decisions on the basis that trial court judgments "feel" right; that is, without specific findings, simply basing the review upon the trial court's broad discretion and upon the conclusion that the trial court had not abused that discretion. RC 3105.171 requires the trial court to provide carefully thought out and accurately presented analyses upon which rational settlement advice can be given and solid appeals can be constructed.[34]

The only circumstance under which transmutation may occur under the provisions of RC 3105.171 is in the case where a party is not able to trace his or her separate property.[35] This is not to say that resulting inequitable separate property awards must stand unfettered. Separate property awards, if inequitable, must be balanced by a statutory

---

[31]Kuehn v. Kuehn, 55 Ohio App. 3d 245, 564 N.E.2d 97 (12th Dist. Clinton County 1988).

[32]Kahn v. Kahn, 42 Ohio App. 3d 61, 536 N.E.2d 678 (2d Dist. Montgomery County 1987).

[33]Morgan v. Morgan, 1993 WL 418495 (Ohio Ct. App. 11th Dist. Portage County 1993); Shewring v. Shewring, 2006-Ohio-3247, 2006 WL 1728059 (Ohio Ct. App. 5th Dist. Fairfield County 2006); Moschella v. Moschella, 2006-Ohio-3635, 2006 WL 1976316 (Ohio Ct. App. 7th Dist. Mahoning County 2006).

[34]The results in Kuehn v. Kuehn, 55 Ohio App. 3d 245, 564 N.E.2d 97 (12th Dist. Clinton County 1988), for example, could be similar after RC 3105.171, but pursuant only to a rationale different from transmutation. The court might have divided the property unequally in favor of wife, or the court might have granted wife a distributive award, based on explicit findings of fact, in order to render equitable the overall property division. See Text § 12:3, Equitable distribution. See also Roberts v. Roberts, 1993 WL 49461 (Ohio Ct. App. 4th Dist. Highland County 1993); Stafford v. Stafford, 1995 WL 118172 (Ohio Ct. App. 2d Dist. Greene County 1995); Modon v. Modon, 115 Ohio App. 3d 810, 686 N.E.2d 355 (9th Dist. Summit County 1996); Randall v. Randall, 1997 WL 133342 (Ohio Ct. App. 6th Dist. Williams County 1997).

[35]But see Black v. Black, 1996 WL 752885 (Ohio Ct. App. 5th Dist. Stark County 1996); Valentine v. Valentine, 1996 WL 72608 (Ohio Ct. App. 5th Dist. Ashland County 1996); Grosnickle v. Grosnickle, 2007-Ohio-3613, 2007 WL 2028919 (Ohio Ct. App. 12th Dist. Warren County 2007).

means other than a summary finding that transmutation has occurred.

The precedent evolving throughout Ohio demonstrates that a body of law on the matter of separate property has rapidly developed with the advent of RC 3105.171. Generally, Ohio courts have acknowledged and followed the clear legislative mandates of the statute. In *Tupler v. Tupler*,[36] the First District Court of Appeals followed the mandates of the statute, finding that husband had traced separate assets, notwithstanding their having been commingled. The Second District has held likewise in *Murphy v. Murphy*.[37]

In *Landry v. Landry*,[38] the Third District Court held that, where the proponent of a separate property claim failed to trace to premarital assets the funds existing on date of valuation, the assets were marital.[39]

The Fourth District Court of Appeals in *Rinehart v. Rinehart*[40] held as follows: "Of course, without making a determination as to the 'traceability' of a disputed asset as is required by RC 3105.171(A)(6)(b), the trial court cannot determine whether the asset is separate or marital property, and thus cannot comply with RC 3105.171(B). "[41]

The Sixth District held that "the trial court must focus on the traceability of the separate property in determining whether it was transmuted into marital property."[42]

The Seventh District Court of Appeals reversed the decision of the

---

[36]Tupler v. Tupler, 1994 WL 6003 (Ohio Ct. App. 1st Dist. Hamilton County 1994).

[37]Murphy v. Murphy, 1996 WL 629522 (Ohio Ct. App. 2d Dist. Montgomery County 1996). See also Stafford v. Stafford, 1995 WL 118172 (Ohio Ct. App. 2d Dist. Greene County 1995).

[38]Landry v. Landry, 105 Ohio App. 3d 289, 663 N.E.2d 1026 (3d Dist. Auglaize County 1995).

[39]See also Mayer v. Mayer, 110 Ohio App. 3d 233, 673 N.E.2d 981 (3d Dist. Allen County 1996); Bucalo v. Bucalo, 2005-Ohio-6319, 2005 WL 3193851 (Ohio Ct. App. 9th Dist. Medina County 2005) (separate property funds deposited into joint checking account from which household bills were paid and employment checks were also deposited).

[40]Rinehart v. Rinehart, 1995 WL 762925 (Ohio Ct. App. 4th Dist. Gallia County 1995).

[41]See also Nance v. Nance, 1996 WL 104741 (Ohio Ct. App. 4th Dist. Pike County 1996); Wilson v. Wilson, 1995 WL 695063 (Ohio Ct. App. 4th Dist. Washington County 1995); Winters v. Winters, 1994 WL 69885 (Ohio Ct. App. 4th Dist. Scioto County 1994).

[42]Landphair v. Landphair, 1996 WL 420876, at *3 (Ohio Ct. App. 6th Dist. Huron County 1996). See also Bockelman v. Bockelman, 1995 WL 358605 (Ohio Ct. App. 6th Dist. Lucas County 1995) (case remanded where trial court awarded wife entire marital home as separate property due to her contribution of part of downpayment from her premarital assets; husband showed that he, too, had contributed premarital assets, marital labor, and marital payments toward reduction of the mortgage balance); Nafziger v. Nafziger, 1996 WL 608537 (Ohio Ct. App. 6th Dist. Fulton County 1996); Cataline v. Cataline, 1993 WL 452093 (Ohio Ct. App. 6th Dist. Sandusky County

trial court in *Fritz v. Fritz*,[43] because the trial court had not addressed the source of funds used to acquire property, the character of which as marital or separate property, was in dispute.

The Eighth District Court of Appeals ruled that the trial court erred in finding that $74,000 was wife's separate property because she had traced only $44,000.[44]

The Ninth District, in *Pruitt v. Pruitt*,[45] held that, since the *Kuehn*[46] decision, amendments to the Revised Code have "restricted, if not rendered obsolete," the application of the *Kuehn* test.[47] See also *Lancione v. Lancione*, Tenth District Court of Appeals.[48]

In *Balogh v. Balogh*, the Eleventh District held that "traceability" is the focus in determining whether separate property is separate after it has been commingled.[49]

In *Stern v. Stern*,[50] the Twelfth District Court of Appeals held as follows: "We begin by observing that with the enactment of R.C. 3105.171 the concept of "transmutation" of separate property to mari-

---

1993) (unless the financial history of an asset cannot be traced, there is no longer commingling or transmutation in Ohio).

[43]Fritz v. Fritz, 1995 WL 75405 (Ohio Ct. App. 7th Dist. Columbiana County 1995).

[44]Bartak v. Bartak, 1993 WL 58613 (Ohio Ct. App. 8th Dist. Cuyahoga County 1993). See also Wyum v. Wyum, 1997 WL 97235 (Ohio Ct. App. 8th Dist. Cuyahoga County 1997); Stepich v. Stepich, 1993 WL 266954 (Ohio Ct. App. 8th Dist. Cuyahoga County 1993); Parr v. Parr, 1997 WL 97231 (Ohio Ct. App. 8th Dist. Cuyahoga County 1997).

[45]Pruitt v. Pruitt, 1996 WL 221893, at *2 (Ohio Ct. App. 9th Dist. Medina County 1996).

[46]Kuehn v. Kuehn, 55 Ohio App. 3d 245, 564 N.E.2d 97 (12th Dist. Clinton County 1988).

[47]See also Franklin v. Franklin, 1994 WL 246156 (Ohio Ct. App. 9th Dist. Summit County 1994); Bauman v. Bauman, 1994 WL 232894 (Ohio Ct. App. 9th Dist. Wayne County 1994); Guenther v. Guenther, 1994 WL 577751 (Ohio Ct. App. 9th Dist. Wayne County 1994); Walker v. Walker, 1994 WL 395286 (Ohio Ct. App. 9th Dist. Summit County 1994); Wolfangel v. Wolfangel, 1995 WL 312697 (Ohio Ct. App. 9th Dist. Summit County 1995). But see Moore v. Moore, 83 Ohio App. 3d 75, 613 N.E.2d 1097 (9th Dist. Summit County 1992) (spouses who executed to each other deeds to their separate property converted their separate property to marital property).

[48]Lancione v. Lancione, 1994 WL 521242 (Ohio Ct. App. 10th Dist. Franklin County 1994).

[49]Balogh v. Balogh, 1995 WL 815504, at *2 (Ohio Ct. App. 11th Dist. Portage County 1995). See also Morgan v. Morgan, 1993 WL 418495 (Ohio Ct. App. 11th Dist. Portage County 1993); Boyles v. Boyles, 2003-Ohio-5351, 2003 WL 22290895 (Ohio Ct. App. 11th Dist. Portage County 2003) (fact that ex-wife managed ex-husband's separate property during marriage was not a sufficient basis to convert the increase in property value to marital property, and thus, appreciation of property value was not marital property, where there was no evidence that increased value was anything other than passive appreciation, and neither party testified they engaged in any renovation or remodeling).

[50]Stern v. Stern, 1996 WL 451056, at *2 (Ohio Ct. App. 12th Dist. Clinton County 1996).

tal property has been 'virtually abolished as a rule of law in Ohio.' [citation omitted] Rather, . . . the focus when deciding whether one spouse's separate property has lost its separate character after being commingled with the couple's marital property is whether the property remains traceable as separate property."[51]

Some courts continue to resist the language of RC 3105.171(A)(6)(b), which provides

The commingling of separate property with other property of any type does not destroy the identity of the separate property, except when the separate property is not traceable.

RC 3105.171(D), stating:

Except as otherwise provided in division (E) of this section or by another provision of this section, the court shall disburse a spouse's separate property to that spouse. If a court does not disburse a spouse's separate property to that spouse, the court shall make written findings of fact that explain the factors that it considered in making its determination that the spouse's separate property should not be disbursed to that spouse.

and RC 3105.171(H), providing that:

Except as otherwise provided in this section, the holding of title to property by one spouse individually or by both spouses in a form of co-ownership does not determine whether the property is marital property or separate property.

Citing *Kuehn v. Kuehn*,[52] which was decided prior to the enactment of RC 3105.171, the Fifth District Court of Appeals in *Black v. Black*[53] held that "the fact that property can be traced back to appellee is not a factor the trial court should consider in addressing the issue of transmutation." Intentional intervening acts of a spouse, such as the giving of separate property of one spouse to the other spouse as a gift, can convert his or her separate property into marital property.[54] "We

---

[51]See also Peck v. Peck, 96 Ohio App. 3d 731, 645 N.E.2d 1300 (12th Dist. Butler County 1994); Greene v. Greene, 1996 WL 263634 (Ohio Ct. App. 12th Dist. Clermont County 1996); Freytag v. Freytag, 1994 WL 424135 (Ohio Ct. App. 12th Dist. Butler County 1994); Lewis v. Lewis, 1995 WL 70200 (Ohio Ct. App. 12th Dist. Clermont County 1995); Wollum v. Wollum, 1993 WL 268879 (Ohio Ct. App. 12th Dist. Clermont County 1993); Cox v. Cox, 1995 WL 399419 (Ohio Ct. App. 12th Dist. Clermont County 1995) (evidence of intent not to transmute is not an element necessary to support a claim to separate property); Moore v. Moore, 2000 WL 1782328 (Ohio Ct. App. 12th Dist. Brown County 2000).

[52]Kuehn v. Kuehn, 55 Ohio App. 3d 245, 564 N.E.2d 97 (12th Dist. Clinton County 1988).

[53]Black v. Black, 1996 WL 752885, at *3 (Ohio Ct. App. 5th Dist. Stark County 1996).

[54]Helton v. Helton, 114 Ohio App. 3d 683, 683 N.E.2d 1157 (2d Dist. Montgomery County 1996); Valentine v. Valentine, 1996 WL 72608 (Ohio Ct. App. 5th Dist. Ashland County 1996).

have determined . . . that the doctrine of transmutation still exists, even after the enactment of R.C. 3105.171(A)(6)(a)(i–vii)."[55]

Thus, notwithstanding the mandatory language of RC 3105.171(A), (D), and (H), in some Ohio jurisdictions, even when separate property can be traced, factors other than those set forth in the statute may render the property marital.[56]

Other Fifth District cases include: *Wells v. Wells*,[57] in which the court combined the theory of transmutation with the tenets of RC 3105.171 regarding gifts; *Renac v. Renac*,[58] which held that the separate property was not sufficiently traced, but the question of whether it was a gift was not addressed at trial or on appeal; *Smith v. Smith*,[59] where appellant failed in his argument that expert testimony was required to establish the direct cause of the increase in value during marriage; and *Slutzker v. Slutzker*,[60] finding that where the appellee conceded that the appellant's property was separate, the court erred in holding that the separate property could not be traced, even if there was no documentary evidence offered.

Notwithstanding that *Kuehn v. Kuehn*,[61] *Kahn v. Kahn*,[62] and *King v. King*[63] were decided prior to the enactment of RC 3105.171, Ohio courts continue to cite to these cases to support findings of transmutation. They disregard the superseding language of RC 3105.171, and cite to *Starr v. Starr*.[64] which expressly states that it is applying RC 3105.18, the predecessor to RC 3105.171, because the latter does not apply to cases filed before its effective date of January 1, 1991. Some courts still rely upon treatises which predate the enact-

---

[55]Black v. Black, 1996 WL 752885, at *2 (Ohio Ct. App. 5th Dist. Stark County 1996).

[56]Bouillon v. Bouillon, 1996 WL 65600, at *2 (Ohio Ct. App. 3d Dist. Seneca County 1996) (after husband invested his premarital $12,000 into farm property, it "ceased to be separate;" although trial court did not award husband his traceable $24,000 inheritance, the overall distribution of property was "within the parameters of the trial court's discretion").

[57]Wells v. Wells, 1994 WL 22888 (Ohio Ct. App. 5th Dist. Coshocton County 1994).

[58]Renac v. Renac, 1996 WL 752554 (Ohio Ct. App. 5th Dist. Knox County 1996).

[59]Smith v. Smith, 1995 WL 499009 (Ohio Ct. App. 5th Dist. Stark County 1995).

[60]Slutzker v. Slutzker, 1994 WL 822539 (Ohio Ct. App. 5th Dist. Stark County 1994).

[61]Kuehn v. Kuehn, 55 Ohio App. 3d 245, 564 N.E.2d 97 (12th Dist. Clinton County 1988).

[62]Kahn v. Kahn, 42 Ohio App. 3d 61, 536 N.E.2d 678 (2d Dist. Montgomery County 1987).

[63]King v. King, 78 Ohio App. 3d 599, 605 N.E.2d 970 (12th Dist. Warren County 1992).

[64]Starr v. Starr, 1995 WL 338496 (Ohio Ct. App. 9th Dist. Summit County 1995).

ment of the statute,[65] and they apply the law of transmutation as it was known prior to January 1, 1991.[66]

§ 12:11 Contribution to the marriage

The property division statute provides that each party must be considered to have contributed equally to the production and acquisition of marital assets.[1] The interpretation of the committee that drafted the statute[2] was that differences between spouses in the fulfillment of their marital duties and in the contribution of effort or earnings to acquisition of assets should be disregarded by the court in favor of the concept of the equal marital partnership set out in *Wolfe*

---

[65]Such as court's reliance upon *Principles and Guidelines for the Division of Property in Actions for Divorce in Ohio*, 54 Ohio B. 491 (1981).

[66]Barker v. Barker v. Kaiser, 1996 WL 529534 (Ohio Ct. App. 7th Dist. Belmont County 1996) (either husband failed to show by clear and convincing evidence that the cash was a gift to him alone, or the gift was to husband and the funds transmuted; regardless, the court found no abuse of discretion); Croftcheck v. Croftcheck, 1996 WL 492261 (Ohio Ct. App. 8th Dist. Cuyahoga County 1996) (court held that wife's premarital home as transmuted because the parties lived in it for 20 years, husband had made repairs, and wife had deeded a half interest to husband; other real estate purchased with wife's inheritance also transmuted because wife purchased it during the marriage, rent was deposited to the joint account, and repairs were made); Henderson v. Henderson, 1995 WL 653827 (Ohio Ct. App. 1st Dist. Hamilton County 1995) (separate funds deposited in children's accounts transmuted to marital property); Kane v. Kane, 1995 WL 869955 (Ohio Ct. App. 11th Dist. Lake County 1995) (where husband testified that most of his inheritance was used to purchase marital home, his inheritance was transmuted to marital property); Paluch v. Paluch, 1995 WL 752661 (Ohio Ct. App. 9th Dist. Summit County 1995) (simple commingling of assets may result in transmutation); Wolf v. Wolf, 1996 WL 563997 (Ohio Ct. App. 2d Dist. Greene County 1996) (wife received one-third interest in real estate from husband and his mother to avoid taxes upon death of husband or his mother; because this was beneficial to husband, his separate interest was transmuted to wife); Wright v. Wright, 1994 WL 649271 (Ohio Ct. App. 4th Dist. Hocking County 1994) (overruled by, Liming v. Liming, 2005-Ohio-2228, 2005 WL 1056263 (Ohio Ct. App. 4th Dist. Athens County 2005)); Wright v. Wright, 1996 WL 1767 (Ohio Ct. App. 9th Dist. Medina County 1996) (transmutation occurred when a spouse invested separate property for a porch, carpet, and pond at the marital home); Smith v. Smith, 1995 WL 499009 (Ohio Ct. App. 5th Dist. Stark County 1995); Renac v. Renac, 1996 WL 752554 (Ohio Ct. App. 5th Dist. Knox County 1996); Black v. Black, 1996 WL 752885 (Ohio Ct. App. 5th Dist. Stark County 1996); Valentine v. Valentine, 1996 WL 72608 (Ohio Ct. App. 5th Dist. Ashland County 1996); Wells v. Wells, 1994 WL 22888 (Ohio Ct. App. 5th Dist. Coshocton County 1994); Bouillon v. Bouillon, 1996 WL 65600 (Ohio Ct. App. 3d Dist. Seneca County 1996) (after husband invested his premarital $12,000 into the farm property, it "ceased to be separate;" although the trial court did not award husband his traceable $24,000 inheritance, the overall distribution of property was "within the parameters of the trial court's discretion"); Alteno v. Alteno, 2002-Ohio-302, 2002 WL 99538 (Ohio Ct. App. 11th Dist. Trumbull County 2002).

[Section 12:11]

[1]RC 3105.171(C)(2).

[2]Ohio State Bar Association Family Law Committee.

v. Wolfe.[3] The statute is conspicuously silent as to whether marital fault, other than financial fault,[4] should impact the division of property.[5] Thus, the case law still governs.[6] The trend is in the direction of disallowing financial punishment for marital misconduct which is not itself financial in nature. Fault "should not be the sole or primary evaluating factor."[7] There should not be a separate award in compensation for aggressions.[8] Therefore, marital fault is rarely a decisive factor in property awards.[9]

§ 12:12   Division without regard to support

A division of property must be made prior to and without regard to any award of spousal support.[1] This assures that the "equal unless inequitable" provision[2] will be effective by directing that there will be no blurring of the awards of support and property division or of the criteria applied to each distinct award.[3]

Confusion between property division and spousal support can occur

---

[3]Wolfe v. Wolfe, 46 Ohio St. 2d 399, 75 Ohio Op. 2d 474, 350 N.E.2d 413 (1976), superseded by statute as stated in Heslep v. Heslep, 2000 WL 818909 (Ohio Ct. App. 7th Dist. Monroe County 2000).

[4]See RC 3105.171(E)(3). See also Berish v. Berish, 69 Ohio St. 2d 318, 23 Ohio Op. 3d 296, 432 N.E.2d 183 (1982); Houck v. Houck, 1992 WL 132469 (Ohio Ct. App. 10th Dist. Franklin County 1992); Corpac v. Corpac, 1992 WL 41244 (Ohio Ct. App. 10th Dist. Franklin County 1992) (awards from marital property for financial misconduct).

[5]The drafting committee reached an impasse on whether to include the words, "without regard to marital misconduct" on the property division and spousal support statutes, RC 3105.171 and RC 3105.18.

[6]Zimmie v. Zimmie, 11 Ohio St. 3d 94, 464 N.E.2d 142, 53 A.L.R.4th 75 (1984); Gage v. Gage, 101 Ohio App. 483, 1 Ohio Op. 2d 413, 73 Ohio L. Abs. 277, 129 N.E.2d 486 (8th Dist. Cuyahoga County 1955), judgment aff'd, 165 Ohio St. 462, 60 Ohio Op. 117, 136 N.E.2d 56 (1956); Esteb v. Esteb, 173 Ohio St. 259, 19 Ohio Op. 2d 80, 181 N.E.2d 462 (1962); Farone v. Farone, 1989 WL 6551 (Ohio Ct. App. 11th Dist. Lake County 1989); Mokris v. Mokris, 1986 WL 6975 (Ohio Ct. App. 8th Dist. Cuyahoga County 1986); Baker v. Baker, 1987 WL 6238 (Ohio Ct. App. 11th Dist. Lake County 1987); Zaller v. Zaller, 1984 WL 7417, at *2 (Ohio Ct. App. 11th Dist. Lake County 1984); Warren v. Warren, 1981 WL 6662 (Ohio Ct. App. 3d Dist. Hancock County 1981); Hammond v. Brown, 1995 WL 546903 (Ohio Ct. App. 8th Dist. Cuyahoga County 1995).

[7]Zaller v. Zaller, 1984 WL 7417 (Ohio Ct. App. 11th Dist. Lake County 1984).

[8]Baker v. Baker, 1987 WL 6238 (Ohio Ct. App. 11th Dist. Lake County 1987).

[9]Warren v. Warren, 1981 WL 6662 (Ohio Ct. App. 3d Dist. Hancock County 1981). But see Zimmie v. Zimmie, 11 Ohio St. 3d 94, 464 N.E.2d 142, 53 A.L.R.4th 75 (1984).

[Section 12:12]

[1]RC 3105.171(C)(3). Moore v. Moore, 83 Ohio App. 3d 75, 613 N.E.2d 1097 (9th Dist. Summit County 1992).

[2]RC 3105.171(C).

[3]See RC 3105.171(F)(1) to (9) and RC 3105.18(C)(1)(a) to (n) for a list of factors to be applied to property and spousal support. See Text § 12:2, Evolution of RC 3105.171; Text § 12:13, Factors to be considered.

in various contexts. In one case, a trial court erred in treating the husband's retirement benefits as income rather than as marital property. The wife's unvested retirement benefits that accumulated during the marriage were not valued at all. The appellate court found that the trial court "inextricably intertwined the issues of spousal support and property division."[4] In another instance, a trial court erred in assigning all of the marital debt to the husband for the reason that the husband was going to pay a "minimum amount of spousal support." In dividing property, a court can consider a party's inability to pay debt, but the court must decide the division of property without regard to spousal support.[5]

§ 12:13 Factors to be considered

Under former RC 3105.18, the court was required to consider all relevant factors, including these eleven factors:

(1) The relative earning abilities of the parties;

(2) The ages, and the physical and emotional conditions of the parties;

(3) The retirement benefits of the parties;

(4) The expectancies and inheritances of the parties;

(5) The duration of the marriage;

(6) The extent to which it would be inappropriate for a party, because he will be custodian of a minor child of the marriage, to seek employment outside the home;

(7) The standard of living of the parties established during the marriage;

(8) The relative extent of education of the parties;

(9) The relative assets and liabilities of the parties;

(10) The property brought to the marriage by either party; and

(11) The contribution of a spouse as homemaker.

It was within the discretion of the court to apply any one of these factors as a criterion for support or for property division, as the court saw fit.[1] Under RC 3105.171(F), there are nine factors that pertain only to the division of property, not to the award of support. These factors are as follows:

(1) The duration of the marriage;[2]

(2) The assets and liabilities of the parties;

---

[4]Levine v. Levine, 1997 WL 583565 (Ohio Ct. App. 4th Dist. Washington County 1997).

[5]Meliher v. Meliher, 1997 WL 772952 (Ohio Ct. App. 11th Dist. Portage County 1997).

[Section 12:13]

[1]Cherry v. Cherry, 66 Ohio St. 2d 348, 20 Ohio Op. 3d 318, 421 N.E.2d 1293 (1981); Slorgie v. Slorgie, 5 Ohio App. 3d 202, 450 N.E.2d 721 (9th Dist. Wayne County 1982).

[2]See Text § 12:6, Statutory terms of art—During the marriage.

(3) The desirability of awarding the family home, or the right to reside in the family home for reasonable periods of time, to the spouse with custody of the children of the marriage;[3]

(4) The liquidity of the property to be distributed;

(5) The economic desirability of retaining intact an asset or an interest in an asset;

(6) The tax consequences of the property division upon the respective awards to be made to each party;[4]

(7) The costs of sale, if it is necessary that an asset be sold to effectuate an equitable distribution of property;

(8) Any division or disbursement of property made in a separation agreement that was voluntarily entered into by the parties; and

(9) Any other factor that the court expressly finds to be relevant and equitable.[5]

Nine factors under the old statute were deleted, and six new factors were added. Both the former and current statutes direct the court to consider all other relevant factors.

The liquidity of an asset[6] may render it more or less valuable to a particular party.[7] For example, if a spouse takes an individual retirement account at age forty-five which is not accessible without penalty until age fifty-nine and one-half, and the other spouse takes an equivalent amount of cash, the ability of the latter to make ready use of the cash could heighten its value. In some instances expert testimony is required to prove the effect of liquidity or lack of liquidity upon the value of the asset. This example also raises the issue of pre-tax dollars under RC 3105.171(F)(6). The cash might or might not have been taxed as of date of division, while the proceeds of the IRA are tax deferred and will at a later time be diminished by the amount of the tax actually paid.

---

[3]See Text § 12:15, Other equitable orders.

[4]Swaney v. Swaney, 2003-Ohio-4641, 2003 WL 22049132 (Ohio Ct. App. 5th Dist. Tuscarawas County 2003) (trial court acted within its discretion in offsetting pension plan against the equity in marital residence, for purposes of property division in divorce proceedings, despite claim that there would be disparate tax consequences upon liquidation of each). Equalization of after property division by use of retirement asset transfer was abuse of discretion by not accounting to taxes and penalties of retirement asset liquidation. Harris v. Harris, 2007-Ohio-1232, 2007 WL 826131 (Ohio Ct. App. 5th Dist. Licking County 2007).

[5]Terry v. Terry, 99 Ohio App. 3d 228, 650 N.E.2d 184 (8th Dist. Cuyahoga County 1994) (court did not err in awarding husband the growth assets where court also awarded all high risk assets to husband).

[6]RC 3105.171(F)(4).

[7]Ralston v. Ralston, 61 Ohio App. 3d 346, 572 N.E.2d 791 (1st Dist. Hamilton County 1989); Andras v. Andras, 1996 WL 157355 (Ohio Ct. App. 8th Dist. Cuyahoga County 1996).

It may be equitable to preserve an asset, rather than dividing it. This is an issue that the court is now mandated to consider.[8] For example, if it is proved to the court that an intact art collection is more valuable than any part of the collection by itself, the court would likely strive to fashion an order allowing one party to retain the entire asset, rather than physically dividing it. This might require that an offsetting asset be awarded the other spouse.

Since the enactment of RC 3105.171(F)(6), not only are expert witnesses more likely than before to be called on the issue of the effect of liquidity or taxation on value, but it is likely that the failure to offer competent evidence to prove the tax impact or the effect of liquidity would, under some facts, constitute legal malpractice. If it is the client's choice not to retain an expert witness to testify on these matters, it is especially wise to obtain written instructions to that effect for permanent placement in the client's file. Taxation issues have been addressed in case law decided before as well as since the enactment of RC 3105.171.[9]

Clearly, under RC 3105.171(F)(7), the costs of sale of an asset will be considered by the court only if sale of the asset is ordered in the decree. This resolves the argument between negotiating counsel as to whether an asset value should be reduced by the anticipated costs of a later sale. RC 3105.171(F)(7) also limits the evidence which would be admissible at trial.[10]

Although retirement benefits have been deleted from RC 3105.171(F)

---

[8]RC 3105.171(F)(5). Babka v. Babka, 83 Ohio App. 3d 428, 615 N.E.2d 247 (9th Dist. Summit County 1992).

[9]Birath v. Birath, 53 Ohio App. 3d 31, 558 N.E.2d 63 (10th Dist. Franklin County 1988); Guidubaldi v. Guidubaldi, 64 Ohio App. 3d 361, 581 N.E.2d 621 (11th Dist. Portage County 1990); Josselson v. Josselson, 52 Ohio App. 3d 60, 557 N.E.2d 835 (8th Dist. Cuyahoga County 1988); Noll v. Noll, 55 Ohio App. 3d 160, 563 N.E.2d 44 (6th Dist. Sandusky County 1989); Cicchini v. Cicchini, 1990 WL 29304 (Ohio Ct. App. 5th Dist. Stark County 1990). James v. James, 101 Ohio App. 3d 668, 656 N.E.2d 399 (2d Dist. Greene County 1995) and Day v. Day, 40 Ohio App. 3d 155, 532 N.E.2d 201 (10th Dist. Franklin County 1988) (where tax consequences are speculative, court not bound to take the impact of taxes into consideration); Frost v. Frost, 84 Ohio App. 3d 699, 618 N.E.2d 198 (10th Dist. Franklin County 1992) (court properly considered tax attributes of assets when dividing marital property); Guziak v. Guziak, 80 Ohio App. 3d 805, 610 N.E.2d 1135 (9th Dist. Summit County 1992) (where divorce decree is silent as to tax liability for pension payments, and the payments qualify as "alimony" because they terminate on death, recipient, not payor, is obligated to pay the tax); Burma v. Burma, 1994 WL 530876 (Ohio Ct. App. 8th Dist. Cuyahoga County 1994) (trial court erred in ordering husband's employer to pay the gross dollar amount of husband's bonus to wife, where employer was obligated by federal regulation to withhold taxes). See also Deborah Akers, *The Valuation of Stock Options in Divorce and Dissolution Cases*, 2 Dom. Rel. J. Ohio 69 (Sept./Oct. 1990); Deborah Akers, *The Valuation of Limited Partnerships in Divorce and Dissolution Matters*, 3 Dom. Rel. J. Ohio 141 (Nov./Dec. 1991); Stanley Morganstern, *Deferred Property Division Payments*, 4 Dom. Rel. J. Ohio 86 (Sept./Oct. 1992); Stanley Morganstern, *Disposition of the Marital Home*, 3 Dom. Rel. J. Ohio 113 (Sept./Oct. 1991).

[10]But see Jameson v. Jameson, 1995 WL 42395 (Ohio Ct. App. 5th Dist. Stark County 1995). See also Text § 12:25, Specific types of property—Real property.

as a factor to be considered in disbursing property, RC 3105.171(A)(3)(a) specifically refers to retirement benefits as part of the marital estate. Thus, although the provision covering retirement benefits is misplaced in the statute, its effect is the same as if it were listed under RC 3105.171(F). Notwithstanding that the earnings of the parties are not a factor listed in RC 3105.171(F), but are a factor under RC 3105.18 for determination of spousal support, the court of appeals expressly considered earnings in ruling that a property division was inequitable.[11]

RC 3105.171(F)(9) allows the court to consider "[a]ny other factor that the court expressly finds to be relevant and equitable." Under this broad discretion, courts often implement RC 3105.171(E)(3) by considering the financial misconduct of one spouse in awarding the other spouse a greater award of marital property. Where a trial court awarded 72% of the assets to the wife and 94% of debt to husband, the decision was not an abuse of discretion when considering the marital estate in its entirety and husband's financial misconduct.[12] Where a trial court awarded each spouse his or her own pension, even though the values were vastly different, the division was equitable where the husband's smaller pension resulted from his voluntary misconduct, i.e., being fired from his job for drug use and thereby losing his opportunity to increase his pension's value.[13]

As of January 1, 1991,[14] expectancies and inheritances[15] are no longer listed as factors to be considered in dividing marital property; nor is property brought into the marriage.[16] Both inheritances and premarital property are defined as separate property;[17] case law decided prior to the statute was conflicting.[18] Property brought into the marriage, if traceable, is separate property.[19]

---

[11]Neel v. Neel, 113 Ohio App. 3d 24, 680 N.E.2d 207 (8th Dist. Cuyahoga County 1996).

[12]Loeffler v. Loeffler, 1998 WL 800951 (Ohio Ct. App. 6th Dist. Lucas County 1998).

[13]Leadingham v. Leadingham, 120 Ohio App. 3d 496, 698 N.E.2d 465 (12th Dist. Warren County 1997).

[14]The effective date of RC 3105.171.

[15]Inheritances and expectancies were deemed by the drafting committee to be speculative, remote, contingent, and not readily valued. They are therefore not to be included in the marital estate. However, an inheritance already received or any interest which has vested is addressed under RC 3105.171(A)(6)(a)(i).

[16]See former RC 3105.18(F)(4) and (10).

[17]RC 3105.171(A)(6)(a)(i), (ii).

[18]In the Matter of Shapiro, 1976 WL 188303 (Ohio Ct. App. 6th Dist. Lucas County 1976); Richardson v. Richardson, 1981 WL 6854 (Ohio Ct. App. 3d Dist. Crawford County 1981); Mcdade v. Mcdade, 1981 WL 5203 (Ohio Ct. App. 12th Dist. Warren County 1981); Halter v. Halter, 1981 WL 4752 (Ohio Ct. App. 7th Dist. Carroll County 1981); Black v. Black, 1981 WL 10393 (Ohio Ct. App. 8th Dist. Cuyahoga County 1981).

[19]See Text § 12:10, Statutory terms of art—Separate property.

§ 12:14 Modification

The future modification of a property division, whether marital or separate, is expressly prohibited.[1] This provision follows the Supreme Court dictate that contingent property awards constitute an unconstitutional deprivation of property.[2]

An agreement providing for payment of monthly household expenses when interpreted to be a division of property is not modifiable.[3] A provision establishing a minimum sales price for the parties' home, which could only be modified by further agreement of the parties, is a division of property. A trial court lacks jurisdiction to modify the agreement despite finding the provision to be "impracticable."[4]

Where a separation agreement incorporated into a dissolution decree expressly allows for modification by court order, a trial court may grant relief from judgment under Civ. R. 60(B) as to the property division without vacating the entire dissolution.[5] Remarriage of the opposing party is not a complete bar to relief, but may be considered by the trial court in determining whether relief is equitable.

A trial court may not provide that a division of property will become spousal support if the payor files bankruptcy in order to guard against discharge in bankruptcy.[6]

When an appellate court remands an action on the limited issue of child support, a trial court is without authority to change the property division that it had previously entered. It is error to modify the distribution of a pension where, eight years post decree, the trial court changes the numerator of the coverture fraction applied at time of

---

[Section 12:14]

[1]RC 3105.171(I).

[2]Zimmie v. Zimmie, 11 Ohio St. 3d 94, 464 N.E.2d 142, 53 A.L.R.4th 75 (1984); Thomas v. Thomas, 5 Ohio App. 3d 94, 449 N.E.2d 478 (5th Dist. Licking County 1982); Finomore v. Finomore, 1992 WL 136501 (Ohio Ct. App. 8th Dist. Cuyahoga County 1992); Teall v. Teall, 1990 WL 162674 (Ohio Ct. App. 6th Dist. Wood County 1990); Tasin v. Tasin, 1978 WL 218166 (Ohio Ct. App. 8th Dist. Cuyahoga County 1978); Dailey v. Dailey, 171 Ohio St. 133, 12 Ohio Op. 2d 161, 167 N.E.2d 906 (1960). But see Schoonover v. Schoonover, 1992 WL 217986 (Ohio Ct. App. 10th Dist. Franklin County 1992); McNair v. McNair, 1992 WL 393155 (Ohio Ct. App. 9th Dist. Summit County 1992).

[3]In Matter of Leonhart v. Nees, 1993 WL 313604 (Ohio Ct. App. 6th Dist. Erie County 1993); Caudill v. Everett, 1993 WL 169158 (Ohio Ct. App. 3d Dist. Union County 1993) (where property division consists of mortgage payments made by husband to mortgage company on behalf of wife, it is not a prohibited modification to substitute wife as payee when the debt to the original payee is satisfied).

[4]Proctor v. Proctor, 122 Ohio App. 3d 56, 701 N.E.2d 36 (3d Dist. Allen County 1997).

[5]In re Whitman, 81 Ohio St. 3d 239, 1998-Ohio-466, 690 N.E.2d 535 (1998).

[6]Reitano v. Reitano, 1994 WL 369412 (Ohio Ct. App. 5th Dist. Fairfield County 1994).

divorce.[7] The original property division remains the law of that case for all subsequent proceedings in the case at both the trial and reviewing levels.[8]

The court has the power to modify the method of payment, but not the property right itself.[9]

The trial court has jurisdiction to correct a clerical error in a QDRO as to the date of division of the pension plan. Civ. R. 60(A) corrections do not amount to a modification of a property division.[10] However, an order adopting a modified QDRO that is inconsistent with the terms of the parties' divorce decree is void ab initio. The requisites of Civ. R. 60(B) do not have to be met where the court modifies a property division without jurisdiction.[11]

At times, decisions made by a trial court intended to remedy a problem raised by the parties are found to be prohibited modifications of a property division, although not intended as such. For example, where the parties' separation agreement specified that the wife would refinance the marital home by a certain date or else the property would be sold, the trial court granted her an extension in order to complete the refinancing. The appellate court reversed, holding that the trial court did not have jurisdiction to extend the time despite strong equitable considerations, because to do so would be a modification of the parties' property division and, thus, is prohibited by RC 3105.17(I).[12]

A trial court did not err in appointing a receiver, three years after the decree, to appraise, sell, and distribute marital property pursuant to parties' separation agreement, because the parties failed to do so as required under the agreement. The court did err, however, by modifying the property division to include hypothetical "rents" payable from one party to the other to make up an alleged loss of investment income due to the delay.[13]

Where a husband was held in contempt for removing certain fixtures from the marital residence, the trial court's sanctions included an order that he pay the wife an additional sum of money. The appellate

---

[7]Ricketts v. Ricketts, 109 Ohio App. 3d 746, 673 N.E.2d 156 (12th Dist. Butler County 1996) (abrogated by, Erb v. Erb, 91 Ohio St. 3d 503, 2001-Ohio-104, 747 N.E.2d 230 (2001)).

[8]Singleton v. Singleton, 95 Ohio App. 3d 467, 642 N.E.2d 708 (9th Dist. Summit County 1994).

[9]Courtright v. Courtright, 1996 WL 570895 (Ohio Ct. App. 5th Dist. Fairfield County 1996).

[10]Peterson v. Peterson, 1998 WL 166475 (Ohio Ct. App. 12th Dist. Butler County 1998).

[11]Doolin v. Doolin, 123 Ohio App. 3d 296, 704 N.E.2d 51 (6th Dist. Lucas County 1997).

[12]Jakubek v. Jakubek, 1998 WL 668164 (Ohio Ct. App. 7th Dist. Mahoning County 1998).

[13]Ratliff v. Ratliff, 1998 WL 514039 (Ohio Ct. App. 10th Dist. Franklin County 1998).

court held this to be error, as a modification of their property division, even though it was intended as a contempt sanctions.[14]

An order which allowed a PERS recipient to change the beneficiary of the remaining portion of the death benefits under his account, after his divorce decree awarded a partial interest in those benefits to his former spouse, was held to be a prohibited modification.[15]

§ 12:15   Other equitable orders

RC 3105.171(J) allows the issuance of orders to achieve equity in general. An order permitting the use by the nonowner spouse of marital or separate property for a reasonable period of time, and an order requiring the sale or encumbrance of any property and directing the disposition of proceeds, are specifically authorized.[1]

In another instance, a trial court ordered that the wife's payment to the husband for his share of the property division be delayed, without interest, until 2002. The appellate court upheld the decision because an immediate payment would have required the wife to sell the marital home in which the minor children resided.[2]

§ 12:16   Retroactive effect of RC 3105.171

Cases filed prior to January 1, 1991, the effective date of RC 3105.171, but argued or decided after that date, are not controlled by the statute, but by RC 3105.18 and prior case law.[1] In cases where the transmutation of separate property is at issue, the matter is espe-

---

[14]Schlueter v. Schlueter, 1998 WL 901733 (Ohio Ct. App. 3d Dist. Auglaize County 1998).

[15]Callihan v. Callihan, 1998 WL 518505 (Ohio Ct. App. 5th Dist. Guernsey County 1998).

[Section 12:15]

[1]See prestatute case Van Fossen v. Van Fossen, 47 Ohio App. 3d 175, 547 N.E.2d 1237 (9th Dist. Summit County 1988). See also RC 3105.171(F)(3) regarding use of the marital home by the spouse to whom custody is granted.

[2]Arthur v. Arthur, 1998 WL 515911 (Ohio Ct. App. 5th Dist. Ashland County 1998).

[Section 12:16]

[1]Schulte v. Schulte, 71 Ohio St. 3d 41, 1994-Ohio-459, 641 N.E.2d 719 (1994); Starr v. Starr, 1995 WL 338496 (Ohio Ct. App. 9th Dist. Summit County 1995); Dunlap v. Dunlap, 1996 WL 134543 (Ohio Ct. App. 1st Dist. Hamilton County 1996); Lyon v. Lyon, 86 Ohio App. 3d 580, 621 N.E.2d 718 (4th Dist. Scioto County 1993); Oatey v. Oatey, 83 Ohio App. 3d 251, 614 N.E.2d 1054 (8th Dist. Cuyahoga County 1992); Indoe v. Indoe, 1993 WL 79534 (Ohio Ct. App. 9th Dist. Medina County 1993); Houck v. Houck, 1992 WL 132469 (Ohio Ct. App. 10th Dist. Franklin County 1992); Hahn v. Hahn, 1992 WL 24785 (Ohio Ct. App. 12th Dist. Butler County 1992); Lairson v. Lairson, 1992 WL 156121 (Ohio Ct. App. 12th Dist. Butler County 1992). See also Nationwide Ins. Co. v. Ohio Dept. of Transp., 61 Ohio Misc. 2d 761, 584 N.E.2d 1370 (Ct. Cl. 1990).

cially important,[2] because substantial changes have been effected by RC 3105.171. However, this problem is limited in scope, due to the natural attrition of cases falling into this category.

§ 12:17   Property agreements between spouses

RC 3103.06 states:

A husband and wife cannot, by any contract with each other, alter their legal relations, except that they may agree to an immediate separation and make provisions for the support of either of them and their children during the separation.

Ohio upholds antenuptial agreements[1] providing for, among other things, disposition of property. Separation agreements are likewise enforceable.[2] However, contracts during the marriage without the immediate separation of the spouses are prohibited.[3] The rationale is that married persons are embroiled in a highly delicate relationship of trust and interdependence. This interdependence encompasses the most fundamental treatment of one spouse by the other, such as the provision of proper food, clothing, and shelter; abstinence from pervasive physical or psychological abuse; and the proper care of minor children. A contract entered during marriage is likely not to be entered at arms' length. There are often present very serious, though subtle, forms of duress, which influence any agreement between spouses. These factors are rarely discernible by a court and are most commonly not witnessed by a disinterested third party.

Property relationships between spouses are not contractual, but are incident to the statutory marital relation and must be governed not by contract law, but by the law of domestic relations. The legislature, in passing RC 3103.06, intended to protect against "disturbing domestic felicity and the peaceful conjugal relations naturally existing between husband and wife living together."[4]

Joint tenancies with rights of survivorship, however, may be cre-

---

[2]See Text § 12:10, Statutory terms of art—Separate property.

[Section 12:17]

[1]Gross v. Gross, 11 Ohio St. 3d 99, 464 N.E.2d 500, 53 A.L.R.4th 139 (1984). See Text Ch 1, Antenuptial Agreements.

[2]RC 3105.10(B). Reynolds v. Reynolds, 1993 WL 29058 (Ohio Ct. App. 12th Dist. Clinton County 1993). See Text Ch 19, Child Support.

[3]RC 3103.06. Du Bois v. Coen, 100 Ohio St. 17, 24, 125 N.E. 121 (1919); Hoagland v. Hoagland, 113 Ohio St. 228, 3 Ohio L. Abs. 388, 148 N.E. 585 (1925); Mendelson v. Mendelson, 123 Ohio St. 11, 8 Ohio L. Abs. 754, 173 N.E. 615 (1930); Brewsaugh v. Brewsaugh, 23 Ohio Misc. 2d 19, 491 N.E.2d 748 (C.P. 1985); Smith v. Smith, 50 Ohio Op. 175, 67 Ohio L. Abs. 489, 112 N.E.2d 346 (C.P. 1953); Dalgarn v. Leonard, 41 Ohio Op. 506, 55 Ohio L. Abs. 149, 87 N.E.2d 728 (Prob. Ct. 1948), judgment aff'd, 55 Ohio L. Abs. 405, 90 N.E.2d 159 (Ct. App. 2d Dist. Franklin County 1949); Tefft v. Tefft, 73 Ohio App. 399, 29 Ohio Op. 99, 54 N.E.2d 423 (9th Dist. Summit County 1943); Pashko v. Pashko, 45 Ohio Op. 498, 63 Ohio L. Abs. 82, 101 N.E.2d 804 (C.P. 1951). But see Wischmeier v. Wischmeier, 1984 WL 5056 (Ohio Ct. App. 8th Dist. Cuyahoga County 1984).

[4]Du Bois v. Coen, 100 Ohio St. 17, 24, 125 N.E. 121 (1919).

ated between husband and wife[5] and cannot be altered by assignment[6] to another or by will[7] to defeat the spouse's rights. The early common law regarding survivorship tenancies has been codified in RC 5302.20 (for transfers after 4-4-85) and RC 5302.21 (for transfers prior to 4-4-85). These sections have altered the common law, however, particularly in the area of creditors' rights.

Courts are frequently called upon to interpret and/or enforce agreements entered by spouses prior to marriage or after their separation. Antenuptial agreements are frequently challenged in divorce proceedings, and courts rely in part on contract law to determine the agreement's effect. In one instance, an antenuptial agreement provided for a lump-sum property settlement of $20,000 per year for each full year of marriage. Nine months after the marriage, the husband was convicted of domestic violence and removed from the marital home. The trial court granted summary judgment for husband in his divorce action, holding that he owed nothing to his wife under the antenuptial agreement because the marriage terminated de facto when he vacated the marital residence before the end of the first full year of marriage. The appellate court reversed, holding that the wife was entitled to her rights under the contract until their marriage was terminated de jure, which occurred on a date more than one year after the marriage. Equity did not allow the husband to limit or extinguish his contract obligations by his own actions.[8]

Separation agreements entered before the marriage is terminated are often at issue in post-decree proceedings. Sometimes the dispute is a question of interpretation of the agreement. As under contract law generally, a trial court may interpret the terms of a separation agreement only if the agreement is ambiguous. Where the parties disputed the meaning of their agreement as it related to the division of pension benefits, the trial court determined that the parties intended a division based upon coverture as opposed to a "benefit freeze."[9]

A court's interpretation of an agreement may unintentionally result in an improper modification of the agreement. Where a separation agreement specified that the wife would refinance the marital home

---

[5]Tax Commission of Ohio v. Hutchison, 120 Ohio St. 361, 166 N.E. 352 (1929); Gladieux v. Parney, 93 Ohio App. 117, 50 Ohio Op. 246, 63 Ohio L. Abs. 289, 106 N.E.2d 317 (6th Dist. Lucas County 1951); Bowerman v. Bowerman, 67 Ohio App. 425, 21 Ohio Op. 364, 34 Ohio L. Abs. 112, 35 N.E.2d 1012 (3d Dist. Henry County 1941).

[6]Schwartz v. Sandusky County Savings & Loan Co., 65 Ohio App. 437, 19 Ohio Op. 43, 30 N.E.2d 556 (6th Dist. Sandusky County 1939).

[7]Bennett v. Bennett, 70 Ohio App. 187, 24 Ohio Op. 510, 45 N.E.2d 614 (9th Dist. Summit County 1942).

[8]Langer v. Langer, 123 Ohio App. 3d 348, 704 N.E.2d 275 (2d Dist. Montgomery County 1997), cause dismissed, 80 Ohio St. 3d 1473, 687 N.E.2d 470 (1997).

[9]Owens v. Owens, 1998 WL 887216 (Ohio Ct. App. 9th Dist. Wayne County 1998).

by a certain date or else the property would be sold, the trial court granted her a short extension of time to permit the transaction to close, reasoning that the parties' intent was that she fulfill the agreement and an extension of time was consistent with that purpose. The appellate court reversed, holding that the trial court did not have jurisdiction to extend the time within which she was to act, despite strong equitable considerations, because to do so would be a modification of their property division and thus is prohibited by RC 3105.171(I).[10]

The manner in which a court enforces an agreement may or may not constitute a modification. Where the parties to a separation agreement failed to carry out its terms, three years after the decree, the trial court appointed a receiver to appraise, sell, and distribute marital property pursuant to the agreement. The appellate court held that this order was proper, but an order modifying the property division to include hypothetical "rents" payable from one party to the other, to compensate for an alleged loss of investment income due to the delay, was improper.[11]

On a motion for contempt and to force the sale of the marital home as provided by a separation agreement, a trial court does not have jurisdiction to enforce the agreement by ordering the parties to accept a lower offer for sale of the marital home than the amount specified in their agreement, as this improperly modifies the parties' property division.[12]

The reconciliation of the parties after separation does not invalidate the provisions of their separation agreement relative to property division.[13]

---

[10]Jakubek v. Jakubek, 1998 WL 668164 (Ohio Ct. App. 7th Dist. Mahoning County 1998).

[11]Ratliff v. Ratliff, 1998 WL 514039 (Ohio Ct. App. 10th Dist. Franklin County 1998).

[12]Proctor v. Proctor, 122 Ohio App. 3d 56, 701 N.E.2d 36 (3d Dist. Allen County 1997).

[13]Fields v. Fields, 39 Ohio App. 3d 187, 530 N.E.2d 933 (2d Dist. Montgomery County 1987); In re Price's Estate, 1 Ohio Op. 459, 22 Ohio L. Abs. 639, 1 Ohio Supp. 173 (Prob. Ct. 1935).

§ 12:18 Specific types of property—Retirement funds and other deferred compensation

The basis for classifying as marital property retirement funds[1] and other forms of deferred compensation, such as stock options,[2] accounts receivable, and professional contingency fees,[3] which are payable after divorce, is that the payments were earned during the marriage, although received subsequent to the divorce. The monetary or labor contribution of either spouse during the marriage which results in a payment after divorce[4] renders the payment marital. A series of cases decided prior to the enactment of RC 3105.171 detail the reasoning involved in valuing and classifying the retirement fund as marital or separate property.[5]

The trial court was correct in concluding that a deferred compensation agreement which was contingent upon husband's continuation as consultant after retirement and which included a non-competition agreement was not divisible as a marital asset.[6]

Trial court did not err in holding that a 1.5 million dollar settlement of an employment dispute was husband's separate property when the uncontroverted evidence established that the sole consideration of the settlement was a non-compete agreement.[7]

A trial court errs as a matter of law when it fails to review and divide the retirement benefits of the parties.[8]

In distributing retirement benefits, the court must consider the cir-

---

[Section 12:18]

[1]See Text Ch 29, Government Retirement Benefits; Text Ch 30, Dividing Private Retirement Benefits in Divorce. See also Judge Judith Nicely and Stanley Morganstern, *Dividing Retirement Benefits: Suggested Clauses*, 8 Dom. Rel. J. Ohio 89 (Nov./Dec. 1996). See also Henry H. Foster, Jr., & Dorias Jonas Freed, *Spousal Rights in Retirement and Pension Benefits*, 16 J. Fam. L. 187 (1977–78).

[2]See Text § 12:21, Specific types of property—Stock options.

[3]Rabbitt v. Rabbitt, 43 Ohio App. 3d 38, 539 N.E.2d 684 (6th Dist. Lucas County 1988).

[4]See Text § 12:6, Statutory terms of art—During the marriage; Text § 12:29, Valuation date. See also RC 3105.171(A)(3)(a).

[5]Hoyt v. Hoyt, 53 Ohio St. 3d 177, 559 N.E.2d 1292 (1990); Holcomb v. Holcomb, 44 Ohio St. 3d 128, 541 N.E.2d 597 (1989); Teeter v. Teeter, 18 Ohio St. 3d 76, 479 N.E.2d 890 (1985); Diefenthaler v. Diefenthaler, 63 Ohio App. 3d 845, 580 N.E.2d 477 (6th Dist. Ottawa County 1989); Powell v. Powell, 49 Ohio App. 3d 56, 550 N.E.2d 538 (6th Dist. Lucas County 1989); Day v. Day, 40 Ohio App. 3d 155, 532 N.E.2d 201 (10th Dist. Franklin County 1988); Blair v. Blair, 11 Ohio App. 3d 117, 463 N.E.2d 423 (10th Dist. Franklin County 1983) (rejected by, Frieden v. Frieden, 1990 WL 82299 (Ohio Ct. App. 8th Dist. Cuyahoga County 1990)); Moser v. Moser, 5 Ohio App. 3d 193, 450 N.E.2d 741 (9th Dist. Lorain County 1982).

[6]Brusaw v. Brusaw, 2000 WL 554516 (Ohio Ct. App. 12th Dist. Warren County 2000).

[7]Gergacz v. Gergacz, 2000 WL 429613 (Ohio Ct. App. 1st Dist. Hamilton County 2000).

[8]Bisker v. Bisker, 69 Ohio St. 3d 608, 1994-Ohio-307, 635 N.E.2d 308 (1994). RC 3105.171(A)(3)(a). McClelland v. McClelland, 2001-Ohio-3302, 2001 WL 674200 (Ohio

cumstances of the case, the status of the parties, the nature, terms, and conditions of the retirement benefits, and the reasonableness of the results, among other factors.[9]

The circumstances of each case dictate a court's decision on two important issues: (1) whether determination of present value is necessary for the court to decide whether to offset the present value with other property or to defer distribution (by reserving jurisdiction or entering a qualified domestic relations order);[10] and (2) when distinguishing the premarital (or post-separation) component of a retirement fund from the marital component, whether to subtract the actual fund value on the date of marriage (or separation or other equitable date, as the case may be) from the total value of the fund, or use a ratio of marital years to total years of participation.[11] A formula for division of retirement benefits that gives the non-participant any portion of the participant's after-divorce contributions is in error. Those contributions are the participant's separate property.[12]

Most Ohio courts agree that retirement benefits are an important and often formidable part of marital estates that must be distributed equitably and, in most cases, must be valued.[13] In the absence of sufficient evidence presented by the parties, the court must order the

---

Ct. App. 7th Dist. Jefferson County 2001). But see Workman v. Workman, 1995 WL 434441 (Ohio Ct. App. 9th Dist. Summit County 1995).

[9]Erb v. Erb, 75 Ohio St. 3d 18, 661 N.E.2d 175 (1996); Hoyt v. Hoyt, 53 Ohio St. 3d 177, 559 N.E.2d 1292 (1990).

[10]Hoyt v. Hoyt, 53 Ohio St. 3d 177, 559 N.E.2d 1292 (1990); Connolly v. Connolly, 70 Ohio App. 3d 738, 591 N.E.2d 1362 (8th Dist. Cuyahoga County 1990); Callahan v. Callahan, 1991 WL 76069 (Ohio Ct. App. 8th Dist. Cuyahoga County 1991); Powell v. Powell, 49 Ohio App. 3d 56, 550 N.E.2d 538 (6th Dist. Lucas County 1989); Diefenthaler v. Diefenthaler, 63 Ohio App. 3d 845, 580 N.E.2d 477 (6th Dist. Ottawa County 1989); Frieden v. Frieden, 1990 WL 82299 (Ohio Ct. App. 8th Dist. Cuyahoga County 1990); Day v. Day, 40 Ohio App. 3d 155, 532 N.E.2d 201 (10th Dist. Franklin County 1988); Little v. Little, 1993 WL 205005 (Ohio Ct. App. 7th Dist. Columbiana County 1993); Sprankle v. Sprankle, 87 Ohio App. 3d 129, 621 N.E.2d 1310, 86 Ed. Law Rep. 387 (9th Dist. Medina County 1993); Bakota v. Bakota, 2001 WL 542330 (Ohio Ct. App. 9th Dist. Summit County 2001).

[11]Hoyt v. Hoyt, 53 Ohio St. 3d 177, 559 N.E.2d 1292 (1990); Connolly v. Connolly, 70 Ohio App. 3d 738, 591 N.E.2d 1362 (8th Dist. Cuyahoga County 1990). The results of the two methods can be startlingly different. The latter method treats each year with equal emphasis; the former method gives each year the weight that the actual contributions dictate.

[12]Hamlin v. Hamlin, 1999 WL 397328 (Ohio Ct. App. 2d Dist. Darke County 1999).

[13]Hoyt v. Hoyt, 53 Ohio St. 3d 177, 559 N.E.2d 1292 (1990); Diefenthaler v. Diefenthaler, 63 Ohio App. 3d 845, 580 N.E.2d 477 (6th Dist. Ottawa County 1989); Connolly v. Connolly, 70 Ohio App. 3d 738, 591 N.E.2d 1362 (8th Dist. Cuyahoga County 1990); Callahan v. Callahan, 1991 WL 76069 (Ohio Ct. App. 8th Dist. Cuyahoga County 1991); Powell v. Powell, 49 Ohio App. 3d 56, 550 N.E.2d 538 (6th Dist. Lucas County 1989); Frieden v. Frieden, 1990 WL 82299 (Ohio Ct. App. 8th Dist. Cuyahoga County 1990); Day v. Day, 40 Ohio App. 3d 155, 532 N.E.2d 201 (10th Dist. Franklin County 1988); Ralston v. Ralston, 61 Ohio App. 3d 346, 572 N.E.2d 791 (1st Dist. Hamilton County 1989); Guidubaldi v. Guidubaldi, 64 Ohio App. 3d 361, 581 N.E.2d 621 (11th Dist. Portage County 1990); Willis v. Willis, 19 Ohio App.

presentation of valuation evidence.[14] The trial court errs in neither assigning a value nor reserving jurisdiction to later divide a retirement fund.[15] The marital and separate portions must be determined.[16] Pension benefits are a divisible asset, in accord with RC 3105.171(A)(3)(a)(i) and (ii), not a stream of income.[17]

In deciding whether to use the present value, to retain jurisdiction to later rule, or to distribute by qualified domestic relations order, the court must consider the equities, including comparative liquidity of the parties' property awards;[18] status of the parties (age, assets, and other factors); contingencies which may warrant a reservation of jurisdiction or a percentage qualified domestic relations order; the tax impact on each party[19] and on the marital unit as a whole; preservation of the asset at its maximum value to the marital unit, including all benefits attendant to the retirement fund; and economic disentanglement of the parties.[20] Courts have differed in their choices of methods of distribution;[21] the method used must be supported by the evidence.[22]

Pensions in pay status have been ruled to be an interest in

3d 45, 482 N.E.2d 1274 (11th Dist. Geauga County 1984); Mochko v. Mochko, 63 Ohio App. 3d 671, 579 N.E.2d 773 (8th Dist. Cuyahoga County 1990).

[14]RC 3105.171(A)(3)(a)(i) and (ii); Bisker v. Bisker, 69 Ohio St. 3d 608, 1994-Ohio-307, 635 N.E.2d 308 (1994); Connolly v. Connolly, 70 Ohio App. 3d 738, 591 N.E.2d 1362 (8th Dist. Cuyahoga County 1990); Callahan v. Callahan, 1991 WL 76069 (Ohio Ct. App. 8th Dist. Cuyahoga County 1991); Guidubaldi v. Guidubaldi, 64 Ohio App. 3d 361, 581 N.E.2d 621 (11th Dist. Portage County 1990); Willis v. Willis, 19 Ohio App. 3d 45, 482 N.E.2d 1274 (11th Dist. Geauga County 1984); Mochko v. Mochko, 63 Ohio App. 3d 671, 579 N.E.2d 773 (8th Dist. Cuyahoga County 1990); Schoonover v. Schoonover, 1992 WL 217986 (Ohio Ct. App. 10th Dist. Franklin County 1992). But see Workman v. Workman, 1995 WL 434441 (Ohio Ct. App. 9th Dist. Summit County 1995).

[15]Bradley v. Bradley, 1993 WL 381466 (Ohio Ct. App. 6th Dist. Wood County 1993).

[16]Scheiben v. Scheiben, 1990 WL 173154 (Ohio Ct. App. 7th Dist. Columbiana County 1990).

[17]Levine v. Levine, 1997 WL 583565 (Ohio Ct. App. 4th Dist. Washington County 1997); Hall v. Hall, 1994 WL 39051 (Ohio Ct. App. 6th Dist. Wood County 1994).

[18]Ralston v. Ralston, 61 Ohio App. 3d 346, 572 N.E.2d 791 (1st Dist. Hamilton County 1989).

[19]Meinke v. Meinke, 1990 WL 187548 (Ohio Ct. App. 2d Dist. Miami County 1990).

[20]Hoyt v. Hoyt, 53 Ohio St. 3d 177, 559 N.E.2d 1292 (1990).

[21]Lemon v. Lemon, 42 Ohio App. 3d 142, 537 N.E.2d 246 (4th Dist. Hocking County 1988); Troccolo v. Troccolo, 1987 WL 11970 (Ohio Ct. App. 8th Dist. Cuyahoga County 1987); Hoyt v. Hoyt, 53 Ohio St. 3d 177, 559 N.E.2d 1292 (1990); O'Harra v. O'Harra, 1988 WL 139130 (Ohio Ct. App. 12th Dist. Madison County 1988); Frieden v. Frieden, 1990 WL 82299 (Ohio Ct. App. 8th Dist. Cuyahoga County 1990); Sprankle v. Sprankle, 87 Ohio App. 3d 129, 621 N.E.2d 1310, 86 Ed. Law Rep. 387 (9th Dist. Medina County 1993).

[22]Mattice v. Mattice, 1998 WL 879208 (Ohio Ct. App. 2d Dist. Montgomery County 1998); Apanovitch v. Apanovitch, 1989 WL 92122 (Ohio Ct. App. 11th Dist. Geauga County 1989); Campitelli v. Campitelli, 65 Ohio App. 3d 307, 583 N.E.2d

property.[23] A pension which is not yet vested is an interest in property to which a value must be assigned.[24] Including the post-divorce accumulations of retirement benefits as marital property is prohibited.[25]

Absent evidence that an increase in wife's retirement account was passive income, a trial court properly divided the accrued pension benefits.[26]

Where no proof of the premarital value of husband's pension plan was in existence at the time of trial and there was no evidence offered that husband in fact participated in the plan prior to marriage, the court did not err in dividing the entire value of the pension as marital property. Under those circumstances, the court will not employ the *Hoyt* formula,[27] crediting husband with a share of the fund as separate property proportional to the percentage of years of total employment that he worked prior to marriage.[28]

In *Wollum v. Wollum*,[29] the trial court properly applied the formula prescribed in *Hoyt v. Hoyt*.[30] Husband's claim that, because his early retirement incentive payments (supplemental retirement) were negotiated prior to marriage, they were separate property, was not well taken. The early retirement incentive payments were earned throughout husband's employment.[31]

A distributive award to wife from husband's separate portion of the proceeds of the sale of the marital dwelling is appropriate to offset wife's interest in husband's pension in order to protect the pension from penalties for early withdrawal.[32]

RC 3105.18 does not govern the distribution of pension benefits, which is controlled by the provisions of RC 3105.171. Therefore, the age of the parties is not a factor which the court is required to consider

---

1322 (5th Dist. Stark County 1989). See Text Ch 29, Government Retirement Benefits; Text Ch 30, Dividing Private Retirement Benefits in Divorce, for a detailed discussion of the QDRO.

[23]Holcomb v. Holcomb, 44 Ohio St. 3d 128, 541 N.E.2d 597 (1989); Hannah v. Hannah, 2000 WL 1133198 (Ohio Ct. App. 2d Dist. Clark County 2000).

[24]Lemon v. Lemon, 42 Ohio App. 3d 142, 537 N.E.2d 246 (4th Dist. Hocking County 1988).

[25]Cox v. Cox, 1999 WL 58098 (Ohio Ct. App. 12th Dist. Warren County 1999); McIntire v. McIntire, 1989 WL 137205 (Ohio Ct. App. 7th Dist. Carroll County 1989).

[26]Burkholder v. Burkholder, 1994 WL 90385 (Ohio Ct. App. 9th Dist. Wayne County 1994).

[27]Hoyt v. Hoyt, 53 Ohio St. 3d 177, 559 N.E.2d 1292 (1990).

[28]Blaner v. Blaner, 1995 WL 407158 (Ohio Ct. App. 11th Dist. Trumbull County 1995).

[29]Wollum v. Wollum, 1993 WL 268879 (Ohio Ct. App. 12th Dist. Clermont County 1993).

[30]Hoyt v. Hoyt, 53 Ohio St. 3d 177, 559 N.E.2d 1292 (1990).

[31]Wollum v. Wollum, 1993 WL 268879 (Ohio Ct. App. 12th Dist. Clermont County 1993).

[32]Babka v. Babka, 83 Ohio App. 3d 428, 615 N.E.2d 247 (9th Dist. Summit County 1992).

in dividing retirement funds.[33] However, one court has held that, where the divorce decree is silent as to tax liability for pension payments, and the payments qualify as "alimony" because they terminate on death; recipient, not payor, is obligated for the tax.[34]

Disability benefits are paid in lieu of wages and are, therefore, treated in divorce proceedings as income, not as a divisible asset.[35]

Although the value of participant's plan changed substantially between date of separation and date of trial, the lower court did not abuse its discretion in employing the date of trial for purposes of valuation.[36]

Husband failed to remove Wife as beneficiary of his 401(k) benefits and then passed away. The Executrix of Husband's estate asked the trial court to require Wife to pay to the estate the difference between the dollar amount Wife was to receive from the property division and the larger amount Wife received from the 401(k). The trial court declined to do so on the theory that a QDRO was never requested and Husband had opportunity to change his beneficiary before his death.[37]

A qualified domestic relations order (QDRO) is a tool made available by federal law[38] because of the urgent need in divorce matters. Tax qualified plans with prohibitions against alienation were once not subject to attachment or direct distribution to a participant's spouse. The exception to prohibition against alienation is now explicit for divorce matters where an approved QDRO is used.[39]

A decree of divorce is a final, appealable order in accord with RC 2505.02, even where the qualified domestic relations order which is mandated in the decree has not yet been submitted or recorded on the journals of the court.[40] On the other hand, the issuance of a QDRO is

---

[33]Babka v. Babka, 83 Ohio App. 3d 428, 615 N.E.2d 247 (9th Dist. Summit County 1992). But see Coats v. Coats, 63 Ohio Misc. 2d 299, 626 N.E.2d 707 (C.P. 1993).

[34]Guziak v. Guziak, 80 Ohio App. 3d 805, 610 N.E.2d 1135 (9th Dist. Summit County 1992).

[35]Koba v. Koba, 1996 WL 732547 (Ohio Ct. App. 8th Dist. Cuyahoga County 1996); Hyder v. Hyder, 2006-Ohio-5285, 2006 WL 2864115 (Ohio Ct. App. 9th Dist. Wayne County 2006); Burkhart v. Burkhart, 2009-Ohio-1307, 2009 WL 737394 (Ohio Ct. App. 12th Dist. Clermont County 2009), appeal not allowed, 122 Ohio St. 3d 1503, 2009-Ohio-4233, 912 N.E.2d 107 (2009); Abernathy v. Abernathy, 2009-Ohio-2263, 2009 WL 1348094 (Ohio Ct. App. 8th Dist. Cuyahoga County 2009).

[36]Wilson v. Wilson, 1996 WL 411631 (Ohio Ct. App. 9th Dist. Wayne County 1996).

[37]Clay v. Clay, 2007-Ohio-4638, 2007 WL 2582211 (Ohio Ct. App. 7th Dist. Belmont County 2007).

[38]I.R.C. § 414(p).

[39]See Text Ch 30, Dividing Private Retirement Benefits in Divorce, for a detailed discussion of the QDRO.

[40]Wright v. Wright, 1994 WL 649271 (Ohio Ct. App. 4th Dist. Hocking County 1994) (overruled by, Liming v. Liming, 2005-Ohio-2228, 2005 WL 1056263 (Ohio Ct. App. 4th Dist. Athens County 2005)).

not a final and appealable order. The divorce decree, not the QDRO, determines the rights of the parties.[41]

Courts are in conflict regarding the treatment of social security benefits in certain contexts.[42] State court distribution of social security benefits is preempted by federal law.[43] While the court cannot order division of social security benefits, the parties may agree to divide their benefits and that agreement is enforceable.[44]

The Ohio Supreme Court in *Neville v. Neville*,[45] held that in making an equitable division of marital property in a divorce proceeding may consider the parties' future Social Security benefits in relation to all marital assets. While *Neville* purports to restate existing law, the Supreme Court upheld a division of property at trial which explicitly balanced the value of the marital residence against Social Security benefits. The decision has led to litigation of the present value of Social Security benefits in many trial courts.[46]

While government sponsored retirement plans are exempt from the provisions of ERISA.[47] and, by statute,[48] are protected from alienation, including attachment, House Bill 535, effective January 1, 2001, provides for their division by court order.[49]

Where one spouse has not participated in social security but has contributed to a public service pension such as Public Employees

---

[41]Lamb v. Lamb, 1998 WL 833606 (Ohio Ct. App. 3d Dist. Paulding County 1998); McGee v. McGee, 168 Ohio App. 3d 512, 2006-Ohio-4417, 860 N.E.2d 1054 (9th Dist. Lorain County 2006); Houchins v. Houchins, 2007-Ohio-1450, 2007 WL 926479 (Ohio Ct. App. 5th Dist. Stark County 2007); Wilson v. Wilson, 116 Ohio St. 3d 268, 2007-Ohio-6056, 878 N.E.2d 16 (2007); Bagley v. Bagley, 181 Ohio App. 3d 141, 2009-Ohio-688, 908 N.E.2d 469 (2d Dist. Greene County 2009), appeal not allowed, 122 Ohio St. 3d 1455, 2009-Ohio-3131, 908 N.E.2d 946 (2009).

[42]Brent Danninger & Andrew Buland, *Making Social Security a Marital Asset*, 14 Fam. Advoc. 55 (Fall 1991).

[43]42 U.S.C.A. § 659, 42 U.S.C.A. § 662.

[44]Bowman v. Bowman, 1999 WL 8365 (Ohio Ct. App. 12th Dist. Warren County 1999).

[45]Neville v. Neville, 99 Ohio St. 3d 275, 2003, 2003-Ohio-3624, 791 N.E.2d 434 (2003).

[46]On remand from the Court of Appeals, a trial court was directed to reconsider its distribution of Husband's Social Security benefits when he began to receive them. The appeal reversed the trial court's handling of the benefits as a spousal support item and ordered the trial court to determine what sums Husband should pay, if any, in lieu of social security benefits as part of the overall property division. Mulliken v. Mulliken, 2008-Ohio-2752, 2008 WL 2332597 (Ohio Ct. App. 11th Dist. Geauga County 2008), appeal not allowed, 120 Ohio St. 3d 1417, 2008-Ohio-6166, 897 N.E.2d 652 (2008).

[47]Erb v. Erb, 75 Ohio St. 3d 18, 661 N.E.2d 175 (1996).

[48]See RC 145.56 (PERS), RC 742.47 (PFDPF), RC 3307.71 (STRS), RC 3309.66 (PSERS), and RC 5505.22 (HPRS).

[49]RC 3105.80 et seq.

Retirement System (PERS),[50] State Teachers Retirement System (STRS),[51] Police and Fireman's Disability and Pension Fund (PFDPF),[52] Highway Patrol Retirement System (HPRS),[53] or Public School Employees Retirement System (PSERS),[54] while the other spouse is entitled only to social security benefits, the courts have recognized a fundamental inequity in including the public service pension in the marital estate and excluding the social security benefits.[55]

The remedy proposed by several courts involves determining a hypothetical social security value for the public plan participant and reducing the public service pension by that amount.[56]

Other courts have held that the appropriate method for treatment of social security benefits under different circumstances is to compute the current value of the social security benefits of the spouse who is not the public plan participant and apply the value of the social security as a setoff against the value of the public plan;[57] or to compute and set off against each other the public plan participant's potential monthly benefit and his or her spouse's potential monthly social secu-

---

[50]RC Ch. 145.

[51]RC Ch. 3307.

[52]RC Ch. 742.

[53]RC Ch. 5505.

[54]RC Ch. 3309.

[55]Schaefers v. Schaefers, 1994 WL 631660 (Ohio Ct. App. 7th Dist. Columbiana County 1994); Cornbleth v. Cornbleth, 397 Pa. Super. 421, 580 A.2d 369 (1990) (rejected by, Hayden v. Hayden, 284 N.J. Super. 418, 665 A.2d 772 (App. Div. 1995)); Eickelberger v. Eickelberger, 93 Ohio App. 3d 221, 638 N.E.2d 130 (12th Dist. Butler County 1994) (rejected by, In re Marriage of Crook, 211 Ill. 2d 437, 286 Ill. Dec. 141, 813 N.E.2d 198 (2004)). See Pamela J. MacAdams, Eighth District Defines Social Security Offset Formulas, 8 Dom. Rel. J. Ohio 4 (July/Aug. 1996); Robert Piron, Suggestions for Better Evaluation of Pensions in Divorce Hearings, 7 Dom. Rel. J. Ohio 5 (Sept./Oct. 1995); Dickinson v. Dickinson, 2001 WL 1518044 (Ohio Ct. App. 6th Dist. Wood County 2001).

[56]Cornbleth v. Cornbleth, 397 Pa. Super. 421, 580 A.2d 369 (1990) (rejected by, Hayden v. Hayden, 284 N.J. Super. 418, 665 A.2d 772 (App. Div. 1995)); Stovall v. Stovall, 1992 WL 236770 (Ohio Ct. App. 9th Dist. Summit County 1992); Neel v. Neel, 113 Ohio App. 3d 24, 680 N.E.2d 207 (8th Dist. Cuyahoga County 1996); Simmons v. Simmons, No. 91-04-0834 (Ohio Ct. C.P. 9th Dist. Summit County 1992); Stovall v. Stovall, 1992 WL 236770 (Ohio Ct. App. 9th Dist. Summit County 1992); Brubaker v. Brubaker, No. 91-04-0911 (Ohio Ct. C.P. 9th Dist. Summit County 1992); Coats v. Coats, 63 Ohio Misc. 2d 299, 626 N.E.2d 707 (C.P. 1993) (court suggested that the formula is equitable in long-term marriages where parties are near retirement, but not as equitable in short marriages with young spouses); Neville v. Neville, 2002-Ohio-2901, 2002 WL 1307405 (Ohio Ct. App. 5th Dist. Holmes County 2002), judgment rev'd, 99 Ohio St. 3d 275, 2003, 2003-Ohio-3624, 791 N.E.2d 434 (2003); Hurte v. Hurte, 164 Ohio App. 3d 446, 2005-Ohio-5967, 842 N.E.2d 1058 (4th Dist. Washington County 2005) (holding that no "social security offset" is required for a public pension when Social Security benefits are also considered); Walker v. Walker, 2007-Ohio-331, 2007 WL 196534 (Ohio Ct. App. 2d Dist. Greene County 2007).

[57]Coats v. Coats, 63 Ohio Misc. 2d 299, 626 N.E.2d 707 (C.P. 1993).

rity benefit.[58] In considering the values of the parties' Social Security benefits, a trial court rejected as too speculative any assumptions regarding Wife's remarriage and window benefits.[59]

One court held that a trial court did not err in failing to assign a dollar value to an STRS account where the division of this asset will take place upon its payout to the employee spouse.[60]

Where husband's expert witness conceded that it was speculative that wife would remain with her current employer through a full thirty years and that the witness rarely assumed continued employment in valuing PERS benefits, the trial court did not abuse its discretion in rejecting husband's "thirty and out" valuation method and setting off husband's share of wife's PERS with funds from wife's individual retirement account.[61]

A trial court may order a PERS participant to make immediate payments to his or her spouse to compensate for the value of a fund allocated to the participant.[62] However, a trial court does not err in ordering a QDRO to divide the husband's pension even though there were sufficient assets to accomplish an immediate offset of the wife's interest in the pension.[63]

Trial court did not err in awarding wife one-half of the marital portion of husband's pension benefit commencing when he retired, elected to take his benefits or reached 65 years of age, whichever first occurred.[64]

A contrary holding may be found in *Luedtke v. Luedtke*,[65] where the trial court erred in dividing husband's police and fireman's pension fund through a "stalking order" which required payments from husband to wife upon their receipt by husband. There were sufficient assets to make an immediate division of property.

---

[58]Back v. Back, 1999 WL 174249 (Ohio Ct. App. 5th Dist. Richland County 1999); Eickelberger v. Eickelberger, 93 Ohio App. 3d 221, 638 N.E.2d 130 (12th Dist. Butler County 1994) (rejected by, In re Marriage of Crook, 211 Ill. 2d 437, 286 Ill. Dec. 141, 813 N.E.2d 198 (2004)); Smith v. Smith, 91 Ohio App. 3d 248, 632 N.E.2d 555 (10th Dist. Franklin County 1993); Streeter v. Streeter, 1991 WL 151215 (Ohio Ct. App. 10th Dist. Franklin County 1991).

[59]Dunham v. Dunham, 171 Ohio App. 3d 147, 2008, 2007-Ohio-1167, 870 N.E.2d 168 (10th Dist. Franklin County 2007), appeal not allowed, 115 Ohio St. 3d 1408, 2007-Ohio-4884, 873 N.E.2d 1314 (2007).

[60]Sprankle v. Sprankle, 87 Ohio App. 3d 129, 621 N.E.2d 1310, 86 Ed. Law Rep. 387 (9th Dist. Medina County 1993).

[61]Wolfangel v. Wolfangel, 1995 WL 312697 (Ohio Ct. App. 9th Dist. Summit County 1995).

[62]Whipple v. Whipple, 1994 WL 140725 (Ohio Ct. App. 5th Dist. Knox County 1994).

[63]Haynes v. Haynes, 1998 WL 114424 (Ohio Ct. App. 9th Dist. Summit County 1998).

[64]Cain v. Cain, 1999 WL 386654 (Ohio Ct. App. 1st Dist. Hamilton County 1999).

[65]Luedtke v. Luedtke, 2000 WL 569941 (Ohio Ct. App. 2d Dist. Montgomery County 2000).

A trial court does not err in equally dividing a husband's retirement benefits in pay out status even though wife's earnings and share of the benefits give her more disposable income than husband.[66]

Likewise in *Perorazio v. Perorazio*,[67] the trial court did not err in ordering husband to pay wife one-half of his pension benefits in monthly installments for her life, even though such payments might exceed one-half of the present dollar value.

It is not an abuse of discretion for a trial court to retain jurisdiction to divide a participant's PERS account until he terminates his employment or retires.[68]

The trial court abused its discretion in ordering husband to secure wife's award of her share of his STRS with insurance to the extent of only half of husband's contributions.[69] The matter was remanded with instructions to redetermine the amount of life insurance sufficient to protect wife's marital interest in the plan; to include findings; and to provide for termination of the insurance upon husband's providing substitute security.

The trial court erred in its division of pension and retirement benefits when it did not consider wife's social security benefits in dividing husband's PERS and deferred compensation benefits.[70]

Several courts of appeal have determined that the present value of public employee vested health insurance benefits and accrued sick leave are subject to equitable division.[71]

A trial court abused its discretion when, before determining the value of wife's Public Employees Retirement System benefits which are subject to division as marital property, it failed to deduct from the value of the PERS fund the hypothetical value of wife's social security benefits, determined as though she had not participated in PERS. The dissent stated that it is within the trial court's discretion to determine the method used to offset the PERS with the social security value,

---

[66]Hannah v. Hannah, 2000 WL 1133198 (Ohio Ct. App. 2d Dist. Clark County 2000).

[67]Perorazio v. Perorazio, 1999 WL 159218 (Ohio Ct. App. 7th Dist. Columbiana County 1999).

[68]Reynolds v. Reynolds, 1999 WL 514039 (Ohio Ct. App. 9th Dist. Wayne County 1999).

[69]Nordhaus v. Nordhaus, 1996 WL 740896 (Ohio Ct. App. 3d Dist. Putnam County 1996); Hiscox v. Hiscox, 2009 WL 4456964 (Ohio App. 7th Dist.).

[70]Smith v. Smith, 91 Ohio App. 3d 248, 632 N.E.2d 555 (10th Dist. Franklin County 1993); Streeter v. Streeter, 1991 WL 151215 (Ohio Ct. App. 10th Dist. Franklin County 1991).

[71]Weller v. Weller, 2002-Ohio-7125, 2002 WL 31862681 (Ohio Ct. App. 11th Dist. Geauga County 2002); Pearson v. Pearson, 1997 WL 275496 (Ohio Ct. App. 10th Dist. Franklin County 1997); Dave Kelly, Are Retirement Health Benefits Marital Property? 14 Dom. Rel. J. Ohio 34 (May/June 2002).

and the court of appeals, therefore, should not have specified the method to be used upon remand.[72]

The court in *Franjesh v. Berg*[73] considered actuarial tables, rates of interest, coverture fractions, and the calculation of the current value of husband's Police and Firemen's Disability and Pension Fund benefits. The court of appeals affirmed the trial court's decision to exclude from the marital estate the value of husband's options to purchase military credits in the PFDPF because he had served in the military prior to marriage. In a case involving consideration of the coverture method as opposed to the "frozen method," the difference being that the alternate payee would not receive any interest on the portion of the benefit to be received between the date the dollar amount was determined and the payment due date, the Court of Appeals affirmed use of the coverture date.[74]

Participant accounts in state and municipal deferred compensation plans[75] are expressly included in the definition of martial property, but only to the extent that any funds therefrom have been transmitted to the deferred compensation board or other governing board during marriage; provided, however, that all income derived from the investment of those funds during the marriage is included.[76]

The Railroad Retirement Solvency Act, 45 U.S.C.A. § 231, authorizes state courts to distribute railroad retirement funds. I.R.C. § 408(d)(6) and I.R.C. § 1041 provide that individual retirement accounts can be distributed pursuant to a decree of divorce. Railroad retirement benefits known as Tier I benefits continue to be treated as separate, nonmarital property. Tier I benefits are analogous to social security benefits. They are distinguishable from Tier II benefits which are similar to pension benefits paid in other industries and are divisible marital assets.[77]

The Uniformed Services Former Spouses Protection Act, 10 U.S.C.A. §§ 1401 et seq., provides for attachment of military retirement benefits for purposes of property division and support. Military pension benefits are therefore distributed in the same manner as other pensions.[78]

---

[72]Neel v. Neel, 113 Ohio App. 3d 24, 680 N.E.2d 207 (8th Dist. Cuyahoga County 1996).

[73]Franjesh v. Berg, 1996 WL 556899 (Ohio Ct. App. 9th Dist. Summit County 1996).

[74]Schroer v. Schroer, 2007-Ohio-4927, 2007 WL 2753272 (Ohio Ct. App. 5th Dist. Richland County 2007).

[75]RC 145.71; RC 145.74.

[76]RC 3105.171(A)(3)(a)(iv).

[77]Tarbet v. Tarbet, 97 Ohio App. 3d 674, 647 N.E.2d 254 (9th Dist. Summit County 1994).

[78]Baker v. Baker, 1996 WL 16888 (Ohio Ct. App. 3d Dist. Seneca County 1996); citing Teeter v. Teeter, 18 Ohio St. 3d 76, 479 N.E.2d 890 (1985); Siler v. Siler, 1994

In *Erb v. Erb*,[79] the trial court entered a QDRO against the Police and Firemen's Disability and Pension Fund. On appeal, the matter was reversed on the basis that the trial court could not immediately distribute wife's interest in husband's government pension, where husband had not chosen to retire even though he was eligible. Such a distribution would violate the terms of the plan, which provides for distribution only upon retirement. Retirement benefits cannot be distributed until they mature; they mature when they are due and payable and subject to distribution according to the terms of the plan. Government plans are exempt from ERISA provisions which allow premature distribution of benefits in divorce cases.[80]

Upon remand, a subpoena of the records of the Police and Fireman's Disability and Pension Fund demonstrated that the husband had retired from the fund and had received a substantial amount of monthly benefits without disbursement of any funds to the wife. Prior to trial on remand, the husband and wife reached an agreement, which provided that the wife would receive a monthly payment directly from the fund itself. The trial court incorporated the terms of the agreement into an entry and issued a domestic relations order to the fund to carry its judgment into effect. The fund appealed and the matter reached the Ohio Supreme Court.

In *Erb v. Erb*,[81] the Ohio Supreme Court framed the issue before it as whether the terms of administration of the fund precluded it from complying with a domestic relations order requiring it to pay a portion of a member's monthly benefit to a former spouse pursuant to a division of marital assets. The court concluded that the fund was not precluded from paying benefits directly to the former spouse and reinstated the trial court's domestic relations order.

The Ohio Supreme Court considered the issue of whether, pursuant to a 1989 divorce case, a constructive trust over STRS survivor benefits could be imposed for the benefit of the former wife after the death of the former husband. The former husband had remarried and his surviving spouse qualified as the statutory beneficiary of STRS survivor benefits. The court held by a four to three vote that a constructive trust is an inappropriate remedy that is contrary to the statutory mandate of STRS to pay survivor benefits to a qualified surviving spouse.[82]

The Supreme Court analyzed the language of the antialienation provision, RC 742.47, which provides that the sums of money in the

---

WL 386106 (Ohio Ct. App. 12th Dist. Warren County 1994); Kutzke v. Kutzke, 1996 WL 173399 (Ohio Ct. App. 2d Dist. Greene County 1996).

[79]Erb v. Erb, 75 Ohio St. 3d 18, 661 N.E.2d 175 (1996).

[80]Erb v. Erb, 75 Ohio St. 3d 18, 661 N.E.2d 175 (1996). The Supreme Court did not reach the issue of whether government plans are subject to qualified domestic relations orders.

[81]Erb v. Erb, 91 Ohio St. 3d 503, 2001-Ohio-104, 747 N.E.2d 230 (2001).

[82]Cosby v. Cosby, 96 Ohio St. 3d 228, 2002-Ohio-4170, 773 N.E.2d 516 (2002).

fund due to "any person" are not subject to attachment and concluded that the term "any person" is not limited to a member of the fund. Finding that the purpose of RC 742.47 is to protect fund benefits against creditors of persons to whom benefits are due, the court opined that a spouse of a member has a property interest in the fund and, is therefore not a creditor. Consequently, the antialienation provision does not apply to a division of benefits pursuant to a division of marital property.

H. B. 535 codified the principle that state government retirement benefits may be divided by order to the pension fund. RC 3105 specifically defines a "party in an action for divorce, legal separation, annulment, or dissolution of marriage" as an alternate payee who may receive payments from a fund. RC 3105.82 provides the elements of a division of property order pursuant to which the state retirement systems have developed a uniform form for submission for payment of benefits. House Bill 535, however, does not provide the same extent of division of a participant's benefits as does ERISA. State division of property orders may not provide for cost-of-living adjustments or survivorship benefits and are limited to a division of fifty-percent of the total of the benefit.[83]

§ 12:19 Specific types of property—Business interests

Generally, the valuation of a business interest requires the opinion of a qualified expert witness.[1] The methodology used by the expert varies according to the availability of comparable sales; specific industrial standards for valuation; history of the business; risks involved in the particular business;[2] and other factors. In *Amigo v. Amigo*, the court found no error where the husband offered no expert opinion of the value of his medical practice and the trial court adopted

---

[83]RC 3105.85. See, Dave Kelly, DOPOs After One Year (Parts I), 14 Dom. Rel. J. Ohio 78 (November/December 2002) and Dave Kelly, DOPOs After One Year (Parts II), 15 Dom. Rel. J. Ohio 17 (March/April 2003); Tobias v. Tobias, 2003-Ohio-6679, 2003 WL 22927842 (Ohio Ct. App. 2d Dist. Greene County 2003); Green v. Green, 2006-Ohio-2534, 2006 WL 1391079 (Ohio Ct. App. 10th Dist. Franklin County 2006); Kinney v. Kinney, 2005-Ohio-5712, 2005 WL 2806667 (Ohio Ct. App. 5th Dist. Stark County 2005); Hurte v. Hurte, 164 Ohio App. 3d 446, 2005-Ohio-5967, 842 N.E.2d 1058 (4th Dist. Washington County 2005); Lawson v. Lawson, 2005-Ohio-6565, 2005 WL 3361099 (Ohio Ct. App. 5th Dist. Coshocton County 2005); Gregory v. Kottman-Gregory, 2005-Ohio-6558, 2005 WL 3359162 (Ohio Ct. App. 12th Dist. Madison County 2005); Lepowsky v. Lepowsky, 2006-Ohio-667, 2006 WL 337059 (Ohio Ct. App. 7th Dist. Columbiana County 2006).

[Section 12:19]

[1]Hosford v. Hosford, 1982 WL 5930 (Ohio Ct. App. 8th Dist. Cuyahoga County 1982). See Bernard Agin, *Marital v. Non-Marital Interests, Valuing Closely Held Corporations*, 8 Dom. Rel. J. Ohio 37 (May/June 1996); Bernard Agin, *When Experts Disagree*, 4 Dom. Rel. J. Ohio (July/Aug. 1992). See also Webb v. Webb, 1996 WL 355059 (Ohio Ct. App. 3d Dist. Marion County 1996).

[2]See Jay Fishman et al., *Guide to Business Valuations* (Practitioners Publ'g Co. 1991); Perocchi & Walsh, *Putting a Value on Closely Held Corporations*, 2 Fam. Advoc. 32 (1979); Bernard Agin, *Marital v. Non-Marital Interests, Valuing Closely*

a modified version of wife's expert's opinions giving reasons for the modification.[3]

It is within the discretion of the court to adopt the most credible and sound of two or more evaluations presented.[4] It is not an abuse of discretion to average valuations to arrive at a conclusion of value.[5] However, there must be sufficient competent, credible evidence to support the court's valuation.[6] For example, a decision was reversed where the record did not support the court's finding that the parties' business was worth $20,000, because there was no expert testimony, the husband opined that it was worth $100, but the wife claimed it was worth $1,000,000.[7]

A court may not adopt an opinion of an expert witness which is not supported by an adequate rationale and evidentiary basis; nor may a court choose a value between the experts' valuations without citing to the evidence which supports that conclusion.[8]

The potential for error when comparing different expert valuations calculated using different methods is illustrated by *Gest v. Gest*.[9] The trial court in *Gest* erred in determining the value of a family farm by: (1) finding the husband's expert valuation based on capitalization of earnings (which method assumes the continued operation of the business and receipt of income) did not include the value of the farm equipment, machinery, or livestock; (2) accepting the wife's expert valuation under an asset-based method (which values the assets at prices expected if sold at auction) as a separate component that was not included in the husband's valuation using the capitalization method; and (3) combining the two valuations as its overall valuation

---

Held Corporations, 8 Dom. Rel. J. Ohio 8 (May/June 1996). Paul Perocchi & Joseph Walsh, *Putting a Value on Closely Held Corporations*, 2 Fam. Advoc. 32 (1979).

[3]Amigo v. Amigo, 1995 WL 366367 (Ohio Ct. App. 4th Dist. Washington County 1995).

[4]Kelch v. Kelch, 1987 WL 10343 (Ohio Ct. App. 9th Dist. Lorain County 1987); Briggs v. Briggs, 1989 WL 13563 (Ohio Ct. App. 11th Dist. Geauga County 1989).

[5]Bredenfoerder v. Bredenfoerder, 1990 WL 61992 (Ohio Ct. App. 12th Dist. Clermont County 1990); Matter of Erre, 1988 WL 59536 (Ohio Ct. App. 5th Dist. Richland County 1988); Jesionowski v. Jesionowski, 1987 WL 14959 (Ohio Ct. App. 6th Dist. Lucas County 1987).

[6]McCoy v. McCoy, 91 Ohio App. 3d 570, 632 N.E.2d 1358 (8th Dist. Cuyahoga County 1993); Zimmerman v. Zimmerman, 1990 WL 82588 (Ohio Ct. App. 12th Dist. Clermont County 1990), dismissed, 55 Ohio St. 3d 720, 564 N.E.2d 496 (1990); Rodriguez v. Rodriguez, 1990 WL 47458 (Ohio Ct. App. 11th Dist. Geauga County 1990); Hoopingarner v. Hoopingarner, 1985 WL 6824 (Ohio Ct. App. 8th Dist. Cuyahoga County 1985); Apanovitch v. Apanovitch, 1989 WL 92122 (Ohio Ct. App. 11th Dist. Geauga County 1989).

[7]Long v. Long, 1997 WL 458042 (Ohio Ct. App. 6th Dist. Lucas County 1997).

[8]McCoy v. McCoy, 91 Ohio App. 3d 570, 632 N.E.2d 1358 (8th Dist. Cuyahoga County 1993). See also Gannett v. Booher, 12 Ohio App. 3d 49, 465 N.E.2d 1326 (6th Dist. Huron County 1983); Rodriguez v. Rodriguez, 1990 WL 47458 (Ohio Ct. App. 11th Dist. Geauga County 1990).

[9]Gest v. Gest, 1998 WL 208872 (Ohio Ct. App. 9th Dist. Lorain County 1998).

of the family farm. The capitalization method presumes the use of the
assets for generating income, so the assets are necessarily included as
part of the valuation by this method. Further, the court did not
consider the tax consequences, the costs of sale, or the economic desirability of retaining the asset intact when it ordered payments that
exceeded the husband's ability to pay without liquidating part or all of
the farm operation.

A reviewing court is not required to accept any particular valuation
method over another, but is required to decide whether, under the
facts of the case, the trial court abused its discretion in arriving at its
value.[10] A reviewing court cannot substitute its judgment for that of
the trial court on issues of valuation, which are almost purely questions of fact.[11]

Fair market value is the required standard of valuation of a
corporation.[12] The trial court's use of the corporation's buy-sell agreement is a valid form of valuation where it is consistent with the history of the business and based on independent market factors.[13] Valuation methods for closely held corporations that have been found to be
equitable include the market approach and the use of the price named
in the stock purchase agreement.[14]

Goodwill is a divisible marital asset distinguishable from future
earning capacity.[15] However, some courts have held that goodwill
represents a duplication of earning ability considered for purposes of
support,[16] and, prior to the enactment of RC 3105.171, courts held
that if the owner spouse was adequately compensated for work done
in a premarital business, the other spouse would not share in the

---

[10]Focke v. Focke, 83 Ohio App. 3d 552, 615 N.E.2d 327 (2d Dist. Montgomery
County 1992).

[11]Farley v. Farley, 1993 WL 311392 (Ohio Ct. App. 8th Dist. Cuyahoga County
1993).

[12]Masheter v. Brewer, 40 Ohio St. 2d 31, 69 Ohio Op. 2d 202, 318 N.E.2d 849
(1974); Hunker v. Hunker, 1987 WL 25257 (Ohio Ct. App. 12th Dist. Butler County
1987); Roberts v. Roberts, 113 Ohio App. 33, 17 Ohio Op. 2d 38, 177 N.E.2d 281 (6th
Dist. Lucas County 1961).

[13]Kell v. Kell, 1993 WL 525003 (Ohio Ct. App. 4th Dist. Ross County 1993).

[14]Montisano v. Montisano, 1993 WL 208324 (Ohio Ct. App. 9th Dist. Summit
County 1993); Jacobs v. Jacobs, 2003-Ohio-3466, 2003 WL 21500026 (Ohio Ct. App.
4th Dist. Scioto County 2003).

[15]Kahn v. Kahn, 42 Ohio App. 3d 61, 536 N.E.2d 678 (2d Dist. Montgomery
County 1987); See also Haas v. Haas, 1992 WL 103738 (Ohio Ct. App. 9th Dist.
Summit County 1992); Karis v. Karis, 1992 WL 323888 (Ohio Ct. App. 9th Dist.
Summit County 1992); Wichman v. Wichman, 1996 WL 125914 (Ohio Ct. App. 2d
Dist. Greene County 1996); Bunkers v. Bunkers, 2007-Ohio-561, 2007 WL 431418
(Ohio Ct. App. 6th Dist. Wood County 2007), appeal not allowed, 114 Ohio St. 3d
1480, 2007, 2007-Ohio-3699, 870 N.E.2d 732 (2007).

[16]Flexman v. Flexman, 1985 WL 8075 (Ohio Ct. App. 2d Dist. Montgomery
County 1985).

increase in value of the business during marriage.[17] Goodwill is defined in *Spayd v. Turner, Granzow & Hollenkamp.*[18]

Capitalization of income may be an appropriate method to value a sole proprietorship.[19]

Where husband's salary was lower than an entry level accountant's, and there existed a buy-sell agreement limiting the marketability of his accounting business, the trial court erred in failing to take those factors into consideration, blindly employing the gross receipts formula of wife's expert.[20]

Commissions earned on insurance policy renewals are marital property because the renewals were obtained during marriage, notwithstanding that the original policies were sold before marriage.[21]

In *West v. West,*[22] the trial court erred in including income from a partnership as gross income for child support calculation rather than dividing the income stream as a marital asset. The trial court did not err, however, in failing to award wife some portion of the residual value upon sale or liquidation of the partnership interest.

Future earnings are not a marital asset; however, a purchase price of $60,000 for a dental practice, which produces $120,000 in annual personal income, defies logic and constitutes an abuse of discretion, where the purchase price includes equipment, all patient records, lease rights, and goodwill; the price of the covenant not to compete is $225,000; the doctor is selling in order to relocate out of state; and the doctor's start-up cost will be at least $100,000. Upon remand, the fair market value of the practice would be marital property; the balance

---

[17]Zimmie v. Zimmie, 11 Ohio St. 3d 94, 464 N.E.2d 142, 53 A.L.R.4th 75 (1984); Oatey v. Oatey, 83 Ohio App. 3d 251, 614 N.E.2d 1054 (8th Dist. Cuyahoga County 1992) (because the case was filed prior to the enactment of RC 3105.171, the court held that the statute did not apply); Black v. Black, 1981 WL 10393 (Ohio Ct. App. 8th Dist. Cuyahoga County 1981); Flexman v. Flexman, 1985 WL 8075 (Ohio Ct. App. 2d Dist. Montgomery County 1985). The theory set forth in the *Black* and *Flexman* decisions is faulty because, in the valuation of a business, an amount for reasonable compensation of the owners is allowed before the excess compensation is used to determine the value. There is therefore a clear distinction between the owner's earned income and the company earnings which determine the company value. Only the reasonable compensation figure should be considered for purposes of support so that there is no "double-dipping."

[18]Spayd v. Turner, Granzow & Hollenkamp, 19 Ohio St. 3d 55, 59-60, 482 N.E.2d 1232 (1985).

[19]Carter v. Carter, 1990 WL 145736 (Ohio Ct. App. 11th Dist. Geauga County 1990).

[20]James v. James, 101 Ohio App. 3d 668, 656 N.E.2d 399 (2d Dist. Greene County 1995).

[21]Sherman v. Sherman, 1989 WL 117421 (Ohio Ct. App. 8th Dist. Cuyahoga County 1989).

[22]West v. West, 2000 WL 331823 (Ohio Ct. App. 2d Dist. Greene County 2000).

would be attributable to the covenant not to compete, which is in the nature of future earnings, a nonmarital asset.[23]

The employment contract of a physician employed by a corporation is comprised of future earnings and, as such, is not an asset. The concepts of reasonable compensation and excess earnings do not apply where the employee is not an owner. The goodwill of a corporation generated by an employee is an asset of the corporation, not the employee. The trial court erred in determining a value for husband's employment contract and dividing it between the parties.[24]

The income used to determine current value of husband's law practice, including accounts receivable from which husband will pay support, will be regenerated in the future; therefore, it is not error to award to wife her share of the marital value of the practice, as well as support.[25]

A trial court errs in valuing an optometrist's practice according to its balance sheet without considering the value of the income-producing potential of the business; furthermore, it is not plausible that the optometrist would agree to sell for the value shown on the balance sheet.[26]

The trial court's adjustment of the expert's capitalization rate was substantiated by the evidence and the findings. It is within the discretion of the trial court to rule that a discount for minority holding does not apply to the value of corporate stock, where, although he is a minority shareholder, husband effectively controls the company through family ownership.[27]

Where the purchase price of a business includes an incentive payment, that is, payment contingent upon the performance of the company after sale, and it includes payment for a covenant not to compete, the former is simply additional purchase price and is a marital asset; the latter is husband's nonmarital property.[28]

Retained earnings held in a corporation and not distributed to the shareholders are a component of value, not income to the

---

[23]Hoeft v. Hoeft, 74 Ohio App. 3d 809, 600 N.E.2d 746 (6th Dist. Lucas County 1991).

[24]Burma v. Burma, 1994 WL 530876 (Ohio Ct. App. 8th Dist. Cuyahoga County 1994).

[25]Turner v. Turner, 90 Ohio App. 3d 161, 628 N.E.2d 110 (10th Dist. Franklin County 1993); Lancione v. Lancione, 1994 WL 521242 (Ohio Ct. App. 10th Dist. Franklin County 1994).

[26]Collier v. Collier, 36 Ohio App. 3d 130, 521 N.E.2d 849 (3d Dist. Crawford County 1987).

[27]Oatey v. Oatey, 83 Ohio App. 3d 251, 614 N.E.2d 1054 (8th Dist. Cuyahoga County 1992).

[28]Blodgett v. Blodgett, 1988 WL 110926 (Ohio Ct. App. 9th Dist. Summit County 1988), judgment rev'd, 49 Ohio St. 3d 243, 551 N.E.2d 1249 (1990).

shareholder.[29] Wife's method of valuing husband's law practice did not constitute an abuse of discretion, where her expert added the checking account balance; accounts receivable; accounts advanced; value of furnishings, equipment, and library materials; and work in progress.[30]

A professional business may be deemed not to have a marital value, particularly if the ethical rules of the profession prohibit transfer of clients; however, a bank account in the name of that business may be a marital asset.[31]

The trial court must consider a significant tax impact on the value of a business.[32] The value of a 501(C)(3) not-for-profit corporation cannot be a marital asset and divided in a divorce proceeding.[33]

§ 12:20   Specific types of property—Professional licenses and degrees

Although in other jurisdictions professional licenses and degrees are subject to valuation and distribution by offset,[1] Ohio courts have ruled to the contrary,[2] stating, "Although not an asset, the future *value* of a professional degree or license acquired by one of the parties during the marriage is an element to be considered in reaching an eq-

---

[29]Riepenhoff v. Riepenhoff, 64 Ohio App. 3d 135, 580 N.E.2d 846 (4th Dist. Jackson County 1990).

[30]Capper v. Capper, 1995 WL 762923 (Ohio Ct. App. 4th Dist. Lawrence County 1995).

[31]Josselson v. Josselson, 52 Ohio App. 3d 60, 557 N.E.2d 835 (8th Dist. Cuyahoga County 1988). But see Turner v. Turner, 90 Ohio App. 3d 161, 628 N.E.2d 110 (10th Dist. Franklin County 1993) (finding the analysis of the Josselson court is unpersuasive), Navicky v. Cambridge S. & L. Assn., 68 Ohio St. 3d 1430, 624 N.E.2d 1067 (1994); Gary Skoloff & Theodore Orenstein, *When a Lawyer Divorces: How to Value a Professional Practice, How to Get Extraordinary Remedies* (ABA Press 1986); Martin M. Shenkman & Georgia Kramer, *Approaches to Valuing Law Firm Interests*, 10 Matrimonial Strategist 1 (May 1992); Shenkman & Fell, *How to Value Spousal Interest in a Law Firm*, 9 Matrimonial Strategist 1 (Oct. 1991).

[32]RC 3105.171(F)(6); Cicchini v. Cicchini, 1990 WL 29304 (Ohio Ct. App. 5th Dist. Stark County 1990).

[33]MacFarlane v. MacFarlane, 2006-Ohio-3155, 2006 WL 1704531 (Ohio Ct. App. 8th Dist. Cuyahoga County 2006).

[Section 12:20]

[1]O'Brien v. O'Brien, 66 N.Y.2d 576, 498 N.Y.S.2d 743, 489 N.E.2d 712 (1985); Woodworth v. Woodworth, 126 Mich. App. 258, 337 N.W.2d 332 (1983); Washburn v. Washburn, 101 Wash. 2d 168, 677 P.2d 152 (1984). See also Margaret McGovern, *Licenses v. Degrees: Is There a Difference?*, 9 Fam. Advoc. 14 (Fall 1986).

[2]Stevens v. Stevens, 23 Ohio St. 3d 115, 492 N.E.2d 131 (1986) (emphasis added); Pacht v. Jadd, 13 Ohio App. 3d 363, 469 N.E.2d 918 (10th Dist. Franklin County 1983); Ranz v. Ranz, 51 Ohio App. 3d 66, 554 N.E.2d 142 (1st Dist. Hamilton County 1988); Kahn v. Kahn, 42 Ohio App. 3d 61, 536 N.E.2d 678 (2d Dist. Montgomery County 1987); Gebhart v. Gebhart, 14 Ohio App. 3d 107, 470 N.E.2d 205 (2d Dist. Montgomery County 1984).

uitable award of alimony in accordance with RC 3105.18."[3] RC 3105.18(C)(1)(j) provides that if a spouse contributes to the acquisition of the other's professional license, that factor must be considered in the award of spousal support. Thus, the court may determine a value of the professional degree for purposes of determining the amount of the spousal support award, but not in order to offset the value of the license with a property award.[4]

Where the professional is engaged in a practice, although his or her license has no value in Ohio, the practice may have value.[5]

§ 12:21   Specific types of property—Stock options

Domestic matters have generally involved stock options issued by the same company on whose stock the option is a call. The options described in the case law[1] were issued to executives and other key employees for various purposes during the course of their employment. They were issued in return for past, current, or the promise of future services, in order to provide maximum tax benefit and bonus compensation or to subsidize cash compensation. Such options are considered fringe benefits of employment, similar in character to deferred compensation, medical insurance payments, and retirement plans. They differ from other fringe benefits, such as free parking, the latter having no residual value for distribution in a divorce matter.

The options generally carry substantial restrictions. The primary reason for such restrictions is two-fold. The Internal Revenue Code allows tax deferral so long as there remains a risk of forfeiture and the options are not granted for the pure monetary compensation of the employee, as stock the employee would buy and sell for immediate profit, but in part, to give key personnel a direct participation in the company's success.

In the states where the issue has been considered,[2] options have been held to be property subject to allocation in divorce and dissolution actions. They are contractual rights, earned by the employee-spouse, not gifts from the employer. Their contingent nature renders them a chose in action, not a mere expectancy.

Once a court has decided that the option is property, it must then

---

[3]Stevens v. Stevens, 23 Ohio St. 3d 115, 492 N.E.2d 131 (1986) (footnote omitted, emphasis added); Cox v. Cox, 1994 WL 613858 (Ohio Ct. App. 8th Dist. Cuyahoga County 1994).

[4]Ranz v. Ranz, 51 Ohio App. 3d 66, 554 N.E.2d 142 (1st Dist. Hamilton County 1988).

[5]See Text § 12:19, Specific types of property—Business interests.

[Section 12:21]

[1]Demo v. Demo, 101 Ohio App. 3d 383, 655 N.E.2d 791 (12th Dist. Butler County 1995); Birath v. Birath, 53 Ohio App. 3d 31, 558 N.E.2d 63 (10th Dist. Franklin County 1988).

[2]Deborah Akers, *Valuation of Stock Options in Divorce and Dissolution Cases*, 2 Dom. Rel. J. Ohio 69 (Sept./Oct. 1990).

determine whether it has value and what that value is and define the period of service in exchange for which the option was granted. It must find whether the period of service fell within the period of marriage, as defined in the particular state. Once the marital or community component is found, the court must formulate a feasible method of distribution.[3]

Some courts have held that it is impossible to value an option which cannot be exercised until a future date; others have held that valuation is mandatory. The methods employed are almost as numerous as the courts rendering the decisions.[4]

The status of the option on date of valuation (date of hearing, separation, or otherwise) dictates the treatment. There are three primary conditions in which we find options (1) exercised; (2) exercisable, but not exercised; (3) and not yet exercisable, although there are others, such as the exercised option subject to forfeiture.[5]

§ 12:22 Specific types of property—Limited partnerships

The problems that accompany the valuation of limited partnerships are unique and perplexing. Neither the limited partner nor the spouse is active in the business, by definition of the limited partnership, and, therefore, neither party has firsthand knowledge of the workings or status. There is often little information in the hands of the parties, but for a prospectus, describing projections for the business. Nor is documentation on the partnership activity readily available from the general partner or partners, who may be across country and not located at a partnership business office, as such.

Limited partnerships are generally formed for reasons different from other business entities that are created for profit; there is high risk attached to the activities in which limited partnerships usually engage, and the tax treatment of limited partnership interests is also

---

[3]Landefeld v. Landefeld, 2002-Ohio-1801, 2002 WL 471941 (Ohio Ct. App. 2d Dist. Greene County 2002).

[4]Deborah Akers, *Valuation of Stock Options in Divorce and Dissolution Cases*, 2 Dom. Rel. J. Ohio 69 (Sept./Oct. 1990); Daugherty v. Daugherty, 2003-Ohio-6019, 2003 WL 22664211 (Ohio Ct. App. 5th Dist. Stark County 2003) (former husband was required to determine value of stock options as of the date they became exercisable, which was date when former wife should have received full payment, where value of options had risen and fallen).

[5]Deborah Akers, *Valuation of Stock Options in Divorce and Dissolution Cases*, 2 Dom. Rel. J. Ohio 69 (Sept./Oct. 1990) (in-depth discussion of these three primary conditions plus classification of marital and separate, methods of distribution, taxation and relevant case law). See also Ammon v. Ammon, 1989 WL 18871 (Ohio Ct. App. 12th Dist. Clermont County 1989), dismissed, 44 Ohio St. 3d 704, 541 N.E.2d 623 (1989).

distinct.[1] Therefore, traditional methods of valuation are not strictly applicable.[2] The speculative nature of discounts for lack of liquidity for minority interests held by the limited partner adds to the difficulty of valuation.[3]

§ 12:23   Specific types of property—Tax exemptions

Before the amendment of RC 3113.21 to address the issue, dependency exemptions recognized for income tax purposes were characterized by the courts as property rights.[1] Therefore, once granted, the award of the exemption could not be modified.[2] However, under RC 3113.21(B)(10), the exemption must be awarded as part of the child support determination.[3] The court therefore retains jurisdiction to modify the exemption award as it does any child support order. The failure to consider the exemption in awarding child support is not error.[4]

[Section 12:22]

[1]David Untract, *Who Gets Custody of the Passive Losses?*, 13 Fam. Advoc. 50 (Fall 1990).

[2]Oatey v. Oatey, 83 Ohio App. 3d 251, 614 N.E.2d 1054 (8th Dist. Cuyahoga County 1992) (husband's negative account balance was the basis for the court's valuation; that aspect of the decision was affirmed).

[3]For detailed discussion including definitions, valuation, tax impact, distribution, significant case law, and related articles see Deborah Akers, *The Valuation of Limited Partnerships in Divorce and Dissolution Matters*, 3 Dom. Rel. J. Ohio 141 (Nov./Dec. 1991).

[Section 12:23]

[1]Hughes v. Hughes, 35 Ohio St. 3d 165, 518 N.E.2d 1213 (1988) (holding modified by, Singer v. Dickinson, 63 Ohio St. 3d 408, 588 N.E.2d 806 (1992)); Hodges v. Hodges, 43 Ohio App. 3d 113, 539 N.E.2d 709 (2d Dist. Clark County 1988) (these cases also held that U.S. Code does not preempt award of exemption by state court). See also Gunkel v. Gunkel, 1989 WL 52895 (Ohio Ct. App. 6th Dist. Lucas County 1989); Lamberjack v. Lamberjack, 1988 WL 100614 (Ohio Ct. App. 3d Dist. Seneca County 1988), cause dismissed, 41 Ohio St. 3d 713, 535 N.E.2d 316 (1989); Mettler v. Mettler, 61 Ohio App. 3d 14, 572 N.E.2d 127 (4th Dist. Ross County 1988).

[2]RC 3105.171(I); Hughes v. Hughes, 35 Ohio St. 3d 165, 518 N.E.2d 1213 (1988) (holding modified by, Singer v. Dickinson, 63 Ohio St. 3d 408, 588 N.E.2d 806 (1992)); Mettler v. Mettler, 61 Ohio App. 3d 14, 572 N.E.2d 127 (4th Dist. Ross County 1988).

[3]See Text Ch 19, Child Support. Dunlap v. Dunlap, 2008-Ohio-3201, 2008 WL 2582924 (Ohio Ct. App. 9th Dist. Summit County 2008); Schaefer v. Schaefer, 2008-Ohio-3960, 2008 WL 3009856 (Ohio Ct. App. 5th Dist. Stark County 2008); Branden v. Branden, 2009-Ohio-866, 2009 WL 478383 (Ohio Ct. App. 8th Dist. Cuyahoga County 2009); Hubbard v. Hubbard, 2009-Ohio-2194, 2009 WL 1272644 (Ohio Ct. App. 3d Dist. Defiance County 2009).

[4]Connolly v. Connolly, 70 Ohio App. 3d 738, 591 N.E.2d 1362 (8th Dist. Cuyahoga County 1990); Wohleber v. Wohleber, 2009-Ohio-995, 2009 WL 580729 (Ohio Ct. App. 9th Dist. Lorain County 2009).

§ 12:24 Specific types of property—Insurance

Insurance policies are generally classified as assets subject to distribution in divorce cases, where the premiums have been paid from marital funds. The face value or death benefit payable under a life insurance policy is not necessarily an indication of value. It is generally the cash surrender value which is the measure of worth. It can be argued that, where a lump-sum or other premium was paid from marital income, the insurance payable under the policy is a marital asset. Courts differ on whether term insurance is an asset. When the insured becomes uninsurable during the marriage, the continuation of an existing policy may thereby attain a special value to the parties.[1]

A trial court abuses its discretion in failing to evaluate and divide the value of life insurance.[2] The portion of husband's premarital insurance policies for which the parties paid with marital funds is marital property.[3]

Federal courts have held that the cash surrender value of national service life insurance is not a marital asset subject to distribution by state courts because federal law preempts.[4]

The right to be named or to remain as the beneficiary of the death benefits or survivorship rights of a former spouse is not technically a property division question, but at times can resemble those issues. In *Clarkston v. Hubbard*,[5] the parties' divorce decree provided that the husband would name their daughter as the beneficiary of his life insurance policies. After his death, summary judgment for the daughter was affirmed because the provisions of the divorce decree qualified as a QDRO, an exception to the preemptive provisions of ERISA. Similarly, a separation agreement provision requiring the husband to maintain a life insurance policy for the benefit of the wife and a child was held to be enforceable against the assets of the husband's estate when he failed to maintain the policy.[6] The Court of Appeals for the Third Appellate District has found that insurance proceeds from lost jewelry were marital property, even though jewelry may have been

---

[Section 12:24]

[1] For a discussion of life, health, and other insurances, see Thomas Mulroy, *Protect Family Insurance after the Divorce*, 13 Fam. Advoc. 6 (1990).

[2] Ingle v. Ingle, 1994 WL 667183 (Ohio Ct. App. 2d Dist. Clark County 1994).

[3] Babka v. Babka, 83 Ohio App. 3d 428, 615 N.E.2d 247 (9th Dist. Summit County 1992).

[4] Wissner v. Wissner, 338 U.S. 655, 70 S. Ct. 398, 94 L. Ed. 424 (1950).

[5] Clarkston v. Hubbard, 1998 WL 127588 (Ohio Ct. App. 2d Dist. Montgomery County 1998).

[6] Hornak v. Hornak, 1997 WL 440950 (Ohio Ct. App. 9th Dist. Summit County 1997).

separate property, where premiums for insurance on jewelry were paid from marital funds.[7]

§ 12:25   Specific types of property—Real property

The marital home is the most significant asset in some divorce cases.[1] In the absence of a recent sale of the subject property, the valuation by a qualified expert is generally required. The professionally accepted approaches to valuation of real estate include the cost method, market comparable method, and income method. Market data is generally used for residential property and for commercial property, where comparables are available, although a commercial appraiser will most commonly conduct valuations by all three methods and assign weights to each or choose the method which is in his or her opinion most reliable under the circumstances.[2]

Where a party is awarded real estate in a divorce decree, no lien is created in favor of the recipient unless and until the decree or a deed is recorded.[3] It is an often-made assumption that the existence of the judgment entry on the court records creates a lien. Although a title company might call such a judgment into question, if it is missed, the party seeking to establish the lien is unprotected.

The court may order the sale of real estate to effect a property division.[4]

It is an abuse of discretion to order real estate sold at auction without allowing the parties to make reasonable efforts to sell it at its fair market value.[5]

In determining the value of the marital share of premarital real estate, a court errs in dividing the current equity by the number of years it was owned in total, multiplied by the number of years of

---

[7]Warner v. Warner, 2003-Ohio-5132, 2003 WL 22229412 (Ohio Ct. App. 3d Dist. Union County 2003). See also RC 3105.171.

[Section 12:25]

[1]See Text § 12:7, Statutory terms of art—Marital property; Text § 12:10, Statutory terms of art—Separate property. See also Stanley Morganstern, *Appreciation of Pre-Marital Real Estate*, 9 Dom. Rel. J. Ohio 21 (March/April 1997). Stanley Morganstern, *Disposition of the Marital Home*, 3 Dom. Rel. J. Ohio 113 (Sept./Oct. 1991).

[2]Bertram Brown, *Putting a Value on Real Estate*, 2 Fam. Advoc. 18 (Summer 1979).

[3]RC 3105.171(J); Vickroy v. Vickroy, 44 Ohio App. 3d 210, 542 N.E.2d 700 (5th Dist. Fairfield County 1988).

[4]Winkler v. Winkler, 117 Ohio App. 3d 247, 690 N.E.2d 109 (7th Dist. Monroe County 1997); Smith v. Smith, 1987 WL 8021 (Ohio Ct. App. 6th Dist. Sandusky County 1987); Cox v. Cox, 1995 WL 399419 (Ohio Ct. App. 12th Dist. Clermont County 1995).

[5]Van Fossen v. Van Fossen, 47 Ohio App. 3d 175, 547 N.E.2d 1237 (9th Dist. Summit County 1988); Lang v. Lang, 1995 WL 494582 (Ohio Ct. App. 7th Dist. Columbiana County 1995) (order for sale of property at auction was reversed, as was order to pay liens from sale where liens were result of one spouse's separate debt).

marriage. An appropriate formula is based on evidence of the property value at the date of marriage and at the date of divorce.[6]

However, in *Nine v. Nine*,[7] the court ruled that, because all of the appreciation in wife's premarital house that had occurred during marriage could not be directly attributed to efforts of either party, the trial court erred in dividing the appreciation as a marital asset. Regular maintenance and payment of property taxes do not directly cause an increase in value of real estate.[8]

The burden is not upon the party asserting that appreciation of a premarital asset during marriage is marital property. To award as separate property all appreciation on premarital real estate would be to erroneously ignore the reduction in the mortgage balance, as well as the maintenance and improvements made by the parties during marriage.[9]

It is error to prorate the value of the marital dwelling according to the percent paid down in premarital funds; if traced, the amount of the downpayment should be categorized as separate property, and the entire balance should be divided as marital property, where the parties lived in the home, contributed to its maintenance, and used marital funds to reduce the mortgage balance.[10]

Where the equity in the marital home is "built" during marriage, it is not an abuse of discretion for the trial court to award husband his

---

[6]Rodgers v. Rodgers, 1993 WL 208296 (Ohio Ct. App. 9th Dist. Summit County 1993); Hamlin v. Hamlin, 2006-Ohio-6117, 2006 WL 3350687 (Ohio Ct. App. 2d Dist. Darke County 2006).

[7]Nine v. Nine, 1995 WL 89478 (Ohio Ct. App. 9th Dist. Summit County 1995); Hutchins v. Hutchins, 2000 WL 1336616 (Ohio Ct. App. 12th Dist. Preble County 2000).

[8]Nine v. Nine, 1995 WL 89478 (Ohio Ct. App. 9th Dist. Summit County 1995) (the value on date of marriage divided by the sum of [value on date of marriage plus the reduction in mortgage balance during marriage] multiplied by the market appreciation during marriage equals the premarital portion of market appreciation during marriage; the reduction in mortgage balance during marriage divided by the sum of [value on date of marriage plus reduction in mortgage balance during marriage] multiplied by the market appreciation during marriage equals the marital portion of market appreciation during marriage. There is a dissenting opinion relating to this calculation.) See also Holman v. Holman, 1997 WL 458046 (Ohio Ct. App. 6th Dist. Ottawa County 1997); Sauer v. Sauer, 1996 WL 284873 (Ohio Ct. App. 8th Dist. Cuyahoga County 1996) (decision reversed where no part of market appreciation during marriage was divided as marital asset); Demo v. Demo, 101 Ohio App. 3d 383, 655 N.E.2d 791 (12th Dist. Butler County 1995).

[9]Hansen v. Hansen, 1992 WL 366885 (Ohio Ct. App. 11th Dist. Lake County 1992); Salmon v. Salmon, 2006-Ohio-1557, 2006 WL 826328 (Ohio Ct. App. 9th Dist. Summit County 2006).

[10]Henderson v. Henderson, 1995 WL 653827 (Ohio Ct. App. 1st Dist. Hamilton County 1995).

premarital contribution thereto and to divide the entire balance of the equity in the home as marital property.[11]

Improvements made to real estate with marital funds contribute to the appreciation for purposes of RC 3105.171(A)(3)(a).[12] Where the husband's separate real estate experienced a significant increase in value due to zoning changes, the court erred in holding it to be his sole property. He was entitled to the value of the property when he inherited it, but the fortuitous abnormal appreciation was marital.[13]

RC 3105.171(F)(7) mandates that a court consider costs of sale of an asset "if it is necessary that an asset be sold to effectuate an equitable distribution of property." Notwithstanding, the Fifth District Court of Appeals has held that a trial court does not err in deducting costs of sale of real estate before dividing its value, even where there is no evidence of likely sale, so long as the division is generally equitable.[14]

A trial court's "somewhat unique" order granting the husband first option to purchase the marital residence from the wife at a stated price, plus reasonable cost of wife's improvements, did not constitute an abuse of discretion.[15]

§ 12:26 Specific types of property—Other types of property

Household items and personal effects are frequently divided by agreement, such that a value need not be assigned to each item. Some courts have allowed division by lot, but only by agreement.[1] In the absence of an appraisal by a qualified expert, the opinion of a party as to the value of his own personal property may suffice.[2] In the absence of some evidence of value of household furnishings, the matter will be

---

[11]Babka v. Babka, 83 Ohio App. 3d 428, 433, 615 N.E.2d 247 (9th Dist. Summit County 1992).

[12]Friend v. Friend, 1998 WL 831471 (Ohio Ct. App. 9th Dist. Summit County 1998); Stafford v. Stafford, 1995 WL 118172 (Ohio Ct. App. 2d Dist. Greene County 1995).

[13]Esterline v. Esterline, 1997 WL 464740 (Ohio Ct. App. 2d Dist. Clark County 1997).

[14]Jameson v. Jameson, 1995 WL 42395 (Ohio Ct. App. 5th Dist. Stark County 1995); Meeks v. Meeks, 2008-Ohio-2015, 2008 WL 1886315 (Ohio Ct. App. 10th Dist. Franklin County 2008).

[15]Underwood v. Underwood, 1995 WL 43624, at *1 (Ohio Ct. App. 5th Dist. Delaware County 1995).

[Section 12:26]

[1]Bokovitz v. Bokovitz, 1981 WL 4166 (Ohio Ct. App. 9th Dist. Medina County 1981).

[2]Evid. R. 701; Construction and effect of provisions of will relied upon as affecting the burden of taxation, 37 A.L.R.2d 7 (secs. 39-52 superseded by Construction and effect of will provisions not expressly mentioning payment of death taxes but relied on as affecting the burden of estate or inheritance taxes, 70 A.L.R.3d 630).; Brookhart v. Brookhart, 1993 WL 483206 (Ohio Ct. App. 4th Dist. Athens County 1993) (trial court's acceptance of a party's valuation of a homemade vehicle affirmed). See also Stout v. Stout, 1993 WL 140494 (Ohio Ct. App. 7th Dist. Columbiana County 1993).

reversed.[3] The National Automobile Dealers Association Official Used Car Guide, known as the "blue book," value of an automobile is admissible.[4] Art and antiques may require valuation by a specialized appraiser.[5]

The Third District Court of Appeals in *Burden v. Burden*[6] held that, where a lottery ticket is purchased from marital funds, lottery winnings are marital property.

Paid vacation time which has not been used but will result in payment is marital if accumulated during the marriage.[7] Disability benefits are paid in lieu of wages and are, therefore, treated in divorce proceedings as income, not as a divisible asset.[8] "Likewise, proceeds of a lawsuit for compensation for lost earnings is a marital asset subject to division."[9]

It has been held that a trial court abuses its discretion in failing to value and divide marital debt.[10] While division of the marital debts is not specifically addressed by RC 3105.171, courts generally consider and assign responsibility for the parties' debts together with the division of their property. Where a trial court assigned all of the parties' marital debt to the husband for the reason that he was going to pay a "minimum amount of spousal support," its decision was reversed. In dividing property, a court can consider a party's inability to pay debt, but the court must decide the division of property without regard to spousal support.[11]

---

[3]Rogers v. Rogers, 1995 WL 461262 (Ohio Ct. App. 2d Dist. Miami County 1995); Carney v. Carney, 2000 WL 1363173 (Ohio Ct. App. 6th Dist. Erie County 2000) (trial court erred in ordering each party to retain all personal property in their respective possession without having determined the value thereof).

[4]Henry v. Serey, 46 Ohio App. 3d 93, 546 N.E.2d 474 (1st Dist. Hamilton County 1989) (overruled by, Dunn v. Westlake, 1990 WL 59262 (Ohio Ct. App. 1st Dist. Hamilton County 1990)) and (disapproved of by, Dunn v. Westlake, 61 Ohio St. 3d 102, 573 N.E.2d 84 (1991)) and (disapproved of by, United Methodist Church of Berea v. Dunlop Const. Products, Inc., 1992 WL 80054 (Ohio Ct. App. 8th Dist. Cuyahoga County 1992)).

[5]Frana Biederman, *Putting a Value on Art and Antiques*, 2 Fam. Advoc. 18 (1979).

[6]Burden v. Burden, 1987 WL 18222 (Ohio Ct. App. 3d Dist. Auglaize County 1987).

[7]Rupp v. Rupp, 1987 WL 20443 (Ohio Ct. App. 6th Dist. Ottawa County 1987).

[8]Koba v. Koba, 1996 WL 732547 (Ohio Ct. App. 8th Dist. Cuyahoga County 1996).

[9]Beagle v. Beagle, 2008-Ohio-764, 2008 WL 501092 (Ohio Ct. App. 10th Dist. Franklin County 2008).

[10]Gibson v. Gibson, 87 Ohio App. 3d 426, 622 N.E.2d 425 (4th Dist. Scioto County 1993); Grime v. Grime, 1996 WL 673516 (Ohio Ct. App. 6th Dist. Fulton County 1996); Ingle v. Ingle, 1994 WL 667183 (Ohio Ct. App. 2d Dist. Clark County 1994).

[11]Meliher v. Meliher, 1997 WL 772952 (Ohio Ct. App. 11th Dist. Portage County 1997).

An option to purchase a $19,000 automobile for $1,183 has value.[12]

Replacement of the lost stone of a wedding ring is a repair to separate property. The ring remains wife's separate property, notwithstanding that marital funds were used for the repair.[13]

A relocation payment made by an employer to defray husband's moving expenses is marital property where it was earned and paid during the marriage and the parties purchased during the marriage the home to which they were moving.[14]

Where wife claimed the tax exemption for a child from her previous relationship, the court did not err in finding that the earned income credit attributable to that exemption was marital property. Husband had provided financial and parental support for the child, and the equities indicated that he was entitled to benefit from the credit.[15]

If the overall distribution of marital property is equitable, a trial court does not abuse its discretion in ordering one spouse to pay the entire income tax liability of both parties.[16] Further, a trial court does not err by assigning the wife the entire burden of her student loan debt. Although the debt was marital, the wife will benefit from the income generated as a result of the degree she obtained during the marriage.[17]

Voluntary separation incentive (VSI) payments made by the U.S. Armed Forces to encourage a reduction in personnel are analogous to severance pay, not retirement benefits. Accordingly, husband's VSI benefits were separate income and not marital property.[18]

With regard to the allocation of companion animals, one court found that notwithstanding the emotional attachment often felt by owners, dogs are considered personal property and will be awarded along with other personal items within the discretion of the court. In one case, despite the desire of the wife to retain the dogs, the court awarded them to the husband because the husband had been awarded the marital residence, the dogs had always lived at the residence, had

---

[12]Wyum v. Wyum, 1997 WL 97235 (Ohio Ct. App. 8th Dist. Cuyahoga County 1997).

[13]Wolfangel v. Wolfangel, 1995 WL 312697 (Ohio Ct. App. 9th Dist. Summit County 1995).

[14]Kelly v. Kelly, 111 Ohio App. 3d 641, 676 N.E.2d 1210 (1st Dist. Hamilton County 1996).

[15]Derr v. Derr, 1996 WL 131156 (Ohio Ct. App. 12th Dist. Preble County 1996); Brewer v. Brewer, 2004-Ohio-3531, 2004 WL 1486781 (Ohio Ct. App. 5th Dist. Licking County 2004); Rosenberger v. Rosenberger, 2005-Ohio-1790, 2005 WL 879270 (Ohio Ct. App. 11th Dist. Geauga County 2005).

[16]Cromberg v. Cromberg, 1995 WL 316526 (Ohio Ct. App. 6th Dist. Lucas County 1995).

[17]Webb v. Webb, 1998 WL 820838 (Ohio Ct. App. 12th Dist. Butler County 1998).

[18]Grooms v. Grooms, 1999 WL 197946 (Ohio Ct. App. 2d Dist. Montgomery County 1999); McClure v. McClure, 98 Ohio App. 3d 27, 647 N.E.2d 832 (2d Dist. Greene County 1994).

ample space to run, and were cared for by an on-premises caretaker.[19] Student loan incurred for the children of the parties have been determined to be a marital debt.[20] Severance payments received as compensation negotiated prior to the termination of employment and for services rendered during the marriage can be divided as marital property. Severance payments intended to compensation for wages lost after the divorce cannot be characterized as marital property.[21] Marital funds transferred to Uniform Transfer to Minors Act (UMTA) accounts cannot be treated as part of the marital estate for distribution.[22]

Even though six Cincinnati Bengals tickets were used more often by husband, the court did not err by awarding them to wife, who lived closer to the stadium, and awarding one half the value to the husband.[23]

§ 12:27 Mandatory valuation of assets

Valuation of all marital assets is mandatory in order for the court of appeals to conduct a meaningful review of a division of property in a divorce case.[1] The value of each piece of marital property must be determined in order for the court to carry out the mandate of RC

---

[19]Green v. Shall, 2004-Ohio-1653, 2004 WL 628649 (Ohio Ct. App. 6th Dist. Lucas County 2004).

[20]Vergitz v. Vergitz, 2007-Ohio-1395, 2007 WL 901597 (Ohio Ct. App. 7th Dist. Jefferson County 2007).

[21]McKenzie v. McKenzie, 2006-Ohio-6841, 2006 WL 3759837 (Ohio Ct. App. 2d Dist. Greene County 2006).

[22]Hyder v. Hyder, 2006-Ohio-5285, 2006 WL 2864115 (Ohio Ct. App. 9th Dist. Wayne County 2006).

[23]Brickner v. Brickner, 2009-Ohio-1164, 2009 WL 683706 (Ohio Ct. App. 12th Dist. Butler County 2009).

[Section 12:27]

[1]Allen v. Allen, 109 Ohio App. 3d 640, 672 N.E.2d 1056 (12th Dist. Butler County 1996); Gibson v. Gibson, 87 Ohio App. 3d 426, 622 N.E.2d 425 (4th Dist. Scioto County 1993); Pawlowski v. Pawlowski, 83 Ohio App. 3d 794, 615 N.E.2d 1071 (10th Dist. Franklin County 1992); Goode v. Goode, 70 Ohio App. 3d 125, 590 N.E.2d 439 (10th Dist. Franklin County 1991); Fritz v. Fritz, 1995 WL 75405 (Ohio Ct. App. 7th Dist. Columbiana County 1995); Dixon v. Dixon, 1995 WL 106137 (Ohio Ct. App. 8th Dist. Cuyahoga County 1995); Rinehart v. Rinehart, 1995 WL 762925 (Ohio Ct. App. 4th Dist. Gallia County 1995); Buckles v. Buckles, 46 Ohio App. 3d 102, 546 N.E.2d 950 (10th Dist. Franklin County 1988); Mochko v. Mochko, 63 Ohio App. 3d 671, 579 N.E.2d 773 (8th Dist. Cuyahoga County 1990); Guidubaldi v. Guidubaldi, 64 Ohio App. 3d 361, 581 N.E.2d 621 (11th Dist. Portage County 1990); Connolly v. Connolly, 70 Ohio App. 3d 738, 591 N.E.2d 1362 (8th Dist. Cuyahoga County 1990); Eisler v. Eisler, 24 Ohio App. 3d 151, 493 N.E.2d 975 (11th Dist. Geauga County 1985); Willis v. Willis, 19 Ohio App. 3d 45, 482 N.E.2d 1274 (11th Dist. Geauga County 1984); Callahan v. Callahan, 1991 WL 76069 (Ohio Ct. App. 8th Dist. Cuyahoga County 1991); Schoonover v. Schoonover, 1992 WL 217986 (Ohio Ct. App. 10th Dist. Franklin County 1992); Conforti v. Conforti, 1992 WL 95751 (Ohio Ct. App. 8th Dist. Cuyahoga County 1992); Roberts v. Roberts, 113 Ohio App. 33, 17 Ohio Op. 2d 38, 177 N.E.2d 281 (6th Dist. Lucas County 1961); Smith v. Smith, 1984 WL 7404 (Ohio Ct. App. 11th Dist. Lake County 1984); Jones v. Jones, 1987 WL 16295 (Ohio

3105.171(C). If neither party submits evidence of the value of an item of property, the court must instruct the parties to do so.[2] If, however, only one party submits evidence of the value of an asset, the court may rely solely on that figure.[3] In some cases, separate property need not be valued.[4]

Where a party filed a motion two years after a decree of divorce was entered, asking for division of retirement benefits which existed on date of divorce but were undisclosed, the court divided the asset.[5] Agricultural Stabilization and Conservation Service payments were undisclosed to the court in the separation agreement; notwithstanding that both parties knew of the asset and there was a clause awarding the " 'balance of the property' " to husband, the court divided the asset upon wife's motion for accounting, holding that all procedural errors were waived upon the appearance of both parties.[6]

The trial court need not accept a stipulation entered by the parties; however, once the court accepts one, the parties have the right to rely on the acceptance in trying their case. Because the parties stipulated that their assets would be divided equally, the court abused its discretion by awarding 25% to one and 75% to the other spouse.[7]

A court may accept testimony of the owner as to the value of an asset.[8]

Where the vast majority of the marital property is distributed by agreement, valuation of specific assets may not be necessary.[9] When the parties enter an agreement settling all issues of property division, the result is an implied waiver of the requirement that the court find

---

Ct. App. 11th Dist. Geauga County 1987); Diefenthaler v. Diefenthaler, 63 Ohio App. 3d 845, 580 N.E.2d 477 (6th Dist. Ottawa County 1989); Keough v. Keough, 1987 WL 18015 (Ohio Ct. App. 11th Dist. Portage County 1987); Phillips v. Phillips, 2006-Ohio-2098, 2006 WL 1118918 (Ohio Ct. App. 5th Dist. Licking County 2006).

[2]Eisler v. Eisler, 24 Ohio App. 3d 151, 493 N.E.2d 975 (11th Dist. Geauga County 1985); Willis v. Willis, 19 Ohio App. 3d 45, 482 N.E.2d 1274 (11th Dist. Geauga County 1984).

[3]Price v. Price, 1999 WL 252722 (Ohio Ct. App. 2d Dist. Montgomery County 1999); Stout v. Stout, 1993 WL 140494 (Ohio Ct. App. 7th Dist. Columbiana County 1993).

[4]Hess v. Peltier, 1996 WL 339972 (Ohio Ct. App. 10th Dist. Franklin County 1996) (not necessary to value separate property when no distributive award is made).

[5]Robbins v. Robbins, 1993 WL 52237 (Ohio Ct. App. 9th Dist. Wayne County 1993).

[6]Schroeder v. Schroeder, 52 Ohio App. 3d 117, 557 N.E.2d 145 (3d Dist. Putnam County 1988).

[7]Miller v. Miller, 1989 WL 1662 (Ohio Ct. App. 9th Dist. Lorain County 1989).

[8]Price v. Price, 1999 WL 252722 (Ohio Ct. App. 2d Dist. Montgomery County 1999); Brookhart v. Brookhart, 1993 WL 483206 (Ohio Ct. App. 4th Dist. Athens County 1993).

[9]Goode v. Goode, 70 Ohio App. 3d 125, 590 N.E.2d 439 (10th Dist. Franklin County 1991); see also Melendrez v. Melendrez, 1993 WL 134893 (Ohio Ct. App. 5th Dist. Delaware County 1993). See Text § 12:3, Equitable distribution.

a value for all property.[10] Where the court orders that property be sold and the proceeds be divided, some courts have held that there is no need to determine the fair market value.[11] Where the court orders the parties to sell the property and divide the proceeds, but the parties fail to comply for three years thereafter, the court does not err by appointing a receiver to appraise, sell, and distribute the property.[12]

Even where the parties own property in a foreign country, and an order regarding that foreign property might not be enforceable overseas, the court must still determine the value of that property and allocate the rights of the parties.[13]

§ 12:28 Methods of valuation

The methods used by a court for valuation of assets are governed by rules of the market place as well as rules of law.[1] The court must have a rational evidentiary basis for assigning a value to a piece of property.[2]

An award of interest on a division of property that is payable over time is not mandatory as a matter of law. RC 1343.03, regarding interest upon judgments, does not apply until an obligation is due and payable.[3] It has been held unreasonable not to award interest on property division payable over eleven years.[4] If property is divided equitably according to statute, but the payment of that equitable amount is extended over time, the longer the time, the lower the current value of the payment. The loss of earnings from the inability to invest as of the date of the award creates a real and measurable diminution in the value of the award.

---

[10]Pawlowski v. Pawlowski, 83 Ohio App. 3d 794, 615 N.E.2d 1071 (10th Dist. Franklin County 1992); Stegawski v. Stegawski, 1994 WL 197232 (Ohio Ct. App. 8th Dist. Cuyahoga County 1994); Melendrez v. Melendrez, 1993 WL 134893 (Ohio Ct. App. 5th Dist. Delaware County 1993).

[11]Bauer v. Bauer, No. 42805 (Ohio Ct. App. 8th Dist. Cuyahoga County 1981); Yesberger v. Yesberger, No. 42560 (Ohio Ct. App. 8th Dist. Cuyahoga County 1981).

[12]Ratliff v. Ratliff, 1998 WL 514039 (Ohio Ct. App. 10th Dist. Franklin County 1998).

[13]Dabis v. Dabis, 1998 WL 391938 (Ohio Ct. App. 3d Dist. Mercer County 1998).

[Section 12:28]

[1]See Text §§ 12:18 to 12:26, Specific types of property.

[2]Kaechele v. Kaechele, 35 Ohio St. 3d 93, 518 N.E.2d 1197 (1988); Campitelli v. Campitelli, 65 Ohio App. 3d 307, 583 N.E.2d 1322 (5th Dist. Stark County 1989); Apanovitch v. Apanovitch, 1989 WL 92122 (Ohio Ct. App. 11th Dist. Geauga County 1989); Meeks v. Meeks, 2006-Ohio-642, 2006 WL 328685 (Ohio Ct. App. 10th Dist. Franklin County 2006).

[3]Koegel v. Koegel, 69 Ohio St. 2d 355, 23 Ohio Op. 3d 320, 432 N.E.2d 206 (1982); Kevdzija v. Kevdzija, 166 Ohio App. 3d 276, 2006-Ohio-1723, 850 N.E.2d 734 (8th Dist. Cuyahoga County 2006); Godar v. Godar, 2006-Ohio-5994, 2006 WL 3290801 (Ohio Ct. App. 5th Dist. Stark County 2006); Hasselback v. Hasselback, 2007-Ohio-762, 2007 WL 549461 (Ohio Ct. App. 10th Dist. Franklin County 2007).

[4]Collier v. Collier, 36 Ohio App. 3d 130, 521 N.E.2d 849 (3d Dist. Crawford County 1987).

Courts have accepted the average of two professional appraisals as a valuation of marital property.[5] However, it is mandatory that the court has a rational basis for its decision to do so.[6]

Comparable sales are readily accepted by courts as evidence of value.[7] The statement of value given by an experienced operator of a like business has been accepted as a valuation in the absence of expert testimony.[8] The opinion of a party as to the fair market value of his own personal property is admissible.[9]

Pursuant to Evidence Rule 803(17), the value shown in the National Automobile Dealers Association Official Used Car Guide (Blue Book) has been accepted as value in the absence of more reliable evidence.[10]

Authority is split on the issue of whether minority discounts should be applied in valuing interests in closely held companies for the purposes of equitable division. Generally, courts which follow a fair market value standard for valuation of business interests allow discounts for minority holdings.[11]

---

[5]Bredenfoerder v. Bredenfoerder, 1990 WL 61992 (Ohio Ct. App. 12th Dist. Clermont County 1990); Jesionowski v. Jesionowski, 1987 WL 14959 (Ohio Ct. App. 6th Dist. Lucas County 1987); Matter of Erre, 1988 WL 59536 (Ohio Ct. App. 5th Dist. Richland County 1988).

[6]Kaechele v. Kaechele, 35 Ohio St. 3d 93, 518 N.E.2d 1197 (1988); Gest v. Gest, 1998 WL 208872 (Ohio Ct. App. 9th Dist. Lorain County 1998); McCoy v. McCoy, 91 Ohio App. 3d 570, 632 N.E.2d 1358 (8th Dist. Cuyahoga County 1993); Zimmerman v. Zimmerman, 1990 WL 82588 (Ohio Ct. App. 12th Dist. Clermont County 1990), dismissed, 55 Ohio St. 3d 720, 564 N.E.2d 496 (1990); Rodriguez v. Rodriguez, 1990 WL 47458 (Ohio Ct. App. 11th Dist. Geauga County 1990); Hoopingarner v. Hoopingarner, 1985 WL 6824 (Ohio Ct. App. 8th Dist. Cuyahoga County 1985); Campitelli v. Campitelli, 65 Ohio App. 3d 307, 583 N.E.2d 1322 (5th Dist. Stark County 1989); Apanovitch v. Apanovitch, 1989 WL 92122 (Ohio Ct. App. 11th Dist. Geauga County 1989); Winter v. Winter, 2002-Ohio-6600, 2002 WL 31711260 (Ohio Ct. App. 5th Dist. Stark County 2002).

[7]Ware v. Ware, 1987 WL 6812 (Ohio Ct. App. 8th Dist. Cuyahoga County 1987); Matter of Erre, 1988 WL 59536 (Ohio Ct. App. 5th Dist. Richland County 1988).

[8]Battler v. Battler, 1990 WL 118697 (Ohio Ct. App. 8th Dist. Cuyahoga County 1990).

[9]Evid. R. 701; Construction and effect of provisions of will relied upon as affecting the burden of taxation, 37 A.L.R.2d 7 (secs. 39-52 superseded by Construction and effect of will provisions not expressly mentioning payment of death taxes but relied on as affecting the burden of estate or inheritance taxes, 70 A.L.R.3d 630).. Brookhart v. Brookhart, 1993 WL 483206 (Ohio Ct. App. 4th Dist. Athens County 1993); Stout v. Stout, 1993 WL 140494 (Ohio Ct. App. 7th Dist. Columbiana County 1993).

[10]Henry v. Serey, 46 Ohio App. 3d 93, 546 N.E.2d 474 (1st Dist. Hamilton County 1989) (overruled by, Dunn v. Westlake, 1990 WL 59262 (Ohio Ct. App. 1st Dist. Hamilton County 1990)) and (disapproved of by, Dunn v. Westlake, 61 Ohio St. 3d 102, 573 N.E.2d 84 (1991)) and (disapproved of by, United Methodist Church of Berea v. Dunlop Const. Products, Inc., 1992 WL 80054 (Ohio Ct. App. 8th Dist. Cuyahoga County 1992)); Hess v. Riedel-Hess, 153 Ohio App. 3d 337, 2003-Ohio-3912, 794 N.E.2d 96 (10th Dist. Franklin County 2003).

[11]Mark B. Bober, *Applying Minority Discounts in Family Law Cases*, 14 Dom. Rel. J. Ohio 1 (January/February 2002); Entingh v. Entingh, 2008-Ohio-756, 2008 WL 498978 (Ohio Ct. App. 2d Dist. Montgomery County 2008).

§ 12:29 Valuation date

The date of valuation of property in a divorce case will vary according to the equities.[1] Prior to RC 3105.171, courts held that date of separation is a more[2] or less[3] equitable date on which to terminate the marriage *de facto* and value the marital property. However, RC 3105.171(A)(2) provides that the date of divorce hearing is determinative unless a different date is expressly found to be equitable.[4]

Husband's unilateral vacation of the marital dwelling did not compel a finding that the marriage had terminated *de facto* as of date of separation. Such a termination must be clear and bilateral, such as is evidenced by the signing of a written separation agreement.[5] The contributions and equitable relations between husband and wife do not necessarily end upon their separation; each case must be decided upon its facts.[6]

The parties cannot pick and choose valuation dates for different items of marital property.[7] Where the trial court selects a variety of dates for valuation and it is not apparent from the record that any logical relationship exists among the duration of the marriage, the valuation dates, and the equities of the case, the court has committed an abuse of discretion.[8] However, where a court sets forth specific reasons, based on the evidence, that valuing certain assets as of different dates will result in a more equitable division, there is no abuse of discretion.[9]

Where all other property is valued approximately at date of hearing or separation, cash wrongfully withdrawn from a joint account and

---

[Section 12:29]

[1]See Text § 12:6, Statutory terms of art—During the marriage.

[2]Candler v. Candler, 1989 WL 2200 (Ohio Ct. App. 2d Dist. Montgomery County 1989); Howard v. Howard, 1989 WL 109745 (Ohio Ct. App. 2d Dist. Montgomery County 1989).

[3]Gerrard v. Gerrard, 1989 WL 68455 (Ohio Ct. App. 2d Dist. Clark County 1989); Frieden v. Frieden, 1990 WL 82299 (Ohio Ct. App. 8th Dist. Cuyahoga County 1990).

[4]See Text § 12:6, Statutory terms of art—During the marriage.

[5]Day v. Day, 40 Ohio App. 3d 155, 532 N.E.2d 201 (10th Dist. Franklin County 1988).

[6]Berish v. Berish, 69 Ohio St. 2d 318, 23 Ohio Op. 3d 296, 432 N.E.2d 183 (1982).

[7]Dabis v. Dabis, 1998 WL 391938 (Ohio Ct. App. 3d Dist. Mercer County 1998); Moll v. Moll, 1993 WL 210512 (Ohio Ct. App. 3d Dist. Wyandot County 1993).

[8]Landry v. Landry, 105 Ohio App. 3d 289, 663 N.E.2d 1026 (3d Dist. Auglaize County 1995).

[9]Green v. Green, 1998 WL 363840 (Ohio Ct. App. 4th Dist. Ross County 1998); DeWitt v. DeWitt, 2003-Ohio-851, 2003 WL 490928 (Ohio Ct. App. 3d Dist. Marion County 2003).

hidden or transferred will have the value which it had on the date of wrongful taking,[10] plus earnings, if the court deems it equitable.

Notwithstanding a long separation of the parties, property acquired during the separation may be designated marital by the court.[11] The unilateral separation of one spouse from the other may be sufficient reason for the court to classify property acquired after separation as marital.[12]

Where husband's complaint for legal separation was filed in 1992, the matter was not converted to a divorce until 1995, and the parties reconciled and resumed living together from November 1992 to June 1993, the trial court did not err in ruling that the termination of marriage occurred in 1995, the date of the divorce trial.[13]

Where a divorce trial began over six years following the date of the parties' separation, there was no attempt at reconciliation, and the parties maintained separate bank accounts, residences, and business activities, the trial court abused its discretion in valuing property as of date of trial, rather than de facto date of termination of the marriage, which was date of separation.[14]

It is error to omit a finding as to whether a marriage is terminated de facto as of date of separation, where evidence of such is advanced by one party.[15]

It is an abuse of discretion to designate a date of valuation which is so arbitrary that its significance with respect to the overall property division could not be determined on appeal.[16]

§ 12:30 Methods of distribution

It is within the discretion of the court, once property is valued, to determine how it must be divided. Certain types of property require

---

[10]Berish v. Berish, 69 Ohio St. 2d 318, 23 Ohio Op. 3d 296, 432 N.E.2d 183 (1982); Josselson v. Josselson, 52 Ohio App. 3d 60, 557 N.E.2d 835 (8th Dist. Cuyahoga County 1988); Guidubaldi v. Guidubaldi, 64 Ohio App. 3d 361, 581 N.E.2d 621 (11th Dist. Portage County 1990); Bachert v. Bachert, 1988 WL 134825 (Ohio Ct. App. 10th Dist. Franklin County 1988).

[11]Esenwein v. Esenwein, 1990 WL 187170 (Ohio Ct. App. 7th Dist. Columbiana County 1990); Nori v. Nori, 58 Ohio App. 3d 69, 568 N.E.2d 730 (12th Dist. Butler County 1989).

[12]Day v. Day, 1985 WL 10789 (Ohio Ct. App. 9th Dist. Lorain County 1985).

[13]Kohler v. Kohler, 1996 WL 455850 (Ohio Ct. App. 9th Dist. Lorain County 1996). But see Murphy v. Murphy, 1996 WL 629522 (Ohio Ct. App. 2d Dist. Montgomery County 1996).

[14]Gullia v. Gullia, 93 Ohio App. 3d 653, 639 N.E.2d 822 (8th Dist. Cuyahoga County 1994), cause dismissed, 70 Ohio St. 3d 1409, 637 N.E.2d 6 (1994).

[15]Connolly v. Connolly, 70 Ohio App. 3d 738, 591 N.E.2d 1362 (8th Dist. Cuyahoga County 1990).

[16]Peters v. Peters, 1992 WL 161450 (Ohio Ct. App. 1st Dist. Hamilton County 1992).

special treatment.[1] The court may deem it equitable to grant the residential parent the use of the marital home,[2] or to award the right to use marital or separate property for a reasonable time.[3] The court may decide which party must take liquid and illiquid assets according to the equities.[4]

Property may be divided in a manner which the court finds to be most conducive to the preservation and management of the property.[5] In *Indoe v. Indoe*,[6] the trial court properly distributed a family business to one spouse, reasoning that in this manner no dissention as to its operation would arise in the future to dissipate the value of the business. The ruling comports with RC 3105.171(F)(5), which directs the court to consider as a factor in its property division the economic desirability of keeping an asset intact.

A trial court may determine, within its discretion, that it would not be economically reasonable to order properties sold when the parties would realize little, if any, profit; an equitable division would be to award one parcel to each party.[7]

A trial court's "somewhat unique" order granting husband first option to purchase the marital residence from wife at a stated price, plus reasonable cost of wife's improvements, did not constitute an abuse of discretion.[8] In another instance, a trial court ordered that the wife's payment to the husband for his share of the property division be delayed, without interest, until 2002. The appellate court upheld the decision because an immediate payment would have required the wife to sell the marital home in which the minor children resided.[9]

A disproportionate award may compensate for financial misconduct.[10]

[Section 12:30]

[1] See Text §§ 12:18 to 12:26, Specific types of property.

[2] RC 3105.171(F)(3).

[3] RC 3105.171(J)(1).

[4] RC 3105.171(F)(4); Andras v. Andras, 1996 WL 157355 (Ohio Ct. App. 8th Dist. Cuyahoga County 1996); Weithman v. Weithman, 1995 WL 363760 (Ohio Ct. App. 3d Dist. Crawford County 1995).

[5] Barrett v. Barrett, 1989 WL 29415 (Ohio Ct. App. 10th Dist. Franklin County 1989).

[6] Indoe v. Indoe, 1993 WL 79534 (Ohio Ct. App. 9th Dist. Medina County 1993).

[7] Gray v. Gray, 1994 WL 695328 (Ohio Ct. App. 8th Dist. Cuyahoga County 1994).

[8] Underwood v. Underwood, 1995 WL 43624 (Ohio Ct. App. 5th Dist. Delaware County 1995).

[9] Arthur v. Arthur, 1998 WL 515911 (Ohio Ct. App. 5th Dist. Ashland County 1998).

[10] Loeffler v. Loeffler, 1998 WL 800951 (Ohio Ct. App. 6th Dist. Lucas County 1998); Leadingham v. Leadingham, 120 Ohio App. 3d 496, 698 N.E.2d 465 (12th Dist. Warren County 1997); Holmes v. Holmes, 1994 WL 68490 (Ohio Ct. App. 6th Dist. Erie County 1994).

A court has statutory authority to invade a spouse's separate property to bring about an equitable distribution of property.[11]

To bring about an equitable property division, it is within the court's discretion to order that future payments be made by a party who was granted an excess of the marital property; the court may require that a loan be taken to facilitate that order.[12] The trial court also has the discretion to assign a wife the entire burden of her student loan debt. Although the debt was marital, the result was equitable because the wife will benefit from the income generated as a result of the degree she obtained during the marriage.[13]

The trial court did not err in allocating approximately 90 percent of a joint tax liability to husband. While wife's claim as an innocent spouse was time barred as to the Internal Revenue Service, she did not waive that right with respect to husband. Husband had actively kept information regarding tax matters from wife.[14]

Credit card charges of about $40,000 incurred by wife after separation were correctly deemed marital debt where husband failed to pay court ordered temporary support payments. The credit charges were for legitimate household and family expenditures.[15]

An order requiring one party to assume a debt and save the other party absolutely harmless is an appropriate sanction for an offending party's financial misconduct.[16]

Trial court did not err in ordering husband to pay a portion of wife's credit card debt incurred solely in her name during the marriage. While husband may not have been aware of the exact amount of the credit card debt, he was aware that some of it existed and there was support in the record for the trial court's finding that husband in some manner acquiesced in the creation of the debt.[17]

The court also has the discretion to interpret and enforce its property division orders when later disagreements arise. In *Kincaid v. Kincaid*,[18] the parties' separation agreement provided that wife would receive a share of the "ultimate value" of the husband's retirement benefits. When the husband elected early retirement and received

---

[11]RC 3105.171(E); see Text § 12:5, Statutory terms of art—Distributive award.

[12]Bohlen v. Bohlen, 1990 WL 77106 (Ohio Ct. App. 9th Dist. Wayne County 1990), cause dismissed, 54 Ohio St. 3d 701, 560 N.E.2d 1318 (1990); RC 3105.171(J)(2).

[13]Webb v. Webb, 1998 WL 820838 (Ohio Ct. App. 12th Dist. Butler County 1998).

[14]Prohaska v. Prohaska, 2000 WL 530359 (Ohio Ct. App. 9th Dist. Medina County 2000).

[15]Glick v. Glick, 133 Ohio App. 3d 821, 729 N.E.2d 1244 (8th Dist. Cuyahoga County 1999).

[16]Forster v. Forster, 1999 WL 561522 (Ohio Ct. App. 8th Dist. Cuyahoga County 1999).

[17]Myers v. Myers, 2000 WL 331573 (Ohio Ct. App. 6th Dist. Lucas County 2000).

[18]Kincaid v. Kincaid, 117 Ohio App. 3d 148, 690 N.E.2d 47 (11th Dist. Ashtabula County 1997).

financial incentives as a result, the court awarded the wife a lump-sum percentage payment for her share. The husband appealed, but the trial court properly interpreted this provision to encompass special early retirement payment and not to be limited to what the husband would have received at normal retirement age.[19]

The court may order the sale of real estate to effect a property division.[20] It is an abuse of discretion to order real estate sold at auction without allowing the parties to make reasonable efforts to sell it at its fair market value.[21]

Contempt is an appropriate sanction for violation of a property division order.[22] Where a wife damaged items of personal property left in her possession, the trial court should have found her in contempt of court because her possession of the property constituted a bailment.[23]

A court may also design an order that ensures that its property division is carried out properly. One trial court ordered the wife's share of property division to be held in escrow until she paid the full amount of credit card debt she fraudulently incurred in both parties' names. Her claim that this order violated her right to file bankruptcy under federal law was rejected.[24] Another trial court ordered that escrowed marital funds be used to pay child support arrearages. This order was reversed in part, however, because it resulted in the support obligee effectively contributing one-half of the support arrearages. The court should have allocated the funds between the parties, and ordered the arrearage paid only from the support obligor's share.[25]

The trial court does not have jurisdiction to enter, as part of its divorce decree, an order restraining husband from transferring assets

---

[19]See also Mattice v. Mattice, 1998 WL 879208 (Ohio Ct. App. 2d Dist. Montgomery County 1998); Keeley v. Keeley, 1997 WL 411607 (Ohio Ct. App. 12th Dist. Clermont County 1997).

[20]Smith v. Smith, 1987 WL 8021 (Ohio Ct. App. 6th Dist. Sandusky County 1987); Savioli v. Savioli, 1996 WL 65854 (Ohio Ct. App. 8th Dist. Cuyahoga County 1996); RC 3105.171(J)(2).

[21]Van Fossen v. Van Fossen, 47 Ohio App. 3d 175, 547 N.E.2d 1237 (9th Dist. Summit County 1988).

[22]Weaver v. Weaver, 36 Ohio App. 3d 210, 522 N.E.2d 574 (4th Dist. Ross County 1987); Henry v. Serey, 46 Ohio App. 3d 93, 546 N.E.2d 474 (1st Dist. Hamilton County 1989) (overruled by, Dunn v. Westlake, 1990 WL 59262 (Ohio Ct. App. 1st Dist. Hamilton County 1990)) and (disapproved of by, Dunn v. Westlake, 61 Ohio St. 3d 102, 573 N.E.2d 84 (1991)) and (disapproved of by, United Methodist Church of Berea v. Dunlop Const. Products, Inc., 1992 WL 80054 (Ohio Ct. App. 8th Dist. Cuyahoga County 1992)); Miller v. Miller, 1993 WL 157705 (Ohio Ct. App. 3d Dist. Allen County 1993); Reedy v. Reedy, 1993 WL 385264 (Ohio Ct. App. 5th Dist. Richland County 1993) (party held in contempt for failure to appear at a coin-toss to decide fair division of personal property).

[23]Vandeventer v. Vandeventer, 132 Ohio App. 3d 762, 726 N.E.2d 534 (12th Dist. Butler County 1999).

[24]Lashley v. Lashley, 1999 WL 100334 (Ohio Ct. App. 5th Dist. Stark County 1999).

[25]Pickerel v. Pickerel, 1999 WL 173678 (Ohio Ct. App. 6th Dist. Sandusky County 1999).

post-decree.[26]

---

[26]RC 2727.03; Gullia v. Gullia, 93 Ohio App. 3d 653, 639 N.E.2d 822 (8th Dist. Cuyahoga County 1994), cause dismissed, 70 Ohio St. 3d 1409, 637 N.E.2d 6 (1994); Hudson v. Hudson, 1989 WL 154862 (Ohio Ct. App. 8th Dist. Cuyahoga County 1989).

Chapter 13

Spousal Support[*]

By Ann Weatherhead and Valerie Brandenberg[**]

---

[*]Updates for the 2007 through 2008–2009 pocket parts are attributed to Magistrate Ann Weatherhead.

[**]Based on the original work of Joel F. Sacco, Esq. and Michael R. Shanabruch, Esq.

Research References

Additional References

FinPlan's Divorce Planner CD-ROM

> **KeyCite®:** Cases and other legal materials listed in KeyCite Scope can be researched
> through the KeyCite service on Westlaw®. Use KeyCite to check citations for form,
> parallel references, prior and later history, and comprehensive citator information,
> including citations to other decisions and secondary materials.

---

§ 13:1 History of spousal support—Change in terminology

By virtue of 1990 House Bill 514,[1] all references to "alimony" have
been replaced throughout the Ohio Revised Code with the words
"spousal support," except in the limited circumstance of reflecting a
prior order using that term when referring to an allowance of money
or property which is not intended as a division of marital property.[2]

§ 13:2 History of spousal support—Development of alimony

In the past, alimony in Ohio included both support and division of
property, distinct concepts which can be traced historically.

In *Piatt v. Piatt*,[1] the Ohio Supreme Court stated that the authority
to grant alimony in this state was derived from sections five and
seven of the act concerning divorce and alimony.[2] The fifth section
provided that where a divorce was decreed in a case of the aggression
of the husband, the woman shall be restored to all her lands and tenements, and be allowed out of her husband's real and personal estate
such share as the court shall think reasonable. In *Piatt*, the Court
distinguished a restoration (lands and tenements held prior to the
marriage) from a transfer (of property from the husband's separate
estate).

As the statute concerning alimony was amended from time to time,
the distinction between division of property and support alimony

---

[Section 13:1]

[1]Eff. 1-1-91.

[2]RC 3105.18(A).

[Section 13:2]

[1]Piatt v. Piatt, 9 Ohio 37, 1839 WL 11 (1839).

[2]29 Ohio Laws 432.

became less discernible. In *Wolfe v. Wolfe*,[3] the Ohio Supreme Court recognized that "the monetary provision made for wives at divorce casts a mixed hue of 'alimony' and a division of property," thus taking note of the confusion in the statute. The *Wolfe* Court quoted from the 1876 case of *Tolerton v. Williard*,[4] where a division of property was deemed to be equitable and "not the less so that it is made under the name of alimony."[5]

> [W]hen the husband receives property of his wife by marriage, or converts his means into real estate, taking the title in his own name, or when the wife, from her industry, economy, and business capacity, contributes largely to the accumulation of a fortune, it is equitable and just that she should have a large share in such property, on divorce for the husband's fault.[6]

In *Soyk v. Soyk*,[7] however, the trial court made a division of the marital property, both real and personal, and ordered each party to pay and hold the other harmless from certain debts. The court characterized the judgment as a division of property rather than as alimony—an important distinction. At the time of the *Soyk* decision there was no statute acknowledging the general equity powers of common pleas courts in domestic relations cases, so they could only apportion assets on the basis of alimony. *Soyk* was reversed.

The legislature has since enacted RC 3105.011, which provides:

> The court of common pleas including divisions of courts of domestic relations, has *full equitable powers and jurisdiction appropriate to the determination of all domestic relations matters*. This section is not a determination by the general assembly that such equitable powers and jurisdiction do not exist with respect to any such matter. (Emphasis added.)

Prior to the passage of 1990 House Bill 514, which enacted RC 3105.171, the distinction between division of property and alimony for support had no practical purpose and was not readily apparent from the reading of a final decree.[8] Former RC 3105.18 had been construed as permitting both spousal support and division of property primarily because the legislature had not created separate designations for division of property and spousal support, having left the matter to be sorted out by the courts. The result was considerable confusion. *Wolfe* took cognizance of the problem but did not resolve it.

House Bill 514 took effect on January 1, 1991. The amendment to

---

[3]Wolfe v. Wolfe, 46 Ohio St. 2d 399, 411, 75 Ohio Op. 2d 474, 350 N.E.2d 413 (1976), superseded by statute as stated in Heslep v. Heslep, 2000 WL 818909 (Ohio Ct. App. 7th Dist. Monroe County 2000).

[4]Tolerton v. Williard, 30 Ohio St. 579, 1876 WL 213 (1876).

[5]Tolerton v. Williard, 30 Ohio St. 579, 587, 1876 WL 213 (1876), supra.

[6]Tolerton v. Williard, 30 Ohio St. 579, 587–88, 1876 WL 213 (1876), ibid.

[7]Soyk v. Soyk, 45 Ohio App. 2d 319, 74 Ohio Op. 2d 532, 345 N.E.2d 461 (9th Dist. Summit County 1975).

[8]See De Milo v. Watson, 166 Ohio St. 433, 2 Ohio Op. 2d 433, 143 N.E.2d 707 (1957).

RC 3105.18 and the enactment of RC 3105.171 constitute the heart of the bill. The primary purpose of House Bill 514 was to divide RC 3105.18, the former alimony statute, into two distinct statutes: one regarding property division—RC 3105.171, and one regarding spousal support—RC 3105.18.

§ 13:3 Necessity of a specific request for spousal support

While it is the better practice to make a specific request for spousal support in the complaint or counterclaim, and in a motion for temporary support, failure to do so is not usually a bar to an order for spousal support.

A demand for alimony was not a prerequisite to the granting of alimony under former RC 3105.18,[1] and a demand for insurance to protect alimony was not a prerequisite for the court to grant it.[2] Even where the defendant-appellee did not file a counterclaim for relief, the Ninth District Court of Appeals found that the prayer of plaintiff's complaint "for such other and further relief as is proper" vested the trial court with discretion to make an allowance for alimony to the defendant.[3] The Ohio Supreme Court held in *Bolinger v. Bolinger* that a trial court acquires subject matter jurisdiction to award spousal support and make a division of marital assets when either party files a complaint for divorce and for an equitable division of such assets.[4]

When the legislature amended RC 3105.18 on January 1, 1991, the drafters added the provision that the trial court may award spousal support "upon the request of either party."[5] While *Bolinger* was decided before RC 3105.18 was amended, the *Bolinger* Court's rationale should still apply. In fact, the Second District Court of Appeals in 1994 affirmed an award of spousal support where no specific request for support was made in the complaint, explaining that the complaint included a general request for "such other relief to which [the wife] may be entitled," and that the husband did not object to evidence of the wife's need for spousal support.[6] The most prudent course, however, is to include a specific request for spousal support in the

---

[Section 13:3]

[1]Bolinger v. Bolinger, 49 Ohio St. 3d 120, 551 N.E.2d 157 (1990).

[2]Stone v. Stone, 1988 WL 125020 (Ohio Ct. App. 4th Dist. Lawrence County 1988).

[3]Carr v. Carr, 46 Ohio App. 3d 132, syl., 546 N.E.2d 226 (9th Dist. Wayne County 1989). See also Garber v. Garber, 1988 WL 4319 (Ohio Ct. App. 2d Dist. Montgomery County 1988).

[4]Bolinger v. Bolinger, 49 Ohio St. 3d 120, 551 N.E.2d 157 (1990).

[5]RC 3105.18(B).

[6]Phillips v. Phillips, 1994 WL 179950, at *3 (Ohio Ct. App. 2d Dist. Montgomery County 1994). But see Woodland v. Woodland, 2007-Ohio-3503, p22, 2007 WL 1976667 (Ohio Ct. App. 7th Dist. Belmont County 2007), which held that the trial court lacked jurisdiction to order spousal support when it was not specifically requested and the opposing party was unaware that spousal support was an issue at trial.

complaint, and to file a motion for temporary spousal support when appropriate. (See section on temporary support below.) A Court may choose not to award spousal support, or may make a minimal award if insufficient evidence is elicited regarding whether a party seeking spousal support can meet his or her reasonable monthly expenses with the income he or she receives without an award of spousal support. A party seeking spousal support who is not forthcoming about his or her income is likely to have little success.[7]

Spousal support may be allowed in the form of real or personal property, or both, or as a sum of money, payable either in a lump sum or by installments or from future income.[8] Criteria for determining the nature of spousal support, the amount of a spousal support award, and the method of payment (in installments or "in gross") are set forth in RC 3105.18. The statute grants jurisdiction to the court of common pleas to determine the reasonableness and appropriateness of spousal support awards in both actions for divorce and legal separation proceedings.

The standard for an award of spousal support under amended RC 3105.18(C) is less strict than that contained in former RC 3105.18.[9] Former RC 3105.18(B) provided that the court must consider all factors, including the eleven listed in the statute, in determining whether alimony was "necessary." RC 3105.18(B), as amended, also requires the court to consider all relevant factors, including fourteen listed in the statute. However, the amended statute directs the trial court to determine not whether spousal support is "necessary," but whether spousal support is "appropriate and reasonable."

The court in *Chaudhry v. Chaudhry*[10] stated that spousal support may be appropriate and reasonable in cases where it is not necessary. Conversely, where spousal support is necessary, it will usually be found to be appropriate and reasonable.

Spousal support should not be confused or commingled with child support, which is an independent matter. Spousal support is property set aside for the specific and definite purpose of supporting and maintaining the former spouse.[11] The distinction may become blurred if, for example, one spouse is ordered to pay the mortgage at the home where the other spouse and the children are living.

---

[7]Vertrees v. Vertrees, 2007-Ohio-2604, 2007 WL 1536818 (Ohio Ct. App. 2d Dist. Clark County 2007); Rockne-Volpe v. Volpe, 2006-Ohio-6235, 2006 WL 3423408 (Ohio Ct. App. 5th Dist. Licking County 2006).

[8]RC 3105.18(B).

[9]Chaudhry v. Chaudhry, 1992 WL 74204 (Ohio Ct. App. 9th Dist. Summit County 1992). Young v. Young, 1993 WL 548765 (Ohio Ct. App. 9th Dist. Lorain County 1993); Simmons v. Simmons, 2002-Ohio-1386, 2002 WL 485769 (Ohio Ct. App. 8th Dist. Cuyahoga County 2002).

[10]Chaudhry v. Chaudhry, 1992 WL 74204 (Ohio Ct. App. 9th Dist. Summit County 1992).

[11]RC 3105.18(A); also see Moell v. Moell, 98 Ohio App. 3d 748, 649 N.E.2d 880 (6th Dist. Ottawa County 1994).

§ 13:4　Defenses to an order of spousal support

There are several defenses to actions for spousal support, e.g., invalidity of the marriage;[1] provision in an antenuptial agreement;[2] spouse's cohabitation[3] (while this is a defense to permanent spousal support, a court may grant temporary spousal support during the pendency of the action).

§ 13:5　Temporary support pendente lite—In general

The obligation to support a spouse is based on the marriage contract and on RC 3103.03, which requires a married person to support his or her spouse. Spousal support is an allowance for nourishment or sustenance which one spouse may be compelled to pay to the other when they are living apart or have been divorced. Spousal support is thus a substitute for support within the marriage relationship and an enforcement of a spouse's legal obligations of support under RC 3103.03. Unlike post decree spousal support awards, which must be "appropriate and reasonable" (See Text § 13:8, Appropriate and reasonable spousal support—In general.) the only guide for spousal support orders is that the award must be "reasonable."[1]

Spousal support pendente lite, or temporary spousal support, is support during the pendency of a divorce or annulment action or a legal separation proceeding. RC 3105.18(B) and Civil Rule 75(N) provide that the court may, for good cause shown, grant temporary spousal support to either of the parties for sustenance and expenses during the suit while the parties are still husband and wife. Permanent spousal support, on the other hand, is that support granted to a former spouse at the conclusion of such proceedings.

§ 13:6　Temporary support pendente lite—When granted

While spousal support pendente lite has traditionally been granted to the wife, Civil Rule 75(N) and RC 3105.18(B) indicate that it may

---

[Section 13:4]

[1]See Text Ch 7, Annulment.

[2]See Text Ch 1, Antenuptial Agreements.

[3]See Wolfe v. Wolfe, 46 Ohio St. 2d 399, 75 Ohio Op. 2d 474, 350 N.E.2d 413 (1976) (alimony modification sought based on payee-wife's cohabitation subsequent to alimony award), superseded by statute as stated in Heslep v. Heslep, 2000 WL 818909 (Ohio Ct. App. 7th Dist. Monroe County 2000). See also Text Ch 14, Modification of Spousal Support.

[Section 13:5]

[1]Keating v. Keating, 2008-Ohio-5345, 2008 WL 4599681, (Ohio Ct. App. 8th Dist. Cuyahoga County 2008), citing Cangemi v. Cangemi, 2006-Ohio-2879, 2006 WL 1555461, (Ohio Ct. App. 8th Dist. Cuyahoga County 2006).

be granted to either party. In fact, equal protection requires that provisions for spousal support be gender neutral.[1]

Temporary spousal support, also known as "temporary alimony" (a holdover from when spousal support was called alimony) or support pendente lite, is not a means of dividing the parties' property. Rather, it is a means of providing sustenance to an economically disadvantaged party during the pendency of the litigation.[2] The theory underlying the temporary spousal support award is that "there is manifest justice . . . which enables the party to a divorce litigation, who is without property or means, to secure funds to prepare and defend or assert rights at the expense of the other party who has property or means."[3] Further, a spouse is responsible for the support of the other, by virtue of the marriage relationship, until the divorce is granted.[4]

A party is not entitled to temporary spousal support as a matter of right.[5] Civil Rule 75(N)(1) provides that the court "may grant spousal support pendente lite." Whether an award should be made is within the sound discretion of the court, giving due consideration to the facts and circumstances of the case.[6]

There is no formula for determining the amount of money or property that will be awarded as temporary spousal support.[7] The court must use its discretion in determining an amount for reasonable support. The factors to be considered are the ability to pay of the party against whom the award is made and the present needs of the party in whose favor the award is given.[8] Present needs are to be

---

[Section 13:6]

[1]Orr v. Orr, 440 U.S. 268, 99 S. Ct. 1102, 59 L. Ed. 2d 306 (1979). See also Henry H. Foster, Jr., and Dorias Jonas Freed, Orr v. Orr, *The Decision That Takes Gender Out of Alimony*, 1 Fam. Advoc. 6 (Spring 1979).

[2]Civ. R. 75(M); Soley v. Soley, 101 Ohio App. 3d 540, 655 N.E.2d 1381 (6th Dist. Lucas County 1995).

[3]Smith v. Smith, 25 Ohio Op. 321, 323, 11 Ohio Supp. 5, 1943 WL 6271 (C.P. 1943).

[4]RC 3103.03(A).

[5]Stone v. Stone, 98 Ohio App. 240, 57 Ohio Op. 267, 122 N.E.2d 404 (8th Dist. Cuyahoga County 1954).

[6]Soley v. Soley, 101 Ohio App. 3d 540, 655 N.E.2d 1381 (6th Dist. Lucas County 1995); Stone v. Stone, 98 Ohio App. 240, 57 Ohio Op. 267, 122 N.E.2d 404 (8th Dist. Cuyahoga County 1954). See also Jackman v. Jackman, 1986 WL 6764 (Ohio Ct. App. 12th Dist. Madison County 1986) (no error to deny hearing on request for relief from temporary order when it was based on affidavit and hearing).

[7]Bair, *How Much Temporary Support is Enough?*, 1 Fam. Advoc. 36 (Spring 1979).

[8]RC 3105.18(B). See Norton v. Norton, 111 Ohio St. 262, 2 Ohio L. Abs. 137, 2 Ohio L. Abs. 628, 145 N.E. 253 (1924).

judged in relation to the standard of living of the parties prior to the time domestic difficulties occurred.[9]

Some appellate courts have suggested that trial courts should consider the factors outlined in RC 3105.18.[10] However, Civ. R. 75(N) does not expressly require so thorough an analysis of the parties' circumstances during the pretrial stage.[11]

Questions have been raised regarding the granting of temporary support when the party seeking support is alleged to be cohabitating or where the terms of an antenuptial agreement provide that no temporary support is to be paid.[12]

While most cases speak to situations where one seeks to terminate spousal support by reason of cohabitation, logic dictates that if cohabitation is grounds for modification or termination of spousal support, then it ought to be a bar to an original award.[13] Logic would also seem to dictate that if cohabitation sufficiently exists to terminate spousal support, it should be a bar to temporary support. Cohabitation of the party seeking temporary spousal support should be considered in the court's determination of granting such support to the degree that the party is being supported by the person with whom he or she is living.

In *Keeley v. Keeley*,[14] the court concluded that wife was cohabiting. It granted the husband's motion to terminate spousal support, filed in March 1999, retroactive to July 1, 1996, the date at which cohabitation commenced.

In affirming the trial court's factual determination of cohabitation and retroactive termination, the Twelfth District Court of Appeals made the following observation:

> When cohabitation is established, the obligation to pay spousal support can be properly terminated even if the relationship between the recipient spouse and the paramour comes to an end prior to the end of the pe-

---

[9]Stone v. Stone, 98 Ohio App. 240, 57 Ohio Op. 267, 122 N.E.2d 404 (8th Dist. Cuyahoga County 1954).

[10]Office v. Office, 1997 WL 18043 (Ohio Ct. App. 2d Dist. Montgomery County 1997); Biggs v. Biggs, 1996 WL 464163 (Ohio Ct. App. 6th Dist. Lucas County 1996); Nastasi v. Nastasi, 1996 WL 297015 (Ohio Ct. App. 11th Dist. Trumbull County 1996).

[11]The Court in Keating v. Keating, 2008-Ohio-5345, 2008 WL 4599681, (Ohio Ct. App. 8th Dist. Cuyahoga County 2008) cites to Cangemi v. Cangemi, 2006-Ohio-2879, 2006 WL 1555461, (Ohio Ct. App. 8th Dist. Cuyahoga County 2006) in making the distinction that temporary spousal support is to be "reasonable" whereas post decree spousal support is to be "appropriate and reasonable."

[12]For a discussion of the antenuptial issue, see Text Ch 1, Antenuptial Agreements.

[13]Vaughan v. Vaughan, 1995 WL 495933 (Ohio Ct. App. 5th Dist. Muskingum County 1995).

[14]Keeley v. Keeley, 2000 WL 431362, at *3 (Ohio Ct. App. 12th Dist. Clermont County 2000).

riod within which the former spouse is required to pay spousal support under the terms of the divorce decree.[15]

The court further noted that the termination of cohabitation cannot revive a spousal support obligation.

An award of temporary spousal support may include expenses for continued support such as housing, food, medical and dental costs, transportation, and attorney fees. Although the court may consider attorney fees in making an allowance for expense money, such allowance must be made to the party; it cannot be made directly to the attorney.[16] (See Text §§ 13:25 to 13:27, Attorney fees.)

§ 13:7 Temporary support pendente lite—Modification and termination

A trial court may not retroactively modify a temporary spousal support award in a final divorce decree in the absence of a motion to modify the temporary spousal support award. However, if a motion to modify is filed, then a trial court can retroactively modify a temporary spousal support award in a final divorce decree to the date the motion was filed.[1]

After a divorce, annulment, or legal separation decree has been granted, temporary spousal support is automatically terminated, with permanent spousal support (if any) substituted.[2] The recipient must be careful not to waive any accrued and unpaid arrearages. Unless the final decree specifies arrearages as due, they will be considered to have merged into the decree and will be uncollectible.[3]

---

[15]Keeley v. Keeley, 2000 WL 431362 (Ohio Ct. App. 12th Dist. Clermont County 2000).

[16]Beach v. Beach, 99 Ohio App. 428, 59 Ohio Op. 187, 134 N.E.2d 162 (2d Dist. Montgomery County 1955) (expenses include attorney fees but they must be paid to spouse); Reynolds v. Reynolds, 22 Ohio Op. 2d 162, 87 Ohio L. Abs. 250, 179 N.E.2d 160 (Ct. App. 4th Dist. Ross County 1961); Sinclair v. Sinclair, 98 Ohio App. 308, 57 Ohio Op. 347, 129 N.E.2d 311 (2d Dist. Preble County 1954); Stout v. Stout, 3 Ohio App. 3d 279, 445 N.E.2d 253 (1st Dist. Hamilton County 1982) (award of attorney fees in divorce action must be entered in favor of litigant, not directly in favor of litigant's attorney); see also Rust v. Takacs, 70 Ohio Misc. 2d 1, 650 N.E.2d 193 (Mun. Ct. 1994).

[Section 13:7]

[1]Lewis v. Lewis, 2008-Ohio-3342, 2008 WL 2609462 (Ohio Ct. App. 7th Dist. Jefferson County 2008) citing Ostmann v. Ostmann, 168 Ohio App. 3d 59, 2006-Ohio-3617, 858 N.E.2d 831 (9th Dist. Medina County 2006), footnote 11; and Didisse v. Didisse, 2004-Ohio-6811, 2004 WL 2914102, (Ohio Ct. App. 7th Dist. Belmont County 2004).

[2]Rahm v. Rahm, 39 Ohio App. 2d 74, 68 Ohio Op. 2d 225, 315 N.E.2d 495 (8th Dist. Cuyahoga County 1974).

[3]Colom v. Colom, 58 Ohio St. 2d 245, 12 Ohio Op. 3d 242, 389 N.E.2d 856 (1979).

Execution of a separation agreement which includes a mutual release of claims for support may constitute a waiver of arrearages accrued under a temporary support order.[4]

§ 13:8   Appropriate and reasonable spousal support—In general

In determining the nature, amount, terms of payment and duration of spousal support, RC 3105.18 directs the court to consider all relevant factors in each case. Effective January 1, 1991, separate statutory factors apply to the award of spousal support,[1] marital property,[2] and distributive awards.[3] In separating property division from support awards, formerly combined in RC 3105.18, the legislature distinguished the factors to be considered for each type of award, with some duplication of factors.

Strictly construed, RC 3105.18(C)(1) does not require a party seeking support to show that an award of support is necessary.[4] The Court in *Cooper v. Cooper*[5] explained the change eloquently as follows: "On January 1, 1991, the legislative changes to RC 3105.18 became effective. Significantly, with respect to spousal support determinations, the amended statute substituted the phrase 'appropriate and reasonable' for 'necessary.' The appropriate and reasonable standard is broader than the necessary standard that was applicable prior to the amendment of RC 3105.18. (citations omitted) Thus, while the 'need' for spousal support may be a factor in a given case, (citations omitted) a court cannot deny a request for spousal support solely on the basis that it is not 'needed' or 'necessary.'" Rather, the statute directs the trial court to use the broader standard of whether support is reasonable and appropriate. Although RC 3105.18 has been changed from requiring a determination as to whether spousal support is necessary to a determination as to whether spousal support is appropriate and reasonable, need continues to be a relevant consideration in that if a person needs spousal support it is likely to be appropriate

---

[4]Swanson v. Swanson, 48 Ohio App. 2d 85, 2 Ohio Op. 3d 65, 355 N.E.2d 894 (8th Dist. Cuyahoga County 1976).

[Section 13:8]

[1]RC 3105.18(B).

[2]RC 3105.171.

[3]RC 3105.171(E).

[4]The legislature amended RC 3105.18 effective January 1, 1991, and removed economic need as one of the factors for consideration in determining spousal support. Christescu v. Christescu, 2008-Ohio-3540, p28, 2008 WL 2764871, (Ohio Ct. App. 8th Dist. Cuyahoga County 2008), appeal not allowed, 120 Ohio St. 3d 1505, 2009-Ohio-361, 900 N.E.2d 623 (2009).

[5]Cooper v. Cooper, 2001 WL 969149 (Ohio Ct. App. 6th Dist. Lucas County 2001).

and reasonable to order spousal support.[6] However, the prior standard of "necessary" has been found to be a higher standard than "appropriate and reasonable."[7] Despite the change in the statute, references to "need" abound, often linking the factors which are in the statute with the concept of need.[8]

Awards of spousal support are not limited to meeting the needs of the obligee.[9] Large awards of spousal support have been affirmed by the courts of appeal on the basis that they are "appropriate and

---

[6]Simoni v. Simoni, 102 Ohio App. 3d 628, 657 N.E.2d 800 (8th Dist. Cuyahoga County 1995); Tomovcik v. Tomovcik, 1997 WL 28548 (Ohio Ct. App. 7th Dist. Jefferson County 1997); Carnahan v. Carnahan, 118 Ohio App. 3d 393, 692 N.E.2d 1086 (12th Dist. Clermont County 1997); Seagraves v. Seagraves, 1996 WL 185332 (Ohio Ct. App. 2d Dist. Montgomery County 1996). Some Courts hold that an award of spousal support "must be underpinned by proof of two matters: the obligee's need for support and the obligor's ability to pay." Shehata v. Shehata, 2005-Ohio-3659, 2005 WL 1685099 (Ohio Ct. App. 2d Dist. Montgomery County 2005), citing Murphy v. Murphy, 1996 WL 629522 (Ohio Ct. App. 2d Dist. Montgomery County 1996) and Layne v. Layne, 83 Ohio App. 3d 559, 615 N.E.2d 332 (2d Dist. Champaign County 1992). Others maintain that "need is not a basis for an award of spousal support." Geitgey v. Farnsworth, 2004-Ohio-6738, 2004 WL 2896424 (Ohio Ct. App. 9th Dist. Medina County 2004), citing Bowen v. Bowen, 132 Ohio App. 3d 616, 626, 725 N.E.2d 1165 (9th Dist. Medina County 1999) and Cronin v. Cronin, 2005-Ohio-301, 2005 WL 188191 (Ohio Ct. App. 2d Dist. Greene County 2005).

[7]Cooper v. Cooper, 2001 WL 969149 (Ohio Ct. App. 6th Dist. Lucas County 2001); Taylor v. Taylor, 1998 WL 904260 (Ohio Ct. App. 9th Dist. Summit County 1998).

[8]The Court in Williams-Booker v. Booker, 2007-Ohio-4717, 2007 WL 2685057 (Ohio Ct. App. 2d Dist. Montgomery County 2007) linked the statutory factors with the concepts of need and ability to pay as follows: "In determining whether spousal support is necessary and reasonable, and in determining the amount and duration of spousal support, the court must consider the factors in RC 3105.18(C)(1)(a) through (n) that are relevant. When applying those factors, the court must balance the needs of one party against the other's ability to pay." Williams-Booker v. Booker, supra, at para. 29. This construct has been adopted in other cases: Pelfrey v. Pelfrey, 2008-Ohio-3012, 2008 WL 2486338 (Ohio Ct. App. 2d Dist. Clark County 2008); Bagnola v. Bagnola, 2003-Ohio-5916, 2003 WL 22501764 (Ohio Ct. App. 5th Dist. Stark County 2003); Slobody v. Friedland-Slobody, 2008-Ohio-3395, 2008 WL 2635496 (Ohio Ct. App. 11th Dist. Geauga County 2008), appeal not allowed, 120 Ohio St. 3d 1422, 2008-Ohio-6166, 897 N.E.2d 655 (2008); Buchal v. Buchal, 2006-Ohio-3879, 2006 WL 2105508 (Ohio Ct. App. 11th Dist. Lake County 2006) (abrogated by, Mandelbaum v. Mandelbaum, 121 Ohio St. 3d 433, 2009-Ohio-1222, 905 N.E.2d 172 (2009)).

[9]Kracker v. Kracker, 2008-Ohio-3751, 2008 WL 2878325 (Ohio Ct. App. 5th Dist. Stark County 2008). Indeed, need is not a factor enumerated in the statute, therefore failing to consider need is not error. Pengov v. Pengov, 2003-Ohio-6755, 2003 WL 22952829 (Ohio Ct. App. 11th Dist. Geauga County 2003); McClellan v. McClellan, 2002-Ohio-6118, 2002 WL 31513584 (Ohio Ct. App. 9th Dist. Summit County 2002); Rukavina v. Rukavina, 2004-Ohio-4210, 2004 WL 1784590 (Ohio Ct. App. 5th Dist. Stark County 2004); Noll v. Noll, 2000 WL 727541 (Ohio Ct. App. 9th Dist. Lorain County 2000). However, need was deemed "a factor to consider" in DeChristefero v. DeChristefero, 2003-Ohio-3065, 2003 WL 21377611 (Ohio Ct. App. 11th Dist. Trumbull County 2003); Tinney v. Tinney, 2004-Ohio-1160, 2004 WL 445947 (Ohio Ct. App. 2d Dist. Montgomery County 2004); Brown v. Brown, 2003-Ohio-304, 2003 WL 164602 (Ohio Ct. App. 4th Dist. Pike County 2003).

reasonable."[10] The court must look to the obligor's ability to comply with a spousal support order. The court should apply the "reasonable and appropriate" standard to the circumstances of the obligor. "A key point to remember is that the issue is not just whether it would be reasonable and appropriate for the one seeking support to receive it but also whether it would be reasonable and appropriate for the other party to have to pay it."[11]

A party's obligations to pay college and automobile expenses for emancipated children are not mandated by law, and do not constitute an inability to pay spousal support. A court does not err in when it prioritizes the wife's needs over those of emancipated children.[12]

By statute, the court must divide the marital property before it addresses the question of spousal support.[13] In determining whether spousal support is appropriate and reasonable, the court must take into account, the value and type of assets being awarded in the property division, in addition to other relevant factors.[14]

The fourteen factors that must be considered when seeking spousal support under current RC 3105.18(C)(1) are as follows:

(a) The income of the parties, from all sources, including, but not limited to, income derived from property divided, disbursed, or distributed under RC 3105.171;

(b) The relative earning abilities of the parties;

(c) The ages and the physical, mental, and emotional conditions of the parties;

(d) The retirement benefits of the parties;

(e) The duration of the marriage;

(f) The extent to which it would be inappropriate for a party, because he will be custodian of a minor child of the marriage, to seek employment outside the home;

(g) The standard of living of the parties established during the marriage;

---

[10]Pruden v. Pruden, 1996 WL 697951 (Ohio Ct. App. 10th Dist. Franklin County 1996); McCoy v. McCoy, 91 Ohio App. 3d 570, 632 N.E.2d 1358 (8th Dist. Cuyahoga County 1993). See also Leslie Herndon Spillane, *Spousal Support: The Other Ohio Lottery*, 24 Ohio N.U. L. Rev. 281 (1998). A person will not be awarded spousal support if he has by his own actions limited his own income. Mullen v. Mullen, 1998 WL 391385 (Ohio Ct. App. 12th Dist. Warren County 1998). Coker v. Ulch, 166 Ohio App. 3d 778, 2006-Ohio-2349, 853 N.E.2d 358 (6th Dist. Lucas County 2006) (No error when trial court ordered wife to pay $200 per month spousal support to ex-husband who is completely disabled and eligible for SSI and Medicaid. Public policy dictates that Medicaid benefits are a last resort, not a device to shift the financial burden to taxpayers where spousal support is otherwise reasonable and necessary.).

[11]White v. White, 2003-Ohio-3279, 2003 WL 21447369 (Ohio Ct. App. 7th Dist. Columbiana County 2003).

[12]Richards v. Richards, 2001-Ohio-1707, 2001 WL 1346043 (Ohio Ct. App. 2d Dist. Montgomery County 2001).

[13]RC 3105.18(B).

[14]See discussion of RC 105.18(i) in Text § 13.19, The statutory factors—(i)—Relative assets and liabilities of the parties including court-ordered payments.

(h) The relative extent of education of the parties;

(i) The relative assets and liabilities of the parties, including but not limited to any court-ordered payments by the parties;

(j) The contribution of each party to the education, training, or earning ability of the other party, including, but not limited to, any party's contribution to the acquisition of a professional degree of the other party;

(k) The time and expense necessary for the spouse who is seeking spousal support to acquire education, training, or job experience so that the spouse will be qualified to obtain appropriate employment provided the education, training, or job experience, and employment is, in fact, sought;

(l) The tax consequences, for each party, of an award of spousal support;

(m) The lost income production capacity of either party that resulted from that party's marital responsibilities; and

(n) Any other factor that the court expressly finds to be relevant and equitable.

The trial court must now divide property before it considers the issue of spousal support.[15] Once the property is divided, the court must determine whether an award of spousal support is reasonable and appropriate, in light of the property division.[16] Therefore, if the division of property is remanded, the trial court must revisit its spousal support order.[17]

RC 3105.18(C)(1)(a) requires the court to consider income that will be derived from the property award to either party as part of the property division. To the extent that property is non-income producing, it is not a factor to be considered under paragraph (a). Non-income producing property should be considered pursuant to paragraph (i), which relates to the relative assets and liabilities of the parties.

In an initial award of spousal support, as opposed to a modification, the court must consider all the factors enumerated in RC 3105.18(C)(1).[18] In paragraph 2 of its syllabus in *Kaechele v. Kaechele*,[19] the Supreme Court held that "in making an award of sustenance alimony, the trial court must indicate the basis for its award in sufficient detail to enable a reviewing court to determine that the award

---

[15]RC 3105.18(B).

[16]RC 3105.18(A), (C).

[17]Smith v. Smith, 182 Ohio App. 3d 375, 2009-Ohio-2326, 912 N.E.2d 1170 (2d Dist. Greene County 2009).

[18]Kucmanic v. Kucmanic, 119 Ohio App. 3d 609, 695 N.E.2d 1205 (8th Dist. Cuyahoga County 1997); Mizenko v. Mizenko, 2001 WL 637563 (Ohio Ct. App. 8th Dist. Cuyahoga County 2001).

[19]Kaechele v. Kaechele, 35 Ohio St. 3d 93, 518 N.E.2d 1197 (1988), superseded by statute as stated in Heslep v. Heslep, 2000 WL 818909 (Ohio Ct. App. 7th Dist. Monroe County 2000).

is fair, equitable and in accordance with the law." This requirement to identify the factors behind an award also should apply to a court's denial of spousal support.[20]

A trial court may be found to err if it issues a spousal support award but fails to specify its consideration of the statutory factors under RC 3105.18. In *Stafinsky v. Stafinsky*,[21] the court's order stated simply that it considered those factors, but did not specify anything about its consideration. The matter was remanded to the trial court for indication of the basis of the spousal support award.

The trial court should make a record of the basis of its spousal support award in compliance with *Kaechele*, however, it need not make findings of fact unless they are requested by a party pursuant to Civ. R. 52. The decision must contain sufficient information to allow a reviewing court to assess the equity of the spousal support award.[22] If there has been no request for findings of fact, a court of appeals is less likely to reverse a trial court because the statutory factors were insufficiently examined.[23] Courts of Appeal range widely in the degree to which they require a trial court to show its consideration of the statutory factors in support of its decisions regarding spousal support. On one extreme, if the trial court says it referred to the factors, and there is no indication that it did not do so, the Court of Appeals will take the trial court at its word.[24] The other extreme not only requires the trial court to refer to the factors, but requires it to evaluate the evidence in light of those factors.[25] If the decision shows facts which support the spousal support award, courts of appeal will rarely reverse the decision solely on the basis that the decision lacks an explicit reference to the statutory factors.[26]

Common pleas judges should be aware of the current practices of

---

[20]Oxyer v. Oxyer, 1993 WL 98038 (Ohio Ct. App. 4th Dist. Gallia County 1993); Kerstetter v. Kerstetter, 1993 WL 98040 (Ohio Ct. App. 4th Dist. Lawrence County 1993).

[21]Stafinsky v. Stafinsky, 116 Ohio App. 3d 781, 689 N.E.2d 112 (11th Dist. Portage County 1996).

[22]Shepherd v. Shepherd, 1995 WL 517051 (Ohio Ct. App. 8th Dist. Cuyahoga County 1995); Clendening v. Clendening, 2005-Ohio-6298, 2005 WL 3150321 (Ohio Ct. App. 5th Dist. Stark County 2005).

[23]Hesseling v. Hesseling, 2009-Ohio-3116, 2009 WL 1830787 (Ohio Ct. App. 4th Dist. Ross County 2009).

[24]Babka v. Babka, 83 Ohio App. 3d 428, 615 N.E.2d 247 (9th Dist. Summit County 1992); Combs v. Combs, 2009-Ohio-1683, 2009 WL 943965 (Ohio Ct. App. 5th Dist. Stark County 2009); Meeks v. Meeks, 2008-Ohio-2015, 2008 WL 1886315 (Ohio Ct. App. 10th Dist. Franklin County 2008); Rodehaver v. Rodehaver, 2009-Ohio-329, 2009 WL 190400 (Ohio Ct. App. 10th Dist. Franklin County 2009).

[25]Branden v. Branden, 2009-Ohio-866, 2009 WL 478383 (Ohio Ct. App. 8th Dist. Cuyahoga County 2009).

[26]Whitmill v. Whitmill, 1997 WL 435703 (Ohio Ct. App. 2d Dist. Montgomery County 1997); Hoffman v. Hoffman, 1999-Ohio-797, 1999 WL 446422 (Ohio Ct. App. 3d Dist. Union County 1999); Taylor v. Taylor, 2006-Ohio-1925, 2006 WL 1029785 (Ohio Ct. App. 8th Dist. Cuyahoga County 2006); Clendening v. Clendening, 2005-Ohio-6298, 2005 WL 3150321 (Ohio Ct. App. 5th Dist. Stark County 2005). But

the appellate courts, which closely scrutinize and sometimes reverse spousal support awards based on mathematical formulae,[27] preferring orders that include a consideration of all the factors listed in RC 3105.18(C).[28] Spousal support determined as a percentage of a payor spouse's income is not favored.[29] In *Kunkle v. Kunkle*,[30] the Ohio Supreme Court held that "absent an agreement between payor and payee spouses, it is improper to include in an award of sustenance alimony a clause requiring the payor to pay alimony based on a fixed

---

see Cooper v. Cooper, 2002-Ohio-7105, 2002 WL 31846267 (Ohio Ct. App. 6th Dist. Lucas County 2002) (the trial court must demonstrate that it considered all of the statutory factors). See also, Kennedy v. Kennedy, 2003-Ohio-1078, 2003 WL 931766 (Ohio Ct. App. 7th Dist. Columbiana County 2003). It is insufficient for the court only to consider the income of the parties and not address any other factor in making its spousal support order. Stychno v. Stychno, 1995 WL 815518 (Ohio Ct. App. 11th Dist. Trumbull County 1995). Hayman v. Hayman, 2003-Ohio-76, 2003 WL 103413 (Ohio Ct. App. 12th Dist. Butler County 2003).

The court's decision must provide some illumination of the facts and reasoning which form the basis of its spousal support award. Stafinsky v. Stafinsky, 116 Ohio App. 3d 781, 689 N.E.2d 112 (11th Dist. Portage County 1996). The trial court must "indicate the basis for its award in sufficient detail to enable a reviewing court to determine whether the award was fair, equitable, and in accordance with the law." White v. White, 2003-Ohio-3279, 2003 WL 21447369 (Ohio Ct. App. 7th Dist. Columbiana County 2003), a spousal support case, citing Heslep v. Heslep, 2000 WL 818909 (Ohio Ct. App. 7th Dist. Monroe County 2000), a property division case.

In addition to citing evidence relevant to the factors, the trial court must explain the basis for its spousal support award. Henderson v. Henderson, 2002-Ohio-2720, 2002 WL 1299770 (Ohio Ct. App. 3d Dist. Mercer County 2002). The trial court must consider all of the factors, however it need not enumerate all of the factors. DeWitt v. DeWitt, 2003-Ohio-851, 2003 WL 490928 (Ohio Ct. App. 3d Dist. Marion County 2003), McConnell v. McConnell, 2000 WL 126730 (Ohio Ct. App. 8th Dist. Cuyahoga County 2000). Reference to some of the statutory factors and how they apply to the spousal support awarded will usually be deemed sufficient by a reviewing court. Earnest v. Earnest, 151 Ohio App. 3d 682, 2003-Ohio-704, 785 N.E.2d 766 (11th Dist. Portage County 2003). "A trial court's decision not to acknowledge all evidence relative to each and every factor listed in R.C. 3105.18(C)(1) does not necessarily mean the evidence was not considered." Miller v. Miller, 2004-Ohio-6141, 2004 WL 2635595 (Ohio Ct. App. 5th Dist. Stark County 2004).

[27]Cherry v. Cherry, 66 Ohio St. 2d 348, 20 Ohio Op. 3d 318, 421 N.E.2d 1293 (1981); Kaechele v. Kaechele, 1986 WL 13922 (Ohio Ct. App. 10th Dist. Franklin County 1986), judgment aff'd and remanded, 35 Ohio St. 3d 93, 518 N.E.2d 1197 (1988); Kunkle v. Kunkle, 51 Ohio St. 3d 64, 554 N.E.2d 83 (1990); Manley v. Manley, 2005-Ohio-129, 2005 WL 78500 (Ohio Ct. App. 2d Dist. Montgomery County 2005). However noting that a spousal support award approaches an equalization of income is appropriate when made in addition to findings on the statutory factors. Flesher v. Flesher, 2004-Ohio-6267, 2004 WL 2674622 (Ohio Ct. App. 9th Dist. Summit County 2004).

[28]Spayd v. Spayd, 1979 WL 208507 (Ohio Ct. App. 2d Dist. Montgomery County 1979) (appellate court found abuse of discretion for trial court not to consider all factors listed in RC 3105.18).

[29]Okey v. Okey, 2001 WL 830441 (Ohio Ct. App. 5th Dist. Stark County 2001); Burner v. Burner, 2000-Ohio-6606, 2000 WL 1533898 (Ohio Ct. App. 9th Dist. Summit County 2000); Edwards v. Edwards, 1991 WL 163651 (Ohio Ct. App. 4th Dist. Jackson County 1991).

[30]Kunkle v. Kunkle, 51 Ohio St. 3d 64, 554 N.E.2d 83 (1990).

percentage of the payor's income, gross or otherwise, when the award is in the form of a penalty or is not based on the payee's need." In *Robiner v. Robiner*,[31] the Eighth District court held that a provision of a spousal support order which required the payor to pay a certain percentage of any income over $100,000 to be reversible error because such an award "is speculative as to the needs of defendant-appellee and deprives the trial court the opportunity to determine if a change in the parties' circumstances would require a modification in the spousal support award." While the court must consider all relevant factors, this does not mean that it must make detailed findings as to each factor vis-a-vis the total award.[32]

Attorneys should conduct their own investigation of the "18(C)" factors and present all relevant factors when they ask for or defend against a spousal support award, be it temporary or permanent.[33] Since the court may make temporary orders on the basis of affidavits,[34] and there often is no hearing on the "18(C)" factors, local court guidelines may be consulted for a practical compromise on emergency support, reserving argument on the "18(C)" factors for the permanent spousal support hearing. Of course, either party may request an oral hearing to modify the temporary spousal support award, and a hearing will then be held on that request.[35] Where a final decree reflects the automatic use of a percentage of income guideline, the award may be challenged.[36]

Yokley v. Yokley[37] involved a dispute over the disposition of alimony, support, and division of property. Mrs. Yokley asserted that the trial court had abused its discretion in resolving these issues. The First District Court of Appeals upheld the trial court's judgment. The appellate court noted that "the position in which she stood was predicated . . . upon the belief that she was entitled to be supported fully by Mr. Yokley, that the court would order him to do so and that she was needed in the home by the children when they returned from school."[38]

---

[31]Robiner v. Robiner, 1995 WL 723269 (Ohio Ct. App. 8th Dist. Cuyahoga County 1995).

[32]Stetler v. Stetler, 6 Ohio App. 3d 29, 452 N.E.2d 344 (3d Dist. Mercer County 1982) (court not required, as to any single factor, to make award based on evidence on that factor, when applying broad discretion to all relevant factors); Lamb v. Lamb, 2002-Ohio-1055, 2002 WL 370037 (Ohio Ct. App. 11th Dist. Portage County 2002).

[33]Hutson v. Hutson, 68 Ohio L. Abs. 131, 120 N.E.2d 618 (C.P. 1954).

[34]Civ. R. 75(N)(1).

[35]Civ. R. 75(N)(2).

[36]Cherry v. Cherry, 66 Ohio St. 2d 348, 20 Ohio Op. 3d 318, 421 N.E.2d 1293 (1981).

[37]Yokley v. Yokley, 1985 WL 6709, at *3–4 (Ohio Ct. App. 1st Dist. Hamilton County 1985).

[38]Yokley v. Yokley, 1985 WL 6709 (Ohio Ct. App. 1st Dist. Hamilton County 1985).

In *Flexman v. Flexman*,[39] the Second District Court of Appeals discussed the practice of awarding limited support alimony to mothers with custody of young children.

[T]he right of the wife to alimony has eroded in recent years because of changes in the status of women and their entrance into the labor market. These changes [have] intensified the already complex problem where the parties have children of tender age for whom a home must be maintained. Allowances for child suport [sic] do not alone fill the bill when children are so young as to make employment outside the home by the custodian impossible, inappropriate, or if they create a condition below the level which such children have experienced. The issue in such cases is not how soon the custodian will readjust and become capable of earning an income; the question is when such spouse may do so under conditions that safely and adequately provide for the welfare of the children according to the standard that the parents have provided in the past.

The point to be made is that the acceptance of a readjustment period of years for the termination of support alimony for a spouse without children or a spouse with older children should not be the same as where one or more issue of the marriage requires constant or more frequent care and attention than can be provided by an employed and absent parent.

The statute states that the court "shall consider all relevant factors," including those listed, indicating that the list is inclusive rather than exclusive. Although RC 3105.18 neither expressly includes nor expressly excludes fault, it is generally accepted that fault is no longer a primary factor in determining whether to award spousal support. In *Lemon v. Lemon*[40] the Fourth District Court of Appeals explained that RC 3105.18 does not require the trial court to consider fault, and that the trial court's failure to take fault into consideration was not an abuse of discretion. Of course, this does not mean that the court may not consider fault. In fact, fault is sometimes considered as a "factor that the court expressly finds to be relevant" pursuant to RC 3105.18(C)(1)(n).[41] Fault may not be the sole basis for an award of spousal support, however.[42]

Two cases have addressed the question of when a prospective

---

[39]Flexman v. Flexman, 1985 WL 8075., at *3–4 (Ohio Ct. App. 2d Dist. Montgomery County 1985) (four-year alimony award subject to further order of court).

[40]Lemon v. Lemon, 42 Ohio App. 3d 142, 537 N.E.2d 246 (4th Dist. Hocking County 1988).

[41]See Becker v. Becker, 1993 WL 358147 (Ohio Ct. App. 12th Dist. Clermont County 1993) (trial court may consider party's criminal conviction as martial fault in making award of spousal support); Esteb v. Esteb, 173 Ohio St. 259, 19 Ohio Op. 2d 80, 181 N.E.2d 462 (1962); Tennent v. Tennent, 1976 WL 188859 (Ohio Ct. App. 9th Dist. Wayne County 1976) (trial court not precluded from considering aggression in determining support); Brulin v. Brulin, 1978 WL 216048 (Ohio Ct. App. 11th Dist. Lake County 1978) (court may consider aggression in determining alimony award).

[42]See Becker v. Becker, 1993 WL 358147 (Ohio Ct. App. 12th Dist. Clermont County 1993) (trial court may consider party's criminal conviction as martial fault in making award of spousal support); Baker v. Baker, 1984 WL 6439 (Ohio Ct. App. 11th Dist. Lake County 1984); Fisher v. Fisher, 1984 WL 6412 (Ohio Ct. App. 11th Dist. Lake County 1984).

spousal support recipient's position should be evaluated. Both held that the time of the award is the appropriate time. In *Savalan v. Savalan*,[43] the Ninth District Court of Appeals held that where four years lapse between separation and divorce, it is error for a trial court not to consider post-separation income in determining spousal support at the time of the divorce.

In *Adler v. Adler*,[44] the Eleventh District Court of Appeals held that it was error for a trial court to award spousal support to a wife when there was no evidence presented of her current living expenses at the time the award was made.

§ 13:9 The statutory factors—(a)—Income of the parties

The first factor listed under RC 3105.18(C)(1), the income of the parties from all sources, including from property division under RC 3105.171 was not a part of former RC 3105.18.

Often, it is difficult to determine what constitutes a party's income for purposes of a spousal support order. In *Freeland v. Freeland*,[1] the Court stated, "Neither the Revised Code nor case law fully defines 'income' for purposes of awarding spousal support. Thus, a trial court appears to possess discretion in determining what constitutes 'income.'" In that court's view, "a trial court should typically use the figures shown on a party's annual income tax return. . . If a trial court chooses not to use a party's annual income tax return in assessing 'income' the court should explain its reasons."[2]

This factor should not be confused with the second factor listed under RC 3105.18(C), the relative earning abilities of the parties. The present income of a party may or may not be the same as a party's earning ability. In cases where a party is underpaid or underemployed, it may be that the earning ability is greater than the present income from all sources. In this situation, counsel should be prepared to argue that income should be imputed to the unemployed or underemployed party. On the other hand, it is also possible that one's income from all sources, including property divided, disbursed, or distributed under RC 3105.171, is presently greater than the earning ability in general. If this is the case, the court should be made aware of such

---

[43]Savalan v. Savalan, 1985 WL 10708 (Ohio Ct. App. 9th Dist. Summit County 1985).

[44]Adler v. Adler, 1985 WL 9947 (Ohio Ct. App. 11th Dist. Lake County 1985) (wife did not present evidence or appear at alimony hearing).

[Section 13:9]

[1]Freeland v. Freeland, 2003-Ohio-5272, 2003 WL 22272603 (Ohio Ct. App. 4th Dist. Jackson County 2003).

[2]*Freeland, supra,* quoted in Taub v. Taub, 2009-Ohio-2762, 2009 WL 1653823 (Ohio Ct. App. 10th Dist. Franklin County 2009).

fact why the party's earning ability is actually less than his or her present income.[3]

The 2nd District Court of Appeals established a three prong test as to whether retained earnings should be included in a party's income for support purposes: First, whether the party exercises sufficient control over the decision to distribute earnings, second, whether the party is using the company to shelter income, and third, whether there is a legitimate business reason for retaining the earnings.[4]

A significant disparity in the parties' incomes, standing alone, will not always result in an award of spousal support. In *Hess v. Riedel-Hess*,[5] the Tenth District Court of Appeals affirmed the trial court's decision not to award the husband spousal support when he earned $37,000 and his wife earned $95,000. The court looked to the short duration of the marriage, the fact that the husband's after-tax income exceeded his stated expenses by $4,000, and the fact that his housing costs were paid as a part of his employment.

Income from property previously divided, disbursed, or distributed under RC 3105.171 is specifically mentioned as income to be considered in an award of spousal support. The court must be provided evidence as to whether the divided assets are income-producing in order to make a spousal support award.[6]

Sufficient income-producing assets may, therefore, be awarded to a party to obviate the need for spousal support, but this factor must be considered by the court in conjunction with the other statutory factors to determine if an award of spousal support is appropriate and reasonable. In any attempt to arrive at a division of property that would impact the income of the parties, counsel must consider RC 3105.171(C)(3), which states that the court must provide for an equitable property division prior to making any award of spousal support and without regard to any spousal support so awarded.

The statute requires that income from all sources must be considered in determining spousal support.[7] Thus, any bonus which a party is

---

[3]See Text § 13:10, Statutory factors—(b)—Relative earning abilities of the parties.

[4]Ulliman v. Ulliman, 2008-Ohio-3876, 2008 WL 2942213 (Ohio Ct. App. 2d Dist. Montgomery County 2008), appeal not allowed, 120 Ohio St. 3d 1488, 2009-Ohio-278, 900 N.E.2d 198 (2009).

[5]Hess v. Riedel-Hess, 153 Ohio App. 3d 337, 2003-Ohio-3912, 794 N.E.2d 96 (10th Dist. Franklin County 2003).

[6]Warner v. Warner, 1991 WL 3858 (Ohio Ct. App. 2d Dist. Miami County 1991).

[7]It may be error to include child support received by a new wife for a step-child as income. Duvall v. Duvall, 2005-Ohio-4685, 2005 WL 2173120 (Ohio Ct. App. 7th Dist. Belmont County 2005). In determining a spousal support obligation of a spouse who has full time employment and is working a second job, a court may decline to consider income from the second job when it makes a spousal support order. Justice v. Justice, 2007-Ohio-5186, 2007 WL 2821794 (Ohio Ct. App. 12th Dist. Warren County 2007). It was error to consider the husband's girlfriend's income, even though they lived together, absent evidence that the husband received income or support

guaranteed to receive must be taken into account.[8] Also, while the expectancies and inheritances of the parties have been deleted from the list of specifically enumerated factors to be considered by the court,[9] and while RC 3105.171 categorizes an inheritance by one party as separate property,[10] income that a party receives from inherited property should be considered when determining spousal support. Similarly, income from a pension, even if that pension has been divided between the parties by a QDRO or otherwise, should be considered by the court in determining the reasonableness and appropriateness of an award of spousal support.[11] The Ninth District Court of Appeals held that a trial court did not err in calculating spousal support award by including the husband's V.A. disability and Social Security benefits in determining his income.[12] The Tenth District Court of Appeals held that income property awarded under RC 3105.171 is a factor that must be considered under RC 3105.18(C).[13]

In determining the amount of spousal support and the income available to pay the support, the court may include income from nonmarital property.[14] Although the court is to consider income from all sources, including income derived from the property allocated, there is no

---

from her. Bell v. Bell, 2008-Ohio-4174, 2008 WL 3845258, (Ohio Ct. App. 5th Dist. Fairfield County 2008).

[8]Kaechele v. Kaechele, 1986 WL 13922 (Ohio Ct. App. 10th Dist. Franklin County 1986), judgment aff'd and remanded, 35 Ohio St. 3d 93, 518 N.E.2d 1197 (1988).

[9]See former RC 3105.18(B)(4).

[10]RC 3105.171(A)(6)(a)(i).

[11]Lindsay v. Curtis, 115 Ohio App. 3d 742, 686 N.E.2d 313 (12th Dist. Butler County 1996). Income from a non-marital asset should be considered in the calculation of a spousal support award. Williams-Booker v. Booker, 2007-Ohio-4717, 2007 WL 2685057 (Ohio Ct. App. 2d Dist. Montgomery County 2007). In Crites v. Crites, 2004-Ohio-6162, 2004 WL 2634627 (Ohio Ct. App. 6th Dist. Wood County 2004), the husband's Veterans' Administration disability pension was earned prior to the marriage, but was a factor in determining his spousal support obligation. In Pelfrey v. Pelfrey, 2008-Ohio-3012, 2008 WL 2486338 (Ohio Ct. App. 2d Dist. Clark County 2008), the trial court noted that although disability income is separate property for purposes of property division, the Court may consider the disability income for purposes of establishing a spousal support order.

[12]Cardone v. Cardone, 1998 WL 224934 (Ohio Ct. App. 9th Dist. Summit County 1998). A party's military Basic Allowance for Subsistence (BAS) and Basic Allowance for Subsistence (BAQ) should be considered as income in determining spousal support. Avery v. Avery, 2003-Ohio-4975, 2003 WL 22159477 (Ohio Ct. App. 2d Dist. Greene County 2003); Simpson v. Simpson, 2007-Ohio-224, 2007 WL 136626 (Ohio Ct. App. 12th Dist. Clermont County 2007) Obligor's income consisted of Social Security benefits.

[13]Thomas v. Thomas, 1999 WL 252483 (Ohio Ct. App. 10th Dist. Franklin County 1999).

[14]Kilcoyne v. Kilcoyne, 1996 WL 86586 (Ohio Ct. App. 8th Dist. Cuyahoga County 1996); Simmons v. Simmons, 1996 WL 297003 (Ohio Ct. App. 11th Dist. Trumbull County 1996) (nonmarital property may be considered by trial court when determining party's ability to pay spousal support). But see Heller v. Heller, 2008-Ohio-3296, 2008 WL 2588064 (Ohio Ct. App. 10th Dist. Franklin County 2008), appeal not

requirement that a party refinance or sell the marital home or any asset to exchange it for an investment to produce income.[15]

The court must have current and full information regarding the parties' earnings. An order of spousal support may be reversed where the court underestimates a party's income.[16] Where one spouse moves for relief from judgment under Civ. R. 60(B), alleging that the other spouse substantially misrepresented his or her income in a prior spousal support proceedings, the trial court errs in overruling the motion without an evidentiary hearing.[17]

§ 13:10   The statutory factors—(b)—Relative earning abilities of the parties

The section of the statute on child support permits income to be imputed to a parent for the purpose of determining child support. RC 3119.01(C)(11)(a).[1] The statutory section on spousal support is less explicit, however some courts have approved the imputation of income for the purpose of determining spousal support.[2]

The Tenth District Court of Appeals has explained that the " '[e]arn-

---

allowed, 120 Ohio St. 3d 1421, 2008-Ohio-6166, 897 N.E.2d 654 (2008). In that case, the Court of Appeals reversed the trial court's decision on the basis that it impermissibly "double dipped." The trial court divided the marital share of a business, whose value had been determined by capitalizing future earnings, then fashioned a spousal support award which ordered the husband to pay a percentage of the profits of that business. The Court of Appeals held that the trial court distributed the husband's interest in the company's future profits twice, once in a division of property, and again in its spousal support order.

[15]Frye v. Frye, 1994 WL 109708 (Ohio Ct. App. 10th Dist. Franklin County 1994); Mizenko v. Mizenko, 2001 WL 637563 (Ohio Ct. App. 8th Dist. Cuyahoga County 2001).

[16]Stefanidis v. Stefanidis, No. 9317 (Ohio Ct. App. 2d Dist. Montgomery County 1985); Gockstetter v. Gockstetter, 2000 WL 818985 (Ohio Ct. App. 6th Dist. Erie County 2000); Hayman v. Hayman, 2003-Ohio-76, 2003 WL 103413 (Ohio Ct. App. 12th Dist. Butler County 2003) (when one party's income is unsubstantiated).

[17]Offenberg v. Offenberg, 1998 WL 274511 (Ohio Ct. App. 8th Dist. Cuyahoga County 1998).

[Section 13:10]

[1]See Text § 19:7, Child support schedules.

[2]Collette v. Collette, 2001 WL 57179 (Ohio Ct. App. 9th Dist. Summit County 2001); Weller v. Weller, 2002-Ohio-7125, 2002 WL 31862681 (Ohio Ct. App. 11th Dist. Geauga County 2002); Motycka v. Motycka, 2001-Ohio-2162, 2001 WL 688886 (Ohio Ct. App. 3d Dist. Van Wert County 2001); Petrusch v. Petrusch, 1997 WL 102014 (Ohio Ct. App. 2d Dist. Montgomery County 1997); Miller v. Miller, 1993 WL 342805 (Ohio Ct. App. 6th Dist. Lucas County 1993); Ranz v. Ranz, 51 Ohio App. 3d 66, 554 N.E.2d 142 (1st Dist. Hamilton County 1988); Koch v. Koch, 2004-Ohio-7192, 2004 WL 3017316 (Ohio Ct. App. 9th Dist. Medina County 2004) (Court found that early retirement could be deemed voluntary underemployment if the party retired early to defeat the other party's claim to spousal support.). Justice v. Justice, 2007-Ohio-5186, 2007 WL 2821794 (Ohio Ct. App. 12th Dist. Warren County 2007); Williams-Booker v. Booker, 2007-Ohio-4717, 2007 WL 2685057 (Ohio Ct. App. 2d Dist. Montgomery County 2007). Income was imputed to the husband in Moore v. Moore, 2007-Ohio-4355, 2007 WL 2410543 (Ohio Ct. App. 12th Dist. Clermont County 2007) where

ing ability' involves both the amount of money one is capable of earning by his or her qualifications, as well as his or her ability to obtain such employment."[3] The statute neither requires actual employment nor does it make the failure to seek employment a determinative factor.[4] The Tenth District Court of Appeals held in *Cary v. Cary*[5] that "a previous earning ability remains the same whether or not employment is sought." The proper focus is on the amount of income a person "could have earned had he made the effort."[6]

There is no longer any question that, in Ohio, professional degrees and licenses are not marital assets,[7] and that earning ability is not a divisible marital asset. The earning capacity of a person possessing such a degree or license is, however, a factor to be considered by a court in awarding spousal support.[8] The value of a [professional practice, degree or license, such as a law practice,] is primarily in its earning capacity rather than as an asset to be divided.[9]

Mere disparity of earning potential alone, however, does not necessarily guarantee an award of spousal support. If, for example, a

---

there was evidence that he listed many of his personal expenses as business expenses and, as a result, had understated his income. A party will not be found to be voluntarily underemployed if her reduced income can be explained by exigent circumstances, for example, that she was working the equivalent of two jobs. Rothman v. Burns, 2007-Ohio-3914, 2007 WL 2206861 (Ohio Ct. App. 8th Dist. Cuyahoga County 2007). The Court will look to other factors, such as health or responsibilities for children to determine whether income should be imputed. Rotte v. Rotte, 2005-Ohio-6269, 2005 WL 3148086 (Ohio Ct. App. 12th Dist. Butler County 2005). Income should not be imputed to a spouse who had no significant employment outside the home during the parties' thirty-year marriage, and who devoted herself to raising the parties' children. Seaburn v. Seaburn, 2005-Ohio-4722, 2005 WL 2174632 (Ohio Ct. App. 5th Dist. Stark County 2005).

[3]Haninger v. Haninger, 8 Ohio App. 3d 286, 288, 456 N.E.2d 1228 (10th Dist. Franklin County 1982). In Ruiz-Bueno v. Ruiz-Bueno, 2008-Ohio-3747, 2008 WL 2875676 (Ohio Ct. App. 11th Dist. Lake County 2008) the Court estimated the obligor's income based on his earning history.

[4]Haninger v. Haninger, 8 Ohio App. 3d 286, 456 N.E.2d 1228 (10th Dist. Franklin County 1982); Bevan v. Bevan, 2006-Ohio-2775, 2006 WL 1519654 (Ohio Ct. App. 11th Dist. Lake County 2006).

[5]Cary v. Cary, 1989 WL 10362, at *2 (Ohio Ct. App. 10th Dist. Franklin County 1989).

[6]Cary v. Cary, 1989 WL 10362 (Ohio Ct. App. 10th Dist. Franklin County 1989); see also Miller v. Miller, No. 89-DR-690 (Ohio Ct. App. 2d Dist. Montgomery County 1994); Donerkiel v. Donerkiel, 1985 WL 11012 (Ohio Ct. App. 9th Dist. Lorain County 1985) (wife who had college degree and post-graduate preparation for CPA exam was found to be capable of supporting herself); Shroyer v. Shroyer, 2001-Ohio-1901, 2001 WL 1548749 (Ohio Ct. App. 5th Dist. Coshocton County 2001); Dahar v. Dahar, 1987 WL 20434 (Ohio Ct. App. 6th Dist. Lucas County 1987) (owner of a floral shop hired an employee rather than performing the work herself).

[7]Stevens v. Stevens, 23 Ohio St. 3d 115, 492 N.E.2d 131 (1986).

[8]Josselson v. Josselson, 52 Ohio App. 3d 60, 557 N.E.2d 835 (8th Dist. Cuyahoga County 1988).

[9]Josselson v. Josselson, 52 Ohio App. 3d 60, 557 N.E.2d 835 (8th Dist. Cuyahoga County 1988).

husband and wife have earning potentials of $100,000 and $50,000, respectively, spousal support will not necessarily be awarded. It is not necessary that an award of spousal support result in an equalization of earnings or earning abilities.[10]

It is not error, however, for the trial court to equalize the parties' incomes where there is a marriage of long duration and the court has considered all proper factors.[11] A finding that the parties' incomes would remain disparate for the foreseeable future, supplemented by other findings regarding training and experience, justified an award of spousal support.[12]

In considering the relative earning ability of the parties, the court may consider the potential income of the obligor spouse who became voluntarily unemployed from his profession, especially where he or she ceased performing his or her trade nearly simultaneously with the divorce action.[13]

The court may also consider the choices a party makes regarding employment and income, and how those decisions affect the parties. Where a husband chose to retire at age 53 while in good health, after 30 years in the automobile industry, his request for spousal support from his wife was properly rejected. She had stayed home to raise their children for most of the marriage and had been working full time for six years when he decided to quit his $60,000 per year job. The fact that wife's income from her employment became greater than husband's retirement benefits, a fact which he knew prior to retire-

---

[10]Kaechele v. Kaechele, 1986 WL 13922 (Ohio Ct. App. 10th Dist. Franklin County 1986), judgment aff'd and remanded, 35 Ohio St. 3d 93, 518 N.E.2d 1197 (1988).

[11]Sollberger v. Sollberger, 1993 WL 84546 (Ohio Ct. App. 9th Dist. Summit County 1993); DiNunzio v. DiNunzio, 2006-Ohio-3888, 2006 WL 2105500 (Ohio Ct. App. 11th Dist. Lake County 2006).

[12]Blatt v. Blatt, 1993 WL 106949 (Ohio Ct. App. 8th Dist. Cuyahoga County 1993).

[13]Gray v. Gray, 1994 WL 695328 (Ohio Ct. App. 8th Dist. Cuyahoga County 1994); Stockman v. Stockman, 2000 WL 1838937 (Ohio Ct. App. 6th Dist. Lucas County 2000) (husband deemed to be voluntarily unemployed, as he quit a job where "he was not respected"); Wagner v. Wagner, 2005-Ohio-226, 2005 WL 121662 (Ohio Ct. App. 5th Dist. Stark County 2005) (Disparity of income, standing alone, is an insufficient basis for an award of spousal support. No spousal support was ordered when wife earned an annual income of $429,562 and husband earned $27,998. The Court found that the husband "made a voluntary choice to be under employed" and was self supporting.). In Meyer v. Meyer, 2005-Ohio-6249, 2005 WL 3120249 (Ohio Ct. App. 6th Dist. Lucas County 2005) the husband's claim of bad health was disproved by a videotape. The court found that his decision to retire was "motivated by his desire to defeat the [appellee's] claim to spousal support." In Rotte v. Rotte, 2005-Ohio-6269, 2005 WL 3148086 (Ohio Ct. App. 12th Dist. Butler County 2005) the court found that the wife's part time work schedule was a matter of choice, even though she was caring for an ill daughter, not issue of the marriage. It imputed income to her to reflect her current wage as earned on a full-time basis. In this case income was being imputed to the wife for the purpose of child support as well as spousal support.

ment, could not justify an award of spousal support to him.[14] If a court finds that a party has voluntarily retired for the purpose of avoiding a spousal support order, a court may find that the party is voluntarily underemployed, and impute additional income to that party.[15]

A trial court did not err by imputing only minimum wages to a wife who had earned substantially more at a job she voluntarily left. Wife was encouraged by husband to retire so the parties could spend more time together and perhaps save a failing marriage. Wife sought, but was unable to find, substantial employment after her retirement.[16] A trial court did not err in refusing to impute income to husband where it found that husband's previous positions had become non-existent or moved from the geographical area in which husband lived. The trial court also concluded that husband could not relocate because of the need for him to continue to care for his parents who were not in good health.[17]

When imputing income for the purpose of spousal support, some courts require a finding as to whether the party seeking spousal support is voluntarily unemployed or underemployed, which is required by RC 3119.01(C)(11), to impute income for the purposes of child support. In *Brown v. Brown*,[18] the Fifth District Court of Appeals specifically rejected the application of RC 3119.01 in a decision to impute income for purposes of spousal support.[19] Other courts make reference to the terms "unemployed" and "underemployed" without referring to the child support statute.[20] Still others impute income for

---

[14]Mullen v. Mullen, 1998 WL 391385 (Ohio Ct. App. 12th Dist. Warren County 1998). In Gordon v. Gordon, 2006-Ohio-51, 2006 WL 39069 (Ohio Ct. App. 11th Dist. Trumbull County 2006) the Court found that the wife lacked the ability or resources to become self-supporting because she was caring for an adult child of the marriage who had special needs. The case did not include an analysis under Castle v. Castle, 15 Ohio St. 3d 279, 473 N.E.2d 803 (1984).

[15]Perry v. Perry, 2008-Ohio-1315, 2008 WL 748370 (Ohio Ct. App. 2d Dist. Clark County 2008) citing to Koch v. Koch, 2004-Ohio-7192, 2004 WL 3017316 (Ohio Ct. App. 9th Dist. Medina County 2004); and Melhorn v. Melhorn, 1989 WL 8452 (Ohio Ct. App. 2d Dist. Montgomery County 1989).

[16]Burress v. Burress, 1999 WL 455787 (Ohio Ct. App. 12th Dist. Clermont County 1999).

[17]Steinmetz v. Steinmetz, 1999 WL 744201 (Ohio Ct. App. 5th Dist. Tuscarawas County 1999); Jacobs v. Jacobs, 2000-Ohio-1771, 2000 WL 1824893 (Ohio Ct. App. 3d Dist. Marion County 2000) (obligor's decision to terminate employment in Wisconsin and return to Ohio to be closer to his family was voluntary; reduction in earnings could not be a basis for modifying spousal support).

[18]Brown v. Brown, 2009-Ohio-3832, 2009 WL 2374335 (Ohio Ct. App. 5th Dist. Fairfield County 2009).

[19]See also Breedlove v. Breedlove, 2008 Ohio 4887, P 14, (4th Dist., Washington Co., Sept. 15, 2008).

[20]Rodehaver v. Rodehaver, 2009-Ohio-329, 2009 WL 190400 (Ohio Ct. App. 10th Dist. Franklin County 2009).

purposes of spousal support without reference to voluntary unemployment or underemployment.[21]

The professional training or earned degree of a wife who has been a homemaker cannot be a determining factor and must be weighed against other factors, including, for example, the possibility for vocational rehabilitation. Spousal support may be paid not only to sustain life or a former lifestyle, but also to permit proper rehabilitation.

Just as the courts will not accept a wife's solicitation of lifetime spousal support merely because she has no actual income,[22] so too will they usually reject a plea by the husband to be relieved of spousal support because he has no actual earnings.[23] In both instances, the court must consider the party's earning ability in addition to their actual income. It is not an abuse of discretion to fail to consider a second job in computing a party's earning ability.[24]

In recognition of the fact that a spousal support order that was valid when issued may subsequently prove inequitable, the Eighth District Court of Appeals held that a trial court abuses its discretion by failing to reserve jurisdiction to modify an indefinite award of spousal support.[25] Similarly, the Fourth District Court of Appeals has held that it is an abuse of discretion for a court to fail to reserve jurisdiction to modify spousal support where the court knows that the parties' financial circumstances are temporary.[26]

In general, in cases where the spouse receiving spousal support has the ability and potential to become self supporting, the court should provide for reasonable termination of the spousal support upon a date certain.[27]

In *Quick v. Quick*,[28] the Sixth District Court of Appeals held that a

---

[21]Brickner v. Brickner, 2009-Ohio-1164, 2009 WL 683706 (Ohio Ct. App. 12th Dist. Butler County 2009).

[22]Com. v. Whiston, 306 Mass. 65, 27 N.E.2d 703 (1940); Morgan v. Morgan, 59 Wash. 2d 639, 369 P.2d 516 (1962); Mattoni v. Mattoni, 1980 WL 351170 (Ohio Ct. App. 6th Dist. Lucas County 1980).

[23]See Text §§ 14:21 to 14:37, Requirements for modification.

[24]Mccoy v. Mccoy, 1985 WL 10504 (Ohio Ct. App. 10th Dist. Franklin County 1985).

[25]Gullia v. Gullia, 93 Ohio App. 3d 653, 639 N.E.2d 822 (8th Dist. Cuyahoga County 1994), cause dismissed, 70 Ohio St. 3d 1409, 637 N.E.2d 6 (1994).

[26]Swank v. Swank, 1990 WL 42310 (Ohio Ct. App. 4th Dist. Athens County 1990).

[27]Kunkle v. Kunkle, 51 Ohio St. 3d 64, 554 N.E.2d 83 (1990); Canfarelli v. Canfarelli, 2000 WL 966165 (Ohio Ct. App. 2d Dist. Montgomery County 2000) (Trial court erred by failing to set a date certain for ending spousal support. Wife was 38 years old and in good health. She had a meaningful opportunity to develop employment outside the home).

[28]Quick v. Quick, 1985 WL 7590 (Ohio Ct. App. 6th Dist. Sandusky County 1985) (forty-six-year-old wife, married for thirty years, employed earning substantially less than husband).

wife with a ninth grade education and a present earning ability of $10,000 had the potential to be self-supporting and awarded her spousal support of $140 per week for five years and said that the trial court had abused its discretion in awarding alimony terminable only upon certain contingencies.

In *Brashear v. Brashear*,[29] the court held that an award of spousal support for a period of four years to allow a wife who had been a homemaker during the nineteen-year marriage to earn a college degree was not an abuse of discretion, even though the wife possessed no marketable skills at the time of the divorce.

A court does err, however, when it awards spousal support that decreases each year but does not set forth its reasoning for the amount and timing of the decreases. In *Roberts v. Roberts*,[30] the wife's only income was less than $10,000 per year in royalties while the husband earned over $150,000 per year. Without an explanation for the "step-down" of the spousal support award, the appellate court could not determine if it was appropriate and reasonable.

In *Michalosky v. Michalosky*,[31] the Eighth District Court of Appeals vehemently disapproved a trial court's allocation of resources and held that it had abused its discretion in awarding an unskilled mother of six, living on welfare, alimony of only $35 per week for six months, when the husband-father was earning over $29,000 per year. The trial court was ordered to "reevaluate its entire award in an attempt to eliminate the appellant from the public dole or welfare roles and make appellee answerable for his responsibilities."[32]

In *Green v. Green*,[33] it was held an abuse of discretion to award sustenance alimony of only $600 per month for five years and child support of $150 per month per child, where the obligor-spouse's earning power (conservatively, $50,000 per year) and financial status made him able to provide more than "poverty-level spousal support of $7,200 per year." The obligee-spouse's earning power was "zero," and the obligor-spouse anticipated a "fairly certain" inheritance from his parents.[34]

In *Furrow v. Furrow*,[35] the parties were sixty-nine and fifty-five years old, and the marriage (a second for both parties) had lasted less

---

[29]Brashear v. Brashear, 1991 WL 54178 (Ohio Ct. App. 12th Dist. Butler County 1991).

[30]Roberts v. Roberts, 1998 WL 421652 (Ohio Ct. App. 6th Dist. Fulton County 1998).

[31]Michalosky v. Michalosky, 1985 WL 8967, at *5 (Ohio Ct. App. 8th Dist. Cuyahoga County 1985).

[32]Michalosky v. Michalosky, 1985 WL 8967 (Ohio Ct. App. 8th Dist. Cuyahoga County 1985) (award of $750 attorney fees to wife also unreasonably low).

[33]Green v. Green, 1985 WL 7152, at *1 (Ohio Ct. App. 5th Dist. Stark County 1985).

[34]Green v. Green, 1985 WL 7152 (Ohio Ct. App. 5th Dist. Stark County 1985).

[35]Furrow v. Furrow, 1985 WL 7947 (Ohio Ct. App. 8th Dist. Cuyahoga County 1985).

than seven years. Even though the retired husband's sole source of income was social security, the court found that he had the ability to earn $45,000 per year, based on his income as an optometrist prior to his retirement.

To determine a party's true earning ability, it is permissible to pierce the corporate veil if the corporation in question has no true identity separate from its shareholder.[36] Lottery winnings, payable over a period of years, while not earnings, are available income on which to base ability to pay spousal support.[37]

§ 13:11 The statutory factors—(c)—Ages and physical and emotional condition of the parties—Age

Inferences based on age alone, such as that young people are capable of supporting themselves while older persons may have problems, do not always apply in specific cases. The age factor, however, in combination with others such as poor health, employability, etc., may be important. Inability to work as a reason to avoid paying spousal support is less credible when advanced by a twenty-five-year-old than by a sixty-year-old.[1] Conversely, older doctors, lawyers, etc., may be more employable than younger ones.

The age of a party is also important in conjunction with consideration of other factors such as the duration of the marriage and the opportunity of a former homemaker-spouse to develop a career.[2]

§ 13:12 The statutory factors—(c)—Ages and physical and emotional condition of the parties—Physical condition

While a party's physical condition does not in and of itself determine earning ability, it is an important factor to be considered. Physical impairments certainly have an impact on economic productivity and personal independence. Even so, it must be shown how the specific

---

[36]Saeks v. Saeks, 24 Ohio App. 3d 67, 493 N.E.2d 280 (2d Dist. Montgomery County 1985).

[37]Howard v. Howard, 1988 WL 55491 (Ohio Ct. App. 2d Dist. Clark County 1988).

[Section 13:11]

[1]Adams v. Adams, 1981 WL 5187 (Ohio Ct. App. 12th Dist. Warren County 1981) (alimony award of $50 per week for one year, $25 per week for following year held abuse of discretion where payee was fifty-two, untrained, had not worked during twenty-six-year marriage, and would probably become public charge).

[2]Noll v. Noll, 55 Ohio App. 3d 160, 563 N.E.2d 44 (6th Dist. Sandusky County 1989); Babeli v. Babeli, 2005-Ohio-2851, 2005 WL 1364597 (Ohio Ct. App. 5th Dist. Stark County 2005) (The husband was eighty-three and the wife was fifty-six. Neither party was employed and they both retained their own pensions. The duration of the marriage was four years, although the parties had a twenty year premarital relationship. The Court of Appeals affirmed the trial court's failure to award spousal support to the wife.).

physical condition interferes with employment and independence.[1] Although it may make finding and keeping some jobs more difficult, physical disability per se, like age, is not necessarily an excuse for unemployment.

An obligee's health problem of osteoarthritis in her shoulder and knees and a marriage of over twenty years, as well as having been a homemaker since the children were born, all combined to justify the trial court's award of $5,000 per month as permanent, modifiable spousal support.[2] The appellate court found no abuse of discretion where the obligee's health seriously impaired her employment opportunities.

Spousal support awards where illness is a factor are particularly fact sensitive. Spousal support for treatment for a substance abuse problem was upheld where the husband admitted that the wife's substance abuse was an illness in *Richards v. Richards*,[3] Other illnesses which have been factors in awards of spousal support are cervical cancer,[4] breast cancer,[5] and multiple sclerosis.[6] It is common for a party who wishes to make the physical condition of either party an issue to rely on the testimony of an expert witness. However, the physical condition of a party may be established by the lay testimony of ei-

---

[Section 13:12]

[1]Crowell v. Crowell, 1981 WL 5793 (Ohio Ct. App. 6th Dist. Fulton County 1981) (five-year alimony award to be reconsidered after five years on motion of either party, not abuse of discretion in light of wife's uncertain emotional and physical condition and inability to hold steady employment); Fairbanks v. Fairbanks, 1981 WL 6417 (Ohio Ct. App. 5th Dist. Richland County 1981) ($300 per month alimony award for sustenance, $100 per month for medical insurance premium, not abuse of discretion, where court considered statutory guidelines indicating twenty-two-year marriage, wife's cancer surgery and poor health, and prospects for full-time or more gainful employment minimal); Reiter v. Reiter, 2001-Ohio-2155, 2001 WL 615729 (Ohio Ct. App. 3d Dist. Hancock County 2001) (court found wife suffered from anorexia, depression, and a nervous condition and that these conditions would prevent her from obtaining better employment).

[2]Turner v. Turner, 90 Ohio App. 3d 161, 628 N.E.2d 110 (10th Dist. Franklin County 1993).

[3]Richards v. Richards, 2001-Ohio-1707, 2001 WL 1346043 (Ohio Ct. App. 2d Dist. Montgomery County 2001). See also DiNunzio v. DiNunzio, 2006-Ohio-3888, 2006 WL 2105500 (Ohio Ct. App. 11th Dist. Lake County 2006) (The court recognized that mental illness may be just as debilitating as physical disability.); Heitzman v. Heitzman, 2005-Ohio-4622, 2005 WL 2129288 (Ohio Ct. App. 3d Dist. Crawford County 2005) (The wife suffered from severe depression, and other mental health problems. The spousal support order was affirmed.).

[4]Allison v. Allison, 2000 WL 1275238 (Ohio Ct. App. 5th Dist. Stark County 2000).

[5]Carroll v. Carroll, 2004-Ohio-6710, 2004 WL 2891928 (Ohio Ct. App. 5th Dist. Delaware County 2004).

[6]Brown v. Brown, 2000 WL CA 00088 (Ohio Ct. App. 5th Dist. Stark County 2000), Titus v. Titus, 1995 WL 228722 (Ohio Ct. App. 9th Dist. Lorain County 1995).

ther party, so long as there is an opportunity for cross-examination.[7] In any event, findings of fact regarding a party's physical condition must be based on evidence adduced from the witness stand.[8] The trial court may not find that a party is disabled solely on the basis of the court's observation of the party during trial when the party does not testify.[9]

§ 13:13 The statutory factors—(c)—Ages and physical and emotional condition of the parties—Emotional condition

The emotional condition of the parties is usually considered along with the physical condition. It should be shown to have an impact on a party's need for or ability to pay spousal support. Both are entwined with the consideration of age, occupation, etc., as previously discussed.[1]

The major difficulty with evaluation of a party's mental or emotional condition involves the use of experts. Expert witnesses in this connection are often challenged and other experts brought in to counter their testimony.[2] The court has the difficult task of resolving this battle of experts and of determining the existence of an emotional problem, its nature and severity, and the occupational and economic impact it will have.

Counsel should note that evidence on this issue may be used later by the court in its ruling on parenting. Evidence of emotional malad-

---

[7]Gullia v. Gullia, 93 Ohio App. 3d 653, 639 N.E.2d 822 (8th Dist. Cuyahoga County 1994), cause dismissed, 70 Ohio St. 3d 1409, 637 N.E.2d 6 (1994); Denney v. Denney, 1985 WL 7628 (Ohio Ct. App. 2d Dist. Montgomery County 1985); Bachtel v. Bachtel, 2004-Ohio-2807, 2004 WL 1194068 (Ohio Ct. App. 7th Dist. Mahoning County 2004). A trial court does not always require medical documentation of a condition which a party claims impairs his or her ability to work full time. Long v. Long, 176 Ohio App. 3d 621, 2008-Ohio-3006, 893 N.E.2d 217 (2d Dist. Greene County 2008).

[8]Graham v. Graham, 98 Ohio App. 3d 396, 648 N.E.2d 850 (2d Dist. Greene County 1994); Dunbar v. Dunbar, 1998 WL 433850 (Ohio Ct. App. 8th Dist. Cuyahoga County 1998).

[9]Graham v. Graham, 98 Ohio App. 3d 396, 648 N.E.2d 850 (2d Dist. Greene County 1994).

[Section 13:13]

[1]Crowell v. Crowell, 1981 WL 5793 (Ohio Ct. App. 6th Dist. Fulton County 1981). Mental illness may be characterized as a physical condition or an emotional condition. The distinction is not important. The focus should be to determine the impact of the problem on earning ability. See DiNunzio v. DiNunzio, 2006-Ohio-3888, 2006 WL 2105500 (Ohio Ct. App. 11th Dist. Lake County 2006); Heitzman v. Heitzman, 2005-Ohio-4622, 2005 WL 2129288 (Ohio Ct. App. 3d Dist. Crawford County 2005).

[2]Federal Power Commission v. Hope Natural Gas Co., 320 U.S. 591, 64 S. Ct. 281, 88 L. Ed. 333 (1944) ("It will not do to say that it must all be left to the skill of experts."); Albert Sherman Osborn, *The Mind of the Juror as Judge of the Facts; or, The Layman's View of the Law* 49 (1937) ("It is well known that the expert witness occupies an unusual position that in numerous ways is of a judicial character. In his testimony in many cases he is in fact deciding the case.").

justment will not help the party seeking to be allocated the parental rights and responsibilities for minor children. Counsel must also be sure that the record reflects the findings of fact upon which the award (or lack of it) was based, for purposes of subsequent motions for modification based on changed circumstances.[3]

Severe mental illness must be considered in an award of spousal support, but should not be taken in isolation; nor should the court limit the spousal support because of a belief that the spouse may never be able to manage her finances due to psychological problems. Such a situation was found, in *Bevens v. Bevens*,[4] to reinforce a need for a greater award of spousal support than awarded by the trial court.

It is not necessary for a party to present expert medical testimony substantiating claims of medical problems and expenses where the party testifies and is thoroughly cross-examined.[5]

§ 13:14   The statutory factors—(d)—Retirement benefits of the parties

The retirement benefits of the parties must be considered in connection with both spousal support and division of marital property. If the need for spousal support extends beyond the obligors retirement, the question of retirement benefits becomes significant. A payor who retires and whose income is thereby reduced may have difficulty paying spousal support to a payee-wife whose need may be increasing.

Married couples often can receive retirement or pension benefits jointly,[1] but after divorce, they are usually pension strangers: a payor may receive limited benefits. Furthermore, if he or she dies, the spouse may get nothing. Postponing a divorce can often prevent hardship. Alternate schemes such as separation or legal separation proceedings should be considered, where the parties desire to live separate lives but wish to keep their pension benefits intact.

With the enactment of the Retirement Equity Act,[2] former spouses need not be pension strangers if each spouse is willing to wait to obtain his or her share of the accumulated benefits. Where the benefits

---

[3]See Text §§ 14:21 to 14:37, Requirements for modification.

[4]Bevens v. Bevens, 1990 WL 313417 (Ohio Ct. App. 6th Dist. Lucas County 1990).

[5]Denney v. Denney, 1985 WL 7628 (Ohio Ct. App. 2d Dist. Montgomery County 1985); Thompson v. Thompson, 1994 WL 144529 (Ohio Ct. App. 8th Dist. Cuyahoga County 1994); Bunjevac v. Bunjevac, 2002-Ohio-2956, 2002 WL 1307437 (Ohio Ct. App. 8th Dist. Cuyahoga County 2002).

[Section 13:14]

[1]20 C.F.R. § 404 (1982); Retirement Equity Act of 1984, Pub. L. No. 98-397 and Technical Corrections to the REA of 1986. See Text Ch 30, Dividing Private Retirement Benefits in Divorce (employee spouse must receive joint and survivor equity unless nonemployed spouse consents to another form).

[2]See 20 C.F.R. pt. 404.

are almost in pay-out status, that is, the participant spouse will soon be fifty-five or the earliest age at which he or she could retire, it may be easier to provide a proportional payment than to find an asset to set off.

It is important to note that although one party may choose to receive pension benefits prior to the age of actual retirement, the other party may not elect to apply for or receive said benefits at that age, which can have a direct impact on spousal support.[3]

A trial court may not order withholding from pension benefits for payment of spousal support in an amount exceeding 60% of the benefit.[4]

If a couple has been married for ten years or more, and one spouse retires on federal social security, the other spouse is eligible for certain benefits.[5] If the parties are divorced before the ten-year mark is reached, the party who has not qualified for social security will not receive any interest in the other party's social security benefits.[6] Again, counsel for the party who does not qualify for social security in his or her own name should consider an informal separation or filing a legal separation action.

One concern in divorce cases has been the appropriateness of dividing the marital pension between the parties and then awarding spousal support based on the income the payor spouse receives from his or her share of the pension.[7] The argument is made by the payor spouse that this is a form of "double dipping." The payee spouse receives (in some fashion) a division of the marital pension and then receives more of the pension via the award of spousal support based at least in part on the pension benefits retained by the payor. RC 3105.18 makes it clear that the retirement benefits of the parties are a factor to be considered by the court in an award of spousal support. This is another area where the division of property has a direct bearing on an award of spousal support.[8] This factor should be considered by counsel when deciding whether to divide a pension via QDRO or via a set-off with other assets.

---

[3]Barth v. Barth, 1998 WL 433830 (Ohio Ct. App. 8th Dist. Cuyahoga County 1998).

[4]RC 3113.21(B)(1)(a); Stewart v. Stewart, 1999 WL 1071976 (Ohio Ct. App. 5th Dist. Stark County 1999).

[5]See Text Ch 30, Dividing Private Retirement Benefits in Divorce.

[6]See Text Ch 30, Dividing Private Retirement Benefits in Divorce.

[7]See Holcomb v. Holcomb, 44 Ohio St. 3d 128, 541 N.E.2d 597 (1989).

[8]See Holcomb v. Holcomb, 44 Ohio St. 3d 128, 541 N.E.2d 597 (1989) (pension plan must be considered when determining spousal support); Roach v. Roach, 61 Ohio App. 3d 315, 572 N.E.2d 772 (8th Dist. Cuyahoga County 1989) (monthly retirement benefits received by husband included in his income for spousal support calculation); Gable v. Gable, 1997 WL 67723 (Ohio Ct. App. 12th Dist. Warren County 1997) (court may include retirement pay in calculation but is not required to do so); Ellman v. Ellman, 1996 WL 562815 (Ohio Ct. App. 2d Dist. Greene County 1996) (court must consider income from pension when considering whether to order spousal support).

§ 13:15 The statutory factors—(e)—Duration of the marriage

Taken alone, the length of a marriage has no necessary relation to whether an award of spousal support is reasonable and appropriate, and an award of spousal support based solely on the duration of the parties' marriage is an abuse of discretion.[1] However, taken together with other factors, such as age, health, and employability, the length of the parties' marriage may have considerable significance.[2]

In *Coreano v. Coreano*,[3] the Eighth District Court of Appeals pointed out that the amount of spousal support should not be determined solely by the length of the marriage, as all of the factors under former RC 3105.18(B) must be considered.

In considering duration of the marriage as a factor in awarding spousal support, counsel should consider RC 3105.171(G), which provides that in any order for the division or disbursement of property or a distributive award, the court must make written findings of fact that support the determination that marital property has been divided equitably and must specify the dates it used in determining the meaning of "during the marriage."[4]

While a trial court must determine the date of marriage and the date of termination for purposes of property valuation, it need only consider the "length of marriage" in determining spousal support. The exact length of the marriage need not be determined.[5] The Eighth District Court of Appeals has held that a trial court need not determine a specific date of termination of the marriage when considering spousal support issues. Rather, the court must only

---

[Section 13:15]

[1]Campbell v. Campbell, 1993 WL 307535 (Ohio Ct. App. 4th Dist. Gallia County 1993).

[2]Fairbanks v. Fairbanks, 1981 WL 6417 (Ohio Ct. App. 5th Dist. Richland County 1981) ($300 per month alimony award for sustenance, $100 per month for medical insurance premium, not abuse of discretion, where court considered statutory guidelines which indicated twenty-two-year marriage, wife's cancer surgery and poor health, and prospects for full-time or more gainful employment minimal). But see Babeli v. Babeli, 2005-Ohio-2851, 2005 WL 1364597 (Ohio Ct. App. 5th Dist. Stark County 2005) (The duration of the marriage was four years, although the parties had a twenty year premarital relationship. The husband was eighty-three; the wife was fifty-six. Neither party was employed and they both retained their own pensions. The Court of Appeals affirmed the trial court's failure to award spousal support to the wife.); McClain v. McClain, 2004-Ohio-2950, 2004 WL 1253297 (Ohio Ct. App. 2d Dist. Champaign County 2004) (trial court was reversed when it awarded no spousal support when the parties had been married for 45 years, the parties were of advanced age, and there was a disparity in the incomes of the parties).

[3]Coreano v. Coreano, 1984 WL 5497 (Ohio Ct. App. 8th Dist. Cuyahoga County 1984) (marriage effectively lasted only three days).

[4]See Text Ch 12, Marital and Separate Property.

[5]Zimmerman v. Zimmerman, 1999 WL 156032 (Ohio Ct. App. 3d Dist. Allen County 1999).

consider the duration of the marriage.[6] However, if "duration of the marriage" had been agreed to or determined for the division of property pursuant to RC 3105.171(2), consistency would seem to demand that the same period of time would constitute the "length of the marriage" for purposes of a spousal support award.

Ordinarily the duration of the marriage will be deemed to be the date of the marriage ceremony until the date of final hearing. But counsel may argue that it would be appropriate and equitable to use other dates to define the duration of the marriage especially when one party has been ordered to pay temporary spousal support to the other.[7]

In *Kunkle v. Kunkle*,[8] the Supreme Court of Ohio held that the lower courts erred in making an order of spousal support with no termination date, and articulated the policy that spousal support orders should end on a date certain, except in cases of a) a long marriage where the party seeking spousal support is b) of advanced age or c) a homemaker-spouse with d) little opportunity to develop meaningful employment outside the home, and no e) resources, ability or potential to be self-supporting. *Kunkle* involved a marriage of 18 years where the wife was 38 when she separated from her husband and 41 at the time of the final decree.

The analysis as to whether indefinite spousal support is warranted should begin with an examination as to whether a spouse has the resources, ability and potential to be self-supporting.[9]

The other *Kunkle* factors must be considered in conjunction with one another, and with the other statutory factors.

Although there is no bright-line rule to determine how long a marriage must be to be considered long-term, it is not uncommon for Ohio courts to affirm permanent spousal support awards in marriages that

---

[6]Kindred v. Kindred, 1999 WL 462370 (Ohio Ct. App. 8th Dist. Cuyahoga County 1999); Bowling v. Bowling, 1998 WL 96440 (Ohio Ct. App. 10th Dist. Franklin County 1998) (The parties had been separated for five years during which time the Defendant supported the wife and their minor child. The trial court's order of three and a half years of spousal support was affirmed because that was the amount of time the wife would need to complete her degree, and the length of the marriage was only one of several factors which were to be considered in setting spousal support.).

[7]See Nori v. Nori, 58 Ohio App. 3d 69, 568 N.E.2d 730 (12th Dist. Butler County 1989); Bacon v. Bacon, 1991 WL 8599 (Ohio Ct. App. 8th Dist. Cuyahoga County 1991); Meadows v. Meadows, 2006-Ohio-2432, 2006 WL 1330937 (Ohio Ct. App. 5th Dist. Stark County 2006) (The court ordered spousal support for a year in a marriage which lasted 294 days. The parties lived together for five years before they were married. After they separated the wife lived in subsidized housing. The husband promised to take care of the wife financially for the rest of her life if she would marry him. The wife gave up her housing and numerous items of personal property prior to the marriage.).

[8]Kunkle v. Kunkle, 51 Ohio St. 3d 64, 554 N.E.2d 83 (1990).

[9]Dissent in Yazdani-Ifehani v. Yazdani-Ifehani, 2008-Ohio-4662, 2008 WL 4193635 (Ohio Ct. App. 4th Dist. Athens County 2008).

have lasted 19 years or longer.[10] Generally, marriages lasting over 20 years have been found to be sufficient to justify spousal support of indefinite duration.[11]

A court of appeals reversed a trial court's finding that a marriage which lasted 17 years before the parties separated and filed for divorce, but was 20 years long before the final decree was filed, was a "marriage of long duration."[12]

In *Krisher v. Krisher*[13] and *Moore v. Moore*,[14] the parties had been married to each other for a long period of time, had terminated their marriage, and shortly thereafter had remarried one another. There was no abuse of discretion in either court's considering the total years the parties spent married to each other in an action to terminate the second marriage. Under appropriate circumstances it is permissible to consider a previous, longstanding, legal, marital relationship as relevant, especially where the separation was for a short period.[15]

A finding of a twenty-seven-year marriage, computed from the date of marriage until the date of divorce, was upheld in spite of the unrefuted testimony that the parties had engaged in no "conjugal relations" for over ten years.[16]

The Sixth District Court of Appeals in *Noll v Noll*[17] stated that where parties had married twenty-nine years, both were of advanced age, and the homemaker-spouse had little opportunity to develop a career since her husband objected to her working during the marriage, the trial court could properly award spousal support terminable only upon the death or remarriage of the recipient or upon further order of court.

§ 13:16 The statutory factors—(f)—Residential parent's duties inconsistent with seeking employment outside the home

In enacting RC 3105.18(C)(1)(f), the Ohio legislature realized that

---

[10]DiBari v. DiBari, 2009-Ohio-3437, 2009 WL 2028444 (Ohio Ct. App. 10th Dist. Franklin County 2009).

[11]Handschumaker v. Handschumaker, 2009-Ohio-2239, 2009 WL 1317874 (Ohio Ct. App. 4th Dist. Washington County 2009) citing to Vanke v. Vanke, 93 Ohio App. 3d 373, 377, 638 N.E.2d 630 (10th Dist. Franklin County 1994).

[12]Yazdani-Ifehani v. Yazdani-Ifehani, 2008-Ohio-4662, 2008 WL 4193635 (Ohio Ct. App. 4th Dist. Athens County 2008).

[13]Krisher v. Krisher, 82 Ohio App. 3d 159, 611 N.E.2d 499 (3d Dist. Logan County 1992).

[14]Moore v. Moore, 83 Ohio App. 3d 75, 613 N.E.2d 1097 (9th Dist. Summit County 1992).

[15]Moore v. Moore, 83 Ohio App. 3d 75, 613 N.E.2d 1097 (9th Dist. Summit County 1992).

[16]Howard v. Howard, 1988 WL 55491 (Ohio Ct. App. 2d Dist. Clark County 1988).

[17]Noll v. Noll, 55 Ohio App. 3d 160, 563 N.E.2d 44 (6th Dist. Sandusky County 1989).

employability and economic independence may be circumscribed by the necessity for child care. Where a nonworking spouse is allocated parental rights and responsibilites for the parties minor children, and the other spouse's income must stretch to support two households, economic reality often dictates that the residential parent go to work, since there is rarely enough income from one spouse to support two households.

In *Ruedele v. Ruedele*,[1] the Tenth District Court of Appeals held that where a husband and wife agree that the wife will leave her full-time position and have children, where she then works around the children's schedule with odd jobs, and where she has credentials that should help her find a full-time position in the future, an order for support alimony for the wife of $100 per month until either her base income equals her husband's or she remarries, is not improper.

In *Goode v. Goode*.[2] The Tenth District Court of Appeals affirmed the trial court's conclusion that the wife's earning ability was what she currently earned working part time, because it would be inappropriate at present for the wife to work full time due to her responsibilities as the residential parent. The Second District Court of Appeals adopted this approach in *West v. West*.[3]

In *Thomas v. Thomas*,[4] the husband appealed an award of spousal support to his wife who was a registered nurse, arguing that she was voluntarily unemployed and that she could make a respectable income. In view of the husband's earning ability and the fact that the wife would be the residential parent for the parties' four children who ranged in age from six to ten, the court found it not unreasonable to expect the wife to remain a full-time mother until the youngest child finished sixth grade.

There is a limitation in the statutory language that the child must be "of the marriage."[5] This would seem to exclude the custodian-at-

---

[Section 13:16]

[1]Ruedele v. Ruedele, 1984 WL 5788 (Ohio Ct. App. 10th Dist. Franklin County 1984).

[2]Goode v. Goode, 70 Ohio App. 3d 125, 590 N.E.2d 439 (10th Dist. Franklin County 1991).

[3]West v. West, 1993 WL 85421 (Ohio Ct. App. 2d Dist. Miami County 1993). Although the trial court enjoys broad discretion in awards of spousal support, in Saluppo v. Saluppo, 2006-Ohio-2694, 2006 WL 1479633 (Ohio Ct. App. 9th Dist. Summit County 2006), the Court of Appeals reversed the trial court's decision not to award spousal support to the mother of small children, stating, "Equity requires that a party receive at least sufficient spousal support to bring him or her to a 'reasonable standard of living, comparable to the standard maintained during the marriage.'" Citing Berthelot v. Berthelot, 154 Ohio App. 3d 101, 114, 2003-Ohio-4519, 796 N.E.2d 541 (9th Dist. Summit County 2003).

[4]Thomas v. Thomas, 1995 WL 137015 (Ohio Ct. App. 2d Dist. Greene County 1995).

[5]RC 3105.18(C)(1)(f).

home factor when the children who need care are from a former marriage.[6]

§ 13:17 The statutory factors—(g)—Standard of living established during the marriage

It is usually not economically feasible to maintain two households at the same standard of living as the marital household was maintained. A trial court must consider the parties' pre-divorce standard of living, but it is not under a duty to insure that standard's continued existence after divorce.[1] For instance, a spouse is not entitled as a matter of law to continue to live the luxurious lifestyle that the parties enjoyed during the marriage.[2] It is not error for a spousal support order to provide the party receiving support a higher standard of living than that which the parties enjoyed during the marriage.[3] While not necessarily applicable to every case, the more frequent scenario after the marriage ends is that the husband's income and standard of living increase above that enjoyed during marriage, while the wife's standard is greatly reduced.[4] After a long marriage, the payee spouse is entitled to maintain the same standard of living as the payor spouse, even if it means that both parties may experience a reduction in their standards of living in order to support two households.[5]

The court can only base a spousal support award on evidence of appropriateness and reasonableness with which it is presented, so

---

[6]See Loucka v. Loucka, 1981 WL 4555 (Ohio Ct. App. 8th Dist. Cuyahoga County 1981).

[Section 13:17]

[1]Carter v. Carter, 1986 WL 3258 (Ohio Ct. App. 9th Dist. Medina County 1986). See also Kaechele v. Kaechele, 1986 WL 13922 (Ohio Ct. App. 10th Dist. Franklin County 1986), judgment aff'd and remanded, 35 Ohio St. 3d 93, 518 N.E.2d 1197 (1988); Chikar v. Chikar, 61 Ohio App. 3d 772, 573 N.E.2d 1160 (12th Dist. Clermont County 1989); Kucmanic v. Kucmanic, 1992 WL 80045 (Ohio Ct. App. 8th Dist. Cuyahoga County 1992). "Obviously, neither party will enjoy exactly the same standard of living now that there are two households to maintain. Neither party is guaranteed the same standard of living enjoyed during the marriage." Dunham v. Dunham, 171 Ohio App. 3d 147, 167, 2007-Ohio-1167, 870 N.E.2d 168 (10th Dist. Franklin County 2007), appeal not allowed, 115 Ohio St. 3d 1408, 2007-Ohio-4884, 873 N.E.2d 1314 (2007).

[2]Simoni v. Simoni, 102 Ohio App. 3d 628, 657 N.E.2d 800 (8th Dist. Cuyahoga County 1995).

[3]Daniels v. Daniels, No. 07AP-709 (Ohio Ct. App. Franklin County Mar. 4, 2008).

[4]Lenore J. Weitzman, *The Divorce Revolution: The Unexpected Social and Economic Consequences for Women and Children in America* (New York: Free Press 1985).

[5]Lepowsky v. Lepowsky, 2007-Ohio-4994, p51–52, 2007 WL 2758608 (Ohio Ct. App. 7th Dist. Columbiana County 2007).

counsel should take care to draw the most complete financial picture possible.[6]

A pattern of living on a reasonable level with prudent savings for the future, as opposed to extravagant spending, does not necessarily require the court to minimize the amount to be paid in spousal support. Savings as well as spending can be a part of the preexisting standard of living, and the trial court may allow adequate spousal support to minimize the injury from the marriage termination.[7] In *Kane v. Kane*,[8] the court found that living modestly and saving for the future constituted a standard of living which the trial court sought to maintain in its award of spousal support. Details as to the impact of a spousal support order on the recipient's standard of living may be necessary to overturn an award deemed insufficient by that recipient. In *Hissa v. Hissa*,[9] the Eight District Court of Appeals stated "[a]bsent a more concrete showing of how her lifestyle would be diminished on $85,000 per year, we find the court did not abuse its discretion when deciding the amount of spousal support."

In *Kaechele v. Kaechele*[10] the Tenth District Court of Appeals held that an award of periodic alimony which gives parity of the disposable income to each party would appear to be in order. The appellate court recognized that while RC 3105.18 mandates consideration of the standard of living established during the marriage, a trial court has difficulty placing the parties on an equal plane as to future lifestyles.

The Supreme Court, while affirming the appellate court's reversal and remand to the trial court also concluded that the appellate court was in error in suggesting that an alimony award must establish an equal standard of living for the parties.[11] The Court did recognize that the income disparity was at least seventy percent to the husband and thirty percent to the wife and, with the inclusion of an installment as-

---

[6]Com. v. Whiston, 306 Mass. 65, 27 N.E.2d 703 (1940); Morgan v. Morgan, 59 Wash. 2d 639, 369 P.2d 516 (1962); Mattoni v. Mattoni, 1980 WL 351170 (Ohio Ct. App. 6th Dist. Lucas County 1980). See also Text Ch 14, Modification of Spousal Support.

[7]Kane v. Kane, 1988 WL 46187 (Ohio Ct. App. 3d Dist. Allen County 1988).

[8]Kane v. Kane, 1988 WL 46187 (Ohio Ct. App. 3d Dist. Allen County 1988).

[9]Hissa v. Hissa, 2002-Ohio-6313, 2002 WL 31618500 (Ohio Ct. App. 8th Dist. Cuyahoga County 2002).

[10]Kaechele v. Kaechele, 1986 WL 13922 (Ohio Ct. App. 10th Dist. Franklin County 1986), judgment aff'd and remanded, 35 Ohio St. 3d 93, 518 N.E.2d 1197 (1988).

[11]Kaechele v. Kaechele, 1986 WL 13922 (Ohio Ct. App. 10th Dist. Franklin County 1986), judgment aff'd and remanded, 35 Ohio St. 3d 93, 518 N.E.2d 1197 (1988). There is no judicial directive which requires that the parties to a divorce must enjoy a post-divorce standard of living comparable to that established during the marriage. The standard of living is just one factor to be considered. Cooper v. Cooper, 2002-Ohio-7105, 2002 WL 31846267 (Ohio Ct. App. 6th Dist. Lucas County 2002). Equity requires that a spouse receive sufficient spousal support for him or her to achieve a reasonable standard of living in light of the standard maintained during the marriage. Glass v. Glass, 2000 WL 896188 (Ohio Ct. App. 11th Dist. Trumbull County 2000).

set, might be as great as seventy-eight percent to the husband and twenty-two percent to the wife.

The standard of living established during the marriage is the highest, but not the lowest, standard to be used in determining need for spousal support. Equity requires that the obligee receive sufficient spousal support to permit a standard of living which is in reasonable relationship to that maintained during marriage. In *Buckles v. Buckles*,[12] despite a large property settlement (approximately $250,000), considering the reduction after paying attorney fees and the non-income-producing nature of some assets, the appellate court found that the income potential of the wife from investment of the cash would not put her living standard anywhere near the husband's, whose income was at least $100,000 per year. The idea that the court should put the parties "on a parity with the marriage standard of living" and so with one another, as articulated in *Buckles v. Buckles*,[13] has been superceded by the modifications to the statute since *Buckles* was decided, although courts can and do equalize incomes, particularly in marriage of long duration.

Citing *Buckles*, the Tenth District Court of Appeals in 1989 stated that "R.C. 3105.18 does not contemplate that, in the absence of extraordinary circumstances, one party will enjoy the same or higher standard of living while the other is forced to live at a standard of living far below that which was established during the marriage."[14] It is appropriate to base an award of spousal support on a need for assistance in maintaining a standard of living approximating that enjoyed during the marriage.[15]

An award of spousal support which does not permit a non-self-sufficient homemaker-spouse to become self-sufficient within a reasonable time, does not meet the spouse's reasonable monthly expenses, has no reasonable relationship to the standard of living enjoyed dur-

---

[12]Buckles v. Buckles, 46 Ohio App. 3d 102, 546 N.E.2d 950 (10th Dist. Franklin County 1988); See also Addy v. Addy, 97 Ohio App. 3d 204, 646 N.E.2d 513 (10th Dist. Franklin County 1994) (at the very least, equity requires that a party receive sufficient spousal support to bring him or her to a reasonable standard of living, comparable to the standard maintained during the marriage).

[13]Buckles v. Buckles, 46 Ohio App. 3d 102, 546 N.E.2d 950 (10th Dist. Franklin County 1988).

[14]Wilder v. Wilder, 1989 WL 43293, at *9 (Ohio Ct. App. 10th Dist. Franklin County 1989). See also Birath v. Birath, 53 Ohio App. 3d 31, 558 N.E.2d 63 (10th Dist. Franklin County 1988); Gerrard v. Gerrard, 1989 WL 68455 (Ohio Ct. App. 2d Dist. Clark County 1989); Cahill v. Patronite, 2003-Ohio-6050, 2003 WL 22672207 (Ohio Ct. App. 8th Dist. Cuyahoga County 2003).

[15]Mills v. Mills, 1999 WL 1082646 (Ohio Ct. App. 2d Dist. Montgomery County 1999); Vanke v. Vanke, 93 Ohio App. 3d 373, 638 N.E.2d 630 (10th Dist. Franklin County 1994).

ing the marriage, and which results in a monthly deficit, is an abuse of discretion.[16]

§ 13:18 The statutory factors—(h)—Relative extent of education of the parties

Usually, more education implies greater earning ability, while less education implies greater need. Education, or lack of it, standing alone does not provide evidence of need or ability to earn.

For instance, a teaching certificate may not assure employability in an area where there is declining enrollment or an economic slump. Evidence beyond simple educational achievement must be presented to give a complete and accurate picture of a party's situation.[1] Where a wife held advanced degrees and her education and work experience led the court to conclude that she was capable of being self-supporting, denial of support was proper.[2]

In *Lira v. Lira*,[3] the court held that a degree or license was not marital property but should be considered for purposes of spousal support.[4] *West v. West*[5] found it to be error not to consider a medical license as an asset in determining the ability of the husband to pay spousal support. These cases indicate that while licenses are not marital property they inevitably affect the appropriateness of an award of spousal support.

---

[16]Henninger v. Henninger, 1993 WL 143765 (Ohio Ct. App. 2d Dist. Darke County 1993); Saluppo v. Saluppo, 2006-Ohio-2694, 2006 WL 1479633 (Ohio Ct. App. 9th Dist. Summit County 2006).

[Section 13:18]

[1]See Adams v. Adams, 1981 WL 5187 (Ohio Ct. App. 12th Dist. Warren County 1981) (alimony award of $50 per week for one year, $25 per week for following year was abuse of discretion where payee was fifty-two, untrained, not worked during twenty-six-year marriage, and would probably become public charge); Lira v. Lira, 68 Ohio App. 2d 164, 22 Ohio Op. 3d 231, 428 N.E.2d 445 (8th Dist. Cuyahoga County 1980) (disapproved of by, Stevens v. Stevens, 23 Ohio St. 3d 115, 492 N.E.2d 131 (1986)) (professional degree not divisible marital asset, but factor to be considered in determining ability to pay future support alimony); Daniels v. Daniels, 20 Ohio Op. 2d 458, 90 Ohio L. Abs. 161, 185 N.E.2d 773 (Ct. App. 2d Dist. Montgomery County 1961) (appellate court sustained alimony award payable from husband's earnings as physician); West v. West, 1978 WL 216236 (Ohio Ct. App. 2d Dist. Montgomery County 1978) (probable future earnings should be considered in evaluating earning ability, making alimony award); Howard, *Educational Degree Does Not Constitute Marital Property Subject to Division Between Spouses Upon Divorce*, 13 Tulsa L. Rev. 652. See also Text Ch 12, Marital and Separate Property.

[2]Kramic-Teuber v. Teuber, 1998 WL 195873 (Ohio Ct. App. 9th Dist. Lorain County 1998).

[3]Lira v. Lira, 68 Ohio App. 2d 164, 22 Ohio Op. 3d 231, 428 N.E.2d 445 (8th Dist. Cuyahoga County 1980) (disapproved of by, Stevens v. Stevens, 23 Ohio St. 3d 115, 492 N.E.2d 131 (1986)).

[4]See also Josselson v. Josselson, 52 Ohio App. 3d 60, 557 N.E.2d 835 (8th Dist. Cuyahoga County 1988).

[5]West v. West, 1978 WL 216236 (Ohio Ct. App. 2d Dist. Montgomery County 1978).

Ohio has refused to consider a spouse's professional degree as marital property. In 1986, the Ohio Supreme Court has spoken clearly on the subject. The syllabus in *Stevens v. Stevens*,[6] provides as follows:

A professional degree or license is not marital property and the present value of the projected future earnings of the degreed spouse is not a marital asset subject to division upon divorce. Although not an asset, the future value of a professional degree or license acquired by one of the parties during the marriage is an element to be considered in reaching an equitable award of alimony in accordance with R.C. 3105.18.

§ 13:19   The statutory factors—(i)—Relative assets and liabilities of the parties including court-ordered payments

The relative assets and liabilities of the parties are a primary factor in the determination of whether spousal support is appropriate and reasonable. The net assets of the parties are identified and valued (liabilities offset against the assets) and their nature as separate property or marital property is determined. Each party's separate property is allocated, then the marital assets are equally or equitably divided, all pursuant to RC 3105.171.[1] By statute, the question of whether spousal support is appropriate and reasonable must be addressed after the property has been divided. RC 3105.18(B) provides as follows: "In divorce and legal separation proceedings, upon the request of either party and after the court determines the division of disbursement of property under section 3105.171 of the Revised Code, the court of common please may award reasonable spousal support to either party."[2] If the facts show the requesting party has sufficient assets to maintain an existing lifestyle indefinitely or until rehabilitation and economic independence are achieved, there will likely be little or no spousal support awarded.[3]

It is proper to include the total of each party's separate property

---

[6]Stevens v. Stevens, 23 Ohio St. 3d 115, 492 N.E.2d 131 (1986).

[Section 13:19]

[1]See Wolfe v. Wolfe, 46 Ohio St. 2d 399, 75 Ohio Op. 2d 474, 350 N.E.2d 413 (1976) (division of property should be court's first order of business, before support alimony dealt with; need for and ability to pay support alimony not determined until of the total assets of each party determined), superseded by statute as stated in Heslep v. Heslep, 2000 WL 818909 (Ohio Ct. App. 7th Dist. Monroe County 2000).

[2]RC 3105.18(B). Jendrusik v. Jendrusik, 2001-Ohio-3377, 2001 WL 1667871 (Ohio Ct. App. 7th Dist. Belmont County 2001) (The Court must divide property first, then determine the appropriateness of a spousal support order.).

[3]Block v. Block, 1981 WL 4126 (Ohio Ct. App. 9th Dist. Medina County 1981) (support alimony not appropriate where wife receives large property settlement, has expectations of substantial salary in near future, and income from sizable financial holding); Reincheld v. Reincheld, 1981 WL 2986 (Ohio Ct. App. 10th Dist. Franklin County 1981) (disallowance of alimony because wife receiving disability income reversible error because facts indicated some alimony warranted in spite of disability payments); Pasterczyk v. Pasterczyk, 1981 WL 4715 (Ohio Ct. App. 8th Dist. Cuyahoga County 1981) (evidence sufficient to sustain inference of necessity for award of alimony, even though decree did not specifically make finding of need);

with the marital property allocated to that party in making the determination as to the reasonableness and appropriateness of an award of spousal support. In addition to determining how much income property may produce, the court may examine whether the property itself is an appreciating or a depreciating asset. In *DeWitt v. DeWitt*,[4] the court noted that the home which the husband was awarded was an appreciating asset.

The trial court may order him or her to pay spousal support out of funds awarded to the obligor as part of the division of property. For instance, an obligor's personal injury settlement might be deemed the obligor's separate property, yet serve as the basis for an award of spousal support.[5]

RC 3105.18 no longer includes expectancies and inheritances as a factor to be considered by the court. The subject of an inheritance that has been received is addressed in RC 3105.171(A)(6)(a)(i), and therefore would be relevant for purposes of determining spousal support. An award of pre-decree support should be considered in establishing post-decree support.[6]

All liabilities including most required to divide property, and child support are to be considered in determining reasonable spousal support.[7] But a payor's voluntary acquisition of additional debt is not necessarily grounds to justify a reduction of spousal support.[8] If one party is paying most of the martial debt, this should be considered

---

White v. White, 2003-Ohio-3279, 2003 WL 21447369 (Ohio Ct. App. 7th Dist. Columbiana County 2003).

[4]DeWitt v. DeWitt, 2003-Ohio-851, 2003 WL 490928 (Ohio Ct. App. 3d Dist. Marion County 2003).

[5]Marcum v. Marcum, 116 Ohio App. 3d 606, 688 N.E.2d 1085 (2d Dist. Montgomery County 1996). A court may also look to when a party will have access to property. Harman v. Harman, 2000 WL 1275258 (Ohio Ct. App. 5th Dist. Tuscarawas County 2000); Wertz v. Wertz, 2003-Ohio-3782, 2003 WL 21658673 (Ohio Ct. App. 2d Dist. Montgomery County 2003) (if spousal support is paid from marital property, the obligee is entitled to an adjustment of the property division to the extent that her own property was used to pay spousal support).

[6]Zimon v. Zimon, 2005-Ohio-271, 2005 WL 156726 (Ohio Ct. App. 9th Dist. Medina County 2005). The Court in O'Grady v. O'Grady, 2004-Ohio-3504, 2004 WL 1486344 (Ohio Ct. App. 11th Dist. Trumbull County 2004) noted the husband's payment of temporary spousal support for almost two years in support of its decision not to award additional spousal support.

[7]White v. White, 2003-Ohio-3279, 2003 WL 21447369 (Ohio Ct. App. 7th Dist. Columbiana County 2003). The court does not err in failing to consider future expenses. Frederick v. Frederick, 2006-Ohio-3234, 2006 WL 1725979 (Ohio Ct. App. 3d Dist. Allen County 2006) (court did not consider wife's future health insurance costs).

[8]Shanley v. Shanley, 46 Ohio App. 3d 100, 546 N.E.2d 477 (8th Dist. Cuyahoga County 1989).

when determining the other party's spousal support obligation, particularly if he or she is also making substantial interest payments.[9]

§ 13:20 The statutory factors—(j)—Contribution to other; (k) education; and (m) lost income production capacity

Three factors added in 1991 relate to the effect of relationship of the spouses during the marriage and the relative advantages and disadvantages to each of the other's contribution to the marriage. These factors are:

(1) The contribution of each party to the education, training, or earning ability of the other party, including, but not limited to, any party's contribution to the acquisition of a professional degree of the other party.[1]

(2) The time and expense necessary for the spouse who is seeking spousal support to acquire education, training, or job experience so that the spouse will be qualified to obtain appropriate employment, provided the education, training, or job experience, and employment is, in fact, sought.[2]

(3) The lost income production capacity of either party that resulted from that party's marital responsibilities.[3]

RC 3105.18(C)(1)(j), (k), and (m) should be read in conjunction with each other. They are all designed to allow a spouse a reasonable and fair chance to improve or maintain his or her standard of living, where the spouse (1) contributed to the other spouse's earning ability; (2) seeks additional education to enhance his or her earning ability; and/or (3) lost earning ability of his or her own.

RC 3105.18(C)(1)(j) requires the court to consider the extent to which one spouse contributed to the earning capacity of the other. The statute codifies the rule the Ohio Supreme Court stated in *Stevens v. Stevens*.[4] In *Stevens*, the Court held that where the wife shouldered the majority of the husband's educational and living expenses while he pursued an education, the wife was entitled to equitable compensation. This rule has been applied in the Seventh District in

---

[9]Myers v. Myers, 2006-Ohio-6252, 2006 WL 3438690 (Ohio Ct. App. 5th Dist. Coshocton County 2006); Rockne-Volpe v. Volpe, 2006-Ohio-6235, 2006 WL 3423408 (Ohio Ct. App. 5th Dist. Licking County 2006).

[Section 13:20]

[1]RC 3105.18(C)(1)(j).

[2]RC 3105.18(C)(1)(k).

[3]RC 3105.18(C)(1)(m). Sutphin v. Sutphin, 2004-Ohio-6844, 2004 WL 2913904 (Ohio Ct. App. 1st Dist. Hamilton County 2004) (affirmed a decision which referred to "compensatory spousal support" on the basis that this was akin to a consideration of "lost income production capacity . . .that resulted from a party's marital responsibilities", and the decision showed that the court considered the other statutory factors as well.).

[4]Stevens v. Stevens, 23 Ohio St. 3d 115, 492 N.E.2d 131 (1986).

the case of *Evans v. Evans*[5] and in the Ninth District in the case of *Flauto v. Flauto*.[6] It is not enough to say that someone got a degree during the marriage. This factor requires the person seeking spousal support to present evidence as to how much the party could earn or is earning using that degree.[7]

RC 3105.18(C)(1)(k) does not provide that support should be granted to allow the recipient to obtain an earning ability equivalent to that of the payor. RC 3105.18(C)(1)(k) requires that education, training, job experience, or employment actually be sought in order to allow an award of support therefor. The Court of Appeals reserved the trial court when it based the duration of spousal support on the time the husband would need to become trained for a betting paying job, after the husband testified that he had no intention of seeking a better paying job.[8]

A request for funds to further one's education should be as specific as possible,[9] and should include the field of study, the cost of the training sought, the amount of time the course of study will take, and the name of the school where the training is to take place. In *Winkelman v. Winkelman*,[10] the trial court did not err in failing to include an award for an advanced degree when the party seeking it "did not show that she had actually made any serious plans to obtain such a degree." In *Franck v. Franck*,[11] the court of appeals upheld the trial court's decision not to award spousal support to pay for the wife's education, despite her testimony as to a specific college, and a course of study, and the cost of that course of study, stating that she had not "even" applied to or been accepted at any college.

The spousal support may be structured as direct payment of, or a reimbursement for, tuition, books, and the like. Because the prerequisite act necessarily occurs after the fact of the award, the court may

---

[5]Evans v. Evans, 1995 WL 752688 (Ohio Ct. App. 9th Dist. Lorain County 1995). But see Carmony v. Carmony, 2004-Ohio-1035, 2004 WL 414922 (Ohio Ct. App. 6th Dist. Lucas County 2004). In Addington v. Addington, 2004-Ohio-6931, 2004 WL 2940897 (Ohio Ct. App. 4th Dist. Scioto County 2004) both parties were trained as pharmacists. The husband went on to medical school while the wife worked and cared for the parties' children. The Court of Appeals affirmed the trial court's award of spousal support until either party's death or the wife's remarriage, citing the standard of living established during the marriage.

[6]Flauto v. Flauto, 1996 WL 242912 (Ohio Ct. App. 7th Dist. Mahoning County 1996).

[7]Taub v. Taub, 2009-Ohio-2762, 2009 WL 1653823 (Ohio Ct. App. 10th Dist. Franklin County 2009).

[8]Long v. Long, 176 Ohio App. 3d 621, 2008-Ohio-3006, 893 N.E.2d 217 (2d Dist. Greene County 2008), Rendered.

[9]Miller v. Miller, 2008-Ohio-4297, 2008 WL 3892154 (Ohio Ct. App. 9th Dist. Wayne County 2008).

[10]Winkelman v. Winkelman, 2008-Ohio-6557, 2008 WL 5205664 (Ohio Ct. App. 11th Dist. Geauga County 2008).

[11]Franck v. Franck, 2008-Ohio-624, 2008 WL 434982 (Ohio Ct. App. 3d Dist. Mercer County 2008).

be burdened with the post-decree responsibility of monitoring the activities of the recipient. In those cases where the support is not spent for the purpose ordered, the court may require the recipient to refund the misappropriated amounts.

RC 3105.18(C)(1)(m) takes into account the fact that in many cases one spouse sacrifices a well-paying job to be a homemaker, to relocate, or to conform with an employer's prohibition against married employees. In *Alder v. Alder*,[12] company policies that prohibited the wife from continuing as her husband's secretary after their marriage led to the parties' agreement that the wife should take early retirement from her employment. As a result of her early departure, her monthly retirement benefits were reduced by $375 per month. The appellate court affirmed the trial court's award of spousal support in the amount of $375 per month, based on the wife's lost income production capacity.

In *Johnston v. Johnston*,[13] the wife sacrificed her career to become a homemaker. The family relocated repeatedly during the husband's military career. The court of appeals held that the trial court properly considered lost income producing capacity that resulted from the wife's family obligations when it determined whether to award spousal support.

A wife who had moved fifteen times with her husband, due to his job-related transfers, although employed at various jobs during the marriage, was properly awarded spousal support with no termination date.[14]

§ 13:21   The statutory factors—(l)—Tax consequences of spousal support on each party

"Tax consequences" was added as a statutory factor in recognition of the fact that taxes and tax considerations play an ever-increasing role in the lives of individuals. While previously a factor that may have been considered by the court as an "other relevant factor," the court now must consider the tax impact of an award of spousal support.

Ordinarily, under Internal Revenue Code Section 71, spousal support is considered ordinary income for the recipient, and a tax deduc-

---

[12]Alder v. Alder, 105 Ohio App. 3d 524, 664 N.E.2d 609 (12th Dist. Butler County 1995) (overruled by, Carnahan v. Carnahan, 118 Ohio App. 3d 393, 692 N.E.2d 1086 (12th Dist. Clermont County 1997)).

[13]Johnston v. Johnston, 1996 WL 648976 (Ohio Ct. App. 11th Dist. Trumbull County 1996).

[14]Frye v. Frye, 1994 WL 109708 (Ohio Ct. App. 10th Dist. Franklin County 1994); Cole v. Cole, 2004-Ohio-6638, 2004 WL 2847820 (Ohio Ct. App. 8th Dist. Cuyahoga County 2004) (court affirmed an award of spousal support, and found that the wife was "substantially dependent upon [the husband] for economic survival and that this dependence resulted from her foregoing employment in order to fulfill her marital responsibilities.").

tion for the payor.[1] In order to be deductible, spousal support must be paid in cash and must terminate upon the death of the recipient spouse. The parties cannot be members of the same household when the payment is made. Payments which otherwise qualify as spousal support are not deductible if they are made voluntarily or if there is a provision in a divorce or separation agreement which states that payments are not deductible by the payer nor taxable income to the recipient.[2]

The Tenth District Court of Appeals has held that tax-shelter consequences may be taken into consideration in an award of spousal support.[3]

The Court need not consider tax consequences if no evidence has been presented on the tax impact of the spousal support award, because in that case the tax consequences would be speculative.[4]

§ 13:22   The statutory factors—(n)—Any other factor

Courts are not limited to the thirteen enumerated factors. RC 3105.18(C)(1)(n) includes "any other factor that the court expressly finds to be relevant and equitable."[1] It is a catchall paragraph which presumably could include factors which appeared in former versions of the statute, or factors arising out of case law, since the statute does not prohibit such consideration. Arguments should focus on the enumerated factors. The court will examine whether and to what extent a contemnor's behavior necessitated attorney fees.[2]

In 1974, when the legislature enacted RC 3105.18 and listed the factors, it also added specific factors to RC 3109.05 for the determination of child support. In the child support statute, there is a specific exclusion for considering marital misconduct. The statute on property

---

[Section 13:21]

[1]See Text Ch 28, Tax Considerations.

[2]Tax Facts 2008, Barbara Porzio.

[3]Birath v. Birath, 53 Ohio App. 3d 31, 558 N.E.2d 63 (10th Dist. Franklin County 1988).

[4]Rice v. Rice, 2007-Ohio-2056, 2007 WL 1241283 (Ohio Ct. App. 11th Dist. Geauga County 2007); Handschumaker v. Handschumaker, 2009-Ohio-2239, 2009 WL 1317874 (Ohio Ct. App. 4th Dist. Washington County 2009).

[Section 13:22]

[1]Chaudhry v. Chaudhry, 1992 WL 74204 (Ohio Ct. App. 9th Dist. Summit County 1992). The fact that the party seeking support has not been allocated the parental rights and responsibilities for the parties' minor children has been deemed a relevant factor. White v. White, 2003-Ohio-3279, 2003 WL 21447369 (Ohio Ct. App. 7th Dist. Columbiana County 2003). In Davis v. Davis, 2004-Ohio-6892, 2004 WL 2924344 (Ohio Ct. App. 6th Dist. Wood County 2004), the trial court found that it had no jurisdiction to enforce the promises the husband made as part of his sponsorship of his wife and her children when she was seeking her citizenship in the U.S. The Court of Appeals reversed, noting that the wife had health problems and a language barrier which would limit her earning ability in the near future.

[2]RC 3105.73

division provides that a distributive award can be made when a party has committed financial misconduct. Since the same legislature did not choose to exclude marital misconduct expressly in regard to establishing spousal support, it would appear to be a permissible other factor, both for payor and payee. It cannot, however, be the sole factor.[3] A court may award greater spousal support to a party if it finds that the other party has, by his actions, limited her ability to earn.[4] The Court may consider the amount of time which a party has been receiving temporary support in its decision to decline to order further spousal support.[5]

A trial court was declared to be within its discretion when it considered, as one of the "other relevant factors," appellant's conduct in diverting marital assets to a nonmember of the family after the couple separated but before the divorce.[6] A party's "gross financial misconduct," when combined with a very real possibility that the obligor spouse will not obey a monthly spousal support order can justify the court in ordering a "lump-sum" spousal support award. This should not be confused with a distributive award under RC 3105.17(A)(1) which is a property division[7] based on financial misconduct. Financial misconduct may not be remedied by an increased amount of spousal support.[8]

In *Fairchild v. Fairchild*,[9] the husband purchased a newer, more expensive residence before separation, then leased a luxury car and purchased a thirty-eight-foot cabin cruiser after separation. The appellate court agreed that the husband cannot retain luxuries and then

---

[3]Baker v. Baker, 1984 WL 6439 (Ohio Ct. App. 11th Dist. Lake County 1984); Zaller v. Zaller, 1984 WL 7417 (Ohio Ct. App. 11th Dist. Lake County 1984); Fisher v. Fisher, 1984 WL 6412 (Ohio Ct. App. 11th Dist. Lake County 1984).

[4]Baker v. Baker, 2000 WL CA 00056 (Ohio Ct. App. 5th Dist. Licking County 2000).

[5]Musil v. Musil, 2007-Ohio-406, 2007 WL 274308 (Ohio Ct. App. 8th Dist. Cuyahoga County 2007); Miller v. Miller, 2008-Ohio-4297, 2008 WL 3892154 (Ohio Ct. App. 9th Dist. Wayne County 2008); Wolf v. Wolf, 2009-Ohio-3687, 2009 WL 2231779 (Ohio Ct. App. 12th Dist. Preble County 2009).

[6]Wilder v. Wilder, 1989 WL 43293, at *3 (Ohio Ct. App. 10th Dist. Franklin County 1989). The trial court was reversed in Kennedy v. Kennedy, 2003-Ohio-495, 2003 WL 220405 (Ohio Ct. App. 7th Dist. Columbiana County 2003), when it refused to award spousal support based on the wife's financial misconduct, and failure to disclose assets. The Court of Appeals stated that financial misconduct could be a reason to increase or decrease spousal support, but should not be a bar to spousal support. Citing Winston v. Winston, 2000 WL 1724287 (Ohio Ct. App. 5th Dist. Stark County 2000). If a party seeking spousal support has committed financial misconduct, and that misconduct has been addressed in the division of property, the misconduct should not act as a bar to spousal support. Utt v. Utt, 2003-Ohio-6720, 2003 WL 22939438 (Ohio Ct. App. 7th Dist. Columbiana County 2003).

[7]Murphy v. Murphy, 1994 WL 75563 (Ohio Ct. App. 5th Dist. Stark County 1994).

[8]Ebner v. Ebner, 2008-Ohio-5335, 2008 WL 4572516 (Ohio Ct. App. 5th Dist. Stark County 2008).

[9]Fairchild v. Fairchild, 38 Ohio St. 3d 723, 533 N.E.2d 1062 (1988).

claim he is unable to pay his former wife what she requires for support.

It is within the discretion of the court setting spousal support to consider that the payor's expenses for basic necessities are reduced because they are shared by another person.[10] The court may also consider the sociological impact and statistical studies of post-decree disparity between standards of living as compared to during marriage.[11]

In *Cohoon v. Cohoon*, the trial court erred in calculating the amount of spousal support to be awarded. The award clearly was insufficient to meet wife's need and there were errors in the calculations presented. The court, however, had a legitimate concern about wife's history of dissipating assets to satisfy a drug habit.[12]

§ 13:23 Form of spousal support

RC 3105.18(B) provides that "spousal support may be allowed in real or personal property, or both." In fashioning a spousal support award, the court must determine both the form of support to be paid and the appropriate time over which the support should be paid. The form of payment may be: (1) a specific sum of money, payable either in a lump[1] sum or in installments; (2) periodic payments of a specific amount; Paragraph B of the statute provides that "An award of support may be allowed . . . from future income" and does not prohibit a percentage of income approach, however a fixed monthly amount serves to disentangle the parties financially. A percentage of income approach puts the spouse who is to receive support at the mercy of the payer spouse's honesty and record keeping. If the payer's income is likely to fluctuate, the court should retain jurisdiction to modify the amount of spousal support.[2] or (3) a transfer of property interests from one spouse to the other. Spousal support may also be in the form of a payment to a third party. In *Montgomery v. Montgomery*, the

---

[10]Mudd v. Mudd, 1988 WL 84416 (Ohio Ct. App. 10th Dist. Franklin County 1988).

[11]Kaechele v. Kaechele, 1986 WL 13922 (Ohio Ct. App. 10th Dist. Franklin County 1986), judgment aff'd and remanded, 35 Ohio St. 3d 93, 518 N.E.2d 1197 (1988).

[12]Cohoon v. Cohoon, 2000 WL 43705 (Ohio Ct. App. 2d Dist. Montgomery County 2000).

[Section 13:23]

[1]Brown v. Brown, 2003-Ohio-304, 2003 WL 164602 (Ohio Ct. App. 4th Dist. Pike County 2003); Lindsey v. Lindsey, 2009-Ohio-2593, 2009 WL 1564805 (Ohio Ct. App. 5th Dist. Tuscarawas County 2009).

[2]Metz v. Metz, 2007-Ohio-549, 2007 WL 431014 (Ohio Ct. App. 1st Dist. Hamilton County 2007), appeal not allowed, 114 Ohio St. 3d 1480, 2007-Ohio-3699, 870 N.E.2d 732 (2007).

court ordered the husband to pay wife's medical insurance until she began receiving social security disability income.[3]

The most frequent form of award, used in both divorce and legal separation actions, is a specific amount of money paid periodically. Spousal support I sometimes paid in a lump sum. This method is often employed when funds are available at the time of the divorce (through a division of property, for example) and the obligor is not a wage earner, or is not considered reliable, and is deemed to be unlikely to comply with the periodic order. In *Miller v. Miller*,[4] the trial court fashioned a lump sum spousal support award by determining what it would have ordered on a periodic basis and adjusting that figure for tax ramifications and present dollar value.

In *Fletcher v. Fletcher*[5] the award of $412, 4121.74 lump-sum spousal support was held to be valid in a marriage which lasted less than ten years where the wife had also received more than $12,148 each month for support between the parties separation and the final decree. In the *Fletcher* case, a valid antenuptial agreement preserved the husband's vast assets. As stated in the opinion, Fletcher was not typical in lifestyle, or in the amount of assets.

Most lump-sum spousal support awards are for attorney fees.[6] *Gest v. Gest*[7] reflects the typical lump-sum award for attorney fees pursuant to RC 3105.18(H), where husband who owned a dairy farm was in a better position to pay these necessary costs of the divorce. A lump-sum spousal support award of $5,000 for attorney fees to be paid in 90 days was held to be valid in *Titus v. Titus*[8] even though husband did not have the funds readily available. The appellate court noted that appellant-husband had the funds available at the beginning of the case, and that he has the ability to obtain the funds. If he dissipated those funds, he did so at his own peril whereas the wife had multiple sclerosis, was confined to a wheelchair, and was unable to work to support herself. Lump-sum awards can also be made payable in installments where the funds to pay the lump-sum are not available.[9]

Lump-sum spousal support awards pursuant to RC 3105.18 are not to be confused with distributive awards pursuant to RC 3105.171(E).

---

[3]Montgomery v. Montgomery, 2004-Ohio-3346, 2004 WL 1433621 (Ohio Ct. App. 12th Dist. Brown County 2004).

[4]Miller v. Miller, 2004-Ohio-923, 2004 WL 370406 (Ohio Ct. App. 3d Dist. Marion County 2004).

[5]Fletcher v. Fletcher, 1995 WL 386818 (Ohio Ct. App. 2d Dist. Montgomery County 1995), case dismissed, 73 Ohio St. 3d 1434, 653 N.E.2d 393 (1995) (the award was a lump-sum to the wife of $200,000 and $212, 421.74 for attorney fees).

[6]For a typical award see Gearig v. Gearig, 1993 WL 93525 (Ohio Ct. App. 6th Dist. Lucas County 1993).

[7]Gest v. Gest, 1998 WL 208872 (Ohio Ct. App. 9th Dist. Lorain County 1998).

[8]Titus v. Titus, 1995 WL 228722 (Ohio Ct. App. 9th Dist. Lorain County 1995).

[9]Motycka v. Motycka, 2001-Ohio-2162, 2001 WL 688886 (Ohio Ct. App. 3d Dist. Van Wert County 2001).

In an unusual case, *Marcum v. Marcum*,[10] the wife received as lump-sum spousal support $50,000 from the husband's settlement proceeds from a severe and disabling motorcycle accident. The trial court went through a pains taking process of apportioning the personal injury settlement proceeds into marital and separate property, and awarded Mr. Marcum his separate property portion of the award. The court then ordered Mr. Marcum to pay spousal support in a lump sum from his separate property award. The court of appeals affirmed this procedure, and held that RC 3105.18(C)(1)(a) and (i) contemplate such an award.

The *Marcum* court further stated as follows:

> Contrary to Mr. Marcum's assertion, the trial court did not make a *distributive award* from his separate property pursuant to R.C. 3105.171. Rather, it ordered him to pay spousal support from property it had divided. The fact that the proceeds to pay for the award of spousal support were to be taken from Mr. Marcum's share of the personal injury proceeds did not transform the spousal support award into a distributive award of separate property.[11]

The court found that this lump-sum award, if invested, would provide for Mrs. Marcum's support until all of her young children were in school, and that she could then seek job training.

Direct payment of spousal support is permitted by RC 3121.441 in limited situations. If the parties do not have any minor children and the spousal support has not been assigned to the department of human services, the obligor can make the spousal support payments directly to the obligee upon proper motion to the court. Section(B) of the statute requires that the payments be made in the manner that "establishes a clear record of payment," such as by check or money order. If the obligee fails to make payment timely, the court can order the payment to be made through the child support collection agency plus poundage.

In awarding support in periodic payments of a specific amount, the court must determine both the amount of each payment, and the duration of time over which these periodic payments will be made. While RC 3105.18 does not require such an award to terminate after any specific period of time or upon the occurrence of any specified event, most orders provide that payments will continue only for a specified number of months or years, or that the payments will cease upon (1) the death of either party; (2) the remarriage of the recipient; (3) the passage of a specific period of time; (4) the recipient's income exceeding a specified amount; or (5) further order of the court.[12]

---

[10]Marcum v. Marcum, 116 Ohio App. 3d 606, 688 N.E.2d 1085 (2d Dist. Montgomery County 1996).

[11]Marcum v. Marcum, 116 Ohio App. 3d 606, 611, 688 N.E.2d 1085, 1088 (2d Dist. Montgomery County 1996) (emphasis in the original).

[12]See Text §§ 13:28 to 13:36, Terminating spousal support; Text Ch 14, Modification of Spousal Support.

§ 13:24 Duration of spousal support

In the past, few limitations were put on the duration of periodic payment awards—they generally terminated only upon the death or remarriage of the recipient.[1] Since the Supreme Court's decision in *Kunkle v. Kunkle*,[2] however, most awards contain some limitation on the duration of the payments.

It may not be error for a trial court to order spousal support for an indefinite period of time where it is difficult to determine how long spousal support will be appropriate and necessary.[3] Often, an order of indefinite spousal support is reasonable and appropriate for an unemployed homemaker-spouse without readily marketable skills. The earning ability, or lack thereof, must be considered. Where the court finds little likelihood that such spouse will become self-supporting, it is inequitable to provide for termination other than for death, remarriage, or further order.[4] The court should retain jurisdiction to modify orders of indefinite or "lifetime" spousal support.

In *Koepke v. Koepke*[5] the Sixth District Court of Appeals held that an award of spousal support for an indefinite period of time, that is terminable only upon the occurrence of certain conditions, may be appropriate where on espouse has no prospect of gaining self sufficiency. The court explained:

> In cases involving marriage of long duration, parties of advanced age, and homemaker-spouse with little opportunity to develop a career, trial court may, in proper exercise of its discretion, award alimony terminable only upon certain contingencies, such as death or remarriage of recoverer of the award of alimony or further order of the court.[6]

[Section 13:24]

[1]See discussion of RC 3105.18(i) in Text § 13:19, The statutory factors—(i)—Relative assets and liabilities of the parties including court-ordered payments.

[2]Kunkle v. Kunkle, 51 Ohio St. 3d 64, 554 N.E.2d 83 (1990).

[3]Gore v. Gore, 27 Ohio App. 3d 141, 499 N.E.2d 1281 (9th Dist. Summit County 1985).

[4]See Mylnek v. Mylnek, 1987 WL 18132 (Ohio Ct. App. 6th Dist. Lucas County 1987) (no abuse found in alimony continuing until death or remarriage of payee or further order, where, after thirty-seven year marriage and five grown children, payee was fifty-six years old and employed part-time for minimal money); Smith v. Smith, 2006-Ohio-2136, 2006 WL 1132850 (Ohio Ct. App. 12th Dist. Butler County 2006). But see Farnsworth v. Farnsworth, 2003-Ohio-2341, 2003 WL 21040707 (Ohio Ct. App. 9th Dist. Medina County 2003).

[5]Koepke v. Koepke, 12 Ohio App. 3d 80, 81, 466 N.E.2d 570 (6th Dist. Lucas County 1983); See also Denney v. Denney, 1985 WL 7628 (Ohio Ct. App. 2d Dist. Montgomery County 1985) (wife had not worked for over twenty-seven years, no current employable skills, and at age where unreasonable to assume she would attain any).

[6]Koepke v. Koepke, 12 Ohio App. 3d 80, 81, 466 N.E.2d 570 (6th Dist. Lucas County 1983), supra. See also the discussion of *Kunkle v. Kunkle* in Text § 13:29, Terminating spousal support—Termination upon date certain.

In *Kunkle v. Kunkle*,[7] the Supreme Court rejected an indefinite award of modifiable alimony, subject to termination only on the occurrence of death, remarriage, or cohabitation, and held as follows:

> except in cases involving a marriage of long duration, parties of advanced age or a homemaker-spouse with little opportunity to develop meaningful employment outside the home, where a payee spouse has the resources, ability and potential to be self-supporting, an award of sustenance alimony should provide for the termination of the award, within a reasonable time and upon a date certain, in order to place a definitive limit upon the parties rights and responsibilities.

In *Winston v. Winston*,[8] the court refused to award indefinite spousal support. It noted the many references in the wife's medical records to her physical complaints being exacerbated by stress and anxiety and found that she needed certainty and security in her financial life while she prepared herself for employment. It concluded that she would not have that security if the court retained jurisdiction to modify the order of spousal support. Indefinite spousal support was found to be warranted, after a nine-year marriage when the wife had multiple sclerosis and required daily care, and so did "not have the resources, ability and potential to be self supporting for the indefinite future."[9] Indefinite spousal support was also approved in a marriage of over thirty years where the obligor's retirement income was projected to be greater than that of the obligee.[10]

The duration of spousal support payments is a frequent topic of dispute. Each case is heavily dependent on its facts. Courts have upheld:

(1) An award of spousal support for two years, consisting of payment of wife's health insurance premiums and kidney medication, even though the marriage was for eighteen years and wife claimed an inability to be self-supporting.[11]

(2) A substantial award to be paid for ten years, where the payee requested lifetime support in an amount sufficient to equalize the parties' income. Although the marriage was of a long duration, a

---

[7]Kunkle v. Kunkle, 51 Ohio St. 3d 64, 554 N.E.2d 83 (1990).

[8]Winston v. Winston, 2000 WL 1724287 (Ohio Ct. App. 5th Dist. Stark County 2000).

[9]Titus v. Titus, 1995 WL 228722 (Ohio Ct. App. 9th Dist. Lorain County 1995); Griffith v. Purcell, 1998 WL 32483 (Ohio Ct. App. 4th Dist. Scioto County 1998); Thomas v. Thomas, 2003-Ohio-5982, 2003 WL 22532883 (Ohio Ct. App. 12th Dist. Butler County 2003).

[10]Carney v. Carney, 2000 WL 1363173 (Ohio Ct. App. 6th Dist. Erie County 2000).

[11]McGee v. McGee, 1997 WL 659009 (Ohio Ct. App. 3d Dist. Union County 1997). See also Clark v. Clark, 2004-Ohio-1577, 2004 WL 615708 (Ohio Ct. App. 7th Dist. Noble County 2004) (A spousal support award short in duration was affirmed where wife had a standing offer of employment for which she needed no additional education.).

substantial award for ten years was appropriate under the circumstances.[12]

(3) The denial of support after a thirty-five year marriage, where wife had no earned income and husband had little income, but wife was living with a man who provided her room and board in exchange for household chores.[13]

(4) An award of $675 per month for 18 months after a 26-year marriage, which was challenged by both parties. Husband argued that because wife cohabited with another male during the parties' marriage, she was not entitled to any support. Wife asserted that the order limiting spousal support to 18 months after a 26-year marriage was an abuse of discretion.[14]

(5) A spousal support award of $1,000 per month for 24 months, where the parties had been married for eight years and wife was in good health and employable.[15]

(6) An award of four years of spousal support at $1,900 per month. The duration of the marriage was ten years. Husband's income was $200,000 per year and wife had no earned income.[16]

However, because equitable principles apply to an award of spousal support, and the court must consider all the factors in RC 3105.18(C), appellate courts have held as error trial court orders requiring spousal support to terminate in the following instances:

(1) After six years, where the payee-spouse would need two years to be able to obtain a current teaching certificate with no promise of a job, had been married for twenty-six years, and had no reservation of jurisdiction.[17]

(2) After six years, where there had been a thirty-year marriage, with payee, at age fifty-four, having diabetes, high blood pressure, and cataract problems, needing special medicines and care, unable

---

[12]Montague v. Montague, 1997 WL 764829 (Ohio Ct. App. 8th Dist. Cuyahoga County 1997).

[13]Moore v. Moore, 1997 WL 727490 (Ohio Ct. App. 12th Dist. Fayette County 1997).

[14]Nemeth v. Nemeth, 117 Ohio App. 3d 554, 690 N.E.2d 1338 (7th Dist. Jefferson County 1997).

[15]Williams v. Williams, 1998 WL 114209 (Ohio Ct. App. 6th Dist. Williams County 1998); Yeazell v. Yeazell, 2000 WL 1064728 (Ohio Ct. App. 2d Dist. Clark County 2000) (an award of spousal support for seven years was held not to be an abuse of discretion although the parties were only married for thirteen years; husband's argument that the court should have followed the "general accepted practice" to award one year of support for every three years of marriage was rejected; there was no evidence in the trial court of any such generally accepted practice), Sowders v. Ohio Liquor Control Comm., 90 Ohio St. 3d 1484, 738 N.E.2d 1256 (2000).

[16]Raphael v. Raphael, 1999 WL 1043726 (Ohio Ct. App. 1st Dist. Hamilton County 1999).

[17]Tissue v. Tissue, 1988 WL 32120 (Ohio Ct. App. 8th Dist. Cuyahoga County 1988).

to qualify for health insurance, and having minimal learning capacity.[18]

(3) After one year, without reservation of jurisdiction to modify, reversed when the reviewing court found that future income was uncertain and could be less than imputed.[19]

(4) After ten years, where recipient spouse had a ninth grade education, her employment during the marriage was at various minimum wage service jobs, and she neither had the resources nor the ability to become self-supporting at present or in the foreseeable future.[20]

(5) When a trial court fails to provide findings regarding a wife's ability to be self-supporting in nine years and fails to indicate how any future employment she might obtain would raise her standard of living to a level similar to that which existed during the marriage, the appellate court was unable to determine the basis for the court's decision to terminate spousal support on a date certain.[21]

(6) When a trial court ordered a twelve month term of spousal support and the parties had been married 20 years. The amount of the award was erroneously based upon imputed income to wife, which the evidence did not support.[22]

(7) When a trial court ordered spousal support for three years when the wife was pursuing a teaching degree which would take approximately four and one-half years to complete.[23]

The court will also note when assets become accessible to each party. In *Harman v. Harman*[24] the retirement benefits earned by the husband were divided equally, yet he was ordered to pay spousal support. He had additional assets which would be available to him sooner than the wife's share of the pension would be available to her.

There is no provision which "authorizes a trial court to continue jurisdiction over the issue of alimony when it made a specific finding that no alimony was warranted at the time of divorce," according to

---

[18]Adams v. Adams, 1987 WL 14409 (Ohio Ct. App. 6th Dist. Wood County 1987).

[19]Leister v. Leister, 1987 WL 18766 (Ohio Ct. App. 10th Dist. Franklin County 1987).

[20]Seawater v. Seawater, 1993 WL 476275 (Ohio Ct. App. 6th Dist. Lucas County 1993).

[21]Arena v. Arena, 1995 WL 571429 (Ohio Ct. App. 10th Dist. Franklin County 1995).

[22]McEaneney v. McEaneney, 2000 WL 141060 (Ohio Ct. App. 9th Dist. Summit County 2000).

[23]Peters v. Peters, 2004-Ohio-2517, 2004 WL 1104003 (Ohio Ct. App. 9th Dist. Lorain County 2004); Wiley v. Wiley, 2004-Ohio-2192, 2004 WL 917388 (Ohio Ct. App. 2d Dist. Montgomery County 2004) (spousal support of 18 months was affirmed in a 22 year marriage when the parties had been separated for 9 years and the wife would graduate within a year with a degree which would permit her to become employed and support herself).

[24]Harman v. Harman, 2000 WL 1275258 (Ohio Ct. App. 5th Dist. Tuscarawas County 2000).

Wolding v. Wolding.[25] Therefore if spousal support is warranted, but at the time of divorce the potential payor does not have the ability to pay, the trial court must make a finding that spousal support is appropriate and set some amount to be modifiable upon a change of circumstances. The trial court cannot award spousal support to commence six years after a divorce decree since a party's situation can change.[26]

It is within the trial court's discretion, when ordering spousal support, to set forth the conditions under which support may be modified in the future. In *Vergon v. Vergon*,[27] the trial court provided a range of income within which the court would not consider a change of income as the sole basis for modification. The appellate court approved the limitations as setting forth monetary income ranges reasonably tailored to the parties' circumstances that would establish what constituted a change for purposes of modification. The Court of Appeals has also dictated that physical conditions, coupled with an inability of a party to work, constitute circumstances allowing the court to retain jurisdiction to modify support pursuant to a divorce decree.[28]

§ 13:25   Attorney fees—Fees as spousal support

RC 3105.73, effective April 27, 2005, provides that attorney fees and litigation expenses may be awarded to either party "if the court finds the award equitable," that this award may be designated as spousal support, and that the Court may make an award of attorney fees under this section in addition to making an award under any other provision of the Revised Code or of the Rules of Civil Procedure. The notes to the statute provide that it applies to cases which had been filed and were pending on the effective date, as well as to cases filed after April 27, 2005.

Courts have often included an allowance for the payment of attorney fees in a decree for spousal support.[1] In the past, Ohio courts have justified awarding attorney fees in alimony actions through lib-

---

[25]Wolding v. Wolding, 82 Ohio App. 3d 235, 239, 611 N.E.2d 860 (3d Dist. Logan County 1992).

[26]Patterson v. Patterson, 1998 WL 880494 (Ohio Ct. App. 4th Dist. Adams County 1998).

[27]Vergon v. Vergon, 1995 WL 444442 (Ohio Ct. App. 8th Dist. Cuyahoga County 1995); Gaines v. Gaines, 2000 WL 1158769 (Ohio Ct. App. 5th Dist. Stark County 2000) (the separation agreement provision which provided for support if wife's monthly income exceeded $2,000 did not give the trial court jurisdiction to modify the amount, only to terminate it if the contingency occurred).

[28]Dunbar v. Dunbar, 1998 WL 433850 (Ohio Ct. App. 8th Dist. Cuyahoga County 1998).

[Section 13:25]

[1]Beach v. Beach, 99 Ohio App. 428, 59 Ohio Op. 187, 134 N.E.2d 162 (2d Dist. Montgomery County 1955); Stone v. Stone, 98 Ohio App. 240, 57 Ohio Op. 267, 122 N.E.2d 404 (8th Dist. Cuyahoga County 1954). See also Text § 25:57, Motions regarding attorneys—Motion for attorney fees, for cases addressing attorney fees.

eral interpretation of RC 3105.18 and the court's general equity powers. The Eighth District Court of Appeals has held that the decision to award attorney fees in an alimony award, and the amount of that particular portion of the award, are within the sound discretion of the trial court.[2] In *Abernethy v. Abernethy*[3] the court of appeals remanded the case because, although the trial court found that Mr. Abernethy had the ability to contribute to Mrs. Abernethy's attorney fees, it did not expressly find that a failure to award reasonable attorney fees would have prevented her from fully litigating her rights and adequately protecting her interests.

Besides affirming that an award of attorney fees is discretionary, the *Swanson* court held that application of a mechanical calculation based on the number of hours asserted multiplied by a specific rate (here, a bar association fee schedule) is error. The court indicated that the quality of the work done during the hours asserted is a proper consideration; i.e., the quality of the work must be determined to justify the rate. Although unstated, the implication is that applicant attorneys must prove quality and quantity of work done, and presumably their evidence and testimony may not be accepted without question. Attorneys are subject to cross-examination by opposing attorneys. The allowance of attorney fees in a spousal support award is not a matter of right, but is within the trial court's discretion.

Swanson also directs trial courts to consider the difficulty of the issues in the case; the professional skill demonstrated in conferences with the client and/or opposing counsel, and whether, in view of the particular facts of the case, the total number of hours spent should be compensable. Testimony on these matters should be in the record of the case, as an award of fees may involve large sums of money.[4] Another essential consideration under *Swanson* is the financial ability of the party in question to meet the demands of any award. As with spousal support in general, not only must the award be within the individual's ability to pay, but also it must leave that individual the means to maintain personal health and well-being by obtaining proper food, shelter, and clothing, and must not be a burden to the extent that incentive to work and pay support is destroyed.

There remains a question as to whether attorney fees may be awarded without direct evidence of the reasonableness of the fee and the time expended. The result may vary from court to court. The Second District Court of Appeals has held that "[w]here the record

---

[2]Swanson v. Swanson, 48 Ohio App. 2d 85, 2 Ohio Op. 3d 65, 355 N.E.2d 894 (8th Dist. Cuyahoga County 1976).

[3]Abernethy v. Abernethy, 2002-Ohio-4193, 2002 WL 1880142 (Ohio Ct. App. 8th Dist. Cuyahoga County 2002).

[4]Swanson v. Swanson, 48 Ohio App. 2d 85, 2 Ohio Op. 3d 65, 355 N.E.2d 894 (8th Dist. Cuyahoga County 1976); Cassaro v. Cassaro, 50 Ohio App. 2d 368, 4 Ohio Op. 3d 320, 363 N.E.2d 753 (8th Dist. Cuyahoga County 1976); Stout v. Stout, 3 Ohio App. 3d 279, 445 N.E.2d 253 (1st Dist. Hamilton County 1982) (error to award attorney fees without hearing).

discloses that alimony awarded as attorney fees by the trial court was determined solely by multiplying the number of hours worked by the minimum hourly fees established by the Bar Association, such an award constitutes prejudicial error which requires reversal."[5] However, the Second District Court of Appeals held in 1994 that where the trial court awards attorney fees in a nominal amount, no evidence of the amount of attorney fees incurred or the reasonableness of the fees incurred is required.[6] The Ninth District Court of Appeals has gone so far as to hold that it is not an abuse of discretion for the trial court to award attorney fees in the absence of direct evidence "where the amount of the attorneys' time and work is evident to the trier of fact."[7] It is the better practice to offer evidence as to the reasonableness of attorney fees. Some local rules have specific requirements about what a fee statement must include, and whether testimony is required. A domestic relations court may, however, use its own knowledge and experience to determine the necessity for and reasonableness of attorney fees, and in these circumstances the party requesting attorney fees is not obligated to offer testimony in support of the request.[8]

In exercising its discretion, the court must give consideration to the financial situation of the parties. In *Stone v. Stone*,[9] a court of appeals held that a party is generally not entitled to an allowance of attorney fees where he or she has sufficient means of his or her own to pay such expenses. In *Cassaro v. Cassaro*,[10] the court of appeals held that the trial court did not abuse its discretion in denying a wife's claim for attorney fees in an alimony award where the evidence showed that the husband was living on a fixed income with certain necessary expenses, and was therefore unable to assist the wife with such fees. The court ordered both parties to pay their respective professional fees.

Where the great bulk of assets awarded to appellant-wife was illiquid and the obligation for attorney fees could not reasonably be met

---

[5]Maze v. Maze, 1985 WL 8757, at *4 (Ohio Ct. App. 2d Dist. Montgomery County 1985).

[6]Woloch v. Foster, 98 Ohio App. 3d 806, 649 N.E.2d 918 (2d Dist. Miami County 1994).

[7]Kreger v. Kreger, 1991 WL 262883, at *2 (Ohio Ct. App. 9th Dist. Lorain County 1991).

[8]Gearig v. Gearig, 1993 WL 93525 (Ohio Ct. App. 6th Dist. Lucas County 1993).

[9]Stone v. Stone, 98 Ohio App. 240, 57 Ohio Op. 267, 122 N.E.2d 404 (8th Dist. Cuyahoga County 1954). See also Spayd v. Spayd, 1979 WL 208507 (Ohio Ct. App. 2d Dist. Montgomery County 1979); Mattoni v. Mattoni, 1980 WL 351170 (Ohio Ct. App. 6th Dist. Lucas County 1980); Cerovski v. Cerovski, 1981 WL 4508 (Ohio Ct. App. 8th Dist. Cuyahoga County 1981); Bowling v. Bowling, 1998 WL 96440 (Ohio Ct. App. 10th Dist. Franklin County 1998).

[10]Cassaro v. Cassaro, 50 Ohio App. 2d 368, 4 Ohio Op. 3d 320, 363 N.E.2d 753 (8th Dist. Cuyahoga County 1976).

from spousal support, the court must consider attorney fees as part of a totality of factors to consider when awarding spousal support.[11]

If the court determines that an award should be made, it must award the attorney fees to the party as part of the spousal support award, not directly to the attorney.[12]

§ 13:26 Attorney fees—Award upon finding contempt

The court's authority to award reasonable attorney fees is not extinguished upon the entering of a final decree of divorce. RC 3105.18(H) indicates that awards of additional attorney fees are appropriate in post-decree enforcement proceedings. In *Blum v. Blum*,[1] the Ohio Supreme Court determined that courts have authority to award attorney fees in the enforcement of child support orders. *Blum* cited *Pretzinger v. Pretzinger*[2] for the principle that the obligation for child support continues beyond the journal date of the divorce decree. Hence, appropriate enforcement must also continue. *Blum* concluded:

Thus, since the trial court can allow attorney fees in its discretion as "expenses during the suit" under Section 3105.14 of the Revised Code, . . . the trial court can allow attorney fees in its discretion as the suit continues. The divorce decree did not exhaust the court's power to award attorney fees.[3]

RC 3105.18(G) provides that where a spousal support obligor is found in contempt for failing to pay spousal support as ordered, "the court that makes the finding . . . shall require the person to pay any reasonable attorney's fees of any adverse party." The plain meaning of this provision is that a spousal support obligee is entitled to recover from the obligor any reasonable attorney fees expended in the effort to enforce the spousal support order that results in a finding of contempt

---

[11]Tissue v. Tissue, 1988 WL 32120 (Ohio Ct. App. 8th Dist. Cuyahoga County 1988).

[12]Reynolds v. Reynolds, 22 Ohio Op. 2d 162, 87 Ohio L. Abs. 250, 179 N.E.2d 160 (Ct. App. 4th Dist. Ross County 1961); Beach v. Beach, 99 Ohio App. 428, 59 Ohio Op. 187, 134 N.E.2d 162 (2d Dist. Montgomery County 1955) (expenses include attorney fees but they must be paid to spouse); Sinclair v. Sinclair, 98 Ohio App. 308, 57 Ohio Op. 347, 129 N.E.2d 311 (2d Dist. Preble County 1954); Stout v. Stout, 3 Ohio App. 3d 279, 445 N.E.2d 253 (1st Dist. Hamilton County 1982) (award of attorney fees in divorce action must be entered in favor of litigant, not directly in favor of litigant's attorney). See also Rust v. Takacs, 70 Ohio Misc. 2d 1, 650 N.E.2d 193 (Mun. Ct. 1994) (right of recovery is personal to the spouse, and spouse's attorney has no right to recover fees against the other spouse).

[Section 13:26]

[1]Blum v. Blum, 9 Ohio St. 2d 92, 38 Ohio Op. 2d 224, 223 N.E.2d 819 (1967).

[2]Pretzinger v. Pretzinger, 45 Ohio St. 452, 15 N.E. 471 (1887) (overruled by, Meyer v. Meyer, 17 Ohio St. 3d 222, 478 N.E.2d 806 (1985)).

[3]Blum v. Blum, 9 Ohio St. 2d 92, 38 Ohio Op. 2d 224, 223 N.E.2d 819 (1967). See also Ward v. Ward, 104 Ohio App. 105, 4 Ohio Op. 2d 177, 74 Ohio L. Abs. 408, 140 N.E.2d 906 (2d Dist. Montgomery County 1956); Keath v. Keath, 78 Ohio App. 517, 34 Ohio Op. 267, 71 N.E.2d 520 (9th Dist. Summit County 1946); Parker v. Parker, 28 Ohio L. Abs. 49, 56 N.E.2d 527 (Ct. App. 2d Dist. Franklin County 1938).

against the obligor. Nothing in the text of the statute suggests that the court may choose not to award attorney fees after finding the obligor in contempt. Thus, the general rule that whether to award attorney fees is a matter within the sound discretion of the trial court[4] does not apply where a finding of contempt for failure to pay spousal support is made. The award of attorney fees is mandatory.

Once a finding of contempt is made, the trial court's discretion in awarding attorney fees is limited to determining the proper amount of the award. In determining what constitutes a reasonable fee for the prosecution of the contempt proceeding, the trial court should consider the factors set forth in *Swanson v. Swanson*[5] that relate to the reasonableness of the fee, such as the attorneys level of experience and expertise, the range of fees in the area in which the case is heard, the difficulty and uniqueness of the issues presented, and the necessity of the services performed. However, because an award of attorney fees is mandatory, and because the award is not an award of additional spousal support under RC 3105.18(H), the court should regard as irrelevant the *Swanson* factors that relate to whether an award of attorney fees should be made, such as the obligee's need for an award of attorney fees and the obligor's ability to pay. The court will examine whether and to what extent a contemnor's behavior necessitated attorney fees.[6]

When awarding attorney fees for the failure to pay spousal support, the court must be careful to distinguish between attorney fees incurred in the prosecution of the obligee's motion to show cause from attorney fees incurred in the prosecution or defense of other motions which may have been consolidated in the same hearing.

In some courts, attorney fees awarded pursuant to RC 3105.18(G) are denominated as "additional spousal support." The purpose for this is to ensure that the award will survive any attempt by the obligor to discharge his obligation by filing for bankruptcy. This is a questionable practice, however, since the award of attorney fees is not additional spousal support pursuant to RC 3105.18(H), but rather a form of restitution. The practice is especially problematic in cases where the trial court did not reserve jurisdiction over the issue of spousal support when it issued the decree. In such cases, it is unlikely that the bankruptcy court will regard the debt as spousal support. Further, calling the award spousal support may make it taxable to the recipient and deductible to the contemnor.

§ 13:27 Attorney fees—Under separation agreement

Parties occasionally provide for payment of attorney fees, in their

---

[4]See Parzynski v. Parzynski, 85 Ohio App. 3d 423, 620 N.E.2d 93 (6th Dist. Erie County 1992).

[5]Swanson v. Swanson, 48 Ohio App. 2d 85, 2 Ohio Op. 3d 65, 355 N.E.2d 894 (8th Dist. Cuyahoga County 1976).

[6]Thomas v. Thomas, 2000 WL 1474446 (Ohio Ct. App. 8th Dist. Cuyahoga County 2000).

separation agreements, including provisions designed to deter default by requiring the payment of attorney fees if subsequent legal action is required to obtain compliance with agreed provisions. The Eighth District Court of Appeals held in *Snyder v. Snyder*[1] that Ohio law did not permit enforcement of this type of clause.

In *Nottingdale Homeowners' Ass'n Inc. v. Darby*,[2] the Ohio Supreme Court subsequently declared that contracts that stipulate the payment of attorney fees are enforceable when assented to in a noncommercial setting by competent parties with equal bargaining positions under neither compulsion nor duress. The Court stated, "It has long been recognized that persons have a fundamental right to contract freely with the expectation that the terms of the contract will be enforced."[3]

The Court continued, stating, "A rule of law which prevents parties from agreeing to pay the other's attorney fees, absent a statute or prior declaration of this court to the contrary, [Footnote omitted.] is outmoded, unjustified and paternalistic."[4]

While not arising out of a domestic action, this case would appear to apply equally to separation agreement provisions[5] that would not violate public policy, so long as the fees awarded are "fair, just and reasonable as determined by the trial court."[6]

In *Wesselman v. Wesselman*,[7] the Twelfth District Court of Appeals held that "[p]rovisions in a dissolution decree requiring a party to pay the other party's attorney fees if legal proceedings are instituted to enforce the terms of the decree are valid and enforceable."

The trial court is not divested of discretion in making its determination of reasonableness of attorney fees just because the parties stipulate to reasonableness. In *Nori v. Nori*,[8] the court held:

> The parties may have agreed to the reasonableness of the fees but the amount of the award is still within the discretion of the trial court. It

---

[Section 13:27]

[1]Snyder v. Snyder, 27 Ohio App. 3d 1, 499 N.E.2d 320 (8th Dist. Cuyahoga County 1985).

[2]Nottingdale Homeowners' Ass'n, Inc. v. Darby, 33 Ohio St. 3d 32, 514 N.E.2d 702 (1987).

[3]Nottingdale Homeowners' Ass'n, Inc. v. Darby, 33 Ohio St. 3d 32, 514 N.E.2d 702 (1987).

[4]Nottingdale Homeowners' Ass'n, Inc. v. Darby, 33 Ohio St. 3d 32, 514 N.E.2d 702 (1987).

[5]See Text § 9:40, Effect of signed agreement—Enforcement.

[6]Nottingdale Homeowners' Ass'n, Inc. v. Darby, 33 Ohio St. 3d 32, 514 N.E.2d 702 (1987).

[7]Wesselman v. Wesselman, 88 Ohio App. 3d 338, 342, 623 N.E.2d 1300 (12th Dist. Butler County 1993), citing Elliott v. Elliott, 1988 WL 38511 (Ohio Ct. App. 12th Dist. Preble County 1988).

[8]Nori v. Nori, 58 Ohio App. 3d 69, 568 N.E.2d 730 (12th Dist. Butler County 1989).

must take into consideration appellant's need following the property division and award of sustenance alimony.[9]

The fact that a trial court awards less than the amount stipulated is not an abuse of discretion.[10]

Of course, RC 3105.18(G) obviates the need for a provision designed to deter the obligor from defaulting on his or her spousal support obligation. However, a provision for the payment of attorney fees may be useful in deterring a party from defaulting on other obligations such as the transfer of property.

§ 13:28 Terminating spousal support—In general

The trial court enjoys broad discretion in determining the duration of an award of spousal support.[1] While the termination of support upon a date certain is preferred, the facts in a given case might warrant an award of support for an indefinite period of time.[2] Generally it is not error for a trial court to refuse to reserve jurisdiction to modify a spousal support award in a marriage of relatively short duration.[3]

There are four ways in which an order for spousal support may terminate:

(1) Spousal support may terminate upon a specified date.

(2) Spousal support may terminate upon the occurrence of a specified event.[4]

(3) The trial court may terminate spousal support as an exercise of its continuing jurisdiction upon finding that a change of circumstances has occurred that warrants the termination of support.

(4) Spousal support may terminate as a matter of law upon the death of either party or upon the remarriage of the obligee.[5]

§ 13:29 Terminating spousal support—Termination upon date certain

The Supreme Court has declared that ordinarily, a court should or-

---

[9]Nori v. Nori, 58 Ohio App. 3d 69, 75, 568 N.E.2d 730 (12th Dist. Butler County 1989).

[10]Arena v. Arena, 1995 WL 571429 (Ohio Ct. App. 10th Dist. Franklin County 1995).

[Section 13:28]

[1]Kunkle v. Kunkle, 51 Ohio St. 3d 64, 554 N.E.2d 83 (1990).

[2]See Text § 13:24, Duration of spousal support; Kunkle v. Kunkle, 51 Ohio St. 3d 64, 554 N.E.2d 83 (1990).

[3]Otis v. Otis, 1999 WL 1127396 (Ohio Ct. App. 2d Dist. Greene County 1999); Brown v. Brown, 2000 WL 1161699 (Ohio Ct. App. 6th Dist. Wood County 2000).

[4]The separation agreement may provide for the occurrence of an event which will terminate spousal support. In Akers v. Akers, 2004-Ohio-2908, 2004 WL 1240574 (Ohio Ct. App. 12th Dist. Butler County 2004) the parties' separation agreement stated that spousal support would end when the husband retired. The husband took early retirement. The spousal support award was terminated.

[5]RC 3105.18(B).

der that spousal support be paid for a specific length of time so that the parties' rights and responsibilities are specifically defined.[1]

The Supreme Court, in *Kunkle v. Kunkle*,[2] reversed the appellate court's affirmance of a trial court's award of modifiable spousal support, subject to termination on the occurrence of death, remarriage, or cohabitation, and held that

> except in cases involving a marriage of long duration, parties of advanced age or a homemaker-spouse with little opportunity to develop meaningful employment outside the home, where a payee spouse has the resources, ability and potential to be self-supporting, an award of sustenance alimony should provide for the termination of the award, within a reasonable time and upon a date certain, in order to place a definitive limit upon the parties rights and responsibilities.

Since equitable principles apply to an award of spousal support, it has been held as error for a trial court to order spousal support to terminate in the following instances:

(1) After six years, where the payee-spouse would need two years to be able to obtain a current teaching certificate with no promise of a job, had been married for twenty-six years, and had no reservation of jurisdiction;[3]

(2) After six years, where there had been a thirty-year marriage, with payee at age fifty-four having diabetes, high blood pressure, and cataract problems, needing special medicines and care, unable to qualify for health insurance, and having minimal learning capacity;[4]

(3) After one year, without reservation of jurisdiction to modify, reversed when the reviewing court found that future income was uncertain and could be less than imputed;[5]

(4) After ten years, where recipient spouse has a ninth grade education, her employment during the marriage was at various minimum wage service jobs, and she neither had the resources nor the ability to become self-supporting at present or in the foreseeable future;[6] and

(5) When a trial court fails to provide findings regarding a wife's ability to be self-supporting in nine years and fails to indicate how any employment she might obtain would raise her standard of living similar to that which existed during the marriage, the appellate

---

[Section 13:29]

[1]Kunkle v. Kunkle, 51 Ohio St. 3d 64, 554 N.E.2d 83 (1990).

[2]Kunkle v. Kunkle, 51 Ohio St. 3d 64, 554 N.E.2d 83 (1990).

[3]Tissue v. Tissue, 1988 WL 32120 (Ohio Ct. App. 8th Dist. Cuyahoga County 1988).

[4]Adams v. Adams, 1987 WL 14409 (Ohio Ct. App. 6th Dist. Wood County 1987).

[5]Leister v. Leister, 1987 WL 18766 (Ohio Ct. App. 10th Dist. Franklin County 1987).

[6]Seawater v. Seawater, 1993 WL 476275 (Ohio Ct. App. 6th Dist. Lucas County 1993).

court was unable to determine the basis for the court's decision to terminate spousal support on a date certain.[7]

The Eleventh District Court of Appeals has held that where the wife was forty-four years old, had never graduated from high school, had not maintained a steady job outside the home during most of her twenty-three-year marriage but instead had devoted her energies to being a homemaker and mother, and, since the parties' separation, had been able to earn only $5 per hour, the trial court's conclusion granting indefinite spousal support was found to be correct.[8] The appellate court found nothing in the wife's background that would permit a finding that she would obtain a job that would pay her sufficient wages to "maintain anything other than genteel poverty."[9]

Courts may continue to award spousal support of indefinite duration, subject to modification, without running afoul of the mandates of *Kunkle*.[10]

§ 13:30   Terminating spousal support—Termination upon specified event—Death or remarriage

Under RC 3105.18(B), spousal support terminates upon the death of either party, unless the decree expressly provides otherwise. If the decree of divorce provides that spousal support is to terminate upon the death of the party paying support, it is illogical to order that spousal support be secured with life insurance. *Waller v. Waller*[1] provides a good analysis of the issue of securing spousal support with insurance, at paragraphs 87 through 89 as follows:

> Five courts have interpreted the aforementioned statutory provision to mean that the trial court must comply with R.C. 3105.18(B) and expressly state that spousal support will continue after the death of the

---

[7]Arena v. Arena, 1995 WL 571429 (Ohio Ct. App. 10th Dist. Franklin County 1995).

[8]Sielaff v. Sielaff, 1990 WL 180636, at *7 (Ohio Ct. App. 11th Dist. Lake County 1990).

[9]Sielaff v. Sielaff, 1990 WL 180636 (Ohio Ct. App. 11th Dist. Lake County 1990).

[10]Corpac v. Corpac, 1992 WL 41244 (Ohio Ct. App. 10th Dist. Franklin County 1992); Karis v. Karis, 1992 WL 323888 (Ohio Ct. App. 9th Dist. Summit County 1992); Leversee v. Leversee, 1993 WL 87005 (Ohio Ct. App. 10th Dist. Franklin County 1993); Halpern v. Halpern, 1993 WL 266904 (Ohio Ct. App. 8th Dist. Cuyahoga County 1993); Wright v. Wright, 1993 WL 471474 (Ohio Ct. App. 12th Dist. Butler County 1993); Poyma v. Poyma, 1993 WL 266840 (Ohio Ct. App. 8th Dist. Cuyahoga County 1993); Reiter v. Reiter, 2001-Ohio-2155, 2001 WL 615729 (Ohio Ct. App. 3d Dist. Hancock County 2001) (no error to order lifetime support for long-term marriage where wife had limited earning ability). But see Canfarelli v. Canfarelli, 2000 WL 966165 (Ohio Ct. App. 2d Dist. Montgomery County 2000) where indefinite spousal support was held to be error. The wife was 38 years old and was in good health and the parties' children were teenagers. The Court of Appeals held that the wife had potential to be self-supporting.

[Section 13:30]

[1]Waller v. Waller, 163 Ohio App. 3d 303, 322-23, 2005-Ohio-4891, 837 N.E.2d 843 (7th Dist. Jefferson County 2005).

obligor in order to justify securing the spousal support award with a life insurance policy.[2]

. . . .

The current consensus of the appellate courts appear to be that a trial court can secure a spousal support order with life insurance, but only if the court makes it clear that it is, in effect, ordering spousal support to extend beyond the death of the obligor.

A trial court may not secure a spousal support order with life insurance, unless the order specifically states that the spousal support continues after the death of the obligor.[3]

Some courts permit an order that the spousal support obligor retain existing insurance to secure the spousal support award.[4] An order for insurance to secure payment of arrearages is proper.[5] The Ohio Supreme Court has held that spousal support ordered in a decree of divorce terminates upon the remarriage of the obligee.[6] In *Kimble v. Kimble*,[7] the Supreme Court of Ohio held the court lacks jurisdiction to terminate spousal support award for a term of years when the obligee remarries if there is no reservation of jurisdiction provision in the divorce decree, and no provision that spousal support shall terminate upon the remarriage of the obligee.

A trial court does not necessarily err in failing to include language in a divorce decree terminating spousal support upon a recipient's remarriage. Instead, a trial court may retain jurisdiction to consider reducing or terminating spousal support upon the recipient's remarriage. Spousal support no longer automatically terminates by

---

[2]See McCoy v. McCoy, 91 Ohio App.3d 570, 632 N.E.2d 1358 (Ohio Ct. App. 8th Dist. Cuyahoga County 1993); Addy v. Addy, 97 Ohio App.3d 204, 646 N.E.2d 513 (Ohio Ct. App. 10th Dist. Franklin County 1994); Pope v. Pope, No. L-96-198, 1997 WL 177697 (Ohio Ct. App. 6th Dist Lucas County 1997); Moore v. Moore, 120 Ohio App.3d 488, 698 N.E.2d 459 (Ohio Ct. App. 9th Dist. Summit County 1997); Vlah v. Vlah, No. 97-G-2049, 1997 WL 750812 (Ohio Ct. App. 11th Dist. Geauga County 1997).

[3]Janosek v. Janosek, 2007-Ohio-68, 2007 WL 64703 (Ohio Ct. App. 8th Dist. Cuyahoga County 2007), appeal not allowed, 114 Ohio St. 3d 1479, 2007-Ohio-3699, 870 N.E.2d 732 (2007); Karis v. Karis, 2007-Ohio-759, 2007 WL 4554454 (Ohio Ct. App. 9th Dist. Summit County 2007), citing Schiesswohl v. Schiesswohl, 2004-Ohio-1615, 2004 WL 626110 (Ohio Ct. App. 9th Dist. Summit County 2004); Moore v. Moore, 120 Ohio App. 3d 488, 492, 698 N.E.2d 459 (9th Dist. Summit County 1997); Sergi v. Sergi, 1996 WL 425914 (Ohio Ct. App. 9th Dist. Summit County 1996) and Pruitt v. Pruitt, 2005-Ohio-4424, 2005 WL 2046422 (Ohio Ct. App. 8th Dist. Cuyahoga County 2005) citing to McCoy v. McCoy, 91 Ohio App. 3d 570, 632 N.E.2d 1358 (8th Dist. Cuyahoga County 1993).

[4]Bertram v. Bertram, 2009-Ohio-55, 2009 WL 50147 (Ohio Ct. App. 2d Dist. Clark County 2009); Skibicki v. Skibicki, 2009-Ohio-390, 2009 WL 223893 (Ohio Ct. App. 6th Dist. Wood County 2009).

[5]Karis v. Karis, 2007-Ohio-759, 2007 WL 4554454 (Ohio Ct. App. 9th Dist. Summit County 2007).

[6]Dunaway v. Dunaway, 53 Ohio St. 3d 227, 560 N.E.2d 171 (1990).

[7]Kimble v. Kimble, 97 Ohio St. 3d 424, 426, 2002-Ohio-6667, 780 N.E.2d 273 (2002).

operation of law when a recipient remarries. When a divorce decree does not provide for the termination of spousal support after the remarriage of a party, a trial court may terminate the support only when the decree contains an express reservation of jurisdiction. Thus, a party's remarriage does not automatically terminate an award of spousal support.[8]

Provisions for the termination of support upon death or remarriage are common. The prudent course is to include a provision in the decree for termination upon death or remarriage.[9] This is especially true in cases involving dissolution of marriage, where the rule that remarriage of the obligee terminates a spousal support order as a matter of law does not apply.[10]

§ 13:31 Terminating spousal support—Termination upon specified event—Cohabitation of obligee

Cohabitation is another factor included in separation agreements and divorce decrees which will trigger a termination of spousal support. The Supreme Court of Ohio found that a woman who continued to receive spousal support while cohabiting was, "attempting to enjoy all of the benefits of a marriage by cohabiting with another man and yet not entering into an actual marriage in order to avoid the loss of alimony."[1]

The *Wolfe v. Wolfe*[2] Court reasoned that cohabitation presents a situation in which either the cohabiter contributes to the ex-wife's support, thus reducing her need for spousal support or the cohabiter is not contributing to household expenses, and is himself supported by a portion of the spousal support.

---

[8]Long v. Long, 176 Ohio App. 3d 621, 2008-Ohio-3006, 893 N.E.2d 217 (2d Dist. Greene County 2008).

[9]Dunaway v. Dunaway, 53 Ohio St. 3d 227, 560 N.E.2d 171 (1990); Taylor v. Taylor, 1998 WL 473340 (Ohio Ct. App. 7th Dist. Belmont County 1998).

[10]In re Adams, 45 Ohio St. 3d 219, 543 N.E.2d 797 (1989).

[Section 13:31]

[1]Wolfe v. Wolfe, 46 Ohio St. 2d 399, 401, 75 Ohio Op. 2d 474, 350 N.E.2d 413 (1976); Brown v. Bordenkircher, 2006-Ohio-3904, 2006 WL 2110746 (Ohio Ct. App. 7th Dist. Jefferson County 2006) (The word "cohabitation" should be used. In this case, court used the term, "take up residency" with an adult male. The wife challenged this language as being void for vagueness. The court of appeals held that the vagueness argument was not ripe, but that if "taking up residency" just meant sharing living space, this would contradict "clearly established law regarding the termination of spousal support."). But see Whittaker v. Whittaker, 1991 WL 273980 (Ohio Ct. App. 7th Dist. Mahoning County 1991) (court of appeals reversed the trial court's termination of spousal support where the separation agreement made no mention of cohabitation as an event which would terminate spousal support).

[2]Wolfe v. Wolfe, 46 Ohio St. 2d 399, 401, 75 Ohio Op. 2d 474, 350 N.E.2d 413 (1976), superseded by statute as stated in Heslep v. Heslep, 2000 WL 818909 (Ohio Ct. App. 7th Dist. Monroe County 2000).

In *State v. Williams*,[3] the Ohio Supreme Court listed two primary factors for determination of cohabitation: (1) the sharing of familial or financial responsibilities; and (2) consortium. Evidence establishing the sharing of familial or financial responsibility includes provisions the parties make for food, shelter, clothing and utilities. Consortium includes consideration of mutual respect, fidelity, affection, society, cooperation, solace, comfort, aid of each other, friendship and conjugal relations.[4]

The determination of cohabitation is a question of fact.[5] The court must consider whether the couple assumed obligations equivalent to those arising from a ceremonial marriage.[6] A finding that a spouse has "legally cohabitated" so as to terminate spousal support is reviewed under a manifest weight of the evidence standard.[7]

While most cases speak to situations where one seeks to terminate spousal support by reason of cohabitation, logic dictates that if cohabitation is grounds for modification or termination of spousal support, then it ought to be a bar to an original award.[8]

---

[3]State v. Williams, 79 Ohio St. 3d 459, 1997-Ohio-79, 683 N.E.2d 1126 (1997).

[4]See also, Moell v. Moell, 98 Ohio App. 3d 748, 649 N.E.2d 880 (6th Dist. Ottawa County 1994); Nelson v. Nelson, 1992 WL 114506 (Ohio Ct. App. 8th Dist. Cuyahoga County 1992); Thurston v. Thurston, 2000 WL 423987 (Ohio Ct. App. 10th Dist. Franklin County 2000) (trial court did not err in denying motion to terminate support by reason of alleged cohabitation by wife as that term was defined in their separation agreement).

[5]Dickerson v. Dickerson, 87 Ohio App. 3d 848, 623 N.E.2d 237 (6th Dist. Lucas County 1993). Rihan v. Rihan, 2006-Ohio-2671, 2006 WL 1461097 (Ohio Ct. App. 2d Dist. Greene County 2006), is unusual because even though the court found cohabitation, it reduced the spousal support order, rather than terminating it. Language in the parties' separation agreement provided that spousal support would terminate upon the wife's remarriage or cohabitation with an unrelated male. The wife lived with a male companion half the time, married him in a Muslim ceremony, albeit before the parties to the case were divorced, and had a child with him, the Court of Appeals affirmed the trial court's decision to modify rather than terminate the spousal support order, because the wife was only living with her companion half the time, and because he did not contribute to her support, only to the support of their child.

[6]Taylor v. Taylor, 11 Ohio App. 3d 279, 465 N.E.2d 476 (1st Dist. Hamilton County 1983).

[7]Clark v. Clark, 168 Ohio App. 3d 547, 2006-Ohio-4820, 860 N.E.2d 1080 (11th Dist. Trumbull County 2006), appeal not allowed, 112 Ohio St. 3d 1471, 2007-Ohio-388, 861 N.E.2d 145 (2007).

[8]Vaughan v. Vaughan, 1995 WL 495933 (Ohio Ct. App. 5th Dist. Muskingum County 1995). The obligee's cohabitation at the time of the divorce may be considered in determining an award of spousal support. Bernard v. Bernard, 2002-Ohio-552, 2002 WL 206411 (Ohio Ct. App. 7th Dist. Columbiana County 2002). But see Tomes v. Tomes, 2005-Ohio-1619, 2005 WL 752424 (Ohio Ct. App. 12th Dist. Butler County 2005) and Watson v. Watson, 2003-Ohio-6350, 2003 WL 22827545 (Ohio Ct. App. 10th Dist. Franklin County 2003) where the trial courts were reversed for failing to consider awarding spousal support because the wife was cohabitating. Cohabitation is not an outright bar to spousal support.

In *Keeley v. Keeley*[9] the court concluded that the wife was cohabitating. The husband's motion to terminate spousal support, filed in March of 1999, was granted retroactive to July 1, 1996, the date when the cohabitation commenced. Note, however, that it is unusual for what is in essence a motion to modify to be granted retroactive to the date of the filing of the motion. (See Text Ch 14, Modification of Spousal Support.)

Courts have found that cohabitation is established when the companion has voluntarily undertaken the duty of total support, or has otherwise assumed obligations equivalent to those arising from a ceremonial marriage.[10]

It has been held that while sexual relations may be one persuasive indicator of cohabitation, sexual relations are not dispositive of the issue.[11]

Awareness of the inequities involved where one party collects spousal support while cohabiting with another person has prompted many parties to include language in their separation agreements that provides for the termination of support upon the obligee's cohabitation with a member of the opposite sex. These provisions are usually enforced. Where the parties fail to agree to such a provision, it is not uncommon for the trial court to include it in its own decree.

The Ohio Supreme Court in *Cherry v. Cherry*[12] found that the court of appeals had "correctly concluded cohabitation with a male should not result in the automatic termination of support, but rather, is only

---

[9]Keeley v. Keeley, 2000 WL 431362 (Ohio Ct. App. 12th Dist. Clermont County 2000).

[10]Perri v. Perri, 79 Ohio App. 3d 845, 608 N.E.2d 790 (2d Dist. Montgomery County 1992); Taylor v. Taylor, 11 Ohio App. 3d 279, 465 N.E.2d 476 (1st Dist. Hamilton County 1983); Moell v. Moell, 98 Ohio App. 3d 748, 649 N.E.2d 880 (6th Dist. Ottawa County 1994). Cohabitation sufficient to terminate spousal support can exist even if the unrelated party does not assume any financial responsibility for the person receiving spousal support. Coe v. Coe, 2004-Ohio-3845, 2004 WL 1620787 (Ohio Ct. App. 9th Dist. Medina County 2004). More often, however, evidence of financial interdependence will be necessary to demonstrate cohabitation which will warrant terminating spousal support. Doody v. Doody, 2007-Ohio-2567, 2007 WL 1532083 (Ohio Ct. App. 11th Dist. Lake County 2007), Clark v. Clark, 168 Ohio App. 3d 547, 2006-Ohio-4820, 860 N.E.2d 1080 (11th Dist. Trumbull County 2006), appeal not allowed, 112 Ohio St. 3d 1471, 2007-Ohio-388, 861 N.E.2d 145 (2007).

[11]Wallenhurst v. Wallenhurst, 116 Ohio App. 3d 823, 689 N.E.2d 586 (7th Dist. Columbiana County 1996); Taylor v. Taylor, 11 Ohio App. 3d 279, 465 N.E.2d 476 (1st Dist. Hamilton County 1983); Graham v. Graham, 2003-Ohio-2123, 2003 WL 1958049 (Ohio Ct. App. 5th Dist. Guernsey County 2003). In Austin v. Austin, 170 Ohio App. 3d 132, 2007-Ohio-676, 866 N.E.2d 74 (9th Dist. Medina County 2007) the wife had a business relationship with a man with whom she had had a sexual relationship in the past. They lived under the same roof and shared financial responsibilities to facilitate the business relationship. The language of the separation agreement was "cohabitates in a relationship akin to a marriage." The Court of Appeals reversed the trial court's finding of cohabitation "akin to marriage" since there was no consortium.

[12]Cherry v. Cherry, 66 Ohio St. 2d 348, 20 Ohio Op. 3d 318, 421 N.E.2d 1293 (1981).

a factor properly considered in an award modification proceeding."[13] It is therefore improper for the court to order future payments to terminate automatically upon cohabitation.[14] The mere fact of a subsequent cohabitation cannot, however, be a per se ground for modification. If it were, the effect would be to control subsequent conduct of the former spouse rather than to achieve economic equity. There must be a hearing to determine the specific limitation posed by *Wolfe*, i.e., the impact of the cohabitation situation on the economic status of the former spouse. Because of this issue of fact, cohabitation does not per se terminate spousal support.[15]

In *Seybert v. Seybert*,[16] the Ninth District Court of Appeals held that the trial court did not abuse its discretion in suspending alimony payments during the period of cohabitation and continuing the alimony payments later. However, in *Miller v. Miller*,[17] the Eighth District Court of Appeals held that where a separation agreement incorporated into a divorce decree provides that alimony will terminate upon the wife's death, remarriage, or cohabitation for longer than one year, the trial court may terminate the alimony upon a finding that such a relationship has lasted more than one year, expenses are shared, and the obligee has attempted to cover up the relationship.

In a case in Montgomery County, the trial court was said to have properly terminated spousal support upon the wife's cohabitation with

---

[13]Cherry v. Cherry, 66 Ohio St. 2d 348, 20 Ohio Op. 3d 318, 421 N.E.2d 1293 (1981), citing Wolfe v. Wolfe, 46 Ohio St. 2d 399, 75 Ohio Op. 2d 474, 350 N.E.2d 413 (1976).

[14]Ruedele v. Ruedele, 1984 WL 5788 (Ohio Ct. App. 10th Dist. Franklin County 1984) (appellate court found error in trial court's ordering cohabitation automatically terminates alimony); Kaufman v. Kaufman, 1990 WL 167401 (Ohio Ct. App. 3d Dist. Marion County 1990), citing Stevens v. Stevens, 23 Ohio St. 3d 115, 492 N.E.2d 131 (1986) (restrictions on cohabitation proper only when award of sustenance alimony sought to be modified and not as automatic termination of alimony); Barrows v. Barrows, 2004-Ohio-7163, 2004 WL 3017232 (Ohio Ct. App. 9th Dist. Summit County 2004). But see Hall v. Hall, 2001 WL 259210 (Ohio Ct. App. 8th Dist. Cuyahoga County 2001) (where the spousal support order was terminated because of the wife's cohabitation, even though that factor was not specifically set forth in the judgment entry of divorce). But see Jeffery v. Jeffery, 2007-Ohio-4482, 2007 WL 2472228 (Ohio Ct. App. 9th Dist. Wayne County 2007), appeal not allowed, 116 Ohio St. 3d 1507, 2008-Ohio-381, 880 N.E.2d 483 (2008), which provides that if cohabitation is not provided in the divorce decree as a basis for termination, it may only be properly used to modify or terminate spousal support if the economic situation of the party receiving the spousal support has changed as a result of the cohabitation. (Citing Barrows v. Barrows, 2004-Ohio-4878, 2004 WL 2050508 (Ohio Ct. App. 9th Dist. Summit County 2004).).

[15]See Text § 14:30, Requirements for modification—Cohabitation of recipient.

[16]Seybert v. Seybert, 1991 WL 2009 (Ohio Ct. App. 9th Dist. Lorain County 1991).

[17]Miller v. Miller, 1985 WL 8602 (Ohio Ct. App. 8th Dist. Cuyahoga County 1985).

an unrelated male, despite the fact that the cohabitant contributed less than the income from the spousal support.[18]

The trial court did not abuse its discretion in concluding that the wife was cohabitating with an adult, unrelated male so as to justify a termination of spousal support where she provided housing, food and laundry services without cost to cohabitant.[19] Monetary support of either the ex-spouse by the cohabitating party or the cohabitating party by the ex-spouse is a key factor in determining whether or not spousal support should be terminated.[20]

§ 13:32 Terminating spousal support—Termination upon specified event—Gainful employment

Frequently, spousal support payments are ordered to terminate upon the payee's obtaining gainful employment. This is especially true in cases where, at the time of the decree, the payee is unemployed but has a significant earning potential. In such cases, it would be inequitable to require the payor spouse to continue to make sustenance payments to the payee who has obtained gainful employment and is thus able to provide for himself.[1]

Where the decree provides for termination on the payee-spouse earning in excess of a given sum per year, it is error to terminate spousal support until the total named sum has been earned, as differentiated from "is earning" and projections based on present income.[2]

§ 13:33 Terminating spousal support—Termination as exercise of continuing jurisdiction

The trial court may terminate spousal support as an exercise of its continuing jurisdiction over the issue of support. As the Ohio Supreme Court held in *Blakemore v. Blakemore*, the authority to modify spousal support includes the authority to terminate spousal support.[1]

The trial court does not have continuing jurisdiction to modify

---

[18]Miller v. Miller, 61 Ohio App. 3d 269, 572 N.E.2d 742 (2d Dist. Montgomery County 1989).

[19]Geitz v. Geitz, 1999 WL 354517 (Ohio Ct. App. 4th Dist. Jackson County 1999).

[20]Schrader v. Schrader, 1999 WL 771882 (Ohio Ct. App. 9th Dist. Medina County 1999).

[Section 13:32]

[1]But see Czap v. Czap, 1985 WL 6905, at *1 (Ohio Ct. App. 7th Dist. Belmont County 1985) (court held obligation to pay sustenance alimony "until such time as the defendant obtains gainful employment" did not terminate when defendant later obtained employment earning $3.50 per hour and worked approximately 100 hours per month).

[2]Harding v. Harding, 1986 WL 12970 (Ohio Ct. App. 5th Dist. Tuscarawas County 1986); Gaines v. Gaines, 2000 WL 1158769 (Ohio Ct. App. 5th Dist. Stark County 2000).

[Section 13:33]

[1]Blakemore v. Blakemore, 5 Ohio St. 3d 217, 450 N.E.2d 1140 (1983).

spousal support in a post-decree proceeding unless the decree includes an express reservation of jurisdiction.[2] It is within the sound discretion of the trial court to reserve jurisdiction to modify support. Moreover, some courts have held that it is an abuse of discretion to award spousal support for an indefinite period of time without reserving jurisdiction to modify.[3]

To terminate spousal support as an exercise of its continuing jurisdiction to modify support, the trial court must find that a change of circumstances has occurred which warrants the termination of support.[4] In considering whether the termination of support is warranted, the trial court should examine whether it is reasonable and appropriate for spousal support to continue in light of the changed circumstances. The analysis of whether the termination of support is warranted should include an analysis of all of the factors set forth in RC 3105.18(C)(1).

The circumstances that warrant the termination of support as an exercise of the court's continuing jurisdiction to modify are often the same circumstances identified in separation agreements providing for the termination of support upon the occurrence of particular events, such as the death of either party, the remarriage of the obligee, cohabitation by the obligee, employment by the obligee, or the reconciliation of the parties. In a given case, any one of these events may warrant the termination of spousal support, even when the decree does not expressly state that support will terminate upon the occurrence of such an event, as long as the trial court reserved jurisdiction to modify support.

Where the parties' separation agreement incorporated into a decree of dissolution does not provide for continuing jurisdiction to modify or terminate spousal support, the remarriage of the party who is receiving the spousal support will not reduce the agreed upon term of spousal support. A separation agreement that provides that no modification can be made unless in writing or by "subsequent court order," is sufficient to confer continuing jurisdiction to modify spousal

---

[2]RC 3105.18(E). See Stackhouse v. Stackhouse, 1997 WL 451471 (Ohio Ct. App. 2d Dist. Clark County 1997); Ujla v. Ujla, 1998 WL 382171 (Ohio Ct. App. 8th Dist. Cuyahoga County 1998). In a dissolution, the court lacks authority to modify the amount of spousal support payments except pursuant to the separation agreement. In an unusual case, the wife remarried and agreed with her first husband that she no longer needed or wanted spousal support. However, neither the parties' separation agreement nor the judgment entry granting the dissolution retained jurisdiction to modify the amount or terms of the spousal support award. The separation agreement did provide that its terms could be modified in a writing signed by both parties. The wife's motion to terminate spousal support was overruled on the basis that the Court lacked jurisdiction to modify spousal support without a writing signed by both parties. Thomas v. Thomas, 159 Ohio App. 3d 761, 2004-Ohio-2928, 825 N.E.2d 626 (11th Dist. Lake County 2004).

[3]Gullia v. Gullia, 93 Ohio App. 3d 653, 639 N.E.2d 822 (8th Dist. Cuyahoga County 1994), cause dismissed, 70 Ohio St. 3d 1409, 637 N.E.2d 6 (1994); Nori v. Nori, 58 Ohio App. 3d 69, 568 N.E.2d 730 (12th Dist. Butler County 1989).

[4]RC 3105.18(E).

support.[5] Where the parties' separation agreement provided for continuing jurisdiction to award spousal support only if one party attempted to succeed in discharging obligations through bankruptcy, wife, who filed bankruptcy but dismissed the action, was not entitled to an award of spousal support. She did not attempt to discharge any of the responsibilities assigned to her under the parties' separation agreement.[6] The Ninth District Court of Appeals has held that a trial court lacks jurisdiction to terminate the husband's spousal support obligation even though the wife has remarried. The separation agreement incorporated into their decree of dissolution did not contain a reservation of jurisdiction.[7]

§ 13:34 Terminating spousal support—Termination as matter of law—In general

Where no provision is made for the termination of support on a date certain or upon the occurrence of a particular event, and support is not terminated as an exercise of the trial court's continuing jurisdiction to modify support, the spousal support order eventually will terminate as a matter of law. Spousal support ordered pursuant to a decree of divorce terminates as a matter of law upon remarriage of the obligee or upon the death of either party, unless the decree expressly provides otherwise.[1]

§ 13:35 Terminating spousal support—Termination as matter of law—Remarriage of obligee

In *Dunaway v. Dunaway*,[1] the Ohio Supreme Court held that "[w]here a dependent divorced spouse remarries, the obligation of the first spouse to pay sustenance alimony terminates as a matter of law, unless: (1) the sustenance alimony constitutes a property settlement, (2) the payment is related to child support, or (3) the parties have executed a separation agreement in contemplation of divorce that expressly provides for the continuation of sustenance alimony after the dependent remarries."[2] Citing as precedent the case of *Hunt v.*

---

[5]Abramovich v. Abramovich, 1999 WL 420144 (Ohio Ct. App. 9th Dist. Summit County 1999), dismissed, 86 Ohio St. 3d 1456, 715 N.E.2d 188 (1999).

[6]McLaughlin v. Cotner, 1999 WL 401585 (Ohio Ct. App. 8th Dist. Cuyahoga County 1999).

[7]Collier v. Collier, 1999 WL 372556 (Ohio Ct. App. 9th Dist. Summit County 1999).

[Section 13:34]

[1]RC 3105.18(B).

[Section 13:35]

[1]Dunaway v. Dunaway, 53 Ohio St. 3d 227, syl., 560 N.E.2d 171 (1990).

[2]Dunaway v. Dunaway, 53 Ohio St. 3d 227, 560 N.E.2d 171 (1990).

Hunt,[3] the Court reasoned that "to hold a first spouse responsible for continued support is tantamount to imposing a legal obligation to support another couple's marriage."[4]

The rule in *Dunaway* is apparently limited to divorce cases. In *In re Adams*,[5] which was decided the year before *Dunaway*, the Ohio Supreme Court held that the trial court may not terminate a spousal support award set forth in a separation agreement incorporated into a decree of dissolution in the absence of an express reservation of jurisdiction to modify support. The Court explained that this is true even if the obligee remarries. The Court distinguished *Adams* from *Hunt*, and stated that *Hunt* involved a divorce, while *Adams* involved a dissolution. The Court reasoned that since dissolutions are contractual in nature, the court is bound by the express terms of the parties' agreement. Where the parties make no provision for post-decree modification of spousal support, the trial court is without the authority to modify or terminate support.

Nothing in the *Dunaway* decision suggests that the court changed its mind about terminating spousal support in dissolution cases in the year after *Adams* was decided. In fact, the Court in *Dunaway* was careful to limit its discussion to the termination of support in divorce cases. Since the Court in *Dunaway* neither expressly overruled *Adams* nor suggested that *Dunaway* is applicable to dissolution cases, *Adams* appears to be good law at this time.[6]

In sum, the remarriage of a spousal support obligee terminates the spousal support order as a matter of law in the absence of an express provision to the contrary only in divorce cases. Where the support order is made pursuant to a decree of dissolution, spousal support cannot be terminated upon the remarriage of the obligee unless the parties provide for termination upon remarriage in their separation agreement, and the trial court expressly reserves jurisdiction over the issue of spousal support.

§ 13:36 Terminating spousal support—Termination as matter of law—Death of either party

RC 3105.18(B) provides that spousal support "shall terminate upon the death of either party, unless the order containing the award expressly provides otherwise." Unlike the rule regarding the remarriage of the spousal support obligee, the rule that the death of either

---

[3]Hunt v. Hunt, 169 Ohio St. 276, 8 Ohio Op. 2d 286, 159 N.E.2d 430 (1959) (overruled by, In re Adams, 45 Ohio St. 3d 219, 543 N.E.2d 797 (1989)).

[4]Dunaway v. Dunaway, 53 Ohio St. 3d 227, 232, 560 N.E.2d 171 (1990). No error not to terminate spousal support when separation agreement permitted termination on obligee's remarriage or "a status thereto" and obligee was involved in a same sex relationship. Cohabitation does not constitute remarriage. Yaeger v. Yaeger, 2004-Ohio-1959, 2004 WL 833187 (Ohio Ct. App. 11th Dist. Geauga County 2004).

[5]In re Adams, 45 Ohio St. 3d 219, 543 N.E.2d 797 (1989).

[6]See Whiteside v. Fowle, 1996 WL 494825 (Ohio Ct. App. 12th Dist. Madison County 1996).

party terminates spousal support as a matter of law applies to both divorces and dissolutions.

Early Ohio law forbade installment payments of spousal support to be satisfied from the estate of the deceased payor.[1] However, a court was allowed to include in its decree an order requiring payment of support in installments, such order to be enforced against the husband's estate upon his death.[2] In the absence of such an order by the court, the parties could agree to bind the payor's estate and hold it liable for spousal support payments upon the death of the payor.[3] Additionally, a wife may execute a judgment for arrearages against the former husband's estate the same as any other creditor.[4]

Distinguishing the 1937 Ohio Supreme Court case of *Snouffer v. Snouffer*,[5] which held that permanent alimony ceased upon the obligor's death, the Second District Court of Appeals in *Denney v. Denney*[6] held that an obligor spouse could be required to designate his ex-spouse as the irrevocable beneficiary of his term life insurance policy for as long as his obligation to pay alimony continued. Such an award is an appropriate means of securing an award of permanent spousal support. The court noted that *Snouffer* was decided before life insurance became a popular device for funding family support after the supporting spouse's death. Further, it is now common practice to insure the support of minor children by naming them as life insurance beneficiaries until they reach majority. Finally, since life insurance proceeds pass outside of probate, there is no prejudice to the estate. It is not error to require a support obligor to maintain an obligee as a beneficiary and to require the obligor to pay the premium so long as the support obligation lasts.[7]

In *Heer v. Heer*,[8] the Tenth District Court of Appeals held that a spouse's need for support does not end when the provider dies. A court has full equitable jurisdiction and may order spousal support payments to be a charge against the provider's estate. Spousal support may also be a charge on the obligor spouse's estate *if* the parties have expressly agreed and such agreement has been incorporated into

---

[Section 13:36]

[1]Graff v. Graff, 99 Ohio St. 448, 125 N.E. 72 (1919); Lockwood v. Krum, 34 Ohio St. 1, 1877 WL 194 (1877).

[2]De Milo v. Watson, 166 Ohio St. 433, 2 Ohio Op. 2d 433, 143 N.E.2d 707 (1957).

[3]White v. White, 48 Ohio App. 2d 72, 2 Ohio Op. 3d 48, 355 N.E.2d 816 (6th Dist. Erie County 1975).

[4]Stemple v. Stemple, 12 Ohio Misc. 147, 41 Ohio Op. 2d 203, 230 N.E.2d 677 (C.P. 1967).

[5]Snouffer v. Snouffer, 132 Ohio St. 617, 9 Ohio Op. 14, 9 N.E.2d 621 (1937).

[6]Denney v. Denney, 1985 WL 7628 (Ohio Ct. App. 2d Dist. Montgomery County 1985).

[7]Gore v. Gore, 27 Ohio App. 3d 141, 499 N.E.2d 1281 (9th Dist. Summit County 1985).

[8]Heer v. Heer, 1985 WL 10066 (Ohio Ct. App. 10th Dist. Franklin County 1985).

a decree, or where, in a decree prior to January 1, 1991, "alimony" is actually a property settlement (debt) owing at the time of death.

A number of appellate courts have held that it is inappropriate for the trial court to order the support obligor to secure his spousal support obligation by naming the obligee as a beneficiary of a life insurance policy where the decree does not expressly provide for the continuation of support after the death of the obligor.[9]

In *Kunkle v. Kunkle*,[10] the Supreme Court held:

> Sustenance alimony awarded in a specific amount for a definite period of time, whether encompassed in an agreement between the payor and payee or decreed by court order, is chargeable against the payor's estate to the extent such award is not fully paid at the death of the payor.

The Court further reiterated its holding in *Ressler v. Ressler*[11] that an award of sustenance alimony for a fixed period of time and for a definite amount is not rendered indefinite even though the award is made subject to the payee's death, remarriage, or cohabitation.

It would appear obvious that spousal support should terminate as a matter of law upon the death of the obligee in all cases. However, the text of RC 3105.18(B) states, "Any award of spousal support made under this section shall terminate upon the death of either party unless the order containing the award expressly provides otherwise." This language suggests that spousal support may continue even after the death of the obligee if the divorce decree so provides. This is an odd provision, since the need for spousal support ends at the time of the obligee's death. Nevertheless, the language is unambiguous and it should be presumed that its inclusion by the legislature was intentional. (The death of a party will result in the dismissal of a divorce case.)

There do not appear to be any appellate cases which involve the continuation of spousal support after the death of the obligee.

The possibility that a court would require an obligor to continue to pay periodic support to a deceased former spouse is remote enough that it can safely be said that the death of the obligee terminates the spousal support order as a matter of law.

Finally, practitioners should keep in mind two points that relate to the death of the obligee:

(1) Death must be identified as a contingency in the decree in order to make the spousal support a tax deduction to the obligor.

(2) Accrued but unpaid installments will likely be viewed as vested, and thus an asset of the estate of the deceased obligee.

---

[9]Addy v. Addy, 97 Ohio App. 3d 204, 646 N.E.2d 513 (10th Dist. Franklin County 1994); McCoy v. McCoy, 91 Ohio App. 3d 570, 632 N.E.2d 1358 (8th Dist. Cuyahoga County 1993); Sergi v. Sergi, 1996 WL 425914 (Ohio Ct. App. 9th Dist. Summit County 1996); Shaw v. Shaw, 1996 WL 551423 (Ohio Ct. App. 12th Dist. Fayette County 1996).

[10]Kunkle v. Kunkle, 51 Ohio St. 3d 64, 554 N.E.2d 83 (1990).

[11]Ressler v. Ressler, 17 Ohio St. 3d 17, 476 N.E.2d 1032 (1985).

§ 13:37   Spousal support forms

◆ *Author's note:* *Forms to request spousal support vary from county to county, but keep track of the forms used to request child support. For spousal support forms, see the child support forms for the county in question.*

Chapter 14

Modification of Spousal Support

By Mark Edward Stone, Esq.[*]

---

[*]Based upon the previous version authored by Don C. Bolsinger, Esq.

Research References

Additional References

FinPlan's Divorce Planner CD-ROM

KeyCite®: Cases and other legal materials listed in KeyCite Scope can be researched through the KeyCite service on Westlaw®. Use KeyCite to check citations for form, parallel references, prior and later history, and comprehensive citator information, including citations to other decisions and secondary materials.

---

§ 14:1   Introduction

Prior to May 2, 1986, what can best be described as a state of confusion existed relative to the issue of modification of "alimony" awards contained in decrees of divorce and dissolution of marriage. That state of confusion is discussed later in greater detail in Text §§ 14:9, Divorce decree, through and including 14:17, and if the award of "alimony" about which the reader is concerned is contained in a decree of divorce or dissolution of marriage that was issued prior to May 2, 1986, the reader should proceed directly to §§ 14:9 through and including 14:17 before reading any other sections of this chapter.

For a brief summary of the history of spousal support known as "alimony," see Text Ch 13, Spousal support and §§ 13:1 and 13:2, History of spousal support. For a much lengthier discussion and analysis, see *Wolfe v. Wolfe*.[1]

Legislation made effective May 2, 1986 (1986 H.B. 358) greatly simplified the determination of whether a trial court has the jurisdiction to modify a spousal support award contained in decrees of divorce and dissolution of marriage. That legislation added the following language to RC 3105.18:

If a continuing order for periodic payments of money . . . is entered on or after May 2, 1986 . . . the court that enters the decree of divorce or dissolution of marriage does not have jurisdiction to modify the amount or terms of the alimony unless the court determines that the circumstances of either party have changed and unless one of the following applies:

(1) In the case of a divorce, the decree or a separation agreement of the

---

[Section 14:1]

[1]Wolfe v. Wolfe, 46 Ohio St. 2d 399, 75 Ohio Op. 2d 474, 350 N.E.2d 413 (1976).

parties to the divorce that is incorporated into the decree contains a provision specifically authorizing the court to modify the amount or terms of alimony.

(2) In the case of a dissolution of marriage, the separation agreement that is approved by the court and incorporated into the decree contains a provision specifically authorizing the court to modify the amount or terms of alimony.[2]

In 1991, additional legislation (1990 H.B. 514; see Text § 12:2, Evolution of RC 3105.171) clarified the distinction between awards that are "property division," not subject to modification at all, and awards that are "spousal support," which may be subject to modification. Such additional legislation also changed the terminology of awards that constituted a "continuing order for periodic payments of money" by calling such awards made on or after its effective date "spousal support" instead of "alimony." And, in what appeared to have been an attempt to define the term "change of circumstances" relative to modification of such awards, such additional legislation in 1991 also added the following language to RC 3105.18:

> (F) For purposes of divisions (D) and (E) of this section, a change in the circumstances of a party includes, but is not limited to, any increase or involuntary decrease in the party's wages, salary, bonuses, living expenses or medical expenses.[3]

Thus, relative to an award of alimony or spousal support contained in a divorce decree, or contained in a separation agreement incorporated into either a divorce decree or a decree of dissolution of marriage, and which decree was issued on or after May 2, 1986, one's analysis of whether that award may be modified should be as follows:

(1) Was language included in the decree that authorized the court to modify the award?

    (a) If the answer is "no", then the court does not have jurisdiction to modify the award.

    (b) If the answer is "yes", then the next question must be answered.

(2) Does the language express an intention to limit or guide the courts' exercise of its continuing jurisdiction?

    (a) If the answer is "yes", then depending upon the language used, and depending upon the appellate jurisdiction, such language may or may not be enforceable.

    (b) If the answer is "no", then in all appellate jurisdictions the next question must be answered.

(3) Do the facts of the case constitute a substantial change in circumstances that was not contemplated at the time of the original decree?

    (a) If the answer is "no", then the court is not permitted to modify the spousal support award.

---

[2]Currently found at RC 3105.18(E).

[3]RC 3105.18(F).

(b) If the answer is "yes", then the court is permitted to modify the spousal support award.

Finally, one must always keep in mind that all awards of spousal support, including those rendered upon modification of the original (or previously modified) award, must be "appropriate and reasonable" as required by the provisions of RC 3105.18(C)(1) and are ultimately subject only to an "abuse of discretion" standard. One commentator, directing his analysis to family law statutes in general and custody and alimony statutes in particular, has characterized statutory standards such as the one embodied in RC 3105.18 as "a governing principle that asks the decision maker to decide as he sees fit."[4] It is hoped that the text and citations to authorities in this chapter give the practitioner a better understanding of the issues involved with modification of spousal support awards. Nevertheless, given the breadth of discretion that RC 3105.18 establishes, the outcome of such cases almost always turn largely on their facts. Thus, as with original awards of spousal support, the answer to the question "under what circumstances, and to what extent, will a court modify an award of spousal support" remains largely unpredictable.[5]

§ 14:2   Procedure

Civil Rule 75(I) sets forth the requirements for invoking the continuing jurisdiction of the court. To modify spousal support, a motion must be filed and service of that motion must be in accordance with Civil Rules 4 to 4.6. Service of modification motions is different from motions filed during the pendency of the case; motions to modify decrees must be served as initial pleadings on the party rather than on counsel. This is true even if other motions are already pending at the time the motion to modify spousal support is filed.[1]

This same rule authorizes discovery procedures in proceedings to modify spousal support. Thus, the use of interrogatories, depositions, etc., may be fully implemented in modification of spousal support

---

[4]See Ira Mark Ellman, *Inventing Family Law*, 32 U.C. Davis L. Rev. 855, 862 (1998 – 1999).

[5]For a detailed and structured analysis of the vast disparity of awards involving identical fact patterns made possible by the "do as you see fit" standard contained in RC 3105.18, as well as a proposed model statute designed to reduce such disparities, see Leslie Spillane, Spousal Support: The Other Ohio Lottery," 24 Ohio N.U. L. Rev. 281 (1998). The American Law Institutes has also produced a model statute, which can be found at Ch. 5, "Compensatory Spousal Payments, Principles of the Law of Family Dissolution: Analysis and Recommendations," American Law Institute (2002); http://www.ali.org., and the Canadian federal Department of Justice has produced what it calls "Spousal Support Advisory Guidelines," and can be found at Carol Rogerson & D.A.R. Thompson, Spousal Support Advisory Guidelines: A Draft Proposal (2005), available at: http://www.justice.gc.ca/en/dept/pub/spousal/project/index.html.

[Section 14:2]

[1]Szymczak v. Szymczak, 136 Ohio App. 3d 706, 737 N.E.2d 980 (8th Dist. Cuyahoga County 2000).

proceedings. In addition to a modification request, the motion may also include a request for attorney fees under RC 3105.73.[2]

§14:3 Motion to modify spousal support—Form⊚

[Title of Court]

[Caption]

Case No.

[_____]

MOTION TO
MODIFY
SPOUSAL
SUPPORT

[Plaintiff/Defendant/Movant, Name] moves this Court for an order *[increasing/ decreasing/ terminating/modifying]* the award of spousal support contained in the *[the Decree of Divorce / Dissolution Decree/ prior order]* entered on *[date]* for the reason that a change of circumstances has occurred since the date of the prior order, as is more fully explained in the *[memorandum/affdavit]* of *[Plaintiff/Defendant/ Movant, Name]* attached hereto and as will be explained more fully to the Court at the oral hearing on the within Motion.

Further, *[Plaintiff/Defendant/Movant, Name]* moves this court for an order awarding *[him/her]* reasonable attorney fees and costs.

_____

Attorney for *[Plaintiff/Defendant/Movant, Name]*

[Notice of Hearing]

[Exhibit "A"—Memorandum/Affidavit of movant giving reasons/ justifications for motion]

[Proof/certificate of service]

NOTES TO FORM

Drafter's Notes

Under the signature line on the motion, counsel should list his or her Supreme Court registration number, business address, and phone number. It is also usually helpful to list a fax number and e-mail address and some courts have local rules requiring them to be listed.

Many courts have promulgated local rules, and often those local rules set forth requirements specific to that court relative to the proper filing and format of post-

_____

[2]For an in-depth discussion of awards of attorney fees, see Text §§ 13:25 to 13:27, Attorney fees.

decree motions. Often those rules also require the filing of a financial affidavit on a separate form required by that court.

A proof/certificate of service is only necessary as set forth in the provisions of Civ. R. 5. Post-decree motions filed at a time when no other matters are pending must be served pursuant to the provisions of Civ. R. 4 through Civ. R. 4.6. Although not specifically addressed by the provisions of Civ. R. 5, it would appear that all pleadings filed subsequent to that post-decree motion and involving the same or related matters may be served by ordinary mail pursuant to the provisions of Civ. R. 5. However, if the subsequent pleading itself raises new issues not related to those already pending, case law exists stating that such motion must be served personally pursuant to the provisions of Civ. R. 4 through Civ. R. 4.6. See Text § 14:2, Procedure.

RC 3105.73 and RC 3123.17(B) (formerly RC 3113.219(B)) grant the court permission to award attorney fees at any stage of the proceeding and when support is modified.

§ 14:4   Judgment entry granting/denying motion for modification—Form⊚

[Title of Court]

[Caption]   Case No. *[_____]*

                                                        AGREED
                                                        JUDGMENT
                                                        ORDER AND
                                                        ENTRY
                                                        MODIFYING
                                                        SPOUSAL
                                                        SUPPORT

This matter came on for hearing on *[date]* upon the motion of *[Plaintiff/ Defendant/Movant, Name]* filed on *[date]* to *[increase/ decrease/terminate]* the award of spousal support contained in the *[the Decree of Divorce / Dissolution Decree/ prior order]* entered on *[date]*. Upon agreement of the parties IT IS HEREBY ORDERED as follows *[specify new terms and/or describe the agreed upon changes]*.

_____

                                                        Judge

[Signature lines for both parties and counsel]

NOTES TO FORM

Drafter's Notes

Under the signature lines for each of the attorneys should be listed the attorney's Supreme Court registration number, business address, and phone number. It is also usually helpful to list one's fax number and e-mail address and some courts have local rules requiring them to be listed.

Although there is no requirement that the parties sign such agreed orders it is usually preferable that they do so.

Only a possible "agreed order" form is being provided. If the modification is the result of a court decision more often than not the court itself will draft the entry. If the court's decision contains language instructing counsel to draft the appropriate judgment entry, more often than not that court will have local rules that contain guidance as to what such judgment entries must contain. And, almost certainly such local rules will also contain guidance as to the provisions agreed orders must contain. Prior to January 25, 2002, all orders for spousal support made or modified after December 1, 1986, were required to be paid by withholding from some source (or bond) and through a support collection agency. However, effective January 25, 2002, new RC 3121.441 permits (but does not require) a court in certain circumstances to order spousal support obligations to be paid directly to the obligee by the obligor. RC 3121.441 still requires that such direct payments be made by some form that establishes a clear record of payment. The practitioner is cautioned to become familiar with the local rules of each court on this issue and on the issue of exactly what language is required by local rules or customs to be contained in any spousal support order.

§ 14:5 Motion for relief from judgment

Proceedings to modify spousal support awards are distinguished from motions for relief from judgment under Civil Rule 60.[1]

Proceedings under Civil Rule 60 include correction by the court of clerical mistakes, as set forth in Civ. R. 60(A), and the specific matters set forth in Civ. R. 60(B) which allow the court to relieve a party from a final judgment.

Civil Rule 60(B)(4) provides a possible legal procedure for use in modification of alimony or spousal support matters. This provision indicates that the court may relieve a party from a final judgment where "the judgment has been satisfied, released or discharged, or a prior judgment upon which it is based has been reversed or otherwise vacated, or it is no longer equitable that the judgment should have prospective application."

McKinnon v. McKinnon[2] held that a court of domestic relations, pursuant to Civ. R. 60(B), may vacate a judgment entry granting sustenance alimony if the court finds it is no longer equitable that the judgment have prospective application. The court in *McKinnon* found that Civ. R. 75(I) is not an exclusive remedy for seeking relief in such matters.

However, in *Knapp v. Knapp*,[3] the Ohio Supreme Court found that Civ. R. 60(B)(4) was not available to relieve a litigant from the consequences of his voluntary, deliberate choice to enter into a separation agreement in a dissolution of marriage proceeding. The court found that to allow a litigant to open such a proceeding through Civ. R.

[Section 14:5]

[1]See Text Ch 24, Relief From Judgment.

[2]McKinnon v. McKinnon, 9 Ohio App. 3d 220, 459 N.E.2d 590 (10th Dist. Franklin County 1983).

[3]Knapp v. Knapp, 24 Ohio St. 3d 141, 493 N.E.2d 1353 (1986); In re Pinkston, 1998 WL 336649 (Ohio Ct. App. 10th Dist. Franklin County 1998); Sidwell v. Sidwell, 1998 WL 346852 (Ohio Ct. App. 5th Dist. Muskingum County 1998).

60(B)(4) would encourage litigants to litigate carelessly. Also, the court found that Ohio public policy did not allow courts to modify periodic alimony payments in dissolution decrees. The *Knapp* case was a dissolution case.

In *Crouser v. Crouser*,[4] alimony was contested and the court issued a spousal support order for a period of two years. The payee appealed and the appellate court affirmed the trial court's decision. The divorce decree was entered on July 3, 1985. The payee then filed a motion to vacate under Civ. R. 60(B)(4) and (B)(5), alleging a change of circumstances. The Supreme Court found that the trial court did not have jurisdiction under Civ. R. 60(B)(4) or (B)(5) to vacate a periodic alimony award which has been litigated. The court found that modification was substantive law subject to the General Assembly and not a procedural mechanism.

Where a party remarried after a decree of dissolution of marriage was entered, and where that same party later filed a motion for relief from judgment, the motion was denied. A party may not "attack the validity of a dissolution after having relied on it for purposes of remarriage."[5] The continuing reliance on these holdings may be reduced in view of the Supreme Court's ruling in *In re Whitman*.[6] It held that Civ. R. 60(B)(1), (2) or (3) motions may be applicable to attack a portion of a decree of dissolution even though one of the parties has remarried.

A separation agreement which has been incorporated into a decree of dissolution of marriage may not be modified pursuant to Civ. R. 60(B) without vacating the entire decree of dissolution.[7] Previously in the same case, *Edwards v. Edwards*, the court had found to the contrary.[8]

In *Crews v. Crews*,[9] the court would not hear the Civ. R. 60(B) motion unless the movant was prepared to have the entire dissolution proceeding set aside. (The court assumed neither party had remarried.)[10]

Civil Rule 60(B)(4) was found to be an inappropriate "mechanism" to reopen the alimony aspects of a previously granted divorce where the former husband's sole request was to add the term "until her

---

[4]Crouser v. Crouser, 39 Ohio St. 3d 177, 529 N.E.2d 1251 (1988).

[5]Anderson v. Anderson, 13 Ohio App. 3d 194, 198, 468 N.E.2d 784 (2d Dist. Greene County 1984); Henry v. Edwards, 1996 WL 220885 (Ohio Ct. App. 2d Dist. Montgomery County 1996) (both parties had remarried).

[6]In re Whitman, 81 Ohio St. 3d 239, 1998-Ohio-466, 690 N.E.2d 535 (1998).

[7]Henry v. Edwards, 1996 WL 220885 (Ohio Ct. App. 2d Dist. Montgomery County 1996).

[8]In Matter of Edwards v. Edwards, 1994 WL 95253 (Ohio Ct. App. 2d Dist. Montgomery County 1994).

[9]Crews v. Crews, 1996 WL 685570 (Ohio Ct. App. 2d Dist. Montgomery County 1996).

[10]But see Whiteside v. Fowle, 1996 WL 494825 (Ohio Ct. App. 12th Dist. Madison County 1996).

death" to the agreed alimony order, so as to qualify for federal income tax deductibility.[11]

A change in the tax laws did not constitute grounds for obtaining relief under Civ. R. 60(B)(4).[12]

Although an award of sustenance alimony is non-modifiable by the terms of a decree, it may be an abuse of discretion to overrule a motion for a new trial based on newly discovered evidence.[13]

In *Whiteside v. Fowle*[14] the court found that the trial court could grant relief from a dissolution of marriage judgment pursuant to Civ. R. 60(B) for the limited purpose of establishing that payor's spousal support obligation terminated upon the payee's remarriage even though a spousal support termination provision was not in the parties' separation agreement. The court further found that a dissolution decree may be vacated for a limited purpose without setting aside the dissolution entirely and restoring the parties' marriage. Distinguishing *Whiteside* on the basis that it did not provide any termination date, the Ninth District Court of Appeals held, in *Abramovich v. Abramovich*,[15] that the remarriage of the recipient spouse did not justify granting Civ. R. 60(B) relief when the spousal support order, not subject to any conditions or reservation of jurisdiction, terminated by its own terms in 12 years.

In *Schaefferkoetter v. Schaefferkoetter*[16] the original divorce decree awarded wife, as property settlement, a portion of the husband's military pension as well as a separate award of spousal support, which award of spousal support was for three years and contained no reservation of continuing jurisdiction. The husband retired a little over three years after the issuance of the decree. When he retired, the husband elected disability retirement, thus substantially reducing the amount the wife received as her share of his military pension. Wife filed a motion to increase her spousal support award, as well as a Civ. R. 60(B) motion to vacate the original award and to ask for a new award that essentially compensated her with spousal support for the retirement benefits she lost. At such hearing the husband testified that he knew at the time of the original divorce that when he retired he was going to retire on disability retirement and that he had no idea whether wife knew this or not. Wife testified that she did not

---

[11]Caughenbaugh v. Caughenbaugh, 1987 WL 9959, at *1 (Ohio Ct. App. 5th Dist. Fairfield County 1987).

[12]Gotshall v. Gotshall, 1993 WL 34514 (Ohio Ct. App. 5th Dist. Stark County 1993).

[13]Marksbury v. Marksbury, 46 Ohio App. 3d 17, 545 N.E.2d 651 (6th Dist. Erie County 1988).

[14]Whiteside v. Fowle, 1996 WL 494825 (Ohio Ct. App. 12th Dist. Madison County 1996).

[15]Abramovich v. Abramovich, 1999 WL 420144 (Ohio Ct. App. 9th Dist. Summit County 1999), dismissed, 86 Ohio St. 3d 1456, 715 N.E.2d 188 (1999).

[16]Schaefferkoetter v. Schaefferkoetter, 2003-Ohio-5529, 2003 WL 22359725 (Ohio Ct. App. 2d Dist. Greene County 2003).

know of these plans. The appellate court affirmed the trial court's refusal to modify the spousal support, on the grounds of lack of continuing jurisdiction, but remanded the case to the trial court with specific instructions to enter an order granting wife's 60(B) motion, further instructing the trial court to take into account the loss of retirement income wife suffered and the gain in income husband realized by taking disability retirement. In *Pappas v. Pappas*[17] the trial court did not abuse its discretion in denying husband's motion under Civ. R. 60(B)(5) for relief from the spousal support provision of divorce decree over which the court did not retain jurisdiction. The motion was based on ex-wife fraudulently obtaining credit cards and theft of husband's identity. His counsel represented that all credit card debt had been reviewed and discussed prior to the divorce decree, no hearing had been requested, husband strongly suspected misuse by wife at the time and Husband neglected to correct own credit report.

In *Barnes v. Barnes*[18] the terms of the parties separation agreement were incorporated into their decree of divorce. In the separation agreement the husband had agreed to pay spousal support of $1,300 per month for 10 years "or until Wife remarries or upon the death of either party." A separate part of their separation agreement contained language reserving continuing jurisdiction but only as it related to the disposition of the parties real estate. Seven months after the decree was filed Husband lost his job and filed a motion to modify his spousal support obligation, and he also filed a motion to vacate the spousal support provision pursuant to Civ. R. 60(B)(4). The trial court overruled both motions. In affirming the trial court's decision, the Barnes court noted that future loss of income is always foreseeable and cannot be the basis for vacating a spousal support provision under Civ. R. 60(B)(4) or (5).

In *Moore v. Moore*[19] the terms of the parties' dissolution decree provided that husband would pay spousal support of an indefinite duration, would terminate "in the event Wife cohabits with a male not related by marriage" and the amount would otherwise be modifiable "in the event of significant change of financial circumstances." Eight years after their dissolution was final Wife had a sex change operation and had a girlfriend. The trial court denied husband's motion for relief pursuant to Civ. R. 60(B)(5). The court of appeals affirmed, holding that the sex change operation alone, without evidence that wife's financial circumstances had also changed, was an insufficient reason to revisit the spousal support provisions of the decree.

A motion labeled as a 60(B)(5) motion, but which simply continues to challenge the sufficiency of the evidence underlying the order being

---

[17]Pappas v. Pappas, 2006-Ohio-1403, 2006 WL 751351 (Ohio Ct. App. 6th Dist. Lucas County 2006).

[18]Barnes v. Barnes, 2005-Ohio-544, 2005 WL 327552 (Ohio Ct. App. 5th Dist. Stark County 2005).

[19]Moore v. Moore, 158 Ohio App. 3d 489, 2004-Ohio-5293, 817 N.E.2d 111 (2d Dist. Montgomery County 2004).

attacked, is a "motion for reconsideration" which is a legal nullity.[20] The Third appellate district has held that with the passage of the amendments to RC 3105.18 in 1986 that specifically addressed the modifiability of spousal support awards, the provisions of Civ. R. 60(B)(4) and (5) "are even less applicable or appropriate" as a vehicle for modifying spousal support awards.[21]

§ 14:6 Decree reserving right to modify

Three types of decrees provide for termination of marriage and may provide for spousal support awards, those being:

(1) Divorce decree not incorporating a separation agreement.

(2) Divorce decree incorporating a separation agreement.

(3) Dissolution of marriage decree incorporating a separation agreement.

As of May 2, 1986 and thereafter, RC 3105.18 grants a court the jurisdiction to modify spousal support awards made in each of such decrees so long as the decree, or the separation agreement incorporated into it, contains a provision specifically authorizing the court to modify the award and a change of circumstances that triggers that jurisdiction has occurred.

There is a conflict of authority over whether a trial court may reserve jurisdiction over the issue of spousal support if it does not enter an order of spousal support in the first place.[1] Cases finding in the affirmative include *Okos v. Okos*,[2] *Aylstock v. Bregenzer*,[3] *Harbert v. Harbert*,[4] *Tomovcik v. Tomovcik*,[5] and *Murphy v. Murphy*.[6] Courts reached contrary opinions in *Durbin v. Durbin*,[7] *Wolding v. Wolding*,[8]

---

[20]Myers v. Myers, 2005-Ohio-3800, 2005 WL 1763608 (Ohio Ct. App. 9th Dist. Summit County 2005).

[21]Jordan v. Jordan, 2005-Ohio-6028, 2005 WL 3031666 (Ohio Ct. App. 3d Dist. Hancock County 2005).

[Section 14:6]

[1]Hall v. Hall, 1994 WL 39051 (Ohio Ct. App. 6th Dist. Wood County 1994).

[2]Okos v. Okos, 137 Ohio App. 3d 563, 739 N.E.2d 368 (6th Dist. Lucas County 2000).

[3]Aylstock v. Bregenzer, 1994 WL 371330 (Ohio Ct. App. 2d Dist. Montgomery County 1994).

[4]Harbert v. Harbert, 1995 WL 643118 (Ohio Ct. App. 2d Dist. Greene County 1995), cause dismissed, 75 Ohio St. 3d 1470, 663 N.E.2d 1298 (1996).

[5]Tomovcik v. Tomovcik, 1997 WL 28548 (Ohio Ct. App. 7th Dist. Jefferson County 1997).

[6]Murphy v. Murphy, 1996 WL 629522 (Ohio Ct. App. 2d Dist. Montgomery County 1996).

[7]Durbin v. Durbin, 1992 WL 32001 (Ohio Ct. App. 9th Dist. Summit County 1992).

[8]Wolding v. Wolding, 82 Ohio App. 3d 235, 611 N.E.2d 860 (3d Dist. Logan County 1992).

and *Vaughn v. Vaughn*[9] The *Harbert* court, finding a conflict with the *Wolding* case, certified the conflict to the Ohio Supreme Court on the issue of whether a trial court may retain jurisdiction over spousal support if it does not order spousal support at the time of the divorce. The Supreme Court found that a conflict existed[10] and accepted the case, but the appellant dismissed the case prior to a decision.[11]

There have been cases where the original decree specifically reserved the court's jurisdiction to modify the spousal support, followed by modification orders which did not specifically re-reserve jurisdiction. Courts have held that the failure to repeat the words does not forfeit the court's jurisdiction.[12]

There have also been cases in which it was held not to be an abuse of discretion for the trial court to refuse to retain continuing jurisdiction to modify the spousal support award after terminating the spousal support award pursuant to a post-decree motion.[13] The Second Appellate District has issued several opinions holding that once a trial court issues an indefinite award of spousal support and retains continuing jurisdiction to modify that award, the trial court never loses jurisdiction to reinstate that award even if it "terminates" the award on a post-decree modification.[14] Subsequently, in the context of an award of spousal support of definite duration, the Ohio Supreme Court stated that the word "modify" as used in RC 3105.18(E) specifically includes "termination" stating they are simply different points or degrees along a continuum.[15] The Ninth appellate district has held that if an event specified in the decree as being a "terminating event" occurs, spousal support must be terminated and the trial court loses jurisdiction over the matter of spousal support, even if the original decree also contained an open ended continuing jurisdiction provision.[16]

RC 3105.18 does not specify the exact words that must be contained in a decree or separation agreement in order for the court to have retained continuing jurisdiction to modify the spousal support award

---

[9]Vaughn v. Vaughn, 2007-Ohio-6569, 2007 WL 4295707 (Ohio Ct. App. 12th Dist. Warren County 2007).

[10]Harbert v. Harbert, 75 Ohio St. 3d 1409, 661 N.E.2d 758 (1996).

[11]Harbert v. Harbert, 75 Ohio St. 3d 1470, 663 N.E.2d 1298 (1996).

[12]Archer v. Archer, 1997 WL 600233 (Ohio Ct. App. 4th Dist. Pickaway County 1997); Foster v. Foster, 1997 WL 583567 (Ohio Ct. App. 4th Dist. Washington County 1997).

[13]Ricketts v. Ricketts, 109 Ohio App. 3d 746, 673 N.E.2d 156 (12th Dist. Butler County 1996) (abrogated by, Erb v. Erb, 91 Ohio St. 3d 503, 2001-Ohio-104, 747 N.E.2d 230 (2001)).

[14]Templeton v. Templeton, 2001 WL 1173340 (Ohio Ct. App. 2d Dist. Montgomery County 2001); Lapierre v. Lapierre, 2001 WL 1018361 (Ohio Ct. App. 2d Dist. Greene County 2001).

[15]Kimble v. Kimble, 97 Ohio St. 3d 424, 2002-Ohio-6667, 780 N.E.2d 273 (2002).

[16]Brubaker v. Brubaker, 2006-Ohio-1035, 2006 WL 551548 (Ohio Ct. App. 9th Dist. Summit County 2006).

contained in that decree or separation agreement. For example, the words "all until further order of the court" placed at the end of a divorce decree, even if the language is not contained in the same paragraph as the award of spousal support, were found to be sufficient to retain jurisdiction to modify spousal support in *Kirkwood v. Kirkwood*.[17] The better practice, of course, is to include language in the separation agreement or decree that specifically and unambiguously authorizes the court to modify the award.

§ 14:7 Divorce decree—Decrees not reserving jurisdiction to modify

The decision whether to retain continuing jurisdiction is within the sound discretion of the trial court.[1] A trial court is not required to retain continuing jurisdiction to modify its own spousal support award.[2] However, failure of a trial court to retain continuing jurisdiction is error if the award is "lengthy," and when the award is indefinite, the trial court must retain continuing jurisdiction.[3] A trial court's failure to retain continuing jurisdiction to modify a court determined

---

[17]Kirkwood v. Kirkwood, 1996 WL 496947, at *1 (Ohio Ct. App. 1st Dist. Hamilton County 1996), which case cites cases supporting this finding as well as those with contrary findings. See also Pierson v. Pierson, 1998 WL 312531 (Ohio Ct. App. 9th Dist. Medina County 1998); Kopich v. Kopich, 126 Ohio App. 3d 332, 710 N.E.2d 350 (1st Dist. Hamilton County 1998) (applying *Kirkwood* holding to divorce decree, where separation agreement used same wording) (Ed. Note: Ohio Supreme Court certified case as conflict 98-815, 6-17-98), appeal dismissed by Kopich v. Kopich, 85 Ohio St.3d 1450, 708 N.E.2d 723 (1999); Phillips v. Phillips, 2007-Ohio-6245, 2007 WL 4148072 (Ohio Ct. App. 11th Dist. Trumbull County 2007). Nor is there any requirement that the language reserving jurisdiction be contained in the spousal support provisions itself. Stadelman-Wells v. Wells, 1995 WL 238419, at *2 (Ohio Ct. App. 10th Dist. Franklin County 1995).

[Section 14:7]
[1]Johnson v. Johnson, 88 Ohio App. 3d 329, 623 N.E.2d 1294 (5th Dist. Knox County 1993); Sutphin v. Sutphin, 2004-Ohio-6844, 2004 WL 2913904 (Ohio Ct. App. 1st Dist. Hamilton County 2004) (trial court did not abuse its discretion in failing to make award of "compensatory spousal support" of $1.4 million payable at $9,000 per month subject to termination upon Wife's remarriage or cohabitation); Shehab v. Shehab, 2004-Ohio-5460, 2004 WL 2293381 (Ohio Ct. App. 11th Dist. Portage County 2004).

[2]Soley v. Soley, 101 Ohio App. 3d 540, 655 N.E.2d 1381 (6th Dist. Lucas County 1995); Sutphin v. Sutphin, 2004-Ohio-6844, 2004 WL 2913904 (Ohio Ct. App. 1st Dist. Hamilton County 2004) (trial court did not abuse its discretion in failing to make award of "compensatory spousal support" of $1.4 million payable at $9,000 per month subject to termination upon Wife's remarriage or cohabitation); Shehab v. Shehab, 2004-Ohio-5460, 2004 WL 2293381 (Ohio Ct. App. 11th Dist. Portage County 2004); Handy v. Handy, 2007-Ohio-4423, 2007 WL 2429735 (Ohio Ct. App. 5th Dist. Tuscarawas County 2007) (8 year award of spousal support and no retention of continuing jurisdiction not an abuse of discretion); Schalk v. Schalk, 2008-Ohio-829, 2008 WL 553283 (Ohio Ct. App. 3d Dist. Seneca County 2008) (6 year award of spousal support and no retention of continuing jurisdiction not an abuse of discretion).

[3]Nori v. Nori, 58 Ohio App. 3d 69, 568 N.E.2d 730 (12th Dist. Butler County 1989); Gullia v. Gullia, 93 Ohio App. 3d 653, 639 N.E.2d 822 (8th Dist. Cuyahoga County 1994), cause dismissed, 70 Ohio St. 3d 1409, 637 N.E.2d 6 (1994). But see,

spousal support award must be attacked on direct appeal or any error will be deemed to have been waived.[4]

The Ohio Supreme Court has made clear the principle that the absence of language reserving jurisdiction to modify in a divorce decree issued by a trial court nullifies the trial court's ability to later modify the spousal support award, even if the grounds for modification is the remarriage of the recipient spouse.[5]

Kimble v. Kimble,[6] involved a divorce decree. The obligor spouse had been ordered to pay spousal support for a period of six years, and in its decree the trial court specifically provided that it was not retaining jurisdiction to modify the award. No appeal was taken from the original decree. Nine months after the issuance of the decree the recipient spouse remarried. The magistrate granted the obligor spouse's motion to terminate spousal support, but was reversed by the trial judge. The court of appeals reversed, and ordered the spousal support to be terminated. In a 7-0 decision, the Ohio Supreme Court reversed, ordering the spousal support award to be reinstated. In rejecting the obligor spouse's argument that the trial court's failure to reserve jurisdiction to "modify" did not prevent the trial court from "terminating" the award, the court stated that a motion to terminate spousal support falls within the definition of a "modification" since "it seeks to alter, change or reduce the support award."[7] The court also rejected the argument that as a matter of public policy the recipient spouse's remarriage is grounds for termination, finding that the passage of RC 3105.18 in 1986 effectively eliminated the holding in *Dunaway*[8] from having any application to decrees issued after May 2, 1986, stating "we can no longer rely on the policy set forth in *Dunaway* which conflicts with and is superseded by statute."

Subsequent to the issuance of the *Kimble* decision, the Ohio Supreme Court reaffirmed this principle in *Wagoner v. Gerbl*,[9] which case involved a negotiated decree that had provided for termination of the spousal support upon the recipient spouse's death but did not otherwise reserve any jurisdiction to modify the award. Again, the re-

---

Jordan v. Jordan, 2003-Ohio-7116, 2003 WL 23018581 (Ohio Ct. App. 3d Dist. Hancock County 2003) (award of spousal support of $6,000 per month for indefinite duration, with specific prohibition against modification within the first 5 years and with limited jurisdiction to modify thereafter held not to be an abuse of discretion under the facts of the case).

[4]McLaughlin v. McLaughlin, 2001-Ohio-2450, 2001 WL 803025 (Ohio Ct. App. 4th Dist. Athens County 2001); Lawson v. Garrison, 1998 WL 614558 (Ohio Ct. App. 6th Dist. Lucas County 1998); Ritchie v. Ritchie, 1999 WL 17675 (Ohio Ct. App. 12th Dist. Warren County 1999).

[5]Kimble v. Kimble, 97 Ohio St. 3d 424, 2002-Ohio-6667, 780 N.E.2d 273 (2002).

[6]Kimble v. Kimble, 97 Ohio St. 3d 424, 2002-Ohio-6667, 780 N.E.2d 273 (2002).

[7]Kimble v. Kimble, 97 Ohio St. 3d 424, 426, 2002-Ohio-6667, 780 N.E.2d 273 (2002).

[8]Dunaway v. Dunaway, 53 Ohio St. 3d 227, 560 N.E.2d 171 (1990).

[9]Wagoner v. Gerbl, 98 Ohio St. 3d 290, 2003-Ohio-739, 783 N.E.2d 899 (2003).

cipient spouse's remarriage was not a valid reason for terminating the award.

§ 14:8 Divorce decree—Decree reserving right to modify— Limiting condition

It does appear that trial courts, and parties, are permitted to limit the reservation of the trial courts' continuing jurisdiction to modify an award of spousal support.[1] A trial court's limited retention of jurisdiction to terminate an award of spousal support on the occurrence of certain events does not confer a general power to modify if such a power is not expressly reserved.[2] The right to modify upon a specifi-

---

[Section 14:8]

[1]Kimble v. Kimble, 97 Ohio St. 3d 424, 2002-Ohio-6667, 780 N.E.2d 273 (2002) (the parties can agree to no continuing jurisdiction to modify at all); Jordan v. Jordan, 2003-Ohio-7116, 2003 WL 23018581, ¶'s 19-22 (Ohio Ct. App. 3d Dist. Hancock County 2003) (the trial court can limit the circumstances that will entitle a party to modification to a finite set of circumstances); McLaughlin v. McLaughlin, 2001-Ohio-2450, 2001 WL 803025, at *4 (Ohio Ct. App. 4th Dist. Athens County 2001) (the parties agreement that provided for modification only if the payor experienced an involuntary reduction in income and which, in that case, provided that the payor's spousal support obligation would be reduced proportionately to his loss of income, and further provided that his obligation would never exceed forty-six percent of his base salary was enforceable); Dzina v. Dzina, 2004-Ohio-4497, 2004 WL 1902566, ¶'s 57-60 (Ohio Ct. App. 8th Dist. Cuyahoga County 2004), subsequent determination, 2005-Ohio-3127, 2005 WL 1484027 (Ohio Ct. App. 8th Dist. Cuyahoga County 2005), judgment aff'd, 108 Ohio St. 3d 385, 2006-Ohio-1195, 843 N.E.2d 1202 (2006) (the separation agreement provided the parties with a "buy-out" option regarding the former wife's spousal support, the trial court found that the former husband validly exercised his buy-out option, and the agreement expressly provided that the former wife was not entitled to future spousal support after she was paid the buy-out amount); Gemmell v. Gemmell, 2007-Ohio-5546, 2007 WL 3026896, ¶ 19 (Ohio Ct. App. 5th Dist. Licking County 2007) (the parties agreement to review of spousal support upon the happening of a certain event was enforceable; to hold otherwise would be to tell the parties they cannot return to court precisely because they agreed it was necessary to do so); Stewart v. Stewart, 1999 WL 1071976, at *3 (Ohio Ct. App. 5th Dist. Stark County 1999) (a prior agreement to modify support at a later date relieves the trial court from the necessity of finding a change of circumstances); and Harbert v. Harbert, 1997 WL 691506, at *3 (Ohio Ct. App. 2d Dist. Greene County 1997) (the language of RC 3105.18 authorizes a court to reserve jurisdiction to modify both amount and duration or either one but not the other). Also compare, in a property division setting, Jordan v. Jordan, 2000 WL 282305, at *2 (Ohio Ct. App. 2d Dist. Greene County 2000) (". . . the trial court was relieved of its authority and responsibility to fashion an equitable division of marital property by the parties themselves who voluntarily entered into an agreement . . ."). See also the discussion at Text § 14:38, Limitations on modification.

[2]Ressler v. Ressler, 17 Ohio St. 3d 17, 476 N.E.2d 1032 (1985); Jordan v. Jordan, 117 Ohio App. 3d 47, 689 N.E.2d 1005 (4th Dist. Scioto County 1996); Ritchie v. Ritchie, 1999 WL 17675 (Ohio Ct. App. 12th Dist. Warren County 1999); Wagoner v. Gerbl, 98 Ohio St. 3d 290, 2003-Ohio-739, 783 N.E.2d 899 (2003). See, also, Yaeger v. Yaeger, 2004-Ohio-1959, 2004 WL 833187 (Ohio Ct. App. 11th Dist. Geauga County 2004) (language in spousal support award "for 72 consecutive months, or sooner upon Wife's death, remarriage or assuming a status thereto" limited court's jurisdiction to

cally referenced event, for instance the commencement of social security benefits, does not confer a general power to modify.[3]

In contrast, in *Moore v. Moore*[4] the final decree issued in 2003
retained continuing jurisdiction to modify spousal support but
prohibited husband from seeking a "reduction in spousal support
based upon an increase in wife's income unless [wife] *earned in excess
of $18,000 per year from employment.*" After husband retired he moved
to reduce his spousal support obligation. The trial court appeared to
have ignored the income wife was to receive as her share of husband's
retirement, which was in excess of $18,000, and did not reduce
husband's spousal support obligation. The appellate court reversed
and remanded, finding that the trial court "erred when it overruled
[husband's] motion to reduce his spousal support obligation the court
had imposed in the divorce decree . . . [t]he source of the error is the
spousal support order in the 2003 divorce decree, from which no appeal was taken . . . [t]he error the court there committed would be
beyond our review herein, *except that as applied in the later order
from which this appeal was taken,* the error denies [husband] the
relief to which he may be currently entitled . . . [t]he error in the
decree's application is therefore preserved for our review."

§ 14:9   Divorce decree—No separation agreement

Case law states that court-ordered alimony or spousal support payments incorporated into a decree entered before May 2, 1986, and not
arising out of a separation agreement, may be modified by the court

---

termination only, not modification, and also did not authorize termination upon evidence of wife's cohabitation with her lesbian partner as such was not shown as being
equivalent to "remarriage or assuming a status thereto"); Jordan v. Jordan,
2005-Ohio-6028, 2005 WL 3031666 (Ohio Ct. App. 3d Dist. Hancock County 2005);
Greene v. Greene, 2008-Ohio-2829, 2008 WL 2572688 (Ohio Ct. App. 5th Dist. Licking
County 2008), appeal not allowed, 120 Ohio St. 3d 1418, 2008-Ohio-6166, 897 N.E.2d
653 (2008) (not abuse of discretion to enforce continuing jurisdiction language in
decree prohibiting consideration of ex-wife's cohabitation or her income).

[3]Keck v. Keck, 2000 WL 1159412 (Ohio Ct. App. 7th Dist. Mahoning County
2000); Gaines v. Gaines, 2000 WL 1158769 (Ohio Ct. App. 5th Dist. Stark County
2000) (condition precedent of wife earning $2,000 per month unambiguous); McLaugh-
lin v. McLaughlin, 2001-Ohio-2450, 2001 WL 803025 (Ohio Ct. App. 4th Dist. Athens
County 2001); Wagoner v. Gerbl, 98 Ohio St. 3d 290, 2003-Ohio-739, 783 N.E.2d 899
(2003). See, also, Yaeger v. Yaeger, 2004-Ohio-1959, 2004 WL 833187 (Ohio Ct. App.
11th Dist. Geauga County 2004) (language in spousal support award "for 72 consecutive months, or sooner upon Wife's death, remarriage or assuming a status thereto"
limited court's jurisdiction to termination only, not modification, and also did not authorize termination upon evidence of wife's cohabitation with her lesbian partner as
such was not shown as being equivalent to "remarriage or assuming a status thereto");
Jordan v. Jordan, 2005-Ohio-6028, 2005 WL 3031666 (Ohio Ct. App. 3d Dist. Hancock
County 2005). See, also, McLaughlin v. McLaughlin, 2007-Ohio-260, 2007 WL 172116
(Ohio Ct. App. 4th Dist. Athens County 2007) (language permitting modification upon
reduction of husband's income did not permit termination of his obligation upon his
reduction of income to zero).

[4]Moore v. Moore, 166 Ohio App. 3d 429, 2006-Ohio-1431, 850 N.E.2d 1265 (2d
Dist. Montgomery County 2006).

even though there is no express reservation of authority to modify.[1] Prior to that date, a court did not have to expressly reserve a right of modification over such alimony or spousal support payments to modify these payments later.[2]

As a result of 1986 House Bill 358, amending RC 3105.18, RC 3105.63, and RC 3105.65, for decrees entered on and after May 2, 1986, there can be no modification of alimony or spousal support decreed in a divorce decree unless the decree "contains a provision specifically authorizing the court to modify the amount or terms of alimony or spousal support."

The words "all until further order of the court" placed at the end of a divorce decree, even if the language is not contained in the same paragraph as the award of spousal support, were found to be sufficient in *Kirkwood v. Kirkwood*[3] to retain jurisdiction to modify spousal support. This case cites cases supporting this finding as well as those with contrary findings.

§ 14:10   Divorce decree—Incorporating separation agreement—In general

The right to modify alimony or spousal support payments awarded in a divorce decree, based on a separation agreement incorporated into the decree, depends upon the date the decree was entered. Decrees entered on or before June 23, 1976, have stricter modification requirements than decrees rendered after that date. Decrees entered on or after May 2, 1986, have even stricter modification requirements.

[Section 14:9]

[1]Corbett v. Corbett, 36 Ohio App. 321, 8 Ohio L. Abs. 286, 173 N.E. 316 (9th Dist. Summit County 1930), judgment aff'd, 123 Ohio St. 76, 9 Ohio L. Abs. 58, 174 N.E. 10 (1930); Popovic v. Popovic, 45 Ohio App. 2d 57, 74 Ohio Op. 2d 94, 341 N.E.2d 341 (8th Dist. Cuyahoga County 1975); Bulloch v. Bulloch, 21 Ohio App. 2d 76, 50 Ohio Op. 2d 142, 255 N.E.2d 299 (10th Dist. Franklin County 1969); Sager v. Sager, 5 Ohio App. 489, 27 Ohio C.D. 559, 1916 WL 1297 (6th Dist. Lucas County 1916); Norris v. Norris, 13 Ohio App. 3d 248, 469 N.E.2d 76 (5th Dist. Stark County 1982); St. Clair v. St. Clair, 9 Ohio App. 3d 195, 459 N.E.2d 243 (9th Dist. Lorain County 1983); McDonagh v. McDonagh, 4 Ohio App. 3d 207, 447 N.E.2d 758 (6th Dist. Lucas County 1982).

[2]Evans v. Evans, 1989 WL 114332 (Ohio Ct. App. 12th Dist. Brown County 1989) (where 1983 decree of sustenance alimony was disputed, alimony award is modifiable even though trial court did not expressly reserve jurisdiction to modify).

[3]Kirkwood v. Kirkwood, 1996 WL 496947, at *1 (Ohio Ct. App. 1st Dist. Hamilton County 1996). See also Pierson v. Pierson, 1998 WL 312531 (Ohio Ct. App. 9th Dist. Medina County 1998); Kopich v. Kopich, 126 Ohio App. 3d 332, 710 N.E.2d 350 (1st Dist. Hamilton County 1998) (applying *Kirkwood* holding to divorce decree, where separation agreement used same wording) (Ed. Note: Ohio Supreme Court certified case as conflict 98-815, 6-17-98), appeal dismissed by Kopich v. Kopich, 85 Ohio St.3d 1450, 708 N.E.2d 723 (1999); Phillips v. Phillips, 2007-Ohio-6245, 2007 WL 4148072 (Ohio Ct. App. 11th Dist. Trumbull County 2007).

§ 14:11 Divorce decree—Incorporating separation agreement—Entered on or before June 23, 1976

These decrees, which incorporate separation agreements entered into by the parties that provide for periodic alimony or spousal support payments and which do not contain an express reservation of jurisdiction to modify[1] are not subject to modification in the absence of mistake, misrepresentation, or fraud.[2]

§ 14:12 Divorce decree—Incorporating separation agreement—Entered after June 23, 1976

The law changed as of June 23, 1976, when *Wolfe v. Wolfe*[1] was decided. The Court stated, "A separation agreement of the parties loses its nature as a contract the moment it is adopted by the court and incorporated into a decree of divorce." When an agreement is incorporated into a decree, the agreement is superseded by the decree, and all obligations with respect to the payment of alimony or spousal support are imposed by decree and not by contract. The Court explicitly stated that the principle of merger applies. The Court then stated that the alimony was no longer a contractual obligation and therefore was no longer inviolable and unassailable; thus, future modification of alimony provisions would not violate contract rights.

The Court continued by defining what type of alimony payments could be modified:

> [W]here an alimony award is for support only, is for an indefinite amount, and where there is no property settlement, or if there is such a settlement, the support award is independent thereof; the jurisdiction of the Court to modify will be implied in the decree irrespective that such support order is based upon an agreement of the parties.[2]

The Court then limited its opinion by stating that this "new allowance" of modification of alimony payments in decrees incorporating

---

[Section 14:11]

[1]Hunt v. Hunt, 169 Ohio St. 276, 8 Ohio Op. 2d 286, 159 N.E.2d 430 (1959) (overruled by, In re Adams, 45 Ohio St. 3d 219, 543 N.E.2d 797 (1989)) (remarriage), In re Adams, 45 Ohio St. 3d 219, 543 N.E.2d 797 (1989); Fahrer v. Fahrer, 36 Ohio App. 2d 208, 65 Ohio Op. 2d 330, 304 N.E.2d 411 (1st Dist. Hamilton County 1973) (common law marriage even though the decree incorporated a separation agreement); White v. White, 1998 WL 101353 (Ohio Ct. App. 4th Dist. Scioto County 1998). See Text § 14:12, Divorce decree—Incorporating separation agreement—Entered after June 23, 1976; § 14:14, Divorce decree—Incorporating oral agreements.

[2]Newman v. Newman, 161 Ohio St. 247, 53 Ohio Op. 135, 118 N.E.2d 649 (1954); Popovic v. Popovic, 45 Ohio App. 2d 57, 74 Ohio Op. 2d 94, 341 N.E.2d 341 (8th Dist. Cuyahoga County 1975); Nash v. Nash, 77 Ohio App. 155, 32 Ohio Op. 409, 65 N.E.2d 728 (9th Dist. Medina County 1945).

[Section 14:12]

[1]Wolfe v. Wolfe, 46 Ohio St. 2d 399, 75 Ohio Op. 2d 474, 350 N.E.2d 413 (1976).

[2]Wolfe v. Wolfe, 46 Ohio St. 2d 399, 419, 75 Ohio Op. 2d 474, 350 N.E.2d 413 (1976).

separation agreements would apply only to those decrees entered after June 23, 1976. Since this prospective application was not set out in the syllabus, some courts of appeals (Lake County and Hamilton County, inter alia) found that the limitation to prospective application was dicta rather than law and thus not applicable. In *Supanick v. Supanick*,[3] the Ohio Supreme Court resolved any misunderstanding in this regard when it made clear that *Wolfe* was to be applied prospectively to those decrees incorporating separation agreements entered after June 23, 1976.

In 1985, the Ohio Supreme Court decided *Ressler v. Ressler*.[4] In that case, the Court found that

> [a] decreeing court does not have continuing jurisdiction to modify a sustenance alimony award that was made for a fixed period of years even though the award is subject to termination in the event of death, remarriage or cohabitation unless the decreeing court expressly reserves jurisdiction to modify.

The Court refused to allow the term of alimony to be extended beyond the term specifically set forth in the decree. Although this decree did not incorporate a separation agreement, the Court found that both types of decrees should be the same and deserved the same finality. This case modified the *Wolfe* decision as to the interpretation of "for an indefinite amount." The Court in *Ressler* found that an alimony award for a fixed period of years, even though subject to termination in the event of death, remarriage, or cohabitation was not an alimony award for an indefinite amount. Therefore, it was not modifiable.

§ 14:13 Divorce decree—Incorporating separation agreement—Entered on or after May 2, 1986

RC 3105.18, RC 3105.63, and RC 3105.65, as amended by 1986 House Bill 358, state that periodic payments of money as alimony or spousal support, whether provided in a divorce decree, a separation agreement incorporated into a decree, or a dissolution of marriage decree, are no longer modifiable, except upon changed circumstances of either party, and the decree or the separation agreement incorporated into the decree contains a provision specifically authorizing the court to modify the amount or terms of alimony or spousal support. These statutes are effective as to decrees entered on or after May 2, 1986.

§ 14:14 Divorce decree—Incorporating oral agreements

The courts have regularly recognized that in enforcement and modification matters there is no distinction between an oral or a writ-

---

[3]Supanick v. Supanick, 66 Ohio St. 2d 360, 20 Ohio Op. 3d 325, 421 N.E.2d 1301 (1981).

[4]Ressler v. Ressler, 17 Ohio St. 3d 17, 476 N.E.2d 1032 (1985).

ten agreement incorporated into a decree.[1] Thus, the June 23, 1976, date has the same application to both oral and written agreements.

§ 14:15 Dissolution of marriage decree—Entered before August 1, 1975

RC 3105.65(D), one of the original dissolution of marriage sections of the Ohio Revised Code, effective September 23, 1974, read, "The Court has full power to enforce its decree, and retains jurisdiction to modify all matters of custody, child support, visitation, *and periodic alimony payments*" (emphasis added).

§ 14:16 Dissolution of marriage decree—Entered on or after August 1, 1975 and before May 2, 1986

Effective August 1, 1975, the General Assembly amended RC 3105.65(B) by deleting the words "and periodic alimony payments" from the statute. The final sentence read, until changed by the General Assembly in 1986,[1] "The Court has full power to enforce its decree, and retains jurisdiction to modify all matters of custody, child support, and visitation."

Since divorce decrees incorporating separation agreements providing for alimony or spousal support payments became modifiable prospectively as of June 23, 1976, as a result of the Ohio Supreme Court's decision in *Wolfe v. Wolfe*,[2] there was some difference of opinion as to whether periodic alimony or spousal support payments set forth in a dissolution of marriage decree incorporating a separation agreement were modifiable or not. The Eighth District Court of Appeals in *Mcclain v. Mcclain*[3] found that alimony payments arising out of a dissolution decree could be modified, even without a clause reserving jurisdiction to do so. The Tenth District Court of Appeals in *Alban v. Alban*[4] found that such alimony payments could not be modified.

[Section 14:14]

[1]Robrock v. Robrock, 167 Ohio St. 479, 5 Ohio Op. 2d 165, 150 N.E.2d 421 (1958) (disapproved of by, Nokes v. Nokes, 47 Ohio St. 2d 1, 1 Ohio Op. 3d 1, 351 N.E.2d 174 (1976)); Mozden v. Mozden, 162 Ohio St. 169, 55 Ohio Op. 4, 122 N.E.2d 295 (1954); Popovic v. Popovic, 45 Ohio App. 2d 57, 74 Ohio Op. 2d 94, 341 N.E.2d 341 (8th Dist. Cuyahoga County 1975). See also Text Ch 9, Separation Agreements. Buder v. Buder, 1989 WL 65093 (Ohio Ct. App. 6th Dist. Erie County 1989).

[Section 14:16]

[1]1986 H.B. 358, eff. 5-2-86.

[2]Wolfe v. Wolfe, 46 Ohio St. 2d 399, 75 Ohio Op. 2d 474, 350 N.E.2d 413 (1976).

[3]Mcclain v. Mcclain, 1983 WL 4638 (Ohio Ct. App. 8th Dist. Cuyahoga County 1983), judgment rev'd, 15 Ohio St. 3d 289, 473 N.E.2d 811 (1984).

[4]Alban v. Alban, 1 Ohio App. 3d 146, 439 N.E.2d 963 (10th Dist. Franklin County 1981).

Mcclain went to the Supreme Court of Ohio.[5] The case involved a post-decree motion to modify alimony payments arising out of a dissolution of marriage decree. The Court held as follows:

> The sole question before this court is whether a court of common pleas may modify a provision for periodic sustenance alimony contained within a dissolution of marriage decree. We answer this question by limiting our holding in *Wolfe* . . . . to divorce cases, and by denying a trial court such jurisdiction to modify when the parties have voluntarily agreed to a dissolution.
>
> . . .
>
> The limitation upon a court's jurisdiction in dissolution cases extends to modifications of separation agreements after a decree is entered. Just as a court lacks authority to set the original amount of alimony payments in a dissolution case, a court also lacks authority to modify the amount of alimony payments originally agreed to by the parties.[6]

Also, in *In re Adams*,[7] the Court found that a court is without jurisdiction to modify or terminate an award of alimony set forth in a separation agreement incorporated into a 1985 decree of dissolution of marriage absent a reservation of jurisdiction in the agreement, even though the payee had remarried.

In *Mcclain*, the Ohio Supreme Court did not address the question of whether parties can bestow jurisdiction to modify alimony or spousal support on a trial court by agreement.

The Supreme Court addressed this issue in *Colley v. Colley*,[8] decided May 24, 1989, and held that

> under R.C. 3105.65(B), as amended effective August 1, 1975, a court may retain jurisdiction to modify alimony payments provided for in a separation agreement by parties to a dissolution where the parties have agreed to such continuing jurisdiction and the agreement has been incorporated in a decree of dissolution of marriage.[9]

§ 14:17 Dissolution of marriage decree—Entered on and after May 2, 1986

As a result of the confusion, conflicting decisions, and unequal treatment of divorce and dissolution decrees, the legislature passed 1986 House Bill 358, effective May 2, 1986. It amended RC 3105.18(D) (now contained in RC 3105.18(E)) to grant the court issuing a divorce or dissolution decree the power to modify alimony or spousal support after determining that the circumstances of either party have changed, but only if as follows:

(1) In the case of a divorce, the decree or a separation agreement

---

[5]McClain v. McClain, 15 Ohio St. 3d 289, 473 N.E.2d 811 (1984).

[6]McClain v. McClain, 15 Ohio St. 3d 289, 473 N.E.2d 811 (1984) (footnote omitted); Villa v. Villa, 1998 WL 241953 (Ohio Ct. App. 8th Dist. Cuyahoga County 1998) (the law at the time of the decree controls).

[7]In re Adams, 45 Ohio St. 3d 219, 543 N.E.2d 797 (1989).

[8]Colley v. Colley, 43 Ohio St. 3d 87, 538 N.E.2d 410 (1989).

[9]Colley v. Colley, 43 Ohio St. 3d 87, 538 N.E.2d 410 (1989).

of the parties to the divorce that is incorporated into the decree contains a provision specifically authorizing the court to modify the amount or terms of alimony or spousal support.

(2) In the case of a dissolution of marriage, the separation agreement that is approved by the court and incorporated into the decree contains a provision specifically authorizing the court to modify the amount or terms of alimony or spousal support.

The amendment is specifically made applicable to decrees entered after its effective date and is declared not to affect prior determinations on modifications. Nothing in the amendment states that courts did not have power to modify alimony or spousal support awards in appropriate circumstances prior to its enactment. After January 1, 1991, payments for sustenance or support are called "spousal support" and are separate from property divisions under RC 3105.171.

However, a court was without jurisdiction to modify or terminate an alimony or a spousal support award set forth in a separation agreement incorporated into a dissolution decree, even after the remarriage of the payee, where the agreement did not provide for termination on remarriage and there is no reservation of jurisdiction in the agreement.[1]

In *Thomas v. Thomas*,[2] the parties obtained a dissolution of their marriage in 1992. Their separation agreement required the husband to pay spousal support, with language increasing the amount as the children became emancipated and terminating the obligation upon the wife's death, but contained no other reservation of jurisdiction to modify the award. Upon the wife's remarriage, the parties verbally agreed that husband's spousal support obligation should terminate. The wife (yes, the wife) filed a motion to terminate the spousal support award, and the husband did not respond to the motion. The trial court denied the motion, finding that it had no jurisdiction to modify or terminate the award based on the wife's remarriage as such jurisdiction had not been retained. The appellate court affirmed this decision, citing *Kimble v. Kimble*.[3] However, the *Thomas* court also noted that "the trial court would have jurisdiction to terminate spousal support if the parties made a joint request in writing," citing as support for this the language in the parties separation agreement that permitted modifications "if done in writing and signed by both parties."

Applying the principle that, under general rules of contract interpretation, a contract should be construed as a whole so as to give effect to every part of the contract, the court in *Stadelman-Wells v.*

[Section 14:17]

[1]Nelson v. Nelson, 1991 WL 18649 (Ohio Ct. App. 11th Dist. Ashtabula County 1991).

[2]Thomas v. Thomas, 159 Ohio App. 3d 761, 2004-Ohio-2928, 825 N.E.2d 626 (11th Dist. Lake County 2004).

[3]Kimble v. Kimble, 97 Ohio St. 3d 424, 2002-Ohio-6667, 780 N.E.2d 273 (2002).

Wells[4] held that the trial court had jurisdiction to modify spousal support even though the paragraphs specifically addressing spousal support did not have language reserving continuing jurisdiction. The agreement did have a sentence in a catchall section called "Further Provisions" that stated the "Agreement is, however, subject to review and modification and to further Order of this Court." The question was whether that language constituted an express reservation of jurisdiction. The court concluded that it was "not possible to view the separation agreement in its entirety, while giving meaning to all the words and phrases, without logically inferring that the modification provision had to have been directed to the issue of alimony."[5] A strong dissent pointed out that the article in the agreement on alimony did not mention any right to modify the dollar amount to be paid, even though it did contain events which would cause termination. The dissenting judge was concerned that the rationale of the majority opinion read the word "specifically" out of RC 3105.18.

A dissolution decree made no provision for modification of spousal support, but called for monthly payments until the payee received a certain percentage of the net worth of a corporation, later found to have a value of over $2,000,000. The appellate court found that there was no authority to order the payor to pay a lump sum in full and final settlement of the support claim, as the support obligation was not subject to modification.[6]

RC 3105.63, as effective January 1, 1991, includes a direction that, if the dissolution petition (which is supposed to incorporate the separation agreement) provides authorization for court modification of spousal support, such modification is to be in accordance with RC 3105.18.

§ 14:18 Legal separation (formerly alimony only) decree— Entered before September 23, 1974

Robertson v. Robertson[1] ruled that where there is no statement retaining jurisdiction over the allowance for further alimony, the court has no jurisdiction to order alimony to a wife on an application for additional alimony. However, *Cummings v. Cummings*[2] and *Gilbert*

---

[4]Stadelman-Wells v. Wells, 1995 WL 238419 (Ohio Ct. App. 10th Dist. Franklin County 1995).

[5]Stadelman-Wells v. Wells, 1995 WL 238419 (Ohio Ct. App. 10th Dist. Franklin County 1995).

[6]Womelsdorf v. Reichert, 1996 WL 61072 (Ohio Ct. App. 1st Dist. Hamilton County 1996).

[Section 14:18]

[1]Robertson v. Robertson, 61 Ohio App. 458, 15 Ohio Op. 286, 22 N.E.2d 744 (4th Dist. Scioto County 1938).

[2]Cummings v. Cummings, 111 Ohio App. 447, 15 Ohio Op. 2d 64, 173 N.E.2d 159 (6th Dist. Erie County 1959).

v. Gilbert[3] found in common law and also under the provisions of RC 3103.03 that a husband has an obligation to support his wife, and that a judgment should not be construed to relieve a husband from this statutory obligation as long as they remain married. Therefore, the court ruled that provision should be made for the retention of jurisdiction for determination of the matter of allowance of alimony upon a showing of changed circumstances. Both of these cases concerned situations where alimony payments had not been ordered in the original decree.

Folz v. Folz[4] stated that an agreement between the parties for alimony when carried into the decree is not subject to modification. Though the court discussed an agreement between the parties at the time of divorce, it apparently applied the rule that such a decree, incorporating an agreement of the parties, is not modifiable. Furthermore, the court stated that oral evidence is permissible to prove an oral agreement between the parties and that this is the agreement carried into the decree. In this case, the court found the decree specifically reserved to the court the right to modify the order. The court made clear that without this reservation of jurisdiction in the decree, the court would not allow an impeachment of the decree through a motion to modify.

In *Pace v. Pace*,[5] the court, finding that execution may not issue on a decree for alimony until the installments have been reduced to a decree in gross, found that "in a suit for alimony alone, that a Decree for allowance of alimony in installments may thereafter be modified not only as to the future installments of alimony, but that such a modification may have a retroactive effect."

In the only Ohio case on the subject, *Bishop v. Bishop*,[6] the court stated that an alimony proceeding affirms the marriage relationship and enforces the support of the wife during the continuance of the marriage. Such a proceeding was found not to contemplate a termination but a continuation of the marriage relationship. The court found that the wife was also asking for the preservation of the marriage, and that the theory of the law indicated that at some time there might be a resumption of the relationship between husband and wife or a reconciliation between the parties. The court also stated that the wife forfeited her right to continued maintenance for any misconduct. Finding misconduct in this case (the wife became pregnant by a man other than her husband), the court terminated all future alimony payments. However, all past due alimony was still owed. The court

---

[3]Gilbert v. Gilbert, 83 Ohio St. 265, 94 N.E. 421 (1911).

[4]Folz v. Folz, 42 Ohio App. 135, 12 Ohio L. Abs. 67, 181 N.E. 658 (1st Dist. Hamilton County 1932).

[5]Pace v. Pace, 41 Ohio App. 130, 137, 11 Ohio L. Abs. 563, 180 N.E. 81 (5th Dist. Morrow County 1931).

[6]Bishop v. Bishop, 18 Ohio Misc. 177, 47 Ohio Op. 2d 417, 248 N.E.2d 641 (C.P. 1969).

followed the general rule that past due alimony is a vested property interest and not modifiable as to such arrearages.[7]

Both *Cummings v. Cummings*[8] and *Gilbert v. Gilbert*[9] provided that an allowance of alimony may be ordered upon a showing of changed circumstances.

§ 14:19 Legal separation (formerly alimony only) decree— Entered on and after September 23, 1974

RC 3105.18(C), effective September 23, 1974, stated, "In an action brought solely for an order for alimony under section 3105.17 of the Revised Code, any continuing order for periodic payments of money entered pursuant to this section is subject to further order of the court upon changed circumstances of either party."

RC 3105.18(C) is now RC 3105.18(D).[1] The wording has remained the same except this section now refers to an action brought for legal separation.

RC 3105.18(D), in providing for modification of periodic payments of money, makes no distinction as to whether the decree incorporates an agreement. The statute appears to grant jurisdiction to consider modification of both decrees.

RC 3105.18(D) is not clear as to whether periodic payments of money for a definite period in the nature of property settlement are subject to modification. Some courts in Ohio followed *Materazzo v. Materazzo*,[2] which held that a court lacks authority to make an equitable division of property in an alimony only proceeding.[3] The issue of property award payments would not be involved in such a decree.[4] However, RC 3105.18(B), as amended effective January 1, 1991, states the court shall equitably divide property pursuant to RC 3105.171 in legal separation proceedings upon the request of either party. The court also has jurisdiction to allocate responsibility for marital debts, in the context of spousal support or property division.

RC 3105.18(F) states for purposes of RC 3105.18(D) that a change in the circumstances of a party includes, but is not limited to, any increase or involuntary decrease in the party's wages, salary, bonuses, living expenses, or medical expenses.

---

[7]See Text § 8:4, Spousal support and division of property.

[8]Cummings v. Cummings, 111 Ohio App. 447, 15 Ohio Op. 2d 64, 173 N.E.2d 159 (6th Dist. Erie County 1959).

[9]Gilbert v. Gilbert, 83 Ohio St. 265, 94 N.E. 421 (1911).

[Section 14:19]

[1]1990 H.B. 514, eff. 1-1-91.

[2]Materazzo v. Materazzo, 139 Ohio St. 36, 21 Ohio Op. 548, 37 N.E.2d 967 (1941).

[3]See also Text § 8:8, Enforcement and modification.

[4]See also Text § 8:4, Spousal support and division of property.

§ 14:20 Unincorporated separation agreement without decree

An unincorporated separation agreement is essentially an interparty contract and is enforceable. It applies to situations where a separation occurred with no contemplation of divorce; where there is a divorce, the parties reached agreement, and the agreement is attached to the judgment, but the judgment does not expressly incorporate the agreement into the judgment by reference; and where the parties expressly intend that the agreement not merge into the judgment. Moreover, an agreement pursuant to a dissolution that was dismissed could survive the dismissal and be enforced as a private contract if the agreement so states.[1]

§ 14:21 Requirements for modification—Factors—Payments as support, not property[1]

Even though the court retains continuing jurisdiction over alimony or spousal support payments, not all such payments are subject to modification. *Wolfe v. Wolfe*[2] not only reviews the history of alimony custom and law, but also specifically sets forth the types of alimony which are modifiable, distinguishing support alimony from a division of marital property.

The Court in *Wolfe* stated, "An alimony award which constitutes a division of the marital assets and liabilities is not subject to modification under the continuing jurisdiction of the court."[3]

Then the Court continued:

> In summary we hold, therefore, that where an alimony award is for support only, is for an indefinite amount, and where there is no property settlement, or if there is such a settlement, the support award is independent thereof, the jurisdiction of the court to modify will be implied in the decree.[4]

As set forth in *Wolfe*, four requirements must be met before alimony can be modified in a post-decree proceeding: (1) the alimony is for support only; (2) it is for an indefinite amount; (3) there is no property settlement; and (4) if there is a property settlement, the support award is independent thereof.

A number of cases prior to *Wolfe* found that a decree is not modifiable where it is for a definite amount payable in installments, or pay-

---

[Section 14:20]

[1]Greiner v. Greiner, 61 Ohio App. 2d 88, 15 Ohio Op. 3d 95, 399 N.E.2d 571 (8th Dist. Cuyahoga County 1979).

[Section 14:21]

[1]AUTHOR'S NOTE: The materials in this section discuss case law that, for the most part if not entirely, is applicable only to decrees issued on or before May 1, 1986.

[2]Wolfe v. Wolfe, 46 Ohio St. 2d 399, 75 Ohio Op. 2d 474, 350 N.E.2d 413 (1976).

[3]Wolfe v. Wolfe, 46 Ohio St. 2d 399, 75 Ohio Op. 2d 474, 350 N.E.2d 413 (1976).

[4]Wolfe v. Wolfe, 46 Ohio St. 2d 399, 419, 75 Ohio Op. 2d 474, 350 N.E.2d 413 (1976).

able only for a limited number of installments, or based upon an agreement of the parties as to a division of property.[5]

Thus, an award which is in fact in the nature of sustenance and support for the former spouse (support alimony) is modifiable as long as it is not a division of property.[6]

---

[5]Clelland v. Clelland, 110 Ohio App. 546, 13 Ohio Op. 2d 354, 82 Ohio L. Abs. 515, 166 N.E.2d 428 (10th Dist. Franklin County 1959); Hunt v. Hunt, 169 Ohio St. 276, 8 Ohio Op. 2d 286, 159 N.E.2d 430 (1959) (overruled by, In re Adams, 45 Ohio St. 3d 219, 543 N.E.2d 797 (1989)); Bulloch v. Bulloch, 21 Ohio App. 2d 76, 50 Ohio Op. 2d 142, 255 N.E.2d 299 (10th Dist. Franklin County 1969); Price v. Price, 4 Ohio App. 3d 217, 447 N.E.2d 769 (8th Dist. Cuyahoga County 1982) (although foreign divorce and alimony decree enforceable, a separation agreement is subject to same general rules governing other contracts, and questions resolved by particular language); Drossman v. Drossman, 48 Ohio App. 2d 81, 2 Ohio Op. 3d 63, 355 N.E.2d 891 (6th Dist. Erie County 1975) (where parties contemplate wife's remarriage and intend decree to be permanent division of property with monthly payments applied to outstanding mortgage and to terminate at fixed date, it is not subject to modification upon remarriage of the wife); Ginsburg v. Ginsburg, 1981 WL 3556 (Ohio Ct. App. 10th Dist. Franklin County 1981) (fixed sum alimony for ten years and one month is in nature of property settlement, not support alimony, and cannot be terminated on basis of remarriage of plaintiff); Kick v. Kick, 1981 WL 4182 (Ohio Ct. App. 9th Dist. Wayne County 1981) (motion to modify alimony denied on ground that payment of $400 per month for sixty months, even though called alimony, is in fact division of marital assets and not subject to modification); Vaught v. Vaught, 2 Ohio App. 3d 264, 441 N.E.2d 811 (12th Dist. Clermont County 1981) (alimony award based on agreement of parties for payment of sum certain in installments over definite period of time without contingencies is part of division of property regardless of how denominated and vests when it is merged into final divorce decree and is accordingly valid claim against estate of deceased spouse), citing Hassaurek v. Hassaurek's Adm'r, 68 Ohio St. 554, 67 N.E. 1066 (1903); Snouffer v. Snouffer, 132 Ohio St. 617, 9 Ohio Op. 14, 9 N.E.2d 621 (1937); Graff v. Graff, 99 Ohio St. 448, 125 N.E. 72 (1919) (alimony award payable in installments, not based on contract, was personal obligation abating on death).

[6]Clelland v. Clelland, 110 Ohio App. 546, 13 Ohio Op. 2d 354, 82 Ohio L. Abs. 515, 166 N.E.2d 428 (10th Dist. Franklin County 1959); Hunt v. Hunt, 169 Ohio St. 276, 8 Ohio Op. 2d 286, 159 N.E.2d 430 (1959) (overruled by, In re Adams, 45 Ohio St. 3d 219, 543 N.E.2d 797 (1989)); Bulloch v. Bulloch, 21 Ohio App. 2d 76, 50 Ohio Op. 2d 142, 255 N.E.2d 299 (10th Dist. Franklin County 1969); Price v. Price, 4 Ohio App. 3d 217, 447 N.E.2d 769 (8th Dist. Cuyahoga County 1982) (although foreign divorce and alimony decree enforceable, a separation agreement is subject to same general rules governing other contracts, and questions resolved by particular language); Drossman v. Drossman, 48 Ohio App. 2d 81, 2 Ohio Op. 3d 63, 355 N.E.2d 891 (6th Dist. Erie County 1975) (where the parties contemplate wife's remarriage and intend decree to be permanent division of property with monthly payments applied to outstanding mortgage and to terminate at fixed date, it is not subject to modification upon remarriage of the wife); Burley v. Burley, 1981 WL 10348 (Ohio Ct. App. 8th Dist. Cuyahoga County 1981) (fact that award in question had element of indefiniteness and that there were other provisions in the decree with respect to division of property was sufficient to indicate that award in question was alimony and court had power to make modifications); Estes v. Estes, 1981 WL 9714 (Ohio Ct. App. 1st Dist. Hamilton County 1981) (where there was separate and independent division of property and statement that alimony would be paid at rate of $100 per month for thirty-six months, the latter division, even though reducible to lump sum, was held to be periodic alimony and subject to modification because of changed circumstance of the plaintiff's remarriage; it would be contrary to public policy to require continued

The next step is to determine whether the award will be modified based on the facts of the situation. There are only two logical requests: the payee may request an increase, or the payor may request a decrease.

On December 31, 1984, the Ohio Supreme Court decided *Colizoli v. Colizoli*,[7] which involved a post-decree motion to modify a combined alimony and child support award because of a substantial change of circumstances. The original award was incorporated into a divorce decree and was based on the husband's income of $43,000 a year. Within four years of the award, the husband's income had risen to $170,000 a year. The Ohio Supreme Court held that the portion of the award representing child support was modifiable, while the portion representing sustenance alimony was not modifiable because there was no express reservation of jurisdiction to do so by the decreeing court and because the sustenance alimony award was for an ascertainable amount over an ascertainable term of years.

> Our decision in this respect should in no way be interpreted as a retreat from our holding in *Wolfe* . . . or our decision in *Blakemore v. Blakemore* . . .. Those decisions continue to be determinative of a court's ability to modify alimony where the amount and/or duration of the alimony award is indefinite. However, where a decree incorporates an agreement of the parties which specifically delineates the amount and duration of sustenance alimony, we find that such a decree should be accorded its proper degree of finality.[8]

In *Ressler v. Ressler*,[9] the Ohio Supreme Court ruled on whether a court has the right to modify periodic alimony payments set forth in a decree for a fixed period of years, even though the payments could be terminated earlier by death, remarriage, or cohabitation of the payee. According to the guidelines of the *Wolfe* case, these alimony payments would be indefinite and therefore would be modifiable; however, the Supreme Court in *Ressler* overruled *Wolfe* in this regard and found

---

support alimony payments under circumstance of remarriage); Ginsburg v. Ginsburg, 1981 WL 3556 (Ohio Ct. App. 10th Dist. Franklin County 1981) (where separation agreement indicated fixed sum alimony for ten years and one month, it is in nature of property settlement rather than support alimony and cannot be terminated on basis of remarriage of plaintiff); Kick v. Kick, 1981 WL 4182 (Ohio Ct. App. 9th Dist. Wayne County 1981) (motion to modify alimony denied on ground that payment of $400 per month for sixty months, even though called alimony, is in fact division of marital assets and not subject to modification); Vaught v. Vaught, 2 Ohio App. 3d 264, 441 N.E.2d 811 (12th Dist. Clermont County 1981) (alimony award based on agreement of parties for payment of sum certain in installments over definite period of time without contingencies is part of division of property regardless of how denominated and vests when it is merged into final divorce decree and is accordingly valid claim against estate of deceased spouse).

[7]Colizoli v. Colizoli, 15 Ohio St. 3d 333, 474 N.E.2d 280 (1984).

[8]Colizoli v. Colizoli, 15 Ohio St. 3d 333, 474 N.E.2d 280 (1984) (footnote omitted). See also Blakemore v. Blakemore, 5 Ohio St. 3d 217, 450 N.E.2d 1140 (1983); Lira v. Lira, 12 Ohio App. 3d 69, 465 N.E.2d 1353 (8th Dist. Cuyahoga County 1983) (fourfold increase in alimony when husband's income had increased sixfold and where court had reserved jurisdiction to review was not abuse of discretion).

[9]Ressler v. Ressler, 17 Ohio St. 3d 17, 476 N.E.2d 1032 (1985).

these alimony payments to be nonmodifiable. The Court did not allow the payments to be extended beyond the original fixed period of years and said:

> A decreeing court does not have continuing jurisdiction to modify a sustenance alimony award that was made for a fixed period of years even though the award is subject to termination in the event of death, remarriage or cohabitation unless the decreeing court expressly reserves jurisdiction to modify.
>
> . . .
>
> In so ruling we are promoting the concept that alimony decrees should possess a degree of finality and certainty.[10]

The fact that the fixed period of alimony payments had been set by the trial court and was not the result of a separation agreement incorporated into the decree did not alter the Court's position. The Court stated, "Divorce decrees determined by court order deserve the same finality as those ordered pursuant to an agreement."[11]

In *Abele v. Abele*,[12] with respect to the court's jurisdiction to modify alimony, the Sixth District Court of Appeals made a distinction between a decree that awarded "$1,200.00 per month for five years, or until her death, remarriage or further order of the Domestic Court"[13] and another decree which read, "for a period of five (5) years, or until her death, remarriage, or further Order of this Court *whichever event should first occur.*"[14] The appellate court held that the wording of the former decree, "until further Order of the . . . Court," gave the court jurisdiction to modify both the amount of and length of time alimony was to be paid, but that the italicized language in the latter decree was a limiting phrase so the alimony could continue no longer than five years.

RC 3105.18(A) codifies the *Wolfe* requirement that "spousal support" does not include any payment made to a spouse or former spouse, or to a third party for the benefit of a spouse or former spouse, that is made as part of a division or distribution of property or a distributive award under RC 3105.171. The Code section further states that spousal support is both for sustenance and support of the spouse or former spouse. Furthermore, RC 3105.18(F), effective May 2, 1986 (formerly RC 3105.18(E)), states that the only payments that may be modified are periodic payments of money as alimony or spousal support. Thus, the statute makes clear that the spousal support award must be independent of the property award to be modifiable.

---

[10]Ressler v. Ressler, 17 Ohio St. 3d 17, 17-18, 476 N.E.2d 1032 (1985).

[11]Ressler v. Ressler, 17 Ohio St. 3d 17, 19, 476 N.E.2d 1032 (1985).

[12]Abele v. Abele, 1989 WL 52892, at *2 (Ohio Ct. App. 6th Dist. Lucas County 1989).

[13]Abele v. Abele, 1989 WL 52892, at *2 (Ohio Ct. App. 6th Dist. Lucas County 1989), quoting Meinke v. Meinke, 56 Ohio App. 3d 171, 565 N.E.2d 875 (6th Dist. Lucas County 1989).

[14]Abele v. Abele, 1989 WL 52892 (Ohio Ct. App. 6th Dist. Lucas County 1989) (emphasis by the court).

§ 14:22 Requirements for modification—Factors—Change in circumstances

Under RC 3105.18(E), trial courts are deprived of jurisdiction to modify spousal support awards unless two conditions are satisfied: (1) the decree must authorize modification; and (2) the court must determine "that the circumstances of either party have changed." RC 3105.18(F) contains the "change of circumstances" definitional language, and it reads as follows:

"(F) For purposes of divisions (D) and (E) of this section, a change in the circumstances of a party includes, but is not limited to, any increase or involuntary decrease in the party's wages, salary, bonuses, living expenses, or medical expenses."

The language set forth in RC 3105.18(F) was enacted as part of Am. H.B. 514, which legislation was approved in August, 1990. The effective date of RC 3105.18(F) was in January, 1991.[1] The language of RC 3105.18(F) has remained the same since its effective date. Prior to the adoption of RC 3105.18(F), no statute had addressed or set forth the meaning of the term "change of circumstances" in the context of alimony or spousal support.

Since the adoption of RC 3105.18(F), and until 2009, appellate courts in Ohio had been divided over its meaning. One line of cases, applying principles that have developed through common law, interpreted the language of RC 3105.18(F) as requiring a finding of "substantial" or "significant" or "drastic" change of circumstances before a trial court is permitted to modify an existing spousal support award.[2] A separate line of cases held that the word "any" as used in RC 3105.18(F) is unambiguous, and that if the Ohio legislature had intended the word "any" to mean "substantial" or "drastic" it would have included or used those words.[3] The Supreme Court of Ohio resolved that conflict, holding that as a jurisdictional requirement to

---

[Section 14:22]

[1]143 Ohio Laws, Part III, 5426, 5457, and 55516–17.

[2]Reveal v. Reveal, 154 Ohio App. 3d 758, 761, 2003-Ohio-5335, 798 N.E.2d 1132 (2d Dist. Montgomery County 2003); Trotter v. Trotter, 2001-Ohio-2122, 2001 WL 390066, at *2 (Ohio Ct. App. 3d Dist. Allen County 2001); Reeves v. Reeves, 2007-Ohio-4988, 2007 WL 2758659, ¶ 18 (Ohio Ct. App. 7th Dist. Jefferson County 2007); Sweeney v. Sweeney, 2006-Ohio-6988, 2006 WL 3825251, ¶ 21 (Ohio Ct. App. 10th Dist. Franklin County 2006); and Carnahan v. Carnahan, 118 Ohio App. 3d 393, 397, 692 N.E.2d 1086, 1089 (12th Dist. Clermont County 1997).

[3]Tsai v. Tien, 162 Ohio App. 3d 89, 93, 2005-Ohio-3520, 832 N.E.2d 809 (5th Dist. Stark County 2005) (abrogated by, Mandelbaum v. Mandelbaum, 121 Ohio St. 3d 433, 2009-Ohio-1222, 905 N.E.2d 172 (2009)); Rollins v. Harvis, 2007-Ohio-6121, 2007 WL 3408230, ¶ 14 (Ohio Ct. App. 6th Dist. Lucas County 2007); Kingsolver v. Kingsolver, 2004-Ohio-3844, 2004 WL 1620723, ¶'s 11-24 (Ohio Ct. App. 9th Dist. Summit County 2004) (abrogated by, Mandelbaum v. Mandelbaum, 121 Ohio St. 3d 433, 2009-Ohio-1222, 905 N.E.2d 172 (2009)); and Buchal v. Buchal, 2006-Ohio-3879, 2006 WL 2105508, ¶ 14 (Ohio Ct. App. 11th Dist. Lake County 2006) (abrogated by, Mandelbaum v. Mandelbaum, 121 Ohio St. 3d 433, 2009-Ohio-1222, 905 N.E.2d 172 (2009)).

modifying a spousal support award a trial court must find that a substantial change in circumstances has occurred, and that such change was not contemplated at the time of the original decree.[4]

In a unanimous decision, the *Mandelbaum* court held that when the legislature enacted changes to RC 3105.18, first in 1986 then again in 1991, the legislature never "suggested an intent to alter longstanding case law requiring a *substantial* change in the parties' circumstances." The *Mandelbaum* decision reasoned that the amendment in 1986, which added the language that is now found at 3105.18(E), was intended to resolve the issues that had arisen in the wake of that court's decision in *Wolfe v. Wolfe*,[5] resolving the question of whether reservation of continuing jurisdiction can be implied or must be expressed in the decree. In noting that the legislature again amended RC 3105.18 in 1991 by adding the language that is now found at section (F), the *Mandelbaum* court reasoned that while those amendments did not expressly codify the "common-law requirement that a trial court is required to find that a substantial change in circumstances has occurred . . . the absence of language [in the statutory amendments] does not demonstrate that the General Assembly intended to abrogate what had become well-settled law." In support of that method of determining legislative intent the *Mandelbaum* opinion then cites the 1907 case of *State ex rel Hunt v. Fronizer*,[6] as standing for the legal principle that "the general assembly will not be presumed to have intended to abrogate a settled rule of the common law unless the language used in a statute clearly supports such intention." (A search in Westlaw for the *Fronizer* case finds that the only other time the Ohio Supreme Court commented on that language from the *Fronizer* case was in 1951 in the case of *In Re McWilson's Estate*,[7] in which the court noted that "[t]here is no expression in the *Fronizer* case that there must be words in an act of the General Assembly expressly abrogating the common law. All that need appear is a provision which clearly does modify or abrogate it . . ." The *Mandelbaum* opinion fails to mention the *In Re McWilson's Estate* case at all.

The *Mandelbaum* opinion also makes no effort to explain why the Supreme Court of Ohio's own other longstanding and well settled approach to the discernment of legislative intent did not apply to the interpretation of the language of RC 3105.18. These long standing principles of statutory interpretation are expressed, among other decisions from the Supreme Court of Ohio, in *Bailey v. Republic*

---

[4]Mandelbaum v. Mandelbaum, 121 Ohio St. 3d 433, 2009-Ohio-1222, 905 N.E.2d 172 (2009).

[5]Wolfe v. Wolfe, 46 Ohio St. 2d 399, 75 Ohio Op. 2d 474, 350 N.E.2d 413 (1976).

[6]State ex rel. Hunt v. Fronizer, 77 Ohio St. 7, 82 N.E. 518 (1907).

[7]In re McWilson's Estate, 155 Ohio St. 261, 44 Ohio Op. 262, 98 N.E.2d 289 (1951).

Engineered Steels, Inc.,[8] *Kimble v. Kimble,*[9] and *Davis v. Davis.*[10] In *Kimble*, the Supreme Court of Ohio had held that these same statutory amendments in 1986 and 1991, by not including "remarriage" as an event automatically terminating spousal support, had abrogated the public policy that alimony awards terminate upon the remarriage of the recipient spouse, stating ". . . the General Assembly subsequently amended RC 3105.18(E), applicable to actions on or after May 2, 1986 . . . [s]ince this appeal involves a post-1986 divorce, we can no longer rely on the policy set forth in *Dunaway,*[11] which conflicts with and is superseded by statute."

In commenting upon its prior case law on spousal support modification the Supreme Court in *Mandelbaum* notes that it and lower appellate courts have previously used terms such as "significant" and "material" and "drastic" and appears to say that such words or terms are either synonymous with "substantial" or are equally acceptable findings for modification purposes. The opinion equates "not contemplated" with "unforeseen" but doesn't say whether that equates to "unforeseeable" as well, and also avoids altogether any discussion of the relevancy or meaning of the term "reasonable or appropriate" contained in the same statute. The opinion makes no attempt to explain how adding the word "substantial" on top of the term "reasonable and appropriate" that is already the standard for every spousal support award provides any gate keeping function that the proponents of the "substantial" standard proclaim it provides.

For a detailed analysis of the evolution of the common law principles the *Mandelbaum* opinion holds to still control the interpretation of the words "change of circumstances," see the appellate opinion it upheld.[12]

§ 14:23 Requirements for modification—Factors—Change not contemplated by parties

See the discussion in Text § 14:22, Requirements for modification—

---

[8]Bailey v. Republic Engineered Steels, Inc., 91 Ohio St. 3d 38, 2001-Ohio-236, 741 N.E.2d 121 (2001) ("In determining legislative intent, a court first looks to the language of the statute . . . In considering statutory language, it is the duty of the court to give effect to the words used in a statute, not to delete words used or to insert words not used . . . If the meaning of a statute is unambiguous and definite, it must be applied as written . . .).

[9]Kimble v. Kimble, 97 Ohio St. 3d 424, 2002-Ohio-6667, 780 N.E.2d 273 (2002) ("A word that is not defined in a statute must be afforded its plain and ordinary meaning.").

[10]Davis v. Davis, 115 Ohio St. 3d 180, 184, 2007-Ohio-5049 ¶ 19, 873 N.E.2d 1305 (2007) ("Importantly, the legislature has chosen to modify "recognized and accredited high school" with the adjective "any." . . . In choosing this adjective, the legislature has manifested its intent that the phrase "recognized and accredited high school" should be construed expansively for purposes of RC 3103.03(B)."

[11]Dunaway v. Dunaway, 53 Ohio St. 3d 227, 560 N.E.2d 171 (1990).

[12]Mandelbaum v. Mandelbaum, 2007-Ohio-6138, 2007 WL 3409307 (Ohio Ct. App. 2d Dist. Montgomery County 2007).

Factors—Change in circumstances, regarding the Supreme Court of Ohio's *Mandelbaum*[1] decision. The specific syllabus holding of *Mandelbaum* is that a trial court has jurisdiction to modify an award of spousal support if "the change was not contemplated at the time of the original decree."[2] But in the body of its opinion the court states the change in circumstances must "be one that had not been contemplated and taken into account by the parties or the court at the time of the prior order."[3] Thus, in relation to an existing order that itself modified the award contained in the original decree, it would appear that the question of whether something had or had not been contemplated is to be viewed from the perspective relative to the order being modified rather than as of the time of the original decree.

Before the issuance of the *Mandelbaum* opinion, a frequently quoted case in this area had been *Leighner v. Leighner*,[4] which held:

> Where modification of an existing order for the payment of sustenance alimony is requested, the threshold determination is whether the order can be modified, which requires a finding of a change in circumstances since the order was entered. The change in circumstances must be substantial and must be such as was not contemplated at the time of the prior order. Only if this necessary prerequisite has been satisfied may the trial court move on to a consideration of whether or not the existing order should be modified. This latter inquiry involves a re-examination of the existing order in the light of the changed circumstances, and requires a two-step determination: First, is sustenance alimony still necessary? And, if so, what amount is reasonable? In addressing the question of whether the existing order should be modified, the trial court's discretion is guided and limited by the consideration of all relevant factors, including those listed in R.C. 3105.18(B).[5]

Although the debate over whether RC 3105.18 limits awards of spousal support to "sustenance" or requires a finding of "need" or "necessary" in light of the use of the words "appropriate and reasonable" is also still ongoing (see Text § 14:25, Requirements for modification—Factors—reasonable and appropriate), it appears that the holding in *Mandelbaum* renders as still good law the remainder of the analysis expressed in the foregoing quote from *Leighner*.

The problems that existed with the "not contemplated" or "foresee-

---

[Section 14:23]

[1]Mandelbaum v. Mandelbaum, 121 Ohio St. 3d 433, 2009-Ohio-1222, 905 N.E.2d 172 (2009).

[2]Mandelbaum v. Mandelbaum, supra, syllabus 2.

[3]Mandelbaum v. Mandelbaum, 121 Ohio St. 3d 433, 2009-Ohio-1222 ¶ 32, 905 N.E.2d 172 (2009).

[4]Leighner v. Leighner, 33 Ohio App. 3d 214, 515 N.E.2d 625 (10th Dist. Franklin County 1986). See also Criner v. Criner, 1997 WL 128922 (Ohio Ct. App. 10th Dist. Franklin County 1997).

[5]Leighner v. Leighner, 33 Ohio App. 3d 214, 215, 515 N.E.2d 625 (10th Dist. Franklin County 1986). See also Blakemore v. Blakemore, 5 Ohio St. 3d 217, 450 N.E.2d 1140 (1983). These factors, formerly listed in RC 3105.18(B), are now found in RC 3105.18(C).

able" standard before the issuance of the *Mandelbaum* decision do not appear to have been resolved or clarified by that decision. In *Birath v. Birath*,[6] at the time of the divorce in 1987, appellee was making $17,316 per year as a schoolteacher. By 1999, appellee was making approximately $34,086 per year as a nurse. This represented a five percent annual increase over 12 years. In affirming the trial court's finding that no change of circumstances had occurred, the appellate court stated "the parties must have anticipated at the time of the award that appellee would receive at least cost of living increases in her salary" and concluded that the "trial court did not abuse its discretion in finding the increase in appellee's wages over the 12-year period is not a change in circumstances as contemplated by R.C. 3105.18(F)." And, in *Palmieri v. Palmieri*,[7] that same court held that husband's "retirement, and the accompanying reduced income, was thoroughly considered at the time of the divorce . . . [b]oth the magistrate and the trial court found retirement was contemplated, discussed, and debated prior to the ultimate agreement on spousal support . . . [n]othing in the record suggests this was not the case . . . [t]he divorce decree lays out three specific terminating events for spousal support . . . Mr. Palmieri's retirement is not one of them . . . [a]t the time of the divorce, Mr. Palmieri could have negotiated a provision regarding modification or termination of spousal support upon retirement . . . [h]e was less than ten years from retirement age at the time of the divorce . . . [h]e did not do so and cannot now ask the court to relieve him of his choice . . . [a] court cannot base modification on a change that was contemplated at the time of the divorce."

In *Strain v. Strain*[8] the decree ordered the husband to pay $833 per month in child support for a 15 year old child and $1,700 per month in spousal support, the latter for a period of six years. Three years after the divorce the minor child was emancipated and the child support obligation was terminated. Wife then filed a motion to increase spousal support, and the trial court increased the spousal support obligation by $300 per month. In affirming the increase in spousal support and finding it not to be an abuse of discretion, the court of appeals rejected Husband's argument that the loss of child support was foreseeable and thus could not be a factor, either as to change of circumstances or as to the reasonableness or appropriateness of an increase, skirting the issue by stating "the record reveals the trial court considered more than just the emancipation of [the child] in rendering its decision . . . [t]he record reveals the court considered the totality of the circumstances, including the parties' salaries, earning capacities, and living expenses." However, the only other specific factors the court

---

[6]Birath v. Birath, 2005-Ohio-2295, 2005 WL 1109657 (Ohio Ct. App. 10th Dist. Franklin County 2005).

[7]Palmieri v. Palmieri, 2005-Ohio-4064, 2005 WL 1869706 (Ohio Ct. App. 10th Dist. Franklin County 2005).

[8]Strain v. Strain, 2005-Ohio-6035, 2005 WL 3031896 (Ohio Ct. App. 12th Dist. Warren County 2005).

noted were that Husband's "current annual income is $98,000, up from $94,909 at the decree . . . [h]is monthly expenses decreased by $883 when his child support obligation ended . . . [a]ppellee's income remained basically unchanged, while her expenses grew . . . [h]er ability to meet her expenses was already suffering and the loss of over $10,000 per year toward these expenses made it impossible."

It seems that courts that use "foreseeability" as a reason for denying a modification do so almost needlessly, especially appellate courts that have rejected the "needs" based analysis and acknowledged that "reasonable and appropriate" is the actual statutory standard. The same result in *Birath*[9] could have been reached by that court simply stating that the increase in income over 12 years from $17,316 per year to $34,086 per year was not a change in circumstances sufficient to justify a decrease, or by stating that even if it were a change in circumstances sufficient to justify a re-evaluation of spousal support that nevertheless the current level of spousal support was still "reasonable and appropriate" in light of all of the other factors, thus avoiding the "foreseeability" issue altogether. The same is true for *Palmieri*,[10] in that the court also noted that "even if retirement had not been contemplated, neither party's income is substantially different now from their income in 1991." And in *Strain*,[11] if that court joined the group of appellate districts that have rejected the purely "needs" based analysis and acknowledged that "reasonable and appropriate" is the actual statutory standard, the court could have stated that "yes, the loss of child support was foreseeable, but the increase in spousal support is still reasonable and appropriate under the totality of the circumstances" and a solid statutory basis for its affirmance of the increase would exist. This appears to be the logic that same appellate court followed in a more recent opinion.[12]

The outer limits of the "foreseeability" argument appear to have been reached in *Howell v. Howell*,[13] a case in which at the time of the original divorce the trial court refused to consider as a factor for spousal support the husband's possible inheritance as being too speculative and uncertain. Subsequently, in a post-decree motion to modify spousal support, the trial court again refused to consider that same inheritance, which husband had actually received after the divorce, for the reason that it was "clearly contemplated at the time of the divorce." The appellate court found "this reasoning process unsound."

---

[9]Birath v. Birath, 2005-Ohio-2295, 2005 WL 1109657 (Ohio Ct. App. 10th Dist. Franklin County 2005).

[10]Palmieri v. Palmieri, 2005-Ohio-4064, 2005 WL 1869706 (Ohio Ct. App. 10th Dist. Franklin County 2005).

[11]Strain v. Strain, 2005-Ohio-6035, 2005 WL 3031896 (Ohio Ct. App. 12th Dist. Warren County 2005).

[12]Derickson v. Derickson, 2007-Ohio-1889, 2007 WL 1174877 (Ohio Ct. App. 12th Dist. Butler County 2007).

[13]Howell v. Howell, 167 Ohio App. 3d 431, 2006-Ohio-3038, 855 N.E.2d 533 (2d Dist. Clark County 2006).

§ 14:24 Requirements for modification—Factors—Burden of proof

The burden of showing that modification of an award of alimony is warranted is upon the spouse who seeks a reduction.[1] Even after the movant demonstrates a change of circumstance, the burden does not shift to the obligee to demonstrate a continuing need for alimony or that the existing award is necessary or reasonable.[2]

The time period to be used to determine changed circumstances is the time period from the order last setting the spousal support until the pending motion. If a previous motion to modify had been denied by the court in that period, the court still must use the time period between the decree and the second motion.[3]

The trial court does not have jurisdiction to reinstate spousal support after the support had been terminated with no continuing order of modification by the Court.[4] However, the Second Appellate District has issued several decisions that hold that once a trial court issues an indefinite award of spousal support and retains continuing jurisdiction to modify that award, the trial court never loses the jurisdiction to reinstate that award even if it "terminates" the award on a post-decree modification.[5]

§ 14:25 Requirements for modification—Factors—Reasonable and appropriate

According to *Griffin v. Griffin*,[1] the standard to be applied is not whether spousal support is necessary, but whether spousal support is reasonable and appropriate under RC 3105.18 as amended effective January 1, 1991. In *Fallang v. Fallang*,[2] the court stated that if a court finds that a change in circumstances has occurred, the court must determine the amount of spousal support that is appropriate

---

[Section 14:24]

[1]Heltzel v. Heltzel, 1990 WL 174152 (Ohio Ct. App. 11th Dist. Trumbull County 1990); Tremaine v. Tremaine, 111 Ohio App. 3d 703, 676 N.E.2d 1249 (2d Dist. Montgomery County 1996).

[2]Guerrero v. Guerrero, 1991 WL 18667 (Ohio Ct. App. 11th Dist. Trumbull County 1991).

[3]Seagraves v. Seagraves, 1996 WL 185332 (Ohio Ct. App. 2d Dist. Montgomery County 1996).

[4]Charlton v. Charlton, 1994 WL 583092 (Ohio Ct. App. 7th Dist. Noble County 1994).

[5]Templeton v. Templeton, 2001 WL 1173340 (Ohio Ct. App. 2d Dist. Montgomery County 2001); Lapierre v. Lapierre, 2001 WL 1018361 (Ohio Ct. App. 2d Dist. Greene County 2001).

[Section 14:25]

[1]Griffin v. Griffin, 1993 WL 69343 (Ohio Ct. App. 10th Dist. Franklin County 1993).

[2]Fallang v. Fallang, 109 Ohio App. 3d 543, 672 N.E.2d 730 (12th Dist. Butler County 1996).

and reasonable and to do so the trial court must consider the factors in RC 3105.18(C)(1). "Need," however, is no longer a statutory standard for awarding or modifying spousal support. Even though the obligor's income in *Fallang* had decreased and obligee's income had increased, a substantial gap continued to exist, and that difference weighed heavily against a reduction in support.

Other courts agree with the statement of law set forth in *Fallang v. Fallang*, while others do not. For example, in *Bowen v. Bowen*,[3] the Ninth District Court of Appeals stated that under the amended version of spousal support statute, "need" is no longer a basis for a spousal support award, nor is it significant whether the spouse "deserves" the support; the only relevant question is what is "appropriate and reasonable" under the circumstances, citing RC 3105.18. Likewise, in *Schultz v. Schultz*,[4] the Tenth District Court of Appeals stated that when considering an award of spousal support, the court should consider all 14 statutory factors and award only an amount which is appropriate and reasonable, not an amount based upon need.

A line of cases has developed that takes a different approach, and in essence hold that need, while no longer specifically mentioned in RC 3105.18, is nevertheless at the core of all spousal support awards and modifications.[5] The Third appellate district appears to be following this approach as well.[6] For an excellent discussion of this issue, see *Billingham v. Billingham*.[7]

In granting or denying a motion to modify spousal support there is no express requirement that the court's order reexamine all of the factors listed in RC 3105.18(C)(1).[8] The court should set forth the basis for its decision with enough details to permit appellate review, but a "rehash of findings" from the initial spousal order is not necessary.

The case of *Carnahan v. Carnahan*,[9] following the "needs vs. ability to pay" analysis and rejecting the "reasonable and appropriate" stan-

---

[3]Bowen v. Bowen, 132 Ohio App. 3d 616, 725 N.E.2d 1165 (9th Dist. Medina County 1999).

[4]Schultz v. Schultz, 110 Ohio App. 3d 715, 675 N.E.2d 55 (10th Dist. Franklin County 1996).

[5]Carnahan v. Carnahan, 118 Ohio App. 3d 393, 692 N.E.2d 1086 (12th Dist. Clermont County 1997); Murphy v. Murphy, 1996 WL 629522 (Ohio Ct. App. 2d Dist. Montgomery County 1996).

[6]Fisher v. Fisher, 2005-Ohio-5615, 2005 WL 2709526 (Ohio Ct. App. 3d Dist. Henry County 2005).

[7]Billingham v. Billingham, 2001 WL 127764 (Ohio Ct. App. 2d Dist. Montgomery County 2001).

[8]Kucmanic v. Kucmanic, 119 Ohio App. 3d 609, 695 N.E.2d 1205 (8th Dist. Cuyahoga County 1997); Flauto v. Flauto, 1999 WL 260890 (Ohio Ct. App. 7th Dist. Mahoning County 1999).

[9]Carnahan v. Carnahan, 118 Ohio App. 3d 393, 692 N.E.2d 1086 (12th Dist. Clermont County 1997).

dard of *Schultz v. Schultz*[10] and its own prior case law, held that while the obligor former husband's new wife's income can be a factor as to whether a change of circumstances has occurred, it is not permissible to consider the obligor's new wife's income when determining whether the former husband has the ability to pay spousal support. At the time of the divorce after a thirty-nine year marriage, the former husband had been earning $72,000 per year and the former wife had been earning $28,000 per year. Former husband was later forced to retire, and he sought a decrease/termination in his support obligation. The evidence showed that former husband was now receiving $19,000 in Social Security retirement and company pension income and that former wife was now earning $36,000 to $40,000 per year, which left her approximately $600 per month short compared to her expenses. Former husband had remarried and his new wife was earning $35,000 per year. The *Carnahan* court reversed the trial court's decision reducing former husband's spousal support obligation from $850 per month to $600 per month. More recently the Twelfth appellate district has indicated it may be taking a different approach.[11]

Somewhat conversely, in *McNutt v. McNutt*[12] the obligor former husband had also been forced to retire and his income was thereby reduced from $99,000 to $17,000. Since the divorce, the former husband had remarried and his new wife had income of approximately $35,000. At the time of the divorce the former wife had been earning $32,000, and at the time of the modification hearing her income from wages and her share of the former husband's pension was approximately $50,000. The original award of spousal support, coming at the end of a 34 year marriage, was for $1,800 per month. On appeal, the former husband claimed that the ongoing award of spousal support would leave him nearly at poverty level. In affirming the trial court's decision to decrease the spousal support to $300 per month but not terminate the obligation, the *McNutt* court held that the "any other factor" language of RC 3015.18(C)(1)(n) renders "the (former husband's) ability to share expenses (with his new wife) relevant in deciding whether an obligor's claim of poverty is well-taken" in a post decree motion filed by the former husband after to modify the obligor's spousal support obligation.

In *Coker v. Ulch*,[13] after the divorce the ex-husband had become almost totally disabled, had been confined to a nursing home for 2 years, received social security disability payments and Medicaid, and was not permitted to retain more than $30 per month as spending

---

[10]Schultz v. Schultz, 110 Ohio App. 3d 715, 675 N.E.2d 55 (10th Dist. Franklin County 1996).

[11]Derickson v. Derickson, 2007-Ohio-1889, 2007 WL 1174877 (Ohio Ct. App. 12th Dist. Butler County 2007).

[12]McNutt v. McNutt, 2005-Ohio-3752, 2005 WL 1714199 (Ohio Ct. App. 2d Dist. Montgomery County 2005).

[13]Coker v. Ulch, 166 Ohio App. 3d 778, 2006-Ohio-2349, 853 N.E.2d 358 (6th Dist. Lucas County 2006).

money, which 'allowance' was being paid from his social security disability benefits by the nursing facility. The trial court overruled the ex-wife's motion to terminate her spousal support payments of $200 per month, and on appeal Wife argued that (1) because the spousal support payments made to the ex-husband are reimbursed to the Medicaid program, they ultimately "do not go to" the ex-husband; and (2) the ex-husband was eligible for Medicaid benefits that were sufficient to cover the full cost of his care, even if the spousal support payments were discontinued. The court of appeals rejected these arguments, and in affirming the trial court's decision noted that while the ex-wife's argument was "somewhat compelling, it requires us to completely ignore the public policy that Medicaid was intended to be the *last resource* of individuals in need of medical care, not a vehicle for avoiding financial obligations which are otherwise appropriate and reasonable, thereby shifting the burden to the taxpayers." Therefore, the court concluded, "under the circumstances presented in this case, the trial court's order for [the ex-wife] to continue to pay $200 in spousal support was not arbitrary, unreasonable, or unconscionable."

§ 14:26 Requirements for modification—Factors—Statutory

Prior to May 2, 1986, the effective date of the statute, case law set forth some specific guidelines as to the modification of alimony or spousal support. Since RC 3105.18(F) refers to a change in the circumstances of the party which *"includes, but is not limited to,"* the factors specifically set out in the statute, and given the holding in *Mandelbaum*[1] that even those portions of RC 3105.18 that appeared to replace common law principles in fact do not, it can be assumed that the factors set forth in prior case law would continue to remain as grounds for modification of alimony or spousal support. Therefore, the following situations would appear to be additional grounds for modification of spousal support:

(1) Changed economic conditions;
(2) Remarriage of the recipient;
(3) Entering into a relationship in another state that would constitute a valid marriage in Ohio;
(4) Cohabitation of recipient;
(5) Payor's increased ability to pay;
(6) Retirement;
(7) Death;
(8) Other circumstances; and
(9) Review of alimony or spousal support at end of term.

[Section 14:26]

[1]Mandelbaum v. Mandelbaum, 121 Ohio St. 3d 433, 2009-Ohio-1222, 905 N.E.2d 172 (2009).

§ 14:27   Requirements for modification—Changed economic conditions

There may be a modification of a former decree upon proper allegations of changed economic circumstances of the parties.[1] This same principle was reaffirmed in *Nash v. Nash*,[2] where the court stated that an alimony judgment may be modified if changed circumstances warrant such action provided the changes are material and not purposely

---

[Section 14:27]

[1]Olney v. Watts, 43 Ohio St. 499, 3 N.E. 354 (1885); Steinbrenner v. Steinbrenner, No. 1609 (Ohio Ct. App. 9th Dist. Wayne County 1979) (motion for increase in alimony based on change in circumstance consisting solely of husband's increase in income is not grounds for an increase in alimony); Fox v. Fox, 1982 WL 2311 (Ohio Ct. App. 8th Dist. Cuyahoga County 1982) (alimony decrease denied where wife has new job and higher income if such income and employment was within expectation of parties at the time, and agreement does not specify that the earnings would be basis for termination); Park v. Park, 1981 WL 3908 (Ohio Ct. App. 9th Dist. Summit County 1981) (not error for trial court to modify alimony pursuant to agreement by decreasing payments to be made by payor); Pappas v. Pappas, 1981 WL 10229 (Ohio Ct. App. 9th Dist. Lorain County 1981) (separation agreement provided for review of alimony if husband's salary decreased to two-thirds of prior level; husband quit his job, court refused to modify alimony; court of appeals held that trial court still exercised its jurisdiction and entered a decree, even though it did not change alimony); Learmonth v. Learmonth, 1981 WL 3030 (Ohio Ct. App. 10th Dist. Franklin County 1981) (court denied reduction of alimony even though plaintiff's wife's income had dramatically increased); Horne v. Horne, 1981 WL 2654 (Ohio Ct. App. 4th Dist. Pike County 1981) (appellate court affirmed order of lifetime alimony to wife which defendant had challenged on grounds that he was receiving only $405 per month from Social Security and $404 from workers' compensation and award indicated only that defendant would pay plaintiff $150 per month alimony without designating source of funds; while workers' compensation awards and Social Security payments are exempt from attachment, court did not designate that the $150 per month would come from these sources, so technically court did not violate exemption); Davis v. Davis, 1981 WL 2576 (Ohio Ct. App. 2d Dist. Clark County 1981) (court affirmed modification of alimony provision agreed to by parties and incorporated into divorce decree and which included provision that it was not to be reduced below $250 per week; court had continuing jurisdiction to modify under *Wolfe* guidelines since alimony was sustenance for wife, further, appellee's employment had been terminated); Arthur v. Arthur, No. 1675 (Ohio Ct. App. 9th Dist. Wayne County 1980) (alimony payments were to terminate upon the wife's becoming employed, but termination did not extinguish arrearages); Connor v. Connor, 1981 WL 6314 (Ohio Ct. App. 5th Dist. Stark County 1981) (where decree ordering alimony provided alimony would terminate when wife earned in excess of $500 gross income for two months, it was not error to grant plaintiff's motion to terminate rather than granting defendant's motion to modify on a sliding scale); Bauer v. Bauer, 1982 WL 3719 (Ohio Ct. App. 2d Dist. Montgomery County 1982) (husband's income was reduced one-half by his retirement, and he sought reduction of court-ordered alimony; court refused modification on grounds that plaintiff, fifty-six years old, had worked thirty years but was not required to retire and therefore change in circumstances was not beyond his control).

[2]Nash v. Nash, 77 Ohio App. 155, 32 Ohio Op. 409, 65 N.E.2d 728 (9th Dist. Medina County 1945).

brought about by the complaining party.[3] The court in *Sager v. Sager*[4] also stated:

> After a decree of divorce and alimony has been granted a wife, the decree awarding alimony may be modified after the term for which it was granted, when the application thereof is based upon new facts, thereafter transpiring, of such character as to make the modification necessary to suit such altered conditions.

In *Haynie v. Haynie*,[5] the Eighth District Court of Appeals held that it is not error to refuse a husband-obligor's request for a reduction in alimony based on changed circumstances, where he is a physician whose income has been substantially reduced (voluntarily) since the original award:

> This story is all too bitterly familiar. A husband pursues a profession; he outgrows his wife in education and experience; he leaves the marriage, literally and figuratively, for a world in which his wife no longer belongs.

> [The husband] has a new life now, but is still bound legally to the needs of the family that saw him through the most difficult years of his life.

The Eighth District Court of Appeals stated in 1975 that the trial court has continuing jurisdiction to modify the award for permanent

---

[3]See also Fox v. Fox, 1982 WL 2311 (Ohio Ct. App. 8th Dist. Cuyahoga County 1982) (a change in financial situation of either party may serve as a basis for modification of alimony award; court will consider earning ability as well as actual earnings); Hutson v. Hutson, 68 Ohio L. Abs. 131, 120 N.E.2d 618 (C.P. 1954) (where moving party has voluntarily brought changed circumstances on himself, it may be consideration in refusing relief); Tydings v. Tydings, 349 A.2d 462 (D.C. 1975); Mileti v. Mileti, 1980 WL 35282 (Ohio App. 2d Dist. Montgomery County 1980) (court will reject alimony modification based on inability to pay where it is determined that person has voluntarily reduced his own income); Parsons v. Parsons, 1981 WL 3921 (Ohio Ct. App. 9th Dist. Summit County 1981) (motion to modify alimony because defendant had suffered a heart attack, bankruptcy, and loss of employment was not tenable because decree was dated prior to the *Wolfe* decision); Singer v. Singer, 1981 WL 4515 (Ohio Ct. App. 8th Dist. Cuyahoga County 1981) (under Civ. R. 60(B)(2) judgment cannot be modified merely because of discovery of heart condition that could have been discovered before trial by careful medical scrutiny); Hayden v. Hayden, 1981 WL 2600 (Ohio Ct. App. 9th Dist. Summit County 1981) (motion to modify alimony denied on basis of exercise of discretion utilizing clean hands doctrine; payor was in contempt of court's order to pay alimony, and the clean hands doctrine was applied to justify the court's refusal to modify alimony); Bauer v. Bauer, 1982 WL 3719 (Ohio Ct. App. 2d Dist. Montgomery County 1982) (husband's income reduced one-half by retirement, and he sought reduction of court-ordered alimony; court refused modification on grounds that plaintiff was not required to retire and therefore change in financial circumstances was not beyond his control); Forkapa v. Forkapa, 1981 WL 5670 (Ohio Ct. App. 6th Dist. Lucas County 1981) (merely because defendant had history of failing to comply with court orders on alimony payments does not mean that court can use this as justification for not terminating alimony).

[4]Sager v. Sager, 5 Ohio App. 489, 27 Ohio C.D. 559, 1916 WL 1297 (6th Dist. Lucas County 1916).

[5]Haynie v. Haynie, 19 Ohio App. 3d 288, 290, 484 N.E.2d 750 (8th Dist. Cuyahoga County 1984) (one-year contract as an emergency room physician ended; husband entered partnership to practice with other physicians).

alimony because of a change of circumstances.[6] In *Wolfe v. Wolfe*,[7] the Court expressed the jurisdiction to modify in the following manner:

> Such initially fair agreements may be rendered manifestly oppressive in countless situations, such as where the custodian of the children fails to provide proper care and guidance, or where the receiver of alimony makes no attempt at self support, or where the economic situation of either or both of the parties drastically changes. The holding in this case, that a court has continuing modification jurisdiction over alimony for sustenance awards, is to assure that such awards are continually just.

Citing to *Leighner v. Leighner*,[8] the appellate court in *Lenick v. Lenick*[9] approved an increase in spousal support from $400 per month to $1,600 per month, holding that a "trial court must be cognizant that the focus in spousal support modification proceedings is upon the standard of living established before the parties' divorce." The increased amount was found to be necessary in order for appellee to maintain her pre-divorce standard of living.

In *Bronson v. Bronson*,[10] the court found that the obligee's failure to further her education or engage in a meaningful attempt at employment was not sufficient grounds for modification of the trial court's original alimony award. The court had previously rejected that argument in *Haninger v. Haninger*.[11] There is no absolute duty imposed on an alimony recipient to become self-sufficient. The fact that the obligee chose to live on the amount of the alimony payment did not result in a change of circumstances to reduce the obligor's alimony obligation.

Under former RC 3105.18(C), now RC 3105.18(D),[12] a trial court which has jurisdiction to modify any continuing order for periodic payments of money under an alimony only or legal separation decree may do so on "changed circumstances of either party." Additionally, effective January 1, 1991, RC 3105.18(F)[13] declares that, for purposes of modifying an award of spousal support arising out of a prior court order, a change in circumstances includes any increase or involuntary decrease in income or expenses. Case law has required the change to be substantial, and has frequently required that it must not have been anticipated at the time of the prior order. Court interpretation of

---

[6]Popovic v. Popovic, 45 Ohio App. 2d 57, 74 Ohio Op. 2d 94, 341 N.E.2d 341 (8th Dist. Cuyahoga County 1975).

[7]Wolfe v. Wolfe, 46 Ohio St. 2d 399, 418-19, 75 Ohio Op. 2d 474, 350 N.E.2d 413 (1976).

[8]Leighner v. Leighner, 33 Ohio App. 3d 214, 515 N.E.2d 625 (10th Dist. Franklin County 1986).

[9]Lenick v. Lenick, 1994 WL 728671, at *1 (Ohio Ct. App. 5th Dist. Richland County 1994).

[10]Bronson v. Bronson, 1992 WL 30781 (Ohio Ct. App. 10th Dist. Franklin County 1992).

[11]Haninger v. Haninger, 8 Ohio App. 3d 286, 456 N.E.2d 1228 (10th Dist. Franklin County 1982).

[12]Amended by 1990 H 514, eff. 1-1-91.

[13]Amended by 1990 H 514, eff. 1-1-91.

this new section will determine whether the change has to be substantial to merit consideration of a modification.

While changes in economic conditions in general can be expected over time, the effects of inflation cannot be predicted. Where inflation significantly reduced an obligee's purchasing power and the obligor had sustained an increase in earnings, modification was proper in *Staehle v Staehle*.[14] An obligor's voluntary decision to incur additional debt does not justify modifying spousal support payments.[15]

In *Fallang v. Fallang*,[16] the court stated that if a trial court finds that a change in circumstances has occurred, and in *Fallang* the payor's income decreased while the payee's income increased, the trial court still must determine the spousal support that is appropriate and reasonable in accordance with RC 3105.18. "Need" is no longer a statutory standard for awarding spousal support. The court found the existing spousal support in *Fallang* was reasonable and appropriate.

In *Lemley v. Lemley*,[17] the payor lost his employment because of theft. The court modified his spousal support payments due to his loss of employment. The court found this was a change of circumstances and the spousal support could be modified. However, in *Brockmeier v. Brockmeier*,[18] the court refused to modify child support where the payor had been found guilty of a felony theft charge and requested a modification. The court found, citing a number of cases, that the substantial decrease in earnings was voluntary. The court stated that the effect of criminal conduct was found to be voluntary and did not give any right to modification of child support obligations. Similarly, in *Willis v. Willis*,[19] the court refused to modify or terminate spousal support where the payor had been found guilty of gross sexual imposition and was incarcerated.

Post-decree lottery winnings, which give obligor the ability to pay an increase in spousal support, may be considered as a change of circumstances to justify an increase where the original decree specifically noted that the obligee's needs exceeded the obligor's ability to pay and the obligee had been forced to subsist at a level below the

---

[14]Staehle v. Staehle, 1992 WL 214354 (Ohio Ct. App. 10th Dist. Franklin County 1992) (increase in spousal support to reflect inflation warranted).

[15]Shanley v. Shanley, 46 Ohio App. 3d 100, 546 N.E.2d 477 (8th Dist. Cuyahoga County 1989); Krause v. Krause, 1995 WL 248527 (Ohio Ct. App. 8th Dist. Cuyahoga County 1995).

[16]Fallang v. Fallang, 109 Ohio App. 3d 543, 672 N.E.2d 730 (12th Dist. Butler County 1996).

[17]Lemley v. Lemley, 1995 WL 758809 (Ohio Ct. App. 7th Dist. Belmont County 1995).

[18]Brockmeier v. Brockmeier, 91 Ohio App. 3d 689, 633 N.E.2d 584 (1st Dist. Hamilton County 1993).

[19]Willis v. Willis, 1998 WL 172618 (Ohio Ct. App. 5th Dist. Stark County 1998).

parties' pre-divorce standard of living.[20] Lottery winnings of $17,000 in one year, being a one-time occurrence, does not reasonably constitute a change of circumstances warranting a reduction in spousal support.[21]

In *Lawrence v. Lawrence*,[22] the court of appeals held that in a modification proceeding it was not improper for the trial court to ignore the payee's post-decree receipt of a $67,000 personal injury settlement since the parties knew at the time of the original divorce that someday the payee would be receiving the settlement. The payor spouse had also complained about the trial court's consideration of the retirement income he was receiving as the result of his involuntary, post-decree retirement because both parties knew at the time of the original divorce that the payor spouse would someday receive that retirement income, which argument the court of appeals rejected.

Conversely, in *Joseph v. Joseph*,[23] the court of appeals held that the income, not existing at the time of the original decree, generated from funds resulting from the post-decree sale of assets awarded in the final decree must be considered as a change along with all other circumstances when determining whether a change of circumstances has occurred sufficient to consider modifying the spousal support award.

While RC 3105.18 lists "income" as one of the factors a court shall consider when making and/or modifying an award of spousal support, unlike the child support statutes no definition of "income" is included. In *Cooper v. Cooper*,[24] in a case where husband was seeking a modification of both his child support and his spousal support modification, the court appears to use the child support statutes definition of income for both issues, without expressly acknowledging that. This decision addresses the treatment of sources of income that husband alleged to be "non-recurring", the issue of whether a bonus received from a past employer within the last 3 years is properly considered as part of income when the husband now has a new employer, as well as the treatment of a "signing bonus" paid to husband as a one-time incentive to accept the new job. This decision also addresses the issue of "voluntary" versus "involuntary" reductions in income in the context of the husband being fired from his job.

---

[20]Foster v. Foster, 1997 WL 583567 (Ohio Ct. App. 4th Dist. Washington County 1997).

[21]Lawler v. Lawler, 1999 WL 417999 (Ohio Ct. App. 11th Dist. Geauga County 1999).

[22]Lawrence v. Lawrence, 144 Ohio App. 3d 454, 760 N.E.2d 846 (2d Dist. Clark County 2001).

[23]Joseph v. Joseph, 122 Ohio App. 3d 734, 702 N.E.2d 949 (2d Dist. Montgomery County 1997).

[24]Cooper v. Cooper, 2004-Ohio-1368, 2004 WL 549784 (Ohio Ct. App. 12th Dist. Clermont County 2004).

§ 14:28 Requirements for modification—Remarriage of recipient

In *Olney v. Watts*,[1] the court found that the remarriage of a wife to a man financially able to support her would be prima facie good cause for modifying a former decree so as to reduce the amount to be paid the wife. Later, in *Hunt v. Hunt*,[2] the Supreme Court found it to be contrary to "good public policy" to require a divorced wife's former husband to continue to make alimony payments after her subsequent marriage to another man capable of supporting her. The support potential of the subsequent spouse is not intended as an evidence factor, but more as a conclusive presumption as a result of choice.[3] This principle also caused or contributed to the subsequent cohabitation findings as shown in *Wolfe* where the issue was not the fact of the subsequent cohabitation, but the continued receipt by the wife of alimony payments from the ex-husband while cohabiting with another man. The Court noted the potential unfairness: "[S]he is, in fact, attempting to enjoy all the benefits of a marriage by cohabiting with an-

---

[Section 14:28]

[1]Olney v. Watts, 43 Ohio St. 499, 3 N.E. 354 (1885).

[2]Hunt v. Hunt, 169 Ohio St. 276, 8 Ohio Op. 2d 286, 159 N.E.2d 430 (1959) (overruled by, In re Adams, 45 Ohio St. 3d 219, 543 N.E.2d 797 (1989)).

[3]See also Lutes v. Lutes, 1981 WL 4085 (Ohio Ct. App. 9th Dist. Summit County 1981) (husband requested modification of divorce decree allowing wife's new husband to live in the marital residence but requiring first husband to pay mortgage and utility bills; divorce decree was sustained, but court of appeals decided that wife upon remarriage must relieve former husband of mortgage and utility obligations); Wyss v. Wyss, 1981 WL 6376 (Ohio Ct. App. 5th Dist. Stark County 1981) (alimony award of $250 per month for six years sustained but modified to provide for termination of alimony upon remarriage of plaintiff, death of either plaintiff or defendant, or further order of the court, whichever occurred first); Maher N.K.A. Danielson v. Maher, 1981 WL 4615 (Ohio Ct. App. 8th Dist. Cuyahoga County 1981) (a separation agreement incorporated into decree to pay alimony for 121 months or until appellee's death not modifiable on grounds of wife's remarriage because remarriage was not one of the contingencies); Drossman v. Drossman, 48 Ohio App. 2d 81, 2 Ohio Op. 3d 63, 355 N.E.2d 891 (6th Dist. Erie County 1975) (where at the time permanent alimony decree is entered, parties contemplate wife's remarriage and intend decree to be permanent division of property with monthly payments applied to outstanding mortgage and to terminate at fixed date, decree not subject to modification at marriage of wife); Estes v. Estes, 1981 WL 9714 (Ohio Ct. App. 1st Dist. Hamilton County 1981) (where there was a separate and independent division of property and a statement that alimony would be paid at rate of $100 per month for thirty-six months, the latter division, even though reducible to lump sum, was held to be periodic alimony and subject to modification because of changed circumstance of plaintiff's remarriage; contrary to public policy to require continued support alimony payments under circumstance of remarriage); Ginsburg v. Ginsburg, 1981 WL 3556 (Ohio Ct. App. 10th Dist. Franklin County 1981) (where separation agreement indicated fixed sum alimony for ten years and one month, it is in nature of property settlement rather than support alimony and cannot be terminated on basis of remarriage of the plaintiff).

other man and yet not entering into an actual marriage in order to avoid the loss of alimony."[4]

The First District Court of Appeals in *Estes v. Estes*[5] held that remarriage terminates alimony unless a contrary intention is stated in the decree.

In *Dunaway v. Dunaway*,[6] the parties were divorced in 1977 and a separation agreement was incorporated into the decree. The agreement did not spell out the circumstances on which the alimony obligation would terminate. The court of appeals found that the alimony was subject to further order of court. On the obligee's remarriage, the obligor moved to terminate the alimony obligation. The trial court found that the remarriage alone did not constitute a sufficient change in circumstances to warrant termination of the alimony obligation. The Supreme Court held where a dependent divorced spouse remarried, the obligation of the first spouse to pay support or alimony terminates as a matter of law, unless:

(1) The alimony payments constitute a property settlement;

(2) The payment is related to child support; or

(3) The parties have executed a separation agreement in contemplation of divorce that expressly provides for the continuation of sustenance alimony after the dependent party remarries.[7]

Subsequent to the *Dunaway*[8] decision, appellate courts generally followed the principle that for decrees issued after May 2, 1986 the absence of an appropriate reservation of jurisdiction deprived the trial court of jurisdiction to terminate a spousal support award based on the obligee's remarriage.[9] In *Kimble v. Kimble*,[10] the Ohio Supreme Court held that the *Dunaway*[11] had involved a decree issued prior to the 1986 revisions to RC 3105.18(E), and that the revisions to RC 3105.18(E) had rendered the *Dunaway*[12] inapplicable to decrees issued after May 2, 1986. The *Kimble* court further held that the term "modify" as used in RC 3105.18(E) specifically includes the term "terminate" and the language in the decree that specifically did not

---

[4]Wolfe v. Wolfe, 46 Ohio St. 2d 399, 401, 75 Ohio Op. 2d 474, 350 N.E.2d 413 (1976).

[5]Estes v. Estes, 1981 WL 9714 (Ohio Ct. App. 1st Dist. Hamilton County 1981).

[6]Dunaway v. Dunaway, 53 Ohio St. 3d 227, 560 N.E.2d 171 (1990).

[7]VonAhlefeld v. VonAhlefeld, 85 Ohio App. 3d 220, 222, 619 N.E.2d 495 (12th Dist. Butler County 1993) (although alimony was originally awarded on basis of "exceptional circumstances," court declined to designate that as a fourth exception to termination upon remarriage).

[8]Dunaway v. Dunaway, 53 Ohio St. 3d 227, 560 N.E.2d 171 (1990).

[9]Alty v. Alty, 1991 WL 217023 (Ohio Ct. App. 2d Dist. Champaign County 1991); McClusky v. Nelson, 94 Ohio App. 3d 746, 641 N.E.2d 807 (9th Dist. Summit County 1994).

[10]Kimble v. Kimble, 97 Ohio St. 3d 424, 2002-Ohio-6667, 780 N.E.2d 273 (2002).

[11]Dunaway v. Dunaway, 53 Ohio St. 3d 227, 560 N.E.2d 171 (1990).

[12]Dunaway v. Dunaway, 53 Ohio St. 3d 227, 560 N.E.2d 171 (1990).

retain continuing jurisdiction to modify also divested the trial court of any jurisdiction to terminate the award. Subsequent to the issuance of the *Kimble* decision, the Ohio Supreme Court reaffirmed this principle in *Wagoner v. Gerbl*.[13]

In *Rihan v. Rihan*[14] it was held that Wife's participation in a religious marriage ceremony after the parties' divorce trial but before the filing of their divorce decree rendered that second marriage "void," and thus did not constitute "remarriage" as grounds for termination of the spousal support award.

In dissolution of marriage proceedings, where the decrees were entered prior to May 2, 1996, *Mcclain v. Mcclain*,[15] and *In re Adams*[16] held that a dissolution decree could not be modified upon the remarriage of the payee absent a reservation of jurisdiction in the agreement. However, in *Whiteside v. Fowle*,[17] where the court granted a motion for relief based on the remarriage of the payee under Rule 60(B) in a dissolution of marriage case where the decree was entered in 1992, and there was no reservation of jurisdiction clause in the agreement.

§ 14:29 Requirements for modification—Entering into relationship in another state that constitutes valid marriage in Ohio

In *Fahrer v. Fahrer*,[1] the court ruled that a party, living in a relationship which would constitute a common law marriage in Ohio but living in a state not recognizing common law marriage, is involved in such a relationship as to terminate alimony payments payable under a separation agreement which provides that such payments cease upon the remarriage of a party. Since a common law marriage in Ohio entered into prior to October 10, 1991, is a legal marriage, and a subsequent legal marriage terminates alimony or spousal support, then the fact that another state does not recognize the common law marriage is not binding on Ohio's view of common law as to status per se and as to alimony or spousal support termination as a consequence.

Since Ohio has abolished common law marriages, as of October 10, 1991,[2] the principles set forth in the *Fahrer* case would no longer be applicable to such relationships that arise after October 10, 1991.

---

[13]Wagoner v. Gerbl, 98 Ohio St. 3d 290, 2003-Ohio-739, 783 N.E.2d 899 (2003).

[14]Rihan v. Rihan, 2006-Ohio-2671, 2006 WL 1461097 (Ohio Ct. App. 2d Dist. Greene County 2006).

[15]McClain v. McClain, 15 Ohio St. 3d 289, 473 N.E.2d 811 (1984).

[16]In re Adams, 45 Ohio St. 3d 219, 543 N.E.2d 797 (1989).

[17]Whiteside v. Fowle, 1996 WL 494825 (Ohio Ct. App. 12th Dist. Madison County 1996).

[Section 14:29]

[1]Fahrer v. Fahrer, 36 Ohio App. 2d 208, 65 Ohio Op. 2d 330, 304 N.E.2d 411 (1st Dist. Hamilton County 1973).

[2]RC 3105.12 as amended by 1991 H.B. 32.

§ 14:30   Requirements for modification—Cohabitation of recipient

In *Wolfe*, the Court stated that unchastity does not per se require, by reason of public policy, a full termination of an alimony award. It is, however, a circumstance that could and should be considered as to modification or termination of alimony payments. The Court quoted from a New Jersey case:

> We have no doubt, however, that where a former wife chooses to co-habit with a paramour, whether in her abode or his, or otherwise consorts with him, the issue may well arise whether, in the circumstances, she has further need for the alimony. If it is shown that the wife is being supported in whole or in part by the paramour, the former husband may come into court for a determination of whether the alimony should be terminated or reduced. Similarly, if the paramour resides in the wife's home without contributing anything toward the purchase of food or the payment of normal household bills, then there may be a reasonable inference that the wife's alimony is being used, at least in part, for the benefit of the paramour, in which case it could be argued with force that the amount thereof should be modified accordingly. In short, the inquiry is whether the former wife's illicit relationship with another man, apart from the misconduct per se, has produced a change of circumstances sufficient to entitle the former husband to relief.[1]

Wolfe made it clear that modification in a subsequent cohabitation situation is a matter within the discretion of the hearing court.[2] A reading of *Wolfe* suggests that unchastity may be the basis for a support alimony or spousal support modification. The morality issue does

---

[Section 14:30]

[1]Wolfe v. Wolfe, 46 Ohio St. 2d 399, 420-21, 75 Ohio Op. 2d 474, 350 N.E.2d 413 (1976), quoting Garlinger v. Garlinger, 137 N.J. Super. 56, 347 A.2d 799 (App. Div. 1975). See also Lester v. Lester, 1981 WL 3186 (Ohio Ct. App. 10th Dist. Franklin County 1981) (subsequent cohabitation not grounds for terminating support alimony where personal relationship did not affect continued need for alimony); Rose v. Rose, 1981 WL 2726 (Ohio Ct. App. 2d Dist. Montgomery County 1981) (even though separation agreement included contingency of cohabitation, it was still matter for trial court to determine whether defendant did in fact cohabit, and not matter for plaintiff to determine for himself; because he did so, finding of contempt not unwarranted); Woods v. Woods, 1980 WL 352680 (Ohio Ct. App. 2d Dist. Fayette County 1980), aff'd, 66 Ohio St. 2d 348, 20 Ohio Op. 3d 318, 421 N.E.2d 1293 (1981) (decree having condition subsequent terminating support upon remarriage or cohabitation with another male was found to be consistent with mandate of *Wolfe*, but stipulation was not grounds for termination per se, or grounds for review by court with respect to need); In the Matter of Heebsch v. Heebsch, 1982 WL 6571 (Ohio Ct. App. 6th Dist. Lucas County 1982) (where alimony decree has contingency of three years, death, remarriage, or cohabitation with a nonrelative male, these acts terminate the alimony).

[2]Wolfe v. Wolfe, 46 Ohio St. 2d 399, 75 Ohio Op. 2d 474, 350 N.E.2d 413 (1976). See also Skidmore v. Skidmore, 1980 WL 352213 (Ohio Ct. App. 11th Dist. Geauga County 1980) (where separation agreement called for alimony in monthly installments for period of time or "until death or remarriage, whichever is first," petitioner's attempt to modify alimony based on subsequent cohabitation denied, because agreement did not include cohabitation; petitioner's attempt to rely on the *Wolfe* mandate was distinguished in that *Wolfe* merely gives trial court authority to modify but does not require that it modify).

not warrant the alimony or spousal support modification, but the co-habitation status as a change in the economic status of the recipient may justify modification. The party requesting the modification must be certain to frame the issue as an economic issue and not a sanction for lifestyle.

"Unchastity is not automatic grounds for termination of [an] alimony award, but it [may] be considered . . . insofar as it is relevant to the issues of continued need for such alimony."[3]

"Cohabitation is manifested by the two persons involved living together in the same household and assuming obligations, including supports [sic] and equivalent to those arising in a ceremonial marriage."[4]

The term "cohabitation" contemplates a relationship that approximates or is the functional equivalent of a marriage.[5] In defining the term "cohabitation," the Ohio Supreme Court has stated the following:

> The essential elements of 'cohabitation' are (1) sharing of familial or financial responsibilities and (2) consortium . . . . Possible factors establishing shared familial or financial responsibilities might include provisions for shelter, food, clothing, utilities, and/or commingled assets. Factors that might establish consortium include mutual respect, fidelity, affection, society, cooperation, solace, comfort, aid of each other, friendship, and conjugal relations.[6]

Once cohabitation is established, support can properly be terminated even if the relationship between the recipient spouse and the par-

---

[3]Savino v. Savino, 1985 WL 7909, at *3 (Ohio Ct. App. 2d Dist. Montgomery County 1985); Wallenhurst v. Wallenhurst, 116 Ohio App. 3d 823, 689 N.E.2d 586 (7th Dist. Columbiana County 1996) citing (Wolfe v. Wolfe, 46 Ohio St. 2d 399, 75 Ohio Op. 2d 474, 350 N.E.2d 413 (1976).

[4]Savino v. Savino, 1985 WL 7909, at *2 (Ohio Ct. App. 2d Dist. Montgomery County 1985); Wallenhurst v. Wallenhurst, 116 Ohio App. 3d 823, 689 N.E.2d 586 (7th Dist. Columbiana County 1996) (cohabitation not found where former wife's friend visited only when in town on business and contributed only to food he ate on those occasional visits; neither had intent to cohabit and there was no continuity of togetherness) citing Wolfe v. Wolfe, 46 Ohio St. 2d 399, 75 Ohio Op. 2d 474, 350 N.E.2d 413 (1976)). See also Fuller v. Fuller, 10 Ohio App. 3d 253, 254, 461 N.E.2d 1348 (10th Dist. Franklin County 1983) ("Cohabitation, then, usually will be manifested by a man and woman living together in the same household and behaving as would a husband and wife, although there need not be an actual assertion of marriage."); Taylor v. Taylor, 11 Ohio App. 3d 279, 465 N.E.2d 476 (1st Dist. Hamilton County 1983) (sexual relationship is strong evidence of cohabitation but it is not dispositive of issue); Hicks v. Hicks, 1982 WL 2709, at *1 (Ohio Ct. App. 9th Dist. Lorain County 1982) ("Cohabiting means living together in one house; a boarding or tabling together; it carries with it the idea of a fixed residence."); Radina v. Radina, 1987 WL 32754 (Ohio Ct. App. 12th Dist. Clermont County 1987) (since decree does not provide that alimony would automatically terminate on cohabitation, it cannot be sole basis for modification).

[5]Piscione v. Piscione, 85 Ohio App. 3d 273, 275, 619 N.E.2d 1030 (9th Dist. Lorain County 1992).

[6]State v. Williams, 79 Ohio St. 3d 459, 1997-Ohio-79, 683 N.E.2d 1126 (1997)

amour comes to an end prior to the end of the period within which the former spouse is required to pay spousal support.[7] At least one court has held that termination of cohabitation neither revives a spousal support obligation nor results in the continuation of spousal support.[8] At least two courts have held that a retroactive order terminating spousal support upon cohabitation is permissible when the decree provides that spousal support shall terminate upon cohabitation.[9]

In *Seybert v. Seybert*,[10] the decree had provided that alimony was to terminate upon the wife's "cohabitation with a person in a state similar to marriage." The court found that even in the absence of a sexual relationship, the wife's living with a prior husband in a relationship of mutual support constituted cohabitation. The trial court, however, affirmed by the appellate court, found full termination of alimony would not be proper and ordered only a suspension of the husband's alimony payments during the period of cohabitation.

In *Evans v. Evans*,[11] the court refused a motion to terminate alimony on the obligor's allegations that the obligee was cohabitating with a person who was providing her with support. The court found that even if the obligee was cohabitating with a third party, the court would only have been justified in modifying the alimony award if it had found that the cohabitation had eliminated or decreased the obligee's need for alimony. Cohabitation is a question of fact. There was competent credible evidence to support the trial court's finding that the obligee and a third party were not cohabiting but were merely "two senior citizens sharing expenses." The evidence did not support appellant's theory that the third party was supporting the obligee as a husband would a wife.

Where the original decree stated that spousal support would terminate upon the wife's entering into "a living arrangement similar to marriage," the trial court erred in terminating support even though the wife and her male friend were involved in a serious relationship, the man spent many nights at the wife's home, they had an ongoing sexual relationship, and he went on vacations with the wife and the children as well as acted as supervisor and protector of her children. In a fact-specific determination, the appellate court in *Piscione v.*

---

[7]Perri v. Perri, 79 Ohio App. 3d 845, 852, 608 N.E.2d 790 (2d Dist. Montgomery County 1992).

[8]Keeley v. Keeley, 2000 WL 431362 (Ohio Ct. App. 12th Dist. Clermont County 2000).

[9]Keeley v. Keeley, 2000 WL 431362 (Ohio Ct. App. 12th Dist. Clermont County 2000); Jennings v. Jennings, 1995 WL 628336 (Ohio Ct. App. 8th Dist. Cuyahoga County 1995).

[10]Seybert v. Seybert, 1991 WL 2009 (Ohio Ct. App. 9th Dist. Lorain County 1991).

[11]Evans v. Evans, 1989 WL 114332 (Ohio Ct. App. 12th Dist. Brown County 1989); Holder v. Holder, 1999 WL 250243 (Ohio Ct. App. 12th Dist. Butler County 1999).

Piscione[12] held the relationship did not rise to a level similar to marriage.

However, in *Miller v. Miller*,[13] the appellate court found the trial court was correct in terminating spousal support when it found that the obligee had cohabitated with an unrelated male who was providing *some* support.[14] While the court must inquire whether the obligee is receiving some sort of monetary support from the new partner,[15] equally important to a finding of cohabitation warranting termination of spousal support is whether the obligee is financially supporting the new partner.[16]

Exemplifying the case-by-case analysis required in cohabitation determination situations, the court in *Moell v. Moell*[17] indicated the trial court may consider behavior and intent of the parties in deciding whether a particular living arrangement rises to the level of "cohabitation" for purposes of a cohabitation clause. Where the former wife and her male friend had not assumed mutual obligations of financial support, even though they contemplated marriage, the trial court was affirmed in its denial of modification or termination.

Living in a "state of concubinage," for purposes of a provision in a divorce decree terminating alimony upon such circumstance, is to be determined on a case-by-case basis. Even though an ex-wife and a man had a sexual relationship and went out socially and the man made some rent, utility, and car payments for the ex-wife, their relationship did not rise to a level of one approximating marriage where the man did not receive mail at the ex-wife's residence and they did not hold themselves out as husband and wife.[18]

---

[12]Piscione v. Piscione, 85 Ohio App. 3d 273, 619 N.E.2d 1030 (9th Dist. Lorain County 1992).

[13]Miller v. Miller, 61 Ohio App. 3d 269, 572 N.E.2d 742 (2d Dist. Montgomery County 1989).

[14]See also King v. King, 1993 WL 489729 (Ohio Ct. App. 12th Dist. Warren County 1993) (where ex-wife paid rent for use of man's half of duplex which she shared with him, court found to be sharing expenses); Nekrosius v. Nekrosius, 1993 WL 265417 (Ohio Ct. App. 2d Dist. Montgomery County 1993) (spousal support reduced where partial support from man should be provided).

[15]Thomas v. Thomas, 76 Ohio App. 3d 482, 602 N.E.2d 385 (10th Dist. Franklin County 1991).

[16]Perri v. Perri, 79 Ohio App. 3d 845, 608 N.E.2d 790 (2d Dist. Montgomery County 1992).

[17]Moell v. Moell, 98 Ohio App. 3d 748, 649 N.E.2d 880 (6th Dist. Ottawa County 1994).

[18]Dial v. Dial, 92 Ohio App. 3d 513, 636 N.E.2d 361 (9th Dist. Summit County 1993); Knowlton v. Knowlton, 1994 WL 10631 (Ohio Ct. App. 7th Dist. Monroe County 1994) (weekend stays for period of three years, use of ex-wife's car, and some clothes in her closet insufficient to establish cohabitation where no obligations for support assumed by man).

In *Synovetz v. Synovetz*,[19] the decree provided for termination on cohabitation. The court found that the payor need not additionally show a change of circumstances to terminate the spousal support since the spousal support terminated on cohabitation by the language in the decree.

In *Daley v. Daley*,[20] although the court did not find cohabitation which would terminate the spousal support order, the court found the payee's living arrangement may provide the payee with such a financial benefit that would have entitled the payor to a modification of his spousal support obligation. Therefore, the appellate court remanded the issue to the trial court to determine what amount of credit, if any, the payor should receive against his spousal support arrearage. The court found that to constitute cohabitation, there must be a voluntary duty undertaken for total support or obligations assumed which were equivalent to those arising from a ceremonial marriage.

Emphasizing that cohabitation, for the purpose of justifying modification or termination of spousal support, must include proof of financial support or assuming responsibility for the other's financial obligations, the appellate court in *In re Dissolution of Marriage of Briggs*[21] reversed the trial court's order of termination. In so doing, the appellate court reviewed the evidence that the former spouse and her male friend each maintained a residence in a different state where both would reside alternately for six months. Since the only financial benefit to either was the purchase of groceries, the appellate court found the trial court's determination of cohabitation to be against the manifest weight of the evidence.

In a case of a payee residing with an adult child, the trial court did not find "cohabitation" for the purpose of terminating the spousal support where the payee was living with her adult child and the child's boyfriend. Query: If cohabitation is defined as an economic issue, why doesn't living in the same household and sharing expenses with someone qualify as cohabitation?[22] The moving party seeking to terminate the spousal support has the burden of proof establishing cohabitation.[23]

In *Dean-Kitts v. Dean*[24] the parties had negotiated and read into the record their agreement in their divorce, including a provision awarding spousal support to wife. Husband sought to terminate his spousal

---

[19]Synovetz v. Synovetz, 1996 WL 199443 (Ohio Ct. App. 9th Dist. Lorain County 1996).

[20]Daley v. Daley, 1997 WL 52919 (Ohio Ct. App. 2d Dist. Miami County 1997).

[21]In re Dissolution of Marriage of Briggs, 129 Ohio App. 3d 346, 717 N.E.2d 1110 (9th Dist. Summit County 1998).

[22]Dickerson v. Dickerson, 87 Ohio App. 3d 848, 623 N.E.2d 237 (6th Dist. Lucas County 1993).

[23]Thurston v. Thurston, 2000 WL 423987 (Ohio Ct. App. 10th Dist. Franklin County 2000).

[24]Dean Kitts v. Dean, 2002-Ohio-5590, 2002 WL 31341601 (Ohio Ct. App. 2d Dist. Greene County 2002).

support obligation on the grounds that wife was cohabiting with another male. The trial court found that in fact the wife was cohabitating, but refused to modify or terminate the spousal support on the grounds that the husband entered into the original agreement to pay spousal support with full knowledge that wife was cohabitating. Husband acknowledged as much in his testimony at the hearing to terminate. On appeal, the court of appeals affirmed, citing principles of estoppel.

Conversely, in *Cleland v. Cleland*[25] in a post decree motion filed by husband seeking to terminate spousal support on grounds of wife's cohabitation, the wife asserted that husband was aware of her cohabitation when he agreed in their negotiated divorce decree to pay spousal support because she testified to living with the other man at a hearing to modify the temporary spousal support held during the divorce proceeding. The court of appeals affirmed the trial court's termination of the spousal support, distinguishing the facts of this case from those found in *Dean-Kitts v. Dean*[26] by noting that a transcript of that temporary support hearing revealed that wife characterized their living together as "temporary" and that the person would be "moving out soon."

Finding that the evidence showed that the recipient former husband was sharing rent and other living expenses with his girlfriend and that he was also apparently contributing to room and board for his girlfriend's daughter, the court in *Barrows v. Barrows*[27] reversed the trial court's refusal to reduce the former wife's spousal support obligation as an abuse of discretion, stating that "the circumstances of Husband have changed—and in a significant way—since the time of the original decree."

The court in *Day v. Day*[28] affirmed the trial court's reduction of the former husband's spousal support obligation by 16%, stating that while it disagreed with the trial court's methodology the evidence nevertheless supported the trial court's finding that the former wife's live-in boyfriend was directly benefiting from the wife's receipt of that much spousal support. The Day court also rejected the former husband's assertion that since his former wife's income had gone from approximately $15,000 at the time of the divorce to approximately $32,000 his spousal support obligation should have been reduced even further, stating "the fact that [the former wife's] income has increased since her divorce from [the former husband] does not by itself provide a sufficient basis or change in circumstance upon which to further reduce [the former husband's] spousal support obligation."

[25]Cleland v. Cleland, 2004-Ohio-561, 2004 WL 234693 (Ohio Ct. App. 7th Dist. Mahoning County 2004).

[26]Dean Kitts v. Dean, 2002-Ohio-5590, 2002 WL 31341601 (Ohio Ct. App. 2d Dist. Greene County 2002).

[27]Barrows v. Barrows, 2004-Ohio-4878, 2004 WL 2050508 (Ohio Ct. App. 9th Dist. Summit County 2004).

[28]Day v. Day, 2005-Ohio-2015, 2005 WL 994693 (Ohio Ct. App. 2d Dist. Greene County 2005).

Although the determination of whether a party is cohabiting is usually a question of fact to be determined by the trial court, subject only to an abuse of discretion under the manifest weight of the evidence standard, it can rise to the level of a question of law if the facts support only one reasonable conclusion. Thus, as a matter of law, the ex-wife and her fiancé were "cohabiting" and sharing expenses so as to warrant termination of ex-husband's spousal support obligation when the fiancé built, paid for, and lived with ex-wife in the home that he transferred to their joint names, the ex-wife's only expense to live in the home was to pay for utilities, groceries, and her own clothing, the ex-wife and her fiancé had a joint checking account, and by providing a rent-free residence to the ex-wife, as well as an automobile, the fiancé supported the ex-wife and her standard of living, and the fact that the fiancé owned another residence where he lived most of the time was irrelevant.[29]

§ 14:31 Requirements for modification—Factors— Cohabitation—Same sex

The specific words employed in the original spousal support order can limit the trial court's power of modification. In *Yaeger v. Yaeger*,[1] the separation agreement and the decree both provided for spousal support "for 72 consecutive months, or sooner upon Wife death, remarriage or assuming a status thereto, ..." Both documents contained a clause that said the court would not retain jurisdiction to modify.

The trial court denied the husband's motion to terminate upon the wife's cohabitation with another woman, in spite of the wife's admission that they were in a sexual relationship, had a joint checking account, and they shared household expenses. The magistrate's rationale was that Ohio does not recognize same-sex marriages; therefore, the wife could not have assumed a status thereto.

Since the court had no jurisdiction to modify, it could not terminate the support unless the specific events occurred. Citing *Kimble v. Kimble*[2] the appeals court affirmed the trial court's refusal to do either. There was no general power to modify, only specific circumstances that would terminate the support, and such triggering factors had not occurred.

---

[29]Clark v. Clark, 168 Ohio App. 3d 547, 2006-Ohio-4820, 860 N.E.2d 1080 (11th Dist. Trumbull County 2006), appeal not allowed, 112 Ohio St. 3d 1471, 2007-Ohio-388, 861 N.E.2d 145 (2007).

[Section 14:31]

[1]Yaeger v. Yaeger, 2004-Ohio-1959, 2004 WL 833187 (Ohio Ct. App. 11th Dist. Geauga County 2004).

[2]Kimble v. Kimble, 97 Ohio St. 3d 424, 2002-Ohio-6667, 780 N.E.2d 273 (2002).

§14:32 Requirements for modification—Payor's increased ability to pay

In *Norris v. Norris*,[1] the court would not grant an increase in alimony where the evidence of a substantial change of circumstances related solely to the payor's ability to pay. Neither party argued any significant change in the needs of the payee. The court held that before alimony can be modified, a determination must be made that there has been a substantial change in the circumstances of the payee relating to the need for sustenance. Only then should the court proceed to determine whether there has been a substantial change in the circumstances of the payor relating to the ability to pay. The court must find changed need first in order to increase an alimony or spousal support award.

The remarriage of the obligor and the income of the obligor's employed second wife are factors the court may consider as change of circumstances in a modification of alimony or spousal support proceeding.[2] Frequently, the obligor's new spouse's income is a factor in maintaining the present order, even if not a cause for an increase.[3]

In *Gross v. Gross*,[4] the obligor's income had increased since the decree was entered ordering periodic payments of alimony.[5] The court would not allow the increase in the obligor's income to be the sole factor for an increase in the alimony payments. The court found as follows:

> Therefore, the general rule is that an increase in the obligor's income alone will not suffice as a change in circumstances sufficient to allow an increase in periodic alimony payments. The exception to this rule is that an increase in income may justify an increase in alimony if the obligor's income was insufficient at the time of the original decree to support the recipient at the standard of living maintained during the marriage and the increase in income will now allow this level to be reached.
>
> . . .
>
> Under the circumstances herein, an increase in income constitutes a change in circumstances only when the increase allows an obligor to afford a higher alimony payment in accordance with R.C. 3105.18(B) than

---

[Section 14:32]

[1]Norris v. Norris, 13 Ohio App. 3d 248, 469 N.E.2d 76 (5th Dist. Stark County 1982).

[2]Roach v. Roach, 61 Ohio App. 3d 315, 572 N.E.2d 772 (8th Dist. Cuyahoga County 1989).

[3]Bishop v. Bishop, 1995 WL 695042 (Ohio Ct. App. 2d Dist. Montgomery County 1995); Bullard v. Bullard, 1995 WL 480625 (Ohio Ct. App. 11th Dist. Lake County 1995).

[4]Gross v. Gross, 64 Ohio App. 3d 815, 582 N.E.2d 1144 (10th Dist. Franklin County 1990).

[5]See also Lodge v. Lodge, 1993 WL 434582 (Ohio Ct. App. 6th Dist. Lucas County 1993) (increase in payor's income, coupled with finding that figure used as income at time of divorce was one-half usual income and thus artificially low, was sufficient change of circumstances).

the obligor could have afforded at the time of the original decree. Absent a change in circumstances, the alimony recipient is collaterally estopped from relitigating the alimony award based upon the obligor's increased income and capacity to pay.[6]

In *Albanese v. Albanese*,[7] the court found applicable the exception noted in *Gross* regarding an inadequate original order based upon temporary unemployment of the obligor. The one dollar a year amount was clearly insufficient then and at the time of the modification hearing. In addition, an obligor's increased income is a change of circumstances, when the obligor's income was initially insufficient to support the obligee spouse at pre-divorce standard of living. The obligee spouse is entitled to an increase corresponding to the obligor's increased income.[8]

An obligor's increased ability to pay spousal support, which occurs because the obligor has increased income post-decree from a professional degree earned during the marriage while the parties lived in a reduced standard, is a valid consideration. The obligee should be permitted to partake of the fruits of the collective efforts.[9]

The trial court does not have jurisdiction to increase an alimony award if the divorce decree only refers to conditions for downward modification and termination.[10]

In *Zahn v. Zahn*,[11] the court held that when imputing income, a trial court is permitted to look at actual evidence regarding a parties' prior work experience and salary, education, voluntary job choices, and consider evidence regarding prevailing job opportunities in the community, and expert testimony is not required to establish prevailing job opportunities in the community. In essence, the *Zahn* court held that the evidence of the party's prior work experience in that community was sufficient evidence of the prevailing job opportunities in the community absent evidence to the contrary, and that the party had had the opportunity to present expert evidence to the contrary but did not do so.

---

[6]Gross v. Gross, 64 Ohio App. 3d 815, 819-20, 582 N.E.2d 1144 (10th Dist. Franklin County 1990).

[7]Albanese v. Albanese, 1999 WL 354361 (Ohio Ct. App. 10th Dist. Franklin County 1999).

[8]McClain v. McClain, 1999 WL 960969 (Ohio Ct. App. 11th Dist. Portage County 1999).

[9]Lira v. Lira, 12 Ohio App. 3d 69, 465 N.E.2d 1353 (8th Dist. Cuyahoga County 1983); Kraska v. Kraska, 1998 WL 964581 (Ohio Ct. App. 11th Dist. Portage County 1998).

[10]Cassavore v. Cassavore, 1990 WL 10968 (Ohio Ct. App. 6th Dist. Lucas County 1990). See also Gable v. Gable, 1997 WL 67723 (Ohio Ct. App. 12th Dist. Warren County 1997).

[11]Zahn v. Zahn, 2004-Ohio-4881, 2004 WL 2050526 (Ohio Ct. App. 9th Dist. Summit County 2004).

§ 14:33   Requirements for modification—Payee's increased income

Increased income of payee spouse does not automatically require termination of spousal support. It can constitute a change of circumstances.[1]

A separation agreement that provides for automatic adjustment of spousal support commensurate with employment income of the payee spouse, with no reservation of jurisdiction to modify, does not permit a trial court to impute income to the obligee spouse.[2]

In *Zahn v. Zahn*,[3] the court held that when imputing income, a trial court is permitted to look at actual evidence regarding a parties' prior work experience and salary, education, voluntary job choices, and consider evidence regarding prevailing job opportunities in the community, and expert testimony is not required to establish prevailing job opportunities in the community. In essence, the *Zahn* court held that the evidence of the party's prior work experience in that community was sufficient evidence of the prevailing job opportunities in the community absent evidence to the contrary, and that the party had had the opportunity to present expert evidence to the contrary but did not do so.

§ 14:34   Requirements for modification—Retirement

In *Roach v. Roach*,[1] the court decided a former husband's retirement at age fifty-nine did not constitute a "voluntary act" barring modification of his alimony obligations where he had merely taken advantage of retirement benefits to which he was entitled, particularly where records suggested that retirement was motivated at least in part by medical reasons. However, he included in his income and expense statement monthly expenses which appeared to be incurred by himself and his second wife. Accordingly, the trial court was required to consider his second wife's income in determining whether his retirement had in fact constituted a substantial change in circumstances. Moreover, his second wife's income should be considered in light of his allegation of changed circumstances.

[Section 14:33]

[1]Franzmann v. Franzmann, 1999 WL 980559 (Ohio Ct. App. 9th Dist. Summit County 1999); Joseph v. Joseph, 122 Ohio App. 3d 734, 702 N.E.2d 949 (2d Dist. Montgomery County 1997).

[2]Maher v. Maher, 1999 WL 1059674 (Ohio Ct. App. 9th Dist. Summit County 1999).

[3]Zahn v. Zahn, 2004-Ohio-4881, 2004 WL 2050526 (Ohio Ct. App. 9th Dist. Summit County 2004).

[Section 14:34]

[1]Roach v. Roach, 61 Ohio App. 3d 315, 572 N.E.2d 772 (8th Dist. Cuyahoga County 1989).

In *Edmondson v. Edmondson*,[2] the court held that a reduction in income due to voluntary retirement is literally a change of circumstances which might justify the termination or suspension of support. In *Edmondson*, however, the payor contemplated retirement when he agreed to the spousal support amount; because the retirement was contemplated, it was not a grounds for a modification.

Where an obligor retired from his law practice due to aggravated health problems and had substantially reduced income, the court held that this was a sufficient change of circumstances to justify a reduction of alimony.[3]

Voluntary retirement does not always constitute a change in circumstance for purposes of modifying alimony or spousal support. In *Guerrero v. Guerrero*,[4] the obligor requested a termination of an alimony obligation after voluntarily retiring after thirty-two years of employment at or about age fifty-two. The obligee relied on several cases in which a voluntary retirement did not constitute a sufficient change of circumstances including *Meyer v. Meyer*[5] and *Williams v. Williams*.[6] In both these cases, the courts found a voluntary retirement not to be a change of circumstances. However, neither of these cases stated that a voluntary retirement could not be a change of circumstance.

The obligee also argued that the court in *Nash v. Nash*[7] stated that changes in circumstances of the parties to be considered must be material and not purposely brought about by the complaining party. The *Guerrero* court then stated that the change of circumstances must be such that it was not contemplated at the time of the prior order, and that a voluntary retirement, not due to some extenuating circumstance, is a circumstance capable of contemplation and consideration, particularly under the facts. The court then found that it "would defy all logic and common sense to conclude" that the potential early retirement was not a consideration for the obligor at the time the separation agreement was negotiated and signed, and the obligor chose not to include or negotiate any provision as to that contingency.[8] The court went on to state that the burden is on the party alleging the

---

[2]Edmondson v. Edmondson, 1996 WL 685783 (Ohio Ct. App. 2d Dist. Montgomery County 1996).

[3]Haase v. Haase, 64 Ohio App. 3d 758, 582 N.E.2d 1107 (8th Dist. Cuyahoga County 1990).

[4]Guerrero v. Guerrero, 1991 WL 18667, at *2 (Ohio Ct. App. 11th Dist. Trumbull County 1991).

[5]Meyer v. Meyer, 1988 WL 59514 (Ohio Ct. App. 5th Dist. Fairfield County 1988).

[6]Williams v. Williams, 1987 WL 11024 (Ohio Ct. App. 11th Dist. Geauga County 1987).

[7]Nash v. Nash, 77 Ohio App. 155, 32 Ohio Op. 409, 65 N.E.2d 728 (9th Dist. Medina County 1945).

[8]Guerrero v. Guerrero, 1991 WL 18667 (Ohio Ct. App. 11th Dist. Trumbull County 1991).

change in circumstances to show that the modification is justified. However, even if such party has established a substantial change, the party seeking a reduction had to show the existing award was unnecessary and unreasonable.

In *Seer v. Seer*,[9] the plaintiff retired and moved to reduce or terminate alimony. The trial court found that spousal support could not be ordered paid from retirement benefits which had been set off in the division of property. The court of appeals reversed that order finding that a trial court may order the payment of spousal support from retirement benefits.[10] In *Meinke v. Meinke*,[11] the divorce decree had awarded the payor his retirement benefits and the payee received property in offset. The payor retired, and the court found that retirement benefits, although awarded in property settlement, could be considered in a spousal support proceeding. The court referred to RC 3105.18(C) which provides that the income of the parties includes retirement benefits. The court found the statute clearly contemplates that a payor spouse may be required to pay spousal support out of the proceeds of an asset awarded to him in the divorce, and specifically requires the court to consider the parties' retirement benefits. In *Gable v. Gable*,[12] the trial court did not include appellee's retirement pay in the income of either party since the retirement was a property right and had already been divided equitably pursuant to the divorce decree. The appellate court, however, said that RC 3105.18(C)(1)(a) permits the court to consider the parties' income from all sources, including pension benefits, when determining whether a spousal support award is appropriate and, thus, found that the trial court could have included the retirement pay in its calculation of the parties' income for spousal support purposes.

Another case in which retirement affected spousal support is *Wefler v. Wefler*.[13] In 1979, the obligor retired and requested a modification of his alimony obligation. The trial court overruled the motion. In 1990, the obligor filed another motion to modify the alimony award. The trial court terminated the alimony. The court of appeals reversed the trial court finding that the assets owned by his second wife should be considered in determining whether there has been a substantial

---

[9]Seer v. Seer, 1991 WL 207290 (Ohio Ct. App. 2d Dist. Montgomery County 1991).

[10]See also Enix v. Enix, 1993 WL 26775 (Ohio Ct. App. 2d Dist. Montgomery County 1993).

[11]Meinke v. Meinke, 1996 WL 748161 (Ohio Ct. App. 6th Dist. Lucas County 1996); Guidubaldi v. Guidubaldi, 1997 WL 585910 (Ohio Ct. App. 11th Dist. Portage County 1997) (payor's income from previously divided pension may still be considered and included in the pool of income from which spousal support can be paid).

[12]Gable v. Gable, 1997 WL 67723 (Ohio Ct. App. 12th Dist. Warren County 1997).

[13]Wefler v. Wefler, 1991 WL 262688 (Ohio Ct. App. 2d Dist. Montgomery County 1991).

change of circumstances.[14] The evidence indicated that the obligor used his own assets and income toward debts and support for his current wife and stepchild. The court made clear that his retirement income should have been considered as well as the assets owned by his second wife. The fact that his retirement had been awarded to him as part of a property settlement would not prevent the court from ordering the payment of spousal support from retirement benefits. The court found the trial court should take into account his wife's assets since the record clearly shows that a portion of the obligor's expenditures were for his new family.

It is not a modification of division of retirement benefits to consider the obligor's retirement income in his ability to pay. There is no statutory exclusion for retirement benefits that were divided as part of the property division in the divorce.[15]

An order denying a reduction in spousal support, after voluntary retirement reduced the payor's gross monthly income by almost one-half, was upheld where the retirement was within the contemplation of the parties and the payor had also received a 401(k) distribution of over $80,000, which he had cavalierly depleted by liquidating the entire account for the purchase of a fishing cabin, truck, boat, and snowmobile.[16]

Voluntary retirement can cause a reduction in income and therefore a change in circumstances. Even though voluntary, where such retirement occurs after an ordinary age of retirement, the trial court may reduce the alimony obligation where the court has retained jurisdiction.[17] Voluntary early retirement is less likely to be viewed as justifying a reduction than at normal retirement age. At the time of the divorce in *Sharp v. Sharp*[18] in 1989, the age was 65. An obligor's early retirement may be only partially contemplated or unforeseen, and thus if the obligor's decrease in income does not actually affect the obligor's ability to meet the support obligations, the court may properly decline to modify the support.

---

[14]Wefler v. Wefler, 1991 WL 262688 (Ohio Ct. App. 2d Dist. Montgomery County 1991).

[15]Boettner v. Boettner, 1998 WL 663219 (Ohio Ct. App. 9th Dist. Summit County 1998); Gamble v. Gamble, 1998 WL 785342 (Ohio Ct. App. 9th Dist. Summit County 1998).

[16]Roberson v. Roberson, 1993 WL 500325 (Ohio Ct. App. 5th Dist. Licking County 1993).

[17]Swogger v. Grimm, 1989 WL 1280 (Ohio Ct. App. 7th Dist. Mahoning County 1989), dismissed, 42 Ohio St. 3d 710, 538 N.E.2d 119 (1989). See also Melhorn v. Melhorn, 1989 WL 8452 (Ohio Ct. App. 2d Dist. Montgomery County 1989); Carnahan v. Carnahan, 118 Ohio App. 3d 393, 692 N.E.2d 1086 (12th Dist. Clermont County 1997); Gable v. Gable, 1997 WL 67723 (Ohio Ct. App. 12th Dist. Warren County 1997).

[18]Sharp v. Sharp, 1995 WL 141071 (Ohio Ct. App. 10th Dist. Franklin County 1995).

In *Sandstrom v. Sandstrom*,[19] the court found that it was equitable to suspend spousal support based upon the change of circumstances of plaintiff's retirement. The spousal support order did remain subject to further order of the court as the court retained continuing jurisdiction.

In *Coder v. Coder*,[20] the payor quit paying when he retired under the impression his spousal support automatically terminated. Fifteen months later payee filed a motion for contempt. The court reduced the spousal support and backdated the modification to the date of retirement even though his motion to modify was not filed until 15 months later. The court found laches on the part of the payee.

Corporations often offer special incentives for early retirement of long-term and higher-paid employees. Additionally, the uncertainty of rumored or actual mergers, layoffs and downsizing has encouraged early retirement. When courts are faced with motions to modify spousal support based on early retirement, the issue is the voluntariness and motive. The courts struggle with whether early retirement is voluntary when the alternative is losing out on other benefits—whether the employee will be credited with additional years, medical insurance, or other incentives.

In *Reed v. Reed*[21] and *Trotter v. Trotter*,[22] the appellate courts reversed the trial court's refusal to consider the early retirement as a change of circumstances and instructed the lower courts to revisit the conclusions that the retirement was designed to avoid spousal support obligation.

However, in *Penewit v. Penewit*,[23] the court found that while the obligor may have taken early retirement due to a transition in ownership of his employer, he still had earning capacity to fulfill his spousal support obligation.

Examples of additional appellate decisions addressing the issue of retirement and its effect upon spousal support modification are *Novick v. Novick*[24] (voluntary versus involuntary and foreseeability), *Billingham v. Billingham*[25] (ability to pay after retirement), *Reed v. Reed*[26] (voluntary versus involuntary and intention to avoid paying support),

---

[19]Sandstrom v. Sandstrom, 1996 WL 354925 (Ohio Ct. App. 2d Dist. Montgomery County 1996).

[20]Coder v. Coder, 1996 WL 257215 (Ohio Ct. App. 2d Dist. Montgomery County 1996).

[21]Reed v. Reed, 2001 WL 127873 (Ohio Ct. App. 2d Dist. Greene County 2001) (husband was 49 with 30 years of service).

[22]Trotter v. Trotter, 2001-Ohio-2122, 2001 WL 390066 (Ohio Ct. App. 3d Dist. Allen County 2001) (husband was 55 with 30 years of service).

[23]Penewit v. Penewit, 2001 WL 9939 (Ohio Ct. App. 2d Dist. Greene County 2001) (husband was 55 and worked for employer for 34 years).

[24]Novick v. Novick, 2001-Ohio-4028, 2001 WL 1591165 (Ohio Ct. App. 1st Dist. Hamilton County 2001).

[25]Billingham v. Billingham, 2001 WL 127764 (Ohio Ct. App. 2d Dist. Montgomery County 2001).

[26]Reed v. Reed, 2001 WL 127873 (Ohio Ct. App. 2d Dist. Greene County 2001).

Trotter v. Trotter[27] (voluntary versus involuntary, foreseeability, and intention to avoid paying support), *Kozlevchar v. Kozlevchar*[28] (retirement due to medical reasons involuntary, support continues at reduced level), and *Kelhoffer v. Kelhoffer*[29] (retirement income still sufficient for continued duty to pay).

In *Koch v. Koch*,[30] the parties entered into an agreed divorce decree. In it the Husband agreed to pay spousal support for a period of 96 months, which coincided with the date the parties expected him to retire. The former husband, an air traffic controller, retired two years later, which was six years earlier than the parties' had expected. At the hearing the former husband testified that he retired "simply because he wanted to stop working." The trial court found that this early retirement constituted a voluntary reduction in his income, imputed income to him at the level he would have been earning had he not retired, and increased the Husband's spousal support obligation. In reversing the trial court, the *Koch* court noted:

> that appellant is an air traffic controller and is in a position of tremendous responsibility. . . [h]is decisions regarding his ability to continue in his duties should be given great respect. . . [i]n this case, the trial court made no finding that appellant retired early for the purpose of defeating spousal support. . . [i]ts sole ground for finding 'voluntary underemployment' was that appellant 'simply wanted to stop working.' . . . [t]his is not a sufficient basis under the foregoing case law in which to find appellant 'voluntarily underemployed' and imputing his pre-retirement income to him. . . The trial court specifically based its award of increased spousal support on two grounds: first, that [Appellee Wife's] expenses have increased and second, that [Appellant Husband's] income has also increased. This Court has declined to consider whether [Appellee Wife's] expenses are an appropriate ground upon which to base additional spousal support. The trial court did not find that [Appellant Husband] retired for the purpose of defeating a spousal support award. As such, the trial court's order is reversed and remanded for proceedings consistent with this opinion.[31]

◆ **Practice Tips:** In drafting provisions for separation agreements and/or in presenting arguments to the court, consideration should be given to the following:[32]

    (1) Include language specifically addressing retirement as an involuntary change of circumstances.

---

[27]Trotter v. Trotter, 2001-Ohio-2122, 2001 WL 390066 (Ohio Ct. App. 3d Dist. Allen County 2001).

[28]Kozlevchar v. Kozlevchar, 2000 WL 640614 (Ohio Ct. App. 8th Dist. Cuyahoga County 2000).

[29]Kelhoffer v. Kelhoffer, 2001-Ohio-8659, 2001 WL 1485835 (Ohio Ct. App. 12th Dist. Butler County 2001).

[30]Koch v. Koch, 2004-Ohio-7192, 2004 WL 3017316 (Ohio Ct. App. 9th Dist. Medina County 2004).

[31]Koch v. Koch, 2004-Ohio-7192, 2004 WL 3017316 (Ohio Ct. App. 9th Dist. Medina County 2004).

[32]With thanks to Cincinnati attorney Barbara Howard.

    (a) Retirement as permitted by employer.
    (b) Retirement as permitted by government.
    (c) Retirement for other specified reasons.
  (2) Specifically define "retirement age" in the Separation Agreement or Decree.

If a court can specifically limit or define its continuing jurisdiction,[33] presumably the court (or the parties) can specifically permit in advance modification upon retirement and/or specifically state under what circumstances an obligor can retire without it being deemed to be a disqualifying "voluntary" act designed to avoid the support obligation.

§ 14:35 Requirements for modification—Death

RC 3105.18(B) specifically states that "[any] award of spousal support made under this section shall terminate upon the death of either party, unless the order containing the award expressly provides otherwise."

§ 14:36 Requirements for modification—Other circumstances

Prior to October 5, 1987, alimony was statutorily modifiable on a showing of interference with visitation.[1] The General Assembly, in 1987 House Bill 231, effective October 5, 1987, deleted that option along with deleting the right to modify child support on such showing. In a case predating 1987 House Bill 231, the Third District Court of Appeals held that where a custodial parent had demonstrated an utter disdain for the order of visitation, the trial court could modify but could not terminate periodic installments of support alimony.[2]

When a payor seeks to terminate alimony or spousal support based on a claim of agreement or waiver of rights to payment, he must show that such agreement was for valuable consideration.[3]

On occasion, a spousal support award can be modified by operation of bankruptcy law. In In re Caughenbaugh,[4] the bankruptcy court applied bankruptcy law[5] to reduce an obligor's spousal support from $130 per week to $80 per week, finding the balance dischargeable. While in some instances the bankruptcy court has held the obligation

---

[33]See Text § 14:8, Decree reserving right to modify—Limiting condition.

[Section 14:36]

[1]RC 3109.05(B).

[2]Deickert v. Deickert, 1987 WL 5846 (Ohio Ct. App. 3d Dist. Marion County 1987).

[3]Mikluscak v. Mikluscak, 1988 WL 30524 (Ohio Ct. App. 8th Dist. Cuyahoga County 1988).

[4]In re Caughenbaugh, 92 B.R. 255 (Bankr. S.D. Ohio 1988).

[5]In re Calhoun, 715 F.2d 1103 (6th Cir. 1983) (rejected by, Draper v. Draper, 790 F.2d 52 (8th Cir. 1986)) and (rejected by, Forsdick v. Turgeon, 812 F.2d 801 (2d Cir. 1987)) and (rejected by, In re Smith, 114 B.R. 457 (Bankr. S.D. Miss. 1990)) and (rejected by, Buccino v. Buccino, 397 Pa. Super. 241, 580 A.2d 13 (1990)) and (rejected

to pay debts is in the nature of spousal support and thus nondischargeable,[6] in others it has permitted them to be discharged, thus modifying the orders in a divorce or dissolution decree.[7]

§ 14:37   Requirements for modification—Review of spousal support at end of term

Not infrequently the court will order spousal support for a specific term and then retain the jurisdiction to review or continue the spousal support at the end of the term.

In *Tansey v. Tansey*,[1] the entry provided for alimony payments for five years. At the end of the five-year period, the alimony order was to be reviewed to determine if the alimony should continue, be modified, or terminated. A month before the end of the five-year period, the obligee filed a motion to continue alimony. The court found that the standard of a substantial change in circumstances was inapplicable to this case because the trial court was not confronted with a mid-term motion for modification. On the contrary, the trial court was presented with a motion, filed at the end of the five-year period, for a continuation of the alimony. The court's jurisdiction was expressly limited to a review at the end of five years and set forth no requirement that either party show a change of circumstances in order to justify a continuation. The court found that requiring a showing of changed circumstances would be contradictory to any possible justification for continuance of an identical award. If one or both of the parties sought modification or termination in addition to a continuance, then a change of circumstances must be demonstrated. In the absence of a request for modification or termination, the court found that the factors to be evaluated by the trial court parallel those considered prior to the original alimony award, that is, RC 3105.18(B).[2]

In *Leighner v. Leighner*,[3] the original order in the decree of divorce stated that the obligor retained the right to request a modification of the alimony order or a review in approximately two years. At the end of the two-year period, the obligor requested a termination of the alimony. The court found that the order in the decree did not obviate a need to establish a change of circumstances. The court stated the

___

by, In re Michaels, 157 B.R. 190 (Bankr. D. Mass. 1993)) and (rejected by, In re Chrusz, 1996 WL 1057950 (Bankr. D. N.H. 1996)).

[6]In re Leupp, 73 B.R. 33 (Bankr. N.D. Ohio 1987); Clark v. Clark, 40 Ohio App. 3d 177, 532 N.E.2d 158 (10th Dist. Franklin County 1987); In re Keeran, 112 B.R. 881 (Bankr. N.D. Ohio 1990) (some debts dischargeable, others nondischargeable).

[7]In re Mallisk, 64 B.R. 39 (Bankr. N.D. Ohio 1986) ($400 per month to spouse dischargeable as in nature of property division).

[Section 14:37]

[1]Tansey v. Tansey, 1989 WL 80945 (Ohio Ct. App. 6th Dist. Lucas County 1989).

[2]Now RC 3105.18(C).

[3]Leighner v. Leighner, 33 Ohio App. 3d 214, 515 N.E.2d 625 (10th Dist. Franklin County 1986).

language was an acknowledgment by the parties that the obligor would request a modification in two years, and that, on such a request, the obligee would be precluded from arguing that an inadequate amount of time had transpired to warrant a review. The trial court did not bind itself to an automatic review of the continuing reasonableness of the sustenance alimony order, in the absence of a demonstration of a substantial change in circumstances.

In *Meinke v. Meinke*,[4] the original court order provided for the payment of alimony for a period of five years or until the obligee's death, remarriage, or further order of this court, whichever event shall first occur. The issue arose as to whether or not the trial court could modify the alimony by extending the alimony beyond the five-year period. The court of appeals found that under the wording of the order, the court had expressly retained jurisdiction to modify both the amount of the alimony and the length of time the alimony is paid.

Where the order for spousal support stated that it was subject to review or termination upon review within two years, and the obligor filed a motion to terminate more than two years after the order, the court was without jurisdiction to modify the spousal support.[5]

The standard of decision for a court in ruling on a motion to continue alimony which was set in a separation agreement to run to a date certain and, following that date, subject to further order of the court is changed circumstances. In *Hukill v. Hukill*,[6] the wife had argued that the court should look de novo at the RC 3105.18 factors as to her need, arguing that the changed circumstances alimony modification standard was no longer viable on the expiration of the alimony award since there was no award in existence to modify.

§ 14:38 Limitations on modification

The trial court does not have jurisdiction to increase an alimony award if the divorce decree only refers to conditions for downward modification and termination.[1] A decree that states that spousal support is modifiable should the recipient remarry or cohabit is a limitation on the court's reservation of jurisdiction.[2] The decrease of the obligor's income is irrelevant when there is a valid limitation that was not appealed.

---

[4]Meinke v. Meinke, 1990 WL 157324 (Ohio Ct. App. 6th Dist. Lucas County 1990).

[5]Williams v. Williams, 1998 WL 15917 (Ohio Ct. App. 6th Dist. Lucas County 1998); Robertson v. Robertson, 1992 WL 328826 (Ohio Ct. App. 6th Dist. Lucas County 1992).

[6]Hukill v. Hukill, 1987 WL 8572 (Ohio Ct. App. 8th Dist. Cuyahoga County 1987).

[Section 14:38]

[1]Nash v. Nash, 77 Ohio App. 155, 32 Ohio Op. 409, 65 N.E.2d 728 (9th Dist. Medina County 1945).

[2]Lawson v. Garrison, 1998 WL 614558 (Ohio Ct. App. 6th Dist. Lucas County 1998).

Where the original decree provided that "this court reserve jurisdiction as to the issue of spousal support", and a subsequent post-decree order issued after husband obtained a job awarded wife spousal support "for a period of 72 months subject to the continuing jurisdiction of the court", the court lost jurisdiction to modify spousal support after the expiration of the 72 months in the absence of express language in the order that the court reserved jurisdiction beyond the 72 month duration of the award.[3]

In *Yeager v. Yeager*[4] the separation agreement incorporated into the divorce decree awarded wife spousal support "for 72 consecutive months, or sooner upon Wife's death, remarriage or assuming a status thereto. . .." The agreement also contained the language "this court shall not retain jurisdiction to modify." Subsequent to the divorce the wife began living with another woman, was involved with her in a sexual relationship, and shared a joint checking account and household expenses including the mortgage. The trial court denied husband's motion to terminate the spousal support award, citing among other reasons its belief that the language in the decree did not give the court continuing jurisdiction. The appellate court affirmed the trial court's refusal to terminate the spousal support award. The appellate court noted that the trial court erred when it said it did not have continuing jurisdiction, noting the distinction between retention of jurisdiction to terminate versus modification. But the appellate court also noted that cohabitation is not the equivalent of remarriage, or even a "status thereto" (whatever that phrase might mean, the court noted), and that if the parties had intended for the court to have jurisdiction to terminate upon evidence of cohabitation the parties should have said that in their agreement. The court specifically declined to decide whether "(a) homosexuals can cohabitate or (b) whether homosexuals can marry."

§ 14:39 Modification of term of spousal support

In a modification hearing, the trial court may consider whether the evidence supports a termination date for spousal support, even where no termination date was provided in the decree.[1] Since modification requires the trial court to consider the same standards it uses in an initial award, the trial court may also consider whether a termination

---

[3]Moore v. Moore, 2003-Ohio-6868, 2003 WL 22966203 (Ohio Ct. App. 8th Dist. Cuyahoga County 2003).

[4]Yaeger v. Yaeger, 2004-Ohio-1959, 2004 WL 833187 (Ohio Ct. App. 11th Dist. Geauga County 2004).

[Section 14:39]

[1]Vanke v. Vanke, 80 Ohio App. 3d 576, 609 N.E.2d 1328 (10th Dist. Franklin County 1992).

date would be appropriate under the rules stated in *Kunkle v. Kunkle.*[2] However, in *Kodish v. Kodish,*[3] where the appellant alleged that the trial court erred when it failed to adopt a date certain for alimony payments to end, the appellate court said that since he did not appeal the judgment entered in 1987, he could not challenge it five years later when his motion to modify spousal support was denied.

The trial court is not required, in a post-decree modification hearing, to establish a definite termination date for spousal support originally awarded for an indefinite term.[4]

When a court awards sustenance alimony for a number of years or "until further order of the court," that court has expressly retained jurisdiction to modify both the amount of the alimony and the length of time the alimony is to be paid.[5]

However, in *Stolar v. Stolar,*[6] the spousal support payments had a termination date of April 1995. The payments were expressly subject to modification by the court. The payee sought to extend the spousal support payments beyond the termination date. The court held that the spousal support payments were modifiable only as to the monthly amount, but not as to the definite term of seven years. The court found that jurisdiction had not been expressly retained to modify the duration of the spousal support award, and cited *Ressler v. Ressler.*[7] The court found a complete absence of any language constituting an express reservation of jurisdiction to extend the term.

A reservation of jurisdiction allowed the trial court, when reducing the amount of spousal support from $2,000 per month to $1,000 per month due to the retirement of the husband, to extend the term of the payments an additional two years.[8]

§ 14:40 Modification of right to remain in marital home

Two unreported decisions have expressed different conclusions on the nature of a former spouse's right to reside in the marital home. In *Hunt v. Hunt,*[1] the Ninth District Court of Appeals held that where a separation agreement is incorporated into a divorce decree, a wife's

[2]Kunkle v. Kunkle, 51 Ohio St. 3d 64, 554 N.E.2d 83 (1990); see also Heuer v. Heuer, 1993 WL 220904 (Ohio Ct. App. 10th Dist. Franklin County 1993).

[3]Kodish v. Kodish, 1993 WL 46654 (Ohio Ct. App. 9th Dist. Summit County 1993).

[4]Johnson v. Johnson, 1997 WL 663319 (Ohio Ct. App. 11th Dist. Lake County 1997).

[5]Meinke v. Meinke, 56 Ohio App. 3d 171, 565 N.E.2d 875 (6th Dist. Lucas County 1989).

[6]Stolar v. Stolar, 1997 WL 43280 (Ohio Ct. App. 6th Dist. Lucas County 1997).

[7]Ressler v. Ressler, 17 Ohio St. 3d 17, 476 N.E.2d 1032 (1985).

[8]Moss v. Moss, 2000-Ohio-1802, 2000 WL 1729288 (Ohio Ct. App. 3d Dist. Allen County 2000).

[Section 14:40]

[1]Hunt v. Hunt, 1984 WL 5127 (Ohio Ct. App. 9th Dist. Summit County 1984).

right under that agreement to live in the marital home until it is sold is in the nature of sustenance alimony, not property division, and is therefore modifiable. The wife in *Hunt* was not living in the home, and the agreement did not address that contingency. However, in *Barcalow v. Barcalow*,[2] the Seventh District Court of Appeals concluded that the right to reside in the family house is in the nature of a property division, rather than alimony, and is therefore not subject to subsequent modification.

---

[2]Barcalow v. Barcalow, 1985 WL 6983 (Ohio Ct. App. 7th Dist. Belmont County 1985).

Chapter 15

Parental Rights and Shared Parenting[*]

By Don W. Martin, Esq.[**]

---

[*]General Editor, Beatrice K. Sowald, acknowledges the assistance of Marilee C. Boroski, Esq., in the preparation of this updated chapter.

[**]Updated for the Fourth Edition by Douglas M. Brill, Esq.

§ 15:1 Allocating parental rights

The enactment of 1990 Senate Bill 3, effective April 11, 1991, altered the substance and terminology of Ohio custody statutes. Pursuant to RC 3109.04, domestic relations courts now allocate parental rights and responsibilities rather than grant custody. A parent granted custody under a court order is designated as the residential parent or residential parent and legal custodian.[1] The noncustodial parent is designated as the parent who is not the residential parent,[2] and shared parenting replaces joint custody.[3] However, RC 2151.23 was not amended by 1990 Senate Bill 3. While this section has been amended numerous times since, the statute continues to refer to awards of custody. For the purposes of this chapter, the above terminology is used interchangeably.

§ 15:2 Motion for temporary custody—Form⊚

[Title of Court]

[Caption]   Case No. *[_____]*
                                     MOTION FOR
                                     TEMPORARY CUSTODY

Now comes *[Plaintiff/Defendant]* in the above captioned case and moves the Court for an Order granting temporary custody, pendente lite, of the *[child/children]* of the parties, *[names and dates of birth]*, for the reasons stated in the accompanying Affidavit in support of the Motion, which is incorporated into this Motion the same as if fully rewritten herein.

_____
                              Attorney for *[Plaintiff/Defendant]*

[Proof/certificate of service]

[Notice of hearing]

[Affidavit of movant giving reasons/justifications for motion]

_____

[Section 15:1]
[1]RC 3109.04(K)(1), (2).
[2]RC 3109.04(K)(3), (4).
[3]RC 3109.041(C).

NOTES TO FORM

Drafter's Notes

In some counties, there is a court form for this motion.

Under his/her signature on the motion, counsel should list his/her business address and phone number and Supreme Court Registration Number.

An affidavit/certificate of service is only necessary when there is opposing counsel. Where the respondent is unrepresented by counsel at the time of filing the motion, the motion papers will be served by the clerk of court pursuant to written instructions filed with the motion.

§ 15:3   Jurisdiction—In general

Upon granting a divorce, annulment, or legal separation, the court has jurisdiction to make an order for the care and maintenance of the minor children of the marriage.[1] The court has the duty to inquire regarding children of the marriage and make an order for their care and maintenance, regardless of whether the issue is raised in the pleadings.[2] Failure to allocate the parental rights and responsibilities may result in the judgment being viewed as interlocutory as to the divorce itself and not a final appealable order.[3] It is questionable whether a final judgment of divorce can be granted when the court enters a physical possession or temporary custody order at the time it grants the divorce, and refers the allocation of parental rights and responsibilities to a magistrate for determination at a later date.[4] Likewise, a separation agreement incorporated into a dissolution decree must allocate parental rights and responsibilities if there are children of the marriage.[5]

While the court may consider the evidence of an expert, the court may not defer its responsibility to make the order to the expert. It is error for a court's decree to provide that visitation would be according to a schedule recommended by a counselor, thus failing to make an express order granting or denying specific visitation.[6]

The court may also enter an order allocating the parental rights and responsibilities when a divorce is dismissed for failure of proof of the causes in the complaint,[7] which also encompasses a dismissal for

---

[Section 15:3]

[1]RC 3105.21(A).

[2]Bower v. Bower, 90 Ohio St. 172, 106 N.E. 969 (1914); Mierowitz v. Mierowitz, 47 Ohio L. Abs. 104, 71 N.E.2d 526 (Ct. App. 7th Dist. Mahoning County 1946).

[3]Ameritrust Company, Trustee, Etc. v. Wright, 1983 WL 4753 (Ohio Ct. App. 8th Dist. Cuyahoga County 1983).

[4]Elkins v. Elkins, 1987 WL 14781 (Ohio Ct. App. 10th Dist. Franklin County 1987).

[5]RC 3105.63.

[6]Mayo v. Mayo, 1995 WL 139747 (Ohio Ct. App. 2d Dist. Darke County 1995).

[7]RC 3105.21(B). Shaffer v. Shaffer, 109 Ohio App. 3d 205, 671 N.E.2d 1317 (3d Dist. Crawford County 1996).

lack of prosecution.[8] The allocation of parental rights and responsibilities must be entered in accordance with RC 3109.04 and be in the child's best interest. However, the dismissal of a petition for a dissolution of marriage under RC 3105.65 does not give the court authority to exercise further jurisdiction if the parties voluntarily dismiss the action.[9]

A court allocating the parental rights and responsibilities following the dismissal of the divorce retains jurisdiction to modify such allocation upon the finding of a change of circumstances.[10] Thereafter, a divorce may be granted in a separate proceeding, but the court granting the divorce lacks jurisdiction over the allocation of parental rights and responsibilities, since continuing jurisdiction was reserved by the court in the original action.[11]

The Uniform Child Custody Jurisdiction Act, RC Ch. 3127, establishes when a court should exercise its jurisdiction, and provides for the resolution of conflicting jurisdiction between courts of concurrent jurisdiction. For the purposes of this chapter, it is assumed that the parents and child are subject to the court's jurisdiction.

Service of process is a condition precedent to the vesting of jurisdiction. In determining which of two courts of concurrent and coextensive jurisdiction has the exclusive right to adjudicate the entire case, the first court to perfect service of process has exclusive jurisdiction, notwithstanding a prior filing in another court.[12] Normally, the court that obtains jurisdiction and enters orders regarding the allocation of parental rights and responsibilities retains continuing jurisdiction over such matters to the exclusion of other courts.[13] The continuing jurisdiction of the court is invoked by a motion filed in the original action.[14] Ohio Rule of Civil Procedure 75(J) provides that service of process must be perfected pursuant to Rules 4 to 4.6 of the Ohio Rules of Civil Procedure. Therefore, post-decree motions served on a parent's former counsel are not proper service to invoke the continuing jurisdiction of the court.

To avoid simultaneous proceedings in more than one jurisdiction, each party to a parenting proceeding in the first pleading or by affidavit attached thereto must provide the following information:

(1) Child's present address and places where the child lived within the last five years;

---

[8]State ex rel. Easterday v. Zieba, 58 Ohio St. 3d 251, 569 N.E.2d 1028 (1991).

[9]State ex rel. Fogle v. Steiner, 74 Ohio St. 3d 158, 1995-Ohio-278, 656 N.E.2d 1288 (1995).

[10]Szymczak v. Szymczak, 136 Ohio App. 3d 706, 737 N.E.2d 980 (8th Dist. Cuyahoga County 2000).

[11]Miller v. Miller, 37 Ohio St. 3d 71, 523 N.E.2d 846 (1988).

[12]State ex rel. Balson v. Harnishfeger, 55 Ohio St. 2d 38, 9 Ohio Op. 3d 21, 377 N.E.2d 750 (1978).

[13]Hardesty v. Hardesty, 16 Ohio App. 3d 56, 474 N.E.2d 368 (10th Dist. Franklin County 1984).

[14]Civ. R. 75(J).

(2) Name and present address of each person with whom the child lived during that period;

(3) Information concerning other parenting proceedings, whether previously adjudicated or currently pending, concerning the same child;

(4) Name of any person not a party to the proceeding who has physical custody of the child, who claims to be the residential parent or custodian, or who claims to have visitation rights; and

(5) Whether the party has pleaded guilty to or been convicted of a criminal offense involving an act that resulted in a child being abused or neglected, or if a child has been adjudicated abused or neglected, the party was the perpetrator of the act that was the basis of the adjudication.[15]

The filing of such an affidavit is a mandatory jurisdictional requirement of a parenting proceeding,[16] although the jurisdictional requirement is satisfied so long as the affidavit is filed prior to the hearing.[17] Where there had not been a suggestion of jurisdictional conflict in any of the post-decree proceedings, the filing of the statutory affidavit at the initiation of the divorce proceedings was sufficient to give the trial court subject matter jurisdiction in the subsequent modification action.[18] Each party is under a continuing duty to supplement the affidavit if additional information is obtained during the course of the proceeding.[19]

Former RC 3109.21(C) defined "parenting proceeding" to include neglect and dependency proceedings, thereby making the filing or the informational affidavit a jurisdictional requirement of such actions in juvenile court. RC 3127.01(B)(4), which replaced repealed RC 3109.21(C), also includes neglect and dependency proceedings, however, the proceeding itself is still addressed as a "child custody proceeding" in this section.

§ 15:4   Jurisdiction—RC 3127.23 affidavit (Franklin)—Form

(Official form, Custody affidavit, rev. 4-2005, Franklin County)

---

[15]RC 3127.23.

[16]Pasqualone v. Pasqualone, 63 Ohio St. 2d 96, 17 Ohio Op. 3d 58, 406 N.E.2d 1121 (1980); Pegan v. Crawmer, 1995 WL 434108 (Ohio Ct. App. 5th Dist. Licking County 1995) (after proper dismissal of custody action for failure to file RC 3127.23 affidavit, trial court had no jurisdiction to stay the court's temporary order).

[17]Mannon v. Mannon, 1984 WL 5692 (Ohio Ct. App. 4th Dist. Lawrence County 1984).

[18]Metcalfe v. Metcalfe, 1996 WL 31148 (Ohio Ct. App. 12th Dist. Clermont County 1996).

[19]RC 3127.23.

**IN THE COURT OF COMMON PLEAS OF FRANKLIN COUNTY, OHIO
DIVISION OF DOMESTIC RELATIONS AND JUVENILE BRANCH**

CASE NO. _____

AFFIDAVIT/R.C. §3127.23

JUDGE _____

_____

PLAINTIFF/PETITIONER   SOCIAL SECURITY NUMBER

_____

ADDRESS

_____

DEFENDANT/RESPONDENT   SOCIAL SECURITY NUMBER

_____

ADDRESS

STATE OF OHIO
FRANKLIN COUNTY, SS:

_____, being first duly sworn, says that he/she is a party to the child custody proceeding hereinabove set forth, concerning the following named child(ren):

1. _____ DOB_____ present _____
                                                address
                                                _____

2. _____ DOB_____ present _____
                                                address
                                                _____

3. _____ DOB_____ present _____
                                                address
                                                _____

4. _____ DOB_____ present _____
                                                address
                                                _____

5. _____ DOB_____ present _____
                                                address
                                                _____

6. _____ DOB_____ present _____
                                                address
                                                _____

Set forth below are the addresses at which said child(ren) resided during the preceding five (5) years, and the name(s) and present address of the person(s) with whom the child resided:

From _____ to _____ With _____

At _____

Current address _____

Custody affidavit (4-2005)   Page 1 of 2

941

From _____ to _____ With _____

At _____

Current address _____

From _____ to _____ With _____

At _____

Current address _____

From _____ to _____ With _____

At _____

Current address _____

From _____ to _____ With _____

At _____

Current address _____

1.　Said Affiant (circle one) HAS/HAS NOT participated as a party, witness or in any other capacity in any other proceeding concerning the allocation, between the parents of the same child, of parental rights and responsibilities for the care of the child including any designation of parenting time rights and the designation of the residential parent and legal custodian of the child or that otherwise concerned the custody of or visitation with the same child. If Affiant has so participated, the court, case number and the date of the child custody determination are stated below.

2.　Said Affiant (circle one) DOES/DOES NOT know of any proceeding that could affect the current proceeding, including proceedings for enforcement of child custody determinations, proceedings relating to domestic violence or protection orders, proceedings to adjudicate the child as an abused, neglected, or dependent child, proceedings seeking termination of parental rights, and adoptions. If Affiant does know of such a proceeding, the court, case number, and the nature of the proceeding are stated below.

3.　Said Affiant (circle one) KNOWS/DOES NOT KNOW of any person who is not a party to the proceeding and has physical custody of the child or claims to be a parent of the child who is designated the residential parent and legal custodian of the child or to have parenting time rights with respect to the child or to be a person other than a parent of the child who has custody or visitation rights with respect to the child. If Affiant knows of such a person, the names and addresses of those persons are stated below.

Said Affiant has the following knowledge regarding information set forth in paragraphs one through three above:

_____

_____

_____

Each party has a continuing duty to inform the court of any child custody proceeding concerning the child in this or any other state that could affect the current proceeding.

Said Affiant says that all the foregoing statements are true.

_____　　_____
Affiant　　　　　　　　　　　　　　　　Attorney

_____　　_____
Notary Public　　　　　　　　　　　　　Address

Sworn to and subscribed by the affiant before me this
_____ day of _____, 20_____.

Custody affidavit (4-2005)　　　　　　　*Page 2 of 2*

NOTES TO FORM

Author's Comment

Always check the local court rules for the specific affidavit required by your court.

§ 15:5 Parentage determinations

1992 Senate Bill 10, effective July 5, 1992, dramatically altered the method of establishing the parent-child relationship. A complainant could not bring an action under RC 3111.01 to RC 3111.19 before an administrative determination of parentage from the child support enforcement agency of the county in which the child or the guardian or legal custodian of the child resides.[1] Effective May 17, 2006, a mother or putative father may file for a parentage determination without first engaging the CSEA.[2] However, if an action is filed for divorce, dissolution of marriage, or legal separation, the domestic relations court retains original jurisdiction to determine whether the parent-child relationship exists without an administrative determination being requested from the child support enforcement agency.[3] Failure to determine the parent-child relationship for children of the parties born prior to the marriage, or children not of the parties born during the marriage, can result in future complications such as the granting of a motion for relief from judgment.[4]

Parentage actions seeking to establish a third party as the father of a child born during the marriage are adversarial in nature. Because dissolution decrees approve and incorporate agreements of the parties,[5] and the parties to a dissolution cannot establish the parent-child relationship between a third party and a child born during the marriage by agreement, they must instead bring an adversarial action against the third party. Thus, parentage actions to establish a third party as the father of the child born during the marriage cannot be heard as part of a dissolution of marriage. However, an administrative determination of parentage may be requested from the child support enforcement agency or an action can be brought in juvenile court, and once the parent-child relationship has been established, the parties can proceed with a dissolution of marriage.

§ 15:6 Best interest standard—In general

For domestic relations courts, the allocation of parental rights and

---

[Section 15:5]

[1]RC 3111.381. Requirement of requesting administrative determination is now found at RC 3111.381 pursuant to 2000 SB 180, eff. 3-22-01. See Text Parentage Ch 3.

[2]2006 HB 136, RC 3111.381(B) and (C).

[3]RC 3111.06(A), RC 3111.381.

[4]See also, Jennifer C. v. Tony M.D., 2005-Ohio-5050, 2005 WL 2335332 (Ohio Ct. App. 12th Dist. Clermont County 2005).

[5]RC 3105.65(B).

responsibilities is governed by RC 3109.04 in substantive matters, RC 3127.01 to RC 3127.53 in jurisdictional disputes, and Civil Rule 75 in procedural matters. The universally applied and recognized standard for determining the allocation of parental rights and responsibilities is the best interest of the child. Ohio courts have long recognized the best interest test to be the controlling principle of a parenting determination.[1] Ohio has codified this standard in RC 3109.04(B)(1), which mandates that the best interest of the child should be the criterion by which the court allocates or modifies the allocation of parental rights and responsibilities. In allocating parental rights and responsibilities, RC 3109.04(F)(1) requires the court to consider all relevant factors, including the ten factors set forth therein.

When considering the relevant factors, the weight of all evidence presented at trial in relation to the best interest of the child, encompasses "the inclination of the *greater amount of credible evidence* offered in a trial to support one side of the issue rather than the other. It indicates clearly to the [fact-finder] that the party having the burden of proof will be entitled to their verdict, if, on weighing the evidence in their minds, they shall find the *greater amount of credible evidence* sustains the issue which is to be established before them. The weight of the ten factors set forth in R.C. 3109.04(F)(1) is not a question of mathematics, but *depends on its effect in inducing belief.*" [Italics sic.][2]

In *Shaffer v. Shaffer*,[3] it was held that the trial court did not abuse its discretion, in proceedings for divorce, in finding overriding reasons, apart from the standard statutory factors considered by it, thereby warranting an award of custody of the parties' child to the husband, where there was testimony from the child's caregiver, police witness, social worker, and the wife's neighbors establishing that the wife abused and neglected the child. The court was not limited to the statutory "best interests" factors in awarding custody.

§ 15:7   Best interest standard—Wishes of parents

Realizing that "[n]o question ever submitted to the court calls for

---

[Section 15:6]

[1]Boyer v. Boyer, 46 Ohio St. 2d 83, 75 Ohio Op. 2d 156, 346 N.E.2d 286 (1976); Godbey v. Godbey, 70 Ohio App. 450, 25 Ohio Op. 184, 36 Ohio L. Abs. 511, 44 N.E.2d 810 (1st Dist. Hamilton County 1942); Ludy v. Ludy, 84 Ohio App. 195, 39 Ohio Op. 241, 53 Ohio L. Abs. 47, 82 N.E.2d 775 (2d Dist. Franklin County 1948); Gishwiler v. Dodez, 4 Ohio St. 615, 1855 WL 28 (1855); Clark v. Bayer, 32 Ohio St. 299, 1877 WL 120 (1877); Trout v. Trout, 73 Ohio L. Abs. 91, 136 N.E.2d 474 (C.P. 1956); Birch v. Birch, 11 Ohio St. 3d 85, 463 N.E.2d 1254 (1984).

[2]See Broadbent v. Broadbent, 2005-Ohio-3227, 2005 WL 1503961, ¶ 7 (Ohio Ct. App. 3d Dist. Union County 2005); citing State v. Thompkins, 78 Ohio St. 3d 380, 387, 1997-Ohio-52, 678 N.E.2d 541 (1997); citing Black's Law Dictionary (6 Ed. 1990) 1594.

[3]Shaffer v. Shaffer, 2005-Ohio-3884, 2005 WL 1797739 (Ohio Ct. App. 3d Dist. Paulding County 2005). See also, Clinard v. Clinard, 2006-Ohio-4188, 2006 WL 2337644 (Ohio Ct. App. 3d Dist. Crawford County 2006).

greater care or wisdom in its decision, and none is more far-reaching in its consequences,"[1] most courts afford parents every opportunity to amicably determine the allocation of parental rights and responsibilities. The court is vested with the discretion to approve the wishes of parents, although it is not bound to do so.[2] The court may also approve and adopt an agreement of the parties as a court order, even though in the absence of such an agreement the court would not have the authority to impose such obligations as are contained in the agreement.[3]

§ 15:8 Best interest standard—Wishes and concerns of child

When the court has interviewed the child and determines that the child has sufficient reasoning ability, it must consider the child's wishes and concerns with respect to the allocation of parental rights and responsibilities. The allocation must be in the best interest of the child, and there is no mandate that the court acquiesce to the child's wishes if they are not in his best interest, regardless of the child's age.[1]

RC 3109.04(B) merely requires trial courts to interview children "regarding their wishes and concerns with respect to the allocation" of parental rights and responsibilities. The statute does not require trial courts to ask any particular questions or employ any particular method of questioning the children. RC 3109.04 does not set forth an exact procedure to be followed in determining the child's wishes and concerns and does not specify when the interview should be conducted. Such matters are left to the discretion of the trial court.[2]

The trial court must make a record of its interview of minor children who are the subject of proceedings involving the award of parental rights when there has been a timely request by a party.[3] An in-camera interview can be requested any time before entry of

---

[Section 15:7]

[1]Searle v. Searle, 115 Colo. 266, 273, 172 P.2d 837 (1946).

[2]Dreitzler v. Dreitzler, 115 Ohio App. 231, 20 Ohio Op. 2d 311, 184 N.E.2d 679 (4th Dist. Ross County 1961). RC 3105.65 provides that the court may approve a separation agreement, thereby making approval discretionary with the court.

[3]Robrock v. Robrock, 167 Ohio St. 479, 5 Ohio Op. 2d 165, 150 N.E.2d 421 (1958) (disapproved of by, Nokes v. Nokes, 47 Ohio St. 2d 1, 1 Ohio Op. 3d 1, 351 N.E.2d 174 (1976)).

[Section 15:8]

[1]RC 3109.04(B). See also Venable v. Venable, 3 Ohio App. 3d 421, 445 N.E.2d 1125 (8th Dist. Cuyahoga County 1981); Watson v. Watson, 76 Ohio L. Abs. 348, 146 N.E.2d 443 (Ct. App. 7th Dist. Columbiana County 1956); Moyer v. Moyer, 1996 WL 729859 (Ohio Ct. App. 10th Dist. Franklin County 1996).

[2]Kellogg v. Kellogg, 2004-Ohio-7202, 2004 WL 3090184 (Ohio Ct. App. 10th Dist. Franklin County 2004); citing Inscoe v. Inscoe, 121 Ohio App. 3d 396, 700 N.E.2d 70 (4th Dist. Meigs County 1997).

[3]Patton v. Patton, 87 Ohio App. 3d 844, 623 N.E.2d 235 (5th Dist. Licking County 1993); Donnell v. Donnell, 1995 WL 557322 (Ohio Ct. App. 6th Dist. Sandusky

judgment.[4] Noting that RC 3109.04 does not specifically state whether the parents of a child have a right to obtain a copy of the transcript of an *in-camera* discussion between the judge and the child, the Ninth District Court of Appeals in *In re Longwell*,[5] affirmed the order sealing the transcript. The court held there is no right of access, stating their belief that "judges should be allowed to keep their private conversations with the children of divorced parents confidential."[6]

In spite of the requirement that a trial court make a record of the interview, for meaningful review by an appellate court, the legislature mandates that no person shall obtain any recorded statement from the child regarding the allocation of parental rights. RC 3109.04(B)(3) permits the sealing of the transcript.[7]

§ 15:9   Best interest standard—Interactions and interrelationships with others

The court must consider the child's interaction and relationships with the parents, siblings, and any other person who may significantly affect the child's best interest.[1] When considering this factor, courts may give strong consideration to which parent provided "primary care" for the child.[2] The primary caregiver doctrine is part of the best interest test and is one way of measuring interaction between the parent and child. However, the question of primary caregiver does not rise to the level of a presumption and should not be used as a substitute for the factual analysis of the relative parental capabilities of the parties and the needs of the child. The court may designate one

---

County 1995) (failure to make a record of interview, when not requested, is not plain error or reversible error); Bowman v. Bowman, 1997 WL 148059 (Ohio Ct. App. 9th Dist. Medina County 1997).

[4]Bauer v. Bauer, 1997 WL 368371 (Ohio Ct. App. 12th Dist. Warren County 1997).

[5]In Matter of Longwell, 1995 WL 520058 (Ohio Ct. App. 9th Dist. Lorain County 1995).

[6]In Matter of Longwell, 1995 WL 520058 (Ohio Ct. App. 9th Dist. Lorain County 1995); Brown v. Brown, 1996 WL 752788 (Ohio Ct. App. 5th Dist. Holmes County 1996) (to permit parties to review testimony is contrary to legislative intent); see contra Inscoe v. Inscoe, 121 Ohio App. 3d 396, 700 N.E.2d 70 (4th Dist. Meigs County 1997) (child's testimony *in camera* must be provided litigants).

[7]Beil v. Bridges, 2000 WL 977221 (Ohio Ct. App. 5th Dist. Licking County 2000).

[Section 15:9]

[1]RC 3109.04(F)(1)(c).

[2]In re Maxwell, 8 Ohio App. 3d 302, 456 N.E.2d 1218, 41 A.L.R.4th 1121 (2d Dist. Darke County 1982). See also Kochersperger v. Kochersperger, 1996 WL 685561 (Ohio Ct. App. 2d Dist. Montgomery County 1996); Marshall v. Marshall, 117 Ohio App. 3d 182, 690 N.E.2d 68 (3d Dist. Allen County 1997).

parent the residential parent even though the other parent was the primary caregiver.[3]

The primary caregiver doctrine evolved from the "tender years doctrine," under which it was presumed that the wife should be awarded custody of infant children. Under earlier common law, the husband was considered the head of the family and was responsible for the care and maintenance of his children. On divorce of the parents, the father's property rights included rights to custody of his minor children. The nature of the legal presumption was that he would love them most, and care for them most wisely.[4] Gradually, the court carved the tender years exception to the common law, whereby custody by the mother was presumed to be in the best interest of a child of tender years, unless the mother was shown to be unfit.[5]

Today, inroads have been made into the tender years doctrine. RC 3109.03 places parents on an equal footing in determining the allocation of parental rights and responsibilities. Further, gender-based distinctions must serve important governmental objectives and be substantially related to the achievement of those objectives in order to withstand judicial scrutiny under the Equal Protection Clause of the Fourteenth Amendment to the U.S. Constitution.[6] To treat the tender years doctrine as a presumption that the mother is entitled to custody constitutes reversible error.[7] However, the tender years doctrine may still be a relevant factor that merits consideration when determining a child's best interest.[8]

The effect of a child having contact with a parent's paramour is commonly raised in a parenting proceeding. In *Wilder v. Wilder*,[9] the court stated that in an initial allocation of parental rights and responsibilities there are three possible rules to apply when a parent is living in a sexual relationship with a person not his or her spouse. The living arrangement (1) automatically disqualifies the parent from being the residential parent; (2) is only a factor to be weighed with all other statutory factors that comprise "best interest"; or (3) is not to be considered at all, absent specific proof of harm to the child. The court then adopted the second option and later held that it is error for a trial court to deny custody to a parent solely because he or she is liv-

---

[3]Thompson v. Thompson, 31 Ohio App. 3d 254, 511 N.E.2d 412 (4th Dist. Washington County 1987).

[4]Hibbette v. Baines, 78 Miss. 695, 29 So. 80 (1900).

[5]Clark v. Bayer, 32 Ohio St. 299, 1877 WL 120 (1877).

[6]Reed v. Reed, 404 U.S. 71, 92 S. Ct. 251, 30 L. Ed. 2d 225 (1971); Caban v. Mohammed, 441 U.S. 380, 99 S. Ct. 1760, 60 L. Ed. 2d 297 (1979).

[7]Charles v. Charles, 23 Ohio App. 3d 109, 491 N.E.2d 378 (10th Dist. Franklin County 1985).

[8]Seibert v. Seibert, 66 Ohio App. 3d 342, 584 N.E.2d 41 (12th Dist. Clermont County 1990).

[9]Wilder v. Wilder, 1985 WL 9844 (Ohio Ct. App. 10th Dist. Franklin County 1985).

ing with an unrelated person of the opposite sex.[10] This rule was also followed when a mother was living in a lesbian relationship.[11]

The court may consider, in awarding custody of a child to the mother, that the mother is living with her parents and that the maternal grandparents have demonstrated a strong commitment to the grandchild.[12] RC 3109.04(F)(1)(c) requires the consideration of the child's interrelationship with various people. The trial court need not find the father "unsuitable" before considering the interaction with the maternal grandparents.

§ 15:10 Best interest standard—Interactions and interrelationships with others—Homosexuality as factor

Unless there is sufficient evidence to support a determination that sexual orientation of a parent directly and adversely affected a child, a trial court must disregard adverse impacts that flow from society's disapproval of a parent's sexual orientation. A parent's sexual orientation, standing alone, has been held to have no relevance to a decision concerning the allocation of parental rights.[1]

§ 15:11 Best interest standard—Adjustment to environment

RC 3109.04(F)(1)(d) examines the child's adjustment to his home, school, and community. School adjustment is often capable of objective determination, and evidence such as school records and the testimony of teachers is easy to obtain. The child's adjustment to the home is also of great importance. Permitting the children to remain in the marital residence often affords stability for the children, and allows them to maintain continuity within their community, school, and with their friends. A parent remaining in the marital residence may be designated residential parent even though the other parent has been the primary caregiver.[1]

A trial court's concerns which centered around the quality of education the children received at a church-run school, selected by the mother, which had problems with teacher staffing, lack of curriculum, and sheltered lifestyle, did not rely on mother's affiliation with the

---

[10]Williams v. Williams, 1985 WL 10133 (Ohio Ct. App. 10th Dist. Franklin County 1985).

[11]Mohrman v. Mohrman, 57 Ohio App. 3d 33, 565 N.E.2d 1283 (6th Dist. Sandusky County 1989).

[12]Davis v. Wilson, 123 Ohio App. 3d 19, 702 N.E.2d 1227 (12th Dist. Warren County 1997).

[Section 15:10]

[1]Inscoe v. Inscoe, 121 Ohio App. 3d 396, 700 N.E.2d 70 (4th Dist. Meigs County 1997).

[Section 15:11]

[1]Pizzino v. Pizzino, 1988 WL 33606 (Ohio Ct. App. 10th Dist. Franklin County 1988).

church. The court had evidence that the public school the children would attend with the father offered programs for the gifted and a wide curriculum.[2]

§ 15:12 Best interest standard—Health of all persons

The mental and physical health of all persons involved in the situation are of concern when determining the child's best interest.[1] RC 3109.04(C) and Civil Rule 35 allow the court to order mental and physical examinations of the parties. Parental disabilities, such as mental illness, do not automatically disqualify a parent from being designated residential parent when the disability can be maintained under satisfactory medical control.[2] The child's health should also be considered as an issue. For example, the fact that a child is placed on Ritalin for attention deficit disorder following a move to another state does not necessarily indicate poor adjustment.[3]

Psychological evaluations may be ordered even after completion of case in chief to assist magistrate in making decision[4]

§ 15:13 Best interest standard—Facilitation of visitation

When parents are cooperative, children generally adapt better to the divorce. A primary factor in parental cooperation is ensuring children maintain continued contact with both parents. The willingness of a parent to facilitate parenting time is a factor that will be considered favorably by the court in determining the child's best interest.[1]

Conversely, refusal to permit visitation in direct violation of a court order, disregarding an order not to take the children out of the state, and requiring the other parent to resort to judicial process to retrieve the children demonstrate an unlikeliness of future facilitation of visitation.[2]

§ 15:14 Best interest standard—Payment of child support

If possible, children are entitled to enjoy the same standard of liv-

---

[2]Arthur v. Arthur, 130 Ohio App. 3d 398, 720 N.E.2d 176 (5th Dist. Fairfield County 1998).

[Section 15:12]

[1]RC 3109.04(F)(1)(e).

[2]Schumeth v. Schumeth, 55 Ohio L. Abs. 376, 86 N.E.2d 798 (Ct. App. 2d Dist. Montgomery County 1949).

[3]Stauffer v. Stauffer, 1989 WL 125680 (Ohio Ct. App. 10th Dist. Franklin County 1989).

[4]Brewer v. Brewer, 2004-Ohio-3531, 2004 WL 1486781 (Ohio Ct. App. 5th Dist. Licking County 2004).

[Section 15:13]

[1]RC 3109.04(F)(1)(f).

[2]Green v. Green, 1993 WL 125454 (Ohio Ct. App. 2d Dist. Montgomery County 1993).

ing they would have enjoyed had the marriage of their parents continued.[1] Parents who fail to support their children often deprive the children of necessary items, and place a much greater burden of support on the other parent. Compliance with a court support order will be viewed favorably, and noncompliance unfavorably, when determining the best interest of the child.[2]

§ 15:15 Best interest standard—Domestic violence, abuse, or neglect

Parents who perpetrate domestic violence on family members act to the detriment of their children. Likewise, parents who are abusive or neglectful of children may not be suitable to be designated as residential parent. In allocating parental rights and responsibilities, the court must consider whether either parent has been convicted of or pleaded guilty to a criminal offense involving an act that resulted in a child being abused or neglected, or whether either parent was the perpetrator of an act that resulted in the child being adjudicated abused or neglected.[1] The abused or neglected child need not be a child of the parent. The court must also consider whether either parent has been convicted of or pleaded guilty to domestic violence against a household member.[2]

If a court grants residential parent status to a parent who has been convicted of a criminal offense under RC 2919.25 of domestic violence involving a victim who was a member of the family that is the subject of the proceeding, the court must not only find that it is in the best interests of the child, but also must make specific written findings to support its decision.[3]

The matter will be reversed when the necessary findings are absent and the cause will be remanded for findings.[4] The court must also issue findings of fact if it orders shared parenting after one of the parents has been found guilty of domestic violence.[5]

In *State ex rel. Thompson v. Spon*,[6] the Ohio Supreme Court held that RC 3109.04(C) does not apply to temporary orders, which are

---

[Section 15:14]

[1]RC 3109.05(A)(1); RC 3113.215(B)(3)(l).

[2]RC 3109.04(F)(1)(g).

[Section 15:15]

[1]RC 3109.04(F)(1)(h).

[2]RC 3109.04(F)(1)(h).

[3]RC 3109.04(C).

[4]Smith v. Smith, 2001 WL 542317 (Ohio Ct. App. 9th Dist. Wayne County 2001).

[5]Schmidt v. Schmidt, 1999 WL 225157 (Ohio Ct. App. 12th Dist. Clermont County 1999).

[6]State ex rel. Thompson v. Spon, 83 Ohio St. 3d 551, 1998-Ohio-298, 700 N.E.2d 1281 (1998).

always interlocutory and subject to modification in the final divorce decree. The dissent criticized the decision not to require findings, by pointing out that the statute expressly refers to "any proceeding."

§ 15:16   Best interest standard—Denial of visitation

1990 Senate Bill 3, effective April 11, 1991, modified RC 3109.04 by deleting the former RC 3109.04(B)(1)(d), which had provided that continuous and willful denial of the other parent's right to parenting time was grounds to modify the allocation of parental rights. Currently, continuous and willful denial of visitation is only one factor to be considered when determining the best interest of the child. For a brief time, between April 12, 1990[1] and April 11, 1991,[2] denial of visitation was a statutory factor for change for custody. In general, however, denial of visitation was held not to be grounds for a change of custody, based upon the reasoning that contempt of court provided the parent denied visitation with an adequate remedy.[3] More recent decisions, however, have upheld the position that repeated interference by the residential parent with the non-residential parent's parenting time may in fact constitute a change of circumstances under RC 3109.04 because it affects the best interest of the child.[4] RC 3109.04(F)(1) states that:

In determining the best interest of a child pursuant to this section, whether on an original decree allocating parental rights and responsibilities for the care of children or a modification of a decree allocating those rights and responsibilities, the court shall consider all relevant factors, including but not limited to:

- The parent more likely to honor and facilitate court-approved parenting time rights or visitation and companionship rights;[5]
- whether the residential parent or one of the parents subject to a shared parenting decree has continuously and willfully denied the other parent's right to parenting time in accordance with an order of the court.[6]

A court can properly conclude that a temporary custodian's acts of interference with the other parent's parenting time are harmful to a child, and therefore, designate the other parent as residential parent.

[Section 15:16]

[1]1990 H.B. 591, eff. 4-12-90, added continuous and willful denial of visitation as grounds to change custody.

[2]1990 S.B. 3, eff. 4-11-91, deleted interference with visitation as a factor or grounds to change custody.

[3]Fitzpatrick v. Fitzpatrick, 4 Ohio App. 2d 279, 31 Ohio Op. 2d 257, 207 N.E.2d 794 (4th Dist. Lawrence County 1965).

[4]See Valentine v. Valentine, 2005-Ohio-6163, 2005 WL 3096587 (Ohio Ct. App. 12th Dist. Butler County 2005); Scaffidi v. Scaffidi, 2005-Ohio-4546, 2005 WL 2087795 (Ohio Ct. App. 9th Dist. Medina County 2005).

[5]RC 3109.04(F)(1)(f).

[6]RC 3109.04(F)(1)(i).

In *Seitz v. Seitz*,[7] although the father had custody for over 5 years, his interference both prior to the divorce filing and while the divorce itself was pending, was a sufficient factor to name the mother the residential parent.

§ 15:17 Best interest standard—Residence out of state

The court must consider whether either party has established a residence, or is planning to establish a residence, outside of Ohio.[1] Children need a stable environment and contact with both parents. Removing the children from Ohio and secreting them from the parent who is not the residential parent has been held to endanger their health and development.[2]

While a trial court may consider nonresidence in determining the best interests of a child, nonresidence alone should not deprive a parent of custody, especially where the evidence is that such parent has been the primary caregiver for the children.[3]

§ 15:18 Best interest standard—Other factors and constitutional issues

A parent may not be denied custody on the basis of his religious practices unless there is probative evidence that those practices will adversely affect the mental or physical health of the child. Evidence that a child will not be permitted to participate in certain social or patriotic activities is not sufficient to prove possible harm.[1] To the extent that a court refuses to award custody to a parent because of his religious beliefs, the court burdens the parent's choice of religion in violation of the Free Exercise Clause of the U.S. Constitution.[2] Although religious beliefs are absolutely protected, the state may regulate the physical acts that result from those beliefs.[3]

---

[7]Seitz v. Seitz, 2007-Ohio-104, 2007 WL 80039 (Ohio Ct. App. 5th Dist. Morrow County 2007).

[Section 15:17]

[1]RC 3109.04(F)(1)(j).

[2]Ross v. Ross, 64 Ohio St. 2d 203, 18 Ohio Op. 3d 414, 414 N.E.2d 426 (1980).

[3]Pennington v. Pennington, 2002 WL 1252173 (Ohio Ct. App. 2d Dist. Montgomery County 2002).

[Section 15:18]

[1]Pater v. Pater, 63 Ohio St. 3d 393, 588 N.E.2d 794 (1992).

[2]Cantwell v. State of Connecticut, 310 U.S. 296, 60 S. Ct. 900, 84 L. Ed. 1213, 128 A.L.R. 1352 (1940).

[3]Employment Div., Dept. of Human Resources of Oregon v. Smith, 494 U.S. 872, 110 S. Ct. 1595, 108 L. Ed. 2d 876 (1990).

The U.S. Constitution prohibits courts from evaluating the merits of religious doctrine or defining the contents of that doctrine.[4] However, a parent's actions are not insulated from the domestic relations court's inquiry merely because they are based on religious beliefs, especially actions that will harm the child's mental or physical health. The court can examine the parent's religious practices to determine the best interest of the child because the law must not ignore a parent's suitability when unsuitability is based on religious practices.[5]

Citing *Pater v. Pater*,[6] the appellate court in *Tsolumba v. Tsolumba*[7] held that there was a distinction between a court's evaluating the merits of religious doctrine and its inquiry into religiously motivated actions. While a court may not burden a parent's choice of religious belief by refusing to award custody on that basis, "neither may a parent shield her actions from the court's scrutiny by claiming religious motivation for those actions."[8]

A court may not restrict the parent who is not the residential parent from exposing the child to religious beliefs, unless such exposure is affecting the child's general welfare.[9] Courts should not interfere unless the child is exhibiting genuine symptoms of distress that are caused by the differences in the parents' religious beliefs. Prohibiting the child from participating in social or patriotic activities is not sufficient to prove possible harm.[10]

Courts cannot implement private prejudices, such as racial prejudices, even if they are widely held by the population. Private biases must be outside the reach of the law, and the law cannot give them effect.[11] Interracial marriage is not grounds to change custody nor will it support a neglect complaint.[12]

§ 15:19 Procedure for allocating parental rights—In general

In actions for divorce, legal separation, or annulment, the court may allocate the parental rights and responsibilities for the care of the children primarily to one parent, designating that parent as the residential parent, and dividing the other rights and responsibilities

---

[4]Thomas v. Review Bd. of Indiana Employment Sec. Division, 450 U.S. 707, 101 S. Ct. 1425, 67 L. Ed. 2d 624 (1981).

[5]Birch v. Birch, 11 Ohio St. 3d 85, 463 N.E.2d 1254 (1984).

[6]Pater v. Pater, 63 Ohio St. 3d 393, 588 N.E.2d 794 (1992).

[7]Tsolumba v. Tsolumba, 1995 WL 366378 (Ohio Ct. App. 9th Dist. Summit County 1995).

[8]Tsolumba v. Tsolumba, 1995 WL 366378 (Ohio Ct. App. 9th Dist. Summit County 1995); Pater v. Pater, 63 Ohio St. 3d 393, 397-98, 588 N.E.2d 794 (1992).

[9]Pater v. Pater, 63 Ohio St. 3d 393, 588 N.E.2d 794 (1992).

[10]Pater v. Pater, 63 Ohio St. 3d 393, 588 N.E.2d 794 (1992).

[11]Palmore v. Sidoti, 466 U.S. 429, 104 S. Ct. 1879, 80 L. Ed. 2d 421 (1984).

[12]In re H., 37 Ohio Misc. 123, 66 Ohio Op. 2d 178, 66 Ohio Op. 2d 368, 305 N.E.2d 815 (C.P. 1973).

between the parents, or the court may issue a shared parenting decree requiring parents to share all or some aspects of physical and legal care of the children.[1] The court must also allocate the parental rights and responsibilities in a dissolution.[2] Because dissolutions are granted pursuant to the agreement of the parties, the court need only determine whether the allocation of parental rights and responsibilities agreed to by the parties is in the best interest of the child.[3]

The designation given to the parenting order is less important than the actual terms of the allocation of parental rights and responsibilities. For example, the court may designate one parent as the residential parent while affording the other parent equal companionship with the child. Conversely, a shared parenting plan approved by the court may award one parent nothing more than possession of the child on alternate weekends.

Courts have many factors to consider when determining the allocation of parental rights and responsibilities.

§ 15:20 Procedure for allocating parental rights—Interviewing the child[1]

In determining the child's best interest, the court has the discretion to interview the child, and on the request of either party the court must interview the child.[2] The request may be propounded by any party properly joined in the action, which may include persons other than the parents of the child. The interview must be conducted in chambers, and no person other than the child, the child's attorney, the judge, necessary court personnel, and, in the judge's discretion, an attorney for each parent may be present.[3]

Prior to the enactment of Senate Bill 3, RC 3109.04(B)(1) allowed any child twelve years of age or older to choose the parent with whom the child was to live. As amended, RC 3109.04(B)(1) abolished the right of a child to make such an election. The court must now interview the child to determine the child's wishes and concerns without regard to the age of the child.

[Section 15:19]

[1]RC 3109.04(A).

[2]RC 3105.63.

[3]RC 3105.65(B).

[Section 15:20]

[1]See also Text § 15:8, Best interest standard—Wishes and concerns of child.

[2]RC 3109.04(B)(1); Leasure v. Leasure, 1998 WL 108137 (Ohio Ct. App. 8th Dist. Cuyahoga County 1998) (reversible error for trial court not to conduct an in-chambers interview when requested); Bauer v. Bauer, 1997 WL 368371 (Ohio Ct. App. 12th Dist. Warren County 1997).

[3]RC 3109.04(B)(2)(c).

If the court interviews the child, it may in its discretion, and on motion of either parent shall, appoint a guardian ad litem for the child.[4]

Although a third party can require the court to interview the child, only a parent can require the court to appoint a guardian ad litem for the child.

When interviewing the child, the court must first determine the child's reasoning ability,[5] which is normally done by determining whether the child is attuned to time, space, and detail. The younger the child, the less likely he is to have sufficient reasoning ability to express his wishes and concerns. If the child lacks sufficient reasoning ability, the court shall not continue the interview to determine his wishes and concerns.

The appellate court in *In re Longwell*[6] addressed the factors that a trial court should consider in assessing a child's reasoning abilities, and looked to Evidence Rule 601, which requires a determination of competency for a child under ten years of age to testify. The court cited *State v. Frazier*[7] as a clarification of five considerations for a trial court in determining competency to testify: "(1) the child's ability to receive accurate impressions of fact or to observe acts about which he or she will testify, (2) the child's ability to recollect those impressions or observations, (3) the child's ability to communicate what was observed, (4) the child's understanding of truth and falsity, and (5) the child's appreciation of his or her responsibility to be truthful."[8] The court also recognized the Supreme Court's adoption of these considerations in a civil context in *Schulte v. Schulte*,[9] and further held that the trial court was not required to make express findings on the considerations.

If the child has sufficient reasoning ability, the court must then determine whether special circumstances exist that would make it not in the child's best interest to determine his wishes and concerns. Normally, such a special circumstance would be the child's fear or reluctance to express his wishes and concerns. If the court determines such special circumstances exist, it shall not proceed to determine the child's wishes and concerns and must enter findings of fact in its journal.[10] If the court determines it is in the best interest of the child to determine his wishes and concerns, it shall proceed to do so. RC

---

[4]RC 3109.04(B)(2)(a); Nentwick v. Nentwick, 1998 WL 78663 (Ohio Ct. App. 7th Dist. Jefferson County 1998) (pro se litigant who fails to request appointment of guardian ad litem during in camera interview is not entitled to reversal just because she had no counsel).

[5]RC 3109.04(B)(2)(b).

[6]In Matter of Longwell, 1995 WL 520058 (Ohio Ct. App. 9th Dist. Lorain County 1995).

[7]State v. Frazier, 61 Ohio St. 3d 247, 574 N.E.2d 483 (1991).

[8]State v. Frazier, 61 Ohio St. 3d 247, 248, 574 N.E.2d 483 (1991).

[9]Schulte v. Schulte, 71 Ohio St. 3d 41, 1994-Ohio-459, 641 N.E.2d 719 (1994).

[10]RC 3109.04(B)(2)(b).

3109.04(B)(3) prohibits all persons from obtaining or attempting to obtain a written or recorded statement or affidavit setting forth the child's wishes and concerns. Although the statute provides no sanctions for obtaining such statements or affidavits, courts are prohibited from considering them.

A trial court does not err in refusing to determine the reasoning capacity of a four-year-old child. Court of appeals held that in *Linger v. Linger*,[11] the Fifth District the trial court does not have to make a record of the interview nor have to make findings of fact with respect to a child's wishes.[12] However, one month later, that same court held that a trial court erred in refusing a timely request to make a record of its interview.[13]

§ 15:21   Procedure for allocating parental rights—Interview procedure

RC 3109.04 does not set forth a procedure to be followed in determining the child's wishes and concerns and does not specify when the interview should be conducted. These matters are left to the discretion of the trial court. In many cases, both parents are unsure as to the child's wishes and concerns but stand ready, albeit reluctantly, to abide by the child's wishes and concerns, as long as they are sure of the true wishes and concerns of the child. In this situation, an interview with the child as the first order of business would be appropriate, but a record should be made in order for the parents to be assured that the child expressed his wishes and concerns freely and independently.

Although there are arguments for keeping children together as a family unit, it does not appear that children should be interviewed jointly when determining their wishes and concerns. Younger siblings may be dominated by older ones, sitting mute, afraid to express themselves, and may later recant their wishes, to the consternation of parents and court alike. When interviewing more than one child, the most articulate and informed child, usually the oldest, should be interviewed first, so that the court may better understand events or things to which the younger children refer.

§ 15:22   Procedure for allocating parental rights—Interview outline—In general

The court should prepare a list of questions to ask the child during the interview. If counsel for the parents will not be present in chambers during the interview, they should be afforded the op-

[11]Linger v. Linger, 1993 WL 274318 (Ohio Ct. App. 5th Dist. Licking County 1993).

[12]Linger v. Linger, 1993 WL 274318 (Ohio Ct. App. 5th Dist. Licking County 1993).

[13]Patton v. Patton, 87 Ohio App. 3d 844, 623 N.E.2d 235 (5th Dist. Licking County 1993).

portunity to submit written questions for the court to pose to the child. However, the court has the discretion to determine which questions will be asked during the interview.

The court may wish to disclose a general outline of the topics that will be covered during the interview to the parents. The court may also advise the parents that (1) this is a matter of supreme importance and will be handled with the utmost sensitivity possible under the circumstances; (2) neither the parents nor the child should view the child's wishes and concerns as a choice between the parents' love; and (3) no retribution should be taken on innocent children, who are forced into expressing their wishes and concerns only by the lack of their parents' ability to resolve the allocation of parental rights and responsibilities. Normally, the court will also inquire into the following matters.

§ 15:23 Procedure for allocating parental rights—Interview outline—Special circumstances

Children sometimes become distraught in the interview setting and do not wish to become involved in their parents' marital dispute. The court should inform the child at the outset that the child need not proceed with the interview, and may terminate the interview at any time. The court should reassure the child that what he has to say is important, and the court is very interested in his wishes and concerns, but that the court does not wish to cause him trauma or pain, and if this interview reaches that level he has the right to terminate it. Such reluctance by a child to express his wishes and concerns would constitute a special circumstance whereby it would not be in his best interest to express his wishes and concerns.

§ 15:24 Procedure for allocating parental rights—Interview outline—Actual experience

The court should inquire into how much time the child spent living with either or both parents at the various times in his life and, more particularly, determine the details of the present living arrangement. An idea of how much time each parent was able to spend with the child is appropriate. This involves asking about babysitters and the hours that the parents were required to be at a place of employment or away from the child for any reason.

§ 15:25 Procedure for allocating parental rights—Interview outline—School and community

The child's perception of how he is getting along in school is very important and sometimes a good indicator of the child's veracity. This may be a good opportunity to develop rapport with the child by discussing school activities, favorite subjects, or favorite teachers and schoolmates. A statement by the child as to which parent helped him with his homework is also illuminating. Inquiry may also be made as to how the child liked the various neighborhoods where he lived, how he related to the neighborhood children, and what physical characteristics of his homes and neighborhoods appealed to him.

§ 15:26   Procedure for allocating parental rights—Interview outline—Family

It is necessary to identify the various family members with whom the child interacts. How the child relates to his brothers and sisters, including half-brothers/sisters and children by a parent's prior marriage, or live-in relatives can be informative.

§ 15:27   Procedure for allocating parental rights—Interview outline—Present situation

There should be a determination as to exactly what the child believes the present situation is between his parents. There may be a misunderstanding in the child's mind that the parents are about to reconcile, or that they are not going through with the divorce.

§ 15:28   Procedure for allocating parental rights—Interview outline—Purpose of interview

Children usually have some prior understanding of the purpose of the interview. The court might inquire as to the sources of his information, and be prepared to handle the answers, to help the child understand the correct status of his parents' relationship and what the interview is supposed to accomplish. The court might specifically ask which parent prepared him for the interview and/or the input from either attorney, school counselor, and any other persons, including peers.

§ 15:29   Procedure for allocating parental rights—Interview outline—Influence

The area of most concern for parents is the possibility of undue influence by the other parent on the child. This generally appears in the form of bribery and/or threats that unduly influence the child. Tangible evidence is relatively straightforward and easy to deal with, but evidence of intangible, psychological, or subtle influence is difficult to discern and weigh. One of the most difficult problems to deal with is the psychological role reversal between parent and child, where the child has assumed the role of protector of the parent and quite firmly believes that the parent cannot get along without the assistance of the child. Therefore, the child is quite straightforward in his wishes. This is one area in which psychological testing and evaluation may help.

§ 15:30   Procedure for allocating parental rights—Interview outline—Incidents

Frequently, one parent will claim that a particular incident, usually involving discipline, will have an inordinate influence over the child's wishes and concerns and should be carefully inquired into, if not discounted entirely. An appropriate question posed to the child, as to how he or she views the incident, could be enlightening.

§ 15:31   Procedure for allocating parental rights—Interview outline—Testing child's reasoning ability

When a child has expressed his wishes and concerns, the court may ask the reasons why. To help this process, the court can inquire into the perceived good and bad points of living with each parent. An idea of how the child believes discipline will be enforced in the respective households may also be useful. Another important factor may be the length of time the child had to develop his wishes and concerns. If the child has been considering his wishes and concerns for a long period of time, the court may be more comfortable than in cases where the child made his decision at the time of the hearing. The court may ask the child if he has informed his parents of his wishes and concerns and heard their reaction. The court should attempt to determine how the child will react if his wishes and concerns are not honored by the court.

§ 15:32   Procedure for allocating parental rights—Interview outline—Confidentiality

Children are sometimes afraid that the court will repeat what they have said in chambers to their parents. A promise of limited confidentiality can help facilitate the interview. However, if a record of the interview is being made, it must be pointed out to the child that his parents will have access to the record. Further, the child must understand that the court will summarize the child's wishes and concerns for his parents or their counsel.

§ 15:33   Procedure for allocating parental rights—Abuse, neglect, or domestic violence

If the court determines that a parent perpetrated an act that resulted in a child being adjudicated neglected, or has been convicted of or pleaded guilty to a criminal offense involving an act that resulted in a child being neglected, or if there is reason to believe a parent acted in a manner resulting in a child being neglected, the court must consider that fact against designating that parent the residential parent and against granting a shared parenting decree.[1] The neglected child need not be a child of the parent.

If the court determines that a parent has been convicted of or pleaded guilty to the offense of domestic violence against a family or household member, or caused physical harm to a family or household

---

[Section 15:33]

[1]RC 3109.04(C).

member during the commission of another offense for which he was convicted or pleaded guilty, or was determined to be the perpetrator of an act that is the basis of a child being adjudicated abused, the court may designate that parent as the residential parent or issue a shared parenting decree only if it is in the best interest of the child and the court enters specific findings of fact supporting that determination.[2]

§ 15:34 Procedure for allocating parental rights— Investigation and report

RC 3109.04(C) and Civil Rule 75(D) permit a court to cause an investigation to be made as to the character, family relations, past conduct, earning ability, and financial worth of each parent. The decision to order an investigation is within the sound discretion of the court.[1] On written request, the report must be made available to either parent or their counsel. The statute and the Civil Rule conflict as to the time when the report must be made available. The statute provides that it must be made available five days prior to hearing, and the Civil Rule provides that it must be made available seven days prior to hearing. The report must be signed by the investigator, who shall be subject to cross-examination by either parent concerning the contents of the report. The court may consider the report, but cannot base its decision solely on the report.[2] Although the earning ability and financial worth of the parents are subject to investigation and inclusion into the report, the court may not give preference to a parent because of his financial status or condition.[3]

The language of both RC 3109.04(C) and Civil Rule 75(D) implicitly gives the trial court the authority to admit custody investigation reports as evidence, since they can be ordered by the court and the investigator is subject to cross examination.[4]

---

[2]RC 3109.04(C).

[Section 15:34]

[1]Stone v. Stone, 9 Ohio App. 3d 6, 457 N.E.2d 919 (12th Dist. Warren County 1983).

[2]Hillard v. Hillard, 29 Ohio App. 2d 20, 58 Ohio Op. 2d 14, 277 N.E.2d 557 (1st Dist. Butler County 1971).

[3]RC 3109.04(F)(3).

[4]Roach v. Roach, 79 Ohio App. 3d 194, 607 N.E.2d 35 (2d Dist. Montgomery County 1992), citing to former RC 3109.04(A); Sayre v. Hoelzle-Sayre, 100 Ohio App. 3d 203, 653 N.E.2d 712 (3d Dist. Seneca County 1994) (RC 2317.39 expressly permits the use of court-ordered investigative reports as long as the report is made readily available to all parties before consideration by the judge); Miller v. Miller, 115 Ohio App. 3d 336, 685 N.E.2d 319 (3d Dist. Seneca County 1996).

Trial courts may consider the report and recommendations of a court appointed investigator despite the hearsay inherent in the report.[5]

§ 15:35 Procedure for allocating parental rights—Expert witnesses

In addition to court-ordered investigations, the court may order the parents of minor children and the children to submit to medical, psychological, and psychiatric examinations.[1]

In *Williams v. Williams*,[2] a marriage counselor, who had never seen the mother or the children, was qualified to give her expert opinion as to how the father related to his children, based upon her questions to the husband.

When a professional has examined or treated a minor, the admissibility of statements made by a minor to the examiner is subject to hearsay and competency rules.[3] The court may, for instance, allow testimony relating to statements made while under stress[4] and for purposes of medical diagnosis or treatment.[5]

§ 15:36 Sole residential parent

The court must designate a sole residential parent in cases where neither parent requests shared parenting, where at least one parent requests shared parenting but does not file a shared parenting plan, or where at least one parent requests shared parenting and files a plan, but shared parenting is not in the best interest of the child.[1]

When allocating parental rights and responsibilities the court shall not give preference to a parent because of his financial status or condition.[2] However, the factors listed in RC 3119.24 must be considered together with the factors listed in RC 3109.04(F)(1) and (2) when determining whether shared parenting is in the best interest of the child.

---

[5]Martin v. Martin, 2004-Ohio-807, 2004 WL 324862 (Ohio Ct. App. 3d Dist. Marion County 2004).

[Section 15:35]

[1]RC 3109.04(C); see Text Ch 37, Mental Health Experts.

[2]Williams v. Williams, 80 Ohio App. 3d 477, 609 N.E.2d 617 (3d Dist. Hardin County 1992).

[3]Evid. R. 601, Evid. R. 801 et seq.

[4]Evid. R. 803(2).

[5]Evid. R. 803(4); Schulte v. Schulte, 1993 WL 197413 (Ohio Ct. App. 6th Dist. Wood County 1993), judgment aff'd, 71 Ohio St. 3d 41, 1994-Ohio-459, 641 N.E.2d 719 (1994).

[Section 15:36]

[1]RC 3109.04(A)(1); Helms v. Helms, 1997 WL 576385 (Ohio Ct. App. 9th Dist. Summit County 1997).

[2]RC 3109.04(F)(3).

§ 15:37   Shared parenting—In general

One or both parents may file a pleading or motion requesting shared parenting and a shared parenting plan. The language throughout RC 3109.04 refers to parents requesting shared parenting, and a strict interpretation would prohibit shared parenting between a parent and a nonparent.

The Ohio Supreme Court in *In re Bonfield*[1] noted that RC 3109.04 specifically uses the term "parent" and this term is defined in RC 3111.01 to mean a narrow class of persons who are statutorily defined as parents for purposes of parentage actions. The court held that the juvenile court could make a "shared custody" order, but not call it "shared parenting."

When the terms of the allocation of parental rights are contested, including where both parties have filed their own written plans, a hearing must be granted where both parents may testify.[2] The trial court has no authority under RC 3109.04(D) to fashion its own shared parenting plan.[3]

§ 15:38   Shared parenting—In general—Parents only

A shared parenting decree that incorporates a plan between a parent and a non-parent is void ab initio.[1] An attempt to impose a child support order according to the guidelines, putting the legal father in the father's column and the biological father under Column II which is captioned "mother," violates the intent of the legislature.[2]

§ 15:39   Shared parenting—Shared parenting plan

The shared parenting plan shall be filed with the petition for dis-

---

[Section 15:37]

[1]In re Bonfield, 96 Ohio St. 3d 218, 2002-Ohio-4182, 773 N.E.2d 507 (2002), opinion superseded on reconsideration, 97 Ohio St. 3d 387, 2002-Ohio-6660, 780 N.E.2d 241 (2002).

[2]Snouffer v. Snouffer, 87 Ohio App. 3d 89, 621 N.E.2d 879 (4th Dist. Meigs County 1993), citing to RC 3109.04(A).

[3]Robbins v. Robbins, 1995 WL 367192 (Ohio Ct. App. 12th Dist. Brown County 1995); Piwinski v. Piwinski, 1999 WL 148483 (Ohio Ct. App. 8th Dist. Cuyahoga County 1999) (trial court cannot order shared parenting plan to be submitted where there is no motion or pleading for shared parenting); Bowen v. Bowen, 132 Ohio App. 3d 616, 725 N.E.2d 1165 (9th Dist. Medina County 1999).

[Section 15:38]

[1]Lorence v. Goeller, 2000 WL 988760 (Ohio Ct. App. 9th Dist. Lorain County 2000); Liston v. Pyles, 1997 WL 467327 (Ohio Ct. App. 10th Dist. Franklin County 1997); Konicek v. Konicek, 144 Ohio App. 3d 105, 759 N.E.2d 801 (9th Dist. Lorain County 2001) (maternal grandfather and natural parents' shared parenting plan in error).

[2]Lorence v. Goeller, 2000 WL 988760 (Ohio Ct. App. 9th Dist. Lorain County 2000).

solution, and in other cases at least thirty days prior to the hearing.[1] The statute does not make clear whether the thirty-day requirement is substantive, and therefore mandatory, or if it is procedural and may be waived. In *Harris v. Harris*,[2] the trial court found that the filing deadline was directory, not mandatory, and that the rule was intended " 'to assure an orderly procedure rather than to foreclose a litigant's options.' "[3] The appellate court agreed that the provision was not intended to divest the trial court of a "reasonable degree of flexibility in considering shared parenting pleas."[4] While it did agree with the appellant that the statutory deadline did implicate her right to due process, in this case the court found she had an adequate opportunity to respond.

A shared parenting plan must include provisions covering all factors relevant to the care of the children, including physical living arrangements, child support obligations, the child's medical and dental care, school placement, and visitation.[5] Unless the plan provides otherwise, both parents are the residential parents and legal custodians when the court issues a shared parenting decree.[6] The parent with whom the child resides at a particular point in time is the residential parent, and the other parent is the non-residential parent, at that point in time.[7] If it is necessary for the purpose of receiving public assistance, the court must designate which one of the parents' residences is to serve as the child's home.[8] The parents may also wish to include provisions in the shared parenting plan for the child's education, religious upbringing, income tax dependency, child care, removal from the state, and use of surname, as well as delineating the authority of each parent.

The court may approve a shared parenting plan only if it is in the best interest of the child.[9] Approval of a plan is discretionary with the court, and the court may not approve more than one plan.[10] The court must approve a plan submitted by one of the parents, and cannot

---

[Section 15:39]

[1]RC 3109.04(G); Bache v. Bache, 1993 WL 171791 (Ohio Ct. App. 5th Dist. Tuscarawas County 1993) (filing of written plan is statutory requirement).

[2]Harris v. Harris, 105 Ohio App. 3d 671, 664 N.E.2d 1304 (2d Dist. Miami County 1995).

[3]Harris v. Harris, 105 Ohio App. 3d 671, 674, 664 N.E.2d 1304 (2d Dist. Miami County 1995).

[4]Harris v. Harris, 105 Ohio App. 3d 671, 674, 664 N.E.2d 1304 (2d Dist. Miami County 1995).

[5]RC 3109.04(G).

[6]RC 3109.04(K)(5).

[7]RC 3109.04(K)(6), (7).

[8]RC 3109.04(A)(2).

[9]RC 3109.04(D)(1)(a).

[10]RC 3109.04(D)(1)(b).

prepare its own plan, or on its own motion amend a plan submitted by a parent.[11]

Whenever possible, the court shall require that a shared parenting plan ensure the opportunity of both parents to have frequent and continuing contact with the child, unless to do so would not be in the best interest of the child.[12] When the court orders shared parenting, child support must be determined in accordance with RC 3119.23.[13]

In the case of *Livermore v. Livermore*,[14] the trial court noted that:

the purpose of a shared parenting plan is to provide the parties the necessary flexibility within the court's order to act in concert in the best interests of their children. As all persons who have raised or are raising children know, matters will arise in the course of their development that cannot necessarily be predicted at the time of divorce. These issues may be educational, emotional, psychological or otherwise. Shared parenting allows divorced parents the ability to cooperate with each other to make parenting decisions as unforeseen needs arise.

§ 15:40   Shared parenting—Joint request and plan—In general

If the parties make a joint request and file a joint shared parenting plan, the court must review the plan. If the court determines the plan is in the best interest of the child, it shall approve the plan. If the plan is not in the best interest of the child, the court may require the parents to make changes. If the changes are made and meet the court's objection, and the plan, as amended, is in the best interest of the child, the court shall approve the amended plan. If changes are not attempted, or the attempted changes are not in the best interest of the child, the court shall deny the request for shared parenting and proceed as if no request had ever been made.[1]

§ 15:41   Shared parenting—Joint request and plan—Joint plan for equal time—Form⊚

SHARED PARENTING PLAN

The parties hereto, *[name]*, mother and *[name]*, father of the minor *[child/children] [name(s)]*, agree that it is in the best interests of the minor *[child/children]* that the parents share in the parenting of the minor *[child/children]*.

The parties acknowledge that each is a caring and appropriate par-

---

[11]RC 3109.04(D)(1)(b); McClain v. McClain, 87 Ohio App. 3d 856, 623 N.E.2d 242 (9th Dist. Summit County 1993) (the statute does not give the court authority to create its own shared parenting plan).

[12]RC 3109.04(D)(1)(c).

[13]RC 3109.04(A)(2).

[14]Livermore v. Livermore, 2006-Ohio-485, 2006 WL 266617 (Ohio Ct. App. 3d Dist. Crawford County 2006).

[Section 15:40]

[1]RC 3109.04(D)(1)(a)(i).

ent, with the ability to provide guidance, concern and a proper home life for the minor *[child/children]*.

[The parties further recognize that the father has a work schedule subject to change each eight weeks in that he changes shifts every eight weeks and days off every eight weeks.] It is with these factors in mind that the parties agree to the following shared parenting plan:

1. The *[child/children]* will make their residence with each parent on an approximately equal basis, with due consideration for the work scheduling of each parent and in order to provide the least disturbance to the *[child/children]* and *[his/her/their]* scheduled activities. For school purposes, the residence of the *[child/children]* will be with the *[father/mother]*. The parties are presently operating under this type of arrangement, and the intention is to continue.

2. So long as the present arrangement continues, and each party has comparable income, and each party is providing approximately equal care, neither party shall be responsible to contribute child support to the other party.

3. Open and free communication, by telephone and otherwise, shall be permitted with the parent with whom a child is not then residing.

4. Arrangements shall be made for holiday and birthday celebrations to be shared or alternated to provide each child with a balance of involvement by each parent.

5. Each parent shall be permitted to have access to the school and medical records of the *[child/children]*.

6. Each parent agrees to consult with the other concerning the education, health and other problems which might involve the *[child/children]*.

7. Each parent shall maintain his/her present health insurance coverage on the minor *[child/children]* so long as it is available through his/her respective place of employment. The uncovered medical, dental, orthodontic and optometric and prescription drug expenses of the minor *[child/children]* not covered by either parent's medical insurance shall be paid one-half by each party. This provision shall cover the *[child/children]* until each is eighteen and out of high school.

8. The appropriateness and need for special expenditures for the *[child/children]*, such as, but not limited to special lessons, activities, outfits and uniforms, musical instruments, sporting equipment, etc., shall be discussed between the parties and the cost of such items deemed necessary shall be equally shared between the parties.

9. Each parent shall be entitled to have the *[child/children]* for at least two consecutive weeks at least once a year, with thirty days' notice to the other parent.

10. In the event the *[child/children]* desire(s) to continue *[his/her/their]* education beyond high school, whether in college or trade school, the parents each agree, to the extent financially able, to contribute at least one-third to such *[child's/children's]* tuition costs, *[with the limitation that such tuition cost not exceed the then cost of a resident*

student in a comparable course of study at the Ohio State University, for a period not to exceed four years].

11. The *[mother/father]* shall have the right to claim the IRS dependency deduction for *[child/children][every year/every other year]* so long as the parties are operating under this shared parenting plan.

_____

Mother

_____

Father

NOTES TO FORM

Drafter's Notes

A shared parenting plan contains no caption in the usual case where it is attached to a separation agreement. However, it is possible that after a divorce is filed, the parties agree to shared parenting and file the plan. In that case, a caption would be required.

The Court may approve provisions agreed upon by the parties in the parenting plan that the Court otherwise would not have authority to order if resolving conflict, provided the provisions are in the best interests of the minor children.

It is always advisable for the parties to attach and incorporate a specific, comprehensive possession schedule if they are unable to maintain the flexible possession schedule described in this plan.

In all parenting plans it is advisable that there be an understanding between the parties regarding any geographical limitations on the change of the child/children's residence.

§ 15:42   Shared parenting—Joint request and plan—Joint plan for specific times—Form⊚

[Title of Court]

[Caption]   Case No. *[_____]*
                                                    SHARED PARENT-
                                                    ING PLAN

The parties hereto, *[name]*, mother and *[name]*, father of the minor *[child/children]* *[names]*, agree that it is in the best interests of the minor *[child/children]* that the parties share in the parenting of their *[child/children]*.

The parties acknowledge that each is a caring and appropriate parent, with the ability to provide guidance, concern and a proper home life for the minor *[child/children]*.

1. Each parent, regardless of where the *[child is/children are]* physically located or with whom the *[child is/children are]* residing at any time, shall be the residential parent and legal custodian of the *[child/children]*.

2. The *[mother/father]* shall be the residential parent and legal custodian for school placement purposes.

3. The father shall have the *[child/children]* with him from *[state]*.

4. The mother shall have the *[child/children]* with her from *[state]*.

5. In addition the *[child/children]* shall reside with each parent for a total of *[five consecutive weeks]* during the summer. During this period, the other parent shall have parenting time rights.

6. The parents shall each have the *[child/children]* on an alternating basis during the following holidays and school breaks: *[list]*.

7. The father shall have the *[child/children]* whenever the mother is unable to care for *[him/her/them]* and the mother shall have the *[child/children]* whenever the father is unable to care for *[him/her/them]*.

8. The parties agree that each shall have the responsibility of sharing and raising the *[child/children]* and both shall have access and input to all academic and medical records and reports, all activities and all major decisions concerning the raising of the *[child/children]*.

9. The *[mother/father]* shall obtain and maintain hospitalization insurance and each shall pay one half of all uncovered medical expenses.

10. The *[mother/father]* shall contribute $*[dollar amount]* per month to assist in the financial needs of the other parent while the *[child/children]* are with that parent. Payment, plus processing charge, shall be made by withholding from the *[wage/bank account/other]* of the *[mother/father]*, through the *[name and address of agency]* until the *[child/children][is/are]* eighteen years of age and out of high school. Said amount of support is *[in compliance with the guidelines/deviates from the guidelines and such deviation is justified by the factors set forth in a separate finding of fact]*.

11. The *[mother/father]*, if otherwise qualified pursuant to IRS regulations, shall be entitled to claim head of household status for *[child's/children's name/names]*.

12. The *[mother/father]* shall be entitled to the income tax dependency exemption for *[child's name]* and the *[mother/father]* shall be entitled to claim *[child's name]* as *[her/his]* dependent.

Mother

Father

NOTES TO FORM

Drafter's Notes

A shared parenting plan contains no caption in the usual case where it is attached to a separation agreement. However, it is possible that after a divorce is filed, the parties agree to shared parenting and file the plan. In that case, a caption would be required.

RC 3109.04(K)(6) provides definitions for parents with shared parenting. RC

3109.04(K)(7) clarifies that a designation for school, income tax, or public assistance benefits purposes does not otherwise affect the designation.

§ 15:43   Shared parenting—Joint request and plan—Alternate clauses—Form⊚

The parties agree that the parental rights and responsibilities for *[child's name/children's names]* will be shared by the parties under the following plan:

The parents shall be the residential parents and legal custodians of the minor children.

Each parent shall have liberal time with the minor *[child/children]*, with the aim of maintaining a close relationship with both parents. The parties agree that the provisions of the *[name of county]* (Local Rule *[number of local rule]*) are adopted by reference. Said time shall be exercised with consideration for the schedule of each party. In the event either party wishes to take the *[child/children]* on vacation, adequate advance notice will be given to the other party.

The *[father/mother]* shall be the residential parent for all school-related purposes.

The *[father/mother]* agrees to contribute child support of $*[dollar amount]* per month. Said payment shall be made, plus processing charge, through the *[name and address of agency]* by payroll withholding from the wages due and owing the *[father/mother]*, and shall continue until the *[child/children][is/are]* eighteen years of age and out of high school.

The parties agree to cooperate in and discuss matters affecting the day-to-day life of the *[child/children]*, including child care, schooling, religion, and medical needs as well as other such matters. In the event of a dispute of this type of matter, the *[father/mother]* will have the final decision.

In the event either party moves out of *[name of county]* County and the parties are unable to agree upon a revised parenting plan, either party may submit the matter to the mediation service of the court, or to the court itself.

The *[child/children]* shall have *[his/her/their]* residence with the *[father/mother]* from *[date]* or the commencement of the *[child's/children's]* school year in the school *[he/she/they]* will be attending when *[he/she/they]* make(s) *[his/her/their]* residence with the *[father/mother]*, whichever comes first, through *[date]* or the end of the *[child's/children's]* academic year, whichever comes last.

The summer months will be shared equally by both parents according to mutual accord over the exact dates. Said dates may vary from summer to summer.

The residence of the *[child/children]* shall not be out of the United States, except by agreement of both parties. Either party may, for vacation periods, take the *[child/children]* out of the United States.

The parties agree to cooperate in the upbringing of the minor *[child/*

children], and to this end agree to encourage love and respect for the other parent.

Each parent shall be permitted to have access to the school records of the *[child/children]*. Each parent agrees to consult with the other concerning the education, health, and other problems which might involve the *[child/children]*, reserving to the residential parent final decisions on such matters.

The parties agree to cooperate to the fullest in making the *[child/children]* available to the other party. The parties agree to attempt to resolve any disputes without the need for intervention of court orders for visitation.

Each parent shall pay for *[his/her]* own transportation costs for parenting time purposes with the *[child/children]*. The *[child's/children's]* transportation costs back and forth between the parents shall be paid proportionately according to their salaries. Should either parent move further than 1,000 miles from the other parent, such parent shall bear the additional travel costs for that excess distance if such amount can be readily ascertainable.

[Optional] [For purposes of computing transportation costs of the *[child/children]*, costs incurred for summer share time, as well as changes of residences, shall be shared proportionately by the parties.]

The *[father/mother]* agrees to continue to provide hospital and surgical and major medical coverage for the minor *[child/children]*. Medical expenses shall also include dental, optometric, and prescription drug costs. Uncovered medical expenses in excess of $100 per year will be shared proportionately by the parties according to their salaries.

The parties agree to share the educational expenses of the minor *[child/children]* proportionately according to the salaries through high school. For purposes of clarification, and not as a limitation, educational expenses include books, trips, uniforms, musical instruments and lessons. In the event said *[child/children][has/have]* private tutors or attend(s) a private school, such expenditures shall be shared only upon mutual accord.

The *[father/mother]* shall be entitled to claim the *[child/children]* as *[his/her]* dependent for IRS dependency exemption purposes.

For purposes of I.R.C. § 152(e), *[name of spouse]* shall be considered the residential parent as to any year during which this shared parenting agreement is in effect, and *[residential parent]* shall execute and deliver to *[non-residential parent]* any declaration required by the Internal Revenue Service to reflect that fact.

§ 15:44   Shared parenting—Separate requests—Separate proposed plans

If each parent requests shared parenting and files a separate plan, the court must review both plans to determine if either plan is in the best interest of the child. If either plan is in the best interest of the child, the court may approve it. If neither plan is in the best interest of the child, the court may order each parent to submit changes to his own plan or to both plans, or may select one plan and order each parent to submit changes.[1] If changes are submitted and the plan, as amended, is in the best interest of the child, the court may approve the amended plan. If changes are not submitted, or the plan as changed continues to be not in the best interest of the child, the court may deny the requests for shared parenting and proceed as if the requests for shared parenting were not made. The court shall journalize findings of fact for approval of a plan or denial of the requests for shared parenting.[2]

§ 15:45 Shared parenting—Separate requests—One proposed plan

If each parent requests shared parenting but only one parent files a plan, or if only one parent requests shared parenting and files a plan, the court may order the other parent to file a plan. The court must then review both plans to determine if either plan is in the best interest of the child, and if so may approve that plan. If neither plan is in the best interest of the child, the court may order each parent to submit changes to his own plan or to both plans, or may select one plan and order each parent to submit changes. If changes are submitted and the plan, as amended, is in the best interest of the child, the court may approve the amended plan. If changes are not submitted, or the plan as changed is not in the best interest of the child, the court may deny the request for shared parenting and proceed as if the request had not been made. The court shall journalize findings of fact for approval of a plan or denial of the request for shared parenting.[1]

§ 15:46 Shared parenting—Separate requests—Motion for shared parenting—Form⊚

[Title of Court]

[Caption]   Case No.
                                                   [_____]
                                                   MOTION FOR
                                                   SHARED
                                                   PARENTING

Now comes *[Plaintiff/Defendant]* and moves this court for an order

---

[Section 15:44]

[1]Foster v. Foster, 1993 WL 57464 (Ohio Ct. App. 6th Dist. Sandusky County 1993) (trial court not required to request revisions in proposed shared parenting plan).

[2]RC 3109.04(D)(1)(a)(ii).

[Section 15:45]

[1]RC 3109.04(D)(1)(a)(iii).

awarding shared parenting to the parties pursuant to the shared parenting plan attached, and for a finding that such plan is in the best interest of the minor *[child / children]*.

_____

Attorney for Movant

SHARED PARENTING PLAN

[Plaintiff / Defendant] proposes the following shared parenting plan for the minor *[child / children]*, namely *[name(s) and date(s) of birth of children]*.

1. The *[child / children]* shall make their residence with both parties as follows:

a. The *[mother / father]* shall have the *[child / children]* with *[her / him]* at reasonable times, including the following: *[times]*.

b. The *[father / mother]* shall have the children all other times.

2. The *[father / mother]* shall pay to the *[mother / father]* the sum of $*[dollar amount]* per month as and for child support. Payments, plus processing charge, shall be made by payroll withholding from *[mother's / father's]* wages and forwarded to the Child Support Enforcement Agency.

[Said sum was computed under the child support guidelines and is in conformity therewith.][or] [Said sum deviates from the child support guidelines. The parties agree that application of the schedule would be unjust or inappropriate to the *[child / children]* or either parent and would not be in the best interest of the child based on the following factors: *[list]*.

NOTES TO FORM

Drafter's Notes

Either parent may file for shared parenting during the pendency of a case or after a decree is rendered. Check local rules for guidelines.

§ 15:47 Shared parenting—Best interest in shared parenting

A court shall not order shared parenting unless it is in the best interest of the child.[1] RC 3109.04(F)(2) provides that in determining whether shared parenting is in the best interest of the child, the court must consider all relevant factors including those set forth in RC 3109.04(F)(1) and 3119.24,[2] as well as the following factors:

_____

[Section 15:47]

[1]RC 3109.04(A)(2).

[2]RC 3109.04(F)(2) also references the factors set forth in RC 3119.23, which is a deviation statute. It is important to first reference the factors enumerated under RC 3119.24 when considering child support under shared parenting orders.

(1) The ability of the parents to cooperate and make decisions jointly with respect to the children;[3]

(2) The ability of each parent to encourage the sharing of love, affection, and contact between the child and the other parent;

(3) Any history of or potential for child abuse, spousal abuse, other domestic violence, or parental kidnapping by either parent;

(4) The geographic proximity of the parents to each other, as the proximity relates to the practical considerations of shared parenting; and

(5) The recommendation of the guardian ad litem of the child, if the child has a guardian ad litem.

None of these factors is more heavily weighted than any other. However, a reading of these factors in conjunction with RC 3109.04(A)(2) clearly shows that the statute intends that parents participating in shared parenting cooperate and share the decisions and responsibilities of caring for their children.

Where the divorce had not been amicable and there was evidence that the hostile relationship between the parties had an adverse effect upon the child's emotional life, forcing the parties into a shared parenting environment could result in a lack of stability and predictability in the child's life.[4]

§ 15:48   Shared parenting—Shared parenting decree

If the court approves a shared parenting plan, it shall incorporate the plan into a final shared parenting decree, which should be issued at the same time as, and appended to, the final decree of divorce, dissolution, annulment, or legal separation.[1] Former RC 3109.04(D)(1)(d), which required the issuance of a provisional decree, was repealed, and a provisional decree is no longer permitted. A shared parenting decree now has immediate effect when issued, but remains subject to modification or termination. A joint custody decree issued prior to the enactment of 1990 Senate Bill 3 is not affected and remains in full force, subject to modification or termination pursuant to RC 3109.04.

---

[3]Cavanaugh v. McCarthy, 1997 WL 781720 (Ohio Ct. App. 8th Dist. Cuyahoga County 1997) (parents' ability to cooperate is just one factor and may be viewed as whether capable of doing so in the future).

[4]Jaegly v. Jaegly, 1993 WL 93476 (Ohio Ct. App. 6th Dist. Wood County 1993); deLevie v. deLevie, 86 Ohio App. 3d 531, 621 N.E.2d 594 (10th Dist. Franklin County 1993) (denial affirmed where parties utterly incapable of cooperating with each other in important decisions concerning child-rearing), appeal dismissed by 67 Ohio St.3d 1409, 615 N.E.2d 1043 (1993); Askin v. Askin, 1995 WL 41600 (Ohio Ct. App. 10th Dist. Franklin County 1995) (communication between the parties was either poor or nonexistent).

[Section 15:48]
[1]RC 3109.04(D)(1)(d).

§ 15:49 Shared parenting—Shared parenting decree—Form⊚

[Title of Court]

[Caption]   Case No. *[_____]*
                                               <u>SHARED PARENTING</u>
                                               <u>DECREE</u>

This Cause came before the Court on *[date]* upon the Motion of the *[Parties/Plaintiff/Defendant]* for an order granting the parties shared parenting of the minor *[child/children]* pursuant to the shared parenting plan submitted by the *[Parties/Plaintiff/Defendant]*.

Wherefore, upon review of the plan, the Court approves said plan and grants the parties shared parenting under the terms of the shared parenting plan and makes the provisions of the plan orders of this Court.

The Court finds that the plan incorporated into this decree is in the best interest of the minor *[child/children]*, namely *[name(s) and date(s) of birth of children]*.

This decree is effective as of the date filed.

                                    _____
                                                Judge

Approved:

_____
Attorney for Husband

_____
Attorney for Wife

NOTES TO FORM

Drafter's Notes

Cuyahoga County Local Rule 18, e.g., specifies the court's requirements and recommendations for a Shared Parenting Plan and Order.

§ 15:50 Shared parenting—Shared parenting decree with waiver—Form⊚

[Title of Court]

[Caption]   Case No. *[Case No.]*

SHARED PARENTING DECREE

This Cause came before the Court on *[date]* upon the Motion of the

[Parties/Plaintiff/Defendant] for an order granting the parties shared parenting of the minor *[child/children]* pursuant to the shared parenting plan submitted by the *[Parties/Plaintiff/Defendant]*.

Wherefore, upon review of the plan, the Court approves said plan and grants the parties shared parenting under the terms of the shared parenting plan and makes the provisions of the plan orders of this Court.

The court, upon request of the parties, hereby waives the 30-day period requirement of filing the plan 30 days prior to hearing.

The Court finds that the plan incorporated into this decree is in the best interest of the minor *[child/children]*, namely *[name(s) and date(s) of birth of children]*.

This decree is effective as of the date filed.

[Signature of Judge]
Judge

Approved:

[Signature of Attorney for Husband]
Attorney for Husband

[Signature of Attorney for Wife]
Attorney for Wife

NOTES TO FORM

Drafter's Notes

Where agreement on shared parenting is reached and signed at or near final hearing date, parties should waive 30 days provision.

§ 15:51   Shared parenting—Child support in shared parenting

When the court orders shared parenting, child support must be determined in accordance with RC 3119.24.[1]

The statute presently provides no separate guideline calculation worksheet adapted to provide for time adjustments to child support where the parties share parenting. Each parent is, by statute, the residential parent of the children, so each would ostensibly be entitled to child support. In *Pauly v. Pauly*,[2] the Sixth District Court of Appeals held that, as a matter of law, a trial court may not automatically deviate from the amount of line 24 of the worksheet to credit a parent's child support obligation for the time the child resides with that parent.

[Section 15:51]

[1]RC 3109.04(A)(2).

[2]Pauly v. Pauly, 1996 WL 199185 (Ohio Ct. App. 6th Dist. Lucas County 1996), judgment aff'd, 80 Ohio St. 3d 386, 1997-Ohio-105, 686 N.E.2d 1108 (1997).

In so holding, the court agreed with the Fifth[3] and Twelfth[4] appellate districts, and rejected the resolutions of the Second[5] and Tenth[6] appellate districts, the latter two which held that under a shared parenting plan, a parent must automatically be credited. The court also rejected a constitutional challenge on the basis of discrimination and found RC 3113.215(B)(6)[7] to be gender neutral. Because of the inconsistency and conflict in the courts' interpretations of the statutes, the court certified the record to the Supreme Court, which affirmed.[8]

Designating one parent as the "obligor" for child support purposes where the parties share parenting equally is not gender discrimination, nor is it a denial of due process and equal protection, especially where one parent earns significantly more than the other.[9]

In addition, there exists a false assumption by parties who share parenting time equally (or even 51% to 49%), that equal parenting time equates to no child support obligation, or a deviation downward from guideline support. In *Spencer v. Spencer*,[10] it was held that "the fact that appellant and appellee equally share time with the children does not in and of itself justify a deviation to '0' of the child-support-guideline amount." The court went on to note that it embraced the theory that such matters are to be determined on a case-by-case basis, and along with all statutory factors as set forth in RC 3119, including but not limited to RC 3109.04, 3119.022, 3119.22, 3119.23 and 3119.24.

---

[3]Wells v. Wells, 1994 WL 22888 (Ohio Ct. App. 5th Dist. Coshocton County 1994).

[4]Critzer v. Critzer, 1995 WL 617487 (Ohio Ct. App. 12th Dist. Butler County 1995); Eickelberger v. Eickelberger, 93 Ohio App. 3d 221, 638 N.E.2d 130 (12th Dist. Butler County 1994) (rejected by, In re Marriage of Crook, 211 Ill. 2d 437, 286 Ill. Dec. 141, 813 N.E.2d 198 (2004)).

[5]Weddell v. Weddell, 1994 WL 312933 (Ohio Ct. App. 2d Dist. Montgomery County 1994).

[6]Looker v. Looker, 1992 WL 394860 (Ohio Ct. App. 10th Dist. Franklin County 1992).

[7]Now RC 3119.24.

[8]Pauly v. Pauly, 80 Ohio St. 3d 386, 1997-Ohio-105, 686 N.E.2d 1108 (1997). See also, Hubin v. Hubin, 92 Ohio St. 3d 240, 2001-Ohio-187, 749 N.E.2d 749 (2001).

[9]Fallang v. Fallang, 109 Ohio App. 3d 543, 672 N.E.2d 730 (12th Dist. Butler County 1996); but see Weinberger v. Weinberger, 1998 WL 241790 (Ohio Ct. App. 1st Dist. Hamilton County 1998) (each parent in shared parenting is a residential parent and each parent's support obligation under the guidelines should be presumed spent on the children), appeal dismissed by 83 Ohio St.3d 1420, 698 N.E.2d 1008 (1998).

[10]Spencer v. Spencer, 2006-Ohio-1913, 2006 WL 1011258 (Ohio Ct. App. 5th Dist. Stark County 2006); citing Glassner v. Glassner, 160 Ohio App. 3d 648, 2005-Ohio-1936, at ¶ 48, 828 N.E.2d 642 (5th Dist. Stark County 2005).

§ 15:52   Award to third party—By parents' agreement

An agreement between parents to place custody of their child with a third person is enforceable, subject only to a judicial determination that the person selected is qualified to be the custodian.[1]

A custodial parent has "legal custody" which vests in the custodian the right to have physical care and control of the child, and to determine where and with whom the child will live.[2] This allows a parent with legal custody the right to decide that her children remain with the stepfather, so long as the parent personally otherwise exercises her responsibilities.[3]

§ 15:53   Award to third party—By parents' agreement—Power of attorney

The legislature has created a method for custodial parents to grant various powers and functions to grandparents by way of a power of attorney.[1]

The required form for the creation of the power is provided in RC 3109.53. Along with specific required notices, the form directs the creator of the power of attorney to file it with the juvenile court of the county where the grandparent resides or any other court that has jurisdiction under a prior proceeding.

While the POA may grant to the attorney in fact the custodian's rights and responsibilities regarding the care, physical custody, and control of the child, including the ability to enroll the child in school, receive information from the school, consent to school related matters and medical treatment, it does not affect the rights of the parent in any future proceedings nor act as a grant of legal custody.

The power of attorney terminates at the latest after one year. There are no statutory restrictions on issuing subsequent powers of attorney, but the RC 3109.53 notice warns, in paragraph 5, that a second or subsequent power triggers a court hearing.

Since the power of attorney is not a custody order, it appears any rights to support might not apply. In *Tuscawaras County, CSEA v. Sanders*[2] the court interpreted RC 3119.07(C) to hold that a child support order could not be set administratively nor adopted by the court on behalf of a caretaker-relative who did not have legal custody.

[Section 15:52]

[1]Clark v. Bayer, 32 Ohio St. 299, 1877 WL 120 (1877); Rowe v. Rowe, 44 Ohio Op. 224, 58 Ohio L. Abs. 497, 97 N.E.2d 223 (Ct. App. 2d Dist. Franklin County 1950).

[2]RC 2151.011(B)(17).

[3]Palmer v. Harrold, 101 Ohio App. 3d 732, 656 N.E.2d 708 (2d Dist. Greene County 1995).

[Section 15:53]

[1]2004 Am. Sub. H.B. 130, RC 3109.51 to 3109.80, eff. 7-20-04.

[2]Tuscarawas County CSEA v. Sanders, 2003-Ohio-5624, 2003 WL 22400729 (Ohio Ct. App. 5th Dist. Tuscarawas County 2003).

The filing of a second or subsequent power of attorney requires the court to set a hearing not later than ten days after filing. The court upon hearing has various options, including in appropriate circumstances, treating the filing as a petition for legal custody and awarding legal custody to the grandparent.[3]

§ 15:54 Award to third party—By the court

Pursuant to RC 3109.04(D)(2), if the court finds that it is in the best interest of the child that neither parent be designated the residential parent, the court may commit the child to a relative, or certify the matter to the juvenile court for further proceedings. Upon certification, the juvenile court has exclusive jurisdiction. A finding of parental unsuitability is no longer required for certification.[1] A finding that it is in the best interest of the child that neither parent be designated residential parent is jurisdictional, and failure to make such a finding will prevent certification to juvenile court.[2] Certification from a domestic relations court to a juvenile court following a finding that it is in the best interest of the child that neither parent be designated the residential parent is a final appealable order.[3]

Custody litigation involving a parent and a nonparent has led to several different results. In *Boyer v. Boyer*,[4] the Ohio Supreme Court found that RC 3109.04(A), as in effect at that time, was clear and unequivocal; that the court need only find custody to neither parent to be in the best interest of the child to certify the matter to juvenile court, and need not find the parents unsuitable. In 1977, the Ohio Supreme Court in *In re Perales*,[5] a child custody proceeding brought in juvenile court pursuant to RC 2151.23(A)(2), held that custody may not be awarded to a nonparent without first making a finding of parental unsuitability. The nonparent must prove by a preponderance of the evidence that the parent (1) abandoned the child, (2) has become totally incapable of supporting or caring for the child, or (3) that an award of custody to the parent would be detrimental to the child. In *Thrasher v. Thrasher*,[6] the Ninth District Court of Appeals extended the holding in *Perales* to a custody dispute brought in domestic relations court under RC 3109.04. There, the court held that a suitable parent has a paramount right to custody so long as such custody is not detrimental to the child. However, other appellate courts do not

---

[3]RC 3109.77(C)(3).

[Section 15:54]

[1]Boyer v. Boyer, 46 Ohio St. 2d 83, 75 Ohio Op. 2d 156, 346 N.E.2d 286 (1976).

[2]State ex rel. Easterday v. Zieba, 58 Ohio St. 3d 251, 569 N.E.2d 1028 (1991).

[3]Robinson v. Robinson, 19 Ohio App. 3d 323, 484 N.E.2d 710 (10th Dist. Franklin County 1984).

[4]Boyer v. Boyer, 46 Ohio St. 2d 83, 75 Ohio Op. 2d 156, 346 N.E.2d 286 (1976).

[5]In re Perales, 52 Ohio St. 2d 89, 6 Ohio Op. 3d 293, 369 N.E.2d 1047 (1977).

[6]Thrasher v. Thrasher, 3 Ohio App. 3d 210, 444 N.E.2d 431 (9th Dist. Summit County 1981).

extend the holding in *Perales* to actions brought in domestic relations court and continue to follow the holding in *Boyer*.[7]

RC 3109.06, which provides for certification of custody cases to juvenile court, was modified in 1984 to provide that the juvenile court shall make disposition of cases certified to it in accordance with RC 3109.04. RC 2151.23 was also modified in 1984 to add section (F) providing that a juvenile court shall exercise its jurisdiction in child custody matters in accordance with RC 3109.04, RC 3109.21 to RC 3109.36[8] and RC 5103.20 to RC 5103.28. These statutes remain in effect today and would appear to bring juvenile and domestic relations courts into conformity, requiring both courts to apply the best interest standard when allocating parental rights and responsibilities. However, in 1986 the Ohio Supreme Court in *Masitto v. Masitto*[9] stated that the general rule in Ohio regarding original custody awards is that suitable parents have a paramount right to custody of their minor children over nonparents. Yet once an original custody award has been made, it will not be modified unless necessary to serve the best interest of the child.

A trial court's finding of a father's abandonment, based on the father's visiting with the minor child, whom he had placed with a co-worker shortly after the child's birth and the child's mother becoming ill, only five times in a three-year period, was upheld by the Supreme Court. In *Reynolds v. Goll*,[10] the Court stated that the right of custody by the biological parents is not absolute and can be forfeited.

§ 15:55 Award to third party—By the court—Jurisdiction

The appellant in *State ex rel. Reeves v. O'Malley*[1] argued that the U.S. Supreme Court in *Troxel v. Granville*[2] recognized the fundamental liberty interest of natural parents and that therefore the judicial respondents did not have the authority to even consider granting custody to anyone else. The appellate court denied the mandamus and prohibition action, finding that *Troxel* did not deprive a court of juris-

---

[7]Rose v. Rose, 1981 WL 6272 (Ohio Ct. App. 5th Dist. Coshocton County 1981); Gwinn v. Gwinn, 1983 WL 3163 (Ohio Ct. App. 4th Dist. Lawrence County 1983); Woosley v. Woosley, 1987 WL 27845 (Ohio Ct. App. 5th Dist. Licking County 1987); Manering v. Manering, 1989 WL 47871 (Ohio Ct. App. 4th Dist. Jackson County 1989).

[8]Now RC 3127.01 to 3127.53.

[9]Masitto v. Masitto, 22 Ohio St. 3d 63, 488 N.E.2d 857 (1986); Matter of Craig S., 1998 WL 336319 (Ohio Ct. App. 6th Dist. Erie County 1998).

[10]Reynolds v. Goll, 75 Ohio St. 3d 121, 1996-Ohio-153, 661 N.E.2d 1008 (1996); In re Combs, 2000 WL 64315 (Ohio Ct. App. 10th Dist. Franklin County 2000).

[Section 15:55]

[1]State ex rel. Reeves v. O'Malley, 2001 WL 664137 (Ohio Ct. App. 8th Dist. Cuyahoga County 2001), as amended nunc pro tunc, (July 5, 2001).

[2]Troxel v. Granville, 530 U.S. 57, 120 S. Ct. 2054, 147 L. Ed. 2d 49 (2000) (see Text § 18:8, Visitation by third parties in domestic relations actions).

diction, but instead raised the issue of the appropriate standards for making such a determination.[3]

Where a child has been placed in the custody of a third party by the juvenile court in a dependency case, any future modification is controlled by a question of best interest and not unsuitability.[4]

In the Ohio Supreme Court case of *Harrold v. Collier*,[5] the Court adopted the plurality view from *Troxel*, stating in the affirmative that Ohio courts are obligated to afford some special weight to the wishes of parents of minor children when considering petitions for nonparental visitation made pursuant to RC 3109.11 or RC 3109.12. Included in these two statutes are references to factors for consideration, including, but not limited to, the factors set forth in RC 3109.051(D).[6] The Court also noted that nothing in *Troxel* suggests that a parent's wishes should be placed before the child's best interest.[7]

Even after evaluating and weighing all the statutory factors on a case by case basis, and after protecting a parent's due-process rights by giving special weight to the parent's objections to a nonparent's request for visitation, a court can still justify a determination that granting a nonparent's request for visitation is warranted under the Revised Code.

§ 15:56   Award to third party—By the court—Constitutional arguments

Numerous U.S. Supreme Court cases have addressed the issue of parental rights, in the context of rearing their children, and interference from government or third parties, under constitutional arguments of due process and fundamental rights to make decisions concerning the care, custody, and control of their children.[1]

---

[3]See Esch v. Esch, 2001 WL 173198 (Ohio Ct. App. 2d Dist. Montgomery County 2001) (custody to grandparent based on RC 3109.04(D)(2) commitment to a relative, reversed, finding statute unconstitutional); Epps v. Epps, 2001 WL 914132 (Ohio Ct. App. 5th Dist. Ashland County 2001) (RC 3109.051 is significantly different from statute reviewed in *Troxel*).

[4]In re A.W.-G., 2004-Ohio-2298, 2004 WL 1040696 (Ohio Ct. App. 12th Dist. Butler County 2004); In re Gales, 2003-Ohio-6309, 2003 WL 22785029 (Ohio Ct. App. 10th Dist. Franklin County 2003).

[5]Harrold v. Collier, 107 Ohio St. 3d 44, 2005-Ohio-5334, 836 N.E.2d 1165 (2005).

[6]See RC 3109.11, RC 3109.12 and RC 3109.051.

[7]See Harrold v. Collier, 107 Ohio St. 3d 44, 2005-Ohio-5334, 836 N.E.2d 1165 (2005).

[Section 15:56]

[1]Meyer v. Nebraska, 262 U.S. 390, 43 S. Ct. 625, 67, 67 L. Ed. 1042, 29 A.L.R. 1446 (1923) (due process liberty rights include parents' rights to establish a home, bring up children, and control their children's education); Pierce v. Society of the Sisters of the Holy Names of Jesus and Mary, 268 U.S. 510, 45 S. Ct. 571, 69 L. Ed. 1070, 39 A.L.R. 468 (1925); Prince v. Massachusetts, 321 U.S. 158, 64 S. Ct. 438, 88 L. Ed. 645 (1944); Stanley v. Illinois, 405 U.S. 645, 92 S. Ct. 1208, 31 L. Ed. 2d 551

§ 15:57 Modifying allocation of parental rights—In general

◆ **Note:** See also Text Ch 16, Modification of Parental Rights and Responsibilities.

Once parental rights and responsibilities are allocated, the focus is on stability for the child.[1] Therefore, a court must not modify a prior allocation of parental rights and responsibilities unless it finds a change occurred in the circumstances of the child, the residential parent,[2] or either parent under a shared parenting decree, and that modification is necessary to serve the best interest of the child.[3] The doctrine of res judicata applies to that part of a decree that allocates parental rights and responsibilities. Therefore, the change of circumstances necessary to modify the allocation of parental rights must be based on facts that have arisen since the prior decree or were unknown to the court at the time of such decree.[4] The court cannot reexamine the facts formerly adjudicated and enter a different order as a result.[5]

Even though a change of circumstances is established, the court may not modify a prior allocation of parental rights and responsibilities unless modification is in the best interest of the child[6] and one of the following applies:

(1) The parents agree to the modification;[7]

(2) The child, with consent of the residential parent or both parents under a shared parenting plan, has become integrated into the family of the other parent;[8] or

(3) The harm likely to be caused by a change of environment is outweighed by the advantage of the change of environment to the child.[9]

Until amended effective April 12, 1990, RC 3109.04(B)(1)(c), the

---

(1972) (denial of due process to presume all unmarried fathers are unfit custodians); Wisconsin v. Yoder, 406 U.S. 205, 92 S. Ct. 1526, 32 L. Ed. 2d 15 (1972) (parents have primary role in their children's upbringing); Parham v. J. R., 442 U.S. 584, 99 S. Ct. 2493, 61 L. Ed. 2d 101 (1979); Santosky v. Kramer, 455 U.S. 745, 102 S. Ct. 1388, 71 L. Ed. 2d 599 (1982) (fundamental liberty interest of natural parents in the care, custody, and management of their child).

[Section 15:57]

[1]Whaley v. Whaley, 61 Ohio App. 2d 111, 15 Ohio Op. 3d 136, 399 N.E.2d 1270 (4th Dist. Lawrence County 1978); In re Rex, 3 Ohio App. 3d 198, 444 N.E.2d 482 (3d Dist. Seneca County 1981).

[2]Ross v. Ross, 64 Ohio St. 2d 203, 18 Ohio Op. 3d 414, 414 N.E.2d 426 (1980).

[3]RC 3109.04(E)(1)(a).

[4]RC 3109.04(E)(1)(a).

[5]Fitzpatrick v. Fitzpatrick, 4 Ohio App. 2d 279, 31 Ohio Op. 2d 257, 207 N.E.2d 794 (4th Dist. Lawrence County 1965).

[6]Masitto v. Masitto, 22 Ohio St. 3d 63, 488 N.E.2d 857 (1986).

[7]RC 3109.04(E)(1)(a)(i).

[8]RC 3109.04(E)(1)(a)(ii).

[9]RC 3109.04(E)(1)(a)(iii).

predecessor of RC 3109.04(E)(1)(a)(iii), also required a moving party to establish that the child's present environment endangered significantly the child's physical health, or his mental, moral, or emotional development in order to prevail in a motion to change custody. That requirement was deleted from the statute, and currently RC 3109.04(E)(1)(a)(iii) is much closer to a best interest test.

§ 15:58　Modifying allocation of parental rights—Temporary orders

Civil Rule 75(N) vests the domestic relations court with authority to issue an order for the temporary allocation of parental rights and responsibilities. These orders are interlocutory, and are subject to modification at the final divorce. The trial court need not find a change of circumstance when entering a final divorce decree that modifies the residential parent designated in the temporary order.[1]

§ 15:59　Modifying allocation of parental rights—Immoral conduct as factor

Modification of the allocation of parental rights and responsibilities cannot properly be used as a penalty for past misconduct where the misconduct is not ongoing and was not shown to adversely affect the child.[1] A court's inquiry into the moral conduct of a residential parent is limited to a determination of the effect of such conduct on the child.[2] While a court should not inquire into competing moral value systems, it can recognize that such moral standards do exist, and that children are harmed by being raised in immoral surroundings. With this standard the court looks not at moral systems, but to the interests of the child.[3] Courts will also consider whether the issue is a legal issue as opposed to a moral issue, such as smoking marijuana.[4]

If a parent's conduct violates common moral principles of the community but is not illegal, such as the mother allowing her boyfriend to reside with her and the child, the court must examine the effect of the

---

[Section 15:58]

[1]Schoffner v. Schoffner, 19 Ohio App. 3d 208, 483 N.E.2d 1190 (3d Dist. Auglaize County 1984); Spence v. Spence, 2 Ohio App. 3d 280, 441 N.E.2d 822 (10th Dist. Franklin County 1981).

[Section 15:59]

[1]Wyss v. Wyss, 3 Ohio App. 3d 412, 445 N.E.2d 1153 (10th Dist. Franklin County 1982).

[2]Wyss v. Wyss, 3 Ohio App. 3d 412, 445 N.E.2d 1153 (10th Dist. Franklin County 1982); Whaley v. Whaley, 61 Ohio App. 2d 111, 15 Ohio Op. 3d 136, 399 N.E.2d 1270 (4th Dist. Lawrence County 1978); In re Rex, 3 Ohio App. 3d 198, 444 N.E.2d 482 (3d Dist. Seneca County 1981).

[3]Whaley v. Whaley, 61 Ohio App. 2d 111, 15 Ohio Op. 3d 136, 399 N.E.2d 1270 (4th Dist. Lawrence County 1978).

[4]Stone v. Stone, 9 Ohio App. 3d 6, 457 N.E.2d 919 (12th Dist. Warren County 1983).

parent's conduct on the child, and will not modify the allocation of parental rights and responsibilities unless it is demonstrated that such conduct is having an adverse impact upon the child.[5] However, if the parent's conduct is illegal, such as the use of controlled substances in the presence of the child, it will in and of itself be sufficient to prove that the advantages of the change of environment outweigh the harm likely to be caused to the child by the change.[6]

§ 15:60   Modifying allocation of parental rights—De facto custody

A change of circumstances is generally required to modify a prior allocation of parental rights and responsibilities, but is not required when establishing an original parenting order. However, in certain cases de facto custody will be found to exist and a change of circumstances must be shown, even to enter an original custody order. For example, prior to RC 3109.042,[1] when the mother of an illegitimate child had raised the child from birth for a substantial time without the father living with her or the child, she had de facto sole legal custody which cannot be changed without proof of circumstances that would permit a change of custody granted in accordance with RC 3109.04.[2] RC 3109.042 provides that the mother of a child born out of wedlock is the sole residential parent and legal custodian of the child until a court issues an order designating another person. Both mother and father have equal standing to seek to be named residential parent.

§ 15:61   Modifying allocation of parental rights—Death of a parent

The court's jurisdiction to allocate the parental rights and responsibilities does not abate on the death of the residential parent.[1] When the residential parent dies, the court may award custody as is in the best interest of the child, and need not find that the surviving parent is unsuitable before awarding custody to another person.[2]

§ 15:62   Modifying allocation of parental rights—Other factors

Courts recognize that children need stability and that modification

---

[5]Kraus v. Kraus, 10 Ohio App. 3d 63, 460 N.E.2d 680 (8th Dist. Cuyahoga County 1983).

[6]Ahlstrom v. Ahlstrom, 1986 WL 15162 (Ohio Ct. App. 10th Dist. Franklin County 1986).

[Section 15:60]

[1]As enacted by 1997 H.B. 352, eff. 1-1-98.

[2]In re Yates, 18 Ohio App. 3d 95, 481 N.E.2d 646 (10th Dist. Franklin County 1984).

[Section 15:61]

[1]RC 3109.06.

[2]Gordon v. Gordon, 33 Ohio App. 2d 257, 62 Ohio Op. 2d 375, 294 N.E.2d 239 (3d Dist. Hardin County 1973).

of a prior custody order is likely to harm a child.[1] Therefore, a moving party must prove that the advantages of a change of environment outweigh the harm resulting therefrom. Moving frequently and being secreted from their father was found to cause emotional instability to the children, which warranted a change of custody.[2]

Socialization and educational development are essential to children. Educating the children at home rather than in a public or private school has been found to warrant a change of custody. When the residential parent possesses no qualifications as a teacher, the children lose socialization and normalization development, and the children over identify with the residential parent in her conflict with the non-residential parent due to excessive time spent with the residential parent.[3]

The election of a child to reside with a non-residential parent has also been found to be a change of circumstances.[4] Although children no longer have the right to elect the parent with whom they will reside, the fact that a child wishes to reside with one parent may constitute a change of circumstances, while at the same time establishing that the advantages of a change of environment outweigh the harm likely to be caused to the child by the change, thereby meeting the statutory requirements to allow the court to modify the allocation of parental rights and responsibilities.

The passage of time is not sufficient to find a change of circumstances. However, the passage of time over a significant portion of the child's life, together with other factors, may constitute a change of circumstances.[5]

§ 15:63 Modifying allocation of parental rights—Sanctions for frivolous motions

A party seeking to modify parental rights under RC 3109.04 (where there was no shared parenting), without the agreement of the other parent, must initially demonstrate that a change in circumstances

---

[Section 15:62]

[1]Whaley v. Whaley, 61 Ohio App. 2d 111, 15 Ohio Op. 3d 136, 399 N.E.2d 1270 (4th Dist. Lawrence County 1978).

[2]Ross v. Ross, 64 Ohio St. 2d 203, 18 Ohio Op. 3d 414, 414 N.E.2d 426 (1980).

[3]Gardini v. Moyer, 61 Ohio St. 3d 479, 575 N.E.2d 423, 68 Ed. Law Rep. 801 (1991).

[4]Dailey v. Dailey, 146 Ohio St. 93, 32 Ohio Op. 29, 64 N.E.2d 246 (1945).

[5]Butler v. Butler, 107 Ohio App. 3d 633, 669 N.E.2d 291 (3d Dist. Auglaize County 1995). See also, In re Tolbert v. McDonald, 2006-Ohio-2377, 2006 WL 1312082 (Ohio Ct. App. 3d Dist. Allen County 2006); In re J.C., 2006-Ohio-2893, 2006 WL 1571056 (Ohio Ct. App. 8th Dist. Cuyahoga County 2006).

has occurred.[1] The change of circumstances claimed must be "substantiated, continuing, and [have] a materially adverse effect upon the child."[2]

When a trial court's factual findings, supported by competent, credible evidence, hold that a party's alleged change of circumstances has no merit or substance and the evidence and/or testimony is insufficient to reallocate parental rights, it lies within the sound discretion of the trial court to assess whether or not to issue a penalty against the moving party. In *Bryan v. Bryan*,[3] the court found the movant-father's motion for reallocation of parental rights and responsibilities to be legally groundless[4] on the basis that the record demonstrated that his action was not warranted under existing law and could not be supported by a good-faith argument for an extension, modification or reversal of existing law.

The trial court in *Bryan* went on to find that "no reasonable lawyer would have brought [and maintained] the [motion] in light of the existing law" that required a demonstration of a change in circumstances to prevail.[5] The *Bryan* court further found the existence of frivolous conduct, thereby justifying the trial court's decision to award attorney fees as a sanction for pursuing the frivolous motion. RC 2323.51 allows a court to award court costs, reasonable attorney fees and expenses to any party who has been adversely affected by frivolous conduct.[6]

Refer also to Text § 15:64, Modifying allocation of parental rights—Shared parenting, which distinguishes modifications which are filed jointly between the parties. If a modification is filed jointly, it must be in the best interest of the child.

[Section 15:63]

[1]Bryan v. Bryan, 161 Ohio App. 3d 454, 2005-Ohio-2739, 830 N.E.2d 1216 (1st Dist. Hamilton County 2005); citing Davis v. Flickinger, 77 Ohio St. 3d 415, 1997-Ohio-260, 674 N.E.2d 1159 (1997).

[2]Schaeffer v. Schaeffer, 2004-Ohio-2032, 2004 WL 869359, at ¶ 21 (Ohio Ct. App. 1st Dist. Hamilton County 2004); quoting Wyss v. Wyss, 3 Ohio App. 3d 412, 416, 445 N.E.2d 1153 (10th Dist. Franklin County 1982).

[3]Bryan v. Bryan, 161 Ohio App. 3d 454, 2005-Ohio-2739, 830 N.E.2d 1216 (1st Dist. Hamilton County 2005).

[4]RC 2323.51(A)(2)(a)(ii).

[5]Bryan v. Bryan, 161 Ohio App. 3d 454, 2005-Ohio-2739, 830 N.E.2d 1216 (1st Dist. Hamilton County 2005); citing Riston v. Butler, 149 Ohio App. 3d 390, at ¶ 21, 2002-Ohio-2308, 777 N.E.2d 857 (1st Dist. Hamilton County 2002).

[6]RC 2323.50(B)(1).

§ 15:64 Modifying allocation of parental rights—Shared parenting

One or both parents under a prior decree allocating parental rights and responsibilities may file a motion requesting shared parenting.[1] Modification is subject to RC 3109.04(E)(1)(a), and the court must determine that a change has occurred in the circumstances of the child or the residential parent that make modification in the best interest of the child, and that one of the factors in RC 3109.04(E)(1)(a) has occurred. The court may then proceed to grant shared parenting if a plan is submitted that is in the best interest of the child.[2]

Both parents to a shared parenting decree may jointly modify the plan at any time.[3] The modification must be filed jointly and must be in the best interest of the child. The modification is effective on inclusion in the plan by the court.

While a change in circumstances is required under RC 3109.04 (E)(1)(a) to modify a prior allocation of parental rights, the same is not statutorily required for a reallocation of parental rights where the parents have shared parenting. Under RC 3109.04(E)(2)(b), the court is authorized to modify the terms of a plan for shared parenting not only upon the request of one or both parents, but also on its own motion, when in the best interest of the children. The court may also terminate a shared parenting decree when it determines that shared parenting is not in the best interest of the children.[4] Thus, a movant for modification of shared parenting does not have the burden of proving a change of circumstances.

When joint parenting was first available, the parties would be advised that the court could not modify the terms without other parties' consent. Over the years, and with the enactment of 1994 House Bill 415, the court's power to modify has basically become unlimited, so long as the court finds a change is in the best interest of the child. Therefore, it is doubtful that parties will be able to construct a plan that is iron-clad and not subject to modification. Consequently a party should not forfeit valuable rights, such as property rights, for more favorable parental rights, because the latter may be taken away or modified at a later time, but the property rights cannot be restored.[5]

The court may modify the terms of a shared parenting plan incorporated into a decree on the request of one or both of the parents

---

[Section 15:64]

[1]RC 3109.04(E)(1)(b).

[2]RC 3109.04(D).

[3]RC 3109.04(E)(2)(a).

[4]RC 3109.04 (E)(2)(c); Myers v. Myers, 153 Ohio App. 3d 243, 2003-Ohio-3552, 792 N.E.2d 770 (7th Dist. Columbiana County 2003).

[5]Compare the wording of RC 3109.04(E)(2)(b) to that contained in RC 3105.18(E) (1) and RC 3105.18(E)(2), which permit modification of spousal support if jurisdiction is reserved.

or upon its own motion if the modification is in the best interest of the child.[6] The court may not modify a joint shared parenting plan or joint custody plan entered prior to April 11, 1991, unless both parents agree to the modification.[7]

The court may terminate a joint custody decree entered prior to April 11, 1991, or a shared parenting decree on the request of one or both of the parents or whenever it determines shared parenting is no longer in the child's best interest.[8] The court may terminate a shared parenting decree that incorporated a separate parenting plan on motion of one or both of the parents, or on the court's own motion, if it determines that shared parenting is no longer in the child's best interest. If the parties attempt to modify a plan and the court rejects the modification, it may terminate the plan if the court finds that shared parenting is no longer in the child's best interest.[9]

Upon termination of a shared parenting decree the court must issue a modified decree allocating the parental rights and responsibilities as if no shared parenting decree had been requested or granted.[10] Because the court must issue a modified decree "as if no request for shared parenting ever had been made,"[11] on termination of a shared parenting decree, the court must designate one parent as residential parent.

§ 15:65 Modifying allocation of parental rights—Relief from judgment

Normally, a motion to modify the allocation of parental rights and responsibilities, rather than a motion for relief from judgment pursuant to Civil Rule 60(B), is the method to determine whether a parenting order should continue to apply.[1] However, relief from judgment may apply to the allocation of parental rights and responsibilities in a divorce decree if the order was obtained by fraud or other recognizable circumstance set forth in Civil Rule 60(B)(1) through (5). The relief obtained by the granting of a motion for relief from judgment is

---

[6]RC 3109.04(E)(2)(b).

[7]Stanton v. Stanton, 1990 WL 118090 (Ohio Ct. App. 3d Dist. Seneca County 1990); Stalker v. Stalker, 1990 WL 129231 (Ohio Ct. App. 9th Dist. Summit County 1990); Martin v. Martin, 1991 WL 268806 (Ohio Ct. App. 11th Dist. Geauga County 1991), judgment rev'd, 66 Ohio St. 3d 110, 609 N.E.2d 537 (1993). But see Miller v. Miller, 1990 WL 150127 (Ohio Ct. App. 12th Dist. Clermont County 1990) (court permitted modification absent agreement pursuant to child support guidelines, now codified as RC 3113.215); Martin v. Martin, 66 Ohio St. 3d 110, 609 N.E.2d 537 (1993).

[8]RC 3109.04(E)(2)(d).

[9]RC 3109.04(E)(2)(c).

[10]RC 3109.04(E)(2)(d).

[11]RC 3109.04(E)(2)(d).

[Section 15:65]

[1]Sexton v. Sexton, 60 Ohio App. 2d 339, 14 Ohio Op. 3d 297, 397 N.E.2d 425 (5th Dist. Morrow County 1978).

an order vacating the previous allocation of parental rights and responsibilities, not a change of custody.[2] The parents would then proceed to litigate the allocation of parental rights and responsibilities as if no order had ever been issued.

§ 15:66 Guardian ad litem—Procedure

RC 3109.04(B)(2)(a) and Civil Rule 75(B)(2) control the appointment of a guardian ad litem in domestic relations cases. The requirements for the appointment of a guardian ad litem pursuant to RC 3109.04(B)(2)(a) differ from those set forth in Civil Rule 75(B)(2). The court may appoint a guardian ad litem on its own motion under the statute or Civil Rules.

While RC 3109.04(B)(1) also applies to proceedings for modification of a prior order and it requires the court upon request to interview the involved children and, if requested, appoint a guardian ad litem, the court is not required to do so where it does not first find the necessary change of circumstance.[1]

When determining the best interest of the child for allocation of parental rights and responsibilities, the court, either on its own motion or on request of either party, may interview the child pursuant to the guidelines set forth in RC 3109.04(B). In the event the court does interview the child, the court is required, by virtue of RC 3109.04(B)(2)(a), to appoint a guardian ad litem for the child if either parent so requests or if the court elects to do so.[2] RC 3109.04(B)(2)(a) does not require the court to join the child as a party or find that the appointment of the guardian ad litem is essential to protect the interests of the child.

If a party moves, in writing or orally, for the court to interview a child, of any age, the court must grant the interview. If a parent requests a guardian ad litem be appointed, the appointment must be made.[3]

Civil Rule 75(B)(2) allows the court to join the child as a party and appoint a guardian ad litem and legal counsel, if necessary, to protect

---

[2]Tatom v. Tatom, 19 Ohio App. 3d 198, 482 N.E.2d 1339 (2d Dist. Montgomery County 1984).

[Section 15:66]

[1]Walsh v. Walsh, 2005-Ohio-3264, 2005 WL 1503707 (Ohio Ct. App. 11th Dist. Geauga County 2005).

[2]State ex rel. Papp v. James, 69 Ohio St. 3d 373, 1994-Ohio-86, 632 N.E.2d 889 (1994) (statute plainly requires appointment of guardian ad litem upon the motion of a parent if the court intends to interview privately a child in a custody dispute).

[3]Badgett v. Badgett, 120 Ohio App. 3d 448, 698 N.E.2d 84 (7th Dist. Mahoning County 1997).

the interests of a child. The appointment can be of great help to the court in protecting the child and in determining his best interest.[4]

Prior to an appointment pursuant to Civil Rule 75(B)(2), there must be a determination that it is essential to protect the interests of the child.[5] While the appointment of a guardian ad litem is usually consented to by one or both of the parties, the court should make a finding on the record that, because of certain circumstances of the case, it is essential to protect the interests of the child. Often one or both of the parents are conducting their marital warfare through the child, and are blind to the psychological damage being done to the child. A guardian ad litem should be appointed whenever there is an apparent conflict of interest between the parent or parents and the child. A court may appoint a guardian ad litem during a trial to protect the interests of minor children called to testify as witnesses regarding financial and parental rights issues in a divorce proceeding, where their testimony was in open court and was not limited to their desires regarding the parent with whom they wish to reside.[6] After determining that it is essential to protect the interests of the child by appointing a guardian, the court may join the child as a party.[7]

An indigent child is entitled to appointed counsel in all juvenile proceedings.[8] Even though an attorney appointed as guardian ad litem may also act as counsel and, absent a conflict, a court should not presume a dual appointment,[9] if a guardian ad litem opposes the wishes of the child, the child in fact has no counsel, contrary to his entitlement.

§ 15:67 Guardian ad litem—Conflict of interest

An attorney may function as both legal counsel and guardian ad litem for a child. However, these two roles may conflict on occasion when the recommendation of the guardian differs from the wishes of the child. As a lawyer, the attorney must zealously represent his cli-

---

[4]Gishwiler v. Dodez, 4 Ohio St. 615, 618, 1855 WL 28 (1855) ("The contending parties may be fairly presumed to be more solicitous to gratify their own interests and feelings, than to develop the whole truth, with a view to the main object of the inquiry; while the child, incapable of judging for itself, and wholly unrepresented in the contest, is in danger of being overlooked."); Foster v. Foster, 40 Ohio App. 2d 257, 69 Ohio Op. 2d 250, 319 N.E.2d 395 (10th Dist. Franklin County 1974) (discussion of the appointment, Civil Rule 75(B), and making a child a party); Barth v. Barth, 12 Ohio Misc. 141, 39 Ohio Op. 2d 83, 41 Ohio Op. 2d 166, 225 N.E.2d 866 (C.P. 1967) (discussion of need for a guardian because of a conflict of interest).

[5]Foster v. Foster, 40 Ohio App. 2d 257, 69 Ohio Op. 2d 250, 319 N.E.2d 395 (10th Dist. Franklin County 1974).

[6]Glimcher v. Glimcher, 29 Ohio App. 2d 55, 58 Ohio Op. 2d 37, 278 N.E.2d 37 (10th Dist. Franklin County 1971).

[7]Civ. R. 75(B)(2).

[8]RC 2151.352.

[9]Matter of Duncan/Walker Children, 109 Ohio App. 3d 841, 673 N.E.2d 217 (5th Dist. Stark County 1996); In re Janie M., 131 Ohio App. 3d 637, 723 N.E.2d 191 (6th Dist. Lucas County 1999).

ent, whereas the duty of the guardian ad litem is to assess the child's situation and act in what he feels to be in the child's best interest. When there is a conflict between the role of the guardian ad litem and the role as attorney, the attorney should request leave to withdraw as guardian ad litem and continue to represent the child as his attorney.[1] However, it is also proper to withdraw as attorney and continue to serve as guardian ad litem.[2] When an attorney acts as both guardian ad litem and attorney for the children, he cannot adequately represent the children if he opposes their election.[3]

In a recent ethics opinion issued by The Supreme Court's Board of Commissioners on Grievances and Discipline on June 9, 2006,[4] the Board addressed 7-104(A)(1) and its restraint on communication with represented persons and parties, as it applies to an attorney who is appointed to serve in a dual role as guardian *ad litem* and attorney for a minor child. This opinion strongly sets forth the fact that it is improper for an attorney, appointed to serve in this dual role, to communicate on the subject of the representation with a represented person or party unless there is consent by counsel or authorization by law (such as through a court rule or court order). It further states that communication which is considered administrative in nature, such as scheduling meetings or appointments, is not communication on the subject of representation.

The procedure in a juvenile court proceeding differs only in the fact that the statute authorizing the appointment of a guardian ad litem, RC 2151.281, specifically refers, in paragraph (H), to the situation where the guardian ad litem is also an attorney. The statute requires the court to relieve the person of duties as a guardian ad litem if the attorney so appointed or the court finds that a conflict may exist between the person's roles as guardian ad litem and counsel. A minor is entitled to counsel in all juvenile proceedings, and to appointed counsel if indigent.[5] Generally, although the roles are different, the attorney may act as both guardian and counsel. However, absent an express dual appointment, the court should neither presume a dual appointment, nor that no conflict exists.[6]

[Section 15:67]

[1]In re Baby Girl Baxter, 17 Ohio St. 3d 229, 479 N.E.2d 257 (1985).

[2]Gallimore v. Gallimore, 1989 WL 33112 (Ohio Ct. App. 2d Dist. Miami County 1989).

[3]Bawidamann v. Bawidamann, 63 Ohio App. 3d 691, 580 N.E.2d 15 (2d Dist. Montgomery County 1989).

[4]Opinion 2006-5.

[5]RC 2151.352; Juv. R. 4.

[6]Matter of Duncan/Walker Children, 109 Ohio App. 3d 841, 673 N.E.2d 217 (5th Dist. Stark County 1996); In re Janie M., 131 Ohio App. 3d 637, 723 N.E.2d 191 (6th Dist. Lucas County 1999).

An attorney for the child must be appointed by the court.[7] Where the court has appointed an attorney, a parent or grandparent cannot have a separate attorney for the child.[8]

§ 15:68   Guardian ad litem—Compensation and costs

Civil Rule 75(B)(2) provides that the cost of the guardian and legal counsel may be taxed as costs, but this will not provide actual compensation in the cases that have very minimal or nonexistent assets. Therefore, it would appear that there should be a fund for payment of legal counsel for children in these circumstances, similar to the funds provided to the juvenile court for representation of juveniles. Courts may also require attorneys accepting appointments as guardian ad litem to perform a designated amount of pro bono guardian ad litem services each year.

The amount of work performed by the guardian ad litem is often disproportionate to the compensation. Payment can be made more likely by virtue of Civil Rule 75(B) which permits compensation for the guardian ad litem to be taxed as costs in the action. Guardian ad litem fees incurred in a divorce case where the husband denied he was the father of the child were properly taxed as reasonable fees and other costs of the action to the co-defendant who was found to be the father.[1] The court noted that the guardian ad litem was vital and significant and had no obligation to serve pro bono.

Where an attorney is appointed to serve as both guardian ad litem and legal counsel for a child, the court is not required to allocate the fees between the services rendered in the different roles nor to require the attorney to distinguish between in-court and out-of-court work.[2] Further, the same hourly rate is a reasonable rate for both services when the attorney has extensive experience as a guardian ad litem as well as an attorney.

Federal bankruptcy courts, addressing the construction of "in the nature of alimony, maintenance, or support" provided in 11 U.S.C.A. § 523(a)(5)(B) as applied to the fees of a guardian ad litem have broadened the meaning of "support" to include any services inuring to

---

[7]Juv. R. 4(C).

[8]State ex rel. Kister-Welty v. Hague, 160 Ohio App. 3d 486, 2005-Ohio-1788, 827 N.E.2d 846 (11th Dist. Ashtabula County 2005).

[Section 15:68]

[1]Sutherland v. Sutherland, 61 Ohio App. 3d 154, 572 N.E.2d 215 (10th Dist. Franklin County 1989). Accord Pruden-Wilgus v. Wilgus, 46 Ohio App. 3d 13, 545 N.E.2d 647 (6th Dist. Lucas County 1988) (all guardian ad litem fees were assessed as costs to party who agreed to be responsible for all costs).

[2]Robbins v. Ginese, 93 Ohio App. 3d 370, 638 N.E.2d 627 (8th Dist. Cuyahoga County 1994).

the benefit of the child in a litigation connected with a matrimonial dispute.[3] Such fees have been held to be a nondischargeable debt.

Where the trial court has been involved in a case over a long period of time and has personal experience with the parties and issues, there is no error in not holding an evidentiary hearing on a guardian-ad-litem application for fees.[4]

§ 15:69 Guardian ad litem—Training

Great care must be exercised in the selection and appointment of the guardian. A customary practice is to use volunteer attorneys, who are trained and experienced to some degree in domestic relations and juvenile matters. As a practical matter, economics is involved, in that the guardian ad litem can be expected to perform legal services without additional cost. If the guardian ad litem is also an attorney, he may participate in the hearing and may call witnesses and examine them.

Juvenile Rule 4(B) requires the appointment of a guardian ad litem to protect the interests of the child when (1) the child has no parent, guardian, or legal custodian; (2) the interests of the child and the parent may conflict; (3) the parent is under eighteen years of age or appears to be mentally incompetent; or (4) appointment is necessary to meet the requirements of a fair hearing. Juvenile Rule 4(C) does not require the guardian ad litem be an attorney.

Although selecting an attorney as a guardian may be expedient, it overlooks a great pool of highly competent persons who would be excellent guardians ad litem, except for the fact that they are not lawyers. Civil Rule 75(B) does not limit guardians to attorneys and even states that an attorney can be appointed in addition to the guardian ad litem. Practically, the choice should not be based on legal training but on competence and objectivity. Ohio courts are using programs such as court appointed special advocates (CASA) to assist the appointed guardian ad litem in their appointed duties.

CASAs are lay guardians who assist the attorney guardian ad litem prepare the case and determine what action is in the child's best interest. CASAs continue to have contact with the child following the trial or disposition, to monitor the child's adjustment and ensure juvenile court case plans are implemented.

§ 15:70 Guardian ad litem—Immunity

A guardian ad litem appointed by the court to represent the interests of the children in a divorce proceeding is "shielded by the umbrella of absolute immunity, as it is afforded to members of the ju-

---

[3]In re Peters, 133 B.R. 291 (S.D. N.Y. 1991), aff'd, 964 F.2d 166 (2d Cir. 1992); In re Lever, 174 B.R. 936 (Bankr. N.D. Ohio 1991); In re Laney, 53 B.R. 231 (Bankr. N.D. Tex. 1985).

[4]Beatley v. Beatley, 2003-Ohio-4375, 2003 WL 21962540 (Ohio Ct. App. 5th Dist. Delaware County 2003).

diciary, due to their quasi-judicial function within the system.""[1] This immunity allows a guardian ad litem " 'to function without the worry of possible later harassment and intimidation from dissatisfied parents.' "[2]

§ 15:71   Guardian ad litem—Testimony by guardian ad litem

A question occasionally arises as to the propriety of a guardian ad litem being required to testify as a witness. Since it is the guardian's function to serve the best interests of the child, it may compromise his or her function when testifying is against the guardian ad litem's better judgment.[1]

A guardian ad litem may testify regarding the guardian's opinion, but not regarding privileged communications made by the child. Where a guardian ad litem testifies as a witness, the trial court may refuse to extend an order of separation of witnesses to include the guardian ad litem. Reasoning that the guardian ad litem should be able to prepare a report based upon all the evidence, including the evidence presented at trial, the court in *Nicewicz v. Nicewicz*[2] found no error in not excluding the guardian ad litem, who did testify, from the courtroom proceedings.

The trial court, in its authority to control discovery, may grant a protective order to prevent the deposing of the guardian ad litem.[3] However, in a case where the guardian ad litem also functioned as an investigator and rendered a report, the appellate court found error in the trial court's sustaining a motion to quash the subpoena for the guardian ad litem.[4] Citing the importance of the right of full cross-examination of an adverse witness, the court found the trial court had relied upon the report, and thus, the appellant had a right to cross-examine the guardian ad litem.

In yet another case in which the guardian ad litem had been given broad investigative authority, a local unwritten policy of the court strictly limited the scope of cross-examination of the guardian ad litem to his or her qualifications and methodology, and the appellate court reversed the trial court's custody determination. In *Lawrence v.*

[Section 15:70]

[1]Penn v. McMonagle, 60 Ohio App. 3d 149, 151-52, 573 N.E.2d 1234 (6th Dist. Huron County 1990).

[2]Penn v. McMonagle, 60 Ohio App. 3d 149, 152, 573 N.E.2d 1234 (6th Dist. Huron County 1990), quoting Kurzawa v. Mueller, 732 F.2d 1456 (6th Cir. 1984).

[Section 15:71]

[1]Frost v. Frost, 84 Ohio App. 3d 699, 618 N.E.2d 198 (10th Dist. Franklin County 1992).

[2]Nicewicz v. Nicewicz, 1995 WL 390800 (Ohio Ct. App. 10th Dist. Franklin County 1995).

[3]Nicewicz v. Nicewicz, 1995 WL 390800 (Ohio Ct. App. 10th Dist. Franklin County 1995).

[4]Rife v. Morgan, 1994 WL 472143 (Ohio Ct. App. 2d Dist. Clark County 1994).

Lawrence,[5] the court found that by denying the mother's rights to a meaningful cross-examination of the guardian ad litem, particularly because the entry indicated the reliance of the court on the guardian's report, the trial court had not complied with RC 3109.04(C).

Making a distinction between the appointment of an attorney to act as guardian-ad-litem and one appointed to serve as legal counsel for a minor child, the appellate court in *Hogan v. Hogan*[6] found that the guardian's files were not entitled to any protection from disclosure under the work product doctrine.[7]

§ 15:72 Alternate dispute resolution—Mediation

In an attempt to remove children from the acrimony that surrounds their parents' marital breakup, 1990 Senate Bill 3 provided alternative methods of resolving disputes regarding the children. RC 3109.052(A) authorizes courts to promulgate local rules setting forth procedures for parents to mediate their differences. In determining whether mediation is appropriate, the court must consider whether either parent has pleaded guilty to or been convicted of domestic violence involving a family or household member, or caused physical harm to a family or household member when committing a criminal offense, or was the perpetrator of an abusive act that was the basis of a child being adjudicated abused. If the court so determines, it may order mediation only if it is in the best interest of the parties and the court enters findings of fact to support its determination.[1]

A court ordering mediation may order parents to file a mediation report and pay the cost of mediation, unless either party files a motion requesting the court to waive the mediation costs. For good cause the court may order one parent to pay the entire cost of mediation.[2]

Mediation reports shall be filed jointly by the parents and the mediator, and shall indicate only whether an agreement was reached on any issues, and if so, the content of the agreement. The mediation report shall not contain background information or details of information discussed during mediation.[3] The mediator shall not be made a party, and shall not testify in any proceeding other than a criminal, delinquency, child abuse, neglect, or dependency action brought

---

[5]Lawrence v. Lawrence, 2001-Ohio-2190, 2001 WL 362308 (Ohio Ct. App. 3d Dist. Allen County 2001).

[6]Hogan v. Hogan, 2003-Ohio-4747, 2003 WL 22073132 (Ohio Ct. App. 12th Dist. Butler County 2003).

[7]Civ. R. 26(B)(3).

[Section 15:72]

[1]RC 3109.052(A). See also Text Ch 6, Mediation and Conciliation.

[2]RC 3109.052(A).

[3]RC 3109.052(B).

against a parent, even if both parties consent to the mediator testifying.[4]

Courts establishing mediation procedures must promulgate local rules establishing standards for conducting mediation.[5]

§ 15:73 Alternate dispute resolution—Arbitration

While mediation is favored as an alternative to court imposed resolution of custody disputes, in *Kelm v. Kelm*,[1] the Supreme Court held that matters of child custody and parental visitation are not subject to arbitration.

§ 15:74 Alternate dispute resolution—Conciliation and family counseling

In actions for divorce, legal separation, or annulment, at any time after thirty days from the service of summons or first publication of notice, or at any time after the filing of a dissolution petition, the court may order the parties to undergo conciliation for a period not to exceed ninety days. If children are involved in the proceeding the court may order the parties to take part in family counseling during the course of the proceeding or for such time as the court may direct.[1] The court may name the counselor, and must designate the type and length of counseling, and the manner in which the costs of counseling or conciliation will be paid. If family counseling or conciliation is ordered, no action for divorce, legal separation, or annulment can be heard or decided until the conciliation or family counseling has been concluded.[2]

§ 15:75 Custody in juvenile court proceedings

Juvenile court has jurisdiction concerning any child alleged to be unruly, delinquent, abused, neglected, or dependent;[1] to determine the custody of any child not a ward of another court of this state;[2] to determine the paternity of any child alleged to have been born out of wedlock;[3] and to hear actions for divorce that are certified to it, includ-

---

[4]RC 2317.02(H), RC 3109.052(C).

[5]RC 3109.052(A).

[Section 15:73]

[1]Kelm v. Kelm, 92 Ohio St. 3d 223, 2001-Ohio-168, 749 N.E.2d 299 (2001).

[Section 15:74]

[1]RC 3105.091(A). See also Text Ch 6, Mediation and Conciliation.

[2]RC 3105.091(B).

[Section 15:75]

[1]RC 2151.23(A)(1).

[2]RC 2151.23(A)(2).

[3]RC 2151.23(B)(2).

ing matters of custody.[4] The grants of jurisdiction in RC 2151.23(A)(1) and (2) are independent of each other, and it is not necessary for a juvenile court to find a child to be dependent, neglected, or abused in order to determine custody.[5] The word "custody" as used in RC 2151.23(A)(2) connotes the sum total of all parental rights.[6]

Although courts have historically distinguished dispositions in abuse, neglect, dependency, unruly, and delinquency cases, from custody matters heard in juvenile court,[7] the disposition statutes for abused, neglected, unruly, and delinquent children permit the juvenile court to award "legal custody" of the child to either parent or any other person who files a motion prior to the dispositional hearing.[8] RC 2151.23(F)(1) requires the juvenile court to exercise its jurisdiction in child custody matters in accordance with RC 3109.04, which applies to any proceeding pertaining to the allocation of parental rights and responsibilities for the care of a child, RC 3127.01 to RC 3127.53, and RC 5103.20 to RC 5103.28. RC 3127.01 defines "child custody proceeding" to include "proceedings in which a parenting determination is one of several issues . . . and includes child neglect and dependency proceedings." It would therefore appear that the historical distinctions are no longer valid.

Pursuant to RC 2151.23(A), the juvenile court has jurisdiction to determine the custody of a child alleged to be abused, neglected, or dependent, and when the child is not a ward of another court in this state. The term "ward" does not include children whose custody is granted pursuant to a divorce decree. Hence the phrase "not a ward of another court" in RC 2151.23(A)(2) cannot be construed to prohibit a juvenile court from changing custody of children subject to a divorce decree entered pursuant to RC 3109.04.[9] While a divorce court has continuing jurisdiction to modify the allocation of parental rights and responsibilities,[10] juvenile court has concurrent jurisdiction to determine custody of children properly subject to its jurisdiction, even though there is a divorce decree granting custody of said children. When the juvenile court seeks to exercise its concurrent jurisdiction and change the custody determination entered in a divorce decree, it

---

[4]RC 2151.23(C), (D).

[5]In re Torok, 161 Ohio St. 585, 53 Ohio Op. 433, 120 N.E.2d 307 (1954).

[6]Kolody v. Kolody, 110 Ohio App. 260, 13 Ohio Op. 2d 25, 169 N.E.2d 34 (9th Dist. Summit County 1960); Patton v. Patton, 1 Ohio App. 2d 1, 30 Ohio Op. 2d 49, 203 N.E.2d 662 (5th Dist. Muskingum County 1963).

[7]In re Small, 114 Ohio App. 248, 19 Ohio Op. 2d 128, 181 N.E.2d 503 (2d Dist. Darke County 1960); Kolody v. Kolody, 110 Ohio App. 260, 13 Ohio Op. 2d 25, 169 N.E.2d 34 (9th Dist. Summit County 1960); In re Snider, 14 Ohio App. 3d 353, 471 N.E.2d 516 (3d Dist. Defiance County 1984); In re Custody of Smelser, 22 Ohio Misc. 41, 51 Ohio Op. 2d 31, 51 Ohio Op. 2d 75, 257 N.E.2d 769 (C.P. 1969).

[8]RC 2151.353(A)(3), RC 2151.354(A)(1), RC 2151.355(A)(1).

[9]In re Poling, 64 Ohio St. 3d 211, 1992-Ohio-144, 594 N.E.2d 589 (1992).

[10]Van Divort v. Van Divort, 165 Ohio St. 141, 59 Ohio Op. 207, 134 N.E.2d 715, 62 A.L.R.2d 538 (1956).

must do so in accordance with RC 2151.23(F)(1), RC 3109.04, RC 3127.01 to RC 3127.53, and RC 5103.20 to RC 5103.28. Specifically, the court must apply RC 3109.04(E)(1)(a) and find that a change of custody is in the best interest of the child, a change has occurred in the circumstances of the minor child or his custodian, and that one of the three events enumerated in RC 3109.04(E)(1)(a)(i), (ii), or (iii) has occurred.[11] RC Chapter 2151 does not envision a scenario which permits the non-residential parent to relitigate an adverse custody determination. Therefore, a finding of abuse, neglect, or dependency standing alone may not be sufficient to warrant modification of custody under RC 3109.04. Such a finding must be decided on a case-by-case basis, depending upon the factual pattern before the court.[12]

In *In re Knisley*,[13] a custody and visitation determination arising out of a dependency, the appellate court distinguished between the RC 3109.04 factors the juvenile court is statutorily required to follow in custody proceedings and the lack of any statutory directive in making a custodial disposition of a dependent pursuant to RC 2151.353(A)(3). It further found that there was no definitive test or set of criteria to apply in determining whether to grant visitation rights to a noncustodial parent in custody proceedings incident to a dependency. The court found no statutory mandate that RC 3109.051 be applied, so technical compliance was not required.

In a juvenile court proceeding between a parent and a nonparent for custody of a child, the juvenile court must consider the paramount rights of a parent, and can only award custody to a nonparent upon a finding that the parent is "unsuitable,"[14] or is considered to have abandoned the child.[15]

Resolving a certified conflict as to whether a juvenile court, in a dependency, abuse or neglect proceeding, must make a separate finding of unsuitability of a parent before awarding legal custody to a

---

[11]In re Poling, 64 Ohio St. 3d 211, 1992-Ohio-144, 594 N.E.2d 589 (1992). See Text §§ 16:10 to 16:15, Change of circumstances.

[12]In re Poling, 64 Ohio St. 3d 211, 1992-Ohio-144, 594 N.E.2d 589 (1992).

[13]Matter of Knisley, 1998 WL 372703 (Ohio Ct. App. 4th Dist. Ross County 1998).

[14]In re Perales, 52 Ohio St. 2d 89, 6 Ohio Op. 3d 293, 369 N.E.2d 1047 (1977); Reynolds v. Goll, 80 Ohio App. 3d 494, 609 N.E.2d 1276 (9th Dist. Lorain County 1992); Harlow by Wheeler v. Harlow-Stevens, 1993 WL 172306 (Ohio Ct. App. 12th Dist. Preble County 1993) (appellate court not only reversed trial court award to nonparent, but also granted custody to mother); Matter of Craig S., 1998 WL 336319 (Ohio Ct. App. 6th Dist. Erie County 1998); In re Wilson, 1999 WL 252799 (Ohio Ct. App. 2d Dist. Miami County 1999) (affirmed award of custody to mother over custodial aunt, since no finding of abandonment or unsuitability); see also Text §§ 15:51 to 15:54, Award to third party.

[15]Reynolds v. Goll, 75 Ohio St. 3d 121, 1996-Ohio-153, 661 N.E.2d 1008 (1996); In re Diedra R., 1999 WL 128380 (Ohio Ct. App. 6th Dist. Erie County 1999) (custody to grandparents is in best interest of child considered abandoned).

non-parent, the Supreme Court in *In re C.R.*,[16] determined the trial court is required to make only a best interest of the child finding at the dispositional hearing. The court distinguished between an award of "permanent custody"[17] and "legal custody,"[18] as well as "temporary custody."[19]

Upon juvenile court assuming jurisdiction over a child, the domestic court no longer has jurisdiction, and a prior order from a divorce proceeding naming the father as custodial parent ceases to exist. The father, therefore, will be subject to a child support order when the juvenile court places the child outside of the prior custodial parent's home.[20]

The grant of legal custody to a non-parent does not automatically divest the natural parent of all parental rights, privileges and obligations toward their children. RC 2151.011(B)(19) defines "legal custody" as a legal status that vests in the custodian the right to have physical care and control of the child and to determine where and with whom the child shall live, and the right and duty to protect, train and discipline the child and to provide the child with food, shelter, education and medical care, *all subject to any residual parental rights, privileges and responsibilities*. (Emphasis added.)[21]

§ 15:76 Custody in juvenile court proceedings—Entry certifying to juvenile court—Form ⊚

[Title of Court]

[Caption]   Case No.
                                                                 [_____]
                                                                 <u>JUDGMENT</u>
                                                                 <u>ENTRY</u>

It appearing to the Court that there is now pending before this Court a *[motion/complaint]* filed *[date]*, relating to the allocation of parental rights and responsibilities for the minor *[child/children]* of the parties hereto, and it further appearing to the Court that *[reasons and necessity for certification to Juvenile Court]*, and it further appearing that the *[Juvenile Court has consented to such certification/ Juvenile Court's consent is not required pursuant to RC 3109.04(D)(2)]*;

IT IS, THEREFORE, ORDERED by the Court that the issues of this case dealing with the allocation of parental rights and responsi-

---

[16]In re C.R., 108 Ohio St. 3d 369, 2006-Ohio-1191, 843 N.E.2d 1188 (2006).

[17]RC 2151.011(B)(30).

[18]RC 2151.011(B)(19).

[19]RC 2151.01(B)(52).

[20]In re Hollaender, 2000 WL 783070 (Ohio Ct. App. 12th Dist. Warren County 2000).

[21]In re S.M., 160 Ohio App. 3d 794, 2005-Ohio-2187, 828 N.E.2d 1044 (8th Dist. Cuyahoga County 2005).

bilities for the parties' minor *[child / children]* are hereby certified to the Juvenile Court of *[name of county]* County, pursuant to RC 3109.04(D)(2), for appropriate action and disposition.

_____

Judge

Approved:

_____

Attorney for Plaintiff

_____

Attorney for Defendant

NOTES TO FORM

Drafter's Notes

This form can usually be obtained from the court.

§ 15:77   Statutory notices for parents—Form⊚

The following Notices are hereby incorporated into the *[shared parenting / separation agreement / judgment decree of divorce]* by agreement of the parties, and made an ORDER of the Court:

All child support and spousal support ordered by this decree shall be withheld or deducted from the wages or assets of the obligor under the order in accordance with RC 3113.21 and shall be forwarded to the obligee under the decree in accordance with RC 3113.21 to RC 3113.214.

I.   RELOCATION NOTICE: Pursuant to RC 3109.051(G), the parties hereto are hereby notified as follows:

If the "residential parent," namely *[name of residential parent]*, intends to move to a residence other than the residence specified in the parties' separation agreement, said "residential parent" shall file a notice of intent to relocate with this court. Except as provided in RC 3109.051(G)(2), (3), and (4), a copy of such notice shall be mailed by the court to *[name of non-residential parent]*. On receipt of the notice, the court, on its own motion or the motion of *[name of non-residential parent]*, may schedule a hearing with notice to both parties to determine whether it is in the best interest of the child or children to revise the visitation or parenting schedule for the child or children.

II.   RECORDS ACCESS NOTICE: Pursuant to RC 3109.051(H) and RC 3319.321(B)(5)(a), the parties hereto are hereby notified as follows:

Excepting as specifically modified or otherwise limited by the parties' separation agreement, and subject to RC 2301.35(G)(2) and RC

3319.321(F), the "non-residential" parent, namely *[name of non-residential parent]*, is entitled to access, under the same terms and conditions as the "residential parent," namely *[name of residential parent]*, to any record that is related to the *[child/children]* and to which said residential parent of the child legally is provided access, including school records. Any keeper of a record, public or private, who knowingly fails to comply with this order, is in contempt of court.

III.   DAY CARE CENTER ACCESS NOTICE: Pursuant to RC 3109.051(I), the parties hereto are hereby notified as follows:

Excepting as specifically modified or otherwise limited by court order, and in accordance with RC 5104.011, *[name of non-residential parent]*, the parent who is not the residential parent, is entitled to access to any day care center that is or will be attended by the child or children with whom visitation is granted, to the same extent that *[name of residential parent]*, the residential parent, is granted access to the center.

IV.   SCHOOL ACTIVITIES NOTICE: Pursuant to RC 3109.051(J), the parties hereto are hereby notified as follows:

Excepting as specifically modified or otherwise limited by the parties' separation agreement, and subject to RC 3319.321, the "non-residential" parent, namely *[name of non-residential parent]*, is entitled to access, under the same terms and conditions as the "residential parent," namely *[name of residential parent]*, to any student activity that is related to the child or children and to which the "residential parent" of the child legally is provided access.

Chapter 16

Modification of Parental Rights and Responsibilities[*]

By Sharon A. Skirbunt, Esq.

KeyCite®: Cases and other legal materials listed in KeyCite Scope can be researched through the KeyCite service on Westlaw®. Use KeyCite to check citations for form, parallel references, prior and later history, and comprehensive citator information, including citations to other decisions and secondary materials.

---

[*]Updated for the Fourth Edition by Laurel G. Stein, Esq.

§ 16:1   Jurisdiction

RC 3109.04 provides that in any divorce, legal separation, or annulment proceeding, and in any proceeding pertaining to the allocation of parental rights and responsibilities, upon hearing testimony and on the consideration of any mediation report filed pursuant to the applicable statutory requirements,[1] the court shall allocate the parental rights and responsibilities for the care of the minor children[2] in one of two ways: (1) primarily to one parent, who will be designated the residential parent and legal custodian of the children, and divide between the parents the other parental rights and responsibilities, including but not limited to support and frequent and continuing contact between the children and the non-residential parent;[3] or, (2) to both parents, and issue a shared parenting order requiring the parents to share some or all of the aspects of physical and legal custody of the children pursuant to a shared parenting plan.[4]

Modification of parental rights and responsibilities refers to the modification of prior decrees allocating parental rights and responsibilities and to the modification of sole custody and joint custody decrees issued prior to the amendments to RC Chapter 3109 enacted by 1990 Senate Bill 3.[5]

Following the journalization of an initial decree providing for the custody of a minor child or for the allocation of parental rights and responsibilities, the court retains jurisdiction to modify the prior decree. The original determination, however, creates a presumption in favor of retaining the current custodian or residential parent, or the current joint custodians or residential parents pursuant to a shared parenting decree.[6]

Civil Rule 75(J) expressly provides for the continuing jurisdiction of the court in divorce, annulment, and legal separation actions. RC 3109.04(B), the court's statutory authority for modification of prior custody decrees, and prior decrees allocating parental rights and responsibilities, implicitly confers jurisdiction on the court that made the prior decree to hear and determine motions to modify that decree. Further, Civil Rule 75(H) provides for the jurisdiction of the trial court to modify, in the best interest of the minor children, a prior or-

---

[Section 16:1]

[1]RC 3109.052; RC 3127.01 to 3127.53; RC 3109.36.

[2]RC 3109.01.

[3]RC 3109.04(A)(1); RC 3109.04(A)(1); RC 3109.04 (does not provide for a "physical custodian" and a trial court errs as a matter of law by awarding "physical custody" of a child to a parent without statutory authority); In Matter of Sadr Ghadar Ghadr, 1997 WL 133299 (Ohio Ct. App. 4th Dist. Hocking County 1997).

[4]RC 3109.04(A)(2).

[5]1990 S.B. 3, eff 4-11-91.

[6]Able v. Able, 1999 WL 234685 (Ohio Ct. App. 2d Dist. Montgomery County 1999); Able v. Able, 1999 WL 234685 (Ohio Ct. App. 2d Dist. Montgomery County 1999); RC 3109.04(E)(1)(a); See Text § 16:10, Change of circumstances—In general.

der allocating parental rights and responsibilities for the period of the pendency of an appeal. Civil Rule 75(H) specifically provides that Civil Rule 62(B)[7] does *not* apply to orders allocating parental rights and responsibilities for the care of children. Thus, a party appealing an order of the trial court modifying the allocation of parental rights and responsibilities may not obtain a stay of execution of the judgment granting the modification.

Ohio case law provides additional authority for a court's continuing jurisdiction to modify decrees allocating parental rights and responsibilities. In *Loetz v. Loetz*,[8] the Ohio Supreme Court held that a court in which a decree of divorce is originally rendered retains continuing jurisdiction over matters relating to the custody, care, and support of the minor children of the parties.[9]

When either one or both parties have become residents of another state, Civil Rule 75(J) does not create exclusive jurisdiction in Ohio over a modification proceeding, as it does not undermine the Uniform Child Custody Jurisdiction and Enforcement Act (UCCJEA) in situations wherein a jurisdictional conflict exists.[10]

The factors to be considered by the court and the evidence admissible in the modification proceeding depend on the nature of the prior decree allocating parental rights and responsibilities; that is, whether (1) one of the parties had sole custody of the minor children or was

---

[7]Rule 62(B) Stay upon appeal. When an appeal is taken, the appellant may obtain a stay of execution of a judgment or any proceeding to enforce a judgment by giving an adequate supersedeas bond. The bond may be given at or after the time of filing the notice of appeal. The stay is effective when the supersedeas bond is approved by the court.

[8]Loetz v. Loetz, 63 Ohio St. 2d 1, 17 Ohio Op. 3d 1, 406 N.E.2d 1093 (1980).

[9]Braatz v. Braatz, 85 Ohio St. 3d 40, 1999-Ohio-203, 706 N.E.2d 1218 (1999). See also Blum v. Blum, 9 Ohio St. 2d 92, 38 Ohio Op. 2d 224, 223 N.E.2d 819 (1967) (court has continuing jurisdiction for purpose of modification of any order or decree relating to support or custody); Bastian v. Bastian, 13 Ohio Op. 2d 267, 81 Ohio L. Abs. 408, 160 N.E.2d 133, 73 A.L.R.2d 1440 (Ct. App. 8th Dist. Cuyahoga County 1959) (court decree); Van Divort v. Van Divort, 165 Ohio St. 141, 59 Ohio Op. 207, 134 N.E.2d 715, 62 A.L.R.2d 538 (1956) (court has continuing jurisdiction over matters relating to custody, care, and support); Selby v. Selby, 69 Ohio L. Abs. 257, 124 N.E.2d 772 (Ct. App. 9th Dist. Summit County 1952) (original court has continuing jurisdiction); Trickey v. Trickey, 158 Ohio St. 9, 47 Ohio Op. 481, 106 N.E.2d 772 (1952) (court has continuing jurisdiction respecting custody); Arnold v. Arnold, 67 Ohio App. 282, 21 Ohio Op. 258, 34 Ohio L. Abs. 92, 36 N.E.2d 430 (2d Dist. Franklin County 1941) (court has continuing jurisdiction because child is ward of court, despite original decree based on agreement of parties); Baxter v. Baxter, 27 Ohio St. 2d 168, 56 Ohio Op. 2d 104, 271 N.E.2d 873 (1971) (appellate court does not have continuing jurisdiction after reversing trial court's decision, trial court retains jurisdiction to modify order at later date). But compare Hall v. Hall, 101 Ohio App. 237, 1 Ohio Op. 2d 177, 139 N.E.2d 60, 71 A.L.R.2d 1366 (4th Dist. Scioto County 1956) (where there is no disposition of custody issue in divorce decree, court granting divorce has no continuing jurisdiction with respect to custody).

[10]See Mayor v. Mayor, 71 Ohio App. 3d 789, 595 N.E.2d 436 (8th Dist. Cuyahoga County 1991); Smith v. Schroeder, 1997 WL 775823 (Ohio Ct. App. 6th Dist. Lucas County 1997) (trial court did not err in declining to exercise jurisdiction under UCCJEA or by failing to hold a full hearing on the question of jurisdiction).

designated the residential parent and legal custodian; (2) the parties had joint custody; (3) the parties were awarded shared parenting pursuant to a separately filed shared parenting plan; or (4) the parties were awarded shared parenting pursuant to a jointly filed shared parenting plan.

§ 16:2   Invoking court's continuing jurisdiction

The court making the original allocation of parental rights and responsibilities has continuing jurisdiction with respect to modification; however, the court's exercise of such jurisdiction is not automatic. The proponent of the modification must properly invoke the continuing jurisdiction of the court pursuant to Civil Rule 75(J), which states, "The continuing jurisdiction of the court shall be invoked by motion filed in the original action, notice of which shall be served in the manner provided for the service of process under Civil Rule 4 through Civil Rule 4.6."[1] Thus, to properly invoke the continuing jurisdiction of the court, the motion, with a full caption, must be served on the opposing *party* through the Clerk of Courts, not upon his or her previous counsel of record.[2] Furthermore, compliance with RC 3127.23, which requires every party in a parenting proceeding to file a parenting proceeding affidavit, or to present in his or her first pleading the information requested in a parenting proceeding affidavit, including whether the party has previously been convicted of or pleaded guilty to any criminal offense involving any act that resulted in a child's being abused or neglected or has previously been determined to be the perpetrator of an abusive or neglectful act that was the basis for an adjudication of a child's being abused or neglected, is a jurisdictional requirement in any action for the allocation of parental rights and responsibilities, and is necessary to properly invoke the continuing jurisdiction of the court in a modification proceeding.[3]

[Section 16:2]

[1]See Awadallah v. Awadallah, 1985 WL 9761 (Ohio Ct. App. 8th Dist. Cuyahoga County 1985) (judge did not give parties notice that he was assuming jurisdiction over custody which had already been determined by another judge; therefore, modification of custody was not properly before court since continuing jurisdiction of court had not been invoked pursuant to Civ. R. 75(J), rendering court lacking in jurisdiction on custody matter; Smith v. Smith, 1981 WL 5635 (Ohio Ct. App. 6th Dist. Lucas County 1981) (court lacks jurisdiction to modify custody where continuing jurisdiction of court has not been properly invoked pursuant to Civ. R. 75(J)); Rauth v. Rauth, 73 Ohio App. 564, 29 Ohio Op. 190, 57 N.E.2d 266 (3d Dist. Defiance County 1943) (as condition to court's jurisdiction to modify, continuing jurisdiction must be invoked by motion).

[2]See Davis v. Davis, 1992 WL 47299 (Ohio Ct. App. 8th Dist. Cuyahoga County 1992).

[3]See Awadallah v. Awadallah, 1985 WL 9761 (Ohio Ct. App. 8th Dist. Cuyahoga County 1985). See also Pasqualone v. Pasqualone, 63 Ohio St. 2d 96, 17 Ohio Op. 3d 58, 406 N.E.2d 1121 (1980). But see Mannon v. Mannon, 1984 WL 5692 (Ohio Ct. App. 4th Dist. Lawrence County 1984) (substantial compliance with RC 3127.23 is

§ 16:3   1990 Senate Bill 3—In general

1990 Senate Bill 3 was one of the most significant acts in the history of Ohio domestic relations law. Senate Bill 3 amended most of the former Ohio statutes addressing custody, visitation, and child support. Some of the amendments to former Ohio domestic relations law impact on the modification of prior decrees, as well as original decrees allocating parental rights and responsibilities.

When making the allocation of parental rights and responsibilities in either an original proceeding or a modification proceeding, the court must take into account the best interest of the child.[1] In determining the child's best interest for purposes of making an allocation of parental rights and responsibilities or for purposes of resolving any issues related to the allocation, the court, in its discretion may and, upon the request of either party, must interview any or all of the involved children regarding their wishes and concerns with respect to the allocation.[2]

§ 16:4   Election abolished

Prior to 1990 Senate Bill 3, children of eleven years of age were given the opportunity to state a preference as to which of their parents should be their custodian. Children twelve years of age or older could make an election as to which parent should be the custodial parent. A child's election could be defeated only if the court determined that the child's choice was not in his or her best interest. 1990 Senate Bill 3 abolished the concept of election.[1]

§ 16:5   Ascertaining the wishes and concerns of the child

Although a child over twelve years of age no longer has a specific right to choose the residential parent, the court now has the authority to ascertain the wishes and concerns of a child, regardless of age, as to the allocation of parental rights and responsibilities. RC 3109.04(B) sets forth the procedure the court must follow to consider a child's wishes and concerns as a factor in determining the child's best interest.

RC 3109.04(B)(1) gives the court discretion to interview a child in

---

sufficient to invoke continuing subject matter jurisdiction of court); May v. May, 1992 WL 2938 (Ohio Ct. App. 9th Dist. Medina County 1992).

[Section 16:3]

[1]RC 3109.04(B)(1).

[2]RC 3109.04(B)(1); Schottenstein v. Schottenstein, 2000 WL 1808327 (Ohio Ct. App. 10th Dist. Franklin County 2000) (Trial court erred by failing to interview the parties' three minor children when deciding issues of contempt for interference with companionship rights. RC 3109.04(B)(1) requires the court to do so when requested by either party.), appeal dismissed by 91 Ohio St.3d 1484, 744 N.E.2d 1196 (2001).

[Section 16:4]

[1]RC 3109.04(B).

chambers upon its own motion, and requires the court to interview the child if so requested by either party. A court does not have the authority to deny a party's motion to interview a child.[1] The court is not required to consider the wishes and concerns expressed by the child unless, after complying with the statutory procedure, the court finds it is in the child's best interest to do so.

If the court intends to interview any child in a proceeding for the allocation or modification of parental rights and responsibilities, the court may, in its discretion, and must, on the motion of either party, appoint a guardian ad litem for the child.[2] The interview must be conducted in chambers, and no person other than the child, the child's attorney, the judge, any necessary court personnel, and, in the judge's discretion, the attorney for each parent, may be present during the interview of the child.[3]

Before ascertaining the child's wishes and concerns, the court must determine whether the child has sufficient reasoning ability to express his or her wishes and concerns with respect to the allocation of parental rights and responsibilities.[4] If the court determines that the child does not have sufficient reasoning ability to express his or her

---

[Section 16:5]

[1]Leasure v. Leasure, 1998 WL 108137 (Ohio Ct. App. 8th Dist. Cuyahoga County 1998); Scassa v. Scassa, 1998 WL 404209 (Ohio Ct. App. 7th Dist. Carroll County 1998); Badgett v. Badgett, 120 Ohio App. 3d 448, 698 N.E.2d 84 (7th Dist. Mahoning County 1997); Schottenstein v. Schottenstein, 2000 WL 1808327 (Ohio Ct. App. 10th Dist. Franklin County 2000); Church v. Church, 2004-Ohio-6215, 2004 WL 2659250 (Ohio Ct. App. 7th Dist. Noble County 2004) (trial court's failure to conduct in camera interview with children, after father has requested such interview, was reversible error); Jackson v. Herron, 2005-Ohio-4046, 2005 WL 1861965 (Ohio Ct. App. 11th Dist. Lake County 2005) (mother's due process rights were not violated by the trial court conducting in camera interviews of the minor children and relying upon the information obtained in the interviews in formulating a decision).

[2]RC 3109.04(B)(2)(a). See Hunter v. Hunter, 1992 WL 193688 (Ohio Ct. App. 12th Dist. Madison County 1992) (court not required under RC 3109.04(B)(2)(a) to appoint guardian ad litem where neither parent filed motion requesting appointment), appeal dismissed by 65 Ohio St.3d 1489, 605 N.E.2d 390 (1993). See also Posey v. Posey, 2008-Ohio-536, 2008 WL 352462 (Ohio Ct. App. 4th Dist. Ross County 2008). The trial court denied a change of residential parent status even though the fourteen year old child expressed his desire to go and live with his father. The child had a guardian ad litem, but not separate counsel. The appellate court held that the trial court did not err by failing to appoint separate counsel for the fourteen year old because the child was not added as a party to the action.

[3]RC 3109.04(B)(2)(a), RC 3109.04(B)(2)(c); Willis v. Willis, 149 Ohio App. 3d 50, 2002-Ohio-3716, 775 N.E.2d 878 (12th Dist. Butler County 2002) (in-camera interviews of children, conducted under statute governing visitation rights, are confidential and not to be disclosed to parties); RC 3109.051.

[4]RC 3109.04(B)(2)(b); RC 3109.04(B)(2)(b); Davis v. Davis, 2000-Ohio-2584, 2000 WL 1617776 (Ohio Ct. App. 7th Dist. Jefferson County 2000) (since the trial court found that the child was a "very bright and articulate child with sufficient recall and reasoning that her preferences should be a consideration," the appellate court found that it was proper for the trial court to consider the child's wishes and concerns when determining her best interests); Dicke v. Dicke, 1995 WL 657112 (Ohio Ct. App. 3d Dist. Allen County 1995) (trial court was within its discretion in finding 8-year-old

wishes and concerns, the court may not proceed to determine the child's wishes and concerns in this regard.[5]

If the court finds that the child has sufficient reasoning ability to express his or her wishes and concerns, the court must then determine whether any special circumstances exist that would render it not in the best interest of the child to determine the child's wishes and concerns with respect to the allocation of parental rights and responsibilities.[6] If the court determines, because of the existence of special circumstances, that it would not be in the best interest of the child to determine the child's wishes and concerns, the court must not make a determination, and it must enter its written findings of fact and opinion in the court's journal.[7]

In *Lynch v. Lynch*,[8] the trial court did not abuse its discretion by determining that the minor child's preference to live with his mother, as indicated during an in-camera interview, was to be accorded little weight in determining that a change in custody from a shared parenting scheme to father as residential parent was in the child's best interest. Although the child expressed a preference to live with his mother, he also expressed a wish to reside with his father and the court considered the fact that at least one parent engaged in a discussion with the child about the in-camera interview.

If the court finds that a child has sufficient reasoning ability, and that it would be in the child's best interest to make a determination as to his or her wishes and concerns, the court must then proceed to

---

child lacked sufficient reasoning ability to make an informed choice of residential parent); Riley v. Riley, 2004-Ohio-5302, 2004 WL 2803229 (Ohio Ct. App. 11th Dist. Portage County 2004) (trial court was required to make independent evaluation as to reasoning ability of child and wishes of child); Andrachik v. Ripepi, 2005-Ohio-6746, 2005 WL 3481486 (Ohio Ct. App. 9th Dist. Summit County 2005) (overruled by, Gunderman v. Gunderman, 2009-Ohio-3787, 2009 WL 2356811 (Ohio Ct. App. 9th Dist. Medina County 2009)) (the trial court concluded that since the time of the parties' divorce, the children were older and able to articulate their preference to remain with their mother in her school community and continue in their extracurricular activities).

[5]RC 3109.04(B)(2)(b); Beatley v. Block, 2000 WL 492127 (Ohio Ct. App. 5th Dist. Delaware County 2000) (Trial court did not err in denying motion to modify when filed six months after the original decree. The trial court had determined, at the time of trial, that the children did not have sufficient reasoning ability to express their wishes and concerns regarding custody.); Quint v. Lomakoski, 167 Ohio App. 3d 124, 2006-Ohio-3041, 854 N.E.2d 225 (2d Dist. Greene County 2006) (trial court interviewed the minor child as part of the modification proceeding, but determined that the child did not have sufficient reasoning ability and his testimony would not have any probative value).

[6]RC 3109.04(B)(2)(b); Dicke v. Dicke, 1995 WL 657112 (Ohio Ct. App. 3d Dist. Allen County 1995) (trial court was within its discretion in finding 8-year-old child lacked sufficient reasoning ability to make an informed choice of residential parent).

[7]RC 3109.04(B)(2)(b).

[8]Lynch v. Lynch, 2003-Ohio-1039, 2003 WL 876566 (Ohio Ct. App. 6th Dist. Huron County 2003).

do so.[9] However, even though a child is able to express his or her wishes, the trial court may disbelieve a child's stated desire to change custody and find it is not in the child's best interest to modify a prior custody decree.[10] Moreover, the trial court is cautioned not to place undue emphasis when considering a child's express wishes. Trial court did not err in rejecting and reversing a Magistrate's decision which denied father's request for modification of custody. The Magistrate did not consider all the relevant factors of RC 3109.04(F)(1). The trial court considered all such factors, including mother's convictions for a drug offense and driving under the influence. The child, who had a learning disability, had failing grades, and was excessively absent and tardy to school. The trial court also believed that the Magistrate put too much emphasis on the child's wishes.[11]

A review of the case law shows that Ohio appellate courts are split on the issue of whether a domestic relations court should be required to provide parents with the transcripts of their child's in-camera interview.[12]

Noting that RC 3109.04 does not specifically state whether the parents of a child have a right to obtain a copy of the transcript of an in-camera discussion between the judge and the child, the Ninth District Court of Appeals, in *In re Longwell*,[13] affirmed the trial court's order sealing the transcript. The court held there is no right of access, stating its belief that "judges should be allowed to keep their private conversations with the children of divorced parents confidential."[14]

---

[9]RC 3109.04(B)(2)(b). See, e.g., Zygela v. Euler, 1997 WL 770972 (Ohio Ct. App. 6th Dist. Lucas County 1997).

[10]Clutter v. Reidy, 1996 WL 342194 (Ohio Ct. App. 7th Dist. Jefferson County 1996). See also Dowell v. Dowell, 2007-Ohio-6026, 2007 WL 3342901 (Ohio Ct. App. 6th Dist. Erie County 2007). A child's wishes to reside with the other parent and his maturity since the prior order were a change of circumstances, but did not outweigh the child's best interests for the custody agreement to remain the same.

[11]Foltz v. Foltz, 1999 WL 211693 (Ohio Ct. App. 12th Dist. Warren County 1999); Ebinger v. Ebinger, 2004-Ohio-4784, 2004 WL 2003948 (Ohio Ct. App. 12th Dist. Warren County 2004) (fact that trial court listed other factors that it considered, in addition to 11 year old child's wishes, did not translate to a failure to give child's expressed wishes appropriate weight).

[12]Willis v. Willis, 149 Ohio App. 3d 50, 2002-Ohio-3716, 775 N.E.2d 878 (12th Dist. Butler County 2002); Inscoe v. Inscoe, 121 Ohio App. 3d 396, 700 N.E.2d 70 (4th Dist. Meigs County 1997). By contrast, the Fifth and Ninth Appellate Districts have held otherwise: Patton v. Patton, 1995 WL 42497 (Ohio Ct. App. 5th Dist. Licking County 1995); In Matter of Longwell, 1995 WL 520058, at *4 Ohio Ct. App. 9th Dist. Lorain County 1995); Chapman v. Chapman, 2007-Ohio-2968, 2007 WL 1721462 (Ohio Ct. App. 2d Dist. Montgomery County 2007) (the trial court did not err in sealing the transcript of the minor child's in-camera interview).

[13]In Matter of Longwell, 1995 WL 520058 (Ohio Ct. App. 9th Dist. Lorain County 1995).

[14]In Matter of Longwell, 1995 WL 520058 (Ohio Ct. App. 9th Dist. Lorain County 1995).

§ 16:6 Written or recorded statements from child

RC 3109.04(B)(3) specifically prohibits any person from obtaining or attempting to obtain from a child a written or recorded statement or affidavit setting forth the child's wishes and concerns regarding the allocation of parental rights and responsibilities. This section of the Revised Code further prohibits any court, in its determination of the child's best interest for the purposes of resolving any issues related to an allocation of parental rights and responsibilities, from accepting or considering any recorded statement or affidavit that purports to set forth a child's wishes and concerns in this regard.[1]

§ 16:7 Investigations and examinations

To aid the court in determining the allocation of parental rights and responsibilities, whether in an original proceeding or a modification proceeding, the court has authority to cause an investigation to be made as to the character, family relations, past conduct, and financial worth of each parent and may order each parent and the children to submit to medical, psychological, and psychiatric examination.[1] The reports resulting from the investigations and examinations must be made available to either parent's counsel of record not less than five days prior to the trial or hearing, upon written request.[2] The reports must be signed, and the investigators and examiners are subject to cross-examination by either parent regarding the contents of the reports.[3] With respect to the expense of each investigation or examination, the court may tax as costs all or part of such expenses.[4]

[Section 16:6]

[1]RC 3109.04(B)(3); RC 3109.04(B)(3); State ex rel. Papp v. James, 69 Ohio St. 3d 373, 1994-Ohio-86, 632 N.E.2d 889 (1994) (Statute prohibiting use in custody and visitation proceedings of statements and affidavits purporting to set forth a child's preference concerning allocation of parental rights and responsibilities also applied in mandamus proceeding which arose out of custody proceeding; harm to child from demand that he choose between his parents is valid concern in any proceeding).

[Section 16:7]

[1]RC 3109.04(C); RC 3109.04(C); Smith v. Smith, 1997 WL 467554 (Ohio Ct. App. 7th Dist. Belmont County 1997). In Citta-Pietrolungo v. Pietrolungo, 2003-Ohio-3357, 2003 WL 21469770 (Ohio Ct. App. 8th Dist. Cuyahoga County 2003), the guardian ad litem's request to the trial court for a forensic evaluation regarding a modification of custody and visitation was proper and based on a showing of good cause, since neither former husband or former wife responded to guardian's request for school and adjustment records. There was also an issue regarding the children's numerous absences from school.

[2]RC 3109.04(C). See Cichanowicz v. Cichanowicz, 2008-Ohio-4779, 2008 WL 4292724 (Ohio Ct. App. 3d Dist. Crawford County 2008). A trial court is not bound by the Guardian ad Litem's or custody evaluator's recommendation.

[3]RC 3109.04(C).

[4]RC 3109.04(C).

§ 16:8 Previous child neglect or child abuse

In a modification proceeding, if the court determines that a parent has been convicted of or has pleaded guilty to any criminal offense involving an act resulting in child neglect, that any parent has been determined to be the perpetrator of the neglectful act that is the basis of an adjudication that a child is a neglected child, or in the event that there is reason to believe that either parent has acted in a manner resulting in a child's being neglected, the court must consider that fact against naming that parent as the residential parent, and against granting a shared parenting decree.[1]

The court must also consider whether either parent has been convicted of or pleaded guilty to a violation of RC 2919.25 involving a victim who, at the time of the offense, was a family member or household member and whether either parent has been convicted of or pleaded guilty to any other offense involving a victim who, at the time of the offense was a family or household member, and caused physical harm to the victim in the commission of the offense, and whether either parent has been determined to be the perpetrator of an abusive act that is the basis of an adjudication that a child is an abused child.[2]

If the court determines the existence of any of the foregoing in the course of making a determination as to the allocation of parental rights and responsibilities, the court may designate that parent as the residential parent and may issue a shared parenting decree or order only if it determines that it is in the best interest of the child, and it makes specific written findings of fact to support its determination.[3] This requirement does not, however, apply to temporary custody orders entered under Civ. R. 53 and Civ. R. 75(N).[4] In a 5-2 per curiam decision, with a dissenting opinion, the Ohio Supreme Court held that because a temporary order is, by its very nature, not a final order and is always subject to modification, the language of RC 3109.04(C) does not apply to such orders.[5]

If the court determines that it would be in the best interest of the minor child for neither parent to be designated the residential parent and legal custodian of the child, the court may commit the child to a relative, or certify a copy of its findings, with as much of the record and further information as it considers necessary, or as the juvenile court requests, to the juvenile court for further proceedings, and, upon

---

[Section 16:8]

[1]RC 3109.04(C).

[2]RC 3109.04(C).

[3]RC 3109.04(C).

[4]Now Civ. R. 75(N).

[5]State ex rel. Thompson v. Spon, 83 Ohio St. 3d 551, 1998-Ohio-298, 700 N.E.2d 1281 (1998).

certification, the juvenile court obtains exclusive jurisdiction over the matter.[6]

§ 16:9 Mediation

In any proceeding involving the allocation of parental rights and responsibilities for the care of a child, if the parents are unable to agree on an appropriate allocation of parental rights and responsibilities, or if they are unable to agree on a specific schedule of visitation, the court may order the parents to mediate their differences pursuant to mediation procedures adopted by the court by local rule.[1] If the court orders the parties to engage in mediation, the court may also order the parties to file a mediation report within a specified period of time and may further order the parties to pay the cost of the mediation, unless either or both of the parties file a motion requesting that the court waive the requirement.[2]

If the mediation order requires the parties to file a mediation report, the mediator and each party must jointly file a report of the results of the mediation process. The report must indicate only whether an agreement has been reached with respect to any of the issues to have been mediated and, if so, the content and details of the agreement.[3] The mediation report must not contain any background information concerning the mediation process or any information that was discussed or presented during the mediation process.[4]

The court must consider the mediation report in its determination as to the allocation of parental rights and responsibilities and as to the establishment of a specific visitation schedule. However, the court is not bound by the mediation report, as the best interest of the child is of paramount importance.[5]

RC 3109.052(C) prohibits the mediator who is undertaking the mediation, pursuant to a mediation order, from being a party and from being called as a witness or to testify in any action or proceeding, other than a criminal, delinquency, child abuse, child neglect, or dependent child action or proceeding, that is brought by or against either parent and that pertains to the mediation process, to any information discussed or presented in the mediation process as to the allocation of parental rights and responsibilities, or to the awarding of visitation rights in relation to the parties' children. Even if both parents give their prior consent to the mediator's being made a party

---

[6]RC 3109.04(D)(2).

[Section 16:9]
[1]RC 3109.052(A).
[2]RC 3109.052(A).
[3]RC 3109.052(B).
[4]RC 3109.052(B).
[5]RC 3109.052(B).

or being called as a witness to testify, the mediator is prohibited from participating in this regard.[6]

A developing issue in the area of modifications of parental rights and responsibilities is the inclusion of mediation clauses in divorce decrees and shared parenting plans. Mediation clauses mandate that the parties shall attempt to resolve through mediation any dispute which may arise regarding the minor children. It still remains to be seen whether courts will entertain post-decree motions to modify the allocation of parental rights and responsibilities or shared parenting if mediation is not first attempted by the parties. In *Spickler v. Spickler*,[7] the Seventh District Court of Appeals addressed the issue and held that the statute empowering the trial court with continuing jurisdiction over matters regarding custody and support of children superceded the provision in the separation agreement requiring that any dispute involving children be addressed in mediation.

§ 16:10 Change of circumstances—In general

RC 3109.04(E)(1)(a) creates a rebuttable presumption that it is in a child's best interest to retain a previously designated residential parent. Specifically, it states "the court shall not modify . . . and . . . shall retain the residential parent" unless certain requirements are met. The statute sets forth a three-step analysis the court must perform in deciding whether to modify an allocation of parental rights and responsibilities.[1]

The first step in a modification proceeding is to determine whether there has been a change of circumstances with respect to the child, the residential parent, or one of the joint custodians or parents subject to a shared parenting decree.[2] Any change of circumstances must be based upon facts that have arisen since the prior decree or that were

---

[6]RC 3109.052(C).

[7]Spickler v. Spickler, 2003-Ohio-3553, 2003 WL 21518732 (Ohio Ct. App. 7th Dist. Columbiana County 2003).

[Section 16:10]

[1]See, e.g., Able v. Able, 1999 WL 234685 (Ohio Ct. App. 2d Dist. Montgomery County 1999).

[2]RC 3109.04(E)(1)(a); RC 3109.04(E)(1)(a); Davis v. Flickinger, 77 Ohio St. 3d 415, 1997-Ohio-260, 674 N.E.2d 1159 (1997) (Statute governing modification of decrees allocating parental rights and responsibilities, while requiring that change of circumstances justifying change of custody be change of substance and not slight or inconsequential, does not require "substantial" change in circumstances; word "substantial" does not appear in the statute, and intent of statute is to spare children from constant tug of war between their parents, and provide stability to custodial status of children.); Moyer v. Moyer, 1993 WL 169098 (Ohio Ct. App. 10th Dist. Franklin County 1993) (change of circumstance is some event, occurrence, or situation that has a material and adverse affect on the children).

In Bauer v. Bauer, 2003-Ohio-2552, 2003 WL 21135483 (Ohio Ct. App. 12th Dist. Clermont County 2003), the appellate court held that a proposed modification of a shared parenting agreement that sought to substantially change the allocation of the parties' parental rights and responsibilities by increasing father's parenting time,

unknown to the court at the time of the prior decree.[3] The Ohio Supreme Court recently upheld the constitutionality of the change of circumstance test set forth in R.C. 3109.04(E). "The provisions of R.C. 3109.04(E) (1) (a) promote stability in the development of children and are not unconstitutional as applied where a non-custodial parent has not evidenced that a change has occurred in the circumstances of the child."[4]

If the court finds that a change of circumstances has occurred, the court then must determine whether the modification is necessary to serve the best interest of the child. Without first finding a change of circumstances, the court may not consider the child's best interest in a request to modify.[5]

The Supreme Court of Ohio recently held that a modification of the designation of residential parent and legal custodian of a child requires a determination that a change of circumstances has occurred, as well as a finding that the modification is in the best interest of the child. The Ohio Supreme Court stated "once a shared parenting decree has been issued, RC 3109.04(E) governs such modifications. The Court specifically held that the designation of residential parent and legal

---

was governed by the statute that governed modification of previously allocated parental rights and responsibilities.

[3]Bragg v. Hatfield, 152 Ohio App. 3d 174, 2003-Ohio-1441, 787 N.E.2d 44 (4th Dist. Vinton County 2003); Alessio v. Alessio, 2006-Ohio-2447, 2006 WL 1351549 (Ohio Ct. App. 10th Dist. Franklin County 2006) (trial court found a change of circumstances occurred because both parents remarried, mother's new husband was in the military and had been placed on active duty for at least two years, mother moved to Virginia and the child had bonded with her step-sister).

[4]In re Brayden James, 113 Ohio St. 3d 420, 2007-Ohio-2335, 866 N.E.2d 467 (2007).

[5]Fetty v. Fetty-Omaits, 2003-Ohio-661, 2003 WL 302399 (Ohio Ct. App. 5th Dist. Tuscarawas County 2003) (1) there must be an initial threshold showing of a change in circumstances; (2) if circumstances have changed, the modification of custody must be in the children's best interests; and (3) any harm to the children from a modification of the plan must be outweighed by the advantages of such modification. In re Carter, 1998 WL 403909 (Ohio Ct. App. 12th Dist. Butler County 1998) (court erred in applying best interest test without first finding a change of circumstance before changing custody); Engelmann v. Engelmann, 2004-Ohio-1530, 2004 WL 609901 (Ohio Ct. App. 11th Dist. Ashtabula County 2004) (modifying parental rights and responsibilities was abuse of discretion where trial court failed to make findings related to change in circumstances or best interests); Green v. Green, 2004-Ohio-185, 2004 WL 77881 (Ohio Ct. App. 3d Dist. Union County 2004) (trial court erred by denying former husband's motion for reallocation of parental rights and responsibilities without first conducting evidentiary hearing to determine whether change of circumstances occurred); Brunip v. Nickerson, 2008-Ohio-5052, 2008 WL 4416456 (Ohio Ct. App. 7th Dist. Columbiana County 2008), appeal not allowed, 120 Ohio St. 3d 1525, 2009-Ohio-614, 901 N.E.2d 245 (2009). A trial court was not required by statute to interview children, though mother had filed a motion seeking such an interview, because the trial court had determined that no change of circumstances had occurred. The statute mandating that the trial court interview the children upon parental request applied when the court was determining best interest, and absent a finding of change of circumstances, there was no reason for the court to consider evidence of best interests.

custodian may only be modified under RC 3109.04(E)(1)(a) and not under RC 3109.04(E)(2)(b), which only allows for the modification of terms of a shared parenting plan."[6]

Once the court determines that a change of circumstances has occurred, and that modifying the allocation of parental rights and responsibilities is in the child's best interest, the court may only order a modification if one of three factors applies:

(1) The residential parent agrees to a change in the residential parent status, or both parents under a shared parenting decree agree to a change in the residential parent;

(2) The child, with the consent of the residential parent, or of both parents under a shared parenting decree, has been integrated into the family of the person seeking to become the residential parent; or

(3) The harm likely to be caused by a change in environment is outweighed by the advantages in the change in environment to the child.[7]

It should be noted that the statute does not state nor suggest that a change of circumstance of the non-residential parent would be sufficient to meet the burden of proving a change. The fact that the non-residential parent improved his or her life or living conditions would not satisfy the first prong in the modification statute.[8] Further, RC 3109.04(E)(1) only requires a finding of a change of circumstances, not a "substantial" change, before a trial court may determine the best interests of a child in a change of custody matter.[9]

---

[6]Fisher v. Hasenjager, 116 Ohio St. 3d 53, 2007-Ohio-5589, 876 N.E.2d 546 (2007). See also Castanias v. Castanias, 2008-Ohio-2909, 2008 WL 2404750 (Ohio Ct. App. 12th Dist. Warren County 2008). See also Sanders-Bechtol v. Bechtol, 2009-Ohio-186, 2009 WL 118084 (Ohio Ct. App. 3d Dist. Hancock County 2009); Barto v. Barto, 2008-Ohio-5538, 2008 WL 4694520 (Ohio Ct. App. 3d Dist. Hancock County 2008). Increase in time that former husband, who was non-residential parent, spent with the children after he moved closer to the children's residence did not constitute a "change in circumstances" of the children, for purposes of statute governing modification of parental rights and responsibilities and thus former husband was not entitled to modification of residential parent status or adoption of shared parenting plan.

[7]RC 3109.04(E)(1)(a)(i) to RC 3109.04(E)(1)(a)(iii); Perz v. Perz, 85 Ohio App. 3d 374, 619 N.E.2d 1094 (6th Dist. Lucas County 1993) (mere passage of time insufficient as change of circumstance before reexamination of custody; passage of time must be significant, such as that from infancy to early adolescence, to warrant further inquiry into best interest).

[8]Matter of Dawson, 1995 WL 434236 (Ohio Ct. App. 5th Dist. Holmes County 1995); Musson v. Musson, 1998 WL 305359 (Ohio Ct. App. 3d Dist. Hardin County 1998).

[9]Davis v. Flickinger, 77 Ohio St. 3d 415, 1997-Ohio-260, 674 N.E.2d 1159 (1997); Willis v. Willis, 1997 WL 272377 (Ohio Ct. App. 8th Dist. Cuyahoga County 1997).

Further, a request to modify only visitation is not governed by RC 3109.04, and, therefore, does not require a change of circumstances. Modification of visitation is governed by RC 3109.051.[10]

§ 16:11 Change of circumstances—Relocation and removal from jurisdiction

A frequently disputed issue is the ability of the residential parent to move the children's residence where the result will cause an interruption or revision of the noncustodial parent's time with the children. Decisions are fact specific but also reveal the uncertainty of the final outcome.[1]

In the event that a residential parent and legal custodian of a minor child intends to remove the child from the jurisdiction of the court, that parent is required to file a notice of intent to relocate.[2] In certain circumstances, the courts have found that the removal of a minor child from the jurisdiction is a change of circumstances sufficient to warrant a modification of parental rights and responsibilities.[3] In *Hauck v. Hauck*,[4] the court determined that, if a divorce decree expressly or impliedly prohibits the custodial parent from removing the child from the jurisdiction, the burden is on the custodial parent to demonstrate that the decree should be modified to permit such removal. If the court determines that the removal may interfere with visitation rights, the court may modify parental rights and responsibilities to designate the parent within the state as the residential par-

---

[10]Braatz v. Braatz, 85 Ohio St. 3d 40, 1999-Ohio-203, 706 N.E.2d 1218 (1999).

[Section 16:11]

[1]See Karner, *Relocation Issues: Part I—Development of Ohio Law*, 5 Dom. Rel. J. Ohio 37 (May/June 1993); Karner, *Relocation Issues: Part II—The Law in Selected States*, 5 Dom. Rel. J. Ohio 57 (July/Aug 1993).

[2]RC 3109.051(G)(1). In re J.C., 2006-Ohio-2893, 2006 WL 1571056 (Ohio Ct. App. 8th Dist. Cuyahoga County 2006) (mother's relocation to California constituted a change of circumstances which warranted the modification of parental rights and responsibilities; the trial court noted that mother's relocation made shared parenting unfeasible).

[3]Lyall v. Lyall, 2004-Ohio-1565, 2004 WL 614990 (Ohio Ct. App. 5th Dist. Muskingum County 2004) (trial court held that change of circumstances had occurred due to mother's relocation out of state with the child, which entitled the court to modify the parties' allocation of parental rights and responsibilities).

[4]Hauck v. Hauck, 1983 WL 5881 (Ohio Ct. App. 8th Dist. Cuyahoga County 1983); Eggleston v. Eggleston, 2007-Ohio-2692, 2007 WL 1584221 (Ohio Ct. App. 11th Dist. Trumbull County 2007), (when a divorce decree expressly or impliedly prohibits the custodial parent's ability to remove the child from the jurisdiction, the burden shifts to the parent wishing to relocate the child to demonstrate that the decree should be modified to permit the child's removal.); Rodkey v. Rodkey, 2006-Ohio-4373, 2006 WL 2441720 (Ohio Ct. App. 8th Dist. Cuyahoga County 2006). Although the act of moving with a child does not, by itself, constitute a substantial change of circumstances to warrant a change of custody, where the shared parenting plan specifically provides that parents may not move the child from the area, the change of circumstance analysis is not applicable. Rather, where such a provision exists, a best interest standard is applied.

ent and legal custodian upon a proper showing of changed circumstances.

Other courts have held that relocation of a child is not, in and of itself, a change of circumstances sufficient to justify a modification of parental rights and responsibilities. There must be a showing of intent to interfere with visitation or of actual harm suffered by the child as a legal basis for establishing a change of circumstances.[5]

Although a change of residence alone does not constitute a change of circumstances, where the mother, the residential parent, used poor judgment in decisions affecting the children during the moving process, disrupting their sleep schedules by continuously traveling back and forth, and failing to recognize the negative effect this disruption had on their education and school attendance, one court held that the overall change in circumstances justified modifying parental rights and responsibilities to name the father as residential parent.[6]

In *Brown v. Brown*,[7] where the siblings were very close and the minor child had already experienced the loss of a sibling due to a prior modification of custody, the court found that the removal of the child from the jurisdiction warranted a modification of parental rights and responsibilities.

In *Rozborski v. Rozborski*,[8] mother seeking to relocate with minor children had the burden of establishing that the relocation was in the children's best interests. The court found that the mother failed to rebut the conclusion of an expert approved by both parties that the children's present residence offered accessibility of day-to-day contact with persons significant to the children and that the relocation would disrupt the children's relationships with their father and other family members.

In *Powe v. Powe*,[9] the mother, who was the custodial parent, filed a motion for an order granting her the authority to remove the minor child to Florida.[10] The prior order prohibited the removal of the child

---

[5]Thatcher v. Thatcher, 1997 WL 619808 (Ohio Ct. App. 3d Dist. Mercer County 1997). See also Campana v. Campana, 2009-Ohio-796, 2009 WL 428580 (Ohio Ct. App. 7th Dist. Mahoning County 2009).

[6]Able v. Able, 1999 WL 234685 (Ohio Ct. App. 2d Dist. Montgomery County 1999). See also Wallace v. Wallace, 2006-Ohio-848, 2006 WL 438678 (Ohio Ct. App. 5th Dist. Guernsey County 2006) (trial court found that parental conflict between mother and step-mother and mother's impending move to Cincinnati were stressors for the minor child and it was in the best interest of the minor child to modify custody to father).

[7]Brown v. Brown, 1984 WL 5398 (Ohio Ct. App. 2d Dist. Montgomery County 1984).

[8]Rozborski v. Rozborski, 116 Ohio App. 3d 29, 686 N.E.2d 546 (8th Dist. Cuyahoga County 1996).

[9]Powe v. Powe, 38 Ohio Misc. 2d 5, 525 N.E.2d 845 (C.P. 1987).

[10]See also Davis v. Davis, 1992 WL 47299 (Ohio Ct. App. 8th Dist. Cuyahoga County 1992) (mother's removal to another state without prior notice sufficient to support modification of custody to father); Thacker v. Thacker, 1995 WL 768556 (Ohio

from the jurisdiction without the consent of both parents or a court order. The agreed pattern and practice of visitation developed over time, so that the child's time became almost evenly divided between the parents, including substantial time with the father during the week. The father objected to the removal in an effort to protect the relationship that had developed between the child and himself as the result of the frequent and ongoing contact they had enjoyed. The mother's request to remove the child to Florida was primarily based upon a mere desire that she and her new husband become Floridians. This was simply something they had always wanted to do, according to the testimony at trial. The thrust of the mother's legal argument in support of her request was grounded in a Constitutional right to travel.

Despite the fact that the court-appointed psychological expert testified that the child was currently very well adjusted, due to the significant and on-going involvment of *both* of his parents, the referee granted the mother's request to remove the child, and the mother moved to Florida with the child as she had planned. Objections to the referee's report were filed by the father, and the judge entertained briefs and oral arguments. The judge rejected the referee's recommendation and issued an opinion and order denying the mother's motion and requiring the mother to return the minor child to Ohio. The judge found that the mother had failed to demonstrate that the removal of the child was in the child's best interest, since she failed to prove that the benefit of the move to the child outweighed the harm that would likely result from such a move. The judge did not, however, order the mother to return to Ohio. The judge simply ordered the mother to promptly place the child in the possession of the father in Cleveland, and to notify the father and the court, in writing, should she elect to stay in Florida. In that event, a hearing would be scheduled to determine "appropriate parental responsibilities under the circumstances."[11]

In *Marsala v. Marsala*,[12] another "constitutional right to travel" case, the trial court ordered the mother, who left the state with the child, to return the child to Cuyahoga county to live with the father unless the mother decided to return also. The court of appeals held that this order did not interfere with the mother's right to travel. The order was essential to protect the child's best interest by preventing the mother from continuing her attempts to alienate the child from the father.

___

Ct. App. 5th Dist. Licking County 1995) (relocation to Florida, deprivation of visitation conduct, and instability of residences supported modification of custody).

[11]Powe v. Powe, 38 Ohio Misc. 2d 5, 11, 525 N.E.2d 845 (C.P. 1987). See also Davis v. Davis, 1992 WL 47299 (Ohio Ct. App. 8th Dist. Cuyahoga County 1992) (mother's removal to another state without prior notice sufficient to support modification of custody to father).

[12]Marsala v. Marsala, 1995 WL 396360, at *1 (Ohio Ct. App. 8th Dist. Cuyahoga County 1995).

In *Hunter v. Hunter*,[13] the trial court held that the mother was permanently restrained from removing the parties' minor child from Ohio and that, should she move from Ohio, her parental rights and responsibilities would be modified so that the father would be designated the residential parent and legal custodian. The trial court took into consideration the fact that the minor child would endure a change of environment with either parent if the mother moved to South Carolina, where she obtained employment. Since the father lived in a different city from the child's current residence, a modification of parental rights and responsibilities would require the child to enroll in a new school. The trial court found that the father has exercised his liberal visitation rights to the fullest extent possible and that he had maintained a "close and loving relationship" with the child. The trial court determined that removal to South Carolina would interrupt the liberal visitation that had been granted to the father, but also that the child's relationship with the mother would be altered, as well, if he were placed in his father's custody. Although the trial court interviewed the minor child, the court determined that the eight-year-old child did not have sufficient reasoning ability to express his wishes and concerns with respect to parental rights and responsibilities.

Taking into account all of the circumstances, the trial court determined that it would be in the minor child's best interest to remain in Ohio where he had already adjusted to his father's home, family, and neighborhood, in the event that his mother moves to South Carolina. The court of appeals affirmed the trial court's decision.

In *Smeltzer v. Smeltzer*,[14] the trial court restricted the custodial parent from relocating the minor children more than 50 miles from the parties' home. The appellate court reversed the trial court's decision, holding that it unconstitutionally restricted the freedom of the mother to live where she chooses.

The court may consider the continuing life processes of children, which are prospective in nature, as well as the circumstances that exist at a particular time and place. Thus, conditioning the retention of custody by the mother upon her reestablishing her residence within 40 miles of the father's home was affirmed as being part of the totality of circumstances.[15]

Ohio courts have also found that repeated moves within the jurisdiction by the custodial parent may, in part, warrant a modification of

---

[13]Hunter v. Hunter, 1992 WL 193688, at *4 (Ohio Ct. App. 12th Dist. Madison County 1992).

[14]Smeltzer v. Smeltzer, 1993 WL 488235 (Ohio Ct. App. 7th Dist. Columbiana County 1993).

[15]Caserta v. Caserta, 1993 WL 544307 (Ohio Ct. App. 5th Dist. Delaware County 1993).

the prior decree. In *Whitmer v. Darrow*,[16] the custodial parent had moved with the child nine times within a seven-year period. This resulted in the child's attending school in six different school districts. The court also relied on other factors as the basis of its decision, such as the child's exposure to alcohol and drug abuse by the custodial parent and excessive use of babysitters.

Another Ohio court, however, denied a request to modify a prior allocation of parental rights and responsibilities, even though the residential parent would be required to periodically relocate due to obligations to the U.S. Navy.[17]

A change of custody from the mother, who had lived with the new husband and the minor child in seven different counties in six different states before the child was four years old, to the father, who had lived in the same residence located near most maternal and paternal relatives, is not an abuse of discretion.[18] While the mother had allowed visitation, nevertheless, the frequent moves caused problems with visitation, even though her intentions were not malicious.

In *Masters v. Masters*,[19] the Supreme Court held that a parent's compliance with a local rule requiring a parent who intends to relocate to notify the court is insufficient to constitute a substantial change in circumstances. Extending the holding of *Masters*, the Fifth District Court of Appeals in *Browne v. Browne*,[20] rejected the appellee's claim of a distinction based upon the appellant's having an actual intention to remove the child. The appellate court disapproved of the trial court's assumption that all prospective changes in the child's life would be negative ones, and rejected an interpretation that *Masters* implies such an assumption by the court.

In *Kolb v. Kolb*,[21] mother's proposed relocation with two of the four children to a different county 210 miles away from where father and siblings resided was not in the best interests of the children. The chil-

---

[16]Whitmer v. Darrow, 1985 WL 4735 (Ohio Ct. App. 9th Dist. Summit County 1985).

[17]Dawes v. Dawes, 1995 WL 152490 (Ohio Ct. App. 7th Dist. Columbiana County 1995).

[18]Gloeckner v. Gloeckner, 1995 WL 763302 (Ohio Ct. App. 7th Dist. Columbiana County 1995).

[19]Masters v. Masters, 69 Ohio St. 3d 83, 1994-Ohio-483, 630 N.E.2d 665 (1994).

[20]Browne v. Browne, 1995 WL 768561 (Ohio Ct. App. 5th Dist. Ashland County 1995).

[21]Kolb v. Kolb, 2003-Ohio-359, 2003 WL 187577 (Ohio Ct. App. 9th Dist. Lorain County 2003); In re Shelton, 2005-Ohio-6148, 2005 WL 3096534 (Ohio Ct. App. 11th Dist. Lake County 2005) (trial court found that father failed to establish that he could provide child with a stable home environment in Colorado and, therefore, the trial court modified the parties' shared parenting plan to name mother as the primary residential parent). But see Valentyne v. Ceccacci, 2004-Ohio-4240, 2004 WL 1799180 (Ohio Ct. App. 8th Dist. Cuyahoga County 2004) (modifying shared parenting plan to grant ex-wife primary residential parenting and permitting mother to relocate with children to California was in children's best interest, where ex-wife could improve her economic circumstances if she moved to California).

dren had no family in the area in which they would relocate; the children enjoyed a close relationship with their father and paternal relatives and friends in the current area. Moreover, mother provided no evidence of benefit to children or occupational opportunities for her by relocating to the proposed location.

§ 16:12   Change of circumstances—Cohabitation or remarriage of residential parent—Heterosexual relationships

The cohabitation of a residential parent with a person of the opposite sex will not automatically constitute a change in circumstances of the child or the residential parent such that the trial court may modify a prior parenting decree. The cohabitation of the residential parent with a nonspouse cannot be the basis for a modification of parental rights and responsibilities without a showing of its material, adverse effect on the child.[1] Where the residential parent engages in nonmarital sexual conduct, it must be shown that such conduct is having a direct, adverse impact on the child before a court will modify the prior parenting order.[2]

Further, remarriage of a parent does not automatically constitute a change of circumstances.[3]

Where the custodial mother had lived with four different men in a five-year period and had moved the principal residence of the child ten to twelve times during the same period, such conduct justified modification of the prior decree.[4] Likewise, where a mother had remarried twice within five years after divorcing the father, the court determined that a modification of parental rights and responsibilities

---

[Section 16:12]

[1]Whaley v. Whaley, 61 Ohio App. 2d 111, 15 Ohio Op. 3d 136, 399 N.E.2d 1270 (4th Dist. Lawrence County 1978) (a court's inquiry into the moral conduct or standards of a custodial parent is limited to a determination of the effect of such conduct on the child); Wyss v. Wyss, 3 Ohio App. 3d 412, 445 N.E.2d 1153 (10th Dist. Franklin County 1982); Kraus v. Kraus, 10 Ohio App. 3d 63, 460 N.E.2d 680 (8th Dist. Cuyahoga County 1983); In re Burrell, 58 Ohio St. 2d 37, 12 Ohio Op. 3d 43, 388 N.E.2d 738 (1979); In the Matter of Demangone Demangone, 1982 WL 3768 (Ohio Ct. App. 2d Dist. Greene County 1982) (impermissible to change custody just to punish mother for conduct court considers morally wrong).

[2]Whaley v. Whaley, 61 Ohio App. 2d 111, 15 Ohio Op. 3d 136, 399 N.E.2d 1270 (4th Dist. Lawrence County 1978); Jasper v. Jasper, 1995 WL 540110 (Ohio Ct. App. 1st Dist. Hamilton County 1995).

[3]Campana v. Campana, 2009-Ohio-796, 2009 WL 428580 (Ohio Ct. App. 7th Dist. Mahoning County 2009).

[4]In the Matter Pilbeam v. Pilbeam, 1984 WL 4378 (Ohio Ct. App. 2d Dist. Montgomery County 1984); Myers v. Myers, 153 Ohio App. 3d 243, 2003-Ohio-3552, 792 N.E.2d 770 (7th Dist. Columbiana County 2003) (change of circumstances occurred where mother had frequent change of addresses and mother exposed child to a sexually charged and possibly dangerous environment).

was appropriate.[5] The court focused on the changing father figures in the life of the child and on the fact that the most recent stepfather had a propensity for violence. The character and personality of a stepparent is certainly relevant to a determination of the custody issue in a modification proceeding.[6]

In *Stone v. Stone*,[7] the court focused on (1) the crowded condition in the parent's home environment where the minor child and two half-siblings shared the same bedroom; (2) the fact that the paramour of the custodial parent had used marijuana in the presence of the child; and (3) the fact that the custodial parent had given birth to a child of the third party while cohabiting with him. These facts distinguish this case from the established line of Ohio cases which conclude that a court's inquiry into the moral conduct or standards of the residential parent is limited to a determination of the effect such conduct has on the child.[8] In *Stone*, these additional factors, coupled with the custodial parent's cohabitation, led the court to conclude that there had been a change in circumstances warranting modification of its prior custody decree, taking into account the best interest of the minor children.

§ 16:13 Change of circumstances—Cohabitation or remarriage of residential parent—Same sex relationships

The cohabitation of a parent with a person of the same gender will not automatically disqualify that parent from being named the residential parent. In approving the termination of joint custody decree and the naming of the mother as sole residential parent, the court in *Large v. Large*[1] held that the mother's lesbian relationship is a negative factor only where it has an adverse impact on the best interests of the children. The court concluded that the mother's partner participated in the children's activities and, while the relationship might not be easy for the children, if there was a supportive family environment, any difficulty could be overridden.

A parent's conduct in engaging in a homosexual relationship with

---

[5]Day v. Day, 1985 WL 10789 (Ohio Ct. App. 9th Dist. Lorain County 1985).

[6]Ross v. Ross, 64 Ohio St. 2d 203, 18 Ohio Op. 3d 414, N.E.2d 426 (1980); Newman v. Newman, 61 Ohio L. Abs. 438, 104 N.E.2d 707 (Ct. App. 8th Dist. Cuyahoga County 1951).

[7]Stone v. Stone, 9 Ohio App. 3d 6, 457 N.E.2d 919 (12th Dist. Warren County 1983).

[8]In re Burrell, 58 Ohio St. 2d 37, 12 Ohio Op. 3d 43, 388 N.E.2d 738 (1979); Whaley v. Whaley, 61 Ohio App. 2d 111, 15 Ohio Op. 3d 136, 399 N.E.2d 1270 (4th Dist. Lawrence County 1978); Kraus v. Kraus, 10 Ohio App. 3d 63, 460 N.E.2d 680 (8th Dist. Cuyahoga County 1983); Wyss v. Wyss, 3 Ohio App. 3d 412, 445 N.E.2d 1153 (10th Dist. Franklin County 1982).

[Section 16:13]

[1]Large v. Large, 1993 WL 498127 (Ohio Ct. App. 10th Dist. Franklin County 1993).

another consenting adult has no relevance to the allocation of parental rights and responsibilities, absent proof that the parent's relationship presently has an adverse collateral impact on the child or children involved. The same test reasonably applies to whether the relationship constitutes a change of circumstances for purposes of RC 3109.04(E)(1)(a).

In *Page v. Page*,[2] the trial court changed the designation of residential parent for two minor boys from mother to father after evidence was presented indicating that mother was in a same-sex relationship and that the children had developed serious anger issues and depression as a result of mother's relationship.

Modification of custody based on a potential negative impact of societal prejudice in the future, without evidence that the residential parent's homosexuality has had a direct and adverse impact on the child, is improper and an order awarding custody to the other parent on that basis will be reversed.[3]

§ 16:14 Change of circumstances—Interference with visitation

If a custodial or residential parent interferes with visitation, a court may modify custody and award residential parent status to the other parent. In *Davis v. Davis*,[1] the court held that it is within the trial court's discretion to modify parental rights and responsibilities and award custody to the father in response to the custodial mother's continuous and willful denial of visitation. The court further held that the mother's removal of the child to another state without notifying the court or the father was sufficient evidence to support the modification.

In *Marshall v. Marshall*,[2] however, the court of appeals held that the trial court erred in awarding custody of the children to their father

---

[2]Page v. Page, 2008-Ohio-3011, 2008 WL 2469176 (Ohio Ct. App. 2d Dist. Clark County 2008).

[3]Inscoe v. Inscoe, 121 Ohio App. 3d 396, 700 N.E.2d 70 (4th Dist. Meigs County 1997).

[Section 16:14]

[1]Davis v. Davis, 1992 WL 47299 (Ohio Ct. App. 8th Dist. Cuyahoga County 1992); Headley v. Headley, 2000 WL 1458961 (Ohio Ct. App. 11th Dist. Ashtabula County 2000) (wife's interference with visitation and hostility toward husband constituted a change of circumstances upon which a change of custody could be granted); Doerfler v. Doerfler, 2006-Ohio-6960, 2006 WL 3825199 (Ohio Ct. App. 9th Dist. Wayne County 2006) (a custodial parent's interference with visitation by a noncustodial parent may be considered a part of a change of circumstances which would allow for modification of the allocation of parental rights and responsibilities); Sheppeard v. Brown, 2008-Ohio-203, 2008 WL 186670 (Ohio Ct. App. 2d Dist. Clark County 2008) (change of designation of residential parent due to mother's failure to allow father visitation); Chelman v. Chelman, 2008-Ohio-4634, 2008 WL 4183979 (Ohio Ct. App. 2d Dist. Greene County 2008).

[2]Marshall v. Marshall, 117 Ohio App. 3d 182, 690 N.E.2d 68 (3d Dist. Allen County 1997).

because of the mother's disobedience of a court order to return to Ohio. The court should have considered other factors, such as the mother having been primary caretaker; the father being physically abusive; and the father having elected not to visit with his children. In *Headley v. Headley*,[3] wife's interference with visitation and hostility toward husband constituted a change of circumstances upon which a change of custody could be granted.

In *Hunter v. Rainer*,[4] the court terminated the parties' shared parenting plan and awarded custody of the children to father. The court found that the parties were not able to cooperate and make decisions jointly and they were not able encourage the sharing of love, affection and contact between the children and the other parent. In particular, the court found that mother continuously and willfully denied father's right to parenting time: "Few custodial parents have laid down more roadblocks and made visitation more difficult than the mother in this case."[5]

The court must look at the totality of the circumstances in determining whether one party's interference with visitation outweighs other factors in deciding whether to modify custody.

§ 16:15   Change of circumstances—Other circumstances addressed by courts

The court in *In re Detwiler*[1] held that the mental illness of a residential parent and legal custodian was a change of circumstances sufficient to warrant a modification of parental rights and responsibilities. In *Boyd v. Boyd*,[2] the court awarded residential parent status to the father in the absence of the mother's appearance at the hearing. The court held that evidence of the child's time spent with his father and the child's withdrawn behavior under the custody of his mother were relevant factors in determining the child's best interest.

In *Lyall v. Lyall*,[3] the court held that the evidence supported the finding that changing the child's residential parent status from mother to father was appropriate when an expert testified that father's profile presented no emotional or psychological problems and mother's profile

---

[3]Headley v. Headley, 2000 WL 1458961 (Ohio Ct. App. 11th Dist. Ashtabula County 2000).

[4]Hunter v. Rainer, 2004-Ohio-1746, 2004 WL 728928 (Ohio Ct. App. 5th Dist. Delaware County 2004).

[5]Hunter v. Rainer, 2004-Ohio-1746, 2004 WL 728928 (Ohio Ct. App. 5th Dist. Delaware County 2004).

[Section 16:15]

[1]Matter of Detwiler, 1991 WL 259557 (Ohio Ct. App. 3d Dist. Marion County 1991).

[2]Boyd v. Boyd, 1992 WL 114596 (Ohio Ct. App. 8th Dist. Cuyahoga County 1992).

[3]Lyall v. Lyall, 2004-Ohio-1565, 2004 WL 614990 (Ohio Ct. App. 5th Dist. Muskingum County 2004).

suggested the possibility of an addictive disorder, impulsiveness and uncontrollable anger under conditions of conflict.

The court considered the impact of drug and alcohol abuse in *Kern v Kern*,[4] and in *Thornton v. Gowins*,[5] the trial court modified custody to the non-residential parent, despite the fact that the non-residential parent had failed to pay child support for a seven-year period. The court of appeals held that the trial court must look at the totality of the circumstances and determine what is in the best interest of the child. Satisfied that the trial court had fulfilled its duty, the court of appeals affirmed the trial court's decision.

The trial court modified parental rights and responsibilities after considering mother's current husband's alcoholism and refusal to seek treatment and the numerous domestic disturbances between mother and her current husband which necessitated police response.[6]

In *Cossin v. Holley*,[7] the trial court terminated a shared parenting plan due to father's alcohol abuse and violent tendencies that could be harmful to the child.

The mere passing of time, however, is not a change of circumstances sufficient to result in a modification of parental rights and responsibilities. Other factors must also exist to warrant such a modification.[8] Poor performance by children on proficiency exams, where children were home-schooled, and a psychologist's evaluation of the children warranted a change of residential parent status to the father in *Sayre v. Hoelzle-Sayre*.[9]

Unsubstantiated allegations of sexual abuse may or may not constitute a change of circumstances to establish grounds to modify a prior custody award. One appellate court held that a trial court erred in modifying custody based upon unsubstantiated allegations of sexual abuse alone.[10] Unsubstantiated allegations of sexual abuse are only one factor that the court can consider in determining whether a

---

[4]Kern v. Kern, 1992 WL 172701 (Ohio Ct. App. 6th Dist. Fulton County 1992).

[5]Thornton v. Gowins, 1992 WL 173283 (Ohio Ct. App. 5th Dist. Tuscarawas County 1992).

[6]Bracy v. Bracy, 2008-Ohio-3888, 2008 WL 2954717 (Ohio Ct. App. 3d Dist. Allen County 2008).

[7]Cossin v. Holley, 2007-Ohio-5258, 2007 WL 2852163 (Ohio Ct. App. 5th Dist. Morrow County 2007).

[8]Butler v. Butler, 107 Ohio App. 3d 633, 669 N.E.2d 291 (3d Dist. Auglaize County 1995).

[9]Sayre v. Hoelzle-Sayre, 100 Ohio App. 3d 203, 653 N.E.2d 712 (3d Dist. Seneca County 1994).

[10]Stover v. Plumley, 113 Ohio App. 3d 839, 682 N.E.2d 683 (4th Dist. Gallia County 1996).

change in circumstances has occurred.[11] Other courts have held that such allegations may be sufficient.[12]

One danger of adopting this strategy is the risk of losing custody if the accusing party cannot prove that the abuse had occurred. This risk may have a "chilling effect" on the reporting of suspected sexual abuse, leaving the child unprotected. Conversely, and also very damaging to the child, is a false allegation of sexual abuse. This circumstance could result in the destruction of the relationship between the child and the accused and could also result in grave criminal and other consequences for the accused, as well. Sexual abuse allegation cases are very delicate matters and should be handled very carefully by practitioners and the courts.

A minor child's apparent gender identity problems constituted a finding of a change of circumstances and permitted the trial court to then consider modifying custody in the best interests of the child.[13]

§ 16:16 Best interest standard

Ohio law creates a rebuttable presumption in favor of retaining the prior custodial or residential parent or the prior joint custodians or parents subject to a shared parenting decree. RC 3109.04(F)(1) provides that not only must the court find that a change of circumstances has occurred, but it must also determine that modification is necessary to serve the best interest of the child.

In determining the best interest of a child, whether in an original proceeding allocating parental rights and responsibilities or in a modification proceeding, the court must consider all relevant factors, including but not limited to, the following:

(1) The wishes of the child's parents regarding his or her care;

(2) The wishes and concerns of the child as expressed to the court, if the court has interviewed the child;

(3) The child's interaction and interrelationship with his parents, siblings, and other person who may significantly affect the child's best interest;

(4) The child's adjustment to his home, school, and community;

(5) The mental and physical health of all persons involved;

(6) The parent more likely to honor and facilitate parenting time and companionship rights approved by the court;

(7) Whether either parent has failed to make all child support payments, including all arrearages, that are required of the parent pursuant to a child support order;

---

[11]In re Nentwick, 2002-Ohio-1560, 2002 WL 924632 (Ohio Ct. App. 7th Dist. Columbiana County 2002).

[12]Beekman v. Beekman, 96 Ohio App. 3d 783, 792, 645 N.E.2d 1332 (4th Dist. Pike County 1994).

[13]Smith v. Smith, 2007-Ohio-1394, 2007 WL 901599 (Ohio Ct. App. 7th Dist. Jefferson County 2007), appeal not allowed, 115 Ohio St. 3d 1409, 2007-Ohio-4884, 873 N.E.2d 1315 (2007).

(8) Whether either parent has been convicted of or pleaded guilty to any criminal offense involving child abuse or child neglect, whether either parent of a child who has been adjudicated as abused or neglected has been determined to be the perpetrator of the abuse or neglect, whether either parent has previously been convicted of or pleaded guilty to a violation of RC 2919.25 involving a victim, who at the time of the offense was a family or household member, whether either parent has been convicted of or pleaded guilty to any offense involving a victim who at the time of the offense was a family or household member and caused physical harm to the victim in the commission of the offense, and whether there is reason to believe that either parent has acted in a manner resulting in a child's being abused or neglected;

(9) Whether the residential parent or one of the parents subject to a shared parenting decree has continuously and willfully denied the other parent the right to parenting time ordered by the court; and

(10) Whether either parent has established, or is planning to establish a residence outside of the state.[1]

§ 16:17   Modification of prior decrees to shared parenting

Either or both parties to any custody decree may file a motion with the original court requesting shared parenting.[1] Modification from sole custody or residential parent status to shared parenting, however, should not be automatic. The court must consider not only the factors set forth in RC 3109.04(E)(1)(a)(i) to RC 3109.04(E)(1)(a)(iii), but also additional relevant factors in this situation. If the court must determine whether modification to shared parenting is in the best interest of the child, the court must consider all relevant factors, including those factors set forth in RC 3109.04(F)(1), the factors enumerated in RC 3109.05(A),[2] and all of the following factors:

(1) The ability of the parents to cooperate and make decisions jointly with respect to the children;[3]

[Section 16:16]

[1]RC 3109.04(F)(1).

[Section 16:17]

[1]RC 3109.041.

[2]RC 3109.05 (factors determining amount of support; support order; medical needs).

[3]The parents' ability to cooperate and make decisions jointly is only one factor to be considered in determining the best interests of the child. It was not error for a trial court to adopt a shared parenting plan despite the parents' past inability to communicate. See Cavanaugh v. McCarthy, 1997 WL 781720 (Ohio Ct. App. 8th Dist. Cuyahoga County 1997). See also Blakeman v. Blakeman, 2008-Ohio-2948, 2008 WL 2429311 (Ohio Ct. App. 4th Dist. Pike County 2008). Trial court granted a change in residential parent status in a shared parenting arrangement because mother had relocated and changed her employment and the father remained in the same school

   (2) The ability of each parent to encourage the sharing of love, affection, and contact between the child and the other parent;

   (3) Any history of, or potential for child abuse, spousal abuse, other domestic violence, or parental kidnapping by either parent;

   (4) The geographic proximity of the parents to each other, as the proximity relates to the practical considerations of shared parenting; and,

   (5) The recommendation of the guardian ad litem of the child, if a guardian ad litem has been appointed.[4]

In its determination as to any allocation of parental rights and responsibilities, including the modification of a prior allocation, the court is prohibited from giving preference to a parent because of that parent's financial status or condition.[5]

When the court is determining whether it should grant shared parenting in a modification proceeding, it must, whenever possible, require the shared parenting plan to ensure the opportunity for both parents to have frequent and continuing contact with the child, unless the court determines that such contact would not be in the best interest of the child.[6] The approval of a shared parenting plan is discretionary with the court, and the court must not approve a shared parenting plan unless it determines that the plan is in the best interest of the child.[7]

If the court approves a shared parenting plan in a modification proceeding, the plan should be incorporated into a final shared parenting decree granting the shared parenting of the children.[8] A shared parenting decree issued as a final resolution of the pending matter has immediate effect as a final decree on the date of its issuance, subject to modification or termination.[9]

Since RC 3109.04(E)(1)(a) requires a demonstration of a sufficient change of circumstances with respect to either the child, the residential parent, or one of the joint custodians or parents subject to a shared parenting decree. If either or both of the parents under a prior parenting decree desire to modify that decree to one of shared parenting, at least one of the parents must file a motion which includes both a request for modification of the prior decree and a request for a shared parenting order, and the movant must submit to the court a proposed

---

district. The trial court's preference for the child to be at home in the mornings before school and in the afternoons after school with father rather than attend a latchkey program in mother's school district was in the child's best interests.

   [4]RC 3109.04(F)(2); Meade v. Meade, 2000-Ohio-1912, 2000 WL 1532872 (Ohio Ct. App. 3d Dist. Marion County 2000) (the trial court did not err in denying father's request for modification of custody, although the child and guardian ad litem supported the change).

   [5]RC 3109.04(F)(3).

   [6]RC 3109.04(D)(1)(c).

   [7]RC 3109.04(D)(1)(b).

   [8]RC 3109.04(D)(1)(d).

   [9]RC 3109.04(D)(1)(d).

shared parenting plan. If the proponent of the modification successfully demonstrates the requisite change of circumstances, the court
approves the submitted shared parenting plan, and, after considering
all relevant circumstances, the court determines that shared parenting would be in the best interest of the child, shared parenting will be
granted.[10]

§ 16:18 Modification of shared parenting plan submitted jointly

Modification of a shared parenting plan is governed by RC
3109.04(E)(2). Prior to November 9, 1994, the procedure to modify a
shared parenting plan that had been submitted jointly by the parties
was different from that to modify a plan that had been submitted by
only one of the parties. 1994 H.B. 415 removed the language that created these distinctions and both types of plans may be modified by essentially the same methods.

The previous version of the statute allowed modification of a shared
parenting plan submitted jointly by the parties only by agreement of
the parties. The court had no authority to modify the plan without the
parties' agreement. When disputes arose under such a plan, the court's
only recourse was to terminate the plan and enter an order designating one party as the residential parent. The 1994 amendment gave
the court much broader discretion in altering the terms of shared
parenting plans, with the only restriction being that any modification
must be in the best interest of the children.

If both parents jointly request that their shared parenting plan be
modified, the court must include the modifications in the plan unless
it finds that they are not in the best interest of the children.[1] In that
event, the court may modify the parties' proposal and adopt it as modified, or reject the proposed modifications and leave the existing plan
in effect or terminate shared parenting, whichever the court finds is
in the best interest of the children.[2]

The court may also modify a shared parenting plan upon its own
motion or upon the request of either or both parties if the court
determines that the modifications are in the best interest of the children,[3] or terminate a shared parenting plan if it finds that shared

---

[10]RC 3109.04(D).

[Section 16:18]

[1]RC 3109.04(E)(2)(a).

[2]RC 3109.04(E)(2)(a), RC 3109.04(E)(2)(c).

[3]RC 3109.04(E)(2)(b); Larkey v. Larkey, 1999 WL 1000688 (Ohio Ct. App. 8th
Dist. Cuyahoga County 1999) (The parties entered into an agreed shared parenting
plan providing for a specific percentage allocation of responsibility for uncovered
medical expenses. The trial court adopted the shared parenting plan, but modified the
distribution of uncovered medical expenses. On appeal, the court of appeals upheld
the modification of the parties' agreed entry reasoning that the trial court can modify

parenting is no longer in the children's best interest.[4] This provision, however, does not give the court unlimited authority to reallocate the parties' parental rights and responsibilities. A trial court's sua sponte finding that a shared parenting plan was "not working" and decision to terminate the plan and name mother as sole residential parent was not supported by the evidence nor requested by either party, and thus was an abuse of discretion.[5] Further, a trial court has no jurisdiction to enforce or interpret a shared parenting plan which, by its terms, terminates upon the filing of a motion by either party.[6]

On termination of a shared parenting decree, the court must proceed and issue a modified decree for the allocation of parental rights and responsibilities for the care of the children as if no shared parenting decree had been granted, and as if no request for shared parenting had ever been made.[7]

This, however, would not preclude the court from issuing a new shared parenting decree adopting a shared parenting plan with different terms, provided that the procedures for obtaining shared parenting set forth in the statute are followed by the parties.

In *Brennaman v. Huber*,[8] the appellate court held that the trial court did not err in terminating the shared parenting plan and awarding custody to the mother. RC 3109.04(E)(2)(c) does not require the trial court to find a change in circumstances to terminate a shared parenting plan.

---

the terms of a shared parenting plan "at any time" and upon its own motion if the modification is in the best interest of the child under RC 3109.04(E)(2)(b).).

[4]Milner v. Milner, 1999 WL 1139965 (Ohio Ct. App. 10th Dist. Franklin County 1999) (Trial court did not err in terminating a shared parenting plan upon appellee-father's motion to modify the allocation of parental rights and responsibilities. The trial court's finding of changed circumstances was based upon the parties' behavior and unwillingness to comply with the terms and spirit of a shared parenting plan. The trial court magistrate concluded that shared parenting was no longer in the children's best interest and that it should be terminated. Once the trial court terminates a shared parenting plan, it must allocate parental rights and responsibilities under RC 3109.04(A), (B) and (C), considering the best interests of the minor children. The appellate court found that the trial court made extensive findings under RC 3109.04(F)(1) as to the best interests of the minor children and that the trial court did not abuse its discretion in designating appellee-father as residential parent and legal custodian.); Dobran v. Dobran, 1999 WL 689220 (Ohio Ct. App. 7th Dist. Mahoning County 1999) (RC 3109.04(E)(2)(c) governs the trial court's authority to terminate a shared parenting plan and does not provide a requirement that a significant change of circumstances exists prior to a determination that the termination is appropriate. Rather, the court must look to the best interests of the child standard in determining whether a termination of the shared parenting plan is warranted.).

[5]Lewis v. Lewis, 1998 WL 719515 (Ohio Ct. App. 3d Dist. Union County 1998).

[6]Boldt v. Boldt, 1998 WL 852717 (Ohio Ct. App. 9th Dist. Summit County 1998).

[7]RC 3109.04(E)(2)(d).

[8]Brennaman v. Huber, 1998 WL 127081 (Ohio Ct. App. 2d Dist. Greene County 1998).

§ 16:19 Appellate review

Where a decision granting or modifying a decree allocating parental rights and responsibilities is appealed, the court of appeals is required to give the case priority on its calendar and to "handle it expeditiously."[1]

In matters of parental rights and responsibilities, the trial court has very broad discretion.[2] Although this discretion is not absolute,[3] once a trial court either grants or denies a request for the modification of parental rights and responsibilities, an appellant is unlikely to be successful in an attempt to persuade a reviewing court to overturn the trial court's decision. A court of appeals will not reverse the judgment of a trial court on a motion for modification unless the judgment constitutes an abuse of discretion by the trial court.[4] If a reviewing court finds any competent, credible evidence supporting a trial court judgment, that judgment will be sustained.[5]

In *Sayre v. Hoelzle-Sayre*,[6] the court of appeals held that the "[a]buse of discretion . . . [standard for review in trial court's decision in child custody matters] means that '[t]he discretion which a trial court enjoys in custody matters should be accorded the utmost respect.' . . . [c]onsequently, it is improper for an appellate court to

---

[Section 16:19]

[1]RC 3109.04(H).

[2]Palladino v. Palladino, 27 Ohio St. 2d 175, 56 Ohio Op. 2d 108, 271 N.E.2d 826 (1971); Trickey v. Trickey, 158 Ohio St. 9, 47 Ohio Op. 481, 106 N.E.2d 772 (1952); Thrasher v. Thrasher, 3 Ohio App. 3d 210, 444 N.E.2d 431 (9th Dist. Summit County 1981).

[3]Trickey v. Trickey, 158 Ohio St. 9, 47 Ohio Op. 481, 106 N.E.2d 772 (1952) (discretion of trial court not unlimited); Palladino v. Palladino, 27 Ohio St. 2d 175, 56 Ohio Op. 2d 108, 271 N.E.2d 826 (1971) (trial court does not have absolute discretion in granting change of custody); Ross v. Ross, 64 Ohio St. 2d 203, 18 Ohio Op. 3d 414, 414 N.E.2d 426 (1980) (judge in custody matter not vested with absolute discretion, elements, standards, and factors of RC 3109.04(B) and (C) limited judge's discretion); Baxter v. Baxter, 27 Ohio St. 2d 168, 56 Ohio Op. 2d 104, 271 N.E.2d 873 (1971) (discretion of trial court not unlimited); Wiley v. Wiley, 1983 WL 2290 (Ohio Ct. App. 4th Dist. Ross County 1983) (extent of court's discretion codified in RC 3109.04(B)); (Voorheis) Cummins v. Voorheis, 1981 WL 5941 (Ohio Ct. App. 4th Dist. Scioto County 1981) (court's discretion limited because court must first find change of circumstances which endangers child; court must also consider harm likely to be caused by change of environment).

[4]Baxter v. Baxter, 27 Ohio St. 2d 168, 56 Ohio Op. 2d 104, 271 N.E.2d 873 (1971) (decision of trial court is subject to reversal on showing of abuse of discretion).

[5]For the Ohio Supreme Court's construction of "abuse of discretion," see Baxter v. Baxter, 27 Ohio St. 2d 168, 56 Ohio Op. 2d 104, 271 N.E.2d 873 (1971) (abuse of discretion connotes something more than merely being against manifest weight of evidence); State v. Adams, 62 Ohio St. 2d 151, 16 Ohio Op. 3d 169, 404 N.E.2d 144, 16 A.L.R.4th 344 (1980) (abuse of discretion connotes more than error of law or judgment; it implies that court's attitude was unreasonable, arbitrary, or unconscionable).

[6]Sayre v. Hoelzle-Sayre, 100 Ohio App. 3d 203, 210, 653 N.E.2d 712 (3d Dist. Seneca County 1994).

independently review the weight of the evidence in the majority of cases."

As the Ohio Supreme Court explained in *Ross v. Ross*,[7] setting forth the standard for reviewing a judgment of the trial court in a modification of custody case, "This court does not undertake to weigh the evidence and pass upon its sufficiency but will ascertain from the record whether there is some competent evidence to sustain the findings of the trial court." Citing *Chicago Ornamental Iron Co. v. Rook*,[8] the Court in *Ross* further stated:

> This case is here "for the determination of all questions presented by the record, except the weight of the evidence. Whether there is any evidence to support the verdict and judgment in the common pleas court is a question that must be answered by this court before it can determine whether the judgment of affirmance [reversal in this cause] in the court of appeals is erroneous."[9]

Although an appellant may assert as error that the trial court's judgment was against the manifest weight of the evidence, the reviewing court will still apply the "any competent, credible evidence" test. In *Ross*, for example, the Court reasoned as follows: the record indicated that all essential elements of the action were supported by some competent, credible evidence; therefore, the trial court's judgment was not against the manifest weight of the evidence.

While a reviewing court may overturn a decision of the trial court on a finding of abuse of discretion, an appellate court may not merely substitute its judgment for that of the trial court.[10] To determine whether a trial court has abused its discretion in a modification case, an appellate court will review the record, considering only matters which were actually presented to the trial court.[11] If there exists any

---

[7]Ross v. Ross, 64 Ohio St. 2d 203, 204, 18 Ohio Op. 3d 414, 414 N.E.2d 426 (1980).

[8]Chicago Ornamental Iron Co. v. Rook, 93 Ohio St. 152, 156–57, 112 N.E. 589 (1915).

[9]Ross v. Ross, 64 Ohio St. 2d 203, 204-05, 18 Ohio Op. 3d 414, 414 N.E.2d 426 (1980); court in *Ross* also cited C. E. Morris Co. v. Foley Const. Co., 54 Ohio St. 2d 279, 8 Ohio Op. 3d 261, 376 N.E.2d 578 (1978) (judgments supported by some competent, credible evidence going to all essential elements of case will not be reversed by reviewing court as being against manifest weight of evidence). See also Franklin v. Franklin, 1984 WL 3850 (Ohio Ct. App. 2d Dist. Montgomery County 1984) (if competent, credible evidence exists, court of appeals will not disturb findings of trial court).

[10]Trickey v. Trickey, 158 Ohio St. 9, 47 Ohio Op. 481, 106 N.E.2d 772 (1952). Bechtol v. Bechtol, 49 Ohio St. 3d 21, 550 N.E.2d 178 (1990), opinion corrected, 51 Ohio St. 3d 701, 554 N.E.2d 899 (1990); Miller v. Miller, 37 Ohio St. 3d 71, 523 N.E.2d 846 (1988).

[11]See Whitmer v. Darrow, 1985 WL 4735 (Ohio Ct. App. 9th Dist. Summit County 1985) (transcript of hearing before referee was not prepared for trial court, it could not be considered by court of appeals); McAlister v. McAlister, 1984 WL 5137 (Ohio Ct. App. 9th Dist. Wayne County 1984).

competent, credible evidence in the record supporting the trial court's decision, the reviewing court will affirm.[12]

Further, when the modification of a prior decree allocating parental rights and responsibilities rests upon the trial court's ascertaining the credibility of witnesses, an appellate court will defer to the trial court's findings on review.[13] In addition, while it is preferable that the trial court expressly state in its judgment entry those standards and guidelines upon which it relied with respect to the evidence supporting its judgment, in the absence of such statements, a reviewing court may assume that the trial court considered that evidence and applied the relevant statutory elements, standards, and factors in making its decision and, thus, will find that the court did not abuse its discretion.[14]

If the trial court fails to make the necessary findings, the appellate court may reverse its decision on that basis.[15] Where a juvenile court modified a custody order that was entered by a domestic relations court in a dissolution of marriage, its decision was reversed because it was not based on the change of circumstances standard as required by RC 3109.04(E)(1)(a).[16]

In *Dilworth v. Dilworth*,[17] the court of appeals held that a trial court's post-decree order forbidding the spouses from having romantic guests stay over night when the children were present was, in fact, a modification of parental rights and responsibilities. Accordingly, the trial court erred by failing to make the necessary findings set forth in RC 3109.04.

§ 16:20   Attorney fees

In post decree modification proceedings, the court, in its discretion,

---

[12]See Whitmer v. Darrow, 1985 WL 4735 (Ohio Ct. App. 9th Dist. Summit County 1985) (transcript of hearing before referee was not prepared for trial court, it could not be considered by court of appeals); McAlister v. McAlister, 1984 WL 5137 (Ohio Ct. App. 9th Dist. Wayne County 1984). See also Ross v. Ross, 64 Ohio St. 2d 203, 18 Ohio Op. 3d 414, 414 N.E.2d 426 (1980); Franklin v. Franklin, 1984 WL 3850 (Ohio Ct. App. 2d Dist. Montgomery County 1984).

[13]See In the Matter Pilbeam v. Pilbeam, 1984 WL 4378 (Ohio Ct. App. 2d Dist. Montgomery County 1984); Ross v. Ross, 64 Ohio St. 2d 203, 18 Ohio Op. 3d 414, 414 N.E.2d 426 (1980); Swanson v. Swanson, 48 Ohio App. 2d 85, 2 Ohio Op. 3d 65, 355 N.E.2d 894 (8th Dist. Cuyahoga County 1976); Joyce v. Joyce, 1993 WL 541596 (Ohio Ct. App. 12th Dist. Warren County 1993) (behavior and credibility of party can be ascertained from listening to and viewing audio and videotapes as well as from courtroom behavior).

[14]Whitmer v. Darrow, 1985 WL 4735 (Ohio Ct. App. 9th Dist. Summit County 1985); Van Blarcum v. Van Blarcum, 1982 WL 4895 (Ohio Ct. App. 9th Dist. Lorain County 1982).

[15]Moauro v. Moauro, 1999 WL 770794 (Ohio Ct. App. 5th Dist. Stark County 1999) (Trial court abused its discretion in failing to issue specific findings of fact and conclusions of law, as required by statute, in support of its denial of husband's motion for shared parenting and proposed shared parenting plan.).

[16]In re Carter, 1998 WL 403909 (Ohio Ct. App. 12th Dist. Butler County 1998).

[17]Dilworth v. Dilworth, 115 Ohio App. 3d 537, 685 N.E.2d 847 (2d Dist. Champaign County 1996).

may award attorney fees to either party. In *Luckino v. Luckino*,[1] the trial court awarded legal expenses incurred in defending against a modification of custody proceeding.

In the event a litigant wishes to appeal a trial court's decision either awarding or denying attorney fees in a modification proceeding, the decision must be a final, appealable order before the court of appeals will accept it for review. In *Kassouf v. Pantona*,[2] numerous post decree motions were filed by both parties, including a motion to modify custody filed by the father and a motion for attorney fees filed by the mother. The mother's motion for attorney fees was denied and the mother appealed. The court of appeals held that, since the mother appealed the court's decision regarding her attorney fees prior to the final disposition of the father's motion to modify custody, the decision of the trial court from which the mother appealed was not a final appealable order and, therefore, was not ripe for review.

§ 16:21 Motion to modify parental rights and responsibilities—Change of circumstances—Form⊚

[Title of Court]

[Caption]

Case No. *[_____]*
MOTION TO MODIFY
CUSTODY/PARENTAL
RIGHTS AND RESPON-
SIBILITIES

[Defendant/Plaintiff] moves that this Court modify the *[divorce/ dissolution/legal separation/annulment]* decree pursuant to RC 3109.04 to change custody/allocation of the minor *[child/children]*, namely, *[name(s) and date(s) of birth of children]* and reallocate parental rights and responsibilities naming *[Defendant/Plaintiff]* the residential parent and legal custodian based on a change of circumstances and a finding that said change is in the best interest of the *[child/children]* and that the advantages of such a change outweigh the disadvantages.

This motion is supported by the affidavit of *[Defendant/Plaintiff]* and is incorporated herein by reference.

[Section 16:20]

[1]Luckino v. Luckino, 1989 WL 29389 (Ohio Ct. App. 10th Dist. Franklin County 1989).

[2]Kassouf v. Pantona, 1992 WL 67617 (Ohio Ct. App. 8th Dist. Cuyahoga County 1992).

Attorney for *[Plaintiff/Defendant]*

[Notice of hearing]

[Exhibit "A"]

State of Ohio   )
)   SS.   <u>AFFIDAVIT</u>
County of *[name*   )
of county]

1. By agreement of the parties as incorporated into the decree of divorce/dissolution, *[respondent]* was *[awarded custody/named residential parent and legal custodian]* of the *[number of minor children]* minor *[child/children]* of the parties, namely *[name(s) and date(s) of birth of minor children]*.

2. Since such prior decree a change has occurred in the circumstances of the *[child/children]* and their *[custodian/residential parent and legal custodian]* and a modification is necessary to serve the best interests of the *[child/children]*. Since the time of the decree, in *[year]*, *[respondent]* has had many different unrelated men living with her, and presently has a man by the name of *[name]* living with her and the *[child/children]* and he has been there for the past five months.

3. Affiant believes that *[respondent]* has on numerous occasions smoked marijuana and had drinking parties while the *[child/children]* were present in the house.

4. Further affiant believes that since *[name]* has been living with *[respondent]* that the police have been out to the residence on numerous occasions to break up domestic violence situations.

5. Affiant further believes that since *[name]* has been in the house that both *[name]* and *[respondent]* have been arrested, convicted and incarcerated for assault and resisting arrest.

6. Affiant believes that the advantages of a *[change of custody/reallocation of parental rights and responsibilities]* to name him the residential parent and legal custodian outweigh any harm caused by such change.

7. Affiant is in a position to provide for his *[child/children]* and wishes to become residential parent and legal custodian of *[him/her/them]*.

Further affiant sayeth naught.

Affiant

[Jurat]

[Proof/certificate of service]

NOTES TO FORM

Drafter's Notes

RC 3109.04(B)(3) now prohibits obtaining or using a written statement from the child regarding the child's wishes and prohibits the court from considering a written statement.

A full caption is required with post-decree motions. The motion must be served by the clerk of court pursuant to written instructions filed with the motion. Counsel should be aware that on post-decree motions service on the respondent will be required unless the respondent has a pending motion.

Under his/her signature on the motion, counsel should list his or her Supreme Court registration number, business address and phone number.

§16:22 Motion to modify parental rights and responsibilities—To leave locale—Form⊚

[Title of Court]

[Caption]

Case No. *[_____]*
MOTION TO MODIFY
CUSTODY/PARENTAL
RIGHTS AND RESPON-
SIBILITIES

[Plaintiff/Defendant] moves that this Court modify the divorce decree, entered on *[date]*, with respect to the *[custody/allocation of parental rights and responsibilities]* of the parties' minor *[child/children]*, namely, *[name(s) and age(s) of children]*, by granting *[Plaintiff/Defendant]* permission to move said *[child/children]* from the state of Ohio to the state of *[name of state]*, for the reasons set forth in the affidavit attached hereto and marked as Exhibit "A."

_____

Attorney for *[Plaintiff/Defendant]*

[Notice of hearing]

[Exhibit "A"—Affidavit of movant giving reasons/justifications for motion]

[Proof/certificate of service]

NOTES TO FORM

Drafter's Notes

A full caption is required with post-decree motions. The motion papers must be served by the clerk of court pursuant to written instructions filed with the motion. Counsel should be aware that on post-decree motions service on the respondent will be required unless the respondent has a pending motion.

§ 16:23 Joint motion to modify parental rights and responsibilities—Shared parenting plan—Form⊚

[Title of Court]

[Caption]

Case No. [_____]
JOINT MOTION TO MODIFY
CUSTODY/PARENTAL RIGHTS
AND RESPONSIBILITIES

Plaintiff and Defendant move that this Court modify the dissolution/ divorce decree, entered on *[date]*, to *[change custody/reallocate parental rights and responsibilities]* of the parties' minor *[child/ children]*, namely, *[name(s) and date(s) of birth of children]*, to both parties under a shared parenting agreement as set forth in the shared parenting plan attached hereto as Exhibit "A." The Affidavits of the parties, attesting to the fact that such a modification is in the best interest of the children are attached hereto as Exhibits B and C.

_____

Attorney for *[Plaintiff/Defendant]*

[Exhibit "A"—Attach an executed shared parenting plan. The plan must be filed thirty days before the entry or decree establishing shared parenting.]

[Notice of hearing]

§ 16:24 Judgment entry modifying parental rights and responsibilities—Form⊚

[Title of Court]

[Caption]

Case No.
[_____]
JUDGMENT
ENTRY

This cause came before the Court on *[date]* upon the motion of *[Defendant]* for an order changing the residential parent and legal custodian of the minor *[child/children]* from *[Plaintiff]* to *[Defendant]*. Both parties appeared with counsel.

Upon the evidence and testimony presented, the Court finds said motion well taken and hereby changes the *[custody/residential parent and legal custodian]* of the minor *[child/children]* from Plaintiff to Defendant.

[Include statutory notices from Text § 15:77, Statutory notices for parents—Form.]

[Further, the prior order of support herein is terminated.]

or

[Further, Plaintiff is ordered to pay the sum of $[dollar amount] as and for support. Payments, plus processing charge, are to be made by withholding $[dollar amount] through the [name and address of county agency].]

_____
Judge

APPROVED:

_____
Attorney for Movant

Chapter 17

Uniform Child Custody Jurisdiction Act; Parental Kidnapping Prevention Act; Uniform Child Custody Jurisdiction and Enforcement Act; International Child Abduction Remedies Act

By Randal S. Bloch, Esq. and Gary J. Gottfried, Esq.

> KeyCite®: Cases and other legal materials listed in KeyCite Scope can be researched through the KeyCite service on Westlaw®. Use KeyCite to check citations for form, parallel references, prior and later history, and comprehensive citator information, including citations to other decisions and secondary materials.

§ 17:1 Uniform Child Custody Jurisdiction Act (UCCJA)— History

Until forty years ago, the question of child custody litigation between parents living in different states was rarely discussed.[1] However, during the 1960s, legal writers began issuing a hue and cry,[2] echoing an entreaty by Professor Geoffrey Hazard, Jr., who stated the problem succinctly when he wrote:

As Justice Rutledge then feared, the struggle between divorced spouses over the custody of their children has transcended the brutality and irregularity of guerrilla warfare. The child is filched from classroom, playground, public street, or his home, transported out of the state and perhaps across country by the abducting parent, there to be held pending a counterforay by the other parent. Meanwhile, each parent recruits the assistance of his home court or of courts elsewhere, seeking by various procedures to strengthen his grip on the child and to lessen that of the other parent.[3]

Since virtually all custody determinations may be modified, historically they have not been considered final judgments and thus not entitled to full faith and credit under Article IV, section 1 of the Ohio Constitution.[4] Further, the United States Supreme Court had failed to rule decisively on matters of jurisdiction and full faith and credit in state custody orders.[5]

The National Conference of Commissioners on Uniform State Laws had long recognized this problem. In an attempt to address the problem and abate the turmoil and confusion, it proceeded to draft uniform legislation. From these efforts came the Uniform Child

---

[Section 17:1]

[1]Brigitte M. Bodenheimer, *Progress Under the Uniform Child Custody Jurisdiction Act and Remaining Problems: Punitive Decrees, Joint Custody and Excessive Modifications,* 65 Cal. L. Rev. 978 (1977); see also Brigitte M. Bodenheimer, *Interstate Custody Initial Jurisdiction and Continuous Jurisdiction Under the UCCJA,* 14 Fam. L.Q. 203 (Winter 1981).

[2]See Brigitte M. Bodenheimer, *Progress Under the Uniform Child Custody Jurisdiction Act and Remaining Problems: Punitive Decrees, Joint Custody and Excessive Modifications,* 65 Cal. L. Rev. 978, 981 n.21 (1977).

[3]Geoffrey C. Hazard, Jr., *May v. Anderson: Preamble to Family Law Chaos,* 45 Va. L. Rev. 379, 392 (1959).

[4]See Ruby, *Modification of an Out of State Child Custody Decree Under the Uniform Child Custody Jurisdiction Act and the Parental Kidnapping Prevention Act,* 16 Rich. L. Rev. 773 (1982).

[5]See Sanford N. Katz, *Child Snatching:* The Legal Response to the Abduction of Children (ABA Sec. Fam. L. 1981); see also Evelyn Leonard Kosicki, Note, *Child Custody Jurisdiction in Ohio Implementing the Uniform Child Custody Jurisdiction Act,* 12 Akron L. Rev. 121 (1978).

Custody Jurisdiction Act (UCCJA). All states, including the District of Columbia, have now passed some version of the UCCJA or Uniform Child Custody Jurisdiction Enforcement Act (UCCJEA).

The act emphasizes ways to deal with the two great injustices under the present law: (1) that the person in possession of the child has the tactical advantage of keeping or obtaining custody regardless of the best interest; and (2) that to obtain this advantage, people will take possession of the child either through guile or ruthlessness.

The UCCJA was created to dissuade child snatchers and to terminate a party's selection of a forum by the imposition of jurisdictional restrictions. Its enactment was also an attempt to alleviate the problems caused by the states' failure to acknowledge and give full faith and credit to sister states' orders.

The Uniform Child Custody Jurisdiction Act was passed by Ohio in 1977 and was codified in RC 3109.21 to RC 3109.37. Although Ohio did not pass section 1, Purposes of the Act: Construction Provisions, the reasons for the legislation are stated in the Uniform Act. "The purpose of the UCCJA is to avoid jurisdictional conflict and to promote cooperation between state courts in custody matters so that a decree is rendered in the state that can . . . best decide the best interest of the child."[6] Ohio has sought to meet the purpose of the UCCJA, with the best interests of the child being of paramount concern, in its adoption of the legislation. This is indicated in the following overview:

(1) The place of the trial should be fair to the litigants.[7]

(2) The forum exercising jurisdiction should be that with maximum access to the relevant evidence.[8]

(3) Issues resolved in a fair hearing should not be redetermined in another forum, and full faith and credit should be given to a sister state court's ruling.[9]

(4) Two courts should not concurrently determine custody.[10]

(5) Removal of the child by either of the parents in disregard of the rights of the other and abduction or retention of the child by either of the parties in violation of a valid decree cannot be condoned.[11]

(6) Parenting determination includes visitation rights.[12]

(7) The state where the child is physically present should have

---

[6]Kachele v. Kachele, 115 Ohio App. 3d 609, 685 N.E.2d 1283 (8th Dist. Cuyahoga County 1996), citing State ex rel. Aycock v. Mowrey, 45 Ohio St. 3d 347, 544 N.E.2d 657 (1989).

[7]RC 3109.24, RC 3109.26, RC 3109.29.

[8]RC 3109.24, RC 3109.25, RC 3127.23, RC 3109.34.

[9]RC 3109.25, RC 3109.30(B), RC 3109.31, RC 3109.32, RC 3109.33(A).

[10]RC 3109.24.

[11]RC 3109.26.

[12]RC 3109.21(B).

authority to protect such child from mistreatment or abuse in an emergency situation.[13]

(8) The respondent or defendant is entitled to have fair notice of all proceedings under the UCCJA.[14]

(9) The tribunal must be advised of all prior and pending litigation concerning the minor child.[15]

(10) Communication between forums is essential.[16]

§ 17:2 UCCJA—Applicability

In any custody determination, now more properly referred to as "parenting determination,"[1] the provisions of the UCCJA are applicable. "Parenting determination" and "parenting proceeding"[2] are defined in RC 3109.21. A court must first determine whether it has jurisdiction and then determine if such jurisdiction should be exercised. The merits of the custody claim, in juvenile court,[3] probate court,[4] (including guardianships)[5] or domestic relations court,[6] cannot be adjudicated until the above-noted two-step jurisdictional test has been passed. Such is the requirement for initial, as well as post-judgment, determinations.

Ohio law requires that a parenting determination be made at the time of any divorce or legal separation. When Senate Bill 3 became effective April 11, 1991, "it became mandatory for the court to make a parenting determination in any divorce, legal separation, or annulment proceeding in which there were minor children. The language of R.C. 3109.04(A) is unequivocal."[7] Thus, the UCCJA is applicable in

---

[13]RC 3109.22(A)(3).

[14]RC 3109.23, RC 3109.28.

[15]RC 3127.23; Sullivan v. Whitten, 2000 WL 1222005 (Ohio Ct. App. 8th Dist. Cuyahoga County 2000).

[16]RC 3109.24, RC 3109.25, RC 3109.31 to RC 3109.34; Daerr v. Daerr, 41 Ohio App. 3d 206, 534 N.E.2d 1229 (9th Dist. Medina County 1987); Andres v. Andres, 1993 WL 155631 (Ohio Ct. App. 6th Dist. Erie County 1993) (court must stay proceedings and contact other state court); Hochmuth v. Hochmuth, 1995 WL 12070 (Ohio Ct. App. 6th Dist. Huron County 1995) (communication required as well as cooperation to avoid jurisdictional conflicts).

[Section 17:2]

[1]RC 3109.21(B).

[2]RC 3109.21(C).

[3]RC 2151.23.

[4]RC 2111.06.

[5]In re Guardianship of Pater, 2002-Ohio-315, 2002 WL 121213 (Ohio Ct. App. 9th Dist. Medina County 2002).

[6]See RC 3109.04.

[7]Schroeder v. Vigil-Escalera Perez, 76 Ohio Misc. 2d 25, 39, 664 N.E.2d 627 (C.P. 1995).

any case involving a parenting determination, including but not limited to all divorce or legal separation proceedings.[8]

Because the juvenile court has original and exclusive jurisdiction of children if they are not wards of another court of this state,[9] initial custody determinations are frequently made by that court. Post-judgment determinations are properly brought in the original forum. The original court may decline to exercise its continuing jurisdiction if none of the factors listed in RC 3109.22 are present and one or more of the factors listed in RC 3109.25 are present. Enforcement of orders of sister states generally occur in juvenile court, although any court of this state that renders custody or parenting decrees is allowed to enforce such orders under the registration provisions of the UCCJA.[10]

The issue of constitutional problems involving the UCCJA and personal jurisdiction is apparent. Subject matter jurisdiction cannot be granted by the parties to the court if it is lacking.[11] As quasi in rem jurisdiction no longer exists, personal jurisdiction and minimum contacts may be necessary prior to any exercise of jurisdiction by a tribunal.[12] "To satisfy the requirements of due process, a valid, enforceable custody adjudication requires *in personam* jurisdiction of the [parties]."[13] In *O'Keeffe v. O'Keeffe*,[14] the Tenth District Court of Appeals indicated that the due process rights of notice and an opportunity to be heard in one's own forum state, pursuant to the UCCJA, make the necessary assertion of in personam jurisdiction both just and fair. In *O'Keeffe*, neither party remained in the state where they had resided together. It was held to be error for the trial court to apply only a minimum contacts test to determine in personam jurisdiction, inasmuch as due process requirements are satisfied by cooperative acts between state courts to protect the opportunity to be heard.

---

[8]Bignell v. Bignell, 1997 WL 254150 (Ohio Ct. App. 2d Dist. Greene County 1997) (a trial court cannot limit the scope of its judgment to award a divorce and not determine custody).

[9]See RC 3109.04. See In re Poling, 64 Ohio St. 3d 211, 1992-Ohio-144, 594 N.E.2d 589 (1992) ("wards of another court of this state" do not include children under divorce decree). See In re West, 2001-Ohio-2634, 2001 WL 1659385 (Ohio Ct. App. 4th Dist. Washington County 2001) (as juvenile court has exclusive original jurisdiction over children who are not wards of this state, when a divorce was granted in West Virginia, and both parents and the child lived in Ohio, the juvenile court had subject matter jurisdiction).

[10]RC 3109.32.

[11]State ex rel. Bond v. Velotta Co., 91 Ohio St. 3d 418, 419, 2001-Ohio-91, 746 N.E.2d 1071 (2001).

[12]See Shaffer v. Heitner, 433 U.S. 186, 97 S. Ct. 2569, 53 L. Ed. 2d 683 (1977); Kulko v. Superior Court of California In and For City and County of San Francisco, 436 U.S. 84, 98 S. Ct. 1690, 56 L. Ed. 2d 132 (1978).

[13]O'Keeffe v. O'Keeffe, 1986 WL 7168, at *4 (Ohio Ct. App. 10th Dist. Franklin County 1986); Pasqualone v. Pasqualone, 63 Ohio St. 2d 96, 17 Ohio Op. 3d 58, 406 N.E.2d 1121 (1980). See also May v. Anderson, 345 U.S. 528, 73 S. Ct. 840, 97 L. Ed. 1221, 67 Ohio L. Abs. 468 (1953).

[14]O'Keeffe v. O'Keeffe, 1986 WL 7168 (Ohio Ct. App. 10th Dist. Franklin County 1986).

The question of jurisdiction is discussed at length in *Broz v. Broz*,[15] "the filing and acceptance of a petition to register a foreign judgment does not confer personal jurisdiction per se. . . . Jurisdiction can be conferred only by constitutional provision or legislative enactment and may not be conferred by consent or acquiescence of the parties. . . . Jurisdiction over the subject matter must be conferred by legislative enactment." Judge Karner stated in *Schroeder v. Vigil-Escalera Perez*,[16] "Therefore, it is clear that R.C. 3109.04, in conjunction with R.C. 2307.385, extends the long-arm jurisdiction to grant in personam jurisdiction in all divorce cases with children, where application of the UCCJA (R.C. 3109.22) indicates that custody jurisdiction is appropriate." This constitutional question of due process will continue to be raised.

In *Smith v. Smith*,[17] the parties had never lived together in Ohio, the children resided in South Carolina with their mother who had not consented to the action, and the plaintiff-father had not filed an affidavit pursuant to RC 3127.23(A). The trial court overlooked all of these defects and awarded the father custody. The appellate court could find no basis for the trial court's order, and held that Ohio was not the home state of the children and, since the court did not acquire personal jurisdiction over the mother, the court was without jurisdiction to make orders regarding custody and support.

§ 17:3 UCCJA—Jurisdiction—Priorities—In general

The heart of the UCCJA, as adopted by Ohio, is RC 3109.22 which sets forth the prerequisites to jurisdiction.

The jurisdictional bases set forth below have been listed according to priority: (1) home state, (2) significant connections, (3) emergency, and (4) no other forum available.[1]

§ 17:4 UCCJA—Jurisdiction—Priorities—Home state

Home state is defined in RC 3109.21(E):

"Home state" means the state in which the child, immediately preceding the time involved, lived with his parents, a parent, or a person acting as parent, for at least six consecutive months, and in the case of a child less than six months old the state in which the child lived from

---

[15]Broz v. Broz, 1995 WL 643938, at *2–3 (Ohio Ct. App. 10th Dist. Franklin County 1995).

[16]Schroeder v. Vigil-Escalera Perez, 76 Ohio Misc. 2d 25, 40, 664 N.E.2d 627 (C.P. 1995) (citing Heckler Co. v. Incorporated Village of Napoleon, 56 Ohio App. 110, 8 Ohio Op. 171, 24 Ohio L. Abs. 85, 10 N.E.2d 32 (3d Dist. Henry County 1937).

[17]Smith v. Smith, 1993 WL 370824 (Ohio Ct. App. 5th Dist. Guernsey County 1993).

[Section 17:3]

[1]Official comments to the UCCJA § 3. See also In re McDonald, 74 Mich. App. 119, 253 N.W.2d 678 (1977); Ruff v. Ruff, 98 Misc. 2d 934, 415 N.Y.S.2d 179 (Fam. Ct. 1979); BNA, *Interstate Custody Litigation Guide* (1981).

birth with any of the persons mentioned. Periods of temporary absence of any of the named persons are counted as part of the six-month or other period.

According to the commissioners of the Uniform Act, jurisdiction should primarily be in the home state.[1]

Where there is conflicting testimony regarding the home state of the child, credibility and weight to be assigned to the evidence are the exclusive province of the trier of fact.[2]

The "home state" of the child was where the child lived for at least six consecutive months, irrespective of whether a parent had established a permanent residence or domicile within that state.[3]

§ 17:5   UCCJA—Jurisdiction—Priorities—Significant connections

A court may exercise jurisdiction if it is in the best interest of the child and where the child and one contestant have significant connections with the state. There must also be available in the state substantial evidence concerning the child's present or future care, protection, training, and personal relationships.[1] In Ohio, this jurisdictional alternative seems to have priority over the other options available under RC 3109.22.[2] In reality, the courts of Ohio look to the factors of RC 3109.22 that can be cumulative in order to exercise jurisdiction.[3] The preferred jurisdiction appears to be the forum which has the "optimum access to relevant evidence about the child and family. There must be maximum rather than minimum contact with the state."[4]

In *Roth v. Hatfield*,[5] the Fourth District Court of Appeals determined that Ohio should not defer to a Michigan custody decree under the "strong contact" provision of the UCCJA. The court noted that the

---

[Section 17:4]

[1]Warman v. Warman, 294 Pa. Super. 285, 439 A.2d 1203 (1982).

[2]Shamblin v. Shamblin, 1989 WL 140178 (Ohio Ct. App. 11th Dist. Trumbull County 1989).

[3]Matter of Brown, 1991 WL 38881 (Ohio Ct. App. 2d Dist. Greene County 1991).

[Section 17:5]

[1]RC 3109.22(A)(2).

[2]In re Wonderly's Guardianship, 67 Ohio St. 2d 178, 21 Ohio Op. 3d 111, 423 N.E.2d 420 (1981).

[3]In re Reynolds, 2 Ohio App. 3d 309, 441 N.E.2d 1141 (1st Dist. Hamilton County 1982); In Re: Heritage, 1981 WL 9973 (Ohio Ct. App. 1st Dist. Hamilton County 1981).

[4]In re Wonderly's Guardianship, 67 Ohio St. 2d 178, 21 Ohio Op. 3d 111, 423 N.E.2d 420 (1981); Matter of Lehman, 1993 WL 171797 (Ohio Ct. App. 5th Dist. Richland County 1993) (children's connection to this state below even a bare minimum).

[5]Roth v. Hatfield, 1983 WL 2300 (Ohio Ct. App. 4th Dist. Gallia County 1983) (guardianship proceeding).

child was living in Ohio and the mother in North Dakota. In *In re Dissolution of Watson*,[6] the Ninth District Court of Appeals held that where the record shows that three states have some degree of connection with the parties and the child, and that Ohio has real and significant contacts with both the parents and the child (having rendered the original judgment and being familiar with the history of the parties and the case), then it is not an abuse of discretion under the UCCJA to assume jurisdiction.

Where a child is in the temporary custody of its grandparents in Ohio, while its mother resides in another jurisdiction (where evidence as to her suitability as a custodian would be located), an Ohio court considering assuming jurisdiction over a custody dispute should declare itself an inconvenient forum.[7]

§ 17:6 UCCJA—Jurisdiction—Priorities—Emergency

There are two reasons for a court to assume jurisdiction under RC 3109.22(A)(3): abandonment of a child, or abuse or threatened abuse or mistreatment of a child physically present within the state.[1] The emergency jurisdiction of the court for the protection of the child must be supported by credible evidence.[2]

"The assumption of emergency jurisdiction, however, only confers jurisdiction to make temporary custody orders."[3] Where an Ohio court had exercised jurisdiction since 1988 and an alleged emergency arose in Florida with allegations of abuse and neglect, the Ohio court indicated that in its exercise of emergency jurisdiction, the Florida court only had authority to enter a temporary custody order. The Florida court did not have authority to make a permanent custody order and its exercise of emergency jurisdiction did not divest Ohio of its jurisdiction.[4]

§ 17:7 UCCJA—Jurisdiction—Priorities—No other forum available

When no other state meets jurisdictional prerequisites or a court in another state has declined to exercise jurisdiction, if it is in the best interest of the child, then Ohio may exercise jurisdiction.

---

[6]In re Marriage of Watson, 13 Ohio App. 3d 344, 469 N.E.2d 876 (9th Dist. Lorain County 1983).

[7]Spencer v. Spencer, 1984 WL 3308 (Ohio Ct. App. 12th Dist. Preble County 1984); Spencer v. Pryor, 1985 WL 7687 (Ohio Ct. App. 12th Dist. Preble County 1985).

[Section 17:6]

[1]Official comment to UCCJA § 3. See also In Re: Heritage, 1981 WL 9973 (Ohio Ct. App. 1st Dist. Hamilton County 1981).

[2]Young v. District Court of Boulder County in 20th Judicial Dist., 194 Colo. 140, 570 P.2d 249 (1977).

[3]In re McClelland, No. 94-L-153 (Ohio Ct. App. 11th Dist. Lake County 1995).

[4]In re McClelland, No. 94-L-153 (Ohio Ct. App. 11th Dist. Lake County 1995) (communication between the two forums is also required).

§ 17:8   UCCJA—Jurisdiction—Continuing jurisdiction and/or concurrent jurisdiction

A split has occurred between the theorists and the courts concerning continuing jurisdiction and concurrent jurisdiction. This split essentially occurs in post-judgment and modification cases. Professor Bodenheimer suggests that there cannot be concurrent jurisdiction and that such theory is incompatible with the Uniform Act.[1] Under her theory, "[once] a court of another state has made a custody decree, a court of this state shall not modify that decree."[2] Exclusive continuing jurisdiction is thus placed in the state granting the initial determination. "Only when the child and all parties have moved away is deference to another state's continuing jurisdiction no longer required."[3]

After stating, "The purpose of the UCCJA is to avoid jurisdictional conflict and to promote cooperation between state courts in custody matters so that a decree is rendered in the state that can best decide the best interest of the child," the Supreme Court in *State ex rel Aycock v. Mowrey*[4] denied a writ of prohibition to prevent an Ohio judge from assuming jurisdiction to change or modify another state's custody decree.[5] Yet, in 2000, the Ohio Supreme Court stated, "once a court of competent jurisdiction has begun the task of deciding the long-term fate of a child, all other courts are to refrain from excercising juridiction over that matter."[6]

The courts have viewed this matter differently. In Ohio, courts have specifically recognized the theory of concurrent jurisdiction.[7] The abundance of litigation under the UCCJA has evolved because two states have exercised their jurisdiction concurrently, and appellate courts must rule on the validity of the jurisdiction. Where trial courts of two states have determined that they meet the jurisdictional

---

[Section 17:8]

[1]Brigitte M. Bodenheimer, *Interstate Custody: Initial Jurisdiction and Continuing Jurisdiction Under the UCCJA*, 14 Fam. L.Q. 203 (Winter 1981).

[2]Brigitte M. Bodenheimer, *Interstate Custody: Initial Jurisdiction and Continuing Jurisdiction Under the UCCJA*, 14 Fam. L.Q. 203, 214 (Winter 1981); RC 3109. 31(A).

[3]Brigitte M. Bodenheimer, *Interstate Custody: Initial Jurisdiction and Continuing Jurisdiction Under the UCCJA*, 14 Fam. L.Q. 203, 214 (Winter 1981); RC 3109. 31(A).

[4]State ex rel. Aycock v. Mowrey, 45 Ohio St. 3d 347, 544 N.E.2d 657 (1989).

[5]See also Knapp v. Knapp, 1990 WL 34104 (Ohio Ct. App. 4th Dist. Ross County 1990).

[6]In re Adoption of Asente, 90 Ohio St. 3d 91, 92, 2000-Ohio-32, 734 N.E.2d 1224 (2000).

[7]In re Wonderly's Guardianship, 67 Ohio St. 2d 178, 21 Ohio Op. 3d 111, 423 N.E.2d 420 (1981); Matter of Prysock, 1995 WL 360311 (Ohio Ct. App. 10th Dist. Franklin County 1995) See In re Absher Children, 141 Ohio App. 3d 118, 2001-Ohio-4197, 750 N.E.2d 188 (12th Dist. Butler County 2001) regarding tribal court jurisdiction.

prerequisites, the first to exercise jurisdiction is entitled to the deference of the other.[8]

In Kachele v. Kachele,[9] the parties lived in Virginia at the time of divorce, where their decree was entered, and the mother and children relocated to Ohio. The father subsequently filed a contempt motion regarding visitation in the Virginia courts, and he was awarded custody of one of the children in the Virginia court. He then moved to Hawaii, where the question of which court had jurisdiction was raised. The Eighth District Court of Appeals viewed this matter as a case of first impression as neither party had any current contact with Virginia, where the decree originated. In following the UCCJA, the court determined that Virginia continued to have jurisdiction, and that Virginia did not decline to exercise its jurisdiction.

Under RC 3109.31, which "strongly encourages modifications of a court order to be made by the same court,"[10] and under RC 3109.04 and Civil Rule 75, which recognize the authority of a court to modify its own order, an Ohio trial court may modify a prior visitation order where the residential parent and the child have moved out of state and another motion is pending in the out-of-state forum. Contrary to theory, therefore, courts have modified sister states' parenting and visitation orders where they believe they have jurisdiction to do so.

In a case which carefully analyzed the jurisdictional issues of the UCCJA, the appellate court in *Fox v. Fox*[11] considered whether the original court with jurisdiction (Hawaii) had continuing jurisdiction to render its modification decree, and further whether the Hawaii court properly exercised jurisdiction under the UCCJA when it awarded a change of custody to the mother. The court recited citations from several jurisdictions, including federal interpretation of the Parental Kidnapping Prevention Act (PKPA),[12] to emphasize the "principle of continuing jurisdiction, i.e., the court that originally decided the issue of custody retains continuing jurisdiction for purposes of modification."[13] Thus, although the child had been living in Ohio for at least one year, the original court was a proper forum. The court declined to impose on the party filing a decree under RC 3109.32, the requirements of the Uniform Enforcement of Foreign Judgments Act

---

[8]Squires v. Squires, 12 Ohio App. 3d 138, 468 N.E.2d 73 (12th Dist. Preble County 1983); Washington v. Smith, 1989 WL 33108 (Ohio Ct. App. 2d Dist. Greene County 1989).

[9]Kachele v. Kachele, 115 Ohio App. 3d 609, 685 N.E.2d 1283 (8th Dist. Cuyahoga County 1996).

[10]Clark v. Clark, 1984 WL 7638, at *2 (Ohio Ct. App. 9th Dist. Lorain County 1984).

[11]Fox v. Fox, 1988 WL 38031, at *3 (Ohio Ct. App. 5th Dist. Tuscarawas County 1988).

[12]Parental Kidnapping Prevention Act of 1980, 28 U.S.C.A. § 1738A. See also Text §§ 17:19 et seq., PKPA.

[13]Fox v. Fox, 1988 WL 38031 (Ohio Ct. App. 5th Dist. Tuscarawas County 1988).

(UEFJA),[14] finding the UEFJA inapplicable to foreign child custody decrees.

The Supreme Court, in *State ex rel. Seaton v. Holmes*[15] in an action for a writ of prohibition, looked beyond the UCCJA and quoted from the PKPA to expand on the definition "such state remains the residence of . . . any contestant." When no party remained in Ohio at the time of the father's filing for a post-decree relief, the trial court erred in exercising continuing jurisdiction.

In *Churchill v. Wood*[16] the appellate court quoted at length a Florida Supreme Court analysis of the UCCJA and the continuing jurisdiction attaching to the state that made the initial determination. However, the appellate court upheld the denial of the grandparents' rights of visitation which arose from the Florida decree under a doctrine of best interests because the child had not lived in Florida for several years.

While Ohio had been the home state of the children for five years prior to the grandparents' filing of a custody complaint in Ohio, the assumption of jurisdiction by a trial court was reversed where Utah had made an earlier original order of custody, Utah would not relinquish jurisdiction, Utah ordered custody to the father, and the father continued to reside in that state.[17]

§ 17:9 UCCJA—Jurisdiction—Decision to exercise jurisdiction—In general

The UCCJA represents a changing attitude by the courts on the subject of a court's jurisdiction. In the past, jurisdiction was thought of as synonymous with the territorial power of a court to act, but this attitude has been changing since *International Shoe Co. v. Washington*,[1] which held that a corporation's sufficient contacts or ties with a state make that corporation amenable to suit in courts of that state. The act represents the furthest step taken from the old physical power concept of jurisdiction. It includes provisions for the court to decline jurisdiction where there is concurrent jurisdiction with a court of another state, where there is a pending parenting action in another

---

[14]RC 2329.021 et seq.

[15]State ex. Rel. Seaton v. Holmes, 100 Ohio St. 3d. 265, 2003-Ohio-5897 (Ohio 2003).

[16]Churchill v. Wood, 1993 WL 102634 (Ohio Ct. App. 2d Dist. Greene County 1993).

[17]Boehn v. Shurtliff, 90 Ohio App. 3d 363, 629 N.E.2d 478 (6th Dist. Huron County 1993); see In re McClelland, No. 94-L-153 (Ohio Ct. App. 11th Dist. Lake County 1995).

[Section 17:9]

[1]International Shoe Co. v. State of Wash., Office of Unemployment Compensation and Placement, 326 U.S. 310, 66 S. Ct. 154, 90 L. Ed. 95, 161 A.L.R. 1057 (1945).

state,[2] where there is a finding of inconvenient forum,[3] or where the petitioner improperly takes or retains a child.[4]

The UCCJA sets forth not only the factors to be considered to establish the court's jurisdiction but also provides a second step to determine whether Ohio should exercise that jurisdiction. The Ohio Supreme Court has ruled that "[t]he Court in which a decree of divorce is originally rendered retains continuing jurisdiction over matters relating to the custody, care and support of the minor children of the parties."[5] However, a jurisdictional dispute may arise when one parent moves out of state with a child. The issue then which must be determined as to which state has the authority to exercise jurisdiction.[6] In its ruling in *Justis v. Justis*, the Ohio Supreme Court indicated that "another state can modify an existing parenting decree if [1] the state seeking to modify the decree has jurisdiction to make a child custody determination, and [2] the original state no longer has jurisdiction, or has declined to exercise such jurisdiction."[7]

In addressing the issue of inconvenient forum, and whether the court of another state is a more appropriate forum, the court in *In re Skrha*[8] approved the trial court's declining to exercise jurisdiction when the children had always lived in Alaska, and only came to Ohio for visits. The court also rejected the appellant's argument that the trial court's initial "ex parte" temporary possession order equated to an "initial decree" which prevented the trial court from later declining to exercise its jurisdiction, stating that "A court issuing an injunction has inherent authority to modify or vacate its own injunctive decree."[9]

Although Ohio was no longer the "home state" of the minor child in *Gordon v. Gordon*[10] and had not been for two years prior to the filing of a motion for change of custody and three years by the time of the hearing, jurisdiction continued from the initial case, and there was

---

[2]RC 3109.24.

[3]RC 3109.25.

[4]RC 3109.26.

[5]Loetz v. Loetz, 63 Ohio St. 2d 1, 2, 17 Ohio Op. 3d 1, 406 N.E.2d 1093 (1980).

[6]Justis v. Justis, 81 Ohio St. 3d 312, 314, 1989-Ohio-626, 691 N.E.2d 264 (1998); Lawrence v. Lawrence, 2002-Ohio-1310, 2002 WL 445055 (Ohio Ct. App. 12th Dist. Clermont County 2002).

[7]Lawrence v. Lawrence, 2002-Ohio-1310, 2002 WL 445055 (Ohio Ct. App. 12th Dist. Clermont County 2002). *Lawrence* provides an in depth analysis of the UCCJA.

[8]In re Skrha, 98 Ohio App. 3d 487, 648 N.E.2d 908 (8th Dist. Cuyahoga County 1994); Flinn v. Flinn, 1996 WL 132389 (Ohio Ct. App. 5th Dist. Fairfield County 1996) (trial court correctly declined to exercise jurisdiction where two other states had more connections; Kansas, the original decreeing state, and Colorado, where the custodial father and the child reside, mere convenience to the mother in Ohio, who has the child in summer, is not sufficient to exercise jurisdiction).

[9]In re Skrha, 98 Ohio App. 3d 487, 497, 648 N.E.2d 908 (8th Dist. Cuyahoga County 1994).

[10]Gordon v. Gordon, 1987 WL 18751 (Ohio Ct. App. 4th Dist. Athens County 1987).

substantial evidence in Ohio available concerning the child's future care, protection, training, and personal relationships. The purpose and procedures of the UCCJA were cited even though there was no action pending in another state.[11]

Citing *In re Guardianship of Wonderly*[12] to require application of the UCCJA when the custody of a minor child is the primary issue or one of several issues in a case, the Tenth District Court of Appeals, in *Snelling v. Gardner*,[13] held that by the very nature of the Act, custody of the child must be disputed before the UCCJA applies. Since there was no indication that custody was disputed, the UCCJA was held inapplicable to the case.

Many cases raising UCCJA jurisdictional issues have confusing and cumbersome fact patterns. In *Galindo v. De Los Santos*,[14] the mother had filed a parentage complaint in the Juvenile Division of the Common Pleas Court of Defiance County, which established paternity and child support. Subsequently the parties moved to Kentucky and married. Upon notice of the marriage, the juvenile court terminated the child support order. A year later, after the mother apparently returned to Defiance County, the trial court awarded custody to the mother and ordered child support. Thereafter, the father dissolved their marriage in Kentucky and agreed that the court in Defiance County would have jurisdiction over all child matters. After several subsequent motions in Defiance County, including after mother had moved to Michigan, the Defiance County court made other custody orders. On appeal, the Third District Court of Appeals, after stating that subject matter jurisdiction cannot be conferred upon the court by the parties, held that the trial court should not have exercised jurisdiction and reversed the judgment.

§ 17:10 UCCJA—Jurisdiction—Decision to exercise jurisdiction—Pending proceedings

If parenting proceedings are pending in another state which has substantially adopted the UCCJA, an Ohio court may not exercise its jurisdiction.[1] It is crucial that the sister state's exercise of jurisdiction be substantially in accordance with the UCCJA before it can be

---

[11]See In re McClelland, No. 94-L-153 (Ohio Ct. App. 11th Dist. Lake County 1995).

[12]In re Wonderly's Guardianship, 67 Ohio St. 2d 178, 21 Ohio Op. 3d 111, 423 N.E.2d 420 (1981).

[13]Snelling v. Gardner, 69 Ohio App. 3d 196, 590 N.E.2d 330 (10th Dist. Franklin County 1990).

[14]Galindo v. DeLosSantos, 2004-Ohio-3343, 2004 WL 1433539 (Ohio Ct. App. 3d Dist. Defiance County 2004).

[Section 17:10]

[1]RC 3109.24(A).

recognized and enforced.[2] When a sister state exercised jurisdiction not in conformity with the UCCJA, the Hamilton County Juvenile Court refused to honor and recognize the out-of-state order and made its own determination.[3]

In *Squires v. Squires*,[4] an Ohio custody decision was voided because it conflicted with an out-of-state custody order (and was therefore not in the child's best interest) and because the Ohio court rendering the decision had failed to communicate with the out-of-state court about the parenting proceedings pending there when it had reason to know of them.

If the exercise of jurisdiction by the sister state is in substantial conformity with the UCCJA, deference will be shown to the sister state.[5] The information required by affidavit under RC 3127.23 is used by an Ohio court to ascertain if there are pending parenting proceedings elsewhere.[6] If the court suspects foreign proceedings, it must make an inquiry to the other state.[7] The clerk of each court that renders a parenting decree shall maintain a parenting and custody registry. All communications regarding pendency of parenting proceedings, findings of inconvenient forum plus other relevant documents are to be entered in the registry along with certified copies of parenting decrees of other states.[8]

There are few cases that discuss the type or the substance of communications required between courts of sister states. In a unique argument, an appellant argued that procedural due process had been violated under the Constitution and the UCCJA, as the courts conducted "ex parte communications."[9] In addressing this argument, the appellate court reflected that jurisdictional discussions between the courts were not substantive in nature but rather procedural. The court further reviewed whether any violation of the Code of Judicial Conduct had occurred when the Ohio and Kentucky courts spoke. "Under Ohio's UCCJA, communications between the courts of different states is clearly encouraged. RC 3109.24 allows, and RC 3109.25

---

[2]Pasqualone v. Pasqualone, 63 Ohio St. 2d 96, 17 Ohio Op. 3d 58, 406 N.E.2d 1121 (1980); In re Marriage of Hopson, 110 Cal. App. 3d 884, 168 Cal. Rptr. 345 (1st Dist. 1980); Williams v. Zacher, 35 Or. App. 129, 581 P.2d 91, 96 A.L.R.3d 959 (1978); Sholty v. Carruth, 126 Ariz. 458, 616 P.2d 918 (Ct. App. Div. 2 1980).

[3]In re Bryan, No. F82-2102 (Ohio Juv. Ct. Hamilton County 1982).

[4]Squires v. Squires, 12 Ohio App. 3d 138, 468 N.E.2d 73 (12th Dist. Preble County 1983) (RC 3109.24 contemplates that Ohio court not exercise jurisdiction in such case until it has communicated with out-of-state court and proper forum has been determined).

[5]Bacon v. Bacon, 97 Mich. App. 334, 293 N.W.2d 819 (1980); Palm v. Superior Court, 97 Cal. App. 3d 456, 158 Cal. Rptr. 786 (4th Dist. 1979).

[6]RC 3109.24(B).

[7]Paltrow v. Paltrow, 37 Md. App. 191, 376 A.2d 1134 (1977), judgment aff'd, 283 Md. 291, 388 A.2d 547 (1978).

[8]RC 3109.33(A).

[9]In re Simons, 1997 WL 102015 (2d Dist. Ct. App., Montgomery, 3-7-97).

mandates, communications between trial courts. Neither statute requires that the parties participate in the conversation. Nor do the statutes require that the communications be recorded."[10] It is thus clear that there is no violation of a party's due process rights when courts communicate regarding the jurisdictional and procedural issues under the UCCJA.

Interstate cooperation is mandated by the act. If the Ohio court learns of concurrent proceedings here and in another state, it must stay the proceedings in order to communicate and exchange information with the foreign court to insure that the issue is litigated in the more appropriate forum.[11] Ohio courts must follow this information exchange requirement even if they do not learn of the pending out-of-state litigation until after a decree is issued in Ohio or until after they have assumed jurisdiction. The statutes comprising the UCCJA in Ohio clearly do not say that in the latter two instances an Ohio court is not required to stay proceedings.[12]

In *Palm v. Superior Court of San Diego County*,[13] the court stated "The state which enjoys priority of time in initiating the proceedings will proceed if the dispute is not resolved by agreement or consent of the other court. . . . The [Uniform] Act permits the state which first obtained jurisdiction to exercise it." The priority of filing rule also has authority from Professor Bodenheimer.[14] Although the UCCJA does not mandate that the winner will be the first to have filed, in effect, a stay of proceedings is required for communication between the courts.

The UCCJA, specifically RC 3109.24, does not address the situation where (1) an out-of-state court has acquired jurisdiction prior to an Ohio filing for custody, (2) communication has repeatedly been attempted by the Ohio court, and (3) the out-of-state court fails or refuses to respond. The Preble County Juvenile Court determined that the statute means the Ohio proceedings should be "stayed for a reasonable time" and further determined that "six months is a more than adequate time for a determination."[15]

The decision of a trial court early in parenting proceedings that jurisdiction exists does not preclude a different decision later. "The jurisdictional issue in custody situations . . . is fluid not static. . . . This wide-ranging discretion is one of the cornerstones of the UCCJA.

---

[10]In re Simons, 118 Ohio App. 3d 622, 632, 693 N.E.2d 1111 (2d Dist. Montgomery County 1997). See also Lawrence v. Lawrence, 2002-Ohio-1310, 2002 WL 445055 (Ohio Ct. App. 12th Dist. Clermont County 2002), where the appellate court discussed substantive vs. procedural communications between courts.

[11]In re Custody of Rector, 39 Colo. App. 111, 565 P.2d 950 (App. 1977).

[12]See In re Marriage of Weinstein, 87 Ill. App. 3d 101, 42 Ill. Dec. 243, 408 N.E.2d 952 (1st Dist. 1980).

[13]Palm v. Superior Court, 97 Cal. App. 3d 456, 466-68, 158 Cal. Rptr. 786 (4th Dist. 1979).

[14]Brigitte M. Bodenheimer, *Interstate Custody: Initial Jurisdiction and Continuing Jurisdiction Under the UCCJA*, 14 Fam. L. Q. 203 (Winter 1981).

[15]Reed v. Reed, 41 Ohio Misc. 2d 13, 14, 535 N.E.2d 761 (C.P. 1987).

The best interest of the child is always the litmus test for determining jurisdiction."[16]

§ 17:11 UCCJA—Jurisdiction—Decision to exercise jurisdiction—Inconvenient forum

The second concept used to insure that only one forum will decide the parenting matter is that of inconvenient forum. To determine the more appropriate forum, the court must consult the guidelines set forth in RC 3109.25(C)(1) to (4). It may also communicate with another court to obtain further data.[1] The court may, upon its own motion or that of a party under RC 3109.25(B), dismiss the proceedings or stay the proceedings upon conditions that may be proper and just.[2]

"'The purpose of this provision is to encourage judicial restraint in exercising jurisdiction whenever another state appears to be in a better position to determine custody of a child. It serves as a second check on jurisdiction once the test of section 3 or 14 has been met.' "[3] In failing to dismiss a suit, the Ohio Supreme Court held that the trial court abused its discretion on the theory of inconvenient forum.[4] The interest of the child is best served when the forum has optimum access to relevant evidence about the child and family. There must be maximum rather than minimum contact with the state.[5] However, in *Spencer v. Pryor*,[6] although the child had been in Ohio with its grandparents for over three years due to court proceedings, and where the custody dispute was between a nonparent Ohio resident and a non-resident parent, the court found that a determination of the parent's ability to care for the child could more appropriately be made in the parent's state.

Where the trial court had proper jurisdiction, and the custodial parent moved to Texas during the pendency, it was inappropriate for the court to abdicate, in its initial decree, future jurisdiction over child support and custody before an actual controversy arose.[7] The trial court should not attempt to predict future events.

The doctrine of inconvenient forum, as found in RC 3109.25, applies

---

[16]Luptak v. Luptak, 1985 WL 10403, at *3 (Ohio Ct. App. 7th Dist. Mahoning County 1985).

[Section 17:11]

[1]RC 3109.25(D).

[2]RC 3109.25(E).

[3]In re Wonderly's Guardianship, 67 Ohio St. 2d 178, 186, 21 Ohio Op. 3d 111, 423 N.E.2d 420 (1981).

[4]In re Wonderly's Guardianship, 67 Ohio St. 2d 178, 21 Ohio Op. 3d 111, 423 N.E.2d 420 (1981).

[5]In re Wonderly's Guardianship, 67 Ohio St. 2d 178, 21 Ohio Op. 3d 111, 423 N.E.2d 420 (1981).

[6]Spencer v. Pryor, 1985 WL 7687 (Ohio Ct. App. 12th Dist. Preble County 1985).

[7]Canales v. Canales, 1989 WL 24187 (Ohio Ct. App. 2d Dist. Greene County 1989).

only to parenting determinations, and is not an appropriate reason to transfer a case where the only issues are child or spousal support.[8]

§ 17:12 UCCJA—Jurisdiction—Decision to exercise jurisdiction—Improper retention

RC 3109.26 deals with the petitioner's improper taking or retention of the child. The court can refuse to exercise jurisdiction if a party enters the court having wrongfully taken or retained the child.[1] The court may not exercise its jurisdiction to modify a parenting decree of another state if there has been an improper retention of the child after a visit or temporary relinquishment.[2] The critical feature of this provision absolutely precludes the court from exercising jurisdiction when the retention of the child is wrongful.[3]

"The mere showing by a Petitioner who wrongfully retains custody that he provides a better or more stable environment for a child as opposed to the party granted custody under the original out of state decree does not per se meet the 'best interest' standard set forth in the Uniform Child Custody Jurisdiction Act."[4] In fact, the court has no jurisdiction where there is wrongful detention of a child; thus, any ruling upon custody by such state is not entitled to full faith and credit and is not made in accordance with the UCCJA.[5]

Where children were taken by the wife ostensibly under a visitation order issued in conjunction with a temporary custody order in a Texas divorce proceeding initiated by the wife, the retention was found to be a wrongful taking.[6] The wife dismissed her divorce after she brought the children to Ohio. The appellate court affirmed the trial court's finding and stated, "The statute was adopted to ensure, in part, that children do not become pawns to their parents' plans and desires to

---

[8]Drucker v. Drucker, 2000 WL 1176514 (Ohio Ct. App. 8th Dist. Cuyahoga County 2000); Durgans v. Durgans, 2001 WL 114983 (Ohio Ct. App. 11th Dist. Portage County 2001), "unlike venue, parties cannot stipulate to a particular court's jurisdiction," citing Beatrice Foods Co. v. Porterfield, 30 Ohio St. 2d 50, 59 Ohio Op. 2d 76, 282 N.E.2d 355 (1972).

[Section 17:12]

[1]RC 3109.26(A).

[2]RC 3109.26(B).

[3]In Re: Heritage, 1981 WL 9973 (Ohio Ct. App. 1st Dist. Hamilton County 1981); In re Marriage of Hopson, 110 Cal. App. 3d 884, 168 Cal. Rptr. 345 (1st Dist. 1980).

[4]Matter of Potter, 56 Ohio Misc. 17, 20, 10 Ohio Op. 3d 214, 377 N.E.2d 536 (C.P. 1978).

[5]In Re: Heritage, 1981 WL 9973 (Ohio Ct. App. 1st Dist. Hamilton County 1981); Warman v. Warman, 294 Pa. Super. 285, 439 A.2d 1203 (1982); Howard v. Howard, 378 So. 2d 1329 (Fla. Dist. Ct. App. 5th Dist. 1980) (if court has no jurisdiction in beginning, it cannot be acquired); Williams v. Zacher, 35 Or. App. 129, 581 P.2d 91, 96 A.L.R.3d 959 (1978); Van Haren v. Van Haren, 171 N.J. Super. 12, 407 A.2d 1242 (App. Div. 1979).

[6]Syrios v. Syrios, 69 Ohio App. 3d 246, 248, 590 N.E.2d 759 (9th Dist. Summit County 1990).

gain custody."[7] The court refused to give "blind adherence to the literal meaning of 'wrongfully taken.'"[8]

§ 17:13 UCCJA—Pleadings and practice

It is mandatory in all cases concerning parenting of children, either initially or post judgment, that an affidavit under RC 3127.23(A) be filed. The information required to be stated in the affidavit is set forth in RC 3127.23(A). An affidavit requires the following:

(A) Each party in a parenting proceeding, in the party's first pleading or in an affidavit attached to that pleading, shall give information under oath as to the child's present address, the places where the child has lived within the last five years, and the name and present address of each person with whom the child has lived during that period. In this pleading or affidavit, each party also shall include all of the following information:

(1) Whether the party has participated as a party, a witness, or in any other capacity in any other litigation, in this or any other state, that concerned the allocation, between the parents of the same child, of parental rights and responsibilities for the care of the child and the designation of the residential parent and legal custodian of the child or that otherwise concerned the custody of the same child;

(2) Whether the party has information of any parenting proceeding concerning the child pending in a court of this or any other state;

(3) Whether the party knows of any person who is not a party to the proceeding and has physical custody of the child or claims to be a parent of the child who is designated the residential parent and legal custodian of the child or to have visitation rights with respect to the child or to be a person other than a parent of the child who has custody or visitation rights with respect to the child;

(4) Whether the party previously has been convicted of or pleaded guilty to any criminal offense involving any act that resulted in a child being an abused child or a neglected child or previously has been determined, in a case in which a child has been adjudicated an abused child or a neglected child, to be the perpetrator of the abusive or neglectful act that was the basis of the adjudication.

Such affidavit must therefore be filed in every divorce, legal separation, dissolution, and parenting proceeding involving minor children, whether filed in juvenile court, domestic relations court, probate court, or general court. The Ohio Supreme Court, in *Pasqualone v. Pasqualone*,[1] held that the filing of the affidavit with the first pleading was a mandatory jurisdictional prerequisite, without which a court was not empowered to act.

---

[7]Syrios v. Syrios, 69 Ohio App. 3d 246, 248, 590 N.E.2d 759 (9th Dist. Summit County 1990).

[8]Syrios v. Syrios, 69 Ohio App. 3d 246, 248, 590 N.E.2d 759 (9th Dist. Summit County 1990).

[Section 17:13]

[1]Pasqualone v. Pasqualone, 63 Ohio St. 2d 96, 17 Ohio Op. 3d 58, 406 N.E.2d 1121 (1980).

The Supreme Court in *In re Palmer*[2] subsequently whittled away at that holding and stated:

> The purpose of the Act is to avoid jurisdictional competition and conflict with courts of other jurisdictions and to facilitate the speedy and efficacious resolution of custody matters so the child or children in question will not be caught in a judicial tug of war between different jurisdictions.

The continued erosion of the mandatory nature of the affidavit is evidenced by the Third District Court of Appeals's decision in *In re Porter*,[3] "a blind adherence to the affidavit requirement in the instant case would frustrate the policy behind the rule."[4]

In *Mercer v. Channell*,[5] the court found *Pasqualone* inapplicable to a case where no proceeding concerning custody of the child was pending in any other jurisdiction. Even though the appellee did not set forth the RC 3127.23(A) information with his first pleading, he did so in an affidavit before the hearing.

Where the complainant in a parenting case fails to file an affidavit and fails to disclose the existence of other proceedings, a party may raise the issue of the court's lack of original jurisdiction to make a parenting order by filing a motion for relief from judgment under Civil Rule 60(B).[6] Challenges to jurisdiction alleging the absence of proper jurisdiction were found properly raised under Rule 60(B)(5) in *Marsh v. Marsh*.[7] In another Civil Rule 60(B) case, the court found that a purported agreed entry regarding custody filed in an action where no UCCJA affidavit had ever been filed was a nullity, because parties may not, by stipulation or agreement, confer subject matter jurisdiction on a court where subject matter jurisdiction is otherwise lacking.[8]

RC 3109.23(A) provides that the contestants are entitled to notice and an opportunity to be heard. Thus a trial court errs in not holding a hearing to determine whether it should accept jurisdiction to modify a parental allocation.[9] In reviewing whether or not a trial court should be required to hold an evidentiary hearing on the issue of subject

---

[2]In re Palmer, 12 Ohio St. 3d 194, 196, 465 N.E.2d 1312 (1984).

[3]In re Porter, 113 Ohio App. 3d 580, 681 N.E.2d 954 (3d Dist. Marion County 1996).

[4]In re Porter, 113 Ohio App. 3d 580, 586, 681 N.E.2d 954 (3d Dist. Marion County 1996).

[5]Mercer v. Channell, 1986 WL 6051 (Ohio Ct. App. 4th Dist. Jackson County 1986).

[6]See Louck v. Louck, 2003-Ohio-5999, 2003 WL 22533679 (Ohio Ct. App. 3d Dist. Marion County 2003).

[7]Matter of Marsh, 1988 WL 135372 (Ohio Ct. App. 11th Dist. Trumbull County 1988).

[8]Louck v. Louck, 2003-Ohio-5999, 2003 WL 22533679 (Ohio Ct. App. 3d Dist. Marion County 2003) (appellate court discussed requirements for filing a UCCJA affidavit and subject matter jurisdiction).

[9]Martin v. Martin, 1992 WL 319293 (Ohio Ct. App. 5th Dist. Licking County 1992); Buchheit v. Watson, 2002-Ohio-7147, 2002 WL 31862198 (Ohio Ct. App. 11th Dist. Lake County 2002).

matter jurisdiction in a UCCJA case, the Second Appellate District joined several other counties in requiring such hearing.[10]

The court may order any party within the state to appear personally before the court and may further order the party to bring the child to court.[11] If the party is outside the state, the court may order notice given pursuant to RC 3109.23(B), which may include a statement that the party personally appear with or without the child.[12] However, it is here that the act adds some teeth to this order, by authorizing the court to warn the out-of-state party that failure to appear may result in an adverse decision under RC 3109.29(B). RC 3109.29(C) becomes an equalizer for parties by giving the court power to require another party to pay the expenses of a party ordered to appear with or without the child from out of state according to RC 3109.29(B). This part of the provision attempts to address the problem of interstate harassment. Adequate and reasonable notice must be given to the following appropriate parties: the contestants, any parent whose parental rights have not been previously terminated, and any person or public agency who has physical custody of the child.[13] Reasonable notice has been held to be twenty days. Service methods are also specified.[14] It is these notice provisions and the process for appearance which establish the due process requirements.[15]

Upon refusal to take jurisdiction, the court has several options. It may dismiss or stay the action.[16] It may charge to the party commencing the proceeding, in addition to the court costs, the necessary travel and other expenses, including attorney fees, incurred by other parties or their witnesses, if it appears that the court is clearly an inappropriate forum.[17] If the initiating party has improperly obtained custody or violated a prior court order in a foreign state, the court may charge to that party all of the responding party's expenses and attorney fees to defend the action.[18] It may also, while declining jurisdiction, retain enough jurisdiction to direct the petitioner with unclean hands to

---

[10]Pruitt v. Taber, 2002-Ohio-1799, 2002 WL 506653 (Ohio Ct. App. 2d Dist. Clark County 2002); Buchheit v. Watson, 2002-Ohio-7147, 2002 WL 31862198 (Ohio Ct. App. 11th Dist. Lake County 2002).

[11]RC 3109.29(A).

[12]RC 3109.29(B).

[13]RC 3109.23.

[14]RC 3109.23; Sontag v. Sontag, 1981 WL 9729 (Ohio Ct. App. 1st Dist. Hamilton County 1981).

[15]See O'Keeffe v. O'Keeffe, 1986 WL 7168 (Ohio Ct. App. 10th Dist. Franklin County 1986).

[16]RC 3109.25(E).

[17]RC 3109.25(G).

[18]RC 3109.26(C); In re Bryan, No. F82-2102 (Ohio Juv. Ct. Hamilton County 1982).

return the child to the other party.[19] The Ohio court must appraise the foreign state court of its actions. This obligation is placed upon the clerk of the appropriate court[20] who must record information received in the registry.[21]

An action to determine the parent-child relationship brought under RC Chapter 3111 is not a custody proceeding, and thus there is no statutory requirement for filing an affidavit pursuant to RC 3127.23 to provide notice of related proceedings in other courts.[22]

§ 17:14 UCCJA—Ancillary proceedings

RC 3109.34 and RC 3109.35 govern the rights and the duties of cooperation between states in obtaining forwarding information necessary to bring custody and parenting litigation to a just conclusion.

RC 3109.34(A) gives a court of this state the right to request another state to hold a hearing and order parties to appear and produce evidence or testimony; to make investigations, social studies, and reports; and to send certified copies of transcripts and other documents regarding the allocation of parental rights and responsibilities for the care of a child, and designation of a parent as the residential parent and legal custodian of a child that is the subject of litigation in this state.[1] Further the same evidence and studies may be requested with respect to the custody of the child by any other person. This right also is permitted any party, guardian, or representative of the child.[2] The court may assess costs of these services against the parties or order them paid by the county treasury and taxed as costs in a case. RC 3109.34(B) gives a court of this state the right to request a court of another state to order a party in that foreign state to attend the hearing in Ohio and, if the party has the child, to bring the child as well. The request may also state how and by whom the expenses shall be paid.

RC 3109.35 governs the reports and duties of a court receiving a request from a foreign state. RC 3109.35(A) gives a court of this state rendering parenting decrees discretionary power to order a person of this state to appear at a hearing in this state and give or produce evidence requested, as well as to order social studies undertaken at the request of the foreign court. It may also order a party in this state to appear at a hearing in another state with or without the child, but

---

[19]Matter of Potter, 56 Ohio Misc. 17, 10 Ohio Op. 3d 214, 377 N.E.2d 536 (C.P. 1978).

[20]RC 3109.25(H).

[21]RC 3109.25, RC 3109.33.

[22]Hardman v. Chiaramonte, 39 Ohio App. 3d 9, 528 N.E.2d 1270 (9th Dist. Summit County 1987).

[Section 17:14]

[1]See also RC 3109.36(B) which authorizes this as well.

[2]RC 3109.34(B). See also In re Davis, 18 Ohio St. 3d 226, 480 N.E.2d 775 (1985).

may condition compliance on an assurance that the expenses will be paid or reimbursed in the fashion it chooses.[3]

RC 3109.34 and RC 3109.35 involve requests made by one court to another for use of discretionary power. The act as a whole encourages cooperation but does not mandate courts to cooperate. Conversely, the act does require clerks of courts[4] to send certified copies of transcripts and other documents to the requesting court.[5] Such may also include pleadings and other documents.[6] Naturally, a party in this state may voluntarily give testimony or a statement in this state to use in an out-of-state hearing.[7]

§ 17:15 UCCJA—Registration of custody decrees and enforcement

A certified copy of another court's custody or parenting decree may be filed in a court of this state which itself renders such decrees. The clerk of court must treat the decree in the same manner as if it were one rendered by the state's court.[1] Thus, until modified, such a decree must be enforced as if it were a decree of an Ohio court.

The clerk of court is to maintain a registry with certified copies of parenting decrees received for filing, plus communications regarding the pendency of parenting proceedings in other states, whether those proceedings affect the local court's jurisdiction, and any pending proceeding of the inconvenient forum.[2]

After the decree is properly filed and registered, it is enforceable by contempt,[3] or by a petition for a writ of habeas corpus.[4] It is also subject to modification if the provisions of RC 3109.31(A) are met, primarily that the original court no longer has jurisdiction under jurisdictional prerequisites of the UCCJA, or that court has declined to assume jurisdiction to modify and the court of this state does have jurisdiction.

In a proceeding for enforcement of a custody decree, as long as the decree has not been modified, full faith and credit must be granted to a sister state's judgment both under the UCCJA and the PKPA. In

---

[3]RC 3109.35(B).
[4]RC 3109.33(B).
[5]RC 3109.35(A).
[6]See RC 3109.36(A).
[7]RC 3109.35(B).

[Section 17:15]

[1]RC 3109.32(A). See In re Marriage of Steiner, 89 Cal. App. 3d 363, 152 Cal. Rptr. 612 (5th Dist. 1979) (foreign modification of domestic custody decree requires enforcement upon its filing in domestic court under this section).

[2]RC 3109.33.
[3]See RC Ch. 2705.
[4]RC 2151.23(A)(3), RC Ch. 2725.

Durgans v. Durgans,[5] the court said "[i]n the past, there were situations where the UCCJA, as enacted in R.C. 3109.22(A), could be interpreted to allow two or more states to exercise concurrent jurisdiction. Congress, however, passed the Parental Kidnapping Prevention Act ("PKPA"), Section 1738A, Title 28, U.S. Code in 1980 to eliminate that possibility. The PKPA prevents 'a second state from modifying a custody decree where the original home state has continuing jurisdiction.'"[6] RC 3109.30 does not provide for a custody hearing to be conducted prior to enforcement.[7]

Where the trial court has properly ascertained that the original court relinquished jurisdiction and that the factors determining the child's home state and significant information about the child are present in Ohio, court's adoption of the decree is not an abuse of discretion. In *Kirby v. Nakanishi*,[8] the resident mother attempted to defeat the non-resident father's "motion to adopt" the foreign decree and concomitant motions for modification of custody and appointment of a guardian ad litem, arguing that the father did not have standing to file and that he had abandoned his rights. The appellate court, with no discussion as to whether the trial court's order accepting jurisdiction was a final appealable order and even though there were pending motions, found that Ohio was the forum with optimum access, was a convenient forum, and that, since the trial court's only action had been to accept jurisdiction, any discussion about enforcement or potential modification would be premature.

In *Shiver v. Shiver*,[9] the mother registered her Ohio decree in Vermont, where she and the children had moved three years earlier. Vermont had assumed jurisdiction but stayed its proceedings pending a decision by the Ohio court whether it intended to retain jurisdiction. In response to the father's motion for contempt in Ohio trial court, the mother filed a motion to dismiss based on loss of jurisdiction. The trial court denied the dismissal motion, and the mother appealed. Noting that generally a denial of a motion to dismiss is not a final appealable order, the appellate court nevertheless stated, in its second footnote, that a case involving child visitation matters between parties residing in different states constitutes a special proceeding affecting substantial rights. A delay in deciding jurisdiction would violate one of the purposes of the UCCJA and the PKPA—to avoid competing claims. The registration in the other state did not defeat nor impede the

---

[5]Durgans v. Durgans, 2001 WL 114983 (Ohio Ct. App. 11th Dist. Portage County 2001).

[6]Durgans v. Durgans, 2001 WL 114983 (Ohio Ct. App. 11th Dist. Portage County 2001), internal citations omitted.

[7]In re McClurg, 78 Ohio App. 3d 465, 605 N.E.2d 418 (12th Dist. Butler County 1992).

[8]Kirby v. Nakanishi, 1995 WL 753944 (Ohio Ct. App. 8th Dist. Cuyahoga County 1995).

[9]Shiver v. Shiver, 1995 WL 757838, at *2 (Ohio Ct. App. 1st Dist. Hamilton County 1995).

continuing jurisdiction of the Ohio court. In Ohio, "[t]he court in which a decree of divorce . . . retains continuing jurisdiction over matters relating to the custody . . . of the [parties'] minor children."[10]

A writ of habeas corpus will not be granted in an original action in the court of appeals, where the petitioner has the remedy in the Ohio divorce action to seek modification or vacation of the decree that awarded respondent custody, even though the petitioner had a decree granted in England awarding her custody.[11] Barring a finding of no jurisdiction in the original Ohio action, or of imminent danger to the children, the writ of habeas corpus will not be granted where there is an adequate remedy at law.

RC 2905.04, which made child stealing a criminal offense, was repealed effective July 1, 1996.[12] The only criminal statutes available would be RC 2905.01, kidnapping, and the lesser criminal charges of abduction and unlawful restraint, under RC 2905.02 and RC 2905.03. A civil action for interference with parental or guardianship interest in a minor child is provided for in RC 2307.50.

§ 17:16 UCCJA—Registration of custody decrees and enforcement—Foreign country decrees

Decrees of foreign nations are not entitled to such enforcement.[1]

When the Ohio General Assembly adopted the [UCCJA] as [RC] 3109.21 through 3109.37, it chose to omit Section 23 of the [UCCJA]. Had our legislature intended to require the recognition of decrees of foreign nations, it could easily have adopted Section 23 of the [UCCJA]. By failing to do so, we believe the legislature expressed its intent not to require the enforcement of such decrees.[2]

§ 17:17 UCCJA—Registration of custody decree and modification

Registering a decree of one state with another state court, for purposes of enforcement, does not necessarily give the registering court jurisdiction to modify the order where the original court never relinquishes jurisdiction. In addition, the filing and acceptance of a petition to register a foreign decree does not confer personal jurisdic-

---

[10]Loetz v. Loetz, 63 Ohio St. 2d 1, 17 Ohio Op. 3d 1, 406 N.E.2d 1093 (1980) (citing Shiver v. Shiver, 1995 WL 757838 (Ohio Ct. App. 1st Dist. Hamilton County 1995)).

[11]Harvey v. Bentley, 74 Ohio App. 3d 375, 599 N.E.2d 284 (2d Dist. Montgomery County 1991).

[12]1995 S.B. 2, eff. 7-1-96.

[Section 17:16]

[1]Minton v. McManus, 9 Ohio App. 3d 165, 166, 458 N.E.2d 1292 (9th Dist. Summit County 1983) ("We will not create such a requirement by judicial construction."); Van Kan v. Mattheus, 1999 WL 476139 (Ohio Ct. App. 11th Dist. Geauga County 1999).

[2]Minton v. McManus, 9 Ohio App. 3d 165, 166, 458 N.E.2d 1292 (9th Dist. Summit County 1983).

tion on a court per se. In *Broz v. Broz*,[1] the mother had registered her Ohio decree in Illinois, where the father lived, for purposes of enforcement of support, presumably under Illinois statutes comparable to former RC 3115.32. Since the Illinois court did not comply with the requirements of UCCJA, the Ohio court held that orders modifying custody and support were not entitled to full faith and credit.

The prerequisites for an Ohio court to exercise modification jurisdiction over another state's decree appear to be flexible enough to stretch to include medical and dental care provided to the child during summer visitation. In *Michael v. Michael*[2] the trial court disregarded the fact that the home state of the child, when the matter was filed in Ohio as a motion for an "ex parte" emergency custody order, was Texas, the decree was in Texas, and the mother continued to reside in Texas. Instead, the court focused on the father's having provided medical, dental, and psychological counseling services for the child in Ohio during summer visitation. In so doing, it analyzed the UCCJA and found justification for the exercise of modification jurisdiction under RC 3109.22(A)(3). This case may be an anomaly since the UCCJA was enacted to avoid juridictional conflict and promote cooperation between the states[3] and the PKPA was to reinforce the UCCJA by mandating full faith and credit valid custody orders of another state.[4]

The UCCJA is not perfect, and in fact the many cases reported reflect sister states' decisions on the validity of each other's orders. When a factual situation presents an irreconcilable conflict between promoting the orderly system of decisions and protecting the best interests of the child before the court, the act makes the best interest of the child predominant.[5] While statutes can be amended and case law distinguished or overruled, judicial notice must be taken of the fact that children grow up only once. When a mistake is made in a custody dispute, the painful effects are irrevocable. To minimize this possibility, the statutes emphasize that the state with the optimum access to the relevant facts should make determinations of this nature.[6] The desire to eliminate the "home court" advantage is a lofty goal yet to be achieved.

§ 17:18   UCCJA—Attorney fees and costs

When the trial court dismisses an action based upon inappropriate

---

[Section 17:17]

[1]Broz v. Broz, 1995 WL 643938 (Ohio Ct. App. 10th Dist. Franklin County 1995).

[2]Michael v. Michael, 1999 WL 1212820 (Ohio Ct. App. 12th Dist. Preble County 1999).

[3]State ex rel. Aycock v. Mowrey, 45 Ohio St. 3d 347, 349, 544 N.E.2d 657 (1989).

[4]Justis v. Justis, 81 Ohio St. 3d 312, 315, 1989-Ohio-626, 691 N.E.2d 264 (1998).

[5]Brock v. Brock, 349 So. 2d 782 (Fla. Dist. Ct. App. 1st Dist. 1977).

[6]In re Wonderly's Guardianship, 67 Ohio St. 2d 178, 21 Ohio Op. 3d 111, 423 N.E.2d 420 (1981).

forum, RC 3109.25(G) permits the court to order the payment by the petitioning party of the attorney fees, necessary travel, and other expenses of the other parties or their witnesses.[1]

RC 3109.32(B) allows a court of this state to require a party violating a parenting decree to pay all necessary travel and other expenses, including attorney fees, incurred by the party entitled to custody, or his witnesses. This provision dovetails with RC 3109.26(B) where a foreign decree is enforced in dismissing an action because the petitioner improperly obtained custody.[2]

§ 17:19   Parental Kidnapping Prevention Act (PKPA)—History

"The problem of child snatching is greater today than ever before. More than 10 million children under the age of 18 live in families headed by a single parent. Although accurate figures are not available, it is estimated that between 25,000 and 100,000 children are victims of interstate child snatchings each year."[1]

Congress responded to this problem with the Parental Kidnapping Prevention Act of 1980 (PKPA).[2] 28 U.S.C.A. § 1738A(a) provides, "The appropriate authorities of every State shall enforce according to its terms, and shall not modify . . . any child custody determination made consistently with the provisions of this section by a court of another state."

The federal legislation attempts to redress the UCCJA pitfalls, namely, lack of adoption by all states and the failure to deter states which were determined to exercise their jurisdiction. The Act does not require that a judgment be final, as does the Full Faith and Credit Clause of the Constitution. Compliance with the Act is mandatory. In *Pierce v. Pierce*,[3] the court stated that the PKPA "elevated the UCCJA jurisdictional standards to a federal level. Custody determinations made in accordance with these standards must now be given full faith and credit." As the PKPA was enacted "to discourage forum shopping for custody determinations and to promote 'interstate cooperation, interstate enforcement of custody decrees and the avoidance of jurisdictional competition and conflict,' " temporary absence from Ohio

---

[Section 17:18]

   [1]Bowen v. Britton, 1993 WL 33315 (Ohio Ct. App. 4th Dist. Jackson County 1993).

   [2]See Matter of Potter, 56 Ohio Misc. 17, 10 Ohio Op. 3d 214, 377 N.E.2d 536 (C.P. 1978).

[Section 17:19]

   [1]*Parental Kidnapping Prevention Act of 1979*, S.105: Joint Hearing before the Subcommittee on Criminal Justice of the Committee on Child and Human Development of the Committee on Labs and Human Resources, 96th Cong., Ind. Sess. 1 (1980) (statement of Senator Matthias).

   [2]Pub. L. No. 96-611, 94 Stat 3568 (1980), codified at 28 U.S.C.A. § 1738A(a).

   [3]Pierce v. Pierce, 197 Mont. 16, 20, 640 P.2d 899 (1982).

did not divest the trial court of jurisdiction over visitation issues arising out of the decree in *Shiver v. Shiver*.[4]

§ 17:20 PKPA—Applicability and jurisdiction

On its face, the PKPA does not expressly authorize federal courts to hear claims involving application of its provisions. Case law has established, however, that federal courts can enforce state compliance with full faith and credit custody determinations made pursuant to the PKPA.[1] In order for a state to exert continuing jurisdiction in a child custody or visitation matter, the PKPA mandates that the state have jurisdiction under its own state law.[2]

Before a custody determination falls under the PKPA, the decision must itself be "consistent with the provisions" of 28 U.S.C.A. § 1738(a). To be consistent, the original state court determination of custody must satisfy the following criteria as set forth in 28 U.S.C.A. § 1738A(c):

(1) The court had jurisdiction under the law of the state; and
(2) One of the following conditions is met:
    (a) The state (i) is the home state of the child on the date of the commencement of the proceeding, and (ii) the child is absent from the state because of his removal or retention by a contestant or for other reasons, and (iii) a contestant continues to live in the state;
    (b) (i) It appears that no other state would have jurisdiction under subparagraph (a), and (ii) it is in the best interest of the child that a court of the state assume jurisdiction because the child and his parents, or the child and at least one contestant, have a significant connection with the state other than mere physical presence, and there is available in the state substantial evidence concerning the child's present or future care, protection, training, and personal relationships;
    (c) The child is physically present in the state and (i) has been abandoned or (ii) it is necessary to protect the child because he has been subjected to or threatened with mistreatment or abuse;
    (d) (i) It appears that no other state would have jurisdiction under subparagraphs (a), (b), (c), or (e), or another state

---

[4]*Shiver v. Shiver*, 1995 WL 757838 (Ohio Ct. App. 1st Dist. Hamilton County 1995).

[Section 17:20]

[1]*Flood v. Braaten*, 727 F.2d 303 (3d Cir. 1984); *DiRuggiero v. Rodgers*, 743 F.2d 1009 (3d Cir. 1984); *McDougald v. Jenson*, 596 F. Supp. 680 (N.D. Fla. 1984), decision aff'd, 786 F.2d 1465 (11th Cir. 1986); *Heartfield v. Heartfield*, 749 F.2d 1138 (5th Cir. 1985).

[2]*Shiver v. Shiver*, 1995 WL 757838 (Ohio Ct. App. 1st Dist. Hamilton County 1995).

has declined to exercise jurisdiction on the ground that the state whose jurisdiction is in issue is the more appropriate forum to determine the custody of the child, and (ii) it is in the best interest of the child that the court assume jurisdiction; or

(e) The court has continuing jurisdiction pursuant to subsection (d) of this section.

Continuing jurisdiction is conferred on the state which made the prior custody decree so long as that state remains the residence of the child or of any contestant. 28 U.S.C.A. § 1738A(d) reads as follows:

The jurisdiction of a court of a State which has made a child custody determination consistently with the provisions of this section continues as long as the requirement of subsection (c)(1) of this section continues to be met and such State remains the residence of the child or of any contestant.

The thrust of the PKPA is to eliminate the problems created by concurrent jurisdiction by granting exclusive jurisdiction for modification purposes upon the state which initially rendered the decree.[3] There is a preference stated in the PKPA for jurisdiction to remain in the home state. According to 28 U.S.C.A. § 1738A(b)(4),

"home State" means the State in which, immediately preceding the time involved, the child lived with his parents, a parent, or a person acting as parent, for at least six consecutive months, and in the case of a child less than six months old, the State in which the child lived from birth with any of such persons. Periods of temporary absence of any such persons are counted as part of the six-month or other period."

The Supreme Court in *Justis v. Justis*[4] held that under the UCCJA and the PKPA, the state court that rendered the initial custody decree has exclusive jurisdiction over an ongoing custody dispute if that state has continuing jurisdiction. In addition, when a second state, with concurrent jurisdiction, attempts to modify the original state's decree, it acts improperly and its orders are not entitled to full faith and credit. The terms of the PKPA prevail over the UCCJA. The Ohio Supreme Court in 2003 stated, "Insofar as the Ohio version of the UCCJA conflicts with the PKPA, the PKPA prevails."[5]

For a modification to occur, the home state must have declined to exercise jurisdiction or must no longer have jurisdiction to render a custody determination. To settle a jurisdictional dispute, a court must

---

[3]See Scott T. Dickens, *The Parental Kidnapping Prevention Act: Application and Interpretation,* 23 J. Fam. L. 419 (April 1985).

[4]Justis v. Justis, 81 Ohio St. 3d 312, 1989-Ohio-626, 691 N.E.2d 264 (1998).

[5]State ex. Rel. Seaton v. Holmes, 100 Ohio St. 3d. 265, 2003-Ohio-5897 (Ohio 2003). The Court followed its reasoning in Justis v. Justis, 81 Ohio St. 3d 312, 1989-Ohio-626, 691 N.E.2d 264 (1998) in recognizing the relationship between the UCCJA and the PKPA.

hold a full evidentiary hearing, and the law of the decree state must be applied in its decision on jurisdiction.[6]

The United States Supreme Court has ruled that the PKPA does not create a private right of action in federal court for the determination of which of two conflicting state child custody decrees is valid.[7] The Act imposes its duty on states to enforce a child custody order entered by another state's court if the determination is consistent with the provisions of the Act, said provisions being similar to those under the UCCJA. Once a state has exercised such jurisdiction, no other state may exercise concurrent jurisdiction even if it would have had that power in the first instance.

The decision arose from a suit filed in federal district court seeking an order to declare a Louisiana decree invalid and a California decree valid and to enjoin the enforcement of the former. The court construed the statute as providing a rule of decisions for state courts.

While a court may decline to exercise its jurisdiction on the basis that the forum is now inconvenient, the purpose of protecting the continuing jurisdiction of the court which issued the original child custody determination is to discourage forum shopping as well as excessive relitigation of child custody matters.[8]

There is no clear indication in the PKPA that it was intended to divest a state court of jurisdiction when there is no jurisdictional conflict nor full faith and credit problem, even when the child is no longer a resident of the original decreeing state. In *Holm v. Smilowitz*[9] the father had moved to North Carolina and the mother had moved to Utah with the child. Utah declined to exercise jurisdiction, so the Ohio court modified its original custody order, finding that neither the PKPA nor the UCCJA sanctioned the mother's move, which was found to have been motivated by an intention to deprive the father of his visitation rights.

§ 17:21 PKPA—Enforcement

Regarding enforcement mechanisms, the PKPA permits states to expand their parent locator services by entering into agreements with the Federal Parental Locator Service. In addition, the Federal Bureau of Investigation can assist in locating parental kidnappers under the

---

[6]Pierce v. Pierce, 197 Mont. 16, 640 P.2d 899 (1982).

[7]Thompson v. Thompson, 484 U.S. 174, 108 S. Ct. 513, 98 L. Ed. 2d 512 (1988).

[8]Zwissler v. Zwissler, 1998 WL 127089 (Ohio Ct. App. 2d Dist. Montgomery County 1998). Reasoning of *Zwissler* differentiated in Miller v. Henry, 2003-Ohio-1511, 2003 WL 1563827 (Ohio Ct. App. 10th Dist. Franklin County 2003).

[9]Holm v. Smilowitz, 83 Ohio App. 3d 757, 615 N.E.2d 1047 (4th Dist. Athens County 1992).

Fugitive Felon Act.[1] The practical effect of these resources has been less than successful.[2]

Federal court enforcement under the PKPA has been more successful. Overcoming the hurdle of the jurisdiction of the federal court to hear the PKPA has been difficult. The Third Circuit was the first appellate court to accept and permit the involvement of the federal court in the compliance of and enforcement of the PKPA.[3] Other courts have followed the precedent and determined that there is federal question jurisdiction to determine PKPA cases.[4]

1. The cases suggest that the clearest situation for obtaining federal relief in an interstate custody case is to file in federal court after two state courts have issued conflicting decrees and thus reached an actual, rather than an anticipated, 'legal impasse.' Use the phrase 'legal impasse' or 'jurisdictional impasse' in your petition.

2. Allege that federal question jurisdiction, 28 U.S.C. 1331, lies to enforce compliance with the PKPA, 28 U.S.C. § 1738A. Cite appropriate case authority.

3. Seek a declaratory judgment to the effect that one of the state courts exercised jurisdiction in conformity with the PKPA and therefore its judgment is entitled to enforcement by the other state court. Request the federal court to issue an injunction directing the state court which improperly exercised jurisdiction in violation of the PKPA to vacate its judgment and to enforce the valid state court order. If an action is still pending in the second state, relief could be sought in the form of an injunction directing the errant state court to dismiss its proceedings.[5]

Perhaps the most significant and effective deterrent is the recognized tort of child snatching. These actions can be brought in state or federal court,[6] and monetary damages can be awarded.

§ 17:22   Uniform Child Custody Jurisdiction and Enforcement Act (1997)

Because of inconsistences in rulings among the 50 states, the District of Columbia and the Virgin Islands, various adoptions by states of the UCCJA, and the passage of the PKPA in 1980, the National Conference of Commissioners on Uniform State Laws has

---

[Section 17:21]

[1]18 U.S.C.A. § 1073.

[2]See Scott T. Dickens, *The Parental Kidnapping Prevention Act: Application and Interpretation,* 23 J. Fam. L. 419 (April 1985).

[3]See, e.g., Flood v. Braaten, 727 F.2d 303 (3d Cir. 1984).

[4]DiRuggiero v. Rodgers, 743 F.2d 1009 (3d Cir. 1984); McDougald v. Jenson, 596 F. Supp. 680 (N.D. Fla. 1984), decision aff'd, 786 F.2d 1465 (11th Cir. 1986); Heartfield v. Heartfield, 749 F.2d 1138 (5th Cir. 1985). But see Siler v. Storey, 587 F. Supp. 986 (N.D. Tex. 1984) (denied relief and took an opposite view of federal jurisdiction).

[5]Patricia M. Hoff, *Federal Court Remedies in Interstate Child Custody and Parental Kidnapping Cases,* 19 Fam. L.Q. 443, 453 (Winter 1986).

[6]See, e.g., Sheltra v. Smith, 136 Vt. 472, 392 A.2d 431 (1978); Lloyd v. Loeffler, 694 F.2d 489 (7th Cir. 1982); Bennett v. Bennett, 682 F.2d 1039, 34 Fed. R. Serv. 2d 697 (D.C. Cir. 1982); Clark v. Bayer, 32 Ohio St. 299, 1877 WL 120 (1877).

proposed the Uniform Child Custody Jurisdiction and Enforcement Act (UCCJEA). Approximately 28 states have adopted the UCCJEA and it has been introduced in others. The UCCJEA requires home state "priority", clarifies emergency jurisdiction, addresses exclusive continuing jurisdiction for the State that entered the decree, clarifies the definition of custody proceeding, and eliminates the term "best interests" to avoid substance as opposed to process in jurisdictional issues. The UCCJEA also provides modifications for enforcement provisions. Although Ohio has not passed this legislation, as it spreads throughout the United States, it is on the horizon.

§ 17:23   History of the UCCJEA

Effective April 11, 2005, Ohio adopted the Uniform Child Custody Jurisdiction and Enforcement Act (UCCJEA) replacing the Uniform Child Custody Jurisdiction Act (UCCJA). By 1981, all 50 states had adopted the UCCJA which was "designed to discourage interstate kidnapping of children by their parents, as it was a common practice for non-custodial parents to take their children across state lines in the hope of securing a favorable custody order."[1] The UCCJA was not as successful in attaining its purpose as there was multi-state custody litigation. Congress, in an effort to dictate the jurisdictional restrictions, passed the Parental Kidnapping Prevention Act in 1980 (PKPA). This legislation did not produce the desired results either. States interpreted their versions of the UCCJA as they wished. The United States Supreme Court in *Thompson v. Thompson*[2] held that while states' decisions were entitled to full faith and credit under the PKPA, Congress did not intend in its legislation to provide a cause of action under the PKPA and that the federal courts were not intended to have an enforcement role. Thus, the UCCJA was more recognized in its breaches than its enforcement. To remedy the dilemma, the National Conference of Commissioners on Uniform State Law became involved again and drafted the UCCJEA "to reconcile the UCCJA with the PKPA and provide for interstate enforcement of custody orders."[3] The draft uniform legislation was completed in 1997 and as of March 1, 2005, 40 states and the District of Columbia had adopted it and the UCCJEA was pending in 5 states.[4]

§ 17:24   The UCCJEA is a jurisdictional statute

The UCCJEA is a jurisdictional granting and enforcement statute.

[Section 17:23]

[1]Bill Analysis of 2004 Ohio Sub. S.B. 185 by the Ohio Legislative Service Commission.

[2]Thompson v. Thompson, 484 U.S. 174, 108 S. Ct. 513, 98 L. Ed. 2d 512 (1988).

[3]Bill Analysis of 2004 Ohio Sub. S.B. 185 by the Ohio Legislative Service Commission.

[4]As of September 1, 2009, the only states which have not adopted the UCCJEA are Massachusetts and Vermont.

It is not a statute that dictates substantive decisions. There is no "best interest" test used and the words are absent in the statute. Rather, the UCCJEA sets forth when a court has jurisdiction to make an initial grant of custody and when a court can modify and enforce a previously entered custody order. The legislation prioritizes the bases upon which jurisdiction is based and provides that the state which makes the initial determination has continuing jurisdiction "so long as a party to the original determination remains in that state [as] [c]ontinuing jurisdiction was not a provision in the original UCCJA. . ."[1] The act also "clarifies how and when emergency jurisdiction should be used."[2] There is a process in the UCCJA for expedited enforcement of custody and visitation orders. Notice provisions are changed from the UCCJA as are the facts to be pleaded in the affidavit. The UCCJEA has prospective application only.[3] The UCCJEA is applicable in dependency of neglect proceedings,[4] and guardianship proceedings.[5]

§ 17:25 Definitions

RC 3127.01 sets forth that the "uniform child custody jurisdiction and enforcement act means the act addressing interstate recognition and enforcement of child custody orders adopted in 1997 by the national conference of commissioners on uniform state laws or any law substantially similar to the act adopted by another state." As the law is so new in Ohio, and as there is precedent in other states that have previously enacted the UCCJEA, reliance can be had on those states' court opinions since the legislation specifically refers to the uniform law as drafted.

"Abandoned" is a new term in the UCCJEA. The definition in the Revised Code differs from the one in the uniform bill.[1] The Ohio definition includes only "parents who have failed to visit or maintain contact for more than ninety days"[2] with the child.

"Child" is defined as an individual who has not attained eighteen

---

[Section 17:24]

[1]Press Release, January, 2000 from the National Conference of Commissioners on Uniform State Laws.

[2]Press Release, January, 2000 from the National Conference of Commissioners on Uniform State Laws.

[3]In re D.H., 2007-Ohio-4069, 2007 WL 2269705, (Ohio Ct. App. 8th Dist. Cuyahoga County 2007).

[4]In re S.S., 2008-Ohio-294, 2009 WL 161333 (Ohio Ct. App. 2d Dist. Montgomery County 2009).

[5]In re Hibshman, 2009-Ohio-1313, 2009 WL 738072 (Ohio Ct. App. 11th Dist. Geauga County 2009).

[Section 17:25]

[1]The uniform bill defines abandoned as "left without provision for reasonable and necessary care or supervision."

[2]RC 3127.01(B)(1).

years of age.[3] Child was not defined in the UCCJA and this definition is taken from the PKPA.

"Child custody determination" encompasses all decisions regarding the custody, allocation of parental rights and responsibilities, permanent, temporary, initial and modification orders.[4] This is an expansion of the UCCJA definition.[5] It does not include support or monetary obligations.[6] A very clear distinction is made here—money and custody are separate.

"Child custody proceeding" is defined as a "proceeding in which custody, physical custody, parenting time, or visitation with respect to a child is an issue."[7] Domestic violence is included in the definition, as is divorce, separation, neglect, abuse, dependency, guardianship, parentage, and termination of parental rights. It does not include juvenile delinquency, contractual emancipation or enforcement under RC 3127.31 to RC 3127.47.[8] Thus, enforcement under the UCCJEA is not a child custody proceeding and is controlled by the specific statutory mandates of RC 3127.31 to RC 3127.47.

"Commencement" is the filing of the first pleading in a proceeding.[9]

"Court" is defined as an entity authorized under law to establish, enforce, or modify a child custody determination.[10]

"Home state" is unchanged from the definition of the UCCJA. It is where the child lived with a parent for at least six consecutive months immediately preceding the commencement of a child custody proceeding.[11] The commentary of the commissioners reflects that no substantive change was intended from the UCCJA.[12]

"Initial determination" means the first custody determination made concerning a child.[13]

"Issuing court" is defined as the court that makes the determination for which enforcement is sought.[14] The term is used also in the Uniform Interstate Family Support Act (UIFSA).

---

[3]RC 3127.01(B)(2).

[4]RC 3127.01(B)(3).

[5]Treneff, Craig, Uniform Child Custody Jurisdiction and Enforcement Act: Part 1, Domestic Relations Journal of Ohio, November/December 2004.

[6]RC 3127.01(B)(3); Smoske v. Sicher, 2007-Ohio-5617, 2007 WL 3052208, (Ohio Ct. App. 11th Dist. Geauga County 2007).

[7]RC 3127.01(B)(4).

[8]RC 3127.01(B)(4).

[9]RC 3127.01(B)(5).

[10]RC 3127.01(B)(6).

[11]RC 3127.01(B)(7).

[12]Uniform Child Custody Jurisdiction and Enforcement Act (1997), Prefatory Notes and Comments.

[13]RC 3127.01(B)(8).

[14]RC 3127.01(B)(9).

"Issuing state" is defined as the state where the custody determination is made.[15]

"Modification" is defined as a child custody determination that changes, replaces, supercedes or is otherwise made after a previous determination concerning the same child, whether or not it is made by the court that made the previous determination.[16]

"Person" is defined extremely broadly and includes, but is not limited to individuals, trusts, public and governmental entities. Thus, an agency which has possession of a child is a person under the UCCJEA.[17]

"Person acting as a parent" must meet both qualifications set forth in the statutory definition. The person must have had physical custody for a period of six months and must have been awarded custody or claim a right to custody under state law.[18]

"Physical custody" is defined as physical care and supervision of a child.[19]

"State" is defined as a state of the United States, territories subject to jurisdiction of the United States, the District of Columbia, the U.S. Virgin Islands and Puerto Rico.[20]

"Tribe" is defined as an Indian tribe of Alaskan Native village recognized by federal or state law.[21]

"Warrant" is defined as an order to take physical custody of a child.[22]

§ 17:26 Non-UCCJEA matters

Adoption proceedings and emergency medical care authorization for a child are not covered under the UCCJEA.[1] As there is a Uniform Adoption Act, adoptions were excluded from the UCCJEA by the uniform law commissioners. Medical authorizations proceedings are not custody determinations and thus were excluded from consideration in the UCCJEA.

---

[15]RC 3127.01(B)(10).
[16]RC 3127.01(B)(11).
[17]RC 3127.01(B)(12).
[18]RC 3127.02(B)(13).
[19]RC 3127.01(B)(14).
[20]RC 3127.01(B)(15).
[21]RC 3127.01(B)(16).
[22]RC 3127.01(B)(17).

[Section 17:26]
[1]RC 3127.02.

§ 17:27   Indian Child Welfare Act

TheUCCJEA does not apply to Indian children if the proceeding is governed by the Indian Child Welfare Act.[1]

§ 17:28   Foreign countries

If a foreign country exercised jurisdiction substantially in compliance with the UCCJEA, the decision will be treated as if it were a state of the United States. However, it may refuse to apply theUCCJEA if the child custody law of the other country violates fundamental principles of human rights.[1]

§ 17:29   Effect of a child custody determination

The determination of a court of this state is binding on all persons served, notified, or who have submitted to the jurisdiction of the court and who have been given an opportunity to be heard.[1]

§ 17:30   Calendar priority

If a party requests it, the question of jurisdiction "shall be given calendar priority and handled expeditiously."[1] This is similar to the language of the UCCJA but was moved to the beginning to "emphasize its importance."[2] The UCCJEA provides that the jurisdictional issue be advanced, and not the entire custody case.[3]

§ 17:31   Notice

Notice given for the exercise of jurisdiction over a person outside of the state is to be governed under the Rules of Civil Procedure or Rules of Juvenile Procedure. It is to be in a manner calculated to give actual notice, but may be by publication.[1] Proof of service is governed

---

[Section 17:27]
    [1]RC 3127.03.

[Section 17:28]
    [1]RC 3127.04.

[Section 17:29]
    [1]RC 3127.05.

[Section 17:30]
    [1]RC 3127.06.

    [2]Uniform Child Custody Jurisdiction and Enforcement Act (1997), Prefatory Notes and Comments.

    [3]Uniform Child Custody Jurisdiction and Enforcement Act (1997), Prefatory Notes and Comments.

[Section 17:31]
    [1]RC 3127.07(A).

by the Rules of Civil Procedure or the Rules of Juvenile Procedure.[2]
Notice is not required if the person submits to the jurisdiction of the
court.[3]

State law now controls the method of notice and proof of service
thereby eliminating the need for the UCCJEA to provide for notice, as
the UCCJA did.

§ 17:32   Personal jurisdiction; immunity

A party to a child custody proceeding, including modification, is not
subject to personal jurisdiction in this state for any other proceeding
or purpose solely by reason of being present for the purpose of
participating in the child custody proceeding.[1] A person who is subject
to personal jurisdiction in this state on a basis other than a physical
presence is not immune from service in this state.[2] The limited immunity in this section does not extend to civil litigation based on acts
unrelated to the UCCJEA committed by the person while in the state.[3]

Participation in a custody proceeding does not give personal jurisdiction over the person for any other issue. As the commentary states,
"Once jurisdiction is proper. . . . a party should not be placed in the
dilemma of choosing between seeking custody or protecting a right not
to be subject to a monetary judgment by a court with no other relationship to the party."[4] This is similar to the immunity provision in
UIFSA.

§ 17:33   Communication between courts

Courts may communicate with each other under the UCCJEA.[1] Parties may be given the opportunity to participate in the communication
and, if they are not able to participate, they can present facts and
legal arguments before a decision concerning jurisdiction is made.[2]
Communication between the courts concerning schedules, calendars,
and court records may occur without notification to the parties and a
record need not be made of the communication.[3] A record shall be
made of the communication, except for scheduling matters, and the

---

[2]RC 3127.07(B).

[3]RC 3127.07(C).

[Section 17:32]

[1]RC 3127.08(A).

[2]RC 3127.08(B).

[3]RC 3127.08(C).

[4]Uniform Child Custody Jurisdiction and Enforcement Act (1997), Prefatory
Notes and Comments.

[Section 17:33]

[1]RC 3127.09(A).

[2]RC 3127.09(B).

[3]RC 3127.09(C).

parties shall be promptly notified of the communication and granted access to the record.[4]

§ 17:34   Methods of taking testimony

Testimony can be taken of witnesses located in another state, including testimony of the parties and the child. The court on its own motion may order that testimony be taken of a person in another state and prescribe the manner that the testimony is to be taken.[1] A court may permit testimony of an individual to be taken by phone, audiovisual means or any other electronic means. The court shall cooperate with courts of other states for deposition or testimony.[2] Documentary evidence from another state transmitted by technological means cannot be excluded based on an objection based on the means of transmission.[3]

§ 17:35   Cooperation between courts

RC 3127.11 is the guiding provision for cooperation between the courts. The court may request a court of another state to hold an evidentiary hearing, order a person to produce or give testimony pursuant to procedures of that state, order an evaluation to be made concerning the allocation of parental rights and responsibilities, forward to the court a certified transcript of the record of the hearing, evidence presented, and any evaluation prepared, and order a party to appear with or without the child.[1] At the request of another state, the court may hold a hearing or enter an order.[2] The court may assess travel and other necessary and reasonable expenses according to the law of Ohio against the parties.[3] At the request of a court or law enforcement, the state shall forward a certified copy of pleadings, orders, decrees, records of hearings, evaluations and other pertinent records to the court or law enforcement of the other state.[4]

§ 17:36   Initial child custody jurisdiction

RC 3127.15 replaces prior RC 3109.22, and provides that an Ohio court has jurisdiction to make an initial determination in a child custody proceeding only if one of the following applies:

---

[4]RC 3127.09(D).

[Section 17:34]

   [1]RC 3127.10(A).
   [2]RC 3127.10(B).
   [3]RC 3127.10(C).

[Section 17:35]

   [1]RC 3127.11(A)(1) to RC 3127.11(A)(5).
   [2]RC 3127.11(B).
   [3]RC 3127.11(C).
   [4]RC 3127.11(D).

(1) Ohio is the home state of the child on the date of the commencement of the proceeding or was the home state within six months
before the commencement of the proceeding and the child is
absent from this state but a parent or person acting as a parent
continues to live in this state;[1]

(2) a court of another state does not have jurisdiction as home state
or the home state has declined to exercise jurisdiction that Ohio
is a more appropriate forum and both of the following are the
case: the child and the child's parents have a significant connection with Ohio other than mere physical presence, and substantial evidence is available in this state concerning the child's
care, protection, training, and personal relationships;[2]

(3) all courts having jurisdiction under (1) or (2) have declined jurisdiction on the ground that this court is the more appropriate
forum to determine custody of the child; or,

(4) no court of any other state would have jurisdiction.[3]

RC 3127.15(A) is the exclusive jurisdictional basis for making a
child custody determination by an Ohio court.[4] Physical presence of,
or personal jurisdiction over, a party or child is not necessary to make
a child custody determination.[5] *In re Craig* held, "Determination of jurisdiction under the UCCJEA is a two-step process. The first step is to
determine if Ohio has jurisdiction, and the second step is to determine
whether Ohio should exercise that jurisdiction. The court may decline
to exercise jurisdiction pursuant to RC 3127.15(A) if it finds that a
court of another state is a more appropriate forum."[6] While Ohio was
the child's home state, the Ohio court was given notice that the North
Carolina court had not relinquished jurisdiction and it was not error
for the Ohio court to decline jurisdiction.

Home state jurisdiction is the priority basis for the exercise of jurisdiction over any other basis. This is the priority in the PKPA, and
with the passage of the UCCJEA, there is no conflict between the two
statutes. There can only be one home state and therefore, competition

---

[Section 17:36]

[1]Home state is the state in which a child lived with a parent or person acting as
a parent for at least six consecutive months immediately preceding the commencement of a child custody proceeding. Rosen v. Celebrezze, 117 Ohio St. 3d 241,
2008-Ohio-853, 883 N.E.2d 420 (2008).

[2]Beck v. Sprik, 2008-Ohio-3197, 2008 WL 2581385 (Ohio Ct. App. 9th Dist.
Medina County 2008), sets forth the determinations a court must make if there is no
home state.

[3]RC 3127.15(A)(1) to RC 3127.15(A)(4).

[4]RC 3127.15(B).

[5]RC 3127.15(C).

[6]In re Craig, 2007-Ohio-3843, 2007 WL 2164532, at ¶ 32 (Ohio Ct. App. 11th
Dist. Trumbull County 2007).

for jurisdiction between the states is avoided.[7] "Best interest" language has been eliminated in the significant connection jurisdictional section of the UCCJEA and significant connection jurisdiction can only be exercised when there is no home state. Emergency jurisdiction has been moved to a subsequent section, RC 3127.18, to make clear that the authority of the court to enter an emergency order does not include the authority to make a permanent order except as that section sets forth.

Neither minimum contacts nor service within the state is required for the state to exercise personal jurisdiction, nor is jurisdiction conferred because there are minimum contacts or service. Jurisdiction is conferred with satisfaction of the requirements of this section of the statute and notice and hearing as required under the UCCJEA. This is also subject matter jurisdiction and, as such, an agreement of the parties to confer jurisdiction on a court that does not otherwise have jurisdiction cannot be accomplished.

§ 17:37 Initial child custody jurisdiction—Default jurisdiction

In *Rosen v. Celebrezze*[1] the court held that the UCCJEA, as codified in Ohio, identified four types of child custody jurisdiction: home state jurisdiction; significant-connection jurisdiction, jurisdiction because of declination of jurisdiction, and default jurisdiction.

Under the default provision, even if a child has not been present in the state for 6 months, a trial court may still have jurisdiction when no other state is exercising jurisdiction and one parent is present in state. Thus, if no other state has assumed jurisdiction, Ohio could assume jurisdiction.[2]

§ 17:38 Exclusive continuing jurisdiction

Exclusive continuing jurisdiction remains with the court until an Ohio court or the court of another state determines that the child, the child's parents, and any other person acting as a parent do not presently reside in this state.[1]

This is an entirely new section. Continuing jurisdiction was not addressed in the UCCJA. The continuing jurisdiction of the state which grants the original decree is exclusive. It continues until that state no

---

[7]Rosen v. Celebrezze, 117 Ohio St. 3d 241, 2008-Ohio-853, 883 N.E.2d 420 (2008); Beck v. Sprik, 2008-Ohio-3197, 2008 WL 2581385 (Ohio Ct. App. 9th Dist. Medina County 2008).

[Section 17:37]

[1]Rosen v. Celebrezze, 117 Ohio St. 3d 241, 2008-Ohio-853, 883 N.E.2d 420 (2008).

[2]Beck v. Sprik, 2008-Ohio-3197, 2008 WL 2581385 (Ohio Ct. App. 9th Dist. Medina County 2008).

[Section 17:38]

[1]RC 3127.16.

longer has significant connections and substantial evidence no longer exists in that state regarding the child, a parent or a person acting as a parent. Exclusive continuing jurisdiction is also lost if the child, the child's parents and any person acting as a parent no longer reside in the original decree state. It is meant to be identical to the PKPA. Continuing jurisdiction may be relinquished to another state is if it is a more convenient forum if exclusive continuing jurisdiction is no longer in existence.[2] Ohio has recognized the theory espoused in the PKPA regarding exclusive continuing jurisdiction[3] and it is likely that the Ohio courts will continue to maintain that the initial state which grants an order will continue to have such jurisdiction. The Ohio Supreme Court recognized that the UCCJEA gives jurisdictional priority and excusive continuing jurisdiction to the home state.[4]

§ 17:39   Jurisdiction to modify

A court of this state may not modify a child custody determination by a court of another state unless the Ohio court has jurisdiction to make an initial determination under RC 3127.15(A)(1) or RC 3127.15(A)(2) and one of the following applies: (A) the court of the other state determines that it no longer has exclusive, continuing jurisdiction or that a court of this state would be a more convenient forum, or (B) the court of this state or the court of another state determines that the child, the child's parents and any other person acting as a parent do not presently reside in the other state.[1]

RC 3127.17 prohibits the court from modifying a custody determination made by another state court unless that state court decides it no longer has exclusive continuing jurisdiction or that this court is a more convenient forum. The modification state cannot determine that the original court lost jurisdiction unless it determines that all parties have moved away from the original state. The modification state must have jurisdiction to grant an initial determination. If Ohio becomes

---

[2]Critzer v. Critzer, 2008-Ohio-5126, 2008 WL 4436777, (Ohio Ct. App. 8th Dist. Cuyahoga County 2008) even though Ohio continued to have exclusive continuing jurisdiction.

[3]Justis v. Justis, 81 Ohio St. 3d 312, 1989-Ohio-626, 691 N.E.2d 264 (1998).

[4]Rosen v. Celebrezze, 117 Ohio St. 3d 241, 2008-Ohio-853, 883 N.E.2d 420 (2008); North v. North, 2008-Ohio-6438, 2008 WL 5159844 (Ohio Ct. App. 9th Dist. Summit County 2008), discussed the need to file a motion to raise the issue of inconvenient forum.

[Section 17:39]

[1]If there is no home state for modification, the court must determine if there is substantial evidence regarding the child's care, protection, training, and personal relationship in Ohio. Which state has "a greater quantity of evidence" does not control. Thebeau v. Thebeau, 2008-Ohio-4751, 2008 WL 4278127 (Ohio Ct. App. 4th Dist. Lawrence County 2008).

the home state, it can modify another state's order[2] In a case involving a custody determination for a child of civil union recognized in Vermont, the tenets PKPA prevailed over the Defense of Marriage Act in the apprehension of jurisdiction. Therefore, the UCCJEA will likely be followed if a jurisdictional issue arises in a custody dispute of same sex partners.[3]

§ 17:40   Temporary emergency jurisdiction

Ohio has temporary emergency jurisdiction if a child is present in the state and either of the following applies: (1) the child has been abandoned, or (2) it is necessary in an emergency to protect the child, because the child, or a sibling or parent of the child, is subjected to or threatened with mistreatment or abuse.[1] If there is no previous child custody determination and a child custody proceeding has not been commenced in another state that has jurisdiction, a child custody determination made under this section remains in effect until an order is obtained from a state court with jurisdiction.[2] If no other state court exercises jurisdiction, then the decision becomes a final determination, if it so provides and Ohio becomes the home state of the child.[3] If there has been a previous child custody determination that is entitled to be enforced, or a child custody proceeding has been commenced, any order issued by this state must specify the period that the court considers adequate for a person seeking an order to obtain an order from the state having jurisdiction. The order remains in effect until an order is obtained from the other state or until the order expires.[4] Communication between the courts shall occur to resolve the emergency, protect the safety of the parties and the child, and determine a period for the duration of the temporary order.[5]

This section broadens what was included in the UCCJA. It is "extraordinary jurisdiction reserved for extraordinary circumstances."[6] The definition of emergency is modified in keeping with the PKPA as neglect has been eliminated. A protective order issued under the Do-

---

[2]McGhan v. Vettel, 122 Ohio St. 3d 227, 2009-Ohio-2884, 909 N.E.2d 1279 (2009).

[3]Miller-Jenkens v. Miller-Jenkens, Court of Appeals of Virginia, decided June 6, 2008, Record No. 070933.

[Section 17:40]

[1]RC 3127.18(A).

[2]RC 3127.18(B).

[3]RC 3127.18(B).

[4]RC 3127.18(C); see In re Collins, 2007-Ohio-4582, 2007 WL 2492731, (Ohio Ct. App. 5th Dist. Guernsey County 2007), which indicates that a court of this state may only issue temporary orders when a previous child custody determination has been issued in another state.

[5]RC 3127.18(D).

[6]Commentary of Professor Bodenheimer to former Section 3(a)(3) of the UCCJA cited in Uniform Child Custody Jurisdiction and Enforcement Act (1997) Prefatory Notes and Comments.

mestic Violence statute must comport with the UCCJEA to be enforceable by another state court. The Violence Against Women's Act, 18 U.S.C.A. § 2265 excludes a custody order from the definition of a protective order under 22 U.S.C.A. § 2266.

As stated in *In re Fluharty*,[7] "An ex parte complaint, by definition, is one filed by or for one party without notice or challenge by the opposing party." The custodial grandparent argued that the court should not consider child's home state in an emergency temporary custody action. While grandparents' complaint was pending, mother filed for divorce in Louisiana. "Commenced," as used in this section, does not mean a proceeding must pre-exist or pre-date the filing of an emergency complaint. "Commenced" simply means the filing of the first pleadings in a proceeding, as defined by RC 3127.01(B)(5).

§ 17:41   Temporary orders

Notice and an opportunity to be heard shall be given to all persons entitled to notice under the law of this state as in child custody proceedings between residents of this state, any parent whose parental rights have not been previously terminated, and any person having physical custody of the child.[1] Revised Code Chapter 3127 does not govern the enforceability of a child custody determination made without notice or an opportunity to be heard.[2] The joinder of parties and the right to intervene as a party are governed by the law of this state as in a child custody proceeding between residents of this state.[3]

Temporary orders which are issued in compliance with the Rules of Civil Procedure and statute of the state are beyond the scope of the UCCJEA. The validity of such orders is governed by the law of the state which authorizes them. Joinder is also dictated by local state law. The requirement of the UCCJEA, like the PKPA, is that there be notice and an opportunity to be heard.

§ 17:42   Simultaneous proceedings

Unless there is an exercise of temporary emergency jurisdiction, a court may not exercise its jurisdiction if, "at the time of the commencement of the proceeding, a child custody proceeding . . . is pending in a court of another state. . . ., unless the proceeding has been

---

[7]In re Fluharty, 2006-Ohio-6529, 2006 WL 3587243, at ¶ 10 (Ohio Ct. App. 11th Dist. Trumbull County 2006).

[Section 17:41]
   [1]RC 3127.19(A).
   [2]RC 3127.19(B).
   [3]RC 3127.19(C).

terminated or is stayed by the court of the other state because a court of this state is a more convenient forum. . . ."[1]

RC 3127.20(B) mandates a court of this state, before hearing a child custody proceeding, to examine documents and information supplied by the parties pursuant to RC 3127.23.[2] If a child custody proceeding is pending in another state, this state's court shall stay its proceedings and communicate with the court of the other state. In accordance with RC 3127.20(B), "If the court of the state having jurisdiction substantially in accordance with this chapter does not determine that the court of this state is a more appropriate forum, the court of this state shall dismiss the proceeding."

RC 3127.20(C) concerns itself with modification jurisdiction. It requires that the Ohio court do any of the following if a proceeding has been commenced in another state: (1) stay the proceeding for modification pending the entry of an order of a court of the other state enforcing, staying, denying or dismissing the proceeding for enforcement; (2) enjoin the parties from continuing with proceeding for enforcement; or (3) if an emergency, proceed with the modification.

RC 3127.20 is the section concerning simultaneous proceedings. As home state jurisdiction is the priority, and exclusive continuing jurisdiction is resolved, and there is a prohibition on modification jurisdiction, the "problem of simultaneous proceeding is no longer a significant issue."[3] The simultaneous proceeding issue will arise only if there is no home state, no state with exclusive continuing jurisdiction, and more than one significant connection state.[4] The cornerstone of theUCCJEA is reflected in this section as there should only be rare instances where there are simultaneous proceedings as the dictates for when jurisdiction should be exercised in a child custody proceeding are set forth in the previous sections of the statute.

§ 17:43   Inconvenient forum considerations

An Ohio court that has jurisdiction may decline to exercise its jurisdiction at any time if it determines that it is an inconvenient forum and that a court of another state is a more convenient forum.[1] The issue may be raised by a party, the Ohio court, or at the request of an-

---

[Section 17:42]

[1]RC 3127.20(A).

[2]RC 3127.20(B).

[3]Uniform Child Custody Jurisdiction and Enforcement Act (1997), National Conference of Commissioners on Uniform State Law, Prefatory Notes and Comment to Section 206.

[4]Uniform Child Custody Jurisdiction and Enforcement Act (1997), National Conference of Commissioners on Uniform State Law, Prefatory Notes and Comment to Section 206.

[Section 17:43]

[1]RC 3127.21(A).

other court.[2] The factors to be considered by the court when making its determination of whether it is an inconvenient forum include the following:

(1) whether domestic violence has occurred and is likely to continue in the future and which state could best protect the parties and the child;

(2) the length of time the child has resided outside Ohio;

(3) the distance between the Ohio court and the court in the state that would assume jurisdiction;

(4) the relative financial circumstances of the parties;

(5) any agreement of the parties as to which state should assume jurisdiction;

(6) the nature and location of the evidence required to resolve the pending litigation, including the testimony of the child;

(7) the ability of the court of each state to decided the issue expeditiously and the procedures necessary to present the evidence;

(8) the familiarity of the court of each state with the facts and issues in the pending litigation.[3]

If an Ohio court determines that it is an inconvenient forum and another state's court is a more appropriate forum, it shall stay the proceedings on the condition that a child custody proceeding be promptly commenced in another state.[4]

RC 3127.21(D) permits a court of this state to decline to exercise jurisdiction if a child custody determination is incidental to an action for divorce or another proceeding while still retaining jurisdiction over the divorce or other proceeding.

This section is similar to the UCCJA as it allows to the court to decide that another state is in a better position to make the custody determination. The list of factors is not meant to be exclusive. To avoid the dilemma that no court would have jurisdiction, a proceeding must be commenced in another state.

In *In re Craig*,[5] the court stated, "Determination of jurisdiction under the UCCJEA is a two-step process. The first step is to determine if Ohio has jurisdiction, and the second step is to determine whether Ohio should exercise that jurisdiction. The court may decline to exercise jurisdiction pursuant to RC 3127.15(A) if it finds that a court of another state is a more appropriate forum." The court considered the following factors in determining that North Carolina was a more convenient and appropriate forum: both parents resided in North Carolina; the parties were granted a divorce in North Carolina; a custody

---

[2]RC 3127.21(A).

[3]RC 3127.21(B). No oral hearing is necessary under the UCCJEA or UCCJA. Critzer v. Critzer, 2008-Ohio-5126, 2008 WL 4436777, (Ohio Ct. App. 8th Dist. Cuyahoga County 2008).

[4]RC 3127.21(C).

[5]In re Craig, 2007-Ohio-3843, 2007 WL 2164532 (Ohio Ct. App. 11th Dist. Trumbull County 2007).

action was pending in North Carolina; and the biological father lacked the funds to hire an attorney in Ohio and was financially unable to travel to and from Ohio for litigation.

§ 17:44   Unjustifiable conduct

An Ohio court which has jurisdiction shall decline to exercise its jurisdiction because a person has engaged in unjustifiable conduct, unless (1) the parents and all persons acting as parents have agreed to the exercise of jurisdiction; (2) a court of the state having jurisdiction determines that this state is a more appropriate forum; (3) no other court would have jurisdiction.[1]

If a court of this state declines to exercise jurisdiction pursuant to this section, it may fashion an appropriate remedy to ensure the safety of the child and prevent a repetition of the unjustifiable conduct.[2]

The court shall assess necessary and reasonable costs, communication expenses, attorney's fess, investigative fees, expenses for witnesses, travel expenses, and child care during the course of the proceedings if a court dismisses or stays a proceeding under this section.[3] Fees may not be assessed if the party establishes that it would be clearly inappropriate, and may not be assessed against a state or political subdivision unless authorized by law.[4]

Unjustifiable conduct is defined as "conduct by a parent or that parent's surrogate that attempts to create jurisdiction in this state by removing the child from the child's home state, secreting the child, retaining the child or restraining or otherwise preventing the child from returning to the child's home state in order to prevent the other parent from commencing a child custody proceeding in the child's home state."[5]

RC 3127.22 "ensures that abducting parents will not receive an advantage for unjustifiable conduct. If the conduct that creates the jurisdiction is unjustified, courts must decline to exercise jurisdiction that is inappropriately invoked by one of the parties."[6] This section focuses on unjustifiable conduct, not justifiable conduct such as domestic violence. If the conduct is unjustifiable, the court must decline to exercise jurisdiction. "It should be noted that the court is not mak-

---

[Section 17:44]

[1]RC 3127.22(A).

[2]RC 3127.22(B).

[3]RC 3127.22(C).

[4]RC 3127.22(C).

[5]RC 3127.22(D).

[6]Uniform Child Custody Jurisdiction and Enforcement Act (1997), National Conference of Commissioners on Uniform State Law, Prefatory Notes and Comments on Section 208.

ing a forum non conveniens analysis in this section."[7] The attorneys'
fee section is similar to the International Child Abduction Remedies
Act, 42 U.S.C.A. § 1607(b)(3).

§ 17:45 Custody affidavit contents

Each party in a child custody proceeding, in the party's first pleading or in an affidavit attached to that pleading, shall give information,
under oath, as to the child's present address or whereabouts, the
places the child has lived within the last five years, and the name and
present address of each person with whom the child has lived during
that period.[1] Subsections (1) to (3) set forth the additional information
required in the affidavit or pleading which includes if the party has
participated in any other proceeding concerning the child; whether
the party knows of any proceeding that could affect the current
proceeding, including enforcement of child custody determinations,
domestic violence, abuse, neglect, dependency, termination of parental
rights and adoptions; and whether any other person who is not a
party has physical custody of the child or claims to be a parent, or
who has custody or visitation rights with the child.[2]

Additional information shall be given as required by the court[3] and
each party has a continuing duty to inform the court of any child
custody proceeding that could affect the current proceeding.[4] If it is alleged that the disclosure of this information would jeopardize the
health, safety, or liberty of a party or child, then the information shall
be sealed and not be disclosed to the other party or public.[5] A public
children services agency is not subject to this section for a complaint
filed under RC 2151.27[6] and an abused, neglected and dependent
child has the meaning as set forth in RC 2151.031, RC 2151.03 and
RC 2151.04 respectively.[7]

An affidavit is required to be filed in the beginning of a child custody
proceeding. The information can be sealed if the safety, health or liberty of a party or child would be jeopardized. Thus, in a domestic
violence proceeding, if appropriate, the information could be sealed.
There is no reason to think that this would not continue to be a

---

[7]Uniform Child Custody Jurisdiction and Enforcement Act (1997), National
Conference of Commissioners on Uniform State Law, Prefatory Notes and Comments
on Section 208.

[Section 17:45]
[1]RC 3127.23(A).
[2]RC 3127.23(A)(1) to RC 3127.23(A)(3).
[3]RC 3127.23(B).
[4]RC 3127.23(C).
[5]RC 3127.23(D).
[6]RC 3127.23(E).
[7]RC 3127.23(F).

jurisdictional requirement in Ohio.[8] The Supreme Court of Ohio indicated that an affidavit is mandatory but the failure to file an affidavit can be remedied with an amended filing. The court indicated that the failure to file does not take from the court subject matter jurisdiction and the failure to file the affidavit can be remedied since the purpose of the affidavit is to provide the court needed information.[9] Filing of the UCCJEA affidavit is jurisdictional in accordance with a recent ruling.[10]

The requirement of an affidavit under RC 3127.23(A), that each party in a child custody proceeding provide information was construed to apply to actions in which the original jurisdiction of an Ohio court to enter orders is invoked. An affidavit is required in a complaint for legal custody and neglect.[11] The court in *Reynolds v. Spicer*[12] found the provisions have no application to requests to enforce relief granted in an action in another state that has appropriate jurisdiction.

§ 17:46 Appearance of parties and child

The court may order any party to appear with or without the child. If a person is within the state, such person may be ordered to appear with the child.[1] The court may enter any orders necessary to ensure the safety of the child and of any person ordered to appear under this section.[2]

§ 17:47 Definitions for enforcement under Hague Convention

RC 3127.31 to RC 3127.47 deal with enforcement of the UCCJEA. RC 3127.31 defines the term "petitioner" as a person who seeks enforcement of an order for return of a child under the Hague Convention or enforcement of a child custody determination. It defines "respondent" as a person against whom a proceeding has been commenced for enforcement of an order for return of a child under the Hague Convention or enforcement of a child custody determination.[1]

---

[8]Pasqualone v. Pasqualone, 63 Ohio St. 2d 96, 17 Ohio Op. 3d 58, 406 N.E.2d 1121 (1980).

[9]In re Complaint for Writ of Habeas Corpus for Goeller, 103 Ohio St. 3d 427, 2004-Ohio-5579, 816 N.E.2d 594 (2004).

[10]Frew v. Frew, 2008-Ohio-4203, 2008 WL 3856300 (Ohio Ct. App. 5th Dist. Coshocton County 2008).

[11]In re S.K., 2008-Ohio-1256, 2008 WL 740573, (Ohio Ct. App. 8th Dist. Cuyahoga County 2008).

[12]Reynolds v. Spicer, 166 Ohio App. 3d 485, 2006-Ohio-1817, 851 N.E.2d 527 (2d Dist. Clark County 2006).

[Section 17:46]
[1]RC 3127.24(A).
[2]RC 3127.24(C).

[Section 17:47]
[1]RC 3127.31(A) and RC 3127.31(B).

§ 17:48   Enforcement under Hague Convention

The Juvenile Court or another court with appropriate jurisdiction may enforce the return of a child under the Hague Convention as if it were a child custody determination.[1] This is a new provision giving the juvenile court jurisdiction for enforcement under the Hague Convention.

§ 17:49   Duty to enforce

An Ohio court shall recognize and enforce a child custody determination of another state if that state exercised jurisdiction in substantial conformity with theUCCJEA or under factual circumstances meeting the jurisdictional standards and the determination has not been modified in accordance with the UCCJEA.[1] Any remedy may be used to enforce a child custody determination. The remedies are cumulative under the UCCJEA and do not affect the availability of other remedies for enforcement.[2]

The Hocking County Court of Appeals has concluded that a writ of habeas corpus was unavailable to a father who sought to enforce a Georgia decree awarding him custody of his children where the UCCJEA provided a mechanism to enforce his custody determination.[3]

The duty to enforce is based upon the UCCJEA and is now consistent with the PKPA. As all remedies are available, contempt, civil suits and other litigation can be accomplished.

§ 17:50   Temporary order for parenting time

A court which does not have jurisdiction to modify a child custody determination may issue a temporary order enforcing either (1) a parenting time or visitation schedule made by a court of another state or (2) the parenting time or vacation provision of a child custody determination of another state that does not provide for a specific parenting time or visitation schedule.[1]

If an Ohio court makes an order, it shall specify in the order a period that it considers adequate for the petitioner to obtain an order

---

[Section 17:48]

[1]RC 3127.32.

[Section 17:49]

[1]RC 3127.33(A).

[2]RC 3127.33(B).

[3]Harris v. Harris, 2005-Ohio-3457, 2005 WL 1579462 (Ohio Ct. App. 4th Dist. Hocking County 2005). However, see In re M.T., 178 Ohio App. 3d 546, 2008-Ohio-5174, 899 N.E.2d 162 (2d Dist. Montgomery County 2008), insofar as habeas corpus as an extraordinary remedy is concerned. The court exercising jurisdiction must have that jurisdiction consistent with the UCCJEA.

[Section 17:50]

[1]RC 3127.34(A).

from the other court.[2] The order remains in effect until an order is obtained from the other court or until the order expires.[3]

This section provides for temporary visitation by the court enforcing another state's court's order. The court may not make a permanent change in visitation or parenting time as that can only be done by the court with exclusive continuing jurisdiction. This provision provides the opportunity for the Ohio court to issue orders for visitation, if none have been made.

§ 17:51   Registration of child custody determination

The clerk of a juvenile court or other court with appropriate jurisdiction may register a child custody determination issued by a court of another state, with or without a simultaneous request for enforcement, on receipt of all of the following:

(1) a letter or other document requesting that the child custody determination be registered;

(2) two copies, including one certified copy, of the determination sought to be registered, and a statement under penalty of perjury, that the order has not been modified;

(3) the name and address of the person seeking registration and any parent who is designated as residential parent and legal custodian, or who has parenting time or who has been awarded custody or visitation sought to be registered; and

(4) the deposit or fee established by the court.[1]

On receipt of the documents, the court shall do both of the following: (1) cause the child custody determination to be filed as a foreign judgment; and (2) serve notice of the registration request on the persons named and provide them with an opportunity to contest the registration in accordance with this section.[2] The notice shall state all of the following:

(1) the registered child custody determination is enforceable as of the date of registration in the same manner as a child custody determination issued by a court of this state;

(2) that a hearing to contest the validity of the registration must be requested within 30 days after service of the notice; and

(3) failure to contest the registration shall result in confirmation of the child custody determination and preclude further contest of that determination with respect to any matter that could have been asserted.[3]

A person seeking to contest the validity of the registered court order shall request a hearing within 30 days after service of the notice.

---

[2]RC 3127.34(B).

[3]RC 3127.34(B).

[Section 17:51]

[1]RC 3127.35(A).

[2]RC 3127.35(B).

[3]RC 3127.35(C).

At the hearing, the court shall confirm the registered order unless one of the following is established: (1) the issuing court did not have jurisdiction; (2) the determination sought to be registered has been vacated, stayed, or modified by a court having jurisdiction; or (3) the person contesting the registration was entitled to notice of the proceeding but notice was not given.[4] If there is no request to contest the validity of the registration, the person requesting registration and all persons served must be notified of the confirmation that occurs as a matter of law.[5] The confirmation of a registered custody determination precludes further contest of the determination that could have been asserted at the time of registration.[6]

RC 3127.35 provides for registration of child custody determinations. The Juvenile Court has the jurisdiction under the UCCJEA and is the court for registration of child custody determinations. The registration provision parallels the process in UIFSA for registration of child support orders. Registration of a custody determination can occur without request for enforcement.

§ 17:52 Registration—Enforcement

A juvenile court or other court may grant any relief normally available to enforce a registered child custody determination.[1] A Juvenile Court and each other court of this state shall recognize and enforce, but may not modify except as acceptable under the UCCJEA, a registered child custody determination of a court of another state.[2]

This is new, but consistent with the premise of the UCCJEA, namely that a court can enforce another state's court's order, but cannot modify it. The other state's court's order remains the order of the granting state.

§ 17:53 Registration—Communication

If a proceeding for enforcement is commenced in this state and the court determines that a proceeding to modify the determination is pending in another state having jurisdiction to modify the determination, the enforcing court shall immediately communicate with the modifying court.[1] The proceeding for enforcement shall continue un-

---

[4]RC 3127.35(D).
[5]RC 3127.35(E).
[6]RC 3127.35(F).
[Section 17:52]
[1]RC 3127.36(A).
[2]RC 3127.36(B).
[Section 17:53]
[1]RC 3127.37.

less the enforcing court, after consultation with the modifying court, stays or dismisses the proceeding.[2]

This section addresses simultaneous proceedings. Pleadings should disclose any pending proceedings. Enforcement normally takes precedence over modification; however, communication is necessary between the courts.

§ 17:54 Registration—Expedited enforcement

A petition for enforcement must be verified and all orders sought to be enforced must be attached to the petition. The attached orders shall be the original or certified copies.[1] A petition for enforcement shall state all of the following:

(1) whether the court that issued the child custody determination identified the jurisdictional basis it relied upon in exercising jurisdiction and, if so, what the basis was;

(2) whether the determination for which enforcement is sought has been vacated, stayed, or modified by a court and, if so, identify the court, case number and nature of the proceeding;

(3) whether any proceeding has been commenced that could affect the current proceeding, and, if so, identify the court, case number and nature of the proceeding;

(4) the present physical address of the child and respondent, if known;

(5) whether relief in addition to the immediate physical custody of the child and attorney's fees is sought, including a request for assistance from law enforcement officials, and the relief sought; and

(6) if the child custody determination has been registered and confirmed, the date and place of registration.[2]

Upon the filing, the court shall issue an order directing the respondent to appear in person, with or without the child, and may enter any order necessary to ensure the safety of the child.[3] If possible the hearing is to be held the next judicial day after service of the order and if that date is impossible, the court shall hold the hearing on the first judicial day possible.[4] The court may extend the date at the request of the petitioner.[5]

An order issued shall state the time and place of the hearing. It shall advise the respondent that the petitioner may take immediate physical custody of the child and that the respondent may pay fees,

---

[2]RC 3127.37.

[Section 17:54]
    [1]RC 3127.38(A).
    [2]RC 3127.38(B).
    [3]RC 3127.38(C).
    [4]RC 3127.38(C).
    [5]RC 3127.38(C).

costs, and expenses and may schedule a hearing to determine whether further relief is appropriate unless the respondent appears and establishes either of the following:

(1) that the child custody determination has not been registered and confirmed and that one of the following circumstances applies:

   (a) the issuing court did not have jurisdiction;

   (b) the child custody determination for which enforcement is sought has been vacated, stayed or modified; or

   (c) the respondent was entitled to notice of the child custody proceeding and notice was not given; or

(2) That the child custody determination for which enforcement is sought was registered and confirmed but has been vacated, stayed or modified.[6]

RC 3127.38 provides for expedited enforcement of child custody determinations. When the initial order is made, consideration must be given to the form, terms and content of the order since enforcement may be necessary in another state's court. As enforcement requires registration and confirmation of the order, the mandates of those sections of the code must be met. Thus any order issued must contemplate the necessary and required pleadings and terms of enforcement. Expeditious enforcement is the standard of the UCCJEA.

§ 17:55 Registration—Enforcement—Service

Service of the petition and order shall be done by any method authorized under the Rules of Civil Procedure upon respondent and any other person who has physical custody of the child.[1]

§ 17:56 Registration—Enforcement—Hearing

Unless a temporary emergency order is issued, upon a finding that a petitioner is entitled to immediate physical custody of the child, the court shall order that the petitioner is entitled to the immediate physical custody of the child unless the respondent establishes either of the following:

(1) That the child custody determination has not been registered and confirmed and that one of the following circumstances apply:

   (a) the issuing court did not have jurisdiction;

   (b) the child custody determination has been vacated, stayed or modified; or

   (c) the respondent was entitled to notice and notice was not given; or

(2) The child custody determination for which enforcement is

---

[6]RC 3127.38(D).

[Section 17:55]

   [1]RC 3127.39.

sought was registered and confirmed but has been vacated, stayed or modified.[1]
Under RC 3127.40(B) the court shall award fees, costs and expenses and additional relief. If a party called to testify refuses to answer on the basis that the testimony may be self-incriminating, the court may draw an adverse inference from the refusal.[2] A privilege against disclosure of communications between spouses and a defense of immunity based on the relationship of husband and wife or parent and child may not be invoked in a proceeding under this chapter.[3]

The "scope of inquiry is quite limited" as the PKPA requires enforcement if the determination was issued in compliance with the federal law.[4] Lack of notice may be the only defense if the order was issued in accordance with the UCCJEA.

§ 17:57   Registration—Enforcement—Warrant

RC 3127.41 prescribes the process for a warrant to take physical custody of the child. Upon the filing of a petition seeking enforcement of a child custody determination, the petitioner may file a verified application for the issuance of a warrant to take physical custody of the child if the child is imminently likely to suffer serious physical harm or be removed from this state.[1] If the court finds this, it may issue a warrant accordingly. This hearing shall be heard on the next judicial day or the first judicial day possible.[2] The application for the warrant shall include statements required under RC 3127.38(B). A warrant shall do all of the following: (1) specify the facts upon which a conclusion of imminent serious physical harm or removal from the jurisdiction is based; (2) direct law enforcement officers to take physical custody of the child immediately; and (3) provide for the placement of the child pending final relief.[3] The respondent shall be served with the petition, warrant and order immediately after the child is taken into physical custody.[4] A warrant is enforceable throughout the state and may authorize the entry by law enforcement officers onto private

---

[Section 17:56]

[1]RC 3127.40(A).

[2]RC 3127.40(C).

[3]RC 3127.40(D).

[4]Uniform Child Custody Jurisdiction and Enforcement Act (1977), National Conference of Commissioners on Uniform State Law, Prefatory Notes and comments Section 310.

[Section 17:57]

[1]RC 3127.41(A).

[2]RC 3127.41(B).

[3]RC 3127.41(C).

[4]RC 3127.41(D).

property and may authorize forcible entry at any hour.[5] The court may also impose conditions upon the placement of a child to ensure the appearance of the child and the child's custodian.[6]

RC 3127.41 provides for emergency action if there is reason to believe that the child will suffer imminent serious physical harm or be removed form the state. Notice requirements can be waived and a warrant to take physical custody can be issued. The court can make any orders to ensure appearance which could include a bond, the holding by the court of passports or the like.

§ 17:58   Registration—Enforcement—Fees and expenses

A court shall award the prevailing party in an action to enforce a child custody determination, including a state, necessary and reasonable expenses, unless the party from whom the fees or expenses are sought establishes that the award would clearly be inappropriate.[1] This shall not be assessed against a state or political subdivision unless authorized by law other than RC Ch. 3127.[2]

This section is derived from the International Child Abduction Remedies Act and the policies of the PKPA.

§ 17:59   Registration—Enforcement—Full faith and credit

An Ohio court shall accord full faith and credit to an order of another state consistent with RC Ch. 3127 that enforces a child custody determination by a court of another state unless the order has been vacated, stayed or modified.[1]

This state must enforce and not modify orders issued by other states, if made in compliance with the UCCJEA. This state must enforce and not modify orders issued by another state if made in compliance with the UCCJEA and so long as the court had jurisdiction to issue an order. In *Ashburn v. Roth*,[2] where an Illinois custody order that was not vacated, stayed or modified, such order did not have to be given full faith and credit because it lacked initial child custody jurisdiction and Ohio was the child's home state.

§ 17:60   Registration—Enforcement—Appellate review

Appeals are authorized under the UCCJEA and an expedited appel-

---

[5]RC 3127.41(E).

[6]RC 3127.41(F).

[Section 17:58]

[1]RC 3127.42(A).

[2]RC 3127.42(B).

[Section 17:59]

[1]RC 3127.43.

[2]Ashburn v. Roth, 2007-Ohio-2995, 2007 WL 1731426 (Ohio Ct. App. 12th Dist. Butler County 2007).

late review must be provided by the Supreme Court of Ohio. Unless an emergency temporary order is issued under RC 3127.18, the enforcing court may not stay an order enforcing a child custody determination pending appeal.[1]

While the trial court cannot stay an order, the Court of Appeals still has the authority to do so.

§ 17:61 Registration—Enforcement—Role of public officers

The prosecutor is authorized to take any lawful action, under the Hague Convention or the UCCJEA, to locate a child, obtain the return of a child, or enforce a child custody determination if there is any of the following: (1) an existing child custody determination; (2) a request to locate a child, obtain the return of a child, or enforce a child custody determination from a court in a pending child custody proceeding; (3) a reasonable belief that a criminal statute has been violated; or (4) a reasonable belief that the child has been wrongfully removed or retained in violation of the Hague Convention.[1] A prosecutor acts on behalf of the court and may not represent any party.[2]

RC 3127.45, RC 3127.46, and RC 3127.47 address the role of public authorities in the civil enforcement of custody and visitation determinations. Their roles are limited to enforcement only and not the determination of jurisdiction.

§ 17:62 Miscellaneous provisions

RC 3127.51 to RC 3127.53 are miscellaneous sections that deal with application and construction, severability and the effective date. The law in effect at the time of filing is the law that governs.[1] If a provision of theUCCJEA is held invalid, it will not affect the entire RC chapter and the provisions are therefore severable.[2]

§ 17:63 Conclusion

The UCCJEA is premised upon the PKPA. Fundamentals have been established by prior court rulings and the commentary of the National Commissioners. The goal is to have only one court able to make an initial determination and only one court to make modifications. Enforcement can be done by a court without modification. The order in an initial custody determination must consider the enforcement

---

[Section 17:60]
   [1]RC 3127.44.

[Section 17:61]
   [1]RC 3127.45(A).
   [2]RC 3127.45(B).

[Section 17:62]
   [1]RC 3127.53.
   [2]RC 3127.52.

provisions to ensure that there can be registration and confirmation and the basis of jurisdiction should be set forth clearly. Emergency orders are only temporary and do not provide any greater jurisdiction to the court to make initial or modification orders. This jurisdictional statute prescribes that only one state can render a child custody determination.

§ 17:64   Chart of comparison

The following tables reprinted from the Bill Analysis of the Ohio Legislative Commission shows the relationship of the sections of the former UCCJA and the new UCCJEA.

Correlation Table
2004 S.B. 185, eff. 4–11–05

New section Number (UCCJEA)	Subject Matter	Former section Number (UCCJA)	Subject Matter
3127.01	Definitions	3109.21	Definitions
3127.01(B)(12)	Definitions	3109.23	Notice of Proceedings
3127.02	Proceedings Governed by Other Law	--	
3127.03	Application to Indian Tribes	--	
3127.04	International Application of Act	--	
3127.05	Effect of Child-Custody Determination	3109.30(A)	Parties Bound by Decrees
3127.06	Priority	3109.37	Priority of Jurisdictional Challenge
3127.07	Notice to Persons	3109.23	Notice of Proceedings
3127.08	Appearance and Limited Immunity	--	
3127.09	Communication Between Courts	--	
3127.10	Taking Testimony in Another State	--	
3127.11(A), (B), and (C)	Cooperation Between Courts	3109.34 and 3109.35	Ancillary Proceedings
3127.11(D)	Preservation/Forwarding of Records	3109.36	Preservation of Records
3127.15	Initial Child-Custody Jurisdiction	3109.22	Prerequisites to Jurisdiction
3127.16	Exclusive, Continuing Jurisdiction	--	
3127.17	Jurisdiction to Modify Determination	3109.31	Modification
3127.18	Temporary Emergency Jurisdiction	3109.22(A)(3)	Prerequisites to Jurisdiction
3127.19(A) and (B)	Notice	3109.23	Notice of Proceedings
3127.19(C)	Joinder	3109.28	Persons Claiming Rights
3127.20	Simultaneous Proceedings	3109.24	Pendency of Proceedings in Another State
3127.21	Inconvenient Forum	3109.25	Inconvenient Forum

New section Number (UCCJEA)	Subject Matter	Former section Number (UCCJA)	Subject Matter
3127.22	Jurisdiction Declined by Reason of Conduct	3109.26	Improperly Obtained Custody
3127.23	Custody Affidavit	3109.27	Custody Affidavit
3127.24	Appearance of Parties and Child	3109.29	Personal Appearance
3127.31	Enforcement Definitions	--	
3127.32	Enforcement under Hague Convention	--	
3127.33(B)	Enforcement Remedies	--	
3127.34	Temporary Visitation	--	
3127.35(A)	Registration	3109.33	Registry
3107.35(B)	Registration Duties	3109.32(A)	Filing from Another State
3127.35(C) to (G)	Notice and Hearing for Registration	--	
3127.36	Enforcement of Registered Determination	--	
3127.37	Simultaneous Proceedings	--	
3127.38	Expedited Enforcement of Child-Custody Determination	--	
3127.39	Service of Petition and Order	--	
3127.40	Hearing and Order	3109.32(B)	Filing from Another State
3127.41	Warrant to take Physical Custody of Child	--	
3127.42	Costs, Fees and Expenses	3109.32(B)	Filing from Another State
3127.43	Recognition and Enforcement	3109.30(B)	Parties Bound by Decree
3127.44	Appeals	--	
3127.45	Role of Prosecutor or Public Official	--	
3127.46	Role of Law Enforcement	--	
3127.47	Costs and Expenses	3109.32(B)	Filing from Another State
3127.51	Application and Construction	--	
3127.52	Severability Clause	--	
3127.53	Effective Date	--	

§ 17:65   International Child Abduction Remedies Act (ICARA)—History—Hague Convention

International child abduction by a parent or another without a legal right to custody has become less unusual than in the past and presents complex issues of national and international law when it occurs.

The Convention on the Civil Aspects of International Child Abduction was adopted at Hague, Switzerland on October 25, 1980. The Hague Convention, as it is commonly referred to, is an international treaty designed to protect custody rights of parents on a global scale.[1] The United States became a signatory nation to the Convention in July of 1988. The International Child Abduction Remedies Act (IC-ARA)[2] was adopted by Congress to provide uniformity in the implementation of the Convention in all jurisdictions in the United States.[3]

The Hague Convention provides the only body of law that governs international custody disputes. Where a country is not a party to the convention when an action is commenced, the convention is inapplicable.[4]

As of June 1996, the Convention is also in force in Argentina, Australia, Austria, The Bahamas, Belize, Bosnia-Herzegovina, Burkina Faso, Canada, Chile, Colombia, Croatia, Cyprus, Denmark, Ecuador, Finland, France, Germany, Great Britain, Greece, Honduras, Hungary, Iceland, Ireland, Israel, Italy, Luxembourg, Former Yugoslavia/Rep. of Macedonia, Mauritius, Mexico, Monaco, Netherlands, New Zealand, Norway, Panama, Poland, Portugal, Romania, Slovenia, Spain, St. Kitts/Nevis, Sweden, Switzerland, The United States, Venezuela, and Zimbabwe. Under the Convention, countries which have adopted the Convention are called contracting states. The treaty is only enforceable between those countries which have signed the treaty at the time of the abduction or wrongful retention.

§ 17:66   ICARA—Objective

The objective of the Convention is to secure the prompt return of children wrongfully removed from or retained in any contracting state. The Convention is not an extradition treaty. The Convention does not provide for any review of the merits of the conflicting custody claims or for enforcement of a foreign custody decree. The conduct which the Convention seeks to remedy is the wrongful removal or retention of children. The Convention offers a civil remedy which is not criminal in nature. The Convention is designed to ensure that rights of custody and of access (visitation) under the law of one contracting state are respected in other contracting states.

The return remedy of the Convention is in addition to any other means such as the international return provisions of the Uniform Child Custody Jurisdiction and Enforcement Act (UCCJEA).

[Section 17:65]

[1] A complete text of the convention on the civil aspects of international child abduction is found in Text Appendix 17-A, Convention on the Civil Aspects of International Child Abduction.

[2] 42 U.S.C.A. § 11601.

[3] A complete text of 42 U.S.C.A. § 11601 is found in Text Appendix 17-B, International Child Abduction Remedies Act.

[4] Taveras v. Taveraz, 477 F.3d 767, 2007 FED App. 0066P (6th Cir. 2007).

§ 17:67   ICARA—Children protected by the Convention

For a child to fall within the protection of the Convention, certain criteria must be established by the party seeking the relief afforded by the Convention. First, both countries must be signatories to the Convention. Second, the child must be under the age of sixteen when the remedies of the Convention are invoked (not at the time of the wrongful removal). Third, in order for the Convention to apply, the child must have been "habitually resident" in a contracting state immediately before any breach of custody or access rights.[1] The Hague conference use of the phrase "habitual residence" was intentionally not defined by the Convention in order to avoid the problem of "domicile" as that term may have been defined and interpreted by each contracting state. Habitual residence is not to be confused with the domicile of a child.[2] A person can have only one habitual residence, and that habitual residence cannot be easily altered. Habitual residence generally refers to the customary residence prior to the removal or retention of the child, and, subject to certain defenses and exceptions, the facts and circumstances subsequent to the child's removal or retention are not relevant to the determination of the child's habitual residence.[3]

A child's habitual residence can be altered by the passage of time, and a change in where the child resides.[4] However, the change in where the child resides (from country to country) must occur prior to the questionable removal.

Generally, however, Courts have defined "habitual residence" as the place that is the center of the child's life, determined by the facts and circumstances presented in each particular case.[5] Further, Ohio courts have rejected the theory relied on by the Ninth Circuit,[6] in which the subjective intent of the parties is paramount to determining the habitual residence of the children. Instead, the court held that the focus was to be solely on the children and not the intentions of the parents, because children are no longer to be considered property of their parents.[7] Fourth, the removal or retention must be wrongful. The removal or retention of a child is considered wrongful where: (1) it is in breach of custody rights attributed to a person, an institution, or another body, either jointly or alone under the law of the state in which the child was habitually resident immediately before the removal or

---

[Section 17:67]

[1]Hague Convention, Article 3.

[2]Robert v. Tesson, 507 F.3d 981, 989 (6th Cir. 2007).

[3]Simcox v. Simcox, 511 F.3d 594, 2007 FED App. 0502P (6th Cir. 2007).

[4]Friedrich v. Friedrich, 983 F.2d 1396, 125 A.L.R. Fed. 703 (6th Cir. 1993).

[5]Friedrich v. Friedrich, 983 F.2d 1396, 125 A.L.R. Fed. 703 (6th Cir. 1993); Ciotola v. Fiocca, 86 Ohio Misc. 2d 24, 684 N.E.2d 763 (C.P. 1997).

[6]Mozes v. Mozes, 239 F.3d 1067 (9th Cir. 2001).

[7]Robert v. Tesson, 507 F.3d 981 (6th Cir. 2007).

retention; and (2) at the time of the removal or retention those rights were actually exercised, either jointly or alone, or would have been so exercised but for the removal or retention.[8] Fifth, the complaint or the return of the child must be brought within one year of the child's alleged wrongful removal or retention.

The District Court, in *Robert v. Tesson*,[9] found Ohio to be the habitual residence of the children, although they had lived with their parents in France before their mother took them to the Ohio, because the United States was considered their habitual residence. In finding that Ohio was the child's habitual residence, the court defined the habitual residence to the "the place where he or she [the children] has been physically present for an amount of time sufficient for acclimatization and which has a 'degree of settled purpose' from the child's perspective."[10]

§ 17:68   ICARA—Judicial proceeding for return of child

When a person's custody rights have been breached by a wrongful removal or retention of the child by another, the Convention establishes two means by which the child may be returned.[1] One is through direct application to a court in the contracting state to which the child has been taken or kept. The other avenue of relief a person may pursue is the filing of an application with the central authority of the contracting state. The Convention requires each contracting state to establish a central authority. In the United States, the Department of State, Office of Consular Services, is the central authority as the term is used under the Convention. These remedies are not mutually exclusive and an aggrieved person may invoke either or both of them.

A petition for return pursuant to the Convention may be filed within one year after the child has been removed or retained. If a person seeks relief through the courts, a return application must be filed with the court and with the central authority. A petition filed with the court seeking return of a child should allege that the child was wrongfully removed or retained in violation of custody rights that were actually being exercised by the petitioner. The petition should state the source of the custody rights, the date of the wrongful conduct, the child's age at the time of the wrongful conduct, and a request for the child's return and an order for payment of fees and expenses to secure the child's return. Attached to the petition can be documents attesting to the return of the child, i.e., affidavits of family or friends, and copies of relevant laws of the country from which the child has been

---

[8]Hague Convention, Article 3.

[9]Robert v. Tesson, 507 F.3d 981 (6th Cir. 2007).

[10]Robert v. Tesson, 507 F.3d 981, 998 (6th Cir. 2007).

[Section 17:68]

[1]Jenkins v. Jenkins, 2008 WL 1990348 (S.D. Ohio 2008), aff'd on other grounds, 569 F.3d 549 (6th Cir. 2009) ("The Hague Convention is effectively a form of forum selection.").

removed. When attached to the petition for return, these documents do not need to be authenticated.[2]

The petition may be filed either in a state court in the county in which the child is located or a federal district court in the jurisdiction where the child is located.[3] There is concurrent jurisdiction between state and federal courts to enforce provisions of 42 U.S.C.A. §§ 11601 et seq., and the Convention. Also, an order issued by either the federal court or a state court ordering the return of a child will be enforced by either court under the doctrine of full faith and credit.

When a petition for the return of a child has been filed with the court, a party to the action or the court may request a social investigation under Article 13 of the Convention. A social investigation under the Convention is to be performed by the Central Authority, or other competent authority, of the country or state that is alleged to be the country or state of the child's habitual residence. The Convention does not specify what is to be in a social investigation, so presumably the content of the social investigation is left to the Central Authority preparing the social investigation. Once a social investigation is completed, the court reviewing the petition shall take into consideration the information contained in social investigation.

A court having jurisdiction to hear a petition for the return of a child may also take judicial notice of the laws of another country or state which is alleged to be the child's country or state of habitual residence. The court may also take judicial notice of court decisions of a jurisdiction which is alleged to be the child's country or state of habitual residence.

Article 15 of the Hague Convention also provides that a court hearing a petition for the return of a child may obtain an advisory opinion from the child's alleged country of habitual residence. This request for an advisory opinion is to be directed to the Central Authority of the alleged country of habitual residence. The issue to be addressed in the Article 15 advisory opinion is whether the removal or retention of the child is wrongful under the laws of the country.

Article 11 of the Convention requires that a court hearing a Hague Convention case is to act "expeditiously" in proceedings to return a child. The phrase "expeditiously" is not defined by either the Hague Convention or 42 U.S.C.A. § 11601. However, both the Convention, Article 11, and 42 U.S.C.A. §§ 11601 et seq. do provide that, if a decision on the return of a child is not made within six weeks, the petitioner-respondent or the Central Authority can request a statement of explanation of the reasons for the delay from the court hear-

---

[2]42 U.S.C.A. § 11605(6).

[3]Crall-Shaffer v. Shaffer, 105 Ohio App. 3d 369, 663 N.E.2d 1346 (1st Dist. Hamilton County 1995) (Hamilton County Domestic Relations Court, as a court of Ohio, had original and concurrent jurisdiction over the Hague petition under 42 U.S.C.A. § 11603(a); father's petition under International Child Abduction Remedies Act (ICARA) could remain pending as a counterclaim after mother's voluntary dismissal of her complaint for legal separation).

ing the case. Although the court is required to give an explanation of why a decision on a case is taking more than six weeks, Article 11 of the Convention and 42 U.S.C.A. § 11601 do not require that a decision be made within six weeks; only that an explanation of the reasons for the delay be provided to the applicant or the Central Authority.

§ 17:69   ICARA—Petition for return of child—Form⊚

[Title of court]

In re the Application of   :
[Plaintiff's name]   :
[Address],   :   Case No. *[_____]*
        Plaintiff,   :   Judge *[_____]*
    vs.   :
[Defendant's name]   :
[Address],   :
       and   :   <u>COMPLAINT FOR RETURN</u>
[Include other defendants],   :   <u>OF CHILD</u>
     Defendants   :   <u>TO PLAINTIFF PURSUANT</u>
                                        <u>TO 42 U.S.C.A. 11601 et seq.,</u>
                                        <u>(THE</u>
                                        <u>INTERNATIONAL CHILD</u>
                                        <u>ABDUCTION REMEDIES</u>
                                        <u>ACT)</u>

COUNT ONE <u>JURISDICTION</u>

1. This action is brought pursuant to The Convention on the Civil Aspects of International Child Abduction, done at the Hague on October 25, 1980, (hereinafter referred to as the Convention) and 42 U.S.C.A. § 11603(b), the International Child Abduction Remedies Act (hereinafter referred to as ICARA). The Convention went into effect in the United States on July 1, 1988. A copy of the Convention and the ICARA are attached to this complaint as Exhibit *[designation of exhibit]* and Exhibit *[designation of exhibit]* respectively and are incorporated as though specifically rewritten herein.

2. The objectives of the convention are under Article 1(a) and are to secure the prompt return of children wrongfully removed to or retained in any Contracting State; and under Article 1(b) to ensure that rights of custody and of access under the law of one Contracting State are effectively respected in the other Contracting States.

3. The United States of America is a Contracting State under the Convention.

4. *[Name of foreign country]* is a Contracting State under the Convention. On *[date]*, the Hague Convention on the Civil Aspects of International Child Abduction (the "Convention") entered into force between the United States and *[name of foreign country]*.

5. This Court has jurisdiction pursuant to 42 U.S.C.A. § 11603.

COUNT TWO <u>PLAINTIFF'S RIGHT TO CUSTODY</u>

6. Plaintiff incorporates as though specifically rewritten herein all of the allegations contained in Plaintiff's complaint paragraphs one (1) through four (4).

7. Plaintiff has a right to custody of the child *[name of child]* within the meaning of Articles Three and Five of the Convention in that Plaintiff is the parent of the child.

8. The Plaintiff at the time of the wrongful removal or retention by Defendant *[name]* and/or Defendant *[name of other defendant]*, was exercising custody within the meaning of Articles Three and Five of the Convention.

9. The Plaintiff, at the time of the application to the Central Authority of the United States of America, was located in *[name of country]*. Plaintiff is and continues to be located in *[name of country]*.

10. The Plaintiff's child *[name of child]* was born on *[date of birth]* and will attain sixteen (16) years of age on *[date]*, approximately *[number of years]* after the date of this application.

11. The child was habitually resident in *[country]* within the meaning of Article Three of the Convention immediately before the removal of the child from *[name of country]* by Defendant. Attached hereto as Exhibit *[designation of exhibit]* is the Declaration Under Uniform Child Custody Jurisdiction and Enforcement Act (DUUCCJEA).

COUNT THREE <u>DEFENDANTS' REMOVAL AND RETENTION OF THE CHILD</u>

12. Plaintiff incorporates the allegations contained in Plaintiff's complaint paragraphs one (1) through ten (10) as though specifically rewritten herein.

13. On *[date]*, Defendant wrongfully removed the child from *[country]* within the meaning of Article Three of the Convention and continues to wrongfully retain the child in the United States of America despite efforts on the part of Plaintiff to have the child returned.

14. The child is presently in the State of Ohio, *[name of county]* County, Country of the United States of America and within the territorial jurisdiction of this Court.

15. The Defendant, at the time of application by the Plaintiff for the Request for Return of the Child to the Central Authority of the United States of America, was a habitual resident (as that term is defined by the Convention) of *[city]*, *[name of county]* County, and the State of Ohio.

COUNT FOUR <u>CUSTODY PROCEEDINGS IN FOREIGN COUNTY</u>

16. Plaintiff incorporates as though specifically rewritten herein all of the allegations contained in Plaintiff's complaint paragraphs one (1) through fourteen (14).

17. The status of custody proceedings in *[country]* are set forth in

the Declaration Under Uniform Child Custody Jurisdiction and Enforcement Act (DUUCCJEA) attached as Exhibit *[designation of exhibit]*.

18. *[Foreign country]* has issued an order for custody of the child in favor of Plaintiff. A copy of the Order is attached hereto as Exhibit *[designation of exhibit]*.

19. The Defendant has filed an action against the Plaintiff seeking a Divorce and custody of the minor child. A copy of the complaint for Divorce is attached hereto as Exhibit *[designation of exhibit]*.

20. Plaintiff requests that this Court issue an order staying any proceedings concerning the custody of the child as required by Article 16 of the Convention.

COUNT FIVE WARRANT IN LIEU OF A WRIT OF HABEAS CORPUS

21. Plaintiff incorporates as though specifically rewritten herein all of the allegations contained in Plaintiff's complaint paragraphs one (1) through nineteen (19).

22. Plaintiff is a person as defined by 42 U.S.C.A. § 11602(5) who has a right of custody of *[name of child]* born on *[date of birth]* for whom this Complaint has been filed. Such right of custody has been breached within the meaning of Article 3 of the Convention.

23. *[Child]* is being illegally held in custody, confinement, or restraint by *[defendant]* and/or *[other defendant]* at *[address of child]*, Ohio.

24. The parents of *[child]* were married on *[date]*.

25. On *[date]*, the Defendant wrongfully removed the child within the meaning of Article 3 of the Convention on the Civil Aspects of International Child Abduction, done at the Hague on *[date]* (Convention) and has since failed to return the child to Plaintiff.

26. Plaintiff believes that the Defendant has previously violated *[citation to relevant law of foreign country]* (see Exhibit *[designation of exhibit]*) in that Defendant brought the child to the United States and *[optional other facts]* without the consent of the Plaintiff. After Defendant refused to return the child to his/her former habitual residence in *[name of country]* on *[date]*, the *[name of foreign court]* rendered a preliminary order transferring custody to the Plaintiff. A further order of the court ordered the Defendant to return the child into the custody of the Plaintiff. Defendant is now in violation of the *[name of country]* order. The Plaintiff believes that the Defendant will further conceal the child unless the child is taken into immediate custody by the court.

27. Plaintiff believes that the child will be carried out of the jurisdiction of the court.

28. No other application for a writ of habeas corpus or a warrant in lieu of writ has been made by or on my behalf of the child in regard to the said restraint.

29. Attached as Exhibit *[designation of exhibit]* is a completed Declaration Under Uniform Child Custody Jurisdiction and Enforcement Act (DUUCCJEA).

WHEREFORE, THE PLAINTIFF REQUESTS THAT THE COURT ISSUE THE FOLLOWING ORDERS:

A. For an order delivering the minor child, *[name of child]*, to the custody of the Plaintiff or his agent.

B. For an Order pursuant to 42 U.S.C.A. § 11604 and, pending further hearing in this court, Plaintiff requests that this court issue instanter an order prohibiting the removal by Defendants *[name of defendant]*, of the minor child *[name of child]* from the jurisdiction of this court.

C. For an order pursuant to 42 U.S.C.A. § 11604(a) and Rule 13 of the Ohio Rules of Juvenile Procedure requiring the Defendants to deliver to the Custody of the United States Marshal or his authorized agent the possession of the minor child *[name of child]* pending a hearing upon this complaint.

D. For an order requiring the Defendants to post a bond in an amount determined by the Court necessary to secure Defendants' compliance with the orders of this Court pending further disposition of this matter. Said bond to remain in effect until further ordered by the court.

E. Pursuant to Article 26 of the Convention and 42 U.S.C.A. § 11607, Plaintiff has attached as Exhibit *[designation of exhibit]*, a copy of all expenditures and costs to date incurred by Plaintiff as a result of the wrongful removal of the child by Defendant. Plaintiff requests that this court award all costs and fees incurred to date, reserving jurisdiction over further costs and fees.

F. For a Warrant in Lieu of a Writ of Habeas Corpus to be issued, directing any peace officer in the State of Ohio to take the child into custody and forthwith bring the child before this court.

Respectfully submitted,

_____

[Name of attorney]
[Address]
[Telephone number]

§ 17:70   ICARA—Duty to return child and exceptions

The judicial duty to order the return of a child is not absolute. There are many exceptions which will limit the return of the child found in Articles 12, 13, and 20 of the Convention. First, a judicial authority may deny an application or petition for return of a child if a person having the care of the child was not actually exercising custody rights at the time of the removal or retention. Second, a court need not order a child returned if there is a grave risk that return would expose the child to physical or psychological harm, or otherwise place the child in an intolerable situation. Third, the return of the child may be refused if this would not be permitted by the fundamental principles of the requested state relating to the protection of human rights and fundamental freedoms. Fourth, the court may refuse to return the child if the person seeking the return acquiesced in the removal. Fifth, that the petitioner had no right of custody or access at the time of the removal or retention.[1] A court hearing a petition for the return of a child has jurisdiction to hear and decide the merits of an abduction or wrongful retention. However, the court hearing a petition for the return of a child does not have jurisdiction to hear and decide the merits of the underlying custody dispute.[2] Sixth, that the child is settled in his or her new environment.[3] Seventh, the child objects to being returned and has attained an age and degree of maturity in which his or her opinion should be considered.[4] Eighth, that the petition for return of the child was not filed within one year of the removal or retention of the child unless the theory of equitable tolling applies.[5]

The burden of proof to establish a defense to the return of a child varies based on the type of defense raised by the person objecting to the return of a child. A defense to the return of a child based upon Acquiescence under Article 13(b) of the Convention, or Violation of Fundamental Freedoms under Article 20 of the Convention must be proven by clear and convincing evidence. Defenses to the return of the child based upon Article 12 of the Convention (i.e., petition not filed within one year) or Article 13 defenses other than Article 13(b) defenses must be proven by a preponderance of the evidence.[6]

In defining when a parent is "exercising" custody rights, the Sixth Circuit U.S. Court of Appeals held that "if a person has valid custody rights to a child under the law of the country of the child's habitual residence, that person cannot fail to 'exercise' those custody rights under the Hague Convention short of acts that constitute clear and

---

[Section 17:70]

[1]Hague Convention, Article 13(b).

[2]Jenkins v. Jenkins, 2008 WL 1990348 (S.D. Ohio 2008), aff'd on other grounds, 569 F.3d 549 (6th Cir. 2009).

[3]Anderson v. Acree, 250 F. Supp. 2d 876 (S.D. Ohio 2002) (Discussion of factors to determine if a child is "settled").

[4]Hague Convention, Article 13 (b); Wasniewski v. Grzelak-Johannsen, 2007 WL 2344760 (N.D. Ohio 2007) (discussion of this narrowly applied exception).

[5]Wasniewski v. Grzelak-Johannsen, 2007 WL 2344760 (N.D. Ohio 2007).

[6]42 U.S.C.A. § 11603(e)(2).

unequivocal abandonment of the child."[7] The question is not whether that parent exercised the rights well or badly.[8]

It is not adequate to establish an affirmative defense of grave risk of psychological harm where the allegation is nothing more than adjustment problems that would attend relocation of most children. There is no "grave" risk, even if the parent's home (in this case, in Germany) "were a grim place to raise a child in comparison to the pretty, peaceful streets of Ironton, Ohio."[9]

Assuming that the court has determined that the removal or retention of the child was wrongful and that no exceptions to the return obligation have been satisfactorily established by the respondent, the court must order the return of the child forthwith. As part of its order returning the child, the court may award to the prevailing party attorney fees and costs.

The scope of a trial court's inquiry when deciding whether to order the return of a child to his or her country of residence under the "grave risk" exception is extremely narrow.[10] The inquiry is not intended to deal with issues which are appropriate in a custody proceeding, such as psychological profiles, evaluations of parental fitness, lifestyle and quality of relationships which are more properly reserved to the tribunal in the place of habitual residence. It is not to be used as a substitute to litigate the issue of the best interest of the child.[11]

§ 17:71   ICARA—Who to contact

In the United States, the function of the central authority is handled by the:

Office of Citizens Consular Services
Department of State
2201 C Street, N.W. Room 4817
Washington, D.C. 20520
Phone: (202) 647-3666

---

[7]Friedrich v. Friedrich, 78 F.3d 1060, 1066, 1996 FED App. 0085P (6th Cir. 1996).

[8]Anderson v. Acree, 250 F. Supp. 2d 876 (S.D. Ohio 2002).

[9]Friedrich v. Friedrich, 78 F.3d 1060, 1068, 1996 FED App. 0085P (6th Cir. 1996).

[10]Simcox v. Simcox, 511 F.3d 594, 2007 FED App. 0502P (6th Cir. 2007).

[11]In re Marriage of Copley, 90 D.R. 1138, (Division B, Colorado 5-8-91).

§ 17:72   ICARA—Costs and fees

While the petitioner may be required to bear the legal costs, court costs, and travel costs,[1] neither the federal government nor state or local governments may impose a fee for administrative processing of applications.[2] Where a court orders the return of a child, the court shall order the respondent to pay necessary expenses. These may include court costs, legal fees, foster home care, and transportation costs, unless the respondent can show such an order is inappropriate.[3]

[Section 17:72]

[1]42 U.S.C.A. § 11607(b)(1).

[2]42 U.S.C.A. § 11607(a).

[3]42 U.S.C.A. § 11607(b)(3); McClary v. McClary, No. 3:07-CV-0845, 2007 WL 3023563 (6th Cir. 2007).

APPENDIX 17-A

Convention on the Civil Aspects of International Child Abduction

The States signatory to the present Convention, Firmly convinced that the interests of children are of paramount importance in matters relating to their custody, Desiring to protect children internationally from the harmful effects of their wrongful removal or retention and to establish procedures to ensure their prompt return to the State of their habitual residence, as well as to secure protection for rights of access,

Have resolved to conclude a Convention to this effect, and have agreed upon the following provisions—

CHAPTER I—SCOPE OF THE CONVENTION

Article 1

The objects of the present Convention are—

(a) to secure the prompt return of children wrongfully removed to or retained in any Contracting State; and

(b) to ensure that rights of custody and of access under the law of one Contracting State are effectively respected in the other Contracting States.

Article 2

Contracting States shall take all appropriate measures to secure within their territories the implementation of the objects of the Convention. For this purpose they shall use the most expeditious procedures available.

Article 3

The removal or the retention of a child is to be considered wrongful where—

(a) it is in breach of rights of custody attributed to a person, an institution or any other body, either jointly or alone, under the law of the State in which the child was habitually resident immediately before the removal or retention; and

(b) at the time of removal or retention those rights were actually exercised, either jointly or alone, or would have been so exercised but for the removal or retention.

The rights of custody mentioned in sub-paragraph a above, may arise in particular by operation of law or by reason of a judicial or administrative decision, or by reason of an agreement having legal effect under the law of that State.

Article 4

The Convention shall apply to any child who was habitually resident in a Contracting State immediately before any breach of custody or access rights. The Convention shall cease to apply when the child attains the age of 16 years.

Article 5

For the purposes of this Convention—

(a) 'rights of custody' shall include rights relating to the care of the person of the child and, in particular, the right to determine the child's place of residence;

(b) 'rights of access' shall include the right to take a child for a limited period of time to a place other than the child's habitual residence.

CHAPTER II—CENTRAL AUTHORITIES

Article 6

A Contracting State shall designate a Central Authority to discharge the duties which are imposed by the Convention upon such authorities.

Federal States, States with more than one system of law or States having autonomous territorial organizations, shall be free to appoint more than one Central Authority and to specify the territorial extent of their powers. Where a State has appointed more than one Central Authority, it shall designate the Central Authority to which applications may be addressed for transmission to the appropriate Central Authority within that State.

Article 7

Central Authorities shall co-operate with each other and promote co-operation amongst the competent authorities in their respective States to secure the prompt return of children and to achieve the other objects of this Convention.

In particular, either directly or through any intermediary, they shall take all appropriate measures—

(a) to discover the whereabouts of a child who has been wrongfully removed or retained;

(b) to prevent further harm to the child or prejudice to interested parties by taking or causing to be taken provisional measures;

(c) to secure the voluntary return of the child or to bring about an amicable resolution of the issues;

(d) to exchange, where desirable, information relating to the social background of the child;

(e) to provide information of a general character as to the law of their State in connection with the application of the Convention;

(f) to initiate or facilitate the institution of judicial or administrative proceedings with a view to obtaining the return of the child and, in a proper case, to make arrangements for organizing or securing the effective exercise of rights of access;

(g) where the circumstances so require, to provide or facilitate the provision of legal aid and advice, including the participation of legal counsel and advisers;

(h) to provide such administrative arrangements as may be necessary and appropriate to secure the safe return of the child;

(i) to keep each other informed with respect to the operation of this Convention and, as far as possible, to eliminate any obstacles to its application.

CHAPTER III—RETURN OF CHILDREN

Article 8

Any person, institution or other body claiming that a child has been removed or retained in breach of custody rights may apply either to the Central Authority of the child's habitual residence or to the Central Authority of any other Contracting State for assistance in securing the return of the child.

The application shall contain—

(a) information concerning the identity of the applicant, of the child and of the person alleged to have removed or retained the child;

(b) where available, the date of birth of the child;

(c) the grounds on which the applicant's claim for return of the child is based;

(d) all available information relating to the whereabouts of the child and the identity of the person with whom the child is presumed to be.

The application may be accompanied or supplemented by—

(e) an authenticated copy of any relevant decision or agreement;

(f) a certificate or an affidavit emanating from a Central Authority, or other competent authority of the State of the child's habitual residence, or from a qualified person, concerning the relevant law of that State;

(g) any other relevant document.

Article 9

If the Central Authority which receives an application referred to in Article 8 has reason to believe that the child is in another Contracting State, it shall directly and without delay transmit the application to the Central Authority of that Contracting State and inform the requesting Central Authority, or the applicant, as the case may be.

Article 10

The Central Authority of the State where the child is shall take or cause to be taken all appropriate measures in order to obtain the voluntary return of the child.

Article 11

The judicial or administrative authorities of Contracting States shall act expeditiously in proceedings for the return of children.

If the judicial or administrative authority concerned has not reached a decision within six weeks from the date of commencement of the proceedings, the applicant or the Central Authority of the requested State, on its own initiative or if asked by the Central Authority of the requesting State, shall have the right to request a statement of the reasons for the delay. If a reply is received by the Central Authority of the requested State, that Authority shall transmit the reply to the Central Authority of the requesting State. or to the applicant, as the case may be.

Article 12

Where a child has been wrongfully removed or retained in terms of Article 3 and, at the date of the commencement of the proceedings before the judicial or administrative authority of the Contracting State where the child is, a period of less than one year has elapsed from the date of the wrongful removal or retention, the authority concerned shall order the return of the child forthwith.

The judicial or administrative authority, even where the proceedings have been commenced after the expiration of the period of one year referred to in the preceding paragraph, shall also order the return of the child, unless it is demonstrated that the child is now settled in its new environment.

Where the judicial or administrative authority in the requested State has reason to believe that the child has been taken to another State, it may stay the proceedings or dismiss the application for the return of the child.

Article 13

Notwithstanding the provisions of the preceding Article, the judicial or administrative authority of the requested State is not bound to order the return of the child if the person, institution or other body which opposes its return establishes that—

(a) the person, institution or other body having the care of the person of the child was not actually exercising the custody rights at the time of removal or retention, or had consented to or subsequently acquiesced in the removal or retention; or

(b) there is a grave risk that his or her return would expose the child to physical or psychological harm or otherwise place the child in an intolerable situation.

The judicial or administrative authority may also refuse to order the return of the child if it finds that the child objects to being returned and has attained an age and degree of maturity at which it is appropriate to take account of its views.

In considering the circumstances referred to in this Article, the judicial and administrative authorities shall take into account the information relating to the social background of the child provided by the Central Authority or other competent authority of the child's habitual residence.

Article 14

In ascertaining whether there has been a wrongful removal or retention within the meaning of Article 3, the judicial or administrative authorities of the requested State may take notice directly of the law of, and of judicial or administrative decisions, formally recognized or not in the State of the habitual residence of the child, without recourse to the specific procedures for the proof of that law or for the recognition of foreign decisions which would otherwise be applicable.

Article 15

The judicial or administrative authorities of a Contracting State may, prior to the making of an order for the return of the child, request that the applicant obtain from the authorities of the State of the habitual residence of the child a decision or other determination that the removal or retention was wrongful within the meaning of Article 3 of the Convention, where such a decision or determination may be obtained in that State. The Central Authorities of the Contracting States shall so far as practicable assist applicants to obtain such a decision or determination.

Article 16

After receiving notice of a wrongful removal or retention of a child in the sense of Article 3, the judicial or administrative authorities of the Contracting State to which the child has been removed or in which it has been retained shall not decide on the merits of rights of custody until it has been determined that the child is not to be returned under this Convention or unless an application under this Convention is not lodged within a reasonable time following receipt of the notice.

Article 17

The sole fact that a decision relating to custody has been given in or is entitled to recognition in the requested State shall not be a ground for refusing to return a child under this Convention, but the judicial or administrative authorities of the requested State may take account of the reasons for that decision in applying this Convention.

Article 18

The provisions of this Chapter do not limit the power of a judicial or administrative authority to order the return of the child at any time.

Article 19

A decision under this Convention concerning the return of the child shall not be taken to be a determination on the merits of any custody issue.

Article 20

The return of the child under the provisions of Article 12 may be refused if this would not be permitted by the fundamental principles of the requested State relating to the protection of human rights and fundamental freedoms.

CHAPTER IV—RIGHTS OF ACCESS

Article 21

An application to make arrangements for organizing or securing the effective exercise of rights of access may be presented to the Central

Authorities of the Contracting States in the same way as an application for the return of a child.

The Central Authorities are bound by the obligations of co-operation which are set forth in Article 7 to promote the peaceful enjoyment of access rights and the fulfillment of any conditions to which the exercise of those rights may be subject. The Central Authorities shall take steps to remove, as far as possible, all obstacles to the exercise of such rights.

The Central Authorities, either directly or through intermediaries, may initiate or assist in the institution of proceedings with a view to organizing or protecting these rights and securing respect for the conditions to which the exercise of these rights may be subject.

CHAPTER V—GENERAL PROVISIONS

Article 22

No security, bond or deposit, however described, shall be required to guarantee the payment of costs and expenses in the judicial or administrative proceedings falling within the scope of this Convention.

Article 23

No legalization or similar formality may be required in the context of this Convention.

Article 24

Any application, communication or other document sent to the Central Authority of the requested State shall be in the original language, and shall be accompanied by a translation into the official language or one of the official languages of the requested State or, where that is not feasible, a translation into French or English.

However, a Contracting State may, by making a reservation in accordance with Article 42, object to the use of either French or English, but not both, in any application, communication or other document sent to its Central Authority.

Article 25

Nationals of the Contracting States and persons who are habitually resident within those States shall be entitled in matters concerned with the application of this Convention to legal aid and advice in any other Contracting State on the same conditions as if they themselves were nationals of and habitually resident in that State.

Article 26

Each Central Authority shall bear its own costs in applying this Convention. Central Authorities and other public services of Contracting States shall not impose any charges in relation to applications submitted under this Convention. In particular, they may not require any payment from the applicant towards the costs and expenses of the proceedings or, where applicable, those arising from the participation of legal counsel or advisers. However, they may require the payment of the expenses incurred or to be incurred in implementing the return of the child.

However, a Contracting State may, by making a reservation in accordance with Article 42, declare that it shall not be bound to assume any costs referred to in the preceding paragraph resulting from the participation of legal counsel or advisers or from court proceedings, except insofar as those costs may be covered by its system of legal aid and advice.

Upon ordering the return of a child or issuing an order concerning rights of access under this Convention, the judicial or administrative authorities may, where appropriate, direct the person who removed or retained the child, or who prevented the exercise of rights of access, to pay necessary expenses incurred by or on behalf of the applicant, including travel expenses, any costs incurred or payments made for locating the child, the costs of legal representation of the applicant, and those of returning the child.

Article 27

When it is manifest that the requirements of this Convention are not fulfilled or that the application is otherwise not well founded, a Central Authority is not bound to accept the application. In that case, the Central Authority shall forthwith inform the applicant or the Central Authority through which the application was submitted, as the case may be, of its reasons.

Article 28

A Central Authority may require that the application be accompanied by a written authorization empowering it to act on behalf of the applicant, or to designate a representative so to act.

Article 29

This Convention shall not preclude any person, institution or body who claims that there has been a breach of custody or access rights within the meaning of Article 3 or 21 from applying directly to the judicial or administrative authorities of a Contracting State, whether or not under the provisions of this Convention.

Article 30

Any application submitted to the Central Authorities or directly to the judicial or administrative authorities of a Contracting State in accordance with the terms of this Convention, together with documents and any other information appended thereto or provided by a Central Authority, shall be admissible in the courts or administrative authorities of the Contracting States.

Article 31

In relation to a State which in matters of custody of children has two or more systems of law applicable in different territorial units—

(a) any reference to habitual residence in that State shall be construed as referring to habitual residence in a territorial unit of that State;

(b) any reference to the law of the State of habitual residence shall be construed as referring to the law of the territorial unit in that State where the child habitually resides.

Article 32

In relation to a State which in matters of custody of children has two or more systems of law applicable to different categories of persons, any reference to the law of that State shall be construed as referring to the legal system specified by the law of that State.

Article 33

A State within which different territorial units have their own rules of law in respect of custody of children shall not be bound to apply this Convention where a State with a unified system of law would not be bound to do so.

Article 34

This Convention shall take priority in matters within its scope over the Convention of 5 October 1961 concerning the powers of authorities and the law applicable in respect of the protection of minors, as between Parties to both Conventions. Otherwise the present Convention shall not restrict the application of an international instrument in force between the State of origin and the State addressed or other law of the State addressed for the purposes of obtaining the return of a child who has been wrongfully removed or retained or of organizing access rights.

Article 35

This Convention shall apply as between Contracting States only to wrongful removals or retentions occurring after its entry into force in those States.

Where a declaration has been made under Article 39 or 40, the reference in the preceding paragraph to a Contracting State shall be taken to refer to the territorial unit or units in relation to which this Convention applies.

Article 36

Nothing in this Convention shall prevent two or more Contracting States, in order to limit the restrictions to which the return of the child may be subject, from agreeing among themselves to derogate from any provisions of this Convention which may imply such a restriction.

CHAPTER VI—FINAL CLAUSES

Article 37

The Convention shall be open for signature by the States which were Members of the Hague Conference on Private International Law at the time of its Fourteenth Session.

It shall be ratified, accepted or approved and the instruments of ratification, acceptance or approval shall be deposited with the Ministry of Foreign Affairs of the Kingdom of the Netherlands.

Article 38

Any other State may accede to the Convention.

The instrument of accession shall be deposited with the Ministry of Foreign Affairs of the Kingdom of the Netherlands.

The Convention shall enter into force for a State acceding to it on the first day of the third calendar month after the deposit of its instrument of accession.

The accession will have effect only as regards the relations between the acceding State and such Contracting States as will have declared their acceptance of the accession. Such a declaration will also have to be made by any Member State ratifying, accepting or approving the Convention after an accession. Such declaration shall be deposited at the Ministry of Foreign Affairs of the Kingdom of the Netherlands; this Ministry shall forward, through diplomatic channels, a certified copy to each of the Contracting States.

The Convention will enter into force as between the acceding State and the State that has declared its acceptance of the accession on the first day of the third calendar month after the deposit of the declaration of acceptance.

Article 39

Any State may, at the time of signature, ratification, acceptance, approval or accession, declare that the Convention shall extend to all the territories for the international relations of which it is responsible, or to one or more of them. Such a declaration shall take effect at the time the Convention enters into force for that State.

Such declaration, as well as any subsequent extension, shall be notified to the Ministry of Foreign Affairs of the Kingdom of the Netherlands.

Article 40

If a Contracting State has two or more territorial units in which different systems of law are applicable in relation to matters dealt with in this Convention, it may at the time of signature, ratification, acceptance, approval or accession declare that this Convention shall extend to all its territorial units or only to one or more of them and may modify this declaration by submitting another declaration at any time.

Any such declaration shall be notified to the Ministry of Foreign Affairs of the Kingdom of the Netherlands and shall state expressly the territorial units to which the Convention applies.

Article 41

Where a Contracting State has a system of government under which executive, judicial and legislative powers are distributed between central and other authorities within that State, its signature or ratification, acceptance or approval of, or accession to this Convention, or its making of any declaration in terms of Article 40 shall carry no implication as to the internal distribution of powers within that State.

Article 42

Any State may, not later than the time of ratification, acceptance, approval or accession, or at the time of making a declaration in terms of Article 39 or 40, make one or both of the reservations provided for in Article 24 and Article 26, third paragraph. No other reservation shall be permitted.

Any State may at any time withdraw a reservation it has made. The withdrawal shall be notified to the Ministry of Foreign Affairs of the Kingdom of the Netherlands.

The reservation shall cease to have effect on the first day of the third calendar month after the notification referred to in the preceding paragraph.

Article 43

The Convention shall enter into force on the first day of the third calendar month after the deposit of the third instrument of ratification, acceptance, approval or accession referred to in Articles 37 and 38.

Thereafter the Convention shall enter into force—

1. for each State ratifying, accepting, approving or acceding to it subsequently, on the first day of the third calendar month after the deposit of its instrument of ratification, acceptance, approval or accession;

2. for any territory or territorial unit to which the Convention has been extended in conformity with Article 39 or 40, on the first day of the third calendar month after the notification referred to in that Article.

Article 44

The Convention shall remain in force for five years from the date of its entry into force in accordance with the first paragraph of Article 43 even for States which subsequently have ratified, accepted, approved it or acceded to it. If there has been no denunciation, it shall be renewed tacitly every five years.

Any denunciation shall be notified to the Ministry of Foreign Affairs of the Kingdom of the Netherlands at least six months before the expiry of the five-year period. It may be limited to certain of the territories or territorial units to which the Convention applies. The denunciation shall have effect only as regards the State which has notified it. The Convention shall remain in force for the other Contracting States.

Article 45

The Ministry of Foreign Affairs of the Kingdom of the Netherlands shall notify the States Members of the Conference, and the States which have acceded in accordance with Article 38, of the following—

(1) the signatures and ratifications, acceptances and approvals referred to in Article 37;

(2) the accessions referred to in Article 38;

(3) the date on which the Convention enters into force in accordance with Article 43;

(4) the extensions referred to in Article 39;

(5) the declarations referred to in Articles 38 and 40;

(6) the reservations referred to in Article 24 and Article 26, third paragraph, and the withdrawals referred to in Article 42;

(7) the denunciations referred to in Article 44.

In witness whereof the undersigned, being duly authorized thereto, have signed this Convention.

Done at The Hague, on the 25th day of October 1980 in the English and French languages, both texts being equally authentic, in a single copy which shall be deposited in the archives of the Government of the Kingdom of the Netherlands, and of which a certified copy shall be sent, through diplomatic channels, to each of the States Members of the Hague Conference on Private International Law at the date of its Fourteenth Session.

APPENDIX 17-B

International Child Abduction Remedies Act

UNITED STATES CODE ANNOTATED

TITLE 42. THE PUBLIC HEALTH AND WELFARE

CHAPTER 121—INTERNATIONAL CHILD ABDUCTION REMEDIES

§ 11601. Findings and declarations 42 U.S.C.A. § 11601

(a) Findings

The Congress makes the following findings:

(1) The international abduction or wrongful retention of children is harmful to their well-being.

(2) Persons should not be permitted to obtain custody of children by virtue of their wrongful removal or retention.

(3) International abductions and retentions of children are increasing, and only concerted cooperation pursuant to an international agreement can effectively combat this problem.

(4) The Convention on the Civil Aspects of International Child Abduction, done at The Hague on October 25, 1980, establishes legal rights and procedures for the prompt return of children who have been wrongfully removed or retained, as well as for securing the exercise of visitation rights. Children who are wrongfully removed or retained within the meaning of the Convention are to be promptly returned unless one of the narrow exceptions set forth in the Convention applies. The Convention provides a sound treaty framework to help resolve the problem of international abduction and retention of children and will deter such wrongful removals and retentions.

(b) Declarations

The Congress makes the following declarations:

(1) It is the purpose of this chapter to establish procedures for the implementation of the Convention in the United States.

(2) The provisions of this chapter are in addition to and not in lieu of the provisions of the Convention.

(3) In enacting this chapter the Congress recognizes—

(A) the international character of the Convention; and

(B) the need for uniform international interpretation of the Convention.

(4) The Convention and this chapter empower courts in the United States to determine only rights under the Convention and not the merits of any underlying child custody claims.

(Pub.L. 100-300, § 2, Apr. 29, 1988, 102 Stat. 437.)

§ 11602. Definitions 42 U.S.C.A. § 11602

For the purposes of this chapter—

(1) the term "applicant" means any person who, pursuant to the Convention, files an application with the United States Central Authority or a Central Authority of any other party to the Convention for the return of a child alleged to have been wrongfully removed or retained or for arrangements for organizing or securing the effective exercise of rights of access pursuant to the Convention;

(2) the term "Convention" means the Convention on the Civil Aspects of International Child Abduction, done at The Hague on October 25, 1980;

(3) the term "Parent Locator Service" means the service established by the Secretary of Health and Human Services under section 653 of this title;

(4) the term "petitioner" means any person who, in accordance with this chapter, files a petition in court seeking relief under the Convention;

(5) the term "person" includes any individual, institution, or other legal entity or body;

(6) the term "respondent" means any person against whose interests a petition is filed in court, in accordance with this chapter, which seeks relief under the Convention;

(7) the term "rights of access" means visitation rights;

(8) the term "State" means any of the several States, the District of Columbia, and any commonwealth, territory, or possession of the United States; and

(9) the term "United States Central Authority" means the agency of the Federal Government designated by the President under section 11606(a) of this title.

(Pub.L. 100-300, § 3, Apr. 29, 1988, 102 Stat. 437.)

§ 11603. Judicial remedies 42 U.S.C.A. § 11603

(a) Jurisdiction of courts

The courts of the States and the United States district courts shall have concurrent original jurisdiction of actions arising under the Convention.

(b) Petitions

Any person seeking to initiate judicial proceedings under the Convention for the return of a child or for arrangements for organizing or securing the effective exercise of rights of access to a child may do so by commencing a civil action by filing a petition for the relief sought in any court which has jurisdiction of such action and which is authorized to exercise its jurisdiction in the place where the child is located at the time the petition is filed.

(c) Notice

Notice of an action brought under subsection (b) of this section shall be given in accordance with the applicable law governing notice in interstate child custody proceedings.

(d) Determination of case

The court in which an action is brought under subsection (b) of this section shall decide the case in accordance with the Convention.

(e) Burdens of proof

(1) A petitioner in an action brought under subsection (b) of this section shall establish by a preponderance of the evidence—

(A) in the case of an action for the return of a child, that the child has been wrongfully removed or retained within the meaning of the Convention; and

(B) in the case of an action for arrangements for organizing or securing the effective exercise of rights of access, that the petitioner has such rights.

(2) In the case of an action for the return of a child, a respondent who opposes the return of the child has the burden of establishing—

(A) by clear and convincing evidence that one of the exceptions set forth in article 13b or 20 of the Convention applies; and

(B) by a preponderance of the evidence that any other exception set forth in article 12 or 13 of the Convention applies.

(f) Application of Convention

For purposes of any action brought under this chapter—

(1) the term "authorities", as used in article 15 of the Convention to refer to the authorities of the state of the habitual residence of a child, includes courts and appropriate government agencies;

(2) the terms "wrongful removal or retention" and "wrongfully removed or retained", as used in the Convention, include a removal or retention of a child before the entry of a custody order regarding that child; and

(3) the term "commencement of proceedings", as used in article 12 of the Convention, means, with respect to the return of a child located in the United States, the filing of a petition in accordance with subsection (b) of this section.

(g) Full faith and credit

Full faith and credit shall be accorded by the courts of the States and the courts of the United States to the judgment of any other such court ordering or denying the return of a child, pursuant to the Convention, in an action brought under this chapter.

(h) Remedies under Convention not exclusive

The remedies established by the Convention and this chapter shall be in addition to remedies available under other laws or international agreements.

(Pub.L. 100-300, 4, Apr. 29, 1988, 102 Stat. 438.)

§ 11604. Provisional remedies 42 U.S.C.A. § 1604

(a) Authority of courts

In furtherance of the objectives of article 7(b) and other provisions of the Convention, and subject to the provisions of subsection (b) of this section, any court exercising jurisdiction of an action brought under section 11603(b) of this title may take or cause to be taken measures under Federal or State law, as appropriate, to protect the well-being of the child involved or to prevent the child's further removal or concealment before the final disposition of the petition.

(b) Limitation on authority

No court exercising jurisdiction of an action brought under section 11603(b) of this title may, under subsection (a) of this section, order a child removed from a person having physical control of the child unless the applicable requirements of State law are satisfied.

(Pub.L. 100-300, § 5, Apr. 29, 1988, 102 Stat. 439.)

§ 11605. Admissibility of documents 42 U.S.C.A. § 11605

With respect to any application to the United States Central Authority, or any petition to a court under section 11603 of this title, which seeks relief under the Convention, or any other documents or information included with such application or petition or provided after such submission which relates to the application or petition, as the case may be, no authentication of such application, petition, document, or information shall be required in order for the application, petition, document, or information to be admissible in court.

(Pub.L. 100-300, § 6, Apr. 29, 1988, 102 Stat. 439.)

§ 11606. United States Central Authority 42 U.S.C.A. § 11606

(a) Designation

The President shall designate a Federal agency to serve as the Central Authority for the United States under the Convention.

(b) Functions

The functions of the United States Central Authority are those ascribed to the Central Authority by the Convention and this chapter.

(c) Regulatory authority

The United States Central Authority is authorized to issue such regulations as may be necessary to carry out its functions under the Convention and this chapter.

(d) Obtaining information from Parent Locator Service

The United States Central Authority may, to the extent authorized by the Social Security Act [42 U.S.C.A. §§ 301 et seq.], obtain information from the Parent Locator Service.

(Pub.L. 100-300, § 7, Apr. 29, 1988, 102 Stat. 439.)

§ 11607. Costs and fees 42 U.S.C.A. § 11607

(a) Administrative costs

No department, agency, or instrumentality of the Federal Government or of any State or local government may impose on an applicant any fee in relation to the administrative processing of applications submitted under the Convention.

(b) Costs incurred in civil actions

(1) Petitioners may be required to bear the costs of legal counsel or advisors, court costs incurred in connection with their petitions, and travel costs for the return of the child involved and any accompanying persons, except as provided in paragraphs (2) and (3).

(2) Subject to paragraph (3), legal fees or court costs incurred in connection with an action brought under section 11603 of this title shall be borne by the petitioner unless they are covered by payments from Federal, State, or local legal assistance or other programs.

(3) Any court ordering the return of a child pursuant to an action brought under section 11603 of this title shall order the respondent to pay necessary expenses incurred by or on behalf of the petitioner, including court costs, legal fees, foster home or other care during the course of proceedings in the action, and transportation costs related to the return of the child, unless the respondent establishes that such order would be clearly inappropriate.

(Pub.L. 100-300, § 8, Apr. 29, 1988, 102 Stat. 440.)

§ 11608. Collection, maintenance, and dissemination of information 42 U.S.C.A. § 11608

(a) In general

In performing its functions under the Convention, the United States Central Authority may, under such conditions as the Central Authority prescribes by regulation, but subject to subsection (c) of this section, receive from or transmit to any department, agency, or instrumentality of the Federal Government or of any State or foreign government, and receive from or transmit to any applicant, petitioner, or respondent, information necessary to locate a child or for the purpose of otherwise implementing the Convention with respect to a child, except that the United States Central Authority—

(1) may receive such information from a Federal or State department, agency, or instrumentality only pursuant to applicable Federal and State statutes; and

(2) may transmit any information received under this subsection notwithstanding any provision of law other than this chapter.

(b) Requests for information

Requests for information under this section shall be submitted in such manner and form as the United States Central Authority may prescribe by regulation and shall be accompanied or supported by such documents as the United States Central Authority may require.

(c) Responsibility of government entities

Whenever any department, agency, or instrumentality of the United States or of any State receives a request from the United States Central Authority for information authorized to be provided to such Central Authority under subsection (a) of this section, the head of such department, agency, or instrumentality shall promptly cause a search to be made of the files and records maintained by such department, agency, or instrumentality in order to determine whether the information requested is contained in any such files or records. If such search discloses the information requested, the head of such department, agency, or instrumentality shall immediately transmit such information to the United States Central Authority, except that any such information the disclosure of which—

(1) would adversely affect the national security interests of the United States or the law enforcement interests of the United States or of any State; or

(2) would be prohibited by section 9 of Title 13;

shall not be transmitted to the Central Authority. The head of such department, agency, or instrumentality shall, immediately upon completion of the requested search, notify the Central Authority of the results of the search, and whether an exception set forth in paragraph (1) or (2) applies. In the event that the United States Central Authority receives information and the appropriate Federal or State department, agency, or instrumentality thereafter notifies the Central Authority that an exception set forth in paragraph (1) or (2) applies to that information, the Central Authority may not disclose that information under subsection (a) of this section.

(d) Information available from Parent Locator Service

To the extent that information which the United States Central Authority is authorized to obtain under the provisions of subsection (c) of this section can be obtained through the Parent Locator Service, the United States Central Authority shall first seek to obtain such information from the Parent Locator Service, before requesting such information directly under the provisions of subsection (c) of this section.

(e) Recordkeeping

The United States Central Authority shall maintain appropriate records concerning its activities and the disposition of cases brought to its attention.

(Pub.L. 100-300, § 9, Apr. 29, 1988, 102 Stat. 440.)

§ 11609. Interagency coordinating group 42 U.S.C.A. § 11609

The Secretary of State, the Secretary of Health and Human Services, and the Attorney General shall designate Federal employees and may, from time to time, designate private citizens to serve on an interagency coordinating group to monitor the operation of the Convention and to provide advice on its implementation to the United States Central Authority and other Federal agencies. This group shall meet from time to time at the request of the United States Central Authority. The agency in which the United States Central Authority is located is authorized to reimburse such private citizens for travel and other expenses incurred in participating at meetings of the interagency coordinating group at rates not to exceed those authorized under subchapter I of chapter 57 of Title 5 for employees of agencies.

(Pub.L. 100-300, § 10, Apr. 29, 1988, 102 Stat. 441.)

§ 11610. Authorization of appropriations 42 U.S.C.A. § 11610

There are authorized to be appropriated for each fiscal year such sums as may be necessary to carry out the purposes of the Convention and this chapter.

(Pub.L.   100-300,   § 12,   Apr.   29,   1988,   102   Stat.   422.)

Chapter 18

Parenting Time and Visitation

By Richard L. Innis, Esq.

§ 18:1 Introduction

Effective March 22, 2001, visitation by a parent became "parenting time" under RC 3109.051(A). The term "visitation" remains for non-parental companionship ordered by the court pursuant to RC 3109.11 and RC 3109.12. Court ordered parenting time and visitation may be referred to as a right of association conferred by state statutes. This right of association has been the subject of judicial scrutiny because it may be in conflict with the due process clause of the 14th Amendment as it relates to the fundamental right to be free from governmental interference in the right to care, custody and control of raising one's own children, and the right to be left alone. This chapter explores the statutory provisions regarding parenting time and visitation and is-sues relating thereto.

§ 18:2 Ohio's statutory scheme

Parenting and visitation rights are created by statute. On May 31, 1990, Ohio adopted a comprehensive statutory scheme for visitation with the enactment of 1990 HB 15. This bill was amended by 2000 SB 180 effective March 22, 2001. RC 3109.051 provides for parenting time and visitation for children of divorce. RC 3109.11 provides for visitation for a child of a deceased parent and RC 3109.12 provides for parenting time and visitation for children born out of wedlock. There is no provision in Ohio law for visitation orders when the nuclear family remains intact.

§ 18:3 Parenting time provisions—Domestic relations actions—By a parent

Pursuant to RC 3109.051(A), the court must in any divorce, dissolution, legal separation, or annulment proceeding, where there is no shared parenting decree, provide a specific schedule of parenting time for the non-residential parent unless the court finds that such parenting time is not in the best interest of the child and supports that finding with findings of fact and conclusions of law. The statute gives wide latitude to the court as to the time and conditions of such parenting time, but also mandates that whenever possible the order should ensure the opportunity for both parents to have "frequent and continuing contact . . . with the child."

This statute requires court and counsel to draft visitation provisions that are realistic and in accordance with the needs, relationships, and personalities of all parties involved, especially the children. Parenting time is recognized as a right of the child, and frequent and continuing contact with the non-residential parent is crucial to the emotional well-being of the children of divorce.[1]

It would appear that little constitutional controversy exists for court ordered parenting time, as once there is a divorce, the state has a compelling interest in ensuring that children have the attention, care and concern that they would have if the family had remained intact.[2]

§ 18:4 Parenting time by non-parents

The Juvenile Court has the authority to determine the custody of any child who is not a ward of a court pursuant to RC 2151.23(A) and whether a shared custody agreement is in the best interests of a child.[1]

§ 18:5 Factors in determining visitation and parenting time issues

Under RC3109.051(A); RC 3109.051(B), RC 3109.11 and RC 3109.12 the court must consider the factors set out in RC 3109.051(D) which are:

(1) The prior interaction and interrelationships of the child with the child's parents, siblings, and other persons related by consanguinity or affinity, and with the person who requested companionship or visitation if that person is not a parent, sibling, or relative of the child;

(2) The geographical location of the residence of each parent and the distance between those residences, and if the person is not a parent, the geographical location of that person's residence and the distance between that person's residence and the child's residence;

(3) The child's and parents' available time, including, but not limited to, each parent's employment schedule, the child's school schedule, and the child's and the parents' holiday and vacation schedule;

(4) The age of the child;

(5) The child's adjustment to his home, school, and community;

(6) If the court has interviewed the child in chambers, pursuant to division (C) of this section, regarding the wishes and concerns of the child as to parenting time by the parent who is not the residential parent or companionship or visitation by the grandparent, relative, or other person who requested companionship or visitation, as to a specific parenting time or visitation schedule or, as to other parenting time or visitation matters, the wishes and concerns of the child, as expressed to the court;

[Section 18:3]

[1]Porter v. Porter, 25 Ohio St. 2d 123, 54 Ohio Op. 2d 260, 267 N.E.2d 299 (1971).

[2]Hollingsworth v. Hollingsworth, 34 Ohio App. 3d 13, 516 N.E.2d 1250 (10th Dist. Franklin County 1986).

[Section 18:4]

[1]In re Bonfield, 96 Ohio St. 3d 218, 2002-Ohio-4182, 773 N.E.2d 507 (2002), opinion superseded on reconsideration, 97 Ohio St. 3d 387, 2002-Ohio-6660, 780 N.E.2d 241 (2002).

(7) The health and safety of the child;

(8) The amount of time that will be available for the child to spend with siblings;

(9) The mental and physical health of all parties;

(10) Each parent's willingness to reschedule missed parenting time and to facilitate the other parent's parenting time rights, and with respect to a person who requested companionship or visitation, the willingness of that person to reschedule missed visitation;

(11) In relation to parenting time, whether either parent previously has been convicted of or pleaded guilty to any criminal offense involving any act that resulted in a child being an abused child or a neglected child; whether either parent, in a case in which a child has been adjudicated an abused child or a neglected child, previously has been determined to be the perpetrator of the abusive or neglectful act that is the basis of the adjudication; and whether there is reason to believe that either parent has acted in a manner resulting in a child being an abused child or a neglected child;

(12) In relation to requested companionship or visitation by a person other than a parent, whether the person previously has been convicted of or pleaded guilty to any criminal offense involving any act that resulted in a child being an abused child or a neglected child; whether the person, in a case in which a child has been adjudicated an abused child or a neglected child, previously has been determined to be the perpetrator of the abusive or neglectful act that is the basis of the adjudication; whether either parent previously has been convicted of or pleaded guilty to a violation of section 2919.25 of the Revised Code involving a victim who at the time of the commission of the offense was a member of the family or household that is the subject of the current proceeding; whether either parent previously has been convicted of an offense involving a victim who at the time of the commission of the offense was a member of the family or household that is the subject of the current proceeding and caused physical harm to the victim in the commission of the offense; and whether there is reason to believe that the person has acted in a manner resulting in a child being an abused child or a neglected child;

(13) Whether the residential parent or one of the parents subject to a shared parenting decree has continuously and willfully denied the other parent his or her right to parenting time in accordance with an order of the court;

(14) Whether either parent has established a residence or is planning to establish a residence outside this state;

(15) In relation to requested companionship or visitation by a person other than a parent, the wishes and concerns of the child's parents, as expressed by them to the court;

(16) Any other factor in the best interest of the child.

While RC 3109.051 does not specify the relative importance of these factors, the court is likely to strongly consider a child's prior interaction with the person seeking visitation under this section, especially for a nonparent. Moreover, the frequency and duration of visits by such nonparents may depend somewhat on what frequency of contact they enjoyed prior to the marriage break-up. RC 3109.051(E) specifically gives the court authority to award visitation to any person regardless of the remarriage of a residential parent. Any person whose motion for visitation is denied is entitled, upon request, to specific findings of fact and conclusions of law by the court in accordance with Civil Rule 52. Under RC 3109.051(F)(1), if the non-residential parent is denied visitation, such findings of fact and conclusions of law appear to be mandatory if such a request is filed.

§18:6 Additional considerations

Ohio courts are required to adhere to certain procedures in determining parenting time and visitation matters pursuant to RC 3109.051, RC 3109.11, and RC 3109.12. The court must consider any mediation report filed pursuant to RC 3109.052. The court must also consider all other relevant factors, including but not limited to the factors set out in RC 3109.051(D). The court may not accept or consider any written or recorded statement or affidavit that purports to set forth the child's wishes or concerns regarding visitation matters. These provisions seem to be mandatory and failure to follow them may be reversible error. The court may, but is not required under this section, interview the child in chambers as to the child's wishes and concerns. The interview must be conducted in chambers and no one may be present except the judge, the child, necessary court personnel, the child's attorney, and, in the judge's discretion, the attorneys for the parties.[1] There is no guidance or restriction as to the age of the child to be interviewed. However, no one may obtain or attempt to obtain a written or recorded statement or affidavit from a child setting forth the child's wishes and concerns regarding visitation matters, per RC 3109.051(C). In *Willis v. Willis*,[2] the appellate court held that the court should make a record of such an interview for the court of appeals but is not required provide a copy to the parties.

§18:7 Constitutional considerations

On June 5, 2000, the United States Supreme Court, in *Troxel v. Granville*,[1] upheld the Washington State Supreme Court's determination that the state statute that provided for any person to petition for visitation rights at any time, and authorized the Washington State superior courts to grant such rights when visitation may serve a child's best interest, to be unconstitutional. The Court held that the 14th Amendment's due process clause required that due process be met before interfering with parents' fundamental right to make decisions concerning the care, custody and control of their children. The

---

[Section 18:6]

[1]Willis v. Willis, 149 Ohio App. 3d 50, 2002-Ohio-3716, 775 N.E.2d 878 (12th Dist. Butler County 2002).

[2]Willis v. Willis, 149 Ohio App. 3d 50, 2002-Ohio-3716, 775 N.E.2d 878 (12th Dist. Butler County 2002).

[Section 18:7]

[1]Troxel v. Granville, 530 U.S. 57, 120, 120 S. Ct. 2054, 147 L. Ed. 2d 49 (2000).

Court noted that the Washington statute was breathtakingly broad and that the decision rendered was nothing more than a simple disagreement between the Court and the mother concerning her children's best interest and therefore that it was an unconstitutional infringement on the mother's right to make decisions regarding the rearing of her child.

The Court did not reach the issue of whether or not the due process clause required all non-parental visitation statutes to include a showing of harm or potential harm to the child as a condition precedent to grant visitation or to decide the precise scope of the parental due process right in the visitation context. The Washington Supreme Court had construed the constitution to permit a state to interfere with the right of parents to rear their children only to prevent harm or potential harm to a child. Most all states have disapproved court ordered visitations when the nuclear family is intact.[2] The Court cited a long line of cases which demonstrate that the right of a parent to rear his or her child is one of the oldest fundamental liberty interests recognized by the United States Supreme Court. The Court did not indicate that it would strike down any non-parental visitation statutes but hinted that such a statute would have to provide that if a fit parent's decision to allow visitation became an issue subject to judicial review, a Court must accord at least some special weight to the parent's own determination and pointed out that many states' statutes expressly provide that courts may not award visitation unless a parent has denied or unreasonably denied visitation to the concerned third party.

The facts in this case were that the grandparents were seeking visitation of children fathered by their deceased son. The mother did not deny visitation to the grandparents but wanted their visitation limited to a much smaller schedule than they had requested. At least one Ohio court of appeals has stated that, under RC 3109.051(D), the courts deciding grandparent cases should also consider the extent to which the autonomy of either parent may be undermined and the impact on the existing family situation under that statute.[3] It certainly is necessary at this point to at least introduce some evidence at trial of the impact that the non-parental visitation would have on the children's nuclear family or the impact of loss of companionship on the child in order to satisfy the 14th Amendment concerns expressed in *Troxel*. Our statute was amended on March 20, 2001 to require the Court to consider the wishes of a parent RC 3109.051(D)(15). Thereafter, *Oliver v. Feldner*,[4] a case which construed Ohio's statute in light of *Troxel* and found our statute unconstitutional based on the facts adduced at trial.

---

[2]Hawk v. Hawk, 855 S.W.2d 573 (Tenn. 1993).

[3]Gaffney v. Menrath, 132 Ohio App. 3d 113, 724 N.E.2d 507 (1st Dist. Hamilton County 1999).

[4]Oliver v. Feldner, 149 Ohio App. 3d 114, 2002-Ohio-3209, 776 N.E.2d 499 (7th Dist. Noble County 2002); see also Sandra Martinez, "The Misinterpretation of Troxell

One Ohio court of appeals stated that, under RC 3109.051(D), the courts deciding grandparent cases should also consider the extent to which the autonomy of either parent may be undermined and the impact on the existing family situation under that statute.[5] Subsequent thereto, *Harrold v. Collier*,[6] a case that was certified to the Supreme Court as in conflict with *Oliver*, resolved these constitutional issues. *Harrold* not only upheld the constitutionality of RC 3109.11, 3109.12 and 3109.051, having considered *Troxel*, but also found them constitutional as applied to the parties. The court held that grandparent visitation can be ordered when it is in the best interest of the children under the narrowly tailored statutory factors. However, counsel may still need to present evidence of negative or positive impact on the child in order to make an appropriate argument as to why such visitation should or should not be granted.

§ 18:8   Visitation by third parties in domestic relations actions

RC 3109.051(B) provides for companionship by grandparents, relatives, or other persons with children of divorce, dissolution, legal separation, annulment, or an action for child support. The statute requires that the person file a motion in the case seeking visitation either when the case is pending, or post-decree on a showing of "changed circumstances." Logically, a change in circumstances will frequently mean a restriction or curtailment of periods of consensual visitation. If the court determines that the person has an interest in the child and that visitation is in the best interest of the child, then the court may order visitation in accordance with the statute. In order to obtain visitation, the moving party shall file a motion to intervene as a party for jurisdictional purposes along with the motion for visitation.

There is no restriction as to who may file a motion for visitation. For example, a stepparent might file a motion in an ex-spouse's previous divorce seeking visitation with a child of that prior marriage.[1] One court of appeals found that a relative by affinity, in this case a step-grandmother had standing to obtain visitation under the statute.[2] This statute is very comprehensive.

At least one court of appeals has allowed a non-parent visitation

---

v. Granville: Construing the New Standard for Third Party Visitation," 36 Fam. L. Q. 487 (2002).

[5]Gaffney v. Menrath, 132 Ohio App. 3d 113, 724 N.E.2d 507 (1st Dist. Hamilton County 1999).

[6]Harrold v. Collier, 107 Ohio St. 3d 44, 2005-Ohio-5334, 836 N.E.2d 1165 (2005).

[Section 18:8]

[1]Hutton v. Hutton, 21 Ohio App. 3d 26, 486 N.E.2d 129 (9th Dist. Lorain County 1984); Shannon v. Shannon, 122 Ohio App. 3d 346, 701 N.E.2d 771 (9th Dist. Summit County 1997).

[2]McFall v. Watson, 178 Ohio App. 3d 540, 2008-Ohio-5204, 899 N.E.2d 158 (4th Dist. Vinton County 2008).

under RC 3109.051 even without the underlying predicate of a child support, divorce, or other enumerated proceeding.[3] The court ruled that a prior case between the same parties involving the issue of child support could serve as a basis for jurisdiction, even though it had been dismissed.

RC 3109.11 provides for visitation for third parties if a parent is deceased, for parents and other relatives if a court determines that it is in the child's best interests regardless of remarriage or stepparent adoption. RC 3109.12 provides the relatives of an unmarried mother may petition for visitation or companionship. The parent of a father of a child may petition for visitation if the father has been determined to be the father per RC 2151.232, RC 3111.04, RC 3111.21 or RC 5101.314, regardless of remarriage of custodial parent.

§ 18:9   The impact of adoption

This area of the law is really misunderstood by many practitioners. However, the current statutory arrangement is very clear. There are two basic rules that apply.

First, adoption including stepparent adoption, will terminate visitation orders of relatives and prevent obtaining such an order where the parents are divorced or were never married. *In re Adoption of Wise* summarizes the current law citing a long line of cases in support of the court's position.[1] *In re Ridenour*[2] also stands for the proposition that grandparents do not have the right to intervene in the adoption process even if they have a visitation order that could be extinguished by granting the adoption.

It is not known if adoption terminates a visitation order granted a non-relative per RC 3109.051(A).

Second, remarriage of a surviving parent or adoption of a child by the spouse of the surviving parent, does not preclude visitation or terminate an existing visitation order by relatives of a deceased parent whose parental rights were not terminated prior to his or her death.[3] RC 3109.11 specifically provides that remarriage of a surviving parent, or adoption by a stepparent does not preclude or terminate

---

[3]Waszkowski v. Lyons, 2009-Ohio-403, 2009 WL 224540 (Ohio Ct. App. 11th Dist. Lake County 2009). But see Liston v. Pyles, 1997 WL 467327 (Ohio Ct. App. 10th Dist. Franklin County 1997), which held the opposite of the holding in the *Waszkowski* case.

[Section 18:9]

[1]In re Adoption of Wise, 2002-Ohio-3785, 2002 WL 1752256 (Ohio Ct. App. 4th Dist. Lawrence County 2002); see In re Adoption of Ridenour, 61 Ohio St. 3d 319, 574 N.E.2d 1055 (1991); Sweeney v. Sweeney, 71 Ohio St. 3d 169, 1994-Ohio-221, 642 N.E.2d 629 (1994); State ex rel. Kaylor v. Bruening, 80 Ohio St. 3d 142, 1997-Ohio-350, 684 N.E.2d 1228 (1997); Foor v. Foor, 133 Ohio App. 3d 250, 727 N.E.2d 618 (12th Dist. Preble County 1999).

[2]In re Adoption of Ridenour, 61 Ohio St. 3d 319, 574 N.E.2d 1055 (1991).

[3]Longwell v. White, 1996 WL 72613 (Ohio Ct. App. 5th Dist. Fairfield County 1996).

visitation, unlike RC 3109.12, which only mentions remarriage, not adoption, for a child born out of wedlock.

Finally, the adoption statute itself[4] provides as follows:

(B) Notwithstanding division (A) of this section, if a parent of a child dies without the relationship of parent and child having been previously terminated and a spouse of the living parent thereafter adopts the child, the child's rights from or through the deceased parent for all purposes, including inheritance and applicability or construction of documents, statutes, and instruments, are not restricted or curtailed by the adoption.

(C) Notwithstanding division (A) of this section, if the relationship of parent and child has not been terminated between a parent and that parent's child and a spouse of the other parent of the child adopts the child, a grandparent's or relative's right to companionship or visitation pursuant to section 3109.11 of the Revised Code is not restricted or curtailed by the adoption.

Both paragraphs (B) and (C) refer to the same situation (i.e. the deceased parent), and this may be the cause for confusion amongst the bar.

§ 18:10 Procedure—Standard visitation guidelines

Each common pleas court in Ohio was required by RC 3109.051(F)(2) to adopt local rules setting forth standard visitation guidelines by July 1, 1991. RC 3109.051(F)(2) now states parenting time guidelines. The statute allows the court to deviate from the guidelines based on the factors in RC 3109.051(D).[1] The reason for the deviation must be evident in the court's decision.[2] To avoid the routine application of these guidelines to each case, counsel may well consider drafting a suggested deviation for submission to the court at the appropriate time in appropriate cases.

§ 18:11 Procedure—Relocation notices, access to records, day care facilities, and school activities

The drafters of RC 3109.051 intended to permit the non-residential parent an opportunity to play a continuing and significant role in the child's development.

RC 3109.051(G) requires a residential parent who intends to move to another residence to file a notice of intent to relocate his or her residence with the court. Unless the court has previously determined that the non-residential parent has been convicted of domestic violence against a member of the subject household, or a crime of physical violence against such a member, or has been determined to be a

---

[4]RC 3107.15(B) and (C).

[Section 18:10]

[1]See, e.g., Carter v. Payer, 1994 WL 620497 (Ohio Ct. App. 9th Dist. Summit County 1994).

[2]See Leas v. Leech, 1996 WL 451374 (Ohio Ct. App. 7th Dist. Jefferson County 1996).

perpetrator of an abusive act that is the basis for an adjudication that a child has been abused, the court must order a copy of the notice sent to the non-residential parent. On motion by the non-residential parent or the court, a hearing may be scheduled after notice to both parents to determine if it is in the child's best interest to revise the visitation schedule.[1]

If the non-residential parent has been a perpetrator, the court can still order the notice of relocation to be sent if the court at the time found that in spite of said activities it is in the child's best interest to order the notice to be sent, supported by specific findings of fact and conclusions of law.[2] There is also a provision in the statute for decrees issued prior to April 11, 1991, regarding the residential parent's request for a hearing to determine if such notice should be sent to the non-residential parent.[3] At this time the court must determine whether or not such notice of relocation should be issued based on the same criteria.

RC 3109.051(H) provides a non-residential parent with equal access to the child's records unless the court finds, based on the child's best interest, that access should be restricted. "Records" are defined as any record, document, files, or other material that contains information directly related to a child including, but not limited to (1) records maintained by public and nonpublic schools; (2) records of day care facilities or preschool services; (3) hospital records or records of facilities or persons that provide medical or surgical treatment for the child; and (4) records maintained by state or political subdivision of the state except the child support enforcement agency.[4]

If a record keeper fails to allow equal access to the non-residential parent, the record keeper is subject to contempt of court. If the record keeper has been presented by the residential parent with an order restricting access but knowingly permits access, that is also contempt of court.

RC 3109.051(I) requires the court to determine whether the non-residential parent should have equal access to day care centers attended or to be attended by the children. Access shall be restricted only where the court clearly specifies the restrictions and supports its ruling by findings of fact and conclusions of law.

RC 3109.051(J) provides equal access to the child's school activities by the non-residential parent unless the court supports any restriction in attending such activities with findings of fact and conclusions of law based on the best interests of the child. The court must include in its order that any school official or employee who knowingly fails to

---

[Section 18:11]

[1]Spain v. Spain, 1995 WL 380067 (Ohio Ct. App. 3d Dist. Logan County 1995).

[2]RC 3109.051(G)(2) to RC 3109.051(G)(4).

[3]RC 3109.051(G)(3).

[4]RC 3109.05(N)(2).

comply with an access order is in contempt of court. Further, school officials and employees must allow equal access to school activities unless the residential parent has provided them with a court order restricting or limiting said access. If said order has been presented and the school official or employee knowingly permits equal access by the non-residential parent, such employee or official is in contempt of court.

All visitation orders should contain specific orders relative to access of day care centers, records, school activities, and notices of intent to relocate that comport to these statutory provisions.[5]

§ 18:12   Procedure—Relocation notices, access to records, day care facilities, and school activities—Form⊚

REQUIRED NOTICES

I. <u>RELOCATION NOTICE</u>: Pursuant to Ohio Revised Code Section 3109.051(G), the parties hereto are hereby notified as follows:

> If the residential parent intends to move to a residence other than the residence specified in the parenting time order or decree of the Court, the residential parent shall file a notice of intent to relocate with this court, addressed to the attention of the relocation officer. Unless otherwise ordered pursuant to ORC Sections RC 3109.051(G)(2), 3109.051(3), and 3109.051(4), a copy of such notice shall be mailed by the court to the parent who is not the residential parent. Upon receipt of the notice, the court, on its own motion or the motion of either party, may schedule a hearing with notice to both parties to determine whether it is in the best interest of the child to revise the parenting time schedule.

II. <u>RECORDS ACCESS NOTICE</u>: Pursuant to Ohio Revised Code Sections 3109.051(H) and 3319.321(B)(5)(a) the parties hereto are hereby notified as follows:

> Excepting as specifically modified or otherwise limited by court order, and subject to ORC Sections 3125.16 and 3319.321(F), the parent who is not the residential parent, is entitled to access to any record that is related to the child, under the same terms and conditions as the residential parent, and to which said residential parent is legally provided access. Any keeper of a record who knowingly fails to comply with this order is in contempt of court.

III. <u>DAY CARE CENTER ACCESS NOTICE</u>: Pursuant to Ohio Revised Code Section 3109.051(I), the parties hereto are hereby notified as follows:

> Excepting as specifically modified or otherwise limited by court order, and in accordance with ORC Section 5104.011, the parent who is not the residential parent, is entitled to access to any day care center that is or will be attended by the child with whom parenting time is granted, to the same extent that the residential parent is granted access to the center.

IV. <u>SCHOOL ACTIVITIES NOTICE</u>: Pursuant to Ohio Revised

---

[5]See Text § 18:12, Procedure—Relocation notices, access to records, day care facilities, and school activities—Form.

Code Section 3109.051(J), the parties hereto are hereby notified as follows:

> Excepting as specifically modified or otherwise limited by court order, and subject to O.RC Section 3319.321(F), the parent who is not the residential parent, is entitled to access, under the same terms and conditions as the residential parent, to any student activity that is related to the child and to which the residential parent of the child legally is provided access. Any school employee or official who knowingly fails to comply with this order is in contempt of court.

NOTES TO FORM

Drafter's Notes

> These notices should be included in any judgment entry establishing or modifying visitation, companionship, or allocation of parental rights and responsibilities.

§ 18:13   Procedure—Contempt provisions

RC 3109.051(K) provides additional penalties besides the court's statutory and inherent powers to enforce its decrees. RC 2705.031(B)(2) provides the remedy of contempt for failure to comply with a visitation order. It requires that summons be issued with notices of possible penalties, per RC 2705.05; notice of right to counsel; and notice that failure to appear may result in arrest. The court also has inherent power to enforce visitation orders.[1] RC 3109.051(K) goes further, however, and mandates that upon conviction for contempt, in addition to any other remedies, the court shall assess all costs against the offending party and order that party to pay any reasonable attorney's fees that the prevailing party paid in relation to the act of contempt. Further, if it is in the best interest of the child, the court may award compensatory visitation to the person whose right of visitation was affected by the contempt. Contempt may not lie, however, where the custodial parent can prove that, despite encouragement to visit, the child is of sufficient age to decide not to visit and has developed a resentment against the visiting parent.[2]

There is no specific designation in the Revised Code as to who may bring a contempt against a record keeper or school official or employee for denying access to the non-residential parent without an order to do so, or for permitting access in violation of an order restricting such access.

§ 18:14   Procedure—Mediation relating to visitation

The mediation statute, RC 3109.052, specifically includes visitation as an issue for which a court may order mediation. The court is

---

[Section 18:13]

[1]Davis v. Davis, 55 Ohio App. 3d 196, 563 N.E.2d 320 (8th Dist. Cuyahoga County 1988).

[2]Pennington v. McCarley, 1996 WL 206761 (Ohio Ct. App. 11th Dist. Portage County 1996).

required to consider a properly filed mediation report in determining visitation.[1]

§ 18:15 Procedure—Affidavit of indigency

RC 3109.051(L) provides that the court may waive the filing fee and costs for an indigent applicant under all three visitation statutes upon the court's determination of indigency and best interests of the child.

§ 18:16 Procedure—Separate cause of action for visitation

In RC 3109.11 and RC 3109.12, the legislature has created a cause of action called a complaint for visitation. The document is styled as a complaint in the statutes and presumably said complaints would have to follow the normal format contained in the Ohio Rules of Civil Procedure. The complaint should name the father, the mother, and the child through its guardian and next friend (the custodial parent) as parties to the action and should allege that the plaintiffs are seeking companionship or visitation and that said visitation would be in the best interest of the child or children with whom they are seeking visitation. The prayer should contain a request for the court to grant reasonable visitation.[1]

Neither RC 3109.11 nor RC 3109.12 specifies in which division of common pleas court said complaints should be filed. Clearly the juvenile division of each court would have jurisdiction to hear complaints under either statute, although it is probable that under proper circumstances, usually where there have been other ancillary proceedings involving the same youth, the probate or domestic divisions might also hear such requests. The court does not have jurisdiction to hear complaints by nonrelatives under either RC 3109.11 or RC 3109.12. Only in the instance of divorce, dissolution, legal separation, or annulment can the court hear a request for visitation by a nonrelative, and that request must be brought by motion in the domestic relations case either during or after the divorce has been granted.[2]

§ 18:17 Procedure—Restrictions on visitation

The court has the authority to restrict visitation both as to duration and under what conditions visitation should take place. These conditions may include the place of visitation or the presence of third

---

[Section 18:14]

[1]RC 3019.051(C). See also Text Ch 6, Mediation and Conciliation.

[Section 18:16]

[1]See Text § 18:30, Visitation provisions—Child of deceased parent—Complaint for visitation—Form; Text § 18:32, Visitation provisions—Child of unmarried mother—Complaint for visitation—Form.

[2]RC 3109.051(B)(1).

parties.[1] It is not uncommon for a court to order that overnight visitation may not take place in the presence of a parent's paramour.[2] Circumstances that create a significant risk of serious physical or emotional harm to the child may justify a denial of visitation.[3] Such circumstances may arise when the visiting parent is unfit by reason of (1) mental illness, (2) immoral behavior, (3) substance abuse, or (4) criminal behavior.[4]

Visitation with an incarcerated parent is not prohibited by statute, and a complete denial of visitation without exploring all options of visitation is an abuse of discretion.[5] However, it has been held that a parent's imprisonment for a period of years is an extraordinary circumstance justifying the denial of visitation in the absence of evidence that visitation is in the child's best interest.[6] A trial court does not abuse its discretion in restricting visitation with the child's homosexual parent,[7] or where the parent has a history of physical violence.[8] Supervised visitation is appropriate when there is credible evidence that the father, a resident alien, would take his child permanently out of the county.[9] However, visitation rights should not be severed absent evidence that a parent is unfit or a showing that visitation would harm the child.[10] In addition, restrictions on visita-

---

[Section 18:17]

[1]RC 3109.051(A).

[2]Irish v. Irish, 102 Mich. App. 75, 300 N.W.2d 739 (1980). See Gray v. Gray, 654 S.W.2d 309, 40 A.L.R.4th 807 (Mo. Ct. App. E.D. 1983); Dilworth v. Dilworth, 115 Ohio App. 3d 537, 685 N.E.2d 847 (2d Dist. Champaign County 1996); Anderson v. Anderson, 47 Ohio App.3d 513, 2002-Ohio-1156 (Carroll 3/12/02).

[3]Pettry v. Pettry, 20 Ohio App. 3d 350, 486 N.E.2d 213 (8th Dist. Cuyahoga County 1984); Smith v. Smith, 70 Ohio App. 2d 87, 24 Ohio Op. 3d 100, 434 N.E.2d 749 (10th Dist. Franklin County 1980); Evans v. Evans, 1992 WL 81303 (Ohio Ct. App. 1st Dist. Hamilton County 1992); Pisani v. Pisani, 1996 WL 28572 (Ohio Ct. App. 8th Dist. Cuyahoga County 1996).

[4]Davis v. Davis, 55 Ohio App. 3d 196, 563 N.E.2d 320 (8th Dist. Cuyahoga County 1988); Thomas v. Thomas, 1993 WL 323637 (Ohio Ct. App. 6th Dist. Lucas County 1993); Schulte v. Schulte, 1993 WL 420109 (Ohio Ct. App. 6th Dist. Wood County 1993).

[5]Tobens v. Brill, 89 Ohio App. 3d 298, 624 N.E.2d 265 (3d Dist. Auglaize County 1993).

[6]Calhoun v. Calhoun, 1996 WL 307128 (Ohio Ct. App. 12th Dist. Fayette County 1996); Simms v. Simms, 1998 WL 156886 (Ohio Ct. App. 11th Dist. Portage County 1998).

[7]Roberts v. Roberts, 22 Ohio App. 3d 127, 489 N.E.2d 1067 (10th Dist. Franklin County 1985).

[8]Bodine v. Bodine, 38 Ohio App. 3d 173, 528 N.E.2d 973 (10th Dist. Franklin County 1988).

[9]Al-Silham v. Al-Silham, 1995 WL 803808 (Ohio Ct. App. 11th Dist. Ashtabula County 1995).

[10]Smiley v. Smiley, 1992 WL 354482 (Ohio Ct. App. 2d Dist. Montgomery County 1992).

tion should not unduly burden the ability of the visiting parent to develop a relationship with his children.[11]

However, the court should order and enforce visitation unless extraordinary circumstances preclude it.[12] For example, homosexuality of the parent in and of itself is not sufficient reason to deny overnight visitation. There must be a showing of harm or probable harm to the child.[13] The burden of proof that visitation would not be in a child's best interest is on the person opposing visitation.[14]

Perhaps the most frequently requested limitation relates to allegations of sexual abuse by the visiting parent. At minimum, supervised visitation should be required when there is competent, credible evidence of a sexual abuse of a minor child.[15] However, unrestricted visitation should be ordered where the only evidence of sexual abuse was the other parent's suspicion uncorroborated by any professional or other witness.[16]

Courts are sometimes faced with the delicate task of accommodating competing religious beliefs of the parents. Most courts, absent a specific showing of physical or emotional harm to the child, exercise restraint in placing limits on visitation due to the other parent's religious activities or observances.[17]

The trial court has broad discretion in determining matters related to visitation as long as its orders are just and reasonable. Its decision will be viewed with deference, and reversed only on a showing of abuse of discretion.[18]

Pursuant to RC 3109.051(F)(1), if the court denies visitation to a parent, or reasonable companionship to a person who files under the statute, and if the parent or movant files a written request for findings of fact, the court must state its findings in writing in accordance

---

[11]Harter v. Harter, 1992 WL 319286 (Ohio Ct. App. 5th Dist. Stark County 1992).

[12]Pettry v. Pettry, 20 Ohio App. 3d 350, 486 N.E.2d 213 (8th Dist. Cuyahoga County 1984).

[13]Conkel v. Conkel, 31 Ohio App. 3d 169, 509 N.E.2d 983 (4th Dist. Pickaway County 1987).

[14]Matter of Nichols, 1998 WL 295937 (Ohio Ct. App. 12th Dist. Clermont County 1998).

[15]Cross v. Cross, 1990 WL 203176 (Ohio Ct. App. 9th Dist. Summit County 1990).

[16]Bardenhagen v. Bardenhagen, 1990 WL 124236 (Ohio Ct. App. 12th Dist. Clermont County 1990).

[17]Pater v. Pater, 63 Ohio St. 3d 393, 588 N.E.2d 794 (1992); In re Marriage of Mentry, 142 Cal. App. 3d 260, 190 Cal. Rptr. 843 (1st Dist. 1983); Morris v. Morris, 271 Pa. Super. 19, 412 A.2d 139 (1979); Holder v. Holder, 171 Ohio App. 3d 728, 2007-Ohio-2354, 872 N.E.2d 1239 (2d Dist. Montgomery County 2007).

[18]See King v. King, 78 Ohio App. 3d 599, 605 N.E.2d 970 (12th Dist. Warren County 1992).

with Civil Rule 52. The court is not required to issue findings of fact when it grants or modifies visitation rights.[19]

§ 18:18 Procedure—Obligation to visit

There is no recognized duty to exercise visitation. Even though visitation has been stated to be the child's right as well as that of the visiting parent, there are no reported cases of a contempt finding for failure to visit. A residential parent may, however, petition the court for additional child support in such a case to cover the cost of additional babysitting. A parent who willfully fails without justification to contact a child for one year loses the right to refuse to consent to adoption under RC 3107.07(A). However, a court cannot force a parent to visit a child.[1]

§ 18:19 Procedure—Effect of support on visitation

Child support and visitation are not concomitant rights.[1] RC 3109.05(D) denies the court the power to withhold support or to escrow support payments because of a refusal to allow visitation.[2] A parent may not be denied visitation for failure to obey a support order due to innocent causes.[3] Failure to comply with a child support order does not rise to the level of egregious conduct that would be harmful to a minor child. Therefore, suspension of a parent's future visitation rights until all arrearages and attorney fees were paid is error.[4]

RC 3109.04(F)(1)(f) provides that the court may consider the residential parent's failure to honor and facilitate visitation in determining the best interest of the child on a motion to modify the allocation of parental rights and responsibilities.

There is some evidence that parents who have frequent visitation are more likely to pay support, and that parents who do not receive regular support are more likely not to encourage visitation. Nevertheless, counsel should explain the independent nature of those two

---

[19]Marchio v. Marchio, 1998 WL 635854 (Ohio Ct. App. 7th Dist. Belmont County 1998).

[Section 18:18]

[1]Hamilton v. Hamilton, 107 Ohio App. 3d 132, 667 N.E.2d 1256 (6th Dist. Lucas County 1995).

[Section 18:19]

[1]Porter v. Porter, 25 Ohio St. 2d 123, 54 Ohio Op. 2d 260, 267 N.E.2d 299 (1971).

[2]Fry v. Fry, 64 Ohio App. 3d 519, 582 N.E.2d 11 (3d Dist. Paulding County 1989); In re Dissolution of Marriage of Al-Faour, 68 Ohio App. 3d 279, 588 N.E.2d 228 (10th Dist. Franklin County 1990).

[3]Johnson v. Johnson, 52 Ohio App. 2d 180, 6 Ohio Op. 3d 170, 368 N.E.2d 1273 (9th Dist. Summit County 1977).

[4]Leasure v. Leasure, 1998 WL 108137 (Ohio Ct. App. 8th Dist. Cuyahoga County 1998).

obligations, especially that failure of one does not excuse performance of the other.

A provision in former RC 3109.05[5] that allowed a court to modify support because of a consistent refusal to comply with visitation orders does not appear in current RC 3105.051, and therefore is no longer considered to be an available remedy to a non-residential parent.[6]

§ 18:20 Procedure—Long distance visitation

Counsel should be aware that RC 3119.23(D) provides that the court may consider "extended times of visitation or extraordinary costs associated with visitation" in a request for deviation from the child support guidelines. Both of these factors may be present in a long distance visitation situation. At minimum, the court should consider ordering that the costs of transportation be shared, preferably with the non-residential parent providing transportation at the beginning of visitation and the residential parent at the conclusion of visitation.

The reason for the geographical move by the custodial party may be considered by the court. Where a trial court found a geographical move by the wife outside of the state, without court permission, and the wife was attempting to influence the child away from the husband, the court did not err in ordering the wife to transport the minor child 600 miles to visit the husband every time the child has a three-day weekend from school.[1]

§ 18:21 Modifying visitation or parenting time orders— Jurisdiction

There is explicit authority to modify the court's visitation orders, now called allocation of parental rights and responsibilities in RC 3109.04(E)(1)(B) and RC 3109.04(F)(1). The court also has inherent power to modify its own judgments regarding custody, support, and visitation.[1]

The continuing jurisdiction of the court must be invoked by filing a motion to modify visitation and by serving process on all other parties as if the matter were a new action per Civil Rule 75(J). Venue is in

---

[5]Repealed, eff. 5-31-90.

[6]See Andrulis v. Andrulis, 26 Ohio App. 3d 164, 498 N.E.2d 1380 (9th Dist. Summit County 1985), but see In re Prenzlin, 2002-Ohio-4161, 2002 WL 1878841 (Ohio Ct. App. 3d Dist. Seneca County 2002) (where appellate court affirmed order which terminated support due to contempt of visitation; order had not been timely appealed, and CSEA was not proper party to bring appeal of later motion to modify).

[Section 18:20]

[1]Corple v. Corple, 123 Ohio App. 3d 31, 702 N.E.2d 1234 (7th Dist. Columbiana County 1997).

[Section 18:21]

[1]Van Divort v. Van Divort, 165 Ohio St. 141, 59 Ohio Op. 207, 134 N.E.2d 715, 62 A.L.R.2d 538 (1956).

the county of original jurisdiction unless that original court relinquishes jurisdiction to a more convenient forum[2] on application of one of the parties or the court in which the action for modification is filed. Pursuant to Civil Rule 75(I), the court may in extraordinary circumstances make an ex parte order modifying parenting time pending the outcome of a formal hearing.

§ 18:22   Modifying parenting time—Basis for modification

RC 3109.04(E)(1)(a), effective April 11, 1991, provides that the court must not modify a prior order allocating parental rights and responsibilities unless there is a showing of changed circumstances since the original decree or facts can be shown that were unknown to the court at the time of the decree, and that the modification is in the best interest of the child. While there was a split of authority among the appellate courts whether a change of circumstances was required to modify visitation, the Supreme Court in *Braatz v. Braatz*[1] held it was not necessary to show that there had been a change of circumstances.[2] The burden is much higher in the event that the motion seeks to change the residential parent named in the original decree. A change in circumstances must be found before the court may consider the best interests of the child.

Once it finds such a change in circumstances, RC 3109.04(F)(1) sets out the specific criteria the court must consider in determining the best interest of the child in this circumstance:

(a) The wishes of the child's parents regarding the child's care;

(b) If the court has interviewed the child in chambers pursuant to division (B) of this section regarding the child's wishes and concerns as to the allocation of parental rights and responsibilities concerning the child, the wishes and concerns of the child, as expressed to the court;

(c) The child's interaction and interrelationship with the child's parents, siblings, and any other person who may significantly affect the child's best interest;

---

[2]Normally, the juvenile court in the county in which the children reside at the time of filing the request for modification per RC 3109.06. See Text Ch 17, Uniform Child Custody Jurisdiction Act; Parental Kidnaping Prevention Act; Uniform Child Custody Jurisdiction and Enforcement Act; International Child Abduction Remedies Act.

[Section 18:22]

[1]Braatz v. Braatz, 85 Ohio St. 3d 40, 1999-Ohio-203, 706 N.E.2d 1218 (1999) (paragraph 2 of syllabus).

[2]Jacobs v. Jacobs, 102 Ohio App. 3d 568, 657 N.E.2d 580 (9th Dist. Wayne County 1995) (abrogated by, Braatz v. Braatz, 85 Ohio St. 3d 40, 1999-Ohio-203, 706 N.E.2d 1218 (1999)) (change in circumstances is required to modify visitation) (abrogated on other grounds by Braatz v. Braatz, 85 Ohio St.3d 40, 706 N.E.2d 1218 (1999); Lillo v. Lillo, 1994 WL 236215 (Ohio Ct. App. 6th Dist. Huron County 1994); Chehayl v. Chehayl, 1994 WL 163986 (Ohio Ct. App. 8th Dist. Cuyahoga County 1994); Walsh v. Walsh, 1994 WL 780879 (Ohio Ct. App. 11th Dist. Geauga County 1994); Wilbanks v. Wilbanks, 1994 WL 371104 (Ohio Ct. App. 2d Dist. Greene County 1994) (a change in circumstances is not required to modify visitation).

(d) The child's adjustment to the child's home, school, and community;

(e) The mental and physical health of all persons involved in the situation;

(f) The parent more likely to honor and facilitate court-appointed parenting time rights or visitation and companionship rights;

(g) Whether either parent has failed to make all child support payments, including all arrearages, that are required of that parent pursuant to a child support order under which that parent is an obligor;

(h) Whether either parent previously has been convicted of or pleaded guilty to any criminal offense involving any act that resulted in a child being an abused child or a neglected child; whether either parent, in a case in which a child has been adjudicated an abused child or a neglected child, previously has been determined to be the perpetrator of the abusive or neglectful act that is the basis of an adjudication; whether either parent previously has been convicted of or pleaded guilty to a violation of section 2919.25 of the Revised Code involving a victim who at the time of the commission of the offense was a member of the family or household that is the subject of the current proceeding; whether either parent previously has been convicted of or pleaded guilty to any offense involving a victim who at the time of the commission of the offense was a member of the family or household that is the subject of the current proceeding and caused physical harm to the victim in the commission of the offense; and whether there is reason to believe that either parent has acted in a manner resulting in a child being an abused child or a neglected child.

(i) Whether the residential parent or one of the parents subject to a shared parenting decree has continuously and willfully denied the other parent's right to parenting time in accordance with an order of the court;

(j) Whether either parent has established a residence, or is planning to establish a residence, outside this state.

The statute does not explain what constitutes a change in circumstances but it includes a "change . . . in the circumstances of the child, the child's residential parent, or either of the parents subject to a shared parenting decree."[3] Examples of changes that are frequently used in modifying preexisting orders are the child's changing age; the child's commencement of formal education;[4] the child's changing interests and desires; the child's extracurricular activities; the parents' changing work habits; and the relocation of either parent. These all fit into one or more of the criteria the court must consider as in the child's best interest. The court has discretion to terminate or modify visitation as the case requires.[5] The parties may also specify in their decree, parenting plan, or separation agreement as to what shall con-

---

[3]RC 3109.04(E)(1)(a).

[4]Scheidler v. Scheidler, 1993 WL 98293 (Ohio Ct. App. 12th Dist. Clermont County 1993).

[5]Angel v. Angel, 2 Ohio Op. 2d 136, 74 Ohio L. Abs. 531, 140 N.E.2d 86 (C.P. 1956); Johnson v. Johnson, 52 Ohio App. 2d 180, 6 Ohio Op. 3d 170, 368 N.E.2d 1273 (9th Dist. Summit County 1977); Beekman v. Beekman, 96 Ohio App. 3d 783, 645 N.E.2d 1332 (4th Dist. Pike County 1994); Davis v. Flickinger, 77 Ohio St. 3d 415, 1997-Ohio-260, 674 N.E.2d 1159 (1997).

stitute a change in circumstances regarding subsequent modification of visitation.[6]

Prior to the enactment of RC 3109.04(E)(1)(a), the court had discretion to modify visitation as defined by the Supreme Court, which held that the standard in Ohio for a modification of visitation is the best interest of the child.[7] The legislature may have intended to change that law in the enactment of RC 3109.04(E)(1)(a) by requiring proof of a "change in circumstance" in modification cases, but because it refers to a "reallocation of parental rights" as opposed to "visitation" or parenting time, some confusion was created.[8]

The Supreme Court of Ohio may have laid to rest the "change in circumstances" issue as it relates to modification of a prior visitation order. The Court held in *Braatz v. Braatz*[9] that:

> The party requesting a change in visitation rights need make no showing that there has been a change in circumstances in order for the court to modify these rights. Pursuant to RC 3109.051(D), the trial court shall consider the fifteen factors enumerated therein, and in its sound discretion shall determine visitation that is in the best interest of the child.

The court construed RC 3109.04(E)(1)(a) as not applicable to requests for modification of visitation (as opposed to modification of custody rights). The court said RC 3109.051, however, pertains to visitation and distinguished custody from visitation as related but separate and distinct legal concepts. The court stated that RC 3109.051 requires no change in circumstances and relied on its reasoning in *Appleby v. Appleby*.[10] The court retains very wide discretion in the modification of its prior visitation orders. However, such discretion is not without limits. For example, it is reversible error to modify visitation where neither party requested it in the pleadings and no evidence was taken on the issue.[11]

For decrees prior to May 31, 1990, a moving party may request a visitation schedule if one is not in place.[12] The moving party may also request access to the child's records, day care, and school activities, as provided per RC 3109.051, if such access has not previously been provided. Courts should grant these changes liberally as provided by statute even though these rights may or may not be cognizable as a change in the legal circumstance of the child.

---

[6]See Brown v. Brown, 78 Ohio App. 3d 416, 604 N.E.2d 1380 (3d Dist. Hancock County 1992).

[7]Appleby v. Appleby, 24 Ohio St. 3d 39, 492 N.E.2d 831 (1986).

[8]In re Brayden James, 113 Ohio St. 3d 420, 2007-Ohio-2335, 866 N.E.2d 467 (2007).

[9]Braatz v. Braatz, 85 Ohio St. 3d 40, 1999-Ohio-203, 706 N.E.2d 1218 (1999).

[10]Appleby v. Appleby, 24 Ohio St. 3d 39, 492 N.E.2d 831 (1986).

[11]Kilbourne v. Kilbourne, 1981 WL 4567 (Ohio Ct. App. 8th Dist. Cuyahoga County 1981).

[12]RC 3109.051(A) requires a schedule of parenting time.

§ 18:23 Modifying parenting time—Evidentiary considerations

Counsel seeking modification of a prior visitation order should present a proposed plan to the court and opposing counsel. Since the court must consider the parent's wishes under RC 3109.04(F)(1)(a), it seems clear that a parent should be able to submit the plan into evidence in the parent's case. Certainly, the parent's testimony as to what is desired should be permitted. Counsel must also be prepared to prove that the change in parenting time is in the best interest of the child. A full evidentiary hearing may be required in modification cases.[1]

One of the most effective ways of accomplishing this is with the use of an expert witness. Psychological testimony is essential in a parenting time case where a party is seeking to terminate or drastically reduce parenting time. A psychologist can also be instrumental in a motion for increased parenting time. The psychologist may indirectly put the child's feelings before the court without putting the child in an adversarial role and may testify as to the benefit of increased contact. Civil Rule 35 allows the court to order the parties and children to undergo a psychological evaluation. Psychiatrists and experts in child development or child abuse are frequently called as expert witnesses with great effect. The failure of the court to give adequate weight to the uncontradicted testimony of a psychologist in a visitation modification may result in a reversal.[2]

The court on motion of either party or its own motion may appoint a guardian ad litem to represent the child's interests in the proceeding under Civil Rule 75(B)(2). The guardian can place the child's feelings before the court without placing the child in a direct adversarial role. The child may be interviewed in chambers as to the child's wishes per RC 3109.04(B). However, current thought is that neither the child nor the child's own analyst should be placed in an adversarial role. A guardian ad litem or psychologist, other than the child's own psychologist, is the appropriate method for putting the child's wishes in evidence. A guardian ad litem will be of little use if the child is of tender years or is otherwise not capable of accurately relating events or feelings.

The court also has authority to order a family investigation in modification cases per Civil Rule 75(D). These reports may have a significant impact on the court's decision to expand or restrict parenting time. Counsel should be prepared to support or rebut by appropriate evidence matters contained in such reports where they are made available prior to hearing.

[Section 18:23]

[1]Quint v. Lomakoski, 167 Ohio App. 3d 124, 2006-Ohio-3041, 854 N.E.2d 225 (2d Dist. Greene County 2006).

[2]Roberts v. Roberts, 22 Ohio App. 3d 127, 489 N.E.2d 1067 (10th Dist. Franklin County 1985).

§ 18:24　Modifying parenting time—Interstate modification

RC 3109.051(G) requires that the residential parent file a notice of relocation with the court if that parent intends to move to another residence. If that move is out of state or to a remote location, the court, on its own motion or that of the non-residential parent, is required to reconsider the parenting time schedule.

It is within the discretion of the trial court to award long distance visitation (including visitation outside the country) when it is in the child's best interest.[1]

If a non-residential parent finds that the child presently is or will be a long distance away, that parent should take immediate steps to ensure a continuing relationship with the child. Many courts have adopted long distance parenting time schedules. However, there may be no reason why a child not yet of school age should not be shared equally under a shared parenting or expanded parenting time plan. Further, if the child is of school age there are good arguments for changing the residential parent if the child will be uprooted and removed from familiar surroundings, supportive family, teachers, friends, and health care providers.

To avoid the problem altogether a contingent long range parenting time schedule should be negotiated at the time of divorce if a long distance move is contemplated by either party. Restrictions against moving from the jurisdiction of the court are rarely upheld if the move is necessitated by a compelling reason such as a job transfer.[2] A restriction on moving will more likely be upheld when it is a specific part of the parties' own agreement.[3]

§ 18:25　Modifying parenting time—Attorney fees

The court may award attorney fees in modification cases to either party.[1] Further, the court may order either party or both to bear as costs the fees of court-appointed psychologists or guardians ad litem.

[Section 18:24]

[1]Mitchell v. Pietrykowski, 1993 WL 308458 (Ohio Ct. App. 6th Dist. Lucas County 1993); Haudenschield v. Brakora, 1993 WL 277846 (Ohio Ct. App. 2d Dist. Montgomery County 1993); Smith v. Smith, 1993 WL 439925 (Ohio Ct. App. 7th Dist. Belmont County 1993); Newsome v. Davis, 1993 WL 350032 (Ohio Ct. App. 2d Dist. Greene County 1993); Snyder v. Snyder, 1993 WL 356939 (Ohio Ct. App. 6th Dist. Sandusky County 1993).

[2]Ross v. Harden, 8 Ohio App. 3d 34, 455 N.E.2d 1313 (10th Dist. Franklin County 1982).

[3]Rozborski v. Rozborski, 1996 WL 673973 (Ohio Ct. App. 8th Dist. Cuyahoga County 11-21-96).

[Section 18:25]

[1]RC 3105.18(H); Cooper v. Cooper, 1990 WL 10980 (Ohio Ct. App. 10th Dist. Franklin County 1990); Blum v. Blum, 9 Ohio St. 2d 92, 38 Ohio Op. 2d 224, 223 N.E.2d 819 (1967); Cohen v. Cohen, 8 Ohio App. 3d 109, 456 N.E.2d 581 (11th Dist. Lake County 1983).

The court usually considers the respective assets of the parties and the merits of their respective cases in awarding fees.

If there has been a failure to comply with visitation or parenting time, the court must assess attorney fees against the offending party under RC 3109.051(K). A modification request may be accompanied by a motion for sanctions in appropriate cases.

§ 18:26 Modifying parenting time—Motion to modify parenting time—Form⊚

[Title of Court]

[Caption] Case No. [_____]

MOTION TO MODIFY PARENTING TIME

[Plaintiff/Defendant] moves that this Court modify the Order heretofore made for parenting time with the minor *[child/children]*, namely, *[name(s) and date(s) of birth of children]*, for the following reasons: *[state reasons]*.

[Plaintiff/Defendant] suggests to the Court that parenting time should take place as follows: *[state requested parenting time schedule/per local parenting time guidelines rule]*.

_____

Attorney for *[Plaintiff/Defendant]*

[Memorandum/Affidavit of movant giving reasons/justifications for motion]

[Notice of Hearing]

[Proof/certificate of service]

NOTES TO FORM

Drafter's Notes

A proof/certificate of service is only necessary when there is opposing counsel. Where the respondent is unrepresented by counsel at the time of filing the motion, the motion papers will be served by the clerk of court pursuant to written instructions filed with the motion.

Under his/her signature on the motion, counsel should list his or her Supreme Court registration number, business address, and phone number.

§ 18:27 Modifying parenting time—Judgment entry modifying visitation—Form⊚

[Title of Court]

[Caption] Case No. [_____]

JUDGMENT ENTRY

This matter came on for hearing on *[date]*, before the Honorable *[name of judge]* upon Plaintiff's motion to modify parenting time previously ordered herein. The Court finds that Defendant has been properly served with said Motion personally according to law.

The Court finds that the parties were divorced on *[date]*, and that Defendant was named residential parent and legal custodian of the parties' minor child and Plaintiff was awarded parenting time until further order of Court as follows: *[description of prior order]*.

The Court finds that there has been a sufficient change of circumstances since the date of the prior Decree that requires a modification of the visitation Order and that the modification is in the best interests of the child.

It is therefore ordered that:

(1) Until further order of Court Plaintiff shall enjoy parenting time with the parties' minor *[child/children]* as follows: *[describe modification/per local guidelines on parenting time, with the following exceptions: [_____];*

(2) Plaintiff shall enjoy parenting time with the parties' minor [child/children] at other times as may be mutually agreed by and between the parties;

(3) Except as expressly modified to the contrary herein, all prior orders of Court with respect to this cause shall remain in full force and effect.

_____
                                                                      Judge

Approved:

_____

Attorney for Movant

PRAECIPE TO THE CLERK OF COURTS: Pursuant to Civil Rule 58(B), you are hereby instructed to serve upon all parties not in default for failure to appear, notice of the judgment and its date of entry upon the journal in the manner prescribed by the attached instructions for service.

§18:28 Modifying visitation or parenting time—Agreed judgment entry modifying visitation or parenting time—Form⊚

[Title of Court]

[Caption] Case No. [_____]

JUDGMENT ENTRY

[Select one of the following, as appropriate]

This cause came on for hearing on *[date]*, upon Petitioner's Motion to modify parenting time. The Court having been advised that the parties to this action have reached an agreement concerning the issues raised in said Motion and the Court having reviewed the agreement of the parties and having found that the agreement is fair, just, and equitable and that by reason thereof the agreement should be approved and made an Order of this Court in its entirety.

or

Upon agreement of the parties and for good cause shown, the Court finding it is in the best interests of the minor *[child / children]*.

It is therefore ordered that:

(1) The prior Order of this Court with respect to visitation privileges of Petitioner for the parties' minor *[child / children]* be amended and that the following schedule is hereby ordered into effect until further Order of the Court: *[description of modified visitation schedule]*;

(2) Except as expressly modified to the contrary herein, all prior Orders of Court with respect to this cause shall remain in full force and effect;

(3) Plaintiff pay the costs of this proceeding for which sum judgment is rendered and execution may issue.

_____
Judge

Approved:

_____
Attorney for Movant

PRAECIPE TO THE CLERK OF COURTS: Pursuant to Civil Rule 52(B), you are hereby instructed to serve upon all parties not in default for failure to appear, notice of the judgment and its date of entry upon the journal in the manner prescribed by the attached instructions for service.

NOTES TO FORM

Drafter's Notes

This form may be used for any agreed modification, i.e., support, allocation of parental rights and responsibilities, etc.

§ 18:29 Visitation provisions—Domestic relations actions— Motion by third party to intervene and visitation request—Forms⊚

[TITLE OF DOMESTIC RELATIONS COURT]

[Caption]   Case No. [_____]

MOTION TO INTERVENE AND REQUEST FOR COMPANIONSHIP OR VISITATION

Now comes the Movant and request that he/she be permitted to intervene in the above styled case as a party and pursuant to RC 3109.051(B) of the Ohio Revised Code, moves the Court for an Order granting him/her visitation or companionship time with the minor child of the parties.

_____

Attorney for Movant

MEMORANDUM IN SUPPORT OF MOTION

Movant states that it is in the best interest of the parties' minor child that he/she be granted visitation or companionship rights as will be more fully shown at the hearing of this cause.

Respectfully submitted,

_____

Attorney for Movant

[NOTICE OF HEARING]

NOTES TO FORM

Drafter's Notes

This motion must be served as if it is a new pleading on all parties pursuant to Civil Rule 4 to Civil Rule 4.6.

§ 18:30 Visitation provisions—Child of deceased parent— Complaint for visitation—Form⊚

[Title of Juvenile Court]

[Name of Relative]:	)
[Address],	)
Plaintiff,	) Case No._____
-vs-	)
[Name of surviving	)
Parent],	
[Address],	)
and	)
[Name of Child], a	)
minor	
by her next friend	)
[Name of Parent],	)
Defendants.	

COMPLAINT FOR COMPANIONSHIP OR VISITATION

1. *[Name of plaintiff-relative]* is the *[type of relationship]* of *[name of deceased parent]*, deceased.

2. *[Name of deceased parent]* was married to *[name of surviving parent]* until his death in *[year]*.

3. *[Name of deceased parent]* and *[name of surviving parent]*, are the parents of *[name of plaintiff-relative]'s [type of relationship]*, *[name of child]*, a minor.

4. Plaintiff states that it is in the best interest of *[name of child]* to have visitation with the Plaintiff, the facts of which will be more fully shown at the trial of this cause.

WHEREFORE, Plaintiff prays pursuant to RC 3109.11 that she may be granted reasonable companionship and visitation rights with *[child]*.

Respectfully submitted,

_____

Attorney for Plaintiff

NOTES TO FORM

Drafter's Notes

This Complaint must be served like any other Complaint under the Civil Rules.

§ 18:31 Visitation provisions—Child of unmarried mother— Venue note

Jurisdiction of the juvenile court to grant visitation rights to grandparents is statutory and requires strict adherence to the statute. Even though parentage and a concomitant child support order is properly established in one county, the juvenile court that issued that order does not have jurisdiction to hear a later request for establishment of grandparent visitation, under RC 3109.12, where the minor child no longer resides in that county.[1]

§ 18:32   Visitation provisions—Child of unmarried mother—Complaint for visitation—Form⊚

[Title of Juvenile Court]

[Name of Relative]	)	
[Address]	)	
Plaintiff	)	Case No._____
-vs-	)	
[Name of Mother]	)	
[Address],	)	
and	)	
[Name of Father],	)	
[Address]	)	
and	)	
[Name of Child], a	)	
minor		
by his next friend	)	
[Name of Mother],	)	
Defendants.		

COMPLAINT TO ESTABLISH COMPANIONSHIP OR VISITATION

1. *[Name of plaintiff-relative]* states that she is the *[type of relationship]* of *[name of child]*, a minor child who was born to *[name of father and relationship to plaintiff, if any]* and the Defendant *[name of mother and relationship to plaintiff, if any]*, on or about *[date]*.

2. Plaintiff states that *[name of father]* acknowledged parentage of this child and the acknowledgment has become final pursuant to affidavit filed in Putative Father Registry on file at the Bureau of Vital Statistics Number 3100015 *[or parentage was determined pursuant to RC Chapter 3111 in case number of the [name of court] Court/ or through the child support enforcement agency in administrative case number [case number].]*

3. Plaintiff states that it is in the best interest of *[name of child]* to have visitation with the Plaintiff, the facts of which will more be fully shown at the trial of this cause.

WHEREFORE, Plaintiff prays, pursuant to RC 3109.12, that she be granted regular companionship or visitation with *[name of child]*.

[Section 18:31]

[1]Borkosky v. Mihailoff, 132 Ohio App. 3d 508, 725 N.E.2d 694 (3d Dist. Wyandot County 1999).

Respectfully submitted,

_____

Attorney for Plaintiff

NOTES TO FORM

Drafter's Notes

This Complaint must be served like any other Complaint on both parents under the Civil Rules.

This Complaint reflects the amendments enacted by 1997 H.B. 352 effective January 1, 1998 and S.B. 180 effective March 21, 2001. Probate court acknowledgments prior to that date were accomplished under former RC 2105.18.

Chapter 19

Child Support

*by Judge Diane M. Palos**

---

*The author gratefully acknowledges the assistance of Daniel M. Newman, bailiff/staff attorney with the Court of Common Pleas of Cuyahoga County, Domestic Relations Division.

KeyCite®: Cases and other legal materials listed in KeyCite Scope can be researched through the KeyCite service on Westlaw®. Use KeyCite to check citations for form, parallel references, prior and later history, and comprehensive citator information, including citations to other decisions and secondary materials.

---

§ 19:1 Introduction

◆ **Note:** See Text Ch 13, Spousal support, for forms involving support.

All child support orders shall comply with Chapter 3119 of the Revised Code.[1] The federal government has mandated that all states have child support guidelines and that the figure reached pursuant to those guidelines be a rebuttable presumption, which can only be rebutted by a finding that the amount is unjust and inappropriate and not in the child's best interest.[2]

The basic child support schedule required to compute child support in Ohio is found at RC 3119.021. The child support worksheet for sole residential parenting and shared parenting is found at RC 3119.022 and RC 3119.023. The use of the schedule and accompanying worksheet is mandatory.[3] However, a trial court has discretion to deviate from the worksheet pursuant to RC 3119.23.

The standard of review in child support matters is abuse of discretion, which, if met, implies the court's attitude is unreasonable, arbitrary, or unconscionable.[4] In all child support proceedings, the court or CSEA shall determine the person or persons responsible for the health care for the children subject to the child support order; provisions for the health care shall be included in the order.[5] Failure to

---

[Section 19:1]

[1] A significant portion of this statute represents a re-codification of the child support statute found at RC 3113.215 prior to 3-22-2001. Some paragraphs and sentences from the repealed RC 3113.215 were also re-codified in Chapters 3121, 3123, and 3125.

[2] RC 3119.03.

[3] Marker v. Grimm, 65 Ohio St. 3d 139, 601 N.E.2d 496 (1992).

[4] Booth v. Booth, 44 Ohio St. 3d 142, 541 N.E.2d 1028 (1989); Blakemore v. Blakemore, 5 Ohio St. 3d 217, 450 N.E.2d 1140 (1983); Wogoman v. Wogoman, 44 Ohio App. 3d 34, 541 N.E.2d 128 (2d Dist. Miami County 1989).

[5] RC 3119.30, RC 3119.38.

issue a health insurance order renders a child support order incomplete, and thus, not a final appealable order.[6]

Whenever a court issues a child support order, a specific visitation schedule shall be included.[7]

§ 19:2 Jurisdiction over child support

Jurisdiction to award child support is conferred to the common pleas court and/or the division of domestic relations court and/or the juvenile court pursuant to several statutes.[1] Continuing jurisdiction is invoked by filing a motion pursuant to Civil Rules 4-4.6. In both the establishment and modification of child support, due process requires that a defending party receive adequate notice of the motion and an opportunity to present evidence in opposition to the motion.[2]

In any proceeding for divorce, dissolution of marriage, legal separation or child support, a common pleas court or domestic relations court may order either or both parents to support or help support their children.[3] If a child is born prior to a marriage, but the parents marry and no juvenile court support or custody order has been issued then the domestic relations court has jurisdiction over the child support at the divorce of the parents.[4]

The parent, guardian, legal custodian of a child, the person with whom a child resides, or the child support agency of the county in which the child, parent, guardian or legal custodian resides, may bring an action in juvenile court or other court with jurisdiction to issue a child support order, all without regard to the marital status of the child's parents.[5] Even if the parents are divorced, if a dependency action is initiated in juvenile court and a third party is granted custody, then child support jurisdiction resides in the juvenile court.[6]

If the domestic relations court exercises its jurisdiction under RC

---

[6]Rahawangi v. Alsamman, 2003-Ohio-3672, 2003 WL 21555173 (Ohio Ct. App. 8th Dist. Cuyahoga County 2003).

[7]RC 3119.08.

[Section 19:2]

[1]RC 2151.23, RC 2151.231 (juvenile court jurisdiction), RC 3103.03, RC 3103.031 (parent's child support obligations), RC 3105.21 (care of dependent children), RC 3109.05 (child support), RC 3113.13(E) (paternity), RC 3113.3l(K)(1) (domestic violence), RC 3115.31 (UIFSA).

[2]Bellamy v. Bellamy, 110 Ohio App. 3d 576, 674 N.E.2d 1227 (6th Dist. Erie County 1996); Carr v. Carr, 1999 WL 598837 (Ohio Ct. App. 9th Dist. Medina County 1999); Hannas v. Hannas, 123 Ohio App. 3d 378, 704 N.E.2d 294 (11th Dist. Trumbull County 1997); Rodriguez v. Rodriguez, 2001 WL 458674 (Ohio Ct. App. 9th Dist. Lorain County 2001).

[3]RC 3109.05(A).

[4]In re Staats, 2007-Ohio-111, 2007 WL 92376 (Ohio Ct. App. 3d Dist. Allen County 2007).

[5]RC 2151.231, RC 3111.78.

[6]Pyle v. Pyle, 2007-Ohio-110, 2007 WL 92377 (Ohio Ct. App. 3d Dist. Allen County 2007).

3109.06 to certify a matter to juvenile court, then after that certification, the juvenile court has permanent, exclusive jurisdiction over all issues, including support.[7]

In addition, the parent, guardian, legal custodian of a child, the person with whom a child resides, or the child support agency of the county in which the child, parent, guardian or legal custodian resides, may request that the child support enforcement agency issue an administrative order for child support.[8]

The court has jurisdiction to order child support to continue through age 18, and the completion of high school, but not later than age 19.[9] Therefore, it is inappropriate for the court to create a college education fund. There have been, however, high-income cases involving professional athletes where a savings fund was ordered by the court due to the finite nature of the income stream.[10]

The domestic relations court retains jurisdiction over funds designated as prepaid child support in a decedent's estate and has the authority to order a lump sum judgment; whereas, the probate court must examine the needs of the child in determining whether to disburse those funds.[11]

In paternity cases pursuant to RC 3111.05 and RC 3111.06 a parent or child may bring a paternity action up to 5 years after the child has reached the age of majority. The Supreme Court of Ohio ruled in *Carnes v. Kemp*,[12] that when such a paternity action is brought by an adult child before he or she reaches age 23, he or she may seek to establish retroactive child support. The decision resolved the split among the appellate districts finding that a juvenile court has subject matter jurisdiction based on a reading *in pari materia* of RC 3111.05 and RC 3111.13(C).

The child support enforcement agency has authority to periodically review child support orders.[13] In addition, the obligor or the obligee may request an administrative hearing at the child support enforcement agency.[14] Absent a request for review of the child support enforcement agency's recommendation or after the review, the agency

---

[7]RC 3109.051(M); McDaniel v. McDaniel, 2007-Ohio-4220, 2007 WL 2350124 (Ohio Ct. App. 12th Dist. Warren County 2007).

[8]RC 3119.20(C).

[9]RC 3103.03, RC 3119.86; see Text § 19:4, Support obligations-Duration; § 19:22, Termination of support obligation-Support past age eighteen, Text § 19:23, Termination of support obligation-Emancipation.

[10]Douglas v. Douglas, 2003-Ohio-2518, 2003 WL 21125427 (Ohio Ct. App. 2d Dist. Greene County 2003); Carr v. Blake, 2000 WL 192138 (Ohio Ct. App. 1st Dist. Hamilton County 2000).

[11]In re Guardianship of Derakhshan, 110 Ohio App. 3d 190, 673 N.E.2d 954 (11th Dist. Lake County 1996).

[12]Carnes v. Kemp, 104 Ohio St. 3d 629, 2004-Ohio-7107, 821 N.E.2d 180 (2004).

[13]RC 3119.60.

[14]RC 3119.61, RC 3119.63.

will submit its recommendation to the trial court with jurisdiction for inclusion in an order.[15] The obligor or the obligee then has an opportunity to request a court hearing on the modification.[16] Any order resulting from an administrative review shall relate back to the first day of the month following the "date certain" on which the review commenced.[17] When a trial court hears the administrative appeal, it is not limited by the issues raised by the parties at the CSEA hearing.[18] The hearing is a *de novo* review, but the order will relate back to the commencement date of the agency modification unless there is evidence to the contrary.[19] A motion to modify parenting does not supersede or divest the CSEA of its jurisdiction in an administrative modification.[20]

The child support enforcement agency has authority to investigate upon notice whether a child is emancipated.[21] Upon administrative review, the parties may request a court hearing to determine whether the support should be terminated.[22] However, a trial court cannot order a CSEA to perform child support calculations.[23]

§ 19:3 Support obligations—In general

The parental duty of support shall be assumed by the following[1]:

(1) A biological parent of a child;

(2) A man determined to be the natural father of the child under RC 3111.01 to RC 3111.19 or RC 3111.20 to 3111.29;

(3) An adoptive parent pursuant to Chapter 3107[2]; or

(4) A parent who signed acknowledgment of paternity which has become final under RC 2151.232, RC 3111.82, or RC 3111.64.

---

[15]RC 3119.61, RC 3119.63.

[16]RC 3119.63, RC 3119.64, RC 3119.66.

[17]RC 3119.71.

[18]Kerbyson v. Kerbyson, 2004-Ohio-3607, 2004 WL 1518612 (Ohio Ct. App. 4th Dist. Washington County 2004); Horvath v. Horvath, 2004-Ohio-6764, 2004 WL 2892372 (Ohio Ct. App. 5th Dist. Stark County 2004) (the trial court shall determine the tax exemption when the issue of child support has been raised in an administrative appeal even where the party requesting the review has withdrawn his request).

[19]RC 3119.71

[20]Cruz v. Kerr, 2009-Ohio-2187, 2009 WL 1272413 (Ohio Ct. App. 9th Dist. Lorain County 2009).

[21]RC 3119.87, RC 3119.89.

[22]RC 3119.92.

[23]In re Hallmon, 2008-Ohio-5454, 2008 WL 4650738 (Ohio Ct. App. 5th Dist. Guernsey County 2008).

[Section 19:3]

[1]RC 3103.031.

[2]Hudgins v. Mitchell, 128 Ohio App. 3d 403, 715 N.E.2d 213 (9th Dist. Summit County 1998) (adoption does not extinguish parent's pre-adoption obligations).

§ 19:4 Support obligations—Duration

The parental duty of support commences upon the birth of the child.[1] However, where the parents are married, the law assumes. that the parents are providing for that support. Therefore, a domestic relations court does not have jurisdiction to award support retroactively prior to a filing date for divorce. In a paternity action, pursuant to RC 3111.13(F), if a parent has failed to previously support a child, child support can be awarded prior to the filing of the action unless the child is over three years of age and the alleged father did not know and had no reason to know of the child's existence. Additionally, birthing expenses can be ordered.[2]

The parental duty of support to the child shall continue beyond the age of majority so long as the child continuously attends on a full-time basis any recognized and accredited high school, or a court-issued child support order provides that the duty of support continues beyond the age of majority. However, except in cases in which the child support order requires the duty of support to continue for any period after the child reaches age nineteen, the order shall not remain in effect after the child reaches age nineteen.[3] That duty of support shall continue during seasonal vacation periods.[4] The Supreme Court of Ohio in *Hoelscher v. Hoelscher*[5] held that support shall continue beyond the age of majority so long as a child continues to attend a recognized and accredited high school on a full-time basis, notwithstanding a provision in the parents' separation agreement to the contrary. This ruling occurred a few months after the effective date of RC 3119.86(C), March 22, 2001, which provided that if a court incorporates a separation agreement into a judgment entry of divorce, legal separation, or dissolution of marriage, the court may not require the duty of support to continue beyond the date the child's parents have agreed support should terminate. Reading the case law and the statute together, the parents may contract to extend support beyond the child's eighteenth birthday and graduation from high school, but may not contract to terminate child support prior to the child's high school graduation, even if that occurs after age eighteen. In the absence of a contract to continue support beyond the high school graduation, child support will terminate upon the child's nineteenth birthday even if the child continues to be enrolled in high school.

[Section 19:4]

[1]Brightwell v. White, 1999 WL 1127392 (Ohio Ct. App. 2d Dist. Montgomery County 1999).

[2]RC 3111.13(C).

[3]RC 3103.03, notwithstanding RC 3101.01.

[4]RC 3119.86.

[5]Hoelscher v. Hoelscher, 91 Ohio St. 3d 500, 2001-Ohio-103, 747 N.E.2d 227 (2001).

§ 19:5   Support obligations—Disabled child

In the case of mentally or physically disabled children, the duty to provide support may continue beyond the age of majority if the children are unable to support themselves.[1] However, the duty of support to a mentally or physically disabled child does not extend to a child who is capable of becoming self-supporting and who holds a part time job, unless that child is not self-sufficient.[2] On the other hand, the court may terminate child support, but retain jurisdiction to modify child support if the adult child receives government benefits due to the disability since the government benefits are unstable.[3] The continuing exercise of jurisdiction by a domestic relations court may preclude the exercise of jurisdiction in a guardianship action by a probate court for an adult disabled child.[4]

Castle v. Castle[5] is a Supreme Court of Ohio case that imposes a continuing duty of support on parents beyond the age of majority, if the children are unable to support themselves because of mental or physical disabilities that existed before attaining the age of majority. A trial court must make a factual determination that a child who is disabled is unable to support himself/herself before extending the obligation of support beyond the age of majority.[6] A trial court may award on-going child support in a divorce for a child disabled under the definition in *Castle*, although the child is over age eighteen at the time of the divorce, because said child has not and will not reach "the

---

[Section 19:5]

[1]RC 3119.86(A)(l)(a); Castle v. Castle, 15 Ohio St. 3d 279, 473 N.E.2d 803 (1984); Yost v. Yost, 2003-Ohio-3754, 2003 WL 21652172 (Ohio Ct. App. 4th Dist. Scioto County 2003); Wiest v. Wiest, 2000 WL 262665 (Ohio Ct. App. 2d Dist. Darke County 2000); Valley v. Armstrong, 1999 WL 803561 (Ohio Ct. App. 7th Dist. Mahoning County 1999); Bowermeister v. Shanks, 1999 WL 252394 (Ohio Ct. App. 2d Dist. Greene County 1999); Abbas v. Abbas, 128 Ohio App. 3d 513, 715 N.E.2d 613 (7th Dist. Mahoning County 1998).

[2]Cooksey v. Cooksey, 55 Ohio App. 3d 135, 562 N.E.2d 934 (6th Dist. Erie County 1988); Traxler v. Traxler, 2003-Ohio-7270, 2003 WL 7270 (Ohio Ct. App. 6th Dist. Williams County 2003); Blacker v. Blacker, 2004-Ohio-2193, 2004 WL 917462 (Ohio Ct. App. 2d Dist. Montgomery County 2004). See also Ulery v. Ulery, 86 Ohio App. 3d 290, 620 N.E.2d 933 (9th Dist. Summit County 1993); Greene v. Greene, 1997 WL 679906 (Ohio Ct. App. 9th Dist. Summit County 1997); Palmer v. Palmer, 1999 WL 22747 (Ohio Ct. App. 2d Dist. Montgomery County 1999) (emotional and behavioral problems do not rise to the level of disability).

[3]Oatey v. Oatey, 1996 WL 200273 (Ohio Ct. App. 8th Dist. Cuyahoga County 1996).

[4]In re Campbell, 2006-Ohio-1764, 2006 WL 890999 (Ohio Ct. App. 7th Dist. Mahoning County 2006).

[5]Castle v. Castle, 15 Ohio St. 3d 279, 473 N.E.2d 803 (1984).

[6]Arthurs v. Arthurs, 2000 WL 1133268 (Ohio Ct. App. 5th Dist. Tuscarawas County 2000).

age of majority" by being self-sufficient or self-sustaining at any fore-seeable point.[7]

There is no equal protection issue involved in extending the award of child support for a disabled child who is not emancipated due to a disability. The statutory and common law duty meets the rational basis test and satisfies the equal protection clause.[8]

§ 19:6   Terminology used in calculating child support

The majority of the definitions for child support terms are located in RC 3119.01.[1]

"Income" is defined as the gross income of an employed parent, or the sum of the gross income and the potential income of the parent when unemployed or underemployed.[2]

"Gross Income" is earned and unearned income,[3] whether taxable or not, and includes income from salaries, wages, overtime pay, bonuses, commissions, royalties, tips, rents, dividends, severance pay,[4] pensions, interest, trust income, annuities, Social Security benefits including retirement, disability, and survivor benefits that are not means tested, workers compensation, disability insurance benefits, non-means tested veterans benefits for any service connected disability,[5] spousal support actually received, and all other sources of income.[6] The statute also lists potential cash flow as another source of gross income.

Potential cash flow is easily confused with potential income as used in the section on imputing income for unemployed and underemployed individuals. An individual does not need to be unemployed or

---

[7]Wiczynski v. Wiczynski, 2006-Ohio-867, 2006 WL 456762 (Ohio Ct. App. 6th Dist. Lucas County 2006).

[8]Bailey v. O'Hare, 2006-Ohio-239, 2006 WL 164917 (Ohio Ct. App. 2d Dist. Montgomery County 2006).

[Section 19:6]

[1]Formerly RC 3113.315(A)(1).

[2]RC 3119.0l(C)(5).

[3]Howell v. Howell, 167 Ohio App. 3d 431, 2006-Ohio-3038, 855 N.E.2d 533 (2d Dist. Clark County 2006) (unearned income includes potential income from sources included in the statutory definition of income such as trust income and interest).

[4]Kerbyson v. Kerbyson, 2004-Ohio-3607, 2004 WL 1518612 (Ohio Ct. App. 4th Dist. Washington County 2004) (severance pay is includable pursuant to the statute by definition and the inclusion is not circumvented by fact that severance pay is nonrecurring by its nature).

[5]Avery v. Avery, 2002-Ohio-1188, 2002 WL 360296 (Ohio Ct. App. 2d Dist. Greene County 2002) (VA disability which is offset against military pension is still received by the obligor and is therefore income).

[6]Bailey v. McCarley, 2004-Ohio-525, 2004 WL 231512, (Ohio Ct. App. 11th Dist. Portage County 2004) (bonus points which are earned by an employee, then redeemed for merchandise, airfare or gift certificates, are income); Streza v. Streza, 2006-Ohio-1315, 2006 WL 709056 (Ohio Ct. App. 9th Dist. Lorain County 2006) (per diems are income for the purpose of child support).

underemployed for potential cash flow to be determined,[7] nor does the potential cash flow need to come only from a non-income producing asset.[8] Potential cash flow would be income that is available to a parent, but which they are not necessarily receiving.[9] The intent of this statutory language is to attempt to prevent a parent from avoiding the payment of child support by shifting income or assets to non-income producing assets.[10] The projected investment account earnings from an inheritance are potential cash flow for child support purposes.[11] Rental property that has been left vacant is an example of property that would be identified as having potential cash flow for the purpose of child support.[12] The interest income potentially generated from personal injury settlement proceeds should be treated as potential cash flow.[13] Stock options available to an employee may be included in income.[14] Monies, paid into an annuity for retirement or hardship, are also gross income.[15]

For members of the armed forces "Gross Income" includes base pay, basic allowance for quarters, basic allowance for subsistence, supplemental subsistence allowance, cost of living adjustment, specialty pay, variable housing allowance, and pay for training or other types of drills.[16]

"Overtime," "bonuses" and "commissions" earned over the last three years are entered on line (1)(b) of the mandated child support worksheet. The figure used for calculation is the lesser of the three-year average or the amount received during the year immediately preceding the year in question.[17] Common sense dictates that averaging occur only where there has been or will continue to be additional income from overtime, commissions or bonuses. For example, if a par-

---

[7]In re Kohlhorst, 2006-Ohio-6481, 2006 WL 3544738 (Ohio Ct. App. 3d Dist. Auglaize County 2006).

[8]Musci v. Musci, 2006-Ohio-5882, 2006 WL 3208558 (Ohio Ct. App. 9th Dist. Summit County 2006).

[9]Wolf v. Wolf, 2009-Ohio-1845, 2009 WL 1040079 (Ohio Ct. App. 12th Dist. Warren County 2009) (the payment of personal taxes by the obligor's corporation is potential cash flow and therefore income for child support purposes).

[10]Howell v. Howell, 167 Ohio App. 3d 431, 2006-Ohio-3038, 855 N.E.2d 533 (2d Dist. Clark County 2006).

[11]Howell v. Howell, 167 Ohio App. 3d 431, 2006-Ohio-3038, 855 N.E.2d 533 (2d Dist. Clark County 2006).

[12]Bishop v. Bishop, 2004-Ohio-4643, 2004 WL 1945637, (Ohio Ct. App. 4th Dist. Scioto County 2004).

[13]Smart v. Smart, 2008-Ohio-1996, 2008 WL 1849631, (Ohio Ct. App. 3d Dist. Shelby County 2008).

[14]Murray v. Murray, 128 Ohio App. 3d 662, 716 N.E.2d 288 (12th Dist. Warren County 1999); Geschke v. Geschke, 2002-Ohio-5426, 2002 WL 31255752 (Ohio Ct. App. 9th Dist. Medina County 2002).

[15]Maio v. Maio, No. 2000-L-073 (Ohio Ct. App. 11th Dist. 2001).

[16]RC 3119.0l(C)(7).

[17]RC 3119.05(D). Peacock v. Peacock, 2000 WL 145168 (Ohio Ct. App. 6th Dist. Erie County 2000). For a comprehensive overview of the handling of unpredictable

ent has recently begun employment that includes commissions, those commissions should not be averaged where the parent previously did not receive commissions;[18] or, if a parent changes employment so that he or she no longer has overtime, the overtime from the previous year's employment should not be averaged and included.[19] Additionally, the court has discretion in the following circumstances: where an obligor fails to provide the breakdown between overtime and base salary, a trial court does not err in averaging the total;[20] or where an obligor testified he may not be able to continue his previous pattern of overtime, the court does not need to reduce his overtime income when he has worked that level of overtime for many years and does not have significant health issues which would preclude the continuation of that pattern.[21] A onetime payment, such as a signing bonus or an incentive payment, are nonrecurring income; as nonrecurring income, these sums are not to be included in the parent's income and are not the type of bonus contemplated by this definition of income.[22]

"Gross Income" also includes self-generated income.[23]

"Self-generated income" means gross receipts received from self-employment, proprietorship of a business, partnership, or closely held corporation, and rents, minus ordinary and necessary business expenses.[24] It also includes reimbursed expenses and in-kind contributions such as a car or car lease, insurance, gas, free housing, reimbursed trips and meals, country club membership, sports season tickets, and other benefits if the reimbursements are significant and

---

income, see Patrice R.T. Yarham, *Averaging Unpredictable Income Under RC 3113.215(B)(5)(h)*, 11 DRJO 38 (May/June 1999).

[18]Walker v. Walker, 2002-Ohio-5293, 2002 WL 31185919 (Ohio Ct. App. 5th Dist. Delaware County 2002).

[19]Thomas v. Thomas, 2004-Ohio-1034, 2004 WL 413657 (Ohio Ct. App. 6th Dist. Lucas County 2004).

[20]Gdula v. Gdula, 2001-Ohio-3329, 2001 WL 911600 (Ohio Ct. App. 7th Dist. Belmont County 2001).

[21]Zornes v. Zornes, 2006-Ohio-877, 2006 WL 456814 (Ohio Ct. App. 12th Dist. Clermont County 2006).

[22]Walker v. Walker, 2002-Ohio-5293, 2002 WL 31185919 (Ohio Ct. App. 5th Dist. Delaware County 2002).

[23]Riepenhoff v. Riepenhoff, 64 Ohio App. 3d 135, 580 N.E.2d 846 (4th Dist. Jackson County 1990) (retained earnings in a closely held corporation are not included in gross income for calculation of child support schedules); McQuinn v. McQuinn, 110 Ohio App. 3d 296, 673 N.E.2d 1384 (12th Dist. Butler County 1996) (income from QDRO received by alternate-payee obligor-spouse from obligee's pension is to be included under the guidelines); Smith v. Smith, 1998 WL 833815 (Ohio Ct. App. 2d Dist. Champaign County 1998) (substantial capital gain on real estate may be a nonrecurring and unsustainable cash flow item); Howell v. Howell, 167 Ohio App. 3d 431, 2006-Ohio-3038, 855 N.E.2d 533 (2d Dist. Clark County 2006) (unearned income includes potential income from sources included in the statutory definition of income such as trust income and interest).

[24]RC 3119.01(C)(13).

reduce personal living expenses.[25] However, it is not appropriate to add back employment related benefits as income to a parent who is not self-employed.[26]

Self-generated income is often not verified or verifiable. The trial court is forced to use the concept of potential or actual cash flow to determine income for self-employed individuals.[27]

Self-employment income earned over a period of years should be averaged where historically the obligor and his partners earned bonuses, but where after his purchase of 100% ownership of the corporation, the obligor continued to pay his former partners bonuses but stopped paying himself bonuses while the company had $172,612 in excess cash flow.[28] Additionally, a trial court erred in using only a two year average when the parent earned substantially less income in one of those years than in the previous years and in the current year.[29] A trial court does not abuse its discretion by using tax-reported income rather than earned income of the obligor which would be reported in the next tax year when actually received.[30] In determining income for child support, it is error to solely rely on the corporate income tax returns for an S-Corporation.[31] It would also be an error to disregard a self employed wage earner's gross receipts as non-recurring income or to average them where the income is earned in the last quarter of one year, but not received until the first quarter of the next year.[32]

Retained earnings from a sub-chapter S corporation may be included as income. The test is how much control that shareholder-parent has over the corporation. A majority shareholder has significant control to hide income or to release funds, whereas a minority shareholder does not.[33] The same test should be used for "phantom income" for a self-employed individual; where the individual has control and, therefore,

---

[25]Zeefe v. Zeefe, 125 Ohio App. 3d 600, 709 N.E.2d 208 (8th Dist. Cuyahoga County 1998).

[26]Spier v. Spier, 2006-Ohio-1289, 2006 WL 696093 (Ohio Ct. App. 7th Dist. Mahoning County 2006).

[27]In re Kohlhorst, 2006-Ohio-6481, 2006 WL 3544738 (Ohio Ct. App. 3d Dist. Auglaize County 2006).

[28]Wright v. Wright, 2009-Ohio-128, 2009 WL 94758 (Ohio Ct. App. 8th Dist. Cuyahoga County 2009).

[29]Worch v. Worch, 2000 WL 376643 (Ohio Ct. App. 2d Dist. Darke County 2000).

[30]Frahlich v. Frahlich-Lerch, 2000 WL 1197022 (Ohio Ct. App. 9th Dist. Summit County 2000).

[31]Offenberg v. Offenberg, 2003-Ohio-269, 2003 WL 152814 (Ohio Ct. App. 8th Dist. Cuyahoga County 2003).

[32]State ex rel. Athens Cty. Child Support Enforcement Agency v. Patel, 2006-Ohio-2951, 2006 WL 1613407 (Ohio Ct. App. 4th Dist. Athens County 2006).

[33]Willman v. Cole, 2001-Ohio-2484, 2001 WL 674191 (Ohio Ct. App. 4th Dist. Adams County 2001); accord, Riepenhoff v. Riepenhoff, 64 Ohio App. 3d 135, 580 N.E.2d 846 (4th Dist. Jackson County 1990); In re Sullivan, 167 Ohio App. 3d 458, 2006-Ohio-3206, 855 N.E.2d 554 (11th Dist. Geauga County 2006).

an ability to manipulate income, said income is properly included for child support purposes.[34]

"Gross Income" does not include benefits from means-tested government administrated programs such as Ohio Works First, prevention, retention and contingency, means tested veteran benefits, Supplemental Security Income,[35] food stamps, disability assistance, or other assistance that is determined on the basis of income or assets. However, the refund a parent receives from the Earned Income Credit (EIC) is distinguishable from other means-tested public assistance programs and therefore can be included in income when calculating child support.[36]

"Gross Income" does not include service-connected benefits under a program that has not been distributed to a veteran who is a beneficiary of benefits that are in the possession of the U.S. Department of Veterans Affairs. "Gross Income" does not include child support received for children who are not born or adopted during the marriage, mandatory deductions for wages such as union dues, but not taxes, Social Security, or retirement in lieu of Social Security. Further, "gross income" does not include adoption and foster care payments per Title IV-E of the "Social Security Act" 94 Stat. 501, 42 U.S.C. 670 (1980), as amended, nor does it include nonrecurring[37] or unsustainable income or cash flow items.

"Nonrecurring or unsustainable income or cash flow" means an item not expected to be received on a regular basis or for fewer than three years. The generic language of "nonrecurring or unsustainable income or cash flow item,"[38] is not to be used to exclude a specifically defined category of gross income. Because the statute specifically includes severance pay in "gross income" the court must construe the specific enumeration as superseding the general language.[39] While capital gains are ordinarily a non-recurring financial event and thus not subject to inclusion in income for the determination of child support,

---

[34]Freeman v. Freeman, 2007-Ohio-6400, 2007 WL 4225425 (Ohio Ct. App. 9th Dist. Wayne County 2007).

[35]Morris v. Morris, 2003-Ohio-5598, 2003 WL 22390092 (Ohio Ct. App. 4th Dist. Meigs County 2003).

[36]Harbour v. Ridgeway, 2005-Ohio-2643, 2005 WL 1252551 (Ohio Ct. App. 10th Dist. Franklin County 2005).

[37]Cooper v. Cooper, 2004-Ohio-1368, 2004 WL 549784 (Ohio Ct. App. 12th Dist. Clermont County 2004); Watral v. Watral, 2005-Ohio-6917, 2005 WL 3537658 (Ohio Ct. App. 9th Dist. Medina County 2005) (lump sum payment for retroactive Social Security Disability payments is not income).

[38]McCoy v. McCoy, 105 Ohio App. 3d 651, 656, 664 N.E.2d 1012 (4th Dist. Meigs County 1995).

[39]McCoy v. McCoy, 105 Ohio App. 3d 651, 656, 664 N.E.2d 1012 (4th Dist. Meigs County 1995).

in the rare instance where a parent is in the business of buying and selling real estate, capital gains should be included in income.[40]

A rollover of a retirement account into an IRA is not income and cannot be included as income for a child support calculation.[41] A self-employed individual's pension contributions are includable as income for child support purposes; however, the portion that represents the employer's contribution should be excluded from income.[42]

"Ordinary and necessary expenses" means actual cash items spent[43] and includes depreciation expenses of business equipment,[44] but does not include other non-cash depreciation expenses that are allowed as deductions on federal tax returns. Only those expenses incurred in the same tax year as the depreciation may be deducted as ordinary and necessary business expenses.[45] It is not appropriate to allow deductions for ordinary and necessary business expenses for parents who are not self-employed.[46] A self-employed obligor's purchase of a shareholder interest in his company is not an ordinary and necessary business expense and the cost is includable in his income for calculating child support.[47] However, where the obligor's payments are for the purchase of a sole proprietorship, they are ordinary and necessary business expenses that should be deducted from income for the purpose of the child support calculation.[48]

---

[40]Conrad v. Conrad, 2007-Ohio-3186, 2007 WL 1806655 (Ohio Ct. App. 7th Dist. Mahoning County 2007).

[41]Rapp v. Rapp, 89 Ohio App. 3d 85, 623 N.E.2d 624 (12th Dist. Warren County 1993).

[42]Lyons v. Bachelder, 2005-Ohio-4966, 2005 WL 2300226 (Ohio Ct. App. 5th Dist. Morrow County 2005); Lyons v. Bachelder, 2005 WL 2266672 (Ohio Ct. App. 5th Dist. Morrow County 2005); Citta-Pietrolungo v. Pietrolungo, 2005-Ohio-4814, 2005 WL 2240953 (Ohio Ct. App. 8th Dist. Cuyahoga County 2005).

[43]Buening v. Buening, 2008-Ohio-6579, 2008 WL 5205674 (Ohio Ct. App. 3d Dist. Mercer County 2008).

[44]RC 3119.01. The changes to the statute commencing 3-22-01 deleted the word "replacement" as an adjective to equipment. There have been two substantive changes to this section of the revised code since its inception: note which version of the statute is interpreted when reviewing the case law. Kamm v. Kamm, 67 Ohio St. 3d 174, 1993-Ohio-60, 616 N.E.2d 900 (1993); Purvis v. Purvis, 2002-Ohio-570, 2002 WL 220067 (Ohio Ct. App. 4th Dist. Adams County 2002) (only the portion of the long term carry-over loss is actually deductible since the loss can be added back as income).

[45]Foster v. Foster, 150 Ohio App. 3d 298, 2002-Ohio-6390, 780 N.E.2d 1041 (12th Dist. Butler County 2002).

[46]Streza v. Streza, 2006-Ohio-1315, 2006 WL 709056 (Ohio Ct. App. 9th Dist. Lorain County 2006).

[47]Citta-Pietrolungo v. Pietrolungo, 2005-Ohio-4814, 2005 WL 2240953 (Ohio Ct. App. 8th Dist. Cuyahoga County 2005).

[48]Weisgerber v. Weisgerber, 2006-Ohio-5628, 2006 WL 3041939 (Ohio Ct. App. 5th Dist. Delaware County 2006).

In some cases, payments of principal on business loans are held to be ordinary and necessary business expenses.[49] In other cases these expenses were added back to the parent's income.[50]

Litigation on these issues tends to be very fact-specific. In *Higgins v. Danvers*,[51] for example, the majority of the court of appeals affirmed the trial court's judgment that, for purposes of computing child support, the husband's gross income should not be reduced by his obligation to acquire a partnership interest in the firm for which he worked. A dissenting opinion argued that the acquisition of a capital asset, though not an ordinary and necessary business expenses, was authorized by the Supreme Court ruling in *Kamm v. Kamm*.[52] The dissent argued that it was in the best interest of the child to allow such a deduction, as the acquisition of the asset generated future income.

Partnership income from separate property used to pay a bankruptcy debt is still income. Repaying oneself for cash previously "borrowed" from a subchapter S Corporation also constitutes income.[53] The value of rent-free housing may be included as income.[54] Subchapter S corporate earnings, depreciation expenses and deductions for meals, entertainment, mileage and parking may be added back to determine gross income.[55] A fully employed wage earner is entitled to a reduction in his gross income when calculating child support for the losses incurred in farm operations deemed by the trial court to be a business rather than a hobby.[56]

However, where a parent who is employed full-time as security system installer had a boat storage "endeavor" which had lost increasing amounts of money each year, the parent is not entitled to a deduction against income for the purposes of the calculation of child

---

[49]See, e.g., DeCapua v. DeCapua, 1992 WL 2917 (Ohio Ct. App. 9th Dist. Wayne County 1992); Woods v. Woods, 95 Ohio App. 3d 222, 642 N.E.2d 45 (3d Dist. Hancock County 1994) (self-employed truck driver's monthly loan payments toward purchase of rig are ordinary and necessary expenditures and deductible from gross income).

[50]See, e.g., Marovich v. Marovich, 1991 WL 268235 (Ohio Ct. App. 12th Dist. Clermont County 1991); Garabedian v. Garabedian, 1990 WL 179592 (Ohio Ct. App. 12th Dist. Butler County 1990); Hite v. Hite, 1990 WL 94636 (Ohio Ct. App. 5th Dist. Stark County 1990). See also Dillbeck, *Effect of Loan Principal Payments on Determination of Income for Support*, 6 Am. J. Fam. L. 2 (1992).

[51]Higgins v. Danvers, 1997 WL 691183 (Ohio Ct. App. 8th Dist. Cuyahoga County 1997); Carr v. Blake, 2000 WL 192138 (Ohio Ct. App. 1st Dist. Hamilton County 2000).

[52]Kamm v. Kamm, 67 Ohio St. 3d 174, 1993-Ohio-60, 616 N.E.2d 900 (1993).

[53]Nicholson v. Nicholson, 2001 WL 1167151 (Ohio Ct. App. 8th Dist. Cuyahoga County 2001).

[54]Green v. Green, 2002-Ohio-2180, 2002-Ohio-2180, 2002 WL 850980 (Ohio Ct. App. 12th Dist. Butler County 2002).

[55]Roblyn M. v. Robert C., 2001 WL 1439526 (Ohio Ct. App. 6th Dist. Wood County 2001).

[56]Beougher v. Beougher, 2000-Ohio-1727, 2000 WL 429900 (Ohio Ct. App. 3d Dist. Mercer County 2000).

support.[57] The determination of income and losses by the Internal Revenue Service is not dispositive in the determination of income in child support cases. Where a parent takes a deduction for loan repayments for the purchase of land which may not be in the ordinary course of business and which lump sum repayments are definitely not in the ordinary course of business, those deductions against income will not be allowed.[58] Deductions for travel expenses, childcare and contributions to a child's college fund are not allowable business deductions.[59]

"Personal earnings" is compensation paid or payable for personal services, however denominated, and includes wages, salary, commissions, bonuses, draws against compensation, profit sharing, vacation pay, or other compensation.

"Potential income" includes imputed income the parent would earn if fully employed and imputed income from any non-income producing assets of a parent, which may be determined from the local passbook savings rate or another appropriate rate not to exceed the statutory rate of interest.[60]

Courts are required to follow a two-step process in imputing income that a parent would earn if fully employed. First, there must be a finding that a parent is voluntarily unemployed or underemployed before income can be imputed.[61] Second, a parent's potential income must be determined by evaluating the parent's prior work experience, education, any physical or mental disabilities, prevailing job opportunities and salary levels in the area where the parent resides, special skills and training, evidence of ability to earn income, special needs of the parent's children, and any other relevant factor.[62]

The court need not find that a parent intends to thwart child support to find that the parent is voluntarily unemployed or

---

[57]Dressler v. Dressler, 2004-Ohio-2072, 2004 WL 877839 (Ohio Ct. App. 12th Dist. Warren County 2004).

[58]Tonti v. Tonti, 2004-Ohio-2529, 2004 WL 1109840 (Ohio Ct. App. 10th Dist. Franklin County 2004).

[59]Kendall v. Kendall, 2005-Ohio-1777, 2005 WL 859447 (Ohio Ct. App. 6th Dist. Ottawa County 2005).

[60]RC 3119.01(C)(11).

[61]Badovick v. Badovick, 128 Ohio App. 3d 18, 713 N.E.2d 1066 (8th Dist. Cuyahoga County 1998); In re Westendorf, 2003-Ohio-5955, 2003 WL 22519535 (Ohio Ct. App. 1st Dist. Hamilton County 2003).

[62]RC 3119 (C)(11)(a); Kiehborth v. Kiehborth, 169 Ohio App. 3d 308, 2006-Ohio-5529, 862 N.E.2d 863 (5th Dist. Delaware County 2006) (use of expert, previous experience and other professionals in the industry can be used to establish the factors for imputation of income). Note that prior to 3-22-2001, the statute provided only three factors to consider to determine potential income. Those were recent work history, occupational qualifications and prevailing opportunities and salaries in the community in which the parent resides.

underemployed.[63] The trial court need not use the highest figure available when imputing income so long as the two-part analysis is followed.

A parent who receives means-tested public assistance benefits shall not be deemed to be voluntarily unemployed or underemployed and no income shall be imputed to that parent. However, if a determination is made that not imputing income would be unjust, inappropriate, and not in the best interest of the child, then income may be imputed to that parent.[64]

"Imputed income" also arises from non-income producing assets as determined from the local passbook savings rate or another appropriate rate as determined by the court, but not exceeding the statutory interest rate of RC 1343.03.[65] A trial court can impute income based on potential income from sources such as interest or trust funds to a person who is fully employed.[66] This does not involve the two-part test for voluntary underemployment or unemployment; therefore, those

---

[63]Rock v. Cabral, 67 Ohio St. 3d 108, 616 N.E.2d 218 (1993). See, Slivka v. Slivka, 1996 WL 100854 (Ohio Ct. App. 8th Dist. Cuyahoga County 1996) (imputation upheld where obligor resigned two weeks before support hearing and court had testimony from union officials as to hourly rate in community); Franke v. Franke, 1996 WL 230570 (Ohio Ct. App. 4th Dist. Highland County 1996) (the trial court did not abuse discretion in not imputing teaching income where there was no testimony regarding what positions were available). Bowlin v. Steele, 2000 WL 146581 (Ohio Ct. App. 12th Dist. Butler County 2000) (trial court did not err in imputing income to father based upon employment he voluntarily left, the father's testimony regarding his previous employment evidence of prevailing opportunities and wages in the community); English v. Rubino, 1996 WL 157342 (Ohio Ct. App. 8th Dist. Cuyahoga County 1996) (imputation of $36,000 per year as an attorney was error where record did not show he failed to seek work as attorney); Marsh v. Marsh, 105 Ohio App. 3d 747, 664 N.E.2d 1353 (3d Dist. Allen County 1995) (income earned by obligor in Saudi Arabia not commensurate with Allen County job opportunities); Hardman v. Hardman, 166 Ohio App. 3d 479, 2006-Ohio-1793, 851 N.E.2d 523 (11th Dist. Trumbull County 2006) (evidence that the obligor was terminated with other like employees and given a severance package supports his involuntary termination and is not outweighed by evidence of poor performance problems on the job a year before); Crookston v. Vanhorn, 2005-Ohio-4081, 2005 WL 1875798 (Ohio Ct. App. 9th Dist. Summit County 2005) (threats to reduce income at an administrative hearing followed by termination of the obligor's employment indicates a voluntary underemployment).

[64]RC 3119.05(I).

[65]RC 3119.01; Schwertner v. Petronzio, 1996 WL 200595 (Ohio Ct. App. 11th Dist. Geauga County 1996) (use of six-month treasury bill yield on obligor's net worth, excluding personal residence, was accurate representation of actual income, thus did not require finding of voluntary unemployment or underemployment).

[66]RC 3119.0l(C)(7). Myers v. Myers, 2006-Ohio-5360, 2006 WL 2925353 (Ohio Ct. App. 6th Dist. Wood County 2006) (withdrawals from a special needs trust for mother are income). But see Styer v. Styer, 2006-Ohio-606, 2006 WL 319248 (Ohio Ct. App. 3d Dist. Hardin County 2006) (proceeds from spend thrift trust are not attachable).

findings are unnecessary since there is no allegation of unemployment or underemployment.[67]

§ 19:7   Child support schedules

In any action in which a child support order is issued or modified, the court shall calculate, on the mandated worksheet, the child support obligation in accordance with the basic child support schedule.[1] It is reversible error to fail to include a completed worksheet as part of the trial court's record. The child support worksheets at RC 3119.022 and RC 3119.023 contain signature lines for the preparer and for the parents, if they have reviewed and agreed to the worksheet. The child support schedules are rebuttably presumed[2] to be the correct amount of child support unless both of the following apply:

(1) The court, after considering the factors and criteria as set forth in RC 3119.23 and RC 3119.24, which are the reasons to deviate, determines that the amount of child support calculated pursuant to the schedules would be unjust, inappropriate, and would not be in the best interest of the child; and,

(2) The court enters in the order the amount of child support calculated pursuant to the basic child support schedule, and then issues findings of fact to support the determination that the amount would be unjust, inappropriate, and would not be in the best interest of the child.

Any deviation by the court from the worksheet amount must be entered by the court in its journal and must include findings of fact to support the determination.

§ 19:8   Medical support

For some time there have been two different procedures to protect the health care needs of a child subject to a child support order in Ohio. These procedures continue in effect but recently have been augmented. One procedure requires the courts to order one or both parents to provide for the health care needs of the child in a child support order. That could include ordering a parent to obtain health insurance coverage. Often this has involved one of the parents obtaining need-based, government subsidized health insurance coverage rather than private health insurance.

The other procedure is related to the child support worksheet. A parent who does obtain non-subsidized health insurance has been able to use the marginal cost of that insurance as an add-on to the child support obligation on the child support worksheet so that the

---

[67]Howell v. Howell, 167 Ohio App. 3d 431, 2006-Ohio-3038, 855 N.E.2d 533 (2d Dist. Clark County 2006).

[Section 19:7]

[1]RC 3119.02.

[2]RC 3119.03.

cost becomes pro-rated between the parents as part of the child support calculation.

These procedures have been determined to be inadequate as they were written and implemented. Legislation was passed on June 30, 2007, which became effective July 21, 2008, which clarified the procedures for ordering health insurance coverage and added an additional cash order to aid a parent in obtaining health insurance coverage and / or to provide for direct costs of health care when no health insurance coverage was in place. The new procedure also will require reimbursement to the state for subsidized health insurance coverage that the state is providing, where one of the parents can afford to contribute to health care costs, but has not been contributing.

In any child support proceeding, the court shall require that one or both parents provide for the health care needs of the children.[1] In determining child support, the court or child support enforcement agency, shall determine the person or persons responsible for the health care of the children and include provisions for the health care in the order.[2] Health care is defined as medical support that includes coverage under a health insurance plan, payment of costs of premiums, co-payments, and deductibles, or payment for medical expenses incurred on behalf of the child.[3]

Where one of the parents provides health insurance at an additional cost to themselves, that additional, or marginal, cost is added to the child support worksheet and it is pro-rated between the parents so that the cost is shared in proportion to the parents' income (line 20a of the child support worksheet). Marginal cost is defined as the contributing cost of private family health insurance, minus the contributing cost of private single health insurance, divided by the total number of dependents covered by the plan, times the number of children who are the subject of the support order.

The recent statutory changes provide that the inquiry into health care shall include whether there is health insurance coverage available to either or both parents.[4] Health insurance coverage is defined as accessible PRIVATE health insurance that provides primary care services within thirty miles from the residence of the child subject to the child support order.[5] Government sponsored, need-based health insurance will no longer be substituted for private insurance if private insurance is available, under the new statutory provisions.

In addition, the court or child support enforcement agency must determine if the health insurance coverage is reasonable. Health in-

---

[Section 19:8]

[1] RC 3109.05(A)(2).

[2] RC 3119.30(A).

[3] RC 3119.29(A)(3).

[4] RC 3119.30(B).

[5] RC 3119.29(A)(4).

surance coverage is deemed reasonable if it does not cost more than five percent of the annual gross income of the parent providing the coverage.[6] These changes are part of a federal and state initiative to ensure that private health care coverage in a child support order can actually be accessed by the child and residential parent, is not a burdensome cost to the parents, and is obtained when appropriate, even though public health insurance may also be available.

The other part of this change includes cash medical support. This is an additional monetary order for which both the obligor and obligee are responsible when there is no private health insurance. It is a specific dollar amount for the obligor to pay. However, the payment is pro-rated between the parties on the child support worksheet. The amount of the obligee's contribution to the cash medical support is deducted from the basic child support obligation so that the obligor is not assessed the obligee's share. This is the same methodology of pro-ration that has been and is part of the child support worksheet calculation for the marginal cost of health insurance and the cost of day care.

The changes mandate a multi-step inquiry before child support can be ordered. A court or child support enforcement agency must obtain information from the parents about the status of the health care coverage. Some of the information from the parents will be entered on the child support worksheet and used in calculating the child support, while other information will be used to determine the parts of the child support order relating to health care.

The first inquiry is whether either parent has private health insurance available. If there is private health insurance available, then the reasonableness of the contributing cost and the accessibility of the health care must be determined. Both inquiries must be made by the court or child support enforcement agency determining child support.

To be reasonable, the contributing cost must not exceed 5% of the gross income of the parent with the coverage. This figure is entered on line 7b of the child support worksheet, but it is only on the worksheet as a help aid and is not part of the ultimate child support calculation. The number to compare to the line 7b figure is called the contributing cost for the child's private health insurance. This is the cost of adding the child to the coverage to the plan participant or the difference between the cost of family coverage and the cost of single coverage. When the cost exceeds 5% of the annual gross of the parent providing the private health insurance, private health insurance may still be ordered if both parents agree that the cost may exceed the limit, the parent with the private health insurance volunteers to maintain it despite its statutory unreasonableness, or the court finds that such an order is in the best interests of the minor child, would not be an

---

[6]RC 3119.29(8).

undue financial burden, and enters findings on the record accordingly.[7] The court also has the option to find that the reasonable private health insurance is not in the best interest of the subject child under the facts of the case. This finding also must be made on the record.

The court or child support enforcement agency must also determine whether the private health insurance is accessible. This inquiry is not part of the calculation of child support on the worksheet. The rule is that private health insurance is accessible when the health care provided is available within 30 miles of the child.[8] There are two exceptions to the accessibility definition; those are that residents in that geographic area customarily travel more than 30 miles for health care or primary health care is only available by public transportation.[9] These findings must be made and supported in the record. And, the information must be determined in addition to the information for the child support worksheet.

If both parents have available private health insurance which is reasonable and accessible, the court or the child support enforcement agency shall order both parents to obtain coverage if dual coverage would provide for coordination of medical benefits without unnecessary duplication.[10] If the private health insurance is available at a more reasonable cost to the obligee, then that parent should be ordered to obtain it and if it is available at a more reasonable cost to the obligor, then that parent should be ordered to obtain it.[11] The authority to order a parent or parents to obtain health insurance has been in effect and the allocation of cost for that health insurance between the parents has been part of the child support worksheet prior to the changes. The difference now is the detailed inquiry that must be made to ensure that the publicly funded health insurance is not substituted when affordable and geographically accessible private health insurance is available.

The other significant change in child support is the addition of cash medical support. Cash medical support is a separate monetary order on the child support obligor to provide a residential parent with funds for the child's medical costs when private health insurance is not available or to pay for the cost of health insurance provided by a public entity, another parent or other person with whom the child resides. In any order for child support, an order for cash medical support shall accompany the child support order.[12]

When no private health insurance is available under the reasonable and accessible analysis, then the child support order will be two figures, a sum for child support and an additional cash medical sup-

---

[7]RC 3119.302(A)(2).

[8]RC 3119.29(A).

[9]RC 3119.302(A)(4).

[10]RC 3119.30(B).

[11]RC 3119.30(B).

[12]RC 3119.30(C), (D).

port order; however, if private health insurance is available, then the child support order will be the sum which includes the line 20 allocation of the marginal cost of the health insurance between the parties. However, even where there is private health insurance, the second child support order, without the allocation of the marginal cost of health insurance, plus a cash medical order, will also be determined in the event the private health insurance is terminated. Thus, any order for child support shall include the amount of child support where there is private health insurance, the amount of child support where there is no private health insurance, and a cash medical amount. If there is private health insurance, the child support order without a private health insurance component and the cash medical support order are merely contingent orders which would only become effective if the private health insurance terminates. But, the child support order without a private health insurance component and the cash medical support order will be the operative orders where there is no private health insurance. These contingent orders, which include three different numbers, are entered into the Support Enforcement Tracking System (SETS) and upon notice of the termination or acquisition of private health insurance, the child support order will change.

Cash medical support will not be ordered unless the obligor's gross income is 150% of the federal poverty level or more. Obligors with income below 150% of the federal poverty level are exempt from paying cash medical support.[13]

The determination for the figure for cash medical support is part of the child support worksheet. Cash medical support is either 5% of the obligor's adjusted gross income on the child support worksheet at line 14a or the obligor's share of the USDA estimated annual health care expenditure per child, whichever is lower.[14] If computer software is used to calculate child support, this comparison will be made by the software and the lower number will appear on line 20b of the child support worksheet, otherwise the person calculating child support will need to manually make this comparison and enter the appropriate figure.

When cash medical support is in effect, the payments through the Office of Child Support will be paid directly to the obligee, if the obligee is not receiving Medicaid health benefits for the child, or to the Office of Child Support, if the obligee is receiving Medicaid health benefits for the child.[15] The cash medical payment is a supplement to child support when private health insurance is unavailable. The amount of the child support is modified when the cash payment amount is paid. The child support worksheets reflect the alternative orders, so that the obligor will be on notice that the order may change. The modified child support and cash medical support payments are

---

[13]RC 3119.30(C).

[14]RC 3119.30(C).

[15]RC 3119.30(D).

due the first month immediately after the month in which the private health insurance terminates.[16] These orders terminate effective the last day of the month immediately before the month in which private health insurance resumes or is obtained.

The prohibition on cash medical support for obligors with an income below 150% of the federal poverty level is unrelated to the parents' duty under the law to provide for the health care needs of their children. Furthermore, both parents are still responsible under the law for health care expenses left unpaid by cash medical support or by health insurance.[17]

The court may enter a separate order for extraordinary medical and dental expenses. Generally, these orders are allocated between the parties in the percentage of income of the parties based on the child support worksheet at line 16, but they may be allocated in another formula ordered by the court.[18] The order on extraordinary expenses can include co-payments or deductible expenses. It would seem that the obligor who is paying cash medical support would be given credit for his/her share of the extraordinary expenses incurred during the year.

The parties providing the coverage must supply the necessary forms, and the insurance company must reimburse the party who paid the costs rather than the party who paid the premium.[19]

The court may order the parties to obtain coverage no later than thirty days after the issuance of the order if neither the obligor nor the obligee has health insurance.[20] An obligor who fails to comply with this order is responsible for paying any medical expenses.[21]

§ 19:9 Computation requirements: information for the child support worksheet

When the court computes the amount of child support required under a child support order, or a child support enforcement agency computes the amount of child support under an administrative paternity or support order, all of the following apply:[1]

The parents shall submit verified current and past income and

---

[16]RC 3119.30(E).

[17]RC 3109.05.

[18]Marek v. Marek, 158 Ohio App. 3d 750, 2004-Ohio-5556, 822 N.E.2d 410 (9th Dist. Summit County 2004) (an obligor should not be ordered to pay 100% of the uninsured expenses); Johnson v. Johnson, 2005-Ohio-55, 2005 WL 38766 (Ohio Ct. App. 2d Dist. Greene County 2005) (an obligor may be ordered to pay 100% of the uninsured expenses, at least until he is current on past due obligations).

[19]RC 3119.31.

[20]RC 3119.32.

[21]RC 3119.56.

[Section 19:9]

[1]RC 3119.05.

personal earnings (tax returns, pay stubs, receipts, vouchers, etc.),[2] Where an obligor is evasive or avoidant in providing his income verification, a court may use available information or previous information to determine the income,[3] or a court may choose to determine income using evidence offered by the other party, such as a loan application rather than tax returns offered by the obligor.[4]

When appropriate, income may be averaged over a reasonable number of years.[5] The averaging of income is appropriate where income is unpredictable or inconsistent.[6] However, it is within the discretion of the trial court to fail to average where income varied, but generally increased over time.[7] It is not appropriate to average income from several years of employment with a year of unemployment where the parent was not voluntarily unemployed,[8] or where the parent was previously employed but now is on Social Security Disability.[9] When averaging income the court does not have to use the lesser of the average or the previous year. That requirement is limited to the averaging of overtime, commissions or bonuses.[10] The trial court may use the last full year of income rather than annualizing based on a partial year.[11] It is less relevant where self-employment income is listed, whether on line 1 or line 2, so long as the total income is reflected on line 7.[12]

The amount of any pre-existing child support obligation of a parent

---

[2]In re Harris, 2006-Ohio-3746, 2006 WL 2037323 (Ohio Ct. App. 2d Dist. Champaign County 2006) (a self-employed obligor may be ordered to provide income and expense verification to the court, otherwise the court will be justified in using a figure it determines for the income).

[3]Cole v. Cole, 2007-Ohio-54, 2007 WL 60670 (Ohio Ct. App. 5th Dist. Stark County 2007).

[4]Johnson v. Tataranowicz, 2006-Ohio-6797, 2006 WL 3746056 (Ohio Ct. App. 5th Dist. Licking County 2006).

[5]RC 3119.05(H).

[6]Marquard v. Marquard, 2001 WL 893451 (Ohio Ct. App. 10th Dist. Franklin County 2001).

[7]Marquard v. Marquard, 2001 WL 893451 (Ohio Ct. App. 10th Dist. Franklin County 2001); Slone v. Slone, 1999 WL 156149 (Ohio Ct. App. 4th Dist. Pike County 1999) (in determining the gross income for child support guideline computation, a trial court may average).

[8]Johnson v. Huddle, 2004-Ohio-410, 2004 WL 193043 (Ohio Ct. App. 4th Dist. Lawrence County 2004).

[9]McGuire v. McGuire, 2002-Ohio-1061, 2002 WL 398725 (Ohio Ct. App. 4th Dist. Scioto County 2002).

[10]Rains v. Rains, 2002-Ohio-654, 2002 WL 337738 (Ohio Ct. App. 8th Dist. Cuyahoga County 2002).

[11]Caniglia v. Caniglia, 2000 WL 630830 (Ohio Ct. App. 12th Dist. Butler County 2000).

[12]Wolfe v. Wolfe, 2005-Ohio-2331, 2005 WL 1118198 (Ohio Ct. App. 10th Dist. Franklin County 2005); Bates v. Bates, 2005-Ohio-3374, 2005 WL 1532424 (Ohio Ct. App. 10th Dist. Franklin County 2005).

under a court order[13] and the amount of any court ordered spousal support[14] shall be deducted from the gross income of that parent to the extent that payments are actually made and verified.

When a parent has other minor children born to him from another relationship who reside with him, the court may deduct from the gross income of the parent an amount equal to the number of children times the federal income tax exemption. However, that amount shall be reduced by child support received for that year, but not less than "0".

When the court calculates gross income that includes overtime, commissions and bonuses, the court must include the lesser of the following as income from overtime, commissions and bonuses: (a) the yearly average of all overtime, commissions and bonuses during the immediate three years;[15] or, (b) the total overtime, commissions and bonuses received in the year immediately prior to the time when the child support is being calculated.

Where a trial court is not offered sufficient evidence to average overtime, commissions or bonuses over three years, it may average total income over any period of time it finds to be appropriate.[16] However, a trial court may not average bonuses from a previous job after the parent is employed at another company and the bonus structure changes.[17]

The child support calculation must not include any income earned by the spouse of a parent. However, this is a factor for consideration in deviating from basic schedules.[18]

In calculating child support, the marginal cost of private health insurance is added on to the basic child support obligation. The marginal cost is defined as the contributing cost of private family health insurance, minus the contributing cost of private single health insurance, divided by the total number of dependents covered by the plan,

[13]Tuscarawas County Child Support Enforcement Agency v. McCamant, 2004-Ohio-443, 2004 WL 203136 (Ohio Ct. App. 5th Dist. Tuscarawas County 2004); Tuscarawas County Child Support Enforcement Agency v. Boggan, 2004-Ohio-444, 2004 WL 203152 (Ohio Ct. App. 5th Dist. Tuscarawas County 2004).

[14]Henderson v. Henderson, 2004-Ohio-1856, 2004 WL 765347 (Ohio Ct. App. 3d Dist. Mercer County 2004) (credit shall be given if value is received in an exchange even if the actual spousal payments are not made).

[15]Hewitt-Totten v. Holt, 1996 WL 748177 (Ohio Ct. App. 6th Dist. Wood County 1996); Peacock v. Peacock, 2000 WL 145168 (Ohio Ct. App. 6th Dist. Erie County 2000); Worch v. Worch, 2000 WL 376643 (Ohio Ct. App. 2d Dist. Darke County 2000).

[16]Gdula v. Gdula, 2001-Ohio-3329, 2001 WL 911600 (Ohio Ct. App. 7th Dist. Belmont County 2001); Worley v. Worley, 2007-Ohio-252, 2007 WL 172118 (Ohio Ct. App. 5th Dist. Licking County 2007).

[17]Cooper v. Cooper, 2004-Ohio-1368, 2004 WL 549784 (Ohio Ct. App. 12th Dist. Clermont County 2004).

[18]Marquard v. Marquard, 2001 WL 893451 (Ohio Ct. App. 10th Dist. Franklin County 2001); Julian v. Julian, 2004-Ohio-1430, 2004 WL 574161 (Ohio Ct. App. 9th Dist. Summit County 2004).

times the number of children who are the subject of the support order.[19] This marginal cost is pro-rated between the parents in accordance with their adjusted gross incomes. In addition to the direct cost of private health insurance, a court shall issue an order for health care needs for a child subject to the child support order.[20] The allocation of extraordinary medical or dental expenses, including, but not limited to, orthodontia, psychological counseling, appropriate private education, and other expenses, may be ordered and can be considered in adjusting child support. The statute deems any expenses over $100 per calendar year per child to be extraordinary.[21]

Another additional cost, which is added on the basic child support obligation, is the amount of any work or school-related day care costs for the child at issue. The amount after application of appropriate tax credits is allocated between the parents based upon their pro-rated shares of adjusted gross income. Note that the State of Ohio has added a state childcare deduction in addition to the federal childcare credit. The trial court may not, however, apply a hypothetical childcare expense in the absence of any evidence of day care costs if a party worked.[22]

The supplement of day care expenses for the parties by a grandparent should not reduce the cost of day care allocated between the parents on the worksheet since that supplement is not guaranteed or legally enforceable.[23] Ultimately, the determination of day care expense and their reasonableness is subject to the approval of the court,[24] and a trial court may accept the testimony of the day care provider.[25]

There is a separate child support worksheet at RC 3119.023 for cases where the parents have split parental rights and responsibilities. This means that there is more than one child subject to the child support order and each parent has primary possession of at least one of the children. When child support is calculated using this worksheet, the child support obligations of each parent is offset, and the court must issue a child support order requiring the parent with the larger

---

[19]RC 3119.022, RC 3119.023.

[20]RC 3109.05.

[21]RC 3119.01(C)(4).

[22]Zaccardelli v. Zaccardelli, 2000 WL 1026687 (Ohio Ct. App. 9th Dist. Summit County 2000). But see, Tonti v. Tonti, 2004-Ohio-2529, 2004 WL 1109840 (Ohio Ct. App. 10th Dist. Franklin County 2004); Beiers v. Phillips, 2009-Ohio-3278, 2009 WL 1912601 (Ohio Ct. App. 5th Dist. Licking County 2009).

[23]Saylor v. Saylor, 2009-Ohio-3109, 2009 WL 1830795 (Ohio Ct. App. 5th Dist. Muskingum County 2009).

[24]Daufel v. Daufel, 2008-Ohio-3868, 2008 WL 2942220 (Ohio Ct. App. 2d Dist. Montgomery County 2008).

[25]Rocky v. Rockey, 2008-Ohio-6525, 2008 WL 5197123 (Ohio App. Ct. 4th Dist. Highland County 2008).

child support obligation to pay the net amount pursuant to the child support order.[26]

If the court issues a child support order where a third party is the legal custodian of the children, the court must issue a child support order requiring each parent to pay his or her child support obligation to the legal custodian.[27]

In calculating child support, it is the standard for the nonresidential parent to pay the support to the residential parent or the practice in shared parenting for the parent with less time to pay the one with more time. However, where the time spent in each household is close to equal, there is a disparity in household incomes, and it is in the best interests of the minor children, the parent with more time and more income can be ordered to pay child support to the other parent.[28]

§ 19:10 Computation requirements: income above and below the child support tables

When the combined annual income of the parents is below $6,600 a year or above $150,000 a year, the court shall consider each case on an individual basis. If the combined gross income is below $6,600, the schedules are to be used as a guideline. Some minimal child support must be issued unless the obligor is totally unable to pay and it would be unjust or inappropriate and not in the best interest of the child.[1] The minimum schedule amount is $50 per month regardless of the number of children.

If the combined gross income of the parents exceeds $150,000 per year, the child support shall be determined on a case-by-case basis considering the needs and standard of living of the parents and the subject children. The order shall be no less than the obligation for a case with a combined gross income of $150,000, unless a finding is made that the amount at a combined gross income of $150,000 is unjust and inappropriate and not in the best interests of the child, or the obligee or obligor.[2]

There are no findings required for an order in excess of the obligation for a combined gross income of $150,000. The court shall use its discretion based upon the needs and standard of living. This methodology represents a modification from the previous statute.[3] The prior statutory language provided for a case-by-case analysis and an

---

[26]RC 3119.07(B).

[27]RC 3119.07(C).

[28]Frey v. Frey, 2007-Ohio-2991, 2007 WL 1731592 (Ohio Ct. App. 3d Dist. Hancock County 2007); Sexton v. Sexton, 2007-Ohio-6539, 2007 WL 4285140 (Ohio Ct. App. 10th Dist. Franklin County 2007); Cameron v. Cameron, 2007-Ohio-3994, 2007 WL 2247593 (Ohio Ct. App. 10th Dist. Franklin County 2007).

[Section 19:10]

[1]RC 3119.04(B).

[2]RC 3119.04(C).

[3]RC 3113.215.

extrapolation based on the percentages of income at the $150,000 level of child support. Under RC 3119.04(C), the obligation for child support at the $150,000 level is not a cap on child support for parents with income exceeding $150,000. It is rather a minimum order.[4]

The court shall consider the needs and standard of living of the children on a case-by case basis.[5] The determination of the needs and standard of living are mandatory.[6] After the considerations, the court may award a figure in excess of the amount at the high end of the current guideline chart,[7] or may use the base level off the chart at $150,000 if the obligor is paying other family debts or expenses.[8]

The statutory change regarding cases where the combined income is in excess of $150,000 did not create an automatic change of circumstances for modification of previous high-income child support orders.[9] There is nothing that precludes a court from using the previous statutory scheme of extrapolation to determine the figure for child support when incomes exceed $150,000;[10] however, the higher the combined

---

[4]Fisher v. Fisher, 2002-Ohio-1297, 2002 WL 444904 (Ohio Ct. App. 3d Dist. Henry County 2002); Deasey v. Deasey, 2003-Ohio-3576, 2003 WL 21525470 (Ohio Ct. App. 5th Dist. Delaware County 2003); Petersen v. Petersen, 2003-Ohio-4189, 2003 WL 21805614 (Ohio Ct. App. 5th Dist. Ashland County 2003).

[5]Cho v. Cho, 2003 WL 23018576 (Ohio Ct. App. 7th Dist. Mahoning County 2003) (the trial court considered the later higher standard of living during the marriage including extracurricular activities and the expectations of the family for the father's career); Beck v. Beck, 2004-Ohio-861, 2004 WL 350958 (Ohio Ct. App. 8th Dist. Cuyahoga County 2004) (the trial court considered private school tuition); Siebert v. Tavarez, 2007-Ohio-2643, 2007 WL 1559565 (Ohio Ct. App. 8th Dist. Cuyahoga County 2007), appeal not allowed, 116 Ohio St. 3d 1412, 2007-Ohio-6140, 876 N.E.2d 969 (2007) (an average standard of living should not be used to determine child support where the income level and standard of living of the obligor is extraordinary).

[6]Gregory v. Kottman-Gregory, 2005-Ohio-6558, 2005 WL 3359162 (Ohio Ct. App. 12th Dist. Madison County 2005); but see, Lyons v. Bachelder, 2005-Ohio-4966, 2005 WL 2300226 (Ohio Ct. App. 5th Dist. Morrow County 2005); Lyons v. Bachelder, 2005 WL 2266672 (Ohio Ct. App. 5th Dist. Morrow County 2005) (where insufficient evidence was provided, there is no error to fail to discuss needs and standard of living).

[7]Deasey v. Deasey, 2003-Ohio-3576, 2003 WL 21525470 (Ohio Ct. App. 5th Dist. Delaware County 2003).

[8]Gerlach v. Gerlach, 2004-Ohio-1607, 2004 WL 625686 (Ohio Ct. App. 10th Dist. Franklin County 2004).

[9]Thompson v. Boivin, 2002-Ohio-4628, 2002 WL 2030862 (Ohio Ct. App. 1st Dist. Hamilton County 2002). Bettinger v. Bettinger, 2005-Ohio-5389, 2005 WL 2514244 (Ohio Ct. App. 9th Dist. Summit County 2005).

[10]Bunkers v. Bunkers, 2007-Ohio-561, 2007 WL 431418 (Ohio Ct. App. 6th Dist. Wood County 2007), appeal not allowed, 114 Ohio St. 3d 1480, 2007-Ohio-3699, 870 N.E.2d 732 (2007).

income, the less this method is accurate or related to needs and standards of living as required by the statute.[11]

The appropriate guide for determining need in a higher income case is to examine the standard of living.[12] The standard of living should be determined by what was the standard of living during the marriage,[13] or at the end of the marriage, if it had increased or was expected to increase.[14] There is some question as to whether a guideline worksheet is strictly required in a case where the parties' income exceeds $150,000 since a court does not have to accept the child support figure on that worksheet.[15]

§ 19:11   Deviation factors regarding child support[1]

The party who wants to rebut the basic child support schedule has the burden of presenting evidence that demonstrates that the calculated award is unjust or inappropriate and would not be in the best interest of the child.[2] To deviate from the basic schedule, the court must specifically state what facts were considered and the reasons why the basic schedule would be unjust or inappropriate and not in the best interest of the child.[3]

The factors for deviation are located at RC 3119.23.[4] In deviating from the amount of support that is mandated from the schedules, the court may consider the following criteria:[5]

---

[11]Siebert v. Tavarez, 2007-Ohio-2643, 2007 WL 1559565 (Ohio Ct. App. 8th Dist. Cuyahoga County 2007), appeal not allowed, 116 Ohio St. 3d 1412, 2007-Ohio-6140, 876 N.E.2d 969 (2007).

[12]O'Neill v. Bowers, 2004-Ohio-6540, 2004 WL 2806331 (Ohio Ct. App. 9th Dist. Summit County 2004); Moore v. Moore, 182 Ohio App. 3d 708, 2009-Ohio-2434, 914 N.E.2d 1097 (3d Dist. Union County 2009) (failure to consider the standard of living is reversible error).

[13]Kendall v. Kendall, 2005-Ohio-1777, 2005 WL 859447 (Ohio Ct. App. 6th Dist. Ottawa County 2005); O'Neill v. Bowers, 2004-Ohio-6540, 2004 WL 2806331 (Ohio Ct. App. 9th Dist. Summit County 2004).

[14]Cho v. Cho, 2003 WL 23018576 (Ohio Ct. App. 7th Dist. Mahoning County 2003).

[15]Cho v. Cho, 2003 WL 23018576 (Ohio Ct. App. 7th Dist. Mahoning County 2003); Farrell v. Farrell, 2009-Ohio-1341, 2009 WL 765185 (Ohio Ct. App. 5th Dist. Licking County 2009).

[Section 19:11]

[1]For citations to numerous cases regarding deviations, please check Westlaw Key Cite for each deviation factor.

[2]RC 3119.22; Halverstadt v. Halverstadt, 1991 WL 168631 (Ohio Ct. App. 7th Dist. Columbiana County 1991).

[3]RC 3119.23.

[4]Formerly RC 3113.215(B)(3).

[5]RC 3119.23.

(A) Special and unusual needs of the children;[6]

(B) Extraordinary obligations for minor children or obligations for handicapped children who are not stepchildren and are not issue of the marriage;

(C) Other court-ordered payments such as spousal support, debts, or property settlements;[7]

(D) Extended times of parenting time or extraordinary costs associated with parenting time, provided that this division does not authorize and shall not be construed as authorizing any deviations from the schedule because of a denial or interference with a right of companionship or parenting time granted by court order;[8]

(E) The obligor obtaining additional employment, after a child support order is issued in order to support a second family;

(F) The financial resources and earnings and earning ability of the child;[9]

(G) Disparity in income between parties or households;[10]

---

[6]Maurer v. Maurer, 1990 WL 103759 (Ohio Ct. App. 5th Dist. Holmes County 1990) (substantial medical expenses reason to deviate); Wilder v. Wilder, 1989 WL 43293 (Ohio Ct. App. 10th Dist. Franklin County 1989) (deviation due to special needs of handicapped children); Kupniewski v. Kupniewski, 1990 WL 75194 (Ohio Ct. App. 8th Dist. Cuyahoga County 1990) (child's participation in extracurricular school activities requiring use of car supported increase); Sullivan v. Sullivan, 2000 WL 1434156 (Ohio Ct. App. 6th Dist. Lucas County 2000) (upward deviation upheld where child is severely handicapped and cannot walk, talk or feed herself); Burns v. May, 133 Ohio App. 3d 351, 728 N.E.2d 19 (12th Dist. Clermont County 1999) (upward deviation held where child failed first grade and was in need of a tutor); Kitchen v. Kitchen, 2004-Ohio-1189, 2004 WL 486105 (Ohio Ct. App. 12th Dist. Butler County 2004) (upward deviation where mother could not work due to daily needs of the child with cerebral palsy and where father provided little or no child care); Marder v. Marder, 2008-Ohio-2500, 2008 WL 2168415, (Ohio Ct. App. 12th Dist. Clermont County 2008) (upward deviation for severely disabled child where obligor has never visited due to time and money spent by obligee without aid from obligor).

[7]Davis v. Davis, 1992 WL 19826 (Ohio Ct. App. 7th Dist. Columbiana County 1992) (no child support where obligee lived in rent-free home with children); Knisley v. Knisley, 1989 WL 74035 (Ohio Ct. App. 2d Dist. Greene County 1989); Fisher v. Fisher, 1990 WL 210797 (Ohio Ct. App. 5th Dist. Morrow County 1990) (no support while obligor making mortgage payments); Lowe v. Lowe, 1990 WL 78864 (Ohio Ct. App. 5th Dist. Fairfield County 1990) (deviation allowed for health insurance); Shultz v. Dimondo, 1991 WL 262885 (Ohio Ct. App. 9th Dist. Summit County 1991).

[8]Bender v. Bender, 2001 WL 808975 (Ohio Ct. App. 9th Dist. Summit County 2001) (a 24.2% deviation from guideline support reflective of parenting time and extraordinary expenses not an abuse of discretion); Karales v. Karales, 2006-Ohio-2963, 2006 WL 1629005 (Ohio Ct. App. 10th Dist. Franklin County 2006) (no error to deviate downward due to obligor/father's additional cost of $16,000 per year for supervised visitation).

[9]Tarr v. Walter, 2002-Ohio-3188, 2002 WL 1396747 (Ohio Ct. App. 7th Dist. Jefferson County 2002) (no deviation to "0" for high school student with employment).

[10]Kimber v. Kimber, 1990 WL 127926 (Ohio Ct. App. 8th Dist. Cuyahoga County 1990) (no support ordered where noncustodial parent had negative cash flow); Vliek v. Myllykoski, 1998 WL 964586 (Ohio Ct. App. 11th Dist. Lake County 1998) (deviation upward was warranted where obligor's refusal to exercise visitation resulted in additional economic burden on the obligee); Tada v. Deleva, 2001 WL 755839 (Ohio Ct.

(H) Benefits that either party receives from remarriage or sharing living expenses with another person;[11]

(I) The amount of federal, state and local taxes actually paid or estimated to be paid by each parent;

(J) Significant in-kind contributions from a parent, including but not limited to direct payment for lessons, sports equipment, schooling, or clothing;[12]

(K) The relative financial resources, assets, and needs of each parent;[13]

(L) The standard of living and circumstances of each parent and the standard of living the child would have enjoyed had the marriage continued;[14]

(M) The physical and emotional condition and needs of the child;[15]

(N) The need and capacity of the child for education, and the educational opportunities that would have been available to him

---

App. 8th Dist. Cuyahoga County 2001) (deviation to 0 upheld where obligor mother had 3 other children, obligee father has limited expenses, and parties shared time extensively with the child); Calvaruso v. Calvaruso, 2004-Ohio-1877, 2004 WL 785454 (Ohio Ct. App. 9th Dist. Summit County 2004) (deviation downward to allow obligee mother funds for visitation allowed even though disparity between households was only approximately $9500 because in lower income cases a small disparity can have a great impact); Karales v. Karales, 2006-Ohio-2963, 2006 WL 1629005 (Ohio Ct. App. 10th Dist. Franklin County 2006) (no error to deviate downward due to disparity in income between households especially where self-employed obligee/mother's company paid many of her expenses directly).

[11]Cameron v. Cameron, 2007-Ohio-3994, 2007 WL 2247593 (Ohio Ct. App. 10th Dist. Franklin County 2007) (new spouse's income is not included in child support, but can be considered for a deviation, but it cannot be used to provide for all the shortfall of expenses for the parties' children); Julian v. Julian, 2004-Ohio-1430, 2004 WL 574161 (Ohio Ct. App. 9th Dist. Summit County 2004) (upward deviation for remarriage of obligor failed where court seemed to believe that the obligor had additional income but only made findings regarding his stated income). See Marvin M. Moore, *The Significance of a Divorced Father's Remarriage in Adjudicating a Motion to Modify Child Support*, 18 Cap. Univ. L. Rev. 483 (1989).

[12]Koffenberger v. Koffenberger, 1990 WL 138357 (Ohio Ct. App. 12th Dist. Clermont County 1990) (trust fund payments to children to be considered); Morosko v. Willis, 2003-Ohio-3360, 2003 WL 21473232 (Ohio Ct. App. 9th Dist. Summit County 2003).

[13]In re Prade, 135 Ohio App. 3d 424, 734 N.E.2d 430 (9th Dist. Summit County 1999) (upward deviation upheld based on father's retirement income where father was imprisoned for murdering mother, even though the children are receiving Social Security death benefits on behalf of their mother).

[14]Schultz v. Schultz, 110 Ohio App. 3d 715, 675 N.E.2d 55 (10th Dist. Franklin County 1996) (less than guideline amount awarded because it was sufficient to maintain the lifestyle of family prior to divorce).

[15]Marder v. Marder, 2008-Ohio-2500, 2008 WL 2168415 (Ohio Ct. App. 12th Dist. Clermont County 2008) (upward deviation where the child has hearing loss, voluntary movement issue, delayed motor skills, learning disabilities, cognitive disabilities and muscle impairment interfering with movement and is in need of daily care by the obligee); Sullivan v. Sullivan, 2000 WL 1434156 (Ohio Ct. App. 6th Dist. Lucas County 2000) (trial court's upward deviation from guidelines for severely handicapped child in need of 24-hour care is not an abuse of discretion).

had the circumstances requiring a court order for his support not arisen;[16]

(O) The responsibility of each parent for the support of others;[17] and

(P) Any other relevant factor.

If the court grants a deviation based on *"any other relevant factor"* it must state specifically what facts are the basis for the deviation.

The court may approve a deviation that assigns a monetary value to the deviation and to which the parties have agreed. Deviations from the guideline amount must comply with RC 3119.22.

The sole and shared custody worksheets each provide a space for an explanation of a deviation. Line 27(A) provides that space if one parent is designated the sole residential parent and legal custodian. In the space, the preparer must provide the specific facts and monetary value for a deviation for sole custody. The same worksheet is used for shared parenting. However, in a shared parenting case, the preparer must complete line 27(B) to justify the deviation. An explanation of the amount of time the child spends with each parent, each parent's ability to maintain adequate housing and each parent's expenses for the child must be stated. The statute provides a separate worksheet for cases where the parents are granted split custody. The explanation of deviation for split custody cases is located on line 25 on that worksheet.

The amount of child support calculated pursuant to the guideline worksheet is "rebuttably presumed" to be the correct amount.[18] A deviation also requires a specific finding that the guideline order would be "unjust and inappropriate" and not in the child's best interest.[19] If the trial court fails to deviate, there is no statutory requirement that the court support its refusal to deviate.[20] However, if there is a deviation, the trial court must include the presumptive

---

[16]Hammel v. Klug, 2004-Ohio-6242, 2004 WL 2675975 (Ohio Ct. App. 12th Dist. Clermont County 2004) (private tuition is a form of child support; if it was in the child's best interest, if the person ordered to pay can afford to pay, if the child had been in private school, and if a child would have continued to attend private school if the marriage had continued, then the court may order it); Roberts v. Roberts, 2005-Ohio-2792, 2005 WL 1324726 (Ohio Ct. App. 12th Dist. Butler County 2005) (private school tuition may be considered in deviating on the order of child support); In re Harris, 2006-Ohio-3746, 2006 WL 2037323 (Ohio Ct. App. 2d Dist. Champaign County 2006) (a gymnastic cost of $600 per year is insufficient to deviate upward on the child support order); Berthelot v. Berthelot, 2006-Ohio-1317, 2006 WL 709025 (Ohio Ct. App. 9th Dist. Summit County 2006) (a dollar for dollar deviation for private school expenses paid directly by the obligor parent may be appropriate).

[17]Johnson v. Johnson, 2004-Ohio-5749, 2004 WL 2426252 (Ohio Ct. App. 4th Dist. Ross County 2004) (obligation to pay secondary education of child from a previous marriage qualifies as support for others).

[18]RC 3119.03.

[19]RC 3119.22.

[20]Warner v. Warner, 2003-Ohio-5132, 2003 WL 22229412 (Ohio Ct. App. 3d Dist. Union County 2003).

amount of child support pursuant to the worksheet in the journal, otherwise its deviation will be reversible error.[21] Deviations have been granted based on the parties' disparity in income.[22] Deviations have also been granted for tuition and tutoring expenses.[23] The order of direct payments for additional expenses is not a deviation pursuant to the statute and does not require the statutory deviation findings.[24]

A local rule that requires abatement of child support during visitation violates the intent and purpose of the guidelines and is arbitrary and unreasonable when applied without individualized consideration.[25] Furthermore, while extraordinary costs associated with visitation may be considered, child support cannot be abated during seasonal vacation periods.[26] The additional costs incurred by the obligee created by the obligor parent's failure to visit may be considered, where the obligor parent was ordered to provide for day care during his visitation, but he failed to visit.[27]

No statutory scheme exists to give credit pursuant to a formula for extended visitation. The reference to extended times of visitation, as a factor, does not automatically entitle a parent, even under a shared parenting agreement, to have a reduction in the support obligation by a percentage corresponding to the visitation.[28] The court may determine that the obligee parent needs the full amount of support to maintain the children in the manner that they would have enjoyed if the marriage continued,[29] or because the obligee parent requires the

---

[21]Ohlemacher v. Ohlemacher, 2003-Ohio-6582, 2003 WL 22900544 (Ohio Ct. App. 9th Dist. Lorain County 2003); Pinchbeck v. Pinchbeck, 2003-Ohio-6125, 2003 WL 22715681 (Ohio Ct. App. 9th Dist. Lorain County 2003); Farmer v. Farmer, 2003-Ohio-4385, 2003 WL 21976091 (Ohio Ct. App. 9th Dist. Medina County 2003).

[22]In re Schreiber Children, 2000 WL 1818548 (Ohio Ct. App. 12th Dist. Butler County 2000).

[23]Luedtke v. Luedtke, 2000 WL 569941 (Ohio Ct. App. 2d Dist. Montgomery County 2000); Burns v. May, 133 Ohio App. 3d 351, 728 N.E.2d 19 (12th Dist. Clermont County 1999).

[24]In re Minnick, 2003-Ohio-4245, 2003 WL 21905088 (Ohio Ct. App. 12th Dist. Madison County 2003).

[25]Gatliff v. Gatliff, 89 Ohio App. 3d 391, 624 N.E.2d 779 (3d Dist. Hancock County 1993); Bowman v. Bowman, 1996 WL 682419 (Ohio Ct. App. 10th Dist. Franklin County 1996).

[26]RC 3119.86(D).

[27]Freed v. Freed, 2000 WL 896285 (Ohio Ct. App. 2d Dist. Greene County 2000) (holding father responsible for additional day care where he failed to visit and he was responsible for costs).

[28]Hubin v. Hubin, 92 Ohio St. 3d 240, 2001-Ohio-187, 749 N.E.2d 749 (2001); Pauly v. Pauly, 80 Ohio St. 3d 386, 1997-Ohio-105, 686 N.E.2d 1108 (1997).

[29]LaLiberte v. LaLiberte, 105 Ohio App. 3d 207, 663 N.E.2d 974 (9th Dist. Medina County 1995). Mueller v. Mueller, 2000 WL 342112 (Ohio Ct. App. 12th Dist. Butler County 2000).

additional funds to maintain adequate housing for the children, especially where there is a disparity in household expenses.[30]

§ 19:12 Shared parenting

In a shared parenting case, the child support must be calculated using the same child support worksheet that is used for a sole residential parent[1] and not the worksheet for split allocation of parenting.[2] The order calculated on the sole residential/shared parenting worksheet is presumed to be the correct child support obligation.[3] However, if the application of the schedule to the shared parenting case would be unjust or inappropriate to the children of either party and would not be in the best interest of the child because of the extraordinary circumstances of the parents, the court may deviate from the amount of the child support that would be ordered in a shared parenting agreement. "Extraordinary circumstances" include, but are not limited to, the following:

(1) The amount of time that the children spend with each parent;

(2) The ability of each parent to maintain adequate housing for the children;

(3) Each parent's expenses, including but not limited to, child care expenses, school tuition, medical expenses, and dental expenses; and

(4) Any other circumstances the court considers relevant.[4]

Although the statute provides that the worksheet for shared parenting cases is the same worksheet to be used for cases where one parent is designated as the sole residential parent, there is a presumption in that the residential parent is presumed to spend his or her child support obligation directly on the child.[5] This has caused confusion in implementing the law in shared parenting cases since both parents are deemed residential parents during the time the child resides with each of them. There is no statutory provision for any credit where there is shared parenting. The Supreme Court of Ohio, in *Pauly v. Pauly*,[6] held that a trial court may not deviate automatically from the worksheet amount to credit a parent's child support obligation for the time the child resides with that parent. As a result, a court must consider the time a child resides with the obligor-parent under a

---

[30]RC 3119.24; Nist v. Nist, 2003-Ohio-3292, 2003 WL 21452876 (Ohio Ct. App. 5th Dist. Delaware County 2003).

[Section 19:12]

[1]RC 3119.022; Copas v. Copas, 2003-Ohio-3473, 2003 WL 21500049 (Ohio Ct. App. 4th Dist. Adams County 2003); Prusia v. Prusia, 2003-Ohio-2000, 2003 WL 1904410 (Ohio Ct. App. 6th Dist. Lucas County 2003).

[2]RC 3119.023.

[3]RC 3119.03.

[4]RC 3119.24.

[5]RC 3119.07(A).

[6]Pauly v. Pauly, 80 Ohio St. 3d 386, 1997-Ohio-105, 686 N.E.2d 1108 (1997).

shared parenting agreement as one of several factors when determining whether the guideline calculation would be in the best interest of the child so as to justify the deviation under RC 3119.24 rather than as a reason for automatic deviation.

A few courts have interpreted *Pauly v. Pauly* to hold that "both" parents are to pay child support as calculated and offset one obligation against the other.[7] This "netting" of each parent's obligation for child support results in a substantially reduced child support order. This issue was presented to the Supreme Court of Ohio in *Hubin v. Hubin*.[8] The Supreme Court of Ohio upheld the Tenth Appellate District's reasoning which rejected the offset of child support in shared parenting cases. The reasoning relied upon by the Supreme Court of Ohio, is found in the appellate opinion.[9]

Furthermore, no child support worksheets are acceptable which are produced from software that performs additional calculations not specified in the statute or which performs offsets;[10] For example, it is error to reduce the father's income by one-half of the tax exemption in order to calculate child support for parents with shared parenting.[11]

Two issues have arisen in shared parenting cases when a modification is requested.[12] One is whether a change of circumstance has occurred when the support ordered is more than the "0" amount in the initial order. Any number more than "0" is a ten percent change of circumstance.[13]

The second issue is which parent should be the obligee and which one becomes the obligor where there is no designation of a residential parent or obligor in a shared parenting agreement.[14] Where the disparity in income between the two households has been significant, the

---

[7]Luke v. Luke, 1998 WL 172813 (Ohio Ct. App. 11th Dist. Lake County 1998); Weinberger v. Weinberger, 1998 WL 241790 (Ohio Ct. App. 1st Dist. Hamilton County 1998).

[8]Hubin v. Hubin, 92 Ohio St. 3d 240, 2001-Ohio-187, 749 N.E.2d 749 (2001).

[9]Hubin v. Hubin, 2000 WL 868590 (Ohio Ct. App. 10th Dist. Franklin County 2000), aff'd, 92 Ohio St. 3d 240, 2001-Ohio-187, 749 N.E.2d 749 (2001); followed in Spencer v. Spencer, 2006-Ohio-1913, 2006 WL 1011258 (Ohio Ct. App. 5th Dist. Stark County 2006); Copas v. Copas, 2003-Ohio-3473, 2003 WL 21500049 (Ohio Ct. App. 4th Dist. Adams County 2003); Prusia v. Prusia, 2003-Ohio-2000, 2003 WL 1904410 (Ohio Ct. App. 6th Dist. Lucas County 2003).

[10]Copas v. Copas, 2003-Ohio-3473, 2003 WL 21500049 (Ohio Ct. App. 4th Dist. Adams County 2003); Prusia v. Prusia, 2003-Ohio-2000, 2003 WL 1904410 (Ohio Ct. App. 6th Dist. Lucas County 2003).

[11]Brown v. Brown, 2003-Ohio-239, 2003 WL 150089 (Ohio Ct. App. 9th Dist. Wayne County 2003).

[12]Mahlerwein v. Mahlerwein, 160 Ohio App. 3d 564, 2005-Ohio-1835, 828 N.E.2d 153 (4th Dist. Hocking County 2005).

[13]DePalmo v. DePalmo, 78 Ohio St. 3d 535, 1997-Ohio-184, 679 N.E.2d 266 (1997); Sapinsley v. Sapinsley, 171 Ohio App. 3d 74, 2007-Ohio-1320, 869 N.E.2d 702 (1st Dist. Hamilton County 2007).

[14]Mahlerwein v. Mahlerwein, 160 Ohio App. 3d 564, 2005-Ohio-1835, 828 N.E.2d 153 (4th Dist. Hocking County 2005).

parent with more time under a shared parenting plan has been designated the obligor based on his income rather than the amount of time he has possession of the children.[15]

§ 19:13 Voluntary unemployment or underemployment[1]

The issue of when to impute income is a fact-sensitive one with proof issues that make the application of the imputation rule difficult. Where the computation involves an unemployed or underemployed parent, the statutory two-part test must be applied. The first question is whether the parent is voluntarily unemployed or underemployed. The second question is whether, under the factors listed in the statute, income can be determined.[2] There is some disagreement in the appellate districts as to how specific the findings of fact must be. The findings as to voluntary unemployment or underemployment must be express[3] or may be implied.[4] And, the reference to the statutory factors in the second part of the test must be specific[5] or just may be considered.[6]

Voluntary unemployment or underemployment takes many forms. Most case law supports that incarceration is voluntary unemployment.[7] An obligor mother who does not work because she has a new baby with her boyfriend is voluntarily unemployed and

---

[15]Sexton v. Sexton, 2007-Ohio-6539, 2007 WL 4285140, (Ohio Ct. App. 10th Dist. Franklin County 2007); Cameron v. Cameron, 2007-Ohio-3994, 2007 WL 2247593 (Ohio Ct. App. 10th Dist. Franklin County 2007).

[Section 19:13]

[1]For citations to numerous cases regarding modification of child support orders due to voluntary unemployment or underemployment, please check Westlaw Key Cite. See also Text § 19:7, Terminology used in calculating child support.

[2]RC 3119.01(C)(11). Badovick v. Badovick, 128 Ohio App. 3d 18, 713 N.E.2d 1066 (8th Dist. Cuyahoga County 1998).

[3]Marek v. Marek, 158 Ohio App. 3d 750, 2004-Ohio-5556, 822 N.E.2d 410 (9th Dist. Summit County 2004).

[4]Wheeler v. Wheeler, 2005-Ohio-1025, 2005 WL 564176 (Ohio Ct. App. 6th Dist. Ottawa County 2005).

[5]Chapman v. Chapman, 2005-Ohio-2801, 2005 WL 1331942 (Ohio Ct. App. 10th Dist. Franklin County 2005).

[6]Keller v. Keller, 2005-Ohio-3302, 2005 WL 1523860 (Ohio Ct. App. 9th Dist. Wayne County 2005).

[7]Matter of Neff, 1998 WL 295576 (Ohio Ct. App. 12th Dist. Clermont County 1998) (even if an obligor is incarcerated, the guidelines must be followed with a deviation finding if the amount would be unjust or inappropriate and not in the best interest of the child); Emmert v. Emmert, 2000 WL 192135 (Ohio Ct. App. 1st Dist. Hamilton County 2000), (the court held that incarceration is a voluntary act, caused by wrongful conduct and cannot justify a modification of child support). See also Kreuzer v. Kreuzer, 2001 WL 468406 (Ohio Ct. App. 2d Dist. Greene County 2001) (holding incarceration is not a valid changed circumstance warranting reduction of support); Rhodes v. Rhodes, 2001-Ohio-3410, 2001 WL 1199877 (Ohio Ct. App. 7th Dist. Belmont County 2001) (no suspension of child support due to incarceration); In re Pease, 2006-Ohio-2785, 2006 WL 1519685 (Ohio Ct. App. 3d Dist. Mercer County

should have income imputed to her.[8] An obligor father was voluntarily underemployed after he quit his $54,974 per year job as a store manager because he refused to work on Sundays and became a building manager for $30,000.[9] An obligee mother is voluntarily underemployed where she is working 16 hours per week for $20,250 when she previously earned $92,000 for a 32-hour workweek and $140,000 for a full time workweek. The parties' plan that she would stay home with the children until they started school was no longer feasible once the parties sought a divorce.[10] It is voluntary underemployment to accept an employee buyout which was not mandatory, would not have resulted in the termination of employment if the obligor father had refused it, and where his salary was $52,000, but was reduced to $26,000 when he obtained new employment.[11]

A trial court may impute income to an obligor where he lost a job and did nothing but "put out feelers" for a new job.[12] However, where an obligor lost his job due to his employer's bankruptcy and he actively sought employment, it is an abuse of discretion to impute income to him.[13] Termination of employment for cause, with or without criminal charges, may be voluntary underemployment.[14]

Voluntary underemployment caused by quitting the former job to start one's own business must be tested not only by whether the change is voluntary, but also whether it was made with due regard to the obligor's income-producing abilities and duty to provide for the continuing needs of the children.[15] Due regard for consequences to the ability to support one's children seem to be a measure in many cases involving modification and voluntary underemployment. Where due regard is not given to the effect on one's ability to meet a child support obligation, a trial court errs in allowing the modification.[16]

It is possible that a consequential reduction in income due to a vol-

---

2006) (support shall not be suspended for incarcerated obligor and his incentive pay in the correction institute is attachable).

[8]Barto v. Barto, 2001 WL 1560903 (Ohio Ct. App. 11th Dist. Lake County 2001).

[9]Cockrell v. Stright, 123 Ohio Misc. 2d 72, 2003-Ohio-2757, 789 N.E.2d 1199 (C.P. 2003).

[10]Justice v. Justice, 2007-Ohio-5186, 2007 WL 2821794 (Ohio Ct. App. 12th Dist. Warren County 2007).

[11]McBryer v. McBryer, 2008-Ohio-5845, 2008 WL 4866610 (Ohio Ct. App. 9th Dist. Summit County 2008).

[12]Barnick v. Barnick, 2002-Ohio-1104, 2002 WL 388906 (Ohio Ct. App. 9th Dist. Summit County 2002).

[13]Badovick v. Badovick, 128 Ohio App. 3d 18, 713 N.E.2d 1066 (8th Dist. Cuyahoga County 1998).

[14]Cesa v. Cesa, 2001 WL 1528911 (Ohio Ct. App. 5th Dist. Coshocton County 2001).

[15]Woloch v. Foster, 98 Ohio App. 3d 806, 649 N.E.2d 918 (2d Dist. Miami County 1994); Moauro v. Moauro, 2000 WL 1682608 (Ohio Ct. App. 5th Dist. Stark County 2000).

[16]Barnard v. Kuppin, 1999 WL 699595 (Ohio Ct. App. 1st Dist. Hamilton County 1999); Castle v. Castle, 2000 WL 1471548 (Ohio Ct. App. 9th Dist. Lorain County

untary change is not voluntary underemployment when it was commenced in good faith and was a reasonable choice in an effort to better the obligor's life in the hope of ultimate benefits to the lives of the children.[17] However, an obligor's termination of employment to enroll as a full-time law student, being a voluntary choice, was not a change of circumstances that would warrant a modification of support. But, the allowance of a partial payment by the trial court while obligor finished law school with the balance accruing as an arrearage payable upon graduation is a reasonable and equitable order.[18]

A father's compassionate role in caring for his sick girlfriend rather than working is voluntary unemployment.[19]

Where a child support obligor took a position within her own community with a salary of about $15,000 less per year than her previous position, but did so for purposes of being able to attend her children's after-school activities and eliminating the time and expense of commuting two-and-a-half hours round trip each day, the trial court erred in finding her to be voluntarily underemployed because there was no evidence that she could have earned more in her home community and opportunities in more distant communities are not relevant.[20] The lack of overtime earnings is not underemployment for imputation purposes.[21]

In the second part of the imputation analysis, the court or child support enforcement agency must determine what the parent would have earned if fully employed using the following criteria:

(1)   The parent's prior employment experience;

(2)   The parent's education;

(3)   The parent's physical and mental disabilities, if any;

(4)   The availability of employment in the geographic area in which the parent resides;

(5)   The prevailing wage and salary levels in the geographic area in which the parent resides;

(6)   The parent's special skills and training;

(7)   Whether there is evidence that the parent has the ability to earn the imputed income;

2000) (no downward modification where obligor terminated employment to attend school so that he could earn the same amount money he earned previously).

[17]Kellogg v. Current, 2002-Ohio-2827, 2002 WL 1299875 (Ohio Ct. App. 3d Dist. Marion County 2002).

[18]Baker v. Grathwohl, 97 Ohio App. 3d 116, 646 N.E.2d 253 (12th Dist. Butler County 1994).

[19]Jefferson County Child Support Enforcement Agency ex rel. Dillon v. Johnston, 2004-Ohio-4904, 2004 WL 2070644 (Ohio Ct. App. 7th Dist. Jefferson County 2004).

[20]Shank v. Shank, 122 Ohio App. 3d 189, 701 N.E.2d 439 (3d Dist. Marion County 1997). Accord, Ramey v. Ramey, 2009-Ohio-2909, 2009 WL 1719366 (Ohio Ct. App. 5th Dist. Fairfield County 2009) (changing from seasonal employment without benefits to a lower-paying city job with benefits was not voluntary underemployment).

[21]Fernback v. Fernback, 2001-Ohio-3482, 2001 WL 1647229 (Ohio Ct. App. 7th Dist. Mahoning County 2001).

(8)   The age and special needs of the child for whom child support is being calculated under this section;

(9)   The parent's increased earning capacity because of experience;

(10) Any other relevant factor.[22]

The second part of the analysis to impute income often fails where little or no evidence is adduced regarding the statutory factors or where the figure used for income is miscalculated.[23] However, a trial court is not required to hear evidence on each statutory factor or discuss each statutory factor.[24]

A trial court may impute income based on former wages when an obligor quits his job. No additional evidence is necessary.[25] The imputation of $65,000 where the obligee is currently earning $20,500, but previously earned $92,000 and $140,000, is appropriate.[26]

The consequence of a finding of voluntary underemployment or unemployment would be the use of that parent's income from previous employment to calculate child support. This results in a child support order based on income not currently being earned. Or, if the unemployed or underemployed parent is seeking a modification, then one would most likely be unwarranted because without a change to the income, the child support would not change more than ten percent and thus no change of circumstance would be found.

It is sometimes difficult to distinguish cases where income is imputed as a matter of fact rather than as a matter of law. The statutory two-part test applies to the imputation of income as a matter of law. However, there are a significant number of cases where income is imputed as a matter of fact. These cases do not involve intentional or unintentional unemployment or underemployment. Rather they involve lifestyle issues and credibility gaps where the trial court disbelieves the stated income of a parent. These cases often involve self-employed individuals. In determining income in these cases, the two-part test is irrelevant.[27] Income should be determined not by statutory imputation, but by using the lifestyle, past practices and debt structure as a gauge for the real amount of income earned.

These cases often involve forensic analysis of the parent's lifestyle or expenses. The statutory two-part test is unnecessary and the use of the word "imputation" confuses the issues on these cases. For example,

---

[22]RC 3119.01(C)(11)(a).

[23]Basham v. Basham, 2002-Ohio-4694, 2002 WL 31007154 (Ohio Ct. App. 3d Dist. Allen County 2002).

[24]Justice v. Justice, 2007-Ohio-5186, 2007 WL 2821794 (Ohio Ct. App. 12th Dist. Warren County 2007).

[25]Bowlin v. Steele, 2000 WL 146581 (Ohio Ct. App. 12th Dist. Butler County 2000).

[26]Justice v. Justice, 2007-Ohio-5186, 2007 WL 2821794 (Ohio Ct. App. 12th Dist. Warren County 2007).

[27]In re Glaser Children, 2000 WL 1682613 (Ohio Ct. App. 5th Dist. Stark County 2000).

the trial court used the two-part imputation test where an obligor father was self-employed in a bar-restaurant business grossing $300,000 per year, but paid himself only $15,000 and his girlfriend $20,000 per year, but did not need to, where it found that he under-reported cash and income and that his income was $75,000 per year.[28] Where an obligor had housing expenses in excess of his claimed income, traveled frequently, made expensive home improvements and had a lifestyle inconsistent with his stated income, the trial court was correct to determine that his income was $36,000.[29] Another example is the determination of the obligor's income from his trucking business by using the normal hourly rate he paid his employees plus his truck depreciation and his interest and dividend income to approximate his earnings.[30] Trial courts have also used averaging of previous income where the current income reported during litigation is significantly less and the lifestyle and expenditures of the party do not harmonize with the stated income.[31]

§ 19:14 Parenting time

All child support orders must include specific parenting time or visitation orders for regular, holiday, vacation, parenting time, and special visitation in accordance with RC 3109.051, RC 3109.11, and RC 3109.12 and RC 3119.08.

Child support must not be withheld because of the denial or interference with the right of parenting time.[1] The appropriate remedy for the denial or interference with parenting time or visitation is an action for contempt against the offending parent. When a court is considering the best interest of a child, whether in an original or a modification proceeding, the court shall consider whether a parent has continuously and willfully denied the other parent any court-ordered parenting time.

---

[28]Calkins v. Calkins, 2002 WL 1009289 (Ohio Ct. App. 12th Dist. Butler County 2002).

[29]Quinn v. Paras, 2003-Ohio-4952, 2003 WL 22146526 (Ohio Ct. App. 8th Dist. Cuyahoga County 2003).

[30]Tate v. Tate, 2004-Ohio-22, 2004 WL 26517 (Ohio Ct. App. 5th Dist. Richland County 2004).

[31]Moore v. Moore, 175 Ohio App. 3d 1, 2008-Ohio-255, 884 N.E.2d 1113 (6th Dist. Ottawa County 2008), appeal not allowed, 118 Ohio St. 3d 1506, 2008-Ohio-3369, 889 N.E.2d 1025 (2008).

[Section 19:14]

[1]RC 3109.05(D), RC 3119.09.

§ 19:15 Tax dependency exemptions

The tax dependency exemption shall be allocated in any establishment or modification of child support.[1] The court may accept the agreement of the parents, if one is offered. If no agreement is proposed, then the court must award the exemption to the parent for whom the award would serve to further the child's best interest. There are specific findings required by RC 3119.82 which include any net tax savings, the relative financial circumstances and needs of the parents and children, the amount of time the children spend with each parent, the eligibility of either or both parents for the federal earned income tax credit, or other state or federal tax credit, and any other relevant factor concerning the best interest of the children.[2] A trial court need not discuss each factor so long as it discusses the operative facts relating to its decision and considers the statute.[3]

A trial court should not automatically award the tax dependency exemption to the parent with the higher income.[4] Where a trial court considers the statutory factors in awarding the tax exemption, such consideration is a best interest analysis.[5] In determining the value of the tax exemption, the court may accept a calculation using the FinPlan software.[6] An agreement by the parties that the tax exemption shall be awarded to the obligor so long as he remains current rather than "substantially current", should be enforced with the equities considered and a $2000 arrearage accrued in a prior year during a lay-off should not prevent the obligor from claiming the tax exemption.[7] The award of the tax exemption is not in the nature of a property division and is always modifiable.[8]

In the absence of an agreement otherwise, the child support pay-

---

[Section 19:15]

[1]RC 3119.82; Horvath v. Horvath, 2004-Ohio-6764, 2004 WL 2892372 (Ohio Ct. App. 5th Dist. Stark County 2004); Piciacchia v. Piciacchia, 2007-Ohio-2328, 2007 WL 1413216 (Ohio Ct. App. 5th Dist. Stark County 2007) (even where no change of circumstances was found by the court to warrant a modification of child support, the court has jurisdiction to modify the tax exemption).

[2]RC 3119.82.

[3]Dunlap v. Dunlap, 2008-Ohio-3201, 2008 WL 2582924 (Ohio Ct. App. 9th Dist. Summit County 2008); Clark v. Clark, 2007-Ohio-5771, 2007 WL 3131941 (Ohio Ct. App. 3d Dist. Union County 2007).

[4]Nist v. Nist, 2003-Ohio-3292, 2003 WL 21452876 (Ohio Ct. App. 5th Dist. Delaware County 2003); Geschke v. Geschke, 2002-Ohio-5426, 2002 WL 31255752 (Ohio Ct. App. 9th Dist. Medina County 2002).

[5]Foster v. Foster, 2004-Ohio-3905, 2004 WL 1662103 (Ohio Ct. App. 6th Dist. Sandusky County 2004).

[6]Cramblett v. Cramblett, 2006-Ohio-4615, 2006 WL 2574561 (Ohio Ct. App. 7th Dist. Harrison County 2006).

[7]McIntire v. Lenarz, 2007-Ohio-2004, 2007 WL 1219488 (Ohio Ct. App. 5th Dist. Guernsey County 2007).

[8]Schott v. Schott, 2004-Ohio-1914, 2004 WL 817364 (Ohio Ct. App. 5th Dist. Tuscarawas County 2004).

ments of the obligor parent must be substantially current for the year that the dependency exemption is claimed by that parent.[9]

The value of the tax dependency exemption has increased significantly in recent years with the addition of the under-17 child tax credit. The Jobs and Growth Tax Relief Reconciliation Act of 2003 increased the value of the under-17 child tax credit to $1000. Parents in the lowest income bracket who are eligible for earned income credit may not receive the full value and parents in the higher income brackets will have the tax dependency exemption and the under-17 child tax credit phased out. The phase out begins at different income levels for the tax dependency exemption and for the under-17 child tax credit.

In awarding the tax dependency exemption, the trial court has the inherent power to order the custodial parent to release the tax dependency exemption to the other parent, or be subject to a finding of contempt of court.[10]

§ 19:16 Attorney fees

The court may include in the support order a statement ordering either party to pay the costs of the action, including but not limited to, attorney fees, fees for genetic tests in contested actions, and court fees.[1]

§ 19:17 Modification of prior orders—Jurisdiction

The child support enforcement agency has the authority to investigate, obtain information, recalculate, and issue administrative orders modifying support.[1]

The trial court retains jurisdiction to modify child support under the Civil Rules and statutes.[2] The process in the trial court requires the filing of a motion with a request for modification and request for service on the other party.[3] If a modification order is made, the order may be made effective from the date the motion for modification was

---

[9]RC 3119.82. See Davis v. Davis, 112 Ohio App. 3d 518, 679 N.E.2d 319 (6th Dist. Lucas County 1996).

[10]RC 3119.82.

[Section 19:16]

[1]RC 3123.17; RC 3105.73; Rowan v. Rowan, 72 Ohio St. 3d 486, 1995-Ohio-110, 650 N.E.2d 1360 (1995) (successful prosecution of claims is key to obtaining funds from which child support can be paid and, therefore, attorney's contingent fee for workers' compensation claim should be paid before remaining funds are released for past due child support).

[Section 19:17]

[1]RC 3119.63.

[2]RC 3109.05, RC 3119.02, RC 3119.79; Civ. R. 75(J).

[3]Civ. R. 4 to 4.6.

filed.[4] But, child support must not commence prior to the actual physical possession of the child.[5]

A trial court cannot modify child support without a pending motion for modification,[6] except in the case of an appeal from an administrative modification from the child support enforcement agency.[7]

A trial court may consider multiple worksheets based on changes in income and status while a motion to modify is pending for the purpose of judicial economy and equity.[8]

A 60(B) motion is not a proper vehicle to modify child support,[9] nor is a collateral attack through a motion to modify the proper vehicle to vacate a judgment.[10]

§ 19:18   Modification of prior orders—Change of circumstance

A two-step analysis is used in a request for modification. Initially the court must decide if a change of circumstances exists.[1] The statute provides that a difference of 10% is deemed a change of circumstances.[2] A court need only find a 10% difference OR an alternative substantial change of circumstance, not both.[3] The 10% difference must be between the amount currently ordered and the new amount calculated pursuant to the guideline worksheet. Other substantial changes of circumstances not contemplated when the last order was issued or modified may also be considered.[4] In determining a change of circumstance,

---

[4]Hamilton v. Hamilton, 107 Ohio App. 3d 132, 667 N.E.2d 1256 (6th Dist. Lucas County 1995); accord, Trump v. Trump, 136 Ohio App. 3d 123, 736 N.E.2d 39 (9th Dist. Summit County 1999). See Text § 19:10, Computation requirements.

[5]Cossin v. Holley, 2007-Ohio-5258, 2007 WL 2852163 (Ohio Ct. App. 5th Dist. Morrow County 2007).

[6]Civ. R. 75(J).

[7]RC 3119.71(B).

[8]Horvath v. Horvath, 2004-Ohio-6764, 2004 WL 2892372 (Ohio Ct. App. 5th Dist. Stark County 2004); Anthony v. Clark, 2009-Ohio-894, 2009 WL 498336 (Ohio Ct. App. 5th Dist. Richland County 2009).

[9]Lawler v. Lawler, 1999 WL 1139916 (Ohio Ct. App. 10th Dist. Franklin County 1999).

[10]In re Marriage of Henson, 2007-Ohio-4376, 2007 WL 2410356 (Ohio Ct. App. 11th Dist. Trumbull County 2007), appeal not allowed, 116 Ohio St. 3d 1478, 2008-Ohio-153, 879 N.E.2d 785 (2008).

[Section 19:18]

[1]RC 3119.79. Yark v. Yark, 2001 WL 27550 (Ohio Ct. App. 6th Dist. Fulton County 2001).

[2]RC 3119.79. Pratt v. McCullough, 100 Ohio App. 3d 479, 654 N.E.2d 372 (12th Dist. Warren County 1995); Smith v. Collins, 107 Ohio App. 3d 100, 667 N.E.2d 1236 (9th Dist. Summit County 1995); Towne v. Towne, 1996 WL 688155 (Ohio Ct. App. 9th Dist. Summit County 1996).

[3]Karales v. Karales, 2006-Ohio-2963, 2006 WL 1629005 (Ohio Ct. App. 10th Dist. Franklin County 2006).

[4]RC 3119.79.

the court shall also consider the cost of health insurance or adequacy of health insurance.[5]

There is an exception to the rule that the 10% difference and the change of circumstances are alternatives. Where the parties entered into an agreement that represented a deviation upward, a court should require both a 10% difference in the child support amount AND a substantial change of circumstances that was not contemplated at the time of the agreement.[6] This modification methodology might also be used in cases where the combined income exceeds $150,000 since there is no statutory guidance for modifications of child support where the original order was issued before the statutory language change in March 2001.

After finding a change of circumstances, the court must determine the appropriate amount of support.[7] It is not necessary to prove an increase in the needs of the child to justify an increase in support.[8]

A trial court errs in failing to grant a modification where income levels at the modification hearing evidence a 10% downward deviation from calculated amount.[9] It is, however, inappropriate for a court to lower a support obligation where it found no substantial change in the parties' circumstances and no decrease in the obligor's income.[10] A trial court errs if it overrules a motion to modify support without explaining why it found no change in circumstances existed and without completing a guideline worksheet.[11]

The statute does not prohibit a party from voluntarily undertaking

---

[5]RC 3119.79.

[6]Bonner v. Bonner, 2005-Ohio-6173, 2005 WL 3111940 (Ohio Ct. App. 3d Dist. Union County 2005) (upward deviation in separation agreement); In re Marriage of Henson, 2007-Ohio-4376, 2007 WL 2410356 (Ohio Ct. App. 11th Dist. Trumbull County 2007), appeal not allowed, 116 Ohio St. 3d 1478, 2008-Ohio-153, 879 N.E.2d 785 (2008), (where obligor agreed to $2250 per month in child support when guideline amount would have been under $700 per month, the support is not modifiable absent a change of circumstances not contemplated by the parties at the time of the agreement); Steggeman v. Steggeman, 2007-Ohio-5482, 2007 WL 2983153, (Ohio Ct. App. 3d Dist. Logan County 2007) (mere passage of time, remarriage of obligee and bankruptcy of obligor are insufficient to be deemed substantial change of circumstance not contemplated at the time of the agreement).

[7]RC 3119.79.

[8]Yark v. Yark, 2001 WL 27550 (Ohio Ct. App. 6th Dist. Fulton County 2001).

[9]Cook v. Cook, 143 Ohio App. 3d 687, 758 N.E.2d 1158 (9th Dist. Lorain County 2001).

[10]Green v. Green, 2002-Ohio-2180, 2002-Ohio-2180, 2002 WL 850980 (Ohio Ct. App. 12th Dist. Butler County 2002); Church v. Gadd, 1999 WL 454466 (Ohio Ct. App. 11th Dist. Geauga County 1999).

[11]Marker v. Grimm, 65 Ohio St. 3d 139, 601 N.E.2d 496 (1992); Zayed v. Zayed, 100 Ohio App. 3d 410, 654 N.E.2d 163 (8th Dist. Cuyahoga County 1995); Seegert v. Zietlow, 95 Ohio App. 3d 451, 642 N.E.2d 697 (8th Dist. Cuyahoga County 1994); Tobens v. Brill, 89 Ohio App. 3d 298, 624 N.E.2d 265 (3d Dist. Auglaize County 1993); Ingalls v. Ingalls, 88 Ohio App. 3d 570, 624 N.E.2d 368 (8th Dist. Cuyahoga County 1993); McClain v. McClain, 87 Ohio App. 3d 856, 623 N.E.2d 242 (9th Dist. Summit County 1993).

a child support obligation in an amount greater than the statutory level. As noted above, however, modification of an increased child support order may be more difficult.

In contrast, previous waivers of child support have been determined to be immaterial, and a later child support order may be construed as an initial order for purposes of deviation calculation.[12] Also, if there was a deviation previously, the amount that would have previously been ordered is not relevant.[13]

Where the parties entered into an agreement to limit the modifiability of the child support, there is conflicting case law. Where an obligor father sought a modification after he had voluntarily agreed to limit the modifiability, the court upheld the limitation and denied the modification.[14] But, where an obligor father resisted a modification using the parties' limitation, the appellate court upheld the right to modify the child support because the parties cannot override the court's duty to review child support.[15] The distinction seems to rest on the direction the child support is being modified: the parties may limit decreases, but not increases in child support.

In a modification proceeding, it is error for the trial court not to complete and include a child support computation worksheet in the record.[16] Adequate documentation must be provided to allow for reduction of child support based upon a reduction in earnings.[17]

§ 19:19 Modification of prior orders—Prior waiver

The Supreme Court of Ohio held in *DePalmo v. DePalmo*[1] that even where no child support was ordered initially, a court must prepare a guideline worksheet in compliance with *Marker v. Grimm* when later

---

[12]DePalmo v. DePalmo, 78 Ohio St. 3d 535, 1997-Ohio-184, 679 N.E.2d 266 (1997).

[13]Fox v. Fox, 2004-Ohio-3344, 2004 WL 1433553 (Ohio Ct. App. 3d Dist. Hancock County 2004); but see, Flanagan v. Flanagan, 174 Ohio App. 3d 77, 2007-Ohio-6209, 880 N.E.2d 962 (9th Dist. Lorain County 2007).

[14]Le v. Bird, 2006-Ohio-204, 2006 WL 156834 (Ohio Ct. App. 12th Dist. Butler County 2006).

[15]Quint v. Lomakoski, 173 Ohio App. 3d 146, 2007-Ohio-4722, 877 N.E.2d 738 (2d Dist. Greene County 2007).

[16]Marker v. Grimm, 65 Ohio St. 3d 139, 601 N.E.2d 496 (1992); Zayed v. Zayed, 100 Ohio App. 3d 410, 654 N.E.2d 163 (8th Dist. Cuyahoga County 1995); Seegert v. Zietlow, 95 Ohio App. 3d 451, 642 N.E.2d 697 (8th Dist. Cuyahoga County 1994); Tobens v. Brill, 89 Ohio App. 3d 298, 624 N.E.2d 265 (3d Dist. Auglaize County 1993); Ingalls v. Ingalls, 88 Ohio App. 3d 570, 624 N.E.2d 368 (8th Dist. Cuyahoga County 1993); McClain v. McClain, 87 Ohio App. 3d 856, 623 N.E.2d 242 (9th Dist. Summit County 1993).

[17]Houts v. Houts, 99 Ohio App. 3d 70, 651 N.E.2d 1031 (Mercer County 1995).

[Section 19:19]

[1]DePalmo v. DePalmo, 78 Ohio St. 3d 535, 1997-Ohio-184, 679 N.E.2d 266 (1997); State ex rel. Lanier v. Rozzi, 1998 WL 114390 (Ohio Ct. App. 9th Dist. Medina County 1998).

considering child support. In so doing, the court expressly rejected the "dual-threshold" test described in earlier case law.[2]

Where a child support order was entered in which the residential parent assumed full responsibility for the child's support, a later request by that parent for payment of support is subject to the 10% standard for finding a change of circumstances. The initial support order was zero dollars, so any amount determined under the guidelines would exceed that amount by more than 10%.[3]

§ 19:20   Modification of prior orders—Lottery winnings

When an individual wins a lottery prize of $600 or more, RC 3770.071 provides that the lottery commission shall require the person entitled to the prize to affirm in writing, under oath, whether or not the person is in default under a support order. If the winner affirms that they are in default, the winnings will be temporarily withheld and a lottery designee will inform the court that issued the support order that the person is entitled to a prize, the amount of the prize and how the prize will be disbursed.[1]

Upon receipt of the information of the winning lottery prize, the court will schedule a hearing to determine if the person is in support default. After the hearing if the lottery winner is in default of support payments, the court shall issue an order to the lottery commission headquarters requiring the lottery designee to deduct from any unpaid winnings a specified amount for child or spousal support to satisfy the unpaid support amount.[2]

A lucky lottery winner was subject to an increase in his child support obligation when the new calculation increased his prior support order of $63 per week to $31,245 per year.[3] The obligor argued that the trial court erred in awarding more child support than was necessary to support the child. The appellate court stated that an increased economic need is not a requirement for obtaining an increase, so long as the increase in the obligor's income would reflect more than a 10% change.

If lottery winnings are paid in a lump sum, or in a series of payments made over a period less than three years, the lottery winnings

---

[2]DePalmo v. DePalmo, 78 Ohio St. 3d 535, 1997-Ohio-184, 679 N.E.2d 266 (1997).

[3]Sapinsley v. Sapinsley, 171 Ohio App. 3d 74, 2007-Ohio-1320, 869 N.E.2d 702 (1st Dist. Hamilton County 2007); Powers v. Powers, 2008-Ohio-3159, 2008 WL 2550765, (Ohio Ct. App. 1st Dist. Hamilton County 2008), appeal not allowed, 120 Ohio St. 3d 1420, 2008-Ohio-6166, 897 N.E.2d 654 (2008).

[Section 19:20]

[1]RC 3770.07.

[2]RC 3770.071.

[3]Pratt v. McCullough, 100 Ohio App. 3d 479, 654 N.E.2d 372 (12th Dist. Warren County 1995).

are "nonrecurring income" and are excluded from gross income.[4] The investment income from such winnings, however, can be used to calculate gross income. A trial court may not order an obligor to create a trust that extends beyond the child's age of majority.[5]

§ 19:21 Commencement date of support modification and retroactive child support

As a general rule, a child support modification will be effective on the date a motion was filed.[1] Commencement of an order prior to a motion filing is generally prohibited.[2] However, the choice of a commencement date subsequent to the filing date is within the discretion of the trial court; but, a trial court errs in failing to make a child support modification retroactive to the date the motion was filed without an explanation for the adoption of some other date.[3] The purpose of this rule is to prevent inequitable results that could occur due to the substantial time, which sometimes elapses before the disposition of the motion.[4]

The trial court, when ruling on a request for judicial review of an administrative modification, shall make the child support order retroactive to the first day of the month after the "date certain" review at the child support enforcement agency.[5] However, the trial court cannot retroactively modify the arrearages accrued under an administrative order issued in a paternity case.[6]

Pursuant to RC 3119.83 and RC 3119.84,[7] a trial court may not retroactively modify an obligor's duty to pay a delinquent support order except those payments due after the filing of a motion to modify

---

[4]RC 3119.01.

[5]Barlow v. Ray, 1997 WL 232241 (Ohio Ct. App. 3d Dist. Marion County 1997).

[Section 19:21]

[1]Bowen v. Bowen, 132 Ohio App. 3d 616, 725 N.E.2d 1165 (9th Dist. Medina County 1999); Hamilton v. Hamilton, 107 Ohio App. 3d 132, 667 N.E.2d 1256 (6th Dist. Lucas County 1995).

[2]RC 3119.84.

[3]Schindler v. Schindler, 1998 WL 46764 (Ohio Ct. App. 9th Dist. Summit County 1998) (a trial court must make a separate finding if child support modification is not effective as of the date of filing); Krzynowek v. Krzynowek, 2000 WL 235756 (Ohio Ct. App. 8th Dist. Cuyahoga County 2000) (a trial court can modify child support several months after the filing where 10% change of circumstances did not occur until then).

[4]State ex rel. Draiss v. Draiss, 70 Ohio App. 3d 418, 591 N.E.2d 354 (9th Dist. Medina County 1990).

[5]RC 3119.71; Willier v. Willier, 175 Ohio App. 3d 793, 2008-Ohio-740, 889 N.E.2d 575 (3d Dist. Mercer County 2008).

[6]Jefferson Cty. Child Support Enforcement Agency ex rel. Gilliam v. DeLauder, 151 Ohio App. 3d 640, 2003-Ohio-693, 785 N.E.2d 482 (7th Dist. Jefferson County 2003).

[7]Formerly RC 3113.21(M)(4) and (5).

child support.[8] However, under the special circumstances where an obligor fraudulently misrepresents his income in a child support hearing and later is found in contempt for not reporting his increase in income, the trial court may retroactively modify his non-delinquent child support obligations.[9] Or, where an obligee fraudulently represented day-care expenses, the child support may be retroactively reduced.[10]

Where the court granted credit to the obligor for the time the children lived with him, it is not a retroactive modification prohibited under RC 3119.83 and RC 3119.84, but rather a permissible credit.[11] Where a domestic relations court granted possession to the father, but a juvenile court subsequently granted him custody, it is not error for a juvenile court to retroactively award the father child support back to the domestic relations court's order of possession.[12]

Where the court reserves jurisdiction to determine child support at the time of the divorce, it is not a retroactive modification to do so upon the proper motion.[13]

§ 19:22 Termination of support obligation—Support past age eighteen

A child support obligation extends beyond a child's eighteenth birthday by operation of law where the child attends, on a full time basis, any recognized and accredited high school, but no later than age nineteen.[1] The Supreme Court of Ohio in *Davis v. Davis*[2] defined "recognized and accredited" by the plain meanings of the words. Thus, "recognized" means "to acknowledge formally" and "accredited" means

---

[8]Danforth v. Danforth, 2001 WL 328556 (Ohio Ct. App. 8th Dist. Cuyahoga County 2001); Kiser v. Quartermaine, 1993 WL 496677, at *2 (Ohio Ct. App. 6th Dist. Wood County 1993) (equitable argument that there was an extra-judicial agreement to modify was held contrary to law); but see, Sprankle v. Sprankle, 1998 WL 159019 (Ohio Ct. App. 9th Dist. Medina County 1998) (RC 3113.2l(M)(4) does not bar a court from making child support retroactive before the motion was filed).

[9]Torbeck v. Torbeck, 2001 WL 1251219 (Ohio Ct. App. 1st Dist. Hamilton County 2001).

[10]Hanes v. Hanes, 2003-Ohio-2131, 2003 WL 1960934 (Ohio Ct. App. 3d Dist. Hancock County 2003).

[11]Gerlach v. Gerlach, 124 Ohio App. 3d 246, 705 N.E.2d 1287 (10th Dist. Franklin County 1997); Peterson v. Hunt, 1998 WL 720690 (Ohio Ct. App. 3d Dist. Allen County 1998); Viox v. Metcalfe, 1998 WL 87579 (Ohio Ct. App. 12th Dist. Clermont County 1998); but see, Bonenfant v. Bonenfant, 2005-Ohio-6037, 2005 WL 3031893 (Ohio Ct. App. 12th Dist. Butler County 2005).

[12]Zamos v. Zamos, 2004-Ohio-2310, 2004 WL 1043673 (Ohio Ct. App. 11th Dist. Portage County 2004).

[13]Brittingham v. Brittingham, 2003-Ohio-812, 2003 WL 434590 (Ohio Ct. App. 12th Dist. Brown County 2003).

[Section 19:22]

[1]RC 3103.03(B), RC 3103.031.

[2]Davis v. Davis, 115 Ohio St. 3d 180, 2007-Ohio-5049, 873 N.E.2d 1305 (2007).

"publicly sanctioned" or "officially authorized"; and, the modifier "any" means "one that is selected without restriction or limitation of choice".[3] This would include schools that are not located within the state of Ohio, such as boarding schools or distance learning facilities, and would include non-traditional education such as home-education or schools located in state youth facilities.[4]

If by a separation agreement incorporated into a decree, a party has agreed to pay child support beyond the age of eighteen, the court may enforce the provision pursuant to the Ohio Revised Code and case law.[5] College clauses have also been interpreted and enforced by the courts.[6]

Pursuant to RC 3119.86, a court ordered child support order shall not continue beyond the child's eighteenth birthday, unless: the child is mentally or physically disabled and is incapable of supporting or maintaining himself or herself; or, the child's parents have agreed to continue support beyond the child's eighteenth birthday pursuant to a separation agreement that was incorporated into a decree of divorce or dissolution; or, the child continuously attends a recognized and accredited high school on a full-time basis on and after the child's eighteenth birthday, but no later than age nineteen. A court does not retain jurisdiction to enforce an award of the tax dependency exemption for emancipated children.[7]

A parent's duty of support to a child imposed pursuant to an administrative child support order also shall not continue beyond the child's eighteenth birthday, unless the child continuously attends a

---

[3]Davis v. Davis, 115 Ohio St. 3d 180, 183, 2007-Ohio-5049, 873 N.E.2d 1305 (2007).

[4]Primack v. Primack, 2005-Ohio-1645, 2005 WL 774040 (Ohio Ct. App. 5th Dist. Stark County 2005) (where 18 year old child is incarcerated, but attending high school on a full-time basis, child support shall continue); Gatchel v. Gatchel, 159 Ohio App. 3d 519, 2005-Ohio-148, 824 N.E.2d 576 (3d Dist. Wyandot County 2005) (where 18 year old child is officially registered for home schooling and is attending classes at the Christian Learning Center, the acceptance of the home schooling status by the state satisfies the requirement that the child attend a recognized and accredited high school); Demcho v. Demcho, 2004-Ohio-4868, 2004 WL 2047363 (Ohio Ct. App. 9th Dist. Medina County 2004) (where 18 year old child is enrolled at his former high school using a friend's address, but the obligee is still supporting him, the lawfulness of his enrollment is irrelevant and child support shall continue).

[5]RC 3119.86(1)(b).

[6]Farra v. Farra, 1996 WL 596536 (Ohio Ct. App. 2d Dist. Montgomery County 1996); Jack v. Jack, 139 Ohio App. 3d 814, 2000-Ohio-2553, 745 N.E.2d 1101 (7th Dist. Jefferson County 2000) (where the terms are overbroad and ambiguous, the trial court has the authority to interpret the terms); In re Petition of Netotea, 2006-Ohio-1445, 2006 WL 763128 (Ohio Ct. App. 11th Dist. Trumbull County 2006) (college provision is not child support and is, therefore, not modifiable; dissenting opinion issued); Gratzmiller v. Gratzmiller, 2007-Ohio-4987, 2007 WL 2758660 (Ohio Ct. App. 7th Dist. Jefferson County 2007) (clear and unambiguous words such as "at a state institution" must be given their ordinary meaning when interpreted and enforced by the trial court).

[7]Chumney v. Scott, 2006-Ohio-439, 2006 WL 242555 (Ohio Ct. App. 5th Dist. Tuscarawas County 2006).

recognized and accredited high school on a full-time basis on and after the child's eighteenth birthday, but no later than age nineteen.[8]

The statute further provides that if a court incorporates a separation agreement into a decree of divorce or dissolution that orders support to terminate on a certain day, the court may not require the duty of support to continue beyond the date the child's parents have agreed support should terminate. However, the Supreme Court of Ohio subsequently contradicted this in *Hoelscher v. Hoelscher*,[9] which held that a child support order may continue beyond the age of majority so long as a child continuously attends a recognized and accredited high school on a full-time basis, even if the continuation is contradicted by the express language of the parties' agreement.[10] Therefore, the parents can contract to extend the support beyond age nineteen, but cannot contract to terminate the support before age 19 if the child is still continuously enrolled on a full-time basis at a recognized and accredited high school.

§ 19:23 Termination of support obligation—Emancipation

The determination of emancipation is decided upon a case-by-case basis dependent upon the individual facts and circumstances of each case.[1]

The party requesting termination of child support bears the burden of proving the emancipation of the child.[2] There is no bright-line standard for determining whether a child has become emancipated.[3]

"Emancipation" has been defined to mean that a child is free from parental control.[4] Emancipation is a relief from the duty of support as it applies to a minor child, but a child may reach the age of majority and still be owed a duty of support.[5] For example, a disabled child over the age of 18 has reached the age of majority, but is not

---

[8]RC 3119.86(A)(2).

[9]Hoelscher v. Hoelscher, 91 Ohio St. 3d 500, 2001-Ohio-103, 747 N.E.2d 227 (2001).

[10]This superseded In re Dissolution of Marriage of Lazor, 59 Ohio St. 3d 201, 572 N.E.2d 66 (1991).

[Section 19:23]

[1]Price v. Price, 12 Ohio App. 3d 42, 465 N.E.2d 922 (2d Dist. Darke County 1983).

[2]Smyers v. Abramovich, 2001 WL 222962 (Ohio Ct. App. 9th Dist. Summit County 2001).

[3]Powell v. Powell, 111 Ohio App. 3d 418, 676 N.E.2d 556 (4th Dist. Athens County 1996); State ex rel. Spencer v. Gatten, 2007-Ohio-4071, 2007 WL 2269693 (Ohio Ct. App. 8th Dist. Cuyahoga County 2007).

[4]Price v. Price, 12 Ohio App. 3d 42, 465 N.E.2d 922 (2d Dist. Darke County 1983).

[5]Swanson v. Swanson, 109 Ohio App. 3d 231, 671 N.E.2d 1333 (2d Dist. Greene County 1996) (a daughter having reached age 18, but still in high school, is owed a duty of support despite having moved out of her mother's house prior to her graduation).

emancipated because he was in high school and in need of support; therefore, his parents' duty of support is not terminated.[6] A temporary absence from the home of a parent will not emancipate a child so long as that child is still dependent on the parent for care.[7] A child who has turned 18 and is not attending high school physically at her school, but who is participating in an off-campus program, is not emancipated.[8]

An obligor may be denied credit for overpaid child support, when obligee successfully asserts defenses of laches and estoppel, even though obligee had a duty to report the emancipation to CSEA.[9]

A trial court errs in terminating support on an ex parte motion without notice or an opportunity to be heard. The child support enforcement agency must conduct a statutory investigation.[10]

§ 19:24 Termination of support obligation—Death of obligor

A child support order in Ohio does not survive the death of the obligor unless the child support order so provides.[1] An order from another state, which state's law does not allow the survival of the order after the death of the obligor, may only be enforced for payments which have accrued and which are not subject to modification retroactively.[2]

§ 19:25 Termination of support obligation—Adoption

Child support will not be due by an obligor whose parental rights are terminated by an adoption of the child subject to the child support order, but past due support is not forgiven by the adoption.[1] The obligation to pay child support shall terminate upon entry of the interlocutory order and shall not be due for the 6-month period of time

---

[6]Risser v. Risser, 173 Ohio App. 3d 430, 2007-Ohio-4936, 878 N.E.2d 1073 (3d Dist. Hardin County 2007), appeal not allowed, 117 Ohio St. 3d 1406, 2008-Ohio-565, 881 N.E.2d 274 (2008).

[7]Matter of Siefker v. Siefker, 1997 WL 658995 (Ohio Ct. App. 3d Dist. Putnam County 1997).

[8]Weber v. Weber, 2001 WL 542319 (Ohio Ct. App. 9th Dist. Lorain County 2001).

[9]Shepherd v. Shepherd, 2000 WL 459700 (Ohio Ct. App. 7th Dist. Jefferson County 2000).

[10]Cox v. Beers, 2000 WL 492450 (Ohio Ct. App. 5th Dist. Fairfield County 2000).

[Section 19:24]

[1]Gilford v. Wurster, 24 Ohio App. 3d 77, 493 N.E.2d 258 (9th Dist. Lorain County 1983).

[2]Barnett v. Barnett, 85 Ohio App. 3d 1, 619 N.E.2d 38 (9th Dist. Lorain County 1993).

[Section 19:25]

[1]Hudgins v. Mitchell, 128 Ohio App. 3d 403, 715 N.E.2d 213 (9th Dist. Summit County 1998).

between the interlocutory and final orders of adoption.[2] The Supreme Court of Ohio held in *Byrd v. Knuckles*[3] that parties may waive past arrearages in an exchange for a consent to adopt where the agreement was reasonable and there are no public funds owed.

§ 19:26 Contempt

An action for contempt of court may be brought against an obligor who has failed to pay child support.[1] The maximum penalties for contempt of court are set forth in RC 2705.05. These are for a first offense, a fine of not more than $250 and/or a definite term of imprisonment for not more than 30 days; for a second offense, a fine of not more than $500 and/or a definite term of imprisonment for not more than 60 days; and, for a third offense, a fine of not more than $1000 and/or a definite term of imprisonment for not more than 90 days.[2]

For orders entered on or after July 1, 1992, if the court determines that failure to pay support is willful, the court must assess interest at the rate specified in RC 1343.03 on the amount of support the obligor failed to pay.[3] The Supreme Court of Ohio in *Dunbar v. Dunbar*[4] held that arrearages, which arose prior to that date which had not been reduced to judgment, were not subject to the statutory award of interest.

If a person is found in contempt for failure to provide support, the court must, in addition to any other remedy or penalty, assess all court costs arising out of that proceeding and require the obligor to pay reasonable attorney fees arising out of the act of contempt as determined by the court.[5]

The inability to pay may be used as a defense at the time of the sentencing; although an inability to pay, coupled with prior opportunities to pay, which were ignored by the obligor, will not be a defense.[6] The obligor's alleged inability to pay coupled with his employers' failure to withhold the child support from his income are not defenses to

---

[2]In re Scheehle, 134 Ohio App. 3d 167, 730 N.E.2d 472 (10th Dist. Franklin County 1999).

[3]Byrd v. Knuckles, 120 Ohio St. 3d 428, 2008-Ohio-6318, 900 N.E.2d 164 (2008).

[Section 19:26]

[1]RC 2705.031.

[2]RC 2705.05.

[3]RC 3123.17.

[4]Dunbar v. Dunbar, 68 Ohio St. 3d 369, 1994-Ohio-509, 627 N.E.2d 532 (1994).

[5]RC 3105.21(C), RC 3109.05(C), RC 3111.13(F); Bergman v. Bergman, 2004-Ohio-584, 2004 WL 249607 (Ohio Ct. App. 10th Dist. Franklin County 2004).

[6]Elkins v. Elkins, 2002-Ohio-1348, 2002 WL 452539 (Ohio Ct. App. 10th Dist. Franklin County 2002).

the imposition of sentence after the obligor agreed to the finding of contempt and failed to purge.[7]

After a finding of contempt, however, a trial court abuses its discretion when it sanctions a child support obligor with a jail sentence, but does not permit him to purge himself of contempt.[8] Furthermore, the purge cannot be used to regulate future behavior, as in pay monthly support as the purge, but the purge may be to perform a separate act, as in pay an amount toward the arrearage.[9]

§ 19:27 Arrearages—Repayment plans

Absent good cause shown, arrearages shall be collected with each payment of support at a rate of at least twenty percent (20%) of the current support payment.[1] A hardship on the obligor might be good cause to reduce the payments on arrears. A current support order that exceeds the limits of collection under the Consumer Credit Protection Act, 15 U.S.C.A. 1673(b), would constitute good cause.[2]

The trial court or child support enforcement agency continues to have jurisdiction to collect past due child support after the current child support order terminates.[3] The amount withheld as payment toward the arrearages shall be at least equal to the amount that was withheld or deducted under the terminated child support order.[4]

Previous case law provided that a repayment plan on arrearages must be equitable, although gradual repayment is allowable under certain proper circumstances.[5] In fashioning a repayment program of support arrears, the trial court erred in allowing 22.5 years to repay the obligation.[6] A trial court did not err in refusing to reduce the arrearage payments below the previous rate of child support where the

---

[7]State ex rel. Brett v. Brett, 2002-Ohio-1841, 2002 WL 561934 (Ohio Ct. App. 5th Dist. Knox County 2002).

[8]Carroll v. Detty, 113 Ohio App. 3d 708, 681 N.E.2d 1383 (4th Dist. Ross County 1996); Burchett v. Miller, 123 Ohio App. 3d 550, 704 N.E.2d 636 (6th Dist. Erie County 1997).

[9]Tucker v. Tucker, 10 Ohio App. 3d 251, 461 N.E.2d 1337 (10th Dist. Franklin County 1983).

[Section 19:27]

[1]RC 3123.21.

[2]RC 3123.21.

[3]RC 3121.36; Cramer v. Petrie, 70 Ohio St. 3d 131, 1994-Ohio-404, 637 N.E.2d 882 (1994).

[4]RC 3121.36.

[5]Inscoe v. Inscoe, 121 Ohio App. 3d 396, 700 N.E.2d 70 (4th Dist. Meigs County 1997); Baird v. Baird, 1990 WL 140668 (Ohio Ct. App. 10th Dist. Franklin County 1990).

[6]State ex rel. Donovan v. Zajac, 2000 WL 816249 (Ohio Ct. App. 11th Dist. Geauga County 2000).

obligor receives Social Security Disability, but the arrearage was $39,000.[7]

§ 19:28 Arrearages—Arrearage defenses

On any arrearage motion, equitable defenses must be pled in an answer or orally argued at the hearing pursuant to Civil Rule 15(B).[1]

A person who claims a defense of laches must show material prejudice by the delay of the person asserting the claim.[2] A trial court does not err in denying a father's defenses of laches or concealment where the evidence did not demonstrate that the mother's interference with visitation prevented the father from visiting, or that the father had been prejudiced by the delay in seeking support.[3] The defense of laches has been allowed on the basis of material prejudice where the obligor was denied contact with the child during the child's minority so as to bar the other parent from a relationship.[4] Delay has also been held to amount to material prejudice.[5] A mother was barred from bringing her claim where there was sufficient evidence she knew of the father's whereabouts during the time in question, there was a 15-year delay in bringing suit, and there was sufficient evidence to support a finding that the father was significantly prejudiced.[6] Additionally, a mother who refused to marry or receive support from her child's father, but

---

[7]Bennett v. Bennett, 2006-Ohio-1305, 2006 WL 709108 (Ohio Ct. App. 9th Dist. Summit County 2006).

[Section 19:28]

[1]Woy v. Lyle, 1992 WL 41290 (Ohio Ct. App. 9th Dist. Summit County 1992).

[2]Smith v. Smith, 168 Ohio St. 447, 7 Ohio Op. 2d 276, 156 N.E.2d 113, 70 A.L.R.2d 1241 (1959); Donelly v. Kashnier, 1991 WL 24961 (Ohio Ct. App. 9th Dist. Medina County 1991); Wright v. Oliver, 35 Ohio St. 3d 10, 517 N.E.2d 883 (1988); Dortch v. Bennett, 1990 WL 235947 (Ohio Ct. App. 9th Dist. Summit County 1990); Ferree v. Sparks, 77 Ohio App. 3d 185, 601 N.E.2d 568 (12th Dist. Warren County 1991); Nelson v. Nelson, 65 Ohio App. 3d 800, 585 N.E.2d 502 (11th Dist. Lake County 1990); Connin v. Bailey, 15 Ohio St. 3d 34, 472 N.E.2d 328 (1984); Kinney v. Mathias, 10 Ohio St. 3d 72, 461 N.E.2d 901 (1984); Seegert v. Zietlow, 95 Ohio App. 3d 451, 642 N.E.2d 697 (8th Dist. Cuyahoga County 1994).

[3]Mondl v. Mondl, 2001-Ohio-1878, 2001 WL 1545638 (Ohio Ct. App. 9th Dist. Summit County 2001) (without proof of an agreement, the father was not materially prejudiced by not exercising visitation).

[4]Park v. Ambrose, 85 Ohio App. 3d 179, 619 N.E.2d 469 (4th Dist. Ross County 1993) (holding modified by, Sexton v. Conley, 2002-Ohio-6346, 2002 WL 31630766 (Ohio Ct. App. 4th Dist. Scioto County 2002)) (holding modified by, Sexton v. Conley, 2002-Ohio-6346, 2002 WL 31630766 (Ohio Ct. App. 4th Dist. Scioto County 2002) (abrogated by, Carnes v. Kemp, 104 Ohio St. 3d 629, 2004-Ohio-7107, 821 N.E.2d 180 (2004))); Bassett v. Bassett, 2002-Ohio-6587, 2002 WL 31716659 (Ohio Ct. App. 11th Dist. Trumbull County 2002) (mother's concealment of the child and denial of visitation amount to material prejudice).

[5]Atwater v. King, 2003-Ohio-53, 2003 WL 77181 (Ohio Ct. App. 2d Dist. Greene County 2003) (a 37 year delay in collecting past due support is a material prejudice to the obligor).

[6]Gerlach v. Gerlach, 124 Ohio App. 3d 246, 705 N.E.2d 1287 (10th Dist. Franklin County 1997).

requested a retroactive order for child support once the child was close to emancipation, is barred from seeking that support by laches.[7]

An additional equitable defense is waiver. Waiver is the "intentional relinquishment . . . of a known right."[8] Both the defenses of waiver and laches failed where an obligor paid double the amount of child support for more than five years; however, where the CSEA had determined arrearages based on the erroneous order, those arrearages should be terminated.[9]

A support obligor cannot assert laches as a defense against the state or child support enforcement agency attempting to recover for back child support.[10]

An obligor cannot receive credit where the obligee was paid funds by a title company she would have received as a consequence of the satisfaction of a judgment lien on the obligor's home, which the title company erroneously released. The obligor should not benefit from the title company's error.[11]

Lost records do no automatically establish the material prejudice necessary to sustain a laches defense[12] especially where no payment records ever existed.[13]

However, a trial court does err in denying a father's motion to vacate a child support arrearage, which accrued during the time he had possession of the children and provided for their needs. This is an equitable exception to RC 3119.83 and 3119.84, which prohibits retroactive modification of child support.[14]

A trial court is not bound to exercise its equitable powers to correct an earlier miscalculation of arrears where obligor failed to assert his

---

[7]Barker v. Jarrell, 2007-Ohio-7024, 2007 WL 4554177 (Ohio Ct. App. 9th Dist. Lorain County 2007).

[8]In re Perme, 2006-Ohio-2771, 2006 WL 1519607 (Ohio Ct. App. 11th Dist. Trumbull County 2006).

[9]In re Perme, 2006-Ohio-2771, 2006 WL 1519607 (Ohio Ct. App. 11th Dist. Trumbull County 2006).

[10]Porter v. Little, 2000 WL 1335876 (Ohio Ct. App. 12th Dist. Butler County 2000); Mizell v. Mizell, 2001-Ohio-3409, 2001 WL 1667865 (Ohio Ct. App. 7th Dist. Jefferson County 2001); contra, Still v. Hayman, 153 Ohio App. 3d 487, 2003-Ohio-4113, 794 N.E.2d 751 (7th Dist. Jefferson County 2003).

[11]Campbell v. Campbell, 2004-Ohio-5553, 2004 WL 2348173 (Ohio Ct. App. 9th Dist. Summit County 2004).

[12]Walker v. Walker, 2006-Ohio-1179, 2006 WL 625969 (Ohio Ct. App. 9th Dist. Summit County 2006).

[13]Watson v. Watson, 2005-Ohio-4195, 2005 WL 1939815 (Ohio Ct. App. 2d Dist. Clark County 2005).

[14]Viox v. Metcalfe, 1998 WL 87579 (Ohio Ct. App. 12th Dist. Clermont County 1998).

rights at the time of former judgment or within a reasonable time thereafter.[15]

Incarceration is not a defense to nonpayment.[16]

§ 19:29 Arrearages—Collection of past due amounts

The termination of a support obligation or support order does not end the power of the court to collect overdue and unpaid support or to punish any person for failure to comply with an order of the court or to pay any support as ordered in the terminated support order.[1] Nor does collection of arrearages due under a terminated temporary order amount to a retroactive modification of a new order.[2]

The trial court or child support enforcement agency shall collect past due support in a monthly amount not less than the amount collected prior to the emancipation of the child.[3] Arrearages can be collected through wage withholding or deduction even after the arrearages have been reduced to judgment.[4]

Additional administrative collection methods are available to the child support enforcement agencies. One method of collection is the authority to intercept an obligor's federal income tax refund to apply toward the obligor's arrearage. Once the tax intercept has occurred, the state court has no jurisdiction to allocate a federal tax refund that was properly intercepted by the child support enforcement agency under RC 3123.81.[5] The obligor may object to the tax intercept only through an administrative review by Ohio Department of Job and Family Services and not through the trial court.[6] Other administrative methods for arrearage collection include liens on real and personal property,[7] suspension of personal and commercial drivers' licenses,[8] suspension of board licenses,[9] and access restrictions on financial

---

[15]Korn v. Korn, 1999 WL 1102691 (Ohio Ct. App. 10th Dist. Franklin County 1999).

[16]State v. Lavelle, 1999 WL 550254 (Ohio Ct. App. 6th Dist. Wood County 1999); Emmert v. Emmert, 2000 WL 192135 (Ohio Ct. App. 1st Dist. Hamilton County 2000).

[Section 19:29]

[1]RC 3121.36; Cramer v. Petrie, 70 Ohio St. 3d 131, 1994-Ohio-404, 637 N.E.2d 882 (1994).

[2]Caron v. Manfresca-Caron, 1997 WL 723262 (Ohio Ct. App. 10th Dist. Franklin County 1997).

[3]RC 3121.36.

[4]Cattren v. Cattren, 83 Ohio App. 3d 111, 614 N.E.2d 770 (8th Dist. Cuyahoga County 1992).

[5]Formerly RC 5101.32.

[6]Davis v. Davis, 1998 WL 258449 (Ohio Ct. App. 1st Dist. Hamilton County 1998); Stapleton v. Holstein, 131 Ohio App. 3d 596, 723 N.E.2d 164 (4th Dist. Scioto County 1998) (a child support enforcement agency has authority to request a tax intercept of an obligor's refund for past due child support).

[7]RC 3123.66; RC 3123.67.

accounts.[10] Other members of an obligor's family cannot claim funds attached in an access restriction where the account is solely in the name of the obligor.[11]

A child support enforcement agency may apply all payments to the current obligations first, rather than to arrearages, and an obligor can be held in contempt for non-compliance to pay arrearages despite the payments.[12] A child support enforcement agency cannot impound any lump sum payment award where the obligor is in compliance with the latest order.[13] Nor may a trial court order a lump-sum judgment on arrears when an obligor is in compliance with a prior agreed entry for installment payments on the arrearage.[14] A trial court cannot order PERS to distribute a lump sum payment to a financial institution for distribution toward child support from the account of an obligor who is no longer employed by the state.[15]

An obligee who is owed past due support may bring an action under the Ohio Uniform Fraudulent Transfer Act in a common pleas court against third parties to set aside fraudulent transfers of assets by a child support obligor.[16]

§ 19:30 Arrearages—Interest on arrearages

Support ordered on or after July 1, 1992, accrues interest at the statutory rate on unpaid installments.[1] Prior to that date, delinquent installments had to be reduced to lump-sum judgment before an execution could be levied on the monies owed.[2]

---

[8]RC 3123.52 et seq.

[9]RC 3123.41 et seq.

[10]RC 3123.24 et seq.

[11]Campbell v. Cuyahoga Cty. Child Support Enforcement Agnecy, 2009-Ohio-3091, 2009 WL 1819437 (Ohio Ct. App. 8th Dist. Cuyahoga County 2009).

[12]Frisina v. Frisina, 1998 WL 553446 (Ohio Ct. App. 11th Dist. Lake County 1998).

[13]Tuscarawas County CSEA v. Maldonado, 1998 WL 400872 (Ohio Ct. App. 5th Dist. Tuscarawas County 1998).

[14]Geauga County Child Support Enforcement Agency v. Miller, 1999 WL 420646 (Ohio Ct. App. 11th Dist. Geauga County 1999).

[15]Goodman v. Goodman, 144 Ohio App. 3d 367, 2001-Ohio-3310, 760 N.E.2d 72 (7th Dist. Columbiana County 2001).

[16]Dinu v. Dinu, 2009-Ohio-2879, 2009 WL 1710735 (Ohio Ct. App. 8th Dist. Cuyahoga County 2009).

[Section 19:30]

[1]RC 3109.05(C).

[2]Dunbar v. Dunbar, 68 Ohio St. 3d 369, 1994-Ohio-509, 627 N.E.2d 532 (1994).

A trial court errs, however, in awarding interest on each install-ment of unpaid child support without making requisite findings under RC 3123.17.[3]

§ 19:31 Effect of agreements between parents

Agreements between parties regarding child support can be problematic. The Supreme Court of Ohio in *DePalmo v. DePalmo*[1] held that while the law favors settlement, not all agreements that benefit parents, benefit children. This tension has often resulted in courts scrutinizing agreements for the motives of the parties and the consequences of the terms. The court scrutiny has resulted in contra-dictory rules and some conflict between the appellate courts. Often the disparate results can only be differentiated by the degree to which the children are protected or might be harmed.

Some decisions have held that children may be deemed third-party beneficiaries whose benefits may not be modified by the parties to the detriment of the children.[2]

An agreement between former spouses to exchange a consent to adopt for forgiveness of arrearages in child support has been held to be an enforceable agreement.[3] The Supreme Court of Ohio held in *Byrd v. Knuckles*[4] that nothing in RC 3119.83 should be construed to prevent parties from reaching agreement on the compromise of child support arrearages. The statutory prohibition in RC 3119.83 is on judges not to modify arrearages. Parents can agree to waive arrear-ages due in exchange for a consent to adopt so long as the agreement is reasonable and no public funds are owed.[5] Future child support is terminated after an adoption.[6] Where the parties make a prospective agreement to terminate the child support, fail to submit it to the court for approval when it is entered into, include language in it that it is

---

[3]Bauer v. Bauer, 2001 WL 877029 (Ohio Ct. App. 6th Dist. Wood County 2001); formerly RC 3113.219(A).

[Section 19:31]

[1]DePalmo v. DePalmo, 78 Ohio St. 3d 535, 1997-Ohio-184, 679 N.E.2d 266 (1997).

[2]Brenneman v. Brenneman, 1991 WL 49998 (Ohio Ct. App. 6th Dist. Wood County 1991); Nelson v. Nelson, 65 Ohio App. 3d 800, 585 N.E.2d 502 (11th Dist. Lake County 1990). See Pamela J. MacAdams, *Validity of Agreements Between Parties to Suspend Support Payments*, Dom. Rel. J. Ohio 12 (Jan/Feb. 1991).

[3]Lawhorn v. Lawhorn, 1990 WL 129287 (Ohio Ct. App. 2d Dist. Montgomery County 1990); Tressler v. Tressler, 32 Ohio App. 2d 79, 61 Ohio Op. 2d 85, 288 N.E.2d 339 (3d Dist. Defiance County 1972).

[4]Byrd v. Knuckles, 120 Ohio St. 3d 428, 2008-Ohio-6318, 900 N.E.2d 164 (2008).

[5]Byrd v. Knuckles, 120 Ohio St. 3d 428, 2008-Ohio-6318, 900 N.E.2d 164 (2008).

[6]In re Scheehle, 134 Ohio App. 3d 167, 730 N.E.2d 472 (10th Dist. Franklin County 1999).

unenforceable, but then submit it to the court at a later time, said agreement, when finally presented to the court, is unenforceable.[7]

A trial court may properly honor the agreement of parents to withhold the filing of a motion to modify child support for a specified term.[8] However, the Second Appellate District held that the trial court has a duty to review support whenever it is asked, despite the parties' agreement to the contrary.[9]

The parents cannot agree to direct payments and reduced child support where the obligee receives public assistance.[10] Despite agreements between the parents, child support obligations cannot be forgiven when the right to collect has been assigned to the state paying child welfare benefits.[11]

A trial court can properly refuse to give a father credit for support payments he made directly to the child or to the college she attended when the support order required payments to be made through the child support enforcement agency.[12] Even where parties requested a child support order that required most of the payment to be made through CSEA, but the court ordered the father to place a certain amount into a bank account jointly controlled by both the father and mother for the children's "necessities" the order was reversed as contrary to RC 3121.44 and RC 3121.45[13] Even by agreement of parties, a court must not deviate from child support enforcement agency procedures.[14]

The parents may agree that the father will pay the mortgage on a residence for the child, but said payments are not in the nature of child support, but are more akin to property division. They are therefore non-modifiable.[15]

---

[7]Day v. Bloom, 2006-Ohio-6957, 2006 WL 3825203 (Ohio Ct. App. 9th Dist. Medina County 2006).

[8]Boraggina v. Boraggina, 2001 WL 304091 (Ohio Ct. App. 6th Dist. Lucas County 2001).

[9]Quint v. Lomakoski, 173 Ohio App. 3d 146, 2007-Ohio-4722, 877 N.E.2d 738 (2d Dist. Greene County 2007).

[10]Harris v. Harris, 2004-Ohio-5561, 2004 WL 2348507 (Ohio Ct. App. 5th Dist. Knox County 2004).

[11]Knorzer v. Snyder, 2000 WL 222105 (Ohio Ct. App. 5th Dist. Stark County 2000); Mudry v. Mudry, 1997 WL 232625 (Ohio Ct. App. 8th Dist. Cuyahoga County 1997).

[12]Rini v. Rini, 1998 WL 213170 (Ohio Ct. App. 8th Dist. Cuyahoga County 1998).

[13]Formerly RC 2301.36(A).

[14]Bowley v. Bowley, 1998 WL 265276 (Ohio Ct. App. 12th Dist. Warren County 1998).

[15]Basista v. Basista, 2004-Ohio-4078, 2004 WL 1752928 (Ohio Ct. App. 8th Dist. Cuyahoga County 2004).

An agreement to pay childcare expenses in addition to computed guideline support amount is enforceable.[16] Where a father agreed to pay child support during his daughter's college education, the agreement is enforceable despite the intervening orders modifying the residential parent from mother to father and back to mother.[17]

Where the parties specifically agreed in the initial divorce decree to divide the medical, optical, dental, orthodontic, prescription drug, psychological or psychiatric expenses, but then modified the provision in a later order deleting the words psychological or psychiatric, expenses for psychological or psychiatric treatment are no longer ordered nor are they considered a part of medical expenses since the intent of the parties as evidenced by the original order was to exclude these treatments from the definition of medical.[18]

A husband agreed to pay for his incompetent adult daughter in a separation agreement. The court had continuing jurisdiction to enforce the agreement even though the child was an adult at the time of the original decree.[19]

§ 19:32 Need-based payments—Benefits for a special needs child

Under RC 3119.23(f), the court may consider the financial resources and earning ability of a child for deviation purposes in calculating child support. However, Supplemental Security Income paid due to a child's disability is a need-based payment that fluctuates based on the other sources of income for that child. Therefore, the Supreme Court of Ohio held in *Paton v. Paton*[1] that Supplemental Security Income benefits received by a disabled child do not constitute a financial resource of the child per RC 3119.23[2] for purposes of justifying a trial court's deviation from the basic child support schedule.

In addition, adoption subsidies received on behalf of special needs children may be treated in the same way as Supplemental Security Income paid on behalf of disabled minor children.[3]

---

[16]Mueller v. Mueller, 2000 WL 342112 (Ohio Ct. App. 12th Dist. Butler County 2000).

[17]Jones v. Brown, 2005-Ohio-3751, 2005 WL 1713321 (Ohio Ct. App. 2d Dist. Greene County 2005).

[18]Randall v. Randall, 2009-Ohio-2070, 2009 WL 1175075 (Ohio Ct. App. 2d Dist. Darke County 2009).

[19]O'Connor v. O'Connor, 71 Ohio App. 3d 541, 594 N.E.2d 1081 (10th Dist. Franklin County 1991).

[Section 19:32]

[1]Paton v. Paton, 91 Ohio St. 3d 94, 2001-Ohio-291, 742 N.E.2d 619 (2001).

[2]Formerly RC 3113.215(B)(3)(D).

[3]In re Caravano Children, 2005-Ohio-1110, 2005 WL 583340 (Ohio Ct. App. 5th Dist. Fairfield County 2005).

§ 19:33   Social Security payments—Benefits to a child from disabled, deceased, or retired parent

The Supreme Court of Ohio, in *Williams v. Williams*,[1] resolved the issue of whether disability payments made to a child on behalf of a parent should be credited directly against that parent's child support obligation or credited against the joint obligation of the parties after which the remainder is proportioned between the parties. The Supreme Court of Ohio resolved the issue in favor of a full credit against either parent's current child support obligation. The term full credit in *Williams* meant full credit for the derivative benefits paid, not full credit for the obligor's other obligations. The *Williams* holding was codified in the definitions in RC 3119.01 and on the child support worksheets.

Any benefits paid to a child on behalf of a parent that are non-means tested including retirement, disability or survivor benefits are treated as a deduction against that parent's child support obligation.[2] This is distinguishable from *Paton*[3] where a means-tested, needs-based benefit was paid to the child.

Where an obligor was ordered to pay more than his Social Security Disability benefits because he had additional income, the amount of child support owed beyond the child's derivative benefits cannot be paid by additional sums paid from Social Security for a different time period.[4] Furthermore, where the obligee received a lump sum for past due benefits for the children based on the obligor's disability, the obligor should receive credit up to the amount of the monthly benefit for the months where current child support was due that correspond to the months represented in the lump sum payment, but not for any remaining arrearages.[5]

§ 19:34   Overpayments and direct payments

Child support payments not made through the CSEA or the Ohio Child Support Payment Central in accordance with an order for child

---

[Section 19:33]

[1]Williams v. Williams, 88 Ohio St. 3d 441, 2000-Ohio-375, 727 N.E.2d 895 (2000).

[2]Breen v. Kraus, 2003-Ohio-505, 2003 WL 231274 (Ohio Ct. App. 12th Dist. Butler County 2003); Church v. Gadd, 2002-Ohio-7129, 2002 WL 31866165 (Ohio Ct. App. 11th Dist. Geauga County 2002).

[3]See Text § 19:32: Need based payments-Benefits for a special needs child.

[4]Slowbe v. Slowbe, 2004-Ohio-2411, 2004 WL 1068418 (Ohio Ct. App. 8th Dist. Cuyahoga County 2004).

[5]Rice v. Rice, 177 Ohio App. 3d 476, 2008-Ohio-3518, 895 N.E.2d 198 (5th Dist. Stark County 2008).

support, are deemed to be gifts.[1] However, this presumption is rebuttable.[2] The party rebutting the presumption has the burden of proof pursuant to Evidence Rule 301.

§ 19:35 Support to third parties

The statute provides that where a third party has custody of the parents' child, the parents each owe his and her respective portions of child support to the third party for that child.[1]

Where a stepparent has taken children into his home and educates and supports them, he stands *in loco parentis,* is responsible for the children's support, and is entitled to receive the child support due for the children. The voluntariness of the stepparents' contribution does not preclude payment.[2] The reasonable value may be the guidelines-calculated child support. Parties cannot avoid child support enforcement agency requirements or reimbursement to the state by making direct payments to the other parent or to third parties on that parent's behalf where the obligee parent is receiving public assistance.[3]

[Section 19:34]

[1]RC 3121.45.

[2]Mihna v. Mihna, 48 Ohio App. 3d 303, 549 N.E.2d 558 (8th Dist. Cuyahoga County 1989); Whitten v. Whitten, 2008-Ohio-3446, 2008 WL 2681139 (Ohio Ct. App. 8th Dist. Cuyahoga County 2008).

[Section 19:35]

[1]RC 3119.07(C).

[2]Palmer v. Harrold, 101 Ohio App. 3d 732, 656 N.E.2d 708 (2d Dist. Greene County 1995), a person who supplies necessities for the support of a minor child whose parent neglects to provide support, is permitted to recover the reasonable value.

[3]Starr v. Starr, 109 Ohio App. 3d 116, 671 N.E.2d 1097 (8th Dist. Cuyahoga County 1996).

Chapter 20

Enforcement of Spousal and Child Support

By Tom H. Nagel, Esq.*

◆ **Editor's Note:** Am. S.B. 180, eff. 3-22-01, amended, enacted, and repealed various sections of the Revised Code that concern child support enforcement agency roles in establishing, enforcing, and modifying child support. The Appendix includes a Correlation Table to assist in identifying and locating the new sections.

---

*General editor, Beatrice K. Sowald, acknowledges the assistance of Eric W. Johnson, Esq., in the preparation of this updated chapter.

III.   THE RUSTY TOOL

IV.   THE AWKWARD TOOL

V.   THE TRENDY TOOL

> **KeyCite®:** Cases and other legal materials listed in KeyCite Scope can be researched through the KeyCite service on Westlaw®. Use KeyCite to check citations for form, parallel references, prior and later history, and comprehensive citator information, including citations to other decisions and secondary materials.

§ 20:1   Statutory history—The advent of withholding

Historically, payment of child support and spousal support was enforced on a case by case basis by counsel for the payee. It was not until 1967 that the General Assembly created bureaus of support. The statute permitted, but did not mandate, that domestic relations courts establish such bureaus.

In 1975, a federal child support program was created through amendments to the Social Security Act.[1] Title IV-D of the act requires all states participating in what was then called the Aid to Families with Dependent Children (AFDC) program to adopt programs whereby absent parents will be located, paternity established, and child support orders enforced. The act imposes upon former AFDC recipients, and beginning October 1, 1997, participants in Ohio Works First,[2] a duty to cooperate in the enforcement procedures and to assign to the state all rights to child support while receiving aid.

The continued failure of many absent parents to pay child support has since led Congress to pass legislation in an attempt to make the child support enforcement program more effective. Results so far have been mixed.

[Section 20:1]

[1]Social Service Amendments, Pub. L. No. 93-647, Part B, § 101(a), 88 Stat 2351 (1974).

[2]1997 H.B. 408.

A series of amendments to the Social Security Act were signed into law as the Child Support Enforcement Amendments.[3] The amendments were generally effective October 1, 1985, and their most important effect was to require automatic wage withholding if the payor fell more than one month behind in making payments.

1984 House Bill 614, effective March 10, 1985, was signed into law on January 8, 1985. It modified existing sections of the Ohio Revised Code in an attempt to insure that child support orders would be enforced more effectively, and to comply with the federal mandates. The state stood to lose substantial federal funding and incur fines without such enforcement provisions.

The amendments to RC 3105.21 and RC 3109.05(C) provided new penalties for contemnors who failed to make support payments as ordered. The amended statute provided:

> If any person required to pay child support under an order made under division (A) of this section on or after April 15, 1985, is found in contempt of court for failure to make support payments under the order, the court that makes the finding, in addition to any other penalty or remedy imposed, shall assess all court costs arising out of the contempt proceeding against the person and require the person to pay any reasonable attorney's fees of any adverse party, as determined by the court, that arose in relation to the act of contempt.[4]

Finally, former RC 3113.21(E) was amended to provide that wage withholding orders, workers' compensation attachment orders, or bank account assignments have priority over all other liens.[5]

The enactment of 1984 House Bill 614 prompted a proliferation of forms and paperwork that still burdens the support collection system. Some courts adopted more than two dozen new multipage local forms merely to attempt compliance with the withholding, attachment, bonding, and notice requirements.

Since each county adopted its own system of forms and procedures, domestic practice quickly became geographically fragmented. Venturing out of a familiar county to handle even a simple divorce or support modification became burdensome, or even risky, for the practitioner.

§ 20:2 Statutory history—Withholding becomes mandatory

The provisions of 1984 House Bill 614, although almost overwhelming to practitioners at the time, were not sufficient to comply with the federal mandates. Also, child support collection did not increase in proportion to the volume of new paperwork.

Effective December 1, 1986, pursuant to 1986 House Bill 509, child support as well as spousal support in the state of Ohio became subject to further strict procedures that all domestic and juvenile courts must follow.

---

[3]Pub. L. No. 98-378 (1984).

[4]Former RC 3109.05(C), as amended by 1984 H.B. 614, eff. 3-10-85.

[5]This provision was amended and recodified as RC 3121.034 by 2000 S.B. 180, eff. 3-22-01.

The bill combined procedures for paying and enforcing child support and spousal support orders. As used in the bill, "support" was defined as "child support, alimony, and support for a spouse or former spouse."[1] 1990 House Bill 514 later eliminated the term "alimony" and replaced it with the term "spousal support." For purposes of clarity, "spousal support" is used hereafter except in direct quotes from prior cases or statutes.

The most immediate effect of 1986 House Bill 509 was a hurried and massive revision of the numerous local forms which had been developed to effect payroll deduction, attachment of funds, bonding, and notification.

The option to defer payroll deduction of support for obligors who stayed in compliance was eliminated in virtually all cases. The only cases without withholding orders now are old cases that have not come back to court for modification and new cases of shared parenting with "zero child support" agreements.

Any order issued under RC 2301.37 or RC 2301.38 is payable at least monthly.[2] No employer may discharge an employee for reason of any order issued under former RC 2301.37, former RC 2301.38, or former RC 3113.21.[3] The Eighth District Court of Appeals has held an employer in contempt for failure to comply with a wage withholding order.[4] The Ohio Supreme Court held that former RC 3113.213(D)[5] created an exception to the employment-at-will doctrine in that an individual has a tort cause of action against an employer for wrongful termination under RC 3113.213(D).[6]

In the few remaining cases with no withholding order, either the obligor or an obligee may file a motion for a withholding order.[7]

◆ **Practice Tip:** If counsel anticipates a contempt filing against the client, the obligor's counsel may file for a withholding order on behalf of the obligor.

This demonstrates good faith on the part of the obligor and eliminates the need for counsel to rely on the obligor to actually write a check to the former spouse. Such an approach may avoid a

---

[Section 20:2]

[1]Former RC 3113.21(O)(7), new RC 3113.21(P)(6).

[2]RC 2301.39(A). Amended and recodified by 2000 S.B. 180, eff. 3-22-01, analogous language in RC 3123.16.

[3]RC 2103.37 and RC 2301.38 amended by 2000 S.B. 180, eff. 3-22-01.

[4]Ankrom v. Ankrom, 30 Ohio App. 3d 47, 506 N.E.2d 259 (8th Dist. Cuyahoga County 1985).

[5]Amended by 2000 S.B. 180, eff. 3-22-01, analogous language in RC 3121.99.

[6]Greeley v. Miami Valley Maintenance Contractors, Inc., 49 Ohio St. 3d 228, 551 N.E.2d 981 (1990) (overruled in part by, Tulloh v. Goodyear Atomic Corp., 62 Ohio St. 3d 541, 584 N.E.2d 729 (1992)); RC 3113.213(D). Amended and recodified by 2000 S.B. 180, eff. 3-22-01, analogous language in RC 3121.39.

[7]RC 3113.21(B).

threatened contempt and get a child support case concluded more easily.

The court, upon issuing or modifying a support order after December 1, 1986, must require all payments to be made through what was then called the bureau of support as trustee for the obligee. Direct payments between the obligor and obligee without going through the bureau of support would not be credited and are legally considered a gift.[8]

Ohio again amended its statutes (in compliance with additional federal requirements in 42 U.S.C.A. § 654) to require each county to designate a child support enforcement agency.[9] Basically, the child support enforcement agencies, or CSEAs, took over the functions of the old bureaus of support, plus a host of new duties.

Contempt procedures for failure to pay support were also amended. RC 2705.031 sets forth contempt procedures for any party who has a legal claim to support for a child, spouse, or former spouse, whether under Title IV-D or otherwise. Per RC 2705.031 contempt proceedings in IV-D cases can be instituted by (1) any party with a legal claim to support, (2) the attorney for the party who has the claim, (3) the prosecuting attorney, (4) the department of human services attorney, or (5) the child support enforcement agency.

The statute requires four specific notices to appear in a summons which accompanies the contempt citation:

(1) A notice that failure to appear may result in an arrest order being issued and in support cases an order for payroll or other type of withholding order.

(2) A notice of right to counsel, and if the defendant is indigent, the right to appointed counsel; and notice that if the defendant believes he is indigent he must apply for a public defender or appointed counsel within three business days of receipt of the summons. (In practice, courts do not always enforce this three-day rule.)

(3) A notice that the court may refuse to grant a continuance at hearing for the defendant to obtain counsel absent a showing of a good faith prior effort to obtain counsel. (Courts often grant continuances without inquiry, despite objection of the moving party.)

(4) A notice of the potential penalties for contempt. Penalties are provided by RC 2705.05, and support obligations remain in effect.

With the enactment of 2000 S.B. 180, the key statute regarding withholding orders for child support and administration of child support orders by the support enforcement agency has been amended and expanded twenty-four times since 1984. Unfortunately, at that point,

---

[8]Former RC 2301.36(A). Amended and recodified by 2000 S.B. 180, eff. 3-22-01, analogous language in RC 3121.45.

[9]Former RC 2301.35 as amended by 1988 H.B. 708 § 6, eff. 6-6-88 (repealing all previous versions of RC 2301.35); 1988 H.B. 708 § 1, eff. 4-19-88; 1987 H.B. 231 § 3, eff. 6-6-88; 1987 H.B. 231 § 1, eff. 10-5-87; 1989 H.B. 111; 1990 H.B. 591; 1990 S.B. 3, eff. 4-11-91.

it left RC 3113.21 some 135 paragraphs long, poorly organized, poorly outlined, and very difficult to comprehend. Also, for reasons known only to the Ohio General Assembly, the entire statutory scheme for support withholding and enforcement plus the rules and tables for child support guidelines resided in the chapter of the Ohio Revised Code dealing with Neglect, Abandonment and Domestic Violence.

§ 20:3   Statutory history—1992 Senate Bill 10, the "poster bill"

Sometimes the simplest ideas are the most effective. In April 1992, the Ohio General Assembly enacted and the governor signed into law 1992 Senate Bill 10. The bill authorized support enforcement agencies to publish and circulate posters featuring the photos of defaulting support obligors. Although the "poster cases" are relatively few, they tend to be tough cases with large arrearages. And the collection results have been impressive.

Originally drafted as a short bill authorizing support enforcement agencies and the department of human services to circulate posters, the final bill included administrative procedures to establish paternity and set child support orders for unmarried parents of minor children.[1]

Under the 1992 amendments of former RC 3111.20(B)[2] the duty of support was imposed on a father if he voluntarily signed a child's birth certificate as an informant or if he signed an acknowledgment of paternity form which was later journalized in the probate court. The parent with custody (more often the mother) or the child's guardian or legal custodian, or even the local support enforcement agency, could then request the issuance of an "administrative support order."[3] If such a request is made, an administrative officer of the agency must schedule an administrative hearing and issue an administrative support order.[4]

The statute was not clear on how the support enforcement agency official, who may not be a lawyer and certainly will not be a judge, would obtain the authority to issue what is basically a wage garnishment order. However, either the father or mother may object to the administrative order, by bringing an action for payment of support in the juvenile court within thirty days of the issuance of the administrative order.[5] After the thirty-day period expires, the support may be

---

[Section 20:3]

[1]See Text Ch 3, Parentage.

[2]Amended and recodified by 2000 S.B. 180, eff. 3-22-01, analogous language in RC 3111.77.

[3]RC 3111.20(C). Amended and recodified by 2000 S.B. 180, eff. 3-22-01, analogous language in RC 3111.78.

[4]Former RC 3111.21(D). Amended and recodified by 2000 S.B. 180, eff. 3-22-01, analogous language in RC 3111.80 and RC 3111.81.

[5]Former RC 3111.20(D). Amended and recodified by 2000 S.B. 180, eff. 3-22-01, analogous language in RC 3111.81 and RC 3111.84.

modified only pursuant to RC 3113.21 to RC 3113.219 or RC 3111.20 to RC 3111.28.[6]

The administrator is required to determine the amount of support in accordance with the statutory child support guidelines and computation forms, but the statute provides that the payments may vary in amount. If it is in the best interests of the child, the administrator may order a lump-sum payment or the purchase of an annuity in lieu of periodic payments.[7]

The final version of the "poster bill" contained a provision allowing the court to assess interest upon delinquent child or spousal support payments, if the court finds willful failure to pay.[8] Specifically, the court is supposed to compute interest in accordance with RC 1343.03 from the date of the first failure to pay to the date of the new court order, and then collect the interest, probably as additional arrearages, under the new payment plan.[9] Except in cases of very large arrearages or arrearages that have persisted for a long time, the extra work of the interest calculations and creation and service of a new withholding order will probably outweigh the benefit of any interest that might actually be collected. As a practical matter, the burden of doing the computations and preparing and filing a new withholding form will fall on counsel for the moving party.[10]

A provision more useful to the private practitioner is RC 3123.17[11] which provides that after July 1, 1992 a court has authority to award either party the costs of the action, including but not limited to attorney fees, court costs, and genetic testing costs, whenever a support order is issued or modified. This provision for attorney fees and costs is not limited to just divorce and dissolution actions but encompasses virtually any proceeding in which support may be ordered, including URESA and UIFSA cases, spousal support motions, dependency and neglect cases, parentage cases, nonparentage child support cases, sentencing procedures following criminal nonsupport convictions, civil protection orders, and commitment of juvenile offenders.

◆ **Practice Tip:** If you are the moving party, always ask for attorney fees and costs. In addition, if the arrearage had previously been reduced to judgment, or the support order was entered on or

---

[6]Amended and recodified by 2000 S.B. 180, eff. 3-22-01, analogous language in Chapters 3119, 3121, 3123 and RC 3111.84.

[7]Former RC 3111.20(D)(1). Amended and recodified by 2000 S.B. 180, eff. 3-22-01, analogous language in RC 3111.81.

[8]Former RC 3113.219; Switzer v. Hyatt, 1999 WL 1206717 (Ohio Ct. App. 2d Dist. Montgomery County 1999) (trial court correctly assessed interest against obligor for a child's medical expenses that obligee paid with loan proceeds).

[9]RC 3113.219(A).

[10]Terrell v. Terrell, 1992 WL 150288 (Ohio Ct. App. 9th Dist. Summit County 1992) (trial court erred in holding request for statutory interest in abeyance until obligee submitted an exact computation of interest owed).

[11]Amended and recodified by 2000 S.B. 180, eff. 3-22-01, analogous language in RC 3111.81.

after July 1, 1992, be sure to request statutory interest on the unpaid amounts. If you do not ask for it, you will not get it.

§20:4 Statutory history—1995 H.B. 167

In 1995, the legislature enacted former RC 2301.373 and RC 2301.374,[1] which began as a proposal to suspend the medical licenses of highly paid physicians who failed to pay their court-ordered support. In a remarkable show of legislative one-upmanship, the bill rapidly evolved into a legislative scheme calling for the suspension of virtually every kind of license issued by the state of Ohio, if the CSEA determines that the license holder is in default of paying support.

The section of the law dealing with suspension of drivers' rights by the Bureau of Motor Vehicles is found in RC 3123.53 to 3123.60. Former RC 2301.373 became effective November 15, 1996, and was immediately put into effect by some CSEAs. Doctors, barbers, real estate agents, and insurance salespeople tended to be the early targets. Beginning January 1, 1998, recreational licenses, such as for hunting and fishing, became subject to suspension as well. The constitutionality of these license suspension statutes has been upheld.[2]

§20:5 Statutory history—1997 H.B. 352

In August 1997, the Ohio General Assembly enacted 1997 House Bill 352, again at the behest of the federal government and under threat of losing federal funds, to comply with some 47 federal mandates dealing with child support enforcement.[1] The most notable change was that the bill called for centralized, statewide collection of support. The garnished employers of obligors would no longer send their payments to 88 different support enforcement agencies, but rather all funds would be sent to the Division of Child Support, within the department of job and family services.

The impact of House Bill 352 on CSEAs throughout the state has occurred gradually, as existing support orders are converted to the SETS system and collection turned over to the ODJFS. Local CSEAs, under rules adopted by the department of job and family services, are still largely responsible for establishing parentage, issuing support orders, and enforcing orders against defaulting obligors. The department of job and family services oversees collection and distribution of support payments, implements the SETS system and support order

---

[Section 20:4]

[1]Amended and recodified by 2000 S.B. 180, eff. 3-22-01, analogous language in RC 3123.43 and RC 3123.53.

[2]See, e.g., State v. Leuvoy, 2004-Ohio-2232, 2004 WL 944387 (Ohio Ct. App. 5th Dist. Fairfield County 2004).

[Section 20:5]

[1]1997 H.B. 352, eff. 1-1-98, was enacted in response to the "Personal Responsibility and Work Reconciliation Act of 1996," also called the "Welfare Reform Act." 110 Stat. 2105.

case registry, coordinates the information it receives (from local agencies, employers, and others) and submits that information (to federal agencies, other states, and others) to comply with federal requirements intended to facilitate support enforcement.

§ 20:6 Statutory history—2000 S.B.180

2000 Senate Bill 180, which became effective on March 22, 2001, drastically changed the organization of the support statutes in the revised code. Before the enactment of 2000 Senate Bill 180 the key code sections regarding withholding orders for child support and administration of child support orders by the support enforcement agency were located in a somewhat random portion of the code, chapter 3113, titled Neglect, Abandonment, or Domestic Violence. The code sections in Chapter 3113 were long, poorly organized and difficult to understand. 2000 Senate Bill 180 restructured and amended the sections regarding support and administration of child support orders and divided them into different chapters that are more organized and easier to comprehend.

2000 Senate Bill 180 also made other important changes to the Revised Code. It recodified and amended chapter 3111, which governed administrative support orders and chapter 5101, which were the general provisions for the department of human services (now the department of job and family services). 2000 Senate Bill 180 also incorporated the previous code sections regarding administrative support orders into the new code sections regarding court ordered support orders. It additionally created four new chapters in the Revised Code for child support laws: chapter 3119 (calculation of support), chapter 3121 (collection and enforcement of support), chapter 3123 (default) and chapter 3125 (state and local administration).

§ 20:7 Tools of the trade for support enforcement

In an attempt to make this chapter more useful to the practitioner, it has been reorganized as a set of tools which may be used in collecting and enforcing support payments—or in defending against such actions. Practice tips and useful forms are integrated with the subject matter text.

I. THE BASIC TOOL

§ 20:8 Continuing jurisdiction—In general

Generally speaking, property divisions by a domestic court are final. But a domestic relations court has continuing jurisdiction to enforce or modify support orders after the final decree, or even after minor children become emancipated.[1]

A domestic relations court has continuing jurisdiction to enforce or modify orders rendered by the court even after the final decree.[2] The concept of continuing jurisdiction of the trial court was referred to as early as 1921 where it was stated that in a divorce or alimony proceeding the court has jurisdiction to allow a specific sum of money per week for the maintenance of minor children and the support can be modified at the discretion of the trial court as the necessity of the case demands.[3]

The continuing jurisdiction of the trial court is the basis of its power to enforce child and spousal support orders. The trial court retains continuing jurisdiction over such orders and is also empowered to modify child support orders throughout their duration.[4] The jurisdiction of the trial court to enforce and to modify child support orders continues until the child support order is properly terminated by the trial court.[5]

Any person or agency ordered to withhold support payments for an obligor pursuant to RC 3121.03 and RC 3121.38 that fails to withhold or deduct the amount of money as ordered by the support order is liable for the amount not withheld.[6] Pursuant to RC 3121.372, any person who has a duty to notify the court on any matter regarding a support order may also be found in contempt of court for failure to comply.

RC 3121.381 provides that any employer under a duty to withhold or deduct support payments that fails to do so shall be fined not more than $200. This also applies if the employer fails to notify the court of any change in circumstances. If the employer fires or disciplines the obligor as a result of the court order, the employer may be fined up to $500.[7]

If any person required to pay child or spousal support under an order made or modified on or after December 1, 1986, is found in contempt, the court that makes the finding, in addition to any other

---

[Section 20:8]

[1]See RC 3105.10, RC 3105.18, RC 3105.65, RC 3109.04, RC 3109.05, RC 3111. 16.

[2]See RC 3105.10, RC 3105.18, RC 3105.65, RC 3109.04, RC 3109.05, RC 3111. 16.

[3]Monahan v. Monahan, 14 Ohio App. 116, 1921 WL 1298 (1st Dist. Hamilton County 1921).

[4]See RC 3105.18, RC 3109.04, RC 3109.05; Civ. R. 75(J).

[5]Nokes v. Nokes, 47 Ohio St. 2d 1, 1 Ohio Op. 3d 1, 351 N.E.2d 174 (1976). See Text Ch 8, Legal Separation; Text Ch 13, Spousal Support.

[6]Former RC 3113.213(B). Carter v. Highland v. Davis, 1997 WL 401565 (Ohio Ct. App. 3d Dist. Marion County 1997) (even though employer denied receiving order due to poor office procedures, employer must pay amount that was to be withheld).

[7]RC 3121.99.

penalty or remedy imposed, must assess all court costs arising out of the contempt proceeding against the person and require the person to pay any reasonable attorney fees of any adverse party, as determined by the court, that arose in relation to the act of contempt.[8]

Additionally, the court has authority under RC 3123.17 and RC 3105.73 to award reasonable attorney fees to either side at any stage of the proceedings to enforce or modify a previous decree. A divided Fifth District Court of Appeals affirmed the trial court's order suspending a jail sentence on the condition that the appellant pay the appellee's attorney fees.[9] The majority characterized the order as a "warning" and the minority as a "threat" of confinement to enforce compliance with a first-time order. A trial court did not err in granting attorney fees on a finding of contempt without holding a hearing, where counsel's affidavit provided a sufficient basis for the fees owed, and the court was familiar with the history of the litigation.[10]

§ 20:9   Continuing jurisdiction—Determining arrearages

An order for support continues until the order is suspended, modified, or terminated.[1] The proper procedure to modify an order requires the filing of an application or motion in the case number of the original divorce action.[2] Arrearages accrue when the obligor does not comply with the order for support. If the obligor never attempted to modify the order legally, the obligor is liable for the full amount of arrearages.

Retroactive modification of delinquent support payments is prohibited by statute except for those payments which become due after notice of a motion to modify the support order.[3] The Sixth District Court of Appeals has held, however, that funds spent by a father in an attempt to obtain visitation were for the benefit of the children and

---

[8]RC 3109.05(C). See also Purden v. Purden, 1994 WL 242523 (Ohio Ct. App. 10th Dist. Franklin County 1994).

[9]McClarren v. McClarren, 1994 WL 313787 (Ohio Ct. App. 5th Dist. Morrow County 1994).

[10]Labriola v. Labriola, 2001-Ohio-1751, 2001 WL 1387748 (Ohio Ct. App. 5th Dist. Stark County 2001); Wilder v. Wilder, 1995 WL 527689 (Ohio Ct. App. 10th Dist. Franklin County 1995).

[Section 20:9]

[1]McClain v. McClain, 26 Ohio App. 2d 10, 55 Ohio Op. 2d 28, 268 N.E.2d 294 (8th Dist. Cuyahoga County 1971) (if a party is unable to maintain alimony payments, arrearages will continue to increase indefinitely and appellee may obtain a judgment for amount of alimony due and unpaid).

[2]Asztalos v. Fortney, 48 Ohio App. 2d 66, 2 Ohio Op. 3d 45, 355 N.E.2d 517 (6th Dist. Lucas County 1975). See also Text Ch 14, Modification of Spousal Support; Text Ch 19, Child Support; Text § 25:56, Post-decree motions—Motion to modify.

[3]RC 3119.83, RC 3119.84.

should be applied against an alleged arrearage in support and this would not be considered a retroactive modification.[4]

Procedurally, if the residential parent is receiving public assistance for the children each month, all money collected by the child support enforcement agency will be disbursed to the public agency involved. If the residential parent is not receiving public assistance for the children, all money shall be distributed to the residential parent. If the residential parent at some time in the past received public assistance for the children but presently does not, the current support collected shall be disbursed to the residential parent and the arrearage payments distributed to the public agency until they are paid in full. Former RC 3113.21(K) was specific as to order of payments of arrears when an obligee was ever a public assistance beneficiary. The priority is now established by reference to federal statutes and rules promulgated by the department of job and family services.[5] Where arrearages are owed to both the residential parent and a public agency, the child support enforcement agency is to pay the arrearage amount first to the obligee until that arrearage is paid in full and then pay toward the agency's arrearage.[6] The order of payment on arrearages does not apply, however, to money collected from income tax intercept.[7]

Through this procedure, the current support order is enforced while at the same time periodic payments are made over a period of time to reduce the money owed a public agency or residential parent. In this manner, the obligor meets his obligation while at the same time has income for his own expenses.

Arrearages are considered as vested. Even though the contempt proceeding may make findings of fact as to the amount of arrearages, and enter those facts into a judgment, it cannot be executed as it is only a judgment of contempt. Arrearages must be reduced to a money judgment for execution.[8]

◆ **Practice Tip:** A party filing a motion for non-payment of child or spousal support should additionally move the court for a determination of arrearages and a reduction of those arrearages to judgment. (For sample language see Text § 20:44, Reduction to judgment and execution—Motion to reduce support arrearage to lump-sum judgment—Form).

---

[4]Miller v. Miller, 92 Ohio App. 3d 340, 635 N.E.2d 384 (6th Dist. Erie County 1993).

[5]RC 3123.19.

[6]Former RC 3113.21(K)(1).

[7]Former RC 3113.21(K)(2).

[8]See Text §§ 20:43 to 20:54, Reduction to judgment and execution; Text § 25:43, Motions by obligee regarding enforcement of judgments—Motion to reduce to judgment.

An emancipated child has a superior claim to child support arrearages when the custodial parent is deceased.[9]

It is not an abuse of discretion for a court to order support arrearages deducted from the obligor's share of the proceeds from the sale of the marital home, even though this results in an unequal distribution of the marital assets.[10]

The basic support withholding statute, RC 3121.03, clearly applies to arrearages and reads in part:

> If a court or child support enforcement agency that issued or modified a support order, or the agency administering the support order, is required by the Revised Code to issue one or more withholding or deduction notices described in this section or other orders described in this section, the court or agency shall issue one or more of the following types of notices or orders, as appropriate, for payment of the support and also, if required by the Revised Code or the court, *to pay any arrearages*:
>
> A(1)(c) Continue the withholding intervals specified in the notice until further notice from the court or child support enforcement agency.
>
> To the extent possible, the amount specified to be withheld shall satisfy the amount ordered for support in the support order *plus any arrearages owed by the obligor under any prior support order that pertained to the same child or spouse*, notwithstanding the limitations of sections 2329.66, 2329.70, 2716.02, 2716.041 and 2716.05 (emphasis added)

The court is not limited by RC 2329.66, RC 2329.70, or RC 2716.13, but at all times the party withholding is subject to the limitations of the Consumer Credit Protection Act.[11] The limitation of percentages of net income subject to withholding by the employer found in said act (50% where new dependents and 60% where no other dependents, plus an additional 5% for arrearages older than 12 weeks) does not constitute a limitation on the amount payable by the obligor nor on the court's ability to enforce an order that exceeds the percentages.

Any assets the obligor has or receives can be voluntarily or involuntarily used toward arrearages unless specifically exempted by the decree or by relevant state or federal execution statutes. Once an arrearage is reduced to judgment and will be enforced by execution, governed by the procedures and exemptions set forth in RC Ch. 2329. While a domestic relations court may consider the exempted assets in determining amounts and award, the court that executes the judgment, and not the domestic relations court, is bound by RC Chapter 2329.

---

[9]In re Estate of Antkowiak, 95 Ohio App. 3d 546, 642 N.E.2d 1154 (6th Dist. Lucas County 1994).

[10]Davis v. Davis, 12 Ohio App. 3d 38, 465 N.E.2d 917 (8th Dist. Cuyahoga County 1983). See also Hendershot v. Hendershot, 1984 WL 4063 (Ohio Ct. App. 2d Dist. Champaign County 1984) (trial court may reduce nonpaying obligor's equity in the marital premises by the amount of arrearages due).

[11]15 U.S.C.A. § 1673(b). But see Calhoun v. Tucker, 1992 WL 127100 (Ohio Ct. App. 5th Dist. Stark County 1992) (CCPA limitations of percentages do not apply to lump-sum payments under RC 3113.21(D)(1)(b)(ix)). Amended and recodified by 2000 S.B. 180, eff. 3-22-01, analogous language in RC 3121.037.

§ 20:10 Continuing jurisdiction—Determining arrearages—In gross order

A child support order that is an order for one amount of support for multiple children is an in-gross order, as opposed to a specific, or per child order, which specifies an amount of support for each child. An in-gross child support order does not automatically abate when custody of a child is changed or emancipation occurs. The obligor must invoke the court's authority, not unilaterally reduce the amount being paid.[1] In general, due and unpaid installments may not be modified retroactively.[2] A trial court may not retroactively modify an in-gross award by recalculating arrearages pro rata as each child becomes emancipated.[3]

However, the Sixth District Court of Appeals held in *Asztalos v. Fortney*[4] that a trial court could retroactively modify an in-gross child support order for four children when one child became emancipated and the custody of a second child was transferred to obligor. Other jurisdictions, however, have declined to follow this holding.[5]

Finally, if the CSEA determines child support for one child should terminate, it will automatically adjust the remaining child support obligation on a *pro rata* basis pursuant to RC § 3119.89(B).

§ 20:11 Continuing jurisdiction—Determining arrearages—Interest on arrears

So long as a delinquent obligor had no penalty or additional cost imposed after becoming delinquent, and only had to pay what was originally ordered, the obligor benefitted from the use of the retained funds. In many instances, the obligor could repay delinquent amounts in small installments. In *Allen v. Allen*,[1] the appellate court held that support orders were judgments when due and interest should be applied to arrearages. The court reasoned that not only had the obligor the use of the money, but also that the obligee may have incurred

---

[Section 20:10]

[1]Lytle v. Lytle, 130 Ohio App. 3d 697, 720 N.E.2d 1007 (10th Dist. Franklin County 1998).

[2]McPherson v. McPherson, 153 Ohio St. 82, 41 Ohio Op. 151, 90 N.E.2d 675 (1950); Morrison v. Morrison, No. 73AP-195 (Ohio Ct. App. 10th Dist. Franklin County 1974).

[3]Swartz v. Roush, 1986 WL 13954 (Ohio Ct. App. 5th Dist. Fairfield County 1986).

[4]Asztalos v. Fortney, 48 Ohio App. 2d 66, 2 Ohio Op. 3d 45, 355 N.E.2d 517 (6th Dist. Lucas County 1975).

[5]See Godfrey v. Godfrey, 1978 WL 215144 (Ohio Ct. App. 9th Dist. Summit County 1978); Lytle v. Lytle, 130 Ohio App. 3d 697, 720 N.E.2d 1007 (10th Dist. Franklin County 1998).

[Section 20:11]

[1]Allen v. Allen, 62 Ohio App. 3d 621, 577 N.E.2d 126 (9th Dist. Summit County 1990).

interest costs in borrowing or otherwise obtaining the funds for support. Subsequently, former RC 3113.219 was enacted in 1992.[2] It provided that on or after July 1, 1992, when a court issued or modified a support order, under a variety of statutes, and an obligor was found to have willfully failed to pay, the court was to assess interest at the statutory rate found in RC 1343.03 from the date of the original order.[3] The Supreme Court in *Dunbar v. Dunbar*,[4] while recognizing the *Allen* case, nevertheless held that for orders entered prior to July 1, 1992, interest would only accumulate on arrearages that had been reduced to judgment.

In enacting RC 3123.17,[5] the legislature omitted any reference to an effective date. Presumably, therefore, the court can determine a default under a prior order entered at any time, and not, as held in *Dunbar*, just an order made subsequent to July 1, 1992.

§ 20:12   Continuing jurisdiction—Determining arrearages— Repayment

At such time as a court support order or administrative child support order terminates, any overdue and unpaid support or arrearage owed under the order is to be withheld in an amount at least equal to the amount withheld under the terminated child support order.[1]

When support orders are ongoing, the arrearage amount is to be ordered collected with each payment of current support in an amount equal to at least twenty percent of the current payment, except upon good cause shown.[2]

§ 20:13   Continuing jurisdiction—Self-employed obligor

The obligor who is self-employed or whose employment is such that his income is derived from a variety of sources is dealt with in RC 3121.03. A wage assignment under such circumstances would be either impractical or unreliable. Hence, the court is given discretion to order automatic deduction from a bank account or the posting of a bond in appropriate circumstances. Such bond may be not less than $500, nor more than $10,000, with sureties approved by the court. This procedure is designed to assure compliance with the order of support and may also be used where the obligor's employer is not subject to the court's jurisdiction.

---

[2]Amended and recodified by 2000 S.B. 180, eff. 3-22-01, analogous language 3123.17.

[3]RC 3113.219 was amended and recodified as RC 3123.17 by 2000 S.B. 180, eff. 3-22-01).

[4]Dunbar v. Dunbar, 68 Ohio St. 3d 369, 1994-Ohio-509, 627 N.E.2d 532 (1994).

[5]2000 S.B. 180.

[Section 20:12]

[1]RC 3121.36.

[2]RC 3123.21.

Bank account withholding only works if there is money in the bank account. Worse, some banks fail to send the child support enforcement agency any money unless the garnished account contains enough to pay the full amount due. This is incorrect, since the RC 3121.03 order is more akin to a garnishment than to a customer's order pre-authorizing withdrawal.

Bonding orders offer the opportunity for creative lawyering. A provision whereby the obligor waives notice and service of summons if the child support enforcement agency records show arrearages would facilitate proceeding against funds posted as bond. Such a provision would eliminate the sometimes difficult task of locating and serving an absconding obligor before the bond money can be turned over to the obligee.

◆ **Practice Tips:** The practitioner should keep in mind that the court has the authority to make more than one kind of order at a time under RC 3121.03. For example, withholding from a bank account plus a bond is a possible combination of orders.

§20:14 Continuing jurisdiction—Nonemployed or underemployed obligor

Practically all resources are available for the payment of child and spousal support by court order. The definition of "payor" in RC 3123.01 was amended to include a broader range of entities and sources of funds, and the definition of income was also broadened. While the preferred method is payroll withholding, where the obligor is unemployed or the amount available for withholding is insufficient to meet the order, the new definitions of "income" and of "payor" permit the court to order funds out of the following:

(1) Workers' compensation, whether paid by state fund or employer;

(2) Pension, annuity, and allowances, where obligor is receiving, is to receive, or has received a warrant from a public employees retirement system, municipal retirement system, police and firemen's disability and pension fund, state teachers' retirement system, school employees retirement system, or state highway patrol retirement system;

(3) Disability or sick pay;

(4) Insurance proceeds;

(5) Lottery prize awards;

(6) Federal, state, or local government benefits to the extent they can be deducted or withheld under the law governing the benefits;

(7) Any trust fund or endowment fund;

(8) Vacation pay;

(9) Commissions and draws against commissions paid on a regular basis;

(10) Bonuses or profit sharing payments or distributions; or

(11)   Funds on deposit in any account in a financial institution under jurisdiction of the court.

Again, a combination of orders is possible and in many cases advisable.

§ 20:15   Continuing jurisdiction—Other resources

An obligor's pension benefits can be used to collect arrearages and to enforce previously decreed support orders, even though the obligee was not awarded direct access to pension benefits.[1] Caution is in order, however. Whenever a court orders support withheld from a fund governed by ERISA, a "qualified domestic relations order" (QDRO) must be prepared by counsel and submitted to the pension fund trustee for approval. This is not a simple withholding order. A careful reading of former RC 3113.21(D)(3)(a) prior to its amendment by 1997 House Bill 352 reveals that the language did not authorize the court to use the regular support withholding procedures as against private pension funds, only against government pension funds.

Accordingly, the nebulous and slow-moving QDRO application procedures have applied to support coming from ERISA-governed pension plans. The client-obligee and the practitioner may well be better off to seek withholding from a different source such as a bank account or even a part-time employer if the dollar amount is small or the duration of the order will be short. The new, broader definitions of "payor," to include "any other person or entity" except the bureau of employment services, and "income," to include "pensions; annuities; allowances; private or governmental retirement benefits," appear to be intended to change this.[2]

All employer orders require the employer to give forty-five days' notice to the child support enforcement agency of any lump-sum payment in excess of $150 to be made to the obligor.[3] The employer must delay payment of such lump sum for thirty days. The employer must then comply with any further order of the court to pay any amount of such lump sum to the child support enforcement agency. If the employer knowingly fails to give appropriate notice, it may be liable for any support payments not made as a result of its failure.[4]

When it is determined that a lump sum will be paid, the court must issue an order either releasing the funds to the obligor if no arrearages exist, or ordering some or all of it paid to the child support

---

[Section 20:15]

[1]Taylor v. Taylor, 44 Ohio St. 3d 61, 541 N.E.2d 55 (1989).

[2]See former RC 3113.21(P)(9), former RC 3113.21(Q); Bacharowski v. Bacharowski, 2000 WL 283087 (Ohio Ct. App. 8th Dist. Cuyahoga County 2000) (trial court may order a levy on obligor's IRA to enforce a support arrearage, although IRA had been awarded to obligor).

[3]RC 3121.12.

[4]RC 3121.12.

enforcement agency.[5] If the amount paid is in excess of the arrearage, the balance must be paid to the obligor within two days.[6] The court has jurisdiction to make a finding of contempt for support arrearages even if the order for support is no longer in effect.[7]

A trial court may impose a jail sentence in both criminal and civil actions to punish a support obligor for contempt of a support order, even if the child has reached majority. An obligation to pay support is not a debt. The imposition of a jail sentence under these circumstances, therefore, does not violate Section 15, Article I of the Ohio Constitution, which prohibits imprisonment for debt.[8]

The goal of the trial court dealing in enforcing support is for the obligor to comply with the support order as well as to pay missed payments, liquidating the arrearages over a reasonable period of time. If the order is to be enforced and the stated goal achieved, the court must take into consideration the income of the non-residential parent who is brought before the court. The order should not be enforced in such a way as to make it impossible for the obligor to comply.

Guideline child support figures carry a presumption of reasonableness, so it is a good argument that if all children are emancipated, arrears should be liquidated at a rate equal to at least the current one child guideline amount for the parties involved.[9]

Generally, trial courts entering judgments dissolving marriages have enforced spousal support awards not only as an exercise of the court's continuing jurisdiction, but as enforcement of the parties' contract.[10] When the separation agreement is incorporated into the final divorce decree, the court that dissolved the marriage has continuing jurisdiction until all obligations have been fulfilled and may enforce the terms of the separation agreement through contempt proceedings.[11]

There are limits on continuing jurisdiction, however. Child and spousal support arrearages may not be modified retroactively unless the divorce decree specifically allows for such modification.[12]

"Judicial enforcement of a separation agreement, incorporated into a divorce decree, which requires a non-custodial parent to pay tuition

---

[5]RC 3121.12.

[6]RC 3121.12.

[7]RC 2705.031(E), as amended by 1990 S.B. 3, eff. 4-11-91.

[8]Cramer v. Petrie, 70 Ohio St. 3d 131, 1994-Ohio-404, 637 N.E.2d 882 (1994).

[9]RC 3121.36. When arrearage exists at time of termination of support, unpaid amount is to be withheld in an amount at least the amount of the last withholding order.

[10]See Greiner v. Greiner, 61 Ohio App. 2d 88, 15 Ohio Op. 3d 95, 399 N.E.2d 571 (8th Dist. Cuyahoga County 1979).

[11]RC 3105.65; Stauffer v. Stauffer, 4 Ohio App. 2d 339, 33 Ohio Op. 2d 395, 212 N.E.2d 622 (4th Dist. Pickaway County 1965).

[12]Armstrong v. Armstrong, 117 Ohio St. 558, 6 Ohio L. Abs. 14, 160 N.E. 34, 57 A.L.R. 1108 (1927).

for his child's religious education, does not offend [the religious freedom provision of] the Ohio Constitution."[13]

Child support enforcement proceedings are typically started by the residential parent or spousal support recipient. When the residential parent or support recipient is receiving public assistance, the department of human services may step in and use contempt to enforce payment. Where a residential parent dies, the child has standing to bring an action to enforce or modify a child support order, even if that child has not been joined as a party, though joining the child would be "the more proper procedure."[14]

Finally, under RC 3103.03(D) if a parent neglects to support his or her minor child and the child is unemancipated, any person supplying the minor child with necessaries in good faith may recover from the neglectful parent the reasonable value of the necessaries supplied. Thus, child support enforcement is even possible at the hands of non-governmental third parties, such as neighbors, grandparents, or other relatives.

§ 20:16 Continuing jurisdiction—Client data needed

Whether support enforcement is sought through private counsel or through the CSEA, counsel needs to obtain a certain minimum amount of information to successfully prepare documents and implement payroll or financial account withholding and other required forms.

All of the following pieces of data are likely to be required on some form, somewhere, sometime, most likely when everyone else on the case has left the courtroom and you are sitting there alone trying to complete the paperwork.

Therefore, gather as much of this data as you can early on, and keep the form in the front of your file. Fill in more blanks via discovery, or when you have the opposing party under oath, or when you meet with opposing counsel.

§ 20:17 Continuing jurisdiction—Client data checklist— Form⊚

SUPPORT DATA CHECKLIST

Payee: Name
                     Address
                     Phone number(s)
                     SSN

---

[13]Rand v. Rand, 18 Ohio St. 3d 356, 481 N.E.2d 609, 26 Ed. Law Rep. 1198 (1985).

[14]Haverland v. Haverland, 1985 WL 6760, at *2 (Ohio Ct. App. 1st Dist. Hamilton County 1985).

Current driver's license number
Date of birth
Employer
Employer address
Payroll office phone number
Current income (attach copy of pay stub, W-2, Tax returns)
Health insurance carrier
Address
Insurance 800 phone number
Group number
Marginal cost for family coverage
Other health care plans (same data needed)

Child(ren): Name
Date of birth
Expected date of emancipation

Payor: Name
Address
Home phone number
Current driver's license number
SSN
Date of birth
Description/photo (for process server)
Employer
Job site address (or hangout)
Employer address
Payroll office phone number
Current income
Old pay records
(attach copies of pay stubs, W-2s, 1099s, Tax returns, old loan applications)
Payor's usual bank, branch, acct. number
Payor's recent home/car purchases?
Payor litigation pending?
Payor family estates pending?
Health insurance carrier
Address
Insurance 800 phone number
Group number
Marginal cost for family coverage
Other health care plans (same data needed)

Other: Prior orders
Worksheets from prior orders

CSEA records, certified copy
Payor deed or mortgage copies
Case number
Judge/Magistrate assigned to case
Likely opposing counsel

§ 20:18 Continuing jurisdiction—Subpoena power

One of the most important powers that the practitioner has under the court's continuing jurisdiction is the subpoena power. Whenever it becomes necessary to invoke the court's continuing jurisdiction, the careful practitioner will use the subpoena power to discover the necessary facts concerning the opposing party's income and insurance coverage. You may make your case for contempt or support modification based only our own client's testimony. You may or may not get discovery from the opposing party. But a subpoena almost always works.

In support enforcement procedures, it is wise to subpoena records from the obligor's employer routinely. Often, counsel can prepare a form to reproduce and staple on to the court's subpoena form:

§ 20:19 Continuing jurisdiction—Subpoena list—Form⊚

EXHIBIT A—Attachment to Subpoena—List of Records Subject to Subpoena

1. Provide a copy of the complete record of wages for years [_____] through the present date for this employee.

2. Provide records *(or fill in blank)* for this employee showing:

Date of hire [_____]
Hourly rate [_____]
Overtime rate [_____]
Pay period [_____]
Date of termination (if applicable) [_____]
Reason for termination (if applicable)

_____

_____

3. If health insurance in available, answer the following questions (or provide records to show) including the name and address of all available plans or carriers, and for each:

a. Cost to employee for individual coverage

b. Cost for family coverage

c. Insurance company name, address, phone number, 800 number, group number.

II. THE ANCIENT TOOL

§ 20:20 Contempt and show cause procedures—In general

The traditional procedure for enforcement of spousal and child support, and indeed all aspects of the decree, was a motion for an order to show cause.[1]

A court has inherent power to enforce its orders through contempt proceedings under RC 2705.02(A).[2]

In practice, a payee, after accumulating an amount of arrearages to warrant retaining an attorney, would bring the action, naming the payor as respondent. Then, a period of time would pass during which service was achieved, notice of hearing was sent, and continuances were requested. Finally, the hearing would be held, and the defaulter would be found to be in contempt of court. A set amount would be determined as arrearages, and the payor would be admonished to pay. Sometimes the respondent would comply, sometimes not. Over a period of time, compliance generally deteriorated.

If the respondent complied, the payments would generally be increased to cover the arrearages, or in some extreme cases, the arrearages would be covered by an extension of the support order. Sometimes this was a useless action where the respondent was in default because of inability to pay. Although this saved a contempt, or a capias,[3] it did not always get the money when and where it was needed. In addition, some of the money was consumed in attorney fees unless the petitioner's attorney also received an order for expense money and costs. If respondent was solvent, the petitioner and counsel would do well. If not, the proceedings were of little use since the attorney did not receive attorney fees and the petitioner did not receive support. Nevertheless, contempt is still a powerful tool for enforcing support orders, because, in the end, the defaulting party knows that the threat of doing jail time is real.

> ◆ **Practice Tip:** It might be best to set support contempt hearings in front of a judge, if that is allowable under the local rules. Some parties seem to react better to "Judge" confrontations than "Magistrate" hearings. The threat of jail time may be more immediate before a judge. If you have multiple motions to file, local rules may specify that some must be heard before a magistrate, and that might be a good reason to set a contempt before the magistrate, to avoid bifurcating the case.

[Section 20:20]

[1]See Text § 25:44, Motions by obligee regarding enforcement of judgments—Motion for order to show cause.

[2]Zakany v. Zakany, 9 Ohio St. 3d 192, 459 N.E.2d 870 (1984) (husband tried to defeat prior court order by various financial maneuvers). See Text § 25:44, Motions by obligee regarding enforcement of judgments—Motion for order to show cause.

[3]Szymkowiak v. Calabrese, 1981 WL 5425 (Ohio Ct. App. 6th Dist. Lucas County 1981) (no abuse of discretion to deny motion for modification because husband had been laid off from his job and being held in contempt while unemployed would have been an unnecessary hardship).

§ 20:21   Contempt and show cause procedures—Contempt under RC 2705.05

Pursuant to RC 2705.031(B), any party who has a legal claim to any support ordered for a child, spouse, or former spouse may initiate a contempt action for failure to pay the support. In Title IV-D cases, the contempt action may also be initiated by an attorney retained by the party, the prosecuting attorney, or an attorney of the Department of Job and Family Services or the local IV-D agency.

Pursuant to RC 2705.05, if the court finds the obligor guilty of contempt, the court may impose any of the following penalties:

(1) For a first offense, a fine of not more than $250, a definite term of imprisonment of not more than thirty days, or both;

(2) For a second offense, a fine of not more than $500, a definite term of imprisonment of not more than sixty days, or both; or

(3) For a third or subsequent offense, a fine of not more than $1,000, a definite term of imprisonment of not more than ninety days, or both.

These are mandatory maximum penalties; there has been some discussion in the Ohio General Assembly of instituting mandatory minimum penalties akin the minimum sentences for drunken driving. The current legislative trend seems to be for the legislature to restrict judicial discretion whenever the perception arises that the courts are not using available penalties to solve societal problems like drunk driving, criminal behavior or non-payment of support.

§ 20:22   Contempt and show cause procedures—Penalties

The penalties for civil contempt do not violate the state and federal constitutional prohibitions against imprisonment for a debt. One of the earliest cases to address this issue was *Slawski v Slawski*.[1] The court found that the duty to support one's children was not a debt, and hence there was no constitutional violation when a jail sentence was imposed for noncompliance. Similarly, Ohio courts have found that the common law and public policy require parents to fulfill their natural duty to provide shelter, food, and clothing for their children. A "debt is a specified sum of money owing to one person from another."[2]

[Section 20:22]

[1]Slawski v. Slawski, 49 Ohio App. 100, 1 Ohio Op. 201, 18 Ohio L. Abs. 515, 195 N.E. 258 (6th Dist. Lucas County 1934).

[2]State v. Ducey, 25 Ohio App. 2d 50, 54 Ohio Op. 2d 80, 266 N.E.2d 233 (10th Dist. Franklin County 1970). See also State v. Wright, 4 Ohio App. 3d 291, 448 N.E.2d 499 (7th Dist. Columbiana County 1982) (imprisonment for the violation of RC 3113.06, failure to pay maintenance costs, a criminal statute, is not imprisonment for a debt in a "civil action" as is prohibited by O. Const. art. I § 15).

The obligation to support one's children is a duty owed to the public generally.[3]

Hence, in the strictest sense, there is no imprisonment for nonpayment of a debt when a delinquent obligor is jailed. Also significant to the resolution of the constitutional question is the fact that the obligor is facing a sentence for civil contempt.

Civil contempt is meant to be remedial and is intended to benefit the aggrieved party by coercing compliance.[4] The defaulting obligor's sentence may be significantly shortened or avoided altogether by a demonstration of compliance. The jail sentence is designed to encourage payment by the defaulting party, and some reasonable effort toward compliance will prevent the defaulter from serving a jail sentence.

In *In re Harper*,[5] the appellant-father contended that the evidence did not support a finding of contempt for failure to pay child support and that the court erred in not applying a "beyond a reasonable doubt" standard. While affirming the trial court, the Seventh District Court of Appeals enunciated the public policy of the state, which imposes a duty on parents to care for their children. There must be a good faith effort to make ordered payments, and the "effort to find employment must be commensurate with their obligation to pay support."[6] Appellant's preference for a life of general relief, ADC, food stamps, and his current wife's child support, rather than his own earned income, was sufficient evidence to sustain the finding of contempt. The court of appeals concluded that failure to pay support is essentially a civil matter and not criminal contempt. Therefore, the burden of proof is not beyond a reasonable doubt.

In setting purge conditions upon a contemnor, it is error for the court to set purge conditions which are void or unreasonable, or impermissibly concern future compliance.[7]

---

[3]State v. Ducey, 25 Ohio App. 2d 50, 54 Ohio Op. 2d 80, 266 N.E.2d 233 (10th Dist. Franklin County 1970). See also State v. Wright, 4 Ohio App. 3d 291, 448 N.E.2d 499 (7th Dist. Columbiana County 1982).

[4]U.S. v. Work Wear Corp., 602 F.2d 110 (6th Cir. 1979).

[5]Matter of Harper, 1989 WL 122537, at *4 (Ohio Ct. App. 7th Dist. Monroe County 1989).

[6]Matter of Harper, 1989 WL 122537 (Ohio Ct. App. 7th Dist. Monroe County 1989).

[7]Burchett v. Miller, 123 Ohio App. 3d 550, 704 N.E.2d 636 (6th Dist. Erie County 1997).

§ 20:23 Contempt and show cause procedures—Hearing procedures

The standard of proof in civil contempt proceedings is clear and convincing evidence.[1] The standard of proof differs from that applied in wholly civil proceedings (preponderance of the evidence) because civil contempt proceedings are quasi-criminal in nature.[2] An initial contempt pleading need only aver a prior order and a default.[3] The elements of civil contempt in a divorce action are (1) a prior order of the court, (2) proper notice given to alleged contemnor, and (3) a failure or refusal to make payment.[4]

An important question raised by the use of contempt to enforce support is whether an indigent party facing a contempt sentence is entitled to legal counsel at state expense. Statutory developments in Ohio have assured an indigent defendant a right to counsel.[5]

An obligor is entitled to basic rights in the civil contempt proceeding. The delinquent party is entitled to adequate notice of the hearing, sufficient time to prepare a defense, and an opportunity to be heard. These rights were found to be encompassed in RC 2705.03 and guaranteed by the due process provisions of the US and Ohio Constitutions.[6] RC 2705.031 requires that the summons served with a contempt motion include a laundry list of notices to the defendant in contempt, advising of the risk of an arrest warrant for failure to appear, the right to counsel, and the possible penalties for being found in contempt.[7] The notice requirements of RC 2705.031 apply only to support issues and not to alleged contempt for violation of restraining orders.[8]

A civil contempt order must allow for purging, otherwise it is void.[9]

[Section 20:23]

[1]Brown v. Executive 200, Inc., 64 Ohio St. 2d 250, 18 Ohio Op. 3d 446, 416 N.E.2d 610 (1980).

[2]Gruebel v. Gruebel, 1987 WL 14302 (Ohio Ct. App. 4th Dist. Pickaway County 1987).

[3]State ex rel. Cook v. Cook, 66 Ohio St. 566, 64 N.E. 567 (1902).

[4]Rossen v. Rossen, 2 Ohio App. 2d 381, 31 Ohio Op. 2d 589, 208 N.E.2d 764 (9th Dist. Summit County 1964).

[5]RC 2705.031(C)(2).

[6]Culberson v. Culberson, 60 Ohio App. 2d 304, 14 Ohio Op. 3d 265, 397 N.E.2d 1226 (1st Dist. Clinton County 1978).

[7]In re Yeauger, 83 Ohio App. 3d 493, 615 N.E.2d 289 (3d Dist. Union County 1992); Benjamin v. Benjamin, 1997 WL 799471 (Ohio Ct. App. 10th Dist. Franklin County 1997); but see Sancho v. Sancho, 114 Ohio App. 3d 636, 683 N.E.2d 849 (3d Dist. Union County 1996) (right to notice of contempt charge may be waived by failing to preserve issue, by proceeding and calling witnesses to defend charge).

[8]Stegawski v. Stegawski, 1994 WL 197232 (Ohio Ct. App. 8th Dist. Cuyahoga County 1994).

[9]McCrea v. McCrea, 1986 WL 13344 (Ohio Ct. App. 8th Dist. Cuyahoga County 1986); Panetta v. Panetta, 1988 WL 57528 (Ohio Ct. App. 9th Dist. Summit County

Likewise a trial court errs by denying one accused of contempt an opportunity to defend or explain his actions.[10] A contemnor must be given an opportunity to be heard, to present available defenses, to call witnesses, and to be represented by counsel.[11] However, a trial court did not err in sentencing a father for contempt without the order containing an opportunity to purge, where the father had ample opportunity to purge himself of the contempt between the filing of the motion and the hearing date, but "failed to make even a token payment."[12] The father had been found in contempt for some of the same failures to comply in earlier proceedings.[13]

In *Tucker v. Tucker*,[14] the court held as follows:

> Offenses against the dignity or process of the court, where the primary purpose of the punishment imposed is to vindicate the authority of the court by punishing the contemnor for his disobedience, are criminal contempts. Violations which are primarily offenses against the party for whose benefit the order was made, and where the primary purpose of the punishment is remedial or coercive and for the benefit of the complainant, are civil contempts, and the sanction must afford the contemnor the opportunity to purge himself of his contempt.[15]

The *Tucker* decision held that the portion of the trial court's judgment that suspended the sentence of incarceration upon condition of keeping future payments of support current was of no effect. There is no error where the purge order allows for the suspension if payor purges the contempt by discharging the support arrearage.[16]

Where there is willful noncompliance, the use of the court's contempt power is the best method of enforcement of a child support

---

1988) (provision in contempt order permitting purging of contempt must match the contempt, i.e., return of household goods, where wrongfully removed, or payment of support where arrearages exist); Pontikos v. Pontikos, 1990 WL 84246 (Ohio Ct. App. 8th Dist. Cuyahoga County 1990).

[10]Cox v. Cox, 1986 WL 14878 (Ohio Ct. App. 5th Dist. Stark County 1986); Moyer v. Moyer, 1988 WL 120776 (Ohio Ct. App. 11th Dist. Geauga County 1988) (trial court did not err at civil contempt hearing in allowing appellee's testimony to go beyond the narrow issues raised in appellant's show cause motion).

[11]In re Yeauger, 83 Ohio App. 3d 493, 615 N.E.2d 289 (3d Dist. Union County 1992); Haren v. Fronsman, 1994 WL 115937 (Ohio Ct. App. 5th Dist. Stark County 1994); Graham v. Graham, 1997 WL 778985 (Ohio Ct. App. 1st Dist. Hamilton County 1997) (form notice of CSEA lacked specificity regarding charges that obligor was voluntarily underemployed).

[12]Goode v. Goode, 1995 WL 458966, at *3 (Ohio Ct. App. 10th Dist. Franklin County 1995).

[13]Goode v. Goode, 1995 WL 458966 (Ohio Ct. App. 10th Dist. Franklin County 1995).

[14]Tucker v. Tucker, 10 Ohio App. 3d 251, 461 N.E.2d 1337 (10th Dist. Franklin County 1983).

[15]Tucker v. Tucker, 10 Ohio App. 3d 251, 252, 461 N.E.2d 1337 (10th Dist. Franklin County 1983).

[16]Williams v. Williams, 1986 WL 5978 (Ohio Ct. App. 10th Dist. Franklin County 1986); Sidwell v. Sidwell, 1997 WL 101680 (Ohio Ct. App. 10th Dist. Franklin County 1997); Stegawski v. Stegawski, 1994 WL 197232 (Ohio Ct. App. 8th Dist. Cuyahoga

or spousal support order. However, the aggrieved party often does not have the money or time off work to pursue a proper contempt motion. This problem is further aggravated if the court ignores the contemnor's duty to make a good faith effort to obtain counsel and grants the contemnor two automatic continuances—one to obtain counsel and one to allow the newly retained counsel to prepare. The aggrieved party then begins to doubt the sincerity of the court's dedication to the enforcement of its own orders.

Sometimes trial courts become frustrated by cases with repeated contempt filings. Nevertheless, the court must allow the parties to present their evidence and may not seek to shortcut the enforcement process. In *Bellamy v. Bellamy*,[17] the Sixth District Court of Appeals held that it was error for the trial court to refuse to hear the parties' evidence, hold the contempt motion "in abeyance," and sua sponte reduce the appellee's child support order as a way of resolving the child support issue. To do so deprived the appellant of her procedural due process right to receive adequate notice and present evidence on the issue.

In the absence of a stay of execution, a trial court retains jurisdiction to enforce its orders, make a finding of contempt and impose sanctions while the underlying decree is on appeal.[18]

§ 20:24   Contempt and show cause procedures—Attorney fees

Attorney fees and court costs must be awarded in an enforcement action, even where the party bringing the action is financially able to pay them.[1] RC 3109.05(C) requires the court to order an award of reasonable attorney fees and all court costs against a party found in contempt of a support order made after April 15, 1985 or modified after December 1, 1986. After July 1, 1992, interest on any arrears may also be assessed if default was willful.[2] The court, of course, determines what fee is reasonable.

◆ **Practice Tip:** Always ask for attorney fees and court costs in your pleadings. If you do not ask for them, you will not get them.

County 1994); Stroud v. Stroud, 1997 WL 703359 (Ohio Ct. App. 11th Dist. Lake County 1997).

[17]Bellamy v. Bellamy, 110 Ohio App. 3d 576, 674 N.E.2d 1227 (6th Dist. Erie County 1996).

[18]RC 2505.09; Mason v. Mason, 1999 WL 253597 (Ohio Ct. App. 3d Dist. Union County 1999).

[Section 20:24]

[1]RC 3109.05(C).

[2]Former RC 3123.17, current RC 3123.17; RC 3123.171.

There is some guidance from prior case law regarding the reasonableness of fees. In *Rand v. Rand*,[3] the Eighth District Court of Appeals noted that

> appellant was aware of his obligations but chose not to adhere to them. Consequently, the appellee had no choice but to institute an action to require the appellant to meet his legal obligations. Had the appellant been properly supporting his son, it would have been unnecessary for the appellee to have hired an attorney to represent her in an enforcement action. Under such circumstances, we do not find it an abuse of discretion for the referee to have awarded attorney fees to the appellee.[4]

In *Linehan v. Linehan*,[5] the Eighth District Court of Appeals refused to award the full amount of fees requested after considering the relative ability of the parties to bear the expense. In *Hamilton v. Hamilton*,[6] the trial court erred in refusing to treat attorney fees and expenses in support enforcement proceedings as additional support and as subject to 1988 House Bill 509 withholding provisions.

In *Moross v. Scott*,[7] it was held to be an abuse of discretion to award only $75 in attorney's fees to a wife earning $6,600 per year and seeking to enforce a prior child support order against a husband earning $23,000 per year, when the wife's attorney had submitted detailed evidence covering the work performed and rates charged in the matter. The court in *Moross* did not require the husband to pay his wife's travel expenses from the state of Washington, noting that she could have avoided those expenses by enforcing the order through URESA proceedings.

Citing *Blum v. Blum*,[8] the Second District Court of Appeals in *Saeks v. Saeks*[9] upheld an award of attorney fees to the wife in an alimony enforcement proceeding, where she was seeking a lump-sum judgment rather than a finding of contempt, saying that as a practical matter, to hold otherwise would insulate an ex-husband from his obligation to pay alimony if the ex-wife could not afford an attorney.

The contempt procedure may never become obsolete as a tool of private counsel representing obligees of support orders. Even given the existence of support enforcement agencies in every county, there

---

[3]Rand v. Rand, 1984 WL 5112, at *6 (Ohio Ct. App. 8th Dist. Cuyahoga County 1984).

[4]Rand v. Rand, 1984 WL 5112 (Ohio Ct. App. 8th Dist. Cuyahoga County 1984). On this point, the *Rand* court took exception to the decision of the Eleventh District Court of Appeals in Cohen v. Cohen, 8 Ohio App. 3d 109, 456 N.E.2d 581 (11th Dist. Lake County 1983). See Text § 13:25, Attorney fees—Fees as spousal support.

[5]Linehan v. Linehan, 34 Ohio App. 3d 124, 517 N.E.2d 967 (8th Dist. Cuyahoga County 1986).

[6]Hamilton v. Hamilton, 40 Ohio App. 3d 190, 532 N.E.2d 213 (10th Dist. Franklin County 1988).

[7]Moross v. Scott, 1985 WL 7055 (Ohio Ct. App. 6th Dist. Lucas County 1985).

[8]Blum v. Blum, 9 Ohio St. 2d 92, 38 Ohio Op. 2d 224, 223 N.E.2d 819 (1967).

[9]Saeks v. Saeks, 24 Ohio App. 3d 67, 493 N.E.2d 280 (2d Dist. Montgomery County 1985).

may not be sympathetic county authorities to supply the funds and personnel to properly staff the agencies. Child support enforcement agencies, which are supposed to act within twenty days of application by the obligee, have six-month backlogs in some jurisdictions. There is still a place for private counsel to assist obligees via contempt filings.

§ 20:25 Contempt defenses—In general

The right to prepare a defense and the opportunity to be heard are essential if the obligor is to present any defenses that might be available to him. However, the right to prepare and to obtain counsel are balanced by the obligor's duty to act in good faith to promptly obtain counsel under RC 2705.031(C)(2). Certain defenses will require documentary proof, and some will be more competently presented with the aid of counsel. Hence, the need for the fair notice requirement becomes obvious. Although there is no defense to an obligor's willful failure to pay support as ordered, there are several other instances in which enforcement would be inequitable.

Possible defenses the obligor may raise include (1) unemployment or inability to pay; (2) forgiving of arrears by the obligee; (3) Social Security benefits to the children; (4) possession of the child by the obligor; (5) remarriage of either party; (6) emancipation; (7) denial of visitation; (8) bankruptcy; (9) agreement of parties; (10) laches or estoppel; (11) church and state arguments; (12) payment in kind; and (13) agreement to mediate or arbitrate.

§ 20:26 Contempt defenses—Unemployment or inability to pay

Although the element of willful noncompliance need not be shown before an individual can be found in contempt, willful noncompliance will be implied when income is received by an obligor and no payments are made. Complete inability to pay may be a possible defense, but, where there is income or the ability to work, the court must look at the obligor's good faith.

In determining arrearages and whether an obligor is in default, all possible defenses must be analyzed.[1]

Inability to pay and comply with a court order is a valid defense if the person charged proves that it is "not in his power to obey the order."[2] In one Eighth District case, a separation agreement required a former husband to pay a lump sum of $4,200, which was intended to

---

[Section 20:26]

[1]Lea v. Lea, 1981 WL 5114 (Ohio Ct. App. 12th Dist. Clinton County 1981).

[2]Courtney v. Courtney, 16 Ohio App. 3d 329, 334, 475 N.E.2d 1284 (3d Dist. Hancock County 1984) (trial court errs and case will be remanded if court does not consider evidence of obligor's alleged inability to pay). See Urbanek v. Urbanek, 1988 WL 37651 (Ohio Ct. App. 9th Dist. Summit County 1988) (trial court failed to consider party's inability to comply with terms of settlement in contempt proceeding); Neff v. Neff, 1989 WL 13531 (Ohio Ct. App. 2d Dist. Montgomery County 1989) (court failed

be paid on the mortgage of the marital residence. The fact that the former wife sold the marital residence and paid off the mortgage before the lump sum was due did not excuse the former husband's refusal to pay.[3] The Seventh District has held that a father who failed to make support payments where the record reflected that he had medical problems and most of his income was from welfare could be found in contempt for not making any effort to comply with the order.[4] Even if there is an inability to pay the full amount ordered, an obligor an obligor must make such partial support payments as are within his or her ability.[5]

Where the record reflects evidence that an obligor had threatened to retire if an increase was substantial, the trial court did not abuse its discretion in refusing to reduce his child support obligation when he took early retirement, and claimed that he suffered from ill health.[6]

One court held that incarceration is an involuntary act so as to constitute a sufficient change of circumstances to terminate a support order.[7] However, another case decided that the acts resulting in an obligor becoming subsequently imprisoned were voluntary and thus no basis for a modification of support.[8] The Sixth District in *Cole v. Cole* suggested, however, that a contempt finding while the obligor was incarcerated was unlikely[9] but neither the trial court nor the Court of Appeals ruled directly on that point.

The length of time afforded to an obligor before imposition of a contempt sentence should be influenced by several considerations such as (1) the extent to which the obligor has in good faith sought employment, (2) efforts the obligor has made to satisfy his support obligation during his period of unemployment, and (3) the obligor's attitude toward his obligation. A chronically unemployed obligor who is unwilling to accept minimum wage employment would not be a good candidate for extended continuances. Conversely, an obligor who is laid off from his place of employment and is making a good faith effort

---

to consider evidence of husband's alleged inability to make hospital insurance payments as required by separation agreement).

[3]Wagner v. Wagner, 1989 WL 21419 (Ohio Ct. App. 8th Dist. Cuyahoga County 1989).

[4]Allen v. Allen, 59 Ohio App. 3d 54, 571 N.E.2d 139 (7th Dist. Columbiana County 1988).

[5]McCree v. McCree, 2009-Ohio-2639, 2009 WL 1581169 (Ohio Ct. App. 7th Dist. Mahoning County 2009).

[6]Engel v. Engel, 1988 WL 70512 (Ohio Ct. App. 5th Dist. Tuscarawas County 1988).

[7]Peters v. Peters, 69 Ohio App. 3d 275, 590 N.E.2d 777 (12th Dist. Warren County 1990) (abrogated by, Richardson v. Ballard, 113 Ohio App. 3d 552, 681 N.E.2d 507 (12th Dist. Butler County 1996)).

[8]Cole v. Cole, 70 Ohio App. 3d 188, 590 N.E.2d 862 (6th Dist. Erie County 1990).

[9]Cole v. Cole, 70 Ohio App. 3d 188, 193, 590 N.E.2d 862 (6th Dist. Erie County 1990).

to meet his support obligation from unemployment or other benefits should be given as much time as fairness and equity dictate. Continued hearings serve both to remind the obligor of his continuing support obligations and to keep the child support enforcement agency apprised of the obligor's employment status, address, and other essential information. The primary concern during the unemployment period is to try to keep any previously incurred arrearages from increasing.

At such time as the obligor secures employment or returns to work, a wage assignment must be ordered. The order should provide for deduction of current support from the obligor's wages, plus an additional amount to be applied toward the arrearage. The amount ordered on arrears should be determined by several factors: (1) the size of the arrearage, (2) the amount of the current order, (3) the obligor's income, and (4) the obligor's other responsibilities. If the arrearage is substantial and the obligor's income is sufficient, an order for arrears that matches or exceeds the order for current support would be reasonable.

A trial court did not err in finding a father in contempt of court for failure to pay child support as ordered. The father did not meet his burden of proof to establish a defense of "inability to pay." The trial court concluded that the father should not have geographically restricted his employment search to be closer to the minor children.[10]

A trial court properly imposed a jail sentence in contempt proceedings where the defendant failed to present any evidence of inability to pay and failed to demonstrate any good faith effort to meet his support obligation.[11] Voluntary termination of employment and subsequent inability to pay child support and to comply with medical orders are not valid defenses to contempt.[12]

The obligor with other family obligations or low income employment poses a different problem. If the deduction for current support represents a significant portion of the obligor's income, anything but a modest order on arrears might remove any motivation to maintain minimum wage employment.

If the obligor still receives income through unemployment compensation, the CSEA can order the bureau of employment services to in effect "payroll deduct" child support from unemployment checks.[13] Child support withheld from unemployment benefits is supplemental and in addition to any withholding order or deduction from other sources throughout Chapter 3121 of the Revised Code.

---

[10]Collins v. Collins, 1995 WL 500511 (Ohio Ct. App. 4th Dist. Athens County 1995).

[11]Stocker v. Couts, 1995 WL 347851 (Ohio Ct. App. 5th Dist. Tuscarawas County 1995).

[12]Jones, by Jones v. Mosley, 1995 WL 739688 (Ohio Ct. App. 10th Dist. Franklin County 1995).

[13]RC 3121.07.

Once it has been established by clear and convincing evidence that a court order has been violated, a defense of inability to pay exists if the inability is real, not self-imposed, nor due to fraud, sharp practices, or intentional avoidance.[14]

When it has been determined that the obligor's unemployment, or at least inability to pay because of lack of income, is because of a deliberate act which positions him in such a way as to avoid income per se and therefore avoid having it attached, and the obligor has no income because of this voluntary act, even though done with counsel's advice, it has been held that the act is no defense to contempt or enforcement.[15]

A parent is considered voluntarily unemployed when she ceases to work in order to have a child of her second marriage, and does not then return to work.[16]

However, where it is the child who is receiving supplemental security income (SSI) directly, rather than receiving Social Security benefits due to a parent's disability, there is no effect on the calculation of the obligor's obligation.[17] In situations where a child is eligible to receive SSI, those benefits are intended to supplement the parents' support obligation, not to reduce it.

§ 20:27 Contempt defenses—Forgiving of arrearages by obligee

As a general rule, arrearages may be forgiven by the obligee as long as public assistance is not involved. If the residential parent and children are not receiving public assistance, the obligee is allowed to forgive arrearages. The obligee may do this voluntarily but should understand that the money forgiven can never be reclaimed. As a practical matter, money should never be forgiven unless the obligee does so in open court and signs the journal entry in evidence of the obligee's understanding and consent. In this situation the obligee may forgive all of the arrearage or any part thereof and may even request that the current support order be suspended or terminated. This should only be allowed where public assistance is not involved.

Where money comes from a governmental agency to support the children, arrearages cannot be forgiven by the parent. The public as-

---

[14]DeWitt v. DeWitt, 1996 WL 125920 (Ohio Ct. App. 2d Dist. Darke County 1996).

[15]Mileti v. Mileti, 1980 WL 352582 (Ohio Ct. App. 2d Dist. Montgomery County 1980); Martin v. Martin, 69 Ohio App. 2d 78, 23 Ohio Op. 3d 102, 430 N.E.2d 962 (9th Dist. Summit County 1980); Boltz v. Boltz, 31 Ohio App. 3d 214, 509 N.E.2d 1274 (9th Dist. Summit County 1986); Haynie v. Haynie, 19 Ohio App. 3d 288, 484 N.E.2d 750 (8th Dist. Cuyahoga County 1984). For a discussion of cases where voluntary reduction of obligor income is not grounds for modification of spousal support, see Text §§ 14:21 to 14:37, Requirements for modification.

[16]Pournaras v. Pournaras, 1993 WL 106973 (Ohio Ct. App. 8th Dist. Cuyahoga County 1993).

[17]Paton v. Paton, 91 Ohio St. 3d 94, 2001-Ohio-291, 742 N.E.2d 619 (2001).

sistance recipient, having already assigned support rights to the department of human services pursuant to 45 C.F.R. § 232.11, cannot waive that unpaid support.

Children may also be considered third party beneficiaries of support provisions. Modification of arrearages should not be granted if it appears to be detrimental to the minor child or causes the minor child to become a public charge.[1]

§ 20:28   Contempt defenses—Social Security benefits

If the obligor's children receive Social Security benefits because of the obligor's disability, then support modification ought to be in order, not a contempt. The dispute centered around how much credit the obligor should be given as against his guideline child support order for the amount of Social Security benefits the children receive. The courts were in conflict on this point. Early on some courts gave credit against the current order in the same amount as the current benefit.[1] As the right to Social Security benefits is in a sense earned, obligors argued that they should be allowed to offset from the order of support the amount their dependents received in Social Security benefits arising out of the obligor's disability.[2]

Other courts relied on the rationale that since the benefits do not come out of the obligor's pocket, or reduce the obligor's own benefits, the amount received by the children should be deducted from the total child support obligation of both parents, and the remainder of the obligation allocated between the parents according to the proportion of their respective incomes.[3]

In 2000, the Supreme Court of Ohio resolved this conflict. In *Williams v. Williams*,[4] the court found that the amount of the Social Security benefits received by the child of a disabled obligor should be set off from the obligor's monthly support obligation, rather than used to reduce the joint support obligation of both parents. Line 23(b) of the Child Support Computation Worksheet [or lines 22(b) and (e) of the

---

[Section 20:27]

[1]Hahn v. Hahn, 1985 WL 9724 (Ohio Ct. App. 9th Dist. Summit County 1985).

[Section 20:28]

[1]Carnutte v. Delarino, No. 2974 (Ohio Ct. App. 9th Dist. Lorain County 1980). See also Loucks v. Loucks, No. OT 79-11 (Ohio Ct. App. 6th Dist. Ottawa County 1980) (Social Security benefits paid for disability must be considered and credited). See also Robinson v. Robinson, 1987 WL 15027 (Ohio Ct. App. 2d Dist. Miami County 1987); Bayne v. Bayne, 1989 WL 13530 (Ohio Ct. App. 2d Dist. Montgomery County 1989); Fugate v. Fugate, 1990 WL 98371 (Ohio Ct. App. 2d Dist. Montgomery County 1990).

[2]Yuhasz v. Yuhasz, No. 42193 (Ohio Ct. App. 8th Dist. Cuyahoga County 1980).

[3]McNeal v. Cofield, 78 Ohio App. 3d 35, 603 N.E.2d 436 (10th Dist. Franklin County 1992).

[4]Williams v. Williams, 88 Ohio St. 3d 441, 2000-Ohio-375, 727 N.E.2d 895 (2000).

split custody worksheet] now provides adjustment to an obligor's support obligation for "[a]ny non-means tested benefits, including Social Security and Veterans' benefits, paid to and received by a child or a person on behalf of the child due to death, disability, or retirement of the parent."

Since Social Security awards are frequently made retroactive to the date of disability, thereby resulting in a lump sum to both the disabled party and children, credit must be given for the period covered by such lump sum award. Arrearages should then be recalculated and a monthly order established for any arrearage accruing prior to the date determined by Social Security to be the onset of disability. The obligor must pay any arrearage out of his monthly Social Security checks, and any arrearage accruing prior to the disability date will not be offset by that amount of the award exceeding the court's order for child support.[5] The current order is suspended and not terminated, because the award may stop in the future at which time the current order would be reinstated on the court's own motion.

If the award pays only a part of the current support, the obligor must be ordered to pay the difference plus an arrearage amount. All should be ordered monthly since the obligor would receive a check once a month.

§ 20:29 Contempt defenses—Possession versus custody of minor children

Physical possession of a child is different from legal custody. A case may arise where the residential parent and legal custodian allows the non-residential parent to keep and care for the child. In such a case, it seems unfair to require payment of a support order when the residential parent is not caring for the child.[1]

The current case law, however, imposes that burden on a parent who takes physical custody but does not seek modification of the court order. Counsel should warn parents of the risk of taking physical possession of children without a change being made in the custody and support orders. Unfortunately, parents often come to counsel having changed physical possession of the children years earlier without having made changes in the custody or support orders. Counsel is then limited to seeking an agreed settlement of the child support arrearage issues during the proceedings to establish a new custody and support order.

Even though giving credit for time spent with the non-residential parent results in a retroactive modification of support, the court can also weigh the in-kind furnishing of support in considering a motion

---

[5]Fuller v. Fuller, 49 Ohio App. 2d 223, 3 Ohio Op. 3d 273, 360 N.E.2d 357 (9th Dist. Summit County 1976).

[Section 20:29]

[1]Gerlach v. Gerlach, 124 Ohio App. 3d 246, 705 N.E.2d 1287 (10th Dist. Franklin County 1997).

to reduce unpaid support to judgment.[2] Another approach would be to use the in-kind furnishing of support as a basis for deviation from the guidelines in regard to future support.[3] Nevertheless, taking physical custody without a change in the court order can leave one parent vulnerable to contempt or other collection procedures.

§ 20:30 Contempt defenses—Remarriage of the parties to each other

The subsequent remarriage of the parties to each other may suspend or terminate the current support order as a matter of law, if the non-residential parent is in the home caring for the child.[1] Good practice should dictate, however, that the obligor seek suspension or termination of the support order through established administrative or court processes.

Should the parties divorce a second time, courts have held it necessary for the original obligee spouse to pursue in the second divorce action any claim for arrearages accumulated prior to the second marriage or be forever barred.[2]

§ 20:31 Contempt defenses—Emancipation

The emancipation of the minor child competent to support himself discharges a parent from an obligation for support.[1] In effect, the court cannot require the non-residential parent to support the child after that child's emancipation. This also applies where there was no prompt effort made to modify an order of support at the time of emancipation. The burden of proving the defense of emancipation rests on the party seeking relief from a support order.[2]

The emancipation of a child may arise in various ways: marriage, entering the armed services, leaving home, becoming employed and self-subsisting, or in any other manner in which the parent consents

---

[2]Gartner v. Gartner, 1984 WL 5850 (Ohio Ct. App. 10th Dist. Franklin County 1984).

[3]See RC 3119.23(J).

[Section 20:30]

[1]Lockard v. Lockard, 49 Ohio Op. 163, 63 Ohio L. Abs. 549, 102 N.E.2d 747 (C.P. 1951). See also, Watchowski v. Watchowski, 1999 WL 769545 (Ohio Ct. App. 6th Dist. Wood County 1999).

[2]Watchowski v. Watchowski, 1999 WL 769545 (Ohio Ct. App. 6th Dist. Wood County 1999); Fout v. Fout, 1993 WL 485119 (Ohio Ct. App. 10th Dist. Franklin County 1993); Annarino v. Annarino, 1991 WL 6208 (Ohio Ct. App. 5th Dist. Licking County 1991), cause dismissed, 63 Ohio St. 3d 1201, 584 N.E.2d 1218 (1992).

[Section 20:31]

[1]Hoffmann v. Hoffmann, 32 Ohio App. 2d 186, 61 Ohio Op. 2d 205, 289 N.E.2d 397 (1st Dist. Hamilton County 1972); Eversman v. Eversman, 1985 WL 7395 (Ohio Ct. App. 3d Dist. Shelby County 1985) (interest may be allowed on unpaid support after date of emancipation).

[2]Daniels v. Daniels, No. 8897 (Ohio Ct. App. 2d Dist. Montgomery County 1985).

to the child's removal from parental control and care. Entry into the armed services does not operate as an automatic emancipation.[3] Marriage of a minor, where the minor continues to live with and be supported by her parent, does not automatically terminate the parent's support obligation.[4]

Child support obligations extend beyond the age of majority if the child continuously attends a recognized and accredited high school on a full time basis. RC 3119.86 is remedial and not substantive. Its retroactive application does not violate Ohio Const. art. II § 28. However, in *Wendling v. Wendling*, the Eighth District Court of Appeals held that RC 3109.05(E)[5] was not controlling on a divorce decree issued years before the enactment of that statute.[6] Support payments terminated upon the child reaching majority although still in high school.

The two most common situations where emancipation may occur before reaching the age of majority is where the minor child marries or the minor child becomes employed. Marriage of a minor child is an act of emancipation that will terminate obligations under domestic relations orders as a matter of law.[7] Employment, however, of the minor child does not terminate obligations of support, as a matter of law. The mere capability of the child to earn money on his own behalf is no ground for termination or reduction of the support order.[8] The test that a court should use is whether there is proof of intent on the part of the residential parent to renounce permanently his or her rights as a parent. Emancipation is the result of an act or omission of the parent and cannot be accomplished by an act of the child alone. It must be noted that emancipation of a child competent to support himself discharges a parent from the obligation to provide support, but if the child later becomes unable to support himself, the parent's duty to provide support revives prior to the child reaching the age of majority.[9]

The Fourth District Court of Appeals held that after a child turned 18 years of age, and withdrew from high school, the obligor's duty of support terminated and was not resurrected by the child's subsequent

---

[3]Omohundro v. Omohundro, 8 Ohio App. 3d 318, 457 N.E.2d 324 (10th Dist. Franklin County 1982).

[4]Abu-Nada v. Abu-Nada, 1999 WL 138667 (Ohio Ct. App. 12th Dist. Clermont County 1999).

[5]Amended and recodified by 2000 S.B. 180, eff. 3-22-01, analogous language RC 3119.86.

[6]Wendling v. Wendling, 1996 WL 50825 (Ohio Ct. App. 8th Dist. Cuyahoga County 1996).

[7]Perry v. Perry, 21 Ohio L. Abs. 577, 1936 WL 2052 (Ct. App. 2d Dist. Franklin County 1936).

[8]Schirtzinger v. Schirtzinger, 95 Ohio App. 31, 52 Ohio Op. 372, 117 N.E.2d 42 (2d Dist. Franklin County 1952).

[9]Townsen v. Townsen, 101 Ohio App. 85, 1 Ohio Op. 2d 49, 137 N.E.2d 789 (9th Dist. Summit County 1954); Ford v. Ford, 109 Ohio App. 495, 12 Ohio Op. 2d 67, 167 N.E.2d 787 (2d Dist. Miami County 1959).

enrollment in vocational school.[10] The obligation continues after age 18 only if the child "continuously" attends high school. However, a child's enrollment in an approved home-education program is the legal equivalent of attending an accredited high school for purposes of RC 3119.86.[11] But the Eleventh District has held that a home-school program that is not approved by Ohio does not constitute a recognized and accredited high school within the meaning of the statute.[12] However, this decision is on appeal before the Supreme Court of Ohio.[13]

◆ **Practice Tip:** Upon the child's emancipation or reaching the age of majority, a written motion to modify[14] or terminate the order should be filed by the obligor.

Currently the obligee has a duty to inform the court of any reason that the support order should terminate, such as emancipation of the child.[15] However, child support withholding orders do not automatically terminate when a child is emancipated, and overworked child support enforcement agencies often do not have a routine in place to promptly terminate support withholding orders upon notification of emancipation. Counsel for obligors should act early to seek an agreed order approved by both obligor and obligee, because there is no statutory mechanism to recover overpayments of child support.

Notice and service of pending motions must be given to all concerned parties. Where the issue is emancipation and the minor child has graduated and is working, but is still under the age of majority, proof of graduation, employment, and conduct by both the residential parent and the child consistent with emancipation should be required by the court. If the minor has married, a marriage certificate should be presented to the court. Finally, if the minor child is eighteen but is still in high school, the motion to modify should not be granted until proof of graduation is made to the court.

In enacting H.B. 352[16] the legislature put a statutory cap on the duty to support a child attending high school after the child had attained 18 years. RC 3103.03(B) was amended to state that "Except in cases in which a child support order requires the duty of support to continue for any period after the child reaches age nineteen, the order shall not remain in effect after the child reaches age nineteen." RC

---

[10]Gleason v. Gleason, 129 Ohio App. 3d 563, 718 N.E.2d 512 (4th Dist. Ross County 1998).

[11]Gatchel v. Gatchel, 159 Ohio App. 3d 519, 2005-Ohio-148, 824 N.E.2d 576 (3d Dist. Wyandot County 2005).

[12]Davis v. Davis, 167 Ohio App. 3d 319, 2006-Ohio-2393, 855 N.E.2d 104 (11th Dist. Geauga County 2006), judgment rev'd, 115 Ohio St. 3d 180, 2007-Ohio-5049, 873 N.E.2d 1305 (2007).

[13]Davis v. Davis, 111 Ohio St. 3d 1410, 2006-Ohio-5083, 854 N.E.2d 1090 (2006).

[14]See Text § 25:56, Post-decree motions—Motion to modify.

[15]RC 3119.87, RC 3119.88.

[16]1997 H.B. 352, eff. 1-1-98.

3103.03(B) was subsequently amended by S.B. 180, which moved the age nineteen limitation language to RC 3119.86(B).[17]

If the parties or the Court intend the support order to extend beyond the age of nineteen years when the child is still attending high school, the order must provide that the duty of support continues after the child reaches age nineteen.[18] An agreement incorporated into a divorce decree that support continue until a child reaches the age of twenty-two, "provided that she was attending a fully accredited institution of secondary education," remains enforceable even where the obligor subsequently became the residential parent for a period of time, only to have the obligee later regain residential parent status.[19]

As support enforcement agencies gradually adopt streamlined procedures to terminate child support withholding orders upon emancipation, the issue will begin to arise less frequently in contempt cases. Emancipation as a partial defense is most likely to be seen in the future in cases where contempt is used to collect arrearages after children turn eighteen and graduate from high school.

In *Thayer v. Thayer*,[20] the Eleventh District Court of Appeals held that it is not an error to enforce a divorce decree which requires a support obligor to pay child support in the form of college tuition beyond the age of majority.

§ 20:32   Contempt defenses—Denial of visitation rights

Child support and spousal support are separate issues from visitation rights given to the obligor. Denial of visitation rights does not automatically affect the support order. Nevertheless, complaints about visitation are commonly raised in defense of contempt motions. Only in extreme situations have child support arrearages been reduced by obligor's expenses incurred in enforcing visitation rights.[1] By statute, the court may not modify, withhold, or escrow child support if visitation rights are violated.[2]

This does not seem to deter many practitioners from responding to a child support contempt with a cross filing for visitation contempt, set on the same hearing date. The burden in such a cross motion is to show that the residential parent willfully violated the court order as it deals with visitation rights. Such a cross filing may have an effect on the negotiating position of the sides, but it is unlikely to have much impression on a judge or magistrate; they have seen it all before.

---

[17]2001 Am. S.B. 180, eff. 3-22-01.

[18]RC 3119.86(B).

[19]Jones v. Brown, 2005-Ohio-3751, 2005 WL 1713321 (Ohio Ct. App. 2d Dist. Greene County 2005).

[20]Thayer v. Thayer, 1984 WL 6512 (Ohio Ct. App. 11th Dist. Lake County 1984) (separation agreement incorporated into divorce decree).

[Section 20:32]

[1]Miller v. Miller, 92 Ohio App. 3d 340, 635 N.E.2d 384 (6th Dist. Erie County 1993).

[2]RC 3109.05(D).

The court should always remember that child support, spousal support, and visitation rights are issues to be kept separate; one should not affect another, as a matter of law.

§ 20:33   Contempt defenses—Bankruptcy of the obligor[1]

In 2005, Congress enacted the Bankruptcy Abuse Prevention and Consumer Protection Act of 2005 ("BAPCPA"), effective October 17, 2005. The effect of BAPCPA on the enforcement of support obligations is as yet untested by the courts, but the language of this sweeping change to the bankruptcy laws provides a certain degree of guidance.

Status Before BAPCPA. Under the law prior to enactment of BAPCPA, alimony, support, and maintenance were non-dischargeable obligations in both Chapter 7 and Chapter 13 bankruptcy proceedings, pursuant to former 11 U.S.C.A. § 523(a)(5). "Other" domestic obligations, as defined in former 11 U.S.C.A. § 523(a)(15), were non-dischargeable in Chapter 7 bankruptcies, but potentially dischargeable under Chapter 13's "superdischarge" provisions. Sections 523(a)(5) and (a)(15) were mutually exclusive and the bankruptcy court retained exclusive jurisdiction to determine dischargeability of debts under § 523(a)(15).[2]

Over time, the U.S. Court of Appeals for the Sixth Circuit developed case law interpreting these sections. In *In re Calhoun*,[3] the court expressed a test for determining whether "alimony, maintenance, or support" was actually "alimony, maintenance, or support." In making this determination, a court was to ascertain (1) the intention of the parties in the domestic case, (2) whether the obligation had the actual effect of providing necessary support, and (3) whether the obligations designated as alimony, maintenance, or support were so excessive as to be unreasonable under traditional concepts of support. If any portion of the obligation was found to be unreasonable, the obligation could be deemed dischargeable.

Believing the district courts were over-reacting to its decision in *Calhoun*, the Sixth Circuit, in *In re Fitzgerald*,[4] directed that a state court's alimony award should be entitled to deference when the obligation was clearly designated and structured as alimony. Notably, both *Calhoun* and *Fitzgerald* were decided prior to the 1994 amendments

---

[Section 20:33]

[1]This section was prepared with substantial reliance upon materials prepared by William B. Logan, Jr. of Luper, Neidenthal & Logan of Columbus, Ohio.

[2]See former 11 U.S.C.A. § 523(c)(1).

[3]In re Calhoun, 715 F.2d 1103 (6th Cir. 1983) (rejected by, Draper v. Draper, 790 F.2d 52 (8th Cir. 1986)) and (rejected by, Forsdick v. Turgeon, 812 F.2d 801 (2d Cir. 1987)) and (rejected by, In re Smith, 114 B.R. 457 (Bankr. S.D. Miss. 1990)) and (rejected by, Buccino v. Buccino, 397 Pa. Super. 241, 580 A.2d 13 (1990)) and (rejected by, In re Michaels, 157 B.R. 190 (Bankr. D. Mass. 1993)) and (rejected by, In re Chrusz, 1996 WL 1057950 (Bankr. D. N.H. 1996)).

[4]In re Fitzgerald, 9 F.3d 517 (6th Cir. 1993).

to the bankruptcy act that established, *inter alia*, the former § 523(a)(15) provisions regarding "other" domestic obligations.

In 1998, the Sixth Circuit decided *In re Sorah*.[5] Although the case was decided subsequent to the 1994 amendments to the act, it only addressed issues under former § 523(a)(5). In *Sorah*, the court developed a three-part test to determine whether a support order was indeed "support":

> [The bankruptcy] court should look to the traditional state law indicia that are consistent with a support obligation. These include, but are not necessarily limited to, (1) a label such as alimony, support or maintenance in the decree or agreement, (2) a direct payment to the former spouse, as opposed to the assumption of a third-party debt, and (3) payments that are contingent upon such events as death, remarriage or eligibility for Social Security benefits.

> An award that is designated as support by the state court and that has the above indicia of a support obligation (along with any others that the state support statute considers) should be conclusively presumed to be a support obligation by the bankruptcy court. A non-debtor [ex-]spouse who demonstrates these indicia are present has satisfied his or her burden of proving that the obligation constitutes support within the meaning of 523 and is thus non-dischargeable.[6]

As mentioned above, Congress amended the former bankruptcy act in 1994 and added former § 523(a)(15) regarding "other" domestic obligations. This section allowed a bankruptcy court to determine that certain obligations incurred in a domestic proceeding that were not in the nature of "alimony, support, or maintenance" were nevertheless non-dischargeable. Under this provision, and in order to prove the dischargeability of a debt incurred in a domestic proceeding, the debtor bore the burden of proving either that (a) he or she did not have the ability to pay the debt or (b) discharging the debt would result in a benefit to the debtor that outweighed the detrimental consequences to the spouse, ex-spouse, or child of the debtor.[7]

Status After BAPCPA. One of the major themes of BAPCPA was to elevate the status and importance of domestic obligations. The new Act sets forth a definition of a "Domestic Support Obligation," or "DSO," that can be found at 11 U.S.C.A. § 101(14A):

> The term "domestic support obligation" means a debt that accrues before, on, or after the date of the order for relief in a case under this title, including interest that accrues on that debt as provided under applicable nonbankruptcy law notwithstanding any other provision of this title, that is—
>
> (A) owed to or recoverable by—
>
>   (i) a spouse, former spouse, or child of the debtor or such child's parent, legal guardian, or responsible relative; or

---

[5]In re Sorah, 163 F.3d 397, 1998 FED App. 0375P (6th Cir. 1998).

[6]In re Sorah, 163 F.3d 397, 401, 1998 FED App. 0375P (6th Cir. 1998).

[7]A good case summarizing pre-BAPCPA law can be found at In re Hammermeister, 270 B.R. 863 (Bankr. S.D. Ohio 2001).

(ii)   a governmental unit;

(B) in the nature of alimony, maintenance, or support (including assistance provided by a governmental unit) of such spouse, former spouse, or child of the debtor or such child's parent, without regard to whether such debt is expressly so designated;

(C) established or subject to establishment before, on, or after the date of the order for relief in a case under this title, by reason of applicable provisions of—

(i)   a separation agreement, divorce decree, or property settlement agreement;

(ii)   an order of a court of record; or

(iii)   a determination made in accordance with applicable nonbankruptcy law by a governmental unit; and

(D) not assigned to a nongovernmental entity, unless that obligation is assigned voluntarily by the spouse, former spouse, child of the debtor, or such child's parent, legal guardian, or responsible relative for the purpose of collecting the debt.

Under BAPCPA, Congress altered § 523(a)(5) to simply provide that Domestic Support Orders are not dischargeable in Chapter 7, 11, 12, or 13 proceedings.[8] Likewise, § 523(a)(15) was amended to remove the tests a bankruptcy court was required to perform to determine whether a domestic obligation other than "alimony, maintenance, or support" was non-dischargeable. That section now provides that a debt is non-dischargeable if it is owed "to a spouse, former spouse, or child of the debtor and not of the kind described in paragraph (5) that is incurred by the debtor in the course of a divorce or separation or in connection with a separation agreement, divorce decree or other order of a court of record, or a determination made in accordance with State or territorial law by a governmental unit."[9]

Therefore, although there is currently no case law interpreting the newly-amended §§ 523(a)(5) and (a)(15), it now appears as though *all* obligations incurred in a domestic relations proceeding are non-dischargeable under BAPCPA in Chapter 7 cases. It is possible, however, that section 523(a)(15) obligations are dischargeable in Chapter 13 cases, even though (a)(5) obligations are not.

Congress's enactment of BAPCPA also empowered state courts with *concurrent* jurisdiction with the federal bankruptcy courts in determining whether a debt is dischargeable. Furthermore, the exceptions to the automatic stay provided to a bankruptcy petitioner were substantially supplemented:

The filing of a petition under section 301, 302, or 303 of this title, or of an application under § 5(a)(3) of the Securities Investor Protection Act of 1970, does not operate as a stay—

(1)   under subsection (a) of this section, of the commencement or

---

[8]11 U.S.C.A. § 523(a)(5).

[9]11 U.S.C.A. § 523(a)(15).

continuation of a criminal action or proceeding against the debtor;

(2) under subsection (a)—

    (A) of the commencement or continuation of a civil action or proceeding—

        (i) for the establishment of paternity;

        (ii) for the establishment or modification of an order for domestic support obligations;

        (iii) concerning child custody or visitation;

        (iv) for the dissolution of a marriage, except to the extent that such proceeding seeks to determine the division of property that is property of the estate; or

        (v) regarding domestic violence;

    (B) of the collection of a domestic support obligation from property that is not property of the estate;

    (C) with respect to the withholding of income that is property of the estate or property of the debtor for payment of a domestic support obligation under a judicial or administrative order or a statute;

    (D) of the withholding, suspension, or restriction of a driver's license, a professional or occupational license, or a recreational license, under State law, as specified in § 466(a)(16) of the Social Security Act;

    (E) of the reporting of overdue support owed by a parent to any consumer reporting agency as specified in § 466(a)(7) of the Social Security Act;

    (F) of the interception of a tax refund, as specified in §§ 464 and 466(a)(3) of the Social Security Act or under an analogous State law; or

    (G) of the enforcement of a medical obligation, as specified under title IV of the Social Security Act.[10]

This section greatly expands the powers of a domestic relations or juvenile court to hear various causes against a debtor without first requiring a party to obtain relief from the automatic stay in the bankruptcy court.

However, while actions to establish or modify domestic support obligations are excepted from the automatic stay, it appears actions to enforce or collect existing domestic support obligations may only be excepted from the automatic stay if the collection is from property that is not property of the debtor's estate. Thus a creditor's use of civil contempt proceedings to collect unpaid prepetition domestic support obligations may well constitute a violation of the automatic stay.[11]

---

[10]11 U.S.C.A. § 362(b).

[11]In re Moore, 2009 WL 1616019, at *5 (Bankr. N.D. Ohio 2009).

§ 20:34   Contempt defenses—Remarriage of the obligor

The subsequent marriage of the obligor, usually the husband, and possible assumption of the obligations of his new family unit, have never been considered as a basis for defense for failure to comply with a support order, nor for relief from judgment, generally, based on the concept that the remarriage was his voluntary assumption of new obligations.

A common argument is that the practical effect is a restraint on the obligor's right to remarry, with no compensatory restraint on the obligee, and thus is a de facto discrimination based on gender. Further, the economic impact on the new family unit could be considered as unreasonable in equity.

An appellate decision held that the subsequent marriage and incident financial obligation must be a consideration in a motion for modification of support.[1] Also, at least one court has found that the obligor's remarriage resulted in an increased ability to pay support.[2] This "defense" may actually backfire.

A modification of support could be in order, however, where the obligor adopted the new spouse's children or if the marriage results in the birth of another child.

§ 20:35   Contempt defenses—Remarriage of the obligee

Occasionally the remarriage of the custodian and the integration of the child into the stepparent's home has been raised as a defense to non-payment of child support. At least one court has, however, rationalized a suspension of support under the extreme circumstances of a case where visitation was purposely denied.[1]

Current practice is to view such subsequent marriage and integration as irrelevant as a defense to failure of the obligor to comply with an order.

The stepparent knows in advance that the new spouse has children. Reality tells us that the children will eventually be integrated into the residential stepparent's home. The new spouse has the companionship of the children but usually does not contemplate having to provide that which another is responsible for providing. One case, *Martin v.*

[Section 20:34]

[1]Martin v. Martin, 69 Ohio App. 2d 78, 23 Ohio Op. 3d 102, 430 N.E.2d 962 (9th Dist. Summit County 1980). For relevant commentary on the impact of the remarriage of the parents, see Text §§ 14:21 to 14:37, Requirements for modification; Text § 19:17, Modification of prior orders—Change of circumstance.

[2]Esber v. Esber, 63 Ohio App. 3d 394, 579 N.E.2d 222 (9th Dist. Medina County 1989).

[Section 20:35]

[1]Miller v. Miller, 92 Ohio App. 3d 340, 635 N.E.2d 384 (6th Dist. Erie County 1993).

Martin,[2] recognized that the economic burden of the second family on the obligor must be taken into consideration.

The second marriage of the residential parent does have an economic advantage to the children. The fact that the children may have a better standard of living by virtue of the residential parent's remarriage and a new income source should have no bearing on the necessity of the non-residential parent's obligation to contribute his fair share. The remarriage may, however, form a basis for deviation from an obligation calculated pursuant to the guideline worksheet if the obligor files a motion to modify support.[3]

§ 20:36 Contempt defenses—Estoppel or agreement of parties

Although rare, a situation could arise where the residential parent reaches an agreement with the obligor to modify the support order and then subsequently changes his or her mind. In one case, the payor's defense was the agreement, waiver, and estoppel against the residential parent who made a deal and then changed his or her mind. The consideration was the obligee's agreement to waive the support in return for the obligor's agreement to waive visitation. The court of appeals held the obligor's surrender of visitation rights was adequate consideration and enforced the agreement of no visitation no support.

In a dissolution case, the separation agreement was modified by the parties approximately one year after the decree whereby husband waived visitation and wife waived support. Two years later the wife elected to bring an action for two years of arrearages for child support and for an increase in child support. The appellate court affirmed the refusal to reduce to judgment the two years of nonpayment as arrearages, holding the wife was bound by the agreement. The court also found that it was not bound by the agreement as to future support payments based on the best interest of child rule.[1]

In a case where the judgment required support payments to the child support enforcement agency, the parties had agreed that the obligor would make the payments directly to his ex-wife who would make the payments to the CSEA. Unknown to the defendant-husband, the ex-wife stopped making payments to the CSEA. On petition by the CSEA, the trial court found the husband to be in contempt of court and cited him for arrearages. The court of appeals reversed giving recognition to the de facto payments made to the wife and allowing them to be credited toward the obligation.[2] Today it would be risky indeed

---

[2]Martin v. Martin, 69 Ohio App. 2d 78, 23 Ohio Op. 3d 102, 430 N.E.2d 962 (9th Dist. Summit County 1980).

[3]RC 3119.23(H).

[Section 20:36]

[1]Saltis v. Frisby, 1982 WL 2883 (Ohio Ct. App. 9th Dist. Summit County 1982).

[2]Carroll County Bureau of Support and Hellyer v. Hellyer, 1981 WL 4779 (Ohio Ct. App. 7th Dist. Carroll County 1981).

for an obligor to make payments directly to the obligee; RC 3121.45 deems such payments to be a gift.

In *Church v. Church*,[3] the plaintiff and her new husband waived child support payments in exchange for the defendant's promise to forego his visitation rights. Both parties performed. Subsequently, the mother filed for contempt and for a lump-sum judgment for the unpaid child support. The court denied it on the grounds that the father's forebearance of his right to visit the child constituted sufficient legal consideration for the agreement. The mother must be held to her promised waiver of support since she accepted defendant's performance of his part of the bargain.

In a subsequent modification of a support and visitation award whereby the husband waived visitation in return for the wife waiving support, the court held that the promise not to bother appellant by exercising visitation rights was a valid consideration for the agreement, and that the wife/mother would be held to that agreement such that the support payments not made would not be reduced to a lump-sum judgment.[4]

The Second District Court of Appeals held that a spousal support obligee may be prevented from recovering unpaid installments under a separation agreement if there has been a subsequent agreement between the parties to relieve the obligation for valuable consideration.[5]

Although child support is for the benefit of the children and cannot be waived by the parents,[6] the Eleventh District Court of Appeals concluded that equitable principles and the evidence, which included a request for consent to adoption, correspondence with the child support enforcement agency, and the relinquishment of visitation, justified enforcing the parties' agreement to waive support.[7] An agreement to relieve a parent of liability for child support must be supported by consideration.[8] The support obligation must be redistributed from one parent to the other, not simply terminated. A separation agreement may provide for suspension of support while the children live with the

---

[3]Church v. Church, 1981 WL 5994 (Ohio Ct. App. 4th Dist. Washington County 1981).

[4]Weppler v. Weppler, 1979 WL 206925 (Ohio Ct. App. 4th Dist. Washington County 1979).

[5]Fox v. Fox, 1987 WL 14256 (Ohio Ct. App. 2d Dist. Montgomery County 1987).

[6]Rhoades v. Rhoades, 40 Ohio App. 2d 559, 69 Ohio Op. 2d 488, 321 N.E.2d 242 (1st Dist. Hamilton County 1974). In practice, however, parties mutually wanting to "waive" child support could conceivably prepare an entry for the court complying with the requirement of RC 3119.22, providing they can prove the asserted reasons for deviation to the court.

[7]Nelson v. Nelson, 65 Ohio App. 3d 800, 585 N.E.2d 502 (11th Dist. Lake County 1990). See also Lawhorn v. Lawhorn, 1990 WL 129287 (Ohio Ct. App. 2d Dist. Montgomery County 1990) (agreement was upheld even though the adoption never took place).

[8]Wise v. Wise, 86 Ohio App. 3d 702, 621 N.E.2d 1213 (12th Dist. Butler County 1993).

support obligor. Failure to pay support during these periods does not justify a finding of contempt.[9]

Estoppel is similar to laches in that it is an equitable defense, there is no time limit, and the case is dismissed without getting to the merits. It is different from laches in that the question at issue is not so much a lapse of time, or a failure to act on the part of the petitioner, but instead is based on a positive act, such as an agreement, consent, or fraud.

The most common use of the estoppel defense would be when the support obligee makes an agreement permitting the support obligor not to make certain payments, then later, after a change of mind, brings an enforcement action for the forgiven payments.

§ 20:37 Contempt defenses—Laches

In addition to the various express statutory and rule defenses, the equitable defenses of laches and estoppel are available, as domestic relations courts are courts of equity.[1] Laches may be a defense to a contempt motion if the delay resulted in material prejudice to the obligor.[2] A defense to a claim for child support arrearages for sixteen years, based on an agreement between the parties for release of support and visitation rights, will be held to be a valid agreement, and the plaintiff will be considered as having been estopped from asserting any claim for arrearages during the period of the agreement.[3] Laches is essentially the equitable statute of limitations that has no time limits. The petitioner can lose his or her rights by waiting too long before bringing the complaint/petition for relief.

Laches is not just passage of time that would precipitate the statute of limitation, but the passage of time that caused a situation that would mean the requested relief would be inequitable under the present circumstances.[4] The wife/custodian may have moved out of state with a new husband; the father stops payment because he can no longer see his children, and the wife does not enforce the support. Years later, the obligee/wife decides to collect the arrearages. The obligor/ex-husband has, in the meantime, established a lifestyle based on the forgiveness of the support, and now, his income is only sufficient to support his new family. He could assert that the length of time for enforcement would be inequitable at this time for him and his new

---

[9]Jarzabek v. Powers, 1996 WL 221170 (Ohio Ct. App. 8th Dist. Cuyahoga County 1996).

[Section 20:37]

[1]RC 3105.011.

[2]Coder v. Coder, 1996 WL 257215 (Ohio Ct. App. 2d Dist. Montgomery County 1996).

[3]See Long v. Long, No. 9590 (Ohio Ct. App. 9th Dist. Summit County 1980).

[4]Connin v. Bailey, 15 Ohio St. 3d 34, 472 N.E.2d 328 (1984); Rhyne v. Rhyne, 1998 WL 180568 (Ohio Ct. App. 10th Dist. Franklin County 1998) (no laches found in spite of seventeen-year delay).

family. If he can prove it, and the judge is familiar with laches, the case would be dismissed for failure to prosecute within a reasonable time.

If, on the other hand, the obligor/ex-husband is currently in excellent financial position, and enforcement of the arrearages would be of more nuisance value than economic disaster, it would be difficult for him to show how the passage of time would cause him economic disaster if he were to comply. In any event, the party asserting the laches defense has the burden of proving the inequities. Although laches may be used as a defense against a lump-sum judgment for child support arrearages, the party invoking the defense of laches has the affirmative burden of proving not only that the other party delayed, but that the delay materially prejudiced the party for whose benefit the doctrine will operate.[5] The fact that a defendant had failed to fulfill his support obligations for a period of nine years does not confer upon him a right to continue to fail to support that child under the concept of laches. There was no change of position to the detriment of the defendant as a result of the mother's inaction. Rather, defendant had benefited from the delay by not being required to pay support over a period of years.[6]

Where the custodial parent brings an action for support arrearages after a lapse of nine years, length of time alone is not sufficient to constitute a material prejudice so as to allow the obligor to invoke laches. The natural father's obligation to support his children was not terminated where children's surname was changed and the obligor's whereabouts were unknown during a nine-year period.[7]

In order for a spousal support obligor to present a viable defense of laches, he must show that the obligee delayed in asserting the right to enforce. The obligor must also show that he has been materially prejudiced by the delay.[8]

---

[5]Heavenridge v. Heavenridge, 1981 WL 5163 (Ohio Ct. App. 12th Dist. Clinton County 1981).

[6]Zaperach v. Beaver, 6 Ohio App. 3d 17, 451 N.E.2d 1249 (10th Dist. Franklin County 1982); Cottrell v. Cottrell, 1985 WL 8226 (Ohio Ct. App. 6th Dist. Lucas County 1985) (laches was properly applied where no action had been taken for four years and obligor believed children had been adopted).

[7]Kinney v. Mathias, 10 Ohio St. 3d 72, 461 N.E.2d 901 (1984).

[8]Fiskness v. Partin, 1989 WL 17282 (Ohio Ct. App. 5th Dist. Richland County 1989) (father materially prejudiced as unable to visit daughter); Crow v. Crow, 1990 WL 44218 (Ohio Ct. App. 12th Dist. Butler County 1990) (refraining of father from seeking support modification after mother moved and his transportation expenses increased; doctrine of laches applicable); Hanney v. Hanney, 1992 WL 9538 (Ohio Ct. App. 6th Dist. Ottawa County 1992); Fossett v. Fossett, 1992 WL 129316 (Ohio Ct. App. 4th Dist. Lawrence County 1992) (where obligees unsuccessfully attempted enforcement after original order).

In *Baker v. Baker*,[9] the Eighth District Court of Appeals held that a five-year gap between the obligee's contempt motions coupled with the obligor's remarriage was insufficient to constitute laches.[10]

Delay in asserting a claim for child support arrearages, even when it is a delay of thirty-five years, does not constitute laches without evidence of material prejudice to the obligor due to the delay. Mere inconvenience is insufficient for this purpose.[11]

It is error for a trial court to grant judgment on an arrearage of child support when the party seeking the arrearage has taken no action for twenty-three years, while knowing the obligor's whereabouts throughout that time, and where the unreasonable and unexplained delay has materially prejudiced the obligor. The appellee-wife in *Mermer v. Clark*[12] induced her former husband to change his position to his detriment. Mr. Clark changed his residence and made several major purchases for the parties' minor son in the belief that his former wife had foregone her right to child support payments. The appellee was denied a judgment for the arrearage because of laches. Other cases have found material prejudice to the obligor where there was active concealment of the child from the parent, loss of evidence, or loss of an available defense.[13]

§ 20:38 Contempt defenses—First Amendment claim

An unusual defense to selective nonpayment is based on the First Amendment requirement of separation of church and state. The obligor may argue that enforcement of his agreed payments for religious school training is illegal. Judicial enforcement of a separation agreement requiring a non-residential parent to pay tuition for his children's religious education at a religiously oriented school is not unconstitutional state support of a religiously oriented school under the free exercise or establishment clause of the First Amendment to the US Constitution nor the religious freedom provision of the Ohio Constitution.[1]

§ 20:39 Contempt defenses—Payment or in-kind contribution

In the past courts have held that, absent a provision in a separation

---

[9]Baker v. Baker, 1985 WL 8999 (Ohio Ct. App. 8th Dist. Cuyahoga County 1985).

[10]See also Smith v. Smith, 168 Ohio St. 447, 7 Ohio Op. 2d 276, 156 N.E.2d 113, 70 A.L.R.2d 1241 (1959).

[11]Connin v. Bailey, 15 Ohio St. 3d 34, 472 N.E.2d 328 (1984).

[12]Mermer v. Clark, 1984 WL 7858 (Ohio Ct. App. 6th Dist. Lucas County 1984); Gerlach v. Gerlach, 124 Ohio App. 3d 246, 705 N.E.2d 1287 (10th Dist. Franklin County 1997).

[13]Lang v. Lang, 2003-Ohio-5445, 2003 WL 22331991 (Ohio Ct. App. 10th Dist. Franklin County 2003).

[Section 20:38]

[1]In re Landis, 5 Ohio App. 3d 22, 448 N.E.2d 845 (10th Dist. Franklin County 1982).

agreement permitting a father to offset his support obligations with voluntary expenditures for clothing, gifts, and entertainment, such expenditures will not offset any amounts owed under the agreement.[1]

Voluntary payments made by a noncustodial parent where the child is not living with the noncustodial parent are not to be considered payments in lieu of support where the divorce decree orders that support payments shall be made through the court or directly to the custodial parent . . .. Direct payments to the child thwart that basic and necessary relationship between a minor child and a custodial parent.[2]

Where the minor child attends a different school from that identified in the separation agreement, the parent with the obligation to pay tuition must pay the equivalent of the tuition at the named institution.[3]

Where a father sought to obtain credit for expenditures made on behalf of his child, other than those provided in the divorce decree, the Eighth District Court of Appeals in *Ferrere v. Ferrere*[4] held that "a father should not be allowed . . . credit for expenditures made voluntarily on behalf of the child which do not specifically conform to the terms of the decree."[5] The court stated that the facts in each case must be examined to determine whether the expenditure is voluntary and the denial of credit appropriate.

The basic rule in regard to in-kind payments for child support is provided by RC 3121.45. If a withholding order is issued, any payment that is not made through the child support enforcement agency shall not be considered as a payment of support and unless the payment is made to discharge an obligation other than support, it is presumed to be a gift.

An obligor may be given credit for payments outside of a child support enforcement agency prior to December 1, 1986, the effective date of former RC 2301.36.[6] The determination of whether the payments are "support payments" or gifts cannot be made without the op-

[Section 20:39]

[1]Rand v. Rand, 1984 WL 5112 (Ohio Ct. App. 8th Dist. Cuyahoga County 1984).

[2]Evans v. Brown, 23 Ohio App. 3d 97, syl. 1–2, 491 N.E.2d 384 (10th Dist. Franklin County 1985) (payments were primarily for travel and other activities, not support, and evidence showed they were designed to "get even" with the custodial parent for denying visitation). But see Gartner v. Gartner, 1984 WL 5850 (Ohio Ct. App. 10th Dist. Franklin County 1984) (child resided with noncustodial parent for a prolonged period and noncustodial parent provided full support, not just money for vacation or visitation purposes).

[3]Evans v. Brown, 23 Ohio App. 3d 97, 491 N.E.2d 384 (10th Dist. Franklin County 1985).

[4]Ferrere v. Ferrere, 20 Ohio App. 3d 82, 484 N.E.2d 753 (8th Dist. Cuyahoga County 1984) (medical insurance premium payments).

[5]Ferrere v. Ferrere, 20 Ohio App. 3d 82, 83, 484 N.E.2d 753 (8th Dist. Cuyahoga County 1984).

[6]Amended and recodified by 2000 S.B. 180, eff. 3-22-01, analogous language RC 3121.44.

portunity to present evidence.[7] Where an obligor was given credit for payments made directly, outside of the bureau of support, and there was no specific objection to the referee's findings of fact, the presumption of gift was deemed waived.[8] The court of appeals could not consider the factual issue of whether the presumption was rebutted.[9] A spousal support obligor may be permitted by the court to make payments directly to the obligee if the parties have no minor children born as the result of the marriage.[10] In this event, payment shall be made in a manner that provides for a clear record.[11] Permission for direct payment of spousal support can be revoked by the court in the event the obligor defaults, and all subsequent payments must then be made to the CSEA.[12]

§ 20:40 Contempt defenses—Agreement to mediate or arbitrate

Shared parenting (or older joint custody) plans frequently contain provisions in which parties agree to settle differences regarding the children through mediation rather than litigation. Such a provision might be raised as a defense in a child support contempt proceeding by the party in default requesting the court to send the contempt motion to mandatory mediation.[1] However, contempt is not a dispute to be mediated between the parties. Contempt is the action of the court to enforce its own orders and vindicate its own authority. RC 2705.05(A) states that in all contempt proceedings the court shall conduct a hearing. The court should not abdicate its authority to enforce support orders by referring contempt issues to alternative dispute resolution.

Unfortunately, orders referring contempt cases to mediation are not final appealable orders, so there is no easy way for the practitioner to avoid the inherent delays caused by court-ordered mediation if a court chooses to move a contempt issue off of its docket by referring it to mediation.[2] On the other hand, orders referring cases to arbitration

---

[7]Drake v. Gozdan, 1997 WL 416471 (Ohio Ct. App. 9th Dist. Wayne County 1997); Jacobs v. England, 1993 WL 414258 (Ohio Ct. App. 12th Dist. Warren County 1993).

[8]Finn v. Finn, 1995 WL 350608 (Ohio Ct. App. 7th Dist. Mahoning County 1995). Civ. R. 53(E)(6).

[9]RC 3121.45.

[10]RC 3121.441(A).

[11]RC 3121.441(B).

[12]RC 3121.441(C).

[Section 20:40]

[1]Springer v. Springer, 1992 WL 328640 (Ohio Ct. App. 10th Dist. Franklin County 1992).

[2]Springer v. Springer, 1992 WL 328640 (Ohio Ct. App. 10th Dist. Franklin County 1992).

are final appealable orders because they in effect determine the outcome of the case.[3]

◆ **Practice Tip:** Counsel should use great caution in including mediation or arbitration clauses in separation agreements and shared parenting plans in order to prevent unintended consequences in matters such as child support enforcement.

§ 20:41   Contempt defenses—Moving party on welfare

A residential parent who has received aid to dependent children from the department of human services or has participated in Ohio Works First, has assigned to the department all of rights regarding support.[1] Accordingly, a parent on welfare loses the right to bring a contempt or show cause action to enforce support.[2] The Court of Appeals for Cuyahoga County held that only the Department of Human Services (later construed to include the CSEA as its agent) could bring a contempt action, because the residential parent was on ADC.

§ 20:42   Contempt defenses—Erroneous order

In *Slone v. Slone*,[1] the appellant argued that the contempt finding against him for failure to pay the child support order was error because that order, as originally imposed, had been reversed as in error. The court held that an erroneous order is no defense to a charge of contempt, regardless of how imprudent or premature the action was, until the order was reversed.

III. THE RUSTY TOOL

§ 20:43   Reduction to judgment and execution—In general

The judgment entry in a contempt proceeding merely finds that the respondent is in contempt of court, and includes a purge order requiring the contemnor to cure the default within a certain time or face penalties of incarceration and fines. Ordinarily, the court will also modify the outstanding withholding order so as to include a method for the obligor to purge himself of contempt by an increase in the amount to be paid, thus amortizing the arrearages. Alternatively, the court might require a lump-sum payment, whichever is appropriate under the circumstances. It may not be necessary to reduce the arrearages to a separate judgment.

---

[3]Kelm v. Kelm, 73 Ohio App. 3d 395, 597 N.E.2d 535 (10th Dist. Franklin County 1992).

[Section 20:41]

[1]RC 5107.20.

[2]Vance v. Banks, 94 Ohio App. 3d 475, 640 N.E.2d 1214 (8th Dist. Cuyahoga County 1994).

[Section 20:42]

[1]Slone v. Slone, 1998 WL 191840 (Ohio Ct. App. 4th Dist. Pike County 1998).

Child support arrearages may be satisfied by installment payments added to current support where financial information justifies such an order.[1]

The CSEA is considered a proper party to all actions for collection of support. Constitutional guarantees of equal protection prohibit dismissal of the agency as a party.[2]

Past due child support may be withheld from federal income tax refunds. Birthing expenses are part of child support and, thus, may also be withheld.[3]

A trial court erred in ordering a father's lump-sum workers' compensation payment to be divided equally between the mother and the father when his child support arrearage exceeded the lump-sum payment. The trial court had no discretion under former RC 3113.21(H)(3)[4] to choose the amounts of lump-sum payments to be allocated to the arrearage and to the obligor. The trial court should have ordered the entire lump sum to be applied to the child support arrearage.[5] A QDRO may order a lump-sum or extended payments to be made to satisfy spousal support arrearages.[6]

However, interest on a support arrearage which accrued before July 1, 1992, the effective date of RC 3109.05(C), only accrues after the arrearage has been reduced to judgment.[7] RC 3123.17 sets forth the prerequisite for ordering interest to accrue on unpaid support orders.

In instances of willful default, or where the obligor has a sketchy employment history or is self employed, the obligee may wish to reduce the arrearages to a money judgment, and collect by execution on the obligor's property, rather than relying on future good behavior and a succession of show cause procedures.[8] Income from a trust that is neither a purely discretionary nor a strict support trust, and that contains no express exclusions of the beneficiaries' children, may be

---

[Section 20:43]

[1]RC 3123.21; Helton v. Helton, 102 Ohio App. 3d 733, 658 N.E.2d 1 (1st Dist. Hamilton County 1994).

[2]State, Cuyahoga Child Support Enforcement Agency v. Seals, 1996 WL 239886 (Ohio Ct. App. 8th Dist. Cuyahoga County 1996). See Text Ch 22, Child Support Enforcement Agencies.

[3]Gladysz v. King, 103 Ohio App. 3d 1, 658 N.E.2d 309 (2d Dist. Clark County 1995).

[4]Amended and recodified by 2000 S.B. 180, eff. 3-22-01, analogous language 3121.12.

[5]Tardona v. Bell, 105 Ohio App. 3d 44, 663 N.E.2d 679 (12th Dist. Butler County 1995).

[6]Myers v. Myers, 1995 WL 360229 (Ohio Ct. App. 10th Dist. Franklin County 1995).

[7]Dunbar v. Dunbar, 68 Ohio St. 3d 369, 1994-Ohio-509, 627 N.E.2d 532 (1994).

[8]See Green v. Green, 120 Ohio App. 112, 28 Ohio Op. 2d 301, 191 N.E.2d 217 (8th Dist. Cuyahoga County 1963).

attached for the purposes of paying a judgment for the beneficiaries' child support.[9]

In *Golick v. Golick*,[10] the Eighth District Court of Appeals upheld a trial court decision appointing a receiver and ordering the sale of stock belonging to a nonpaying obligor.

Pursuant to RC 3123.14 an obligee may request CSEA assistance to obtain a judgment for the support arrearage and execution of that judgment through any available procedure after the termination of the support order. The CSEA, pursuant to RC 3123.15, is supposed to act within twenty days of the obligee's application for help, but it is doubtful that most agencies can act that quickly. While a support order is ongoing an obligee may seek the assistance of the CSEA or the court to obtain a judgment for unpaid support pursuant to RC 3123.18.

◆ **Practice Tips:** It is often wise for the practitioner to seek a lump-sum judgment at the same time as or instead of pursuing a contempt motion. In some counties it may be possible to join both proceedings in one motion before one judge or magistrate. If not, it may be worthwhile to file two separate motions, or even to seek a consent judgment as part of the settlement of a contempt proceeding.

Judgments can be made liens on real estate simply by filing a certificate of judgment in the county where the real estate is located.[11] Even after-acquired real estate can be subject to the lien—all the judgment holder needs to do is re-file the lien. Once a certificate of judgment is filed in a county where the judgment debtor owns real estate, the judgment creditor has a lien that is valid for five years. It can be extended for additional five-year terms by re-filing the certificate of judgment before the current five-year period ends.[12]

◆ **Practice Tip:** In the event the defaulting obligor satisfies the judgment, it is important to file a release of lien to avoid liability in an action to quiet title or for slander of title.

Judgments can be collected against estates of obligors, or out of personal injury settlements, lottery winnings, or even from inheritances of obligors. Judgments do not go away, although they may become dormant and need reviving pursuant to RC 2325.15.[13] Judgments are not subject to the defense of laches. And judgments can easily be made to include statutory interest, pursuant to RC 1343.03, which can be a major benefit in counties where the courts do not

---

[9]Matthews v. Matthews, 5 Ohio App. 3d 140, 450 N.E.2d 278 (10th Dist. Franklin County 1981), on reconsideration, 1982 WL 3990 (Ohio Ct. App. 10th Dist. Franklin County 1982).

[10]Golick v. Golick, 9 Ohio App. 3d 106, 458 N.E.2d 459 (8th Dist. Cuyahoga County 1983).

[11]See RC 2329.02.

[12]See RC 2329.07. Kuehnle and Levey, Ohio Real Estate Law, Ch. 39 (3d ed.).

[13]See Text §§ 20:43 to 20:54, Reduction to judgment and execution; Kuehnle and Levey, Ohio Real Estate Law, Ch. 39 (3d ed.).

automatically add interest to arrearages. The tax commissioner determines the interest rate annually, pursuant to RC 5703.47.

Child support orders do not automatically terminate. Many a chronically defaulting obligor becomes instantly diligent when the time comes for a child to be emancipated. Often, the defaulting obligor will file a motion to terminate child support, or start CSEA proceedings to terminate the order. This brings them before the court, where they can be examined under oath regarding their assets and income, in an effort to collect on old lump-sum judgments and the accumulated interest.

Unfortunately, many domestic relations practitioners are out of the habit of seeking judgments or filing judgment liens. Worse, in counties with separate clerk's offices for domestic cases, the clerk of court's personnel may not know how to issue a certificate of judgment or how to issue execution. In such cases, it may be necessary to arrange a meeting between personnel from both the civil and domestic branches of the clerk's office to get the job done. Do not let the extra effort required here deter you. Every lump-sum judgment filed and certified as a lien is an investment made for the future of your client.

§ 20:44 Reduction to judgment and execution—Motion to reduce support arrearage to lump-sum judgment—Form⊚

[Title of Court]

[Caption]

Case No. *[_____]*
<u>MOTION TO REDUCE
INSTALLMENT
SPOUSAL SUPPORT
AWARD TO LUMP SUM
JUDGMENT</u>

[Plaintiff/Defendant] moves this Court for an order reducing to judgment the unpaid arrearages of *[spousal support/child support]* accrued to date of hearing.

Further, the *[Plaintiff/Defendant]* moves this Court for an order awarding *[him/her]* interest on said arrearage, calculated from the time each payment was due to the present and thereafter until paid in full, at the statutory rate pursuant to RC 1343.03.

Further, *[Plaintiff/Defendant]* moves this Court for an order awarding *[him/her]* attorney fees for bringing this action to enforce the Court's order.

This motion is supported by the affidavit below.

_____

Attorney for *[Plaintiff / Defendant]*

State of Ohio   :
                                                           :   SS.   <u>AFFIDAVIT</u>
County of *[_____]*   :

[Plaintiff / Defendant], being first duly sworn, deposes and says that:

1. By decree herein *[name of payor]* was ordered to pay to *[name of payee]* the sum of $*[dollar amount]* per *[period of time]* as and for *[alimony / spousal support / child support]*.

2. *[Name of payor]* has failed and neglected to comply with said order, in that as of *[date][he / she]* should have paid the sum of $*[dollar amount]*, has paid the sum of $*[dollar amount]* and is in arrears in the amount of $*[dollar amount]* and may accumulate additional amounts of arrearages by time of hearing.

3. Affiant has incurred attorney fees in an amount to be determined at hearing, and *[name of payor / payee]* has the ability to pay, and affiant would not be able to bring this action before the court without payment by *[name of payor / payee]* of *[his / her]* attorney fees.

4. *[Name of payor]* has failed to pay said sum and such failure was willful. *[Name of payor]* should be required to pay the interest which accrued on each installment when due.

Further affiant sayeth naught.

_____

Affiant

[Jurat]

[Notice of hearing]

[Proof / certificate of service]

NOTES TO FORM

Drafter's Notes

A proof/certificate of service is only necessary when there is litigation already pending in the same case number. Where there is no pending litigation (either in the original case or post-decree) irrespective of whether the responding party already has counsel at the time of filing the motion, the motion papers will be served by the clerk of court upon the responding party pursuant to written instructions filed with the motion.

Where the original order was for "alimony," it is not improper to refer to the past order as alimony. It may help to say "alimony, now known as spousal support."

This motion may be combined with other motions such as attorney fees, for contempt, modification, withholding order, etc. Check the local court rules regarding allowable combinations of motions.

§ 20:45 Reduction to judgment and execution—Judgment entry reducing support arrearage to lump-sum judgment—Form⊙

[Title of Court]

[Caption]   Case No. [_____]
                                                   JUDGMENT ENTRY

This cause came before the Court on [date] upon the Motion of [name of payee]. [Name of payor] was duly served pursuant to law and [failed to appear/appeared with counsel/counsel appeared for [name of payor].

WHEREFORE, the Court having considered the testimony and evidence finds said Motion well taken, that as of [date] [name of payor] was in arrears in payment of [spousal support/child support] and [name of payee] is entitled to a judgment in the amount of $[dollar amount] [including interest accrued to date/plus interest accrued to date].

The Court hereby grants to [name of payee] a judgment against [name of payor] in the amount of $[dollar amount] plus interest at the statutory rule.

Effective:

_____
Judge

Approved:

_____
Attorney for payee

NOTES TO FORM

Drafter's Notes

This judgment may be executed upon in the same manner as any other judgment, including garnishment, attachment, and filing a certificate of judgment in common pleas court to create a lien and executing upon the lien. However, in counties with a separate domestic relations division of the clerk's office, counsel may find that the personnel in the domestic clerk's office are unfamiliar with certificates of judgment, garnishment, and attachment. You may need to get someone from the civil division clerk's office to help you get execution paperwork completed.

§ 20:46 Reduction to judgment and execution—Motion for examination of judgment debtor—Form⊚

[Title of Court]

[Caption]   Case No. *[_____]*
                                              MOTION FOR EXAMINATION
                                              OF
                                              JUDGMENT DEBTOR

Now comes Plaintiff by counsel and moves the Court for an order requiring Defendant to appear before a Magistrate of the Court of Common Pleas, Division of Domestic Relations, *[full street address]* and answer concerning *[his/her]* property and that *[he/she]* be enjoined from disposing of *[his/her]* property or any part thereof until further order herein.

                                              _____
                                              Attorney for Plaintiff

State of Ohio   :
                                 :   SS.   AFFIDAVIT
County of *[_____]*   :

   [Name] says that *[he/she]* is the attorney for Plaintiff; that on *[date]* judgment was obtained in the sum of $*[dollar amount]* against Defendant; that said judgment is wholly unpaid; that there is now due an unpaid balance of $*[dollar amount]* plus interest and costs; and that unless restrained, Defendant may dispose of his property.

                                              _____
                                              Affiant

[Jurat]

NOTES TO FORM

Drafter's Notes

   Since a judgment debtor proceeding is generally post-decree, service will be required upon obligor. Do not be surprised if the domestic relations clerk's office has never seen a motion like this.

§ 20:47 Reduction to judgment and execution—Judgment entry ordering examination or judgment debtor—Form⊚

[Title of Court]

[Caption]

Case No. [_____]
ORDER FOR EXAMINATION OF
JUDGMENT DEBTOR

On the motion of Plaintiff, by counsel, in the above entitled action, it is hereby ordered that Defendant, [name of defendant], appear before the Court Magistrate, [full street address] at [time] on [date], to answer under oath concerning [his/her] property and [he/she] is hereby enjoined from disposing of [his/her] property or any part thereof in any manner whatsoever until further order herein.

_____
Judge

APPROVED:

_____
Attorney for Plaintiff

§ 20:48 Reduction to judgment and execution—Praecipe requesting certificate of judgment—Form⊚

[Title of Court]

[Caption]

Case No. [_____]

REQUEST FOR FILING CERTIFICATE OF JUDGMENT LIEN
TO THE CLERK:
PLEASE ISSUE CERTIFICATE OF JUDGMENT LIEN IN FAVOR
OR JUDGMENT CREDITOR [name of creditor]
AGAINST JUDGMENT DEBTOR(S) [name of debtor(s)]
Amount: $[dollar amount] with interest at a rate of [percentage amount]%- from [date]
Costs: $[dollar amount]

_____
Attorney for plaintiff

Please return Certificate of Judgment to [address to which certificate should be mailed].

Issue to Foreign County

NOTES TO FORM

Drafter's Notes

Civil Division clerk's offices will usually have a stock form for requesting Certificates of Judgment. The Domestic Relations Division may not have these on hand and may not know what to do with them if you file one. Take your time, be patient, and suggest the domestic clerk personnel talk to the civil side of the office.

§ 20:49   Reduction to judgment and execution—Motion for conditional order for revivor—Form®

[Title of Court]

[Caption]

Case No. *[_____]*
MOTION FOR CONDITIONAL
ORDER FOR REVIVOR OF
DORMANT JUDGMENT

1. Now comes *[name]*, Plaintiff-Judgment-Creditor, residing at *[address]*, Ohio, and respectfully moves the Court for a conditional order reviving the judgment in *[its/his/her]* favor against *[name of defendant-judgment-debtor]*, Defendant-Judgment-Debtor, residing at *[address of defendant-judgment-debtor]*, Ohio, rendered in the *[Court of Common Pleas of [name of county] County/[name of municipality] Municipal Court]* on *[date]*, in the principal sum of $*[dollar amount]*, with *[percentage amount]%* interest from *[date]*, and costs of $*[dollar amount]*. There is still unpaid the principal sum of $*[dollar amount]*, with *[percentage amount]%* interest per annum from *[date]*.

2. Certificate of this judgment was filed with the Clerk of Courts of *[name of county]* County on *[date]*, in Certificates of Judgment Docket *[designation of docket]*, pages *[designation of pages]*.

3. Writ of Execution was issued to the [Sheriff of *[name of county]* County/Bailiff of the *[name of municipality]* Municipal Court] on *[date]*.

4. The judgment is now dormant.

_____

Attorney for Judgment-Creditor
[Address and Telephone]

State of Ohio   )
)   ss
[County]   )

[Name] being first duly sworn, states that *[he/she]* is the [judgment-creditor in the above proceedings for revivor of dormant judgment/attorney for *[name of corporation]*, an Ohio corporation, the judgment-

creditor in the above proceedings for revivor of dormant judgment], and that the facts contained in the above Motion are true as *[he/she]* verily believes.

[Judgment Creditor]

Sworn to before me and subscribed in my presence this *[date]*.

Notary Public

§ 20:50 Reduction to judgment and execution—Judgment entry ordering conditional revivor of judgment— Form⊚

[Title of Court]

[Caption]   Case No. *[_____]*

Upon Motion of *[name of party filing motion]*, filed on *[date]*, it appearing that the judgment rendered herein on *[date]*, in favor of Plaintiff *[name of plaintiff]* and against Defendant *[name of defendant]*, has become dormant on *[date]*, it is ordered that the judgment be revived in the principal amount of $*[dollar amount]*, with interest at *[percentage amount]%* per annum from *[date]*, which is the amount the Court finds unpaid on the judgment, unless said Defendant *[name of defendant]*, by *[date]*, appears and shows cause why the judgment should not be revived.

It is ordered that this Order be served on Defendant *[name]*, residing at *[address]*, Ohio, at least twenty-eight (28) days before said date.

Judge

§ 20:51 Reduction to judgment and execution—Instructions for service on judgment debtor—Form⊚

[Title of Court]

[Caption]   Case No. *[_____]*

To the Clerk of Court of *[Common Pleas of [name of county] County/ [name of municipality] Municipal Court]*:

Please issue certified copy of the Conditional Order of Revivor of

Dormant Judgment entered on *[date]*, directed to the *[Sheriff of [name of county] County / Bailiff of the [name of municipality] Municipal Court]*, returnable according to law, for service upon Defendant *[name of defendant]*, residing at *[address]*, Ohio.

_____

Attorney for Plaintiff-Judgment-Debtor

[Date]

§ 20:52   Reduction to judgment and execution—Judgment entry final order reviving judgment—Form⊚

[Title of Court]

[Caption]   Case No. *[_____]*

This cause came on to be heard upon Conditional Order for revivor of dormant judgment, and proof of service of certified copy of said Order upon Defendant.

Upon due consideration, the Court finding that Defendant *[name of defendant]* not having shown sufficient cause why the judgment rendered herein on *[date]* against *[him / her]* and in favor of Plaintiff *[name of plaintiff]* should not be revived, it is ordered that said judgment stand revived in the principal amount of $*[dollar amount]*, with *[percentage amount]%* interest from *[date]*, and costs herein; and Certificate of Judgment shall issue for the amount of such revived judgment.

_____

Judge

§ 20:53   Reduction to judgment and execution—Partial satisfaction of judgment—Form⊚

[Title of Court]

[Caption]   Case No. *[_____]*

PARTIAL SATISFACTION OF JUDGMENT

Know All Men by These Presents, That *[name]*, *[address]*, does hereby release and discharge from the operation of the lien of the judgment obtained against *[name]*, *[address]*, entered on *[date]* in the *[title of court]* Court, and the Certificate of which judgment was filed in Judgments Docket *[designation of docket]*, page *[designation of page]* in the office of the Clerk of Courts of *[name of county]* County on *[date]*, and which judgment became a lien upon the following described real property:

Situate in the *[type of locale]* of *[name of locale]*, County of *[name of county]*, State of Ohio.

[Metes-and-bounds description]

Title Reference: Being the premises conveyed to *[name of grantee]* from *[name of grantor]* [with release of dower by *[wife]* by deed of general warranty dated *[date]* and presented for recording in Deed Book *[designation of deed book]*, pages *[designation of pages]* in the office of the Recorder of *[name of county]* County on *[date]*.

Provided, however, that this Release shall not be construed to waive or in any manner affect the lien of the judgment upon the residue of the real estate owned by the judgment debtors subject to the Certificate of Judgment.

In Witness Whereof, *[name of judgment lien creditor]*, the judgment lien creditor, has subscribed his/her name to these presents, this *[date]*.

Executed in presence of:

_____

_____   *[name]*

)

)   SS

[Jurat]

§ 20:54 Reduction to judgment and execution—Attorney fee awards

An award of attorney fees is a prime candidate for being reduced to judgment and made judgment liens. A judgment lien can be assigned by its owner (the client) to the attorney for later collection from the obligor. While an order for attorney fees in favor of one of the parties to a divorce has been recognized as necessary, and hence properly encompassed in an alimony award,[1] the enforcement burden is still upon the recipient of such fees. Such an order may be enforced by other methods previously discussed. The award of fees may be reduced to judgment and execution levied. A contempt motion may also be filed on behalf of the party for whom attorney fees were awarded and in some cases the latter may be a more efficient means of collection. Without initiation by the obligee, however, enforcement of attorney fees will not be actively pursued by the court.

[Section 20:54]

[1]Wolf v. Friedman, 20 Ohio St. 2d 49, 49 Ohio Op. 2d 306, 253 N.E.2d 761 (1969). See also Text § 13:25, Attorney fees—Fees as spousal support.

The Tenth District Court of Appeals has held that an award of attorney fees in support enforcement proceedings is additional support and it is payable through withholding provisions just as any order or arrearage.[2]

In some jurisdictions, the court issues orders indicating that the attorney fee is to be paid to petitioner's counsel as an attorney fee, instead of directing it to the petitioner. This order may be unenforceable.[3]

IV. THE AWKWARD TOOL

§ 20:55   Working with your CSEA—In general

Privately represented clients seeking child support enforcement have the choice of one or more of these three basic options: (1) seeking to have the obligor found in contempt and ordered to purge or be sentenced to jail; (2) seeking a lump-sum judgment and execution upon the judgment; and (3) obtaining a payroll or financial account deduction order, including an order for an additional periodic amount to liquidate arrearages.

The child support enforcement agency (CSEA) is empowered to use the same three basic techniques. In addition, it has at least eight additional options not available to private counsel. These options are (1) administrative review of support orders,[1] (2) federal and state tax refund intercepts,[2] (3) criminal nonsupport prosecutions in cooperation with the county prosecutor,[3] (4) reporting defaulting obligors to credit reporting agencies,[4] (5) printing and circulating "wanted posters" featuring defaulting obligors,[5] (6) license revocation procedures, (7) attaching funds in unclaimed bank[6] accounts, and (8) administrative liens on real and personal property.[7]

Because the past key CSEA statutes[8] were so complex, badly written, and poorly organized, the CSEAs in different counties have developed differing methods of dealing with cases. Generally the county agency will not have a published set of procedures, so the private attorney must resort to attempting to learn the local agency

---

[2]Hamilton v. Hamilton, 40 Ohio App. 3d 190, 532 N.E.2d 213 (10th Dist. Franklin County 1988).

[3]Hamilton v. Hamilton, 40 Ohio App. 3d 190, 532 N.E.2d 213 (10th Dist. Franklin County 1988).

[Section 20:55]

[1]See Text Ch 22, Child Support Enforcement Agencies. RC 3119.61.

[2]RC 3123.81, RC 3123.821, RC 5747.121.

[3]RC 3125.14, RC 2919.21.

[4]RC 3123.92, RC 3123.932.

[5]RC 3123.96, RC 3123.95.

[6]RC 3123.88.

[7]RC 3123.66, RC 3123.67.

[8]Primarily former RC 2301.373, former RC 2301.374, former RC 2301.375.

procedures through experience, asking questions of agency officials, and comparing notes with colleagues.

> ◆ **Practice Tip:** A "Freedom of Information Act" request seeking a copy of the local agency's procedural manual is not out of the question.

Once again, an unfortunate byproduct of the complex new statutes created by recent legislation is the difficulty for counsel to effectively practice outside their own geographic regions.

The advent of the laws creating CSEAs also coincided with the general availability of voice mail systems, the result being the creation of a large agency in control of vital functions where you never can get through to a live person on the phone. If you practice in such a county, this leaves basically two choices:

(1) do all of your business on an agency case on the hearing dates, and forget about trying to resolve anything ahead of time; or

(2) go knock on the agency's door, and confront the agency personnel on their turf. If they get tired of seeing you, they may consent to take phone calls.

The advantages to the client of working through the CSEA include minimal or no cost for representation and access to additional routes for collection. Disadvantages vary, depending upon the level of competence of the local CSEA, and include waiting periods, backlogs, lack of personal attention, inability to get questions answered or to contact an individual handling the client's case, unnecessary court appearances, and difficulty getting the job done due to inadequate staffing.

§ 20:56 Working with your CSEA—Interception of income tax refunds

RC 3123.81 directs the CSEA to work with the Secretary of the Treasury to collect past-due child support from refunds of paid federal taxes that are payable to the individual who owes the past-due support. If the obligor has filed a joint tax return, the other filing party may take action to secure his or her share of the joint refund.[1]

RC 5747.121 permits collection by the department of job and family services of overdue child support payments from interception of refunds of paid state income taxes payable to obligors. This interception can be made even if the obligor is making regular payments on an arrearage pursuant to a court order.[2]

Until the enactment of S.B. 180,[3] there was no reciprocal right for obligors to collect overpaid support. Now, RC 5747.123 requires the tax commissioner to cooperate with the Department of Job and Fam-

---

[Section 20:56]

[1]42 U.S.C.A. § 664.

[2]RC 3123.22, eff. 3-22-01.

[3]S.B. 180, eff. 3-22-01.

ily Services in collecting overpaid child support from refunds of paid state tax that are payable to obligees. However, there is currently no similar statutory provision for the recoupment of overpaid support from an obligee's federal income tax refund.

In the case of persons filing a joint state income tax return, the amount of the refund available for the collection of overdue or overpaid child support shall be based on the proportion of the refund due only to the obligor or obligee, respectively.[4]

§ 20:57 Working with your CSEA—Wanted posters and other approaches

In the spring of 1992 the Ohio General Assembly enacted 1992 Senate Bill 10. Originally offered as a short bill authorizing child support enforcement agencies and the Department of Human Services (now the Department of Job and Family Services) to circulate posters featuring the photos of defaulting obligors, the final bill included an administrative procedure to establish paternity and set child support orders for unmarried parents of minor children.[1]

Former RC 2301.355[2] authorized support enforcement agencies to adopt a program to increase child support collections by identifying, publicizing, and possibly even locating delinquent obligors by publishing and distributing posters. The statute used mandatory "shall" language to specify the contents of the posters, including photos, names, identification information, and a toll-free telephone number that could be called to report information on the whereabouts of the featured defaulters. While the poster program is optional for county support enforcement agencies, RC 3123.95 requires the Department of Job and Family Services to establish such a program.

Both the local and state poster programs apply only to obligors the agency is unable to locate or to obligors whose location cannot be verified by the agency, are not welfare recipients, have not filed bankruptcy, and whose former spouse consents to the program.[3]

The "Wanted Poster" program has been surprisingly effective, and in an appropriate case, counsel can do a real service to the client by facilitating the acceptance of the client's case into the county's poster program. This is best done by gathering as much data on the obligor as possible from old case files, traffic cases in municipal court, and similar sources, and then contacting the local CSEA to set up a meeting with the individual responsible for "Wanted Posters" in the county. These officials are often looking for a few good candidates, but do not

---

[4]RC 5747.121(C).

[Section 20:57]

[1]See Text Ch 3, Parentage.

[2]Amended and recodified by 2000 S.B. 180, eff. 3-22-01, with analogous language at RC 3123.96.

[3]RC 5101.323(B).

have the time available to do the background work. If you do it for them, you may be able to recruit their cooperation.

The same general approach also works for getting the CSEA's help with tax refund intercepts.

Provide the CSEA with the name and address and phone number of the debtor's employer. Give CSEA a copy of its own support payment records. Tell the agency why you think there is a refund coming (e.g., "He always got a refund when we were married," or, "He just changed jobs and I think he is going to pull the money out of the retirement plan,"). And plan ahead. The time window for filing tax refund intercepts closes early, well before the end of the calendar year.

Thus, there are three general rules for working with your CSEA, particularly in large counties:

    1. If you want their help, gather lots of data and do the legwork for them.

    2. If you are defending against an agency's actions, the best way to get things resolved before court is to go knock on their door.

    3. Do not expect a CSEA worker to treat you the same way a fellow attorney would. Do not expect mail to be answered or phone calls to be returned. Do not expect any effort toward settlement any time except hearing dates.

    ◆ **Practice Tip:** If you are representing a client in an effort to enforce support or if you are defending a client against impending CSEA action, it may be possible to "freeze out" the CSEA by filing your own motion. Simply file your own motion to modify support, and then serve a copy on the CSEA. Typically, the agency will not act on a case if a privately filed motion is pending.

V. THE TRENDY TOOL

§ 20:58 License suspension and revocation—In general

Ohio statutes aimed at enforcing support by license suspension are RC 3123.43 (occupational and professional licenses), RC 3123.54 (driver's licenses), and RC 3123.62 (recreational licenses). These provisions started out as part of a proposal to suspend the medical licenses of highly paid physicians who failed to pay their court-ordered support. In a remarkable show of legislative one-upmanship, the bill rapidly evolved into a legislative scheme calling for the suspension of virtually every kind of license issued by the state of Ohio, if the CSEA determines that the license holder is in default of paying support. Effective January 1, 1998, even recreational licenses are included.[1]

Former RC 2301.373[2] became effective November 15, 1996, and was immediately put into effect by some CSEAs. Doctors, barbers, real

---

[Section 20:58]

    [1]RC 3123.62.

    [2]Amended and recodified by 2000 S.B. 180, eff. 3-22-01, analogous language RC 3123.43.

estate agents, and insurance salespeople tended to be the early targets. Many CSEAs are still working out procedures to implement these laws, and the addition of recreational licenses will further complicate the matter.

At present, is seems that CSEAs are using license revocation procedures on big dollar cases, which is probably what the legislature intended, at least initially. If your client is owed a significant sum of money, the obligor has a good income but is self-employed and needs a professional license to work, consider gathering all the necessary data for your CSEA and sending it to them on a form similar to the following:

§ 20:59 License suspension and revocation—Request to agency for license suspension—Form⊚

REQUEST FOR LICENSE SUSPENSION NOTIFICATION

The undersigned requests that the CSEA act under Ohio Revised Code Section 3123.43, 3123.54, and 3123.62 to notify the obligor and all licensing agencies that the court and/or the CSEA has determined the obligor to be in default under a child support order, so that all applicable licenses of the obligor will be suspended or withheld until the obligor is in compliance.

The Obligor
Address
SSN
Court
Case number
CSEA number

Regarding the obligor's default, please note all attached documentation and the following:

    Order finding default:
    Licenses payor holds:
    Agency:

Respectfully submitted,

_____

Attorney for *[name]*
Sup. Ct. Reg. #
Address
City, State, Zip
Phone

NOTES TO FORM

Drafter's Notes

Because this is not a motion filed in court, no certificate of service, notice of hearing date, or service of summons is required. However, sending a copy to the payor or his counsel might well get good results.

Many CSEAs will require constant monitoring by counsel once a request for license suspension is made. The best bet is to give them as much data as you can, and do as much legwork for them as possible ahead of time. Then keep pestering the CSEA to act on your case.

§ 20:60   License suspension and revocation—Procedures in CSEA

RC 3123.42 provides that if a court or CSEA makes a final and enforceable determination that an obligor is in default, then the CSEA *may* "determine" whether the obligor holds any state licenses. RC 3123.53, regarding driver's licenses, and RC 3123.62, regarding recreational licenses, have similar language. Virtually everybody holds some state license.[1]

The use of the word "may" indicates that the CSEA investigation is at their discretion. Query: if you notify them that an obligor is in default and licensed, then what discretion do they have left?

Next, the statute says that if a CSEA finds that a defaulting obligor is licensed, then it *shall* send the obligor a notice that the CSEA *may* be send the various licensing agencies a notice to suspend the licenses until further notice.

The additional "may" language appears to inject further CSEA discretion into the process.

As a practical matter, things may not go that simply. For example, the Franklin County Child Support Enforcement Agency has instituted a procedure whereby an obligor, having been notified that a court or the agency has made a final and enforceable determination that the the obligor is in default, is granted a further hearing. The hearing process can continue with appeals to a hearing officer, a court, an appellate court, etc. until there is a final and enforceable order that there is indeed a final and enforceable order. The statute does not seem to require this redundant procedure.

§ 20:61   License suspension and revocation—Procedures at licensing agency

RC 3123.49 states that, notwithstanding RC 119.06, no licensing board shall hold any hearing in connection with an order suspending or refusing to issue a license on account of child support default.

The licensing agency has no discretion; it is to hold the license in suspension until the CSEA notifies the agency that the obligor is no longer in default.

[Section 20:60]

[1]See Text § 20:68, License suspension and revocation—Licenses included under RC 3123.41.

§ 20:62 License suspension and revocation—Lifting the suspension

The statute uses mandatory language requiring the CSEA to notify licensing agencies that a licensee is no longer in default if:

(1) the obligor pays the arrears in full;

(2) an "appropriate" withholding order is issued, covering current support and liquidation of arrears, and the obligor is complying; or

(3) a "new" child support order has been issued, or the old order has been modified to collect current support and arrears, and the obligor is complying.

An interesting question is how an obligor can comply with a new wage withholding order when the license needed for employment is suspended?

In addition, the statute does not define what constitutes an "appropriate" withholding order, leaving the practitioner to guess if it means one that the CSEA agrees to.

§ 20:63 License suspension and revocation—Constitutional defense

A due process question has arisen, that there is no rational connection between the qualification to practice the profession in question and the issue of child support arrearages. However, at least one court, within the context of RC 3123.54 has determined that the suspension process violates neither substantive nor procedural due process rights.[1]

It may also be argued that the entire license suspension scheme is in violation of the Equal Protection clause of the US Constitution and the equivalent provisions in the Ohio Const. Art. I § 2 and Ohio Const. Art. II § 26. It is arguably a violation of equal protection for a law to prohibit the employment of an individual who needs a state license for his or her profession, while permitting another individual, who does not need a state license to work, to be in child support default with relative impunity.

§ 20:64 License suspension and revocation—Notice defense

License suspension procedures have been collaterally attacked by obligors filing for injunction in the civil division of common pleas courts, arguing that they received improper notification of the

---

[Section 20:63]

[1]State v. Leuvoy, 2004-Ohio-2232, 2004 WL 944387 (Ohio Ct. App. 5th Dist. Fairfield County 2004).

revocation.[1] In order to suspend or revoke a license, the Child Support Enforcement Agency must comply with the notice procedures outlined by RC 3123.43 (occupational and professional licenses), or RC 3123.62 (recreational licenses). Pursuant to RC 3123.63, the director of Job and Family Services has adopted rules to implement the suspension of recreational licenses.[2]

§ 20:65 License suspension and revocation—Slow ball defense

Obligors whose local agencies offer them the opportunity for an additional hearing to determine by way of a final and enforceable order whether there was a previous final and enforceable order finding them in default may well choose to litigate slowly and delay the suspension by means of successive appeals to magistrate, judge, court of appeals, and so forth. In counties where nothing gets heard in court without three prior continuances, the slow-ball technique could buy significant time.

§ 20:66 License suspension and revocation—Checkbook technique

The discretion granted to the CSEA in issuing reinstatement notices seems to suggest that a hefty payment toward arrearages and a new withholding order may be the quickest way to resolve a license suspension.

§ 20:67 License suspension and revocation—Changing the forum

While risky, some licensees might choose to practice with a suspended license, and then litigate the constitutionality and procedural correctness of the license suspension before their own licensing agency, rather than before the CSEA. Making this choice would probably require an assessment of how the licensing agency feels about RC 3123.44

§ 20:68 License suspension and revocation—Licenses included under RC 3123.41

The definition of "license" under RC 3123.41 includes any "license, certificate, permit, registration, or other authorization to engage in an occupation or profession." "Board" is similarly defined to include "any entity" with the authority to issue licenses under Title 47, and any other state agency (except the Supreme Court) with the authority to issue a license permitting an individual to engage in an occupation or

---

[Section 20:64]

[1]LeuVoy v. Franklin County Child Support Enforcement Agency, No. 9VCV005921 (Ohio Ct. C.P. 10th Dist. Franklin County 1997).

[2]Ohio Admin. Code § 5101:1-30-882.

profession, including an administrative officer with such authority. Under these definitions, licenses subject to suspension, revocation, or a refusal to issue would include at least licenses issued under the following regulations:

Type of position	Revised Code reference
Accountants	RC Ch. 4701
Ambulance service operators	RC Ch. 4766
Architects	RC Ch. 4703
Auctioneers	RC Ch. 4707
Barbers	RC Ch. 4709
Chiropractors	RC Ch. 4734
Construction industry certificates	RC Ch. 4740
Cosmetologists	RC Ch. 4713
Counselors and social workers	RC Ch. 4757
Dentists and dental hygienists	RC Ch. 4715
Dietitians	RC Ch. 4759
Embalmers and funeral directors	RC Ch. 4717
Emergency medical service operators	RC Ch. 4765
Hearing aid dealers	RC Ch. 4747
Motor vehicle salvage operators	RC Ch. 4738
Nurses	RC Ch. 4723
Nursing home administrators	RC Ch. 4751
Occupational and physical therapists	RC Ch. 4755
Optometrists and opticians	RC Ch. 4725
Pawnbrokers	RC Ch. 4727
Pharmacists	RC Ch. 4729
Physicians and limited practitioners	RC Ch. 4731
Physicians' assistants	RC Ch. 4730
Precious metals dealers	RC Ch. 4728
Private investigators and security services	RC Ch. 4749
Professional engineers and surveyors	RC Ch. 4733
Psychologists	RC Ch. 4732
Real estate appraisers	RC Ch. 4763
Real estate brokers	RC Ch. 4735
Respiratory care providers	RC Ch. 4761
Sanitarians	RC Ch. 4736
Speech pathologists and audiologists	RC Ch. 4753
Steam engineers and boiler operators	RC Ch. 4739
Veterinarians	RC Ch. 4741
X-ray machine operators; radiographers; radiation therapy and nuclear medicine technologists	RC Ch. 4773

In addition to licenses for occupations and professions regulated under Title 47, licenses issued by other state agencies that would also fall within RC 3123.41 would include licenses authorizing certain occupations such as:

Type of position	Revised Code reference
Bee keepers	RC Ch. 909
Dairy producers	RC Ch. 917
Meat handlers	RC Ch. 918 and Ch. 919
Pesticide service providers	RC Ch. 921
Agricultural commodities dealers	RC Ch. 926
Livestock dealers	RC Ch. 927
Nursery stock dealers	RC Ch. 943
Mortgage brokers	RC Ch. 1322
Small finance company operators	RC Ch. 1321
Various commercial boating, fishing, and hunting activities	RC Ch. 1533 and Ch. 1541
Educators including teachers and administrators	RC Ch. 3301 and Ch. 3319
Safety inspectors and abatement of regulated materials including asbestos, radon, and lead	RC Title 37
Insurance and finance professionals	RC Title 39
Mining industry positions	RC Title 41
Day care operations and MR/DD employees	RC Title 51

§20:69 License suspension and revocation—Attorneys and judges

The legislature does not regulate the practice of law. That function is allocated to the Ohio Supreme Court by Article IV Section 2 of the Ohio Constitution. Accordingly, the Ohio Supreme Court has amended its Rules for Government of the Bar, Rule V, to effect the interim suspension of any judge, justice, or attorney against whom a final and enforceable default determination has been made pursuant to RC 3123.01 to 3123.04.[1]

Gov. Bar R. V, titled "Disciplinary procedures," contains language indicating that the "determination of default" shall be submitted to the Supreme Court regardless of the pendency of an appeal. This indicates that the Supreme Court would interpret "final and enforceable default determination" to be the same as a final appealable order.

[Section 20:69]

[1]See In re Hawkins, 96 Ohio St. 3d 1475, 2002-Ohio-4156, 773 N.E.2d 552 (2002) for interim order.

Presumably, the Court, having written its own rule this way, would rule likewise in appeals from RC 3123.41 et seq., the license suspension statute for nonlawyers.

Query: Since the Ohio Supreme Court has adopted a license suspension rule essentially identical to RC 3123.43, what is the likelihood the Court would find RC 3123.43 to be constitutionally or procedurally defective if challenged?

A judge or attorney under an interim suspension for default of a child support order shall be reinstated upon the filing with, and submission to, the Supreme Court of Ohio of either (a) a certified copy of a judgment entry reversing the finding of default or (b) a notice from a court or CSEA that the judge or attorney is no longer in default or is subject to a withholding or deduction notice, or is subject to a new or modified child support order to collect current support or arrearages due under the defaulted support order, and is complying with such notice or order.[2] However, reinstatement shall not terminate any pending disciplinary proceeding.[3]

Taking the interim suspension process one step further, the Supreme Court of Ohio has suspended attorney licenses as a disciplinary sanction for professional misconduct arising from the non-payment of child support.[4] The suspension is based upon the Court's determination an attorney's non-payment of child support constituted violations of DR 1-102(A)(5) (prohibiting conduct that is prejudicial to the administration of justice) and DR 1-102(A)(6) (prohibiting conduct that adversely reflects on a lawyer's fitness to practice law).[5] In some instances, the Court has been unwilling to grant credit to the attorney for any period of time encompassed by an interim suspension under Gov. Bar R. V, § 5(A)(1)(b) where the attorney has done little to cure the support default or cooperate in the disciplinary process.[6]

The Supreme Court of Ohio adopted the Ohio Rules of Professional Conduct, effective February 1, 2007, thus replacing the Ohio Code of Professional Responsibility. The Court has, however, continued to follow the practice of finding the non-payment of child support may constitute a disciplinary violation and warrant suspension under Prof.Cond.R. 8.4(h), the successor rule to DR 1-102.[7]

---

[2]Gov. Bar R. V, § 5(D)(1)(b), (c).

[3]Gov. Bar R. V, § 5(D)(2).

[4]Disciplinary Counsel v. Geer, 112 Ohio St. 3d 124, 2006-Ohio-6516, 858 N.E.2d 388 (2006); Disciplinary Counsel v. Curry, 112 Ohio St. 3d 130, 2006-Ohio-6517, 858 N.E.2d 392 (2006).

[5]Disciplinary Counsel v. Redfield, 116 Ohio St. 3d 262, 2007-Ohio-6039, 878 N.E.2d 10 (2007).

[6]Disciplinary Counsel v. Geer, 112 Ohio St. 3d 124, 2006-Ohio-6516, 858 N.E.2d 388 (2006); Disciplinary Counsel v. Curry, 112 Ohio St. 3d 130, 2006-Ohio-6517, 858 N.E.2d 392 (2006).

[7]Cincinnati Bar Assn. v. Heisler, 119 Ohio St. 3d 573, 2008-Ohio-5221, 895 N.E.2d 839 (2008).

VI. THE MISSING TOOL

§ 20:70 College education expenses

Once a child reaches age of majority, a trial court is generally held to have no jurisdiction to order support, including college expenses.[1] Further, a trial court has no authority to order a party to set up and fund a trust fund for a child's college education without a separation agreement or any other enforceable agreement.[2] Accordingly, if contribution to college education for the children is a concern of one of the parties, counsel needs to (1) negotiate a settlement rather than take the case to trial; and (2) include in the settlement agreed provisions, in clear and enforceable language, calling for payment of college education expenses. The court then has jurisdiction to enforce the agreement of the parties.

A father was found to be in contempt of court for failure to pay college education expenses in a four-year, undergraduate program for his daughter. While the agreement provided such expenses were to be paid at a college or university of father's approval, the trial court concluded he unreasonably withheld approval under the circumstances, and the court of appeals agreed.[3]

Holding that a trial court has no jurisdiction to modify provisions of a dissolution relating to benefits created for a third party beneficiary after such beneficiary reached the age of majority, without the consent of the third party beneficiary, the appellate court in *Ipson v. Ipson*[4] found that all trial court orders purporting to modify the college-related provisions after majority were void. RC 3105.65(B), which gives the court jurisdiction to modify child support orders, applies only to minor children.[5] The Lake County Court of Appeals reached an opposite position in *Sutherell v. Sutherell*[6] and held that when preliminary thresholds are observed, a court may modify the terms regarding a child, even after that child becomes an adult.

A claim for contempt for failure to pay tuition on behalf of minor children is not barred by the doctrine of res judicata, where a previous contempt motion only addressed a support arrearage. The prior motion was handled through the county prosecutor's office. The mother

---

[Section 20:70]

[1]Troha v. Troha, 105 Ohio App. 3d 327, 663 N.E.2d 1319 (2d Dist. Greene County 1995).

[2]Pratt v. McCullough, 100 Ohio App. 3d 479, 654 N.E.2d 372 (12th Dist. Warren County 1995).

[3]Tapp v. Tapp, 105 Ohio App. 3d 159, 663 N.E.2d 944 (2d Dist. Montgomery County 1995).

[4]Ipson v. Ipson, 1998 WL 767631 (Ohio Ct. App. 8th Dist. Cuyahoga County 1998).

[5]Rohrbacher v. Rohrbacher, 83 Ohio App. 3d 569, 615 N.E.2d 338 (6th Dist. Lucas County 1992).

[6]Sutherell v. Sutherell, 1999 WL 417990 (Ohio Ct. App. 11th Dist. Lake County 1999).

was advised that the prosecutor could only address support arrearages and not other issues such as failure to pay tuition.[7]

VII. THE FINAL TOOL

§ 20:71 Criminal nonsupport

In more extreme cases of economic neglect, the state has available to it the criminal nonsupport statute, RC 2919.21. Under RC 2919.21, one found guilty of failing to support a spouse or minor child may be punished for a first degree misdemeanor. If the failure to support includes 26 weeks out of any 104 weeks, or is a second or subsequent offense, the crime is a fifth-degree felony, and is a fourth-degree felony if the defendant previously was convicted of felony nonsupport. The statutory reference to 104 weeks indicates that support recipients should not expect swift action on the part of prosecuting attorneys to enforce child support via this route.

Though not a proper means of enforcing a support order in a divorce decree, the statute is designed in part to assure that children are adequately supported and do not become public charges, where one or both parents are able to provide such support. However, the federal pressure on states to increase child support collections has recently moved some county sheriffs and county prosecutors to stage highly publicized arrests and prosecutions of individuals with the biggest support arrearages, as disclosed by the support enforcement agency files.

The criminal nonsupport charge is governed by a strict needs and capabilities test, and many of the defenses which are not available in a contempt proceeding are proper in defending against criminal nonsupport. The support ordered in a divorce decree establishes the non-residential parent's obligation to provide adequate support, and compliance with an order made by the domestic relations court has been found to be a meritorious defense to criminal prosecution[1] just as a release in a divorce decree is also a defense from such obligation.[2] The same holds true for juvenile court orders.[3]

Inability to provide adequate support is also available as a defense,

---

[7]Zambory v. Zambory, 1992 WL 189551 (Ohio Ct. App. 8th Dist. Cuyahoga County 1992).

[Section 20:71]

[1]State v. Oppenheimer, 46 Ohio App. 2d 241, 75 Ohio Op. 2d 404, 348 N.E.2d 731 (10th Dist. Franklin County 1975); Rowland v. State, 14 Ohio App. 238, 1921 WL 1100 (3d Dist. Crawford County 1921).

[2]Rowland v. State, 14 Ohio App. 238, 1921 WL 1100 (3d Dist. Crawford County 1921).

[3]State v. Holl, 25 Ohio App. 2d 75, 54 Ohio Op. 2d 114, 266 N.E.2d 587 (3d Dist. Auglaize County 1971); Baugh v. Carver, 3 Ohio App. 3d 139, 444 N.E.2d 58 (1st Dist. Hamilton County 1981) (child support payments pursuant to paternity determination commence with child's date of birth; court did not order child support to begin at date of birth, pursuant to RC 3111.17, it is an abuse of discretion); Edwards v. Sadusky, 4 Ohio App. 3d 297, 448 N.E.2d 506 (9th Dist. Summit County 1982) (sup-

where the defendant has at least provided such support as was within his ability and means.[4] Consequently, evidence as to gifts and outside support from a noncustodial parent would be relevant at a trial for criminal nonsupport.

Courts previously have found relevant the residential parent's ability to independently provide adequate support for the minor child without contribution from the absent parent.[5] Contrary to the holding of the Tenth District Court of Appeals in *State v. Oppenheimer*,[6] the Eighth District Court of Appeals held in *State v. Schaub*[7] that RC 2919.21 requires only that the state prove that a child was not adequately supported by the defendant parent who has the ability to provide.

It is not a proper defense that someone else was providing adequate support, nor is it a defense that the child was receiving Social Security benefits. The criminal nonsupport statute has been rewritten since the 1975 decision in *Oppenheimer*, and the court would be unlikely to uphold that case today.

An obligor's "single act" of nonsupport supports both a criminal contempt and a civil contempt, and sentences pursuant to both actions will not violate the Double Jeopardy Clauses of the Ohio and United States Constitutions.[8] RC 2919.21(E) does not violate a defendant's right to a jury trial.[9]

There is no "mens rea" stated in RC 2919.21, nonsupport of dependents. When a criminal statute does not state the degree of culpability the state must prove, RC 2901.21(B) applies. If the section plainly indicates a purpose to impose strict liability, then culpability is not an issue. When the statute does not specify culpability and does not plainly indicate a purpose to impose strict liability, recklessness is

---

port and maintenance award under RC 3111.17 is function of both mother's needs and father's ability to pay, trial court must award child support from date of child's birth to date of paternity adjudication).

[4]RC 2919.21(B).

[5]State v. Oppenheimer, 46 Ohio App. 2d 241, 75 Ohio Op. 2d 404, 348 N.E.2d 731 (10th Dist. Franklin County 1975).

[6]State v. Oppenheimer, 46 Ohio App. 2d 241, 75 Ohio Op. 2d 404, 348 N.E.2d 731 (10th Dist. Franklin County 1975).

[7]State v. Schaub, 16 Ohio App. 3d 317, 475 N.E.2d 1313 (8th Dist. Cuyahoga County 1984); Tindenberg v. Tinderberg, 1994 WL 477746 (Ohio Ct. App. 5th Dist. Stark County 1994); Vance v. Banks, 94 Ohio App. 3d 475, 640 N.E.2d 1214 (8th Dist. Cuyahoga County 1994).

[8]State v. Jones, 1995 WL 367197 (Ohio Ct. App. 12th Dist. Clermont County 1995).

[9]State v. Jones, 1995 WL 367197 (Ohio Ct. App. 12th Dist. Clermont County 1995).

sufficient culpability. It is the state's burden to prove the defendant acted recklessly.[10]

Nonsupport of dependents is a misdemeanor, fifth degree felony or fourth degree felony, depending on various factors. Pursuant to RC 2929.13(B)(1), the sentencing provisions for fourth or fifth degree felonies require the court to consider community controlled sanctions instead of incarceration unless the court finds the offender is not amenable to available programs, and one of the nine factors listed in the statute applies.

The trial court must follow the sentencing guidelines of RC 2929.11 et seq. in imposing sentence for nonsupport of dependents. When the imposition of any sentence other than imprisonment would be demeaning to the offense, a nine-month prison sentence for the fifth degree felony appropriately balanced the seriousness and recidivism factors.[11] It has also been deemed appropriate to impose restrictions on procreation as a condition of probation in such matters.[12] However, such a restriction is unconstitutionally overbroad if it cannot be lifted once the obligor became curent on the support obligation.[13]

The issuance of an indictment will often result in the sudden liquidation of long-standing child support arrearages. If the case goes to trial, the court has the authority to order restitution as part of an order of probation. However, the court in a criminal case should not refer a defendant to the probation department to have his monthly child support obligation set. That is a function of the support enforcement agency or the domestic relations court, pursuant to RC 3113.21 to former RC 3123.17.[14]

§ 20:72 Criminal nonsupport—Jurisdiction and venue

Jurisdiction of the court for a criminal non-support is present where "the criminal defendant resides because that is where a defendant's failure to perform the required act fairly can be said to occur."[1] The act of failing to provide support occurs in the additional venue of the

---

[10]State v. Collins, 1999 WL 277176 (Ohio Ct. App. 6th Dist. Lucas County 1999), judgment rev'd, 89 Ohio St. 3d 524, 2000-Ohio-231, 733 N.E.2d 1118 (2000).

[11]State v. Hartman, 1999 WL 461750 (Ohio Ct. App. 6th Dist. Wood County 1999).

[12]State v. Talty, 2003-Ohio-3161, 2003 WL 21396835 (Ohio Ct. App. 9th Dist. Medina County 2003), judgment rev'd, 103 Ohio St. 3d 177, 2004-Ohio-4888, 814 N.E.2d 1201 (2004).

[13]State v. Talty, 103 Ohio St. 3d 177, 2004-Ohio-4888, 814 N.E.2d 1201 (2004).

[14]See State v. Lizanich, 93 Ohio App. 3d 706, 639 N.E.2d 855 (10th Dist. Franklin County 1994). Cites former sections RC 3113.21 to RC 3113.219, which were amended and recodified by 2000 S.B. 180, eff. 3-22-01, analogous language RC 3113.21, and RC 3113.219.

[Section 20:72]

[1]State v. Rosenstock, 1995 WL 723535 (Ohio Ct. App. 10th Dist. Franklin County 1995) (abrogated by, State v. Chintalapalli, 88 Ohio St. 3d 43, 2000-Ohio-266, 723 N.E.2d 111 (2000)).

place where the defendant was required to perform a legal obligation.[2]

---

[2]RC 2901.11(A)(4); State v. Chintalapalli, 88 Ohio St. 3d 43, 2000-Ohio-266, 723 N.E.2d 111 (2000); State v. Wood, 2000-Ohio-1641, 2000 WL 140831 (Ohio Ct. App. 3d Dist. Logan County 2000).

Chapter 21

Enforcement of Parenting Time Rights and Allocation of Parental Rights

By Hon. June R. Galvin

> **KeyCite®:** Cases and other legal materials listed in KeyCite Scope can be researched through the KeyCite service on Westlaw®. Use KeyCite to check citations for form, parallel references, prior and later history, and comprehensive citator information, including citations to other decisions and secondary materials.

§ 21:1 Parenting time—In general

Recent trends indicate that one marriage in two is likely to end in divorce. As divorce and dissolution of marriage have become more common, laws have been established to more closely meet the needs of parents and children regarding enforcement of their court orders relating to parenting time and the allocation of parental rights and responsibilities.

Child support enforcement has finally been recognized as such a vital part of the rights of residential parents and minor children that the Ohio Department of Job and Family Services supervises each county's child support enforcement agency (CSEA). The CSEA automatically enforces a support obligation against the non-residential parent.

In contrast, enforcement of parenting time places the full financial burden and initiative to act on the non-residential parent. Two common methods of enforcing parenting time rights have been to seek a modification of parental rights and responsibilities, or to file a motion for contempt. However, legislative changes have codified common sense practices used by Ohio courts into statutory form that should greatly improve the lot of non-residential parents.

§ 21:2 Parenting time—Establishing visitation order

A court in a divorce, dissolution, legal separation, or annulment proceeding "shall make a just and reasonable order or decree" for parenting time at times and upon conditions it decides, unless the court finds it is not in the best interests of the child to do so. The court must make specific findings of facts and conclusions of law if it determines parenting time is not in the child's best interest.[1] In determining parenting time, the court "shall include in its final decree a *specific schedule of parenting time*."[2]

A court may order parents to mediate their differences regarding parenting time and parental rights under mediation procedures

---

[Section 21:2]

[1]RC 3109.051(A).

[2]RC 3109.051(A) (emphasis added).

established by local court rule.[3] If mediation is ordered, the court must consider any mediation report in deciding the issue of parenting time.[4]

A court, in its discretion, may interview a child in chambers regarding the child's wishes and concerns about parenting time. The interview must be conducted in chambers with only the judge, the child, the child's attorney, necessary court personnel, and in the judge's discretion, the attorneys of the parents to be present.[5] No affidavit, written or recorded statement of a child concerning his wishes or concerns shall be obtained, or if obtained, considered by the court.[6]

A court during a divorce, dissolution, legal separation, annulment, or child support proceeding "may grant reasonable companionship or visitation rights . . . if all of the following apply: (a) [t]he grandparent, relative, or other person files a motion with the court seeking companionship or visitation rights. (b) [t]he court determines that the grandparent, relative, or other person has an interest in the welfare of the child. (c) [t]he court determines that the granting of the companionship or visitation rights is in the best interest of the child."[7] After awarding a divorce, dissolution, legal separation, annulment, or child support, the court may award visitation rights to a nonparent as described above if there has been a change in circumstances since the final award.[8]

If parents are unmarried, and one dies, a court may grant parents and other relatives of the deceased parent reasonable companionship or visitation rights upon filing a complaint if it is in the best interests of the child. The remarriage of the surviving parent of the child, or the adoption of the child by the spouse of the surviving parent of the child, does not affect the authority of the court to grant reasonable companionship or visitation rights to a parent or other relative of the child's deceased mother or father.[9]

When a child is born to an unmarried woman, her parents and any of her relatives may file a complaint for reasonable companionship or visitation rights with the child. Likewise, if the father of the child has effected a final acknowledgment pursuant to RC 2151.232, RC 3111.25, or RC 3111.821, or was found to be the father pursuant to an action under Chapter 3111 of the Revised Code, the father, his parents, and his relatives may file a complaint requesting companionship rights. The standard to be applied is the best interest of the child.[10]

Grandparent rights to parenting time were recently addressed in

---

[3]RC 3109.052.

[4]RC 3109.051(C).

[5]RC 3109.051(C).

[6]RC 3109.051(C).

[7]RC 3109.051(B)(1).

[8]RC 3109.051(B)(2).

[9]RC 3109.11.

[10]RC 3109.12(A).

the case of *Troxel v. Granville*,[11] In that case, the parents had two children without benefit of marriage, the father died, and the paternal grandparents petitioned for visitation rights with their grandchildren. There was no prior court involvement before the grandparents filed their petition. The Supreme Court found that Washington Rev. Code section 26.10.160(3) permitting "any person" to petition for visitation rights "at any time" and authorizing state superior courts to grant such rights whenever visitation may serve a child's best interest unconstitutionally infringes on parents' fundamental right to rear their children. It reasoned that the Federal Constitution permits a State to interfere with this right only to prevent harm or potential harm to the child and that this section of Washington's code does not require a threshold showing of harm and sweeps too broadly by permitting any person to petition at any time with the only requirement being that the visitation serve the best interest of the child. The Court reasoned further "so long as a parent adequately cares for his or her children (i.e., is fit), there will normally be no reason for the State to inject itself into the private realm of the family to further question the ability of that parent to make the best decisions concerning the rearing of that parent's children."

The Ohio General Assembly has mandated guidelines establishing orders for parenting time whether under RC 3109.051, RC 3109.11, or RC 3109.12. Those guidelines are as follows:[12]

(1) The prior interaction and interrelationships of the child with his parent, siblings, and other persons related by consanguinity or affinity, and with the person who requested companionship or visitation if that person is not a parent, sibling or relative of the child;

(2) The geographical location of the residence of each parent and the distance between those residences, and if the person requesting companionship or visitation is not a parent, the geographical location of that person's residence and the distance between that person's residence and the child's residence;

(3) The child's and parents' available time, including, but not limited to, each parent's employment schedule, the child's school schedule, and the child's and the parents' holiday and vacation schedule;

(4) The age of the child;

(5) The child's adjustment to home, school, and community;

(6) If the court has interviewed the child in chambers, pursuant to RC 3109.051(C), regarding the wishes and concerns of the child as to parenting time by the parent who is not the residential parent, or companionship or visitation by the grandparent, relative, or other person who requested companionship or

---

[11]Troxel v. Granville, 530 U.S. 57, 120 S. Ct. 2054, 147 L. Ed. 2d 49 (2000).
[12]RC 3109.051(D).

visitation, as to a specific parenting time schedule, or as to the other parenting time matters, the wishes and concerns of the child, as expressed to the court;

(7) The health and safety of the child;

(8) The amount of time that will be available for the child to spend with siblings;

(9) The mental and physical health of all parties;

(10) Each parent's willingness to reschedule missed parenting time rights and to facilitate the other parent's parenting time rights, and with respect to the person who requested companionship or visitation, the willingness of that person to reschedule missed visitation;

(11) In relation to parenting time by a parent, whether either parent previously has been convicted of or pleaded guilty to any criminal offense involving any act that resulted in a child being abused or neglected; whether either parent, in a case in which a child has been adjudicated an abused or a neglected child, previously has been determined to be the perpetrator of the abuse or neglectful act that is the basis of the adjudication; and whether there is reason to believe that either parent has acted in a manner resulting in a child being an abused or neglected child;

(12) Regarding visitation requested by a nonparent, the same considerations as with a parent described in item (11) above, and, in addition, whether there was any conviction or guilty plea under RC 2919.25 involving a family member in the case at bar; whether either parent has been convicted of a violent act involving a family member in the case at bar;

(13) Whether the residential parent or one of the parents subject to a shared parenting decree has continuously and willfully denied the other parent's right to parenting time in accordance with an order of court;

(14) Whether either parent has established a residence or is planning to establish a residence outside this state; and

(15) In relation to requested companionship or visitation by a person other than a parent, the wishes and concerns of the child's parents as expressed by them to the court.

(16) Any other factor in the best interest of the child.

By July 1, 1991, each common pleas court had to adopt by court rule a standard visitation schedule.[13] The guidelines must reserve to the court the right to deviate based on the statutory factors set forth in RC 3109.051(D).

The non-residential parent has the right of access to any record relating to the child, access to a day care center, and access to student activities the other is entitled to, unless not in the child's best

---

[13]RC 3109.051(F)(2).

interests.[14] Record means any record, including those maintained by school, day-care or pre-school, public or nonpublic, hospitals or other medical providers, and any state agency unless confidential.[15]

Another provision requires a residential parent to file a notice of intent to relocate with the court if a parent is changing residences, with certain exceptions.[16] The court may schedule a hearing when it receives the notice to determine if it is necessary to change the visitation order.

§ 21:3   Parenting time—Jurisdiction—In general

Courts with domestic relations jurisdiction have the right to make orders regarding the allocation of parental rights and responsibilities, including parenting time, in proceedings involving divorce, dissolution of marriage, legal separation, annulment,[1] and in parentage proceedings ancillary to divorce, dissolution, or legal separation.[2] In any allocation of parental rights and responsibilities, the court must follow RC 3109.04 to designate the residential parent and legal custodian based on the best interest of the child.[3] The court may also issue a temporary allocation of parental rights and responsibilities, including parenting time, in a domestic violence proceeding if no other court has determined, or is determining, this allocation.[4]

An additional requirement to exercise jurisdiction over parental rights and responsibilities is compliance with the Uniform Child Custody Jurisdiction and Enforcement Act (UCCJEA), set forth in RC 3127.01 to RC 3127.53. The statute was designed to avoid costly and lengthy conflicts between states in establishing and modifying allocations of parental rights and responsibilities, and to prevent forum shopping. In addition to the factual findings required of a court before determining where jurisdiction lies, the UCCJEA requires an affidavit to be filed by each party regarding very specific matters.[5] The affidavit requires a statement as to "whether the party previously has been convicted of or pleaded guilty to any criminal offense involving any act that resulted in a child being an abused child or a neglected child or previously has been determined, in a case in which a child has been adjudicated an abused child or a neglected child, to be the perpetrator of the abusive or neglectful act that was the basis of the

---

[14]RC 3109.051(H)(1), (I), (J).

[15]See RC 3109.051(N)(2).

[16]RC 3109.051(G)(1).

[Section 21:3]

[1]RC 3105.21(A).

[2]RC 3111.06(A).

[3]See also Civ. R. 75(N) relating to temporary orders.

[4]RC 3113.31(E)(1)(d).

[5]RC 3127.23.

adjudication."[6] The information required by RC 3127.23 has been determined to be a mandatory jurisdictional requirement.[7] Attorneys and judges alike must be extremely wary of the consequences if the affidavit is not filed, or not fully completed, prior to the trial of the case or issuance of an order.[8] In juvenile court proceedings, enforcement of the requirement of the parenting affidavit is sometimes less strict. The consequences for counsel or judges may be quite serious if the UCCJEA affidavit is not filed and a parent absconds with a child.

All fifty states had adopted the former UCCJA.[9] An Ohio court has jurisdiction under the UCCJEA in a contempt, visitation, or change of allocation of parental rights and responsibilities matter where the parties previously have entered into a consent order in Ohio, or where Ohio has at least equal family ties as compared to the foreign state and there is available in Ohio substantial evidence concerning the child's care, protection, training, and relationship, even though the children have another home state.[10]

The Parental Kidnapping Prevention Act of 1980 (PKPA) proposes to make the UCCJA applicable in all jurisdictions. Under that act, the term "custody determination" means a judgment, decree, or other order of a court providing for the custody or parenting time of a child, and includes permanent and temporary orders, and initial orders and modifications.[11] Most particularly, the Ohio statute specifies that it applies to "court decisions and court orders" involving allocation of parental rights and responsibilities including "any designation of parenting time rights."[12]

Juvenile courts also award visitation rights pursuant to RC 3109.051 when establishing parentage in compliance with RC Chapter 3111 requirements[13] and in the exercise of its authority as granted by RC 2151.23.

§ 21:4   Parenting time—Jurisdiction—Service of initial documents

The question of service on another party is covered in Civil Rules 4, 5, and 6, and as set out in Civil Rule 75. A court needs to exercise caution, particularly in cases where the other party fails to appear, to

---

[6]RC 3109.27(A)(4).

[7]Pasqualone v. Pasqualone, 63 Ohio St. 2d 96, 17 Ohio Op. 3d 58, 406 N.E.2d 1121 (1980). But see In re Palmer, 12 Ohio St. 3d 194, 465 N.E.2d 1312 (1984); In re Porter, 113 Ohio App. 3d 580, 681 N.E.2d 954 (3d Dist. Marion County 1996).

[8]See Pulliam v. Allen, 466 U.S. 522, 104 S. Ct. 1970, 80 L. Ed. 2d 565 (1984).

[9]See Text Uniform Child Custody Jurisdiction Act; Parental Kidnapping Prevention Act; Uniform Child Custody Jurisdiction and Enforcement Act; International Child Abduction Remedies Act Ch 17.

[10]RC 3127.15; Willis v. Willis, 25 Ohio Misc. 2d 1, 495 N.E.2d 478 (C.P. 1985).

[11]28 U.S.C.A. § 1738A.

[12]RC 3109.21(B).

[13]RC 3111.13(C).

determine that the court has jurisdiction over the minor children prior to deciding issues as to a residential parent, child support, and parenting time. The mere fact of obtaining service, for example, in an uncontested divorce, does not indicate that the other party was ever an Ohio resident, that there are sufficient minimum contacts with Ohio to give the court jurisdiction to issue an "in personam" order,[1] or that the child's home state is Ohio, or that any of the other conditions exist before the court may make an award regarding a minor child.[2] The factual allegations required in divorce pleadings sufficient to award a divorce are often insufficient on their face for the court to determine without further questioning whether jurisdiction attaches for the minor children.

§ 21:5 Parenting time—Jurisdiction—Service after judgment

Civil Rule 75(J) indicates how to obtain service to invoke a court's continuing jurisdiction after that court has entered a judgment. Such service must again be obtained by satisfying Civil Rule 4 to 4.6.

Service is a prerequisite to the attaching of jurisdiction. A court has no jurisdiction to modify a visitation or parenting time decree where a party was not served pursuant to Civil Rule 75(J).[1] Where a father received no notice pursuant to the rules of procedure that the continuing jurisdiction had been invoked to modify his visitation rights, the court of appeals will reverse.[2] A note should be placed in the record on how service was obtained and the date of service prior to the case proceeding on a post-judgment motion.

§ 21:6 Development of statutory requirements

Judges traditionally have relied on their experience in establishing parenting time orders in the average case. They have generally ignored the advice of experts such as Goldstein, Freud, and Solnit, who recommended that "once it is determined who will be the custodial parent, it is that parent, not the court, who must decide under what conditions he or she wishes to raise the child. Thus, the noncustodial parent should have no legally enforceable right to visit the child, and the custodial parent should have the right to decide

---

[Section 21:4]

[1]See Civ. R. 4.3(A)(8). See also Text §§ 27:39 to 27:46, Personal jurisdiction.
[2]See RC 3109.22.

[Section 21:5]

[1]Jenkins v. Jenkins, 1981 WL 2651 (Ohio Ct. App. 4th Dist. Lawrence County 1981).

[2]Harris v. Harris, 1981 WL 2578 (Ohio Ct. App. 2d Dist. Clark County 1981).

whether it is desirable for the child to have such visits."[1] Some judges have assumed that, after divorce, parents could best determine for themselves what was best for their children, and issued standard orders of nonspecific "reasonable visitation and companionship." This left many noncustodial parents negotiating to see their child if the custodial parent did not cooperate. Senate Bill 3[2] initiated the era of "shared parenting," and required specific and standard visitation orders, which may authorize eighty-eight differing visitation schedules.

The Ohio General Assembly has not yet determined what, in its opinion, is in a child's best interests in terms of the amount of time he or she should spend with both parents. That difficult question has been left to the courts on a case by case basis.

Ohio's first cautious and conservative approach to the sensitive issue of post-divorce parenting, called "joint custody," began in March 1984 and generally provided for joint custody only if the parties could agree.[3] In 1990, Senate Bill 3 expanded the concept only slightly, allowing the court to order shared parenting over the objection of one of the parents.[4] The plan for shared parenting must include provisions for the physical living arrangements, child support obligations, medical and dental care, school placement, and the parent with which the children will be physically placed during legal holidays, school holidays, and other days of special importance.[5]

1990 Senate Bill 3 eliminated the age of election, as well as any reference to age in the court determining the wishes of the child. The major statutory change, however, relates to the instruction to the court in allocation of parental rights cases. No longer may the court have total discretion to make a "just and reasonable order" for the parent without custody to visit the children "at the time and under the conditions that the court directs."[6] That short paragraph was replaced by a much more extensive section, RC 3109.051, with very specific instruction to Ohio judges. The Ohio General Assembly set forth its philosophy that "both parents [are] to have frequent and continuing contact with the child, unless frequent and continuing contact by either parent with the child would not be in the best interest of the child."[7]

The clear objective of the General Assembly is to require consider-

---

[Section 21:6]

[1]Joseph Goldstein, et al., *Beyond the Best Interests of the Child*, 38 (Free Press 1973).

[2]1990 S.B. 3, eff. 4-11-91.

[3]Former RC 3109.04(D).

[4]RC 3109.04(A)(2).

[5]RC 3109.04(G).

[6]Former RC 3109.05(B).

[7]RC 3109.051(A).

ation of many factors before making an order in the child's best interests. The order must be specific so that each parent is able to understand and comply with his or her rights and responsibilities. The General Assembly did not, however, address the issue of enforcement by an agency or judicial officer without the parent returning to court. Nor did the General Assembly address the equally vexing issue of a parent who is awarded parenting time rights but either neglects or refuses to comply with that order.

An increasingly important issue in visitation is the matter of grandparents and their desire to be recognized as a specific category of persons entitled by statute to visitation with their grandchildren, separate and apart from other relatives or step-parents. The Ohio General Assembly has responded to the lobbying efforts of grandparents to maintain contact with grandchildren after a divorce by enacting RC 3109.051. While some states permit reasonable visitation rights to grandparents with no prerequisites,[8] some require that there first be a death of a parent, a divorce, or stepparent adoption.[9] Determining the best interest of a child with respect to conflicts between a child's parents is always difficult, and the grandparent issue adds another dimension to this emotionally charged question.

The ability of a court to order mediation[10] for warring parties is an important step, with the potential reward to the parents that they, not the court, not an expert, not a guardian nor other stranger to them or their child, fashion their own visitation arrangement. Even if parents cannot reach a complete resolution, mediation provides a forum to air grievances and a catharsis for the emotions.

The least intrusive method of resolving disputes over visitation is now authorized by the Ohio General Assembly, leaving the courts with the discretion as to how to best enforce visitation rights for the non-residential parent.

While not yet mandatory under Ohio's statutory framework, many domestic relations courts, in cooperation with a local agency, have implemented parent education programs.[11] By local court rule, judges often require divorcing parents to attend class before granting divorces. The programs typically are a minimum of two hours, but may consist of multiple classes over several weeks. The programs educate parents on the legal process, the parent's adjustment to divorce, the emotional and developmental needs of children whose parents are

---

[8]Richard S. Victor, et al., *Statutory Review of Third Party Rights Regarding Custody, Visitation and Support*, 25 Fam. L.Q. 19 (Spring 1991).

[9]See Text Ch 18, Parenting Rights; Richard S. Victor, et al., *Statutory Review of Third Party Rights Regarding Custody, Visitation and Support*, 25 Fam. L.Q. 19 (Spring 1991). Sweeney v. Sweeney, 1994-Ohio-221, 71 Ohio St. 3d 169, 642 N.E.2d 629 (1994) (under RC 3107.15(C), as effective 3-22-01, stepparent adoption forecloses rights of grandparents to obtain court-ordered visitation only if the parent-child relationship had been terminated).

[10]RC 3109.052.

[11]See RC 3109.053, enacted by 1996 H.B. 368, eff. 9-10-96.

going through a divorce, and how to develop better skills for problem solving. Legislation is proposed to make the programs mandatory for all Ohio's divorcing parents.

While research shows mixed results for the parents' future ability to resolve visitation issues as a result of the educational program, one study shows promising results. One program, *Children in the Middle*, "increased client satisfaction and increased awareness of children's needs . . . and in teaching parents the skills they need to adopt new behaviors."[12]

Noting that the most common issue, after child support, for which parents return to court is to request a "change in parenting plan and access problems," the research indicated that a group of parents who had completed the education program within four weeks of filing had a relitigation rate of 12.5%, while those who waited longer than four weeks had a relitigation rate of 60%. This statistic suggests that education programs should be required at the earliest possible point after the plaintiff has filed for divorce.

§ 21:7 Enforcement of parenting time—Comprehensive parenting time order

The most critical step in enforcement of parenting time begins with a comprehensive well-drafted parenting time order whether one parent only is designated as residential parent and legal custodian or parents are awarded shared parenting. The Ohio Revised Code is devoid of requirements to include in parenting time orders or shared parenting plans. Evidently, the Ohio General Assembly expects that the parents, lawyers, and the family law trial courts should determine contents on a case by case basis without standardization. By contrast, the Ohio Revised Code standardized and regulated contents of child support orders. It mandates a comprehensive "to-do" list for *every* (emphasis added) child support order (see RC Chapters 3119, 3121, 3123, and 3125) leaving nothing to chance.

The Revised Code sets forth requirements in the contents of parenting time orders in RC 3119.08:

> Whenever a court issues a child support order, it shall include in the order specific provisions for regular, holiday, vacation, parenting time, and special visitation in accordance with section 3109.052, 3109.11, or 3109.12 of the Revised Code or in accordance with any other applicable section of the Revised Code.

It is unrealistic to expect lay parents weary of lengthy emotional, legal, and financial battles with each other to have the knowledge and the foresight to anticipate appropriate content for parenting time orders. Some courts have adopted minimum parenting time (visitation and companionship) guidelines that are only date and time specific. Some courts supplement specific parenting time orders with solutions

---

[12]Jack Arbuthknot, et al., *Patterns of Relitigation Following Divorce Education*, 35 Fam. & Conciliation L. Rev. (July 1997).

to problems normal to parents who live apart to better inform parents about issues to enable parents to avoid pitfalls and court-based solutions.[1]

Unlike child support, parenting time lost cannot ever be adequately compensated. Orders which are not date and time specific for all exchanges including vacations, and orders which provide no guidelines for issues common to separated parents are bound to create future stress for parent and child, and expensive time-consuming litigation. The expertise of the drafters is essential to deal with predictable child rearing problems and suggest appropriate solutions to avoid parents resorting to self-help, police, attorneys and the courts. This is true whether parents are contentious or agreeable during the course of litigation, whether the parties successfully completed mediation, or participated in parent education courses. Experience in post judgment parenting litigation clearly shows that parents need firm guidance beyond parenting times and dates to successfully implement their order. Experience in family disputes also indicates some parents treat their child as a personal chattel, a bargaining chip, or trump in a card game. That type of parent routinely ignores parenting time orders to settle personal matters with the other parent. Such a parent lacks understanding of children's needs or doesn't care about the terribly harmful effects of his or her behavior. It further indicates that parent's disrespect of the value of on their child's rights to two parents, and failure to understand he or she is teaching their child a lasting lesson about adult dispute resolution techniques.

A basic parenting time order, to minimize disagreements between parents, should minimally include the following:

(1) The detailed rights and responsibilities for each parent, whether or not the residential parent and legal custodian;

(2) A detailed distinguishment between custodial rights and parenting time rights;

(3) Why parents should maintain a regular schedule for themselves and the child, subject to their agreement or unusual circumstances;

(4) The importance of sharing major decisions between parents;

(5) Suggestions for method of and time for parental communication including use of fax machines and e-mail if other methods are unsuccessful or unavailable;

(6) A specific date for parenting time to begin, and the regular schedule, including vacations and holidays and other days of special meaning which must include times, if parents do not otherwise agree (it is critical that summer vacations be date specific as the parties can always agree otherwise);

(7) A parenting time arrangement if the parents live _____

[Section 21:7]

[1]See for example, Text Appendix 21-A.

miles apart which affects the amount of available time and cost of transportation (long distance parenting time plan);

(8) Special problems which may occur over the lifetime of a child;

(9) Potential consequences or prohibitions about the use of alcohol/illegal drugs.

(10) Methods of discipline to be employed by parent/caretaker of the child;

(11) Dealing with a child's illness;

(12) A child's participation in sports or any other potentially hazardous activity;

(13) Methods of dispute resolution other than filing a motion in court.

There are simple effective ways attorneys may assist parents to comply with their court order, the most important being thorough and effective drafting.

Another method to effectuate parenting time is for the attorney to provide an annual calendar[2] at the temporary order or before. A color-coded calendar is a clear visual direction eliminating error and emotional interpretation. It is far more functional than a court order which is highly unlikely to be thoroughly read and retained for future use.

A further aid to parents is for the attorney to reduce the parenting time order to a wallet-sized card[3] for each parent to carry on his or her person.

In cases where one parent claims the other never shows up for companionship, and the other claims that the parent is never home at the time for pick-up, an attorney may provide a parenting log[4]. If both parties comply with the instructions on the log, neither should have any future problems with the other's compliance with a parenting time or shared parenting order. The log is self-authenticating as each parent initials his and her own log each at every exchange of the child, noting the date and time of the exchange. The dates and times are listed pursuant to the court order in the left column.

Today's consumers, when buying any product expect written notice about its correct usage and any safety concerns. When parents divorce or establish parentage, there is no other major source of guidance about parenting after separation other than the attorneys or the courts.

◆ **Practice Tips:** Therefore, an attorney is well advised to provide the parent with the most thorough parenting time order that, in a perfect world, would serve as minimum guide to parents. Providing

---

[2]Text Appendix 21-B. The author gratefully acknowledges the assistance of John Pokorny, of the Cuyahoga County Juvenile Court, for the design and graphics of this calendar.

[3]See Text Appendix 21-C, Figure 2.

[4]Text Appendix 21-C, Figure 1.

a parent with as much useful information as possible in an easy to understand format should significantly reduce stress between parents and post-judgment filings to enforce parenting time rights.

§ 21:8   Enforcement of parenting time—Contempt proceedings in court

The second most effective method of enforcing a parenting time order is the power of the court to enforce through civil contempt. Specifically the threat of incarceration of the residential parent and legal custodian and/or the fear of paying the other parents' attorney fees and court costs for denial of or interfering with the parenting time is a very effective legal remedy.

RC 2705.031(B)(2) expressly authorizes a party to file contempt proceedings for interference with parenting time rights. The statute provides that summons is to issue upon the accused, which summons must include various notices. The notices include consequences of failure to appear, potential penalties as well as right to counsel provisions.[1] The penalties are the same whether the contempt is a failure to comply with a support order or with a parenting time order.[2] One appellate court declined to characterize contempt under RC 2705.031(B)(2) as civil or criminal, as the finding of contempt was justified either by a clear or convincing or beyond a reasonable doubt burden of proof.[3]

Since the court is not available at all hours to either interpret court orders upon request or to enforce orders as needed, the matter of enforcement of parenting time orders has left a gap between what the recipients of these orders want and what is available. Enforcement is complicated, as the parent must file a motion with the court, either by incurring the expense of counsel or by acting pro se, pay court costs, and await both service and a trial date, all the while often having little or no contact with the child. Further, child support in most cases will continue to be deducted from the parent's income which adds to the frustration. It is understandable that so many parents are disillusioned with a legal or judicial process that is expensive in terms of court costs, attorney fees, time off work, loss of income, and the delay in the enforcement of their rights.

The court may award reasonable attorney fees to enforce a court order for parenting time or visitation rights.[4] Where a custodial parent was defiant of the court's order, which necessitated motions to show cause, a hearing and legal expenses to compel compliance, there was no abuse of discretion in including attorney fees as part of the taxable

---

[Section 21:8]

[1]RC 2705.031(C).

[2]RC 2705.05.

[3]Cavaleri v. Cavaleri, 1995 WL 396336 (Ohio Ct. App. 8th Dist. Cuyahoga County 1995).

[4]RC 3109.051(K).

costs.[5] Attorney fees and costs should be awarded under RC 3109.051(K) against a person found in contempt for interfering with companionship or visitation rights.[6] Likewise, fees *may* be awarded within the discretion of the court against one who abuses the court process to deny parenting time.

Enforcement of parenting time rights cases requires significant time and effort on the part of the courts. They frequently involve inter-parental conflict about matters that may or may not have any relevance to a parent-child relationship.

One obligated to pay a sum certain on a date certain should be entitled to parenting time for a specific period of time and on a date certain. Specific parenting time schedules for the majority of the families seen in family court are simply a road map until the road travelled becomes familiar. Specific parenting time schedules for those having minor parenting time disputes provide order in the lives of parents and their children until the problem corrects itself or goes away. A specific parenting time schedule between parents becomes an order which must be complied with under penalty of contempt as a last resort.

While many parents seem to be able to settle for themselves when, where, and how often their children are with each parent, many cannot, and they expect the court to make the decisions. The non-residential parent may claim denial or frustration of the court order; the residential parent may claim that the other parent fails to show up, is inconsistent, or fails to give notice, leaving the children upset, angry, and confused. The Ohio General Assembly has provided no remedy for a residential parent or a child to enforce a court order requiring parenting time by the non-residential parent. Some believe that if the non-residential parent fails to comply with either an agreement or an order for visitation, it would constitute a substantial change of circumstances sufficient to modify an award of child support because the residential parent's expenses for the child's food, transportation, and entertainment will naturally increase. There is an argument that the residential parent is entitled to some freedom from the day-to-day responsibility as a caregiver. However, in *Hamilton v. Hamilton*,[7] the appellate court ruled that the trial court erred in its order forcing a father to exercise his agreed order to have companionship rights with his multi-handicapped daughter, who required twenty-four hour care. The plaintiff was requesting that the defendant care for their child one weekend per month. "On the other hand, visitation is a right or privilege that is normally, but not always,

---

[5]Cavaleri v. Cavaleri, 1995 WL 396336 (Ohio Ct. App. 8th Dist. Cuyahoga County 1995).

[6]Cavagnaro v. Cavagnaro, 1995 WL 375852 (Ohio Ct. App. 12th Dist. Clinton County 1995).

[7]Hamilton v. Hamilton, 107 Ohio App. 3d 132, 138, 667 N.E.2d 1256 (6th Dist. Lucas County 1995).

granted to a non-resident parent. Because it is a right, not a duty, a court cannot force a non-residential parent to visit his or her child."[8]

While the federal government through the office of child support enforcement has provided funding for a variety of research projects relating to child support, there has been little research into the causes of noncompliance with court-ordered visitation. One study, funded by the National Welfare Grants Directorate, Health and Welfare Canada, provides some insight as to why parents drop out of their children's lives. While some have suggested that parents are not interested in custody, the research showed the opposite to be true in the cases where the parent ceased contact. The two most frequent reasons observed for dropping out were:

(1) The adversarial nature of the conflict on the part of counsel limiting communication between the parents; and

(2) Fathers most involved with and attached to their children before divorce are most likely to acutely experience the negative effects of the loss of their children; these fathers had a particularly strong desire to continue to be influential in all aspects of their children's growth and development, values, and life-style which they found difficult to do within the constraints of visiting.

This research questions the appropriateness of sole custody, and indicates that joint custody merits serious consideration.[9]

Once a court has determined that it is in a child's best interests to have parenting time with the non-residential parent, the court is for the most part left to its own ingenuity to resolve the conflict once the non-residential parent seeks to enforce the order. The cases involving enforcement of parenting time are frequently highly emotional, defy simple resolution, and some of the parties are frequenters of the judicial process.

A court has an interest in protecting minor children's best interest and may restrict parenting time to prevent exposure to adulterous situations. Repeated and blatant violations of a no-contact order that prohibited visitation in the presence of non-relative adults of the opposite sex were punishable by a jail sentence, even if it did not afford the contemnor the opportunity to purge.[10]

When uncontroverted evidence indicates that a parent interfered with a visitation order by purposely deceiving the other parent as to a

---

[8]Davis v. Davis, 55 Ohio App. 3d 196, 563 N.E.2d 320 (8th Dist. Cuyahoga County 1988); Bradley v. Bradley, 1995 WL 42405 (Ohio Ct. App. 5th Dist. Stark County 1995).

[9]Kruk, *Psychological and Structural Factors Contributing to the Disengagement of Noncustodial Fathers After Divorce*, 1 Fam. & Conc. Cts. Rev. 98 (January 1992).

[10]Boggs v. Boggs, 118 Ohio App. 3d 293, 692 N.E.2d 674 (5th Dist. Stark County 1997).

child's whereabouts, the trial court erred in finding the interference did not rise to the level of contempt of court.[11]

It is not necessarily a defense to contempt that the non-residential father did not come to the residential mother's house to demand visitation, where the father always called first to confirm visitation. Where he was told by the mother that he could not have visitation, he was not required to perform a "vain and futile" act.[12]

§ 21:9 Enforcement of parenting time—Self-help efforts

The oldest and most common method of enforcement is self-help. Complaints from residential parents would indicate that when negotiation fails, threats, intimidation, and, unfortunately, refusal to return a child after parenting time or taking the child forcefully are not uncommon occurrences.

Probably the most well established method of enforcing parenting time is enlisting the local police to enforce a court order at the time for parenting time to begin. It has the advantage of providing an immediate resolution if the police are sympathetic, the children are willing, and the order is clearly written. It avoids attorneys, court costs, and delay.

Another common self-help method is the refusal of the non-residential parent to make child support payments when denied parenting time. With the passage of a mandatory withholding statute,[1] that self-help method is no longer available to most parents, although the reality is that refusal to pay child support for denial or frustration of parenting time is still occurring. This approach has consistently been held to be contrary to law. In *Flynn v. Flynn*,[2] the court stated, "When a noncustodial parent is denied visitation rights, he shall obtain an appropriate remedy through proper legal channels rather than refusing to make support payments." The court went on to say that visitation and support rights are entitled to separate enforcement.

---

[11]Carpenter v. Jetter, 122 Ohio App. 3d 443, 702 N.E.2d 114 (12th Dist. Clermont County 1997).

[12]Tangeman v. Tangeman, 2000 WL 217284 (Ohio Ct. App. 2d Dist. Greene County 2000).

[Section 21:9]

[1]RC 3105.21(C), RC 3111.13(F)(1).

[2]Flynn v. Flynn, 15 Ohio App. 3d 34, 34-35, 472 N.E.2d 388 (12th Dist. Madison County 1984).

§ 21:10 Enforcement of parenting time—Equitable circumstances

One court found an unusual method of penalizing a non-compliant legal custodian. In *Miller v. Miller*,[1] Ms. Miller, a citizen of Great Britain, returned to her native country after a dissolution of marriage from Mr. Miller. As custodial parent, she took their two children with her. She was awarded child support and Mr. Miller was awarded visitation. Post judgment, the CSEA proceeded on motions to determine arrears against Mr. Miller and he filed motions to suspend, terminate or reduce child support, and cited Ms. Miller for contempt for denial of his rights of visitation. The court affirmed the trial courts' (1) finding of contempt against Ms. Miller; (2) crediting travel expenses incurred for visitation expenses to Great Britain toward child support arrearages; (3) denied repayment on the resulting arrears; (4) finding that Ms. Miller is not in need of financial assistance to rear their children, and suspension of child support until further order of court. The court reasoned that "one who seeks equity must do equity." The opinion is noteworthy in its interpretation of RC 3109.05(D) prohibiting a court from escrowing, impoundment, withholding of any child support payment ordered, because of a denial of or interference with a right of companionship or visitation.

§ 21:11 Enforcement of parenting time—Motion to modify parental rights

For a non-residential parent who has lost patience with the residential parent's frustration of or outright denial of parenting time rights, a more effective method may be filing a motion to change the designation of residential parent. One such case involved allegations of sexual abuse of a child. In *Grant v. Grant*,[1] the appeals court directly addressed the mother's obstruction of the father's visitation rights. The mother was awarded custody of their child, Austin, born in 1981, in the original decree. Three years later, the mother moved to California with Austin without informing the father of the move. The father filed for a change of custody. During the three years of litigation, the mother repeatedly denied visitation, failed to comply with orders for psychological evaluation, and ignored court orders to return the child to Ohio. In 1987, the court awarded temporary custody to the father, and the child was brought back from California. The mother alleged the father sexually abused Austin, but she did not contact child protective services.

Expert testimony was presented by the mother's experts, the

[Section 21:10]

[1]Miller v. Miller, 92 Ohio App. 3d 340, 635 N.E.2d 384 (6th Dist. Erie County 1993).

[Section 21:11]

[1]Grant v. Grant, 1989 WL 80951 (Ohio Ct. App. 6th Dist. Wood County 1989), dismissed, 47 Ohio St. 3d 702, 547 N.E.2d 986 (1989).

father's experts, and a court-appointed psychologist. The court found the mother failed to establish by a preponderance of the evidence that the father sexually abused Austin, and awarded custody to the father. The court did not act punitively but determined that the mother's behavior was endangering the child's mental and emotional development, and emotionally abusing the child. The mother was awarded supervised visitation.

Since *Grant*, the Ohio General Assembly has added "[w]hether the residential parent or one of the parents subject to a shared parenting decree has continuously and willfully denied the other parent his or her right to parenting time in accordance with an order of the court"[2] to the list of factors the court must consider in determining who is to be the residential parent. Where a custodial parent is found to have consistently interfered with parenting time, the court may find that conduct is a sufficient change of circumstances to allow for modification of custody. In *Madden v. Madden*,[3] the mother's extreme hatred for the father, which had a negative effect on the children, justified a change of custody.

In addition to the denial of parenting time being a factor in deciding the best interest of a child, repeated interference constitutes a change of circumstances because it affects the best interests of the child.[4]

Changing custody from the custodial parent to the non-custodial parent may seem to be an extreme consequence of interference with parental times of non-custodial parent, but sometimes it takes draconian measures to stop the violations. The court frequently finds the children are negatively impacted by the ongoing disputes.[5]

§ 21:12 Enforcement of parenting time—Uniform Child Custody Jurisdiction Act

For Ohio residents who have orders emanating from the courts of other states, the method of enforcing those orders may not be through Ohio courts ancillary to an Ohio divorce. In *State ex rel. Adache v. Avellone*,[1] the Eleventh District Court of Appeals granted a writ of prohibition against the trial court to modify a Maryland visitation order. The parties were married in Maryland, the child was born in

---

[2]RC 3109.04(F)(1)(i).

[3]Madden v. Madden, 1996 WL 339941 (Ohio Ct. App. 2d Dist. Montgomery County 1996); see also Thomas v. Freeland, 1997 WL 624331 (Ohio Ct. App. 2d Dist. Greene County 1997).

[4]Valentine v. Valentine, 2005-Ohio-6163, 2005 WL 3096587 (Ohio Ct. App. 12th Dist. Butler County 2005); Mitchell v. Mitchell, 126 Ohio App. 3d 500, 710 N.E.2d 793 (2d Dist. Montgomery County 1998).

[5]Scaffidi v. Scaffidi, 2005-Ohio-4546, 2005 WL 2087795 (Ohio Ct. App. 9th Dist. Medina County 2005).

[Section 21:12]

[1]State, ex rel. Adache, v. Avellone, 70 Ohio App. 3d 521, 591 N.E.2d 420 (11th Dist. Lake County 1991).

Maryland, and the relator and daughter never resided in Ohio. The father filed his divorce action requesting visitation rights with his daughter after the Maryland judgment was issued. The case involved interpretation of the UCCJA, particularly the contention that the child "has significant connection" with Ohio based on the fact that her father resides in this state. The court found that "significant connection" based solely on one parent being a resident of this state would nullify the effect of the UCCJA.

The determination of jurisdiction under the UCCJA is a two-step process. First, the court must determine if Ohio has jurisdiction, and second, the court then determines whether Ohio should exercise that jurisdiction. In *In re Skrha*, the trial court could have exercised jurisdiction, but declined to when it found that Ohio was not the home state of the children, that Alaska, the home state, had substantial evidence concerning the children's present and future care, protection, training, and personal relationships, and that Alaska had already accepted jurisdiction.[2]

§ 21:13   Enforcement of parenting time—UCCJEA

With the enactment of the UCCJEA[1] the enforcement of decrees of other states becomes more specifically effective. The expedited proceeding is intended to restore possession to the legally entitled parent by incorporating the basic features of a habeas corpus procedure, providing for orders of warrants for law enforcement officers to take possession of the child or children,[2] and requiring a prompt hearing, preferably within one day. Habeas hearings, which originally were only to determine who was legally entitled to custody, devolved to permit argument regarding the best interests of a child as would be appropriate in a modification proceeding, and tended to stall the process or even allow time to pass, defeating the overall purpose of a habeas proceeding—immediate action and enforcement.

Following registration pursuant to the requirements of RC 3127.35, with appropriate notice, RC 3127.38 provides expedited hearing on the next judicial day after service of an order to appear.[3] There also is the potential of taking immediate physical custody of the child.[4]

In addition, RC 3127.34(A) purports to provide the court with the power to issue a temporary order enforcing a parenting time or visitation schedule.

---

[2]In re Skrha, 98 Ohio App. 3d 487, 648 N.E.2d 908 (8th Dist. Cuyahoga County 1994).

[Section 21:13]

[1]See Text Ch. 17, Uniform Child Custody Jurisdiction Act; Parental Kidnapping Prevention Act; Uniform Child Custody Jurisdiction and Enforcement Act; International Child Abduction Remedies Act.

[2]RC 3127.41(C) (such a warrant is enforceable throughout the state).

[3]RC 3127.38(C).

[4]RC 3127.38(D).

§ 21:14 Enforcement of parenting time—Interview of child

Another method of enforcing parenting time is requesting the court to interview the child. In *In re Whitaker*,[1] the court held that an *in-camera* interview of a child may be an appropriate method by which the trial court determines the child's best interest in parenting time cases, even if one of the parties objects to such an interview. Arguably, the interview places an undue responsibility on the child, creates conflicting loyalties, and places the child in the middle of adult conflicts. However, a child's point of view is important to the court's determination. Note that in determining parenting time, as differentiated from awarding parental rights, the interview is *discretionary* (emphasis added).[2]

However, in *In re Whitaker*, RC 3109.051(C) specifically authorizes the interview in chambers regarding the child's wishes and concerns about whether to grant visitation rights to a parent, grandparent, relative, or other person. Failure to interview the child when requested by a party to do so is reversible error.[3] The record of the interview, however, is not available to the parents. The interview is confidential.[4]

Even when the children had an attorney and a guardian ad litem representing them, the court committed error in not interviewing the children in a contempt proceeding against their mother. Especially since the children may blame themselves if their mother goes to jail, it is imperative that the court conduct an interview to ascertain the children's view and to explain its ruling on the contempt. While normally the guardian ad litem could fulfill this role, the appellate court in *Schottenstein v. Schottenstein*[5] concluded that the guardian ad litem in the contempt hearing "conducted himself in many ways as if he were a second attorney for the girls' father, cross-examining the mother in very hostile fashion at times."

§ 21:15 Enforcement of parenting time—Defenses—Wishes of child

A common defense to an attempt to enforce a parenting time judgment is that of the child's decision not to visit. A prime concern is that of the child's age.

[Section 21:14]

[1]In re Whitaker, 36 Ohio St. 3d 213, 522 N.E.2d 563 (1988).

[2]RC 3109.051(C). However, in allocating parental rights and regulations, RC 3109.04(B)(1) provides that the court may, and upon the request of either party, shall interview in chambers. RC 3109.051(C) refers to parenting time rights.

[3]Troll v. Troll, 1996 WL 19079 (Ohio Ct. App. 7th Dist. Belmont County 1996).

[4]In Matter of Longwell, 1995 WL 520058 (Ohio Ct. App. 9th Dist. Lorain County 1995); Patton v. Patton, 1995 WL 42497 (Ohio Ct. App. 5th Dist. Licking County 1995), dismissed, appeal not allowed, 72 Ohio St. 3d 1527, 649 N.E.2d 837 (1995); Bell v. Bridges, 2000 WL 977221 (Ohio Ct. App. 5th Dist. Licking County 2000).

[5]Schottenstein v. Schottenstein, 2000 WL 1808327, at *6 (Ohio Ct. App. 10th Dist. Franklin County 2000).

In *Foster v. Foster*,[1] the fifteen-year-old child did not want to visit with her father at any time because of her fear of his violent behavior and bad driving habits. Her mother encouraged the visitation. The child testified of fear of her father. The court refused to find the mother guilty of contempt, finding that all that was required was a bona fide effort to convince the child to visit with the other parent. "She [custodial parent] is not required to force her children to visit with their father when they strongly object to doing so, although defendant [custodial parent] testified she had 'forced them to go on certain occasions.' "[2]

However, with a younger child, the result may be quite the opposite. In Franklin County, eight-year-old and five-year-old children were found required to visit with their father.[3] The mother, who testified she encouraged the children to see their father but that they were reluctant to do so was found guilty of contempt. The court held that

> [i]n the absence of proof showing that visitation with the defendant would cause physical or mental harm to the children or a showing of some justification for preventing visitation, the plaintiff must do more than merely encourage the minor children to visit the defendant. Until the children can affirmatively and independently decide not to have any visitation with the defendant, the plaintiff must follow the court order that she deliver the children to the defendant for purposes of visitation.[4]

In *Canty v. Canty*[5] the custody of the four children was originally divided, with two living with each parent, and all four to be together in the summer, dividing the time between the parents. When the eleven-year-old son in the father's custody refused to go with the mother and his siblings to Tennessee for the second half of summer, the mother filed a contempt motion. The appellate court affirmed the trial court's finding of contempt for the father's failure to compel his son to go and for planning scheduled activities during the mother's time. The court found that the father "at least indirectly, encouraged the boy not to go . . . and nurtured the thought in the boy's mind that

---

[Section 21:15]

[1] Foster v. Foster, 40 Ohio App. 2d 257, 69 Ohio Op. 2d 250, 319 N.E.2d 395 (10th Dist. Franklin County 1974).

[2] Foster v. Foster, 40 Ohio App. 2d 257, 270, 69 Ohio Op. 2d 250, 319 N.E.2d 395 (10th Dist. Franklin County 1974).

[3] Smith v. Smith, 70 Ohio App. 2d 87, 24 Ohio Op. 3d 100, 434 N.E.2d 749 (10th Dist. Franklin County 1980); Newhouse v. Toler, 1997 WL 723385 (Ohio Ct. App. 8th Dist. Cuyahoga County 1997) (in spite of teenage children's expressed unwillingness to visit father, mother found in contempt where there was no legitimate reason for visitation to stop).

[4] Smith v. Smith, 70 Ohio App. 2d 87, 90, 24 Ohio Op. 3d 100, 434 N.E.2d 749 (10th Dist. Franklin County 1980).

[5] Canty v. Canty, 1992 WL 344969 (Ohio Ct. App. 10th Dist. Franklin County 1992).

staying . . . was an acceptable alternative."[6] A trial court did not abuse its discretion in ordering limited supervised visitation, where a father had been in county jail for more than ten months during past three years on contempt charges. The father had also been indicted and convicted of drug abuse, and the child expressed apprehension about visitation.[7]

While recognizing that children as they get older typically have acquired complex schedules and activities as well as friendships and associations that affect the division of their times, the court in *Carver v. Halley*,[8] nevertheless, held that each parent has mutual obligation to ensure that the other parent is afforded the parenting time agreed upon and ordered. Therefore, the trial court's finding of contempt against the mother, who allowed their 10 and 13-year-old to act on their own choice not to be with their father for two days in which he was entitled, was upheld. In addition, an order, compensatory time, attorney fees and costs, and jail time was affirmed.

§ 21:16   Enforcement of parenting time—Defenses—Allegations of abuse

Where a custodial parent's motivation for denial of visitation was based upon a sincere belief that the father had sexually abused the daughter and the custodial parent's actions were designed to protect the child, the court did not find it unreasonable to deny the motion for contempt for denial of visitation filed by the father.[1]

It is within the discretion of the court to decline to issue a contempt citation, notwithstanding uncontroverted evidence that a court order has been violated. Where the custodial parent prevented visitation based upon her "genuinely perceived" threat to her children, such action brought no disrespect to the court nor did it obstruct the court.[2] Thus, the courts appear to be applying a best interests test even with a nonparent and a relative by marriage only. Unsubstantiated allegations of sexual abuse, along with an attempt to poison the relationship between the child and the noncustodial parent, constitute a

---

[6]Canty v. Canty, 1992 WL 344969, at *2 (Ohio Ct. App. 10th Dist. Franklin County 1992).

[7]Kreuzer v. Kreuzer, 1992 WL 171254 (Ohio Ct. App. 2d Dist. Greene County 1992).

[8]Carver v. Halley, 2007-Ohio-2351, 2007 WL 1429628 (Ohio Ct. App. 2d Dist. Greene County 2007).

[Section 21:16]

[1]Clark v. Clark, 1993 WL 119814 (Ohio Ct. App. 12th Dist. Preble County 1993).

[2]Shafer v. Shafer, 1993 WL 524958 (Ohio Ct. App. 4th Dist. Washington County 1993).

change of circumstance that may warrant modification of a prior custody order.[3]

The litigation of sexual abuse as a defense against enforcement of a parenting time order in domestic relations cases has occurred more frequently. Whether fueled by factual events, media exposure of the issue, a parent who is determined to deny the other parent access to a child at all costs, or a creative child who hopes the allegation will limit being with the other parent, the mere allegation of sexual abuse has immediate consequences for the child and the accused, in addition to consuming docket time. Allegations of abuse must be proved to serve as a defense for failure to allow visitation.[4]

In *Mascorro v. Mascorro*[5] the appellate court stated that other courts in Ohio noted that there is a significant percentage of false allegations of sexual abuse in child custody disputes. A reliance on experts is not enough to defeat a contempt of visitation motion against the mother, when the experts were presented with only the mother's view of the situation.[6]

§ 21:17 Enforcement of parenting time—Failure to visit

Ordinarily a court cannot find a parent in contempt for not exercising parenting time, since it is considered a right, not a requirement.[1]

In a case where custody had been granted to the father, the mother's failure to exercise her specific, supervised visits, along with other unfitness finding, resulted in a suspension of the mother's visitation rights.[2]

§ 21:18 Practical methods—Mediation

When a court is faced with a motion over parenting time disputes, it has numerous options available to assist in resolving the dispute. The court has the ability to order the parties who do not agree upon a specific schedule of parenting time to mediation.[1] If mediation is not successful, or the parties are not good candidates, or "[w]hen it is es-

---

[3]Beekman v. Beekman, 96 Ohio App. 3d 783, 645 N.E.2d 1332 (4th Dist. Pike County 1994).

[4]Althaus v. Althaus, 1996 WL 97583 (Ohio Ct. App. 3d Dist. Shelby County 1996).

[5]Mascorro v. Mascorro, 2000 WL 731751 (Ohio Ct. App. 2d Dist. Montgomery County 2000).

[6]Gross v. Gross, 2000 WL 638955 (Ohio Ct. App. 6th Dist. Huron County 2000).

[Section 21:17]

[1]Hamilton v. Hamilton, 107 Ohio App. 3d 132, 667 N.E.2d 1256 (6th Dist. Lucas County 1995).

[2]In re Shackelford, 2005-Ohio-2778, 2005 WL 1322762 (Ohio Ct. App. 3d Dist. Seneca County 2005).

[Section 21:18]

[1]RC 3109.052.

sential to protect the interests of a child," the court may order the appointment of a guardian ad litem, or legal counsel if necessary.[2] The court may also order a psychological examination to include those persons, such as new spouses, to get at the heart of the problem.[3] While there are many approaches to disputes over parenting time, if mediation is not appropriate, the use of experts in finding the problem and recommending solutions appears to be a better solution than litigation, and usually will result in a settled case.

§21:19 Practical methods—Counseling

The court has an additional tool to enforce parenting time by giving explicit authority to order conciliation counseling for the parties, and "if children are involved in the proceeding, the court may order the parties to take part in family counseling during the course of the proceeding or for any reasonable period of time as directed by the court."[1] While RC 3105.091 speaks to actions for "divorce, annulment, or legal separation, and dissolution of marriage," the court may on its own motion order the parties to undergo counseling. The court would also have post-judgment authority to order counseling where appropriate, such as post-divorce adjustment counseling, to help the parties learn to communicate, parent-child counseling where the child and parent are estranged, or in cases of sexual abuse. Some judges believe that the granting of residential parent status or parenting time may be conditioned upon a party entering into and remaining in counseling until released by the counselor for completing the goals of counseling. While a court may order parents to cooperate, the parents' ability to cooperate may be limited by their individual differences which prevent or frustrate parenting time efforts. An order for counseling with a follow-up hearing date in the most difficult cases often resolves the differences between the parties and enables them to get on with the job of parenting.

§21:20 Practical methods—Review hearings

A review hearing of a parenting time order held approximately sixty to ninety days after the divorce is another effective tool for enforcement of parenting time. This hearing sends a signal to the parties that their actions will be monitored by the court, and gives the parties an opportunity to make a bona fide effort to resolve a problem. Often, parenting time problems arising before a divorce frequently disappear completely once the divorce is granted. If the review hearing reveals the problems have either worsened or have not improved, then a guardian ad litem, psychological evaluation, or counseling may be the appropriate solution.

---

[2]Civ. R. 75(B)(2).

[3]RC 3109.04(C); Civ. R. 75(D).

[Section 21:19]

[1]RC 3105.091(A).

§ 21:21   Enforcement problems—In general

While there are many difficult situations posed to a court involving enforcement of parenting time, there are three that require very specific directions for a child's best interests to be served: domestic violence; drug use or alcohol abuse; and chronic lack of communication between the parents.

§ 21:22   Enforcement problems—Domestic violence

One of the more difficult issues is where one parent is in fear of the other as a result of past or current physical violence. During parenting times where parents usually come in contact with each other, the opportunity for violence in front of the children should be minimized by an appropriately drafted order. For example, an order could provide that: "the parent who is not the residential parent is prohibited absolutely from entering upon the property of the residential parent to exchange the children, the residential parent must remain inside the home, and there must be no communication during the exchange of the children. The process of curb-side exchange means the parent who is not the residential parent parks in front of the residential parent's residence, honks the horn to notify the residential parent to send the children to the car. The residential parent shall immediately send the children to the car, making certain the driver is well-known to the children and watch the children enter the car and leave. Upon return after the visitation, the parent who is not the residential parent returns the children at the time for the visitation to end, parks in front of the residential parent's home, honks the horn to signal that the children are returned, watches the children return to the residence, making certain that there is an appropriate person able to care for the children present, unless the parties have agreed otherwise."

In the most extreme scenario, an order for the parties to stay 1,000 feet apart, except for court hearings (if one can see the other, it's a violation), and parenting time is arranged where one parent brings the child to a neutral exchange point leaving the child with a caregiver, and the other parent arrives no more than one-half hour later. Attorneys need to be familiar with local programs available for exchanging children.

§ 21:23   Enforcement problems—Drug use or alcohol abuse

While parents who are alcoholics are not a new issue for family courts, parents who are drug dependent or who have a history of drug use pose a more recent predicament. The court has authority to order a parent drug tested under Civil Rule 75(D). RC 3109.04(C) states "the court may cause an investigation to made as to the character, family relations, . . . and may order the parents . . . to submit to medical, psychological, and psychiatric examinations." A common order restricting parenting time may state that each parent is prohibited from abusing alcohol or using illegal drugs, and being under the influence of alcohol or illegal drugs, during any period of time the parent is with the child.

In more serious cases, further orders may be necessary for parenting time supervised by a parent's relative or friend, including specific orders to the supervisor, such as the child should not be left alone with the parent, the supervisor has the right to refuse parenting time if in their opinion, the parent is under the influence, and the supervisor has the right to terminate the visitation should the other parent become abusive, assaultive, or harass the supervisor or child. The supervisor should always be joined as a party to the action.[1]

In an extreme case, the court may make an order requiring a parent to enter a treatment program and provide proof to the court on completion prior to being awarded unsupervised visitation.

Generally, supervised parenting time in the home of the residential parent should be a last resort. It's not a natural setting for exercise of parenting time for the non-residential parent; the residential parent sometimes resents the obligation and may directly or indirectly impact the quality of the parent-child relationship.

§ 21:24 Enforcement problems—Parents unable to communicate

The parents' inability to communicate over child-related issues is one of the worst case scenarios for a court and a child. Detecting the lack of communication is best done by the court. An appropriate order would be that the parties are prohibited from communicating through the children, and shall communicate, except in emergencies, through a family member or good friend they both have confidence in and who is willing to help the parties adjust. Mediation early in the process, or counseling at any point in time, could be appropriate orders, but should be reviewed in three to six months to determine if the communication is improved.

It is more common to order parents to communicate by fax, which creates a permanent record of their communication, reflects the date and time of transmission, and reveals the tone of the message. Many parents voluntarily opt for e-mail. Unfortunately, neither gets to the heart of their disability.

[Section 21:23]

[1]Hollingsworth v. Hollingsworth, 34 Ohio App. 3d 13, 516 N.E.2d 1250 (10th Dist. Franklin County 1986) (providing that court may add a party to action not originally party to case).

§ 21:25 Enforcement problems—Supervised parenting time order—Form⊙

[Title of Court]

[caption]

Case No. [_____]

JUDGMENT ENTRY TO
APPOINT
SUPERVISOR FOR A MINOR
CHILD

This day this cause came on for hearing on a motion for [_____]
filed by [_____], and upon the evidence.

The Court finds that is necessary to protect the best interests of a
minor child, specifically

NAME   DATE OF BIRTH   AGE
_____   _____   _____

The court finds that supervised parenting time is in the best
interests of a minor child pursuant to the ordered attached hereto and
made a part hereof as if specifically rewritten herein, with the future
times, dates, places of parenting time, and responsibility for
transportation stated therein.

The Court further finds that [_____] is a suitable person, over
eighteen (18) years of age, and not under any disability, to protect the
best interests of said minor child as a supervisor of said parenting
time order which order shall be subject to the further order of the
court.

It is ORDERED, ADJUDGED, and DECREED that [_____] shall
do all of the following in performance of this order of supervision:

1. The supervisor at all dates, times, and places, while supervising,
shall be in the immediate physical presence of the parent being
supervised and the minor child.

2. The supervisor, while supervising, shall closely observe all physical contact between the parent and child, and shall closely observe all
verbal exchange between the parent and child.

3. The supervisor, while supervising, shall prohibit the parent
supervised from being alone out of the immediate presence or out of
the immediate range of hearing of the supervisor.

4. The supervisor, while supervising, shall protect the child from
verbal, emotional, mental, physical abuse and confrontation by the
parent being supervised.

5. The supervisor agreeing to be available for the parenting times,
dates, and places in advance, shall be present for the duration of the
supervision. If an emergency occurs preventing the supervision, the
supervisor shall notify both parents, and reschedule the missed

parenting time. No other person shall be permitted to supervise the child-and-parent parenting time except *[_____]*, the substitute supervisor, who shall comply with all orders herein, and shall enter his/her appearance herein.

6. The supervisor shall notify the Court at [telephone number], [the guardian ad litem], at [telephone number], and the residential parent at [telephone number] of any attempt by the parent being supervised to be alone with the child without supervision, or of any other behavior, actions or words by the parent being supervised that may be or are inappropriate. The supervisor shall have the authority, in such event, to terminate the parenting time with the parent being supervised.

7. The supervisor shall notify the Court and the parties in writing upon desiring to end the responsibility of supervising the Court's parenting time order, and the court shall immediately reschedule this matter to determine an appropriate supervisor without further motion.

8. In signing this order, the supervisor consents to be NAMED A PARTY TO THIS ACTION, AGREES TO COMPLY WITH EACH AND EVERY ORDER HEREIN, WAIVES RECEIPT OF NOTICE OF HEARING AND SERVICE OF SUMMONS, and ACKNOWLEDGES KNOWLEDGE OF THE ACTIONS THAT LED TO THE ORDER OF SUPERVISED VISITATION.

[_____][name and address of residential parent]
[_____][name and address of non-residential parent]
[_____][name and address of guardian ad litem]
[_____][name and address of Supervisor]
[_____][name and address of Substitute Supervisor]

_____
Judge

§ 21:26 Civil sanctions

Under URESA and former RC 3115.21(B) an Ohio court was permitted to impound funds that were paid to the court by the obligor in accordance with the support order upon proof that the obligor had been continuously deprived of a right of visitation. Concomitantly, under former RC 3115.21(C) the court was permitted to suspend the obligor's right of visitation if the obligor willfully failed to provide support. The potential sanction of impoundment of support was repealed in 1987[1]

_____

[Section 21:26]
[1]Sub H.B. 231, eff. 10-5-87.

although the power of the court in a URESA proceeding to suspend visitation was not eliminated by the legislature until 1998.[2]

The Ohio General Assembly has eliminated the court's discretion to impound, escrow, or withhold a child support order as a sanction for denial of parenting time rights.[3] Prior to 1971, there was authority for the modification of child support where visitation was being denied. At one time former RC 3109.05(B) after permitting visitation, also provided for enforcement, authorizing modification where there was proof of continuous or repeated influence with court ordered visitation.[4] There is no authority for the suspension of a support order because of the denial or interference with visitation rights.

Current law equalized the penalties for civil contempt of court for failure to pay support and "failure to comply with, or an interference with, a parenting time order."[5] Summons for civil contempt must be in accordance with the statute. Penalties found in RC 2705.05 provide for a first offense a fine of no more than $250, and imprisonment for no more than thirty days, or both; for a second offense, a fine of no more than $500, and imprisonment of no more than sixty days, or both; for a third or subsequent offense, a fine of no more than $1,000 and imprisonment of no more than ninety days, or both.

The statutory monetary sanctions found in RC 2705.05(A) are not a limitation on the trial court's power to punish contempt. The General Assembly has prescribed procedures for judicial determination of indirect contempt and has outlined penalties, which the trial court has a duty to follow. However, the trial court may exercise its discretion to impose any sanction that is reasonable, including a fine of $1,000.00 for a first offense.[6]

The statute provides a further sanction, in addition to a jail sentence and a fine, for payment of "all court costs and reasonable attorney fees to the adverse party" if a person is found in contempt of court for failing to comply with or interfering with any award of parenting time.[7]

RC 3109.051(K) provides in pertinent part:

If any person is found in contempt of court for failing to comply with or interfering with any order or decree granting companionship or parenting time issued pursuant to this section, section 3109.11 or 3109.12 of the Revised Code, or any other provision of the Revised Code, the court that makes the finding, in addition to any other penalty or remedy imposed, shall assess all court costs arising out of the contempt

---

[2]1997 H.B. 352, eff 1-1-98.

[3]RC 3109.05(D), RC 3119.09.

[4]See also Porter v. Porter, 25 Ohio St. 2d 123, 54 Ohio Op. 2d 260, 267 N.E.2d 299 (1971).

[5]RC 2705.031.

[6]Caldwell v Caldwell, 2003-Ohio-1752, 2003 WL 1795247 (Ohio Ct. App 4th Dist. Gallia County 2003).

[7]RC 3109.051(K).

proceeding against the person and require the person to pay any reasonable attorney's fees of any adverse party, as determined by the court, that arose in relation to the act of contempt.

When considering the question of whether to award reasonable attorney fees in post divorce cases the court must consider:

(1) the earning capacity of the parties;

(2) the time and labor required on the part of the attorney;

(3) the fee customarily charged in the locality for similar legal services;

(4) the experience, reputation, and ability of the attorney performing the services; and

(5) the amount involved and the result obtained.[8]

The final sanction authorized is for an award of compensatory parenting time if in the best interest of the child.[9] The court may not modify an existing order of visitation when the motion is for contempt.[10]

The civil sanction, contempt of court, is often confused by the public with criminal contempt, civil contempt being an act of coercion, and criminal contempt being an act of punishment. In *Tucker v. Tucker*,[11] the court held that criminal contempt may be defined as an offense against the dignity or process of the court, where the primary purpose of punishment imposed upon the contemnor is to vindicate the authority of the court. The court further found a civil contempt order suspending punishment on condition that the contemnor comply in the future with the terms of a preexisting child support order does not properly allow for purging.

§ 21:27 Civil sanctions—Damages

An inventive approach to enforcement of parenting time rights is seeking civil damages against a family member who participated in secreting a minor child. In *Giambrone v. Berger*,[1] the father was awarded temporary custody after a dispute over the jurisdiction being in New York or Ohio, with the proviso that the mother was awarded visitation rights. The wife was helped by members of her family in defying the New York order, and the husband filed suit against the

---

[8]Moross v. Scott, 1985 WL 7055 (Ohio Ct. App. 6th Dist. Lucas County 1985), citing Swanson v. Swanson, 48 Ohio App. 2d 85, 2 Ohio Op. 3d 65, 355 N.E.2d 894 (8th Dist. Cuyahoga County 1976) and Cohen v. Cohen, 8 Ohio App. 3d 109, 456 N.E.2d 581 (11th Dist. Lake County 1983).

[9]RC 3109.051(K).

[10]Andrulis v. Andrulis, 26 Ohio App. 3d 164, 498 N.E.2d 1380 (9th Dist. Summit County 1985).

[11]Tucker v. Tucker, 10 Ohio App. 3d 251, 461 N.E.2d 1337 (10th Dist. Franklin County 1983).

[Section 21:27]

[1]Giambrone v. Berger, 57 Ohio App. 3d 38, 566 N.E.2d 711 (1st Dist. Hamilton County 1989), cause dismissed, 57 Ohio St. 3d 601, 564 N.E.2d 700 (1991).

family member for interference with custody under RC 2307.50, which provides a civil action for a violation of RC 2919.23, which prohibits interference with custody.

RC 2307.50, effective since 1985, provides a civil action for depriving an adult of "parental or guardianship interest" in a minor. This section defines "parental or guardianship interest" as being rights as residential parent and legal custodian, or right of access or custody, and provides for:

(1) full compensatory damages, including, but not limited to, damages for loss of society of the minor, and, if applicable, for loss of minor's services, and damages for expenses incurred by the plaintiff in locating or recovering the minor;

(2) punitive damages;

(3) reasonable attorney fees; and

(4) costs of bringing the civil action.

The statute, however, does not create a civil action for one parent against the other parent who commits a child stealing crime against his own child.[2]

The court in *Giambrone* found that it is not required that the defendant be convicted of or plead guilty to a child stealing crime for the plaintiff to obtain relief, as long as the trier of fact determines that the defendant committed a child stealing crime.

§ 21:28   Civil sanctions—Federal

Often the question of proper jurisdiction arises in a case where one or more defendants are involved. For instance, conflict of law situations are created when the non-residential parent abducts the child and crosses state lines or national borders. If the child, the abductor, and the residential parent are all in the same state, and the wrongful taking originated in that state, the problem is minimized. However, if several states are involved, with conspiratorial defendants being residents of a state other than that of the plaintiffs, the court will have more difficulty determining which state has jurisdiction.[1]

The federal courts were reluctant to serve as an alternative forum, until statutory changes were adopted to assist a party in wrongful taking cases. In *Wasserman v. Wasserman,*[2] the parents were divorced in the state of Maryland, with the court awarding custody of their four children to the wife. The husband removed three of the four children to another state, concealing their location from the wife. She filed an action claiming diversity of citizenship, charging the father

---

[2]RC 2307.50(D).

[Section 21:28]

[1]See Text Uniform Child Custody Jurisdiction Act; Parental Kidnapping Prevention Act; Uniform Child Custody Jurisdiction and Enforcement Act; International Child Abduction Remedies Act Ch 17.

[2]Wasserman v. Wasserman, 671 F.2d 832 (4th Cir. 1982).

and others with child enticement, intentional infliction of emotional distress, and civil conspiracy. The trial court dismissed the actions. On appeal, the court reversed and remanded. The court held it was not being requested to rule on the award of custody, but to rule on whether torts were committed, finding that torts such as child enticement or intentional infliction of emotional distress are not limited to family relationships.

§ 21:29 Criminal sanctions

After the repeal of RC 2905.04,[1] RC 2919.23 is the only criminal statute applicable to interference with custody. The offense is committed when a person, knowing he is without privilege to do so, or being reckless in that regard, entices, takes, keeps or harbors from a parent, guardian, or custodian:

(1) A child under eighteen or a mentally or physically handicapped child under twenty-one. It is an affirmative defense to this enticing or taking that the person who takes the child reasonably believed that his conduct was necessary to preserve the child's health or safety. It is an affirmative defense to a charge of keeping or harboring that the person who takes the child in good faith gave notice to law enforcement or judicial authorities within a reasonable time after the child or committed person came under his shelter, protection or influence;

(2) A person committed by law as delinquent, unruly, neglected, abused, or dependent child to an institution; or

(3) A person committed by law to an institution for the mentally ill or mentally retarded.

With the advent of domestic violence legislation, a natural issue with a victim of domestic violence taking a child to a shelter for safekeeping is whether the shelter must be found guilty of harboring a child in violation of the criminal code as a prerequisite to entitling the other parent to damages under the civil code section relating to depriving an adult of a parental or guardianship interest in a minor. Citing RC 3109.03 which provides that parents stand upon an equality as to the care, custody, and control of their children, that parents have equal rights to custody, it was the decision of the Tenth District Court of Appeals in *Waliser v. Tada*,[2] that the legislature in enacting RC 2919.23 did not intend to make the taking of a child by one parent without the permission of the other when both have equal custody rights a criminal act. The court stated the proper remedy is obtaining a custody order. Ms. Tada had removed their child and gone to a domestic violence shelter. The shelter does not broadcast its address or confirm nor deny the presence of anyone within the shelter. Mr.

[Section 21:29]

[1]RC 2905.04, repealed by 1995 S.B. 2, eff. 7-1-96.

[2]Waliser v. Tada, 1990 WL 20080 (Ohio Ct. App. 10th Dist. Franklin County 1990), cause dismissed, 61 Ohio St. 3d 1405, 573 N.E.2d 1097 (1991).

Walisa visited the shelter and was unable to determine if his child was there. Ms. Tada left for California with their son. Mr. Walisa filed a civil suit under RC 2307.50, complaining of negligent infliction of emotional distress and intentional infliction of emotional distress against the shelter and Ms. Tada. The shelter did not violate the criminal section since both parents have equal custody rights.[3]

The affirmative defenses set forth in the criminal statute can negatively affect the ability of the state to protect children from acts by one parent to deprive the other parent of possession. Experience indicates that a parent seldom acts without some element of the child's best interests in mind, even when the parent takes a child without the permission of the other. Fear of a child being removed from the state or community, fear that the child is being abused physically or sexually, and fear that a child is being neglected are some reasons for the act of removing a child from another parent. The practical effectiveness of the criminal sanctions in the enforcement of visitation rights is questionable, given the defenses.

§ 21:30 Effect of inability to pay support on parenting time

While it may be tempting for a court to limit parenting time rights, while trying to enforce a support obligation against a repeatedly noncomplying obligor, where circumstances indicate an inability on the part of the non-residential parent to pay child support, such parent cannot be deprived of his right of visitation solely by reason of his inability to pay. In *Johnson v. Johnson*,[1] Mr. Johnson was found in contempt on support payments, a suspended jail sentence was imposed, he was ordered to pay $1,959 in back support, and some of his personal property was ordered to be sold to pay the support. On appeal, the court stated, "The vast majority of reported decisions find disfavor with the theory and practice of conditioning visitation on child support."[2]

Interpreting RC 3109.05, the then-existing visitation statute, the court went on to say

> [w]e cannot withhold this right [visitation] simply because the noncustodial parent has not complied with a monetary order of the court. Society holds few favors as precious as the opportunity for a parent to show his care and affection for his child. . . . the right of visitation, of course, should be denied if, in the opinion of the court, the exercise of that right

---

[3]Waliser v. Tada, 1990 WL 20080 (Ohio Ct. App. 10th Dist. Franklin County 1990), cause dismissed, 61 Ohio St. 3d 1405, 573 N.E.2d 1097 (1991).

[Section 21:30]

[1]Johnson v. Johnson, 52 Ohio App. 2d 180, 6 Ohio Op. 3d 170, 368 N.E.2d 1273 (9th Dist. Summit County 1977).

[2]Johnson v. Johnson, 52 Ohio App. 2d 180, 181, 6 Ohio Op. 3d 170, 368 N.E.2d 1273 (9th Dist. Summit County 1977); Leasure v. Leasure, 1998 WL 108137 (Ohio Ct. App. 8th Dist. Cuyahoga County 1998) (trial court cannot suspend visitation conditioned upon payment of child support arrearages).

is harmful to the child. However, if that right is granted on other grounds, then that opportunity for a proper and lasting association between father and child should not be denied simply because support orders in a divorce case are not complied with.[3]

§ 21:31 Custody to non-parent

As required by RC 3109.03, "[w]hen a husband and wife are living separate and apart from each other, or are divorced, and the questions as to the parental rights and responsibilities for the care of their children and the place of residence and legal custodian of their children is brought before a court of competent jurisdiction, they shall stand upon an equality as to the parental rights and responsibilities for the care of their children . . . "

If a court finds that it is in the best interest of a minor child for neither parent to be designated the residential parent and legal custodian, it may commit the child to a relative, or certify a copy of its finding to the juvenile court.

The juvenile court must consent to accept a case involving a minor if the court finds the parents unsuitable to have parental rights and responsibilities for the child's care and unsuitable to provide the place of residence and to be the legal custodian of the child.[1]

§ 21:32 Parental Kidnapping Prevention Act

In a study sponsored by the US Department of Justice, it was estimated that 354,100 children were abducted by a family member during 1988.[1] Prior to Congressional action in enacting the Parental Kidnapping Prevention Act of 1980 (PKPA),[2] the incidence of child snatching by a family member trying to forum-shop for a favorable custody ruling eventually led to a US Supreme Court decision, *May v. Anderson*,[3] dealing with jurisdiction to award custody between two states. Following *May*, the Uniform Laws Commission created the UCCJA to develop a uniform state approach. The final legislative effort was the PKPA in 1980, to promote cooperation between states, to promote the exchange of information, facilitate enforcement of custody and visitation decrees, to discourage controversies over custody, and to avoid jurisdictional competition.

---

[3]Johnson v. Johnson, 52 Ohio App. 2d 180, 182-83, 6 Ohio Op. 3d 170, 368 N.E.2d 1273 (9th Dist. Summit County 1977) (appellate court denied visitation on grounds other than support).

[Section 21:31]

[1]RC 3109.06.

[Section 21:32]

[1]Andrea S. Charlow, *Jurisdictional Gerrymandering and the Parental Kidnapping Prevention Act*, 25 Fam. L.Q. 299 (Fall 1991).

[2]28 U.S.C.A. § 1738A. See also Text Ch 17, Uniform Child Custody Jurisdiction Act; Parental Kidnapping Prevention Act; Uniform Child Custody Jurisdiction and Enforcement Act; International Child Abduction Remedies Act.

[3]May v. Anderson, 345 U.S. 528, 73 S. Ct. 840, 97 L. Ed. 1221, 67 Ohio L. Abs. 468 (1953).

It does not appear that the UCCJA nor the PKPA remedies have been fully successful in their purpose of avoiding jurisdictional disputes, preventing parental kidnapping, and reducing expensive and extensive litigation.

§ 21:33 Habeas corpus

The original authority in Ohio for habeas corpus is the Ohio Constitution, Article IV § 2 which invests the Ohio Supreme Court with original jurisdiction in habeas corpus; and in Article IV, § 3, which gives courts of appeals original jurisdiction in habeas corpus. In addition to these courts, the common pleas courts and probate courts may hear and decide an action in habeas corpus.[1]

However, it is the juvenile court that has exclusive original jurisdiction to hear and determine any application for a writ of habeas corpus involving the custody of a minor child.[2] Nonetheless, despite the legislative directive providing the juvenile court as the jurisdictional home of habeas corpus in child custody proceedings, a litigant retains the right to file an action in accord with the Ohio constitutional provision with the court of appeals.[3]

Habeas corpus is a seldom used method of seeking an award of child custody, probably due to the conditions that must be met before a court will grant the relief requested. Habeas corpus is an extraordinary remedy and, as with every extraordinary remedy, it is not available as a means of relief when there is an adequate remedy in the ordinary course of the law.[4] Habeas corpus may not be used as a substitute for appeal nor may it be used where an adequate statutory remedy for review of the questions presented exists.[5]

In *Hughes v. Scaffide*,[6] when a father provided no support for nine years for a child, leaving all parental duties to be supplied by maternal grandparents, the court found that he had abandoned the child after fathering him out-of-wedlock, even though he had married the mother, and a writ of habeas corpus was denied as the child was always reared by the maternal grandparents.

On the same day that *Hughes* was decided, the Supreme Court, under slightly different facts, came to the same conclusion. A mother left the two-year-old child with the stepfather who supported the child. The mother visited infrequently for seven years, then began regular visitation, and sought return of the child, filing for a writ of

---

[Section 21:33]

[1] RC 2725.02.

[2] RC 2151.23(A)(3).

[3] In re Black, 36 Ohio St. 2d 124, 65 Ohio Op. 2d 308, 304 N.E.2d 394 (1973).

[4] In re Piazza, 7 Ohio St. 2d 102, 36 Ohio Op. 2d 84, 218 N.E.2d 459 (1966).

[5] In re Piazza, 7 Ohio St. 2d 102, 36 Ohio Op. 2d 84, 218 N.E.2d 459 (1966).

[6] Hughes v. Scaffide, 58 Ohio St. 2d 88, 12 Ohio Op. 3d 92, 388 N.E.2d 1233 (1979).

habeas corpus because she had an order of custody from her first marriage. The court denied the writ and was affirmed.[7] Thus, the courts appear to be applying a best interests test even with a nonparent and a relative by marriage only.

Regardless of the judicial forum chosen by the applicant, the burden is on the applicant to establish that he or she is legally entitled to have custody and that it in the best interest of the child to be in the custody of the applicant. The burden of proof is by preponderance of the evidence.[8]

With the enactment of the UCCJEA[9] parties will not be entitled to habeas corpus proceedings to enforce parental rights since they have an adequate legal remedy under RC 3127.31 to RC 3127.47 which provides a mechanism for regulating and enforcing parenting rights issued by another state.[10]

§ 21:34 Technology and parenting time

In the legal profession, we tend to see parenting time cases that are problematic. We may not have experience with successful parenting techniques. With the explosion of communications technology, we need to be aware of new ways for parent and child or parent and parent to communicate when they live apart, sometimes referred to as "virtual parenting."

In the article on "Top Tips for Long Distance Parenting," author Pamela Payne[1] makes a series of recommendations for parents:

- use the Internet for communication (cost estimated initially at $1,000);
- use Web cams to allow parent and child to have face to face conversations (cost estimated for about $100 for each computer);
- purchasing digital cameras to allow parent and child to exchange photos (cost estimated at $300);
- using cell phones with long distance carriers providing unlimited night and weekend rates.

Given the common usage of telephone answering devices and voice mail, parental personal communications (especially those who will not or cannot communicate) in separated busy families suffers even further. Fortunately, the availability and the affordability of fax machines can provide some assistance in communicating. Faxes tend

---

[7]In re Young, 58 Ohio St. 2d 90, 12 Ohio Op. 3d 93, 388 N.E.2d 1235 (1979).

[8]In re Perales, 52 Ohio St. 2d 89, 6 Ohio Op. 3d 293, 369 N.E.2d 1047 (1977).

[9]2004 Sub S.B. 185, eff. 4-11-05.

[10]Harris v. Harris, 2005-Ohio-3457, 2005 WL 1579462 (Ohio Ct. App. 4th Dist. Hocking County 2005).

[Section 21:34]

[1]Pamela Payne, *Building a Bridge: A Divorced Parent's Guide to Long-Distance Loving*; see www.longdistancefamilies.com to obtain copies of the cited material. The author makes no assertion regarding the remaining contents of this website.

to receive higher priority than returning phone calls in the scheme of things. Faxes can be used to verify or modify time and date for parenting time, notice of changes in plans during parenting time requiring changes in needed clothing, notice of a child's illness or conditions which require attention during parenting times, providing activity information, grade cards, medical bills, a change of phone number, employment, etc. The benefits are instant delivery, and proof of time, content, and delivery of the message. Given the amount of litigation over access to a child's school and medical records, attorneys are well advised to consider the many uses that fax communication may benefit the parents and the child in drafting parenting time and shared parenting plans.

§ 21:35   Research on post-divorce family

Judith Wallerstein in her book, *Second Chances*, chronicled lives of children and parents in California after divorce. Her findings concluded that "These families . . . need help in making decisions about living arrangements, visiting schedules, and sole or joint custody. And they need help in implementing these decisions over many years—and in modifying them as the children grow and the family changes."[1]

Another survey of California families indicated

Generally, parents reported lower conflict in families where the children spend significant amounts of time with both parents than in families in which the father has more limited contact. Also, both mothers and father view de facto joint physical custody fathers as more involved in a range of activities with children than de facto non-residential fathers. . . . These findings suggest that, in de facto joint physical custody families, the level of each parent's perceived involvement with the children and satisfaction with parenting may be more equal than in primary physical custody families (although, neither parent may be as satisfied as they would be with primary physical custody).[2]

While research results cannot be a basis for decisions in individual cases as each family is different, it does form a basis for the development of and the foundation for specific visitation schedules in the first step in enforcement of visitation if that schedule provides considerable contact with each parent. Once again, the courts determine on a case by case basis how much time is in the child's best interests to spend with each parent.

Unfortunately, no panacea has emerged from either the mental health community, the Ohio General Assembly, the courts, or the legal community to alleviate the problems of enforcing parenting time rights.

[Section 21:35]

[1]Judith S. Wallerstein & Sandra Blakeslee, *Second Chances, Men, Women and Children a Decade after Divorce* (Ticknor & Fields 1989).

[2]Little, *The Impact of the Custody Plan on the Family: A Five-Year Follow-up*, 30 Fam. & Conc. Cts. Rev. 248 (April 1992).

APPENDIX 21-A
Standard Companionship Schedule

EXHIBIT "A " - Standard Companionship Schedule

I.   ORIENTATION

to Allocation of Parental Rights and Responsibilities for the Care of Children [R.C. 3109.04(A-G)], and Companionship or Parenting Time [R.C. 3109.051(D)(1)]

When parents give birth to or adopt a child, the mother and the father assume long term legal and moral obligations to the child and to each other whether or not the parents were married or lived together. From birth until adulthood, a child is physically helpless and completely dependent on both father and mother for survival and emotional growth. Most parents are also dependent on each other to share the child-rearing burden whether they live together or not.

Society's moral code imposes obligations on both parents to provide for a child's physical and emotional needs such as feeding, clothing, sheltering, providing medical attention, educating, guidance, nurturing, protecting, keeping a child safe from harm, providing a philosophical or religious base, and teaching a child to respect both his or her parents. A parent is not excused from his or her moral responsibilities because the parents never married or are no longer married, one parent loves another person, because the child has a parental-like relationship with another man or woman, because one parent assumed more duties to a child, because the parents married, divorced, and only one is awarded custody, because the public (welfare) supports a child, because the child is born from a casual encounter between parents, because one parent is or was unhappy about the pregnancy, because one parent has responsibilities to another child, because a parent (or his or her spouse) dislikes, is indifferent to, or hates the other parent, or because a Court has issued an order. _The Court expects parents to put their children first over personal problems between them and their child by not relating any differences between the parents. The Court expects parents to take appropriate steps to settle their differences peacefully outside the child's presence. The Court expects parents not to let any other person or relative interfere with the parent-child relationship._

To answer the daily demands of taking care of a child, each parent should ideally be able to count on emotional support from the other. Without it, one parent can become overwhelmed and be incapable of parenting to the best of his or her ability.

Ohio's laws impose obligations on both parents when either files a complaint to determine parentage of a child, for legal separation, custody, or divorce. The law requires a Court to (1) determine what is in the "best interests of the child" based on the evidence supplied by parents, (2) designate one or both parents as residential parent(s) and legal custodian(s) (subject to exceptions), (3) determine the times and events that the parent who is not designated the residential parent and legal custodian shall be awarded with their son or daughter, (4) calculate child support based on each parent's earning ability, (5) issue a child support order, (6) order a parent to, provide health insurance if available at a reasonable cost, and (7) determine division of and a procedure for payment of the child's future medical expenses.

In designating one parent as residential parent and legal custodian, the Court is not punishing nor rewarding either parent, or is the Court forcing a child to choose between parents. The Court is not deciding that a child loves one parent more than the other or that one parent is fit and one is not.

The State's purpose in mandating that courts designate one parent to the apparent exclusion of the other parent is _only_ to protect the best interest of the child by promoting important State interests. A major interest is the State could not timely and expeditiously hear and decide all the disputes that many separated parents have day-to-day about child rearing if both parents legally shared all decision making. If parents can't agree on meeting a child's needs (ie. food, housing, education, medical treatment, prescriptions), and each parent has equal authority to make decisions, the result could be parental gridlock, the child's needs may go wanting, and courts could be overloaded. Other examples of State interest are as follows: the State of Ohio must determine which parent to hold responsible for failing, refusing or neglecting to feed, clothe, and shelter the child, require the child to attend school, provide all necessary medical and related treatment, and for liability for a child's destructive acts or theft. Additionally, a doctor and other *related personnel must know which parent may authorize medical treatment; school and child care providers must know which parent may enroll a child; the State must know which parent can receive welfare or Social Security benefits.* **The Court expects that parents will cooperate with each other and act in the best interest of their child.**

II.   QUESTIONS AND ANSWERS
WHAT DOES BEING DESIGNATED THE "RESIDENTIAL PARENT AND LEGAL CUSTODIAN" MEAN?

The residential parent and legal custodian has the rights, responsibilities, and obligation to do all of the following:

1. To actively promote, encourage, and nurture the child to respect and love the other parent, and the other parent's family (even if the parents do not get along); and

2. To have possession of their child only on days and times not awarded to the non-residential parent as set forth in the Judgment Entry and this schedule **or as the parties agree**, free of any interference by the non-residential parent or any other person, and

3. To have the non-residential parent take their child to the non-residential parent's residence and timely return their child to the residential parent and legal custodian's residence at such days and times set forth in the Judgment Entry and this schedule, **or as the parties agree**, together with all clothing and child's possessions provided for the companionship period, **and the residential parent and legal custodian may be sentenced to jail and/or fined, and required to pay the non-residential parent's attorney fees and court costs, among other legal remedies, if (s)he fails, refuses or neglects to comply with the Court order for parenting time and companionship**; and

4. To have the non-residential parent prepare their child physically and emotionally for returning to the residential parent at the end of each companionship time; and

5. To have the right to consult with the non-residential parent on matters involving their child so that both parents have knowledge of their child's needs and make their best effort to agree about their child's education, maintaining and treating their child's physical and emotional health, form a united front on matters of moral training and consistent appropriate discipline, determine their child's religion, moral training, and standard of conduct, agree on safety matters such as sports and/or activities either parent may consider risky, and on other important matters, free of interference from any new spouse, "significant other," or any other person; and

6. To the regular receipt of child support from the non-residential parent to whom the residential parent shall supply such additional monies required by the Ohio Child Support Guideline and in the Judgment Entry to pay **all** their child's financial and (extraordinary) medical needs, including, but not limited to, child care for employment or training purposes, groceries, restaurant, school lunches, housing, home maintenance and insurance, heat, electric, water and telephone service, transportation expenses, car insurance, gasoline, maintenance, clothing, social activities, sports participation, life or personal property insurance, entertainment, lessons, sports, clubs, educational expenses such as tuition, tutors, school supplies and programs, activities, fees and books, personal grooming, allowance to their child, vacation, and furniture, furnishings and appliances, out-of-pocket medical, dental, surgical, hospital, or optical, psychological, psychiatric, counseling and prescription expense, directly to their providers of services; and

7. To establish their child's standard of living and house rules in her or his own home; and

8. To determine their child's activities not in conflict with their child's education, energy or time with the non-residential parent **without the express agreement** of the non-residential parent; and

9. To make final decisions about all matters for their child, including but not limited to their child's medical, dental,

surgical, hospital, optical, psychological, psychiatric, counseling and prescription needs (the non-residential parent **must** administer prescriptions and/or medical treatments exactly as directed by their child's physician during companionship, or risk having the companionship schedule changed); to set standards for their child's behavior, set discipline standards that are not child abuse; enroll their child in day care, pre-school, school, whether public or private, religious or secular; to determine their child's religious affiliation and moral training; to set their child's standard for grooming, body piercing or adornment, and dressing, to take whatever steps are necessary to provide access to school and child care provider facility and records, and medical and related records. The non-residential parent may make emergency medical and related treatment decisions for their child which arise during companionship periods provided that communication is attempted to reach the residential parent and legal custodian; and

10. To represent their child in any legal proceeding and make decisions of a substantial legal significance concerning their child, unless the Court appoints a guardian ad litem for their child and orders otherwise. The residential parent and legal custodian, does not have the right to legally change the last name of their child in any other Court or to use another last name for their child other than that determined by a Court of law.

11. The right to know the non-residential parent's personal and business telephone number and address, and any new address or telephone number. If the residential parent intends to move the residence address, the residential parent shall immediately file a **NOTICE OF INTENT TO RELOCATE WITH THIS COURT.**

Commentary

The above appears to give the residential parent absolute control over the child with the sole exception of time and events with the other parent. As stated earlier that is not the intent of the law, and parents who act without consulting the other parent are more likely to be defending his or her actions in court. The State expects that parents regularly communicate about their child, make compromises of their differing parenting styles, and <u>that neither parent has a license to speak ill of nor display an attitude against, or influence a child's beliefs, attitudes or feelings negatively toward the other parent, his or her family, "significant other," or friends, or permit any other person or relative to do so. Such actions cannot be in the child's best interests. Some parents do not realize how harmful it is for children to hear one parent's negative beliefs or opinions about the other parent. Over time, the child may come to believe that if the other parent is full of faults, he or she too is flawed. A parent who cannot control his or her criticism of the other parent to a child needs to enter into counseling. Parents are expected to put aside their legitimate differences with each other for the benefit of their child no matter how difficult it may be to do so. As much as possible, a child needs his or her parents communicating and compromising their viewpoints to establish one, not two different standards.</u> Common areas of consensus needed from parents are major medical, prescription, or related treatment, toilet-training, major educational decisions, standards of conduct and discipline, moral training, religious affiliation, grooming and related standards, safety matters (ie. participation in sporting events and/or activities that either parent may view as potentially risky), or such other matters important to their child's physical and emotional growth and development.

WHAT IS COMPANIONSHIP?

Companionship is the times and events given to the parent who is not the residential parent and legal custodian to enjoy a parental relationship of equal quality as that between the child and residential parent. The non-residential parent has the right (subject to the restrictions in the Judgment Entry <u>and</u> this Companionship Schedule) to have their child(ren) participate in the parent's life with family, friends, and acquaintances of the parent's choosing, to live at, visit with, and travel to any place, and to participate in any activity in the child's best interests free of objection and/or interference from the residential parent and legal custodian.

The non-residential parent and legal custodian has the rights, responsibilities, and obligation to do all of the following:

A. To actively promote, encourage, and nurture the child to respect and love the other parent, and the other parent's family (even if the parents do not get along); and

B. To have their child at each day and time awarded to the non-residential parent as stated in the Judgment Entry <u>and</u> this schedule, **or as the parties agree**, free of any interference by the residential parent and legal custodian or any other person, and to have their child timely available to her or him at the beginning of every companionship period as set forth in the Judgment Entry <u>and</u> schedule, **or as the parties may agree;** and

C. To have the residential parent physically and emotionally prepare their child for the non-residential parent to take their child to his or her residence's residence, together with sufficient clothing and other important possessions to comfort the child during the companionship period; and

D. To consult with the residential parent on major medical or related treatment, education, standards of conduct and discipline, moral training, religious affiliation, grooming and related standards, safety matters (ie. participation in sporting events and/or activities that either parent may find risky), or such other matters important to their child's physical and emotional growth and development, so that the parents have knowledge about their child's needs and development, and the residential parent has the benefit of the non-residential parent's wisdom and experience before making a decision; and

E. To contribute to the cost of rearing their child by fully and regularly paying that portion of the child support obligation assigned to the parent based on the Ohio Child Support Guideline as approved in the Judgment Entry so that the residential parent and legal custodian can maintain their child's ongoing needs for food, shelter, transportation, medical treatment, clothing, and miscellaneous needs set forth above, and the portion of (extraordinary) medical and related expenses noted in the Judgment Entry so that their child is not denied medical and related treatment; to obtain emergency medical and related treatment for their child which need arises during companionship periods; and

F. To determine their child's activities which do not conflict with, or adversely affect, their child's energy or time with the residential parent and legal custodian, or for his or her education, **without the express agreement of the residential parent;** (the non-residential parent **must** administer prescriptions and/or medical treatments exactly as directed by their child's physician during companionship, subject only to informing the other parent/child's physician if the prescription is having an adverse effect on the child); and

G. To establish their child's standard of living and house rules in her or his own home;

H. To have full access to their child's records (school, health, or agency related to their child only), access to any child day care center which their child attends, and any student activity in which their child participates, including the right to consult with school officials and professionals treating their child, and the cooperation of the residential parent and legal custodian's cooperation to obtain the above, unless the court orders otherwise; and

I. The right to know the residential parent's personal and business telephone number and address, and any new address or telephone number. If the residential parent intends to move to another residence, the residential parent and legal custodian shall immediately file a **NOTICE OF INTENT TO RELOCATE with this Court.**

<u>Commentary</u>

The above appears to give the parent not designated the residential parent and legal custodian the legal responsibility to have companionship with the child. However, the law does not permit the Court to order the parent to exercise companionship time and events. The parent's failure, refusal or neglect is not in the child's best interests. The common effect of such failure is to upset the child as most children eagerly look forward to being with the other parent. Long term, the child may suffer from the belief that he or she is disliked by the other parent. Over time, the child may refuse any future contact with the parent. Sometimes a parent who refuses to spend time with a child doesn't realize how important he or she is to the child, and how hurt the child is by the parent's actions. The residential parent and legal custodian who cannot convince the non-residential parent to exercise companionship times and events needs to enter the child in counseling. The parent's failure to exercise the companionship ordered may be reason to increase child support because the residential parent's expenses will increase.

WHY SHOULD PARENTS USE A SCHEDULE?

A regular schedule is preferable to no routine which leaves the parents constantly trying to prioritize parent and children's current events with court-ordered parent-child time. A schedule insures that the parent-child relationship is the primary priority, reduces communication conflicts, and makes the future predictable and less chaotic for all concerned. The best companionship schedule is the parents' own plan based on their work hours and other responsibilities in consideration of their child's school and activities. If the times and days herein do not fit with the parents' work days/hours, holiday celebrations, traditions, and religious preferences, the parties shall develop their own written schedule.

By law, every Ohio Court must have a written general companionship schedule. It is not the Court's intention to impose its will upon parents or a child by establishing this schedule, the times and events. This schedule is not intended to be an absolute standard **if the parties agree to have a different schedule.**

HOW DOES THE COURT DETERMINE WHAT IS IN A CHILD'S BEST INTEREST IN ESTABLISHING A COMPANIONSHIP SCHEDULE?

Before issuing this specific order, the Court provided notice of hearing and an opportunity for each parent to present evidence about their child's welfare, the child's developmental needs, physical and emotional health, parenting skills, any substance abuse, emotional instability, child or domestic violence, or any other matter of importance. The Court may order or permit the parties to mediate, or appoint experts such as a guardian ad litem or psychologist to investigate and issue a report and recommendation. **Based on the evidence, this Companionship Schedule is in the child's best interests but <u>parents should comply with a court order which contradicts part of this schedule</u>.**

WHAT CAN PARENTS DO TO HELP THEIR CHILD(REN) WHEN PARENTS DON'T LIVE TOGETHER?

Being a parent is difficult even when parents live together, more difficult, when parents separate and live in the same community, and more difficult still if parents live so far apart that a child lacks frequent physical contact. Being a child is difficult when parents are separated and don't communicate, communicate with each other through a child, or are hostile and angry to each other. If conditions don't improve, the parents should be in counseling. If one parent refuses, there are techniques parents might try to relieve their (temporary) communication problems:

(1) <u>Parenting Time Outs</u>

Two days before every companionship period of two days or more, the non-residential parent calls the residential parent to discuss the upcoming needs of the companionship period, ie. clothing, the child's physical and emotional health or school problems or activities of note, any problems the child may be having, etc. During "parenting time outs," parents never criticize each other or others important to the other parent. Children should not be within hearing range.

(2) <u>Parenting Planning Times</u>

Within seven (7) days of the residential parent receiving a child's school/day care written evaluation or grade card, the parent calls the other parent, they jointly schedule a meeting at a public place, meet and review their child's progress as reported by the school/day care provider, and determine if any remedial steps need to be taken based on the evaluation or report. During "Parenting Planning Times," the parents never criticize each other or others important to the other parent. Children should not be present.

(3) Communication

Parents may find that using home fax machines to provide proof of notices, provide copies of grade cards, school activities, doctor visits, etc. Other methods may be e-mail.

III. COMPANIONSHIP AND PARENTING TIME FOR PARENTS LIVING *LESS* THAN 100 MILES APART

Unless agreed otherwise, parenting time and companionship shall not be less than the following:

A.   WEEKENDS

Every other weekend Friday at 7:00 p.m. to Sunday at 7:00 p.m. The residential parent shall provide dinner Friday. If the non-residential parent works second or third shift, then beginning on Saturday at 9:00 a.m. to Sunday at 7:00 p.m. The cycle shall repeat itself indefinitely despite interruption for holidays, birthdays, vacations, days of special meaning and special events, and make-up parenting times.

NOTICE REQUIRED?

No, unless (1) special clothing is needed; (2) the non-residential parent fails to exercise every other weekend companionship; (3) the non-residential parent works a swing shift, or (4) to cancel or change the time/day. Oral notice of 48 hours is sufficient.

B.   and WEEKDAYS

One day every week, with the non-residential parent to provide dinner, at the following times:

5:00 p.m. to 7:30 p.m. for children under six years of age;

5:00 p.m. to 8:00 p.m. for children six years to thirteen years;

5:00 p.m. to 9:00 p.m. for children fourteen years and older.

If the parents cannot agree on the day, the day shall be Wednesday.

If the parents have more than one child, the hour of returning the child shall be the hour for the youngest child. The cycle shall repeat itself indefinitely. Holidays, birthdays, vacations out of the parent's community, days of special meaning and special events shall take precedence over weekday companionship.

NOTICE REQUIRED?

No, unless (1) special clothing is needed; (2) the non-residential parent fails to exercise every week companionship; (3) the non-residential parent works a swing shift, or (4) to cancel or change the time/day. Oral notice of 48 hours is sufficient.

C.   and HOLIDAYS

The companionship schedule assumes that parents will assume traditional or religious holidays with their children by alternating the holidays. *Days of special meaning such as Passover, Rosh Hashana, Kwanzaa, Ramadan, Presidents' Day, Martin Luther King Day, and Christmas and Easter school vacation breaks should be added by the parties.* If the parties do not agree otherwise, the holidays, days, and times are as follows:

	Odd-numbered Years	Even-numbered years	Days-Times
Easter	Father	Mother	Sat., 7:00 p.m. - Sun. 7:00 p.m.
Memorial Day	Mother	Father	Sun., 7:00 p.m.-Mon., 7:00 p.m.
July 4th	Father	Mother	7/4, 9:00 a.m. - 7/5, 9:00 a. m.
Labor Day	Mother	Father	Sun., 7:00 p.m.-Mon., 7:00 p.m.
Halloween	Father	Mother	5:00 p.m. - 8:30 p.m.
Thanksgiving	Mother	Father	Thurs., 9:00 a.m.- Fri. 9:00 a.m.
Christmas Eve	Father	Mother	12/23, 9:00 p.m.- 12/24, 9:00 p.m.
Christmas Day	Mother	Father	12/24, 9:00 p.m.-12/25, 9:00 p.m.
New Year's	Father	Mother	12/31, 5:00 p.m. - 1/1, 9:00 p.m.

_____ _____   _____ _____

Christmas   vacation: from ____ p.m. on _____ to _____p.m.   on _____
_____

Easter   vacation: from   _____p.m. on _____ to _____p.m. on _____

If a holiday falls on a weekend, then the child shall spend the holiday with the parent set forth above, and spend the rest of the weekend with the parent who is entitled to that weekend. Holiday times spent with a parent are not made up at a later day. If a holiday occurs during a parent's scheduled vacation, then the child shall spend the holiday with the parent designated above.

The cycle shall repeat itself indefinitely.
NOTICE REQUIRED?

Yes, because these holidays are very important to parent, child, and extended family. Parents may wish to change times and days to suit their individual needs over the years but the non-residential parent shall be given a minimum of <u>seven (7) days oral notice.</u>

D.   and DAYS OF SPECIAL MEANING

1. **Mother's Day** shall be spent with mother, **Father's Day** shall be spent with father. For parents who cannot agree on the times, the time is <u>10:00 a.m. to 7:00 p.m.</u> The parent entitled to that weekend shall have the child for the duration of the Mother-Father's Day weekend. If either Mother or Father's day is during a scheduled vacation, then the child shall spend the day with the parent designated in this paragraph even though the child is on vacation with the other parent.

2. The **child's birthday** shall be spent with the mother in the even-numbered calendar years and with the father in the odd-numbered calendar years. _If the child's birthday occurs on a weekend, weekday, holiday, mother or father's day, any other day of special meaning, and vacation for either parent, the child shall spend the birthday with the parent designated in this paragraph._ The missed companionship shall not be made up. Biological sisters and brothers shall also attend the birthday event. If the parents cannot agree on the time, the time shall be as follows:

<u>10:00 a.m. to 8:00 p.m. for a child not in school on the birthday</u>
<u>5:00 p.m. to 8:00 p.m. for a child in school on the birthday</u>
The cycle shall repeat itself indefinitely.
NOTICE REQUIRED?

Yes, because these events are very special to parent, child, and extended family. The parent entitled to Mother's day, Father's Day and the child's birthday shall give <u>seven (7) days oral notice</u> to the other parent.

E.   and VACATION PERIODS

<u>1. Four weeks vacation in not less than two week segments.</u>

     For children not in kindergarten, vacation with the non-residential parent may not exceed a block of two consecutive weeks. An additional two week block period of vacation may be exercised after a minimum of two weeks with the residential parent and legal custodian.

     2. The non-residential parent's choice of vacation shall take precedence over the residential parent and legal custodian's choice, unless the latter has a mandatory employer shut down.

     3. **Summer school necessary for the child to pass to the next grade or graduate must be attended, and vacation plans must be scheduled to permit summer school attendance.**

     4. At any time that either parent removes or cause the child to be removed from the parent's community of residence, that parent shall provide <u>seven (7) days advance notice</u> to the other parent of the name, telephone number and address of the travel destination, method of travel, times of arrival and departure (airplane, flight number).

     5. The residential parent and legal custodian is entitled to weekend and midweek companionship during the non-residential parent's exercise of vacation, if the child is not traveling out of the community. Conversely, the non-residential parent is entitled to weekend and midweek companionship during the residential parent's vacation with the child, if the child is not traveling out of the community.

     6. If the parents cannot agree on the vacation periods, they are as follows:

For any child and siblings not in Kindergarten, from **9:00 a.m. June 16 to 9:00 p.m. June 30**.
and 9:00 a.m. August 1 to 9:00 p.m. August 14
For any other child with no siblings below Kindergarten age, **9:00 a.m. July 5 to 9:00 p.m. August 1**.
The cycle shall repeat itself indefinitely.

7.   During vacation periods, holiday, birthday, and days of special meaning will be spent with the parent designated in the above paragraphs (see pp. 6-7).

NOTICE REQUIRED?

Each parent must give the other written (unless the parties agree to oral notice) notice of intent to take summer vacation no later than May 1 of each year.

F.   SPECIAL DAYS/EVENTS

Unusual, unique, and unanticipated events and opportunities, such as graduations, weddings, funerals, religious ceremonies, family reunions, and family illnesses, and special events with a child's friends, are an important part of childhood. This companionship schedule assumes that parents will accommodate the needs of parents to have their children be able to participate in important events and unusual opportunities, provided that sufficient notice is provided to the other parent. If the parents cannot agree, **each parent shall have one 24 hour period each calendar year to have the child with them only to participate in a special event or circumstances which do not conflict with the child's birthday, Mother or Father's day, holidays, or vacations that are out of the community provided that the parent gives the other parent at least 24 hours notice, if possible.**

Commentary

If the residential parent arbitrarily refuses or frustrates the other parent's exercise of this companionship order, then such actions are not in the child's best interests, and may be contempt of court. Some parents believe because they dislike the other parent or his or her spouse or friends that (s)he can refuse the other parent companionship times and events. A parent who denies or frustrates companionship for his or her own benefit is more likely to be defending his or her actions in court. And sometimes, a parent does not want to tell the other parent or the Court the reasons he or she wants to deny companionship (as examples only, a reasoned belief that a parent is abusive to a child, there is domestic violence in the other parent's home life placing a child at risk, the child's health needs are neglected). A residential parent who wishes to protect a child needs to file a motion with the Clerk of Courts of the Court that issued the order. **A parent who arbitrarily refuses to give companionship without seeking a Court protective order risks many penalties, including but not limited to imposition of a jail sentence, a fine, payment of attorney fees, payment of travel expenses, reimbursement of vacation travel expenses, modification of the companionship order, and/or a reallocation of parental rights and responsibilities.** The failure of a parent to regularly pay child support is not a legal defense if the residential parent denies or frustrates companionship.

If parents argue about whether the residential parent is denying companionship or the non-residential parent's consistent exercise of companionship, the parents should each keep a written calendar of the dates and times of companionship that do occur. Each parent should sign his or her name, the date, and time in the other's calendar at the exchange. The calendar signed by each party is proof of whether or not the residential parent and the non-residential parent are complying with an agreement and/or court order if one parent files a motion in Court.

If the other parent fails, refuses or neglects to exercise this minimum order/companionship schedule, generally those actions are not in the child's best interests, unless the reason is work or health related, or an emergency occurs. Some parents don't want to tell the other parent or a Court the reasons he or she does not exercise the court schedule of companionship (ie. guilt over inability to pay child support, fear of consequences for introducing the child to a "significant other," inability to peacefully communicate with the residential parent, not being emotionally disentangled from the residential parent, the parent and child do not have a good relationship, threats from the other parent if he or she tries to see the child). Notwithstanding the reason, the parent who voluntarily chooses not to comply with the minimum order/schedule should take appropriate steps to resolve the problem so that the child does not believe he or she is the cause or was abandoned. If face-to-face meeting between parents is troubling a parent, the parents shall agree upon a neutral site for the pick up and delivery of the child (ie. a relative's home or public place).

If either parent fails, refuses or neglects to comply with this order/companionship schedule, and neither files to change or require the other parent to comply with the order, there may be long term ill effects on the emotional well-being of the child.

Curbside Exchange

When parents can't exchange the child for companionship times without emotional outbursts upsetting to parent and child, parents should consider using a "curbside exchange." The process requires the following:
1. the non-residential parent phones the other parent giving an estimated time of arrival;
2. upon arrival, remains in the vehicle, briefly honks the horn and waits for the child to walk alone to the vehicle;
3. the residential parent stays in his/her home, and watches the child walk to the vehicle;
4. the parents do not communicate with each other.
5. upon return, the non-residential parent calls, returns the child, waits until the child is safely in the residence.
This technique cannot be used for a child who cannot carry his/her belongings to a vehicle.

IV. COMPANIONSHIP AND Parenting time FOR PARENTS LIVING *MORE* THAN 100 MILES APART

Unless agreed otherwise, companionship and parenting time shall not be less than the following and the cycle shall repeat itself indefinitely:

A.   **WEEKENDS (if the child's travel time is less than 3.5 hours) and**
Beginning on _____, one weekend a month. If the parties do not agree on the weekend, then the weekend shall begin the **second Friday** each month. The days and times are as follows:
Friday at 5:00 p.m. (or as soon thereafter as the parties agree) to Sunday at 8:00 p.m. (or as the parties agree), unless Monday is a non-school day, then the weekend ends Monday at 8:00 p.m. (or as the parties agree). The non-residential parent shall provide dinner.
The cycle shall repeat itself indefinitely despite interruption for holidays, birthdays, vacations, days of special meaning and special events.

B.   **SUMMER VACATION PERIOD and**
1. **For a child up to five year's old**
Four (4) weeks vacation in consecutive two (2) week segments. If the parties do not agree, then the days and times are as follows:
The third Friday in June at 7 p.m. for fourteen (14) consecutive days until 7 p.m
and the third Friday in July for fourteen (14) consecutive days until 7 p.m.
2. **For a child five years and older**
Six (6) weeks vacation in not less than consecutive two (2) week segments. If the parties do not agree, then the days and times are as follows:
(a)   The second Friday in July at 7 p.m. for six (6) consecutive weeks ending at 7 p.m., unless (b) is chosen in writing no later than May 1ˢᵗ by the non-residential parent.
(b)   Or The third Friday in June at 7 p.m. for fourteen (14) consecutive days ending at 7 p.m. and the third Friday in July at 7 p.m. for twenty-eight (28) consecutive days ending at 7 p.m.
3. For vacation periods, the following applies:
(a) The non-residential parent's choice of vacation dates and times shall take priority over the residential parent and legal custodian's choice, unless the residential parent has a mandatory employer shut down.
(b) Summer school necessary for the child to pass to the next grade or graduate must be attended and vacation plans must be scheduled to permit summer school attendance for these purposes.
(c) At any time that either parent removes or causes the child to be removed from the parent's residential community,

that parent shall provide seven (7) days advance notice to the other parent of the name, telephone number and address of the travel destination, method of travel, times of arrival and departure (airline, flight number).

(d) During vacation periods, holidays, birthdays, and days of special meaning shall be spent with the parent designated on pages.6-7.

NOTICE REQUIRED?

YES, EACH PARENT MUST GIVE THE OTHER WRITTEN NOTICE OF INTENT TO TAKE SUMMER VACATION NO LATER THAN <u>MAY 1 EACH YEAR</u>. Failure to give notice timely shall mean that the parties agree to the vacation days and times above stated. If the non-residential parent and legal custodian does not intend to exercise vacation companionship, notice must be given no later than May 1 of each year.

C.

SPRING VACATION and

The non-residential parent shall be entitled to the entire school vacation in the odd-numbered calendar years. Unless otherwise agreed, the days and times are as follows:

<u>from 10:00 a.m. the day after school is out to 7 p.m. the day before school begins</u>

If a child is too young to attend school, the days and times are as follows:

<u>the third Friday in April at 7 p.m. to the fourth Sunday in April at 7 p.m</u>

Notice required?

Yes, the non-residential parent shall give written notice thirty (30) days in advance.

D.

HOLIDAY VACATION and

1. Thanksgiving - the non-residential parent is entitled to the Thanksgiving holiday every other year. Unless otherwise agreed, the days and times are as follows:

<u>in the odd numbered calendar years, Wednesday at 7 p.m. to Sunday at 7 p.m.</u>

<u>in the even-numbered calendar years, Friday at 10:00 a.m. following Thanksgiving to Sunday at 7 p.m.</u>

2. Winter vacation - unless otherwise agreed, the non-residential parent is entitled to the following:

<u>in the odd numbered calendar years, December 23 at 7 p.m. to December 28 at 7 p.m.</u>

<u>in the even numbered calendar years, December 26 at 7 p.m. to January 1 at 10:00 a.m.</u>

Notice required?

Yes, the non-residential parent shall give written notice thirty (30) days in advance.

E.

ADDITIONAL Parenting time

1. The parties shall comply with the order for the child's birthday, if practical, and shall comply with Mother and Father's Day, if practical (see pages 6-7).

2. The residential parent shall at all times notify the non-residential parent when the child will be in the non-residential parent's community and provide two (2) days advance oral notice. The residential parent shall provide reasonable parenting time and companionship to the non-residential parent for the duration of the stay.

3. The non-residential parent shall be entitled to telephone/Internet contact, at reasonable times, with the child three times weekly for fifteen (15) minutes per call, unless agreed otherwise. The residential parent shall not be entitled to listen, nor interfere with telephone contact, nor permit any other person to do so.

4. The child may telephone either parent at reasonable times provided that any long distance call is paid for by the parent receiving the call, unless otherwise agreed.

5. **If the travel time between the parents' residences is more than 3.5 hours <u>and</u> the child is five years or older <u>and</u> if the non-residential parent cannot afford to exercise the monthly weekend parenting time and companionship specified in section B(2) above, then instead of monthly weekend parenting time and companionship, the non-residential parent shall have the right to summer parenting time and companionship beginning at 7:00 p.m. on the seventh day after the last day of school and ending 7:00 p.m. on the seventh day before school begins for the fall term. In order to exercise this option for extended summer vacation, the non-residential parent shall give <u>written</u> notice to be received by the residential parent by January 15th each year. If the residential parent does not receive written notice by January 15th, then the failure to give timely written notice shall be a waiver of the right to extended summer parenting time and companionship for that year only.** The residential parent and legal custodian is entitled to weekend parenting time and companionship during the non-residential parent's exercise of summer vacation, if the child is not traveling out of the community as set forth in section

"A" above.

V.   <u>**SPECIAL PROBLEMS**</u>

<u>Commentary</u>

In order that separated parents are better informed about the realities of parenting, the Court has identified a number of problem areas common to some parents' who live apart. When faced with choices for a child, a single parent may be influenced by the parent's past relationship with the other parent as much as the best interests of the child. The purpose of including these problems in the schedule is to assist parents in making choices for their child and avoid returning to court for answers. It is not the Court's intent in providing this information to interfere in parents' decisions.

1. Introductory Period

A.   For a child who is not well acquainted with a parent, there should be an introductory period where the child is in familiar surroundings with a person well known to the child to supervise the introduction to that parent, and the non-residential parent learns about the child's physical and developmental needs and abilities. Generally, the supervisor should not be the residential parent due to the possibility of emotional conflicts between two parents. The length of the introductory period depends on the age of the child, his or her physical and emotional maturity, and the circumstances of each case.

B.   Unless agreed otherwise parties agree otherwise, for a child six years and under, the introductory period should occur for not less than eight (8) companionship periods of not less than three hours each. The supervisor selected should be present for the first three hours of each of the eight visits. After the first visit, one hour should be added to each visit (ie. 3 hours, first visit; 4 hours, second visit, etc.). New spouses, other siblings, other family members, or friends should not be included in the introductory period unless specifically agreed in advance by the supervisor and both parents. The eighth period should be an overnight with the child returned no later than 8:30 a.m. to the other parent's residence. The parties may agree to reduce the supervisor's three hour period of supervision. Thereafter, the Court's companionship schedule should begin with a midweek companionship and weekend companionship the following weekend. Transportation should be provided by the residential parent to and from the supervisor's residence, except for the last supervised visit.

C.   Unless agreed otherwise, for a child seven years and older, the introductory period should occur for at least six visits of three hour periods. The person supervising should be present for the first three hours of each of the six visits. The sixth visit should be an overnight with the child returned no later than 8:30 a.m. to the other parent's residence. After the first visit, two hours should be added to each visit (ie. 3 hours, first visit; 5 hours, second visit, etc.). Thereafter, the Court's companionship schedule should begin with a midweek companionship and weekend companionship the following weekend. New spouses, other siblings or other family members or friends should not be included in the introductory period unless specifically agreed in advance by the supervisor and both parents. Transportation should be provided by the residential parent to and from the supervisor's residence, except for the last supervised visit.

The introductory period shall be as follows: Beginning on_____

_____

The supervisor for the introduction is _____

The supervisor in the event of the unavailability of the primary supervisor is_____

The place of the supervised companionship is _____

Mother's phone #_____ Father's #_____Supervisors' #(1)_____(2)_____

The person responsible for the transportation to the supervisor is_____

D.   For parents who cannot agree on days or time, the introductory period shall be as follows:
On the first [] Saturday or []Sunday (check one) following the court hearing days establishing companionship, at 9:00

a.m. to 12 noon; on the second and each successive visit during the introductory period, the parent being introduced should have the right to take the child out of the supervisor's residence for the duration of that companionship period.

E. **For any child who resists companionship, the parents should immediately select a professional counselor to assist the child's introduction to a parent.**

2. Child's Reaction to Companionship

At times, a child may state opposition to companionship (or returning to the residential parent), or give the impression of opposing companionship (or returning to the residential parent). A baby or toddler, particularly one adjusting to the parents' separation for the first time, may be or appear to be emotionally upset or oppose leaving one parent to return to the other. An older child may be emotionally upset upon leaving or returning after a long period of separation from one parent.

A parent may easily misinterpret the child's responses as evidence that the parent-child relationship needs to be supervised or terminated. A child may quickly adjust if the parents comfort the child. When an older child verbalizes opposition or refusal to be with a parent, the parent should discuss the issue with the other parent out of the child's presence. If the parents cannot find a solution, some parent needs to consult with a counselor or psychologist if the child continues to object to companionship.

3. Companionship Procedure

A. This companionship schedule presumes that both parents are competent to care for the child, and neither the Parent nor any member of their household is a risk or danger to the child; that all blood or adopted siblings shall be together, not separated, except for special events; that the residential parent and legal custodian understands that the payment of child support is not a condition that (s)he may impose prior to any companionship period.

B. **This companionship schedule presumes that the residential parent always encourages a positive emotional relationship between the child and the other parent, and the other parent always encourages a positive emotional relationship between the child and the residential parent, regardless of their personal differences.**

C. The schedule presumes that the non-residential parent shall arrive at the times and days agreed upon or ordered by this schedule *without having to provide prior notice* to the residential parent unless prior notice is agreed or ordered in this schedule. Therefore, the residential parent cannot require that the non-residential parent call in advance or confirm companionship times for companionship except as noted previously. Vacation, holidays, the child's birthday, or special days or events shall always be with prior notification because of their special importance and the possibility of misunderstandings.

D. The schedule presumes that the non-residential parent will be prompt in arriving for and returning the child. Courtesy requires that a non-residential parent who is late notify the residential parent. The residential parent has no obligation to wait, or keep the child waiting, more than thirty (30) minutes for the other parent to arrive for a companionship period, unless agreed otherwise parent agrees otherwise. A parent more than thirty (30) minutes late for a companionship period without prior notification forfeits that companionship period, and the companionship does not have to be made up. A non-residential parent who habitually is late in arriving without reason risks having the schedule modified by the Court. A non-residential parent who fails to return the child on the time and/or day to be returned risks the Court imposing a jail sentence and a modification of the companionship schedule, among other remedies.

The schedule assumes that the residential parent shall be flexible with a non-residential parent employer's work demands and family or personal emergencies, and vice versa.

E.   This schedule presumes that the non-residential parent shall not return the child prior to the time or days agreed for return, or ordered by the schedule. This schedule presumes that the residential parent shall have the child at the residential parent's home, not any other address, for the non-residential parent to pick up the child, at the time either agreed upon or ordered by this schedule. This schedule presumes that the residential parent will be at the residence for the return of the child at the days and times agreed upon, or as ordered by the schedule.

F.   This companionship schedule presumes that the non-residential parent shall transport the child to and from the residential parent's residence, unless agreed otherwise parties agree otherwise. If the non-residential parent is transporting the child, the parent shall use a driver well-known to the child and the other parent. Any parent or person designated by a parent to drive a child shall possess a valid driver's license and comply with state laws on having car insurance. Any parent or person designated by a parent to drive the child shall comply with all child restraint laws (seat belts and child seats). No parent or person authorized by a parent to drive a child shall violate a state's laws concerning use of drugs or alcohol, or allow any other person to drive the child who has been convicted of driving under the influence.

G.   This companionship schedule presumes that each parent in caring for and supervising the child shall have the child's safety and stability as his and her paramount concern. *This issue is more likely than any other to cause parent's concern, fear for their child, and future litigation.*

No parent shall use any drug not prescribed by a physician for the parent's sole use and no parent shall abuse any drug (alcohol included) before forty-eight hours of having or during the times of possession of their child, and no parent shall cause the child to be left in the care of any person using illegal drugs or abusing any drug (including alcohol).

Other problem areas are the following: a parent, other child, or another adult not adequately supervising a child; permitting a child to participate in an activity that one parent believes is unsafe or inappropriate to the child's age, physical or emotional condition; allowing the child to violate the law (allowing a child to have a sexual relationship, use alcohol or drugs, drive without a license or insurance); a parent, stepparent, "significant other" or other hitting or otherwise abusing the child; allowing the child to be in the presence of persons with known criminal records who one parent believes is a danger to a child; a parent who fails, refuses or neglects to require the child to attend school; and exposing a child to a home environment where the adults engage in domestic violence.

One parent's belief that the other parent failed to adequately provide for a child's safety or stability may result in a strained parental relationships and litigation. Legal remedies may include changing an order designating the residential parent or the companionship schedule, ordering supervised companionship, counseling, psychological or psychiatric evaluation, appointing a guardian ad litem and/or attorney for a child, or terminating companionship, in addition to the possibility of criminal charges against the parent.

H.   This schedule presumes that it is in the best interest of a child that the methods of discipline used by parents and every caretaker shall be discussed and agreed upon by and between the parents. Unless stated otherwise hereafter, the methods of discipline DO NOT INCLUDE ANY FORM OF PHYSICAL DISCIPLINE, and are STRICTLY limited to the following :

EXPLAINING THE REASON THE CHILD'S BEHAVIOR IS INAPPROPRIATE
TIME OUT
TAKING AWAY A PRIVILEGE (Include other methods below)

_____

_____

I.   The schedule presumes that a child shall have a sleeping area separate from other adults in the non-residential parent's household and to ensure a child's need for privacy.

J.   The schedule presumes that each parent must provide time and place of the child to study, complete homework assignments, papers or other assigned school projects even if doing so interferes with the parent's plans for the child. It is the residential parent's responsibility, not the child's, to notify the non-residential parent of the school work to be completed at the non-residential parent's home.

K.   The schedule presumes that the residential parent shall give timely written notice to the other parent of the child's chronic medical or emotional conditions, and allergies to drugs, food, or other substances immediately. The schedule presumes that if a child is ill or injured, each parent shall always inform the other. *Failure or refusal to give notice may cause the other parent to fear that the child has been intentionally hurt or neglected while in the other parent's care.* If the child becomes ill or injured prior to a companionship period, the residential parent shall notify the non-residential parent, and discuss whether the companionship shall take place. Parents should consider the comfort of the child, the exposure of an illness to others, the care necessary and ability to provide that level of care, and the impact on special companionship plans, etc.

If the parents decide that the companionship should occur, the residential parent must provide all medical necessities required by the treating physician with written instructions for treatment. The non-residential parent must comply with the treating physician's directions for treatment, and notify the residential parent if the child's physical condition deteriorates, if the child is responding poorly to the medication or treatment, or does not improve as is expected.

If the parents decide that the child shall remain with the residential parent, the non-residential parent has the right to visit the child daily for at least one (1) hour during the days of companionship. This provision does not apply if there is an existing court order prohibiting the non-residential parent from being in the home of the residential parent. If the parents have more than one biological child together, then the other child shall go for the period of the companionship.

The companionship missed due to illness or injury shall be made up within sixty (60) days of the illness.

Failure, refusal or neglect to provide a child with medical, dental, or other related necessary treatment may result in criminal charges against a parent, changing the residential parent and legal custodian, or changing the companionship order, among other legal remedies.

If the child is ill or injured during companionship times, the non-residential parent shall notify the other parent, obtain necessary emergency medical treatment, and provide instructions provided by the medical doctor to the residential parent, including all prescriptions upon returning the child.

If a child habitually is too ill for participating in companionship, then the non-residential parent shall have the right at his or her expense to have a physical exam at the medical doctor of his or her choice with advance notice to the residential parent who shall transport the child to the medical doctor. The non-residential parent has the right to consult with the medical doctor concerning the findings.

NO SCHEDULE CAN DIRECT APPROPRIATE PARENTAL ACTION WHEN A CHILD IS SICK OR INJURED. IT IS THE PARENT'S RESPONSIBILITY TO SECURE APPROPRIATE MEDICAL AND RELATED TREATMENT FOR A CHILD AND CONSULT WITH EACH OTHER.

L.   This schedule presumes that a child will have friends, activities, employment and relationships with others which conflict with parent's time. It is not the child's responsibility to negotiate with a parent to participate in activities important to him or her, or to have relationships and friends. It is solely the residential parent's responsibility to inform the non-residential parent of events that may impact on companionship times. The residential parent shall not permit the child or cause the child to engage in activities that fall within the non-residential parent's companionship time consistently, unless agreed otherwise parties agree otherwise (ie. Saturday lessons). It is both parents' responsibility to discuss in advance activities important to the child, so that the child is not discouraged from nor deprived of friends, relationships, or activities. The parent who has the child during the time of the activity is responsible for the transportation and cost thereof, attendance or other arrangements, unless parties agree otherwise. The residential parent shall provide written notice to the other parent of the name, address and phone number of the person in charge of the activity, if known. Both parents are encouraged to attend a child's activities if open to parents. ANY ACTIVITY THAT IS POTENTIALLY HAZARDOUS MUST BE DISCUSSED BETWEEN THE PARENTS, ie. sporting activities,

M.   This schedule presumes that the child has the right to phone or communicate with both parents at any reasonable time (collect only, if long distance). This schedule presumes that each parent can call with a child at the home of the other parent. If the parents do not agree, the non-residential parent can call the child twice a week, and residential parent once per week. The non-residential parent may call a child too ill to participate in companionship once a day for the duration of the missed companionship or once a day for any missed companionship period.

The residential parent shall have the right to call the child during any weekend or vacation with the other parent as the parties can agree. If there is no agreement, then the residential parent shall have the right to call the child twice per week during vacation if the vacation takes place at the non-residential parent's home.

No telephone call shall be made from either parent within one hour of the child's bedtime, or before 9:00 a.m. Each parent shall ensure that the child returns all calls within 24 hours.

N.   This schedule presumes that the non-residential parent has weekends free for companionship and is available for midweek companionship. If the non-residential parent is unavailable for any portion of the weekend or midweek companionship periods, the parents shall attempt to reach an agreement on an alternative companionship schedule to compensate the child and non-residential parent. Alternative schedule:_____
_____
_____

O.   This schedule presumes that both parents, not a child and parent, communicate changes in the companionship schedule necessary to affect what is in the child's best interests. Parents who cannot communicate with each other shall not communicate through a child regarding whether, when, where or under what circumstances companionship shall occur. Parents who cannot communicate should jointly ask a trusted person or secure the service of a professional counselor to assist the parents in communicating. *Failure of parents to communicate concerning their child is not in the child's best interests. It is the parents' responsibility to find a solution if this is a problem.*

P.   This schedule presumes that both parents shall at all times provide the other parent with a residence and employment address and telephone number for contact in the event of an emergency.

Q.   This schedule presumes that when a parent designates a day care provider or babysitter to care for the child that the parent has sufficient knowledge of the day care provider or baby sitter to know that there is no risk of danger posed to the child by the person chosen, and that the parent has given sufficient instructions to the day care provider and babysitter as to the child's needs, and procedures. Therefore, it is unnecessary that the parent notifies the other parent when the other parent is not personally present to care for the children. However, each parent shall always leave the telephone number at work and at home for every school and every day care provider or babysitter for emergency procedures.

R.   This schedule presumes that it is in the best interests of a child to have only one mother and one father, and neither parent shall encourage nor direct or allow the child to make reference to any other person as if that person was a mother or a father. Neither parent shall permit any person from encouraging or directing or allowing a child to make reference to a person as if the person was the child's mother or father.

S.   The schedule presumes that the residential parent and legal custodian shall make available sufficient clean clothing for the companionship period giving consideration of the outdoors temperature and usual companionship activities. If the non-residential parent plans extraordinary activity with the child during any companionship period, it is that parent's responsibility to inform the residential parent what special clothing is needed at least two (2) days in advance. If the non-residential parent fails to provide two days notice or if the child does not have the type of clothing necessary, the residential parent is under no obligation to provide the clothing.

The non-residential parent shall return all clothing immediately at the end of a companionship period in the same condition that it was received from the residential parent.

The schedule presumes that the child is free to remove from the residential parent's home treasured possessions (ie. Teddy bear, favorite blanket, etc.) for companionship periods to ease the transition between his or her homes and comfort the child. The non-residential parent shall return all of the child's treasured possessions immediately at the end of a companionship period.

NOTICE OF RELOCATION

The residential parent and legal custodian shall provide the Court and the non-residential parent written notice of relocation thirty (30) days in advance of moving his or her residence from her or his current residence with the minor child. The parent shall give notice of the day of moving, the new address and telephone number, and shall make a good faith attempt to develop a new companionship schedule. Either party may file a motion with the Clerk of Courts to change the order.

ACCESS TO RECORDS, DAY CARE, STUDENT ACTIVITIES

The non-residential parent is entitled to access of any school, health or agency record or reports relating to the minor child, any student activity related to the minor child, and/or any day current or future day care facility attended by their child, under the same terms and conditions as the residential parent is entitled to access to these records. The residential parent shall timely <u>mail, call, or physically deliver</u> (not through a child) the names and addresses of all health care providers, all notices, grade cards, deficiency notices, etc. received from health care providers, school, activities, or day care center, and also the name of any activity leader, telephone number and address if known by the residential parent. A residential parent may seek a protective order to prevent release of any record from the Court, upon written motion (note, it is not the responsibility of a residential parent to provide notice of activities not related to school-sponsored events involving a child).

WHEN COMPANIONSHIP IS TROUBLESOME TO A CHILD OR PARENT

For parents or a child having difficulty implementing their companionship schedule, there are a number of options: (1) seeking joint private counseling; (2) seeking joint mediation, or call the Court that issued the order to see what services are available; (3) filing a motion with the Clerk of Courts.

APPENDIX 21-B

Standard Companionship & Visitation Calendar

2002 Standard Companionship & Visitation Schedule

Beginning On _____ for____ [FATHER] _____ [MOTHER]

JANUARY						
S	M	T	W	T	F	S
	1	2	3	4	5	
	8	9	10	11	12	13
14	15	16	17	18	19	
	22	23	24	25	26	27
28	29	30	31			

FEBRUARY						
S	M	T	W	T	F	S
				1	2	
	5	6	7	8	9	10
11	12	13	14	15	16	
	19	20	21	22	23	24
25	26	27	28			

MARCH						
S	M	T	W	T	F	S
				1	2	
	5	6	7	8	9	10
11	12	13	14	15	16	
	19	20	21	22	23	24
25	26	27	28	29	30	31

APRIL						
S	M	T	W	T	F	S
	2	3	4	5	6	7
8	9	10	11	12	13	
	16	17	18	19	20	21
22	23	24	25	26	27	
	30					

MAY						
S	M	T	W	T	F	S
		1	2	3	4	5
6	7	8	9	10	11	
	14	15	16	17	18	19
20	21	22	23	24	25	
	28	29	30	31		

JUNE						
S	M	T	W	T	F	S
					1	2
3	4	5	6	7	8	
	11	12	13	14	15	16
17	18	19	20	21	22	
	25	26	27	28	29	30

JULY						
S	M	T	W	T	F	S
1	2	3	4	5	6	
	9	10	11	12	13	14
15	16	17	18	19	20	
	23	24	25	26	27	28
29	30	31				

AUGUST						
S	M	T	W	T	F	S
			1	2	3	
	6	7	8	9	10	11
12	13	14	15	16	17	
	20	21	22	23	24	25
26	27	28	29	30	31	

SEPTEMBER						
S	M	T	W	T	F	S
	3	4	5	6	7	8
9	10	11	12	13	14	
	17	18	19	20	21	22
23	24	25	26	27	28	

OCTOBER						
S	M	T	W	T	F	S
	1	2	3	4	5	6
7	8	9	10	11	12	
	15	16	17	18	19	20
21	22	23	24	25	26	
	29	30	31			

NOVEMBER						
S	M	T	W	T	F	S
				1	2	3
4	5	6	7	8	9	
	12	13	14	15	16	17
18	19	20	21	22	23	
	26	27	28	29	30	

DECEMBER						
S	M	T	W	T	F	S
1	2	3	4	5	6	7
8	9	10	11	12	13	
	16	17	18	19	20	21
22	23	24	25	26	27	
	30	31				

F	Father's Time	Mother's Time	Residential Parent & Legal Custodian
TD =	Transition Day	Father's Holiday	= Mother's Holiday

For Details, See Reverse Side

Other: _____
_____
_____
_____
_____
_____

A. **WEEKENDS**: Every other weekend Friday at 7:00 p.m. to Sunday at 7:00 p.m. If the non-residential parent works second or third shift, then Saturday at 9:00 a.m. to Sunday at 7:00 p.m. the cycle shall repeat itself indefinitely despite interruption for holidays, birthdays, vacations, days of special meaning and special events, and make-up visitations.
NOTICE REQUIRED? No, unless (1) special clothing is needed; (2) the non-residential parent fails to exercise every other weekend companionship; (3) the non-residential parent works a swing shift, or (4) to cancel or change the time/day. Oral notice of <u>48 hours</u> is sufficient.

B. **WEEKDAYS**: One day every week thereafter at the following times:
5:00 p.m. to 7:30 p.m. for children not yet in mandatory kindergarten;
5:00 p.m. to 8:00 p.m. for children in grades K-8;
5:00 p.m. to 9:00 p.m. for high school aged children.
If the parents cannot agree on the day, the day shall be <u>Wednesday</u>. If the parents have more than one child, the hour of returning the child shall be the hour for the youngest child. The cycle shall repeat itself indefinitely. Holidays, birthdays, vacations out of the parent's community, days of special meaning and special events shall take precedence over weekday companionship. NOTICE REQUIRED? No, unless (1) special clothing is needed; (2) the non-residential parent finals to exercise every other weekend companionship; (3) the non-residential parent works a swing shift, or (4) to cancel or change the time/day. Oral notice of <u>48 hours</u> is sufficient.

C. **HOLIDAYS**: The companionship schedule assumes that parents will assume traditional or religious holidays with their children by alternating the holidays. Days of special meaning such as Passover, Rosh Hashana, Kwanza, Ramadan, President's Day, Martin Luther King Day, and Christmas and Easter school vacation breaks should be added by the parties. If the parties do not agree otherwise, the holidays, days, and times are as follows:

Odd-numbered Years		Even-numbered Years	Days-Times
Easter	Father	Mother	Sat., 7:00 p.m.-Sun., 7:00 p.m.
Memorial Day	Mother	Father	Sun., 7:00 p.m. – Mon., 7:00 p.m.
July 4th	Father	Mother	7/4, 9:00 a.m. – 7/5, 9:00 a.m.
Labor Day	Mother	Father	Sun., 7:00 p.m. – Mon., 7:00 p.m.
Halloween	Father	Mother	5:00 p.m. – 8:30 p.m.
Thanksgiving	Mother	Father	Thurs., 9:00 a.m. – Fri. 9:00 a.m.
Christmas Eve	Father	Mother	12/23, 9:00 p.m. – 12/24, 9:00 p.m.
Christmas Day	Mother	Father	12/24, 9 p.m. – 12/25, 9:00 p.m.
New Year's	Father	Mother	12/31, 5:00 p.m. – 1/1, 9:00 p.m.

If a holiday falls on a weekend, then the child shall spend the holiday with the parent set forth above, and spend the rest of the weekend with the parent who is entitled to that weekend. Holiday times spent with a parent are not made up at a later day. If a holiday occurs during a parent's scheduled vacation, then the child shall spend the holiday with the parent designated above. The cycle shall repeat itself indefinitely.
NOTICE REQUIRED? Yes, because these holidays are very important to parent, child and extended family. Parents may wish to change times and days to suit their individual needs over the years but the non-residential parent shall give a minimum of <u>seven (7) days oral notice.</u>

D. **DAYS OF SPECIAL MEANING**: Mother's Day shall always be with the mother, Father's Day shall always be with the father. For parents who cannot agree on the times, the time is 10:00 a.m. to 7:00 p.m. The parent entitled to that weekend shall have the child for the duration of the Mother-Father's Day weekend. If either Mother or Father's day is during a scheduled vacation, then the child shall spend the day with the parent designated in this paragraph even though the child is on vacation with the other parent. The child's birthday shall be spent with the mother in the even-numbered calendar years and with the father in the odd-numbered calendar years. *If the child's birthday occurs on a weekend, weekday, holiday, mother or father's day, any other day of special meaning, and vacation for either parent, the child shall spend the birthday with the parent designated in this paragraph.* The missed companionship shall not be made up. Biological sisters and brothers shall also attend the birthday event. If the parents cannot agree on the time, the time shall be as follows:
10:00 a.m. to 8:00 p.m. for a child not in school on the birthday
5:00 p.m. to 8:00 p.m. for a child in school on the birthday
The cycle shall repeat itself indefinitely. NOTICE REQUIRED? Yes, because these events are very special to parent, child, and extended family. The parent entitled to Mother's day, Father's Day and child's birthday shall give <u>seven (7) days oral notice</u> to the other parent.

E. **VACATION PERIODS**

1. <u>Four weeks vacation in not less than two-week segments.</u>
    For children not in kindergarten, vacation with the non-residential parent may not exceed a block of two consecutive weeks. An additional two-week block period of vacation may be exercised after a minimum of two weeks with the residential parent and legal custodian.
2. The non-residential parent's choice of vacation shall take precedence over the residential parent and legal custodian's choice, unless the latter has a mandatory employer shutdown.
3. Summer school necessary for the child to pass to the next grade or graduate must be attended, and vacation plans must be scheduled to permit summer school attendance.
4. At any time that either parent removes or causes the child to be removed from the parent's community of residence, that parent shall provide <u>seven (7) days' advance notice</u> to the other parent of the name, telephone number and address of the travel destination, method of travel, times of arrival and departure (airplane, flight number).
5. The residential parent and legal custodian is entitled to weekend and midweek companionship during the non-residential parent's exercise of vacation, if the child is not traveling out of the community. If out of the community, the missed companionship must be made up within 60 days of return. Conversely, the non-residential parent is entitled to weekend and midweek companionship during the residential parent's vacation with the child, if the child is not traveling out of the community. If out of the community, the missed companionship must be made up within 60 days of return.
6. If the parents cannot agree on the vacation periods, they are as follows:
    For any child and siblings not in Kindergarten, from 9:00 a.m. June 16 to 9:00 p.m. June 30, and 9:00 a.m. August 1 to 9:00 p.m. August 14. For any child with no siblings below Kindergarten age, 9:00 a.m. July 5 to 9:00 p.m. August 1. The cycle shall repeat itself indefinitely.
7. During vacation periods, holiday, birthday, and days of special meaning will be spent with the parent designated in the above paragraphs. NOTICE REQUIRED? Each parent must give the other written (unless the parties agree to oral notice) notice of intent to take summer vacation no later than May 1 of each year.

F. **SPECIAL DAYS/EVENTS**: Unusual, unique, and unanticipated events and opportunities, such as graduations, weddings, funerals, religious ceremonies, family reunions, and family members' illnesses, and special events with a child's friends, are an important part of childhood. This companionship schedule assumes that parents will accommodate the needs of parents to have their children be able to participate in important events and unusual opportunities, provided that sufficient notice is provided to the other parent. If the parents cannot agree, each parent shall have one 24 hour period each calendar year to have the child with them only to participate in a special event or circumstances which does not conflict with the child's birthday, Mother or Father's day, holidays, or vacations that are out of the community provided that the parent gives the other parent at least <u>24 hours</u> notice, if possible.
(Parents should thoroughly read the full visitation and companionship schedule prior to the visitation to avoid disputes).

APPENDIX 21-C

Parenting Log and Parenting Time Reminder

Figure 1

Page____

PARENTING LOG FOR [] the Mother [] the Father

To avoid disagreements/mistakes and to maintain a permanent record of parenting rights and times exercised, (1) First, make blank copies for future use; then (2) on one copy, in the first column on the left, write in date and time of future parenting exchanges and returns based on the Court's order for **one year**; (3) Make a second copy, and give one to each parent for future use; (3) Each time the child is delivered from one to the other, the parents (persons) temporarily exchange the logs. The parent (person) <u>delivering</u> the child writes in the actual date/time, that parent's address, initials **both** logs and presents the log for completion by the parent (person). The parent (person) receiving the child verifies the time and date by initialing **both** logs and writing in the address where that parent lives. When the parenting time is ended, the parents repeat the process. **Each parent should keep his/her own log as proof of compliance with the Court's order.**

<u>Date & Time</u> <u>per order</u>	<u>Actual Date//Time</u>	<u>Address of Parent</u> <u>delivering child</u>	<u>Address of Parent</u> <u>returning child</u>	<u>Parents</u> <u>Initials</u>

Figure 2

Parenting Time Reminder
(to be photocopied and folded for wallet-sized card)

MONTH	WEEKENDS (7 PM to 7PM)	MIDWEEK*
January	11-13, 25-27	2, 9, 16, 23, 30
February	8-10, 22-24	6, 13, 20, 27
March	8-10, 22-24	6, 13, 20, 27
April	5-7, 19-21	3, 10, 17, 24
May**	3-5, 17-19, 5/31-6/2	1, 8, 15, 22, 29
June**	14-16, 28-30	5, 12, 19, 26
July	12-14, 26-28	3, 10, 17, 24, 31
August	9-11, 23-25	7, 14, 21, 28
September** 6-8, 20-22		4, 11, 18, 25
October	4-6, 18-20	2, 9, 16, 23, 30
November **1-3, 15-16, 11/29-12/1		6, 13, 20, 27
December** 13-15, 27-29		4, 11, 18

PARENTING TIME REMINDER 2002
Holidays and Vacation**
May 1-give written dates for summer vacation to other parent
May 26, Sun. 7 PM (Memorial Day) to May 27, Mon. 7 PM
June 16, Sun. (Father's Day) 10 AM to7 PM
Sept. 1, Sun. 7 PM (Labor Day) to Sept. 2, Mon. 7 PM
Nov. 28, Thur., 9AM (Thanksgiving) to Nov. 29, Fri. 9AM
Dec. 24, Tu. 9PM (Christmas Day) to Dec.25 Wed. 9PM and
(for child 5 and under) 4 weeks vacation at 2 weeks each., June 16-June
30, Aug.1-Aug.14. Exchange child at 9PM. For child 6 and older. *See Court Order for details.* **Parties may change schedule if both agree. Court order prevails otherwise.***5-7:30 PM if child 5 years and under, 5-8PM for child 6-13 years; 5-9 PM for child 14years and older.